Published by

# THE
# ROYAL AIR FORCE
# RETIRED LIST

# 2002

LONDON: The Stationery Office

Applications for reproduction should be made in writing to The Copyright Unit, Her Majesty's Stationery Office, St. Clements House, 2-16 Colegate, Norwich, NR3 1BQ

ISBN 0 11 772971 X

# CONTENTS

# NOTES

The Royal Air Force Retired List is published biennially, showing officers who have retired from permanent commissions.

Officers are placed on the Retired List in their substantive ranks. Where the Defence Council has permitted officers to retain as courtesy titles in civil life ranks higher than their substantive ranks, this is shown by "rtg ........."

The Branches shown against Retired officers' names are those in which they were serving on leaving the Active List.

The ranks shown in respect of former Royal Air Force Chaplains are the relative ranks which the Defence Council has permitted them to retain on retirement.

Retired officers who succeed to peerages, baronetcies or courtesy titles should notify the Editor for inclusion in the Retired List and records of the Ministry of Defence.

Readers who may notice errors or omissions are invited to communicate with the Editor quoting the relevant page. To enable correction of entries for the next edition, all notifications should reach the Editor by 27 June 2002. Such communications should not be sent to the publishers or printers.

Correspondence for the editor should be addressed to:

The Editor of Air Force Lists
PMA(Sec)1a(1)
Personnel Management Agency
Room 5 Bldg 248A
RAF Innsworth
Gloucester
GL3 1EZ

The following abbreviations are used throughout the book:

## Ranks

| | |
|---|---|
| Air Chief Marshal | ACM |
| Air Marshal | AM |
| Air Vice-Marshal | AVM |
| Air Commodore | A Cdre |
| *Air Commandant PMRAFNS | A Cdt |
| Group Captain | Gp Capt |
| *Group Officer PMRAFNS | Gp Offr |
| Wing Commander | Wg Cdr |
| *Wing Officer PMRAFNS | Wg Offr |
| Squadron Leader | Sqn Ldr |
| *Squadron Officer PMRAFNS | Sqn Offr |
| Flight Lieutenant | Flt Lt |
| *Flight Officer PMRAFNS | Flt Offr |
| Flying Officer | Fg Offr |
| Pilot Officer | Plt Offr |

*These ranks are also held by WRAF officers who retired before 1 August 1968.

## Branches

| | |
|---|---|
| ACB | Airfield Construction |
| ADMIN | Administrative |
| ASD | Administrative and Special Duties |
| *CAT | Catering |
| DEL | Dental |
| DM | Director of Music |
| *EDN | Education |
| ENG | Engineer and former Technical |
| GD | General Duties |
| ***(GD(G) | General Duties (Ground and former Aircraft Control, Balloon and Fighter Control) |
| OPS SPT | Operations Support |
| LGL | Legal |
| MAR | Marine |
| MED | Medical |
| MED(SEC) | Medical Secretarial |
| ****MED SPT | Medical Support |
| *PE | Physical Education and former Physical Fitness |
| PI | Photographic Interpretation |
| **PRT | Provost |
| ***RGT | Royal Air Force Regiment |
| SEC | Secretarial and former Accountant |
| SUP | Supply and former Equipment |
| SY | Security |

*These branches shown as ADMIN after 1975.
**This branch shown as ADMIN after April 1997.
***These branches shown as OPS SPT after April 1997.
****This branch shown as MED SPT after April 2000.

# LIST OF RETIRED OFFICERS OF THE ROYAL AIR FORCE

## A

ABBERSTEIN K. A. Born 18/11/30. Commd 13/2/64. Flt Lt 13/2/69. Retd GD 1/8/74.
ABBEY A. S. Born 18/2/56. Commd 17/7/75. Flt Lt 17/1/81. Retd GD 1/4/84.
ABBOTT C. J. A., MBE MB BS MRCGP MHSM MRCS LRCP DObstRCOG DAvMed AFOM. Born 11/7/48. Commd 29/9/69. Gp Capt 1/1/96. Retd MED 12/7/98.
ABBOTT H. M. Born 13/2/40. Commd 28/11/69. Fg Offr 28/11/69. Retd SEC 4/12/71.
ABBOTT J. A. Born 13/6/20. Commd 3/6/44. Flt Lt 26/3/60. Retd GD(G) 22/6/70.
ABBOTT J. A. Born 11/2/20. Commd 6/6/46. Sqn Ldr 1/1/60. Retd SEC 30/3/69.
ABBOTT J. H. Born 23/9/45. Commd 17/10/71. Sqn Ldr 1/7/85. Retd ENG 1/7/88.
ABBOTT J. W., ACIS. Born 21/6/22. Commd 17/1/51. Wg Cdr 1/1/70. Retd ADMIN 21/6/77.
ABBOTT L. E. Born 11/7/35. Commd 30/5/69. Sqn Ldr 1/7/91. Retd ENG 1/7/94.
ABBOTT L. S., MBE. Born 17/6/20. Commd 21/7/55. Sqn Ldr 1/7/66. Retd ENG 18/9/74.
ABBOTT M. J., BSc. Born 4/10/47. Commd 28/2/69. Flt Lt 28/5/74. Retd ENG 4/10/85.
ABBOTT M. J. Born 25/6/44. Commd 5/3/65. A Cdre 1/7/92. Retd GD 25/6/94.
ABBOTT N. J. Born 9/8/63. Commd 2/9/84. Flt Lt 2/9/89. Retd SUP 6/1/97.
ABBOTT R. E. Born 22/9/27. Commd 2/3/49. Sqn Ldr 1/7/59. Retd GD 22/9/65.
ABBOTT R. J., MBE. Born 24/1/41. Commd 20/7/78. Sqn Ldr 1/1/90. Retd ADMIN 2/4/95.
ABBOTT W. T. Born 18/11/11. Commd 25/3/43. Fg Offr 29/1/44. Retd ENG 13/3/46 rtg Flt Lt.
ABBOTT-WRIGHT J. C. Born 11/10/49. Commd 13/1/72. Flt Lt 22/6/78. Retd ADMIN 14/3/97.
ABEL G. W. Born 15/4/26. Commd 20/12/46. Flt Lt 29/6/50. Retd GD 15/4/64.
ABEL W. G. Born 29/1/24. Commd 3/9/43. Gp Capt 1/1/69. Retd GD 5/2/77.
ABELA P. P., MIMgt. Born 26/6/46. Commd 21/10/66. Sqn Ldr 1/1/81. Retd ENG 26/6/84.
ABELL The Rev P. J. Born 8/1/45. Commd 1/9/74. Retd 2/12/98. Wg Cdr.
ABER C. P. Born 3/4/44. Commd 22/2/63. Wg Cdr 1/7/88. Retd GD 3/4/99.
ABEY-KOCH L. K., MA BA LLB. Born 17/6/50. Commd 16/12/79. Sqn Ldr 1/1/88. Retd ADMIN 16/12/95.
ABLETT S. G. Born 4/6/10. Commd 15/5/47. Fg Offr 15/5/47. Retd SUP 1/3/52 rtg Flt Lt.
ABLITT B. P., BA. Born 30/10/57. Commd 16/6/92. Flt Lt 16/6/94. Retd ADMIN 14/3/97.
ABRAHAM W. B., BSc. Born 27/3/44. Commd 22/7/68. Sqn Ldr 22/1/76. Retd ADMIN 22/7/84.
ABRAM C. J. Born 10/5/46. Commd 18/8/67. Flt Lt 18/8/70. Retd GD 31/5/75.
ABRAM E. A., BA. Born 13/11/66. Commd 11/11/90. Flt Lt 11/5/93. Retd ADMIN 14/3/97.
ABREY J. W., OBE FIMgt. Born 13/2/24. Commd 26/1/45. Gp Capt 1/1/73. Retd GD 13/2/75.
ABROOK R. H., BEM. Born 18/9/06. Commd 15/2/40. Wg Cdr 1/7/47. Retd ENG 18/9/58.
ACHILLES J. C. P. Born 11/10/41. Commd 23/11/78. Sqn Ldr 1/1/88. Retd ENG 2/6/94.
ACKERS J. R. Born 3/3/00. Commd 3/12/27. Sqn Ldr 1/12/44. Retd SEC 2/4/48 rtg Wg Cdr.
ACKLAM G. Born 13/7/30. Commd 30/1/52. Wg Cdr 1/1/81. Retd GD 13/7/85.
ACKROYD A. C. C., MA. Born 10/6/37. Commd 5/1/60. Sqn Ldr 13/3/71. Retd ADMIN 25/6/76.
ACKROYD D. F. W., MMedSci MB BS MRCGP MFOM DRCOG DAvMed. Born 4/1/54. Commd 17/2/80. Wg Cdr 18/8/91. Retd MED 4/12/97.
ACKROYD D. G. S. Born 2/4/42. Commd 5/9/69. Wg Cdr 1/7/83. Retd GD(G) 2/3/96.
ACKROYD E. Born 25/11/22. Commd 26/4/43. Flt Lt 20/10/46. Retd GD 15/2/58.
ACKROYD S. J. Born 30/3/44. Commd 1/4/65. Flt Lt 1/10/70. Retd GD 31/7/75.
ACONS E. G. N. Born 1/5/45. Commd 9/12/65. Wg Cdr 1/7/89. Retd OPS SPT 1/5/00.
ACRES J. Born 30/6/21. Commd 11/6/42. Flt Lt 14/9/46. Retd SUP 27/10/55.
ADAIR P. J. Born 9/10/31. Commd 6/12/51. Flt Lt 17/4/57. Retd GD 29/4/78.
ADAM A. E., MA MB BS MRCPath. Born 7/6/39. Commd 23/1/67. Sqn Ldr 14/8/75. Retd MED 12/5/83.
ADAM G. W. Born 7/9/14. Commd 9/3/43. Flt Lt 9/9/46. Retd ENG 31/3/62.
ADAM I. W., BSc. Born 24/5/44. Commd 28/9/64. Sqn Ldr 1/7/78. Retd ENG 24/5/99.
ADAM J., BSc. Born 2/12/62. Commd 3/5/83. Flt Lt 15/1/87. Retd GD 2/3/01.
ADAM J. H. M. Born 26/2/35. Commd 14/1/54. Flt Lt 7/3/62. Retd GD 26/8/93.
ADAMS A. C. T. Born 20/5/49. Commd 5/3/11/73. Retd GD 31/5/11.
ADAMS A. H. D. Born 2/3/30. Commd 19/12/63. Flt Lt 19/12/68. Retd ENG 2/3/92.
ADAMS A. W. Born 14/8/19. Commd 7/11/46. Sqn Ldr 1/7/63. Retd ENG 14/8/74.
ADAMS B. S., BA. Born 13/5/56. Commd 18/11/79. Flt Lt 18/2/81. Retd GD 19/11/88.
ADAMS C. J. Born 30/5/39. Commd 1/8/61. Sqn Ldr 1/1/74. Retd GD 1/1/98.
ADAMS C. M. Born 29/7/21. Commd 19/3/42. Sqn Ldr 1/7/60. Retd SEC 16/7/61.
ADAMS C. R. Born 18/1/36. Commd 6/2/54. Wg Cdr 1/1/86. Retd GD 18/1/91.
ADAMS C. R., CBE AFC FCIPD. Born 1/4/40. Commd 1/8/61. A Cdre 1/1/90. Retd GD 1/4/95.

ADAMS D. Born 11/1/24. Commd 2/1/50. Wg Cdr 1/7/66. Retd GD 11/1/79.
ADAMS D. A., MIMgt. Born 27/8/49. Commd 6/10/69. Wg Cdr 1/7/89. Retd ENG 17/1/97.
ADAMS D. B., MA PhD BSc. Born 26/4/27. Commd 19/10/49. Wg Cdr 1/4/69. Retd EDN 31/3/74.
ADAMS E. R. Born 26/3/34. Commd 12/8/59. Sqn Ldr 1/9/68. Retd EDN 12/8/75.
ADAMS J. H. Born 25/8/32. Commd 17/1/52. Flt Lt 29/4/59. Retd GD 20/10/70.
ADAMS J. H. A. Born 30/8/35. Commd 30/7/57. Sqn Ldr 1/7/68. Retd GD 31/8/74.
ADAMS K. M. Born 18/5/46. Commd 31/8/78. Sqn Ldr 1/1/88. Retd ENG 6/12/96.
ADAMS K. S. Born 24/4/58. Commd 1/12/77. Flt Lt 1/6/83. Retd GD 30/9/88.
ADAMS M. K., CB AFC FRAeS. Born 23/1/34. Commd 18/3/53. AVM 1/7/83. Retd GD 2/10/88.
ADAMS M. P., MRAeS MIMgt. Born 22/10/40. Commd 13/2/60. Wg Cdr 1/1/93. Retd GD 1/1/96.
ADAMS M. T. H., DFC. Born 20/1/20. Commd 30/5/39. Sqn Ldr 1/7/55. Retd GD 20/1/69.
ADAMS N. J. Born 5/11/30. Commd 26/7/51. Flt Lt 14/11/56. Retd GD 5/11/68.
ADAMS N. M. Born 22/4/59. Commd 20/9/79. Sqn Ldr 1/1/95. Retd GD 1/10/98.
ADAMS N. R. Born 30/6/48. Commd 23/3/68. Sqn Ldr 1/7/82. Retd GD 28/2/93.
ADAMS P. B. Born 16/6/33. Commd 30/1/52. Flt Lt 13/11/57. Retd GD 16/6/88.
ADAMS P. G., DFC. Born 29/4/18. Commd 22/5/48. Sqn Ldr 1/7/55. Retd GD 29/4/61.
ADAMS P. S. G., MBE. Born 10/4/47. Commd 10/6/66. Sqn Ldr 1/1/80. Retd GD 14/3/96.
ADAMS R. C., MBE Born 20/3/49. Commd 20/9/68. Sqn Ldr 1/1/90. Retd GD(G) 20/3/93.
ADAMS R. H. D. Born 19/11/33. Commd 10/9/52. Sqn Ldr 1/7/69. Retd GD 19/9/84.
ADAMS R. J. Born 29/12/28. Commd 5/12/51. Flt Lt 6/6/60. Retd GD 29/12/86.
ADAMS R. M., MB ChB. Born 6/7/62. Commd 13/11/84. Sqn Ldr 1/8/93. Retd MED 8/1/97.
ADAMS R. W. G. Born 28/5/37. Commd 16/12/58. Sqn Ldr 1/1/69. Retd SUP 5/6/82.
ADAMS S. J. Born 28/3/27. Commd 6/6/57. Flt Lt 6/12/60. Retd GD 28/3/82.
ADAMS S. M., MCIPS. Born 5/10/30. Commd 30/3/61. Wg Cdr 1/1/79. Retd SUP 1/4/85.
ADAMS T. F. Born 27/4/30. Commd 4/2/71. Flt Lt 4/2/74. Retd ENG 1/10/84.
ADAMS W. H. Born 29/11/17. Commd 20/11/42. Flt Lt 20/5/46. Retd GD 23/10/55.
ADAMSON A. N. G., BSc CEng MIERE MIEE MIMgt. Born 20/11/33. Commd 6/10/60. Flt Lt 25/11/62. Retd ENG 1/11/80.
ADAMSON D. E., MA. Born 14/3/20. Commd 4/8/42. Wg Cdr 1/7/64. Retd SEC 30/9/67.
ADAMSON D. T. Born 29/5/25. Commd 1/4/45. Sqn Ldr 1/10/55. Retd GD 1/9/62.
ADAMSON E., DFM. Born 9/4/22. Commd 3/3/44. Flt Lt 29/6/50. Retd ADMIN 9/4/77.
ADAMSON G. N., BTech. Born 16/5/55. Commd 2/9/73. Sqn Ldr 1/1/87. Retd ENG 16/5/93.
ADAMSON N. C. Born 5/9/38. Commd 28/7/59. Flt Lt 7/3/62. Retd GD 31/7/69.
ADAMSON W. M. Born 19/3/34. Commd 18/3/52. Flt Lt 15/2/65. Retd GD 1/1/69.
ADCOCK B. R. Born 7/2/39. Commd 11/7/64. Flt Lt 26/7/67. Retd GD 7/2/77.
ADCOCK C. B., BA FIMgt. Born 5/4/41. Commd 31/7/62. Gp Capt 1/1/91. Retd GD 1/1/97.
ADCOCK D. F. Born 6/5/21. Commd 9/10/42. Sqn Ldr 1/7/54. Retd GD 8/5/64.
ADCOCK K. C. Born 20/3/27. Commd 4/6/52. Flt Lt 9/7/59. Retd GD 20/3/65.
ADCOCK T. L. Born 19/4/38. Commd 24/4/56. Wg Cdr 1/7/76. Retd GD 30/9/84.
ADCOCK T. R., OBE MRAeS. Born 1/10/43. Commd 22/5/64. Sqn Ldr 1/1/78. Retd GD 1/10/81.
   Re-entered 28/4/82. Sqn Ldr 29/7/78. Retd GD 18/4/99.
ADDAMS J. R., AFC. Born 3/3/04. Commd 17/12/24. Wg Cdr 1/1/40. Retd GD 3/7/46 rtg Gp Capt.
ADDINGTON F. F., DFC. Born 19/7/13. Commd 7/4/40. Wg Cdr 1/1/54. Retd GD 19/9/60.
ADDIS M. H., MSc BSc. Born 6/5/55. Commd 31/8/75. Sqn Ldr 1/7/87. Retd ENG 6/5/94.
ADDIS P. J. Born 28/8/24. Commd 14/11/51. Flt Lt 20/6/55. Retd GD(G) 28/8/82.
ADDISON T. Born 23/10/46. Commd 1/10/65. Sqn Ldr 1/7/85. Retd SY 1/11/87.
ADE G. C. H. Born 18/4/18. Commd 3/4/39. Flt Lt 10/2/47. Retd SUP 12/5/67 rtg Wg Cdr.
ADES A. V., MBE MBA FIMgt. Born 29/11/43. Commd 10/11/61. Gp Capt 1/7/96. Retd GD 1/7/99.
ADHEMAR P. N. Born 7/2/47. Commd 25/2/66. Flt Lt 25/8/71. Retd GD 12/4/76.
ADKINSON C. R. Born 7/3/64. Commd 27/3/88. Fg Off 27/3/88. Retd ENG 6/7/89.
ADLINGTON L. E., AFM. Born 6/6/26. Commd 28/1/60. Flt Lt 28/7/63. Retd GD 31/3/74.
ADOLPH M. P. N., MSc MB BCh BAO DAvMed. Born 8/3/31. Commd 16/7/62. Wg Cdr 25/10/74.
   Retd MED 16/7/78.
ADRIAN G. K. Born 27/3/56. Commd 1/7/90. Flt Lt 9/12/85. Retd ADMIN 1/7/96.
AEDY K. J. Born 29/5/24. Commd 8/3/45. Sqn Ldr 1/1/58. Retd GD 29/5/73.
AGER S. M., DPhysEd. Born 14/5/42. Commd 14/9/65. Sqn Ldr 1/7/80. Retd GD 14/9/87.
AGER W. G. A. Born 26/4/22. Commd 24/2/43. Flt Lt 24/8/46. Retd GD 26/4/65.
AGNEW B. M. Born 23/7/34. Commd 5/5/55. Sqn Ldr 1/7/69. Retd SUP 25/9/88.
AGNEW R., BA MIMgt. Born 7/1/46. Commd 6/11/64. Wg Cdr 1/7/88. Retd GD 14/9/96.
AGNEW R. Born 28/7/12. Commd 19/11/42. Flt Lt 19/5/46. Retd ENG 3/7/58.
AHERNE R. B., MBE. Born 8/2/35. Commd 5/11/70. Sqn Ldr 1/1/84. Retd ENG 8/1/86.
AHMED R. R. A., BA. Born 7/7/63. Commd 30/8/81. Flt Lt 15/10/85. Retd GD 14/3/96.
AIKEN R. Born 14/5/32. Commd 28/1/53. Flt Lt 17/6/58. Retd GD 14/5/92.
AIKEN Sir John., KCB. Born 22/12/21. Commd 22/11/41. ACM 8/7/76. Retd GD 31/3/78.
AINGE D. B. Born 7/7/43. Commd 17/12/64. Sqn Ldr 1/1/78. Retd GD 7/7/81.
AINGE D. R., CEng MIEE MIMgt. Born 26/4/44. Commd 15/7/65. Gp Capt 1/1/92. Retd ENG 26/4/99.

AINLEY M. Born 8/4/22. Commd 30/8/51. Flt Offr 30/8/57. Retd SEC 1/10/60.
AINLEY P., DFC. Born 4/11/23. Commd 26/5/43. Sqn Ldr 1/1/54. Retd GD 5/7/66 rtg Wg Cdr.
AINSLIE E. J., BEM. Born 14/2/35. Commd 12/7/79. Flt Lt 12/7/84. Retd ENG 14/2/85.
AINSWORTH D. P., BSc. Born 4/12/63. Commd 8/5/88. Flt Lt 8/11/90. Retd GD 8/5/00.
AINSWORTH H. Born 2/10/17. Commd 27/2/47. Flt Lt 27/8/51. Retd SUP 1/12/61.
AINSWORTH J. Born 8/3/19. Commd 10/12/42. Sqn Ldr 1/1/57. Retd ENG 8/3/74.
AINSWORTH J. C., CEng MRAeS MIMgt. Born 4/9/26. Commd 4/3/54. Gp Capt 1/7/73. Retd ENG 3/9/77.
AINSWORTH S. J., MDA BSc MCIPS MCIT MILT MIMgt. Born 19/11/61. Commd 31/8/80. Sqn Ldr 1/7/91. Retd SUP 13/12/99.
AIREY F. C., MBE. Born 26/6/16. Commd 26/4/43. Wg Cdr 1/1/61. Retd ENG 26/6/72.
AIREY I. S., BSc. Born 23/2/43. Commd 14/12/62. Flt Lt 14/12/65. Retd GD 31/12/71.
AIREY N. D. Born 11/7/58. Commd 11/1/79. Sqn Ldr 1/1/95. Retd GD 5/7/98.
AIRS K. A. Born 28/10/41. Commd 28/9/62. Flt Lt 28/3/68. Retd GD 23/10/79.
AITKEN A. I. Born 7/11/38. Commd 23/6/61. Flt Lt 1/4/66. Retd GD 7/11/76.
AITKEN W. M., BEd. Born 25/2/54. Commd 9/10/77. Sqn Ldr 1/7/87. Retd ADMIN 29/8/96.
AKDENIZ S. O., BSc. Born 12/2/63. Commd 2/9/84. Flt Lt 2/3/88. Retd SY 1/10/91
AKED G. A. Born 20/6/25. Commd 17/8/50. Flt Lt 17/2/55. Retd GD 20/6/71.
AKEHURST C. S. L., MIMgt. Born 1/12/21. Commd 17/3/55. Sqn Ldr 1/7/69. Retd ENG 1/1/72.
AKEHURST DE VISME P. M. Born 7/6/48. Commd 1/8/69. Fg Offr 1/2/70. Retd GD 30/11/72.
AKEROYD W. S., DFM FIMgt. Born 23/10/20. Commd 29/10/42. Gp Capt 1/1/70. Retd GD(G) 23/10/76.
AKERS S. J., MBA GradInstPS. Born 4/12/58. Commd 13/12/79. Sqn Ldr 1/7/92. Retd SUP 14/3/97.
AKERS-DOUGLAS A. A. Born 17/9/43. Commd 24/6/65. Flt Lt 9/2/68. Retd GD 11/4/73.
AKHURST D. H. Born 9/12/39. Commd 17/5/63. Flt Lt 17/11/68. Retd GD 6/10/79.
AKISTER W. H. Born 5/8/32. Commd 27/8/52. Flt Lt 12/2/58. Retd GD 5/8/87.
ALABASTER J. C. Born 4/3/36. Commd 10/3/60. Fg Offr 10/9/61. Retd ENG 24/1/65.
ALBONE D. P. J. F. Born 10/2/23. Commd 22/8/63. Flt Lt 22/8/66. Retd GD 16/2/73.
ALCOCK A. J. H., MBE. Born 3/5/44. Commd 22/5/64. Gp Capt 1/7/90. Retd GD 3/5/99.
ALCOCK G. R., AFC. Born 2/3/43. Commd 10/12/65. Flt Lt 1/7/69. Retd GD 2/3/81.
ALCOCK J. M., MRAeS. Born 3/10/32. Commd 14/7/54. Wg Cdr 1/7/72. Retd GD 3/10/90.
ALCOCK Sir Michael, GCB KBE DSc FEng FIMechE FRAeS. Born 11/7/36. Commd 30/12/58. ACM 30/6/93. Retd ENG 25/6/96.
ALCOCK M. R. Born 2/1/41. Commd 19/6/64. Flt Lt 19/12/69. Retd GD 2/3/80. Reinstated 4/6/84. Flt Lt 15/4/74. Retd GD 3/1/91.
ALCOCK R. C. K. Born 3/3/34. Commd 31/12/52. Flt Lt 6/6/61. Retd GD 5/9/76.
ALDEN D. R. Born 14/1/45. Commd 28/4/65. Flt Lt 28/10/70. Retd GD 11/11/75.
ALDEN L. S. Born 1/5/22. Commd 10/3/44. Flt Lt 10/9/47. Retd GD 3/2/68.
ALDERSMITH M. F. Born 13/9/26. Commd 14/6/46. Wg Cdr 1/7/69. Retd GD 13/9/81.
ALDERSON B. Born 29/1/41. Commd 24/2/61. Flt Lt 24/8/71. Retd GD 29/1/96.
ALDERSON G. L. D., MEd BA BSc(Econ). Born 31/7/31. Commd 3/1/61. Wg Cdr 1/7/78. Retd ADMIN 3/5/84.
ALDERSON M. J. D. Born 16/10/29. Commd 1/8/51. Flt Lt 1/8/56. Retd SEC 30/1/60.
ALDERSON N. C. Born 15/4/44. Commd 28/4/67. Flt Lt 28/10/72. Retd GD 16/1/83.
ALDERSON O. W., AFC. Born 16/5/31. Commd 28/12/51. Sqn Ldr 1/7/72. Retd GD 16/11/93.
ALDINGTON J. D. Born 23/12/42. Commd 28/10/81. Sqn Ldr 1/7/87. Retd GD 14/10/90.
ALDOUS D. I. Born 14/3/44. Commd 19/4/63. Sqn Ldr 1/7/75. Retd GD 14/3/88.
ALDRED J. D. Born 14/4/33. Commd 24/1/52. Sqn Ldr 1/1/86. Retd GD 14/4/91.
ALDRED J. R. Born 15/5/42. Commd 19/6/64. Flt Lt 19/12/69. Retd GD 15/5/80.
ALDRED R. H. Born 22/8/40. Commd 6/4/72. Flt Lt 6/4/74. Retd ADMIN 23/10/90.
ALDRICH E. W. Born 21/5/09. Commd 17/12/41. Flt Lt 1/7/46. Retd ENG 3/11/46.
ALDRICH J. R. A., MSc BSc CEng MIEE. Born 30/7/57. Commd 30/8/78. Sqn Ldr 1/7/89. Retd ENG 30/7/95.
ALDRIDGE B. Born 25/7/18. Commd 11/8/40. Sqn Ldr 1/8/47. Retd GD 27/6/58.
ALDRIDGE B. J., MSc MRAeS. Born 6/8/35. Commd 2/10/61. Sqn Ldr 1/7/70. Retd GD 11/6/76.
ALDRIDGE F. S. J. Born 26/6/24. Commd 17/6/54. Sqn Ldr 1/7/71. Retd GD 30/9/75.
ALDRIDGE H. V. Born 7/2/29. Commd 24/9/59. Sqn Ldr 1/1/73. Retd ADMIN 9/2/82.
ALDRIDGE K. Born 14/5/46. Commd 21/1/66. Flt Lt 21/7/71. Retd GD 27/7/91.
ALDWINCKLE J. P., MA. Born 13/9/22. Commd 13/3/50. Wg Cdr 1/1/68. Retd ADMIN 13/9/77.
ALEXANDER C. R. Born 15/12/49. Commd 14/3/72. Flt Lt 15/10/74. Retd ENG 1/6/79.
ALEXANDER C.D., FHCIMA. Born 1/5/39. Commd 28/7/60. Gp Capt 1/1/88. Retd SUP 3/4/92.
ALEXANDER D. A. M. Born 27/2/26. Commd 22/8/43. Sqn Ldr 1/7/64. Retd GD(G) 27/2/76.
ALEXANDER G., BSc. Born 6/6/42. Commd 14/9/64. Sqn Ldr 1/1/75. Retd GD 14/9/80.
ALEXANDER G. B. Born 25/2/25. Commd 29/5/52. Sqn Ldr 1/7/72. Retd GD 30/11/75.
ALEXANDER J. G. Born 2/5/47. Commd 27/3/80. Flt Lt 27/3/82. Retd GD(G) 17/7/95.
ALEXANDER J. R., DFC DFM. Born 6/6/22. Commd 9/9/43. Sqn Ldr 1/7/63. Retd GD 6/6/73.
ALEXANDER R. D., OBE AFC. Born 7/4/23. Commd 27/6/51. Wg Cdr 1/1/72. Retd GD 7/4/78.
ALEXANDER R. S. Born 28/2/37. Commd 14/5/60. Flt Lt. 14/11/65. Retd GD 26/4/75.
ALEXANDER-BOWEN M. Born 7/10/54. Commd 18/12/80. Flt Lt 18/6/87. Retd ADMIN 14/4/96.
ALFORD B. J. Born 1/11/48. Commd 28/4/67. Flt Lt 28/10/72. Retd GD 5/4/86.

ALFORD J., BA. Born 23/8/32. Commd 2/8/68. Sqn Ldr 2/8/76. Retd ADMIN 31/12/83.
ALFORD R. Born 27/3/44. Commd 9/8/63. Flt Lt 9/2/69. Retd GD(G) 27/3/82.
ALFORD T. A., BA. Born 4/11/32. Commd 23/11/56. Sqn Ldr 23/8/65. Retd EDN 23/11/74.
ALGAR H. K. M. Born 18/2/24. Commd 27/1/55. Flt Lt 27/1/61. Retd GD 30/4/68.
ALISON R. H., MBE. Born 28/8/24. Commd 12/6/45. Wg Cdr 1/7/73. Retd SEC 28/8/79.
ALISTER-JONES N. A. Born 29/9/42. Commd 14/1/65. Flt Lt 8/3/72. Retd SY 1/10/77.
ALLAIN A. M. Born 9/3/36. Commd 30/3/61. Flt Lt 1/4/71. Retd GD(G) 9/3/93.
ALLAM C. M. Born 29/1/56. Commd 21/4/77. Sqn Ldr 1/7/87. Retd GD 29/1/94.
ALLAM J. W. Born 3/10/24. Commd 6/2/44. Flt Lt 6/8/47. Retd GD 29/8/54.
ALLAMBY W. L. R. Born 21/5/32. Commd 2/6/77. Flt Lt 2/6/82. Retd ENG 1/4/84.
ALLAN A. S. M. Born 16/3/32. Commd 14/12/50. Flt Lt 14/12/56. Retd SEC 16/9/70.
ALLAN C. F. Born 4/4/56. Commd 21/4/77. Flt Lt 21/10/82. Retd GD 21/9/87.
ALLAN D. Born 26/9/46. Commd 16/12/66. Sqn Ldr 1/1/91. Retd SUP 14/3/97.
ALLAN D. D. Born 9/7/46. Commd 2/8/73. Gp Capt 1/7/94. Retd ENG 31/8/98.
ALLAN D. R., MBE BSc. Born 25/9/47. Commd 22/9/65. Gp Capt 1/1/91. Retd ENG 9/7/94.
ALLAN G. L. A. Born 16/8/40. Commd 14/1/65. Flt Lt 14/7/70. Retd GD 7/7/80.
ALLAN J. McM., MSc BA CEng MIEE. Born 12/11/53. Commd 23/5/85. Sqn Ldr 1/1/92. Retd 23/5/99.
ALLAN N. Born 5/2/52. Commd 4/4/96. Flt Lt 4/4/00. Retd ADMIN 9/12/00.
ALLAN P. H. W., ACIS. Born 6/8/30. Commd 28/7/49. Sqn Ldr 1/7/64. Retd SEC 25/7/75.
ALLARD D. Born 26/3/31. Commd 12/3/64. Flt Lt 12/3/70. Retd PE 1/9/73.
ALLARD S. Born 15/6/11. Commd 6/10/41. Flt Lt 30/4/44. Retd ENG 7/2/46 rtg Sqn Ldr.
ALLARDYCE D. C. Born 12/11/43. Commd 17/7/64. Flt Lt 22/5/69. Retd GD 27/8/76.
ALLAWAY W. J. Born 12/1/45. Commd 30/4/81. Sqn Ldr 1/1/89. Retd GD 7/10/97.
ALLBON J. D. Born 11/3/42. Commd 5/6/67. Fg Offr 5/6/69. Retd SEC 5/6/71.
ALLCHIN B. C. Born 21/4/38. Commd 4/12/56. Sqn Ldr 1/1/70. Retd GD 1/10/87
ALLCORN B. E. Born 12/8/41. Commd 2/9/63. Wg Cdr 1/7/82. Retd SY 9/9/96.
ALLDIS C. A., CBE DFC AFC MA. Born 28/9/18. Commd 3/10/39. Gp Capt 1/7/59. Retd GD 26/1/66 rtg A Cdre.
ALLDRITT D. P. G. Born 9/4/60. Commd 11/9/86. Flt Lt 11/9/88. Retd SY 12/12/95.
ALLEN A. F. Born 17/9/37. Commd 31/1/66. Swn Ldr 1/1/74. Retd ADMIN 21/3/78.
ALLEN A. G. Born 19/8/32. Commd 22/7/71. Flt Lt 22/7/73. Retd SUPPLY 19/8/87.
ALLEN A. R. Born 11/4/18. Commd 21/4/42. Flt Lt 21/10/45. Retd GD 18/11/53 rtg Sqn Ldr.
ALLEN B. J. Born 30/12/12. Commd 24/9/44. Flt Lt 24/9/50. Retd SEC 29/9/58.
ALLEN B. R. Born 12/4/32. Commd 3/2/65. Flt Lt 3/2/65. Retd GD(G) 3/2/73.
ALLEN C. Born 8/8/55. Commd 27/2/75. Wg Cdr 1/1/93. Retd ADMIN 8/8/99.
ALLEN C. R. Born 15/6/47. Commd 8/9/77. Sqn Ldr 1/1/85. Retd ENG 16/6/97.
ALLEN D. F. Born 29/5/63. Commd 12/3/87. Flt Lt 12/9/92. Retd 27/5/96.
ALLEN D. G. Born 18/1/24. Commd 28/1/45. Flt Lt 22/7/51. Retd GD 12/4/68.
ALLEN D. G. Born 18/10/40. Commd 26/10/61. Flt Lt 23/8/68. Retd REGT. 18/10/78.
ALLEN D. M., CEng MIEE MRAeS CDip AF. Born 23/2/43. Commd 15/7/64. Wg Cdr 1/7/79. Retd ENG 23/2/87.
ALLEN D. R., MSc BDS MGDSRCS (Edin). Born 23/12/42. Commd 16/9/62. Wg Cdr 15/6/80. Retd DEL 1/4/91.
   Re-entered 1/9/92. Gp Capt 1/1/94. Retd DEL 23/12/00.
ALLEN D. W. Born 30/10/33. Commd 23/7/52. Sqn Ldr 1/1/71. Retd GD 30/10/93.
ALLEN F. Born 22/11/32. Commd 20/3/52. Gp Capt 1/1/82. Retd GD 2/9/83.
ALLEN F. D., MSc BSc CEng MIMechE. Born 14/6/35. Commd 4/9/59. Sqn Ldr 4/3/70. Retd EDN 4/9/75.
ALLEN F. G., BA MInstAM MIMgt. Born 7/5//29. Commd 11/2/65. Sqn Ldr 1/7/77. Retd GD 31/3/85.
ALLEN F. G. Born 8/12/38. Commd 25/7/60. Wg Cdr 1/7/78. Retd SUP 8/12/93.
ALLEN G. E. Born 24/3/38. Commd 4/10/63. Flt Lt 4/4/69. Retd GD 18/6/79.
ALLEN G. H. Born 5/11/14. Commd 9/10/42. Sqn Ldr 1/1/60. Retd GD(G) 5/11/64.
ALLEN G. H. Born 8/9/36. Commd 9/3/62. Flt Lt 1/4/66. Retd GD 8/9/74.
ALLEN G. P. Born 9/8/35. Commd 4/4/57. Sqn Ldr 1/7/75. Retd ADMIN 9/4/90.
ALLEN H., MIMgt. Born 4/4/14. Commd 26/4/45. Wg Cdr 1/7/65. Retd SEC 4/4/69.
ALLEN H. A. Born 18/5/57. Commd 6/7/80. Flt Lt 6/1/85. Retd ADMIN 31/3/97.
ALLEN J. Born 9/12/34. Commd 10/10/63. Sqn Ldr 1/1/85. Retd GD 1/9/88.
ALLEN J. D. Born 18/3/61. Commd 28/2/80. Wg Cdr 1/1/98. Retd SUP 1/1/01.
ALLEN J. G. Born 26/10/58. Commd 3/11/77. Flt Lt 3/5/83. Retd GD 1/10/89.
ALLEN J. H., DFC. Born 30/7/23. Commd 28/7/44. Flt Lt 10/8/54. Retd SEC 1/1/75.
ALLEN J. H. Born 10/12/45. Commd 1/4/66. Flt Lt 6/10/71. Retd GD 1/5/87
ALLEN J. W. Born 10/6/31. Commd 7/11/51. Sqn Ldr 1/1/66. Retd GD 6/9/85.
ALLEN K. E. Born 26/7/24. Commd 22/6/45. Wg Cdr 1/1/67. Retd GD 24/7/76.
ALLEN L. J. Born 30/3/18. Commd 18/10/51. Flt Offr 18/4/56. Retd GD(G) 30/3/68.
ALLEN M. D. P. Born 29/5/50. Commd 1/4/71. Sqn Ldr 1/1/84. Retd GD(G) 1/10/92.
ALLEN M. J. W., BSc.Born 15/10/49. Commd 26/2/71. Flt Lt 26/11/75. Retd ENG 15/10/87.
ALLEN M. K. C. Born 25/7/52. Commd 22/5/75. Flt Lt 22/11/80. Retd GD 3/2/91.
ALLEN M. S. Born 26/10/56. Commd 16/9/76. Flt Lt 16/3/82. Retd GD 11/10/88.
ALLEN N. E., MSc BSc(Econ) MIMgt. Born 8/7/34. Commd 4/1/56. Sqn Ldr 5/3/69. Retd EDN 1/10/79.
ALLEN N. J. Born 11/10/60. Commd 20/6/91. Flt Lt 20/6/93. Retd ADMIN 14/9/96.

ALLEN P. Born 2/10/23. Commd 27/8/64. Flt Lt 27/8/67. Retd GD 30/6/73.
ALLEN P. J. Born 19/2/34. Commd 30/1/58. Flt Lt 30/7/62. Retd GD 21/7/72.
ALLEN R., MBE BA. Born 28/2/59. Commd 17/8/80. Sqn Ldr 1/1/93. Retd ADMIN 5/11/00.
ALLEN R. A. E., AFC* MIIM MIMgt. Born 28/11/22. Commd 9/11/44. Wg Cdr 1/7/62. Retd GD 28/11/77.
ALLEN R. C., CBE BSc. Born 21/8/31. Commd 18/3/53. A Cdre 1/1/82. Retd GD 21/8/86.
ALLEN R. L., BEM. Born 23/10/25. Commd 4/11/48. Wg Cdr 1/7/66. Retd SEC 5/3/71.
ALLEN R. N. G., CBE DFC. Born 8/11/20. Commd 17/4/41. Gp Capt 1/7/61. Retd GD 8/2/73.
ALLEN R. R. Born 16/11/42. Commd 6/4/62. Flt Lt 6/10/67. Retd GD 31/12/85. Re-entered 2/12/90. Flt Lt 7/9/72.
   Retd GD 31/3/99.
ALLEN S. Born 24/3/18. Commd 10/9/43. Flt Lt 10/3/47. Retd GD 10/7/58.
ALLEN S. B., BA. Born 5/2/57. Commd 14/1/79. Flt Lt 14/10/80. Retd GD 14/1/87.
ALLEN T. J., ACIS MIMgt. Born 1/5/37. Commd 25/7/60. Sqn Ldr 1/7/72. Retd ADMIN 1/9/82.
ALLEN T. N., BSc. Born 23/9/44. Commd 28/9/64. Sqn Ldr 1/1/80. Retd GD 14/1/87
ALLEN W. G. Born 30/9/25. Commd 6/2/50. Flt Lt 11/11/68. Retd GD 30/9/77.
ALLENBY W., BSc. Born 14/8/25. Commd 29/8/51. Flt Lt 30/4/53. Retd GD 13/11/57.
ALLERTON R. C., CB. Born 7/12/35. Commd 9/12/54. AVM 1/7/87. Retd SUP 15/4/90.
ALLFREE D. N. Born 29/12/15. Commd 8/3/45. Fg Offr 3/5/46. Retd SEC 21/9/53 rtg Flt Lt.
ALLGOOD R. S., MBE FAAI MInstAM(Dip) MCIPD. Born 28/12/34. Commd 17/6/54. Wg Cdr 1/7/78. Retd ADMIN
   1/10/87.
ALLIES E. M., MBE DFC BA. Born 11/4/20. Commd 6/8/40. Gp Capt 1/1/72. Retd EDN 11/4/75.
ALLIN G. R. Born 5/8/33. Commd 30/4/52. Flt Lt 6/11/57. Retd GD 5/8/71.
ALLINSON J. E. Born 10/10/31. Commd 16/5/51. Flt Lt 16/2/57. Retd GD 10/10/69.
ALLINSON P. A. Born 18/1/26. Commd 4/9/49. Flt Lt 11/12/56. Retd GD 26/7/65.
ALLISON C., BA. Born 13/11/39. Commd 19/9/71. Sqn Ldr 1/7/88. Retd ADMIN 13/11/94.
ALLISON D., CBE. Born 5/8/31. Commd 15/12/53. A Cdre 1/7/83. Retd GD 4/8/85.
ALLISON D., CB. Born 15/10/32. Commd 6/4/54. AVM 1/7/85. Retd GD 12/1/87.
ALLISON H., MC. Born 8/11/23. Commd 4/9/61. Flt Lt 4/9/61. Retd SUP 16/2/74.
ALLISON J. Born 27/7/21. Commd 27/5/54. Flt Lt 27/5/60. Retd GD 28/9/68.
ALLISON Sir John, KCB CBE FRAeS. Born 24/03/43. Commd 28/7/64. ACM 8/3/96. Retd GD 6/9/99.
ALLISON J. S., BSc. Born 12/3/49. Commd 28/2/72. Flt Lt 28/5/75. Retd PI 24/10/82.
ALLISON R. M., BEd. Born 30/3/57. Commd 9/10/79. Sqn Ldr 1/1/90. Retd ADMIN 9/10/95.
ALLISON R. W. I. Born 17/12/42. Commd 24/6/65. Flt Lt 24/12/67. Retd GD 23/12/72.
ALLISON T. S. Born 15/10/52. Commd 22/9/88. Flt Lt 22/9/92. Retd SUP 31/3/94.
ALLISSTONE M. J., CBE FInstPet FIMgt MCIPS. Born 13/2/33. Commd 27/7/54. Air Cdre 1/1/84. Retd SUP 2/4/88.
ALLKINS C. R. Born 4/10/44. Commd 9/10/64. Sqn Ldr 1/7/80. Retd GD 1/5/92.
ALLKINS R. D. Born 28/6/47. Commd 11/1/81. Sqn Ldr 1/1/91. Retd ADMIN 1/1/94.
ALLOTT M. G., CB FIMgt. Born 28/12/18.Commd 12/1/44. A Cdre 1/7/73. Retd SUP 28/12/76.
ALLOWAY H. V. Born 25/6/14. Commd 1/9/33. Wg Cdr 1/7/47. Retd GD 22/9/57.
ALLPORT D. K., DSO DFC*. Born 13/4/17. Commd 26/3/42. Wg Cdr 1/7/65. Retd GD 13/4/72.
ALLPORT M. K., MBE. Born 6/3/44. Commd 24/1/65. Wg Cdr 1/1/91. Retd GD 6/9/99.
ALLSO C. E., MBE. Born 30/7/21. Commd 13/12/43. Sqn Ldr 1/7/60. Retd GD 25/4/75.
ALLSOP K. Born 8/1/26. Commd 7/10/48. Flt Lt 7/4/52. Retd GD 8/1/69.
ALLSOP N. G. Born 20/4/23. Commd 26/8/45. Flt Lt 27/5/54. Retd GD 3/10/67.
ALLSOPP R. F. Born 8/9/35. Commd 27/1/67. Flt Lt 27/1/69. Retd PRT 27/1/75.
ALLSOPP W. Born 20/3/16. Commd 6/10/38. Sqn Ldr 1/1/54. Retd GD 25/4/59.
ALM G. A. Born 11/7/48. Commd 20/9/79. Flt Lt 20/9/81. Retd SUP 20/9/87.
ALMOND G. Born 10/5/30. Commd 11/2/81. Sqn Ldr 1/4/76. Retd SUP 10/5/92.
ALMOND J. S., BEM. Born 1/6/21. Commd 12/12/46. Sqn Ldr 1/1/69. Retd SUP 14/12/74.
ALSFORD J. E., BSc. Born 24/3/54. Commd 26/10/75. Sqn Ldr 1/7/85. Retd GD 1/4/88.
ALSOP D. Born 9/7/46. Commd 24/6/71. Flt Lt 24/6/73. Retd ENG 9/7/93.
ALSOP The Rev E. G., ALCD. Born 19/4/12. Commd 13/9/39. Retd 19/4/67 Gp Capt.
ALTERSKYE J. A. Born 20/11/44. Commd 5/12/63. Flt Lt 4/5/72. Retd GD(G) 30/12/72.
ALTON V. E. G., OBE. Born 18/9/17. Commd 16/6/41. Wg Cdr 1/1/52. Retd RGT 25/9/67.
AMBLER J., BEng MRAeS. Born 1/3/39. Commd 2/10/61. Wg Cdr 1/7/82. Retd GD 4/10/91.
AMBLER K. T. W., MBE. Born 22/3/32. Commd 12/12/51. Sqn Ldr 1/7/69. Retd GD 27/2/76.
AMBLER M. J. Born 2/9/42. Commd 16/9/71. Sqn Ldr 16/9/78. Retd ADMIN 1/10/87.
AMBRIDGE E. G. Born 28/9/07. Commd 8/1/32. Wg Cdr 1/7/48. Retd SUP 28/9/60.
AMBRIDGE F. Born 15/7/29. Commd 1/6/72. Flt Lt 1/6/76. Retd ENG 10/12/84.
AMBROSE D. W. Born 22/3/34. Commd 4/7/69. Flt Lt 4/7/73. Retd ENG 22/3/94.
AMBROSE E. A., AFC. Born 25/2/26. Commd 31/8/50. Flt Lt 27/5/54. Retd GD 31/1/76.
AMBROSE M. D. Born 17/12/36. Commd 20/5/82. Flt Lt 20/5/85. Retd ADMIN 18/12/88.
AMBROSE M. P. W. Born 25/3/35. Commd 8/5/56. Flt Lt 8/11/61. Retd GD 10/2/89.
AMDOR J. A. R., BSocSc MCIPD MIMgt. Born 13/12/40. Commd 5/1/65. Sqn Ldr 1/7/76. Retd ADMIN 26/4/91.
AMES J. G. Born 5/5/21. Commd 30/9/54. Flt Lt 10/3/59. Retd ENG 21/1/69.
AMEY P. N., BSc. Born 30/7/54. Commd 17/9/72. Sqn Ldr 1/1/87. Retd ENG 30/7/92.

AMIES D. R., MB BS FRCS(Edin) MRCS LRCP. Born 18/10/34. Commd 30/9/62. Wg Cdr 14/8/71. Retd MED 1/10/74.
AMIES J. N. Born 14/8/38. Commd 7/6/68. Flt Lt 7/6/70. Retd ENG 30/10/76. Reinstated 18/6/80. Flt Lt 24/1/74. Retd ENG 14/8/88.
AMIES N. F., CEng MIMechE. Born 22/11/40. Commd 4/2/64. Sqn Ldr 1/7/77. Retd ENG 22/11/95.
AMIN J. S. Born 24/10/44. Commd 4/10/63. Flt Lt 4/4/69. Retd GD 1/9/76.
AMOR G., MBE. Born 7/10/22. Commd 30/5/45. Wg Cdr 1/7/65. Retd GD 7/10/77.
AMOR R. L., AFC. Born 31/7/10. Commd 1/4/40. Sqn Ldr 1/7/51. Retd GD(G) 31/7/60 rtg Wg Cdr.
AMOR S. R. W. Born 19/10/15. Commd 23/1/39. Sqn Ldr 1/7/48. Retd SUP 23/10/64 rtg Wg Cdr.
AMOR T. J., MB ChB. Born 6/8/57. Commd 5/9/78. Wg Cdr 1/8/94. Retd MED 6/8/95.
AMOS A. K. Born 3/7/30. Commd 26/3/52. Gp Capt 1/7/73. Retd GD 31/12/77.
AMOS D. G., MBE. Born 8/4/32. Commd 29/10/64. Flt Lt. 29/10/69. Retd ENG 1/9/86.
AMOS S. A. Born 9/10/62. Commd 22/11/84. Flt Lt 3/11/87. Retd ADMIN 9/10/00.
AMOS V. E. Born 24/9/33. Commd 31/3/59. Sqn Ldr 31/10/67. Retd EDN 31/3/75.
AMROLIWALLA F. K., BSc MB BS FRCP DPH DIH DAvMed. Born 21/2/33. Commd 2/5/66. A Cdre 19/11/91. Retd MED 21/2/98.
ANCELL G. Born 12/11/53. Commd 18/1/73. Sqn Ldr 1/7/92. Retd GD 23/12/95.
ANDERS J. N., BSc. Born 3/7/40. Commd 9/9/63. Flt Lt 9/12/64. Retd GD 9/9/79.
ANDERS R. G. Born 9/7/39. Commd 25/10/73. Flt Lt 25/10/75. Retd SEC 25/10/81.
ANDERSON A. Born 9/2/34. Commd 15/7/53. Flt Lt 5/10/60. Retd GD 10/12/87.
ANDERSON A. F., DSO* DFC. Born 21/11/10. Commd 15/1/34. Gp Capt 1/7/52. Retd GD 19/12/57.
ANDERSON A. J., CEng MIEE MRAeS. Born 19/1/42. Commd 7/5/63. Sqn Ldr 1/1/73. Retd ENG 19/1/80.
ANDERSON A. W. Born 25/6/43. Commd 10/12/65. Flt Lt 6/10/71. Retd GD 31/1/76.
ANDERSON B. E. Born 4/8/32. Commd 27/1/67. Flt Lt 27/1/69. Retd SUP 27/1/75.
ANDERSON B. M., MIMgt. Born 2/12/36. Commd 8/5/56. Flt Lt 7/3/62. Retd GD 2/12/94.
ANDERSON B. R. Born 4/2/34. Commd 12/3/60. Flt Lt 12/9/65. Retd GD 5/2/77.
ANDERSON B. S. Born 21/2/32. Commd 14/5/57. Sqn Ldr 1/1/68. Retd GD 1/1/71.
ANDERSON C. G., BEd. Born 8/1/56. Commd 30/3/86. Flt Lt 30/9/89. Retd SUP 14/3/96.
ANDERSON C. McK., BA. Born 28/5/62. Commd 30/10/83. Flt Lt 30/4/87. Retd ADMIN 22/10/89.
ANDERSON C. S. M., MBE. Born 30/4/39. Commd 13/12/60. Sqn Ldr 1/1/73. Retd GD 13/12/85.
ANDERSON D. D., MBE. Born 22/2/33. Commd 27/3/52. A Cdre 1/1/84. Retd SY 22/8/87.
ANDERSON D. J. Born 2/1/32. Commd 17/12/52. Sqn Ldr 1/1/75. Retd SUP 2/1/75.
ANDERSON D. M., BSc CEng MRAeS. Born 24/6/46. Commd 28/9/64. A Cdre 1/1/93. Retd ENG 1/12/95.
ANDERSON D. S., BSc. Born 9/5/61. Commd 11/12/83. Flt Lt 11/6/86. Retd GD 11/12/99.
ANDERSON E. W. Born 19/4/24. Commd 23/3/62. Flt Lt 29/3/67. Retd ENG 7/7/79.
ANDERSON G. G., MHCIMA. Born 28/1/54. Commd 11/10/84. Flt Lt 11/10/86. Retd ADMIN 14/3/96.
ANDERSON H. C. N. Born 7/2/23. Commd 1/2/49. Sqn Ldr 1/7/58. Retd GD 4/4/64.
ANDERSON H. S. Born 26/9/23. Commd 12/9/60. Flt Lt 12/9/66. Retd GD 4/10/68.
ANDERSON I. V., MB ChB DPH. Born 14/3/29. Commd 2/2/58. Wg Cdr 23/3/70. Retd MED 2/2/74.
ANDERSON J. A. Born 2/5/29. Commd 4/7/51. Flt Lt 17/10/56. Retd GD 3/5/71.
ANDERSON J. D. Born 22/4/22. Commd 18/11/53. Flt Lt 18/11/58. Retd GD(G) 31/1/73.
ANDERSON J. D., BSc. Born 20/10/40. Commd 5/12/66. Flt Lt 5/9/68. Retd GD 7/11/82.
ANDERSON J. D., MBE. Born 18/3/57. Commd 20/5/82. Sqn Ldr 1/1/91. Retd ADMIN 18/3/98.
ANDERSON J. D., BSc. Born 20/10/40. Commd 5/12/66. Flt Lt 5/9/68. Retd GD 1/4/94.
ANDERSON J. E., MIMgt. Born 20/9/17. Commd 22/9/55. Flt Lt 22/9/61. Retd ENG 3/10/72.
ANDERSON J. G., BSc. Born 23/4/39. Commd 3/12/61. Sqn Ldr 1/7/74. Retd GD 23/4/94.
ANDERSON J. P., OBE. Born 23/11/43. Commd 14/8/64. Wg Cdr 1/7/85. Retd GD 23/11/98.
ANDERSON K. L., MIMgt. Born 4/11/47. Commd 1/8/69. Sqn Ldr 1/1/81. Retd ADMIN 4/11/88.
ANDERSON L. E. Born 19/11/46. Commd 11/6/81. Sqn Ldr 1/1/89. Retd ADMIN 19/5/01.
ANDERSON L. J., MBE CEng MIEE MIMgt. Born 30/11/29. Commd 5/12/51. Wg Cdr 1/1/75. Retd ENG 1/10/82.
ANDERSON M., DPhysEd. Born 1/1/39. Commd 15/8/65. Flt Lt 19/3/68. Retd ADMIN 1/9/76.
ANDERSON M. F. Born 6/3/43. Commd 8/11/68. Fg Offr 22/3/71. Retd SUP 28/7/73.
ANDERSON M. I. S., MVO. Born 22/9/31. Commd 25/9/52. Sqn Ldr 1/7/83. Retd GD 22/4/92.
ANDERSON M. J., MSc BSc. Born 1/7/53. Commd 25/9/74. Sqn Ldr 1/7/87. Retd ENG 1/12/92.
ANDERSON M. N., BSc. Born 22/1/64. Commd 20/8/89. Flt Lt 20/3/92. Retd ENG 4/5/92.
ANDERSON N. J. C. Born 9/9/54. Commd 28/11/74. Sqn Ldr 1/7/89. Retd GD 15/7/93.
ANDERSON R. Born 27/11/29. Commd 12/3/52. Flt Lt 12/9/56. Retd GD 27/11/67.
ANDERSON R. C., BSc. Born 12/3/42. Commd 30/9/61. Sqn Ldr 1/7/73. Retd ENG 12/3/80.
ANDERSON R. W. Born 8/9/46. Commd 21/4/67. Flt Lt 4/5/72. Retd GD 1/10/76.
ANDERSON S. E. Born 5/6/47. Commd 6/9/68. Flt Lt 9/11/74. Retd SEC 22/1/79.
ANDERSON T. L., BSc MRAeS. Born 20/2/31. Commd 9/7/54. Sqn Ldr 1/7/70. Retd GD 1/7/73.
ANDERSZ S. T. R. Born 16/3/18. Commd 1/9/39. Flt Lt 1/7/46. Retd SEC 1/4/73.
ANDERSZ T., DFC. Born 27/9/18. Commd 1/3/41. Flt Lt 15/3/53. Retd GD(G) 27/9/73.
ANDERTON D. J. Born 13/2/44. Commd 28/10/66. Flt Lt 28/4/72. Retd GD 7/10/78.
ANDERTON M. B. Born 12/4/42. Commd 29/11/63. Flt Lt 29/5/69. Retd GD 14/1/76. Re-instated 6/10/72 to 21/12/82.

ANDREW A. G. Born 29/10/60. Commd 15/10/81. Flt Lt 15/4/87. Retd GD 27/12/98.
ANDREW D. Born 25/5/21. Commd 26/10/43. Flt Lt 4/6/53. Retd GD 31/7/68.
ANDREW D., MBE AFC. Born 26/1/23. Commd 14/7/44. Sqn Ldr 1/7/58. Retd GD 26/1/72.
ANDREW D. Born 5/11/40. Commd 8/11/68. Sqn Ldr 1/1/77. Retd GD 1/1/91.
ANDREW D. R., MB ChB. Born 20/6/55. Commd 24/10/78. Sqn Ldr 1/2/87. Retd MED 24/10/94.
ANDREW J. M. T. Born 25/8/54. Commd 6/7/80. Flt Lt 6/7/85. Retd ADMIN 1/10/88.
ANDREW R., MBE. Born 12/6/24. Commd 26/2/44. Sqn Ldr 1/7/71. Retd SEC 12/6/79.
ANDREWS A., MSc BSc(Eng) CEng ACGI MRAeS. Born 9/7/34. Commd 22/12/55. A Cdre 1/1/83.
    Retd ENG 3/11/85.
ANDREWS A. E. Born 6/12/30. Commd 8/11/62. Sqn Ldr 1/1/80. Retd ENG 15/3/83.
ANDREWS C. W., BSc DCAe CEng MRAeS MIEE. Born 3/3/34. Commd 2/2/56. Sqn Ldr 2/8/66. Retd EDN 3/3/72.
ANDREWS D. C., MBE FRIN. Born 1/4/44. Commd 12/7/63. A Cdre 1/1/96. Retd GD 1/4/99.
ANDREWS F. L., BA. Born 6/1/55. Commd 16/9/73. Flt Lt 15/10/79. Retd SUP 15/7/88.
ANDREWS F. S. Born 8/9/37. Commd 11/6/60. Flt Lt 26/7/67. Retd GD(G) 19/1/76.
ANDREWS G. D. Born 28/5/37. Commd 29/7/58. Sqn Ldr 1/1/69. Retd GD 24/10/69.
ANDREWS G. N. Born 14/1/43. Commd 10/11/80. Sqn Ldr 1/7/91. Retd ADMIN 14/1/98.
ANDREWS G. R. Born 1/12/38. Commd 30/10/57. Flt Lt 18/2/64. Retd PRT 31/7/65.
ANDREWS J. Born 20/9/35. Commd 15/2/62. Flt Lt 1/4/66. Retd GD 20/9/73.
ANDREWS J. B., CEng MIEE FRAeS. Born 25/4/36. Commd 23/7/58. Gp Capt 1/7/79. Retd ENG 28/5/83.
ANDREWS J. W. T., TD CEng MIMechE. Born 25/4/33. Commd 20/2/72. Wg Cdr 1/7/82. Retd ENG 25/6/91.
ANDREWS M. A. Born 27/12/32. Commd 4/9/58. Flt Lt 4/12/64. Retd ADMIN 30/9/67. Re-employed 1/3/71.
    Sqn Ldr 1/7/74. Retd 1/6/83.
ANDREWS M. L. Born 19/5/60. Commd 11/1/79. Flt Lt 11/7/84. Retd GD 19/5/98.
ANDREWS P. D., BEM. Born 26/7/57. Commd 26/9/91. Flt Lt 26/9/93. Retd ADMIN 14/3/96.
ANDREWS R., BA. Born 15/10/33. Commd 18/10/55. Sqn Ldr 1/7/64. Retd GD 18/10/71.
ANDREWS R. C. Born 21/9/18. Commd 14/8/43. Flt Lt 14/2/47. Retd GD 21/9/68.
ANDREWS R. M. Born 6/9/50. Commd 10/9/70. Flt Lt 10/3/77. Retd GD(G) 6/9/88.
ANDREWS S. A. Born 12/10/47. Commd 28/11/69. Flt Lt 28/5/75. Retd GD 12/10/85.
ANDREWS S. C. Born 26/9/42. Commd 3/1/72. Flt Lt 13/1/74. Retd GD 14/4/96.
ANDREWS The Rev E. R. Born 17/8/33. Commd 29/12/69. Retd 1/5/88 Wg Cdr.
ANDREWS W. D. B. Born 8/3/32. Commd 30/9/53. Sqn Ldr 1/7/82. Retd GD 23/8/88.
ANDRZEIEWSKI S. J., AFC. Born 21/11/17. Commd 1/3/41. Flt Lt 1/9/45. Retd GD(G) 1/7/69.
ANFIELD J. E. Born 16/2/52. Commd 8/9/83. Flt Lt 8/9/85. Retd ADMIN 8/9/92.
ANGEL B. L. Born 27/4/33. Commd 29/5/56. Flt Lt 13/4/60. Retd GD 1/12/83.
ANGEL R. Born 10/12/53. Commd 3/1/78. Flt Lt 3/1/80. Retd GD 31/7/93.
ANGELA D. W. F. Born 19/7/38. Commd 19/9/60. Gp Capt 1/1/86. Retd GD 17/5/95.
ANGELL A. P. Born 27/5/44. Commd 28/6/79. Flt Lt 28/6/82. Retd GD 31/12/93.
ANGELL E. E. M., AFC. Born 18/9/14. Commd 10/2/36. Wg Cdr 1/7/47. Retd GD 10/11/61.
ANGELL H. E., DFC. Born 1/11/16. Commd 29/6/36. Wg Cdr 1/7/52. Retd GD 1/11/71.
ANGELL K. G. Born 18/4/20. Commd 17/7/43. Flt Lt 14/11/56. Retd GD 20/2/68.
ANGELL T. J., BSc CEng MIEE. Born 6/6/12. Commd 28/1/43. Fg Offr 29/1/44. Retd ENG 28/3/46 rtg Flt Lt.
ANGUS G. Born 27/10/25. Commd 6/7/45. Flt Lt 1/3/61. Retd GD 7/5/73.
ANGUS I. J. McI. Born 2/7/39. Commd 23/9/66. Sqn Ldr 1/7/91. Retd GD 2/7/94.
ANGUS J. A. Born 29/3/47. Commd 1/3/68. Plt Offr 1/3/68. Retd GD 20/11/68.
ANGUS P. J. M., MBE BA. Born 15/2/55. Commd 9/12/76. Wg Cdr 1/7/93. Retd OPS SPT 6/4/01.
ANGUS S. G. Born 28/3/58. Commd 9/12/76. Flt Lt 9/6/83. Retd ADMIN 30/12/86.
ANNABLE K. Born 6/8/22. Commd 19/6/44. Sqn Ldr 1/1/62. Retd GD 5/9/69.
ANNAL E., CEng MIEE MRAeS. Born 23/10/33. Commd 5/5/60. Sqn Ldr 1/7/72. Retd ENG 2/4/85.
ANNAN R. H., DSO. Born 8/8/17. Commd 3/11/40. Wg Cdr 1/7/52. Retd GD 12/3/55.
ANNAND K.P., MA MSc. Born 9/7/37. Commd 30/9/55. Sqn Ldr 1/1/67. Retd ENG 9/7/75.
ANNE G. C., OBE. Born 11/2/06. Flt Lt 21/1/25. Retd SUP 11/8/26 rtg Sqn Ldr.
ANNING J. A., BA. Born 9/10/36. Commd 6/4/62. Fg Offr 6/10/62. Retd GD 30/8/65.
ANNING T. V. Born 24/12/42. Commd 17/5/79. Flt Lt 17/5/84. Retd GD 17/4/93.
ANSCOMBE M. R. J. Born 7/9/38. Commd 30/5/59. Sqn Ldr 1/1/74. Retd GD 1/4/79.
ANSCOMBE P. C., AFC DFM. Born 24/10/13. Commd 19/5/42. Flt Lt 19/5/44. Retd GD 8/6/47.
ANSDELL D. J. Born 19/5/27. Commd 3/11/51. Flt Lt 14/5/58. Retd GD 19/5/65.
ANSELL A. N. Born 8/8/24. Commd 23/1/50. Flt Lt 21/12/59. Retd GD 12/7/65.
ANSELL V. B., DFC. Born 29/4/15. Commd 2/6/44. Flt Lt 2/6/50. Retd GD(G) 23/8/61.
ANSELL W. T. K. Born 15/2/30. Commd 6/4/50. Flt Lt 19/11/53. Retd GD 20/8/71.
ANSLEY J. H. Born 3/11/32. Commd 2/7/52. Flt Lt 27/11/57. Retd GD 3/11/70.
ANSLEY R. J. H. Born 27/1/22. Commd 25/5/44. Flt Lt 25/11/47. Retd GD 27/1/65.
ANSTEAD E. W. Born 4/3/34. Commd 11/6/52. Flt Lt 28/9/60. Retd GD 9/9/79.
ANSTEAD J. S. Born 15/10/46. Commd 28/4/67. Flt Lt 28/4/72. Retd GD 1/3/75.
ANSTEE R. E., AFC AFM. Born 11/2/24. Commd 23/1/64. Flt Lt 23/1/67. Retd GD 1/9/73.
ANSTEY B. G., MInstAM. Born 10/12/37. Commd 26/3/59. Gp Capt 1/7/83. Retd SY(PRT) 10/12/87.

ANSTISS R., DipTech DipSoton MPhil CPhys CEng MInstP MIEE. Born 30/1/40. Commd 13/2/72. Sqn Ldr 1/1/78. Retd ENG 13/2/88.
ANTHONY E., MD ChB FRCPsych DCH DPM. Born 26/10/30. Commd 3/2/57. Gp Capt 3/2/80. Retd MED 30/8/89.
ANTHONY J. D. E. Born 7/2/57. Commd 28/10/76. Flt Lt 28/4/82. Retd GD 1/8/94.
ANTHONY K., MIMgt. Born 5/12/26. Commd 14/11/51. Sqn Ldr 1/1/62. Retd GD 12/11/73.
ANTHONY K. F. Born 1/3/43. Commd 2/6/77. Flt Lt 2/6/79. Retd GD 2/6/85.
ANTHONY S. T. Born 30/8/58. Commd 17/7/87. Flt Lt 17/8/90. Retd OPS SPT 30/8/99.
ANTLIFF D. M. Born 28/3/48. Commd 24/11/67. Flt Lt 24/5/73. Retd GD 28/3/86.
ANTON D. J., MSc MB BS MFOM MRCS LRCP DAvMed. Born 25/1/46. Commd 27/1/69. Wg Cdr 25/5/85. Retd MED 1/4/93.
ANTONIAK T. P. Born 26/6/20. Commd 17/5/56. Sqn Ldr 1/1/72. Retd GD 26/6/75.
APIAFI H. Born 8/9/41. Commd 23/9/66. Flt Lt 1/7/69. Retd GD 8/9/79.
APPLEBOOM K. J., MIMgt. Born 18/5/26. Commd 3/5/46. Wg Cdr 1/7/69. Retd GD 18/5/81.
APPLEBY B. K. Born 12/5/46. Commd 6/5/66. Sqn Ldr 1/7/96. Retd GD 12/5/01.
APPLEBY M. W. Born 29/9/47. Commd 31/7/86. Flt Lt 31/7/90. Retd ENG 1/10/93.
APPLEBY N. E. Born 31/12/44. Commd 26/9/62. Flt Lt 4/11/70. Retd GD 31/12/82.
APPLEFORD K. E., AFC. Born 11/2/25. Commd 6/1/55. Sqn Ldr 1/1/70. Retd GD 11/2/83.
APPLEGARTH E. W. Born 20/5/22. Commd 30/8/43. Flt Lt 4/1/51. Retd PE 20/5/70.
APPLEGARTH G. F. Born 23/11/24. Commd 30/7/64. Flt Lt 20/7/67. Retd GD 18/8/73.
APPLEGARTH P. N. J., BSc. Born 29/10/57. Commd 5/9/76. Flt Lt 15/4/81. Retd GD 6/1/89.
APPLEGATE D. S. Born 2/10/31. Commd 23.9/53. Sqn Ldr 1/7/65. Retd ENG 2/10/69.
APPLETON J. G. Born 8/6/17. Commd 7/5/53. Sqn Ldr 1/7/62. Retd ENG 5/8/67.
APPLETON J. H. Born 18/4/19. Commd 23/10/43. Flt Lt 23/4/47. Retd GD 18/4/62.
APPLETON S. G. Born 1/5/48. Commd 1/8/69. Gp Capt 1/7/94. Retd ADMIN 14/3/96.
APPLETON W. A., OBE. Born 16/12/15. Commd 3/10/43. Wg Cdr 1/1/60. Retd ENG 16/12/70.
APPLEYARD B. Born 11/8/22. Commd 29/10/43. Flt Lt 7/1/52. Retd GD 11/8/77.
APPLEYARD D. R. Born 22/4/32. Commd 22/5/75. Flt Lt 22/5/78. Retd GD 7/9/83.
APPLEYARD F., FIMgt. Born 4/7/37. Commd 18/4/51. Gp Capt 1/1/78. Retd GD 4/7/86.
APPLEYARD G. K., BA. Born 7/4/35. Commd 12/7/57. Sqn Ldr 15/3/65. Retd EDN 18/4/78.
APPLEYARD K. D. Born 24/3/48. Commd 11/5/78. Sqn Ldr 1/1/85. Retd SUP 11/5/92.
APPLEYARD R. J., MSc BEng CEng MRAeS. Born 12/6/55. Commd 5/9/76. Sqn Ldr 1/1/90. Retd ENG 12/6/93.
APPS R. M. Born 25/2/45. Commd 11/4/85. Sqn Ldr 1/7/96. Retd ENG 25/8/00.
ARAM G. D., MBE. Born 10/6/43. Commd 12/1/62. Sqn Ldr 1/7/81. Retd GD 10/6/98.
ARBER J. C. Born 23/4/28. Commd 25/5/50. Sqn Ldr 1/1/62. Retd GD 22/6/74.
ARBER R. C. Born 2/2/53. Commd 20/9/79. Flt Lt 20/9/81. Retd GD 2/2/91.
ARCHBELL T. H., DFC. Born 23/10/14. Commd 16/5/38. Sqn Ldr 1/9/45. Retd GD 11/7/47 rtg Wg Cdr.
ARCHBOLD D. A., BA MIMgt. Born 20/2/45. Commd 15/7/66. Sqn Ldr 1/1/76. Retd ADMIN 20/2/89. rtg Acting Wg Cdr.
ARCHBOLD F. Born 29/6/21. Commd 16/6/44. Flt Lt 16/12/47. Retd GD 28/6/70.
ARCHBOLD J. F. P. Born 28/8/21. Commd 1/4/45. Sqn Ldr 1/7/66. Retd GD(G) 28/8/76.
ARCHER D. F. Born 10/8/27. Commd 22/8/63. Flt Lt 22/8/68. Retd ENG 29/8/75.
ARCHER H. D., DFC. Born 10/7/22. Commd 5/9/42. Wg Cdr 1/1/61. Retd GD 10/7/77.
ARCHER H. M., AFC MRAeS. Born 25/3/27. Commd 21/3/52. Gp Capt 1/1/73. Retd GD 2/9/80.
ARCHER J. A. Born 28/11/47. Commd 11/10/84. Flt Lt 11/10/88. Retd ENG 31/12/96.
ARCHER J. P. Born 18/8/37. Commd 29/12/76. Sqn Ldr 1/1/86. Retd GD 2/8/95.
ARCHER L. G., CEng FIMgt MIEE. Born 6/11/44. Commd 17/12/64. Gp Capt 1/1/91. Retd ENG 1/5/94.
ARCHER M. G., BSc. Born 3/12/62. Commd 30/1/81. Flt Lt 15/10/87. Retd ENG 1/6/92.
ARCHER P. J. Born 19/2/10. Commd 18/9/41. Flt Lt 1/9/45. Retd ENG 4/10/59 rtg Sqn Ldr.
ARCHER R. N., OBE. Born 24/12/22. Commd 24/5/44. Wg Cdr 1/7/65. Retd GD 24/12/77.
ARCHER-JONES K. E., BSc. Born 6/6/54. Commd 16/9/73. Gp Capt 1/1/97. Retd ENG 1/5/99.
ARCHIBALD D. Born 23/2/50. Commd 3/1/69. Flt Lt 1/6/76. Retd SUP 23/4/77.
ARDEN R. W., ACA. Born 2/9/47. Commd 7/3/71. Flg Offr 7/9/71. Retd SEC 30/11/74.
ARDLEY B. Born 10/12/34. Commd 19/12/59. Gp Capt 1/1/84. Retd SY 20/1/87.
ARGALL I. H. A., MCIPS MIMgt. Born 5/4/38. Commd 5/3/57. Sqn Ldr 1/7/70. Retd SUP 5/4/96.
ARGUE D. W., BEM. Born 3/4/31. Commd 8/11/68. Sqn Ldr 1/7/82. Retd ENG 29/9/86.
ARKELL-HARDWICK G. H. Born 20/5/40. Commd 23/12/58. Sqn Ldr 1/1/70. Retd GD 1/2/79.
ARKIESON D. S. Born 13/8/56. Commd 22/5/75. Flt Lt 22/11/81. Retd GD(G) 13/8/85.
ARKLEY J. D., BA. Born 11/9/36. Commd 31/8/62. Flt Lt 15/2/64. Retd GD 23/11/82.
ARM D. A. Born 19/5/25. Commd 21/4/44. Sqn Ldr 1/10/55. Retd GD 30/1/76.
ARMIGER B., OBE. Born 5/8/18. Commd 17/4/39. Wg Cdr 1/7/59. Retd SUP 31/12/68.
ARMIGER N. S. Born 21/4/39. Commd 23/12/58. Sqn Ldr 1/1/84. Retd GD(G) 21/4/94.
ARMITAGE A. Born 3/12/30. Commd 13/8/52. Flt Lt 20/2/58. Retd GD 3/12/88.
ARMITAGE A., BA. Born 2/4/47. Commd 13/10/85. Sqn Ldr 1/7/89. Retd ADMIN 22/10/94.
ARMITAGE F. S. Born 3/6/29. Commd 6/5/65. Flt Lt 6/5/68. Retd GD 3/6/87
ARMITAGE G. D. Born 6/2/31. Commd 10/8/59. Flt Lt 27/6/61. Retd GD (G) 6/2/86.
ARMITAGE H., MIMgt. Born 20/12/24. Commd 20/7/45. Wg Cdr 1/1/68. Retd GD 31/5/72.

ARMITAGE J. Born 9/4/16. Commd 12/6/58. Sqn Ldr 6/7/67. Retd MED(T) 1/5/70.
ARMITAGE Sir Michael, KCB CBE. Born 25/8/30. Commd 14/4/53. ACM 1/7/86. Retd GD 5/4/90.
ARMITAGE-MADDOX S. E. Born 11/11/56. Commd 20/7/78. Flt Lt 12/1/85. Retd SUP 20/7/86.
ARMOUR A. E., MIMgt. Born 25/4/31. Commd 19/1/66. Sqn Ldr 1/1/80. Retd ENG 25/4/91.
ARMOUR P. MacD. Born 12/5/28. Commd 5/4/50. Flt Lt 5/10/52. Retd GD 15/10/54.
ARMSON The Rev B. R., AIB. Born 21/6/46. Commd 17/8/86. Retd 31/7/87 Flt Lt.
ARMSTRONG B., BA. Born 19/11/56. Commd 16/12/79. Sqn Ldr 1/7/89. Retd GD 7/12/97.
ARMSTRONG B. R. Born 9/9/56. Commd 23/11/78. Wg Cdr 1/1/95. Retd GD 31/7/98.
ARMSTRONG C., MIMgt. Born 22/5/23. Commd 20/4/50. Wg Cdr 1/1/73. Retd SUP 31/3/77.
ARMSTRONG C., CEng MIMechE MRAeS. Born 18/3/35. Commd 2/11/62. Sqn Ldr. 1/7/69. Retd ENG 7/11/78.
ARMSTRONG C. Born 24/4/52. Commd 16/3/73. Sqn Ldr 1/1/81. Retd GD 24/4/90.
ARMSTRONG D. Born 3/11/37. Commd 24/9/59. Flt Lt 1/4/66. Retd ENG 3/11/75.
ARMSTRONG E. P. Born 19/3/36. Commd 19/9/59. Flt Lt 19/3/65. Retd GD 15/10/88.
ARMSTRONG G. P. Born 3/2/39. Commd 19/2/76. Flt Lt 19/2/81. Retd ENG 12/12/83.
ARMSTRONG G. R., BSc. Born 28/2/55. Commd 25/2/79. Flt Lt 25/5/80. Retd GD 1/6/99.
ARMSTRONG G. W. Born 30/10/11. Commd 31/12/42. Flt Lt 6/1/57. Retd SEC 30/10/66.
ARMSTRONG J. Born 4/2/35. Commd 13/12/55. Sqn Ldr 1/1/68. Retd GD 4/2/73.
ARMSTRONG J. D., MBE. Born 9/3/37. Commd 19/9/57. Wg Cdr 1/7/81. Retd GD 9/3/92.
ARMSTRONG J. G. Born 12/11/23. Commd 13/4/44. Sqn Ldr 1/1/55. Retd GD 12/11/61.
ARMSTRONG J. M. Born 29/5/60. Commd 28/6/79. Flt Lt 28/12/84. Retd GD 31/7/98.
ARMSTRONG J. S. Born 30/9/29. Commd 8/11/51. Flt Lt 24/4/68. Retd GD 16/5/81.
ARMSTRONG L. I., MCIPS. Born 4/5/43. Commd 24/4/70. Sqn Ldr 1/7/84. Retd SUP 2/5/89.
ARMSTRONG M. J., FHCIMA. Born 23/6/45. Commd 9/11/65. Gp Capt 1/7/90. Retd ADMIN 14/3/96.
ARMSTRONG N. I., BA. Born 7/2/34. Commd 21/6/56. Sqn Ldr 21/12/66. Retd EDN 30/6/72.
ARMSTRONG N. J., MCIPS. Born 9/11/44. Commd 3/10/69. Sqn Ldr 1/1/83. Retd SUP 14/3/96.
ARMSTRONG P. J. Born 15/4/30. Commd 11/4/51. Sqn Ldr 1/1/62. Retd GD 5/12/75.
ARMSTRONG P. W. Born 4/5/41. Commd 3/1/64. Sqn Ldr 1/1/74. Retd GD 13/8/79.
ARMSTRONG P. W. Born 20/9/60. Commd 7/8/87. Flt Lt 27/9/90. Retd ENG 23/4/94.
ARMSTRONG R., MBE. Born 13/12/23. Commd 12/6/44. Flt Lt 3/7/48. Retd GD 21/12/61.
ARMSTRONG R. L., CEng MIEE. Born 26/1/20. Commd 18/11/43. Sqn Ldr 1/1/56. Retd ENG 17/12/73.
ARMSTRONG S. W. Born 3/1/31. Commd 20/6/51. Flt Lt 20/12/55. Retd GD 3/1/69.
ARMSTRONG T., CEng MIEE. Born 9/5/30. Commd 27/4/65. Flt Lt 27/1/67. Retd ENG 1/10/76.
ARMSTRONG W., MBE. Born 29/1/44. Commd 17/5/79. Sqn Ldr 1/1/88. Retd ADMIN 28/5/94.
ARMSTRONG W. J. A. Born 26/5/23. Commd 11/9/42. Flt Lt 29/3/51. Retd GD 28/1/68.
ARNAUD J. R., DFC. Born 23/8/20. Commd 11/1/43. Sqn Ldr 1/1/68. Retd GD 23/8/75.
ARNEY J. W. Born 22/6/14. Commd 27/7/35. Wg Cdr 1/7/47. Retd GD 31/10/57.
ARNOLD A. V. Born 22/7/34. Commd 28/4/61. Flt Lt 9/2/68. Retd GD 21/12/76.
ARNOLD C. Born 12/3/35. Commd 7/1/71. Flt Lt 7/1/73. Retd SUP 7/1/79.
ARNOLD D. J. B. Born 25/11/36. Commd 27/3/56. Flt Lt 1/8/62. Retd GD(G) 3/4/80.
ARNOLD M., OBE BSc(Eng) CEng MRAeS MIMgt. Born 24/12/38. Commd 12/9/61. Gp Capt 1/1/85.
    Retd GD 24/12/93.
ARNOLD M. D. Born 24/2/28. Commd 15/8/51. Flt Lt 15/5/57. Retd GD 25/1/67.
ARNOLD M. E. Born 9/10/62. Commd 25/2/82. Flt Lt 25/8/87. Retd GD 9/8/91.
ARNOLD P. Born 7/6/49. Commd 2/5/69. Sqn Ldr 1/7/84. Retd SUP 7/6/93.
ARNOLD S., MBE MIMgt. Born 14/12/18. Commd 26/4/45. Sqn Ldr 1/7/55. Retd RGT 14/12/73.
ARNOLD S. P. Born 18/10/63. Commd 28/7/88. Flt Lt 24/5/92. Retd GD(G) 14/3/96.
ARNOLD W. J. Born 7/3/21. Commd 21/10/54. Sqn Ldr 1/7/69. Retd ENG 7/6/73.
ARNOTT R. D., CBE FIMgt MCIPD. Born 4/3/39. Commd 7/1/58. A Cdre 1/7/87. Retd GD 28/6/96.
ARNOTT R. M. H. Born 28/9/40. Commd 22/5/64. Flt Lt 22/11/69. Retd GD 1/6/86.
ARNOTT W., AFC. Born 13/3/16. Commd 31/8/40. Flt Lt 1/9/45. Retd GD(G) 13/3/71 rtg Sqn Ldr.
ARROWSMITH F. B., BSc. Born 25/3/30. Commd 15/11/51. Sqn Ldr 25/3/63. Retd EDN 25/3/68.
ARROWSMITH R. H., BEM. Born 8/11/41. Commd 19/7/84. Sqn Ldr 1/7/91. Retd ENG 2/7/93.
ARSCOTT J. R. D. Born 19/4/47. Commd 23/3/66. AVM 1/7/99. Retd OPS SPT 18/4/01.
ARSCOTT K. M. Born 15/1/43. Commd 21/10/64. Flt Lt 21/10/70. Retd SEC 1/3/73.
ARSCOTT P. M. Born 13/7/49. Commd 27/2/70. Flt Lt 28/8/75. Retd GD 23/5/81.
ARSCOTT R. H., CBE. Born 18/9/24. Commd 18/1/44. Gp Capt. 1/1/70. Retd GD 3/4/79.
ARTHUR J. R. G., BSc. Born 9/6/54. Commd 6/5/76. Sqn Ldr 1/1/90. Retd GD 14/9/96.
ARTHUR L., DFC. Born 15/10/19. Commd 28/7/43. Flt Lt 28/1/47. Retd GD 2/7/47.
ARTHUR L. T. Born 9/5/35. Commd 2/1/54. Sqn Ldr 1/1/68. Retd GD 9/5/73.
ARTHUR P. J., MBE. Born 17/4/36. Commd 23/7/58. Gp Capt 1/1/81. Retd ENG 17/4/90.
ARTUS E. D. Born 22/4/20. Commd 7/3/47. Flt Lt 7/9/51. Retd SUP 27/5/56.
ARTUS E. G., BSc CEng MIOSH MRAeS MIMgt. Born 22/12/46. Commd 22/9/65. Wg Cdr 1/1/91.
    Retd ENG 14/3/97.
ARULANANDAM E. A. A. Born 12/7/44. Commd 25/8/67. Flt Lt 25/2/74. Retd SUP 7/2/83. Re-entered 6/7/90.
    Flt Lt 6/7/90. Retd SUP 6/7/96.
ARUNDEL I., BEM. Born 2/1/54. Commd 16/2/89. Flt Lt 16/2/89. Retd ENG 1/1/93.

ARUNDELL W. H. Born 10/1/21. Commd 10/5/44. Flt Lt 1/9/45. Retd PE 10/1/76.
ASBURY M. J. A. Born 30/4/39. Commd 24/9/59. Flt Lt 1/7/68. Retd GD 30/4/77.
ASH C. S., BSc. Born 8/8/52. Commd 3/9/72. Flt Lt 15/4/76. Retd GD 14/9/96.
ASH The Rev J. R. L. Born 13/6/17. Commd 10/2/50. Retd 13/9/72 Wg Cdr.
ASH J. S., BA. Born 15/7/53. Commd 17/6/79. Flt Lt 17/9/82. Retd SUP 2/1/85.
ASH P. D. Born 8/7/31. Commd 5/12/51. Flt Lt 5/6/56. Retd GD 31/10/75.
ASHBY D. W. Born 12/6/24. Commd 8/6/44. Sqn Ldr 1/9/65. Retd GD 13/6/74.
ASHBY M. F. Born 14/11/33. Commd 7/5/52. Flt Lt 2/10/57. Retd GD 14/11/71.
ASHBY P. McE. Born 15/3/60. Commd 5/4/79. Flt Lt 5/10/84. Retd GD 1/5/91.
ASHCROFT J. B., MB BCh FRCR DMR(D). Born 29/1/47. Commd 27/1/69. Wg Cdr 26/7/84. Retd MED 29/1/85.
ASHDOWN B. Born 23/8/19. Commd 15/4/43. Sqn Ldr 1/1/57. Retd ENG 23/8/68.
ASHE M. J. Born 23/12/23. Commd 13/3/46. Sqn Ldr 1/1/60. Retd RGT 23/12/68.
ASHFORD A. M., BSc. Born 7/4/65. Commd 15/9/86. Flt Lt 15/1/90. Retd GD 15/7/99.
ASHFORD F., FTCL ARCM. Born 30/10/36. Commd 15/6/83. Flt Lt 15/3/81. Retd DM 31/10/89.
ASHFORD R. G., CBE LLB. Born 2/5/31. Commd 27/2/52. AVM 1/7/83. Retd GD 12/9/85.
ASHFORD-SMITH R. P. Born 10/5/25. Commd 29/4/53. Flt Lt 29/4/59. Retd GD 10/5/63.
ASHFORTH-SMITH A. J., BA. Born 8/2/54. Commd 11/9/83. Sqn Ldr 1/7/94. Retd SUP 14/3/97.
ASHLEIGH-THOMAS P. D., BSc BSc CEng MIEE MRAeS MIMgt. Born 29/1/40. Commd 6/3/63. Sqn Ldr 1/7/75.
    Retd ENG 7/8/88. Rtg Wg Cdr.
ASHLEY B. A., AFC. Born 10/1/28. Commd 21/3/51. Wg Cdr 1/1/69. Retd GD 6/5/77.
ASHLEY G. M., MInstAM(Dip). Born 20/12/34. Commd 20/6/63. Flt Lt 17/3/71. Retd ADMIN 20/12/89.
ASHLEY M. S. Born 1/7/42. Commd 26/8/81. Flt Lt 25/9/69. Retd GD 12/1/93.
ASHLEY N. J. Born 6/9/42. Commd 25/1/63. Flt Lt 6/3/68. Retd GD 6/9/80.
ASHLEY, K. F., OBE BDS FDSRCS FRCS LRCP. Born 3/4/34. Commd 29/2/60. Gp Capt 19/4/82. Retd DEL 1/9/88.
ASHMAN G. C., AIIP. Born 17/10/35. Commd 11/11/65. Sqn Ldr 1/7/79. Retd ENG 25/8/82.
ASHMAN J.K. Born 6/6/30. Commd 20/12/51. Flt Lt 22/5/57. Retd GD 6/6/68.
ASHMORE P. A., MRIN. Born 2/6/38. Commd 3/7/56. Sqn Ldr 1/1/73. Retd GD 2/6/88.
ASHMORE P. E., BSc. Born 14/7/51. Commd 25/2/72. Sqn Ldr 1/1/84. Retd ENG 1/6/91.
ASHOVER D. R., AFC. Born 8/6/31. Commd 17/5/51. Flt Lt 6/9/56. Retd GD 5/4/72.
ASHTON D. Born 20/6/49. Commd 3/10/69. Sqn Ldr 1/1/90. Retd GD(G) 1/10/95.
ASHTON E. R. Born 28/4/21. Commd 29/4/45. Flt Lt 10/11/55. Retd GD 14/12/69.
ASHTON J. M. Born 25/11/39. Commd 26/10/66. Sqn Ldr 1/7/76. Retd GD 18/7/88. Reinstated 15/8/90. Sqn Ldr
    29/7/78. Retd GD 25/11/94.
ASHTON J. T. Born 15/8/46. Commd 21/1/66. Flt Lt 21/7/71. Retd GD 26/8/77.
ASHTON The Venerable L. J., CB. Born 27/6/15. Commd 15/5/45. Retd 1/7/73. AVM.
ASHTON M. A., MB BS MRCPath. Born 6/3/57. Commd 20/9/81. Wg Cdr 20/9/94. Retd MED 14/3/96.
ASHTON M. D. Born 3/3/43. Commd 22/2/63. Flt Lt 22/8/68. Retd GD 3/3/81.
ASHTON R. Born 16/2/36. Commd 14/8/56. Flt Lt 14/2/62. Retd GD 16/2/91.
ASHTON T. Born 2/9/28. Commd 11/1/50. Flt Lt 30/11/55. Retd GD 2/9/66.
ASHTON-JONES K. Born 12/5/42. Commd 12/6/62. Gp Capt 1/7/87. Retd ADMIN 2/4/94.
ASHURST D. Born 25/11/46. Commd 27/6/71. Flt Lt 27/3/74. Retd ENG 18/10/75.
ASHWORTH A. D. Born 23/10/26. Commd 25/7/52. Flt Lt 5/12/55. Retd GD 19/6/73.
ASHWORTH J. Born 9/8/42. Commd 11/8/77. Sqn Ldr 1/1/91. Retd GD(G) 22/4/94.
ASHWORTH J. N. L., BA. Born 11/9/48. Commd 5/10/75. Wg Cdr 5/10/85. Retd LGL 5/10/91.
ASHWORTH K. Born 15/9/63. Commd 10/5/90. Flt Lt 10/5/92. Retd SUP 14/3/96.
ASHWORTH R. C. B. Born 3/8/28. Commd 11/4/51. Sqn Ldr 1/7/72. Retd GD 17/6/77.
ASHWORTH S. P. Born 24/4/66. Commd 4/7/85. Flt Lt 4/1/90. Retd GD 12/5/97.
ASKER H. A., DFC DFM. Born 22/4/20. Commd 8/11/41. Sqn Ldr 1/7/51. Retd GD 22/4/63.
ASKHAM W. D., OBE CEng FIMgt MRAeS. Born 19/3/31. Commd 12/2/53. Gp Capt 1/1/74. Retd ENG 20/6/88.
ASPIN P. D. Born 15/11/31. Commd 7/6/68. Sqn Ldr 1/7/78. Retd ENG 15/4/82.
ASPINALL K. P. Born 5/6/45. Commd 19/12/79. Sqn Ldr 1/1/87. Retd SUP 1/5/90.
ASPINALL M., BA. Born 30/5/59. Commd 4/7/82. Sqn Ldr 1/7/91. Retd ADMIN 4/1/97.
ASPLIN D. J. Born 30/7/56. Commd 27/3/75. Wg Cdr 1/1/93. Retd GD(G) 1/1/96.
ASPY J. T. Born 12/9/16. Commd 10/6/44. Flt Lt 4/1/51. Retd SEC 12/9/65.
ASSHETON W. R., DFC. Born 12/12/17. Commd 6/3/39. Sqn Ldr 1/8/47. Retd GD 22/11/57.
ASTLE J. Born 23/8/10. Commd 9/5/41. Sqn Ldr 1/8/47. Retd SEC 23/8/59.
ASTLE M. H., MBE. Born 29/4/43. Commd 12/1/62. Sqn Ldr 1/7/91. Retd GD 3/5/94.
ASTLEY P. M. Born 27/11/15. Commd 1/8/36. Wg Cdr 12/9/45. Retd GD 15/12/47 rtg Gp Capt.
ASTLEY-COOPER N. F., BEng. Born 11/7/49. Commd 16/11/72. Sqn Ldr 1/1/83. Retd ENG 16/1/91.
ASTON A. A. Born 1/9/37. Commd 17/5/56. Sqn Ldr 1/7/69. Retd SUP 1/4/77.
ASTON A. B. Born 2/3/44. Commd 13/6/74. Flt Lt 13/6/76. Retd GD 13/6/84.
ASTON A. J. Born 14/2/13. Commd 21/2/46. Flt Lt 21/8/50. Retd SUP 14/2/62 rtg Sqn Ldr.
ASTON B. J. Born 7/9/29. Commd 19/8/71. Sqn Ldr 1/1/81. Retd ENG 7/5/88.
ASTON C. J. Born 29/8/48. Commd 13/9/70. Sqn Ldr 1/1/81. Retd ADMIN 13/9/86.
ASTON F. C., DFC TD. Born 12/9/19. Commd 1/9/45. Sqn Ldr 1/7/53. Retd RGT 29/3/58.
ATCHISON I. W., BDS. Born 20/12/26. Commd 29/9/50. Wg Cdr 17/7/63. Retd DEL 29/9/66.

ATHERLEY D. M. K. Born 11/4/31. Commd 30/7/52. Wg Cdr 1/7/80. Retd GD 11/4/86.
ATHERTON D. A., FIMgt. Born 2/4/31. Commd 9/4/52. A. Cdre 1/7/82. Retd ADMIN 1/8/84.
ATHERTON D. W. Born 26/8/36. Commd 11/1/79. Sqn Ldr 1/1/89. Retd MED(SEC) 1/6/93.
ATHERTON S. P. Born 16/5/57. Commd 9/8/79. Wg Cdr 1/1/96. Retd SUP 21/11/98.
ATKIN C. H. Born 26/4/21. Commd 7/9/44. Flt Lt 12/12/52. Retd GD 29/1/63.
ATKINS A. R., CEng MIEE. Born 30/4/26. Commd 25/5/50. Wg Cdr 1/1/67. Retd ENG 1/5/74.
ATKINS C. V. Born 14/2/29. Commd 7/12/49. Flt Lt 27/12/55. Retd GD 14/2/67.
ATKINS C. W. F. Born 6/11/45. Commd 11/3/65. Flt Lt 11/9/71. Retd ENG 12/3/75.
ATKINS D. MacD. Born 2/9/40. Commd 5/11/59. Flt Lt 9/2/68. Retd SEC 21/8/68.
ATKINS P. B., OBE MIMgt. Born 31/5/43. Commd 9/3/62. Wg Cdr 1/7/85. Retd GD 17/3/93.
ATKINS P. C. Born 30/7/37. Commd 29/7/58. Gp Capt 1/7/86. Retd SUP 30/7/92.
ATKINS P. J. Born 8/11/40. Commd 18/12/62. Sqn Ldr 1/1/77. Retd GD 8/11/95.
ATKINS W. A. Born 10/2/21. Commd 11/6/45. Flt Lt 19/6/52. Retd GD 25/2/65.
ATKINSON A. B. Born 26/3/43. Commd 17/5/63. Flt Lt 17/11/68. Retd GD 2/10/73.
ATKINSON A. J. Born 16/11/36. Commd 12/11/80. Flt Lt 25/2/67. Retd GD 16/11/93.
ATKINSON A. R. Born 2/4/14. Commd 3/2/44. Flt Lt 3/8/47. Retd ENG 24/10/53.
ATKINSON A. T., OBE MIMgt. Born 20/4/35. Commd 25/10/61. Wg Cdr 1/7/72. Retd GD 20/4/93.
ATKINSON A. W. W., OBE AFC. Born 4/9/24. Commd 9/6/45. Gp Capt 1/1/74. Retd GD 31/3/78.
ATKINSON B. C., OBE. Born 20/6/36. Commd 7/12/61. Wg Cdr 1/7/76. Retd ADMIN 20/6/94.
ATKINSON Sir David, KBE MB ChB FRCP(Edin) FFCM FFOM. Born 29/9/24. Commd 3/3/49. AM 1/7/81. Retd MED 29/9/84.
ATKINSON D. M., BEng CEng FIIE(elec) MIEE. CDipAF. Born 30/3/58. Commd 13/9/81. Flt Lt 15/7/86 ENG 30/3/97. Retd ENG 30/3/97.
ATKINSON D. R. Born 17/3/29. Commd 9/4/52. Sqn Ldr 1/7/62. Retd GD 14/5/76. Reinstated 9/7/80. Sqn Ldr 26/8/66. Retd GD 17/3/89.
ATKINSON E. J., CEng FIEE DipEl. Born 21/10/23. Commd 1/9/45. Wg Cdr 1/1/67. Retd ENG 17/3/78.
ATKINSON E. L., MBE. Born 7/9/25. Commd 14/11/51. Wg Cdr 1/1/71. Retd ADMIN 7/9/80.
ATKINSON G. B., BSc CEng MIMechE MRAeS. Born 20/2/45. Commd 15/7/65. Flt Lt 15/4/70. Retd ENG 31/7/76.
ATKINSON G. E. Born 27/9/18. Commd 22/2/44. Flt Lt 24/2/50. Retd SEC 6/2/65.
ATKINSON H. E., IEng. Born 11/11/30. Commd 31/10/69. Flt Lt 31/10/74. Retd ENG 9/1/91.
ATKINSON J. Born 26/6/26. Commd 25/6/53. Flt Lt 25/12/56. Retd GD 26/6/64.
ATKINSON J. Born 11/5/33. Commd 30/1/52. Flt Lt 13/11/57. Retd GD 11/5/71.
ATKINSON J. A. Born 10/6/20. Commd 11/10/41. Sqn Ldr 1/1/53. Retd GD 10/6/63.
ATKINSON J. C., CBE FIMgt. Born 15/10/28. Commd 27/7/49. A Cdre 1/1/77. Retd GD 12/11/83.
ATKINSON K. R. Born 5/9/52. Commd 2/1/75. Sqn Ldr 1/1/91. Retd GD 5/9/94.
ATKINSON M. R. Born 13/7/42. Commd 17/12/64. Sqn Ldr 1/1/80. Retd GD 1/4/96.
ATKINSON P. Born 19/2/31. Commd 2/7/64. Sqn Ldr 1/7/76. Retd GD(AEO) 30/4/89.
ATKINSON P. R. Born 31/7/59. Commd 25/8/80. Flt Lt 25/8/86. Retd GD 31/7/97.
ATKINSON R. C., BSc. Born 4/4/54. Commd 17/9/72. Flt Lt 15/10/76. Retd GD 15/7/87.
ATKINSON R. C., AFC. Born 4/12/41. Commd 9/10/64. Sqn Ldr 1/1/82. Retd GD 11/10/97.
ATKINSON R. E. Born 9/5/34. Commd 17/12/52. Sqn Ldr 1/7/65. Retd GD 10/5/74.
ATKINSON R. F. Born 5/9/24. Commd 21/4/44. Sqn Ldr 1/4/55. Retd GD 3/7/76.
ATKINSON S. D. Born 17/2/36. Commd 30/8/62. Sqn Ldr 1/7/75. Retd ADMIN 1/10/82.
ATKINSON T. E. Born 15/11/48. Commd 22/9/69. Flt Lt 22/3/76. Retd ENG 15/11/86.
ATLAY P. A. Born 15/9/43. Commd 20/6/63. Wg Cdr 1/1/90. Retd GD(G) 14/9/96.
ATTARD A. M., DFM. Born 28/2/20. Commd 18/4/45. Flt Lt 4/12/52. Retd SUP 28/2/69.
ATTENBOROUGH R. G., MRCS LRCP. Born 25/2/28. Commd 18/7/54. Flt Lt 18/7/55. Retd MED 8/10/60 rtg Sqn Ldr.
ATTERWILL H. G. Born 24/9/13. Commd 12/2/42. Sqn Ldr 1/7/53. Retd ENG 22/4/58.
ATTLEE D. L., CB MVO DL. Born 2/9/22. Commd 28/1/44. AVM 1/7/75. Retd GD 2/9/77.
ATTON D. H. Born 30/1/45. Commd 30/5/71. Sqn Ldr 1/7/82. Retd ENG 30/5/90.
ATTON T. W. Born 23/3/30. Commd 25/6/66. Flt Lt 25/6/71. Retd SUP 1/5/75.
ATTRIDGE A. R., MBE. Born 21/3/29. Commd 28/7/60. Wg Cdr 1/1/77. Retd Admin 21/3/84.
ATTRILL A. J. Born 27/6/34. Commd 30/7/59. Wg Cdr 1/7/76. Retd SUP 30/6/84.
ATTRYDE R A J. Born 30/8/43. Commd 30/7/59. Flt Lt 18/12/84. Retd GD 30/3/94.
ATTWOOD A. I., MB BS FRCS(Edin) MRCS LRCP. Born 6/5/48. Commd 29/7/68. Wg Cdr 30/8/85. Retd MED 1/1/94.
ATTWOOD D. J. Born 11/4/50. Commd 15/9/69. Flt Lt 26/8/75. Retd GD 22/10/94.
AUBREY K. Born 21/3/52. Commd 28/7/88. Flt Lt 28/7/92. Retd MED(SEC) 10/10/95.
AUBREY N., BSc CEng MIMechE MINucE. Born 30/9/36. Commd 15/1/63. Sqn Ldr 1/7/70. Retd 6/11/76.
AUBREY-REES G. W. Born 17/7/18. Commd 21/2/42. Flt Lt 17/12/48. Retd GD(G) 28/4/63.
AUDHLAM-GARDINER B. G. P., MMar MIMgt. Born 22/1/34. Commd 22/10/63. Sqn Ldr 22/10/63. Retd GD(G) 22/1/92.
AUDLEY H. M. Born 19/3/30. Commd 3/2/52. Flt Lt 9/2/62. Retd SEC 22/6/75.
AUDSLEY D. MacR. Born 20/5/38. Commd 26/5/61. Flt Lt 26/11/66. Retd GD 16/7/68.
AUKETT J. Born 14/1/35. Commd 29/4/54. Sqn Ldr 1/7/75. Retd ADMIN 14/1/90.

AULT J., DFC. Born 3/9/33. Commd 8/6/59. Wg Cdr 1/1/76. Retd GD 29/1/87.
AUST W. F. Born 23/11/24. Commd 9/12/48. Flt Lt 3/12/52. Retd GD 23/11/62.
AUSTEN-SMITH Sir Roy, KBE CB DFC. Born 28/6/24. Commd 7/4/44. AM 1/7/79. Retd GD 1/11/81.
AUSTIN C. Born 7/3/25. Commd 18/5/45. Sqn Ldr 1/1/61. Retd GD 28/9/68.
AUSTIN D. A. Born 11/5/23. Commd 12/4/45. Sqn Ldr 1/1/56. Retd GD 14/5/66.
AUSTIN F. H. P., OBE. Born 11/8/16. Commd 7/9/40. Wg Cdr 1/1/54. Retd GD 3/4/65.
AUSTIN G. P., BA. Born 22/11/46. Commd 4/6/72. Flt Lt 4/9/73. Retd GD 4/6/88.
AUSTIN J. A. G. Born 21/7/12. Commd 24/8/40. Flt Offr 1/9/45. Retd SEC 21/7/61.
AUSTIN J. R. Born 26/12/44. Commd 28/2/64. Flt Lt 12/11/69. Retd GD 26/6/82.
AUSTIN J. W. Born 26/7/21. Commd 23/8/56. Flt Lt 23/8/59. Retd GD 27/9/68.
AUSTIN K. P. Born 3/1/34. Commd 14/12/54. Sqn Ldr 1/1/66. Retd SEC 29/7/75.
AUSTIN M. F., MA FCII MIMgt DMS. Born 30/1/33. Commd 22/2/55. Flt Lt 25/2/57. Retd GD(G) 30/1/93.
AUSTIN P. D. A., AFC. Born 20/7/31. Commd 4/4/51. Wg Cdr 1/7/69. Retd GD 23/7/74.
AUSTIN P. G. Born 20/1/43. Commd 8/12/61. Sqn Ldr 1/1/80. Retd GD 26/4/84.
AUSTIN R. A. Born 30/1/30. Commd 25/5/50. Wg Cdr 1/7/75. Retd GD(G) 30/1/85.
AUSTIN S. P., FCA. Born 16/4/13. Commd 17/4/39. Wg Cdr 1/7/54. Retd SEC 17/4/68.
AUSTIN Sir Roger., KCB AFC FRAeS. Born 9/3/40. Commd 18/2/58. AM 6/4/92. Retd GD 22/5/97.
AUSTIN T. S. Born 14/9/38. Commd 8/1/57. Sqn Ldr 1/7/73. Retd GD 14/9/93.
AUSTIN W. R., BSc. Born 24/4/46. Commd 28/2/72. Flt Lt 28/5/73. Retd GD 14/9/96.
AUSTIN-VAUTIER S. W., BSc. Born 16/2/53. Commd 14/9/75. Wg Cdr 1/7/90. Retd ADMIN 2/12/93.
AUTIE P. G. Born 25/9/39. Commd 6/4/62. Sqn Ldr 1/7/73. Retd SUP 26/9/94.
AUTON K. N. Born 2/11/32. Commd 12/7/51. Flt Lt 20/2/62. Retd GD 1/10/75.
AVENS R. B., MCIPD MIMgt. Born 27/4/38. Commd 28/2/57. Sqn Ldr 1/1/72. Retd SY 1/10/86.
AVERY D. G. Born 7/5/47. Commd 31/10/69. Sqn Ldr 1/1/92. Retd GD 14/12/98.
AVERY J. D., PhD BSc. Born 18/2/45. Commd 14/11/71. Sqn Ldr 6/8/76. Retd ADMIN 14/11/90.
AVERY V. G. Born 12/9/29. Commd 19/6/52. Flt Lt 19/12/55. Retd GD 21/6/80.
AVISS H. G., MBE. Born 1/6/11. Commd 2/4/53. Sqn Ldr 1/1/62. Retd ENG 1/6/68.
AVORY I. H. Born 8/5/47. Commd 3/5/60. Flt Lt 3/11/73. Retd GD 8/5/85.
AWAD H. H. F., MB ChB MRCOG. Born 20/6/52. Commd 19/11/89. Sqn Ldr 19/11/87. Retd MED 13/9/96.
AXFORD R., MBE. Born 3/8/36. Commd 12/4/73. Sqn Ldr 1/1/82. Retd ENG 6/5/87.
AYEE P. C., CBE CEng FIEE FRAeS. Born 14/1/42. Commd 5/12/63. A Cdre 1/1/94. Retd ENG 14/1/97.
AYERS C. R. Born 1/3/42. Commd 28/3/63. Sqn Ldr 1/7/84. Retd SUP 1/3/97.
AYERS J. R. Born 28/10/32. Commd 28/7/53. Flt Lt 28/1/56. Retd GD 28/10/70.
AYERS P. S. Born 25/1/56. Commd 9/5/91. Flt Lt 9/5/95. Retd ADMIN 14/12/96.
AYERS-BERRY R. L. W. Born 4/3/50. Commd 2/8/68. Flt Lt 18/1/75. Retd GD(G) 1/5/75.
AYERST P. V., DFC MIMgt. Born 4/11/20. Commd 14/12/38. Wg Cdr 1/7/68. Retd GD 5/5/73.
AYKROYD G. M. Born 5/4/43. Commd 21/12/62. Sqn Ldr 1/7/74. Retd GD 14/12/82.
AYLETT G. J., CBE CEng FIMgt MRAeS. Born 28/6/21. Commd 8/2/45. Gp Capt 1/1/69. Retd ENG 30/8/75.
AYLETT G. L., OBE. Born 8/12/35. Commd 31/7/56. Wg Cdr 1/1/80. Retd GD 8/12/90.
AYLING C. J., MHCIMA. Born 26/5/39. Commd 23/10/59. Sqn Ldr 1/1/72. Retd ADMIN 26/5/77.
AYLING L. J., MBE. Born 13/1/25. Commd 6/5/46. Sqn Ldr 1/1/60. Retd SEC 1/7/67.
AYLING R. J. Born 30/8/18. Commd 26/12/46. Flt Lt 26/12/52. Retd SEC 30/8/73.
AYLOTT L. H. Born 29/10/37. Commd 28/5/57. Flt Lt 21/8/63. Retd GD 29/10/94.
AYLWARD A. J. Born 19/4/35. Commd 9/12/53. Wg Cdr 1/1/73. Retd SUP 2/4/80.
AYLWARD D. Born 31/7/41. Commd 8/1/62. Wg Cdr 1/7/78. Retd GD 31/7/85.
AYLWARD G. A. S. Born 4/2/11. Commd 24/10/45. Flt Lt 4/1/51. Retd SEC 29/7/59.
AYO J. E. Born 21/5/36. Commd 19/8/71. Flt Lt 19/8/72. Retd ADMIN 21/5/86.
AYRE G. A., BA. Born 1/2/41. Commd 23/6/63. Flt Lt 1/7/67. Retd GD 30/3/69.
AYRE K. W. A. Born 8/9/24. Commd 9/11/45. Sqn Ldr 1/7/69. Retd GD 2/7/73.
AYRES G. A. Born 22/2/14. Commd 2/6/49. Sqn Ldr 1/1/63. Retd SEC 3/7/64.
AYRES M. L., MB BS FRCS. Born 1/2/39. Commd 14/3/70. Wg Cdr 13/9/78. Retd MED 13/4/86.
AYRES N. Born 23/10/27. Commd 2/12/53. Flt Lt 2/12/57. Retd PE 30/11/68.
AYRES S. A., MSc BSc CPhys MInstP. Born 5/12/54. Commd 19/6/83. Flt Lt 19/12/82. Retd ADMIN 5/1/91.
AYRES V. E., BA. Born 25/3/45. Commd 24/6/65. Sqn Ldr 1/1/78. Retd GD 25/3/83.
AYRIS F. R. S., AFM. Born 25/1/38. Commd 4/7/69. Flt Lt 4/5/72. Retd GD 4/7/77.
AYSHFORD J. M. Born 12/11/21. Commd 8/4/41. Gp Capt 1/1/66. Retd GD 12/11/76.
AZIZ S. I., BSc DMS FIMgt. Born 3/10/37. Commd 24/6/68. Fg Offr 5/9/67. Retd SEC 31/10/70.
AZZARO P. G. Born 19/12/41. Commd 30/7/63. Flt Lt 13/10/69. Retd GD 30/5/94.

# B

BAATZ A. P. Born 21/3/60. Commd 10/2/83. Flt Lt 10/8/88. Retd GD 14/3/96.
BABBINGTON F. T. Born 17/9/19. Commd 5/1/64. Flt Lt 5/1/64. Retd GD(G) 17/9/69.
BABBINGTON J. D., BTech. Born 21/6/51. Commd 15/9/71. Sqn Ldr 1/1/87. Retd GD 1/1/90.
BABLER P. E. O., CEng MRAeS. Born 29/7/38. Commd 30/7/59. Sqn Ldr 1/1/71. Retd ENG 4/8/76.
BABRAFF J. K. L. Born 25/11/46. Commd 22/12/67. Sqn Ldr 1/7/82. Retd GD 1/7/85.
BACH G. I., BSc CEng MRAeS MIEE MIMgt. Born 5/5/33. Commd 7/9/56. Gp Cpt 1/1/77. Retd ENG 22/8/78.
BACK A. H. C., MBE AFC MA BSc. Born 30/5/30. Commd 21/10/51. Sqn Ldr 1/7/60. Retd GD 21/7/69.
BACK R. C., BA. Born 23/8/48. Commd 24/9/67. Flt Lt 15/10/71. Retd GD 23/8/86.
BACKHOUSE D. H. W., BTech. Born 19/3/45. Commd 27/10/70. Wg Cdr 1/1/88. Retd ENG 31/10/00.
BACON A. Born 28/6/42. Commd 19/8/71. Wg Cdr 1/1/86. Retd ADMIN 1/2/89.
BACON C. E. Born 13/3/41. Commd 25/8/67. Sqn Ldr 1/1/78. Retd GD(G) 13/3/96.
BACON F. C. G. Born 27/3/31. Commd 21/10/66. Sqn Ldr 1/1/86. Retd ENG 27/12/91.
BACON G. A. Born 19/8/51. Commd 3/8/75. Fg Offr 3/2/76. Retd GD 6/9/77.
BACON G. McA. Born 16/6/30. Commd 20/6/52. A Cdre 1/1/79. Retd GD 3/9/84.
BACON J. C. Born 9/3/60. Commd 15/8/85. Flt Lt 12/5/88. Retd ADMIN 29/3/91.
BACON S. H. Born 7/4/19. Commd 19/8/42. Sqn Ldr 1/7/53. Retd ENG 7/4/68.
BACON S. W. G., ACMA MIMgt. Born 25/10/38. Commd 1/3/68. Wg Cdr 1/7/86. Retd ADMIN 25/10/88.
BACON T. J., OBE. Born 30/5/42. Commd 12/7/79. Wg Cdr 1/1/92. Retd ADMIN 3/6/96.
BADCOCK H. F. Born 16/1/22. Commd 22/10/59. Sqn Ldr 1/7/71. Retd ENG 16/7/75.
BADDELEY E. S., CEng FRAeS FIMgt. Born 6/12/23. Commd 16/9/43. A Cdre 1/1/74. Retd ENG 25/3/78.
BADDOCK R. J. Born 30/9/33. Commd 30/12/55. Flt Lt 30/6/61. Retd GD 30/9/71.
BADLEY P. I. Born 18/6/22. Commd 20/11/43. Flt Lt 5/7/49. Retd GD(G) 30/3/77.
BAERSELMAN J. C. K. Born 7/8/36. Commd 4/4/57. Sqn Ldr 1/7/67. Retd GD 8/1/77.
BAFF R. N. Born 27/2/27. Commd 9/1/50. Flt Lt 11/11/54. Retd GD 7/10/65.
BAGG W. L., OBE DFC. Born 17/9/20. Commd 12/9/42. Wg Cdr 1/1/64. Retd SUP 17/4/75.
BAGGALEY W. N. Born 4/1/24. Commd 3/1/46. Sqn Ldr 1/7/74. Retd GD(G) 7/5/76.
BAGGLEY K. J. Born 31/1/60. Commd 11/1/79. Sqn Ldr 1/7/90. Retd GD 31/1/98.
BAGGOTT J. P., MBE MA MSc CEng MIEE. Born 18/1/57. Commd 5/9/76. Sqn Ldr 1/1/88. Retd ENG 18/1/95.
BAGGULEY W. Born 9/7/36. Commd 29/4/58. Flt Lt 7/8/64. Retd GD 10/4/88.
BAGLEY C. Born 27/2/39. Commd 2/2/78. Sqn Ldr 1/1/88. Retd ENG 2/9/93.
BAGLEY D. C. Born 6/10/60. Commd 16/2/89. Flt Lt 16/2/91. Retd ENG 6/10/98.
BAGLEY L., BA. Born 1/7/39. Commd 6/9/61. Fg Offr 6/9/63. Retd SEC 23/4/65.
BAGLEY W. K., BA. Born 13/2/32. Commd 9/9/54. Sqn Ldr 17/2/63. Retd EDN 9/9/70.
BAGNALL A. C., BA. Born 11/12/62. Commd 7/12/86. Flt Lt 7/6/90. Retd ADMIN 14/3/97.
BAGNALL J. C., BSc. Born 11/11/45. Commd 27/10/70. Sqn Ldr 1/1/84. Retd GD 1/5/96.
BAGNALL R. A. Born 17/7/44. Commd 14/8/64. Sqn Ldr 1/1/95. Retd GD 17/7/99.
BAGSHAW D. R., AFC. Born 28/2/37. Commd 4/6/62. Sqn Ldr 1/7/82. Retd GD 28/2/92.
BAGSHAW F. Born 15/10/06. Commd 23/4/53. Flt Lt 23/4/56. Retd ENG 23/4/63.
BAGSHAW G. Born 13/1/32 Commd 14/1/53. Sqn Ldr 1/7/63. Retd GD 13/1/87.
BAGSHAW M., MB BCh MRCS LRCP DAvMed AFOM MRAeS. Born 9/7/46. Commd 29/11/70. Sqn Ldr 26/7/79.
  Retd MED 29/11/86.
BAGSHAW T. W., MRAeS MIMgt. Born 26/7/20. Commd 15/4/43. Sqn Ldr 1/1/63. Retd ENG 25/5/73.
BAIGENT P. Born 22/2/33. Commd 19/8/53. Flt Lt 15/8/62. Retd GD 22/2/71.
BAILEY A. A. Born 6/4/36. Commd 26/3/64. Flt Lt 16/6/69. Retd GD(G) 14/12/77.
BAILEY A. A. Born 2/7/47. Commd 8/4/82. Sqn Ldr 1/1/90. Retd ENG 31/3/94.
BAILEY A. C. Born 11/2/33. Commd 11/11/71. Sqn Ldr 1/1/81. Rtd ENG 6/4/83.
BAILEY B. J., MSc BSc CEng MRAeS. Born 22/8/51. Commd 15/9/69. Sqn Ldr 1/1/84. Retd ENG 12/12/89.
BAILEY C. Born 27/11/46. Commd 1/4/66. Flt Lt 1/10/71. Retd GD 6/12/75.
BAILEY C. A., BEM MIMgt. Born 24/4/28. Commd 11/3/65. Flt Lt 11/3/70. Retd ENG 16/1/79. Reinstated 17/9/80
  to 12/12/86
BAILEY C. T. Born 8/1/55. Commd 15/12/88. Flt Lt 15/12/30. Retd GD 1/8/96.
BAILEY D. A., DFC. Born 28/4/20. Commd 2/11/42. Sqn Ldr 1/7/63. Retd GD 12/6/69.
BAILEY D. A. F., MIMgt ACIS. Born 3/10/41. Commd 24/9/64. Wg Cdr 1/7/80. Retd ADMIN 5/4/93.
BAILEY D. G., CB CBE FIMgt. Born 12/9/24. Commd 26/1/48. AVM 1/7/76. Retd GD 28/7/80.
BAILEY D. J. Born 27/10/49. Commd 3/12/70. Flt Lt 27/4/75. Retd GD 27/10/87.
BAILEY D. M., MB BS. Born 5/2/66. Commd 26/2/92. Sqn Ldr 1/8/95. Retd MED 7/2/96.
BAILEY E. A., MBE. Born 25/5/13. Commd 20/5/43. Fg Off 23/7/46. Retd SUP 17/12/47 rtg Flt Lt.
BAILEY G., MSc CBiol MIBiol FIMLS MIMgt. Born 31/10/32. Commd 2/1/70. Wg Cdr 1/7/75. Retd MED(T) 1/7/88.
BAILEY G. H. Born 30/3/25. Commd 6/2/50. Flt Lt 6/2/54. Retd MAR 1/3/59.
BAILEY G. M., AFC. Born 11/4/25. Commd 1/4/45. Sqn Ldr 1/7/56. Retd GD 28/2/68.

BAILEY G. P. B. Born 28/3/22. Commd 16/6/44. Wg Cdr 1/7/64. Retd GD 19/10/67.
BAILEY I. C. Born 20/5/43. Commd 26/5/67. Flt Lt. 15/9/70. Retd ENG 20/5/82.
BAILEY J. D. Born 18/4/47. Commd 29/2/66. Flt Lt 25/8/71. Retd GD 18/4/85.
BAILEY J. F., BSc. Born 15/3/36. Commd 28/11/58. Sqn Ldr 18/8/68. Retd EDN 30/8/75.
BAILEY J. H. Born 8/2/53. Commd 16/9/76. Sqn Ldr 1/7/88. Retd ENG 1/7/91.
BAILEY J. W. Born 16/1/47. Commd 20/10/83. Sqn Ldr 1/1/92. Retd MED(SEC) 14/3/96.
BAILEY K. J. Born 25/7/30. Commd 1/10/55. Sqn Ldr 1/1/64. Retd GD 2/10/83
BAILEY L. M., MBE. Born 16/10/23. Commd 14/12/45. Sqn Ldr 1/7/59. Retd GD 16/10/66.
BAILEY M. J. Born 3/3/24. Commd 10/3/44. Flt Lt 10/9/47. Retd GD 15/3/67.
BAILEY N. P. Born 24/9/56. Commd 8/10/87. Flt Lt 8/10/89. Retd GD(G) 8/10/95.
BAILEY R., MRAeS. Born 1/7/51. Commd 4/7/69. Sqn Ldr 1/1/87. Retd GD 1/1/90.
BAILEY R., AFC. Born 1/10/14. Commd 13/6/40. Sqn Ldr 1/8/47. Retd SEC 14/12/68.
BAILEY R., FHCIMA MCIPD. Born 28/4/35. Commd 9/6/54. Sqn Ldr 1/1/68. Retd ADMIN 28/4/93.
BAILEY R. C. Born 28/9/35. Commd 15/9/60. Flt Lt 15/3/65. Retd GD 28/9/73.
BAILEY R. C. Born 21/4/52. Commd 16/3/73. Flt Lt 16/3/76. Retd GD 21/4/90.
BAILEY The Rev R. W. Born 30/1/49. Commd 29/6/75. Retd 29/6/99 Wg Cdr.
BAILEY S. W. Born 13/5/09. Commd 7/11/41. Flt Lt 1/9/45. Retd ENG 13/5/58.
BAILEY T. G., BA BEd. Born 27/6/43. Commd 21/7/65. Flt Lt 15/4/70. Retd GD 30/4/76. Reinstated 3/7/79.
   Flt Lt 3/7/79. Retd ADMIN 30/4/90.
BAILEY W. B. Born 13/8/46. Commd 30/1/70. Fg Offr 30/1/72. Retd GD 3/8/76.
BAILLIE M. B. Born 7/8/39. Commd 24/8/72. Flt Lt. 24/8/74. Retd GD 15/4/82.
BAILLIE S., OBE. Born 17/9/22. Commd 15/9/44. A Cdre 1/1/74. Retd SUP 31/3/77.
BAIN C. J. Born 5/4/44. Commd 28/9/62. Sqn Ldr 1/7/81. Retd GD 1/10/94.
BAIN G. D. Born 1/1/22. Commd 16/10/43. Sqn Ldr 1/7/70. Retd GD 1/7/73.
BAIN G. D. P., LLB. Born 27/7/45. Commd 31/10/66. Flt Lt 31/7/68. Retd GD 1/3/75.
BAINBRIDGE A. C. Born 23/8/61. Commd 13/3/80. Sqn Ldr 1/7/94. Retd OPS SPT 26/12/99.
BAINBRIDGE A. R., BA. Born 1/7/29. Commd 6/2/52. Flt Offr 6/8/57. Retd SEC 1/1/58.
BAINBRIDGE B., MBE DFC. Born 20/12/22. Commd 7/7/44. Wg Cdr 1/7/62. Retd GD(G) 20/12/71.
BAINBRIDGE R. G. Born 12/4/24. Commd 12/2/46. Flt Lt 26/5/55. Retd GD 12/4/67.
BAINBRIDGE R. T., AFC. Born 21/6/16. Commd 22/6/41. Wg Cdr 1/1/55. Retd GD 23/7/66.
BAINBRIDGE S. W., OBE MRAeS. Born 25/7/26. Commd 27/3/52. Gp Capt 1/1/78. Retd GD 25/7/81.
BAINES A. P. Born 2/12/33. Commd 1/12/59. Flt Lt 11/10/63. Retd GD 23/1/78.
BAINES W. S. Born 18/11/44. Commd 15/7/66. Sqn Ldr 1/7/86. Retd GD 29/2/96.
BAIRD B. S. McI. Born 2/11/58. Commd 28/2/82. Flt Lt 28/2/87. Retd ENG 1/3/90.
BAIRD G. M. Born 28/10/13. Commd 13/3/39. Flt Lt 1/9/45. Retd GD 12/2/63.
BAIRD Sir John., KBE MB ChB FRCP(Edin) FRCS(Edin) FFOM FRAeS DAvMed. Born 25/7/37. Commd 3/11/63.
   AM 24/2/97. Retd MED 16/6/00.
BAIRD P. D. A. Born 19/1/20. Commd 12/11/43. Flt Lt 30/6/57. Retd GD(G) 6/9/64.
BAIRD W. R. Born 11/10/03. Commd 29/5/26. Sqn Ldr 1/8/38. Retd GD 9/1/43.
BAIRSTO Sir Peter, KBE CB AFC CIMgt. Born 3/8/26. Commd 10/5/46. AM 1/7/81. Retd GD 17/4/84.
BAIRSTOW G. Born 27/5/47. Commd 1/8/69. Flt Lt 1/2/72. Retd GD 27/5/91.
BAKER A. C., BSc MRAeS MIMgt. Born 25/4/36. Commd 30/11/58. Sqn Ldr 1/1/72. Retd GD 23/9/75.
BAKER A. J. R. Born 24/5/23. Commd 2/3/61. Flt Lt 2/3/64. Retd GD 13/4/73.
BAKER A. K., MIMgt. Born 17/1/24. Commd 31/7/58. Sqn Ldr 1/7/74. Retd ENG 6/5/78.
BAKER A. R. Born 20/11/36. Commd 11/5/62. Flt Lt 1/7/68. Retd GD(G) 8/1/79. Reinstated 5/3/80. Flt Lt 6/1/70.
   Retd ADMIN 20/11/91.
BAKER B. A. F. Born 13/4/47. Commd 26/8/66. Flt Lt 17/12/72. Retd OPS SPT 7/4/98.
BAKER B. P., DFM. Born 3/7/16. Commd 1/5/42. Sqn Ldr 1/4/58. Retd SEC 15/11/62.
BAKER C. Born 24/10/42. Commd 29/4/63. Flt Lt 24/10/68. Retd PRT 2/9/72.
BAKER C. Born 15/4/47. Commd 20/8/65. Flt Lt 20/2/71. Retd GD 1/6/77.
BAKER C. C. M., OBE FIMgt MCIPD. Born 7/10/19. Commd 29/11/37. A Cdre 1/7/68. Retd GD 31/7/71.
BAKER C. H. Born 4/4/15. Commd 30/7/47. Wg Cdr 1/1/56. Retd RGT 28/4/65.
BAKER C. P., CB FIMgt FCIPS. Born 14/6/38. Commd 2/10/58. AVM 1/1/90. Retd SUP 14/6/93.
BAKER D. M., OBE FIMgt. Born 4/1/48. Commd 8/9/69. Gp Capt 1/1/92. Retd ADMIN 8/9/00.
BAKER D. V. Born 29/8/33. Commd 22/7/55. Wg Cdr 1/7/74. Retd ENG 31/8/83
BAKER D.H.G., MBE BA. Born 12/4/39. Commd 30/9/58. Gp Capt 1/1/81. Retd ENG 1/5/88.
BAKER E. J., OBE MIMgt MCIPS. Born 29/4/23. Commd 24/6/43. Wg Cdr 1/7/64. Retd SUP 30/9/77.
BAKER E. J. Born 2/9/28. Commd 8/7/54. Flt Lt 1/10/67. Retd GD 2/9/83.
BAKER E. M. Born 11/9/10. Commd 24/2/43. Sqn Offr 1/7/59. Retd SEC 1/7/62.
BAKER F. Born 11/4/32. Commd 13/8/52. Flt Lt 9/1/58. Retd GD 11/4/70.
BAKER F. J. Born 24/7/24. Commd 26/11/53. Flt Lt 26/5/57. Retd GD 3/11/63.
BAKER F. M. A. Born 1/2/25. Commd 26/8/45. Sqn Ldr 1/7/64. Retd SUP 1/3/68.
BAKER F. T., BEM. Born 5/5/19. Commd 26/9/57. Sqn Ldr 1/1/67. Retd ENG 5/5/74.
BAKER G. G. Born 1/8/09. Commd 27/7/53. Flt Lt 27/1/47. Retd ENG 20/5/62.
BAKER G. H. Born 24/10/32. Commd 28/7/53. Sqn Ldr 1/7/61. Retd GD 1/9/62.
BAKER H., MBE DFC. Born 15/9/14. Commd 16/12/40. Flt Lt 16/6/44. Rtd GD(G) 15/9/69.

BAKER H. G. Born 14/3/11. Commd 21/7/41. Sqn Ldr 1/7/50. Retd SEC 14/2/59.
BAKER H. M. Born 24/4/46. Commd 2/11/88. Flt Lt 2/11/92. Retd OPS SPT 28/4/97.
BAKER I. I. Born 25/5/14. Commd 1/9/45. Flt Offr 1/9/45. Retd SEC 31/7/52.
BAKER J. D. Born 17/10/25. Commd 16/4/47. Sqn Ldr 1/1/57. Retd GD 12/1/68.
BAKER J. E. Born 1/4/64. Commd 24/3/83. Flt Lt 24/9/89. Retd SY 7/3/93.
BAKER J. F. Born 21/2/11. Commd 10/8/44. Sqn Ldr 1/1/53. Retd SUP 3/4/60.
BAKER J. M. Born 1/7/13. Commd 18/8/41. Flt Offr 1/9/45. Retd SEC 30/4/54.
BAKER J. T. Born 27/12/45. Commd 26/5/57. Flt Lt 18/2/70. Retd GD 7/10/75.
BAKER J. W. Born 12/12/45. Commd 5/2/65. Flt Lt 5/8/70. Retd GD 26/4/75.
BAKER L. A. B., AFC. Born 25/4/33. Commd 3/9/52. Wg Cdr 1/7/71. Retd GD 25/4/88.
BAKER L. J. Born 1/8/13. Commd 12/8/54. Flt Lt 12/8/57. Retd ENG 1/8/68.
BAKER L. M. Born 2/4/45. Commd 19/10/80. Flt Lt 26/2/87. Retd ADMIN 5/12/91.
BAKER M. E. Born 25/1/36. Commd 23/11/78. Flt Lt 23/11/83. Retd ENG 1/9/89.
BAKER M. G., MVO. Born 15/4/23. Commd 10/3/44. Sqn Ldr 1/9/65. Retd GD 30/9/69.
BAKER M. J. Born 18/9/32. Commd 30/1/58. Flt Lt 30/7/62. Retd GD 30/11/72.
BAKER M. J., BA. Born 4/3/39. Commd 25/3/60. Sqn Ldr 1/7/77. Retd GD 4/3/94.
BAKER M. P. C. Born 20/9/44. Commd 6/11/64. Flt Lt 4/5/72. Retd GD 22/10/94.
BAKER N. G. Born 21/7/24. Commd 29/9/45. Flt Lt 29/3/49. Retd GD 4/2/70.
BAKER P. Born 1/7/53. Commd 8/8/74. Flt Lt 8/2/81. Retd GD 1/7/91.
BAKER P., BA. Born 13/10/59. Commd 5/10/79. Flt Lt 15/4/83. Retd GD 31/1/99.
BAKER P. F. Born 29/7/37. Commd 22/7/62. Sqn Ldr 1/7/73. Retd ENG 22/1/80.
BAKER P. H., FCA Born 31/12/15. Commd 10/6/38. Sqn Ldr 1/1/50. Retd SEC 31/12/60.
BAKER P. J. Born 13/7/41. Commd 22/5/75. Flt Lt 22/5/77. Retd GD 22/5/85.
BAKER P. P., AFC. Born 2/9/25. Commd 19/10/45. Sqn Ldr 1/7/56. Retd GD 17/7/59.
BAKER P. T., MBE. Born 13/12/43. Commd 17/12/65. Wg Cdr 1/1/86. Retd GD 1/2/93.
BAKER R., OBE BSc (Eng) CEng MRAeS MIMgt. Born 25/8/38. Commd 28/11/66. Wg Cdr 1/7/80. Retd ENG 29/11/90.
BAKER R. A. H. Born 29/6/33. Commd 1/8/69. Flt Lt 1/8/73. Retd ENG 1/8/75.
BAKER R. F., BSc. Born 31/5/37. Commd 15/3/60. Sqn Ldr 15/9/70. Retd EDN 15/3/76.
BAKER R. F. Born 30/7/33. Commd 27/3/70. Flt Lt 27/3/75. Retd SEC 3/4/78.
BAKER R. J., BSc. Born 6/7/33. Commd 11/4/57. Wg Cdr 1/1/75. Retd ENG 29/10/85
BAKER R. P. Born 14/6/34. Commd 7/6/68. Flt Lt 7/6/70. Retd ENG 1/11/80.
BAKER S., DSO* DFC*. Born 19/11/18. Commd 24/11/41. Wg Cdr 1/7/75. Retd GD 20/6/66.
BAKER S. E. Born 10/6/39. Commd 15/7/58. Wg Cdr 1/7/78. Retd SUP 6/4/90.
BAKER S. E., MSc BSc CEng MIEE MIMgt. Born 2/3/59. Commd 11/9/77. Sqn Ldr 1/1/90. Retd ENG 19/7/98.
BAKER T. H., DFC DFM. Born 16/8/13. Commd 9/4/41. Wg Cdr 1/1/55. Retd GD 28/1/58.
BAKER V. W. Born 25/3/40. Commd 14/10/71. Flt Lt 14/10/73. Retd GD 14/10/81.
BAKER W. E., DFC. Born 24/3/24. Commd 17/5/47. Flt Lt 29/6/50. Retd GD 24/10/55.
BAKER W. J., MSc CEng MIEE MRAeS. Born 7/4/34. Commd 30/8/62. Sqn Ldr 23/5/70. Retd ADMIN 12/1/86.
BAKER W. J., BA. Born 1/7/26. Commd 19/10/49. Flt Offr 19/4/53. Retd EDN 8/4/60.
BALCHIN D. P. G. Born 9/8/20. Commd 21/2/46. Flt Lt 21/8/50. Retd SUP 9/8/69.
BALCHIN R. G. Born 21/3/15. Commd 3/10/46. Sqn Ldr 1/7/63. Retd SUP 21/3/70.
BALCOMBE F. J., BSc. Born 17/7/06. Commd 16/5/39. Sqn Ldr 1/10/46. Retd EDN 8/2/60.
BALD G. Born 10/6/38. Commd 16/9/76. Flt Lt 16/9/77. Retd ADMIN 16/9/84.
BALDCHIN L. A. Born 9/3/23. Commd 21/8/42. Sqn Ldr 1/10/55. Retd GD 9/3/66.
BALDIE I. S. Born 25/6/44. Commd 31/1/64. Flt Lt 31/7/69. Retd GD 1/3/75.
BALDING P. D. M. Born 29/4/42. Commd 11/5/62. Sqn Ldr 1/7/80. Retd GD(G) 29/4/86.
BALDING R. Born 4/8/46. Commd 24/2/67. Wg Cdr 1/1/90. Retd SUP 14/3/97.
BALDOCK E. J., MBE. Born 27/9/13. Commd 10/5/45. Sqn Ldr 1/1/58. Retd SEC 27/9/62.
BALDOCK K. W., OBE. Born 23/9/40. Commd 28/7/67. Wg Cdr 1/7/90. Retd ADMIN 30/4/96.
BALDOCK S. D., MBE DFM MIMgt. Born 19/2/21. Commd 14/6/43. Wg Cdr 1/7/62. Retd GD 19/2/76.
BALDWIN C. C. Born 9/5/48. Commd 1/8/69. Flt Lt 4/5/72. Retd GD 9/5/86.
BALDWIN C. F., DFM. Born 8/3/24. Commd 23/12/52. Flt Lt 23/6/56. Retd GD(G) 5/4/74.
BALDWIN C. J., AFC. Born 19/11/37. Commd 3/7/56. Sqn Ldr 1/1/73. Retd GD 19/11/92.
BALDWIN D. A. M. Born 3/9/32. Commd 31/5/51. Flt Lt 28/11/56. Retd GD 1/5/61.
BALDWIN D. J., BA. Born 18/6/48. Commd 3/1/69. Sqn Ldr 1/1/82. Retd GD 18/6/86.
BALDWIN E., DSO OBE DFC DFM. Born 11/2/16. Commd 5/11/41. Wg Cdr 1/7/54. Retd GD 11/2/71.
BALDWIN G. F. Born 5/10/32. Commd 2/7/52. Flt Lt 27/11/57. Retd GD 4/1/71.
BALDWIN N. B., CB CBE. Born 20/9/41. Commd 31/7/62. AVM 1/7/93. Retd GD 20/6/96.
BALDWIN P. A. Born 10/1/64. Commd 28/7/88. Flt Lt 18/4/91. Retd SUP 3/1/96.
BALDWIN P. H., OBE MA. Born 24/9/17. Commd 16/11/37. Gp Capt 1/1/57. Retd GD 24/9/67.
BALDWIN R. M. Born 27/11/35. Commd 9/4/57. Sqn Ldr 1/1/63. Retd GD 26/8/76.
BALDWIN S. A., MBE. Born 17/9/42. Commd 11/5/62. A Cdre 1/7/90. Retd GD 14/9/96.
BALDWYN M., MILT. Born 17/5/58. Commd 15/8/85. Flt Lt 15/8/87. Retd SUP 14/9/96.
BALEAN P. B. Born 25/8/20. Commd 23/12/39. Sqn Ldr 1/8/47. Retd GD 12/6/50.
BALES S. S., DPhysEd. Born 11/7/48. Commd 13/9/70. Sqn Ldr 1/7/82. Retd ADMIN 13/9/86.

BALFOUR A. J. C., CBE MA MB BChir FRCPath LMSSA DCP DTM&H MRAeS. Born 19/11/26. Commd 15/3/54. A Cdre 22/9/89. Retd MED 19/11/91.
BALFOUR T. Born 10/11/29. Commd 6/12/51/ Flt Lt 30/6/57. Retd GD 10/11/67.
BALFRE A. L. J. Born 26/6/49. Commd 16/9/71. Flt Lt 16/3/77. Retd GD 25/6/87.
BALGARNIE N., MBE. Born 29/1/44. Commd 12/4/73. Sqn Ldr 1/1/82. Retd ADMIN 31/1/96.
BALL A. J. W. Born 11/1/43. Commd 19/8/66. Flt Lt 16/6/69. Retd GD 11/1/81.
BALL Sir Alfred, KCB DSO DFC. Born 18/1/21. Commd 23/12/39. AM 1/7/75. Retd GD 7/4/79.
BALL B. J., DFC. Born 20/5/27. Commd 5/4/50. Wg Cdr 1/7/63. Retd GD 31/10/78.
BALL B. W., OBE MCIT MILT MIMgt. Born 16/4/39. Commd 4/6/59. Wg Cdr 1/1/77. Retd SUP 16/9/91.
BALL C. A. Born 15/1/32. Commd 2/7/52. Flt Lt 27/11/57. Retd GD 17/1/52.
BALL D. Born 23/3/20. Commd 21/2/49. Wg Cdr 1/1/66. Retd ENG 30/12/72.
BALL D. Born 13/10/29. Commd 23/8/51. Wg Cdr 1/1/72. Retd GD 9/8/83.
BALL D. B. Born 5/4/51. Commd 28/10/76. Sqn Ldr 1/7/85. Retd ENG 5/4/89.
BALL D. C. Born 27/3/31. Commd 26/3/53. Sqn Ldr 1/1/77. Retd PI 2/4/81.
BALL D. E., BSc. Born 1/11/61. Commd 29/4/84. Sqn Ldr 1/1/97. Retd OPS SPT 29/4/00.
BALL E., MBE. Born 25/11/22. Commd 5/11/53. Sqn Ldr 1/7/63. Retd SEC 18/4/69.
BALL E. H., BSc. Born 14/8/52. Commd 13/9/70. Sqn Ldr 1/7/83. Retd GD 1/7/86.
BALL F. C., DFC. Born 9/2/20. Commd 1/12/42. Flt Lt 1/6/46. Retd GD 3/3/54.
BALL J. A. Born 22/4/40. Commd 10/2/72. Flt Lt 10/2/74. Retd GD(G) 22/4/95.
BALL J. A. C. Born 11/7/40. Commd 20/9/59. Sqn Ldr 3/8/70. Retd DEL 11/7/78.
BALL J. C. Born 20/10/41. Commd 19/12/63. Sqn Ldr 1/7/73. Retd SUP 20/10/79.
BALL J. F. Born 28/12/10. Commd 2/9/43. Sqn Ldr 1/1/56. Retd ENG 28/12/65.
BALL K. A. Born 11/5/32. Commd 9/9/54. Flt Lt 9/6/56. Retd GD 9/9/70.
BALL L. A. Born 6/12/17. Commd 2/6/49. Flt Lt 2/12/52. Retd SEC 1/4/55.
BALL M. G., DFC. Born 7/4/63. Commd 24/3/83. Sqn Ldr 1/1/95. Retd GD 7/4/01.
BALL M. J. Born 4/10/37. Commd 9/11/55. Sqn Ldr 1/7/78. Retd GD(G) 4/10/92.
BALL M. W., AFC. Born 22/4/47. Commd 2/8/68. Gp Capt 1/7/91. Retd GD 23/4/97.
BALL P. G., CEng MIMechE MRAeS. Born 5/1/26. Commd 5/4/71. Sqn Ldr 5/4/71. Retd ENG 11/9/87.
BALL S. M., MInstAM ACIS. Born 29/10/50. Commd 12/12/71. Sqn Ldr 1/1/83. Retd ADMIN 2/2/92.
BALL T. A. Born 9/6/28. Commd 20/4/55. Sqn Ldr 1/1/65. Retd CAT 10/5/71.
BALL T. F., BSc MRAeS. Born 4/6/46. Commd 26/5/67. Sqn Ldr 1/1/80. Retd ENG 4/6/90.
BALLANTINE A. G. Born 18/4/24. Commd 28/9/61. Flt Lt 28/9/66. Retd GD 18/4/82.
BALLANTYNE A., MB ChB. Born 23/1/34. Commd 6/1/63. Sqn Ldr 13/8/64. Retd MED 1/6/68.
BALLANTYNE J. A. Born 3/8/40. Commd 3/10/74. Sqn Ldr 1/7/83. Retd ENG 3/8/85.
BALLINGER F. G. Born 26/3/34. Commd 14/12/72. Fg Offr 14/12/72. Retd GD(G) 8/7/75.
BALLINGER J. Born 11/2/44. Commd 22/3/63. Sqn Ldr 1/7/76. Retd GD 11/2/82.
BALMER C. H. Born 5/9/19. Commd 2/4/53. Sqn Ldr 1/1/62. Retd ENG 5/9/74.
BALMFORD D. E. Born 6/7/34. Commd 6/6/56. Flt Lt 6/3/63. Retd GD(G) 2/8/72.
BALMFORTH P. Y., CEng MRAeS MIMgt. Born 27/11/21. Commd 24/9/59. Sqn Ldr 1/1/69. Retd ENG 1/11/73.
BALMFORTH-SLATER D. L. Born 2/12/62. Commd 24/3/83. Flt Lt 24/9/89. Retd OPS SPT 2/12/00.
BALSHAW J. K., BSc. Born 9/3/30. Commd 20/8/52. Sqn Ldr 9/3/63. Retd ADMIN 20/8/80.
BAMBERGER C. S., DFC*. Born 4/5/19. Commd 9/2/42. Sqn Ldr 1/1/57. Retd/GD 29/1/59.
BAMBERGER J. Born 8/11/55. Commd 1/9/74. APO 1/9/74. Retd GD 3/11/77.
BAMFIELD R. H., MBE MIMgt. Born 3/7/43. Commd 8/10/70. Wg Cdr 1/1/90. Retd ADMIN 1/7/93.
BAMFORD M. N. Born 2/8/55. Commd 20/1/80. Sqn Ldr 1/7/88. Retd ADMIN 20/1/96.
BAMPTON A. F. Born 5/5/36. Commd 10/11/61. Flt Lt 28/4/66. Retd GD 25/6/77.
BANCE A. E., AFC. Born 12/11/23. Commd 19/11/53. Flt Lt 19/11/59. Retd GD 8/3/68.
BANCE D. E. Born 2/11/31. Commd 18/4/74. Sqn Ldr 1/1/84. Retd ENG 1/1/94.
BANCROFT J. J. Born 12/9/36. Commd 24/2/61. Sqn Ldr 1/1/85. Retd GD 12/9/91.
BANCROFT J. K. Born 13/12/29. Commd 11/6/52. Flt Lt 18/12/57. Retd GD 13/12/72. Re-instated 21/5/81 to 13/12/84.
BANCROFT-PITMAN G. Born 7/11/35. Commd 20/10/65. Wg Cdr 1/1/78. Retd GD(G) 2/4/94 rtg Gp Capt.
BANCROFT-PITMAN S. C. Born 29/10/44. Commd 6/11/80. Sqn Ldr 1/1/92. Retd GD 29/10/99.
BANCROFT-WILSON A., BSc. Born 3/2/58. Commd 26/7/81. Flt Lt 26/10/84. Retd ADMIN 28/4/88.
BANCROFT-WILSON H. A., BEng. Born 6/2/55. Commd 26/7/81. Flt Lt 26/1/82. Retd ENG 1/12/96.
BANEY T. H. Born 29/10/35. Commd 2/10/58. Flt Lt 2/4/69. Retd GD 2/10/74.
BANFIELD A.F. Born 8/2/38. Commd 23/10/56. Sqn Ldr 1/7/77. Retd GD 1/7/88.
BANFIELD E. L., AFC. Born 23/8/32. Commd 14/4/60. Sqn Ldr 1/7/87. Retd GD 21/8/92.
BANFIELD M. W. F. Born 18/4/32. Commd 6/12/51. Sqn Ldr 1/1/64. Retd GD 1/8/79.
BANGAY J. M., MIMgt. Born 21/10/21. Commd 24/10/45. Sqn Ldr 1/7/64. Retd SY 21/10/76.
BANGAY W. G. E. Born 7/5/30. Commd 6/7/50. Flt Lt 6/7/56. Retd SEC 7/5/68.
BANGOR-JONES E. R. Born 26/6/20. Commd 1/5/42. Sqn Ldr 1/7/54. Retd GD 26/6/65 rtg Wg Cdr.
BANKS A. J. R., OBE FCIS FCIPD. Born 29/6/47. Commd 4/5/72. Gp Capt 1/7/92. Retd ADMIN 10/12/96.
BANKS C. O. Born 13/6/54. Commd 22/2/79. Sqn Ldr 1/1/90. Retd GD 2/8/93.
BANKS D. R. Born 29/9/47. Commd 27/2/70. Flt Lt 14/5/74. Retd ENG 4/4/85.
BANKS E., OBE FLCM LRAM LGSM ARCM. Born 2/4/32. Commd 20/12/62. Wg Cdr 1/7/83. Retd DM 2/4/89.

BANKS E. F., FIMgt. Born 29/4/29. Commd 11/4/51. Gp Capt 1/1/75. Retd SUP 29/4/84.
BANKS F. W. J. Born 8/8/31. Commd 6/12/51. Flt Lt 27/6/57. Retd GD 8/8/74.
BANKS G. D. Born 11/3/44. Commd 19/7/84. Flt Lt 19/7/88. Retd ENG 1/4/93.
BANKS G. E., MA. Born 17/2/41. Commd 6/11/64. Flt Lt 6/2/66. Retd GD 17/7/93.
BANKS G. F. Born 9/10/24. Commd 11/3/65. Flt Lt 11/3/68. Retd GD 31/7/73.
BANKS I. N. Born 24/7/53. Commd 2/10/72. Sqn Ldr 1/7/91. Retd ADMIN 12/4/94.
BANKS K. J. Born 9/2/45. Commd 20/9/79. Flt Lt 20/9/81. Retd. ENG 20/9/87.
BANKS L. F., DFC AFC. Born 9/2/20. Commd 6/6/42. Wg Cdr 1/1/57. Retd GD 10/11/63.
BANKS M. C. F. Born 11/10/30. Commd 19/1/50. Wg Cdr 1/7/75. Retd SUP 11/10/85.
BANKS M. L. Born 18/9/33. Commd 24/3/61. Fg Offr 21/3/58. Retd GD 16/8/66.
BANKS M. R., MB ChB DO. Born 10/9/44. Commd 11/1/65. Sqn Ldr 12/8/73. Retd MED 1/8/80.
BANKS P. C., MBE BSc CertEd. Born 10/11/45. Commd 20/5/79. Sqn Ldr 1/1/90. Retd ADMIN 30/4/99.
BANKS R. L. Born 3/9/39. Commd 20/11/60. Flt Lt 20/5/65. Retd GD 3/9/77.
BANKS R. W. Born 5/3/24. Commd 25/8/60. Flt Lt 25/8/63. Retd ENG 6/12/74.
BANKS S. Born 6/8/07. Commd 20/1/44. Fg Offr 20/1/44. Retd ENG 12/1/46.
BANNARD R. J., FIMgt. Born 8/6/30. Commd 9/4/52. Gp Capt 1/7/71. Retd GD 15/10/81.
BANNATYNE J. A., CBE BA. Born 12/2/11. Commd 27/1/40. Gp Offr 1/7/60. Retd SEC 6/12/64.
BANNERMAN A. Born 1/1/29. Commd 25/8/52. Flt Lt 25/3/56. Retd GD 1/1/72.
BANNERMAN H., MB BS DOMS. Born 9/10/08. Commd 8/1/33. Wg Cdr 1/10/46. Retd MED 1/6/55.
BANNING D. C. Born 12/11/37. Commd 22/5/70. Sqn Ldr 1/7/82. Rtd GD(G) 13/11/88.
BANNISTER A. J., MIMgt. Born 25/10/18. Commd 17/4/39. Wg Cdr 1/7/67. Retd SUP 25/10/73.
BANNISTER D. R. Born 2/8/48. Commd 20/12/73. Wg Cdr 1/7/89. Retd GD 3/12/99.
BANNISTER M., BA. Born 26/2/39. Commd 31/12/79. Sqn Ldr 11/7/77. Retd ADMIN 1/9/85.
BANNISTER P. Born 15/5/37. Commd 16/12/58. Sqn Ldr 1/1/69. Retd SUP 15/5/75.
BANNISTER R. A. Born 19/1/54. Commd 1/7/76. Sqn Ldr 1/7/90. Retd GD 1/2/98.
BANNISTER S. W. Born 2/9/07. Commd 23/11/42. Flt Lt 23/5/47. Retd GD(G) 1/1/54.
BANNON R. P., BSc MB BS FRCR MRCS LRCP DCH. Born 6/1/47. Commd 27/4/70. Sqn Ldr 22/8/79. Retd MED 28/10/86.
BANYARD A. E., CEng MIMechE. Born 8/5/42. Commd 10/10/63. Sqn Ldr 1/7/78. Retd ENG 8/5/86.
BANYARD G. F., OBE. Born 23/7/21. Commd 23/10/43. Wg Cdr 1/7/61. Retd GD 23/7/76.
BAPTISTE P. J. Born 9/3/62. Commd 28/2/85. Flt Lt 16/2/89. Retd GD(G) 19/12/95.
BAPTY P. C., BEng. Born 12/5/59. Commd 4/7/82. Flt Lt 4/10/83. Retd GD 14/3/97.
BARBER A. F. H. Born 31/10/20. Commd 9/6/43. Flt Lt 9/3/47. Retd ENG 1/11/61.
BARBER A. W., BSc. Born 14/11/33. Commd 25/6/55. Flt Lt 25/6/58. Retd GD 25/9/72.
BARBER D. J. Born 22/8/12. Commd 1/1/37. Wg Cdr 1/1/50. Retd SUP 1/1/60.
BARBER D. J. Born 11/12/44. Commd 25/3/64. Sqn Ldr 1/1/82. Retd GD 1/1/85.
BARBER D. W., OBE. Born 11/3/22. Commd 2/1/42. Gp Capt 1/7/72. Retd GD 11/3/77.
BARBER F. W. A. Born 14/9/19. Commd 19/7/56. Sqn Ldr 1/1/66. Retd ENG 14/9/77.
BARBER G. M., BA. Born 23/1/25. Commd 5/9/48. Sqn Ldr 1/1/62. Retd GD 1/1/65.
BARBER J. Born 18/5/56. Commd 9/10/75. Flt Lt 9/4/81. Retd GD 18/5/94.
BARBER J. C., DFM. Born 10/6/21. Commd 28/9/45. Sqn Ldr 1/1/70. Retd GD(G) 1/5/75.
BARBER J. R., BA. Born 22/1/60. Commd 8/5/83. Sqn Ldr 1/7/91. Retd SUP 8/5/99.
BARBER K. Born 31/3/24. Commd 24/1/52. Sqn Ldr 1/7/62. Retd ENG 1/7/65.
BARBER L. A., OBE AFC. Born 18/1/10. Commd 21/2/30. Wg Cdr 1/10/46. Retd GD 18/1/57 rtg Gp Capt.
BARBER M. I., BEng. Born 19/2/60. Commd 1/8/86. Flt Lt 25/7/90. Retd ENG 31/3/99.
BARBER N. J. H. Born 13/9/62. Commd 5/2/81. Flt Lt 5/8/86. Retd GD 14/3/96.
BARBER P., OBE DFC. Born 2/5/23. Commd 19/9/42. Wg Cdr 1/1/60. Retd GD 2/5/70.
BARBER P. Born 6/2/52. Commd 27/9/73. Flt Lt 1/4/93. Retd GD 27/3/79.
BARBER R. Born 23/9/59. Commd 5/4/79. Sqn Ldr 1/1/91. Retd GD 23/9/97.
BARBER R. E., BSc CEng MIEE. Born 5/8/40. Commd 2/9/73. Sqn Ldr 1/1/83. Retd ENG 2/9/89.
BARBER R. H. Born 17/9/47. Commd 27/1/67. Flt Lt 25/5/73 Retd GD(G) 17/9/85.
BARBER R. S. Born 21/4/45. Commd 3/1/64. Flt Lt 3/7/69. Retd GD 21/4/83.
BARBER R. V. W. Born 10/4/47. Commd 21/10/66. Flt Lt 25/2/73. Retd GD(G) 10/4/85.
BARBER W. D. Born 20/3/21. Commd 14/3/46. Flt Lt 10/8/55. Retd GD 18/7/64.
BARBER W. J. Born 31/8/42. Commd 16/9/71. Flt Lt 16/9/73. Retd ENG 31/8/80.
BARBOUR T. M., BA. Born 31/5/55. Commd 30/4/78. Flt Lt 30/1/80. Retd GD 14/3/97.
BARCILON R. L., AFC. Born 17/3/34. Commd 5/4/55. Air Cdre 1/7/86. Retd GD 13/7/87.
BARCLAY A. B. G. Born 11/2/17. Commd 8/5/41. Flt Lt 10/11/55. Retd CAT 7/4/64.
BARCLAY B. N. Born 14/9/24. Commd 14/4/49. Flt Lt 14/10/52. Retd GD 30/3/68.
BARCLAY R. T. Born 21/12/21. Commd 28/2/57. Flt Lt 27/8/60. Retd GD 6/4/68.
BARCLAY S. J., OBE MCIPD. Born 15/5/42. Commd 6/5/65. Gp Capt 1/7/90. Retd ADMIN 14/3/96.
BARCROFT A. M. L. Born 15/10/49. Commd 31/7/70. Wg Cdr 1/1/89. Retd SUP 14/3/97.
BARDELL T. Born 22/9/46. Commd 9/12/65. Sqn Ldr 1/7/91. Retd GD(G) 14/3/96.
BARDEN D. W. Born 15/5/39. Commd 23/12/58. Wg Cdr 1/7/77. Retd GD 7/4/82.
BARDEN J. A. Born 11/5/54. Commd 2/6/77. Flt Lt 2/12/82. Retd GD. 14/4/93.

BARDON P. J., DFC AFC. Born 15/4/29. Commd 14/12/49. Wg Cdr 1/1/65. Retd GD 31/7/68.
BARDON R. T. Born 20/4/54. Commd 3/11/77. Flt Lt 3/5/80. Retd GD 20/10/92.
BARDSLEY A., BSc. Born 13/5/31. Commd 3/8/55. Sqn Ldr 1/1/65. Retd ENG 25/6/85.
BARFIELD D. B. Born 11/5/34. Commd 11/11/71. Flt Lt. 11/11/75. Retd SY 11/5/82.
BARFOOT D. B. Born 5/12/23. Commd 6/7/44. Sqn Ldr 1/7/55. Retd GD 25/2/72.
BARFOOT S. E. Born 12/12/14. Commd 17/12/53. Sqn Ldr 1/7/65. Retd SEC 12/12/69.
BARFOOT W. E. Born 31/10/19. Commd 27/3/43. Sqn Ldr 1/1/53. Retd GD 5/6/59.
BARGEWELL T. A., IEng MIIE. Born 19/3/46. Commd 8/9/83. Sqn Ldr 1/1/93. Retd ENG 3/3/99.
BARGH R. A., BSc. Born 31/7/31. Commd 8/12/59. Flt Lt. 18/3/64. Retd ENG 22/9/89.
BARHAM C. L. Born 7/7/47. Commd 26/4/84. Flt Lt 26/4/88. Retd GD 1/4/90.
BARHAM D. G. A., MA. Born 22/5/37. Commd 7/10/48. Wg Cdr 25/5/68. Retd EDN 24/11/75.
BARHAM E. M. Born 29/7/29. Commd 17/5/62. Sqn Ldr 1/7/73. Retd PRT 2/4/81.
BARHAM M. W. Born 13/7/34. Commd 21/9/62. Wg Cdr 1/1/83. Retd SUP 26/2/89.
BARKEL J. Born 31/10/22. Commd 11/4/57. Flt Lt 14/2/66. Retd GD(G) 31/10/77.
BARKER A. Born 11/3/44. Commd 4/12/64. Flt Lt 4/6/70. Retd GD 18/8/76.
BARKER A. C., MBE MSc. Born 9/7/53. Commd 18/4/76. Wg Cdr 1/7/93. Retd ENG 31/5/01.
BARKER A. M. Born 22/6/55. Commd 3/7/80. Sqn Ldr 1/1/89. Retd ADMIN 15/11/92.
BARKER B. G. Born 22/12/35. Commd 11/11/65. Sqn Ldr 11/8/73. Retd EDN 22/12/73.
BARKER D., BSc. Born 6/4/57. Commd 26/11/78. Flt Lt 26/8/80. Retd GD 6/4/95.
BARKER D. H., MSc BSc BSc MRAeS AFIMA. Born 16/7/45. Commd 22/9/65. Sqn Ldr 15/1/78. Retd ADMIN 16/7/89.
BARKER D. J. Born 28/3/41. Commd 16/9/71. Flt Lt 16/9/73. Retd ENG 16/9/79.
BARKER D. S., MA BSc MIMgt. Born 27/7/34. Commd 23/9/55. Sqn Ldr 1/7/66. Retd SEC 16/11/68.
BARKER H. Born 31/5/34. Commd 13/8/52. Flt Lt 29/4/59. Retd GD 31/5/72.
BARKER J. Born 9/8/35. Commd 24/1/63. Sqn Ldr 1/7/72. Retd GD(G) 1/4/86.
BARKER J. Born 14/6/45. Commd 31/1/64. Wg Cdr 1/1/93. Retd GD 31/3/99.
BARKER J. A., MB ChB DLO MRAeS. Born 13/12/39. Commd 21/1/63. Wg Cdr 2/8/76. Retd MED 3/4/82.
BARKER J. E., CEng FIMgt MIEE. Born 10/1/30. Commd 30/9/54. Gp Capt 1/1/82. Retd ENG 10/1/88.
BARKER J. L., CB CBE DFC BA. Born 12/11/10. Commd 6/7/31. Gp Capt 1/1/53. Retd GD 26/2/63 rtg AVM.
BARKER J. S. Born 2/12/21. Commd 23/8/56. Sqn Ldr 1/1/69. Retd ENG 4/12/71.
BARKER M. A., BSc. Born 9/8/55. Commd 15/9/74. Sqn Ldr 1/1/87. Retd ENG 1/4/95.
BARKER N. C. W. Born 17/5/43. Commd 17/12/65. Sqn Ldr 1/7/73. Retd GD 27/4/93.
BARKER R. Born 19/9/08. Commd 1/3/41. Flt Lt 1/9/45. Retd ENG 30/5/48.
BARKER R. A. Born 29/7/32. Commd 25/1/66. Flt Lt 9/12/66. Retd EDN 9/12/73.
BARKER R. A., BSc. Born 23/2/52. Commd 13/9/70. Sqn Ldr 1/1/84. Retd ENG 10/8/90.
BARKER R. H. C. Born 21/10/17. Commd 3/8/42. Flt Lt 31/12/50. Retd SEC 29/4/61.
BARKER R. J. Born 29/12/57. Commd 17/7/87. Flt Lt 17/7/89. Retd OPS SPT 19/2/01.
BARKER R. P. Born 6/11/47. Commd 2/12/66. Flt Lt 2/6/72. Retd GD 22/10/94.
BARKER S. J., CEng DipSoton MIEE. Born 1/2/34. Commd 22/7/55. Wg Cdr 1/7/77. Retd ENG 1/2/87.
BARKER W. W., BSc. Born 24/9/30. Commd 15/10/52. Sqn Ldr 1/1/65. Retd GD 12/5/85
BARKWAY A. F. Born 2/8/44. Commd 18/4/74. Sqn Ldr 1/7/84. Retd SUP 14/3/96.
BARKWAY R. J. Born 26/7/37. Commd 1/4/65. Flt Lt 26/7/92. Retd SUP 26/7/92.
BARLEE L. W. Born 24/5/19. Commd 21/9/50. Sqn Ldr 1/7/59. Retd ENG 24/5/68.
BARLEX A. N. Born 29/12/31. Commd 12/9/51. Wg Cdr 1/7/79 Retd GD 29/12/86.
BARLOW D. E. Born 23/7/59. Commd 15/8/85. Flt Lt 5/9/88. Retd OPS SPT 23/7/97.
BARLOW I. G., MIMgt. Born 5/10/38. Commd 14/4/49. Sqn Ldr 1/7/70. Retd GD 1/4/78.
BARLOW J. F., BA. Born 9/3/27. Commd 24/1/56. Fg Offr 24/7/56. Retd ENG 7/6/60.
BARLOW J. R. Born 2/1/23. Commd 22/5/43. Flt Lt 25/11/58. Retd GD 18/8/67.
BARLOW M. A., BEng. Born 7/11/65. Commd 6/11/88. Flt Lt 6/5/90. Retd GD 14/3/97.
BARLOW P. E. C. Born 4/5/51. Commd 15/2/73. Wg Cdr 1/1/91. Retd ADMIN 13/1/97.
BARLOW R. A. G. Born 22/11/23. Commd 7/11/46. Flt Lt 30/7/48. Retd ENG 12/4/62 rtg Sqn Ldr.
BARLOW R. C. Born 26/12/17. Commd 14/10/41. Flt Lt 1/9/45. Retd GD 26/2/55.
BARLOW T. F. Born 7/2/10. Commd 22/7/43. Flt Lt 22/1/48. Retd SEC 30/5/64.
BARLTROP D. F., MBE. Born 1/1/34. Commd 16/9/71. Sqn Ldr 1/1/82. Retd ENG 1/1/94.
BARLTROP W. S. Born 1/3/40. Commd 29/10/64. Sqn Ldr 1/7/81. Retd GD(G) 1/3/95.
BARMBY A. S. Born 15/3/35. Commd 24/6/53. Flt Lt 25/11/58. Retd GD 15/3/73.
BARMBY J. Born 16/2/63. Commd 25/2/82. Flt Lt 26/8/88. Retd GD(G) 7/8/89.
BARNARD E. F. E. Born 21/1/09. Commd 30/4/35. Wg Cdr 1/10/46. Retd GD 13/4/56.
BARNARD J. Born 7/6/20. Commd 6/1/55. Flt Lt 6/1/58. Retd GD(G) 7/6/75.
BARNARD J. B., BA. Born 22/8/33. Commd 6 Apr 54. Flt Lt 11/3/60. Retd GD 22/8/93.
BARNARD J. B. Born 3/5/44. Commd 6/7/62. Sqn Ldr 1/7/88. Retd GD 1/6/98.
BARNARD J. O., CBE. Born 21/5/17. Commd 3/7/38. AC 1/7/67. Retd GD 14/12/68.
BARNARD M. H. Born 21/7/38. Commd 9/4/60. Sqn Ldr 1/7/71. Retd GD 21/7/76.
BARNARD P. J. Born 5/4/31. Commd 1/9/52. Flt Lt 1/3/57. Retd GD 5/4/69.
BARNARD P. Q., MBE IEng. Born 4/5/43. Commd 23/11/78. Sqn Ldr 1/1/87. Retd ENG 4/5/00.
BARNARD R. G. Born 18/6/30. Commd 24/1/52. Flt Lt 15/5/57. Retd GD 3/8/76.

BARNARD T. A. Born 29/12/40. Commd 4/4/59. Flt Lt 4/10/64. Retd GD 29/12/78.
BARNARD W. G. Born 4/3/29. Commd 4/6/52. Flt Lt 20/3/58. Retd. MAR 15/1/68.
BARNDEN R. J. Born 24/1/30. Commd 21/3/51. Gp Capt 1/7/71. Retd GD 5/4/80.
BARNES C. H. Born 16/5/37. Commd 24/9/64. Sqn Ldr 1/7/72. Retd GD 1/10/85.
BARNES D. A. W., BA. Born 30/5/36. Commd 3/1/58. Sqn Ldr 23/3/68. Retd EDN 30/5/74.
BARNES D. H., OBE. Born 28/3/37. Commd 30/3/61. Gp Capt 1/1/82. Retd GD 5/4/85
BARNES D. J., MBE CEng MRAeS MIMgt. Born 1/10/20. Commd 13/4/44. Wg Cdr 1/7/68. Retd ENG 3/6/78.
BARNES D. J. Born 6/8/44. Commd 29/7/83. Sqn Ldr 1/7/92. Retd ADMIN 2/12/97.
BARNES F., AFC MRAeS MIMgt. Born 29/9/22. Commd 25/3/44. Wg Cdr 1/7/69. Retd GD 1/5/72.
BARNES F. G., BSc. Born 12/3/35. Commd 10/10/56. Flt Lt 18/3/64. Retd SUP 29/11/74.
BARNES G. A., FIMgt. Born 3/4/36. Commd 19/4/55. Gp Capt 1/1/84. Retd GD 25/4/86.
BARNES G. T., MIMgt. Born 8/2/20. Commd 11/6/53. Sdn Ldr 1/7/63. Retd ENG 8/8/73.
BARNES H. Born 19/4/23. Commd 23/12/45. Flt Lt 19/6/52. Retd ENG 16/9/76.
BARNES H. J. C. Born 31/3/26. Commd 21/12/45. Sqn Ldr 1/1/57. Retd GD 1/4/68.
BARNES I. A. Born 8/4/22. Commd 11/5/48. Flt Lt 11/5/52. Retd SUP 9/5/62.
BARNES J. Born 9/2/20. Commd 25/6/53. Flt Lt 25/6/56. Retd SEC 30/5/64.
BARNES J. A. Born 27/5/42. Commd 17/5/63. Flt Lt 17/11/68. Retd GD 31/5/72.
BARNES J. H. Born 1/5/44. Commd 11/9/64. Sqn Ldr 1/7/77. Retd GD 1/5/82.
BARNES K. M. Born 20/10/38. Commd 10/2/72. Flt Lt 10/2/74. Retd GD(G) 11/8/81.
BARNES M. Born 10/8/39. Commd 22/3/63. A Cdre 1/7/89. Retd GD 22/4/92.
BARNES N. I. Born 15/9/55. Commd 25/2/82. Flt Lt 20/12/84. Retd ENG 15/9/99.
BARNES P. E. Born 23/6/44. Commd 6/11/64. Plt Offr 6/11/65. Retd 13/5/67.
BARNES S. G., DFC BSc. Born 22/3/62. Commd 14/9/80. Wg Cdr 1/7/97. Retd GD 24/4/01.
BARNES W. H., MSc. Born 9/10/36. Commd 31/10/71. Sqn Ldr 31/10/71. Retd ENG 3/10/75.
BARNES-MOSS J. D. Born 10/12/21. Commd 14/5/44. Sqn Ldr 1/1/66. Retd GD 10/12/76.
BARNETT A., DFM. Born 8/1/22. Commd 21/11/43. Flt Lt 21/5/47. Retd ENG 10/9/59.
BARNETT C. A. Born 11/10/42. Commd 23/11/62. A Cdre 1/7/94. Retd GD(G) 1/12/95.
BARNETT G. W. Born 16/3/18. Commd 29/10/43. Sqn Ldr 1/1/63. Retd ENG 30/3/68.
BARNETT J. C. Born 12/4/38. Commd 22/5/64. Flt Lt 22/5/68. Retd GD 3/2/80. Re-entered 6/3/85. Flt Lt 21/6/73.
   Retd GD 12/4/98.
BARNETT J. J. Born 6/6/49. Commd 31/7/70. Wg Cdr 1/7/86. Retd GD 14/11/89.
BARNETT J. N., BSc. Born 6/1/62. Commd 2/9/84. Flt Lt 2/3/86. Retd GD 3/1/93.
BARNETT M. J. R. Born 30/1/44. Commd 12/7/63. Sqn Ldr 1/7/83. Retd GD 2/4/93.
BARNETT R. E. J. Born 12/5/23. Commd 26/8/43. Wg Cdr 1/7/65. Retd ENG 31/12/77.
BARNETT W. Born 24/2/45. Commd 23/9/65. Gp Capt 1/1/97. Retd ADMIN 24/2/00.
BARNEY J. S., MB ChB. Born 12/9/59. Commd 29/3/83. Wg Cdr 1/8/97. Retd MED 29/3/00.
BARNFATHER B. J. Born 19/12/63. Commd 24/3/83. Flt Lt 24/9/88. Retd GD 31/12/92.
BARNFATHER C. L., BA CEng MIEE MRAeS MIMgt. Born 21/6/37. Commd 23/7/58. Wg Cdr 1/7/84.
   Retd ENG 21/6/92.
BARNICOAT D. R., MIMgt. Born 21/7/25. Commd 19/10/45. Wg Cdr 1/1/67. Retd GD 1/11/75.
BARNINGHAM R. A. Born 17/11/54. Commd 8/9/83. Sqn Ldr 1/7/91. Retd SUP 14/3/96.
BARNOWSKI B. Born 15/9/22. Commd 25/1/51. Flt Lt 10/11/55. Retd GD 17/8/73.
BARNWELL L. M. L., BA. Born 12/8/43. Commd 3/2/73. Flt Lt 3/2/78. Retd SEC 22/9/81.
BARON D. A., OBE. Born 3/2/41. Commd 24/2/61. Gp Capt 1/1/85. Retd GD 3/2/96.
BARON G. Born 14/9/46. Commd 10/6/66. Flt Lt 10/6/71. Retd GD 29/6/83.
BARON R. A. Born 13/8/53. Commd 6/4/72. Flt Lt 6/10/77. Retd GD 23/10/80.
BARON R. J. M., MBE. Born 5/6/26. Commd 15/11/45. Flt Lt 10/10/51. Retd GD 1/7/57.
BARR D. M., FRAeS FIMgt. Born 17/9/47. Commd 1/4/66. Gp Capt 1/1/94. Retd GD 3/1/97.
BARR J. J. Born 25/7/21. Commd 19/8/39. Gp Capt 1/1/67. Retd GD 30/4/72.
BARR J. W. Born 20/7/42. Commd 28/8/75. Flt Lt 28/8/77. Retd ENG 28/8/83.
BARR-SIM I. E. Born 11/8/29. Commd 13/12/50. Flt Lt 19/11/53. Retd GD 18/7/56.
BARRACLOUGH Sir John., KCB CBE DFC AFC FRAeS FRSA. Born 2/5/18. Commd 7/5/38. ACM 3/9/73. Retd GD
   3/4/76.
BARRACLOUGH R. H. Born 27/10/30. Commd 8/2/51. Sqn Ldr 1/1/63. Retd GD 6/5/77. Reinstated 15/10/80.
   Sqn Ldr 12/6/66. Retd GD 16/6/91.
BARRACLOUGH S. M. Born 2/4/17. Commd 28/6/41. Sqn Ldr 1/8/47. Retd GD 28/5/58.
BARRADELL D. J. Born 27/2/44. Commd 12/1/62. Flt Lt 12/7/67. Retd GD 28/9/98.
BARRAS-SMITH D. I. Born 6/11/20. Commd 25/2/43. Flt Lt 25/8/46. Retd GD 6/11/63 rtg Sqn Ldr.
BARRASS J. A., BSc. Born 31/3/59. Commd 18/10/81. Wg Cdr 1/7/98. Retd GD 10/4/01.
BARRASS K. Born 10/7/58. Commd 15/2/90. Flt Lt 15/2/92. Retd ENG 15/2/98.
BARRATT J. F. Born 25/12/31. Commd 21/4/67. Flt Lt 21/4/70. Retd GD 1/8/74.
BARRATT K. J. Born 8/10/23. Commd 11/6/45. Gp Capt 1/1/68. Retd GD 22/7/77.
BARRATT M. A. Born 4/9/31. Commd 12/8/54. Sqn Ldr 1/1/83. Retd GD 4/9/89.
BARRATT The Rev P. Born 25/3/56. Commd 5/4/79. Flt Lt 20/9/82. Retd GD 2/9/87. Re-entered 2/7/90.
   Retd 31/12/97 Sqn Ldr.

BARRATT P. C. S., MBE BSc. Born 10/3/50. Commd 19/11/72. Sqn Ldr 1/1/83. Retd GD 1/4/90.
BARRATT S. G. Born 18/7/25. Commd 30/8/55. Flt Lt 16/11/64. Retd ADMIN 18/7/84.
BARRETT A. Born 31/3/47. Commd 1/7/82. Sqn Ldr 1/1/91. Retd ENG 14/3/96.
BARRETT A. H., BSc. Born 24/1/60. Commd 19/6/83. Sqn Ldr 1/1/92. Retd ENG 19/6/99.
BARRETT A. W. B. Born 17/7/08. Commd 30/4/34. Gp Capt 1/1/52. Retd GD 17/7/58.
BARRETT B. C. Born 26/3/46. Commd 26/5/67. Sqn Ldr 1/1/80. Retd ENG 26/3/84.
BARRETT B. D. Born 1/11/17. Commd 17/7/42. Sqn Ldr 1/7/60. Retd PRT 30/9/70 rtg Wg Cdr.
BARRETT C. J. Born 19/8/44. Commd 27/1/74. Flt Lt 27/1/74. Retd GD(G) 19/8/82.
BARRETT D. C. Born 1/6/53. Commd 9/9/81. Flt Lt 21/1/80. Retd ADMIN 11/11/87.
BARRETT D. G. Born 4/8/37. Commd 7/6/73. Flt Lt 7/6/75. Retd GD(G) 7/6/81.
BARRETT D. W. R. Born 12/1/31. Command 19/1/50. Wg Cdr 1/7/75. Retd ADMIN 26/9/83.
BARRETT E. Born 18/10/13. Commd 22/4/43. Sqn Ldr 1/4/56. Retd ENG 1/5/63.
BARRETT E. A., MIMgt. Born 2/7/21. Commd 1/5/47. Sqn Ldr 1/1/61. Retd ENG 4/9/76.
BARRETT F. J. Born 18/5/27. Commd 7/10/48. Sqn Ldr 1/7/59. Retd GD 7/9/68.
BARRETT F. O., CBE DFC. Born 2/12/18. Commd 25/10/38. A Cdre 1/1/70. Retd GD 8/2/73.
BARRETT H., CEng MIMechE MRAeS MIMgt. Born 27/7/26. Commd 30/4/51. Sqn Ldr 1/1/61. Retd ENG 7/9/74.
BARRETT J. H. Born 21/7/13. Commd 4/3/35. Sqn Ldr 1/9/40. Retd GD 15/8/47.
BARRETT P., BSc ARSM. Born 20/11/53. Commd 23/9/73. Sqn Ldr 1/1/88. Retd GD 20/11/91.
BARRETT R. J., BA. Born 28/2/31. Commd 16/12/54. Flt Lt 1/3/71. Retd Pl 6/7/74.
BARRETT R. J. Born 6/8/37. Commd 28/7/59. Wg Cdr 1/7/83. Retd GD 6/8/92.
BARRETT R. T., CEng MIEE MRAes. Born 1/9/40. Commd 18/7/61. Sqn Ldr 1/7/70. Retd ENG 1/9/78.
BARRETT R. W. Born 27/3/43. Commd 31/10/70. Flt Lt 31/10/76. Retd ADMIN 31/10/82.
BARRETT S. A. Born 7/9/21. Commd 23/10/43. Sqn Ldr 1/4/55. Retd GD 5/3/65.
BARRETT S. T., BSc. Born 10/8/61. Commd 2/9/84. Flt Lt 12/4/89. Retd ENG 2/5/94.
BARRETT T. Born 20/2/34. Commd 30/9/52. Wg Cdr 1/7/74. Retd GD 31/5/83.
BARREY C. J., DFC AFC DFM. Born 13/12/19. Commd 10/7/43. Sqn Ldr 1/7/61. Retd GD 13/12/74.
BARRIBALL E. R. Born 4/9/33. Commd 9/6/69. Wg Cdr 1/7/79. Retd GD(G) 31/12/86.
BARRINGER M. J. Born 25/10/38. Commd 25/7/60. Sqn Ldr 1/1/70. Retd GD 1/11/80.
BARRINGTON A. Born 13/8/23. Commd 9/3/44. Sqn Ldr 1/7/57. Retd SEC 1/9/67.
BARRINGTON D. E. Born 27/9/54. Commd 3/1/88. Flt Lt 3/1/88. Retd ADMIN 16/2/97.
BARRINGTON F. N. Born 31/10/16. Commd 31/5/45. Sqn Ldr 1/10/56. Retd SEC 31/10/65.
BARRITT J. B., MIMgt. Born 10/4/30. Commd 22/7/66. Sqn Ldr 1/7/82. Retd ENG 10/4/85.
BARRON J. Born 1/2/33. Commd 6/2/52. Flt Lt 22/1/58. Retd GD 11/1/75.
BARRON J. D. Born 12/12/56. Commd 14/10/84. Flt Lt 14/4/90. Retd ADMIN 14/3/97.
BARROW B. A. J., MB BS MRCS LRCP DPM. Born 26/12/29. Commd 18/7/54. Wg Cdr 5/7/67. Retd MED 18/7/70.
BARROW J. F. V. Born 7/8/20. Commd 4/6/59. Sqn Ldr 1/7/70. Retd GD 7/8/75.
BARROW J. I. Born 2/10/34. Commd 13/12/55. Gp Capt 1/1/85. Retd SUP 21/7/89.
BARROW J. L. Born 24/11/44. Commd 26/11/64. Sqn Ldr 1/1/82. Retd GD 1/1/85.
BARROW P. A. Born 9/7/34. Commd 14/12/54. Flt Lt 14/6/57. Retd GD 9/7/72.
BARRY G. P., FIMgt. Born 18/4/20. Commd 18/1/45. Gp Capt 1/7/70. Retd SUP 18/4/75.
BARRY J. S., MBE. Born 4/8/44. Commd 31/8/78. Wg Cdr 1/1/92. Retd GD(G) 30/11/94.
BARRY M. Born 1/7/09. Commd 7/4/43. Flt Offr 7/4/49. Retd SUP 2/10/51.
BARSBY N. H. Born 27/5/13. Commd 27/5/43. Flt Lt 27/11/46. Retd ENG 8/5/54.
BARTER C. Born 11/9/39. Commd 17/9/57. Sqn Ldr 1/1/91. Retd GD 11/9/94.
BARTER G. B. Born 6/11/33. Commd 5/10/58. Sqn Ldr 1/1/71. Retd CAT 15/10/74.
BARTER J. F. Born 21/4/61. Commd 5/2/81. Sqn Ldr 1/1/94. Retd OPS SPT 22/4/98.
BARTHOLOMEW E., DFC. Born 29/11/22. Commd 24/11/44. Flt Lt 24/5/48. Retd GD 1/9/62.
BARTHOLOMEW J. Born 21/8/48. Commd 28/11/69. Flt Lt 28/5/75. Retd GD 31/5/75.
BARTHROPP P. P. C., DFC AFC. Born 9/11/20. Commd 31/10/38. Sqn Ldr 1/8/47. Retd GD 28/12/57 rtg Wg Cdr.
BARTLE C. J. Born 19/9/41. Commd 20/8/65. Sqn Ldr 1/7/87. Retd GD 19/9/96.
BARTLE D. G. Born 29/7/33. Commd 29/3/56. Wg Cdr 1/1/78. Retd GD(G) 2/5/88.
BARTLE G. L. Born 18/8/44. Commd 14/2/63. Fg Offr 14/8/30. Retd GD 10/10/66.
BARTLE M., BSc. Born 27/11/41. Commd 22/5/64. Sqn Ldr 1/7/72. Retd GD 4/2/80.
BARTLE S. J., BEng. Born 3/11/73. Commd 7/2/92. Fg Offr 15/1/95. Retd ENG 16/4/97.
BARTLETT C., AFC. Born 27/10/20. Commd 8/9/44. Wg Cdr 1/1/64. Retd GD 27/10/75.
BARTLETT C. S. McD. Born 31/8/23. Commd 24/5/46. Sqn Ldr 1/1/58. Retd GD 2/9/66.
BARTLETT G. C. C., AFC. Born 19/8/12. Commd 29/6/36. Wg Cdr 1/10/46. Retd GD 29/9/59.
BARTLETT J. Born 1/3/32. Commd 23/8/51. Sqn Ldr 1/7/78. Retd Pl 8/11/84.
BARTLETT J. E. Born 26/1/47. Commd 13/1/67. Flt Lt 13/1/72. Retd GD 27/1/90.
BARTLETT J. W. Born 24/11/37. Commd 6/9/63. Flt Lt 26/7/67. Retd GD 24/11/75.
BARTLETT K. W., BA MBCS. Born 9/3/57. Commd 25/2/82. Flt Lt 25/8/85. Retd ADMIN 16/11/96.
BARTLETT L. H., DSO. Born 26/6/16. Commd 31/7/41. Gp Capt 1/1/60. Retd GD 20/6/66.
BARTLETT M. A. Born 6/3/45. Commd 20/10/67. Flt Lt 4/5/72. Retd GD 1/4/76.
BARTLETT M. S., MVO CEng MIMechE. Born 15/1/45. Commd 11/2/65. Wg Cdr 1/1/82. Retd ENG 18/9/84.
BARTLETT M. T. Born 24/2/23. Commd 30/3/45. Sqn Ldr 1/7/59. Retd GD 26/2/66.
BARTLETT R. J. Born 23/11/12. Commd 30/10/41. Wg Cdr 1/7/58. Retd ENG 23/11/66.

BARTLETT S. E. J. Born 27/1/14. Commd 15/1/43. Flt Lt 15/7/47. Retd PE 27/1/62.
BARTLETT T. R., CEng MIEE. Born 13/1/24. Commd 7/12/61. Sqn Ldr 13/9/68. Retd EDN 13/9/78.
BARTLETT W. E., MBE. Born 25/12/11. Commd 26/4/41. Flt Lt 1/9/45. Retd ENG 31/1/53 rtg Sqn Ldr.
BARTLETT W. R. J. Born 10/1/55. Commd 28/7/88. Flt Lt 27/7/90. Retd ENG 28/7/96.
BARTLEY D. C. Born 31/10/42. Commd 16/8/68 Fg Offr 16/8/70. Retd GD 20/12/72.
BARTMAN C. D. Born 21/5/22. Commd 10/3/43. Sqn Ldr 1/1/53. Retd GD 21/5/65.
BARTON A. D. Born 17/5/36. Commd 19/12/59. Flt Lt 19/6/64. Retd GD 17/5/74.
BARTON A. E. MacK., CEng MRAeS. Born 31/1/24. Commd 14/10/44. Sqn Ldr 1/1/58. Retd GD 31/8/67.
BARTON D. H., MIMgt. Born 16/8/25. Commd 21/4/45. Sqn Ldr 1/7/58. Retd SEC 25/4/78.
BARTON D. I. Born 14/10/22. Commd 15/6/44. Flt Lt 19/6/52. Retd GD(G) 18/4/56.
BARTON E. J. Born 9/2/38. Commd 3/8/62. Flt Lt 1/4/66. Retd GD 1/9/78.
BARTON L. Born 3/2/32. Commd 2/1/56. Sqn Ldr 1/1/70. Retd GD(G) 4/2/82.
BARTON M. A. Born 22/9/59. Commd 13/12/79. Flt Lt 13/6/85. Retd GD 14/9/96.
BARTON N. Born 14/12/48. Commd 31/7/70. Flt Lt 31/7/73. Retd GD 14/12/86.
BARTON P.C., BSc. Born 17/6/51. Commd 15/8/69. Flt Lt 15/4/74. Retd GD 1/4/86.
BARTON R. A., OBE DFC* Born 7/6/16. Commd 27/1/36. Wg Cdr 1/7/47. Retd GD 27/2/59.
BARTON R. H. Born 28/6/39. Commd 24/2/61. Flt Lt 24/8/66. Retd GD 1/3/77.
BARTRUM J., AFC. Born 12/4/24. Commd 27/2/47. Flt Lt 11/11/54. Retd GD 12/4/62.
BARWELL C. H. Born 16/5/23. Commd 19/2/44. Sqn Ldr 1/4/56. Retd GD 16/5/68.
BARWELL J. D., AFC. Born 31/3/31. Commd 17/10/51. Sqn Ldr 1/1/60. Retd SEC 19/5/68.
BARWELL R.D., BA. Born 6/11/35. Commd 10/10/58. Sqn Ldr 10/4/69. Retd ADMIN 30/6/87.
BARWICK F. W. Born 14/3/19. Commd 21/4/55. Flt Lt 23/6/53. Retd SEC 19/5/68.
BARWOOD A. J., OBE MRCS LRCP DPH DIH FRAeS. Born 1/4/15. Commd 7/2/41. Gp Capt 1/7/59.
   Retd MED 1/4/80.
BARWOOD A. T., MRCS LRCP DPH. Born 7/7/24. Commd 3/8/50. Wg Cdr 3/8/62. Retd MED 24/11/66.
BASCOMBE A. R. H., BSc. Born 25/12/54. Commd 2/9/73. Flt Lt 15/10/77. Retd GD 5/11/86.
BASEY P. A. B. Born 3/9/59. Commd 8/9/83. Sqn Ldr 1/1/95. Retd GD 29/7/99.
BASHAARAT A., MSc BDS LDSRCS. Born 25/2/42. Commd 18/9/60. Wg Cdr 23/12/77. Retd DEL 25/2/80.
BASHALL I. Born 31/5/34. Commd 18/3/53. Flt Lt 3/9/58. Retd GD 15/8/64.
BASHFORD G. J. Born 20/5/22. Commd 5/2/44. Flt Lt 15/9/65. Retd GD 20/5/77.
BASKERVILLE G. J., BSc. Born 16/3/35. Commd 2/11/56. Sdn Ldr 10/3/65. Retd EDN 16/3/73.
BASKETT C. A., DFC. Born 19/9/11. Commd 16/11/36. Wg Cdr 1/1/51. Retd GD 13/1/58.
BASNETT M. A., CBE. Born 1/4/46. Commd 1/4/65. Gp Capt 1/1/90. Retd SY 3/7/93.
BASS G. C. Born 7/2/21. Commd 22/9/55. Flt Lt 22/9/61. Retd ENG 30/6/73.
BASS J. Born 22/1/42. Commd 19/12/85. Flt Lt 19/12/89. Retd SY 22/1/92.
BASS J. M. Born 28/7/30. Commd 11/6/52. Flt Lt 18/12/57. Retd GD 28/7/68.
BASS R. H. Born 14/10/66. Commd 19/11/87. Flt Lt 19/5/94. Retd SUP 14/3/96.
BASSETT J. W. Born 17/11/31. Commd 17/5/62. Flt Lt 17/5/68. Retd GD 8/1/77.
BASSETT R. G. Born 21/3/38. Commd 2/4/56. Sqn Ldr 1/7/69. Retd GD 21/3/76.
BASSFORD P. G. Born 2/5/30. Commd 19/1/50. Flt Lt 17/1/57. Retd GD 2/5/68.
BASSINGTHWAIGHTE K. Born 19/1/43. Commd 11/3/68. Wg Cdr 11/3/81. Retd LGL 11/3/84 rtg Gp Capt.
BASTABLE A. W. R. Born 26/1/38. Commd 10/3/77. Sqn Ldr 1/7/87. Retd ENG 1/4/94.
BASTARD L. G. A., AFC. Born 3/5/23. Commd 12/2/43. Gp Capt 1/1/68. Retd GD 31/3/78.
BASTEN P. F. Born 25/9/36. Commd 9/4/60. Flt Lt 9/10/65. Retd GD 25/9/74.
BASTIAN M. A. Born 2/10/35. Commd 5/12/63. Fg Offr 1/4/64. Retd GD(G) 26/10/67.
BASTIN J. E., LLB. Born 8/3/29. Commd 12/12/51. Sqn Ldr 1/1/62. Retd SUP 8/3/67.
BASTON I. J. Born 5/5/61. Commd 16/9/79. Flt Lt 10/5/86. Retd GD 5/5/99.
BATCHELAR E. Born 7/9/21. Commd 10/6/41. Gp Capt 1/7/66. Retd GD 7/7/72.
BATCHELDER A. A. N. Born 26/12/23. Commd 8/6/42. Flt Lt 20/12/51. Retd GD 27/2/65.
BATCHELOR L. E. Born 23/10/35. Commd 21/12/62. Flt Lt 1/4/66. Retd GD 31/3/69.
BATCHELOR P. D. Born 4/10/44. Commd 23/1/64. Sqn Ldr 1/7/78. Retd GD(G) 4/10/82.
BATCHELOR P. J., MB BS FRCS DLO. Born 31/8/26. Commd 29/6/53. Wg Cdr 29/6/64. Retd MED 29/6/69.
BATCHELOR W. A., BEd DPhysEd. Born 6/5/26. Commd 5/9/51. Wg Cdr 1/7/71. Retd PE 16/11/79.
BATCHELOR W. B. Born 19/6/08. Commd 19/9/40. Flt Lt 1/1/43. Retd ENG 19/7/48 rtg Sqn Ldr.
BATE L. C. Born 3/8/46. Commd 2/8/68. Sqn Ldr 1/7/84. Retd ENG 14/3/96.
BATEMAN A. J., BSc. Born 20/9/55. Commd 1/9/74. Sqn Ldr 1/7/88. Retd GD 30/6/94.
BATEMAN J. M., MB BS MRCP(UK). Born 31/1/58. Commd 17/3/80. Sqn Ldr 1/8/88. Retd MED 14/3/96.
BATEMAN R. H., BA. Born 18/5/24. Commd 11/2/44. Flt Lt 10/11/55. Retd GD 6/4/65.
BATEMAN R.E., MBE MIMgt. Born 11/10/29. Commd 11/2/65. Sqn Ldr 1/7/75. Retd ENG 11/10/87.
BATES C., BSc. Born 24/12/33. Commd 7/12/56. Sqn Ldr 7/6/67. Retd EDN 1/1/75.
BATES C. R., BSc CEng FIEE. Born 2/8/39. Commd 12/9/61. Gp Capt 1/1/87. Retd ENG 2/8/94.
BATES D. F., CB FIMgt. Born 10/4/28. Commd 9/4/50. AVM 1/1/80. Retd ADMIN 11/12/82.
BATES D. L. Born 23/3/33. Commd 8/11/51. Wg Cdr 1/1/80. Retd GD 23/3/88.
BATES E. Born 7/6/28. Commd 15/7/52. Flt Lt 15/4/58. Retd GD 7/6/66.
BATES G. A., MBE. Born 19/4/24. Commd 25/8/60. Sqn Ldr 1/7/74. Retd ENG 30/4/76.
BATES J. Born 13/7/38. Commd 19/8/58. Flt Lt 15/2/65. Retd GD 18/10/75.

BATES J., BA. Born 16/12/44. Commd 1/3/68. Sqn Ldr 1/1/80. Retd ENG 1/1/83.
BATES J. F. Born 15/4/31. Commd 13/8/52. Flt Lt 9/1/58. Retd GD 15/4/69.
BATES J. L. Born 30/10/30. Commd 5/12/51. Flt Lt 14/11/56. Retd GD 30/10/68.
BATES J. O., BSc CEng MIEE MRAeS. Born 8/9/45. Commd 9/10/67. Wg Cdr 1/1/85. Retd ENG 8/9/00.
BATES J. S. Born 29/12/28. Commd 10/4/52. Sqn Ldr 1/1/65. Retd GD 29/12/83.
BATES P. F. Born 27/11/36. Commd 14/11/59. Flt Lt 14/5/65. Retd GD 27/11/74.
BATES R. Born 7/10/30. Commd 28/5/66. Sqn Ldr 1/7/84. Retd ENG 7/10/88.
BATES R. C., BSc. Born 28/2/55. Commd 16/9/73. Sqn Ldr 1/7/87. Retd ENG 28/8/94.
BATES R. D., AFC FIMgt. Born 13/3/34. Commd 27/7/54. Gp Capt 1/1/76. Retd GD 5/5/86.
BATES R. G. Born 28/8/47. Commd 15/6/83. Sqn Ldr 1/1/92. Retd ENG 14/3/97.
BATES R. J. S., BA CEng MRAeS. Born 21/2/39. Commd 30/9/57. Wg Cdr 1/7/75. Retd ENG 9/5/79.
BATES W. N. Born 17/4/62. Commd 29/7/83. Flt Lt 29/1/89. Retd GD 17/4/00.
BATESON A. M. Born 21/1/53. Commd 3/1/88. Flt Lt 3/1/94. Retd ADMIN 14/3/97.
BATESON D. Born 12/6/60. Commd 15/3/79. Flt Lt 8/7/85. Retd ADMIN 14/3/96.
BATESON W. Born 17/1/04. Commd 9/5/40. Sqn Ldr 1/6/45. Retd ENG 18/6/50 rtg Wg Cdr.
BATEY R. Born 3/7/11. Commd 19/8/43. Flt Lt 19/2/47. Retd ENG 3/7/48.
BATH D. S. G., MB ChB DLO. Born 8/3/35. Commd 6/11/60. Sqn Ldr 16/10/65. Retd MED 7/3/69.
BATHE M. L. L. Born 9/8/14. Commd 2/12/40. Wg Cdr 1/1/58. Retd ENG 1/6/66.
BATHER R. A. Born 18/6/58. Commd 18/10/79. Flt Lt 28/6/83. Retd GD 16/8/96.
BATHO C. J. Born 10/10/13. Commd 9/5/40. Flt Lt 1/1/43. Retd GD 18/3/48 rtg Sqn Ldr.
BATSTONE A. E., PhD BSc. Born 9/11/30. Commd 2/9/53. Sqn Ldr 1/1/63. Retd GD 2/9/69.
BATT B. B., FIMgt. Born 26/7/35. Commd 21/4/54. A Cdre 1/7/88. Retd GD 2/4/91.
BATT K. F. Born 25/6/20. Commd 2/3/61. Flt Lt 7/5/65. Retd (MED(T) 30/4/69.
BATT M. K., MBE. Born 23/4/33. Commd 20/7/59. Gp Capt 1/1/85. Retd SY (RGT) 23/4/88.
BATT W. L. Born 16/2/22. Commd 13/8/46. Flt Lt 30/4/53. Retd GD 1/4/65.
BATTEN H. G. Born 4/8/14. Commd 21/2/40. Sqn Ldr 1/8/47. Retd SEC 5/8/63.
BATTEN J. Born 22/11/18. Commd 30/1/47. Flt Lt 30/7/51. Retd SUP 19/6/55.
BATTEN R. L. Born 30/5/21. Commd 8/12/48. Flt Lt 8/12/48. Retd GD 17/5/66.
BATTEN R. M. Born 7/12/21. Commd 29/10/41. Flt Lt 19/6/51. Retd GD(G) 20/9/66.
BATTERSBY R. S. H., BA. Born 15/5/59. Commd 5/2/84. Sqn Ldr 1/7/95. Retd ADMIN 5/2/00.
BATTEY E. F., BA. Born 23/8/36. Commd 19/12/59. Sqn Ldr 1/1/75. Retd GD 23/8/86.
BATTEY F. J., BA. Born 11/1/62. Commd 11/9/83. Flt Lt 15/1/88. Retd ADMIN 11/8/00.
BATTLE J. B. R. Born 24/10/21. Commd 14/11/42. Sqn Ldr 1/7/54. Retd GD 24/10/64.
BATTY P. Born 8/11/35. Commd 28/11/69. Flt Lt 4/5/72. Retd GD(G) 28/11/77. Re-instated 1/2/80 to 16/11/85.
BATTY P. H. Born 7/3/25. Commd 26/5/60. Sqn Ldr 1/1/69. Retd GD(G) 7/3/83.
BATTY S. T., MILT. Born 16/6/68. Commd 8/10/87. Fg Offr 8/4/90. Retd SUP 1/5/93.
BATTY W. G., MB ChB DObstRCOG DAvMed. Born 12/2/29. Commd 21/11/54. Wg Cdr 8/3/69. Retd MED 16/5/77.
BAUCHOP J. S. Born 2/2/11. Commd 4/1/45. Fg Offr 4/7/45. Retd ASD 3/7/46 rtg Flt Lt.
BAUGH D. L., OBE. Born 18/8/43. Commd 28/7/64. Gp Capt 1/7/89. Retd GD 2/6/97.
BAUGH S. P., BA. Born 5/5/64. Commd 2/9/84. Flt Lt 15/1/88. Retd GD 14/9/96.
BAUGHAN D. S., IEng MIEIE. Born 10/4/54. Commd 8/10/87. Flt Lt 8/10/89. Retd ENG 15/12/00.
BAUGHAN M. J. Born 27/7/34. Commd 26/8/66. Flt Lt 26/8/67. Retd EDN 26/8/74.
BAUGHAN R. D., OBE. Born 30/10/13. Commd 8/6/36. Wg Cdr 1/7/47. Retd GD 12/5/58.
BAUMGARTNER H. N. Born 7/4/50. Commd 29/3/68. Flt Lt 29/9/73. Retd GD 21/8/76.
BAVERSTOCK M. J., BEd. Born 29/9/60. Commd 13/2/83. Flt Lt 13/11/84. Retd GD 13/2/99.
BAVERSTOCK T. Born 15/7/46. Commd 2/3/70. Flt Lt 2/9/75. Retd GD 27/9/80.
BAXANDALL J. D. C., MB BS FRCOG. Born 21/3/32. Commd 17/6/57. A Cdre 17/10/88. Retd MED 14/9/96.
BAXTER A. Born 1/5/46. Commd 21/11/74. Sqn Ldr 1/7/84. Retd OPS SPT 1/12/99.
BAXTER G. G., BSc. Born 23/12/34. Commd 20/12/57. Sqn Ldr 20/6/67. Retd EDN 12/9/73.
BAXTER G. R., MA BA FIMgt. Born 16/12/25. Commd 7/10/48. Gp Capt 1/7/66. Retd GD 7/5/80.
BAXTER H., MBE. Born 18/2/28. Commd 20/10/49. Gp Capt 1/7/81. Retd GD 18/2/83.
BAXTER J. J. Born 8/11/16. Commd 27/8/59. Flt Lt 27/8/62. Retd SUP 8/11/71.
BAXTER J. T. Born 3/4/20. Commd 21/6/56. Flt Lt 21/6/62. Retd GD(G) 11/8/67.
BAXTER J. W. Born 29/1/24. Commd 17/7/51. Sqn Ldr 1/1/71. Retd GD 10/11/78.
BAXTER P. R. Born 21/9/36. Commd 16/9/55. Sqn Ldr 1/7/67. Retd GD 15/5/81.
BAXTER P. S., CEng MIEE. Born 23/3/35. Commd 24/6/58. Sqn Ldr 1/1/69. Retd ENG 17/4/74.
BAXTER S. G. L. Born 26/2/61. Commd 3/7/80. Flt Lt 17/12/86. Retd SUP 1/10/89.
BAXTER W. J. Born 2/9/18. Commd 26/5/60. Flt Lt 26/5/63. Retd ENG 2/9/73.
BAXTER W. L. Born 10/9/22. Commd 12/2/44. Sqn Ldr 1/1/55. Retd GD 10/9/71.
BAYES C. R. Born 16/2/46. Commd 15/10/81. Sqn Ldr 1/7/94. Retd ENG 14/3/96.
BAYLEY J. L. Born 13/11/17. Commd 23/9/44. Wg Cdr 1/7/68. Retd GD 2/12/72.
BAYLEY S. G. Born 1/4/14. Commd 4/4/45. Flt Lt 4/4/51. Retd RGT 29/12/57 rtg Sqn Ldr.
BAYLEY W. J., FAAI MIMgt. Born 2/8/31. Commd 27/9/51. Sqn Ldr 1/7/68. Retd ADMIN 1/9/85.
BAYLISS G. G., DFC AFC. Born 28/4/29. Commd 19/4/60.Flt Lt 19/4/60. Retd GD 19/9/71.
BAYLISS J. A., MBE. Born 3/4/41. Commd 18/12/62. Wg Cdr 1/1/89. Retd GD 3/4/96.
BAYLISS V., MIMgt. Born 28/5/24. Commd 23/12/44. Wg Cdr 1/1/70. Retd GD(G) 28/5/79.

BAYLY A. E., BSc CEng MIEE. Born 27/6/43. Commd 30/9/62. Sqn Ldr 1/1/74. Retd ENG 15/5/76.
BAYLY R. C., MBE. Born 9/1/24. Commd 18/9/44. Sqn Ldr 1/1/70. Retd PE 9/1/79.
BAYNE D. P. Born 3/6/37. Commd 28/7/67. Flt Lt 4/5/72. Retd GD 4/6/74.
BAYNE R. M. Born 28/2/39. Commd 13/12/60. Sqn Ldr 1/7/74. Retd GD 1/9/79.
BAYNES K. G. Born 16/3/32. Commd 24/9/52. Gp Capt 1/7/80. Retd GD 31/3/85.
BAYNTON J. G., BSc. Born 6/3/53. Commd 14/1/73. Sqn Ldr 1/7/84. Retd GD 6/3/90.
BAYNTON W. G. Born 18/10/24. Commd 27/5/44. Sqn Ldr 1/4/55. Retd GD 30/3/68.
BAZALGETTE L. C. Born 27/10/21. Commd 13/4/42. Sqn Ldr 1/1/54. Retd GD 1/12/70.
BEACH M. D. Born 6/10/32. Commd 6/2/57. Flt Lt 21/8/63. Retd ADMIN 30/9/83.
BEACHAM W. J. Born 4/1/30. Commd 31/8/50. Sqn Ldr 1/7/68. Retd GD 4/1/88.
BEADLE P. J. C. Born 30/7/57. Commd 24/7/81. Sqn Ldr 1/1/92. Retd GD 14/3/96.
BEADLE T. Born 18/4/48. Commd 23/2/68. Flt Lt 23/8/73. Retd GD 18/4/86.
BEADLE T. C., LLB. Born 28/3/61. Commd 17/7/81. Flt Lt 15/10/83. Retd GD 19/10/87.
BEADLE W. W. Born 4/10/18. Commd 26/2/54. Flt Lt 26/2/59. Retd ENG 5/1/62.
BEADMAN J. F. Born 4/10/44. Commd 29/10/64. Sqn Ldr 1/1/84. Retd SUP 4/10/92.
BEAK P., BEd. Born 9/3/49. Commd 18/11/79. Flt Lt 18/11/83. Retd ADMIN 18/11/95.
BEAL D. G., OBE CEng MRAeS MinstP FINucE. Born 6/4/18. Commd 7/1/43. Wg Cdr 1/1/62. Retd ENG 6/7/73.
BEAL M. J. Born 9/11/41. Commd 24/3/61. Flt Lt 10/2/67. Retd GD 9/11/79.
BEAL R. V., FACCA. Born 17/8/06. Commd 15/9/39. Sqn Ldr 1/8/47. Retd SEC 15/9/58.
BEALER R. A. Born 17/6/45. Commd 3/3/67. Wg Cdr 1/1/91. Retd GD 17/6/00.
BEAMENT H. T. Born 22/7/43. Commd 31/1/64. Flt Lt 4/11/70. Retd GD 1/8/75.
BEAMISH D. T., CBE MMAR MIMgt. Born 25/9/20. Commd 19/10/49. Gp Capt 1/1/71. Retd MAR 25/9/75.
BEAMISH O. T. Born 30/12/38. Commd 19/2/76. Sqn Ldr 1/7/85. Retd GD 30/12/93.
BEAN E., MBE. Born 1/4/18. Commd 3/8/44. Sqn Ldr 1/10/55. Retd ENG 1/4/69.
BEAN J. D. Born 25/7/44. Commd 27/2/75. Flt Lt 27/2/77. Retd GD 27/2/83.
BEANE D. Born 5/9/38. Commd 7/12/61. Flt Lt 1/4/66. Retd GD 5/9/76.
BEANE M. J. Born 7/5/39. Commd 9/9/58. Sqn Ldr 1/7/92. Retd GD 7/5/94.
BEANEY G. P. E., FRCS MB BS MRCS LRCP DLO. Born 8/4/33. Commd 4/1/59. Sqn Ldr 4/7/63. Retd MED 1/5/68.
BEAR E. A., BSc(Eng) CEng FIMgt MRAeS MIMechE. Born 7/3/29. Commd 24/9/52. A Cdre 1/1/78.
    Retd ENG 7/3/84.
BEARBLOCK C. D. A. F., BSc. Born 3/1/66. Commd 16/9/84. Flt Lt 15/1/90. Retd GD 15/7/99.
BEARD A. F. P., MBE. Born 12/11/18. Commd 20/7/43. Wg Cdr 1/1/64. Retd SUP 1/2/69.
BEARD A. J. Born 16/11/39. Commd 12/7/79. Sqn Ldr 1/1/89. Retd ENG 18/9/91.
BEARD D. H. Born 17/8/26. Commd 5/12/63. Sqn Ldr 1/7/73. Retd PE 30/6/81.
BEARD D. J. R. Born 6/3/30. Commd 11/10/51. Sqn Ldr 1/7/64. Retd GD 6/3/68.
BEARD D. M. Born 5/11/43. Commd 13/12/79. Ft Lt 13/12/84. Retd SUP 5/11/99.
BEARD J. N. Born 8/8/23. Commd 10/4/52. Flt Lt 10/11/55. Retd GD 8/8/78.
BEARD J. S. Born 8/11/45. Commd 6/5/66. Flt Lt 6/11/71. Retd GD 2/4/90.
BEARD M. E. Born 13/10/34. Commd 19/11/52. Flt Lt 15/4/58. Retd GD 30/9/77.
BEARD S. W. B. Born 24/3/35. Commd 16/6/69. Flt Lt 16/6/71. Retd PRT 5/1/73.
BEARDMORE J., CEng MIEE. Born 4/3/23. Commd 27/5/43. Sqn Ldr 1/10/55. Retd ENG 6/7/63.
BEARDON D. F., AFC. Born 24/5/15. Commd 5/4/37. Gp Capt 1/7/56. Retd GD 5/7/65.
BEARDS J. B. Born 9/9/43. Commd 24/6/65. Flt Lt 24/12/67. Retd GD 13/4/73.
BEARDSALL, D. H. Born 20/3/34. Commd 17/12/64. Flt Lt 17/12/70. Retd SEC 1/11/75.
BEARDSLEY R. A., DFC. Born 9/1/20. Commd 28/6/41. Sqn Ldr 1/7/63. Retd GD(G) 1/8/70.
BEARDSMORE J., BA DPhysEd. Born 30/6/46. Commd 7/8/67. Sqn Ldr 1/7/79. Retd ADMIN 30/6/90.
BEARNE G., CB. Born 5/11/08. Commd 28/6/29. AVM 1/7/56. Retd GD 5/11/61.
BEARRYMAN F. G. Born 13/5/25. Commd 19/7/57. Sqn Ldr 1/1/71. Retd ENG 10/6/75.
BEASANT N.C.A., BSc. Born 9/7/50. Commd 18/4/71. Sqn Ldr 1/1/83. Retd GD 16/7/88.
BEASLEY D. A., MBE FHCIMA. Born 13/2/21. Commd 11/5/53. Wg Cdr 1/1/67. Retd CAT 31/8/73.
BEASLEY G. J. Born 24/3/43. Commd 8/12/61. Flt Lt 9/2/68. Retd GD 1/6/94.
BEATON A. J. Born 12/12/47. Commd 27/2/67. Sqn Ldr 1/1/81. Retd GD 3/8/85.
BEATON H. B. Born 6/1/63. Commd 20/10/83. Plt Offr 19/8/84. Retd ADMIN 15/12/85.
BEATON H. W. Born 25/8/31. Commd 6/12/51. Sqn Ldr 1/7/67. Retd GD 20/8/76.
BEATON J. Born 28/6/19. Commd 9/9/39. Flt Lt 30/1/47. Retd SUP 19/11/60. rtg Sqn Ldr.
BEATON J. L., BA MMar. Born 5/12/32. Commd 11/4/61. Sqn Ldr 11/7/72. Retd ADMIN 11/4/77.
BEATON K. A. Born 20/3/48. Commd 1/7/82. Flt IT 1/7/84. Retd ADMIN 1/6/94.
BEATON M. J. Born 13/8/52. Commd 25/2/79. Sqn Ldr 1/1/93. Retd ADMIN 14/3/96.
BEATON P. K. Born 20/6/35. Commd 27/10/65. Flt Lt 27/10/69. Retd GD 27/10/75.
BEATON W. McB. G. Born 2/10/09. Commd 22/8/41. Flt Lt 1/1/44. Retd SUP 28/6/47 rtg Sqn Ldr.
BEATSON B. F., DTM DPH. Born 7/4/90. Commd 13/10/22. Sqn Ldr 31/1/24. Retd MED 13/10/46.
BEATSON R. MacL. Born 15/11/33. Commd 11/6/52. Flt Lt 14/5/58. Retd GD 15/11/71.
BEATSON T. R., MB BS FRCS LRCP. Born 4/3/28. Commd 5/8/52. Wg Cdr 5/7/64. Retd MED 5/8/68.
BEATTIE A. C. Born 11/5/12. Commd 16/6/41. Flt Lt 1/9/45. Retd ENG 24/10/53 rtg Sqn Ldr.
BEATTIE D. L. Born 5/1/32. Commd 22/9/55. Flt Lt 5/10/60. Retd GD 29/1/70.
BEATTIE J. G. Born 31/1/41. Commd 16/1/60. Flt Lt 28/7/65. Retd GD 31/1/79.

BEATTIE N. G. Born 10/4/44. Commd 13/12/79. Sqn Ldr 1/1/91. Retd ENG 3/1/97.
BEATTIE T. W. Born 4/2/23. Commd 6/3/53. Sqn Ldr 1/1/66. Retd GD 31/8/68.
BEAUGEARD G. G. Born 6/11/21. Commd 5/7/44. Gp Capt 1/7/73. Retd GD 6/11/76.
BEAUMONT D. Born 20/11/18. Commd 17/7/45. Sqn Ldr 1/1/57. Retd SEC 22/5/65.
BEAUMONT D. L. Born 26/4/41. Commd 17/5/63. Flt Lt 8/1/69. Retd GD 26/4/79.
BEAUMONT K. M., MA. Born 4/11/19. Commd 1/9/41. Sqn Ldr 1/3/56. Retd EDN 1/2/58.
BEAUTEMENT P., MSc BSc PGCE. Born 14/6/51. Commd 2/9/84. Sqn Ldr 1/7/91. Retd ADMIN 14/3/97.
BEAVAN A. J. P. Born 18/6/43. Commd 11/8/67. Flt Lt 4/5/72. Retd GD 10/2/77.
BEAVERS F. P. P., MSc BChD LDSRCS MGDSRCS(Ed). Born 2/6/53. Commd 9/4/78. Wg Cdr 15/5/89.
     Retd DEL 9/4/94.
BEAVES B. R., BA DPhysEd. Born 1/6/43. Commd 13/9/70. Sqn Ldr 13/3/74. Retd ADMIN 13/9/86.
BEAVIS Sir Michael, KCB CBE AFC CBIM. Born 13/8/29. Commd 25/8/49. ACM 1/7/84. Retd GD 3/1/87.
BEAZLEY F., IEng. Born 18/4/31. Commd 26/5/67. Sqn Ldr 1/1/80. Retd ENG 1/5/89.
BEAZLEY R. H., CBE AFC FRAeS. Born 15/9/41. Commd 5/3/65. Gp Capt 1/1/90. Retd GD 15/12/96.
BEBBINGTON F. S. Born 22/10/43. Commd 9/3/62. Sqn Ldr 1/1/77. Retd GD 31/1/82.
BEBBINGTON H. A. Born 29/4/37. Commd 31/10/69. Flt Lt 4/5/72. Retd GD 31/10/77.
BEBBINGTON J. K. Born 9/1/35. Commd 23/9/66. Flt Lt 23/9/71. Retd ENG 6/9/74.
BECK B. Born 6/8/12. Commd 1/9/41. Flt Lt 10/1/45. Retd ENG 13/1/46 rtg Sqn Ldr.
BECK C. O. Born 6/8/14. Commd 12/8/42. Sqn Ldr 1/1/55. Retd GD(G) 9/11/61.
BECK G., BSc. Born 7/3/66. Commd 12/2/95. Flt Lt 12/8/98. Retd ADMIN 18/4/00.
BECK H. W. B. Born 10/6/33. Commd 15/5/58. Sqn Ldr 1/1/72. Retd GD 5/5/78.
BECK M. P., BA MRAeS. Born 22/7/36. Commd 21/4/67. Wg Cdr 1/7/79. Retd ENG 8/5/86.
BECK P. R. Born 26/6/44. Commd 28/10/66. Flt Lt 28/4/72. Retd GD 7/12/72.
BECK S. R. Born 17/1/16. Commd 13/6/44. Flt Lt 7/6/51. Retd SEC 16/5/54 rtg Sqn Ldr.
BECKER A. F. Born 19/1/29. Commd 31/1/52. Flt Lt 31/1/57. Retd ENG 6/8/60.
BECKER B. H., CEng MRAeS. Born 12/6/12. Commd 17/7/33. Gp Capt 1/7/53. Retd ENG 1/5/55.
BECKER K. H. Born 18/10/43. Commd 29/11/63. Sqn Ldr 1/7/80. Retd GD 18/10/99.
BECKETT G. A. J., CEng MIEE. Born 2/12/23. Commd 5/12/51. Wg Cdr 1/7/69. Retd ENG 21/12/73.
BECKETT J. D. Born 28/8/35. Commd 23/2/60. Sqn Ldr 11/7/71. Retd EDN 23/2/76.
BECKETT J. H., MIMgt. Born 7/12/23. Commd 15/9/60. Sqn Ldr 1/7/74. Retd ADMIN 6/8/77.
BECKETT J. R., MCIPS. Born 18/9/42. Commd 23/9/66. Sqn Ldr 1/7/74. Retd SUP 18/9/97.
BECKINGHAM A. T. H. Born 27/6/39. Commd 8/6/60. Flt Lt 16/10/67. Retd ADMIN 18/7/77.
BECKLEY D. H. Born 4/5/30. Commd 30/5/69. Flt Lt 30/5/73. Retd GD(G) 4/5/80.
BECKLEY P. A., FIMgt. Born 17/7/29. Commd 9/8/51. Gp Capt 1/7/81. Retd ADMIN 1/12/83.
BECKLEY R. B. Born 9/10/20. Commd 2/2/45. Flt Lt 7/6/56. Retd GD 9/6/64.
BECKNELLE P. V. Born 15/1/39. Commd 27/1/61. Flt Lt 27/7/66. Retd GD 28/4/72.
BEDDOES A. B. Born 28/6/45. Commd 17/1/85. Sqn Ldr 1/1/94. Retd ENG 14/3/97.
BEDDOW W. D., AFC. Born 19/9/12. Commd 30/7/42. Retd GD 10/4/47.
BEDDOWS A. J. Born 28/1/46. Commd 26/5/67. Flt Lt 26/11/73. Retd ADMIN 28/1/84.
BEDFORD A. W., AFC. Born 18/11/20. Commd 14/11/42. Flt Lt 14/5/46. Retd GD 15/9/51.
BEDFORD B. Born 11/3/29. Commd 2/7/52. Flt Lt 8/1/58. Retd GD 21/1/68.
BEDFORD B. K. Born 2/2/32. Commd 28/11/51. Flt Lt 28/5/56. Retd GD 2/2/70.
BEDFORD D. J. Born 5/2/63. Commd 2/2/84. Flt Lt 2/8/89. Retd GD 28/4/00.
BEDFORD E. Born 28/10/46. Commd 28/2/69. Flt Lt 6/10/71. Retd GD 10/6/91.
BEDFORD G. R., MB ChB. Born 30/7/12. Commd 2/5/41. Gp Capt 1/7/62. Retd MED 2/8/70.
BEDFORD P. A., AFC MRAeS. Born 28/5/46. Commd 26/5/67. Gp Capt 1/1/92. Retd GD 17/1/99.
BEDFORD R., MBE BSc DCAe MRAeS. Born 10/8/34. Commd 22/11/56. Sqn Ldr 1/1/66. Retd ENG 16/8/72.
BEDFORD S. H. Born 22/2/51. Commd 17/7/70. Sqn Ldr 1/1/87. Retd GD 1/5/89.
BEDNALL M. P., BSc MRAeS. Born 24/2/43. Commd 30/9/62. Wg Cdr 1/1/79. Retd ENG 1/1/82.
BEDWELL R. S. W. Born 26/9/23. Commd 17/10/57. Sqn Ldr 1/1/71. Retd ENG 7/4/78.
BEDWIN P. G. W., MBE. Born 4/11/43. Commd 4/11/64. Sqn Ldr 1/1/79. Retd GD 1/1/82.
BEDWORTH M. A., BSc. Born 23/1/40. Commd 4/7/63. Flt Lt 4/7/67. Retd EDN 1/10/71.
BEE M. E., AFC. Born 31/12/37. Commd 29/7/58. Wg Cdr 1/1/73. Retd GD 11/7/78.
BEEBE A. S., MBE. Born 26/10/16. Commd 27/8/59. Sqn Ldr 1/7/68. Retd SUP 26/10/72.
BEEBE P. S. J. Born 17/1/33. Commd 14/11/57. Gp Capt 1/7/79. Retd ADMIN 11/9/82.
BEEBY C. W., BA. Born 20/7/48. Commd 28/12/80. Sqn Ldr 1/1/89. Retd SUP 14/3/96.
BEEBY J. M., MRAeS MIMgt. Born 6/6/20. Commd 17/11/49. Sqn Ldr 1/1/58. Retd ENG 2/1/71.
BEECH M. D., AFC BSc. Born 21/10/51. Commd 13/9/70. Sqn Ldr 1/7/82. Retd GD 20/11/88.
BEECH P. D., BSc. Born 19/5/53. Commd 11/7/76. Flt Lt 11/10/77. Retd GD 11/7/88.
BEECH-ALLAN M. D. Born 13/8/47. Commd 28/4/67. Flt Lt 28/10/72. Retd GD 1/4/76.
BEECHAM R. S., OBE. Born 28/1/33. Commd 21/8/52. Gp Capt 1/7/79. Retd ADMIN 3/4/82.
BEECHING J. Born 18/8/16. Commd 20/3/52. Flt Offr 20/3/58. Retd SEC 9/8/67.
BEECROFT J., DFM. Born 25/9/20. Commd 8/6/43. Flt Lt 8/12/46. Retd GD 25/9/63.
BEEDIE W., FInstAM MIMgt. Born 17/9/48. Commd 8/11/68. Wg Cdr 1/7/87. Retd ADMIN 14/3/97.
BEEDIE W. A., CEng MRAeS. Born 29/7/23. Commd 2/9/43. Wg Cdr 1/7/73. Retd ENG 24/12/76.
BEENY R. E., OBE. Born 11/1/14. Commd 17/1/38. Gp Capt 1/1/58. Retd ENG 10/9/66.

BEER The Rev D. V., PhL STL. Born 21/5/31. Commd 11/1/66. Retd 21/5/86 Wg Cdr.
BEER. G. C. Born 12/6/43. Commd 4/12/64. Flt Lt 8/1/69. Retd GD 30/10/76.
BEER M. E., MBE. Born 10/2/44. Commd 19/4/63. Sqn Ldr 1/7/82. Retd GD 9/9/95.
BEER P. G., CB CBE LVO. Born 16/7/41. Commd 11/5/62. AVM 1/7/91. Retd GD 16/11/95.
BEER R. B. E. Born 2/11/24. Commd 12/9/63. Sqn Ldr 1/1/74. Retd ENG 28/8/79.
BEES R. G., BSc. Born 6/11/56. Commd 14/10/76. Sqn Ldr 1/7/88. Retd GD 6/11/94.
BEESLEY J. H. Born 19/7/28. Commd 17/7/58. Sqn Ldr 1/7/77. Retd GD 2/4/85.
BEET G. T. W., BSc. Born 20/5/60. Commd 6/9/81. Sqn Ldr 1/1/95. Retd GD 20/5/99.
BEETLESTONE T. J. Born 30/11/35. Commd 6/4/72. Flt Lt 6/4/75. Retd GD 30/11/93.
BEGG A., MBE. Born 27/9/25. Commd 21/11/51. Flt Lt 21/5/56. Retd GD 28/3/69.
BEGG A. L. Born 24/5/39. Commd 13/2/60. Sqn Ldr 1/7/72. Retd GD 25/5/76.
BEGG G. I., BSc. Born 15/3/56. Commd 14/9/75. Flt Lt 15/10/76. Retd GD 1/5/88.
BEGG W., ACCS. Born 18/10/23. Commd 23/12/61. Flt Lt 23/12/64. Retd SEC 17/1/68.
BEGGS B. D. Born 20/1/36. Commd 9/4/57. Flt Lt 9/10/59. Retd GD 27/10/67.
BEGLAN P. M. Born 11/4/43. Commd 28/2/64. Flt Lt 13/6/72. Retd GD 11/4/81.
BEHRENS R. W., CEng MIEE. Born 14/2/42. Commd 26/5/64. Sqn Ldr 1/7/75. Retd ENG 8/7/83.
BEILBY I.D.C. Born 14/12/29. Commd 11/2/65. Flt Lt 11/2/70. Retd ENG 14/12/89.
BEILL A., CB. Born 14/2/31. Commd 30/7/52. AVM 1/1/85. Retd SUP 1/4/87.
BEITH-JONES H., OBE FIMgt. Born 21/3/44. Commd 28/3/63. Wg Cdr 1/1/85. Retd ADMIN 27/3/96.
BELBEN M. J., BA CEng MIEE MRAeS MIMgt. Born 21/11/37. Commd 27/1/67. Flt Lt 27/1/69. Retd ENG 21/11/75.
BELBIN A.T., CEng MRAeS. Born 7/10/41. Commd 11/3/68. Flt Lt 11/11/70. Retd ENG 30/9/86.
BELCHAMBER N. W. Born 4/11/30. Commd 30/3/61. Flt Lt 30/3/66. Retd GD 4/11/85.
BELCHER D. Born 28/10/29. Commd 12/3/52. Sqn Ldr 1/7/64. Retd GD 5/12/75.
BELCHER F. D. Born 3/4/33. Commd 30/5/69. Flt Lt 30/5/75. Retd GD(G) 4/4/79.
BELCHER H. G. Born 13/7/15. Commd 17/8/39. Wg Cdr 1/7/54. Retd SUP 28/6/58.
BELDING V. C., MBE. Born 18/9/20. Commd 6/9/51. Sqn Ldr 1/1/63. Retd SUP18/6/73.
BELFITT F., DFM. Born 10/8/17. Commd 18/2/43. Flt Lt 18/8/46. Retd GD(G) 10/8/69.
BELFORD J. C. Born 31/5/94. Commd 9/5/18. Flt Lt 1/1/30. Retd GD 13/5/32. Recalled 25/8/39 to 24/4/40.
BELK P. Born 16/12/38. Commd 15/6/83. Sqn Ldr 1/1/90. Retd ENG 20/1/95.
BELL A. A. Born 8/2/36. Commd 5/5/60. Flt Lt 5/11/64. Retd GD 8/2/74.
BELL A. E. Born 2/12/23. Commd 3/1/44. Flt Lt 29/6/50. Retd SEC 12/11/50.
BELL A. G. Born 6/8/57. Commd 21/1/78. Sqn Ldr 1/7/92. Retd SY 1/4/97.
BELL A. J. Born 2/7/25. Commd 18/10/51. Flt Lt 18/4/55. Retd GD(G) 2/7/80.
BELL A. MacD., BSc CEng MIEE MIMgt. Born 19/10/30. Commd 4/11/53. Sqn Ldr 1/1/65. Retd ENG 4/11/69.
BELL A. P., MRAeS. Born 1/4/43. Commd 9/2/62. Wg Cdr 1/1/83. Retd GD 2/4/93.
BELL A. R. Born 27/10/39. Commd 25/7/60. Flt Lt 25/1/63. Retd GD 27/10/94.
BELL C. G., BA MRAeS MRIN MIMgt. Born 25/8/33. Commd 5/11/52. Wg Cdr 1/7/79. Retd GD 25/8/88.
BELL C. J. Born 15/8/23. Commd 27/5/54. Sqn Ldr 1/1/71. Retd GD 12/5/73.
BELL C. R. Born 10/9/23. Commd 20/10/46. Flt Lt 20/4/50. Retd GD 15/1/62.
BELL C. R. L., BSc CEng MIMechE. Born 6/8/44. Commd 15/7/65. Wg Cdr 1/1/86. Retd ENG 6/8/99.
BELL C.E., BA, Born 12/6/36. Commd 26/10/79. Sqn Ldr 26/10/76. Retd ENG 7/7/87
BELL D. A. Born 24/1/33. Commd 29/12/54. Flt Lt 29/6/60. Retd GD 28/11/71.
BELL D. A. Born 5/4/39. Commd 11/11/64. Sqn Ldr 1/1/86. Retd GD(G) 1/5/89.
BELL D. A. J., MBE. Born 13/10/24. Commd 28/7/67. Flt Lt 28/7/70. Retd ENG 13/10/79.
BELL D. W. E. Born 9/3/24. Commd 22/11/44. Flt Lt 19/6/52. Retd SEC 31/3/62.
BELL E., AFC. Born 21/2/16. Commd 23/11/42. Sqn Ldr 1/7/54. Retd GD 13/3/59.
BELL F. W. Born 3/4/22. Commd 21/2/44. Flt Lt 21/2/50. Retd SEC 3/4/71.
BELL G., MMar MNI. Born 26/6/33. Commd 11/3/68. Wg Cdr 1/7/84. Retd ADMIN 4/6/90.
BELL G. Born 2/1/35. Commd 28/6/79. Sqn Ldr 1/1/88. Retd ENG 30/4/90.
BELL G. B., AFC. Born 6/12/24. Commd 25/8/49. Sqn Ldr 1/7/58. Retd GD 8/4/74.
BELL G. B. M., OBE. Born 18/10/14. Commd 14/9/34. Wg Cdr 1/7/47. Retd GD 7/2/59 rtg Gp Capt.
BELL G. E. Born 13/12/36. Commd 23/3/55. Flt Lt 1/1/67. Retd GD 13/12/74.
BELL G. F. Born 23/7/41. Commd 30/8/64. Sqn Ldr 1/7/87. Retd GD 23/7/96.
BELL G. F. A. Born 16/2/52. Commd 29/7/83. Flt Lt 29/7/85. Retd GD(G) 29/7/91.
BELL H., ACIS. Born 13/1/30. Commd 11/3/65. Sqn Ldr 1/7/74. Retd SEC 5/9/79.
BELL H. W., BA. Born 23/12/48. Commd 1/11/71. Flt Lt 1/2/73. Retd GD 1/11/83.
BELL J., MBE. Born 14/2/41. Commd 11/5/78. Sqn Ldr 1/7/88. Retd SUP 14/6/96.
BELL J. A., OBE FIMgt. Born 16/9/34. Commd 26/7/55. Air Cdre 1/7/87. Retd GD 1/10/89.
BELL J. D., BA. Born 1/4/48. Commd 16/8/70. Sqn Ldr 1/7/79. Retd ENG 16/8/86.
BELL J. D., OBE. Born 21/5/45. Commd 11/8/77. Wg Cdr 1/7/90. Retd ADMIN 30/6/00.
BELL J. H., CEng MRAeS MIMgt, Born 5/2/22. Commd 16/5/57. Sqn Ldr 1/7/70. Retd ENG 26/8/72.
BELL J. J. Born 19/8/40. Commd 23/1/64. Flt Lt 20/6/70. Retd GD(G) 9/1/80.
BELL J. J. Born 19/8/40. Commd 24/11/80. Sqn Ldr 1/7 87. Retd SUP 10/12/92.
BELL J. L. Born 30/7/43. Commd 8/6/62. Flt Lt 8/12/67. Retd GD 15/5/72
BELL J. R., DFC MBE. Born 25/3/23. Commd 22/2/44. Wg Cdr 1/7/72. Retd PI 31/3/77.
BELL J. S., BSc. Born 27/10/42. Commd 7/10/63. Sqn Ldr 1/1/74. Retd GD 27/10/80.

BELL J. S. W., OBE, AFC. Born 29/3/24. Commd. 24/3/44. Gp Capt 1/7/71. Retd GD 29/6/78.
BELL J. T. Born 7/2/40. Commd 15/9/61. Flt Lt 15/3/72. Retd GD 7/8/90.
BELL J. V., CBE. Born 29/10/40. Commd 5/3/65. Gp Capt 1/7/87. Retd GD 29/7/96.
BELL K. Born 8/1/29. Commd 13/2/64. Sqn Ldr 1/7/75. Retd ADMIN 8/7/82.
BELL K. Born 26/2/41. Commd 6/5/83. Sqn Ldr 1/7/92. Retd SY 26/2/96.
BELL M. A., BA. Born 16/3/59. Commd 18/10/81. Sqn Ldr 1/1/93. Retd SUP 14/9/96.
BELL M. C., BSc. Born 16/5/54. Commd 3/9/72. Flt Lt 15/4/79. Retd ENG 16/5/92.
BELL M. F. Born 20/7/41. Commd 26/5/61. Wg Cdr 1/1/94. Retd GD 20/7/96.
BELL M. J. Born 4/1/43. Commd 1/7/82. Flt Lt 1/3/87. Retd ENG 16/5/93.
BELL P., MBE. Born 28/9/22. Commd 1/5/47. Flt Lt 4/6/53. Retd PE 30/4/70.
BELL P. A., BSc. Born 22/6/62. Commd 27/10/82. Sqn Ldr 1/1/98. Retd GD 1/1/01.
BELL P. G., CEng MRAeS. Born 11/9/39. Commd 18/7/61. Wg Cdr 1/1/77. Retd ENG 21/6/85.
BELL P. J. Born 20/7/58. Commd 20/7/78. Flt Lt 20/1/84. Retd GD 20/7/96.
BELL R. L. B. Born 17/9/36. Commd 12/1/55. Sqn Ldr 1/7/69. Retd GD 17/9/74.
BELL S. H. Born 5/5/26. Commd 14/11/51. Flt Lt 14/5/56. Retd GD 5/5/81.
BELL W. A., BA. Born 6/4/40. Commd 1/10/62. Wg Cdr 1/1/80. Retd GD 1/10/89.
BELL W. E. B. Born 1/9/33. Commd 26/8/52. Flt Lt 31/7/57. Retd GD 1/1/65.
BELL W. G. Born 21/10/23. Commd 27/1/55. Flt Lt 27/1/61. Retd GD 31/8/68.
BELL., M. J. BSc. Born 12/7/48. Commd 3/1/69. Flt Lt 15/10/70. Retd GD 1/1/82.
BELLAMY D. W. Born 17/8/63. Commd 13/8/82. Flt Lt 13/2/88. Retd GD 1/4/92.
BELLAMY R. M., BTech. Born 1/2/44. Commd 30/12/69. Flt Lt 30/3/73. Retd ENG 11/5/79.
BELLAMY S. R. J., MB BS DCP. Born 22/10/34. Commd 1/1/64. Gp Capt 4/2/86. Retd MED 14/9/96.
BELLAMY-KNIGHTS P. G. Born 21/4/32. Commd 19/3/52. Wg Cdr 1/7/75. Retd GD 13/10/86.
BELLERGY P. A. Born 27/12/20. Commd 4/6/45. Gp Capt 1/7/71. Retd SEC 30/4/74.
BELLERS W. R. Born 1/2/36. Commd 13/7/61. Flt Lt 1/4/66. Retd RGT 14/10/75.
BELLINGALL J. E. Born 7/12/43. Commd 25/4/69. Flt Lt 25/10/74. Retd GD 7/12/00.
BELLWOOD B., BA DPhysEd. Born 22/8/31. Commd 25/3/54. Flt Lt 7/3/62. Retd SUP 30/8/75.
BELSHAM P. M. Born 30/8/33. Commd 18/6/52. Flt Lt 1/3/61. Retd GD 30/4/76.
BELSON D. J. Born 13/7/31. Commd 9/4/52. Sqn Ldr 1/7/61. Retd GD 13/7/69.
BEMAN K. Born 22/2/37. Commd 31/12/62. Flt Lt 22/4/68. Retd GD 23/2/75.
BENBOW G. T. Born 1/4/32. Commd 5/3/57. Flt Lt 21/8/63. Retd GD 1/4/94.
BENCKE R. G. Born 2/9/40. Commd 19/12/61. Sqn Ldr 1/1/76. Retd GD 1/7/80.
BENDELL A. J., OBE AFC. Born 30/3/36. Commd 3/3/54. Wg Cdr 1/7/74. Retd GD 19/6/87.
BENDELL T. W. Born 4/4/44. Commd 8/9/77. Flt Lt 8/9/79. Retd ENG 8/9/85.
BENDY R. A. Born 26/3/50. Commd 28/11/74. Flt Lt 28/5/80. Retd GD 12/8/90.
BENDYSHE-BROWN W. J., BA. Born 7/11/47. Commd 29/3/68. Wg Cdr 1/1/89. Retd SUP 25/6/94.
BENFIELD D. Born 25/1/32. Commd. 23/6/67. Flt Lt 23/6/72. Retd GD(G) 8/4/78.
BENFIELD J. M. Born 25/10/43. Commd 26/10/62. Flt Lt 26/4/68. Retd GD 20/8/76.
BENFORD T. J., BA MCIPS. Born 22/4/47. Commd 1/3/68. Sqn Ldr 1/7/79. Retd SUP 22/4/85.
BENHAM D. I., OBE DFC* AFC. Born 30/12/17. Commd 21/3/41. Sqn Ldr 1/8/47. Retd GD 30/12/57. rtg Wg Cdr.
BENJAMIN C. Born 20/7/09. Commd 13/9/45. Flt Lt 1/1/52. Retd PRT 25/7/54.
BENN L.V., BA. Born 31/3/48. Commd 28/2/69. Flt Lt 28/2/72. Retd GD 14/10/86.
BENNEDIK P. R., MBE. Born 16/3/21. Commd 4/9/58. Sqn Ldr 1/7/70. Retd ENG 1/3/78.
BENNETT A. R., MVO. Born 24/12/41. Commd 29/11/63. Flt Lt 29/5/69. Retd GD 22/5/93.
BENNETT A. W., BEM MIMgt. Born 2/9/20. Commd 30/9/54. Sqn Ldr 1/7/66. Retd ENG 2/2/76.
BENNETT B. C., AFC. Born 9/10/17. Commd 14/12/38. A Cdre 1/1/66. Retd GD 25/10/71.
BENNETT C. R., MIIE. Born 21/3/61. Commd 1/5/80. Sqn Ldr 1/7/96. Retd ENG 1/11/99.
BENNETT D. Born 25/3/47. Commd 10/1/69. Sqn Ldr 1/1/86. Retd GD 26/5/01.
BENNETT D. A., MBE. Born 10/10/27. Commd 26/5/60. Wg Cdr 1/1/75. Retd ENG 26/4/78.
BENNETT D. G. Born 25/6/43. Commd 22/2/63. Flt Lt 22/8/68. Retd GD 13/12/75.
BENNETT D. H. Born 4/4/27. Commd 22/7/47. Wg Cdr 1/7/66. Retd GD 4/4/82.
BENNETT D. J. C. Born 30/1/46. Commd 10/6/66. Sqn Ldr 1/1/84. Retd GD 2/10/94.
BENNETT D. P. Born 18/7/26. Commd 6/3/52. Wg Cdr 1/1/76. Retd GD 18/7/81.
BENNETT Sir Erik, KBE CB. Born 3/9/26. Commd 22/1/48. AVM 1/1/82. Retd GD 10/6/91.
BENNETT F. R. Born 26/6/30. Commd 13/2/52. Flt Lt. 1/10/67. Retd GD 9/7/68.
BENNETT F. W. Born 3/9/20. Commd 6/5/43. Sqn Ldr 1/7/69. Retd SEC 31/8/73.
BENNETT G., CEng MRAeS. Born 16/2/29. Commd 30/1/52. Wg Cdr 1/1/76. Retd ENG 12/4/79.
BENNETT G. Born 20/7/32. Commd 27/7/71. Sqn Ldr 22/7/79. Retd EDN 1/11/83.
BENNETT G. A. Born 6/1/19. Commd 13/6/46. Flt Lt 13/12/50. Retd RGT 1/7/58.
BENNETT G. W. Born 23/12/17. Commd 5/3/53. Flt Lt 5/3/56. Retd ENG 25/6/60.
BENNETT H. E. Born 23/10/22. Commd 9/8/47. Flt Lt 9/2/51. Retd GD 8/11/77.
BENNETT H. F. G. Born 1/11/15. Commd 29/1/46. Flt Lt 11/11/54. Retd RGT 30/12/57.
BENNETT H. T. Born 26/10/10. Commd 26/12/30. Gp Capt 1/7/50. Retd GD 23/6/61.
BENNETT I., BSc FCIPD. Born 4/3/43. Commd 19/9/71. Wg Cdr 1/1/93. Retd ADMIN 13/4/96.
BENNETT I. M. H., BSc. Born 2/2/49. Commd 12/12/71. Flt Lt 12/3/72. Retd GD 28/10/88.
BENNETT I. T. Born 18/6/30. Commd 7/5/52. Flt Lt 13/4/60. Retd SEC 18/3/66.

BENNETT J. Born 19/9/22. Commd 10/12/43. Flt Lt 7/6/51. Retd GD 31/1/62.
BENNETT J. A. Born 17/9/41. Commd 17/4/68. Flt Lt 16/11/74. Retd SUP 16/11/80.
BENNETT J. C., LDSRCS. Born 27/5/41. Commd 20/9/59. Flt Lt 10/6/65. Retd DEL 27/7/68.
BENNETT J. F., MRAeS AIIP. Born 19/4/33. Commd 26/3/52. Sqn Ldr 1/7/71. Retd ENG 27/8/86.
BENNETT J. N., BSc CEng MIEE. Born 21/5/52. Commd 23/1/74. Flt Lt 23/4/77. Retd ENG 30/4/83.
BENNETT J. R. Born 9/11/09. Commd 3/8/44. Flt Lt 3/2/47. Retd ENG 14/7/48.
BENNETT J. S., AFC. Born 20/3/22. Commd 22/3/50. Sqn Ldr 1/7/68. Retd GD 20/3/77.
BENNETT J. S. Born 2/3/49. Commd 21/4/77. Fg Offr 4/8/79. Retd ADMIN 2/6/82.
BENNETT J. W. Born 27/1/49. Commd 30/10/79. Flt Lt 30/10/79. Retd GD 30/10/87.
BENNETT K. Born 17/11/30. Commd 11/9/56. Flt Lt 11/3/62. Retd GD 5/6/72 rtg Sqn Ldr.
BENNETT K. Born 3/4/61. Commd 16/2/86. Fg Offr 16/2/88. Retd SY 1/11/91.
BENNETT K. G., BSc CEng MIEE. Born 10/1/41. Commd 30/9/60. Gp Capt 1/1/87. Retd ENG 27/8/90.
BENNETT K. J. Born 28/8/36. Commd 3/4/58. Sqn Ldr 1/1/75. Retd SUP 28/8/91.
BENNETT K. M. Born 15/12/70. Commd 9/5/91. Flt Lt 9/11/97. Retd ADMIN 17/2/00.
BENNETT K. N. Born 24/9/55. Commd 1/7/82. Flt Lt 1/7/84. Retd GD 1/2/00.
BENNETT L., DFC*. Born 4/6/11. Commd 14/4/40. Sqn Ldr 1/8/47. Retd GD(G) 4/6/61.
BENNETT M. G., DFC. Born 7/1/25. Commd 7/7/49. Wg Cdr 1/1/65. Retd GD 10/5/69.
BENNETT N. H., BSc CEng MRAeS. Born 5/3/50. Commd 10/1/72. Flt Lt 15/4/77. Retd ENG 5/3/88.
BENNETT P. B. Born 27/7/57. Commd 26/11/81. Flt Lt 29/9/84. Retd ADMIN 27/7/95.
BENNETT P. D. S., DFC*. Born 18/3/18. Commd 20/10/37. Sqn Ldr 1/9/45. Retd GD 31/12/57 rtd Wg Cdr.
BENNETT P. G. N. Born 20/6/40. Commd 10/12/65. Flt Lt 14/7/71. Retd GD 26/7/84.
BENNETT P. J. Born 14/5/47. Commd 2/8/68. Sqn Ldr 1/1/84. Retd GD 1/1/87.
BENNETT R. J. Born 20/7/35. Commd 9/4/57. Gp Capt 1/1/82. Retd ADMIN 1/3/86.
BENNETT R. J., BSc. Born 4/1/54. Commd 30/9/73. Wg Cdr 1/1/95. Retd GD 1/11/98.
BENNETT R. L., AFC. Born 14/8/27. Commd 7/7/49. Wg Cdr 1/7/66. Retd GD 14/5/82.
BENNETT R. P., FCA. Born 7/1/13. Commd 11/6/37. Wg Cdr 1/1/63. Retd SEC 31/3/68.
BENNETT R. R. Born 28/12/01. Commd 21/3/24. Fg Offr 28/12/28. Retd GD 15/9/34. Recalled 26/8/39 to
    11/4/41.
BENNETT R. W., BEM. Born 7/9/40. Commd 11/10/84. Flt Lt 11/10/88. Retd SY 7/9/94.
BENNETT S. C. S. Born 28/4/23. Commd 20/4/50. Sqn Ldr 1/7/66. Retd GD 9/4/73.
BENNETT T. Born 25/2/12. Commd 15/10/43. Flt Lt 15/4/47. Retd ENG 15/7/48.
BENNETT T. A., CBE. Born 21/12/28. Commd 27/7/49. A Cdre 1/1/82. Retd GD 1/1/84.
BENNETT T. R., MMar. Born 12/8/52. Commd 2/3/80. Flt Lt 2/3/80. Retd GD 14/3/97.
BENNETT W. G. Born 4/9/20. Commd 1/1/43. Sqn Ldr 1/7/58. Retd GD 15/5/61.
BENNETT W. R. Born 31/12/45. Commd 28/2/64. Flt Lt 28/8/69. Retd GD 1/1/84.
BENNINGTON G. W., DFM MIMgt. Born 4/5/23. Commd 24/7/44. A Cdre 1/1/73 Retd SUP 31/1/76.
BENNISON S. Born 18/11/49. Commd 1/8/69. Sqn Ldr 1/1/91. Retd ADMIN 19/10/92.
BENNISON S. W., BSc CEng MIEE. Born 10/11/59. Commd 6/9/81. Sqn Ldr 1/1/91. Retd ENG 10/11/97.
BENOIST J. D. Born 12/10/46. Commd 27/2/75. Sqn Ldr 1/1/88. Retd OPS SPT 2/4/98.
BENSAID K. A. Born 23/8/20. Commd 24/1/63. Flt Lt 24/1/68. Retd ENG 23/8/75.
BENSLEY D., BA. Born 26/11/34. Commd 25/4/63. Sqn Ldr 10/2/68. Retd ADMIN 12/6/82.
BENSON A. N. W. Born 28/10/49. Commd 22/5/70. Flt Lt 22/11/75. Retd GD 28/10/87
BENSON G., MIMgt. Born 12/9/40. Commd 12/1/61. Sqn Ldr 1/1/74. Retd ADMIN 12/9/86.
BENSON G. E., CEng MRAeS. Born 30/3/37. Commd 23/2/60. Sqn Ldr 1/1/71. Retd ENG 23/2/76.
BENSON J. W., BA. Born 21/3/32. Commd 25/11/53. Sqn Ldr 6/6/65. Retd EDN 6/11/72.
BENSON N. R., BSc. Born 27/11/61. Commd 5/2/84. Sqn ldr 1/1/96. Retd GD 5/2/00.
BENSON R. Born 26/5/23. Commd 26/4/44. Flt Lt 15/8/48. Retd GD 30/4/57.
BENSON T. E. Born 1/9/31. Commd 12/6/31. A Cdre 1/1/85. Retd GD 15/4/87.
BENSON T. J., BSc. Born 14/6/55. Commd 7/11/76. Sqn Ldr 1/1/90. Retd GD 14/6/93.
BENSTEAD A. H. Born 2/6/44. Commd 2/6/77. Flt Lt 2/6/79. Retd GD 14/3/96.
BENT B., DFC. Born 22/8/19. Commd 24/4/43. Flt Lt 27/5/54. Retd GD(G) 5/12/70.
BENT R. C. T., MVO BSc ACGI. Born 17/5/47. Commd 22/9/65. Wg Cdr 1/7/87. Retd ENG 31/3/94.
BENT R. W. Born 21/8/17. Commd 21/8/43. Flt Lt 21/2/48. Retd GD(G) 21/8/67.
BENTHAM P., BEng. Born 5/1/40. Commd 2/10/61. Wg Cdr 1/1/91. Retd GD 5/11/95.
BENTLEY A. C. Born 6/5/11. Commd 13/10/41. Fg Offr 1/10/42. Retd ASD 3/12/45 rtg Flt lt.
BENTLEY A. J., BSc CEng FIEE. Born 26/3/42. Commd 15/7/63. A Cdre 1/7/92. Retd ENG 25/7/94.
BENTLEY A. M., OBE AFC. Born 28/1/16. Commd 1/8/36. Wg Cdr 1/7/47. Retd GD 9/5/49 rtg Gp Capt.
BENTLEY D. E. Born 25/5/47. Commd 17/1/69. Wg Cdr 1/1/90. Retd ADMIN 7/5/01.
BENTLEY I. Born 24/3/37. Commd 29/7/58. Plt Offr 29/7/58. Retd GD 5/12/59.
BENTLEY J. P. Born 14/6/22. Commd 1/5/42. Sqn Ldr 1/1/73. Retd SUP 14/2/76.
BENTLEY M. J. Born 3/7/50. Commd 7/1/80. Sqn Ldr 1/1/87. Retd ADMIN 7/1/96.
BENTLEY T. H. J. Born 24/3/24. Commd 12/2/45. Sqn Ldr 1/1/56. Retd GD 24/4/64.
BENTLEY W. H., OBE FIMgt. Born 4/10/13. Commd 6/9/40. Wg Cdr 1/1/54. Retd SEC 4/10/65.
BERESFORD J. D., OBE. Born 20/6/15. Commd 29/10/41. Wg Cdr 1/1/55. Retd GD 27/6/70.
BERESFORD S. E. Born 24/2/53. Commd 12/3/87. Flt Lt 12/3/89. Retd ENG 31/10/97.
BERGGREN J. V., DFC. Born 30/11/15. Commd 25/11/37. Flt Lt 19/10/44. Retd GD 26/9/58 rtg Sqn Ldr.

BERGH I. Le C. Born 9/8/26. Commd 19/6/47. Flt Lt 4/7/56. Retd GD 12/2/65.
BERGIN J. P. Born 26/5/56. Commd 18/12/80. Sqn Ldr 1/7/92. Retd SUP 14/3/97.
BERGIN T. A. Born 30/9/21. Commd 3/8/50. Sqn Ldr 1/7/68. Retd GD(G) 30/9/76.
BERGMAN V., DFC. Born 28/8/15. Commd 12/7/40. Sqn Ldr 1/1/63. Retd GD(G) 30/4/69.
BERKELEY P. R. A. Born 31/12/30. Commd 5/3/57. Flt Lt 5/9/62. Retd GD 31/12/68.
BERNARD D. H., MBE CEng MIEE MIMgt. Born 23/5/20. Commd 12/6/47. Wg Cdr 1/1/67. Retd ENG 23/5/75.
BERNAU K. H. Born 8/9/22. Commd 26/5/67. Flt Lt 15/12/70. Retd GD(G) 30/5/81.
BERNERS-PRICE C. Born 13/1/57. Commd 27/1/77. Flt Lt 27/7/82. Retd GD 1/3/89.
BERRESFORD C. S. Born 28/11/43. Commd 23/2/68. Flt Lt 23/8/73. Retd GD 14/3/96.
BERRIDGE A. D. Born 12/10/46. Commd 31/10/69. Flt Lt 30/4/75. Retd GD 7/8/76.
BERRIMAN S. C., BTech CEng MIMechE. Born 20/9/52. Commd 26/7/81. Sqn Ldr 1/1/88. Retd ENG 14/10/98.
BERRY A. J., CEng MIEE CDipAF. Born 10/9/47. Commd 12/12/71. Wg Cdr 1/1/86. Retd ENG 1/1/89.
BERRY C. C., OBE DFC CEng MRAeS. Born 5/1/19. Commd 18/9/44. Wg Cdr 1/7/66. Retd ENG 5/1/74.
BERRY D. E. de, BEd. Born 26/9/33. Commd 7/5/52. Flt Lt 2/10/57. Retd GD 14/10/75. Reinstated 31/8/78. Sqn Ldr 1/7/86. Retd 26/9/91.
BERRY E. R. Born 8/8/38. Commd 24/6/71. Flt Lt 24/6/73. Retd SUP 24/6/79.
BERRY K. H. Born 15/4/41. Commd 1/10/52. Flt Lt 1/4/67. Retd GD 12/9/70.
BERRY L. G., DFC MIMgt. Born 4/6/22. Commd 15/10/43. Sqn Ldr 1/4/56. Retd GD 4/6/77.
BERRY M. A. Born 23/3/37. Commd 28/6/60. Sqn Ldr 1/1/69. Retd ENG 20/3/92.
BERRY N. A. Born 25/5/30. Commd 9/3/66. Sqn Ldr 1/1/78. Retd SUP 31/5/80.
BERRY R. D. Born 18/3/48. Commd 21/3/69. Sqn Ldr 1/1/89. Retd SUP 14/3/97.
BERRYMAN J. A. Born 8/3/44. Commd 28/2/64. Flt Lt 12/11/69. Retd. GD 7/11/75.
BERRYMAN K. F., BSc. Born 5/3/44. Commd 11/10/70. Sqn Ldr 11/4/78. Retd EDN 11/10/79.
BERRYMAN N. W. Born 13/12/45. Commd 26/5/67. Sqn Ldr 1/7/79. Retd GD 7/3/91.
BERTHON P. L. A. Born 20/9/06. Commd 11/12/26. Plt Offr 11/12/26. Retd GD 2/11/27.
BERTRAM J. S. Born 17/8/10. Commd 8/10/53. Flt Lt 8/10/56. Retd ENG 19/8/64.
BERTRAM S. Born 21/7/11. Commd 21/11/44. Flt Lt 29/11/51. Retd GD(G) 1/10/64.
BERTRAND F. R., BDS. Born 8/1/24. Commd 16/12/60. Sqn Ldr 2/1/62. Retd DEL 7/8/66.
BESANT J. H. Born 26/2/23. Commd 11/1/44. Flt Lt 7/6/51. Retd GD 18/8/73.
BESLEY J., FCA AMCIPD. Born 19/3/33. Commd 16/5/57. Sqn Ldr 1/1/67. Retd SEC 22/9/71.
BESSANT D. E. L. Born 27/2/38. Commd 4/7/69. Flt Lt 4/7/71. Retd ENG 4/7/79.
BESSANT P. Born 9/1/41. Commd 13/7/61. Sqn Ldr 1/1/86. Retd SY 10/1/91.
BESSEY C. L. Born 2/8/07. Commd 10/4/41. Flt Lt 29/4/45. Retd ENG 10/1/46 rtg Sqn Ldr.
BEST B. V., BA. Born 3/4/38. Commd 9/8/60. Sqn Ldr 9/2/69. Retd ADMIN 9/8/76.
BEST E. F. Born 17/10/38. Commd 2/5/69. Flt Lt 2/5/71. Retd GD 2/5/77.
BEST G. L., OBE. Born 19/8/09. Commd 26/11/30. Wg Cdr 1/10/46. Retd ENG 24/8/47 rtg Gp Capt.
BEST I. G. Born 26/11/16. Commd 22/8/41. Wg Cdr 1/7/64. Retd SEC 26/11/71.
BEST M. A. Born 10/5/53. Commd 29/6/72. Sqn Ldr 1/1/87. Retd GD(G) 5/7/91.
BEST P. A. Born 1/10/22. Commd 21/1/55. Flt Lt 21/10/59. Retd GD 1/10/77.
BEST R. M., CEng MIMechE MIProdE. Born 22/10/42. Commd 16/8/70. A Cdre 1/1/91. Retd ENG 14/9/96.
BESWETHERICK A. T. Born 14/11/25. Commd 11/3/53. Flt Lt 11/12/58. Retd GD 29/1/66.
BESZANT G. W., BSc. Born 9/3/49. Commd 2/7/72. Flt Lt 2/4/76. Retd PI 2/7/84.
BETHELL R. A. Born 9/4/22. Commd 7/2/42. Flt Lt 19/11/48. Retd GD 28/6/55.
BETSON C. Born 12/6/43. Commd 30/5/69. Flt Lt 30/11/74. Retd GD 1/7/75.
BETTEL D.C. Born 24/8/21. Commd 19/7/44. Sqn Ldr 1/7/70. Retd SUP 24/8/76.
BETTELL M. J., OBE. Born 12/3/44. Commd 28/9/62. A Cdre 1/7/89. Retd GD 16/4/99.
BETTERIDGE A. J. Born 20/7/39. Commd 1/8/69. Flt Lt 4/5/72. Retd ADMIN 1/8/77.
BETTERIDGE H. Born 31/5/28. Commd 11/2/65. Flt Lt 11/2/70. Retd ENG 12/12/74.
BETTERIDGE J. Born 14/1/24. Commd 6/5/47. Flt Lt 20/1/54. Retd GD 14/1/62.
BETTERIDGE M. P., BDS. Born 4/9/54. Commd 16/11/75. Wg Cdt 8/4/91. Retd DEL 4/9/92.
BETTERIDGE R. S. J. Born 22/11/23. Commd 11/8/54. Sqn Ldr 1/1/68. Retd DG 1/4/73.
BETTERIDGE T. J., MB ChB MRCPath DCP. Born 8/10/31. Commd 10/7/60. Wg Cdr 18/8/71. Retd MED 10/7/76.
BETTERTON B. D. Born 19/12/38. Commd 30/4/57. Gp Capt 1/7/88. Retd GD 19/12/93.
BETTERTON T. J. Born 5/4/36. Commd 18/8/54. Flt Lt 18/2/60. Retd GD 5/4/96.
BETTINSON L. G., DFC. Born 2/10/19. Commd 25/8/40. Flt Lt 25/8/46. Retd GD 1/5/50.
BETTS C. J., BSc. Born 26/3/60. Commd 11/12/83. Flt Lt 11/6/85. Retd GD 11/12/95.
BETTS C. S., CBE MA. Born 8/4/19. Commd 11/7/41. AVM 1/1/72. Retd ENG 8/4/74.
BETTS D. E. Born 3/8/31. Commd 23/10/80. Sqn Ldr 12/6/75. Retd GD 3/8/91.
BETTS D. J., MSc CEng MBCS MIMgt AIDPM. Born 20/11/45. Commd 26/5/67. Sqn Ldr 1/1/77. Retd SUP 20/2/92.
BETTS J. E. Born 6/5/19. Commd 7/3/46. Flt Lt 19/6/52. Retd SUP 6/6/68.
BETTS J. W., MBE. Born 30/9/23. Commd 24/5/51. Sqn Ldr 1/1/69. Retd GD 30/9/78.
BETTS L. J., BSc. Born 8/7/54. Commd 7/11/76. Flt Lt 7/2/78. Retd GD 7/11/88.
BETTS M. Born 22/7/42. Commd 28/2/64. Sqn Ldr 1/7/75. Retd GD 22/7/80.
BETTS N. G. Born 31/5/48. Commd 28/2/69. Flt Lt 28/8/74. Retd ENG 5/1/82.

BETTS P. J., BSc(Econ). Born 22/7/48. Commd 2/2/70. Fg Offr 2/2/72. Retd SEC 2/2/76. Re-entered 31/10/77.
Wg Cdr 1/1/92. Retd SY 14/9/96.
BETTS R. C., BA. Born 7/1/42. Commd 30/7/63. Wg Cdr 1/7/77. Retd GD 18/1/83.
BEVAN A. W., BEM. Born 12/3/29. Commd 15/6/61. Sqn Ldr 1/7/75. Retd ENG 12/3/84.
BEVAN B. Born 28/10/28. Commd 2/3/61. Flt Lt 2/3/66. Retd DG 1/3/68.
BEVAN D. C. Born 9/12/44. Commd 12/7/63. Sqn Ldr 1/7/93. Retd GD 30/4/94.
BEVAN D. L., BSc. Born 14/2/49. Commd 1/11/71. Sqn Ldr 1/7/79. Retd ENG 1/11/87.
BEVAN E. W. J. Born 21/2/13. Commd 5/12/47. Sqn Ldr 1/7/51. Retd RGT 19/10/57.
BEVAN G. G. Born 15/2/14. Commd 15/4/43. Sqn Ldr 1/1/57. Retd ENG 15/2/63.
BEVAN J. H. Born 26/1/44. Commd 31/8/78. Sqn Ldr 1/7/86. Retd GD(G) 2/3/94.
BEVAN M. Born 4/2/20. Commd 20/4/44. Flt Lt 20/10/47. Retd ENG 4/2/69.
BEVAN S. J., BEM. Born 7/11/20. Commd 23/12/60. Flt Lt 23/12/66. Retd ENG 15/7/67.
BEVAN T. E. Born 11/4/49. Commd 10/3/77. Flt Lt 7/5/56. Retd GD 11/4/87.
BEVAN W. J., BA. Born 30/11/38. Commd 1/9/64. Wg Cdr 1/1/87. Retd ADMIN 21/10/91.
BEVAN-JOHN D. R. S., OBE. Born 25/2/17. Commd 30/7/38. Gp Capt 1/1/57. Retd GD 30/1/59.
BEVERIDGE A. W., BSc. Born 18/8/45. Commd 13/2/72. Sqn Ldr 19/12/76. Retd ADMIN 13/2/88.
BEVERIDGE D. A. Born 1/3/53. Commd 29/4/71. Flt Lt 29/10/76. Retd GD 1/3/91.
BEVERIDGE G. J. Born 4/11/29. Commd 8/7/54. Wg Cdr 1/1/80. Retd ADMIN 4/11/84.
BEVERLEY O. E. Born 3/1/25. Commd 1/3/62. Flt Lt 1/3/57. Retd GD 15/1/76.
BEVIS C. G. S. Born 10/2/15. Commd 7/5/56. Flt Lt 7/5/56. Retd MAR 30/9/67.
BEWLEY D. I. W., MHCIMA MIMgt. Born 29/12/30. Commd 25/9/52. Wg Cdr 1/1/74. Retd ADMIN 16/6/82.
BEYNON G. G. Born 9/3/48. Commd 17/7/87. Flt Lt 17/7/89. Retd GD 30/9/94.
BHATIA R. J. Born 14/5/62. Commd 28/5/85. Flt Lt 23/11/90. Retd GD 21/1/01.
BIANCO D. Born 23/5/43. Commd 21/2/74. Sqn Ldr 1/1/83. Retd SUP 23/5/93.
BIBBEY A. Born 16/5/22. Commd 4/9/58. Sqn Ldr 1/7/73. Retd ENG 16/5/77.
BIBBY G. Born 29/3/39. Commd 25/9/80. Fg Offr 25/9/79. Retd PI 1/10/85.
BIBBY G. T., BA Born 21/3/27. Commd 7/10/48. Flt Lt 4/12/52. Retd GD 23/1/60.
BIBBY G. W. Born 25/1/22. Commd 23/8/50. Sqn Ldr 1/7/66. Retd GD(G) 25/1/72.
BIBBY M. J., OBE. Born 3/12/44. Commd 2/6/67. Wg Cdr 1/1/87. Retd GD 14/3/96.
BIBBY W. W. Born 12/8/22. Commd 1/10/43. Sqn Ldr 1/7/54. Retd GD 20/5/68.
BIBEY M. A. Born 13/7/50. Commd 9/5/91. Flt Lt 9/5/95. Retd ENG 1/6/96.
BICHARD K., OBE. Born 23/7/33. Commd 27/7/54. Wg Cdr 1/1/74. Retd GD 23/7/89.
BICKERS R. A. Born 9/1/43. Commd 27/2/75. Sqn Ldr 1/1/90. Retd GD 12/1/96.
BICKERS R. L. T. Born 5/7/17. Commd 22/7/43. Flt Lt 22/7/50. Retd GD(G) 16/8/57.
BICKERS S. M. Born 27/9/61. Commd 24/3/83. Sqn Ldr 1/7/96. Retd SUP 1/1/01.
BICKERSTAFF G. G. F., DFC. Born 1/2/20. Commd 9/10/42. Flt Lt 9/4/46. Retd GD 6/6/53.
BICKFORD-SMITH D. G. Born 5/11/22. Commd 16/2/43. Sqn Ldr 1/1/57. Retd GD(G) 1/6/67.
BICKNELL D. W., AFC. Born 31/1/17. Commd 13/5/43. Flt Lt 13/11/46. Retd GD 15/9/53.
BICKNELL J. Born 15/2/17. Commd 23/3/50. Wg Cdr 1/1/67. Retd SEC 3/4/70.
BIDDINGTON D. V. W. Born 13/4/47. Commd 23/4/87. Sqn Ldr 1/1/97. Retd ENG 24/2/01.
BIDDISCOMBE P. G. Born 10/7/32. Commd 26/7/55. Sqn Ldr 1/7/65. Retd GD 7/9/85.
BIDIE C. H., AFC* MIMgt. Born 27/3/26. Commd 9/3/50. Wg Cdr 1/1/66. Retd GD 30/3/77.
BIDSTON P.M. Born 30/8/49. Commd 17/7/72. Flt Lt 17/1/76. Retd GD 30/8/87.
BIEBER S. M., FRCS LRCP DIH DPH DTM&H. Born 27/7/12. Commd 9/7/38. Wg Cdr 1/1/58. Retd MED 1/9/60.
BIGGAR G. Born 5/12/27. Commd 29/6/48. Gp Capt 1/1/76. Retd SY 5/12/82.
BIGGIE C. J. R. Born 21/8/39. Commd 24/9/63. Flt Lt 24/11/67. Retd ENG 24/9/79.
BIGGS D. Born 20/2/64. Commd 29/7/91. Flt Lt 27/11/93. Retd GD(G) 14/3/96.
BIGGS J. P. C., IEng AMRAeS. Born 12/12/61. Commd 16/2/89. Flt Lt 7/11/91. Retd ENG 14/3/96.
BIGGS M. J. Born 12/8/24. Commd 27/2/58. Sqn Ldr 1/1/72. Retd GD 12/8/83.
BIGGS R. V. A. Born 3/8/30. Commd 22/12/49. Flt Lt 22/6/53. Retd GD 29/3/69.
BIGGS T. W. G. Born 20/4/57. Commd 29/1/79. Flt Lt 21/4/85. Retd GD 7/9/88.
BIGLANDS S., BSc. Born 24/6/48. Commd 17/1/72. Flt Lt 17/4/73. Retd GD 17/1/88.
BIGMORE H. J. Born 2/7/11. Commd 18/3/43. Fg Offr 19/9/46 rtg Flt Lt. Retd ENG 9/8/46 rtg Flt Lt.
BILLETT R. T. Born 11/1/16. Commd 22/4/41. Wg Cdr 1/7/52. Retd GD 21/2/71.
BILLING M. Born 2/4/27. Commd 30/7/59. Flt Lt 18/8/64. Retd ENG 15/1/72.
BILLINGE P. A. Born 14/7/38. Commd. 15/12/59. Flt Lt 15/6/62. Retd GD 1/12/78.
BILLINGS E. H. Born 14/1/43. Commd 22/5/80. Flt Lt 22/5/83. Retd GD 14/1/98.
BILLINGS G. J. Born 24/6/50. Commd 24/4/70. Sqn Ldr 1/7/83. Retd SUP 24/6/88.
BILLINGS N. G. Born 17/1/36. Commd 4/7/69. Sqn Ldr 1/7/75. Retd ENG 1/7/78.
BILLINGS S. J., BSc DipEd. Born 26/9/54. Commd 6/9/81. Flt Lt 6/3/84. Retd ENG 6/9/97.
BILLINGTON D. P. Born 25/6/60. Commd 30/8/84. Sqn Ldr 1/1/97. Retd GD 30/4/00.
BILLS D. T., FCIPD ACIS. Born 30/6/47. Commd 1/8/69. Wg Cdr 1/1/86. Retd SY 14/3/96.
BILLS M. A. Born 6/7/54. Commd 31/8/78. Flt Lt 18/11/80. Retd GD 18/7/85.
BILLSON R. A. Born 17/6/37. Commd 11/5/78. Flt Lt 11/5/81. Retd GD 17/6/92.
BILTCLIFFE A. J. Born 20/4/27. Commd 13/2/52. Flt Lt 12/6/57. Retd GD 20/4/65.
BINDLOSS K. M. Born 1/7/15. Commd 3/6/42. Flt Offr 3/12/46. Retd SEC 16/11/53.

BINDON T. R. Born 17/6/25. Commd 10/10/63. Flt Lt 10/10/68. Retd GD 28/2/78.
BINEDELL A. C. G., DFC. Born 9/3/17. Commd 1/9/45. Flt Lt 1/9/45. Retd GD(G) 27/3/63.
BING N. J. Born 6/12/41. Commd 18/12/62. Flt Lt 28/7/65. Retd GD 6/12/79.
BINGHAM D. C. Born 7/5/32. Commd 11/12/51. Flt Lt 17/10/56. Retd GD 1/10/83.
BINGHAM J. H. Born 6/11/67. Commd 14/1/88. Flt Lt 14/7/93. Retd GD 10/9/00.
BINGHAM P. C. Born 8/3/47. Commd 21/1/66. Gp Capt 1/1/96. Retd GD 14/9/96.
BINGHAM S. A., BA. Born 22/11/55. Commd 3/5/81. Sqn Ldr 1/1/93. Retd GD(G) 14/3/96.
BINGHAM W. G. Born 15/12/23. Commd 24/9/64. Sqn Ldr 1/7/73. Retd SUP 15/12/78.
BINHAM P. P. Born 6/2/53. Commd 30/9/73. Sqn Ldr 1/1/86. Retd GD 21/11/91.
BINKS A. F., DFC. Born 3/4/16. Commd 12/4/37. Wg Cdr 1/1/51. Retd GD 29/4/59.
BINKS E., DFM. Born 21/2/18. Commd 5/3/51. Sqn Ldr 1/7/52. Retd GD 26/9/59.
BINKS H. Born 11/8/26. Commd 11/11/50. Wg Cdr 1/1/70. Retd GD 16/8/75.
BINNIE D., AFC. Born 4/3/46. Commd 14/8/64. Sqn Ldr 1/1/78. Retd GD 10/12/86.
BINNINGTON A. W. Born 19/6/39. Commd 23/6/61. Flt Lt 1/4/66. Retd GD 14/2/94.
BINNS C. C. Born 7/4/12. Commd 18/6/52. Sqn Offr 1/4/58. Retd SEC 1/10/63.
BINNS C. G. Born 29/1/38. Commd 2/2/60. Sqn Ldr 1/7/71. Retd CAT 2/2/76.
BINNS H., OBE MInstPkg MCIPS MILT. Born 17/8/40. Commd 15/2/62. Wg Cdr 1/1/85. Retd SUP 20/11/92.
BINNS J. H., MB ChB FRCS. Born 27/4/31. Commd 30/1/57. Wg Cdr 30/1/70. Retd MED 3/3/73.
BIRBECK S. Born 20/12/42. Commd 29/6/72. Flt Lt 29/6/74. Retd ENG 21/7/83.
BIRCH C. N., AFC. Born 27/11/18. Commd 14/11/38. Sqn Ldr 1/8/47. Retd GD 28/3/58.
BIRCH D. B. T., OBE CEng FIMechE FIMgt MRAeS. Born 9/6/33. Commd 7/11/58. Gp Capt 1/1/85.
    Retd ENG 9/6/93.
BIRCH D. N. Born 15/12/35. Commd 14/7/63. Flt Lt 1/7/68. Retd GD 1/9/86.
BIRCH J. L., BSc. Born 27/11/24. Commd 24/11/48. Wg Cdr 1/7/74. Retd SY 31/7/76.
BIRCH J. Y. Born 7/9/11. Commd 5/5/52. Flt Lt 30/11/45. Retd ENG 14/11/62.
BIRCH P. H. B., BEng. Born 30/5/63. Commd 3/8/88. Flt Lt 15/7/91. Retd ENG 30/5/01.
BIRCH R. F., MBE. Born 6/12/38. Commd 25/7/60. Sqn Ldr 1/1/69. Retd GD 27/8/76.
BIRCH R. J., BA. Born 24/1/41. Commd 1/10/62. Sqn Ldr 1/7/75. Retd GD 24/1/79.
BIRCHALL P. Born 14/4/46. Commd 11/10/84. Flt Lt 11/10/88. Retd ENG 30/8/96.
BIRCHALL R. A. Born 28/9/30. Commd 1/8/51. Plt Offr 1/8/51. Retd SEC 24/12/52.
BIRD C. Born 8/3/48. Commd 23/4/87. Flt Lt 23/4/91. Retd ADMIN 14/3/97.
BIRD D. L. Born 10/11/30. Commd 19/1/50. Sqn Ldr 1/1/66. Retd SEC 31/8/68.
BIRD G. D. Born 12/5/25. Commd 19/1/45. Wg Cdr 1/1/68. Retd GD 8/5/76.
BIRD H. Born 15/3/19. Commd 5/10/50. Sqn Ldr 1/7/61. Retd ENG 27/3/71.
BIRD H. S. Born 3/11/38. Commd 3/5/68. Sqn Ldr 1/7/78. Retd SUP 14/11/81. Reinstated 1/7/87. Sqn Ldr 15/2/84.
    Retd SUP 3/11/91.
BIRD J. B., BSc. Born 5/12/34. Commd 20/12/57. Sqn Ldr 20/6/67. Retd EDN 19/9/73.
BIRD J. C. Born 26/1/60. Commd 28/6/79. Flt Lt 28/12/84. Retd GD 26/8/98.
BIRD J. K. Born 21/5/33. Commd 7/5/52. Sqn Ldr 1/7/74. Retd ADMIN 21/5/91.
BIRD J. O. Born 4/1/66. Commd 11/5/89. Fg Offr 11/5/91. Retd GD 1/7/93.
BIRD J. R. Born 15/4/28. Commd 11/5/51. Flt Lt 6/9/56. Retd GD 31/3/70.
BIRD J. S. Born 3/7/39. Commd 5/2/65. Flt Lt 14/5/68. Retd GD 3/7/94.
BIRD L. A. Born 11/9/30. Commd 4/2/53. Sqn Ldr 1/1/62. Retd CAT 18/10/69.
BIRD M. J., MHCIMA. Born 5/9/31. Commd 24/9/63. Sqn Ldr 1/7/77. Retd ADMIN 5/9/86.
BIRD P. D. Born 9/10/20. Commd 22/5/42. Gp Capt 1/7/67. Retd GD 9/4/71.
BIRD P. R. Born 20/11/47. Commd 11/8/67. Sqn Ldr 1/7/80. Retd SY 14/3/96.
BIRD R. C. Born 7/7/44. Commd 22/5/70. Sqn Ldr 1/1/92. Retd GD 7/1/01.
BIRD R. V. Born 1/4/44. Commd 11/9/64. Flt Lt 4/5/72. Retd GD 1/4/82.
BIRD T. E. Born 2/12/11. Commd 29/6/50. Fg Offr 29/6/50. Retd MED(T) 23/7/53.
BIRD W. F. Born 2/10/34. Commd 25/5/61. Flt Lt 1/10/67. Retd GD 25/5/77.
BIRD W. J., MBE MA. Born 13/4/52. Commd 2/2/75. Sqn Ldr 1/1/87. Retd GD 2/2/91.
BIRD-WILSON H. A. C., CBE DSO DFC* AFC*. Born 20/11/19. Commd 30/11/37. AVM 1/1/70. Retd GD 1/6/74.
BIRDLING W. R., DFC. Born 10/9/22. Commd 30/6/45. Flt Lt 30/12/47. Retd GD 21/3/61.
BIRKETT C. R., BSc. Born 6/2/57. Commd 14/9/75. Plt Off 15/7/78. Retd GD 5/5/79.
BIRKETT G. M. R. Born 25/9/15. Commd 1/5/52. Wg Cdr 19/6/68. Retd MED(T) 25/9/70.
BIRKS B. G. Born 6/12/42. Commd 6/7/62. Flt Lt 6/1/68. Retd GD 30/4/85.
BIRLISON R. K. Born 7/8/22. Commd 6/9/56. Sqn Ldr 1/1/70. Retd ENG 13/1/73.
BIRNIE J. Born 10/10/26. Commd 24/1/52. Flt Lt 24/7/55. Retd GD 14/9/68.
BIRRELL D. Born 26/6/21. Commd 25/1/43. Flt Lt 25/7/46. Retd GD 2/6/48.
BIRRELL W. D., MSc BSc MCIPD MIMgt. Born 9/10/36. Commd 8/8/60. Sqn Ldr 11/8/69. Retd EDN 1/10/78.
BIRSE D. L. Born 18/8/20. Commd 21/9/50. Sqn Ldr 1/1/64. Retd SUP 18/18/70.
BIRSE R. C. G., BSc. Born 9/6/43. Commd 4/6/67. Flt Lt 4/3/69. Retd GD 4/6/83.
BIRT A. E., BSc. Born 11/3/37. Commd 25/9/62. Sqn Ldr 14/12/74. Retd ADMIN 11/4/93.
BIRTLES R., MA MCIPD MInstAM MIMgt. Born 4/5/49. Commd 12/12/71. Wg Cdr 1/1/89. Retd ADMIN 12/12/93.
BIRTLES T. D., MBE MB ChB DAvMed AFOM. Born 24/12/35. Commd 28/4/64. Wg Cdr 3/4/74. Retd MED
    28/4/80.

BISBEY J. Born 4/9/21. Commd 9/12/48. Flt Lt 9/6/52. Retd GD 4/9/64.
BISH D. Born 25/6/26. Commd 25/10/46. Sqn Ldr 1/1/60. Retd GD 1/3/68.
BISHOP A. M. Born 14/7/47. Commd 23/10/86. Flt Lt 23/10/88. Retd GD 15/7/97.
BISHOP B. M., BDS LDSRCS. Born 28/3/37. Commd 19/7/57. Wg Cdr 28/2/76. Retd DEL 1/10/77.
BISHOP D. A., BSc. Born 5/9/58. Commd 29/8/77. Sqn Ldr 1/1/92. Retd ENG 5/9/96.
BISHOP D. G. Born 4/4/50. Commd 25/2/72. Flt Lt 25/8/77. Retd SUP 1/4/79.
BISHOP G. M. Born 12/1/26. Commd 19/1/56. Flt Offr 5/10/60. Retd SEC 5/12/67.
BISHOP J. H. Born 30/4/28. Commd 12/12/51. Gp Capt 1/1/73. Retd SEC 11/1/75.
BISHOP J. L., AFC BA MRAeS. Born 6/3/45. Commd 3/3/67. Wg Cdr 1/1/83. Retd GD 22/7/91.
BISHOP J. M., MA FIL. Born 9/7/48. Commd 3/1/69. Wg Cdr 1/7/86. Retd ADMIN 16/3/93.
BISHOP J. M., MIMgt. Born 11/10/43. Commd 10/5/73. Sqn Ldr 1/1/86. Retd GD(G) 14/3/96.
BISHOP J. N., MBE. Born 5/7/21. Commd 15/9/60. Sqn Ldr 1/7/71. Retd ENG 31/3/74.
BISHOP J. S. V. C. Born 21/11/24. Commd 21/6/56. Flt Lt 21/6/62. Retd GD 21/11/74.
BISHOP M. J., BSc. Born 17/5/38. Commd 1/10/62. Sqn Ldr 1/1/71. Retd GD 1/10/78.
BISHOP M. R. M. Born 22/9/23. Commd 29/7/44. Sqn Ldr 1/1/69. Retd GD 22/9/81.
BISHOP N. A., BEng. Born 27/2/65. Commd 10/5/86. Flt Lt 15/1/89. Retd GD 21/2/96.
BISHOP R. G., BChD LDSRCS. Born 6/9/40. Commd 20/9/59. Sqn Ldr 21/9/70. Retd DEL 2/4/78.
BISHOP R. J., BA. Born 2/4/43. Commd 9/10/75. Flt Lt 9/10/77. Retd ENG 3/4/93.
BISHOP R. J. Born 23/10/38. Commd 22/8/61. Flt Lt 22/8/65. Retd ADMIN 22/8/77.
BISHOP R. S. Born 19/11/44. Commd 11/10/84. Sqn Ldr 1/7/95. Retd ADMIN 19/11/99.
BISHOP T. R. Born 28/9/20. Commd 1/5/42. Flt Lt 1/11/46. Retd GD(G) 1/4/65.
BISSELL N. Born 1/1/31. Commd 27/8/52. Flt Lt 5/2/58. Retd GD 1/1/69.
BISSHOPP G. W. Born 19/4/41. Commd 21/1/73. Flt Lt 21/1/75. Retd ENG 20/4/84.
BITHELL W. R. N. Born 15/10/07. Commd 9/10/39. Flt Lt 7/7/42. Retd SEC 8/5/47 rtg Sqn Ldr.
BITTEL E., BSc(Eng) ACGI. Born 29/6/48. Commd 2/8/71. Sqn Ldr 1/7/83. Retd ENG 22/6/96.
BLACK A. W., MB ChB FRCPsych DPM. Born 6/5/25. Commd 24/11/52. Gp Capt 22/10/74. Retd MED 6/5/85.
BLACK E. J., FRAeS FIMgt. Born 12/7/46. Commd 25/2/66. A Cdre 1/7/97. Retd GD 5/5/99.
BLACK F. A. Born 7/12/21. Commd 27/4/41. Flt Lt 1/9/45. Retd GD 7/12/55 rtg Sqn Ldr.
BLACK F. S., MB BCh BAO MFCM DPH. Born 15/4/24. Commd 2/12/62. Wg Cdr 1/5/67. Retd MED 1/12/76.
BLACK G. P., CB OBE AFC. Born 10/7/32. Commd 19/1/53. AVM 1/1/85. Retd 10/7/87.
BLACK I. C. Born 11/5/59. Commd 22/2/79. Flt Lt 20/6/84. Retd GD 11/5/97.
BLACK J. B., OBE DFC. Born 20/4/14. Commd 16/3/34. Wg Cdr 1/7/47. Retd GD 17/2/49 rtg Gp Capt.
BLACK J. B. Born 26/6/33. Commd 29/6/59. Flt Lt 29/6/59. Retd GD 31/8/87.
BLACK J. H. W., MBE. Born 14/8/35. Commd 2/10/58. Wg Cdr 1/1/80. Retd GD 14/9/90.
BLACK The Rev J. McL., MA BD. Born 11/7/36. Commd 20/10/69. Retd 11/7/91 Wg Cdr.
BLACK M., BA. Born 7/9/54. Commd 7/11/76. Sqn Ldr 1/1/92. Retd GD 23/9/93.
BLACK MacD. V., MIMgt. Born 14/11/20. Commd 1/4/43. Sqn Ldr 3/11/59. Retd ENG 18/6/82.
BLACK P. D., BSc MB BS FRCS LRCP DO. Born 14/11/43. Commd 11/1/65. Sqn Ldr 3/2/74. Retd MED 14/11/81.
BLACK S. C., MM. Born 4/10/92. Commd 18/9/18. Flt Lt 10/10/28. Retd GD 18/11/28 rtg Sqn Ldr.
BLACK W. Born 13/6/29. Commd 25/6/53. Flt Lt 25/12/56. Retd GD 13/6/67.
BLACK W. A. Born 23/7/33. Commd 13/8/52. Sqn Ldr 1/7/84. Retd GD 23/7/93.
BLACK-ROBERTS J. D. Born 25/9/32. Commd 26/6/57. Fg Offr 26/6/57. Retd SUP 10/1/65.
BLACKBURN A. M. Born 29/4/25. Commd 21/1/45. Flt Lt 1/10/48. Retd GD 29/4/63.
BLACKBURN D. A. Born 3/2/30. Commd 28/11/51. Flt Lt 28/5/56. Retd GD 3/2/68.
BLACKBURN G. J., MBE. Born 25/9/35. Commd 16/11/59. Sqn Ldr 1/1/72. Retd GD 31/8/86.
BLACKBURN G. J., BA. Born 3/10/60. Commd 20/1/85. Flt Lt 3/5/91. Retd ADMIN 20/1/01.
BLACKBURN L. E., MBE. Born 4/4/28. Commd 20/12/51. Sqn Ldr 1/7/68. Retd GD 4/4/83.
BLACKBURN N. J. S. Born 21/10/57. Commd 14/8/80. Flt Lt 14/2/86. Retd GD 14/4/96.
BLACKBURN R., MBE. Born 29/4/32. Commd 19/4/51. Sqn Ldr 1/1/68. Retd GD 25/9/78.
BLACKBURN R. H., BSc. Born 3/5/47. Commd 13/9/71. Sqn Ldr 1/7/88. Retd GD 14/9/96.
BLACKBURN R. M., BSc. Born 17/11/57. Commd 8/2/81. Sqn Ldr 1/1/90. Retd SUP 1/6/96.
BLACKBURN S. A. Born 19/7/50. Commd 27/3/70. Sqn Ldr 1/1/86. Retd ADMIN 6/4/88.
BLACKFORD B. M. Born 10/1/45. Commd 22/5/64. Wg Cdr 1/1/90. Retd GD 16/8/93.
BLACKFORD D. W. Born 9/6/33. Commd 10/9/52. Flt Lt 13/4/60. Retd GD(G) 9/6/88.
BLACKFORD J. L. Born 26/10/35. Commd 31/7/56. Sqn Ldr 1/1/67. Retd GD 1/3/77.
BLACKFORD P., MB ChB MRCGP DRCOG DAvMed. Born 22/5/54. Commd 22/7/75. Wg Cdr 30/8/91. Retd MED 22/5/92.
BLACKFORD P. F. Born 22/11/20. Commd 23/12/39. Sqn Ldr 1/8/47. Retd GD 1/5/58.
BLACKHAM T. H., OBE DFC DL. Born 11/7/22. Commd 7/2/42. A Cdre 1/7/74. Retd GD 11/7/77.
BLACKHAM W., DPhysEd. Born 8/9/24. Commd 13/8/52. Flt Lt 13/8/56. Retd PE 7/3/66.
BLACKLAW J. Born 9/6/11. Commd 17/6/43. Sqn Ldr 1/1/56. Retd ENG 31/7/60.
BLACKLEY A. B., CBE AFC BSc. Born 28/9/37. Commd 16/11/59. AVM 1/1/89. Retd GD 30/11/93.
BLACKLOCK D. W. Born 5/9/34. Commd 10/3/60. Flt Lt 10/9/64. Retd GD 30/9/87.
BLACKLOCK G. B., OBE DFC DFM. Born 23/6/14. Commd 28/8/40. Gp Capt 1/7/56. Retd GD 28/8/61.
BLACKMAN A. L., BA. Born 6/4/28. Commd 9/12/48. Flt Lt 7/6/51. Retd GD 6/8/56.
BLACKMAN J. P., OBE MSc BSc MIMgt. Born 24/5/46. Commd 22/2/71. Wg Cdr 1/7/85. Retd ENG 7/1/96.

BLACKMORE D. J., MBE MPhil MIBiol. Born 24/9/32. Commd 18/10/62. Flt Lt 11/10/68. Retd MED(T) 1/6/73.
BLACKMORE F. C., AFC. Born 16/2/16. Commd 9/4/41. Sqn Ldr 1/8/47. Retd GD 27/6/59 rtg Wg Cdr.
BLACKMORE-HEAL D. C., IEng MIIE. Born 4/5/53. Commd 29/3/90. Flt Lt 29/3/94. Retd ENG 2/10/00.
BLACKNEY A. B., MBA CEng FIMechE FIMgt. Born 29/11/34. Commd 3/1/61. Gp Capt 1/1/80. Retd ENG 9/12/85.
BLACKSHAW S. G. Born 26/9/48. Commd 8/10/70. Flt Lt 8/4/76. Retd GD 22/10/94.
BLACKWELL A. W. Born 14/8/43. Commd 14/6/63. Sqn Ldr 1/1/84. Retd GD 29/1/96.
BLACKWELL J., AFC. Born 13/1/50. Commd 21/3/69. Wg Cdr 1/1/85. Retd GD 11/12/88.
BLACKWELL J. G. Born 31/7/17. Commd 15/9/54. Flt Lt 15/9/59. Retd ENG 30/11/63.
BLACKWELL S. A. Born 19/2/22. Commd 26/9/57. Flt Lt 1/4/63. Retd ENG 30/4/66.
BLACKWOOD T. V. Born 20/12/46. Commd 23/3/67. Sqn Ldr 1/1/84. Retd GD 20/12/90.
BLACKWOOD W. D., BDS. Born 24/1/34. Commd 11/1/59. Wg Cdr 19/11/71. Retd DEL 11/1/75.
BLAGBROUGH R. B. Born 6/5/43. Commd 17/12/64. Sqn Ldr 1/7/75. Retd GD 6/5/81.
BLAGDEN A. G. Born 13/2/12. Commd 9/5/40. Flt Lt 9/5/42. Retd GD 14/12/45.
BLAGROVE C. N., MBE BSc. Born 13/1/56. Commd 30/10/77. Sqn Ldr 1/7/87. Retd GD 13/1/00.
BLAIK M. A. Born 19/9/42. Commd 27/1/67. Wg Cdr 1/1/83. Retd SUP 19/9/86.
BLAIN A. A., BSc. Born 15/1/41. Commd 6/8/63. Sqn Ldr 1/1/73. Retd ENG 6/8/79.
BLAIN D. F., ACA. Born 2/12/10. Commd 4/9/36. Sqn Ldr 1/6/45. Retd SEC 1/8/47 rtg Wg Cdr.
BLAIR D. A. Born 16/10/22. Commd 12/4/45. Flt Lt 4/1/51. Retd GD 16/10/65.
BLAIR H. Born 22/2/23. Commd 3/8/50. Sqn Ldr 1/1/69. Retd ADMIN 22/2/78.
BLAIR J., DFM. Born 19/7/18. Commd 4/10/43. Sqn Ldr 1/7/67. Retd SUP 19/7/73.
BLAIR J. C., DFC AFC. Born 8/4/20. Commd 15/11/42. Wg Cdr 1/7/58. Retd GD 13/5/64.
BLAIR J. J., DFC Born 16/2/19. Commd 28/1/44. Flt Lt 28/7/47. Retd GD 30/7/63.
BLAIR M. J., BSc. Born 18/3/43. Commd 17/5/62. Sqn Ldr 1/7/77. Retd ENG 1/5/93.
BLAIR-HICKMAN W. N. Born 11/9/42. Commd 30/7/63. Flt Lt 30/1/66. Retd GD 23/8/75.
BLAKE A. H. Born 17/12/14. Commd 29/7/41. Wg Cdr 1/1/53. Retd RGT 30/6/55.
BLAKE A. H. Born 1/10/40. Commd 18/12/62. Sqn Ldr 1/7/73. Retd GD 1/5/79.
BLAKE B. J. Born 29/10/20. Commd 27/10/55. Sqn Ldr 1/7/69. Retd ENG 29/3/75.
BLAKE C. Born 21/7/38. Commd 11/5/62. Sqn Ldr 1/7/71. Retd GD 8/8/78.
BLAKE D. J. Born 6/8/40. Commd 9/2/62. Flt Lt 20/7/70. Retd PRT 6/8/78.
BLAKE H. R. Born 25/12/11. Commd 1/11/45. Sqn Ldr 9/7/57. Retd MED(T) 26/12/66.
BLAKE J. D. Born 5/8/39. Commd 14/5/57. Sqn Ldr 1/7/75. Retd GD 13/6/84.
BLAKE P., OBE. Born 13/12/28. Commd 1/5/52. Wg Cdr 1/1/77. Retd GD 3/1/84.
BLAKE P. G., FIMgt. Born 20/8/38. Commd 28/7/59. Gp Capt 1/7/85. Retd GD 20/8/93.
BLAKE V. R. H. Born 7/11/33. Commd 26/5/54. Flt Lt 7/3/62. Retd GD 7/11/71.
BLAKELEY J., OBE BSc CEng FRAeS. Born 26/10/42. Commd 15/7/63. A Cdre 1/1/90. Retd ENG 1/5/91.
BLAKELEY J. B., OBE. Born 19/12/32. Commd 9/4/52. Gp Capt 1/7/79. Retd GD 2/4/85.
BLAKEMAN G., OBE MIMgt. Born 26/7/21. Commd 23/10/42. Wg Cdr 1/1/60. Retd GD 26/7/68.
BLAKEMORE R. C. Born 30/7/39. Commd 28/1/60. Sqn Ldr 1/7/71. Retd ADMIN 1/10/84.
BLAKEY J. H. N. M., BSc. Born 16/10/46. Commd 27/10/68. Flt Lt 27/7/70. Retd GD 12/8/77.
BLAKEY R. W. Born 18/8/32. Commd 13/8/52. Flt Lt 9/1/58. Retd GD 18/8/69.
BLAKLEY R. J. Born 28/11/22. Commd 1/1/62. Flt Lt 24/11/65. Retd ENG 27/8/77.
BLANCHFIELD G., BSc. Born 23/10/48. Commd 13/1/745. Wg Cdr 1/1/90. Retd GD 13/12/96.
BLANE D. C., PhD BA FIMA MIMgt. Born 20/7/35. Commd 31/12/58. Sqn Ldr 31/8/69. Retd EDN 28/11/79.
BLANK K. R. Born 3/5/32. Commd 5/7/68. Flt Lt 5/7/73. Retd ADMIN 3/5/92.
BLANN A. D., BSc. Born 28/10/30. Commd 17/12/52. Flt Lt 17/3/54. Retd GD 28/10/68.
BLASZAK R. M. Born 1/2/15. Commd 1/3/41. Flt Lt 1/7/46. Retd PE 4/4/69.
BLATCH J. R., AFC Born 23/2/31. Commd 6/12/51. Sqn Ldr 1/1/64. Retd GD 27/8/76.
BLATCHFORD K. G. Born 10/3/42. Commd 27/1/61. Flt Lt 27/7/66. Retd. GD 10/3/80.
BLAYMIRES M. E. F. Born 12/2/19. Commd 10/6/43. Flt Lt 10/12/46. Retd ENG 30/7/60 rtg Sqn Ldr.
BLEACH D. G., MIMgt. Born 12/2/23. Commd 10/9/43. Wg Cdr 1/1/70. Retd GD 1/8/74.
BLEADEN J. A. Born 2/7/40. Commd 28/7/60. Flt Lt 10/2/67. Retd GD 2/7/78.
BLEASDALE P. D. Born 11/9/41. Commd 16/7/62. Flight Lt 16/1/68. Retd GD 2/4/76.
BLEASE S. C. P., MB ChB. Born 14/11/58. Commd 12/1/82. Sqn Ldr 1/8/88. Retd MED 30/1/96.
BLEE W. H. P., MIMgt. Born 5/12/23. Commd 28/3/45. Wg Cdr 1/7/68. Retd ADMIN 30/19/76.
BLENCOE The Rev C. D., BA. Born 11/11/17. Commd 10/3/63. Sqn Ldr 18/9/61 rtg Wg Cdr.
BLENCOWE M. R. Born 25/10/45. Commd 19/8/65. Flt Lt 2/12/71. Retd SEC 25/10/83.
BLENKINSOP C. M. Born 14/9/47. Commd 10/5/73. Flt Lt 10/11/79. Retd ADMIN 25/9/88.
BLENKINSOP G. E., MIFireE. Born 22/5/47. Commd 8/11/68. Flt Lt 20/9/74. Retd SY 22/5/85.
BLENKIRON T. J. Born 13/3/49. Commd 29/6/72. Flt Lt 29/12/78. Retd ADMIN 13/3/88.
BLEVINS D. Born 16/5/38. Commd 7/9/80. Sqn Ldr 1/1/88. Retd SUP 16/5/93.
BLEVINS S. J. Born 19/3/58. Commd 20/1/80. Flt Lt 20/1/85. Retd ADMIN 21/12/87.
BLEW D. Born 22/9/18. Commd 18/5/37. Flt Lt 26/8/46. Retd SUP 5/3/63.
BLEZARD D. N. Born 8/4/49. Commd 2/8/68. Flt Lt 18/1/75. Retd GD(G) 1/4/78.
BLICQ R. S. Born 2/5/25. Commd 20/10/52. Flt Lt 26/5/55. Retd GD 16/5/57.
BLINMAN M. G. Born 29/12/34. Commd 10/4/56. Sqn Ldr 1/7/69. Retd SUP 30/4/92.
BLINMAN T. V. Born 15/7/17. Commd 30/1/44. Flt Lt 30/7/47. Retd SEC 15/7/61.

BLISS D.A. Born 31/5/16. Commd 15/11/46. Sqn Ldr 1/1/52. Retd RGT 23/3/58.
BLISS J. E., ACIS. Born 4/6/13. Commd 29/8/46. Sqn Ldr 1/1/58. Retd SEC 7/5/61.
BLISS N. A. Born 24/12/56. Commd 30/4/81. Sqn Ldr 1/7/91. Retd GD(G) 24/12/94.
BLISS R. J. Born 9/5/44. Commd 3/8/62. Sqn Ldr 1/7/78. Retd GD 26/8/92.
BLISS W. E., CBE. Born 4/10/28. Commd 7/7/49. Gp Capt 1/1/76. Retd GD 4/10/85.
BLISSETT H. Born 17/12/22. Commd 19/7/51. Sqn Ldr 1/7/61. Retd ENG 21/12/78. Re-instated 13/6/62 to 17/12/82.
BLOCKEY J. W. Born 3/4/37. Commd 17/12/57. Wg Cdr 1/7/79. Retd GD 2/4/92.
BLOCKEY P. D. Born 16/7/33. Commd 9/10/56. Sqn Ldr 1/7/68. Retd GD 16/7/71.
BLOCKI J. Born 24/12/21. Commd 15/4/47. Flt Lt 1/7/47. Retd GD(G) 24/12/76.
BLOME-JONES L. M., DFC. Born 17/1/12. Commd 17/2/36. Sqn Ldr 9/6/47. Retd SEC 8/3/58 rtg Wg Cdr.
BLOMFIELD O. H. D. Born 28/9/12. Commd 14/8/34. Wg Cdr 1/10/46. Retd GD 10/3/49.
BLOMLEY D. L., MBE. Born 22/10/43. Commd 17/12/65. Sqn Ldr 1/1/75. Retd SUP 22/10/81. Re-entered 18/7/84. Wg Cdr 1/7/92. Retd SUP 31/8/00.
BLOOD D. M. W., BSc. Born 23/11/61. Commd 31/8/80. Flt Lt 15/10/84. Retd GD 1/9/00.
BLOODWORTH, LLO MB BCh MRCP. Born 17/3/52. Commd 26/6/73. Sqn Ldr 17/8/81. Retd MED 13/3/86.
BLOOM P. G. Born 14/4/31. Commd 25/5/50. Flt Lt 25/5/56. Retd SUP 14/4/69.
BLOOMFIELD J. N. Born 2/8/33. Commd 3/4/58. Sqn Ldr 1/7/69. Retd GD 11/11/81.
BLOOMFIELD P. B. Born 24/5/30. Commd 18/6/52. Flt Lt 13/11/57. Retd GD 24/5/68.
BLOOR R. N., MRCPsych MRCS LRCP. Born 20/12/49. Commd 14/2/71. Sqn Ldr 24/9/80. Retd MED 20/12/87.
BLORE C. E. Born 23/10/50. Commd 12/10/78. Sqn Ldr 1/1/88. Retd ENG 1/1/91.
BLOUNT C. C., MVO. Born 2/2/25. Commd 19/10/45. Sqn Ldr 1/1/56. Retd GD 18/10/60.
BLOW G. J. Born 18//5/51. Commd 25/2/72. Wg Cdr 1/1/90. Retd SUP 29/2/92.
BLOWER A. P., MB MChir FRCS DMRD. Born 31/1/27. Commd 30/3/53. Wg Cdr 5/3/65. Retd MED 19/3/70.
BLOWERS A. L. Born 1/5/29. Commd 14/12/70. Flt Lt 14/12/70. Retd ADMIN 16/5/84.
BLOWFIELD G. E. Born 17/8/16. Commd 28/3/46. Sqn Ldr 1/7/68. Retd SUP 17/8/71.
BLOXAM J. R., OBE DFC. Born 20/3/18. Commd 14/1/39. Wg Cdr 1/7/52. Retd GD 20/3/65.
BLUNDELL M. D., MB ChB FFARCS DA. Born 13/2/41. Commd 28/9/64. Wg Cdr 8/8/81. Retd MED 15/3/83.
BLUNDEN D. Born 10/4/30. Commd 5/3/52. Flt Lt 5/9/56. Retd GD 31/3/70.
BLUNDEN D. G., MBE. Born 3/10/29. Commd 3/11/51. Wg Cdr 1/1/76. Retd GD 1/2/84.
BLUNKELL M. E., MBE CEng MIEE. Born 17/6/42. Commd 14/2/63. Wg Cdr 1/7/83. Retd ENG 17/4/93.
BLUNT A. S. Born 17/8/41. Commd 18/7/61. Wg Cdr 1/7/85. Retd ENG 17/4/89.
BLUNT C. A., MIMgt MCIPD. Born 9/1/31. Commd 9/11/50. Wg Cdr 1/7/72. Retd SEC 4/4/81.
BLUNT I. R. Born 26/8/40. Commd 30/7/64. Gp Capt 1/7/86. Retd ENG 1/5/91.
BLYTH A. G. Born 22/1/21. Commd 14/3/49. Flt Lt 4/6/56. Retd GD 2/2/70.
BLYTH A. J. G., MIMgt. Born 29/5/42. Commd 21/7/61. Sqn Ldr 1/7/78. Retd GD 1/7/81.
BLYTH C. I., DFC* AFC*. Born 1/4/25. Commd 24/5/45. Sqn Ldr 1/1/56. Retd GD 1/4/63.
BLYTH G. F. Born 27/5/11. Commd 24/3/43. Flt Lt 24/9/46. Retd ENG 8/3/47.
BLYTH G. G., BA. Born 2/11/48. Commd 24/9/67. Flt Lt 15/10/73. Retd SUP 2/11/86.
BLYTH I. D. Born 22/3/37. Commd 15/9/60. Wg Cdr 1/7/82. Retd GD(AEO) 1/1/90.
BLYTHE A. C., DFC Born 26/7/21. Commd 11/5/41. Gp Capt 1/1/60. Retd GD 18/5/70.
BLYTHE W. D. Born 10/7/17. Commd 11/7/46. Sqn Ldr 1/1/58. Retd SEC 31/1/63.
BLYTHE-BROOK D. Born 10/3/40. Commd 21/4/67. Sqn Ldr 1/7/82. Retd SUP 10/3/95.
BOAGEY J. G., MBE. Born 1/10/19. Commd 28/2/46. Wg Cdr 1/1/63. Retd ENG 1/6/70.
BOAK D. C., MIMgt. Born 14/8/39. Command 19/1/66. Wg Cdr 1/1/85. Retd ADMIN 4/1/87.
BOALCH C. J. Born 3/6/16. Commd 26/8/41. Sqn Ldr 1/1/52. Retd ENG 3/6/65.
BOARDMAN C. L. Born 2/10/36. Commd 12/6/58. Sqn Ldr 1/1/70. Retd CAT 12/8/75.
BOARDMAN H. J., MBE BSc CEng MIMechE MIMgt. Born 12/12/50. Commd 26/2/71. Sqn Ldr 1/1/82. Retd ENG 12/12/88.
BOARDS D. A., DFM. Born 1/2/17. Commd 13/8/43. Sqn Ldr 1/4/56. Retd GD 5/2/60.
BOAST R. S., CBE DFC AE. Born 21/12/20. Commd 16/6/40. Gp Capt 1/7/61. Retd GD 24/7/65.
BOATWRIGHT P.H., CBE FIMgt FRAeS. Born 4/3/37. Commd 26/3/64. Gp Capt 1/1/87. Retd GD(G) 3/4/92.
BOBART R. Born 29/6/22. Commd 11/8/44. Flt Lt 26/5/55. Retd GD 23/6/67.
BOBISHKO-BIGGS P. V., BDS. Born 20/12/57. Bommd 1/4/84. Flt Lt 7/8/82. Retd DEL 28/7/86.
BOCKING I. Born 6/10/47. Commd 29/1/87. Flt Lt 29/1/91. Retd OPS SPT 29/7/98.
BODDINGTON J. A., BA DPhysED MIMgt. Born 12/5/43. Commd 8/10/65. Sqn Ldr 1/1/77. Retd PE 10/8/81.
BODDY G.M., OBE. Born 16/9/37. Commd 5/2/56. A Cdre 1/1/90. Retd GD(G) 1/7/92.
BODEN A. N., BA FRSA LHSM. Born 21/4/38. Commd 19/1/66. Gp Capt 1/7/87. Retd MED(SEC) 1/7/89.
BODEN D. E. G. Born 13/7/29. Commd 20/11/51. Flt Lt 28/8/56. Retd GD 13/7/84.
BODEN G. R. Born 5/8/28. Commd 1/7/52. Sqn Ldr 1/1/63. Retd GD 5/8/66.
BODEN J. Born 9/4/40. Commd 24/11/67. Flt Lt 15/4/70. Retd SEC 9/4/78.
BODEN J. M., MIMgt. Born 28/6/30. Commd 30/7/52. Wg Cdr 1/1/76. Retd ADMIN 28/2/78.
BODEN R. A. Born 28/9/46. Commd 21/2/74. Flt Lt 3/2/77. Retd GD(G) 14/3/96.
BODENHAM B. Born 8/11/50. Commd 15/8/85. Flt Lt 15/8/87. Retd ENG 15/8/93.
BODIAM A. R., BSc. Born 8/6/51. Commd 26/9/69. Sqn Ldr 1/1/88. Retd GD 1/3/91.
BODIE J. W. Born 14/11/52. Commd 15/3/73. Sqn Ldr 1/7/86. Retd ADMIN 14/12/90.

BODY W. R. S., CEng MRAeS. Born 13/9/22. Commd 4/11/58. Sqn Ldr 1/7/70. Retd ENG 13/9/73.
BOE I. C. C. Born 3/5/48. Commd 11/8/67. Flt Lt 11/2/74. Retd SY (RGT) 3/5/88.
BOETIUS J. M., CEng MRAeS MIMechE. Born 4/6/33. Commd 28/10/57. Flt Lt 28/10/62. Retd ENG 28/10/73.
BOETIUS P. A. Born 1/7/34. Commd 11/8/55. Flt Offr 11/8/61. Retd SEC 16/12/61.
BOFFEY B. G. A. Born 28/10/31. Commd 20/11/58. Flt Lt 14/4/65. Retd SUP 17/3/71.
BOGG R. Born 14/6/42. Commd 11/5/62. A Cdre 11/5/62. Retd GD 14/6/97.
BOGGIA R., BDS MGDSRCS(Ed) MGDSRCS(Eng) LDSRCS. Born 7/2/39. Commd 30/6/63. Sqn Ldr 22/12/67. Retd DEL 30/6/66. Re-entered 22/6/75. Gp Capt 1/1/91. Retd DEL 7/2/97.
BOGGIS M. F. Born 8/3/35. Commd 6/2/54. Flt Lt 6/8/59. Retd GD(G) 14/9/87
BOGGIS P. J. S., DFC. Born 29/9/18. Commd 8/8/39. Flt Lt 1/9/45. Retd GD(G) 7/10/67 rtg Sqn Ldr.
BOGUE P. J. Born 24/11/30. Commd 30/7/52. Flt Lt 30/1/55. Retd GD 25/11/68.
BOHL M. J., BA. Born 23/9/61. Commd 11/9/83. Flt Lt 11/3/86. Retd ADMIN 14/3/97.
BOHM E. B., ACIS. Born 23/7/48. Commd 17/5/79. Wg Cdr 1/7/95. Retd ADMIN 1/12/98.
BOLAM G. D., MA BSc CEng MIEE DUS. Born 1/8/19. Commd 24/8/49. Wg Cdr 24/9/66. Retd EDN 17/11/71.
BOLD G. Born 15/1/25. Commd 29/6/50. Sqn Ldr 1/1/62. Retd GD 31/1/75.
BOLER F. F. Born 5/6/25. Commd 9/6/44. Flt Lt 9/6/50. Retd GD(G) 1/10/69.
BOLEY P. G., IEng MIIE(elec) MILT. Born 17/1/43. Commd 26/9/82. Sqn Ldr 1/7/92. Retd ENG 26/9/98.
BOLINGBROKE P. V. Born 26/9/22. Commd 22/6/50. Flt Lt 22/6/56. Retd SEC 1/5/74.
BOLLANS G. D. Born 26/9/57. Commd 17/5/79. Flt Lt 17/11/84. Retd GD 13/12/95.
BOLT C. R., MBE MCIPS. Born 29/3/47. Commd 2/8/68. Wg Cdr 1/1/91. Retd SUP 14/9/96.
BOLT J. L. Born 8/7/35. Commd 7/5/60. Sqn Ldr 1/1/70. Retd ENG 17/5/76.
BOLTON A. W. Born 5/5/12. Commd 13/3/47. Fg Offr 13/3/48. Retd SUP 8/1/55.
BOLTON C. A. Born 5/11/20. Commd 3/7/57. Sqn Ldr 1/1/64. Retd SEC 29/12/73.
BOLTON C. A., BSc CEng MIEE AMBCS MIDPM. Born 23/4/50. Commd 17/10/71. Sqn Ldr 1/7/84. Retd ENG 23/4/88.
BOLTON C. A. Born 15/6/45. Commd 5/12/63. Gp Capt 1/1/92. Retd ADMIN 2/12/96.
BOLTON C. C. I. Born 12/1/46. Commd 6/11/64. Flt Lt 4/5/72. Retd GD 16/10/76.
BOLTON D., MIMgt. Born 15/4/32. Commd 22/10/53. Gp Capt 1/7/78. Retd SY 23/9/80.
BOLTON F. H. Born 3/10/1900. Commd 14/3/40. Flt Lt 1/2/43. Retd ENG 21/12/45 rtg Sqn Ldr.
BOLTON J. A. Born 6/5/37. Commd 2/5/59. Sqn Ldr 1/7/71. Retd GD 1/10/78.
BOLTON J. F. Born 3/8/28. Commd 22/7/50. Flt Lt 22/7/55. Retd RGT 12/1/68.
BOLTON J. W. A., BSc MRAeS. Born 17/12/44. Commd 30/8/66. Gp Capt 1/1/89. Retd GD 1/10/93.
BOLTON P. M. Born 30/1/44. Commd 22/3/63. Flt Lt 22/9/68. Retd GD 29/3/74.
BOLTON R. A. Born 7/9/48. Commd 29/11/68. Flt Lt 29/5/74. Retd GD 14/10/78.
BOLTON R. J. Born 26/3/36. Commd 24/9/64. Flt Lt 24/9/66. Retd GD 24/8/74.
BOLTON W. Born 22/12/20. Commd 9/10/42. Flt Lt 26/5/55. Retd GD 31/1/68.
BOLTON-KING J. Born 9/7/36. Commd 23/12/58. Flt Lt 7/8/64. Retd GD 9/9/72.
BOLTON-KING R., BA. Born 23/2/40. Commd 17/8/64. Sqn Ldr 1/1/75. Retd GD 17/8/80.
BOMBER K. J. Born 6/10/45. Commd 22/5/64. Sqn Ldr 1/7/77. Retd GD 6/10/83.
BONAS R. H. Born 6/6/34. Commd 29/10/73. Sqn Ldr 1/1/80. Retd GD 13/2/87
BOND A. D. Born 21/9/48. Commd 19/6/70. Flt Lt 1/12/74. Retd GD 21/9/86.
BOND C., BEng. Born 29/1/42. Commd 9/9/63. Sqn Ldr 1/7/78. Retd GD 29/1/97.
BOND C. C. Born 22/2/33. Commd 9/4/52. Flt Lt 17/4/61. Retd GD 17/10/75.
BOND C. F., DFC. Born 7/10/18. Commd 22/1/43. Flt Lt 15/7/52. Retd SEC 7/10/73.
BOND C. P. Born 21/4/60. Commd 21/6/90. Flt Lt 21/6/92. Retd GD 21/6/98.
BOND E. D. B. Born 23/6/31. Commd 22/12/53. Flt Lt 7/3/62. Retd GD 1/9/69.
BOND F. E. Born 1/5/95. Commd 1/4/18. Wg Cdr 1/1/39. Retd REG 27/1/42 rtg Gp Capt.
BOND G. Born 15/11/46. Commd 25/2/82. Flt Lt 25/2/85. Retd GD 1/10/91.
BOND G. H., BSc. Born 17/4/56. Commd 21/10/79. Flt Lt 21/1/81. Retd GD 6/6/89.
BOND M. N. Born 16/10/38. Commd 16/5/60. Sqn Ldr 1/1/71. Retd GD 16/10/76.
BOND N. P. Born 14/12/47. Commd 23/9/66. Flt Lt 18/3/73. Retd SUP 1/1/76.
BOND P. R. Born 29/5/33. Commd 3/9/52. Gp Capt 1/7/81. Retd GD 9/7/91.
BOND R. A. V., MILT. Born 13/8/47. Commd 1/3/68. Wg Cdr 1/1/91. Retd SUP 17/7/96.
BOND R. N. Born 24/12/23. Commd 6/12/56. Flt Lt 6/12/62. Retd GD 2/4/68.
BOND T. A. M. Born 14/12/32. Commd 14/12/54. Sqn Ldr 1/7/69. Retd SUP 1/7/72.
BOND T. M. Born 17/11/36. Commd 30/12/54. Flt Lt 1/3/61. Retd GD 17/11/74.
BONE A. L. Born 27/6/26. Commd 21/11/51. Flt Lt 21/5/56. Retd GD 31/12/69.
BONE D. J. Born 15/7/61. Commd 15/8/85. Flt Lt 15/2/91. Retd GD 6/8/94.
BONE J. H., FINucE. Born 23/6/27. Commd 4/2/48. Flt Lt 4/2/54. Retd SEC 1/2/78.
BONE R. D., MBE. Born 29/1/24. Commd 19/11/53. Flt Lt 19/11/59. Retd GD 29/1/79.
BONELLA T. R., MSc BSc. Born 24/5/52. Commd 25/9/71. Wg Cdr 1/7/91. Retd ENG 2/12/98.
BONFIELD F. W. L. Born 17/9/41. Commd 26/5/61. Sqn Ldr 1/7/73. Retd GD 17/9/79.
BONFIELD K. M. Born 3/2/64. Commd 23/5/85. Fg Offr 23/5/87. Retd GD 1/7/90.
BONHAM-SMITH I. H. Born 1/3/40. Commd 23/6/60. Flt Lt 23/9/66. Retd ADMIN 1/3/78.
BONNER W. H. McC., OBE MCIPD MIMgt. Born 12/12/33. Commd 13/9/51. Wg Cdr 1/7/73. Retd GD 9/2/86.
BONNEY G. W. Born 25/10/25. Commd 5/11/46. Flt Lt 4/11/53. Retd GD 30/6/65.

BONNEY K. G. B., CEng FRAeS FInstMC FIMgt. Born 27/6/22. Commd 9/3/50. Wg Cdr 1/1/70. Retd ENG 27/6/77.
BONNOR N., FRIN FRAeS. Born 29/7/39. Commd 25/7/60. A Cdre 1/1/89. Retd GD 2/4/91.
BONNY G. L., MIMgt Born 18/2/24. Commd 26/8/48. Wg Cdr 1/7/64. Retd GD 1/3/73.
BONSALL P. J., BSc CEng MRAeS MIMgt. Born 11/11/49. Commd 4/10/68. Sqn Ldr 1/1/87. Retd ENG 1/1/90.
BONSER C. E. B., MCIT MILT MIMgt. Born 14/4/29. Commd 26/9/51. Wg Cdr 1/1/80. Retd SUP 29/7/82.
BONSEY J. D. Born 8/4/33. Commd 26/9/52. GD(G) 8/4/93. Retd GD(G) 8/4/93.
BOOKER E. J., OBE MM MIMgt. Born 6/11/20. Commd 5/4/43. Wg Cdr 1/7/59. Retd ENG 6/11/75.
BOOKER G. S. F., BSc CEng MIMechE MRAeS. Born 16/11/47. Commd 27/2/70. Wg Cdr 1/7/88. Retd ENG 14/3/97.
BOOKER H. J. Born 21/5/23. Commd 2/7/64. Flt Lt 2/7/67. Retd GD 21/5/78.
BOOKER L. A. J., BEM. Born 29/10/17. Commd 26/9/57. Flt Lt 26/9/60. Retd ENG 23/11/63.
BOOKER R., BA. Born 24/2/21. Commd 3/5/49. Wg Cdr 1/1/65. Retd EDN 1/5/73.
BOOKER S. A., MBE. Born 25/4/22. Commd 18/5/43. Sqn Ldr 1/1/72. Retd GD 30/6/73.
BOOKER T. T. Born 3/3/44. Commd 21/4/77. Sqn Ldr 1/7/86. Retd MED(SEC) 3/3/99.
BOOLY M. I. E. Born 30/8/54. Commd 7/11/91. Flt Lt 7/11/95. Retd SUP 1/10/98.
BOON J. F., CBE FCIPD FIMgt. Born 27/4/35. Commd 18/2/54. Air Cdre 1/7/85. Retd ADMIN 28/4/93.
BOON T. R. Born 26/8/46. Commd 23/3/67. Sqn Ldr 1/1/85. Retd GD 15/9/00.
BOONHAM A., OBE CEng MIEE. Born 24/9/16. Commd 29/3/41. Gp Capt 1/1/64. Retd ENG 24/9/71.
BOORMAN P. Born 11/3/35. Commd 13/9/50. Flt Lt 15/3/65. Retd GD 1/3/73.
BOORMAN P. S. Born 19/7/49. Commd 6/11/80. Sqn Ldr 1/1/91. Retd OPS SPT 1/10/97.
BOOTH A. E. Born 17/6/35. Commd 24/4/70. Flt Lt 12/7/74. Retd MED(T) 1/9/76.
BOOTH C. B. K. Born 10/6/11. Commd 12/8/41. Flt Lt 1/9/45. Retd ENG 15/9/58 rtg Sqn Ldr.
BOOTH C. J. Born 26/6/40. Commd 1/8/61. Wg Cdr 1/7/91. Retd GD 26/6/95.
BOOTH D. P. Born 15/7/45. Commd 18/8/67. Sqn Ldr 1/7/79. Retd SUP 7/12/98.
BOOTH E. D. Born 14/5/23. Commd 10/3/44. Flt Lt 24/6/54. Retd SEC 28/8/64.
BOOTH E. M., MSc MB ChB MFCM MFOM DIH. Born 29/1/32. Commd 6/1/63. Wg Cdr 23/12/71. Retd MED 31/10/81.
BOOTH F. Born 27/8/31. Commd 23/8/51. Sqn Ldr 1/7/65. Retd GD 27/8/86.
BOOTH K. S., OBE AFC. Born 20/12/20. Commd 8/8/41. Wg Cdr 1/1/59. Retd GD 20/12/75 rtg Gp Capt.
BOOTH L. W. N., DFC. Born 2/9/18. Commd 20/3/43. Sqn Ldr 1/7/62. Retd SUP 31/8/72.
BOOTH M. R. Born 18/2/56. Commd 24/6/76. Flt Lt 24/12/81. Retd GD 29/5/88.
BOOTH P., MB ChB MRCP DCH. Born 14/10/54. Commd 22/7/75. Wg Cdr 1/8/92. Retd MED 14/10/92.
BOOTH P. M., BSc. Born 8/10/23. Commd 3/1/61. Sqn Ldr 14/2/66. Retd ADMIN 3/1/77.
BOOTH R. Born 27/9/37. Commd 16/9/55. Sqn Ldr 1/1/72. Retd GD 27/9/75.
BOOTH R. E. Born 19/11/38. Commd 9/7/60. Sqn Ldr 1/7/78. Retd GD 19/11/93.
BOOTH R. I. Born 31/8/42. Commd 2/2/62. Flt Lt 9/8/67. Flt Lt 9/8/67. Retd GD 1/4/76.
BOOTH R. S. Born 27/5/51. Commd 25/2/72. Sqn Ldr 1/1/88. Retd SY 2/6/93.
BOOTH T. A. Born 18/9/44. Commd 31/8/62. Flt Lt 1/7/69. Retd GD 3/7/82.
BOOTH T. I. Born 19/11/43. Commd 12/1/62. Flt Lt 1/7/68. Retd GD 19/11/81.
BOOTHBY A., MIMgt. Born 18/12/22. Commd 25/8/43. Sqn Ldr 1/1/68. Retd RGT 18/6/79.
BOOTHBY H. E., OBE BA. Born 1/11/22. Commd 2/6/43. Gp Capt 1/7/72. Retd ADMIN 1/11/77.
BOOTHBY P. E. Born 16/10/56. Commd 20/9/79. Flt Lt 20/3/85. Retd GD 2/3/98.
BOOTHROYD P. V. Born 27/12/46. Commd 5/2/65. Flt Lt 4/11/70. Retd GD 14/3/96.
BOOTLE C. H. Born 6/6/29. Commd 23/7/52. Sqn Ldr 1/7/68. Retd SUP 6/6/84. Reinstated 7/11/84. Sqn Ldr 2/12/68. Retd SUP 6/6/89.
BORE J. E., OBE. Born 14/10/32. Commd 13/9/51. A Cdre 1/7/81. Retd GD 1/7/83.
BOREHAM P. J. Born 30/7/37. Commd 3/4/59. Wg Cdr 1/1/80. Retd ENG 30/7/87.
BOREHAM P. M. Born 8/9/43. Commd 8/9/63. Sqn Ldr 1/1/79. Retd GD 1/1/82.
BOREHAM R. J. Born 2/7/31. Commd 19/8/71. Flt Lt 19/8/74. Retd GD(G) 1/3/83.
BORLAND D. A., AFM. Born 5/11/22. Commd 26/11/53. Flt Lt 26/11/59. Retd GD 5/11/72.
BORRILL C. P., BSc. Born 20/7/61. Commd 14/10/84. Sqn Ldr 1/7/92. Retd SUP 14/10/00.
BORROWS K., BSc CEng MRAeS MIMgt. Born 3/11/37. Commd 4/9/59. Sqn Ldr 1/1/67. Retd ENG 4/9/89.
BOSANCO-MITCHELL D. W. Born 7/6/44. Commd 4/7/85. Sqn Ldr 1/1/94. Retd ENG 13/4/99.
BOSANQUET C. C. Born 19/12/46. Commd 4/5/70. Flt Lt 15/4/72. Retd GD 13/9/75.
BOSELEY K. Born 9/1/58. Commd 19/12/91. Flt Lt 19/12/93. Retd SUP 14/3/96.
BOSHER J. H. Born 18/10/32. Commd 23/8/51. Flt Lt 22/5/57. Retd GD 29/5/72.
BOSLEY G. Born 29/4/32. Commd 2/6/77. Flt Lt 2/6/82. Retd GD(G) 1/2/86.
BOSSY M. J. Born 31/10/45. Commd 1/6/72. Wg Cdr 1/7/96. Retd GD 31/10/00.
BOSTOCK S. N., MSc FIMgt. Born 9/8/43. Commd 17/12/65. A Cdre 1/7/94. Retd GD 23/12/96.
BOSTON F. Born 12/11/03. Commd 14/5/23. Flt Lt 17/7/29. Retd GD 8/8/34.
BOSTON G. A. Born 12/7/26. Commd 22/2/47. Flt Lt 7/6/51. Retd GD 12/7/69.
BOSTON J. Born 27/4/45. Commd 30/8/84. Sqn Ldr 1/1/96. Retd ADMIN 27/4/00.
BOSWORTH G. W. Born 24/3/58. Commd 15/12/88. Flt Lt 15/12/90. Retd ADMIN 23/4/92.
BOSWORTH J. Born 28/8/31. Commd 18/2/53. Flt Lt 20/7/58. Retd GD(G) 28/8/89.
BOSWORTH J. M. Born 20/4/63. Commd 8/12/83. Flt Lt 8/6/90. Retd SUP 1/10/90.
BOTELER W. E., DFC. Born 13/6/20. Commd 4/6/43. Sqn Ldr 1/10/55. Retd GD 13/6/63.

BOTHAM J. A. Born 26/3/48. Commd 2/12/66. Sqn Ldr 1/1/85. Retd GD 26/3/92.
BOTHAMS J. Born 4/10/21. Commd 17/3/49. Wg Cdr 1/1/66. Retd SEC 1/5/74.
BOTSFORD F. A., AFM. Born 19/8/23. Commd 30/11/50. Flt Lt 30/5/54. Retd GD 31/8/68.
BOTT A. K. Born 17/2/20. Commd 16/1/47. Flt Lt 30/9/57. Retd SEC 28/10/67.
BOTT J. M. Born 5/5/21. Commd 14/9/44. Flt Lt 27/5/54. Retd GD 30/7/69.
BOTTELEY R. J., BSc. Born 9/12/43. Commd 3/10/66. Sqn Ldr 3/4/77. Retd ADMIN 3/10/82.
BOTTERILL P.G., CBE AFC FIMgt. Born 14/1/32. Commd 14/11/51. Gp Capt 1/1/77. Retd GD 14/1/87.
BOTTERY P.A. Born 8/8/49. Commd 1/8/69. Sqn Ldr 1/1/85. Retd ENG 1/1/88.
BOTTING L. E., CBE DFC. Born 29/7/13. Commd 16/8/41. Gp Capt 1/1/57. Retd GD 31/8/60.
BOTTOME N. L. Born 21/6/20. Commd 7/1/42. Sqn Ldr 1/7/54. Retd GD 21/6/63.
BOTTOMLEY M. V. Born 5/5/39. Commd 27/8/64. Wg Cdr 1/7/81. Retd SUP 5/5/94.
BOTWRIGHT P. Born 28/2/30. Commd 14/11/51. Flt Lt 22/5/57. Retd GD 28/2/68.
BOUCAUT R. P. Born 29/9/45. Commd 29/3/68. Fg Offr 29/3/70. Retd GD 30/11/72.
BOUCH P. A. Born 23/10/35. Commd 1/2/56. Sqn Ldr 1/7/88. Retd GD 1/7/91.
BOUCH R. Born 10/7/58. Commd 10/3/77. Sqn Ldr 1/1/90. Retd GD 10/7/96.
BOUCHARD A. M., MBE. Born 15/1/51. Commd 5/7/73. Sqn Ldr 1/7/88. Retd GD(G) 19/3/95.
BOUCHER J. F. Born 3/10/29. Commd 24/10/51. Flt Lt 24/4/56. Retd GD 26/9/75.
BOUGHTON A. H. Born 18/6/08. Commd 3/1/41. Sqn Ldr 1/7/48. Retd SEC 4/12/58.
BOUGHTON T. V. J., MBE. Born 19/7/20. Commd 15/4/43. Flt Lt 15/10/46. Retd ENG 18/7/73.
BOULD G. R., CEng MIMechE MRAeS. Born 7/4/41. Commd 10/1/70. Flt Lt 10/4/73. Retd ENG 14/1/82.
BOULDING N. J., BA. Born 28/11/53. Commd 3/9/72. Sqn Ldr 1/7/84. Retd ENG 28/11/91.
BOULIND P. R., MB ChB MRCOG. Born 11/3/43. Commd 27/1/69. Wg Cdr 11/8/83. Retd MED 27/1/85.
BOULNOIS D. P. Born 25/10/21. Commd 11/5/41. Sqn Ldr 1/7/52. Retd GD 20/7/58.
BOULT R. de V. Born 27/8/31. Commd 17/12/52. Sqn Ldr 1/7/61. Retd GD 16/10/76.
BOULTER P. A. Born 9/11/38. Commd 30/5/69. Flt Lt 4/5/72. Retd GD 30/5/77.
BOULTON D. H. Born 4/3/46. Commd 30/1/75. Flt Lt 7/6/81. Retd GD 15/7/90.
BOULTON R. D. B. Born 11/12/29. Commd 20/12/51. Flt Lt 4/4/57. Retd GD 11/12/67.
BOUNDY B. M. Born 21/4/30. Commd 19/4/50. Flt Lt 19/10/54. Retd GD 21/4/68.
BOUNDY P. J., BSc. Born 7/8/61. Commd 13/2/83. Flt Lt 13/5/84. Retd GD 23/3/01.
BOUNTIFF A. Born 30/1/24. Commd 14/4/49. Sqn Ldr 1/7/61. Retd GD 15/5/75.
BOURKE D., MBE. Born 19/6/15. Commd 11/6/53. Sqn Ldr 1/1/64. Retd ENG 19/6/70.
BOURKE D. L. Born 17/12/16. Commd 18/11/53. Flt Lt 18/11/58. Retd ENG 24/12/66.
BOURN J. J. Born 18/10/28. Commd 14/12/49. Sqn Ldr 1/1/62. Retd GD 5/2/71.
BOURNE A., MBE. Born 4/4/24. Commd 4/10/60. Sqn Ldr 1/1/72. Retd GD(G) 4/4/79.
BOURNE A. G., AFM. Born 9/1/25. Commd 6/9/56. Flt Lt 13/4/60. Retd GD 21/4/70.
BOURNE B. A. Born 19/10/21. Commd 30/1/44. Sqn Ldr 1/4/55. Retd GD 19/10/70.
BOURNE D. R. Born 23/1/33. Commd 6/4/54. Sqn Ldr 1/1/73. Retd GD 19/4/83.
BOURNE E. Born 5/8/29. Commd 9/4/52. Fg Offr 9/4/52. Retd GD 27/7/54.
BOURNE G. F., BA BSc. Born 31/12/44. Commd 1/4/76. Sqn Ldr 1/7/82. Retd GD 1/9/98.
BOURNE The Rev H. Born 1/2/34. Commd 7/8/67. Retd 7/1/88. Wg Cdr.
BOURNE L. Born 16/10/54. Commd 31/1/80. Sqn Ldr 1/1/94. Retd OPS SPT 31/10/97.
BOUSFIELD F. P. Born 13/6/18. Commd 25/8/60. Flt Lt 25/8/65. Retd ENG 7/10/68.
BOUTIN J. L. B., MIMgt. Born 17/1/34. Commd 7/11/60. Sqn Ldr 1/7/66. Retd GD 7/11/76.
BOWART P. Born 10/5/44. Commd 20/5/82. Flt Lt 1/3/87. Retd ADMIN 14/3/97.
BOWATER M. V., MIMgt. Born 7/10/28. Commd 7/6/51. Sqn Ldr 1/7/81. Retd ADMIN 12/1/82.
BOWD S. K. Born 27/2/23. Commd 24/9/59. Sqn Ldr 1/7/74. Retd ENG 29/5/76.
BOWDEN A. J. Born 2/2/48. Commd 9/3/72. Flt Lt 9/9/78. Retd GD(G) 1/10/92.
BOWDEN D. B. Born 23/6/47. Commd 27/2/70. Sqn Ldr 1/7/80. Retd SUP 23/6/85.
BOWDEN G. S., BSc DipEl CEng MIEE. Born 13/9/31. Commd 19/8/43. Sqn Ldr 17/2/65. Retd ADMIN 19/6/76.
BOWDEN M. W. Born 20/9/47. Commd 1/3/68. Flt Lt 6/7/74. Retd GD(G) 20/9/85.
BOWDITCH K. H. Born 21/11/32. Commd 21/11/51. Flt Lt 21/5/56. Retd GD 31/8/74.
BOWDREY D. C. Born 20/7/44. Commd 7/2/71. Flt Lt 7/2/75. Retd ENG 1/3/78.
BOWELL S. J. P., MBA BSc. Born 1/4/61. Commd 2/9/79. Flt Lt 15/10/83. Retd GD 1/4/99.
BOWEN A. Born 22/6/34. Commd 10/12/52. Sqn Ldr 1/7/82. Retd GD 22/6/92.
BOWEN A. J. Born 1/11/44. Commd 5/2/65. Sqn Ldr 1/7/90. Retd GD 31/3/94.
BOWEN D. E. Born 13/12/24. Commd 9/11/44. Wg Cdr 1/7/68. Retd GD(G) 3/4/73.
BOWEN D. E. Born 31/5/37. Commd 27/9/73. Flt Lt 27/9/78. Retd SEC 2/10/81.
BOWEN G. A. Born 9/6/20. Commd 27/6/46. Sqn Ldr 1/7/57. Retd SEC 1/5/68.
BOWEN J. B., BSc. Born 16/1/59. Commd 11/9/77. Sqn Ldr 1/1/98. Retd GD 18/12/00.
BOWEN J. L. Born 4/6/44. Commd 4/6/64. Flt Lt 24/12/70. Retd SUP 1/2/77.
BOWEN N. E. Born 30/4/23. Commd 30/9/43. Wg Cdr 1/7/59. Retd GD 29/11/72.
BOWEN R. D. F. Born 22/4/25. Commd 19/10/45. Flt Lt 15/12/49. Retd GD 1/10/52.
BOWEN R. N., MSc BSc CEng MInstNDT DIC. Born 27/12/58. Commd 23/10/80. Sqn Ldr 1/1/92. Retd ENG 27/12/96.
BOWEN The Rev T. R., BA. Born 30/6/20. Commd 30/12/53. Retd 26/7/75 Gp Capt.
BOWEN W. V. Born 7/8/17. Commd 7/6/44. Flt Lt 7/12/48. Retd GD(G) 7/8/67.

BOWEN-EASLEY F., OBE FIMgt. Born 3/8/21. Commd 19/3/43. Gp Capt 1/7/65. Retd GD 1/1/70.
BOWER A. H., AFC. Born 6/7/34. Commd 24/9/52. Flt Lt 21/5/58. Retd GD 6/7/72.
BOWER A. W., OBE DFC. Born 12/7/20. Commd 19/8/42. Wg Cdr 1/7/58. Retd GD 28/8/67.
BOWER D., CBE AFC. Born 6/1/20. Commd 6/11/42. AVM 1/1/73. Retd GD 6/1/75.
BOWER K. A. Born 3/5/24. Commd 28/7/67. Flt Lt 28/7/72. Retd ENG 3/5/79.
BOWER R., MA CEng MIEE. Born 26/4/48. Commd 1/12/69. Sqn Ldr 1/7/83. Retd ENG 1/7/86.
BOWERMAN G. T., BSc. Born 25/11/49. Commd 23/9/68. Flt Lt 15/10/72. Retd GD 6/9/80.
BOWERS D. V. Born 16/10/35. Commd 23/8/65. Flt Lt 23/9/67. Retd SEC 16/1/74.
BOWERS R. C., MBE. Born 18/5/22. Commd 5/10/50. Wg Cdr 1/7/70. Retd ENG 18/5/77.
BOWES F. T. Born 11/2/20. Commd 9/2/42. Flt Lt 7/6/51. Retd GD 7/2/66.
BOWES J. M. B. Born 11/7/32. Commd 15/12/53. Fg Offr 15/12/53. Retd GD 1/3/56.
BOWES J. W., BEM. Born 13/2/33. Commd 19/6/70. Flt Lt 19/6/72. Retd GD 1/3/56.
BOWES R. E. M., BSc. Born 31/5/51. Commd 15/9/69. Sqn Ldr 1/7/84. Retd ENG 9/9/96.
BOWHILL K. R., OBE BA. Born 31/1/22. Commd 16/9/42. Wg Cdr 1/7/58. Retd GD 31/1/69.
BOWIE The Rev A. G., CBE BA BSc. Born 10/5/28. Commd 7/1/55. Retd 22/10/84 Gp Capt.
BOWIE J. J. Born 10/2/29. Commd 4/8/49. Flt Lt 23/11/55. Retd GD 10/2/67.
BOWIE R., MBE. Born 21/5/26. Commd 3/5/46. Sqn Ldr 1/7/56. Retd GD 21/5/84.
BOWKER M.P. Born 7/9/33. Commd 16/7/52. Sqn Ldr 1/1/67. Retd GD 17/7/87.
BOWLES D. J. Born 21/2/58. Commd 12/8/79. Sqn Ldr 1/1/96. Retd ADMIN 1/1/99.
BOWLES E. B. Born 20/8/24. Commd 18/8/69. Flt Lt 1/8/72. Retd GD(G) 20/8/76.
BOWLES G. E. Born 26/7/33. Commd 26/3/52. Wg Cdr 1/7/73. Retd GD 26/7/88.
BOWLEY J. L. A. Born 31/5/30. Commd 5/4/36. Flt Lt 25/1/57. Retd GD 31/5/68.
BOWMAN A. M., MBE. Born 5/4/36. Commd 18/2/58. Gp Capt 1/7/84. Retd GD 3/4/89.
BOWMAN D. H. J., BSc, MRAeS. Born 12/7/40. Commd 14/9/64. Flt Lt 14/6/66. Retd GD 14/9/80.
BOWMAN D. W., MBE. Born 31/1/27. Commd 29/3/50. Sqn Ldr 1/1/62. Retd GD 19/6/79.
BOWMAN J. C. Born 7/8/43. Commd 15/7/64. Flt Lt 15/7/69. Retd ENG 10/8/73.
BOWMAN J. H. Born 16/12/13. Commd 2/12/43. Flt Lt 2/6/48. Retd GD(G) 16/12/63.
BOWMAN J. R. Born 18/9/35. Commd 23/2/54. Flt Lt 1/10/67. Retd GD 18/9/90.
BOWMAN M. A. Born 9/7/48. Commd 27/3/86. Flt Lt 27/3/90. Retd ADMIN 13/10/00.
BOWMAN M. N., BSc(Eng). Born 1/9/60. Commd 4/9/78. Sqn Ldr 1/1/94. Retd GD 1/9/98.
BOWMER J. L., DFC DFM. Born 10/5/23. Commd 14/6/44. Flt Lt 14/12/47. Retd GD 1/9/73 rtg Sqn Ldr.
BOWN J. A. Born 10/9/25. Commd 4/10/56. Flt Lt 4/10/62. Retd GD 1/12/85.
BOWNS A., ARRC SRN RNT. Born 6/3/37. Commd 20/10/68. Sqn Ldr 20/10/80. Retd MED(SEC) 30/1/81.
BOWRING C. M., DFM. Born 12/5/19. Commd 10/3/43. Flt Lt 10/9/47. Retd SEC 12/5/68.
BOWRING D. J., BSc. Born 22/4/53. Commd 22/8/76. Flt Lt 22/2/82. Retd GD 22/8/92.
BOWRING J. I. R., CB CBE CEng FIMgt FRAeS. Born 28/3/23. Commd 27/4/44. AVM 1/7/74. Retd ENG 4/1/78.
BOWRING R. T., AFC. Born 1/1/20. Commd 13/12/42/ Sqn Ldr 1/1/52. Retd GD 15/7/66.
BOWSHER D. S. Born 24/7/59. Commd 17/5/79. Flt Lt 17/11/84. Retd GD 24/7/97.
BOWYER E. C. Born 2/3/32. Commd 13/8/52. Flt Lt 9/1/58. Retd GD 2/3/70.
BOWYER R. G., FIMgt. Born 29/8/32. Commd 14/4/53. Gp Capt 1/7/79. Retd GD 18/7/80.
BOX A. G., BSc. Born 24/10/33. Commd 25/6/57. Sqn Ldr 1/7/66. Retd GD 30/9/75.
BOXALL C. J. Born 22/3/41. Commd 31/8/62. Flt Lt 29/2/68. Retd GD 22/3/79.
BOXALL K. Y. Born 14/8/45. Commd 27/2/75. Flt Lt 27/2/77. Retd GD 13/8/84.
BOXALL-HUNT A. E. Born 23/1/48. Commd 24/11/67. Sqn Ldr 1/1/64. Retd GD 1/1/87.
BOXELL R., MBE BEM. Born 27/3/29. Commd 14/8/70. Flt Lt 14/8/75. Retd ADMIN 1/9/84.
BOXER H. E. C., CB OBE. Born 28/7/14. Commd 27/7/35. A Cdre 1/1/59. Retd GD 29/11/67.
BOXER J. A. Born 21/3/52. Commd 9/3/72. Flt Lt 9/9/77. Retd GD 21/3/90.
BOXER W. D. Born 20/4/30. Commd 11/4/63. Flt Lt 11/4/69. Retd ADMIN 31/10/84.
BOXSEY C. R., MIMgt. Born 13/8/19. Commd 26/9/57. Sqn Ldr 1/1/67. Retd ENG 16/8/69.
BOXX P. J., MB ChB FRCOG. Born 5/5/39. Commd 28/4/65. Gp Capt 22/7/88. Retd MED 1/1/91.
BOYACK C., AFC MIMgt. Born 24/6/33. Commd 9/4/52. Wg Cdr 1/7/85. Retd GD 24/6/88.
BOYCE J. Born 23/5/56. Commd 28/6/79. Flt Lt 10/3/82. Retd GD 23/5/94.
BOYCE J. S. Born 14/11/12. Commd 22/8/45. Flt Offr 17/5/56. Retd SEC 23/1/62.
BOYCE M. D., BA. Born 21/11/35. Commd 13/10/64. Sqn Ldr 5/11/72. Retd EDN 5/5/81.
BOYCE S. G. J. Born 7/1/57. Commd 22/2/79. Flt Lt 22/2/84. Retd GD 10/10/89.
BOYCE T. S. B., MIMgt. Born 8/4/31. Commd 15/12/53. Wg Cdr 1/1/76. Retd GD 2/12/85.
BOYD A. F., OBE DFC. Born 11/4/21. Commd 30/3/42. Wg Cdr 1/1/62. Retd GD 20/2/71.
BOYD J. Mcl. Born 26/11/30. Commd 5/7/53. Sqn Ldr 1/1/77. Retd GD 26/11/91.
BOYD K. L. Born 9/8/28. Commd 22/10/53. Sqn Ldr 1/1/74. Retd GD 9/8/83.
BOYD M. N. R. Born 19/1/58. Commd 28/6/79. Flt Lt 28/12/84. Retd GD 1/9/96.
BOYD P. C., BDS. Born 6/9/42. Commd 26/1/66. Wg Cdr 26/1/79. Retd DEL 26/1/82.
BOYD P. M. Born 5/12/44. Commd 5/7/73. Wg Cdr 1/1/90. Retd ENG 9/12/94.
BOYDE G. W. Born 31/7/23. Commd 14/1/44. Flt Lt 17/5/65. Retd GD 30/8/68.
BOYDELL F., IEng. Born 12/2/52. Commd 1/7/82. Flt Lt 1/7/84. Retd ENG 1/3/90.
BOYENS A. R. Born 10/9/50. Commd 13/10/72. Flt Lt 13/4/78. Retd GD 1/12/85.
BOYER K. Born 23/11/60. Commd 24/4/80. Flt Lt 24/10/85. Retd GD 13/9/99.

BOYES D. R., MA. Born 24/4/41. Commd 1/4/66. Sqn Ldr 1/7/72. Retd GD 26/1/84.
BOYES R. Born 9/12/25. Commd 16/9/71. Flt Lt 16/9/74. Retd GD 9/12/83.
BOYLE A. A. Born 20/4/35. Commd 10/4/56. Flt Lt 10/10/58. Retd. GD 29/1/64.
BOYLE E. J. Born 8/12/45. Commd 18/8/67. Flt Lt 18/8/70. Retd GD 1/5/94.
BOYLE J. S. Born 12/6/30. Commd 14/4/53. Flt Lt 22/5/57. Retd GD 12/6/68.
BOYLE M. S. Born 17/12/32. Commd 9/1/57. Flt Lt 15/8/62. Retd GD 9/1/73.
BOYLE P., BSc MB ChB MRCGP. Born 3/6/49. Commd 28/9/86. Wg Cdr 28/9/92. Retd MED 14/9/96.
BOYLE P. R., BSc CEng MIEE MRAeS. Born 19/2/49. Commd 1/9/70. Flt Lt 1/12/71. Retd GD 17/12/87.
BOYLES M. L., BTech. Born 24/5/54. Commd 3/9/72. Sqn Ldr 1/7/88. Retd ENG 24/5/92.
BOYMAN R. S. Born 16/10/27. Commd 29/3/62. Flt Lt 29/3/67. Retd ENG 16/10/85.
BOYNE H. G. Born 12/9/29. Commd 12/11/51. Sqn Ldr 1/1/67. Retd GD 28/11/75.
BOYNE R. Born 1/2/39. Commd 27/7/72. Sqn Ldr 1/7/81. Retd ADMIN 29/7/91.
BOYNS J. H. A. Born 25/6/18. Commd 18/3/42. Flt Lt 18/9/42. Retd SUP 31/1/65.
BOYS D. R. Born 13/6/34. Commd 7/5/64. Sqn Ldr 1/1/77. Retd ENG 13/6/89.
BOYS-STONES P. A. Born 27/10/28. Commd 15/10/52. Sqn Ldr 1/7/61. Retd GD 20/5/68.
BOZIER V. Born 3/9/47. Commd 1/3/68. Flt Lt 3/9/74. Retd GD(G) 3/9/88.
BRABAN R. L. Born 28/5/38. Commd 1/3/68. Wg Cdr 1/1/88. Retd ADMIN 2/6/90.
BRABBINS R. W., BTech. Born 17/11/50. Commd 15/9/69. Sqn Ldr 1/1/86. Retd GD 1/1/89.
BRACE E. A., MBE. Born 30/9/20. Commd 23/1/45. Flt Lt 21/10/55. Retd SEC 17/10/70.
BRACE F. E. Born 17/2/50. Commd 20/12/73. Flt Lt 27/9/77. Retd GD(G) 17/2/88.
BRACEBRIDGE M. C., MB BS. Born 30/9/44. Commd 24/4/67. Sqn Ldr 24/7/75. Retd MED 24/4/83.
BRACKEN E. W. Born 3/3/39. Commd 9/12/65. Sqn Ldr 1/1/75. Retd ENG 25/8/84.
BRACKENBOROUGH F. A. Born 29/5/23. Commd 29/7/65. Flt Lt 29/7/70. Retd GD 1/6/73.
BRACKENBURY I., CB OBE BSc CEng FIMechE. Born 28/8/45. Commd 26/5/67. AVM 1/1/98. Retd ENG 28/8/00.
BRACKENBURY S. Born 27/5/54. Commd 10/5/732. Sqn Ldr 1/1/86. Retd GD(G) 27/5/92.
BRACKETT J. E., MIMgt. Born 3/3/38. Commd 14/3/57. Wg Cdr 1/1/75. Retd SUP 7/4/91 rtg Gp Capt.
BRACKLEY M. J. Born 7/6/35. Commd 30/4/62. Sqn Ldr 1/7/74. Retd ADMIN 7/6/85.
BRACKPOOL M. J., BA. Born 31/7/46. Commd 15/10/81. Sqn Ldr 1/1/88. Retd ENG 26/5/98.
BRACKSTONE K. G., LLB. Born 17/10/53. Commd 3/9/72. Sqn Ldr 1/7/94. Retd ADMIN 18/10/98.
BRADBEER R. Born 15/3/19. Commd 20/4/44. Sqn Ldr 1/1/67. Retd GD(G) 30/3/74.
BRADBURN N. P. Born 7/2/60. Commd 5/2/84. Flt Lt 5/2/89. Retd ADMIN 14/3/96.
BRADBURY T. J. Born 22/10/26. Commd 14/2/27. Flt Lt 14/8/50. Retd GD 8/7/68.
BRADEN E. G. A., BEM. Born 13/12/28. Commd 7/9/61. Sqn Ldr 1/1/76. Retd ENG 13/12/83.
BRADFORD D. A., BA. Born 16/7/42. Commd 30/7/63. Flt Lt 30/10/65. Retd GD 16/7/00.
BRADFORD D. P. Born 21/2/08. Commd 10/12/42. Fg Offr 10/12/42. Retd ENG 31/7/47 rtg Flt Lt.
BRADFORD G. Born 31/5/25. Commd 21/3/51. Flt Lt 10/11/55. Retd GD 30/6/77.
BRADFORD M. R. Born 20/11/18. Commd 18/11/54. Sqn Ldr 1/1/67. Retd ENG 21/11/70.
BRADFORD M. W. B., MBE. Born 31/1/41. Commd 19/4/64. Sqn Ldr 1/7/78. Retd GD 29/9/95.
BRADFORD T. Born 16/8/17. Commd 14/2/46. Flt Lt 15/12/49. Retd ENG 24/4/54.
BRADING R. Born 10/1/33. Commd 3/11/53. Flt Lt 21/1/59. Retd GD 27/2/71.
BRADLEY B. R., AFM. Born 3/12/24. Commd 21/7/55. Flt Lt 21/7/61. Retd GD 3/12/74.
BRADLEY C. E. Born 11/5/15. Commd 1/5/39. Sqn Ldr 1/8/47. Retd SUP 11/5/64 rtg Wg Cdr.
BRADLEY D. J., BSc. Born 9/12/39. Commd 23/10/62. Sqn Ldr 23/4/71. Retd EDN 23/10/78.
BRADLEY D. L. Born 26/7/35. Commd 19/8/71. Sqn Ldr 26/10/82. Retd MED(T) 21/6/86.
BRADLEY G. M., BSc. Born 1/12/64. Commd 1/2/87. Flt Lt 1/8/89. Retd GD 1/2/99.
BRADLEY H. Born 1/7/23. Commd 14/10/42. Flt Offr 14/10/47. Retd SEC 3/4/54.
BRADLEY J. D., AFC. Born 12/2/22. Commd 26/5/47. Flt Lt 26/5/55. Retd GD 1/12/61.
BRADLEY J. F., BSc(Eng) BSc CEng MIEE. Born 25/6/47. Commd 2/2/75. Sqn Ldr 1/1/88. Retd ENG 2/2/91.
BRADLEY K., OBE MA MCIPD. Born 16/7/35. Commd 30/1/58. Gp Capt 1/1/85. Retd ADMIN 16/7/91.
BRADLEY M. G., AFC BA. Born 22/9/28. Commd 12/10/50. Wg Cdr 1/7/66. Retd GD 22/9/83.
BRADLEY M. J., MB BCh BAO. Born 30/4/34. Commd 20/8/61. Flt Lt 20/8/61. Retd MED 17/2/66.
BRADLEY M. M. Born 22/10/19. Commd 10/11/41. Sqn Ldr 1/1/63. Retd SEC 1/11/69.
BRADLEY P. J. Born 7/9/23. Commd 1/4/65. Sqn Ldr 1/7/75. Retd ADMIN 29/3/78.
BRADLEY P. L. F. Born 4/3/33. Commd 26/1/55. Flt Lt 15/8/62. Retd TD 1/10/71.
BRADLEY R. M. Born 4/4/08. Commd 12/8/32. Wg Cdr 1/1/45. Retd GD 3/3/54.
BRADLEY R. W., MBE. Born 5/4/24. Commd 21/2/52. Sqn Ldr 1/1/65. Retd GD 5/4/72.
BRADLEY T., MBE BA MRAeS. Born 19/4/41. Commd 13/1/67. Wg Cdr 1/7/86. Retd GD 10/11/91.
BRADLEY T. J., BEng. Born 25/3/36. Commd 1/1/57. Flt Lt 12/11/63. Retd GD 12/2/78.
BRADLEY W. G., MBE MSc(Eng) MSc CEng MRAeS. Born 17/10/38. Commd 27/4/65. Wg Cdr 1/7/83. Retd ENG 17/10/93.
BRADLEY W. H. M., MIMgt. Born 26/2/33. Commd 18/2/63. Sqn Ldr 1/7/72. Retd ADMIN 26/2/83.
BRADLY P., MRIN. Born 10/7/43. Commd 26/10/62. Gp Capt 1/1/91. Retd GD 10/5/93.
BRADSHAW A., DFC. Born 22/8/22. Commd 13/1/43. Flt Lt 13/7/46. Retd GD 22/8/65.
BRADSHAW E. Born 1/3/38. Commd 5/11/70. Flt Lt 5/11/72. Retd GD(G) 6/11/75. Reinstated 12/11/80. Flt Lt 12/11/77. Retd GD(G) 1/10/94.
BRADSHAW G. W. Born 20/10/28. Commd 23/9/81. Flt Lt 4/7/65. Retd GD 20/10/88.

BRADSHAW J. C., MSc BSc. Born 13/5/49. Commd 1/8/69. Sqn Ldr 1/1/85. Retd ENG 13/11/00.
BRADSHAW J. R., MCIPS MIDPM MIMgt. Born 26/3/30. Commd 17/12/52. Gp Capt 1/7/78. Retd SUP 26/3/85.
BRADSHAW J. T. Born 10/6/44. Commd 23/9/66. Sqn Ldr 1/7/80. Retd SY 1/7/85.
BRADSHAW K. M. J., BEng. Born 26/11/57. Commd 6/7/80. Sqn Ldr 1/7/89. Retd ENG 9/6/97.
BRADSHAW P. N., MSc. Born 2/1/52. Commd 25/5/80. Sqn Ldr 1/1/89. Retd GD(G) 25/5/96.
BRADSHAW P. R., BSc. Born 11/4/54. Commd 3/10/76. Flt Lt 30/1/80. Retd GD(G) 3/10/92.
BRADSHAW W. H. A., DFC. Born 21/2/21. Commd 19/1/42. Gp Capt 1/1/68. Retd GD(G) 1/5/71.
BRADY D. Born 12/4/60. Commd 29/7/83. Flt t 29/1/90. Retd GD(G) 21/1/92.
BRADY G. A. Born 10/6/46. Commd 2/4/65. Flt Lt 8/3/72. Retd GD 10/6/84.
BRADY J. P., BA. Born 16/5/47. Commd 19/8/66. Wg Cdr 1/1/86. Retd GD 16/5/97.
BRADY J. W. Born 19/3/33. Commd 15/7/53. Sqn Ldr 1/1/71. Retd GD 19/3/91.
BRADY N. H. Born 21/9/60. Commd 31/1/80. Sqn Ldr 1/1/96. Retd GD 1/1/99.
BRADY R. P., BSc. Born 15/10/54. Commd 2/9/73. Flt Lt 15/4/78. Retd GD 15/7/88.
BRADY T. A. Born 24/10/45. Commd 7/1/71. Sqn Ldr 1/7/85. Retd ADMIN 24/10/00.
BRAGG E. J. Born 2/1/31. Commd 2/4/57. Fg Offr 9/4/59. Retd GD 2/4/62.
BRAGG G. W. Born 11/11/64. Commd 19/12/91. Flt Lt 12/3/95. Retd ADMIN 1/11/96.
BRAGG R. H. Born 8/5/30. Commd 12/12/51. Wg Cdr 1/1/70. Retd GD 29/9/72.
BRAILSFORD E. E., BEM Born 12/7/20. Commd 10/1/57. Flt Lt 10/1/63. Retd SUP 18/7/70.
BRAIN A. S. Born 10/5/08. Commd 8/6/42. Flt Lt 2/9/45. Retd ENG 10/5/57.
BRAIN J., AFC. Born 11/1/16. Commd 4/3/39. Wg Cdr 1/1/53. Retd GD 9/2/63.
BRAIN P. M. Born 2/8/34. Commd 26/11/60. Sqn Ldr. 1/1/80. Retd GD 2/8/89.
BRAIN R. J., AFC. Born 31/5/21. Commd 30/5/44. Sqn Ldr 1/1/55. Retd GD 31/5/61.
BRAITHWAITE R. G., AFC. Born 11/7/39. Commd 29/4/58. Sqn Ldr 1/7/87. Retd GD 1/8/92.
BRAITHWAITE S. H. Born 13/2/15. Commd 25/8/44. Sqn Ldr 1/1/56. Retd SEC 17/2/65.
BRAITHWAITE S. M. Born 13/10/63. Commd 24/3/83. Flt Lt 24/9/88. Retd GD 1/10/97.
BRAKES D. M. P. Born 10/12/53. Commd 17/9/72. Fg Off 6/4/77. Retd GD(G) 31/3/79.
BRAMALL D. C., MSc BEng CEng MIMechE MIMgt. Born 28/1/42. Commd 13/10/64. Wg Cdr 1/1/78. Retired ENG 13/10/83.
BRAMBLEY F. R., AFC. Born 21/4/33. Commd 6/12/51. Wg Cdr 1/1/79. Retd GD 5/11/84.
BRAMELD I. N. Born 25/1/39. Commd 28/7/60. Wg Cdr 1/7/79. Retd SUP 2/4/82.
BRAMHAM P. M. Born 21/10/52. Commd 3/7/83. Sqn Ldr 1/1/89. Retd GD 1/1/92.
BRAMLEY D. W., DPhysEd. Born 5/8/41. Commd 16/4/63. Wg Cdr 1/7/79. Retd GD 5/8/85.
BRAMLEY P. A. McC. Born 21/3/29. Commd 31/7/50. Flt Lt 26/3/56. Retd GD 21/3/67.
BRAMMER P. H. Born 26/5/43. Commd 14/6/63. Flt Lt 4/5/72. Retd GD 2/12/75.
BRAMWELL R. W., MRCS LRCP. Born 7/4/32. Commd 4/11/62. Sqn Ldr 1/7/69. Retd MED 23/9/68.
BRAMWELLS W. H., LDS. Born 16/12/27. Commd 27/3/60. Gp Capt 1/1/79. Retd DEL 1/3/85.
BRANCH K. G., MB ChB FFARCS Dip Soton DA. Born 23/10/32. Commd 2/2/58. Wg Cdr 2/2/71. Retd MED 2/2/74.
BRAND G. Born 27/4/17. Commd 16/11/44. Sqn Ldr 1/10/57. Retd SEC 24/1/69.
BRAND M. S. Born 16/11/45. Commd 4/7/85. Flt Lt 4/7/87. Retd GD 31/10/95.
BRAND R. S., DFC. Born 28/7/26. Commd 16/4/47. Sqn Ldr 1/1/59. Retd GD 3/5/68.
BRANDIE W. J. Born 25/7/49. Commd 30/5/69. Flt Lt 30/11/74. Retd GD 2/4/01.
BRANDON J. H. Born 16/10/35. Commd 18/2/58. Wg Cdr 1/1/85. Retd GD 16/10/93.
BRANKIN W. R., BEM. Born 28/10/29. Commd 20/6/63. Sqn Ldr 1/1/80. Retd PE 1/8/80.
BRANNAN E. S. Born 24/2/60. Commd 6/5/83. Sqn Ldr 1/1/96. Retd GD 5/1/99.
BRANSBURY J. M. Born 8/12/47. Commd 1/10/65. Flt Lt 1/4/71. Retd GD 14/3/96.
BRANSON R. A., AFC. Born 18/6/16. Commd 14/5/44. Flt Lt 14/11/47. Retd GD(G) 5/10/63.
BRANT J. M., CEng MRAeS. Born 15/9/31. Commd 6/7/50. Gp Capt 1/1/79. Retd ENG 15/9/86.
BRANTHWAITE P. A. Born 8/4/47. Commd 6/5/66. Flt Lt 6/11/71. Retd GD 22/4/01.
BRANTON G. J. Born 14/12/46. Commd 28/7/73. Flt Lt 19/6/76. Retd GD(G) 14/12/84.
BRANTON J. F., BSc. Born 16/1/32. Commd 1/3/56. Gp Capt 1/7/78. Retd ENG 24/1/84.
BRASSINGTON C. S. Born 25/5/35. Commd 21/10/66. Flt Lt 21/10/72. Retd ENG 27/7/74.
BRATBY M. J., MSc BA. Born 25/2/45. Commd 27/10/70. Wg Cdr 1/1/89. Retd SUP 25/2/00.
BRATLEY D. B. Born 4/10/47. Commd 8/12/83. Flt Lt 27/7/88. Retd ADMIN 1/10/99.
BRAUEN P. D., MBE MIMgt. Born 6/11/30. Commd 31/8/50. Sqn Ldr 1/7/67. Retd SEC 6/11/80.
BRAUN E. R., BEM CEng MRAeS MIMgt. Born 30/7/22. Commd 29/9/49. Wg Cdr 1/1/73. Retd ENG 5/1/74.
BRAUN P. D. Born 15/7/48. Commd 2/5/69. Sqn Ldr 1/1/83. Retd ENG 16/7/89.
BRAUND R. E. Born 5/3/27. Commd 11/4/51. Flt Lt 11/1/57. Retd GD 22/11/65.
BRAWN F. R., MBE. Born 24/3/21. Commd 3/6/65. Flt Lt 3/6/70. Retd ENG 30/6/77.
BRAWN R. H. Born 14/12/41. Commd 31/1/80. Fg Offr 30/7/63. Retd GD 25/2/66.
BRAY A. M. J. Born 28/2/59. Commd 3/11/77. Sqn Ldr 1/7/89. Retd GD 10/10/99.
BRAY A. N. Born 24/3/13. Commd 17/12/32. Plt Offr 17/12/32. Retd GD 6/12/33.
BRAY D. B. Born 27/12/44. Commd 22/5/64. Sqn Ldr 1/1/81. Retd GD 2/12/97.
BRAY D. R. M. Born 16/3/21. Commd 14/2/47. Fg Offr 14/2/47. Retd RGT 24/6/50.
BRAY H. S., AFC. Born 21/4/32. Commd 15/4/55. Flt Lt 1/3/61. Retd GD 2/11/70.
BRAY J. H. Born 2/12/42. Commd 14/2/63. Flt Lt 2/12/69. Retd ENG 2/12/80.
BRAY J. J., DFC. Born 20/7/18. Commd 15/1/42. Flt Lt 1/9/45. Retd GD 30/8/53 rtg Sqn Ldr.

BRAY M. S. Born 2/4/47. Commd 10/12/65. Flt Lt 10/6/71. Retd GD 30/9/77.
BRAY R. W., LHA. Born 12/7/32. Commd 7/2/70. Flt Lt 7/2/74. Retd MED (SEC) 17/1/76.
BRAY R. W. Born 1/7/28. Commd 6/4/50. Wg Cdr 1/1/66. Retd GD 1/7/83.
BRAY-SMITH A. J. Born 5/6/58. Commd 8/9/77. Flt Lt 8/3/83. Retd GD 14/1/96.
BRAYSHAW S., BSc CEng MIEE. Born 29/12/41. Commd 15/7/63. Wg Cdr 1/1/88. Retd ENG 19/12/98.
BRAYSHER S. P. Born 25/6/52. Commd 14/10/71. Fg Offr 14/4/74. Retd SUP 22/4/75.
BRAZENDALE H. Born 17/6/09. Commd 11/3/43. Flt Lt 11/9/46. Retd ENG 30/5/47.
BRAZENDALE S. R. L., BSc. Born 8/9/49. Commd 2/7/72. Sqn Ldr 1/1/85. Retd ENG 2/7/88.
BRAZIEL C. J. Born 13/1/50. Commd 15/8/85. Flt Lt 15/8/89. Retd SY 28/2/94.
BRAZIER J. A. Born 29/8/34. Commd 19/10/79. Sqn Ldr 17/1/76. Retd SUPPLY 1/11/87.
BRAZIER J. F., OBE. Born 23/10/32. Commd 9/2/55. Wg Cdr 1/7/74. Retd GD 1/8/85.
BRAZIER P. D. Born 26/5/53. Commd 9/3/72. Flt Lt 5/8/78. Retd GD(G) 2/12/90.
BREADMORE K. G. W. Born 5/12/49. Commd 21/3/69. Flt Lt 21/9/74. Retd GD 1/6/78.
BREADNER D. G. J., BSc CEng FIEE FIMechE FIIM FRAeS FIMgt. Born 26/7/36. Commd 7/8/58. Air Cdre 1/7/83.
    Retd ENG 30/11/89.
BREADNER J. H. Born 28/3/23. Commd 12/12/45. Wg Cdr 1/1/69. Retd ENG 28/3/78.
BREAKES A., MBE MIMgt. Born 12/7/28. Commd 5/4/50. Wg Cdr 1/7/74. Retd 3/4/79.
BREALEY D. J., MSc BSc. Born 3/7/52. Commd 2/10/72. Sqn Ldr 15/1/84. Retd ADMIN 3/7/90.
BREARLEY R. H., MA MSc AFIMA MIMgt. Born 17/9/40. Commd 8/12/64. Sqn Ldr 8/6/75. Retd ADMIN
    8/12/80
BRECKEN S. Born 24/6/25. Commd 4/7/57. Sqn Ldr 1/7/68. Retd GD 4/11/75.
BRECKENRIDGE M. J. Born 16/1/42. Commd 14/1/82. Sqn Ldr 1/1/93. Retd ENG 16/1/97.
BREDDY P. B., BSc. Born 22/6/66. Commd 1/9/85. Flt Lt 15/1/91. Retd GD 15/7/00.
BREDENKAMP J. Born 24/3/34. Commd 5/4/55. Wg Cdr 1/1/75. Retd GD 24/3/89.
BREEZE A. Born 13/2/32. Commd 7/5/52. Flt Lt 2/10/57. Retd GD 13/2/92.
BREEZE R. S., DFM. Born 17/9/15. Commd 20/9/45. Sqn Ldr 1/7/64. Retd SEC 8/2/69.
BREGEON G. E. Born 31/5/32. Commd 27/5/53. Wg Cdr 1/7/78. Retd GD 4/6/86.
BREMNER C. M. Born 22/11/50. Commd 4/5/72. Flt Lt 4/11/77. Retd GD 13/8/82.
BREMNER D. A. G. Born 11/9/45. Commd 18/8/67. Gp Capt 1/1/91. Retd OPS SPT 11/9/00.
BREMNER J. A. Born 6/4/42. Commd 14/2/63. Sqn Ldr 1/7/79. Retd SY 1/7/87.
BREMNER-YOUNG J. E. Born 22/2/25. Commd 6/8/52. Flt Lt 7/2/57. Retd GD 5/9/66.
BRENNAN C. Born 6/3/57. Commd 16/6/88. Flt Lt 21/4/94. Retd MED(T) 15/8/97.
BRENNAN D. E. Born 6/4/30. Commd 4/7/51. Flt Lt 14/11/56. Retd GD 6/4/68.
BRENNAN D. H., MA MB LMSSA DO. Born 30/7/30. Commd 5/5/57. Wg Cdr 5/5/70. Retd MED 1/1/75.
BRENNAN D. J. Born 15/3/29. Commd 24/9/59. Flt Lt 24/9/64. Retd GD 1/1/77.
BRENNAN J. P. Born 8/9/52. Commd 8/6/84. Flt Lt 8/6/86. Retd ADMIN 31/3/94.
BRENNAN V. T. Born 4/5/33. Commd 17/1/52. Flt Lt 8/5/57. Retd GD 4/5/71.
BRENT E. A. Born 16/2/20. Commd 24/5/48. Flt Lt 28/11/60. Retd GD 29/8/67.
BRENT M. J. Born 16/7/33. Commd 10/4/56. Flt Lt 10/10/61. Retd GD 21/3/75.
BRERETON MARTIN W. S., CBE. Born 6/5/43. Commd 24/6/65. Gp Capt 1/1/89. Retd SY 5/5/94.
BRESLIN C. J., BSc. Born 1/6/53. Commd 10/11/85. Sqn Ldr 1/1/91. Retd ADMIN 1/11/96.
BRESSEY M. C. Born 14/3/06. Commd 11/11/42. Flt Offr 11/11/47. Retd SEC 16/1/54.
BRETON P. M. Born 14/12/23. Commd 25/6/43. Flt Lt 20/6/48. Retd GD 15/8/55.
BRETT D. E. Born 15/9/32. Commd 13/9/51. Wg Cdr 1/1/75. Retd GD 15/2/84.
BRETT G. A. Born 23/4/64. Commd 22/11/84. Flt Lt 22/5/90. Retd GD 14/9/96.
BRETT J. D., MA. Born 11/7/35. Commd 23/2/60. Wg Cdr 1/7/79. Retd ADMIN 31/7/85.
BRETT W. H. Born 3/4/03. Commd 7/3/40. Sqn Ldr 1/8/47. Retd SEC 6/12/53.
BRETT W. J. Born 20/2/12. Commd 25/3/43. Sqn Ldr 1/7/61. Retd. ENG 20/2/67.
BRETTELL I. C. B. Born 6/10/31. Commd 17/12/52. Sqn Ldr 1/1/63. Retd GD 6/10/69.
BREW R. A. Born 1/4/34. Commd 10/9/52. Flt Lt 7/2/58. Retd GD 1/4/72.
BREWER A. Born 11/11/31. Commd 17/5/51. Flt Lt 6/9/56. Retd GD 11/11/69.
BREWER A. F., AFC. Born 3/1/33. Commd 13/5/53. Sqn Ldr 1/7/73. Retd GD 3/1/93.
BREWER A. R., BEng. Born 13/11/44. Commd 9/10/67. Flt Lt 9/1/71. Retd ENG 17/7/88.
BREWER C. W. Born 6/8/45. Commd 29/12/69. Wg Cdr 1/7/90. Retd SUP 30/10/92.
BREWER F. R. Born 27/10/20. Commd 14/10/57. Sqn Ldr 1/1/66. Retd CAT 28/1/75.
BREWER H. E., DFC. Born 31/1/16. Commd 9/10/42. Sqn Ldr 1/1/66. Retd SEC 28/11/69.
BREWER R. B., MIMgt. Born 9/4/49. Commd 27/10/67. Wg Cdr 1/7/86. Retd GD(G) 1/10/89.
BREWERTON N., BA MRAeS MIMgt. Born 7/11/54. Commd 30/9/73. Gp Capt 1/7/97. Retd GD 23/5/01.
BREWIN E. Born 29/1/20. Commd 5/5/44. Sqn Ldr 1/7/55. Retd GD 8/7/66.
BREWINGTON A. H. Born 1/5/34. Commd 26/10/61. Flt Lt 1/4/66. Retd GD(G) 31/7/87. Reinstated 9/4/90. Flt Lt
    9/12/68. Retd GD(G) 9/4/93.
BREWSTER D. Born 22/12/22. Commd 3/12/44. Flt Lt 2/2/51. Retd SEC 1/11/68.
BREWSTER E. M. Born 1/7/14. Commd 9/12/42. Flt Offr 9/12/47. Retd SEC 13/12/51.
BREWSTER M. G. Born 14/12/54. Commd 20/9/79. Sqn Ldr 1/1/91. Retd SUP 14/3/96.
BREWSTER R. W. Born 22/6/19. Commd 27/1/43. Flt Lt 27/7/47. Retd PRT 22/10/64.
BREX J. T. Born 14/11/37. Commd 5/2/57. Flt Lt 15/8/62. Retd GD 9/8/76.

BRICE D. V., AFC. Born 9/6/30. Commd 31/7/58. Sqn Ldr 1/1/70. Retd GD 9/6/85.
BRICE E. J., CBE MRAeS DPhysEd. Born 12/2/17. Commd 28/6/40. A Cdre 1/1/69. Retd PE 17/4/71.
BRICE W. R., FCIS. Born 7/11/41. Commd 11/11/65. Gp Capt 1/7/87. Retd ADMIN 1/6/94.
BRICKWOOD Sir Basil Bt. Born 21/5/23. Commd 10/5/45. Flt Lt 14/5/58. Retd RGT 26/2/60.
BRICKWOOD R., MBE MIEE. Born 18/8/18. Commd 20/12/45. Sqn Ldr 1/1/56. Retd ENG 29/6/63.
BRIDGE A. J., MIMgt. Born 27/3/32. Commd 21/1/53. Sqn Ldr 1/7/68. Retd SEC 1/7/71.
BRIDGE B. J. Born 25/9/47. Commd 8/12/83. Sqn Ldr 1/7/93. Retd ENG 2/4/98.
BRIDGE D. Born 8/1/38. Commd 30/9/63. Sqn Ldr 1/7/83. Retd GD 1/1/87.
BRIDGE R. W., AFC. Born 3/3/34. Commd 16/7/52. Sqn Ldr 1/7/66. Retd GD 3/3/72.
BRIDGEMAN D. A., MIMgt ACIS. Born 6/2/35. Commd 24/2/67. Flt Lt 24/2/69. Retd SEC 1/9/73.
BRIDGER C., MBBS FRCP. Born 3/9/39. Commd 10/6/63. Gp Capt 27/11/87. Retd MED 1/7/96.
BRIDGER D. G. Born 17/12/28. Commd 26/3/52. Sqn Ldr 1/7/76. Retd GD 25/5/83.
BRIDGER P. S. Born 21/10/25. Commd 18/1/46. Wg Cdr 1/1/69. Retd GD 26/3/76.
BRIDGES A.G., CBE. Born 4/4/35. Commd 26/7/55. Gp Capt 1/7/78. Retd GD 4/4/92.
BRIDGES B. S., MIMgt. Born 2/3/26. Commd 17/1/49. Wg Cdr 1/7/75. Retd SY 2/3/83.
BRIDGES F. W., AIIP. Born 31/1/23. Commd 19/5/49. Flt Lt 19/11/53. Retd ENG 12/5/73.
BRIDGES G. E. Born 15/9/40. Commd 1/8/61. Sqn Ldr 1/1/72. Retd GD 16/12/79.
BRIDGES J. D. Born 26/5/62. Commd 5/10/81. APO 5/10/81. Retd GD 10/1/85.
BRIDGES M. D., MBE. Born 11/5/50. Commd 15/8/85. Sqn Ldr 1/1/94. Retd SUP 14/3/97.
BRIDGES R. B. Born 27/3/34. Commd 23/5/63. Gp Capt 1/7/83. Retd GD(G) 27/3/89.
BRIDGES R. C. Born 5/10/62. Commd 19/12/85. Flt Lt 19/6/91. Retd GD 14/3/96.
BRIDGES S. J. Born 31/10/60. Commd 30/8/84. Flt Lt 1/3/91. Retd OPS SPT 30/4/00.
BRIDGEWATER K., MA CEng MIEE. Born 31/10/27. Commd 29/12/53. Sqn Ldr 1/1/63. Retd ENG 29/12/69.
BRIDGHAM T. H. Born 23/1/45. Commd 19/8/66. Sqn Ldr 1/7/84. Retd GD 29/2/96.
BRIDLE A. L. M., BEd. Born 8/9/56. Commd 21/10/79. Flt Lt 21/10/83. Retd ADMIN 21/10/95.
BRIDLE D. W. Born 14/3/40. Commd 6/10/69. Sqn Ldr 1/7/84. Retd PRT 1/2/91.
BRIDLE N. H. Born 25/12/21. Commd 7/9/44. Flt Lt 27/6/55. Retd SUP 27/2/65.
BRIDSON D. S., AFC. Born 20/7/31. Commd 14/11/51. Sqn Ldr 1/1/67. Retd GD 31/8/73.
BRIDSON D. W., MSc. Born 31/3/37. Commd 30/9/58. Sqn Ldr 1/7/71. Retd ENG 21/10/78.
BRIDSON G. T. Born 3/8/33. Commd 13/9/51. Flt Lt 4/1/57. Retd GD 3/8/76.
BRIERLEY G., MIMgt. Born 14/2/28. Commd 8/11/51. Wg Cdr 1/1/77. Retd SUP 14/2/83.
BRIERLEY G. N., OBE AFC BA DPhysEd. Born 4/11/25. Commd 25/8/52. Gp Capt 1/1/71. Retd PE 3/4/79.
BRIERS D. J. Born 21/3/40. Commd 31/10/63. Flt Lt 15/2/70. Retd GD(G) 21/3/95.
BRIERTON A. A. Born 7/12/24. Commd 13/6/46. Flt Lt 27/5/54. Retd RGT 31/8/58.
BRIGDEN K. Born 9/11/39. Commd 26/3/64. Flt Lt 25/7/70. Retd GD(G) 1/1/80. Reinstated 1/4/81. Flt Lt 23/10/71. Retd GD(G) 1/4/91.
BRIGGS C. D. C. Born 14/5/27. Commd 24/9/47. Sqn Ldr 1/1/57. Retd GD 6/5/77.
BRIGGS D. A. Born 9/4/32. Commd 26/7/51. Flt Lt 6/10/56. Retd GD 9/4/70.
BRIGGS D. W., DFC. Born 7/5/24. Commd 30/9/44. Flt Lt 30/3/48. Retd GD 8/12/73.
BRIGGS E. H., CEng MIEE. Born 26/9/21. Commd 23/12/43. Wg Cdr 1/7/67. Retd ENG 2/4/75.
BRIGGS J. F., BSc. Born 23/10/48. Commd 8/9/74. Sqn Ldr 1/1/91. Retd GD 2/9/97.
BRIGGS K. R. Born 17/7/33. Commd 27/7/54. Gp Capt 1/1/81. Retd GD 12/12/85
BRIGGS P. N. Born 28/2/53. Commd 22/7/71. Fg Offr 11/12/73. Retd GD(G) 1/10/75.
BRIGGS R. Born 21/1/23. Commd 25/8/60. Flt Lt 25/8/65. Retd ENG 13/4/74.
BRIGGS R. Born 28/10/51. Commd 4/2/71. Sqn Ldr 1/1/86. Retd GD 28/10/89.
BRIGGS T., CEng MIEE MIMgt. Born 2/2/34. Commd 22/10/59. Sqn Ldr 1/7/69. Retd ENG 31/1/76.
BRIGHT A. Born 12/1/33. Commd 15/12/53. Sqn Ldr 1/1/67. Retd SUP 12/1/71.
BRIGHT D. M. F., MSc BA CEng MRAeS. Born 26/10/34. Commd 26/9/53. Wg Cdr 1/7/71. Retd ENG 9/12/86.
BRIGHT P. T. Born 24/1/48. Commd 28/2/69. Fg Offr 28/2/71. Retd SUP 3/8/75.
BRIGHT S. Born 18/11/18. Commd 9/8/45. Sqn Ldr 1/7/57. Retd SEC 18/11/68.
BRIGHT T. A. G. Born 16/6/43. Commd 24/3/83. Flt Lt 24/3/87. Retd ENG 31/4/92.
BRIGHTON P., BSc CEng MRAeS MIMgt. Born 26/3/33. Commd 3/8/55. Wg Cdr 1/7/68. Retd ENG 3/8/71.
BRIGHTON R. H. Born 10/6/25. Commd 26/3/52. Sqn Ldr 1/7/68. Retd GD 1/5/76.
BRIGHTWELL P. M. Born 16/9/42. Commd 6/4/62. Flt Lt 6/4/69. Retd SUP 1/5/76.
BRIGNALL T. A., MBE. Born 14/7/56. Commd 26/4/84. Wg Cdr 1/1/97. Retd OPS SPT 1/2/01.
BRIMELOW B., BA DCAe. Born 31/1/35. Commd 25/9/54. Sqn Ldr 1/7/65. Retd ENG 31/1/73 rtg Wg Cdr.
BRIMMELL B. D. Born 23/4/58. Commd 10/12/88. Flt Lt 15/12/90. Retd ENG 15/12/96.
BRIMSON C. D. Born 5/12/36. Commd 4/7/57. Sqn Ldr 1/1/71. Retd GD 21/11/78.
BRIMSON I. D., MIMgt. Born 10/2/34. Commd 27/7/54. Gp Capt 1/7/74. Retd GD 3/4/81.
BRINDLE A., AFC. Born 21/12/25. Commd 24/7/52. Flt Lt 17/5/56. Retd GD 31/1/74.
BRINDLE C. F., BA. Born 28/12/41. Commd 4/8/64. Sqn Ldr 4/2/73. Retd ADMIN 4/8/80.
BRINDLE P. J., MPhil FIMgt MInstD. Born 5/6/48. Commd 20/12/73. Gp Capt 1/7/94. Retd ADMIN 21/8/96.
BRINDLEY J., BSc CEng MRAeS. Born 9/4/49. Commd 11/3/73. Sqn Ldr 1/1/81. Retd ENG 11/3/89.
BRINDLEY P. R. H., CEng MIMechE. Born 31/1/39. Commd 13/6/71. Wg Cdr 1/7/84. Retd ENG 31/1/89.
BRINE K. C., CEng MIEE MRAes MIMgt. Born 20/2/33. Commd 22/7/55. Wg Cdr 1/7/74. Retd ENG 22/2/83.
BRINICOMBE P. M., MEd BA. Born 27/3/45. Commd 11/5/71. Sqn Ldr 1/1/90. Retd ADMIN 1/1/93.

BRIODY P. J. Born 8/4/41. Commd 17/7/62. Sqn Ldr 1/7/76. Retd ENG 1/7/79.
BRISBANE G. M., DSO DFC DFM. Born 11/1/11. Commd 21/8/40. Wg Cdr 1/7/53. Retd GD 3/3/58.
BRISCOE L. B. Born 18/6/22. Commd 14/11/57. Sqn Ldr 1/7/70. Retd ENG 13/8/73.
BRISDION G. A., MSc BSc. Born 10/11/54. Commd 20/1/85. Flt Lt 20/7/88. Retd OPS SPT 20/1/01.
BRISTOW C. F. Born 8/3/35. Commd 19/4/93. Flt Lt 27/9/61. Retd GD 8/3/93.
BRISTOW G. A. Born 1/5/15. Commd 13/7/43. Sqn Ldr 1/4/56. Retd ENG 1/5/64.
BRISTOW J., BTech CEng MIMechE. Born 12/8/50. Commd 8/1/73. Wg Cdr 1/7/87. Retd ENG 8/1/95.
BRISTOW J. C. Born 4/3/31. Commd 29/10/52. Flt Lt 24/3/58. Retd GD(G) 29/10/83.
BRISTOW P. A. Born 9/8/34. Commd 16/7/52. Flt Lt 6/2/58. Retd GD 9/8/72.
BRISTOW P. D., BSc. Born 18/11/52. Commd 28/3/76. Sqn Ldr 1/1/90. Retd ADMIN 2/12/00.
BRITTAIN A. A. Born 18/4/43. Commd 12/2/64. Flt Lt 6/4/69. Retd SEC 19/8/78.
BRITTAIN D. R. Born 9/2/33. Commd 4/10/51. Sqn Ldr 1/1/81. Retd GD 9/2/93.
BRITTAIN E. A., AFC. Born 11/8/21. Commd 11/6/43. Sqn Ldr 1/7/53. Retd GD 11/8/64.
BRITTAIN J. N. Born 13/8/38. Commd 23/10/56. Flt Lt 21/8/63. Retd GD 13/8/76.
BRITTAIN R. D., CBE FIMgt MCIPS. Born 26/6/30. Commd 11/4/51. A Cdre 1/1/80. Retd SUP 27/6/85.
BRITTAIN R. E. G. Born 27/2/09. Commd 16/3/31. Gp Capt 1/7/51. Retd GD 5/4/54.
BRITTAN J. R. Born 6/1/06. Commd 20/5/41. Sqn Ldr 1/8/47. Retd ENG 3/10/56.
BRITTON D., MIMgt. Born 8/3/35. Commd 18/10/62. Flt Lt 10/2/67. Retd Sec 18/7/78.
BRITTON G. E. Born 5/4/37. Commd 6/4/62. Sqn Ldr 1/1/88. Retd GD 30/4/91.
BRITTON J. P. Born 10/4/18. Commd 5/4/43. Sqn Ldr 1/7/54. Retd GD 29/1/58.
BRITTON P. D. Born 13/6/46. Commd 12/7/79. Sqn Ldr 1/1/87. Retd SUP 22/10/00.
BRITTON R. D. Born 23/6/32. Commd 25/11/55. Sqn Ldr 1/1/71. Retd GD 22/12/80.
BRITTON R. E. Born 13/5/25. Commd 27/3/57. Sqn Ldr 1/7/72. Retd SUP 17/6/77.
BRITTON R. T. Born 19/1/22. Commd 25/9/43. Sqn Ldr 1/7/59. Retd GD(G) 14/7/62.
BROAD B. A. Born 24/11/33. Commd 20/11/75. Sqn Ldr 1/1/89. Retd ENG 1/1/92.
BROAD L. C., MSc CEng MRAeS. Born 21/5/35. Commd 26/4/60. Sqn Ldr 5/3/73. Retd ADMIN 26/4/76. Re-instated 3/9/79 to 21/6/85.
BROAD M. H. D. Born 1/2/30. Commd 12/12/51. Flt Lt 12/12/56. Retd SUP 30/9/75.
BROAD R. N., MA. Born 7/7/29. Commd 7/7/49. Sqn Ldr 1/7/59. Retd GD 7/7/67.
BROADBENT A. C. Born 4/7/62. Commd 19/11/87. Flt Lt 19/11/89. Retd GD 2/2/97.
BROADBENT J. A., DSO. Born 14/9/47. Commd 24/4/70. Gp Capt 1/1/93. Retd GD 12/12/96.
BROADBENT J. W. Born 27/1/36. Commd 22/7/65. Flt Lt 22/7/71. Retd GD(G) 2/4/80.
BROADBENT M. E., CEng MIMechE MRAeS. Born 31/3/39. Commd 24/9/63. Sqn Ldr 1/7/71. Retd ENG 24/9/79.
BROADBENT R., DFC. Born 23/8/19. Commd 1/9/45. Wg Cdr 1/1/56. Retd GD 30/11/63.
BROADHEAD R. Born 2/9/28. Commd 19/7/50. Flt Lt 19/1/61. Retd GD 2/9/66.
BROADHURST I., BA. Born 23/4/55. Commd 29/9/85. Flt Lt 29/3/89. Retd SUP 3/4/93.
BROADHURST P. W. T. Born 27/12/34. Commd 10/12/52. Sqn Ldr 1/7/76. Retd SUP 9/2/89.
BROADLEY D. F. Born 15/3/27. Commd 9/6/48. Sqn Ldr 1/1/66. Retd SY 15/7/77.
BROADMEADOW H., MIMgt. Born 18/6/24. Commd 22/9/44. Wg Cdr 1/1/69. Retd GD 18/6/79.
BROADWITH D. T. Born 17/11/35. Commd 24/6/55. Sqn Ldr 1/7/68. Retd GD 14/12/74.
BROATCH K. A., BEd. Born 20/4/64. Commd 5/1/92. Flt Lt 5/7/94. Retd ADMIN 14/9/96.
BROCK I. R. Born 15/2/34. Commd 26/7/56. Flt Lt 1/3/61. Retd GD 15/2/77.
BROCKLEBANK A. Born 2/6/41. Commd 4/5/72. Flt Lt 28/10/78. Retd SUP 17/1/88.
BROCKLEBANK B. A. Born 3/7/27. Commd 24/2/64. Sqn Ldr 1/7/75. Retd SUP 8/10/81.
BROCKLEBANK R. A. Born 25/4/43. Commd 11/5/62. Flt Lt 11/11/66. Retd GD 25/10/00.
BROCKLESBY P. M., BA. Born 10/2/50. Commd 25/7/71. Flt Lt 25/10/74. Retd SUP 16/4/77.
BROCKLEY R. S., PhD MSc BSc. Born 2/12/52. Commd 6/11/80. Sqn Ldr 1/7/90. Retd GD 6/7/96.
BROCKMAN R. F., BSc. Born 18/3/41. Commd 11/9/86. Flt Lt 11/9/88. Retd GD 18/3/96.
BRODERICK H. J. Born 14/9/23. Commd 12/9/63. Flt Lt 12/9/66. Retd GD 14/9/78.
BRODERICK J. A., OBE MCIT MILT MIMgt. Born 23/3/42. Commd 23/9/65. Wg Cdr 1/7/89. Retd SUP 23/6/98.
BRODIE I. M. Born 2/6/17. Commd 9/3/36. Sqn Ldr 1/7/62. Retd GD(G) 12/1/74.
BRODIE J. G., MBE AFC. Born 6/12/22. Commd 29/11/44. Wg Cdr 1/1/66. Retd GD 6/12/77.
BRODIE R. C. G., BSc MRAeS. Born 25/12/39. Commd 1/2/61. Sqn Ldr 1/7/73. Retd GD 1/10/84.
BROEKHUIZEN P. Born 3/5/44. Commd 4/9/81. Sqn Ldr 1/1/87. Retd ADMIN 3/1/89.
BROGAN G. E. Born 23/12/65. Commd 8/1/89. Flt Lt 8/7/90. Retd GD 7/3/91.
BROGAN J. A. Born 9/10/41. Commd 27/5/71. 14/10/77. Retd ADMIN 18/4/94.
BROGAN L. J., CEng MIEE. Born 24/6/32. Commd 5/12/63. Flt Lt 10/2/67. Retd ENG 5/12/72.
BROGAN M. J. Born 13/5/15. Commd 20/8/42. Flt Lt 15/5/56. Retd GD(G) 21/1/69.
BROMIDGE H. D., BA. Born 1/6/44. Commd 5/7/73. Sqn Ldr 1/7/81. Retd ENG 1/7/84.
BROMLEY C. J. Born 22/6/20. Commd 9/8/47. Flt Lt 9/2/52. Retd SUP 22/6/69.
BROMLEY D. Born 19/7/31. Commd 17/12/52. Sqn Ldr 1/1/66. Retd GD 1/9/73.
BROMLEY H. Born 10/4/26. Commd 15/11/48. Flt Lt 9/6/52. Retd GD 31/3/74.
BROMLEY P. E. Born 15/8/45. Commd 3/3/65. Flt Lt 5/9/70. Retd GD 25/9/75. Re-Instated 27/8/80 to 16/3/82 GD(G).
BROOK C. J. Born 6/8/50. Commd 25/2/72. Flt Lt 25/2/75. Retd GD 25/8/82.
BROOK D. C. G., CB CBE. Born 23/12/35. Commd 31/7/56. AVM 1/7/86. Retd GD 22/12/89.

BROOK E. D. C. Born 28/1/29. Commd 23/9/65. Flt Lt 23/9/70. Retd ENG 13/10/73.
BROOK J. M., CB MB ChB FRCGP MFOM DAvMed. Born 26/5/34. Commd 15/2/59. AVM 1/1/92. Retd MED 26/5/94.
BROOK P. A. Born 15/11/30. Commd 12/3/52. Flt Lt 10/7/57. Retd GD 15/11/68.
BROOKE C. L. Born 5/6/44. Commd 22/8/71. Sqn Ldr 1/1/85. Retd ADMIN 31/3/94.
BROOKE D. J. Born 25/6/31. Commd 7/11/51. Flt Lt 17/5/56. Retd GD 1/9/77.
BROOKE G. U. Born 2/8/26. Commd 4/5/50. Flt Lt 26/5/55. Retd GD 2/8/64.
BROOKE K. Born 7/12/24. Commd 24/9/64. Flt Lt 24/9/67. Retd GD 14/10/75.
BROOKE M. C., AFC. Born 22/4/44. Commd 11/5/62. Wg Cdr 1/7/86. Retd GD 31/3/94.
BROOKE R., MCIPS MIMgt. Born 24/8/48. Commd 30/5/69. Wg Cdr 1/7/91. Retd SUP 31/3/94.
BROOKE-SMITH B. A. Born 6/8/46. Commd 29/4/71. Flt Lt 29/10/75. Retd GD 9/8/87.
BROOKER J. A. Born 4/8/10. Commd 19/6/41. Flt Lt 25/7/47. Retd SEC 1/3/51.
BROOKES A. J., MBA BA FRSA. Born 16/2/45. Commd 5/1/66. Wg Cdr 1/1/88. Retd GD 25/6/99.
BROOKES Rev D. M., MA. Born 28/5/17. Commd 20/9/44. Retd 28/10/72 Wg Cdr.
BROOKES M. Born 11/9/42. Commd 4/10/63. Flt Lt 11/3/68. Retd GD 3/1/80.
BROOKES M. W., BA. Born 25/2/38. Commd 7/8/59. Wg Cdr 1/1/78. Retd ADMIN 4/4/85.
BROOKFIELD C. Born 24/12/42. Commd 30/8/84. Flt Lt 38/8/88. Retd ENG 2/5/93.
BROOKING C. H. Born 25/7/09. Commd 13/3/47. Plt Offr 13/3/47. Retd SUP 25/5/48.
BROOKING D. Born 5/5/47. Commd 28/2/69. Sqn Ldr 1/7/84. Retd GD 1/7/87.
BROOKS A. Born 26/10/27. Commd 28/7/67. Flt Lt 28/7/70. Retd GD 26/10/82.
BROOKS A. J. Born 11/3/33. Commd 21/11/51. Sqn Ldr 1/1/84. Retd GD 11/3/91.
BROOKS C. A., BDS MGDSRCS(Eng). Born 17/12/41. Commd 17/9/61. Wg Cdr 22/12/79. Retd DEL 14/3/97.
BROOKS C. L. Born 22/10/20. Commd 7/1/42. Sqn Ldr 1/7/50. Retd GD 1/10/61 rtg Wg Cdr.
BROOKS D., BSc. Born 12/1/43. Commd 14/9/64. Sqn Ldr 1/7/76. Retd GD 10/5/99.
BROOKS D. Born 13/11/15. Commd 24/1/45. Sqn Offr 1/7/60. Retd SUP 30/11/62.
BROOKS D. A., BSc CEng MIMechE MRAeS MIMgt. Born 20/3/34. Commd 20/12/57. Sqn Ldr 4/5/67. Retd ADMIN 9/11/85.
BROOKS D. G. Born 13/3/31. Commd 28/6/51. Flt Lt 10/10/56. Retd GD 13/3/69.
BROOKS F. J. T., DFC DFM. Born 7/12/13. Commd 5/9/42. Flt Lt 5/9/44. Retd GD 11/12/46.
BROOKS J. L. Born 8/5/39. Commd 23/7/65. Flt Lt 6/4/74. Retd GD 6/4/80.
BROOKS K. A. Born 25/10/53. Commd 10/5/90. Sqn Ldr 1/1/99. Retd GD 31/5/01.
BROOKS L. M. Born 26/8/31. Commd 3/5/51. Flt Lt 23/11/57. Retd GD 12/11/71.
BROOKS M. A. Born 26/7/49. Commd 10/9/70. Sqn Ldr 1/7/86. Retd GD 1/7/90.
BROOKS N. J., BSc. Born 21/10/45. Commd 8/9/69. Flt Lt 8/12/70. Retd GD 18/11/88.
BROOKS N. N., BA. Born 12/2/52. Commd 13/2/92. Flt Lt 13/2/94. Retd ADMIN 7/8/00.
BROOKS P. Born 9/10/58. Commd 27/3/80. Flt Lt 27/9/86. Retd GD(G) 15/5/89.
BROOKS P. E., BA. Born 15/11/48. Commd 28/8/72. Flt Lt 29/11/75. Retd ADMIN 29/8/88.
BROOKS R. Born 3/9/31. Commd 7/11/51. Flt Lt 7/5/56. Retd P.I. 2/7/82.
BROOKS R. F., DFM. Born 1/2/25. Commd 27/10/67. Flt Lt 27/10/70. Retd GD(G) 1/2/83.
BROOKS W. J. Born 26/11/28. Commd 3/5/51 Sqn Ldr 1/1/64 Retd GD(G) 28/2/79.
BROOKS W. T., OBE DSO AFC. Born 8/1/17. Commd 12/7/37. A Cdre 1/1/64. Retd GD 8/4/65.
BROOKWICK T. R. W., BSc. Born 26/3/61. Commd 13/2/83. Flt Lt 13/5/84. Retd GD 17/8/95.
BROOM B. A. Born 31/7/45. Commd 15/10/81. Sqn Ldr 1/7/91. Retd ADMIN 1/1/97.
BROOM C. J. Born 12/9/56. Commd 6/10/77. Sqn Ldr 1/7/90. Retd GD 12/9/94.
BROOM C. J., MBE. Born 4/12/22. Commd 24/1/52. Sqn Ldr 1/1/68. Retd GD 4/12/77.
BROOM Sir Ivor, KCB CBE DSO DFC** AFC. Born 2/6/20. Commd 9/11/41. AM 1/7/74. Retd GD 6/7/77.
BROOM T. A. Born 16/4/31. Commd 5/5/51. Flt Lt 5/11/55. Retd GD 16/4/69.
BROOME M. J., BA. Born 28/9/60. Commd 4/1/83. Sqn Ldr 1/1/96. Retd GD 4/1/99.
BROOMFIELD A. J. E., DFC. Born 19/2/95. Commd 1/4/18. Flt Lt 1/1/26. Retd GD 29/10/30. Recalled 6/12/40 to 25/1/41.
BROOMFIELD J. D. Born 26/8/47. Commd 22/9/67. Flt Lt 23/12/73. Retd ADMIN 30/9/77.
BROOMFIELD W. T. H. Born 21/8/28. Commd 22/7/66. Flt Lt 22/7/69. Retd ENG 1/1/85.
BROTHERHOOD W. R., CBE. Born 22/1/12. Commd 17/2/32. A Cdre 1/7/56. Retd GD 13/2/61.
BROTHERS P. M., CBE DSO DFC*. Born 30/9/17. Commd 23/3/36. A Cdre 1/7/66. Retd GD 4/4/73.
BROTHERTON C. Born 16/7/06. Commd 24/11/41. Flt Lt 1/9/45. Retd ENG 31/8/53.
BROTHERTON I. P. Born 6/11/30. Commd 29/11/50. Sqn Ldr 1/1/64. Retd GD 18/3/77.
BROTHERTON J. Born 17/4/25. Commd 13/7/45. Sqn Ldr 20/6/63. Retd EDN 28/8/70.
BROTHERTON S. C. D. Born 28/3/45. Commd 6/4/72. Flt Lt 6/4/74. Retd GD(G) 23/11/76.
BROUGH G. Born 11/10/58. Commd 19/3/81. Sqn Ldr 1/1/92. Retd GD 1/1/97.
BROUGH I. S., BSc. Born 14/11/59. Commd 27/3/83. Flt Lt 27/6/86. Retd ADMIN 31/3/92.
BROUGH J. E., MIMgt. Born 9/3/17. Commd 2/9/44. Wg Cdr 1/1/64. Retd SEC 30/3/73.
BROUGH J. H. Born 20/1/62. Commd 26/4/84. Sqn Ldr 1/1/97. Retd GD 20/4/00.
BROUGH S. G., BEng CEng MRAeS. Born 27/7/54. Commd 8/10/75. Sqn Ldr 1/1/88. Retd ENG 31/1/01.
BROUGHTON A., MSc MB ChB MRCPath DCP DTM&H. Born 19/6/35. Commd 4/9/60. Wg Cdr 4/9/72. Retd MED 4/9/73.
BROUGHTON D. W., MBE BA FRIN. Born 27/12/39. Commd 28/9/60. Gp Capt 1/1/90. Retd GD 5/4/91.

BROUGHTON J., FIMgt. Born 18/2/34. Commd 24/9/52. Air Cdre 1/7/86. Retd GD 1/1/89.
BROUGHTON J. C. W. Born 18/11/41. Commd 3/5/68. Sqn Ldr 1/1/87. Retd GD(G) 1/5/93.
BROUGHTON K. Born 26/8/30. Commd 11/4/51. Flt Lt 11/1/57. Retd GD 14/9/70.
BROUGHTON P. J. Born 1/7/18. Commd 11/8/41. Sqn Offr 1/1/52. Retd SEC 5/10/52.
BROUGHTON R. P. Born 30/6/32. Commd 19/7/51. Flt Lt 13/4/60. Retd GD 30/6/70.
BROUGHTON T. W. Born 24/7/36. Commd 5/11/70. Flt Lt 5/11/72. Retd GD 31/7/76.
BROWN A., DFC. Born 16/1/20. Commd 9/5/40. Gp Capt 1/7/66. Retd GD 31/7/68.
BROWN A. Born 9/12/16. Commd 27/9/37. Sqn Ldr 1/9/45. Retd GD 8/1/58 retg Wg Cdr.
BROWN A., MIIM MIMgt. Born 15/12/31. Commd 29/7/63. Sqn Ldr 29/4/73. Retd ADMIN 15/12/91.
BROWN A. C. Born 2/5/25. Commd 28/12/43. Flt Lt 18/9/54. Retd GD 11/12/65.
BROWN A. C. Born 15/3/38. Commd 11/5/78. Sqn Ldr 1/1/89. Retd SUP 29/3/90.
BROWN A. D., MBE AFC. Born 12/9/48. Commd 10/9/70. Flt Lt 10/3/76. Retd GD 29/4/89.
BROWN A. D. Born 19/5/63. Commd 23/5/85. Sqn Ldr 1/1/98. Retd GD 19/5/01.
BROWN A. M. Born 18/11/19. Commd 19/7/57. Flt Lt 19/7/60. Retd GD 26/2/68.
BROWN A. P. Born 13/3/20. Commd 22/9/44. Flt Lt 22/3/48. Retd GD 13/3/63.
BROWN A. S. Born 7/9/37. Commd 20/8/55. Sqn Ldr 1/1/69. Retd GD 7/9/74.
BROWN A. S. Born 18/2/56. Commd 31/1/80. Flt Lt 8/3/84. Retd ADMIN 25/10/94.
BROWN A. W. J. Born 14/12/30. Commd 9/9/54. Sqn Ldr 1/1/76. Retd GD 3/4/84.
BROWN B., OBE. Born 28/11/11. Commd 28/8/41. Wg Cdr 1/1/61. Retd ENG 27/10/62.
BROWN C. Born 26/2/27. Commd 8/11/68. Flt Lt 8/11/73. Retd ENG 17/12/77.
BROWN C. B., CBE AFC. Born 17/1/21. Commd 11/10/41. A Cdre 1/1/67. Retd GD 17/1/72.
BROWN C. G., BA. Born 25/12/43. Commd 23/9/68. Flt Lt 23/3/73. Retd ENG 20/9/87.
BROWN C. J., MILT MCIPD. Born 23/8/50. Commd 8/5/86. Flt Lt 8/5/90. Retd SUP 2/4/93.
BROWN C. J. T., MIMgt. Born 23/7/36. Commd 25/9/46. Flt Lt 25/9/52. Retd SUP 23/7/81.
BROWN C. McD. Born 11/5/35. Commd 28/2/57. Sqn Ldr 1/1/67. Retd GD 11/5/73.
BROWN C. N. A., BSc CEng MIMechE. Born 27/8/52. Commd 22/6/75. Sqn Ldr 1/1/84. Retd ENG 2/6/97.
BROWN C. R. Born 14/10/41. Commd 14/10/71. Sqn Ldr 14/10/77. Retd ADMIN 19/4/83.
BROWN C. R. Born 16/5/46. Commd 10/6/66. Flt Lt 10/12/71. Retd GD 16/5/84.
BROWN D. A. Born 15/9/27. Commd 15/6/50. Sqn Ldr 1/7/62. Retd SUP 15/9/65.
BROWN D. A. Born 8/12/36. Commd 7/12/54. Sqn Ldr 1/1/90. Retd GD 8/12/94.
BROWN D. A. Born 3/5/56. Commd 2/2/78. Wg Cdr 1/1/97. Retd GD 10/7/00.
BROWN D. C., OBE. Born 20/4/45. Commd 31/10/63. Gp Capt 1/1/90. Retd SUP 22/4/94.
BROWN D. G. P., MB ChB. Born 3/10/24. Commd 12/1/52. Wg Cdr 12/1/64. Retd MED 28/1/78.
BROWN D. J. Born 20/5/44. Commd 22/2/63. Sqn Ldr 1/7/75. Retd GD 30/5/88.
BROWN D. J. Born 8/11/45. Commd 31/1/64. Flt Lt 28/3/70. Retd GD 31/3/94.
BROWN D. M. H. Born 14/9/33. Commd 27/3/75. Sqn Ldr 1/1/84. Retd ENG 14/12/92.
BROWN D. N., MBE. Born 27/12/28. Commd 28/9/61. Wg Cdr 1/1/80. Retd ENG 1/7/83.
BROWN D. O. Born 9/8/18. Commd 16/8/41. Sqn Ldr 1/7/49. Retd GD 14/4/58.
BROWN D. P. Born 25/2/31. Commd 14/9/54. Flt Lt 14/3/59. Retd GD 14/9/70.
BROWN D. P. Born 8/1/57. Commd 11/6/81. Flt Lt 11/12/86. Retd GD 10/11/96.
BROWN D. P. Born 21/1/54. Commd 6/11/80. Sqn Ldr 1/1/90. Retd ADMIN 31/8/94.
BROWN D. S., BA MCIPD MIMgt DipEd. Born 6/8/36. Commd 7/8/63. Gp Capt 1/7/90. Retd ADMIN 1/7/93.
BROWN D. T., MRAeS. Born 2/4/19. Commd 19/8/42. Wg Cdr 1/1/63. Retd ENG 13/1/71.
BROWN D. W. Born 2/3/46. Commd 26/5/67. Flt Lt 4/11/70. Retd GD 5/5/79.
BROWN D. W., BEM MInstAM. Born 15/1/41. Commd 6/5/83. Sqn Ldr 1/7/92. Retd ADMIN 15/1/96.
BROWN E., MRAeS. Born 21/4/17. Commd 15/4/43. Wg Cdr 1/7/64. Retd ENG 1/11/68.
BROWN E. A. Born 6/11/36. Commd 23/11/78. Sqn Ldr 1/1/87. Retd ENG 6/11/94.
BROWN E. F., DFC AFC. Born 23/12/23. Commd 14/5/43. Wg Cdr 1/7/59. Retd GD 23/9/68.
BROWN E. G. Born 15/8/35. Commd 4/8/53. Sqn Ldr 1/1/68. Retd GD 15/4/77.
BROWN E. J. B. Born 16/12/18. Commd 4/4/49. Wg Cdr 1/7/63. Retd RGT 24/12/68.
BROWN E. M., MA MCIPD. Born 3/4/44. Commd 16/1/72. Sqn Ldr 16/3/77. Retd ADMIN 16/1/88.
BROWN E. McN. Born 2/11/39. Commd 19/6/61. Flt Lt 19/12/66. Retd GD 28/6/73.
BROWN E. N. L. Born 30/12/23. Commd 10/7/52. Flt Offr 10/7/58. Retd SEC 2/5/68.
BROWN E. W. Born 26/2/32. Commd 4/6/52. Sqn Ldr 1/1/84. Retd GD 26/2/87.
BROWN F., BSc CEng DipSoton FIMgt MIEE. Born 10/3/34. Commd 22/11/56. GP Capt 1/1/83. Retd ADMIN 30/11/84.
BROWN F. D. Born 5/8/18. Commd 6/3/52. Flt Lt 6/9/56. Retd SUP 13/7/59.
BROWN F. J. Born 7/8/31. Commd 10/10/63. Flt Lt 10/10/68. Retd CAT 29/9/73.
BROWN F. L. Born 30/6/17. Commd 6/6/57. Sqn Ldr 1/7/69. Retd ENG 30/6/72.
BROWN G. A. Born 1/3/34. Commd 10/5/52. Flt Lt 17/9/58. Retd GD 30/9/75.
BROWN G. G. Born 16/11/21. Commd 6/1/44. Sqn Ldr 1/7/55. Retd ENG 9/8/69.
BROWN G. G. Born 3/9/30. Commd 7/12/61. Flt Lt 7/12/66. Retd GD 21/4/77.
BROWN G. H. Born 8/2/14. Commd 16/3/45. Flt Lt 19/12/51. Retd SUP 6/9/58.
BROWN G. J. Born 1/4/39. Commd 21/10/66. Sqn Ldr 1/7/80. Retd ENG 4/5/90.
BROWN G. P. Born 3/11/47. Commd 2/12/66. Sqn Ldr 1/7/84. Retd GD 1/7/87.
BROWN G. R., CEng MRAeS MIEE. Born 8/8/32. Commd 14/1/54. Wg Cdr 1/7/74. Retd ENG 15/1/76.

BROWN The Rev G S. Born 4/8/51. Commd 10/5/87. Retd 10/5/93. Sqn Ldr.
BROWN H. J. Born 4/12/35. Commd 9/8/60. Sqn Ldr 1/1/71. Retd ADMIN 9/8/76.
BROWN H. J. R. Born 25/9/10. Commd 11/2/43. Flt Lt 14/7/54. Retd SUP 26/10/65.
BROWN H. M., MSc BA. Born 17/7/51. Commd 17/11/81. Sqn Ldr 1/7/86. Retd ADMIN 14/3/96.
BROWN H. M. K., MIMgt. Born 5/4/28. Commd 27/7/49. Sqn Ldr 1/1/61. Retd GD 25/6/76.
BROWN H. P. Born 31/10/96. Commd 19/7/40. Flt Lt 1/9/42. Retd ASD 30/4/46 rtg Sqn Ldr.
BROWN H. T., DFC MIMgt. Born 17/2/22. Commd 7/8/47. Wg Cdr 1/1/61. Retd GD 28/7/76.
BROWN I. Born 23/9/54. Commd 8/4/82. FO 8/10/84. Retd GD 26/6/87
BROWN I. P. Born 30/5/59. Commd 31/1/80. Sqn Ldr 1/7/91. Retd ADMIN 30/6/98.
BROWN J. Born 4/4/33. Commd 27/2/52. Wg Cdr 1/1/80. Retd GD(G) 4/4/88.
BROWN J. Born 16/10/13. Commd 24/2/55. Flt Lt 24/2/58. Retd SEC 16/10/68.
BROWN J. Born 3/8/21. Commd 26/9/57. Sqn Ldr 1/7/72. Retd ENG 29/3/74.
BROWN J. Born 18/8/28. Commd 4/9/58. Sqn Ldr 1/1/78. Retd GD 18/8/86.
BROWN J., BA. Born 12/5/47. Commd 17/7/70. Sqn Ldr 1/1/80. Retd ENG 12/5/91.
BROWN J. Born 21/2/44. Commd 15/6/83. Flt Lt 15/6/87. Retd ENG 10/7/98.
BROWN J. A. Born 15/4/47. Commd 2/12/66. Sqn Ldr 1/7/78. Retd GD 15/4/85.
BROWN J. C. Born 2/3/32. Commd 15/12/53. Sqn Ldr 1/7/64. Retd GD 11/3/70.
BROWN J. C. Born 6/3/20. Commd 18/7/51. Flt Lt 18/7/57. Retd GD(G) 15/3/70.
BROWN J. D. Born 5/9/31. Commd 29/12/51. Flt Lt 25/4/57. Retd GD(G) 25/6/77.
BROWN J. E. Born 20/10/21. Commd 30/10/44. Sqn Ldr 1/1/68. Retd GD 19/4/73.
BROWN J. E. Born 7/1/38. Commd 16/12/58. Wg Cdr 1/1/80. Retd GD 1/6/84.
BROWN J. E. Born 4/10/61. Commd 6/5/83. Sqn Ldr 1/7/95. Retd GD 4/10/99.
BROWN J. G. V. Born 14/2/40. Commd 1/7/82. Flt Lt 1/7/85. Retd GD(G) 31/3/95.
BROWN J. H. Born 31/1/41. Commd 2/3/61. Sqn Ldr 1/1/74. Retd SUP 2/4/93.
BROWN J. H. F., SSC. Born 11/1/29. Commd 19/6/52. Wg Cdr 1/1/80. Retd GD 11/1/84.
BROWN J. D., MA CEng MRAeS DCAe. Born 8/8/35. Commd 25/9/54. Wg Cdr 1/1/75. Retd ENG 8/8/90.
BROWN J. L. L. Born 16/10/41. Commd 28/4/67. Flt Lt 6/12/69. Retd GD 16/10/79.
BROWN J. M., OBE CEng FIEE MIMgt. Born 17/9/33. Commd 26/9/71. Wg Cdr 1/7/76. Retd ENG 17/9/88.
BROWN J. M. Born 31/5/34. Commd 10/9/70. Flt Lt 10/9/73. Retd GD 5/8/77.
BROWN J. McC., BSc. Born 22/2/46. Commd 20/1/80. Fg Offr 20/1/78. Retd ADMIN 20/2/82.
BROWN J. R. Born 2/9/21. Commd 11/2/65. Sqn Ldr 1/1/76. Retd ENG 24/3/78.
BROWN J. R. Born 12/1/45. Commd 25/3/64. Wg Cdr 1/1/88. Retd GD 8/12/97.
BROWN J. S. Born 2/7/18. Commd 16/1/44. Sqn Ldr 1/7/67. Retd ENG 12/7/69.
BROWN J. S. Born 18/11/47. Commd 3/10/74. Flt Lt 3/10/76. Retd ENG 18/11/85.
BROWN J. W. J., MCSP MIMgt. Born 30/7/30. Commd 1/6/72. Sqn Ldr 1/7/85. Retd MED (SEC) 23/11/88.
BROWN K., DFC. Born 28/11/23. Commd 17/9/43. Sqn Ldr 1/7/72. Retd GD 28/11/73.
BROWN K. C. Born 11/4/14. Commd 24/3/43. Sqn Ldr 1/1/66. Retd SEC 15/5/69.
BROWN K. M. A. Born 1/5/46. Commd 9/3/72. Sqn Ldr 1/7/90. Retd ADMIN 1/1/98.
BROWN The Rev K. R., BA. Born 17/3/48. Commd 22/4/79. Retd 22/4/95 Wg Cdr.
BROWN L., MBE. Born 29/8/36. Commd 7/5/64. Wg Cdr 1/7/85. Retd ENG 29/8/88.
BROWN L. B. Born 20/8/37. Commd 2/8/68. Sqn Ldr 1/1/76. Retd ADMIN 20/8/87.
BROWN L. B., AFM. Born 13/2/17. Commd 3/8/50. Flt Lt 1/8/55. Retd GD 26/5/62.
BROWN L. G. Born 23/12/13. Commd 1/2/45. Fg Offr 1/8/45. Retd ASD 18/10/48.
BROWN L. I. Born 14/1/23. Commd 20/10/43. Sqn Ldr 1/7/71. Retd GD(G) 14/1/78.
BROWN L. W. Born 1/3/45. Commd 1/2/65. Flt Lt 28/8/70. Retd GD(G) 1/3/83.
BROWN M. Born 2/7/33. Commd 12/11/57. Sqn Ldr 1/1/70. Retd GD 15/2/76.
BROWN M. J., BA MIMgt. Born 3/1/37. Commd 11/10/65. Sqn Ldr 1/7 77. Retd SUP 3/1/93.
BROWN M. J. D., MA CEng MRAeS MRIN. Born 9/5/36. Commd 25/9/54. AVM 1/7/86. Retd ENG 9/5/91.
BROWN M. R. Born 31/5/35. Commd 17/9/57. Sqn Ldr 1/7/71. Retd GD 28/9/88.
BROWN M. R., MIIM MIMgt. Born 2/6/43. Commd 4/11/82. Sqn Ldr 1/1/91. Retd ENG 2/6/98.
BROWN M. S. Born 16/3/50. Commd 22/5/70. Flt Lt 22/11/75. Retd GD 16/6/80.
BROWN M. S., BA. Born 11/2/32. Commd 17/12/52. Sqn Ldr 1/7/65. Retd ADMIN 2/6/84.
BROWN M. T. Born 16/10/35. Commd 17/7/59. Flt Lt 7/7/64. Retd EDN 19/6/65.
BROWN M. W. Born 10/5/45. Commd 3/3/67. Flt Lt 3/9/69. Retd GD 11/5/76.
BROWN N. Born 19/12/50. Commd 3/7/80. Flt Lt 3/7/82. Retd GD 1/9/86.
BROWN N. A. Born 28/4/65. Commd 2/11/88. Flt Lt 2/5/94. Retd GD 14/3/97.
BROWN N. F. Born 14/12/19. Commd 19/2/45. Flt Lt 23/9/47. Retd GD 27/7/63.
BROWN N. J. B. Born 18/9/52. Commd 8/10/87. Fg Off 8/10/87. Retd ENG 25/4/93 rtg Flt Lt.
BROWN O. C. Born 18/7/13. Commd 23/2/43. Flt Lt 27/5/54. Retd GD(G) 14/2/62.
BROWN P. A. Born 24/4/47. Commd 24/4/80. Flt Lt 24/4/82. Retd ENG 24/4/88.
BROWN P. A. Born 8/1/57. Commd 2/2/84. Flt Lt 8/5/86. Retd Flt Lt 23/6/95.
BROWN P. C. Born 24/2/37. Commd 10/2/59. Sqn Ldr 1/1/90. Retd GD 1/1/93.
BROWN P. J., BSc. Born 18/10/40. Commd 9/9/63. Sqn Ldr 1/7/78. Retd GD 9/3/93.
BROWN P. S., DFC. Born 1/12/23. Commd 22/2/45. Flt Lt 29/12/55. Retd GD(G) 30/6/69.
BROWN R. Born 1/7/35. Commd 28/7/67. Flt Lt 28/7/69. Retd GD 7/1/75.
BROWN R. Born 2/12/47. Commd 16/8/68. Flt Lt 2/12/74. Retd SUP 1/1/76.

BROWN R. Born 29/12/31. Commd 11/10/69. Sqn Ldr 1/12/79. Retd MED(T) 30/5/85.
BROWN R. Born 21/7/34. Commd 4/3/71. Flt Lt 4/3/73. Retd SUP 4/3/79.
BROWN R. Born 18/1/33. Commd 12/3/52. Sqn Ldr 1/7/68. Retd GD 13/11/84.
BROWN R., McN. Born 3/12/32. Commd 15/12/53. Wg Cdr 1/1/71. Retd GD 1/5/85.
BROWN R. A. Born 4/5/28. Commd 21/12/48. Flt Lt 22/1/55. Retd PI 31/8/78.
BROWN R. A. Born 19/4/47. Commd 26/8/66. Flt Lt 17/12/72. Retd GD(G) 27/1/79.
BROWN R. A., CEng MIEE MRAeS MIMgt. Born 16/6/34. Commd 24/7/57. Sqn Ldr 1/1/68. Retd ENG 1/2/83 rtg
  Wg Cdr.
BROWN R. A., MA. Born 23/3/44. Commd 31/10/71. Flt Lt 30/7/72. Retd ADMIN 12/9/85.
BROWN R. D. Born 11/12/41. Commd 29/1/63. Flt Lt 3/6/69. Retd GD 3/2/79. Reinstated 19/1/83. Sqn Ldr 1/1/93.
  Retd GD 1/5/96.
BROWN R. E. Born 2/6/24. Commd 8/8/51. Sqn Ldr 1/1/67. Retd GD 2/6/84.
BROWN R. F., MA BM BCh FRCS (Eng). Born 11/9/25. Commd 3/3/52. Air Cdre 1/7/83. Retd MED 9/4/89.
BROWN R. G. H. Born 4/1/41. Commd 17/7/64. Flt Lt 6/10/71. Retd GD 2/9/80.
BROWN R. J. Born 9/3/14. Commd 25/4/40. Sqn Ldr 22/4/45. Retd ENG 12/5/47 rtg Wg Cdr.
BROWN R. J. Born 27/12/60. Commd 20/5/82. Flt Lt 20/11/87. Retd GD 14/9/96.
BROWN R. S., MBE MCIPD MIMgt. Born 26/1/23. Commd 4/6/44 Wg Cdr 1/7/63. Retd ADMIN 4/9/76.
BROWN R. W. Born 10/6/31. Commd 3/6/65. Sqn Ldr 1/9/76. Retd MED(SEC) 10/2/79.
BROWN R. W. Born 10/4/30. Commd 30/8/62. Sqn Ldr 1/1/77. Retd ENG 1/5/80.
BROWN S. D. Born 17/12/48. Commd 23/3/67. Flt Lt 23/9/72. Retd GD 17/12/86.
BROWN S. K. Born 11/4/46. Commd 22/5/64. Flt Lt 15/4/70. Retd GD 11/4/01.
BROWN S. P., BSc CEng MRAeS. Born 28/5/51. Commd 15/9/69. Sqn Ldr 1/7/87. Retd ENG 29/5/01.
BROWN T. C. L., GM MB BS MRCS LRCP DPH DIH. Born 1/9/24. Commd 31/10/47. Wg Cdr 1/4/62. Retd MED
  1/5/64.
BROWN T. H. Born 8/11/48. Commd 27/2/70. Flt Lt 27/2/73. Retd GD 22/9/87.
BROWN T. L., BEM. Born 9/1/21. Commd 15/9/60. Sqn Ldr 1/1/72. Retd ENG 7/4/73.
BROWN The Rev R. R., BA BD. Born 24/3/36. Commd 7/8/67. Retd 31/10/94 Gp Capt.
BROWN W. Born 1/7/31. Commd 11/11/65. Sqn Ldr 15/7/73. Retd EDN 15/10/74.
BROWN W. A., CEng MRAeS. Born 9/12/47. Commd 3/5/68. Sqn Ldr 1/7/82. Retd ENG 9/12/85.
BROWN W. G. Born 24/10/11. Commd 26/7/45. Flt Lt 4/1/51. Retd SEC 1/7/54.
BROWN W. H. P., FIIP MIMgt. Born 10/3/31. Commd 29/10/52. Sqn Ldr 1/7/69. Retd PI 11/4/81.
BROWN W. J., CEng MRAeS MIEE. Born 8/8/32. Commd 14/1/54. Wg Cdr 1/7/74. Retd ENG 15/1/76.
BROWN W. P. W., BSc. Born 5/12/53. Commd 7/3/76. Sqn Ldr 1/1/88. Retd GD 7/3/92.
BROWNBRIDGE S. M., BA. Born 29/7/52. Commd 25/9/71. Flt Lt 15/4/79. Retd SY 11/6/80.
BROWNE B. R. Born 3/3/23. Commd 25/5/43. Sqn Ldr 1/1/60. Retd GD 13/6/72.
BROWNE C. D. A., CB DFC FIMgt. Born 8/7/22. Commd 1/6/41. A Cdre 1/1/68, Retd GD 8/1/73.
BROWNE D. F. M., CBE AFC* FIMgt. Born 3/7/24. Commd 14/1/44. A Cdre 1/1/74. Retd GD 30/9/77.
BROWNE D. K. Born 7/3/42. Commd 7/6/73. Flt Lt 7/6/75. Retd GD 7/3/97.
BROWNE G. B., OBE. Born 30/3/35. Commd 26/7/55. Wg Cdr 1/1/78. Retd GD 30/3/93.
BROWNE J. F. P., MBE MIMgt AIDPM. Born 10/5/37. Commd 25/7/60. Wg Cdr 1/7/78. Retd SUP 28/2/89.
BROWNE J. P. R., CBE BSc(Eng) CEng FRAeS FICE FIMgt. Born 27/4/37. Commd 17/9/58. AVM 1/7/89. Retd ENG
  27/4/92.
BROWNE K. C. Born 14/12/17. Commd 22/9/40. Sqn Ldr 1/8/47. Retd GD 11/12/57. rtg Wg Cdr.
BROWNE P. H. Born 6/3/58. Commd 1/12/77. Flt Lt 6/3/96. Retd GD 6/3/96.
BROWNE P. J. Born 10/10/30. Commd 17/5/62. Sqn Ldr 1/1/74. Retd ENG 19/1/82.
BROWNE R. D. Born 4/4/31. Commd 23/7/52. Flt Lt 25/7/66. Retd GD 4/4/74.
BROWNE R. McV., BSc CEng MRAeS MIMgt. Born 16/8/40. Commd 14/9/65. Gp Capt 1/1/86. Retd ENG 16/8/95.
BROWNE W. E., LHA. Born 16/6/27. Commd 7/12/61. Wg Cdr 1/7/75. Retd MED(SEC) 16/6/82.
BROWNING B. E. L., OBE BA. Born 2/6/27. Commd 31/7/56. Sqn Ldr 1/1/73. Retd SEC 4/6/77.
BROWNING D. A. V. Born 14/2/33. Commd 27/3/70. Flt Lt 27/3/76. Retd SEC 30/9/83.
BROWNING G. R. C. Born 2/5/46. Commd 28/10/66. Flt Lt 4/5/72. Retd GD 4/5/75.
BROWNING H. H. J. Born 11/7/30. Commd 14/4/51. Sqn Ldr 1/7/61. Retd GD 15/10/71.
BROWNING I. M. R., DFC. Born 17/9/20. Commd 6/2/39. Sqn Ldr 1/8/47. Retd GD 18/9/58.
BROWNING N. J. Born 1/12/46. Commd 18/11/66. Flt Lt 6/5/73. Retd SY 1/12/84.
BROWNLEE A. A. Born 12/12/13. Commd 11/11/42. Flt Offr 11/11/47. Retd SUP 11/3/63.
BROWNLOW B., CB OBE AFC FRAeS. Born 13/1/29. Commd 7/7/49. AVM 1/1/80. Retd GD 13/1/84.
BROWNLOW R. P. Born 9/9/39. Commd 19/9/59. Gp Capt 1/1/91. Retd GD 9/9/94.
BROWNLOW S. M. Born 12/12/62. Commd 26/4/84. Sqn Ldr 1/7/97. Retd GD 16/3/01.
BROWNRIGG H. C. Born 11/1/09. Commd 19/6/41. Flt Lt 1/9/45. Retd SUP 11/1/64 rtg Sqn Ldr.
BROWSE C. R. Born 6/2/38. Commd 26/5/61. Flt Lt 26/11/71. Retd GD 29/11/76.
BROWSE J. S. A. McM. Born 12/8/38. Commd 8/12/61. Flt Lt 8/6/67. Retd GD 22/8/77.
BRUCE A., MA AHSM. Born 27/10/49. Commd 26/11/81. Sqn Ldr 1/1/90. Retd MED SEC 2/4/93.
BRUCE A. I., DPhysEd. Born 11/12/22. Commd 25/9/45. Wg Cdr 1/7/69. Retd PE 1/7/73.
BRUCE A. J. Born 2/10/43. Commd 27/2/70. Wg Cdr 1/7/88. Retd ADMIN 26/11/94.
BRUCE C. W., OBE. Born 28/11/35. Commd 10/4/56. A Cdre 1/1/88. Retd GD 2/4/91.
BRUCE D. Born 14/10/45. Commd 25/2/66. Wg Cdr 1/7/90. Retd GD 25/11/00.

BRUCE D. A. Born 2/6/48. Commd 5/8/76. Sqn Ldr 1/1/88. Retd ENG 31/10/00.
BRUCE D. V. Born 25/8/58. Commd 22/6/89. Flt Lt 22/6/91. Retd ENG 22/6/97.
BRUCE L. Born 21/4/32. Commd 3/11/60. Sqn Ldr 1/7/76. Retd GD 2/12/86.
BRUCE M. J. Born 20/8/46. Commd 8/1/65. Gp Capt 1/7/91. Retd GD 14/3/96.
BRUFF S. A. F., BSc. Born 27/6/55. Commd 13/4/80. Flt Lt 13/4/83. Retd ENG 7/5/96.
BRUMAGE M. W., MA CertEd. Born 15/2/46. Commd 18/11/79. Wg Cdr 1/7/94. Retd ADMIN 2/11/00.
BRUMBY F. Born 24/10/36. Commd 8/4/82. Flt Lt 8/4/85. Retd ENG 31/7/91.
BRUNGER W. D. Born 3/4/27. Commd 21/11/51. Sqn Ldr 1/7/63. Retd GD 6/2/76.
BRUNING M. P. W. C. E. W. M. Born 1/11/42. Commd 6/11/67. Sqn Ldr 1/7/85. Retd OPS SPT 1/11/97.
BRUNNING R. Born 25/4/43. Commd 10/9/70. Sqn Ldr 1/1/84. Retd GD(G) 1/1/87.
BRUNSDEN J. P. Born 14/3/43. Commd 28/4/65. Sqn Ldr 1/7/79. Retd GD 14/3/98.
BRUNSDEN-BROWN R. A. T. Born 25/8/32. Commd 28/6/51. Flt Lt 14/5/58. Retd GD 25/8/70.
BRUNSKILL F. Born 13/11/11. Commd 27/5/54. Flt Lt 27/5/57. Retd SEC 13/11/66.
BRUNSKILL J. Born 7/9/32. Commd 4/6/52. Flt Lt 14/10/53. Retd GD 1/1/76.
BRUNT R. Born 7/4/43. Commd 21/5/65. Flt Lt 8/3/72. Retd GD 7/11/75.
BRUNTON F. A. McK. Born 10/10/22. Commd 3/9/43. Wg Cdr 1/1/71. Retd GD(G) 10/10/77.
BRUNTON I. A. J. Born 2/6/45. Commd 18/8/67. Flt Lt 1/7/69. Retd GD 30/12/75.
BRUSHNEEN R. P. Born 11/1/45. Commd 27/1/77. Flt Lt 10/9/79. Retd ADMIN 30/4/83.
BRUSTER A. G. Born 12/7/40. Commd 20/7/78. Flt Lt 20/7/81. Retd GD 4/1/95.
BRUYN A. A. Born 28/4/36. Commd 9/2/55. Sqn Ldr 1/7/89. Retd GD 1/7/92.
BRYAN A. S. Born 24/11/58. Commd 3/7/80. Flt Lt 17/12/86. Retd SUP 13/3/92.
BRYAN C. J., BEM. Born 17/3/29. Commd 23/9/66. Flt Lt 23/9/68. Retd ENG 23/9/74.
BRYAN D. R. Born 9/12/24. Commd 26/4/50. Sqn Ldr 1/1/61. Retd GD 31/5/67.
BRYAN G., OBE MIMgt. Born 5/9/25. Commd 25/8/49. Wg Cdr 1/7/67. Retd GD 8/4/78.
BRYAN J. H., CEng FIEE FIMgt MRAeS MIIM. Born 14/11/33. Commd 30/4/59. Wg Cdr 1/7/76. Retd ENG 1/11/87.
BRYAN The Rev N. A., BA. Born 7/9/39. Commd 11/8/69. Retd 7/9/94 Wg Cdr.
BRYAN P. S. Born 21/4/34. Commd 31/10/69. Sqn Ldr 1/7/80. Retd ENG 21/4/84.
BRYAN W. A. M. Born 17/6/40. Commd 20/9/79. Flt Lt 20/9/81. Retd ADMIN 20/9/87.
BRYAN W. J. Born 19/6/22. Commd 3/12/59. Flt Lt 3/12/65. Retd ENG 19/6/73.
BRYANS J. C. W., MSc BA BSc CEng MIEE. Born 9/3/45. Commd 1/11/79. Wg Cdr 1/7/94. Retd ADMIN 21/12/99.
BRYANT D. T., CB OBE. Born 1/11/33. Commd 23/7/52. AVM 1/1/85. Retd GD 7/4/89.
BRYANT F. P., MSc. Born 29/12/43. Commd 9/8/63. Sqn Ldr 1/1/74. Retd GD 6/12/82.
BRYANT J. M. Born 17/4/45. Commd 14/7/66. Wg Cdr 1/7/84. Retd GD 28/4/90.
BRYANT M. K., DLUT. Born 18/12/42. Commd 5/11/70. Sqn Ldr 1/7/80. Retd ENG 1/7/83.
BRYANT P. N. R. Born 1/11/53. Commd 30/8/84. Sqn Ldr 1/7/94. Retd ADMIN 30/8/98.
BRYANT R. F. Born 17/5/29. Commd 5/5/51. Wg Cdr 1/1/75. Retd GD 14/10/83.
BRYANT S. H. Born 17/12/10. Commd 27/12/43. Fg Offr 27/12/43. Retd ASD 20/1/46.
BRYDEN R. W. Born 12/7/41. Commd 3/5/65. Gp Capt 1/7/89. Retd ADMIN 17/9/94.
BRYDON R. J., AFC AFM. Born 10/3/22. Commd 15/3/44. Flt Lt 7/3/62. Retd GD 10/3/77.
BRYETT D. B., BSc. Born 1/8/33. Commd 2/11/56. Sqn Ldr 2/5/66. Retd ADMIN 12/1/87
BRYSON L. C. Born 12/7/48. Commd 29/11/68. Flt Lt 29/5/74. Retd GD 1/9/85.
BUCHAN A. Born 21/12/46. Commd 7/1/71. Gp Capt 1/7/93. Retd SUP 14/3/97.
BUCHAN D. J. Born 20/9/42. Commd 3/8/62. Sqn Ldr 1/7/80. Retd OPS SPT 20/9/97.
BUCHAN F. N. Born 17/5/25. Commd 27/5/54. Flt Lt 27/11/57. Retd GD 17/5/63.
BUCHAN J. E., DFM. Born 25/12/21. Commd 15/9/43. Flt Lt 15/3/48. Retd SY 25/12/76.
BUCHAN J. T. Born 2/11/19. Commd 18/12/43. Flt Lt 29/6/50. Retd GD(G) 2/11/74.
BUCHAN T. G. Born 2/11/20. Commd 23/3/66. Flt Lt 23/3/72. Retd SUP 20/11/73.
BUCHANAN D. R., MIMgt. Born 18/8/22. Commd 4/5/53. Wg Cdr 1/7/71. Retd SEC 12/10/75.
BUCHANAN J. L. Born 21/8/57. Commd 9/8/79. Flt Lt 20/12/85. Retd SUP 25/7/93.
BUCHANAN N. W. Born 14/11/44. Commd 21/10/63. Gp Capt 1/1/87. Retd SUP 10/4/90.
BUCHER T. J. P., MB BS FRCS(Edin). Born 19/4/33. Commd 17/8/58. Flt Lt 17/8/59. Retd MED 16/8/61.
    Reinstated 1/9/63. A Cdre 3/12/91. Retd MED 2/5/94.
BUCK B. W. Born 15/1/23. Commd 13/9/44. Flt Lt 13/3/48. Retd GD 31/3/62.
BUCK D. G., BSc. Born 15/1/42. Commd 14/9/64. Flt Lt 14/12/65. Retd GD 14/9/80.
BUCKBY D. M. Born 7/3/58. Commd 18/10/81. Flt Lt 18/10/85. Retd ADMIN 18/10/97.
BUCKE P. J. Born 27/2/44. Commd 21/12/62. Flt Lt 21/6/68. Retd GD 13/7/76.
BUCKEL A. K. Born 28/2/47. Commd 15/10/81. Flt Lt 15/10/86. Retd ENG 1/5/93.
BUCKELL E. A. C., MB BS MRCS LRCP DObstRCOG. Born 23/3/30. Commd 27/6/54. Sqn Ldr 1/4/62. Retd MED 27/6/64.
BUCKELS R. D., BA. Born 13/9/15. Commd 11/8/47. Sqn Ldr 11/4/49. Retd EDN 1/1/55.
BUCKHAM H. Born 18/12/34. Commd 9/4/57. Sqn Ldr 1/1/67. Retd GD 18/12/72.
BUCKINGHAM A. E. Born 12/12/34. Commd 21/3/69. Sqn Ldr 1/7/79. Retd GD(G) 12/12/89.
BUCKINGHAM C. F. Born 15/4/49. Commd 11/4/85. Flt Lt 11/4/89. Retd GD 15/4/00.
BUCKINGHAM C. W., MBE. Born 25/7/07. Commd 25/11/41. Flt Lt 1/9/45. Retd ENG 25/7/56 rtg Sqn Ldr.
BUCKLAND C. E., MIMgt. Born 5/5/19. Commd 14/3/57. Flt Lt 21/10/59. Retd SEC 7/5/74.
BUCKLAND E. S., DFC. Born 10/1/23. Commd 26/11/42. Flt Lt 26/11/48. Retd GD(G) 10/1/68.

BUCKLAND J. R. Born 6/7/31. Commd 12/8/54. Flt Lt 12/2/59. Retd GD 6/7/69.
BUCKLAND N. A. Born 26/11/48. Commd 28/2/69. Gp Capt 1/7/89. Retd GD 14/3/96.
BUCKLAND P. G. Born 13/4/45. Commd 15/7/66. Sqn Ldr 1/7/83. Retd GD 13/4/89.
BUCKLAND P. J. L. Born 3/12/43. Commd 11/8/77. Flt Lt 11/8/79. Retd ADMIN 11/8/91.
BUCKLE D. M. Born 27/2/49. Commd 7/6/68. Sqn Ldr 1/7/83. Retd SY(RGT) 1/10/89.
BUCKLE E. Born 16/7/29. Commd 12/9/57. Flt Lt 12/12/63. Retd SEC 4/4/73.
BUCKLE F. G., CEng MRAeS MIEE. Born 10/2/29. Commd 9/7/59. Wg Cdr 1/1/75. Retd ENG 18/11/78.
BUCKLEY E., DFM. Born 4/9/14. Commd 29/3/43. Flt Lt 29/9/47. Retd SEC 9/5/54.
BUCKLEY G. C. A., DFC. Born 15/3/54. Commd 2/6/77. Wg Cdr 1/1/98. Retd GD 14/2/00.
BUCKLEY J. Born 19/1/22. Commd 26/7/45. Gp Capt 1/7/73. Retd SEC 26/9/75.
BUCKLEY J. E. D. Born 23/3/25. Commd 14/3/46. Flt Lt 27/5/54. Retd SUP 23/3/63.
BUCKLEY J. N. G. Born 25/11/32. Commd 9/4/52. Flt Lt 29/4/59. Retd SEC 19/5/71.
BUCKLEY J. W. Born 3/11/19. Commd 27/2/46. Flt Lt 30/8/48. Retd GD 22/11/62.
BUCKLEY M. Born 22/4/36. Commd 23/6/67. Flt Lt 4/5/72. Retd GD 23/6/75.
BUCKLEY N. J. Born 1/10/47. Commd 13/1/67. Gp Capt 1/7/88. Retd OPS SPT 7/4/01.
BUCKLEY R. W. W., CEng MIEE MRAeS. Born 18/12/14. Commd 10/12/42. Flt Lt 4/9/46. Retd ENG 29/11/54.
BUCKLEY T. P., MIMgt. Born 18/5/43. Commd 3/1/64. Wg Cdr 1/7/92. Retd ADMIN 18/5/98.
BUDD A. W. Born 20/1/13. Commd 21/2/42. Fg Offr 29/12/42. Retd ENG 24/8/46 rtg Flt Lt.
BUDD C. B., BSc CEng DIC MIMechE MRAeS ACGI. Born 18/10/26. Commd 20/11/47. Gp Capt 1/1/77. Retd ENG
    30/8/80.
BUDD G. E. Born 11/3/42. Commd 19/4/63. Flt Lt 19/10/68. Retd GD 11/3/80.
BUDDEN W. C. G., MBE BEM. Born 18/6/19. Commd 28/7/49. Flt Lt 5/11/58. Retd ENG 18/6/68.
BUDDIN N. C. P. Born 1/1/24. Commd 1/10/43. Sqn Ldr 1/1/55. Retd GD 1/1/62.
BUDDIN T. Born 2/7/43. Commd 8/1/65. Flt Lt 4/11/70. Retd GD 29/11/75. Reinstated 22/9/78. Flt Lt 28/8/73.
    Retd GD 2/2/92.
BUDKIEWICZ K. S. Born 12/8/46. Commd 8/6/84. Flt Lt 8/6/88. Retd ENG 4/10/00.
BUFTON K. D. Born 2/8/56. Commd 27/1/77. Sqn Ldr 1/1/92. Retd GD 29/9/96.
BUGG S. L., MSc CEng MIMechE MRAeS MIIM MIMgt. Born 7/5/29. Commd 25/9/52. Wg Cdr 1/1/77. Retd ENG
    7/5/84.
BUICK A. E. F. Born 21/6/24. Commd 29/5/46. Sqn Ldr 1/1/58. Retd GD 31/12/73.
BUICK F. D., BSc. Born 6/3/31. Commd 23/9/53. Wg Cdr 1/7/71. Retd ENG 10/12/85.
BUICK J. M. Born 7/11/30. Commd 25/8/54. Flt Lt 5/10/60. Retd GD 31/1/69.
BUIST L. J. Born 15/11/32. Commd 20/3/52. Flt Lt 27/9/57. Retd GD 1/3/70 rtg Sqn Ldr.
BULFORD P. J., DFC. Born 6/8/30. Commd 26/9/51. Sqn Ldr 1/7/61. Retd GD 6/8/88.
BULFORD S. E., AFC. Born 2/9/19. Commd 29/12/40. Sqn Ldr 1/7/49. Retd GD 19/9/58.
BULL A. E. Born 16/12/16. Commd 4/4/38. Sqn Ldr 1/1/53. Retd GD 1/1/58.
BULL B. S., AFM. Born 28/3/24. Commd 7/7/54. Sqn Ldr 1/7/73. Retd GD 26/2/77.
BULL E. F., BEM. Born 6/6/29. Commd 24/11/60. Sqn Ldr 1/1/78. Retd ENG 6/6/79.
BULL M. Born 11/2/45. Commd 15/2/90. Flt Lt 15/2/94. Retd ENG 1/2/00.
BULL N. J. Born 1/12/16. Commd 15/4/44. Flt Lt 1/1/58. Retd GD(G) 30/12/71.
BULL R. M. Born 21/12/48. Commd 27/5/78. Sqn Ldr 1/7/90. Retd OPS SPT 1/9/00.
BULL R. P., BSc CEng MRAeS. Born 17/2/48. Commd 28/2/69. Wg Cdr 1/1/89. Retd ENG 10/2/97.
BULLEN A. G., MBE. Born 26/7/15. Commd 16/10/44. Wg Cdr 1/7/65. Retd PRT 30/6/69.
BULLEN P., MILT. Born 14/12/58. Commd 30/3/89. Flt Lt 30/3/91. Retd SUP 25/8/96.
BULLEN R., CB GM MA FIMgt. Born 19/10/20. Commd 28/6/42. AVM 1/7/72. Retd SEC 19/10/75.
BULLEN R. J. Born 13/3/43. Commd 13/2/64. Sqn Ldr 1/1/75. Rtd ADMIN 13/3/81.
BULLEN R. K. Born 31/1/43. Commd 19/3/81. Sqn Ldr 1/1/90. Retd ENG 31/7/98.
BULLERS R. F. Born 18/11/29. Commd 27/3/57. Sqn Ldr 1/7/75. Retd GD(G) 18/11/89.
BULLEY B., BSc. Born 25/4/45. Commd 28/9/64. Sqn Ldr 1/1/78. Retd GD 25/4/89.
BULLEY R. A., MBE. Born 3/12/41. Commd 30/5/69. Flt Lt 30/5/71. Retd GD 1/7/94.
BULLEY W. B. Born 5/1/32. Commd 18/4/51. Sqn Ldr 1/7/72. Retd GD 1/12/75.
BULLIFENT A. D., BSc. Born 9/7/65. Commd 14/5/89. Flt Lt 14/11/91. Retd GD 14/3/97.
BULLIVENT A. E. Born 24/1/23. Commd 28/7/49. Sqn Ldr 1/1/60. Retd ADMIN 24/1/78.
BULLOCK A. B., MBE. Born 3/12/32. Commd 29/10/52. Sqn Ldr 1/7/74. Retd GD(G) 3/12/87.
BULLOCK C. Born 17/9/41. Commd 25/3/64. Flt Lt 25/9/69. Retd GD 12/8/75.
BULLOCK C. T. Born 15/4/36. Commd 11/6/81. Flt Lt 11/6/84. Retd GD 11/6/91.
BULLOCK E., BSc. Born 12/5/32. Commd 18/11/54. Wg Cdr 1/1/75. Retd ENG 11/7/84.
BULLOCK G., BA MIMgt. Born 12/12/46. Commd 6/1/69. Sqn Ldr 1/1/77. Retd ADMIN 6/1/85.
BULLOCK J. M., BSc. Born 18/9/20. Commd 6/9/50. Wg Cdr 1/7/64. Retd EDN 16/4/71.
BULLOCK J. P., CEng MRAeS MIMgt. Born 22/1/20. Commd 19/8/42. Wg Cdr 1/7/61. Retd ENG 22/1/75.
BULLOCK J. P. L. Born 31/3/38. Commd 8/10/70. Sqn Ldr 1/7/79. Retd SUP 31/3/96.
BULLOCK J. S. Born 4/11/33. Commd 18/2/53. Wg Cdr 1/1/77. Retd GD 4/11/88.
BULLOCK K. W. Born 25/9/23. Commd 14/1/44. Flt Lt 27/5/54. Retd GD 15/12/64.
BULLOCK M. C., BSc. Born 14/11/49. Commd 12/12/71. Wg Cdr 1/7/87. Retd ADMIN 12/12/99.
BULLOCK M. J., BSc. Born 26/6/43. Commd 6/10/69. Sqn Ldr 1/7/76. Retd ENG 8/4/78.
BULLOCK R. W. Born 5/8/28. Commd 10/10/63. Sqn Ldr 1/7/77. Retd ADMIN 5/8/80.

BULLOCK S. L. Born 11/5/53. Commd 27/8/87. Flt Lt 27/8/89. Retd ENG 27/8/95.
BULLOCKE M. B. Born 24/7/38. Commd 25/7/60. Wg Cdr 1/7/77. Retd GD 24/7/93.
BULMAN J. C., BA. Born 12/3/43. Commd 17/7/75. Sqn Ldr 1/1/88. Retd ENG 19/8/94.
BULPETT E. H. Born 3/7/39. Commd 28/8/75. Sqn Ldr 1/1/88. Retd GD(G) 3/1/90.
BULPORT C. E. Born 26/1/14. Commd 28/6/45. Sqn Ldr 1/1/57. Retd SEC 15/2/67.
BUMSTEAD G. E. S., FIMgt. Born 24/9/21. Commd 9/8/48. A Cdre 1/1/73. Retd SY 24/9/76.
BUNCE D. F., BSc. Born 24/9/36. Commd 3/1/58. Sqn Ldr 3/7/66. Retd EDN 24/9/74.
BUNCE J. B. L., MA. Born 21/4/14. Commd 20/12/47. Sqn Ldr 20/6/54. Retd EDN 1/10/63.
BUNCE S. C. Born 2/5/61. Commd 15/10/81. Retd GD 13/6/82.
BUNCE S. M., BEd. Born 31/8/61. Commd 29/9/85. Flt Lt 29/3/88. Retd ADMIN 3/3/89.
BUNCE T. N. Born 13/10/41. Commd 17/7/87. Flt Lt 17/7/89. Retd ENG 2/9/93.
BUNCH B. R. Born 14/10/39. Commd 3/8/62. Flt Lt 1/7/68. Retd GD 10/4/78.
BUNCHER C. P. Born 9/6/49. Commd 19/6/70. Sqn Ldr 1/1/85. Retd GD 1/1/88.
BUNCHER R. H. Born 16/4/41. Commd 1/10/65. Flt Lt 1/10/68. Retd GD 28/9/74.
BUNKHALL E. W., CDipAF Born 21/2/24. Commd 9/8/45. Wg Cdr 1/1/66. Retd GD 30/6/78.
BUNN O. G., CBE. Born 16/4/41. Commd 15/9/61. Gp Capt 1/1/88. Retd GD 2/4/93.
BUNNER A. J. Born 29/11/20. Commd 14/2/46. Flt Lt 16/12/51. Retd ENG 5/9/56.
BUNNEY C. J. Born 29/6/38. Commd 10/9/70. Sqn Ldr 1/7/81. Retd ADMIN 29/6/88.
BUNNEY K. M. Born 18/6/52. Commd 1/6/72. Flt Lt 1/12/78. Retd ADMIN 26/7/86.
BUNNING F. W. Born 2/2/26. Commd 27/6/51. Flt Lt 27/3/57. Retd GD 26/5/66.
BUNTING H. V., OBE. Born 6/6/13. Commd 1/4/40. Wg Cdr 1/7/52. Retd GD 6/6/68.
BUNTING M. C., MBE. Born 23/1/18. Commd 13/11/41. Gp Capt 1/7/62. Retd GD 5/3/73.
BUNTING P. J. Born 15/8/45. Commd 1/10/65. Flt Lt 4/5/72. Retd GD 7/11/75.
BUNTING V. G. Born 31/3/40. Commd 28/4/65. Flt Lt 9/2/68. Retd GD 31/3/78.
BURBOROUGH W. R. Born 14/7/43. Commd 28/11/69. Flt Lt 12/8/73. Retd GD 14/7/81.
BURCH J. C., MIMgt. Born 16/10/20. Commd 17/4/44. Sqn Ldr 1/4/55. Retd GD 16/10/69.
BURCH M. W. Born 6/3/57. Commd 5/8/76. Sqn Ldr 1/1/95. Retd GD(G) 14/3/96.
BURCH P. F. R. Born 6/2/44. Commd 6/4/72. Flt Lt 6/10/78. Retd SUP 6/2/99.
BURCH R. M. Born 27/8/35. Commd 18/5/61. Sqn Ldr 1/1/73. Retd GD(G) 27/8/90.
BURCHALL R. F. Born 21/3/46. Commd 9/8/79. Flt Lt 9/8/80. Retd ADMIN 9/8/87.
BURCHELL C. R. Born 13/9/34. Commd 22/12/53. Flt Lt 23/6/59. Retd GD(G) 13/9/91.
BURCHELL D. J. Born 11/12/45. Commd 8/7/65. Sqn Ldr 1/1/87. Retd GD(G) 14/3/96.
BURD T. F., OBE. Born 11/11/21. Commd 10/10/46. Gp Capt 1/1/68. Retd SUP 11/11/76.
BURDEKIN P. A. Born 20/11/45. Commd 28/10/66. Flt Lt 28/4/72. Retd GD 31/3/95.
BURDEN A. R., MISM MIMgt. Born 26/2/27. Commd 16/5/57. Sqn Ldr 1/1/70. Retd GD(G) 26/2/82.
BURDEN D. S., MBE AFC MRIN. Born 18/11/30. Commd 23/4/53. Sqn Ldr 1/1/76. Retd GD 18/11/88.
BURDEN F. W., BSc CEng MIEE. Born 15/3/48. Commd 24/2/74. Sqn Ldr 1/1/84. Retd ENG 24/2/90.
BURDEN G. H. St. J. Born 28/3/27. Commd 27/6/51. Flt Lt 29/7/63. Retd GD 29/7/71.
BURDEN R. A. Born 29/2/56. Commd 23/10/86. Flt Lt 23/10/88. Retd GD(G) 23/10/94.
BURDEN R. C. Born 7/6/53. Commd 7/6/73. Sqn Ldr 1/1/91. Retd GD 7/6/94.
BURDESS A. R. E., MSc BSc CEng MIEE. Born 15/10/61. Commd 11/9/83. Sqn Ldr 1/7/92. Retd ENG 15/10/99.
BURDESS C. R. Born 25/12/51. Commd 22/5/75. Flt Lt 22/11/80. Retd GD 1/6/92.
BURDESS S. B., BEng CEng FRAeS. Born 17/9/46. Commd 28/9/64. A Cdre 1/7/95. Retd ENG 2/1/97.
BURDETT B. B. Born 11/9/36. Commd 18/8/54. Flt Lt 5/10/60. Retd GD 11/9/73 rtg Sqn Ldr.
BURDETT P. N. Born 24/8/57. Commd 4/11/82. Flt Lt 4/5/85. Retd GD 24/8/95.
BURDETT R. E. Born 3/6/41. Commd 6/5/66. Flt Lt 17/3/71. Retd SUP 2/2/74.
BURDETT T. F., MBE CEng MIMechE. Born 10/10/40. Commd 10/1/71. Sqn Ldr 1/1/86. Retd ENG 10/10/95.
BUREAU P. Born 19/4/30. Commd 30/7/52. Flt Lt 10/11/55. Retd GD 19/4/68.
BURFORD K. A. Born 7/5/44. Commd 9/7/72. Wg Cdr 1/1/89. Retd GD(G) 30/12/93.
BURGE F. G., MIMgt. Born 13/6/44. Commd 16/6/69. Wg Cdr 1/1/89. Retd SY 1/8/96.
BURGE W. J., MBE. Born 15/10/34. Commd 24/1/74. Flt Lt 24/1/77. Retd GD(G) 1/2/85.
BURGES J. R., BSc CEng FIEE FRAeS. Born 18/10/19. Commd 13/9/40. A Cdre 1/7/70. Retd ENG 18/10/74.
BURGESS A. E. Born 12/1/20. Commd 2/12/43. Sqn Ldr 1/4/56. Retd ENG 19/10/68.
BURGESS A. S., MB BS. Born 4/2/60. Commd 6/10/81. Sqn Ldr 1/8/90. Retd MED 1/3/91.
BURGESS A. V., MIMgt. Born 10/4/33. Commd 18/7/63. Wg Cdr 1/7/82. Retd SY 10/4/91.
BURGESS G. H., CBE FIMgt. Born 16/5/22. Commd 26/6/42. Gp Capt 1/7/68. Retd GD 30/3/77.
BURGESS I. A. Born 26/4/16. Commd 1/1/43. Flt Lt 1/1/43. Retd GD(G) 10/8/63.
BURGESS J. G. Born 28/11/51. Commd 16/3/73. Flt Lt 16/3/76. Retd GD 28/11/89.
BURGESS J. H. Born 17/9/46. Commd 31/10/74. Wg Cdr 14/3/96. Retd ENG 14/3/96.
BURGESS J. N., MMar MNI FIMgt. Born 24/12/30. Commd 29/6/56. Gp Capt 1/7/76. Retd MAR 1/4/82.
BURGESS K. J. Born 10/12/27. Commd 18/10/51. Sqn Ldr 1/7/62. Retd GD 28/11/75. Re-instated 3/9/80 to 14/4/85.
BURGESS M. J. Born 18/8/23. Commd 16/4/43. Sqn Ldr 1/1/53. Retd RGT 7/4/64.
BURGESS P. Born 25/9/30. Commd 1/2/62. Flt Lt 1/2/68. Retd PE 30/9/80
BURGESS P. O'D., MIMgt. Born 14/12/22. Commd 3/9/43. Wg Cdr 1/1/68. Retd ADMIN 14/12/77.
BURGESS R. W. Born 5/10/29. Commd 5/4/50. Flt Lt 5/10/52. Retd GD 31/12/75 rtg Sqn Ldr.

BURGESS S. D. Born 17/7/29. Commd 6/12/56. Flt Lt 16/8/61. Retd PI 28/2/73.
BURGESS S. F., BSc. Born 22/11/62. Commd 2/9/84. Flt Lt 2/3/88. Retd ADMIN 31/1/97.
BURGHAM A. P., BA. Born 3/12/55. Commd 27/3/80. Sqn Ldr 1/1/91. Retd SUP 21/1/97.
BURGIS W. S. Born 21/4/52. Commd 4/3/71. Flt Lt 4/9/76. Retd GD 21/4/90.
BURKBY J. A. Born 9/4/41. Commd 1/10/65. Sqn Ldr 1/7/87. Retd GD 9/4/96.
BURKE B. Born 25/8/46. Commd 20/11/75. Sqn Ldr 1/1/86. Retd GD 31/3/94.
BURKE E. S. R. Born 9/11/42. Commd 25/1/63. Flt Lt 4/11/68. Retd GD 22/10/94.
BURKE H. R. Born 24/5/59. Commd 19/6/86. Flt Lt 6/12/92. Retd GD(G) 14/3/96.
BURKE J. J., BSc CEng FIEE DipEL MRAeS. Born 12/4/30. Commd 12/11/53. A Cdre 1/1/78. Retd ENG 12/4/85.
BURKE K. S., MSc BSc. Born 28/11/58. Commd 17/1/82. Sqn Ldr 1/1/91. Retd ENG 17/1/98.
BURKE O. G. Born 16/4/14. Commd 23/8/44. Sqn Offr 1/1/58. Retd PRT 28/4/61.
BURKE R. H. Born 28/6/39. Commd 21/7/61. Sqn Ldr 1/1/74. Retd GD 28/6/97.
BURKE T. A., DFC. Born 1/7/20. Commd 21/5/41. Flt Lt 12/7/46. Retd GD 29/3/58 rtg Sqn Ldr.
BURKE T. E., BA CEng MIMechE MRAeS. Born 11/3/34. Commd 14/5/63. Sqn Ldr 1/7/75. Retd ENG 14/5/79.
BURKE T. F. Born 16/4/40. Commd 10/6/63. Gp Capt 1/7/94. Retd GD(G) 16/4/95.
BURKE T. J. d'E., BA. Born 30/3/27. Commd 13/1/49. Sqn Ldr 1/7/59. Retd ENG 30/3/85.
BURKEY J. W. Born 19/2/40. Commd 28/6/79. Flt Lt 28/6/82. Retd GD 19/2/95.
BURLEIGH G. H., AFC. Born 31/12/31. Commd 30/7/52. Gp Capt 1/1/76. Retd GD 31/12/86.
BURLES D. R. Born 17/10/31. Commd 28/7/53. Flt Lt 28/1/56. Retd GD 18/4/70.
BURLEY B. M. Born 27/6/30. Commd 11/4/51. Gp Capt 1/1/81. Retd GD 26/5/83.
BURLINGTON-GREEN E. A. Born 3/8/18. Commd 18/7/46. Sqn Ldr 1/7/63. Retd ENG 3/8/73.
BURLOW N. E., DFC. Born 3/8/22. Commd 25/8/55. Flt Lt 25/8/58. Retd GD 12/8/72.
BURMAN B. G. Born 16/11/41. Commd 12/9/63. Wg Cdr 1/7/83. Retd SY 3/7/93.
BURMAN M. H., BSc. Born 21/5/61. Commd 30/10/83. Flt Lt 30/4/86. Retd GD 30/10/99.
BURN N. Born 1/6/57. Commd 6/10/77. Sqn Ldr 1/1/95. Retd GD 1/6/01.
BURNELL C. M. Born 11/6/55. Commd 11/7/74. Flt Lt 11/1/81. Retd SUP 28/2/81.
BURNESS S. A. Born 10/12/16. Commd 17/3/49. Sqn Ldr 1/4/58. Retd SEC 10/4/70.
BURNET-SMITH W. J. Born 29/12/22. Commd 28/3/44. Flt Lt 30/10/58. Retd GD 1/1/73.
BURNETT Sir Brian, GCB DFC AFC BA. Born 10/3/13. Commd 27/6/32. ACM 7/10/67. Retd GD 11/3/72.
BURNETT B. StL. Born 27/12/45. Commd 5/3/65. Flt Lt 5/9/70. Retd GD 30/12/82.
BURNETT D. J. Born 3/4/45. Commd 17/12/65. Flt Lt 1/7/68. Retd GD 17/9/97.
BURNETT P., DSO DFC. Born 13/2/14. Commd 23/9/36. Gp Capt 1/7/54. Retd GD 13/11/60.
BURNETT P. G. Born 2/1/42. Commd 17/7/62. Flt Lt 15/4/72. Retd ENG 2/1/80.
BURNETT R. J. Born 31/8/35. Commd 30/1/58. Sqn Ldr 1/7/69. Retd GD 31/8/73.
BURNETT W. J., DSO OBE DFC AFC. Born 8/11/15. Commd 5/9/37. AC 1/7/63. Retd GD 21/5/68.
BURNETT W. M. Born 19/7/44. Commd 24/1/65. Gp Capt 1/1/91. Retd GD 8/7/93.
BURNHAM A. F. R. Born 3/11/29. Commd 16/12/49. Flt Lt 16/12/54. Retd RGT 3/11/67.
BURNINGHAM J. Born 1/4/31. Commd 26/5/60. Flt Lt 26/5/66. Retd GD 15/4/84.
BURNINGHAM J. K., MBE Dip Soton. Born 22/11/31. Commd 29/12/53. Gp Capt 1/7/74. Retd 24/2/80.
BURNS A. H. F. Born 20/5/44. Commd 8/5/86. Sqn Ldr 1/7/93. Retd ADMIN 14/3/96.
BURNS F. W., DPhysEd. Born 14/3/36. Commd 17/7/62. Flt Lt 17/7/66. Retd PE 5/9/78.
BURNS G. F. Born 5/5/47. Commd 1/4/71. Flt Lt 1/10/76. Retd GD 30/9/77.
BURNS I. D., MIMgt. Born 4/8/34. Commd 15/3/60. Sqn Ldr 1/7/76. Retd ADMIN 1/10/84.
BURNS I. D. Born 13/11/48. Commd 30/5/69. Flt Lt 30/11/74. Retd GD 8/10/81.
BURNS J., CBE. Born 27/7/33. Commd 9/4/52. Gp Capt 1/7/79. Retd GD 27/7/93.
BURNS J. C. Born 27/9/43. Commd 26/3/64. Flt Lt 25/7/70. Retd GD(G) 27/9/82.
BURNS J. G. Born 27/11/27. Commd 8/4/49. Flt Lt 8/10/51. Retd GD 12/2/58.
BURNS J. R. Born 24/2/23. Commd 12/11/43. Sqn Ldr 1/1/67/ Retd GD 24/2/78.
BURNS K. D. Born 21/8/46. Commd 1/3/68. Wg Cdr 1/1/90. Retd GD 31/12/93.
BURNS M. H. C. Born 7/4/19. Commd 1/7/46. Flt Lt 1/7/46. Retd RGT 1/5/58.
BURNS N. J. Born 9/5/38. Commd 9/11/64. Sqn Ldr 1/7/84. Retd SUP 23/7/92.
BURNS P. Born 20/7/37. Commd 18/12/56. Sqn Ldr 1/1/83. Retd GD 1/12/89.
BURNS P. J. Born 13/5/59. Commd 22/2/79. Flt Lt 22/8/84. Retd GD 24/2/91.
BURNS P. R. S., MB ChB. Born 11/3/42. Commd 14/5/74. Sqn Ldr 1/8/82. Retd MED 27/4/89.
BURNS R. E., CBE DFC* BSc CEng MRAeS. Born 5/10/12. Commd 28/4/34. Gp Capt 1/1/54. Retd GD 2/6/67.
BURNS S. Born 4/4/47. Commd 6/5/66. Flt Lt 6/11/71. Retd GD 4/6/76.
BURNS T. J. Born 25/5/35. Commd 13/12/55. Sqn Ldr 1/1/71. Retd GD 1/1/74.
BURNS T. P. Born 17/5/33. Commd 21/5/52. Wg Cdr 1/1/85. Retd GD(G) 17/11/91.
BURNS W. L. Born 14/5/25. Commd 6/5/65. Flt Lt 6/5/71. Retd SUP 1/8/84.
BURNSIDE D. H., OBE DSO DFC*. Born 26/1/12. Commd 28/10/35. Gp Capt 1/7/54. Retd GD 23/3/62.
BURNSIDE P. A. L., BSc. Born 18/1/54. Commd 15/1/74. Sqn Ldr 1/1/88. Retd GD 18/1/92.
BURR R. A. M. Born 2/10/38. Commd 30/5/59. Flt Lt 19/1/65. Retd GD 2/10/76.
BURR R. H., DFM. Born 3/9/16. Commd 28/11/43. Flt Lt 28/5/47. Retd GD 24/10/57.
BURRAGE P. A. Born 14/11/26. Commd 21/1/53. Flt Lt 21/7/56. Retd GD 13/7/79.
BURRAGE W. C. Born 12/6/21. Commd 22/10/59. Flt Lt 22/10/62. Retd ENG 12/6/71.
BURRELL A. G. Born 4/8/42. Commd 6/11/80. Sqn Ldr 1/1/91. Retd ENG 30/4/97.

BURRELL J. D. Born 6/3/37. Commd 24/4/70. Wg Cdr 1/7/84. Retd ADMIN 15/6/87.
BURRELLS J. S. S. Born 1/10/37. Commd 19/12/63. Sqn Ldr 1/7/73. Retd SUP 2/5/79.
BURRETT I. C. Born 21/3/60. Commd 11/10/78. Wg Cdr 1/1/96. Retd GD 2/5/00.
BURREY J. D. Born 6/12/50. Commd 22/5/75. Flt Lt 22/11/80. Retd GD 3/2/91.
BURRIDGE J., MIMgt. Born 6/11/24. Commd 1/12/44. Gp Capt 1/1/72. Retd SUP 31/3/78.
BURRILL B. C. Born 12/9/45. Commd 20/10/83. Sqn Ldr 1/1/91. Retd ADMIN 23/4/94.
BURROWS A. R. Born 21/4/68. Commd 21/12/89. Fg Offr 21/12/91. Retd GD 25/4/93.
BURROWS C. E. Born 22/7/28. Commd 25/2/53. Flt Lt 10/6/59. Retd GD 22/8/75.
BURROWS D. S. Born 22/9/31. Commd 30/7/52. Wg Cdr 1/7/76. Retd GD 22/9/86.
BURROWS H. C., MIMgt. Born 5/6/31. Commd 7/3/51. Sqn Ldr 1/7/64. Retd GD 17/7/74.
BURROWS J. S., BSc. Born 22/8/50. Commd 13/9/71. Sqn Ldr 1/1/81. Retd ENG 22/12/88.
BURROWS N. Born 23/6/44. Commd 24/6/65. Flt Lt 24/12/67. Retd GD 6/4/74.
BURROWS P. G. Born 27/6/56. Commd 17/7/75. Flt Lt 17/1/81. Retd GD 15/4/01.
BURROWS R. S., AFC FRAeS FIMgt. Born 18/10/43. Commd 3/8/62. Gp Capt 1/7/86. Retd GD 1/7/88.
BURROWS S. E. Born 17/12/68. Commd 28/7/88. Flt Lt 20/12/94. Retd ADMIN 28/1/97.
BURROWS T. G. Born 19/8/39. Commd 3/7/80. Flt Lt 3/7/85. Retd SUP 19/8/94.
BURROWS W. D. Born 9/11/32. Commd 4/7/51. Sqn Ldr 1/7/67. Retd SEC 9/11/70.
BURRY S. J., BSc(Eng) CEng MRAeS. Born 7/1/53. Commd 25/9/71. Wg Cdr 1/1/94. Retd ENG 7/1/97.
BURSCOUGH B. Born 22/11/48. Commd 16/6/88. Flt Lt 16/6/92. Retd SUP 14/3/97.
BURT A. G. Born 7/12/16. Commd 19/7/57. Sqn Ldr 1/1/66. Retd ENG 8/12/71.
BURT A. T. Born 26/7/32. Commd 13/9/51. Sqn Ldr 1/7/69. Retd GD 17/9/76.
BURT S. J. Born 27/7/25. Commd 25/8/55. Flt Lt 25/8/61. Retd GD 27/7/80.
BURT V. A. Born 21/6/43. Commd 5/3/65. Flt Lt 5/9/70. Retd GD 21/6/81.
BURTENSHAW A. J. Born 19/4/57. Commd 21/4/77. Sqn Ldr 1/1/88. Retd GD 9/12/95.
BURTON A. A. Born 15/4/40. Commd 11/6/60. Flt Lt 10/2/67. Retd GD 15/4/78.
BURTON A. R. K., BSc CEng MRAeS MIEE. Born 17/8/23. Commd 14/10/42. Wg Cdr 1/1/62. Retd ENG 8/6/68.
BURTON B. E. Born 3/3/28. Commd 5/11/53. Wg Cdr 1/1/75. Retd GD 3/3/83.
BURTON B. H. Born 30/6/53. Commd 15/2/90. Flt Lt 15/2/94. Retd ENG 14/3/97.
BURTON B. M. Born 6/6/35. Commd 11/11/71. Flt Lt 11/11/74. Retd GD 12/11/76.
BURTON D. E. Born 16/2/24. Commd 1/4/45. Flt Lt 17/3/49. Retd GD 31/8/63.
BURTON D. O. Born 22/9/47. Commd 22/11/84. Flt Lt 22/11/88. Retd SUP 1/10/93.
BURTON D. P. Born 4/12/60. Commd 23/10/86. Flt Lt 23/10/88. Retd GD 4/12/98.
BURTON F. Born 20/11/21. Commd 21/2/44. Sqn Ldr 1/7/65. Retd GD(G) 10/11/76 rtg Wg Cdr.
BURTON G. E. W., BSc MRCS LRCP. Born 16/1/48. Commd 9/7/81. Sqn Ldr 3/7/90. Retd MED 6/5/96.
BURTON G. O. Born 23/7/45. Commd 19/6/70. Gp Capt 1/7/90. Retd ENG 23/7/00.
BURTON H. M. Born 22/9/59. Commd 5/4/79. Flt Lt 5/10/84. Retd GD 25/9/89.
BURTON J. C. Born 14/6/44. Commd 24/6/65. Sqn Ldr 1/1/74. Retd SUP 14/6/82.
BURTON J. E. Born 24/2/24. Commd 27/6/45. Wg Cdr 1/1/67. Retd GD 26/4/74.
BURTON J. K. Born 14/2/35. Commd 22/7/66. Flt Lt 22/7/68. Retd ENG 22/7/74.
BURTON J. M., MBE. Born 4/2/50. Commd 31/8/78. Sqn Ldr 1/7/86. Retd ENG 1/10/96.
BURTON J. M. Born 15/4/57. Commd 15/10/78. Sqn Ldr 1/7/91. Retd ADMIN 14/3/97.
BURTON K. C., SRN RNT. Born 4/9/22. Commd 12/6/58. Flt Lt 27/5/64. Retd MED(T) 10/11/68.
BURTON K. W. Born 7/6/29. Commd 30/7/64. Sqn Ldr 1/1/77. Retd GD(G) 23/5/83.
BURTON M., JC OBE FRIN FIMgt. Born 12/8/32. Commd 30/1/52. A Cdre 1/1/85. Retd GD 12/8/87.
BURTON N., MBE. Born 1/9/09. Commd 11/12/44. Sqn Ldr 1/7/52. Retd PRT 9/2/63.
BURTON P. F. J., AFC MIMgt. Born 22/10/40. Commd 1/8/61. Wg Cdr 1/7/76. Retd GD 30/7/80.
BURTON R. K., BSc. Born 2/6/38. Commd 1/10/62. Sqn Ldr 1/6/74. Retd EDN 1/10/78.
BURTWELL K. W. Born 10/12/44. Commd 24/1/77. Flt Lt 24/6/79. Retd ADMIN 16/2/87.
BURTWELL P. A., BSc. Born 19/7/50. Commd 22/10/72. Sqn Ldr 1/1/86. Retd ADMIN 1/1/89.
BURWELL C. C. N., MBE. Born 12/9/51. Commd 25/2/72. Gp Capt 1/7/93. Retd GD 27/7/99.
BURWOOD M. K. Born 23/8/42. Commd 19/8/65. Fg Offr 29/12/67. Retd GD 23/4/70.
BURY H. Born 3/7/07. Commd 28/10/42. Flt Offr 6/2/50. Retd CAT 10/10/61.
BURY J. E., CEng MIEE MIMgt. Born 6/12/17. Commd 12/9/42. Flt Lt 12/3/46. Retd ENG 6/12/69.
BURY R. F., BSc MB BS FRCS. Born 10/8/48. Commd 8/8/71. Wg Cdr 22/11/87. Retd MED 6/2/88.
BURY T. M. G., CB OBE. Born 11/9/18. Commd 22/4/42. A Cdre 1/7/68. Retd ENG 11/9/73.
BUSBY C. A., BSc. Born 18/4/60. Commd 20/1/85. Flt Lt 20/7/88. Retd OPS SPT 20/1/01.
BUSCH W. Born 13/11/43. Commd 11/11/71. Flt Lt 11/11/73. Retd GD(G) 13/11/81.
BUSFIELD D. B. Born 22/2/42. Commd 11/6/60. Flt Lt 11/12/65. Retd GD 22/2/80.
BUSH G. R. Born 21/10/48. Commd 17/3/67. Gp Capt 1/7/94. Retd OPS SPT 7/4/98.
BUSH J. D. Born 28/5/68. Commd 21/12/89. Fg Offr 23/5/92. Retd ADMIN 30/7/96.
BUSH M. J. Born 31/8/40. Commd 5/6/62. Sqn Ldr 1/7/73. Retd GD 31/8/78.
BUSH P. J. Born 12/5/48. Commd 12/10/78. Wg Cdr 1/1/90. Retd MED(SEC) 23/8/98.
BUSH R. F. J. Born 20/6/44. Commd 12/2/68. Flt Lt 7/9/71. Retd EDN 4/4/78.
BUSH T. H., BSc CEng FIMechE MRAeS MIMgt. Born 29/12/40. Commd 15/7/63. Wg Cdr 1/1/79. Retd ENG 17/4/88.
BUSHELL C. T. Born 20/3/19. Commd 16/5/57. Flt Lt 1/4/63. Retd PE 20/3/74.

BUSHELL G. K., OBE. Born 18/4/22. Commd 5/3/43. Wg Cdr 1/7/62. Retd GD 3/4/73.
BUSHNELL D. C., BEM. Born 11/12/19. Commd 29/10/64. Flt Lt 29/10/67. Retd ENG 11/12/74.
BUSSEREAU V. R. D. Born 7/7/42. Commd 21/5/65. Wg Cdr 1/7/94. Retd GD 7/7/97.
BUSSEY J. E., MBE. Born 7/8/34. Commd 7/9/61. Wg Cdr 1/7/80. Retd GD 18/9/82.
BUSSEY W. T., MVO OBE BEM. Born 13/12/13. Commd 23/12/43. Wg Cdr 1/1/62. Retd ENG 1/9/67.
BUSUTTIL W., MB ChB. Born 5/11/59. Commd 9/7/81. Wg Cdr 1/8/97. Retd MED 5/11/97.
BUSWELL B. D. Born 26/12/27. Commd 19/5/49. Flt Lt 19/11/53. Retd GD 26/12/65.
BUTCHARD J. E. Born 2/6/41. Commd 15/9/61. Flt Lt 2/12/66. Retd GD 1/10/86.
BUTCHER The Rev A. J., MA. Born 20/10/43. Commd 26/3/72. Retd 26/3/88. Wg Cdr.
BUTCHER A. J., BSc. Born 3/8/55. Commd 2/1/77. Wg Cdr 1/1/91. Retd ADMIN 1/1/94.
BUTCHER C. A. Born 1/7/39. Commd 26/3/59. Flt Offr 29/5/65. Retd GD(G) 3/12/66.
BUTCHER D. J. Born 18/10/45. Commd 26/5/67. Sqn Ldr 1/1/87. Retd GD(G) 1/10/96.
BUTCHER E. Born 12/1/20. Commd 21/10/54. Flt Lt 21/10/57. Retd GD 12/1/70.
BUTCHER E. R., OBE. Born 28/10/06. Commd 16/5/40. Wg Cdr 1/7/47. Retd ENG 31/3/58.
BUTCHER E. T. Born 11/2/20. Commd 27/3/41. Flt Lt 27/3/43. Retd GD(G) 11/2/75.
BUTCHER E. V. Born 12/5/18. Commd 15/11/44. Flt Lt 15/5/47. Retd ENG 3/9/69.
BUTCHER F. A. Born 23/3/33. Commd 17/1/52. Flt Lt 8/5/57. Retd GD 11/5/76.
BUTCHER H. R., MCIPS. Born 18/4/39. Commd 31/10/69. Sqn Ldr 1/7/80. Retd SUP 18/4/94.
BUTCHER P. C., OBE BA MRAeS MIMgt. Born 9/12/47. Commd 1/3/68. Gp Capt 1/1/93. Retd GD 4/10/94.
BUTCHER T. A. Born 12/12/42. Commd 6/7/62. Flt Lt 6/1/68. Retd GD 12/12/80.
BUTLAND J. E. Born 26/1/19. Commd 1/5/39. Sqn Ldr 1/7/48. Retd SUP 8/5/53.
BUTLER A. A. Born 12/10/32. Commd 6/9/68. Flt Lt 1/1/73. Retd GD 12/10/92.
BUTLER B. J. McG. Born 19/12/37. Commd 5/11/70. Sqn Ldr 1/1/83. Retd SY (RGT) 18/6/88.
BUTLER B. R. M. Born 30/11/23. Commd 23/9/43. Flt Lt 30/10/52. Retd MAR 29/10/58.
BUTLER C. G. M. Born 13/3/40. Commd 3/9/60. Flt Lt 3/3/66. Retd GD 13/5/77.
BUTLER C. W. J. Born 17/1/36. Commd 30/12/54. Sqn Ldr 1/1/71. Retd GD 17/1/91.
BUTLER D. J. Born 9/2/41. Commd 30/5/59. Flt Lt 15/2/65. Retd GD 13/10/94.
BUTLER D. O., DFC. Born 19/7/15. Commd 9/3/36. Wg Cdr 1/7/47. Retd GD 3/2/58.
BUTLER D. P., MSc BSc. Born 30/1/61. Commd 4/1/83. Sqn Ldr 1/1/92. Retd ENG 30/1/99.
BUTLER D. W., AFC. Born 26/6/22. Commd 27/3/43. Sqn Ldr 1/7/54. Retd GD 25/8/60.
BUTLER D. W. J., DFC MHCIMA. Born 27/4/20. Commd 25/8/43. Sqn Ldr 1/1/69. Retd CAT 30/9/72.
BUTLER H. W. T. Born 18/9/31. Commd 3/11/51. Flt Lt 3/5/56. Retd GD 18/9/86
BUTLER I. B., DFC AFC. Born 22/7/17. Commd 25/8/40. Gp Capt 1/1/61. Retd GD 2/9/72.
BUTLER J. C. Born 3/5/29. Commd 27/9/51. Sqn Ldr 1/7/64. Retd GD 1/3/74.
BUTLER J. G. Born 10/5/32. Commd 7/5/53. Flt Lt 7/11/57. Retd GD 10/5/70.
BUTLER M .A., BA. Born 31/1/42. Commd 10/3/77. Wg Cdr 1/7/91. Retd GD 31/1/97.
BUTLER M. B. Born 2/9/32. Commd 28/6/51. Sqn Ldr 1/7/67. Retd GD 3/6/77.
BUTLER M. J. Born 26/2/42. Commd 23/12/60. A Cdre 1/7/90. Retd GD 26/2/97.
BUTLER M. P. J., BSc. Born 17/3/51. Commd 19/2/73. Sqn Ldr 1/7/84. Retd GD 17/3/89.
BUTLER P. Born 15/11/26. Commd 24/1/52. Flt Lt 15/5/57. Retd GD 15/11/69.
BUTLER P. P., MBE. Born 28/9/14. Commd 2/1/39. Sqn Ldr 1/1/49. Retd SUP 24/2/62.
BUTLER P. W. P. Born 23/12/55. Commd 30/1/75. Sqn Ldr 1/7/94. Retd GD 14/3/97.
BUTLER R. A., BSc. Born 9/5/55. Commd 6/11/77. Flt Lt 6/8/79. Retd GD 6/11/89.
BUTLER R. L. S. Born 16/5/40. Commd 1/8/61. Flt Lt 1/2/64. Retd GD 16/5/78.
BUTLER R. M., QHDS MSc BDS FFGDP(UK) MGDSRCS(Ed). Born 20/5/44. Commd 21/7/68. A Cdre 1/7/97. Retd DEL 20/5/01.
BUTLER S. J., MBE. Born 8/4/52. Commd 27/7/89. Sqn Ldr 1/7/96. Retd ADMIN 4/10/99.
BUTLER T. G. W., BSc. Born 28/1/56. Commd 27/4/74. Flt Lt 15/10/79. Retd GD 20/11/94.
BUTLER W. C. Born 20/4/23. Commd 1/8/44. Flt Lt 4/4/51. Retd SUP 20/5/55.
BUTLER W. F. Born 28/1/18. Commd 31/7/58. Sqn Ldr 1/1/67. Retd ENG 28/4/70.
BUTT A. G. M. Born 29/1/20. Commd 21/4/44. Wg Cdr 1/1/65. Retd GD(G) 14/9/68.
BUTT L. A. K. Born 31/7/96. Commd 1/4/18. Flt Lt 24/11/25. Retd SUP 1/1/29. Recalled 1/9/39 to 6/2/46 rtg Gp Capt.
BUTT L. C. Born 24/11/45. Commd 24/4/64. Sqn Ldr 1/7/79. Retd GD 24/11/00.
BUTT M. R. D. Born 13/3/34. Commd 14/1/54. Sqn Ldr 1/7/71. Retd GD 13/3/89.
BUTT P. C. Born 24/4/47. Commd 1/3/68. Gp Capt 1/1/88. Retd ADMIN 24/4/91.
BUTT R. H. S. Born 1/11/20. Commd 9/10/47. Sqn Ldr 1/7/70. Retd ENG 6/1/74.
BUTT W. E., FIMLT. Born 20/5/34. Commd 5/9/69. Flt Lt 20/5/74. Retd MED(T) 1/4/77.
BUTTAR M. S., MIMgt. Born 30/1/32. Commd 12/7/62. Sqn Ldr 1/7/73. Retd SUP 30/1/87.
BUTTER H. A. J., MIMgt. Born 19/12/32. Commd 24/8/56. Sqn Ldr 24/2/64. Retd EDN 6/4/78.
BUTTERFIELD C. T., BSc. Born 17/10/56. Commd 14/1/76. Flt Lt 14/4/80. Retd GD 14/1/87.
BUTTERFIELD D. I. Born 22/7/22. Commd 15/9/60. Flt Lt 15/9/63. Retd GD 22/7/77.
BUTTERFIELD L. J., CEng MIMechE. Born 3/12/30. Commd 6/8/52. Sqn Ldr 1/7/66. Retd ENG 21/8/74.
BUTTERISS J., MBE. Born 6/3/21. Commd 21/11/43. Sqn Ldr 1/1/64. Retd GD(G) 1/6/74.
BUTTERISS M., BA MB BChir MRCGP MRCS LRCP DRCOG DAVMED. Born 10/8/45. Commd 24/7/67. Sqn Ldr 2/8/76. Retd MED 24/1/84.

BUTTERS D. J., DFC* MIMgt. Born 19/7/22. Commd 21/8/44. Sqn Ldr 1/1/63. Retd SUP 19/9/73.
BUTTERS G. K. Born 2/5/42. Commd 18/10/62. Sqn Ldr 1/7/79. Retd ENG 2/5/86.
BUTTERWORTH B., BA. Born 18/3/31. Commd 18/11/53. Sqn Ldr 1/1/69. Retd GD 30/9/74.
BUTTERWORTH J. D. T., MBE. Born 14/5/36. Commd 12/4/73. Sqn Ldr 1/7/82. Retd ENG 14/5/92.
BUTTERWORTH R., BSc. Born 16/12/48. Commd 23/9/68. Flt Lt 15/4/72. Retd GD 22/10/94.
BUTTERWORTH R. J. Born 16/12/44. Commd 7/7/67. Flt Lt 7/7/72. Retd GD 28/3/83.
BUTTERWORTH W. D. Born 9/5/42. Commd 21/7/61. Wg Cdr 1/7/93. Retd GD 5/12/98.
BUTTERWORTH W. H. Born 7/11/23. Commd 26/10/48. Flt Lt 19/6/52. Retd GD(G) 15/7/63.
BUTTLE E. R. Born 2/3/17. Commd 19/7/56. Flt Lt 25/10/59. Retd GD(G) 2/3/73.
BUTTON A. H. Born 2/2/05. Commd 19/5/30. Sqn Ldr 1/10/38. Retd GD 25/5/40.
BUTTON D. H., DFM. Born 21/1/18. Commd 19/1/43. Sqn Ldr 1/7/54. Retd ENG 22/6/68.
BUXEY M. R. Born 10/10/41. Commd 27/1/61. Sqn Ldr 1/1/82. Retd GD 20/8/94.
BUXTON C. T. Born 14/4/56. Commd 27/2/75. Sqn Ldr 1/1/91. Retd GD 14/4/94.
BUXTON D. G. Born 25/4/56. Commd 28/10/76. Flt Lt 28/2/82. Retd GD 25/4/94.
BUXTON D. O., MRAeS. Born 31/10/19. Commd 27/4/44. Sqn Ldr 1/1/55. Retd ENG 20/1/61.
BYCROFT P. C. Born 22/1/39. Commd 9/2/62. Flt Lt 1/4/66. Retd GD 17/10/77.
BYE F. W. G. Born 20/9/11. Commd 1/9/44. Fg Offr 1/3/45. Retd ASD 30/1/46.
BYERS C. W. Born 4/4/26. Commd 23/4/52. Flt Lt 5/9/62. Retd GD 12/11/75.
BYRAM P. A., MBE. Born 14/12/45. Commd 21/1/66. Sqn Ldr 1/7/86. Retd GD 1/12/95.
BYRNE B. N. Born 13/7/23. Commd 26/2/43. Sqn Ldr 1/4/55. Retd GD 11/11/61.
BYRNE E. G. Born 9/4/45. Commd 4/12/86. Flt Lt 4/12/90. Retd ENG 14/9/96.
BYRNE G. C. H. Born 22/9/36. Commd 2/8/66. Sqn Ldr 1/7/78. Retd SY 12/6/81.
BYRNE H. D., AFC. Born 24/11/17. Commd 1/9/45. Wg Cdr 1/1/57. Retd GD 26/11/64.
BYRNE J. J. Born 11/2/33. Commd 19/8/53. Fg Offr 20/8/55. Retd GD 31/1/64.
BYRNE J. T. C., CEng MIMechE Born 20/2/19. Commd 23/8/40. Sqn Ldr 1/7/52. Retd ENG 30/5/69.
BYRNE K. C. Born 16/10/48. Commd 28/2/69. Sqn Ldr 1/7/80. Retd ENG 16/10/86.
BYRNE M. J. Born 27/12/17. Commd 19/9/46. Fg Offr 19/9/46. Retd RGT 27/12/48.
BYRNE R. F., MBE. Born 11/7/33. Commd 4/6/52. Sqn Ldr 1/7/79. Retd GD 11/5/84.
BYRNE-BURNS P. J. Born 20/6/45. Commd 28/4/65. Flt Lt 4/11/70. Retd GD 21/6/94.
BYRNE-BURNS R. M. Born 22/8/43. Commd 23/1/64. Sqn Ldr 1/7/79. Retd ADMIN 1/7/82.
BYRON A. N., MSc CEng MRAeS. Born 12/6/22. Commd 3/3/43. Sqn Ldr 1/1/55. Retd ENG 12/6/82.
BYWATER D.L., FRAeS FIMgt. Born 16/7/37. Commd 1/4/58. A Cdre 1/1/89. Retd GD 1/8/92.
BYWATER E. B. Born 28/9/34. Commd 19/11/52. Wg Cdr 1/1/83. Retd GD 28/9/92.
BYWATER R. D. Born 20/3/64. Commd 30/8/84. Flt Lt 20/2/90. Retd GD 30/3/98.

# C

CABLE B. F., MBE. Born 30/1/43. Commd 26/5/61. Wg Cdr 1/1/91. Retd GD 22/4/94.
CABLE E. D. Born 25/9/21. Commd 14/8/41. Sqn Ldr 1/7/58. Retd GD 25/9/64.
CABLE J. A. Born 8/7/22. Commd 5/12/43. Sqn Ldr 1/7/62. Retd SUP 8/7/77.
CABORN J. R. Born 25/10/43. Commd 17/12/64. Sqn Ldr 1/1/77. Retd GD 25/10/81.
CABOURNE P. J., BA FIMgt. Born 4/8/27. Commd 12/10/52. A Cdre 1/1/81. Retd GD 5/2/83.
CADAMY W. H. Born 24/2/21. Commd 10/3/45. Wg Cdr 1/7/62. Retd GD 10/4/72.
CADE A. S., OBE. Born 16/9/17. Commd 24/10/41. Wg Cdr 1/7/58. Retd GD 16/9/72.
CADIOT C. J., BSc. Born 25/1/51. Commd 28/10/73. Flt Lt 1/6/81. Retd SUP 28/10/92.
CADLE C. P. Born 7/11/46. Commd 15/9/67. Fg Offr 15/9/69. Retd GD 14/2/71.
CADMAN P., OBE MSc CEng MIMechE MRAeS. Born 19/6/22. Commd 15/4/43. Gp Capt 1/7/67. Retd ENG 30/3/77.
CADOGAN C. I. G. Born 26/6/41. Commd 28/2/80. Sqn Ldr 1/7/88. Retd ENG 1/2/96.
CADOGAN C. V., MBE. Born 5/8/12. Commd 8/7/54. Sqn Ldr 1/7/64. Retd ENG 5/8/67.
CADOGAN S. W. Born 23/7/47. Commd 5/1/70. Gp Capt 1/7/94. Retd ADMIN 14/9/96.
CADWALLADER D. G. Born 2/12/44. Commd 3/3/67. Sqn Ldr 1/1/79. Retd GD 19/10/97.
CAFFERKY P. W. P. Born 25/1/62. Commd 8/9/83. Sqn Ldr 1/7/95. Retd GD 25/1/00.
CAHILL I. G. Born 28/8/61. Commd 4/11/82. Sqn Ldr 1/1/87. Retd GD 1/1/00.
CAIGER A. B. E. Born 9/12/34. Commd 9/4/57. Sqn Ldr 1/7/67. Retd SUP 9/12/72.
CAIGER J. J. Born 8/2/1900. Commd 20/2/22. Flt Lt 1/1/29. Retd SEC 31/3/31 rtg Sqn Ldr. Re-employed 26/8/39 to 22/12/44.
CAILES C. P. Born 6/12/63. Commd 19/11/87. Flt Lt 26/10/93. Retd ADMIN 14/3/97.
CAILLARD D. P. Born 10/8/61. Commd 4/8/82. Fg Off 10/8/84. Retd SY 1/4/86.
CAILLARD H. A., CB. Born 16/4/27. Commd 8/4/49. AVM 1/1/80. Retd GD 8/5/82.
CAIN B. W., BA. Born 9/6/47. Commd 1/11/70. Flt Lt 1/5/73. Retd ADMIN 1/7/77.
CAIN P. T. Born 14/1/45. Commd 24/6/76. Flt Lt 24/6/78. Retd ENG 6/4/84.
CAINES C. J. Born 24/1/49. Commd 25/9/80. Flt Lt 25/9/82. Retd ENG 24/1/99.
CAINES J. Born 12/7/49. Commd 13/1/72. Flt Lt 13/7/77. Retd GD 20/9/87.
CAINEY D. J., BA MIMgt ACIS. Born 25/7/33. Commd 1/9/64. Sqn Ldr 11/12/73. Retd ADMIN 3/2/83.
CAIRD A. R. Born 18/11/47. Commd 27/10/67. Flt Lt 27/4/74. Retd SUP 18/11/85.
CAIRD M. S. Born 10/5/50. Commd 2/1/70. Wg Cdr 1/7/94. Retd SUP 14/3/97.
CAIRD R., CEng MRAeS MIMgt. Born 21/9/22. Commd 26/8/43. Wg Cdr 1/7/62. Retd ENG 28/4/73.
CAIRNES A. E. Born 6/7/13. Commd 16/12/33. Sqn Ldr 1/1/42. Retd GD 6/6/46 rtg Wg Cdr.
CAIRNS A. Born 8/10/33. Commd 9/10/67. Sqn Ldr 1/1/79 Retd MAR 11/10/83.
CAIRNS D. R., MA. Born 21/5/63. Commd 2/4/84. Flt Lt 15/1/87. Retd GD 23/10/89.
CAIRNS F. T. V., DFC. Born 3/12/18. Commd 25/10/42. Flt Lt 11/5/46. Retd GD(G) 17/7/62.
CAIRNS G. C., CBE AFC MRAeS. Born 21/5/26. Commd 22/2/46. AVM. 1/1/75. Retd GD 21/5/80.
CAIRNS H. W. D. Born 15/9/42. Commd 15/12/60. Gp Capt 1/7/88. Retd ADMIN 2/7/94.
CAIRNS J. D. Born 18/5/36. Commd 9/2/66. Sqn Ldr 1/1/74. Retd ENG 1/1/77.
CAIRNS J. G. Born 29/10/44. Commd 23/9/66. Sqn Ldr 1/1/90. Retd GD 30/9/94.
CAIRNS J. P. W., DFC*. Born 19/2/16. Commd 3/6/42. Flt Lt 2/11/51. Retd GD(G) 1/5/68.
CAIRNS J. W. McL. Born 9/5/42. Commd 17/2/64. Flt Lt 9/11/67. Retd GD 1/10/75.
CAIRNS W. D., MIMgt. Born 21/1/21. Commd 25/8/55. Flt Lt 25/8/61. Retd ENG 30/6/73.
CAIRNS W. J., FInstPet. Born 9/11/31. Commd 28/5/66. Flt Lt 1/2/72. Retd SUP 31/1/83.
CAKEBREAD J. R. G., DFC. Born 18/4/22. Commd 27/10/43. Flt Lt 27/4/47. Retd ENG 1/9/61.
CALAME M. R. Born 25/3/42. Commd 19/8/66. Sqn Ldr 1/7/90. Retd GD 1/10/94.
CALDER G. R. D., MSc CEng FIMechE FRAeS FIMgt. Born 16/9/23. Commd 27/4/44. A Cdre 1/7/73. Retd ENG 2/4/74.
CALDER I. M., MBE. Born 15/1/33. Commd 17/1/52. Sqn Ldr 1/1/71. Retd GD 15/1/83.
CALDER R. J. G. Born 13/9/48. Commd 1/8/69. Fg Offr 1/2/70. Retd GD 7/9/72.
CALDER-JONES H. L., OBE FIMgt. Born 20/8/24. Commd 15/10/43. Gp Capt 1/7/65. Retd GD 21/11/69.
CALDON M., MA BA. Born 19/9/48. Commd 25/2/79. Flt Lt 25/2/80. Retd ADMIN 1/10/85.
CALDOW W. F., DSO AFC DFM. Born 12/3/21. Commd 20/10/42. Flt Lt 20/4/46. Retd GD 21/7/55 rtg Sqn Ldr.
CALDWELL D. E. Born 28/7/32. Commd 13/9/51. A Cdre 1/7/84. Retd GD 10/6/85.
CALDWELL T. S., MIMgt. Born 28/3/39. Commd 11/9/64. Sqn Ldr 1/1/79. Retd GD 29/10/91.
CALEY J. R., MBE. Born 17/1/22. Commd 13/6/46. Flt Lt 4/6/53. Retd SY 11/7/77.
CALEY M. C., BTech CEng MIMechE. Born 28/7/38. Commd 9/7/61. Sqn Ldr 1/1/72. Retd ENG 9/7/79.
CALEY P. R., BEM. Born 22/5/28. Commd 10/9/60. Sqn Ldr 1/7/71. Retd GD(G) 31/8/82.
CALFORD A. J., DPhysEd. Born 19/2/29. Commd 18/4/56. Flt Lt 18/4/60. Retd SUP 25/12/71.
CALIGARI K. V. S., DFM. Born 31/7/22. Commd 19/12/44. Flt Lt 29/6/50. Retd ENG 31/3/62.
CALLADINE W. J., CEng MIEE. Born 17/2/32. Commd 9/9/54. Gp Capt 1/7/73. Retd ENG 17/1/76.

CALLAGHAN G. G., FIMgt. Born 28/12/30. Commd 6/9/56. Wg Cdr 1/1/72. Retd SEC 1/10/74.
CALLAGHAN J., BA MIL. Born 19/3/49. Commd 11/8/74. Sqn Ldr 1/7/8/36. Retd ADMIN 30/6/92.
CALLAGHAN J. F. Born 24/3/38. Commd 10/9/62. Sqn Ldr 1/1/78. Retd GD 16/5/80.
CALLAGHAN P. R. Born 21/1/37. Commd 30/9/55. Sqn Ldr 1/7/67. Retd GD 21/1/95.
CALLAN P., BA. Born 11/9/34. Commd 18/7/63. Gp Capt 1/7/84. Retd ADMIN 1/11/85.
CALLAWAY A. Born 16/9/32. Commd 19/10/67. Wg Cdr 1/8/85. Retd GD 17/4/87.
CALLAWAY A. B., CEng FIMechE FIMgt. Born 8/7/34. Commd 24/4/59. Gp Capt 1/7/81. Retd ENG 20/2/87.
CALLEJA A. A. Born 16/9/43. Commd 28/4/67. Flt Lt 28/6/73. Retd ADMIN 31/12/83.
CALLEY Sir Henry, DSO DFC. Born 9/12/14. Commd 1/11/41. Wg Cdr 1/7/47. Retd GD 10/8/48.
CALLIS A., BEM MIMgt. Born 30/11/20. Commd 25/8/60. Sqn Ldr 1/7/72. Retd SEC 30/11/75.
CALLISTER C. W., BA DipEd. Born 14/6/40. Commd 24/9/63. Sqn Ldr 24/3/71. Retd ADMIN 14/6/95.
CALLISTER J. W. Born 11/8/58. Commd 9/11/89. Flt Lt 9/11/91. Retd ENG 1/10/94.
CALNAN J.M.P., CB CEng FIMechE. Born 22/4/36. Commd 25/10/57. AVM 1/7/90. Retd ENG 10/7/92.
CALTON S., AFC. Born 21/5/51. Commd 27/3/70. Sqn Ldr 1/1/85. Retd GD 21/5/89. Re-entered 13/5/91. Sqn Ldr 24/12/86. Retd GD 4/12/98.
CALVERT C. J., DFC. Born 2/8/18. Commd 16/12/44. Flt Lt 10/11/55. Retd GD 13/11/63.
CALVERT D. J. Born 23/2/41. Commd 9/3/62. Flt Lt 1/7/68. Retd GD 23/2/79.
CALVERT D. T. Born 4/1/44. Commd 15/9/67. Wg Cdr 1/1/87. Retd GD 11/10/97.
CALVERT J. A., MIMgt. Born 15/4/33. Commd 15/11/51. Wg Cdr 1/7/76. Retd ADMIN 3/4/79.
CALVERT L. G., MC. Born 25/6/23. Commd 4/2/48. Flt Lt 4/8/52. Retd RGT 29/3/59.
CALVERT R. A. Born 26/7/31. Commd 14/4/53. Sqn Ldr 1/7/61. Retd GD 26/7/69.
CALVERT R. D., BA. Born 12/2/47. Commd 21/1/66. Sqn Ldr 1/7/83. Retd GD 1/7/86.
CALVERT S. A. Born 3/2/70. Commd 28/3/91. Fg Offr 28/9/93. Retd ADMIN 15/12/96.
CALVERT S. E. Born 29/5/62. Commd 7/11/85. Flt Lt 4/12/90. Retd OPS SPT 29/5/00.
CAMBRIDGE F. W. J. Born 17/1/16. Commd 27/2/47. Flt Lt 27/8/51. Retd SEC 10/1/56.
CAMERON A. D. C. Born 25/8/56. Commd 27/1/77. Wg Cdr 1/7/95. Retd ADMIN 15/4/00.
CAMERON A. F., BSc. Born 10/3/50. Commd 29/8/72. Sqn Ldr 1/7/85. Retd GD 29/8/89.
CAMERON C. H. Born 13/2/24. Commd 16/5/57. Flt Lt 1/4/63. Retd GD 1/10/68.
CAMERON D. A. Born 18/8/14. Commd 10/3/45. Flt Lt 10/3/51. Retd SUP 20/6/64.
CAMERON D. F., BSc MB ChB MFOM DAvMed. Born 25/3/29. Commd 1/9/63. Wg Cdr 16/2/71. Retd MED 15/10/82.
CAMERON D. G., MIMgt. Born 16/3/26. Commd 20/1/45. Wg Cdr 1/1/71. Retd GD(G) 16/3/86.
CAMERON D. N. Born 29/7/34. Commd 9/4/53. Wg Cdr 1/7/79. Retd GD 1/8/85.
CAMERON J. J. C. Born 19/2/23. Commd 7/9/61. Flt Lt 7/9/66. Retd ENG 19/11/77.
CAMERON K. A., MB ChB MFCM DipSocMed. Born 4/4/29. Commd 1/1/62. Wg Cdr 9/11/66. Retd MED 7/12/75.
CAMERON M. J. Born 11/6/43. Commd 2/5/71. Sqn Ldr 1/7/85. Retd SY 18/12/93.
CAMERON S., AFC DPhysEd. Born 26/10/30. Commd 7/1/57. Sqn Ldr 1/7/67. Retd PE 31/7/75.
CAMMELL G. W. Born 11/5/23. Commd 3/9/51. Flt Lt 3/9/51. Retd GD 4/9/67.
CAMP A. J., AFC. Born 12/9/21. Commd 9/12/46. Flt Lt 26/5/55. Retd GD 1/4/62.
CAMP P. J., DFM. Born 13/11/16. Commd 25/8/40. Sqn Ldr 1/8/47. Retd GD 1/8/58.
CAMPBELL A. D. K. Born 8/6/41. Commd 18/12/62. Wg Cdr 1/7/84. Retd GD 8/6/96.
CAMPBELL C. Born 17/3/34. Commd 28/7/60. Sqn Ldr 1/1/70. Retd GD 1/1/73.
CAMPBELL C., FIMgt. Born 16/9/32. Commd 30/7/52. Wg Cdr 1/1/79. Retd GD 4/4/88.
CAMPBELL C. A., MB BS FRCS(Edin) MRCS LRCP. Born 15/1/42. Commd 15/10/62. Wg Cdr 3/1/80. Retd MED 31/12/83.
CAMPBELL C. C. W. Born 14/2/58. Commd 8/9/77. Flt Lt 8/3/83. Retd GD 16/2/95.
CAMPBELL C. D. Born 6/10/46. Commd 25/6/65. Sqn Ldr 1/1/76. Retd GD 6/10/84.
CAMPBELL C. H. Born 21/10/41. Commd 17/1/85. Sqn Ldr 1/1/93. Retd ENG 21/10/96.
CAMPBELL C. J. A. Born 17/12/60. Commd 28/9/89. Sqn Ldr 1/1/98. Retd ADMIN 1/1/01.
CAMPBELL C. T. Born 18/7/34. Commd 19/12/63. Wg Cdr 1/7/77. Retd ADMIN 15/9/84.
CAMPBELL D. Born 20/3/22. Commd 10/4/45. Fg Offr 10/4/46. Retd GD 20/3/55.
CAMPBELL D. Born 8/8/32. Commd 16/7/52. Flt Lt 12/12/57. Retd GD 8/10/70.
CAMPBELL D. A. Born 23/11/58. Commd 2/3/78. Sqn Ldr 1/1/94. Retd GD 1/9/97.
CAMPBELL D. H. Born 1/11/28. Commd 1/10/54. Flt Lt 4/1/56. Retd GD 12/8/80.
CAMPBELL D. M. Born 12/6/32. Commd 22/10/59. Flt Lt 28/7/65. Retd GD 12/6/70.
CAMPBELL E. C. Born 26/3/46. Commd 13/9/70. Flt Lt 13/3/75. Retd ENG 31/3/94.
CAMPBELL G. Born 2/12/19. Commd 31/12/42. Sqn Ldr 6/3/63. Retd EDN 28/6/66.
CAMPBELL G. F. Born 2/12/41. Commd 3/11/60. Sqn Ldr 1/1/75. Retd GD 2/12/78.
CAMPBELL H. D., DFM. Born 3/4/23. Commd 17/3/45. Flt Lt 12/7/54. Retd GD(G) 20/11/61.
CAMPBELL I. R., CB CBE AFC. Born 5/10/20. Commd 12/5/40. AVM 1/7/70. Retd GD 5/10/75.
CAMPBELL J. Born 23/2/36. Commd 20/12/73. Sqn Ldr 1/1/86. Retd GD(G) 28/12/89.
CAMPBELL J. A. Born 30/8/35. Commd 22/1/54. Flt Lt 22/7/59. Retd GD 30/9/84.
CAMPBELL J. R. Born 19/2/22. Commd 6/4/47. Flt Lt 26/5/55. Retd GD 1/1/66.
CAMPBELL J. T., BSc. Born 15/12/62. Commd 30/8/81. Flt Lt 15/10/85. Retd GD 7/2/96.
CAMPBELL K. A., CB MSc BSc CEng MRAeS. Born 3/5/36. Commd 25/9/54. AVM 1/7/85. Retd ENG 2/2/90.
CAMPBELL M., BSc CEng. Born 6/4/48. Commd 18/4/69. Sqn Ldr 1/7/83. Retd ENG 1/7/87.

CAMPBELL M. C. Born 24/10/54. Commd 22/5/75. Sqn Ldr 1/1/89. Retd GD(G) 24/10/92.
CAMPBELL M. R., MIMgt. Born 8/2/30. Commd 1/8/51. Wg Cdr 1/1/71. Retd SUP 31/3/77.
CAMPBELL N., MCIPS MCIT MILT MIMgt. Born 16/2/45. Commd 3/3/67. Sqn Ldr 1/7/76. Retd SUP 1/5/86.
CAMPBELL The Rev P. P., BD. Born 26/2/55. Commd 27/2/83. Retd 31/3/90 Sqn Ldr.
CAMPBELL R. D. Born 25/4/60. Commd 3/7/80. Flt Lt 3/1/87. Retd OPS SPT 25/4/98.
CAMPBELL R. I. Born 29/11/32. Commd 6/5/52. Wg Cdr 1/1/80. Retd GD 1/7/86.
CAMPBELL R. MCL. Born 24/12/41. Commd 24/3/61. Wg Cdr 1/1/90. Retd GD 24/12/96.
CAMPBELL R. S. Born 7/6/45. Commd 3/7/80. Sqn Ldr 1/7/91. Retd ENG 6/2/98.
CAMPBELL W. M. Born 20/8/47. Commd 2/8/68. Flt Lt 6/10/71. Retd GD 1/5/76.
CAMPBELL W. M. Born 5/7/44. Commd 25/6/65. Flt Lt 25/12/70. Retd GD 1/6/89.
CAMPBELL W. MC., AFC. Born 12/6/40. Commd 10/11/61. Sqn Ldr 1/1/88. Retd GD 15/12/92.
CAMPBELL-VOULLAIRE E. G., DFC. Born 10/6/12. Commd 14/9/34. Wg Cdr 1/10/46. Retd GD 15/4/52.
CAMPEY A., AFC. Born 22/10/23. Commd 20/5/44. Sqn Ldr 1/7/55. Retd GD 27/4/68.
CAMPIN C. G. Born 15/9/25. Commd 13/3/52. Flt Lt 13/3/56. Retd RGT 26/2/67.
CAMPING R. A., BSc. Born 21/9/44. Commd 14/9/65. Gp Capt 1/1/94. Retd ENG 18/9/98.
CAMPION A. J., DFC. Born 14/12/38. Commd 18/8/61. Flt Lt 18/8/66. Retd GD 28/7/72.
CAMPION G. E. Born 1/7/22. Commd 13/10/41. Sqn Offr 1/1/53. Retd SEC 3/7/56.
CAMPION N. J., BSc. Born 27/11/55. Commd 19/9/76. Flt Lt 15/10/78. Retd GD 15/7/89.
CAMPION P. Born 6/2/39. Commd 22/5/75. Sqn Ldr 1/7/90. Retd ADMIN 6/2/94.
CAMPION W. D., MBE. Born 12/3/22. Commd 2/10/58. Sqn Ldr 1/1/70. Retd ENG 12/3/78.
CAMPLING K. R. Born 6/2/45. Commd 16/8/68. Flt Lt 16/2/74. Retd GD 6/5/84.
CAMPODONIC B. P. Born 1/7/22. Commd 18/10/44. Flt Offr 1/3/52. Retd SEC 22/12/53.
CANAVAN G. R. Born 24/4/03. Commd 10/10/30. Flt Lt 1/4/36. Retd GD 30/7/39.
CANAVAN M. B. M., MA. Born 20/10/41. Commd 17/12/63. Wg Cdr 1/1/86. Retd GD 20/10/96.
CANAWAY J. F. Born 21/1/21. Commd 13/3/45. Flt Lt 12/3/51. Retd SEC 21/8/67.
CANDLISH E. G. J., MRIN MIMgt. Born 24/11/42. Commd 29/11/68. Sqn Ldr 1/7/84. Retd GD 24/11/00.
CANDY G. R. Born 17/8/22. Commd 3/12/59. Sqn Ldr 1/1/74. Retd ENG 17/8/77.
CANDY S. N. Born 5/4/21. Commd 21/7/55. Flt Lt 21/7/58. Retd GD 15/4/76.
CANE P. J. Born 13/6/51. Commd 11/5/89. Fg Off 11/5/89. Retd SY 2/1/93.
CANE R. Born 26/10/41. Commd 31/7/62. Flt Lt 31/1/65. Retd GD 3/4/73.
CANFER B. J. Born 1/12/46. Commd 21/1/66. Sqn Ldr 1/1/83. Retd GD 11/2/95.
CANN B. S. Born 12/5/20. Commd 8/7/43. Sqn Ldr 1/7/68. Retd ENG 24/4/73.
CANN M. L., MIMgt. Born 8/5/29. Commd 13/12/50. Wg Cdr 1/1/76. Retd SUP 8/5/84.
CANN M. R. Born 15/10/43. Commd 28/10/66. Flt Lt 28/4/72. Retd GD 31/1/76.
CANNELL F. G., BSc. Born 19/7/57. Commd 14/12/75. Flt Lt 15/10/79. Retd GD 15/7/90.
CANNELL J. M. B. Born 6/5/21. Commd 13/2/47. Wg Cdr 1/1/70. Retd SUP 6/5/76.
CANNIFORD B. J. Born 20/7/37. Commd 3/5/56. Flt Lt 28/3/63. Retd SEC 22/7/72.
CANNING E. J., MIMgt. Born 5/1/26. Commd 1/5/47. Flt Lt 28/2/66. Retd SUP 6/3/74.
CANNING J. J., DFC. Born 28/1/20. Commd 31/7/42. Sqn Ldr 1/1/54. Retd GD 1/5/71.
CANNING J. W. Born 8/8/35. Commd 31/7/56. Wg Cdr 1/7/77. Retd GD 16/4/89.
CANNING P. F. A. Born 24/3/39. Commd 13/12/60. Gp Capt 1/1/88. Retd ADMIN 31/8/93.
CANNOCK N. J. M., BSc. Born 3/1/55. Commd 6/7/80. Flt Lt 6/4/82Retd. Retd ENG 22/12/84.
CANNON B. O. Born 21/1/11. Commd 6/1/36. Sqn Ldr 1/6/43. Retd SUP 24/3/50 rtg Wg Cdr.
CANNON G. J., BSc. Born 18/11/61. Commd 21/1/82. Flt Lt 15/10/85. Retd GD 20/12/98.
CANNON G. T., AFC. Born 6/9/30. Commd 17/8/50. Wg Cdr 1/1/70. Retd GD 10/1/72.
CANNON M. R. Born 27/3/36. Commd 13/10/61. Wg Cdr 1/1/86. Retd ADMIN 4/4/90.
CANNON M. R., BEng. Born 9/11/54. Commd 16/9/73. Sqn Ldr 1/1/91. Retd SY 14/3/96.
CANNON P. Born 8/10/35. Commd 10/3/77. Flt Lt 10/3/81. Retd ENG 10/10/86.
CANNON S. J. Born 4/11/40. Commd 12/3/64. Flt Lt 12/9/70. Retd ENG 15/5/71.
CANT A. F Born 24/11/47. Commd 1/8/69. Sqn Ldr 1/1/88. Retd SUP 24/11/91.
CANT C. I. H. Born 1/2/43. Commd 28/7/64. Flt Lt. 28/1/67. Retd GD 3/10/78.
CANTON B. V., CEng MRAeS MIEE. Born 24/2/41. Commd 26/5/65. Sqn Ldr 1/7/77. Retd ENG 1/7/80.
CANTON E. J., DFC. Born 30/11/20. Commd 24/4/43. Flt Lt 4/12/52. Retd GD 1/8/68.
CANTON N. E., MBE DFC. Born 16/9/15. Commd 10/7/39. Sqn Ldr 1/8/47. Retd GD 10/1/58 rtg Wg Cdr.
CANTWELL E. W. Born 12/5/21. Commd 11/11/65. Flt Lt 11/11/70. Retd ENG 12/5/76.
CANTWELL P. J., BSc. Born 26/2/63. Commd 30/8/81. Flt Lt 15/10/85. Retd GD 14/3/97.
CAPE G. A. Born 15/10/32. Commd 31/1/62. Sqn Ldr 1/1/81. Retd GD 30/9/88.
CAPE N. J., OBE. Born 22/8/21. Commd 25/5/44. Wg Cdr 1/7/62. Retd GD 18/6/72.
CAPEWELL H. J. Born 3/4/27. Commd 13/2/52. Flt Lt 12/6/57. Retd GD 1/4/74.
CAPP C. H. Born 28/9/24. Commd 28/2/57. Flt Lt 28/2/63. Retd GD 28/9/74.
CAPP T. R., BSc. Born 23/2/34. Commd 8/8/65. Sqn Ldr 1/1/67. Retd GD 8/8/72.
CAPPER A. C., AFC. Born 25/11/23. Commd 8/10/45. Flt Lt 29/6/50. Retd GD 8/3/52.
CAPPUCCITTI E. G. N., MIMgt. Born 30/4/25. Commd 25/8/45. Wg Cdr 1/1/75. Retd GD(G) 30/4/80.
CAPSTICK R. A., BEM MCIPS MIMgt. Born 20/11/35. Commd 2/8/68. Wg Cdr 1/1/85. Retd SUP 1/8/90.
CARD D. E., CEng MRAeS MIEE MIMgt. Born 8/6/23. Commd 12/4/51. Wg Cdr 1/7/69. Retd ENG 29/9/77.
CARD D. R. Born 23/1/48. Commd 11/8/67. Flt Lt 11/2/73. Retd GD 16/8/77.

CARD J. Born 15/5/21. Commd 10/3/44. Flt Lt 10/9/47. Retd GD 15/5/54.
CARD R. W. F. Born 8/1/38. Commd 19/8/65. Flt Lt 19/8/67. Retd ADMIN 1/10/77. Reinstated 23/11/79. Sqn Ldr 1/7/84. Retd ADMIN 1/11/90.
CARD S. J. G. Born 21/10/34. Commd 13/12/55. Flt Lt 5/11/58. Retd GD 21/10/72.
CARDALE B. B. Born 3/6/16. Commd 17/11/41. Flt Offr 1/9/45. Retd SEC 25/8/65.
CARDEN D. R., AFC. Born 17/2/39. Commd 14/8/64. Wg Cdr 1/1/88. Retd GD 17/2/94.
CARDEN H. C. Born 4/9/59. Commd 26/11/81. Flt Lt 8/5/86. Retd SY 14/3/96.
CARDER A. M., BA. Born 28/5/31. Commd 21/1/54. Sqn Ldr 17/2/63. Retd ADMIN 2/1/77.
CARDER A. S. Born 5/4/33. Commd 17/1/52. Sqn Ldr 1/7/67. Retd GD 2/12/85.
CARDUS D. M. Born 22/1/47. Commd 1/4/66. Flt Lt 1/10/71. Retd GD 22/1/88.
CARDWELL J. B., MB ChB MRCGP DTM&H. Born 30/8/30. Commd 14/10/56. Wg Cdr 17/11/69 Retd MED 19/1/73.
CARDWELL J. S., MRCS LRCP. Born 24/1/25. Commd 1/5/52. Sqn Ldr 19/7/58. Retd MED 4/8/62.
CARDY D. K. J. Born 6/8/29. Commd 2/3/61. Flt Lt 2/3/67. Retd SY 6/8/87.
CARDY J. B., FInstPet MCIPS MIMgt. Born 25/3/35. Commd 7/7/55. Sqn Ldr 1/1/68. Retd SUP 11/6/85.
CARDY K. T. Born 24/3/33. Commd 3/5/68. Sqn Ldr 1/7/80. Retd ENG 3/4/85.
CARE J., DFC. Born 26/11/21. Commd 29/10/42. Sqn Ldr 1/1/52. Retd GD 1/9/72.
CARELESS R. J. Born 27/1/27. Commd 12/3/52. Flt Lt 12/12/57. Retd GD 21/11/66.
CAREY D. J. Born 24/6/45. Commd 18/3/73. Sqn Ldr 1/1/86. Retd GD 2/3/93.
CAREY D. K. Born 30/12/43. Commd 4/7/69. Sqn Ldr 1/7/78. Retd SUP 14/9/96.
CAREY F. R., CBE DFC** AFC DFM. Born 7/5/12. Commd 1/4/40. Gp Capt 1/7/56. Retd GD 2/6/60.
CAREY I. Born 25/9/43. Commd 1/11/79. Sqn Ldr 1/9/90. Retd ADMIN 25/9/98.
CAREY R. Born 14/4/48. Commd 20/12/73. Flt Lt 20/6/76. Retd GD 14/4/86.
CARFOOT B. G., OBE. Born 5/5/14. Commd 12/9/38. Wg Cdr 13/2/45. Retd SUP 22/3/46. rtg Gp Capt.
CARGILL J. Born 27/11/21. Commd 7/7/55. Sqn Ldr 1/7/66. Retd ENG 11/8/73.
CARGILL N. S., MIMgt. Born 30/8/38. Commd 14/5/57. Sqn Ldr 1/7/72. Retd GD(G) 30/8/76.
CARLE F. G., OBE. Born 14/9/10. Commd 28/8/36. Wg Cdr 1/7/48. Retd SUP 10/6/58.
CARLE G. S. Born 15/2/44. Commd 17/3/67. Sqn Ldr 1/1/83. Retd GD(G) 1/12/88.
CARLESS D. Born 16/8/46. Commd 24/11/67. Flt Lt 24/5/73. Retd GD 27/4/77.
CARLETON G. W., CB. Born 22/9/35. Commd 18/6/59. Plt Offr 24/12/59. Retd LGL 12/7/61. Re-entered 31/5/65. AVM 1/1/93. Retd LGL 22/9/97.
CARLEY K. J. Born 8/1/34. Commd 3/7/67. Wg Cdr 1/1/80. Retd SUP 1/10/87.
CARLEY T. E. Born 29/9/21. Commd 17/4/50. Flt Lt 23/10/56. Retd GD 24/11/66.
CARLING G. Born 5/8/54. Commd 10/5/90. Flt Lt 10/5/90. Retd ENG 1/8/93.
CARLISLE P. H. Born 17/5/44. Commd 14/6/63. Sqn Ldr 1/1/76. Retd GD 12/12/84.
CARLSON I. O. B. Born 26/1/12. Commd 15/7/41. Sqn Ldr 1/8/47. Retd RGT 26/1/57 rtg Wg Cdr.
CARLSON J. E. Born 18/3/36. Commd 28/1/58. Flt Lt 30/7/63. Retd GD 18/3/74.
CARLTON T. W. G., FIMgt FRAeS. Born 75/37. Commd 29/7/58. Air Cdre 1/7/86. Retd GD 8/5/88.
CARMAN R., MBE CEng MIEE MIMgt. Born 4/7/20. Commd 6/6/46. Sqn Ldr 1/7/59. Retd ENG 4/7/75.
CARMAN R. D. Born 24/10/44. Commd 24/8/71. Flt Lt 24/8/73. Retd GD(G) 24/8/83.
CARMEN T. R. E. Born 17/1/44. Commd 17/12/65. Sqn Ldr 1/7/75. Retd SUP 17/1/00.
CARMICHAEL A. G. Born 2/4/25. Commd 5/5/55. Sqn Ldr 1/1/64. Retd GD 1/4/74.
CARMICHAEL B. K., BSc. Born 13/9/45. Commd 27/4/69. Wg Cdr 1/7/90. Retd GD 14/9/96.
CARMICHAEL W. J., MCIPD. Born 19/2/50. Commd 7/3/76. Sqn Ldr 1/7/86. Retd ADMIN 7/3/93.
CARN P. E. Born 29/8/20. Commd 24/7/61. Flt Lt 27/4/66. Retd ENG 2/10/71.
CARNAZZA C. J. Born 26/5/59. Commd 28/6/79. Flt Lt 28/12/84. Retd GD 21/10/96.
CARNEGIE D. N. Born 4/7/44. Commd 17/5/63. Flt Lt 17/11/68. Retd GD 28/1/76.
CARNERIS L. Born 12/12/15. Commd 26/8/43. Flt Lt 26/2/47. Retd ENG 14/11/53.
CAROLAN A. J. Born 9/12/46. Commd 5/11/65. Flt Lt 20/7/71. Retd GD 9/12/84.
CARPENTER C. J., MSc BSc MCIPD MRAeS. Born 3/11/44. Commd 13/9/70. Sqn Ldr 13/3/79. Retd ADMIN 13/9/86.
CARPENTER D. R. Born 28/5/38. Commd 25/6/66. Sqn Ldr 1/1/83. Retd GD(G) 1/7/92.
CARPENTER D. W., BSc. Born 22/9/46. Commd 22/2/71. Flt Lt 22/11/72. Retd GD 7/2/88.
CARPENTER H. J. Born 27/6/34. Commd 19/11/52. Flt Lt 15/4/58. Retd GD 27/6/72.
CARPENTER J. M. V., DFC*. Born 9/4/21. Commd 1/5/39. Flt Lt 1/9/45. Retd GD 31/12/59 rtg Sqn Ldr.
CARPENTER R. R. T. Born 4/4/29. Commd 26/2/53. Sqn Ldr 1/7/67. Retd SUP 4/4/84. Reinstated 27/4/84. Sqn Ldr 24/7/67. Retd SUP 4/9/88.
CARPENTER R. ST. G., AFC. Born 8/11/35. Commd 23/9/81. Sqn Ldr 1/1/89. Retd GD 8/11/93.
CARPENTER T. H. Born 3/2/33. Commd 15/6/53. Flt Lt 17/9/58. Retd GD 3/1/85.
CARPENTER W. C. A. Born 13/2/26. Comm 30/7/59. Flt Lt 30/7/64. Retd ENG 1/6/76.
CARPMAEL R. M. Born 28/9/30. Commd 1/11/56. Sqn Ldr 1/1/72. Retd GD(G) 20/9/85.
CARR B. M., BSc. Born 12/9/32. Commd 2/2/55. Flt Lt 2/11/59. Retd SUP 2/9/71.
CARR C. L. J., BSc. Born 6/11/41. Commd 27/2/63. Flt Lt 17/5/66. Retd PI 19/8/77.
CARR C. P. Born 4/4/37. Commd 28/11/69. Flt Lt 4/5/72. Retd GD 1/1/75.
CARR D. R., MIMgt. Born 12/1/26. Commd 24/5/53. Sqn Ldr 1/1/63. Retd GD 12/1/84.
CARR E., MILT MCIPD. Born 15/4/46. Commd 8/12/83. Sqn Ldr 1/7/94. Retd SUP 14/3/96.

CARR E. W., DCAe. Born 12/11/25. Commd 3/8/45. Sqn Ldr 1/7/57. Retd ENG 12/11/63.
CARR I. R. Born 22/6/40. Commd 22/2/63. Flt Lt 22/8/68. Retd GD 30/10/78.
CARR J. H., MSc BSc (Eur Ing) CEng MIMechE. Born 3/9/62. Commd 14/10/84. Flt Lt 14/4/87. Retd ENG 14/10/00.
CARR J. V., BTech. Born 23/6/57. Commd 6/9/81. Sqn Ldr 1/7/96. Retd GD 1/7/99.
CARR M. C. Born 21/11/45. Commd 1/4/65. Sqn Ldr 1/7/84. Retd SUP 21/11/00.
CARR M. J. I. Born 28/4/36. Commd 21/4/54. Flt Lt 13/4/60. Retd GD 1/1/76.
CARR N. J., MB BS MRCPath. Born 11/1/60. Commd 8/10/84. Wg Cdr 22/9/97. Retd MED 8/10/00.
CARR P. G., BSc. Born 6/4/59. Commd 15/1/79. Flt Lt 15/4/82. Retd GD 24/11/98.
CARR P. H. Born 7/11/59. Commd 11/6/81. Sqn Ldr 1/7/91. Retd GD 4/1/98.
CARR P. S. Born 17/5/33. Commd 27/3/70. Sqn Ldr 1/1/80. Retd ENG 12/3/86.
CARR P. W., AFC. Born 30/3/25. Commd 4/9/46. Sqn Ldr 1/7/58. Retd GD 27/2/60.
CARR P. W., BA. Born 14/5/48. Commd 1/2/87. Flt Lt 1/2/92. Retd ADMIN 5/2/96.
CARR R. H., DFM. Born 15/9/16. Commd 23/12/42. Flt Lt 4/6/53. Retd GD(G) 19/9/71.
CARR S. E. Born 11/9/29. Commd 24/9/64. Flt Lt 24/9/69. Retd ENG 29/4/78.
CARR S. J. Born 9/6/42. Commd 4/7/69. Flt Lt 21/2/73. Retd GD 1/1/89.
CARR T. J. Born 4/2/41. Commd 17/7/62. Sqn Ldr 1/7/73. Retd ENG 2/3/79.
CARR W. Born 27/12/11. Commd 30/1/47. Fg Offr 30/1/47. Retd SUP 21/8/48.
CARR W. G., CBE. Born 12/11/16. Commd 30/8/45. A Cdre 1/7/69. Retd SUP 6/4/72.
CARR W. R., OBE FInstPet MIMgt. Born 25/5/29. Commd 24/9/59. Wg Cdr 1/7/76. Retd SUP 2/7/82.
CARR-GLYNN K. A. Born 4/3/42. Commd 5/3/65. Flt Lt 9/2/68. Retd GD 6/3/79.
CARR-WHITE C. I. Born 23/6/37. Commd 6/12/58. Sqn Ldr 1/1/70. Retd GD 11/12/77.
CARRAN R. J. Born 9/6/38. Commd 18/7/63. Flt Lt 1/4/66. Retd GD 10/6/75.
CARRELL P. C., CEng MIMgt MRAeS. Born 12/5/41. Commd 19/1/66. Sqn Ldr 1/7/75. Retd ENG 12/11/95.
CARREY R. A. J. Born 8/11/31. Commd 31/10/51. Flt Lt 31/7/57. Retd GD 8/11/69.
CARRINGTON C. J. M., BA. Born 16/9/41. Commd 30/7/63. Wg Cdr 1/7/83. Retd GD 31/12/91.
CARRINGTON D. Born 2/8/32. Commd 3/11/51. Flt Lt 3/5/56. Retd GD 2/8/70.
CARRINGTON D. J., BSc(Eng) CEng MRAeS ACGI. Born 21/4/48. Commd 20/9/66. Wg Cdr 1/1/88. Retd ENG 21/4/92.
CARRINGTON P. C. R. Born 7/7/18. Commd 19/7/46. Wg Cdr 1/7/62. Retd RGT 31/10/64.
CARRINGTON P. J., BSc. Born 16/1/34. Commd 16/12/56. Sqn Ldr 6/6/67. Retd EDN 30/8/72.
CARRINGTON W., CEng MRAeS MIMgt. Born 10/6/13. Commd 2/8/51. Sqn Ldr 1/7/62. Retd ENG 11/6/68.
CARROLL B., BSc MRAeS MIMgt. Born 22/2/31. Commd 6/2/52. Wg Cdr 1/7/68. Retd GD 22/9/84.
CARROLL B. P. Born 20/10/32. Commd 13/5/51. Flt Lt 4/1/57. Retd GD 15/9/73.
CARROLL D. Born 26/1/41. Commd 25/8/60. Flt Lt 25/11/66. Retd ADMIN 1/9/91.
CARROLL F. A., BEM. Born 29/3/43. Commd 11/10/84. Sqn Ldr 1/1/90. Retd SUP 21/8/93.
CARROLL M. J., MB ChB D AvMed. Born 16/1/53. Commd 23/1/74. Wg Cdr 15/8/90. Retd MED 31/7/91.
CARROLL M. J., BChD FDSRCS. Born 14/5/41. Commd 24/3/63. Sqn Ldr 20/3/70. Retd DEL 7/3/78.
CARROLL P. Born 9/7/59. Commd 7/8/87. Flt Lt 15/7/91. Retd ENG 9/7/97.
CARROLL P. A. Born 21/6/21. Commd 21/8/43. Sqn Ldr 1/7/66. Retd GD 11/12/73.
CARROLL P. J. Born 21/4/51. Commd 27/3/70. Flt Lt 27/9/75. Retd GD 21/4/89.
CARROLL P. T. J. Born 14/3/42. Commd 15/9/67. Wg Cdr 1/7/89. Retd GD 15/11/92.
CARROLL R. M., MSc BSc. Born 9/10/52. Commd 3/7/83. Flt Lt 1/5/78. Retd ADMIN 25/3/92.
CARROLL S. D. Born 7/9/68. Commd 28/7/88. Fg Offr 28/1/91. Retd SY 20/8/93.
CARROLL T. F. Born 5/8/23. Commd 3/9/44. Flt Lt 11/12/54. Retd GD(G) 12/11/64.
CARROLL W. H. Born 9/4/30. Commd 26/3/52. Flt Lt 31/7/57. Retd GD 1/4/76.
CARROTT I. C. Born 31/10/27. Commd 14/4/49. Sqn Ldr 1/7/61. Retd GD 24/2/79.
CARRUTHERS J. A., MA CEng MIEE. Born 6/7/37. Commd 8/7/59. Wg Cdr 1/7/79. Retd ENG 6/7/92.
CARRUTHERS J. B., BSc. Born 15/9/26. Commd 20/11/47. Wg Cdr 1/1/66. Retd GD 15/12/82.
CARRUTHERS R. Born 20/7/40. Commd 15/6/83. Flt Lt 15/6/87. Retd ADMIN 31/10/93.
CARSON A. V. Born 24/12/61. Commd 12/3/87. Sqn Ldr 1/7/97. Retd ENG 1/7/00.
CARSON G. P., BEd FIMgt DPhysEd. Born 13/2/46. Commd 11/8/69. Gp Capt 1/1/92. Retd ADMIN 8/9/95.
CARSON T. A., DFC Born 14/7/23. Commd 3/8/44. Flt Lt 13/12/48. Retd GD 5/10/61.
CARSTAIRS T., BEM. Born 31/3/37. Commd 1/6/72. Sqn Ldr 1/7/83. Retd ENG 1/7/92.
CARTER A. J. R. Born 9/2/45. Commd 24/4/64. Flt Lt 24/10/69. Retd GD 1/2/71.
CARTER A. M. Born 3/12/37. Commd 31/1/64. Wg Cdr 1/1/87. Retd GD 30/6/93.
CARTER A. R. Born 20/5/38. Commd 17/7/56. Sqn Ldr 1/7/68. Retd GD 20/5/76.
CARTER B. R. Born 11/11/32. Commd 27/1/55. Sqn Ldr 1/7/68. Retd GD 31/1/70.
CARTER C. G. Born 29/2/44. Commd 19/4/63. Flt Lt 19/10/68. Retd GD 14/9/96.
CARTER C. L., MHCIMA. Born 6/1/32. Commd 14/11/66. Sqn Ldr 1/1/79. Retd ADMIN 14/11/82.
CARTER C. N., BSc. Born 3/6/52. Commd 22/3/81. Flt Lt 22/9/84. Retd OPS SPT 6/3/99.
CARTER C. S. Born 25/9/44. Commd 11/1/79. Flt Lt 11/1/81. Retd GD 11/1/87.
CARTER D. E. Born 21/6/42. Commd 18/12/62. Flt Lt 18/6/65. Retd GD 29/12/73.
CARTER D. E. Born 14/2/41. Commd 11/6/60. Flt Lt 14/2/66. Retd GD 14/2/79.
CARTER D. J. Born 9/2/42. Commd 3/8/62. Flt Lt 3/2/68. Retd GD 9/2/80.
CARTER D. McG. Born 8/12/23. Commd 30/7/61. Sqn Ldr 1/1/73. Retd ADMIN 9/12/77.

CARTER E. M. A., MBA BA. Born 9/10/59. Commd 4/1/83. Sqn Ldr 1/7/97. Retd OPS SPT 1/10/99.
CARTER E. R. Born 29/8/27. Commd 11/4/57. Sqn Ldr 1/7/69. Retd GD 2/6/76.
CARTER G. H., AFC. Born 1/6/17. Commd 14/3/45. Flt Lt 29/6/50. Retd GD(G) 13/8/64.
CARTER G. R. Born 13/9/24. Commd 27/5/54. Flt Lt 27/5/60. Retd GD 29/1/72.
CARTER G. R. Born 31/5/44. Commd 2/2/68. Flt Lt 12/4/74. Retd SEC 10/10/83.
CARTER G. W. Born 28/6/22. Commd 16/4/52. Flt Lt 7/3/62. Retd SEC 15/5/69.
CARTER I. C. Born 17/2/32. Commd 25/2/63. Flt Lt 24/11/67. Retd GD(G) 17/2/89.
CARTER J. A. Born 16/11/36. Commd 12/9/63. Wg Cdr 1/1/78. Retd ADMIN 1/9/87
CARTER J. A. Born 28/11/24. Commd 16/4/44. Flt Lt 23/1/49. Retd GD 31/12/55.
CARTER J. A. Born 7/2/30. Commd 30/6/54. Flt Lt 5/10/60. Retd GD 2/12/68.
CARTER J. C. Born 10/7/59. Commd 29/8/77. APo. 29/8/77. Retd ENG 28/9/78.
CARTER J. D. Born 13/9/61. Commd 1/7/82. Sqn Ldr 1/1/93. Retd GD 13/9/99.
CARTER J. F. Born 10/9/35. Commd 31/7/59. Fg Offr 31/7/59. Retd GD 15/5/66.
CARTER J. G., MA CEng MIEE MRAeS. Born 30/9/35. Commd 25/9/54. Sqn Ldr 1/1/67. Retd ENG 30/9/73.
CARTER J. G. Born 28/9/28. Commd 4/6/52. Wg Cdr 1/1/75. Retd GD 1/1/82.
CARTER J. H., AFC. Born 29/4/34. Commd 8/4/53. Wg Cdr 1/7/78. Retd GD 1/10/84.
CARTER J. S. R. B. Born 25/1/29. Commd 20/6/63. Flt Lt 20/6/66. Retd GD 14/11/79.
CARTER J. V. E. P. Born 17/3/26. Commd 22/2/46. Wg Cdr 1/7/63. Retd GD 17/3/81.
CARTER J. W., DFM. Born 16/8/18. Commd 14/12/46. Flt Lt 7/6/51. Retd GD 1/1/54.
CARTER M. A. Born 11/8/58. Commd 21/4/77. Flt Lt 21/10/82. Retd GD 22/3/91.
CARTER N. T., OBE. Born 6/4/42. Commd 24/1/63. A Cdre 1/1/90. Retd SUP 1/10/94.
CARTER P. Born 29/12/33. Commd 13/12/55. Gp Capt 1/1/78. Retd GD 15/11/85.
CARTER P. R. Born 24/4/35. Commd 2/4/65. Flt Lt 4/11/70. Retd GD 30/1/73.
CARTER P. R. Born 16/9/46. Commd 18/11/66. Wg Cdr 1/7/88. Retd GD(G) 14/3/96.
CARTER R. Born 2/8/35. Commd 23/6/67. Sqn Ldr 1/7/80. Retd ENG 10/7/86.
CARTER R. A. C., CB DSO DFC MRAeS. Born 15/9/10. Commd 23/7/32. A Cdr 1/7/56. Retd GD 25/4/64.
CARTER R. F., MIMgt. Born 27/2/21. Commd 29/8/46. Wg Cdr 1/1/67. Retd SUP 27/2/76.
CARTER S. J., MB BS DA FFARCS. Born 5/4/32. Commd 16/6/57. Gp Capt 17/11/79. Retd MED 16/10/85.
CARTER T. F., MBE AFC. Born 5/9/31. Commd 2/7/52. Sqn Ldr 1/7/77. Retd GD 3/10/91.
CARTER V. W., IEng. Born 24/2/45. Commd 8/6/84. Flt Lt 8/6/88. Retd ENG 1/9/94.
CARTLICH S. A. Born 11/6/23. Commd 24/5/59. Flt Lt 24/9/64. Retd ENG 1/9/77.
CARTLIDGE A. W. F. Born 9/10/29. Commd 13/12/50. Flt Lt 13/12/55. Retd SUP 9/10/67.
CARTLIDGE J. K. Born 1/4/48. Commd 1/8/69. Flt Lt 1/2/75. Retd ENG 15/7/77.
CARTLIDGE P. F. Born 30/11/36. Commd 23/6/61. Fg Offr 23/6/63. Retd GD 30/4/69.
CARTMELL A. E., BA MA. Born 15/8/32. Commd 14/7/55. Wg Cdr 1/1/75. Retd EDN 5/1/82.
CARTNER E., DPhysEd. Born 3/12/39. Commd 26/5/64. Wg Cdr 1/7/90. Retd 11/8/93.
CARTWRIGHT A. A., MA. Born 9/1/28. Commd 23/2/50. Gp Capt 1/1/74. Retd ADMIN 20/9/80.
CARTWRIGHT A. W. P. Born 18/5/04. Commd 23/12/43. Flt Lt 23/6/47. Retd ENG 11/8/48.
CARTWRIGHT B. A. Born 30/1/32. Commd 28/7/67. Flt Lt 15/4/70. Retd GD 17/11/75. Reinstated 18/12/79. Retd GD 15/5/90.
CARTWRIGHT J., OBE. Born 22/4/23. Commd 9/7/43. Wg Cdr 1/1/63. Retd GD 27/3/76.
CARTWRIGHT J. Born 8/2/37. Commd 1/4/58. Flt Lt 8/10/63. Retd GD 26/6/69.
CARTWRIGHT J. B., BSc. Born 5/4/32. Commd 8/8/56. Sqn Ldr 22/7/64. Retd ADMIN 17/8/84.
CARTWRIGHT J. E. Born 16/2/38. Commd 5/11/70. Sqn Ldr 1/7/77. Retd GD(G) 16/2/93.
CARTWRIGHT R. J., MRIN MIMgt. Born 17/11/44. Commd 14/6/63. Wg Cdr 1/1/88. Retd GD 31/3/94.
CARTWRIGHT S. A., BA. Born 29/4/52. Commd 22/10/72. Flt Lt 22/7/76. Retd SUP 22/10/84.
CARTWRIGHT-TERRY I. S. Born 27/4/49. Commd 26/2/71. Flt Lt 26/2/74. Retd GD 14/3/97.
CARTY P. J. Born 26/11/25. Commd 3/5/46. Sqn Ldr 1/7/60. Retd GD 1/9/72.
CARUANA P. A. Born 5/10/53. Commd 2/7/81. Flt Lt 2/11/92. Retd SUP 8/6/93.
CARUS D. A., BSc. Born 14/10/51. Commd 13/9/70. Flt Lt 15/10/76. Retd ENG 22/1/80.
CARVELL C. J. Born 9/4/45. Commd 5/11/70. Sqn Ldr 1/1/88. Retd GD(G) 14/3/96.
CARVELL D. R., AFC. Born 28/10/46. Commd 3/8/68. Flt Lt 3/1/71. Retd GD 28/10/84.
CARVELL R. M., BA. Born 22/4/56. Commd 6/11/77. Flt Lt 6/2/80. Retd ADMIN 2/2/86.
CARVELLO P. E. Born 24/2/37. Commd 25/9/59. Flt Lt 28/7/65. Retd ENG 25/9/75.
CARVER H. D., FIMgt. Born 14/1/24. Commd 3/3/45. Gp Capt 1/1/74. Retd GD 29/4/78.
CARVER H. S., CBE LVO FIMgt. Born 30/9/28. Commd 5/4/50. A Cdre 1/7/77. Retd GD 1/3/84.
CARVER M. J. Born 24/8/38. Commd 28/4/65. Flt Lt 8/1/69. Retd GD 29/8/75.
CARVER N. J., AFC. Born 5/8/22. Commd 3/7/42. Gp Capt 1/7/62. Retd GD 31/8/63.
CARVOSSO A. F. Born 18/1/23. Commd 3/7/42. Wg Cdr 1/1/62. Retd GD 29/11/72.
CARVOSSO K. G. Born 1/11/46. Commd 29/4/71. Sqn Ldr 1/1/86. Retd GD 1/1/89.
CARWARDINE A. J. Born 5/3/16. Commd 28/6/45. Flt Lt 28/12/49. Retd SEC 5/3/65.
CASANO M. P., MC. Born 7/6/13. Commd 12/6/35. Flt Lt 1/6/45. Retd SEC 24/3/58. Sqn Ldr 1/6/42.
CASE G. A. Born 7/8/52. Commd 13/9/70. Sqn Ldr 1/7/85. Retd GD 7/8/90.
CASE R. A. Born 6/3/51. Commd 15/9/69. Flt Lt 13/3/76. Retd GD 5/10/88.
CASE V. L. Born 11/12/57. Commd 27/1/77. Flt Lt 4/6/83. Retd GD(G) 11/12/95.
CASE W. C., BA. Born 9/3/38. Commd 2/10/61. Sqn Ldr 14/8/68. Retd ADMIN 2/10/77.

CASEMENT P. R., DSO DFC* AFC. Born 22/5/21. Commd 21/7/40. Gp Capt 1/1/60. Retd GD 29/6/68.
CASEY B. J. Born 18/6/50. Commd 14/1/79. Fg Offr 14/1/79. Retd ADMIN 23/11/82.
CASEY D. M. Born 18/10/42. Commd 18/4/74. Wg Cdr 1/1/89. Retd GD 31/10/92.
CASEY H., BSc. Born 9/6/57. Commd 2/3/80. Flt Lt 2/6/83. Retd GD(G) 7/9/83.
CASEY L., MBE. Born 31/5/15. Commd 25/5/44. Sqn Ldr 1/1/64. Retd GD(G) 31/7/70.
CASEY R. F., DFC. Born 10/2/96. Commd 1/5/18. Fg Offr 1/5/18. Retd GD 1/4/27. Re-employed 30/8/39 to 14/4/41.
CASEY T. M. Born 8/5/39. Commd 25/6/66. Flt Lt 12/11/69. Retd GD 31/7/73.
CASEY W. M. Born 23/7/23. Commd 15/9/47. Flt Lt 25/11/53. Retd GD 23/7/66.
CASEY W. P. Born 3/4/48. Commd 23/3/67. Sqn Ldr 1/1/85. Retd GD(G) 3/4/92.
CASH P. B. Born 8/3/31. Commd 28/7/53. Wg Cdr 1/7/80. Retd GD. 8/3/86.
CASKIE J. Born 13/9/39. Commd 9/2/62. Flt Lt 9/8/67. Retd GD 17/10/77.
CASLEY V. G. S. Born 16/6/16. Commd 6/9/42. Sqn Ldr 1/1/55. Retd GD 1/7/58.
CASS A. C., MBE. Born 15/2/39. Commd 5/2/57. Sqn Ldr 1/1/91. Retd GD 15/2/94.
CASS J. M., BA. Born 25/3/61. Commd 27/3/83. Sqn Ldr 1/1/96. Retd GD 18/3/00.
CASS R. P., BSc CEng MIEE MIMechE MRAeS. Born 29/5/28. Commd 15/7/52. Wg Cdr 1/1/66. Retd ENG 29/5/83.
CASSEL J., OBE. Born 20/3/08. Commd 2/8/41. Wg Cdr 1/1/55. Retd ENG 20/3/60.
CASSELL D. B. Born 17/4/24. Commd 15/8/51. Flt Lt 28/3/57. Retd GD(G) 31/8/68. Re-instated 10/6/71 to 17/4/82.
CASSELS C. McI. Born 11/8/23. Commd 10/7/44. Sqn Ldr 1/7/53. Retd GD 11/8/66.
CASSELS J. R., DFC*. Born 2/4/22. Commd 21/7/43. Sqn Ldr 1/1/53. Retd GD 2/4/65.
CASSELS J. R. G. Born 10/9/41. Commd 28/4/61. Sqn Ldr 1/1/75. Retd GD 8/3/76.
CASSELY A. A. Born 2/3/23. Commd 21/4/67. Flt Lt 21/4/70. Retd GD(G) 2/7/48.
CASSELY I. H., BSc. Born 10/8/53. Commd 6/3/77. Flt Lt 6/3/93. Retd GD 8/3/93.
CASSIA S. H., MA. Born 1/5/57. Commd 5/9/76. Flt Lt 15/10/82. Retd ENG 25/4/86.
CASSIDY A. C., MA CEng MRAeS. Born 7/4/49. Commd 15/9/69. Sqn Ldr 1/7/80. Retd ENG 7/2/90. rtg Wg Cdr.
CASSIDY A. J. Born 6/3/48. Commd 21/1/66. Flt Lt 21/7/71. Retd GD 30/10/74.
CASSIDY E. M. Born 26/3/47. Commd 13/5/73. Flt Lt 13/11/74. Retd SEC 24/5/75.
CASSIDY The Rt Rev Mgr M.J.V. Born 15/2/37. Commd 3/9/68. Retd 11/4/92. Gp Capt.
CASSIDY P. J., MA BSc. Born 29/3/48. Commd 5/2/84. Sqn Ldr 1/7/91. Retd ADMIN 14/2/97.
CASSON D. S. Born 3/2/23. Commd 21/1/45. Flt Lt 7/12/49. Retd GD 10/6/59.
CASSON E. A., DMS. Born 9/3/32. Commd 22/1/55. Sqn Ldr 1/1/66. Retd GD 1/11/76.
CASTAGNOLA J., DSO DFC*. Born 20/4/22. Commd 13/12/43. Sqn Ldr 1/7/55. Retd GD 15/11/61.
CASTLE D. J. D. Born 11/12/32. Commd 21/5/52. Sqn Ldr 1/7/70. Retd GD 13/11/75.
CASTLE G., BA. Born 9/2/48. Commd 13/9/70. Gp Capt 1/1/93. Retd SY 2/6/95.
CASTLE K. A. Born 24/9/41. Commd 9/3/62. Flt Lt 9/9/67. Retd GD 26/11/76.
CASTLE L. L. G. Born 14/6/13. Commd 7/7/55. Flt Lt 7/7/58. Retd ENG 1/7/67.
CASTLE R. C., MILT MCIPD MIMgt. Born 3/6/49. Commd 22/5/70. Sqn Ldr 1/7/83. Retd SUP 3/6/87.
CASTLE R. G. Born 10/7/30. Commd 5/3/53. Flt Lt 5/9/57. Retd GD 31/3/70.
CASTLE T. B. Born 6/10/36. Commd 26/10/61. Flt Lt 4/8/66. Retd GD 6/10/74.
CASTLE. D. E. Born 8/7/36. Commd 25/1/63. Flt Lt 26/7/67. Retd GD 3/9/78.
CASTLING D. P., MB ChB. Born 3/12/56. Commd 17/7/80. Sqn Ldr 1/8/88. Retd MED 14/3/96.
CASTLING H. C. Born 19/3/22. Commd 25/9/46. Flt Lt 4/12/52. Retd SY 26/3/77.
CASTLING S. H. P., LLB. Born 20/11/53. Commd 17/9/72. Flt Lt 30/3/80. Retd LGL 1/9/83.
CASWELL A. G. Born 2/7/37. Commd 28/2/57. Flt Lt 21/8/63. Retd SY 2/7/92.
CATER G., CEng MIMechE. Born 27/12/34. Commd 7/12/34. Sqn Ldr 1/1/73. Retd ENG 9/8/86.
CATER J. H., AFC. Born 10/11/16. Commd 16/10/40. Sqn Ldr 1/7/58. Retd ENG 28/11/65.
CATER K. P., MBE CEng MRAeS. Born 3/1/20. Commd 15/4/43. Sqn Ldr 1/7/54. Retd ENG 16/7/73.
CATER M. J. G. Born 21/9/43. Commd 22/3/63. Flt Lt 17/3/71. Retd GD 27/11/76.
CATER R. L., MBE CEng MRAeS. Born 6/10/17. Commd 29/9/41. Sqn Ldr 1/1/54. Retd ENG 6/10/72.
CATER R. S. C., MA MRAeS. Born 10/11/11. Commd 4/4/39. Gp Capt 1/7/64. Retd EDN 8/8/70.
CATLIN B., MIMgt. Born 10/2/19. Commd 5/10/50. Sqn Ldr 1/7/61. Retd ENG 10/12/77.
CATLOW M. W. Born 2/7/41. Commd 14/8/64. Flt Lt 14/2/70. Retd GD 11/7/80.
CATON G. Born 2/1/49. Commd 29/11/68. Sqn Ldr 1/7/84. Retd GD 14/9/96.
CATON J. E. Born 22/1/17. Commd 9/9/43. Sqn Ldr 1/7/58. Retd SEC 22/1/66.
CATON T. G. C. Born 31/10/28. Commd 5/4/50. Flt Lt 27/2/55. Retd GD 31/10/83.
CATT D. G. Born 14/11/36. Commd 4/2/63. Flt Lt 4/2/63. Retd GD 14/11/86.
CATT R. D. Born 3/5/30. Commd 22/3/51. Flt Lt 22/3/57. Retd SEC 30/12/61.
CATT W. R. Born 28/12/39. Commd 9/11/84. Sqn Ldr 1/1/93. Retd GD 31/3/95.
CATTERSON D. G., BSc. Born 12/1/51. Commd 8/7/73. Sqn Ldr 1/1/86. Retd GD 14/9/96.
CATTLE A. P. Born 26/9/37. Commd 9/2/62. Sqn Ldr 1/7/89. Retd GD 26/9/97.
CATTLE F. H. P., AFC MIMgt. Born 29/6/26. Commd 14/6/46. Wg Cdr 1/1/66. Retd GD 23/2/79.
CATTLEY J. E. Born 7/2/21. Commd 23/4/46. Flt Lt 23/9/48. Retd GD 7/2/64.
CAULFIELD W., BA. Born 13/3/33. Commd 31/10/61. Sqn Ldr 9/3/66. Retd ADMIN 31/10/77.
CAUSER D. R., BSc ACGI. Born 7/12/50. Commd 24/3/74. Flt Lt 2/2/76. Retd GD 2/4/92.
CAUSTON A. C. A. Born 3/3/10. Commd 20/10/41. Wg Offr 1/7/56. Retd SEC 10/5/62.

CAUSTON M. J. Born 19/4/40. Commd 2/6/77. Flt Lt 2/6/81. Retd GD(G) 1/5/90. Reinstated 9/9/91. Flt Lt 11/10/82. Retd GD(G) 1/8/94.
CAVANAGH J. C., BSc MIMgt. Born 5/12/52. Commd 28/12/71. Sqn Ldr 1/7/84. Retd GD 5/12/90.
CAVANAGH J. P. Born 17/2/42. Commd 11/3/65. Sqn Ldr 15/2/83. Retd GD 31/3/94.
CAVE A. P. D., MB ChB FRCR DRCOG. Born 19/3/50. Commd 28/9/70. Wg Cdr 16/4/87. Retd MED 14/3/96.
CAVE G. S., BSc. Born 19/4/58. Commd 12/8/79. Sqn Ldr 1/7/95. Retd ADMIN 14/3/97.
CAVE L. W., MBE. Born 8/5/30. Commd 13/7/61. Sqn Ldr 1/1/71. Retd SUP 8/2/73.
CAVE R. A. Born 7/3/48. Commd 23/3/67. Flt Lt 23/9/72. Retd GD 7/3/86
CAVE T. S., BA. Born 2/8/58. Commd 22/3/81. Flt Lt 22/6/82. Retd GD 22/11/93.
CAVEY V. W. Born 25/3/28. Commd 22/9/55. Wg Cdr 1/7/74. Retd ADMIN 1/12/82.
CAWDERY P. H., MSc BSc. Born 18/10/43. Commd 30/9/63. Sqn Ldr 1/1/76. Retd ENG 18/10/81.
CAWDRON K. R. Born 26/1/35. Commd 5/7/53. Sqn Ldr 1/7/65. Retd GD 26/1/73.
CAWRSE R. C. Born 26/10/20. Commd 15/5/47. Sqn Ldr 1/1/58. Retd SEC 12/6/65.
CAWSEY A. W. Born 26/7/35. Commd 10/2/54. Flt Lt 10/8/59. Retd GD 2/1/73.
CAWSEY M. J. Born 20/9/25. Commd 27/1/55. Sqn Ldr 1/7/66. Retd GD 20/9/75.
CAWSEY M. J. Born 21/5/32. Commd 9/12/71. Sqn Ldr 1/1/82. Retd GD 1/8/87.
CAWTHORN P. F. Born 16/5/27. Commd 2/7/47. Flt Lt 19/11/53. Retd RGT 16/5/65.
CAWTHORNE C. A., DFM CEng MRAeS MIMgt. Born 22/2/24. Commd 11/5/44. Wg Cdr 1/1/67. Retd ENG 4/7/74.
CAYGILL M. N. Born 1/12/44. Commd 3/3/67. Gp Capt 1/7/86. Retd GD 23/4/90.
CEMM N. A., BSc. Born 20/8/60. Commd 12/2/80. Sqn Ldr 1/7/93. Retd GD 20/8/98.
CHABROWSKI H. B. Born 4/8/47. Commd 16/12/66. Flt Lt 16/6/73. Retd SUP 3/10/78.
CHACKSFIELD A. W. Born 4/8/47. Commd 1/8/69. Flt Lt 1/8/70. Retd RGT 18/10/74.
CHADDERTON A. P. Born 29/3/59. Commd 3/7/80. Flt Lt 3/1/86. Retd GD 29/3/97.
CHADWICK D. Born 5/10/39. Commd 10/11/61. Flt Lt 10/11/66. Retd GD 5/10/77.
CHADWICK D. B., CEng MIMechE. Born 12/4/43. Commd 22/8/71. Flt Lt 22/7/74. Retd ENG 5/4/90.
CHADWICK D. P. C. Born 12/9/46. Commd 19/1/66. Sqn Ldr 1/7/78. Retd SUP 9/7/90.
CHADWICK P. Born 8/8/25. Commd 6/7/45. Flt Lt 12/10/51. Retd GD 28/9/68.
CHADWICK P. J., AFC FIMgt MRAeS. Born 22/11/44. Commd 14/7/63. Wg Cdr 1/1/86. Retd GD 31/3/94.
CHAFER S. N., BA. Born 23/4/59. Commd 4/11/82. Flt Lt 4/5/88. Retd GD 5/7/98.
CHAFFE R. Born 29/12/31. Commd 2/1/64. Sqn Ldr 2/1/69. Retd EDN 24/10/74.
CHAFFEY W. K. T., CEng MRAeS. Born 13/2/39. Commd 30/1/70. Sqn Ldr 1/1/77. Retd ENG 13/2/94.
CHAIKIN D. Born 26/11/22. Commd 22/5/54. Flt Lt 27/5/54. Retd GD 26/11/77.
CHAKRAVERTY A. C., MB BS MChOrth FRCSEd. Born 5/9/36. Commd 1/7/91. Gp Capt 31/5/89. Retd MED 7/3/99.
CHALKLEY K. B., MBE. Born 19/1/45. Commd 15/7/66. Sqn Ldr 1/7/80. Retd GD 9/12/96.
CHALKLEY W. G. Born 18/10/22. Commd 19/8/65. Flt Lt 19/8/70. Retd GD 18/10/77.
CHALLANS P. G., BSc CEng MIEE. Born 17/4/46. Commd 31/3/70. Wg Cdr 1/1/91. Retd ENG 1/11/96.
CHALLEN J. M. Born 24/8/32. Commd 6/12/51. Flt Lt 27/3/57. Retd GD(G) 24/8/93.
CHALLINOR J. A., MVO DFM. Born 12/6/23. Commd 5/8/44. Sqn Ldr 1/1/68. Retd GD 12/6/78.
CHALLIS P., BSc. Born 5/12/47. Commd 6/10/69. Wg Cdr 1/1/88. Retd GD 27/6/94.
CHALMERS B. L. Born 23/3/21. Commd 15/5/52. Sqn Ldr 1/7/70. Retd SEC 1/1/75.
CHALMERS G. A., DFC DFM. Born 12/2/21. Commd 27/6/43. Flt Lt 27/12/46. Retd GD 12/8/54.
CHALMERS G. S. Born 27/11/21. Commd 24/4/42. Sqn Ldr 1/10/54. Retd GD 27/11/70.
CHALMERS I. G. C., MIMgt. Born 15/8/33. Commd 16/7/52. Wg Cdr 1/7/75. Retd GD 17/1/86.
CHALMERS I. MacD. Born 31/3/29. Commd 2/7/52. Flt Lt 22/8/59. Retd GD 1/9/86.
CHALMERS R. D. Born 13/4/36. Commd 3/11/77. Flt Lt 3/11/81. Retd ENG 1/1/90.
CHALONER C. R., AFC. Born 10/9/47. Commd 11/11/71. Flt Lt 16/8/74. Retd GD 10/9/85.
CHALONER J., DFM. Born 3/6/21. Commd 19/1/44. Flt Lt 19/7/47. Retd GD(G) 30/12/67.
CHAMBERLAIN D. B., BSc. Born 20/1/50. Commd 15/9/69. Sqn Ldr 1/1/84. Retd GD 20/1/88.
CHAMBERLAIN E. J. Born 29/3/27. Commd 28/6/51. Flt Lt 10/8/56. Retd GD 21/11/75.
CHAMBERLAIN K. G., DFC MCIPD. Born 24/3/21. Commd 3/9/42. Wg Cdr 1/7/64. Retd SEC 24/3/76.
CHAMBERLAIN N., AFC. Born 20/10/27. Commd 27/7/49. Sqn Ldr 1/1/62. Retd GD 28/9/76.
CHAMBERS B. R. G., BSc CEng MIMechE MRAeS. Born 23/1/43. Commd 25/11/68. Wg Cdr 1/1/88. Retd ENG 23/1/98.
CHAMBERS D. C. Born 7/5/21. Commd 26/9/57. Flt Lt 1/4/63. Retd ENG 9/12/71.
CHAMBERS H. Born 9/1/19. Commd 30/4/59. Sqn Ldr 15/3/68. Retd MED(SEC) 9/1/74.
CHAMBERS H. J. Born 1/9/30. Commd 5/12/51. Flt Lt 22/5/57. Retd GD 22/8/75.
CHAMBERS J. A. R. Born 10/1/23. Commd 28/5/43. Sqn Ldr 1/7/58. Retd SEC 10/1/73.
CHAMBERS P. J. Born 17/3/44. Commd 6/4/92. Sqn Ldr 1/1/86. Retd GD(G) 1/6/93.
CHAMBERS R. Born 15/12/28. Commd 19/1/66. Sqn Ldr 1/7/79. Retd ENG 15/12/83.
CHAMBERS R. C., AFC. Born 17/1/36. Commd 19/1/61. Sqn Ldr 1/7/67. Retd GD 17/1/69.
CHAMBERS S. P., BSc. Born 31/8/58. Commd 5/9/76. Sqn Ldr 1/1/88. Retd GD 31/8/96.
CHAMBERS S. P. Born 20/10/58. Commd 20/7/78. Flt Lt 20/1/84. Retd GD 2/4/92.
CHAMBRE A. C. F., BSc DipEl. Born 7/8/20. Commd 5/8/42. Wg Cdr 4/9/62. Retd EDN 1/6/65.
CHAMP M. L., MIMgt. Born 3/11/27. Commd 1/2/62. Sqn Ldr 1/7/77. Retd ENG 3/11/85.
CHAMP R. A. Born 8/2/41. Commd 24/2/67. Flt Lt 12/11/69. Retd GD(G) 8/2/96.
CHAMPION B. R., CEng MRAeS FINucE. Born 25/8/21. Commd 7/3/40. Sqn Ldr 1/7/56. Retd ENG 25/8/70.

CHAMPION J. H. Born 14/11/32. Commd 27/11/54. Sqn Ldr 1/1/68. Retd SUP 2/6/84.
CHAMPION J. L. Born 24/10/30. Commd 18/3/63. Flt Lt 18/3/63. Retd GD 18/3/71.
CHAMPION M. Born 23/9/48. Commd 3/5/68. Sqn Ldr 1/7/78. Retd GD 10/2/86.
CHAMPION M. C. Born 2/10/43. Commd 15/7/64. Sqn Ldr 1/1/74. Retd ENG 2/10/81.
CHAMPION R. S. Born 16/10/22. Commd 9/3/53. Flt Lt 9/3/57. Retd SEC 12/11/65.
CHAMPNEYS B., DFC. Born 5/9/20. Commd 28/2/42. Wg Cdr 1/5/57. Retd GD 7/4/64.
CHAMPNISS P. H., AFC. Born 1/2/33. Commd 6/4/54. Gp Capt 1/1/74. Retd GD 30/9/78.
CHANCE J. P., BSc CEng DipSoton MRAeS. Born 3/9/34. Commd 23/9/55. Wg Cdr 1/7/76. Retd ENG 10/5/86.
CHANDLER C. C. Born 18/3/47. Commd 2/8/68. Sqn Ldr 1/7/80. Retd GD 1/5/90.
CHANDLER D. H. M., OBE MIMgt. Born 15/5/23. Commd 10/2/45. Gp Capt 1/7/74. Retd GD 15/5/78.
CHANDLER D. N. Born 17/9/38. Commd 26/4/84. Flt Lt 26/4/88. Retd ENG 26/4/94.
CHANDLER H. A., MSc MB BS FRCPath MRCS(Eng) LRCP. Born 18/9/38. Commd 5/11/90. Gp Capt 30/6/91. Retd MED 14/9/96.
CHANDLER H. C. H. Born 1/9/14. Commd 3/2/45. Flt Lt 17/9/55. Retd SEC 14/5/62.
CHANDLER H. F. Born 14/10/24. Commd 17/11/44. Flt Lt 17/5/48. Retd GD 14/10/82.
CHANDLER H. T. Born 21/11/46. Commd 1/3/68. Flt Lt 1/3/71. Retd GD 1/5/90.
CHANDLER J. A. W. Born 19/10/32. Commd 28/6/51. Flt Lt 10/10/56. Retd GD(G) 19/10/82.
CHANDLER M. F. Born 31/10/34. Commd 21/10/66. Flt Lt 21/10/71. Retd GD 31/3/87.
CHANDLER N. R., MBE LLB. Born 25/10/58. Commd 17/8/80. Gp Capt 1/1/98. Retd SUP 1/5/01.
CHANDLER P. L., BSc. Born 10/11/53. Commd 27/7/75. Sqn Ldr 1/1/86. Retd GD 10/11/94.
CHANDLER P. M. Born 27/12/56. Commd 18/10/79. Flt Lt 8/10/83. Retd GD 1/1/91.
CHANDLER R. F. Born 19/10/19. Commd 1/5/42. Flt Lt 13/7/49. Retd GD 1/2/58.
CHANDLER R. J. Born 18/3/61. Commd 15/10/81. Flt Lt 18/4/87. Retd GD 17/10/92.
CHANDLER R. M. Born 26/9/45. Commd 2/4/65. Flt Lt 2/10/70. Retd GD 26/9/83.
CHANDLER R. W. Born 12/7/36. Commd 9/4/57. Sqn Ldr 1/7/69. Retd GD 1/12/75.
CHANEY P. D., MIMgt. Born 14/6/49. Commd 29/11/68. Sqn Ldr 1/7/84. Retd GD 14/3/96.
CHANNON J. H., MBE. Born 11/11/43. Commd 6/4/72. Wg Cdr 1/1/90. Retd GD 11/11/98.
CHANTLER A. H. Born 4/9/23. Commd 17/10/51. Flt Lt 24/7/55. Retd GD 31/2/62.
CHAPLE P. J. S. Born 20/3/21. Commd 22/4/42. Flt Lt 18/9/51. Retd GD(G) 17/10/66.
CHAPLIN A. J. Born 22/11/36. Commd 17/12/57. Gp Capt 1/7/84. Retd GD 22/11/91.
CHAPLIN J. H., DSO DFC BA. Born 18/6/11. Commd 3/6/34. Gp Capt 1/1/51. Retd GD 3/3/60 rtg A Cdre.
CHAPMAN A. Born 15/3/34. Commd 24/9/52. Flt Lt 1/4/58. Retd GD 4/7/85.
CHAPMAN A. D. Born 13/4/46. Commd 6/5/66. Flt Lt 8/3/72. Retd GD 13/4/01.
CHAPMAN A. R., BA. Born 24/10/67. Commd 12/11/89. Flt Lt 12/5/92. Retd GD 14/9/96.
CHAPMAN B., AEO. Born 16/8/19. Commd 9/2/43. Sqn Ldr 1/1/63. Retd SUP 16/10/70.
CHAPMAN C. H. Born 6/4/21. Commd 1/2/62. Sqn Ldr 1/1/72. Retd GD 31/5/75.
CHAPMAN D. Born 29/3/26. Commd 21/12/45. Sqn Ldr 1/4/56. Retd GD 30/3/68.
CHAPMAN D. J. W., ERD. Born 13/6/32. Commd 12/2/71. Sqn Ldr 5/12/71. Retd SUP 5/12/87.
CHAPMAN D. P. Born 30/7/59. Commd 8/11/90. Flt Lt 8/11/92. Retd ENG 25/6/96.
CHAPMAN D. R. Born 19/9/44. Commd 7/6/68. Flt Lt 7/12/73. Retd GD 26/2/84.
CHAPMAN D. S. J., CEng MIEE. Born 19/10/16. Commd 11/6/53. Sqn Ldr 1/7/61. Retd ENG 6/5/67.
CHAPMAN D. ST.J. Born 6/1/37. Commd 20/12/73. Sqn Ldr 1/1/83. Retd GD 6/1/94.
CHAPMAN E. G., CEng MIEE. Born 21/3/38. Commd 30/7/64. Sqn Ldr 1/7/73. Retd ENG 21/3/93.
CHAPMAN F. N. Born 19/3/29. Commd 26/5/60. Sqn Ldr 1/7/72. Retd ENG 9/8/79.
CHAPMAN F. W., BA. Born 18/11/58. Commd 11/9/77. Flt Lt 15/4/82. Retd GD 18/11/96.
CHAPMAN G. C. Born 3/11/32. Commd 31/5/51. Sqn Ldr 1/1/71. Retd GD 3/11/92.
CHAPMAN G. H. Born 16/11/35. Commd 12/7/63. Flt Lt 12/1/69. Retd GD 26/3/79.
CHAPMAN G. K. Born 19/7/15. Commd 19/8/44. Sqn Ldr 1/1/54. Retd RGT 29/9/57.
CHAPMAN I. J. Born 20/5/56. Commd 14/1/88. Flt Lt 29/6/90. Retd ENG 30/3/93.
CHAPMAN J. H., BSc. Born 19/3/16. Commd 3/12/42. Wg Cdr 1/7/62. Retd EDN 30/11/70.
CHAPMAN J. R., MIMgt. Born 16/8/21. Commd 4/9/43. Sqn Ldr 1/10/55. Retd GD 16/8/70.
CHAPMAN J. S. Born 27/10/42. Commd 6/11/64. Flt Lt 6/5/70. Retd GD 27/10/80.
CHAPMAN K., MPhil BA. Born 21/3/39. Commd 24/2/61. Gp Capt 7/7/84. Retd GD 21/3/94.
CHAPMAN N. S., OBE. Born 23/6/12. Commd 25/4/40. Wg Cdr 1/1/60. Retd SEC 23/6/67.
CHAPMAN P. E. Born 11/5/20. Commd 17/6/54. Flt Lt 1/6/57. Retd ENG 11/8/62.
CHAPMAN P. G. Born 12/1/35. Commd 15/7/53. Flt Lt 8/1/59. Retd GD 12/1/73.
CHAPMAN P. R. C. Born 31/7/44. Commd 19/4/63. Sqn Ldr 1/7/75. Retd GD 30/6/84.
CHAPMAN R., BSc. Born 5/10/22. Commd 10/7/42. Sqn Ldr 4/3/59. Retd EDN 18/3/64.
CHAPMAN R. C., DFC MRAeS. Born 10/5/18. Commd 21/2/43. Sqn Ldr 1/1/63. Retd GD 1/2/68.
CHAPMAN R. H. Born 21/12/33. Commd 25/2/53. Flt Lt 17/8/58. Retd GD 21/12/71.
CHAPMAN R. W., RMN RNT. Born 9/5/29. Commd 24/2/67. Fg Offr 24/2/69. Retd MED(T) 27/2/71.
CHAPMAN S. D. Born 13/3/35. Commd 9/7/57. Sqn Ldr 1/1/73. Retd GD 12/3/93.
CHAPMAN S. M., BA. Born 22/5/29. Commd 26/3/52. Sqn Ldr 1/7/63. Retd SEC 26/6/69.
CHAPMAN T. W., DFC MIMgt. Born 30/11/23. Commd 24/6/44. Sqn Ldr 1/1/60. Retd ENG 31/10/70.
CHAPMAN-ANDREWS D.F.J., BDS FDS RCS. Born 21/10/33. Commd 3/3/63. Gp Capt 15/12/80. Retd DEL 31/12/91.

CHAPPELL The Rev E. R., MA. Born 11/3/08. Retd 29/3/63 Wg Cdr.
CHAPPELL J. D. Born 4/6/38. Commd 10/11/61. Flt Lt 10/5/67. Retd GD 25/7/77.
CHAPPELL M. J. Born 9/6/37. Commd 4/7/57. Sqn Ldr 1/7/74. Retd ADMIN 9/6/89.
CHAPPELL P. D. W. Born 25/3/21. Commd 24/11/40. Sqn Ldr 1/1/53. Retd GD 30/8/61.
CHAPPELL R. Born 2/1/20. Commd 25/5/50. Sqn Ldr 1/1/68. Retd SUP 30/1/70.
CHAPPLE B. A. C., AFC. Born 30/10/41. Commd 18/6/63. Sqn Ldr 1/7/80. Retd GD 30/10/96.
CHAPPLE M. W. P., OBE AFC. Born 11/10/43. Commd 22/9/63. Wg Cdr 1/1/89. Retd GD 5/8/96.
CHAPPLE R., CB MB BS MFPHM MFOM MRCS MIMgt LRCP DPH. Born 2/5/34. Commd 6/11/60. AVM 1/1/92. Retd MED 1/7/94.
CHAPPLE R. C. Born 5/6/36. Commd 3/8/68. Sqn Ldr 1/1/90. Retd GD 1/1/92.
CHAPPLE S. C. Born 5/6/21. Commd 2/1/43. Flt Lt 25/8/46. Retd GD 29/7/54.
CHARLES G. Born 11/12/42. Commd 9/12/65. Flt Lt 9/6/72. Retd ENG 28/2/76.
CHARLES G. A., MBE. Born 16/10/19. Commd 17/9/43. Flt Lt 28/5/50. Retd GD 25/10/68 rtg Sqn Ldr.
CHARLES G. W. F., MRAeS. Born 14/4/29. Commd 26/7/50. Gp Capt 1/1/78. Retd GD 2/2/83.
CHARLES M. M., AFC. Born 27/10/41. Commd 28/4/61. Sqn Ldr 1/7/73. Retd GD 27/10/79.
CHARLES N. W., BSc. Born 11/6/56. Commd 15/9/74. Flt Lt 15/4/79. Retd GD 15/7/89.
CHARLESWORTH A. M., DFC. Born 9/8/22. Commd 6/7/41. Sqn Ldr 1/7/57. Retd GD 30/9/67.
CHARLESWORTH J. M., FIMgt. Born 29/4/31. Commd 24/1/52. Gp Capt 1/1/81. Retd GD 29/4/86.
CHARLESWORTH P. B., BSc. Born 24/9/56. Commd 28/9/80. Sqn Ldr 1/1/90. Retd ENG 28/9/96.
CHARLETT-GREEN J. A., MBE. Born 15/8/39. Commd 22/7/66. Wg Cdr 1/1/79. Retd ENG 15/8/94.
CHARLICK S. F. Born 10/2/29. Commd 24/1/52. Flt Lt 15/5/57. Retd GD 15/2/75.
CHARLTON A. R., BSc. Born 19/11/50. Commd 13/9/70. Sqn Ldr 1/7/83. Retd ENG 25/7/90.
CHARLTON B. J., CEng MIEE. Born 13/3/38. Commd 28/7/67. Wg Cdr 1/7/85. Retd ENG 13/3/93.
CHARLTON D. Born 8/5/49. Commd 8/5/86. Wg Cdr 1/7/96. Retd ADMIN 1/7/97.
CHARLTON E. M., BSc. Born 9/4/58. Commd 17/1/82. Flt Lt 17/4/82. Retd GD 28/10/95.
CHARLTON G. K., BSc. Born 24/3/47. Commd 1/9/70. Sqn Ldr 1/7/86. Retd GD 25/9/97.
CHARLTON J. P. Born 21/7/41. Commd 16/1/60. Sqn Ldr 1/1/77. Retd ENG 1/1/80.
CHARLTON M. C. Born 30/3/45. Commd 26/5/67. Wg Cdr 1/1/90. Retd ENG 14/9/96.
CHARLTON P. E., MC MIMgt. Born 13/4/25. Commd 20/9/48. Sqn Ldr 1/1/55. Retd SY 30/9/78.
CHARLTON R. A. Born 31/10/39. Commd 9/2/62. Flt Lt 9/8/67. Retd GD 31/10/77.
CHARLTON-BROWN T. H. Born 9/12/13. Commd 23/12/43. Sqn Ldr 1/7/56. Retd ENG 23/1/63.
CHARMAN C. A. Born 4/3/23. Commd 3/9/53. Flt Lt 22/5/57. Retd GD(G) 4/3/78.
CHARMAN J. W. Born 9/8/24. Commd 8/9/44. Flt Lt 8/3/48. Retd GD 9/8/62.
CHARMAN K. P. Born 9/9/24. Commd 6/2/44. Flt Lt 7/6/51. Retd GD 20/11/63.
CHARNLEY N. S., BSc. Born 24/5/62. Commd 14/9/80. Flt Lt 15/4/85. Retd GD 24/5/01.
CHARNOCK P. M. Born 27/7/59. Commd 26/9/90. Flt Lt 26/9/92. Retd ADMIN 26/9/98.
CHARTERS S. J. D. Born 2/6/12. Commd 18/2/42. Flt Lt 1/9/45. Retd ENG 2/6/61 rtg Sqn Ldr.
CHARTRES R. W., AFC. Born 12/5/23. Commd 30/9/42. Wg Cdr 1/7/66. Retd GD 2/8/68.
CHASE M. H. Born 14/8/16. Commd 1/8/46. Flt Lt 14/11/56. Retd SUP 14/8/73.
CHASE R. J. Born 2/6/34. Commd 2/7/52. Flt Lt 16/8/61. Retd GD 2/6/72.
CHASE S. W., BA FCIPD FBIFM FIMgt MInstAM. Born 22/5/55. Commd 16/9/73. Gp Capt 1/1/95. Retd ADMIN 10/7/97.
CHASEMORE R. A., QGM. Born 31/5/24. Commd 6/2/44. Sqn Ldr 1/1/78. Retd SY 30/9/81.
CHATER H. A., AFC. Born 6/4/17. Commd 3/5/37. Wg Cdr 1/7/55. Retd GD 6/4/72 rtg Gp Capt.
CHATFIELD F. H. Born 28/6/25. Commd 16/9/53. Flt Lt 16/9/60. Retd SEC 28/6/63.
CHATFIELD R. M., DFC. Born 20/10/19. Commd 14/10/40. Sqn Ldr 1/7/53. Retd GD 27/3/59.
CHATTAWAY A. M., BA. Born 24/7/61. Commd 30/10/83. Flt Lt 30/4/87. Retd SY 14/3/96.
CHATTAWAY C. Born 12/5/57. Commd 20/1/76. Flt Lt 16/4/84. Retd GD 1/4/92.
CHATTERTON M., LLB. Born 19/6/54. Commd 5/1/76. Sqn Ldr 1/1/88. Retd GD 13/2/97.
CHEADLE B. B. Born 11/10/32. Commd 12/9/63. Flt Lt 12/9/69. Retd SEC 1/11/72.
CHEAL T. Born 31/7/59. Commd 20/7/78. Sqn Ldr 1/1/91. Retd GD 31/7/97.
CHEATER B. J. Born 16/5/38. Commd 28/7/59. Sqn Ldr 1/7/68. Retd GD 16/5/76.
CHECKETTS Sir David., CVO. Born 23/8/30. Commd 31/8/48. Sqn Ldr 1/7/61. Retd GD 23/8/67.
CHEEK W. H., DFC. Born 2/9/12. Commd 11/2/43. Flt Lt 11/8/47. Retd SEC 4/9/67.
CHEESBROUGH J. Born 6/12/26. Commd 4/7/57. Flt Lt 4/1/62. Retd GD 4/4/81.
CHEESEBROUGH D. Born 24/10/37. Commd 1/10/60. Sqn Ldr 1/1/84. Retd GD 24/10/95.
CHEESEMAN H. J. R., MIMgt. Born 27/5/23. Commd 15/12/60. Sqn Ldr 1/1/74. Retd ENG 28/5/77.
CHEESEMAN R. J. Born 26/5/40. Commd 14/10/71. Sqn Ldr 14/10/79. Retd EDN 14/7/80.
CHEESEMAN S. B., BSc. Born 30/3/51. Commd 15/9/69. Sqn Ldr 1/1/84. Retd GD 30/3/89.
CHEESLEY A. T. Born 16/1/18. Commd 4/7/57. Flt Lt 1/8/60. Retd ENG 18/1/72.
CHEESMAN C. J., BSc CEng MIEE. Born 8/1/37. Commd 11/9/62. Gp Capt 1/7/89. Retd ENG 1/7/92.
CHEESMAN G. J. Born 4/1/45. Commd 23/5/64. Wg Cdr 1/7/85. Retd ADMIN 4/1/89.
CHEESMAN M., MIMgt. Born 17/1/37. Commd 23/7/58. Wg Cdr 1/1/77. Retd ENG 13/5/91.
CHEESMAN P. F. Born 8/2/36. Commd 6/8/60. Flt Lt 6/2/66. Retd GD 12/4/76.
CHEETHAM G. E. Born 23/7/53. Commd 2/2/84. Flt Lt 2/2/86. Retd ADMIN 2/2/92.
CHEETHAM J. D. Born 21/3/38. Commd 21/3/74. Flt Lt 21/3/77. Retd GD 22/9/90.

CHEETHAM J. L. Born 10/2/45. Commd 12/7/63. Flt Lt 12/1/69. Retd GD 26/8/76.
CHEETHAM P. D., BSc. Born 13/5/58. Commd 9/11/80. Flt Lt 9/2/82. Retd GD 9/11/96.
CHELMICK. E., MBE. Born 20/6/20. Commd 24/4/45. Wg Cdr 1/7/64. Retd SUP 6/4/68.
CHELU R. Born 13/7/54. Commd 12/7/79. Flt Lt 12/7/81. Retd GD 15/2/01.
CHERRY A. V. Born 5/12/32. Commd 9/4/52. Flt Lt 5/9/57. Retd GD 5/12/70.
CHERRY P. Born 14/9/21. Commd 17/12/43. Sqn Ldr 1/1/56. Retd GD 14/9/64.
CHERRY P. D., OBE DFC DFM. Born 21/4/19. Commd 31/12/41. Wg Cdr 1/1/60. Retd ENG 27/4/68 rtg Gp Capt.
CHERRY R. A., MBE BEng CEng MIEE MIMgt. Born 28/5/42. Commd 30/5/69. Sqn Ldr 1/1/77. Retd ENG 28/5/97.
CHESHER B. C. Born 17/11/24. Commd 26/1/45. Wg Cdr 1/7/76. Retd GD(G) 30/3/78.
CHESHIRE C. Born 27/7/25. Commd 19/1/45. Wg Cdr 1/7/64. Retd GD 23/3/69.
CHESHIRE R. C. Born 7/8/40. Commd 13/2/72. Flt Lt 13/11/73. Retd ENG 7/8/95.
CHESHIRE Sir John., KBE CB FRAeS. Born 4/9/42. Commd 17/12/63. ACM 11/3/97. Retd GD 4/9/00.
CHESNEY A., BSc. Born 15/11/56. Commd 2/9/73. Sqn Ldr 1/1/90. Retd SY 15/11/94.
CHESSALL M. P. Born 9/10/44. Commd 22/5/64. Flt Lt 22/11/69. Retd GD 21/12/76.
CHESSHIRE A., MB BS DA. Born 22/5/21. Commd 9/6/63. Wg Cdr 15/12/67. Retd MED 9/6/82.
CHESTERMAN W. G. Born 16/10/18. Commd 21/9/43. Wg Cdr 1/7/62. Retd SEC 1/5/73.
CHESWORTH G. A., CB OBE DFC. Born 4/6/30. Commd 1/10/53. AVM 1/1/81. Retd GD 3/6/84.
CHETWYND K. J., BSc CEng MIEE. Born 26/8/63. Commd 13/9/81. Flt Lt 15/10/87. Retd ENG 11/3/94.
CHEVERTON B. J. Born 20/12/36. Commd 28/4/61. Flt Lt 1/4/66. Retd GD 1/1/75.
CHEVIN R. W. Born 10/7/47. Commd 19/7/84. Sqn Ldr 1/7/93. Retd MED 14/3/96.
CHEW C. P., BA BArch. Born 19/8/56. Commd 6/9/81. Flt Lt 6/12/82. Retd GD 6/9/97.
CHEW J. W. T. Born 10/3/37. Commd 11/6/60. Fg Offr 11/6/63. Retd SEC 10/12/65.
CHEW S. R. Born 12/4/42. Commd 17/12/63. Flt Lt 17/6/66. Retd GD 13/4/79.
CHEYNE J. J. Born 27/5/44. Commd 8/6/62. Sqn Ldr 1/7/75. Retd GD 27/5/82.
CHICHESTER-CONSTABLE G. R., BSc. Born 25/11/55. Commd 28/9/80. Flt Lt 28/12/83. Retd ENG 15/7/88.
CHICK J. F. H. Born 9/1/29. Commd 13/12/50. Wg Cdr 1/7/70. Retd GD 9/1/84. rtg Gp Capt.
CHICK R. Born 19/3/32. Commd 15/8/51. Sqn Ldr 1/1/70. Retd GD 8/5/90.
CHICK S. D., BSc. Born 11/3/64. Commd 17/11/83. Flt Lt 15/1/88. Retd GD 15/7/97.
CHICKEN R. Born 26/8/10. Commd 6/9/40. Sqn Ldr 1/8/47. Retd SEC 7/9/59.
CHICKEN S. H., BSc. Born 17/8/60. Commd 4/8/78. Sqn Ldr 1/7/94. Retd ENG 23/1/98.
CHIGNALL G. N. V., MBE FIMgt. Born 24/3/20. Commd 13/11/42. Gp Capt 1/7/68. Retd SUP 4/5/74.
CHILCOTT C. J. M., BEM. Born 5/8/12. Commd 6/1/55. Sqn Ldr 1/7/64. Retd ENG 5/8/67.
CHILCOTT P. Born 4/12/09. Commd 25/4/42. Flt Lt 19/11/53. Retd GD(G) 2/1/62.
CHILD J. G. Born 14/12/49. Commd 26/10/62. Sqn Ldr 1/1/78. Retd GD 14/12/88.
CHILDS A. P. Born 21/10/45. Commd 26/5/67. Wg Cdr 1/7/91. Retd GD 21/10/00.
CHILDS I. J., 24/6/42. 17/12/64. Wg Cdr 1/7/89. Retd GD 24/6/97.
CHILDS L. A. Born 12/8/13. Commd 25/12/41. Sqn Ldr 1/7/51. Retd RGT 23/9/58.
CHILDS M., BSc. Born 22/1/31. Commd 21/10/54. Wg Cdr 1/7/75. Retd ENG 2/4/85.
CHILLAS I. S. Born 6/4/34. Commd 10/9/70. Sqn Ldr 1/7/83. Retd GD 6/4/94.
CHILLERY B. J. Born 13/6/40. Commd 18/8/66. Flt Lt 19/8/68. Retd GD(G) 30/6/90.
CHILTON T. B. Born 7/3/31. Commd 5/11/52. Flt Lt 24/3/58. Retd GD(G) 7/3/86.
CHILVERS A., BSc CEng MRAeS. Born 28/1/47. Commd 26/5/57. Sqn Ldr 1/7/81. Retd ENG 17/2/99.
CHILVERS H. S. Born 10/10/37. Commd 6/7/62. Flt Lt 1/4/66. Retd GD 11/10/91.
CHIMES B. V., BSc. Born 12/7/56. Commd 15/10/78. Sqn Ldr 1/7/91. Retd GD 14/3/96.
CHINERY M. A. Born 15/12/61. Commd 8/9/83. Flt Lt 8/3/90. Retd OPS SPT 15/12/99.
CHINN C. W., BTech. Born 9/7/49. Commd 23/9/68. Sqn Ldr 1/7/85. Retd ENG 1/7/88.
CHINN D. Born 10/9/49. Commd 4/7/69. Flt Lt 4/7/74. Retd GD 1/4/77.
CHINNERY H. M., MVO AFC. Born 10/1/23. Commd 5/9/42. Gp Capt 1/7/63. Retd GD 6/3/65.
CHIPP M. J. Born 28/6/48. Commd 16/8/68. Sqn Ldr 1/1/85. Retd GD 1/1/88.
CHIPPINGTON C. J., BSc. Born 16/12/43. Commd 15/7/65. Sqn Ldr 1/1/77. Retd ENG 16/12/81.
CHIPPINGTON D. W. B., MBE. Born 7/2/32. Commd 13/6/60. Gp Captain 1/7/78. Retd GD(G) 7/2/87.
CHIPPS B. G. Born 21/11/48. Commd 24/7/81. Flt Lt 24/7/83. Retd GD(ENG) 18/8/88.
CHISHOLM C. G. Born 5/12/32. Commd 28/3/63. Sqn Ldr 1/7/80. Retd GD(AEO) 5/12/87.
CHISHOLM I. M., MCIPD. Born 27/5/40. Commd 26/5/61. Sqn Ldr 1/7/83. Retd GD 25/4/94.
CHISHOLM J., DFC. Born 25/4/23. Commd 17/6/44. Flt Lt 17/6/50. Retd SEC 5/10/58.
CHISLETT C. Born 14/7/60. Commd 5/4/79. Fg Offr 5/10/81. Retd GD(G) 3/7/85.
CHISLETT P. J. A., CBE. Born 31/10/32. Commd 6/12/54. Air Cdre 1/1/85. Retd GD(G) 31/10/87.
CHISWICK D. H. Born 20/7/33. Commd 29/12/51. Flt Lt 22/5/57. Retd GD 20/7/76.
CHIVERS F. A. E., DipEE. Born 28/1/23. Commd 21/10/65. Sqn Ldr 1/1/75. Retd ENG 28/1/83.
CHIVERS J. Born 10/12/32. Commd 28/2/57. Flt Lt 28/8/61. Retd GD 30/4/84.
CHIVERS R. A. Born 17/4/48. Commd 28/2/69. Flt Lt 4/5/72. Retd GD 28/1/96.
CHIVERS T. A., MA. Born 7/9/33. Commd 14/2/66. Flt Lt 14/2/66. Retd ADMIN 4/4/85.
CHO-YOUNG C., DipSoton MSc CEng FIMgt FRAeS MIEE AFIMA. Born 9/5/45. Commd 19/8/71. Gp Capt 1/7/91. Retd ADMIN 14/3/96.
CHOLERTON P.W., BSc. Born 13/10/49. Commd 26/2/71. Flt Lt 26/5/76. Retd ENG 13/10/87.
CHORLEY A. A., AIIP. Born 1/7/18. Commd 2/10/58. Sqn Ldr 1/1/69. Retd ENG 1/7/73.

CHORLTON I., MB BS MRCPath DCP. Born 31/7/37. Commd 27/8/62. Wg Cdr 22/8/75. Retd MED 27/8/78.
CHOTHIA G. M. Born 31/1/44. Commd 28/7/67. Wg Cdr 1/7/96. Retd OPS SPT 10/4/98.
CHOWN B. A. J. Born 1/5/43. Commd 7/7/67. Sqn Ldr 1/1/80. Retd GD 3/1/83.
CHOWN J. F., BEM. Born 14/11/32. Commd 14/3/52. Flt Lt 14/11/75. Retd PI 1/10/81.
CHOY E. Born 22/8/23. Commd 15/10/43. Flt Lt 15/10/45. Retd GD 17/9/73.
CHRISP C. R., CEng MRAeS. Born 9/3/24. Commd 21/10/63. Sqn Ldr 10/2/67. Retd EDN 21/10/79.
CHRISPIN D. S. Born 30/10/34. Commd 31/12/52. Sqn Ldr 1/7/66. Retd GD 30/10/72.
CHRISTIAN D. A. Born 7/6/35. Commd 10/4/56. Flt Lt 29/4/59. Retd GD 7/6/73.
CHRISTIAN D. A. Born 31/8/26. Commd 27/4/59. Flt Lt 15/2/65. Retd SEC 9/12/71.
CHRISTIE A., BSc Born 14/6/30. Commd 11/10/52. Flt Lt 1/6/57. Retd ENG 4/9/63.
CHRISTIE A. M., AFC MRAeS. Born 20/10/28. Commd 12/12/51. Gp Capt 1/1/77. Retd GD 20/10/83.
CHRISTIE C. M., FIMgt. Born 3/5/32. Commd 2/7/52. Gp Capt 1/1/82. Retd GD 3/9/87.
CHRISTIE D. Born 20/4/36. Commd 22/10/54. Flt Lt 5/10/60. Retd GD 20/4/74.
CHRISTIE D. D., CBE AFC. Born 17/12/07. Commd 19/5/30. Gp Capt 1/7/47. Retd GD 1/1/57.
CHRISTIE G., BSc. Born 26/1/43. Commd 27/3/80. Flt Lt 27/3/82. Retd ENG 27/3/88.
CHRISTIE J. L., BSc MB ChB MRCPath DCP DMJ. Born 13/12/39. Commd 3/10/66. Wg Cdr 15/10/78. Retd MED 3/10/82.
CHRISTIE J. McL., MSc BSc. Born 17/5/42. Commd 30/8/66. Sqn Ldr 28/2/74. Retd ADMIN 10/2/90.
CHRISTIE M. R. Born 10/11/37. Commd 18/4/74. Sqn Ldr 1/7/85. Retd GD 1/10/95.
CHRISTIE N. G. Born 25/9/47. Commd 14/7/66. Flt Lt 4/5/72. Retd GD 25/9/85.
CHRISTIE S. G., MSc BSc. Born 10/12/49. Commd 15/9/69. Sqn Ldr 1/7/81. Retd ENG 10/3/88.
CHRISTIE S. J. Born 7/5/47. Commd 6/5/83. Sqn Ldr 1/7/91. Retd ADMIN 1/12/00.
CHRISTIE-MILLER I. R. Born 4/5/42. Commd 18/12/62. Flt Lt 18/6/65. Retd GD 24/11/77.
CHRISTISON J. D., MBE. Born 21/8/33. Commd 2/7/52. Sqn Ldr 1/7/80. Retd GD 21/8/93.
CHRISTMAS D. F. Born 5/4/31. Commd 28/6/51. Flt Lt 22/5/77. Retd GD 3/7/77.
CHRISTY M. G. Born 24/7/43. Commd 28/7/64. Flt Lt 26/7/67. Retd GD 24/7/88.
CHRISTY M. P., BSc. Born 2/5/60. Commd 28/1/82. Sqn Ldr 1/1/95. Retd GD 2/5/98.
CHUBB A. B., BSc. Born 3/2/81. Commd 19/2/73. Sqn Ldr 1/7/85. Retd GD 19/2/89.
CHURCH F. W., MBE. Born 18/1/17. Commd 11/3/43. Sqn Ldr 1/7/54. Retd ENG 18/1/74.
CHURCH J. E. H. Born 2/11/24. Commd 15/9/60. Sqn Ldr 1/1/72. Retd ENG 2/11/79.
CHURCH J. M., BA. Born 12/9/33. Commd 21/11/56. Sqn Ldr 1/7/67. Retd SEC 21/11/72.
CHURCHER C. F. S., MBE CEng MRAeS. Born 12/8/18. Commd 19/8/42. Sqn Ldr 1/1/54. Retd ENG 12/8/76.
CHURCHER D. A. Born 24/4/25. Commd 24/5/44. Flt Lt 4/12/52. Retd GD 28/7/66.
CHURCHER L. C. Born 14/10/20. Commd 2/11/44. Flt Lt 2/7/53. Retd GD 20/5/75.
CHURCHER R. G., DSO MVO DFC*. Born 9/5/22. Commd 29/5/41. Gp Capt 1/1/70. Retd GD 31/3/77.
CHURCHER T. F. C. Born 12/2/20. Commd 4/4/38. Sqn Ldr 1/8/47. Retd GD 12/2/63.
CHURCHER W. J. Born 25/2/27. Commd 19/1/49. Wg Cdr 1/7/76. Retd RGT 7/4/79.
CHURCHILL A. W. Born 23/12/38. Commd 2/5/68. Flt Lt 10/2/74. Retd GD(G) 10/2/80.
CHURCHILL E. J., AFC. Born 20/4/21. Commd 27/9/43. Sqn Ldr 1/4/55. Retd GD 20/4/64.
CHURCHILL J. H., BA MRAeS. Born 25/12/40. Commd 10/11/61. Gp Capt 1/7/88. Retd GD(G) 2/4/93.
CHURCHILL P. S. Born 11/11/59. Commd 5/4/79. Flt Lt 5/10/84. Retd GD 27/6/88.
CHURCHMAN S. C. Born 25/12/30. Commd 19/6/70. Sqn Ldr 1/1/80. Retd ADMIN 2/6/84.
CHURCHWARD A. J. Born 30/6/14. Commd 13/5/43. Sqn Ldr 1/1/55. Retd ENG 3/7/63.
CHURMS T. G. E., BSc DUS CEng MIEE MInstP MRAeS. Born 1/1/31. Commd 3/8/55. Wg Cdr 17/2/73. Retd ADMIN 30/9/76.
CLACK A. S. A. Born 9/1/39. Commd 2/1/70. Flt Lt 2/1/72. Retd GD 2/10/80.
CLACK S. B. Born 13/3/20. Commd 16/11/61. Flt Lt 16/11/67. Retd ENG 3/8/68.
CLACKETT M. R. Born 23/11/47. Commd 8/9/77. Sqn Ldr 1/1/86. Retd ENG 14/6/88.
CLAMP W. E. Born 22/3/36. Commd 3/12/54. Flt Lt 3/6/60. Retd GD 22/3/91.
CLAMPITT C. H. J. Born 17/9/04. Commd 24/4/41. Flt Lt 1/9/45. Retd ENG 17/9/59 rtg Sqn Ldr.
CLANCY L. J., BSc MRAeS DCAe. Born 15/3/29. Commd 22/8/51. Sqn Ldr 1/4/61. Retd EDN 22/8/67.
CLAPHAM J. R., CEng MRAeS. Born 8/2/19. Commd 27/4/44. Sqn Ldr 1/10/55. Retd ENG 8/2/74.
CLAPP B. D., BA. Born 3/6/45. Commd 3/8/66. Flt Lt 3/12/67. Retd GD 5/3/75.
CLAPPERTON W. T. Born 17/9/21. Commd 31/7/58. Sqn Ldr 1/1/69. Retd ENG 17/8/73.
CLARE A. J., MIMgt. Born 18/11/45. Commd 11/11/65. Wg Cdr 1/1/96. Retd OPS SPT 18/11/00.
CLARE B. G. Born 2/1/21. Commd 2/1/56. Flt Lt 22/5/57. Retd SEC 2/10/74.
CLARE D., DFC. Born 6/4/20. Commd 16/8/41. Gp Capt 1/1/63. Retd GD 25/6/74.
CLARE H. R. Born 23/5/21. Commd 29/10/43. Flt Lt 19/11/53. Retd GD 11/5/68.
CLARIDGE G. J. B., CBE. Born 23/2/30. Commd 1/11/50. ACdre 1/1/79. Retd GD 27/2/84.
CLARIDGE J. G., DFC AFC. Born 13/5/20. Commd 28/8/43. Wg Cdr 1/1/59. Retd GD 26/3/59.
CLARIDGE P. G., BSc CEng MIEE. Born 23/6/35. Commd 10/10/58. Sqn Ldr 10/7/68. Retd ADMIN 23/6/93.
CLARIDGE R. V. Born 26/11/30. Commd 27/2/52. Flt Lt 7/3/62. Retd GD 23/6/69.
CLARK A. Born 5/12/43. Commd 8/1/76. Sqn Ldr 1/1/87. Retd ADMIN 5/12/98.
CLARK A. A., BSc CEng MRAeS ACGI. Born 7/9/37. Commd 2/10/58. Sqn Ldr 1/7/70. Retd GD 7/9/75.
CLARK A. B., MIMgt ACIS. Born 30/9/36. Commd 12/7/62. Wg Cdr 1/1/80. Retd ADMIN 8/12/87.
CLARK A. J. C. Born 17/3/29. Commd 10/12/52. Flt Lt 5/5/58. Retd GD 15/7/68.

CLARK A. M., BA. Born 19/12/49. Commd 4/7/69. Flt Lt 18/10/75. Retd ADMIN 17/12/87.
CLARK A. R. Born 18/9/42. Commd 28/7/64. Flt Lt 28/1/76. Retd GD 18/9/80.
CLARK B. E., MBE. Born 19/3/39. Commd 27/8/64. Sqn Ldr 1/1/76. Retd PRT 1/1/79.
CLARK B. J., BSc. Born 27/8/62. Commd 1/7/93. Sqn Ldr 1/7/93. Retd SUP 27/8/00.
CLARK B. S. Born 2/10/19. Commd 9/7/53. Sqn Ldr 1/1/62. Retd ENG 30/11/73.
CLARK B. S. Born 6/9/38. Commd 14/8/56. Flt Lt 25/1/71. Retd GD 25/1/79.
CLARK C. D. Born 5/7/17. Commd 29/5/47. Flt Lt 29/11/51. Retd SUP 19/8/60.
CLARK C. E. Born 27/2/25. Commd 29/12/51. Flt Lt 26/2/58. Retd GD 11/1/66.
CLARK C. F., MSc MILT. Born 10/11/46. Commd 9/2/66. Sqn Ldr 1/7/83. Retd SUP 14/3/97.
CLARK C. J. J., BEM. Born 1/9/39. Commd 7/1/71. Flt Lt 7/1/73. Retd ADMIN 1/10/77.
CLARK C. P. Born 1/5/43. Commd 6/4/62. Flt Lt 6/10/67. Retd GD 21/2/72.
CLARK C. W. Born 2/1/21. Commd 15/9/44. Wg Cdr 1/1/61. Retd GD 2/1/76.
CLARK D., MSc BA. Born 13/12/43. Commd 12/8/79. Sqn Ldr 1/1/88. Retd ADMIN 1/11/97.
CLARK D. H. Born 25/9/40. Commd 26/5/61. Sqn Ldr 1/7/79. Retd GD 25/9/95.
CLARK The Rev D. H. G. Born 17/1/26. Commd 13/2/61. Retd 15/9/82. rtg Gp Capt.
CLARK D. J. Born 27/12/56. Commd 13/2/77. Sqn Ldr 1/1/90. Retd SUP 14/3/97.
CLARK D. M. Born 10/2/48. Commd 3/5/68. Sqn Ldr 1/7/79. Retd GD 26/4/86.
CLARK D. P. C. V., BA. Born 7/2/62. Commd 2/9/84. WgCdr 1/1/97. Retd ADMIN 2/9/00.
CLARK D. R. Born 15/7/28. Commd 30/7/59. Sqn Ldr 1/7/73. Retd SY 30/7/77.
CLARK D. S. J. Born 31/7/22. Commd 2/4/43. Flt Lt 2/10/46. Retd GD 16/11/61.
CLARK E., BEM. Born 13/4/18. Commd 20/10/55. Sqn Ldr 1/1/70. Retd ENG 1/6/72.
CLARK E., BA. Born 9/2/50. Commd 15/9/69. Flt Lt 15/4/77. Retd SY(RGT) 9/8/88.
CLARK E. G., MBE. Born 18/11/22. Commd 7/4/44. Sqn Ldr 1/7/68. Retd SUP 18/11/77.
CLARK E. S. C. Born 9/2/23. Commd 12/3/53. Fg Offr 12/3/55. Retd SEC 9/11/57.
CLARK F. D. G., CBE BA. Born 2/11/29. Commd 1/7/53. AVM 1/1/80. Retd GD 10/11/84.
CLARK F. J. Born 27/9/34. Commd 27/1/67. Sqn Ldr 1/1/75. Retd SUP 27/9/92.
CLARK G. Born 15/9/39. Commd 10/6/66. Flt Lt 10/12/71. Retd GD 14/5/82.
CLARK G. Born 28/11/45. Commd 19/6/64. Flt Lt 19/12/69. Retd GD 3/12/98.
CLARK G. F. Born 31/1/24. Commd 7/4/44. Wg Cdr 1/1/61. Retd GD 31/1/79.
CLARK G. J., AFC. Born 26/4/23. Commd 26/5/45. Sqn Ldr 1/7/65. Retd GD 26/4/78.
CLARK G. S., IEng MCIT MILT MRAeS MHSM. Born 25/2/45. Commd 26/3/72. Wg Cdr 1/1/90. Retd SUP 25/2/00.
CLARK H. G., MBE. Born 5/6/25. Commd 6/7/45. Wg Cdr 1/7/67. Retd GD 4/10/75.
CLARK H. J., BA. Born 24/11/42. Commd 27/2/75. Flt Lt 27/2/77. Retd GD 28/11/87.
CLARK I. F., LLB. Born 11/11/44. Commd 15/7/66. Flt Lt 15/1/69. Retd GD 11/11/82.
CLARK I. G. Born 5/10/21. Commd 22/7/66. Flt Lt 22/7/69. Retd SEC 6/2/76.
CLARK J. Born 23/5/21. Commd 27/1/44. Sqn Ldr 1/1/63. Retd ENG 28/4/73.
CLARK J. B. Born 29/5/53. Commd 22/5/75. Flt Lt 22/11/80. Retd GD 18/9/93.
CLARK J. C. Born 28/8/38. Commd 4/2/64. Sqn Ldr 1/7/83. Retd ENG 1/5/91.
CLARK J. D. Born 4/2/41. Commd 26/5/61. Flt Lt 26/11/66. Retd GD 4/8/79.
CLARK J. F. Born 19/8/30. Commd 24/9/52. Sqn Ldr 1/7/62. Retd ENG 24/9/68.
CLARK J. M., BSc MRAeS. Born 8/10/56. Commd 31/8/75. Sqn Ldr 1/7/89. Retd GD 8/10/94.
CLARK J. R. T. Born 16/5/47. Commd 2/8/68. Flt Lt 8/3/72. Retd GD 11/10/75.
CLARK K. Born 4/8/30. Commd 17/9/52. Plt Offr 16/12/53. Retd GD 1/1/55.
CLARK K. A., BSc MRAeS. Born 13/2/37. Commd 16/11/59. Sqn Ldr 1/7/69. Retd GD 13/2/95.
CLARK L. D., BA BSc MRAeS. Born 3/3/45. Commd 28/9/64. Sqn Ldr 1/7/75. Retd GD 12/12/83.
CLARK M. B., BSc DipEl ARCS. Born 27/6/33. Commd 24/1/56. Wg Cdr 26/7/74. Retd ADMIN 30/9/76.
CLARK M. J. Born 25/11/31. Commd 1/1/63. Flt Lt 1/10/71. Retd CAT 1/1/79.
CLARK M. V. Born 21/6/45. Commd 25/3/64. Flt Lt 6/10/69. Retd GD 21/6/83.
CLARK P., AFM. Born 21/1/25. Commd 21/10/54. Flt Lt 21/10/60. Retd GD 30/4/68.
CLARK P. C., FIMgt. Born 18/5/33. Commd 22/1/53. Gp Capt 1/7/76. Retd SY 26/7/83.
CLARK P. D., CB BA CEng FRAeS. Born 19/3/39. Commd 28/7/60. AVM 1/7/91. Retd ENG 25/4/94.
CLARK P. J. W. Born 12/12/42. Commd 22/2/63. Flt Lt 22/8/68. Retd GD 12/12/80.
CLARK P. S. Born 7/12/18. Commd 14/8/45. Flt Lt 25/8/53. Retd GD 20/12/61.
CLARK R., BEM. Born 28/10/47. Commd 14/8/80. Sqn Ldr 1/7/87. Retd ADMIN 14/8/91.
CLARK R. Born 20/10/22. Commd 25/9/46. Flt Lt 25/9/52. Retd SY 20/10/82.
CLARK R., MBE. Born 21/10/22. Commd 2/10/47. Flt Lt 27/5/54. Retd PE 22/10/65.
CLARK R. E. V., MSc BA BSc. Born 23/2/52. Commd 23/1/74. Wg Cdr 1/1/96. Retd ADMIN 15/9/00.
CLARK R. I. Born 5/12/25. Commd 29/1/62. Flt Lt 29/1/62. Retd GD 21/1/72.
CLARK R. J. Born 10/3/29. Commd 26/8/66. Sqn Ldr 1/7/79. Retd ENG 10/3/84.
CLARK R. W., OBE CEng FIEE. Born 6/4/44. Commd 7/6/68. A Cdre 1/7/96. Retd ENG 22/7/00.
CLARK S. E., BSc CEng MRAeS. Born 8/12/44. Commd 28/9/4. A Cdre 1/7/91. Retd ENG 2/8/93.
CLARK S. J. Born 13/7/32. Commd 22/3/51. Flt Lt 1/9/59. Retd GD 1/12/65.
CLARK T. B. Born 2/11/21. Commd 11/5/43. Flt Lt 2/6/48. Retd GD 20/11/64.
CLARK T. J. Born 18/6/61. Commd 25/9/83. Flt Lt 29/6/89. Retd OPS SPT 25/9/99.
CLARKE A. J., AFC MRAeS. Born 30/7/23. Commd 18/11/46. Sqn Ldr 1/7/57. Retd GD 30/7/66.
CLARKE A. K. Born 23/8/49. Commd 31/7/70. Sqn Ldr 1/7/83. Retd GD 7/3/87.

CLARKE B. R. Born 17/6/25. Commd 29/3/45. Wg Cdr 1/1/66. Retd ADMIN 25/10/77.
CLARKE C. C. Born 9/2/53. Commd 1/6/72. Flt Lt 1/12/78. Retd ENG 1/4/83.
CLARKE C. H., FIMgt. Born 25/11/23. Commd 1/3/43. A Cdre 1/1/74. Retd SUP 25/11/78.
CLARKE C. J. G. Born 26/4/42. Commd 16/6/88. Flt Lt 16/6/92. Retd SUP 2/4/93.
CLARKE C. J. V. Born 1/9/33. Commd 14/8/61. Flt Lt 14/8/61. Retd GD 8/9/71.
CLARKE D. B., BA DipEd MIPM MIMgt. Born 9/5/33. Commd 25/8/55. Sqn Ldr 25/2/65. Retd EDN 25/8/71.
CLARKE D. E. Born 6/2/38. Commd 22/5/70. Flt Lt 22/5/74. Retd GD 30/4/76.
CLARKE D. F. A. Born 3/6/96. Commd 28/4/24. Sqn Ldr 1/12/41. Retd SEC 15/12/44 rtg Wg Cdr.
CLARKE D. J., LDS RCS. Born 8/11/21. Commd 6/1/63. Wg Cdr 6/1/69. Retd DEL 6/1/79.
CLARKE D. J., MB ChB FRCS. Born 11/12/34. Commd 21/7/65. Wg Cdr 21/10/75. Retd MED 1/6/83.
CLARKE E. J. Born 24/3/20. Commd 22/5/45. Flt Lt 22/11/48. Retd GD 22/6/54.
CLARKE F. Born 13/5/30. Commd 12/9/63. Sqn Ldr 1/7/78. Retd ENG 1/5/81.
CLARKE F. A. Born 28/6/11. Commd 18/1/45. Fg Offr 18/1/45. Retd ASD 15/3/46.
CLARKE F. J., BSc. Born 10/11/51. Commd 13/9/70. Wg Cdr 1/7/95. Retd ENG 30/12/96.
CLARKE G., MA. Born 18/9/27. Commd 19/9/51. Wg Cdr 1/7/64. Retd GD 31/12/69.
CLARKE G., MA MSc. Born 17/2/49. Commd 28/1/79. Flt Lt 28/1/79. Retd ADMIN 28/1/95.
CLARKE G. J. Born 8/4/35. Commd 21/3/74. Sqn Lr 21/3/86. Retd MED(T) 8/4/90.
CLARKE H. O. Born 13/3/33. Commd 18/8/61. Fg Offr 18/8/63. Retd GD 13/3/71.
CLARKE H. S. Born 29/8/26. Commd 2/7/52. Sqn Ldr 1/1/72. Retd GD(G) 29/8/81.
CLARKE J. L. Born 12/9/24. Commd 1/6/45. Flt Lt 7/6/51. Retd SEC 1/6/57.
CLARKE J. L. Born 2/9/32. Commd 29/7/65. Flt Lt 29/7/66. Retd EDN 13/8/73.
CLARKE J. P. Born 20/5/30. Commd 11/6/52. Flt Lt 11/12/56. Retd GD 20/5/68.
CLARKE K. A., BA. Born 12/9/36. Commd 8/8/74. Sqn Ldr 1/1/84. Retd ENG 11/10/86.
CLARKE K. P., BEng MSc MRAeS. Born 14/9/37. Commd 23/9/59. Sqn Ldr 20/5/74. Retd EDN 1/10/79.
CLARKE L. G., BA MCIPS. Born 23/5/47. Commd 10/5/73. Wg Cdr 1/1/92. Retd SUP 20/7/96.
CLARKE M. C. A. Born 12/12/42. Commd 6/7/62. Sqn Ldr 1/1/85. Retd OPS SPT 12/12/97.
CLARKE M. F. O. Born 19/8/19. Commd 17/9/41. Flt Lt 19/11/53. Retd SEC 9/1/65.
CLARKE M. G. A. Born 7/12/25. Commd 25/5/50. Sqn Ldr 1/7/62. Retd ENG 1/7/65.
CLARKE N. E. Born 10/5/07. Commd 24/11/41. Sqn Offr 1/7/52. Retd SEC 26/8/56.
CLARKE N. K. Born 17/11/40. Commd 9/3/72. Flt Lt 9/3/74. Retd GD(G) 9/3/80.
CLARKE P. C. Born 13/4/25. Commd 5/7/53. Flt Lt 13/4/60. Retd GD 13/4/83.
CLARKE P. J. Born 10/11/45. Commd 26/5/64. Flt Lt 22/11/69. Retd GD 10/11/83.
CLARKE P. M., MSc. Born 17/2/49. Commd 6/4/72. Flt Lt 6/10/78. Retd ADMIN 7/4/99.
CLARKE P. S. Born 14/4/45. Commd 26/5/67. Flt Lt 26/11/71. Retd GD 19/4/88.
CLARKE R. D. Born 29/8/43. Commd 11/4/63. Wg Cdr 1/7/80. Retd SY 29/8/87.
CLARKE R. D., BA. Born 23/10/58. Commd 27/3/83. Flt Lt 27/6/86. Retd GD(G) 11/8/89.
CLARKE R. E. Born 26/12/24. Commd 24/10/49. Flt Lt 10/10/55. Retd GD 5/10/57.
CLARKE R. E. Born 29/11/46. Commd 30/5/69. Flt Lt 30/11/74. Retd GD 31/1/76.
CLARKE R. G. Born 14/7/44. Commd 5/7/73. Sqn Ldr 1/7/86. Retd ENG 14/9/96.
CLARKE R. J. Born 31/8/28. Commd 12/7/50. Flt Lt 14/5/56. Retd GD 31/8/66.
CLARKE R. J., MSc MInst PS MIDPM MIMgt. Born 20/6/48. Commd 25/8/67. Sqn Ldr 1/7/83. Retd ADMIN 15/12/87.
CLARKE R. P. Born 25/8/44. Commd 10/2/72. Flt Lt 10/2/74. Retd ADMIN 26/8/94.
CLARKE S. Born 14/6/44. Commd 4/7/69. Flt Lt 24/1/73. Retd GD 1/7/75.
CLARKE S. M., CEng MRAeS. Born 6/4/24. Commd 22/9/49. G Capt 1/1/72. Retd ENG 5/9/78.
CLARKE T. J. R., BSc. Born 20/9/33. Commd 22/11/57. Sqn Ldr 22/5/68. Retd EDN 22/11/73.
CLARKE T. M. Born 12/3/33. Commd 24/1/52. Flt Lt 29/5/57. Retd GD 12/3/71.
CLARKE V. F. Born 15/2/17. Commd 26/9/41. Wg Cdr 1/7/61. Retd SUP 9/2/68.
CLARKE V. G. Born 16/5/22. Commd 12/5/44. Wg Cdr 1/7/62. Retd GD 18/5/65.
CLARKIN B. T. Born 13/10/42. Commd 3/11/77. Sqn Ldr 1/1/88. Retd ADMIN 3/1/97.
CLARKSON J., AFC. Born 30/11/45. Commd 5/2/65. Wg Cdr 1/1/91. Retd GD 22/4/94.
CLARKSON T. W., DFC. Born 16/4/43. Commd 16/4/43. Flt Lt 5/5/63. Retd GD 1/7/76.
CLAUSE D. M., AFC FIMgt MRAeS. Born 1/8/23. Commd 20/2/43. Gp Capt 1/1/65. Retd GD 31/10/76.
CLAXTON J. F., MA. Born 23/1/32. Commd 26/9/53. Sqn Ldr 1/7/65. Retd ENG 23/1/70.
CLAXTON K. Born 1/4/53. Commd 7/7/73. Wg Cdr 1/7/89. Retd GD 14/7/92.
CLAY A. R. F., BA. Born 9/6/57. Commd 14/9/75. Flt Lt 15/10/79. Retd GD 15/7/90.
CLAY E. F. Born 24/11/13. Commd 9/8/47. Flt Lt 9/2/52. Retd SEC 1/3/68.
CLAY F. A. W., DFC*. Born 24/1/22. Commd 29/5/43. Sqn Ldr 1/7/66. Retd GD 28/9/68.
CLAY J. M. Born 30/7/36. Commd 14/10/71. Flt Lt 14/10/75. Retd ENG 14/8/84.
CLAY L. S. Born 11/6/52. Commd 18/12/80. Flt Lt 18/2/82. Retd ADMIN 18/12/96.
CLAY P., BSc, CEng MRAeS. Born 12/6/23. Commd 8/6/44. Sqn Ldr 1/10/56. Retd ENG 12/6/78.
CLAYDON K. W. Born 12/6/29. Commd 14/11/51. Sqn Ldr 1/7/62. Retd GD 4/2/73.
CLAYFIELD W. E., DFC. Born 11/10/19. Commd 28/1/43. Wg Cdr 1/7/70. Retd SEC 11/10/74.
CLAYPHAN A. A. A. Born 11/2/32. Commd 21/5/52. Sqn Ldr 1/7/67. Retd GD 12/1/74.
CLAYSON J. L., MBE FIMgt. Born 21/11/31. Commd 21/8/52. Gp Capt 1/7/76. Retd ADMIN 30/7/84. rtg A Cdre.
CLAYTON B. A., AFC. Born 6/3/29. Commd 8/9/47. Flt Lt 23/12/58. Retd SUP 6/3/67.

CLAYTON C. P. Born 24/10/45. Commd 29/7/65. Sqn Ldr 1/1/89. Retd ENG 24/12/95.
CLAYTON D. A., CEng MIMechE MRAeS. Born 9/6/33. Commd 25/7/56. Gp Capt 1/1/79. Retd ENG 9/12/87.
CLAYTON J. D., BSc. Born 10/7/30. Commd 19/9/51. Sqn Ldr 1/7/61. Retd GD 10/7/68.
CLAYTON J. McK. Born 24/3/25. Commd 15/6/61. Flt Lt 15/6/64. Retd GD 1/10/75.
CLAYTON L. C. F. Born 22/3/43. Commd 27/1/61. Flt Lt 27/7/66. Retd GD 3/12/68.
CLAYTON N. Born 13/3/22. Commd 30/10/44. Flt Lt 30/4/48. Retd GD 1/6/62.
CLAYTON R. H. Born 9/3/37. Commd 14/10/71. Flt Lt 14/10/73. Retd ENG 17/7/81.
CLAYTON R. J. Born 25/7/44. Commd 4/2/71. Fg Offr 4/8/73. Retd SUP 3/1/76.
CLAYTON R. M. Born 3/4/38. Commd 18/12/56. Gp Capt 1/7/87. Retd GD 3/7/93.
CLAYTON S. Born 3/6/63. Commd 26/11/81. Sqn Ldr 1/7/96. Retd GD 10/1/00.
CLAYTON-JONES G. S., MRAeS. Born 22/3/42. Commd 14/5/60. Wg Cdr 1/1/85. Retd GD 22/3/97.
CLEARY G. A. L. Born 23/1/45. Commd 14/1/82. Flt Lt 1/3/87. Retd GD(G) 1/10/89.
CLEAVE N. H. L. W. Born 13/9/39. Commd 31/7/62. Flt Lt 15/2/65. Retd GD 13/9/94.
CLEAVER A. A. B., DFC. Born 29/4/15. Commd 10/6/41. Sqn Ldr 1/8/47. Retd GD 21/5/58.
CLEAVER A. G. Born 4/7/39. Commd 21/7/61. Gp Capt 1/7/89. Retd GD 4/7/94.
CLEAVER L. D. Born 27/9/23. Commd 26/2/46. Sqn Ldr 1/1/67. Retd GD(G) 16/3/74.
CLEAVER R. B. Born 8/8/98. Commd 20/7/34. Wg Cdr 1/7/47. Retd ENG 14/8/50.
CLEE P. A. Born 28/5/36. Commd 30/12/54. Sqn Ldr 1/1/71. Retd GD 1/8/88.
CLEE R. B. Born 2/12/22. Commd 6/2/44. Flt Lt 4/12/52. Retd GD 28/11/67.
CLEGG D. Born 1/7/20. Commd 22/9/41. Flt Offr 1/9/45. Retd SEC 21/5/55.
CLEGG J. R. Born 26/9/43. Commd 25/6/66. Flt Lt 25/12/72. Retd ENG 1/9/83.
CLEGG M. A. Born 10/8/42. Commd 17/12/64. Gp Capt 1/1/91. Retd GD 2/4/98.
CLEIFE V. E. Born 22/12/10. Commd 23/3/42. Flt Lt 23/3/44. Retd GD 29/9/46.
CLELLAND D. H. Born 23/3/26. Commd 9/4/52. Flt Lt 21/8/57. Retd GD 23/3/76.
CLEMAS L. H. Born 17/2/17. Commd 23/1/39. Flt Lt 18/2/52. Retd SUP 17/2/66 rtg Sqn Ldr.
CLEMENTS A. J. B., CEng FIMgt MIEE DipEl. Born 2/12/21. Commd 9/8/45. A Cdre 1/7/74. Retd ENG 2/12/76.
CLEMENTS A. N., BSc(Eng) ACGI. Born 19/5/51. Commd 19/2/73. Sqn Ldr 1/1/83. Retd GD 19/5/89.
CLEMENTS D. M., BA. Born 17/12/33. Commd 12/7/57. Sqn Ldr 12/1/65. Retd ADMIN 29/3/87.
CLEMENTS G. D. Born 2/11/52. Commd 1/4/76. Flt Lt 1/10/81. Retd GD 8/12/91.
CLEMENTS H. E., OBE MIMgt. Born 3/1/28. Commd 14/12/49. Wg Cdr 1/1/69. Retd GD 1/11/75.
CLEMENTS H. H. Born 22/1/15. Commd 5/8/43. Sqn Ldr 1/7/54. Retd ENG 10/1/62.
CLEMENTS J. B. Born 20/1/41. Commd 15/3/84. Sqn Ldr 1/1/92. Retd SY 20/6/96.
CLEMENTS J. MacS. Born 14/9/45. Commd 25/6/65. Flt Lt 8/3/72. Retd GD 14/9/86.
CLEMENTS M. F., DUS. Born 31/5/36. Commd 23/7/58. Sqn Ldr 1/7/68. Retd ENG 31/5/74.
CLEMENTS M. P. M., BSc CEng MRAeS ACGI. Born 20/2/52. Commd 24/9/76. Sqn Ldr 1/1/89. Retd ENG 24/9/92.
CLEMENTS P. H. R. Born 10/6/38. Commd 14/8/64. Flt Lt 1/7/68. Retd GD 10/6/76.
CLEMENTS R. D., MBA BSc. Born 1/3/46. Commd 12/7/70. Wg Cdr 1/1/88. Retd GD 14/9/96.
CLEMENTS R. E. Born 18/6/43. Commd 3/5/68. Sqn Ldr 1/7/79. Retd GD 21/9/97.
CLEMENTS S. H., MBA MIMgt. Born 29/12/48. Commd 8/1/78. Sqn Ldr 1/7/88. Retd ADMIN 8/1/94.
CLEMENTSON J., MA. Born 29/5/36. Commd 30/7/80. Sqn Ldr 28/8/77. Retd ADMIN 1/4/92.
CLEMITSON J. M., OBE. Born 29/10/35. Commd 27/2/70. Wg Cdr 1/7/82. Retd GD(G) 13/2/87.
CLERICI A. E. Born 19/4/16. Commd 24/11/41. Flt Offr 1/9/45. Retd SEC 4/9/60.
CLERK R. D. Born 13/2/20. Commd 1/7/43. Flt Lt 1/1/47. Retd ENG 23/12/56.
CLEVERLEY D. H. H., DFM. Born 15/6/20. Commd 1/5/42. Flt Lt 1/11/46. Retd GD(G) 19/5/54 rtg Sqn Ldr.
CLEVERLEY J. W., BA. Born 2/10/27. Commd 24/4/59. Sqn Ldr 28/6/64. Retd EDN 31/12/75.
CLEVERLEY N. A. Born 2/12/51. Commd 16/9/71. Flt Lt 16/3/77. Retd GD 4/9/81.
CLEVERLEY R. A. R. Born 4/5/19. Commd 1/3/62. Flt Lt 1/3/65. Retd ENG 4/5/74.
CLEVERLY A. J. Born 19/2/34. Commd 26/11/52. Sqn Ldr 1/7/84. Retd GD(G) 19/2/89.
CLEVERLY R. K. Born 2/5/36. Commd 30/11/55. Flt Lt 28/8/61. Retd GD 25/5/66.
CLEVERLY R. M. Born 20/7/49. Commd 25/8/67. Flt Lt 3/2/74. Retd GD(G) 3/4/76.
CLEVES K. G., BA. Born 10/11/31. Commd 15/7/54. Sqn Ldr 15/1/65. Retd EDN 15/7/70.
CLEWS J. D. Born 2/3/17. Commd 16/2/44. Sqn Ldr 1/1/69. Retd SEC 2/3/72.
CLIFF F. H. Born 26/1/37. Commd 19/6/70. Flt Lt 1/7/75. Retd ENG 19/6/78. Reinstated 1/7/81. Sqn Ldr 1/1/89. Retd ENG 26/1/95.
CLIFF M. E. Born 13/3/38. Commd 8/1/76. Flt Lt 8/1/81. Retd ADMIN 31/8/89.
CLIFF M. J. H. Born 24/9/60. Commd 13/12/79. Sqn Ldr 1/7/93. Retd GD 24/9/98.
CLIFF P. D., OBE. Born 19/3/35. Commd 17/6/53. Wg Cdr 1/7/79. Retd GD 17/7/82.
CLIFFE R. B. Born 30/10/52. Commd 24/6/76. Wg Cdr 1/1/93. Retd ENG 1/11/98.
CLIFFE S.M., BEd. Born 29/7/59. Commd 29/11/81. Sqn Ldr 1/1/91. Retd ADMIN 14/3/96.
CLIFFORD A. W. Born 20/10/22. Commd 10/5/46. Flt Lt 19/11/53. Retd GD 31/3/70.
CLIFFORD B. B. Born 27/8/34. Commd 24/9/52. Flt Lt 17/9/58. Retd GD 27/8/92.
CLIFFORD B. J. Born 1/6/43. Commd 17/12/65. Sqn Ldr 1/1/73. Retd GD 1/6/81.
CLIFFORD D. P. Born 30/9/54. Commd 16/5/74. Flt Lt 5/10/80. Retd OPS SPT 30/9/99.
CLIFFORD G. F. Born 16/10/49. Commd 25/2/72. Sqn Ldr 1/1/88. Retd GD 16/10/93.
CLIFFORD G. M., BSc. Born 16/6/58. Commd 28/2/82. Flt Lt 28/8/85. Retd ADMIN 31/10/87.
CLIFFORD G. R. M. Born 14/3/03. Commd 15/8/28. Wg Cdr 1/1/40. Retd GD 14/3/53 rtg Gp Capt.

CLIFFORD J. M., MSc MB BChir. Born 17/4/29. Commd 21/11/54. Wg Cdr 21/11/67. Retd MED 28/10/73.
CLIFFORD J. N. Born 25/12/46. Commd 27/5/71. Flt Lt 7/1/75. Retd PI 25/12/85.
CLIFFORD K. C., MBE. Born 28/3/33. Commd 4/6/64. Sqn Ldr 1/1/76. Retd ENG 28/10/93.
CLIFFORD M. W. A. Born 4/6/34. Commd 26/4/60. Sqn Ldr 18/9/69. Retd EDN 23/1/76.
CLIFFORD P., MBE. Born 12/12/19. Commd 27/2/43. Flt Lt 27/2/45. Retd GD(G) 12/12/74.
CLIFFORD P. H. R., MIMgt. Born 1/6/33. Commd 26/3/52. Sqn Ldr 1/1/63. Retd GD 1/6/71.
CLIFFORD R. I., MIMgt. Born 25/4/44. Commd 25/6/65. Flt Lt 25/12/70. Retd GD 26/1/73. Re-entered 6/6/74. Sqn
  Ldr 1/7/87. Retd ADMIN 5/1/98.
CLIFFORD T. W. P., MBE DFC. Born 6/6/24. Commd 31/10/44. Gp Capt. 1/1/76. Retd SEC 6/6/79.
CLIFFORD-JONES W. E., MB BS MRCS LRCP DO. Born 13/9/29. Commd 1/5/55. Gp Capt 26/3/78. Retd MED
  3/5/78.
CLIFT D. G. Born 15/3/19. Commd 1/4/39. Sqn Ldr 1/1/71. Retd GD(G) 2/7/74.
CLIFTON A. G. Born 21/9/32. Commd 29/9/54. Fg Offr 30/12/56. Retd GD 9/7/57.
CLIFTON D. J. Born 17/9/51. Commd 27/3/75. Flt Lt 27/9/80. Retd GD 2/12/90.
CLIFTON P. J. Born 16/10/22. Commd 8/6/43. Sqn Ldr 1/10/55. Retd GD 16/10/65.
CLINCH B. A. Born 12/12/51. Commd 18/12/80. Flt Lt 18/12/82. Retd SUP 12/12/89.
CLINCH B. F. A. Born 13/2/36. Commd 5/5/54. Flt Lt 5/10/60. Retd GD 30/3/74.
CLINCH C. W. Born 5/10/12. Commd 8/4/43. Sqn Ldr 1/4/56. Retd ENG 5/10/68.
CLINGAN B. R. Born 30/5/42. Commd 19/6/70. Flt Lt 19/6/72. Retd ENG 20/5/88.
CLINGING D., MBE. Born 15/11/49. Commd 20/12/73. Sqn Ldr 1/7/89. Retd GD(G) 31/8/92.
CLINKER S. P. Born 21/12/53. Commd 30/8/84. Flt Lt 30/8/86. Retd SUP 14/9/96.
CLINKSKEL J. W. C. Born 23/8/57. Commd 23/3/81. Fg Off 23/3/83. Retd SUP 1/10/86.
CLINTON E. M., MBE. Born 17/7/31. Commd 11/2/65. Flt Lt 11/2/71. Retd SUP 17/7/89.
CLINTON H. V. Born 28/1/24. Commd 25/8/60. Sqn Ldr 1/1/72. Retd ENG 30/3/74.
CLINTON I. J. Born 5/2/38. Commd 15/6/61. Flt Lt 1/4/66. Retd SEC 5/2/76.
CLIPSHAM J. R., AMCIPD. Born 8/8/58. Commd 18/4/74. Sqn Ldr 1/7/88. Retd GD(G) 14/9/96.
CLISBY B. E., CEng MIEE. Born 16/3/37. Commd 23/10/59. Sqn Ldr 1/7/71. Retd ENG 23/10/75.
CLISH R. E. Born 11/12/11. Commd 27/3/44. Flt Lt 7/6/51. Retd SUP 28/9/53.
CLITHEROW A. F., BSc. Born 1/12/57. Commd 19/9/76. Flt Lt 15/10/80. Retd GD 11/11/96.
CLIVE-GRIFFIN J. B. Born 1/7/14. Commd 30/6/51. Flt Offr 30/6/55. Retd CAT 18/4/64.
CLIVE-SPENCER J. L. S. Born 28/12/17. Commd 19/7/51. Flt Lt 19/1/56. Retd SEC 1/4/61.
CLODE R. F. Born 12/4/41. Commd 7/6/68. Flt Lt 28/2/72. Retd SD 31/7/94.
CLOETE D., MC AFC. Born 11/7/88. Commd 1/4/18. Sqn Ldr 1/1/26. Retd GD 16/3/27. Re-employed 18/9/40 to
  15/3/45.
CLOGGER P. A., CEng MRAeS. Born 17/6/45. Commd 13/2/64. Wg Cdr 1/7/83. Retd ENG 17/6/89.
CLOHERTY J. K., MB BCh FRCS(Edin) FCOphth DO. Born 8/12/28. Commd 11/8/57. A Cdre 3/4/89. Retd
  MED 8/12/93.
CLOKE B. E. Born 13/4/43. Commd 16/6/69. Wg Cdr 1/7/89. Retd SY 14/4/93.
CLOKE J. A., BSc. Born 8/3/47. Commd 28/7/67. Sqn Ldr 1/1/80. Retd ENG 8/3/85.
CLOKE R., AFC FIMgt. Born 8/7/38. Commd 28/7/59. Gp Capt 1/1/88. Retd GD 21/6/89.
CLOKE S. R., MSc BA FCIT FILT FCIPD. Born 3/6/58. Commd 4/9/81. Sqn Ldr 1/1/90. Retd SUP 23/10/98.
CLOSE A. P. Born 27/10/34. Commd 23/9/65. Sqn Ldr 1/7/73. Retd SY(PRT) 1/6/88.
CLOSE J. A. Born 12/4/39. Commd 2/5/59. Flt Lt 28/7/65. Retd 12/11/70. Reinstated 16/9/71. Sqn Ldr 1/1/87. Retd
  ENG 12/4/94.
CLOSE T. D. Born 15/11/51. Commd 19/6/70. Flt Lt 19/12/75. Retd GD 29/1/82.
CLOSE W. E. Born 21/7/32. Commd 15/12/53. Wg Cdr 1/1/72. Retd GD 1/12/84.
CLOTHIER P. R., MB ChB FRCS. Born 14/4/49. Commd 10/1/71. Wg Cdr 9/9/87. Retd MED 25/2/95.
CLOUDER B. E. W. Born 25/9/45. Comm 14/10/71. Flt Lt 14/4/74. Retd GD 25/9/83.
CLOUGH D. B. Born 19/8/47. Commd 14/7/66. Flt Lt 4/5/72. Retd GD 28/2/78. Re-entered 30/8/85. Flt Lt 2/11/79.
  Retd OPS SPT 18/11/97.
CLOUGH J. H., DFC. Born 27/10/19. Commd 8/3/41. Flt Lt 1/9/45. Retd GD 30/10/48 rtg Wg Cdr.
CLOUGH P. J., BSc CEng MIEE. Born 1/3/46. Commd 15/7/66. Wg Cdr 1/7/83. Retd ENG 1/7/86.
CLOUTMAN D. H. Born 26/6/40. Commd 1/4/77. Sqn Ldr 1/7/77. Retd SUP 14/8/95.
CLOVER W. H. Born 6/10/82. Commd 1/4/18. Flt Lt 1/4/18. Retd GD 20/3/20.
CLOVIS M. Born 6/4/48. Commd 28/2/69. Sqn Ldr 1/7/83. Retd ENG 1/7/86.
CLOWES R. G. Born 1/11/59. Commd 19/3/81. Flt Lt 10/10/84. Retd GD 14/3/97.
CLUBB J. A. W. Born 14/5/29. Commd 15/12/49. Sqn Ldr 1/1/61. Retd GD 6/5/76.
CLUBBE H. M. Born 7/5/12. Commd 2/8/45. Sqn Ldr 1/7/62. Retd SUP 7/5/68.
CLUBBE P., OBE FIMgt MCIPS. Born 30/1/28. Commd 7/10/48. Gp Capt 1/1/77. Retd SUP 30/1/83.
CLUBLEY G., DFC. Born 24/10/22. Commd 2/4/44. Sqn Ldr 1/10/54. Retd GD 1/6/70.
CLUCAS B. P., MInstPet. Born 17/6/46. Commd 18/8/67. Sqn Ldr 1/7/80. Retd SUP 6/12/99.
CLUCAS R. D. Born 27/8/40. Commd 13/12/79. Sqn Ldr 1/7/89. Retd ENG 1/5/93.
CLUER C. B. Born 17/9/37. Commd 28/10/63. Sqn Ldr 1/1/71. Retd GD 1/4/75.
CLUER R. J. Born 22/6/57. Commd 16/9/76. Sqn Ldr 1/7/94. Retd GD 22/6/99.
CLULOW M. A. Born 20/8/39. Commd 28/8/75. Wg Cdr 1/1/91. Retd GD(G) 20/8/94.
CLUTTERBUCK A. N. Born 30/12/53. Commd 30/4/81. Flt Lt 1/11/84. Retd SY 7/12/92.

CLUTTON N. A., BSc. Born 27/5/49. Commd 1/9/70. Flt Lt 1/12/71. Retd GD 1/4/91.
CLYDE G. A., BSc. Born 18/11/48. Commd 6/3/77. Wg Cdr 1/7/92. Retd ADMIN 9/10/99.
COAK A. F. H., DipPE. Born 11/12/43. Commd 16/8/70. Sqn Ldr 1/7/81. Retd ADMIN 16/8/86.
COALES M. R. Born 16/3/43. Commd 19/6/64. Flt Lt 19/12/69. Retd GD 16/3/81.
COATES A. Born 20/8/16. Commd 18/3/43. Sqn Ldr 1/7/56. Retd SEC 20/8/65.
COATES A. N. Born 15/10/34. Commd 24/2/67. Flt Lt. 24/2/69. Retd PRT 24/2/75.
COATES B. C., DFC DFM. Born 5/1/21. Commd 11/12/42. Sqn Ldr 1/10/55. Retd GD 5/1/70.
COATES D. J., MBE. Born 6/10/29. Commd 19/8/53. Sqn Ldr 1/7/67. Retd GD 5/11/73.
COATES F. B. Born 24/11/20. Commd 2/10/58. Sqn Ldr 1/7/69. Retd ENG 23/5/73.
COATES H., DFC. Born 10/10/18. Commd 5/4/43. Sqn Ldr 1/7/54. Retd GD 3/5/59.
COATES J. Born 30/12/50Commd 5/8/76. Commd 5/8/76Flt Lt 6/6/79. Flt Lt 6/6/79 ADMIN 18/5/83. Retd ADMIN 18/5/83.
COATES J. B., BSc CEng MIEE. Born 10/4/46. Commd 15/7/66. Flt Lt 15/10/70. Retd ENG 10/4/84.
COATES J. G., BSc CEng MRAeS. Born 19/4/49. Commd 27/2/70. Wg Cdr 1/7/90. Retd ENG 14/9/96.
COATES R. A. Born 31/1/55. Commd 8/8/74. Flt Lt 8/2/79. Retd GD 9/11/87.
COATES S. G., BEng. Born 11/12/62. Commd 16/9/84. Flt Lt 7/4/89. Retd ENG 1/1/96.
COATESWORTH G. A., MIMgt. Born 8/11/31. Commd 17/12/52. Sqn Ldr 1/1/66. Retd GD 8/11/69.
COBB D. C., MSc DPhysEd CDipAF. Born 20/11/43. Commd 10/8/65. Sqn Ldr 1/7/77. Retd ADMIN 18/6/82.
COBB F. Born 8/10/16. Commd 2/6/49. Sqn Ldr 1/4/58. Retd SEC 8/4/72.
COBB H. J., DSO DFC AFC. Born 31/5/22. Commd 7/1/43. Wg Cdr 1/1/62. Retd GD 3/12/67.
COBB J. A., MIMgt. Born 11/8/48. Commd 19/2/76. Sqn Ldr 1/1/84. Retd GD(G) 2/2/96.
COBB J. W., MBE. Born 20/9/41. Commd 11/8/69. Sqn Ldr 1/7/90. Retd SY 9/12/96.
COBB N. A. Born 26/1/60. Commd 30/4/81. Sqn Ldr 1/1/96. Retd GD 1/1/99.
COBB R. D., BSc. Born 2/5/64. Commd 5/9/82. APO 5/9/82. Retd GD 11/12/85.
COBB S. D. Born 12/5/61. Commd 1/7/82. Flt Lt 1/1/89. Retd ADMIN 11/12/96.
COBBOLD C. H. Born 21/7/07. Commd 7/10/41. Flt Lt 1/9/45. Retd SUP 9/12/49 rtg Sqn Ldr.
COBBOLD J. W. Born 21/1/21. Commd 15/5/47. Flt Lt 15/11/51. Retd SEC 21/1/70.
COBLEY R. A. Born 25/9/34. Commd 1/4/71. Sqn Ldr 1/1/80. Retd SUP 25/9/89.
COBURN E. W., CBE CEng FIMechE MRAeS. Born 29/12/25. Commd 22/4/53. A.Cdre 1/7/76. Retd ENG 25/4/80.
COBURN K., BA CEng MIEE MRAeS. Born 11/12/42. Commd 22/7/71. Wg Cdr 1/7/86. Retd ENG 31/3/94.
COCHRAN D. Born 17/12/45. Commd 6/5/66. Flt Lt 17/6/71/ Retd GD 30/9/77.
COCHRANE C. G., BSc CEng MIEE. Born 2/7/44. Commd 15/7/65. Sqn Ldr 1/1/74. Retd ENG 2/7/82.
COCHRANE J. Born 26/7/30. Commd 9/4/52. Sqn Ldr 1/7/60. Retd GD 29/9/62.
COCHRANE J. Born 24/8/47. Commd 28/7/88. Flt Lt 28/7/90. Flt Lt 7/1/74. Retd OPS SPT 1/9/00.
COCHRANE J. E. Born 13/12/25. Commd 7/1/71. Flt Lt 7/1/74. Retd GD 7/1/84.
COCHRANE R. A. Born 14/2/30. Commd 24/9/59. Flt Lt 24/9/64. Retd GD 12/8/77.
COCHRANE R. B. S. Born 2/8/16. Commd 30/1/47. Sqn Ldr 1/1/67. Retd SUP 2/8/70.
COCKARILL T. J. Born 31/5/47. Commd 28/4/65. Flt Lt 17/3/71. Retd GD 8/11/75.
COCKAYNE W. N. Born 16/4/18. Commd 28/1/43. Flt Lt 28/7/46. Retd ENG 7/8/54.
COCKBURN D. Born 29/4/48. Commd 2/8/68. Flt Lt 2/8/71. Retd GD 22/10/94.
COCKCROFT W. Born 28/1/29. Commd 28/7/60. Sqn Ldr 1/1/82. Retd ENG 28/1/89.
COCKER F. S., DFC CEng MIEE. Born 3/2/20. Commd 1/5/42. Wg Cdr 1/7/68. Retd ENG 30/11/77.
COCKERAM J. L. Born 27/11/10. Commd 6/3/52. Flt Lt 23/8/54. Retd MED(T) 29/11/60.
COCKERELL T. F., AFC. Born 13/5/39. Commd 26/5/61. Gp Capt 1/1/89. Retd GD 1/2/90.
COCKERILL G. W., MRIN MIMgt. Born 29/6/24. Commd 23/10/47. Sqn Ldr 1/7/73. Retd GD 15/5/76. Reinstated 22/10/80 to 29/6/84.
COCKERILL L. G. Born 26/1/30. Commd 9/4/52. Flt Lt 9/10/54. Retd GD 26/1/68.
COCKFIELD G. Born 5/5/29. Commd 28/2/57. Sqn Ldr 1/1/76. Retd GD 5/5/84.
COCKFIELD J. E., OBE. Born 20/11/21. Commd 21/6/44. Gp Capt 1/7/69. Retd GD 13/12/76.
COCKING J. S. Born 20/12/38. Commd 23/6/67. Wg Cdr 1/7/86. Retd ENG 2/4/93.
COCKLE A. V. Born 12/1/28. Commd 26/8/66. Flt Lt 26/8/72. Retd SUP 12/1/89.
COCKLE C. E. Born 18/1/18. Commd 23/9/43. Wg Cdr 1/7/69. Retd ENG 18/1/73.
COCKLE J. A. Born 29/4/37. Commd 28/6/67. Flt Lt 27/5/73. Retd SEC 29/1/81.
COCKMAN A., FCA. Born 3/1/15. Commd 25/7/41. Sqn Ldr 1/1/50. Retd SEC 3/4/64 rtg Wg Cdr.
COCKMAN P. S. Born 28/9/23. Commd 9/11/50. Sqn Ldr 1/1/61. Retd GD 29/6/68.
COCKRAM H. Born 25/12/11/ Commd 21/11/44. Fg Offr 21/5/45. Retd GD(G) 18/12/45. Recalled 18/8/47. Flt Lt 7/6/51. Retd 25/12/61.
COCKRELL D.J., BSc ACGI DIC. Born 28/3/26. Commd 20/11/47. Flt Lt 28/3/51. Retd EDN 31/7/55.
COCKRILL M. J., MBE. Born 1/10/46. Commd 25/6/65. Wg Cdr 1/1/89. Retd GD 1/10/96.
COCKS A. J. Born 17/6/14. Commd 27/8/41. Flt Lt 1/9/45. Retd ENG 28/9/53 rtg Sqn Ldr.
COCKS G. Born 5/5/25. Commd 9/6/55. Flt Lt 9/12/58. Retd GD 24/9/70.
COCKS J. H. Born 16/6/14. Commd 2/1/39. Wg Cdr 1/7/52. Retd SUP 8/2/60.
COCKS J. H. Born 3/3/51. Commd 31/10/74. Flt Lt 1/5/81. Retd GD(G) 15/7/90.
COCKSEDGE M. P. Born 17/9/48. Commd 27/2/70. Wg Cdr 1/7/89. Retd GD 20/1/00.
COCKSEDGE R. D. Born 7/11/42. Commd 6/11/64. Flt Lt 6/5/70. Retd GD 23/8/74.
COCKSHOTT C. R. G. Born 8/4/37. Commd 30/3/61. Sqn Ldr 1/7/71. Retd SUP 1/9/83.

CODD M. H., OBE. Born 26/3/39. Commd 14/12/72. Wg Cdr 1/1/87. Retd ADMIN 26/8/94.
CODY A., DFC AFC DFM. Born 15/5/18. Commd 15/6/41. Flt Lt 1/9/45. Retd GD 30/9/64.
CODY C. F. K. Born 22/3/54. Commd 29/6/72. Fg Offr 9/12/74. Retd GD(G) 1/8/75.
CODY C. T. K. Born 4/8/22. Commd 13/6/42. Wg Cdr 1/7/69. Retd GD 31/3/73.
COE M. J. Born 18/10/42. Commd 11/5/78. Sqn Ldr 1/1/92. Retd ENG 18/10/97.
COE M. R., AFC. Born 22/11/44. Commd 15/7/66. Wg Cdr 1/1/86. Retd GD 31/3/94.
COFFEY P. V., MBE. Born 24/9/27. Commd 5/4/52. Sqn Ldr 1/1/65. Retd GD 29/9/87.
COGAN L. E. Born 23/2/17. Commd 5/6/42. Sqn Ldr 1/1/52. Retd GD 1/3/58.
COGGINS M. G. Born 15/10/38. Commd 28/7/60. Gp Capt 1/7/81. Retd ENG 22/11/88.
COGGON B., CEng MIEE MRAeS. Born 15/11/29. Commd 3/12/54. Wg Cdr 1/1/75. Retd ENG 15/11/84.
COGILL J. C., DSO DFC. Born 17/7/20. Commd 20/6/42. Wg Cdr 1/1/58. Retd GD 17/10/68.
COHEN A. G., MBE BSc. Born 12/8/55. Commd 30/8/78. Flt Lt 28/2/79. Retd GD 30/8/94.
COHEN G. A. Born 10/11/24. Commd 25/8/55. Flt Lt 25/8/61. Retd GD 10/5/77.
COHU J. M., CBE. Born 29/4/04. Commd 15/3/24. A. Cdre 1/1/50. Retd GD 10/5/57 rtg AVM.
COHU T. R. Born 15/3/34. Commd 26/7/55. Wg Cdr 1/1/84. Retd GD 14/2/87.
COIA E. G. Born 6/11/35. Commd 7/5/64. Sqn Ldr 1/7/75. Retd ENG 9/9/81.
COKE A. F. G. Born 23/5/07. Commd 1/5/47. Fg Offr 1/5/47. Retd SUP 2/8/48 rtg Flt Lt.
COKER C. A. J., BSc. Born 1/3/58. Commd 22/3/81. Flt Lt 22/12/82. Retd GD 22/3/97.
COKER J. D. Born 5/10/43. Commd 20/12/64. Flt Lt 20/6/70. Retd GD 22/10/94.
COKER R. T. Born 21/1/35. Commd 6/2/54. Flt Lt 6/8/59. Retd GD 21/1/73.
COLAM G. Born 1/7/34. Commd 1/7/53. Flt Lt 7/3/62. Retd GD 1/7/72.
COLBECK R. Born 22/4/26. Commd 22/2/46. A.Cdre 1/7/78. Retd GD 22/4/81.
COLBECK W. J., MA MB BCh FFARCS Dip Soton. Born 26/1/28. Commd 31/8/53. Wg Cdr 29/8/65. Retd MED 31/8/69.
COLBOURNE G. A. Born 25/11/26. Commd 22/8/51. Flt Lt 22/8/55. Retd GD 21/12/69.
COLBOURNE R., GM. Born 26/5/19. Commd 27/5/54. Flt Lt 27/5/57. Retd GD(G) 26/5/76.
COLBOURNE S. J., IEng. Born 23/12/40. Commd 19/2/76. Sqn Ldr 1/1/87. Retd ENG 23/12/95.
COLCHESTER A. C. F., BA BM BCh MRCP. Born 4/10/47. Commd 18/6/72. Sqn Ldr 24/7/80. Retd MED 11/9/81.
COLCLOUGH D. H., BA BSc MCIPD CertEd. Born 28/9/47. Commd 2/11/88. Flt Lt 2/11/90. Retd ADMIN 31/1/97.
COLDICOTT T. StG. Born 10/9/45. Commd 26/5/67. Flt Lt 18/2/70. Retd GD 10/9/82.
COLDICUTT D. C. Born 13/3/42. Commd 12/1/62. Sqn Ldr 1/7/74. Retd GD 10/8/76.
COLDREY M. J. M. Born 28/2/45. Commd 5/2/65. Flt Lt 5/8/70. Retd GD 30/10/75.
COLE A. J., CEng MIEE MRAeS MBCS. Born 12/4/33. Commd 23/9/55. Wg Cdr 1/1/76. Retd ENG 24/9/83.
COLE B. C., OBE. Born 12/3/48. Commd 22/11/73. Wg Cdr 1/1/89. Retd ADMIN 1/1/97.
COLE C. L. P., BSc DUS. Born 18/3/25. Commd 3/1/46. Wg Cdr 1/1/71. Retd EDN 19/4/69.
COLE D. J. Born 16/10/42. Commd 10/9/70. Sqn Ldr 1/7/79. Retd GD 1/7/82.
COLE D. J. R., BA DPhysEd. Born 21/12/44. Commd 7/8/67. Wg Cdr 1/7/89. Retd ADMIN 21/6/97.
COLE E. J. Born 16/1/02. Commd 14/3/40. Flt Lt 1/3/45. Retd ENG 10/1/56 rtg Sqn Ldr.
COLE G. E. Born 5/12/59. Commd 27/3/80. Flt Lt 27/9/86. Retd OPS SPT 5/12/97.
COLE G. H. Born 2/10/30. Commd 2/2/56. Flt Lt 2/8/60. Retd GD 2/10/85.
COLE I. Born 3/4/19. Commd 20/10/40. Sqn Offr 1/1/54. Retd SEC 17/12/62.
COLE J. B. Born 19/9/32. Commd 29/5/56. Sqn Ldr 1/1/71. Retd GD 10/8/84.
COLE J. G., DFC. Born 11/2/20. Commd 28/12/38. Sqn Ldr 1/8/47. Retd GD 29/5/58 rtg Wg Cdr.
COLE J. M. Born 1/10/58. Commd 12/10/78. Flt Lt 3/3/85. Retd GD(G) 14/3/96.
COLE J. M. Born 16/12/32. Commd 27/9/51. Flt Lt 11/1/57. Retd GD 16/12/70.
COLE J. T. Born 20/4/15. Commd 20/10/44. Flt Lt 20/4/49. Retd CAT 20/4/64.
COLE K. N. Born 25/12/25. Commd 7/1/49. Flt Lt 11/11/54. Retd GD 25/12/68.
COLE L. R., DFC. Born 9/10/19. Commd 9/6/44. Flt Lt 9/12/47. Retd GD 29/11/58.
COLE M. E., OBE DPhysEd. Born 10/4/35. Commd 25/9/62. Sqn Ldr 1/7/73. Retd ADMIN 30/9/87.
COLE M. J. Born 10/10/61. Commd 24/10/81. Flt Lt 24/4/86. Retd GD 1/12/91.
COLE P. E. Born 11/1/51. Commd 31/8/78. Sqn Ldr 1/7/85. Retd ADMIN 18/8/89.
COLE P. L. Born 12/5/46. Commd 26/4/84. Sqn Ldr 1/7/92. Retd ENG 12/5/98.
COLE P. S. Born 28/3/32. Commd 27/9/51. Wg Cdr 1/7/70. Retd GD 15/1/87.
COLE R. D. Born 26/7/41. Commd 31/7/62. Flt Lt 31/1/65. Retd GD 26/7/79.
COLE W. L. Born 18/5/11. Commd 17/9/42. Sqn Ldr 1/7/52. Retd SUP 28/5/59.
COLEBROOK R. Born 18/11/21. Commd 4/12/42. Flt Lt 23/4/51. Retd GD 1/10/68.
COLEBY B. F., MBE. Born 11/8/45. Commd 2/6/77. Sqn Ldr 1/7/91. Retd GD 6/7/96.
COLEMAN A. H. Born 10/10/31. Commd 9/4/52. Flt Lt 9/10/55. Retd GD 10/10/69.
COLEMAN C. J. F., MA. Born 10/8/46. Commd 18/9/66. Flt Lt 15/4/70. Retd GD 31/3/86.
COLEMAN D. A., BSc. Born 10/10/50. Commd 21/1/73. Sqn Ldr 1/1/85. Retd ENG 21/1/89.
COLEMAN D. E. Born 19/12/23. Commd 1/11/43. Sqn Ldr 1/1/57. Retd GD 31/12/61.
COLEMAN D. R. Born 18/8/48. Commd 16/8/70. Sqn Ldr 1/1/82. Retd ADMIN 30/9/87.
COLEMAN E. R. T. Born 26/4/53. Commd 3/9/72. Flt Lt 4/5/80. Retd GD 26/4/91.
COLEMAN F. A., MA MRAeS. Born 18/7/14. Commd 4/4/39. Gp Capt 1/1/67. Retd EDN 18/7/74.
COLEMAN The Rev J. F., BD. Born 25/10/53. Commd 1/9/78. Retd 1/9/94 Wg Cdr.
COLEMAN J. R. Born 21/8/30. Commd 1/8/51. Flt Lt 1/2/54. Retd GD 21/8/68.

COLEMAN K. H. Born 18/2/30. Commd 30/7/64. Flt Lt 30/7/70. Retd SUP 19/2/77.
COLEMAN P. T. Born 14/6/42. Commd 29/6/72. Wg Cdr 1/1/96. Retd ENG 14/6/97.
COLEMAN R. H. Born 3/3/40. Commd 10/11/61. Flt Lt 10/5/67. Retd GD 19/10/67.
COLEMAN R. J., MMS MIMgt. Born 26/1/34. Commd 25/2/53. Gp Capt 1/1/80. Retd GD 26/1/90.
COLES A., BA. Born 9/10/37. Commd 23/6/61. Sqn Ldr 1/1/72. Retd GD 31/1/87. rtg Wg Cdr.
COLES A. J. Born 15/3/32. Commd 21/11/51. Sqn Ldr 1/1/64. Retd GD 15/3/70.
COLES G. B. Born 9/11/36. Commd 4/10/63. Flt Lt 9/2/68. Retd GD 9/11/74.
COLES G. T. Born 25/1/25. Commd 2/7/52. Flt Lt 27/11/57. Retd GD 25/9/75.
COLES J. G. Born 11/6/23. Commd 1/5/52. Sqn Ldr 1/1/69. Retd GD 11/6/71.
COLES P. K. L., MB ChB MRCGP DRCOG DAvMed AFOM. Born 31/1/48. Commd 20/2/72. Gp Capt 1/7/94. Retd
   MED 31/7/99.
COLES R. E., BSc. Born 20/10/57. Commd 19/9/76. Sqn Ldr 1/1/91. Retd ENG 1/10/97.
COLES R. G. Born 30/11/41. Commd 22/2/63. Flt Lt 12/11/69. Retd GD(G) 1/10/75. Re-entered 8/7/81. Sqn Ldr
   1/7/87. Retd OPS SPT 8/7/97.
COLES S. E., BSc. Born 7/9/47. Commd 22/9/65. Flt Lt 1/3/71. Retd GD 23/9/75.
COLESKY A. D. Born 19/3/38. Commd 9/3/62. Flt Lt 1/7/69. Retd GD 13/6/70.
COLEY D. G. L. Born 19/2/20. Commd 29/8/45. Sqn Ldr 1/7/55. Retd RGT 19/11/60.
COLEY N. Born 3/4/56. Commd 17/7/75. Sqn Ldr 1/7/91. Retd GD 14/3/97.
COLGAN F. J. Born 27/2/20. Commd 23/9/46. Sqn Ldr 1/7/53. Retd RGT 31/7/61.
COLHOUN D. N. T. Born 23/12/48. Commd 29/3/68. Flt Lt 29/9/73 Retd GD 23.12.86.
COLHOUN M. S. Born 12/8/42. Commd 8/12/61. Flt Lt 8/6/67. Retd GD 12/8/83.
COLL J. G. M. Born 15/11/18. Commd 2/3/50. Retd SEC 14/5/54.
COLLARD R. Born 20/7/35. Commd 1/12/54. Flt Lt 1/6/60. Retd GD 20/7/73.
COLLARD R. H. B. Born 23/11/22. Commd 3/9/43. Flt Lt 18/7/52. Retd GD 31/3/62.
COLLEN B. A., DFM. Born 20/11/23. Commd 27/4/61. Flt Lt 27/4/64. Retd GD 30/9/73.
COLLENETTE M. C. J. Born 11/11/44. Commd 19/12/63. Wg Cdr 1/7/87. Retd ADMIN 18/11/89.
COLLENETTE R. M. C. Born 6/5/16. Commd 25/1/51. Flt Lt 25/1/57. Retd SEC 6/5/73.
COLLETT D. M. Born 25/8/38. Commd 8/12/61. Flt Lt 28/5/66. Retd GD 2/5/77.
COLLEY D. T. Born 30/9/55. Commd 31/8/78. Flt Lt 14/9/83. Retd PI 1/9/89.
COLLEY P. J. Born 3/9/48. Commd 25/10/68. Sqn Ldr 1/7/81. Retd SY(RGT) 31/12/87.
COLLIER C. P. Born 24/7/41. Commd 11/2/65. Flt Lt 12/11/69. Retd SUP 25/7/91.
COLLIER D. S., AFC. Born 19/3/23. Commd 11/2/44. Sqn Ldr 1/10/55. Retd GD 19/3/66.
COLLIER J. C. Born 23/9/37. Commd 9/12/65. Gp Capt 1/7/85. Retd ENG 3/1/90.
COLLIER J. D. D., DSO DFC*. Born 10/11/16. Commd 29/6/36. Wg Cdr 1/7/47. Retd GD 9/3/59 rtg Gp Capt.
COLLIER J. M. Born 5/5/43. Commd 28/7/64. Wg Cdr 1/7/87. Retd GD 5/11/98.
COLLIER N. D. Born 11/8/37. Commd 12/9/56. Fg Offr 15/10/59. Retd SUP 19/3/63.
COLLIER P. G. Born 25/10/34. Commd 26/11/64. Sqn Ldr 3/9/72. Retd EDN 26/11/72.
COLLIER V. Born 1/11/33. Commd 3/6/65. Flt Lt 3/6/71. Retd ENG 17/11/72. Reinstated 7/5/80. Sqn Ldr 1/7/85.
   Retd ENG 1/11/88.
COLLIER-BAKER A. D. Born 6/2/57. Commd 15/2/90. Flt Lt 15/2/92. Retd ENG 15/2/98.
COLLIER-WEBB D. R., AE. Born 4/6/32. Commd 13/2/52. Wg Cdr 1/7/74. Retd GD 4/6/85.
COLLIN M. A. B. Born 22/6/38. Commd 25/7/60. Sqn Ldr 1/7/69. Retd GD 7/4/77.
COLLINGE M. J. Born 2/4/62. Commd 26/4/84. Sqn Ldr 1/7/93. Retd ENG 2/4/00.
COLLINGE R. A., MBE MIMgt. Born 23/4/35. Commd 29/4/54. Wg Cdr 1/7/79. Retd SY 29/7/85.
COLLINGS J. C., MB BS(Lond) HRCS(Eng) LRCP(Lond). Born 20/2/34. Commd 2/7/62. Wg Cdr 20/2/74. Retd
   MED 2/7/78.
COLLINGS S. J. Born 5/5/38. Commd 28/11/69. Flt Lt 28/11/71. Retd PI 28/11/77.
COLLINGWOOD D. C. Born 1/2/38. Commd 25/6/62. Flt Lt 25/6/62. Retd GD 20/12/68.
COLLINGWOOD D. J. Born 8/7/30. Commd 4/7/51. Flt Lt 13/11/57. Retd GD 8/7/73.
COLLINGWOOD W. Born 30/3/13. Commd 7/10/43. Sqn Ldr 1/4/56. Retd ENG 30/3/62.
COLLINS A., AFC DFM. Born 26/10/19. Commd 10/8/43. Sqn Ldr 1/10/54. Retd GD 15/8/68 rtg Wg Cdr.
COLLINS A. C. Born 4/9/36. Commd 4/9/61. Wg Cdr 1/1/83. Retd GD 4/4/90.
COLLINS A. D., DPhysEd. Born 1/3/25. Commd 11/8/52. Sqn Ldr 1/1/64. Retd PE 14/1/68.
COLLINS A. F., MLitt BA. Born 19/9/45. Commd 20/8/67. Sqn Ldr 1/1/92. Retd GD 16/3/98.
COLLINS A. J. Born 29/1/44. Commd 4/10/63. Sqn Ldr 1/1/94. Retd GD 24/1/01.
COLLINS A. J. F. Born 8/11/44. Commd 31/10/74. Flt Lt 31/10/76. Retd ADMIN 8/11/82.
COLLINS B. E. Born 11/4/32. Commd 3/11/51. Flt Lt 3/5/56. Retd GD(G) 1/9/77. Reinstated 7/1/80. Flt Lt 27/8/62.
   Retd GD(G) 1/8/89.
COLLINS D. Born 26/8/33. Commd 9/4/52. Flt Lt 21/8/57. Retd GD 11/4/78. Reinstated 19/11/80. Flt Lt 31/3/60.
   Retd GD 26/8/88.
COLLINS D. A. I. Born 21/2/46. Commd 3/10/69. Flt Lt 3/4/75. Retd GD 19/5/85.
COLLINS D. G. Born 8/7/30. Commd 29/10/64. Sqn Ldr 1/7/84. Retd ENG 8/7/88.
COLLINS D. S., MCIPD. Born 13/3/48. Commd 15/6/83. Flt Lt 15/6/87. Retd SY 5/1/97.
COLLINS D.C., MCIPS MIMgt. Born 22/6/38. Commd 2/9/57. A Cdre 1/1/90. Retd SUP 4/4/92.
COLLINS E. A. H. Born 7/4/20. Commd 19/1/53. Flt Lt 19/1/53. Retd SEC 7/4/65.
COLLINS E. P. Born 31/10/31. Commd 11/8/57. A Cdre 5/4/89. Retd MED 31/10/91.

COLLINS E. T., CEng MRAeS MIEE. Born 20/10/34. Commd 28/11/69. Flt Lt 28/11/71. Retd ENG 28/11/77.
COLLINS G. Born 5/2/21. Commd 14/4/44. Flt Lt 9/5/58. Retd GD(G) 2/3/71.
COLLINS G. E. Born 19/1/51. Commd 5/2/81. Flt Lt 5/2/83. Retd GD(G) 5/2/95.
COLLINS G. P. Born 18/4/49. Commd 10/9/70. Wg Cdr 1/7/88. Retd GD 2/6/90.
COLLINS H. B., MA MRAeS. Born 23/3/07. Commd 28/9/28. Gp Capt 1/1/49. Retd ENG 16/6/58.
COLLINS I. S. Born 20/1/57. Commd 19/11/87. Flt Lt 19/11/89. Retd ENG 19/11/95.
COLLINS J. B. V. Born 6/4/35. Commd 31/7/56. Sqn. Ldr 1/7/70. Retd GD 1/7/73.
COLLINS J. H. Born 15/8/36. Commd 13/12/68. Sqn Ldr 1/1/78. Retd GD(G) 1/10/80.
COLLINS J. P. Born 7/5/36. Commd 10/11/61. Flt Lt 10/2/67. Retd GD 7/5/74.
COLLINS J. R. Born 5/12/35. Commd 21/10/66. Flt Lt 21/10/68. Retd GD 5/12/73.
COLLINS K., BSc. Born 25/1/50. Commd 25/11/73. Flt Lt 25/5/74. Retd GD 22/10/94.
COLLINS L. J. Born 2/6/24. Commd 26/11/43. Flt Lt 4/6/53. Retd GD(G) 13/4/66.
COLLINS M. A. Born 8/11/33. Commd 28/4/61. Flt Lt 1/4/66. Retd GD 8/5/91.
COLLINS M. W. F., MBE. Born 24/4/47. Commd 1/12/69. Sqn Ldr 1/1/83. Retd SUP 10/12/99.
COLLINS M. W. G. Born 14/4/24. Commd 19/4/44. Gp Capt 1/7/73. Retd SEC 14/4/79.
COLLINS P. I. Born 26/4/52. Commd 3/10/74. Flt Lt 25/8/78. Retd GD 26/4/90.
COLLINS P. J., BSc. Born 22/4/54. Commd 3/9/72. Sqn Ldr 1/1/87. Retd GD 1/1/93.
COLLINS P. J. Born 21/4/48. Commd 16/9/76. Flt Lt 14/12/78. Retd ENG 21/4/86.
COLLINS P. M. Born 29/5/34. Commd 18/2/58. Flt Lt 20/8/63. Retd GD 30/5/83.
COLLINS P. S., CB AFC BA FIMgt. Born 19/3/30. Commd 17/10/51. AVM 1/7/83. Retd GD 1/7/85.
COLLINS R. Born 26/4/56. Commd 28/7/93. Flt Lt 28/7/97. Retd ENG 9/8/98.
COLLINS R. D. Born 18/7/43. Commd 19/6/64. Sqn Ldr 1/7/90. Retd GD 18/7/00.
COLLINS R. M., MIMgt. Born 28/12/39. Commd 28/11/69. Sqn Ldr 1/1/85. Retd GD 4/5/92.
COLLINS S. M. StC., MBE. Born 7/5/41. Commd 24/3/61. Sqn Ldr 1/7/74. Retd GD 7/5/79.
COLLINS S. P. Born 26/11/63. Commd 10/5/90. Flt Lt 10/5/92. Retd ADMIN 14/3/96.
COLLINS T. J. Born 24/12/55. Commd 14/7/77. Flt Lt 12/6/83. Retd GD 1/10/98.
COLLINS W. R. Born 23/5/26. Commd 3/5/46. Sqn Ldr 1/7/58. Retd GD 27/8/76.
COLLIS D. J. Born 25/11/39. Commd 12/12/59. Flt Lt 12/6/65. Retd GD 14/3/78.
COLLIS L., BA. Born 10/11/40. Commd 26/11/62. Sqn Ldr 1/7/72. Retd GD 1/10/87.
COLMAN A. E. Born 8/1/31. Commd 10/7/52. Sqn Ldr 1/1/67. Retd GD 21/5/76.
COLMAN M. H. J. Born 13/2/24. Commd 28/1/44. Wg Cdr 1/1/66. Retd GD 13/10/70.
COLMAN N. A., MSc MCIT MILT MCIPS MIMgt. Born 22/8/45. Commd 4/6/64. Gp Capt 1/7/91. Retd SUP
    30/3/94.
COLQUHOUN C. I., MBE DFC AFC. Born 25/8/23. Commd 18/12/43. Wg Cdr 1/1/69. Retd ENG 30/6/78.
COLQUHOUN I. F. Born 6/10/31. Commd 17/3/55. Sqn Ldr 1/7/64. Retd PE 22/9/70.
COLSON E. B., DSO. Born 26/5/10. Commd 30/5/50. Sqn Ldr 30/5/50. Retd RGT 11/8/55.
COLSTON J. F. A., BSc. Born 13/12/26. Commd 28/6/51. Sqn Ldr 1/7/69. Retd GD 2/9/75.
COLSTON R. J. Born 4/7/22. Commd 1/9/45. Sqn Ldr 1/7/54. Retd GD 6/7/61.
COLSTON W. B. Born 7/10/30. Commd 17/5/51. Flt Lt 17/5/53. Retd GD 7/10/68.
COLTART G. Born 6/3/21. Commd 19/5/44. Sqn Ldr 1/1/69. Retd ENG 15/9/73.
COLTERJOHN E. D., MB ChB DObstRCOG. Born 6/8/30. Commd 10/10/56. Sqn Ldr 1/4/62. Retd MED 3/10/67.
COLTMAN J. D. Born 22/6/34. Commd 18/3/53. Wg Cdr 1/1/76. Retd GD 1/5/82.
COLTON R. A., BSc. Born 27/12/40. Commd 10/9/63. Flt Lt 26/7/67. Retd ENG 10/9/79.
COLVER R. J., OBE. Born 12/4/45. Commd 13/8/65. Gp Capt 1/1/94. Retd GD 14/3/96.
COLVIN N. G. Born 22/1/31. Commd 25/5/50. Gp Capt 1/7/76. Retd GD(G) 13/11/82.
COLWELL G. P., BA. Born 6/8/38. Commd 14/8/59. Wg Cdr 1/7/86. Retd GD 6/8/93.
COLWELL V. W. E. Born 6/4/23. Commd 1/8/50. Flt Lt 5/9/56. Retd GD 17/12/66.
COLWILL D. P. Born 20/5/19. Commd 15/7/45. Flt Lt 15/1/50. Retd SEC 25/4/70.
COLWILL S. J., FRAeS. Born 20/8/51. Commd 27/3/70. Gp Capt 1/7/94. Retd GD(G) 19/10/96.
COLYER D. R. Born 29/7/37. Commd 11/9/56. Flt Lt 11/3/62. Retd GD 29/7/75.
COLYER R. B., MIMgt. B. Born 27/12/39. Commd 23/3/66. Sqn Ldr 1/1/75. Retd ENG 10/4/90.
COMBER N. Born 25/12/23. Commd 4/11/45. Sqn Ldr 1/1/56. Retd GD 31/7/69.
COMINA B. J. Born 19/6/52. Commd 27/5/71. Flt Lt 14/10/77. Retd ADMIN 20/7/79. Re-entered 20/8/80. Gp Capt
    1/7/98. Retd ADMIN 30/4/01.
COMMANDER R. J. Born 16/5/48. Commd 23/3/67. Flt Lt 23/9/72. Retd GD 1/6/85.
COMMON W. W. Born 17/11/27. Commd 9/1/51. Flt Lt 26/9/56. Retd GD 20/2/66.
COMPTON D. Born 23/4/29. Commd 26/5/60. Sqn Ldr 1/1/76. Retd ENG 1/5/79.
COMPTON J. F. Born 1/10/14. Commd 5/5/44. Flt Lt 29/6/50. Retd CAT 1/10/66 rtg Sqn Ldr.
COMPTON P. J. Born 21/2/48. Commd 1/4/66. Sqn Ldr 1/1/87. Retd GD 1/9/94.
COMPTON P.A.G. Born 20/6/47. Commd 4/2/71. Flt Lt 21/7/74. Retd ENG 20/7/86.
COMRIE A. C. Born 20/3/39. Commd 4/3/71. Flt Lt 4/3/73. Retd SUP 3/9/77.
CONANT G. T. G. Born 7/10/24. Commd 8/7/46. Flt Lt 8/7/52. Retd GD(G) 6/3/53.
CONBA T. W. T., ACIS. Born 20/8/33. Commd 25/8/67. Flt Lt 25/8/69. Retd SEC 2/2/74.
CONCHIE B. J., AFC. Born 11/9/30. Commd 2/7/52. Sqn Ldr 1/1/77. Retd GD 1/1/80.
CONDIE J. P. Born 26/4/36. Commd 8/1/76. Flt Lt 8/1/79. Retd GD 27/4/86.
CONDIE R. H. Born 1/9/32. Commd 11/4/58. Sqn Ldr 11/10/67. Retd EDN 11/4/74.

CONDLIFF T. D. Born 28/8/44. Commd 5/11/70. Flt Lt 1/4/74. Retd GD 28/8/82.
CONDON R., FRGS MInstAM MIMgt. Born 19/2/46. Commd 18/8/67. Wg Cdr 1/1/89. Retd ADMIN 2/4/95.
CONGDON P. S. M. Born 1/3/46. Commd 18/11/66. Sq Ldr 1/7/84. Retd SY 11/7/87.
CONLON G. D. Born 24/12/36. Commd 14/5/80. Flt Lt 14/5/74. Retd SY 16/7/87.
CONLON T. P. Born 11/9/44. Commd 12/7/68. Sqn Ldr 1/7/88. Retd GD 6/8/96.
CONNARTY A. O. Born 21/11/48. Commd 8/8/74. Wg Cdr 1/1/94. Retd GD(G) 14/3/96.
CONNELL E. Born 13/11/22. Commd 11/1/45. Flt Lt 6/4/53. Retd GD 8/8/64.
CONNELL J. A., OBE MIMgt. Born 19/1/30. Commd 30/3/61. Wg Cdr 1/1/77. Retd SEC 1/10/83.
CONNELL J. L., BSc. Born 17/5/57. Commd 15/3/87. Sqn Ldr 1/1/95. Retd ADMIN 14/3/97.
CONNELL M. B. Born 30/5/50. Commd 30/5/69. Sqn Ldr 1/7/84. Retd GD 19/5/90.
CONNELLY J. S., BA MIMgt. Born 19/10/34. Commd 10/4/56. Sqn Ldr 1/1/76. Retd GD(G) 1/10/85.
CONNING W. J. J. Born 16/5/32. Commd 23/4/52. Flt Lt 19/9/57. Retd GD 16/5/87.
CONNOLLY G. A. W., LLB. Born 26/11/50. Commd 20/10/74. Flt Lt 20/7/76. Retd GD 20/10/90.
CONNOLLY T. V. Born 25/6/22. Commd 19/12/54. Sqn Ldr 1/7/71. Retd GD(G) 25/6/77.
CONNOR E. L., MIMgt. Born 29/12/22. Commd 1/10/43. Wg Cdr 1/7/63. Retd GD 2/10/73.
CONNOR J. P., AFC BSc(Eng). Born 11/10/46. Commd 20/8/67. Sqn Ldr 1/7/81. Retd GD 11/10/90.
CONNOR M. R. H., OBE MSc. Born 22/3/45. Commd 8/7/65. Gp Capt 1/7/92. Retd SUP 18/4/00.
CONNORS J. J. Born 20/10/23. Commd 29/3/45. Flt Lt 29/11/51. Retd GD 16/12/64.
CONNORTON J. Born 2/12/43. Commd 27/7/72. Sqn Ldr 1/1/89. Retd ENG 2/12/98.
CONOLLY R. G. Born 3/11/47. Commd 19/5/67. Sqn Ldr 1/1/84. Retd GD 21/1/94.
CONQUER N. P. W. Born 16/2/21. Commd 24/8/41. Wg Cdr 1/7/58. Retd GD 16/2/68.
CONRAD J. A. Born 7/11/48. Commd 29/8/72. Sqn Ldr 1/1/84. Retd ADMIN 14/3/96.
CONRADI I. G., BSc. Born 19/4/37. Commd 27/10/57. Flt Lt 2/4/63. Retd GD 19/4/75.
CONRADI K. R., BSc. Born 14/2/62. Commd 14/9/80. Flt Lt 15/10/84. Retd GD 17/12/96.
CONRAN-SMITH D. R. Born 5/11/39. Commd 19/12/61. Sqn Ldr 1/1/72. Retd GD 5/11/83.
CONRY J. D. Born 29/8/23. Commd 7/11/44. Sqn Ldr 1/4/55. Retd GD 9/12/67.
CONSTABLE D. C. J. Born 7/3/45. Commd 30/5/69. Sqn Ldr 1/1/97. Retd GD 1/12/99.
CONSTABLE F. G., DFM. Born 19/12/19. Commd 16/4/41. Sqn Ldr 1/7/53. Retd GD 17/1/59.
CONSTABLE J. E., BA. Born 20/5/57. Commd 19/9/76. Flt Lt 15/10/82. Retd SY 1/10/87.
CONSTABLE P. F., AFC. Born 19/6/37. Commd 24/6/55. Wg Cdr 1/7/80. Retd GD 1/2/90.
CONSTABLE R. E. Born 19/4/35. Commd 30/8/62. Sqn Ldr 1/1/71. Retd SUP 3/5/78.
CONSTANTI D. Born 11/1/31. Commd 18/6/52. Flt Lt 13/11/57. Retd GD 30/1/69.
CONSTANTINE K. W. Born 13/6/22. Commd 19/7/51. Sqn Ldr 1/7/67. Retd ADMIN 13/6/77.
CONWAY A. G., DFC MCIPD. Born 18/3/22. Commd 20/8/41. Wg Cdr 1/1/56. Retd. GD 18/3/77.
CONWAY D. B. Born 18/11/37. Commd 9/2/62. Flt Lt 25/7/66. Retd GD 4/3/88.
CONWAY H. D., MB ChB DPH DIH. Born 11/11/10. Commd 30/3/35. Wg Cdr 1/7/47. Retd MED 9/11/63.
CONWAY L. B. J. Born 25/11/24. Commd 12/3/52. Sqn Ldr 1/7/72. Retd GD 25/5/76.
CONWAY S. D. Born 12/5/45. Commd 21/7/65. Flt Lt 21/1/71. Retd GD 16/2/77.
CONYERS G. G. Born 29/7/17. Commd 4/3/43. Sqn Ldr 1/4/56. Retd ENG 29/7/66.
COODE I. C. S. M. Born 25/2/32. Commd 6/5/65. Flt Lt 26/7/67. Retd SUP 6/5/73.
COOK A. K., DFC. Born 7/10/11. Commd 1/4/40. Flt Lt 1/4/42. Retd GD 15/12/45 rtg Sqn Ldr.
COOK B. H. Born 14/5/32. Commd 21/5/52. Flt Lt 15/10/57. Retd GD(G) 4/11/75.
COOK B. W. Born 14/2/23. Commd 19/3/52. Sqn Ldr. 1/7/65. Retd GD 5/3/76.
COOK C. E., BSc. Born 20/2/46. Commd 28/9/64. Sqn Ldr 1/1/83. Retd GD 14/3/97.
COOK C. J. Born 22/11/42. Commd 14/2/69. Sqn Ldr 1/1/88. Retd GD 22/11/00.
COOK C. M. Born 14/6/54. Commd 16/9/76. Sqn Ldr 1/7/92. Retd ADMIN 14/6/00.
COOK D., OBE MIMgt. Born 27/9/30. Commd 19/4/50. Gp Capt 1/1/76. Retd GD 27/9/85.
COOK D. A., MILT. Born 7/1/46. Commd 11/5/78. Sqn Ldr 1/1/88. Retd SUP 20/4/96.
COOK D. E., MMedSci MB ChB DIH DAvMed AFOM MRAeS. Born 31/5/56. Commd 18/1/77. Wg Cdr 1/8/93. Retd MED 18/6/97.
COOK D. F. Born 1/4/49. Commd 27/2/70. Sqn Ldr 1/1/81. Retd GD 1/1/01.
COOK D. G. Born 28/4/29. Commd 18/7/63. Sqn Ldr 1/7/77. Retd GD(G) 1/8/79.
COOK E. J., MBE. Born 1/7/18. Commd 30/9/42. Sqn Offr 1/7/50. Retd SEC 5/5/54.
COOK E. W. W. Born 16/10/11. Commd 3/1/47. Fg Offr 3/1/47. Retd SUP 27/1/49.
COOK F. A. Born 26/9/43. Commd 9/2/66. Flt Lt 18/6/72. Retd GD(G) 9/11/81.
COOK F. J. Born 13/1/32. Commd 2/2/63. Flt Lt 25/7/66. Retd GD 24/8/76.
COOK G. H. Born 18/1/26. Commd 20/10/59. Flt Lt 22/10/65. Retd ENG 26/11/76.
COOK H. T., BSc. Born 31/12/51. Commd 13/9/70. Sqn Ldr 1/7/85. Retd GD 20/4/90.
COOK J. Born 20/2/21. Commd 26/9/45. Sqn Ldr 1/7/59. Retd GD 2/2/71.
COOK J. A. Born 18/11/26. Commd 24/1/63. Flt Lt 24/1/68. Retd GD(G) 18/11/87.
COOK J. B., MILDM. Born 26/6/34. Commd 21/10/65. Sqn Ldr 1/7/78. Retd SUP 30/4/90.
COOK J. D., BA. Born 1/6/23. Commd 14/8/43. Sqn Ldr 1/10/55. Retd GD 11/11/61.
COOK J. F. Born 21/4/17. Commd 30/7/39. Sqn Ldr 1/7/43. Retd GD 1/11/57.
COOK J. H., CEng MIEE MRAeS MIMgt. Born 31/5/24. Commd 21/6/56. Wg Cdr 1/1/70. Retd ENG 1/1/72.
COOK J. K. Born 4/5/18. Commd 6/10/44. Flt Lt 6/4/48. Retd GD 17/7/54.
COOK J. R. Born 13/10/34. Commd 29/4/71. Sqn Ldr 1/7/85. Retd ENG 13/10/92.

COOK K. H. H., DFC. Born 9/4/23. Commd 22/1/43. Wg Cdr 1/1/60. Retd GD 13/1/68.
COOK L. Born 29/6/18. Commd 15/11/40. Sqn Ldr 1/10/57. Retd SEC 19/6/61.
COOK M. E. Born 26/11/32. Commd 26/3/52. Flt Lt 7/8/57. Retd GD 26/11/70.
COOK M. J., BSc(Eng). Born 19/12/63. Commd 11/9/83. Flt Lt 15/1/89. Retd GD 15/7/98.
COOK N. C., MILAM. Born 20/1/47. Commd 19/1/66. Wg Cdr 1/1/86. Retd RGT 20/1/91.
COOK P. Born 17/2/35. Commd 18/2/54. Flt Lt 1/3/61. Retd CAT 17/2/73.
COOK P. J. Born 28/7/40. Commd 18/12/80. Flt Lt 18/12/83. Retd GD(ENG) 23/5/89.
COOK R. M. Born 3/8/38. Commd 8/12/61. Flt Lt 28/11/67. Retd SUP 1/5/77.
COOK R. M. S., MBE. Born 23/1/41. Commd 28/4/61. Wg Cdr 1/1/88. Retd GD 24/7/95.
COOK R. T. Born 20/2/26. Commd 20/11/50. Flt Lt 26/5/55. Retd GD 30/6/69.
COOK W. Born 3/3/54. Commd 13/1/72. Plt Offr 6/5/72. Retd GD(G) 2/10/72.
COOKE A. J. Born 3/7/31. Commd 3/6/65. Flt Lt 3/6/71. Retd GD(G) 3/7/89.
COOKE A. K., BTech BEng. Born 19/1/60. Commd 11/9/83. Flt Lt 11/3/86. Retd ADMIN 11/9/95.
COOKE B. H., MIMgt. Born 4/3/30. Commd 5/11/53. Sqn Ldr 1/1/74. Retd SEC 24/10/81.
COOKE C. K. Born 15/4/24. Commd 1/10/43. Gp Capt 1/7/71. Retd GD 29/5/75.
COOKE D. Born 4/7/21. Commd 10/5/43. Flt Lt 10/11/46. Retd GD 4/7/64.
COOKE F. I., CEng MIEE. Born 22/4/35. Commd 25/8/60. Flt Lt 14/2/66. Retd ENG 22/4/73.
COOKE The Rev G. Born 11/1/38. Commd 2/10/67. Retd 20/10/71 Sqn Ldr.
COOKE G. H. Born 11/8/15. Commd. 11/6/53. Flt Lt 11/6/56. Retd ENG 30/8/70.
COOKE H. Born 23/7/44. Commd 16/12/66. Flt Lt 16/3/73. Retd PI 24/1/76.
COOKE I. E., BSc PhD. Born 1/5/48. Commd 22/10/72. Flt Lt 22/10/73. Retd EDN 28/11/75.
COOKE J. Born 20/4/28. Commd 23/1/64. Flt Lt 23/1/69. Retd GD 20/4/88.
COOKE J. D., BA. Born 1/8/23. Commd 2/7/51. Sqn Ldr 1/1/64. Retd PE 31/5/73.
COOKE J. M. Born 17/1/38. Commd 24/6/71. Flt Lt 24/6/73. Retd ENG 21/9/89.
COOKE J. M. Born 7/8/21. Commd 19/7/44. Flt Lt 19/1/48. Retd GD 12/6/51.
COOKE J. N. C., CB OBE MD BS FRCP FRCP(Edin) MFOM MRCS. Born 16/1/22. Commd 1/11/45. AVM 1/9/79. Retd MED 15/6/85.
COOKE J.J., BA. Born 21/10/45. Commd 9/6/68. Gp Capt 1/7/90. Retd SUP 24/10/92.
COOKE M. S. Born 20/6/37. Commd 18/1/56. Flt Lt 18/7/61. Retd GD 26/4/64.
COOKE P. K. Born 12/5/27. Commd 19/7/51. Flt Lt 19/1/55. Retd GD 12/5/65.
COOKSEY J. R. Born 7/12/12. Commd 9/5/40. Flt Lt 9/5/42. Retd GD 2/7/47.
COOKSLEY A. G. Born 5/6/08. Commd 11/5/42. Flt Lt 1/7/46. Retd SUP 11/3/47.
COOKSON F. D. Born 14/4/30. Commd 11/11/65. Flt Lt 11/11/68. Retd GD 17/11/77. Reinstated 2/9/81. Flt Lt 27/8/72. Retd GD 14/4/88.
COOLE A. M. Born 24/7/09. Commd 20/3/41. Flt Lt 1/9/45. Retd ENG 4/8/58 rtg Sqn Ldr.
COOLEDGE R. C. Born 10/9/18. Commd 26/1/45. Flt Lt 26/7/48. Retd GD 23/11/57.
COOMBES C. Born 19/7/34. Commd 10/4/56. Flt Lt 1/3/61. Retd GD 18/6/81.
COOMBES D. L. Born 8/10/67. Commd 31/7/86. Flt Lt 21/1/93. Retd ADMIN 27/6/96.
COOMBES D. W. Born 9/11/25. Commd 20/4/50. Sqn Ldr 1/1/68. Retd GD 9/7/76.
COOMBES L. D. W. Born 4/8/19. Commd 21/11/41. Sqn Ldr 1/1/59. Retd ENG 4/8/77.
COOMBES P. K. Born 5/11/27. Commd 9/8/51. Flt Lt 28/11/56. Retd 5/11/82.
COOMBES S. R. A., BSc. Born 4/8/60. Commd 26/9/82. Sqn Ldr 1/1/94. Retd GD 26/9/98.
COOMBS B., BA. Born 21/7/47. Commd 30/1/70. Wg Cdr 1/7/98. Retd OPS SPT 1/12/00.
COOMBS C. J. T., BSc MRAeS MIMgt. Born 1/9/26. Commd 20/11/47. Wg Cdr 1/7/74. Retd EDN 28/7/79.
COOMBS M. J. Born 2/8/36. Commd 21/1/67. Flt Lt 27/1/69. Retd PRT 27/1/75.
COON W. J. B., BSc CEng MRAeS. Born 14/9/32. Commd 22/1/55. Wg Cdr 1/7/75. Retd ENG 1/10/82.
COONEY E. F. Born 1/7/15. Commd 22/6/50. Fg Offr 22/6/52. Retd SEC 16/7/55.
COONEY P. J. Born 17/3/61. Commd 1/11/79. Sqn Ldr 1/1/94. Retd GD 17/3/99.
COOPER A. C., MBE. Born 4/6/14. Commd 29/11/43. Sqn Ldr 1/1/56. Retd ENG 4/6/69.
COOPER A. D. Born 30/3/43. Commd 22/5/75. Sqn Ldr 1/7/87. Retd GD 14/3/96.
COOPER A. F. Born 9/3/54. Commd 17/7/75. Flt Lt 9/9/79. Retd GD 14/3/96.
COOPER A. H. Born 23/2/29. Commd 24/9/64. Sqn Ldr 1/1/77. Retd ENG 3/4/79.
COOPER A. R. C. Born 23/6/83. Commd 1/4/18. Sqn Ldr 1/4/18. Retd GD 22/8/28 rtg Wg Cdr. Recalled 26/10/39 to 28/10/43.
COOPER B. C. Born 30/3/10. Commd 14/2/46. Flt Lt 14/8/48. Retd ENG 30/3/65.
COOPER B. F., MSc BSc CEng MRAeS. Born 8/10/37. Commd 10/8/65. Sqn Ldr 1/1/75. Retd ENG 8/2/96.
COOPER B. V. Born 24/5/27. Commd 20/12/62. Flt Lt 20/12/68. Retd ADMIN 24/5/85.
COOPER C. A., MA. Born 3/7/33. Commd 26/9/53. Wg Cdr 1/7/74. Retd ENG 3/7/88.
COOPER C. C. F., DFC. Born 16/7/16. Commd 19/2/38. Wg Cdr 1/7/53. Retd GD 29/8/63.
COOPER C. E. F. Born 16/8/28. Commd 12/1/51. Sqn Ldr 1/7/71. Retd SUP 6/9/78.
COOPER C. F., CBE BA MIMgt MCIPS. Born 5/10/44. Commd 11/11/71. A Cdre 1/7/93. Retd SUP 2/5/01.
COOPER C. G., BTech. Born 6/4/51. Commd 9/5/69. Sqn Ldr 1/7/84. Retd ENG 6/4/89.
COOPER C. R., OBE FIMgt CertEd. Born 05/03/45. Commd 30/1/70. Gp Capt 1/7/93. Retd ADMIN 8/9/99.
COOPER D. A., AFC. Born 27/9/30. Commd 12/12/51. Wg Cdr 1/7/67. Retd GD 1/7/70.
COOPER D. F., BSc. Born 26/3/36. Commd 9/8/57. Sqn Ldr 12/8/70. Retd ADMIN 1/11/76.
COOPER D. R., MSc BSc. Born 18/7/43. Commd 5/1/70. Sqn Ldr 5/3/75. Retd ADMIN 18/7/98.

COOPER E. E. Born 22/12/12. Commd 12/9/46. Sqn Ldr 1/1/63. Retd SUP 22/12/67.
COOPER E. W. Born 16/3/09. Commd 19/8/41. Flt Lt 1/7/45. Retd ENG 21/4/46 rtg Sqn Ldr.
COOPER F. A. Born 27/4/23. Commd 1/7/44. Sqn Ldr 1/1/62. Retd GD 26/2/65.
COOPER F. B., CEng MIMechE MIQA MRAeS. Born 30/9/37. Commd 1/1/62. Wg Cdr 1/1/84. Retd ENG 30/9/91.
COOPER F. T. Born 13/2/23. Commd 3/2/45. Sqn Ldr 1/7/56. Retd GD 13/2/66.
COOPER G. Born 14/8/46. Commd 18/1/73. Sqn Ldr 1/1/90. Retd GD 14/8/98.
COOPER G. B., DPhysEd. Born 12/3/28. Commd 6/8/52. Flt Lt 6/8/56. Retd PE 6/8/68.
COOPER G. D., MBE. Born 7/11/19. Commd 31/12/41. Wg Cdr 1/1/58. Retd ENG 7/11/74.
COOPER G. E. Born 15/5/39. Commd 16/9/71. Flt Lt 16/9/73. Retd GD 15/5/94.
COOPER G. M. G., BSc CEng FRAeS FIMgt. Born 12/9/31. Commd 24/9/52. A Cdre 1/7/81. Retd ENG 30/11/82.
COOPER G. P. Born 25/6/52. Commd 16/3/73. Sqn Ldr 1/7/86. Retd SUP 25/6/90.
COOPER G. S., OBE. Born 25/10/25. Commd 21/12/45. A Cdre 1/7/75. Retd GD 1/9/78.
COOPER H., BDS LDS RCS MGDSRCS(Eng). Born 31/1/42. Commd 18/6/60. Wg Cdr 5/1/78. Retd DEL 31/3/88.
COOPER I. D. Born 9/9/55. Commd 13/12/79. Flt Lt 19/1/84. Retd GD 1/4/89.
COOPER J., DPhysEd. Born 30/9/39. Commd 5/1/65. Flt Lt 5/7/70. Retd GD 15/9/77.
COOPER J. A. Born 5/12/22. Commd 10/9/44. Flt Lt 10/3/48. Retd GD 12/5/73.
COOPER J. E. Born 22/5/33. Commd 6/4/54. Gp Capt 1/7/85. Retd SUP 18/5/88.
COOPER J. G., OBE DFC. Born 27/7/20. Commd 4/7/41. Wg Cdr 1/7/63. Retd GD(G) 1/5/73.
COOPER J. H. Born 12/2/51. Commd 14/10/71. Sqn Ldr 1/7/85. Retd GD 12/2/89.
COOPER J. J., OBE MIMgt. Born 12/1/23. Commd 6/8/44. Wg Cdr 1/1/64. Retd GD 12/1/78.
COOPER J. W., BA. Born 16/8/30. Commd 18/6/52. Flt Lt 13/11/57. Retd 16/9/90.
COOPER J. W. Born 21/1/17. Commd 10/5/47. Flt Lt 10/11/51. Retd SUP 21/1/72.
COOPER K. C. Born 27/12/23. Commd 19/7/51. Flt Lt 19/1/55. Retd GD(G) 1/10/77.
COOPER K. G. Born 1/1/31. Commd 4/1/56. Flt Lt 4/7/61. Retd GD 1/12/70.
COOPER K. J., MHCIMA. Born 12/10/21. Commd 17/10/57. Flt Lt 1/4/63. Retd CAT 18/10/75.
COOPER L. A., BSc. Born 16/12/38. Commd 31/10/60. Flt Lt 31/7/62. Retd GD 12/11/77.
COOPER M. A. Born 12/7/46. Commd 21/5/80. Flt Lt 21/3/74. Retd GD 25/2/87.
COOPER M. B. Born 30/11/14. Commd 2/1/39. Sqn Ldr 1/6/45. Retd GD 28/4/49.
COOPER P. A., BSc CEng DipEl MIEE. Born 30/1/28. Commd 23/2/50. Sqn Ldr 1/4/61. Retd EDN 9/10/73.
COOPER P. A. L. Born 29/8/18. Commd 9/9/39. Wg Cdr 1/1/55. Retd SEC 31/12/60.
COOPER P. R., BEng. Born 12/7/50. Commd 17/1/72. Sqn Ldr 1/7/85. Retd GD 12/7/88.
COOPER R. A., BA. Born 6/3/50. Commd 13/9/70. Flt Lt 15/4/73. Retd GD 6/3/88.
COOPER R. A. Born 24/2/38. Commd 7/6/68. Sqn Ldr 1/1/78. Retd ENG 21/4/83.
COOPER R. B. A. Born 16/12/28. Commd 8/2/51. Flt Lt 1/1/66. Retd SUP 1/1/69.
COOPER R. E., BEM. Born 21/1/32. Commd 4/7/64. Sqn Ldr 4/7/71. Retd EDN 4/7/74.
COOPER R. H. Born 27/6/29. Commd 18/9/50. Flt Lt 5/10/60. Retd GD 27/6/67.
COOPER R. H. Born 29/9/19. Commd 21/10/54. Sqn Ldr 1/1/63. Retd ENG 1/9/70.
COOPER R. M. Born 8/12/41. Commd 29/10/60. Sqn Ldr 1/1/72. Retd GD 8/12/79.
COOPER R. S. Born 5/8/15. Commd 21/7/40. Flt Lt 21/7/42. Retd GD 14/5/63.
COOPER R. W. L. Born 4/2/45. Commd 4/7/69. Flt Lt 14/11/75. Retd GD(G) 11/3/85.
COOPER S. H. Born 26/7/20. Commd 27/8/59. Flt Lt 27/9/64. Retd SUP 26/1/71.
COOPER S. R. Born 17/9/35. Commd 1/8/69. Flt Lt 1/8/71. Retd ADMIN 10/9/76.
COOPER T. K. N. Born 20/10/43. Commd 11/5/86. Sqn Ldr 29/12/86. Retd MED(T) 1/7/88.
COOPER T. W., AFM. Born 21/5/24. Commd 29/6/50. Sqn Ldr 1/1/61. Retd GD 23/4/76.
COOPER W. P. Born 11/7/22. Commd 25/2/44. Flt Lt 4/1/51. Retd PE 6/8/67 rtg Sqn Ldr.
COOTE C. H. Born 23/5/58. Commd 5/4/79. Flt Lt 5/10/84. Retd GD 5/4/87.
COOTER C. E., BA. Born 15/8/34. Commd 9/8/60. Sqn Ldr 24/5/69. Retd EDN 16/7/74.
COPE LEWIS R. Born 25/6/35. Commd 9/6/54. Flt Lt 9/12/59. Retd GD 5/10/73.
COPE S. E. Born 13/4/20. Commd 1/5/47. Flt Lt 1/11/51. Retd SUP 3/10/59.
COPE-LEWIS M. M. Born 24/7/39. Commd 20/12/62. Sqn Ldr 1/7/73. Retd SEC 26/9/78.
COPELAND P. J. Born 22/7/34. Commd 19/1/66. Sqn Ldr 1/1/74. Retd ENG 7/9/88.
COPELAND S. J. Born 23/9/60. Commd 26/4/84. Flt Lt 27/9/90. Retd ADMIN 11/12/96.
COPLAND J. H., MIMgt. Born 17/3/33. Commd 4/5/53. Sqn Ldr 1/1/67. Retd GD 19/3/76.
COPLESTON D. J. Born 6/4/23. Commd 22/8/46. Flt Lt 22/2/50. Retd ENG 6/4/56.
COPNALL P. I., BSc. Born 20/4/63. Commd 29/9/85. Flt Lt 29/3/93. Retd GD 15/12/92.
COPPARD E. G. Born 11/11/26. Commd 18/3/52. Flt Lt 22/5/57. Retd GD 7/8/67.
COPPING G. C. A. Born 26/8/55. Commd 22/5/75. Sqn Ldr 1/7/91. Retd ADMIN 12/6/98.
COPPINS D. V. H. Born 2/2/26. Commd 22/8/63. Flt Lt 22/8/66. Retd GD 2/2/84.
COPSEY G. J., MBA BSc CEng MRAeS MIMgt. Born 11/2/51. Commd 25/2/72. Sqn Ldr 1/1/85. Retd ENG 26/2/90.
COPSEY J. E. Born 6/1/44. Commd 2/8/66. Flt Lt 17/3/71. Retd GD 6/1/82.
CORBELL B. Born 23/11/32. Commd 10/9/79. Sqn Ldr 20/5/76. Retd ADMIN 10/9/80.
CORBET D. J. Born 13/12/22. Commd 14/6/44. Wg Cdr 1/7/62. Retd GD 30/7/66.
CORBETT A. F. Born 31/1/31. Commd 6/9/56. Flt Lt 6/3/61. Retd GD 31/1/91.
CORBETT A. J., BA. Born 12/7/60. Commd 7/11/82. Flt Lt 7/5/86. Retd ADMIN 5/11/95.
CORBIN C. J., MRCS LRCP. Born 24/3/53. Commd 22/1/74. Sqn Ldr 1/8/82. Retd MED 1/4/90.
CORBIN L. G. Born 10/7/20. Commd 26/9/43. Flt Lt 26/3/47. Retd GD 10/7/75.

CORBITT A. G. Born 13/6/48. Commd 27/2/70. Wg Cdr 1/7/90. Retd SUP 1/6/95.
CORBITT A. L. Born 30/5/49. Commd 1/3/68. Flt Lt 1/6/74. Retd SEC 1/3/78.
CORBRIDGE W. Born 16/5/25. Commd 24/4/70. Flt Lt 24/4/76. Retd MED(T) 16/5/80.
CORBY J. Born 9/2/38. Commd 25/3/70. Sqn Ldr 1/1/81. Retd GD 9/2/93.
CORCK R. G. Born 3/5/26. Commd 7/12/48. Flt Lt 15/12/53. Retd GD 14/1/66.
CORDEN A. M. Born 22/2/46. Commd 5/2/65. Flt Lt 5/2/71. Retd GD 1/10/75.
CORDEN J. S., BSc ACGI. Born 3/6/57. Commd 23/9/79. Sqn Ldr 1/1/92. Retd GD 31/12/96.
CORDEROY, Rev G.T., BA. Born 15/4/31. Commd 1/1/62. Retd 23/10/87. Rel Gp Capt
CORDERY J. V., MBE AFC BA. Born 19/3/25. Commd 17/4/46. Sqn Ldr 1/1/60. Retd GD 19/3/63. Re-instated Flt Lt 19/3/58 to 19/3/83.
CORDING R. F. Born 20/4/28. Commd 20/4/48. Flt Lt 28/6/60. Retd GD 29/1/68.
CORDUROY F. G., MSc. BSc. Born 23/10/30. Commd 10/10/51. Flt Lt 10/4/66. Retd GD 23/10/68.
CORFE A. G. Born 24/7/25. Commd 29/12/44. Sqn Ldr 1/1/58. Retd GD 3/12/76.
CORFIELD B. T. Born 6/12/20. Commd 3/11/44. Flt Lt 3/5/48. Retd GD 6/12/63.
CORFIELD J. Born 28/2/23. Commd 17/10/57. Sqn Ldr 1/1/78. Retd ENG 28/2/83.
CORFIELD P. W. Born 21/11/40. Commd 10/9/70. Flt Lt 10/9/72. Retd SEC 21/11/78.
CORIAT H., BA. Born 9/10/37. Commd 15/12/59. Gp Capt 1/1/86. Retd GD 31/10/88.
CORKE B. C., MB ChB. Born 16/2/38. Commd 16/7/62. Sqn Ldr 16/7/67. Retd MED 3/4/74.
CORKE D. Born 1/7/18. Commd 19/12/41. Sqn Offr 1/7/51. Retd SEC 1/2/54.
CORKER R. C., DFC. Born 10/11/20. Commd 5/7/44. Sqn Ldr 1/7/69. Retd GD(G) 10/11/75.
CORKERTON W. C. Born 27/8/30. Commd 5/12/51. Flt Lt 5/6/56. Retd GD 27/8/68.
CORKETT A. H. Born 9/8/17. Commd 15/4/39. Flt Lt 1/9/52. Retd GD(G) 15/1/62 rtg Sqn Ldr.
CORLEY B. R. Born 4/4/34. Commd 8/10/52. Flt Lt 6/3/58. Retd GD 4/4/72.
CORMACK B. A., BTech CEng MRAeS MIMgt. Born 5/8/53. Commd 25/9/71. Sqn Ldr 1/1/86. Retd ENG 5/8/91.
CORMACK B. G., MA. Born 5/7/40. Commd 1/8/66. Sqn Ldr 1/3/73. Retd ADMIN 1/8/88.
CORMACK P. G., MIMgt. Born 23/1/36. Commd 5/5/55. Wg Cdr 1/7/74. Retd RGT 9/5/81.
CORNABY P. J., DPhysEd MIMgt. Born 9/7/30. Commd 16/1/57. Wg Cdr 1/1/74. Retd SUP 3/9/83.
CORNALL C. J. Born 23/9/51. Commd II/4/85. Flt Lt 11/4/87. Retd GD 22/1/95.
CORNELIUS J. Born 2/8/17. Commd 4/11/43. Flt Lt 4/5/47. Retd ENG 31/10/63.
CORNELIUS S. J. Born 24/2/39. Commd 6/12/59. Sqn Ldr 1/1/86. Retd GD 24/2/94.
CORNES S. W., CEng MIEE. Born 16/1/16. Commd 5/8/43. Wg Cdr 1/1/62. Retd ENG 26/2/71.
CORNFORD A. L. Born 29/8/14. Commd 8/1/39. Wg Cdr 1/7/53. Retd SUP 17/11/64.
CORNFORD D. A. Born 21/2/45. Commd 23/5/85. Flt Lt 23/5/89. Retd ENG 1/9/99.
CORNISH A. H. P. Born 1/1/30. Commd 1/8/51. Sqn Ldr 1/1/64. Retd GD 5/3/76.
CORNISH C. W. Born 20/5/23. Commd 28/5/43. Wg Cdr 1/7/59. Retd GD 10/9/68.
CORNISH C. W., CEng MINucE MRAeS. Born 11/3/21. Commd 17/5/56. Sqn Ldr 1/1/68. Retd ENG 10/8/74.
CORNISH E. J. Born 22/5/32. Commd 28/1/60. Flt Lt 28/7/64. Retd SEC 22/5/70.
CORNISH J. H. Born 7/3/27. Commd 13/2/64. Sqn Ldr 1/7/74. Retd ENG 7/3/85.
CORNTHWAITE J. D. Born 14/4/34. Commd 17/7/70. Sqn Ldr 1/7/80. Retd ENG 31/10/86.
CORNWELL M. R. Born 16/10/45. Commd 21/7/65. Flt Lt 21/1/71. Retd GD 16/10/83.
CORNWELL N. H. Born 12/9/24. Commd 12/9/63. Flt Lt 12/9/68. Retd ENG 12/9/79.
CORP G. G. Born 30/5/14. Commd 27/5/54. Flt Lt 27/5/57. Retd GD 28/2/59.
CORPS S. G. Born 2/11/29. Commd 1/4/53. Flt Lt 3/9/58. Retd GD 20/12/62.
CORRANS K. D., MIMgt. Born 28/10/38. Commd 18/2/81. Wg Cdr 1/7/91. Retd ADMIN 18/2/97.
CORRIE H. C. D. Born 31/10/16. Commd 3/9/43. Sqn Ldr 1/1/65. Retd SUP 1/11/71.
CORRIN J. E. Born 17/9/42. Commd 2/1/75. Sqn Ldr 1/7/82. Retd SUP 24/7/93.
CORSER V. J., MIMgt. Born 23/1/18. Commd 13/2/47. Wg Cdr 1/1/64. Retd SUP 23/1/73.
CORSER W. J. L., BA. Born 5/1/44. Commd 22/5/64. Sqn Ldr 1/7/90. Retd GD 30/4/96.
CORSER W. P. Born 10/10/15. Commd 27/1/55. Sqn Ldr 1/1/64. Retd ENG 4/8/67.
CORSON J. P. Born 4/4/31. Commd 19/4/51. Flt Lt 17/10/56. Retd GD 4/4/69.
CORTON S. Born 3/3/38. Commd 12/1/62. Flt Lt 1/7/66. Retd GD 3/3/88.
COSBY D. R., AFC. Born 7/12/43. Commd 9/2/62. Flt Lt 12/11/69. Retd GD 7/12/81.
COSGROVE J. A., CBE. Born 13/10/43. Commd 21/7/65. Gp Capt 1/1/92. Retd GD 22/5/98.
COSHAM A. R. Born 6/1/47. Commd 28/11/69. Flt Lt 17/8/73. Retd GD 2/9/75.
COSTAIN H. D., MBE MIMgt. Born 27/3/22. Commd 6/3/43. Wg Cdr 1/1/70. Retd GD 27/3/77.
COSTELLO J. M. Born 12/4/19. Commd 31/10/43. Flt Lt 3/4/47. Retd GD(G) 12/4/63.
COSTICK E. H., QGM. Born 5/10/28. Commd 6/4/64. Sqn Ldr 1/7/76. Retd ENG 5/10/83.
COSTIN W. J. Born 13/12/47. Commd 14/8/70. Flt Lt 14/2/76. Retd GD 13/12/85.
COSTLEY J. A. Born 2/3/32. Commd 23/1/64. Flt Lt 23/1/69. Retd GD 16/8/75.
COSTLEY J. M., BSc. Born 8/3/31. Commd 11/2/54. Sqn Ldr 11/8/64. Retd EDN 28/10/69.
COTTAM B. M. Born 19/3/45. Commd 26/5/67. Gp Capt 1/1/92. Retd GD 5/12/96.
COTTAM J., MB BS LMSSA FRCS(Edin). Born 25/3/30. Commd 26/9/54. Wg Cdr 3/9/67. Retd MED 26/9/70.
COTTER J. D., DFC. Born 21/9/23. Commd 4/11/43. Sqn Ldr 1/10/55. Retd GD 21/3/62.
COTTERELL S. C. Born 6/6/20. Commd 21/5/49. Flt Lt 6/3/63. Retd GD(G) 11/1/69.
COTTERILL F., BSc. Born 14/8/20. Commd 31/10/41. Sqn Ldr 1/1/52. Retd ENG 27/2/62.
COTTERILL P. A. S. Born 23/7/30. Commd 2/6/49. Flt Lt 6/3/56. Retd GD 23/7/68.

COTTEW T. F. Born 23/1/24. Commd 14/3/57. Flt Lt 15/8/62. Retd GD 1/1/65. Re-instated 18/7/66 Sqn Ldr 1/1/74. Retd CAT 2/6/83.
COTTINGHAM A. S. Born 25/10/34. Commd 17/12/57. Sqn Ldr 1/1/70. Retd GD 25/11/75.
COTTON A. E., MIMgt. Born 24/9/32. Commd 15/5/58. Flt Lt 15/5/64. Retd SUP 24/6/73.
COTTON G. J. Born 31/1/50. Commd 4/7/69. Sqn Ldr 1/7/85. Retd GD 1/7/88.
COTTON M. J., IEng AMRAeS. Born 28/4/58. Commd 11/9/86. Flt Lt 11/9/88. Retd ENG 28/4/96.
COTTON R. J. Born 4/10/33. Commd 11/10/51. Sqn Ldr 1/7/63. Retd GD 3/1/89.
COTTON S. J. Born 26/10/41. Commd 8/4/70. Fl Lt 8/3/72. Retd GD 19/5/80.
COTTON W. F. Born 3/6/41. Commd 14/8/70. Sqn Ldr 1/7/80. Retd SUP 2/4/92.
COTTRELL A. Born 7/9/15. Commd 25/8/44. Sqn Ldr 1/7/58. Retd PRT 24/5/69.
COTTRELL F. R. Born 11/9/23. Commd 2/4/45. Flt Lt 28/6/56. Retd GD(G) 15/12/60.
COUBAN S. J., ACA. Born 26/12/05. Commd 30/5/41. Sqn Ldr 1/8/47. Retd SEC 30/11/58.
COUCH A. P., BTech. Born 19/5/50. Commd 23/9/68. Wg Cdr 1/7/86. Retd GD 14/11/89.
COUCH Rev. J. H. Born 6/5/22. Commd 1/3/56. Retd 6/5/77 Gp Capt.
COUCH S. J., BSc. Born 20/10/60. Commd 13/2/83. Flt Lt 15/5/86. Retd ENG 13/2/93.
COUCH T. J. Born 15/6/36. Commd 24/2/55. Sqn Ldr 1/1/72. Retd SUP 30/4/77.
COUCHER J. J., AFM. Born 24/11/21. Commd 7/2/57. Flt Lt 7/2/60. Retd GD 29/10/68.
COUCHMAN A. J., AFC. Born 5/10/19. Commd 5/3/43. Sqn Ldr 1/1/70. Retd GD 5/10/74.
COUCHMAN C. M., MBE. Born 23/5/54. Commd 8/9/83. Flt Lt 8/9/85. Retd GD(G) 23/5/92.
COUCHMAN H. M. C. Born 3/7/45. Commd 6/5/65. Sqn Ldr 1/1/85. Retd GD 14/3/97.
COUCHMAN M. J. Born 26/12/47. Commd 23/1/87. Flt Lt 23/1/93. Retd GD(G) 14/3/96.
COUCILL G. C., BSc. Born 18/10/29. Commd 10/4/52. Sqn Ldr 1/7/63. Retd GD 21/1/77.
COUGHLAN D. A. Born 16/11/43. Commd 26/10/62. Flt Lt 26/4/68. Retd GD 14/6/77.
COUGHLIN C. C., BA. Born 20/12/55. Commd 15/9/74. Flt Lt 15/10/80. Retd ADMIN 1/10/83.
COUKHAM A. T., FIMLS. Born 18/8/32. Commd 13/1/72. Flt Lt 26/9/74. Retd MED(T) 31/12/76.
COULCHER C. P. J., MIMgt. Born 17/3/37. Commd 17/12/57. Wg Cdr 1/7/77. Retd GD 17/3/92.
COULES E. W. Born 26/10/26. Commd 6/6/51. Flt Lt 22/5/57. Retd GD 1/12/66.
COULSON D. L. Born 10/5/63. Commd 27/8/87. Flt Lt 4/10/89. Retd GD 14/9/96.
COULSON L. R., IEng MIIE(mech) AMRAeS. Born 14/2/44. Commd 26/4/84. Sqn Ldr 1/1/94. Retd ENG 14/3/96.
COULSON P. Born 6/9/41. Commd 18/12/62. Flt Lt 28/7/65. Retd GD 15/2/74.
COULSON P. A. Born 13/5/54. Commd 4/7/85. Sqn Ldr 1/7/92. Retd GD 1/7/95.
COULSON P. G., MBE AFC. Born 19/10/21. Commd 12/7/44. Wg Cdr 1/7/64. Retd GD 30/7/76.
COULSON R. L. S., CBE. Born 18/2/20. Commd 5/11/41. Gp Capt 1/1/65. Retd GD 18/2/70.
COULSON S. P., DSO DFC. Born 6/7/16. Commd 19/12/36. Gp Capt 1/1/57. Retd GD 30/9/65.
COULSON T. M. Born 26/9/25. Commd 28/11/49. Sqn Ldr 1/1/66. Retd GD 31/7/68.
COULTER D. N. Born 26/12/37. Commd 13/2/58. Flt Lt 21/8/63. Retd GD 26/12/75.
COULTON R. G. Born 7/6/21. Commd 27/4/49. Flt Lt 27/4/55. Retd SEC 28/10/65. Re-instated 28/4/71 to 28/4/74.
COUMBE D. J. Born 16/1/35. Commd 9/2/66. Sqn Ldr 1/1/80. Retd (GD(G) 13/9/86.
COUNTER R. T., MB BS FRCS(Edin) MRCS LRCP DLO. Born 10/4/45. Commd 19/7/65. Sqn Ldr 18/7/74. Retd MED 27/4/77.
COUPAR W. G. Born 27/9/30. Commd 23/4/52. Sqn Ldr 1/1/84. Retd GD 27/9/88.
COUPER J. L. Born 7/1/25. Commd 29/3/45. Flt Lt 27/1/54. Retd GD 19/12/81.
COURCHEE J. W. Born 3/9/37. Commd 22/7/71. Sqn Ldr 1/7/78. Retd ENG 1/1/88.
COURCOUX J. Born 24/6/46. Commd 1/4/66. Sqn Ldr 1/7/78. Retd GD 21/10/78.
COURSE P. K. Born 16/3/45. Commd 9/3/72. Flt Lt 9/3/74. Retd GD 31/3/78.
COURSE R. H. Born 24/8/16. Commd 3/9/45. Sqn Ldr 1/1/56. Retd ENG 2/9/65.
COURT A. R. Born 15/6/32. Commd 9/4/52. Flt Lt 12/2/58. Retd GD 15/6/70.
COURT C. J., BSc MBA MCIPD. Born 18/3/50. Commd 11/5/75. Sqn Ldr 1/7/84. Retd ADMIN 11/5/91.
COURT D. M., BSc. Born 2/8/60. Commd 4/1/83. 4/4/84. Retd GD 12/12/95.
COURT D. T. Born 23/3/31. Commd 21/3/49. Flt Lt 7/11/57. Retd GD 2/8/68.
COURT F. J. Born 28/5/11. Commd 30/7/53. Flt Lt 1/12/56. Retd ENG 28/5/66.
COURT J. M. A., BSc. Born 25/7/17. Commd 1/9/48. Sqn Ldr 1/6/56. Retd EDN 1/9/56.
COURT L. R. Born 20/3/23. Commd 9/11/43. Sqn Ldr 1/10/55. Retd GD 26/7/57.
COURT-SMITH D. St. J. Born 5/2/32. Commd 21/5/52. Sqn Ldr 1/7/78. Retd GD 6/2/90.
COURTENAY L. M., CEng MIEE. Born 2/5/22. Commd 3/4/57. Sqn Ldr 1/7/58. Retd ENG 24/10/64.
COURTENAY R. T., MB BS DAvMed. Born 29/9/59. Commd 18/6/81. Wg Cdr 1/8/97. Retd MED 29/9/97.
COURTMAN B. Born 10/9/35. Commd 3/3/54. Sqn Ldr 1/1/73. Retd GD 1/5/88.
COURTNAGE K., OBE AFC. Born 7/2/23. Commd 1/5/45. Gp Capt 1/7/68. Retd GD 30/4/75.
COURTNEY G. H. H. Born 30/11/41. Commd 2/2/68. Flt Lt 27/4/74. Retd GD(G) 10/10/83.
COUSENS R. J. Born 17/4/59. Commd 5/2/81. Flt Lt 5/8/86. Retd GD 5/2/96.
COUSINS Sir David, KCB AFC BA. Born 20/1/42. Commd 17/12/63. ACM 1/8/97. Retd GD 11/11/98.
COUSINS E. S. J. Born 2/3/24. Commd 19/7/57. Flt Lt 1/4/63. Retd GD 7/4/79.
COUSINS L. D. Born 6/9/09. Commd 2/4/53. Flt Lt 2/4/56. Retd ENG 6/9/64.
COUSINS L. W. J., CEng MIEE. Born 7/10/20. Commd 5/11/42. Wg Cdr 1/1/67. Retd ENG 7/10/75.
COUSINS P. Born 22/7/33. Commd 29/3/56. Flt Lt 1/10/67. Retd SEC 22/7/71.
COUTHARD C. W., CB AFC* FRAeS. Born 27/2/21. Commd 2/8/41. AVM 1/7/72. Retd GD 27/2/76.

COUTTS J. Born 16/10/33. Commd 23/7/52. Flt Lt 29/4/59. Retd GD(G) 16/10/93.
COUTTS J. A., MA. Born 11/1/41. Commd 9/6/62. Flt Lt 9/6/65. Retd GD 11/9/79.
COUTTS-SMITH A. Born 25/2/26. Commd 7/7/49. Sqn Ldr 1/7/58. Retd GD 30/3/68.
COUZENS E. L. Born 13/11/19. Commd 21/4/45. Flt Lt 15/12/49. Retd GD(G) 28/5/66.
COVELL R. G., BA MB BChir MFCM MRCS LRCP DPH. Born 17/11/26. Commd 1/4/52. Gp Capt 1/1/73. Retd MED 29/1/76.
COVENEY A. J. Born 21/2/43. Commd 6/11/67. Sqn Ldr 1/1/78. Retd SUP 5/12/97.
COVENEY D. L., MBE MSc. Born 9/4/30. Commd 29/12/53. Wg Cdr 1/7/70. Retd ENG 3/6/80.
COVENTRY J. F., MSc BDS LDSRCS. Born 1/6/41. Commd 18/9/60. Wg Cdr 23/12/77. Retd DEL 1/6/79.
COVENTRY P. P. Born 11/8/22. Commd 20/9/41. Sqn Ldr 1/7/57. Retd GD 29/7/63.
COVENTRY W. C. Born 21/6/33. Commd 1/9/54. Flt Lt 30/11/61. Retd GD 6/1/66.
COVERDALE A. T. L. Born 3/3/43. Commd 17/12/65. Flt Lt 17/6/68. Retd GD 1/8/71.
COWAN A. Born 19/10/22. Commd 10/3/44. Sqn Ldr 1/1/66. Retd GD 19/10/77.
COWAN C. W., DFC DFM. Born 24/9/19. Commd 19/6/41. Sqn Ldr 1/7/54. Retd GD 2/4/59.
COWAN D. M. Born 12/5/28. Commd 3/11/51. Sqn Ldr 1/7/64. Retd GD 31/7/71.
COWAN J. A., MBE BA. Born 8/10/45. Commd 27/2/70. Sqn Ldr 1/1/86. Retd GD 23/4/98.
COWAN J. L., MRCS LRCP DTM&H. Born 10/5/24. Commd 29/6/50. Wg Cdr 28/12/62. Retd MED 7/10/69.
COWAN R. C., BEM CEng MRAeS. Born 16/8/16. Commd 23/3/50. Sqn Ldr 1/7/62. Retd ENG 16/8/71.
COWAP M., MBE. Born 10/11/32. Commd 25/8/52. Flt Lt 18/5/72. Retd PRT 30/6/73.
COWAP M. J. Born 24/4/39. Commd 3/6/58. Flt Lt 7/8/64. Retd GD 26/9/77.
COWARD D. J., OBE FInstAM. Born 20/5/37. Commd 4/6/64. Wg Cdr 1/1/89. Retd ADMIN 26/11/92.
COWARD J. B., AFC. Born 18/5/15. Commd 28/1/37. A Cdre 1/7/62. Retd GD 8/9/69.
COWARD M. R., BA MIMgt. Born 17/4/53. Commd 25/9/71. Sqn Ldr 1/1/89. Retd ADMIN 28/7/91.
COWBURN L. Born 11/4/08. Commd 25/3/54. Flt Lt 25/3/57. Retd ENG 25/3/64.
COWDEN E. M. L. Born 28/6/28. Commd 26/3/59. Flt Lt 26/6/65. Retd ADMIN 18/11/80.
COWE J. F. L. Born 20/8/22. Commd 24/3/44. Wg Cdr 1/1/70. Retd GD(G) 1/3/75.
COWELL D. H. Born 12/2/26. Commd 4/7/51. Flt Lt 17/5/56. Retd GD 14/12/69. Re-instated 13/4/58 to 12/2/83.
COWELL J. R. Born 28/7/41. Commd 8/11/68. Sqn Ldr 1/1/80. Retd GD 1/12/84.
COWELL J. R. D. Born 21/4/22. Commd 26/3/43. Flt Lt 26/3/47. Retd GD 31/5/52.
COWELL R. W. Born 8/2/47. Commd 14/7/66. Sqn Ldr 1/7/85. Retd GD(G) 2/7/94.
COWEN H. E. Born 6/5/17. Commd 22/12/44. Flt Lt 22/6/48. Retd Sec 6/5/61.
COWEN P. G. Born 23/8/40. Commd 1/8/61. Sqn Ldr 1/7/73. Retd GD 6/12/75.
COWEN R. I., BA. Born 30/12/48. Commd 2/7/72. Flt Lt 2/10/75. Retd SEC 1/4/78.
COWEY P. A. Born 1/7/29. Commd 2/9/54. Flt Offr 2/9/60. Retd SEC 19/11/60.
COWEY W. H. Born 24/6/24. Commd 20/10/44. Flt Lt 1/4/63. Retd GD 31/7/73.
COWHAM A. T. Born 11/9/33. Commd 1/11/56. Flt Lt 9/2/63. Retd GD(G) 6/8/72.
COWIE A. J., BSc. Born 8/3/67. Commd 18/8/91. Flt Lt 18/2/94. Retd GD 14/3/01.
COWIE C. Born 9/9/41. Commd 9/8/63. Flt Lt 9/2/69. Retd GD 9/9/79.
COWIE I. W. Born 13/5/46. Commd 2/8/68. Flt Lt 4/5/72. Retd GD(G) 13/5/90.
COWIE T. F., MA. Born 24/3/24. Commd 30/4/62. Sqn Ldr 6/2/68. Retd EDN 30/4/78.
COWLAND R. A., CEng MIMechE. Born 2/8/29. Commd 28/11/51. Sqn Ldr 12/3/67. Retd EDN 12/9/79.
COWLES G. W. Born 10/9/31. Commd 23/4/52. Flt Lt 19/9/57. Retd GD 10/9/92.
COWLEY A., BSc. Born 10/3/60. Commd 13/2/83. Sqn Ldr 1/1/91. Retd ENG 5/1/93.
COWLEY A. T. Born 1/4/47. Commd 23/3/67. Flt Lt 23/9/72. Retd GD 3/9/77.
COWLEY D. A., AFC BA. Born 15/4/36. Commd 30/7/57. A Cdre 1/7/86. Retd GD 15/4/91.
COWLEY G. R. Born 30/1/51. Commd 5/8/76. Fg Offr 5/8/78. Retd ADMIN 27/2/82.
COWLING G. C. Born 9/6/23. Commd 30/7/44. Sqn Ldr 1/1/72. Retd GD 28/3/75.
COWLING R. A. Born 19/7/29. Commd 12/3/52. Sqn Ldr 1/1/70. Retd GD 12/7/84.
COWMEADOW G. V., MSc BSc(Eng). Born 8/2/21. Commd 17/10/41. Wg Cdr 1/1/58. Retd ENG 8/2/77.
COWNIE A. G. H., BSc. Born 20/10/56. Commd 1/2/79. Sqn Ldr 1/7/91. Retd GD 4/4/98.
COWPE R. A., BSc. Born 9/11/47. Commd 18/8/68. Flt Lt 9/5/70. Retd GD 22/8/80.
COWPER P. M. Born 16/8/39. Commd 9/12/76. Sqn Ldr 1/1/83. Retd ADMIN 16/8/94.
COWPER R. Born 30/9/48. Commd 3/7/80. Sqn Ldr 1/1/88. Retd SUP 14/3/97.
COWTON J. B. Born 31/3/25. Commd 1/4/45. Wg Cdr 1/1/69. Retd GD 27/3/76.
COX A. F., MA BSc CEng MIEE MIMgt. Born 3/5/62. Commd 31/8/80. Wg Cdr 1/1/98. Retd ENG 1/1/01.
COX A. H., MB.BS. Born 21/11/27. Commd 4/2/52. Wg Cdr 2/2/64. Retd MED 11/11/80.
COX B. F. Born 9/8/06. Commd 18/7/27. Plt Offr 31/1/28. Retd GD 6/11/29.
COX B. G. Born 2/3/33. Commd 6/4/54. Sqn Ldr 1/7/64. Retd GD 2/3/71.
COX B. R. A., OBE AFC MIMgt. Born 4/9/26. Commd 20/9/48. Gp Capt 1/1/73. Retd GD 4/9/81.
COX C. S. Born 21/8/55. Commd 28/2/82. Flt Lt 28/8/86. Retd GD 1/12/95.
COX C. W., MA Born 5/11/20. Commd 2/5/49. Wg Cdr 1/1/66. Retd EDN 21/7/71.
COX D. J. Born 28/7/30. Commd 27/8/52. Sqn Ldr 1/1/79. Retd GD 28/7/85.
COX D. N. Born 13/4/62. Commd 29/7/83. Flt Lt 29/1/89. Retd GD 1/5/99.
COX D. S. Born 19/4/36. Commd 7/5/64. Flt Lt 1/4/67. Retd ENG 19/4/74.
COX E. M. P. S. Born 20/2/44. Commd 17/5/63. Plt Offr 17/5/64. Retd GD 30/9/65.
COX E. R. Born 9/11/39. Commd 13/12/60. Gp Capt 1/7/87. Retd GD 9/11/94.

COX F. W. P. Born 20/4/22. Commd 27/6/45. Sqn Ldr 1/1/71. Retd GD 20/4/77. Re-instated 14/9/79 to 20/4/82.
COX G. Born 3/3/42. Commd 21/12/66. Flt Lt 21/6/70. Retd GD 3/3/80.
COX G. L. Born 21/5/43. Commd 28/4/67. Fg Offr 28/4/69. Retd GD 26/9/69.
COX H. F., AFC. Born 16/6/16. Commd 31/7/37. Wg Cdr 1/7/48. Retd GD 1/5/59.
COX H. R. Born 8/1/45. Commd 17/2/67. Sqn Ldr 1/7/81. Retd GD 8/1/89.
COX J. C., MIMgt. Born 15/7/21. Commd 25/11/41. Wg Cdr 1/1/60. Retd GD 15/7/68.
COX J. E. Born 25/4/37. Commd 13/6/74. Sqn Ldr 1/1/89. Retd ADMIN 25/4/94.
COX J. R. Born 11/4/25. Commd 7/4/44. Sqn Ldr 1/1/62. Retd ENG 28/9/68.
COX M. G. T., BEng. Born 20/5/61. Commd 1/8/86. Flt Lt 15/7/89. Retd ENG 20/5/99.
COX P. Born 9/7/25. Commd 18/5/61. Flt Lt 18/5/66. Retd GD 16/12/67.
COX P. A. Born 25/7/42. Commd 30/7/63. Flt Lt 30/1/66. Retd GD 22/10/94.
COX R. A. P. Born 3/11/42. Commd 24/9/64. Wg Cdr 1/1/83. Retd SUP 18/2/86.
COX R. E. N. Born 13/10/44. Commd 2/12/66. Sqn Ldr 1/7/83. Retd OPS SPT 1/12/00.
COX R. M., CEng FINucE MIEE MIMgt. Born 1/12/22. Commd 11/12/43. Sqn Ldr 1/7/62. Retd ENG 28/2/78.
COX R. S. Born 13/6/26. Commd 24/1/52. Flt Lt 15/5/57. Retd GD 31/7/68.
COX R. S. S. Born 26/1/38. Commd 14/8/56. Flt Lt 14/2/62. Retd GD 10/10/64.
COX S. B., BSc. Born 25/11/42. Commd 24/1/66. Sqn Ldr 1/1/88. Retd GD 25/11/97.
COX S. C., DFC DFM. Born 16/12/17. Commd 17/4/42. Flt Lt 26/5/48. Retd GD(G) 13/3/55.
COX S. H. Born 28/10/24. Commd 1/7/44. Sqn Ldr 1/4/56. Retd GD 28/10/67.
COX T. J. Born 19/5/36. Commd 17/3/67. Flt Lt 17/3/71. Retd SUP 17/3/75.
COX W. C. Born 29/6/25. Commd 16/4/47. Sqn Ldr 1/1/60. Retd GD 7/5/76.
COXELL D. J. Born 12/8/21. Commd 25/5/43. Flt Lt 26/5/55. Retd GD 8/8/68.
COXELL W. J. Born 29/4/15. Commd 24/6/43. Flt Lt 8/10/52. Retd GD(G) 28/8/65.
COXHEAD D. J. M., AFC. Born 1/11/16. Commd 14/8/43. Flt Lt 15/11/48. Retd GD 2/9/58.
COY A., BA. Born 20/10/48. Commd 1/9/70. Sqn Ldr 1/1/96. Retd GD 1/5/99.
COY S. J., OBE. Born 29/11/44. Commd 15/7/66. Gp Capt 1/7/92. Retd GD 29/11/99.
COY-BURT R. H. E. Born 14/3/54. Commd 19/2/76. Flt Lt 3/7/82. Retd GD(G) 14/3/92.
COYLE P. J. Born 15/3/57. Commd 22/3/81. Sqn Ldr 1/1/91. Retd ENG 22/9/97.
COYLE W. L. J., BSc CEng MRAeS. Born 14/12/48. Commd 27/2/70. Sqn Ldr 1/7/80. Retd ENG 14/12/86.
COYNE N. A. Born 27/10/58. Commd 6/10/94. Fg Offr 1/1/89. Retd ADMIN 14/9/96.
COYNE T., AIIP. Born 17/12/32. Commd 13/2/52. Sqn Ldr 1/7/82. Retd ENG 3/3/85.
COZENS G. A. Born 26/9/22. Commd 10/12/45. Flt Lt 7/6/51. Retd GD 29/11/66.
COZENS G. T. J. Born 19/1/37. Commd 4/1/60. Sqn Ldr 4/7/70. Retd EDN 4/1/76.
COZENS R. S. G. Born 23/12/20. Commd 8/7/54. Sqn Ldr 1/1/69. Retd GD 30/11/73.
COZENS R. W., DFC. Born 27/7/21. Commd 24/11/43. Flt Lt 4/1/51. Retd GD(G) 10/8/76.
CRABB A. S. G. Born 23/11/60. Commd 14/9/80. Sqn Ldr 1/7/94. Retd GD 1/7/99.
CRABB C. M. Born 23/2/24. Commd 9/9/44. Sqn Ldr 1/7/68. Retd GD 20/6/73.
CRABB G. A., OBE CEng FIMgt MRAeS MIProdE. Born 16/3/18. Commd 29/4/42. Gp Capt 1/1/69. Retd ENG 21/4/73.
CRABTREE R. A. K., OBE. Born 26/7/38. Commd 13/12/60. Wg Cdr 1/7/79. Retd GD 5/6/85.
CRABTREE S., SRN. Born 3/4/50. Commd 26/5/74. Flt Lt 26/3/81. Retd GD(G) 22/3/84.
CRACROFT H. G. Born 23/12/36. Commd 1/4/58. Wg Cdr 1/1/76. Retd GD 1/3/85.
CRACROFT P. D., CB AFC. Born 29/11/07. Commd 19/3/27. AVM 1/7/54. Retd GD 29/12/58.
CRADDEN B. P. Born 26/9/42. Commd 31/1/90. Flt Lt 31/1/84. Retd ENG 1/6/93.
CRADDEN C. M., BSc. Born 14/8/48. Commd 27/10/70. Flt Lt 27/7/74. Retd SUP 27/10/86.
CRADDOCK N. J. B. Born 5/12/45. Commd 21/10/66. Sqn Ldr 1/1/87. Retd ENG 1/10/89.
CRAGG J. Born 18/10/26. Commd 2/4/54. Flt Lt 22/9/72. Retd GD 18/10/84.
CRAGGS F. T. Born 22/9/24. Commd 23/6/60. Flt Lt 23/6/66. Retd SUP 22/9/79.
CRAGGS M. B. Born 6/1/47. Commd 12/12/78. Sqn Ldr 1/1/84. Retd ADMIN 12/12/94.
CRAGHILL W. M. Born 29/3/40. Commd 18/2/58. A Cdre 1/7/90. Retd GD 29/7/93.
CRAIG A. J. Born 1/7/51. Commd 13/9/70. Flt Lt 22/4/78. Retd GD 1/7/90.
CRAIG A. J., CEng MRAeS MIMechE. Born 1/5/40. Commd 18/7/61. Sqn Ldr 1/7/70. Retd ENG 4/9/79.
CRAIG A. R., MIMgt. Born 17/8/32. Commd 14/12/54. Wg Cdr 1/7/79. Retd ADMIN 16/7/88.
CRAIG C. N. Born 25/12/35. Commd 2/1/67. Sqn Ldr 14/10/72. Retd ADMIN 24/12/86.
CRAIG G. J. Born 27/12/36. Commd 6/4/32. Sqn Ldr 1/1/72. Retd ADMIN 7/4/87.
CRAIG G. P. Born 7/7/26. Commd 7/5/52. Flt Lt 2/10/57. Retd GD 6/7/76.
CRAIG J. Born 20/9/37. Commd 10/11/61. Flt Lt 10/5/67. Retd GD 22/8/77.
CRAIG J. B. Born 20/4/33. Commd 29/8/51. Flt Lt 29/5/57. Retd GD 12/5/60.
CRAIG J. McD., DFC. Born 18/7/20. Commd 21/1/42. Wg Cdr 1/1/57. Retd GD 26/1/63.
CRAIG J. S. D. Born 1/4/33. Commd 25/10/51. Flt Lt. 22/5/57. Retd GD 1/4/71.
CRAIG K. D., MB BCh MRCPsych. Born 9/7/49. Commd 21/11/71. Wg Cdr 28/7/88. Retd MED 31/1/96.
CRAIG R., DFC. Born 14/11/20. Commd 7/4/44. Sqn Ldr 1/1/70. Retd SUP 31/5/73.
CRAIG R. Born 4/11/41. Commd 20/10/83. Flt Lt 20/10/87. Retd ENG 2/3/93.
CRAIG R. F. Born 28/1/35. Commd 25/7/67. Sqn Ldr 1/1/77. Retd ADMIN 28/1/85.
CRAIGEN R. K. Born 1/9/44. Commd 9/8/63. Flt Lt 9/2/69. Retd GD 1/9/93.
CRAIGIE R. A. Born 29/10/14. Commd 23/8/37. Wg Cdr 1/7/57. Retd SEC 23/11/66.

CRAIGMYLE A. A. Born 12/3/22. Commd 9/7/59. Sqn Ldr 1/1/70. Retd ENG 12/3/77.
CRAMB B. L. Born 5/8/44. Commd 24/7/81. Flt Lt 1/3/87. Retd MED(SEC) 31/8/89.
CRAMER V. N., OBE FIMgt. Born 22/9/23. Commd 28/6/45. Gp Capt 1/1/68. Retd GD 23/9/73.
CRAMP C. Born 8/6/14. Commd 15/6/42. Sqn Ldr 1/7/54. Retd ENG 8/6/69.
CRAMP D. C., BSc. Born 27/2/52. Commd 27/1/70. Flt Lt 15/4/76. Retd ADMIN 27/2/93.
CRAMPTON J., DFC AFC*. Born 21/8/21. Commd 1/9/41. Sqn Ldr 1/7/50. Retd GD 1/6/57.
CRAMPTON P. P. Born 21/12/21. Commd 20/4/50. Sqn Ldr 1/1/68. Retd GD 21/12/76.
CRANE C. D. Born 3/7/57. Commd 5/4/79. Sqn Ldr 1/7/90. Retd GD(G) 3/7/95.
CRANE D. L. Born 24/2/35. Commd 6/5/53. Sqn Ldr 1/1/71. Retd GD 8/8/88.
CRANE G. D. Born 19/5/20. Commd 5/5/60. Flt Lt 5/5/65. Retd ENG 6/6/70.
CRANE J., OBE CEng MRAeS. Born 4/7/19. Commd 19/8/42. Wg Cdr 1/7/59. Retd ENG 4/7/74.
CRANE J. S. Born 21/5/33. Commd 17/1/52. Sqn Ldr 1/1/66. Retd GD 29/6/74.
CRANE R. Born 25/7/23. Commd 21/4/45. Flt Lt 4/12/52. Retd GD 12/8/66.
CRANE T. Born 19/4/49. Commd 17/5/79. Flt Lt 17/5/81. Retd GD 17/5/87.
CRANFIELD J. T. O'B., MB BS FFARCS MRCS LRCP. Born 9/10/44. Commd 23/1/67. Wg Cdr 3/7/83. Retd MED 27/10/85.
CRAVEN A. H., PhD MSc DCAe. Born 23/7/27. Commd 4/12/47. Sqn Ldr 1/4/61. Retd EDN 28/8/65.
CRAVEN I. W. Born 19/3/62. Commd 15/3/84. Flt Lt 15/9/89. Retd GD 19/1/01.
CRAVEN J. K. Born 14/7/26. Commd 7/5/52. Wg Cdr 1/7/68. Retd GD 22/5/77.
CRAVEN J. T. Born 29/6/42. Commd 17/12/63. Sqn Ldr 1/1/76. Retd GD 1/10/86.
CRAVEN Sir Robert, KBE CB DFC FIMgt. Born 16/1/16. Commd 5/7/37. AM 1/1/70. Retd GD 28/4/72.
CRAVEN-GRIFFITHS J. K., OBE BA MINSTPS. Born 29/4/31. Commd 9/4/52. Gp Capt 1/1/82. Retd SUP 9/11/83.
CRAWFORD A. G. S. Born 27/12/21. Commd 21/1/53. Flt Lt 21/1/53. Retd SEC 4/4/64 rtg Sqn Ldr.
CRAWFORD A. I., MA. Born 18/11/56. Commd 5/2/76. Flt Lt 15/4/82. Retd ADMIN 28/12/87.
CRAWFORD A. J. Born 10/11/55. Commd 4/7/85. Flt Lt 4/7/87. Retd GD 20/10/93.
CRAWFORD B. Born 15/10/14. Commd 10/6/38. Flt Lt 10/6/42. Retd SEC 19/3/50 rtg Sqn Ldr.
CRAWFORD B. J., MVO. Born 29/3/34. Commd 26/11/52. Sqn Ldr 1/7/81. Retd GD 29/3/92.
CRAWFORD C. W., AFC. Born 27/12/11. Commd 24/1/45. Flt Lt 29/6/50. Retd GD(G) 28/6/57.
CRAWFORD D., BSc. Born 3/10/49. Commd 2/9/73. Flt Lt 2/9/76. Retd ENG 2/9/89.
CRAWFORD D. E. G. Born 30/10/33. Commd 16/12/66. Sqn Ldr 1/1/80. Retd ADMIN 30/10/91.
CRAWFORD G. J., MIMgt MRAeS. Born 25/10/55. Commd 11/8/77. Wg Cdr 1/1/95. Retd GD 25/10/99.
CRAWFORD J. A., BSc. Born 14/6/60. Commd 4/9/78. Sqn Ldr 1/7/94. Retd GD 14/6/98.
CRAWFORD J. S. Born 31/5/21. Commd 20/2/43. Sqn Ldr 1/7/62. Retd GD 26/7/71.
CRAWFORD J. S. Born 29/4/21. Commd 4/4/45. Flt Lt 30/6/49. Retd GD 29/4/76.
CRAWFORD P. A., AFC BSc. Born 11/1/50. Commd 3/10/68. A Cdre 1/7/96. Retd GD 10/11/00.
CRAWFORD P. D. Born 17/2/57. Commd 11/1/81. Flt Lt 18/10/84. Retd ADMIN 17/2/95.
CRAWFORD R. S. Born 4/5/18. Commd 15/3/37. Flt Lt 1/12/42. Retd GD 28/8/51 rtg Sqn Ldr.
CRAWLEY M., BSc CEng MRAeS. Born 5/1/53. Commd 25/9/71. Sqn Ldr 1/7/83. Retd ENG 5/1/91.
CRAWLEY H. L., DFC. Born 7/9/29. Commd 26/3/52. Flt Lt 7/8/57. Retd GD 2/8/71.
CRAWLEY I. C. Born 15/2/43. Commd 7/3/68. Flt Lt 4/11/70. Retd SY 21/5/84.
CRAWLEY L. F., MBE. Born 5/8/17. Commd 16/7/43. Wg Cdr 1/1/65. Retd SEC 5/8/72.
CRAWLEY M. A., MB ChB MRCP DPhysMed. Born 15/1/34. Commd 17/8/58. Wg Cdr 2/8/71. Retd MED 1/7/77.
CRAWLEY T. W. Born 6/6/58. Commd 29/7/83. Sqn Ldr 1/7/93. Retd MED SEC 14/3/96.
CRAWSHAW J. A. L., MBE MIMgt. Born 13/7/29. Commd 12/12/51. Sqn Ldr 1/7/63. Retd SEC 14/7/74.
CRAWSHAW P. H., MBE. Born 22/1/30. Commd 21/3/51. Sqn Ldr 1/1/67. Retd GD 31/7/80.
CRAWSHAW R. D. Born 22/9/45. Commd 31/1/64. Flt Lt 31/7/69. Retd GD 23/6/73.
CRAWSHAY-WILLIAMS P. G. Born 20/11/23. Commd 3/9/43. Flt Lt 3/3/47. Retd GD 20/11/61.
CRAXTON L. V. Born 4/3/21. Commd 27/3/41. Wg Cdr 1/1/60. Retd GD 4/3/68.
CRAY R. D., BSc. Born 12/11/60. Commd 11/12/83. Fg Off 11/12/82. Retd GD 7/8/86.
CREAGH P. W. M. Born 13/10/43. Commd 15/4/61. Sqn Ldr 1/1/88. Retd ADMIN 1/1/91.
CREASEY G. Born 29/1/18. Commd 12/6/47. Flt Lt 12/12/51. Retd SUP 29/1/67.
CREASEY B. R., MIMgt. Born 16/8/29. Commd 20/6/63. Flt Lt 20/6/68. Retd ENG 21/8/76.
CREASEY W. A., OBE CEng MIMechE. Born 6/1/37. Commd 26/2/71. A Cdre 1/7/89. Retd ENG 6/1/92.
CREE T. S. Born 2/9/44. Commd 19/3/81. Flt Lt 19/3/84. Retd GD(ALM) 30/6/89.
CREED T. Born 27/1/45. Commd 1/4/66 Sqn Ldr 1/7/79. Retd GD 27/1/83.
CREIGH P. J. W. Born 20/5/37. Commd 4/5/58. Sqn Ldr 1/7/70. Retd GD 25/9/73.
CREIGHTON W. H. Born 30/7/43. Commd 11/5/78. Flt Lt 11/5/80. Retd GD 31/7/99.
CRESSWELL A. P., BSc. Born 16/6/56. Commd 15/9/74. Flt Lt 15/4/79. Retd GD 15/7/89.
CRESSWELL G. J., MB ChB. Born 6/5/49. Commd 26/6/73. Sqn Ldr 8/7/81. Retd MED 26/6/89.
CRESSWELL J. S. Born 17/10/33. Commd 5/4/53. Wg Cdr 1/1/69. Retd GD 17/10/88.
CRESSWELL J. V. Born 29/5/42. Commd 22/2/63. Flt Lt 9/2/68. Retd GD 29/5/80.
CRESSWELL K. N. A. B. Born 25/12/27. Commd 10/3/60. Flt Lt 10/3/65. Retd GD 3/5/77.
CRESSWELL R. F., BA MCIPS MILT MIMgt. Born 23/4/44. Commd 15/7/66. Sqn Ldr 1/7/77. Retd SUP 27/10/97.
CRESSWELL T. J. Born 1/8/30. Commd 1/8/51. Flt Lt 1/2/54. Retd GD 1/8/68.
CRESSY F. J. Born 18/2/12. Commd 13/9/43. Flt Lt 13/3/48. Retd SUP 15/11/55.
CRETNEY F. D. Born 24/4/33. Commd 30/4/53. Sqn Ldr 1/7/64. Retd GD 1/10/70.

CREW E. D., CB DSO* DFC* MA. Born 24/12/17. Commd 3/10/39. AVM 1/7/69. Retd GD 3/3/73.
CREWE G. P. Born 18/5/44. Commd 14/2/69. Flt Lt 14/8/74. Retd GD 20/8/76.
CREWS P. Born 30/5/23. Commd 6/10/60. Flt Lt 6/10/63. Retd GD 24/3/78.
CRIBB P. H., CBE DSO* DFC. Born 28/9/18. Commd 30/7/38. A Cdre 1/1/62. Retd GD 28/9/66.
CRIGHTON S. M. Born 7/5/63. Commd 12/11/89. Fg Offr 12/11/90. Retd SUP 15/5/95.
CRILLEY D. J. F. Born 26/1/40. Commd 21/2/69. Flt Lt 21/2/71. Retd GD(G) 30/9/82.
CRIPPS A. G., CEng MIMechE MRAeS. Born 4/3/42. Commd 8/11/62. Sqn Ldr 1/1/97. Retd ENG 4/3/97.
CRIPPS B. D. Born 14/5/37. Commd 21/10/65. Flt Lt 9/2/68. Retd GD(G) 14/5/87.
CRIPPS J. S., CEng MIEE MIMechE. Born 3/7/37. Commd 1/8/63. Sqn Ldr 1/7/70. Retd ENG 3/7/75.
CRIPPS R. H. Born 4/7/27. Commd 29/7/65. Sqn Ldr 21/10/70. Retd EDN 29/7/73.
CRIPPS R. W. Born 29/7/37. Commd 4/7/69. Wg Cdr 1/7/86. Retd ENG 29/7/92.
CRIPPS S. T. B., DFC. Born 8/3/99. Commd 1/4/18. Flt Lt 1/7/25. Retd GD 5/2/29.
CRIPPS T. P. Born 15/6/37. Commd 30/9/55. Sqn Ldr 1/1/68. Retd GD 15/6/75.
CRIPPS T.M., BA. Born 21/1/38. Commd 25/9/62. Sqn Ldr 14/9/72. Retd ADMIN 1/5/87.
CRISPIN J. A. Born 9/6/24. Commd 10/3/44. Sqn Ldr 1/10/54. Retd GD 9/6/67.
CRISPIN P., BA MRIN MIMgt. Born 22/4/45. Commd 15/7/66. Sqn Ldr 1/1/80. Retd GD 22/4/89.
CRISTINACCE G. Born 30/7/23. Commd 23/7/51. Flt Lt 8/1/58. Retd GD 23/7/67.
CRITCHLEY F. J. E. Born 15/2/51. Commd 28/11/69. Flt Lt 28/5/75. Retd GD 8/2/79.
CRITCHLEY P. G. Born 19/4/53. Commd 9/3/72. Sqn Ldr 1/1/85. Retd GD 19/4/91.
CRITTENDEN B. Born 5/1/35. Commd 15/4/55. Sqn Ldr 1/1/67. Retd GD 5/1/73.
CROASDALE G. P. H. Born 4/10/52. Commd 4/5/72. Sqn Ldr 1/7/86. Retd GD 4/10/90.
CROCKATT A. B., AFC. Born 12/9/50. Commd 26/2/71. Wg Cdr 1/1/91. Retd GD 5/4/01.
CROCKATT D. R., MRCS LRCP DAvMed FIMgt. Born 12/7/27. Commd 8/4/56. Gp Capt 1/1/79. Retd MED 2/4/85.
CROCKER A. E. Born 15/1/21. Commd 30/5/46. Flt Lt 7/6/51. Retd GD(G) 5/10/68.
CROCKER A. P. Born 14/4/66. Commd 22/11/84. Plt Offr 22/5/85. Retd GD(G) 24/6/86.
CROCKER C. E. Born 23/9/23. Commd 6/5/44. Sqn Ldr 1/7/60. Retd SUP 1/4/73.
CROCKER L. R., BA. Born 15/6/32. Commd 28/10/54. Sqn Ldr 1/7/67. Retd SUP 1/7/82.
CROCKER R. G., DFC. Born 2/3/21. Commd 28/8/42. Flt Lt 6/5/46. Retd GD 12/3/47.
CROCKETT T. Born 23/3/39. Commd 9/2/62. Sqn Ldr 1/7/79. Retd GD 23/3/94.
CROCKFORD B. W. Born 17/4/39. Commd 30/3/65. Flt Lt 15/4/70. Retd ENG 30/3/81.
CROCKFORD W. C. Born 5/3/01. Commd 1/7/41. Sqn Ldr 1/1/49. Retd ENG 3/4/54.
CROFT G. J. Born 30/11/43. Commd 31/10/74. Flt Lt 31/10/76. Retd GD(G) 31/10/82.
CROFT I., BSc CEng MICE MRAeS. Born 11/12/39. Commd 25/2/64. Sqn Ldr 1/1/71. Retd ENG 25/2/80.
CROFT K. F., BSc MB ChB DRCOG. Born 22/1/48. Commd 17/9/74. Wg Cdr 3/8/91. Retd MED 14/3/96.
CROFT M. H. Born 8/12/56. Commd 4/9/81. Flt Lt 4/3/88. Retd OPS SPT 4/5/97.
CROFT P. A. Born 2/8/42. Commd 6/2/67. Sqn Ldr 1/7/74. Retd SY 6/2/83.
CROFT R., MIMgt. Born 7/9/23. Commd 6/11/58. Sqn Ldr 1/7/71. Retd ENG 26/3/77.
CROFTS P. G. Born 24/9/34. Commd 23/10/56. Flt Lt 23/4/62. Retd ENG 24/9/72.
CROFTS R. Born 11/8/50. Commd 8/11/90. Flt Lt 6/11/92. Retd ENG 2/7/93.
CROIZAT J. P., MBE. Born 15/8/32. Commd 7/5/53. Sqn Ldr 1/7/63. Retd CAT 15/8/70.
CROMACK B. J., MSc BSc. Born 1/7/29. Commd 28/9/80. Sqn Ldr 1/7/87. Retd ADMIN 7/2/88.
CROMACK R., BSc. Born 18/2/40. Commd 8/9/69. Sqn Ldr 8/3/73. Retd ADMIN 8/9/87.
CROMAR A. D. Born 5/1/12. Commd 13/1/42. Fg Offr 1/10/42. Retd ENG 8/1/46 rtg Flt Lt.
CROMAR R. Born 2/5/14. Commd 8/9/42. Flt Lt 14/3/51. Retd GD(G) 29/8/64.
CROMARTY I. J., MSc MB ChB MRCGP DRCOG DAvMed. Born 20/2/56. Commd 2/9/75. Wg Cdr 1/8/92. Retd MED 20/2/00.
CROMARTY J. I., MB ChB MFCM DPH. Born 28/12/28. Commd 29/9/52. Gp Capt 1/7/74. Retd MED 6/8/76.
CROMBIE G. J., MBE. Born 11/12/45. Commd 26/5/67. Sqn Ldr 1/1/97. Retd GD 1/5/99.
CROMBIE K. S. Born 16/8/53. Commd 25/4/82. Sqn Ldr 1/1/94. Retd GD 25/4/98.
CROMPTON D. J., BA MBCS. Born 28/11/32. Commd 24/8/56. ACdre 1/7/83. Retd ADMIN 31/1/86.
CROMPTON D. M. Born 24/10/28. Commd 13/8/58. Sqn Ldr 1/7/70. Retd SUP 24/10/83.
CROMPTON J. W. Born 15/8/27. Commd 9/12/48. Flt Lt 28/2/55. Retd GD 7/10/61.
CROMPTON R. M. Born 1/7/29. Commd 16/10/52. Flt Offr 16/10/58. Retd SEC 7/7/61.
CROMWELL O. Born 21/11/09. Commd 10/12/42. Sqn Ldr 1/1/54. Retd ENG 21/11/58.
CRONE H. J., AFC, MIMgt. Born 16/2/41. Commd 9/12/61. Sqn Ldr 1/1/71. Retd GD 16/2/79.
CRONING D. I. R. Born 21/11/41. Commd 3/10/74. Flt Lt 3/10/76. Retd SUP 3/10/82.
CROOK B. A., MPhil. Born 30/5/44. Commd 17/5/63. Wg Cdr 1/7/83. Retd GD 30/5/88.
CROOK C., MBE. Born 17/10/31. Commd 30/7/52. Sqn Ldr 1/7/64. Retd EF 17/10/69.
CROOK G. C. Born 13/9/25. Commd 23/9/52. Flt Lt 26/2/64. Retd GD 23/9/68.
CROOK G. D. W., MB ChB MRCP(UK). Born 1/2/56. Commd 10/3/77. Wg Cdr 1/8/93. Retd MED 1/2/94.
CROOK G. T., LDSRCS. Born 7/6/23. Commd 22/8/46. A Cdre 1/7/80. Retd DEL 1/7/82.
CROOK M. R. W. Born 24/5/45. Commd 3/3/67. Sqn Ldr 1/7/79. Retd GD 30/11/85.
CROOK P. W. Born 22/2/41. Commd 18/12/62. Sqn Ldr 1/1/73. Retd GD 22/2/79.
CROOKS F. R. Born 9/8/35. Commd 5/7/68. Sqn Ldr 1/7/76. Retd ENG 9/8/90.
CROPPER E. S. G., AE BSc CEng FIEE. Born 6/12/07. Commd 4/4/39. Wg Cdr 1/7/57. Retd EDN 6/12/67.
CROPPER E. W. Born 15/12/23. Commd 30/1/44. Gp Capt 1/7/70. Retd GD 23/3/74.

CROSBIE J. C. Born 20/9/14. Commd 1/5/42. Flt Lt 26/11/45. Retd GD(G) 20/9/64 rtg Sqn Ldr.
CROSBIE J. L., OBE. Born 31/7/14. Commd 15/12/34. Gp Capt 1/1/53. Retd GD 31/7/64.
CROSBIE J. P. Born 8/5/56. Commd 8/10/87. Flt Lt 8/10/89. Retd ENG 8/10/95.
CROSBY B. W., CEng MIEE MRAeS. Born 26/8/37. Commd 13/10/64. Flt Lt 13/10/69. Retd ENG 13/10/80.
CROSBY C. R. C. Born 18/7/41. Commd 31/8/62. Flt Lt 18/1/67. Retd GD 29/6/78.
CROSBY K. B., FIMgt MCIT MILT MRAeS. Born 21/7/19. Commd 23/9/43. Gp Capt 1/7/70. Retd GD(G) 21/7/74.
CROSBY M. A. Born 20/12/63. Commd 24/3/83. Sqn Ldr 1/7/94. Retd GD 31/12/97.
CROSLAND M. R. Born 2/12/31. Commd 22/7/53. Flt Lt 7/1/59. Retd GD 4/12/69.
CROSS A. R. D., BA. Born 23/12/59. Commd 19/6/83. Sqn Ldr 1/7/94. Retd ENG 19/6/99.
CROSS E. J. Born 27/12/32. Commd 11/4/51. Flt Lt 11/1/57. Retd GD 11/10/61.
CROSS J. A. Born 18/5/49. Commd 29/4/71. Flt Lt 14/8/77. Retd ADMIN 18/5/87.
CROSS Sir Kenneth., KCB CBE DSO DFC. Born 4/10/11. Commd 11/4/30. ACM 1/10/65. Retd GD 24/2/67.
CROSS K. J., MIMgt. Born 13/10/34. Commd 6/10/60. Sqn Ldr 1/1/72. Retd GD(G) 9/4/80.
CROSS M. J., BA. Born 7/1/59. Commd 11/4/82. Sqn Ldr 1/1/92. Retd ADMIN 11/4/98.
CROSS M. W., AFC. Born 18/5/24. Commd 6/11/46. Flt Lt 20/10/53. Retd GD 11/2/59.
CROSS P. A. Born 31/12/44. Commd 8/12/83. Sqn Ldr 1/7/92. Retd ENG 1/1/93.
CROSS P. B. Born 28/3/26. Commd 5/9/56. Flt Lt 13/4/60. Retd GD 5/5/81.
CROSS P. D. Born 28/8/39. Commd 22/5/75. Sqn Ldr 1/1/83. Retd GD(G) 1/1/85.
CROSS P. R. Born 22/4/47. Commd 16/8/68. Flt Lt 16/2/73. Retd GD 22/10/94.
CROSS R. A. Born 31/10/32. Commd 19/7/51. Sqn Ldr 1/7/81. Retd GD 31/10/87.
CROSS T., CEng MIEE. Born 25/6/20. Commd 3/6/43. Wg Cdr 1/1/62. Retd ENG 27/3/71.
CROSS W. E. J. Born 30/11/12. Commd 6/5/43. Fg Offr 26/2/44. Retd ENG 8/2/46.
CROSS W. M. N., OBE. Born 26/2/42. Commd 31/7/62. Gp Capt 1/1/93. Retd GD 26/5/97.
CROSSE J. P., MA. Born 25/1/56. Commd 10/10/77. Flt Lt 15/10/81. Retd SY 1/3/86.
CROSSFIELD R. J. Born 8/3/66. Commd 13/2/92. Flt Lt 14/4/92. Retd ADMIN 14/9/96.
CROSSLEY C., BSc. Born 16/9/57. Commd 26/7/81. Flt Lt 26/1/85. Retd GD(G) 4/3/93.
CROTTY M. P., CBE MSc BA FCIT FILT FILDM. MCIPS. Born 14/4/41. Commd 17/7/62. A Cdre 1/1/89. Retd SUP 18/10/95.
CROUCH A. M. Born 1/7/21. Commd 3/5/44. Flt Offr 8/8/54. Retd SEC 31/7/60.
CROUCH A. W. Born 4/6/20. Commd 3/10/42. Flt Lt 3/4/46. Retd GD 11/9/53.
CROUCH C. A. Born 8/1/50. Commd 8/8/69. Sqn Ldr 1/7/85. Retd GD 27/9/87.
CROUCH I. A. Born 18/4/50. Commd 25/2/72. Fg Offr 25/2/73. Retd SUP 3/7/76.
CROUCH J. R., MSc BSc. Born 8/4/48. Commd 11/8/74. Sqn Ldr 1/7/84. Retd ADMIN 11/8/90.
CROUCH P. C., AFM. Born 29/6/23. Commd 5/9/57. Sqn Ldr 1/7/71. Retd GD 29/6/78.
CROUCH P. T. Born 27/6/56. Commd 2/1/75. Wg Cdr 1/7/92. Retd GD(G) 1/7/95.
CROUCHEN D. H., DFC. Born 3/8/21. Commd 9/3/41. Flt Lt 13/11/57. Retd GD(G) 14/10/67 rtg Sqn Ldr.
CROUCHER D. G. Born 6/6/24. Commd 11/2/44. Gp Capt 1/1/70. Retd GD 28/5/76.
CROW A. T. Born 23/2/39. Commd 15/9/60. Flt Lt 1/4/66. Retd SUP 10/1/90.
CROW J. T. M. D. O'D. Born 25/10/37. Commd 10/8/60Flt. Flt Lt 4/5/72. Retd CAT 7/12/73.
CROW M. F. Born 31/3/21. Commd 21/4/45. Sqn Ldr 1/1/57. Retd GD 2/2/68.
CROW T. Born 24/11/11. Commd 22/4/43. Sqn Ldr 1/1/54. Retd SUP 24/11/66.
CROWDEN-LONGSTREATH P. D. Born 11/1/16. Commd 18/7/44. Flt Lt 13/11/57. Retd SUP 25/2/71.
CROWDER R. B., MIMgt. Born 22/1/39. Commd 28/7/59. Wg Cdr 1/1/76. Retd GD 2/4/89.
CROWE G. V. Born 21/9/44. Commd 13/6/74. Flt Lt 13/6/76. Retd ENG 21/9/82.
CROWE H. G., CBE MC. Born 11/6/97. Commd 1/4/18. Gp Capt 1/1/43. Retd GD 28/12/45 rtg A Cdre.
CROWE J. B., MA MB BChir DMRD FFSR. Born 18/1/31. Commd 5/3/57. Wg Cdr 5/3/70. Retd MED 31/3/73.
CROWE M. Born 14/2/25. Commd 20/3/52. Flt Lt 1/1/56. Retd SEC 14/2/63. Re-appointed 1/11/67 to 1/11/72.
CROWE P. Born 4/8/29. Commd 31/12/52. Flt Lt 26/5/58. Retd GD(G) 9/4/76.
CROWE P. A., BSc(Eng) MMS MIMgt. Born 3/11/42. Commd 30/9/62. Sqn Ldr 1/1/78. Retd GD 3/11/97.
CROWHURST G., MIDPM. Born 9/3/39. Commd 2/2/70. Wg Cdr 1/1/80. Retd GD(G) 1/4/86.
CROWHURST J. H. Born 14/1/32. Commd 5/9/57. Wg Cdr 1/7/80. Retd ADMIN 9/5/86.
CROWHURST T. Born 30/12/44. Commd 5/9/57. Wg Cdr 1/1/80. Retd GD(G) 1/10/92.
CROWLE A. J. W. Born 26/8/61. Commd 8/11/90. Flt Lt 8/11/92. Retd ENG 26/8/99.
CROWLE J. D. Born 15/8/41. Commd 6/10/60. Wg Cdr 1/7/78. Retd SUP 15/8/96.
CROWLE P. W. Born 4/2/49. Commd 2/7/78. Flt Lt 20/7/80. Retd ENG 4/2/87.
CROWLESMITH J. D., MB BS MRCS MFCM LRCP DCH FIMgt. Born 10/2/26. Commd 3/7/50. Gp Capt 1/1/71. Retd MED 30/3/77.
CROWLEY A. C. Born 4/10/55. Commd 2/11/88. Flt Lt 2/11/90. Retd SUP 2/4/93.
CROWLEY J. M., AFC CEng MRAeS. Born 30/8/27. Commd 8/4/49. Wg Cdr 1/1/63. Retd GD 31/8/68.
CROWLEY K. A., BA. Born 3/2/44. Commd 24/6/65. Flt Lt 24/3/67. Retd GD 19/6/71.
CROWLEY L. J. Born 24/1/36. Commd 22/1/57. Sqn Ldr 1/7/70. Retd GD 24/1/74.
CROWLEY M. B. Born 2/10/15. Commd 25/7/45. Sqn Offr 1/7/58. Retd SUP 2/10/64.
CROWLEY R. J., BSc. Born 31/12/55. Commd 1/9/74. Flt Lt 15/10/78. Retd GD 10/6/88.
CROWSON D., MBE. Born 25/3/36. Commd 26/9/57. Sqn Ldr 1/7/72. Retd GD 25/3/86.
CROWSON F. J. Born 14/8/38. Commd 1/4/65. Sqn Ldr 1/7/79. Retd GD(G) 1/10/85.
CROWTHER A. J. Born 23/3/45. Commd 29/11/63. Flt Lt 4/11/70. Retd GD 23/3/83.

CROY A. O. Born 6/4/20. Commd 8/6/54. Flt Lt 8/6/59. Retd ENG 6/4/62.
CROYDON W. H., CBE. Born 8/9/33. Commd 9/4/52. Air Cdre 1/1/84. Retd GD 8/8/88.
CROZIER I. D., AFC MRAeS. Born 18/1/22. Commd 7/7/42. Wg Cdr 1/7/59. Retd GD 1/11/67.
CROZIER P. C. Born 10/3/42. Commd 23/12/60. Fg Offr 19/6/63. Retd GD 24/12/65.
CROZIER W. J., AFC. Born 23/3/17. Commd 9/10/42. Flt Lt 24/3/47. Retd GD(G) 24/5/66.
CRUICKSHANK A. Born 22/8/16. Commd 22/2/44. Sqn Ldr 1/1/52. Retd RGT 1/4/58.
CRUICKSHANK J. H., MBE. Born 12/4/20. Commd 27/8/59. Sqn Ldr 1/1/70. Retd ENG 12/4/75.
CRUICKSHANK L. W. Born 24/1/24. Commd 16/3/45. Sqn Ldr 1/7/70. Retd SUP 24/1/79.
CRUICKSHANKS C. J., AFC* FRaeS. Born 7/1/45. Commd 17/12/65. A Cdre 1/7/94. Retd GD 7/1/00.
CRUICKSHANKS R. E., BSc. Born 27/7/32. Commd 22/12/55. Sqn Ldr 14/2/66. Retd EDN 15/9/71.
CRUMBIE G. C. Born 30/5/40. Commd 13/12/60. Sqn Ldr 1/1/69. Retd GD 30/5/80.
CRUMPTON R. H., MBE. Born 2/4/29. Commd 7/5/52. Sqn Ldr 1/1/64. Retd GD 19/12/75.
CRUSE C. Born 12/3/47. Commd 1/6/69. Wg Cdr 1/1/87. Retd SUP 12/3/97.
CRUSE J. G., AFC. Born 2/6/27. Commd 22/3/51. Sqn Ldr 1/1/61. Retd GD 9/8/61.
CRUSH M. W. A. Born 28/8/49. Commd 25/4/69. Flt Lt 25/10/74. Retd GD 9/10/76.
CRUTCHLOW R. L. Born 9/12/33. Commd 3/12/59. Wg Cdr 1/1/85. Retd GD 8/4/88.
CRUWYS G. E. Born 27/2/20. Commd 12/5/40. Sqn Ldr 1/7/53. Retd GD 27/2/63.
CRWYS-WILLIAMS D. O., CB FCIPD. Born 24/12/40. Commd 1/8/61. AVM 1/7/88. Retd GD 1/4/93.
CRYMBLE M. J. Born 24/3/54. Commd 24/8/72. Flt Lt 24/2/78. Retd GD 5/4/00.
CUBBERLEY F. J. Born 11/6/33. Commd 10/3/60. Sqn Ldr 1/7/81. Retd GD 8/8/88.
CUBBY G., MBE. Born 20/12/20. Commd 12/12/42. Gp Capt 1/1/67. Retd SEC 16/1/71.
CUBIN A., MBE. Born 9/10/62. Commd 26/11/81. Sqn Ldr 1/1/98. Retd GD 1/1/01.
CUBITT R. J. Born 4/12/51. Commd 8/9/83. Flt Lt 8/9/85. Retd SUP 8/9/91.
CUDMORE A. F. J. Born 19/7/58. Commd 7/11/91. Flt Lt 7/11/93. Retd SUP 31/3/94.
CUDMORE M. C. Born 8/2/62. Commd 20/5/90. Flt Lt 10/1/88. Retd GD 1/8/00.
CUDWORTH J. E. Born 30/4/27. Commd 28/2/57. Flt Lt 28/5/63. Retd SEC 5/11/69.
CUGLEY J., OBE MB BS. Born 13/10/46. Commd 9/4/85. Wg Cdr 8/2/95. Retd MED 17/9/99.
CUGNONI K. F., BA. Born 11/9/34. Commd 23/10/59. Flt Lt 23/2/64. Retd SEC 6/9/78.
CULL M. S. Born 3/12/35. Commd 2/3/61. Sqn Ldr 1/7/72. Retd GD 11/9/81.
CULLEN A. M. Born 25/11/45. Commd 26/11/81. Sqn Ldr 1/1/89. Retd ADMIN 25/11/00.
CULLEN G. M., AFC. Born 11/9/24. Commd 11/6/53. Sqn Ldr 1/7/81. Retd GD 11/9/84.
CULLEN H. G., DFC. Born 1/9/21. Commd 1/5/46. Sqn Ldr 1/1/51. Retd GD 1/9/64.
CULLEN J. J. Born 11/2/19. Commd 19/7/57. Sqn Ldr 1/1/69. Retd ENG 31/8/74.
CULLEN P. G. Born 27/9/31. Commd 8/5/53. Flt Lt 18/8/58. Retd GD(G) 27/9/88.
CULLEN R. J., BTh CertEd Dip Pas Th. Born 27/4/55. Commd 30/4/78. Flt Lt 30/6/82. Retd ADMIN 30/4/83.
   Re-entrant 9/5/84. Sqn Ldr 1/1/91. Retd ADMIN 14/9/96.
CULLEY E. R. Born 20/9/23. Commd 30/8/59. Flt Lt 30/8/65. Retd GD 1/12/67.
CULLIFORD F. J. Born 2/5/23. Commd 17/8/43. Wg Cdr 1/7/63. Retd ENG 2/8/77.
CULLIFORD J. Born 27/1/16. Commd 16/9/35. Sqn Ldr 1/1/50. Retd SEC 7/3/71.
CULLIGAN S. A. Born 12/8/50. Commd 9/10/75. Sqn Ldr 1/1/92. Retd SUP 31/3/94.
CULLING S. R., BSc CEng MIMechE MRAeS MIMgt. Born 12/2/40. Commd 30/9/59. Sqn Ldr 1/1/74. Retd ENG
   1/4/87.
CULLINGTON G. G., CBE AFC BSc. Born 8/5/44. Commd 28/9/64. Gp Capt 1/1/91. Retd GD 8/2/00.
CULLINGWORTH R. Born 29/8/51. Commd 16/3/73. Sqn Ldr 1/1/88. Retd GD 1/1/91.
CULLIS C. Born 9/10/37. Commd 21/10/66. Sqn Ldr 1/7/80. Retd GD 9/10/95.
CULLUM G. W. Born 1/6/24. Commd 15/6/50. Sqn Ldr 1/1/70. Retd GD 31/8/73.
CULLUM W. B. J. Born 18/10/27. Commd 26/8/66. Flt Lt 26/8/71. Retd ENG 31/3/78.
CULMER A. W., MBE MSc BSc CEng FIMechE FRAeS ACGI. Born 19/2/23. Commd 21/1/45. Gp Capt 1/7/69. Retd
   ENG 19/3/77.
CULMER B. E. Born 4/11/43. Commd 22/5/75. Flt Lt 22/5/77. Retd OPS SPT 3/4/98.
CULMER D. R., CEng MIEE qs. Born 4/4/39. Commd 23/3/66. Gp Capt 22/12/92. Retd ENG.
CULPAN J. Born 18/5/16. Commd 12/4/45. Flt Lt 12/10/49. Retd SEC 13/8/55.
CULPIN B. W., DSO DFC. Born 27/12/21. Commd 11/7/43. Sqn Ldr 1/7/55. Retd GD 27/12/76.
CULPITT G. E., OBE. Born 1/6/36. Commd 9/2/55. Gp Capt 1/7/84. Retd GD 1/5/90.
CULVERHOUSE P. C., MBE. Born 18/9/43. Commd 9/10/64. Sqn Ldr 1/7/79. Retd GD 18/9/98.
CUMBERLAND T., MIMgt. Born 18/10/38. Commd 13/12/60. Wg Cdr 1/1/77. Retd SUP 1/1/81.
CUMMING D. Born 18/6/45. Commd 4/3/71. Flt Lt 4/3/73. Retd GD 16/8/95.
CUMMING F. G., MBE MB ChB. Born 5/3/25. Commd 15/7/48. Wg Cdr 1/4/62. Retd MED 1/6/67.
CUMMING J., CEng MIEE MRAeS. Born 4/4/36. Commd 10/8/55. Sqn Ldr 1/7/77. Retd ENG 16/7/82.
CUMMING J. A., MB BS. Born 18/2/40. Commd 24/9/62. Sqn Ldr 17/6/69. Retd MED 3/1/73.
CUMMING L. L., BSc. Born 18/10/29. Commd 26/11/49. Sqn Ldr 1/7/60. Retd GD 17/9/68.
CUMMING P. L., BDS. Born 18/12/30. Commd 3/1/60. Gp Capt 1/1/80. Retd DEL 18/12/88.
CUMMING R. G. Born 11/2/45. Commd 1/4/71. Wg Cdr 1/7/91. Retd GD 3/5/99.
CUMMING R. G. F. Born 10/9/34. Commd 27/2/70. Sqn Ldr 1/7/87. Retd ENG 10/9/92.
CUMMINGS A. E., BA. Born 4/8/40. Commd 21/2/63. Sqn Ldr 26/10/71. Retd EDN 19/2/79.
CUMMINGS C. J., MBCS MIDPM. Born 3/2/44. Commd 12/3/64. Wg Cdr 1/1/88. Retd SUP 10/5/94.

CUMMINGS D., CEng MIEE MRAeS. Born 26/1/30. Commd 20/12/51. Gp Capt 1/1/78. Retd ENG 30/8/80.
CUMMINGS L. M. Born 12/10/46. Commd 9/2/66. Sqn Ldr 1/1/78. Retd ADMIN 12/10/84.
CUMMINGS W. J. Born 15/3/51. Commd 4/5/72. Sqn Ldr 1/1/89. Retd GD 15/3/95.
CUMMINS J. B. Born 1/5/28. Commd 11/3/53. Flt Lt 24/11/58. Retd GD 20/1/69.
CUMMINS P. D. Born 5/12/19. Commd 9/9/48. Flt Lt 4/6/53. Retd PE 30/9/62.
CUMMINS R. P. Born 14/5/13. Commd 31/12/42. Sqn Ldr 1/1/54. Retd SEC 14/5/62.
CUMMINS T. M. Born 12/4/31. Commd 6/8/63. Flt Lt 12/11/69. Retd GD(G) 12/4/92.
CUNDALL H. J., CBE DSO DFC AFC. Born 7/4/19. Commd 17/12/38. Gp Capt 1/1/57. Retd GD 27/11/61.
CUNDY P. J., DSO DFC AFC TD. Born 3/10/16. Commd 11/4/40. Wg Cdr 1/1/52. Retd GD 3/10/63.
CUNLIFFE D. A., BA MRIN. Born 15/12/38. Commd 6/7/59. Sqn Ldr 1/1/70. Retd GD 25/11/89.
CUNLIFFE R. D., BSc. Born 24/2/62. Commd 9/12/84. Flt Lt 16/12/85. Retd GD 14/3/96.
CUNLIFFE Rev T. F. G. Born 13/6/23. Commd 8/9/53. Retd 13/6/78. Rtg Wg Cdr.
CUNLIFFE V. Born 25/8/55. Commd 13/12/79. Flt Lt 13/6/85. Retd GD 31/5/91.
CUNNANE A. Born 17/9/35. Commd 5/5/60. Sqn Ldr 1/7/73. Retd GD 2/10/84.
CUNNIFFE T. J., LLB. Born 2/5/38. Commd 13/11/62. Wg Cdr 1/7/79. Retd ADMIN 17/9/90.
CUNNINGHAM D. R. Born 25/2/19. Commd 26/11/53. Sqn Ldr 1/7/67. Retd SEC 1/7/69.
CUNNINGHAM F. McK. Born 7/9/30. Commd 6/5/53. Flt Lt 6/2/59. Retd GD 7/9/68.
CUNNINGHAM G. W., MSc BSc CEng MRAeS. Born 3/2/50. Commd 23/9/68. Wg Cdr 1/7/88. Retd ENG 18/5/96.
CUNNINGHAM J. A. D. J., FRCS FRCS(I) LRCP&S. Born 21/1/24. Commd 1/1/51. Wg Cdr 1/4/62. Retd MED 1/3/67.
CUNNINGHAM M. J., OBE. Born 22/5/43. Commd 5/11/65. Gp Capt 1/7/88. Retd GD 2/5/89.
CUNNINGHAM M. R. C., MA. Born 11/12/26. Commd 10/5/54. Sqn Ldr 2/3/63. Retd EDN 11/12/81.
CUNNINGHAM M. R. S., MBE MIMgt. Born 1/1/24. Commd 19/9/43. Sqn Ldr 1/7/55. Retd GD 1/7/72.
CUNNINGHAM P. D., MBE. Born 5/9/35. Commd 22/7/71. Sqn Ldr 1/7/80. Retd SUP 5/9/92.
CUNNINGHAM P. J., DFM. Born 7/1/35. Commd 5/5/60. Flt Lt 5/11/64. Retd GD 7/1/73.
CUNNINGHAM P. W. J. Born 1/9/37. Commd 30/7/59. Sqn Ldr 1/7/71. Retd ENG 1/6/78.
CUNNINGHAM R. A., MRAeS MIEE. Born 30/3/23. Commd 27/2/44. Sqn Ldr 1/1/61. Retd ENG 1/1/64.
CUNNINGHAM R. H. Born 22/4/33. Commd 27/9/51. Flt Lt 26/1/57. Retd GD 1/4/75 rtg Sqn Ldr.
CUNNINGHAM Rev T. Born 28/11/31. Commd 24/9/62. Retd 24/9/78. Rel Wg Cdr.
CUNNINGHAM S. P., GM. Born 29/8/08. Commd 27/5/43. Flt Lt 27/11/45. Retd ENG 30/9/58.
CUNNINGHAM V. A. L. M. Born 18/3/52. Commd 15/2/84. Flt Lt 18/8/78. Retd GD(G) 23/9/89.
CUNNINGHAM-SMITH H. C. Born 23/2/44. Commd 12/3/72. Flt Lt 29/5/74. Retd ADMIN 12/3/88.
CUNNINGTON G. H., OBE. Born 5/5/26. Commd 20/7/50. Wg Cdr 1/7/70. Retd GD 4/2/81.
CUNNINGTON P. C., MA. Born 5/5/40. Commd 30/9/59. Sqn Ldr 1/7/74. Retd ENG 5/5/95.
CUPPLES J. M. Born 1/7/19. Commd 7/4/41. Sqn Offr 1/7/51. Retd SEC 4/11/53.
CUPPLES S. E., MB BCh DPH. Born 10/6/18. Commd 20/3/42. Wg Cdr 1/7/56. Retd MED 18/9/71.
CURD B. R. Born 18/6/37. Commd 28/7/67. Flt Lt 28/7/69. Retd GD 28/7/75.
CURE A. G., MA. Born 9/9/46. Commd 22/9/74. Wg Cdr 1/1/94. Retd ADMIN 14/3/96.
CURETON C. Born 7/10/38. Commd 5/3/57. Sqn Ldr 1/1/73. Retd GD 27/10/78.
CURLEY M. T., AFC. Born 26/2/46. Commd 3/1/64. Sqn Ldr 1/7/86. Retd GD 31/12/86.
CURNOW J. Born 25/8/42. Commd 31/8/62. Flt Lt 15/4/70. Retd GD 25/8/80.
CURRAN E. T., MBE BSc CEng DCAe MIMechE MRAeS. Born 13/1/30. Commd 10/2/49. Wg Cdr 1/1/66. Retd ENG 14/1/69.
CURRANT C. F., DSO DFC*. Born 14/12/11. Commd 1/4/40. Wg Cdr 1/7/47. Retd GD 14/12/58.
CURRASS A. E. Born 29/9/21. Commd 18/11/66. Flt Lt 18/11/71. Retd ENG 31/3/76.
CURREY K. F., BA CEng MIEE MRAeS MIMgt. Born 14/2/20. Commd 29/3/45. Sqn Ldr 1/7/64. Retd ENG 14/3/80.
CURRIE H. Born 30/8/23. Commd 18/6/44. Wg Cdr 1/7/68. Retd GD 17/3/78.
CURRIE I. Born 30/6/46. Commd 15/9/67. Flt Lt 15/3/73. Retd GD 30/6/84.
CURRIE I. A., MIMgt. Born 14/12/50. Commd 1/4/71. Flt Lt 1/7/77. Retd ADMIN 14/12/88.
CURRIE I. G., MB ChB. Born 20/1/29. Commd 24/10/54. Gp Capt 1/1/77. Retd MED 5/1/83.
CURRIE J., CEng MIMechE MRAeS. Born 20/6/26. Commd 3/10/61. Sqn Ldr 1/1/68. Retd ENG 30/9/81.
CURRIE J. H. Born 2/7/41. Commd 31/7/62. Flt Lt 31/1/65. Retd GD 22/10/94.
CURRIE J. W. A. Born 17/2/34. Commd 25/1/60. Sqn Ldr 1/7/67. Retd GD 17/2/72.
CURRIE P. R. Born 8/1/30. Commd 7/10/52. Flt Lt 30/12/57. Retd GD 7/10/68.
CURRUMS G. D. Born 2/9/53. Commd 9/10/75. Sqn Ldr 1/1/88. Retd GD 17/10/94.
CURRY A. C., OBE FIMgt. Born 13/1/34. Commd 7/5/52. A Cdre 1/1/87. Retd GD 13/1/89.
CURRY B. G. Born 25/9/43. Commd 8/9/83. Sqn Ldr 1/7/90. Retd ADMIN 31/3/94.
CURRY D. J. Born 22/11/39. Commd 1/8/61. Sqn Ldr 1/1/72. Retd GD 22/11/77.
CURRY J. M. Born 28/8/35. Commd 19/8/53. Gp Capt 1/1/79. Retd GD 24/2/88.
CURRY P. M. Born 22/6/47. Commd 19/8/66. Sqn Ldr 1/1/91. Retd GD 10/2/98.
CURRY R. G. Born 7/5/41. Commd 27/6/59. A Cdre 1/7/89. Retd GD 5/8/96.
CURTIES D. M., BSc. Born 4/2/52. Commd 22/9/72. Sqn Ldr 1/1/86. Retd GD 22/12/91.
CURTIN P. B., AFC. Born 7/6/37. Commd 1/4/58. Sqn Ldr 1/7/70. Retd GD 1/10/77.
CURTIS A. L. Born 1/10/35. Commd 1/11/53. Wg Cdr 1/7/74. Retd GD 1/6/87.
CURTIS C. F. A. Born 13/12/26. Commd 16/1/48. Sqn Ldr 1/7/57. Retd GD 11/10/62.
CURTIS D. G., MBE. Born 21/6/44. Commd 1/7/82. Sqn Ldr 1/1/92. Retd GD(G) 14/3/96.

CURTIS D. J., MBE. Born 30/11/23. Commd 23/1/45. Sqn Ldr 1/7/68. Retd GD 31/3/74.
CURTIS F. A. Born 25/8/62. Commd 26/9/85. Flt Lt 22/9/90. Retd ADMIN 14/9/96.
CURTIS J. A. B., DFC. Born 23/6/12. Commd 1/3/43. Flt Lt 1/3/48. Retd GD(G) 29/3/59.
CURTIS K. J., BSc. Born 20/12/52. Commd 13/8/70. Sqn Ldr 1/1/85. Retd ENG 20/12/90.
CURTIS K. R. Born 21/11/22. Commd 18/11/53. Sqn Ldr 1/1/72. Retd GD 2/5/75.
CURTIS M. I. M., BA CEng MIEE DipEE. Born 1/1/41. Commd 31/3/64. Sqn Ldr 1/7/83. Retd ENG 31/7/95.
CURTIS M. R., MBE. Born 21/6/37. Commd 19/7/56. Wg Cdr 1/1/74. Retd SEC 16/1/79.
CURTIS N. F., OBE. Born 30/1/22. Commd 25/9/43. Gp Capt 1/7/66. Retd GD 19/4/71.
CURTIS P. H. Born 26/9/15. Commd 2/1/39. Sqn Ldr 8/6/45. Retd SUP 14/5/50 rtg Wg Cdr.
CURTIS R. A., BSc. Born 27/3/43. Commd 2/5/71. Flt Lt 2/5/73. Retd ENG 2/5/87.
CURTIS R. R. Born 24/7/34. Commd 26/5/60. Sqn Ldr 1/7/70. Retd GD 2/10/79.
CURTIS R. S. Born 17/4/42. Commd 4/6/64. Wg Cdr 1/7/88. Retd GD(G) 16/4/94.
CURTIS R. W. J., BA. Born 5/2/57. Commd 27/8/87. Flt Lt 27/8/89. Retd ADMIN 7/3/97.
CURTIS S. A., MBE. Born 21/10/28. Commd 9/8/51. Sqn Ldr 1/1/68. Retd GD 21/10/83.
CURTIS W. A. Born 11/7/46. Commd 22/5/64. Flt Lt 22/11/69. Retd GD 1/11/72.
CURTISS Sir John., KCB KBE CIMgt. Born 6/12/24. Commd 27/10/44. AM 1/1/81. Retd GD 13/6/83.
CURZON F. Born 21/4/31. Commd 22/8/63. Flt Lt 22/8/66. Retd SEC 29/9/73.
CURZON H. N., MA. Born 22/1/62. Commd 11/9/83. Flt Lt 11/3/87. Retd ADMIN 11/9/89.
CUSHION B. C. Born 10/3/47. Commd 1/3/68. Flt Lt 1/3/71. Retd GD 9/7/90.
CUSSEN O. A., DFC*. Born 20/3/16. Commd 8/5/43. Flt Lt 6/11/45. Retd GD(G) 1/4/63.
CUTBUSH D. H. D. Born 20/3/45. Commd 28/7/88. Flt Lt 28/7/92. Retd ENG 31/1/97.
CUTCHEY P. H., DFC. Born 8/6/22. Commd 28/3/42. Flt Lt 28/9/45. Retd GD(G) 11/8/66.
CUTHBERT-JOHNSTONE E. Born 12/1/08. Commd 19/3/41. Fg Offr 8/4/42. Retd ASD 25/6/46 rtg Flt Lt.
CUTHBERTSON D. Born 6/5/59. Commd 13/12/79. Sqn Ldr 1/7/91. Retd GD 6/5/97.
CUTHEW J. Born 23/5/33. Commd 27/2/52. Flt Lt 26/6/57. Retd GD 23/5/71.
CUTHILL C. R., DFC AFC. Born 12/5/23. Commd 30/9/44. Flt Lt 30/3/48. Retd GD 12/5/61.
CUTHILL J., DFC. Born 28/6/23. Commd 16/10/44. Flt Lt 26/5/55. Retd GD 29/8/69.
CUTHILL R. T. Born 19/1/46. Commd 1/3/68. Wg Cdr 1/7/86. Retd GD 15/6/97.
CUTHILL S. M., BA BA BSc(Eng) CEng MRAeS. Born 19/4/47. Commd 10/4/68. Sqn Ldr 1/1/80. Retd ENG 15/7/88.
CUTLER A., BSc. Born 12/5/50. Commd 3/9/72. Flt Lt 15/4/80. Retd ENG 3/9/88.
CUTLER A. M., MHCIMA. Born 20/6/51. Commd 8/7/73. Sqn Ldr 1/1/85. Retd ADMIN 8/7/89.
CUTLER D. P. Born 28/7/47. Commd 21/10/65. Flt Lt 4/5/72. Retd GD(G) 14/2/88.
CUTLER D. R. Born 1/7/44. Commd 20/11/64. Sqn Ldr 1/7/79. Retd GD(G) 1/7/82.
CUTLER P. E. C. Born 2/6/33. Commd 4/7/51. Flt Lt 19/7/58. Retd RGT 2/6/64.
CUTLER P. S., BA. Born 4/4/44. Commd 16/1/72. Flt Lt 16/10/75. Retd GD(G) 1/4/77.
CUTTER N. F. Born 22/6/30. Commd 23/8/56. Flt Lt 23/2/61. Retd GD 22/6/68.
CUTTILL D. A., ACIS. Born 24/7/31. Commd 19/6/52. Sqn Ldr 1/7/64. Retd SEC 24/7/69.
CUTTING D. J., BA. Born 20/6/36. Commd 20/1/64. Sqn Ldr 1/1/72. Retd GD 20/1/80.
CUTTLE D. A., CEng MIMechE MRAeS. Born 23/10/41. Commd 24/1/63. Sqn Ldr 1/1/75. Retd ENG 23/10/96.
CUTTS P. D. Born 29/4/47. Commd 29/3/68. Wg Cdr 1/1/87. Retd ENG 1/9/91.
CYSTER C. D. Born 23/3/44. Commd 20/10/67. Sqn Ldr 1/7/80. Retd GD 10/7/89.
CZARNECKI Z. H. Born 12/1/21. Commd 26/9/57. Flt Lt 26/9/60. Retd GD 12/1/71.

# D

D'ARCY R. S. G. Born 19/10/40. Commd 13/10/61. Flt Lt 13/4/72. Retd GD 19/10/95.
D'ARCY S. H. R. L. Born 19/11/29. Commd 11/4/51. Sqn Ldr 1/7/61. Retd GD 1/5/76. Reinstated 5/11/80 to 30/7/87.
D'AUTHREAU A. Born 1/7/26. Commd 28/8/52. Flt Offr 28/8/58. Retd SEC 1/11/67.
D'AVOINE J. A. S. Born 18/5/21. Commd 10/7/44. Flt Lt 8/7/60. Retd GD 2/4/68.
D'OLIVEIRA B., OBE. Born 5/2/28. Commd 4/5/50. Wg Cdr 1/7/69. Retd GD 1/11/75.
DABIN V. R. Born 28/12/31. Commd 6/2/61. Sqn Ldr 1/1/75. Retd GD 1/11/86.
DACE P. A. Born 25/3/25. Commd 27/4/45. Sqn Ldr 1/1/58. Retd GD 1/4/70.
DACHTLER. A. H., BSc. Born 15/6/43. Commd 12/7/63. Flt Lt 15/6/66. Retd GD 15/6/81.
DACRE J. P. Born 22/7/41. Commd 22/2/63. Gp Capt 1/1/90. Retd GD 12/1/95.
DADD R. S. M., BSc. Born 6/3/27. Commd 15/3/49. Sqn Ldr 1/1/62. Retd ENG 26/10/65.
DADSWELL L. D., BSc DIC. Born 16/3/13. Commd 1/1/34. Gp Capt 1/1/56. Retd ENG 1/10/63.
DAFTER E. J. Born 21/5/29. Commd 5/12/51. Flt Lt 5/6/55. Retd GD(G) 21/5/89.
DAGG M. Born 13/12/25. Commd 19/12/63. Flt Lt 19/12/68. Retd ENG 18/8/78.
DAGGER The Rev J. H. K., MA. Born 16/11/07. Commd 20/5/40. Retd 20/11/61 Wg Cdr.
DAIMOND The Rev J. E., BA. Born 19/11/39. Commd 6/1/66. Retd 4/10/91 Wg Cdr.
DAINTY G. P. Born 6/3/45. Commd 5/3/65. Flt Lt 5/9/70. Retd GD 6/3/82.
DAINTY J. D. G. Born 30/8/39. Commd 12/9/63. Wg Cdr 1/1/81. Retd SUP 21/7/91.
DAINTY P. C., OBE. Born 12/10/14. Commd 10/10/40. Gp Capt 1/1/62. Retd SEC 9/10/67.
DAISH J. R. Born 18/3/39. Commd 11/12/61. Wg Cdr 1/1/87. Retd GD 16/5/94.
DALBY D., MRAeS. Born 28/5/20. Commd 23/9/43. Sqn Ldr 1/7/54. Retd ENG 28/5/69.
DALE A. A. Born 29/4/45. Commd 20/8/65. Flt Lt 29/10/70. Retd GD(G) 29/4/89.
DALE A. J. Born 18/1/58. Commd 24/7/81. Flt Lt 21/1/84. Retd GD 18/1/96.
DALE B. H. Born 3/2/36. Commd 22/1/55. Wg Cdr 1/7/79. Retd GD 18/8/87.
DALE D. C. Born 31/3/56. Commd 10/5/90. Flt Lt 10/5/92. Retd SUP 27/1/00.
DALE D. M., BSc. Born 6/2/38. Commd 24/5/59. Sqn Ldr 1/7/72. Retd GD 28/3/77.
DALE H. L. Born 21/9/12. Commd 1/6/42. Fg Offr 14/12/42. Retd ENG 31/5/46 rtg Flt Lt.
DALE I. P., MSc BA. Born 3/3/59. Commd 29/8/77. Sqn Ldr 1/7/92. Retd ENG 29/9/98.
DALE J. Born 12/5/57. Commd 6/10/77. Wg Cdr 1/7/99. Retd ADMIN 2/4/01.
DALE J. D. Born 14/3/44. Commd 17/12/65. Sqn Ldr 1/1/75. Retd SY 8/5/82. Reinstated 14/5/84. Wg Cdr 1/1/85. Retd SY 1/8/87.
DALE J. R. F. Born 13/3/51. Commd 24/4/70. Flt Lt 8/8/76. Retd GD(G) 28/5/82.
DALE P. G. Born 13/3/23. Commd 20/9/44. Flt Offr 1/7/51. Retd PRT 23/7/56.
DALE P. P. Born 6/11/30. Commd 31/12/52. Flt Lt 15/2/65. Retd GD 22/11/70.
DALE R. M. Born 27/9/32. Commd 5/1/54. Flt Lt 5/11/60. Retd GD 4/1/75.
DALE R. W., ACIS. Born 19/5/35. Commd 20/6/63. Flt Lt 1/4/66. Retd SEC 19/5/73.
DALE T. B., BA MInstAM MIMgt. Born 6/10/38. Commd 17/11/59. Wg Cdr 1/7/87. Retd ADMIN 6/10/93.
DALE T. E. Born 28/3/31. Commd 26/8/66. Sqn Ldr 1/1/79. Retd ENG 20/1/84.
DALES M. Born 7/9/40. Commd 30/7/63. Sqn Ldr 1/1/72. Retd GD 7/9/78. Reinstated 1/4/82. Sqn Ldr 26/7/75. Retd GD 7/9/95.
DALEY F. W. Born 19/6/33. Commd 10/4/56. Sqn Ldr 1/7/67. Retd GD 30/9/73.
DALGLEISH A. H. L. Born 27/2/28. Commd 31/7/61. Wg Cdr 1/7/76. Retd SUP 1/8/79.
DALGLEISH J. W. O., OBE. Born 20/3/88. Commd 1/4/18. Wg Cdr 1/4/18. Retd GD 9/10/20.
DALGLEISH R. F. Born 22/11/46. Commd 17/7/70. Flt Lt 22/4/74. Retd GD 1/12/89.
DALGLEISH W. H. Born 18/1/26. Commd 22/2/46. Sqn Ldr 1/7/56. Retd GD 18/1/64.
DALGLIESH D. C. Born 27/5/47. Commd 23/3/67. Flt Lt 23/9/72. Retd GD 27/5/85.
DALKIN J. L. Born 26/5/33. Commd 17/12/64. Sqn Ldr 2/10/74. Retd ADMIN 1/2/84.
DALLAS G. C. Born 10/9/52. Commd 2/2/84. Flt Lt 2/2/86. Retd ENG 14/3/97.
DALLEY J. O., OBE DFM. Born 7/4/20. Commd 28/8/42. Gp Capt 1/7/62. Retd GD 26/4/75.
DALLEY K. P. Born 25/3/42. Commd 2/3/61. Flt Lt 9/2/68. Retd GD 24/3/80. Re-entered 11/3/81. Sqn Ldr 1/1/87. Rtd GD 15/4/00.
DALLIMORE G. Born 26/1/37. Commd 24/9/63. Sqn Ldr 1/7/71. Retd ENG 5/4/91.
DALLIMORE J. M. Born 26/11/38. Commd 7/5/64. Sqn Ldr 1/7/73. Retd ENG 26/11/76.
DALLISON D. M. Born 14/1/26. Commd 18/4/50. Flt Lt 11/6/53. Retd GD 15/12/57.
DALLISON P. M., MCIPD MIMgt. Born 21/7/45. Commd 5/3/65. Sqn Ldr 1/1/83. Retd GD 14/3/96.
DALTON B. Born 31/8/27. Commd 26/3/64 Sqn Ldr 1/1/75. Retd ADMIN 31/8/85
DALTON C. Born 15/12/57. Commd 27/7/89. Flt Lt 27/7/91. Retd ADMIN 14/3/96.
DALTON G. Born 13/11/46. Commd 7/7/67. Sqn Ldr 1/1/93. Retd GD(G) 1/4/94.
DALTON I. R., MBE. Born 21/4/45. Commd 19/3/81. Sqn Ldr 1/1/90. Retd ADMIN 22/4/97.
DALTON J. A. H. Born 16/11/21. Commd 30/12/43. Flt Lt 7/9/47. Retd GD(G) 16/11/76.
DALTON J. G. Born 23/11/15. Commd 30/3/53. Flt Lt 11/11/54. Retd SEC 23/11/73.
DALTON R. W., DFM. Born 24/8/18. Commd 27/1/42. Sqn Ldr 1/4/56. Retd GD 31/3/58.
DALTON-MORRIS S. E. J. Born 24/6/34. Commd 24/9/52. Sqn Ldr 1/7/76. Retd GD 18/12/86.

DALY G. J., DFC. Born 7/6/20. Commd 29/5/43. Wg Cdr 1/1/66. Retd GD 7/6/75.
DALY J. H. D. Born 3/4/29. Commd 30/7/52. Sqn Ldr 1/7/62. Retd GD 3/4/67.
DALY M. J., MBE. Born 27/12/52. Commd 12/7/79. Sqn Ldr 1/1/90. Retd SY 1/1/93.
DALY M. J. Born 16/6/33. Commd 13/2/52. Sqn Ldr 1/7/66. Retd GD(G) 19/7/81.
DALY P. K. Born 28/6/60.Commd 28/2/80. Plt Offr 28/2/81. Retd GD 9/5/82.
DALY R. J. Born 16/3/23. Commd 25/2/44. Sqn Ldr 1/1/70. Retd SEC 30/6/73.
DALY W. O. Born 27/3/20. Commd 3/8/50. Wg Cdr 1/7/61. Retd SUP 27/3/75.
DALZELL S. R. Born 29/10/55. Commd 26/9/85. Sqn Ldr 1/7/92. Retd ENG 1/7/95.
DALZIEL L. McA., BA. Born 14/7/56. Commd 11/4/82. Flt Lt 11/10/85. Retd GD(G) 15/9/89.
DALZIEL S. M., BSc. Born 11/6/48. Commd 18/7/66. Flt Lt 25/11/73. Retd ENG 11/6/86.
DAMMENT J. F. D. Born 12/3/32. Commd 17/12/53. Sqn Ldr 1/7/69. Retd SUP 18/12/84
DAMPIER E. P. Born 23/3/87. Commd 1/4/18. Fg Offr 1/10/19. Retd GD 23/12/22 rtg Flt Lt.
DANBY C. I. Born 10/12/42. Commd 20/12/62. Flt Lt 15/2/70. Retd GD 9/10/94.
DANBY J. E. Born 28/10/20. Commd 26/7/45. Sqn Ldr 1/1/68. Retd SEC 1/12/70.
DANBY T. Born 31/3/33. Commd 2/4/57. Sqn Ldr 1/7/79. Retd GD 14/4/85.
DANCE N. R. Born 1/2/48. Commd 17/2/67. Flt Lt 17/8/72. Retd GD 30/9/85.
DANCKWARDT F. P. J. L. Born 20/7/24. Commd 21/8/44. Sqn Ldr 1/4/56. Retd GD 20/6/74.
DANDEKER K., DFC. Born 14/12/17. Commd 6/1/43. Wg Cdr 1/7/67. Retd ENG 1/6/72.
DANDEKER P. Born 15/2/46. Commd 1/10/65. Sqn Ldr 1/1/86. Retd GD 1/10/89.
DANDO D. F. Born 31/1/34. Commd 18/6/52. Flt Lt 29/4/59. Retd GD(G) 15/8/85.
DANDY G. T. Born 30/4/26. Commd 16/7/52. Sqn Ldr 1/1/75. Retd GD 30/6/76.
DANDY R. Born 6/7/46. Commd 3/5/68. Flt Lt 3/11/73. Retd GD 4/5/77.
DANE M. B., MBE. Born 15/2/35. Commd 15/2/73. Sqn Ldr 1/7/81. Retd GD 15/2/93.
DANIEL C. R. D., MCIT MILT. Born 12/9/45. Commd 14/1/65. Sqn Ldr 1/1/77. Retd SUP 12/9/83.
DANIEL J. A. Born 8/12/37. Commd 2/1/75. Flt Lt 8/12/92. Retd GD(G) 8/12/92.
DANIEL J. M., DFC. Born 30/8/23. Commd 26/4/43. Grp Capt 1/1/69. Retd GD 30/6/71.
DANIEL M. P. Born 26/12/40. Commd 22/9/67. Sqn Ldr 1/7/78. Retd ADMIN 7/1/86.
DANIEL N. S. Born 28/2/41. Commd 17/5/79. Flt Lt 17/5/84. Retd GD(G) 28/2/96.
DANIEL T. P. Born 8/4/32. Commd 4/10/51. Flt Lt 4/4/57. Retd GD 8/4/70.
DANIELI G. A. Born 19/9/39. Commd 27/1/61. Flt Lt 10/2/67. Retd GD 19/9/77.
DANIELL D. H., BA. Born 18/12/25. Commd 28/7/60. Sqn Ldr 1/1/73. Retd SEC 18/12/757.
DANIELL P. A., BSc BA CEng MIEE MIMgt. Born 8/3/28. Commd 5/12/51. Wg Cdr 1/1/76. Retd ENG 18/3/78.
DANIELS B. A., CEng MIEE MRAeS. Born 20/7/34. Commd 24/7/57. Sqn Ldr 1/7/66. Retd ENG 20/7/72.
DANIELS B. V., BSc. Born 29/7/59. Commd 27/4/54. Wg Cdr 1/1/69. Retd ENG 5/9/81.
DANIELS G. A. Born 2/10/44. Commd 5/11/70. Sqn Ldr 1/1/84. Retd GD 2/10/99.
DANIELS J. G. Born 19/11/28. Commd 22/1/54. Sqn Ldr 1/1/79. Retd GD 16/8/87.
DANIELS K. R., MA MSc MB BChir MRCGP DCH DRCOG DAvMed. Born 23/11/47. Commd 27/7/70. Wg Cdr 9/9/87. Retd MED 14/3/96.
DANIELS L. F. Born 20/11/22. Commd 24/1/63. Flt Lt 24/1/68. Retd ENG 20/11/77.
DANIELS M. E. J. Born 22/1/30. Commd 24/2/67. Sqn Ldr 1/7/80. Retd ENG 22/6/92.
DANIELS P. J. Born 20/5/43. Commd 23/9/66. Flt Lt 8/3/72. Retd GD 30/9/77.
DANIELS R. E. Born 8/11/29. Commd 13/8/52. Wg Cdr 1/1/77. Retd GD 8/11/84.
DANKS E. T. M. Born 24/1/45. Commd 3/3/67. Sqn Ldr 1/1/76. Retd GD 24/1/89.
DANKS P. I., BSc CEng MRAeS MIMgt. Born 17/12/48. Commd 4/11/73. Wg Cdr 1/7/97. Retd ENG 6/11/99.
DANN G. H. Born 6/10/23. Commd 10/3/45. Flt Lt 14/7/58. Retd GD(G) 9/2/68.
DANNING J. M. Born 9/10/44. Commd 10/1/69. Sqn Ldr 1/1/81. Retd GD 16/11/91.
DANTON B. E. Born 20/12/34. Commd 14/1/53. Flt Lt 3/6/58. Retd GD 20/12/89.
DANVERS K. V., BTech. Born 27/12/55. Commd 20/11/78. Flt Lt 20/2/79. Retd GD 20/11/86.
DARBY B. T. Born 3/10/37. Commd 22/3/63. Flt Lt 1/7/69. Retd GD(G) 8/4/91.
DARBY J. E. Born 11/9/44. Commd 19/6/64. Sqn Ldr 1/7/80. Retd GD 11/9/88.
DARBY K. Born 7/10/28. Commd 13/8/52. Flt Lt 3/71/55. Retd GD 7/10/66.
DARBY M. C., MVO BSc(Eng) CEng FIMechE FRAeS. Born 1/8/37. Commd 30/9/56. A Cdre 1/1/86. Retd ENG 7/4/90.
DARBYSHIRE P., MA BSc. Born 19/8/50. Commd 17/7/77. Wg Cdr 1/7/91. Retd ADMIN 14/9/96.
DARGAN J. C. Born 8/7/26. Commd 25/10/46. Sqn Ldr 1/7/60. Retd GD 8/7/64.
DARK C. J. Born 9/1/40. Commd 21/8/58. Sqn Ldr 1/1/88. Retd GD 9/1/95.
DARK M. E. Born 9/10/30. Commd 9/4/52. Sqn Ldr 1/1/63. Retd GD 24/7/70.
DARKE C. Born 29/7/95. Commd 8/1/37. Flt Lt 8/1/40. Retd SUP 29/7/50 rtg Wg Cdr.
DARLING D., OBE CEng FRAeS. Born 2/5/31. Commd 11/2/53. Gp Capt 1/1/76. Retd ENG 4/4/80.
DARLING J. G. A., MIMgt. Born 20/12/18. Commd 12/6/58. Sqn Ldr 1/7/66. Retd ENG 2/1/71.
DARLING M. H. O. Born 5/12/41. Commd 22/2/63. Sqn Ldr 1/1/91. Retd GD 5/12/96.
DARLING S. J., BEd. Born 25/1/63. Commd 10/11/85. Flt Lt 10/5/88. Retd ADMIN 31/3/95.
DARLING T., BEM. Born 24/8/39. Commd 22/11/84. Flt Lt 29/3/93. Retd ENG 22/4/93.
DARLINGTON G. C., BTech. Born 21/8/50. Commd 13/9/70. Sqn Ldr 1/7/86. Retd ENG 1/7/89.
DARLOW T., MBE. Born 26/10/23. Commd 29/10/64. Sqn Ldr 1/1/80. Retd ENG 26/10/83.
DARNELL A. R., BEM. Born 12/5/19. Commd 30/7/59. Flt Lt 30/7/64. Retd ENG 31/12/69.

DARNELL E. A. Born 27/12/14. Commd 2/1/39. Wg Cdr 1/7/51. Retd SUP 4/7/61.
DARNELL R. Born 28/10/44. Commd 31/1/64. Flt Lt 12/11/69. Retd GD(G) 14/3/96.
DARNEY D. H. Born 22/6/21. Commd 14/8/42. Flt Lt 21/9/46. Retd GD 9/5/66.
DARRANT D. E. Born 1/7/20. Commd 27/9/42. Flt Offr 29/1/47. Retd SEC 30/6/54.
DARROCH D. G. Born 3/1/44. Commd 31/1/64. Flt Lt 31/7/69. Retd GD 1/4/77.
DARROCH T. J., BSc. Born 15/4/33. Commd 17/7/55. Sqn Ldr 17/2/65. Retd EDN 14/9/72.
DART A. C. Born 21/2/57. Commd 30/4/88. Flt Lt 11/10/81. Retd GD 30/4/96.
DART A. P., CBE DSO DFC. Born 4/4/16. Commd 7/10/41. Gp Capt 1/1/61. Retd GD 4/4/71.
DART C. J. Born 9/7/43. Commd 20/8/65. Flt Lt 4/5/72. Retd GD 27/10/89.
DART R. E., BSc. Born 7/10/27. Commd 24/7/52. Sqn Ldr 1/4/61. Retd EDN 15/4/68.
DART W. A. C. Born 1/3/55. Commd 11/7/74. Flt Lt 11/1/80. Retd GD 24/8/82.
DARWENT W. Born 14/12/34. Commd 16/9/71. Flt Lt 16/9/75. Retd ENG 15/12/84.
DARWIN R. B., BSc. Born 20/12/39. Commd 14/5/63. Sqn Ldr 1/1/74. Retd GD 19/11/90.
DASH D. M., BSc. Born 9/10/47. Commd 17/1/72. Flt Lt 17/10/73. Retd GD 2/6/79.
DASTON H. N. M. Born 11/8/14. Commd 18/5/40. Flt Lt 18/5/46. Retd SEC 11/8/69.
DATTNER D., OBE AFC. Born 20/1/22. Commd 6/6/44. Sqn Ldr 1/1/60. Retd GD 30/1/65.
DAULBY D. J., BSc. Born 13/2/46. Commd 11/5/71. Sqn Ldr 1/1/85. Retd GD 1/7/94.
DAUM R. E. O., MB BS FFARCS. Born 13/6/54. Commd 19/11/74. Wg Cdr 1/2/92. Retd MED 13/6/92.
DAUNCEY R. H. H., MIMgt. Born 21/2/31. Commd 9/4/52. Wg Cdr 1/1/76. Retd ADMIN 29/2/84.
DAVENPORT A. Born 27/7/43. Commd 5/11/65. Flt Lt 5/5/71. Retd GD 6/7/77.
DAVENPORT R. J., CBE AFC MIMgt. Born 15/2/25. Commd 27/7/45. A Cdre 1/1/78. Retd GD 2/4/81.
DAVENPORT-GOOD A. M. Born 2/12/61. Commd 11/6/81. Sqn Ldr 1/7/93. Retd OPS SPT 1/8/97.
DAVEY C., MIMgt. Born 20/4/41. Commd 25/2/63. Sqn Ldr 1/1/77. Retd ENG 1/1/80.
DAVEY D. N. Born 18/11/31. Commd 18/7/63. Sqn Ldr 1/7/74. Retd ENG 31/1/88.
DAVEY G. G. Born 17/9/23. Commd 9/9/54. Flt Lt 9/3/58. Retd GD 19/1/63.
DAVEY G. W. Born 14/1/22. Commd 27/8/59. Sqn Ldr 1/1/77. Retd ENG 21/12/77.
DAVEY H. A. Born 13/2/31. Commd 28/1/60 Sqn Ldr 1/1/79 Retd GD(G) 19/9/85.
DAVEY J. M. Born 15/12/43. Commd 24/9/90. Sqn Ldr 1/1/88. Retd SUP 26/7/93.
DAVEY K. E. Born 7/7/22. Commd 19/5/45. Flt Lt 29/11/51. Retd GD(G) 1/6/62.
DAVEY K. M., DFC. Born 27/4/20. Commd 26/1/43. Flt Lt 26/7/46. Retd GD 3/5/63.
DAVEY L. B., OBE FIMgt. Born 26/11/19. Commd 30/4/43. A Cdre 1/1/71. Retd SUP 3/1/73.
DAVEY P. J. O. Born 9/9/35. Commd 22/1/55. Sqn Ldr 1/7/83. Retd GD(G) 9/9/90.
DAVEY R. C. Born 3/3/47. Commd 17/3/67. Sqn Ldr 1/1/78. Retd ADMIN 3/10/88.
DAVEY R. G. Born 10/4/31. Commd 9/4/52. Wg Cdr 1/1/81. Retd SUP 10/4/86.
DAVEY R. J. Born 25/3/34. Commd 24/9/90. Sqn Ldr 3/7/81. Retd GD 25/3/93.
DAVEY S. B. Born 30/7/44. Commd 31/8/62. Wg Cdr 1/7/83. Retd SY(RGT) 30/7/88.
DAVID E. W., DPhysEd. Born 17/9/36. Commd 6/7/62. Sqn Ldr 1/1/73. Retd GD 31/5/79.
DAVID J. M. Born 6/12/34. Commd 19/10/60. Flt Lt 19/10/60. Retd GD 19/10/76.
DAVID K. F., MBE. Born 22/9/33. Commd 26/8/66. Flt Lt 26/8/71. Retd GD 3/5/72.
DAVID R. J. M. Born 14/4/34. Commd 19/8/53. Gp Capt 1/1/83. Retd GD 14/4/89.
DAVID W. D., CBE DFC* AFC. Born 25/7/18. Commd 4/4/38. Gp Capt 1/7/60. Retd GD 26/5/67.
DAVID W. I. Born 12/12/31. Commd 23/1/52. Flt Lt 14/11/56. Retd GD 13/1/71.
DAVIDGE E. H., MCIPD. Born 12/3/50. Commd 14/1/88. Flt Lt 14/1/92. Retd ADMIN 13/11/97.
DAVIDGE M. C. F., MA MIISec. Born 1/10/47. Commd 13/4/80. Sqn Ldr 1/1/89. Retd SY 31/10/96.
DAVIDSON A. Born 27/9/34. Commd 26.3.53. Sqn Ldr 1/7/69. Retd GD 29/9/87.
DAVIDSON A. C. Born 2/12/49. Commd 19/6/70. Sqn Ldr 1/7/87. Retd SY(RGT) 1/10/89.
DAVIDSON C. A., DFM. Born 6/4/18. Commd 26/4/43. Flt Lt 26/10/47. Retd SEC 6/4/67.
DAVIDSON C. W. H. Born 6/11/20. Commd 15/6/50. Sqn Ldr 1/1/67. Retd GD 6/5/73.
DAVIDSON D. K. Born 21/2/60. Commd 5/5/88. Flt Lt 28/7/90. Retd ADMIN 13/10/96.
DAVIDSON F. R., DFC MIMgt. Born 17/3/21. Commd 26/1/43. Wg Cdr 1/1/68. Retd GD 17/3/76.
DAVIDSON G., OBE. Born 5/3/14. Commd 25/4/40. Wg Cdr 1/1/56. Retd SEC 6/3/64.
DAVIDSON G. McG. Born 20/1/18. Commd 23/12/43. Flt Lt 23/5/56. Retd GD(G) 27/9/67.
DAVIDSON H., OBE. Born 10/10/30. Commd 12/6/51. A Cdre 1/7/79. Retd GD 8/8/81.
DAVIDSON I. Born 7/2/55. Commd 28/10/76. Flt Lt 28/4/82. Retd GD 9/6/99.
DAVIDSON I. F., BA. Born 3/4/66. Commd 8/1/65. Wg Cdr 1/1/94. Retd GD 3/4/01.
DAVIDSON I. W. B., MIMgt. Born 12/5/49. Commd 24/9/67. Flt Lt 25/5/74. Retd GD 1/10/89.
DAVIDSON J., DFC. Born 8/1/23. Commd 26/6/45. Flt Lt 4/1/51. Retd GD 28/2/62.
DAVIDSON J. C. Born 6/3/51. Commd 29/1/87. Flt Lt 29/1/91. Retd ENG 3/4/93.
DAVIDSON J. E., DFC AFC. Born 30/9/22. Commd 19/9/44. Flt Lt 3/3/49. Retd GD(G) 30/6/61.
DAVIDSON J. J. Born 15/7/52. Commd 28/8/75. Sqn Ldr 1/7/86. Retd GD(G) 12/5/91
DAVIDSON J. N., BTech MCIT MILT. Born 30/5/53. Commd 26/11/78. Flt Lt 26/11/79. Retd SUP 16/12/84.
DAVIDSON M. F. Born 10/6/38. Commd 4/7/57. Sqn Ldr 1/1/75. Retd SY(RGT) 10/6/88.
DAVIDSON M. W. Born 8/6/37. Commd 18/2/58. Flt Lt 7/8/64. Retd GD 20/12/68.
DAVIDSON N. Born 28/3/33. Commd 7/1/71. Flt Lt 7/1/76. Retd SEC 1/10/83.
DAVIDSON P. M. Born 17/10/51. Commd 19/8/71. Flt Lt 18/12/77. Retd SUP 19/8/81. Re-entered 14/9/83. Sqn Ldr 1/1/91. Retd SUP 9/1/00.

DAVIDSON R. Born 21/2/51. Commd 16/3/73. Sqn Ldr 1/7/88. Retd ADMIN 15/4/92.
DAVIDSON R. B., DFC MIMgt. Born 9/5/20. Commd 24/11/41. Wg Cdr 1/1/64. Retd GD 9/5/75.
DAVIDSON R. H. C., MA. Born 27/1/47. Commd 18/9/66. Sqn Ldr 1/1/79. Retd GD 11/7/89.
DAVIDSON R. N. Born 6/1/34. Commd 11/6/52. Sq Ldr 1/7/70. Retd GD(G) 2/7/87.
DAVIDSON S. Born 9/4/33. Commd 14/5/53. Flt Lt 13/4/60. Retd SEC 9/4/71 rtg Sqn Ldr.
DAVIDSON S. M., CBE CEng FIEE. Born 1/11/22. Commd 7/8/42. AVM 1/1/75. Retd ENG 31/3/77.
DAVIDSON S. M. Born 1/9/56. Commd 20/7/78. Flt Lt 20/1/84. Retd GD 1/9/94.
DAVIDSON T. J. Born 25/7/56. Commd 5/8/76. Sqn Ldr 1/7/88. Retd GD 25/7/94.
DAVIDSON W. Born 7/7/19. Commd 2/10/41. Flt Lt 1/9/45. Retd ENG 14/11/53.
DAVIE D. Born 25/9/28. Commd 18/9/47. Flt Lt 19/12/55. Retd GD 25/9/66.
DAVIE J. R. Born 2/10/20. Commd 20/4/50. Flt Lt 20/10/53. Retd GD 9/11/64.
DAVIE P. E., BA MBCS. Born 10/8/30. Commd 28/11/51. A Cdre 1/1/80. Retd SEC 28/11/81.
DAVIE R. C., MB BS DA DAvMed. Born 9/6/32. Commd 10/7/60. Gp Capt 1/7/81. Retd MED 31/12/87.
DAVIES A. Born 24/8/48. Commd 31/7/70. Flt Lt 31/7/73. Retd GD 31/3/94.
DAVIES A., MA BA. Born 25/1/66. Commd 2/9/84. Flt Lt 15/1/90. Retd GD 2/12/96.
DAVIES A. B., BEng. Born 15/8/61. Commd 16/9/84. Flt Lt 11/8/88. Retd ENG 2/5/94.
DAVIES A. C., MBE CEng MIProdE MIMgt. Born 11/2/41. Commd 7/12/65. Wg Cdr 1/7/81. Retd ENG 11/2/91.
DAVIES A. C. Born 17/1/39. Commd 2/2/68. Flt Lt 4/11/70. Retd SUP 17/1/77.
DAVIES A. D. Born 13/10/27. Commd 7/10/48. Sqn Ldr 1/1/61. Retd GD 28/6/68.
DAVIES A. E. Born 21/1/38. Commd 19/1/66. Wg Cdr 1/1/90. Retd ENG 21/1/93.
DAVIES A. J. Born 20/9/43. Commd 5/11/70. Flt Lt 5/11/72. Retd GD(G) 20/9/81.
DAVIES A. J., BA. Born 8/6/36. Commd 23/9/59. Wg Cdr 1/1/81. Retd GD 2/3/87.
DAVIES A. J. I., BA MIMgt. Born 6/11/30. Commd 15/7/54. Sqn Ldr 17/2/63. Retd EDN 22/10/73.
DAVIES B. Born 27/5/25. Commd 17/11/44. Flt Lt 17/11/50. Retd GD 15/10/64.
DAVIES B. D., AFC. Born 11/7/20. Commd 5/9/42. Sqn Ldr 1/7/54. Retd GD 11/7/63.
DAVIES B. J., BSc. Born 23/11/44. Commd 16/2/69. Flt Lt 16/11/70. Retd GD 17/8/74.
DAVIES C. Born 8/7/16. Commd 21/2/46. Wg Cdr 1/7/62. Retd SUP 28/11/64.
DAVIES C. G. Born 17/6/23. Commd 23/3/50. Fg Offr 23/3/51. Retd ENG 27/3/54.
DAVIES C. W. Born 8/3/40. Commd 2/8/73. Flt Lt 2/8/75. Retd ENG 2/8/82.
DAVIES D., DFC. Born 10/2/22. Commd 6/11/42. Flt Lt 6/11/48. Retd SEC 2/10/65.
DAVIES D. Born 28/9/14. Commd 12/8/54. Flt Lt 12/8/57. Retd SUP 28/3/70.
DAVIES D. A., BA. Born 19/8/34. Commd 9/8/57. Wg Cdr 1/7/81. Retd ADMIN 19/8/84.
DAVIES D. B. A. L., BSc MB BS FRCGP MFCM MFOM MRCS LRCP DRCOG DAvMed. Born 4/2/32. Commd 29/1/58. AVM 1/1/89. Retd MED 4/2/92.
DAVIES D. C., OBE BSc MInstP. Born 24/7/21. Commd 2/9/42. Wg Cdr 24/7/63. Retd ADMIN 24/7/76.
DAVIES D. E., DFC AFC*. Born 6/2/17. Commd 29/3/39. Sqn Ldr 1/9/45. Retd GD 4/3/58 rtg Wg Cdr.
DAVIES D. E. Born 23/11/35. Commd 19/8/71. Flt Lt 19/8/76. Retd ENG 10/10/93.
DAVIES D. G. Born 10/11/47. Commd 11/11/71. Flt Lt 8/6/75. Retd GD(G) 1/11/85.
DAVIES D. I., MRCS LRCP. Born 1/6/21. Commd 27/7/50. Gp Capt. 1/7/71. Retd MED 7/4/79.
DAVIES D. S. Born 14/1/36. Commd 28/9/61. Sqn Ldr 1/7/76. Retd SUP 1/5/89.
DAVIES D. T., FIMgt. Born 6/3/39. Commd 8/6/62. A Cdre 1/1/91. Retd ADMIN 6/3/94.
DAVIES E. Born 17/1/11. Commd 23/2/43. Fg Offr 20/10/43. Retd ENG 15/3/46 rtg Flt Lt.
DAVIES E. A. Born 5/2/33. Commd 15/11/51. Flt Lt 22/5/57. Retd GD 5/2/71.
DAVIES E. H. Born 20/7/23. Commd 21/5/46. Flt Lt 4/12/53. Retd GD 20/7/68.
DAVIES E. J. L. Born 16/7/16. Commd 16/3/44. Flt Lt 16/9/47. Retd ENG 24/7/65.
DAVIES E. L. J. Born 11/8/22. Commd 29/8/44. Flt Lt 17/5/56. Retd GD 10/8/64.
DAVIES E. O. Born 23/12/31. Commd 13/12/51. Sqn Ldr 1/1/63. Retd SUP 1/1/66.
DAVIES F. H. Born 10/12/36. Commd 3/12/54. Flt Lt 3/6/60. Retd GD 10/12/91.
DAVIES F. R., DFC BA. Born 11/9/15. Commd 17/10/42. Flt Lt 7/5/47. Retd GD(G) 11/9/70.
DAVIES F. W. J., BA MIMgt. Born 18/3/24. Commd 3/5/46. Sqn Ldr 1/7/56. Retd GD 27/5/78.
DAVIES G. Born 22/3/24. Commd 19/5/45. Flt Lt 19/5/51. Retd GD 9/3/63.
DAVIES G., MBE BA. Born 19/9/33. Commd 9/4/53. Flt Lt 14/5/62. Retd GD 12/9/93.
DAVIES G. E., DFC. Born 24/9/23. Commd 5/5/44. Sqn Ldr 1/7/55. Retd GD 31/3/62.
DAVIES G. G., AFC. Born 23/1/29. Commd 2/7/52. Wg Cdr 1/7/70. Retd GD 2/10/73.
DAVIES G. J. Born 3/12/70. Commd 14/2/93. Plt Offr 14/2/93. Retd ENG 10/5/94.
DAVIES G. M. D. Born 12/6/20. Commd 22/2/44. Fg Offr 5/2/47. Retd PE 7/2/56 rtg Flt Lt.
DAVIES G. R. Born 14/1/24. Commd 2/2/44. Sqn Ldr 1/7/69. Retd GD(G) 29/1/77.
DAVIES G. W., BM BS BMedSci MRCGP DRCOG DAvMed. Born 25/6/52. Commd 16/7/74. Wg Cdr 27/7/89. Retd MED 16/1/97.
DAVIES H. A., BSc. Born 10/1/56. Commd 30/8/78. Sqn Ldr 1/1/88. Retd GD 30/8/94.
DAVIES H. D. Born 2/3/25. Commd 22/10/44. Sqn Ldr 1/1/67. Retd GD 4/6/73.
DAVIES H. D. Born 21/2/41. Commd 20/5/82. Sqn Ldr 1/1/90. Retd SUP 21/2/96.
DAVIES H. J. Born 29/6/27. Commd 16/1/47. Sqn Ldr 1/1/57. Retd GD 30/9/68.
DAVIES H. L., MB BCh FRCS(Edin) FRCS LRCP. Born 30/8/35. Commd 6/11/60. Wg Cdr 8/8/73. Retd MED 6/11/76.
DAVIES H. M., BA. Born 5/7/39. Commd 12/2/62. Sqn Ldr 1/7/74. Retd GD 5/7/94.

DAVIES H. M. F., BA DipEd. Born 7/6/31. Commd 15/8/65. Sqn Ldr 15/2/67. Retd ADMIN 21/10/88.
DAVIES H. N. R. Born 26/7/51. Commd 25/10/73. Flt Lt 30/6/80. Retd GD(G) 26/7/89.
DAVIES I. J., MBE FIMgt. Born 3/11/17. Commd 5/10/44. Gp Capt 1/7/66. Retd SUP 27/12/72.
DAVIES I. K., MA PhD MSc. Born 19/12/30. Commd 25/8/55. Wg Cdr 17/2/71. Retd EDN 23/2/72.
DAVIES I. T. Born 10/2/51. Commd 12/3/87. Flt Lt 12/3/91. Retd SUP 1/10/93.
DAVIES J., BSc. Born 26/6/42. Commd 22/10/72. Sqn Ldr 1/1/81. Retd ENG 22/10/91.
DAVIES J., BA. Born 21/8/20. Commd 15/7/43. Sqn Ldr 5/11/58. Retd EDN 7/4/72.
DAVIES J., CEng MIMechE. Born 1/7/34. Commd 20/7/65. Sqn Ldr 1/1/72. Retd ENG 20/7/79.
DAVIES J. Born 11/4/58. Commd 14/7/77. Sqn Ldr 1/1/94. Retd GD 28/7/98.
DAVIES J., MIDPM MIMgt. Born 20/8/51. Commd 15/9/69. Sqn Ldr 1/1/86. Retd SUP 14/3/97.
DAVIES J. A., DFC BA. Born 24/10/22. Commd 26/1/45. Sqn Ldr 23/4/57. Retd EDN 14/8/63.
DAVIES J. A. M., MBE. Born 5/8/21. Commd 13/4/45. Sqn Ldr 1/1/61. Retd PE 31/5/73.
DAVIES J. B. Born 10/3/38. Commd 16/4/57. Flt Lt 7/8/64. Retd GD 10/3/76.
DAVIES J. C. Born 31/1/41. Commd 17/5/63. Sqn Ldr 1/7/82. Retd GD 31/1/96.
DAVIES J. C. W. Born 18/2/14. Commd 11/1/43. Sqn Ldr 1/7/52. Retd GD 18/2/57.
DAVIES J. D. Born 27/9/30. Commd 27/10/54. Flt Lt 21/10/59. Retd GD 24/6/69.
DAVIES J. D. E. Born 16/2/14. Commd 2/1/39. Wg Cdr 1/7/51. Retd SUP 5/10/59.
DAVIES J. E. Born 29/8/37. Commd 16/2/61. Flt Lt 1/4/66. Retd SEC 29/8/75.
DAVIES J. F. Born 5/2/34. Commd 8/10/52. Flt Lt 6/3/58. Retd GD 5/2/89.
DAVIES J. F. Born 20/3/35. Commd 9/5/54. Wg Cdr 1/7/83. Retd GD 28/4/89.
DAVIES J. G. Born 18/2/46. Commd 26/5/67. Flt Lt 18/2/70. Retd GD 18/2/90.
DAVIES J. G., AFC. Born 28/9/27. Commd 28/11/51. Flt Lt 28/5/56. Retd GD 3/8/76.
DAVIES J. H. Born 25/1/26. Commd 18/5/61. Sqn Ldr 1/7/73. Retd ADMIN 1/6/77.
DAVIES J. I., CBE MIMgt. Born 8/6/30. Commd 15/6/50. Wg Cdr 1/7/67. Retd GD 29/6/74.
DAVIES J. L., OBE MA MRIN. Born 9/5/46. Commd 28/9/64. Gp Capt 1/7/92. Retd GD 30/7/94.
DAVIES J. M. Born 6/3/35. Commd 14/10/71. Flt Lt 14/10/73. Retd SUP 14/10/78.
DAVIES J. M. B., BA MCIPS. Born 13/6/47. Commd 2/8/68. Gp Capt 1/7/92. Retd SUP 16/4/94.
DAVIES J. P. Born 21/6/54. Commd 19/12/85. Sqn Ldr 1/1/92. Retd SY 2/1/95.
DAVIES J. R., MInstAM. Born 13/2/30. Commd 30/7/52. Wg Cdr 1/7/72. Retd SUP 13/2/85.
DAVIES J. T. Born 3/2/31. Commd 2/7/52. Flt Lt 14/5/58. Retd GD 3/2/69.
DAVIES J. W. Born 27/12/38. Commd 21/10/65. Wg Cdr 1/1/85. Retd ADMIN 27/12/93.
DAVIES J. W. A. Born 24/3/35. Commd 4/7/69. Flt Lt 4/4/71. Retd ENG 4/7/77.
DAVIES K. F. Born 16/7/28. Commd 23/3/66. Sqn Ldr 1/7/78. Retd ENG 16/7/83.
DAVIES K. W. Born 23/10/09. Commd 7/6/51. Sqn Ldr 1/7/59. Retd ENG 23/10/64.
DAVIES L., AFC. Born 15/2/20. Commd 26/6/43. Wg Cdr 1/7/65. Retd GD 3/7/73.
DAVIES L. H., BA. Born 28/12/39. Commd 31/3/64. Flt Lt 30/12/65. Retd GD 1/5/90.
DAVIES L. J. Born 5/7/23. Commd 26/3/44. Wg Cdr 1/1/70. Retd GD(G) 21/8/73.
DAVIES L. K., BEd. Born 9/8/53. Commd 13/4/80. Flt Lt 13/2/82. Retd ADMIN 31/8/89.
DAVIES L. V., DFM. Born 7/7/19. Commd 7/8/41. Flt Lt 1/9/45. Retd SEC 29/2/64 rtg Sqn Ldr.
DAVIES L. W. Born 8/8/19. Commd 29/11/37. Sqn Ldr 1/8/47. Retd GD 2/12/57.
DAVIES M., MSc BSc CEng MIMechE. Born 11/1/49. Commd 1/8/69. Gp Capt 1/7/93. Retd ENG 13/9/96.
DAVIES M. J., BSc. Born 10/7/60. Commd 19/8/84. Flt Lt 19/12/85. Retd ENG 19/6/99.
DAVIES M. J. Born 4/11/50. Commd 22/5/70. Flt Lt 22/11/75. Retd GD 8/8/81.
DAVIES M. J. Born 17/5/59. Commd 20/7/78. Fg Offr 12/1/81. Retd SUP 31/7/82.
DAVIES M. J. A., DPhysEd. Born 3/2/33. Commd 17/1/52. Sqn Ldr 1/7/72. Retd PE 15/9/75.
DAVIES M. J. P. Born 7/4/21. Commd 18/4/45. Sqn Ldr 1/1/56. Retd GD 27/4/64.
DAVIES M. P. Born 2/3/25. Commd 26/2/46. Sqn Ldr 1/7/56. Retd GD 12/3/63.
DAVIES N. A. Born 20/12/27. Commd 7/12/48. Flt Lt 22/4/54. Retd GD 20/12/65.
DAVIES N. C. Born 18/12/22. Commd 26/10/44. Sqn Ldr 1/7/70. Retd PI 28/3/78.
DAVIES N. E., BSc CEng MRAeS. Born 8/7/36. Commd 30/9/58. Sqn Ldr 1/1/76. Retd ENG 8/7/94.
DAVIES P. Born 24/12/41. Commd 26/3/69. Sqn Ldr 1/7/79. Retd SUPPLY 22/5/93.
DAVIES P. A., BA CertEd. Born 13/9/39. Commd 17/7/62. Sqn Ldr 8/10/75. Retd ADMIN 17/7/78.
DAVIES P. A., BSc. Born 5/3/58. Commd 18/10/81. Flt Lt 18/1/81. Retd GD 1/8/93.
DAVIES P. A. G., BSc. Born 9/1/46. Commd 5/12/71. Sqn Ldr 1/7/80. ADMIN 18/4/01.
DAVIES P. F. Born 24/5/57. Commd 11/6/81. Flt Lt 11/12/87. Retd GD 1/10/88.
DAVIES P. J., BTech. Born 6/2/55. Commd 15/9/74. Flt Lt 27/3/80. Retd ENG 1/10/83.
DAVIES P. V. Born 4/4/48. Commd 17/7/70. Flt Lt 17/1/76. Retd GD 4/4/86.
DAVIES R., FIMgt. Born 25/6/22. Commd 16/2/45. Gp Capt 1/7/72. Retd SUP 13/7/74.
DAVIES R. Born 8/11/42. Commd 17/12/64. Flt Lt 9/2/68. Retd GD 29/4/94.
DAVIES R. E. Born 4/9/30. Commd 31/5/50. Sqn Ldr 1/7/61. Retd GD 16/9/76.
DAVIES R. J., MB BCh MRC Psych DPM. Born 13/2/33. Commd 20/8/65. Wg Cdr 28/8/72. Retd MED 8/11/80.
DAVIES R. M. Born 23/5/43. Commd 26/11/60. Flt Lt 26/5/666. Retd GD 4/7/75.
DAVIES R. McQ. Born 4/10/23. Commd 14/7/44. Sqn Ldr 1/7/71. Retd ADMIN 30/10/76.
DAVIES R. W. Born 30/8/49. Commd 3/12/70. Flt Lt 3/6/76. Retd GD 22/10/94.
DAVIES Rev. S. W., AKC. Born 12/8/26. Commd 24/10/61. Retd 24/10/77. Rel Sqn Ldr.
DAVIES S. Born 26/4/13. Commd 28/6/45. Flt Lt 4/1/51. Retd SEC 26/4/62.

DAVIES S. H. Born 18/3/37. Commd 22/1/55. Sqn Ldr 1/7/73. Retd GD 18/3/94.
DAVIES S. J. Born 12/2/15. Commd 30/1/47. Sqn Ldr 1/7/63. Retd SEC 4/12/65.
DAVIES S. P. Born 21/5/48. Commd 23/3/67. Flt Lt 23/9/72. Retd GD 14/10/77.
DAVIES S. R. Born 23/5/15. Commd 30/5/46. Flt Lt 30/11/50. Retd SEC 23/5/65.
DAVIES T. C., MSc BSc CEng MIEE. Born 4/1/40. Commd 24/9/63. Flt Lt 24/3/66. ADMIN 24/9/82.
DAVIES T. C., BSc CEng FIEE FRAeS MInstP. Born 21/10/42. Commd 13/4/64. A Cdre 1/1/91. Retd ENG 21/10/97.
DAVIES T. K. Born 5/5/48. Commd 4/3/71. Flt Lt 4/9/76. Retd GD 22/10/94.
DAVIES T. N., CEng MIMechE MRAeS. Born 2/8/37. Commd 5/1/60. Sqn Ldr 5/1/70. Retd EDN 5/1/76.
DAVIES T. V., CEng FIMechE FRAeS. Born 20/10/38. Commd 3/2/69. Gp Capt 1/7/87. Retd ENG 20/10/93.
DAVIES W. C. S., CEng MRAeS. Born 26/11/20. Commd 19/10/49. Flt Lt 11/11/54. Retd ENG 3/4/69.
DAVIES W. G. Born 10/6/42. Commd 2/6/77. Sqn Ldr 1/7/87. Retd ADMIN 28/11/92.
DAVIES W. I. Born 4/5/19. Commd 17/3/49. Flt Lt 17/9/53. Retd GD(G) 4/5/62.
DAVIES W. J. Born 17/1/33. Commd 13/9/51. Flt Lt 24/3/57. Retd GD 17/1/76.
DAVIES W. J. Born 27/11/26. Commd 17/10/51. Flt Lt 7/8/55. Retd GD 18/3/65.
DAVIES-THOMAS J. B. Born 30/9/34. Commd 30/5/59. Sqn Ldr 1/7/71. Retd ADMIN 1/10/84.
DAVIS A. H. Born 23/8/43. Commd 9/9/63. Sqn Ldr 1/7/92. Retd GD 23/8/98.
DAVIS A. McB., OBE. Born 24/11/44. Commd 22/5/64. Wg Cdr 1/1/90. Retd GD 24/11/99.
DAVIS A. R. Born 13/6/33. Commd 13/2/52. Sqn Ldr 1/1/64. Retd GD 13/6/71.
DAVIS B. Born 12/11/14. Commd 6/9/56. Flt Lt 6/9/59. Retd SEC 19/6/72.
DAVIS C. A. Born 9/2/55. Commd 8/8/74. Sqn Ldr 1/1/89. Retd GD(G) 9/2/93.
DAVIS C. G. Born 1/1/21. Commd 15/4/43. Sqn Ldr 1/7/73. Retd ENG 1/1/76.
DAVIS C. H., FIMgt. Born 11/3/29. Commd 27/2/52. Wg Cdr 1/7/73. Retd SEC 18/10/83.
DAVIS C. H. Born 11/11/31. Commd 29/4/53. Flt Lt 30/9/58. Retd GD 11/11/69.
DAVIS C. J. Born 16/1/33. Commd 8/5/53. Sqn Ldr 1/7/78. Retd GD 27/3/89.
DAVIS C. K. Born 22/10/16. Commd 19/2/45. Sqn Ldr 1/1/66. Retd ENG 22/10/73.
DAVIS C. L. Born 31/8/39. Commd 10/12/57. Sqn Ldr 1/1/88. Retd GD 31/8/95.
DAVIS D. Born 27/12/23. Commd 26/5/60. Flt Lt 26/5/65. Retd GD 4/6/73.
DAVIS D. A., MBE. Born 6/7/28. Commd 30/7/59. Sqn Ldr 1/1/72. Retd ENG 6/7/78.
DAVIS F. W. T. Born 20/6/22. Commd 22/9/43. Flt Lt 15/12/49. Retd GD 20/6/77.
DAVIS G. Born 21/4/45. Commd 2/5/71. Flt Lt 2/6/75. Retd GD 2/5/87.
DAVIS J. Born 6/5/24. Commd 20/5/44. Flt Lt 20/11/47. Retd GD 30/11/68.
DAVIS J. A. S. Born 4/11/22. Commd 27/5/54. Flt Lt 27/11/57. Retd GD 30/5/64.
DAVIS J. D. Born 23/3/34. Commd 18/3/53. Wg Cdr 1/7/73. Retd GD 30/9/88.
DAVIS J. D., BSc. Born 13/10/35. Commd 8/4/57. Flt Lt 18/6/61. Retd ENG 6/4/66.
DAVIS J. D. Born 22/6/37. Commd 16/12/66. Flt Lt 16/12/68. Retd GD 23/8/74.
DAVIS J. F., OBE DFC AFC. Born 28/2/17. Commd 10/4/40. A Cdre 1/1/64. Retd GD 1/1/65.
DAVIS J. H. W., OBE. Born 1/12/39. Commd 7/1/58. A Cdre 1/1/90. Retd GD 30/6/91.
DAVIS J. L., AFC. Born 3/9/26. Commd 15/10/50. Sqn Ldr 1/1/69. Retd GD 26/8/76.
DAVIS J. S. C. Born 16/3/31. Commd 27/2/52. Flt Lt 27/11/57. Retd GD 16/3/69.
DAVIS K. G. Born 28/7/71. Commd 10/5/90Plt. Plt Offr 10/11/90. Retd ENG 26/3/93.
DAVIS K. J. M., MIMgt. Born 23/2/29. Commd 1/8/51. Sqn Ldr 1/1/62. Retd GD 1/2/75.
DAVIS L. A. Born 7/10/13. Commd 16/9/43. Flt Lt 16/3/47. Retd SUP 29/12/48.
DAVIS L. A. E. Born 28/4/34. Commd 24/9/52. Flt Lt 21/2/58. Retd GD 1/5/76.
DAVIS M. C. A. Born 6/12/34. Commd 17/12/52. Gp Capt 1/1/80. Retd GD 10/9/89.
DAVIS M. L. Born 24/9/61. Commd 11/4/85. Flt Lt 4/2/88. Retd GD 14/3/97.
DAVIS M. R. Born 6/12/51. Commd 16/2/89. Sqn Ldr 1/1/98. Retd GD 4/2/00.
DAVIS N. B. Born 11/10/12. Commd 10/12/42. Fg Offr 11/8/43. Retd ENG 29/6/46 rtg Flt Lt.
DAVIS N. W. Born 7/8/46. Commd 5/2/65. Flt Lt 5/8/71. Retd GD(G) 16/10/96.
DAVIS P. H. Born 19/4/46. Commd 23/3/67. Flt Lt 23/9/72. Retd GD 19/4/84.
DAVIS P. P. Born 11/5/43. Commd 2/12/66. Flt Lt 15/4/70. Retd GD 31/22/75.
DAVIS P. R., ACIS. Born 2/4/34. Commd 26/7/55. Wg Cdr 1/7/78. Retd ADMIN 22/8/83.
DAVIS R., MSc BSc CEng MIMechE. Born 24/10/54. Commd 14/6/81. Sqn Ldr 1/1/90. Retd ENG 7/2/00.
DAVIS R. C. Born 26/11/22. Commd 25/3/54. Sqn Ldr 1/1/71. Retd GD 10/11/73.
DAVIS R. F., DFM. Born 19/9/16. Commd 1/1/42. Sqn Ldr 1/7/54. Retd SUP 19/9/76.
DAVIS R. G., BSc. Born 11/5/35. Commd 2/10/58. Flt Lt 14/2/66. Retd GD 2/10/74.
DAVIS R. G., BSc. Born 5/7/44. Commd 30/9/64. Sqn Ldr 1/1/76. Retd GD 23/2/84.
DAVIS R. K. Born 8/8/56. Commd 20/9/79. Sqn Ldr 1/1/93. Retd ADMIN 1/1/96.
DAVIS R. L., CB. Born 22/3/30. Commd 17/12/52. AVM 1/1/81. Retd GD 13/7/83.
DAVIS R. N., DPhysEd. Born 25/5/46. Commd 22/8/71. Sqn Ldr 1/7/85. Retd ADMIN 23/4/94.
DAVIS R. S. Born 10/8/26. Commd 26/11/64. Flt Lt 26/11/67. Retd GD 2/4/76.
DAVIS S. L. Born 6/2/61. Commd 24/7/81. Flt Lt 8/12/86. Retd GD 27/3/92.
DAVIS W., MBE. Born 27/3/43. Commd 17/7/87. Flt Lt 17/7/91. Retd ADMIN 1/8/96.
DAVISON Rev C. F. MA. Born 7/8/21. Commd 1/7/47. Retd 7/8/76 Gp Capt.
DAVISON C. M., BSc CEng FIEE MIMgt. Born 24/09/48. Commd 27/2/70. A Cdre 1/7/97. Retd ENG 4/4/01.
DAVISON D. Born 3/3/44. Commd 30/3/89. Flt Lt 14/1/87. Retd DM 1/4/95.
DAVISON D. P. Born 8/10/30. Commd 30/7/52. Flt Lt 26/5/55. Retd GD 8/10/68.

DAVISON F. Born 29/5/09. Commd 30/7/53. Flt Lt 30/7/56. Retd ENG 29/5/64.
DAVISON F. W. Born 2/8/21. Commd 1/9/45. Wg Cdr 1/1/58. Retd GD 21/9/68.
DAVISON G., DFC AFC. Born 1/5/14. Commd 24/10/40. Sqn Ldr 1/8/47. Retd GD 24/2/57.
DAVISON J. L., MBE MSc MCIPS. Born 14/2/48. Commd 27/2/70. Sqn Ldr 1/1/81. Retd SUP 16/9/86.
DAVISON T. A., MIMgt Born 1/11/47. Commd 20/8/65. Wg Cdr 1/7/88. Retd GD(G) 1/11/91.
DAVY A. M. J., BA. Born 31/12/45. Commd 24/11/67. Sqn Ldr 1/7/88. Retd GD 31/12/00.
DAVY J. W., MCIPD MIMgt. Born 12/8/44. Commd 21/12/62. Sqn Ldr 1/7/75. Retd GD 12/8/82.
DAVY P. J., BDS LDSRCS. Born 27/2/42. Commd 18/9/60. Wg Cdr 23/12/77. Retd DEL 14/3/97.
DAVY T. H. Born 6/6/22. Commd 28/3/45. Flt Lt 8/2/53. Retd GD 1/8/68.
DAW F. G., DFC AFC. Born 30/12/17. Commd 19/1/39. Wg Cdr 1/7/55. Retd GD 7/5/65.
DAW N. Born 3/4/42. Commd 5/11/65. Flt Lt 5/5/71. Retd GD 26/7/81.
DAW S. Born 3/12/09. Commd 25/3/43. Flt Lt 4/2/52. Retd SUP 21/3/62.
DAWE D. T., LDS DPD. Born 4/6/30. Commd 4/1/54. Wg Cdr 21/8/66. Retd DEL 29/3/72.
DAWES A. D. R., MIMgt. Born 4/11/30. Commd 12/12/51. Sqn Ldr 1/1/62. Retd GD 5/11/80.
DAWES D. J. Born 26/3/35. Commd 25/2/53. Wg Cdr 1/7/74. Retd GD 26/3/90.
DAWES E. L. Born 1/2/37. Commd 23/11/78. Sqn Ldr 1/7/88. Retd ENG 1/2/95.
DAWES J. P. H., BSc. Born 25/5/37. Commd 2/10/58. Sqn Ldr 1/7/73. Retd GD 1/7/76.
DAWES L. H. Born 16/9/10. Commd 6/8/40. Flt Lt 1/9/45. Retd SUP 12/3/55 rtg Sqn Ldr.
DAWES L. H., DFC. Born 11/2/21. Commd 21/11/41. Sqn Ldr 1/10/55. Retd GD 1/5/58.
DAWES M. R., BSc. Born 12/4/48. Commd 13/9/71. Sqn Ldr 1/7/81. Retd ENG 14/12/96.
DAWES P., MBE. Born 3/6/23. Commd 22/9/44. Sqn Ldr 1/10/55. Retd GD 3/6/72.
DAWES P. A., BSc. Born 29/5/44. Commd 6/9/65. Sqn Ldr 1/7/78. Retd ENG 29/5/82.
DAWKES A. Born 9/4/66. Commd 11/4/85. Fg Off 11/4/87. Retd GD 31/1/90.
DAWKINS B. D., MSc BSc BSc CEng FIIP MRAeS. MIMgt. Born 16/7/44. Commd 4/6/64. Sqn Ldr 1/1/75. Retd ENG 22/7/82.
DAWKINS T. G. D. Born 10/10/25. Commd 25/9/50. Flt Lt 4/12/52. Retd GD 8/8/57.
DAWS A. ST. J. Born 2/6/65. Commd 19/6/86. Flt Lt 19/12/91. Retd GD 14/3/96.
DAWSON A., MIMgt. Born 9/9/36. Commd 6/5/55. Wg Cdr 1/1/75. Retd GD 12/7/77.
DAWSON A. F. Born 12/5/44. Commd 31/1/64. Wg Cdr 1/1/86. Retd GD 8/10/98.
DAWSON A. N., MBE BEM. Born 1/4/22. Commd 17/5/56. Sqn Ldr 1/7/70. Retd ENG 1/4/77.
DAWSON C. L. Born 13/5/52. Commd 29/4/71. Wg Cdr 1/7/90. Retd ADMIN 10/10/00.
DAWSON D. A. Born 15/8/28. Commd 10/2/49. Sqn Ldr 1/1/74. Retd SEC 15/11/78.
DAWSON D. J. Born 17/1/41. Commd 10/11/61. Flt Lt 10/5/67. Retd GD 31/10/73.
DAWSON D. M. Born 29/10/42. Commd 20/6/63. Sqn Ldr 1/7/75. Retd ADMIN 29/10/80.
DAWSON E., CBE BSc Dip Soton CEng FIEE MRAeS FIMgt. Born 17/12/28. Commd 20/12/51. A Cdre 1/1/74. Retd ENG 1/1/81.
DAWSON F. P. Born 2/10/13. Commd 1/1/37. Wg Cdr 1/7/50. Retd SUP 28/11/57.
DAWSON G. P. M., IEng MIIE. Born 10/5/50. Commd 4/7/85. Sqn Ldr 1/7/93. Retd ENG 9/4/01.
DAWSON G. S Born 1/4/48. Commd 16/9/76. Flt Lt 20/12/79. Retd ENG 1/3/91.
DAWSON G. W., DFM. Born 14/10/17. Commd 24/7/42. Sqn Ldr 1/1/53. Retd SEC 14/10/66.
DAWSON H. H., MIMgt. Born 1/11/14. Commd 17/7/58. Flt Lt 17/7/63. Retd ENG 1/11/69.
DAWSON H. M. Born 14/5/42. Commd 26/11/60. Flt Lt 14/5/52. Retd OPS SPT 14/5/97.
DAWSON J. B., MSc CEng MIEE. Born 20/7/34. Commd 3/6/65. Sqn Ldr 3/3/73. Retd EDN 1/10/75.
DAWSON L. Born 19/9/22. Commd 27/9/42. Flt Lt 27/9/44. Retd GD(G) 7/6/74.
DAWSON M. E. H., DFC* DFM FIMgt. Born 9/9/19. Commd 24/11/41. Gp Capt 1/1/66. Retd GD 9/9/74.
DAWSON M. J. Born 9/8/50. Commd 8/1/76. Sqn Ldr 1/1/88. Retd GD(G) 1/1/91.
DAWSON M. J. Born 21/11/27. Commd 7/3/51. Wg Cdr 1/7/70. Retd GD 3/7/78.
DAWSON R., BSc MS DCAe CEng MRAeS. Born 13/4/27. Commd 28/8/48. Wg Cdr 1/1/70. Retd ENG 1/6/78.
DAWSON R. D., BEng. Born 27/11/62. Commd 30/6/84. Flt Lt 30/12/86. Retd GD 1/6/93.
DAWSON R. J. C., OBE. Born 25/9/47. Commd 28/2/69. Wg Cdr 1/7/87. Retd ENG 7/12/91.
DAWSON R. T., CBE. Born 6/8/30. Commd 1/7/57. AVM 1/1/90. Retd LGL 6/11/92.
DAWSON S. Born 28/7/47. Commd 17/2/67. Flt Lt 17/8/72. Retd GD 1/4/87.
DAWSON S. C. Born 15/6/20. Commd 19/8/41. Wg Cdr 1/7/57. Retd ENG 11/7/68.
DAWSON S. D., BSc. Born 10/3/57. Commd 1/10/75. Flt Lt 15/10/81. Retd ENG 1/4/87.
DAWSON T. L. I. Born 21/2/38. Commd 7/2/57. Sqn Ldr 1/1/69. Retd SUP 3/5/75.
DAWSON W. E., BEng. Born 13/2/57. Commd 20/11/78. Flt Lt 20/8/80. Retd GD 1/12/97.
DAWSON W. H. Born 9/9/44. Commd 14/11/82. Flt Lt 1/3/87. Retd ENG 29/11/91.
DAY A. C., ACII. Born 28/6/55. Commd 25/5/80. Plt Offr 25/5/80. Retd ADMIN 7/10/81.
DAY B. G. Born 22/4/32. Commd 19/4/51. Flt Lt 17/10/56. Retd GD 22/10/70.
DAY C. G. Born 18/2/17. Commd 26/8/43. Sqn Ldr 1/7/54. Retd ENG 7/9/68.
DAY D. A. G. Born 30/10/34 Commd 9/8/60. Wg Cdr 1/1/81. Retd GD 1/11/84.
DAY F. J. Born 26/4/08. Commd 28/10/41. Flt Lt 1/9/45. Retd ENG 24/7/54.
DAY G. C. Born 19/5/24. Commd 13/9/45. Flt Lt 29/11/51. Retd GD 19/5/62.
DAY G. R., BA. Born 31/5/46. Commd 28/9/70. Sqn Ldr 1/7/85. Retd GD 1/7/88.
DAY J. G. Born 17/11/50. Commd 27/5/71. Flt Lt 27/11/76. Retd GD 30/5/81.
DAY L. J., DFC. Born 17/7/23. Commd 20/5/46. Sqn Ldr 1/7/59. Retd GD 31/1/62.

DAY M. Born 12/9/42. Commd 14/8/80. Flt Lt 14/8/83. Retd GD 12/9/00.
DAY P. Born 30/5/50. Commd 8/8/74. Flt Lt 8/2/81. Retd OPS SPT 29/1/99.
DAY P., OBE AFC. Born 4/4/42. Commd 6/4/62. Sqn Ldr 1/7/76. Retd GD 2/4/01.
DAY P. J. Born 23/8/45. Commd 28/2/64. Wg Cdr 1/7/84. Retd GD 8/6/90.
DAY P. W., AFC. Born 25/1/44. Commd 19/4/63. Gp Capt 1/1/90. Retd GD 25/1/99.
DAY P.A. Born 1/7/36. Commd 12/9/63. Wg Cdr 1/7/82. Retd SUP 1/7/91.
DAY R. F. Born 3/2/36. Commd 22/5/55. Wg Cdr 1/7/73. Retd GD(G) 1/7/76.
DAY R. H. Born 10/1/39. Commd 19/1/66. Wg Cdr 1/7/91. Retd ENG 1/7/94.
DAY S. H. Born 18/8/51. Commd 27/3/70. Flt Lt 27/9/75. Retd GD 1/6/77.
DAY T. H. Born 3/5/43. Commd 18/5/61. Flt Lt 1/7/68. Retd GD(G) 3/5/81.
DAYAN-SMITH C. H. Born 26/4/07. Commd 11/8/31. Wg Cdr 1/10/46. Retd ENG 18/1/48 rtg Gp Capt.
DAYBELL D. J., MA. Born 9/10/18. Commd 5/8/47. Sqn Ldr 5/8/52. Retd EDN 5/8/65.
DAYBELL P. J., MBE MA BA. Born 14/10/50. Commd 15/9/69. Wg Cdr 1/7/91. Retd ADMIN 28/1/00.
DAYKIN K. F., MBE MSc BSc CEng MRAeS. Born 8/10/46. Commd 2/5/71. Wg Cdr 1/7/85. Retd ENG 31/3/89.
DAYKIN V. Born 18/9/21. Commd 15/7/45. Flt Lt 10/2/58. Retd GD(G) 16/4/68.
DAYMON C. P. F. Born 3/6/52. Commd 6/4/72. Flt Lt 6/10/77. Retd GD 11/6/84.
DAYSH R. E. Born 7/7/27. Commd 3/2/49. Sqn Ldr 1/1/59. Retd GD 7/7/65.
de BELDER K. R. J., OBE MB BS FRCS LRCP. Born 3/6/27. Commd 1/9/52. Gp Capt 3/11/70. Retd MED 30/11/73.
de BELDER M. J. K., MA MB BChir MRCGP DAvMed. Born 3/7/52. Commd 26/6/73. Wg Cdr 1/8/90. Retd MED 1/8/91.
DE BLAC I. J. M.A. Born 16/6/24. Commd 24/7/50. Flt Lt 22/8/60. Retd GD 25/5/68.
DE BURCA P. J. Born 3/2/41. Commd 22/2/63. Flt Lt 17/3/71. Retd GD(G) 3/2/79. Reinstated 6/8/80. Flt Lt 17/9/72. Retd GD(G) 3/2/96.
de BURGH M., MIMgt. Born 11/3/29. Commd 17/5/51. Wg Cdr 1/7/67. Retd GD 9/4/79.
DE BURIATTE A. H. Born 8/2/24. Commd 12/9/50. Flt Lt 26/5/55. Retd GD(G) 8/2/62. Re-appointed 25/4/66 to 8/2/79.
DE BURLET R. P. A. J. Born 12/4/21. Commd 23/10/39. Sqn Ldr 1/7/52. Retd ENG 31/3/62.
DE CAMPS P. S. Born 7/10/50. Commd 8/8/74. Flt Lt 8/2/81. Retd ADMIN 14/3/96.
de COURCIER M. H. Born 1/5/53. Commd 13/1/72. Flt Lt 13/7/77. Retd GD 1/5/91.
DE FLEURY C. G. Born 7/2/41. Commd 22/7/71. Sqn Ldr 1/7/80. Retd ENG 7/6/99.
DE GARIS D. R. W. Born 16/10/37. Commd 16/10/58. Wg Cdr 1/7/80. Retd GD 16/10/92.
de GARIS L., AFC. Born 16/11/26. Commd 14/6/46/ Wg Cdr 1/1/63. Retd GD 1/4/68.
DE GARIS M. G. Born 23/10/33. Commd 10/9/52. Flt Lt 7/2/58. Retd GD 23/10/71 rtg Sqn Ldr.
DE GRUCHY N. E. Born 5/4/18. Commd 1/5/39. Sqn Ldr 1/8/47. Retd SUP 26/8/67 rtg Wg Cdr.
de IONGH B. E. Born 15/5/24. Commd 10/6/44. Gp Capt 1/1/70. Retd GD 31/3/76.
DE LA COUR G., OBE BSc. Born 12/6/62. Commd 7/10/82. Sqn Ldr 1/1/97. Retd GD 12/9/00.
de la HAYE G. E. Born 23/3/20. Commd. 15/1/40. Wg Cdr 1/1/69. Retd SUP 23/3/75.
de la HOYDE D. E. Born 29/10/16. Commd 29/11/37. Flt Lt 3/8/46. Retd GD(G) 30/3/60.
de LABAT A. C. P. Born 1/7/52. Commd 6/1/76. Sqn Ldr 1/7/87. Retd ADMIN 1/1/91.
DE LAURIER D. R. P. Born 5/12/21. Commd 31/7/43. Sqn Ldr 1/10/55. Retd GD 25/11/58.
DE LEACY J. R. Born 3/4/28. Commd 15/5/61. Flt Lt 30/8/88. Retd SEC 1/10/74.
De MARCO M. L. Born 19/12/44. Commd 9/10/64. Flt Lt 9/4/70. Retd GD 1/5/76.
DE NAEYER P. J. Born 10/4/17. Commd 23/12/61. Flt Lt 23/12/66. Retd SUP 30/4/71.
de NAEYER R. E. S. Born 8/8/19. Commd 17/8/50. Sqn Ldr 1/7/61. Retd SUP 10/4/70.
DE PROCHNOW N. S. H. Born 12/7/48. Commd 8/12/70. Flt Lt 8/12/76. Retd ADMIN 8/12/86.
DE ROSBOURG A. E. G., AFC. Born 17/8/20. Commd 1/8/44. Flt Lt 19/11/53. Retd GD 21/1/68.
DE SALIS J. P. F. Born 28/4/28. Commd 16/9/50. Flt Lt 16/3/55. Retd GD 28/4/66.
DE SALIS T. W. F., OBE AFC. Born 13/7/26. Commd 14/6/46. Wg Cdr 1/1/66. Retd GD 13/7/81.
DE SOUZA R. G. Born 5/5/24. Commd 26/3/59. Flt Lt 26/3/65. Retd GD 25/11/67.
de SOUZA T. P. Born 1/7/40. Commd 11/7/74. Flt Lt 11/7/76. Retd ENG 11/7/82.
De SOYZA A. A., MSc DUS CEng MRAeS. Born 6/7/36. Commd 30/7/59. Sqn Ldr 1/7/69. Retd ENG 29/5/76.
de THIER L. R., CEng MRAeS. Born 3/6/20. Commd 19/8/42. Sqn Ldr 1/7/53. Retd ENG 22/2/78.
DE VECCHIS B. Born 25/1/42. Commd 23/6/67. Flt Lt 8/10/69. Retd SEC 23/6/72.
de VERTEUIL R. A. P. Born 4/12/40. Commd 2/10/61. Flt Lt 2/4/67. Retd GD 4/12/78.
de VILLE F. Born 1/11/43. Commd 6/1/69. Plt Offr 6/1/69. Retd SEC 7/1/72.
DE'ATH J. G., MBE MA FIIM FIMgt. Born 29/4/32. Commd 6/4/54. A Cdre 1/1/83. Retd SUP 4/2/86.
DE'ATH J. J. D., CEng MIEE. Born 17/12/31. Commd 29/12/53. Sqn Ldr 1/7/66. Retd ENG 29/12/69.
de'NAHLIK A. J. J. A., MIMgt. Born 27/2/20. Commd 13/9/43. Wg Cdr 1/1/65. Retd SEC 14/9/68.
de-ROHAN-WILLNER G. P., BSc. Born 16/2/64. Commd 11/5/84. Plt Off 15/7/86. Retd ENG 20/2/87.
DE-SALIS M. S. F. Born 12/5/65. Commd 22/11/84. Fg Off 22/5/91. Retd SY 1/4/93.
DEACON C. E., MBE CEng MRAeS MIMgt. Born 16/2/21. Commd 10/1/57. Sqn Ldr 1/7/66. Retd ENG 1/3/74.
DEACON D. F., BSc. Born 24/6/60. Commd 12/10/78. Flt Lt 15/10/82. Retd GD 15/7/93.
DEACON E. W., DSO DFC AFC. Born 13/12/12. Commd 7/9/40. Gp Capt 1/7/63. Retd GD 13/12/67.
DEACON ELLIOTT R. C. Born 30/5/49. Commd 1/8/69. Flt Lt 1/8/72. Retd GD 30/5/87.
DEACON R. J. S., MCIPS. Born 5/11/34. Commd 23/3/66. Wg Cdr 1/9/81. Retd SUP 1/5/85.
DEACON R. L. Born 9/4/22. Commd 25/5/46. Flt Lt 19/1/55. Retd GD 1/12/61.

DEACON V. H. W., MHCIMA. Born 10/10/26. Commd 28/9/51. Sqn Ldr 1/1/72. Retd ADMIN 31/1/78.
DEACON-ELLIOTT A. S., BSc. Born 4/11/50. Commd 13/9/70. Sqn Ldr 1/1/88. Retd GD 1/1/91.
DEADMAN C. D. Born 5/8/27. Commd 13/8/52. Flt Lt 20/2/58. Retd GD 14/4/82.
DEADMAN D. E., AFC. Born 1/11/32. Commd 29/5/52. Flt Lt 27/8/57. Retd GD 1/11/70.
DEAKIN P. J., MIMgt MCIPD. Born 6/10/30. Commd 30/7/52. Sqn Ldr 1/1/63. Retd GD 26/8/77.
DEAKIN P. V. Born 5/4/40. Commd 19/12/61. Sqn Ldr 1/1/74. Retd GD 5/4/95.
DEAKIN P. V. Born 5/10/39. Commd 1/8/61. Gp Capt 1/1/90. Retd GD 5/10/94.
DEAKIN S. J. Born 8/3/43. Commd 4/7/69. Sqn Ldr 1/1/95. Retd GD 16/4/96.
DEAL J. P. Born 28/2/21. Commd 6/12/44. Flt Lt 11/11/54. Retd GD 28/2/76.
DEALTRY R. A. Born 2/10/45. Commd 16/9/76. Flt Lt 16/9/77. Retd ADMIN 16/9/84.
DEAN B., MBE. Born 1/6/46. Commd 1/4/71. Sqn Ldr 1/7/84. Retd SUP 1/8/96.
DEAN B. T. Born 2/5/32. Commd 12/3/52. Flt Lt 10/7/57. Retd GD 31/10/68.
DEAN G. M., LLB. Born 3/12/53. Commd 18/4/76. Wg Cdr 1/1/93. Retd ADMIN 14/9/96.
DEAN G. W., BA. Born 30/7/36. Commd 23/5/63. Flt Lt 23/5/64. Retd EDN 21/8/71.
DEAN H. M., BSc CEng MRAeS MinstP. Born 30/1/22. Commd 9/1/43. Gp Capt 1/7/71. Retd EDN 1/7/73.
DEAN H. P. E. Born 19/2/06. Commd 8/11/40. Flt Lt 1/9/45. Retd ENG 14/12/47 rtg Sqn Ldr.
DEAN J. D. E., BSc. Born 19/3/52. Commd 2/10/72. Flt Lt 15/4/76. Retd GD 19/3/90.
DEAN J. H. Born 23/2/32. Commd 1/3/62. Sqn Ldr 1/7/72. Retd GD(G) 23/2/90.
DEAN M. H. Born 6/4/38. Commd 3/2/63. Wg Cdr 21/9/76. Retd MED 17/7/82.
DEAN M. J. Born 3/8/38. Commd 29/4/58. Sqn Ldr 1/7/78. Retd GD 24/11/90.
DEAN M. S., MBE. Born 20/7/43. Commd 15/7/66. Sqn Ldr 1/7/76. Retd ENG 31/3/93.
DEAN O. V. C. Born 8/7/22. Commd 26/2/42. Flt Lt 26/6/46. Retd GD 31/3/62.
DEAN R. C. Born 26/6/44. Commd 21/12/62. Sqn Ldr 1/7/79. Retd GD 17/2/84.
DEAN R. H., DFC. Born 10/7/10. Commd 26/3/43. Flt Lt 18/7/49. Retd SEC 4/8/58 rtg Sqn Ldr.
DEAN R. J. H. Born 12/2/34. Commd 4/6/59. Sqn Ldr 1/7/79. Retd SY 23/6/84.
DEAN W. G. Born 15/12/43. Commd 21/4/77. Sqn Ldr 1/1/84. Retd SUP 21/4/91.
DEANS D. A. Born 19/2/46. Commd 20/11/75. Flt Lt 20/11/77. Retd GD 14/3/96.
DEAR C. A., DFC. Born 17/7/20. Commd 30/10/42. Sqn Ldr 1/1/67. Retd GD(G) 19/7/75.
DEARDEN A. Born 27/10/30. Commd 24/2/55. Sqn Ldr 1/7/66. Retd ENG 20/11/91.
DEARDS S. J. Born 26/8/23. Commd 10/3/44. Wg Cdr 1/1/67. Retd GD 26/8/78.
DEARMAN K. J. Born 29/12/39. Commd 25/7/60. Gp Capt 1/1/88. Retd GD 29/12/94.
DEARN I. E. M. Born 4/7/35. Commd 18/5/55. Sqn Ldr 1/7/69. Retd GD 4/7/73.
DEARSLEY E., BEM. Born 8/6/39. Commd 29/7/83. Sqn Ldr 1/7/90. Retd ENG 8/6/94.
DEAS R. P. Born 1/12/33. Commd 7/5/52. Flt Lt 5/5/61. Retd GD 6/7/74.
DEBELLE F. A. Born 7/12/28. Commd 1/9/54. Flt Lt 13/4/60. Retd GD 8/1/73.
DEBENHAM B. C., BA. Born 26/9/52. Commd 25/9/71. Wg Cdr 1/7/91. Retd ADMIN 26/9/96.
DEBNAM A. F. H. Born 20/10/21. Commd 24/6/43. Flt Lt 27/5/54. Retd GD 27/3/64.
DEBNAM C. Born 31/7/41. Commd 3/5/68. Sqn Ldr 1/7/80. Retd ENG 30/6/82.
DEBNEY P. J. Born 6/10/42. Commd 17/10/65. Flt Lt 30/11/67. Retd GD 30/8/82.
DEBUSE A. W., MSc BSc CEng MIMechE MCIPD MRAeS CertEd. Born 23/10/45. Commd 19/9/71. Sqn Ldr 22/4/75. Retd ADMIN 31/3/94.
DECKER D. W. M. Born 19/10/36. Commd 20/10/65. Sqn Ldr 1/1/77. Retd CAT 1/1/80.
DEDMAN N. J. P. Born 10/3/57. Commd 14/9/84. Sqn Ldr 1/7/91. Retd GD 10/3/95.
DEE D. H. Born 29/9/25. Commd 31/8/45. Flt Lt 2/3/49. Retd GD 29/9/68.
DEEBANK A. E., BSc. Born 28/2/54. Commd 23/9/79. Sqn Ldr 1/7/94. Retd ADMIN 14/9/96.
DEEBLE D. C., BSc(Eng) CEng FEANI. MRAeS. Born 18/1/40. Commd 19/2/63. Wg Cdr 1/7/78. Retd ENG 19/2/85.
DEEKS F. J., DFC. Born 10/4/22. Commd 17/5/42. Flt Lt 25/11/49. Retd GD 19/10/61.
DEEKS N. B. Born 27/2/33. Commd 28/11/69. Sqn Ldr 26/9/80. Retd MED(SEC) 30/7/83.
DEELEY C. R., FRIN FIAP MIMgt. Born 20/3/36. Commd 30/5/59. Wg Cdr 1/1/86. Retd GD 20/3/94.
DEEMAN S. H. Born 28/12/29. Commd 17/3/67. Sqn Ldr 12/10/76. Retd MED(SEC) 28/12/84.
DEEN R. J. E. Born 16/1/52. Commd 17/5/79. Flt Lt 15/5/81. Retd SY(PRT) 16/1/90
DEEPAN K. V. Born 16/3/40. Commd 20/10/64. Sqn Ldr 1/1/76. Retd GD 16/3/95.
DEERE W. Born 27/3/30. Commd 24/1/52. Flt Lt 15/5/57. Retd GD 27/3/68.
DEFFEE H. McL. D. Born 8/1/15. Commd 4/2/44. Flt Lt 5/4/54. Retd GD(G) 8/1/65.
DEIGHTON G. B. Born 30/7/25. Commd 6/7/45. Flt Lt 6/1/49. Retd GD 30/7/68.
DELAFIELD J., MRAeS. Born 31/1/38. Commd 16/12/58. A Cdre 1/1/89. Retd GD 11/5/91.
DELAHAYE P. F. Born 2/10/23. Commd 27/5/44. Flt Lt 22/4/48. Retd GD 2/10/66.
DELAHUNT-RIMMER P. R. Born 27/11/55. Commd 20/7/78. Sqn Ldr 20/7/83. Retd GD 20/3/94.
DELANEY D. D. Born 10/12/23. Commd 18/1/50. Sqn Ldr 1/1/61. Retd GD 1/1/64 rtg Sqn Ldr.
DELANY D. B., AFC. Born 10/12/21. Commd 3/4/41. Wg Cdr 1/7/59. Retd GD 10/12/68.
DELANY J. F. B., AFC. Born 8/5/22. Commd 4/5/50. Sqn Ldr 1/7/72. Retd GD 29/3/77.
DELANY O. D. L., OBE BA FBIFM FIMgt. Born 12/10/49. Commd 13/9/70. A Cdre 1/7/97. Retd ADMIN 14/12/98.
DELAP D. V. MA. Born 8/10/37. Commd 30/9/56. Wg Cdr 1/1/76. Retd ENG 30/9/82.
DELAP T. H. F. Born 6/11/35. Commd 17/12/57. Sqn Ldr 1/7/65. Retd GD 6/11/73.
DELBRIDGE K. S., DFC. Born 8/9/22. Commd 22/11/43. Sqn Ldr 1/10/55. Retd SUP 8/9/60.
DELDERFIELD V. A. J. Born 3/6/58. Commd 13/8/82. Sqn Ldr 1/1/91. Retd ENG 3/6/96.

DELL C. J., BSc. Born 31/10/58. Commd 17/8/80. Sqn Ldr 1/7/94. Retd SUP 8/12/98.
DELL G. F. Born 30/12/94. Commd 4/9/37. Sqn Ldr 1/6/45. Retd SUP 30/1/48 rtg Wg Cdr.
DELL J. L., OBE. Born 23/8/24. Commd 15/11/44. Sqn Ldr 1/7/55. Retd GD 12/12/59.
DELL P. E. Born 29/3/34. Commd 26/11/52. Flt Lt 2/6/58. Retd GD 29/3/93.
DELLBRIDGE J. H. Born 27/2/09. Commd 4/12/40. Sqn Ldr 1/1/51. Retd ENG 27/2/58.
DELLOW J. E. Born 29/4/25. Commd 5/2/51. Flt Lt 16/11/60. Retd GD 8/8/66.
DELMEGE G. H. Born 19/2/45. Commd 28/2/64. Flt Lt 28/8/69. Retd GD 14/3/96.
DELVE H. Born 22/12/43. Commd 25/1/63. Gp Capt 1/7/95. Retd GD 22/7/00.
DELVE K., BA. Born 7/7/54. Commd 17/9/72. Flt Lt 15/10/76. Retd GD 1/11/94.
DEMERY N. J. Born 30/1/54. Commd 3/9/72. Flt Lt 9/3/80. Retd GD 8/4/88.
DEMMER P. S., BA FIMgt. Born 23/7/32. Commd 31/5/51. Gp Capt 1/7/84. Retd GD 3/11/85.
DEMPSEY J. Born 15/10/56. Commd 15/12/88. Flt Lt 20/9/91. Retd SY 24/5/93.
DEMPSTER H. McI. Born 20/4/28. Commd 5/7/68. Flt Lt 5/7/71. Retd GD 1/11/75.
DENCER S. D., BSc. Born 1/3/56. Commd 5/9/77. Flt Lt 5/6/81. Retd ENG 12/1/88.
DENCH K. V. Born 6/6/27. Commd 22/8/63. Sqn Ldr 1/7/74. Retd SUP 6/5/78.
DENCH R. L. H. Born 22/10/22. Commd 20/7/43. Flt Lt 1/1/52. Retd GD 22/10/77.
DENHAM D. C., BA CEng MIMechE. Born 21/1/44. Commd 15/7/66. Wg Cdr 1/1/82. Retd ENG 1/5/96.
DENHAM E. Born 2/5/22. Commd 24/2/55. Flt Lt 23/2/60. Retd GD 3/12/73.
DENHAM J. D. Born 14/8/35. Commd 20/11/56. Sqn Ldr 1/7/69. Retd GD 31/12/73.
DENISON D. F. Born 7/1/27. Commd 20/6/50. Sqn Ldr 1/7/55. Retd GD 7/1/87.
DENISON D. M., MB BS BSc PhD. Born 7/3/33. Commd 1/9/63. Wg Cdr 15/10/75. Retd MED 1/3/76.
DENMAN K. R. Born 4/2/37. Commd 26/3/64. Sqn Ldr 1/1/83. Retd GD 1/9/92.
DENMAN W. J., MBE. Born 12/7/41. Commd 7/1/71. Sqn Ldr 1/7/77. Retd GD 26/1/84.
DENNAY V. R., BEng. Born 3/8/55. Commd 5/9/76. Sqn Ldr 1/7/90. Retd ENG 3/8/99.
DENNEHEY R. T. M., MBE. Born 4/6/21. Commd 26/1/45. Sqn Ldr 1/10/57. Retd SEC 4/6/70.
DENNEHY J. Born 19/12/26. Commd 26/8/66. Sqn Ldr 4/3/72. Retd EDN 30/8/74.
DENNETT J. A., BSc CEng MRAeS. Born 9/10/38. Commd 30/9/58. Wg Cdr 1/1/81. Retd ENG 10/10/88.
DENNETT T. A. Born 14/5/50. Commd 19/8/71. Sqn Ldr 1/7/86. Retd ADMIN 28/1/93.
DENNEY J. A., BEd. Born 18/9/55. Commd 15/10/78. Flt Lt 15/7/80. Retd GD 21/8/82.
DENNEY R. A. Born 22/5/22. Commd 26/7/43. Sqn Ldr 1/7/66. Retd GD 1/10/68.
DENNING J. R. Born 4/8/48. Commd 21/4/67. Flt Lt 21/10/73. Retd SUP 1/3/78.
DENNING L. A., BDS LDSRCS. Born 14/10/52. Commd 9/12/84. Wg Cdr 20/12/91. Retd DEL 14/3/97.
DENNING R. J., BSc. Born 31/1/63. Commd 30/8/81. Flt Lt 15/10/87. Retd ENG 1/5/92.
DENNING T. W. E. Born 13/7/44. Commd 24/11/67. Sqn Ldr 1/1/94. Retd GD 13/7/00.
DENNIS B. W., MBE MA PhD CEng MIEE MIMechE MRAeS MIMgt. Born 9/9/37. Commd 30/9/57. Wg Cdr 1/1/76. Retd ENG 3/1/86.
DENNIS D. E. P. Born 30/6/46. Commd 15/10/81. Flt Lt 1/3/87. Retd ADMIN 1/10/87.
DENNIS N. C. H. Born 23/7/42. Commd 9/2/62. Flt Lt 9/2/67. Retd GD 23/7/80.
DENNIS R. V. Born 2/6/18. Commd 28/5/43. Sqn Ldr 1/7/68. Retd GD(G) 1/8/71.
DENNIS S. Born 7/7/36. Commd 22/7/71. Sqn Ldr 1/1/86. Retd GD 7/7/94.
DENNIS T. E. Born 29/11/32. Commd 28/2/52. Flt Lt 5/9/57. Retd GD 29/11/70.
DENNISON J. P. Born 29/5/29. Commd 1/3/56. Flt Lt 1/4/60. Retd GD 30/12/68.
DENNY A. C. H., OBE BA FCIS FCIPD FIMgt. Born 13/2/30. Commd 28/7/53. Wg Cdr 1/7/78. Retd ADMIN 26/2/82.
DENNY G. R. Born 27/4/40. Commd 19/9/59. Flt Lt 19/3/65. Retd GD 27/6/69.
DENNY I. J. Born 20/1/47. Commd 29/7/83. Flt Lt 29/7/83. Retd ADMIN 31/1/97.
DENNY J. R., MBE DFC. Born 9/5/13. Commd 25/4/40. Wg Cdr 1/7/53. Retd GD 19/7/58.
DENNY T. O., BSc MRAeS. Born 22/1/29. Commd 2/1/52. Wg Cdr 1/7/78. Retd ADMIN 22/1/84.
DENOVEN A., MBE DFM. Born 3/3/22. Commd 27/3/43. Flt Lt 25/6/49. Retd ADMIN 5/11/77.
DENT B. Born 4/12/32. Commd 10/9/52. Flt Lt 9/3/70. Retd GD 7/5/64. Reinstated 9/3/70. Sqn Ldr 2/3/92.
DENT B. J. Born 9/11/33. Commd 20/3/57. Flt Lt 3/2/61. Retd GD 9/11/91.
DENT C. R. Born 24/7/38. Commd 25/7/60. Flt Lt 17/4/65. Retd GD 24/7/93.
DENT F. T., MSc CEng MIMechE. Born 11/9/22. Re-commissioned 6/10/47. Wg Cdr 1/7/65. Retd ENG 24/6/80.
DENT L., BA MIMgt. Born 10/6/31. Commd 6/4/54. Flt Lt 6/4/59. Retd SEC 10/2/70.
DENT R. A. Born 5/3/11. Commd 12/11/42. Flt Lt 12/5/46. Retd ENG 1/9/50.
DENTON C. A. F., CEng MIEE MIMgt. Born 5/2/22. Commd 25/4/46. Sqn Ldr 1/10/56. Retd ENG 5/2/77.
DENTON P. K. Born 4/1/51. Commd 27/3/70. Flt Lt 27/9/75. Retd GD 4/1/89.
DENTON-POWELL F. M., MBE FCIPD MIMgt. Born 31/7/42. Commd 24/1/74. Wg Cdr 2/4/93. Retd ENG 2/4/93.
DENYER L. S. Born 25/1/23. Commd 16/9/43. Sqn Ldr 1/1/55. Retd ENG 25/1/83.
DEPOLO M. J. Born 7/7/49. Commd 4/12/86. Sqn Ldr 1/1/98. Retd OPS SPT 8/7/99.
DERBYSHIRE E. G., BSc. Born 9/5/28. Commd 6/1/53. Flt Lt 6/7/57. Retd GD 6/1/69.
DERBYSHIRE P. N. Born 26/4/48. Commd 1/8/69. Flt Lt 1/8/72. Retd GD 26/4/92.
DERRICK J. W. Born 9/7/45. Commd 10/1/69. Flt Lt 10/7/74. Retd GD 8/3/84.
DERRICK T. Born 29/12/19. Commd 12/7/44. Flt Lt 1/1/48. Retd GD 1/12/67.
DERRINGTON T. F. Born 21/7/52. Commd 10/2/72. Flt Lt 10/8/77. Retd GD 14/9/79.
DESMOND G. J. Born 16/9/18. Commd 9/7/42. Sqn Ldr 1/1/57. Retd GD 18/1/58.
DESMOND P., MBE. Born 25/3/33. Commd 13/8/52. Wg Cdr 1/7/80. Retd GD 25/3/88.

DETAIN L. W. G. Born 20/2/21. Commd 13/2/47. A Cdre 1/7/73. Retd SUP 20/2/76.
DEUBERT R. A. Born 3/3/46. Commd 2/4/65. Flt Lt 2/10/70. Retd GD 3/5/84.
DEVEREUX J. G., BA CertEd MIL. Born 21/2/49. Commd 2/2/75. Sqn Ldr 1/1/91. Retd ADMIN 2/7/94.
DEVEREUX P. Born 1/9/36. Commd 15/10/78. Flt Lt 15/10/84. Retd ENG 6/4/89.
DEVEREUX R. O. Born 16/7/39. Commd 4/10/63. Sqn Ldr 1/7/74. Retd GD 16/7/89.
DEVERILL J. J. Born 24/2/22. Commd 26/4/41. Sqn Ldr 1/7/54. Retd GD 24/2/65 rtg Wg Cdr.
DEVERSON M. Born 22/6/25. Commd 8/7/54. Flt Lt 8/1/58. Retd GD 22/6/76.
DEVERSON P. O. Born 15/1/23. Commd 9/4/43. Flt Lt 28/5/51. Retd GD 11/3/67.
DEVESON K. H., BA BSc MRAeS. Born 24/9/47. Commd 18/9/66. Sqn Ldr 1/7/85. Retd GD 8/2/99.
DEVEY SMITH T. W. A., MIMgt. Born 2/9/29. Commd 11/4/51. Sqn Ldr 1/1/61. Retd GD 14/5/76.
DEVILLEZ E. A. Born 26/3/22. Commd 19/9/47. Sqn Ldr 1/1/58. Retd GD 14/8/71.
DEVINE D. Born 10/4/46. Commd 28/5/66. Wg Cdr 1/7/87. Retd GD 30/1/96.
DEVINE S. P. Born 13/11/48. Commd 31/10/69. Fg Offr 31/10/71. Retd GD 30/1/75.
DEVLIN H. T. Born 2/5/47. Commd 26/7/70. Sqn Ldr 1/7/93. Retd GD 2/9/98.
DEVONSHIRE C. H., BSc. Born 7/8/51. Commd 15/9/69. Flt Lt 15/4/77. Retd SUP 1/10/84. rtg Sqn Ldr.
DEW R. S. Born 21/3/47. Commd 29/4/71. Flt Lt 29/10/75. Retd GD 11/1/87.
DEWAR R. Born 9/5/12. Commd 23/3/50. Flt Lt 23/9/54. Retd SUP 9/5/67.
DEWELL F. W., AFC. Born 9/1/12. Commd 1/4/40. Wg Cdr 1/7/58. Retd GD 9/1/65.
DEWEY G. F., DFM. Born 17/4/16. Commd 17/9/42. Sqn Ldr 1/7/54. Retd GD 10/5/59.
DEWHURST D. P. Born 1/8/31. Commd 27/10/54. Flt Lt 27/4/60. Retd GD 7/12/54.
DEXTER G., BA. Born 8/1/61. Commd 29/4/84. Flt Lt 29/10/86. Retd ADMIN 14/2/92.
DEXTER R. A., MCIPD MIMgt. Born 21/12/29. Commd 14/7/55. Wg Cdr 1/1/76. Retd ADMIN 21/12/84.
DEXTER R. W. Born 21/7/32. Commd 5/11/70. Flt Lt 5/11/73. Retd GD 19/7/75.
DEYTRIKH A., AFC. Born 24/10/21. Commd 5/11/41. Sqn Ldr 1/1/57. Retd GD 24/10/67 rtg Wg Cdr.
DEZONIE L. J. Born 6/10/60. Commd 3/7/80. Sqn Ldr 1/1/91. Retd ADMIN 6/10/98.
DEZONIE V. C. Born 25/3/27. Commd 21/10/65. Flt Lt 21/10/71. Retd ADMIN 25/3/82.
DHENIN Sir Geoffrey., KBE AFC* GM MA MD MChir MRCS LRCP FFCM DPH FRAeS. Born 2/4/18. Commd 11/2/43. AM 1/1/74. Retd MED 31/3/78.
DHESE I. R. Born 17/4/43. Commd 24/7/81. Sqn Ldr 1/1/89. Retd ADMIN 17/4/98.
DIACK H. W. Born 6/12/43. Commd 23/9/68. Flt Lt 23/6/72. Retd CAT 1/4/78.
DIAMANDOPOULOS D., BSc CEng MRAeS. Born 14/1/43. Commd 15/7/60. Wg Cdr 1/7/88. Retd ENG 1/10/91.
DIAPER E. D. J., MB ChB DAvMed AFOM. Born 18/11/30. Commd 2/2/58. Gp Capt 1/1/85. Retd MED 16/10/92.
DIAPER G. H. H., MBE. Born 2/2/23. Commd 15/6/61. Sqn Ldr 1/1/75. Retd ENG 4/12/82.
DIBB P. G. R. Born 9/7/60. Commd 12/9/86. Sqn Ldr 1/1/94. Retd GD 2/12/97.
DIBBENS D. T. Born 19/9/52. Commd 28/10/76. Flt Lt 28/4/82. Retd GD 12/7/92.
DIBBERN R. V. Born 5/7/22. Commd 24/8/44. Flt Lt 7/6/51. Retd GD 29/5/58.
DICK A. H. Born 4/3/24. Commd 23/8/44. Wg Cdr 1/7/64. Retd GD 31/3/75.
DICK A. R., MSc BSc. Born 16/6/47. Commd 3/8/80. Sqn Ldr 1/1/92. Retd ADMIN 14/9/96.
DICK E. A. Born 15/10/20. Commd 27/6/43. Sqn Ldr 1/1/59. Retd GD 9/4/71.
DICK I. C. H., MBE AFC. Born 23/7/42. Commd 18/12/62. Gp Capt 1/7/86. Retd GD 23/11/97.
DICK I. R. Born 2/2/26. Commd 29/7/48. Sqn Ldr 1/1/75. Retd GD 26/2/81.
DICK N. McL. Born 16/4/32. Commd 9/4/52. Flt Lt 9/1/58. Retd GD 2/6/66.
DICK R., CB. Born 18/10/31. Commd 30/7/52. AVM 1/1/85. Retd GD 15/8/88.
DICK R. Born 21/3/45. Commd 29/7/65. Flt Lt 28/10/71. Retd ADMIN 21/3/83.
DICK-CLELAND A. S. Born 28/1/35. Commd 27/6/59. Flt Lt 27/12/64. Retd GD 6/3/75.
DICKEN A. B., MIMgt. Born 13/4/30. Commd 8/7/54. Wg Cdr 1/1/80. Retd GD 13/10/85.
DICKEN M. J. C. W., CB FIMgt. Born 13/7/35. Commd 29/7/58. AVM 1/7/89. Retd ADMIN 3/4/92.
DICKENS B. C., BSc CEng MRAeS MIMgt. Born 8/2/45. Commd 31/1/64. Gp Capt 1/7/92. Retd ENG 15/5/01.
DICKENS J. S., AFC. Born 10/7/45. Commd 3/5/65. Flt Lt 28/10/70. Retd GD 10/7/83.
DICKENS M. D. Born 18/11/55. Commd 22/5/80. Flt Lt 22/2/86. Retd GD 25/5/90.
DICKENS R. E. Born 20/10/15. Commd 20/5/46. Flt Lt 4/1/51. Retd SEC 20/9/70.
DICKENSON P. M. Born 11/4/36. Commd 23/2/55. Sqn Ldr 1/7/71. Retd GD 28/11/75.
DICKER A. H. G. Born 21/5/24. Commd 26/1/45. Flt Lt 26/1/48. Retd GD 17/7/62.
DICKER R. W. Born 30/6/31. Commd 3/8/51. Gp Capt 1/7/76. Retd SY 20/9/80.
DICKIE D. G., AFM. Born 18/3/24. Commd 11/1/47. Flt Lt 7/6/56. Retd GD 31/8/67.
DICKINS T. P., CEng MIEE MRAeS. Born 19/8/31. Commd 4/3/58. Wg Cdr 1/1/76. Retd ENG 1/4/83.
DICKINSON B. Born 15/9/50. Commd 27/2/70. Flt Lt 18/7/76. Retd SUP 15/9/88.
DICKINSON B., MBE MA DCAe CEng FIMA FInstP MRAeS. Born 15/8/27. Commd 13/1/49. Wg Cdr 15/8/68. Retd EDN 5/2/72.
DICKINSON D. P. Born 15/9/42. Commd 24/3/83. Flt Lt 24/3/87. Retd ENG 15/9/97.
DICKINSON D. W. K. Born 8/6/53. Commd 22/5/75. Sqn Ldr 1/1/89. Retd GD(G) 17/10/89.
DICKINSON H. E. Born 7/11/17. Commd 25/3/54. Sqn Ldr 1/1/63. Retd ENG 7/11/67.
DICKINSON J. H. Born 15/6/55. Commd 22/5/75. Wg Cdr 1/7/91. Retd GD 15/6/96.
DICKINSON M. J. Born 6/4/46. Commd 30/8/84. Sqn Ldr 1/1/94. Retd ENG 5/1/96.
DICKINSON N. M., BSs. Born 4/5/56. Commd 15/9/74. Flt Lt 15/10/78. Retd GD 15/7/90.
DICKINSON R. H., BA. Born 21/4/59. Commd 22/10/76. Sqn Ldr 1/1/94. Retd GD 21/4/97.

DICKINSON R. J. F., AFC. Born 19/8/26. Commd 20/12/46. Gp Capt 1/1/73. Retd GD 19/8/81.
DICKINSON W. D. Born 3/4/26. Commd 25/5/50. Sqn Ldr 1/7/58. Retd GD 31/7/70.
DICKISON L. V. W. Born 19/2/17. Commd 14/8/50. Flt Lt 26/5/55. Retd GD(G) 19/2/67.
DICKS E. C. R., MRAeS. Born 19/4/44. Commd 17/12/64. Wg Cdr 1/1/91. Retd GD 19/4/99.
DICKSON E. D. Born 9/4/21. Commd 11/11/45. Flt Lt 7/6/51. Retd SEC 23/6/56.
DICKSON E. I. D., MIMgt. Born 30/1/24. Commd 11/1/51. Sqn Ldr 1/1/62. Retd ENG 24/3/78.
DICKSON H. M. Born 16/9/37. Commd 1/6/61. Wg Cdr 1/1/86. Retd ADMIN 16/9/88.
DICKSON J. A., BA. Born 9/8/36. Commd 30/9/58. Flt Lt 9/4/64. Retd GD 9/8/94.
DICKSON J. J. H., LVO MBE AE. Born 11/4/34. Commd 5/11/52. Wg Cdr. 1/7/76. Retd GD 10/8/85.
DICKSON L. G. Born 23/1/28. Commd 8/4/49. Sqn Ldr 1/7/61. Retd GD 24/1/73.
DICKSON M. W. Born 27/10/62. Commd 4/7/85. Flt Lt 4/1/92. Retd OPS SPT 4/3/01.
DIFFEY G. E., MBE. Born 29/5/52. Commd 20/7/78. Wg Cdr 1/1/99. Retd OPS SPT 28/2/01.
DIFFEY K. S., BA. Born 22/3/34. Commd 8/8/56. Wg Cdr 1/1/77. Retd ADMIN 22/3/89.
DIGBY A. P. Born 16/4/47. Commd 15/2/73. Flt Lt 15/2/75. Retd GD 1/4/92.
DIGBY B. N., ACIS. Born 8/1/35. Commd 6/10/60. Sqn Ldr 1/1/72. Retd ADMIN 31/12/77.
DIGBY J. R. Born 19/8/36. Commd 16/12/58. Wg Cdr 1/7/86. Retd ADMIN 8/4/89.
DIGGANCE P. J. Born 4/10/39. Commd 20/12/57. Flt Lt 30/6/63. Retd GD 4/10/77.
DIGGLE G. Born 28/10/43. Commd 2/6/77. Sqn Ldr 1/7/90. Retd ADMIN 2/7/93.
DIGINGS N. L., BSc. Born 5/8/51. Commd 13/9/70. Flt Lt 15/4/75. Retd GD 5/8/89.
DIGMAN J. I. S., OBE DFC. Born 4/9/23. Commd 25/6/43. Gp Capt 1/1/69. Retd GD 4/9/71.
DIGNAN J. C. Born 14/7/46. Commd 28/4/67. Sqn Ldr 1/7/82. Retd GD 19/12/86.
DIGNAN P. B. Born 14/7/19. Commd 4/1/48. Sqn Ldr 1/10/55. Retd GD 8/7/64 rtg Wg Cdr.
DIGNEN B. Born 16/9/30. Commd 28/6/51. Flt Lt 1/6/57. Retd GD 16/9/68.
DILLINGHAM G. G. Born 15/8/21. Commd 17/3/44. Flt Lt 4/6/53. Retd GD 15/8/76.
DILLON J. L., MIMgt. Born 29/3/29. Commd 12/9/50. Gp Capt 1/7/76. Retd GD 28/8/83.
DILLON J. Y., BEd. Born 30/5/57. Commd 23/7/78. Flt Lt 23/1/82. Retd GD(G) 14/3/96.
DILLON J.A. Born 2/10/45. Commd 2/8/68. Flt Lt 6/10/71. Retd GD 1/7/76.
DILLON K. Born 6/12/46. Commd 2/8/68. Wg Cdr 1/1/92. Retd GD 14/3/96.
DILLON R. B. R. Born 28/11/31. Commd 8/10/52. Flt Lt 27/6/59. Retd SEC 28/11/69.
DILWORTH R. L., BSc. Born 26/4/44. Commd 28/9/64. Flt Lt 15/4/68. Retd GD 27/5/81.
DIMENT A. J. Born 16/9/47. Commd 27/10/67. Wg Cdr 1/7/91. Retd SY 30/9/94.
DIMES D. C. J. Born 8/4/40. Commd 11/7/74. Flt Lt 11/7/76. Retd ENG 8/4/93.
DIMMER A. H. Born 22/8/46. Commd 1/4/65. Sqn Ldr 1/1/78. Retd SUP 22/8/84.
DIMMER F. J. L. Born 18/3/33. Commd 26/3/52. Flt Lt 31/7/57. Retd GD 18/3/71.
DIMMER G. E. Born 12/2/17. Commd 3/9/39. Wg Cdr 1/7/60. Retd SUP 22/4/72.
DIMMER J. F. E., BSc. Born 25/8/51. Commd 17/11/74. Flt Lt 17/2/75. Retd GD 17/11/90.
DIMMER T. W. Born 13/11/30. Commd 17/11/59. Sqn Ldr 8/3/72. Retd EDN 17/11/75.
DIMOCK D. H. T. Born 2/7/25. Commd 22/6/45. Wg Cdr 1/1/66. Retd GD 14/2/76.
DIMOND G. F., BEM. Born 7/11/19. Commd 24/9/59. Sqn Ldr 1/1/71. Retd ENG 3/8/74.
DINEEN M. G. Born 7/9/43. Commd 9/9/63. Wg Cdr 1/1/91. Retd GD 1/9/93.
DINGWALL P. C., BA ACIS. Born 10/1/48. Commd 13/9/70. Wg Cdr 1/1/88. Retd ADMIN 14/3/97.
DINGWALL R. H. Born 2/5/30. Commd 17/6/54. Flt Lt 17/12/58. Retd GD 2/5/90.
DINGWALL R. L. Born 20/2/39. Commd 16/12/66. Sqn Ldr 1/1/88. Retd GD(G) 20/2/94.
DINMORE D., MBE. Born 11/8/44. Commd 17/12/65. Flt Lt 17/6/68. Retd GD 31/3/80.
DINMORE G. W. Born 4/3/38. Commd 30/1/75. Wg Cdr 1/1/91. Retd GD(G) 31/8/92.
DINNING G. A., BSc. Born 19/2/66. Commd 15/9/86. Flt Lt 15/1/90. Retd GD 14/3/96.
DINNIS J. J. J. Born 13/4/32. Commd 27/7/54. Sqn Ldr 1/7/69. Retd SUP 1/7/72.
DIPPER O. D. Born 16/6/34. Commd 11/11/53. Sqn Ldr 1/1/72. Retd GD 1/1/85.
DIPROSE D. A., BA. Born 23/8/42. Commd 18/8/67. Flt Lt 18/8/70. Retd GD 23/6/90.
DISBREY W. D., CB CBE AFC CEng FIMechE FRAeS. Born 23/8/12. Commd 15/7/33. AVM 1/7/65. Retd ENG 15/6/70.
DISCOMBE F. H. Born 30/3/23. Commd 25/5/43. Flt Lt 26/5/57. Retd GD 30/3/66.
DISNEY H. A. S., OBE MA. Born 9/7/17. Commd 8/3/38. Gp Capt 1/1/58. Retd GD 23/8/63.
DISNEY R. H. Born 8/4/32. Commd 28/9/61. Flt Lt 28/9/67. Retd GD 14/8/70.
DITCHBURN A. Born 15/4/44. Commd 31/10/69. Flt Lt 20/7/73. Retd GD 1/1/76.
DITCHBURN A. W., BA IEng AMRAeS. Born 20/5/54. Commd 30/3/89. Flt Lt 30/3/91. Retd ENG 30/3/97.
DITCHFIELD G. F., BEM. Born 30/10/34. Commd 5/11/70. Flt Lt 5/11/75. Retd SY 1/4/77.
DIVE L. S., BEng. Born 27/4/29. Commd 17/12/52. Sqn Ldr 28/1/66. Retd EDN 2/4/81.
DIVERS A. R., MB BS. Born 30/11/52. Commd 20/2/73. Wg Cdr 26/9/89. Retd MED 30/11/90.
DIVERS D. M., MVO. Born 11/2/24. Commd 20/4/50. Wg Cdr 1/1/68. Retd GD 30/1/73.
DIVERS J. M. Born 10/5/56. Commd 22/9/88. Flt Lt 22/9/90. Retd ENG 22/9/96.
DIX K. J., OBE AFC MIEE MRAeS MIMgt . Born 12/9/30. Commd 25/9/52. Wg Cdr 1/7/71. Retd GD 1/1/83.
DIX M., BSc. Born 15/3/52. Commd 15/9/71. Sqn Ldr 1/7/87. Retd RGT 1/7/90.
DIX R. E. Born 13/1/61. Commd 19/12/91. Flt Lt 19/12/93. Retd OPS SPT 19/12/99.
DIX R. J. Born 29/7/42. Commd 29/11/63. Sqn Ldr 1/7/76. Retd GD 29/7/80.
DIXON A. Born 2/12/32. Commd 25/10/51. Flt Lt 25/4/57. Retd GD 30/3/73.

DIXON A., BSc. Born 8/8/55. Commd 23/9/73. Flt Lt 15/4/78. Retd GD 4/1/00.
DIXON A. H. Born 5/12/21. Commd 29/9/57. Flt Lt 1/4/63. Retd ADMIN 5/12/76.
DIXON A. J. Born 20/8/57. Commd 22/5/80. Flt Lt 22/11/85. Retd GD 1/4/00.
DIXON C. F., MSc MIMgt. Born 7/10/39. Commd 19/12/61. Wg Cdr 1/1/77. Retd SUP 1/12/89.
DIXON D. J. Born 21/3/31. Commd 22/7/66. Flt Lt 22/7/67. Retd EDN 22/7/74.
DIXON D. P. Born 23/4/65. Commd 16/6/88. Flt Lt 24/6/91. Retd GD 13/3/97.
DIXON E. R. Born 1/7/15. Commd 15/7/42. Flt Offr 15/1/47. Retd SEC 6/10/56.
DIXON G. K. Born 11/1/58. Commd 11/10/84. Flt Lt 6/11/88. Retd ADMIN 3/6/96.
DIXON H. M. Born 5/11/23. Commd 7/2/48. Flt Lt 25/3/56. Retd GD 7/5/67.
DIXON H. P. Born 3/1/33. Commd 18/1/52. Wg Cdr 1/1/77. Retd GD(G) 3/1/88.
DIXON J., MA. Born 19/2/37. Commd 22/8/58. Wg Cdr 1/7/76. Retd ADMIN 24/10/89.
DIXON J. E. Born 1/12/45. Commd 5/2/65. Flt Lt 5/8/70. Retd GD 1/12/84.
DIXON J. E. Born 18/10/22. Commd 1/5/44. Sqn Ldr 1/7/70. Retd ADMIN 17/10/77.
DIXON J. M. Born 16/7/45. Commd 3/3/67. Flt Lt 3/9/69. Retd OPS SPT 16/7/00.
DIXON J. P. S. Born 29/6/32. Commd 6/4/54. Flt Lt 14/11/56. Retd GD 29/6/70.
DIXON K. R., BA BEd. Born 13/3/45. Commd 20/1/80. Flt Lt 20/1/81. Retd ADMIN 20/1/96.
DIXON M. Born 21/12/45. Commd 2/8/68. Flt Lt 2/2/71. Retd GD 1/7/89.
DIXON M., BA. Born 23/11/36. Commd 15/10/58. Wg Cdr 1/1/77. Retd ADMIN 26/2/83.
DIXON M. E. Born 1/7/18. Commd 27/10/43. Flt Offr 19/6/52. Retd SEC 15/2/55.
DIXON N. D. Born 22/7/48. Commd 2/3/78. Sqn Ldr 1/7/85. Retd ENG 1/7/88.
DIXON N. G., BA. Born 1/2/41. Commd 30/9/61. Wg Cdr 1/7/81. Retd ENG 31/3/96.
DIXON R., OBE MCIPS MIMgt. Born 8/3/44. Commd 17/12/65. Gp Capt 1/7/88. Retd SUP 7/3/94.
DIXON R. H. B. Born 15/5/25. Commd 8/12/45. Wg Cdr 1/7/61. Retd GD 24/3/77 rtg Gp Capt.
DIXON R. S. Born 11/3/47. Commd 2/12/66. Sqn Ldr 1/1/87. Retd GD 30/12/91.
DIXON R. T., OBE. Born 29/5/32. Commd 19/2/51. Gp Capt 1/7/78. Retd GD 19/9/87.
DIXON R. T. Born 15/4/46. Commd 27/7/72. Sqn Ldr 1/7/88. Retd ENG 13/9/96.
DIXON S. R., DFC AFC. Born 31/7/20. Commd 24/11/41. Sqn Ldr 1/1/53. Retd GD 31/7/75.
DIXON T. S. J. Born 14/12/32. Commd 2/7/52. Flt Lt 27/11/57. Retd GD 14/12/70.
DJUMIC M., MSc BSc. Born 3/6/59. Commd 18/10/81. Wg Cdr 1/1/97. Retd SUP 1/1/00.
DOBB A. L., BSc. Born 25/11/41. Commd 26/5/70. Sqn Ldr 1/1/83. Retd ENG 2/7/93.
DOBBIE D. A., AFC. Born 18/6/21. Commd 28/3/43. Sqn Ldr 1/7/53. Retd GD 18/6/70.
DOBBIE J. A. A., BSc Born 30/11/38. Commd 28/9/60. Flt Lt 28/3/65. Retd GD 31/5/90.
DOBBIE J. B. Born 16/2/20. Commd 14/12/44. Flt Lt 14/6/48. Retd ENG 16/2/69.
DOBBS A. C. Born 29/5/43. Commd 24/6/65. Sqn Ldr 1/7/83. Retd GD 26/6/98.
DOBBS P. F. Born 26/12/46. Commd 1/3/68. Sqn Ldr 1/7/80. Retd ENG 12/11/90.
DOBBS S. S., OBE. Born 10/3/12. Commd 22/4/43. Wg Cdr 1/7/59. Retd ENG 10/3/67.
DOBBY V. Born 20/3/43. Commd 11/6/81. Flt Lt 11/6/84. Retd GD 12/10/97.
DOBEL M. J. Born 29/4/42. Commd 1/3/68. Sqn Ldr 1/1/74. Retd SEC 29/4/81.
DOBIE I. M. Born 3/4/46. Commd 15/6/83. Sqn Ldr 1/7/91. Retd ENG 14/12/96.
DOBIE T. G., OBE MD ChB. Born 23/6/23. Commd 23/7/43. Gp Capt 1/7/69. Retd MED 30/9/72.
DOBLE L. A., OBE FRAeS. Born 6/1/47. Commd 28/4/67. A Cdre 1/1/96. Retd GD 29/12/00.
DOBSON B. S. Born 8/8/30. Commd 9/8/51. Flt Lt 30/11/56. Retd GD 8/8/68.
DOBSON C. W. Born 27/4/21. Commd 13/2/47. Flt Lt 13/2/53. Retd SEC 1/8/64.
DOBSON G. C. Born 7/3/31. Commd 20/1/51. Flt Lt 10/11/55. Retd GD 8/5/85.
DOBSON G. J., DFC BSc. Born 22/5/63. Commd 13/9/81. Flt Lt 15/1/87. Retd GD 21/7/98.
DOBSON G. M. Born 4/5/50. Commd 29/4/71. Flt Lt 29/10/76. Retd GD 1/6/91.
DOBSON J. B. Born 22/8/40. Commd 15/9/67. Sqn Ldr 1/7/82. Retd GD 22/8/95.
DOBSON J. B. M. Born 3/7/33. Commd 27/7/54. Sqn Ldr 1/1/65. Retd GD 3/7/71.
DOBSON L., MBE. Born 7/5/21. Commd 6/9/56. Sqn Ldr 1/1/69. Retd ENG 11/2/78.
DOBSON M. Born 2/8/22. Commd 3/1/46. Flt Lt 22/5/57. Retd GD 1/10/68.
DOBSON M. F. H., AFC. Born 10/9/24. Commd 7/7/49. Sqn Ldr 1/7/59. Retd GD 9/10/73.
DOBSON M. H. Born 31/5/47. Commd 1/3/68. Sqn Ldr 1/1/81. Retd GD 31/5/91.
DOBSON R. G. R. Born 17/5/26. Commd 22/12/49. Flt Lt 22/6/53. Retd GD 18/5/64.
DOBSON W. J. Born 13/8/25. Commd 26/9/51. Flt Lt 26/3/56. Retd GD 1/10/68.
DOBSON W. J. Born 27/12/33. Commd 27/2/52. Flt Lt 26/6/57. Retd GD 20/12/75.
DOCHERTY J. Born 26/7/36. Commd 1/4/65. Flt Lt 1/4/67. Retd GD 17/12/74.
DOCHERTY J., BDS. Born 27/8/32. Commd 21/7/55. Sqn Ldr 21/8/62. Retd DEL 30/8/66.
DOCKER C. E., BSc. Born 6/11/61. Commd 29/4/84. Flt Lt 29/10/86. Retd GD 29/4/00.
DOCKER C. E. Born 25/7/59. Commd 13/3/80. Flt Lt 24/7/86. Retd SUP 31/8/91.
DOCKERTY R. Born 11/9/28. Commd 25/6/66. Flt Lt 25/6/69. Retd GD 1/1/77.
DODD B. J. H., LHA AMIMgt. Born 3/6/36. Commd 21/2/69. Sqn Ldr 1/5/80. Retd MED (SEC) 5/1/84.
DODD C. G., MA. Born 16/3/35. Commd 25/10/57. Sqn Ldr 25/4/65. Retd EDN 25/10/73.
DODD D. Born 19/7/33. Commd 17/10/59. Sqn Ldr 1/1/77. Retd GD 3/11/84.
DODD J. B. Born 31/8/46. Commd 18/8/67. Sqn Ldr 1/1/87. Retd GD 14/9/96.
DODD L. Born 27/4/35. Commd 27/4/61. Sqn Ldr 1/7/73. Retd ADMIN 4/11/85.
DODD M. T. B. Born 28/4/39. Commd 28/1/60. Sqn Ldr 1/1/72. Retd ADMIN 28/4/77.

DODD R. L. Born 21/10/36. Commd 3/11/60. Sqn Ldr 1/1/74. Retd GD 1/6/89.
DODDS A., BEM AIIP. Born 18/3/30. Commd 30/7/64. Sqn Ldr 1/7/78. Retd ENG 23/8/80.
DODDS C. N. Born 23/11/40. Commd 12/1/62. Sqn Ldr 1/7/76. Retd GD 1/6/82.
DODDS G., BSc. Born 1/4/40. Commd 2/10/61. Sqn Ldr 1/7/70. Retd GD 26/3/79.
DODDS K. M. Born 29/10/36. Commd 6/4/72. Flt Lt 6/4/78. Retd ADMIN 29/10/86.
DODDS L. W. M. Born 11/2/26. Commd 16/2/49. Flt Lt 19/11/53. Retd GD 8/10/57.
DODDS T. E. D. Born 11/1/38. Commd 9/1/57. Flt Lt 14/1/64. Retd SUP 28/9/67.
DODGSON H. J. Born 12/11/22. Commd 18/4/42. Flt Lt 29/12/46. Retd GD 31/3/62 rtg Sqn Ldr.
DODHY B. M. A., MB ChB. Born 15/6/39. Commd 24/2/75. Wg Cdr 1/8/81. Retd MED 7/4/94.
DODIMEAD D. J., OBE. Born 13/12/24. Commd 24/10/46. Cp Capt 1/7/71. Retd GD 13/12/79.
DODKINS W. J. Born 17/4/23. Commd 19/9/44. Sqn Ldr 1/1/68. Retd SUP 17/4/78.
DODSON G. A. F. Born 2/2/60. Commd 16/12/82. Flt Lt 16/6/88. Retd GD 13/12/99.
DODSON H. J., AFC. Born 29/8/21. Commd 3/5/42. Gp Capt 1/1/62. Retd GD 9/9/65.
DODWORTH P., CB OBE AFC BSc. Born 12/9/40. Commd 2/10/61. AVM 1/1/91. Retd GD 1/10/96.
DOE R. F. T., DSO DFC*. Born 10/3/20. Commd 20/3/39. Wg Cdr 1/1/56. Retd GD 1/4/66.
DOE R. J. Born 17/8/34. Commd 9/4/53. Flt Lt 18/8/58. Retd GD 17/8/72.
DOEL J. E. Born 11/10/39. Commd 14/8/80. Sqn Ldr 1/1/88. Retd ENG 11/10/94.
DOGGART J. M. Born 8/6/47. Commd 28/2/69. Sqn Ldr 1/7/79. Retd GD 3/12/90.
DOGGETT A. C. Born 1/6/31. Commd 17/12/52. Sqn Ldr 1/1/63. Retd ENG 1/9/73.
DOGGETT P. G. Born 19/10/35. Commd 11/11/71. Sqn Ldr 1/1/83. Retd SUP 1/8/86.
DOHERTY F. W. Born 10/12/22. Commd 23/7/43. Wg Cdr 1/7/61. Retd GD 21/8/70.
DOHERTY I. E. Born 21/8/44. Commd 14/2/63. Sqn Ldr 1/7/74. Retd ENG 21/8/88.
DOHERTY J., MSc. Born 7/6/38. Commd 12/9/61. Sqn Ldr 1/1/71. Retd ENG 12/9/77.
DOHERTY M. R. Born 20/4/30. Commd 14/11/51. Flt Lt 14/5/56. Retd GD 20/4/85.
DOHERTY M. V., BA MRCS LRCP DAvMed. Born 12/7/19. Commd 27/8/62. Wg Cdr 22/11/65. Retd MED 27/8/78.
DOHERTY M. V., LLB. Born 16/12/35. Commd 18/8/57. Sqn Ldr 1/1/68. Retd GD 29/6/85.
DOIG U. M. Born 9/5/46. Commd 11/8/77. Flt Lt 11/2/84. Retd GD(G) 11/8/93.
DOLAN D. M. Born 6/12/50. Commd 14/8/70. Flt Lt 14/2/76. Retd GD 31/1/98.
DOLBY J. R., MBE. Born 24/1/16. Commd 25/4/43. Sqn Ldr 1/1/63. Retd ENG 17/2/72.
DOLE T. F., MIMgt. Born 27/1/37. Commd 1/11/56. Gp Capt 1/7/85. Retd ADMIN 27/1/92.
DOLEMAN R. A. Born 21/3/46. Commd 23/9/66. Flt Lt 14/1/73. Retd GD 21/3/84.
DOLING G. J. Born 31/5/51. Commd 29/6/72. Flt Lt 29/12/77. Retd GD 31/5/89.
DOLING G. J. Born 31/5/51. Commd 29/6/72. Flt Lt 29/12/77. Retd GD 31/5/89.
DOLING P. E. Born 28/4/34. Commd 30/5/58. Sqn Ldr 3/10/68. Retd EDN 6/10/79.
DOLLIMORE R. P., MA. Born 7/7/27. Commd 4/11/48. Wg Cdr 1/7/69. Retd ENG 16/5/78.
DOLMAN A. T., MBE BSc. Born 27/5/47. Commd 16/1/72. Wg Cdr 1/7/89. Retd ENG 21/5/91.
DOLMAN G. H. Born 30/6/34. Commd 26/3/53. Sqn Ldr 1/1/80. Retd GD 30/6/89.
DOLPHIN L. Born 17/6/23. Commd 24/4/47. Sqn Ldr 1/1/73. Retd GD 1/7/78.
DOLTON D. J., BSc. Born 14/2/60. Commd 6/9/81. Flt Lt 6/12/84. Retd GD(G) 15/2/91.
DOMMETT J. B. Born 5/2/33. Commd 14/8/70. Sqn Ldr 1/7/80. Retd ENG 3/4/84.
DONACHY J., OBE FCCA. Born 12/6/37. Commd 5/6/67. Wg Cdr 1/7/84. Retd ADMIN 7/8/92.
DONALD A. W. M. Born 16/4/60. Commd 20/10/77. Flt Lt 14/2/85. Retd GD 1/2/93.
DONALD B. Born 6/3/40. Commd 2/5/69. Flt Lt 18/10/75. Retd GD(G) 6/9/90.
DONALD Sir John, KBE QHS MB ChB FRCGP FFOM MFCM DTM&H FIMgt. Born 7/11/27. Commd 31/8/53.
    AM 1/7/84. Retd MED 31/7/86.
DONALD M. Born 5/6/35. Commd 29/7/54. Flt Lt 5/10/60. Retd GD 1/11/68.
DONALDSON M. P., MBE. Born 22/7/43. Commd 22/2/63. AVM 1/7/93. Retd GD 14/9/96.
DONALDSON W. F. Born 7/9/29. Commd 11/10/51. Flt Lt 25/1/57. Retd GD 30/11/68.
DONALDSON-DAVIDSON D. Born 28/2/23. Commd 26/11/53. Sqn Ldr 1/1/70. Retd GD 7/1/72.
DONDERS B. Born 22/12/32. Commd 8/11/51. Sqn Ldr 1/7/77. Retd GD 20/1/84.
DONEY G. E. Born 15/7/45. Commd 11/6/81. Sqn Ldr 1/1/91. Retd ENG 22/4/94.
DONKIN P. E. Born 15/5/48. Commd 28/4/67. Flt Lt 28/10/72. Retd GD 17/5/93.
DONLAN P. Born 8/2/38. Commd 26/8/66. Wg Cdr 1/7/80. Retd GD(G) 8/2/93.
DONMALL N. E. G. Born 12/12/22. Commd 8/11/41. Flt Lt 17/5/56. Retd GD(G) 12/12/77.
DONNELLY B. Born 14/2/41. Commd 13/10/61. Flt Lt 13/4/67. Retd GD 14/12/79.
DONNELLY D. A., MRIN. Born 6/2/45. Commd 15/7/66. Wg Cdr 1/1/90. Retd GD 6/6/00.
DONNELLY D. V. Born 29/1/17. Commd 1/11/44. Flt Lt 1/5/48. Retd GD(G) 23/2/67. Re-commissioned 26/8/68 to
    29/1/75.
DONNELLY G. L., DFM. Born 29/10/20. Commd 29/3/45. Flt Lt 7/6/51. Retd GD(G) 18/12/66.
DONNELLY J. M. Born 29/7/43. Commd 6/11/64. Wg Cdr 1/1/86. Retd GD 1/2/94.
DONNELLY W. D., BSc. Born 4/5/16. Commd 7/12/48. Sqn Ldr 7/2/52. Retd EDN 9/3/61.
DONNISON E., BSc BDS BA LDSRCS. Born 12/5/38. Commd 7/8/59. Gp Capt 1/1/92. Retd DEL 12/5/96.
DONOGHUE E. C., AFC. Born 27/10/22. Commd 29/3/45. Flt Lt 29/9/48. Retd GD 27/10/65.
DONOHOE W. J. Born 26/10/30. Commd 30/7/52. Sqn Ldr 1/1/68. Retd ENG 31/8/69.
DONOHUE A. Born 5/4/36. Commd 5/9/69. Flt Lt 5/9/71. Retd PRT 28/2/75.
DONOHUE P. F., MIMgt. Born 1/4/28. Commd 24/12/53. Sqn Ldr 1/7/68. Retd ADMIN 1/4/80.

DONOVAN C. P. Born 18/12/24. Commd 27/1/45. Gp Capt 1/7/72. Retd GD 18/12/82.
DONOVAN F. T. Born 28/2/13. Commd 9/12/54. Flt Lt 9/12/57. Retd SEC 22/6/64.
DOOLE W. J. Born 28/7/48. Commd 25/8/67. Fg Offr 21/12/70. Retd RGT 12/5/74.
DOONAN D. K., BSc. Born 22/3/61. Commd 30/10/83. Flt Lt 30/4/87. Retd ADMIN 30/10/99.
DOONAN J. S., MIMgt. Born 24/10/34. Commd 28/4/61. Sqn Ldr. 1/7/76. Retd GD 24/10/89.
DOORNE R. L., BA. Born 2/3/34. Commd 26/9/53. Sqn Ldr 1/7/67. Retd ENG 2/3/72.
DOPSON J. S. Born 20/1/29. Commd 19/4/51. Flt Lt 17/10/68. Retd GD 2/2/67.
DORA M. J., MSc BSc MIMgt. Born 11/5/54. Commd 3/9/72. Sqn Ldr 1/7/87. Retd SUP 14/3/97.
DORAN A. P. Born 20/10/33. Commd 19/1/56. Sqn Ldr 1/7/71. Retd SEC 20/11/81.
DORAN F. E., OBE. Born 8/9/22. Commd 28/4/45. G Capt 1/1/75. Retd GD(G) 30/3/78.
DORANS J. C. Born 8/12/16. Commd 4/7/57. Sqn Ldr 18/5/66. Retd MED 10/4/70.
DOREY A. J. Born 20/2/48. Commd 27/2/70. Flt Lt 27/8/72. Retd GD 28/8/93.
DORLING R. F., BMedSci MB ChB MRCGP DRCOG DAvMed AFOM. Born 3/4/49. Commd 21/11/71. Sqn Ldr 4/9/80. Retd MED 18/7/88.
DORMAN T. R., BA. Born 27/4/55. Commd 15/9/74. Sqn Ldr 1/1/88. Retd SUP 31/10/00.
DORMAN-JACKSON C. I. Born 20/3/38. Commd 10/12/57. Sqn Ldr 1/7/77. Retd GD 21/11/88.
DORN A. Born 13/2/49. Commd 2/2/68. Flt Lt 23/5/74. Retd GD(G) 13/2/87.
DORNAN C. R. Born 7/2/35. Commd 1/2/60. Flt Lt 1/2/60. Retd GD 1/2/76.
DORRETT I. Born 27/4/39. Commd 25/7/60. Gp Capt 1/7/87. Retd SUP 28/2/95.
DORRICOTT G. H. Born 3/3/30. Commd 7/5/52. Sqn Ldr 1/1/70. Retd GD 27/7/73.
DORRINGTON B. Born 27/11/30. Commd 24/1/52. Flt Lt 15/5/57. Retd GD 27/11/88.
DORSETT R. C. T. Born 4/1/24. Commd 21/7/55. Flt Lt 21/7/61. Retd GD 13/7/74.
DORWARD D. B., BEM. Born 26/11/29. Commd 19/12/65. Flt Lt 9/12/71. Retd EDN 1/9/73.
DORWARD P. J. G. Born 11/8/57. Commd 9/5/91. Fg Off 26/3/84. Retd ENG 2/4/93.
DORWARD S. G., FIMgt. Born 6/2/49. Commd 26/5/67. Wg Cdr 1/1/86. Retd GD(G) 14/3/96.
DOSWELL B. E. Born 25/4/42. Commd 20/9/68. Flt Lt 12/5/72. Retd GD 1/11/75.
DOUBEK J. Born 24/1/14. Commd 2/8/40. Flt Lt 10/11/55. Retd SEC 24/1/65.
DOUBLE J., DFC. Born 23/11/21. Commd 27/2/44. Flt Lt 27/8/47. Retd GD 23/11/64.
DOUBLE L. Born 11/6/20. Commd 10/8/44. Flt Lt 30/6/49. Retd SUP 14/2/50.
DOUBLEDAY M., CEng MIEE. Born 1/2/22. Commd 20/4/54. Flt Lt 20/4/59. Retd ENG 5/2/72.
DOUBLEDAY M., BA. Born 20/6/34. Commd 27/9/57. Sqn Ldr 27/3/65. Retd EDN 29/6/68.
DOUCE R. J. Born 26/6/55. Commd 29/4/81. Flt Lt 30/4/83. Retd GD 1/2/91.
DOUCH A. J., MA MRAeS FIMgt. Born 26/10/17. Commd 25/6/38. Wg Cdr 1/1/53. Retd GD 8/6/72.
DOUGAN W. W. Born 22/10/17. Commd 6/1/55. Flt Lt 6/1/58. Retd GD 18/7/68.
DOUGHTY N. A. R. Born 5/4/19. Commd 13/9/38. Sqn Ldr 1/8/47. Retd GD 6/1/58.
DOUGLAS A. G., CBE MC. Born 6/2/17. Commd 14/12/38. A Cdre 1/1/67. Retd RGT 7/8/70.
DOUGLAS AND CLYDESDALE The Marquess of, BA. Born 13/9/38. Commd 28/9/60. Flt Lt 28/6/62. Retd GD 27/12/67.
DOUGLAS G. A., MB ChB FFARCS. Born 13/2/48. Commd 30/9/68. Wg Cdr 8/8/85. Retd 12/7/87.
DOUGLAS G. J., IEng AMRAeS. Born 26/7/58. Commd 29/1/87. Flt Lt 29/1/89. Retd ENG 26/7/96.
DOUGLAS G. S. A. Born 24/7/14. Commd 21/1/43. Flt Lt 21/7/47. Retd GD(G) 24/7/64.
DOUGLAS I. Born 7/10/35. Commd 2/8/68. Sqn Ldr 1/7/80. Retd ENG 7/10/93.
DOUGLAS I. A. MCC. Born 7/1/39. Commd 1/4/58. Wg Cdr 1/7/85. Retd GD 7/1/94.
DOUGLAS J. C., DFC. Born 30/5/18. Commd 23/2/43. Wg Cdr 1/1/63. Retd GD 30/5/73.
DOUGLAS J. P. Born 17/6/27. Commd 9/12/48. Sqn Ldr 1/1/60. Retd GD 17/6/61.
DOUGLAS J. R. H., BSc CEng MRAeS. Born 9/6/49. Commd 23/9/68. Sqn Ldr 1/1/81. Retd ENG 9/6/88.
DOUGLAS J. S., OBE. Born 24/4/45. Commd 25/3/64. Wg Cdr 1/1/89. Retd GD 24/4/00.
DOUGLAS O. C. Born 10/11/22. Commd 16/3/45. Flt Lt 16/9/48. Retd GD 28/2/62.
DOUGLAS R. M. Born 24/1/45. Commd 20/9/68. Flt Lt 10/7/71. Retd GD 1/5/76.
DOUGLAS S. Born 1/2/64. Commd 23/5/85. Fg Offr 31/7/86. Retd GD(G) 25/9/89.
DOUGLAS S. S. Born 3/3/23. Commd 7/4/44. Sqn Ldr 1/7/55. Retd GD 4/4/66.
DOUGLAS-BEVERIDGE A. J., CEng MRAeS MIEE. Born 10/3/40. Commd 18/7/61. Sqn Ldr 1/7/70. Retd ENG 10/3/78.
DOUGLASS A. G., OBE AFC. Born 29/10/18. Commd 9/4/43. Sqn Ldr 1/7/54. Retd GD 31/10/58.
DOUGLASS M. P., AFC. Born 11/9/49. Commd 8/9/69. Sqn Ldr 1/7/87. Retd GD 1/7/90.
DOUTY P. A., OBE CEng MIMechE MRAeS. Born 8/5/34. Commd 25/7/56. Wg Cdr 1/1/73. Retd ENG 7/11/85.
DOUXCHAMPS F. Born 11/11/15. Commd 15/3/50. Flt Offr 15/3/56. Retd GD(G) 11/11/65.
DOVE A. N. E., BSc. Born 18/12/62. Commd 8/12/87. Flt Lt 28/2/89. Retd GD 14/9/96.
DOVE B., AFC. Born 25/11/43. Commd 8/12/61. Wg Cdr 1/7/81. Retd GD 18/10/97.
DOVE-DIXON B. W. Born 19/2/33. Commd 4/10/51. Sqn Ldr 1/1/71. Retd GD(G) 13/4/79.
DOVER I. P. Born 22/5/62. Commd 22/11/84. Flt Lt 22/5/90. Retd GD 22/5/00.
DOVESTON A. E. J., MIDPM. Born 28/4/37. Commd 17/7/70. Sqn Ldr 1/7/84. Retd SUP 27/6/88.
DOVEY A. R. Born 17/2/31. Commd 12/11/54. Flt Lt 16/8/61. Retd GD 1/8/82.
DOW A. M. Born 7/7/32. Commd 11/10/51. Flt Lt 25/1/57. Retd GD 12/11/86.
DOW E. M., OBE. Born 1/7/15. Commd 17/6/40. Wg Offr 1/1/50. Retd SEC 17/10/54 rtg Gp Offr.
DOW I. H. Born 24/11/46. Commd 2/8/68. Sqn Ldr 1/1/76. Retd GD 24/11/96.

DOWD R. K., BSc. Born 23/9/45. Commd 22/9/65. Flt Lt 15/4/69. Retd GD 1/4/85.
DOWDALL N. P., MB ChB MRCGP DRCOG DAvMed. Born 1/8/57. Commd 1/1/79. Wg Cdr 1/8/95. Retd MED 31/12/96.
DOWDESWELL D., MIMgt. Born 17/1/27. Commd 2/6/61. Gp Capt 1/1/80. Retd MED(SEC) 1/1/83.
DOWDS T., MSc BA. Born 20/6/48. Commd 2/3/78. Sqn Ldr 1/1/86. Retd ENG 14/5/01.
DOWELL A McL., BA MCSP DipTP. Born 14/11/31. Commd 6/9/68. Sqn Ldr 23/10/79. Retd MED(T) 2/6/81.
DOWER N. S., FIMgt. Born 11/4/21. Commd 3/8/43. Gp Capt 1/1/67. Retd GD(G) 16/6/72.
DOWER W. D. K. Born 10/11/21. Commd 4/10/60. Flt Lt 4/10/63. Retd GD(G) 30/5/70.
DOWLER R. R. J. Born 9/10/46. Commd 1/3/68. Flt Lt 1/3/71. Retd GD 3/10/78.
DOWLING B. R. C., CEng MRAes MIMechE. Born 17/6/39. Commd 28/7/60. Sqn Ldr 1/1/70. Retd ENG 7/8/84.
DOWLING D. E. Born 13/4/23. Commd 13/2/64. Flt Lt 13/2/69. Retd ENG 1/10/74.
DOWLING D. E. B., AFC. Born 18/6/30. Commd 11/4/51. Gp Capt 1/7/74. Retd GD 12/6/81.
DOWLING F. J., MIMgt. Born 10/10/30. Commd 30/1/70. Sqn Ldr 1/7/80. Retd ADMIN 31/8/85.
DOWLING F. N. Born 3/9/41. Commd 28/3/66. Flt Lt 15/4/70. Retd RGT 31/3/73.
DOWLING F. W., OBE. Born 30/5/15. Commd 25/4/40. Wg Cdr 1/7/57. Retd SEC 30/5/67.
DOWLING J. E. Born 20/4/51. Commd 8/8/69. Sqn Ldr 1/7/87. Retd GD 1/7/90.
DOWN A. M. Born 7/8/46. Commd 14/8/64. Sqn Ldr 1/1/84. Retd GD 1/1/91.
DOWN B. J. Born 24/5/36. Commd 23/6/67. Flt Lt 4/11/70. Retd ENG 23/6/75.
DOWN J. L. Born 23/12/99. Commd 25/11/41. Flt Lt 1/9/45. Retd ENG 23/12/58.
DOWN L. M., MSc BEng CEng MIMechE. Born 15/10/50. Commd 22/4/71. Wg Cdr 1/1/87. Retd ENG 30/9/90.
DOWNER R. R. Born 31/5/44. Commd 4/11/82. Sqn Ldr 1/7/89. Retd ADMIN 1/6/97.
DOWNER S. V. B. Born 29/1/33. Commd 12/11/54. Flt Lt 26/2/64. Retd GD 29/1/71.
DOWNES B. R. Born 8/8/31. Commd 13/9/51. Sqn Ldr 1/7/66. Retd ADMIN 1/12/83.
DOWNES C. B. W. Born 14/1/23. Commd 30/5/44. Sqn Ldr 1/1/55. Retd GD 27/10/61.
DOWNES D. R. Born 18/9/08. Commd 28/1/43. Flt Lt 1/9/47. Retd SUP 4/1/54.
DOWNES D. T. Born 13/5/45. Commd 16/5/74. Sqn Ldr 1/7/81. Retd ENG 10/8/98.
DOWNES M. Born 16/12/16. Commd 7/4/44. Sqn Ldr 1/10/54. Retd GD 6/3/58.
DOWNES N. J. Born 22/1/42. Commd 20/8/65. Flt Lt 20/2/71. Retd GD 3/5/81.
DOWNES R. N., BSc MB BS. Born 29/4/52. Commd 22/1/74. Wg Cdr 23/1/91. Retd MED 10/8/92.
DOWNEY D. B. G., MBE. Born 10/10/35. Commd 5/5/54. Sqn Ldr 1/7/85. Retd GD 12/10/88.
DOWNEY J. C. T., CB DFC AFC. Born 26/11/20. Commd 24/6/39. AVM 1/1/70. Retd GD 13/12/75.
DOWNEY T. R. Born 20/1/30. Commd 13/2/52. Sqn Ldr 1/7/67. Retd GD 24/2/76.
DOWNEY W. R. H., MB BCh FRCP DCH. Born 8/2/30. Commd 6/1/57. Gp Capt 8/1/79. Retd MED 3/4/85.
DOWNING J. W., CEng MIEE MRAeS. Born 19/6/40. Commd 15/12/60. Sqn Ldr 1/1/72. Retd ENG 30/7/77.
DOWNING M. R. Born 25/5/43. Commd 9/3/62. Flt Lt 9/9/67. Retd GD 27/5/76.
DOWNING P. W. Born 22/12/24. Commd 19/5/49. Flt Lt 19/11/52. Retd GD 13/3/64.
DOWNING R. E. Born 10/7/32. Commd 22/1/54. Flt Lt 22/7/59. Retd GD 10/7/70.
DOWNING W. G. Born 6/3/20. Commd 22/2/51. Sqn Ldr 1/1/66. Retd GD 31/7/68.
DOWNS D. E. Born 22/1/35. Commd 19/11/63. Flt Lt 1/4/66. Retd GD 22/1/73.
DOWNS D. H., OBE. Born 13/6/22. Commd 4/12/42. Wg Cdr 1/7/67. Retd GD 31/7/73.
DOWNS E. J., MBE. Born 24/9/21. Commd 23/11/43. Sqn Ldr 1/4/55. Retd GD 24.9/70.
DOWNS E. J. R. Born 19/6/25. Commd 27/11/46. Sqn Ldr 1/1/61. Retd GD 30/8/68.
DOWNS E. L., BSc. Born 11/1/62. Commd 31/8/80. Flt Lt 15/4/85. Retd GD 1/4/96.
DOWNS J. W. Born 11/4/31. Commd 3/1/54. Flt Lt 21/7/61. Retd GD(G) 11/4/69.
DOWNS R. D. Born 10/8/31. Commd 30/12/54. Sqn Ldr 1/1/71. Retd GD 11/1/84.
DOYE C. C. Born 2/2/45. Commd 8/4/82. Wg Cdr 1/7/95. Retd ENG 10/4/98.
DOYLE A. J. R., AFC. Born 17/1/34. Commd 19/12/58. Sqn Ldr 1/7/68. Retd GD 19/1/73.
DOYLE B. J. Born 27/4/44. Commd 17/12/64. Flt Lt 17/6/67. Retd GD 1/1/76.
DOYLE B. M., OBE. Born 10/10/40. Commd 29/11/63. Wg Cdr 1/7/84. Retd GD 26/12/95.
DOYLE J. F. Born 21/4/35. Commd 3/2/63. Sqn Ldr 26/8/64. Retd MED 1/2/72.
DOYLE K. Born 2/5/51. Commd 7/11/91. Fg Offr 7/11/91. Retd ENG 2/4/93.
DOYLE L. Born 23/11/65. Commd 28/9/89. Flt Lt 19/1/94. Retd SUP 14/3/96.
DOYLE P. E. Born 3/6/24. Commd 17/6/54. Sqn Ldr 1/7/73. Retd GD 2/4/80.
DOYLE-DAVIDSON M. J. S., MIMgt. Born 16/1/38. Commd 1/4/58. Gp Capt 1/1/92. Retd GD 16/1/93.
DRABBLE J. E. L. Born 14/3/01. Commd 21/12/20. Flt Lt 1/7/28. Retd GD 14/12/32.
DRABBLE K. W. Born 11/3/18. Commd 20/12/43. Sqn Ldr 1/1/58. Retd ENG 11/3/73.
DRAGE F. L. G. Born 17/1/24. Commd 8/9/44. Sqn Ldr 1/7/58. Retd GD 17/1/84.
DRAKE B., DSO DFC*. Born 20/12/17. Commd 7/9/36. Wg Cdr 1/1/53. Retd GD 1/7/63 rtg Gp Capt.
DRAKE B. R. Born 5/9/40. Commd 9/10/64. Sqn Ldr 1/7/73. Retd GD 30/9/82.
DRAKE D. A. Born 1/9/47. Commd 7/7/67. Flt Lt 7/1/73. Retd GD 30/9/75.
DRAKE D. R. Born 8/5/44. Commd 22/2/63. Flt Lt 12/11/69. Retd GD 8/5/82.
DRAKE E. L. D., DFC* AFC. Born 10/10/20. Commd 27/3/42. Wg Cdr 1/7/58. Retd GD 16/7/66.
DRAKE H. Born 8/2/35. Commd 31/12/52. Flt Lt 5/11/58. Retd GD 8/2/73.
DRAKE P. H., MB BS MRCS LRCP MRCOG. Born 21/6/25. Commd 1/6/58. Gp Capt 1/7/74. Retd MED 4/8/77.
DRAKE R. J. Born 9/2/22. Commd 22/2/67. Flt Lt 22/9/70. Retd ENG 9/2/82.
DRAKE W. M. Born 25/10/25. Commd 29/3/45. Sqn Ldr 1/1/60. Retd GD 28/1/77.

DRANE S. A. Born 2/4/24. Commd 1/4/52. Wg Cdr 1/1/72. Retd ADMIN 1/4/77.
DRAPER A. B. Born 14/3/39. Commd 23/12/60. Flt Lt 23/6/66. Retd GD 5/4/84.
DRAPER A. R. Born 3/12/28. Commd 2/3/49. Flt Lt 9/9/60. Retd SUP 3/12/66.
DRAPER E. E. J. Born 18/4/42. Commd 5/1/70. Sqn Ldr 1/1/81. Retd ENG 17/4/93.
DRAPER W. J. B. P. Born 21/2/38. Commd 28/2/56. Flt Lt 15/2/65. Retd GD 11/12/72.
DRAYTON D. L. J. A. Born 8/7/30. Commd 22/7/66. Fg Offr 22/7/66. Retd SUP 8/9/68.
DREA T. A. F. Born 31/7/19. Commd 6/6/57. Flt Lt 1/4/63. Retd ENG 17/12/67.
DREVER T. A. Born 3/6/16. Commd 23/1/45. Flt Lt 23/7/48. Retd GD 13/1/53.
DREW C. D. Born 1/6/36. Commd 30/7/57. Flt Lt 30/7/62. Retd SEC 1/6/74.
DREW C. D. Born 6/11/49. Commd 1/12/77. Sqn Ldr 1/7/87. Retd ENG 1/7/90.
DREW F. R., CBE. Born 2/5/09. Commd 27/7/29. Gp Capt 1/7/47. Retd GD 1/6/57.
DREW G., BA MIMgt. Born 25/10/31. Commd 14/7/55. Sqn Ldr 17/2/65. Retd EDN 14/7/71.
DREW H. A. W., AFC FIMgt. Born 17/11/38. Commd 2/5/59. Gp Capt 1/1/87. Retd GD 20/4/90.
DREW J. K. Born 15/3/36. Commd 4/5/59. Flt Lt 28/6/64. Retd GD 4/5/75.
DREW J. M. Born 6/11/22. Commd 23/6/60. Flt Lt 23/6/63. Retd GD 6/11/73.
DREWERY C. C. Born 28/2/63. Commd 13/8/82. Sqn Ldr 1/1/94. Retd GD 28/5/01.
DREWITT B., MA CEng MRAeS. Born 9/12/40. Commd 30/9/59. Sqn Ldr 1/1/73. Retd ENG 9/5/81.
DRING B. N. Born 31/7/37. Commd 8/10/79. Sqn Ldr 5/10/78. Retd GD 6/10/87.
DRING C. A. Born 29/7/50. Commd 19/3/81. Flt Lt 19/3/83. Retd OPS SPT 16/9/00.
DRING G. Born 23/6/12. Commd 1/5/41. Flt Lt 4/1/51. Retd SUP 23/10/61 rtg Sqn Ldr.
DRINKELL W. G., DFC AFC. Born 23/11/21. Commd 26/4/43. Sqn Ldr 1/10/54. Retd GD 20/4/68.
DRINKWATER E. Born 18/7/32. Commd 6/12/51. Flt Lt 13/11/57. Retd GD 18/7/90.
DRINKWATER R. Born 8/2/36. Commd 6/4/72. Flt Lt 6/4/77. Retd ADMIN 1/10/77.
DRISCOLL G. P., BSc. Born 15/7/54. Commd 17/9/72. Sqn Ldr 1/7/84. Retd ENG 18/9/92.
DRISSELL P., BA. Born 2/5/57. Commd 28/9/80. Sqn Ldr 1/1/87. Retd ADMIN 14/3/96.
DRIVER A. C. Born 2/7/16. Commd 17/10/42. Fg Offr 28/12/49. Retd GD 1/3/51 rtg Flt Lt.
DRIVER D. F. Born 22/7/30. Commd 2/7/52. Flt Lt 8/1/58. Retd GD 29/8/64.
DRIVER J. W., DFC. Born 21/1/12. Commd 6/7/44. Flt Lt 6/7/50. Retd GD(G) 29/1/62.
DRIVER K. C. Born 14/5/30. Commd 11/11/65. Wg Cdr 1/7/84. Retd ENG 14/5/88.
DRIVER R. E. A. Born 26/1/24. Commd 22/3/51. Flt Lt 14/11/56. Retd GD 26/1/82.
DRIVER V. R., BA. Born 15/10/41. Commd 3/10/74. Sqn Ldr 1/7/81. Retd ENG 8/1/96.
DRIVER W. F. Born 29/6/10. Commd 22/5/43. Flt Lt 20/11/46. Retd ENG 30/5/50.
DROWN R. W. Born 6/11/21. Commd 6/5/44. Sqn Ldr 1/7/73. Retd GD 6/11/76. Re-instated 29/12/76 to 4/12/82.
DRU DRURY S. G., MBE CEng MIEE. Born 29/4/39. Commd 24/9/59. Gp Capt 1/1/87. Retd ENG 29/4/94.
DRUMMOND G. K. Born 11/8/34. Commd 10/10/63. Flt Lt 10/10/69. Retd GD 26/10/74.
DRUMMOND J. A., BSc AMBCS. Born 2/6/42. Commd 19/8/68. Wg Cdr 1/1/88. Retd ADMIN 2/10/90.
DRUMMOND J. M. Born 16/5/33. Commd 15/12/53. Flt Lt 15/12/58. Retd SEC 27/1/68.
DRUMMOND-HAY P. D. F. Born 28/8/21. Commd 19/8/44. Sqn Ldr 1/1/61. Retd GD(G) 28/9/70.
DRUREY S. J. Born 25/12/58. Commd 28/6/79. Sqn Ldr 1/1/95. Retd GD 1/1/98.
DRURY K. A., DFM. Born 9/6/23. Commd 12/5/44. Sqn Ldr 1/7/73. Retd GD 9/6/83.
DRURY R. G., BSc. Born 26/2/54. Commd 17/9/72. Flt Lt 15/10/78. Retd ENG 15/7/87.
DRYBURGH G. D. Born 6/5/46. Commd 11/10/84. Flt Lt 11/10/88. Retd ENG 2/4/99.
DRYBURGH J. Born 15/12/25. Commd 6/1/55. Flt Lt 22/1/62. Retd GD 20/7/68.
DRYBURGH J. J. Born 27/1/32. Commd 1/2/62. Sqn Ldr 1/7/73. Retd ENG 7/10/83.
DRYDEN D. W., MIMgt. Born 1/2/48. Commd 2/6/67. Sqn Ldr 1/1/81. Retd GD(G) 2/6/94.
DRYDEN W. E. Born 4/12/41. Commd 31/8/78. Sqn Ldr 1/1/90. Retd SY 11/7/94.
DRYLAND G. N. Born 12/12/44. Commd 15/7/66. Flt Lt 15/1/69. Retd GD 30/4/76.
DRYSDALE J. D., CBE FIMgt. Born 1/8/33. Commd 1/9/54. Gp Capt 1/7/80. Retd GD 1/11/87.
DRYSDALE P. A. Born 20/4/27. Commd 14/11/51. Flt Lt 14/5/56. Retd GD 20/4/70.
DRYSDALE S. C. Y. Born 1/12/28. Commd 2/1/52. Flt Lt 2/10/57. Retd GD 1/6/67.
du BOULAY F. H., CBE DFC. Born 1/1/13. Commd 17/12/32. Wg Cdr 1/6/41. Retd GD 3/6/46 rtg Gp Capt.
DU FEU D. F. Born 7/5/30. Commd 8/11/51. Flt Lt 23/2/57. Retd GD 7/6/68.
DU PLESSIS R. P. Born 22/3/30. Commd 2/7/52. Sqn Ldr 1/7/66. Retd GD 1/7/69.
DUBIENIEC A. P. Born 2/6/56. Commd 28/2/80. Flt Lt 15/4/84. Retd ADMIN 2/6/94.
DUBOCK R. M., OBE AFC. Born 20/10/22. Commd 29/1/43. Wg Cdr 1/1/69. Retd GD 30/4/77.
DUCKENFIELD B. L., AFC. Born 15/4/17. Commd 1/4/40. Gp Capt 1/1/66. Retd GD 28/6/69.
DUCKER M. G. Born 22/6/53. Commd 27/7/72. Flt Lt 27/1/78. Retd GD 1/9/79.
DUCKETT E. T. Born 1/6/21. Commd 29/6/44. Wg Cdr 1/7/71. Retd SEC 1/6/74.
DUCKETT R. B., CVO AFC. Born 5/6/42. Commd 30/7/63. A Cdre 1/7/88. Retd GD 4/5/96.
DUCKHAM J. L., BSc. Born 3/7/51. Commd 26/9/69. Sqn Ldr 1/7/87. Retd GD 1/7/90.
DUCKMANTON G. R. Born 24/5/46. Commd 24/4/70. Sqn Ldr 1/7/84. Retd SUP 16/7/94.
DUCKWORTH C., CEng MRAeS MIMgt. Born 8/9/20. Commd 3/8/50. Sqn Ldr 1/1/60. Retd ENG 8/9/70.
DUCKWORTH D. J., MIMgt. Born 28/1/44. Commd 5/5/69. Sqn Ldr 1/1/81. Retd ADMIN 11/1/96.
DUCKWORTH P., MBE. Born 26/6/38. Commd 22/2/63. Sqr Ldr 1/7/73. Retd GD 3/7/84.
DUDDY J. Born 4/11/42. Commd 4/7/85. Sqn Ldr 27/6/93. Retd MED(T) 24/4/96.
DUDGEON A. G., CBE DFC. Born 6/2/16. Commd 14/12/35. A Cdre 1/1/62. Retd GD 6/4/68 rtg AVM.

DUDGEON M. G., OBE. Born 6/11/43. Commd 17/12/65. Wg Cdr 1/1/92. Retd GD 6/11/00.
DUDLEY E. E. Born 3/8/33. Commd 28/1/53. Flt Lt 17/6/58. Retd GD 3/8/71.
DUDLEY M. J. Born 29/9/58. Commd 13/12/79. Flt Lt 13/6/85. Retd GD 18/3/91.
DUDLEY P. T. McD. Born 25/3/27. Commd 14/11/51. Flt Lt 14/5/56. Retd GD 25/3/65.
DUDLEY T. H. Born 25/9/16. Commd 12/9/46. Flt Lt 27/5/54. Retd SUP 13/5/55.
DUFF I. R. Born 6/8/40. Commd 25/11/68. Sqn Ldr 1/1/81. Retd ADMIN 25/11/84.
DUFF L. Born 31/12/46. Commd 11/2/65. Wg Cdr 1/1/92. Retd ADMIN 31/8/96.
DUFF M. C. Born 14/2/34. Commd 8/1/57. Flt Lt 1/7/62. Retd GD 1/11/75.
DUFFIELD A. F. Born 29/2/20. Commd 27/12/43. Sqn Ldr 1/7/56. Retd GD 1/6/62.
DUFFILL G. E. Born 30/11/22. Commd 2/10/58. Flt Lt 2/10/64. Retd ENG 10/11/77.
DUFFIN P. A. R., BA BA MRIN MRAeS. Born 14/3/44. Commd 24/7/63. Wg Cdr 1/1/91. Retd GD 14/3/99.
DUFFIN S. V., BSc(Eng) CEng MRAeS ACGI. Born 29/9/46. Commd 22/9/65. Wg Cdr 1/7/85. Retd ENG 29/9/90.
DUFFUS J. C. Born 9/9/57. Commd 20/1/80. Sqn Ldr 1/7/90. Retd ADMIN 19/8/96.
DUFFY J., DFM. Born 25/9/21. Commd 4/6/44. Sqn Ldr 1/7/58. Retd GD(G) 25/9/76.
DUFFY M. G., MMar. Born 27/6/39. Commd 28/2/66. Sqn Ldr 1/7/75. Retd MAR 28/2/82.
DUFTON A., MCIPD MIMgt. Born 23/11/32. Commd 27/7/54. Wg Cdr 1/7/73. Retd ADMIN 29/1/77.
DUFTON H., FIMgt MCIPS. Born 16/11/21. Commd 16/1/50. Gp Capt 1/7/70. Retd SUP 16/11/76.
DUGDALE A. Born 27/11/17. Commd 5/3/53. Flt Lt 12/8/58. Retd ENG 31/8/68.
DUGDALE A. T., DFC. Born 27/6/22. Commd 22/6/44. Flt Lt 22/12/47. Retd GD 31/12/61.
DUGDALE J. A. Born 7/10/09. Commd 7/10/43. Flt Lt 7/4/47. Retd ENG 31/10/53.
DUGDALE K. R., MSc BSc ARCS. Born 15/9/46. Commd 13/9/70. Sqn Ldr 13/3/77. Retd ADMIN 13/9/86.
DUGDALE M. R., MB ChB MRCS LRCP DRCOG. Born 28/7/49. Commd 16/4/72. Wg Cdr 14/9/86. Retd MED 14/10/88.
DUGGAN C. E. Born 30/5/64. Commd 7/11/91. Flt Lt 7/11/93. Retd SUP 2/12/96.
DUGGAN G. H. Born 9/1/30. Commd 7/12/56. Sqn Ldr 1/7/67. Retd CAT 3/8/69.
DUGGAN T. E. Born 1/5/47. Commd 28/2/69. Sqn Ldr 1/7/81. Retd GD 1/6/98.
DUGUID A. G., MA. Born 14/1/25. Commd 12/7/50. Gp Capt 1/1/76. Retd ADMIN 14/1/80.
DUGUID M. D., MA MIMgt. Born 18/4/47. Commd 24/9/67. Wg Cdr 1/1/88. Retd SUP 19/2/97.
DUKE P. M. Born 29/5/43. Commd 6/7/62. Flt Lt 6/1/68. Retd GD 1/1/73.
DUKE R. C. E. Born 23/9/32. Commd 4/7/51. Flt Lt 22/5/57. Retd GD 23/9/77. Re-instated 8/4/81. Retd 8/5/87.
DULAKE E. A. Born 1/10/57. Commd 3/5/81. Sqn Ldr 1/1/91. Retd ADMIN 5/7/91.
DULAKE I. G. L. Born 9/7/47. Commd 2/1/77. Sqn Ldr 1/1/88. Retd ADMIN 2/1/93.
DULSON P. P. Born 8/2/48. Commd 14/8/70. Flt Lt 14/8/75. Retd GD 31/3/86.
DULY S. V., MBE. Born 23/8/38. Commd 5/12/63. Sqn Ldr 1/7/74. Retd SUP 23/8/93.
DUMMER F. G., CEng MRAeS MIMgt. Born 17/7/19. Commd 15/4/43. Wg Cdr 1/7/59. Retd ENG 17/7/74.
DUMMER P. J., BA. Born 30/10/38. Commd 28/9/60. Sqn Ldr 1/7/73. Retd GD 10/10/97.
DUNBAR R. C., DFM MIMgt MCIPD. Born 7/10/21. Commd 20/11/42. Wg Cdr 1/7/68. Retd SEC 15/4/72.
DUNCALF R. J. Born 3/1/56. Commd 27/1/77. Flt Lt 27/7/82. Retd GD 1/10/97.
DUNCAN A., BSc DCAe CEng MIEE. Born 31/1/34. Commd 2/4/59. Sqn Ldr 11/10/65. Retd ENG 24/4/75.
DUNCAN B. C. Born 4/7/60. Commd 20/12/90. Flt Lt 20/12/92. Retd ENG 20/12/98.
DUNCAN D. Born 23/7/22. Commd 27/2/58. Flt Lt 27/2/61. Retd ENG 23/7/77.
DUNCAN D., MSc CEng MRAeS. Born 27/10/22. Commd 26/8/43. Wg Cdr 1/7/63. Retd ENG 27/10/77.
DUNCAN E. C. D., BSc CEng MRAeS. Born 2/10/62. Commd 2/8/85. Flt Lt 15/3/90. Retd ENG 2/10/00.
DUNCAN G. Born 20/6/60. Commd 8/5/86. Flt Lt 16/2/89. Retd GD 31/8/98.
DUNCAN G. D. Born 18/8/32. Commd 26/12/51. Sqn Ldr 1/1/80. Retd GD 18/8/93.
DUNCAN H. K. A., BSc. Born 29/6/65. Commd 3/1/88. Sqn Ldr 1/7/94. Retd ADMIN 2/3/97.
DUNCAN I. B. Born 28/1/32. Commd 30/1/52. Flt Lt 30/10/57. Retd GD 25/8/70.
DUNCAN J. C. Born 26/8/28. Commd 21/3/51. Wg Cdr 1/7/75. Retd GD 8/5/81.
DUNCAN M. J. Born 21/1/60. Commd 26/11/81. Flt Lt 26/5/88. Retd ADMIN 19/1/96.
DUNCAN P. J. Born 30/9/51. Commd 9/3/72. Sqn Ldr 1/7/87. Retd GD 30/9/90.
DUNCAN R. Born 1/1/31. Commd 17/5/51. Flt Lt 6/9/56. Retd GD 1/1/69.
DUNCAN R. F. Born 2/8/30. Commd 31/3/60. Flt Lt 31/3/66. Retd GD 28/9/76.
DUNCAN R. J. Born 3/12/45. Commd 6/5/66. Flt Lt 6/11/71. Retd GD 13/1/76.
DUNCAN R. P., BSc. Born 28/1/42. Commd 24/1/66. Flt Lt 24/10/67. Retd GD 24/1/82.
DUNCAN T. F. Born 27/6/21. Commd 2/3/45. Flt Lt 2/9/48. Retd GD 28/11/55.
DUNCAN W. Born 19/12/35. Commd 6/9/68. Flt Lt 6/3/71. Retd GD 18/9/76.
DUNCOMBE D. J., BA. Born 23/6/35. Commd 10/9/63. Sqn Ldr 27/2/66. Retd EDN 31/8/72.
DUNCOMBE J. J., AFC. Born 13/6/23. Commd 29/10/45. Wg Cdr 1/1/63. Retd GD 28/2/78.
DUNCOMBE R. A. Born 23/4/21. Commd 27/10/43. Flt Lt 25/1/46. Retd GD 31/8/54.
DUNCOMBE R. F. Born 30/6/20. Commd 15/11/48. Sqn Ldr 1/1/52. Retd RGT 1/11/61.
DUNDAS H. S. L., DSO* DFC. Born 22/7/20. Commd 1/12/42. Wg Cdr 1/5/45. Retd GD 25/1/47 rtg Gp Capt.
DUNFORD B. E., MBE. Born 60/11/40. Commd 26/5/67. Wg Cdr 1/7/91. Retd GD 30/11/95.
DUNGATE J., MBE AFM. Born 17/7/40. Commd 14/8/70. Sqn Ldr 1/1/87. Retd GD 17/7/95.
DUNKLEY P. A. Born 21/2/61. Commd 23/10/86. Flt Lt 23/10/88. Retd GD 25/4/00.
DUNKLEY R. L., MBE. Born 25/8/22. Commd 26/7/44. Sqn Ldr 1/4/56. Retd GD 25/8/65.
DUNLEAVY B. T., MBE. Born 22/6/51. Commd 23/4/87. Sqn Ldr 1/1/95. Retd ADMIN 1/1/99.

DUNLOP J. G., MA. Born 11/8/27. Commd 5/11/52. Sqn Ldr 5/5/63. Retd EDN 5/11/68.
DUNLOP J. S., BSc. Born 22/1/56. Commd 8/1/89. Flt Lt 8/7/92. Retd ADMIN 14/9/96.
DUNLOP K. E., MBE. Born 20/7/46. Commd 19/8/71. Sqn Ldr 1/1/82. Retd GD(G) 5/4/88.
DUNLOP P., AFC*. Born 14/12/48. Commd 4/2/71. Wg Cdr 1/7/86. Retd GD 14/10/90.
DUNN A., MBE BSc. Born 15/6/23. Commd 19/12/42. Wg Cdr 1/1/65. Retd GD 31/3/78.
DUNN A. P. Born 15/12/23. Commd 16/6/44. Sqn Ldr 1/1/56. Retd GD 31/3/62.
DUNN D. J., BA. Born 1/3/47. Commd 31/8/78. Sqn Ldr 1/7/85. Retd ADMIN 1/7/88.
DUNN Sir Eric, KBE CB BEM CEng MRAeS. Born 27/11/27. Commd 12/2/53. AM 1/7/83. Retd ENG 1/7/86.
DUNN E. H. Born 1/11/45. Commd 23/9/66. Wg Cdr 1/1/91. Retd GD 14/3/96.
DUNN G. A., BSc. Born 7/8/43. Commd 14/9/64. Sqn Ldr 1/7/74. Retd GD 15/9/94.
DUNN I., BDS LDSRCS. Born 18/3/41. Commd 26/2/78. Wg Cdr 29/9/80. Retd DEL 1/4/89.
DUNN I. L., LLB. Born 5/6/20. Commd 11/6/42. Wg Cdr 1/1/60. Retd GD 23/12/64.
DUNN J. C. Born 28/6/31. Commd 17/12/52. Gp Capt 1/7/85. Retd GD 21/9/86.
DUNN J. H., BSc. Born 1/10/52. Commd 25/9/71. Flt Lt 15/4/77. Retd GD 1/10/90.
DUNN J. R. Born 10/5/61. Commd 15/6/83. Sqn Ldr 1/1/95. Retd OPS SPT 10/5/99.
DUNN J. S. Born 13/7/42. Commd 28/9/62. Flt Lt 28/3/68. Retd GD 13/11/80.
DUNN M. Born 2/3/43. Commd 21/12/62. Sqn Ldr 1/7/79. Retd GD(G) 2/3/84. Re-entered 17/4/89. Sqn Ldr 1/7/93. Retd OPS SPT 17/4/99.
DUNN M. Born 7/12/37. Commd 27/5/71. Sqn Ldr 1/1/90. Retd GD 1/6/92.
DUNN M. J. Born 7/12/41. Commd 8/11/70. Flt Lt 30/11/78. Retd SUP 7/1/84.
DUNN Sir Patrick, KBE CB DFC. Born 31/12/12. Commd 3/3/33. AM 1/1/65. Retd GD 1/3/67.
DUNN R. A. E. Born 12/10/32. Commd 27/9/51. Sqn Ldr 1/7/78. Retd GD 3/4/85.
DUNN R. E. L. Born 3/5/36. Commd 28/5/66. Flt Lt 1/7/68. Retd PI 28/5/74.
DUNN S. F. Born 14/8/17. Commd 18/11/53. Flt Lt 18/11/58. Retd GD(G) 9/3/66.
DUNN T. U., MRAeS. Born 22/11/12. Commd 9/8/40. Wg Cdr 1/1/59. Retd ENG 7/12/67.
DUNN W. A. Born 13/1/43. Commd 6/4/62. Flt Lt 29/6/69. Retd GD(G) 1/1/74.
DUNN W. H. Born 21/10/30. Commd 6/6/57. Sqn Ldr 1/1/69. Retd GD 1/11/80.
DUNNACHIE D. J. Born 1/3/33. Commd 7/7/66. Sqn Ldr 1/1/85. Retd GD 1/6/91.
DUNNE J. Born 23/1/23. Commd 7/9/61. Flt Lt 7/9/66. Retd GD(G) 1/7/76.
DUNNE J. M. Born 21/10/33. Commd 31/10/63. Sqn Ldr 1/7/79. Retd ENG 18/2/85.
DUNNE P. F. Born 12/2/36. Commd 9/10/75. Sqn Ldr 1/7/87. Retd SUP 12/4/90.
DUNNE T. E. M., MIMgt. Born 21/6/25. Commd 14/10/44. Wg Cdr 1/7/66. Retd GD 21/6/80.
DUNNE W. Born 24/6/06. Commd 23/12/48. Fg Offr 23/12/48. Retd SUP 25/4/51.
DUNNETT J. B. Born 25/12/19. Commd 28/5/42. Flt Lt 15/10/51. Retd GD(G) 30/4/66.
DUNNETT E. W. Born 18/1/26. Commd 10/10/63. Flt Lt 10/10/68. Retd SEC 1/2/69.
DUNNETT N. A. W., CEng MIMechE MRAeS. Born 15/10/39. Commd 28/4/64. Sqn Ldr 1/7/72. Retd ENG 28/4/82.
DUNNING A., DFC. Born 2/2/13. Commd 9/8/41. Sqn Ldr 1/7/53. Retd PRT 26/3/55.
DUNNINGHAM N. J. J. Born 4/1/23. Commd 14/8/43. Sqn Ldr 1/7/64. Retd GD 28/8/74.
DUNNINGTON N., FIMgt. Born 12/2/38. Commd 5/7/68. Wg Cdr 1/1/81. Retd ADMIN 2/10/85.
DUNPHY D. G., CEng MIMechE MRAeS MIMgt. Born 11/7/18. Commd 22/10/41. Wg Cdr 1/7/58. Retd ENG 15/4/67.
DUNSCOMBE F. L. Born 26/10/23. Commd 10/3/44. Sqn Ldr 1/1/62. Retd GD(G) 30/4/66.
DUNSFORD E. C., BEM MIMgt. Born 20/10/31. Commd 19/12/63. Sqn Ldr 1/1/75. Retd GD(AEO) 20/10/89.
DUNSMORE M. Born 23/5/37. Commd 22/10/59. Sqn Ldr 1/7/69. Retd GD 14/5/71.
DUNSMUIR D. B., DPhysEd. Born 5/3/49. Commd 13/9/70. Sqn Ldr 1/1/87. Retd ADMIN 1/1/93.
DUNSTAN P. N. Born 16/4/37. Commd 31/10/63. Sqn Ldr 1/1/73. Retd GD 17/4/87.
DUNSTONE D. J. Born 12/4/33. Commd 8/5/53. Flt Lt 1/3/61. Retd GD 29/9/70.
DUNTON D. B. Born 13/11/45. Commd 25/6/66. Sqn Ldr 1/7/77. Retd GD 13/11/83.
DUNWOODIE A. Born 24/2/42. Commd 16/9/76. Flt Lt 16/9/77. Retd ADMIN 16/9/84.
DUNWOODIE J. S. Born 28/6/34. Commd 8/5/53. Flt Lt 18/4/67. Retd GD 10/3/71.
DUPENOIS N. G., Sol. Born 29/4/47. Commd 1/3/71. Flt Lt 1/3/71. Retd LGL 1/3/73.
DUPERE J. G., MB BS. Born 28/8/42. Commd 6/4/64. Flt Lt 10/7/68. Retd MED 10/7/73.
DUPRE R. A. C. Born 26/5/19. Commd 17/9/43. Sqn Ldr 1/10/57. Retd SEC 29/5/67.
DURACK C. B. Born 11/7/41. Commd 6/11/80. Sqn Ldr 1/1/92. Retd ENG 11/7/96.
DURAND B. E. Born 2/9/37. Commd 6/8/60. Wg Cdr 1/1/84. Retd GD 2/9/92.
DURANT-LEWIS J. A., MSc BSc CEng MRAeS MIMgt. Born 8/7/45. Commd 28/9/64. Sqn Ldr 1/7/75. Retd ENG 8/7/83.
DURBIDGE K., DFC DFM. Born 1/6/21. Commd 28/2/43. Sqn Ldr 1/4/55. Retd GD 1/6/64.
DURBIN W. Born 10/2/44. Commd 15/10/81. Flt Lt 15/10/86. Retd ENG 6/5/93.
DURBRIDGE C. J. Born 19/1/50. Commd 29/8/72. Flt Lt 1/3/78. Retd GD 19/1/91.
DURHAM A. ST J. L. Born 2/2/52. Commd 15/2/73. Sqn Ldr 1/7/89. Retd ADMIN 1/7/92.
DURHAM E. Born 29/12/35. Commd 21/4/54. Gp Capt 1/1/87. Retd GD 17/7/89.
DURHAM M. W., MSc BSc DIC. Born 19/10/54. Commd 30/8/78. Flt Lt 30/11/79. Retd GD 1/1/95.
DURHAM W., BTech. Born 21/6/49. Commd 1/11/71. Flt Lt 1/8/72. Retd GD 3/12/92.
DURKIN G. E. Born 26/2/38. Commd 17/1/69. Flt Lt 17/1/71. Retd ENG 17/1/77.

DURKIN P. Born 7/9/42. Commd 19/8/71. Flt Lt 20/7/75. Retd GD(G) 19/12/82. Re-entered 30/11/87. Flt Lt 1/7/80. Retd OPS SPT 7/9/98.
DURKIN Sir Herbert, KBE CB MA CEng FIEE FRAeS FIMgt. Born 31/3/22. Commd 24/10/41. AM 1/7/76. Retd ENG 1/7/78.
DURLING A. M. Born 9/9/16. Commd 26/4/45. Sqn Ldr 1/10/56. Retd SEC 3/4/69.
DURLING D. F. Born 16/4/34. Commd 24/9/52. Flt Lt 14/5/58. Retd GD(G) 16/4/72. Reinstated 26/10/79. Flt Lt 23/11/65. Retd GD(G) 17/5/88.
DURLING D. H. Born 11/12/21. Commd 5/3/43. Flt Lt 5/9/46. Retd GD 11/12/64.
DURMAN P. M. Born 22/10/19. Commd 20/4/44. Wg Cdr 1/7/67. Retd ENG 3/5/74.
DURN I. P., MSc BSc CEng MIEE. Born 20/10/48. Commd 26/2/71. Sqn Ldr 1/1/80. Retd ENG 1/1/91.
DURNAN C. J. Born 9/6/44. Commd 12/9/63. Flt Lt 12/12/69. Retd SEC 29/9/73.
DURNFORD A. C. Born 21/6/51. Commd 27/3/70. Flt Lt 27/9/75. Retd GD 22/1/85.
DURNFORD H. T. M., MIMgt. Born 2/9/33. Commd 10/4/56. Sqn Ldr 1/1/70. Retd SUP 30/9/84.
DUROSE C. G., MSc BSc MIMgt. Born 16/3/44. Commd 8/9/69. Sqn Ldr 8/3/75. Retd ADMIN 8/9/85.
DURRANT C. Born 17/3/28. Commd 11/10/51. Sqn Ldr 1/1/65. Retd GD 28/5/76.
DURRANT D. B. Born 25/5/28. Commd 1/8/51. Flt Lt 1/2/54. Retd GD 25/5/66.
DURRANT F. J., MBE. Born 1/1/21. Commd 26/9/57. Sqn Ldr 1/7/66. Retd ENG 1/1/75.
DURRANT J. H. Born 30/7/24. Commd 19/12/63. Flt Lt 19/12/66. Retd SEC 31/10/72.
DURRANT P. J., BSc(Eng) CEng MIMechE MRAes. Born 26/10/43. Commd 22/9/63. Wg Cdr 1/7/78. Retd ENG 2/12/83.
DURSTON I. Born 27/9/46. Commd 21/7/65. Flt Lt 4/5/72. Retd GD 1/3/85.
DURSTON L. S. W., MBE. Born 5/10/19. Commd 20/6/46. Sqn Ldr 1/7/60. Retd ENG 30/5/70.
DUTHIE A. B., MA. Born 17/7/45. Commd 22/9/63. Flt Lt 15/10/68. Retd GD 17/7/83.
DUTTON A. D., BSc. Born 29/7/41. Commd 8/1/68. Sqn Ldr 1/7/78. Retd ENG 29/7/93.
DUTTON A.G.B., MB ChB FRCOG. Born 6/11/38. Commd 26/9/71. Gp Capt 1/10/88. Retd MED 6/11/92.
DUTTON F. R. Born 18/5/35. Commd 21/10/61. Sqn Ldr 1/1/74. Retd CAT 2/9/80.
DUTTON J. J., OBE. Born 13/4/18. Commd 23/1/40. Wg Cdr 1/1/55. Retd SUP 20/9/56.
DUTTON L. M., MSc BA MRIN MRAeS. Born 1/10/46. Commd 7/7/67. Wg Cdr 1/1/90. Retd GD 15/1/96.
DUTTON M. J. R. Born 13/8/35. Commd 1/7/53. Flt Lt 7/3/62. Retd GD 20/12/91.
DUTTON M. R. G. Born 15/7/49. Commd 14/8/70. Flt Lt 14/8/75. Retd GD 12/3/88.
DUVAL D. V. Born 27/9/36. Commd 30/7/57. Wg Cdr 1/7/74. Retd GD 27/10/89.
DWELLY J. F. Born 30/3/17. Commd 20/10/41. Flt Lt 1/9/45. Retd ENG 2/12/50.
DWYER M. W. Born 7/3/36. Commd 14/8/70. Sqn Ldr 1/7/80. Retd ENG 7/3/94.
DYCHE R., BSc CEng MRAeS MIEE MIMgt. Born 14/1/32. Commd 27/9/57. Wg Cdr 1/1/76. Retd ENG 2/5/78.
DYDE S. A. J. Born 19/2/60. Commd 28/2/80. Flt Lt 1/1/91. Retd GD 30/6/97.
DYE P. D., AFC BSc. Born 18/9/49. Commd 15/9/69. Sqn Ldr 1/1/85. Retd GD 1/1/88.
DYE R. M. Born 4/11/24. Commd 11/8/44. Sqn Ldr 1/1/56. Retd GD 4/11/67.
DYE R. P. Born 5/12/26. Commd 16/9/50. Sqn Ldr 1/7/72. Retd GD 5/12/82.
DYER B., BSc. Born 2/9/46. Commd 25/11/68. Sqn Ldr 25/5/78. Retd ADMIN 25/11/84.
DYER B. H. Born 18/11/44. Commd 29/11/63. Flt Lt 29/5/69. Retd GD 21/12/74.
DYER G. C., MBE BA FRIN MIMgt. Born 5/4/34. Commd 5/7/53. Wg Cdr 1/1/73. Retd GD 19/6/78.
DYER G. L. S., MA. Born 2/9/37. Commd 30/9/56. Flt Lt 15/10/62. Retd GD 2/9/75.
DYER H. W. Born 31/3/17. Commd 11/1/51. Sqn Ldr 1/7/62. Retd GD(G) 31/3/72.
DYER J. Born 21/5/45. Commd 24/6/71. Wg Cdr 1/7/89. Retd ADMIN 21/5/00.
DYER J. H., MA MIMgt. Born 28/4/23. Commd 23/10/42. Wg Cdr 1/1/68. Retd GD 1/8/75.
DYER J. T. F., BSc. Born 22/12/52. Commd 27/7/75. Flt Lt 27/10/76. Retd GD 29/9/84.
DYER N. R. Born 31/3/44. Commd 24/6/65. Flt Lt 24/12/67. Retd GD 5/7/74.
DYER P. C., MIMgt. Born 22/3/38. Commd 3/12/62. Flt Lt 14/2/66. Retd GD(G) 22/3/93.
DYER R. A., BSc CEng. Born 14/6/49. Commd 16/9/73. Flt Lt 30/11/76. Retd ENG 14/6/87.
DYKE Rev. K. A. Born 27/7/30. Commd 3/10/66. Retd 3/10/82. Wg Cdr.
DYKES P. H. Born 5/11/26. Commd 30/7/59. Flt Lt 16/9/64. Retd ENG 5/11/81.
DYMOND F. E. Born 6/3/20. Commd 16/1/42. Sqn Ldr 1/10/54. Retd GD 6.3.69.
DYMOND J. N. Born 20/12/32. Commd 6/4/54. Flt Lt 22/5/57. Retd GD 20/12/70.
DYNES D. R. Born 7/5/39. Commd 29/4/71. Flt Lt 29/4/73. Retd SEC 29/4/79.
DYSON C. J. F. Born 18/6/38. Commd 9/9/59. Flt Lt 19/3/70. Retd GD 18/6/76.
DYSON J. B. Born 19/11/45. Commd 28/10/66. Flt Lt 28/4/72. Retd GD 19/11/83.
DYSON K. F. Born 8/12/31. Commd 1/6/72. Flt Lt 1/6/74. Retd MED(SEC) 30/9/87.
DYSON M. L., MRCS LRCP DMRT. Born 13/5/22. Commd 27/10/50. Sqn Ldr 27/1/55. Retd MED 26/2/60.
DYSON R. E., DFC. Born 3/9/21. Commd 8/8/42. Sqn Ldr 1/7/51. Retd GD 3/9/76 rtg Wg Cdr.
DYSON T. M. Born 20/1/35. Commd 13/1/56. Flt Lt 1/7/67. Retd GD 12/4/74.

# E

EACOPO M. J. Born 4/1/48. Commd 23/2/68. Sqn Ldr 1/1/91. Retd GD 14/3/96.
EADES G. O. Born 31/1/30. Commd 11/4/51. Wg Cdr 1/1/67. Retd GD 1/3/75.
EADES J. A. Born 15/3/30. Commd 22/6/50. Flt Offr 22/5/57. Retd SEC 23/6/58.
EADIE C. J., BL LLB FCIS. Born 18/9/34. Commd 25/4/58. Gp Capt 1/1/79. Retd LGL 26/12/89.
EADON W. R., MIMgt. Born 6/1/29. Commd 6/10/60. Sqn Ldr 1/1/74. Retd ENG 6/7/79.
EADY C. J., MSc BSc. Born 5/2/63. Commd 2/9/84. Sqn Ldr 1/1/97. Retd ENG 5/2/01.
EAGERS C. J. Born 7/10/46. Commd 31/10/74. Wg Cdr 1/7/89. Retd SUP 14/9/96.
EAGLES T. W. Born 23/3/44. Commd 9/3/72. Flt Lt 7/2/75. Retd GD(G) 23/3/94.
EAMES P. F. Born 23/4/16. Commd 31/5/38. Sqn Ldr 1/8/47. Retd GD 1/11/57.
EARL A. C. Born 29/12/63. Commd 20/10/83. Flt Lt 20/4/90. Retd GD(G) 1/10/90.
EARL D. L. T. Born 18/3/43. Commd 17/12/63. Wg Cdr 1/1/84. Retd GD 1/10/88.
EARLAND J. M. Born 23/9/22. Commd 27/3/43. Flt Lt 10/9/47. Retd GD 31/3/62.
EARLE B.P. Born 16/5/31. Commd 5/5/51. Gp Capt 1/1/76. Retd GD 17/4/86.
EARLE D. J. Born 30/8/45. Commd 15/7/66. Sqn Ldr 1/7/75. Retd ENG 31/12/77.
EARLE-WELBY G. R., MA. Born 14/8/21. Commd 10/10/49. Sqn Ldr 14/8/55. Retd EDN 14/9/68.
EARLY V. G., BSc. Born 16/2/34. Commd 8/2/57. Sqn Ldr 9/1/67. Retd ADMIN 16/2/89.
EARNSHAW C. W., DFC. Born 7/3/23. Commd 13/3/44. Flt Lt 13/9/47. Retd ENG 11/3/53.
EARNSHAW E., OBE AMInstMunE. Born 12/10/12. Commd 11/7/41. Gp Capt 1/1/63. Retd ACB 16/10/67.
EARNSHAW P. T. Born 17/11/49. Commd 13/6/74. Flt Lt 13/12/79. Retd GD 25/2/90.
EARP D. A. Born 21/5/51. Commd 14/8/70. Sqn Ldr 1/1/88. Retd GD 1/1/91.
EARP J. R. Born 16/8/47. Commd 7/1/71. Flt Lt 1/4/74. Retd GD 6/1/76.
EASBY M, BSc. Born 2/5/40. Commd 27/10/62. Wg Cdr 1/7/85. Retd ADMIN 2/5/95.
EASEY J. A. Born 8/4/39. Commd 5/2/57. Sqn Ldr 1/7/84. Retd GD 9/4/88.
EASLEY M. J. Born 26/1/49. Commd 4/7/69. Flt Lt 4/1/75. Retd GD 26/1/87.
EASON R. F. Born 10/8/35. Commd 1/6/72. Flt Lt 1/6/74. Retd MED(SEC) 2/10/76.
EAST A., BSc. Born 22/10/59. Commd 4/9/78. Flt Lt 15/10/82. Retd GD 1/10/99.
EAST A. C., AFC. Born 21/4/34. Commd 7/5/52. Flt Lt 2/10/57. Retd GD 31/12/72.
EAST D. R. Born 4/2/56. Commd 27/8/87. Flt Lt 27/8/89. Retd ADMIN 27/8/95.
EAST F. C., CEng MIEE. Born 26/1/42. Commd 9/3/66. Sqn Ldr 1/1/78. Retd ENG 1/1/81.
EAST M. J. Born 10/1/47. Commd 5/3/65. Wg Cdr 1/1/90. Retd GD 14/3/96.
EAST R. T. Born 23/10/17. Commd 15/11/50. Sqn Ldr 31/7/61. Retd EDN 1/9/65.
EASTER G. K. Born 26/3/18. Commd 18/8/45. Flt Lt 18/2/48. Retd GD 21/6/61.
EASTERBROOK R. L. Born 17/7/24. Commd 6/6/46. Gp Capt. 1/1/71. Retd GD 17/10/79.
EASTERBROOK T. Born 17/6/44. Commd 4/5/72. Flt Lt 4/11/76. Retd GD 27/10/81.
EASTERBROOK W. J. Born 14/8/20. Commd 15/11/51. Flt Lt 26/5/55. Retd GD 28/6/67.
EASTERLING G. G. Born 28/1/25. Commd 25/8/44. Flt Lt 13/3/51. Retd GD(G) 28/1/63.
EASTMEAD B. P. Born 5/7/29. Commd 13/12/50. Sqn Ldr 1/7/64. Retd SUP 13/9/67.
EASTMENT R. M., OBE MRAeS. Born 16/3/49. Commd 12/7/68. Wg Cdr 1/7/89. Retd GD 4/12/98.
EASTMOND D. H. Born 20/11/40. Commd 24/4/64. Sqn Ldr 1/1/75. Retd GD 3/2/80.
EASTON B. R. L., MA CEng FIMechE MRAeS. Born 14/6/34. Commd 25/9/54. A Cdre 1/7/80. Retd ENG 11/6/88.
EASTON I. F., CEng FRAeS FIMgt. Born 11/2/21. Commd 19/8/42. Gp Capt 1/7/70. Retd ENG 11/2/76.
EASTON J. H. Born 26/10/43. Commd 19/8/66. Wg Cdr 1/1/87. Retd GD 26/10/98.
EASTON S. J., BSc. Born 14/7/64. Commd 29/9/83. Flt Lt 15/1/88. Retd GD 15/7/97.
EASTWOOD D. Born 12/10/37. Commd 10/10/58. Sqn Ldr 6/10/71. Retd ADMIN 12/4/76.
EASTWOOD E. S., MA. Born 24/2/39. Commd 1/7/61. Wg Cdr 1/1/79. Retd GD 3/4/82.
EASTWOOD J. C. E. Born 16/4/41. Commd 25/1/63. Flt Lt 25/7/68. Retd GD 1/10/74.
EASTWOOD S. P. Born 10/1/60. Commd 29/1/87. Flt Lt 29/1/89. Retd GD(G) 14/3/96.
EASY C. A. Born 19/3/45. Commd 3/6/56. Flt Lt 25/7/72. Retd ADMIN 13/2/84.
EASY R. C. H. Born 1/10/20. Commd 30/5/45. Sqn Ldr 1/10/55. Retd GD 1/10/69.
EASY W. R., MB ChB DCH. Born 23/1/44. Commd 24/7/67. Wg Cdr 21/10/86. Retd MED 31/1/89.
EATON C. W., DFC*. Born 18/11/22. Commd 17/4/44. Flt Lt 17/10/47. Retd GD 18/11/65.
EATON K. A., MSc BDS MGDS RCS LDSRCS. Born 20/4/45. Commd 11/12/78. Wg Cdr 25/7/81. Retd DEL 29/4/90.
EATON K. C. Born 25/3/54. Commd 18/1/73. Sqn Ldr 1/7/87. Retd GD 25/3/92.
EATON N. G., MIMgt. Born 9/1/36. Commd 9/3/55. Sqn Ldr 1/7/66. Retd GD 9/1/74.
EATON S. J., DFC. Born 4/12/21. Commd 25/9/42. Wg Cdr 1/1/61. Retd GD 15/7/70.
EATON-SHORE J. H., CEng MRAeS MIMgt. Born 19/5/21. Commd 9/12/43. Wg Cdr 1/1/67. Retd ENG 19/5/76.
EATWELL E. E., FRIN. Born 11/8/31. Commd 26/11/69. Wg Cdr 1/1/80 Retd GD 11/8/86.
EAVES J. G. Born 21/10/29. Commd 16/7/52. Flt Lt 16/11/64. Retd GD(G) 16/11/72.
EBBAGE D. A. Born 1/9/42. Commd 25/3/64. Flt Lt 25/9/69. Retd GD 9/1/76.

ECCLES G. Born 16/4/16. Commd 28/10/43. Flt Lt 4/6/53. Retd SEC 1/3/69.
ECCLES H. H., MA MRAeS. Born 5/6/19. Commd 26/9/39. Gp Capt 1/1/60. Retd GD 10/7/64.
ECCLES J. V. R. Born 22/1/30. Commd 6/12/51. Wg Cdr 1/7/76. Retd ADMIN 1/10/80.
ECCLES R., AFC. Born 2/2/45. Commd 21/5/65. Sqn Ldr 1/1/82. Retd GD 1/1/85.
ECKEL A. M. Born 28/9/32. Commd 24/9/52. Flt Lt 21/2/58. Retd GD 28/9/70.
ECKERT P. M., BSc CEng MIEE MRAeS. Born 23/10/49. Commd 24/9/67. Sqn Ldr 1/7/83. Retd ENG 23/10/87.
EDDELL J. P., BSc. Born 6/10/49. Commd 7/12/75. Sqn Ldr 1/1/86. Retd ADMIN 7/12/91.
EDDY G. P. Born 24/5/23. Commd. 12/7/62. Flt Lt 12/7/67. Retd GD 24/5/78.
EDELSTEN P., MIMgt MCIPD. Born 23/5/23. Commd 5/9/42. Sqn Ldr 1/1/55. Retd GD 23/5/72.
EDEN D. F. E., MBE. Born 10/1/34. Commd 30/1/45. Sqn Ldr 1/1/67. Retd GD(G) 6/10/72.
EDEN F. R. Born 6/10/21. Commd 30/1/45. Sqn Ldr 1/1/67. Retd GD(G) 6/10/72.
EDEN N. C. Born 1/10/50. Commd 25/2/72. Flt Lt 25/2/74. Retd GD 1/10/88.
EDEN P. C. Born 11/7/28. Commd 15/12/47. Sqn Ldr 1/1/63. Retd GD 12/8/78.
EDENBROW G. R., MBE. Born 8/9/23. Commd 8/9/44. Wg Cdr 1/1/70. Retd PE 31/3/74.
EDENBROW R. A. O., BSc. Born 30/4/50. Commd 15/9/69. Flt Lt 15/12/73. Retd GD 14/3/97.
EDGAR C. H., MBE AE. Born 15/3/21. Commd 17/7/46. Sqn Ldr 1/7/72. Retd RGT 29/11/75.
EDGCUMBE G. D. T. Born 3/5/55. Commd 11/9/86. Sqn Ldr 1/7/96. Retd 14/4/00.
EDGE F. D., MBE. Born 16/3/19. Commd 4/5/50. Flt Lt 1/7/54. Retd PRT 30/6/62.
EDGE G. Born 28/9/57. Commd 9/12/76. Flt Lt 9/6/82. Retd GD 9/1/95.
EDGE P. M. Born 10/9/23. Commd 26/3/53. Sqn Ldr 1/1/73. Retd GD 10/4/78.
EDGELEY C. V. Born 2/7/40. Commd. 11/11/65. Flt Lt 7/6/68. Retd ENG 2/7/78.
EDGELL J. A. Born 10/4/54. Commd 30/4/81. Sqn Ldr 1/1/89. Retd SUP 10/9/92.
EDGERLEY A. G. Born 26/3/23. Commd 9/11/43. Sqn Ldr 1/7/60. Retd GD 26/3/78.
EDGINGTON J. F., FIMgt. Born 27/9/36. Commd 6/5/55. Gp Capt 1/1/78. Retd ADMIN 30/9/80.
EDINGTON D. J. Born 3/11/48. Commd 31/7/70. Flt Lt 31/1/76. Retd SUP 21/3/78.
EDINGTON J. A. Born 28/4/20. Commd 17/11/44. Flt Lt 17/5/48. Retd GD(G) 5/11/73.
EDKINS A. C. Born 31/12/46. Commd 21/3/74. Flt Lt 29/6/80. Retd OPS SPT 6/7/97.
EDKINS A. J. A., CEng MRAeS MIMgt. Born 4/12/38. Commd 17/7/62. Sqn Ldr 1/7/71. Retd ENG 17/7/78.
EDMONDS A. C. Born 21/8/42. Commd 9/8/79. Sqn Ldr 1/1/85. Retd ADMIN 21/8/94.
EDMONDS D. L., CVO AFC*. Born 13/11/23. Commd 21/6/44. G Capt 1/1/68. Retd GD 31/3/78.
EDMONDS K. R., FIMgt. Born 14/4/34. Commd 17/12/52. Gp Capt 1/7/84. Retd GD 14/4/89.
EDMONDS M. A. Born 16/3/36. Commd 7/12/54. Sqn Ldr 1/1/71. Retd GD 16/6/74.
EDMONDS P. J. Born 27/12/35. Commd 21/10/66. Flt Lt 21/10/68. Retd SEC 21/10/74.
EDMONDS R. J., DFM. Born 29/9/17. Commd 8/9/42. Wg Cdr 1/1/60. Retd ENG 30/6/65.
EDMONDS R. J. Born 18/2/11. Commd 24.4.41. Flt Lt 1/9/45. Retd ENG 8/12/49.
EDMONDSON C. S. Born 3/7/45. Commd 17/5/79. Sqn Ldr 1/1/86. Retd ENG 3/4/89.
EDMONDSON F. R., DFC. Born 12/9/21. Commd 6/4/47. Flt Lt 4/1/51. Retd GD 12/9/64.
EDMONDSON S., DFC. Born 6/4/21. Commd 1/11/43. Flt Lt 19/11/53. Retd GD 14/9/68.
EDMONDSON-JONES J. R. Born 23/1/28. Commd 14/12/49. Plt Offr 14/12/49. Retd GD 31/7/52.
EDMONSTON A. C. Born 31/3/62. Commd 30/4/81. Flt Lt 30/10/86. Retd GD 31/3/93.
EDMUND R. C. P., BSc CEng MIEE. Born 9/12/41. Commd 30/9/61. Sqn Ldr 1/7/73. Retd ENG 9/12/96.
EDMUNDS A. C. Born 23/9/35. Commd 30/7/57. Wg Cdr 1/1/85. Retd GD 23/9/93 .
EDMUNDS A. R. Born 22/12/35. Commd 16/9/55. Flt Lt 6/3/63. Retd GD 22/12/78.
EDMUNDS D. J., BA. Born 28/12/41. Commd 31/8/78. Sqn Ldr 1/1/89. Retd GD(G) 19/2/94.
EDMUNDSON M. Born 29/6/49. Commd 11/3/79. Flt Lt 11/3/88. Retd SY 31/5/95.
EDNEY P. A., BSc. Born 28/6/39. Commd 23/9/59. Sqn Ldr 8/4/73. Retd ADMIN 28/6/76.
EDSALL K. C., MB BS MRCS LRCP. Born 30/5/40. Commd 18/6/72. Wg Cdr 26/5/89. Retd MED 9/1/95.
EDWARD A. F., BA MCIPS MIMgt. Born 12/1/48. Commd 27/10/67. Sqn Ldr 1/1/80. Retd SUP 12/1/86.
EDWARDE J. D. Born 1/1/74. Commd 21/7/65. Flt Lt 21/1/73. Retd GD 21/3/77.
EDWARDS A., BSc. Born 22/10/60. Commd 16/9/79. Sqn Ldr 1/1/94. Retd GD 1/6/99.
EDWARDS A. E. Born 7/4/23. Commd 14/1/54. Sqn Ldr 1/1/71. Retd GD 23/2/78.
EDWARDS A. K., MBE. Born 1/4/21. Commd 13/8/44. Flt Lt 13/2/48. Retd GD 1/4/64.
EDWARDS A. W. Born 25/5/44. Commd 29/3/68. Flt Lt 4/5/72. Retd GD(G) 25/5/82. Reinstated 20/3/90. Flt Lt 20/3/84. Retd GD(G) 14/3/96.
EDWARDS B. Born 2/8/37. Commd 3/8/62. Flt Lt 1/4/71. Retd GD 2/8/75.
EDWARDS B. M. Born 26/12/47. Commd 13/5/73. Sqn Ldr 1/1/86. Retd ENG 1/5/91.
EDWARDS C. B. F. Born 12/12/19. Commd 28/7/60. Flt Lt 28/7/63. Retd SEC 22/3/69.
EDWARDS C. J., OBE. Born 17/5/17. Commd 28/2/46. Sqn Ldr 1/7/57. Retd SEC 17/5/67 rtg Wg Cdr.
EDWARDS C. R. Born 19/11/38. Commd 26/8/66. Wg Cdr 1/1/80. Retd PI 4/5/84.
EDWARDS D. Born 20/3/24. Commd 23/4/44. Sqn Ldr 1/7/60. Retd GD 30/6/78.
EDWARDS D. A. Born 31/12/65. Commd 30/3/89. Fg Offr 30/3/91. Retd SUP 14/3/96.
EDWARDS D. A. H., CEng MIEE MRAeS. Born 23/3/38. Commd 24/9/59. Gp Capt 1/7/85. Retd ENG 31/10/90.
EDWARDS D. G. Born 29/8/36. Commd 9/6/55. Sqn Ldr 1/1/73. Retd ADMIN 29/8/87.
EDWARDS D. L. Born 13/1/34. Commd 12/3/53. Gp Capt 1/7/79. Retd GD 13/1/84.
EDWARDS D. M., MCIPS MIMgt. Born 22/10/33. Commd 17/9/53. Gp Capt. 1/1/76. Retd SUP 10/5/79.
EDWARDS D. P. Born 4/4/33. Commd 24/2/67. Flt Lt 24/2/72. Retd ENG 24/10/75.

EDWARDS D. W. J. Born 19/11/46. Commd 24/4/70. Sqn Ldr 1/7/80. Retd ENG 19/11/84.
EDWARDS E. J., BA. Born 6/1/28. Commd 30/6/54. Sqn Ldr 7/9/61. Retd EDN 30/9/73.
EDWARDS E. T. D. Born 12/7/32. Commd 21/5/52. Flt Lt 16/10/57. Retd GD 12/7/70.
EDWARDS F. G. Born 19/12/37. Commd 19/6/70. Flt Lt 19/6/72. Retd ENG 19/12/87.
EDWARDS G. Born 21/1/09. Commd 26/12/46. Fg Offr 26/12/46. Retd SUP 31/5/48.
EDWARDS G. C. Born 12/3/45. Commd 25/2/66. Flt Lt 1/11/72. Retd GD 12/3/83.
EDWARDS G. G. Born 7/9/31. Commd 5/9/49. Flt Lt 14/11/56. Retd GD(G) 7/9/69. Re-instated 31/12/70 to
    30/6/82.
EDWARDS H., DFC MIMgt. Born 7/6/22. Commd 4/10/41. Wg Cdr 1/1/60. Retd SEC 1/1/74.
EDWARDS H. J. Born 31/8/49. Commd 31/10/69. Flt Lt 27/3/76. Retd SUP 1/11/78.
EDWARDS H. J. B., DFM. Born 18/4/21. Commd 27/3/45. Flt Lt 27/3/51. Retd ADMIN 18/4/76.
EDWARDS I. P., BSc. Born 4/6/64. Commd 18/8/85. Flt Lt 18/2/88. Retd GD 18/8/97.
EDWARDS J. A. Born 26/6/31. Commd 30/8/50. Flt Lt 26/5/55. Rtd GD 31/12/68.
EDWARDS J. A. F. Born 5/3/39. Commd 11/8/69. Flt Lt 11/8/71. Retd ENG 9/12/81.
EDWARDS J. A. K., MBE MCIPD. Born 9/5/31. Commd 14/1/54. Sqn Ldr 1/7/74. Retd SY(RGT) 9/5/89.
EDWARDS J. D. Born 21/1/35. Commd 3/3/54. Flt Lt 3/9/59. Retd GD 14/2/76.
EDWARDS J. D. Born 19/7/22. Commd 16/7/43. Wg Cdr 1/1/70. Retd ENG 5/9/75.
EDWARDS J. M., MInstAM MIMgt. Born 21/8/41. Commd 24/2/67. Wg Cdr 1/7/90. Retd ADMIN 2/4/93.
EDWARDS J. M. Born 5/5/29. Commd 26/3/59. Fg Offr 26/6/61. Retd SEC 5/5/67.
EDWARDS J. R. W. Born 20/4/33. Commd 17/9/57. Wg Cdr 1/7/80. Retd SUP 11/2/85.
EDWARDS J. W. Born 17/9/51. Commd 13/9/70. Sqn Ldr 1/1/88. Retd ADMIN 1/1/91.
EDWARDS K., MBE FCIPD. Born 8/11/40. Commd 25/8/67. Gp Capt 1/1/88. Retd ADMIN 5/4/91.
EDWARDS K., BA(Econ). Born 10/7/44. Commd 8/5/67. Gp Capt 1/1/90. Retd ADMIN 11/4/95.
EDWARDS K. A., BSc. Born 12/3/51. Commd 13/9/70. Fg Offr 15/10/72. Retd GD 5/7/75. Re-entered 22/5/83.
    Sqn Ldr 1/7/90. Retd SUP 15/10/99.
EDWARDS M. Born 22/5/32. Commd 14/4/53. Sqn Ldr 1/1/63. Retd GD 14/4/65.
EDWARDS M. C., BTech. Born 10/6/53. Commd 13/2/77. Sqn Ldr 1/1/88. Retd ENG 13/2/93.
EDWARDS M. J., BA. Born 26/3/32. Commd 29/3/56. Sqn Ldr 23/6/71. Retd ADMIN 30/9/73. Reinstated 7/5/80 to
    26/3/87.
EDWARDS The Rev M. S., BD. Born 13/2/44. Commd 25/4/82. Retd 19/1/96 Sqn Ldr.
EDWARDS P. Born 22/1/43. Commd 12/7/63. Gp Capt 1/7/90. Retd GD 12/2/01.
EDWARDS P. A. Born 1/4/45. Commd 1/4/65. Flt Lt 1/7/71. Retd ADMIN 1/4/83.
EDWARDS P. G. C. Born 29/12/32. Commd 27/9/51. Flt Lt 13/11/57. Retd GD 29/12/70.
EDWARDS P. J. Born 10/11/26. Commd 3/5/46. Flt Lt 3/11/49. Retd GD 19/3/53.
EDWARDS P. W. Born 17/4/53. Commd 31/10/74. Sqn Ldr 1/1/91. Retd GD 14/3/97.
EDWARDS R. A., OBE, 30/1/32. Commd 15/12/53. Gp Capt 1/1/81. Retd GD 30/1/87.
EDWARDS R. M., BSc. Born 7/5/34. Commd 20/9/57. Sqn Ldr 20/3/67. Retd EDN 20/9/73.
EDWARDS S. A., OBE. Born 24/11/34. Commd 9/4/57. Gp Capt 1/1/83. Retd GD 2/1/85.
EDWARDS T. A., BSc. Born 23/6/63. Commd 10/11/85. Flt Lt 10/5/88. Retd GD 28/11/97.
EDWARDS T. A. Born 16/1/25. Commd 15/9/60. Flt Lt 15/9/65. Retd GD 1/11/73.
EDWARDS T. P. Born 16/3/21. Commd 11/2/44. Flt Lt 11/8/47. Retd GD 25/11/61.
EDWARDS W., AFC. Born 14/8/26. Commd 20/12/46. Gp Capt 1/7/74. Retd GD 29/10/80.
EDWARDS W. A. Born 17/11/35. Commd 31/7/56. Sqn Ldr 1/7/69. Retd SUP 17/11/73.
EDWORTHY P. J. Born 16/2/38. Commd 28/7/59. Sqn Ldr 1/7/71. Retd GD 3/1/85.
EEDLE D. S., BSc. Born 25/5/28. Commd 25/5/50. Gp Capt 1/7/79. Retd GD 25/5/83.
EELES J. S. Born 5/5/25. Commd 26/3/53. Flt Lt 26/9/56. Retd GD 16/12/70.
EELES T., BA. Born 14/9/42. Commd 30/7/63. Gp Capt 1/7/90. Retd GD 14/9/97.
EGAN I., BSc. Born 24/6/58. Commd 5/9/76. Sqn Ldr 1/7/91. Retd GD 24/6/96.
EGAN J. J., DFC. Born 30/10/23. Commd 14/6/50. Flt Lt 10/11/53. Retd GD 19/8/64.
EGAN-WYER D. G., ACCS. Born 6/12/26. Commd 9/11/59. Sqn Ldr 1/7/68. Retd SUP 8/1/71.
EGGINTON J. T., AFC. Born 14/3/33. Commd 7/5/52. Sqn Ldr 1/1/73. Retd GD 1/11/73.
EGGLESTONE B. J. Born 21/12/43. Commd 19/12/63. Flt Lt 4/11/70. Retd GD(G) 25/12/80.
EGGLETON M. B. Born 10/4/34. Commd 4.2.53. Flt Lt 24/6/58. Retd GD 1/7/68.
EGGLETON M. H. A. Born 14/1/33. Commd 23/8/51. Flt Lt 25/2/57. Retd GD 26/11/72.
EGLINGTON W. D. S. Born 6/6/25. Commd 24/1/52. Flt Lt 13/11/57. Retd GD 16/3/68.
EGRE C. H. Born 30/5/49. Commd 27/2/70. Sqn Ldr 1/1/91. Retd GD(G) 1/4/94.
EIDSFORTH A. R. J. Born 18/5/39. Commd 19/12/61. Flt Lt 19/12/66. Retd SUP 18/5/77.
EISLER J. J. Born 27/12/39. Commd 21/10/64. Flt Lt 21/10/64. Retd GD 21/10/80.
EKE D. V., BA MSRG. Born 21/3/38. Commd 9/7/60. Flt Lt 9/1/60. Retd GD 21/3/93.
EKE P. Born 27/3/34. Commd 5/7/53. Flt Lt 15/8/62. Retd GD 6/10/84.
EKINS D. J., BSc. Born 14/1/61. Commd 15/8/82. Sqn Ldr 1/7/93. Retd GD 14/1/99.
ELBURN A. J., BA. Born 25/4/33. Commd 2/10/61. Flt Lt 2/4/67. Retd GD 28/8/79.
ELDER P. R. Born 28/8/41. Commd 2/10/61. Flt Lt 2/4/67. Retd GD 28/8/79.
ELDER R. D., CBE FRAeS. Born 27/5/46. Commd 1/3/68. AVM 1/7/96. Retd GD 8/2/99.
ELDER W. J., MB BS DCH MRCP. Born 8/9/29. Commd 3/4/55. Wg Cdr 5/3/68. Retd MED 3/4/71.
ELEY D. L. Born 27/1/26. Commd 21/12/45. Wg Cdr 1/1/65. Retd GD 7/2/77.

ELEY M. M. Born 9/10/48. Commd 8/8/74. Sqn Ldr 1/1/88. Retd GD 22/4/94.
ELEY T. E. A. Born 15/3/36. Commd 28/9/61. Wg Cdr 1/1/79. Retd GD 16/3/86.
ELFORD C. B., FCIPD MIMgt. Born 11/10/19. Commd 26/3/42. Wg Cdr 1/7/62. Retd 22/10/74.
ELIAS J. W. A. Born 2/2/31. Commd 9/9/55. Sqn Ldr 1/7/72. Retd GD 27/5/84.
ELING C. I. Born 28/5/50. Commd 20/9/79. Flt Lt 20/9/81. Retd GD 28/10/87.
ELIOT R. C. Born 7/5/60. Commd 13/12/79. Flt Lt 13/6/85. Retd GD 7/5/98.
ELISTON J. A., AFM. Born 7/5/24. Commd 29/7/65. Sqn Ldr 1/1/75. Retd GD 9/1/80.
ELKINGTON J. F. D. Born 23/12/20. Commd 14/7/40. Wg Cdr 1/7/61. Retd GD 23/12/75.
ELKINGTON K. A. Born 16/7/43. Commd 21/7/61. Sqn Ldr 1/1/79. Retd GD 1/1/82.
ELKINS C. A., MSc BSc. Born 5/10/50. Commd 15/9/69. Wg Cdr 1/7/90. Retd ENG 14/3/96.
ELLACOMBE J. L.W., CB DFC* FIMgt. Born 28/2/20. Commd 23/3/40. A Cdre 1/7/68. Retd GD 16/4/73.
ELLAM C., CEng MIMechE MRAeS. Born 28/6/32. Commd 26/9/71. Sqn Ldr 26/9/71. Retd ENG 28/6/92.
ELLAM D. J., MB BS MRCS LRCP DA. Born 15/5/34. Commd 7/2/60. Wg Cdr 7/2/73. Retd MED 1/11/84.
ELLENDER A. R. Born 3/8/42. Commd 28/7/64. Sqn Ldr 1/7/74. Retd GD 3/8/86.
ELLERBECK H. W. Born 28/11/26. Commd 12/8/54. Flt Lt 12/2/59. Retd GD 16/12/70.
ELLERD-STYLES L., BSc CEng MIMechE MRAeS DCAe. Born 31/10/14. Commd 3/10/41. Gp Capt 1/1/64. Retd ENG 31/10/69.
ELLERTON D. R. D. Born 9/7/22. Commd 11/5/43. Sqn Ldr 1/7/53. Retd GD 1/1/56.
ELLES-HILL W. J. Born 16/2/33. Commd 20/3/52. Fg Offr 6/8/61. Retd GD 10/4/66.
ELLICOTT R. A. C. Born 25/8/30. Commd 4/4/51. Sqn Ldr 1/1/75. Retd GD 21/8/84.
ELLIMAN J. N. Born 6/2/25. Commd 7/9/46. Sqn Ldr 1/1/61. Retd GD 30/4/73.
ELLINGWORTH R. A. Born 17/12/35. Commd 17/5/56. Sqn Ldr 1/1/75. Retd GD(G) 25/7/89.
ELLIOT A. H. Born 14/9/24. Commd 15/11/44. Flt Lt 18/5/64. Retd GD 31/8/73.
ELLIOT D. Born 28/12/37. Commd 18/4/73. Sqn Ldr 1/7/84. Retd ENG 28/12/92.
ELLIOT J. R. Born 29/9/33. Commd 22/1/53. Flt Lt 16/12/59. Retd SEC 29/9/71 rtg Sqn Ldr.
ELLIOT T. F., BEM. Born 1/5/19. Commd 15/5/58. Flt Lt 15/5/63. Retd ENG 1/5/74.
ELLIOT-WILLIAMS B. H. Born 5/4/36. Commd 22/7/66. Flt Lt 1/7/69. Retd GD(G) 23/7/74.
ELLIOTT C. B. Born 15/6/32. Commd 8/5/56. Flt Lt 8/11/61. Retd GD 15/6/70.
ELLIOTT D. G. Born 5/10/48. Commd 27/2/75. Flt Lt 16/3/77. Retd GD 5/10/86.
ELLIOTT F. C. P. Born 17/3/21. Commd 5/2/44. Wg Cdr 1/7/65. Retd GD 17/3/76.
ELLIOTT G. C. Born 2/9/41. Commd 4/3/71. Flt Lt 4/9/77. Retd SUP 9/11/86.
ELLIOTT H. J. Born 18/10/61. Commd 19/3/81. Sqn Ldr 1/1/98. Retd GD 1/1/01.
ELLIOTT J. E. Born 24/5/42. Commd 13/12/79. Sqn Ldr 1/7/90. Retd ENG 20/7/93.
ELLIOTT J. H. Born 16/6/24. Commd 29/3/45. Wg Cdr 1/1/67. Retd GD 18/4/70.
ELLIOTT K. T. Born 18/6/51. Commd 2/1/70. Flt Lt 7/3/76. Retd ADMIN 18/6/89.
ELLIOTT L. C., MBE. Born 1/4/14. Commd 22/8/41. Sqn Ldr 1/7/60. Retd ENG 1/4/69.
ELLIOTT M. R. Born 27/3/47. Commd 1/4/71. Flt Lt 1/10/76. Retd GD 30/4/88.
ELLIOTT N. P. G., MSc BSc. Born 21/8/47. Commd 8/1/73. Sqn Ldr 1/7/84. Retd ENG 8/1/89.
ELLIOTT P. Born 22/1/47. Commd 31/7/86. Flt Lt 31/7/90. Retd ENG 2/4/93.
ELLIOTT P. J. B., MBE. Born 16/9/41. Commd 2/1/70. Sqn Ldr 1/7/76. Retd GD 16/9/96.
ELLIOTT P. W., MIISec. Born 17/6/47. Commd 14/10/71. Flt Lt 17/11/74. Retd SY 17/6/85.
ELLIOTT R. L. Born 3/5/29. Commd 26/9/51. Flt Lt 23/9/70. Retd GD 1/5/76.
ELLIOTT R. P., DSO DFC*. Born 13/4/17. Commd 1/3/37. Sqn Ldr 1/7/52. Retd GD 20/12/57 rtg Wg Cdr.
ELLIOTT R. T. Born 27/7/41. Commd 10/4/67. Flt Lt 10/4/71. Retd ADMIN 1/10/87.
ELLIOTT T. E., MINucE. Born 4/12/20. Commd 26/9/57. Sqn Ldr 1/7/68. Retd ENG 2/1/71.
ELLIOTT T. J. Born 3/10/44. Commd 29/11/63. Flt Lt 1/7/69. Retd GD 22/10/94.
ELLIS A. C., BSc. Born 15/10/46. Commd 23/9/68. Flt Lt 23/3/70. Retd EDN 9/10/71.
ELLIS A. G., MBE. Born 29/6/26. Commd 20/12/46. Wg Cdr 1/7/73. Retd GD 5/4/79.
ELLIS A. I. Born 24/4/23. Commd 3/7/45. Flt Lt 4/1/51. Retd SEC 24/4/78.
ELLIS D. Born 25/11/28. Commd 5/12/51. Flt Lt 5/6/56. Retd GD(G) 25/11/88.
ELLIS D. Born 5/8/43. Commd 12/1/62. Flt Lt 12/7/67. Retd GD 5/8/76.
ELLIS D. C., MSc BSc CEng MIMechE. Born 18/9/57. Commd 23/9/79. Sqn Ldr 1/1/89. Retd ENG 30/4/00.
ELLIS D. J. A. Born 23/6/25. Commd 15/6/61. Sqn Ldr 1/7/74. Retd ENG 3/6/78.
ELLIS E., BA. Born 31/7/21. Commd 11/10/50. Sqn Ldr 2/2/60. Retd EDN 1/11/64.
ELLIS G. L. Born 25/9/30. Commd 6/9/68. Flt Lt 6/9/74. Retd SEC 17/9/78.
ELLIS H. R. W. Born 15/8/38. Commd 12/11/57. Flt Lt 15/2/65. Retd GD 11/9/76.
ELLIS H. W., BSc. Born 16/10/54. Commd 2/9/73. Flt Lt 15/10/77. Retd GD 15/7/88.
ELLIS J., CBE DFC*. Born 28/2/17. Commd 23/3/36. Gp Capt 1/1/59. Retd GD 28/2/67.
ELLIS J. C., OBE CEng MIMechE MRAeS. Born 15/6/15. Commd 23/9/43. Wg Cdr 1/7/61. Retd ENG 25/11/67.
ELLIS J. C. Born 13/10/62. Commd 26/9/90. Flt Lt 26/9/92. Retd ADMIN 3/3/96.
ELLIS J. D. Born 2/12/40. Commd 23/12/58. Flt Lt 1/7/64. Retd GD 15/5/76.
ELLIS J. R. Born 3/8/56. Commd 24/2/87. Flt Lt 23/4/89. Retd ADMIN 23/4/95.
ELLIS L. E., DFC. Born 19/6/12. Commd 12/7/37. Sqn Ldr 1/1/45. Retd GD 19/6/55 rtg Wg Cdr.
ELLIS P. W., DFC. Born 19/4/23. Commd 23/1/43. Sqn Ldr 1/1/54. Retd GD 13/3/58.
ELLIS R. Born 5/9/40. Commd 22/5/70. Sqn Ldr 1/1/77. Retd GD(G) 1/1/80.
ELLIS R. A. Born 10/7/24. Commd 22/2/60. Sqn Ldr 1/7/65. Retd SUP 2/12/71.

ELLIS R. A. Born 12/11/58. Commd 2/6/77. Flt Lt 2/12/82. Retd GD 7/12/00.
ELLIS R. H., MB BChir MRCOG. Born 8/7/32. Commd 16/2/59. Wg Cdr 16/2/72. Retd MED 16/2/75.
ELLIS R. M. Born 10/3/46. Commd 26/11/81. Flt Lt 16/10/86. Retd SUP 6/5/95.
ELLIS S. Born 30/5/52. Commd 30/1/75. Flt Lt 30/5/79. Retd GD(G) 29/5/81.
ELLIS T. D. Born 4/10/36. Commd 28/7/67. Flt Lt 28/7/69. Retd GD 5/8/75.
ELLIS T. J., MA. Born 18/8/52. Commd 2/1/74. Flt Lt 15/1/75. Retd GD 23/11/75.
ELLISON C. O., DFC. Born 28/9/19. Commd 19/3/43. Sqn Ldr 1/1/54. Retd GD 16/3/59.
ELLISON I., MIMgt. Born 12/7/45. Commd 8/7/65. Wg Cdr 1/7/90. Retd ADMIN 12/7/00.
ELLISON J. T., ACIS. Born 30/7/19. Commd 22/3/43. Sqn Ldr 1/7/55. Retd SEC 1/7/71.
ELLISON T. B. Born 8/2/59. Commd 8/4/82. Flt Lt 8/4/87. Retd GD 8/3/96.
ELMER J. C. Born 17/7/20. Commd 6/10/60. Flt Lt 6/10/63. Retd GD 12/9/75.
ELMES T. J. W. Born 30/6/26. Commd 23/4/47. Sqn Ldr 1/1/69. Retd SY 31/7/76.
ELMITT J. W. Born 5/12/32. Commd 13/9/51. Flt Lt 11/6/57. Retd GD 5/12/75.
ELPHICK A. P. Born 5/7/25. Commd 4/7/50. Sqn Ldr 1/7/72. Retd GD 31/8/73.
ELRICK A. D. Born 7/1/48. Commd 23/4/87. Flt Lt 23/4/91. Retd ADMIN 7/5/94.
ELSAM M. B., FIMgt. Born 28/10/40. Commd 2/5/59. Gp Capt 1/7/84. Retd GD 11/6/90.
ELSDEN L. P. Born 22/11/23. Commd 6/6/45. Flt Lt 6/6/51. Retd RGT 31/12/59.
ELSDON I. J. Born 1/7/20. Commd 25/8/41. Flt Offr 1/9/45. Retd SEC 14/5/50 rtg Sqn Offr.
ELSDON T. A. F., OBE DFC. Born 22/1/17. Commd 8/12/37. Wg Cdr 1/1/49. Retd GD 22/10/59. rtg Gp Capt.
ELSEGOOD A. W. Born 25/3/33. Commd 17/12/52. Flt Lt 12/5/58. Retd GD 25/3/71.
ELSEGOOD W. W. Born 30/9/33. Commd 8/5/53. Sqn Ldr 1/1/70. Retd GD 1/1/73.
ELSOM B. Born 13/10/36. Commd 18/11/64. Flt Lt 18/11/64. Retd GD 20/5/67.
ELTON D. H. Born 20/3/31. Commd 28/8/57. Fg Offr 28/8/57. Retd GD 26/2/64.
ELTON P. Born 24/9/32. Commd 5/9/69. Sqn Ldr 1/7/79. Retd GD(G) 5/4/85.
ELTON P. H., MIMgt. Born 14/4/33. Commd 14/4/53. Gp Capt 1/1/81. Retd GD 1/3/86.
ELTON P. J. G., BA MCIPD MIMgt. Born 17/8/29. Commd 26/7/50. Sqn Ldr 1/7/61. Retd GD 31/12/80.
ELVIN E. A., MIMgt. Born 15/6/20. Commd 27/2/58. Flt Lt 1/4/63. Retd ENG 25/6/75.
ELWAY D. R. Born 1/11/33. Commd 21/1/53. Sqn Ldr 1/1/67. Retd ADMIN 30/9/80.
ELWELL R. F. Born 21/5/36. Commd 1/2/56. Flt Lt 1/8/61. Retd GD(G) 21/5/91.
ELWIG R. H., CEng MRAeS. Born 27/4/40. Commd 17/7/62. A Cdre 1/1/90. Retd ENG 27/4/95.
ELWORTHY The Honourable Sir Timothy., KCVO CBE. Born 27/1/38. Commd 28/7/59. A Cdre 1/7/87. Retd GD 27/1/93.
ELWY W. N., MRAeS. Born 6/8/12. Commd 10/4/31. Wg Cdr 1/7/48. Retd ENG 1/11/57. rtg Gp Capt.
ELY P., MInst AM MIMgt. Born 22/12/35. Commd 5/9/69. Sqn Ldr 1/7/76. Retd ADMIN 16/7/86.
EMANUEL M. H., MIMgt. Born 30/8/31. Commd 30/1/58. Sqn Ldr 1/1/68. Retd GD 27/8/76.
EMBERLEY S. E. Born 29/1/20. Commd 11/8/44. Sqn Ldr 1/1/57. Retd SEC 28/2/62.
EMBERSON K. J. Born 4/9/58. Commd 30/8/84. Flt Lt 30/8/86. Retd GD 4/9/96.
EMBLETON G. A. Born 11/10/31. Commd 26/9/51. Flt Lt 17/5/56. Retd GD 11/10/89.
EMERSON C., MBE. Born 19/12/48. Commd 19/6/86. Sqn Ldr 1/7/93. Retd ENG 1/1/97.
EMERSON J. E. Born 24/9/43. Commd 8/6/84. Sqn Ldr 1/7/93. Retd ENG 12/10/97.
EMERSON J. R. Born 4/2/25. Commd 4/9/58. Flt Lt 4/9/63. Retd ENG 5/2/75.
EMERSON K. J., MPhil BSc. Born 3/7/60. Commd 13/2/83. Sqn Ldr 1/1/94. Retd GD 13/2/99.
EMERY D. A. Born 27/10/32. Commd 3/12/56. Wg Cdr 1/1/76. Retd GD(G) 27/10/87.
EMERY E. W. C. Born 3/12/08. Commd 5/6/41. Flt Lt 1/9/45. Retd ENG 29/5/54 rtg Sqn Ldr.
EMERY J. V., OBE CEng MRAeS MIMgt. Born 5/12/39. Commd 30/9/59. Wg Cdr 1/7/77. Retd ENG 5/12/89.
EMERY M. J. R. Born 12/4/38. Commd 14/6/63. Flt Lt 8/1/69. Retd GD 20/11/88.
EMMERSON D., CBE AFC. Born 6/9/39. Commd 30/7/57. AVM 1/1/90. Retd GD 1/5/91.
EMMERSON D. E. Born 3/6/17. Commd 26/5/43. Flt Lt 4/6/53. Retd GD(G) 3/6/71.
EMMERSON J. G. Born 21/5/43. Commd 6/9/65. Flt Lt 6/9/69. Retd GD 6/9/81. Re-entered 3/11/86. Sqn Ldr 1/7/94. Retd GD 21/5/98.
EMMERSON R. J. Born 7/5/37. Commd 24/2/61. Flt Lt 25/7/66. Retd GD 5/5/74.
EMMETT W. A. C. Born 3/7/16. Commd 15/3/37. Sqn Ldr 1/1/54. Retd SUP 30/4/58.
EMMITT R. Born 19/8/34. Commd 8/10/70. Flt Lt 8/10/74. Retd ENG 1/10/84.
EMPSON D. K., MBE. Born 14/6/31. Commd 12/9/51. Gp Capt 1/1/81. Retd GD 16/6/83.
EMPSON H. G., CEng MRAeS MIMgt. Born 10/2/28. Commd 25/8/60. Wg Cdr 1/1/76. Retd ENG 8/9/82.
EMPTAGE J. A., BSc. Born 4/7/52. Commd 19/10/75. Flt Lt 19/1/76. Retd GD 1/3/99.
EMRYS-EVANS S., DFC MIMgt. Born 3/6/20. Commd 3/7/44. Sqn Ldr 1/7/68. Retd GD(G) 9/6/75.
ENDACOTT R. Born 14/1/31. Commd 21/11/51. Flt Lt 21/5/56. Retd GD 14/7/68.
ENDERBY G. Born 11/2/42. Commd 12/7/62. Gp Capt 1/7/87. Retd RGT 30/5/90.
ENGLAND D. C. E., MA. Born 5/7/33. Commd 6/4/54. Sqn Ldr 1/7/69. Retd GD 1/7/72.
ENGLAND H. G. C. Born 4/1/38. Commd 30/7/64. Sqn Ldr 1/7/81. Retd ADMIN 4/1/93.
ENGLAND H.A., DFC. Born 14/1/19. Commd 9/7/38. Wg Cdr 1/1/54. Retd GD 14/1/74.
ENGLAND K. Born 11/8/22. Commd 25/2/44. Flt Lt 17/5/56. Retd GD(G) 11/8/77.
ENGLAND R. J. Born 24/4/62. Commd 4/9/81. Flt Lt 4/3/87. Retd GD 1/3/89.
ENGLISH D. F. Born 15/9/40. Commd 15/10/81. Sqn Ldr 1/1/91. Retd ENG 1/10/93.
ENGLISH D. P. Born 11/8/29. Commd 1/8/51. Sqn Ldr 1/7/66. Retd GD 30/9/77.

ENGLISH H. A., MIMgt. Born 10/1/21. Commd 9/9/54. Sqn Ldr 1/7/69. Retd ENG 9/4/73.
ENGLISH J. P. Born 16/2/54. Commd 13/9/80. Sqn Ldr 1/7/90. Retd GD 31/12/94.
ENGLISH K. A. Born 11/9/16. Commd 27/10/55. Flt Lt 27/10/58. Retd ENG 12/9/63.
ENGLISH N., CEng MRAeS. Born 12/5/18. Commd 3/8/44. Sqn Ldr 1/4/56. Retd ENG 19/9/70.
ENGLISH R. G., DFC. Born 10/7/14. Commd 31/10/38. Sqn Ldr 1/8/47. Retd GD 3/8/57.
ENKEL P. A., AIIP. Born 27/4/35. Commd 21/10/66. Flt Lt 21/10/68. Retd ENG 21/10/84. Re-instated 2/6/77 to
    2/6/85.
ENRIGHT P. T. Born 19/11/02. Commd 25/11/43. Flt Lt 25/5/47. Retd ENG 7/10/57.
ENSOR Rev K. V. Born 11/3/08. Commd 10/10/39. Retd 9/4/63. Wg Cdr.
ENSTON J. N. Born 7/8/45. Commd 2/4/65. Flt Lt 2/10/70. Retd GD 7/8/00.
ENSTONE A. W. J., MBE. Born 29/12/20. Commd 29/1/46. Flt Lt 27/5/54. Retd RGT 29/12/75.
ENTICKNAP R. G. Born 6/10/15. Commd 1/12/40. Sqn Ldr 1/7/50. Retd ENG 8/12/51.
ENTWISLE B. Born 24/4/33. Commd 13/2/52. Gp Capt 1/1/85. Retd GD 20/6/87.
ENTWISLE P. A. Born 1/8/23. Commd 27/2/58. Sqn Ldr 1/7/75. Retd ADMIN 1/8/83.
ENVIS I. F. C. Born 10/3/49. Commd 27/3/70. Sqn Ldr 1/7/86. Retd SUP 1/7/89.
EPISCOPO S., MBE. Born 16/1/38. Commd 11/6/60. Sqn Ldr 1/7/87. Retd GD 14/4/93.
EPPS E. J. G. Born 29/2/20. Commd 26/2/45. Flt Lt 26/8/48. Retd GD 28/11/53.
EPPS W. R. Born 22/2/35. Commd 15/5/61. Flt Lt 15/5/62. Retd RGT 1/7/70.
EPTON O. W. Born 24/8/41. Commd 24/6/65. Sqn Ldr 1/7/74. Retd GD 30/9/78.
ERNSTING J., CB OBE PhD MB BS BSc FRAeS FRCP MFOM MRCS. Born 21/4/28. Commd 27/6/54. AVM
    18/7/90. Retd MED 21/4/93.
ERRINGTON J. H. Born 26/10/21. Commd 14/7/44. Sqn Ldr 1/1/68. Retd GD(G) 26/10/76.
ERRY D. S., BEng. Born 14/12/65. Commd 14/8/88. Flt Lt 14/2/91. Retd GD 14/8/00.
ERSKINE C. E. Born 18/12/32. Commd 24/2/67. Sqn Ldr 1/7/76. Retd ENG 1/8/84.
ERSKINE CRUM W. S., OBE. Born 26/3/42. Commd 30/7/63. Wg Cdr 1/1/86. Retd GD 26/6/97.
ERSKINE H. G. Born 22/3/45. Commd 14/7/66. Flt Lt 14/1/72. Retd GD 11/12/76.
ERVINE T. E. Born 12/9/20. Commd 5/4/43. Flt Lt 24/2/50. Retd GD 17/6/54.
ERWICH J. A. Born 12/3/25. Commd 19/11/52. Flt Lt 20/10/60. Retd SEC 9/7/68.
ERWIN P. G. Born 8/8/42. Commd 23/11/78. Sqn Ldr 1/1/89. Retd ENG 20/4/96.
ERWOOD T. K. Born 26/5/21. Commd 7/7/49. Sqn Ldr 1/1/73. Retd GD 26/5/76.
ESCOTT B. E., BA MIMgt. Born 23/12/29. Commd 15/2/61. Sqn Ldr 12/10/70. Retd ADMIN 23/12/85.
ESPLEY R. H., BEM. Born 27/12/06. Commd 5/11/42. Flt Lt 5/5/46. Retd ENG 28/12/61.
ESPLIN I. G., CB OBE DFC MA BEc. Born 22/2/14. Commd 19/10/40. AVM 1/1/63. Retd GD 8/9/65.
ESSAI R. I., OBE. Born 17/9/33. Commd 9/7/60. Wg Cdr 1/1/77. Retd GD 17/9/88.
ESSERY J. C., AFC BEM. Born 2/7/45. Commd 1/4/85. Sqn Ldr 1/7/88. Retd GD 1/10/91.
ESSEX B. J. N., AFC. Born 28/9/44. Commd 28/2/64. Wg Cdr 1/7/81, Retd GD 2/11/85.
ESSON D. G. Born 5/6/47. Commd 23/9/66. Sqn Ldr 1/7/82. Retd GD 1/7/85.
ETCHELLS K. Born 3/12/22. Commd 17/2/45. Flt Lt 17/8/48. Retd GD 1/3/61.
ETCHES R. A. W. Born 25/2/58. Commd 31/8/78. Flt Lt 29/2/84. Retd GD 1/10/98.
ETHEREDGE G. H. Born 29/4/08. Commd 5/8/41. Flt Lt 12/5/44. Retd ENG 14/1/46 rtg Sqn Ldr.
ETHERIDGE E. K. Born 22/7/13. Commd 9/3/44. Flt Lt 19/6/52. Retd SUP 22/7/60.
ETHERINGTON R. F. Born 2/2/24. Commd 25/3/45. Flt Lt 25/9/48. Retd GD 26/11/55.
ETKINS J. Born 11/10/25. Commd 11/5/45. Sqn Ldr 1/7/61. Retd GD 1/7/64.
ETTRIDGE A. G. Born 8/8/35. Commd 30/7/57. Sqn Ldr 1/1/66. Retd GD 8/8/73.
EUSTACE P. H. Born 5/8/42. Commd 12/1/62. A Cdre 1/1/91. Retd GD 3/4/98.
EVA H. J. Born 24/2/36. Commd 30/4/59. Wg Cdr 1/1/78. Retd ADMIN 24/2/91.
EVA V. J. Born 23/4/11. Commd 19/1/50. Flt Lt 19/7/52. Retd ENG 1/5/59.
EVANS A. Born 19/3/23. Commd 25/8/60. Flt Lt 25/8/65. Retd GD 1/3/68.
EVANS A. Born 6/11/35. Commd 1/4/58. Flt Lt 26/2/64. Retd GD 5/2/77.
EVANS A., BSc. Born 6/11/45. Commd 1/3/68. Sqn Ldr 1/1/83. Retd ENG 20/7/96.
EVANS A. A. Born 23/5/22. Commd 15/5/45. Sqn Ldr 1/7/58. Retd GD 23/5/65.
EVANS A. E. Born 9/11/16. Commd 30/6/43. Flt Lt 27/5/54. Retd SEC 30/9/67.
EVANS A. J. Born 18/2/46. Commd 1/3/68. Flt Lt 8/3/72. Retd GD 18/2/84.
EVANS A. M. Born 12/7/48. Commd 27/2/70. Flt Lt 27/8/75. Retd GD 12/7/89.
EVANS B., MBE MRAeS. Born 4/2/34. Commd 11/2/64. Sqn Ldr 1/7/75. Retd ENG 4/2/94.
EVANS B. A., BSc. Born 13/4/65. Commd 11/10/84. Flt Lt 15/1/89. Retd GD 15/7/98.
EVANS B. D. Born 18/6/43. Commd 27/2/70. Flt Lt 25/9/72. Retd GD(G) 18/6/81.
EVANS B. K. J., BSc. Born 18/6/40. Commd 22/10/63. Sqn Ldr 22/4/73. Retd EDN 22/10/79.
EVANS C., MBE. Born 7/11/38. Commd 27/6/59. Flt Lt 14/2/66. Retd GD 7/11/93.
EVANS C. D., MB BS MRCP DObstRCOG DPhysMed. Born 15/11/32. Commd 21/6/59. Wg Cdr 24/9/71. Retd MED
    21/6/75.
EVANS C. E., CBE. Born 21/4/37. Commd 4/5/53. AVM 1/1/89. Retd GD 21/4/92.
EVANS C. H. Born 24/3/36. Commd 9/7/57. Flt Lt 26/5/69. Retd SUP 9/2/77.
EVANS C. J., BSc. Born 12/12/51. Commd 18/3/84. Flt Lt 18/9/80. Retd ADMIN 18/3/00.
EVANS C. R., OBE. Born 21/6/25. Commd 29/3/45. Wg Cdr 1/1/64. Retd GD 12/2/77.
EVANS C. W. Born 10/2/23. Commd 28/7/45. Wg Cdr 1/1/74. Retd ADMIN 13/1/78.

EVANS D., AFC. Born 16/6/24. Commd 5/5/45. Flt Lt 5/11/47. Retd GD 16/6/67.
EVANS D. A. T. Born 21/9/39. Commd 29/11/63. Flt Lt 15/10/66. Retd GD 21/9/80.
EVANS D. C., MB ChB MRCOG. Born 15/3/47. Commd 21/11/71. Wg Cdr 6/8/88. Retd MED 21/11/88.
EVANS D. C. Born 12/10/26. Commd 18/7/63. Sqn Ldr 1/1/78. Retd PRT 1/9/79.
EVANS D. C. Born 19/4/58. Commd 26/9/90. Flt Lt 26/9/92. Retd ADMIN 26/9/98.
EVANS D. G. Born 8/2/38. Commd 4/12/64. Flt Lt 8/1/69. Retd GD 30/6/72.
EVANS D. J. Born 17/4/29. Commd 11/6/53. Flt Lt 11/12/56. Retd GD 17/4/67.
EVANS D. K. Born 16/4/35. Commd 25/7/56. Sqn Ldr 1/1/80. Retd ENG 16/4/93.
EVANS D. M. Born 8/3/36. Commd 29/3/56. Sqn Ldr 1/7/70. Retd SEC 1/5/79.
EVANS D. N., MCIPD MRIN. Born 28/8/34. Commd 30/7/52. Sqn Ldr 1/1/80. Retd GD 1/10/85.
EVANS D. O. Born 10/12/23. Commd 1/10/43. Sqn Ldr 1/1/61. Retd GD 25/2/65.
EVANS D. R. Born 4/9/24. Commd 15/4/50. Flt Lt 1/7/59. Retd GD 4/9/66.
EVANS D. R. Born 20/2/31. Commd 29/3/50. Flt Lt 29/9/54. Retd GD 15/3/69.
EVANS D. R. J., MA CEng MIEE DipEL. Born 27/4/31. Commd 26/9/53. Wg cdr 1/7/69. Retd ENG 27/4/83.
EVANS D. S. Born 7/2/50. Commd 2/5/69. Flt Lt 2/5/72. Retd PI 1/2/73.
EVANS D. T., OBE. Born 17/10/24. Commd 16/2/45. Wg Cdr 1/1/68. Retd GD 17/10/82.
EVANS E. Born 11/2/57. Commd 24/4/80. Flt Lt 24/10/85. Retd GD 30/6/89.
EVANS E., OBE. Born 5/9/21. Commd 3/7/42. Wg Cdr 1/7/59. Retd GD 6/8/66.
EVANS E. E. Born 25/10/29. Commd 7/1/61. Flt Lt 27/2/72. Retd ADMIN 27/2/78.
EVANS E. G. Born 24/1/16. Commd 27/1/45. Flt Lt 27/3/51. Retd GD(G) 30/1/65.
EVANS E. J. Born 26/12/20. Commd 27/10/55. Sqn Ldr 1/7/67. Retd ENG 9/6/73.
EVANS F. E. Born 16/4/13. Commd 12/8/40. Wg Cdr 1/1/57. Retd SEC 16/4/65.
EVANS G. A. Born 20/5/38. Commd 28/1/60. Flt Lt 28/7/66. Retd ENG 20/5/76.
EVANS G. E. W., MIMgt. Born 2/10/31. Commd 5/11/52. Wg Cdr 1/1/77, Retd GD 4/10/85.
EVANS G. H., MSc BSc CEng MIEE MRAeS. Born 4/2/55. Commd 28/7/88. Flt Lt 28/7/90. Retd ENG 29/9/98.
EVANS G. H., BSc. Born 25/11/59. Commd 6/9/81. Flt Lt 6/12/82. Retd GD 25/11/97.
EVANS G. H. D., DSO DFC. Born 29/6/17. Commd 18/12/37. Wg Cdr 1/1/49. Retd GD 29/5/68.
EVANS G. M. Born 6/10/21. Commd 12/8/47. Flt Lt 12/2/52. Retd SEC 27/10/55.
EVANS G. P. Born 28/8/49. Commd 31/7/70. Flt Lt 31/7/73. Retd GD 2/9/81.
EVANS G. R., MRAeS. Born 12/6/56. Commd 20/7/78. Gp Capt 1/1/98. Retd GD 7/4/00.
EVANS H. J. Born 12/2/61. Commd 15/8/85. Flt Lt 30/1/89. Retd GD 14/3/96.
EVANS H. N. Born 22/2/32. Commd 3/11/51. Flt Lt 17/5/56. Retd GD 30/12/63.
EVANS I. Born 22/3/48. Commd 17/2/67. Gp Capt 1/1/95. Retd GD 1/3/00.
EVANS I. H. Born 15/8/23. Commd 15/12/49. Flt Lt 15/6/53. Retd GD(G) 15/8/78.
EVANS I. M. Born 5/7/40. Commd 16/6/83. Sqn Ldr 1/7/92. Retd ENG 5/7/95.
EVANS J. Born 5/10/39. Commd 1/8/61. Gp Capt 1/1/90. Retd GD 5/10/94.
EVANS J. A., BA. Born 3/1/44. Commd 31/10/63. Wg Cdr 1/1/88. Retd ADMIN 22/6/94.
EVANS J. C. Born 15/1/18. Commd 7/1/43. Flt Lt 15/6/53. Retd SEC 15/1/67.
EVANS J. E. C., MB BCh DAvMed. Born 5/9/49. Commd 23/1/72. Wg Cdr 14/7/88. Retd MED 26/7/90.
EVANS J. G., MBE MBA BA. Born 1/5/55. Commd 16/9/73. Wg Cdr 1/1/94. Retd OPS SPT 7/5/00.
EVANS J. J., BA. Born 19/8/32. Commd 30/9/54. Sqn Ldr 15/2/65. Retd EDN 30/9/71.
EVANS J. L. D. Born 2/8/23. Commd 29/6/50. Fg Offr 29/6/51. Retd RGT 15/7/55.
EVANS J. M., DFC. Born 5/12/33. Commd 24/1/52. Flt Lt 29/5/57. Retd GD 15/10/73.
EVANS J. M. Born 28/12/14. Commd 13/3/35. Sqn Ldr 1/3/45. Retd GD(G) 30/4/61 rtg Wg Cdr.
EVANS J. P. Born 20/12/39. Commd 6/4/62. Wg Cdr 1/7/91. Retd GD 3/7/93.
EVANS J. R., MDA BSc CEng MRAeS. Born 30/9/60. Commd 2/9/79. Sqn Ldr 1/1/93. Retd ENG 15/12/98.
EVANS J. R. Born 13/8/19. Commd 6/11/45. Flt Lt 6/11/50. Retd SEC 5/11/55.
EVANS J. V. Born 30/3/43. Commd 9/6/63. Flt Lt 6/3/69. Retd GD 3/3/84.
EVANS J. V., MCIPS MIMgt. Born 12/7/26. Commd 6/8/63. Sqn Ldr 1/1/69. Retd SUP 6/11/85.
EVANS J. W. Born 24/9/35. Commd 25/6/67. Flt Lt 26/5/69. Retd SUP 19/7/74.
EVANS K. Born 18/12/41. Commd 30/7/63. Sqn Ldr 1/1/74. Retd GD 17/5/79.
EVANS K. A. D. Born 30/8/41. Commd 14/8/62. Flt Lt 14/2/68. Retd GD 31/8/79.
EVANS K. B. G. Born 24/1/20. Commd 18/9/47. Flt Lt 29/11/51. Retd PI 24/1/75.
EVANS K. R. Born 10/2/40. Commd 27/3/63. Flt Lt 27/9/66. Retd GD 31/10/70.
EVANS K. W. S., DFC. Born 24/12/19. Commd 10/6/42. Flt Lt 23/4/51. Retd GD 6/10/64.
EVANS L., DPhysEd. Born 29/11/38. Commd 25/9/62. Flt Lt 25/9/66. Retd PE 25/9/78.
EVANS L. H. Born 11/2/11. Commd 12/3/42. Sqn Ldr 1/1/53. Retd ENG 19/6/65.
EVANS L. N. Born 8/6/59. Commd 24/3/83. Flt Lt 24/9/88. Retd GD 5/7/98.
EVANS M. Born 16/12/49. Commd 4/2/71. Flt Lt 1/4/75. Retd GD 1/10/90.
EVANS M. C. Born 18/1/41. Commd 26/8/66. Flt Lt 28/1/73. Retd ADMIN 18/1/96.
EVANS M. D. Born 26/2/39. Commd 25/7/60. Sqn Ldr 1/7/70. Retd GD 9/8/85.
EVANS M. E. S. Born 24/11/26. Commd 14/6/46. Flt Lt 15/12/49. Retd GD 24/11/64.
EVANS M. H., IEng FSERT. Born 4/10/44. Commd 25/10/73. Sqn Ldr 1/1/85. Retd ENG 4/10/99.
EVANS M. J., CEng MIMechE MRAeS. Born 12/6/35. Commd 23/7/58. A.Cdre 1/7/84. Retd ENG 1/7/86.
EVANS M. N. Born 5/4/40. Commd 4/4/59. Gp Capt 1/1/86. Retd GD 5/4/95.
EVANS M. R., BSc. Born 3/3/58. Commd 3/5/77. Flt Lt 15/10/80. Retd GD 26/11/96.

EVANS M. W., BA. Born 22/10/59. Commd 28/2/82. Flt Lt 28/8/85. Retd ADMIN 17/6/89.
EVANS N. Born 27/11/44. Commd 19/6/64. Flt Lt 15/4/70. Retd GD 1/7/76.
EVANS N. M. Born 26/2/50. Commd 30/5/69. Gp Capt 1/7/93. Retd GD(G) 5/4/96.
EVANS N. V. Born 31/1/37. Commd 21/4/64. Fg Offr 21/10/64. Retd ENG 1/3/68.
EVANS P. A. Born 5/5/53. Commd 29/6/72. Sqn Ldr 1/7/89. Retd GD 1/5/01.
EVANS P. G., CEng MRAeS MIEE. Born 29/12/30. Commd 22/12/55. Sqn Ldr 1/7/66. Retd ENG 7/9/71.
EVANS P. I., MSc MBA BSc. Born 15/2/60. Commd 23/11/80. Sqn Ldr 1/1/92. Retd ENG 15/2/98.
EVANS P. L. Born 19/9/39. Commd 27/2/75. Flt Lt 12/6/70. Retd ADMIN 27/2/83.
EVANS P. R., AFC. Born 13/9/34. Commd 26/7/55. Flt Lt 26/1/58. Retd GD 13/9/72.
EVANS P. R. Born 16/6/29. Commd 15/6/61. Fg Offr 15/6/61. Retd ENG 17/12/66.
EVANS R. Born 4/8/30. Commd 4/9/58. Wg Cdr 1/1/80. Retd GD 1/9/85.
EVANS R. Born 30/10/57. Commd 10/3/77. Flt Lt 10/9/82. Retd GD 29/3/95.
EVANS R. C. Born 11/8/23. Commd 24/11/44. Flt Lt 18/2.49. Retd GD 16/1/60.
EVANS R. J., CEng MRAeS. Born 29/7/35. Commd 4/1/60. Sqn Ldr 1/1/76. Retd ENG 29/7/89.
EVANS R. W. D. Born 15/9/24. Commd 9/9/44. Sqn Ldr 1/4/56. Retd GD 5/10/63.
EVANS S. J. R. Born 22/4/18. Commd 29/10/42. Sqn Ldr 1/7/53. Retd ENG 22/4/73.
EVANS S. M., BSc. Born 24/9/51. Commd 13/9/70. Sqn Ldr 1/1/89. Retd GD 1/1/92.
EVANS S. R., BA. Born 3/7/46. Commd 2/10/67. Flt Lt 15/10/69. Retd GD 1/7/90.
EVANS Sir David., GCB CBE CIMgt. Born 14/7/24. Commd 7/4/44. ACM 31/3/78. Retd GD 9/8/83.
EVANS T. E. W., BA. Born 4/7/15. Commd 20/5/41. Sqn Ldr 29/9/51. Retd EDN 1/9/66.
EVANS T. L., BSc. Born 24/7/51. Commd 28/9/70. Sqn Ldr 1/1/85. Retd GD 24.7.89.
EVANS T. N. Born 14/11/44. Commd 13/2/86. Flt Lt 13/2/90. Retd GD(G) 7/12/96.
EVANS T. W., BSc. Born 1/10/24. Commd 12/9/61. Sqn Ldr 12/3/65. Retd ADMIN 12/9/77.
EVANS W. D. Born 13/12/12. Commd 8/8/40. Flt Lt 8/8/42. Retd GD 23/5/47.
EVANS W. E., DFC. Born 4/9/21. Commd 26/7/43. Sqn Ldr 1/4/56. Retd GD 4/9/64.
EVANS W. E. Born 1/10/13. Commd 14/3/46. Sqn Ldr 1/7/58. Retd SUP 16/10/62.
EVANS W. H., DFC AFC. Born 15/12/16. Commd 24/10/44. Flt Lt 29/11/51. Retd GD(G) 16/12/71.
EVANS W. J. Born 17/7/40. Commd 20/5/82. Flt Lt 1/3/87. Retd ENG 17/7/95.
EVE J. Born 19/8/12. Commd 24/6/40. Flt Lt 1/9/45. Retd GD(G) 31/8/64 rtg Sqn Ldr.
EVE J. S. Born 24/2/52. Commd 12/10/78. Flt Lt 25/4/81. Retd GD 24/2/90.
EVELEIGH G. C., CB OBE. Born 25/10/12. Commd 16/12/33. AVM 1/1/61. Retd GD 27/3/65.
EVELEIGH M., OBE. Born 9/12/48. Commd 7/6/68. Wg Cdr 1/7/92. Retd SY 14/3/97.
EVERALL S., MA. Born 23/5/20. Commd 11/8/53. Wg Cdr 11/3/66. Retd EDN 5/11/74.
EVEREST K. Born 1/11/39. Commd 19/4/63. Sqn Ldr 1/1/86. Retd GD 1/11/94.
EVEREST L. H. Born 11/4/23. Commd 11/4/44. Flt Lt 8/1/49. Retd GD(G) 30/3/77.
EVERETT B. D., MBE BA FIMgt MCIPS MInstAM(Dip) MRAeS. Born 17/6/35. Commd 26/9/57. Wg Cdr 1/1/75. Retd SUP 1/9/85.
EVERETT E. W. Born 25/6/18. Commd 30/12/42. Sqn Ldr 1/7/54. Retd SEC 25/6/73.
EVERITT A. J., MSc BEd DIC. Born 11/7/45. Commd 20/1/80. Sqn Ldr 1/7/88. Retd ADMIN 10/8/91.
EVERITT G. H., CBE DSO DFC*. Born 29/12/17. Commd 9/6/40. Gp Capt 1/7/58. Retd GD 29/12/67.
EVERITT J. W., MBE MIMgt. Born 12/3/24. Commd 9/11/44. Wg Cdr 1/7/67. Retd GD 12/3/79.
EVERITT W. G. C. Born 12/1/93. Commd 29/6/50. Flt Lt 24/1/54. Retd MED(T) 19/3/60.
EVERITT W. M., CEng MRAeS. Born 31/10/39. Commd 17/7/62. Wg Cdr 1/1/78. Retd ENG 1/2/94.
EVERS E. D. Born 6/11/36. Commd 5/3/55. Sqn Ldr 1/7/67. Retd GD 1/1/74.
EVERSHED T. A., BA MB BCh MRCS MFCM LRCP DPH DIH. Born 17/10/21. Commd 18/4/46. A Cdre 19/10/74. Retd MED 18/1/75.
EVERSON D. G., DFM. Born 13/12/21. Commd 8/2/43. Flt Lt 8/8/46. Retd GD(G) 13/12/76.
EVERSON R. C., OBE AFC. Born 16/2/20. Commd 29/5/43. Wg Cdr 1/1/59. Retd GD 16/2/67.
EVERSON R. M. Born 13/11/57. Commd 5/4/79. Flt Lt 5/10/84. Retd GD 13/5/96.
EVERY T. Born 18/2/22. Commd 19/9/43. Flt Lt 27/5/54. Retd GD 24/10/63.
EVES D. G. E. D. Born 28/7/49. Commd 24/11/67. Flt Lt 24/5/74. Retd ADMIN 1/8/94.
EVES D. V. Born 2/1/29. Commd 10/3/59. Flt Lt 10/3/65. Retd GD(G) 2/1/67.
EVESHAM D. A., MSc BSc MBCS. Born 11/7/53. Commd 2/3/80. Sqn Ldr 1/1/89. Retd ADMIN 2/3/96.
EVETTS P. C. Born 8/11/33. Commd 29/12/51. Flt Lt 25/10/57. Retd GD 2/7/65.
EVETTS R. Born 19/11/20. Commd 11/4/57. Sqn Ldr 1/7/68. Retd ENG 19/11/73.
EWAN J., MA. Born 25/1/30. Commd 28/6/55. Wg Cdr 1/1/72. Retd GD 25/6/85.
EWENS A. V. Born 25/11/31. Commd 2/6/52. Flt Lt 27/11/57. Retd GD 11/4/91.
EWENS W. W. H., MIMgt. Born 23/11/35. Commd 19/8/54. Sqn Ldr 1/7/69. Retd GD 21/8/76.
EWER A. C. Born 16/1/37. Commd 25/7/59. Sqn Ldr 1/7/72. Retd GD 1/9/94.
EWER R. M. Born 8/6/63. Commd 25/2/82. Flt Lt 25/8/87. Retd GD 1/2/96.
EWING M. I. H. Born 3/2/27. Commd 17/1/49. Sqn Ldr 1/7/70. Retd SY 1/6/77.
EWING P. M. M., CEng MRAeS. Born 20/3/30. Commd 15/7/54. Sqn Ldr 2a/2/64. Retd ADMIN 1/10/77.
EXELL P. F. Born 10/7/33. Commd 23/12/53. Sqn Ldr 1/7/68. Retd ENG 10/7/71.
EXLER R. W. Born 21/2/51. Commd 4/7/69. Flt Lt 4/1/75. Retd GD 2/8/89.
EXLEY B. J. A. Born 13/5/36. Commd 7/3/65. Flt Lt 8/3/72. Retd ADMIN 30/1/78. Reinstated 19/10/83. Sqn Ldr 1/1/89. Retd ADMIN 31/10/91.

EXLEY D. Born 4/12/33. Commd 11/6/52. Flt Lt 18/12/57. Retd GD 4/12/71.
EXLEY D. A., MBE. Born 3/1/26. Commd 22/8/63. Sqn Ldr 1/1/74. Retd GD(G) 31/1/86.
EXTON M. H., DFC. Born 8/12/16. Commd 6/11/42. Sqn Ldr 1/1/52. Retd. GD 3/5/59.
EXTON S. W. Born 24/10/49. Commd 18/4/74. Wg Cdr 1/1/94. Retd GD 24/10/99.
EXWOOD I. W. R., CEng MRAeS. Born 10/1/38. Commd 28/7/60. Sqn Ldr 1/7/60. Retd ENG 10/1/76.
EYLES E. J., MSc CEng MIEE. Born 21/2/31. Commd 25/9/62. Sqn Ldr 4/1/68. Retd EDN 27/9/83.
EYLES J. S. Born 24/3/15. Commd 28/9/44. Flt Lt 28/3/48. Retd ENG 31/10/53.
EYNON A. V. Born 6/7/12. Commd 31/12/41. Flt Lt 22/10/45. Retd ENG 30/12/57 rtg Sqn Ldr.
EYNON J. F. Born 21/2/28. Commd 5/11/52. Sqn Ldr 1/1/72. Retd ADMIN 29/11/80.
EYRE A. W., BSc CEng FRAeS ARSM FIMgt. Born 8/10/18. Commd 19/12/41. A Cdre 1/7/69. Retd ENG 8/10/73.
EYRE J. W., AFC. Born 8/10/32. Commd 6/12/51. Flt Lt 13/11/57. Retd GD 9/10/79.
EYRE T. Born 23/11/33. Commd 24/11/67. Flt Lt 4/5/72. Retd PE 24/11/75.
EZRA W. A. Born 25/6/17. Commd 6/8/44. Sqn Ldr 1/7/65. Retd SUP 12/7/72.

# F

FABIAN G. C., MSc BSc CEng MRAeS. Born 28/11/56. Commd 17/8/80. Sqn Ldr 1/1/91. Retd ENG 1/1/97.
FACE P. P., CEng MRAeS MIMgt. Born 26/12/23. Commd 28/3/46. Wg Cdr 1/1/72. Retd ENG 31/3/78.
FACER J. L., MB BS MRCS LRCP MRCP(E)MFCM DPH DIH. Born 11/4/27. Commd 27/7/50. Gp Capt 1/7/72. Retd MED 25/10/75.
FACER P. Born 1/3/56. Commd 1/7/82. Flt Lt 1/7/84. Retd GD 1/3/94.
FACEY D. E., FCA. Born 11/5/32. Commd 4/7/57. Sqn Ldr 1/7/70. Retd ADMIN 11/5/82.
FAGG A. J. Born 11/8/52. Commd 10/2/72. Sqn Ldr 1/1/86. Retd GD(G) 11/8/90.
FAGG G. A., BSc. Born 31/1/59. Commd 13/10/77. Flt Lt 15/10/81. Retd GD 31/1/97.
FAGG P. S., MB BS. Born 2/3/51. Commd 19/2/74. Wg Cdr 7/9/89. Retd MED 22/8/90.
FAHY P. E., DFC AFC. Born 14/6/21. Commd 18/5/44. Flt Lt 6/2/48. Retd GD 9/8/58.
FAIERS J. H. Born 19/4/43. Commd 14/8/80. Sqn Ldr 1/1/90. Retd ENG 19/4/98.
FAINT P. E. Born 16/2/38. Commd 30/11/56. Flt Lt 24/5/63. Retd GD 13/7/78.
FAIR G. P. Born 24/8/48. Commd 11/8/77. Sqn Ldr 1/7/92. Retd GD 1/8/94.
FAIR P. C. Born 18/5/06. Commd 15/11/26. Flt Lt 1/8/33. Retd GD 8/4/37.
FAIRBAIRN A. D. Born 16/2/45. Commd 24/2/67. Sqn Ldr 1/7/80. Retd SUP 14/3/97.
FAIRBAIRN D., BSc. Born 26/8/21. Commd 14/2/49. Sqn Ldr 1/7/67. Retd GD 26/8/76.
FAIRBAIRN D. I., OBE. Born 2/12/23/ Commd 9/5/44. Wg Cdr 1/7/66. Retd GD 11/8/76.
FAIRBAIRN J. M. Born 7/1/59. Commd 25/9/80. Sqn Ldr 1/1/95. Retd GD 6/10/97.
FAIRBROTHER E. A. Born 9/4/16. Commd 10/12/44. Flt Lt 10/6/48. Retd GD(G) 9/4/66.
FAIRCHILD F. Born 4/12/13. Commd 20/4/43. Flt Lt 20/10/46. Retd GD(G) 6/12/63.
FAIREY M. J. Born 25/7/31. Commd 22/1/54. Flt Lt 22/7/59. Retd GD(G) 6/10/69.
FAIRFOOT C. F. Born 20/1/17. Commd 20/10/41. Sqn Ldr 1/7/52. Retd SUP 1/8/64.
FAIRGRIEVE J. C., DFC. Born 17/2/18. Commd 1/5/42. Flt Lt 1/11/45. Retd GD 4/1/54.
FAIRGRIEVE P. J. Born 14/5/38. Commd 2/6/77. Flt Lt 2/6/82. Retd GD(G) 30/7/90.
FAIRHEAD I. F., BSc(Eng). Born 29/8/39. Commd 1/1/63. Sqn Ldr 1/1/71. Retd ENG 29/8/94.
FAIRHURST E. A., DFC TD. Born 14/4/18. Commd 13/5/40. Wg Cdr 1/1/55. Retd GD 22/5/65.
FAIRHURST G. L. Born 21/6/52. Commd 27/3/86. Flt Lt 27/3/88. Retd GD(ENG) 10/10/89.
FAIRHURST P., MBE. Born 7/4/27. Commd 27/9/50. Sqn Ldr 1/1/62. Retd ENG 7/4/82 rtg Wg Cdr.
FAIRWEATHER A. J., BSc(Eng) ACGI. Born 31/12/38. Commd 2/10/61. Gp Capt 1/1/93. Retd GD 1/1/96.
FAIRWEATHER J. M. Born 23/4/30. Commd 2/56. Sqn Ldr 1/1/70. Retd PRT 1/4/76.
FAITH M. M. Born 1/7/12. Commd 17/11/41. Sqn Off 1/1/50. Retd SEC 10/12/61.
FALCONER D. G. Born 28/5/11. Commd 2/11/44. Flt Lt 2/2/52. Retd GD(G) 28/5/61.
FALCONER G., BEM. Born 14/4/23. Commd 22/7/63. Flt Lt 22/7/69. Retd SEC 14/4/73.
FALCONER N., BSc MRAeS FIS. Born 9/7/33. Commd 18/10/55. Flt Lt 18/7/57. Retd GD 18/1/72.
FALCONER N. A. Born 13/12/14. Commd 13/6/46. Flt Lt 29/11/51. Retd RGT 28/11/57.
FALCONER R. J. Born 29/12/33. Commd 10/3/82. Flt Lt 10/3/82. Retd ENG 16/11/87.
FALK V. S. Born 1/7/16. Commd 5/4/44. Flt Offr 4/1/51. Retd SUP 1/7/54.
FALKINER R. J. T. Born 28/8/41. Commd 28/7/64. Sqn Ldr 1/7/75. Retd SUP 28/8/79.
FALL L. A. Born 21/10/46. Commd 6/5/65. Flt Lt 5/8/71. Retd SEC 31/1/73.
FALL R. M., FHCIMA MIMgt. Born 5/12/46. Commd 11/8/69. Sqn Ldr 1/1/79. Retd ADMIN 11/8/85
FALLAS G. D. Born 9/3/23. Commd 9/11/43. Sqn Ldr 1/4/55. Retd GD 25/1/64.
FALLON F., MRAeS. Born 12/1/20. Commd 19/8/42. Sqn Ldr 1/1/61. Retd ENG 13/1/68.
FALLON P., BA. Born 25/7/37. Commd 7/8/59. Sqn Ldr 7/2/67. Retd EDN 7/8/75.
FALLOW D. Born 25/12/55. Commd 22/9/88. Sqn Ldr 1/7/97. Retd ENG 2/4/01.
FANNING D. M., OBE MB BS MRCS LRCP DPH DIH. Born 12/4/28. Commd 5/1/53. Wg Cdr 8/4/65. Retd MED 12/10/70.
FANNING M., MB BS FFARCS DA. Born 9/8/28. Commd 29/8/54. Wg Cdr 31/1/66. Retd MED 29/8/70.
FANNON J. V. Born 29/2/16. Commd 30/1/47. Flt Lt 30/7/51. Retd SUP 1/3/65.
FARAGHER G. E., CEng MIEE MRAeS. Born 5/9/37. Commd 28/7/60. Sqn Ldr 1/7/69. Retd ENG 5/9/75.
FARCI V. I. A. Born 14/6/57. Commd 5/9/91. Sqn Ldr 1/7/97. Retd GD 1/7/00.
FARDELL J. B. Born 12/9/35. Commd 3/5/60. Flt Lt 3/3/66. Retd GD 12/9/73.
FARES D. B., MInstAM MHSM MIMgt. Born 20/3/48. Commd 8/9/77. Wg Cdr 1/7/89. Retd MED SEC 14/3/96.
FAREY M. J. Born 26/11/41. Commd 17/5/62. Sqn Ldr 1/7/77. Retd SY 1/7/83.
FARISH T. J., BSc. Born 26/12/55. Commd 15/9/74. Sqn Ldr 1/7/87. Retd GD 26/12/93.
FARLAM G. A., BSc. Born 14/3/34. Commd 26/7/55. Flt Lt 26/1/58. Retd GD 14/3/72.
FARLEY G. G. Born 29/7/26. Commd 7/10/48. Sqn Ldr 1/7/60. Retd GD 16/2/79.
FARLEY G. H., AFC. Born 10/4/22. Commd 24/5/44. Flt Lt 11/11/54. Retd GD 17/10/61.
FARLEY J. F., AFC. Born 17/4/33. Commd 21/9/55. Flt Lt 14/6/61. Retd GD 6/9/67.
FARLEY R. H., MIMgt. Born 14/2/30. Commd 12/12/51. Sqn Ldr 1/7/69. Retd SEC 30/8/80.
FARLEY R. M. Born 31/3/34. Commd 18/2/53. Wg Cdr 1/7/76. Retd GD(G) 10/11/88.

FARMAN R. J., BSc. Born 18/6/52. Commd 13/9/70. Sqn Ldr 1/1/90. Retd ENG 18/6/93.
FARMER A. T. Born 22/1/39. Commd 19/1/66. Sqn Ldr 1/1/81. Retd GD 15/1/93.
FARMER B. L., BSc CEng MIMechE MRAeS MIMgt. Born 3/10/45. Commd 23/8/83. Sqn Ldr 1/7/89. Retd ENG 1/7/93.
FARMER H. A. Born 11/1/60. Commd 8/6/84. Flt Lt 8/12/90. Retd SUP 31/3/94.
FARMER H. T. C. Born 1/10/28. Commd 6/9/51. Gp Capt 1/1/74. Retd GD 2/4/77.
FARMER L. R., MBE. Born 16/4/22. Commd 2/10/58. Sqn Ldr 1/1/70. Retd ENG 21/7/73.
FARMER M. E. Born 26/12/39. Commd 27/3/75. Sqn Ldr 1/7/87. Retd ENG 26/12/94.
FARMER M. J. Born 22/4/45. Commd 16/9/76. Sqn Ldr 1/7/84. Retd ENG 22/4/00.
FARMER R. A. Born 4/2/42. Commd 9/12/71. Flt Lt 9/6/78. Retd GD(G) 28/6/88.
FARMER R. G., BSc. Born 23/9/31. Commd 23/9/55. Sqn Ldr 23/3/65. Retd EDN 23/9/71.
FARMER T. J., CEng MIEE. Born 1/6/38. Commd 11/4/63. Flt Lt 10/6/68. Retd ENG 10/8/76.
FARMER-WRIGHT I. P. Born 15/11/29. Commd 17/12/52. Sqn Ldr 1/1/72. Retd ADMIN 15/11/87.
FARMERY H. R., OBE MIMgt. Born 4/1/19. Commd 18/12/43. Wg Cdr 1/1/70. Retd PRT 1/12/72.
FARNES P. C. P., DFM. Born 16/7/18. Commd 27/11/40. Sqn Ldr 1/9/45. Retd GD 27/6/58 rtg Wg Cdr.
FARNES R. H. Born 7/3/41. Commd 20/8/65. Flt Lt 1/7/68. Retd GD 13/7/74.
FARNFIELD K. D. Born 6/9/50. Commd 14/8/70. Sqn Ldr 1/1/85. Retd GD 6/9/88.
FARNLEY L. A. Born 4/9/08. Commd 20/2/43. Flt Lt 20/8/46. Retd ENG 29/8/57.
FARQUHAR D. B., AFC MA. Born 20/2/49. Commd 10/4/68. Wg Cdr 1/7/86. Retd GD 31/3/95.
FARQUHAR J. G. Born 20/9/34. Commd 11/3/57. Sqn Ldr 1/1/67. Retd GD 1/10/87.
FARQUHAR K. G. Born 17/3/18. Commd 4/10/56. Flt Lt 4/10/59. Retd SEC 29/9/62.
FARQUHAR W. E. Born 28/5/41. Commd 3/5/68. Fl Lt 21/9/74. Retd GD 7/11/83.
FARQUHAR-SMITH H. W., BA FIL MRAeS MIMgt. Born 7/11/39. Commd 30/1/61. Gp Capt 1/1/91. Retd GD 7/11/94.
FARQUHARSON A. J. M. Born 5/2/23. Commd 12/6/47. Sqn Ldr 1/7/60. Retd SEC 1/7/63.
FARQUHARSON D., BSC. Born 6/7/46. Commd 27/4/69. Flt Lt 27/10/73. Retd GD 31/12/76.
FARQUHARSON F. H. K. Born 23/1/51. Commd 16/9/76. Wg Cdr 1/7/95. Retd ENG 14/3/97.
FARQUHARSON G. M. Born 2/7/36. Commd 14/8/70. Flt Lt 14/8/72. Retd SUP 14/8/78. Reinstated 14/1/80. Sqn Ldr 1/1/88. Retd SUP 5/8/91.
FARQUHARSON W. L., DFC* FIMgt. Born 28/9/20. Commd 14/2/42. Gp Capt 1/7/66. Retd GD 28/1/76.
FARR J. L., OBE. Born 8/6/24. Commd 10/12/43. Sqn Ldr 1/1/59. Retd GD 8/7/67.
FARR P. G. D., CB OBE DFC FIMgt. Born 26/8/17. Commd 12/7/37. AVM 1/7/70. Retd GD 6/11/72.
FARR-VOLLER G. E. A., BA. Born 5/7/47. Commd 30/3/89. Flt Lt 30/3/91. Retd GD 14/7/96.
FARRAND B. M. Born 1/7/26. Commd 9/6/55. Fg Offr 9/6/57. Retd SUP 1/3/61.
FARRANDS R. A., FCIS MIMgt. Born 19/4/23. Commd 5/3/45. Gp Capt 1/1/74. Retd ADMIN 19/3/77.
FARRANT E. H. Born 5/12/32. Commd 17/5/70. Flt Lt 17/7/74. Retd GD 5/12/87.
FARRAR A. MCK. Born 12/5/46. Commd 29/6/72. Flt Lt 29/12/77. Retd GD 22/10/94.
FARRAR-HOCKLEY H. A. Born 14/10/54. Commd 20/9/79. Flt Lt 26/11/84. Retd ADMIN 14/10/93.
FARRELL B. G. Born 26/4/44. Commd 13/12/79. Sqn Ldr 1/1/90. Retd ENG 26/4/99.
FARRELL C. L., MA. Born 14/4/38. Commd 30/9/57. Wg Cdr 1/7/80. Retd ENG 14/4/93.
FARRELL J. A. J. Born 4/6/24. Commd 4/5/50. Sqn Ldr 1/1/69. Retd GD 16/7/73.
FARRELL W. Born 10/7/23. Commd 6/9/56. Flt Lt 6/9/62. Retd GD 28/3/68.
FARRER B. C., MBE. Born 25/7/34. Commd 9/4/53. Air Cdre 1/1/86. Retd GD 25/7/89.
FARRER W. R., AFM. Born 20/2/24. Commd 17/5/56. Flt Lt 17/5/62. Retd GD 20/2/74 rtg Sqn Ldr.
FARRIER C. D., MB BS FRCS FRCS(Edin) LRCP, Born 30/11/30. Commd 21/8/55. Wg Cdr 26/12/68. Retd MED 10/9/76.
FARRINGTON J. A. Born 18/1/34. Commd 23/2/55. Flt Lt 23/8/60. Retd GD 18/1/72.
FARROW A. G. Born 29/3/44. Commd 11/9/78. Flt Lt 11/5/80. Retd GD 1/4/85.
FARROW H., BEM. Born 16/4/15. Commd 4/7/57. Flt Lt 1/4/63. Retd SEC 10/7/69.
FARROW P. J. Born 21/9/40. Commd 22/2/63. Sqn Ldr 1/7/74. Retd GD 21/9/95.
FARTHING D. E. Born 27/12/26. Commd 6/1/71. Flt Lt 7/1/75. Retd GD 27/12/81
FARTHING P. J., MA. Born 26/5/38. Commd 23/10/59. Sqn Ldr 1/7/69. Retd SEC 23/10/75.
FARWELL J. Born 6/10/33. Commd 27/7/54. Wg Cdr 1/1/74. Retd GD 6/10/88.
FAUCHON F. T. Born 20/9/35. Commd 21/6/56. Wg Cdr 1/1/77. Retd GD(G) 20/9/90.
FAULKNER B. E. F., OBE FIMgt. Born 17/6/29. Commd 11/4/51. Gp Capt 1/1/77. Retd SEC 17/5/80.
FAULKNER E. C. H., MBE. Born 2/1/09. Commd 19/9/41. Sqn Ldr 1/8/47. Retd ENG 2/1/58.
FAULKNER J. H. Born 24/1/27. Commd 8/6/53. Flt Lt 17/5/56. Retd GD 26/3/67.
FAULKNER K. O. Born 1/10/49. Commd 19/3/81. Flt Lt 19/3/83. Retd GD 19/6/89.
FAULKNER M., BA. Born 28/6/49. Commd 24/9/72. Sqn Ldr 1/7/89. Retd GD 10/8/94.
FAULKNER V., BSc. Born 29/9/35. Commd 19/10/58. Flt Lt 23/3/64. Retd GD 23/9/75.
FAUSCH A. V. Born 15/6/28. Commd 30/5/51. Flt Lt 30/11/55. Retd GD 30/1/67.
FAWCETT J. H., AFC BSc MRAeS. Born 8/4/40. Commd 27/7/62. Flt Lt 9/12/64. Retd GD 1/1/76.
FAWCETT K. A. Born 17/1/31. Commd 8/9/57. Sqn Ldr 1/7/74. Retd ADMIN 19/5/76.
FAWCETT M., MBE MIMgt. Born 31/3/22. Commd 24/3/55. Sqn Ldr 1/1/69. Retd SUP 31/3/77.
FAWCETT P. Born 9/9/39. Commd 1/8/39. Wg Cdr 1/7/90. Retd GD(G) 29/4/93.
FAWCETT W. J. Born 13/2/39. Commd 13/12/79. Sqn Ldr 1/7/90. Retd ENG 29/10/93.

FAWCUS K. A. Born 16/11/46. Commd 29/7/68. Flt Lt 4/5/72. Retd SY 16/11/84.
FAWCUS P. C. A. Born 17/12/43. Commd 25/2/66. Flt Lt 25/8/71. Retd GD 17/12/81.
FAWCUS T. F. Born 11/9/21. Commd 30/5/45. Flt Lt 1/12/51. Retd SUP 30/4/73.
FAWSON S. E., CEng MRAeS FIMgt. Born 25/7/22. Commd 13/9/43. Gp Cpt 1/7/71. Retd ENG 25/7/82.
FAZACKERLEY M. D. Born 17/7/53. Commd 10/2/72. Fg Offr 10/2/74. Retd GD 11/11/77.
FAZAKERLEY I. Born 25/5/41. Commd 31/7/62. Wg Cdr 1/1/85. Retd SUP 25/5/96.
FAZEY F. Born 18/8/18. Commd 26/11/42. Sqn Ldr 1/1/54. Retd ENG 1/8/64.
FEAKES G. W. Born 30/9/34. Commd 20/8/53. Flt Lt 22/5/61. Retd GD 30/9/72.
FEAKES R. Born 25/8/35. Commd 9/4/57. Sqn Ldr 1/7/65. Retd GD 27/8/85.
FEALEY P. E., MIMgt. Born 28/2/28. Commd 26/4/60. Sqn Ldr 1/1/73. Retd SUP 28/2/88.
FEAR F. L. Born 28/2/23. Commd 12/10/44. Sqn Ldr 1/1/68. Retd GD(G) 28/2/78.
FEAR T. J., CEng MIMechE. Born 11/4/50. Commd 26/2/71. Sqn Ldr 1/7/87. Retd ENG 30/6/90.
FEAR T. J. Born 26/3/45. Commd 9/8/63. Flt Lt 9/2/69. Retd GD 29/6/74.
FEARN M. H. Born 4/2/58. Commd 25/9/80. Flt Lt 18/11/84. Retd GD(G) 4/2/96.
FEAST D. T. H., MIMgt. Born 15/1/31. Commd 18/10/62. Sqn Ldr 1/1/69. Retd ADMIN 18/1/84
FEAST R. C. Born 26/6/50. Commd 21/3/69. Wg Cdr 1/7/90. Retd GD 1/3/97.
FEATHER D. R. Born 30/9/25. Commd 6/7/45. Sqn Ldr 1/7/58. Retd GD 30/9/63.
FEATHERSTONE A. J., OBE MMS MIMgt. Born 23/12/37. Commd 5/6/56. Wg Cdr 1/7/82. Retd GD 23/12/92.
FEATHERSTONE D. F. W. Born 20/2/38. Commd 19/6/64. Flt Lt 9/2/68. Retd GD 20/2/76.
FEATHERSTONE J. C. Born 15/4/43. Commd 17/12/64. Gp Capt 1/7/91. Retd ADMIN 15/4/98.
FEATHERSTONE J. R., MSc BA. Born 18/8/46. Commd 17/10/71. Sqn Ldr 1/7/86. Retd SUP 1/9/96.
FEATONBY W. G. Born 28/9/34. Commd 24/5/53. Sqn Ldr 1/1/68. Retd GD 18/5/86.
FEEK C. D. Born 9/10/45. Commd 3/3/67. Wg Cdr 1/1/86. Retd SY 2/9/93.
FEELEY H. J., MBE MRAeS. Born 8/5/30. Commd 30/3/61. Sqn Ldr 1/7/74. Retd ENG 8/5/80.
FEENEY C. M. Born 7/3/54. Commd 24/7/81. Flt Lt 24/7/83. Retd RGT 7/3/92.
FEENEY J. Born 23/3/42. Commd 14/7/66. Sqn Ldr 1/1/92. Retd GD 14/8/96.
FEESEY J. D. L., AFC MRAeS. Born 11/10/42. Commd 12/1/62. AVM 1/1/94. Retd GD 30/1/99.
FEETHAM G. C. Born 27/4/34. Commd 18/7/54. Sqn Ldr 1/7/67. Retd GD(G) 31/8/69.
FEIRN R., MIMgt. Born 12/4/21. Commd 18/5/61. Sqn Ldr 1/1/73. Retd ENG 12/4/82.
FEIST M. Born 12/12/44. Commd 14/6/63. Flt Lt 15/4/70. Retd GD 16/5/92.
FEIST N. R. Born 30/10/37. Commd 29/11/63. Flt Lt 25/7/66. Retd GD 1/10/76.
FELIX R., LVO MIMgt. Born 30/9/39. Commd 9/7/57. Wg Cdr 1/7/78. Retd GD 15/3/83.
FELL C. M., CBE AFC. Born 12/10/18. Commd 26/1/41. A Cdr 1/7/68. Retd GD 12/8/71.
FELL E. E., AFC* MIMgt. Born 20/4/22. Commd 5/3/53. Sqn Ldr 1/1/67. Retd GD 23/4/74.
FELL H. Born 26/1/20. Commd 5/12/43. Sqn Ldr 1/4/55. Retd GD 27/1/69.
FELL J. C., BSc CEng MRAeS. Born 15/8/21. Commd 1/8/43. Sqn Ldr 1/10/56. Retd ENG 25/1/69.
FELL M. C. Born 27/9/49. Commd 19/6/70. Flt Lt 14/11/76. Retd GD(G) 27/9/87.
FELL P. A. Born 18/3/26. Commd 19/7/56. Flt Lt 19/7/62. Retd GD 1/11/75.
FELL W. B., MIMgt. Born 7/9/22. Commd 24/7/52. Sqn Ldr 1/7/74. Retd SUP 7/9/77.
FELLOWES D., MSc BSc. Born 28/10/41. Commd 13/9/70. Wg Cdr 1/7/87. Retd ADMIN 7/12/91.
FELLOWES T. P. Born 25/6/07. Commd 17/1/49. Sqn Ldr 1/7/50. Retd RGT 1/2/54.
FELLOWS K. Born 30/5/38. Commd 14/2/64. Flt Lt 14/2/70. Retd SUPPLY 1/9/80.
FELLOWS L., BEd MIL. Born 22/4/46. Commd 22/3/81. Sqn Ldr 1/1/89. Retd ADMIN 14/3/97.
FELLOWS T. A. Born 3/1/57. Commd 13/12/79. Sqn Ldr 1/7/94. Retd SUP 13/7/97.
FELMING P. C. H. Born 24/12/23. Commd 8/8/51. Sqn Ldr 1/1/63. Retd CAT 30/9/67.
FELSTEAD L. S. Born 21/12/09. Commd 20/5/42. Flt Offr 26/7/51. Retd SEC 18/2/62.
FELTON F. Born 25/9/36. Commd 29/7/65. Flt Lt 29/7/67. Retd PRT 25/9/74.
FELTON M. C. D. Born 28/3/33. Commd 23/8/51. Wg Cdr 1/7/75. Retd ADMIN 25/2/84.
FELTS P. A., BA. Born 22/8/47. Commd 2/3/80. Flt Lt 2/12/83. Retd SUP 2/3/96.
FELTS W. Born 4/6/46. Commd 20/9/79. Flt Lt 20/9/80. Retd ADMIN 20/9/87.
FELWICK D. L. Born 9/11/44. Commd 24/6/65. Wg Cdr 1/1/80. Retd SY 1/1/83.
FENBOW C. G. Born 12/9/38. Commd 25/7/59. Flt Lt 22/2/65. Retd GD 15/8/68.
FENECH F. Born 12/12/22. Commd 12/6/47. Flt Lt 7/8/56. Retd SUP 9/8/64.
FENLON K. S. Born 29/1/36. Commd 27/3/75. Flt Lt 27/3/80. Retd ENG 29/1/94.
FENLON-SMITH P. A. Born 4/5/60. Commd 12/7/79. Sqn Ldr 1/1/93. Retd GD 4/5/98.
FENN A. A. Born 18/7/15. Commd 26/1/42. Flt Lt 27/4/49. Retd GD(G) 20/9/61.
FENN A. K., BDS. Born 20/3/58. Commd 1/9/86. Sqn Ldr 28/6/93. Retd DEL 20/3/98.
FENN M. G. Born 15/8/33. Commd 11/10/51. Flt Lt 27/7/59. Retd GD 15/8/71 rtg Sqn Ldr.
FENN R. J. Born 31/10/45. Commd 11/9/64. Flt Lt 4/11/70. Retd GD 31/10/85
FENNELL G. R. Born 27.1.30. Commd 13/9/51. Flt Lt 30/4/57. Retd GD 3/2/76.
FENNELL J., MBE AFC. Born 7/1/25. Commd 24/7/47. Gp Capt. 1/7/69. Retd GD 7/1/80.
FENNELL J. R. Born 9/6/42. Commd 31/8/62. Sqn Ldr 1/7/94. Retd GD 9/6/97.
FENNELL P. R. Born 2/4/39. Commd 22/2/64. Wg Cdr 1/7/86. Retd GD 2/4/94.
FENNELL S. M. Born 9/6/44. Commd 24/9/64. Flt Lt 10/12/70 fenwick. Retd SEC 5/5/73.
FENNER M. D., MIMgt. Born 16/2/29. Commd 5/4/50. Gp Capt 1/1/74. Retd GD 31/3/77.
FENNESSY D. C., LLB. Born 24/11/37. Commd 14/5/63. Sqn Ldr 31/3/73. Retd EDN 14/5/79.

FENNING R. C. Born 4/3/31. Commd 24/1/52. Flt Lt 5/11/58. Retd GD 10/6/71.
FENNY D. R. Born 5/2/61. Commd 29/7/83. Flt Lt 29/1/89. Retd GD 28/3/99.
FENTON G. N. Born 2/5/48. Commd 2/8/68. Flt Lt 8/3/72. Retd GD 20/5/85.
FENTON M. J., CEng MIMechE. Born 28/9/42. Commd 23/12/61. Flt Lt 23/6/68. Retd ENG 28/9/82.
FENTON S.C. Born 22/2/43. Commd 8/9/83. Flt Lt 8/9/87. Retd ENG 30/11/88.
FENTON W. J. F. Born 15/1/17. Commd 9/9/39. Wg Cdr 1/7/56. Retd SUP 10/8/61.
FENTUM M. D. Born 12/7/48. Commd 20/10/67. Sqn Ldr 1/1/86. Retd GD 1/11/96.
FENWICK T., ACIS AIM. Born 1/3/22. Commd 17/6/44. Flt Lt 17/12/47. Retd GD(G) 27/8/75.
FENWICK-WILSON R. M., AFC. Born 29/7/14. Commd 24/8/34. Sqn Ldr 1/9/40. Retd GD 11/3/46 rtg Wg Cdr.
FEREDAY W. L. Born 1/7/14. Commd 3/6/42. Sqn Offr 1/1/53. Retd SEC 30/6/59.
FERENCZY G. I., CEng FIEE FIMgt. Born 15/6/34. Commd 12/6/58. A Cdre 1/7/80. Retd ENG 11/6/85.
FERGUSON A., FIMgt. Born 24/7/44. Commd 20/6/66. Gp Capt 1/1/89. Retd GD 16/10/93.
FERGUSON A. D. Born 3/11/12. Commd 15/7/33. Plt Offr 15/7/33. Retd GD 4/4/34.
FERGUSON A. M., CEng FIEE. Born 21/3/44. Commd 15/7/65. A Cdre 1/1/95. Retd ENG 14/7/99.
FERGUSON A. P., BSc CEng MRAeS MIMgt. Born 2/7/53. Commd 3/9/72. Sqn Ldr 1/7/85. Retd ENG 2/7/91.
FERGUSON C. G. Born 11/4/41. Commd 14/5/60. Sqn Ldr 1/7/76. Retd GD 11/7/93.
FERGUSON D. A. Born 4/3/35. Commd 19/8/54. Flt Lt 7/3/62. Retd GD 1/10/86 rtg Sqn Ldr.
FERGUSON D. C., AFC. Born 9/6/33. Commd 27/2/52. Wg Cdr 1/1/76. Retd GD 9/6/88.
FERGUSON D. W. B., BSc. Born 29/9/55. Commd 26/5/85. Flt Lt 26/11/86. Retd ENG 31/3/94.
FERGUSON G. A., CB CBE. Born 15/4/38. Commd 28/7/60. AVM 1/7/91. Retd SUP 1/7/94.
FERGUSON I. C., BA. Born 19/2/60. Commd 11/9/83. Flt Lt 11/3/85. Retd GD 29/2/96.
FERGUSON I. J. Born 9/2/54. Commd 5/2/81. Sqn Ldr 1/7/90. Retd GD(G) 2/7/96.
FERGUSON I. K. Born 16/4/51. Commd 7/6/73. Flt Lt 7/12/78. Retd GD 30/9/91.
FERGUSON J. Born 8/6/26. Commd 8/7/65. Sqn Ldr 31/8/74. Retd MED(SEC) 30/4/77.
FERGUSON J. Born 10/3/24. Commd 9/7/59. Flt Lt 9/7/64. Retd GD 29/3/69.
FERGUSON L. H., DFM. Born 1/5/21. Commd 23/10/42. Flt Lt 13/12/48. Retd GD 1/5/64 rtg Sqn Ldr.
FERGUSON M. C., MBE. Born 26/3/22. Commd 19/1/50. Gp Capt 1/1/71. Retd ENG 8/6/74.
FERGUSON P. D. Born 11/6/24. Commd 15/12/44. Sqn Ldr 1/1/69. Retd GD 28/4/79.
FERGUSON R. A. W., MBE. Born 17/8/18. Commd 17/5/56. Flt Lt 17/5/59. Retd ENG 30/5/64.
FERN B. E. Born 26/9/23. Commd 29/7/44. Sqn Ldr 1/7/59. Retd GD 9/9/67.
FERN R. A. Born 22/11/62. Commd 26/11/81. Flt Lt 26/5/88. Retd GD(G) 22/4/89.
FERNEE M. F. Born 14/3/44. Commd 3/8/62. Flt Lt 3/2/68. Retd GD 4/8/81.
FERNIE J. E. Born 21/8/57. Commd 31/8/75. Sqn Ldr 1/1/89. Retd GD 21/8/95.
FERNIE W. A., MSc BSc(Eng) CEng MRAeS. Born 2/11/49. Commd 4/10/71. Sqn Ldr 1/1/85. Retd ENG 1/1/90.
FERREN T. B. Born 23/11/29. Commd 21/10/66. Sqn Ldr 1/7/82. Retd ENG 23/11/89.
FERRIDAY D. W., MSc MMedSci MB BCh FFOM MRCGP DRCOG. Born 13/10/52. Commd 4/9/73. Sqn Ldr 4/8/82.
  Retd MED 1/2/83. Re-entered 13/2/87. Wg Cdr 13/2/93. Retd MED 21/9/00.
FERRILL B., BEM. Born 13/3/32. Commd 3/6/65. Flt Lt 3/6/71. Retd ADMIN 29/6/84.
FERRILL M. B. A., BSc. Born 8/3/62. Commd 31/8/80. Flt Lt 15/10/86. Retd SUP 8/12/96.
FERRIS R. B., DPhysEd. Born 21/1/29. Commd 28/9/55. Sqn Ldr 1/7/68. Retd SUP 28/9/71.
FEWELL D. J. Born 23/11/32. Commd 21/5/52. Flt Lt 16/10/57. Retd GD 31/7/76.
FEWING W. R. J., CBE MA MSc CEng MRAeS MIMgt. Born 30/5/34. Commd 26/9/53. Air Cdre 1/7/85. Retd ENG
  30/5/89.
FEWTRELL C. G. Born 14/4/31. Commd 15/6/53. Flt Lt 14/10/58. Retd GD 14/4/69.
FEWTRELL E. C. S., DFC. Born 3/7/16. Commd 23/3/36. Wg Cdr 1/1/52. Retd GD 3/7/71 rtg Gp Capt.
FEWTRELL G. H. S. Born 26/12/24. Commd 21/4/45. Flt Lt 11/6/53. Retd GD 15/5/68.
FFRENCH-CONSTANT M. C., BA BM BCh. Born 27/9/29. Commd 4/4/55. Wg Cdr 4/4/68. Retd MED 4/4/71.
FIDLER P. P. Born 13/1/42. Commd 8/9/83. Flt Lt 8/9/87. Retd ENG 10/3/93.
FIELD B. C., FInstPet MCIPS. Born 7/8/34. Commd 26/5/64. Sqn Ldr 1/1/73. Retd SUP 12/10/79.
FIELD C. P. Born 5/3/33. Commd 15/12/53. Fg Offr 15/12/53. Retd GD 25/11/59.
FIELD C. R. Born 6/7/45. Commd 1/4/65. Sqn Ldr 1/1/81. Retd SY 1/10/85.
FIELD D., MA PhD. Born 17/1/21. Commd 17/10/41. Gp Capt 1/7/67. Retd SUP 17/1/76.
FIELD H. O. Born 14/4/29. Commd 1/6/51. Sqn Ldr 1/7/62. Retd GD 14/4/67.
FIELD J., DPhysEd. Born 13/6/45. Commd 3/10/66. Wg Cdr 1/7/88. Retd ADMIN 14/9/96.
FIELD J., MBE. Born 5/10/30. Commd 13/7/61. Sqn Ldr 1/7/74. Retd ENG 6/8/83.
FIELD J. L., CBE MA. Born 3/3/26. Commd 21/12/45. A Cdre 1/1/78. Retd GD 20/4/81.
FIELD M. J. G. Born 10/3/39. Commd 6/9/68. Flt Lt 6/9/70. Retd GD 10/3/77.
FIELD M. K., BA. Born 24/12/34. Commd 14/5/60. Flt Lt 14/2/63. Retd GD 24/12/72.
FIELD P. A., MBE MIMgt. Born 4/9/34. Commd 23/3/64. Wg Cdr 1/7/79. Retd ADMIN 8/4/88.
FIELD P. V., BSc CEng MRAeS. Born 3/3/28. Commd 25/5/50. Wg Cdr 1/1/67. Retd ENG 1/11/73.
FIELD S. E. B. Born 10/6/43. Commd 15/7/64. Flt Lt 15/7/69. Retd ENG 1/10/74.
FIELD W. H. J. Born 5/6/08. Commd 25/11/43. Flt Lt 25/11/48. Retd ENG 15/9/53.
FIELD-RICHARDS N. J., CEng MRAeS. Born 7/7/39. Commd 28/7/60. Wg Cdr 1/7/75. Retd ENG 26/3/79.
FIELDING D. Born 24/8/52. Commd 28/9/89. Flt Lt 28/9/91. Retd ENG 5/4/99.
FIELDING F. W., MBE AFC. Born 1/9/25. Commd 23/4/53. Sqn Ldr 1/1/68. Retd GD 1/9/79.
FIELDING J. G., OBE MIMgt. Born 7/11/28. Commd 22/9/49. Wg Cdr 1/1/73. Retd ADMIN 7/11/84.

FIELDING P. Born 11/8/44. Commd 11/2/65. Sqn Ldr 1/7/78. Retd ADMIN 11/8/82.
FIELDING S. Born 23/7/32. Commd 12/10/54. Flt Lt 16/8/61. Retd GD 23/10/70.
FIGGINS P. D. Born 21/3/40. Commd 1/11/79. Sqn Ldr 1/7/91. Retd SY 21/2/95.
FIGGURES J. M. F., BSc CEng MIEE. Born 26/11/44. Commd 28/9/64. Sqn Ldr 1/1/85. Retd ENG 26/5/00.
FILBEY C. H. Born 2/9/21. Commd 27/2/47. Sqn Ldr 1/7/66. Retd SUP 13/9/68.
FILDES R. A. Born 30/8/22. Commd 28/7/60. Flt Lt 28/7/65. Retd SEC 1/1/76.
FILING T. J., AFC. Born 3/11/33. Commd 11/6/52. Flt Lt 18/12/57. Retd GD 3/11/71.
FILLINGHAM A. P. Born 5/3/61. Commd 8/12/83. Flt Lt 8/6/89. Retd GD 14/3/96.
FILLINGHAM K., DFC. Born 16/5/23. Commd 3/4/44. Flt Lt 19/11/53. Retd GD 13/12/67.
FINCH A. J., MA MEd BA MCIPD DipEd PGCE. Born 4/10/57. Commd 11/9/83. Sqn Ldr 1/1/91. Retd ADMIN 14/3/97.
FINCH C. R., MIExpE. Born 28/9/47. Commd 13/9/70. Sqn Ldr 1/1/91. Retd ENG 12/10/96.
FINCH E. D. Born 15/6/27. Commd 8/4/49. Sqn Ldr 1/7/57. Retd GD 15/6/65.
FINCH F. W. Born 11/7/12. Commd 7/5/53. Sqn Ldr 1/7/61. Retd ENG 1/8/64.
FINCH G. P. Born 19/2/47. Commd 18/8/67. Flt Lt 11/2/73. Retd GD 19/4/92.
FINCH J., CBE DFC AFC. Born 18/8/20. Commd 13/4/41. Gp Capt 1/7/61. Retd GD 6/1/68.
FINCH J. E., BSc. Born 17/5/28. Commd 4/10/50. Flt Lt 19/6/52. Retd GD 23/4/55.
FINCH J. S. G. Born 15/7/32. Commd 25/3/52. Flt Lt 7/8/57. Retd GD 15/7/87.
FINCH P. F. Born 10/5/28. Commd 9/12/65. Flt Lt 9/12/71. Retd SUP 24/5/75.
FINCH P. S. Born 2/3/59. Commd 23/10/86. Flt Lt 17/11/88. Retd SY 2/3/97.
FINCH R. B. Born 3/11/49. Commd 27/2/75. Flt Lt 27/8/80. Retd GD 3/11/90.
FINCH R. I., FCIPD FSCA. Born 24/11/35. Commd 9/4/57. Wg Cdr 1/7/77. Retd ADMIN 24/11/90.
FINCH R. T. A., BSc MCIPS Born 20/9/49. Commd 15/9/69. Flt Lt 15/10/75. Retd SUP 1/7/78.
FINCHAM P. J. Born 26/7/44. Commd 15/3/73. Sqn Ldr 1/1/80. Retd ENG 26/7/88.
FINCHER H. Born 28/8/12. Commd 11/12/41. Sqn Ldr 1/1/52. Retd ENG 13/11/64.
FINCHER J. F., CEng MIMechE. Born 7/7/32. Commd 15/7/54. Sqn Ldr 1/1/65. Retd ENG 7/7/92.
FINDING A. R. Born 19/8/51. Commd 4/2/71. Sqn Ldr 1/1/86. Retd ADMIN 6/3/89.
FINDING P., CEng MRAes MIMgt. Born 12/5/22. Commd 10/12/43. Sqn Ldr 1/1/62. Retd ENG 9/11/74.
FINDLATER J. Born 22/10/33. Commd 27/2/56. Wg Cdr 1/7/80. Retd GD 11/6/86.
FINDLAY D. W., MA. Born 12/3/55. Commd 9/6/54. Flt Lt 15/4/77. Retd GD 15/7/87.
FINDLAY G. S., OBE BSc FIMgt. Born 21/11/35. Commd 22/8/61. Gp Capt 1/7/89. Retd ADMIN 2/7/91.
FINDLAY J. Born 2/3/13. Commd 14/11/46. Plt Offr 14/11/46. Retd SUP 13/6/48.
FINDLAY M. D. de R. Born 22/7/42. Commd 28/7/64. Flt Lt 26/7/67. Retd GD 17/9/71.
FINE B. H. P. Born 24/11/35. Commd 14/6/63. Flt Lt 25/7/66. Retd GD 24/11/73.
FINEGAN C. M., BSc MIMgt. Born 25/1/33. Commd 7/12/65. Sqn Ldr 1/1/74. Retd SUP 25/1/91.
FINELY N. H. M. Born 16/10/44. Commd 30/8/73. Wg Cdr 1/1/96. Retd OPS SPT 28/4/01.
FINKLE R. Born 2/1/34. Commd 12/7/57. Sqn Ldr 1/7/66. Retd ENG 12/7/73.
FINLAY D., CBE. Born 4/1/12. Commd 15/7/33. Gp Capt 1/7/50. Retd GD 15/1/67 rtg A Cdre.
FINLAY D. L. A., MIMgt. Born 25/1/24. Commd 8/8/44. Sqn Ldr 1/4/57. Retd SEC 22/11/75.
FINLAY G., BSc. Born 8/7/57. Commd 26/7/81. Flt Lt 26/10/81. Retd GD 14/3/96.
FINLAY J. I., MIMgt. Born 26/11/24. Commd 17/8/50. Sqn Ldr 1/7/62. Retd GD 1/10/73.
FINLAYSON J. S., MA. Born 20/1/44. Commd 16/1/67. Sqn Ldr 1/7/77. Retd GD 25/11/93.
FINLAYSON P. J. S., AFC. Born 9/12/20. Commd 14/1/39. Wg Cdr 1/1/54. Retd GD 9/12/75 rtg Gp Capt.
FINN B. B. Born 23/2/19. Commd 1/4/46. Flt Lt 9/2/51. Retd ENG 18/9/54.
FINN-KELCEY C. J., MBE. Born 26/8/51. Commd 17/7/70. Flt Lt 17/1/76. Retd GD 29/6/82.
FINNERON T. J., MIMgt. Born 14/9/50. Commd 25/2/72. Sqn Ldr 1/1/82. Retd GD 9/12/90.
FINNEY P., BSc(Eng) MSc CEng MRAeS. Born 5/10/39. Commd 9/7/63. Wg Cdr 1/1/78. Retd ENG 9/7/85.
FINNEY S. F., MBE. Born 5/8/50. Commd 29/6/72. Sqn Ldr 1/7/85. Retd ADMIN 5/8/00.
FINNIE A. J., BA MCIPD. Born 23/6/30. Commd 8/2/52. Wg Cdr 1/1/75. Retd SEC 4/2/78.
FINNIE J. B. Born 13/12/41. Commd 20/8/65. Flt Lt 1/7/68. Retd GD 24/8/74.
FINNIS J. F. S. Born 21/1/22. Commd 28/7/44. Flt Lt 27/5/54. Retd GD 21/1/77.
FIRMIN P. A., BSc. Born 18/3/61. Commd 5/2/84. Flt Lt 5/8/85. Retd GD 1/12/00.
FIRMSTON-WILLIAMS R. A. Born 28/12/57. Commd 5/2/81. Flt Lt 5/8/86. Retd GD 29/4/97.
FIRTH C. J. Born 11/7/29. Commd 24/1/52. Flt Lt 29/10/57. Retd GD 29/3/69.
FIRTH J. F., MBE MIMgt. Born 26/10/20. Commd 14/3/46. Sqn Ldr 1/7/65. Retd ENG 31/8/78.
FIRTH J. R. Born 2/8/41. Commd 18/8/61. Flt Lt 22/9/68. Retd GD 2/4/81.
FIRTH J. V., MA BA. Born 1/1/30. Commd 11/12/52. Gp Capt 1/7/83. Retd ADMIN 1/1/85.
FIRTH P. A. Born 28/2/33. Commd 24/5/53. Sqn Ldr 1/7/68. Retd GD 28/2/88.
FISH D. Born 22/1/24. Commd 6/7/50. Sqn Ldr 1/1/62. Retd GD 22/3/68.
FISH I. D., BSc. Born 3/10/46. Commd 13/9/70. Sqn Ldr 1/7/85. Regd GD(G) 31/10/90.
FISH L., DFC DFM. Born 5/2/20. Commd 25/6/42. Flt Lt 20/1/47. Retd GD(G) 3/3/70.
FISH M. A., MBE. Born 4/2/31. Commd 23/5/51. Sqn Ldr 1/7/69. Retd GD 26/10/76.
FISH P. A. Born 20/10/41. Commd 27/1/61. Flt Lt 15/4/70. Retd GD 20/10/79.
FISHBURN A. Born 8/5/23. Commd 9/11/43. Flt Lt 6/9/62. Retd GD 31/1/68.
FISHER A., AFC MRAeS. Born 19/8/33. Commd 9/4/52. Sqn Ldr 1/1/70. Retd GD 31/12/73.
FISHER A. Born 22/9/50. Commd 4/3/71. Sqn Ldr 1/1/86. Retd SY(PRT) 1/1/89.

FISHER B. N. M. S. Born 17/6/41. Commd 10/6/66. Flt lt 10/12/71. Retd GD 22/2/96.
FISHER C. Born 28/5/32. Commd 22/7/66. Flt Lt 22/7/68. Retd SEC 30/9/78.
FISHER C. J. Born 5/3/43. Commd 24/11/67. Sqn Ldr 1/7/81. Retd SUP 1/7/84. Re-entered 17/2/89. Sqn Ldr 17/2/86. Retd SUP 5/3/98.
FISHER C. R., BSc. Born 20/7/49. Commd 17/1/72. Flt Lt 17/4/73. Retd GD 17/1/88.
FISHER D. Born 30/12/20. Commd 17/6/54. Flt Lt 27/8/57. Retd GD 30/3/68.
FISHER D. J., AFC. Born 9/8/46. Commd 26/5/67. Sqn Ldr 1/7/80. Retd GD 31/10/89.
FISHER D. W., lEng MIIE(elec) MIMgt. Born 31/5/47. Commd 16/12/66. Sqn Ldr 1/7/83. Retd ENG 31/5/91.
FISHER E. H. Born 27/5/20. Commd 26/9/57. Sqn Ldr 18/4/67. Retd DEL 30/8/69.
FISHER E. T. Born 4/5/19. Commd 2/3/45. Flt Lt 4/1/51. Retd GD 31/8/68.
FISHER G. W. O., OBE DFC*. Born 10/7/21. Commd 19/8/39. Wg Cdr 1/1/55. Retd GD 5/5/61.
FISHER H. M., AFC. Born 18/7/28. Commd 28/6/51. Flt Lt 10/10/56. Retd GD 16/10/66.
FISHER H. W. H., DFC. Born 19/3/17. Commd 6/2/39. Wg Cdr 1/7/52. Retd GD 27/2/56.
FISHER J. A., CEng MIEE. Born 5/2/30. Commd 18/5/65. Wg Cdr 1/1/75. Retd ENG 4/4/81.
FISHER J. F., AFC MRAeS. Born 5/6/43. Commd 17/12/63. Sqn Ldr 1/1/78. Retd GD 5/6/81.
FISHER J. R. Born 21/10/16. Commd 3/4/39. Sqn Ldr 1/8/47. Retd SUP 21/10/66.
FISHER J. S., BSc CEng MIEE. Born 27/3/47. Commd 6/9/71. Flt Lt 6/3/74. Retd 6/9/87.
FISHER J. W. Born 8/4/52. Commd 3/12/70. Sqn Ldr 1/1/88. Retd SUP 1/1/91.
FISHER M., BA. Born 18/8/36. Commd 10/10/58. Sqn Ldr 10/4/67. Retd EDN 11/10/75.
FISHER M. G. P., BA MB BChir MFOM DRCOG DCH DAvMed. Born 21/11/30. Commd 14/10/56. Gp Capt 1/7/79. Retd MED 29/8/85.
FISHER M. G. W. Born 31/3/43. Commd 29/10/64. Sqn Ldr 1/7/77. Retd ADMIN 31/3/84. Re-entered 16/1/87. Wg Cdr 1/7/90. Retd ADMIN 1/10/00.
FISHER P. A. Born 22/5/44. Commd 22/3/63. Flt Lt 22/9/68. Retd GD 1/6/77.
FISHER P. T. Born 15/1/59. Commd 6/5/83. Flt Lt 23/10/86. Retd GD(G) 26/9/89.
FISHER R. A. Born 19/9/44. Commd 28/2/64. Flt Lt 28/8/69. Retd GD 3/1/76.
FISHER R. I. Born 9/5/43. Commd 28/4/67. Wg Cdr 1/1/94. Retd GD 9/5/98.
FISHER R. J. Born 6/8/33. Commd 21/5/52. Flt Lt 26/11/57. Retd GD 6/8/71.
FISHER W. Born 28/9/27. Commd 21/4/67. Flt Lt 21/4/70. Retd GD 28/9/82.
FISHER W. I. J. Born 17/12/38. Commd 14/8/70. Flt Lt 14/8/76. Retd MED(SEC) 28/8/76.
FISHWICK H., MBE FIMgt. Born 4/3/20. Commd 28/6/43. Gp Capt 1/1/72. Retd ENG 4/3/75.
FISK D. C. Born 31/12/23. Commd 29/4/44. Flt Lt 5/11/58. Retd GD(G) 19/4/69.
FISK M. P., BSc. Born 22/11/61. Commd 31/8/80. Flt Lt 15/10/84. Retd GD 22/11/99.
FITCHARD R. H., MRIN MMS MIMgt. Born 25/12/36. Commd 29/9/55. Sqn Ldr 1/1/72. Retd GD 25/12/94.
FITCHEN E. E., DFC. Born 24/2/12/ Commd 16/10/40. Flt Lt 1/9/45. Retd SEC 1/1/54 rtg Sqn Ldr.
FITCHEW K. E. Born 28/6/27. Commd 16/7/52. Flt Lt 12/12/57. Retd GD 18/11/75.
FITHEN G., BSc FIMgt. Born 7/1/28. Commd 21/1/55. A Cdre 1/7/77. Retd EDN 3/11/81.
FITNESS P. M., BSc. Born 19/7/58. Commd 4/7/82. Fg Off 4/1/82. Retd GD(G) 10/12/84.
FITT G. R. Born 26/8/45. Commd 15/7/69. Fg Offr 15/7/71. Retd SUP 15/7/75. Re-entered 11/12/77. Sqn Ldr 1/7/86. Retd SUP 11/12/99.
FITTON J. Born 1/10/13. Commd 9/9/54. Sqn Ldr 1/1/64. Retd ENG 9/11/68.
FITTON K. Born 27/6/17. Commd 28/9/44. Sqn Ldr 1/1/66. Retd SUP 29/6/68.
FITTON K. B., DFC. Born 24/2/24. Commd 28/11/49. Flt Lt 19/11/53. Retd GD 24/2/82.
FITTON M. M., AFM. Born 6/8/34. Commd 4/2/71. Flt Lt 4/2/74. Retd GD(G) 6/8/89.
FITTUS J. C. Born 25/3/41. Commd 31/7/62. Flt Lt 14/2/66. Retd GD 10/10/70.
FITZ-GERALD S. F. Born 14/3/57. Commd 1/11/81. Flt 1/4/85. Retd GD(G) 31/3/96.
FITZCHARLES M. Born 18/2/35. Commd 19/8/65. Flt Lt 19/8/70. Retd GD 1/5/73.
FITZGERALD D., MBE DFC MRAeS. Born 1/9/22. Commd 2/9/42. Wg Cdr 1/1/64. Retd GD 1/9/68.
FITZGERALD M. A. Born 1/4/43. Commd 31/10/69. Flt Lt 8/9/74. Retd SY 16/1/83.
FITZGERALD P. E., BSc. Born 8/8/46. Commd 1/10/70. Sqn Ldr 1/1/83. Retd GD 22/4/94.
FITZGERALD-LOMBARD D. A. I., MBE. Born 29/10/47. Commd 30/1/70. Sqn Ldr 1/1/86. Retd SUP 29/10/91.
FITZGERALD-LOMBARD D. M. B. Born 5/8/06. Commd 18/10/37. Sqn Ldr 1/7/48. Retd MAR 21/6/58 rtg Wg Cdr.
FITZGERALD-LOMBARD R. M. S., CEng FIEE MRAeS. Born 9/10/39. Commd 18/7/61. A Cdre 1/7/90. Retd ENG 9/10/94.
FITZPATRICK A. G. Born 15/8/41. Commd 18/8/62. Flt Lt 8/1/69. Retd GD 15/8/79.
FITZPATRICK C. Born 12/2/49. Commd 27/2/70. Sqn Ldr 1/7/95. Retd GD 1/10/98.
FITZPATRICK D. Born 2/10/27. Commd 21/11/51. Flt Lt 29/4/59. Retd GD 16/5/67.
FITZPATRICK H. G. Born 4/8/19. Commd 29/3/44. Flt Lt 25/11/51. Retd GD(G) 5/1/68.
FITZPATRICK K. L. Born 18/12/42. Commd 30/7/63. Wg Cdr 1/7/78. Retd GD 1/7/81.
FITZPATRICK P. Born 14/2/27. Commd 24/2/66. Flt Lt 24/2/72. Resigned SUP 2/4/77. Reinstated 13/8/80. Retd 14/2/87.
FITZPATRICK P., MBE. Born 21/7/33. Commd 9/2/55. Flt Lt 10/8/60. Retd GD 29/11/76.
FITZPATRICK P. J. Born 30/3/47. Commd 17/3/67. Sqn Ldr 1/1/80. Retd SUP 1/6/87.
FITZPATRICK Sir John., KBE CB. Born 15/12/29. Commd 28/7/53. AM 1/1/84. Retd GD 31/3/86.
FITZROY K. C. Born 20/9/28. Commd 30/1/52. Flt Lt 18/4/57. Retd GD 30/1/68.
FITZSIMMONS A. P., BA. Born 30/1/50. Commd 10/6/73. Flt Lt 10/9/76. Retd GD(G) 10/6/89.

FITZSIMMONS D. J., AFC. Born 12/4/42. Commd 13/2/60. Flt Lt 13/8/65. Retd GD 12/4/79.
FIXTER S. R. Born 23/11/58. Commd 7/8/87. Flt Lt 15/7/90. Retd ENG 23/11/96.
FLACK G. G., MBE. Born 27/12/37. Commd 4/10/56. Sqn Ldr 1/1/70. Retd SY 20/2/77.
FLACK G. N., BSc. Born 12/1/54. Commd 3/9/72. Flt Lt 15/10/76. Retd GD 15/7/87. Reinstated 3/12/90. Sqn Ldr 1/7/92. GD 1/7/95.
FLACK R. P. B. Born 3/12/40. Commd 9/9/63. Flt Lt 9/3/69. Retd GD 23/12/80.
FLAHERTY S. D. Born 7/8/51. Commd 13/1/72. Sqn Ldr 1/7/84. Retd GD 18/9/85.
FLAKE A. J., CEng MIEE. Born 1/5/15. Commd 25/11/41. Sqn Ldr 1/1/52. Retd ENG 1/11/64.
FLANAGAN N. G., MB ChB MRCP MRCPath DCP DMJ. Born 3/4/36. Commd 28/4/63. Wg Cdr 31/10/75. Retd MED 28/4/79.
FLANAGAN R. C. Born 10/3/18. Commd 30/10/41. Flt Lt 19/2/46. Retd ENG 10/3/67.
FLANAGAN T. C., MSc BA MIMgt. Born 11/4/33. Commd 10/7/52. Gp Capt 1/1/81. Retd GD 4/5/83.
FLANDERS J. R., CEng MIEE. Born 10/10/40. Commd 2/8/68. Flt Lt 2/8/70. Retd ENG 10/10/78.
FLANNERY T. J. Born 24/5/20. Commd 12/7/46. Flt Lt 10/6/54. Retd ENG 22/10/61.
FLAVELL D. M. Born 21/4/43. Commd 11/4/85. Sqn Ldr 1/7/95. Retd ENG 24/4/98.
FLAVELL E. J. G., AFC. Born 25/4/22. Commd 24/10/44. Sqn Ldr 1/1/56. Retd GD 1/6/68.
FLAVIN J. Born 9/4/63. Commd 1/7/82. Flt Lt 13/11/88. Retd ADMIN 1/3/91.
FLAXMAN D. J. Born 24/2/37. Commd 30/11/56. Sqn Ldr 1/7/75. Retd GD(G) 1/7/78.
FLECKNEY W. T. H., DFC LLB MIMgt. Born 27/6/22. Commd 15/9/44. Sqn Ldr 1/7/70. Retd GD 26/6/73.
FLEET S. J. Born 31/8/39. Commd 20/8/65. Flt Lt 20/2/70. Retd GD 3/5/81.
FLEGG H. G., MA DCAe MRAeS. Born 10/6/24. Commd 11/1/45. Sqn Ldr 6/9/60. Retd EDN 12/5/65.
FLEMING A. W. P. Born 14/5/31. Commd 27/2/70. Flt Lt 27/2/76. Retd ADMIN 1/7/77.
FLEMING C. J., BSc. Born 27/12/61. Commd 11/9/83. Flt Lt 11/3/86. Retd GD 14/3/96.
FLEMING E. M. Born 18/12/25. Commd 23/5/63. Flt Lt 23/5/69. Retd GD(G) 17/8/79.
FLEMING H. C., FCA. Born 16/12/11. Commd 12/6/36. Wg Cdr 1/7/53. Retd SEC 15/6/59.
FLEMING J. B. A., OBE. Born 23/2/16. Commd 13/5/40. Wg Cdr 1/7/53. Retd GD 5/3/63.
FLEMING J. H. Born 14/3/17. Commd 17/10/57. Sqn Ldr 1/1/69. Retd SUP 9/7/73.
FLEMING J. McL. Born 18/8/26. Commd 27/5/53. Fg Off 19/2/58. Retd SUP 4/2/64.
FLEMING P., OBE. Born 14/9/15. Commd 16/3/34. Gp Capt 1/1/55. Retd GD 14/10/65.
FLEMING P. J., MCSP DPhysEd. Born 13/5/47. Commd 11/8/69. Sqn Ldr 1/7/86. Retd ADMIN 14/3/96.
FLEMING R. B., DFC AFC MIMgt. Born 17/5/16. Commd 14/1/39. Wg Cdr 1/1/53. Retd GD 17/5/71.
FLEMING W. B. Born 30/3/10. Commd 2/9/32. Wg Cdr 1/1/49. Retd SEC 3/3/58.
FLEMMINGS M. S. Born 28/12/52. Commd 16/3/73. Sqn Ldr 1/1/85. Retd GD 28/12/90.
FLETCHER A. Born 11/12/44. Commd 8/11/70. Sqn Ldr 1/1/88. Retd ENG 2/4/93.
FLETCHER The Rev A. P. R., BTh DipPasTh. Born 7/9/46. Commd 14/5/78. Retd 14/5/00 Wg Cdr.
FLETCHER The Rev A. W. G., BA. Born 23/4/24. Commd 6/6/61. Retd 31/7/72 Wg Cdr.
FLETCHER B., MIMgt. Born 22/10/35. Commd 27/10/67. Sqn Ldr 1/1/75. Retd SEC 1/1/78.
FLETCHER B. M. G. Born 22/3/38. Commd 1/3/62. Sqn Ldr 1/7/74. Retd SUP 1/7/77.
FLETCHER C. F. Born 23/10/20. Commd 30/4/44. Flt Lt 26/6/51. Retd GD(G) 23/10/70.
FLETCHER C. W. Born 17/11/15. Commd 29/5/41. Sqn Ldr 1/1/54. Retd ENG 1/4/60.
FLETCHER D. B. Born 17/8/35. Commd 19/8/53. Flt Lt 21/10/59. Retd GD 17/8/73.
FLETCHER D. K. Born 8/7/52. Commd 5/8/76. Sqn Ldr 1/1/91. Retd GD 10/5/97.
FLETCHER E. B. Born 23/2/25. Commd 30/1/52. Flt Lt 29/4/59. Retd GD 6/11/70.
FLETCHER E. M. D. Born 18/5/09. Commd 18/8/41. Sqn Offr 1/7/50. Retd SEC 31/5/58.
FLETCHER G. R. K., AFC. Born 11/12/26. Commd 8/4/49. Wg Cdr 1/1/64. Retd GD 1/8/68.
FLETCHER J. T. Born 15/7/21. Commd 3/8/50. Sqn Ldr 1/1/61. Retd ENG 15/8/73.
FLETCHER K. D., BSc MB ChB. Born 6/11/55. Commd 5/9/78. Sqn Ldr 1/8/87. Retd MED 5/9/94.
FLETCHER L. A., CEng MIEE MRAeS. Born 13/8/32. Commd 13/8/52. Flt Lt 20/5/58. Retd ENG 30/5/71.
FLETCHER L. S. Born 9/12/23. Commd 6/3/52. Flt Lt 6/9/56. Retd SUP 23/1/68.
FLETCHER L. W. Born 26/2/18. Commd 2/8/45. Wg Cdr 1/7/65. Retd SEC 2/3/74.
FLETCHER M. D. Born 22/12/43. Commd 14/1/82. Flt Lt 14/1/84. Retd ENG 14/9/90.
FLETCHER M. J. Born 7/5/34. Commd 18/5/53. Sqn Ldr 1/7/85. Retd GD 3/7/86.
FLETCHER N., MA. Born 25/3/22. Commd 19/6/42. Wg Cdr 1/1/64. Retd GD 26/9/68.
FLETCHER N. K. Born 5/6/46. Commd 20/11/75. Flt Lt 20/11/77. Retd GD 1/10/84.
FLETCHER P., DPhysEd. Born 19/4/30. Commd 24/4/57. Sqn Ldr 1/1/68. Retd SUP 1/9/74.
FLETCHER P. G. C., BA. Born 20/7/30. Commd 15/4/54. Flt Lt 15/4/60. Retd RGT 29/7/60.
FLETCHER P. J., ACIS. Born 4/3/50. Commd 19/6/70. Sqn Ldr 1/7/81. Retd ADMIN 4/3/88.
FLETCHER R. B. Born 5/11/43. Commd 2/5/69. Flt Lt 3/8/71. Retd SUP 5/11/81.
FLETCHER R. C. Born 27/4/46. Commd 19/7/84. Flt Lt 19/7/86. Retd ADMIN 19/7/92.
FLETCHER R. H., BSc CEng MIMechE MRAeS. Born 17/2/47. Commd 26/5/67. A Cdre 1/7/95. Retd ENG 7/8/99.
FLETCHER R. N. Born 14/10/47. Commd 14/10/71. Sqn Ldr 1/1/89. Retd ADMIN 1/9/96.
FLETCHER R. S., MSc BSc(Eng) CEng MIEE. Born 1/4/47. Commd 16/1/72. Sqn Ldr 1/1/80. Retd ENG 16/1/88.
FLETCHER T., DFC DFM*. Born 7/9/14. Commd 12/9/43. Flt Lt 12/3/47. Retd GD(G) 7/9/64.
FLETCHER W. D. M., CEng MRAeS. Born 12/7/42. Commd 7/12/65. Wg Cdr 1/7/82. Retd ENG 12/7/97.
FLETT K. McD. Born 22/8/26. Commd 1/10/50. Sqn Ldr 1/1/59. Retd GD 22/8/81.
FLETTON R. J. Born 20/12/45. Commd 28/11/69. Flt Lt 28/5/75. Retd GD 22/10/94.

FLEWITT A. J., BSc CEng MIEE MRAeS. Born 25/2/51. Commd 13/11/72. Sqn Ldr 1/7/81. Retd ENG 25/2/89.
FLIGHT J. P., MMS MIMgt. Born 4/7/31. Commd 15/9/71. Sqn Ldr 1/7/80. Retd ADMIN 2/4/86.
FLINN P. W. Born 4/5/27. Commd 8/4/49. Flt Lt 8/10/51. Retd GD 4/5/65.
FLINN T. J. Born 12/1/49. Commd 27/2/70. Wg Cdr 1/7/86. Retd GD 1/7/89.
FLINT C. J., MILT MIMgt. Born 22/2/43. Commd 26/5/67. Wg Cdr 1/7/84. Retd SUP 22/2/98.
FLINT C. J. Born 20/9/33. Commd 5/5/54. Fg Offr 18/5/65. Retd GD(G) 20/11/66.
FLINT D. A., MIMgt. Born 14/7/21. Commd 25/3/43. Gp Capt 1/1/61. Retd ENG 5/4/75.
FLINT H. P. Born 29/8/30. Commd 26/3/52. Flt Lt 31/7/57. Retd GD 11/9/68.
FLINT P. A. Born 27/2/48. Commd 28/11/69. Sqn Ldr 1/7/86. Retd GD 22/12/00.
FLIPPANT F. W. J., DFC. Born 25/2/25. Commd 14/11/57. Flt Lt 1/4/63. Retd GD(G) 1/8/79.
FLITCROFT K. W. Born 21/3/40. Commd 23/11/78. Sqn Ldr 1/7/88. Retd ENG 21/3/95.
FLOATE N. J., BSc. Born 20/12/33. Commd 11/4/58. Sqn Ldr 11/10/67. Retd EDN 11/4/74.
FLOCKHART D. Born 11/4/38. Commd 7/1/71. Flt Lt 7/1/73. Retd SUP 11/4/93.
FLOOD D. M. Born 12/1/21. Commd 25/1/51. Sqn Ldr 1/7/71. Retd SEC 12/1/76.
FLOOD F. J. Born 21/5/25. Commd 23/8/56. Flt Lt 23/8/62. Retd GD 1/8/68.
FLOOD J. Born 10/7/46. Commd 26/5/67. Sqn Ldr 1/7/83. Retd GD 1/7/86.
FLOOD P. J. Born 21/2/57. Commd 28/2/80. Flt Lt 26/8/83. Retd SY 21/2/95.
FLOOD R. G. Born 6/5/28. Commd 10/10/63. Flt Lt 10/10/68. Retd ENG 19/10/68.
FLOOD R. P., AFC. Born 6/10/25. Commd 5/6/45. Wg Cdr 1/7/68. Retd GD 2/10/75.
FLOOD T. Born 13/10/35. Commd 20/6/63. Flt Lt 1/4/66. Retd GD 13/10/90.
FLORCZAK F., MBE BA MIMgt. Born 12/8/19. Commd 16/7/41. Sqn Ldr 1/1/63. Retd ENG 12/8/77.
FLORENCE W. H. Born 16/8/28. Commd 29/3/62. Sqn Ldr 1/7/74. Retd ENG 16/8/83.
FLOWER R. G. Born 21/3/23. Commd 3/8/61. Flt Lt 3/8/64. Retd GD 30/6/73.
FLOYD J. M., BSc CEng MRAeS. Born 24/11/43. Commd 3/10/66. Sqn Ldr 1/7/81. Retd ENG 1/7/84.
FLOYDD W. F., MBE BEM. Born 29/1/32. Commd 28/5/66. Wg Cdr 1/1/84. Retd SY 2/11/85.
FLYNN C. T., MBE MB ChB MRCP. Born 13/11/30. Commd 25/2/64. Wg Cdr 1/3/72. Retd MED 16/1/76.
FLYNN J. B. Born 7/7/34. Commd 11/4/63. Sqn Ldr 1/1/77. Retd GD 7/7/84.
FLYNN J. R. Born 17/2/27. Commd 27/3/70. Flt Lt 11/7/73. Retd DEL 17/8/82.
FLYNN M. R. Born 12/2/44. Commd 1/1/62. Sqn Ldr 1/1/82. Retd GD 12/2/88.
FOALE C. H. Born 10/6/30. Commd 12/12/51. A Cdre 1/1/77. Retd GD 14/7/79.
FOARD D. J. S. Born 27/8/25. Commd 25/8/49. Sqn Ldr 1/1/60. Retd GD 30/3/68.
FODEN D., MBE. Born 17/10/42. Commd 17/5/79. Sqn Ldr 1/1/86. Retd ENG 1/11/95.
FODEN J. B., BA FHCIMA MIMgt AMRSH. Born 7/5/26. Commd 17/1/49, Wg Cdr 1/1/70. Retd ADMIN 7/5/84.
FOERS R., MBE MHCIMA. Born 30/12/35. Commd 6/6/57. Sqn Ldr 1/1/76. Retd ADMIN 30/12/92.
FOGARTY M., BEM. Born 11/11/26. Commd 2/2/68. Flt Lt 2/2/73. Retd ADMIN 11/11/84.
FOGARTY R. J., BCom. Born 11/10/62. Commd 16/2/85. Flt Lt 18/10/87. Retd GD 25/9/98.
FOGG W. G. Born 4/2/39. Commd 4/10/63. Flt Lt 1/2/70. Retd GD 18/6/79.
FOGGIE P. R., BSc CEng MIEE. Born 4/9/44. Commd 15/7/65. Sqn Ldr 1/7/77. Retd ENG 4/9/82.
FOGGIN R. W. Born 6/12/29. Commd 18/7/63. Flt Lt 18/7/68. Retd ENG 7/12/79.
FOGGO R. C. Born 8/7/40. Commd 6/11/80. Sqn Ldr 1/7/90. Retd ENG 30/11/95.
FOGGO W. N. Born 22/5/43. Commd 19/2/76. Sqn Ldr 1/1/91. Retd GD 2/4/93.
FOLEY A. J. Born 11/5/44. Commd 21/12/62. Flt Lt 15/4/70. Retd GD 5/4/77.
FOLEY H. A. W. Born 27/9/28. Commd 17/6/54. Flt Lt 17/12/59. Retd GD 9/2/70.
FOLEY J. F., MBE BSc. Born 6/6/50. Commd 13/9/71. Sqn Ldr 1/7/86. Retd GD 14/9/96.
FOLEY J. W. A. Born 9/5/45. Commd 31/1/64. Flt Lt 4/5/72. Retd GD 30/7/76.
FOLEY T. Born 4/7/40. Commd 27/9/73. Sqn Ldr 1/7/80. Retd ADMIN 1/1/91.
FOLLETT P. Born 15/2/36. Commd 27/2/75. Sqn Ldr 1/1/84. Retd SUP 16/8/89.
FOLLEY R. F. Born 15/11/11. Commd 6/1/36. Gp Capt 1/7/54. Retd SUP 6/4/67.
FOLLIS R. G. C., DFC. Born 13/9/23. Commd 12/9/42. Sqn Ldr 1/7/59. Retd GD(G) 15/9/63.
FOLLIS R. J. C. Born 7/1/44. Commd 17/5/62. Flt Lt 2/9/69. Retd GD 7/1/81.
FONFE F. D. C. Born 16/8/49. Commd 27/10/67. Fg Offr 14/3/70. Retd RGT 26/3/72.
FONFE M. D. C., MBE. Born 21/2/45. Commd 26/5/67. Wg Cdr 1/7/87. Retd OPS SPT 21/2/00.
FOORD I. A., BSc. Born 24/6/51. Commd 15/9/69. Flt Lt 15/10/73. Retd GD 4/7/80.
FOOT C. W. J. Born 28/12/34. Commd 18/3/53. Flt Lt 6/2/59. Retd GD 28/12/72.
FOOT F. G., OBE. Born 29/3/13. Commd 4/4/38. Wg Cdr 1/7/52. Retd GD 14/1/58 rtg Gp Capt.
FOOT G. E. P., MBE. Born 21/11/23. Commd 29/11/44. Sqn Ldr 1/10/55. Retd GD 21/11/66.
FOOT W. J. Born 13/11/31. Commd 5/11/53. Flt Lt 5/5/58. Retd GD 13/11/76. Reinstated 22/6/79. Flt Lt 12/12/60. Retd GD 13/11/88.
FOPP D., AFC AE MIMgt. Born 13/3/20. Commd 3/11/41. Sqn Ldr 1/9/65. Retd GD 13/3/75.
FORBEAR J. S. Born 30/4/46. Commd 23/3/66. Fg Offr 23/9/68. Retd ENG 19/12/70.
FORBES D. J., FIMgt. Born 26/3/45. Commd 24/9/64. Gp Capt 1/7/90. Retd SUP 7/7/96.
FORBES D. L. Born 23/9/22. Commd 25/9/46. Flt Lt 29/11/51. Retd GD 30/9/58.
FORBES D. M. Born 8/4/44. Commd 6/5/65. Flt Lt 4/5/72. Retd GD(G) 8/1/82.
FORBES F. A. Born 7/12/21. Commd 15/9/60. Sqn Ldr 1/1/73. Retd ENG 31/7/74.
FORBES G. A., BSc. Born 11/10/50. Commd 15/9/69. Sqn Ldr 1/1/85. Retd GD 30/1/88.
FORBES G. S. Born 12/10/49. Commd 4/2/71. Sqn Ldr 1/1/83. Retd GD 12/10/87.

FORBES J. C., DFM MIMgt. Born 20/8/21. Commd 18/12/41. Gp Capt 1/1/65. Retd GD 20/8/76.
FORBES J. M. Born 10/8/16. Commd 16/3/45. Sqn Ldr 1/7/53. Retd SUP 7/4/62.
FORBES K. J., MBE. Born 12/8/22. Commd 6/6/57. Sqn Ldr 1/7/66. Retd ENG 10/9/77.
FORBES L. J. C., MCIPD MRAeS. Born 23/6/51. Commd 29/6/72. Sqn Ldr 1/7/88. Retd GD 1/7/91.
FORBES P. B., MB ChB MRCOG. Born 29/1/51. Commd 16/5/72. Wg Cdr 6/8/88. Retd MED 31/7/91.
FORBES R. C. Born 10/1/20. Commd 9/9/44. Flt Lt 9/3/48. Retd GD 11/6/53.
FORBES S. J. Born 27/3/44. Commd 17/12/64. Flt Lt 17/6/71. Retd ENG 10/3/73.
FORBES S. M. Born 21/10/19. Commd 7/4/44. Flt Lt 11/3/48. Retd GD(G) 1/8/62.
FORD A. T. Born 18/12/45. Commd 26/5/67. A Cdre 1/7/97. Retd ADMIN 23/5/99.
FORD C. G. Born 7/12/41. Commd 24/3/61. Sqn Ldr 1/1/75. Retd GD 7/12/96.
FORD C. P. Born 31/12/22. Commd 30/4/59. Flt Lt 30/4/62. Retd GD 1/3/68.
FORD F. R. Born 22/11/23. Commd 30/1/45. Flt Lt 10/8/48. Retd GD 3/12/66.
FORD G. C., BA. Born 7/7/50. Commd 15/9/69. Flt Lt 15/10/73. Retd GD 28/4/74.
FORD G. W., AFM. Born 12/9/24. Commd 26/5/54. Fg Offr 26/5/56. Retd GD 31/7/57.
FORD H. A. Born 28/7/30. Commd 31/12/52. Wg Cdr 1/7/77. Retd GD 28/7/85.
FORD J., OBE CEng MRAeS. Born 24/1/20. Commd 15/4/43. Wg Cdr 1/7/61. Retd ENG 24/1/75.
FORD J. A., BSc. Born 7/6/57. Commd 8/2/81. Flt Lt 8/5/81. Retd GD 8/2/97.
FORD J. A. F., FIMgt. Born 19/6/44. Commd 24/6/65. A Cdre 1/7/94. Retd GD 24/5/98.
FORD J. M. Born 27/10/30. Commd 18/6/52. Flt Lt 17/8/58. Retd GD 14/6/71.
FORD J. P., AFC. Born 16/6/21. Commd 16/3/47. Wg Cdr 1/1/62. Retd GD 16/6/76 rtg Gp Capt.
FORD M. A., MBE BDS FDRCS. Born 19/4/36. Commd 19/2/61. Wg Cdr 21/6/73. Retd DEL 30/9/77.
FORD M. A. Born 24/11/56. Commd 20/7/78. Flt Lt 20/1/84. Retd GD 14/3/97.
FORD N. A., BSc. Born 1/7/60. Commd 4/9/78. Flt Lt 15/10/84. Retd ENG 28/5/89.
FORD N. L. Born 19/11/41. Commd 21/12/62. Sqn Ldr 1/7/74. Retd GD 19/11/79.
FORD P. C. C., BSc. Born 15/6/47. Commd 1/1/67. Flt Lt 15/6/70. Retd GD 15/6/85.
FORD P. J. Born 14/7/44. Commd 22/3/63. Flt Lt 20/11/68. Retd GD 14/10/82.
FORD P. M. Born 6/10/38. Commd 23/6/67. Wg Cdr 1/1/87. Retd ENG 6/10/93.
FORD Sir Geoffrey, KBE CB BSc FEng FIEE DipEl. Born 6/8/23. Commd 21/10/42. AM 1/7/78. Retd ENG 6/4/81.
FORD W. A., MBE BA ACIS. Born 14/1/34. Commd 19/10/59. Wg Cdr 1/1/75. Retd ADMIN 14/1/89.
FORDE W. L. T. Born 2/8/41. Commd 18/12/62. Sqn Ldr 1/7/74. Retd ADMIN 19/12/94.
FORDER R. A. Born 10/11/44. Commd 15/7/66. Flt Lt 1/7/69. Retd GD 10/8/72.
FORDER R. M., CEng MIMechE MRAeS. Born 28/9/39. Commd 28/5/66. Sqn Ldr 1/1/77. Retd ENG 28/9/94.
FORDHAM A., MA. Born 24/3/25. Commd 29/3/45. Sqn Ldr 1/7/57. Retd GD 5/6/65.
FORDHAM G. C., BSc. Born 18/9/45. Commd 26/5/67. Sqn Ldr 1/7/76. Retd ENG 1/10/87.
FORDHAM K. Born 4/8/44. Commd 5/1/70. Sqn Ldr 1/1/81. Retd GD 5/1/86.
FOREMAN M. C. Born 3/8/59. Commd 29/8/77. Sqn Ldr 1/7/97. Retd GD 3/8/97.
FOREMAN R. Born 17/3/36. Commd 6/1/64. Sqn Ldr 1/1/85. Retd GD 17/3/94.
FORESHEW W. P. Born 30/12/12. Commd 23/3/50. Flt Lt 23/9/53. Retd SEC 17/11/58.
FORMAN G. N., CB. Born 30/11/30. Commd 27/11/57. AVM 1/7/82. Retd LGL 3/11/89.
FORMBY M. L., MRAeS. Born 19/6/13. Commd 12/3/34. Wg Cdr 1/7/53. Retd ENG 20/5/67.
FORREST J. E. N. Born 21/1/20. Commd 9/8/47. Flt Lt 7/6/51. Retd GD(G) 21/1/75.
FORREST M. J. Born 9/12/31. Commd 7/12/51. Flt Lt 16/2/57. Retd GD 2/10/65.
FORREST P. F., MSc BSc CEng MIEE. Born 22/1/59. Commd 14/10/84. Sqn Ldr 1/7/92. Retd ENG 14/10/00.
FORREST P. G. Born 28/4/63. Commd 22/6/89. Flt Lt 22/6/91. Retd ADMIN 28/8/96.
FORREST S. A. E., MBE CEng MIEE. Born 4/8/24. Commd 15/1/63. Sqn Ldr 1/12/65. Retd EDN 4/8/79.
FORRESTER A. J., BSc. Born 8/1/68. Commd 3/8/88. Flt Lt 30/6/92. Retd GD 7/2/96.
FORRESTER A. J., BSc. Born 18/2/56. Commd 29/4/84. Flt Lt 29/10/83. Retd ADMIN 14/3/97.
FORRESTER C. Born 25/8/30. Commd 19/7/51. Flt Lt 30/10/56. Retd GD 25/8/92.
FORRESTER I. C. Born 29/6/29. Commd 7/5/52. Flt Lt 2/10/57. Retd GD 16/10/67.
FORRESTER P. A. W. Born 2/8/24. Commd 3/5/56. Sqn Ldr 1/7/71. Retd GD 3/5/73.
FORRESTER R. A., OBE BA. Born 2/6/44. Commd 22/3/63. Wg Cdr 1/7/87. Retd GD 17/10/98.
FORROW T. H., AMCIPD. Born 24/6/52. Commd 28/11/74. Sqn Ldr 1/1/89. Retd GD(G) 1/1/92.
FORSHAW D. J. Born 1/7/41. Commd 13/12/79. Flt Lt 13/12/85. Retd ENG 31/3/94.
FORSHAW J. F., ACIS MCIPD MIMgt. Born 5/3/37. Commd 27/4/55. Wg Cdr 1/1/76. Retd SEC 5/1/82.
FORSHAW T. H. T. Born 29/8/16. Commd 17/8/36. Sqn Ldr 1/8/47. Retd GD 29/11/57.
FORSHAW T. K. G. Born 19/6/23. Commd 20/4/50. Flt Lt 19/11/53. Retd GD 19/12/63.
FORSSANDER D. R. Born 19/12/14. Commd 20/6/41. Sqn Ldr 1/1/49. Retd SUP 1/1/50.
FORSTER A. D., DFC. Born 17/4/14. Commd 31/5/38. Wg Cdr 1/7/47. Retd GD 24/4/62.
FORSTER B. J. Born 29/3/65. Commd 15/3/84. Flt Lt 15/9/89. Retd GD 7/10/92.
FORSTER B. R. W., MBE DFC AFC. Born 7/7/17. Commd 19/5/42. Wg Cdr 1/7/56. Retd GD 30/7/60.
FORSTER C. P. Born 1/7/25. Commd 6/12/50. Flt Offr 6/6/56. Retd SEC 28/8/56.
FORSTER E. A. G. Born 8/1/35. Commd 14/11/59. Flt Lt 14/5/65. Retd GD 8/1/78.
FORSTER F. O. Born 24/5/22. Commd 1/8/42. Flt Lt 2/3/50. Retd GD 22/6/65.
FORSTER I., DPhysEd. Born 31/1/49. Commd 16/8/70. Fg Offr 31/1/71. Retd PE 1/9/73.
FORSTER I. H., OBE BA FCIPD FIMgt. Born 2/8/33. Commd 12/9/56. A Cdre 1/1/56. Retd ADMIN 1/12/87.
FORSTER J. A. Born 1/7/34. Commd 1/6/72. Flt Lt 1/6/78. Retd SY 1/6/85.

FORSTER J. A. F. Born 20/5/24. Commd 6/9/56. Flt Lt 6/9/62. Retd GD 16/11/67.
FORSTER J. B. Born 25/8/41. Commd 25/2/66. Flt Lt 25/8/72. Retd GD(G) 25/8/87.
FORSTER P. J. Born 7/1/41. Commd 1/4/65. Sqn Ldr 1/1/73. Retd SEC 7/1/79.
FORSTER P. R. Born 21/9/35. Commd 13/11/62. Sqn Ldr 1/1/75. Retd SEC 13/11/78.
FORSTER R. A. A., BA MILT MIMgt. Born 7/5/48. Commd 17/1/72. Sqn Ldr 1/1/88. Retd SUP 14/3/97.
FORSTER R. D. Born 5/6/42. Commd 5/1/78. Flt Lt 5/1/80. Retd ENG 5/1/86.
FORSYTH B., BA. Born 24/11/45. Commd 17/12/64. Wg Cdr 1/7/83. Retd ENG 24/11/89.
FORSYTH D. R. G., MBE MSc FCIPS MIL. Born 25/11/47. Commd 2/8/68. Gp Capt 1/1/90. Retd SUP 13/7/95.
FORSYTH J. G. Born 12/5/42. Commd 27/4/70. Sqn Ldr 1/7/89. Retd ENG 1/9/93.
FORSYTHE J. R., CBE DFC. Born 10/7/20. Commd 10/11/42. A Cdre 1/1/71. Retd GD 10/11/75.
FORTEATH J. H. Born 18/1/31. Commd 1/10/55. Gp Capt 1/7/79. Retd GD 14/4/84.
FORTESCUE D. C. Born 11/9/17. Commd 21/6/45. Wg Cdr 1/1/64. Retd SEC 18/2/66.
FORTEY R. G. Born 13/6/29. Commd 15/3/57. Flt Lt 15/9/61. Retd GD 11/10/71.
FORTUNE D. B., CEng MIMechE. Born 7/12/28. Commd 13/6/60. Wg Cdr 1/1/77. Retd ENG 24/7/82.
FORTUNE M. B. Born 22/7/37. Commd 6/7/62. Flt Lt 6/1/67. Retd GD 23/6/68.
FORWARD B. M. E., OBE MRAeS. Born 20/10/35. Commd 10/2/59. Wg Cdr 1/7/80. Retd GD 18/5/86.
FORWARD C. W. Born 17/9/08. Commd 3/1/41. Flt Lt 1/9/45. Retd SUP 23/10/54 rtg Sqn Ldr.
FOSH J. S., CBE MMAR MNI. Born 28/5/35. Commd 16/4/63. Gp Capt 1/7/84. Retd MAR 25/5/85.
FOSKETT G. W. Born 25/5/25. Commd 2/1/48. Sqn Ldr 1/7/54. Retd RGT 25/5/63 rtg Wg Cdr.
FOSKETT L. B., OBE AFC. Born 17/8/21. Commd 1/1/43. Gp Capt 1/1/65. Retd GD 17/8/76.
FOSTER A. Born 11/11/37. Commd 2/9/55. Flt Lt 2/3/61. Retd GD 24/3/65.
FOSTER A., BSc CEng MIEE. Born 18/7/48. Commd 7/9/70. Sqn Ldr 1/1/79. Retd ENG 1/9/92.
FOSTER A. F. Born 21/11/36. Commd 6/5/65. Flt Lt 6/5/71. Retd GD 21/11/94.
FOSTER A. R., BSc. Born 24/6/47. Commd 6/10/69. Flt Lt 6/1/71. Retd GD 6/10/85.
FOSTER B. G. A. Born 21/11/46. Commd 16/9/76. Sqn Ldr 1/1/87. Retd ENG 14/3/97.
FOSTER D. F., MB ChB MFOM DRCOG DAvMed. Born 17/4/31. Commd 14/11/66. Gp Capt 1/1/82. Retd MED 11/1/85.
FOSTER D. J. G., AFC BSc CEng MRAeS. Born 24/7/36. Commd 23/3/55. Wg Cdr 1/1/76. Retd GD 1/1/79.
FOSTER D. R. Born 1/4/23. Commd 19/8/44. Sqn Ldr 1/1/66. Retd GD 31/3/74.
FOSTER F. R. Born 23/3/16. Commd 14/12/35. Sqn Ldr 1/9/40. Retd GD 23/12/57 rtg Wg Cdr.
FOSTER F. W. Born 21/1/48. Commd 1/8/69. Sqn Ldr 1/7/80. Retd GD 30/12/89.
FOSTER G. Born 2/11/31. Commd 2/7/52. Flt Lt 2/3/58. Retd GD 29/4/71.
FOSTER G. R. Born 15/3/21. Commd 12/1/45. Sqn Ldr 1/1/72. Retd GD 15/3/76.
FOSTER G. R. Born 6/6/36. Commd 20/1/64. Flt Lt 20/1/64. Retd SUP 4/6/67.
FOSTER G. R. Born 17/8/47. Commd 17/2/67. Flt Lt 17/8/72. Retd GD 31/1/85.
FOSTER G. S. Born 29/1/37. Commd 17/10/59. Sqn Ldr 1/1/77. Retd GD 9/10/89.
FOSTER J. A. Born 16/10/44. Commd 1/4/66. Flt Lt 1/10/71. Retd GD 16/10/82.
FOSTER J. A. Born 23/11/40. Commd 28/4/61. Flt Lt 28/10/66. Retd GD 23/11/95.
FOSTER J. E., MRIN MIMgt. Born 17/7/40. Commd 8/12/61. Sqn Ldr 1/7/74. Retd GD 17/7/95.
FOSTER J. E. Born 24/1/29. Commd 11/4/63. Flt Lt 11/4/66. Retd GD 4/6/68.
FOSTER J. M., BA. Born 22/6/55. Commd 23/9/73. Flt Lt 15/10/77. Retd GD 1/10/87.
FOSTER J. P. Born 22/12/54. Commd 1/11/79. Sqn Ldr 1/1/90. Retd Retd SY 1/1/93.
FOSTER J. W., DFC AFC. Born 1/8/22. Commd 18/9/42. Gp Capt 1/1/67. Retd GD 14/9/75.
FOSTER K. C., OBE. Born 14/10/42. Commd 27/1/61. Wg Cdr 1/1/82. Retd GD 3/1/93.
FOSTER L. B. P. Born 4/2/19. Commd 15/10/42. Sqn Ldr 1/1/63. Retd ENG 4/2/74.
FOSTER L. L. Born 18/4/20. Commd 23/8/56. Flt Lt 23/8/59. Retd GD 1/10/64.
FOSTER M. A. Born 3/5/48. Commd 27/9/73. Sqn Ldr 1/1/86. Retd GD(G) 19/3/89.
FOSTER M. G. L., AFC. Born 15/4/13. Commd 24/2/37. Wg Cdr 1/10/46. Retd GD 15/4/60.
FOSTER M. M., OBE. Born 20/11/29. Commd 1/8/51. Wg Cdr 1/7/71. Retd GD 20/11/84.
FOSTER P. J., BSc. Born 13/4/48. Commd 17/10/71. Flt Lt 17/7/75. Retd ADMIN 17/10/87.
FOSTER P. G. Born 1/10/22. Commd 11/8/44. Flt Lt 11/2/48. Retd GD 1/10/65.
FOSTER R. K., BSc. Born 14/2/36. Commd 23/6/61. Flt Lt 23/12/66. Retd GD 28/3/77.
FOSTER R. W. J. Born 5/2/65. Commd 16/2/89. Flt Lt 16/8/94. Retd GD 14/3/96.
FOSTER S. F., BEng. Born 27/3/62. Commd 2/8/89. Flt Lt 15/7/92. Retd ENG 7/5/01.
FOSTER S. R. Born 1/5/49. Commd 24/6/71. Flt Lt 24/12/76. Retd GD 1/5/87.
FOSTER V. A. Born 27/8/29. Commd 18/10/62. Flt Lt 18/10/68. Retd ENG 31/7/71.
FOSTER W. E. Born 30/5/19. Commd 30/7/59. Sqn Ldr 1/1/70. Retd ENG 1/1/76.
FOSTER W. H. Born 3/5/32. Commd 15/5/58. Flt Lt 15/5/64. Retd SEC 3/5/70.
FOSTER W. R. Born 8/1/11. Commd 6/5/43. Flt Lt 7/6/51. Retd SUP 21/2/62.
FOSTER-PEGG R. I. Born 16/2/66. Commd 23/5/88. Flt Lt 23/11/90. Retd GD 14/3/96.
FOTHERGILL W. T., MB BS DipSoton DA FFARCS. Born 11/3/29. Commd 1/10/53. Wg Cdr 10/9/65. Retd MED 1/10/69.
FOULGER D. A., MBE. Born 28/11/44. Commd 15/7/66. Sqn Ldr 1/7/79. Retd GD 6/3/93.
FOULKES B. V., MIMgt. Born 30/7/37. Commd 26/5/67. Flt Lt 26/5/73. Retd MED(SEC) 3/10/75.
FOULKES D. D. Born 3/10/41. Commd 26/3/64. Flt Lt 3/10/68. Retd SEC 14/9/73.
FOULKES R. L., BSc. Born 12/3/54. Commd 13/5/76. Flt Lt 15/10/77. Retd GD 13/5/92.

FOUND D. G. Born 15/1/41. Commd 3/8/62. Fg Offr 3/8/64. Retd GD 25/11/66.
FOUNTAIN C., FIMgt. Born 9/10/25. Commd 14/11/49. A Cdre 1/1/76. Retd GD 1/5/79.
FOUNTAIN J. S. Born 19/5/43. Commd 24/6/65. Flt Lt 29/11/70. Retd GD 26/8/76.
FOURIE V. H. Born 1/10/24. Commd 29/8/45. Sqn Ldr 1/1/57. Retd GD 18/12/62.
FOVARQUE A. J., BSc. Born 4/9/46. Commd 17/1/72. Wg Cdr 1/7/94. Retd GD 16/1/99.
FOWLE A. P. D. Born 10/4/76. Commd 5/10/95. Plt Offr 5/10/96. Retd GD 16/2/98.
FOWLE C. J. D., BSc CEng MInstP MRAeS MIMgt. Born 15/5/22. Commd 5/8/42. Wg Cdr 1/7/68. Retd ENG
    20/8/77.
FOWLE M. D. Born 13/7/48. Commd 7/10/69. Wg Cdr 1/1/92. Retd ADMIN 14/9/96.
FOWLER A. K. Born 13/8/57. Commd 27/3/80. Flt Lt 15/5/84. Retd GD(G) 7/1/97.
FOWLER C. R. Born 19/11/45. Commd 28/11/69. A Cdre 1/1/96. Retd ADMIN 19/12/00.
FOWLER D., BSc CEng MRAeS. Born 7/8/45. Commd 15/7/66. Sqn Ldr 1/1/76. Retd ENG 7/8/83.
FOWLER D. Born 9/7/47. Commd 19/6/70. Sqn Ldr 1/7/84. Retd GD 1/7/87.
FOWLER D. F. Born 27/2/21. Commd 18/12/44. Flt Lt 18/6/47. Retd GD 2/3/54.
FOWLER D. J., AFC. Born 19/3/20. Commd 22/4/44. Sqn Ldr 1/10/54. Retd GD 19/3/69.
FOWLER F. A. Born 11/2/20. Commd 5/3/53. Sqn Ldr 1/7/67. Retd ENG 11/2/78.
FOWLER F. B. L., MRAeS. Born 2/7/15. Commd 10/6/43. Sqn Ldr 1/7/54. Retd ENG 2/8/64.
FOWLER G. A. Born 12/12/35. Commd 2/2/60. Wg Cdr 1/1/79. Retd EDN 1/4/81.
FOWLER J. Born 21/5/26. Commd 20/7/50. Wg Cdr 1/1/69. Retd GD 24/4/77.
FOWLER J. C., MSc BA MCIPS. Born 23/4/48. Commd 26/5/70. Sqn Ldr 1/7/82. Retd SUP 14/3/96.
FOWLER J. G., MA MB BChir MRCGP DAvMed. Born 22/12/37. Commd 15/10/62. Wg Cdr 2/9/76. Retd MED
    15/10/78.
FOWLER J. W. Born 7/10/10. Commd 5/5/55. Flt Lt 5/5/58. Retd ENG 13/1/65.
FOWLER K. E., BSc. Born 8/10/61. Commd 16/9/79. Sqn Ldr 1/1/98. Retd GD 8/5/01.
FOWLER L. W., MBE MIMgt. Born 31/3/25. Commd 10/8/45. Sqn Ldr 1/1/63. Retd GD 31/3/78.
FOWLER M. S. Born 9/2/46. Commd 21/7/65. Flt Lt 21/1/71. Retd GD 21/9/84.
FOWLER R., AFC. Born 2/2/38. Commd 25/1/63. Gp Capt 1/1/84. Retd GD 29/12/89.
FOWLER R. O. Born 11/12/20. Commd 2/10/58. Flt Lt 2/10/64. Retd ENG 11/7/73.
FOWLER S. Born 5/8/38. Commd 31/7/58. Wg Cdr 1/1/83. Retd ADMIN 23/9/88.
FOWLER S. M. Born 4/7/45. Commd 28/11/69. Flt Lt 28/5/75. Retd GD 14/5/00.
FOWLER T. A. M. Born 5/4/41. Commd 22/12/61. Flt Lt 18/4/67. Retd RGT 9/8/72.
FOWLIE D. G., MB ChB MRCPsych. Born 16/1/46. Commd 29/9/67. Sqn Ldr 6/8/76. Retd MED 12/11/83.
FOWNES P. W. Born 28/2/31. Commd 18/10/62. Sqn Ldr 1/7/80. Retd GD 3/10/81.
FOX A. M. Born 17/8/50. Commd 1/11/81. Flt Lt 9/2/79. Retd GD 15/1/93.
FOX A. R., OBE DCAe CEng MRAeS DipEl. Born 2/6/24. Commd 24/10/51. Gp Capt 1/1/73. Retd ENG 12/9/78.
FOX B. C. A., OBE LLB FIMgt. Born 7/9/16. Commd 17/4/39. Gp Capt 1/7/67. Retd SUP 1/9/70.
FOX B. L. Born 16/4/33. Commd 8/7/65. Flt Lt 8/7/71. Retd MED(T) 1/10/75.
FOX C. J. H., MBE. Born 28/1/23. Commd 3/8/50. Sqn Ldr 1/1/64. Retd GD 1/6/79.
FOX C. W., BEM. Born 10/9/35. Commd 21/9/72. Sqn Ldr 1/7/85. Retd ENG 21/5/90.
FOX D. A. Born 23/5/40. Commd 12/3/60. Flt Lt 12/9/65. Retd GD 2/4/93.
FOX E. A. Born 31/8/33. Commd 30/7/64. Flt Lt 30/7/70. Retd SEC 5/9/73.
FOX E. D., MIMgt. Born 15/12/16. Commd 21/2/46. Sqn Ldr 1/7/70. Retd SUP 1/7/73.
FOX G. H. Born 17/10/49. Commd 26/2/71. Sqn Ldr 1/1/85. Retd SY 14/3/96.
FOX J., MIIM. Born 11/6/48. Commd 17/5/79. Flt Lt 17/5/81. Retd Eng 17/5/87.
FOX J. A. Born 31/12/41. Commd 10/5/73. Flt Lt 1/5/75. Retd ENG 10/5/81.
FOX J. B., CEng MIEE MIMgt. Born 3/5/33. Commd 11/1/57. Sqn Ldr 1/7/66. Retd ENG 15/5/84.
FOX J. E. Born 24/10/42. Commd 19/4/63. Flt Lt 19/10/68. Retd GD 31/7/76.
FOX M. A. Born 22/11/41. Commd 2/4/65. Flt Lt 4/11/70. Retd GD 7/12/80.
FOX M. J. Born 22/4/55. Commd 27/2/75. Sqn Ldr 1/7/87. Retd GD 22/4/93.
FOX N. A., MIMgt. Born 18/9/35. Commd 31/7/56. Wg Cdr 1/1/75. Retd SUP 23/5/89.
FOX N. H., BSc. Born 8/2/49. Commd 7/5/72. Flt Lt 7/2/74. Retd GD 7/5/88.
FOX O. A., DFM. Born 27/7/17. Commd 21/6/43. Flt 21/12/46. Retd PE 21/7/66.
FOX R., MBE BEM. Born 28/8/17. Commd 7/12/61. Flt Lt 7/12/64. Retd PE 10/10/72.
FOX R. G. Born 17/4/35. Commd 31/7/56. Sqn Ldr 1/7/65. Retd GD 17/4/73. Reinstated 23/9/81. Sqn Ldr 7/12/73.
    Retd GD 17/4/95.
FOX R. O., BSc. Born 27/8/46. Commd 20/4/71. Flt Lt 20/7/71. Retd GD 20/4/87.
FOX R. W. Born 7/6/44. Commd 22/2/63. Flt Lt 8/1/69. Retd GD 14/3/96.
FOX R. W. Born 18/8/29. Commd 12/12/51. Flt Lt 12/6/54. Retd GD 18/8/67.
FOX-EDWARDS A., BSocSc. Born 13/7/62. Commd 14/9/80. Sqn Ldr 1/7/94. Retd GD 13/7/00.
FOXLEY-NORRIS Sir Christopher., GCB DSO OBE AE MA. Born 16/3/17. Commd 22/12/36. ACM 1/12/70. Retd GD
    22/4/74.
FOY M. A., BM FRCS(Edin). Born 8/12/52. Commd 18/11/85. Wg Cdr 4/8/91. Retd MED 30/11/93.
FOYLE D. A. Born 16/8/19. Commd 21/2/55. Flt Lt 21/2/55. Retd SEC 1/12/64.
FOYLE D. J. Born 30/7/44. Commd 11/7/74. Sqn Ldr 1/1/81. Retd ENG 30/7/88.
FRADLEY D. Born 7/12/40. Commd 31/7/62. Sqn Ldr 1/1/72. Retd GD 5/2/80.
FRAGEL N. J. Born 17/9/64. Commd 15/3/84. Fg Off 15/9/86. Retd ADMIN 1/10/89.

FRAME L. S., BSc. Born 24/8/38. Commd 1/1/61. Wg Cdr 1/1/77. Retd GD 1/1/80.
FRAME O. S. Born 27/3/19. Commd 5/8/42. Flt Lt 19/3/51. Retd GD(G) 28/6/69.
FRAME P. J. Born 13/1/33. Commd 13/9/51. Sqn Ldr 1/7/64. Retd GD 28/1/77. Reinstated 30/3/83. Sqn Ldr 30/8/70. Retd GD 13/1/91.
FRAMPTON J. H. Born 25/2/19. Commd 4/3/38. Sqn Ldr 1/1/51. Retd GD 24/2/59.
FRANCE B. N. Born 30/6/42. Commd 4/7/69. Flt Lt 4/5/72. Retd RGT 12/11/73.
FRANCE J. D. Born 21/11/37. Commd 22/1/57. Sqn Ldr 1/1/78. Retd GD(G) 2/4/92.
FRANCE L. K., PhD BSc CEng MIM MIEE. Born 30/11/42. Commd 6/1/69. Wg Cdr 1/1/81. Retd ADMIN 6/1/85.
FRANCEY A. I. Born 28/3/47. Commd 1/4/66. Fg Off 1/4/68. Retd GD 26/10/71.
FRANCEY M. D., BSc. Born 4/6/60. Commd 8/5/92. Flt Lt 7/11/85. Retd GD 9/5/00.
FRANCIS A. D. Born 28/7/38. Commd 28/2/80. Flt Lt 28/2/84. Retd ENG 19/9/88.
FRANCIS C. Born 11/7/63. Commd 28/3/91. Flt Lt 28/3/93. Retd ADMIN 11/11/96.
FRANCIS C. F. Born 9/5/13. Commd 12/12/46. Flt Lt 12/6/50. Retd SUP 27/8/58.
FRANCIS C. P. Born 12/5/28. Commd 27/7/49. Sqn Ldr 1/7/58. Retd GD 1/4/67.
FRANCIS C. V. Born 24/4/35. Commd 6/9/55. Flt Lt 6/3/61. Retd GD 1/3/69.
FRANCIS G., DFC AFC*. Born 4/9/16. Commd 16/3/47. Flt Lt 5/2/48. Retd GD(G) 4/9/74.
FRANCIS G. A. Born 16/10/26. Commd 3/5/46. Sqn Ldr 1/1/57. Retd GD 30/12/67.
FRANCIS G. R. Born 5/1/37. Commd 30/7/57. Sqn Ldr 1/7/70. Retd GD 1/4/87.
FRANCIS H. T., DFC. Born 3/3/15. Commd 1/1/43. Sqn Ldr 1/8/47. Retd GD 7/5/58.
FRANCIS I. C., DPhysEd MIMgt. Born 8/5/31. Commd 24/2/55. Sqn Ldr 1/7/68. Retd SUP 26/2/74.
FRANCIS I. E. Born 31/3/38. Commd 26/5/60. Wg Cdr 1/1/78. Retd GD 23/6/90.
FRANCIS I. P., BA. Born 16/2/37. Commd 7/8/59. Sqn Ldr 7/2/67. Retd EDN 7/8/75.
FRANCIS L. E., CEng MRAeS FIMgt. Born 9/8/18. Commd 1/12/41. Gp Capt 1/7/69. Retd ENG 9/8/72.
FRANCIS N. J. Born 30/11/48. Commd 21/3/69. Fg Offr 20/9/71. Retd GD(G) 23/12/74.
FRANCIS N. P., BSc. Born 7/8/61. Commd 29/4/84. Flt Lt 29/10/86. Retd GD 14/9/96.
FRANCIS P. H. Born 25/10/18. Commd 28/7/49. Sqn Ldr 1/7/58. Retd ENG 26/10/67.
FRANCIS R. H., BA. Born 23/7/30. Commd 22/9/49. Sqn Ldr 1/7/75. Retd SEC 23/7/80.
FRANCIS R. J. Born 12/3/43. Commd 20/7/78. Sqn Ldr 1/7/86. Retd ENG 15/1/95.
FRANCIS R. W., DFC. Born 18/1/25. Commd 11/11/44. Sqn Ldr 1/7/69. Retd GD 30/8/75.
FRANCIS T. Born 25/6/56. Commd 29/5/90. Flt Lt 29/3/92. Retd ENG 28/3/94.
FRANCIS W. G. Born 25/5/39. Commd 22/10/59. Wg Cdr 1/7/89. Retd ADMIN 21/8/90.
FRANCIS W. K. Born 10/12/29. Commd 13/7/61. Flt Lt 13/7/67. Retd SEC 19/8/67.
FRANK A. D., CB CBE DSO DFC BA. Born 27/7/17. Commd 29/12/36. AVM 1/7/65. Retd GD 27/10/70.
FRANK C. G. H., BSc CEng MRAeS MIEE. Born 26/5/27. Commd 6/11/47. Wg Cdr 1/7/71. Retd ENG 1/3/79.
FRANK E. A. Born 1/7/20. Commd 4/10/44. Flt Offr 9/11/52. Retd SEC 13/1/55.
FRANK M. J. C. Born 6/4/45. Commd 15/9/67. Sqn Ldr. 1/7/80. Retd GD 1/11/89.
FRANKCOM G. P., BA. Born 15/4/42. Commd 17/9/67. Sqn Ldr 1/7/77. Retd GD 17/9/83.
FRANKLAND M. J. Born 26/9/51. Commd 29/4/71. Sqn Ldr 1/7/85. Retd GD 14/3/97.
FRANKLAND R. Born 11/8/53. Commd 5/8/76. Flt Lt 5/2/82. Retd GD 20/4/92.
FRANKLIN C. E. Born 6/9/34. Commd 14/10/71. Flt Lt 14/10/75. Retd ENG 17/9/84.
FRANKLIN D. B. Born 12/8/32. Commd 27/9/51. Flt Lt 29/4/57. Retd GD 12/8/87.
FRANKLIN D. G. T., AFC. Born 25/5/26. Commd 20/4/50. Sqn Ldr 1/7/58. Retd GD 31/5/76.
FRANKLIN D. J. P. Born 26/1/48. Commd 26/5/67. Flt Lt 26/11/72. Retd GD 29/11/75.
FRANKLIN G. S., AFC. Born 25/11/35. Commd 10/11/63. Flt Lt 25/7/66. Retd GD 7/12/74.
FRANKLIN H. J., AFC. Born 10/11/16. Commd 31/7/42. Sqn Ldr 1/1/54. Retd GD 29/1/58.
FRANKLIN K. T. Born 1/7/20. Commd 20/10/4. Sqn Offr 1/1/55. Retd SEC 11/12/55.
FRANKLIN N. E. Born 7/10/28. Commd 25/6/66. Sqn Ldr 1/7/79. Retd ENG 2/4/82.
FRANKLIN P. R. Born 19/7/40. Commd 22/5/70. Flt Lt 22/5/72. Retd GD(G) 17/9/78.
FRANKLIN T. J. Born 21/10/32. Commd 24/9/64. Flt Lt 24/9/69. Retd ENG 1/2/73.
FRANKLIN-JONES A., BSc MRAeS. Born 3/11/13. Commd 22/8/39. Wg Cdr 1/1/58. Retd EDN 17/9/66.
FRANKLING M. B., MSc CEng MRAeS. Born 22/12/43. Commd 16/9/76. Sqn Ldr 1/1/87. Retd ADMIN 16/9/90.
FRANKLYN R. V. B. Born 8/7/13. Commd 1/1/37. Wg Cdr 1/1/50. Retd SUP 4/5/59.
FRANKS C. Born 27/12/41. Commd 10/3/77. Sqn Ldr 1/7/91. Retd ENG 27/6/93.
FRANKS D. M. Born 15/9/45. Commd 6/9/68. Flt Lt 6/3/75. Retd GD 12/3/84.
FRANKS J. N. Born 3/6/34. Commd 18/5/55. Flt Lt 23/11/60. Retd GD 3/6/89.
FRAPWELL J. R. Born 13/3/22. Commd 17/5/62. Flt Lt 17/5/67. Retd ENG 13/3/77.
FRASER A. L., CEng MIMechE. Born 28/12/33. Commd 28/10/55. Wg Cdr 1/7/73. Retd ENG 29/11/85.
FRASER A. L. Born 30/9/40. Commd 5/12/63. Sqn Ldr 1/1/80. Retd ENG 30/9/95.
FRASER A. W. Born 15/3/34. Commd 18/3/53. A Cdre 1/7/77. Retd GD 24/7/79.
FRASER B., BA DPhysEd. Born 30/1/46. Commd 15/12/70. Sqn Ldr 1/1/88. Retd ADMIN 30/1/01.
FRASER B. A., MIMgt MRIN AMRAeS. Born 11/10/21. Commd 14/7/44. Sqn Ldr 1/1/59. Retd GD(G) 11/10/76.
FRASER B. F. J. Born 4/5/35. Commd 4/7/69. Flt Lt 4/7/71. Retd ADMIN 4/7/77.
FRASER E. M. Born 1/7/19. Commd 17/5/41. Flt Offr 1/9/45. Retd SEC 15/8/50.
FRASER G. W., MA MA. Born 13/5/44. Commd 4/9/67. Wg Cdr 1/1/83. Retd ADMIN 1/1/86.
FRASER I. Born 16/8/29. Commd 18/2/53. Wg Cdr 1/1/71. Retd GD 24/5/75.
FRASER I. Born 13/6/35. Commd 23/1/64. Flt Lt 1/4/66. Retd SEC 13/6/73.

FRASER J. Born 6/8/41. Commd 6/9/63. Sqn Ldr 1/7/91. Retd GD 6/8/98.
FRASER J. C. A., BSc. Born 23/10/56. Commd 15/9/74. Sqn Ldr 1/7/90. Retd GD 23/10/00.
FRASER J. J. S. Born 22/2/22. Commd 8/11/62. Flt Lt 8/11/65. Retd ENG 12/6/75.
FRASER J. W., MBE. Born 11/10/24. Commd 3/6/53. Sqn Ldr 1/7/62. Retd CAT 9/8/69.
FRASER K. Born 26/9/05. Commd 3/6/29. Sqn Ldr 1/12/43. Retd SEC 7/5/46 rtg Wg Cdr.
FRASER N. A. S. Born 10/9/62. Commd 24/7/81. Sqn Ldr 1/7/94. Retd OPS SPT 10/9/00.
FRASER N. M. J. Born 14/3/35. Commd 13/12/55. Wg Cdr 1/7/80. Retd GD 22/2/89.
FRASER N. N. Born 24/12/37. Commd 25/1/63. Flt Lt 25/7/68. Retd GD 2/10/78.
FRASER Sir Paterson, KBE CB AFC BA FRaeS. Born 15/7/07. Commd 7/9/29. AM 1/7/59. Retd GD 20/11/64.
FRASER R. G., BSc. Born 8/6/53. Commd 14/11/76. Wg Cdr 1/1/99. Retd GD 31/7/00.
FRASER W. A., MBE MIMgt. Born 31/10/19. Commd 5/5/60. Sqn Ldr 1/7/68. Retd ENG 31/10/74.
FRATER S., MCIPD MIMgt. Born 12/3/45. Commd 4/5/72. Wg Cdr 1/7/88. Retd ADMIN 1/4/92.
FRAY F. G., DFC. Born 13/4/20. Commd 24/1/42. Sqn Ldr 1/7/50. Retd GD 13/10/63.
FRAYN F. E., CBE. Born 28/10/12. Commd 14/1/40. Gp Capt 1/7/59. Retd SEC 31/12/66.
FRAZER C. F. Born 20/9/45. Commd 3/3/64. Flt Lt 17/3/71. Retd GD 30/4/76.
FRAZER K. D. Born 18/7/42. Commd 16/9/71. Sqn Ldr 1/7/79. Retd ENG 18/7/97.
FRAZER W. M., BSc. Born 28/12/46. Commd 6/10/69. Flt Lt 6/7/71. Retd GD 23/5/91.
FREARSON W. C., MIMgt. Born 13/1/21. Commd 5/12/42. Sqn Ldr 1/1/70. Retd SEC 13/1/76.
FREARY W. T. W., BEM. Born 31/3/36. Commd 27/10/67. Sqn Ldr 1/1/75. Retd ADMIN 29/4/77.
FREEBORN A. J. Born 16/10/28. Commd 2/3/49. Wg Cdr 1/1/70. Retd GD 4/9/76.
FREEGUARD T. S. Born 24/4/40. Commd 14/10/71. Sqn Ldr 1/1/78. Retd ADMIN 1/7/82.
FREEMAN A. R. Born 4/3/41. Commd 30/7/63. Sqn Ldr 1/1/72. Retd GD 20/12/80.
FREEMAN B. G., OBE. Born 20/3/45. Commd 27/5/71. Gp Capt 1/1/94. Retd GD 1/1/98.
FREEMAN G. Born 18/9/32. Commd 12/7/51. Flt Lt 20/5/64. Retd GD 1/2/72.
FREEMAN K. S., DFM. Born 22/1/18. Commd 25/4/43. Flt Lt 25/10/46. Retd GD 2/8/53.
FREEMAN N. B., AFC. Born 15/4/19. Commd 27/7/40. Wg Cdr 1/7/56. Retd GD 23/4/66.
FREEMAN R. E. M. Born 30/7/37. Commd 16/12/58. Wg Cdr 1/1/79. Retd GD 20/6/83.
FREEMAN R. G. E. P. Born 23/2/22. Commd 14/12/43. Sqn Ldr 1/1/56. Retd SEC 10/11/65.
FREEMAN S. J., BSc. Born 2/2/30. Commd 6/8/63. Sqn Ldr 15/4/70. Retd ADMIN 6/8/79.
FREEMAN T. J., CEng MIEE. Born 26/4/40. Commd 19/1/66. Flt Lt 23/1/70. Retd ENG 26/4/78.
FREER Sir Robert., GBE KCB CIMgt. Born 1/9/23. Commd 25/9/43. ACM 1/1/80. Retd GD 3/4/82.
FREESTON D. J. Born 23/9/29. Commd 24/9/52. Flt Lt 1/4/58. Retd GD 29/9/84.
FREESTONE-WALKER A. Born 28/5/41. Commd 8/11/68. Sqn Ldr 1/1/77. Retd SUP 1/1/80.
FREKE C. J. Born 26/11/55. Commd 13/8/82. Fg Off 13/2/85. Retd GD(G) 1/2/87.
FRENCH A., OBE FRIN MRAeS. Born 11/6/32. Commd 7/6/54. Gp Capt 1/7/77. Retd GD 8/4/87.
FRENCH A. P. W. Born 22/2/58. Commd 19/9/76. Flt Lt 12/3/83. Retd GD 22/2/96.
FRENCH B. T. A. Born 24/2/31. Commd 22/8/71. Sqn Ldr 22/8/71. Retd SUP 26/11/88.
FRENCH D R., CB MBE CEng MRAeS. Born 11/12/37. Commd 6/10/60. AVM 1/7/91. Retd ENG 1/1/94.
FRENCH E. G., BSc. Born 19/12/25. Commd 24/4/49. Sqn Ldr 19/11/63. Retd ADMIN 24/4/75.
FRENCH H. F. Born 8/6/36. Commd 24/6/71. Sqn Ldr 1/1/84. Retd ENG 30/4/88.
FRENCH J. F. Born 13/11/42. Commd 28/2/64. Sqn Ldr 1/7/88. Retd GD 22/5/93.
FRENCH K. G. H. Born 29/3/44. Commd 24/6/65. Flt Lt 24/12/67. Retd GD 29/1/82.
FRENCH K. H. Born 15/6/38. Commd 9/4/60. Flt Lt 9/10/65. Retd GD 1/10/76.
FRENCH M. R. Born 19/6/39. Commd 1/4/58. Gp Capt 1/1/85. Retd GD 16/9/88.
FRENCH P. F. G., MSc BSc CEng MIEE. Born 17/12/52. Commd 19/3/78. Sqn Ldr 1/1/85. Retd ADMIN 19/3/94.
FRENCH R. Born 17/11/26. Commd 3/5/46. Flt Lt 28/2/50. Retd GD(G) 17/1/73.
FRENCH R. A. Born 3/12/41. Commd 26/5/61. Flt Lt 26/11/66. Retd GD 22/10/94.
FRENCH R. E. Born 27/1/40. Commd 23/6/61. Fg Offr 23/6/63. Retd GD 5/8/66.
FRENCH T. H., MBE. Born 28/2/15. Commd 29/11/43. Flt Lt 24/4/50. Retd SUP 28/2/64. Re-commissioned 7/3/66 to 7/3/69.
FRENCH T. J., CEng MRAeS MIEE. Born 24/3/33. Commd 25/7/56. Wg Cdr 1/1/76. Retd ENG 24/3/87.
FREWER P. J. Born 3/9/34. Commd 9/12/53. Flt Lt 3/9/61. Retd GD 3/9/72.
FREYNE Rev T. Born 25/11/17. Commd 28/7/42. Retd 15/3/62. Wg Cdr.
FRIAR P. D., MSc BSc (Eur Ing) CEng MRAeS. Born 25/2/56. Commd 4/1/81. Sqn Ldr 1/1/90. Retd ENG 4/1/97.
FRICKER C. J. Born 2/1/42. Commd 2/8/68. Sqn Ldr 1/1/78. Retd ENG 1/1/87. Re-entered 21/12/87. Sqn Ldr 21/12/87. Retd ENG 2/1/97.
FRICKER G. A., OBE. Born 26/10/08. Commd 9/9/41. Wg Cdr 1/7/54. Retd ENG 26/10/60.
FRIDAY S. J. Born 25/8/63. Commd 25/2/82. Flt Lt 25/8/87. Retd GD 4/4/92.
FRIDGE A. R. Born 6/12/32. Commd 21/10/66. Sqn Ldr 1/1/78. Retd GD(G) 1/8/83.
FRIEND N., MBE. Born 28/4/20. Commd 15/3/47. Gp Capt 1/1/69. Retd SUP 1/11/72.
FRIPP A. G. Born 13/6/14. Commd 12/6/47. Sqn Ldr 1/1/64. Retd ENG 13/6/69.
FRIPP M. D., BA. Born 28/5/37. Commd 30/9/56. Sqn Ldr 1/1/69. Retd ENG 28/5/75.
FRIPP W. A., DFC. Born 20/10/21. Commd 25/8/44. Flt Lt 21/1/53. Retd SUP 10/6/61.
FRISCH M. A. F. Born 1/9/43. Commd 15/12/88. Flt Lt 15/12/90. Retd ENG 1/9/98.
FRITCHLEY E., BSc. Born 16/10/53. Commd 26/10/75. Flt Lt 26/7/79. Retd ENG 26/10/91.
FRITH E. D., CBE AFC*. Born 12/9/33. Commd 27/7/54. Gp Capt 1/7/78. Retd GD 12/9/88.

FRITH E. L., CB ACIS. Born 18/3/19. Commd 20/8/38. AVM 1/7/71. Retd SEC 18/3/74.
FRITH J. E., BSc CEng MIEE DipEl. Born 1/2/21. Commd 22/8/41. Gp Capt 1/7/61. Retd ENG 9/8/69.
FRITH M. C., IEng. Born 24/4/44. Commd 5/7/73. Wg Cdr 1/7/88. Retd ENG 7/11/98.
FRIZZELL J. S. Born 12/7/46. Commd 23/9/66. Sqn Ldr 1/1/83. Retd GD 18/1/90.
FRIZZELLE Rev D. St C. A. Born 1/8/17. Commd 10/12/45. Retd 10/9/72 Wg Cdr.
FROELICH B. Born 21/5/14. Commd 7/1/45. Fg Offr 7/7/45. Retd GD(G) 18/12/45. Re-commissioned 14/5/50. Flt Lt 19/11/53. Retd 24/4/66.
FROGGATT D. G. Born 9/4/56. Commd 3/11/77. Sqn Ldr 1/7/88. Retd GD 9/4/94.
FROGLEY R. T., CBE DFC MRAeS. Born 30/5/16. Commd 31/7/37. Gp Capt 1/7/55. Retd GD 30/5/66.
FROST A. F. Born 15/1/23. Commd 3/7/42. Flt Lt 5/10/60. Retd GD(G) 15/1/78 rtg Sqn Ldr.
FROST A. K., BSc. Born 6/5/56. Commd 20/10/86. Sqn Ldr 1/7/90. Retd ENG 1/10/91.
FROST C. V. Born 14/11/96. Commd 11/6/42. Flt Lt 4/11/46. Retd MED(T) 25/5/46.
FROST D. F., BA CEng MIMechE. Born 22/2/35. Commd 1/3/71. Sqn Ldr 1/3/71. Retd ENG 22/4/93.
FROST D. J. C. Born 13/2/10. Commd 20/2/41. Sqn Ldr 1/8/47. Retd ENG 13/2/60.
FROST G. B. Born 24/1/36. Commd 21/12/62. Flt Lt 25/7/66. Retd SEC 24/1/74.
FROST G. L. Born 13/5/30. Commd 16/11/51. Sqn Ldr 1/7/77. Retd GD 13/5/88.
FROST I. E. Born 24/3/46. Commd 6/11/64. Sqn Ldr 1/7/83. Retd GD 1/7/86.
FROST I. M. Born 10/8/51. Commd 25/2/72. Sqn Ldr 1/7/84. Retd GD 10/8/89.
FROST J. Born 12/10/34. Commd 10/3/60. Sqn Ldr 1/1/69. Retd ENG 13/10/77. Re-instated 28/7/82. Sqn Ldr 15/10/73. Retd ENG 12/10/92.
FROST J. R., MIMgt. Born 15/11/13. Commd 21/1/43. Sqn Ldr 1/7/54. Retd ENG 20/11/68.
FROST J. W., CBE DFC DL. Born 30/7/21. Commd 8/5/42. A Cdre 1/7/68. Retd GD 11/10/76.
FROST P. C. Born 17/2/46. Commd 19/8/66. Flt Lt 17/2/73. Retd ENG 17/2/84.
FROST R. G. Born 6/6/51. Commd 4/5/72. Flt Lt 4/11/77. Retd GD 22/10/94.
FROST T. P. Born 23/2/23. Commd 16/7/48. Flt Lt 4/11/53. Retd GD 29/7/55.
FROST W. S., CEng MRAeS MIMgt. Born 30/5/18. Commd 9/3/44. Wg Cdr 1/7/62. Retd ENG 30/9/72.
FROUD J. R. J. Born 14/10/31. Commd 4/6/52. Sqn Ldr 1/7/82. Retd GD 14/10/91.
FROUD T. R. W. Born 10/1/20. Commd 21/2/42. Sqn Ldr 1/7/54. Retd GD 10/1/63.
FROUDE H., RM. Born 23/1/51. Commd 10/11/74. Sqn Offr 1/6/85. Retd MED 10/11/93.
FROW B. G., DSO DFC*. Born 6/10/22. Commd 3/7/41. A Cdre 1/1/73. Retd GD 6/10/77.
FRUIN-BALL V. C. Born 22/2/28. Commd 18/6/52. Sqn Ldr 1/1/67. Retd SEC 1/1/70.
FRY A. B., DFC. Born 30/6/15. Commd 12/7/41. Flt Lt 13/3/51. Retd GD(G) 28/6/64 rtg Sqn Ldr.
FRY B. J., DFC. Born 16/6/24. Commd 24/3/45. Sqn Ldr 1/4/56. Retd GD 16/6/67.
FRY D. J. Born 16/6/61. Commd 22/5/80. Sqn Ldr 1/7/95. Retd GD 16/6/99.
FRY F. J. Born 2/1/25. Commd 2/1/49. Flt Lt 23/10/56. Retd GD 2/1/63.
FRY G. P., MBE BSc MIMgt. Born 24/5/30. Commd 20/8/52. Wg Cdr 1/1/71. Retd ADMIN 1/10/77.
FRY J. R. Born 5/11/38. Commd 29/7/65. Flt Lt 29/7/67. Retd GD 5/11/76.
FRY P., OBE. Born 5/8/33. Commd 18/7/53. Wg Cdr 1/1/81. Retd GD 6/8/83.
FRY P. J., DFC. Born 19/12/22. Commd 26/11/44. Sqn Ldr 1/7/55. Retd GD 1/2/61.
FRY R. D., MHCIMA. Born 22/2/55. Commd 30/3/75. Wg Cdr 1/7/92. Retd ADMIN 14/9/96.
FRY W. E. C. Born 23/11/30. Commd 30/7/59. Sqn Ldr 1/7/72. Retd GD(G) 30/8/75.
FRYER A. H. Born 29/9/24. Commd 19/5/44. Sqn Ldr 1/10/55. Retd GD 29/9/67.
FRYER D. F. Born 19/4/44. Commd 25/3/64. Flt Lt 25/9/69. Retd GD 2/6/76.
FRYER J. A. Born 4/1/30. Commd 11/4/51. Sqn Ldr 1/1/62. Retd GD 4/1/70.
FRYER J. M., DFM. Born 2/1/22. Commd 5/6/43. Wg Cdr 1/7/71. Retd GD(G) 3/1/73.
FRYER T. P. Born 10/10/52. Commd 18/4/74. Sqn Ldr 1/1/89. Retd GD(G) 1/1/92.
FRYER W. C. Born 13/2/25. Commd 20/4/50. Flt Lt 20/10/53. Retd GD 1/10/68.
FRYETT B. W. Born 1/4/54. Commd 11/9/86. Flt Lt 11/9/88. Retd ADMIN 11/9/96.
FRYETT D. B. Born 22/6/39. Commd 26/10/62. Flt Lt 26/4/68. Retd GD 10/7/78. Reinstated 28/7/81. Sqn Ldr 1/1/90. Retd ADMIN 30/9/91.
FUDGE R. A., BEM. Born 14/5/30. Commd 11/2/65. Sqn Ldr 1/7/75. Retd SEC 1/8/80.
FULENA P. N. Born 28/2/45. Commd 17/7/64. Flt Lt 17/1/70. Retd GD 1/5/76.
FULFORD J. W., BA MIMgt. Born 1/9/35. Commd 23/10/56. Wg Cdr 1/7/80. Retd GD 1/9/90.
FULFORD K. T., BEM. Born 25/12/28. Commd 13/2/64. Sqn Ldr 1/7/74. Retd ENG 30/12/78.
FULLARTON B. M. Born 27/4/39. Commd 26/6/61. Flt Lt 1/4/71. Retd GD 28/11/73.
FULLBROOK D. J., MPhil CEng MIMechE MRAeS. Born 2/12/39. Commd 6/10/74. Sqn Ldr 1/1/80. Retd ENG 5/5/99.
FULLER A. B. Born 18/2/40. Commd 5/3/65. Sqn Ldr 1/1/77. Retd GD 27/4/98.
FULLER B. A., MSc CEng MRAeS. Born 8/6/37. Commd 25/4/60. Sqn Ldr 18/8/70. Retd EDN 1/7/78.
FULLER B. G. Born 18/9/32. Commd 1/4/53. Wg Cdr 1/7/76. Retd SUP 18/9/87.
FULLER D. P., BA. Born 26/6/40. Commd 30/9/59. Sqn Ldr 1/1/71. Retd ENG 26/6/78.
FULLER G. D., FIMgt. Born 23/6/24. Commd 20/10/44. Gp Capt. 1/1/76. Retd GD 23/6/79.
FULLER J. D. Born 13/3/39. Commd 6/4/62. Fg Offr 6/4/64. Retd GD 19/3/66.
FULLER J. H. Born 13/5/16. Commd 5/7/45. Fg Offr 30/8/47. Retd CAT 12/8/50 rtg Flt Lt.
FULLER K. Born 8/11/34. Commd 3/3/65. Flt Lt 30/4/68. Retd SUP 9/12/86.
FULLER K. D. J. Born 13/8/31. Commd 21/5/52. Flt Lt 16/10/57. Retd GD 13/8/69.

FULLER M. J. D. Born 2/5/38. Commd 28/7/59. Sqn Ldr 1/1/71. Retd GD 2/4/76.
FULLER N. D., DFC. Born 6/7/22. Commd 8/10/43. Flt Lt 8/4/47. Retd GD 31/3/62.
FULLER R. F. Born 9/10/46. Commd 2/8/68. Sqn Ldr 1/1/80. Retd ENG 9/10/84.
FULLER R. L., AFC*. Born 20/5/20. Commd 14/1/39. Gp Capt 1/7/63. Retd GD 13/3/70.
FULLER S. C., OBE BEM. Born 21/10/44. Commd 16/8/70. Gp Capt 1/7/94. Retd SY 21/8/96.
FULLER W. Born 16/1/45. Commd 3/3/67. Flt Lt 3/9/69. Retd GD 26/10/73.
FULLERTON Rev J. A., MA. Born 9/8/25. Commd 8/1/53. Retd 20/2/69 Wg Cdr.
FULLFORD A. C. Born 10/12/58. Commd 23/11/78. Flt Lt 23/5/84. Retd GD 10/12/94.
FULLILOVE W. G. Born 26/9/28. Commd 21/5/52. Flt Lt 2/3/58. Retd GD 10/6/71.
FULLUCK D. J. Born 7/8/35. Commd 10/2/54. Flt Lt 10/2/61. Retd GD 5/4/74.
FULTON M. J. Born 14/7/43. Commd 25/6/65. Flt Lt 1/7/69. Retd GD 24/3/94.
FULTON T. J. N., BSc. Born 10/2/42. Commd 30/8/66. Wg Cdr 1/1/89. Retd GD 10/2/98.
FUNNELL I. S. Born 30/3/32. Commd 24/9/52. Flt Lt 29/4/59. Retd GD 24/4/72.
FUNNELL S. N. G. Born 24/5/44. Commd 31/7/86. Flt Lt 31/7/90. Retd ENG 24/5/94.
FURLONG C. D. Born 10/11/37. Commd 4/12/56. Sqn Ldr 1/7/72. Retd GD 10/11/75.
FURLONG J. A., MA BSc. Born 28/4/37. Commd 22/10/59. Sqn Ldr 1/4/70. Retd EDN 1/10/78.
FURLONG R. Born 5/7/49. Commd 31/7/70. Flt Lt 31/7/73. Retd GD 17/9/81.
FURNEAUX S. J. Born 9/4/13. Commd 9/8/41. Sqn Ldr 1/8/47. Retd RGT 19/5/58 rtg Wg Cdr.
FURNELL P. C. Born 26/5/43. Commd 15/8/85. Flt Lt 15/8/89. Retd ADMIN 26/5/93.
FURNER D. J., CBE DFC AFC. Born 14/11/21. Commd 31/7/42. AVM 1/1/74. Retd GD 31/1/76.
FURNESS M. J. Born 3/6/36. Commd 12/3/64. Sqn Ldr 1/7/71. Retd GD 3/6/78.
FURNESS T. H-B., MIMgt. Born 6/1/23. Commd 30/5/45. Sqn Ldr 1/7/61. Retd ADMIN 6/1/78.
FURNEY J. G. L. Born 13/6/43. Commd 18/7/63. Sqn Ldr 1/1/79. Retd SUP 1/1/85.
FURNISS P., DFC. Born 16/7/19. Commd 31/1/42. AVM 1/1/79. Retd LGL 1/4/82.
FURSE D. C., DFC. Born 21/6/21. Commd 9/3/41. Wg Cdr 1/7/61. Retd GD 1/5/72.
FURZE H. MacA., AFC MIMgt. Born 9/11/28. Commd. 27/7/49. Wg Cdr 1/7/66. Retd GD 9/11/83.
FUSSELL A. L., BSc CEng MIEE MRAeS. Born 2/10/19. Commd 18/6/40. Wg Cdr 1/7/57. Retd ENG 6/7/68.
FYFE I., BA. Born 16/9/35. Commd 30/9/55. Flt Lt 1/10/67. Retd ENG 6/11/76.
FYFE J. N. MCD, MA. Born 16/5/57. Commd 27/9/78. Flt Lt 15/4/81. Retd GD 15/1/92.
FYNES C. J. S., AFC. Born 21/9/44. Commd 11/8/77. Sqn Ldr 1/7/91. Retd GD 24/3/01.
FYNES P. N. S. Born 16/2/43. Commd 19/12/63. Flt Lt 9/5/70. Retd GD(G) 1/6/82.

# G

GADD N. Born 5/5/40. Commd 8/9/68. Wg Cdr 1/1/89. Retd GD(G) 5/5/95.
GADD R. P., BL LLB. Born 5/7/33. Commd 17/5/62. Flt Lt 17/5/68. Retd GD 31/8/74.
GAGE P. S. Born 5/12/15. Commd 18/10/41. Wg Cdr 1/7/58. Retd ENG 5/3/71.
GAGE V., ACIS MIMgt. Born 3/10/43. Commd 27/1/67. Wg Cdr 1/1/83. Retd ADMIN 6/11/87.
GAINE M. L., DSO AFC MRAeS. Born 24/10/10. Commd 24/2/38. Gp Capt 1/1/59. Retd ENG 24/10/65.
GAIR G. A. Born 28/9/35. Commd 28/9/62. Flt Lt 8/1/69. Retd GD 9/10/73.
GAIT B. Born 17/9/24. Commd 26/8/45. Flt Lt 4/6/53. Retd GD 20/12/66.
GAIT-SMITH F. E. Born 20/8/37. Commd 1/1/64. Flt Lt 1/1/64. Retd GD 26/8/66.
GAJOWSKYJ J. B. Born 27/1/54. Commd 31/7/86. Fg Offr 6/9/88. Retd RGT 18/6/91.
GALBRAITH E. A. Born 4/7/20. Commd 12/6/57. Flt Lt 12/6/57. Retd CAT 1/6/63.
GALBRAITH T. F. Born 10/11/16. Commd 22/10/41. Flt Lt 8/5/51. Retd SEC 1/8/53.
GALBRAITH-GUNNER R. V. Born 7/6/20. Commd 3/12/44. Flt Lt 3/12/50. Retd SEC 19/8/67.
GALE B. D. Born 2/5/22. Commd 14/10/43. Flt Lt 27/5/54. Retd GD 2/9/67.
GALE D. W., MVO. Born 27/12/46. Commd 14/7/66. Sqn Ldr 1/7/83. Retd GD 27/12/90
GALE I. T. Born 4/2/60. Commd 12/7/79. Sqn Ldr 1/7/91. Retd GD 4/2/98.
GALE J., OBE. Born 22/6/23. Commd 11/8/44. Wg Cdr 1/7/66. Retd GD 29/9/72.
GALE J. F. Born 19/5/30. Commd 13/12/50. Sqn Ldr 1/7/62. Retd GD 5/3/85.
GALE J. O. Born 19/8/15. Commd 2/1/39. A Cdre 1/7/67. Retd SUP 24/4/70.
GALE R. A. A. Born 14/12/32. Commd 14/11/57. Sqn Ldr 1/7/69. Retd SUP 30/9/78.
GALEA A. P., MIMgt. Born 23/7/42. Commd 28.7.64. Sqn Ldr 1/1/75. Retd GD 28/7/79.
GALKOWSKI R. A., MSc BEng MRAeS. Born 6/3/63. Commd 2/8/85. Sqn Ldr 1/7/96. Retd ENG 6/3/01.
GALLACHER A. S., BSc. Born 26/2/56. Commd 16/12/73. Sqn Ldr 1/7/88. Retd GD 26/2/94.
GALLAFENT M. D. Born 22/10/32. Commd 29/12/51. Flt Lt 22/5/57. Retd GD 26/6/78.
GALLAGHER A. J. K., LRCP. Born 25/1/17. Commd 28/5/43. Wg Cdr 28/5/58. Retd MED 29/2/64.
GALLAGHER H. Born 14/7/31. Commd 14/7/69. Flt Lt 14/7/72. Retd PRT 7/1/75.
GALLAGHER R. Born 11/1/43. Commd 6/9/63. Sqn Ldr 1/7/84. Retd GD 11/1/98.
GALLAGHER S. F., BSc. Born 12/5/39. Commd 14/9/65. Wg Cdr 1/1/86. Retd GD 12/5/94.
GALLAGHER T. A. Born 14/4/16. Commd 1/1/43. Sqn Ldr 1/1/54. Retd GD 21/8/57.
GALLAGHER W., LVO AFC. Born 20/7/15. Commd 16/5/42. Wg Cdr 1/7/62. Retd SUP 10/2/72.
GALLAGHER W. F. Born 8/10/39. Commd 1/4/66. Flt Lt 1/10/71. Retd GD 13/12/81.
GALLANDERS P. A. Born 27/7/46. Commd 23/9/65. Wg Cdr 1/7/89. Retd GD(G) 30/3/95.
GALLETLY G. E. G., MIMgt. Born 27/5/24. Commd 20/3/45. Sqn Ldr 1/7/57. Retd GD 27/5/73.
GALLETTI I. Born 26/4/33. Commd 24/4/56. Flt Lt 24/10/61. Retd GD(G) 26/4/71. reinstated 24/5/73 to 27/2/84.
GALLEY B. W. Born 6/11/43. Commd 10/1/71. Sqn Ldr 1/7/86. Retd ADMIN 10/1/01.
GALLEY J. Born 21/8/29. Commd 28/11/51. Flt Lt 28/5/56. Retd GD 21/8/84.
GALLIENNE W. C. Born 24/5/22. Commd 24/2/67. Flt Lt 24/2/72. Retd ENG 30/3/77.
GALLIVER D. R., MIMgt. Born 29/1/17. Commd 21/2/46. Wg Cdr 1/1/68. Retd SUP 29/1/72.
GALLON J. D. Born 20/5/43. Commd 4/6/64. Sqn Ldr 1/7/82. Retd GD(G) 31/6/85. Reinstated 17/7/89. Flt Lt 17/7/89. Retd GD(G) 1/9/95.
GALLOP G. A. M., DFC. Born 15/1/13. Commd 4/7/42. Sqn Ldr 1/7/53. Retd ENG 15/1/62.
GALLOP H. J. Born 13/3/41. Commd 24/4/70. Flt Lt 4/5/72. Retd GD 1/10/80.
GALLOW A. F. A. Born 8/9/33. Commd 24/7/61. Wg Cdr 1/7/79. Retd GD 4/11/88.
GALLOW N. R. A. Born 11/4/62. Commd 18/12/80. Flt Lt 18/6/86. Retd GD 21/3/89.
GALLOWAY E. W., BA. Born 27/1/49. Commd 6/5/83. Flt Lt 6/5/84. Retd ADMIN 6/5/91.
GALLOWAY T. A. Born 29/6/50. Commd 26/2/71. Flt Lt 26/2/74. Retd GD 25/9/89.
GALLWEY I. D. Born 2/5/36. Commd 30/7/57. Sqn Ldr 1/1/68. Retd GD 2/5/74. Reinstated 28/11/84. Sqn Ldr 30/7/78. Retd GD 19/5/89.
GALPIN D. N., MRIN. Born 13/4/29. Commd 15/12/49. Gp Capt 1/1/77. Retd GD 13/4/84.
GALYER J. T. Born 8/1/43. Commd 10/11/61. Sqn Ldr 1/7/74. Retd GD 8/1/81.
GALYER R. P. Born 6/1/36. Commd 1/10/54. Sqn Ldr 1/1/68. Retd GD 6/12/75.
GAMBLE A. T. Born 9/10/20. Commd 28/7/44. Flt Lt 28/1/48. Retd GD(G) 9/10/70.
GAMBLE D. H. Born 23/6/29. Commd 30/7/52. Wg Cdr 1/7/76. Retd SUP 4/8/79.
GAMBLE J. L. Born 4/6/45. Commd 14/6/63. Sqn Ldr 1/1/82. Retd GD 26/4/85.
GAMBLE R. Born 23/9/16. Commd 28/10/43. Flt Lt 22/2/48. Retd ENG 14/10/54.
GAMBLE R. E. Born 17/6/30. Commd 13/12/50. Flt Lt 19/11/53. Retd GD 17/6/69.
GAMBLE W. M., BSc. Born 13/5/49. Commd 30/9/79. Sqn Ldr 1/1/84. Retd. ENG 30/4/90.
GAMBLIN R. W., AFC. Born 8/9/44. Commd 31/8/62. Wg Cdr 1/7/81. Retd GD 1/7/84.
GAMBOLD W. G. Born 23/11/38. Commd 9/4/60. A Cdre 1/7/91. Retd GD(G) 23/11/93.
GAME D. I. Born 27/6/25. Commd 21/5/46. Flt Lt 1/4/63. Retd GD 29/3/69.
GAMMAGE P. A. Born 17/9/46. Commd 6/4/70. Flt Lt 17/4/78. Retd GD(G) 6/4/92.

GAMMON N. W. Born 4/12/21. Commd 8/9/44. Sqn Ldr 1/1/71. Retd GD(G) 30/4/76.
GAMMON R. M. Born 5/3/32. Commd 22/8/51. Sqn Ldr 1/1/63. Retd GD 5/3/70.
GAMSON J. A. Born 5/12/32. Commd 12/7/51. Wg Cdr 1/7/84. Retd SUP 5/12/87.
GANN M. D., LDS RCS. Born 18/11/36. Commd 6/1/63. Wg Cdr 17/3/75. Retd DEL 6/1/79.
GANNON D. H., DFC AFC. Born 5/8/23. Commd 10/12/43. Flt Lt 7/6/51. Retd GD 5/8/66.
GANT J., MBE DFM DPhysEd. Born 10/2/23. Commd 5/9/51. Sqn Ldr 1/1/63. Retd PE 24/5/70.
GAPPER L. F., AFM. Born 8/9/24. Commd 28/1/60. Sqn Ldr 1/7/75. Retd GD 8/9/82.
GARBUTT M. J. B. Born 18/1/31. Commd 14/11/59. Fg Offr 14/11/61. Retd GD 20/2/65.
GARBUZ T. Born 19/2/24. Commd 17/12/64. Flt Lt 17/12/67. Retd GD 4/4/73.
GARDEN S. R., AFC. Born 27/3/18. Commd 10/3/45. Flt Lt 30/6/49. Retd GD 30/3/68.
GARDEN Sir Timothy., KCB MA MPhil FRAeS. Born 23/4/44. Commd 22/9/63. AM 21/3/94. Retd GD 23/4/96.
GARDENER A. M. Born 31/8/29. Commd 21/5/52. Flt Lt 16/10/57. Retd GD 31/8/84.
GARDENER J. I. Born 28/1/32. Commd 18/10/62. Sqn Ldr 1/7/88. Retd GD 28/1/93.
GARDHAM R. H. Born 1/7/23. Commd 6/9/44. Flt Offr 19/6/52. Retd SUP 13/10/54.
GARDINER A. Born 5/2/24. Commd 30/7/59. Sqn Ldr 1/1/73. Retd ENG 29/6/78.
GARDINER C. A., BA MCIPS. Born 14/5/45. Commd 15/7/66. Gp Capt 1/1/96. Retd SUP 14/5/00.
GARDINER D. R. Born 1/7/12. Commd 5/5/41. Sqn Offr 1/1/50. Retd SEC 16/3/53.
GARDINER G. J., BA. Born 10/7/53. Commd 7/11/82. Wg Cdr 1/7/96. Retd ADMIN 8/11/99.
GARDINER I. F., BEd. Born 16/2/61. Commd 19/6/88. Flt Lt 19/12/88. Retd ADMIN 1/10/94.
GARDINER J. C, MBE. Born 1/9/50. Commd 19/12/85. Sqn Ldr 1/1/94. Retd SUP 24/5/01.
GARDINER J. C., BA DPhysEd. Born 7/1/46. Commd 22/8/71. Wg Cdr 1/1/92. Retd ADMIN 7/1/01.
GARDINER P. M., MIMgt. Born 31/10/44. Commd 1/4/65. Wg Cdr 1/7/87. Retd GD(G) 20/1/94.
GARDINER P. M. R. Born 3/7/42. Commd 21/12/64. Flt Lt 1/7/68. Retd GD 31/1/76.
GARDINER P. O. Born 26/10/50. Commd 21/2/74. Sqn Ldr 1/1/88. Retd GD 1/1/91.
GARDINER R. J., MIMgt. Born 15/5/20. Commd 3/5/51. Sqn Ldr 1/1/61. Retd SEC 9/1/71.
GARDINER S. V. Born 5/4/49. Commd 29/6/72. Wg Cdr 1/7/94. Retd ADMIN 14/9/96.
GARDNER A. J., LLB. Born 18/9/32. Commd 27/6/58. Sqn Ldr 27/4/68. Retd ADMIN 18/9/92.
GARDNER B. R. Born 19/7/47. Commd 5/11/70. Flt Lt 12/7/74. Retd GD 1/4/92.
GARDNER C. M. S., OBE DFC. Born 7/10/13. Commd 1/9/45. Wg Cdr 1/7/47. Retd GD 22/4/52.
GARDNER D. F. Born 21/3/26. Commd 17/10/57. Sqn Ldr 1/7/75. Retd GD 21/9/84.
GARDNER G. Born 26/6/46. Commd 10/6/66. Sqn Ldr 1/7/76. Retd GD 1/7/85.
GARDNER J. Born 18/6/32. Commd 10/9/52. Sqn Ldr 1/7/64. Retd GD 1/7/69.
GARDNER J. A. Born 13/6/42. Commd 15/7/63. Sqn Ldr 1/1/75. Retd ENG 30/10/82.
GARDNER J. E. Born 28/11/20. Commd 2/10/42. Sqn Ldr 1/1/72. Retd GD 28/11/75.
GARDNER J. R. Born 14/6/18. Commd 1/4/39. Wg Cdr 1/1/54. Retd GD 14/6/65 rtg Gp Capt.
GARDNER M. J. Born 26/11/41. Commd 15/9/67. Sqn Ldr 1/1/93. Retd GD 26/11/96.
GARDNER N., CEng MRAeS MIMechE DCAe. Born 19/1/29. Commd 28/11/51. Sqn Ldr 1/7/61. Retd ENG 28/11/67.
GARDNER N. T. Born 29/12/32. Commd 30/7/52. Flt Lt 2/12/58. Retd GD 29/12/75.
GARDNER P. B. Born 16/9/39. Commd 24/3/61. Wg Cdr 1/1/84. Retd GD 1/3/92.
GARDNER P. M., DFC. Born 1/7/18. Commd 29/11/37. Sqn Ldr 1/8/47. Retd GD 31/7/48.
GARDNER R., BEM. Born 26/8/24. Commd 5/5/60. Sqn Ldr 1/7/70. Retd ENG 2/12/75.
GARDNER R. C. Born 25/3/35. Commd 5/11/70. Flt Lt 5/11/72. Retd SUP 5/11/78.
GARDNER R. M. Born 23/11/60. Commd 11/4/85. Flt Lt 31/1/88. Retd SY 23/2/93.
GARDNER R. S. Born 3/3/51. Commd 22/5/70. Flt Lt 22/11/76. Retd OPS SPT 6/8/99.
GARDNER T. R. Born 13/4/34. Commd 28/1/53. Sqn Ldr 1/1/76. Retd GD(G) 19/12/85.
GARFIELD R. F. Born 1/5/43. Commd 17/5/63. Flt Lt 1/11/68. Retd GD 1/5/76.
GARGETT J. P. Born 31/5/44. Commd 26/11/81. Sqn Ldr 1/7/90. Retd ENG 3/12/97.
GARLAND A. H. Born 13/11/11. Commd 12/9/30. Gp Capt 1/1/50. Retd GD 30/4/58.
GARLAND A. R., MBE BSc FRGS MIMgt. Born 1/5/43. Commd 24/2/67. Wg Cdr 1/7/88. Retd GD(G) 1/9/94.
GARLAND D. J., AE BSc MIEE. Born 11/9/14. Commd 22/8/39. Gp Capt 1/1/67. Retd EDN 11/9/69.
GARLAND R. Born 18/9/27. Commd 27/6/51. Flt Lt 10/7/55. Retd GD 7/1/73.
GARLICK J. Born 12/7/34. Commd 17/6/53. Flt Lt 7/3/62. Retd GD 12/7/72.
GARLICK R. J., BA CEng MRAeS. Born 26/3/36. Commd 25/7/56. GpCapt 1/1/87. Retd ENG 26/5/91.
GARNER B. L., DFC AFC. Born 25/11/18. Commd 11/9/41. Sqn Ldr 1/7/51. Retd GD 22/11/57.
GARNER B. R., BSc. Born 14/10/35. Commd 5/1/60. Sqn Ldr 27/3/68. Retd ADMIN 14/10/92.
GARNER J. T. Born 10/4/34. Commd 14/1/65. Sqn Ldr 1/1/87. Retd GD 10/4/92.
GARNER P. J. Born 16/5/62. Commd 29/7/91. Fg Offr 29/7/93. Retd MED(T) 8/12/95.
GARNETT C. H., BSc CEng MRAeS MIEE. Born 21/2/35. Commd 24/11/55. Sqn Ldr 1/7/64. Retd ENG 29/5/71.
GARNETT P. E. Born 1/7/21. Commd 8/8/45. Flt Offr 30/6/52. Retd SUP 16/9/52.
GARNONS-WILLIAMS J. S., BSc. Born 3/8/46. Commd 18/8/68. Sqn Ldr 1/1/81. Retd GD 18/8/84.
GARRARD-COLE E., MC. Born 21/5/17. Commd 5/7/37. Wg Cdr 1/1/53. Retd GD 21/11/60.
GARRATT D. R. Born 13/5/47. Commd 31/8/75. Gp Capt 1/7/90. Retd LGL 1/7/93.
GARRETT G. E., BA MCIPD MIMgt CertEd. Born 15/5/47. Commd 1/7/79. Sqn Ldr 1/1/85. Retd ADMIN 1/7/89.
GARRETT K. A. S. Born 12/8/30. Commd 15/6/50. Flt Lt 26/4/56. Retd GD 12/8/68.
GARRETT S. J., BSc. Born 3/11/58. Commd 29/11/81. Sqn Ldr 1/1/95. Retd GD 11/9/98.

GARRETTS A., MBE. Born 3/4/22. Commd 13/10/45. Sqn Ldr 1/7/57. Retd GD 3/4/71.
GARRETY M. J. Born 26/6/68. Commd 16/6/88. Fg Offr. Retd GD 19/2/93.
GARRIGAN M., CEng MIMechE. Born 4/12/39. Commd 4/7/66. GpCapt 1/1/89. Retd ENG 26/8/91.
GARRITT P. C., CEng MIEE. Born 2/7/34. Commd 28/7/67. Flt Lt 28/7/69. Retd ENG 28/7/75. Reinstated 29/4/81. Sqn Ldr 1/1/87. Retd ENG 2/7/94.
GARRITY M. J. Born 6/3/32. Commd 2/1/52. Sqn Ldr 1/1/79. Retd GD 6/3/92.
GARRITY R. D. Born 21/3/62. Commd 24/7/81. Flt Lt 24/1/88. Retd OPS SPT 21/3/00.
GARROCH A. W., OBE MPhil BSc(Eng) MRAeS. Born 25/8/47. Commd 18/9/66. Wg Cdr 1/7/86. Retd GD 1/1/94.
GARROD A. E. Born 8/4/12. Commd 14/6/40. Flt Lt 1/9/45. Retd GD(G) 8/4/67.
GARROD S. J. Born 6/8/51. Commd 16/5/74. Flt Lt 16/11/79. Retd GD 28/1/90.
GARSIDE M. Born 12/4/64. Commd 27/8/87. Flt Lt 27/2/94. Retd ADMIN 14/3/97.
GARSIDE P. Born 13/7/40. Commd 2/12/66. Flt Lt 2/6/72. Retd GD 22/8/82.
GARSTIN A. Born 1/7/29. Commd 18/10/50. Flt Offr 21/1/55. Retd CAT 19/10/60.
GARSTIN L. K., MB BS MRCS LRCP. Born 7/5/23. Commd 2/4/51. Gp Capt 1/1/74. Retd MED 3/1/81.
GARTH P. A., BA. Born 20/6/34. Commd 7/9/56. Gp Capt 1/7/85. Retd ADMIN 20/6/89.
GARTHWAITE B. Born 28/8/57. Commd 27/1/77. Sqn Ldr 1/1/90. Retd GD 28/8/95.
GARTON A. C. Born 8/9/45. Commd 10/6/66. Sqn Ldr 1/1/78. Retd GD 28/10/97.
GARTON I. H. A., BA. Born 30/11/42. Commd 30/9/62. Flt Lt 15/4/69. Retd ENG 1/5/74.
GARTON R. T., MBE. Born 10/1/20. Commd 22/9/55. Sqn Ldr 1/7/68. Retd ENG 15/9/73.
GARTON-HORSLEY C. I. M. Born 4/12/17. Commd 10/11/41. Flt Offr 1/9/45. Retd SEC 11/1/67.
GARWOOD H. G. Born 16/8/18. Commd 22/10/44. Sqn Ldr 1/7/55. Retd GD 15/8/58.
GARWOOD R. H., DFC. Born 26/8/22. Commd 10/5/43. Sqn Ldr 1/9/55. Retd GD 1/11/73.
GASCOIGNE W. F. Born 16/12/12. Commd 12/2/43. Fg Offr 4/11/44. Retd ENG 13/3/46.
GASCOYNE A. W. Born 2/8/22. Commd 6/3/52. Flt Lt 6/9/56. Retd SEC 28/10/60.
GASCOYNE B. A., BA. Born 4/5/42. Commd 3/5/68. Sqn Ldr 1/7/84. Retd SUP 4/5/97.
GASH C. A. Born 13/6/50. Commd 25/2/72. Flt Lt 25/2/74. Retd GD 22/10/94.
GASH R. F., MRAeS. Born 11/12/20. Commd 21/9/44. Sqn Ldr 1/1/56. Retd ENG 26/9/64.
GASH W. J. Born 18/9/18. Commd 14/11/46. Wg Cdr 1/7/65. Retd ENG 1/10/70.
GASKELL D. Born 15/7/41. Commd 19/4/63. Sqn Ldr 1/7/91. Retd SUP 15/7/96.
GASSON D. R., MBE. Born 21/11/44. Commd 31/3/68. Sqn Ldr 1/1/81. Retd GD 31/3/84. Re-entered 2/6/86. Wg Cdr 1/7/90. Retd GD 15/8/97.
GASSON T. P. Born 16/4/31. Commd 15/10/52. Flt Lt 22/4/58. Retd GD 16/4/69.
GASTRELL D. Born 31/3/28. Commd 23/6/60. Flt Lt 23/6/65. Retd GD 23/5/68.
GATELEY P., BSc. Born 5/1/50. Commd 17/1/72. Flt Lt 17/10/73. Retd GD 17/1/88.
GATENBY M. H., BSc. Born 3/8/58. Commd 28/9/80. Sqn Ldr 1/1/94. Retd ADMIN 28/9/99.
GATES A. C. Born 24/11/38. Commd 4/10/71. Flt Lt 6/10/76. Retd ENG 14/10/79. Reinstated 6/10/82. Sqn Ldr 1/7/88. Retd ENG 24/8/94.
GATES E. S., DFC MA. Born 25/3/22. Commd 19/6/43. Wg Cdr 1/4/69. Retd EDN 1/7/73.
GATES F. G., MBE. Born 20/4/30. Commd 27/8/64. Sqn Ldr 1/7/76. Retd SUP 1/10/84.
GATES J. A., MBE. Born 9/1/33. Commd 3/7/55. Gp Capt 1/1/83. Retd GD(G) 15/1/89.
GATES M., BEng. Born 16/1/65. Commd 7/8/87. Flt Lt 21/2/92. Retd ENG 17/8/00.
GATES P., CEng MRAeS. Born 31/10/42. Commd 10/4/67. Sqn Ldr 1/1/78. Retd ENG 10/4/89.
GATES P. N. Born 11/6/26. Commd 15/9/60. Sqn Ldr 1/7/74. Retd ENG 7/4/81.
GATES W. Born 27/5/27. Commd 9/2/50. Flt Lt 24/3/56. Retd GD 10/9/72.
GATHERAL G. H. Born 18/7/12. Commd 1/11/33. Wg Cdr 1/10/46. Retd GD 18/2/58.
GATHERAL H. E. M. Born 15/3/09. Commd 16/6/42. Sqn Offr 1/7/53. Retd SEC 15/3/58.
GATHERCOLE D. C. Born 14/8/30. Commd 12/9/51. Sqn Ldr 1/1/67. Retd GD 1/1/70.
GATHERER, J. A. Born 9/11/43. Commd 10/11/61. Flt Lt 4/5/72. Retd GD 9/11/81.
GATHERER G. Born 28/4/42. Commd 11/7/74. Sqn Ldr 1/1/89. Retd ENG 1/7/93.
GATISS J. W. Born 26/5/45. Commd 8/7/65. Flt Lt 7/10/71. Retd SY 11/6/82.
GATLAND A. J. Born 13/6/50. Commd 31/7/70. Flt Lt 31/7/73. Retd GD 31/3/79.
GATTER P. G. E., BSc. Born 10/6/34. Commd 6/9/55. Sqn Ldr 1/1/71. Retd GD 9/10/79.
GATTRELL R. L. B. Born 4/5/38. Commd 19/6/64. Wg Cdr 1/7/82. Retd SUP 4/5/93.
GATWARD V. J. Born 14/5/33. Commd 30/1/52. Flt Lt 29/5/57. Retd GD 14/5/91.
GAUDEN-ING R. Born 23/11/41. Commd 10/4/63. Flt Lt 19/3/73. Retd GD 30/12/72.
GAUGHAN P. J. Born 14/3/63. Commd 22/11/84. Flt Lt 22/5/90. Retd GD 14/3/01.
GAULT A. J. Born 2/12/40. Commd 21/12/62. Flt Lt 4/11/70. Retd GD 2/12/78.
GAULT I. Born 6/6/48. Commd 26/6/77. Sqn Ldr 1/1/87. Retd GD(G) 14/3/96.
GAULT J. Born 6/6/25. Commd 28/9/61. Flt Lt 28/9/68. Retd MAR 6/6/83.
GAULT R. W. Born 25/9/44. Commd 5/2/65. Gp Capt 1/7/90. Retd GD 25/9/99.
GAULT W., MBE. Born 18/2/46. Commd 1/4/66. Sqn Ldr 1/1/84. Retd GD 8/6/99.
GAUNT D. Born 23/1/47. Commd 19/3/81. Flt Lt 19/3/83. Retd GD 14/3/96.
GAUNTLETT D. W. Born 26/3/63. Commd 21/12/89. Flt Lt 21/12/91. Retd GD 26/3/01.
GAUSDEN P. H., AFC. Born 2/4/37. Commd 3/3/57. Sqn Ldr 1/1/86. Retd GD 2/4/95.
GAUTREY D. H. Born 8/3/16. Commd 3/1/51. Sqn Ldr 14/11/56. Retd EDN 1/6/66.
GAUTREY M. S. Born 5/5/33. Commd 23/7/52. Wg Cdr 1/1/73. Retd GD 30/3/77.

GAVIN G. A. Born 20/7/26. Commd 13/2/64. Flt Lt 13/2/69. Retd ENG 2/11/76.
GAWN I. L., MIMgt. Born 17/2/44. Commd 30/4/80. Wg Cdr 1/7/91. Retd ADMIN 1/9/93.
GAY A., CEng MIMechE. Born 8/11/41. Commd 19/10/65. Flt Lt 12/11/69. Retd ENG 19/10/81.
GAY L. W. J. Born 12/1/20. Commd 16/11/42. Flt Lt 16/5/46. Retd SUP 11/11/55.
GAYER W. A. Born 23/3/33. Commd 29/12/51. Sqn Ldr 1/7/67. Retd GD 23/3/71.
GAYFER H. W. Born 30/12/19. Commd 14/2/46. Fg Offr 14/8/47. Retd ENG 23/3/49.
GAYFORD W. M. Born 25/6/29. Commd 14/10/51. Flt Lt 14/4/56. Retd GD 30/6/79.
GAYLER L. W., CEng MIEE. Born 7/11/18. Commd 30/5/42. Sqn Ldr 1/1/54. Retd ENG 15/12/73.
GAZZARD T. A. Born 14/6/44. Commd 6/9/63. Flt Lt 17/3/71. Retd GD 14/6/82.
GC SINCLAIR Sir Laurence., KCB CBE DSO*. Born 13/6/08. Commd 28/7/28. AVM 1/7/52. Retd GD 29/7/60.
GEACH C. R. Born 25/11/37. Commd 25/7/60. Sqn Ldr 1/1/72. Retd GD 25/11/93.
GEACH S. R. Born 22/2/54. Commd 28/2/85. Flt Lt 25/1/87. Retd ADMIN 28/2/93.
GEAR K. C. Born 7/10/25. Commd 5/5/55. Flt Lt 5/11/58. Retd ADMIN 30/7/77.
GEAREY D. T., MSc. Born 28/12/47. Commd 16/5/74. Wg Cdr 1/1/89. Retd ENG 1/11/95.
GEARING J. N., BA DCAe. Born 12/7/34. Commd 25/10/57. Wg Cdr 1/7/83. Retd ADMIN 12/7/92.
GEARS H. Born 29/8/17. Commd 17/4/47. Flt Lt 17/10/51. Retd SUP 10/1/57.
GEARY N. F. Born 10/7/25. Commd 7/4/55. Sqn Ldr 1/1/74. Retd GD 10/7/76.
GEDDES E. I. G. Born 29/7/34. Commd 3/12/59. Sqn Ldr 1/1/71. Retd ADMIN 26/1/86.
GEDDES M. S. Born 7/8/32. Commd 7/6/51. Sqn Ldr 1/7/70. Retd SUP 7/8/73.
GEDDES R. G., BSc. Born 4/5/47. Commd 14/11/71. Sqn Ldr 1/1/95. Retd GD 1/3/01.
GEDGE P. W. Born 19/12/42. Commd 28/4/67. Sqn Ldr 1/7/90. Retd SUP 19/12/97.
GEE B. J., BSc. Born 11/9/30. Commd 25/2/53. Wg Cdr 1/7/70. Retd GD 1/7/73.
GEE E. J., MIMgt. Born 26/9/26. Commd 17/1/49. Sqn Ldr 1/7/66. Retd RGT 14/4/78.
GEE F. W. Born 24/2/22. Commd 21/6/56. Flt Lt 21/6/62. Retd ENG 31/7/68.
GEE G. S., MRAeS. Born 5/1/20. Commd 15/4/43. Sqn Ldr 1/1/54. Retd SUP 5/1/75.
GEE P. W., MBE AFC. Born 4/1/25. Commd 20/10/49. Sqn Ldr 1/1/65. Retd GD 25/6/76.
GEENTY W. J., MIMgt. Born 1/4/24. Commd 16/3/47. Wg Cdr 1/7/67. Retd GD 1/4/79.
GEESON J. A., BEng. Born 19/6/75. Commd 6/10/96. Fg Offr 6/4/97. Retd ENG 6/12/99.
GEFFRYES S. D. Born 12/2/27. Commd 27/6/51. Flt Lt 27/3/57. Retd GD 6/3/67.
GELBHAUER M., DFC. Born 12/1/21. Commd 11/1/51. Flt Lt 11/7/54. Retd GD(G) 5/4/74.
GELDARD A. P. Born 26/8/64. Commd 8/9/83. Flt Lt 8/3/89. Retd GD 1/9/98.
GELDART M. B. Born 2/7/30. Commd 27/7/51. Flt Lt 13/11/57. Retd GD 30/7/83.
GENESE H. N. H., MRCS LRCP. Born 17/12/18. Commd 19/7/43. Sqn Ldr 19/7/51. Retd MED 1/9/55.
GENT B. Born 10/1/34. Commd 19/6/70. Sqn Ldr 1/7/84. Retd SUP 10/1/94.
GENT E. W. Born 22/2/42. Commd 10/11/61. Flt Lt 10/5/67. Retd GD 26/1/74.
GENT J. B. Born 4/11/35. Commd 26/8/66. Sqn Ldr 1/1/78. Retd ADMIN 17/9/92.
GENTLE D. H. Born 3/7/32. Commd 26/12/51. Sqn Ldr 1/1/63. Retd GD 3/7/88.
GENTLEMAN J. Born 8/1/44. Commd 15/9/67. Sqn Ldr 1/7/79. Retd GD 1/10/91.
GEOGHEGAN M. Born 3/7/52. Commd 22/10/72. Sqn Ldr 1/7/89. Retd ADMIN 1/5/99.
GEOGHEGAN M. F. C. Born 20/11/50. Commd 14/10/71. Flt Lt 14/4/77. Retd GD 14/3/97.
GEORGE B. Born 12/3/29. Commd 13/2/64. Sqn Ldr 1/7/74. Retd ENG 12/7/79.
GEORGE D. R., MIMgt. Born 17/4/23. Commd 21/8/43. Wg Cdr 1/1/67. Retd GD 26/10/77.
GEORGE E. V., DFM. Born 2/2/24. Commd 7/6/68. Flt Lt 7/6/71. Retd GD 2/2/84.
GEORGE G. H. E. Born 9/7/46. Commd 22/7/71. Flt Lt 11/12/77. Retd OPS SPT 7/4/98.
GEORGE N., OBE. Born 10/5/22. Commd 28/7/49. Wg Cdr 1/1/67. Retd ADMIN 30/3/77.
GEORGE R. B. W. A. Born 9/6/28. Commd 27/7/49. Sqn Ldr 1.7/59. Retd GD 17/3/77.
GEORGE R. C. E. Born 29/3/23. Commd 23/4/45. Flt Lt 23/10/48. Retd GD 25/3/77.
GEORGE R. J. Born 26/8/47. Commd 9/3/72. Flt Lt 9/9/77. Retd GD 14/9/96.
GEORGE W. G., AFC. Born 9/8/47. Flt Lt 7/6/51. Retd GD 1/9/73.
GERIG C. M., MVO MSc BSc CEng MRAeS ACGI. Born 6/1/46. Commd 28/9/64. Sqn Ldr 1/1/78. Retd ENG 6/1/84.
GERMAIN D. J., MIMgt. Born 11/8/32. Commd 28/6/51. Sqn Ldr 1/7/64. Retd GD 11/8/87.
GERMAN A. Born 21/6/33. Commd 30/9/55. Sqn Ldr 1/7/73. Retd GD 21/6/91.
GERMAN R. D. Born 19/12/50. Commd 12/8/76. Flt Lt 21/5/80. Retd GD 5/8/90.
GERMANEY R. C. Born 31/3/52. Commd 20/7/78. Sqn Ldr 1/7/96. Retd OPS SPT 20/3/00.
GERRARD D. W. Born 15/9/40. Commd 30/5/59. Gp Capt 1/1/90. Retd GD 15/9/95.
GERRARD T. J., BA MIMgt ACIS. Born 29/7/50. Command 20/9/75. Wg Cdr 1/1/88. Retd ADMIN 1/1/91.
GERRARD W. G. Born 26/5/23. Commd 6/11/42. Flt Lt 13/1/55. Retd SUP 17/6/68.
GERRY B. T. Born 16/8/39. Commd 6/4/62. Flt Lt 6/10/67. Retd GD 12/12/77.
GETGOOD L. V. Born 7/1/21. Commd 7/10/43. Flt Lt 19/10/50. Retd SEC 3/1/59.
GETHING R. T., CB OBE AFC. Born 11/8/11. Commd 15/3/32. Gp Capt 1/7/50. Retd GD 29/1/60 rtg A Cdre.
GETHINGS T. M. Born 10/4/20. Commd 12/11/43. Sqn Ldr 1/7/56. Retd SEC 10/4/69.
GEVAUX W. G., BSc. Born 12/1/38. Commd 5/8/59. Flt Lt 28/6/62. Retd GD 28/9/76.
GHAIL R. S. Born 22/11/39. Commd 20/11/67. Flt Lt 20/11/67. Retd ENG 22/11/77.
GHENT P. W. B. Born 2/9/49. Commd 4/7/85. Flt Lt 4/7/89. Retd ENG 1/5/93.
GIBB A. H., FIMgt. Born 27/2/20. Commd 29/12/40. Gp Capt 1/1/69. Retd GD 23/4/71.
GIBB G. P., MRAeS. Born 7/8/33. Commd 4/2/53. Wg Cdr 1/7/82. Retd GD 2/4/85.

GIBB I. B., MBE DipTechEd MILT MInstPet. Born 2/6/44. Commd 30/5/69. Wg Cdr 1/7/91. Retd SUP 2/6/00.
GIBB P. W. Born 26/12/15. Commd 19/3/42. Sqn Ldr 1/10/55. Retd ENG 20/10/68.
GIBB R. W. Born 7/4/40. Commd 1/8/61. Wg Cdr 1/1/88. Retd GD 7/4/95.
GIBBARD B. D. Born 14/1/42. Commd 17/2/66. Wg Cdr 1/1/85. Retd SY(PRT) 17/2/88.
GIBBARD C. P. Born 24/12/49. Commd 11/11/71. Fg Offr 22/4/74. Retd SUP 1/11/75.
GIBBARD R. W., MBE. Born 8/3/29. Commd 19/11/52. Sqn Ldr 1/7/66. Retd GD 15/4/76.
GIBBINS P. Born 27/1/38. Commd 14/12/70. Wg Cdr 1/1/84. Retd SUP 1/5/92.
GIBBON A. J. Born 4/9/47. Commd 29/6/72. Flt Lt 29/12/77. Retd GD 14/3/96.
GIBBON Rev E. H. M., BA. Born 5/4/15. Commd 15/1/47. Retd 14/5/66 Wg Cdr.
GIBBON J., MBE. Born 8/4/34. Commd 22/12/53. Wg Cdr 1/1/75. Retd GD 9/1/81.
GIBBON P. C. Born 21/5/43. Commd 5/2/65. Flt Lt 5/8/70. Retd GD 16/9/76.
GIBBON R. M. Born 3/6/43. Commd 17/7/75. Wg Cdr 1/1/91. Retd ENG 3/6/98.
GIBBONS B. K. W., BCom MIMgt ACIS ACCA. Born 6/11/26. Commd 7/5/56. Sqn Ldr 1/1/67. Retd SUP 1/10/73.
GIBBONS C. Born 4/3/48. Commd 17/3/67. Sqn Ldr 1/1/88. Retd GD 1/10/90.
GIBBONS D. B., DPhysEd. Born 8/1/39. Commd 14/9/65. Flt Lt 1/7/68. Retd ADMIN 8/1/94.
GIBBONS D. G. Born 25/10/24. Commd 9/8/51. Flt Lt 13/11/57. Retd GD 2/4/68.
GIBBONS D. R. Born 4/6/49. Commd 27/3/70. Flt Lt 27/9/75. Retd GD 4/6/87.
GIBBONS G. Born 5/7/24. Commd 23/8/56. Flt Lt 23/8/59. Retd GD 1/10/68.
GIBBONS G. R. Born 5/8/47. Commd 17/2/67. Flt Lt 17/8/72. Retd GD 1/5/01.
GIBBONS J. R., AFC. Born 24/10/23. Commd 9/4/43. Gp Capt 1/7/63. Retd GD 9/3/67.
GIBBONS J. S. Born 17/3/20. Commd 22/12/44. Sqn Ldr 1/9/65. Retd GD 17/3/75.
GIBBONS M. J. Born 5/9/37. Commd 16/12/58. Sqn Ldr 1/7/70. Retd GD 5/9/93.
GIBBONS P. C. Born 18/11/39. Commd 31/10/63. Flt Lt 31/1/70. Retd SEC 16/4/79.
GIBBONS T. E. Born 13/6/45. Commd 19/3/81. Sqn Ldr 1/1/90. Retd ENG 13/6/00.
GIBBS A. G. Born 21/1/18. Commd 30/1/47. Flt Lt 30/3/52. Retd SEC 16/2/57.
GIBBS A. J., BSc. Born 14/6/43. Commd 30/9/61. Flt Lt 14/12/67. Retd ENG 14/6/74.
GIBBS B., FCIS MIMgt. Born 5/12/32. Commd 15/7/53. Wg Cdr 1/1/72. Retd SEC 1/5/75.
GIBBS C. M., CB CBE DFC. Born 11/6/21. Commd 16/1/47. AVM 1/7/74. Retd GD 1/7/76.
GIBBS D. J. Born 28/7/29. Commd 1/2/62. Flt Lt 1/2/68. Retd PE 27/9/75.
GIBBS F. Born 11/11/11. Commd 9/12/41. Sqn Ldr 1/7/54. Retd ENG 11/11/60.
GIBBS I. C. Born 18/7/36. Commd 30/5/59. Sqn Ldr 1/7/71. Retd GD 30/9/78.
GIBBS I. W. B. Born 4/12/42. Commd 11/5/62. Flt Lt 11/11/67. Retd GD 4/12/80.
GIBBS J. S., MBE CEng MRAeS MIMgt. Born 17/1/21. Commd 4/6/43. Sqn Ldr 1/1/63. Retd ENG 17/1/76.
GIBBS P. H. Born 5/4/19. Commd 24/4/42. Sqn Ldr 1/1/51. Retd GD 3/1/59.
GIBBS R. P. M., DSO DFC*. Born 2/4/15. Commd 1/8/36. Sqn Ldr 1/9/42. Retd GD 24/2/44 rtg Wg Cdr.
GIBLEN J. T. Born 10/6/33. Commd 6/6/57. Sqn Ldr 1/7/86. Retd GD 10/6/91.
GIBLIN B. J. Born 30/7/41. Commd 6/11/64. Flt Lt 4/5/72. Retd GD 15/9/80.
GIBSON A. D., AFC DFM. Born 7/1/23. Commd 15/9/47. Sqn Ldr 1/1/57. Retd GD 7/1/72.
GIBSON A. J. Born 15/9/35. Commd 17/12/57. Sqn Ldr 1/7/71. Retd GD 29/12/88.
GIBSON A. J. Born 11/3/45. Commd 6/4/72. Sqn Ldr 1/1/82. Retd GD 11/3/89.
GIBSON The Rev A. W. M. Born 6/7/34. Commd 6/6/66. Retd 6/7/89. Wg Cdr.
GIBSON B., DFC DPhysEd. Born 3/1/23. Commd 30/10/43. Flt Lt 26/8/53. Retd PE 1/5/65.
GIBSON B. M. Born 17/5/25. Commd 29/1/46. Flt Lt 19/6/52. Retd RGT 12/10/59.
GIBSON B. S. Born 28/5/13. Commd 14/9/41. Sqn Ldr 1/8/47. Retd GD 28/5/56 rtg Wg Cdr.
GIBSON D. A., MRAeS. Born 24/8/08. Commd 16/8/32. Gp Capt 1/7/49. Retd ENG 1/11/52.
GIBSON D. W. Born 19/8/34. Commd 16/5/74. Sqn Ldr 1/7/83. Retd ADMIN 1/6/87.
GIBSON E. E. Born 17/7/10. Commd 8/1/44. Flt Lt 10/8/48. Retd SUP 3/2/58.
GIBSON G. G., BSc. Born 16/1/32. Commd 30/9/54. Gp Capt 1/7/83. Retd ADMIN 16/1/89.
GIBSON G. M. Born 28/5/35. Commd 9/12/65. Flt Lt 1/7/68. Retd ENG 9/12/73.
GIBSON G. W., CBE. Born 19/1/41. Commd 17/1/69. Gp Capt 1/7/89. Retd ENG 14/12/96.
GIBSON J. A., BSc. Born 31/3/62. Commd 16/2/84. Flt Lt 15/1/87. Retd GD 1/5/01.
GIBSON J. A. A., DSO DFC. Born 24/8/16. Commd 16/5/38. Sqn Ldr 1/1/53. Retd GD 31/12/54.
GIBSON J. D., AFC. Born 20/2/26. Commd 22/3/51. Flt Lt 22/9/54. Retd GD 20/2/64.
GIBSON J. H. Born 6/11/55. Commd 28/4/85. Sqn Ldr 1/7/91. Retd GD(G) 1/7/94.
GIBSON J. M. M., BA. Born 10/3/61. Commd 27/8/87. Sqn Ldr 1/1/95. Retd ENG 10/10/00.
GIBSON J. N. Born 9/12/23. Commd 9/9/59. Sqn Ldr 21/2/70. Retd ADMIN 11/5/76.
GIBSON K. S. Born 6/3/31. Commd 4/2/53. Flt Lt 24/6/58. Retd PI 6/3/86.
GIBSON L. Born 4/3/36. Commd 25/9/59. Sqn Ldr 1/1/72. Retd SUP 5/11/76.
GIBSON L., BSc. Born 24/9/41. Commd 1/8/66. Sqn Ldr 1/1/77. Retd GD 24/9/96.
GIBSON M. J., CB OBE BSc FRAeS ACGI. Born 2/1/39. Commd 13/7/59. AVM 1/7/91. Retd GD 2/1/94.
GIBSON M. T. Born 3/6/22. Commd 18/12/50. Flt Lt 1/9/54. Retd GD 29/10/62.
GIBSON P. G., OBE. Born 17/2/28. Commd 22/7/50. Gp Capt 1/1/83. Retd SY 1/9/84.
GIBSON P. H., MBE MA FIMgt. Born 10/12/30. Commd 28/5/55. Wg Cdr 1/7/69. Retd ADMIN 1/3/77 rtg Gp Capt.
GIBSON P. J. Born 4/11/44. Commd 12/7/63. Flt Lt 15/4/70. Retd GD 4/11/82.
GIBSON R. H. Born 19/7/38. Commd 1/8/61. Flt Lt 26/2/64. Retd GD 31/12/68.
GIBSON S. J., MBE. Born 21/3/47. Commd 17/7/75. Sqn Ldr 1/7/84. Retd ENG 21/3/91.

GIBSON T. Born 29/5/27. Commd 8/11/62. Sqn Ldr 1/7/79. Retd ENG 29/5/88.
GIBSON T. C. Born 8/10/62. Commd 29/1/87. Flt Lt 29/7/92. Retd GD 14/3/96.
GIBSON T. J., MBA BSc. Born 17/2/50. Commd 11/8/74. Sqn Ldr 1/1/88. Retd ENG 1/12/97.
GIBSON V. S. Born 20/12/20. Commd 4/11/44. Flt Lt 4/5/48. Retd GD 30/8/68.
GIBSON W. Born 20/5/21. Commd 3/3/45. Flt Lt 19/11/53. Retd GD 20/5/76.
GIBSON W. R. Born 9/7/30. Commd 9/8/51. Sqn Ldr 1/1/66. Retd GD 1/4/83.
GIDDENS P. J. Born 26/2/30. Commd 11/4/51. Wg Cdr 1/1/68. Retd GD 3/10/81.
GIDDINGS Rev H. W., AKC. Born 7/10/30. Commd 2/1/67. Retd 1/5/83 Wg Cdr.
GIDDINGS Sir Michael, KCB OBE DFC AFC* MRAeS. Born 27/8/20. Commd 1/11/41. AM 1/1/74. Retd GD 19/6/76.
GIDNEY A. J., BEng. Born 19/7/44. Commd 22/6/64. Flt Lt 30/5/68. Retd GD 8/9/73.
GIFFIN N. C. W. Born 18/11/50. Commd 19/6/70. Flt Lt 19/12/76. Retd ADMIN 1/7/84.
GIFFIN N. H. Born 13/5/31. Commd 30/7/52. Flt Lt 30/1/55. Retd GD 13/5/69.
GIFFORD F. C. M. Born 16/8/49. Commd 3/12/70. Sqn Ldr 1/1/88. Retd OPS SPT 16/8/99.
GIFFORD R. Born 18/3/35. Commd 23/9/53. Flt Lt 6/6/61. Retd GD 13/11/65.
GIGGINS R. P. Born 28/11/46. Commd 16/8/68. Flt Lt 28/5/72. Retd GD 1/7/85.
GIGGS A. F. Born 31/5/39. Commd 24/6/76. Sqn Ldr 1/7/88. Retd ADMIN 2/10/92.
GILBERT A. C., DFC. Born 5/10/21. Commd 26/10/44. Sqn Ldr 1/1/64. Retd ADMIN 5/10/76.
GILBERT B. H. T., BA. Born 22/6/38. Commd 19/1/66. Sqn Ldr 1/7/75. Retd ENG 7/5/89.
GILBERT C. D. Born 26/9/32. Commd 6/12/51. Sqn Ldr 1/1/63. Retd GD 1/10/76.
GILBERT D. J., MSc BSc(Eng) DIC MBCS. Born 26/2/45. Commd 28/9/64. Sqn Ldr 1/7/80. Retd ENG 26/2/89.
GILBERT D. M. Born 1/7/15. Commd 9/12/42. Flt Offr 9/12/47. Retd GD(G) 16/1/57.
GILBERT E. G. Born 4/11/12. Commd 26/8/40. Flt Lt 27/10/47. Retd GD(G) 4/11/62 rtg Sqn Ldr.
GILBERT E. J., MIMgt. Born 2/12/19. Commd 4/9/58. Flt Lt 4/9/63. Retd ENG 27/4/73.
GILBERT E. L., LMSSA. Born 22/8/20. Commd 2/3/53. Wg Cdr 1/4/62. Retd MED 7/2/78.
GILBERT E. S. Born 8/6/34. Commd 8/10/52. Wg Cdr 1/1/75. Retd GD(G) 4/4/80.
GILBERT G. H., AFC FIMgt. Born 8/11/30. Commd 30/11/50. Gp Capt 1/7/74. Retd GD 8/11/85.
GILBERT J. Born 16/1/49. Commd 21/3/69. Sqn Ldr 1/1/85. Retd GD 7/2/01.
GILBERT Sir Joseph., KCB CBE BA CIMgt. Born 15/6/31. Commd 17/9/52. ACM 1/1/87. Retd GD 9/8/89.
GILBERT J. C., MBE BSc. Born 22/1/45. Commd 28/9/64. Gp Capt 1/7/91. Retd ENG 22/1/00.
GILBERT J. L., CVO DFC. Born 19/12/21. Commd 28/10/43. Gp Capt 1/1/66. Retd GD 31/1/68.
GILBERT J. S., MA. Born 8/7/32. Commd 3/8/55. Sqn Ldr 10/2/67. Retd EDN 19/11/71.
GILBERT J. W., BDS LDSRCS. Born 2/7/33. Commd 5/5/57. Wg Cdr 22/1/70. Retd DEL 31/10/88.
GILBERT J. W. Born 30/10/41. Commd 14/10/71. Sqn Ldr 1/1/81. Retd SY 2/4/93.
GILBERT K. V. E. Born 2/12/29. Commd 5/4/50. Sqn Ldr 1/7/60. Retd GD 2/12/67.
GILBERT M. STJ. J., BSc. Born 8/1/61. Commd 11/12/83. Flt Lt 11/6/86. Retd GD 9/10/00.
GILBERT P. G., BSc. Born 7/1/32. Commd 18/11/54. Sqn Ldr 1/1/65. Retd ENG 18/11/70.
GILBERT P. N. Born 4/3/59. Commd 28/2/85. Flt Lt 2/11/87. Retd OPS SPT 4/8/97.
GILBERT R., BA MIMgt. Born 14/4/42. Commd 22/10/63. Sqn Ldr 22/4/72. Retd ADMIN 14/4/83.
GILBERT R. M. R. Born 16/9/21. Commd 25/8/40. Sqn Ldr 1/7/54. Retd SUP 16/9/70.
GILBERT R. W. Born 26/2/49. Commd 3/10/74. Flt Lt 3/4/79. Retd GD 17/6/90.
GILBERT T. J., MB BS. Born 26/6/62. Commd 11/12/84. Wg Cdr 10/9/99. Retd MED 11/12/00.
GILBODY P. G. A. Born 19/9/50. Commd 30/8/73. Flt Lt 10/11/79. Retd GD(G) 14/5/89.
GILBY D. A. Born 23/5/20. Commd 30/1/47. Sqn Ldr 1/7/58. Retd SUP 17/4/65.
GILCHRIST A. B. Born 19/4/46. Commd 19/3/80. Flt Lt 9/5/77. Retd SY 26/6/86.
GILCHRIST A. J., MSc BSc MRAeS. Born 5/3/46. Commd 24/9/67. Sqn Ldr 15/1/78. Retd ADMIN 6/1/97.
GILCHRIST C. C. R. Born 16/7/48. Commd 28/2/69. Flt Lt 28/2/72. Retd GD 16/7/86.
GILCHRIST J. I. Born 28/6/46. Commd 2/8/68. Sqn Ldr 1/1/91. Retd GD(G) 31/3/95.
GILCHRIST J. K. Born 24/2/23. Commd 23/4/51. Sqn Ldr 1/7/73. Retd GD(G) 24/2/83.
GILCHRIST N. S. F., AFC. Born 8/8/56. Commd 5/8/76. Sqn Ldr 1/7/90. Retd GD 14/9/96.
GILDING A. R. Born 16/6/10. Commd 18/12/41. Sqn Ldr 1/1/51. Retd ENG 16/6/60 rtg Wg Cdr.
GILDING C. R., CEng MRAeS CDipAF. Born 14/1/40. Commd 28/7/60. Sqn Ldr 1/7/76. Retd ENG 14/1/95.
GILDING J. L. Born 2/10/44. Commd 26/6/63. Flt Lt 20/12/69. Retd ENG 3/4/71.
GILDING M. J., MSc BSc BA CEng FIEE. Born 8/8/47. Commd 22/9/65. A Cdre 1/7/96. Retd ENG 5/5/01.
GILES A. F., BSc CEng MIMechE MIEE MRAeS ACGI. Born 17/11/37. Commd 14/5/63. Sqn Ldr 1/7/71. Retd ENG 14/5/79.
GILES D., DFC. Born 27/5/22. Commd 30/1/42. Sqn Ldr 1/1/51. Retd GD 3/10/64.
GILES J. A., BSc. Born 9/7/48. Commd 5/1/70. Sqn Ldr 1/7/84. Retd GD 1/7/87.
GILES J. A., BSc. Born 20/8/52. Commd 25/7/76. Flt Lt 25/4/78. Retd GD 20/8/92.
GILES R. W. Born 3/10/41. Commd 18/12/62. Flt Lt 18/12/67. Retd SEC 27/5/74.
GILES W. J., BA. Born 15/6/44. Commd 16/9/76. Sqn Ldr 1/7/85. Retd ENG 1/12/98.
GILL A. A. Born 17/8/48. Commd 7/10/73. Wg Cdr 1/7/91. Retd GD(G) 17/3/92.
GILL A. M., OBE DFC AE MRAeS MCIPD MIMgt. Born 24/2/16. Commd 6/9/40. Wg Cdr 1/7/55. Retd GD 3/3/71.
GILL C. Born 29/8/23. Commd 27/1/55. Flt Lt 27/1/61. Retd GD 29/8/73.
GILL D. A. Born 27/4/45. Commd 22/5/64. Flt Lt 22/11/69. Retd GD 29/3/73.
GILL D. N., BA BSc CEng MRAeS. Born 25/4/62. Commd 11/9/83. Sqn Ldr 1/7/93. Retd ENG 25/4/00.

GILL F. Born 11/5/30. Commd 3/11/51. Flt Lt 3/5/56. Retd GD 1/5/68.
GILL H., CB OBE. Born 30/10/22. Commd 1/1/43. AVM 1/1/77. Retd SUP 25/8/79.
GILL J. Born 1/2/42. Commd 20/7/78. Flt Lt 20/7/83. Retd GD 1/2/97.
GILL L. W. G., DSO MCIPD. Born 31/3/18. Commd 28/11/37. AVM 1/1/68. Retd GD 31/3/73.
GILL M., MIMgt. Born 18/11/29. Commd 11/4/51. Sqn Ldr 1/7/60. Retd GD 31/3/75.
GILL N. J., BSc. Born 14/4/36. Commd 23/9/59. Flt Lt 23/3/64. Retd GD 23/9/75.
GILL P. Born 7/10/24. Commd 5/5/44. Sqn Ldr 1/7/56. Retd GD 7/10/62.
GILL P. H. R., MSc MFOM MRCS LRCP DAvMed. Born 30/1/42. Commd 11/1/65. Gp Capt 5/9/92. Retd MED 14/1/98.
GILL P. J., BSc. Born 19/6/51. Commd 13/6/74. Sqn Ldr 1/7/88. Retd GD 1/8/91.
GILL P. W. R. Born 18/6/32. Commd 2/1/52. Flt Lt 2/7/56. Retd GD 4/4/77.
GILL R. A., CBE MS BSc. Born 22/5/40. Commd 30/9/60. A Cdre 1/7/90. Retd ENG 1/1/94.
GILL R. E., DFC. Born 17/3/21. Commd 8/7/44. Flt Lt 8/1/48. Retd GD 17/3/54.
GILL R. L., BSc. Born 10/4/60. Commd 2/9/79. Wg Cdr 1/1/96. Retd ENG 1/1/99.
GILL T. E., MBE BSc MRAeS. Born 26/5/31. Commd 7/10/53. Sqn Ldr 1/7/64. Retd GD 24/6/73.
GILL V. A. Born 7/5/38. Commd 24/8/72. Flt Lt 24/2/79. Retd ADMIN 8/5/88.
GILL W., DFC. Born 27/3/21. Commd 15/2/45. Fg Offr 15/11/46. Retd GD 11/5/54.
GILL W. A. Born 29/4/26. Commd 9/1/50. Flt Lt 9/11/54. Retd GD 9/1/66.
GILL W. A. Born 17/4/42. Commd 4/7/85. Flt Lt 4/7/89. Retd GD(G) 17/4/92.
GILL W. G., LDSRCS. Born 15/2/45. Commd 21/7/74. Wg Cdr 22/12/83. Retd DEL 21/8/87.
GILLAN A. M. F. Born 9/9/44. Commd 5/7/68. Flt Lt 21/11/74. Retd RGT 4/12/74.
GILLANDERS D. C. Born 29/2/40. Commd 4/4/59. Sqn Ldr 1/7/71. Retd GD 26/3/79.
GILLARD E. P. Born 28/6/32. Commd 23/1/52. Flt Lt 23/7/56. Retd GD 28/9/70.
GILLARD L. F., CEng MRAeS. Born 18/5/29. Commd 19/2/53. Sqn Ldr 1/7/64. Retd ENG 4/7/70.
GILLARD N. J., BA. Born 14/11/49. Commd 24/9/72. Sqn Ldr 1/1/83. Retd ADMIN 1/12/89.
GILLATT D. G. Born 8/2/24. Commd 28/5/63. Flt Lt 28/5/69. Retd GD 1/4/73.
GILLEN D. Born 27/11/31. Commd 3/12/61. Fg Offr 16/8/92. Retd PRT 3/12/69.
GILLEN J. M. Born 22/7/07. Commd 2/6/43. Wg Cdr 1/7/53. Retd PRT 11/5/61.
GILLESPIE A. V. I., MB ChB MRCOG. Born 13/7/50. Commd 9/5/71. Wg Cdr 31/7/87. Retd MED 31/8/89.
GILLESPIE I. R., MBE BA. Born 26/8/41. Commd 9/9/63. Sqn Ldr 1/7/88. Retd GD 26/8/96.
GILLESPIE J. P., AE BL. Born 22/8/39. Commd 6/9/65. Sqn Ldr 1/7/76. Retd GD 22/8/94.
GILLESPIE J. R. Born 10/1/45. Commd 20/5/82. Sqn Ldr 1/7/90. Retd ADMIN 10/1/00.
GILLESPIE M., BSc Dip Soton. Born 13/6/37. Commd 19/2/63. Sqn Ldr 3/3/68. Retd ADMIN 19/2/83.
GILLETT A. F. Born 1/6/53. Commd 1/6/72. Flt Lt 1/12/77. Retd GD 14/1/85.
GILLETT B. T. Born 20/11/61. Commd 12/1/92. Flt Lt 30/5/86. Retd SUP 1/12/95.
GILLETT M. J. Born 26/12/40. Commd 24/4/64. Flt Lt 8/3/72. Retd GD 3/2/80.
GILLIATT P., OBE. Born 26/2/30. Commd 26/7/50. Wg Cdr 1/7/69. Retd GD 28/11/80.
GILLIATT Z. E. Born 9/2/39. Commd 28/4/60. Sqn Ldr 1/1/74. Retd ADMIN 30/6/77.
GILLIES C. D. Born 9/7/07. Commd 18/10/40. Sqn Ldr 1/8/47. Retd SEC 18/10/58.
GILLIES E., DFC*. Born 20/8/20. Commd 2/2/43. Sqn Ldr 1/7/52. Retd GD 20/8/69.
GILLING T., BA. Born 12/12/31. Commd 17/12/64. Sqn Ldr 1/1/75. Retd ADMIN 9/11/85.
GILLMORE J. N. Born 29/12/36. Commd 17/7/56. Sqn Ldr 1/7/72. Retd GD 25/4/90.
GILLOW C. H. P., BA. Born 11/8/57. Commd 3/10/77. Sqn Ldr 1/1/89. Retd GD 12/12/95.
GILMER W. N., OBE AFC. Born 7/5/23. Commd 17/7/44. Wg Cdr 1/1/61. Retd GD 12/8/75.
GILMORE T. K. Born 11/8/37. Commd 3/6/58. Flt Lt 5/12/63. Retd GD 13/10/73.
GILMOUR A. Born 19/9/49. Commd 30/8/73. Flt Lt 29/2/76. Retd GD 31/1/90.
GILMOUR K. C. Born 14/1/18. Commd 19/9/47. Flt Lt 16/9/50. Retd GD(G) 14/1/73.
GILMOUR P. S. Born 12/10/53. Commd 8/1/85. Sqn Ldr 1/1/89. Retd GD 1/1/92.
GILPIN H. V., DPhysEd. Born 2/4/28. Commd 27/10/54. Flt Lt 1/3/61. Retd SUP 28/11/70.
GILPIN J., MBE. Born 16/11/31. Commd 12/3/64. Flt Lt 12/3/69. Retd GD 2/6/84.
GILPIN P. W., CBE DFC. Born 30/9/22. Commd 19/6/42. Gp Capt 1/7/65. Retd GD 30/9/77.
GILPIN R. C. Born 28/11/32. Commd 28/7/53. Flt Lt 28/1/56. Retd GD 30/11/62.
GILRAY G., MB ChB MFCM DPH. Born 6/11/29. Commd 1/5/55. Wg Cdr 5/4/66. Retd MED 8/1/76.
GILROY C. N., BSc. Born 18/8/45. Commd 20/2/67. Sqn Ldr 1/1/80. Retd GD 18/8/85.
GILROY J. W. Born 31/1/49. Commd 5/7/68. Flt Lt 14/12/74. Retd GD(G) 31/1/87.
GILROY P. P. Born 29/6/41. Commd 30/7/63. Sqn Ldr 1/7/72. Retd GD 6/10/73.
GILSON J. I. Born 26/2/42. Commd 12/1/62. Wg Cdr 1/1/87. Retd ADMIN 30/9/92.
GILSON M. Q. Born 17/7/44. Commd 5/3/65. Sqn Ldr 1/1/82. Retd GD 17/7/88.
GILVARY R. B. Born 19/5/37. Commd 1/4/58. Wg Cdr 1/1/76. Retd GD 1/4/90.
GIMBLETT G. R. G., MBE. Born 6/3/20. Commd 25/11/42. Sqn Ldr 1/1/72. Retd GD 6/3/75.
GINGELL A. S., BSc. Born 15/11/55. Commd 15/9/74. Sqn Ldr 1/1/87. Retd SUP 15/11/93.
GINGELL Sir John, GBE KCB. Born 3/2/25. Commd 16/4/51. ACM 1/1/82. Retd GD 22/6/84.
GINGELL R. R. Born 20/2/50. Commd 6/1/71. Sqn Ldr 1/1/86. Retd GD 1/1/89.
GINN A. W. Born 22/7/32. Commd 14/4/53. Sqn Ldr 1/7/64. Retd GD 1/9/84.
GINN M. C., AFC. Born 15/10/35. Commd 31/7/56. Sqn Ldr 1/7/64. Retd GD 1/2/68.
GINNS J. L. Born 23/2/19. Commd 6/12/41. Sqn Ldr 1/7/54. Retd GD 1/1/59.

GIRDLER E. E. G. Born 8/7/37. Commd 14/8/64. Flt Lt 26/7/67. Retd GD 8/7/75.
GIRDWOOD W. S., FCIPS. Born 22/1/36. Commd 7/7/55. Gp Capt 1/1/84. Retd SUP 6/4/90.
GIRVEN C. F., BSc. Born 8/8/61. Commd 2/9/84. Flt Lt 2/3/87. Retd GD 2/3/01.
GISSING H. C. Born 26/9/24. Commd 16/2/45. Flt Lt 21/11/48. Retd GD 30/9/67.
GITSHAM G. T. Born 1/5/24. Commd 23/12/43. Flt Lt 21/7/61. Retd GD 29/3/69.
GJERTSEN A. B., BSc. Born 2/12/48. Commd 28/2/72. Flt Lt 28/5/73. Retd GD 6/10/77.
GLADDING R. E., CBE. Born 17/6/29. Commd 9/4/52. ACdre 1/1/76. Retd SUP 17/6/84.
GLADSTONE J., AFC*. Born 6/9/22. Commd 12/6/51. Sqn Ldr 1/9/65. Retd GD 6/9/73.
GLADSTONE P. G. Born 13/10/20. Commd 6/2/45. Sqn Ldr 1/7/56. Retd GD 21/11/63.
GLADWELL B. N. Born 2/9/28. Commd 22/7/66. Flt Lt 22/7/69. Retd GD 2/9/83.
GLADWELL I. M., DFM. Born 28/2/23. Commd 7/6/43. Flt Lt 7/12/46. Retd GD 28/2/66.
GLADWIN D. W. Born 4/10/44. Commd 3/8/62. Flt Lt 3/2/68. Retd GD 29/12/73.
GLAISTER D. H., PhD BSc MB BS. Born 13/3/34. Commd 21/6/59. Gp Capt 21/6/82. Retd MED 23/12/94.
GLAISTER J. L. G., DFC. Born 28/12/15. Commd 26/6/39. Flt Lt 1/9/45. Retd SEC 5/8/52 rtg Sqn Ldr.
GLANCY W. C. Born 2/5/52. Commd 11/4/83. Flt Lt 11/4/87. Retd ENG 9/2/93.
GLANFIELD P., ACT(Batt) MHCIMA. Born 21/7/34. Commd 8/12/59. Sqn Ldr 1/7/70. Retd CAT 8/12/75.
GLAS J. A., BA. Born 25/9/50. Commd 3/1/71. Sqn Ldr 1/7/85. Retd GD 25/9/88.
GLASER E. D., DFC. Born 20/4/21. Commd 11/7/40. Flt Lt 1/9/45. Retd GD 26/6/53 rtg Sqn Ldr.
GLASGOW G. H. Born 14/3/39. Commd 10/12/57. Sqn Ldr 1/1/75. Retd GD 1/1/78.
GLASIER J. Born 26/4/60. Commd 26/9/91. Fg Offr 5/3/94. Retd ADMIN 14/3/97.
GLASS E. S. A. Born 2/6/41. Commd 1/12/77. Flt Lt 1/12/82. Retd ADMIN 1/4/87.
GLASS J. R., CEng MIMechE MRAeS MIMgt. Born 10/2/36. Commd 2/2/60. Sqn Ldr 1/1/68. Retd ENG 2/2/76.
GLASS M. R., BEng CEng MIMechE. Born 1/9/60. Commd 8/8/85. Sqn Ldr 1/7/95. Retd ENG 1/9/98.
GLASS N. J. Born 15/1/31. Commd 12/12/51. Sqn Ldr 1/7/66. Retd GD 1/7/69.
GLASSPOOL I. D. Born 13/8/41. Commd 17/1/69. Sqn Ldr 1/7/76. Retd GD(G) 13/8/96.
GLAZIER D. W. Born 28/10/35. Commd 30/5/69. Flt Lt 30/5/71. Retd ENG. 30/9/78.
GLAZIER M. J. Born 27/4/31. Commd 4/6/64. Sqn Ldr 1/7/74. Retd ENG 6/4/83.
GLAZIER W. T. Born 6/12/10. Commd 21/1/43. Sqn Ldr 1/1/54. Retd ENG 6/12/59.
GLEADEN A. W., BSc. Born 21/11/28. Commd 10/11/54. Sqn Ldr 1/7/62. Retd GD 8/11/75.
GLEBOCKI J. Born 4/1/13. Commd 1/1/37. Flt Lt 1/7/46. Retd SEC 8/10/61.
GLEDHILL J. P. Born 8/8/24. Commd 9/12/48. Sqn Ldr 1/1/58. Retd GD 11/5/68.
GLEDHILL J. S. Born 29/5/30. Commd 19/8/65 Sqn Ldr 1/7/75. Retd ENG 9/10/81.
GLEDHILL T. C., AFC. Born 20/12/24. Commd 28/10/44. Gp Capt 1/7/66. Retd GD 27/9/75.
GLEED D. R., MIMgt. Born 27/4/45. Commd 10/10/63. Wg Cdr 1/1/86. Retd GD(G) 28/2/94.
GLEN J. G., OBE. Born 20/11/08. Commd 12/1/32. Gp Capt 1/7/51. Retd GD 1/4/55.
GLEN M. C., CEng MIIM MRAeS MIMgt. Born 29/12/36. Commd 24/7/57. Wg Cdr 1/7/77. Retd ENG 1/2/87.
GLENDINNING B. W. Born 9/8/40. Commd 19/8/65. Sqn Ldr 1/1/79. Retd SY 1/10/82.
GLENDINNING H. D. Born 29/6/21. Commd 8/7/54. Sqn Ldr 1/1/68. Retd GD 30/8/76.
GLENN G. H. W., DFC*. Born 19/10/20. Commd 17/12/41. Sqn Ldr 1/1/55. Retd GD 10/10/63.
GLENN H. Born 19/4/20. Commd 17/6/43. Flt Lt 19/8/51. Retd SUP 25/8/53.
GLENN J. A., BSc DPhysEd. Born 1/12/32. Commd 4/7/57. Sqn Ldr 20/9/66. Retd ADMIN 1/12/92.
GLENN W. J., AFC DFM. Born 28/9/19. Commd 17/11/42. Flt Lt 17/5/46. Retd GD 20/4/63.
GLENNIE D. J. Born 21/10/43. Commd 3/5/68. Sqn Ldr 1/7/87. Retd GD 21/1/92.
GLENNIE J., BSc. Born 9/6/40. Commd 9/11/65. Sqn Ldr 1/1/79. Retd ENG 1/1/82.
GLENNIE W. G. Born 25/3/38. Commd 10/12/58. Sqn Ldr 1/7/71. Retd SUP 5/5/83.
GLENTON J. A. Born 25/1/43. Commd 28/9/62. Flt Lt 1/7/68. Retd GD 25/1/98.
GLEW W. Born 26/4/54. Commd 16/5/74. Sqn Ldr 1/1/89. Retd SUP 8/8/96.
GLIDLE C. S. Born 18/8/29. Commd 26/3/52. Sqn Ldr 1/7/67. Retd GD 28/11/75.
GLINN J. W. Born 16/3/15. Commd 18/9/41. Flt Lt 1/9/45. Retd ENG 1/9/50.
GLOAG A. D. Born 12/7/40. Commd 9/2/64. Flt Lt 14/3/69. Retd GD 21/4/81.
GLOVER A. G. Born 20/9/43. Commd 28/9/62. Flt Lt 8/1/69. Retd GD 3/8/76.
GLOVER G. H., CEng FIMechE MRAeS. Born 7/12/36. Commd 17/7/59. Gp Capt 1/7/84. Retd ENG 16/4/90.
GLOVER H. F., CEng MRAeS. Born 27/3/23. Commd 7/10/43. A Cdre 1/7/75. Retd ENG 27/3/78.
GLOVER J. Born 29/10/42. Commd 4/7/85. Flt Lt 4/7/89. Retd ADMIN 29/10/94.
GLOVER J. W., BA. Born 2/4/54. Commd 3/9/72. Sqn Ldr 1/1/86. Retd GD 15/12/96.
GLOVER N. D. Born 5/8/22. Commd 24/11/44. Flt Lt 11/11/54. Retd PI 5/8/77.
GLOVER P. B. Born 25/9/45. Commd 26/5/67. Flt Lt 4/5/72. Retd GD 13/12/75.
GLOVER R. A. H. Born 8/1/21. Commd 27/8/64. Flt Lt 27/8/69. Retd ENG 8/1/76.
GLOVER R. B. Born 18/2/31. Commd 1/9/70. Sqn Ldr 1/7/76. Retd SUP 25/8/84.
GLOVER R. E., DFC. Born 29/3/18. Commd 17/8/40. Wg Cdr 1/7/54. Retd GD 29/3/73.
GLOVER R. B. Born 27/6/65. Commd 26/4/84. Flt Lt 26/10/89. Retd GD 28/2/93.
GLOVER R. G. Born 6/7/42. Commd 21/12/62. Flt Lt 21/6/68. Retd GD 6/7/80 rtg Sqn Ldr.
GLOVER R. W., BSc. Born 27/5/33. Commd 12/1/53. Sqn Ldr 1/1/62. Retd GD 27/5/71.
GLUNING S. L. Born 26/8/34. Commd 22/5/75. Sqn Ldr 1/7/85. Retd ENG 26/8/92.
GOADBY A. Born 18/8/31. Commd 9/5/51. Flt Lt 9/11/55. Retd GD 18/2/71.

GOADBY J. W., MRCS LRCP MFOM DRCOG DAvMed. Born 14/3/38. Commd 22/4/63. Wg Cdr 23/8/80. Retd MED 19/5/83.
GOATER J. N., BA. Born 12/1/53. Commd 14/4/86. Flt Lt 22/10/80. Retd SUP 19/1/92.
GOATHAM J. R. Born 24/7/34. Commd 19/1/66. Flt Lt 19/1/71. Retd GD 1/6/73.
GOATLEY B. J., MBCS. Born 23/4/28. Commd 11/4/51. Wg Cdr 1/7/73. Retd SUP 1/12/77.
GOBLE T. J. L., BA. Born 26/4/57. Commd 11/5/77. Plt Off 15/7/79. Retd GD 26/2/79.
GODBY P. R. Born 27/8/14. Commd 6/3/39. Wg Cdr 1/7/55. Retd GD 6/9/61.
GODDARD A. F., BSc CEng MRAeS. Born 24/1/37. Commd 23/7/58. Wg Cdr 1/7/74. Retd ENG 18/9/82 rtg Gp Capt.
GODDARD B. Born 5/10/48. Commd 9/12/71. Flt Lt 9/6/77. Retd GD 29/1/96.
GODDARD D. E. Born 12/9/31. Commd 26/3/53. Flt Lt 5/8/58. Retd GD(G) 12/9/91.
GODDARD G. M., MSc BSc CEng MIMechE ACGI. Born 13/12/45. Commd 28/9/64. Wg Cdr 1/1/86. Retd ENG 13/12/00.
GODDARD J. A., BSc. Born 17/8/48. Commd 6/4/70. Sqn Ldr 1/7/83. Retd GD 7/2/87.
GODDARD J. F., BSc DipEl CEng MIEE. Born 27/1/25. Commd 9/6/45. Wg Cdr 11/12/68. Retd ADMIN 3/4/76.
GODDARD J. J., BSc. Born 9/5/29. Commd 4/10/51. Sqn Ldr 9/5/61. Retd ADMIN 9/5/86.
GODDARD J. S. Born 30/1/44. Commd 31/12/62. Fg Offr 21/12/64. Retd GD 10/7/65.
GODDARD M. J. S., BSc. Born 17/6/49. Commd 14/1/79. Wg Cdr 1/1/91. Retd ADMIN 14/3/96.
GODDARD P. J., CB AFC. Born 17/10/43. Commd 22/3/63. AVM 1/1/94. Retd GD 17/4/98.
GODDARD P. R. Born 9/2/52. Commd 22/5/80. Flt Lt 22/5/82. Retd GD 14/3/96.
GODDARD R., BA. Born 10/9/57. Commd 19/9/76. Fg Off 15/4/78. Retd GD 5/6/80.
GODDARD S. G. A., MBE. Born 8/6/20. Commd 17/3/49. Gp Capt 1/7/70. Retd ENG 8/6/75.
GODDEN D. R. P., BDS MB ChB FDSRCS(Eng) FRCS(Eng). Born 28/12/58. Commd 13/1/80. Plt Offr 13/1/80. Retd DEL 8/12/86. Re-entered 28/8/88. Sqn Ldr 1/8/92. Retd DEL 28/9/97.
GODFREY A., MIMgt. Born 1/4/51. Commd 24/6/76. Sqn Ldr 1/1/87. Retd ADMIN 1/1/90.
GODFREY A. G. Born 16/4/13. Commd 16/3/44. Sqn Ldr 1/7/55. Retd ENG 16/6/62.
GODFREY A. R. Born 20/11/40. Commd 1/8/69. Sqn Ldr 1/7/80. Retd ADMIN 20/11/95.
GODFREY A. V. Born 17/1/23. Commd 22/6/45. Flt Lt 30/6/49. Retd GD 21/11/64.
GODFREY C. B. Born 19/6/92. Commd 1/4/18. Fg Offr 1/4/18. Retd GD 31/12/24 rtg Flt Lt.
GODFREY I. P. Born 1/8/48. Commd 10/6/66. Flt Lt 4/5/72. Retd GD 1/7/90.
GODFREY M. F., BSc. Born 28/5/49. Commd 19/9/71. Sqn Ldr 1/1/89. Retd ADMIN 23/12/00.
GODFREY R. W. Born 9/8/36. Commd 1/2/65. Flt Lt 26/7/67. Retd GD 9/8/74.
GODFREY S. H. Born 15/7/10. Commd 1/11/45. Flt Lt 1/11/51. Retd SUP 15/7/65.
GODFREY S. J. G. Born 22/4/40. Commd 25/3/64. Flt Lt 25/9/69. Retd GD 3/12/79.
GODFREY T. W., MBE. Born 1/7/34. Commd 28/5/66. Gp Capt 1/1/87. Retd SY(PRT) 17/6/89.
GODLEY P. R. Born 16/5/46. Commd 4/7/69. Flt Lt 4/1/76. Retd ADMIN 24/3/85.
GODMAN M. E. Born 25/2/39. Commd 10/2/59. Flt Lt 12/8/64. Retd GD 21/8/78.
GODSALL-STANTON J. R. Born 16/4/31. Commd 5/5/51. Flt Lt 10/11/55. Retd GD 16/4/92.
GODSELL S. J., LLB. Born 25/8/53. Commd 16/2/86. Flt Lt 16/8/87. Retd ADMIN 1/1/93.
GODSMARK F. R. Born 23/5/18. Commd 4/3/39. Sqn Ldr 1/1/60. Retd SEC 23/5/73.
GODWIN A. F. Born 13/6/22. Commd 25/6/43. Flt Lt 25/12/46. Retd GD 1/2/59.
GODWIN C. L., AFC. Born 3/5/24. Commd 20/8/43. A Cdre 1/1/70. Retd GD 2/5/79.
GOFF J. H. Born 24/9/29. Commd 31/3/60. Sqn Ldr 1/7/68. Retd GD 26/8/74.
GOFF R. Born 23/2/44. Commd 3/1/64. Flt Lt 7/7/69. Retd GD 1/5/76.
GOGGIN T. E., MIMgt. Born 6/9/28. Commd 11/4/63. Sqn Ldr 1/7/77. Retd SUP 30/11/78.
GOLBY D. H., MA MIMgt. Born 3/4/37. Commd 14/8/61. Sqn Ldr 1/1/70. Retd ADMIN 2/2/91.
GOLD E. J., BSc DCAe CEng MRAeS. Born 16/3/34. Commd 5/9/57. Wg Cdr 14/1/73. Retd ADMIN 30/9/76.
GOLDBY J. L., DFC. Born 28/6/22. Commd 28/12/42. Sqn Ldr 1/1/56. Retd GD 30/6/62.
GOLDBY M. B. Born 9/12/49. Commd 4/9/81. Sqn Ldr 1/7/90. Retd ENG 14/9/96.
GOLDEN E. Born 26/4/49. Commd 30/5/69. Sqn Ldr 1/7/85. Retd GD 1/7/88. Re-entered 21/4/89. Sqn Ldr 21/4/86. Retd GD 29/5/00.
GOLDEN M. J. Born 7/2/46. Commd 26/1/66. Sqn Ldr 1/7/90. Retd GD 7/2/01.
GOLDFIELD R. H. Born 7/1/48. Commd 13/6/74. Sqn Ldr 1/7/83. Retd GD(G) 29/4/88.
GOLDIE J. Born 25/12/61. Commd 23/10/86. Flt Lt 19/2/90. Retd SY 20/3/93.
GOLDIE J. M. Born 27/5/21. Commd 22/9/48. Flt Lt 22/9/54. Retd SEC 27/5/70.
GOLDING C. G. L. Born 14/2/24. Commd 20/8/43. Flt Lt 7/11/47. Retd GD 4/1/49.
GOLDS A. F. Born 8/11/34. Commd 14/11/59. Flt Lt 14/5/65. Retd GD 8/11/89.
GOLDS C. C., AFC. Born 16/9/36. Commd 29/12/54. Sqn Ldr 1/7/66. Retd GD 13/2/71.
GOLDSMITH T. W. Born 16/10/19. Commd 27/12/44. Flt Lt 7/6/51. Retd SEC 16/10/52.
GOLDSTEIN M., MBE BA. Born 17/6/34. Commd 12/7/57. Wg Cdr 1/1/77. Retd ADMIN 7/4/86.
GOLDSWORTHY G. R. Born 18/4/23. Commd 18/6/62. Sqn Ldr 1/1/80. Retd CAT 18/4/83.
GOLDTHORPE S. D. Born 10/8/19. Commd 17/10/57. Flt Lt 1/4/63. Retd ENG 10/8/74.
GOLLAN A., OBE CA. Born 30/6/09. Commd 9/6/34. A Cdre 1/7/62. Retd SY 1/7/65.
GOLLINS J. H. Born 1/10/34. Commd 3/10/60. Sqn Ldr 1/7/73. Retd SY 17/1/87.
GOMES R. S. Born 11/9/41. Commd 22/5/80. Flt Lt 22/5/86. Retd ENG 9/5/87.
GOMMO R. D., MA CEng. Born 14/6/34. Commd 25/9/54. Gp Capt 1/1/78. Retd ENG 16/6/81.

GOOCH J. E. Born 5/4/30. Commd 25/8/60. Sqn Ldr 1/7/74. Retd ENG 5/4/88.
GOOCH N. W. Born 17/10/18. Commd 31/7/58. Flt Lt 31/7/63. Retd ENG 30/11/68.
GOOD R. J. A. Born 9/4/20. Commd 13/4/42. Sqn Ldr 1/1/51. Retd GD 9/4/69.
GOODACRE F. H., AFC. Born 23/12/15. Commd 10/11/42. Flt Lt 10/5/46. Retd (GD(G) 30/12/65.
GOODALL J., MBE. Born 18/10/21. Commd 26/9/57. Sqn Ldr 1/7/69. Retd ENG 18/10/81.
GOODALL J. F. Born 1/7/32. Commd 2/1/52. Sqn Ldr 1/7/69. Retd GD 1/7/72.
GOODALL M. P. Born 16/5/51. Commd 17/1/85. Sqn Ldr 1/7/92. Retd ENG 13/12/99.
GOODALL P. J., MIMgt. Born 27/6/30. Commd 14/4/53. Wg Cdr 1/7/67. Retd GD 15/8/75.
GOODE A. G., MIMgt. Born 31/10/20. Commd 13/6/43. Sqn Ldr 1/1/69. Retd SUP 1/11/74.
GOODE G. E. F., OBE DFC. Born 8/4/17. Commd 17/11/40. Wg Cdr 1/7/56. Retd GD 15/6/68.
GOODE M. J. A. Born 16/2/57. Commd 25/4/82. Flt Lt 8/2/82. Retd GD 14/3/97.
GOODE The Rev A. T. R., MA. Born 10/12/42. Commd 18/7/71. Retd 10/12/97 Wg Cdr.
GOODENOUGH P. J. Born 19/2/28. Commd 8/8/51. Flt Lt 8/5/57. Retd GD 10/7/67.
GOODEY L. G., DFC. Born 26/4/16. Commd 23/8/42. Wg Cdr 1/1/60. Retd ENG 16/5/71.
GOODFELLOW B. H. Born 6/4/41. Commd 23/1/64. Sqn Ldr 1/1/75. Retd SEC 6/4/79.
GOODFELLOW J. H., MA CEng MIEE MIMgt. Born 19/7/37. Commd 2/2/60. Sqn Ldr 1/1/71. Retd ENG 2/2/76.
GOODFELLOW J. V., MSc BSc CEng MRAeS AFIMA. Born 10/6/38. Commd 25/9/59. Sqn Ldr 25/3/68. Retd
    ADMIN 10/6/76.
GOODFELLOW M. S. Born 15/3/30. Commd 16/1/52. Sqn Ldr 1/7/60. Retd GD 15/3/68.
GOODFELLOW W. Born 4/2/38. Commd 5/12/63. Sqn Ldr 1/1/73. Retd SEC 4/2/76.
GOODHEAD D. G. C., CEng MRAeS MIMgt MIProdE. Born 16/6/30. Commd 11/6/53. Sqn Ldr 1/7/64. Retd ENG
    1/7/78.
GOODHEW A. N. Born 31/10/29. Commd 5/12/51. Flt Lt 5/6/56. Retd GD 31/10/67.
GOODING D. J. Born 14/6/50. Commd 25/2/72. Flt Lt 25/8/77. Retd ADMIN 14/6/88.
GOODING J. Born 11/6/33. Commd 13/12/68. Flt Lt 13/12/73. Retd ENG 11/6/92.
GOODING P. J., AFC. Born 23/11/43. Commd 24/6/65. Gp Capt 1/1/90. Retd GD 28/2/99.
GOODINSON H. J. Born 20/5/34. Commd 18/11/58. Sqn Ldr 1/7/68. Retd ADMIN 3/4/85.
GOODLIFFE I. R. Born 6/8/38. Commd 16/12/66. Sqn Ldr 1/7/73. Retd ADMIN 1/5/82.
GOODMAN A. G. Born 5/11/51. Commd 5/7/68. Flt Lt 4/11/70. Retd GD 5/11/96.
GOODMAN A. M. Born 14/4/37. Commd 16/12/58. Sqn Ldr 1/1/71. Retd GD 14/10/97.
GOODMAN E. J. Born 25/4/33. Commd 8/7/65. Gp Capt 1/1/83. Retd MED 30/6/87.
GOODMAN G. N. Born 26/12/05. Commd 22/7/43. Flt Lt 22/1/47. Retd ENG 13/12/55.
GOODMAN J. R., DFC* AFC AE. Born 10/1/21. Commd 6/5/42. Gp Capt 1/1/66. Retd SEC 10/1/76.
GOODMAN K. M. Born 21/4/10. Commd 11/7/45. Flt Offr 19/11/53. Retd SEC 3/7/59.
GOODMAN L. S. Born 24/9/20. Commd 24/4/42. Sqn Ldr 1/1/61. Retd GD 1/1/64.
GOODMAN P. Born 15/8/37. Commd 18/2/64. Wg Cdr 1/1/81. Retd GD 15/8/92.
GOODMAN P. J. Born 3/10/38. Commd 13/12/60. Sqn Ldr 1/1/72. Retd GD 3/10/96.
GOODMAN R. N., BSc. Born 14/5/53. Commd 17/9/72. Flt Lt 15/4/78. Retd GD 5/4/00.
GOODRIDGE V. D. Born 21/3/42. Commd 19/2/76. Sqn Ldr 13/2/87. Retd MED(T) 6/4/92.
GOODRIDGE W. M. Born 25/6/38. Commd 29/1/72. Sqn Ldr 1/7/82. Retd ENG 1/10/84.
GOODRUM J. R. Born 14/4/40. Commd 24/4/80. Sqn Ldr 1/7/89. Retd GD 14/4/95.
GOODRUM S. Born 23/1/31. Commd 5/11/52 Wg Cdr 1/1/76. Retd GD 1/10/85.
GOODSELL B. D. Born 16/2/29. Commd 13/12/50. Flt Lt 13/12/55. Retd SEC 16/2/67 rtg Sqn Ldr.
GOODSELL B. H. Born 23/9/20. Commd 15/4/43. Flt Lt 20/3/48. Retd ENG 23/9/69.
GOODSIR D. H., AFC. Born 20/2/32. Commd 28/2/52. Flt Lt 14/5/58. Retd GD 7/7/73.
GOODSON J. C., DFM. Born 9/4/20. Commd 5/4/43. Flt Lt 5/4/45. Retd GD(G) 9/4/75.
GOODWILL J. P., BSc. Born 18/2/32. Commd 25/8/55. Sqn Ldr 25/2/63. Retd EDN 19/1/74.
GOODWILL W. M. G., BSc. Born 12/10/62. Commd 22/6/86. Flt Lt 22/12/88. Retd GD 22/6/98.
GOODWIN B. E. Born 20/3/17. Commd 18/9/39. Wg Cdr 1/7/65. Retd SUP 20/3/67.
GOODWIN B. M. P. Born 20/8/55. Commd 14/7/77. Sqn Ldr 1/1/91. Retd SY 1/1/94.
GOODWIN C. W. D. Born 3/8/57. Commd 29/7/76. Sqn Ldr 1/1/91. Retd GD 1/6/98.
GOODWIN D. Born 7/6/40. Commd 11/10/84. fLT IT 11/10/88. Retd ENG 7/6/95.
GOODWIN D. M. Born 17/5/31. Commd 14/11/51. Wg Cdr 1/1/70. Retd GD 21/5/86.
GOODWIN D. M. Born 4/2/35. Commd 12/1/55. Flt Lt 1/3/61. Retd GD 14/7/73.
GOODWIN F. W., AFC. Born 8/2/24. Commd 23/5/63. Flt Lt 23/5/66. Retd PI 31/5/78.
GOODWIN G. J. Born 8/1/14. Commd 21/7/55. Flt Lt 27/1/59. Retd ENG 8/1/69.
GOODWIN J. Born 7/7/30. Commd 5/11/52. Flt Lt 1/3/61. Retd GD 7/7/85.
GOODWIN K. J., CBE AFC. Born 2/5/28. Commd 7/7/49. A Cdre 1/7/80. Retd GD 1/7/82.
GOODWIN M. F. Born 14/7/27. Commd 3/2/49. Flt Lt 3/8/52. Retd GD 29/8/65.
GOODWIN M. J. Born 25/3/38. Commd 14/3/57. Flt Lt 12/1/66. Retd GD 19/8/75.
GOODWIN M. J. Born 7/5/59. Commd 11/8/74. Flt Lt 11/8/78. Retd ADMIN 11/8/90.
GOODWIN N. P. Born 11/9/46. Commd 27/10/67. Fg Offr 11/9/69. Retd RGT 6/12/72.
GOODWIN P. M. Born 13/8/32. Commd 10/12/52. Flt Lt 15/11/61. Retd GD 1/3/65.
GOODWIN W. A. Born 20/1/18. Commd 20/4/54. Flt Lt 20/4/59. Retd ENG 1/5/64.
GOODWYN C. R., BA. Born 28/11/58. Commd 27/3/83. Flt Lt 27/6/86. Retd OPS SPT 27/3/99.
GOODYER G. C. D., MVO. Born 25/11/27. Commd 15/12/49. A Cdre 1/1/75. Retd GD 26/6/79.

GOORNEY A. B., BSc MB ChB DIH DPM. Born 16/1/27. Commd 1/5/51. Wg Cdr 18/8/63. Retd MED 1/9/67.
GOOSE E. J. T., MA. Born 23/7/23. Commd 9/9/43. A Cdre 1/1/73. Retd ENG 23/3/78.
GOPSILL W. G. Born 2/6/32. Commd 17/7/58. Flt Lt 17/1/63. Retd GD 31/10/75.
GORDDARD R. C. Born 23/12/09. Commd 3/1/41. Flt Lt 8/1/45. Retd SUP 24/7/46 rtg Sqn Ldr.
GORDINE G. A. P. Born 23/4/27. Commd 16/12/50. Sqn Ldr 1/1/66. Retd GD 16/10/76. Reinstated 12/11/79 to 17/9/84.
GORDON A. D., BEM. Born 30/8/14. Commd 10/12/42. Flt Lt 10/6/46. Retd ENG 18/9/53 rtg Sqn Ldr.
GORDON A. L., BSc MIMgt. Born 22/7/43. Commd 6/9/65. Wg Cdr 1/1/91. Retd GD 2/4/93.
GORDON A. McP., MA. Born 18/10/52. Commd 11/11/71. Wg Cdr 1/7/94. Retd ADMIN 7/2/99.
GORDON A. T., BSc. Born 15/8/43. Commd 14/12/65. Flt Lt 28/1/67. Retd GD 15/8/81.
GORDON C. R., MVO MIMgt. Born 9/7/23. Commd 6/10/44. Gp Capt 1/1/68. Retd GD 29/1/76.
GORDON D. C. Born 4/4/23. Commd 5/12/42. Sqn Ldr 1/7/56. Retd GD 23/4/64.
GORDON D. F. M. Born 12/8/43. Commd 12/1/62. Sqn Ldr 1/7/78. Retd GD 1/4/90.
GORDON D. J. Born 21/3/25. Commd 25/9/45. Wg Cdr 1/1/64. Retd GD 2/7/68.
GORDON E. D., MA. Born 24/4/26. Commd 13/11/62. Sqn Ldr 13/5/64. Retd EDN 28/11/64.
GORDON E. N. Born 9/9/56. Commd 4/7/85. Fg Offr 4/1/88. Retd GD(G) 7/8/88.
GORDON E. R., AFC. Born 23/12/22. Commd 6/11/47. Flt Lt 27/5/54. Retd GD 14/10/61.
GORDON G. D. Born 10/8/48. Commd 1/6/72. Flt Lt 1/12/77. Retd GD 22/10/94.
GORDON J. A., CEng MIMechE MRAeS. Born 7/11/40. Commd 18/7/61. Flt Lt 15/4/66. Retd ENG 1/8/70.
GORDON K. D. M., CEng MIMechE MRAeS. Born 24/9/37. Commd 30/7/59. Wg Cdr 1/1/77. Retd ENG 20/2/88.
GORDON M. A., MBE DFC BA. Born 27/4/57. Commd 26/11/78. Wg Cdr 1/7/92. Retd GD 1/7/95.
GORDON M. H. Born 6/9/37. Commd 10/5/73. Flt Lt 10/5/78. Retd END 1/10/81.
GORDON P. Born 12/12/40. Commd 26/4/84. Flt Lt 26/4/88. Retd ENG 12/12/95.
GORDON R. W. Born 20/3/25. Commd 1/4/52. Sqn Ldr 1/1/62. Retd GD 20/7/80.
GORDON R. W. A. Born 29/3/42. Commd 4/10/63. Sqn Ldr 1/7/75. Retd GD 1/4/93.
GORDON S. L., CEng MIEE MIMgt. Born 31/10/36. Commd 29/1/43. Gp Capt 1/1/69. Retd ENG 7/2/74.
GORDON W., MBE. Born 17/11/30. Commd 8/4/53. Sqn Ldr 1/1/68. Retd SUP 5/11/84.
GORDON W. Born 13/6/32. Commd 28/3/66. Flt Lt 4/5/72. Retd ADMIN 13/6/92.
GORDON W. H., MBE DFC. Born 16/4/22. Commd 5/9/42. Flt Lt 5/3/46. Retd ENG 31/3/77, rtg Sqn Ldr.
GORDON-CUMMING A. R. Born 10/9/24. Commd 3/9/44. Gp Capt 1/7/63. Retd GD 16/11/69.
GORDON-HALL P. J., DFC. Born 16/12/20. Commd 12/6/39. Sqn Ldr 1/7/51. Retd GD 24/12/53.
GORDON-JOHNSON P. Born 11/11/44. Commd 12/7/63. Sqn Ldr 1/7/74. Retd GD 1/12/79.
GORDON-JONES Sir Edward, KCB CBE DSO DFC. Born 31/8/14. Commd 7/10/35. AM 1/7/67. Retd GD 22/8/69.
GORDON-SMITH G. E. Born 9/7/35. Commd 10/4/62. Flt Lt 10/4/62. Retd RGT 6/7/68.
GORE P. C. Born 26/40/20. Commd 26/8/43. Flt Lt 15/12/49. Retd GD(G) 26/1/71.
GOREY S. N., BEng. Born 18/6/58. Commd 16/9/84. Flt Lt 11/2/87. Retd ENG 18/6/96.
GORMAN A., BSc. Born 23/10/56. Commd 17/1/82. Flt Lt 17/4/85. Retd OPS SPT 17/1/98.
GORMAN E. B. T. Born 6/5/37. Commd 30/9/58. Sqn Ldr 1/7/72. Retd GD 1/7/75.
GORMAN K., MBCS MIDPM. Born 31/12/47. Commd 2/8/68. Sqn Ldr 1/7/81. Retd GD(G) 31/12/85.
GORMAN M. J. Born 20/8/49. Commd 27/7/89. Flt Lt 27/7/93. Retd ADMIN 14/3/97.
GORNALL J. H., MIMgt. Born 14/2/39. Commd 7/6/68. Sqn Ldr 1/7/79. Retd ENG 14/2/89.
GORRIE W. G. K., DFC. Born 9/4/14. Commd 26/1/42. Wg Cdr 1/1/55. Retd GD 24/5/61.
GORRINGE-SMITH P. L. Born 16/5/24. Commd 10/8/45. Flt Lt 10/8/51. Retd SUP 16/5/62.
GORTON S. H. Born 11/10/57. Commd 14/9/75. Sqn Ldr 1/7/89. Retd GD 2/1/97.
GOSLING J. R. Born 24/6/61. Commd 24/4/80. Sqn Ldr 1/1/94. Retd GD 24/6/99.
GOSLING S. J. Born 24/11/47. Commd 10/12/65. Wg Cdr 1/1/87. Retd GD 25/11/90.
GOSLYN H. I. Born 30/3/42. Commd 26/11/64. Fg Offr 26/11/64. Retd GD 30/6/69.
GOSNEY G. A. Born 5/11/19. Commd 5/11/43. Flt Lt 5/5/47. Retd GD 21/12/53.
GOSS A. R., MBE Born 16/5/26. Commd 26/12/51. Sqn Ldr 1/7/66. Retd GD 16/5/84.
GOSS C. R. J. Born 22/12/49. Commd 3/10/69. Wg Cdr 1/1/87. Retd SUP 1/1/90.
GOSS E. J. Born 17/5/25. Commd 3/2/49. Wg Cdr 1/7/71. Retd SUP 17/5/80.
GOSS J. P., BA. Born 7/2/49. Commd 6/7/80. Flt Lt 6/10/83. Retd ADMIN 31/3/94.
GOSS M. E. Born 8/10/25. Commd 25/5/50. Wg Cdr 1/1/75. Retd ENG 2/9/77.
GOSS T. A., BEng CEng MIEE. Born 26/6/47. Commd 13/2/72. Sqn Ldr 1/1/84. Retd ENG 13/2/91.
GOSSE P. M., MC. Born 16/5/19. Commd 1/9/45. Wg Cdr 1/7/55. Retd RGT 29/9/60.
GOSSLAND D. M. Born 20/5/21. Commd 23/1/41. Flt Lt 28/3/47. Retd SU 31/10/56.
GOSTELOW T. F. Born 19/2/23. Commd 4/6/64. Flt Lt 4/6/67. Retd GD 6/4/68.
GOSTLING A. E., BSc. Born 2/10/29. Commd 24/9/52. Sqn Ldr 24/3/63. Retd EDN 24/9/68.
GOSWELL G. A. Born 25/7/32. Commd 7/5/52. Flt Lt 1/10/67. Retd GD 25/7/70.
GOTHARD A. Born 2/9/31. Commd 7/6/68. Flt Lt 7/6/73. Retd ENG 19/6/93.
GOTHARD E. L., MBE. Born 11/2/39. Commd 13/12/60. Flt Lt 15/2/65. Retd GD 6/2/94.
GOTTS S. Born 4/1/13. Commd 1/11/56. Flt Lt 1/11/59. Retd SEC 4/1/68.
GOUCHER D. Born 7/10/36. Commd 29/7/58. Gp Capt 1/7/79. Retd ADMIN 22/9/87.
GOUCK R. F., MMS. Born 10/5/41. Commd 27/3/70. Sqn Ldr 1/7/79. Retd SUP 1/2/83.
GOUGH D. C. Born 23/9/45. Commd 13/8/82. Sqn Ldr 1/1/90. Retd 1/1/93.
GOUGH E. C. Born 29/7/23. Commd 7/5/43. Sqn Ldr 1/1/54. Retd GD 29/7/66.

GOUGH H. G. Born 17/4/22. Commd 8/11/46. Flt Lt 9/6/52. Retd GD 30/11/60.
GOUGH J. W., BSc. Born 2/4/48. Commd 4/1/68. Flt Lt 22/6/71. Retd GD 17/2/81.
GOUGH P. D. Born 1/3/24. Commd 10/12/43. Flt Lt 29/6/55. Retd GD(G) 9/12/65.
GOUGH V. A., AFC MCIPD MIMgt. Born 14/12/21. Commd 8/4/44. Wg Cdr 1/7/67. Retd GD 14/12/76.
GOUGH V. R., MIMgt. Born 29/12/33. Commd 24/6/71. Flt Lt 24/6/76. Retd ENG 1/10/79.
GOULBORN M. C. Born 12/2/59. Commd 2/2/78. Flt Lt 17/6/84. Retd SUP 31/8/86.
GOULBORN P. A. G. Born 7/8/24. Commd 30/5/69. Sqn Ldr 1/7/76. Retd GD(G) 7/8/79.
GOULD C. E. Born 23/5/38. Commd 3/7/56. Gp Capt 1/7/81. Retd GD 1/2/87.
GOULD D. J. Born 1/4/09. Commd 18/12/40. Fg Offr 1/10/41. Retd SEC 20/8/46 rtg Flt Lt.
GOULD E. A. Born 24/7/47. Commd 1/4/66. Sqn Ldr 1/1/84. Retd GD 1/1/87.
GOULD M. B., LLB. Born 1/8/51. Commd 13/9/71. Sqn Ldr 1/7/86. Retd ADMIN 6/9/89.
GOULD R. H., CBE MA FRAeS. Born 22/1/45. Commd 5/1/66. A Cdre 1/1/92. Retd GD 22/1/00.
GOULD R. J. Born 7/2/15. Commd 2/8/45. Flt Lt 18/5/56. Retd CAT 10/3/66.
GOULD T. C. Born 18/3/20. Commd 13/4/42. Sqn Ldr 1/1/51. Retd SUP 11/4/64 rtg Wg Cdr.
GOULD T. D. Born 24/4/41. Commd 10/9/70. Sqn Ldr 1/1/87. Retd SUP 24/4/96.
GOULDEN A. A. Born 30/8/37. Commd 4/3/71. Sqn Ldr 1/1/79. Retd SUP 8/10/88.
GOULDING B. S. Born 16/2/57. Commd 26/9/90. Flt Lt 13/5/95. Retd MED(T) 12/10/97.
GOULDING G., BSc. Born 4/2/35. Commd 9/8/57. Wg Cdr 1/1/81. Retd ADMIN 20/6/88.
GOULT B. L. Born 8/10/12. Commd 24/6/43. Sqn Ldr 1/10/55. Retd ENG 8/10/61.
GOULT J. P., BSc. Born 14/3/52. Commd 27/7/75. Flt Lt 27/10/76. Retd GD 27/7/87.
GOULTHORPE P. J., CBE MA MRAeS CEng. Born 20/4/30. Commd 6/10/53. A Cdre 1/7/78. Retd ENG 13/2/84.
GOURD D. A., MBE. Born 21/6/22. Commd 27/10/67. Flt Lt 27/10/70. Retd SY 23/6/82.
GOVAN M. G. Born 1/7/21. Commd 30/5/45. Flt Offr 16/12/51. Retd SUP 1/10/59.
GOVER P. D. L., AFC BSc FRAeS FIMgt. Born 17/7/38. Commd 28/11/60. A Cdre 1/1/87. Retd GD 17/7/93.
GOW F. J. Born 17/10/21. Commd 26/5/60. Sqn Ldr 1/7/72. Retd ENG 17/12/76.
GOW J. A., LDSRCS. Born 13/8/22. Commd 22/8/46. Sqn Ldr 22/4/54. Retd DEL 2/3/57.
GOWANS J. W. Born 31/1/24. Commd 6/3/50. Sqn Ldr 1/7/64. Retd SUP 1/10/76.
GOWER S. D. Born 27/5/57. Commd 26/4/84. Flt Lt 11/8/89. Retd ENG 31/3/94.
GOWER-JONES J. E., BA MIMgt. Born 16/6/20. Commd 17/4/47. Wg Cdr 1/1/68. Retd SUP 17/4/75.
GOWERS A. E., BSc CEng MIEE. Born 2/1/50. Commd 4/3/74. Sqn Ldr 1/7/84. Retd ENG 4/3/90.
GOWERS C. J. Born 28/11/53. Commd 5/7/73. Wg Cdr 1/7/91. Retd GD 9/5/95.
GOWERS C. S. Born 20/12/52. Commd 11/8/77. Sqn Ldr 1/7/93. Retd GD 31/12/93.
GOWERS K. G. Born 12/6/31. Commd 1/4/53. Sqn Ldr 1/7/69. Retd GD 12/6/91.
GOWING A. J. Born 28/11/40. Commd 14/1/63. Flt Lt 20/5/67. Retd GD 1/3/73.
GOWING D. Born 5/11/20. Commd 27/9/12. Flt Lt 19/11/53. Retd GD 7/7/67.
GOWING K., MA CEng MIMechE MRAeS. Born 14/5/45. Commd 28/9/64. Gp Capt 1/7/91. Retd ENG 14/5/00.
GOWING W. H., BSc. Born 12/2/50. Commd 15/9/69. Flt Lt 15/10/72. Retd GD 2/4/87.
GOWLING B. J., MBE. Born 23/11/31. Commd 21/5/52. Wg Cdr 1/1/81. Retd GD 23/11/89.
GOWRING R. J., CBE. Born 29/6/40. Commd 16/1/60. Gp Capt 1/1/88. Retd GD 29/6/95.
GOY G. S. W., MSc BSc (Eur Ing) CEng FRAeS. Born 14/2/32. Commd 19/8/54. Wg Cdr 17/2/71. Retd ADMIN 4/12/76.
GRACE E. T., BA. Born 27/4/48. Commd 25/2/88. Flt Lt 25/2/90. Retd ENG 25/2/96.
GRACE I. B., BSc. Born 18/2/57. Commd 26/11/78. Flt Lt 26/2/80. Retd ENG 26/11/87.
GRACE J. W. Born 10/6/35. Commd 14/10/71. Sqn Ldr 1/7/89. Retd GD 1/7/92.
GRACE R. Born 17/1/46. Commd 4/7/85. Flt Lt 4/8/89. Retd ENG 31/10/98.
GRACE T., DFC. Born 28/4/22. Commd 13/6/42. Sqn Ldr 1/7/62. Retd GD 28/4/77.
GRACIE K. M. R., BSc. Born 3/8/42. Commd 15/7/63. Sqn Ldr 1/1/73. Retd ENG 13/9/75.
GRADDON L. G. R. Born 6/10/16. Commd 26/3/53. Sqn Ldr 1/1/62. Retd ENG 10/10/70.
GRADLEY J. A. Born 25/3/36. Commd 8/1/76. Sqn Ldr 1/1/86. Retd ENG 11/11/88.
GRAEME-COOK B. G. Born 1/3/60. Commd 4/9/81. Sqn Ldr 1/1/95. Retd GD 1/5/98.
GRAFHAM A. C. Born 9/3/35. Commd 27/10/54. Flt Lt 1/3/61. Retd GD 9/3/93.
GRAFTON G., MBE. Born 1/3/46. Commd 1/7/69. Sqn Ldr 1/7/76. Retd GD 24/9/84.
GRAHAM A. Born 21/2/44. Commd 31/10/63. Flt Lt 17/12/72. Retd ADMIN 8/1/84.
GRAHAM A. R. Born 11/4/41. Commd 6/9/63. Sqn Ldr 1/1/88. Retd GD 11/4/96.
GRAHAM B. S., CEng MRAeS. Born 31/1/39. Commd 23/3/66. Wg Cdr 1/1/78. Retd ENG 1/7/83.
GRAHAM D. Born 16/10/46. Commd 23/10/86. Sqn Ldr 1/7/95. Retd ENG 17/10/96.
GRAHAM D. Born 11/8/30. Commd 24/10/51. Wg Cdr 1/1/79. Retd GD(G) 1/1/81.
GRAHAM D. F. Born 29/5/31. Commd 17/3/55. Flt Lt 17/9/59. Retd GD 30/7/76.
GRAHAM D. H. M., OBE. Born 27/9/12. Commd 6/1/36. Gp Capt 1/1/57. Retd SUP 6/10/61.
GRAHAM D. J. Born 27/5/31. Commd 26/3/52. Flt Lt 1/10/57. Retd GD 27/5/69.
GRAHAM D. M. Born 20/1/46. Commd 12/7/68. Sqn Ldr 1/7/81. Retd GD 14/9/96.
GRAHAM E. C., CEng MIEE. Born 5/3/39. Commd 28/7/60. Sqn Ldr 1/1/71. Retd ENG 5/3/77.
GRAHAM G. G., DFM MIMgt. Born 26/4/17. Commd 20/5/43. Flt Lt 20/11/46. Retd SEC 3/4/71.
GRAHAM G. W. Born 12/12/32. Commd 7/5/52. Flt Lt 13/4/60. Retd GD 9/10/86.
GRAHAM I. J. A., BSc. Born 16/9/48. Commd 28/2/72. Flt Lt 28/11/72. Retd GD 30/9/84.
GRAHAM I. S. Born 19/5/47. Commd 23/3/67. Flt Lt 23/9/72. Retd GD 7/12/76.

GRAHAM J. Born 3/6/38. Commd 28/7/59. Wg Cdr 1/1/75. Retd GD 9/12/85.
GRAHAM J. C., DFC*. Born 28/6/17. Commd 17/9/38. Wg Cdr 1/7/53. Retd GD 25/7/61.
GRAHAM K. H. Born 24/10/37. Commd 8/12/61. Flt Lt 10/2/67. Retd GD 24/10/75.
GRAHAM K. M. Born 6/2/50. Commd 31/7/70. Flt Lt 31/7/73. Retd GD 6/2/88.
GRAHAM K. P., BSc. Born 3/11/59. Commd 20/3/79. Flt Lt 15/10/82. Retd GD 3/11/97.
GRAHAM M. B. Born 3/7/46. Commd 21/3/74. Sqn Ldr 1/7/81. Retd GD 3/7/94.
GRAHAM M. G., MIMgt. Born 26/11/32. Commd 4/4/62. Sqn Ldr 1/1/70. Retd ADMIN 26/11/92.
GRAHAM M. G. C. Born 25/8/63. Commd 8/9/83. Sqn Ldr 1/7/95. Retd GD 15/12/00.
GRAHAM N. P. Born 21/4/33. Commd 9/12/53. Flt Lt 16/8/61. Retd GD 26/5/72.
GRAHAM P. J. Born 30/11/46. Commd 29/1/87. Flt Lt 29/1/91. Retd SY 1/10/93.
GRAHAM R. Born 28/4/47. Commd 21/1/66. Sqn Ldr 1/1/81. Retd GD 4/9/97.
GRAHAM R. H. Born 21/2/35. Commd 11/11/53. Flt Lt 15/4/59. Retd GD 29/4/72.
GRAHAM-CUMMING A. N., MB BS MRCGP MRCS MFOM LRCP DAvMed MRAeS. Born 17/12/48. Commd
    23/1/72. Gp Capt 1/1/98. Retd MED 6/8/00.
GRAHAM-WILSON E. B. Born 1/7/21. Commd 10/3/43. Flt Offr 29/5/53. Retd SEC 5/1/63.
GRAINGE R. J., CEng MRAeS MIMechE. Born 20/11/30. Commd 16/6/55. Sqn Ldr 1/1/65. Retd ENG 1/1/72.
GRAINGER B. J. Born 2/6/37. Commd 18/5/55. Sqn Ldr 1/7/68. Retd GD 1/8/87.
GRAINGER D. Born 24/7/43. Commd 23/11/78. Flt Lt 23/11/82. Retd ENG 24/3/89.
GRAINGER P. D. Born 12/11/49. Commd 6/11/80. Sqn Ldr 1/1/88. Retd ENG 1/1/91.
GRAND-SCRUTTON J. Born 29/7/37. Commd 10/9/63. Sqn Ldr 1/7/84. Retd ENG 29/7/95.
GRANDY N., BA. Born 5/10/54. Commd 22/1/77. Flt Lt 2/4/78. Retd GD 2/1/89.
GRANGE M. Born 24/7/71. Commd 26/9/90. Fg Offr 26/9/92. Retd GD 30/3/94.
GRANGE M. J. Born 2/6/38. Commd 18/2/60. Wg Cdr 1/1/89. Retd GD 5/2/93.
GRANGE R. J. Born 10/3/46. Commd 28/4/67. Flt Lt 28/10/72. Retd GD 27/4/76.
GRANGER D. W., MBE BSc MIMgt. Born 5/9/33. Commd 20/9/57. Sqn Ldr 20/3/67. Retd EDN 1/1/74.
GRANGER H. J., CEng MIEE. Born 10/6/22. Commd 16/1/47. Wg Cdr 1/1/67. Retd ENG 30/3/77.
GRANSHAW S. H. Born 28/7/50. Commd 29/8/83. Flt Lt 19/8/85. Retd ENG 3/4/93.
GRANT B. C. E. Born 6/8/44. Commd 18/11/66. Wg Cdr 1/1/95. Retd OPS SPT 6/8/99.
GRANT B. N. Born 7/6/08. Commd 27/6/46. Flt Lt 4/1/51. Retd SEC 12/11/53.
GRANT B. P., MCIPS MIMgt. Born 19/5/35. Commd 7/3/56. Gp Capt 1/1/81. Retd SUP 3/4/82.
GRANT D., MCIPS MCIT MILT. Born 7/7/44. Commd 9/2/66. Gp Capt 1/7/93. Retd SUP 7/7/94.
GRANT D. I. G., ACMA. Born 24/8/36. Commd 27/8/64. Sqn Ldr 1/7/71. Retd SEC 2/10/79 rtg Wg Cdr.
GRANT D. R. Born 16/1/16. Commd 30/9/41. Flt Lt 1/9/45. Retd ENG 1/6/61.
GRANT D. S., MRCS LRCP. Born 6/7/13. Commd 11/4/41. Gp Capt 1/7/65. Retd MED 11/5/72.
GRANT H. J. Born 9/5/14. Commd 1/1/45. Sqn Ldr 1/1/63. Retd SEC 9/5/69.
GRANT H. S., MB ChB MFOM MRAeS DRCOG DAvMed. Born 23/8/47. Commd 29/7/68. Gp Capt 1/7/95. Retd
    MED 30/4/96.
GRANT I. Born 11/4/41. Commd 3/8/62. Flt Lt 11/10/66. Retd GD 11/4/79.
GRANT I. H. Born 26/10/22. Commd 26/10/43. Sqn Ldr 1/1/71. Retd GD 12/4/74.
GRANT J. A., MBE MIMgt. Born 27/1/18. Commd 2/4/53. Wg Cdr 28/8/70. Retd MED(T) 27/1/73.
GRANT J. C., IEng FIEIE. Born 7/12/38. Commd 31/1/80. Sqn Ldr 1/7/89. Retd ENG 7/12/93.
GRANT J. D. Born 17/1/23. Commd 4/8/44. Flt Lt 19/11/53. Retd GD 29/8/63.
GRANT K. R. Born 26/11/38. Commd 3/10/69. Wg Cdr 1/7/87. Retd MED(SEC) 3/7/89.
GRANT L. J. Born 10/6/22. Commd 24/3/44. Flt Lt 24/9/47. Retd GD 31/3/74.
GRANT N. G. Born 16/10/31. Commd 20/11/52. Wg Cdr 1/1/79. Retd ADMIN 16/10/86.
GRANT P. Born 27/7/30. Commd 26/3/57. Sqn Ldr 1/1/74. Retd GD(G) 27/7/85.
GRANT P. A. Born 24/5/25. Commd 6/10/60. Flt Lt 6/10/65. Retd GD(G) 5/10/74.
GRANT P. R. M. Born 12/5/52. Commd 4/2/71. Flt Lt 4/8/76. Retd GD 4/8/89.
GRANT P. W. Born 20/7/25. Commd 21/6/56. Flt Lt 16/8/61. Retd GD 5/6/70.
GRANT R. Born 4/5/25. Commd 17/7/46. Sqn Ldr 1/7/60. Retd SY 25/6/77.
GRANT R. G. H. Born 29/10/20. Commd 4/6/64. Flt Lt 4/6/69. Retd ENG 29/5/71.
GRANT T., DFC. Born 12/7/20. Commd 25/6/48. Flt Lt 16/10/57. Retd GD(G) 21/10/66.
GRANT T. A., MSc BA. Born 3/10/49. Commd 24/8/72. Sqn Ldr 1/1/85. Retd SUP 1/4/99.
GRANT T. A. Born 10/6/25. Commd 3/4/58. Flt Lt 3/10/62. Retd GD 4/12/81.
GRANT T. J., BSc CEng MRAeS. Born 18/6/47. Commd 18/9/66. Sqn Ldr 1/7/78. Retd ENG 1/10/87.
GRANT-DAVIE R. H. Born 1/8/13. Commd 10/2/44. Flt Lt 10/8/47. Retd ENG 4/8/68.
GRANTHAM A. R. A. Born 27/6/46. Commd 10/12/65. Flt Lt 10/6/71. Retd GD 1/2/73.
GRANTHAM G. L., DFC. Born 31/12/16. Commd 11/5/43. Flt Lt 11/11/46. Retd GD(G) 16/5/63.
GRANVILLE B., MIMgt. Born 15/7/43. Commd 27/1/77. Wg Cdr 1/7/91. Retd ADMIN 31/3/94.
GRANVILLE-MARTIN H. Born 1/7/12. Commd 7/11/49. Flt Lt 7/11/49. Retd SUP 16/6/58.
GRANVILLE-WHITE C., CBE. Born 3/7/41. Commd 31/7/62. Gp Capt 1/7/87. Retd GD 3/7/96.
GRATER C. L., MHCIMA. Born 3/6/39. Commd 23/6/60. Sqn Ldr 1/7/71. Retd ADMIN 3/6/77.
GRATTAN R. C. Born 19/1/42. Commd 17/7/61. Flt Lt 26/7/67. Retd GD 28/8/76.
GRATTAN R. F., BA. Born 21/8/31. Commd 1/11/50. Gp Capt 1/1/78. Retd GD 30/6/79.
GRATTAN W. J. Born 24/12/39. Commd 1/11/79. Sqn Ldr 1/1/89. Retd SUP 1/1/94.
GRATTON J. B. Born 5/2/33. Commd 15/12/53. Sqn Ldr 1/7/67. Retd GD 5/2/71.

GRATTON L. G. Born 7/1/17. Commd 18/12/42. Flt Lt 25/8/46. Retd GD(G) 7/1/75 rtg Sqn Ldr.
GRAVELEY A. F. Born 22/4/45. Commd 14/2/63. Wg Cdr 1/7/88. Retd SY 1/7/93.
GRAVELL S. W. Born 7/2/32. Commd 14/1/53. Flt Lt 3/6/58. Retd GD 7/2/70.
GRAVES A. W. Born 2/6/52. Commd 16/6/88. Flt Lt 16/6/90. Retd GD 14/3/97.
GRAVES J. R. C. H., OBE. Born 15/4/22. Commd 27/4/41. Wg Cdr 1/7/60. Retd GD 6/7/68.
GRAVES O. W., FCA. Born 27/6/35. Commd 5/5/60. Flt Lt 5/5/66. Retd SEC 26/10/75.
GRAVES P. L., MSc BSc. Born 18/1/41. Commd 23/10/62. Gp Capt 1/1/91. Retd ADMIN 18/1/96.
GRAVES S. C. Born 19/4/53. Commd 7/6/73. Flt Lt 7/12/78. Retd GD 1/7/87.
GRAY A. J. Born 24/4/27. Commd 28/7/49. Wg Cdr 1/1/68. Retd ADMIN 20/5/82.
GRAY A. R. Born 15/3/47. Commd 30/4/81. Sqn Ldr 1/7/88. Retd ADMIN 1/7/91.
GRAY A. R. N. Born 26/10/46. Commd 28/11/74. Flt Lt 28/11/79. Retd ADMIN 26/10/86.
GRAY A. S. Born 2/7/17. Commd 29/5/46. Sqn Ldr 1/7/57. Retd SEC 31/8/63.
GRAY C. R., BSc. Born 1/1/39. Commd 10/11/64. Sqn Ldr 30/4/73. Retd ADMIN 15/10/90.
GRAY C. W. Born 26/4/23. Commd 1/3/62. Flt Lt 1/3/65. Retd GD 26/4/78.
GRAY D., BA. Born 27/9/43. Commd 6/5/83. Wg Cdr 1/7/94. Retd ADMIN 14/3/96.
GRAY D. S. Born 13/6/39. Commd 16/12/65. Flt Lt 19/6/72. Retd SEC 19/6/78.
GRAY D. V. M. Born 14/2/10. Commd 30/4/41. Sqn Offr 1/1/50. Retd SEC 17/2/59 rtg Wg Offr.
GRAY E. G. Born 3/10/30. Commd 10/12/52. Flt Lt 5/5/58. Retd GD 3/10/68.
GRAY G. Born 13/9/54. Commd 16/12/82. Flt lt 16/12/84. Retd GD 13/9/94.
GRAY G., DFC AFC. Born 23/8/16. Commd 8/5/42. Sqn Ldr 1/7/50. Retd GD 19/12/51.
GRAY G., MBE. Born 2/9/24. Commd 8/6/44. Sqn Ldr 1/4/56. Retd GD 2/9/73.
GRAY G., BSc. Born 16/5/40. Commd 22/10/63. Sqn Ldr 23/2/73. Retd ADMIN 16/5/95.
GRAY G. B. Born 2/11/49. Commd 25/2/72. Sqn Ldr 1/7/83. Retd GD 2/11/87.
GRAY H., BA. Born 3/12/18. Commd 3/8/48. Sqn Ldr 3/5/54. Retd EDN 15/9/70.
GRAY H. B. Born 26/9/26. Commd 7/6/48. Flt Lt 1/6/52. Retd SY 26/10/77.
GRAY J. Born 27/7/23. Commd 4/10/56. Flt Lt 4/4/60. Retd GD 5/9/71.
GRAY J. Born 6/6/41. Commd 4/5/72. Sqn Ldr 1/7/88. Retd ENG 7/10/91.
GRAY J. Born 13/10/11. Commd 10/6/42. Sqn Offr 1/1/60. Retd SEC 16/11/66.
GRAY J. C., MSc BSc BDS. Born 10/7/33. Commd 27/1/56. Wg Cdr 8/10/73. Retd DEL 7/5/85.
GRAY J. T. W., DFC. Born 4/1/19. Commd 21/12/43. Flt Lt 26/5/55. Retd GD(G) 25/1/63.
GRAY M. Born 1/7/19. Commd 2/9/42. Flt Offr 20/5/48. Retd SEC 11/8/50.
GRAY M. C. Born 12/12/27. Commd 8/7/54. Flt Lt 8/1/58. Retd GD 12/12/86.
GRAY M. J., AFC. Born 16/8/44. Commd 12/7/63. Wg Cdr 1/1/85. Retd GD 16/8/88.
GRAY P., DFC. Born 3/10/24. Commd 5/12/51. Flt Lt 5/6/56. Retd GD 12/8/68.
GRAY P. B., MHCIMA. Born 20/2/31. Commd 25/2/64. Sqn Ldr 1/1/77. Retd ADMIN 20/2/89.
GRAY P. J. Born 25/9/40. Commd 19/9/59. Gp Capt 1/1/85. Retd GD(G) 1/9/89.
GRAY P. L. Born 9/1/32. Commd 14/4/53. Grp Capt 1/1/76. Retd GD 28/5/87.
GRAY R. Born 13/3/38. Commd 2/10/58. Sqn Ldr 1/1/73. Retd GD 11/5/88.
GRAY R. J., BSc. Born 2/3/72. Commd 9/10/94. Fg Offr 9/10/93. Retd GD 17/4/98.
GRAY R. K., MIEH. Born 4/8/29. Commd 5/11/52. Wg Cdr 5/5/70. Retd ADMIN 1/8/78.
GRAY R. W. Born 1/9/21. Commd 16/7/45. Flt Lt 27/5/54. Retd GD 1/9/76.
GRAY T. L. Born 21/8/21. Commd 3/5/56. Flt Lt 3/5/62. Retd SEC 30/11/67.
GRAY W. A. Born 26/9/26. Commd 16/7/52. Flt Lt 12/5/62. Retd GD 26/9/69.
GRAY W. G. Born 2/3/19. Commd 11/2/43. Flt Lt 11/2/45. Retd GD(G) 2/3/74.
GRAYDON G. O., OBE. Born 10/1/30. Commd 26/4/50. Gp Capt 1/1/80. Retd GD 30/4/84.
GRAYSON R. J. Born 23/8/40. Commd 21/12/62. Flt Lt 21/6/68. Retd GD 10/12/91.
GRAYSON S. Born 7/4/19. Commd 4/10/56. Flt Lt 12/10/60. Retd PRT 22/4/69.
GREALY P. G. R. Born 9/11/23. Commd 18/6/43. Sqn Ldr 1/1/54. Retd GD 9/11/72.
GREAVES A. J., BA. Born 23/11/51. Commd 1/6/83. Flt Lt 15/10/76. Retd ADMIN 1/4/81. Reinstated 1/6/83.
   Sqn Ldr 1/7/87. Retd ADMIN 23/1/91.
GREAVES C. Born 19/10/22. Commd 23/5/45. Flt Lt 16/8/61. Retd GD(G) 25/6/68.
GREAVES C. G. R., CEng MRAeS. Born 28/11/40. Commd 28/1/60. Wg Cdr 1/7/79. Retd ENG 28/11/95.
GREAVES J. R. Born 27/5/19. Commd 14/1/43. Flt Lt 14/7/47. Retd SEC 27/5/69.
GREAVES K. F. Born 15/3/31. Commd 6/12/51. Flt Lt 27/3/57. Retd GD 15/3/69.
GREAVES R. B., MIMgt. Born 15/8/35. Commd 4/2/71. Flt Lt 4/2/73. Retd SUP 4/2/79.
GREEN A. Born 4/2/41. Commd 19/12/61. Wg Cdr 1/1/79. Retd GD 1/1/82.
GREEN A. J. Born 4/7/31. Commd 27/2/52. Flt Lt 27/2/56. Retd GD 4/7/69.
GREEN A. J. Born 28/12/57. Commd 18/10/81. Sqn Ldr 1/1/91. Retd ENG 10/5/99.
GREEN A. J., LLM MB BS MRCPath MRCS LRCP. Born 5/4/50. Commd 14/5/78. Wg Cdr 27/2/89. Retd MED
   14/9/96.
GREEN A. N., BA. Born 29/9/54. Commd 11/5/70. Wg Cdr 1/1/92. Retd MED SEC 14/3/96.
GREEN A. P. Born 18/3/59. Commd 19/10/80. Sqn Ldr 1/7/90. Retd GD(G) 18/3/97.
GREEN A. R. Born 9/7/36. Commd 24/2/67. Flt Lt 24/2/73. Retd ADMIN 3/4/76.
GREEN B. B., BSc CEng MIMechE MRAeS MIMgt. Born 16/4/34. Commd 23/9/55. Wg Cdr 1/7/76. Retd ENG
   4/10/78.
GREEN B. N. Born 27/4/28. Commd 11/4/63. Sqn Ldr 1/7/84. Retd ENG 1/9/86.

GREEN B. W. Born 7/9/15. Commd 1/4/45. Sqn Ldr 1/1/54. Retd PRT 5/1/64.
GREEN C. L. D. Born 4/10/34. Commd 19/12/54. Flt Lt 9/2/68. Retd GD 15/5/85.
GREEN D. A. Born 29/10/46. Commd 18/8/67. Sqn Ldr 1/7/83. Retd SUP 3/7/00.
GREEN D. D. G. Born 6/6/23. Commd 20/10/43. Flt Lt 14/11/56. Retd GD 28/5/67.
GREEN D. E., CEng FIEE MRAeS. Born 5/2/21. Commd 25/8/60. Flt Lt 25/8/65. Retd ENG 26/6/71.
GREEN D. G. P. Born 27/7/51. Commd 30/1/75. Sqn Ldr 1/1/93. Retd GD(G) 14/3/96.
GREEN D. J., FIMgt. Born 29/10/22. Commd 10/7/43. Gp Capt 1/1/72. Retd GD 29/10/77.
GREEN D. J., CEng MRAeS. Born 23/12/39. Commd 17/7/62. Sqn Ldr 1/1/72. Retd ENG 23/12/77.
GREEN D. L. Born 21/2/29. Commd 15/2/51. Flt Lt 15/8/54. Retd GD 21/2/84.
GREEN D. R., OBE. Born 17/9/42. Commd 30/7/63. Wg Cdr 1/1/78. Retd GD 31/12/85.
GREEN D. W. Born 22/12/38. Commd 17/5/63. Flt Lt 7/6/67. Retd GD 22/12/76.
GREEN D. W., BA. Born 2/6/33. Commd 9/8/57. Sqn Ldr 9/2/65. Retd ADMIN 23/8/89.
GREEN D. W. J., BSc. Born 18/7/58. Commd 29/11/81. Sqn Ldr 1/1/95. Retd SY 13/1/96.
GREEN E. Born 7/2/35. Commd 9/6/54. Flt Lt 9/12/59. Retd GD 7/2/72.
GREEN E. B., OBE MC. Born 8/7/97. Commd 30/9/18. Retd GD 20/5/25. Recalled 31/8/39. Sqn Ldr 8/2/42. Retd 27/3/46 rtg Wg Cdr.
GREEN G. P., BSc. Born 15/9/58. Commd 28/12/80. Flt Lt 1/11/84. Retd REGT 11/5/91.
GREEN H. E., MBE. Born 6/5/14. Commd 9/11/42. Sqn Ldr 1/7/62. Retd GD(G) 1/5/65.
GREEN H. M. S. Born 22/9/20. Commd 1/4/41. Wg Cdr 1/1/56. Retd GD 22/9/67.
GREEN J., MIMgt. Born 8/7/32. Commd 8/10/70. Sqn Ldr 27/2/81. Retd MED(SEC) 11/7/84.
GREEN J., BSc. Born 6/9/44. Commd 15/7/66. Sqn Ldr 1/7/79. Retd ENG 6/9/82.
GREEN J. B., BA. Born 3/10/68. Commd 8/2/90. Plt Offr. Retd GD(G) 15/1/93.
GREEN J. C. Born 2/7/31. Commd 2/7/52. Flt Lt 20/7/58. Retd GD 27/2/64. Reinstated 2/11/65. Flt Lt 2/11/65. Retd GD 2/7/93.
GREEN J. D. Born 17/3/44. Commd 25/6/66. Flt Lt 15/10/72. Retd GD(G) 17/3/82.
GREEN J. E., MIMgt. Born 13/3/19. Commd 4/8/43. Sqn Ldr 1/4/56. Retd ENG 18/10/69.
GREEN J. E. Born 9/4/34. Commd 22/1/57. Sqn Ldr 1/7/76. Retd GD 19/4/94.
GREEN J. H., BSc(Econ). Born 14/4/54. Commd 16/9/73. Wg Cdr 1/1/91. Retd ADMIN 10/1/97.
GREEN K. W. J. Born 22/6/44. Commd 28/10/76. Wg Cdr 1/7/94. Retd ADMIN 22/6/99.
GREEN M. J., DPhysEd. Born 4/9/39. Commd 1/9/64. Wg Cdr 1/1/80. Retd ADMIN 1/7/88.
GREEN M. K., MBE. Born 10/10/47. Commd 7/6/68. Flt Lt 10/10/74. Retd GD(G) 1/10/90.
GREEN M. R., OBE. Born 8/7/14. Commd 8/7/42. Wg Cdr 1/7/61. Retd SEC 14/7/69.
GREEN N. E. Born 12/5/27. Commd 10/10/63. Sqn Ldr 1/7/77. Retd GD 12/5/82.
GREEN P., MBE. Born 3/6/18. Commd 15/10/42. Wg Cdr 1/1/59. Retd ENG 3/6/73.
GREEN P. F. Born 11/10/31. Commd 16/9/71. Sqn Ldr 1/7/81. Retd ENG 11/10/91.
GREEN P. F. Born 7/8/30. Commd 25/5/50. Wg Cdr 1/1/81. Retd ADMIN 1/2/85.
GREEN P. F., DPhysEd. Born 28/9/39. Commd 7/6/39. Sqn Ldr 1/1/79. Retd ADMIN 13/2/84.
GREEN P. G. Born 24/9/41. Commd 2/6/77. Flt Lt 2/6/81. Retd GD 11/8/92.
GREEN P. L Born 11/11/31. Commd 1/3/62. Sqn Ldr 1/7/74. Retd ENG 15/12/84.
GREEN P. O. V., AFC FIMgt. Born 16/6/20. Commd 20/8/38. A Cdre 1/1/67. Retd GD 1/12/73.
GREEN P. S. Born 31/7/42. Commd 13/3/80. Flt Lt 13/3/83. Retd GD 1/11/89.
GREEN R., BA. Born 23/6/32. Commd 16/9/71. Sqn Ldr 16/9/78. Retd ADMIN 16/9/80.
GREEN R., OBE. Born 20/5/33. Commd 6/4/54. Gp Capt 1/7/79. Retd SEC 1/7/81.
GREEN R. A. Born 16/5/47. Commd 9/8/79. Sqn Ldr 1/7/87. Retd ADMIN 1/7/90.
GREEN R. A. Born 2/12/19. Commd 28/8/42. Flt Lt 10/11/55. Retd SEC 20/12/68.
GREEN R. A. S. Born 3/8/51. Commd 2/3/80. Flt Lt 2/3/84. Retd ENG 2/3/96.
GREEN R. C. Born 21/4/18. Commd 18/1/45. Sqn Ldr 1/7/66. Retd GD(G) 21/4/74.
GREEN R. C. E. Born 3/4/44. Commd 25/3/64. Flt Lt 29/10/69. Retd GD 2/6/76.
GREEN R. D. Born 28/12/60. Commd 30/4/81. Sqn Ldr 1/1/94. Retd SUP 28/12/98.
GREEN R. E., CEng MIEE MRAeS. Born 15/7/40. Commd 18/7/61. Sqn Ldr 1/1/71. Retd ENG 15/7/78.
GREEN R. J. Born 26/5/19. Commd 27/10/55. Sqn Ldr 1/1/68. Retd ENG 26/5/74.
GREEN R. J. Born 28/5/23. Commd 17/2/44. Flt Lt 17/8/47. Retd ENG 28/5/56.
GREEN R. J. C., MRIN MIMgt. Born 27/1/40. Commd 10/2/59. Wg Cdr 1/1/81. Retd GD 27/1/95.
GREEN R. M. Born 16/12/43. Commd 30/7/64. Flt Lt 28/11/70. Retd GD(G) 14/3/96.
GREEN R. T. Born 26/6/32. Commd 25/11/53. Flt Lt 25/5/59. Retd GD 26/6/70.
GREEN R. W. Born 11/2/38. Commd 25/2/82. Flt Lt 25/2/87. Retd ADMIN 11/12/93.
GREEN S. D. J., BA. Born 10/11/53. Commd 2/9/73. Flt Lt 15/10/77. Retd GD 15/7/88.
GREEN S. J. Born 2/7/47. Commd 28/2/69. Flt Lt 28/2/72. Retd GD 25/5/76.
GREEN S. J., BSc (Eur Ing) CEng CPhys. MInstP MRAeS. Born 13/6/54. Commd 30/9/73. Sqn Ldr 1/1/89. Retd ENG 9/8/92.
GREEN W. Born 16/10/21. Commd 29/4/45. Flt Lt 25/2/54. Retd GD(G) 16/2/62.
GREEN W. L., OBE DFC. Born 24/5/23. Commd 15/1/44. Gp Capt 1/1/71. Retd GD 2/11/75.
GREEN W. S., AFC. Born 12/4/21. Commd 12/7/45. Flt Lt 4/1/51. Retd GD 12/4/64.
GREENALL P., MBE MMAR MIMgt. Born 14/12/26. Commd 23/11/56. Wg Cdr 1/1/81. Retd MAR 1/1/84.
GREENAWAY P. C. Born 21/2/40. Commd 22/3/63. Flt Lt 22/9/68. Retd GD 2/10/78.
GREENE B. A., BSc. Born 26/9/47. Commd 18/9/66. Flt Lt 15/4/72. Retd GD 26/8/74.

GREENFIELD M. D., BSc. Born 25/1/61. Commd 26/9/82. Flt Lt 26/12/83. Retd GD 14/2/86.
GREENFIELD N., MSc BA FCMA ACIS. Born 12/10/53. Commd 17/9/72. Wg Cdre 1/7/84. Retd ADMIN 31/12/91.
GREENHALGH B. S. Born 5/7/29. Commd 12/12/51. Flt Lt 4/7/59. Retd GD 7/3/62.
GREENHALGH J. Born 31/3/16. Commd 16/4/35. Wg Cdr 1/7/47. Retd GD 18/9/53. rtg Gp Capt.
GREENHALGH J. L., MBE. Born 23/12/44. Commd 27/1/67. Wg Cdr 1/7/90. Retd ADMIN 2/12/98.
GREENHALGH J. S., BA MIRTE MIMgt. Born 1/1/33. Commd 21/10/66. Sqn Ldr 1/7/78. Retd ENG 1/1/93.
GREENHALGH N. Born 7/10/24. Commd 22/6/45. Wg Cdr 1/7/67. Retd GD 7/10/84.
GREENHALGH S. A., MRCS LRCP DPH DTM&H. Born 10/9/27. Commd 4/3/56. Wg Cdr 4/3/69. Retd MED 1/9/73.
GREENHALGH S. B. Born 20/11/46. Commd 22/5/80. Flt Lt 22/5/82. Retd GD 14/9/96.
GREENHALGH W. R. Born 13/5/43. Commd 23/1/64. Sqn Ldr 1/7/79 . Retd SY 1/7/83.
GREENHALL R. L., CEng MRAeS MIProdE MIMechE MIMgt. Born 13/7/34. Commd 23/6/58. Wg Cdr 1/1/76. Retd ENG 10/9/85.
GREENHILL J. G., FIMgt. Born 10/10/26. Commd 14/6/46. A Cdre 1/1/80. Retd GD 1/1/82.
GREENHILL-HOOPER T. J. Born 15/11/32. Commd 15/12/53. Sqn Ldr 1/7/66. Retd GD 15/11/70.
GREENHOUGH G. H., BA BD. Born 3/4/36. Commd 7/11/58. Sqn Ldr 16/1/69. Retd EDN 2/2/75.
GREENHOW M., DPhysEd. Born 5/7/33. Commd 19/9/59. Sqn Ldr 1/1/71. Retd GD 14/10/83.
GREENHOW N. Born 16/1/25. Commd 25/5/50. Sqn Ldr 1/7/72. Retd GD 15/9/77.
GREENHOW S. Born 7/3/21. Commd 27/8/44. Sqn Ldr 1/4/55. Retd GD 10/3/64.
GREENLAND B. J. L., AFC. Born 20/12/22. Commd 19/4/43. Sqn Ldr 1/7/55. Retd GD 29/1/62.
GREENLAND J. M. Born 3/9/28. Commd 11/11/50. Flt Lt 26/5/55. Retd GD 3/9/83.
GREENLEAF E. J., DSO DFC. Born 7/2/15. Commd 19/1/42. Sqn Ldr 1/8/47. Retd GD 21/2/58.
GREENLEAF G. F. Born 1/3/20. Commd 2/12/43. Flt Lt 27/2/51. Retd GD(G) 2/4/70.
GREENSLADE F. W. Born 27/1/31. Commd 30/1/70. Sqn Ldr 1/1/82. Retd ENG 27/1/89.
GREENSLADE R. E. Born 11/7/30. Commd 29/3/62. Flt Lt 29/3/67. Retd GD 6/9/75.
GREENSTREET G. G., MBE. Born 21/9/34. Commd 29/10/52. Sqn Ldr 1/1/67. Retd GD 21/9/89.
GREENWAY D. F., MIMgt. Born 31/8/34. Commd 24/9/52. Sq Ldr 1/7/77. Retd PI 7/4/87.
GREENWAY D. H. A., OBE FIMgt. Born 15/2/39. Commd 26/6/57. Gp Capt 1/1/86. Retd GD 15/2/94.
GREENWAY J. Born 6/2/44. Commd 28/2/85. Sqn Ldr 1/7/94. Retd ADMIN 16/2/97.
GREENWAY T. C. Born 20/11/38. Commd 11/5/78. Sqn Ldr 26/5/88. Retd MED(T).
GREENWOOD A. S. Born 16/6/32. Commd 14/5/53. Wg Cdr 1/7/80. Retd ADMIN 2/7/83.
GREENWOOD A. W. Born 1/10/32. Commd 27/2/52. Wg Cdr 1/7/84. Retd GD(G) 1/9/88.
GREENWOOD B., BSc CEng MRAeS. Born 3/11/49. Commd 5/1/75. Sqn Ldr 1/1/84. Retd ENG 30/4/00.
GREENWOOD B. J., MHCIMA MIMgt. Born 24/9/31. Commd 5/7/54. Wg Cdr 1/7/83. Retd ADMIN 24/9/86.
GREENWOOD D., BSc. Born 28/4/42. Commd 1/9/64. Sqn Ldr 1/7/86. Retd ADMIN 28/4/97.
GREENWOOD D. E. Born 23/9/31. Commd 25/6/66. Flt Lt 25/6/71. Retd ADMIN 7/5/77.
GREENWOOD D. F., CEng MRAeS MIEE. Born 27/3/24. Commd 19/7/51. Wg Cdr 1/1/67. Retd ENG 7/9/74.
GREENWOOD D. J., AFM. Born 21/1/34. Commd 28/9/61. Flt Lt 28/3/66. Retd GD 6/7/79.
GREENWOOD E. W., BSc. Born 9/4/32. Commd 11/8/52. Sqn Ldr 1/7/67. Retd GD 31/1/74.
GREENWOOD J. Born 22/8/25. Commd 7/7/44. Flt Lt 19/11/53. Retd GD 1/8/73.
GREENWOOD R. K. Born 26/11/44. Commd 22/3/63. Sqn Ldr 1/1/81. Retd GD 1/7/93.
GREEP D. F. Born 26/8/46. Commd 14/7/69. Wg Cdr 1/7/91. Retd ENG 15/7/93.
GREETHURST A. P. L. Born 30/3/25. Commd 8/7/54. Flt Lt 21/10/59. Retd GD 30/3/63.
GREEVES A. G., MBE. Born 12/12/12. Commd 8/7/54. Flt Lt 1/7/64. Retd SUP 12/12/67.
GREEVES B. J., BSc. Born 28/4/50. Commd 15/9/69. Flt Lt 15/6/73. Retd GD 8/12/81.
GREGG J. L. Born 11/10/30. Commd 2/5/51. Wg Cdr 1/1/67. Retd GD 11/3/78.
GREGORY A., BA. Born 22/3/37. Commd 14/3/57. Sqn Ldr 1/7/69. Retd GD 17/2/77.
GREGORY B. Born 4/1/30. Commd 6/6/57. Flt Lt 6/12/61. Retd GD  8/6/62.
GREGORY C. M., MSc BSc CEng MIEE. Born 3/4/58. Commd 6/9/81. Sqn Ldr 1/1/89. Retd ENG 6/9/97.
GREGORY D. G., FCIPD FIMgt. Born 24/7/30. Commd 11/4/51. A Cdre 1/7/79. Retd SEC 27/4/81.
GREGORY E. J. Born 4/4/49. Commd 21/2/69. Flt Lt 12/7/75. Retd GD(G) 4/6/80.
GREGORY E. J. W., MCIPD ACGI. Born 4/11/34. Commd 26/10/61. Sqn Ldr 1/7/80. Retd GD 4/11/92.
GREGORY H. Born 28/8/23. Commd 20/10/55. Flt Lt 20/10/61. Retd GD 28/9/68.
GREGORY H. E. Born 15/3/24. Commd 14/7/44. Flt Lt 29/9/48. Retd GD 1/10/68.
GREGORY J. Born 1/7/21. Commd 10/12/43. Flt Lt 5/5/53. Retd GD(G) 16/12/66.
GREGORY J. J. Born 1/8/21. Commd 13/7/45. Flt Lt 26/5/55. Retd GD 14/8/65.
GREGORY J. L. Born 7/6/27. Commd 27/9/51. Flt Lt 21/10/59. Retd PI 19/12/81. rtg Sqn Ldr.
GREGORY J. M., MHCIMA. Born 16/7/24. Commd 19/4/48. Flt Lt 1/10/51. Retd CAT 25/10/78.
GREGORY L. C., DFC. Born 7/8/20. Commd 12/12/40. Sqn Ldr 1/1/57. Retd GD. 8/5/65. rtg Wg Cdr.
GREGORY M. J., MA MSc CEng MRAeS MIEE. Born 30/10/40. Commd 30/9/59. Wg Cdr 1/1/84. Retd ENG 1/5/96.
GREGORY P. S. Born 17/3/47. Commd 21/9/72. Flt Lt 21/3/78. Retd GD 8/2/89.
GREGORY R. D. Born 10/5/49. Commd 31/7/70. Sqn Ldr 1/1/91. Retd GD 9/5/01.
GREGORY R. G. Born 1/2/23. Commd 10/3/60. Flt Lt 10/3/65. Retd GD 17/1/68.
GREGORY R. P., BM. Born 17/4/59. Commd 19/12/79. Sqn Ldr 1/8/88. Retd MED 23/2/96.
GREGORY W. G. Born 31/10/23. Commd 26/11/53. Sqn Ldr 1/1/68. Retd GD 1/5/73.
GREGORY W. J., DSO DFC* DFM. Born 23/11/13. Commd 22/1/42. Wg Cdr 1/1/59. Retd GD(G) 1/6/64.
GREGSON B. P. Born 6/5/48. Commd 19/2/76. Sqn Ldr 1/1/87. Retd GD(G) 27/10/91.

GREGSON O. G., OBE. Born 25/2/96. Commd 4/6/18. Flt Lt 30/6/22. Retd GD 18/11/28. Recalled 10/9/39, Sqn Ldr 4/5/42. Retd 25/8/46 rtg Wg Cdr.
GREIG J. R., BM BS. Born 26/2/69. Commd 6/9/89. Flt Lt 1/8/93. Retd MED 31/5/96.
GREIG J. R., OBE MSc MB ChB MFOM DIH. Born 14/5/36. Commd 30/9/62. A Cdre 1/7/91. Retd MED 30/9/96.
GREIG K. D., BA CEng MIEE. Born 31/8/38. Commd 11/4/63. Wg Cdr 1/1/86. Retd ENG 31/8/93.
GREIG R. C. C. Born 24/5/36. Commd 24/4/70. Sqn Ldr 1/7/81. Retd GD 24/5/91.
GREIG S. A. Born 28/5/51. Commd 9/12/71. Flt Lt 9/6/77. Retd GD 28/11/89.
GREIG S. McN. Born 14/1/14. Commd 12/9/38. Wg Cdr 1/1/60. Retd SUP 10/10/64.
GRENFELL J. Born 16/12/38. Commd 1/10/60. Sqn Ldr 1/7/76. Retd GD 1/7/81.
GRESHAM J. L. W. Born 31/1/19. Commd 3/5/56. Flt Lt 3/5/59. Retd GD(G) 16/4/65.
GRESWELL J. H., CB CBE DSO DFC. Born 28/7/16. Commd 30/9/35. A Cdre 1/1/62. Retd GD 28/7/68.
GREVES E. W. Born 24/3/41. Commd 14/5/60. Flt Lt 14/11/65. Retd GD 24/3/96.
GREVILLE N. Born 17/8/22. Commd 4/7/42. Flt Lt 4/1/46. Retd GD 22/11/55.
GREW P. E. Born 5/7/15. Commd 29/8/46. Flt Lt 28/2/51. Retd SUP 29/7/60 rtg Sqn Ldr.
GREY D. M. Born 15/2/46. Commd 22/5/64. Wg Cdr 1/1/84. Retd GD 10/8/85.
GREY P. R., FCA. Born 8/10/15. Commd 10/6/39. Sqn Ldr 1/8/47. Retd SEC 8/10/70.
GREY S. H., BA. Born 2/5/29. Commd 5/9/51. Sqn Ldr 1/4/61. Retd EDN 30/3/74.
GRIBBLE W. L. Born 18/8/21. Commd 10/2/45. Fg Offr 4/6/47. Retd GD 3/12/48.
GRICE P. W., BA. Born 12/6/52. Commd 2/10/72. Sqn Ldr 1/1/87. Retd GD 13/8/89.
GRIERSON M. J. Born 7/12/45. Commd 7/7/67. Flt Lt 5/2/75. Retd GD 22/4/94.
GRIERSON-JACKSON M. W. Born 19/12/20. Commd 18/5/41. Flt Lt 1/9/45. Retd GD 1/1/53 rtg Sqn Ldr.
GRIESHABER D. C. Born 12/4/33. Commd 19/8/71. Flt Lt 19/8/76. Retd ENG 4/2/88.
GRIEVE A. J. M. Born 13/2/41. Commd 8/12/61. Flt Lt 26/7/67. Retd GD 13/2/96.
GRIEVE B. S. Born 17/10/36. Commd 29/12/54. Flt Lt 15/8/62. Retd GD 15/12/67.
GRIEVE D. J. W., BA. Born 23/12/54. Commd 18/3/84. Flt Lt 18/9/86. Retd ADMIN 18/3/00.
GRIEVE I. P. Born 9/6/42. Commd 3/8/62. Sqn Ldr 1/1/75. Retd GD 28/12/93.
GRIFFIN A. J., AFC. Born 3/8/45. Commd 15/7/66. A Cdre 1/7/92. Retd GD 14/3/96.
GRIFFIN C. A., BEng. Born 14/4/59. Commd 29/11/81. Flt Lt 29/2/84. Retd ENG 29/11/97.
GRIFFIN E. K. Born 4/5/48. Commd 26/5/70. Flt Lt 26/11/75. Retd GD 20/6/93.
GRIFFIN F. J. Born 23/5/19. Commd 11/4/46. Sqn Ldr 1/7/59. Retd ENG 23/5/68.
GRIFFIN J. Born 13/3/51. Commd 3/7/80. Flt Lt 3/7/82. Retd MED(SEC) 13/3/89.
GRIFFIN K. G. Born 13/8/48. Commd 2/6/67. Sqn Ldr 1/1/84. Retd GD 1/1/87.
GRIFFIN M. E. L., BSc. Born 15/12/62. Commd 7/12/86. Flt Lt 7/6/90. Retd GD(G) 1/10/91.
GRIFFIN The Rev N. P., BA. Born 23/1/37. Commd 24/2/69. Retd 24/2/85. Wg Cdr.
GRIFFIN S. A., BSc CEng MRAeS. Born 10/7/59. Commd 10/10/79. Wg Cdr 1/1/96. Retd ENG 1/1/99.
GRIFFIN S. E. Born 28/8/46. Commd 2/8/68. Flt Lt 2/8/71. Retd GD 28/8/84.
GRIFFIN T. E. Born 29/4/15. Commd 24/12/42. Flt Lt 16/8/47. Retd ENG 2/3/68.
GRIFFITH D. V., BSc. Born 27/6/63. Commd 13/9/81. Flt Lt 15/10/85. Retd GD 15/7/96.
GRIFFITH H. D., BSc. Born 2/5/29. Commd 17/9/52. Sqn Ldr 1/1/63. Retd ENG 8/7/84.
GRIFFITH M. D. Born 7/12/46. Commd 11/10/84. Flt Lt 11/10/88. Retd MED SEC 14/3/96.
GRIFFITH R. J., BA. Born 30/10/49. Commd 29/1/87. Flt Lt 29/1/89. Retd ADMIN 29/1/95.
GRIFFITH-JONES G. L. S., CBE MA. Born 3/5/11. Commd 7/4/32. Gp Capt 1/7/52. Retd ENG 3/5/66.
GRIFFITHS A. Born 19/10/41. Commd 27/1/67. Wg Cdr 1/7/81. Retd SY 20/4/93.
GRIFFITHS A., BSc DUS CEng MIEE MInstP. Born 19/11/35. Commd 4/9/59. Wg Cdr 4/3/75. Retd ADMIN 17/5/76.
GRIFFITHS A., CB AFC. Born 22/8/22. Commd 10/9/42. AVM 1/7/72. Retd GD 22/8/77.
GRIFFITHS A. W., OBE. Born 26/5/23. Commd 29/10/43. Wg Cdr 1/7/60. Retd GD 30/9/69.
GRIFFITHS B. T., MBE BA MIMgt. Born 29/9/30. Commd 3/9/52. Wg Cdr 17/2/71. Retd EDN 18/11/73.
GRIFFITHS C. E. Born 13/6/46. Commd 3/5/65. Flt Lt 4/11/70. Retd GD 19/9/75.
GRIFFITHS D. A. Born 12/3/39. Commd 27/8/64. Flt Lt 4/12/66. Retd SUP 12/3/77.
GRIFFITHS D. A., OBE AFC. Born 20/7/42. Commd 30/7/63. Gp Capt 1/1/85. Retd GD 22/7/86.
GRIFFITHS D. A., BSc CEng MIEE MIMgt. Born 8/5/33. Commd 30/4/72. Sqn Ldr 30/4/72. Retd ENG 8/5/93.
GRIFFITHS D. B. Born 25/4/16. Commd 31/1/43. Wg Offr 1/7/55. Retd SEC 29/6/63.
GRIFFITHS D. F. Born 8/6/21. Commd 3/10/46. Flt Lt 3/4/51. Retd SUP 19/6/54.
GRIFFITHS D. I., DFC. Born 29/12/21. Commd 23/5/42. Sqn Ldr 1/7/57. Retd GD 29/12/64.
GRIFFITHS D. J. Born 4/4/32. Commd 16/12/66. Sqn Ldr 1/1/79. Retd ENG 12/12/85.
GRIFFITHS D. J., AFC BSc. Born 21/8/41. Commd 8/1/65. Sqn Ldr 1/1/75. Retd GD 21/8/96.
GRIFFITHS D. P. L., DPhysEd. Born 15/10/46. Commd 18/10/79. Sqn Ldr 1/7/90. Retd ADMIN 1/11/96.
GRIFFITHS D. W., DFC*. Born 7/8/21. Commd 27/7/42. Sqn Ldr 1/1/57. Retd GD 7/8/64.
GRIFFITHS E. J., MIMgt. Born 26/8/20. Commd 1/5/42. Sqn Ldr 1/4/57. Retd SEC 26/8/69.
GRIFFITHS E. P. Born 30/11/11. Commd 18/1/45. Sqn Ldr 1/7/57. Retd SEC 2/3/59.
GRIFFITHS E. R., OBE MB BS FRCS(E). Born 10/7/24. Commd 7/2/51. Wg Cdr 1/4/62. Retd MED 6/8/67.
GRIFFITHS F. P. Born 11/6/44. Commd 10/3/77. Flt Lt 10/3/79. Retd GD(G) 30/9/86.
GRIFFITHS G., OBE. Born 7/1/23. Commd 9/3/44. Wg Cdr 1/1/71. Retd GD(G) 7/1/78.
GRIFFITHS G. Born 24/4/46. Commd 9/3/66. Wg Cdr 1/7/88. Retd ADMIN 14/3/96.
GRIFFITHS G. B. Born 9/2/41. Commd 28/11/74. Sqn Ldr 1/7/83. Retd ENG 30/9/94.

GRIFFITHS G. D., MSc BSc. Born 24/6/62. Commd 23/4/87. Sqn Ldr 1/1/97. Retd ENG 9/9/00.
GRIFFITHS H. M. Born 1/5/18. Commd 23/3/50. Sqn Ldr 1/7/59. Retd PRT 31/7/64.
GRIFFITHS H. M., MB ChB DPhysMed. Born 15/9/43. Commd 25/7/66. Wg Cdr 27/8/83. Retd MED 19/5/84.
GRIFFITHS H. W., BSc. Born 13/4/53. Commd 3/9/78. Wg Cdr 1/7/92. Retd ADMIN 14/9/96.
GRIFFITHS H.A. Born 16/6/34. Commd 3/3/54. Gp Capt 1/7/87. Retd GD 16/6/92.
GRIFFITHS J. Born 25/11/17. Commd 28/3/46. Sqn Ldr 1/1/57. Retd SUP 15/9/62.
GRIFFITHS J. D., MBE. Born 4/11/21. Commd 15/5/58. Sqn Ldr 1/7/69. Retd ENG 30/6/76.
GRIFFITHS J. D., BSc. Born 8/6/46. Commd 7/2/71. Flt Lt 7/11/74. Retd GD(G) 7/2/87.
GRIFFITHS J. D. Born 11/8/48. Commd 21/4/67. Sqn Ldr 1/1/85. Retd GD 1/1/88.
GRIFFITHS M. J. Born 15/12/34. Commd 13/12/55. Flt Lt 13/6/58. Retd GD 10/2/62.
GRIFFITHS M. J., BSc MB BS. Born 30/5/63. Commd 13/11/85. Sqn Ldr 1/8/94. Retd MED 14/3/96.
GRIFFITHS M. L. Born 4/4/38. Commd 2/2/60. Sqn Ldr 24/7/71. Retd ADMIN 4/4/76.
GRIFFITHS N. A. Born 3/12/21. Commd 12/6/47. Sqn Ldr 1/7/69. Retd ENG 3/12/76.
GRIFFITHS N. M., BA FCIPS FIMgt. Born 27/4/44. Commd 15/7/66. A Cdre 1/1/93. Retd SUP 2/12/98.
GRIFFITHS N. T. Born 6/4/19. Commd 5/8/47. Sqn Ldr 5/1/56. Retd EDN 31/8/63.
GRIFFITHS P. Born 30/10/61. Commd 7/8/87. Flt Lt 15/7/90. Retd ENG 16/1/94.
GRIFFITHS P. A. Born 10/3/43. Commd 28/7/64. Wg Cdr 1/1/91. Retd GD 31/3/94.
GRIFFITHS P. D. Born 16/4/50. Commd 12/4/73. Sqn Ldr 1/7/85. Retd SUP 1/7/88.
GRIFFITHS P. R., BSc. Born 2/12/51. Commd 13/8/70. Sqn Ldr 1/7/83. Retd ENG 2/12/90.
GRIFFITHS P. S. Born 15/4/47. Commd 2/4/65. Flt Lt 2/10/70. Retd GD 28/9/84.
GRIFFITHS R. D. Born 17/1/25. Commd 5/11/59. Flt Lt 5/11/65. Retd SUP 1/5/69.
GRIFFITHS R. E., MSc BSc(Eng) ACGI. Born 22/10/39. Commd 30/9/58. Wg Cdr 1/7/87. Retd ENG 22/10/94.
GRIFFITHS R. G. E., CEng MRAeS. Born 23/10/16. Commd 4/11/43. Sqn Ldr 1/7/54. Retd ENG 23/3/68.
GRIFFITHS R. H. Born 19/7/41. Commd 30/3/61. Wg Cdr 1/1/87. Retd ENG 19/7/96.
GRIFFITHS R. P. A., BSc. Born 22/4/54. Commd 2/1/77. Fh Offr 2/7/74. Retd ADMIN 1/5/79.
GRIFFITHS S. C., BEng. Born 12/1/63. Commd 31/7/90. Flt Lt 15/7/93. Retd ENG 12/1/01.
GRIFFITHS S. G., MBE MBA. Born 2/6/48. Commd 28/2/69. Wg Cdr 1/1/87. Retd GD 29/2/00.
GRIFFITHS W. Born 15/9/23. Commd 18/5/44. Sqn Ldr 1/7/62. Retd SUP 3/3/78.
GRIFFITHS W. Born 28/3/44. Commd 14/1/65. Sqn Ldr 1/7/78. Retd GD 28/3/82.
GRIFFITHS W. L. Born 10/10/21. Commd 5/6/42. Sqn Ldr 1/1/54. Retd GD 14/11/64.
GRIGG G. A. F., BA. Born 16/11/32. Commd 15/7/54. Flt Lt 26/2/64. Retd EDN 30/6/65.
GRIGG R. F. Born 11/10/28. Commd 12/9/63. Sqn Ldr 1/1/74. Retd ENG 10/11/78.
GRIGGS D. S., AFC BA. Born 1/9/50. Commd 6/4/70. Gp Capt 1/1/96. Retd GD 1/9/00.
GRIGGS R. W. R. Born 5/2/24. Commd 6/12/56. Flt Lt 6/6/66. Retd GD 5/2/67.
GRIGGS T. C. Born 15/5/48. Commd 25/10/73. Flt Lt 25/4/79. Retd GD 22/10/94.
GRIGOR H. S. Born 19/1/50. Commd 15/9/69. Flt Lt 15/3/77. Retd GD 19/1/88.
GRIGSON M. W. S., OBE MA DipEl CEng MIEE. Born 13/12/33. Commd 26/9/53. Wg Cdr 1/1/73. Retd ENG 1/8/79. Reinstated 22/10/80. Wg Cdr 24/3/74. Retd ENG 18/4/88.
GRILLI P. J. P. Born 15/3/38. Commd 20/12/62. Wg Cdr 1/7/81. Retd ADMIN 3/5/90.
GRIMA F.X., MD MSc MRCGP MFOM MIMgt DPH. Born 28/8/31. Commd 9/7/61. Gp Capt 1/7/85. Retd MED 28/8/92.
GRIME G. H., BDS. Born 19/5/38. Commd 26/1/66. WgCdr 13/1/79. Retd DEL 21/4/92.
GRIMER J. O. Born 25/9/43. Commd 28/2/66. Wg Cdr 1/7/87. Retd SUP 14/3/96.
GRIMES M. K. Born 28/8/48. Commd 7/6/68. Flt Lt 7/12/74. Retd GD(G) 28/8/86.
GRIMSDALE G. E. Born 14/3/26. Commd 17/10/57. Flt Lt 1/4/63. Retd GD 21/9/68.
GRIMSEY J. M. Born 1/7/31. Commd 12/3/53. Flt Offr 12/3/59. Retd SEC 12/3/61.
GRIMSHAW E. B. Born 9/12/30. Commd 2/1/70. Flt Lt 2/1/76. Retd SUP 14/2/76.
GRIMSHAW F. Born 3/7/31. Commd 20/12/51. Flt Lt 4/4/57. Retd GD 15/1/70.
GRIMSHAW G. Born 24/11/31. Commd 11/8/53. Flt Lt 6/2/59. Retd GD 24/11/69.
GRIMSHAW J. D. Born 16/4/22. Commd 14/5/43. Sqn Ldr 1/7/57. Retd GD 30/3/62.
GRIMSTON D. F., CEng MIEE. Born 17/4/37. Commd 30/7/59. Wg Cdr 1/1/90. Retd ENG 21/4/92.
GRINDLEY G. L., OBE. Born 20/12/33. Commd 13/8/52. Gp Capt 1/1/87. Retd SY 2/7/87.
GRINDON J. E., CVO DSO AFC. Born 30/9/17. Commd 31/7/37. Gp Capt 1/7/56. Retd GD 1/9/59.
GRINTER R. K., CEng MIMechE MRAeS. Born 26/3/35. Commd 24/4/59. Wg Cdr 1/1/83. Retd ENG 1/4/85.
GRIPTON M. J. Born 24/6/56. Commd 15/12/88. Flt Lt 15/12/90. Retd ENG 2/4/93.
GRISBROOK D., MBE BSc. Born 25/8/29. Commd 5/11/52. Sqn Ldr 5/5/63. Retd EDN 5/11/68.
GRIST M. J., CEng MIMechE MIMgt. Born 2/9/36. Commd 5/7/60. Sqn Ldr 1/1/70. Retd ENG 5/7/76.
GRISTWOOD P. E. Born 28/9/25. Commd 28/6/51. Flt Lt 10/10/56. Retd GD 1/1/76.
GROBELNY W., AFC. Born 21/5/19. Commd 24/1/52. Sqn Ldr 1/7/67. Retd GD 1/8/73.
GROCOTT D. F. H., CBE AFC. Born 8/2/23. Commd 15/10/43. A Cdre 25/9/76. Retd GD 29/9/77.
GROCOTT J. C. Born 24/4/48. Commd 17/2/67. Sqn Ldr 1/1/86. Retd GD 1/1/89.
GROCOTT R. G. Born 7/6/24. Commd 25/3/44. Wg Cdr 1/7/81. Retd GD(G) 3/12/77.
GROGAN C. D., AFC. Born 10/5/23. Commd 5/3/53. Flt Lt 5/9/56. Retd GD 23/2/63.
GROGAN J. B. Born 15/7/46. Commd 4/12/64. Wg Cdr 1/7/81. Retd GD 15/7/87.
GROOCOCK D. W., AFC. Born 28/6/22. Commd 1/1/44. Gp Capt 1/1/70. Retd GD 1/6/74.
GROOM G. R. Born 8/5/15. Commd 3/3/44. Sqn Ldr 1/7/55. Retd SEC 3/6/65.

GROOM J. A., MHCIMA. Born 4/8/50. Commd 19/11/72. Flt Lt 19/12/76. Retd CAT 3/10/79.
GROOMBRIDGE P. L., MBE. Born 2/12/31. Commd 30/7/64. Wg Cdr 1/7/82. Retd SUP 1/8/84.
GROOMBRIDGE R. C. Born 17/11/39. Commd 6/10/60. Sqn Ldr 1/7/74. Retd GD 17/11/77. Re-entrant 3/12/79.
Sq Ldr 17/7/76. Retd GD 14/12/97.
GROSE G. M., BSc MCIPS. Born 11/10/53. Commd 3/9/72. Sqn Ldr 1/1/85. Retd SUP 11/10/91.
GROSE N. J., AFC. Born 17/4/53. Commd 22/7/71. Flt Lt 22/1/77. Retd GD 1/6/83.
GROSE R. J., BEM. Born 15/1/23. Commd 26/9/57. Sqn Ldr 1/1/68. Retd ADMIN 1/5/76.
GROSS A. J., BEng. Born 25/8/40. Commd 16/10/61. Gp Capt 1/1/92. Retd GD 25/8/95.
GROSSE H. M., AFC. Born 23/2/44. Commd 6/7/62. Wg Cdr 1/7/82. Retd GD 23/2/88.
GROSSET M. J. Born 9/12/47. Commd 23/6/67. Sqn Ldr 1/1/78. Retd ADMIN 15/2/85.
GROSSET P. M., MIMgt. Born 7/5/43. Commd 17/12/65. Gp Capt 1/1/90. Retd ADMIN 22/4/94.
GROSVENOR D. E. Born 20/11/32. Commd 20/12/51. Wg Cdr 1/7/72. Retd ADMIN 2/4/85.
GROSVENOR L. Born 9/1/44. Commd 23/9/66. Flt Lt 23/3/72. Retd GD 5/2/84. Re-entered 3/4/85. Flt Lt 18/5/73.
Retd GD 9/7/00.
GROUT D. L., AFC. Born 23/1/06. Commd 13/11/40. Sqn Ldr 1/8/47. Retd GD(G) 1/1/57.
GROUT M. D. Born 1/7/16. Commd 20/10/41. Sqn Offr 1/7/50. Retd SEC 16/10/51.
GROVE N., DFM. Born 13/1/24. Commd 28/2/57. Flt Lt 28/2/63. Retd GD 11/2/73.
GROVER P. E. Born 26/2/32. Commd 6/6/57. Flt Lt 6/12/61. Retd GD 26/2/70.
GROVES B. A. Born 24/3/36. Commd 10/2/72. Flt Lt 10/2/74. Retd ADMIN 10/2/82.
GROVES B. A., BSc. Born 16/5/48. Commd 7/12/75. Flt Lt 7/3/77. Retd GD 7/12/91.
GROVES E. R. Born 8/6/29. Commd 30/3/61. Sqn Ldr 1/7/79. Retd MED 8/6/87.
GROVES F. J., MBE MB BCh MRCGP DRCOG DAvMed MRAeS. Born 30/9/56. Commd 9/7/81. Wg Cdr 10/8/94.
Retd MED 9/7/98.
GROVES J. A. Born 28/4/54. Commd 22/6/89. Sqn Ldr 1/7/97. Retd ADMIN 1/7/00.
GROVES R. L. Born 15/6/22. Commd 19/7/51. Wg Cdr 1/7/66. Retd ENG 17/2/73.
GROVES W. R., MBE. Born 17/11/15. Commd 24/3/45. Wg Cdr 1/7/66. Retd SUP 12/6/70.
GROZIER J. Born 10/11/22. Commd 4/5/50. Flt Lt 4/11/53. Retd GD 11/7/72.
GRUBB D. W. Born 12/4/24. Commd 9/8/47. Sqn Ldr 1/1/62. Retd GD 9/7/76.
GRUMBLEY K. G. Born 4/12/45. Commd 18/8/67. Wg Cdr 1/1/86. Retd GD 4/12/00.
GRUNDON B. I., MCIPD. Born 11/9/36. Commd 19/9/71. Flt Lt 19/9/73. Retd ENG 19/9/87.
GRUNDY B. G., OBE. Born 28/9/20. Commd 1/9/45. A Cdre 1/7/71. Retd SEC 30/11/72.
GRUNDY F. H. Born 25/9/56. Commd 27/2/75. Sqn Ldr 1/7/90. Retd GD 1/10/96.
GRUNDY L. V., MIPM. Born 25/5/44. Commd 4/6/64. Sqn Ldr 1/7/75. Retd ADMIN 1/8/91.
GRUNDY R. Born 11/2/32. Commd 22/12/53. Flt Lt 21/10/59. Retd GD 11/2/70.
GRUNDY R. C., MMS. Born 19/12/40. Commd 21/7/70. Sqn Ldr 1/1/82. Retd ADMIN 2/1/93.
GRUNDY R. M. Born 15/7/95. Commd 1/4/18. Flt Lt 1/1/24. Retd SEC 19/12/29.
GRUNDY R. W., MBE BTech. Born 8/2/51. Commd 13/9/71. Sqn Ldr 1/7/87. Retd GD 14/3/97.
GRUNDY W. L. Born 23/10/31. Commd 17/5/62. Sqn Ldr 1/1/74. Retd ENG 5/11/83.
GRUNER S. C. Born 18/2/45. Commd 3/3/67. Sqn Ldr 1/7/80. Retd GD 21/9/84.
GUARD F. R. Born 10/10/32. Commd 25/10/53. Wg Cdr 1/1/85. Retd GD 1/1/88.
GUBBINS R. B., FIMgt. Born 4/6/32. Commd 27/7/54. Gp Capt 1/1/76. Retd GD 9/3/87.
GUEST C. A., MIMgt. Born 4/9/18. Commd 11/11/43. Sqn Ldr 1/7/54. Retd ENG 7/8/71.
GUEST C. B. Born 15/1/42. Commd 3/9/62. Sqn Ldr 1/1/75. Retd GD 15/1/80.
GUEST G. R. Born 21/11/14. Commd 16/5/42. Flt Lt 16/11/46. Retd SEC 9/12/63 rtg Sqn Ldr.
GUEST M. J., MA MSc CEng MRAeS. Born 20/5/34. Commd 26/9/53. Gp Capt 1/1/76. Retd ENG 17/6/92.
GUEST N. E., BSc. Born 27/9/25. Commd 15/11/45. Sqn Ldr 1/10/56. Retd ENG 25/11/72.
GUEST R., MSc MB ChB MRCGP DIH MFOM. Born 14/12/54. Commd 30/3/76. Wg Cdr 6/8/84. Retd MED
14/12/92.
GUILE H. W., MIMgt. Born 15/5/24. Commd 20/12/48. Wg Cdr 1/7/66. Retd GD 3/4/79.
GUILFOYLE A. A. Born 5/8/37. Commd 20/7/78. Flt Lt 20/7/81. Retd GD 30/9/85.
GUILFOYLE D., BA. Born 6/6/41. Commd 7/6/68. Sqn Ldr 1/1/76. Retd ENG 1/10/87.
GULLICK R., BSc. Born 31/7/53. Commd 1/9/75. Sqn Ldr 1/1/88. Retd ENG 1/10/93.
GULLIVER M. B. Born 23/4/29. Commd 24/8/48. Fg Offr 20/7/51. Retd GD 10/12/55.
GULLIVER M. C. H., BSc CEng MIMechE ACGI MIMgt. Born 24/1/41. Commd 20/7/65. Sqn Ldr 1/7/73. Retd ENG
20/7/81.
GUNDRY A. F. Born 8/12/23. Commd 28/7/60. Flt Lt 28/7/63. Retd GD 8/12/81.
GUNN A. C., MA LLB(EDIN) LLB(LOND) BL. Born 6/2/30. Commd 5/9/57. Wg Cdr 1/7/58. Retd LGL 1/7/71.
GUNN A. J. Born 19/10/29. Commd 30/7/52. Flt Lt 27/12/57. Retd GD 1/8/73.
GUNN A. R. Born 9/8/24. Commd 29/1/46. Flt Lt 29/1/52. Retd RGT 29/2/60.
GUNN D. J. Born 27/5/60. Commd 20/5/82. Sqn Ldr 1/1/96. Retd GD 18/8/00.
GUNN G. A. Born 4/5/26. Commd 15/6/48. Sqn Ldr 1/7/58. Retd GD 30/12/59.
GUNN J. Born 26/4/42. Commd 24/3/63. Sqn Ldr 1/1/92. Retd ENG 1/7/79.
GUNN R. H. Born 15/9/34. Commd 24/2/55. Flt Lt 24/2/61. Retd SEC 10/7/64.
GUNNELL P. Born 4/7/44. Commd 29/4/71. Flt Lt 29/4/73. Retd SUP 1/9/77.
GUNNELL S. D., DFM. Born 2/12/22. Commd 23/3/43. Flt Lt 9/3/47. Retd GD 1/10/66.
GUNNING R. D. Born 23/4/38. Commd 28/7/59. Flt Lt 28/1/62. Retd GD 22/5/66.

GUNNS P. E., CEng MIMechE MRAeS MIMgt. Born 18/5/36. Commd 23/7/58. Wg Cdr 1/1/74. Retd ENG 18/5/91.
GUNTRIP J. J. Born 23/5/28. Commd 14/12/49. Flt Lt 14/6/52. Retd GD 23/5/66.
GUNYON H. W. Born 16/2/28. Commd 4/8/53. Flt Lt 23/10/57. Retd GD 24/2/68.
GURNEY D. J. Born 20/1/43. Commd 29/5/64. Sqn Ldr 1/1/75. Retd GD 20/1/81.
GURNEY J. A. Born 14/1/44. Commd 17/2/67. Flt Lt 17/8/72. Retd GD 16/12/76.
GUTHRIE D. Born 26/5/28. Commd 27/7/49. Sqn Ldr 1/1/60. Retd GD 26/5/66.
GUTHRIE I., BA. Born 7/9/57. Commd 8/5/83. Sqn Ldr 1/7/93. Retd SUP 8/5/99.
GUTHRIE P. F. Born 11/11/59. Commd 4/7/82. Sqn Ldr 1/1/92. Retd ENG 4/7/98.
GUTTERIDGE A. C. Born 1/5/45. Commd 28/4/65. Sqn Ldr 1/7/77. Retd GD 1/5/89.
GUTTERIDGE J. L., BEM CEng MRAeS. Born 16/8/22. Commd 26/2/53. Sqn Ldr 1/1/63. Retd ENG 1/11/75.
GUTTRIDGE A. H., MVO MBE. Born 27/10/43. Commd 2/12/66. Sqn Ldr 1/1/91. Retd GD 27/10/98.
GUTTRIDGE D. A. E. Born 10/10/34. Commd 17/11/59. Wg Cdr 1/7/78. Retd ENG 1/8/87.
GUY B. T., MRAeS. Born 17/7/26. Commd 29/3/56. Flt Lt 29/9/59. Retd GD 8/9/76.
GUY E. L. Born 8/5/29. Commd 17/12/64. Sqn Ldr 1/1/78. Retd GD 8/5/84.
GUY L. Born 11/8/58. Commd 24/4/80. Sqn Ldr 1/1/91. Retd ADMIN 11/8/96.
GUY P. N., BA. Born 4/2/39. Commd 23/10/62. Sqn Ldr 23/4/72. Retd EDN 13/12/79.
GUY R. F. B., FCIS. Born 3/11/12. Commd 1/1/37. Wg Cdr 1/1/53. Retd SUP 1/7/60.
GUY R. J. Born 11/4/24. Commd 17/7/58. Sqn Ldr 1/7/69. Retd GD 9/4/77.
GUY R. W., CEng MIEE MRAeS. Born 26/10/34. Commd 25/7/56. Wg Cdr 1/1/73. Retd ENG 26/8/89.
GUYATT D. J. Born 26/12/48. Commd 10/1/69. Flt Lt 26/6/74. Retd GD 14/9/96.
GUYER M. L. Born 10/8/32. Commd 19/4/51. Flt Lt 17/10/55. Retd GD 4/6/65.
GWINNELL E. B. C. Born 17/4/30. Commd 18/8/54. Flt Lt 18/1/60. Retd GD 23/5/70.
GWYNNE G. B. Born 5/9/31. Commd 1/10/55. Gp Capt 1/1/82. Retd GD 15/9/84.
GWYNNE R. C. Born 19/5/30. Commd 28/11/69. Sqn Ldr 1/1/80. Retd GD 2/1/84.
GWYTHER H. V. Born 30/5/19. Commd 31/7/42. Sqn Ldr 1/7/54. Retd GD 7/11/58.
GWYTHER V. R. Born 9/5/22. Commd 28/2/57. Sqn Ldr 1/7/73. Retd GD 31/3/77.
GYLES S. W. Born 27/9/46. Commd 11/1/66. Sqn Ldr 1/1/87. Retd GD 10/10/90.

# H

HAARHOFF H. A., DFC. Born 25/9/12. Commd 17/1/40. Sqn Ldr 1/1/50 . Retd ENG 29/11/59.
HACK D. R. Born 19/7/58. Commd 2/2/78. Sqn Ldr 1/1/93. Retd GD(G) 16/12/96.
HACK K. S. Born 15/5/43. Commd 17/5/79. Sqn Ldr 1/1/88. Retd SY 31/3/94.
HACKE L. E. A. Born 29/1/22. Commd 3/6/44. Sqn Ldr 1/7/57. Retd GD 29/1/65.
HACKE N. S., BSc. Born 7/11/61. Commd 29/4/84. Flt Lt 29/10/86. Retd GD 31/7/89.
HACKETT A. D. B. P. Born 13/8/42. Commd 29/3/68. Flt Lt 11/11/73. Retd SUP 13/8/80.
HACKETT G. R. Born 22/12/43. Commd 28/9/62. Flt Lt 28/1/70. Retd GD 22/4/94.
HACKETT T. H., MA BLitt. Born 19/6/31. Commd 24/4/57. Sqn Ldr 17/2/63. Retd EDN 24/4/73.
HACKFORD D. M. MCC. Born 18/7/44. Commd 22/8/63. Sqn Ldr 1/7/75. Retd SUP 18/8/82. Re-entered 5/8/83.
    Sqn Ldr 20/7/76. Retd SUP 14/9/96.
HACKMAN G. E. H., AFC. Born 9/8/19. Commd 20/6/42. Sqn Ldr 1/1/53. Retd GD 6/2/59 rtg Wg Cdr.
HACKNEY A. C. Born 18/5/36. Commd 6/4/55. Flt Lt 6/10/60. Retd GD 18/5/94.
HACKNEY P. S., BSc. Born 9/7/53. Commd 4/10/71. Flt Lt 15/10/75. Retd GD 9/7/92.
HACKNEY R. G., MB ChB. Born 2/9/57. Commd 30/1/79. Wg Cdr 1/5/96. Retd MED 1/12/99.
HADDOCK P. Born 2/7/22. Commd 5/2/45. Flt Lt 19/6/52. Retd GD(G) 6/3/64.
HADDOW R. W., OBE AFM MSc CEng MIEE MRAeS. Born 20/5/36. Commd 4/9/67. Sqn Ldr 13/10/72. Retd
    ADMIN 4/9/83.
HADLAND J. V., DFC. Born 23/5/14. Commd 17/8/41. Sqn Ldr 1/1/49. Retd SUP 20/12/58.
HADLEY D., BSc. Born 13/3/47. Commd 27/10/70. Flt Lt 27/7/74. Retd GD(G) 6/12/74.
HADLEY T. G. Born 7/8/33. Commd 5/8/54. Sqn Ldr 1/1/67. Retd RGT 8/9/73.
HADLINGTON P. B. Born 5/10/31. Commd 19/11/52. Flt Lt 15/4/58. Retd GD(G) 5/10/88.
HADLOW R. K. J. Born 20/4/35. Commd 21/4/54. Sqn Ldr 1/7/66. Retd GD 20/4/73.
HAFFENDEN N. C. Born 23/12/36. Commd 23/11/78. Flt Lt 23/11/83. Retd ENG 24/12/90.
HAGAN G. E. Born 26/9/23. Commd 27/5/54. Flt Lt 27/5/60. Retd GD 31/1/69.
HAGAN P. V. Born 12/3/65. Commd 28/9/89. Flt Lt 21/1/94. Retd SUP 14/9/96.
HAGE A. E. Born 20/4/29. Commd 13/2/64. Flt Lt 13/2/69. Retd ENG 11/3/75. Re-employed 21/5/80. Retd
    25/10/83.
HAGEL G. Born 16/11/32. Commd 11/10/51. Sqn Ldr 1/7/69. Retd GD 25/2/77.
HAGGAR H. T., MBE DFM FIMgt. Born 7/5/17. Commd 6/4/43. Gp Capt 1/1/69. Retd SEC 7/5/72.
HAGGAR N. A. T. Born 4/11/47. Commd 23/3/67. Flt Lt 23/9/72. Retd GD 27/7/00.
HAGGERTY F. M., MBE. Born 17/11/43. Commd 12/7/63. Flt Lt 12/11/69. Retd GD 22/10/94.
HAGGERTY M. E. O. Born 5/5/33. Commd 29/12/51. Sqn Ldr 1/7/64. Retd GD 5/5/71.
HAGGETT N. L., MBE MRAeS DPhysEd. Born 8/7/26. Commd 8/8/56. Sqn Ldr 1/1/68. Retd ADMIN 8/3/85.
HAGUE L., OBE MIMgt. Born 4/3/21. Commd 23/10/43. Wg Cdr 1/1/65. Retd GD 14/12/74.
HAGUE S. J. Born 20/8/59. Commd 14/1/81. Flt Lt 6/3/86. Retd SUP 31/3/94.
HAIG J. C. H., BA. Born 6/1/38. Commd 5/6/56. Flt Lt 5/12/61. Retd GD 6/1/81.
HAIG T. L. Born 1/9/40. Commd 16/9/71. Sqn Ldr 1/1/84. Retd GD(G) 1/9/95.
HAIGH A. J., MIEE MIMgt. Born 22/6/49. Commd 15/9/69. Sqn Ldr 1/1/83. Retd ENG 22/6/87.
HAIGH C. F., MBE. Born 7/2/43. Commd 2/9/63. Sqn Ldr 1/7/85. Retd GD 7/2/98.
HAIGH D. Born 16/10/17. Commd 23/6/44. Sqn Ldr 1/7/58. Retd SEC 16/10/66.
HAIGH I. G. Born 3/12/33. Commd 23/7/52. Flt Lt 29/1/58. Retd GD 3/12/71.
HAIGH J. P. C. Born 29/3/49. Commd 20/9/68. Flt Lt 20/3/74. Retd GD 16/11/74.
HAIGH P., BTech. Born 21/2/43. Commd 22/2/71. Flt Lt 22/5/72. Retd SUP 22/2/87.
HAIGH-JONES R. C. Born 2/7/46. Commd 4/2/71. Sqn Ldr 1/1/82. Retd GD(G) 1/1/85.
HAIL I. S. Born 3/2/47. Commd 25/2/66. Flt Lt 8/3/72. Retd GD 3/2/85. Reinstated 23/9/87. Flt Lt 26/10/74. Retd
    GD 23/12/95.
HAILE J. E. T. Born 8/3/18. Commd 30/7/38. Wg Cdr 1/7/49. Retd GD 31/7/54.
HAIMES R. C. Born 4/5/23. Commd 13/7/61. Flt Lt 13/7/64. Retd GD(G) 31/3/77.
HAINE R. C., OBE DFC FIMgt. Born 1/10/16. Commd 1/4/40. Gp Capt 1/7/62. Retd GD 1/10/70.
HAINES C. V., AFC*. Born 11/3/12. Commd 1/4/40. Sqn Ldr 1/7/55. Retd SEC 29/3/59.
HAINES F. C. Born 11/11/21. Commd 25/12/43. Sqn Ldr 1/4/55. Retd GD 11/11/64.
HAINES G. C., LDSRCS. Born 10/3/33. Commd 19/8/62. Wg Cdr 3/9/72. Retd DEL 10/9/91.
HAINES G. S. Born 22/1/16. Commd 3/12/42. Sqn Ldr 1/7/53. Retd SEC 28/12/62.
HAINES H. G., AFC. Born 2/4/24. Commd 18/11/55. Sqn Ldr. 1/7/63. Retd GD 2/4/79.
HAINES P. W. R. Born 17/8/47. Commd 1/3/68. Flt Lt 6/7/74. Retd GD(G) 17/8/85.
HAINES R. A. Born 4/10/28. Commd 17/5/51. Flt Lt 22/5/57. Retd GD 4/10/66.
HAIR W. J. Born 29/1/51. Commd 16/3/73. Flt Lt 16/3/76. Retd GD 29/1/89.
HAISELDEN J. C. Born 7/11/38. Commd 28/10/76. Flt Lt 28/10/78. Retd ENG 28/10/84.
HAISLEY J. R., LLB. Born 13/5/37. Commd 2/10/67. Flt Lt 2/10/67. Retd GD(G) 2/10/75.
HAKIN L., OBE. Born 9/7/42. Commd 6/9/63. Gp Capt 1/7/90. Retd GD 9/7/97.

HALDANE G. E., BA. Born 5/11/47. Commd 4/6/72. Flt Lt 4/3/74. Retd GD 4/6/88.
HALDANE I. Born 14/5/42. Commd 1/4/66. Flt Lt 4/5/72. Retd GD 8/11/77.
HALE A., OBE BEM. Born 5/7/20. Commd 14/11/46. A Cdre 1/1/73. Retd SUP 5/7/75.
HALE E. J., DFC AFC. Born 6/12/13. Commd 26/10/42. Flt Lt 26/4/47. Retd GD(G) 31/3/60 rtg Sqn Ldr.
HALE M. W. Born 14/12/24. Commd 21/4/44. Sqn Ldr 1/4/56. Retd GD 14/12/62.
HALE R. A. Born 28/3/25. Commd 30/4/46. Wg Cdr 1/1/67. Retd GD 27/3/76.
HALE R. M. Born 23/12/46. Commd 14/7/66. Sqn Ldr 1/7/80. Retd GD 23/12/84.
HALEEM S. A. B. A. Born 19/7/43. Commd 10/7/64. Flt Lt 19/1/69. Retd GD 18/3/69.
HALEEM S. M. Born 22/6/67. Commd 16/6/88. Flt Lt 16/12/93. Retd GD 14/3/97.
HALES A. E. G., MIMgt. Born 10/11/33. Commd 31/10/62. A Cdre 1/1/85. Retd SY 1/1/87.
HALEY J. W. J., MIMgt. Born 31/1/25. Commd 26/8/45. Wg Cdr 1/1/67. Retd SUP 4/9/79.
HALEY M. J. B. Born 1/4/37. Commd 7/1/58. Flt Lt 21/8/63. Retd SY 25/9/76.
HALEY R. C., BSc. Born 23/4/62. Commd 11/9/83. Flt Lt 11/3/86. Retd GD 11/9/95.
HALFACREE K. D. Born 27/9/23. Commd 20/5/44. Flt Lt 26/5/55. Retd ENG 30/6/78.
HALFORD W. T. H. Born 9/6/40. Commd 6/8/63. Flt Lt 26/7/67. Retd SUP 6/8/79.
HALFPENNY The Rev B. N., CB MA. Born 7/6/36. Commd 20/10/65. Retd AVM 7/10/91.
HALKES J. S. Born 17/7/39. Commd 17/7/60. Sqn Ldr 1/7/68. Retd GD 1/1/71.
HALL A. N. C. M-M. Born 4/7/47. Commd 21/7/65. Sqn Ldr 1/7/94. Retd GD 4/7/00.
HALL A. T. Born 3/10/50. Commd 5/4/91. Sqn Ldr 5/4/89. Retd ENG 14/7/97.
HALL A. V. Born 29/10/45. Commd 1/3/68. Gp Capt 1/7/91. Retd ENG 14/9/96.
HALL B. E. Born 23/12/37. Commd 14/8/64. Flt Lt 3/2/70. Retd ADMIN 6/4/89.
HALL B. J. Born 21/8/38. Commd 8/1/57. Wg Cdr 1/7/75. Retd GD 10/4/92.
HALL C. A. Born 15/1/47. Commd 1/4/71. Flt Lt 1/10/76. Retd GD 24/4/82.
HALL C. R. Born 26/10/37. Commd 28/2/64. Flt Lt 10/2/67. Retd GD 1/8/73.
HALL C. R. Born 14/11/43. Commd 8/9/69. Wg Cdr 1/7/89. Retd SY 23/4/94.
HALL C. S. Born 15/7/41. Commd 28/2/66. Sqn Ldr 1/1/78. Retd ENG 28/2/82.
HALL D. Born 23/1/46. Commd 26/5/67. Flt Lt 4/11/70. Retd GD 23/1/90.
HALL D. Born 28/3/31. Commd 30/7/52. Flt Lt 21/1/58. Retd GD(G) 28/3/89.
HALL D. B. Born 25/7/34. Commd 14/1/53. Flt Lt 3/6/58. Retd PI 5/12/85.
HALL D. C. Born 5/5/28. Commd 28/4/51. Flt Lt 13/10/60. Retd GD 6/5/69.
HALL D. I. Born 5/8/31. Commd 19/8/54. Sqn Ldr 1/7/67. Retd ENG 19/8/81.
HALL E. Born 9/11/34. Commd 11/9/56. Flt Lt 15/8/62. Retd GD 25/6/65.
HALL F. P., CEng MRAeS. Born 13/5/39. Commd 11/10/70. Sqn Ldr 1/7/81. Retd ENG 12/11/91.
HALL G. A., AFM. Born 23/11/23. Commd 27/1/55. Sqn Ldr 1/1/72. Retd GD 1/10/73.
HALL G. G. Born 1/7/16. Commd 16/9/42. Sqn Offr 1/4/57. Retd SEC 1/9/58.
HALL G. H. E. Born 5/7/33. Commd 18/11/66. Flt Lt 18/11/68. Retd GD(G) 18/11/74.
HALL G. R., BEng. Born 27/4/65. Commd 15/9/86. Fg Off 15/7/86. Retd GD 17/5/88.
HALL G. T. Born 30/11/33. Commd 16/7/52. Flt Lt 21/10/59. Retd GD 30/11/76.
HALL G. W. B., BEng. Born 8/7/37. Commd 4/4/61. Sqn Ldr 1/7/72. Retd GD 16/12/79.
HALL H. B. Born 15/2/37. Commd 5/3/57. Flt L5 5/9/62. Retd GD 4/5/74.
HALL H. D., CB CBE AFC FIMgt. Born 3/6/25. Commd 20/9/48. AVM 1/7/79. Retd GD 6/12/82.
HALL H. R., OBE DFC BCom. Born 21/10/13. Comm 1/1/43. Wg Cdr 1/1/54. Retd GS 1/6/68 rtg Gp Capt.
HALL H. W., CBE. Born 28/2/39. Commd 28/4/65. A Cdre 1/7/89. Retd GD 1/6/94.
HALL I., MBE. Born 15/5/40. Commd 1/4/58. Sqn Ldr 1/7/70. Retd GD 15/5/78.
HALL I. S., BA. Born 9/9/48. Commd 13/1/67. Gp Capt 1/1/96. Retd GD 1/10/98.
HALL J. Born 28/12/34. Commd 17/9/52. Flt Lt 17/6/58. Retd GD 20/8/66.
HALL J. A., BA. Born 2/7/49. Commd 27/2/70. Wg Cdr 1/7/86. Retd GD 14/4/97.
HALL J. D. Born 15/2/45. Commd 15/8/85. Flt Lt 15/8/89. Retd ENG 2/4/93.
HALL J. D. Born 9/8/51. Commd 9/5/91. Flt Lt 9/5/93. Retd ADMIN 2/12/96.
HALL J. D. M. Born 21/4/34. Commd 23/1/59. Flt Lt 27/8/62. Retd GD 23/1/71.
HALL J. F., OBE FIIP CEng MRAeS MIMgt. Born 28/6/20. Commd 28/7/43. Wg Cdr 1/7/66. Retd ENG 28/6/75.
HALL J. H. Born 20/10/45. Commd 15/9/67. Flt Lt 15/3/73. Retd GD 14/2/77.
HALL J. R. Born 26/3/35. Commd 10/4/56. Flt Lt 10/10/58. Retd GD 26/3/73.
HALL J. S., CBE MSc MB BS FFOM DIH DAvMed. Born 25/10/31. Commd 3/3/57. A Cdre 1/7/87. Retd MED 4/4/92.
HALL K., BSc. Born 23/7/46. Commd 13/9/67. Sqn Ldr 15/1/76. Retd ADMIN 23/7/84.
HALL M. E. Born 8/11/34. Commd 26/5/54. Flt L5 26/11/59. Retd GD 8/11/72.
HALL M. G. Born 12/10/31. Commd 29/12/51. Flt Lt 25/4/57. Retd GD 18/7/73. Re-employed 11/3/81 to 20/2/82.
HALL M. R., BA. Born 6/1/43. Commd 13/4/66. Wg Cdr 1/1/86. Retd GD 17/10/97.
HALL N. A. Born 2/1/63. Commd 20/1/85. Flt Lt 20/7/88. Retd OPS SPT 20/1/01.
HALL P. M., BA. Born 28/12/40. Commd 17/3/67. Gp Capt 1/7/88. Retd ADMIN 1/7/94.
HALL P. T., MBE. Born 7/8/24. Commd 1/5/45. Wg Cdr 1/7/66. Retd GD 31/7/76.
HALL R. D. Born 15/10/28. Commd 6/7/49. Sqn Ldr 1/7/66. Retd GD 16/7/73.
HALL R. J. J. Born 5/6/19. Commd 20/6/46. Sqn Ldr 1/1/65. Retd ENG 5/6/74.
HALL S. C. Born 11/11/36. Commd 9/2/55. Sqn Ldr 1/7/66. Retd GD 11/11/74.

HALL S. R., MA BA MCIPD MRIN. Born 27/12/43. Commd 9/4/72. Sqn Ldr 12/3/74. Retd ADMIN 27/12/98.
HALL T. D. Born 22/4/20. Commd 19/7/44. Wg Cdr 1/7/74. Retd ENG 18/1/50.
HALLAM G. P. Born 5/5/36. Commd 9/2/66. Flt Lt 1/7/68. Retd ENG 1/10/75.
HALLAM J. R. Born 21/2/18. Commd 30/3/61. Flt Lt 30/3/66. Retd GD(G) 31/1/69.
HALLAM M. E., MEng BSc CEng MIMechE. Born 18/7/37. Commd 7/5/72. Sqn Ldr 1/6/74. Retd ADMIN 26/10/90.
HALLAM W. B. L., MA. Born 9/2/35. Commd 25/9/54. Flt L5 15/8/62. Retd ENG 9/2/73.
HALLATT W. H. Born 12/3/22. Commd 5/11/45. Sqn Ldr 1/4/56. Retd GD 12/11/60.
HALLER D. Born 5/10/37. Commd 28/7/59. Sqn Ldr 1/1/69. Retd GD 1/8/80.
HALLETT A. C. Born 24/11/48. Commd 21/12/67. Sqn Ldr 1/1/86. Retd SY(RGT) 1/1/89.
HALLETT A. W., MBE DFC AFC. Born 12/11/21. Commd 24/4/44. Flt Lt 24/4/50. Retd CAT 12/11/70.
HALLETT C. A. Born 26/2/33. Commd 16/9/71. Flt Lt 16/9/74. Retd GD 26/2/88.
HALLIDAY B. W., BSc. Born 27/6/32. Commd 6/1/55. Sqn Ldr 1/1/65. Retd EDN 23/9/70.
HALLIDAY N. G., MSc MBCS. Born 30/12/34. Commd 27/5/53. Wg Cdr 1/7/83. Retd GD 2/11/85.
HALLING G. R., MBE. Born 31/7/17. Commd 8/7/43. Flt Lt 8/1/47. Retd ENG 14/8/65.
HALLION G. Born 17/7/31. Commd 29/12/51. Flt Lt 13/11/57. Retd GD 17/7/69.
HALLIWELL N. J. Born 23/9/54. Commd 16/5/74. Sqn Ldr 1/7/89. Retd GD 23/9/92.
HALLIWELL S., DFC* MIMgt. Born 25/7/21. Commd 19/4/43. Wg Cdr 1/7/68. Retd GD 10/8/76.
HALLORAN G. M. Born 28/7/44. Commd 6/9/68. Sqn Ldr 1/7/84. Retd ADMIN 17/1/91.
HALLOWAY I., BEng. Born 26/2/64. Commd 1/8/86. Flt Lt 27/2/91. Retd ENG 14/9/96.
HALLOWS B. R. W., OBE DFC. Born 3/6/16. Commd 7/3/40. Wg Cdr 1/1/52. Retd GD 16/6/60.
HALLS B. J. Born 21/2/31. Commd 13/8/52. Flt Lt 9/1/58. Retd GD 21/2/69.
HALLS B. R. Born 10/2/41. Commd 19/1/68. Flt Lt 29/6/74. Retd ENG 29/6/80.
HALLS B. R. Born 10/2/41. Commd 10/7/87. Sqn Ldr 1/1/91. Retd ENG 31/3/93.
HALLS M. D. Born 22.1.38. Commd 25/7/59. Flt Lt 25/1/65. Retd GD(G) 6/4/79.
HALLS R. A. Born 31/1/19. Commd 29/8/46. Flt Lt 7/6/51. Retd SUP 8/5/56.
HALLUMS P. L. Born 8/6/18. Commd 6/12/56. Flt Lt 6/12/59. Retd ENG 8/6/73.
HALLWORTH B., MSc BSc. Born 30/12/35. Commd 3/1/61. Sqn Ldr 17/6/70. Retd ADMIN 3/1/77.
HALSALL M. C., MBCS MIEE. Born 13/3/53. Commd 1/7/82. Flt Lt 1/7/84. Retd ENG 13/3/91.
HALSEY J. C., MSc BSc(Eng) ACGI. Born 14/11/54. Commd 2/9/73. Sqn Ldr 1/7/89. Retd ENG 15/11/91.
HALSTEAD J. S. Born 22/8/46. Commd 20/10/67. Flt Lt 22/2/72. Retd GD 12/10/93.
HALSTEAD R. G., DFC. Born 10/6/22. Commd 7/1/44. Flt Lt 4/12/52. Retd GD 28/10/64.
HAMBIDGE C. D., BEM. Born 19/4/22. Commd 26/8/66. Flt Lt 26/8/68. Retd SEC 26/8/74.
HAMBIDGE J. E., MB BS. Born 14/9/58. Commd 29/8/80. Sqn Ldr 1/8/89. Retd MED 1/3/96.
HAMBLETON J. R. Born 24/2/39. Commd 31/7/62. Flt Lt 15/2/65. Retd GD 20/12/82.
HAMBLIN B. E. Born 22/4/46. Commd 28/4/65. Flt Lt 4/11/70. Retd GD 12/11/76. Re-instated 4/8/78. Flt Lt 28/7/72. Retd GD 1/4/90.
HAMBLING B. F. Born 29/11/46. Commd 3/12/70. Sqn Ldr 1/7/78. Retd ENG 29/11/84.
HAMBLY F. E. W. Born 11/6/31. Commd 21/5/52. Sqn Ldr 1/7/85. Retd GD 1/5/90.
HAMBLY P. F. Born 1/7/59. Commd 5/2/81. Sqn Ldr 1/7/92. Retd SUP 14/3/97.
HAMBRY E. V. Born 23/12/11. Commd 6/6/40. Sqn Ldr 1/8/47. Retd SEC 23/12/60.
HAMER J. L. Born 16/8/47. Commd 1/8/69. Flt Lt 1/2/75. Retd ENG 22/6/79.
HAMER N. J. T. Born 29/3/43. Commd 13/12/79. Sqn Ldr 1/1/90. Retd GD 14/9/96.
HAMER T. L., BSc. Born 19/1/51. Commd 21/1/73. Sqn Ldr 1/7/82. Retd GD(G) 21/1/89.
HAMER T. M., AFC AFM. Born 10/11/23. Commd 24/2/55. Sqn Ldr 1/1/69. Retd GD 24/1/82.
HAMES C. S. Born 29/9/22. Commd 1/1/43. Flt Lt 1/7/46. Retd GD 28/9/55.
HAMILL J. I. Born 16/4/23. Commd 6/7/44. Wg Cdr 1/1/63. Retd GD 16/10/75.
HAMILL J. W. Born 31/10/40. Commd 26/5/61. Sqn Ldr 1/1/88. Retd GD 2/12/92.
HAMILL P. A. Born 31/12/29. Commd 19/4/56. Wg Cdr 1/1/74. Retd GD 18/4/84.
HAMILL R., BSc. Born 7/4/51. Commd 5/5/71. Flt Lt 15/4/74. Retd GD 7/4/89.
HAMILL-KEAYS W. J. P. Born 11/3/40. Commd 16/9/76. Sqn Ldr 1/7/84. Retd ADMIN 1/7/87.
HAMILTON A. F., DSO DFC. Born 15/12/12. Commd 12/8/32. Wg Cdr 1/10/46. Retd GD 23/12/59.
HAMILTON A. G., MIMgt. Born 3/2/29. Commd 30/7/52. Sqn Ldr 1/7/63. Retd SEC 8/9/72.
HAMILTON A. G. Born 23/12/47. Commd 2/12/66. Flt Lt 2/6/72. Retd GD 15/6/76.
HAMILTON A. R. Born 12/3/46. Commd 54/7/79. Flt Lt 5/4/81. Retd SUP 5/4/89.
HAMILTON B., CBE DFC AFC FRIN MRAeS FIMgt. Born 18/10/23. Commd 1/7/46. A Cdre 1/7/69. Retd GD 9/6/78.
HAMILTON B. I. L., MRAeS. Born 7/10/34. Commd 10/2/54. Sqn Ldr 1/1/72. Retd GD 4/5/88.
HAMILTON D. R. Born 24/7/48. Commd 28/4/67. Gp Capt 1/1/95. Retd GD 12/9/97.
HAMILTON F. B. Born 28/4/21. Commd 28/7/43. Sqn Ldr 1/1/56. Retd GD 11/5/64.
HAMILTON F. J., MIMgt. Born 21/6/36. Commd 2/4/57. Gp Capt 1/1/86. Retd GD 21/6/91.
HAMILTON G. Born 18/4/47. Commd 1/9/86. Flt Lt 15/10/73. Retd GD 2/4/93.
HAMILTON I. B. Born 23/6/33. Commd 24/5/53. Sqn Ldr 1/1/66. Retd GD 23/6/71.
HAMILTON I. B. Born 30/3/37. Commd 23/1/64. Flt Lt 1/4/66. Retd PRT 30/3/75.
HAMILTON J. M., BSc. Born 19/6/53. Commd 17/9/72. Sqn Ldr 1/7/88. Retd ENG 30/11/92.
HAMILTON M. B. Born 3/4/11. Commd 19/12/31. Wg Cdr 1/10/46. Retd GD 2/6/48 rtg Gp Capt.
HAMILTON M. L., DFC. Born 31/1/18. Commd 25/9/42. Sqn Ldr 1/10/55. Retd GD 22/10/57.
HAMILTON N. I. Born 13/8/43. Commd 10/5/64. A Cdre 1/1/96. Retd GD 1/2/98.

HAMILTON P. D., BMet. Born 23/3/61. Commd 29/1/82. Flt Lt 15/4/84. Retd GD 23/3/99.
HAMILTON R. C. F. Born 31/8/27. Commd 12/6/51. Flt Lt 17/5/56. Retd GD(G) 14/12/74.
HAMILTON R. J., BSc. Born 2/1/50. Commd 22/10/72. Sqn Ldr 1/1/84. Retd GD 22/10/88.
HAMILTON R. McC. Born 16/8/23. Commd 11/8/44. Flt Lt 15/5/48. Retd GD 16/8/68 rtg Sqn Ldr.
HAMILTON T. A. P., BSc DCAe CEng MRAeS. Born 10/8/35. Commd 30/9/55. Wg Cdr 1/7/72. Retd ENG 1/7/75.
HAMILTON T. E. Born 29/11/44. Commd 21/10/65. Gp Capt 1/1/95. Retd GD(G) 14/9/96.
HAMILTON T. S. Born 6/11/60. Commd 30/3/89. Flt Lt 30/3/91. Retd ENG 6/5/94.
HAMILTON-BROWN T. H. Born 25/6/17. Commd 26/11/42. Sqn Ldr 1/7/56. Retd ENG 25/6/66.
HAMILTON-GREY D. Born 24/3/38. Commd 12/11/63. Wg Cdr 1/7/79. Retd SUP 9/4/83.
HAMILTON-IRVINE W. D. Born 27/7/41. Commd 8/12/61. Flt Lt 10/2/67. Retd GD 18/7/72.
HAMILTON-RUMP D. J. Born 23/4/43. Commd 17/12/64. A Cdre 1/1/93. Retd GD 8/1/94.
HAMLETT D. M., BA. Born 23/9/12. Commd 30/8/51. Sqn Offr 1/1/65. Retd SEC 4/2/68.
HAMLEY D. B. D. Born 9/4/27. Commd 7/4/48. Wg Cdr 1/1/65. Retd GD 1/6/78.
HAMLEY P. O. V. Born 24/3/22. Commd 22/2/45. Flt Lt 19/6/52. Retd GD 30/5/56.
HAMLIN D. E., MA. Born 21/4/32. Commd 28/9/54. Flt Lt 28/12/55. Retd GD 28.9.70.
HAMLIN D. P. A., BA. Born 18/9/59. Commd 11/9/77. Flt Lt 15/10/81. Retd GD 8/8/00.
HAMLYN K. Born 12/4/46. Commd 13/12/79. Sqn Ldr 1/1/91. Retd SUP 14/3/97.
HAMM D. J. Born 16/4/36. Commd 22/4/68. Flt Lt 15/8/73. Retd ADMIN 22/4/84.
HAMMANS G. D. Born 4/7/28. Commd 11/4/51. Fg Offr 11/4/53. Retd SUP 12/4/56.
HAMMANS M. P. Born 3/8/59. Commd 20/1/81. Sqn Ldr 1/1/95. Retd GD 1/1/98.
HAMMATT D. A., AFC DFM*. Born 17/11/19. Commd 30/3/42. Sqn Ldr 1/7/50.Retd GD 12/12/58.
HAMMETT R. J., BSc. Born 27/6/50. Commd 24/9/72. Wg Cdr 1/7/91. Retd SY 14/3/96.
HAMMOND B. G., FCA. Born 23/4/34. Commd 11/4/57. Gp Capt 1/1/81. Retd ADMIN 15/9/84.
HAMMOND D. J., FHCIMA MIMgt. Born 9/10/36. Commd 5/10/56. Wg Cdr 1/7/76. Retd ADMIN 11/2/85.
HAMMOND D. R. Born 2/10/51. Commd 21/9/72. Sqn Ldr 1/1/87. Retd GD 1/1/90.
HAMMOND E. J., CEng MRAeS MIEE. Born 24/7/33. Commd 30/4/59. Wg Cdr 1/1/74. Retd ENG 26/7/83.
HAMMOND L. C. Born 16/6/42. Commd 9/11/70. Sqn Ldr 1/1/80. Retd SUP 16/6/97.
HAMMOND L. J. C. Born 26/7/35. Commd 22/1/54. Sqn Ldr 1/1/71. Retd GD 1/1/74.
HAMMOND M. K., BSc CEng MIEE. Born 1/3/58. Commd 17/8/80. Sqn Ldr 1/1/90. Retd ENG 17/8/96.
HAMMOND O. M. Born 30/10/45. Commd 8/1/65. Flt Ltd 8/7/70. Retd GD 31/12/75.
HAMMOND P. R. A. Born 30/11/41. Commd 1/4/71. Fg Offr 1/10/73. Retd SUP 22/11/74.
HAMMOND R. J. Born 21/4/34. Commd. 14/1/53. Flt Lt 21/10/59. Retd GD 21/4/72.
HAMMOND S. H. J., BEM. Born 7/7/14. Commd 27/10/55. Flt Lt 27/10/61. Retd ENG 23/7/69.
HAMMOND T. L. Born 7/6/53. Commd 5/7/73. Flt Lt 5/1/79. Retd GD 12/8/90.
HAMMOND T. M., MB ChB MRCGP DRCOG DAvMed. Born 12/9/58. Commd 19/12/80. Sqn Ldr 1/2/90. Retd MED 19/12/96.
HAMMOND-DOUTRE G. I. Born 15/2/36. Commd 22/8/59. Sqn Ldr 1/1/81. Retd GD 15/2/91.
HAMON S. Born 13/5/47. Commd 2/11/88. Flt Lt 2/11/92. Retd GD(G) 14/3/96.
HAMPER K. L., BSc. Born 7/7/56. Commd 23/9/79. Flt Lt 23/12/82. Retd GD(G) 23/9/95.
HAMPSON L., MIMgt. Born 23/7/24. Commd 13/5/44. Gp Capt 1/7/76. Retd GD 24/4/79.
HAMPSON S. T. J. Born 20/4/21. Commd 11/8/43. Sqn Ldr 1/7/56. Retd ENG 20/4/71.
HAMPTON A. A. Born 5/11/21. Commd 11/5/44. Flt Lt 4/6/53. Retd GD(G) 13/11/71.
HAMPTON A. G. N. Born 13/3/30. Commd 30/7/52. Flt Lt 30/1/55. Retd GD 1/10/58.
HAMPTON D. J. Born 6/10/26. Commd 25/10/46. Flt Lt 25/4/50. Retd GD 6/10/64.
HAMPTON G., OBE DFC. Born 26/8/19. Commd 28/11/42. Wg Cdr 1/1/58. Retd GD 28/8/66.
HAMPTON R., AFC. Born 1/5/24. Commd 3/8/45. Gp Capt. 1/7/71. Retd GD 1/5/79.
HANAFIN B. D., DFC. Born 1/1/21. Commd 10/4/41. Sqn Ldr 1/7/55. Retd GD 17/2/61.
HANAGAN R. M., MBE. Born 26/6/12. Commd 23/4/53. Flt Lt 1/6/56. Retd CAT 16/7/68 rtg Sqn Ldr.
HANBURY T. J., BDS LDSRCS. Born 26/9/37. Commd 18/9/60. Wg Cdr 6/8/74. Retd DEL 31/12/82.
HANCOCK C. S. Born 10/8/38. Commd 13/10/61. Sqn Ldr 1/1/80. Retd ADMIN 10/4/86.
HANCOCK D. J. Born 23/10/24. Commd 14/2/45. Flt Lt 14/8/48. Retd GD 23/10/67.
HANCOCK J. E. G., DFC AE. Born 18/6/11. Commd 5/5/40. Sqn Ldr 1/7/50. Retd GD(G) 2/9/61.
HANCOCK L.T. F. Born 1/9/13. Commd 12/11/42. Sqn Ldr 1/7/53. Retd ENG 1/9/68.
HANCOCK N. P. W., DFC. Born 4/8/19. Commd 6/2/39. Sqn Ldr 1/8/47. Retd GD 12/8/58 rtg Wg Cdr.
HANCOCK P. W. Born 3/5/19. Commd 14/11/43. Sqn Ldr 1/4/56. Retd ENG 30/3/77.
HANCOCK R. A., OBE CEng MRAeS MIEE. Born 26/12/30. Commd 16/11/51. Wg Cdr 1/1/72. Retd ENG 12/8/85.
HANCOX I. R., BSc CEng MRAeS. Born 18/2/49. Commd 24/1/73. Flt Lt 24/4/75. Retd ENG 24/4/82.
HAND G. J., AFC DPhysEd. Born 4/6/47. Commd 11/8/69. Sqn Ldr 1/7/81. Retd ADMIN 14/3/96.
HANDFIELD R. Born 19/4/49. Commd 31/7/70. Flt Lt 31/7/73. Retd GD 2/2/82.
HANDLEY C., MA BM BCh FRCS(Edin). Born 15/10/49. Commd 20/2/73. Wg Cdr 16/7/88. Retd MED 20/2/95.
HANDLEY D. J. Born 17/7/46. Commd 4/7/85. Flt Lt 4/7/89. Retd ADMIN 14/3/97.
HANDLEY F. M. Born 22/8/12. Commd 26/9/41. Flt Lt 17/10/47. Retd SUP 22/8/67.
HANDLEY R. Born 12/4/30. Commd 9/12/65. Sqn Ldr 27/12/72. Retd EDN 9/12/73.
HANDS E. C. Born 30/12/47. Commd 17/7/75. Flt Lt 17/7/77. Retd ENG 30/12/85.
HANDS G. T. Born 19/11/13. Commd 18/2/43. Sqn Ldr 1/1/54. Retd ENG 19/5/72.
HANDS M. W. Born 30/5/42. Commd 27/1/61. Flt Lt 27/7/66. Retd GD 15/2/80.

HANDS P. J. F., IEng MIMgt. Born 20/10/40. Commd 23/11/78. Sqn Ldr 1/1/88. Retd ENG 1/5/95.
HANDSCOMB K. L. Born 26/12/29. Commd 11/1/55. Sqn Ldr 1/7/83. Retd GD 26/12/87.
HANDY R. B., MCIPD. Born 4/10/43. Commd 30/7/64. Sqn Ldr 1/1/87. Retd OPS SPT 19/4/99.
HANFORD F. J., BA. Born 26/8/41. Commd 14/11/71. Flt Lt 14/5/74. Retd SUP 23/6/96.
HANKIN E. C. H. Born 23/6/07. Commd 16/1/47. Flt Lt 4/1/51. Retd SUP 8/11/55.
HANKINSON K. Born 18/9/24. Commd 23/4/53. Flt Lt 23/10/56. Retd GD 13/12/78.
HANKINSON K. W., BA. Born 19/4/52. Commd 12/1/75. Flt Lt 12/4/76. Retd GD 1/10/91.
HANKINSON R. C. D., MSc BA MBCS. Born 12/7/52. Commd 24/6/71. Sqn Ldr 1/1/84. Retd SUP 12/7/90.
HANLEY-LANDERS J. E. Born 5/1/50. Commd 14/10/71. Flt Lt 11/3/78. Retd GD(G) 5/1/88.
HANLON D. J., BSc. Born 15/8/49. Commd 22/10/72. Flt Lt 22/7/73. Retd GD 22/10/88.
HANLON R. E. Born 7/8/41. Commd 12/7/68. Sqn Ldr 1/7/80. Retd GD 5/4/93.
HANLON T. G., FRAes FIMgt. Born 10/7/47. Commd 5/11/65. Gp Capt 1/1/95. Retd GD 26/4/00.
HANMORE D. Born 22/2/25. Commd 9/6/45. Flt Lt 27/5/54. Retd GD 24/4/66.
HANN D. W. Born 22/8/35. Commd 9/7/54. AVM 1/1/85. Retd GD 17/8/89.
HANN M. P., BA. Born 24/8/37. Commd 7/10/63. Sqn Ldr 1/7/76. Retd GD 7/10/79.
HANN P. G., BEM CEng MRAeS MIMgt. Born 13/8/16. Commd 12/4/51. Wg Cdr 1/1/68. Retd ENG 5/9/71.
HANNA M. A. Born 6/8/59. Commd 20/7/78. Flt Lt 20/1/84. Retd GD 8/10/88.
HANNA R. G., AFC*. Born 28/8/28. Commd 2/ 5/51. Sqn Ldr 1/1/68. Retd GD 14/5/71.
HANNAFORD A. G. Born 19/2/38. Commd 23/10/59. Sqn Ldr 1/7/72. Retd SEC 19/2/76.
HANNAFORD E. R. Born 27/8/43. Commd 9/2/62. Wg Cdr 1/1/90. Retd GD 4/12/98.
HANNAFORD R. Born 25/8/21. Commd 11/3/43. Flt Lt 11/3/49. Retd SUP 12/9/50. Re-employed 28/4/52. Wg Cdr
    1/1/69. Retd 31/7/75.
HANNAH F. J. Born 18/7/20. Commd 25/4/43. Flt Lt 29/11/51. Retd GD 11/5/57.
HANNAH K. J. E., MVO AFC. Born 16/8/26. Commd 3/5/46. Wg Cdr 1/1/70. Retd GD 14/2/76.
HANNAH M. Born 16/8/22. Commd 10/9/43. Wg Cdr 1/7/72. Retd GD 16/8/77.
HANNAM G. I. Born 1/8/48. Commd 29/4/71. Sqn Ldr 1/1/85. Retd GD 1/1/88.
HANNANT J. W., DFC. Born 19/2/15. Commd 5/1/42. Flt Lt 1/9/45. Retd PE 26/4/69.
HANNAY T. J. Born 2/9/29. Commd 14/8/53. Flt Lt 12/4/59. Retd GD 30/9/75.
HANNEY J. P. Born 12/12/33. Commd 7/2/57. Flt Lt 12/12/57. Retd GD 26/10/62.
HANNIGAN C. R. Born 28/1/23. Commd 13/1/52. Flt Lt 13/7/55. Retd GD 14/3/68.
HANNIGAN The Rev J. B. Born 20/4/30. Commd 18/10/61. Retd 18/10/81 Wg Cdr.
HANNINGTON R. H., CEng MRAeS. Born 8/7/40. Commd 17/7/62. Sqn Ldr 1/7/72. Retd ENG 8/7/78.
HANNINGTON R. P. H., MBA BEng CEng MIEE MIMgt. Born 27/11/52. Commd 21/1/75. Wg Cdr 1/7/89. Retd ENG
    12/1/97.
HANNS D. W. G. Born 3/12/37. Commd 17/5/79. Sqn Ldr 1/7/89. Retd GD 3/12/93.
HANSEN E. J. Born 3/5/32. Commd 8/10/52. Flt Lt 6/3/58. Retd GD 14/11/71.
HANSLIP N. C., MSc MRAeS DCAe. Born 14/5/23. Commd 9/8/50. Sqn Ldr 9/7/57. Retd EDN 3/2/65.
HANSON B. Born 22/8/39. Commd 10/12/65. Sqn Ldr 1/7/75. Retd GD 18/7/83.
HANSON B. T. Born 28/10/29. Commd 23/3/51. Flt Lt 13/2/57. Retd GD 30/7/70.
HANSON J. H. Born 16/6/35. Commd 24/6/53. Flt Lt 29/4/59. Retd GD 8/3/73.
HANSON P. C. Born 26/1/54. Commd 11/2/93. Flt Lt 11/2/97. Retd ADMIN 15/9/97.
HANSON T. H., CEng MRAeS. Born 10/10/05. Commd 26/6/41. Sqn Ldr 1/8/47. Retd ENG 25/11/54.
HARBISON W., CB CBE AFC. Born 11/4/22. Commd 6/11/42. AVM 1/1/75. Retd GD 31/3/77.
HARBORD H. R., CEng MRAeS MIMgt. Born 12/5/22. Commd 19/6/52. Wg Cdr 1/1/71. Retd ENG 31/3/77.
HARBORNE M. P., BSc. Born 29/5/56. Commd 15/9/74. Flt Lt 15/4/79. Retd GD 29/5/94.
HARCOMBE R. T. Born 18/12/31. Commd 24/1/63. Sqn Ldr 1/1/77. Retd ENG 18/1/84.
HARCOURT-SMITH B. Born 18/7/34. Commd 18/6/52. Wg Cdr 1/7/73. Retd GD 25/2/85.
HARCOURT-SMITH Sir David., GBE KCB DFC FRAeS. Born 14/10/31. Commd 30/7/52. ACM 1/1/87. Retd GD
    20/5/89.
HARDAKER S. Born 5/5/21. Commd 28/9/61. Sqn Ldr 1/1/72. Retd ENG 30/3/76.
HARDCASTLE H., CEng MRAeS. Born 28/8/20. Commd 3/8/50. Wg Cdr 1/7/69. Retd ENG 28/8/71.
HARDCASTLE J. E. F. Born 15/9/30. Commd 19/4/50. Sqn Ldr 1/1/62. Retd GD 15/9/68.
HARDCASTLE W. D. Born 20/2/32. Commd 27/1/77. Flt Lt 27/1/80. Retd ADMIN 28/5/82.
HARDEN K. J. Born 16/4/44. Commd 12/7/79. Wg Cdr 1/7/91. Retd ADMIN 16/4/99.
HARDEN R. H. Born 16/2/43. Commd 14/2/69. Flt Lt 6/10/71. Retd GD 18/2/81.
HARDHAM J. A. Born 18/10/28. Commd 8/9/53. Flt Lt 22/5/57. Retd GD 25/10/66.
HARDIE C. B. H. Born 30/4/40. Commd 19/12/61. Flt Lt 19/6/64. Retd GD 29/9/83.
HARDIE C. H. C. Born 27/10/33. Commd 16/7/52. Flt Lt 12/12/57. Retd GD 27/10/71.
HARDIE J. D. V. Born 8/9/48. Commd 1/8/69. Flt Lt 1/8/72. Retd GD 3/2/81.
HARDIE J. W. Born 5/9/37. Commd 4/3/71. Flt Lt 4/3/73. Retd GD 4/3/79.
HARDIE P. D. Born 23/1/49. Commd 2/12/66. Sqn Ldr 1/1/85. Retd GD 14/3/96.
HARDIE T. J., AFC. Born 22/8/29. Commd 12/6/51. Flt Lt 12/12/55. Retd GD 22/8/67.
HARDING A. G., MSc BSc. Born 10/6/48. Commd 27/2/70. Sqn Ldr 1/7/84. Retd ENG 1/10/89.
HARDING C. D. E. Born 14/9/64. Commd 15/3/84. Flt Lt 15/9/90. Retd OPS SPT 14/3/00.
HARDING D. A. W. Born 14/4/37. Commd 23/9/66. Flt Lt 23/9/68. Retd GD 14/12/85.
HARDING J. J. H., BEM. Born 1/7/08. Commd 24/1/43. Sqn Ldr 1/7/53. Retd SUP 28/7/60.

HARDING J. V., CBE. Born 9/5/40. Commd 31/7/62. Gp Capt 1/1/90. Retd GD 9/8/95.
HARDING J. W. Born 15/1/34. Commd 27/5/53. Flt Lt 29/4/59. Retd GD 15/1/72.
HARDING J. W. W. Born 14/10/45. Commd 7/7/67. Sqn Ldr 1/1/82. Retd GD(G) 8/11/93.
HARDING K. A. Born 10/4/65. Commd 19/7/84. Flt Lt 19/1/90. Retd GD 29/7/96.
HARDING K. O., OBE. Born 10/12/37. Commd 19/2/57. Gp Capt 1/1/86. Retd GD 2/4/91.
HARDING M. S. Born 6/7/60. Commd 27/3/80. Flt Lt 27/9/85. Retd GD 12/7/99.
HARDING P. E., DPhysEd. Born 27/3/42. Commd 11/8/69. Sqn Ldr 1/7/84. Retd ADMIN 15/8/94.
HARDING P. G., MBE. Born 3/6/20. Commd 18/7/49. Flt Lt 4/1/51. Retd RGT 19/12/51.
HARDING P. J., MIMgt. Born 13/7/39. Commd 4/9/58. Sqn Ldr 1/1/70. Retd SUP 13/7/77.
HARDING P. J. Born 5/7/48. Commd 1/8/69. Sqn Ldr 1/1/81. Retd SY 5/7/87.
HARDING P. J., CB CBE AFC. Born 1/6/40. Commd 12/3/60. AVM 1/1/89. Retd GD 1/6/98.
HARDING P. M. Born 1/7/25. Commd 6/10/51. Flt Offr 12/3/59. Retd SEC 6/5/61.
HARDING R. M., PhD BSc MB BS DAvMed AFOM MRAeS. Born 17/7/50. Commd 5/3/72. Wg Cdr 12/7/89. Retd MED 21/4/95.
HARDING R. R. Born 16/3/26. Commd 1/10/54. Wg Cdr 1/7/67. Retd GD 16/3/84.
HARDING S. J. Born 19/11/41. Commd 24/4/80. Sqn Ldr 1/7/90. Retd ENG 29/7/95.
HARDING S. J. Born 4/11/57. Commd 28/2/80. Sqn Ldr 1/1/93. Retd ADMIN 1/1/96.
HARDING W. H. Born 4/10/12. Commd 11/1/45. Flt Lt 23/5/55. Retd GD(G) 24/4/64.
HARDING-MORRIS S. Born 31/3/56. Commd 10/5/90. Flt Lt 2/9/95. Retd MED(T) 14/3/96.
HARDINGE N. G. Born 26/3/36. Commd 6/7/62. Flt Lt 1/4/66. Retd GD 23/6/74.
HARDISTY R. W. Born 29/4/44. Commd 22/2/63. Flt Lt 22/8/68. Retd GD 28/4/76.
HARDLESS J. W. Born 16/8/30. Commd 17/1/51. Flt Lt 17/7/55. Retd GD 16/8/68.
HARDMAN C. Born 29/3/21. Commd 21/9/43. Sqn Ldr 1/7/63. Retd GD 31/7/68.
HARDMAN K. P., BSc CEng MRAeS. Born 17/3/28. Commd 30/11/50. Sqn Ldr 17/2/65 Retd EDN 14/7/73.
HARDS P. H. Born 9/4/17. Commd 24/4/43. Sqn Ldr 1/7/56. Retd GD 28/10/72.
HARDSTAFF J., MBE. Born 28/2/35. Commd 27/5/53. Air Cdre 1/1/84. Retd GD 1/4/88.
HARDWICK B. J. Born 7/10/30. Commd 24/2/67. Flt Lt 24/2/72. Retd GD 12/3/77.
HARDWICK E. A. Born 17/8/47. Commd 26/5/67. Sqn Ldr 1/7/81. Retd ENG 17/8/86.
HARDWICK J. R. Born 13/10/33. Commd 17/12/52. Gp Capt 1/7/80. Retd GD 6/5/88.
HARDY A. J., BPhil MCIPD DPhysEd DipTM CertEd. Born 6/6/35. Commd 14/9/79. Sqn Ldr 1/7/86. Retd ADMIN 6/6/93.
HARDY E. Born 25/5/18. Commd 12/7/62. Flt Lt 12/7/65. Retd ENG 2/9/72.
HARDY F. O. C. Born 26/3/29. Commd 27/2/50. Flt Lt 22/4/66. Retd GD 26/3/67.
HARDY M. J. Born 15/3/34. Commd 12/1/52. Gp Capt 1/7/74. Retd GD 26/11/76.
HARDY O. L., DFC* AFC. Born 31/7/22. Commd 1/9/45. Wg Cdr 1/1/59. Retd GD 20/8/69.
HARDY R., MBE. Born 14/6/27. Commd 4/2/48. Wg Cdr 1/1/70. Retd SY 31/7/76.
HARDY R. A. Born 25/5/49. Commd 8/9/77. Flt Lt 8/3/84. Retd SUP 23/5/93.
HARDY R. J. Born 24/7/51. Commd 13/9/70. Fg Offr 13/9/73. Retd GD 24/12/74.
HARDY W. W. G. Born 21/6/37. Commd 26/9/57. Sqn Ldr 1/1/71. Retd SY 21/6/77.
HARDY-SMITH B. A. Born 10/12/41. Commd 11/7/64. Flt Lt 4/5/72. Retd GD 10/12/79.
HARE C. M. Born 23/11/09. Commd 17/1/41. Flt Lt 1/9/45. Retd GD(G) 17/1/60.
HARE E. W. F., OBE MRAeS FIMgt. Born 12/9/23. Commd 12/11/43. Gp Capt 1/7/69. Retd GD 12/9/73.
HARE J. M. Born 22/7/33. Commd 30/9/53. Sqn Ldr 1/1/64. Retd GD 14/9/73.
HARE M. W. J., AFC LLB. Born 9/1/55. Commd 16/9/73. Sqn Ldr 1/1/86. Retd GD 12/4/88.
HARGRAVE G. W. Born 11/1/24. Commd 1/1/63. Flt Lt 1/1/63. Retd EDN 31/8/67.
HARGREAVES A. S. Born 24/9/43. Commd 17/7/64. Wg Cdr 1/1/88. Retd ADMIN 6/1/97.
HARGREAVES D. A. Born 28/9/57. Commd 19/12/76. Sqn Ldr 1/7/93. Retd GD 1/1/97.
HARGREAVES D. J. Born 1/4/44. Commd 17/12/65. Sqn Ldr 1/1/78. Retd GD 1/4/94.
HARGREAVES G., CEng MRAeS C Chem MRSC. Born 1/12/35. Commd 2/1/62. Wg Cdr 1/7/78. Retd ENG 1/6/86.
HARGREAVES J. G., CBE. Born 17/3/37. Commd 6/8/58. A Cdre 1/1/93. Retd SUP 1/1/93.
HARGREAVES K. Born 10/7/43. Commd 14/6/63. Flt Lt 14/12/68. Retd GD 10/7/81. Re-entered 19/5/82. Sqn Ldr 1/7/90. Retd GD 10/7/99.
HARGREAVES L. J. Born 18/3/34. Commd 30/7/52. Sqn Ldr 1/1/65. Retd GD 22/3/72.
HARGREAVES L. N. M., PhD BSc MB ChB DAvMed. Born 25/9/50. Commd 5/9/78. Wg Cdr 4/8/95. Retd MED 14/9/96.
HARGREAVES M. Born 3/7/44. Commd 14/6/63. Flt Lt 14/12/69. Retd SUP 3/7/82.
HARGREAVES R. S., BSc(Eng) MRAeS. Born 26/1/33. Commd 4/4/59. Wg Cdr 1/7/80. Retd GD 3/5/85.
HARKER F. G. Born 8/8/19. Commd 27/10/55. Flt Lt 27/10/61. Retd SUP 3/10/64.
HARKER W. D. Born 12/9/18. Commd 29/6/54. Flt Lt 29/6/59. Retd ENG 22/10/61.
HARKIN A. G., BSocSc. Born 20/8/63. Commd 26/4/87. Flt Lt 26/10/89. Retd ADMIN 14/9/96.
HARKIN D. J., BA. Born 25/1/52. Commd 20/9/71. Sqn Ldr 1/1/85. Retd GD 25/1/90.
HARLAND A. J., CEng MIMechE MRAeS. Born 16/6/33. Commd 20/2/55. Wg Cdr 1/7/79. Retd ENG 12/7/88.
HARLAND L. L., DFC*. Born 12/2/20. Commd 19/7/42. Wg Cdr 1/1/58. Retd GD 24/2/67.
HARLAND Sir Reginald E. W., KBE CB AE MA CEng FIMechE FIEE FRAeS CBIM. Born 30/5/20. Commd 3/10/39. AM 1/1/74. Retd ENG 8/8/77.
HARLAND W. G. F., BA. Born 27/5/48. Commd 1/10/70. Flt Lt 1/7/71. Retd GD 14/5/96.

HARLE D. D. Born 28/3/51. Commd 25/2/72. Flt Lt 25/2/75. Retd GD 28/3/89.
HARLEY G. P. Born 28/10/64. Commd 4/12/86. Flt Lt 4/6/92. Retd GD 14/3/97.
HARLING R., DFC. Born 25/10/20. Commd 14/1/45. Flt Lt 14/7/48. Retd GD 31/3/62.
HARLOW D. M. Born 8/1/41. Commd 14/5/62. Flt Lt 9/2/68. Retd GD 31/7/76.
HARLOW E. J. A. Born 10/3/43. Commd 17/7/64. Flt Lt 17/1/70. Retd GD 10/3/98.
HARLOW J. Born 16/9/21. Commd 21/4/44. Flt Lt 16/2/48. Retd GD 1/9/60.
HARLOW R. A., MB BS LMSSA MRCOG. Born 3/3/32. Commd 13/4/58. Wg Cdr 4/7/70. Retd MED 13/4/74.
HARMAN G. T. Born 19/12/16. Commd 9/8/41. Sqn Ldr 1/8/47. Retd GD 30/5/58.
HARMAN H. T. Born 10/2/99. Commd 6/11/40. Flt Lt 1/3/45. Retd ENG 17/10/48 rtg Sqn Ldr.
HARMAN J. D. Born 17/12/45. Commd 14/8/64. Flt Lt 14/2/70. Retd GD 23/11/83.
HARMAN P. J. Born 5/4/45. Commd 28/2/64. Flt Lt 28/8/69. Retd GD 21/1/76.
HARMSTON R. W. Born 15/4/37. Commd 24/2/67. Flt Lt 24/2/69. Retd SEC 15/4/75.
HARNETT E. E. Born 25/6/40. Commd 30/1/70. Sqn Ldr 1/1/79. Retd ADMIN 31/7/90.
HARPER A., AFC, CEng MRAeS MIMgt. Born 20/2/24. Commd 22/9/45. Wg Cdr 1/1/62. Retd GD 20/2/79.
HARPER B. A. H., CEng MRAeS. Born 5/2/41. Commd 30/8/66. Flt Lt 30/1/71. Retd ENG 30/8/82.
HARPER B. J. Born 22/4/37. Commd 24/6/55. Sqn Ldr 1/1/67. Retd GD 17/8/87.
HARPER B. L. S. Born 9/3/43. Commd 10/11/61. Sqn Ldr 1/7/81. Retd GD 9/3/98.
HARPER D. J., OBE AFC MIMgt. Born 28/3/24. Commd 8/11/44. Wg Cdr 1/7/62. Retd GD 1/9/76.
HARPER D. J. Born 9/5/27. Commd 2/3/49. Flt Lt 2/2/55. Retd GD 1/10/68.
HARPER D. P. Born 10/9/48. Commd 30/1/70. Fg Offr 18/7/72. Retd SUP 20/5/76.
HARPER H. R. Born 25/1/46. Commd 8/1/65. Sqn Ldr 1/1/89. Retd GD 14/3/96.
HARPER J. R. Born 18/5/31. Commd 17/12/52. Sqn Ldr 1/7/67. Retd GD 1/7/70.
HARPER J. W., DFC. Born 25/5/20. Commd 13/1/43. Sqn Ldr 1/1/64. Retd GD(G) 25/5/75.
HARPER K. I. Born 7/4/57. Commd 25/2/82. Flt Lt 13/2/86. Retd GD(G) 7/4/95.
HARPER N. B. Born 18/6/29. Commd 14/3/57. Flt Lt 14/9/61. Retd GD(G) 18/6/87.
HARPER P. J. C., DFC. Born 15/1/16. Commd 26/3/38. Flt Lt 3/9/45. Retd GD(G) 15/1/66 rtg Sqn Ldr.
HARPER R. A. Born 22/1/37. Commd 26/6/57. Flt Lt 28/7/65. Retd GD 1/5/75.
HARPER R. B. B., DPhysEd. Born 20/9/19. Commd 27/8/52. Flt Lt 27/8/56. Retd PE 28/4/69.
HARPER R. D. Born 12/1/47. Commd 3/10/69. Sqn Ldr 1/1/87. Retd GD 22/4/94.
HARPER S. E. R. Born 29/6/24. Commd 22/6/46. Flt Lt 4/1/51. Retd GD 29/6/67.
HARPER S. R. J., DFC BA. Born 15/10/21. Commd 16/7/44. Flt Lt 5/8/53. Retd SEC 4/11/61.
HARPHAM S. T., DFM. Born 6/6/16. Commd 29/10/42. Flt Lt 29/4/47. Retd SEC 28/9/63.
HARPUR W. Born 30/7/36. Commd 9/3/62. Flt Lt 22/5/68. Retd SUP 4/8/76. Reinstated 7/1/81. Flt Lt 25/10/72. Retd SUP 1/10/89.
HARRALL M. R. M. Born 13/1/40. Commd 25/7/59. Flt Lt 25/1/65. Retd GD 14/11/74.
HARRELD J. J. Born 14/7/33. Commd 17/1/52. Flt Lt 8/5/57. Retd GD 14/7/72.
HARRIDENCE R. P. S., DFC MIMgt. Born 12/7/22. Commd 20/11/42. Sqn Ldr 1/1/67. Retd GD(G) 1/10/74.
HARRIES G. O. Born 19/8/46. Commd 3/5/68. Sqn Ldr 1/1/81. Retd GD 19/8/90.
HARRIES The Rev H. R. M., MBE. Born 6/6/30. Commd 30/10/58. Retd GD 30/10/72. Wg Cdr.
HARRIES J. M., BA. Born 11/11/39. Commd 3/10/61. Sqn Ldr 11/5/71. Retd ADMIN 30/1/78.
HARRIES K. J., MA ACIS. Born 10/2/27. Commd 7/10/48. Sqn Ldr 1/1/62. Retd SEC 10/2/65.
HARRIES W. D. Born 15/5/34. Commd 25/2/53. Flt Lt 14/7/58. Retd GD 15/5/77.
HARRIES W. J. L., OBE MB BS FRCS LRCP. Born 17/10/21. Commd 2/1/47. Gp Capt 3/1/69. Retd MED 1/9/82.
HARRIES-JENKINS G., MA MPhil LLB. Born 13/7/31. Commd 18/11/53. Sqn Ldr 13/4/63. Retd EDN 11/3/70.
HARRILD D. J., DFC. Born 9/5/20. Commd 21/4/44. Sqn Ldr 1/1/69. Retd GD(G) 9/5/75.
HARRINGTON B. R. Born 17/11/20. Commd 24/6/44. Flt Lt 20/5/55. Retd SEC 17/11/75.
HARRINGTON D. G., BA CEng FIEE MIMgt. Born 14/1/38. Commd 23/7/58. Air Cdre 1/1/87. Retd ENG 2/4/89.
HARRINGTON D. H., BSc Dip Soton CEng MIEE. Born 31/10/33. Commd 23/9/55. Sqn Ldr 29/4/65. Retd EDN 17/1/76.
HARRINGTON J. Born 9/12/48. Commd 31/7/70. Flt Lt 31/7/73. Retd GD 18/6/76.
HARRINGTON L. Born 16/7/26. Commd 23/8/46. Sqn Ldr 1/7/56. Retd GD 16/7/64.
HARRINGTON M. V. P. H., CVO BA FIMgt. Born 19/9/36. Commd 17/12/57. Gp Capt 1/7/81. Retd GD 19/9/91.
HARRINGTON R. G., AFM. Born 6/12/23. Commd 23/8/56. Flt Lt 23/8/62. Retd GD 29/5/70.
HARRINGTON W. T., OBE. Born 31/5/07. Commd 30/6/41. Wg Cdr 1/1/54. Retd ENG 31/5/58.
HARRIS A., MCIPS. Born 10/7/23. Commd 22/9/44. Wg Cdr. Retd SUP 30/3/78.
HARRIS A. D. Born 19/6/30. Commd 25/10/51. Flt Lt 14/5/58. Retd GD 2/7/68.
HARRIS A. D. Born 30/7/55. Commd 8/6/84. Sqn Ldr 1/1/94. Retd GD 14/3/96.
HARRIS A. E., BSc. Born 6/11/43. Commd 10/7/67. Wg Cdr 1/7/83. Retd ADMIN 1/10/93.
HARRIS A. J., AFC. Born 11/10/22. Commd 4/5/50. Flt Lt 4/11/53. Retd GD 11/1/63.
HARRIS A. J. Born 28/12/16. Commd 22/9/55. Flt Lt 22/9/58. Retd SEC 12/2/72.
HARRIS A. J. Born 2/3/47. Commd 2/8/68. Sqn Ldr 1/1/80. Retd GD(G) 2/3/85.
HARRIS A. J., MSc BSc. Born 11/11/62. Commd 8/9/81. Sqn Ldr 1/1/94. Retd ENG 11/11/00.
HARRIS The Rt Rev Mgr A. J., VG. Born 6/5/40. Commd 24/10/77. Retd 5/4/94 BGp Capt.
HARRIS B. Born 21/6/31. Commd 22/7/55. Wg Cdr 1/1/70. Retd ENG 2/4/82.
HARRIS B. Born 13/10/37. Commd 22/8/59. Flt Lt 22/2/65. Retd GD 13/10/75.
HARRIS B. H. Born 26/12/27. Commd 27/2/52. Flt Lt 11/5/58. Retd GD 26/12/65.

HARRIS C. P. A., BSc. Born 31/7/44. Commd 22/12/71. Flt Lt 22/5/72. Retd GD 22/10/94.
HARRIS D. B. R. Born 8/3/29. Commd 1/10/53. Wg Cdr 1/1/71. Retd GD 8/3/84.
HARRIS D. J., MBE MSc. Born 1/11/38. Commd 29/3/62. Sqn Ldr 1/7/73. Retd ENG 3/1/78.
HARRIS D. P., CEng MIMarE. Born 29/8/35. Commd 27/7/70. Sqn Ldr 1/1/75. Retd ENG 30/4/82.
HARRIS E. A. Born 7/8/47. Commd 3/10/69. Wg Cdr 1/1/91. Retd GD(G) 14/9/96.
HARRIS E. A., MBE. Born 5/3/37. Commd 30/12/55. Gp Capt 1/7/89. Retd GD 5/8/92.
HARRIS E. C., DFC. Born 18/9/21. Commd 13/12/48. Flt Lt 11/11/54. Retd GD 22/3/68.
HARRIS E. H., BA MITD MIMgt. Born 30/9/32. Commd 24/12/64. Sqn Ldr 24/8/70. Retd ADMIN 22/11/84.
HARRIS G., OBE. Born 29/1/47. Commd 2/2/68. Wg Cdr 1/7/86. Retd ADMIN 11/6/96.
HARRIS H. J. Born 26/10/17. Commd 15/9/60. Flt Lt. 15/9/63. Retd SEC 27/10/72.
HARRIS H. S. T., DFC. Born 16/7/23. Commd 17/10/44. Flt Lt 17/4/48. Retd GD 1/5/68.
HARRIS I. W., DFC. Born 16/10/20. Commd 18/10/41. Sqn Ldr 1/1/55. Retd GD 16/10/63.
HARRIS J., OBE DFC. Born 21/9/20. Commd 2/8/41. Wg Cdr 1/1/58. Retd GD 21/9/67.
HARRIS J. Born 25/7/41. Commd 22/2/63. Sqn Ldr 1/1/74. Retd GD 25/7/79.
HARRIS The Rt Rev Mgr J. B. Born 17/9/31. Commd 6/6/66. Retd 25/3/88. Gp Capt.
HARRIS J. F. Born 26/11/27. Commd 7/8/59. Sqn Ldr 29/5/67. Retd ADMIN 1/4/77.
HARRIS J. G. Born 16/12/25. Commd 13/6/46. Flt Lt 15/8/62. Retd RGT 19/9/71.
HARRIS J. H. Born 21/10/22. Commd 25/8/60. Sqn Ldr 1/7/72. Retd ENG 23/7/73.
HARRIS J. P. Born 25/1/34. Commd 4/2/71. Sqn Ldr 1/7/84. Retd ENG 25/1/93.
HARRIS J. S. Born 31/3/57. Commd 20/5/82. Flt Lt 2/2/85. Retd ENG 31/3/95.
HARRIS J. V. Born 21/12/31. Commd 26/5/60. Flt Lt 26/5/66. Retd GD 17/2/67.
HARRIS K. Born 30/11/38. Commd 19/2/76. Sqn Ldr 1/1/85. Retd GD(G) 16/9/90.
HARRIS K. A. Born 6/10/30. Commd 7/1/71. Sqn Ldr 1/1/84. Retd ENG 4/10/86.
HARRIS K. B., MBE. Born 9/8/25. Commd 22/8/63. Sqn Ldr 1/1/76. Retd ENG 9/8/83.
HARRIS K. J., BSc CEng MIEE. Born 20/3/46. Commd 26/5/67. Wg Cdr 1/1/89. Retd ENG 20/3/01.
HARRIS L., MIMgt. Born 25/3/32. Commd 16/7/52. Wg Cdr 1/1/77. Retd GD(G) 25/3/87.
HARRIS L. R., BEM AIIP. Born 6/10/20. Commd 6/10/60. Sqn Ldr 1/7/71. Retd ENG 24/11/73.
HARRIS M. C. Born 18/6/40. Commd 12/8/63. Fg Offr 26/10/65. Retd GD(G) 11/2/67.
HARRIS M. C. S. Born 11/12/40. Commd 18/12/62. Flt Lt 1/2/67. Retd GD 10/1/79.
HARRIS M. G., DFC DFM. Born 18/8/19. Commd 3/7/41. Flt Lt 16/12/46. Retd GD 18/8/77.
HARRIS M. J., MA. Born 16/6/56. Commd 1/9/74. Flt Lt 15/10/78. Retd GD 16/6/94.
HARRIS N. G., DFC. Born 27/11/20. Commd 31/8/44. Flt Lt 28/2/49. Retd GD(G) 27/11/70.
HARRIS N. J. Born 13/3/44. Commd 27/3/70. Flt Lt 27/9/75. Retd GD 1/2/88.
HARRIS N. M. W. Born 9/5/09. Commd 9/10/39 Sqn Ldr 1/8/47. Retd SEC 13/10/51.
HARRIS P. C., BEM. Born 21/9/38. Commd 11/6/81. Flt Lt 11/6/85. Retd ENG 7/4/89.
HARRIS P. F., MBE. Born 11/7/29. Commd 10/2/55. Wg Cdr 1/7/75. Retd GD 11/7/84.
HARRIS P. I. Born 13/5/40. Commd 21/5/65. Flt Lt 26/7/67. Retd GD 21/9/74.
HARRIS P. T. Born 5/7/47. Commd 10/12/65. Sqn Ldr 1/1/84. Retd GD(G) 1/9/94.
HARRIS R., ACIS MIMgt. Born 27/11/35. Commd 18/11/66. Sqn Ldr 1/1/75. Retd SEC 3/7/79.
HARRIS R. C., BSc. Born 28/10/50. Commd 23/9/68. Flt Lt 15/10/72. Retd GD 28/10/88.
HARRIS R. C. Born 14/5/49. Commd 18/12/80. Wg Cdr 1/7/96. Retd SUP 1/6/01.
HARRIS R. D. Born 27/5/37. Commd 23/7/58. Sqn Ldr 1/1/70. Retd ENG 27/5/92.
HARRIS R. F., OBE MB ChB FRCP DCH. Born 22/6/42. Commd 16/9/63. Wg Cdr 7/8/80. Retd MED 19/3/89.
HARRIS R. G., MBE. Born 23/1/38. Commd 5.9.57. Sqn Ldr 1/1/76. Retd PI 3/8/78.
HARRIS R. G. StJ. Born 5/3/26. Commd 4/4/51. Sqn Ldr 1/1/69. Retd GD 31/12/73.
HARRIS R. J. L., FRSH MIDSH. Born 10/8/30. Commd 16/12/66. Wg Cdr 1/1/80. Retd MED(T) 10/8/85.
HARRIS R. W., MIMgt. Born 15/11/52. Commd 24/4/80. Flt Lt 24/7/83. Retd ADMIN 23/4/93.
HARRIS S. A., DFC. Born 8/6/21. Commd 2/10/44. Sqn Ldr 1/7/55. Retd GD 8/6/70.
HARRIS S. G. Born 7/10/19. Commd 22/9/55. Sqn Ldr 1/1/66. Retd ENG 31/3/77.
HARRIS S. W. Born 19/1/58. Commd 4/11/82. Flt Lt 22/10/85. Retd ENG 2/9/93.
HARRIS Sir John., KCB CBE. Born 3/6/38. Commd 25/6/58. AM 1/5/92. Retd GD 29/6/96.
HARRIS T. S., DFC. Born 2/12/22. Commd 9/5/42. Sqn Ldr 1/7/51. Retd GD 30/11/54.
HARRIS T. W. P. Born 31/7/45. Commd 3/6/65. Flt Lt 4/5/72. Retd SEC 3/5/78.
HARRIS V. Born 13/8/99. Commd 4/7/22. Wg Cer 1/1/40. Retd GD 15/2/45 rtg Gp Capt.
HARRIS W. C., BA. Born 23/12/41. Commd 5/11/65. Flt Lt 5/8/67. Retd GD 21/6/81.
HARRIS W. H. Born 25/1/20. Commd 21/4/45. Flt Lt 21/10/48. Retd GD 25/1/75.
HARRISON A., BA. Born 23/7/43. Commd 15/9/67. Sqn Ldr 1/7/79. Retd GD 1/7/85.
HARRISON A. J., CB CBE. Born 9/11/43. Commd 22/2/63. AVM 1/1/95. Retd GD 4/5/98.
HARRISON A. J. Born 9/10/42. Commd 17/5/63. Flt Lt 17/5/69. Retd GD 9/10/80.
HARRISON The Rev A. L., ALCD. Born 6/2/22. Commd 24/8/54. Retd 3/8/67 Sqn Ldr.
HARRISON A. R. Born 13/7/49. Commd 9/3/72. Flt Lt 9/9/77. Retd GD 15/11/87.
HARRISON B. P., BA. Born 29/8/56. Commd 28/9/80. Flt Lt 28/3/84. Retd ADMIN 28/9/96.
HARRISON D. E. Born 8/12/63. Commd 25/6/89. Flt Lt 25/6/93. Retd ADMIN 4/5/01.
HARRISON D. J. Born 13/7/42. Commd 2/4/65. Flt Lt 4/5/72. Retd PI 9/11/80.
HARRISON D. J., CBE FIMgt. Born 2/7/37. Commd 5/10/56. A Cdre 1/7/86. Retd ADMIN 2/7/92.
HARRISON E. G. G. Born 8/4/21. Commd 29/7/44. Sqn Ldr 1/4/55. Retd GD 1/8/68.

HARRISON E. M. Born 7/3/20. Commd 5/6/43. Sqn Ldr 1/1/55. Retd SEC 7/3/69.
HARRISON G. J. Born 26/9/50. Commd 28/7/88. Flt Lt 28/7/90. Retd SUP 8/5/93.
HARRISON G. S., BA. Born 8/6/44. Commd 30/5/71. Wg Cdr 1/1/87. Retd SUP 8/9/94.
HARRISON G. S., BA. Born 9/5/63. Commd 13/9/81. Sqn Ldr 1/7/95. Retd GD 9/5/01.
HARRISON H., AFC. Born 20/4/26. Commd 1/10/50. Gp Capt 1/1/74. Retd GD 27/4/81.
HARRISON I. Born 20/12/41. Commd 2/5/69. Flt Lt 8/3/72. Retd SEC 20/12/79.
HARRISON I. R. Born 12/10/33. Commd 18/11/65. Flt Lt 1/5/72. Retd GD(G) 1/5/80.
HARRISON J. A. Born 26/12/25. Commd 6/10/50. Sqn Ldr 1/1/61. Retd GD 15/1/67 rtg Wg Cdr.
HARRISON J. B. Born 5/9/08. Commd 6/6/40. Sqn Ldr 1/8/47. Retd SEC 5/9/57.
HARRISON J. D., BA. Born 22/1/53. Commd 6/3/77. Flt Lt 6/12/78. Retd GD 1/10/97.
HARRISON J. D., MIL. Born 18/7/46. Commd 28/11/69. Flt Lt 27/4/74. Retd ADMIN 12/6/84.
HARRISON J. G., AFC. Born 22/12/18. Commd 4/12/42. Sqn Ldr 1/1/52. Retd GD 20/1/54.
HARRISON J. G. M., MRCS LRCP. Born 3/2/25. Commd 26/11/63. Retd MED 26/11/67.
HARRISON J. L. Born 22/6/31. Commd 17/12/52. Flt Lt 17/6/55. Retd GD 22/6/69.
HARRISON J. R., BSc. Born 5/7/52. Commd 2/1/77. Flt Lt 2/11/78. Retd ENG 1/8/83.
HARRISON K. A., BSc. Born 7/12/38. Commd 31/7/59. Flt Lt 28/3/65. Retd GD 7/12/76.
HARRISON L. H. Born 8/9/29. Commd 10/8/50. Flt Lt 16/5/56. Retd GD 1/3/69.
HARRISON M. E. J., BSc. Born 30/10/33. Commd 5/9/57. Sqn Ldr 1/1/69. Retd ENG 29/4/77.
HARRISON N. A., MMedSci MB BS MRCP(UK) DTM&H DAvMed. Born 27/9/54. Commd 12/2/79. Wg Cdr 1/8/93. Retd MED 9/7/96.
HARRISON N. F., DSO AFC*. Born 5/5/20. Commd 17/12/51. Wg Cdr 1/7/62. Retd GD 1/12/66.
HARRISON P. J., CEng MIMechE MRAeS MIMgt. Born 23/12/44. Commd 15/7/66. Sqn Ldr 1/1/79. Retd ENG 23/12/82.
HARRISON P. M., BEng. Born 19/10/66. Commd 16/9/84. Fg Off 15/1/87. Retd ENG 6/2/90.
HARRISON R. Born 12/2/31. Commd 9/12/65. Flt Lt 9/12/70. Retd ENG 30/4/74.
HARRISON R. A., CEng MIMechE MRAeS. Born 4/8/29. Commd 16/6/55. Wg Cdr 1/1/69. Retd ENG 5/7/75.
HARRISON R. A. W., DFC. Born 25/6/24. Commd 18/7/44. Sqn Ldr 1/7/58. Retd GD 10/5/66.
HARRISON R. B. Born 25/4/16. Commd 21/11/39. Wg Cdr 1/1/60. Retd SUP 21/4/64.
HARRISON R. F. J. Born 18/1/44. Commd 12/7/63. Sqn Ldr 1/1/79. Retd GD 18/1/82.
HARRISON R. J. Born 29/8/11. Commd 26/11/41. Sqn Ldr 1/8/47. Retd GD 29/8/56.
HARRISON R. M. Born 13/3/44. Commd 5/7/67. Wg Cdr 1/7/94. Retd ENG 13/3/99.
HARRISON R. S. Born 19/9/37. Commd 6/8/63. Flt Lt 6/8/66. Retd EDN 31/12/69.
HARRISON R. S., MMS MIMgt. Born 27/11/46. Commd 21/4/67. Flt Lt 21/10/73. Retd ENG 27/11/84.
HARRISON S. E., DFC DFM. Born 13/9/19. Commd 2/7/42. Sqn Ldr 1/7/50. Retd GD 28/8/59.
HARRISON T. E., BA. Born 9/6/28. Commd 6/9/50. Sqn Ldr 1/1/61. Retd SEC 23/9/67.
HARRISON W. A. S., OBE MIMgt. Born 22/8/24. Commd 27/12/44. Wg Cdr 1/1/63 Retd GD 29/9/72.
HARRISON W. E. Born 26/10/21. Commd 27/10/44. Flt Lt 19/11/53. Retd GD 26/10/64.
HARRISON W. P. Born 10/6/44. Commd 1/10/65. Flt Lt 1/4/71. Retd GD 4/10/85.
HARROD J. B. Born 8/3/27. Commd 29/9/51. Flt Lt 13/2/57. Retd GD 8/3/65.
HARROP D., CEng MRAeS. Born 27/11/40. Commd 13/10/64. Sqn Ldr 1/7/92. Retd ENG 13/4/95.
HARROP D. R., MRAeS MIDPM. Born 17/11/38. Commd 22/6/60. Wg Cdr 1/7/90. Retd GD(G) 17/11/93.
HARROP G. G. Born 9/12/32. Commd 20/12/51. Flt Lt 4/4/57. Retd GD 9/12/90.
HARROP P. A., MA BA MIPM MIMgt. Born 12/10/51. Commd 20/6/72. Sqn Ldr 1/1/85. Retd ADMIN 12/10/88.
HARROP W. S., CEng MRAeS MIMgt. Born 10/4/22. Commd 23/8/56. Sqn Ldr 1/1/69. Retd ENG 31/12/75.
HARROW C. T., BSc CEng MRAeS. Born 26/3/42. Commd 15/7/63. Gp Capt 1/1/91. Retd ENG 26/3/94.
HARROW J. F. Born 2/3/27. Commd 23/4/47. Wg Cdr 1/1/79. Retd SY 2/3/84.
HARRYMAN M. J. Born 29/6/40. Commd 5/8/76. Sqn Ldr 1/1/88. Retd ADMIN 29/6/95.
HART C. M., BA MIMgt. Born 19/8/36. Commd 10/5/73. Sqn Ldr 1/1/84. Retd ENG 19/8/93.
HART D. Born 17/2/45. Commd 31/8/78. Sqn Ldr 1/7/85. Retd ADMIN 31/3/94.
HART D. C., BSc. Born 14/3/59. Commd 29/8/77. Sqn Ldr 1/1/92. Retd GD 14/3/97.
HART E. M. Born 24/5/45. Commd 26/4/84. Flt Lt 26/4/88. Retd ENG 23/4/94.
HART F. K., CEng MIMechE MRAeS. Born 22/3/27. Commd 23/1/52. Sqn Ldr 1/7/67. Retd ENG 22/3/87.
HART G. Born 27/9/32. Commd 20/8/52. Flt Lt 26/5/58. Retd GD 27/9/70.
HART I. B. Born 7/8/14. Commd 22/12/43. Flt Offr 22/12/49. Retd SEC 9/9/63.
HART J. S., FIMgt. Born 21/9/22. Commd 20/9/41. Gp Capt 1/7/67. Retd GD 31/5/71.
HART K. L. Born 2/9/37. Commd 2/9/55. Sqn Ldr 1/1/71. Retd GD 3/9/76.
HART L. R. Born 25/1/39. Commd 4/2/71. Sqn Ldr 1/7/89. Retd ADMIN 25/1/94.
HART P. I., DFC. Born 7/6/22. Commd 1/5/42. Sqn Ldr 1/4/55. Retd GD 8/10/66.
HART P. J. Born 1/8/31. Commd 31/12/52. Flt Lt 26/5/58. Retd GD 1/8/69.
HART P. T. Born 8/9/61. Commd 8/9/83. Sqn Ldr 1/1/94. Retd ADMIN 8/9/99.
HART R. E. E., OBE. Born 19/3/46. Commd 4/6/64. A Cdre 1/7/91. Retd ADMIN 30/6/94.
HART R. J. A. Born 30/3/43. Commd 23/3/67. Flt Lt 23/9/72. Retd GD(G) 5/12/85.
HARTE C. S. W. Born 22/3/15. Commd 12/9/38. Wg Cdr 1/1/51. Retd SUP 2/3/59.
HARTE J. K., OBE. Born 14/10/43. Commd 24/4/70. Wg Cdr 1/7/92. Retd GD 14/10/98.
HARTILL D. R. Born 24/3/51. Commd 27/3/75. Sqn Ldr 1/1/90. Retd GD 1/10/98.
HARTLAND D. V., MBE. Born 19/2/33. Commd 21/11/51. Sqn Ldr 1/1/70. Retd SUP 19/2/93.

HARTLEY I. G. Born 21/5/46. Commd 18/8/67. Sqn Ldr 1/7/86. Retd GD 12/6/99.
HARTLEY J., CEng MRAeS MIMgt MBE. Born 24/11/17. Commd 15/11/45. Wg Cdr 1/7/69. Retd ENG 24/11/72.
HARTLEY J. Born 24/9/43. Commd 19/5/69. Wg Cdr 1/7/88. Retd ADMIN 31/1/92.
HARTLEY J. C. Born 28/9/42. Commd 15/7/63. Fg Offr 15/1/64. Retd ENG 18/5/68.
HARTLEY J. W. Born 10/2/37. Commd 29/7/58. Flt Lt 13/5/64. Retd GD 1/1/76.
HARTLEY K. A. Born 26/8/48. Commd 27/2/70. Flt Lt 27/2/73. Retd GD 22/12/79.
HARTLEY M., CEng FRAeS MIMgt. Born 15/8/35. Commd 24/7/57. Sqn Ldr 1/1/67. Retd ENG 28/4/89.
HARTLEY R. P. H. Born 27/7/45. Commd 11/8/67. Flt Lt 11/2/73. Retd GD 1/10/87.
HARTLEY R.M., MBE Born 14/12/21. Commd 10/10/44. Sqn Ldr 15/2/65. Retd ADMIN 10/8/76.
HARTLEY S. McK. Born 25/11/47. Commd 17/7/70. Flt Lt 17/1/77. Retd GD(G) 5/1/89.
HARTLEY V., MA BA. Born 18/12/47. Commd 13/9/70. Sqn Ldr 15/1/81. Retd ADMIN 13/9/86.
HARTLEY-WOOLLEY A. H. Born 30/6/45. Commd 17/5/79. Sqn Ldr 1/1/89. Retd GD(G) 17/5/93.
HARTMAN G., DFC. Born 24/10/17. Commd 13/7/40. Sqn Ldr 1/1/57. Retd GD 27/2/59.
HARTNELL-PARKER B. K. Born 17/7/18. Commd 29/5/47. Sqn Ldr 1/1/62. Retd SUP 21/9/68.
HARTNETT F. E. L., OBE BSc. Born 3/9/40. Commd 10/8/65. Wg Cdr 1/1/80. Retd ADMIN 1/7/87.
HARTRIDGE B. W. A. Born 9/10/31. Commd 14/8/70. Flt Lt 14/8/73. Retd GD 15/7/75.
HARTWELL N. R. G. Born 6/7/23. Commd 26/8/43. Sqn Ldr 1/7/57. Retd ENG 30/6/78.
HARTY C. J. Born 8/9/62. Commd 23/10/86. Fg Off 23/10/88. Retd GD 23/10/89.
HARTY T. A. Born 21/9/20. Commd 2/4/53. Flt Lt 1/6/56. Retd RGT 2/9/72.
HARVARD I. C. Born 14/8/56. Commd 22/11/84. Flt Lt 22/11/86. Retd OPS SPT 14/8/00.
HARVATT B. E. Born 29/4/25. Commd 20/10/49. Sqn Ldr 1/1/59. Retd GD 30/1/76.
HARVEY A. D., MBE. Born 27/6/21. Commd 28/11/46. Wg Cdr 1/7/63. Retd SUP 27/6/66.
HARVEY B. Born 26/3/23. Commd 13/5/44. Flt Lt 1/5/52. Retd GD 1/4/64.
HARVEY D. L. Born 22/9/20. Commd 4/3/39. Wg Cdr 1/1/57. Retd GD 3/8/66.
HARVEY The Rev D. V. R., MTh BA. Born 2/4/37. Commd 9/12/65. Retd 2/4/92. Wg Cdr.
HARVEY G. C., MSc BSc AFIMA. Born 22/7/29. Commd 10/11/64. Wg Cdr 10/5/74. Retd ADMIN 30/9/77.
HARVEY G. F. Born 13/4/22. Commd 25/5/60. Flt Lt 26/5/63. Retd GD(G) 13/4/77.
HARVEY H. Born 20/3/13. Commd 28/12/40. Wg Cdr 1/7/56. Retd ENG 16/4/68.
HARVEY H., GM. Born 14/6/22. Commd 13/7/48. Flt Lt 19/6/52. Retd GD 9/5/66.
HARVEY H. Born 22/11/05. Commd 9/5/40. Flt Lt 1/9/45. Retd GD(G) 22/5/57. rtg Sqn Ldr.
HARVEY H. A., MIMgt. Born 26/1/28. Commd 2/3/49. Wg Cdr 1/7/65. Retd GD 2/11/76.
HARVEY H. G., MA MIMgt. Born 15/7/36. Commd 23/9/59. Wg Cdr 1/7/86. Retd GD 1/5/90.
HARVEY I. R., MBE BSc. Born 15/8/51. Commd 15/9/69. Wg Cdr 1/1/88. Retd GD 18/6/91.
HARVEY J. C., CEng MRAeS. Born 23/1/41. Commd 17/7/62. Sqn Ldr 1/7/74. Retd ENG 23/1/79.
HARVEY J. D. Born 26/5/32. Commd 26/7/55. Wg Cdr 1/1/74. Retd GD 10/3/84.
HARVEY J. F. Born 1/7/20. Commd 24/1/44. Flt Lt 24/1/50. Retd GD(G) 16/9/67.
HARVEY J. J. Born 30/10/26. Commd 8/10/52. Flt Lt 6/3/58. Retd GD 27/5/68.
HARVEY J. T. Born 18/5/32. Commd 29/12/51. Sqn Ldr 1/1/63. Retd GD 18/6/70.
HARVEY K. L. Born 12/10/60. Commd 30/4/81. Flt Lt 30/10/87. Retd GD(G) 1/6/93.
HARVEY M. A. Born 16/9/36. Commd 30/12/65. A Cdre 1/7/86. Retd GD(G) 2/4/91.
HARVEY M. J. A. Born 28/1/42. Commd 24/6/65. Flt Lt 8/3/72. Retd GD(G) 21/1/80.
HARVEY M. McD. Born 26/10/28. Commd 14/12/49. Sqn Ldr 1/7/61. Retd GD 30/9/74.
HARVEY P. J. R., MSc BSc. Born 3/2/46. Commd 1/11/81. Sqn Ldr 1/1/91. Retd ENG 3/2/01.
HARVEY P. M., FIMgt. Born 16/2/23. Commd 17/9/43. Gp Capt 1/1/70. Retd GD 29/7/74.
HARVEY S., BSc. Born 8/1/61. Commd 14/4/85. Sqn Ldr 1/7/96. Retd ADMIN 14/4/01.
HARVEY S. R. Born 10/5/47. Commd 25/6/65. Flt Lt 4/5/72. Retd GD 18/11/99.
HARVEY T. Born 24/10/52. Commd 9/5/91. Flt Lt 9/5/95. Retd MED(SEC) 4/4/96.
HARVEY T. J. Born 26/6/36. Commd 31/8/62. Flt Lt 25/7/66. Retd GD 5/3/90.
HARVEY T. R. D. Born 11/7/36. Commd 4/8/59. Flt Lt 25/6/66. Retd SEC 6/3/81.
HARVEY V. N. W. Born 4/7/14. Commd 29/10/43. Flt Lt 17/5/56. Retd GD(G) 7/10/67.
HARVEY-BENNETT P. G., BSc(Eng) Dip Soton. Born 30/3/40. Commd 30/9/58. Sqn Ldr 1/7/69. Retd ENG 1/9/83.
HARWOOD A. R. Born 28/4/40. Commd 26/3/64. Sqn Ldr 1/7/81. Retd GD 29/4/90.
HARWOOD C. A. Born 15/1/38. Commd 28/8/56. Wg Cdr 1/7/79. Retd GD(G) 18/1/90.
HARWOOD R. A. Born 13/1/17. Commd 15/12/44. Flt Lt 29/6/50. Retd SEC 13/1/73.
HARWOOD-GRAYSON M., MA. Born 4/12/52. Commd 14/11/76. Wg Cdr 1/1/90. Retd ADMIN 1/1/93.
HASKELL G. P., MCIPS. Born 26/6/39. Commd 9/3/66. Sqn Ldr 1/1/74. Retd SUP 6/5/85.
HASKINS S. W. Born 5/1/61. Commd 31/1/80. Flt Lt 31/7/85. Retd GD 7/6/98.
HASLAM J. A. G., MC DFC. Born 24/9/96. Commd 2/5/18. Flt Lt 1/1/22. Retd GD 10/6/27. Recalled 9/9/39. Wg Cdr 1/12/41. Retd 25/12/45 rtg Gp Capt.
HASLAM R. J. Born 11/2/23. Commd 5/9/57. Flt Lt 5/9/60. Retd GD 31/5/68.
HASLER P. R. Born 8/4/38. Commd 20/11/75. Sqn Ldr 1/7/89. Retd ENG 8/4/96.
HASSALL M. G. Born 8/11/33. Commd 27/3/75. Flt Lt 27/3/80. Retd ENG 28/3/85.
HASSAN W. E., MB BS MFCM DPH. Born 24/2/24. Commd 16/5/46. Gp Capt 1/7/68. Retd MED 22/11/75.
HASSELL R. S. Born 24/2/29. Commd 5/6/50. Flt Lt 5/9/56. Retd GD 24/9/67.
HASSELSTROM W. H. Born 29/8/20. Commd 17/4/42. Sqn Ldr 1/1/54. Retd SEC 30/12/67.
HASTINGS A. Born 6/10/48. Commd 24/4/80. Sqn Ldr 1/1/87. Retd ADMIN 1/8/95.

HASTINGS C. N., BSc. Born 31/1/63. Commd 30/8/81. Sqn Ldr 1/1/98. Retd GD 31/1/01.
HASTINGS M. C. Born 23/4/30. Commd 21/11/51. Flt Lt 21/5/56. Retd GD 23/4/68.
HASTINGS T. A., OBE. Born 14/8/29. Commd 18/6/52. Gp Capt 1/1/78. Retd GD 13/2/82.
HASTINGS W. J. G., BEM. Born 15/4/13. Commd 25/8/55. Flt Lt 25/8/58. Retd ENG 15/4.68.
HASZELDINE D. R., MSc BSc. Born 5/4/53. Commd 3/9/72. Sqn Ldr 1/7/84. Retd ENG 5/4/91.
HATCHER A. I. Born 2/5/54. Commd 20/6/91. Flt Lt 20/6/93. Retd ENG 2/9/00.
HATCHER F. J. Born 27/1/42. Commd 12/2/68. Sqn Ldr 1/7/80. Retd ENG 12/2/84.
HATCHER L. Born 5/12/43. Commd 28/4/65. Flt Lt 28/10/70. Retd GD 5/6/82.
HATCHER P. J. Born 29/11/24. Commd 23/9/66. Flt Lt 23/9/69. Retd GD 30/6/72.
HATCHER R. G., CEng MIEE MRAeS. Born 20/12/44. Commd 15/7/65. Sqn Ldr 1/7/74. Retd ENG 20/12/82.
HATCHER T. M. Born 28/2/66. Commd 30/8/84. Flt Lt 28/2/90. Retd GD 29/2/96.
HATHAWAY J. H. T. Born 10/7/39. Commd 29/3/68. Sqn Ldr 1/1/81. Retd GD 10/7/94.
HATHAWAY R. L. S., AFC MIMgt. Born 30/4/21. Commd 25/10/47. Sqn Ldr 1/7/62. Retd GD 30/4/76.
HATHAWAY R. T. Born 1/1/20. Commd 28/8/42. Flt Lt 28/2/47. Retd SEC 1/1/69.
HATLEY E. M., MHCIMA. Born 5/9/42. Commd 7/12/65. Gp Capt 1/7/91. Retd ADMIN 30/7/95.
HATT G. D. Born 18/4/24. Commd 24/8/44. Flt Lt 6/10/63. Retd GD 16/10/75.
HATTEN A. F., BEM. Born 15/4/43. Commd 13/12/79. Sqn Ldr 1/1/88. Retd ENG 20/10/95.
HATTER A. J. Born 14/9/45. Commd 29/7/65. Flt Lt 4/5/72. Retd SUP 16/3/74.
HATTON D. Born 19/10/38. Commd 14/5/60. Flt Lt 8/1/69. Retd GD(G) 30/9/82.
HATTON G. A. Born 26/8/18. Commd 10/3/44. Sqn Ldr 1/7/67. Retd GD(G) 26/8/73.
HATTON J. F. Born 7/7/20. Commd 23/12/39. Wg Cdr 1/1/54. Retd GD 7/7/67.
HATTON M. F., OBE CEng FIMgt MRAeS. Born 18/9/21. Commd 20/5/42. Gp Capt 1/1/66. Retd ENG 25/5/74.
HATTON P. A. Born 11/5/48. Commd 8/11/68. Sqn Ldr 1/1/89. Retd SY 25/7/96.
HATTON S., OBE. Born 5/10/22. Commd 11/8/44. Wg Cdr 1/7/65. Retd GD 19/7/75.
HAUGHTON D. J. Born 12/6/46. Commd 10/12/65. Sqn Ldr 1/1/82. Retd GD 12/6/90.
HAVEN R. C. Born 7/7/32. Commd 21/5/52. Sqn Ldr 1/7/70. Retd GD 12/8/77.
HAW C., DFC DFM. Born 8/5/20. Commd 6/3/42. Flt Lt 10/2/46. Retd GD 19/9/51 rtg Sqn Ldr.
HAW D. G. Born 28/1/27. Commd 3/8/61. Sqn Ldr 1/7/73. Retd PE 4/8/81.
HAWARD C. W. A. Born 8/11/45. Commd 2/4/65. Flt Lt 2/10/70. Retd GD 9/12/95.
HAWARD F. W. W., DFC. Born 31/1/20. Commd 5/12/42. Flt Lt 26/5/59. Retd GD(G) 31/1/70.
HAWARD P. J., MBE. Born 17/11/46. Commd 10/12/65. Sqn Ldr 1/7/93. Retd GD 1/10/94.
HAWES A. S. Born 20/3/21. Commd 25/9/46. Fg Offr 25/9/48. Retd PE 23/10/55.
HAWES C. D., BDS. Born 22/5/41. Commd 30/12/62. Wg Cdr 23/12/77. Retd DEL 22/5/79.
HAWES K. N. J. Born 28/11/38. Commd 30/7/57. Sqn Ldr 1/1/72. Retd GD 11/12/77.
HAWES M. J., LVO. Born 18/10/32. Commd 4/7/51. Sqn Ldr 1/7/73. Retd GD 18/10/92.
HAWES R. G. O. Born 22/3/24. Commd 4/9/58. Flt Lt 22/9/61. Retd ENG 12/4/75.
HAWES The Rev M. R., AKC. Born 28/10/31. Commd 15/6/65. Retd 28/10/86 Wg Cdr.
HAWES W. G. Born 21/12/33. Commd 15/10/52. Flt Lt 21/10/58. Retd GD 21/12/92.
HAWKE J. M., BA MIMgt. Born 30/8/32. Commd 23/9/55. Wg Cdr 1/1/74. Retd SUP 3/10/78.
HAWKEN P. H. G., BA. Born 26/4/40. Commd 29/4/58. Sqn Ldr 1/1/72. Retd PRT 26/4/78.
HAWKER H. C. V., DFC. Born 25/9/22. Commd 28/2/42. Flt Lt 5/12/47. Retd GD 13/1/58.
HAWKER P. B., AFM. Born 16/3/25. Commd 29/7/52. Flt Lt 3/11/59. Retd GD 15/3/69.
HAWKER S. R., BEd. Born 12/12/55. Commd 9/11/86. Flt Lt 9/5/82. Retd ADMIN 1/7/86.
HAWKES A. J. Born 28/2/37. Commd 21/9/55. Flt Lt 30/6/61. Retd GD 1/10/68.
HAWKEY J. A. Born 24/4/23. Commd 18/6/44. Sqn Ldr 1/7/59. Retd GD 3/3/62.
HAWKHEAD H. Born 13/5/11. Commd 24/12/44. Sqn Ldr 1/1/56. Retd PRT 13/5/60.
HAWKINS A. J. J., BA. Born 31/1/23. Commd 1/1/63. Sqn Ldr 14/2/66. Retd ADMIN 31/1/78.
HAWKINS B. J. R. Born 6/3/56. Commd 17/5/79. Sqn Ldr 1/7/88. Retd OPS SPT 6/3/00.
HAWKINS C. H., DFC AFC. Born 7/12/16. Commd 1/11/41. Flt Lt 16/7/51. Retd GD(G) 28/2/62.
HAWKINS D. E., CB CBE DFC*. Born 27/12/19. Commd 7/5/38. AVM 1/7/69. Retd GD 31/7/74.
HAWKINS D. G., PhD BSc. Born 1/6/41. Commd 21/1/68. Gp Capt 1/1/87. Retd GD 3/12/97.
HAWKINS D. G. Born 16/5/19. Commd 12/9/63. Flt Lt 12/9/68. Retd SEC 31/12/68.
HAWKINS D. J. Born 24/2/46. Commd 13/3/80. Flt Lt 13/3/82. Retd GD 1/2/96.
HAWKINS D. R., CB MBE FCIPD FIMgt. Born 5/4/37. Commd 17/12/59. AVM 1/7/91. Retd SY 1/7/93.
HAWKINS I. P. W., MIMgt. Born 21/10/24. Commd 29/3/45. Wg Cdr 1/7/65. Retd GD 1/11/75.
HAWKINS J. D., AFC. Born 30/12/99. Commd 24/4/41. Sqn Ldr 1/7/53. Retd GD 11/2/59.
HAWKINS J. W. J., CEng MIEE MRAeS. Born 24/7/30. Commd 17/12/52. Wg Cdr 1/1/75. Retd ENG 14/4/84.
HAWKINS M. J. Born 1/9/31. Commd 12/4/51. Flt Lt 1/1/64. Retd GD 1/9/69.
HAWKINS M. L., BSc CEng FRAeS MIMechE. Born 28/9/40. Commd 30/9/60. Gp Capt 1/7/87. Retd ENG 28/9/95.
HAWKINS N. M., BA. Born 7/9/32. Commd 5/12/60. Sqn Ldr 29/1/72. Retd ADMIN 31/5/84.
HAWKINS P. R. Born 30/3/19. Commd 12/6/47. Sqn Ldr 1/4/58. Retd SEC 14/8/65.
HAWKSLEY P. Born 20/7/42. Commd 14/8/64. Flt Lt 14/2/70. Retd GD 1/8/68.
HAWKSWORTH J. Born 6/5/20. Commd 11/3/43. Flt Lt 2/1/50. Retd EDN 7/2/57.
HAWKSWORTH P. R. Born 18/12/40. Commd 19/4/63. Gp Capt 1/1/91. Retd GD 6/6/93.
HAWLEY N. H. Born 19/12/35. Commd 4/4/71. Flt Lt 4/4/73. Retd ENG 19/12/85.
HAWORTH D. A. Born 2/9/32. Commd 19/4/51. Sqn Ldr 1/1/73. Retd GD(G) 1/3/89.

HAWORTH G., DFC DFM. Born 4/9/15. Commd 17/7/41. Sqn Ldr 1/8/47. Retd GD 28/12/57.
HAWORTH T. D. Born 16/4/24. Commd 29/3/45. Flt Lt 7/7/63. Retd SEC 25/7/73.
HAWRYLOWICZ A. S. Born 6/7/16. Commd 12/10/43. Sqn Ldr 1/7/60. Retd SEC 12/7/71.
HAWTHORN I. E., MB BS FRCS(Edin) MRCS LRCP. Born 22/3/57. Commd 18/10/77. Wg Cdr 1/8/94. Retd MED 22/3/95.
HAWTHORNE J. F., CEng MIEE MRAeS. Born 27/2/20. Commd 10/12/42. Sqn Ldr 1/10/55. Retd ENG 31/10/63.
HAWTIN J. D. C. Born 9/12/33. Commd 26/7/55. Wg Cdr 1/7/73. Retd GD 9/12/88.
HAY A. A., BEM. Born 28/5/05. Commd 16/10/40. Sqn Ldr 1/8/47. Retd Eng 28/1/54.
HAY A. W. Born 16/3/12. Commd 21/2/46. Sqn Ldr 1/1/57. Retd SUP 30/5/61.
HAY H. W., MIMgt. Born 18/3/16. Commd 23/10/43. Sqn Ldr 1/7/70. Retd SUP 8/7/72.
HAY I. J. Born 20/11/36. Commd 10/9/70. Flt Lt 10/9/72. Retd SEC 10/9/78.
HAY J. B. Born 18/10/11. Commd 1/10/40. Flt Lt 10/6/45. Retd ASD 12/12/47.
HAY J. S. S., AFC. Born 2/12/23. Commd 29/3/45. Sqn Ldr 1/9/65. Retd GD 1/10/68.
HAY M. Born 19/10/53. Commd 15/2/73. Sqn Ldr 1/7/90. Retd GD(G) 1/7/93.
HAY P. Born 17/9/42. Commd 10/12/765. Flt Lt 10/6/71. Retd GD 1/9/81.
HAY P. G. Born 1/5/38. Commd 10/2/59. Fg Offr 12/2/61. Retd GD 11/2/66.
HAY P. MCN. Born 24/5/33. Commd 20/3/52. Sqn Ldr 1/1/69. Retd GD 24/5/93.
HAY W. P. Born 22/10/33. Commd 19/11/57. Flt Lt 7/8/64. Retd GD(G) 22/10/88.
HAY W. T. H. Born 6/4/22. Commd 23/4/45. Flt Lt 23/4/51. Retd PE 30/4/58.
HAYCOCK M. Born 15/3/40. Commd 24/11/67. Flt Lt 24/11/69. Retd P.E. 15/9/78.
HAYDAY J. C. Born 15/11/32. Commd 4/6/52. Flt Lt 30/10/57. Retd GD 15/11/70.
HAYDEN B., BSc. Born 12/7/57. Commd 11/9/83. Flt Lt 11/3/85. Retd ADMIN 31/10/86.
HAYDEN M. J. Born 16/5/33. Commd 16/7/52. Wg Cdr 1/7/76. Retd GD 23/11/87.
HAYDON D. A. Born 12/2/47. Commd 1/1/67. Flt Lt 1/7/72. Retd GD 28/2/76.
HAYES A. P. Born 11/5/50. Commd 25/2/72. Wg Cdr 1/1/89. Retd GD 11/5/94.
HAYES C. G. Born 19/7/62. Commd 19/12/91. Flt Lt 21/11/94. Retd ENG 23/10/00.
HAYES C. W., OBE. Born 11/5/17. Commd 6/5/42. Gp Capt 1/1/68. Retd GD 15/3/70.
HAYES D. T. C. Born 31/3/26. Commd 21/9/50. Sqn Ldr 1/7/62. Retd GD 28/11/75.
HAYES E., MBE. Born 22/3/34. Commd 17/3/67. Flt Lt 17/3/72. Retd GD 22/6/92.
HAYES E. Born 1/7/13. Commd 13/1/43. Flt Offr 13/1/48 SUP. Retd SUP 21/8/55.
HAYES E. C. Born 25/3/13. Commd 3/12/41. Flt Lt 9/9/45. Retd ENG 3/10/53 rtg Sqn Ldr.
HAYES K., BSc. Born 26/11/30. Commd 17/10/51. Sqn Ldr 1/1/61. Retd GD 26/11/68.
HAYES L. J. Born 6/4/47. Commd 19/3/81. Flt Lt 19/3/83. Retd GD 1/6/95.
HAYES N. C., AFM. Born 21/12/20. Commd 6/4/50. Sqn Ldr 1/1/71. Retd GD 21/12/75.
HAYES N. R. Born 14/3/24. Commd 6/9/68. Flt Lt 6/9/71. Retd GD 14/9/78.
HAYES S. G. Born 6/6/51. Commd 24/4/70. Sqn Ldr 1/7/85. Retd SUP 6/6/89.
HAYHOW K. J. Born 12/4/23. Commd 23/12/43. Flt Lt 10/11/55. Retd SEC 11/8/65.
HAYLER P. Born 29/11/33. Commd 25/6/66. Flt Lt 25/6/68. Retd SUP 25/6/74.
HAYLETT M. Born 16/11/18. Commd 27/11/52. Flt Offr 27/11/58. Retd SUP 21/1/60.
HAYLETT M. G. Born 7/5/50. Commd 6/11/80. Flt Lt 6/11/82. Retd GD(ENG) 6/11/88.
HAYLEY C. A., DFC. Born 15/4/21. Commd 16/4/43. Flt Lt 16/10/46. Retd GD 15/4/67.
HAYLEY J. T. Born 21/12/23. Commd 22/7/63. Sqn Ldr 1/7/75. Retd GD 21/12/81.
HAYLOCK E. K. A., MIMgt. Born 18/12/22. Commd 15/10/43. Sqn Ldr 1/7/67. Retd ADMIN 18/12/77.
HAYMAN D. J., BA. Born 26/9/42. Commd 28/7/64. Wg Cdr 1/7/87. Retd SUP 26/9/93.
HAYMAN J. Born 12/8/31. Commd 1/3/62. Flt Lt 1/3/68. Retd ENG 1/6/77.
HAYMAN M. J. Born 24/9/47. Commd 24/6/71. Flt Lt. 14/10/77. Retd SEC 1/8/78.
HAYMAN W. F., MBE MRAeS. Born 23/12/31. Commd 10/10/63. Sqn Ldr 1/7/76. Retd ENG 23/12/92.
HAYNE R. D. Born 26/4/58. Commd 15/6/83. Flt Lt 15/6/85. Retd ENG 26/4/96.
HAYNES C. J. P., BSc MIMgt. Born 24/12/46. Commd 22/9/65. Sqn Ldr 1/1/78. Retd ENG 24/12/84.
HAYNES D. M., ACIS MIMgt. Born 8/11/40. Commd 27/8/59. Sqn Ldr 1/7/78. Retd SEC 1/7/81.
HAYNES F. J. P. Born 17/4/18. Commd 18/9/39. Wg Cdr 1/1/61. Retd SUP 10/4/69.
HAYNES F. M. Born 13/3/30. Commd 13/2/52. Flt Lt 12/6/57. Retd GD 13/3/68.
HAYNES H. M., BA BEd. Born 17/7/56. Commd 7/11/85. Flt Lt 7/5/87. Retd ADMIN 14/3/97.
HAYNES J. H. Born 25/3/38. Commd 14/3/57. Flt Lt 5/8/64. Retd SUP 8/8/67.
HAYNES P. C. Born 26/5/66. Commd 21/6/90. Flt Lt 21/12/95. Retd GD 14/3/97.
HAYNES P. W. Born 26/9/47. Commd 23/6/67. Sqn Ldr 1/1/79. Retd SY 26/9/85.
HAYNES R. Born 6/6/19. Commd 6/11/43. Flt Lt 6/5/47. Retd GD(G) 6/6/76.
HAYNES R. G. Born 23/9/44. Commd 28/9/62. Flt Lt 28/3/68. Retd GD 23/9/82.
HAYS L. Born 5/7/23. Commd 4/9/44. Flt Lt 4/9/50. Retd ADMIN 6/7/76.
HAYSOM C. C. Born1/10/41. Commd 30/7/63. Flt Lt 30.1.66. Retd GD 6/1/79.
HAYSOM K. J. Born 13/8/46. Commd 1/11/79. Flt Lt 1/11/81. Retd GD 31/3/94.
HAYTER A. J., MIMgt. Born 11/3/22. Commd 10/7/44. Sqn Ldr 1/7/60. Retd GD 11/3/71.
HAYTER D. E. F. Born 4/2/23. Commd 29/6/50. Sqn Ldr 1/7/60. Retd ENG 15/8/64.
HAYTER F. E. G. Born 1/5/15. Commd 13/10/37. Flt Lt 17/3/47. Retd SEC 6/1/61 rtg Sqn Ldr.
HAYTER L. A. Born 6/4/20. Commd 3/2/44. Flt Lt 27/7/55. Retd GD(G) 8/12/71.
HAYTER M. D. Born 1/3/50. Commd 10/9/70. Flt Lt 10/3/76. Retd GD 22/10/94.

HAYTER R. J., CEng MIMechE MRAeS. Born 3/8/29. Commd 18/7/51. Wg Cdr 1/7/79. Retd ENG 3/8/84.
HAYTER S. J. Born 12/12/47. Commd 10/6/66. Sqn Ldr 1/7/78. Retd SUP 11/12/85.
HAYTER-PRESTON P. Born 19/12/21. Commd 7/1/42. Flt Lt 8/5/51. Retd GD(G) 17/7/57.
HAYTON P., MA. Born 11/4/50. Commd 5/5/71. Flt Lt 15/1/73. Retd GD 12/5/78.
HAYWARD B. A., MBE. Born 9/11/32. Commd 7/12/61. Flt Lt 7/12/66. Retd GD 2/9/72.
HAYWARD D. Born 3/7/31. Commd 1/6/72. Sqn Ldr 19/8/81. Retd MED(T) 3/7/89.
HAYWARD D., OBE. Born 22/2/45. Commd 15/7/66. Gp Capt 1/1/89. Retd GD 14/3/96.
HAYWARD E. J. N. Born 15/6/40. Commd 25/9/80. Flt Lt 15/12/82. Retd GD 19/7/85.
HAYWARD F. Born 22/5/26. Commd 21/6/56. Sqn Ldr 1/7/74. Retd GD 22/5/84.
HAYWARD H. R. Born 26/6/29. Commd 10/10/63. Flt Lt 10/10/68. Retd GD 29/3/69.
HAYWARD K. R., AFC. Born 15/5/21. Commd 30/9/54. Sqn Ldr 1/1/66. Retd GD 28/8/68.
HAYWARD L. C. Born 13/10/24. Commd 25/8/49. Flt Lt 25/2/53. Retd GD 13/10/67.
HAYWARD N. R., AFC. Born 4/5/40. Commd 1/8/61. Wg Cdr 1/7/75. Retd GD 1/7/78.
HAYWARD R. Born 11/11/44. Commd 12/7/68. Sqn Ldr 1/1/81. Retd GD 30/5/97.
HAYWARD R. A., AFC. Born 12/7/23. Commd 15/1/45. Flt Lt 15/7/48. Retd GD 12/7/66.
HAYWARD T. F., OBE MRIN MIMgt. Born 23/9/36. Commd 20/8/55. Wg Cdr 1/7/76. Retd GD 20/7/84.
HAYWARD V. F., BA. Born 12/5/33. Commd 25/8/55. Wg Cdr 1/7/77. Retd ADMIN 9/5/87.
HAYWOOD J. W., MSc BEng CEng. Born 29/4/44. Commd 28/11/76. Sqn Ldr 1/1/84. Retd ADMIN 4/1/99.
HAYWOOD K. M., MIMgt. Born 27/9/39. Commd 17/5/79. Sqn Ldr 1/1/90. Retd ADMIN 7/7/93.
HAYWOOD V. M., MA MCIPD MBIFM CertEd AdvDipEd(Open) DPhysEd. Born 17/9/52. Commd 2/1/77. Sqn Ldr
   1/1/90. Retd ADMIN 13/12/99.
HAZAN T. S. W. Born 15/11/50. Commd 15/9/69. Flt Lt 30/1/78. Retd GD 14/3/97.
HAZELL A. R. E., BSc. Born 14/1/34. Commd 5/10/56. Sqn Ldr 5/4/66. Retd ADMIN 2/1/87.
HAZLEHURST N. R., BSc(Eng) ACGI. Born 23/8/54. Commd 6/11/77. Flt Lt 6/8/79. Retd GD 6/11/89.
HAZLEWOOD F. S., CB CBE AFC* FRAeS FIMgt. Born 13/5/21. Commd 16/4/43. AVM 1/1/73. Retd GD 15/1/77.
HEAD D. Born 9/7/42. Commd 24/4/70. Flt Lt 4/5/72. Retd GD 9/7/80.
HEAD D. A. Born 17/6/52. Commd 19/8/71. Flt Lt 19/2/77. Retd GD 17/6/90.
HEAD D. G. Born 23/10/37. Commd 11/11/65. Sqn Ldr 1/1/78. Retd GD 23/10/92.
HEAD G. J. A. Born 4/11/22. Commd 14/7/44. Sqn Ldr 1/1/75. Retd ADMIN 4/11/77.
HEAD I. C. Born 16/1/33. Commd 5/3/59. Flt Lt 18/3/64. Retd ENG 15/9/74.
HEAD J. W. M. Born 13/1/43. Commd 28/7/64. Flt Lt 9/2/68. Retd GD 6/4/80.
HEAD M. G. Born 6/7/40. Commd 19/12/61. Wg Cdr 1/1/81. Retd GD 1/5/93.
HEAD M. J., MMar. Born 19/11/36. Commd 2/1/67. Sqn Ldr 2/1/75. Retd MAR 2/1/83.
HEAD R. A. Born 27/10/43. Commd 22/5/64. Flt Lt 22/11/69. Retd GD 1/6/82.
HEADLAND M. J., BSc. Born 7/7/50. Commd 26/4/72. Flt Lt 15/4/77. Retd ENG 1/9/77.
HEADLAND R. J. Born 17/3/26. Commd 21/6/56. Sqn Ldr 1/1/73. Retd GD 31/12/75.
HEADLEY I. S., OBE. Born 24/12/33. Commd 26/3/52. Wg Cdr 1/1/81. Retd GD 24/12/91.
HEADLEY P. J. Born 26/2/40. Commd 1/8/61. Flt Lt 7/8/64. Retd GD 27/5/73.
HEAL C. W. C., OBE FInst Pet FIMgt. Born 24/11/32. Commd 8/8/58. Gp Capt 1/7/80. Retd SUP 23/11/86.
HEAL H. J., DFC*. Born 22/9/15. Commd 14/1/39. Sqn Ldr 1/8/47. Retd SEC 22/9/64 rtg Wg Cdr.
HEAL J. C. F. Born 2/7/64. Commd 27/8/87. Flt Lt 27/2/93. Retd GD 14/3/97.
HEALD M. A. R., MBE. Born 14/7/25. Commd 5/10/50. Flt Lt 5/4/54. Retd GD 14/7/80.
HEALEY D. E. Born 3/1/19. Commd 30/9/41. Sqn Ldr 1/1/53. Retd RGT 29/8/59.
HEALEY J. A. Born 6/8/43. Commd 25/1/63. Flt Lt  1/7/69. Retd GD 31/3/94.
HEALEY N. V. O., MCIPS MInstAM MIMgt. Born 31/12/35. Commd 27/4/61. Sqn Ldr 1/1/71. Retd SUP 21/1/78.
HEALEY P. M. Born 9/2/42. Commd 4/6/62. Sqn Ldr 1/1/77. Retd GD 22/4/94.
HEALY D., BSc ACGI. Born 24/5/23. Commd 16/9/43. Sqn Ldr 1/7/54. Retd ENG 31/8/61.
HEALY D. J., BSc. Born 6/6/61. Commd 2/9/84. Flt Lt 2/3/87. Retd SUP 14/3/96.
HEALY P. C. F., CEng MIEE MIMgt. Born 15/3/34. Commd 31/12/64. Sqn Ldr 1/1/69. Retd ENG 1/10/80.
HEANEY R. C. Born 21/1/52. Commd 27/2/75. Flt Lt 27/8/81. Retd GD(G) 4/11/90.
HEAP E. Born 14/5/56. Commd 11/5/78. Sqn Ldr 1/7/88. Retd GD 14/5/94.
HEAP F. W. Born 1/5/26. Commd 17/5/62. Sqn Ldr 1/1/76. Retd GD 1/5/84.
HEAP P. J. Born 31/3/42. Commd 11/5/78. Flt Lt 11/5/83. Retd SUP 2/10/85.
HEARD A. W. Born 7/1/59. Commd 25/2/62. Flt Lt 25/8/87. Retd GD 19/10/97.
HEARD L. J. Born 18/5/12. Commd 21/2/46. Fg Offr 1/11/47. Retd SUP 17/3/48.
HEARD N. J., BSc. Born 21/12/59. Commd 4/9/78. Sqn Ldr 1/7/93. Retd GD 21/12/97.
HEARLE Rev D. C., MA BD. Born 20/4/20. Commd 23/8/44. Retd 20/4/75. Gp Capt.
HEARMON P. C. Born 8/5/31. Commd 13/9/51. Flt Lt 4/1/57. Retd GD 8/5/71.
HEARN M. P. Born 9/1/48. Commd 4/7/69. Flt Lt 4/1/75. Retd GD 9/1/89.
HEARN P. G., AFC BA. Born 31/8/32. Commd 25/8/53. Gp Capt 1/1/80. Retd ADMIN 31/8/87.
HEARN P. J. Born 9/1/21. Commd 19/2/43. Sqn Ldr 1/7/51. Retd SUP 9/8/70.
HEARN P. J. Born 1/12/44. Commd 6/9/68. Flt Lt 8/2/75. Retd SUP 20/5/84.
HEARN P. J., MBE MIMgt. Born 28/2/42. Commd 2/4/65. Sqn Ldr 1/1/82. Retd GD 31/12/97.
HEARNDEN D. M. Born 4/6/06. Commd 8/7/42. Flt Offr 8/1/47. Retd SEC 23/1/57.
HEARNE P. J. Born 6/2/19. Commd 28/7/42. Sqn Ldr 1/7/54. Retd GD 24/2/62.
HEARNSHAW T., BA. Born 8/8/34. Commd 7/2/57. Sqn Ldr 7/8/65. Retd EDN 25/10/72.

HEASMAN D. A. Born 28/7/22. Commd 11/12/45. Flt Lt 19/11/53. Retd RGT 30/9/61.
HEATH A. D. Born 9/4/47. Commd 28/2/69. Flt Lt 8/3/72. Retd GD 1/4/88.
HEATH B. D. Born 8/2/38. Commd 20/11/75. Sqn Ldr 1/7/90. Retd ENG 1/7/93.
HEATH B. P. Born 2/8/27. Commd 6/6/51. Flt Lt 5/9/56. Retd GD 4/5/76.
HEATH E. L. Born 30/4/22. Commd 3/7/43. Sqn Ldr 1/7/54. Retd GD 30/4/69.
HEATH F. G. Born 28/5/14. Commd 15/10/53. Sqn Ldr 22/2/63. Retd MED(T) 31/12/66.
HEATH G. Born 11/3/45. Commd 28/10/66. Sqn Ldr 1/7/89. Retd GD 9/1/96.
HEATH G. F., BA. Born 27/10/38. Commd 23/6/61. Flt Lt 23/12/66. Retd GD 27/10/93.
HEATH J. G. Born 11/10/44. Commd 11/9/64. Flt Lt 15/4/70. Retd GD 31/3/93.
HEATH J. R., MBE. Born 27/6/37. Commd 4/11/82. Sqn Ldr 1/1/89. Retd ENG 4/11/92.
HEATH J. W. H. Born 27/7/31. Commd 31/12/52. Flt Lt 13/4/60. Retd GD 31/8/68.
HEATH L. S. Born 12/12/14. Commd 6/10/40. Flt Lt 19/6/52. Retd GD(G) 11/10/61.
HEATH Sir Maurice, KBE CB CVO DL. Born 12/8/09. Commd 27/7/29. AM 1/1/63. Retd GD 17/7/65.
HEATH P. G., BSc. Born 16/6/49. Commd 19/5/74. Flt Lt 19/8/75. Retd GD 19/5/90.
HEATH P. J. Born 14/4/40. Commd 22/5/75. Sqn Ldr 1/1/90. Retd ENG 2/4/93.
HEATH R. A. J. Born 29/3/55. Commd 11/1/79. Sqn Ldr 1/1/89. Retd GD 30/9/98.
HEATH R. O. Born 3/4/11. Commd 12/6/35. Fg Offr 12/6/36. Retd SEC 9/12/39. Recalled 7/10/40. Flt Lt 13/11/42. Retd 9/6/47 rtg Sqn Ldr.
HEATH-SMITH G. M., MBE. Born 10/7/18. Commd 16/6/42. Wg Cdr 1/1/60. Retd SEC 1/5/64.
HEATH-WHYTE R. W., BSc CEng MIEE MRAeS. Born 24/5/40. Commd 30/9/59. Sqn Ldr 1/7/73. Retd ENG 24/5/78.
HEATHCOTE D. F., MCIPD MRIN MIMgt. Born 10/1/37. Commd 6/10/60. Wg Cdr 1/7/87. Retd GD 31/7/93.
HEATHCOTE E. Born 9/2/15. Commd 8/9/41. Sqn Ldr 1/7/52. Retd ENG 9/2/62.
HEATHER G. A. Born 13/11/21. Commd 10/3/44. Flt Lt 10/9/47. Retd ADMIN 13/11/76.
HEATHER G. W. Born 21/12/09. Commd 9/10/31. Wg Cdr 1/10/46. Retd GD 1/8/56.
HEATHER R. L. Born 9/3/32. Commd 14/11/51. Flt Lt 17/7/56. Retd GD 9/3/70.
HEATHERILL J. A., OBE MIMgt. Born 27/11/22. Commd 26/11/43. Wg Cdr 1/7/61. Retd GD 27/11/77.
HEATON A. Born 7/4/34. Commd 10/8/60. Flt Offr 14/2/66. Retd CAT 22/9/67.
HEATON E. A. Born 22/7/41. Commd 20/9/68. Sqn Ldr 1/1/91. Retd GD 23/4/96.
HEATON M. G., BA. Born 23/2/57. Commd 8/12/77. Sqn Ldr 1/1/90. Retd GD 23/2/95.
HEAVER P. L. Born 25/7/33. Commd 28/1/53. Flt Lt 14/12/61. Retd GD 25/7/71.
HEAVERS I. D. Born 25/9/26. Commd 2/10/50. Flt Lt 13/5/56. Retd GD 24/3/66.
HEAVERY F. C., AFC DFM. Born 4/1/23. Commd 23/4/43. Flt Lt 23/10/46. Retd GD 4/1/66.
HEAVISIDE W. Born 13/10/18. Commd 3/5/56. Sqn Ldr 1/7/66. Retd ENG 13/10/73.
HEBBEN S. J. Born 17/3/65. Commd 15/8/85. Plt Off 15/2/86. Retd ADMIN 24/2/89.
HEBBES D. G., BEd. Born 16/11/57. Commd 18/8/85. Flt Lt 18/8/86. Retd ADMIN 2/11/96.
HEBBLETHWAITE J. E. Born 8/1/43. Commd 28/9/62. Flt Lt 28/3/68. Retd GD 8/1/81.
HEBBORN K., MBE BSc CEng DipEL MIEE. Born 1/2/31. Commd 5/8/53. Gp Capt 1/7/76. Retd ADMIN 31/12/84.
HEBDEN W. S. Born 23/2/09. Commd 27/7/29. A Cdre 1/7/52. Retd GD 3/10/58.
HEDGCOCK T. J. Born 30/11/36. Commd 8/12/61. Flt Lt 1/4/66. Retd GD 30/11/91.
HEDGECOCK B. Born 23/9/32. Commd 29/6/72. Sqn Ldr 1/1/84. Retd ENG 14/9/89.
HEDGECOCK R. B. G., MSc. Born 11/7/35. Commd 20/2/59. Wg Cdr 1/7/74. Retd ENG 3/3/87.
HEDGELAND P. M. S., CB OBE BSc CEng FIEE FCGI. Born 24/11/22. Commd 10/6/42. AVM 1/1/75. Retd ENG 31/3/78.
HEDGER J. H. Born 15/4/23. Commd 13/12/42. Gp Capt 1/7/73. Retd GD(G) 31/3/78.
HEDGER S. C. Born 21/1/19. Commd 1/9/64. Flt Lt 30/10/65. Retd GD(G) 21/1/74.
HEDGES A. G. F. Born 19/4/32. Commd 14/1/53. Flt Lt 3/6/58. Retd GD 1/10/75.
HEDGES J. W. Born 23/2/10. Commd 1/5/42. Flt Lt 20/11/45. Retd ENG 17/1/50.
HEDGES R. W. H., CBE. Born 2/5/44. Commd 17/12/65. Gp Capt 1/7/87. Retd GD 1/11/91.
HEDLEY B. Born 12/8/28. Commd 26/3/64. Flt Lt 26/3/69. Retd PE 12/8/83.
HEDLEY C. H., DFC. Born 30/4/21. Commd 1/5/44. Flt Lt 1/11/47. Retd GD 17/5/54.
HEELEY W. J. Born 25/2/21. Commd 21/11/42. Wg Cdr 1/7/65. Retd GD 26/8/68.
HEGARTY J. F. Born 24/7/31. Commd 28/10/81. Flt Lt 22/5/75. Retd GD. Re-instated 23/11/82 to 24/7/87.
HEGLAND G., DSC. Born 15/5/17. Commd 17/10/49. Sqn Ldr 17/10/57. Retd MAR 17/10/65.
HEGLEY I. S. Born 8/6/47. Commd 23/2/68. Sqn Ldr 1/1/83. Retd SUP 8/6/91.
HEITHUS C., MCIPS MILT MIMgt. Born 13/1/44. Commd 3/3/67. Wg Cdr 1/7/94. Retd SUP 13/1/99.
HELD F. P. Born 20/1/26. Commd 30/10/61. Flt Lt 30/10/61. Retd ADMIN 20/1/86.
HELLAWELL K., FIMgt. Born 14/10/20. Commd 1/5/42. A Cdre 1/1/73. Retd ENG 14/10/75.
HELLEN R. A., MBE. Born 15/7/28. Commd 23/9/66. Sqn Ldr 1/7/79. Retd ENG 15/7/86.
HELLINGS K. E. Born 28/8/24. Commd 4/3/45. Flt Lt 4/9/48. Retd GD 29/6/69.
HELLYER C., MRIN. Born 5/12/43. Commd 3/1/64. Wg Cdr 1/7/92. Retd GD 31/3/94.
HELLYER R. J. Born 21/5/44. Commd 27/3/75. Sqn Ldr 1/7/89. Retd GD 26/1/93.
HELPS D. W., DFM. Born 1/7/20. Commd 14/2/52. Flt Lt 1/7/56. Retd GD 30/6/73.
HELSBY C. M., CEng. Born 25/8/34. Commd 27/11/58. Sqn Ldr 17/1/69. Retd ADMIN 22/10/76.
HELSBY E. W., BA MinstAM DPhysEd. Born 16/10/29. Commd 4/9/59. Retd ADMIN 16/11/84.
HELY M. H. M., MA DUS CEng MIEE. Born 12/12/36. Commd 30/9/55. Sqn Ldr 1/7/67. Retd SUP 12/12/74.

HEMBROW S. P. Born 24/2/61. Commd 11/10/84. Flt Lt 11/10/90. Retd GD 14/3/96.
HEMINGWAY J. A., DFC. Born 17/7/19. Commd 7/5/38. Gp Capt 1/1/69. Retd GD 12/9/69.
HEMMING B. H. Born 12/7/36. Commd 21/1/74. Flt Lt 21/2/77. Retd GD 1/1/85.
HEMMING I. G. S., CB CBE FIMgt. Born 11/12/11. Commd 18/9/39. A Cdre 1/7/62. Retd SUP 2/4/68.
HEMMING W. J., DFC. Born 23/11/20. Commd 21/10/43. Flt Lt 21/4/47. Retd GD(G) 23/11/66.
HEMMINGS D. J., AFC. Born 2/10/45. Commd 5/2/64. Sqn Ldr 1/1/77. Retd GD 4/11/83.
HEMMINGS J. A. Born 3/4/24. Commd 18/7/63. Flt Lt 18/7/66. Retd GD 5/6/73.
HEMMINGS W. J. Born 18/9/20. Commd 21/6/56. Flt Lt 21/6/62. Retd GD(G) 18/9/75.
HEMPSEED J. C. Born 21/8/17. Commd 17/10/46. Fg Offr 17/10/46. Retd ENG 26/10/54.
HEMPSTEAD M. C., AFC. Born 15/5/28. Commd 28/6/51. Sqn Ldr 1/7/68. Retd GD 15/3/77.
HEMSLEY H. C. Born 5/3/27. Commd 11/3/65. Flt Lt 11/3/70. Retd SUP 30/9/72.
HEMSLEY S. E. Born 15/8/36. Commd 31/7/56. Flt Lt 16/8/61. Retd PRT 15/8/74.
HEMSLEY T., AFC. Born 19/8/20. Commd 17/12/44. Flt Lt 4/12/52. Retd GD 7/8/64.
HEMSLEY W. A. C. Born 21/4/23. Commd 6/9/56. Sqn Ldr 1/1/73. Retd GD(G) 3/6/76.
HEMSLEY-HALL H. S. Born 9/8/13. Commd 14/8/40. Sqn Ldr 1/7/50. Retd GD(G) 31/3/60.
HEMSON E. A. Born 11/7/42. Commd 9/9/63. Flt Lt 9/9/67. Retd GD 11/10/80.
HEMSWORTH J. R. Born 13/8/18. Commd 3/6/44. Sqn Ldr 1/4/55. Retd GD 31/1/58.
HENCE R. H. J., CEng MIEE MIMgt. Born 13/12/24. Commd 28/9/45. Wg Cdr 1/1/68. Retd ENG 13/12/81 rtg Gp Capt.
HENCHIE S. D. Born 13/5/38. Commd 28/4/61. Sqn Ldr 1/1/84. Retd GD(G) 3/7/90.
HENCHOZ A. T. Born 18/1/46. Commd 9/3/66. Flt Lt 30/7/72. Retd SUP 18/1/84.
HENCKEN D. C., BSocSc. Born 10/3/43. Commd 22/9/63. Gp Capt 1/7/91. Retd GD 20/9/98.
HENDERSON A. E., AFC. Born 24/11/19. Commd 1/9/45. Sqn Ldr 1/10/54. Retd GD 24/11/62.
HENDERSON C., BSc DipEl CEng MIEE. Born 28/4/28. Commd 11/10/50. Wg Cdr 1/4/69. Retd ADMIN 29/9/76.
HENDERSON C. J. Born 21/9/44. Commd 23/3/67. Wg Cdr 1/1/92. Retd GD 27/8/94.
HENDERSON D. Born 9/8/33. Commd 21/4/54. Flt Lt 7/3/62. Retd GD 9/8/71.
HENDERSON D. F. A., CBE. Born 24/4/48. Commd 28/2/69. AVM 1/7/94. Retd GD 2/1/96.
HENDERSON D. I. Born 21/12/57. Commd 9/8/79. Flt Lt 2/2/84. Retd GD 21/12/95.
HENDERSON E. C., MBE. Born 15/4/17. Commd 12/9/46. Sqn Ldr 1/7/57. Retd SEC 15/4/66.
HENDERSON H. R. Born 28/6/56. Commd 23/9/79. Sqn Ldr 1/1/90. Retd ADMIN 23/9/98.
HENDERSON I., AFC. Born 2/9/36. Commd 1/4/58. Sqn Ldr 1/7/68. Retd GD 12/2/75 rtg Wg Cdr.
HENDERSON J. A. Born 3/5/50. Commd 13/1/72. Sqn Ldr 1/7/85. Retd ADMIN 1/7/88.
HENDERSON J. H., CEng MIEE. Born 19/4/20. Commd 6/5/43. Sqn Ldr 1/1/63. Retd ENG 19/4/75.
HENDERSON J. S. Born 18/9/42. Commd 1/11/63. Flt Lt 4/5/72. Retd OPS SPT 18/9/97.
HENDERSON K., MIMgt. Born 28/12/33. Commd 24/9/80. Sqn Ldr 22/10/70. Retd GD 28/12/89.
HENDERSON K., MA MSc DIC CEng MIEE. Born 9/9/50. Commd 6/3/77. Sqn Ldr 1/7/85. Retd ADMIN 31/12/94.
HENDERSON P. G. R. Born 3/10/22. Commd 5/9/60. Flt Lt 5/5/63. Retd GD(G) 15/1/70.
HENDERSON P. W., CB MBE BSc CEng FRAeS. Born 5/11/45. Commd 26/5/67. AVM 1/1/98. Retd ENG 5/11/00.
HENDERSON R., OBE. Born 20/4/15. Commd 28/2/46. Wg Cdr 1/7/62. Retd ENG 30/4/67.
HENDERSON R. C. Born 12/12/36. Commd 30/10/61. Sqn Ldr 1/7/86. Retd GD 12/12/94.
HENDERSON R. M. W. Born 16/9/17. Commd 23/1/39. Wg Cdr 1/1/59. Retd SUP 30/11/68.
HENDERSON T. A. Born 20/10/57. Commd 8/5/83. Sqn Ldr 1/1/96. Retd SUP 8/5/99.
HENDERSON W. J. T. Born 26/5/22. Commd 6/12/41. Sqn Ldr 1/7/53. Retd GD 31/3/62.
HENDLEY I. F., FIDPM MILT MBCS. Born 22/4/44. Commd 27/2/70. Gp Capt 22/4/99. Retd ADMIN 22/4/99.
HENDRA T. H. Born 15/1/17. Commd 28/10/43. Flt Lt 14/2/57. Retd GD(G) 20/4/69.
HENDRICK R. J. Born 8/4/32. Commd 8/10/70. Flt Lt 8/10/73. Retd GD(ENG) 2/8/77. Reinstated 14/1/81. Flt Lt 22/3/77. Retd GD(ENG) 21/11/89.
HENDRICK R. O. Born 30/1/46. Commd 30/1/70. Flt Lt 30/7/75. Retd GD 14/9/96.
HENDRIE A., PhD BSc MB ChB MRCGP DRCOG DAvMed. Born 2/12/46. Commd 5/9/72. Wg Cdr 3/8/89. Retd MED 3/12/96.
HENDRY L. J. T., MBE. Born 26/6/53. Commd 18/1/73. Sqn Ldr 1/1/87. Retd ENG 16/8/91.
HENDRY R. Born 11/7/32. Commd 21/5/52. Flt Lt 11/5/58. Retd GD 19/4/71.
HENDRY R. W. Born 18/11/54. Commd 12/1/92. Flt Lt 15/5/86. Retd GD 12/2/00.
HENDY C. Born 3/12/20. Commd 20/10/55. Flt Lt 20/10/58. Retd GD(G) 9/7/66.
HENDY J. V. Born 3/3/44. Commd 10/9/70. Flt Lt 10/9/72. Retd GD(G) 3/3/83.
HENLEY B. S. Born 28/11/52. Commd 10/2/72. Sqn Ldr 1/1/85. Retd GD 28/11/90.
HENLEY I. M. Born 8/6/43. Commd 8/6/62. Wg Cdr 1/1/87. Retd GD 8/6/98.
HENLEY J. F. Born 25/5/19. Commd 8/3/45. Fg Offr 8/3/46. Retd GD 15/5/54.
HENLEY P. Born 30/6/30. Commd 16/4/57. Wg Cdr 1/1/75. Retd GD 1/1/78.
HENLEY P. G. Born 28/2/61. Commd 8/4/82. Flt Lt 8/10/88. Retd OPS SPT 28/2/99.
HENLY J. D. E. Born 3/12/29. Commd 2/7/52. Flt Lt 27/11/57. Retd GD 3/12/67.
HENNESSEY M. A. Born 18.11.46. Commd 26/8/66. Flt Lt 26/2/73. Retd SUP 1/1/76.
HENNESSEY P. de P. Born 1/9/23. Commd 31/8/45. Sqn Ldr 1/1/57. Retd GD 1/6/68.
HENNESSEY P. L. M., MBE MIMgt. Born 1/3/25. Commd 29/12/52. Gp Capt 1/7/83. Retd SY 1/9/84.
HENNESSEY W. A. Born 24/4/27. Commd 3/11/60. Flt Lt 3/11/65. Retd GD 24/4/82.
HENNESSY B. M. Born 16/5/46. Commd 13/1/72. Flt Lt 22/6/78. Retd ADMIN 23/8/89.

HENNESSY D. F., DPhysEd. Born 31/8/45. Commd 13/9/70. Sqn Ldr 1/7/85. Retd ADMIN 1/3/91.
HENNESSY D. M. Born 22/4/26. Commd 20/6/50. Sqn Ldr 1/7/63. Retd GD 9/1/76.
HENNINGTON J. T., MBE BSc CEng MRAeS. Born 12/11/46. Commd 22/9/65. Wg Cdr 1/7/85. Retd ENG 1/3/90.
HENRY A. W. Born 27/9/26. Commd 3/5/46. Flt Lt 4/1/51. Retd GD 27/9/64.
HENRY E. J., MIMgt. Born 16/4/48. Commd 9/12/76. Sqn Ldr 1/1/86. Retd ADMIN 1/1/89.
HENRY K. Born 17/4/31. Commd 2/1/52. Sqn Ldr 1/7/64. Retd GD 10/5/80.
HENRY L. C., BSc. Born 4/12/70. Commd 9/12/97. Fg Offr 9/8/96. Retd ADMIN 23/4/00.
HENRY P. G., BEng. Born 13/11/59. Commd 2/9/84. Flt Lt 23/6/87. Retd ENG 13/11/97.
HENRY R. G. Born 15/12/21. Commd 17/11/49. Flt Lt 17/11/49. Retd GD 30/9/58.
HENRY R. W. Born 20/11/52. Commd 14/12/72. Gp Capt 1/1/98. Retd GD 13/1/99.
HENRY The Rev B. G., BA. Born 28/5/30. Commd 1/5/63. Retd 27/6/81 Wg Cdr.
HENRY W. M., BSc. Born 18/11/46. Commd 1/11/71. Sqn Ldr 1/1/79. Retd ENG 1/11/87.
HENSHAW A. E. Born 29/4/47. Commd 24/6/76. Sqn Ldr 1/7/86. Retd ADMIN 2/6/93.
HENSHAW J. A., OBE MCIPD. Born 10/7/20. Commd 11/7/43. Gp Capt 1/1/72. Retd SEC 10/7/75.
HENSHAW M. J. Born 7/2/49. Commd 29/8/72. Wg Cdr 1/7/89. Retd ADMIN 1/10/96.
HENSHAW W. R. Born 30/8/44. Commd 14/7/66. Sqn Ldr 1/1/82. Retd GD 1/10/86.
HENSON J. M., OBE. Born 20/9/40. Commd 3/8/62. Wg Cdr 1/7/91. Retd GD 2/4/93.
HENSON W. J. Born 22/9/24. Commd 20/10/55. Flt Lt 20/10/61. Retd GD 22/9/82.
HENWOOD B. N. Born 17/3/35. Commd 8/7/53. Sqn Ldr 1/1/81. Retd GD 10/5/85.
HEPBURN R. M., BSocSc. Born 6/10/54. Commd 2/9/73. Fg Offr 15/4/75. Retd ADMIN 4/2/78.
HEPPENSTALL S., BSc. Born 7/8/50. Commd 27/1/70. Flt Lt 15/4/73. Retd GD 7/8/88.
HEPPENSTALL S. G. Born 14/6/47. Commd 25/1/71. Wg Cdr 1/7/90. Retd GD 14/9/96.
HEPTONSTALL P. Born 4/2/19. Commd 22/8/46. Flt Lt 22/2/50. Retd ENG 4/2/68.
HEPWORTH M. E. Born 31/7/44. Commd 15/3/84. Sqn Ldr 1/1/91. Retd ENG 31/12/98.
HERBERT C. Born 20/10/01. Commd 12/6/39. Sqn Ldr 1/6/45. Retd ENG 21/10/50 rtg Gp Capt.
HERBERT C. A. Born 30/8/34. Commd 5/4/55. Gp Capt 1/7/77. Retd GD 30/6/86.
HERBERT G. J., BSc. Born 7/3/62. Commd 31/7/83. Sqn Ldr 1/7/97. Retd GD 17/5/01.
HERBERT J. R. Born 12/12/43. Commd 11/8/67. Flt Lt 11/2/73. Retd GD 15/12/85.
HERBERT P. C. J., OBE MIMgt. Born 12/2/42. Commd 12/3/60. Wg Cdr 1/7/82. Retd GD 12/2/97.
HERBERT S. J. Born 3/9/41. Commd 3/9/60. Flt Lt 9/2/68. Retd GD 1/5/73.
HERBERT W. R. Born 15/8/20. Commd 7/1/42. Wg Cdr 1/7/65. Retd GD 15/8/75.
HERBERTSON J. M. Born 28/11/51. Commd 16/3/73. Flt Lt 16/3/76. Retd GD 15/8/81.
HERBERTSON J. N. Born 28/12/38. Commd 15/12/59. Wg Cdr 1/1/78. Retd GD 5/1/91.
HERCLIFFE F. Born 8/5/22. Commd 2/4/51. Sqn Ldr 1/1/71. Retd GD 1/8/73.
HERCUS W. G. Born 8/9/41. Commd 5/2/65. Flt Lt 21/8/67. Retd GD 8/9/79.
HERD H. D., OBE. Born 25/6/36. Commd 15/12/59. Wg Cdr 1/1/80. Retd ADMIN 21/12/88.
HERDMAN A. Born 18/7/42. Commd 30/8/73. Sqn Ldr 1/7/85. Retd ADMIN 20/4/93.
HERDMAN I. A., MRAeS MIMgt. Born 15/12/45. Commd 3/6/65. Sqn Ldr 1/7/79. Retd GD(G) 4/7/89.
HERDMAN T. J. Born 29/5/35. Commd 18/11/53. Flt Lt 23/8/59. Retd GD 29/11/60.
HEREFORD J. N., MA. Born 25/7/32. Commd 31/1/66. Sqn Ldr 31/7/69. Retd ADMIN 25/7/87.
HERITAGE M. J. H., BEM MCIPS. Born 13/7/33. Commd 22/5/70. Flt Lt 22/5/74. Retd SUP 14/7/83.
HERMAN J. E. Born 10/2/24. Commd 18/7/63. Flt Lt 18/7/66. Retd GD 10/2/82.
HERMER G. P., AFC MRAeS. Born 28/8/45. Commd 26/5/67. Sqn Ldr 1/1/81. Retd GD 1/7/84.
HERMISTON D. L. Born 22/4/14. Commd 20/4/49. Sqn Ldr 1/7/63. Retd PE 22/4/69.
HERMISTON M., MBE CEng FRAeS MIMechE. Born 29/12/15. Commd 5/7/40. Gp Capt 1/7/61. Retd ENG 4/1/71.
HERMITAGE G. M. Born 17/7/26. Commd 7/4/48. Gp Capt 1/7/69. Retd GD 29/9/76.
HERMOLLE M. A. Born 7/8/43. Commd 11/6/81. Flt Lt 11/6/84. Retd GD 2/4/93.
HERN H. R. Born 25/11/19. Commd 17/9/45. Flt Lt 17/3/48. Retd GD 22/2/64.
HERN J. M. Born 21/12/32. Commd 13/2/57. Flt Lt 13/2/63. Retd SEC 1/7/75.
HERN P. Born 20/9/45. Commd 10/12/65. Flt Lt 20/3/71. Retd GD 20/9/83.
HERN R. W. Born 2/2/20. Commd 11/4/57. Flt Lt 1/4/63. Retd ENG 2/8/64.
HEROLD C. J. W., MBE FIIP. Born 5/11/20. Commd 13/11/43. Gp Capt 1/1/71. Retd ENG 31/8/74.
HERON Rev. A. F., BA LTh. Born 11/2/28. Commd 1/2/62. Retd 1/2/78 Wg Cdr.
HERON A. V., MBE. Born 27/7/28. Commd 10/10/63. Sqn Ldr 1/1/77. Retd ENG 27/7/86.
HERON J. D., OBE. Born 14/6/36. Commd 17/12/57. Gp Capt 1/7/83. Retd GD 14/5/87.
HERON S. W. Born 5/1/60. Commd 1/7/82. Sqn Ldr 1/7/91. Retd ENG 5/1/98.
HERON-WEEBER D. R. Born 1/11/20. Commd 6/12/54. Flt Lt 6/12/54. Retd PRT 31/3/62.
HERRETT D. E. Born 28/6/31. Commd 28/6/51. Sqn Ldr 1/7/72. Retd GD 28/6/89.
HERRICK N., BEng. Born 12/1/60. Commd 16/9/84. Flt Lt 1/8/87. Retd ENG 1/5/88.
HERRIDGE W. E. Born 27/4/34. Commd 6/10/77. Flt Lt 6/10/80. Retd PI 1/8/86.
HERRIGTON W. J., CB FIMgt. Born 18/5/28. Commd 27/7/49. AVM 1/7/78. Retd GD 3/4/82.
HERRING G. R. Born 8/7/43. Commd 17/12/63. Sq Ldr 1/1/74. Retd GD 8/7/87.
HERRING K. Born 2/2/10. Commd 13/9/41. Sqn Ldr 1/8/47. Retd GD 2/2/59.
HERRING K. A. Born 4/9/46. Commd 25/2/88. Flt Lt 25/2/92. Retd ENG 3/4/93.
HERRING P. Born 26/11/22. Commd 23/3/66. Flt Lt 23/3/71. Retd ENG 26/11/82.
HERSEY G. H. Born 20/12/11. Commd 29/6/42. Flt Lt 1/3/46. Retd ENG 29/4/58.

HESELWOOD R. Born 24/8/46. Commd 27/3/70. Flt Lt 4/12/73. Retd GD 12/3/92.
HESKETH P. M., BA. Born 6/2/31. Commd 4/11/53. Sqn Ldr 26/2/64. Retd EDN 1/2/75.
HESKETT D. Born 27/12/46. Commd 11/10/84. Flt Lt 11/10/88. Retd SUP 11/7/93.
HESLAM-ELEY D. Born 4/9/42. Commd 19/6/64. Flt Lt 8/3/72. Retd GD 4/9/80.
HESLOP G. Born 21/7/23. Commd 29/4/44. Flt Lt 9/7/48. Retd GD 21/7/66.
HESLOP J. Born 27/2/25. Commd 1/2/62. Sqn Ldr 1/1/73. Retd GD(G) 4/4/75.
HESMONDHALGH E. J. Born 10/7/21. Commd 17/4/47. Flt Lt 17/10/51. Retd SUP 1/6/61.
HESSEY B. Born 7/1/24. Commd 19/7/57. Flt Lt 1/10/67. Retd GD 28/6/72.
HESTER E. R. Born 5/2/22. Commd 19/8/41. Sqn Ldr 1/7/52. Retd ENG 10/9/52.
HESTER V. A., DFC. Born 16/11/19. Commd 25/11/41. Sqn Ldr 11/7/53. Retd GD 16/11/58.
HETHERINGTON A. J., MA. Born 12/11/38. Commd 9/5/66. Flt Lt 9/2/68. Retd GD 10/4/86.
HETHERINGTON D. T. Born 4/1/46. Commd 28/4/67. Sqn Ldr 1/1/91. Retd GD 14/3/96.
HETHERINGTON H., BA. Born 4/8/20. Commd 30/9/52. Sqn Ldr 30/12/58. Retd EDN 9/3/73.
HETHERINGTON J. M., BSc. Born 23/4/56. Commd 14/8/77. Wg Cdr 1/7/94. Retd GD 1/1/98.
HETHERINGTON R. Born 10/10/21. Commd 26/9/57. Wg Cdr 1/7/72. Retd ENG 7/9/76.
HEWARD M. Born 15/11/09. Commd 1/12/41. Flt Offr 1/12/47. Retd CAT 29/5/62.
HEWETT B. P. G., MBE. Born 3/1/37. Commd 28/2/56. Sqn Ldr 1/1/73. Retd SY 3/1/92.
HEWETT G. M., MBE. Born 20/5/61. Commd 25/9/80. Wg Cdr 1/1/98. Retd GD 1/1/01.
HEWETT-HICKS P. E. Born 9/7/20. Commd 23/2/48. Flt Lt 22/7/48. Retd SEC 9/7/75.
HEWITT A. R. Born 23/10/22. Commd 3/10/43. Plt Offr 3/10/48. Retd SEC 7/5/51.
HEWITT D. N. Born 10/11/39. Commd 2/3/65. Sqn Ldr 1/7/74. Retd ENG 2/3/81. Re-entered 4/10/90. Sqn Ldr 4/10/90. Retd ENG 10/7/96.
HEWITT F. P., OBE. Born 7/6/08. Commd 28/7/28. Fg Offr 28/1/30. Retd GD 17/8/32. Recalled 21/9/39 to 20/4/46 rtg Sqn Ldr.
HEWITT H. B. Born 15/5/17. Commd 15/9/60. Flt Lt 15/9/65. Retd ENG 27/6/72.
HEWITT I. S. Born 10/1/43. Commd 25/3/64. Flt Lt 12/11/69. Retd GD 31/5/80. Re-instated 8/12/82. Flt Lt 21/5/72. Retd GD 25/6/93.
HEWITT J. A. Born 21/7/36. Commd 26/5/67. Sqn Ldr 1/1/75. Retd ENG 31/8/90.
HEWITT J. G. F., DSM. Born 4/1/30. Commd 9/4/52. Gp Capt 1/7/77. Retd GD 5/4/83.
HEWITT M. Born 30/12/45. Commd 11/8/67. Flt Lt 30/6/71. Retd GD 14/3/96.
HEWITT P. A. Born 24/10/45. Commd 22/7/71. Flt Lt 21/7/74. Retd GD 14/3/96.
HEWITT R. C. Born 14/12/46. Commd 21/1/66. Sqn Ldr 1/1/83. Retd GD 12/1/92.
HEWITT S. G., AFC*. Born 18/12/22. Commd 28/5/43. Sqn Ldr 1/7/53. Retd GD 25/12/61.
HEWLETT R. E., DFC. Born 12/10/17. Commd 2/9/42. Sqn Ldr 1/7/69. Retd GD(G) 12/10/72.
HEWLETT T. C., OBE. Born 9/2/49. Commd 27/2/70. Gp Capt 1/1/95. Retd GD 29/4/01.
HEWLETT W. H. Born 30/3/20. Commd 26/11/41. Flt Lt 1/9/45. Retd GD(G) 30/3/75.
HEXT J. H. G. Born 12/4/30. Commd 9/6/54. Sqn Ldr 1/7/76. Retd GD 3/10/79.
HEXTALL R. Born 3/11/34. Commd 23/5/63. Wg Cdr 1/1/79. Retd SUP 3/4/82.
HEYES E. R. Born 23/11/32. Commd 19/6/70. Flt Lt 19/6/75. Retd ENG 1/10/77. Reinstated 21/5/80. Sqn Ldr 1/1/87. Retd ENG 23/11/90.
HEYES M. R. H., MA MSc CEng FIEE FIMgt MRAeS. Born 22/7/34. Commd 25/9/54. Gp Capt 1/1/79. Retd ENG 10/4/87.
HEYES T. A. Born 27/12/47. Commd 17/2/67. Sqn Ldr 1/1/80. Retd GD 27/12/85.
HEYLAND C. R. K. Born 12/10/45. Commd 9/12/65. Sqn Ldr 1/1/83. Retd SUP 1/1/92.
HEYS P. J., IEng FIIE(elec). Born 6/1/47. Commd 1/3/68. Sqn Ldr 1/1/83. Retd ENG 14/3/96.
HEYWARD P. J. Born 25/6/23. Commd 22/9/49. Flt Lt 22/3/54. Retd SEC 24/10/61.
HEYWOOD D. G. L., MIMgt. Born 20/11/26. Commd 25/10/46. Gp Capt 1/1/70. Retd GD 1/10/76.
HEYWOOD J. N. Born 25/12/45. Commd 23/3/67. Sqn Ldr 1/7/84. Retd SY 16/8/93.
HEYWOOD T. D. L. Born 2/2/48. Commd 9/3/72. Flt Lt 24/6/78. Retd GD(G) 15/11/89.
HIBBERD N. R. W., AFC. Born 8/10/44. Commd 28/2/64. Sqn Ldr 1/1/80. Retd GD 1/6/97.
HIBBERT C. J., BA. Born 18/8/44. Commd 15/7/66. Flt Lt 15/7/69. Retd GD 18/8/77.
HIBBERT W. J., DFC. Born 12/7/20. Commd 13/4/42. Sqn Ldr 1/1/54. Retd GD 15/11/61.
HIBBIN D. J. Born 13/6/37. Commd 3/11/77. Flt Lt 3/11/81. Retd ENG 4/8/93.
HICK A. R. Born 20/11/23. Commd 18/9/44. Flt Lt 13/11/57. Retd GD 1/5/68.
HICK M. R., FIMgt MCIPD. Born 4/4/37. Commd 13/9/60. Gp Capt 1/7/75. Retd ADMIN 2/10/87.
HICKEY C. D. Born 4/9/20. Commd 14/11/46. Flt Lt 14/5/51. Retd SUP 30/5/64.
HICKEY G. A., MIMgt. Born 23/1/33. Commd 1/10/57. Gp Capt 1/1/79. Retd SY 1/5/81.
HICKEY J. J. Born 6/6/16. Commd 16/5/47. Sqn Ldr 1/7/65. Retd SUP 6/6/71.
HICKEY L. D., AFC. Born 19/7/21. Commd 6/7/50. Flt Lt 10/11/55. Retd GD 10/4/68.
HICKEY P. L., CBE MSc MB BS DObstRCOG DAvMed. Born 21/6/45. Commd 19/7/65. Gp Capt 1/7/92. Retd MED 10/10/94.
HICKEY S. A., OBE FRAeS FIMgt. Born 23/5/46. Commd 16/12/66. Gp Capt 1/7/95. Retd GD 6/4/01.
HICKIE J. A. Born 9/5/29. Commd 22/7/66. Sqn Ldr 1/1/79. Retd ENG 9/5/87.
HICKLEY P. A. M., BA. Born 29/1/44. Commd 31/1/64. Flt Lt 31/7/69. Retd GD 01/10/92.
HICKLING A. I. Born 29/8/27. Commd 30/11/59. Flt Lt 30/11/59. Retd GD 3/1/69.
HICKMAN C. St.J. Born 8/8/39. Commd 19/4/63. Flt Lt 19/10/68. Retd GD 8/8/94.

HICKMAN K. P. Born 6/10/43. Commd 11/7/74. Sqn Ldr 1/1/86. Retd ENG 6/4/96.
HICKMORE G. G. A., MBE. Born 25/11/35. Commd 4/5/55. Sqn Ldr 1/7/82. Retd GD 25/11/93.
HICKMOTT J. A. Born 7/10/34. Commd 8/7/53. Sqn Ldr 1/1/70. Retd GD 1/1/73.
HICKMOTT M. E. J., DFC MRAeS. Born 11/7/24. Commd 26/8/45. Sqn Ldr 1/1/59. Retd GD 11/6/73.
HICKOX A. J. L., DFC*. Born 3/6/22. Commd 1/5/42. Flt Lt 29/3/49. Retd GD 30/10/62.
HICKS A. G., MA CEng MIEE MRAeS. Born 18/2/36. Commd 9/8/57. A Cdre 1/7/87. Retd GD 18/10/91.
HICKS A. V. J. Born 3/3/19. Commd 27/5/43. Sqn Ldr 1/7/55. Retd ENG 3/3/68.
HICKS B., MBE. Born 3/10/44. Commd 14/7/69. Wg Cdr 1/1/88. Retd PRT 14/7/91.
HICKS D. Born 2/10/33. Commd 2/7/52. Flt Lt 14/5/58. Retd GD(G) 2/10/88.
HICKS D. B. J., DFC CEng MIEE MIMgt. Born 20/11/22. Commd 20/8/44. Sqn Ldr 1/1/59. Retd ENG 20/11/77.
HICKS D. S. Born 4/5/33. Commd 27/5/69. Sqn Ldr 1/1/82. Retd GD 4/5/91.
HICKS F. H. Born 15/5/21. Commd 24/10/45. Flt Lt 15/12/49. Retd GD 1/10/57.
HICKS G. A. Born 15/9/28. Commd 20/5/63. Flt Lt 23/5/68. Retd GD(G) 15/9/83.
HICKS G. C. Born 6/8/07. Commd 25/4/40. Sqn Ldr 1/8/47. Retd SEC 7/8/57.
HICKS G. F. Born 23/9/23. Commd 21/7/55. Sqn Ldr 1/7/75. Retd GD 1/7/82.
HICKS H., MBE BA. Born 13/7/23. Commd 31/1/45. Gp Capt 1/7/72. Retd ADMIN 31/3/76.
HICKS J. S. R., MA. Born 6/11/35. Commd 5/3/60. Sqn Ldr 1/7/71. Retd GD 1/4/80. Reinstated 4/2/81. Sqn Ldr
　　6/5/72. Retd GD 30/9/89.
HICKS P. Born 21/7/30. Commd 31/7/58. Flt Lt 31/1/62. Retd GD 1/4/77.
HICKS P. K. V. Born 9/7/22. Commd 11/11/44. Wg Cdr 1/7/64. Retd GD 1/9/67.
HICKS T. P., MBE. Born 9/9/48. Commd 8/6/84. Sqn Ldr 1/1/91. Retd ENG 5/4/96.
HICKSON C. Born 3/3/44. Commd 6/4/62. Flt Lt 6/10/67. Retd GD 31/10/94.
HIDE D. C. Born 14/12/42. Commd 28/4/65. Flt Lt 28/10/70. Retd GD 12/1/81.
HIDE W. R., DFC. Born 10/7/17. Commd 14/10/42. Flt Lt 14/4/47. Retd GD(G) 10/7/72.
HIFLE R. Born 24/4/39. Commd 13/1/72. Sqn Ldr 1/7/85. Retd GD 8/11/89.
HIGGINBOTTOM D. H. Born 20/8/48. Commd 27/5/48. Sqn Ldr 1/1/87. Retd GD(G) 7/12/92.
HIGGINS B. H. Born 21/6/37. Commd 9/2/62. Wg Cdr 1/7/89. Retd ADMIN 21/6/92.
HIGGINS C. R. M., BA. Born 1/9/32. Commd 27/2/61. Flt Lt 1/5/61. Retd GD(G) 9/12/92.
HIGGINS E. B. Born 8/8/19. Commd 6/9/56. Flt Lt 6/9/62. Retd GD(G) 31/10/72.
HIGGINS J. E. N. Born 31/8/20. Commd 20/11/58. Sqn Ldr 1/7/67. Retd ENG 1/9/73.
HIGGINS J. W., CEng MRAeS MIMgt. Born 12/5/21. Commd 28/7/49. Wg Cdr 1/1/73. Retd ENG 12/5/76.
HIGGINS M. P. Born 22/9/34. Commd 4/6/64. Flt Lt 10/2/67. Retd SEC 22/9/72.
HIGGINSON A. G., MB ChB MRCPath. Born 19/4/43. Commd 11/1/65. Wg Cdr 7/9/80. Retd MED 9/11/81.
HIGGINSON F. W., DFC DFM. Born 17/2/13. Commd 18/9/40. Wg Cdr 1/7/53. Retd GD 5/4/56.
HIGGOTT G. D., CEng MRAeS. Born 20/10/40. Commd 4/12/67. Flt Lt 4/12/72. Retd ENG 4/12/83.
HIGGS A. R. N., OBE MA. Born 6/2/34. Commd 3/1/58. Wg Cdr 1/7/80. Retd ADMIN 10/4/93.
HIGGS B., CBE. Born 22/8/34. Commd 19/11/52. AVM 1/1/86. Retd GD 29/10/87.
HIGGS D. M. Born 30/11/36. Commd 6/7/45. Wg Cdr 1/1/81. Retd ADMIN 27/4/84.
HIGGS E. L. C., MIMgt. Born 11/1/25. Commd 6/7/45. Wg Cdr 1/1/70. Retd SUP 3/4/79.
HIGGS J. F., MIMgt. Born 8/9/33. Commd 3/6/65. Sqn Ldr 1/7/78. Retd ADMIN 6/4/83.
HIGGS P. R., BSc. Born 22/6/54. Commd 3/1/88. Flt Lt 3/7/88. Retd ENG 23/9/95.
HIGH M. N. S. Born 11/10/56. Commd 9/12/76. Flt Lt 9/6/82. Retd GD 11/10/94.
HIGH R. Born 3/12/20. Commd 7/10/44. Flt Lt 19/11/53. Retd GD(G) 1/3/68.
HIGH W. D. Born 1/7/10. Commd 10/6/42. Flt Offr 10/12/46. Retd SEC 29/10/50.
HIGHAM D., MBE. Born 13/9/31. Commd 22/9/55. Sqn Ldr 1/7/66. Retd ENG 1/3/85.
HIGHAM F. J., OBE DFC. Born 2/5/15. Commd 14/7/41. Wg Cdr 1/7/55. Retd GD 2/5/62.
HIGHAM P. Born 2/12/48. Commd 19/6/86. Flt Lt 19/6/90. Retd ADMIN 14/3/96.
HIGHMAN P. Born 26/7/22. Commd 7/6/51. Flt Lt 7/12/55. Retd MAR 18/9/76.
HIGHMORE H. G. Born 14/8/30. Commd 3/6/65. Sqn Ldr 1/1/77. Retd ENG 2/6/82.
HIGHTON P. T. Born 13/1/34. Commd 28/9/54. Sqn Ldr 1/1/69. Retd GD 31/7/73.
HIGLEY G. R. Born 7/7/34. Commd 28/1/53. Flt Lt 29/4/59. Retd GD 7/7/72.
HIGNELL A. F., OBE MA MB BChir MFCM MRCGP DPH. Born 6/7/28. Commd 26/9/54. Gpn Capt 1/7/77. Retd
　　MED 1/4/80.
HIGNELL R. A., BSc. Born 23/8/54. Commd 2/9/73. Flt Lt 15/10/79. Retd ENG 1/5/83.
HIGNETT D. R. Born 2/3/46. Commd 22/9/65. Flt Lt 28/8/72. Retd ENG 2/3/84.
HIGSON D. J., BA. Born 14/2/49. Commd 30/7/72. Sqn Ldr 1/7/79. Retd ADMIN 30/7/88.
HIGSON E. M. Born 17/5/23. Commd 25/6/43. Wg Cdr 1/7/64. Retd GD 30/3/78.
HILDAGE A. R., MIMgt. Born 31/12/52. Commd 8/9/83. Wg Cdr 1/7/96. Retd ADMIN 1/5/98.
HILDITCH C. H., BSc. Born 24/9/34. Commd 20/11/56. Flt Lt 20/8/58. Retd GD 24/9/89.
HILDITCH L. E. Born 22/9/47. Commd 27/10/67. Fg Offr 24/2/70. Retd GD(G) 15/9/73. Re-entered 31/10/84. Flt Lt
　　31/10/87. OPS SPT 31/10/00.
HILDRETH P. Born 15/4/22. Commd 23/1/43. Flt Lt 23/1/48. Retd RGT 25/6/58 rtg Sqn Ldr.
HILES A. N., BA. Born 11/3/41. Commd 10/11/64. Flt Lt 10/8/68. Retd SEC 1/7/75.
HILL A. G. Born 23/4/44. Commd 2/2/68. Wg Cdr 1/1/94. Retd ADMIN 14/3/96.
HILL A. J. Born 17/6/17. Commd 6/3/39. Sqn Ldr 1/8/47. Retd GD 25/10/57.
HILL A. M. Born 20/3/47. Commd 14/1/82. Sqn Ldr 1/7/91. Retd SY 2/12/96.

HILL A. R. Born 6/9/31. Commd 14/4/53. Flt Lt 14/10/55. Retd GD 6/9/69.
HILL A. R. Born 22/6/38. Commd 6/5/66. Flt Lt 4/11/70. Retd GD(G) 18/11/77.
HILL A. R., BSc. Born 10/7/45. Commd 2/8/71. Wg Cdr 1/1/92. Retd ENG 13/1/95.
HILL B. H. Born 30/6/42. Commd 12/4/73. Wg Cdr 1/1/92. Retd GD 30/6/97.
HILL C. Born 29/1/39. Commd 28/10/63. Flt Lt 20/12/67. Retd GD 31/1/84.
HILL D. Born 15/7/45. Commd 2/6/67. Sqn Ldr 1/1/80. Retd GD 1/6/98.
HILL D., CEng MRAeS. Born 15/3/21. Commd 19/8/42. Gp Capt 1/7/71. Retd ENG 15/9/73.
HILL D. B. R. Born 8/3/26. Commd 3/5/46. Fg Offr 3/5/47. Retd GD 15/6/49.
HILL D. F. E., BA. Born 28/12/33. Commd 22/5/62. Sqn Ldr 26/7/65. Retd EDN 22/5/78.
HILL D. H. Born 3/5/13. Commd 7/5/53. Sqn Ldr 1/7/62. Retd ENG 3/5/68.
HILL D. P. Born 4/11/39. Commd 16/12/66. Sqn Ldr 1/1/91. Retd GD 4/11/94.
HILL D. S., BEM. Born 7/8/31. Commd 7/9/61. Flt Lt 7/9/67. Retd ENG 1/12/81.
HILL D. W., BEM. Born 26/12/24. Commd 18/5/61. Flt Lt 18/5/66. Retd ENG 1/1/77.
HILL Dame Felicity., DBE. Born 12/12/15. Commd 25/4/41. A Cdre 1/4/66. Retd SEC 9/8/69.
HILL E. G. F., CBE. Born 1/10/17. Commd 3/4/39. A Cdre 1/1/70. Retd SUP 3/1/73.
HILL E. J. Born 23/1/30. Commd 30/8/62. Sqn Ldr 1/7/84. Retd ENG 23/1/88.
HILL The Rev Mgr E. P. Born 8/4/43. Commd 14/9/82. Retd 5/5/00 Gp Capt.
HILL F. Born 3/9/11. Commd 20/4/44. Flt Lt 20/10/47. Retd ENG 2/6/48.
HILL G. J., BSc. Born 24/9/60. Commd 11/9/83. Flt Lt 11/3/85. Retd GD 11/9/99.
HILL H. F. Born 21/2/24. Commd 20/11/58. Flt Lt 1/2/63. Retd GD(G) 21/2/82.
HILL I. J. C. Born 20/10/38. Commd 20/9/59. Sqn Ldr 1/1/72. Retd GD 1/2/73. Re-employed 13/11/78. Retd 1/11/83.
HILL I. R., OBE MA PhD MD MB BChir MRC Path AMRAeS LDS. Born 26/11/39. Commd 25/11/68. Wg Cdr 29/3/84. Retd MED 28/5/91.
HILL J. Born 23/11/98. Commd 30/10/40. Fg Offr 30/10/40. Retd ENG 30/9/45 rtg Flt Lt.
HILL J. B., AFC. Born 14/5/43. Commd 24/6/65. Gp Capt 1/7/86. Retd GD 13/5/93.
HILL J. E., BA. Born 16/5/59. Commd 18/10/81. Flt Lt 14/5/83. Retd ADMIN 14/3/97.
HILL J. G., MA. Born 7/1/33. Commd 25/8/55. Sqn Ldr 25/2/63. Retd EDN 31/10/73.
HILL J. R. E. Born 21/5/40. Commd 8/12/64. Sqn Ldr 1/1/76. Retd ENG 8/12/87.
HILL L. C. V. Born 21/7/23. Commd 19/12/63. Flt Lt 19/12/68. Retd ENG 21/7/77.
HILL L. R. Born 3/3/23. Commd 19/11/45. Flt Lt 30/6/49. Retd GD 3/3/62.
HILL M. A., BEng. Born 13/11/46. Commd 24/7/68. Flt Lt 1/6/72. Retd GD 5/4/75.
HILL M. D. Born 18/8/34. Commd 17/3/54. Flt Lt 15/8/62. Retd GD 28/3/77.
HILL M. J. Born 23/10/51. Commd 16/3/73. Sqn Ldr 1/7/85. Retd GD 23/10/89.
HILL P. A., MIMgt. Born 18/11/32. Commd 25/9/52. Sqn Ldr 1/1/69. Retd ADMIN 18/11/87.
HILL P. F. Born 25/3/38. Commd 24/2/61. Flt Lt 1/4/66. Retd GD 2/9/75.
HILL P. G. Born 14/3/22. Commd 30/4/41. Gp Capt 1/1/67. Retd GD 14/3/77.
HILL P. J. R. Born 1/2/43. Commd 26/5/61. Sqn Ldr 1/1/81. Retd GD 1/1/84.
HILL P. M. Born 16/11/23. Commd 21/7/55. Flt Lt 21/7/61. Retd GD 16/11/73.
HILL P. R., MBE. Born 26/6/22. Commd 29/9/44. Wg Cdr 1/1/74. Retd GD(G) 30/6/76.
HILL R., MRAeS. Born 1/10/17. Commd 19/11/42. Sqn Ldr 1/7/53. Retd ENG 1/10/67.
HILL R. Born 11/2/23. Commd 25/8/49. Sqn Ldr 1/1/73. Retd GD 10/9/77.
HILL R., DPhysEd. Born 17/8/42. Commd 22/9/64. Fg Offr 22/9/64. Retd ADMIN 22/9/82.
HILL R. A. Born 2/6/44. Commd 14/7/66. Wg Cdr 1/7/83. Retd GD 10/6/88.
HILL R. B., MHCIMA. Born 27/5/25. Commd 7/5/56. Flt Lt 5/11/58. Retd CAT 7/6/75.
HILL R. G., MIMgt LHA. Born 2/3/34. Commd 22/7/66. Sqn Ldr 21/9/77. Retd MED(SEC) 2/5/84.
HILL R. L. Born 28/8/50. Commd 27/1/77. Flt Lt 27/7/81. Retd GD 30/3/94.
HILL S. C. A. Born 19/4/34. Commd 2/7/52. Sqn Ldr 1/7/67. Retd SEC 19/4/72.
HILL S. J., MSc BSc. Born 1/8/47. Commd 30/5/71. Sqn Ldr 1/1/80. Retd ENG 30/5/87.
HILL S. R., OBE BA CEng FIMechE FIMgt FRAeS CertDipAF. Born 27/3/42. Commd 28/11/66. A Cdre 1/7/89. Retd ENG 28/2/91.
HILL W. Born 4/2/33. Commd 1/12/54. Wg Cdr 1/7/78. Retd GD 11/5/87.
HILL W. W. Born 16/8/32. Commd 26/3/52. Flt Lt 26/12/63. Retd GD 2/1/76.
HILL W. W., MBE. Born 8/3/30. Commd 17/5/51. Sqn Ldr 1/1/67. Retd GD 18/3/88.
HILL-TREVOR N. E. Born 25/4/31. Commd 25/5/50. Fg Offr 30/1/54. Retd RGT 16/7/60.
HILLARY R. D. Born 9/8/24. Commd 25/6/51. Gp Capt. 1/1/74. Retd GD 9/8/79.
HILLEN R. G. Born 26/4/17. Commd 17/5/45. Sqn Ldr 1/1/59. Retd SEC 27/4/72.
HILLER D. W., CEng MRAeS MIMgt. Born 24/3/35. Commd 16/5/57. Gp Capt 1/1/85. Retd ENG 1/12/89.
HILLIARD A. J. Born 22/9/35. Commd 3/3/54. Flt Lt 3/9/59. Retd GD 22/9/90.
HILLIARD F. H. Born 3/1/26. Commd 6/3/52. Flt Lt 6/9/55. Retd GD 3/1/76.
HILLIARD G. H. Born 28/10/56. Commd 28/10/76. Flt Lt 28/4/82. Retd GD(G) 28/10/96.
HILLIARD T. Born 6/6/32. Commd 23/4/52. Sqn Ldr 1/1/64. Retd GD 2/8/69.
HILLIER B. E. Born 18/11/44. Commd 8/10/70. Flt Lt 28/1/73. Retd ENG 18/11/82.
HILLIER C. Born 8/3/18. Commd 5/10/50. Sqn Ldr 1/1/62. Retd ENG 8/3/69.
HILLIER D. J., CEng MRAeS. Born 12/3/43. Commd 15/7/65. Sqn Ldr 1/7/74. Retd ENG 30/6/81.
HILLIER P. F. J. Born 23/11/22. Commd 2/3/45. Flt Lt 29/11/51. Retd GD 25/5/61.

HILLIKER C. Born 6/6/46. Commd 6/5/66. Wg Cdr 1/1/91. Retd GD 31/7/00.
HILLMAN C. G., MILAM DPhysEd. Born 19/3/48. Commd 13/9/70. Wg Cdr 1/1/89. Retd ADMIN 13/9/92.
HILLMAN R. Born 20/4/35. Commd 16/9/53. Sqn Ldr 1/7/67. Retd GD 31/12/91.
HILLS B. F., MBE. Born 18/7/25. Commd 3/9/46. Wg Cdr 1/7/71. Retd GD 18/7/80.
HILLS C. C. Born 2/3/34. Commd 15/10/52. Flt Lt 22/4/58. Retd GD 11/4/72.
HILLS D. G. M., CB OBE MB BS MFCM DPH. Born 28/2/25. Commd 29/6/50. AVM 1/4/83. Retd MED 1/4/85.
HILLS D. W., CEng MIEE. Born 25/8/21. Commd 6/6/46. Wg Cdr 1/1/66. Retd ENG 1/2/78.
HILLS E. D., CB CBE. Born 26/1/17. Commd 23/1/39. AVM 1/7/71. Retd SUP 1/9/73.
HILLS J. Born 5/12/46. Commd 7/1/71. Sqn Ldr 1/7/81. Retd GD 31/5/85.
HILLS N. G. R. Born 29/10/63. Commd 23/4/87. Flt Lt 21/8/93. Retd ADMIN 14/3/96.
HILLS P. L., MIMgt. Born 13/10/20. Commd 26/9/57. Sqn Ldr 1/1/68. Retd ENG 17/10/70.
HILLS R. J. Born 31/10/62. Commd 11/10/87. Flt Lt 11/10/93. Retd ADMIN 29/1/97.
HILLS T. A. Born 7/8/56. Commd 17/7/75. Flt Lt 17/1/81. Retd GD 7/8/94.
HILLSMITH K. R. Born 30/12/62. Commd 20/10/83. Flt Lt 20/4/89. Retd GD 30/1/01.
HILTON A. A. Born 9/8/26. Commd 4/7/51. Flt Lt 24/4/57. Retd GD 25/8/71.
HILTON A. P. Born 16/9/33. Commd 5/4/55. Sqn Ldr 1/1/70. Retd GD 1/1/73.
HILTON B. S. Born 18/12/33. Commd 15/3/55. Flt Lt 24/3/58. Retd ADMIN 1/4/84.
HILTON D. E. Born 20/1/36. Commd 2/12/55. Flt Lt 2/6/61. Retd GD 20/1/91.
HILTON J. B. S. Born 11/4/48. Commd 27/2/70. Flt Lt 27/8/75. Retd ADMIN 1/10/90.
HILTON L. J. Born 26/7/14. Commd 16/4/42. Wg Cdr 1/1/64. Retd GD(G) 26/7/69.
HILTON P. W. Born 3/9/37. Commd 21/10/65. Gp Capt 1/7/89. Retd SUP 3/9/92.
HILTON R. B., BSc. Born 9/7/51. Commd 25/9/71. Fg Off 15/4/74. Retd ENG 10/4/79.
HILTON T. F. Born 19/7/45. Commd 26/5/67. Flt Lt 4/5/72. Retd GD 26/9/72.
HINCHCLIFFE P. M. Born 22/11/28. Commd 6/12/50. Flt Lt 6/9/56. Retd GD 27/11/66.
HINCHLIFFE D. A. R. Born 6/5/40. Commd 10/2/59. Sqn Ldr 1/1/79. Retd GD 6/5/95.
HINCHLIFFE N. B. Born 24/9/53. Commd 20/1/80. Flt Lt 20/1/81. Retd ADMIN 20/1/99.
HINCHLIFFE P. C. Born 20/8/24. Commd 26/3/45. Flt Lt 16/3/57. Retd GD(G) 10/8/67.
HIND J. M., MIMgt. Born 15/6/32. Commd 6/1/51. Sqn Ldr 1/7/67. Retd SUP 1/7/77.
HIND K. Born 2/12/33. Commd 22/7/55. Fg Offr 15/10/56. Retd ENG 16/10/59.
HIND L. Born 10/11/42. Commd 27/9/73. Flt Lt 27/9/75. Retd GD 1/5/93.
HIND P. J. Born 8/12/35. Commd 14/1/65. Flt Lt 26/7/67. Retd GD 30/6/77.
HINDE C. J., MBA MIMgt. Born 25/4/46. Commd 11/5/75. Flt Lt 11/2/79. Retd ADMIN 11/5/91.
HINDLE I., MSc BDS FDSRCS FFDRCSIrel. Born 28/7/45. Commd 31/7/66. Flt Lt 18/12/68. Retd DEL 18/12/73.
    Re-entered 2/4/79. Gp Capt 20/12/91. Retd DEL 3/4/97.
HINDLE M. P., ACIS. Born 19/12/45. Commd 25/8/67. Wg Cdr 1/7/85. Retd ADMIN 19/12/89.
HINDLEY A., OBE AFC. Born 19/3/15. Commd 23/10/39. Wg Cdr 1/7/54. Retd GD 1/1/58.
HINDLEY F., MBE. Born 24/6/37. Commd 21/10/66. Flt Lt 1/7/69. Retd GD 24/6/95.
HINDLEY M. A. Born 25/3/43. Commd 22/2/63. Sqn Ldr 1/7/74. Retd GD 25/3/94.
HINDMARSH A. D., AFC. Born 22/7/15. Commd 9/4/43. Sqn Ldr 1/7/52. Retd GD 21/11/58.
HINDMARSH J. Born 2/2/29. Commd 20/6/63. Sqn Ldr 1/7/74. Retd ENG 2/2/84.
HINDMARSH T.J., OBE BA. Born 19/9/37. Commd 24/4/64. Gp Capt 1/1/89. Retd GD 24/10/92.
HINDS C. D., BSc. Born 4/2/45. Commd 15/7/66. Sqn Ldr 1/7/75. Retd ENG 6/11/76.
HINE A. T. Born 27/2/47. Commd 19/8/66. Flt Lt 8/3/72. Retd GD 27/2/85.
HINE D. J. Born 22/4/35. Commd 26/5/54. Air Cdre 1/1/87. Retd GD 18/11/88.
HINE Sir Patrick., GCB GBE FRAeS CIMgt. Born 14/7/32. Commd 22/3/51. ACM 1/7/85. Retd GD 1/9/91.
HINES F. M. A. Born 14/3/33. Commd 5/4/55. Wg Cdr 1/7/70. Retd GD 27/10/84.
HING T. J. Born 18/8/50. Commd 30/1/70. Fg Offr 18/7/72. Retd SUP 31/3/76.
HINGE C. J. Born 2/2/39. Commd 21/10/65. Flt Lt 29/7/68. Retd GD 2/2/77.
HINGLEY H. B., OBE BMus LRAM ARCM. Born 4/3/38. Commd 24/3/67. Wg Cdr 1/7/89. Retd DM 4/3/95.
HINGSTON-JONES G. F., OBE MInst FIMgt. Born 20/4/31. Commd 18/6/71. Wg Cdr 1/1/79. Retd SUP 18/7/87.
HINKLEY SMITH K. L., MA. Born 12/10/39. Commd 27/4/65. Sqn Ldr 1/7/79. Retd ADMIN 1/4/97.
HINNELL K. G. Born 10/10/19. Commd 15/11/45. Sqn Ldr 1/7/66. Retd ENG 10/10/74.
HINSHELWOOD W. E. D., MSc BTech. Born 22/12/48. Commd 18/4/69. Sqn Ldr 1/7/83. Retd ENG 1/10/88.
HINTON D. H. E. Born 29/6/32. Commd 17/12/52. Flt Lt 17/5/56. Retd GD 29/1/70. Reinstated 14/9/79 to 29/1/84.
HINTON N .G., CEng MRAeS. Born 3/10/37. Commd 10/8/65. Sqn Ldr 1/7/74. Retd ENG 10/8/81.
HINTON P. N., MIMgt. Born 5/5/47. Commd 1/4/66. Sqn Ldr 1/7/83. Retd GD 1/9/00.
HINTON R. H. Born 12/4/22. Commd 15/3/45. Sqn Ldr 1/1/59. Retd GD 14/4/65.
HINWOOD J. A. Born 5/6/22. Commd 12/3/43. Flt Lt 19/11/53. Retd GD(G) 5/6/77.
HIPKINS B. G. Born 17/10/25. Commd 9/8/47. Sqn Ldr 1/7/70. Retd ADMIN 7/10/78.
HIPKINS J. R. D. Born 29/11/68. Commd 15/12/88. Fg Offr 15/6/91. Retd SUP 1/5/93.
HIPPERSON D. G. Born 22/4/35. Commd 18/8/54. Flt Lt 26/2/60. Retd GD 22/4/73.
HIPPERSON G. Born 17/6/41. Commd 23/6/63. Flt Lt 22/9/68. Retd GD 17/6/82.
HIRD D. W. Born 14/1/25. Commd 10/4/52. Flt Lt 10/4/52.Retd GD 14/1/83.
HIRD R. Born 8/12/57. Commd 22/9/88. Flt Lt 22/9/90. Retd ENG 22/9/96.
HIRONS P. J. Born 22/3/37. Commd 26/5/67. Sqn Ldr 1/7/75. Retd ENG 31/5/77.
HIRPARA R. H., MB BS MIMgt DAvMed. Born 2/4/43. Commd 1/2/80. Wg Cdr 22/5/92. Retd MED 14/9/96.

HIRST C. A. R., BSc. Born 9/4/50. Commd 28/2/72. Flt Lt 28/5/73. Retd GD 9/4/88.
HIRST C. W. Born 24/6/52. Commd 27/1/77. Flt Lt 7/12/80. Retd OPS SPT 1/10/97.
HIRST F. Born 16/8/20. Commd 28/2/46. Sqn Ldr 1/1/63. Retd ENG 28/4/68.
HIRST J. K. Born 6/1/37. Commd 24/11/60. Sqn Ldr 6/11/69. Retd ADMIN 30/5/76.
HIRST K. L. Born 5/6/26. Commd 14/6/46. Sqn Ldr 1/7/59. Retd GD 1/10/73.
HIRST P. B. Born 2/2/40. Commd 28/7/60. Sqn Ldr 1/7/74. Retd ENG 2/2/78.
HIRST P. J. Born 12/4/32. Commd 24/1/52. Wg Cdr 1/7/74. Retd GD 10/2/86.
HISCOCK P. G. Born 7/12/33. Commd 22/5/59. Sqn Ldr 20/8/68. Retd ADMIN 24/5/77. Reinstated 2/1/80 to
    13/7/84.
HISLOP I. G. Born 20/6/33. Commd 8/7/54. Sqn Ldr 1/1/70. Retd SUP 3/3/76.
HITCHCOCK C. W. Born 13/5/48. Commd 17/3/67. Flt Lt 17/9/73. Retd SUP 12/7/80.
HITCHCOCK J. E. Born 11/11/28. Commd 24/10/51. Flt Lt 24/4/56. Retd GD 11/11/66.
HITCHCOCK K. J., CBE. Born 23/8/25. Commd 22/9/49. A Cdre 1/7/76. Retd SEC 17/11/79.
HITCHCOCK P. G. Born 23/9/47. Commd 6/5/66. Wg Cdr 1/7/87. Retd GD 13/5/99.
HITCHEN G. P., BA. Born 2/10/31. Commd 23/9/53. Sqn Ldr 17/2/63. Retd ADMIN 1/5/76.
HITCHEN N. Born 25/12/32. Commd 11/10/51. Sqn Ldr 1/7/76. Retd PI 27/4/84.
HITCHEN S., MVO AFC. Born 8/5/35. Commd 11/2/55. Wg Cdr 1/1/75. Retd GD 4/4/80.
HITCHEN S. T. Born 18/8/19. Commd 17/7/57. Sqn Ldr 17/2/64. Retd EDN 18/8/74.
HITCHING J. T., AFC. Born 18/1/18. Commd 21/9/42. Sqn Ldr 1/1/52. Retd GD 15/2/58.
HITCHINGS G. M., CEng FIEE FIMgt MRAeS. Born 25/7/38. Commd 23/7/58. Gp Capt 1/7/89. Retd ENG 25/7/93.
HITCHINS D. K., MSc CEng MIEE MRAeS. Born 28/6/35. Commd 30/7/59. Sqn Ldr 1/7/68. Retd ENG 1/1/74.
HIVES D. B. Born 9/6/31. Commd 14/4/53. Gp Capt 1/1/79. Retd GD 9/6/86.
HOAD N. E., CVO CBE AFC* FIMgt. Born 28/7/23. Commd 1/5/43. AVM 1/7/74. Retd GD 31/3/78.
HOAR B. A. Born 5/2/34. Commd 27/3/70. Sqn Ldr 1/7/81. Retd SY 4/7/84.
HOAR L. J. Born 26/5/25. Commd 1/12/44. Flt Lt 1/6/48. Retd GD 26/5/68.
HOAR R. J. Born 2/7/42. Commd 2/6/67. Sqn Ldr 1/1/88. Retd GD 2/7/97.
HOARE D. S. Born 22/10/17. Commd 16/11/36. Gp Capt 1/7/60. Retd GD 22/7/67.
HOARE M. G. N., BA. Born 17/12/34. Commd 1/10/63. Sqn Ldr 1/7/69. Retd GD 1/2/84.
HOARE P., DMS FRIN. Born 30/6/23. Commd 28/1/44. Sqn Ldr 1/7/59. Retd GD 30/6/72.
HOARE P. F., BA. Born 9/7/48. Commd 27/10/70. Sqn Ldr 1/7/83. Retd GD 27/10/86.
HOARE P. H. Born 31/7/43. Commd 23/11/78. Flt Lt 23/11/83. Retd ENG 1/5/85.
HOARE R. Born 13/8/32. Commd 15/12/53. Flt Lt 15/6/56. Retd GD 13/8/70.
HOARE W. A. Born 5/4/37. Commd 12/1/61. Wg Cdr 1/1/79. Retd GD 30/6/81.
HOARE W. H. C. Born 29/8/45. Commd 15/7/66. Sqn Ldr 1/7/75. Retd ENG 29/8/00.
HOBBS D. J. Born 10/9/49. Commd 2/5/69. Flt Lt 19/7/75. Retd SEC 21/6/81.
HOBBS E. J., MIMgt MCIPD. Born 20/5/32. Commd 22/3/51. Sqn Ldr 1/7/68. Retd SEC 1/10/74.
HOBBS E. W., BSc MCGI. Born 23/5/53. Commd 4/7/82. Flt Lt 4/4/86. Retd OPS SPT 4/7/98.
HOBBS J. Born 2/7/28. Commd 19/7/50. Flt Lt 14/5/56. Retd GD 2/7/66.
HOBBS J. B. Born 26/2/50. Commd 11/11/71. Flt Lt 11/5/77. Retd GD 13/6/89.
HOBBS J. R. Born 21/3/47. Commd 12/7/68. Flt Lt 12/1/74. Retd GD 1/10/75.
HOBBS L. G. Born 24/12/21. Commd 21/12/43. Flt Lt 21/6/47. Retd GD 17/2/56 rtg Sqn Ldr.
HOBBS M. A. A. Born 6/9/30. Commd 24/5/53. Sqn Ldr 1/1/66. Retd GD 10/4/75.
HOBBS P. C., OBE CEng FRAeS MCIPD MIMgt. Born 21/3/41. Commd 2/3/65. Gp Capt 1/1/91. Retd ENG 4/4/93.
HOBBS P. F. Born 10/4/33. Commd 25/1/54. Sqn Ldr 1/1/80. Retd GD 10/4/93.
HOBBS R. K. Born 4/5/21. Commd 17/3/44. Flt Lt 17/9/47. Retd GD(G) 30/3/76.
HOBBS S., BEd. Born 27/8/61. Commd 30/8/83. Sqn Ldr 1/7/94. Retd ADMIN 14/3/97.
HOBBS W. H. Born 25/8/06. Commd 31/12/46. Fg Offr 31/12/46. Retd SUP 8/10/48.
HOBBY W. E., AFC. Born 23/2/32. Commd 17/3/55. Wg Cdr 1/1/78. Retd GD 27/8/86.
HOBDAY D. E. Born 9/11/30. Commd 1/8/51. Flt Lt 27/8/54. Retd GD 9/11/68.
HOBDAY P., MSc BA. Born 5/12/48. Commd 10/6/84. Sqn Ldr 1/1/91. Retd ADMIN 5/7/98.
HOBDEN M. F., OBE. Born 12/3/22. Commd 20/3/42. Gp Capt 1/7/70. Retd RGT 5/7/72.
HOBGEN C. W. Born 31/10/22. Commd 23/1/44. Gp Capt 1/1/73. Retd PRT 18/1/75.
HOBKINSON J. T., LDSRCS. Born 1/7/40. Commd 27/12/61. Wg Cdr 13/7/77. Retd DEL 1/7/98.
HOBLYN F. J. Born 22/2/17. Commd 7/7/42. Sqn Ldr 1/7/62. Retd ENG 29/3/73.
HOBSON J. F., MB ChB MFCM MFOM DPH DIH. Born 5/3/25. Commd 27/10/50. A Cdre 1/7/76. Retd MED
    20/12/83.
HOBSON M. E., CBE AFC FIMgt. Born 1/12/26. Commd 23/8/46. Gp Capt 1/7/66. Retd GD 1/8/73.
HOBSON R. M., MIMgt. Born 23/11/40. Commd 2/6/77. Flt Lt 2/6/81. Retd ADMIN 23/11/86.
HOBSON W. R. T. Born 6/4/34. Commd 24/8/54. Flt Lt 29/6/59. Retd GD 7/4/72.
HOCHMAL A. Born 18/12/14. Commd 2/8/40. Flt Lt 12/11/49. Retd GD(G) 29/1/70 rtg Sqn Ldr.
HOCKIN J. W. Born 29/5/44. Commd 14/8/64. Flt Lt 4/11/70. Retd GD 29/5/82. Re-entered 1/4/85. Flt Lt 28/10/73.
    Retd GD 29/5/99.
HOCKING E. J. Born 12/4/34. Commd 5/11/52. Flt Lt 1/4/66. Retd SEC 24/7/74.
HOCKING J. M. Born 5/5/23. Commd 13/11/45. Sqn Ldr 1/7/56. Retd GD 5/5/72.
HOCKING M. C. Born 1/10/57. Commd 28/2/80. Flt Lt 28/8/85. Retd GD 22/10/95.
HOCKNELL J. S., OBE MSc BSc CertEd. Born 13/9/42. Commd 10/7/67. Wg Cdr 1/1/85. Retd ADMIN 13/9/00.

HOCTOR B. P., CEng MIEE. Born 3/9/43. Commd 15/7/65. Sqn Ldr 1/1/75. Retd ENG 3/9/98.
HODDER C. A. Born 25/4/10. Commd 3/2/41. Flt Lt 1/7/43. Retd ENG 5/1/46 rtg Sqn Ldr.
HODDER R. W. Born 1/2/15. Commd 7/11/43. Sqn Ldr 1/4/56. Retd ENG 1/2/64.
HODDINOTT G., BEM. Born 15/7/23. Commd 2/7/47. Sqn Ldr 1/7/58. Retd RGT 15/7/68.
HODGE A. J., BEM. Born 23/9/19. Commd 21/7/55. Sqn Ldr 1/7/65. Retd ENG 23/9/74.
HODGE B. J., BEng. Born 26/4/63. Commd 13/9/81. Flt Lt 15/1/87. Retd GD 15/7/96.
HODGE D. J. Born 2/6/45. Commd 1/4/65. Gp Capt 1/1/97. Retd OPS SPT 3/5/99.
HODGE K. B., IEng MIIE(elec). Born 19/9/44. Commd 19/6/86. Flt Lt 19/6/90. Retd ENG 1/4/93.
HODGE M. V. Born 14/2/22. Commd 22/7/42. Wg Cdr 1/1/65. Retd GD 20/9/67.
HODGE T. D. A., BSc. Born 28/2/63. Commd 13/2/81. Flt Lt 15/4/86. Retd GD 15/7/96.
HODGES F. A. Born 21/7/12. Commd 14/10/43. Sqn Ldr 1/7/56. Retd GD(G) 27/5/61.
HODGES F. G., BA. Born 22/4/27. Commd 25/8/54. Flt Lt 25/8/60. Retd SEC 3/12/68.
HODGES J. T. Born 10/10/22. Commd 28/2/42. Flt Lt 1/9/45. Retd GD 4/6/54.
HODGES Sir Lewis, KCB CBE DSO* DFC*. Born 1/3/18. Commd 17/12/38. ACM 1/5/71. Retd GD 2/5/76.
HODGES M. G. M. Born 11/2/41. Commd 9/2/62. Wg Cdr 1/7/91. Retd GD(G) 28/2/95.
HODGES M. T., CEng MIEE. Born 5/5/41. Commd 17/7/62. Gp Capt 1/1/89. Retd ENG 2/4/96.
HODGES R., BA MCIPD ACIS. Born 29/1/38. Commd 18/7/61. Sqn Ldr 1/10/69. Retd ADMIN 18/7/77.
HODGETTS P. N. Born 18/8/36. Commd 19/7/57. Sqn Ldr 1/7/70. Retd SUP 18/8/74.
HODGKIN C. W. Born 13/5/21. Commd 17/3/55. Sqn Ldr 1/1/69. Retd ENG 1/8/73.
HODGKINS W. M. Born 22/6/39. Commd 6/11/66. Flt Lt 29/9/67. Retd GD 4/11/80.
HODGKINSON Sir Derek, KCB CBE DFC AFC. Born 27/12/17. Commd 25/1/37. ACM 22/4/74. Retd GD 8/5/76.
HODGKINSON V. A. Born 14/2/30. Commd 9/4/52. Wg Cdr 1/7/69. Retd ADMIN 4/3/78.
HODGKINSON W. J. Born 14/2/30. Commd 14/4/53. Sqn Ldr 1/7/67. Retd GD 1/7/70.
HODGSON G. F., BA. Born 19/10/47. Commd 1/8/69. Sqn Ldr 1/1/85. Retd GD 21/9/99.
HODGSON J., MIMgt. Born 5/4/32. Commd 17/12/52. Wg Cdr 1/7/73. Retd GD 5/4/87.
HODGSON J., MBE. Born 17/12/18. Commd 14/11/57. Sqn Ldr 1/7/70. Retd ENG 17/12/73.
HODGSON J. W. Born 2/5/41. Commd 17/5/63. Sqn Ldr 1/7/80. Retd GD 2/3/92.
HODGSON K. C. Born 17/2/27. Commd 13/8/52. Sqn Ldr 1/1/70. Retd GD 3/8/76.
HODGSON M. Born 19/12/45. Commd 10/6/66. Sqn Ldr 1/1/93. Retd GD 14/3/96.
HODGSON M. W. Born 1/12/36. Commd 30/9/55. Sqn Ldr 1/7/79. Retd GD(G) 1/8/91.
HODGSON N., LDS. Born 7/4/22. Commd 30/1/47. Gp Capt 1/7/73. Retd MED 7/4/80.
HODGSON P. E. Born 28/9/35. Commd 12/1/61. Flt Lt 12/7/65. Retd GD 28/9/73.
HODGSON R. E. Born 25/2/36. Commd 12/9/63. Flt Lt 29/1/70. Retd SUP 12/6/79.
HODGSON R. P. Born 30/3/53. Commd 3/1/82. Flt Lt 30/4/78. Retd GD 30/3/91.
HODGSON S. W. S., MSc BSc CEng MRAeS. Born 23/1/52. Commd 25/9/71. Sqn Ldr 1/1/86. Retd ENG 1/10/92.
HODGSON T. G. Born 14/3/18. Commd 25/5/44. Sqn Ldr 1/1/62. Retd ENG 14/3/73.
HODGSON T. H. Born 18/11/21. Commd 28/6/46. Flt Lt 4/1/51. Retd SEC 18/11/61.
HODKINSON C. G. Born 9/8/23. Commd 25/8/55/ Flt Lt 25/8/61. Retd GD 9/8/78.
HODKINSON R. G. W. Born 8/7/20. Commd 27/1/55. Flt Lt 27/1/58. Retd GD 10/2/68.
HODNETT N. J. G., CBE. Born 3/6/37. Commd 2/12/56. A Cdre 1/1/88. Retd GD 3/6/92.
HODSON B. T. Born 31/5/26. Commd 27/3/47. Sqn Ldr 1/7/64. Retd SUP 1/7/67.
HODSON I. Born 15/2/43. Commd 7/6/68. Sqn Ldr 1/7/82. Retd GD 30/11/99.
HODSON K. G., OBE. Born 28/5/19. Commd 25/11/42. Sqn Ldr 1/1/57. Retd GD 28/5/74.
HODSON N. Born 1/7/15. Commd 27/10/43. Flt Offr 18/5/56. Retd SEC 8/11/64.
HOFFLER I. H., BSc. Born 21/12/49. Commd 13/9/71. Flt Lt 13/12/72. Retd GD 1/6/94.
HOFFMAN DE VISME G. F. A., BSc DipEl. Born 3/5/23. Commd 30/1/50. Sqn Ldr 3/5/57. Retd EDN 20/11/62.
HOFFORD D. H. Born 25/4/25. Commd 27/5/44. Flt Lt 4/6/54. Retd GD 26/1/66.
HOGAN B. E. Born 18/5/20. Commd 31/12/41. Wg Cdr 1/7/71. Retd GD 17/8/73.
HOGAN F. J. Born 16/10/25. Commd 6/12/50. Flt Lt 6/9/56. Retd GD 20/1/66.
HOGAN G. J. C., DFC AFC FIMgt. Born 19/6/20. Commd 9/7/38. Gp Capt 1/7/65. Retd GD 17/5/72.
HOGAN J. S. Born 25/3/48. Commd 4/4/71. Wg Cdr 1/1/89. Retd ADMIN 4/4/93.
HOGAN P. J. Born 15/1/21. Commd 15/1/44. Sqn Ldr 1/7/66. Retd GD(G) 15/1/76.
HOGARTH P. W. F. Born 15/7/33. Commd 2/4/57. Flt Lt 6/3/63. Retd GD 15/7/71.
HOGG A. W., BSc. Born 11/9/59. Commd 13/2/83. Flt Lt 13/8/84. Retd GD 14/11/95.
HOGG J. E. Born 26/11/28. Commd 27/5/53. Flt Lt 11/11/58. Retd GD 20/1/69.
HOGG J. S. Born 12/1/30. Commd 26/3/59. Flt Lt 26/3/65. Retd GD 12/1/85.
HOGG M. C. Born 12/2/42. Commd 28/2/64. Flt Lt 28/8/69. Retd GD 12/2/80.
HOGG P. F., MB BS MRCS MRCP DMRD. Born 20/5/39. Commd 29/12/65. Wg Cdr 25/9/76. Retd MED 22/7/80.
HOGG R. I. Born 14/3/46. Commd 26/5/67. Gp Capt 1/1/95. Retd GD 31/3/01.
HOGG R. P. Born 6/9/20. Commd 13/6/44. Sqn Ldr 1/1/52. Retd RGT 27/11/61.
HOILE J. F., CEng MIMechE. Born 5/7/33. Commd 7/2/57. Sqn Ldr 1/7/65. Retd ENG 20/1/86.
HOLBEN F. B. Born 7/1/45. Commd 17/12/65. Flt Lt 17/6/69. Retd GD 7/1/83.
HOLBOURN A. C. E., OBE BA MRAeS. Born 7/3/36. Commd 1/4/58. Wg Cdr 1/7/82. Retd GD 3/4/86.
HOLBOURN A. S. Born 26/4/16. Commd 12/6/47. Flt Lt 26/5/55. Retd PE 19/5/64.
HOLBOURN P. E. Born 5/5/31. Commd 7/11/51. Sqn Ldr 1/7/65. Retd GD(G) 5/5/69.
HOLBROOK G. F., DFC. Born 17/9/21. Commd 12/7/44. Sqn. Ldr 1/7/69. Retd GD 1/9/73.

HOLBROOK T. H. Born 3/6/27. Commd 1/8/69. Sqn Ldr 1/1/81. Retd ENG 3/6/87.
HOLBURN R. T., OBE. Born 26/7/27. Commd 26/9/49. Wg Cdr 1/7/73. Retd RGT 1/10/79.
HOLCROFT D., OBE. Born 17/9/36. Commd 19/1/66. Wg Cdr 1/7/85. Retd ENG 26/5/91.
HOLDEN A. E. Born 4/6/24. Commd 1/7/53. Flt Lt 11/7/57. Retd GD(G) 6/7/66.
HOLDEN A. P. G., OBE. Born 19/10/16. Commd 14/12/38. Wg Cdr 1/1/58. Retd SEC 19/10/71.
HOLDEN B. D. Born 20/5/34. Commd 27/4/61. Flt Lt 27/10/65. Retd GD 20/5/72.
HOLDEN D. J., CEng MIMechE. Born 3/4/38. Commd 19/5/69. Flt Lt 19/5/71. Retd ENG 1/8/74.
HOLDEN G., BA. Born 29/1/56. Commd 5/2/84. Flt Lt 5/8/87. Retd ADMIN 13/5/96.
HOLDEN G. A., MMar. Born 27/11/41. Commd 16/6/69. Sqn Ldr 1/7/84. Retd ADMIN 1/5/96.
HOLDEN J. F. Born 24/8/21. Commd 14/4/49. Flt Lt 14/10/52. Retd GD(G) 27/2/65. Reappointed 10/10/66 to 24/8/76.
HOLDEN P. J., MA MSc. Born 12/11/60. Commd 2/9/79. Sqn Ldr 1/7/96. Retd ENG 1/7/99.
HOLDEN P. J., AIB. Born 14/8/54. Commd 23/9/79. Wg Cdr 1/7/93. Retd ADMIN 4/4/97.
HOLDEN R. E., BSc. Born 5/6/50. Commd 15/9/69. Sqn Ldr 1/1/85. Retd GD 5/12/88.
HOLDEN T. C. W., DipEurHum. Born 13/12/50. Commd 14/8/88. Flt Lt 14/8/90. Retd ADMIN 14/8/96.
HOLDEN W. V., MBE BSc MRAeS. Born 7/11/26. Commd 24/8/50. Wg Cdr 1/1/66. Retd ENG 7/11/81.
HOLDEN-RUSHWORTH P. Born 11/12/29. Commd 27/2/58. Sqn Ldr 1/7/75. Retd GD 1/8/80.
HOLDER E. H. M. Born 25/4/29. Commd 18/5/55. Sqn Ldr 5/3/70. Retd EDN 5/9/74.
HOLDER M. T. Born 31/12/45. Commd 5/3/65. Flt Lt 5/9/70. Retd GD 31/1/96.
HOLDER N. R. Born 24/12/45. Commd 26/5/67. Sqn Ldr 1/7/78. Retd GD 24/12/83.
HOLDER R. R., BSc(Eng) Born 13/9/12. Commd 15/3/35. A Cdre 1/1/64. Retd ENG 15/9/67.
HOLDING B. C., AFC. Born 6/12/52. Commd 22/7/71. Wg Cdr 1/7/90. Retd GD 8/9/00.
HOLDING J. Born 4/4/22. Commd 12/2/53. Flt Lt 12/2/56. Retd ENG 4/4/77. Rtg Sqn Ldr.
HOLDSTOCK A. C., MA CEng MIMechE. Born 11/12/51. Commd 25/9/71. Sqn Ldr 1/1/88. Retd ENG 1/1/91.
HOLDSTOCK A. J. Born 25/5/16. Commd 20/10/48. Flt Lt 29/3/56. Retd GD(G) 31/8/60.
HOLDSWORTH A. D. Born 31/7/58. Commd 18/9/89. Flt Lt 6/2/88. Retd GD 26/6/96.
HOLDSWORTH M. T., BA. Born 17/1/47. Commd 2/8/68. Sqn Ldr 1/1/79. Retd ADMIN 17/1/85.
HOLDSWORTH P. Born 20/5/58. Commd 8/4/82. Flt Lt 8/7/87. Retd GD 1/12/99.
HOLDSWORTH T. M. J., MIMgt. Born 7/10/43. Commd 23/6/67. Wg Cdr 1/1/86. Retd GD(G) 6/7/94. rtg Gp Capt.
HOLDWAY J. C. Born 1/11/33. Commd 5/4/55. Sqn Ldr 1/1/68. Retd GD 2/11/83.
HOLE E. M., OBE. Born 10/2/20. Commd 23/9/42. Wg Offr 1/7/61. Retd SEC 16/5/63.
HOLE J. D. Born 25/4/42. Commd 30/9/60. Flt Lt 17/7/67. Retd ENG 24/5/70.
HOLE P. K. Born 20/11/40. Commd 19/9/59. Flt Lt 10/2/67. Transferred to Reserve 10/4/71. Reinstated 13/2/80. Flt Lt 16/12/75. Retd GD 30/9/88.
HOLES D. G. Born 9/8/33. Commd 27/10/54. Flt Lt 5/10/60. Retd GD 25/4/74.
HOLF J. V. Born 20/6/20. Commd 17/8/43. Sqn Ldr 1/1/72. Retd GD 20/6/75.
HOLKHAM-JENNER E. G., MIMgt. Born 30/8/20. Commd 9/10/43. Sqn Ldr 1/7/68. Retd GD(G) 10/6/71.
HOLLAND B. C., MA. Born 9/2/36. Commd 23/11/59. Sqn Ldr 1/1/71. Retd GD 9/8/91.
HOLLAND D. T., BA. Born 12/2/34. Commd 6/12/56. Sqn Ldr 6/6/64. Retd ADMIN 29/5/76.
HOLLAND G. M. Born 12/6/53. Commd 19/3/81. Flt Lt 15/3/84. Retd ADMIN 12/6/91.
HOLLAND J. E., DFC. Born 18/4/20. Commd 11/7/40. Wg Cdr 1/7/56. Retd GD 18/4/67.
HOLLAND J. P. Born 14/11/46. Commd 2/6/67. Flt Lt 2/12/72. Retd GD(D) 12/11/94.
HOLLAND J. P., BA. Born 11/7/30. Commd 11/12/58. Flt Lt 11/12/63. Retd GD 1/12/82.
HOLLAND N. T. H. Born 11/4/21. Commd 26/11/41. Sqn Ldr 1/1/66. Retd GD(G) 30/3/76.
HOLLAND P., MBE. Born 7/3/35. Commd 17/6/54. Gp Capt 1/7/86. Retd SUP 7/3/90.
HOLLAND P., BSc. Born 7/12/31. Commd 29/10/59. Sqn Ldr 29/4/64. Retd EDN 29/10/72.
HOLLAND P. Born 16/4/42. Commd 4/2/71. Flt Lt 4/2/73. Retd ADMIN 16/4/83.
HOLLAND P. L., BSc. Born 26/7/62. Commd 11/9/83. Sqn Ldr 1/7/95. Retd OPS SPT 26/7/00.
HOLLAND R. M. J. Born 13/5/46. Commd 28/6/65. Wg Cdr 1/7/92. Retd GD 13/5/96.
HOLLAND T. R., AFC. Born 9/4/26. Commd 20/12/46. Wg Cdr 1/1/67. Retd GD 3/4/76.
HOLLAND V. G., AFM. Born 1/3/33. Commd 7/9/61. Fg Offr 7/9/61. Retd GD 22/3/69.
HOLLAND W. H., AInstAM. Born 10/11/34. Commd 24/1/74. Flt Lt 24/1/76. Retd GD(G) 10/11/89.
HOLLAND-SMITH T. R. M. Born 28/2/42. Commd 18/8/61. Flt Lt 8/1/69. Retd GD 28/2/80.
HOLLANDS K. E. H., MIMgt. Born 19/9/40. Commd 11/11/71. Wg Cdr 1/7/87. Retd ADMIN 3/1/91.
HOLLETT G. K. A., OBE MIMgt. Born 14/4/20. Commd 7/10/43. Wg Cdr 1/1/68. Retd SEC 20/4/72.
HOLLETT R. A. F. Born 31/12/42. Commd 4/11/82. Sqn Ldr 1/1/89. Retd ENG 31/12/97.
HOLLETT R. L. Born 21/6/40. Commd 6/7/62. Wg Cdr 1/1/85. Retd GD 21/6/95.
HOLLEY J. C. Born 26/8/11. Commd 29/4/42. Flt Lt 3/12/45. Retd ENG 2/6/48.
HOLLIDAY A. M. R. Born 10/3/52. Commd 24/4/70. Sqn Ldr 1/1/82. Retd SUP 10/3/90.
HOLLIDAY D. J. Born 13/11/41. Commd 14/12/63. Wg Cdr 1/1/91. Retd GD 31/3/94.
HOLLIDAY D. M., AFC CDipAF MIMgt. Born 9/1/36. Commd 6/4/55. Wg Cdr 1/1/80. Retd GD 9/1/86.
HOLLIDAY G. S. C. Born 14/2/17. Commd 2/5/38. Sqn Ldr 1/8/47. Retd GD 13/2/58.
HOLLIDAY H. L., DFC. Born 30/9/19. Commd 8/5/41. Sqn Ldr 1/7/51. Retd GD 6/3/59.
HOLLIDAY R. A. Born 1/2/27. Commd 22/7/66. Flt Lt 22/7/71. Retd SEC 8/11/75.
HOLLIDAY R. C., DCAe CEng MRAeS MIMechE. Born 15/11/35. Commd 18/7/71. Sqn Ldr 18/7/71. Retd ENG 20/3/89.

HOLLIDAY R. E., OBE. Born 5/9/38. Commd 11/9/56. Gp Capt 1/7/83. Retd GD 5/9/93.
HOLLIDAY R. W. D. C., BA CEng MIEE. Born 25/9/38. Commd 30/9/57. Wg Cdr 1/1/74. Retd ENG 25/9/93.
HOLLIN D., MIMgt. Born 6/4/44. Commd 8/11/68. Gp Capt 1/7/94. Retd OPS SPT 1/11/99.
HOLLINGDALE M. D., BSc(Eng) ACGI. Born 10/7/57. Commd 21/10/79. Flt Lt 21/1/81. Retd GD21/10/87.
HOLLINGSWORTH A. Born 8/11/21. Commd 24/4/43. Sqn Ldr 1/7/66. Retd GD 8/11/76.
HOLLINGSWORTH A. C. Born 18/2/22. Commd 21/8/42. Gp Capt 1/1/65. Retd GD 2/4/73.
HOLLINGSWORTH D. Born 22/6/27. Commd 23/8/56. Flt Lt 23/8/62. Retd GD 16/4/73.
HOLLINGTON H. B., CEng MIEE MRaeS. Born 23/9/31. Commd 25/8/55. Sqn Ldr 1/1/68. Retd GD 11/2/77.
HOLLINGWORTH I., BSc. Born 11/12/55. Commd 19/9/76. Flt Lt 15/10/79. Retd GD 14/10/88.
HOLLINGWORTH M. Born 11/12/35. Commd 6/9/68. Flt Lt 6/9/70. Retd GD 6/9/76.
HOLLIS D. J., BSc LLB MIMgt. Born 4/12/32. Commd 14/12/54. Gp Capt 1/7/74. Retd SUP 21/9/77.
HOLLIS I. A., CEng MIERE. Born 15/11/35. Commd 9/10/67. Flt Lt 4/11/70. Retd ENG 15/11/90.
HOLLOWAY A. F. Born 1/7/15. Commd 29/9/41. Flt Offr 16/4/52. Retd SEC 31/10/59.
HOLLOWAY E. J., DFC. Born 3/4/18. Commd 6/12/41. Wg Cdr 1/7/56. Retd GD 1/9/61.
HOLLOWAY G. M. N., MB ChB FRCS. Born 19/11/45. Commd 17/9/72. Wg Cdr 28/10/83. Retd MED 16/10/92.
HOLLOWAY R. A. Born 6/5/53. Commd 11/6/81. Flt Lt 11/6/83. Retd GD 29/12/96.
HOLLOWAY R. E., MBE. Born 16/11/32. Commd 12/7/51. Wg Cdr 1/7/81. Retd GD 16/11/90.
HOLLOWAY R. J. B. Born 1/2/50. Commd 3/12/70. Flt Lt 3/6/76. Retd GD 10/1/80.
HOLLOWAY T. M., MRAeS. Born 5/1/45. Commd 18/11/66. Gp Capt 1/7/91. Retd SUP 14/3/96.
HOLLOWAY W. F. J., MBE MIMgt. Born 5/9/30. Commd 18/5/61. Sqn Ldr 1/7/72. Retd ENG 7/9/76. Re-instated 2/1/80. Retd ENG 5/9/85.
HOLLOWOOD J. W. Born 1/10/45. Commd 1/3/68. Gp Capt 1/7/94. Retd SUP 14/9/96.
HOLMAN A. C. Born 26/12/47. Commd 2/8/68. Sqn Ldr 1/1/82. Retd GD 1/10/96.
HOLMAN C. V. Born 15/2/27. Commd 30/11/50. Sqn Ldr 1/7/67. Retd GD 1/2/75.
HOLMAN D. C. L. Born 21/7/31. Commd 14/4/53. Sqn Ldr 1/7/67. Retd SEC 1/7/70.
HOLMAN P. J. Born 17/8/34. Commd 23/6/67. Sqn Ldr 1/1/76. Retd ENG 20/4/83.
HOLMAN R. A., OBE. Born 9/10/35. Commd 12/9/63. Gp Capt 1/7/85. Retd ADMIN 9/10/90.
HOLME B. P. Born 30/9/32. Commd 22/8/59. Flt Lt 22/2/65. Retd GD 28/7/78. Reinstated 30/1/80. Flt Lt 27/8/66. Retd GD 30/9/92.
HOLME D. Born 31/3/39. Commd 23/9/59. Sqn Ldr 1/1/79. Retd GD 27/5/89.
HOLME H., MBE. Born 8/3/10. Commd 26/8/41. Sqn Ldr 1/1/56. Retd ENG 8/3/59.
HOLMES A. E. Born 17/4/16. Commd 2/5/45. Fg Offr 2/5/45. Retd RGT 17/1/56.
HOLMES E., DFC. Born 29/1/21. Commd 4/9/43. Flt Lt 4/3/47. Retd GD 1/2/62.
HOLMES E. F. O., MBE. Born 22/11/22. Commd 2/5/50. Sqn Ldr 1/7/66. Retd GD 22/11/73.
HOLMES F. M. Born 19/8/44. Commd 8/11/68. Sqn Ldr 1/1/84. Retd SUP 23/7/90.
HOLMES G., ACCA ACIS. Born 3/11/32. Commd 19/7/56. Sqn Ldr 1/7/65. Retd SEC 21/11/71.
HOLMES J. A., DFC* Born 30/6/17. Commd 17/12/38. Gp Capt 1/1/57. Retd GD 30/6/67 rtg A Cdre.
HOLMES J. W. Born 3/12/15. Commd 21/10/43. Sqn Ldr 1/1/55. Retd ENG 3/12/64.
HOLMES J. W. Born 12/2/07. Commd 6/6/40. Sqn Ldr 1/8/47. Retd SEC 12/12/53.
HOLMES K. Born 22/6/48. Commd 6/9/68. Flt Lt 21/12/74. Retd GD(G) 15/3/77.
HOLMES K. W., MBE. Born 15/9/23. Commd 22/9/44. Wg Cdr 1/1/68. Retd GD(G) 1/5/75.
HOLMES L. G., OBE DFC AFC FIMgt. Born 15/4/21. Commd 10/10/42. Gp Capt 1/7/63. Retd GD 18/2/75.
HOLMES M. E. Born 12/1/22. Commd 19/7/57. Flt Lt 19/7/60. Retd ENG 2/12/67.
HOLMES M. K. Born 29/9/58. Commd 11/6/81. Sqn Ldr 1/7/91. Retd GD 9/2/97.
HOLMES M. R. Born 17/11/28. Commd 21/2/49. Flt Lt 16/3/55. Retd GD 17/11/66.
HOLMES M. S. Born 11/10/45. Commd 3/3/65. Gp Capt 1/1/94. Retd GD 11/4/01.
HOLMES P. B. Born 10/3/32. Commd 28/6/51. Wg Cdr 1/1/77. Retd ADMIN 10/2/87.
HOLMES R., BEng. Born 29/3/60. Commd 2/8/89. Flt Lt 15/7/92. Retd ENG 29/3/01.
HOLMES R. D., MIMgt. Born 28/9/21. Commd 26/4/45. Sqn Ldr 1/7/58. Retd SEC 29/6/78.
HOLMES R. G. Born 15/1/45. Commd 6/9/63. Flt Lt 6/3/69. Retd GD 15/1/00.
HOLMES R. H. Born 7/5/39. Commd 15/12/59. Sqn Ldr 1/1/70. Retd GD 7/5/77.
HOLMES R. L., MBE. Born 5/7/33. Commd 6/4/54. Wg Cdr 1/7/75. Retd GD 5/7/88.
HOLMES R. M. Born 27/4/24. Commd 17/2/45. Fg Offr 14/1/50. Retd GD 4/2/56.
HOLMES S. W., MIMgt. Born 21/4/31. Commd 24/7/52. Wg Cdr 1/1/72. Retd GD 26/7/84.
HOLMES V. R. Born 15/7/30. Commd 30/7/52. Flt Lt 30/3/58. Retd GD 30/4/76.
HOLMES W. G., AFC. Born 24/11/21. Commd 5/12/56. Flt Lt 5/12/61. Retd GD 1/2/68.
HOLMES W. G. Born 3/12/27. Commd 7/10/48. Wg Cdr 1/1/68. Retd GD 3/11/79.
HOLMYARD D. P. Born 13/5/47. Commd 16/8/68. Sqn Ldr 1/1/95. Retd GD 2/1/97.
HOLROYD J. Born 24/7/40. Commd 20/11/75. Sqn Ldr 1/1/86. Retd ENG 24/7/95.
HOLROYD., KBE CB MSc CEng FIEE FRAeS CBIM. Born 30/8/35. Commd 10/1/57. AM 4/7/88. Retd ENG 5/12/91.
HOLT G. F. Born 26/3/41. Commd 13/2/60. Flt Lt 14/2/66. Retd GD 26/6/91.
HOLT I. W. Born 14/1/44. Commd 27/1/67. Sqn Ldr 1/1/87. Retd GD(G) 31/7/96.
HOLT The Rev K. J., BD. Born 28/10/08. Commd 15/5/42. Retd 4/8/66 Gp Capt.
HOLT R. J., MSc BSc CEng MIEE. Born 14/8/45. Commd 22/9/63. A Cdre 1/1/94. Retd ENG 14/3/97.
HOLT S. D. H., MA MB BChir FRCS. Born 16/7/51. Commd 22/1/74. Sqn Ldr 14/9/82. Retd MED 7/8/90.
HOLTBY H. Born 28/10/41. Commd 21/2/69. Sqn Ldr 1/7/87. Retd GD 28/10/96.

HOLTBY P. R., MBE CEng FIEE FRAeS. Born 19/7/39. Commd 18/7/61. Gp Capt 1/7/87. Retd ENG 19/7/90.
HOLTON J. P. L., MIMgt. Born 17/3/36. Commd 12/7/62. Sqn Ldr 1/1/71. Retd SUP 2/4/76.
HOLYOAKE A. A., AFC. Born 28/9/26. Commd 13/2/60. Sqn Ldr 1/1/75. Retd GD 28/9/86.
HOLYOAKE A. P., MBE. Born 1/7/78. Commd 9/3/66. Sqn Ldr 1/7/78. Retd ENG 27/11/86.
HOME S. M., BSc. Born 27/10/46. Commd 27/6/70. Flt Lt 27/3/75. Retd ADMIN 27/6/87.
HOMER C. R. C. Born 9/9/37. Commd 28/7/60. Sqn Ldr 1/1/88. Retd GD(G) 9/9/92.
HOMER D. St John. Born 8/3/36. Commd 30/7/57. Gp Capt 1/7/78. Retd GD 31/5/87.
HOMES C. J., AFC. Born 20/2/19. Commd 19/2/44. Sqn Ldr 1/10/54. Retd GD 19/2/59.
HONE A. J. Born 10/8/25. Commd 21/6/45. Sqn Ldr 1/1/59. Retd SUP 10/8/63.
HONE B. S. Born 10/2/49. Commd 12/10/78. Flt Lt 12/10/80. Retd GD(G) 10/2/87.
HONE D. H., AE. Born 30/9/17. Commd 9/6/40. Flt Lt 9/6/42. Retd GD(G) 30/9/75.
HONE S. J. Born 19/7/20. Commd 12/8/54. Sqn Ldr 1/7/72. Retd ENG 19/7/75.
HONEY A., MRCS LRCP. Born 16/10/27. Commd 31/8/53. Wg Cdr 6/6/65. Retd MED 31/8/72.
HONEY G. W., OBE. Born 22/5/35. Commd 29/7/55. Wg Cdr 1/7/77. Retd GD 1/11/87.
HONEY R. J., CB CBE FCIPD. Born 3/12/36. Commd 26/1/55. AVM 1/7/87. Retd GD 12/6/94.
HONEY R. O. H. Born 28/7/40. Commd 3/8/62. Flt Lt 3/5/66. Retd GD 28/7/78.
HONEYBALL D. C. Born 23/4/46. Commd 5/1/78. Flt Lt 5/1/80. Retd GD(G) 5/1/89.
HONEYMAN D. B. Born 1/6/29. Commd 7/6/68. Sqn Ldr 1/1/83. Retd ENG 1/12/89.
HONEYMAN G. Born 17/2/24. Commd 10/5/45. Sqn Ldr 1/10/55. Retd GD 17/2/73.
HONLEY A. D. A., CBE AFC FIMgt. Born 5/12/25. Commd 19/12/45. A Cdre 1/7/79. Retd GD 3/4/82.
HONOUR G. W. Born 4/6/30. Commd 26/10/61. Flt Lt 26/10/67. Retd GD 25/8/69.
HOOD B. Born 19/2/41. Commd 19/6/64. Flt Lt 26/11/67. Retd GD 19/9/81. Reinstated 14/3/88. Flt Lt 21/5/74. Retd GD 19/2/96.
HOOD E. J., AFC. Born 12/6/29. Commd 13/9/51. Flt Lt 4/1/57. Retd GD 3/4/70.
HOOD E. J. R. F. Born 7/7/41. Commd 18/12/62. Flt Lt 28/7/65. Retd GD 20/6/68.
HOOD I. A. Born 1/8/45. Commd 2/5/71. Sqn Ldr 1/7/86. Retd ENG 9/8/98.
HOOD J. Born 25/11/47. Commd 30/1/75. Flt Lt 28/6/81. Retd GD(G) 15/7/90.
HOOD J. H. G. Born 27/4/20. Commd 24/1/42. Flt Lt 21/11/48. Retd PI 5/8/72.
HOOD P. R. Born 15/8/28. Commd 6/12/56. Flt Lt 6/12/62. Retd GD 27/9/68.
HOOK L. Born 26/7/23. Commd 12/8/54. Sqn Ldr 1/7/73. Retd GD 26/7/83.
HOOK N. B. Born 21/4/28. Commd 26/3/64. Flt Lt 26/6/70. Retd SEC 8/1/80.
HOOKS R. K., CBE BSc(Eng) CEng FRAeS. Born 7/8/29. Commd 5/9/51. AVM 1/1/81. Retd ENG 5/5/84.
HOOLEY D. P. Born 29/11/43. Commd 2/8/68. Sqn Ldr 1/7/77. Retd GD(G) 29/3/83.
HOOLEY D. R. A., MCIPS MIMgt. Born 28/9/24. Commd 9/3/45. Sqn Ldr 1/1/60. Retd SUP 31/12/76.
HOOLEY T. M., MA BA. Born 5/1/36. Commd 22/6/65. Sqn Ldr 5/3/67. Retd EDN 21/8/81.
HOOPER A. L. Born 17/11/38. Commd 15/12/59. Sqn Ldr 1/7/71. Retd GD 28/6/98.
HOOPER C. A. Born 1/3/46. Commd 26/5/67. Sqn Ldr 1/7/82. Retd GD 1/6/01.
HOOPER The Rev G. M. Born 11/5/39. Commd 15/9/69. Retd 4/4/74 Sqn Ldr.
HOOPER H. Born 10/11/46. Commd 23/4/87. Flt Lt 23/4/91. Retd ENG 2/4/93.
HOOPER J. E. Born 18/9/37. Commd 27/10/67. Flt Lt 15/4/70. Retd GD 28/9/74.
HOOPER R. C., MBE. Born 20/5/22. Commd 20/6/42. Sqn Ldr 1/7/67. Retd GD 20/3/74.
HOOPER-SMITH C. J., BSc. Born 30/6/45. Commd 13/4/67. Flt Lt 15/4/71. Retd GD 1/2/89.
HOPE A. H., MIMgt. Born 15/4/17. Commd 15/8/41. Wg Cdr 1/7/60. Retd ENG 16/4/72.
HOPE V. G., DFC. Born 27/11/18. Commd 19/1/43. Flt Lt 19/7/46. Retd GD 27/10/47 rtg Sqn Ldr.
HOPER B. P. Born 8/2/51. Commd 31/7/86. Sqn Ldr 1/1/95. Retd ADMIN 3/4/01.
HOPGOOD M. S. Born 7/12/42. Commd 10/11/61. Flt Lt 1/7/69. Retd GD 7/12/80.
HOPKIN P. M. A., BSc. Born 8/6/44. Commd 19/8/68. Sqn Ldr 19/2/76. Retd ADMIN 19/8/84.
HOPKINS A. F. Born 24/2/48. Commd 11/1/79. Sqn Ldr 1/7/86. Retd GD 14/9/96.
HOPKINS A. J., AFC. Born 11/5/35. Commd 26/5/55. Wg Cdr 1/1/71. Retd GD 1/1/74.
HOPKINS B. Born 17/9/34. Commd 28/1/53. Sqn Ldr 1/7/66. Retd GD 17/9/72.
HOPKINS C. C. Born 29/10/31. Commd 19/8/54. Wg Cdr 1/1/76. Retd ENG 1/3/80.
HOPKINS C. W. R. Born 8/11/23. Commd 25/8/44. Sqn Ldr 1/4/55. Retd GD 8/11/61.
HOPKINS D. B. Born 8/12/30. Commd 29/4/53. Flt Lt 10/9/58. Retd GD 8/12/68.
HOPKINS E. E., AFC. Born 13/8/17. Commd 3/5/43. Flt Lt 29/11/51. Retd GD(G) 1/1/62.
HOPKINS E. W. Born 16/1/33. Commd 25/10/51. Flt Lt 25/4/57. Retd GD 16/1/71.
HOPKINS G. H. Born 1/7/33. Commd 5/4/55. Sqn Ldr 1/7/68. Retd SUP 1/7/71.
HOPKINS H. E., CBE DFC AFC. Born 29/8/12. Commd 12/10/36. Gp Capt 1/7/63. Retd GD 29/8/62.
HOPKINS H. E. Born 23/2/20. Commd 6/9/47. Flt Lt 6/3/52. Retd SEC 30/11/68.
HOPKINS H. L., MSc BSc CEng MRAeS MInstP. Born 25/11/30. Commd 28/10/55. Wg Cdr 20/2/74. Retd ADMIN 30/9/77.
HOPKINS J. D. N. Born 20/11/37. Commd 10/2/56. Wg Cdr 1/1/76. Retd GD 30/4/91. rtg Gp Capt.
HOPKINS J. M. Born 5/4/96. Commd 28/4/24. Flt Lt 1/7/30. Retd SEC 7/6/33.
HOPKINS J. P., MB ChB DRCOG. Born 8/3/52. Commd 15/1/89. Wg Cdr 15/1/95. Retd MED 14/3/97.
HOPKINS L., MBE. Born 20/4/19. Commd 19/5/49. Sqn Ldr 1/7/58. Retd ENG 23/7/66.
HOPKINS N. K., MBE. Born 21/7/30. Commd 11/4/51. Sqn Ldr 1/7/62. Retd SEC 21/7/68.
HOPKINS P. A. Born 22/3/51. Commd 25/2/72. Sqn Ldr 1/7/81. Retd GD 28/9/85.

HOPKINS P. J. A., BA. Born 16/8/50. Commd 19/2/73. Sqn Ldr 1/1/83. Retd GD 19/2/89.
HOPKINS R. J., DSO MIMgt. Born 17/12/21. Commd 19/9/42. Wg Cdr 1/7/61. Retd GD 9/12/75.
HOPKINS R. S. A. E. Born 28/7/37. Commd 11/1/79. Flt Lt 11/1/82. Retd GD 28/7/94.
HOPKINS W. B. G., AFC. Born 29/5/34. Commd 2/7/52. Gp Capt 1/1/79. Retd GD 1/2/86.
HOPKINSON F. E. Born 15/9/21. Commd 29/6/43. Flt Lt 30/8/47. Retd GD 25/11/67.
HOPKINSON M. I. T. Born 16/5/49. Commd 3/5/68. Flt Lt 3/11/73. Retd GD 24/1/76. Re-entered 6/8/80. Flt Lt 16/5/78. Retd GD 14/3/97.
HOPKINSON M. J., BSc. Born 13/6/61. Commd 31/8/80. Sqn Ldr 1/7/93. Retd GD 30/8/98.
HOPKIRK J. A. C., BA MB BChir MRCP. Born 3/3/43. Commd 11/1/65. Wg Cdr 4/9/81. Retd MED 3/3/87.
HOPPER A. G. Born 30/12/44. Commd 15/11/65. Gp Capt 1/7/91. Retd GD 14/3/96.
HOPPER B. Born 13/6/42. Commd 7/1/63. Fg Offr 7/1/65. Retd GD 15/5/66.
HOPPER H. E. Born 25/8/18. Commd 4/11/44. Flt Lt 4/5/48. Retd GD(G) 25/8/68.
HOPPER I. G., CEng MRAeS. Born 6/2/41. Commd 17/7/62. Sqn Ldr. 1/7/73. Retd ENG 6/2/79.
HOPPER K., MA CEng MIEE MRAeS. Born 11/7/35. Commd 9/5/54. Sqn Ldr 1/1/66. Retd ENG 15/6/75.
HOPPS D. Born 22/11/27. Commd 1/8/69. Flt Lt 1/8/72. Retd GD 1/5/75.
HOPTON D., MBE. Born 9/12/18. Commd 26/8/60. Sqn Ldr 1/1/69. Retd ENG 31/5/74.
HOPTON D. StJ. Born 10/3/29. Commd 6/12/56. Sqn Ldr 1/7/66. Retd PRT 1/10/74.
HOPWOOD P. G., BSc. Born 22/9/39. Commd 3/1/64. Sqn Ldr 1/1/78. Retd GD 1/1/81.
HORAH D. E. Born 6/12/22. Commd 25/5/45. Flt Lt 16/10/61. Retd GD(G) 1/7/75.
HORAN J. F. Born 4/7/39. Commd 18/12/80. Sqn Ldr 18/12/80. Retd ENG 17/8/93.
HORDER G. E. Born 2/6/45. Commd 5/1/66. Fg Offr 15/10/66. Retd GD 31/8/68.
HORDLEY M. J., BSc. Born 5/6/55. Commd 2/9/73. Flt Lt 15/4/80. Retd ENG 30/9/83.
HORDLEY W. G. J. Born 21/2/25. Commd 15/1/45. Sqn Ldr 1/7/70. Retd SEC 31/3/78.
HORE C. Born 12/8/18. Commd 27/10/44. Flt Lt 27/4/48. Retd GD(G) 30/7/60.
HORE N. E. Born 21/5/14. Commd 9/5/40. Flt Lt 1/1/43. Retd 23/7/53 rtg Sqn Ldr.
HORLEY G. E. Born 5/8/17. Commd 10/2/43. Flt Lt 10/8/47. Retd SEC 18/10/53 rtg Sqn Ldr.
HORLOCK G. L. Born 10/10/48. Commd 21/3/69. Sqn Ldr 1/7/83. Retd ENG 10/10/86.
HORLOCK K. J. Born 29/5/51. Commd 16/5/72. Flt Lt 15/4/77. Retd ADMIN 30/5/88.
HORLOCK R. E., BA. Born 24/10/57. Commd 18/10/81. Sqn Ldr 1/1/90. Retd ENG 18/10/97.
HORN C., MBE. Born 6/4/21. Commd 21/12/43. Sqn Ldr 1/9/65. Retd GD 11/5/68.
HORN G. W. Born 24/2/32. Commd 22/7/66. Sqn Ldr 1/7/83. Retd ENG 24/2/87.
HORNE A. W., DFC AFC. Born 25/10/19. Commd 7/3/38. Wg Cdr 1/7/55. Retd GD 10/9/68.
HORNE C. J. L. Born 9/12/37. Commd 15/2/60. Flt Lt 15/8/65. Retd GD 15/2/76.
HORNE D. A. Born 13/10/48. Commd 21/3/69. Sqn Ldr 1/1/86. Retd SY(RGT) 1/1/89.
HORNE G. E. Born 29/12/15. Commd 21/2/36. Wg Cdr 1/7/47. Retd GD 29/12/62.
HORNE M. J., MSc CEng MIEE. Born 3/3/44. Commd 15/7/65. Sqn Ldr 1/7/74. Retd ENG 3/3/82.
HORNE R., BA PGCE MCIPD. Born 27/6/42. Commd 14/11/71. Sqn Ldr 14/5/79. Retd ADMIN 28/5/93.
HORNE R. J., BEd MILAM. Born 18/9/47. Commd 29/8/72. Sqn Ldr 1/7/88. Retd ADMIN 16/11/92.
HORNE S. L. Born 4/11/45. Commd 5/3/65. Flt Lt 6/10/71. Retd GD 4/11/84.
HORNE W. J., MBE. Born 12/4/34. Commd 8/5/53. Sqn Ldr 1/1/78. Retd GD 28/11/88.
HORNING G.B. Born 17/4/30. Commd 21/11/51. Sqn Ldr 1/7/83. Retd GD 17/4/88.
HORNSBY I. L. I. Born 29/9/09. Commd 28/7/41. Sqn Offr 1/5/50SEC. Retd SEC 14/5/59.
HORNSBY N. A. Born 27/8/62. Commd 18/3/84. Flt Lt 18/9/87. Retd OPS SPT 27/8/00.
HORNSBY The Rev E., AKC. Born 25/12/23. Commd 16/9/55. Retd 14/5/69 Sqn Ldr.
HORNSBY-SMITH F. C., OBE. Born 8/10/04. Commd 26/7/39. Wg Cdr 1/1/49. Retd SEC 22/6/58.
HORNSEY R. Born 26/9/34. Commd 8/5/56. Flt Lt 8/11/61. Retd GD 26/9/72.
HOROBIN C. Born 16/12/41. Commd 1/10/65. Flt Lt 14/3/69. Retd GD 16/12/79.
HORRELL J. A., OBE BSc. Born 1/10/28. Commd 10/1/51. Gp Capt 1/7/80. Retd GD 18/5/84.
HORROCKS C. A. Born 16/6/56. Commd 17/1/85. Flt Lt 17/1/87. Retd GD(G) 16/6/94.
HORROCKS I. Born 10/3/34. Commd 26/11/52. Air Cdre 1/7/85. Retd GD 22/12/89.
HORROCKS J., DFC. Born 25/6/22. Commd 21/12/43. Flt Lt 4/6/53. Retd GD 25/6/73.
HORROCKS J. S. Born 8/7/23. Commd 17/3/55. Flt Lt 17/3/61. Retd GD 8/7/78. Rtg Sqn Ldr.
HORSCROFT H. M. Born 17/8/31. Commd 30/5/69. Sqn Ldr 1/7/77. Retd GD 30/9/81.
HORSCROFT J. R. Born 28/7/45. Commd 12/7/63. Flt Lt 12/1/69. Retd GD 31/7/76.
HORSFALL G. J. Born 24/12/11. Commd 25/3/44. Flt Lt 25/3/50. Retd GD(G) 1/9/64.
HORSFALL J. A., AFC. Born 21/3/38. Commd 15/12/59. Sqn Ldr 1/7/70. Retd GD 2/4/88.
HORSFALL J. E. Born 8/6/24. Commd 3/2/49. Sqn Ldr 1/1/59. Retd GD 8/6/67.
HORSFIELD R. Born 19/10/34. Commd 5/4/55. Wg Cdr 1/7/70. Retd GD 1/11/77.
HORSHAM-BATLEY D. J. W., BTech. Born 18/4/58. Commd 29/3/90. Flt Lt 29/3/92. Retd MED(SEC) 29/3/98.
HORSLEY C. J. Born 8/7/37. Commd 15/12/59. Wg Cdr 1/1/85. Retd GD 8/7/92.
HORSLEY Sir Peter, KCB CBE MVO AFC. Born 26/3/21. Commd 8/4/41. AM 1/7/73. Retd GD 2/8/75.
HORSLEY R. G. Born 29/9/49. Commd 4/5/72. Flt Lt 4/11/78. Retd GD(G) 17/10/90.
HORSLEY R. M., DFC AFC. Born 4/5/21. Commd 20/4/42. Wg Cdr 1/7/60. Retd GD 1/7/68.
HORSLEY-HEATHER J. S. B. Born 21/2/35. Commd 25/7/56. Sqn Ldr 1/7/69. Retd ENG 21/2/73.
HORSTED K. T. Born 26/5/59. Commd 22/6/89. Flt Lt 22/6/91. Retd ENG 22/6/97.
HORTH H. S., MBE AFC. Born 26/1/21. Commd 25/2/44. Sqn Ldr 1/10/54. Retd GD 26/1/76.

HORTON B. A. Born 30/8/44. Commd 31/3/64. Wg Cdr 1/7/85. Retd GD 31/8/99.
HORTON G. R., BA BSc. Born 2/3/51. Commd 5/8/73. Flt Lt 5/11/74. Retd GD 15/12/95.
HORTON M. P., MIMgt. Born 16/3/45. Commd 26/5/67. Sqn Ldr 1/7/75. Retd GD 16/3/83.
HORTON T. W., DSO DFC*. Born 29/12/19. Commd 6/5/43. Wg Cdr 1/1/56. Retd GD 29/12/66.
HORWOOD A. W., MBE. Born 11/7/06. Commd 14/1/43. Flt Lt 1/7/46. Retd ENG 7/10/46.
HORWOOD J. V., MIMgt. Born 11/8/26. Commd 24/9/47. Wg Cdr 1/1/63. Retd GD 1/11/75.
HOSE P. S. Born 13/8/18. Commd 15/8/46. Wg Cdr 1/7/65. Retd SUP 13/8/73.
HOSIER J. D. Born 26/4/38. Commd 17/1/69. Flt Lt 17/1/71. Retd GD 17/1/77.
HOSKIN D. P. Born 23/7/44. Commd 29/7/83. Flt Lt 29/7/87. Retd ENG 23/7/99.
HOSKINS B. R., AFC MRaeS MIMgt. Born 14/9/43. Commd 22/5/64. Gp Capt 1/1/89. Retd GD 14/9/94.
HOSKINS F. D. Born 25/12/29. Commd 12/12/51. Wg Cdr 1/1/70. Retd GD 25/11/75.
HOSKINS J. H., DSO DFC. Born 20/1/16. Commd 17/5/41. Wg Cdr 1/1/52. Retd GD 24/2/63.
HOSKINS J. W. Born 19/2/36. Commd 1/4/58. Sqn Ldr 1/7/71. Retd GD 1/10/75.
HOSKINS P. A., ACIS. Born 24/5/30. Commd 12/12/51. Sqn Ldr 1/1/65. Retd SEC 20/10/73.
HOSKINS P. J., BA MIL. Born 6/2/48. Commd 28/2/69. Gp Capt 1/7/91. Retd GD 1/5/98.
HOTCHKISS A. E. Born 12/3/32. Commd 19/4/51. Gp Capt 1/1/79. Retd GD 12/3/87.
HOTCHKISS E. L. Born 18/10/21. Commd 11/3/46. Flt Lt 7/6/51. Retd GD 18/10/76.
HOTSON C. C. J. Born 4/6/31. Commd 22/10/53. Flt Lt 22/4/58. Retd GD 21/2/76.
HOUCHIN C. R. Born 30/7/44. Commd 31/1/64. Flt Lt 31/7/69. Retd GD 31/5/75.
HOUGH A. E. Born 21/3/21. Commd 9/8/47. Sqn Ldr 1/7/62. Retd ENG 28/3/68.
HOUGH A. L., BA. Born 7/6/41. Commd 30/8/84. Flt Lt 30/8/88. Retd ENG 19/1/93.
HOUGH J. D., MMAR. Born 27/12/46. Commd 8/9/74. Sqn Ldr 1/7/81. Retd MAR 1/4/86.
HOUGH J. M. P. Born 13/3/40. Commd 29/10/60. Sqn Ldr 1/7/72. Retd GD 8/9/78.
HOUGH R. J. Born 3/3/25. Commd 21/12/45. Sqn Ldr 1/1/56. Retd GD 2/3/60.
HOUGHAM R. W. Born 7/6/18. Commd 9/8/48. Sqn Ldr 1/7/69. Retd RGT 7/6/73.
HOUGHTON A. J. Born 15/11/43. Commd 11/8/67. Flt Lt 4/12/71. Retd GD 24/10/84.
HOUGHTON A. W. Born 8/9/36. Commd 30/12/55. Wg Cdr 1/7/73. Retd GD 5/5/88.
HOUGHTON F. A., MBE MRaeS. Born 7/4/18. Commd 26/7/41. Sqn Ldr 1/7/52. Retd ENG 7/1/63 rtg Wg Cdr.
HOUGHTON J. E., AFC FIMgt. Born 25/5/40. Commd 27/6/59. A Cdre 1/7/87. Retd GD 25/5/95.
HOUGHTON N. B. Born 26/2/47. Commd 10/2/72. Flt Lt 10/8/77. Retd GD 2/3/93.
HOUGHTON P. F. Born 16/7/24. Commd 27/8/60. Flt Lt 28/7/63. Retd GD 16/7/82.
HOUGHTON P. G., BA. Born 19/7/51. Commd 15/9/69. Sqn Ldr 1/1/83. Retd GD 19/7/89.
HOUGHTON R., MBE. Born 8/2/23. Commd 11/7/44. Wg Cdr 1/1/73. Retd GD 8/2/78.
HOUGHTON R. Born 7/5/34. Commd 17/12/52. Wg Cdr 1/1/83. Retd GD 7/5/92.
HOUGHTON R. W. J. Born 16/7/25. Commd 1/7/53. Flt Lt 11/12/58. Retd GD 23/2/65.
HOULBROOK L. Born 3/3/60. Commd 19/11/87. Flt Lt 19/11/89. Retd OPS SPT 3/3/98.
HOULGATE F. V. Born 26/1/23. Commd 10/2/44. Flt Lt 25/4/48. Retd GD 9/8/57.
HOULSTON P. Born 17/3/48. Commd 13/1/67. Fg Offr 16/2/69. Retd GD 3/4/71.
HOUNSELL G. E. Born 4/9/30. Commd 11/5/55. Sqn Ldr 1/7/66. Retd GD 1/7/69.
HOUNSELL L. J. Born 27/11/32. Commd 28/2/80. Sqn Ldr 1/7/89. Retd ENG 27/11/98.
HOURIGAN Rev T. Born 29/8/05. Commd 2/9/38. Retd 2/9/60 Gp Capt.
HOURSTON D. I. Born 14/12/59. Commd 5/4/79. Sqn Ldr 1/1/92. Retd SUP 14/12/97.
HOURSTON I. M., MB ChB. Born 29/10/31. Commd 31/3/57. A Cdre 1/7/85. Retd MED 1/7/87.
HOURY R. Born 17/5/40. Commd 26/5/61. Flt Lt 1/11/67. Retd GD 2/4/76.
HOUSBY G., BSc. Born 14/8/61. Commd 26/3/92. Flt Lt 26/3/94. Retd ENG 26/3/00.
HOUSBY S. J. Born 20/5/52. Commd 4/5/72. Flt Lt 4/11/77. Retd GD 4/8/89.
HOUSE C. W. Born 7/10/19. Commd 28/12/42. Flt Lt 1/11/51. Retd GD(G) 22/11/66.
HOUSE E. D. Born 1/4/16. Commd 27/6/43. Sqn Ldr 1/1/57. Retd SUP 4/5/65.
HOUSE G. W. Born 12/8/45. Commd 5/12/63. Wg Cdr 1/7/88. Retd GD(G) 14/3/96.
HOUSE J. R. Born 25/4/29. Commd 27/8/59. Sqn Ldr 1/1/76. Retd ENG 23/11/82.
HOUSE L. G. Born 23/5/22. Commd 9/7/59. Flt Lt 9/7/64. Retd ENG 23/9/73.
HOUSEMAN W. A., BSc. Born 12/7/47. Commd 1/8/69. Sqn Ldr 1/1/83. Retd GD 19/7/89.
HOUSLEY T. J., BA. Born 2/6/59. Commd 29/8/77. Flt Lt 15/10/83. Retd SUP 1/10/88.
HOUSTON E., BA LLB. Born 14/7/46. Commd 18/9/66. Flt Lt 15/10/69. Retd GD 1/10/85.
HOUTHEUSEN H. J., DFC. Born 16/5/15. Commd 4/8/42. Sqn Ldr 1/1/63. Retd GD(G) 8/4/66.
HOVER R. A. Born 6/7/40. Commd 24/9/63. Sqn Ldr 1/1/75. Retd ENG 6/7/95.
HOW A. J. Born 19/7/29. Commd 13/8/52. Flt Lt 9/1/58. Retd GD 28/3/70.
HOW D. Born 30/8/53. Commd 30/5/82. Sqn Ldr 1/1/91. Retd SUP 14/3/96.
HOW J. D. Born 11/4/09. Commd 8/7/43. Fg Offr 21/4/44. Retd ENG 13/1/46. Recalled 12/5/49. Flt Lt 4/1/51. Retd 7/2/64.
HOW M. S. F. Born 31/7/37. Commd 12/12/59. Sq Ldr 1/7/71. Retd GD 31/7/75.
HOWARD A. C., LLB. Born 1/11/60. Commd 25/10/87. Sqn Ldr 25/10/91. Retd LGL 15/7/99.
HOWARD A. E. Born 17/5/32. Commd 25/11/53. Flt Lt 25/5/59. Retd GD 17/5/72 rtg Sqn Ldr.
HOWARD A. H. Born 12/1/35. Commd 5/11/70. Sqn Ldr 1/7/79. Retd ADMIN 7/3/90.
HOWARD B. H., DFC. Born 8/4/24. Commd 10/7/43. Wg Cdr 1/7/61. Retd GD 16/8/68.
HOWARD E., BSc. Born 11/11/55. Commd 14/8/77. Flt Lt 14/11/77. Retd GD 14/8/89.

HOWARD E. E. Born 5/3/29. Commd 11/1/50. Flt Lt 3/5/56. Retd GD 5/3/67.
HOWARD G. Born 31/3/45. Commd 15/7/66. Flt Lt 12/11/69. Retd GD 10/9/76.
HOWARD H. J. Born 27/3/44. Commd 22/5/70. Flt Lt 7/1/74. Retd GD 27/3/00.
HOWARD H. R. Born 17/11/26. Commd 1/8/50. Flt Lt 26/3/56. Retd GD 17/11/69.
HOWARD M. R., BSc. Born 4/3/49. Commd 28/12/71. Flt Lt 15/10/76. Retd ENG 28/12/87.
HOWARD N. R. S. Born 27/3/30. Commd 24/10/51. Wg Cdr 1/1/72. Retd GD 14/5/83.
HOWARD P., CB OBE PhD MB BS FRCP FFOM FRAeS. Born 15/12/25. Commd 20/8/51. AVM 1/8/85. Retd MED 17/10/88.
HOWARD P. Born 2/4/46. Commd 24/3/83. Sqn Ldr 1/7/91. Retd ENG 2/4/01.
HOWARD P. D. Born 19/10/23. Commd 27/8/59. Sqn Ldr 1/7/73. Retd SEC 30/8/75.
HOWARD P. E. S. Born 17/9/23. Commd 5/5/14. Flt Lt 17/3/54. Retd GD(G) 30/7/64.
HOWARD P. I., BDS MGDSRCS(Eng) MCIPD. Born 7/12/58. Commd 13/1/80. Wg Cdr 5/12/94. Retd DEL 7/12/96.
HOWARD P. J., ACIS. Born 24/11/38. Commd 28/12/66. Wg Cdr 1/1/87. Retd ADMIN 14/5/89.
HOWARD P. V. Born 17/2/15. Commd 17/9/43. Flt Lt 29/6/50. Retd GD(G) 26/3/70.
HOWARD R. F. G., BEM FCIPS FIMgt. Born 23/3/23. Commd 1/7/72. Retd ADMIN 23/3/78.
HOWARD R. J., AFC. Born 9/11/38. Commd 25/7/60. Gp Capt 1/7/87. Retd GD 9/11/93.
HOWARD R. T., AFC. Born 28/9/20. Commd 18/2/44. Sqn Ldr 1/1/58. Retd GD 28/9/69.
HOWARD W. J. Born 14/7/39. Commd 25/7/60. Sqn Ldr 1/7/72. Retd GD 3/11/81.
HOWARD W. T., BEM. Born 1/1/23. Commd 13/7/61. Sqn Ldr 1/7/73. Retd ENG 15/1/77.
HOWARD-JONES G. M., DFC FIMgt MCIPD. Born 11/9/19. Commd 24/6/39. Gp Capt 1/7/69. Retd SEC 27/4/74.
HOWARTH G. W. L., PGCE BTech. Born 30/11/53. Commd 6/9/81. Sqn Ldr 1/1/89. Retd ADMIN 14/3/97.
HOWARTH P., BSc CEng MRAeS. Born 8/7/41. Commd 1/8/66. Retd ENG 1/8/82.
HOWARTH P. D. Born 17/2/44. Commd 1/4/66. Flt Lt 18/1/76. Retd GD 13/12/77. Re-entered 1/4/81. Wg Cdr 1/7/95. Retd ADMIN 14/12/96.
HOWARTH R. Born 25/8/37. Commd 1/3/68. Sqn Ldr 6/11/75. Retd EDN 1/3/76.
HOWAT A. H. Born 21/5/48. Commd 24/2/67. Flt Lt 24/8/72. Retd GD 18/6/74.
HOWAT M. C. M., BSc. Born 17/6/42. Commd 26/3/63. Flt Lt 17/6/65. Retd GD 9/10/77.
HOWAT T. MCC. Born 15/4/41. Commd 27/6/59. Sqn Ldr 1/7/87. Retd GD 15/4/96.
HOWDEN M. J., BSc. Born 1/7/19. Commd 16/6/43. Flt Offr 6/8/50. Retd SEC 4/5/63.
HOWDEN R. I. C. Born 31/7/35. Commd 11/2/55. Wg Cdr 1/1/73. Retd GD 1/2/75.
HOWE E. J. Born 31/3/41. Commd 18/8/61. Flt Lt 30/9/66. Retd GD 31/3/79.
HOWE I. MCG. G. Born 11/5/57. Commd 5/8/76. Wg Cdr 1/7/94. Retd GD 1/12/97.
HOWE J. F. G., CB CBE AFC. Born 26/3/30. Commd 4/10/54. AVM 1/7/80. Retd GD 30/11/85.
HOWE J. L., BSc. Born 28/2/43. Commd 13/4/64. Sqn Ldr 1/7/74. Retd GD 28/2/81. Re-instated 14/11/84. Retd GD 7/3/86.
HOWE R. Born 11/2/46. Commd 27/1/67. Flt Lt 15/7/73. Retd SUP 11/2/84.
HOWE R. S. Born 9/9/45. Commd 26/5/67. Sqn Ldr 1/7/92. Retd GD 9/9/00.
HOWE R. S. L., MSc CEng MIEE. Born 23/3/30. Commd 18/2/54. Sqn Ldr 18/6/64. Retd EDN 18/2/70.
HOWELL A. J. Born 18/12/04. Commd 10/1/29. Sqn Ldr 1/8/39. Retd SUP 23/8/46.
HOWELL E. A., BEd. Born 21/3/56. Commd 3/9/78. Sqn Ldr 1/1/89. Retd ADMIN 3/9/00.
HOWELL E. M. T., CBE CEng FRAeS. Born 11/9/13. Commd 15/12/34. AVM 1/1/66. Retd ENG 17/3/67.
HOWELL F. C. Born 19/1/19. Commd 19/7/45. Flt Lt 19/1/50. Retd SEC 11/10/53.
HOWELL G. P., MB BS FRCS(Edin) LMSSA. Born 12/12/53. Commd 18/2/75. Wg Cdr 16/2/92. Retd MED 30/10/96.
HOWELL J. K., MB ChB DCH DObstRCOG. Born 12/9/30. Commd 17/2/56. Wg Cdr 17/2/69. Retd MED 4/3/73.
HOWELL M. D. Born 18/6/51. Commd 25/2/72. Flt Lt 25/2/75. Retd GD 1/9/83.
HOWELL R. A. Born 30/12/59. Commd 3/7/80. Flt Lt 31/12/83. Retd GD 14/1/91.
HOWELL R. T. Born 7/3/38. Commd 20/11/56. Sqn Ldr 1/1/74. Retd GD 1/10/80.
HOWELL W. W., FC. Born 14/9/20. Commd 15/6/45. Sqn Ldr 1/7/72. Retd GD 14/9/75.
HOWELLS J. R., BSc CEng MRAeS. Born 24/4/39. Commd 30/9/59. Wg Cdr 1/7/76. Retd ENG 1/7/79.
HOWELLS M. A., BA FInstPet MIMgt. Born 9/10/32. Commd 27/7/54. Wg Cdr 1/7/72. Retd SUP 30/7/83.
HOWELLS P. M., BA. Born 20/12/40. Commd 2/2/65. Sqn Ldr 1/7/77. Retd SEC 2/2/81.
HOWELLS R. L. Born 27/10/50. Commd 19/6/70. Flt Lt 13/2/77. Retd GD(G) 18/7/81.
HOWELLS V. B., CBE. Born 14/2/38. Commd 15/12/59. A Cdre 1/7/88. Retd SUP 14/8/95.
HOWES A. M. McC. Born 19/7/30. Commd 12/12/51. Sqn Ldr 1/7/69. Retd SUP 1/9/82.
HOWES C. E., OBE. Born 25/5/15. Commd 8/12/41. Wg Offr 1/7/56. Retd SEC 28/3/61.
HOWES G. P. Born 3/1/59. Commd 30/4/81. Sqn Ldr 1/1/92. Retd GD 3/1/97.
HOWES H. L. Born 20/11/28. Commd 9/5/51. Sqn Ldr 1/7/63. Retd GD 28/11/75.
HOWES M. Born 19/8/45. Commd 2/6/67. Sqn Ldr 1/1/80. Retd GD 19/8/89.
HOWES M. E. Born 18/11/43. Commd 21/12/62. Flt Lt 1/7/69. Retd GD 18/11/81.
HOWES Rev M. J. N., BA. Born 17/4/43. Commd 22/10/72. Retd 22/10/88. Wg Cdr.
HOWEY J. H. Born 6/12/34. Commd 30/5/59. Flt Lt 10/2/67. Retd GD(G) 5/12/74.
HOWIE A. Born 11/9/30. Commd 12/9/50. Wg Cdr 1/1/72. Retd GD 11/9/85.
HOWIE D. G. Born 21/7/33. Commd 15/3/60. Sqn Ldr 1/1/73. Retd GD 21/7/88.
HOWIE T. D. Born 17/11/61. Commd 19/3/81. Flt Lt 19/9/87. Retd OPS SPT 17/11/99.
HOWITT J. S., AFC MRCS LRCP. Born 24/12/16. Commd 10/9/40. Gp Capt 1/1/59. Retd MED 11/9/64.

HOWLAND R. J. L., BSc. Born 3/10/66. Commd 16/9/84. Fg Off 15/1/87. Retd ENG 15/6/88.
HOWLES P. A. H. Born 6/1/33. Commd 28/1/53. Sqn Ldr 1/1/71. Retd GD 1/1/74.
HOWLETT N. S., CB. Born 17/4/27. Commd 2/10/47. AVM 1/1/79. Retd GD 17/4/82.
HOWLETT P. C. Born 7/2/31. Commd 21/12/67. Sqn Ldr 1/7/83. Retd ENG 7/2/93.
HOWLETT P. W., AFC. Born 19/2/46. Commd 21/5/65. Sqn Ldr 1/7/93. Retd GD 19/2/01.
HOWORTH D. M., OBE. Born 28/7/19. Commd 27/7/40. Wg Cdr 1/7/66. Retd GD(G) 28/7/74.
HOWSEGO G. M. Born 6/5/62. Commd 11/6/81. Flt Lt 11/12/87. Retd SY 14/3/96.
HOWSON G., BSc. Born 1/5/49. Commd 14/11/73. Sqn Ldr 1/1/82. Retd ENG 14/11/89.
HOXEY K. H. Born 28/5/23. Commd 15/12/44. Sqn Ldr 1/7/74. Retd GD 28/5/78.
HOY S. L. Born 2/10/43. Commd 14/8/70. Flt Lt 14/8/72. Retd ENG 2/10/81.
HOY W., DFC AFC. Born 23/12/18. Commd 8/10/39. Wg Cdr 1/1/51. Retd GD 5/4/66.
HOYER W. Born 9/10/33. Commd 8/11/51. Flt Lt 23/2/57. Retd GD 14/6/74.
HOYES M. P., BSc. Born 5/1/48. Commd 13/9/70. Sqn Ldr 1/1/89. Retd ENG 13/9/92.
HOYLAND P. Born 15/7/04. Commd 1/9/45. Sqn Ldr 1/8/47. Retd RGT 2/11/54.
HOYLE A. Born 16/10/39. Commd 26/5/61. Sqn Ldr 1/1/83. Retd GD 17/10/89.
HRUSKA A. L. Born 23/6/15. Commd 2/8/40. Sqn Ldr 1/7/60. Retd GD(G) 23/6/70.
HUARD S. C. Born 3/10/04. Commd 21/9/44. Flt Lt 4/5/48. Retd GD(G) 20/1/57.
HUBBARD A. J. Born 8/11/21. Commd 25/3/54. Flt Lt 6/3/58. Retd GD 3/5/68.
HUBBARD F. W., MBE MIMgt. Born 14/9/21. Commd 8/6/44. Wg Cdr 1/1/62. Retd GD 26/4/74.
HUBBARD G. E. F., RD. Born 9/7/21. Commd 8/5/57. Flt Lt 8/5/57. Retd MAR 3/5/71.
HUBBARD K. G., OBE DFC AFC. Born 26/2/20. Commd 6/5/41. Gp Capt 1/7/61. Retd GD 1/1/66.
HUBBARD L. H. Born 16/6/42. Commd 22/5/68. Flt Lt 22/5/74. Retd GD(G) 11/6/75.
HUBBARD M. R., MSc BSc CEng MIEE. Born 18/12/47. Commd 21/4/67. Sqn Ldr 1/7/80. Retd ENG 18/12/88.
HUBBARD P. U. Born 14/12/24. Commd 7/7/49. Sqn Ldr 1/7/58. Retd GD 14/12/62.
HUBBARD R. G. M., MIMgt. Born 10/4/22. Commd 10/5/46. Wg Cdr 1/7/65. Retd SY 26/3/77.
HUBBARD S. J., DFC AFC* MRAeS. Born 25/3/21. Commd 15/7/44. Wg Cdr 1/1/60. Retd GD 30/6/65.
HUBBARD W. Born 2/3/05. Commd 13/3/43. Flt Lt 13/9/45. Retd ENG 19/6/57.
HUBBLE C. M., BSc. Born 7/12/50. Commd 13/9/71. Flt Lt 15/10/76. Retd ENG 1/10/81.
HUBBLE Rev R. C. Born 11/10/30. Commd 11/6/64. Retd 11/10/85 Wg Cdr.
HUCKER Rev M. F., MBE MA BD. Born 1/5/33. Commd 1/9/62. Retd 10/11/90. Gp Capt.
HUDDLESTON C. J. Born 6/7/60. Commd 22/7/84. Flt Lt 22/7/90. Retd SUP 22/7/00.
HUDDLESTON Rev G. R., MA. Born 22/1/36. Commd 7/7/69. Retd 7/7/85 Wg Cdr.
HUDGELL E. E. L. Born 22/6/13. Commd 1/3/41. Sqn Offr 1/7/54. Retd SEC 10/4/56.
HUDGELL P. H., MBE. Born 4/12/23. Commd 15/6/45. Sqn Ldr 1/10/55. Retd GD 4/12/72.
HUDSON A. Born 8/6/23. Commd 1/5/47. Flt Lt 4/1/51. Retd ENG 8/6/56.
HUDSON D. B., BSc. Born 26/8/48. Commd 27/2/70. Sqn Ldr 1/7/83. Retd ENG 26/8/92.
HUDSON E. G. Born 15/11/35. Commd 1/4/58. Sqn Ldr 1/7/90. Retd GD 15/11/95.
HUDSON F. B. Born 18/4/16. Commd 23/9/44. Flt Lt 23/3/49. Retd GD(G) 18/4/71.
HUDSON J. A. Born 18/8/42. Commd 21/12/62. Flt Lt 8/1/69. Retd GD 18/8/80.
HUDSON K. B. Born 23/1/45. Commd 24/6/76. Flt Lt 24/6/78. Retd GD 24/6/84.
HUDSON M., MA BA. Born 10/11/49. Commd 30/10/83. Flt Lt 30/4/87. Retd ADMIN 10/1/01.
HUDSON M. E., MIMgt. Born 13/2/49. Commd 11/5/78. Sqn Ldr 1/7/86. Retd ADMIN 13/2/93.
HUDSON N. R., BSc. Born 25/12/47. Commd 7/6/71. Sqn Ldr 1/1/79. Retd ENG 7/6/87.
HUDSON R., MB BS DAvMed. Born 10/12/55. Commd 28/3/84. Wg Cdr 1/6/95. Retd MED 14/3/97.
HUDSON R. A. Born 9/11/19. Commd 24/3/44. Sqn Ldr 1/4/57. Retd SEC 10/2/68.
HUDSON R. A. H. R., DFM. Born 20/5/24. Commd 2/5/45. Flt Lt 2/11/48. Retd GD 2/1/68.
HUDSON R. I. Born 5/10/24. Commd 10/12/44. Flt Lt 4/12/52. Retd SEC 22/11/68.
HUDSON R. J. S. Born 14/8/28. Commd 27/9/50. Flt Lt 27/9/53. Retd GD 5/9/56.
HUDSON R. S. Born 29/6/37. Commd 16/9/71. Sqn Ldr 1/7/91. Retd SUP 1/7/94.
HUDSON S. Born 25/12/21. Commd 7/4/44. Sqn Ldr 1/1/56. Retd GD 31/8/68.
HUDSON S. G. Born 15/4/60. Commd 1/11/79. Flt Lt 1/5/86. Retd SY 16/4/87.
HUDSON T. F. H. Born 26/8/15. Commd 3/4/39. Wg Cdr 1/1/52. Retd SUP 31/8/59.
HUDSPETH J. D. Born 9/12/45. Commd 17/7/70. Flt Lt 25/2/74. Retd GD 11/12/75.
HUES C. F. Born 18/10/38. Commd 20/2/72. Flt Lt 21/8/73. Retd ADMIN 20/2/83.
HUETT P. S. Born 20/1/46. Commd 6/5/66. Sqn Ldr 1/7/79. Retd GD 7/12/86.
HUGGARD W. M. Born 6/1/16. Commd 8/6/43. Flt Lt 17/9/51. Retd GD(G) 5/12/62.
HUGGETT D. F., AFC. Born 12/12/33. Commd 20/5/52. Flt Lt 20/2/58. Retd GD 4/12/65.
HUGGETT W. D. F., DFC. Born 31/5/15. Commd 6/3/42. Flt Lt 16/10/50. Retd GD(G) 21/4/63.
HUGGINS A. G. Born 24/1/06. Commd 15/2/40. Sqn Ldr 1/8/47. Retd ENG 1/5/57 rtg Wg Cdr.
HUGGINS D. G., DPhysEd. Born 23/6/49. Commd 22/8/71. Sqn Ldr 1/7/88. Retd ADMIN 1/3/94.
HUGGINS J. C. Born 3/7/48. Commd 2/2/68. Flt Lt 22/6/74. Retd SUP 11/11/77.
HUGGINS W., MBE. Born 11/12/31. Commd 17/1/69. Flt Lt 17/1/73. Retd ADMIN 31/1/88.
HUGH J. A. C., MPhil BSc CEng MIEE. Born 15/10/41. Commd 6/10/69. Sqn Ldr 1/1/76. Retd ENG 6/10/85.
HUGHES A. G. Born 12/6/46. Commd 4/7/85. Flt Lt 4/7/89. Retd GD(G) 6/1/97.
HUGHES B. Born 2/3/30. Commd 11/4/51. A Cdre 1/1/76. Retd SUP 2/3/85.
HUGHES B., BSc(Eng) CEng MIEE MRAeS. Born 30/11/40. Commd 30/9/60. Wg Cdr 1/1/79. Retd ENG 1/4/86.

HUGHES B. J., MSc MRAeS MIMgt. Born 27/4/37. Commd 21/8/61. Wg Cdr 1/7/78. Retd GD 1/9/82.
HUGHES B. J. Born 10/1/47. Commd 8/7/65. Gp Capt 1/1/91. Retd SY 22/6/94.
HUGHES B. M. Born 7/3/64. Commd 18/11/90. Flt Lt 25/1/93. Retd GD 21/4/98.
HUGHES C. E. Born 4/1/47. Commd 27/2/70. Flt Lt 18/4/74. Retd ADMIN 4/1/85.
HUGHES C. J., AFC. Born 14/12/37. Commd 19/4/63. Flt Lt 1/4/66. Retd GD 14/12/75.
HUGHES C. O. Born 1/12/32. Commd 18/6/52. Flt 13/11/57. Retd GD(G) 1/12/87.
HUGHES C. W. G. Born 2/4/34. Commd 30/7/52. Sqn Ldr 1/7/73. Retd GD 2/4/92.
HUGHES D. G. M., BSc. Born 12/6/43. Commd 4/4/66. Flt Lt 4/1/68. Retd GD 4/4/82.
HUGHES D. H., CEng MRAeS MIMgt MIIM. Born 20/7/26. Commd 21/2/51. Wg Cdr 1/7/73. Retd ENG 20/7/84.
HUGHES D. J. S., FIFA. Born 6/6/40. Commd 18/7/63. Sqn Ldr 1/7/76. Retd ADMIN 8/7/90.
HUGHES D. N. Born 4/8/59. Commd 11/6/81. Flt Lt 11/12/87. Retd OPS SPT 4/8/97.
HUGHES E. J. A., MBE. Born 14/10/33. Commd 11/10/51. Sqn Ldr 1/7/84. Retd GD 14/10/89.
HUGHES F., MA MSc. Born 1/9/41. Commd 1/9/64. Sqn Ldr 30/3/71. Retd GD 1/9/75.
HUGHES G. F., BA. Born 12/2/55. Commd 1/9/74. Wg Cdr 1/7/94. Retd ADMIN 21/12/96.
HUGHES G. G. Born 26/3/42. Commd 4/10/63. Flt Lt 4/4/69. Retd GD 26/3/80.
HUGHES G. T. Born 5/8/25. Commd 11/11/50. Flt Lt 11/2/55. Retd GD 4/7/65.
HUGHES H. W., BSc. Born 24/12/38. Commd 28/9/60. Wg Cdr 1/1/80. Retd GD 24/12/93.
HUGHES I. C. J. Born 19/9/41. Commd 30/7/63. Wg Cdr 1/7/83. Retd GD 1/1/93.
HUGHES J. Born 5/2/43. Commd 28/7/64. Flt Lt 28/1/67. Retd GD 5/3/80.
HUGHES J. A. Born 6/4/46. Commd 30/5/69. Sqn Ldr 1/1/94. Retd GD 14/3/96.
HUGHES J. C., BDS. Born 8/4/41. Commd 20/9/59. Wg Cdr 23/6/77. Retd DEL 8/4/01.
HUGHES J. G. Born 21/7/41. Commd 6/7/62. Flt Lt 9/2/68. Retd GD 21/7/79.
HUGHES J. G. Born 11/6/38. Commd 26/11/81. Flt Lt 10/3/87. Retd SY(PRT) 10/11/89.
HUGHES J. H., BA MCIPD. Born 25/12/38. Commd 12/9/61. Sqn Ldr 1/7/73. Retd ADMIN 12/9/85.
HUGHES J. M. Born 27/9/26. Commd 23/4/52. Flt Lt 29/4/59. Retd GD 31/10/67.
HUGHES J. P. Born 22/12/15. Commd 16/5/57. Flt Lt 16/5/60. Retd ENG 22/12/70.
HUGHES K. A. Born 5/7/28. Commd 26/11/64. Flt Lt 26/11/67. Retd GD 5/7/78.
HUGHES K. L., DFC. Born 27/8/21. Commd 11/4/43. Sqn Ldr 1/7/52. Retd GD 11/2/56.
HUGHES K. L., AFC. Born 2/11/23. Commd 17/9/43. Sqn Ldr 1/10/54. Retd GD 31/12/61.
HUGHES K. R. Born 30/3/15. Commd 16/10/39. Flt Lt 1/1/43. Retd GD 1/7/50.
HUGHES L. J. Born 19/6/29. Commd 20/5/53. Flt Lt 6/3/63. Retd SUP 19/6/90.
HUGHES M. Born 5/3/30. Commd 1/8/51. Wg Cdr 1/1/69. Retd GD 25/10/80.
HUGHES M. J. Born 18/1/43. Commd 17/12/63. Flt Lt 17/6/66. Retd GD 31/3/73.
HUGHES M. K. Born 4/3/60. Commd 16/6/88. Flt Lt 16/6/90. Retd GD(G) 4/12/95.
HUGHES M. S., MSc MB BS FRIPHH MRCS LRCP DAvMed DIH MFOM. Born 21/12/32. Commd 2/9/64. Wg Cdr 25/4/75. Retd MED 5/1/83.
HUGHES N. D., OBE. Born 13/1/45. Commd 22/2/63. Wg Cdr 1/1/86. Retd GD 31/3/94.
HUGHES N. J. Born 24/3/41. Commd 18/12/62. Wg Cdr 1/1/87. Retd GD 24/3/96.
HUGHES N. J., BA. Born 12/2/67. Commd 29/9/91. Flt Lt 29/3/95. Retd ADMIN 30/9/96.
HUGHES P. Born 30/8/47. Commd 5/11/65. Flt Lt 3/9/71. Retd GD 30/9/77.
HUGHES P. A., CBE DFC. Born 18/11/18. Commd 29/7/39. Gp Capt 1/1/61. Retd GD 11/6/68 rtg A Cdre.
HUGHES R. Born 18/2/32. Commd 17/7/58. Flt Lt 17/1/63. Retd GD 18/11/71.
HUGHES R. P., BSc. Born 22/8/59. Commd 19/6/83. Flt Lt 19/12/84. Retd GD 19/6/99.
HUGHES R. W. A. Born 19/6/22. Commd 20/4/50. Sqn Ldr 1/1/70. Retd GD 30/3/77.
HUGHES S. D. Born 4/10/59. Commd 15/10/81. Sqn Ldr 1/7/93. Retd GD 4/10/97.
HUGHES S. G., BL. Born 16/2/31. Commd 27/8/59. Flt Lt 27/11/65. Retd SEC 28/4/73.
HUGHES S. J. Born 25/2/57. Commd 20/9/79. A.P.O. 20/9/79. Retd GD 29/11/80.
HUGHES S. J., BDS. Born 13/10/45. Commd 30/8/66. Wg Cdr 13/9/81. Retd DEL 14/3/97.
HUGHES S. P. Born 1/8/42. Commd 17/12/63. Flt Lt 17/6/66. Retd GD 18/4/68.
HUGHES T. Born 1/10/29. Commd 28/2/52. Sqn Ldr 1/7/67. Retd SUP 14/1/85.
HUGHES T. F. Born 15/5/38. Commd 8/12/61. Sqn Ldr 1/1/76. Retd GD(G) 28/12/88.
HUGHES W. Born 29/10/22. Commd 20/11/44. Sqn Ldr 1/7/73. Retd GD 10/6/77.
HUGHES W. D. Born 13/3/28. Commd 2/7/52. Flt Lt 27/11/57. Retd GD 26/6/68.
HUGHES W. F. Born 19/7/35. Commd 21/7/55. Gp Capt 1/7/83. Retd ADMIN 19/7/90.
HUGHES W. H. Born 27/10/30. Commd 28/7/67. Sqn Ldr 1/1/81. Retd ADMIN 27/10/85.
HUGHES W. O., BSc. Born 30/11/31. Commd 9/9/54. Sqn Ldr 1/7/65. Retd GD 9/9/70.
HUGHES W. P. G. Born 11/12/46. Commd 8/10/70. Sqn Ldr 1/7/83. Retd ADMIN 1/7/86.
HUGHES-LEWIS A. B. Born 20/3/44. Commd 17/12/64. Wg Cdr 1/1/86. Retd GD 3/4/89.
HUGHESDON A. D. Born 6/8/33. Commd 16/7/52. Flt Lt 1/11/61. Retd GD 1/11/77.
HUGILL J., DFC. Born 30/5/19. Commd 13/7/43. Flt Lt 13/7/45. Retd GD(G) 30/5/74.
HUGILL J. Born 24/6/31. Commd 15/2/51. Flt Lt 13/4/50. Retd GD 7/9/70.
HUGO V., MRIN. Born 15/7/38. Commd 22/8/59. Sqn Ldr 1/1/72. Retd GD 2/12/77.
HUIE R. G., FCIPD MIMgt. Born 13/10/23. Commd 6/6/45. Wg Cdr 1/1/67. Retd SEC 13/10/78.
HULBERT J., DFM. Born 23/1/21. Commd 21/6/45. Flt Lt 7/6/51. Retd GD 13/2/64.
HULIN W. H. Born 7/2/20. Commd 9/4/43. Flt Lt 15/12/49. Retd SEC 4/11/53.
HULL A. F. R. Born 13/8/23. Commd 26/9/51. Flt Lt 30/4/62. Retd GD 13/8/66.

HULL D. Born 1/5/38. Commd 19/4/63. Sqn Ldr 1/7/84. Retd GD 1/5/93.
HULL D. H., MA MB BChir FRCP. Born 21/8/31. Commd 11/8/57. AVM 28/4/94. Retd MED 21/8/96.
HULL G. N. Born 12/3/34. Commd 10/9/52. Flt Lt 7/2/58. Retd GD 31/3/77.
HULL P. M. A. Born 4/5/21. Commd 11/4/44. Flt Lt 27/5/54. Retd GD 24/5/65.
HULL W. B., BSc. Born 22/7/37. Commd 12/9/61. Sqn Ldr 12/3/69. Retd ADMIN 22/6/88.
HULLAH D. Born 20/10/25. Commd 28/5/66. Flt Lt 28/5/71. Retd SY 1/11/77.
HULM F. R., BDS. Born 10/5/31. Commd 16/6/63. A Cdre 1/7/83. Retd DEL 11/7/86.
HULME A. N., MBE. Born 16/4/33. Commd 6/9/54. Wg Cdr 1/1/77. Retd GD 28/1/82.
HULME L. M. Born 29/6/45. Commd 30/1/70. Sqn Ldr 1/7/95. Retd GD 29/6/00.
HULME S. Born 18/9/38. Commd 25/8/60. Sqn Ldr 1/1/72. Retd ENG 18/9/76.
HULSE D. S. Born 9/1/37. Commd 30/11/55. Flt Lt 30/5/61. Retd GD 9/1/95.
HULSE K. G. Born 3/10/45. Commd 16/8/68. Flt Lt 15/4/72. Retd GD 3/10/83.
HULYER M. C., MIMgt. Born 2/6/45. Commd 5/3/65. Sqn Ldr 1/1/83. Retd GD 1/10/88.
HUMAN P. R. Born 11/2/44. Commd 23/4/87. Flt Lt 23/4/91. Retd ENG 5/5/93.
HUMBERSTONE G. F. Born 18/11/35. Commd 23/6/61. Flt Lt 1/4/66. Retd GD 1/9/76.
HUMBLE B., OBE BSc(Eng). Born 11/9/37. Commd 8/10/61. Wg Cdr 1/1/81. Retd ENG 9/8/88.
HUMBLE T. L. Born 10/3/19. Commd 28/3/46. Sqn Ldr 1/7/63. Retd ENG 28/6/69.
HUME D. Born 20/7/45. Commd 6/5/83. Flt Lt 6/5/87. Retd ADMIN 15/11/93.
HUME D. C., BSc CEng MIEE. Born 1/10/54. Commd 2/9/73. Sqn Ldr 1/7/88. Retd ENG 1/10/92.
HUME J. W., OBE CEng MRAeS. Born 6/10/20. Commd 19/8/42. Gp Capt 1/7/68. Retd ENG 6/10/75.
HUMPHERSON R. Born 27/3/32. Commd 17/12/52. Flt Lt 17/6/55. Retd GD 27/3/70.
HUMPHREY A. S. Born 1/7/22. Commd 2/9/42. Flt Offr 2/9/47. Retd SEC 16/4/52.
HUMPHREY C. A. Born 24/1/45. Commd 3/3/67. Wg Cdr 1/1/88. Retd GD 14/3/96.
HUMPHREY J. A. Born 23/4/62. Commd 71/11/85. Flt Lt 22/10/89. Retd MED 31/8/90.
HUMPHREY M., BA MIMgt. Born 16/7/49. Commd 5/9/69. Flt Lt 17/1/76. Retd GD(G) 1/9/90.
HUMPHREY R. Born 8/12/37. Commd 4/12/56. Flt Lt 12/6/62. Retd GD 1/7/88.
HUMPHREY R. Born 11/5/37. Commd 29/7/58. Sqn Ldr 1/1/71. Retd GD 1/10/96.
HUMPHREY R. C., BSc MSc CEng MRAeS. Born 4/12/35. Commd 7/11/58. Sqn Ldr 12/3/68. Retd ADMIN 4/12/80.
HUMPHREY R. J. Born 29/11/36. Commd 21/12/67. Wg Cdr 1/7/85. Retd GD 16/5/87.
HUMPHREY S. F. Born 28/5/24. Commd 11/11/47. Flt Lt 10/11/55. Retd GD 13/7/67.
HUMPHREYS G. A., BSc. Born 17/7/58. Commd 11/9/77. Sqn Ldr 1/7/89. Retd GD 1/12/97.
HUMPHREYS M. W. Born 14/5/40. Commd 2/7/64. Wg Cdr 1/7/88. Retd ADMIN 1/7/90.
HUMPHREYS R. E. Born 2/3/09. Commd 22/5/43. Sqn Ldr 1/1/60. Retd ENG 2/3/64.
HUMPHREYS-EVANS D. H., AFC. Born 8/1/40. Commd 9/2/62. Sqn Ldr 1/1/87. Retd GD 12/8/90.
HUMPHREYSON R. C., MBE AFC. Born 9/6/38. Commd 30/10/58. Gp Capt 1/7/80. Retd GD 1/2/90.
HUMPHRIES A. G., BA. Born 1/1/46. Commd 28/2/80. Flt Lt 28/2/82. Retd GD 14/3/96.
HUMPHRIES B. M., CBE BSc CEng MIMechE. Born 13/3/43. Commd 15/7/63. A Cdre 1/1/89. Retd ENG 10/1/90.
HUMPHRIES H. V. J. Born 23/12/47. Commd 8/9/83. Flt Lt 8/9/87. Retd ENG 14/9/96.
HUMPHRIES J. R. Born 28/5/35. Commd 27/5/73. Flt Lt 24/3/62. Retd GD(G) 2/4/90.
HUMPHRIES J. S. Born 13/10/21. Commd 15/2/51. Flt Lt 15/8/54. Retd ENG 13/10/70.
HUMPHRIES P. J., FIMLT. Born 12/1/29. Commd 7/12/61. Sqn Ldr 13/2/73. Retd MED(T) 6/12/73.
HUMPHRIES R. L., MSc BDS. Born 12/6/39. Commd 27/12/61. Wg Cdr 29/11/76. Retd DEL 2/10/80.
HUMPHRYS P. J. C. Born 24/4/48. Commd 17/7/70. Flt Lt 17/1/76. Retd GD 3/11/88.
HUMPSTON E. A. R., CEng MRAeS. Born 17/9/29. Commd 3/3/54. Wg Cdr 1/1/72. Retd ENG 17/9/84.
HUNKIN E. Born 25/11/49. Commd 31/7/70. Sqn Ldr 1/1/85. Retd GD 1/1/88.
HUNNISETT S. P. Born 17/8/51. Commd 5/4/79. Sqn Ldr 1/7/85. Retd SUP 31/3/94.
HUNT A. Born 27/10/47. Commd 11/10/70. Sqn Ldr 1/7/85. Retd ENG 1/7/88.
HUNT A. Born 21/4/21. Commd 13/8/44. Flt Lt 13/8/48. Retd RGT 2/9/60.
HUNT A. A. Born 23/2/47. Commd 20/10/83. Flt Lt 20/10/87. Retd GD(G) 21/10/90.
HUNT A. J. F. Born 1/8/41. Commd 31/7/62. Flt Lt 31/1/65. Retd GD 20/9/75.
HUNT B. Born 1/10/40. Commd 30/5/69. Wg Cdr 1/1/88. Retd GD 31/10/93.
HUNT B. Born 3/7/43. Commd 21/1/73. Sqn Ldr 1/7/83. Retd ENG 28/1/95.
HUNT B. C., BSc. Born 23/4/39. Commd 1/10/62. Wg Cdr 1/7/87. Retd GD 23/4/94.
HUNT C., MB ChB BAO MRCGP DAvMed. Born 15/12/52. Commd 24/6/84. Wg Cdr 20/11/90. Retd MED 14/3/96.
HUNT C. C., BDS. Born 24/7/53. Commd 14/5/74. Wg Cdr 25/11/89. Retd DEL 24/7/91.
HUNT C. D. Born 12/12/44. Commd 3/1/64. Flt Lt 3/7/69. Retd GD 12/12/82.
HUNT D. Born 5/5/34. Commd 10/12/52. Flt Lt 20/7/58. Retd GD 5/6/72.
HUNT D. Born 13/3/33. Commd 22/7/66. Sqn Ldr 1/7/76. Retd ADMIN 10/6/85.
HUNT F. H. Born 17/7/08. Commd 18/3/44. Fg Offr 18/9/44. Retd ASD 8/1/46.
HUNT G. K. Born 31/3/20. Commd 15/6/61. Sqn Ldr 1/7/69. Retd SUP 15/9/72.
HUNT H. A., MB ChB FRCGP DRCOG DCH. Born 16/3/33. Commd 5/4/59. Gp Capt 1/1/82. Retd MED 5/4/85.
HUNT H. E., MBE. Born 27/10/17. Commd 23/1/43. Wg Cdr 1/7/56. Retd RGT 27/10/68.
HUNT J. L. Born 23/1/11. Commd 8/3/41. Flt Lt. Commd 25/9/51. Retd SEC 21/2/59.
HUNT K. D., BEM. Born 5/3/22. Commd 6/11/58. Flt Lt 6/11/63. Retd ENG 31/12/66.
HUNT M. L., MInstPet. Born 18/3/46. Commd 26/8/66. Sqn Ldr 16/6/83. Retd SUP 31/3/94.
HUNT N. B., MSc. Born 19/8/50. Commd 26/2/71. Sqn Ldr 1/1/85. Retd SUP 30/9/90.

HUNT N. B., BSc. Born 1/8/59. Commd 11/9/77. Sqn Ldr 1/1/95. Retd GD 1/1/98.
HUNT N. J. Born 15/7/59. Commd 24/7/81. Flt Lt 24/1/87. Retd GD 20/12/96.
HUNT P. A. Born 27/2/20. Commd 19/5/40. Flt Lt 1/9/45. Retd GD 27/2/63.
HUNT P. C. Born 7/10/21. Commd 14/11/42. Flt Lt 14/5/46. Retd SEC 7/10/70.
HUNT P. E. Born 3/11/47. Commd 19/7/84. Flt Lt 19/7/84. Retd ENG 25/8/93.
HUNT P. M. Born 26/9/31. Commd 14/1/65. Flt Lt 14/1/68. Retd SEC 30/1/75.
HUNT R. G. Born 13/1/41. Commd 11/6/60. Flt Lt 11/12/65. Retd GD 13/1/79.
HUNT R. G. T., MBE MIMgt. Born 5/10/45. Commd 8/10/70. Wg Cdr 1/1/91. Retd ADMIN 14/3/96.
HUNT S. D. Born 2/5/60. Commd 23/11/78. Flt Lt 23/5/84. Retd GD 2/5/97.
HUNT S. J. Born 21/5/22. Commd 19/6/43. Sqn Ldr 23/6/65. Retd EDN 26/9/75.
HUNT S. W., CBE. Born 21/10/47. Commd 1/8/69. Gp Capt 1/7/90. Retd GD 14/9/96.
HUNTER A. Born 23/5/15. Commd 21/8/41. Flt Lt 27/2/63. Retd ENG 23/5/64.
HUNTER A. F. C., CBE AFC MA LLB. Born 8/3/39. Commd 1/10/62. AVM 1/7/89. Retd GD 1/7/93.
HUNTER B. J., OBE CEng FIEE MRAeS. Born 22/2/41. Commd 18/7/61. Gp Capt 1/7/81. Retd ENG 1/6/89.
HUNTER B. L., MBE. Born 12/4/23. Commd 3/7/42. Wg Cdr 1/1/72. Retd PI 31/3/78.
HUNTER B. V. Born 19/12/21. Commd 6/9/41. Sqn Ldr 1/10/55. Retd GD 1/10/58.
HUNTER C. E. Born 12/9/16. Commd 16/10/43. Flt Lt 16/4/47. Retd GD 17/7/53.
HUNTER D. A. Born 25/12/54. Commd 16/9/73. Sqn Ldr 1/1/91. Retd GD 1/1/94.
HUNTER D. A., BA. Born 7/2/58. Commd 14/4/85. Sqn Ldr 1/1/95. Retd ADMIN 14/4/01.
HUNTER D. I. Born 18/10/50. Commd 27/3/70. Flt Lt 18/7/76. Retd SUP 1/12/79.
HUNTER D. M. Born 4/3/47. Commd 19/6/70. Flt Lt 19/12/75. Retd GD 22/3/87.
HUNTER F. J. W. Born 14/5/35. Commd 28/2/56. Sqn Ldr 1/1/70. Retd GD 16/1/76.
HUNTER I. Born 13/1/48. Commd 21/4/67. Sqn Ldr 1/7/81. Retd SUP 13/1/92.
HUNTER I. M., MA. Born 2/3/51. Commd 4/6/70. Sqn Ldr 1/1/86. Retd GD 2/3/89.
HUNTER I. P. N. M. Born 11/7/43. Commd 20/2/64. Flt Lt 11/5/69. Retd RGT 11/7/81.
HUNTER J. Born 23/8/34. Commd 14/1/54. Flt Lt 14/7/59. Retd GD 31/8/72.
HUNTER J. Born 28/10/46. Commd 15/3/73. Wg Cdr 1/1/91. Retd ADMIN 31/3/94.
HUNTER J. A. L. Born 12/7/20. Commd 9/3/44. Sqn Ldr 1/7/63. Retd ENG 12/7/75.
HUNTER K., BSc. Born 27/10/27. Commd 16/6/53. Wg Cdr 1/1/69. Retd GD 20/9/78.
HUNTER K. Born 30/4/44. Commd 2/11/88. Flt Lt 2/11/92. Retd ENG 5/10/00.
HUNTER K. E. Born 14/9/37. Commd 25/7/71. Sqn Ldr 1/1/86. Retd ENG 30/4/89.
HUNTER K. G., CBE FIMgt. Born 18/4/26. Commd 25/8/49. Gp Capt 1/1/77. Retd GD 18/7/83.
HUNTER M. R. Born 2/2/41. Commd 14/6/63. Flt Lt 4/5/72. Retd GD 2/2/96.
HUNTER N. Born 1/7/17. Commd 22/9/39. Gp Offr 1/7/50. Retd SEC 17/11/51.
HUNTER N. B. Born 21/10/48. Commd 1/8/69. Sqn Ldr 1/7/85. Retd GD 1/7/88.
HUNTER P. Born 9/6/68. Commd 26/9/90. Plt Off 26/3/91. Retd SY 24/3/93.
HUNTER S. C. Born 7/6/48. Commd 7/9/80. Flt Lt 7/9/80. Retd GD(G) 1/2/91.
HUNTER S. J., BSc MB BS. Born 12/9/33. Commd 16/1/83. Sqn Ldr 17/3/85. Retd MED 22/11/91.
HUNTER W. D., OBE CEng FRAeS. Born 20/4/20. Commd 19/8/42. A Cdre 1/7/72. Retd ENG 5/10/74.
HUNTER W. J., MIMgt. Born 13/1/20. Commd 28/12/40. Wg Cdr 1/1/72. Retd GD 13/1/75.
HUNTER W. K. Born 23/8/09. Commd 30/3/42. Flt Lt 26/12/46. Retd RGT 6/6/56 rtg Sqn Ldr.
HUNTER-TOD G. R. A. Born 21/2/20. Commd 8/8/45. Sqn Offr 1/10/57. Retd SEC 25/5/60.
HUNTER-TOD J. F. Born 3/12/60. Commd 8/6/84. Flt Lt 6/12/90. Retd SUP 1/8/99.
HUNTLEY A. S. Born 18/11/43. Commd 22/5/64. Wg Cdr 1/1/83. Retd OPS SPT 18/11/98.
HUNTLEY L. S., MB BCh. Born 31/8/58. Commd 9/1/79. Sqn Ldr 1/8/87. Retd MED 14/3/96.
HUNWICK P. F. Born 11/1/34. Commd 26/7/55. Flt Lt 14/5/58. Retd GD(G) 30/7/72.
HUPPLER A. B. Born 21/2/33. Commd 24/6/53. Flt Lt 21/10/59. Retd GD 21/2/71.
HURCOMBE M. J. L. Born 9/1/46. Commd 26/5/67. Wg Cdr 1/7/85. Retd ENG 18/10/96.
HURLEY D., LVO AFC. Born 5/8/32. Commd 12/7/51. Sqn Ldr 1/7/78. Retd GD 30/11/88.
HURLEY J. B. Born 2/2/28. Commd 6/8/49. Flt Lt 25/9/58. Retd GD 2/2/66.
HURLEY K. Born 30/10/48. Commd 20/9/68. Sqn Ldr 1/7/79. Retd GD 17/1/87.
HURLEY P. R. J. Born 24/4/50. Commd 9/12/76. Sqn Ldr 1/1/90. Retd ADMIN 24/4/94.
HURLEY W. J., OBE FIMgt. Born 20/1/23. Commd 2/9/44. Gp Capt 1/7/74. Retd GD 31/3/77.
HURLOCK W. J., MIBM MCIPD. Born 15/10/21. Commd 30/8/44. Gp Capt 1/1/73. Retd SEC 27/3/76.
HURLOW-JONES W. P. F., MSc CEng MIMechE MRAeS. Born 1/6/36. Commd 23/7/58. Flt Lt 15/4/63. Retd ENG 26/9/80.
HURRELL A. J., BSc. Born 7/5/54. Commd 30/9/73. Sqn Ldr 1/7/90. Retd GD 14/9/96.
HURRELL A. J., BA. Born 28/6/50. Commd 15/9/69. Sqn Ldr 1/1/90. Retd GD 14/3/97.
HURRELL D. A., CB AFC FRAeS. Born 29/04/43. Commd 2/12/63. AVM 1/7/95. Retd GD 29/4/98.
HURRELL F. C., CB OBE FFOM MB BS MRCS LRCP DAvMed. Born 24/4/28. Commd 27/4/53. AVM 1/7/84. Retd MED 24/4/88.
HURRELL I. E., CEng MIEE. Born 7/12/45. Commd 18/11/66. Sqn Ldr 1/1/79. Retd ENG 7/12/89.
HURRELL L. G. Born 27/4/22. Commd 30/10/43. Sqn Ldr 1/1/55. Retd GD 27/4/65.
HURRELL M. C. Born 26/9/45. Commd 29/4/71. Flt Lt 29/10/76. Retd GD 11/1/87.
HURRELL M. D. Born 21/1/35. Commd 4/12/56. Flt Lt 12/6/62. Retd GD 16/12/68.
HURRELL T. Born 20/9/33. Commd 1/4/53. Sqn Ldr 1/7/66. Retd GD 20/9/88.

HURREN D. G., MBA BA. Born 14/12/52. Commd 8/5/83. Sqn Ldr 1/1/94. Retd SUP 8/5/99.
HURRY D. P. Born 3/9/33. Commd 25/10/57. Flt Lt 1/1/62. Retd PRT 25/10/73.
HURRY J., DSO DFC FIMgt. Born 2/1/20. Commd 23/10/39. Gp Capt 1/7/64. Retd GD 2/1/74.
HURST A. J., MCIPS. Born 19/8/45. Commd 1/3/68. Sqn Ldr 1/7/78. Retd SUP 19/8/83.
HURST J. P. Born 16/1/24. Commd 7/8/46. Flt Lt 4/1/51. Retd GD 2/7/55.
HURST L. Born 12/8/41. Commd 27/1/61. Flt Lt 27/6/66. Retd GD 12/8/79.
HURST M. W. M., BA CEng MIMechE. Born 2/9/42. Commd 30/9/62. Wg Cdr 1/1/79. Retd ENG 1/1/85.
HURST R. H., BSc. Born 5/4/49. Commd 30/1/75. Sqn Ldr 1/7/87. Retd ENG 29/7/90.
HURST R. W. Born 13/7/13. Commd 19/9/40. Gp Capt 1/1/63. Retd SEC 15/7/65.
HURST W., MBE. Born 28/6/21. Commd 2/9/44. Flt Lt 2/3/49. Retd SEC 29/6/71.
HURST W. E. B., CEng MRAeS MIMgt. Born 1/6/18. Commd 7/1/43. Wg Cdr 1/7/66. Retd ENG 1/6/76.
HURST W. J., AFC. Born 26/3/21. Commd 12/7/41. Sqn Ldr 1/7/51. Retd GD 31/8/61.
HURWORTH P. W. J. Born 26/5/31. Commd 28/7/67. Flt Lt 28/7/ 69. Retd SY 1/4/77.
HUSBAND A. J., CEng MIEE. Born 26/4/38. Commd 12/9/61. Sqn Ldr 1/1/80. Retd ENG 30/4/92.
HUSBAND G. S., BA. Born 16/2/44. Commd 30/5/69. Flt Lt 7/1/72. Retd ENG 16/2/82.
HUSBAND R. E., MBE. Born 14/4/41. Commd 11/5/78. Sqn Ldr 1/1/88. Retd SUP 14/4/96.
HUSHER R. P. Born 24/5/44. Commd 24/4/70. Flt Lt 24/4/72. Retd GD 24/5/82.
HUSKISSON N. D., BSc. Born 12/4/65. Commd 28/8/83. Flt Lt 15/1/89. Retd GD 15/7/98.
HUSSEY G. T. Born 11/8/34. Commd 16/9/53. Flt Lt 16/3/59. Retd GD 1/11/61.
HUSSEY K. Born 24/10/52. Commd 2/11/88. Flt Lt 2/11/92. Retd ADMIN 1/12/95.
HUSSEY R. J. C., BSc. Born 6/2/58. Commd 21/10/79. Sqn Ldr 1/1/90. Retd ENG 6/2/96.
HUSTON J. T., BSc CEng MIEE MIMgt. Born 6/8/38. Commd 18/7/61. Sqn Ldr 1/7/70. Retd ENG 18/7/77.
HUSTWAYTE W. R. Born 21/3/33. Commd 25/10/51. Flt Lt 22/5/57. Retd GD 21/3/91.
HUSTWITH R. H. C., OBE BA. Born 8/10/22. Commd 2/4/43. Wg Cdr 1/1/66. Retd GD 2/7/68.
HUTCHESON R. J., BSc. Born 16/7/34. Commd 16/4/59. Sqn Ldr 1/7/73. Retd GD 16/7/91.
HUTCHINGS Rev F. O., BA. Born 16/5/35. Commd 30/8/66. Retd 1/8/88. Wg Cdr.
HUTCHINGS J. Born 11/2/48. Commd 17/3/67. Wg Cdr 1/1/88. Retd SUP 11/2/92.
HUTCHINGS P. J. P. Born 1/5/38. Commd 8/7/65. Gp Capt 1/1/87. Retd GD(G) 1/5/93.
HUTCHINGS R. G., BSc. Born 13/4/51. Commd 13/9/70. Sqn Ldr 1/1/83. Retd ADMIN 13/4/89.
HUTCHINS B. R. J. Born 18/8/50. Commd 19/2/76. Sqn Ldr 1/1/93. Retd GD 14/3/96.
HUTCHINS G. I. Born 20/12/62. Commd 12/1/92. Flt Lt 3/5/91. Retd GD 30/3/01.
HUTCHINS M. B. Born 13/11/43. Commd 17/12/65. Wg Cdr 1/1/92. Retd GD 13/11/99.
HUTCHINS P., OBE. Born 5/11/25 Commd 13/6/46. Gp Capt 1/1/74. Retd RGT 16/1/79.
HUTCHINS P. F. W., CEng MIEE. Born 14/6/42. Commd 15/6/65. Wg Cdr 1/7/88. Retd ENG 14/6/97.
HUTCHINS T. J., BA. Born 14/12/53. Commd 24/7/81. Sqn Ldr 1/7/90. Retd OPS SPT 14/12/97.
HUTCHINSON A. A., MA. Born 21/1/27. Commd 9/12/48. Wg Cdr 1/7/72. Retd GD 21/1/82.
HUTCHINSON A. C., BSc AIIP CEng MRAeS. Born 12/2/40. Commd 21/10/66. Sqn Ldr 1/7/76. Retd ENG 1/10/86.
HUTCHINSON B., MSc CEng MIMechE MRAeS. Born 18/1/36. Commd 5/1/60. Sqn Ldr 1/7/68. Retd EDN 5/1/76.
HUTCHINSON C. R. Born 6/11/32. Commd 30/7/57. Flt Lt 15/2/63. Retd GD 3/5/73.
HUTCHINSON D. W. Born 14/6/21. Commd 19/8/42. Sqn Ldr 1/4/56. Retd GD 14/6/76.
HUTCHINSON G. C. Born 23/3/25. Commd 8/9/45. Flt Lt 4/12/52. Retd GD 13/11/57.
HUTCHINSON H. W. F., CEng MIMechE MRAeS. Born 2/8/38. Commd 18/7/61. Sqn Ldr 1/7/71. Retd ENG 25/9/76.
HUTCHINSON I. Born 13/11/18. Commd 5/8/41. Sqn Ldr 1/1/55. Retd GD 1/12/57.
HUTCHINSON I. F. C. Born 17/11/38. Commd 15/12/59. Sqn Ldr 1/1/70. Retd GD 30/10/70.
HUTCHINSON J. C. Born 24/12/58. Commd 11/4/82. Flt Lt 11/4/87. Retd ENG 11/4/98.
HUTCHINSON J. D. Born 14/8/34. Commd 14/12/54. Gp Capt 1/1/80. Retd GD 26/11/85.
HUTCHINSON L. H. Born 29/6/23. Commd 9/11/43. Flt Lt 31/7/50. Retd GD(G) 31/3/62.
HUTCHINSON R. S., MIMgt. Born 19/12/29. Commd 17/12/52. Wg Cdr 1/1/72. Retd SUP 3/1/81.
HUTCHINSON T. H. Born 8/5/21. Commd 20/2/43. Sqn Ldr 1/7/54. Retd GD 8/5/70 rtg Wg Cdr.
HUTCHINSON W. R. Born 18/6/18. Commd 13/2/45. Flt Lt 13/8/48. Retd GD 12/6/58.
HUTCHISON A. G. L. Born 26/3/31. Commd 29/10/52. Gp Capt 1/1/75. Retd GD 2/12/80.
HUTCHISON A. S. Born 8/11/33. Commd 16/7/52. Flt Lt 29/4/59. Retd GD 8/11/71.
HUTCHISON C., BSc. Born 24/1/54. Commd 30/4/78. Plt Off 30/4/78 Retd GD(G) 20/9/78.
HUTCHISON G. W., MSc BSc CEng DipSoton FIMgt MIEE MCIPD. Born 12/8/35. Commd 11/4/58. Wg Cdr 11/10/76. Retd ADMIN 1/9/84.
HUTCHISON J. C. Born 24/12/58. Commd 11/4/82. Flt Lt 11/4/87. Retd ENG 11/4/98.
HUTCHISON P. D. J., BSc. Born 8/3/63. Commd 13/9/81. Flt Lt 15/10/85. Retd GD 15/7/97.
HUTCHISON P. J. I., BSc. Born 20/8/51. Commd 24/1/74. Sqn Ldr 1/7/88. Retd PRT 1/7/91.
HUTCHISON R. C. Born 9/9/24. Commd 25/2/44. Flt Lt 7/3/48. Retd GD 29/3/69.
HUTSON P. J. Born 20/3/27. Commd 7/5/57. Sqn Ldr 1/7/69. Retd SUP 20/3/77.
HUTT H. G. Born 1/4/31. Commd 21/10/66. Flt Lt 4/5/72. Retd SUP 21/10/74.
HUTTON A. Born 19/1/21. Commd 5/9/57. Sqn Ldr 1/1/71. Retd GD(G) 19/1/76.
HUTTON J. C., DFC. Born 27/1/21. Commd 16/3/41. Wg Cdr 1/1/56. Retd GD 31/1/64.
HUTTON J. H., CEng MIMechE. Born 21/1/36. Commd 17/10/57. Wg Cdr 1/1/76. Retd ENG 3/7/87.
HUTTON L. Born 13/11/20. Commd 25/8/45. Sqn Ldr 1/10/56. Retd ENG 13/3/64.

HUTTON L. H. Born 27/9/37. Commd 20/6/61. Sqn Ldr 1/7/73. Retd ENG 20/6/77.
HUTTON P. A. J. Born 4/1/46. Commd 3/3/67. Flt Lt 3/9/69. Retd GD 1/8.72.
HUTTON P. C. Born 7/6/24. Commd 30/8/51. Flt Offr 30/8/57. Retd SEC 31/5/62.
HUTTON T. W. A., OBE DFC FIMgt. Born 27/4/23. Commd 1/9/45. Gp Capt 1/1/66. Retd GD 11/2/78.
HUXLEY B., CB CBE. Born 14/9/31. Commd 17/12/52. AVM 1/1/85. Retd GD 21/3/87.
HUXLEY-JONES R. J. Born 11/6/59. Commd 30/4/81. Flt Lt 11/8/85. Retd SUP 13/8/85.
HUYTON H. G. Born 6/10/22. Commd 17/3/45. Sqn Ldr 1/1/59. Retd GD 16/10/65.
HUZZARD I. J. Born 17/1/49. Commd 17/7/70. Sqn Ldr 1/7/83. Retd GD 17/1/87.
HYAM C. Born 6/11/34. Commd 23/2/54. Sqn Ldr 1/1/74. Retd GD 1/10/77.
HYATT C. J., MA CEng MRAeS MIMgt. Born 25/12/34. Commd 25/9/54. Wg Cdr 1/7/76. Retd ENG 26/9/78.
HYDE C. B. Born 6/7/41. Commd 23/6/61. Wg Cdr 1/1/85. Retd SY 1/10/95.
HYDE J. A. Born 23/4/33. Commd 7/1/57. Sqn Ldr 1/7/79. Retd GD 28/4/91.
HYDE J. H., MCIPD MIMgt. Born 27/9/30. Commd 14/7/52. Wg Cdr 1/7/75. Retd GD(G) 2/4/82.
HYDE K. Born 26/7/43. Commd 28/6/79. Flt Lt 28/6/82. Retd GD 26/7/98.
HYDE O. L., CEng MRAeS. Born 22/2/20. Commd 30/8/40. Gp Capt 1/1/72. Retd ENG 22/2/75.
HYDE T. J. G. Born 2/7/35. Commd 9/12/53. Flt Lt 7/3/62. Retd GD(G) 3/11/81.
HYDER C. W. Born 20/4/35. Commd 6/6/57. Sqn Ldr 1/1/73. Retd GD 20/4/93.
HYGATE J. P. Born 3/1/43. Commd 3/11/77. Flt Lt 3/11/79. Retd ENG 3/1/98.
HYLAND A. D. Born 24/11/15. Commd 24/11/41. Sqn Offr 1/1/54. Retd SEC 15/12/64.
HYLAND D. M. Born 29/9/42. Commd 23/5/63. Sqn Ldr 1/1/75. Retd SUP 25/7/81.
HYLAND N. E. Born 27/7/31. Commd 9/4/52. Flt Lt 5/9/57. Retd GD 27/4/71.
HYLTON B. R. V., MBE BSc CEng MIEE. Born 25/2/40. Commd 30/9/59. Wg Cdr 1/7/75. Retd ENG 1/7/78.
HYMAN D. M. Born 25/1/25. Commd 14/1/44. Sqn Ldr 1/1/71. Retd GD(G) 25/1/83.
HYMANS J. A., BSc. Born 4/9/63. Commd 29/9/85. Flt Lt 29/3/87. Retd GD 14/3/96.
HYMANS R. E. Born 9/10/36. Commd 9/2/55. Sqn Ldr 1/1/70. Retd GD 9/10/74. Reinstated 21/11/79. Retd GD 7/9/87.
HYMERS A. W. Born 3/3/33. Commd 6/4/54. Flt Lt 6/10/56. Retd GD 22/7/57.
HYNDS H. A., AFC. Born 15/4/24. Commd 27/1/55. Sqn Ldr 1/1/72. Retd GD 15/4/84.
HYNES G. P., MBE MCIPS. Born 18/1/36. Commd 22/7/66. Sqn Ldr 1/7/74. Retd SUP 18/1/86.
HYNES V. S. Born 6/8/13. Commd 22/9/41. Flt Offr 1/9/45. Retd SEC 27/6/60.
HYSLOP J. S. D. Born 7/12/11. Commd 24/12/41. Sqn Ldr 1/7/48. Retd RGT 1/3/58.
HYSON P. G., FIMgt. Born 5/12/23. Commd 6/1/46. Gp Capt 1/7/75. Retd GD 15/3/78.

# I

IBBETSON B. Born 13/7/34. Commd 17/12/64. Flt Lt 10/2/67. Retd SUP 17/12/72.
IBBETSON H. E. Born 18/1/36. Commd 3/10/69. Sqn Ldr 3/10/77. Retd ADMIN 1/12/87.
IBBOTT R. I. Born 7/2/47. Commd 4/12/64. Flt Lt 4/6/70. Retd GD 7/2/85.
IBISON G. B. Born 15/1/29. Commd 19/6/52. Flt Lt 19/3/56. Retd GD 28/6/68.
IDDON B. R. Born 19/3/56. Commd 20/7/78. Flt Lt 11/1/82. Retd GD 19/3/93.
IDE J. M. Born 5/7/31. Commd 4/1/60. Flt Lt 4/1/60. Retd GD 5/7/86.
IFOULD K. W., CBE AFC FRAeS MIL. Born 14/1/46. Commd 5/2/65. Gp Capt 1/7/94. Retd GD 14/1/01.
IGNATOWSKI K., AFC DFM. Born 28/11/19. Commd 24/5/49. Sqn Ldr 1/7/71. Retd GD 28/11/74.
IKIN D. R., MIMgt. Born 5/4/32. Commd 23/7/52. Sqn Ldr 1/1/70. Retd GD 19/5/90.
ILBERT J. C. Born 24/11/43. Commd 17/7/64. Flt Lt 6/10/71. Retd GD 22/11/75.
ILCHESTER The Earl of, CEng FINucE MRAeS FIMgt. Born 1/4/20. Commd 28/3/46. Wg Cdr 1/7/66. Retd ENG
    27/3/76 rtg Gp Capt.
ILES M. G. Born 11/8/41. Commd 22/5/64. Flt Lt 22/11/69. Retd GD 12/3/80.
ILES R. G., AFC. Born 3/2/22. Commd 12/7/43. Sqn Ldr 1/7/58. Retd GD 3/2/77.
ILES W. A. J. Born 27/9/13. Commd 11/9/42. Wg Cdr 1/1/62. Retd SUP 2/7/66.
ILETT R. P. Born 20/2/60. Commd 28/6/79. Sqn Ldr 1/1/91. Retd GD 31/7/98.
ILEY C. Born 11/11/28. Commd 11/3/65. Flt Lt 11/3/68. Retd GD 31/5/75.
ILEY L. A. Born 6/10/44. Commd 4/6/64. Flt Lt 29/8/70. Retd GD(G) 12/4/75.
ILIFFE C. R. Born 11/5/15. Commd 2/1/39. Wg Cdr 1/7/51. Retd SUP 27/2/59.
ILLINGWORTH P. F. Born 29/4/17. Commd 21/12/36. Sqn Ldr 1/8/47. Retd GD 16/4/58.
ILSLEY C. W. Born 30/5/43. Commd 30/8/66. Wg Cdr 1/7/90. Retd GD 10/12/98.
ILSLEY D. J. Born 23/10/31. Commd 28/7/53. Sqn Ldr 1/1/67. Retd GD 1/1/70.
ILSLEY J. M., BSc. Born 27/11/25. Commd 12/3/49. Flt Lt 19/11/53. Retd GD 20/8/60.
IMBER H. Mack., BEng. Born 1/3/66. Commd 25/9/88. Flt Lt 25/3/90. Retd GD 14/9/96.
IMPEY A. C., FCIPS. Born 6/9/36. Commd 3/5/56. A Cdre 1/1/85. Retd SUP 23/3/93.
IMS M. K. Born 28/3/61. Commd 1/7/82. Flt Lt 1/1/88. Retd GD 28/6/99.
INCE E. K. P., DFC. Born 3/1/16. Commd 3/1/41. Sqn Ldr 1/7/51. Retd RGT 1/7/54.
INCE J. B. Born 1/7/41. Commd 15/9/67. Flt Lt 12/11/69. Retd GD 1/7/79.
INCE J. G. Born 1/2/29. Commd 14/4/49. Sqn Ldr 1/7/64. Retd GD 3/2/72.
INCE-JONES H. Born 5/11/32. Commd 7/7/69. Flt Lt 7/7/69. Retd GD(G) 7/7/85.
INCH J. D. R. Born 4/8/49. Commd 2/2/68. Flt Lt 18/7/74. Retd SEC 4/2/78.
INCLEDON-WEBBER G. Born 19/2/30. Commd 4/7/51. Flt Lt 3/11/56. Retd GD 19/8/68.
INGALLS R. D. Born 8/8/24. Commd 1/11/56. Sqn Ldr 1/7/71. Retd GD 8/8/79.
INGAMELLS J. R. Born 13/11/38. Commd 22/2/63. Wg Cdr 1/1/81. Retd GD 17/5/89.
INGELBRECHT A. C. Born 13/11/59. Commd 20/9/79. Flt Lt 20/3/85. Retd GD 14/9/96.
INGHAM B. H. Born 30/3/37. Commd 26/5/67. Sqn Ldr 1/1/81. Retd ENG 30/3/92.
INGHAM D. B. Born 26/7/24. Commd 10/10/63. Flt Lt 10/10/66. Retd ENG 31/7/74.
INGHAM G. R. Born 13/3/40. Commd 1/4/65. Sqn Ldr 1/1/85. Retd ADMIN 13/3/95.
INGHAM J. E. Born 7/1/40. Commd 14/8/70. Flt Lt 14/8/72. Retd GD(G) 30/3/77. Re-instated. 24/8/80. Flt Lt
    4/11/75. Retd. GD(G) 1/11/92.
INGHAM R. A., AFC BEng. Born 14/2/51. Commd 19/11/72. Sqn Ldr 1/7/84. Retd GD 14/1/96.
INGLE C. M. Born 28/8/46. Commd 2/12/66. Flt Lt 2/6/72. Retd GD 26/8/77.
INGLE M. W., CEng MRAeS. Born 29/7/36. Commd 27/3/58. Sqn Ldr 1/7/68. Retd ENG 27/9/74.
INGLIS M. J. Born 27/1/65. Commd 19/7/87. Flt Lt 19/7/93. Retd ADMIN 14/9/96.
INGOE P. Born 13/6/46. Commd 2/8/68. Sqn Ldr 1/1/84. Retd GD 13/6/90.
INGOLD S. L. Born 21/12/32. Commd 24/4/70. Flt Lt 4/5/72. Retd SEC 24/4/78.
INGOLDBY A. C. R. Born 12/7/36. Commd 17/12/57. Gp Capt 1/1/84. Retd GD 12/7/91.
INGRAM J., BSc CEng MIMechE. Born 25/2/35. Commd 31/10/71. Sqn Ldr 31/10/71. Retd ENG 25/8/93.
INGRAM J. A., DFC. Born 19/7/13. Commd 24/8/36. Sqn Ldr 1/8/47. Retd GD 19/10/56.
INGRAM The Rev J. R. Born 20/3/24. Commd 14/12/48. Retd 26/4/77 Wg Cdr.
INGRAM J. W. Born 26/7/24. Commd 29/3/45. Flt Lt 29/9/48. Retd GD 31/7/64.
INGRAM J. W. Born 3/9/40. Commd 6/7/62. Sqn Ldr 1/7/87. Retd GD 3/9/95.
INGRAM The Rev M. Born 27/5/28. Commd 6/1/60. Retd 6/1/76. Wg Cdr.
INGWELL S. M., BSc CEng MIEE. Born 14/6/45. Commd 20/10/71. Sqn Ldr 1/1/79. Retd ENG 20/10/87.
INIONS E. T. Born 17/5/22. Commd 14/8/45. Flt Lt 1/7/52. Retd PRT 26/3/62.
INNES B. M. C. Born 10/8/48. Commd 3/10/69. Flt Lt 14/3/76. Retd GD(G) 10/8/86.
INNES C. R. Born 31/8/12. Commd 7/8/49. Flt Lt 7/8/49. Retd SUP 30/12/57.
INNES D. S. Born 10/3/34. Commd 28/7/55. Flt Lt 6/3/62. Retd GD 30/11/68.
INNES G., CBE FIMgt. Born 26/11/23. Commd 31/3/45. A Cdre 1/7/76. Retd SY 1/7/78.
INNES G. A. R. Born 18/10/47. Commd 26/5/67. Sqn Ldr 1/7/87. Retd GD(G) 18/6/91.

INNES P. E., MA BSc. Born 18/1/28. Commd 24/9/52. Sqn Ldr 24/3/63. Retd EDN 24/9/68.
INNES R. A. Born 15/6/18. Commd 5/3/41. Sqn Ldr 1/8/47. Retd GD 31/8/61.
INNES R. T. A. Born 29/9/28. Commd 30/1/52. Flt Lt 29/5/57. Retd GD 28/11/69.
INNES W. J. A., MA. Born 11/10/34. Commd 28/7/54. Sqn Ldr 1/7/65. Retd GD 11/10/72.
INNES-SMITH N. A., OBE. Born 7/6/30. Commd 12/12/51. Wg Cdr 1/1/68. Retd GD 7/6/88.
INNISS A. R. de L., DFC. Born 21/11/16. Commd 6/3/39. Sqn Ldr 1/9/45. Retd GD 18/12/57 rtg Wg Cdr.
INVERARITY A. D., BA. Born 24/11/44. Commd 6/10/69. Flt Lt 6/1/71. Retd GD 22/4/94.
INVERARITY G. A., DFC. Born 23/9/19. Commd 28/8/43. Sqn Ldr 1/7/69. Retd GD(G) 16/7/72.
IONS G. Born 27/5/37. Commd 30/7/64. Sqn Ldr 1/7/71. Retd SUP 30/9/82.
IONS G. W. Born 10/9/06. Commd 14/7/41. Fg Offr 14/9/42. Retd ASD 26/1/46 rtg Flt Lt.
IREDALE R. D. Born 27/5/47. Commd 2/4/65. Gp Capt 1/1/94. Retd GD 27/5/01.
IREDALE T. P. Born 7/3/43. Commd 9/2/66. Flt Lt 29/4/70. Retd SUP 7/7/75.
IRELAND B. J. Born 24/4/49. Commd 4/5/72. Flt Lt 4/11/77. Retd GD 31/5/01.
IRELAND D. S. J. Born 3/7/21. Commd 23/9/44. Flt Lt 27/5/54. Retd GD 31/7/76.
IRELAND H. Born 23/2/09. Commd 15/6/44. Flt Lt 15/12/48. Retd SUP 17/4/58 rtg Sqn Ldr.
IRELAND N. C. V. Born 22/8/39. Commd 13/12/60. Flt Lt 7/8/64. Retd GD 22/8/77. Reinstated 2/8/91. Flt Lt
   2/8/81. Retd ENG 22/8/94.
IRELAND W. S., OBE. Born 16/7/27. Commd 13/2/52. Wg Cdr 1/7/72. Retd GD 20/9/80.
IREMONGER J. H., DFC. Born 31/3/18. Commd 30/7/38. Gp Capt 1/1/57. Retd GD 1/1/61.
IRISH R. G. V., FIMgt MCIPS. Born 24/5/33. Commd 27/2/52. Wg Cdr 1/1/77. Retd SUP 1/12/87.
IRONS A. J. Born 1/3/61. Commd 15/10/81. APO 15/10/81. Retd GD 10/4/83.
IRONSIDE H. H. A. Born 31/8/15. Commd 16/4/35. Flt Lt 1/3/45. Retd GD(G) 23/12/45. Re-employed 24/12/49.
   Sqn Ldr 1/1/52. Retd 31/8/65 rtg Wg Cdr.
IRONSIDE J. J. N. A. Born 26/3/42. Commd 6/4/62. Flt Lt 6/10/67. Retd GD 26/3/80.
IRVIN J. H., OBE. Born 30/5/15. Commd 21/10/35. Wg Cdr 1/7/47. Retd GD 20/6/60 rtg Gp Capt.
IRVINE H. R. Born 17/3/25. Commd 11/2/57. Flt Lt 11/2/57. Retd ADMIN 7/4/83.
IRVINE K. F., MIMgt. Born 20/4/29. Commd 7/9/61. Flt Lt 7/9/66. Retd ENG 31/5/74.
IRVINE M. C. G., MB BS. Born 28/6/60. Commd 25/6/89. Sqn Ldr 8/6/91. Retd MED 14/3/96.
IRVINE T. G., BSc. Born 3/7/59. Commd 29/8/77. Flt Lt 15/9/83. Retd GD 14/9/00.
IRVINE W. G. Born 8/7/31. Commd 28/9/51. Flt Lt 28/3/56. Retd GD 8/7/69.
IRVINE-BROWN M. Born 4/5/49. Commd 9/12/71. Fg Offr 9/6/74. Retd GD(G) 1/11/75.
IRVING H. J. Born 16/7/25. Commd 9/6/44. Wg Cdr 1/1/72. Retd GD 23/8/75.
IRVING J. Born 24/3/33. Commd 23/8/51. Flt Lt 3/12/57. Retd GD 10/10/75.
IRVING J. N. B., MBE PhD BSc CEng FRAeS. Born 31/5/30. Commd 11/11/56. Gp Capt 1/7/73. Retd ENG 3/5/79.
IRVING N. R., AFC. Born 19/2/47. Commd 23/3/67. A Cdre 1/1/95. Retd GD 19/2/99.
IRWIN A. F., BSc. Born 5/12/50. Commd 15/9/69. Sqn Ldr 1/1/85. Retd GD 5/12/88.
IRWIN G. S. Born 10/2/41. Commd 1/4/84. Wg Cdr 1/1/94. Retd MED(SEC) 4/4/96.
IRWIN R. H. Born 29/5/25. Commd 24/9/64. Fg Offr 24/9/64. Retd SUP 20/4/70.
IRWIN S. R. C., BA IEng MISM AMRAeS. Born 16/2/48. Commd 2/8/90. Flt Lt 2/8/92. Retd ADMIN 14/3/97.
ISAAC P. N. Born 20/3/14. Commd 12/6/36. Wg Cdr 1/7/49. Retd SEC 31/7/56.
ISAACSON A. Born 5/6/23. Commd 14/7/51. Sqn Ldr 1/5/65. Retd EDN 21/9/73.
ISABEL J. R. Born 12/12/45. Commd 23/9/66. Flt Offr 23/9/67. Retd GD 12/12/68.
ISHAM D. C., CEng MIMgt MIEE. Born 26/6/26. Commd 26/9/57. Wg Cdr 1/1/71. Retd ENG 15/7/77.
ISHAM L. J. Born 4/3/20. Commd 22/9/55. Sqn Ldr 1/7/67. Retd ENG 4/3/75.
ISHERWOOD P. B. Born 14/7/37. Commd 4/1/56. Sqn Ldr 1/1/70. Retd GD 31/5/75.
ISHERWOOD R. Born 1/11/22. Commd 14/3/42. Sqn Ldr 1/9/65. Retd GD 29/11/77.
IVELAW P. I., BSc CEng MIMechE MIEE MRAeS. Born 21/8/20. Commd 1/4/42. Sqn Ldr 1/4/56. Retd ENG
   31/10/64.
IVELAW-CHAMPAN J. Born 4/9/36. Commd 29/2/56. Flt Lt 17/3/62. Retd GD 4/9/73.
IVES P. F., BSc. Born 15/6/31. Commd 7/9/56. Sqn Ldr 7/3/66. Retd EDN 15/6/73.
IVES R. C. Born 10/2/40. Commd 15/6/61. Flt Lt 6/8/68. Retd GD(G) 24/2/87.
IVES W. J., CBE MIMgt. Born 8/11/21. Commd 11/11/42. Gp Capt 1/1/71. Retd GD 8/11/76.
IVESON R. D., AFC. Born 18/8/47. Commd 2/6/67. Gp Capt 1/1/94. Retd GD 19/8/99.
IVESON T. C., DFC. Born 11/9/19. Commd 1/5/42. Flt Lt 11/4/48. Retd GD 12/7/49.
IWACHOW K. J. W. Born 15/6/21. Commd 25/5/50. Flt Lt 11/11/54. Retd GD 15/6/64.
IZZARD J., OBE CEng FIMechE. Born 18/4/45. Commd 14/4/69. Wg Cdr 1/1/85. Retd ENG 18/4/00.
IZZARD J. Born 21/8/13. Commd 24/5/45. Fg Offr 24/11/45. Retd SEC 17/5/47 rtg Flt Lt.
IZZARD P. W., MBE. Born 10/11/42. Commd 4/10/63. Wg Cdr 1/1/94. Retd GD 10/11/97.

# J

JACEWICZ J., DFM. Born 24/4/20. Commd 1/9/48. Sqn Ldr 1/1/57. Retd GD 24/4/69.
JACK D. A. Born 13/7/42. Commd 5/9/69. Wg Cdr 1/7/87. Retd SUP 2/4/97.
JACK J., MBE. Born 15/10/33. Commd 24/2/67. Sqn Ldr 1/7/74. Retd SY 1/7/77.
JACK J. M. A., ACIS. Born 28/1/46. Commd 1/4/65. Sqn Ldr 1/7/80. Retd ADMIN 28/1/90.
JACKLIN D. Born 7/5/42. Commd 29/4/71. Sqn Ldr 29/10/77. Retd ADMIN 1/10/80.
JACKMAN L. C. Born 11/3/47. Commd 29/4/71. Sqn Ldr 1/1/92. Retd GD 31/3/94.
JACKSON A., DPhysEd. Born 11/9/41. Commd 7/8/67. Sqn Ldr 1/7/78. Retd ADMIN 7/8/83.
JACKSON A. E. Born 30/9/61. Commd 31/1/80. Sqn Ldr 1/1/94. Retd GD 1/5/95.
JACKSON A. F., OBE. Born 22/7/34. Commd 25/9/59. Gp Capt 1/7/86. Retd ADMIN 22/7/94.
JACKSON A. I. Born 2/7/45. Commd 28/2/64. Flt Lt 28/8/69. Retd GD 31/8/94.
JACKSON A.D., CBE BSc CEng FIEE AInstP. Born 16/10/15. Commd 25/4/39. A Cdre 1/1/63. Retd ENG 17/10/70.
JACKSON C. Born 15/11/39. Commd 2/3/61. Flt Lt 19/3/67. Retd GD 3/10/70.
JACKSON C. Born 5/2/43. Commd 21/5/65. Flt Lt 1/7/94. Retd GD 5/2/84.
JACKSON C. F. Born 7/1/23. Commd 16/3/45. Flt Lt 4/6/53. Retd SEC 31/3/62.
JACKSON C. S., MBE FIMgt MInstPS. Born 11/3/26. Commd 16/1/47. Gp Capt 1/7/75. Retd SUP 11/3/81.
JACKSON D. E. Born 23/11/31. Commd 23/4/52. Flt Lt 25/9/57. Retd GD 23/11/69.
JACKSON D. H., BSc. Born 3/11/42. Commd 6/8/63. Wg Cdr 1/1/94. Retd GD 3/11/97.
JACKSON D. L. Born 30/4/29. Commd 18/6/52. Flt Lt 13/11/57. Retd GD 18/5/84.
JACKSON D. L. Born 15/3/49. Commd 11/4/85. Sqn Ldr 1/7/94. Retd ENG 4/12/96.
JACKSON D. S. Born 15/12/35. Commd 30/7/62. Flt Lt 30/7/62. Retd GD 15/12/93.
JACKSON D. V., MIMgt. Born 21/5/30. Commd 17/12/52. Sqn Ldr 1/1/63. Retd SUP 21/5/68.
JACKSON E. D., MIMgt. Born 18/12/22. Commd 22/9/49. Wg Cdr 1/1/66. Retd ENG 7/8/76.
JACKSON G., AFM. Born 11/10/20. Commd 4/9/58. Flt Lt 4/9/61. Retd GD(G) 11/10/75.
JACKSON G. W., DFC. Born 9/10/20. Commd 16/4/43. Flt Lt 16/4/45. Retd GD(G) 9/10/75.
JACKSON H. M. Born 1/7/13. Commd 7/9/42. Sqn Ldr 1/7/55. Retd GD(G) 1/7/63.
JACKSON H. McL. M. Born 8/11/22. Commd 9/4/45. Flt Lt 11/11/54. Retd GD 8/11/65.
JACKSON I. A., DFC. Born 21/1/14. Commd 4/4/43. Flt Lt 4/1/51. Retd SEC 16/2/63.
JACKSON I. R. Born 14/11/44. Commd 23/1/64. Gp Capt 1/7/87. Retd PRT 24/8/90.
JACKSON J. Born 24/8/46. Commd 28/8/75. Sqn Ldr 1/1/84. Retd ENG 1/1/87.
JACKSON J. D., BA. Born 5/7/40. Commd 17/7/64. Sqn Ldr 3/7/74. Retd ADMIN 5/7/95.
JACKSON J. D., BSc DUS. Born 15/12/34. Commd 25/9/54. Flt Lt 15/4/61. Retd ENG 27/7/68.
JACKSON J. G., BA. Born 8/5/39. Commd 15/6/61. Sqn Ldr 1/1/73. Retd SUP 1/7/79.
JACKSON J. J. Born 6/7/30. Commd 13/9/51. Flt Lt 13/4/60. Retd GD 2/9/83.
JACKSON J. K., MBE MHCIMA. Born 13/2/28. Commd 22/9/49/ Gp Capt 1/7/73. Retd CAT 11/3/75.
JACKSON J. M. Born 4/5/41. Commd 28/4/67. Flt Lt 28/10/72. Retd GD 17/1/83.
JACKSON J. R., AFC. Born 19/10/29. Commd 1/7/52. Wg Cdr 1/1/78. Retd GD 19/10/84.
JACKSON J. W. Born 20/2/40. Commd 27/6/59. Flt Lt 27/12/64. Retd GD 29/10/90.
JACKSON K. Born 12/8/35. Commd 15/10/81. Flt Lt 15/10/86. Retd ENG 12/8/93.
JACKSON K. F. Born 4/10/30. Commd 1/7/53. Sqn Ldr 1/7/61. Retd GD 30/12/68.
JACKSON K. R., MBE AFC. Born 5/9/23. Commd 12/4/51. Sqn Ldr 1/1/74. Retd GD 5/9/83.
JACKSON L. J. Born 3/4/31. Commd 24/2/67. Flt Lt 4/5/72. Retd PE 24/2/75.
JACKSON M. A. Born 24/12/26. Commd 27/2/70. Sqn Ldr 1/7/81. Retd ENG 25/5/88.
JACKSON M. L. Born 29/6/71. Commd 29/3/90. Fg Offr 29/3/92. Retd GD 25/5/93.
JACKSON M. L., OBE MA FCIPD. Born 29/03/46. Commd 29/7/65. A Cdre 1/1/92. Retd ADMIN 14/3/97.
JACKSON M. R., CB. Born 28/12/41. Commd 17/12/63. AVM 1/7/96. Retd GD 1/7/98.
JACKSON N., CBE CEng FRAeS FIMechE. Born 16/11/35. Commd 27/9/57. A Cdre 1/1/79. Retd ENG 2/1/81.
JACKSON P. H. Born 26/4/07. Commd 30/7/26. Plt Offr 30/7/26. Retd GD 15/2/28.
JACKSON Sir Ralph, KBE CB FRCP(Edin) FRCP(Lond) MRCS. Born 22/6/14. Commd 16/5/36. AVM 1/9/69. Retd MED 30/9/75.
JACKSON R., MBE DFM CEng MIEE MIMgt. Born 3/6/20. Commd 25/11/43. Wg Cdr 1/7/69. Retd ENG 28/4/73.
JACKSON R. Born 4/7/15. Commd 17/4/47. Flt Lt 17/10/51. Retd SEC 12/5/56.
JACKSON R. A. Born 12/2/33. Commd 5/4/55. Sqn Ldr 1/7/65. Retd GD 12/2/91.
JACKSON R. A. Born 1/5/52. Commd 29/6/72. Sqn Ldr 1/1/88. Retd GD 1/1/90.
JACKSON R. K. Born 4/4/44. Commd 15/7/66. Sqn Ldr 1/1/82. Retd GD 1/6/89.
JACKSON R. M. Born 16/11/31. Commd 11/4/63. Flt Lt 11/4/69. Retd SEC 1/1/72.
JACKSON S., MBE MIMgt. Born 14/7/21. Commd 2/7/44. Wg Cdr 1/1/70. Retd SUP 30/12/75.
JACKSON T. A., MVO AFC. Born 30/10/22. Commd 23/7/43. Sqn Ldr 1/9/65. Retd GD 30/10/77.
JACKSON T. H. Born 24/1/23. Commd 23/9/43. Wg Cdr 1/1/70. Retd ENG 24/1/78.
JACKSON T. W. Born 28/10/42. Commd 25/6/65. Flt Lt 4/10/68. Retd GD 28/10/80.
JACKSON V. L., DFC. Born 11/4/22. Commd 2/4/43. Flt Lt 2/10/46. Retd GD(G) 14/10/64.

JACKSON W. S. Born 6/8/22. Commd 30/4/43. Wg Cdr 1/1/65. Retd ADMIN 25/3/77.
JACOBS G. H. Born 1/1/39. Commd 2/2/68. Sqn Ldr 1/7/78. Retd SY(RGT) 1/10/88.
JACOBS R. Born 23/7/43. Commd 6/9/63. Sqn Ldr 1/7/85. Retd GD 23/7/98.
JACOBS V. K. Born 18/9/18. Commd 1/9/45. Sqn Ldr 1/1/49. Retd GD 15/12/57.
JACOBS W. Born 3/7/20. Commd 29/2/47. Sqn Ldr 1/7/66. Retd SUP 15/6/73.
JACOBS W. F. Born 26/4/30. Commd 13/12/50. Sqn Ldr 1/7/60. Retd GD 26/4/68.
JACOTINE A. E. D. Born 19/12/32. Commd 2/1/70. Flt Lt 2/1/73. Retd GD 3/4/85.
JACQUES B. Born 15/12/46. Commd 6/5/65. Sqn Ldr 1/1/84. Retd GD(G) 15/12/90.
JAGO P. Born 15/8/55. Commd 5/1/78. Sqn Ldr 1/7/89. Retd OPS SPT 12/9/99.
JAGO W. P. Born 4/8/37. Commd 29/7/58. Sqn Ldr 1/1/68. Retd GD 6/8/74.
JAKEMAN C. M., BM MB BS BMedSci FRCS(Edin). Born 18/10/56. Commd 12/2/80. Wg Cdr 1/8/94. Retd MED 12/2/96.
JAMES A., OBE. Born 4/4/14. Commd 1/4/40. Wg Cdr 1/7/54. Retd SEC 1/6/59.
JAMES A. G. T., OBE. Born 8/8/15. Commd 16/3/35. Wg Cdr 1/7/47. Retd GD 28/3/58.
JAMES A. J. S. Born 17/10/37. Commd 13/1/56. Flt Lt 26/2/64. Retd GD 17/10/74.
JAMES A. S. L., BA. Born 20/2/19. Commd 26/10/49. Flt Lt 26/10/49. Retd SEC 7/4/68.
JAMES B. Born 29/11/41. Commd 25/9/80. Sqn Ldr 1/1/89. Retd ENG 1/10/91.
JAMES B. A., MC. Born 17/4/15. Commd 1/5/39. Flt Lt 1/1/43. Retd RGT 11/6/58 rtg Sqn Ldr.
JAMES B. E. Born 12/4/31. Commd 2/7/52. Sqn Ldr 1/7/69. Retd GD 11/12/76.
JAMES B. P., BMet CEng MIEE DipEl. Born 8/8/29. Commd 22/11/50. Sqn Ldr 1/1/62. Retd ENG 22/8/67.
JAMES C. P., FCIPS. Born 10/7/31. Commd 27/7/54. A Cdre 1/7/78. Retd SUP 1/10/83.
JAMES D. A. Born 10/6/54. Commd 2/8/73. Sqn Ldr 1/1/91. Retd GD 1/1/94.
JAMES D. A. Z., AFC. Born 13/4/44. Commd 17/12/64. Flt Lt 17/6/67. Retd GD 13/5/89.
JAMES D. J., MVO. Born 27/2/33. Commd 4/7/51. Sqn Ldr 1/1/80. Retd GD 27/2/93.
JAMES E. R. Born 11/8/22. Commd 12/5/44. Sqn Ldr 1/1/73. Retd GD 11/8/77.
JAMES E. W. Born 27/4/23. Commd 14/3/57. Flt Lt 14/3/63. Retd GD 29/3/78.
JAMES E. W. Born 20/6/32. Commd 27/8/52. Flt Lt 23/1/58. Retd GD 24/4/92.
JAMES F. Born 27/6/25. Commd 20/12/51. Wg Cdr 1/7/76. Retd PI 27/6/80.
JAMES F. D. Born 7/2/34. Commd 24/9/64. Flt Lt 9/2/68. Retd GD(G) 12/12/73.
JAMES F. R. Born 11/1/25. Commd 17/3/45. Sqn Ldr 1/1/67. Retd GD 15/9/73.
JAMES G. H. J. Born 18/6/29. Commd 22/10/59. Sqn Ldr 1/1/72. Retd SEC 28/9/74.
JAMES G. R., MIMgt. Born 4/6/43. Commd 21/12/62. Gp Capt 1/1/88. Retd SUP 30/4/91.
JAMES G. T., BSc. Born 26/11/52. Commd 17/8/72. Sqn Ldr 1/1/86. Retd ENG 26/11/90.
JAMES H. G., AFC* DFM. Born 3/10/21. Commd 12/2/44. Sqn Ldr 1/10/54. Retd GD 31/7/65.
JAMES H. M. Born 17/10/25. Commd 4/5/50. Sqn Ldr 1/7/69. Retd GD 17/10/80.
JAMES I., MHCIMA MRSH. Born 16/7/59. Commd 27/3/83. Flt Lt 27/9/87. Retd ADMIN 27/3/99.
JAMES J. M. Born 22/12/31. Commd 13/3/65. Flt Lt 11/3/71. Retd SEC 13/11/74.
JAMES J. N. Born 6/10/45. Commd 8/7/65. Flt Lt 7/10/71 Retd SY 2/10/85.
JAMES J. R., BA. Born 6/9/41. Commd 22/5/80. Sqn Ldr 1/1/90. Retd ADMIN 1/9/95.
JAMES J. W. G., DFC. Born 3/11/20. Commd 11/2/42. Sqn Ldr 1/7/56. Retd GD 31/3/62.
JAMES M. F. C., OBE MSc BSc CEng MRAeS. Born 20/4/46. Commd 7/1/71. Wg Cdr 1/7/89. Retd ENG 25/8/97.
JAMES M. J. Born 20/8/37. Commd 5/7/73. Flt Lt 5/7/78. Retd ENG 19/8/78. Reinstated 27/8/80. Flt Lt 13/7/80. Retd ENG 4/3/88.
JAMES M. K. B. Born 7/6/19. Commd 1/9/45. Sqn Ldr 1/1/59. Retd SEC 3/10/64.
JAMES M. N., FIMLS. Born 14/11/31. Commd 3/10/74. Sqn Ldr 28/12/82. Retd MED(T) 14/11/86.
JAMES The Rev N. B. W. Born 23/9/39. Commd 13/8/72. Retd 12/11/93 Wg Cdr.
JAMES N. G. R., BA. Born 17/6/48. Commd 24/9/72. Gp Capt 1/7/92. Retd ADMIN 4/4/96.
JAMES N. H., MSc BDS BPharm. Born 25/12/36. Commd 23/10/59. Air Cdre 1/1/91. Retd DEL 24/10/93.
JAMES N. K. Born 25/3/44. Commd 7/3/71. Flt Lt 7/9/74. Retd ENG 7/3/87.
JAMES P. H. D. Born 29/10/21. Commd 23/7/43. Flt Lt 29/6/50. Retd GD(G) 29/10/65.
JAMES P. W. S. Born 21/3/23. Commd 26/11/43. Flt Lt 26/5/47. Retd GD 27/6/55 rtg Sqn Ldr.
JAMES R. Born 19/4/25. Commd 14/7/45. Sqn Ldr 1/1/60. Retd GD 25/6/76.
JAMES R., BA. Born 21/1/48. Commd 6/10/69. Sqn Ldr 1/7/80. Retd GD 21/1/86.
JAMES R. A. B., CEng MRAeS. Born 28/8/19. Commd 19/8/42. Wg Cdr 1/7/60. Retd ENG 7/2/74.
JAMES R. P., MBE. Born 30/9/22. Commd 14/8/42. Sqn Ldr 1/1/52. Retd GD 30/9/65.
JAMES S. L., BSc. Born 26/11/51. Commd 22/9/73. Flt Lt 15/10/74. Retd GD 17/7/90.
JAMES S. P. Born 28/7/56. Commd 8/11/89. Flt Lt 9/11/91. Retd ENG 91/3/94.
JAMES T. Born 23/12/18. Commd 27/9/37. Sqn Ldr 1/1/54. Retd GD 23/12/57.
JAMES T. A. Born 12/6/40. Commd 11/5/78. Sqn Ldr 1/1/88. Retd SUP 12/6/95.
JAMES T. A. L. Born 24/2/29. Commd 1/5/52. Sqn Ldr 17/2/65. Retd EDN 28/8/67.
JAMES T. M. Born 14/1/48. Commd 5/1/78. Flt Lt 5/1/80. Retd GD 1/12/99.
JAMES W. A. Born 19/10/19. Commd 27/5/43. Sqn Ldr 1/7/55. Retd ENG 30/4/74.
JAMES W. B. Born 11/11/37. Commd 2/1/70. Flt Lt 2/1/72. Retd GD 11/11/92.
JAMES W. C., MBE MA. Born 15/2/26. Commd 6/11/47. Wg Cdr 1/1/62. Retd ENG 1/1/65.
JAMES W. D. Born 2/9/33. Commd 4/7/69. Flt Lt 4/7/75. Retd ENG 12/6/84.
JAMES W. D. Born 19/9/46. Commd 16/8/70. Sqn Ldr 16/2/77. Retd ADMIN 11/2/97.

JAMES W. J. M., AFC. Born 2/4/38. Commd 23/12/60. Sqn Ldr 1/7/84. Retd GD 2/10/99.
JAMESON S. V. Born 8/9/44. Commd 4/7/85. Sqn Ldr 1/1/94. Retd ENG 8/9/99.
JAMIESON A. D., MLITT BSc. Born 8/11/40. Commd 7/10/63. Flt Lt 7/1/65. Retd GD 7/10/79.
JAMIESON D. W. Born 27/10/13. Commd 2/9/45. Sqn Ldr 1/10/57. Retd SEC 11/1/63.
JAMIESON E. C., MB ChB DAvMed. Born 19/4/43. Commd 25/7/66. Sqn Ldr 2/8/73. Retd MED 31/8/74.
JAMIESON H. C., OBE MRAeS. Born 31/3/30. Commd 28/1/53. Wg Cdr 1/1/69. Retd ENG 1/1/72.
JAMIESON J. Born 6/2/23. Commd 5/5/60. Sqn Ldr 1/7/71. Retd ENG 6/2/76.
JAMIESON J. G., BSc CEng MRAeS. Born 4/9/45. Commd 26/5/67. Sqn Ldr 1/7/77. Retd ENG 1/10/86.
JAMIESON L. K. Born 11/9/25. Commd 22/10/59. Flt Lt 22/10/65. Retd ADMIN 12/4/76.
JAMIESON M. J. Born 13/9/46. Commd 1/4/66. Flt Lt 8/3/72. Retd GD 13/9/84.
JAMIESON R. Born 14/10/09. Commd 15/6/44. Flt Lt 15/12/47. Retd SUP 14/10/66 rtg Sqn Ldr.
JAMISON D., BA. Born 18/5/36. Commd 25/9/62. Sqn Ldr 18/11/67. Retd EDN 17/9/83.
JANE R. D., DPhysEd. Born 11/10/24. Commd 23/8/50. Sqn Ldr 1/7/61. Retd PE 30/5/70.
JANERING B. D. Born 6/2/42. Commd 24/12/67. Flt Lt 11/11/73. Retd GD(G) 6/2/80.
JANES J. E. Born 30/4/21. Commd 3/6/44. Sqn Ldr 1/7/55. Retd ADMIN 30/4/76.
JANES M. F. Born 14/9/30. Commd 25/5/50 Flt Lt 21/10/56. Retd RGT 14/9/68.
JANES P. J. Born 8/4/33. Commd 15/9/60. Flt Lt 1/4/66. Retd SEC 12/11/72.
JANIUREK J. D. Born 16/11/55. Commd 1/11/79. Sqn Ldr 1/1/92. Retd GD 2/7/95.
JANKIEWICZ M. Born 18/1/23. Commd 24/5/48. Flt Lt 7/2/61. Retd GD 21/8/67.
JAQUARELLO A. R. Born 6/1/39. Commd 24/2/67. Flt Lt 24/2/69. Retd GD 6/1/77.
JAQUES A. F. Born 3/8/28. Commd 30/9/54. Flt Lt 21/10/59. Retd GD 11/12/71.
JAQUES P., BA. Born 7/4/45. Commd 9/8/79. Sqn Ldr 1/7/85. Retd ADMIN 9/8/93.
JAQUES P. S., BA. Born 9/3/47. Commd 11/10/70. Sqn Ldr 1/7/84. Retd GD(G) 11/10/92.
JAQUES S. A. Born 7/3/23. Commd 30/10/45. Flt Lt 23/10/55. Retd GD 28/3/70.
JARDINE D. Born 4/7/22. Commd 22/3/51. Flt Lt 22/9/54. Retd ENG 13/10/61.
JARDINE J. A., BA. Born 20/9/44. Commd 27/2/75. Flt Lt 27/2/77. Retd GD(G) 27/2/83. Re-entered 30/4/90. Flt Lt 30/4/86. Retd OPS SPT 22/5/98.
JARMAN B. C., MHCIMA MIMgt. Born 14/2/53. Commd 27/3/77. Sqn Ldr 1/1/90. Retd ADMIN 1/10/94.
JARMY J. F. D., DFC. Born 26/4/22. Commd 20/11/42. Sqn Ldr 1/1/53. Retd SUP 26/4/77.
JARRETT F. Born 22/8/22. Commd 12/8/54. Sqn Ldr 1/1/71. Retd GD 1/1/74.
JARRETT H. W. Born 29/1/10. Commd 12/1/42. Sqn Ldr 1/1/53. Retd ENG 20/4/59.
JARRETT R. W. E. Born 26/11/11. Commd 6/4/45. Fg Offr 6/4/45. Retd GD 17/4/46.
JARRON T. E. L. Born 21/12/42. Commd 17/12/63. A Cdre 1/1/92. Retd GD 21/4/94.
JARVIS A. G., OBE AFC. Born 15/4/98. Commd 1/4/18. Flt Lt 1/1/24. Retd GD 10/6/29 rtg Gp Capt.
JARVIS A. J. Born 20/10/32. Commd 27/2/58. Sqn Ldr 1/1/69. Retd SEC 25/12/74.
JARVIS A. S., MBE. Born 3/8/27. Commd 14/8/51. Flt Lt 14/8/57. Retd SEC 18/7/64.
JARVIS D. Born 7/11/31. Commd 18/7/63. Sqn Ldr 1/7/78. Retd SY 9/2/82.
JARVIS D. B., DFC. Born 11/8/21. Commd 25/9/42. Flt Lt 25/9/44. Retd GD 8/5/47.
JARVIS E. A. Born 29/7/17. Commd 1/9/45. Flt Lt 1/9/45. Retd GD(G) 29/7/67.
JARVIS G. H. Born 13/7/26. Commd 10/5/50. Wg Cdr 1/1/70. Retd GD 10/7/76.
JARVIS G. J. Born 12/7/32. Commd 11/2/65. Flt Lt 11/2/71. Retd SUP 16/1/74.
JARVIS K. W. Born 3/7/42. Commd 30/7/63. Wg Cdr 1/1/81. Retd GD 3/7/86.
JARVIS N. C. S. Born 13/3/28. Commd 29/3/62. Sqn Ldr 1/1/75. Retd ENG 1/5/80. Reinstated 4/11/81. Sqn Ldr 7/7/76. Retd ENG 19/3/90.
JARVIS R. C. Born 17/2/39. Commd 17/1/69. Flt Lt 17/1/71. Retd GD(G) 30/9/82. Reinstated 8/9/86. Flt Lt 25/12/74. Retd GD(G) 4/8/91.
JARVIS R. H. Born 6/6/28. Commd 18/10/62. Flt Lt 18/10/68. Retd SUP 30/7/82.
JARVIS R. H. Born 8/8/37. Commd 14/12/55. Sqn Ldr 1/7/71. Retd GD 24/11/81. Re-entered 13/3/87. Sqn Ldr 18/10/76. Retd GD 8/8/98.
JARVIS R. J., OBE. Born 5/1/23. Commd 28/5/43. Gp Capt 1/7/71. Retd GD 23/1/78.
JARVIS R. M. Born 3/1/34. Commd 19/1/66. Sqn Ldr 1/7/83. Retd ENG 1/8/95.
JARVIS S. G. Born 19/8/36. Commd 27/6/60. Flt Lt 1/10/67. Retd GD 27/6/76.
JARVIS T. Born 9/7/59. Commd 1/7/82. Flt Lt 1/1/88. Retd GD 1/3/01.
JARVIS W. D., AFC. Born 14/6/22. Commd 16/12/43. Flt Lt 16/6/47. Retd GD 14/6/55.
JASKE J. A. Born 30/1/13. Commd 17/8/40. Flt Lt 26/5/48. Retd GD(G) 31/5/68 rtg Sqn Ldr.
JASPER N. J. Born 28/2/33. Commd 8/11/51. Flt Lt 22/5/57. Retd GD 28/2/71.
JAWORSKI J. T. Born 21/9/21. Commd 9/7/54. Sqn Ldr 1/7/70. Retd GD 21/9/76.
JAY J. B., MIMgt. Born 23/4/24. Commd 11/4/44. Wg Cdr 1/7/62. Retd GD 15/1/72.
JAY J. M. Born 3/8/33. Commd 8/7/54. Sqn Ldr 1/7/68. Retd GD 3/8/76.
JAY R. H. Born 5/10/29. Commd 16/7/52. Flt Lt 15/4/59. Retd SUP 14/9/68.
JAY W. J. Born 19/7/15. Commd 12/11/42. Flt Lt 12/5/46. Retd ENG 19/10/60.
JAYAKODY-ARACHCHIGE D., MSc BSc(Eng) CEng MIMechE MRAeS. Born 10/12/45. Commd 2/8/68. Sqn Ldr 1/1/81. Retd ENG 1/10/87. Re-entered 15/2/88. Sqn Ldr 5/8/81. Retd ENG 14/9/96.
JEAKES J. K. A., DFC. Born 18/1/99. Commd 1/4/18. Flt Lt 1/7/24. Retd GD 13/11/45 rtg Sqn Ldr.
JEAPES J. M. Born 14/6/33. Commd 4/2/71. Flt Lt 4/2/74. Retd GD 27/12/83.
JEE E. A. Born 28/8/22. Commd 21/9/42. Sqn Ldr 1/7/54. Retd GD 1/5/74.

JEFFERIES D. J. Born 24/12/31. Commd 23/12/61. Sqn Ldr 1/7/74. Retd SUP 24/12/82.
JEFFERIES R. E., OBE AFC. Born 6/7/23. Commd 25/8/49. Wg Cdr 1/1/67. Retd GD 20/12/75.
JEFFERS J. Born 14/9/22. Commd 6/6/57. Sqn Ldr 1/7/73. Retd ENG 24/3/78.
JEFFERSON B. Born 1/9/46. Commd 24/4/70. Flt Lt 24/10/75. Retd 1/12/85.
JEFFERY E. Born 10/12/47. Commd 28/7/88. Flt Lt 28/7/92. Retd ENG 26/3/96.
JEFFERY E. G. P. Born 13/8/26. Commd 14/6/46. A Cdre 1/1/77. Retd GD 13/8/81.
JEFFERY J. M. Born 2/9/52. Commd 9/3/72. Sqn Ldr 1/7/86. Retd ADMIN 6/1/01.
JEFFERYS A. D. Born 24/8/33. Commd 30/7/52. Flt Lt 27/12/57. Retd GD 24/8/71.
JEFFORD C. G., MBE BA. Born 13/9/40. Commd 16/1/60. Wg Cdr 1/7/87. Retd GD 11/9/91.
JEFFORD C. W. Born 28/4/13. Commd 12/11/42. Sqn Ldr 1/1/54. Retd ENG 28/4/68.
JEFFORD J. E., MBE. Born 16/7/43. Commd 7/6 73. Sqn Ldr 1/1/82. Retd ENG 1/1/85.
JEFFREY E. Born 10/12/47. Commd 28/7/88. Flt Lt 28/7/92. Retd ENG 26/3/96.
JEFFREY J. E., BA MRAeS. Born 31/1/44. Commd 17/12/64. Gp Capt 1/7/97. Retd GD 31/1/99.
JEFFREY T. M. Born 14/8/34. Commd 6/2/54. Sqn Ldr 1/1/69. Retd GD 1/12/86.
JEFFRIES A. H. Born 2/9/17. Commd 7/5/53. Sqn Ldr 1/1/67. Retd ENG 15/4/72.
JEFFRIES R. K., OBE. Born 2/11/14. Commd 14/12/35. Gp Capt 1/7/57. Retd ENG 14/3/65.
JEFFS F. R., AFC. Born 7/12/13. Commd 11/5/36. Wg Cdr 1/7/47. Retd GD 31/10/56.
JEFFS W. J. Born 28/9/47. Commd 13/1/82. Flt Lt 13/1/87. Retd GD(G) 18/4/96.
JELL R. A., DFC AFC. Born 28/7/19. Commd 23/4/41. Wg Cdr 1/7/55. Retd GD 28/7/74.
JELLIE J. M. E. Born 1/5/24. Commd 27/8/52. Sqn Ldr 1/1/67. Retd SEC 25/9/73.
JENKING D., MIMgt. Born 13/7/43. Commd 5/11/70. Wg Cdr 1/7/84. Retd ADMIN 13/7/87.
JENKINS B., OBE MIMgt. Born 9/4/26. Commd 21/5/47. Wg Cdr 1/1/67. Retd GD 9/4/81.
JENKINS B., BEng CEng MRAeS MIEE. Born 15/10/40. Commd 30/9/59. Wg Cdr 1/1/84. Retd ENG 1/1/87.
JENKINS D. S. Born 29/12/37. Commd 20/7/78. Sqn Ldr 1/1/88. Retd GD 29/12/92.
JENKINS D. T. Born 24/5/20. Commd 25/9/45. Flt Lt 10/11/55. Retd RGT 24/5/65.
JENKINS D. V. Born 28/1/17. Commd 5/6/43. Flt Lt 19/11/53. Retd PI 28/1/72.
JENKINS E. H., CBE CEng FRAeS FIMgt. Born 13/2/20. Commd 19/8/42. A Cdre 1/7/71. Retd ENG 15/8/73.
JENKINS G. R., BA. Born 7/10/32. Commd 27/10/55. Sqn Ldr 1/2/64. Retd EDN 27/10/71.
JENKINS H. A., DFC. Born 15/11/20. Commd 21/7/40. Wg Cdr 1/1/52. Retd GD 1/1/66.
JENKINS H. H. Born 19/11/17. Commd 8/2/43. Sqn Ldr 1/7/52. Retd GD 1/3/60.
JENKINS H. J. F. Born 13/1/50. Commd 11/10/70. Sqn Ldr 1/1/81. Retd ADMIN 13/1/88.
JENKINS J. Born 21/12/43. Commd 22/11/84. Flt Lt 1/3/87. Retd GD 31/3/94.
JENKINS J. C., MB ChB DPM MRCPsych. Born 17/9/34. Commd 30/9/62. Sqn Ldr 2/10/64. Retd MED 29/4/72.
JENKINS J. C. Born 15/8/39. Commd 28/1/60. Flt Lt 25/7/66. Retd GD(G) 2/4/75.
JENKINS J. K., DPhysEd. Born 15/6/28. Commd 6/8/52. Sqn Ldr 1/1/69. Retd ADMIN 1/5/80.
JENKINS J. R. Born 20/2/38. Commd 2/10/58. Wg Cdr 1/7/82. Retd GD(G) 4/4/89.
JENKINS L. H., MBE DPhysEd. Born 1/7/31. Commd 4/9/59. Wg Cdr 1/7/79. Retd ADMIN 1/7/86.
JENKINS M., MIMgt. Born 4/3/31. Commd 4/7/51. Wg Cdr 1/7/69. Retd GD 2/4/81.
JENKINS M. D. Born 12/1/41. Commd 12/7/63. Flt Lt 12/1/69. Retd GD 26/3/79.
JENKINS N., BSc. Born 27/3/51. Commd 15/9/69. Sqn Ldr 1/7/85. Retd ADMIN 9/11/00.
JENKINS P., MSc BSc MIMechE MIMgt. Born 20/12/46. Commd 1/9/71. Wg Cdr 1/7/90. Retd ENG 1/9/93.
JENKINS P. G., MA MS. Born 14/8/45. Commd 28/9/64. Sqn Ldr 1/7/76. Retd ENG 12/5/84.
JENKINS P. J., BSc ACGI. Born 24/11/50. Commd 15/9/69. Sqn Ldr 1/1/85. Retd ENG 24/11/88.
JENKINS P. R., CEng MRAeS. Born 24/10/36. Commd 16/4/63. Sqn Ldr 1/1/72. Retd ENG 9/6/78. Reinstated 19/3/80. Sqn Ldr 11/10/73. Retd ENG 24/10/93.
JENKINS R. Born 1/3/07. Commd 6/3/41. Sqn Ldr 1/1/57. Retd SEC 30/3/62.
JENKINS R. M., AFC*, FIMgt. Born 20/12/23. Commd 2/10/47. Gp Capt 1/1/70. Retd GD 20/12/78.
JENKINS T. J., CEng MIEE. Born 2/10/26. Commd 9/5/66. Wg Cdr 1/7/78. Retd ENG 9/5/82.
JENKINS V., BSc. Born 14/1/36. Commd 29/2/63. Sqn Ldr 26/2/70. Retd EDN 19/2/79.
JENKINSON C. R. D., BA. Born 6/6/59. Commd 28/9/80. Flt Lt 14/10/81. Retd GD 31/8/96.
JENKINSON D., BSc MCIPD. Born 6/8/34. Commd 7/9/56. Sqn Ldr 7/3/64. Retd EDN 7/9/72.
JENKINSON J. D. Born 13/8/31. Commd 12/2/53. Wg Cdr 1/1/78. Retd GD(G) 12/8/83.
JENKINSON T. R., MB ChB. Born 11/11/58. Commd 14/8/83. Sqn Ldr 14/8/88. Retd MED 19/2/96.
JENKS M. W., BSc. Born 6/8/64. Commd 7/6/87. Flt Lt 7/12/89. Retd SY(PRT) 19/4/92.
JENKYNS The Rev. T. J. B., BA. Born 18/10/31. Commd 1/6/64. Retd 31/12/85 Wg Cdr.
JENNER P. W. I., AFC. Born 1/3/23. Commd 25/5/50. Flt Lt 25/11/53. Retd GD 28/3/61.
JENNER Sir Timothy., KCB FRAeS. Born 31/12/45. Commd 26/5/67. AM 17/9/98. Retd GD 24/5/01.
JENNER T. R. Born 30/3/38. Commd 12/2/62. Sqn Ldr 1/1/91. Retd GD 12/2/96.
JENNINGS B. A. T., MA CEng MIEE MIMgt. Born 19/1/34. Commd 26/9/53. Sqn Ldr 1/1/67. Retd ENG 19/1/72.
JENNINGS B. L. Born 25/2/27. Commd 21/9/46. Flt Lt 19/6/52. Retd RGT 25/2/65.
JENNINGS D. C. Born 17/10/24. Commd 2/6/44. Sqn Ldr 1/1/70. Retd GD(G) 23/7/76.
JENNINGS D. R. Born 13/5/36. Commd 2/5/69. Flt Lt 8/3/72. Retd GD 2/5/74.
JENNINGS E. N. Born 18/6/12. Commd 21/8/41. Sqn Ldr 1/7/54. Retd ENG 18/6/61.
JENNINGS J. K. Born 27/3/33. Commd 27/7/54. Flt Lt 27/1/57. Retd GD 27/3/71.
JENNINGS J. T., DFC FInstAM FIMgt. Born 22/2/24. Commd 4/7/46. Gp Capt 1/7/67. Retd GD 22/2/79.

JENNINGS L. M., BA. Born 6/3/52. Commd 14/6/81. Sqn Ldr 1/1/92. Retd SUP 27/11/96.
JENNINGS R. T. Born 21/4/33. Commd 9/4/52. Flt Lt 5/9/57. Retd PI 6/4/82.
JENNINGS S. A., DFC. Born 27/7/17. Commd 6/11/42. Flt Lt 6/11/48. Retd GD(G) 27/7/74.
JENNINGS S. G. Born 20/11/44. Commd 5/3/65. Wg Cdr 1/7/84. Retd GD 1/10/89.
JENNISON G. M. Born 27/6/59. Commd 23/9/79. Flt Lt 23/6/83. Retd ADMIN 9/8/89.
JENNISON R. W., BSc. Born 29/7/53. Commd 30/9/73. Flt Lt 15/4/76. Retd GD 3/1/94.
JENSEN F. D., MSc BSc CEng MIEE. Born 21/10/49. Commd 24/9/72. Wg Cdr 1/7/91. Retd ENG 1/10/97.
JENSEN T. A., BSc. Born 31/12/47. Commd 12/5/70. Flt Lt 12/2/72. Retd GD 14/6/74.
JENVEY M. D. Born 20/9/57. Commd 17/5/79. Flt Lt 22/3/83. Retd GD 20/9/95.
JEPSON H. Born 29/5/25. Commd 8/7/45. Sqn Ldr 1/7/57. Retd GD 28/9/68.
JERMYN P. Born 6/9/20. Commd 8/7/43. Sqn Ldr 1/7/57. Retd GD(G) 4/9/65.
JERRUM E. W. Born 14/3/24. Commd 31/10/65. Flt Lt 31/10/66. Retd GD 1/1/74.
JERVIS D. A. Born 19/10/49. Commd 27/2/70. Flt Lt 27/8/75. Retd GD 31/3/77.
JERVIS N. Born 12/4/23. Commd 2/12/46. Flt Lt 3/8/52. Retd GD 31/8/66.
JERVIS W. L. A. Born 5/10/29. Commd 18/6/52. Flt Lt 7/3/62. Retd GD 27/6/74 rtg Sqn Ldr.
JERVIS-HUNTER G. Born 3/3/05. Commd 8/2/42. Flt Lt 2/9/45. Retd ENG 7/1/50 rtg Sqn Ldr.
JESSIMAN W. Born 24/1/35. Commd 7/7/54. Flt Lt 17/3/61. Retd GD(G) 2/2/90.
JESSON F. Born 26/9/18. Commd 17/7/43. Wg Cdr 1/1/61. Retd GD(G) 31/7/62.
JESSOP H. V., LDS. Born 18/10/13. Commd 31/10/39. Wg Cdr 1/7/52. Retd DEL 18/10/71.
JESSOP I. J. Born 31/5/12. Commd 27/5/42. Flt Offr 27/11/46. Retd SEC 7/7/67.
JESSUP A. B. Born 10/4/39. Commd 24/11/67. Flt Lt 4/11/70. Retd ENG 17/3/84.
JEVONS P. J. Born 22/5/42. Commd 9/7/60. Wg Cdr 1/1/85. Retd GD 22/5/97.
JEVONS R. C., MBE BSc. Born 22/1/46. Commd 7/5/72. Flt Lt 7/5/74. Retd SUP 1/4/81.
JEW I. T. Born 19/11/41. Commd 21/2/74. Sqn Ldr 1/7/84. Retd PRT 21/11/91.
JEWELL B. D. Born 25/12/41. Commd 8/1/65. Flt Lt 6/10/71. Retd GD 14/9/80.
JEWELL B. R., MSc BSc CEng MRAeS. Born 20/9/29. Commd 1/5/52. Gp Capt. 1/1/78. Retd ENG 20/9/79.
JEWELL C. G. Born 23/7/55. Commd 8/10/87. Flt Lt 8/10/89. Retd ENG 8/10/95.
JEWELL P. M. Born 22/9/33. Commd 3/12/54. Sqn Ldr 1/7/85. Retd GD 22/9/91.
JEWISS J. O. Born 18/8/37. Commd 2/4/57. Wg Cdr 1/7/75. Retd GD 24/5/80.
JEWITT R. E. R. Born 12/7/13. Commd 6/11/58. Flt Lt 6/11/64. Retd GD 13/11/68.
JEWKES P. Born 21/3/44. Commd 18/4/74. Sqn Ldr 1/1/87. Retd ENG 4/8/96.
JEWSBURY S. J., MIMgt. Born 20/12/29. Commd 7/4/55. Sqn Ldr 1/1/69. Retd SUP 14/11/81.
JEWSBURY T. A., MIMgt. Born 6/5/37. Commd 1/6/72. Sqn Ldr 1/7/79. Retd ADMIN 29/7/88.
JEWSON J. A. Born 10/10/17. Commd 19/3/58. Sqn Ldr 19/3/58. Retd SUP 10/10/72.
JINMAN J. A. V. Born 11/8/32. Commd 27/8/52. Sqn Ldr 1/1/79. Retd GD 11/8/87.
JOBLING K. A. Born 19/10/42. Commd 17/5/63. Flt Lt 17/11/68. Retd GD 2/4/93.
JOBLING P. L. Born 29/10/36. Commd 9/7/55. Flt Lt 1/3/61. Retd GD 29/10/74.
JOCE D. J. Born 30/4/20. Commd 9/4/43. Flt Lt 9/10/46. Retd GD 30/4/63.
JOCELYN M. A., BSc. Born 12/9/53. Commd 3/9/72. Wg Cdr 1/7/91. Retd GD 12/9/97.
JOHN G. A., BA CEng MIEE MRAeS MIMgt. Born 4/2/38. Commd 30/9/58. Wg Cdr 1/7/77. Retd ENG 9/7/89.
JOHN The Rev H. Born 11/5/28. Commd 12/6/62. Retd 12/6/78. Retd Wg Cdr.
JOHN H. M. S. Born 6/4/40. Commd 10/2/59. Flt Lt 30/6/66. Retd GD 6/4/78.
JOHN J. L., MBE. Born 27/8/29. Commd 28/11/69. Sqn Ldr 1/7/89. Retd ENG 8/10/92.
JOHN L. Born 1/7/19. Commd 22/12/42. Flt Lt 22/6/46. Retd GD 5/7/63.
JOHN L. O. Born 19/5/31. Commd 14/5/53. Flt Lt 14/5/59. Retd SEC 19/5/69.
JOHN P. D. M., MBE MCIPS MIMgt. Born 17/2/45. Commd 8/7/65. Wg Cdr 1/1/85. Retd SUP 17/2/89.
JOHN P. S., BSc. Born 7/7/52. Commd 13/9/70. Flt Lt 15/4/75. Retd GD 7/7/90.
JOHN R. S., BSc CEng MIMechE MRAeS. Born 11/2/63. Commd 29/9/84. Flt Lt 2/3/88. Retd ENG 11/2/01.
JOHNCOCK E. D., MBE. Born 15/3/25. Commd 2/7/59. Sqn Ldr 1/7/72. Retd ADMIN 15/3/85.
JOHNS L. T. Born 22/4/36. Commd 17/11/65. Sqn Ldr 1/7/87. Retd ADMIN 22/4/94.
JOHNS R. A. Born 13/7/21. Commd 17/10/41. Flt Lt 17/4/46. Retd SEC 13/7/70.
JOHNSON A., AFC. Born 13/12/18. Commd 12/4/45. Sqn Ldr 1/1/56. Retd PE 13/1/58.
JOHNSON A., MBE. Born 24/6/07. Commd 11/9/43. Fg Offr 11/9/43. Retd ENG 31/1/46 rtg Flt Lt.
JOHNSON A. A. B., DPhysEd. Born 1/11/36. Commd 11/4/61. Sqn Ldr 1/1/73. Retd PE 26/3/79.
JOHNSON A. F., DFC MA. Born 30/5/13. Commd 14/3/37. Gp Capt 1/7/53. Retd GD 17/7/68 rtg A Cdre.
JOHNSON A. F., MSc MB BS MRCGP MRCS LRCP DObstRCOG DAvMed AFOM. Born 15/5/41. Commd 22/4/68.
  A Cdre 1/1/92. Retd MED 15/12/95.
JOHNSON A. K., BSc DPhysEd. Born 14/3/33. Commd 20/9/57. Sqn Ldr 20/3/67. Retd ADMIN 14/3/88.
JOHNSON A. R. Born 4/3/48. Commd 21/1/66. Flt Lt 21/7/71. Retd GD 4/3/86.
JOHNSON A. R. A., BSc. Born 18/12/59. Commd 19/6/83. Flt Lt 19/12/85. Retd GD 25/8/00.
JOHNSON A. T., MB ChB FRAeS MFCM MFOM DAvMed. Born 3/3/31. Commd 11/8/57. AVM 1/1/89. Retd MED
  11/8/91.
JOHNSON B., BSc. Born 7/1/31. Commd 2/2/56. Sqn Ldr 2/8/65. Retd EDN 21/9/72.
JOHNSON B., Phd MSc BSc MinstP. Born 20/2/41. Commd 23/9/68. Gp Capt 1/7/88. Retd ADMIN 4/4/92.
JOHNSON B. A. Born 4/2/49. Commd 4/7/69. Flt Lt 4/1/75. Retd GD 22/10/94.
JOHNSON B. B., MIMgt. Born 23/9/16. Commd 23/1/39. Wg Cdr 1/1/55. Retd SUP 23/10/72.

JOHNSON B. C., OBE. Born 21/3/39. Commd 25/7/60. Gp Capt 1/7/84. Retd GD 21/6/96.
JOHNSON B. D., MCIPS MIMgt. Born 9/3/38. Commd 1/4/58. Gp Capt 1/7/87. Retd SUP 1/7/91.
JOHNSON B. H. Born 24/8/37. Commd 23/1/64. Flt Lt 13/4/69. Retd GD(G) 3/12/82.
JOHNSON B. L. Born 10/12/40. Commd 12/12/59. Sqn Ldr 1/1/71. Retd ENG 10/12/78.
JOHNSON B. L. Born 24/8/49. Commd 4/5/72. Flt Lt 4/11/77. Retd GD 17/1/88.
JOHNSON B. M. Born 26/9/16. Commd 5/9/5. Fg Offr 5/3/53. Retd SEC 25/8/54.
JOHNSON B. W. Born 21/6/43. Commd 19/1/64. Wg Cdr 1/1/88. Retd GD 21/6/00.
JOHNSON C., BSc. Born 4/12/49. Commd 14/7/74. Flt Lt 14/4/76. Retd GD 14/7/90.
JOHNSON C. I., OBE CEng MIEE MRAeS. Born 25/2/40. Commd 28/7/60. Gp Capt 1/7/83. Retd ENG 4/6/86.
JOHNSON C. R., OBE AFC MIMgt. Born 20/2/21. Commd 3/9/43. Wg Cdr 1/1/61. Retd GD 30/6/73.
JOHNSON D. Born 6/12/34. Commd 22/5/59. Sqn Ldr 3/9/68. Retd ADMIN 31/8/86.
JOHNSON D. A. V., BSc. Born 6/10/31. Commd 29/9/55. Sqn Ldr 1/1/63. Retd GD 7/6/71.
JOHNSON D. B. W. Born 30/12/23. Commd 14/3/45. Flt Lt 29/11/51. Retd GD 25/5/68.
JOHNSON D. L., MCIPD MIMgt. Born 6/12/38. Commd 12/9/61. Sqn Ldr 4/3/93. Retd ADMIN 1/4/93.
JOHNSON D. M. Born 13/3/39. Commd 12/4/66. Sqn Ldr 1/7/86. Retd GD 5/4/89.
JOHNSON D. R., BA. Born 16/8/60. Commd 13/2/83. Flt Lt 13/5/83. Retd GD 13/2/91.
JOHNSON D. T. Born 25/11/46. Commd 27/9/73. Sqn Ldr 1/7/84. Retd ENG 1/7/87.
JOHNSON F. Born 7/12/11. Commd 1/7/43. Fg Offr 26/2/44. Retd ASD 4/2/46.
JOHNSON F. A., DFC. Born 6/10/19. Commd 3/2/45. Sqn Ldr 1/7/54. Retd GD 7/11/58.
JOHNSON F. S. R., CB OBE CIMgt. Born 4/8/17. Commd 9/4/43. AVM 1/1/71. Retd SUP 1/1/74.
JOHNSON G. L., DFM. Born 25/11/21. Commd 29/11/43. Sqn Ldr 1/4/55. Retd GD 15/9/62.
JOHNSON G. L. Born 11/1/27. Commd 28/11/51. Flt Lt 28/11/55. Retd GD 28/4/69.
JOHNSON G. S., BA. Born 18/10/26. Commd 18/11/52. Flt Lt 18/11/58. Retd SUP 30/8/67.
JOHNSON G. W., DFC*, MRAeS. Born 8/1/23. Commd 5/3/45. Wg Cdr 1/1/60. Retd GD 18/4/69.
JOHNSON H. D., DFC. Born 10/6/18. Commd 16/3/42. Sqn Ldr 1/1/52. Retd GD 14/3/58.
JOHNSON H. R., BSc. Born 30/4/58. Commd 2/3/80. Flt Lt 2/12/81. Retd GD 14/3/97.
JOHNSON H. S., LDS. Born 14/5/07. Commd 8/8/41. Sqn Ldr 8/8/49. Retd DEL 26/5/54.
JOHNSON I. A. Born 21/8/29. Commd 18/8/61. Flt Lt 16/8/61. Retd GD 16/8/69.
JOHNSON J. D. Born 8/1/15. Commd 11/4/45. Flt Lt 4/1/51. Retd SEC 8/1/64.
JOHNSON J. E., CB CBE DSO** DFC*. Born 9/3/15. Commd 10/8/40. AVM 1/1/63. Retd GD 15/3/66.
JOHNSON J. F. Born 10/9/15. Commd 1/12/42. Flt Lt 19/2/45. Retd GD 12/8/47.
JOHNSON J. H., DFC. Born 26/11/20. Commd 9/5/41. Wg Cdr 1/1/56. Retd GD 10/12/57.
JOHNSON J. R. Born 28/7/31. Commd 14/4/53. Wg Cdr 1/1/74. Retd GD 28/7/86.
JOHNSON K. Born 26/3/23. Commd 26/6/44. Wg Cdr 1/7/61. Retd GD 27/9/68.
JOHNSON K. W., DFC. Born 18/9/24. Commd 1/4/45. Sqn Ldr 1/1/59. Retd GD 15/10/67.
JOHNSON L. F., OBE. Born 9/10/09. Commd 20/6/41. Sqn Ldr 1/1/61. Retd SUP 9/10/64.
JOHNSON M. Born 8/5/55. Commd 2/3/80. Sqn Ldr 1/1/88. Retd ADMIN 14/3/96.
JOHNSON M. Born 17/10/46. Commd 20/5/82. Sqn Ldr 1/7/94. Retd SUP 17/10/99.
JOHNSON M. Born 13/6/48. Commd 1/7/82. Sqn Ldr 1/1/91. Retd ADMIN 1/7/96.
JOHNSON M., MSc BSc(Eng) CEng MRAeS ACGI. Born 16/11/55. Commd 15/9/74. Sqn Ldr 1/1/88. Retd ENG 5/4/96.
JOHNSON M. A. Born 14/5/47. Commd 22/11/84. Flt Lt 22/11/88. Retd ADMIN 14/3/96.
JOHNSON M. A. Born 17/5/39. Commd 15/12/59. Flt Lt 15/6/62. Retd GD 11/6/91.
JOHNSON M. C. Born 28/10/47. Commd 13/1/67. Sqn Ldr 1/1/80. Retd GD 28/10/85. Re-entered 23/8/88. Sqn Ldr 26/10/82. Retd GD 14/3/97.
JOHNSON M. H., CEng MRAeS. Born 12/4/36. Commd 16/11/61. Sqn Ldr 1/7/71. Retd ENG 26/8/75.
JOHNSON M. K., AFC. Born 16/7/50. Commd 19/8/71. Sqn Ldr 1/7/82. Retd GD 16/7/88.
JOHNSON M. W. Born 12/4/32. Commd 26/3/52. Flt L. 7/8/57. Retd GD 5/1/68.
JOHNSON M. W., MIMgt, BD. Born 9/5/48. Commd 2/8/68. Sqn Ldr 1/7/84. Retd ADMIN 1/7/87.
JOHNSON N., BSc. Born 20/5/49. Commd 18/4/71. Flt Lt 15/4/72. Retd GD 2/12/91.
JOHNSON P. Born 26/3/49. Commd 17/12/72. Wg Cdr 1/7/91. Retd ENG 31/10/98.
JOHNSON P. G., OBE BA FRAeS FIMgt. Born 08/06/44. Commd 14/6/63. A Cdre 1/7/94. Retd GD 24/8/99.
JOHNSON P. J. Born 6/10/30. Commd 24/9/64. Flt Lt 24/9/69. Retd ENG 7/10/80.
JOHNSON R. Born 10/6/34. Commd 31/12/52. Flt Lt 5/11/58. Retd GD 10/6/72.
JOHNSON R. Born 6/7/37. Commd 6/8/60. Flt Lt 6/2/66. Retd GD 6/7/92.
JOHNSON R. A., BSc CEng MRAeS. Born 19/10/51. Commd 25/9/71. Sqn Ldr 1/7/85. Retd ENG 14/3/97.
JOHNSON R. D., BSc. Born 31/3/49. Commd 3/1/69. Wg Cdr 1/7/86. Retd SUP 1/7/89.
JOHNSON R. H., DL. Born 17/1/24. Commd 29/7/43. Wg Cdr 1/1/61. Retd ENG 1/1/64.
JOHNSON R. H., CEng MRAeS. Born 24/6/45. Commd 19/8/65. Sqn Ldr 1/1/80. Retd ENG 24/6/83.
JOHNSON R. H. O. Born 3/2/44. Commd 24/6/65. A Cdre 1/1/96. Retd SUP 3/2/99.
JOHNSON R. S. Born 22/2/39. Commd 10/11/61 Flt Lt 1/7/68. Retd GD 3/11/72.
JOHNSON S. Born 19/7/49. Commd 25/2/72. Sqn Ldr 1/7/84. Retd ADMIN 19/7/87.
JOHNSON S., BEd. Born 2/9/55. Commd 14/4/85. Sqn Ldr 1/1/96. Retd OPS SPT 14/4/01.
JOHNSON S. A. Born 14/7/66. Commd 11/4/85. Flt Lt 11/10/90. Retd GD 14/3/96.
JOHNSON S. D., BEM. Born 18/12/19. Commd 20/10/55. Sqn Ldr 1/7/67. Retd ENG 18/7/70.
JOHNSON S. P., DFC BEM. Born 28/2/22. Commd 10/11/43. Sqn Ldr 1/10/54. Retd GD 28/2/71.

JOHNSON S. R., BSc(Econ). Born 12/2/48. Commd 27/4/70. Sqn Ldr 1/1/80. Retd GD 27/4/86.
JOHNSON T. E., DFC. Born 23/6/22. Commd 13/11/43. Sqn Ldr 1/10/54. Retd GD 23/6/71.
JOHNSON W. A., BSc. Born 16/6/43. Commd 17/8/64. Wg Cdr 1/7/87. Retd GD 16/6/98.
JOHNSON W. C., BEM. Born 7/3/20. Commd 3/5/56. Flt Lt 7/10/60. Retd PRT 11/3/75.
JOHNSON W. H. Born 17/2/22. Commd 29/7/45. Sqn Ldr 1/1/70. Retd GD 23/2/72.
JOHNSON W. R. Born 29/3/38. Commd 24/4/64. Flt Lt 24/10/69. Retd GD 7/1/80.
JOHNSTON B. Born 10/2/38. Commd 16/12/58. Flt Lt 6/3/63. Retd GD 1/8/89.
JOHNSTON B. E., BSc. Born 18/12/41. Commd 30/7/63. Gp Capt 1/7/86. Retd GD 1/4/97.
JOHNSTON C. K. Born 10/8/20. Commd 22/12/44. Flt Lt 22/6/49. Retd GD(G) 10/8/70.
JOHNSTON E. A., OBE. Born 9/10/18. Commd 17/12/38. Gp Capt 1/1/57. Retd GD 9/10/68.
JOHNSTON G. Born 24/4/24. Commd 20/4/50. Sqn Ldr 1/7/69. Retd GD 24/4/84.
JOHNSTON G. A. Born 19/7/47. Commd 1/3/68. Sqn Ldr 1/1/79. Retd ENG 1/8/91.
JOHNSTON G. MacA. Born 6/10/51. Commd 15/2/73. Flt Lt 15/8/79. Retd GD(G) 12/12/81.
JOHNSTON H. Born 18/10/47. Commd 2/6/67. Wg Cdr 1/1/95. Retd GD 31/7/99.
JOHNSTON J. A., DPhysEd. Born 13/1/43. Commd 23/2/68. Wg Cdr 1/7/89. Retd ADMIN 14/3/96.
JOHNSTON N. M. Born 10/6/50. Commd. 8/8/69. Fg Offr 8/8/71. Retd GD(G) 25/10/72. Reinstated 8/11/74. Flt Lt 22/8/77. Retd GD(G) 24/6/89.
JOHNSTON P. J. C. Born 11/2/38. Commd 3/11/77. Wg Cdr 1/7/90. Retd ADMIN 2/4/92.
JOHNSTON R. Born 5/6/31. Commd 19/11/52. Fl Lt 15/4/58. Retd GD 5/6/69.
JOHNSTON R. A. Born 29/9/37. Commd 16/12/58. Sqn Ldr 1/1/72. Retd GD 29/9/95.
JOHNSTON R. C. R., MBE BA CEng MIEE. Born 3/4/42. Commd 15/7/64. Gp Capt 1/1/88. Retd ENG 4/4/93.
JOHNSTON R. C., MBE MIMgt. Born 6/9/19. Commd 4/6/59. Sqn Ldr 1/7/67. Retd ENG 27/11/71.
JOHNSTON S. B., MIMgt. Born 12/8/38. Commd 15/12/59. Sqn Ldr 1/1/68. Retd GD 31/8/79.
JOHNSTON T. A. Born 18/3/38. Retd 25/3/64. Fg Offr 25/3/66. Retd GD 22/6/69.
JOHNSTONE A. Born 31/10/42. Commd 9/8/63. Flt Lt 9/2/69. Retd GD 1/11/79.
JOHNSTONE D. B. Born 11/9/22. Commd 4/8/54. Flt Lt 4/8/59. Retd ENG 11/9/64.
JOHNSTONE D. N., BA MB BCh BAO MRCP MRCPsych DPM. Born 27/11/29. Commd 3/6/50. Gp Capt 3/6/79. Retd MED 1/1/89.
JOHNSTONE F. E., MBE. Born 13/12/22. Commd 18/11/66. Flt Lt 18/11/69. Retd ENG 26/2/78.
JOHNSTONE J. C. Born 28/1/32. Commd 3/11/60. Sqn Ldr 1/1/79. Retd GD(G) 2/4/83.
JOHNSTONE N. D., MIMgt DPhysEd. Born 4/3/28. Commd 6/4/50. Wg Cdr 1/7/68. Retd ADMIN 30/8/80.
JOHNSTONE T. Born 13/3/24. Commd 9/3/60. Sqn Ldr 1/1/72. Retd GD 31/8/73.
JOINT J. M., BSc CEng MIMechE. Born 1/3/47. Commd 22/9/65. Wg Cdr 1/7/84. Retd ENG 1/7/87.
JOLL W. I. Born 28/11/08. Commd 12/9/46. Flt Lt 12/3/51. Retd SUP 21/1/58 rtg Sqn Ldr.
JOLLEY M. S. Born 1/7/25. Commd 12/3/53. Fg Offr 12/3/55. Retd SEC 1/12/63.
JOLLIE P. McF. O., MRCS LRCP DObstRCOG. Born 28/4/30. Commd 11/11/56. Wg Cdr 30/8/69. Retd MED 11/1/72.
JOLLIFFE F. S. W. Born 27/7/23. Commd 20/3/45. Wg Cdr 1/7/66. Retd GD 1/10/77.
JOLLY D. Born 2/9/28. Commd 1/8/51. Fg Offr 1/8/51. Retd GD 25/3/54.
JOLLY P. D. R., BA FIMgt. Born 19/9/45. Commd 3/1/64. Wg Cdr 1/7/85. Retd GD 1/10/94.
JOLLY R. M., CBE CIMgt. Born 4/8/20. Commd 7/1/43. A Cdre 1/1/71. Retd SEC 4/8/75.
JONAS C. A. C., BA. Born 27/5/27. Commd 27/7/47. Flt Lt 27/7/50. Retd GD 15/12/53.
JONATHAN P. W. Born 14/12/46. Commd 7/1/73. Flt Lt 7/1/73. Retd GD 22/4/94.
JONES A., MBE. Born 31/5/50. Commd 3/10/74. Wg Cdr 1/7/92. Retd ADMIN 15/9/00.
JONES A. Born 3/12/11. Commd 17/6/43. Flt Lt 23/9/48. Retd SUP 25/11/53.
JONES A. C., MA. Born 10/11/23. Commd 27/9/50. Sqn Ldr 1/1/65. Retd SUP 31/3/74.
JONES A. C. Born 5/2/30. Commd 23/4/52. Sqn Ldr 1/7/69. Retd ENG 5/2/88.
JONES A. D. G., AFC DipPE. Born 12/4/39. Commd 30/8/66. Wg Cdr 1/7/90. Retd ADMIN 14/7/91.
JONES A. E., MBE. Born 10/8/33. Commd 3/8/53. Sqn Ldr 1/1/74. Retd RGT 10/6/91.
JONES A. E. Born 26/11/10. Commd 23/2/50. Fg Offr 23/2/50. Retd SEC 4/3/58.
JONES A. E. Born 16/10/48. Commd 27/2/70. Flt Lt 27/2/73. Retd GD 1/3/78.
JONES A. F. Born 18/1/45. Commd 18/8/67. Sqn Ldr 1/1/80. Retd GD 18/1/83.
JONES A. G. Born 24/4/49. Commd 27/1/77. Flt Lt 27/1/79. Retd GD 24/4/99.
JONES A. H. Born 19/8/41. Commd 31/7/62. Wg Cdr 1/1/87. Retd GD 10/5/92.
JONES A. J. Born 20/4/58. Commd 8/5/91. Flt Lt 9/5/93. Retd ADMIN 7/8/96.
JONES A. M., BSc. Born 23/6/55. Commd 2/9/73. Flt Lt 15/4/78. Retd GD 13/2/80.
JONES A. P. S. Born 9/7/39. Commd 15/12/59. Flt Lt 21/8/63. Retd GD 28/9/70.
JONES A. S. Born 11/9/61. Commd 15/3/84. Flt Lt 15/9/90. Retd OPS SPT 11/9/99.
JONES A. T. Born 21/11/41. Commd 17/7/70. Sqn Ldr 1/7/85. Retd GD 21/4/93.
JONES A. W., BSc. Born 22/5/36. Commd 25/10/57. A Cdre 1/7/85. Retd ENG 25/6/90.
JONES A. W. Born 26/12/09. Commd 20/6/40. Wg Cdr 1/7/57. Retd SEC 26/12/61.
JONES A. W. Born 2/5/44. Commd 10/6/66. Flt Lt 4/5/72. Retd GD 1/11/75.
JONES A. W., BSc MCIPD. Born 28/5/44. Commd 6/1/69. Sqn Ldr 6/3/76. Retd ADMIN 6/1/85.
JONES B. A., BSc. Born 27/3/47. Commd 22/2/71. Wg Cdr 1/1/87. Retd ENG 30/9/99.
JONES B. B. Born 9/2/36. Commd 12/11/57. Wg Cdr 1/1/84. Retd GD(G) 9/2/91.
JONES B. C. Born 4/3/35. Commd 21/11/61. Sqn Ldr 1/7/75. Retd GD(G) 1/7/78.

JONES B. C. E., BSc CEng MRAeS. Born 6/7/28. Commd 11/10/50. Wg Cdr 1/1/67. Retd ENG 13/8/77.
JONES B. C. S. Born 22/7/34. Commd 28/7/55. Wg Cdr 1/7/78. Retd SY(RGT) 10/5/89.
JONES B. D., OBE FHCIMA. Born 7/9/37. Commd 17/11/59. A Cdre 1/1/90. Retd ADMIN 7/9/92.
JONES B. E. Born 15/5/52. Commd 30/4/81. Sqn Ldr 1/7/89. Retd ADMIN 4/1/93.
JONES B. E. Born 14/10/41. Commd 18/8/61. Flt Lt 9/2/68. Retd GD 14/10/79.
JONES B. H. Born 6/2/33. Commd 14/12/54. Sqn Ldr 1/1/67. Retd GD 6/2/93.
JONES B. J. Born 27/8/32. Commd 4/8/53. Flt Lt 5/10/60. Retd GD 27/8/70.
JONES B. L., BA. Born 15/4/33. Commd 26/3/52. Sqn Ldr 1/1/74. Retd SUP 15/4/93.
JONES B. L., BSc. Born 12/9/30. Commd 21/10/66. Flt Lt 21/10/71. Retd GD 15/11/75.
JONES B. R. Born 9/4/40. Commd 2/1/58. Fg Offr 13/8/61. Retd SUP 28/4/65.
JONES B. R. R. Born 6/4/48. Commd 2/8/68. Sqn Ldr 1/1/80. Retd GD 24/11/86.
JONES C., AFC DFM. Born 19/9/20. Commd 6/9/56. Flt Lt 6/9/59. Retd GD(G) 28/6/68.
JONES C. A. Born 26/5/54. Commd 2/1/75. Sqn Ldr 1/1/90. Retd GD 14/9/96.
JONES C. A., BSc. Born 12/10/54. Commd 19/3/78. Flt Lt 19/9/79. Retd ADMIN 14/3/96.
JONES C. B. S. Born 12/2/47. Commd 31/7/83. Flt Lt 31/7/83. Retd ENG 16/1/89.
JONES C. C. Born 14/9/48. Commd 29/11/68. Sqn Ldr 1/7/84. Retd GD 1/7/87.
JONES C. F. J., CEng MIMechE. Born 26/6/38. Commd 17/7/62. Sqn Ldr 1/7/69. Retd ENG 18/10/74.
JONES C. L. Born 1/9/16. Commd 23/3/44. Flt Lt 30/6/49. Retd SUP 8/5/54.
JONES C. M. Born 9/1/24. Commd 16/10/52. Flt Offr 2/11/61. Retd SEC 19/10/65.
JONES C. V., MHCIMA. Born 19/11/52. Commd 11/9/77. Flt Lt 11/3/81. Retd ADMIN 11/9/93.
JONES D. Born 30/5/31. Commd 8/11/68. Sqn Ldr 1/7/83. Retd ENG 6/4/87.
JONES D. A., BA DPhysEd. Born 4/5/30. Commd 20/8/52. Flt Lt 20/11/56. Retd SUP 20/8/68 rtg Sqn Ldr.
JONES D. B., MSc BSc. Born 9/11/49. Commd 24/4/77. Sqn Ldr 1/7/84. Retd ADMIN 24/4/93.
JONES D. C. Born 28/5/60. Commd 24/7/81. Sqn Ldr 1/1/94. Retd GD 28/5/98.
JONES D. C., DFC. Born 26/4/22. Commd 12/6/44. Sqn Ldr 1/4/56. Retd GD 26/4/65.
JONES D. C. Born 17/3/30. Commd 20/1/51. Flt Lt 14/11/56. Retd GD 24/9/80.
JONES D. G. Born 30/10/32. Commd 20/9/55. Flt Lt 7/3/62. Retd GD 17/4/72.
JONES D. G., MIMgt FINucE. Born 31/5/32. Commd 20/5/53. Sqn Ldr 1/7/67. Retd RGT 2/7/71.
JONES D. G., MRCS LRCP DLO. Born 16/2/17. Commd 18/4/46. Gp Capt 18/4/68. Retd MED 19/4/80.
JONES D. G. Born 29/6/46. Commd 8/9/69. Flt Lt 8/12/70. Retd GD 8/9/85.
JONES D. H. S., BSc. Born 1/5/44. Commd 30/8/66. Flt Lt 30/5/68. Retd GD 30/8/82.
JONES D. I. P. Born 10/12/36. Commd 30/12/55. Flt Lt 30/6/61. Retd GD 24/4/77.
JONES D. J. Born 5/8/44. Commd 14/1/65. Gp Capt 1/1/90. Retd GD 14/3/96.
JONES D. J., MB BS FRCS LRCP DRCOG. Born 11/1/51. Commd 17/10/71. Wg Cdr 2/12/87. Retd MED 12/8/90.
JONES D. J., MBE. Born 1/1/15. Commd 8/7/54. Sqn Ldr 1/7/66. Retd PE 2/7/68.
JONES D. J. C. Born 25/12/19. Commd 25/8/60. Sqn Ldr 1/1/71. Retd ENG 25/12/74.
JONES D. J. R. Born 2/1/45. Commd 30/1/75. Flt Lt 9/3/94. Retd GD(G) 6/4/94.
JONES D. L. Born 2/5/39. Commd 7/1/58. Flt Lt 9/7/63. Retd GD 2/5/77.
JONES D. L., BEng. Born 27/5/62. Commd 15/9/85. Flt Lt 15/3/90. Retd ENG 3/12/96.
JONES D. M., BSc. Born 21/8/56. Commd 11/9/83. Sqn Ldr 1/1/92. Retd ADMIN 11/9/99.
JONES D. M. Born 31/7/34. Commd 18/5/56. Sqn Ldr 1/1/69. Retd GD 20/8/76.
JONES D. M. Born 15/2/50. Commd 17/1/69. Flt Lt 19/4/75. Retd SEC 30/11/75.
JONES D. McK. Born 21/6/48. Commd 22/8/71. Sqn Ldr 1/7/85. Retd ADMIN 1/7/88.
JONES D. R. Born 22/7/38. Commd 2/1/61. Wg Cdr 1/7/80. Retd GD 5/9/90.
JONES D. R. C., BA. Born 26/9/42. Commd 1/4/66. Flt Lt 1/7/67. Retd GD 14/3/96.
JONES D. R. H. Born 12/1/15. Commd 8/4/41. Sqn Ldr 1/1/55. Retd PRT 18/1/64.
JONES E., LDS. Born 9/5/16. Commd 30/12/43. Flt Lt 30/12/44. Retd DEL 14/6/50.
JONES E. Born 17/6/20. Commd 28/3/46. Sqn Ldr 1/1/65. Retd SUP 16/2/68.
JONES E. Born 18/5/18. Commd 13/6/45. Sqn Ldr 1/7/59. Retd SUP 18/5/62.
JONES E. A., AMCIPD. Born 16/10/43. Commd 24/6/65. Wg Cdr 1/7/85. Retd GD 2/8/93.
JONES E. A., DFM. Born 18/3/24. Commd 16/10/44. Sqn Ldr 1/7/73. Retd ADMIN 30/6/78.
JONES E. E., AFC. Born 6/10/32. Commd 17/3/54. Wg Cdr 1/1/78. Retd GD 8/5/87.
JONES E. G., OBE BSc MB ChB. Born 2/2/53. Commd 30/8/78. Wg Cdr 1/7/93. Retd GD 30/8/97.
JONES F. H. Born 15/5/26. Commd 13/9/51. Flt Lt 4/1/57. Retd GD 1/10/83.
JONES F. J., BSc. Born 6/3/39. Commd 11/9/64. Flt Lt 26/11/68. Retd GD(G) 5/1/83.
JONES G. Born 23/7/39. Commd 27/8/59. Sqn Ldr 1/1/71. Retd ADMIN 1/9/76.
JONES G. Born 3/6/29. Commd 31/5/51. Wg Cdr 1/1/69. Retd GD 3/4/81.
JONES The Rev G. Born 19/5/35. Commd 22/4/68. Retd 1/1/86 Wg Cdr.
JONES G. A. Born 6/5/32. Commd 15/9/60. Flt Lt 15/9/66. Retd GD 6/5/87.
JONES G. C. Born 14/12/46. Commd 28/4/65. Wg Cdr 1/1/85. Retd GD 26/10/90.
JONES G. G., BSc. Born 29/9/35. Commd 31/7/56. Sqn Ldr 1/7/69. Retd GD 15/10/80.
JONES G. M., BEd. Born 25/1/59. Commd 6/9/81. Sqn Ldr 1/1/92. Retd SY 14/3/96.
JONES G. M. Born 23/7/17. Commd 3/6/42. Flt Offr 3/12/46. Retd SEC 1/5/73.
JONES G. P. Born 5/5/48. Commd 1/6/72. Flt Lt 1/12/78. Retd GD(G) 14/2/88.
JONES G. W. Born 21/5/31. Commd 8/7/54. Flt Lt 8/1/59. Retd GD 23/5/69.
JONES The Rev G. W. H. Born 30/5/24. Commd 12/5/52. Retd 25/4/67 rtg Wg Cdr.

JONES H. Born 21/9/30. Commd 6/8/52. Flt Lt 6/2/57. Retd GD 21/9/68.
JONES H., MBE. Born 28/3/39. Commd 5/8/76. Sqn Ldr 1/7/87. Retd ADMIN 1/5/92.
JONES H. D., MB BS FFARCS Dip Soton DA. Born 3/6/27. Commd 29/8/54. Wg Cdr 30/1/66. Retd MED 29/8/70.
JONES H. G. Born 1/8/28. Commd 9/5/55. Wg Cdr 1/1/72. Retd SEC 1/9/73.
JONES H. V. Born 7/6/39. Commd 31/1/64. Sqn Ldr 1/1/85. Retd GD 1/1/91.
JONES H. W. Born 9/3/60. Commd 15/3/84. Flt Lt 15/9/90. Retd OPS SPT 31/10/99.
JONES I., AFC. Born 28/12/23. Commd 4/9/46. Flt Lt 7/3/62. Retd SUP 13/6/74.
JONES I., CEng MIMechE MRAeS FIEE MIMgt. Born 31/12/24. Commd 27/6/51. Sqn Ldr 1/1/63. Retd ENG 27/6/67.
JONES I. Born 20/4/56. Commd 24/4/80. Fg Offr 24/10/82. Retd SUP 30/6/84.
JONES I. M. Born 28/6/44. Commd 11/10/70. Sqn Ldr 1/1/79. Retd ENG 11/10/89.
JONES I. M. Born 5/9/61. Commd 8/11/90. Flt Lt 8/11/92. Retd ENG 31/3/94.
JONES I. R. Born 11/9/48. Commd 11/8/77. Flt Lt 11/8/79. Retd ADMIN 11/10/86.
JONES J. Born 8/11/40. Commd 7/6/68. Flt Lt 7/6/70. Retd ENG 30/6/78.
JONES J. B. L., BSc. Born 10/5/63. Commd 30/8/81. Flt Lt 15/4/86. Retd GD 15/7/96.
JONES J. B. M. Born 7/4/35. Commd 29/4/54. Gp Capt 1/1/84. Retd ADMIN 7/4/90.
JONES J. D., MBE MA DUS. Born 27/2/27. Commd 24/11/48. A Cdre 1/7/74. Retd ENG 15/3/78.
JONES The Rev J. D. M., MA. Born 17/8/24. Commd 17/11/59. Retd 29/4/66. Sqn Ldr.
JONES J. E., DCM. Born 7/4/20. Commd 26/5/51. Flt Lt 31/3/59. Retd SEC 1/12/64.
JONES J. H. Born 26/8/21. Commd 27/8/43. Flt Lt 27/2/47. Retd GD 26/8/67.
JONES J. H., DFM. Born 9/4/17. Commd 4/3/44. Flt Lt 4/3/49. Retd SEC 18/9/65.
JONES J. H. Born 21/10/39. Commd 23/5/63. Flt Lt 1/12/69. Retd SUP 20/2/79.
JONES J. H. Born 1/10/33. Commd 17/7/58. Sqn Ldr 4/1/69. Retd ADMIN 1/10/93.
JONES J. I., BSc. Born 21/1/20. Commd 24/4/42. Flt Lt 19/11/53. Retd GD 13/3/64.
JONES J. L., BSc MInstP MBCS. Born 14/11/44. Commd 13/8/72. Sqn Ldr 29/3/78. Retd ADMIN 13/8/88.
JONES J. M., BEng. Born 21/6/66. Commd 30/8/87. Flt Lt 28/2/90. Retd GD 30/8/99.
JONES J. M., CB BDS FDSRCS(Eng). Born 27/1/31. Commd 16/10/55. AVM 1/7/83. Retd DEL 26/2/88.
JONES J. M., MB BCh DAvMed AFOM. Born 14/10/46. Commd 30/9/68. Gp Capt 1/7/96. Retd MED 2/4/01.
JONES J. M. R. Born 12/11/13. Commd 22/9/44. Flt Lt 22/3/49. Retd GD(G) 26/12/66.
JONES J. McK. Born 20/6/24. Commd 2/7/47. Flt Lt 23/11/60. Retd GD 1/1/69.
JONES J. N. Born 15/3/40. Commd 1/4/58. Sqn Ldr 1/7/74. Retd GD 15/3/95.
JONES J. R., MB BCh MRCGP DRCOG DAvMed. Born 6/9/56. Commd 5/11/79. Wg Cdr 1/8/94. Retd MED 5/11/95.
JONES J. S., CBE BSc CEng MRAeS. Born 10/12/40. Commd 13/10/64. A Cdre 1/1/92. Retd ENG 10/12/95.
JONES J. T. Born 4/5/40. Commd 13/12/68. Flt Lt 13/12/70. Retd GD 7/10/77.
JONES J. V. Born 2/7/29. Commd 15/6/48. Flt Lt 6/9/55. Retd GD(G) 2/7/67.
JONES J. W. H. Born 12/6/17. Commd 22/9/49. Sqn Ldr 1/7/59. Retd ENG 2/3/68.
JONES K. A., BSc. Born 18/3/62. Commd 30/10/83. Flt Lt 30/4/86. Retd GD 18/3/00.
JONES K. A., MBE. Born 27/3/47. Commd 14/7/66. Sqn Ldr 1/7/93. Retd GD 7/4/01.
JONES K. C. Born 24/7/46. Commd 7/6/68. Flt Lt 24/1/72. Retd GD 6/7/84.
JONES K. E. Born 18/1/38. Commd 30/11/55. Sqn Ldr 1/1/72. Retd GD 18/1/76.
JONES K. G. Born 16/1/24. Commd 19/10/44. Sqn Ldr 1/7/59. Retd GD 16/1/79.
JONES K. H. R., DFC. Born 5/1/23. Commd 11/12/45. Sqn Ldr 1/1/74. Retd GD(G) 5/1/78.
JONES K. W. P. Born 22/9/30. Commd 21/10/65. Sqn Ldr 1/7/79. Retd ENG 14/9/84.
JONES L. Born 19/12/27. Commd 25/7/47. Flt Lt 14/4/53. Retd SEC 1/12/65.
JONES M., OBE. Born 16/8/47. Commd 21/4/67. Wg Cdr 1/7/87. Retd PRT 1/9/90.
JONES M. Born 22/8/21. Commd 24/1/42. Sqn Ldr 1/1/52. Retd GD 22/8/64 rtg Wg Cdr.
JONES M. A. Born 19/9/38. Commd 7/5/64. Wg Cdr 1/7/82. Retd ENG 20/9/88.
JONES M. D. Born 5/11/43. Commd 17/5/63. Plt Offr 17/5/64. Retd GD 11/3/65.
JONES The Rev M. F. Born 20/7/44. Commd 2/9/73. Retd 1/5/81 Sqn Ldr.
JONES M. G. Born 30/11/27. Commd 29/3/50. Flt Lt 29/9/54. Retd GD 14/9/68.
JONES M. H. Born 2/12/41. Commd 28/9/62. Sqn Ldr 1/7/79. Retd GD 2/12/79.
JONES M. H., BSc CEng MIEE. Born 10/2/48. Commd 28/2/69. Sqn Ldr 1/7/79. Retd ENG 10/2/86.
JONES M. J., OBE MIMgt. Born 2/8/41. Commd 20/12/62. Wg Cdr 1/1/81. Retd SUP 31/3/97.
JONES M. J. Born 9/10/27. Commd 13/3/47. Sqn Ldr 1/1/75. Retd SUP 6/5/76.
JONES M. J. Born 29/5/39. Commd 14/8/64. Flt Lt 15/4/70. Retd GD 20/8/81.
JONES M. P., BSc. Born 19/7/63. Commd 22/7/84. Flt Lt 22/1/87. Retd GD 12/2/01.
JONES M. S., BSc. Born 22/4/63. Commd 22/7/84. Flt Lt 22/1/87. Retd GD 23/7/00.
JONES M. S. Born 5/2/41. Commd 3/8/62. Fg Offr 3/8/64. Retd GD 8/9/65.
JONES M. S. Born 18/2/48. Commd 2/8/68. Flt Lt 2/8/71. Retd GD 4/9/73.
JONES N., BSc. Born 10/2/29. Commd 19/4/51. Wg Cdr 1/1/66. Retd GD 1/1/69.
JONES N. E. Born 9/5/47. Commd 28/2/69. Flt Lt 28/2/72. Retd GD 1/1/75.
JONES N. G., DFC BSc. Born 13/5/20. Commd 6/12/41. Sqn Ldr 1/4/56. Retd GD 17/5/68.
JONES N. H. Born 1/6/50. Commd 24/4/70. Flt Lt 24/10/75. Retd GD 1/6/88.
JONES N. M. Born 23/1/18. Commd 10/12/42. Sqn Ldr 1/7/53. Retd ENG 27/4/68.
JONES O. Born 16/12/24. Commd 6/9/56. Flt Lt 6/9/62. Retd GD 16/12/83.

JONES O. N., CGM MIMgt. Born 25/12/23. Commd 18/3/44. Sqn Ldr 1/7/62. Retd GD(G) 19/1/74.
JONES P. Born 24/11/29. Commd 4/8/54. Flt Lt 22/8/59. Retd GD 12/10/69.
JONES P. A., BTech. Born 14/3/62. Commd 2/9/84. Sqn Ldr 1/7/96. Retd GD 2/9/00.
JONES P. A. R., BSc. Born 22/4/41. Commd 9/9/63. Sqn Ldr 1/1/74. Retd GD 9/9/79.
JONES P. D., BA. Born 5/10/32. Commd 29/12/53. Sqn Ldr 17/2/63. Retd EDN 5/10/70.
JONES P. D. Born 17/6/55. Commd 2/3/78. Flt Lt 2/9/83. Retd GD 25/1/88.
JONES P. F. P., BSc. Born 17/3/48. Commd 11/8/74. Sqn Ldr 1/7/86. Retd GD 13/4/98.
JONES P. H., MBE. Born 21/10/22. Commd 3/6/46. Sqn Ldr 1/7/63. Retd PE 21/7/73.
JONES P. J. Born 21/2/34. Commd 12/7/66. Retd GD(G) 1/10/82.
JONES P. K., BEng. Born 9/10/61. Commd 20/1/85. Flt Lt 20/7/87. Retd GD 30/9/97.
JONES P. M., BA. Born 10/7/30. Commd 13/2/64. Sqn Ldr 1/7/84. Retd ENG 4/7/86.
JONES P. N. Born 29/9/32. Commd 24/2/67. Flt Lt 24/2/73. Retd ENG 1/4/82.
JONES P. N. Born 13/2/41. Commd 11/9/64. Sqn Ldr 1/1/83. Retd GD 13/2/96.
JONES P. R., BSc. Born 25/8/67. Commd 18/9/85. Flt Lt 15/1/91. Retd GD 15/7/00.
JONES P. R., DFC MIMgt. Born 21/10/20. Commd 28/2/44. Sqn Ldr 1/7/66. Retd GD(G) 23/9/75.
JONES P. R. Born 26/10/65. Commd 28/2/85. Flt Lt 28/2/91. Retd GD 14/3/96.
JONES P. R. C. Born 9/7/40. Commd 18/12/62. Sqn Ldr 1/7/72. Retd GD 9/7/78.
JONES P. W., MIMgt. Born 20/12/53. Commd 5/4/79. Sqn Ldr 1/7/88. Retd SY 14/9/96.
JONES R. Born 20/6/28. Commd 28/11/51. Sqn Ldr 1/1/64. Retd GD 25/10/75.
JONES R., BA. Born 30/12/33. Commd 1/11/56. Sqn Ldr 1/5/64. Retd EDN 30/8/72.
JONES R. Born 19/3/30. Commd 6/12/51. Flt Lt 28/1/58. Retd GD 29/3/69.
JONES R. Born 10/8/40. Commd 11/11/71. Flt Lt 11/11/73. Retd GD 30/9/89.
JONES R. A., BA. Born 30/7/60. Commd 20/10/83. Flt Lt 18/4/90. Retd ADMIN 20/6/99.
JONES R. A. Born 11/6/25. Commd 25/9/50. Gp Capt 1/7/72. Retd LGL 28/8/75.
JONES R. A. Born 24/4/37. Commd 22/2/71. Wg Cdr 1/1/90. Retd MED(SEC) 1/1/92.
JONES R. A. J., MBE CEng MRAeS. Born 27/3/33. Commd 26/3/59. Wg Cdr 1/1/76. Retd ENG 28/9/85.
JONES R. B. Born 15/6/34. Commd 17/3/67. Flt Lt 4/4/69. Retd GD(G) 15/11/78.
JONES R. C., BA. Born 13/11/32. Commd 12/7/57. Sqn Ldr 1/7/63. Retd EDN 13/10/74.
JONES R. F. Born 12/2/10. Commd 9/5/40. Flt Lt 10/3/42. Retd GD 6/12/45 rtg Sqn Ldr.
JONES R. G. Born 7/8/29. Commd 28/11/51. Sqn Ldr 1/1/82. Retd GD 7/8/84.
JONES R. G. A., CEng MRAeS. Born 12/12/21. Commd 20/12/57. Sqn Ldr 1/1/70. Retd ENG 12/12/76.
JONES R. I. Born 30/4/30. Commd 1/7/60. Wg Cdr 1/7/68. Retd SUP 2/5/75.
JONES R. J. A. Born 12/4/20. Commd 19/8/42. Wg Cdr 1/1/63. Retd ENG 12/4/75.
JONES R. L., MCIPD CertEd. Born 8/12/45. Commd 15/10/81. Sqn Ldr 1/1/87. Retd ADMIN 15/10/92.
JONES R. M., CEng MIMechE MRAeS. Born 25/1/44. Commd 15/7/65. Sqn Ldr 1/1/75. Retd ENG 25/1/82.
JONES R. M. Born 7/10/28. Commd 23/6/67. Flt Lt 23/6/70. Retd GD 7/10/88.
JONES R. M., MSc MB BS MRCP MRCPath DRCOG. Born 9/5/48. Commd 4/6/80. Wg Cdr 28/8/85. Retd MED 27/9/89.
JONES R. M. G. Born 19/5/61. Commd 16/9/79. Flt Lt 2/9/85. Retd GD 11/4/91.
JONES R. N. Born 17/12/47. Commd 13/1/72. Flt Lt 13/7/77. Retd GD 20/9/87.
JONES R. N., IEng MIIE(elec). Born 21/4/45. Commd 9/8/79. Sqn Ldr 1/1/87. Retd ENG 20/8/98.
JONES R. O., MBE. Born 20/6/32. Commd 5/11/52. Sqn Ldr 1/1/77. Retd PI 30/12/84.
JONES R. O. M., MB BS MFCM DPH. Born 28/9/16. Commd 14/11/41. Wg Cdr 1/7/54. Retd MED 28/9/74.
JONES R., MSc BA. Born 2/12/44. Commd 9/10/67. Sqn Ldr 1/7/75. Retd SUP 12/12/84.
JONES R. T., AFC. Born 11/12/22. Commd 11/2/44. Flt Lt 11/8/47. Retd GD 31/3/62.
JONES R. T. B., CB FRCS LRCP. Born 16/11/25. Commd 1/9/52. AVM 17/9/87. Retd MED 18/7/90.
JONES R. W. Born 19/4/29. Commd 27/8/59. Flt Lt 27/8/65. Retd ENG 19/4/74.
JONES R. W., BChD LDS. Born 18/9/42. Commd 20/10/74. Wg Cdr 17/3/80. Retd DEL 14/3/87.
JONES R. W. Born 31/5/54. Commd 15/3/73. Sqn Ldr 1/7/91. Retd GD(G) 14/3/96.
JONES S. Born 10/12/42. Commd 21/7/61. Flt Lt 9/2/68. Retd GD 22/10/94.
JONES S. A. Born 2/6/54. Commd 13/6/74. Wg Cdr 1/7/90. Retd GD(G) 1/7/93.
JONES S. A., CBE BA. Born 30/9/34. Commd 18/10/62. A Cdre 1/1/87. Retd ADMIN 20/1/90.
JONES S. B. Born 29/3/48. Commd 28/2/69. Sqn Ldr 1/1/84. Retd SUP 14/3/97.
JONES S. J. Born 11/1/62. Commd 7/5/92. Flt Lt 7/5/94. Retd ENG 7/5/00.
JONES S. O. Born 3/2/52. Commd 13/1/72. Flt Lt 13/7/77. Retd GD 3/2/90.
JONES S. W. Born 11/12/26. Commd 12/1/61. Sqn Ldr 1/1/76. Retd ENG 11/12/82.
JONES T. Born 15/2/13. Commd 26/6/42. Sqn Ldr 1/1/52. Retd SUP 15/2/68.
JONES T., BA. Born 2/12/34. Commd 17/5/76. Sqn Ldr 5/4/66. Retd ADMIN 17/5/76.
JONES T. C., MBE. Born 20/2/23. Commd 26/5/60. Sqn Ldr 1/1/72. Retd ENG 31/3/78.
JONES T. E., BSc. Born 22/5/34. Commd 8/8/56. Wg Cdr 1/7/79. Retd ADMIN 22/5/89.
JONES T. L., MA. Born 18/5/33. Commd 28/2/56. Sqn Ldr 1/7/84. Retd GD 1/1/88.
JONES T. P. F. Born 3/10/45. Commd 31/10/63. Wg Cdr 1/1/81. Retd SY 1/1/84.
JONES T. R. Born 16/5/39. Commd 20/1/69. Gp Capt 1/1/87. Retd LGL 3/11/97.
JONES T. S. C., AFC. Born 31/5/33. Commd 27/2/52. Wg Cdr 1/7/72. Retd GD 12/6/81.
JONES T. W. Born 11/2/30. Commd 10/10/63. Flt Lt 10/10/68. Retd ENG 1/10/77.
JONES T. W. Born 20/8/46. Commd 17/7/64. Sqn Ldr 1/1/84. Retd GD 1/1/87.

JONES V. G. Born 18/2/50. Commd 22/11/73. Flt Lt 22/5/80. Retd SUP 6/8/89.
JONES W. C., MBE. Born 3/7/48. Commd 16/6/92. Flt Lt 16/6/94. Retd ADMIN 1/9/97.
JONES W. D. Born 8/10/29. Commd 28/4/64. Gp Capt 1/1/80. Retd GD 8/10/84.
JONES W. J. C., MIMgt. Born 23/12/19. Commd 15/1/43. Sqn Ldr 1/1/58. Retd GD 23/12/74.
JONES W. O. Born 27/11/11. Commd 7/11/33. Wg Cdr 1/7/47. Retd RGT 1/2/58.
JONES W. R., MIMgt. Born 10/4/23. Commd 15/5/47. Wg Cdr 1/7/69. Retd ENG 28/3/78.
JONES W. R., AFC. Born 22/11/11. Commd 2/9/40. Flt Lt 1/9/45. Retd GD(G) 28/1/59 rtg Sqn Ldr.
JONES W. R. D. Born 14/7/43. Commd 12/7/63. Sqn Ldr 1/1/82. Retd GD 14/7/00.
JONKLAAS C. G. D. Born 10/10/30. Commd 11/12/51. Sqn Ldr 1/1/67. Retd GD 10/10/85.
JONSON J. R. Born 30/7/36. Commd 11/12/58. Wg Cdr 1/1/77. Retd ADMIN 10/9/88.
JOOSSE C. A. Born 2/1/44. Commd 11/1/79. Sqn Ldr 1/7/89. Retd ENG 2/12/97.
JORDAN A. D. G., FCA. Born 9/5/16. Commd 23/8/40. Sqn Ldr 1/8/47. Retd SEC 9/5/65.
JORDAN A. G., BSc. Born 21/5/48. Commd 27/2/70. Sqn Ldr 1/7/80. Retd ENG 21/5/86.
JORDAN A. R. Born 26/6/23. Commd 11/9/43. Sqn Ldr 1/7/58. Retd GD 26/9/66.
JORDAN C., CEng MIEE MIMgt. Born 24/7/14. Commd 29/4/42. Sqn Ldr 1/1/53. Retd ENG 24/7/69.
JORDAN E. I. R., MBE BEM. Born 26/11/22. Commd 25/8/60. Sqn Ldr 1/1/72. Retd ENG 26/11/77.
JORDAN H. E. Born 13/12/31. Commd 2/7/52. Flt Lt 27/11/57. Retd GD 31/12/69.
JORDAN J. Born 21/4/16. Commd 12/5/43. Sqn Ldr 1/7/54. Retd ENG 27/6/70.
JORDAN J. B. Born 23/6/33. Commd 28/5/57. Flt Lt 6/12/62. Retd GD 23/6/71.
JORDAN K., MB BS FRCS(Edin) DO. Born 28/10/47. Commd 23/2/70. Wg Cdr 6/2/86. Retd MED 9/6/89.
JORDAN M. F. Born 1/10/43. Commd 14/6/63. Wg Cdr 1/1/88. Retd ADMIN 3/4/00.
JORDAN M. W. Born 24/6/38. Commd 24/2/61. Flt Lt 24/2/68. Retd RGT 30/11/68.
JORDAN P. A. Born 17/5/25. Commd 31/3/44. Sqn Ldr 1/7/67. Retd GD 15/5/76.
JORDAN R. J. B., BSc. Born 3/2/60. Commd 11/12/83. Flt Lt 11/6/86. Retd GD 11/12/95.
JORDAN R. K. Born 1/1/41. Commd 6/8/60. Flt Lt 4/2/67. Retd GD(G) 1/1/79.
JORDAN R. W., DFC AFC. Born 2/9/23. Commd 5/3/43. Gp Capt 1/7/65. Retd GD 13/4/70.
JORDAN T. A., BA. Born 18/3/35. Commd 7/9/56. Sqn Ldr 7/3/65. Retd EDN 7/9/74.
JORDAN T. E., MB BS MRCS LRCP. Born 15/12/44. Commd 28/9/64. Sqn Ldr 6/9/73. Retd MED 23/6/77.
JOSEPH M. M., CEng MIEE. Born 26/4/30. Commd 3/10/66. Sqn Ldr 6/10/71. Retd EDN 3/10/83.
JOSEPHY T. W. Born 2/7/48. Commd 23/3/67. Sqn Ldr 1/7/96. Retd GD 1/6/99.
JOSEY D. A., DFC. Born 1/6/20. Commd 22/5/42. Flt Lt 19/12/48. Retd GD(G) 7/7/68.
JOSLIN J. M., CEng MIMechE MRAeS MIMgt. Born 7/7/38. Commd 28/7/60. Sqn Ldr 1/1/73. Retd ENG 18/10/75.
JOSS D. A., MBE JP MCIPD MIMgt. Born 15/5/21. Commd 24/9/44. Sqn Ldr 1/7/56. Retd SEC 27/6/69.
JOY A. Born 11/2/30. Commd 25/10/51. Flt Lt 27/4/57. Redt GD 11/2/68.
JOY A. I. P., MIMgt. Born 12/12/44. Commd 1/9/70. Flt Lt 8/12/72. Retd GD 30/1/84.
JOY H. F. Born 21/7/25. Commd 27/5/54. Sqn Ldr 1/7/68. Retd GD 31/3/74.
JOY R. M., MBE. Born 15/8/44. Commd 3/3/67. Sqn Ldr 1/1/78. Retd GD 22/11/96.
JOYCE C. J. Born 27/8/28. Commd 17/12/52. Flt Lt 5/11/58. Retd GD 15/10/72.
JOYCE M. H., BA. Born 2/6/38. Commd 30/9/57. Wg Cdr 1/7/80. Retd ENG 2/6/93.
JOYCE M. P. R. Born 28/5/37. Commd 20/9/61. Flt Lt 1/10/67. Redt GD 20/9/71.
JOYCE R. L., PhD BSc CEng MIM MRAeS. Born 28/3/37. Commd 11/12/61. Gp Capt 1/7/83. Retd GD 13/12/87.
JOYCE W. T., MBE MIMgt. Born 15/9/20. Commd 16/8/46. Wg Cdr 1/1/69. Retd SEC 30/7/73.
JOYNER C. D., MBE. Born 7/5/47. Commd 1/8/69. Wg Cdr 1/1/91. Retd GD 1/1/97.
JUDD J. A. Born 15/1/23. Commd 14/4/49. Sqn Ldr 1/7/59. Retd GD 22/1/71.
JUDD L. J. Born 4/10/41. Commd 28/9/62. Sqn Ldr 1/7/78. Retd GD 4/10/96.
JUDGE A. M. Born 19/3/59. Commd 9/8/79. Flt Lt 9/2/85. Retd GD 30/11/96.
JUDSON G. W. Born 16/2/29. Commd 11/4/51. Flt Lt 11/4/56. Retd SEC 28/3/58.
JUDSON M. T. Born 8/3/11. Commd 5/1/43. Sqn Ldr 1/7/54. Retd ENG 8/3/60.
JUKES A. R., BDS MIMgt. Born 19/7/39. Commd 12/12/76. Sqn Ldr 6/2/76. Retd DEL 12/12/84.
JUKES B. A. Born 10/12/46. Commd 10/12/65. Sqn Ldr 1/7/89. Retd GD 14/3/96.
JUKES G., AFC. Born 17/10/24. Commd 9/3/45. Sqn Ldr 1/7/69. Retd GD 10/10/76.
JUNGMAYR E. W., MBE RSCN. Born 9/4/58. Commd 14/8/83. Sqn Ldr 1/1/93. Retd MED SEC 14/3/96.
JUNOR I. O. Born 7/9/40. Commd 18/12/62. Gp Capt 1/1/86. Retd GD 2/4/93.
JUPE D. B. Born 12/4/56. Commd 22/2/79. Flt Lt 20/7/82. Retd GD 10/1/99.
JUPP M. F. Born 24/6/42. Commd 8/6/62. Wg Cdr 1/7/80. Retd GD 6/11/89.
JUPP S. K. Born 20/2/12. Commd 2/9/43. Fg Offr 13/7/44. Retd ENG 12/1/46 rtg Flt Lt.
JURY A. R., IEng AMRAeS. Born 13/3/41. Commd 21/9/72. Sqn Ldr 1/1/91. Retd ENG 13/3/96.
JUST E. J., BSc ARCS CEng MRAeS MIEE. Born 10/4/32. Commd 24/11/54. Sqn Ldr 1/1/67. Retd ENG 24/11/70.

# K

KAIN K. V. Born 1/7/20. Commd 7/10/42. Flt Offr 7/10/47. Retd SEC 7/7/54.
KALKHOVEN D. G. Born 21/7/17. Commd 18/10/43. Flt Lt 29/6/50. Retd SEC 1/9/60.
KANAGASABAY S., MSc MB BS MFCM. Born 9/7/28. Commd 15/11/59. Wg Cdr 6/6/69. Retd MED 27/8/76.
KANE E. J. Born 27/5/23. Commd 1/5/45. Sqn Ldr 1/1/72. Retd GD 31/8/73.
KANE J. H. Born 12/5/45. Commd 26/3/64. Sqn Ldr 1/7/76. Retd ADMIN 12/5/87.
KANE T. M., MIMgt. Born 9/10/20. Commd 17/9/38. Wg Cdr 1/7/69. Retd GD(G) 29/5/74.
KANE W. B. Born 24/10/46. Commd 28/7/67. Wg Cdr 1/7/87. Retd ADMIN 24/10/90.
KARL H. L. Born 12/2/51. Commd 20/9/69. Sqn Ldr 1/7/84. Retd GD 12/2/89.
KARLE D. Born 7/3/51. Commd 20/12/90. Flt Lt 20/12/94. Retd OPS SPT 22/5/99.
KARRAN J. A. C., AFC. Born 24/3/13. Commd 16/4/35. Sqn Ldr 1/9/41. Retd GD 12/1/48 rtg Wg Cdr.
KATON R. C., CEng MIMechE MRAeS. Born 2/7/41. Commd 17/7/62. Sqn Ldr 1/1/72. Retd ENG 31/8/78.
KAY A. F. G. Born 5/11/23. Commd 6/3/52. Flt Lt 6/9/56. Retd SEC 31/3/62.
KAY D. Born 29/7/39. Commd 5/11/70. Flt Lt 5/11/72. Retd SEC 5/11/78.
KAY D. J. Born 18/3/29. Commd 6/7/49. Flt Lt 23/10/57. Retd GD 19/8/67.
KAY E. Born 6/5/15. Commd 20/6/41. Flt Lt 26/5/55. Retd SEC 30/9/61.
KAY G. C. Born 25/10/46. Commd 21/1/66. Flt Lt 21/7/71. Retd GD 25/10/84.
KAY M. I., LLB. Born 17/8/48. Commd 1/9/70. Flt Lt 1/6/72. Retd GD 15/11/87.
KAY N. Born 22/11/21. Commd 14/3/46. Sqn Ldr 1/1/63. Retd ENG 8/1/65.
KAY R. Born 20/12/15. Commd 15/10/42. Sqn Ldr 1/7/56. Retd ENG 20/12/64.
KAY R. Born 14/1/21. Commd 7/10/43. Flt Lt 7/4/48. Retd SUP 17/10/58.
KAY R. P. Born 2/2/19. Commd 12/4/45. Sqn Ldr 1/7/59. Retd ENG 2/2/74.
KAYE D. G. Born 20/6/33. Commd 4/2/53. Flt Lt 24/6/58. Retd GD 25/6/76.
KAYE G. Born 11/6/33. Commd 26/3/52. Sqn Ldr 1/7/77. Retd SUP 14/5/86.
KAYE J. F. M., BSc. Born 13/11/47. Commd 27/10/70. Flt Lt 27/1/71. Retd GD 27/10/86.
KAYE M. Born 4/4/21. Commd 7/4/43. Wg Cdr 1/1/71. Retd GD 31/5/75.
KAYE M. P., BA. Born 2/4/44. Commd 17/12/64. Sqn Ldr 1/7/76. Retd GD 2/4/82.
KEAM P. C. Born 15/4/38. Commd 29/7/72. Sqn Ldr 29/8/78. Retd ADMIN 27/7/86.
KEAN T. F., MBE CEng MIMechE MRAeS. Born 25/4/39. Commd 28/7/60. Sqn Ldr 1/7/69. Retd ENG 10/7/89.
KEANE A. M. Born 10/12/41. Commd 28/10/63. Sqn Ldr 1/7/77. Retd GD 1/7/80.
KEANE L. Born 20/3/61. Commd 20/10/83. Flt Lt 20/4/89. Retd GD 1/10/90.
KEAREY J. A. Born 29/9/14. Commd 26/12/46. Flt Lt 26/6/51. Retd SUP 18/2/61.
KEAREY J. R., BSc CEng MRAeS. Born 7/1/48. Commd 2/8/68. Sqn Ldr 1/7/80. Retd ENG 1/10/87.
KEARL I. A. R. Born 23/11/33. Commd 27/7/54. Sqn Ldr 1/1/69. Retd SUP 29/5/76.
KEARN S. C., CEng MRAeS. Born 17/8/18. Commd 23/9/43. Wg Cdr 1/7/68. Retd ENG 17/8/73.
KEARNEY A. J., CBE BSc(Econ). Born 26/5/45. Commd 3/3/67. Gp Capt 1/1/93. Retd GD 26/5/00.
KEARNEY C. J. Born 6/1/59. Commd 6/10/94. Fg Offr 19/10/89. Retd ADMIN 29/11/96.
KEARNEY J. J., MBE. Born 19/4/28. Commd 21/1/52. Sqn Ldr 1/1/64. Retd GD 30/6/77.
KEARNS D. C. L., AFC DSC. Born 24/12/16. Commd 23/4/43. Sqn Ldr 1/7/54. Retd GD 17/3/60.
KEARNS M. E., BA. Born 4/2/36. Commd 28/11/58. Sqn Ldr 28/5/69. Retd EDN 1/7/75.
KEARSEY M. H. Born 8/10/58. Commd 1/12/77. Plt Offr 1/6/78. Retd SUP 6/3/79.
KEARY D. H., DFC. Born 1/4/16. Commd 1/5/41. Wg Cdr 1/7/56. Retd SEC 30/5/64.
KEAST R. J., BSc CEng MRAeS. Born 20/8/37. Commd 30/9/57. Sqn Ldr 1/7/69. Retd ENG 20/8/75.
KEATING P. J., BA MRIN. Born 6/11/41. Commd 21/7/61. Sqn Ldr 1/1/89. Retd GD 6/9/94.
KEATING S. F. Born 12/3/24. Commd 17/5/02. Flt Lt 17/5/65. Retd ENG 12/3/79.
KEATLEY R. F. Born 6/11/22. Commd 23/12/43. Sqn Ldr 1/4/55. Retd GD 6/11/65.
KEATS D. J. B. Born 10/1/31. Commd 12/1/51. Sqn Ldr 1/7/61. Retd GD 10/1/69.
KEATS T. S. Born 5/12/40. Commd 31/7/62. Sqn Ldr 1/7/73. Retd GD 5/12/78.
KEAY V. C. Born 21/5/23. Commd 20/11/42. Sqn Ldr 1/1/60. Retd GD 21/9/73.
KEDAR A., BSc CEng MRAeS MIMgt. Born 16/9/30. Commd 23/9/53. Gp Capt 1/1/74. Retd ENG 16/9/85.
KEDDIE D. G. Born 23/5/09. Commd 5/9/31. Gp Capt 1/7/50. Retd GD 25/1/57.
KEDDIE J. B. F. Born 29/1/20. Commd 8/2/44. Flt Lt 8/8/47. Retd GD 26/12/58.
KEDDIE W. M. Born 21/11/04. Commd 11/3/32. Wg Cdr 1/10/46. Retd ENG 14/8/47 rtg Gp Capt.
KEE W. Born 18/3/18. Commd 6/5/43. Flt Lt 6/11/47. Retd SEC 1/1/55.
KEEBLE P. N. Born 9/11/45. Commd 18/8/67. Flt Lt 4/5/72. Retd GD 1/1/76. Re-entered 22/4/81. Flt Lt 24/11/75.
   Retd GD 2/3/97.
KEEBLE P. W. Born 16/5/47. Commd 6/5/66. Flt Lt 6/11/71. Retd GD 1/6/94.
KEECH A. J., BEM MIMgt. Born 27/7/28. Commd 7/6/68. Sqn Ldr 1/7/83. Retd ENG 27/7/86.
KEECH J. E. Born 19/8/21. Commd 19/6/42. Flt Lt 24/9/49. Retd GD(G) 5/3/65.
KEECH R. A., BSc. Born 9/3/52. Commd 30/10/72. Sqn Ldr 1/1/87. Retd GD 9/3/90.
KEEDLE B. D. Born 15/11/33. Commd 23/7/52. Flt Lt 29/1/58. Retd GD 15/4/71.

KEELEY A. F. W. Born 27/10/31. Commd 17/12/52. Flt Lt 17/6/55. Retd GD 21/1/73.
KEELEY T. J. Born 31/1/29. Commd 4/6/64. Flt Lt 4/6/67. Retd GD 31/1/84.
KEELING A. G., BSc CEng MRAeS. Born 7/2/43. Commd 22/10/70. Flt Lt 22/10/70. Retd ENG 26/6/83.
KEELING R. F. N. Born 6/4/25. Commd 24/9/56. Sqn Ldr 1/1/64. Retd PRT. 1/1/67.
KEELING T. W. Born 16/1/45. Commd 13/9/70. Sqn Ldr 1/7/84. Retd ENG 9/6/97.
KEEN R. D., MBCS. Born 30/8/46. Commd 9/12/65. Sqn Ldr 1/7/78. Retd GD 15/7/87.
KEEN S. S. Born 5/2/46. Commd 22/7/71. Sqn Ldr 1/1/80. Retd ENG 31/3/85. Re-entered 8/3/91. Wg Cdr 1/1/96.
  Retd ENG 11/12/98.
KEEN W. H. Born 14/11/19. Commd 20/1/44. Sqn Ldr 1/7/63. Retd GD(G) 14/11/69.
KEENAN E. J., DFC. Born 21/11/19. Commd 29/5/41. Flt Lt 27/4/54. Retd SEC 1/8/63.
KEENAN J. F. Born 19/9/44. Commd 5/11/70. Flt Lt 21/7/74. Retd GD 21/11/75.
KEENE D. A., BDS DOrthRCS. Born 26/3/40. Commd 20/9/59. Wg Cdr 29/7/77. Retd DEL 26/3/78.
KEEP M. G. Born 1/11/25. Commd 25/8/55. Flt Lt·25/8/61. Retd GD 30/3/68.
KEEP R. P. Born 22/11/61. Commd 25/2/83. Sqn Ldr 1/7/95. Retd SUP 22/11/99.
KEER D. C. Born 15/4/33. Commd 27/2/70. Sqn Ldr 1/1/79. Retd ENG 16/4/83.
KEEVES J. E. Born 6/12/21. Commd 28/9/61. Flt Lt 28/9/66. Retd ENG 6/12/76.
KEFALAS D., LLB BA. Born 26/6/35. Commd 4/6/58. Flt Lt 9/11/70. Retd SEC 22/6/73.
KEHOE P., BSc. Born 21/4/59. Commd 15/3/79. Flt Lt 15/10/84. Retd GD(G) 20/9/87
KEHOE S. Born 25/6/29. Commd 22/8/51. Flt Lt 22/2/56. Retd GD(G) 25/6/87.
KEILLER D. E. S. Born 19/3/31. Commd 3/7/56. Flt Lt 3/1/62. Retd GD 17/1/64.
KEILLER F. E. S., MBE MB ChB FRCS(Edin) FRCS. Born 20/7/27. Commd 1/7/56. Wg Cdr 21/8/68. Retd MED
  1/7/72.
KEILY J. A. Born 15/10/28. Commd 11/4/51. Sqn Ldr 1/7/62. Retd SUP 15/10/66.
KEITCH M. P., BA CDipAF IEng. Born 10/5/42. Commd 9/5/66. Sqn Ldr 1/1/80. Retd ENG 1/1/83. Re-entered
  12/5/86. Sqn Ldr 12/5/83. Retd ENG 10/5/97.
KEITH G. T. Born 10/4/47. Commd 28/5/66. Gp Capt 1/7/89. Retd OPS SPT 15/6/98.
KEKEWICH H. C., BA. Born 27/8/56. Commd 10/6/84. Flt Lt 10/12/86. Retd SUP 14/9/96.
KEKWICK A. R. Born 17/7/33. Commd 7/11/52. Sqn Ldr 1/7/66. Retd RGT 13/6/70.
KELL G. W. Born 10/3/53. Commd 11/5/78. Sqn Ldr 1/1/97. Retd OPS SPT 1/8/98.
KELLAWAY H. Born 24/7/10. Commd 11/2/43. Flt Lt 11/8/46. Retd SEC 3/3/58.
KELLEHER K. P. Born 22/10/23. Commd 9/8/45. Sqn Ldr 1/1/71. Retd GD 22/10/78.
KELLETT B. M., MSc BSc. Born 29/9/55. Commd 15/9/74. Wg Cdr 1/7/93. Retd SUP 29/9/99.
KELLETT M., DFC. Born 25/9/17. Commd 7/9/40. Sqn Ldr 1/9/45. Retd GD 19/6/56 rtg Wg Cdr.
KELLEY J. W. D., BA. Born 27/11/30. Commd 10/1/61. Sqn Ldr 1/9/68. Retd ADMIN 17/12/74.
KELLEY W. E. J. Born 22/3/30. Commd 21/2/69. Flt Lt 21/2/72. Retd GD 1/11/76.
KELLY A. F. Born 10/11/37. Commd 28/4/61. Flt Lt 1/4/66. Retd GD 16/1/75.
KELLY A. G. Born 6/3/20. Commd 9/7/47. Flt Lt 9/1/52. Retd SUP 4/4/64.
KELLY A. W., BSc. Born 31/8/54. Commd 27/3/83. Flt Lt 27/3/84. Retd ADMIN 14/3/96.
KELLY B. J. Born 11/3/37. Commd 29/6/72. Sqn Ldr 1/1/80. Retd ENG 19/5/90.
KELLY C. J. Born 9/4/47. Commd 21/1/66. Flt Lt 4/5/72. Retd GD 1/12/73.
KELLY D. J. Born 3/9/21. Commd 19/9/44. Fg Offr 1/7/46. Retd RGT 25/9/50 rtg Flt Lt.
KELLY G. Born 13/11/42. Commd 10/6/66. Flt Lt 4/5/72. Retd GD 30/4/76.
KELLY G. C. Born 14/4/43. Commd 28/10/66. Flt Lt 28/4/72. Retd GD 18/1/83.
KELLY H. B., CB MVO MD BS FRCP MRCS DCH. Born 12/8/21. Commd 23/11/53. AVM 1/9/78. Retd MED
  26/3/83.
KELLY J. D. C., BM BCh MRCS LRCP FRCS. Born 15/3/30. Commd 16/10/55. Wg Cdr 16/10/68. Retd MED
  16/10/71.
KELLY L. E., CEng MRAeS. Born 12/4/32. Commd 28/10/55. Wg Cdr 1/7/75. Retd ENG 12/4/90.
KELLY M. Born 18/5/39. Commd 25/7/59. Flt Lt 25/1/65. Retd GD 18/5/77.
KELLY P. Born 14/10/46. Commd 21/7/65. Sqn Ldr 1/7/77. Retd GD 12/8/80.
KELLY P. A., OBE. Born 30/1/38. Commd 30/7/59. A Cdre 1/7/89. Retd ENG 2/7/91.
KELLY P. N. Born 22/8/38. Commd 9/10/75. Sqn Ldr 31/3/86. Retd MED(T) 25/4/91.
KELLY R. H., DPhysEd. Born 27/8/28. Commd 5/9/51. Flt Lt 5/9/55. Retd PE 26/3/67.
KELLY R. V. Born 4/6/26. Commd 1/3/62. Sqn Ldr 1/7/72. Retd SUP 4/6/84.
KELLY R. W., MIMgt. Born 20/3/22. Commd 24/12/44. Wg Cdr 1/7/71. Retd GD(G) 30/3/78.
KELLY Rev W. E., MA. Born 25/5/31. Commd 6/6/66. Retd 6/6/82 Wg Cdr
KELLY W. E. Born 9/4/28. Commd 26/7/50. Gp Capt 1/1/71. Retd GD 30/6/78.
KELLY W. W., DFC. Born 26/1/23. Commd 2/5/49. Flt Lt 17/5/56. Retd PI 31/1/75.
KELSEY H. C., DSO DFC*. Born 19/10/20. Commd 25/6/41. Wg Cdr 1/7/56. Retd GD 19/10/67.
KELSEY R. J. Born 17/7/17. Commd 29/6/36. Wg Cdr 1/7/50. Retd GD 15/6/59.
KELSEY W., MRAeS. Born 10/12/27. Commd 15/2/51. Flt Lt 15/11/54. Retd ENG 25/9/66.
KELSON G. M. Born 3/5/35. Commd 3/1/64. Flt Lt 4/5/72. Retd GD 10/9/79.
KELSON M. Born 7/3/31. Commd 21/6/56. Sqn Ldr 1/1/71. Retd GD 7/4/88.
KEMBALL Sir John., KCB CBE DL BA. Born 31/1/39. Commd 12/11/57. AM 10/11/89. Retd GD 30/4/93.
KEMBLE R. Born 13/1/41. Commd 9/10/64. Flt Lt 6/10/71. Retd GD 26/9/75. Reinstated 18/5/79. Flt Lt 28/5/75.
  Retd GD 13/1/96.

KEMLEY M. J., BA. Born 5/3/55. Commd 16/9/73. Wg Cdr 1/7/96. Retd ADMIN 18/8/00.
KEMMETT R. J. Born 19/1/35. Commd 23/3/66. Sqn Ldr 1/7/84. Retd GD 19/1/93.
KEMP C. A. Born 27/5/44. Commd 8/10/70. Flt Lt 8/4/76. Retd GD 1/4/92.
KEMP E. A. Born 20/8/43. Commd 18/10/62. Fg Offr 18/1/65. Retd SEC 17/10/68.
KEMP E. W. W., MBE CEng MIEE. Born 25/12/19. Commd 15/11/45. Wg Cdr 1/1/62. Retd ENG 1/6/70.
KEMP G. G. J. N., BSc MRAeS. Born 17/8/31. Commd 6/3/52. Sqn Ldr 4/3/65. Retd EDN 17/5/74.
KEMP G. J., CB. Born 14/7/21. Commd 3/12/41. AVM 1/7/73. Retd SEC 8/11/75.
KEMP H. A. Born 30/8/51. Commd 16/9/71. Plt Offr 23/12/71. Retd RGT 24/7/73.
KEMP I. H., CEng MRAeS. Born 7/4/26. Commd 21/6/56. Sqn Ldr 1/1/64. Retd ENG 7/4/84.
KEMP J. A. Born 28/9/15. Commd 18/11/41. Sqn Ldr 1/8/47. Retd RGT 28/5/58.
KEMP M. J. Born 30/4/34. Commd 20/1/64. GD Sqn Ldr 1/1/82. Retd GD 30/4/92.
KEMP N. L. D., DFC. Born 24/7/19. Commd 7/9/40. Flt Lt 25/9/48. Retd GD 31/8/66.
KEMP P., BSc. Born 12/2/47. Commd 1/11/71. Flt Lt 1/5/76. Retd GD 1/11/87.
KEMP P. J. Born 16/1/39. Commd 25/7/60. Gp Capt 1/7/83. Retd GD 1/10/89.
KEMP P. J. Born 26/7/36. Commd 31/7/61. Flt Lt 10/2/67. Retd RGT 31/7/77.
KEMP R. G., QVRM AE FRIN. Born 24/3/47. Commd 21/1/66. Sqn Ldr 1/1/78. Retd GD 24/3/85.
KEMP R. J. M., MBE BSc. Born 14/11/52. Commd 3/10/76. Sqn Ldr 1/7/87. Retd SY 2/4/93.
KEMP W. J. Born 21/12/40. Commd 18/12/62. Sqn Ldr 1/1/75. Retd GD 21/12/90.
KEMPEN E. McM. Born 7/1/15. Commd 13/3/46. Flt Lt 7/6/51. Retd RGT 17/4/54.
KEMPSELL A. J., BSc. Born 30/9/53. Commd 29/7/72. Flt Lt 15/10/79. Retd ENG 30/9/91.
KEMPSTER M. J., BSc. Born 22/7/41. Commd 13/6/66. Sqn Ldr 1/1/82. Retd GD 22/7/96.
KEMSLEY A. H. Born 7/4/98. Commd 15/10/40. Flt Lt 1/12/44. Retd SEC 5/3/47. rtg Sqn Ldr.
KEMSLEY R. W. Born 15/3/20. Commd 9/2/43. Wg Cdr 1/1/71. Retd ENG 26/2/77.
KENDAL S. R. Born 14/9/18. Commd 26/3/38. Flt Lt 27/11/45. Retd GD 1/11/61 rtg Sqn Ldr.
KENDALL E. P., MBE MIMgt. Born 19/10/37. Commd 17/7/56. Wg Cdr 1/1/87. Retd GD 19/10/92.
KENDALL F. M. Born 31/3/12. Commd 9/5/41. Flt Lt 1/9/45. Retd SUP 20/7/57 rtg Sqn Ldr.
KENDALL P. J. Born 21/10/38. Commd 12/10/63. Flt Lt 10/2/67. Retd GD 25/7/85.
KENDRA P. G. Born 2/7/18. Commd 9/7/53. Sqn Ldr 1/1/65. Retd ENG 5/10/68.
KENDRICK C. E. Born 19/8/39. Commd 6/9/63. Flt Lt 15/4/70. Retd GD 21/5/79. Reinstated 1/8/90. Flt Lt 1/8/84.
   Retd GD 19/8/94.
KENDRICK D. A., BA. Born 5/3/45. Commd 15/7/66. Wg Cdr 1/1/85. Retd ENG 16/9/89.
KENDRICK D. I., MIDPM. Born 4/2/47. Commd 4/3/71. Gp Capt 1/1/97. Retd SUP 18/5/01.
KENDRICK E. C. Born 8/9/31. Commd 7/10/57. Sqn Ldr 1/7/68. Retd GD 1/7/71.
KENDRICK F. W. Born 11/10/21. Commd 9/7/44. Sqn Ldr 1/1/59. Retd PRT 11/10/68 rtg Wg Cdr.
KENDRICK I., LRCM ARCM. Born 17/2/40. Commd 21/4/77. Sqn Ldr 5/10/86. Retd DM 8/5/90.
KENDRICK J. D. Born 5/10/42. Commd 30/7/63. Sqn Ldr 1/7/73. Retd GD 5/10/80.
KENDRICK J. M. Born 20/5/45. Commd 26/9/72. Flt Lt 10/5/79. Retd GD(G) 27/6/92.
KENDRICK K. R., IEng. Born 4/12/42. Commd 9/2/66. Sqn Ldr 1/7/79. Retd ENG 4/7/97.
KENDRICK L., CBE MRAeS. Born 16/4/19. Commd 5/11/41. Gp Capt 1/1/64. Retd ENG 1/8/67.
KENDRICK O. M. J. Born 17/10/32. Commd 19/9/59. Flt Lt 19/3/70. Retd GD 17/10/70.
KENDRICK V. B., BA FIMgt. Born 27/6/32. Commd 24/8/56. Gp Capt 1/7/77. Retd ADMIN 1/9/83.
KENEFICK J. H. P. Born 16/3/24. Commd 27/2/44. Flt Lt 27/2/50. Retd ADMIN 16/3/82.
KENNEDY A. J. Born 3/3/11. Commd 5/2/32. Wg Cdr 1/10/46. Retd GD 29/8/47.
KENNEDY A. K. M. Born 16/12/13. Commd 6/10/41. Flt Offr 1/9/45. Retd SEC 14/8/52.
KENNEDY B. J. O. Born 13/11/49. Commd 9/10/75. Wg Cdr 1/7/92. Retd ADMIN 13/5/00.
KENNEDY C. G., MSc MB BS MRCGP DRCOG DAvMed. Born 8/6/54. Commd 20/8/78. Wg Cdr 20/8/91. Retd MED
   31/7/97.
KENNEDY C. J. Born 28/12/48. Commd 31/7/70. Sqn Ldr 1/1/97. Retd GD 31/5/00.
KENNEDY C. W. N., MBE. Born 28/8/27. Commd 31/5/50. Wg Cdr 1/7/71. Retd GD 1/5/79.
KENNEDY D. A. Born 19/6/49. Commd 10/5/73. Flt Lt 10/11/78. Retd GD 22/1/89.
KENNEDY E. O. Born 1/6/20. Commd 4/4/45. Wg Cdr 1/7/69. Retd PRT 31/1/73.
KENNEDY G., AFC DFM. Born 11/4/12. Commd 1/4/40. Wg Cdr 1/1/54. Retd GD 11/4/59.
KENNEDY G. A. A. Born 23/4/33. Commd 2/3/61. Flt Lt 2/9/65. Retd GD 30/5/86.
KENNEDY G. F., Sol. Born 30/7/12. Commd 5/9/55. Wg Cdr 5/9/68. Retd LGL 5/9/72.
KENNEDY G. S. Born 9/2/44. Commd 21/12/62. Sqn Ldr 1/7/75. Retd GD 9/3/97.
KENNEDY I. D., BSc. Born 21/3/52. Commd 14/9/75. Flt Lt 14/12/76. Retd GD 14/9/87.
KENNEDY J. Born 9/10/29. Commd 16/9/71. Sqn Ldr 1/7/79. Retd ADMIN 16/6/83.
KENNEDY K. T. Born 9/4/39. Commd 9/3/66. Wg Cdr 1/1/80. Retd GD(G) 22/10/86.
KENNEDY M. Born 17/5/36. Commd 31/10/69. Flt Lt 4/5/72. Retd ENG 31/10/77.
KENNEDY M. H. Born 20/11/44. Commd 4/7/69. Flt Lt 4/1/75. Retd GD 6/10/98.
KENNEDY P. A., DSO DFC AFC. Born 15/5/17. Commd 7/3/42. A Cdre 1/7/67. Retd GD 15/12/67.
KENNEDY P. J. Born 4/2/56. Commd 27/2/75. Flt Lt 27/8/80. Retd GD 1/10/89.
KENNEDY P. R. Born 30/10/37. Commd 8/11/68. Flt Lt 29/11/71. Retd SUP 20/6/78.
KENNEDY R. N. Born 16/1/43. Commd 6/4/62. Flt Lt 6/10/67. Retd GD 1/2/75.
KENNEDY R. R. Born 10/5/19. Commd 26/8/42. Flt Lt 7/6/51. Retd GD 28/6/68.
KENNEDY S. Born 25/12/56. Commd 30/4/81. Sqn Ldr 1/7/94. Retd GD 14/3/96.

KENNEDY Sir Thomas., GCB AFC*. Born 19/5/28. Commd 8/4/49. ACM 1/7/83. Retd GD 10/5/86.
KENNEDY T. Born 7/5/44. Commd 22/11/84. Sqn Ldr 1/6/94. Retd ENG 7/5/99.
KENNEDY T., MBE DFC* MIMgt. Born 22/2/23. Commd 21/7/44. Wg Cdr 1/7/66. Retd GD 1/11/72.
KENNELL J. M., MSc. Born 11/11/42. Commd 26/11/60. Gp Capt 1/7/93. Retd GD 11/5/98.
KENNELLY B. C. Born 28/2/33. Commd 4/10/51. Sqn Ldr 1/7/65. Retd GD 19/11/73.
KENNETT P. Born 16/1/30. Commd 30/7/52. Flt Lt 17/5/56. Retd GD 16/1/68.
KENNETT R. J., MSc BA FInstPet MCIPS MIMIS. Born 11/7/44. Commd 15/7/66. Wg Cdr 1/1/96. Retd SUP
    11/7/99.
KENNETT R. J. Born 12/1/31. Commd 20/5/57. Flt Lt 13/12/59. Retd SEC 2/3/69.
KENNEY E. StB., BA BAI. Born 14/7/20. Commd 4/1/45. Wg Cdr 1/1/65. Retd ACB 19/7/75.
KENNEY K. L. Born 20/5/36. Commd 12/11/54. Flt Lt 12/5/60. Retd GD 20/5/74.
KENNY T. J. Born 9/6/37. Commd 29/7/55. Flt Lt 7/3/62. Retd GD 9/6/75.
KENRICK M. E. Born 4/2/32. Commd 27/2/52. Sqn Ldr 1/1/89. Retd GD 9/2/90.
KENT A. J., BSc CEng MIEE. Born 1/1/45. Commd 15/7/66. Wg Cdr 1/1/82. Retd ENG 1/1/89.
KENT H. M., MSc CEng MRAeS. Born 7/2/29. Commd 17/1/51. Gp Capt 1/1/83. Retd ENG 7/2/84.
KENT J. W. L., CEng MIMechE. Born 23/3/37. Commd 17/11/59. Wg Cdr 1/7/77. Retd ENG 2/10/84.
KENT K. J. Born 26/9/42. Commd 31/7/86. Flt Lt 31/7/90. Retd OPS SPT 26/9/97.
KENT L. D. Born 11/11/12. Commd 10/12/42. Fg Offr 10/6/43. Retd ENG 15/6/47 rtg Flt Lt.
KENT P. E. M. Born 15/7/37. Commd 16/12/58. Wg Cdr 1/7/74. Retd SUP 19/1/79.
KENT P. L., MB ChB MRCGP DRCOG DAvMed. Born 5/8/49. Commd 6/7/86. Wg Cdr 6/7/92. Retd MED 14/3/97.
KENT R. J. Born 11/10/44. Commd 22/5/64. Sqn Ldr 1/1/81. Retd SUP 31/3/94.
KENT W., AFC. Born 14/1/21. Commd 9/7/43. Gp Capt 1/1/66. Retd GD 14/1/71.
KENT W. W. Born 1/9/24. Commd 12/9/51. Flt Lt 12/6/56. Retd GD 21/9/65.
KENTISH L. Born 6/10/28. Commd 3/4/59. Sqn Ldr 1/1/71. Retd ENG 7/4/79.
KENVYN I. P., BSc. Born 17/8/50. Commd 15/9/69. Sqn Ldr 1/1/84. Retd GD 17/8/88.
KENWARD The Rev R. N., MA. Born 12/6/34. Commd 1/1/64. Retd 12/6/89. Wg Cdr.
KENWORTHY F. C., BA. Born 13/8/16. Commd 3/1/51. Sqn Ldr 3/11/54. Retd EDN 1/11/64.
KENWORTHY J. M. Born 10/3/20. Commd 11/4/44. Flt Lt 11/4/46. Retd SEC 12/3/74.
KENYON A. Born 2/4/21. Commd 17/9/43. Flt Lt 18/10/65. Retd GD 30/3/68.
KENYON B. Born 7/8/31. Commd 4/3/71. Flt Lt 4/3/75. Retd ADMIN 19/2/88.
KENYON G. B., CEng MIMechE. Born 25/10/35. Commd 27/11/58. Wg Cdr 1/1/74. Retd ENG 11/7/88.
KEOGH J. McK. Born 19/12/17. Commd 6/10/44. Sqn Ldr 1/1/60. Retd SEC 12/1/73.
KEOGH R. P. Born 3/8/25. Commd 8/10/57. Flt Lt 7/6/51. Retd GD 17/12/57.
KEOGH T. C. Born 6/5/29. Commd 15/9/60. Flt Lt 15/9/66. Retd PE 14/9/68.
KEPPEL-COMPTON R. W. Born 24/1/38. Commd 6/6/57. Gp Capt 1/1/85. Retd ADMIN 1/12/88.
KEPPIE I. H., AFC. Born 22/7/33. Commd 27/7/54. Gp Capt 1/1/73. Retd GD 29/3/75.
KER N. R. Born 14/11/12. Commd 16/2/49. Flt Lt 3/7/49. Retd GD 14/11/64.
KER R. F. Born 17/12/37. Commd 21/7/61. Flt Lt 25/7/66. Retd GD 31/1/70.
KERBY R. S. Born 8/9/22. Commd 24/1/42. Wg Cdr 1/1/62. Retd GD 16/9/68.
KERMEEN R. W., MSc BSc FBCS PGCE. Born 1/4/41. Commd 30/8/66. Sqn Ldr 1/3/73. Retd ADMIN 30/8/82.
    Reinstated 4/5/83. Wg Cdr 1/1/87. Retd ADMIN 1/10/95.
KERMODE R. E. T. Born 9/7/23. Commd 3/2/44. Sqn Ldr 1/10/55. Retd ENG 4/4/69.
KERNS R. K., MSc BTECH. Born 5/9/48. Commd 1/9/71. Sqn Ldr 1/7/79. Retd ENG 1/9/87.
KERR C., MIMgt. Born 7/3/17. Commd 21/10/54. Sqn Ldr 1/1/66. Retd ENG 7/6/74.
KERR D. B. Born 12/5/33. Commd 6/5/53. Flt Lt 7/3/62. Retd GD 9/4/72.
KERR D. C. Born 6/12/33. Commd 8/9/54. Flt Lt 6/3/63. Retd GD 1/6/77.
KERR G. J. A., AFC. Born 21/2/24. Commd 25/9/52. Sqn Ldr 1/1/70. Retd GD 21/2/79.
KERR H. R., OBE. Born 6/2/20. Commd 29/5/42. Wg Cdr 1/7/58. Retd GD 6/3/63.
KERR J. L., MA ARCM. Born 25/11/16. Commd 1/1/43. Wg Cdr 1/7/57. Retd GD 1/4/668.
KERR K. J. Born 26/9/28. Commd 28/2/51. Flt Lt 28/11/56. Retd GD 26/9/66.
KERR R. G. Born 16/5/35. Commd 17/12/57. Sqn Ldr 1/7/66. Retd GD 16/5/73.
KERR T. Born 26/10/48. Commd 11/5/78. Sqn Ldr 1/1/87. Retd SUP 31/10/96.
KERRIDGE G. E. Born 12/2/18. Commd 10/8/40. Sqn Ldr 1/7/51. Retd GD 11/12/57.
KERRIDGE M. H. Born 12/1/41. Commd 11/8/77. Flt Lt 11/8/78. Retd ADMIN 11/8/85.
KERRIDGE R. S., BEng. Born 30/5/38. Commd 23/10/59. Flt Lt 2/7/63. Retd GD 2/10/77.
KERRIGAN C. P. Born 13/6/53. Commd 15/8/85. Sqn Ldr 1/1/93. Retd ENG 15/11/96.
KERRIGAN E., CEng MRAeS. Born 29/9/15. Commd 25/3/43. Sqn Ldr 1/7/54. Retd ENG 5/11/64.
KERRIGAN J. G. Born 8/4/33. Commd 27/7/54. Gp Capt 1/7/84. Retd SEC 8/12/86.
KERRISON P. I., BSc CEng MIMechE MRAeS. Born 24/10/42. Commd 15/7/64. Sqn Ldr 1/7/77. Retd ENG
    24/10/99.
KERSHAW J. B., MB ChB MRCPath. Born 17/4/47. Commd 27/4/70. Sqn Ldr 13/8/78. Retd MED 14/7/86.
KERSHAW M. E., DPhysEd MIMgt. Born 6/3/47. Commd 19/8/68. Sqn Ldr 1/1/82. Retd ADMIN 21/5/01.
KERSHAW R. M. Born 24/2/20. Commd 29/6/50. Sqn Ldr 1/7/61. Retd SUP 15/10/70.
KERSLEY J. A., MB ChB MRCS LRCP FRCS(E) DLO. Born 25/4/06. Commd 18/7/31. Wg Cdr 1/12/43. Retd MED
    21/12/46.
KERSS T. J., MBE BSc. Born 29/6/57. Commd 31/8/75. Wg Cdr 1/7/93. Retd GD 1/7/96.

KERSWELL R. H. Born 9/2/22. Commd 21/7/44. Flt Lt 29/6/50. Retd GD 15/10/62.
KERTLAND R. J., MIMgt. Born 13/1/19. Commd 22/3/51. Sqn Ldr 1/7/62. Retd ENG 14/4/72.
KESSELER P. J. Born 11/5/37. Commd 5/11/59. Gp Capt 1/1/86. Retd SUP 11/5/92.
KESTERTON P., BA. Born 17/1/54. Commd 7/6/73. Flt Lt 7/12/79. Retd GD(G) 23/4/82.
KETCHER L. S., AFM. Born 14/11/23. Commd 4/3/44. Sqn Ldr 1/1/75. Retd GD 30/9/77.
KETTELL L. P. Born 3/12/60. Commd 31/1/80. Sqn Ldr 1/1/91. Retd SUP 3/12/98.
KETTLE A., MBE. Born 22/11/19. Commd 25/8/55. Sqn Ldr 1/7/74. Retd GD(G) 8/9/77.
KETTLE J. D. N., MA CEng FIEE. Born 5/4/36. Commd 30/9/56. Gp Capt 1/1/79. Retd ENG 7/5/90.
KETTLEWELL G. V. W. Born 30/1/16. Commd 31/7/37. Wg Cdr 1/1/49. Retd GD 1/4/59.
KEVAN R. G., BA. Born 14/12/38. Commd 15/1/63. Sqn Ldr 29/4/70. Retd EDN 15/1/79.
KEWIN J. A. Born 22/1/43. Commd 9/3/62. Flt Lt 9/9/67. Retd GD 27/5/96.
KEY G. C., OBE DFC MA. Born 1/1/14. Commd 4/5/36. Gp Capt 1/7/55. Retd GD 1/1/64.
KEY S. W. R. A. Born 12/9/34. Commd 26/7/55. Sqn Ldr 1/1/66. Retd GD 12/9/94.
KEYS A. R., DFC BSc. Born 21/2/29. Commd 29/12/51. Wg Cdr 1/1/66. Retd GD 2/7/70.
KEYS D. Born 22/4/28. Commd 12/1/55. Flt Lt 29/4/59. Retd GD 18/6/66.
KEYS P. E. Born 2/12/34. Commd 19/8/65. Flt Lt 19/8/70. Retd GD 3/4/79.
KEYTE H. W. Born 1/11/16. Commd 4/1/47. Sqn Ldr 1/7/62. Retd SUP 1/11/74.
KEYTE S.W., OBE BA. Born 27/12/41. Commd 6/7/62. Wg Cdr 1/7/86. Retd GD 3/4/93. Rtg Gp Capt.
KEYWORTH G. Born 2/1/47. Commd 25/2/66. Flt Lt 25/8/72. Retd SUP 2/1/85.
KHAN F. A., MSc BSc CEng MIExpE MIMechE. Born 24/6/48. Commd 15/6/71. Sqn Ldr 1/1/83. Retd ENG 14/3/97.
KHAN R., BEng. Born 4/7/60. Commd 1/8/86. Flt Lt 3/7/91. Retd ENG 5/7/99.
KHAREGAT R. P. Born 16/2/36. Commd 31/7/56. Sqn Ldr 1/1/72. Retd GD 16/2/74.
KIDD A. M., BSc. Born 25/7/56. Commd 30/10/77. Sqn Ldr 1/7/89. Retd ENG 25/7/00.
KIDD B. J. G., MIMgt. Born 20/3/32. Commd 2/2/56. Gp Capt 1/1/77. Retd ENG 1/4/85.
KIDD C. Born 8/6/20. Commd 10/8/43. Flt Lt 10/11/55. Retd GD 1/11/61.
KIDD D. A., MBE CEng MIERE. Born 17/8/33. Commd 6/6/57. Gp Capt 1/1/85. Retd ENG 17/8/88.
KIDD E. A. Born 7/5/45. Commd 22/5/83. Flt Lt 27/7/76. Retd GD 1/8/94.
KIDD M. A. M. Born 13/7/44. Commd 25/10/63. Gp Capt 1/7/94. Retd ADMIN 14/7/96.
KIDD W. R. Born 21/3/37. Commd 25/6/57. Flt Lt 3/1/63. Retd GD 5/4/75.
KIDDLE P. G. Born 5/3/45. Commd 31/1/64. Sqn Ldr 1/1/82. Retd GD 5/3/89.
KIDNEY R., AFC. Born 9/11/35. Commd 30/7/57. Gp Capt 1/1/87. Retd GD 16/7/88.
KIERNAN A. H. Born 1/4/13. Commd 7/1/43. Flt Lt 7/7/47. Retd PE 21/4/68.
KIGGELL L. J. Born 18/4/41. Commd 22/7/66. Wg Cdr 1/7/85. Retd GD(G) 5/2/96.
KIGGELL P. S., OBE. Born 27/4/43. Commd 3/1/64. Gp Capt 1/1/92. Retd GD 2/1/94.
KILBURN P., BSc. Born 29/1/30. Commd 21/12/52. Sqn Ldr 21/6/63. Retd ADMIN 1/11/86.
KILBY K. R. Born 5/3/54. Commd 8/12/83. Flt Lt 8/12/85. Retd ENG 2/4/93.
KILCOYNE J. G. Born 20/5/39. Commd 18/10/79. Sqn Ldr 1/1/88. Retd SY 20/5/94.
KILDUFF J. E., CBE FIMgt MRIN. Born 23/2/22. Commd 24/7/42. Gp Capt 1/1/68. Retd GD 23/2/77.
KILFORD P. C. Born 8/11/54. Commd 24/4/80. Sqn Ldr 1/1/89. Retd ENG 31/3/94.
KILFORD R. I., BSc. Born 6/1/59. Commd 29/8/77. Sqn Ldr 1/1/90. Retd ENG 6/1/97.
KILGORE D. I. Born 14/4/44. Commd 2/4/65. Flt Lt 4/5/72. Retd GD(G) 2/12/77.
KILLICK M. R. Born 4/10/38. Commd 30/4/57. Gp Capt 1/7/87. Retd GD 4/10/93.
KILLINGRAY A. J. Born 24/5/44. Commd 3/7/80. Sqn Ldr 1/1/90. Retd ENG 19/11/97.
KILMINSTER M. R. Born 25/6/47. Commd 27/11/68. Fg Offr 12/10/69. Retd GD 31/5/73.
KILNER A. Born 23/9/34. Commd 30/6/66. Flt Lt 30/8/66. Retd PI 4/3/78.
KILPATRICK N. D., BA MB BChir MRCS LRCP FRCOG. Born 8/12/31. Commd 4/1/59. Wg Cdr 2/2/71. Retd MED 2/11/78.
KIMBER A. B. Born 6/11/40. Commd 17/5/63. Fg Offr 17/5/65. Retd GD 6/4/66.
KIMBER P. L. Born 24/9/20. Commd 18/3/45. Flt Lt 22/10/48. Retd GD 20/7/65.
KIMBERLEY R. G. Born 10/8/48. Commd 29/10/68. Flt Lt 29/5/74. Retd GD 19/10/80.
KIMBREY C. G. Born 29/7/07. Commd 1/12/41. Wg Cdr 1/7/53. Retd ENG 29/9/62.
KIME A. B. Born 24/6/34. Commd 27/2/70. Sqn Ldr 1/1/78. Retd ENG 24/6/92.
KIME K. C. Born 17/9/33. Commd 16/2/59. Sqn Ldr 1/1/83. Retd GD(G) 31/12/85.
KIME K. G. Born 25/4/37. Commd 19/2/76. Sqn Ldr 1/1/89. Retd ENG 25/4/95.
KIMMINGS R. W., MBE. Born 29/4/22. Commd 24/2/55. Sqn Ldr 1/1/71. Retd GD 29/4/77.
KINCH D. G., DFM. Born 6/6/29. Commd 9/9/54. Sqn Ldr 1/1/65. Retd GD 8/6/79.
KINDELL F. J., BA. Born 3/1/62. Commd 25/11/84. Flt Lt 25/5/87. Retd ADMIN 25/11/00.
KINDER C. T. Born 4/8/28. Commd 27/2/52. Flt Lt 7/3/62. Retd GD 4/2/67.
KINDER E., FCIS MIMgt. Born 3/5/31. Commd 15/6/50. Gp Capt 1/7/76. Retd SEC 7/10/81.
KINDER J. R. Born 31/10/62. Commd 8/4/82. Flt Lt 8/10/87. Retd GD 30/11/00.
KINDER R. Born 9/10/23. Commd 7/7/49. Sqn Ldr 1/7/59. Retd GD 9/10/72.
KING A. D. Born 16/9/23. Commd 21/11/56. Flt Lt 22/5/60. Retd GD 27/2/82.
KING A. F., CEng MIMechE. Born 23/3/33. Commd 30/5/61. Sqn Ldr 1/7/69. Retd ENG 27/5/83.
KING A. J., MInstPet MCIPS. Born 25/6/43. Commd 12/7/63. Sqn Ldr 1/1/76. Retd SUP 17/7/93.
KING A. R., MIMgt. Born 19/8/31. Commd 21/11/56. Wg Cdr 1/7/76. Retd GD 19/4/85.
KING A. S., CEng MRACS MIEE. Born 15/3/35. Commd 2/10/57. Wg Cdr 1/7/75. Retd ENG 1/4/87.

KING A. V. Born 26/5/16. Commd 1/11/45. Flt Lt 4/1/51. Retd ENG 17/7/54.
KING B. Born 15/3/33. Commd 21/10/65. Sqn Ldr 1/1/78. Retd SUP 15/5/80.
KING B. A. R. Born 1/4/19. Commd 1/5/47. Flt Lt 1/11/51. Retd SUP 31/7/64.
KING B. H. Born 25/3/38. Commd 21/7/61. Flt Lt 9/5/66. Retd GD 25/3/76.
KING B. J. Born 8/8/33. Commd 4/6/52. Flt Lt 30/10/57. Retd GD 8/8/70.
KING B. M. Born 1/7/10. Commd27/1/43. Flt Offr 27/1/48. Retd SEC 5/1/50.
KING B. W. Born 12/2/48. Commd 28/2/69. Flt Lt 28/2/72. Retd GD 12/8/92.
KING C., OBE CEng MRAeS MIMgt. Born 2/9/21. Commd 24/5/51. Gp Capt 1/1/71. Retd ENG 2/10/75.
KING C. Born 13/12/49. Commd 28/11/69. Sqn Ldr 1/7/90. Retd GD 22/4/94.
KING C. H. Born 16/3/19. Commd 29/8/45. Flt Lt 4/12/52. Retd SEC 29/4/69.
KING D. Born 13/9/30. Commd 28/2/51. Flt Lt 20/12/56. Retd GD 31/7/62.
KING D. Born 20/9/34. Commd 24/2/61. Flt Lt 1/4/66. Retd GD 20/9/72.
KING E., DFC. Born 8/3/19. Commd 3/4/48. Flt Lt 3/4/48. Retd GD 31/3/62.
KING E. Born 20/1/36. Commd 16/9/71. Flt Lt 17/8/76. Retd MED(T) 21/1/78.
KING E. H., OBE. Born 6/3/18. Commd 15/4/39. Wg Cdr 1/7/56. Retd GD 6/3/65.
KING E. T., MB BS DPH LMSSA. Born 21/3/22. Commd 29/6/50. Wg Cdr 15/12/62. Retd MED 30/10/73.
KING E. T. I., MRAeS MIMgt. Born 26/5/44. Commd 3/1/64. Gp Capt 1/1/86. Retd 20/4/87.
KING F. G. Born 23/10/22. Commd 3/5/56. Sqn Ldr 1/7/71. Retd GD(G) 23/10/77.
KING F. G. H. Born 13/12/20. Commd 31/7/61. Flt Lt 31/7/61. Retd SEC 13/12/70.
KING G. A., MIMgt. Born 28/6/32. Commd 5/2/53. Wg Cdr 1/1/74. Retd GD 12/9/83.
KING G. A. Born 13/8/47. Commd 28/6/79. Sqn Ldr 1/1/86. Retd ADMIN 27/11/95.
KING G. H., MBE. Born 6/3/10. Commd 21/1/43. Sqn Ldr 1/7/54. Retd ENG 6/3/65.
KING H., OBE. Born 11/5/18. Commd 9/12/42. Gp Capt 1/1/64. Retd GD 11/5/73.
KING J. Born 6/11/20. Commd 12/6/43. Sqn Ldr 1/4/55. Retd GD 1/3/62.
KING J. Born 14/6/30. Commd 13/8/52. Sqn Ldr 1/7/66. Retd GD 1/1/69.
KING J., BSc. Born 29/12/50. Commd 14/11/69. Flt Lt 15/10/73. Retd GD 1/2/88.
KING J. A., AFC. Born 31/12/43. Commd 22/2/63. Gp Capt 1/1/91. Retd GD 31/12/98.
KING J. A. Born 13/9/31. Commd 6/9/56. Sqn Ldr 1/1/83. Retd GD 13/9/88.
KING J. F., BEM. Born 27/4/16. Commd 31/7/58. Flt Lt 31/7/61. Retd SEC 7/11/65.
KING J. G. Born 30/8/42. Commd 22/7/71. Sqn Ldr 1/7/80. Retd ENG 7/6/97.
KING J. G., MRCS. Born 26/7/30. Commd 28/8/56. Gp Capt 28/8/79. Retd MED 10/4/87.
KING J. H., BA. Born 4/11/13. Commd 6/9/40. Wg Cdr 1/7/58. Retd SUP 13/4/67.
KING J. K., MIMgt. Born 21/6/20. Commd 30/1/58. Wg Cdr 7/9/72. Retd MED(SEC) 21/6/75.
KING J. M., MBE. Born 16/2/24. Commd 6/6/45. Sqn Ldr 1/1/74. Retd GD(G) 16/2/82.
KING J. M. Born 15/1/35. Commd 1/2/62. Sq Ldr 1/1/77. Retd SEC 4/4/87.
KING J. N. Born 23/12/14. Commd 26/7/45. Sqn Ldr 1/1/57. Retd SEC 23/12/63.
KING J. P. Born 12/6/37. Commd 9/3/66. Flt Lt 9/3/68. Retd GD 9/4/76.
KING J. S. Born 3/2/44. Commd 4/11/82. Sqn Ldr 1/7/91. Retd ENG 14/3/96.
KING J. W., DFC DFM FCIS. Born 26/5/22. Commd 8/12/42. Gp Capt 1/7/67. Retd GD 26/10/73.
KING M. D. J., BSc MIL. Born 20/5/51. Commd 2/1/70. Wg Cdr 1/1/92. Retd GD 20/5/95.
KING M. G. Born 28/11/30. Commd 1/8/51. Wg Cdr 1/7/72. Retd GD 29/11/80.
KING N. A. Born 1/1/62. Commd 26/11/81. Flt Lt 26/5/87. Retd GD 9/8/91.
KING N. M. Born 6/1/54. Commd 11/5/78. Flt Lt 11/11/83. Retd GD 10/10/93.
KING P., CBE FIMgt. Born 3/4/35. Commd 27/10/54. Air Cdre 1/7/85. Retd GD 27/5/88.
KING P. F., CB OBE FRCS(Edin) MFOM MRCS LRCP DLO MRAeS. Born 17/9/22. Commd 14/8/45. AVM 1/7/83. Retd MED 17/9/87.
KING P. T., MB BS FRCR DMRD. Born 24/7/36. Commd 21/1/63. Wg Cdr 4/12/77. Retd MED 19/11/78.
KING R. Born 31/8/23. Commd 6/6/57. Flt Lt 1/4/63. Retd GD 28/2/70.
KING R. A. D. Born 15/11/45. Commd 20/9/68. Flt Lt 20/3/74. Retd GD 17/10/86.
KING R. J. Born 4/9/12. Commd 22/4/43. Sqn Ldr 1/7/54. Retd ENG 30/4/66.
KING R. P. J. Born 27/8/29. Commd 12/12/51. Sqn Ldr 1/1/61. Retd GD 26/12/67.
KING R. S., BA. Born 12/3/32. Commd 11/12/52. Sqn Ldr 1/2/69. Retd EDN 1/5/80.
KING S. E. Born 29/4/22. Commd 3/8/61. Flt Lt 3/8/64. Retd ENG 29/4/72.
KING S. E. Born 3/7/31. Commd 28/7/53. A Cdre 1/1/79. Retd GD 29/11/82.
KING T. A. Born 31/1/48. Commd 4/10/78. Flt Lt 19/7/74. Retd GD(G) 21/2/93.
KING T. N. Born 2/10/34. Commd 10/4/56. Wg Cdr 1/7/82. Retd GD 2/10/89.
KING The Rev F. W. Born 4/2/24. Commd 20/5/55. Retd 18/6/70 Wg Cdr.
KING V. D., OBE. Born 25/2/33. Commd 8/10/56. Wg Cdr 1/1/74. Retd SUP 25/2/88.
KING W. C., AFC. Born 23/2/26. Commd 7/5/53. Flt Lt 7/11/56. Retd GD 3/8/64.
KING W. F. Born 18/1/43. Commd 21/2/74. Sqn Ldr 1/1/87. Retd ADMIN 18/1/98.
KING W. J., MBE. Born 26/12/19. Commd 30/7/59. Flt Lt 30/7/64. Retd ENG 31/5/73.
KINGAN J. G., MB ChB MFCM AFOM DPH. Born 27/11/23. Commd 2/6/49. Gp Capt 1/7/76. Retd MED 27/11/81.
KINGDOM A. A. Born 2/11/30. Commd 8/11/62. Sqn Ldr 1/7/72. Retd GD 2/11/85.
KINGDOM R. J., MBE. Born 12/5/22. Commd 11/6/45. Flt Lt 4/1/51. Retd GD 13/6/67.
KINGDON R. C. N. Born 21/10/32. Commd 26/3/52. Flt Lt 18/9/57. Retd GD(G) 21/10/88.
KINGHORN D. B. Born 20/5/31. Commd 27/4/61. Flt Lt 27/4/66. Retd GD 5/5/87.

KINGHORN R. A., MIMgt. Born 4/6/32. Commd 19/4/51. Wg Cdr 1/1/77. Retd SUP 1/10/84.
KINGON A. M., MBE MB BS MRCP MRCS. Born 1/9/20. Commd 12/4/49. Wg Cdr 1/4/62. Retd MED 1/10/67.
KINGS A. F., BSc. Born 2/7/59. Commd 3/9/79. Sqn Ldr 1/1/91. Retd ENG 2/7/97.
KINGS R. A. Born 22/10/14. Commd 3/8/40. Flt Lt 1/9/45. Retd GD(G) 27/10/64 rtg Sqn Ldr.
KINGSFORD P. G., BSc. Born 30/6/50. Commd 1/11/71. Sqn Ldr 1/1/84. Retd GD 30/6/88.
KINGSHOTT K., CBE DFC. Born 8/7/24. Commd 21/1/46. AVM 1/1/78. Retd GD 29/1/80.
KINGSLEY J. T. Born 21/11/36. Commd 10/8/55. Flt Lt 15/2/65. Retd GD 23/11/73.
KINGSTON D. W. Born 8/8/23. Commd 25/10/44. Flt Lt 25/4/48. Retd GD 8/8/66.
KINGSTON J. M., MB BS MRCS LRCP DAvMed. Born 20/5/43. Commd 11/5/80. Wg Cdr 11/5/86. Retd MED 14/3/96.
KINGSTON R. Born 10/11/44. Commd 17/12/65. Sqn Ldr 1/1/76. Retd GD 10/11/82.
KINGSTON R. A. Born 7/9/34. Commd 21/12/67. Sqn Ldr 1/1/77. Retd GD(G) 4/9/79.
KINGSTON-BROWN D. Born 29/7/51. Commd 16/9/76. Sqn Ldr 1/7/92. Retd ADMIN 31/8/95.
KINGSWOOD C. J. Born 12/12/58. Commd 11/1/79. Flt Lt 11/7/84. Retd GD 12/12/96.
KINGTON-BLAIR-OLIPHANT D. N., CB OBE BA. Born 22/12/11. Commd 17/3/33. A Cdre 1/7/58. Retd ENG 14/4/66 rtg AVM.
KINGWILL P. N. Born 24/11/14. Commd 9/5/54. Wg Cdr 1/7/59. Retd SUP 14/8/65.
KINNAIRD S., BA. Born 30/1/61. Commd 16/9/79. Sqn Ldr 1/7/92. Retd GD 1/9/99.
KINNARD R. M. Born 28/9/17. Commd 29/6/50. Sqn Ldr 1/7/65. Retd SUP 28/9/72.
KINNEAR J. T. Born 16/8/26. Commd 4/6/64. Flt Lt 4/6/67. Retd ENG 1/6/74.
KINNIN V. Born 18/5/42. Commd 22/5/80. Sqn Ldr 1/1/90. Retd ENG 18/5/97.
KINVER J. A. Born 15/10/19. Commd 20/8/43. Flt Lt 31/12/47. Retd GD 20/6/64.
KINZETT R. H., BA FCIPD MInstAM. Born 23/9/49. Commd 17/1/72. Gp Capt 1/7/97. Retd ADMIN 1/10/00.
KIRBY B. C., BA. Born 24/12/37. Commd 23/7/58. Wg Cdr 1/7/80. Retd ENG 29/5/89.
KIRBY E. F., MIMgt. Born 23/6/25. Commd 6/10/44. Wg Cdr 1/7/62. Retd GD 19/6/76.
KIRBY M. A. Born 25/12/45. Commd 2/2/68. Flt Lt 2/8/74. Retd SUP 5/5/79.
KIRBY N. R. Born 29/5/46. Commd 5/2/65. Sqn Ldr 1/7/79. Retd GD 29/5/90.
KIRBY R. A. Born 5/9/44. Commd 17/7/64. Sqn Ldr 1/1/79. Retd GD 5/9/84.
KIRBY R. S. Born 6/1/05. Commd 3/8/40. Flt Lt 1/9/45. Retd SUP 9/10/48.
KIRBY R. S., BA. Born 11/9/52. Commd 25/9/71. Flt Lt 15/4/78. Retd ADMIN 1/2/83.
KIRBY W. J., MBE. Born 8/10/36. Commd 15/2/56. Wg Cdr 1/7/79. Retd GD 8/4/87.
KIRK A. C. Born 23/1/23. Commd 10/12/43. Wg Cdr 1/1/65. Retd SEC 2/12/67.
KIRK A. N. Born 20/12/31. Commd 7/12/54. Sqn Ldr 1/1/63. Retd ENG 9/12/70.
KIRK A. P. Born 9/5/47. Commd 20/9/68. Wg Cdr 1/1/93. Retd GD 5/1/01.
KIRK A. W., MB ChB DAvMed DRCOG ALCM. Born 13/12/52. Commd 22/1/74. Wg Cdr 7/2/91. Retd MED 22/7/93.
KIRK E. A. Born 21/7/26. Commd 17/12/52. Flt Lt 12/5/58. Retd GD 2/1/64.
KIRK G. H. Born 17/11/43. Commd 9/3/62. Flt Lt 9/9/67. Retd GD 17/11/81. Re-entrant 14/9/83. Sqn Ldr 1/7/90. Retd GD 17/11/98.
KIRK J. E., OBE. Born 18/9/03. Commd 28/7/34. Gp Capt 1/1/53. Retd GD 18/9/58.
KIRK J. M., MB ChB MRCGP. Born 16/5/43. Commd 18/4/66. Sqn Ldr 1/8/74. Retd MED 18/4/82.
KIRK J. S., MBE. Born 16/5/34. Commd 13/8/52. Sqn Ldr 1/7/79. Retd GD 30/12/84.
KIRK J. S. Born 28/6/50. Commd 31/10/69. Flt Lt 30/4/75. Retd GD 28/6/88.
KIRK M. A. Born 2/2/44. Commd 24/6/65. Flt Lt 1/7/68. Retd GD 10/9/76.
KIRK R., MIMgt. Born 13/6/33. Commd 23/3/55. Sqn Ldr 1/1/66. Retd GD 13/6/71.
KIRK W. E. Born 8/2/31. Commd 9/4/52. Wg Cdr 1/1/73. Retd GD 20/5/83.
KIRKBRIDE R. Born 10/5/24. Commd 2/6/44. Flt Lt 10/11/55. Retd GD 30/11/78.
KIRKHAM A. J. A., BSc. Born 20/1/57. Commd 2/3/80. Flt Lt 2/6/83. Retd GD(G) 2/3/96.
KIRKHAM R. N. Born 19/1/43. Commd 21/7/65. Flt Lt 12/11/69. Retd GD 19/8/81.
KIRKHAM R. R. Born 15/7/33. Commd 1/7/83. Sqn Ldr 1/7/83. Retd ENG 28/11/86.
KIRKLAND B. S. Born 18/2/41. Commd 3/10/61. Sqn Ldr 1/1/72. Retd SEC 18/2/79.
KIRKLAND D. W. Born 29/10/33. Commd 27/3/56. Flt Lt 7/7/63. Retd GD 24/7/73.
KIRKLAND G., BSc. Born 23/10/43. Commd 26/9/66. Flt Lt 26/6/68. Retd GD 26/9/82.
KIRKMAN W. G. Born 20/6/29. Commd 26/11/53. Flt Lt 26/5/58. Retd GD 16/1/64.
KIRKPATRICK P. S. Born 29/1/47. Commd 27/1/77. Flt Lt 27/1/79. Retd MED 29/1/85.
KIRKPATRICK W. J., BA. Born 10/8/53. Commd 19/10/75. Wg Cdr 1/7/91. Retd GD 1/2/98.
KIRKPATRICK W. J., BSc. Born 26/2/53. Commd 30/10/72. Flt Lt 15/10/75. Retd GD 30/10/84.
KIRKWOOD A. S., MA. Born 12/4/11. Commd 20/9/48. Sqn Ldr 12/2/53. Retd EDN 22/8/61.
KIRTLEY S. Born 6/11/21. Commd 25/4/42. Wg Cdr 1/1/61. Retd GD 1/9/68.
KIRTON P. A. M. Born 8/3/61. Commd 14/1/88. Flt Lt 14/1/90. Retd GD 2/1/96.
KIRTON P. J., BEng. Born 22/9/49. Commd 18/4/71. Flt Lt 15/10/73. Retd GD 22/9/87.
KISSANE R. C. Born 2/1/33. Commd 12/10/54. Flt Lt 12/4/60. Retd GD(G) 26/4/87.
KITCHEN S. Born 27/2/16. Commd 19/3/44. Flt Lt 19/9/47. Retd GD 9/5/58.
KITCHENER B. Born 8/9/35. Commd 21/7/61. Fg Offr 21/7/63. Retd GD 23/7/66.
KITCHENER D. H. Born 8/3/86. Commd 4/8/64. Sqn Ldr 1/7/82. Retd SUP 13/9/86.
KITCHIN J. S. F. Born 15/8/46. Commd 25/6/65. Flt Lt 25/12/70. Retd GD 1/3/77.
KITCHING D. J. Born 7/10/42. Commd 1/8/69. Wg Cdr 1/1/91. Retd GD 2/4/93.

KITCHING R. Born 23/5/33. Commd 5/9/57. Flt Lt 5/3/62. Retd GD 23/5/71.
KITCHINGMAN B. F. Born 27/11/23. Commd 2/3/61. Flt Lt 2/3/66. Retd SEC 10/9/68.
KITLEY A. J. H., MIMgt. Born 15/7/22. Commd 18/11/41. Wg Cdr 1/1/59. Retd GD 15/7/69.
KITSON D. A. Born 27/2/31. Commd 17/12/52. Fg Offr 17/12/54. Retd SEC 17/12/55.
KIVER P. A., BSc. Born 9/4/57. Commd 26/11/78. Sqn Ldr 1/1/90. Retd GD(G) 9/4/95.
KLEBOE D. E. Born 19/10/21. Commd 24/12/41. Flt Lt 1/9/45. Retd ENG 19/10/76 rtg Sqn Ldr.
KLEIN C. J. Born 23/12/58. Commd 24/7/81. Fg Offr 24/1/82. Retd GD(G) 29/5/85.
KLEYNHANS J. W. Born 7/8/28. Commd 7/5/57. Flt Lt 7/11/61. Retd GD 7/5/73.
KLIDJIAN A., MB BS FRCS FRCP. Born 22/4/18. Commd 17/6/48. A Cdre 1/1/70. Retd MED 22/4/83.
KNAPP J. D., AFC. Born 15/12/30. Commd 8/10/52. Sqn Ldr 1/1/81. Retd GD 15/12/91.
KNAPP P. D. Born 21/1/50. Commd 16/11/72. Sqn Ldr 1/1/91. Retd GD 14/3/96.
KNAPPER W. F., OBE. Born 6/7/28. Commd 5/4/50. Gp Capt 1/1/72. Retd GD 14/1/83.
KNAPTON P. A., OBE DFC. Born 4/5/21. Commd 19/2/42. Wg Cdr 1/7/60. Retd GD 8/4/75.
KNELL C. L. F. Born 1/8/21. Commd 24/9/43. Flt Lt 2/1/48. Retd GD(G) 1/8/71.
KNELL J. C. Born 4/9/30. Commd 4/7/51. Flt Lt 17/10/56. Retd GD 4/9/68.
KNEVITT H. J., BSc DCAe MIMechE MRAeS ACGI. Born 20/1/17. Commd 20/11/39. Wg Cdr 1/1/56. Retd ENG 10/
  3/62.
KNIGHT The Rev A. C. E., BSc. Born 22/3/42. Commd 2/9/73. Retd 2/9/95 Wg Cdr.
KNIGHT A. E. Born 17/9/61. Commd 8/9/83. Flt Lt 8/89. Retd GD 17/9/99.
KNIGHT A. F. H. Born 7/10/23. Commd 20/9/60. Sqn Ldr 20/9/68. Retd ADMIN 20/9/76.
KNIGHT B. C., MBE. Born 10/4/32. Commd 17/5/51. Sqn Ldr 1/7/62. Retd GD 30/4/81.
KNIGHT B. J. S. Born 24/12/25. Commd 5/2/48. Sqn Ldr 1/1/59. Retd GD 4/8/76.
KNIGHT B. R. R., CEng MRAeS. Born 12/9/35. Commd 7/2/58. Sqn Ldr 1/7/66. Retd ENG 7/2/74.
KNIGHT D., MSc BSc. Born 27/2/43. Commd 31/10/66. Sqn Ldr 10/8/73. Retd ADMIN 31/10/82.
KNIGHT D. A., MBE MA BA. Born 23/5/55. Commd 2/9/73. Wg Cdr 1/1/94. Retd ENG 15/11/00.
KNIGHT D. A. Born 18/8/54. Commd 17/9/72. Flt Lt 12/2/80. Retd GD 18/8/92.
KNIGHT D. E. Born 12/9/20. Commd 3/5/51. Flt Lt 10/11/55. Retd ENG 11/7/73.
KNIGHT F. K. Born 10/10/20. Commd 6/12/41. Wg Cdr 1/7/71. Retd SUP 10/10/75.
KNIGHT J. Born 5/1/39. Commd 3/8/62. Flt Lt 3/2/68. Retd GD 10/4/78.
KNIGHT J., BSc. Born 9/7/49. Commd 2/1/74. Flt Lt 2/1/76. Retd ADMIN 1/4/82.
KNIGHT J. C. Born 29/1/32. Commd 27/3/52. Sqn Ldr 1/7/63. Retd CAT 29/1/70.
KNIGHT J. M. Born 29/11/35. Commd 25/8/67. Flt Lt 4/5/72. Retd GD 31/8/73.
KNIGHT J. S. Born 25/5/26. Commd 7/7/49. Flt Lt 4/6/53. Retd GD 3/10/73.
KNIGHT K. A. R. Born 15/4/43. Commd 9/8/63. Sqr Ldr 1/7/79. Retd GD 25/4/87.
KNIGHT Sir Michael., KCB AFC DLitt BA FRAeS. Born 23/11/32. Commd 28/9/54. ACM 1/7/86. Retd GD 18/11/89.
KNIGHT M. F. J. Born 26/1/15. Commd 27/5/45. Sqn Ldr 1/7/60. Retd SEC 26/1/68.
KNIGHT M. H., MA BA. Born 15/5/39. Commd 12/9/61. Sqn Ldr 12/3/72. Retd EDN 1/10/79.
KNIGHT M. J. Born 16/1/49. Commd 27/2/70. Flt Lt 27/2/73. Retd GD 16/1/87.
KNIGHT O. J. A. Born 21/6/38. Commd 6/10/59. Wg Cdr 1/7/83. Retd GD 25/9/93.
KNIGHT P. C., MSc. Born 29/9/45. Commd 11/11/65. Wg Cdr 1/7/88. Retd SUP 1/12/99.
KNIGHT P. G. Born 18/5/37. Commd 25/7/71. Flt Lt 25/11/74. Retd ENG 31/12/87.
KNIGHT P. N., MB BS DObstRCOG DPhysMed. Born 5/2/31. Commd 26/6/55. Wg Cdr 26/6/68. Retd MED 26/3/73.
KNIGHT R. Born 3/4/27. Commd 20/12/46. Sqn Ldr 1/7/57. Retd GD 4/4/64.
KNIGHT R. Born 26/7/26. Commd 23/8/46. Sqn Ldr 1/4/56. Retd GD 26/7/64.
KNIGHT R. Born 23/5/36. Commd 22/10/59. Sqn Ldr 1/1/72. Retd GD 23/5/92.
KNIGHT R. I. Born 14/9/43. Commd 21/4/77. Flt Lt 21/4/79. Retd MED(SEC) 21/4/85.
KNIGHT S. M. Born 28/1/61. Commd 27/3/80. Flt Lt 27/9/85. Retd GD 14/9/96.
KNIGHT T. B., CEng MIMechE MRAeS. Born 2/12/43. Commd 15/7/65. Sqn Ldr 1/1/75. Retd ENG 2/12/81.
KNIGHTON E. A., AFC MIMgt. Born 11/10/23. Commd 20/11/45. Wg Cdr 1/1/61. Retd GD 15/3/78.
KNIGHTS E. C. R. Born 25/10/20. Commd 15/7/43. Fg Offr 24/12/45. Retd ENG 24/11/47 rtg Flt Lt.
KNIGHTS P. R. Born 20/12/50. Commd 10/5/73. Flt Lt 10/11/78. Retd GD 22/10/94.
KNIGHTS P. W. Born 2/6/38. Commd 4/3/71. Flt Lt 4/3/73. Retd GD 4/3/79.
KNILL A. P. Born 3/8/55. Commd 2/9/73. Sqn Ldr 1/1/87. Retd GD(G) 3/8/93.
KNILL T. S., MSc BSc(Eng). Born 30/1/60. Commd 4/9/78. Sqn Ldr 1/7/91. Retd ENG 30/1/98.
KNOPP G. E. Born 16/9/33. Commd 18/6/52. Flt Lt 15/4/70. Retd GD 13/10/74.
KNOTT K. S. Born 25/12/21. Commd 21/10/54. Sqn Ldr 1/7/64. Retd GD 12/2/76.
KNOTT L. J. Born 24/4/23. Commd 5/11/53. Flt Lt 4/11/58. Retd GD(G) 24/4/78.
KNOTT R. G., CB DSO DFC AFC*. Born 19/12/17. Commd 31/1/37. AVM 1/7/67. Retd GD 18/3/72.
KNOTTS R. M. H., MBA BA. Born 14/1/36. Commd 1/4/71. Sqn Ldr 1/7/78. Retd ENG 1/10/89.
KNOWLDEN W. E. Born 16/2/98. Commd 1/4/18. Flt Lt 1/7/25. Retd GD 3/1/33 recalled 22/5/40. Sqn Ldr 19/6/42.
  Retd 1/3/45 rtg Wg Cdr.
KNOWLES J. R., BSc. Born 21/2/51. Commd 28/2/72. Flt Lt 28/5/73. Retd GD 5/10/76.
KNOWLES M. C. Born 10/3/38. Commd 19/2/63. Sqn Ldr 1/7/73. Retd ENG 1/12/90.
KNOWLES P. A. Born 26/1/42. Commd 3/11/77. Sqn Ldr 1/7/87. Retd ENG 31/5/96.
KNOWLES S. J. R., BSc. Born 18/8/47. Commd 25/7/71. Sqn Ldr 1/1/85. Retd ENG 1/1/88.
KNOWLES W. J., CEng FRAeS FIMgt FINucE. Born 27/2/18. Commd 3/6/43. Gp Capt 1/7/66. Retd ENG 30/5/70.

KNOX A. G., MSc BA. Born 3/9/45. Commd 23/3/66. Wg Cdr 1/7/87. Retd SUP 13/9/94.
KNOX A.E., MBE MIMgt. Born 3/4/39. Commd 28/5/66. A Cdre 1/1/88. Retd GD(G) 12/10/92.
KNOX G. J. Born 4/10/47. Commd 12/7/68. Flt Lt 12/1/74. Retd GD 1/4/78.
KOCH M. E. J. Born 15/12/33. Commd 17/7/56. Flt Lt 7/3/62. Retd GD 1/10/84.
KOCHER C. J., AIIP. Born 18/11/32. Commd 24/10/51. Flt Lt 22/5/57. Retd GD 18/11/70.
KOGUT S. A. Born 13/8/16. Commd 9/9/54. Flt Lt 8/9/59. Retd GD(G) 13/8/71.
KOPP A. K. Born 12/5/50. Commd 18/10/79. Sqn Ldr 1/1/88. Retd SUP 11/9/91.
KORNER J. R. Born 15/9/37. Commd 17/7/56. Flt Lt 21/8/63. Retd GD(G) 6/8/89.
KORNICKI F. Born 18/12/16. Commd 25/6/51. Sqn Ldr 1/1/61. Retd CAT 8/1/72.
KOTLARZ M. Born 14/7/19. Commd 1/9/48. Sqn Ldr 1/1/54. Retd GD 14/7/74.
KRECKELER M. K., BSc. Born 18/12/60. Commd 2/9/79. Flt Lt 15/9/86. Retd ENG 18/12/00.
KRISTER S. J., MRCS LRCP DPH DIH. Born 12/2/23. Commd 17/10/46. Wg Cdr 3/3/61. Retd MED 17/10/62.
KUIPERS R. D. Born 4/7/39. Commd 27/1/61. Flt Lt 10/2/67. Retd GD 4/7/79.
KUUN D. R. Born 14/12/37. Commd 29/7/58. Wg Cdr 1/1/74. Retd GD 14/12/92.
KYFFIN R. G. M., BA. Born 9/2/61. Commd 19/6/83. Flt Lt 19/12/86. Retd OPS SPT 19/6/99.
KYLE J., DFM. Born 20/9/22. Commd 1/5/44. Flt Lt 19/11/53. Retd GD(G) 20/9/74.
KYLE J. W. P., MBE MIMgt. Born 14/4/32. Commd 15/5/58. Wg Cdr 1/1/78. Retd SY 1/6/85.
KYLE R. H., CB MBE BSc(Eng) CEng FRAeS. Born 4/1/43. Commd 30/9/61. AVM 1/1/92. Retd ENG 8/9/97.
KYLE V. T. Born 20/3/32. Commd 26/8/66. Flt Lt 26/8/71. Retd ENG 2/10/79. Reinstated 11/2/81. Flt Lt 6/1/73. Retd ENG 20/3/89.
KYLES J. G., MIMgt. Born 7/3/22. Commd 5/5/44. Wg Cdr 1/1/68. Retd SUP 4/3/77.
KYRKE-SMITH V. J., DFM. Born 2/12/21. Commd 30/6/44. Flt Lt 1/3/61. Retd GD 27/5/63.

# L

L'ESTRANGE J. P., AFC AFM. Born 26/4/26. Commd 26/9/51. Sqn Ldr 1/7/67. Retd GD 24/8/84.
LA TOUCHE T. P. D. Born 28/3/25. Commd 1/11/48. Wg Cdr 1/1/68. Retd GD 28/3/82.
LABERCOMBE A. J., MIMgt. Born 14/12/44. Commd 3/3/67. Wg Cdr 1/7/91. Retd GD 14/9/96.
LABOUCHERE C. M., MA. Born 2/12/38. Commd 30/9/57. Sqn Ldr 1/1/69. Retd ENG 1/1/77.
LACE F. J. Born 18/2/33. Commd 21/11/51. Flt Lt 6/3/57. Retd GD 6/4/76. Re-instated 4/3/81 to 3/6/85.
LACEY K. M. Born 28/8/56. Commd 11/5/78. Flt Lt 30/9/84. Retd GD(G) 9/1/97.
LACEY M., BSc(Eng) CEng MIMechE ACGI. Born 28/10/36. Commd 30/9/56. Wg Cdr 1/7/75. Retd ENG 15/5/90.
LACEY N. V., BTech. Born 17/5/52. Commd 13/9/70. Sqn Ldr 1/1/89. Retd GD 25/7/96.
LACEY W. Born 17/7/51. Commd 13/1/72. Wg Cdr 1/7/92. Retd SY 14/3/97.
LACY F. S., MBE AE BA MIMgt. Born 27/5/18. Commd 17/9/42. Sqn Ldr 1/1/60. Retd SEC 27/5/75.
LACY P. A. Born 8/8/41. Commd 14/10/71. Sqn Ldr 1/10/76. Retd EDN 14/10/79.
LADBROOKE D. R. Born 5/3/42. Commd 4/10/63. Flt Lt 5/9/67. Retd GD 16/6/85.
LADMORE W. Born 28/6/35. Commd 26/5/67. Sqn Ldr 1/7/73. Retd ENG 1/7/76.
LADRO E. A., DFC*. Born 17/7/13. Commd 1/9/44. Flt Lt 1/9/44. Retd GD 29/8/58.
LAGNADO E. J. Born 4/9/28. Commd 17/12/53. Flt Lt 17/12/59. Retd SEC 5/1/69.
LAIDLAY A. M., DFC. Born 14/8/24. Commd 24/3/44. Sqn Ldr 1/1/61. Retd GD 26/3/76.
LAIDLER A. J. Born 23/2/43. Commd 4/10/63. Sqn Ldr 1/1/83. Retd GD 23/2/00.
LAIDLER W. J., MRAeS FIMgt. Born 22/4/24. Commd 3/6/44. Gp Capt 1/7/68. Retd GD 25/3/77.
LAINES C. J. Born 24/1/49. Commd 25/9/80. Flt Lt 25/9/82. Retd ENG 24/1/99.
LAING C. W. Born 5/5/14. Commd 17/8/39. Sqn Ldr 1/8/47. Retd SUP 17/5/63.
LAING D. Born 31/12/57. Commd 22/9/88. Flt Lt 22/9/90. Retd ADMIN 14/9/96.
LAING J. S. Born 2/3/33. Commd 28/11/60. Flt Lt 28/11/60. Retd GD 2/3/71.
LAING S. J. Born 6/1/65. Commd 8/9/83. Flt Lt 8/7/90. Retd GD(G) 1/6/91.
LAIRD B. C. Born 7/2/41. Commd 16/1/60. Flt Lt 14/2/66. Retd GD 7/2/79.
LAIRD D., MMAR MNI MIMgt. Born 10/4/33. Commd 14/8/62. Sqn Ldr 14/8/70. Retd MAR. 14/8/78.
LAIRD P. E., DFC AFC. Born 24/2/18. Commd 13/7/43. Flt Lt 13/1/47. Retd GD 1/6/61 rtg Sqn Ldr.
LAITE B. C. Born 8/6/44. Commd 19/4/63. Air Cdre 1/1/94. Retd GD 4/6/98.
LAITHWAITE L. J. Born 18/8/35. Commd 17/3/67. Flt Lt 17/3/73. Retd SY 18/12/76.
LAKE C. T. Born 28/6/30. Commd 27/6/51. Flt Lt 27/12/55. Retd GD 28/6/68.
LAKE E. E., MVO CEng MRAeS MIMgt. Born 3/2/23. Commd 1/10/44. Gp Capt 1/1/75. Retd ENG 3/2/78.
LAKE H. B., MBE. Born 30/7/35. Commd 12/12/59. Wg Cdr 1/7/79. Retd GD 1/3/84.
LAKE P. Born 1/10/29. Commd 24/6/52. Flt Lt 5/11/58. Retd GD 1/10/67.
LAKEN D. E. Born 17/7/28. Commd 7/1/71. Flt Lt 7/1/74. Retd GD(G) 10/8/82.
LAKER J. G. S., MIMgt. Born 25/5/48. Commd 8/11/68. Sqn Ldr 1/1/87. Retd OPS SPT 25/5/98.
LAKEY M. J., GM. Born 23/9/47. Commd 25/2/66. Sqn Ldr 1/1/84. Retd GD 1/1/87. Re-entrant 16/8/91. Sqn Ldr 16/8/88. Retd GD 1/10/00.
LAMB C. A. Born 9/10/34. Commd 16/12/66. Flt Lt 16/12/68. Retd ENG 31/12/74.
LAMB D., MIEE. Born 5/2/35. Commd 24/9/64. Flt Lt 28/3/67. Retd ENG 5/2/73.
LAMB E. Born 2/6/38. Commd 10/4/67. Flt Lt 4/5/72. Retd ENG 10/4/83.
LAMB E. W., MVO MIMgt. Born 18/1/23. Commd 27/4/44. Wg Cdr 1/7/63. Retd ENG 28/4/76.
LAMB F. Born 24/12/19. Commd 8/9/52. Flt Lt 26/5/55. Retd SEC 31/1/68.
LAMB F. N., MBE. Born 22/6/16. Commd 6/12/56. Sqn Ldr 1/1/65. Retd GD(G) 28/2/70.
LAMB G. C., CB CBE AFC FIMgt. Born 23/7/23. Commd 4/12/42. AVM 1/7/75. Retd GD 31/3/78.
LAMB G. J. Born 10/7/46. Commd 18/11/66. Flt Lt 18/5/72. Retd GD 10/7/84.
LAMB I. C., BA. Born 12/11/54. Commd 15/3/87. Flt It 15/3/92. Retd ADMIN 13/9/96.
LAMB J. Born 11/10/33. Commd 3/9/52. Sqn Ldr 1/7/72. Retd GD(G) 30/1/77.
LAMB J. A. Born 6/4/30. Commd 7/5/53. Sqn Ldr 1/1/64. Retd GD 19/3/76.
LAMB J. R., MSc BSc. Born 22/6/33. Commd 8/8/56. Sqn Ldr 8/2/66. Retd ADMIN 2/4/85.
LAMB K. Born 17/8/40. Commd 9/3/62. Flt Lt 1/7/68. Retd GD 17/8/78.
LAMB M. P., MBBS MRCOG MRCS LRCP. Born 26/3/45. Commd 25/7/66. Sqn Ldr 2/6/75. Retd MED 26/3/83.
LAMB N. Born 14/10/25. Commd 6/9/56. Sqn Ldr 1/1/66. Retd GD 14/10/83.
LAMB R. Born 27/5/30. Commd 8/3/61. Flt Lt 3/8/67. Retd GD 23/3/69.
LAMB R. B., BA MIMgt. Born 27/7/31. Commd 18/10/55. Sqn Ldr 1/7/63. Retd GD 24/9/84.
LAMB T. D., AFC. Born 4/11/18. Commd 19/4/45. Sqn Ldr 1/7/59. Retd GD 2/7/62.
LAMB W. D. R. Born 5/12/27. Commd 8/4/49. Flt Lt 8/10/51. Retd GD 1/1/69.
LAMBDIN G. S. Born 19/4/17. Commd 22/9/55. Flt Lt 22/9/58. Retd ENG 21/2/61.
LAMBDON S. G. Born 17/1/31. Commd 27/5/53. Flt Lt 1/3/61. Retd GD 30/9/83.
LAMBE G. F. Born 8/12/44. Commd 17/7/64. Sqn Ldr 1/7/82. Retd GD 8/4/89.
LAMBE M. T., BA MIMgt. Born 8/4/32. Commd 21/10/54. Sqn Ldr 16/10/66. Retd ADMIN 9/4/82.
LAMBERT A. D., DFC. Born 6/8/19. Commd 15/6/40. Sqn Ldr 1/8/47. Retd GD 19/5/56.

LAMBERT A. J. Born 29/9/52. Commd 25/9/71. Flt Lt 19/5/78. Retd GD 29/9/90.
LAMBERT A. R. Born 31/3/54. Commd 5/8/76. Sqn Ldr 1/1/89. Retd SY 14/9/96.
LAMBERT C. R., BSc. Born 19/12/55. Commd 15/9/74. Flt Lt 15/10/78. Retd GD 15/7/89.
LAMBERT C. R. Born 24/6/54. Commd 20/8/80. Wg Cdr 1/7/94. Retd SY 14/9/96.
LAMBERT E. V. Born 13/5/32. Commd 23/9/66. Sqn Ldr 1/7/80. Retd ADMIN 3/5/85.
LAMBERT G. D., AFC. Born 16/5/31. Commd 19/8/53. Sqn Ldr 1/1/82. Retd GD 16/5/93.
LAMBERT The Rev I. A., MTh BA. Born 9/2/43. Commd 5/11/75. Retd 10/2/98. Wg Cdr.
LAMBERT J. D., MIMgt. Born 1/1/32. Commd 6/12/51. Wg Cdr 1/7/74. Retd SUP 15/9/86.
LAMBERT J. R., OBE MA MRAeS. Born 3/2/30. Commd 17/12/52. A Cdre 1/1/77. Retd SUP 4/2/87.
LAMBERT K. M. Born 1/7/24. Commd 23/5/51. Flt Offr 23/5/55. Retd CAT 10/12/57.
LAMBERT L. H., DFC AFC. Born 21/10/19. Commd 13/2/42. Wg Cdr 1/7/56. Retd GD 13/2/61.
LAMBERT P. C. Born 29/4/38. Commd 6/5/65. Sqn Ldr 1/7/86. Retd GD 29/7/94.
LAMBERT R. W. Born 2/2/25. Commd 15/6/50. Flt Lt 27/5/54. Retd GD 2/2/63.
LAMBERT T. M., MA. Born 6/9/17. Commd 19/5/48. Sqn Ldr 1/1/65. Retd SUP 6/9/72.
LAMBLE D. A. Born 29/10/28. Commd 3/11/60. Flt Lt 3/11/66. Retd ENG 1/10/75.
LAMBOURNE A. J. Born 19/10/43. Commd 6/4/62. Sqn Ldr 1/1/77 Retd GD 24/10/80.
LAMBOURNE C. F. Born 4/12/23. Commd 2/4/53. Flt Lt 14/5/58. Retd GD 7/8/64.
LAMBTON D., MB ChB MRCGP MFOM DRCOG DAvMed. Born 30/8/31. Commd 3/3/57. Gp Capt. 1/7/80. Retd
    MED 25/6/83.
LAMBTON K. P. Born 28/5/52. Commd 2/1/75. Flt Lt 7/10/79. Retd GD 6/6/80.
LAMING H. J. Born 17/7/18. Commd 10/8/43. Flt Lt 10/2/47. Retd ENG 14/11/53.
LAMMING B. Born 18/1/32. Commd 27/2/70. Sqn Ldr 1/7/79. Retd ENG 31/7/84.
LAMOND A. J., BA. Born 2/12/58. Commd 7/11/82. Flt Lt 7/8/84. Retd GD 4/11/95.
LAMOND H. W. Born 26/8/15. Commd 4/1/39. Wg Cdr 1/7/53. Retd GD 15/9/62.
LAMONT C. R. Born 27/9/36. Commd 4/5/55. Sqn Ldr 30/11/78. Retd GD 27/9/94.
LAMONT J. P. Born 25/7/40. Commd 11/5/62. Flt Lt 9/2/68. Retd GD 25/7/78.
LAMONT-TURNER A. R. Born 12/6/20. Commd 12/8/44. Flt Lt 12/8/48. Retd RGT 1/3/58.
LAMPARD I. B. Born 23/8/35. Commd 9/9/54. Sqn Ldr 1/7/70. Retd SUP 23/8/90.
LAMPER C. G., BEM. Born 30/11/44. Commd 22/5/80. Sqn Ldr 1/7/94. Retd ADMIN 10/7/96.
LAMPITT M. L. Born 22/1/47. Commd 27/7/72. Sqn Ldr 1/7/86. Retd GD 9/6/92.
LAMPKIN E. A. Born 22/7/22. Commd 7/6/44. Flt Lt 11/1/48. Retd GD 20/4/63.
LANCASTER D. E., BSc. Born 13/9/62. Commd 30/8/81. Flt Lt 15/10/85. Retd GD 1/4/00.
LANCASTER D. W. Born 1/10/30. Commd 10/12/52. Flt Lt 5/5/58. Retd GD 1/10/68.
LANCASTER J. E. Born 15/4/33. Commd 27/5/53. Flt Lt 28/10/58. Retd GD 15/10/71.
LANCASTER J. S. R. Born 31/1/35. Commd 1/10/63. Flt Lt 7/3/66. Retd GD 31/1/73.
LANCASTLE G. J., BSc. Born 19/2/43. Commd 23/9/68. Sqn Ldr 23/3/76. Retd ADMIN 18/9/94.
LANCE R. M., MIMgt. Born 24/2/39. Commd 22/10/59. Sqn Ldr 1/7/74. Retd ADMIN 1/7/77.
LANCE V. R. Born 2/9/60. Commd 14/10/84. Flt Lt 14/10/89. Retd SUP 14/10/96.
LANCHBURY G. J. Born 25/8/42. Commd 25/1/63. Wg Cdr 1/1/90. Retd GD 1/8/93.
LANCHBURY R. W. Born 25/2/35. Commd 21/4/67. Flt Lt 21/4/69. Retd GD 1/6/74.
LAND W. A., MBE AFC. Born 15/1/20. Commd 28/6/42. Flt Lt 10/5/51. Retd SEC 1/6/63.
LANDELLS A. B., MBE DFC. Born 23/3/24. Commd 19/9/44. Wg Cdr 1/7/65. Retd GD 30/1/73.
LANDELLS S. H. Born 13/10/66. Commd 23/10/86. Flt Lt 23/4/92. Retd GD 14/3/96.
LANDER P. J., BTech. Born 6/1/51. Commd 2/10/72. Sqn Ldr 1/1/88. Retd GD 1/1/91.
LANDERYOU J. N., BA FIMgt MIL. Born 30/12/38. Commd 5/3/57. Wg Cdr 1/1/79. Retd GD 14/4/94.
LANDESS L. Born 20/12/32. Commd 16/11/64. Flt Lt 16/11/64. Retd GD 20/12/89.
LANDON E. P., DFC FIMgt. Born 4/9/20. Commd 24/4/42. Gp Capt 1/1/64. Retd GD 15/7/71.
LANDREY C. J. Born 17/4/21. Commd 13/4/43. Sqn Ldr 1/1/53. Retd GD 17/4/70.
LANDY J. N., MSc MBCS MIMgt. Born 18/3/44. Commd 26/8/66. Sqn Ldr 1/7/78. Retd SUP 1/10/85.
LANE The Rev A. H. J., MBE BA. Born 13/9/49. Commd 20/8/78. Retd 20/8/92. Wg Cdr.
LANE C. B. Born 24/4/38. Commd 6/12/61. Sqn Ldr 1/1/73. Retd SY 15/4/77.
LANE C. D. Born 1/7/39. Commd 25/5/80. Flt Lt 22/5/83. Retd ADMIN 2/5/93.
LANE H. R. Born 24/12/23. Commd 3/11/44. Flt Lt 27/5/54. Retd GD 23/11/65.
LANE I. E. P., BA. Born 1/7/30. Commd 20/1/60. Flt Offr 18/3/64. Retd EDN 29/8/64.
LANE J. F. Born 23/8/46. Commd 6/5/66. Flt Lt 6/11/71. Retd GD 6/12/76.
LANE J. G. A., MBE. Born 13/3/17. Commd 12/12/46. Sqn Ldr 1/7/60. Retd PE 14/3/72.
LANE K. Born 1/6/47. Commd 13/12/68. Sqn Ldr 1/1/81. Retd SUP 1/6/85.
LANE L. S., BSc. Born 19/6/43. Commd 10/4/58. Sqn Ldr 19/6/63. Retd EDN 13/10/83.
LANE M. J., MIMgt. Born 17/11/34. Commd 14/1/54. Gp Capt. 1/7/82. Retd ADMIN 17/11/90.
LANE M. T. Born 28/3/46. Commd 2/6/67. Flt Lt 2/12/72. Retd GD 28/3/84.
LANE P. D. Born 27/11/43. Commd 22/3/63. Flt Lt 22/9/68. Retd GD 27/11/98.
LANE R., BSc. Born 24/7/47. Commd 8/1/84. Flt Lt 8/1/83. Retd LGL 1/4/85.
LANE R. G. Born 12/5/42. Commd 23/6/67. Sqn Ldr 1/1/77. Retd ENG 12/5/80.
LANE R. J., MSc BDS DGDPRCS. Born 25/11/39. Commd 23/2/66. Gp Capt 1/1/87. Retd DEL 30/4/94.
LANE R. W. Born 28/1/44. Commd 11/8/77. Sqn Ldr 1/1/85. Retd ENG 15/8/97.
LANE S. E. J. Born 9/1/44. Commd 9/3/62. Wg Cdr 1/7/90. Retd GD(G) 1/2/95.

LANE W. A. N. Born 22/2/36. Commd 21/7/55. Sqn Ldr 1/7/69. Retd GD 31/12/71.
LANE W. F., BEM MIMgt. Born 3/8/20. Commd 9/9/54. Sqn Ldr 1/7/67. Retd ENG 26/6/71.
LANFORD J. B. Born 26/5/33. Commd 21/10/66. Sqn Ldr 1/1/79. Retd ENG 31/1/86.
LANG A. G., DFC. Born 26/10/19. Commd 17/12/41. Sqn Ldr 1/1/50. Retd GD 18/2/58.
LANG A. J. Born 11/5/63. Commd 11/10/84. Flt Lt 11/10/89. Retd GD 18/7/92.
LANG B. Born 30/6/47. Commd 17/7/70. Wg Cdr 1/1/90. Retd SY 1/9/94.
LANG D. E. R., AFC. Born 6/4/25. Commd 5/12/43. Flt Lt 1/8/53. Retd GD 26/3/64.
LANG J. A., BA. Born 2/4/37. Commd 1/9/70. Sqn Ldr 1/7/78. Retd ADMIN 2/4/96.
LANG K. R. Born 23/4/25. Commd 28/4/44. Sqn Ldr 1/1/57. Retd GD 8/9/72.
LANG R. A. M. Born 22/12/23. Commd 27/11/43. Flt Lt 4/6/53. Retd SUP 21/12/59.
LANGAN P. J. Born 18/4/40. Commd 27/2/70. Flt Lt 27/2/72. Retd GD(G) 20/4/90.
LANGAN-FOX C. P. Born 18/11/44. Commd 9/3/72. Flt Lt 9/3/74. Retd GD(G) 18/11/82.
LANGDON A. C., OBE. Born 26/12/20. Commd 25/5/42. Wg Cdr 1/1/57. Retd GD 26/12/67.
LANGDON L. M. Born 20/12/36. Commd 27/1/77. Flt Lt 27/1/83. Retd ADMIN 20/12/86.
LANGDON N. R., BEM MIMgt. Born 14/6/38. Commd 19/8/66. Sqn Ldr 1/7/74. Retd GD 10/9/88.
LANGDON P. G., DFM. Born 10/2/22. Commd 4/12/43. Sqn Ldr 1/7/69. Retd GD 30/3/77.
LANGDOWN P. Born 17/12/37. Commd 30/9/58. Flt Lt 9/4/64. Retd GD 12/8/76.
LANGER J. F., CBE AFC FIMgt MRAeS. Born 24/6/25. Commd 6/2/44. A Cdre 1/7/73. Retd GD 29/9/79.
LANGFORD T. W. R. Born 17/7/36. Commd 30/7/57. Flt Lt 30/1/60. Retd GD 17/7/94.
LANGHAM M. B. Born 11/9/42. Commd 17/12/64. Wg Cdr 1/1/80. Retd GD 31/3/94.
LANGHAM R. T. Born 20/9/18. Commd 18/11/53. Flt Lt 18/11/58. Retd GD(G) 20/9/68.
LANGLEY A. Born 22/4/33. Commd 5/11/70. Sqn Ldr 1/1/80. Retd ADMIN 22/4/83.
LANGLEY J. D., BA. Born 12/3/32. Commd 6/4/54. Flt Lt 6/10/56. Retd GD 24/9/91.
LANGLEY M. J. Born 15/2/44. Commd 9/3/62. Wg Cdr 1/1/85. Retd GD 2/3/98.
LANGLEY P. J., DFC. Born 24/10/24. Commd 14/1/44. Flt Lt 19/11/53. Retd GD 26/2/66.
LANGLEY W. F., BEM. Born 13/8/20. Commd 12/9/46. Sqn Ldr 1/1/59. Retd SUP 11/5/63.
LANGRIDGE H. A., OBE MIMgt. Born 12/5/23. Commd 10/7/51. Wg Cdr 1/1/69. Retd SEC 13/5/75.
LANGRILL P., OBE. Born 22/7/38. Commd 11/6/60. Gp Capt 1/1/90. Retd GD 22/7/93.
LANGSTAFF R., OBE AFC. Born 17/1/28. Commd 27/6/51. Gp Capt 1/1/80. Retd GD 20/11/82.
LANGSTAFF R. J., MA BA MB BCh FRCS(Edin). Born 29/2/56. Commd 25/8/77. Wg Cdr 11/8/95. Retd MED 30/11/95.
LANGSTAFF-ELLIS J. W., BEd. Born 6/1/50. Commd 17/8/80. Flt Lt 17/2/84. Retd ADMIN 7/1/00.
LANGSTON J., CBE. Born 30/6/24. Commd 22/9/44. A Cdre 1/7/75. Retd GD 26/7/79.
LANGTON R. P., BA. Born 3/6/31. Commd 19/10/59. Wg Cdr 1/7/77. Retd ADMIN 9/9/88.
LANGWORTHY W. A., AFC. Born 16/4/35. Commd 21/10/53. Sqn Ldr 1/7/78. Retd GD 29/11/85.
LANIGAN D. S. Born 29/6/41. Commd 31/7/62. Flt Lt 31/1/65. Retd GD 29/6/79.
LANNEN C. A., BSc. Born 21/4/50. Commd 15/9/69. Sqn Ldr 1/1/81. Retd ENG 26/10/90.
LANNING G. E. Born 15/2/20. Commd 22/4/42. Flt Lt 30/8/50. Retd GD(G) 31/12/64.
LANNING H., DFC. Born 7/12/19. Commd 24/9/42. Sqn Ldr 1/7/56. Retd ENG 7/12/74.
LANNON P. M. H. Born 6/1/29. Commd 25/8/60. Sqn Ldr 1/7/72. Retd ENG 11/4/80.
LANSDELL C. H. Born 23/12/33. Commd 30/6/54. Flt Lt 16/8/61. Retd GD 25/12/71.
LANYON J. C. Born 16/2/22. Commd 31/1/42. Flt Lt 23/4/51. Retd GD 16/2/77.
LAPHAM E. F., MBE MIMgt. Born 7/9/21. Commd 11/9/42. Sqn Ldr. 1/1/58. Retd SEC 12/9/70.
LAPPIN K. E., BA. Born 13/7/37. Commd 11/10/60. Sqn Ldr 31/3/71. Retd ADMIN 11/10/76.
LAPRAIK R. D., BSc(Eng). Born 1/10/49. Commd 24/9/67. Sqn Ldr 1/7/79 Retd GD 18/11/86.
LAPSLEY J. C. W. Born 25/6/48. Commd 28/2/69. Sqn Ldr 1/7/80. Retd ENG 25/6/86.
LAPWOOD G . E. Born 1/8/19. Commd 7/7/55. Sqn Ldr 1/7/67. Retd GD(G) 1/5/71.
LARARD F. N., DFM. Born 19/1/24. Commd 5/9/44. Flt Lt 5/9/50. Retd SEC 19/1/62.
LARBEY J. P. S. Born 10/10/42. Commd 7/5/64. Flt Lt 4/11/70. Retd OPS SPT 10/10/97.
LARKIN D. E., CBE MRAeS. Born 11/7/33. Commd 25/7/59. Gp Capt 1/1/86. Retd GD 11/7/94.
LARKIN W. J. Born 13/2/21. Commd 2/3/45. Flt Lt 4/1/51. Retd GD 30/3/68.
LARKING R. G. Born 12/8/53. Commd 15/3/73. Sqn Ldr 1/1/88. Retd GD 12/8/91.
LARKINS G. S. Born 17/5/33. Commd 6/4/54. Flt Lt 6/4/59. Retd SUP 16/9/64.
LARKWORTHY L. T. Born 17/10/25. Commd 19/6/52. Sqn Ldr 1/7/67. Retd ENG 17/6/77.
LARKWORTHY W., MB, BS, FRCP, DCH. Born 29/3/33 Commd 20/9/59. Wg Cdr 3/9/71. Retd MED 20/9/78.
LARNER J. Born 28/4/24. Commd 1/8/69. Flt Lt 1/8/72. Retd RGT 1/11/74.
LARNEY G. K., DFC MRAeS. Born 18/10/12. Commd 29/6/39. Sqn Ldr 1/7/56. Retd ENG 19/11/61.
LARTER P. J. Born 7/9/44. Commd 2/2/71. Sqn Ldr 1/1/85. Retd SUP 30/8/96.
LASHBROOK W. I., DFC AFC DFM. Born 3/1/13. Commd 27/5/41. Flt Lt 10/10/42. Retd GD 23/11/48 rtg Sqn Ldr.
LASSETER W. Born 4/9/52. Commd 6/4/72. Sqn Ldr 1/6/84. Retd GD 14/3/97.
LAST R. W., BA. Born 21/1/59. Commd 16/9/79. Sqn Ldr 1/1/95. Retd GD 24/6/98.
LAST V. E., DPhysEd. Born 8/1/44. Commd 7/8/67. Flt Lt 8/3/72. Retd ADMIN 1/1/87.
LATCHAM J., BSc MInstP DipEl. Born 22/12/17. Commd 24/8/49. Wg Cdr 24/8/66. Retd EDN 22/12/72.
LATCHEM R. E. Born 21/4/33. Commd 17/1/52. Flt Lt 24/7/57. Retd GD 21/4/88.
LATHAM F., OBE DSc MD ChB. Born 7/3/20. Commd 23/5/46. Wg Cdr 23/1/58. Retd MED 23/5/60.
LATHAM P. A., CB AFC. Born 18/6/25. Commd 22/2/46. AVM 1/1/78 Retd GD 2/4/81.

LATHAM P. E. S. Born 14/10/61. Commd 8/10/87. Flt Lt 8/10/89. Retd GD 14/10/99.
LATHAM T., BSc. Born 9/8/59. Commd 29/8/77. Sqn Ldr 1/7/88. Retd ENG 1/10/90.
LATIMER M. B. Born 10/11/37. Commd 24/9/59. Flt Lt 1/4/66. Retd ENG 10/11/75.
LATIN R. V., BSc MS CEng MIEE. Born 15/5/39. Commd 30/9/58. Sqn Ldr 1/1/69. Retd ENG 15/5/77. rtg Wg Cdr.
LATTER B. Born 25/4/38. Commd 30/4/57. Wg Cdr 1/1/79. Retd GD 6/7/85.
LATTIMER B. C., BCom. Born 20/3/44. Commd 3/11/69. Flt Lt 3/8/71. Retd GD 1/3/75.
LATTIMER D. N., MBE. Born 11/5/19. Commd 5/11/59. Wg Cdr 8/10/70. Retd MED(SEC) 11/5/74.
LATTON K. B., BA FRAeS. Born 6/3/41. Commd 18/12/62. A Cdre 1/1/90. Retd GD 28/1/94.
LAU G. S., OBE MCIPD MIMgt. Born 7/5/19. Commd 7/5/45. Sqn Ldr 1/4/56. Retd GD 6/10/69.
LAUCHLAN J. P. Born 6/3/64. Commd 19/7/84. Flt Lt 13/12/90. Retd ADMIN 14/3/96.
LAUGHLIN M., BSc. Born 5/4/41. Commd 3/7/62. Sqn Ldr 1/7/72. Retd GD 29/3/77.
LAUGHTON L. S., OBE. Born 30/8/22. Commd 28/3/42. Wg Cdr 1/1/59. Retd GD 7/7/73.
LAUNDY M. J. Born 11/1/45. Commd 15/7/66. Flt Lt 15/1/69. Retd GD 11/1/89.
LAURANCE M. A., MIMgt. Born 27/5/35. Commd 17/3/55. Sqn Ldr 1/7/66. Retd ADMIN 28/6/85.
LAURENSON J. A. W. S. Born 13/5/40. Commd 19/12/61. Sqn Ldr 1/1/74. Retd GD 13/5/95.
LAURIE G. H., MVO. Born 15/12/45. Commd 8/1/65. Sqn Ldr 1/7/77. Retd GD 15/12/00.
LAURIE I. H., AFC. Born 16/11/27. Commd 7/7/55. Sqn Ldr 1/1/83. Retd GD 16/11/85.
LAURIE R. I. Born 9/11/34. Commd 4/3/71. Flt Lt 4/3/74. Retd GD 2/10/79.
LAVELLE P. J. Born 25/3/30. Commd 29/3/68. Sqn Ldr 1/7/83. Retd ENG 31/5/89.
LAVENDER B. W., OBE AFC FIMgt. Born 25/4/35. Commd 16/9/53. Gp Capt 1/7/78. Retd GD 18/12/89.
LAVENDER N. D., BDS LDSRCS. Born 31/5/34. Commd 17/8/58. Gp Capt 1/1/80. Retd MED 27/4/91.
LAVER R. A., CEng MIEE. Born 18/3/42. Commd 15/7/64. Sqn Ldr 1/1/91. Retd ENG 18/3/97.
LAVERACK W. P. Born 29/9/27. Commd 12/3/64. Sqn Ldr 10/4/74. Retd MED(T) 19/7/79.
LAW A. B. Born 8/12/37. Commd 20/7/64. Sqn Ldr 1/1/83. Retd GD 2/8/89.
LAW A. L., DFC AFC*. Born 28/11/15. Commd 2/5/40. Sqn Ldr 1/7/49. Retd GD 27/5/57.
LAW A. W. Born 18/5/31. Commd 9/4/52. Gp Capt 1/7/76. Retd SEC 29/1/81.
LAW B. A. Born 9/3/08. Commd 20/4/41. Flt Lt 1/9/45. Retd SEC 20/1/58 rtg Sqn Ldr.
LAW G. A. Born 29/1/21. Commd 10/12/43. Sqn Ldr 1/7/57. Retd GD 29/1/64.
LAW J., AFM. Born 8/7/19. Commd 1/11/56. Sqn Ldr 1/7/71. Retd GD 8/7/74.
LAW J. Born 4/1/31. Commd 16/12/51. Flt Lt 14/5/58. Retd GD 4/1/86.
LAW J. S., MA. Born 23/6/90. Commd 8/9/74. Sqn Ldr 1/1/87. Retd GD(G) 8/9/90.
LAW M. D. Born 25/1/30. Commd 13/12/51. Sqn Ldr 1/1/77. Retd SY 8/4/81.
LAW P. A., CEng MIEE. Born 24/11/27. Commd 14/12/49. Gp Capt 1/1/74. Retd ENG 25/11/76.
LAW R. C. E., DSO DFC MA. Born 2/11/17. Commd 21/2/39. Wg Cdr 1/1/52. Retd GD 28/4/60 rtg Gp Capt.
LAW S. A. T., BA MB ChB MRCGP DA DAvMed. Born 21/12/53. Commd 14/8/83. Wg Cdr 14/8/92. Retd MED 15/12/97.
LAW S. H. Born 6/2/59. Commd 12/7/79. Flt Lt 12/1/86. Retd SY 6/2/97.
LAWER A., BSc MRAeS. Born 3/3/56. Commd 14/1/79. Sqn Ldr 1/1/89. Retd GD 14/1/97.
LAWES J. W., FIMgt MInstAM. Born 23/6/37. Commd 8/7/65. Gp Capt 1/1/84. Retd GD(G) 16/1/90.
LAWLEY B. J., MB ChB. Born 18/5/28. Commd 3/7/52. Sqn Ldr 3/7/59. Retd MED 26/2/61.
LAWLEY R. L. Born 10/7/18. Commd 26/12/46. Sqn Ldr 1/7/62. Retd ENG 15/10/66.
LAWLOR W. J., BA. Born 21/9/36. Commd 22/10/63. Sqn Ldr 9/3/72. Retd EDN 22/10/79.
LAWN B. E. T., CEng MIEE. Born 9/1/38. Commd 12/9/61. Sqn Ldr 1/1/74. Retd ENG 3/4/82.
LAWRANCE M. J. B., MBE. Born 11/4/35. Commd 10/4/56. Sqn Ldr 1/7/72. Retd GD 11/4/93.
LAWRENCE A. Born 14/4/09. Commd. 20/10/41. Flt Lt 1/9/45. Retd SUP 25/4/58 rtg Sqn Ldr.
LAWRENCE A. G. E. Born 16/4/27. Commd 17/10/57. Flt Lt 1/4/63. Retd GD 16/4/76.
LAWRENCE A. J. Born 19/6/41. Commd 22/7/71. Flt Lt 22/7/73. Retd SUP 22/7/79.
LAWRENCE B. Born 17/5/43. Commd 17/12/65. Flt Lt 17/6/68 Retd GD 17/5/81.
LAWRENCE C. G. Born 8/8/20. Commd 1/5/42. Flt Lt 20/8/46. Retd GD(G) 1/4/69.
LAWRENCE C. M. Born 12/4/57. Commd 22/11/84. Flt Lt 15/3/87. Retd SY 12/4/95.
LAWRENCE C. T., MBE BSc. Born 11/9/56. Commd 30/10/77. Sqn Ldr 1/7/87. Retd GD 11/9/94.
LAWRENCE D., ACIS MIMgt. Born 30/8/38. Commd 15/12/59. Sqn Ldr 1/7/70. Retd ADMIN 1/9/95.
LAWRENCE D. B. Born 10/3/30. Commd 23/5/51. Flt Lt 13/11/57. Retd GD 10/3/68.
LAWRENCE D. F., CBE CEng MIMechE. Born 29/4/35. Commd 19/7/57. A Cdre 1/7/84. Retd ENG 29/6/90.
LAWRENCE G. F., OBE BA CEng MIEE MRAeS. Born 22/4/39. Commd 18/7/61. Gp Capt. 1/1/81. Retd ENG 3/10/89.
LAWRENCE H. H., DFC. Born 30/7/19. Commd 19/10/43. Flt Lt 17/5/47. Retd GD 30/7/62.
LAWRENCE I. C. Born 26/5/35. Commd 5/7/53. Sqn Ldr 1/1/81. Retd GD 27/11/89.
LAWRENCE J. Born 23/1/59. Commd 17/9/84. Sqn Ldr 1/7/94. Retd SUP 4/7/96.
LAWRENCE J. Born 26/2/19. Commd 12/6/47. Sqn Ldr 1/1/61. Retd SUP 5/3/69.
LAWRENCE J. T., CB CBE AFC. Born 16/4/20. Commd 5/8/41. AVM 1/7/71. Retd GD 16/4/75.
LAWRENCE P., BSc. Born 30/8/63. Commd 14/4/85. Flt Lt 14/10/88. Retd PI 28/4/91.
LAWRENCE P. J., LLB. Born 20/5/52. Commd 13/9/70. Sqn Ldr 1/7/82. Retd GD 20/5/89.
LAWRENCE P. W. F. Born 10/2/43. Commd 17/7/64. Flt Lt 17/1/70. Retd GD 13/1/79.
LAWRENCE R. F. Born 3/2/33. Commd 11/4/51. Flt Lt 15/1/57. Retd GD 9/7/65.
LAWRENCE R. J., MBE. Born 31/1/33. Commd 13/2/52. Flt Lt 30/6/57. Retd GD 31/1/88.

LAWRENCE R. N. Born 11/11/47. Commd 1/8/69. Fg Offr 1/2/71. Retd RGT 27/11/73.
LAWRENCE V. J. W. Born 1/9/28. Commd 11/4/51. Wg Cdr 1/7/72. Retd SEC 13/7/75.
LAWRENCE W. T. J. Born 11/8/45. Commd 18/8/67. Flt Lt 18/2/73. Retd SUP 11/8/83.
LAWRENSON A. J., BA. Born 6/4/67. Commd 19/2/89. Flt Lt 19/8/91. Retd GD 14/3/97.
LAWRENSON R. F., DFM. Born 28/10/21. Commd 21/7/44. Flt Lt 19/6/52. Retd GD 2/3/63.
LAWRENSON R. I., FHCIMA FIMgt. Born 14/9/32. Commd 29/5/52. Gp Capt 1/1/76. Retd ADMIN 16/9/82.
LAWRIE J. D. C. Born 18/1/27. Commd 6/12/56. Sqn Ldr 1/1/68. Retd GD 31/10/75.
LAWRIE J. R. G., MIMgt. Born 8/10/24. Commd 1/10/52. Wg Cdr 1/7/79. Retd SY 8/10/82.
LAWRY K. J. Born 21/4/47. Commd 2/6/67. Sqn Ldr 1/1/82. Retd GD 21/6/00.
LAWS A. P., MBE. Born 24/5/63. Commd 20/10/83. Sqn Ldr 1/1/97. Retd OPS SPT 24/5/01.
LAWS D. F. Born 14/6/32. Commd 28/9/51. Flt Lt 28/3/56. Retd GD 15/11/75.
LAWS L. R. Born 11/3/40. Commd. 24/6/71. Flt Lt 13/11/77. Retd GD(G) 8/3/87.
LAWS P. E. Born 17/9/25. Commd 21/5/52. Sqn Ldr 1/7/74. Retd PI 17/9/80.
LAWSON A. Born 6/10/17. Commd 7/2/43. Sqn Ldr 1/7/52. Retd SUP 15/11/66.
LAWSON A. A. Born 17/2/32. Commd 22/2/52. Flt Lt 5/9/57. Retd GD 29/5/65.
LAWSON A. J., MBE ChB. Born 26/1/27. Commd 1/4/52. Wg Cdr 5/8/64. Retd MED 3/12/69.
LAWSON D. Born 1/1/50. Commd 27/3/70. Flt Lt 1/7/75. Retd GD 1/11/88.
LAWSON D. E. Born 11/4/43. Commd 2/8/68. Flt Lt 10/6/74. Retd ENG 11/4/81.
LAWSON E. A., MA. Born 17/2/54. Commd 2/1/77. Sqn Ldr 1/1/86. Retd ADMIN 2/1/93.
LAWSON E. R. W. Born 7/12/23. Commd 10/12/43. Wg Cdr 1/7/65. Retd GD 29/5/76.
LAWSON E. W., MBE CEng MRAeS MIMgt. Born 16/7/21. Commd 6/3/52. Sqn Ldr 1/1/62. Retd ENG 16/7/71.
LAWSON G. C., AInstAM. Born 18/3/54. Commd 19/3/81. Flt Lt 19/9/87. Retd ADMIN 10/11/96.
LAWSON G. G., BA. Born 25/7/37. Commd 24/4/56. Wg Cdr 1/1/79. Retd GD 25/7/92.
LAWSON K. W. Born 31/10/24. Commd 30/6/45. Flt Lt 30/12/48. Retd GD(G) 31/10/79.
LAWSON M. C. Born 1/7/10. Commd 23/8/44. Flt Offr 1/5/50. Retd PRT 11/3/60.
LAWSON P. G. Born 17/9/27. Commd 23/4/52. Flt Lt 27/8/58. Retd GD 17/9/70.
LAWSON P. W., AFM. Born 4/2/25. Commd 30/7/64. Flt Lt 30/7/67. Retd GD 21/3/78.
LAWTON D. G., MBE. Born 24/7/25. Commd 26/6/66. Flt Lt 26/8/69. Retd GD 15/1/80.
LAWTON G. C. S. Born 21/7/15. Commd 7/2/42. Flt Lt 9/9/46. Retd MAR 21/7/64.
LAWTON H. J. Born 18/6/37. Commd 25/6/66. Flt Lt 1/7/68. Retd GD 18/6/75.
LAWTON J. M. Born 12/5/44. Commd 3/11/77. Flt Lt 3/11/78. Retd ADMIN 3/11/85.
LAWTON J. V. Born 30/12/43. Commd 17/5/63. Sqn Ldr 1/7/78. Retd GD 30/6/84.
LAWTON J. W. H. Born 13/9/28. Commd 9/2/66. Sqn Ldr 1/7/78. Retd ENG 13/9/84.
LAWTON M. C. Born 10/3/52. Commd 9/3/72. Sqn Ldr 1/7/88. Retd GD 1/7/91.
LAWTON R. E. Born 11/2/42. Commd 21/7/61. Flt Lt 21/1/67. Retd GD 11/7/85.
LAWTON R. E. Born 31/7/51. Commd 13/2/86. Flt Lt 13/2/88. Retd ENG 22/8/91.
LAX B., CEng MIEE MRAeS MIMgt. Born 15/9/24. Commd 14/2/45. Wg Cdr 1/7/70. Retd ENG 30/10/76.
LAX F. C. Born 3/3/11. Commd 14/12/44. Flt Lt 15/12/49. Retd SEC 25/5/56.
LAX I. A. W. Born 24/3/60. Commd 18/10/79. Flt Lt 18/4/85. Retd GD 16/2/94.
LAXON P. B. Born 10/12/19. Commd 13/10/41. Flt Lt 1/9/45. Retd SEC 10/12/68.
LAYBOURN R. A., OBE BEM BA. Born 20/11/43. Commd 25/2/82. Wg Cdr 1/1/96. Retd ENG 13/6/98.
LAYBOURNE K. R. Born 5/11/57. Commd 24/7/81. Flt Lt 3/12/84. Retd SY 14/3/96.
LAYCOCK A. D. Born 21/11/30. Commd 28/6/51. Sqn Ldr 1/7/65. Retd GD 21/5/76.
LAYCOCK F. Born 20/4/30. Commd 8/2/51. Flt Lt 25/7/57. Retd GD 20/4/68.
LAYCOCK J. Born 25/4/38. Commd 28/7/59. Gp Capt 1/7/80. Retd GD 1/11/89.
LAZZARI J. N. Born 8/9/49. Commd 28/6/79. Sqn Ldr 1/1/95. Retd GD 2/4/01.
LE BAIGUE E. A. Born 20/11/31. Commd 6/6/57. Sqn Ldr 1/7/67. Retd GD 1/12/71.
Le BROCQ R. H. B., AFC. Born 15/1/36. Commd 17/12/57. Sqn Ldr 1/7/71. Retd GD 29/5/76.
Le BRUN J. L. J. C., AFC. Born 2/3/38. Commd 1/11/61. Flt Lt 26/7/67. Retd GD 24/12/82.
LE CHEMINANT Sir Peter, GBE KCB DFC*. Born 17/6/20. Commd 23/12/39. ACM 2/2/76. Retd GD 27/8/79.
LE CLERCQ L. R. W., MIMgt. Born 31/7/48. Commd 2/8/73. Sqn Ldr 1/7/86. Retd GD(G) 31/7/92.
LE CORNU C. C. Born 16/9/39. Commd 25/7/60. Wg Cdr 1/1/84. Retd GD 16/9/94.
LE COUNT E. W. Born 23/9/37. Commd 10/9/70. Sqn Ldr 1/7/90. Retd GD 1/7/93.
Le CRERAR J. L. Born 6/1/18. Commd 27/1/44. Flt Lt 27/7/47. Retd ENG 30/6/54. rtg Sqn Ldr.
LE CUDENEC R., DFC. Born 13/12/22. Commd 13/12/42. Wg Cdr 1/1/61. Retd GD 13/8/77.
LE DIEU N., CEng MRAeS. Born 26/9/39. Commd 4/9/61. Gp Capt 1/1/91. Retd ENG 26/9/94.
LE DREW L. R. Born 20/11/36. Commd 18/6/62. Flt Lt 18/6/62. Retd GD 18/6/78.
Le GRAS J. M. Born 26/8/32. Commd 24/10/51. Flt Lt 16/2/57. Retd GD 26/8/70.
Le GRESLEY A. I. Born 11/3/28. Commd 1/3/49. Sqn Ldr 1/1/63. Retd GD 11/3/66.
LE HEUZE D. P. J. Born 11/10/55. Commd 9/5/91. Flt Lt 9/5/93. Retd ADMIN 14/3/97.
LE JEUNE P. V. Born 31/10/46. Commd 28/2/69. Flt Lt 4/5/72. Retd GD 2/11/76.
LE LORRAIN R. C. Born 31/1/28. Commd 28/6/51. Flt Lt 28/6/57. Retd SUP 31/1/83.
LE MARIE M. J. Born 5/9/49. Commd 7/6/68. Sqn Ldr 1/7/84. Retd ADMIN 1/7/87.
LE MARQUAND P. E. Born 18/12/35. Commd 15/2/56. Gp Capt 1/1/86. Retd GD 5/7/88.
LE MOINE J. Born 16/6/35. Commd 11/11/71. Sqn Ldr 1/1/80. Retd ADMIN 16/1/87.
Le ROUGETEL S. Born 18/5/12. Commd 9/5/37. Sqn Ldr 1/8/47. Retd GD 11/2/58 rtg Wg Cdr.

LE-MONNIER P. R. Born 26/3/69. Commd 28/7/88. Fg Offr 28/1/91. Retd SY 31/3/93.
LEA R. F. Born 2/4/44. Commd 3/8/62. Flt Lt 3/2/68. Retd GD 2/4/81.
LEA R. G. Born 14/10/12. Commd 14/7/44. Fg Offr 14/1/45. Retd GD 2/1/46.
LEA R. J., BSc. Born 17/5/63. Commd 2/9/84. Sqn Ldr 1/7/95. Retd GD 17/5/01.
LEA S. M., BSc. Born 5/4/63. Commd 2/9/84. Sqn Ldr 1/1/94. Retd SUP 5/4/01.
LEA T. C. Born 28/2/24. Commd 14/4/49. Flt Lt 14/10/52. Retd GD 15/4/59.
LEACH A. J., CEng MIEE MRAeS. Born 21/12/43. Commd 15/7/65. Flt Lt 15/10/70. Retd ENG 21/12/81.
LEACH C. W., CEng MIEE. Born 19/2/21. Commd 15/7/43. Wg Cdr 1/1/63. Retd ENG 19/2/76.
LEACH D. Q. R. Born 11/12/43. Commd 10/1/69. Flt Lt 10/7/74. Retd GD 2/12/91.
LEACH P. A. G., MBE CEng MIEE MRAeS. Born 20/5/39. Commd 2/3/65. Wg Cdr 1/1/85. Retd ENG 20/5/94.
LEACH R. E., MBE BA MIMgt. Born 10/2/36. Commd 27/6/59. Sqn Ldr 1/7/74. Retd GD 28/8/88.
LEACH R. M., BSc. Born 23/9/35. Commd 30/4/58. Sqn Ldr 1/1/69. Retd GD 22/12/69.
LEACH W. T., BSc. Born 23/4/62. Commd 31/8/80. Flt Lt 15/10/84. Retd GD 23/4/00.
LEADBEATER R. A. L. Born 17/1/40. Commd 13/12/79. Sqn Ldr 1/7/92. Retd ENG 17/1/95.
LEADON F. R. Born 9/1/23. Commd 11/10/44. Flt Lt 17/5/56. Retd GD 1/10/68.
LEAH L. E., ACIS. Born 30/7/20. Commd 1/6/43. Flt Lt 6/12/49. Retd SEC 1/10/60.
LEAH M. H. Born 2/4/29. Commd 27/8/59. Sqn Ldr 1/1/73. Retd ENG 22/11/85.
LEAHY A. McL. Born 31/5/57. Commd 25/2/82. Sqn Ldr 1/1/90. Retd ENG 31/5/95.
LEAHY J. J., BA FIMgt. Born 26/8/38. Commd 28/5/66. Gp Capt 1/1/88. Retd SUP 26/8/93.
LEANEY G. Born 18/6/45. Commd 3/3/67. Sqn Ldr 1/7/80. Retd ADMIN 18/6/89.
LEANING P. T. W., FILT MCIPS. Born 6/2/48. Commd 19/6/70. A Cdre 1/7/98. Retd SUP 2/8/00.
LEAR G. G. Born 9/6/35. Commd 27/2/70. Sqn Ldr 1/7/77. Retd GD(G) 27/2/86.
LEARMONTH, C., MBE MIMgt. Born 13/6/33. Commd 23/6/67. Wg Cdr 1/7/80. Retd SY 18/9/86.
LEARMOUNT D. W. Born 3/5/47. Commd 8/10/70. Flt Lt 8/4/75. Retd GD 1/6/79.
LEARNER R. H., CEng MIProdE MRAeS. Born 23/8/48. Commd 14/9/75. Wg Cdr 1/7/90. Retd ENG 19/7/93.
LEARY J. D. Born 1/6/32. Commd 14/4/53. Gp Capt 1/1/85. Retd GD 1/6/88.
LEARY J. M., AFC BSc. Born 29/5/28. Commd 25/11/54. Sqn Ldr 1/1/63. Retd GD 30/1/76.
LEARY M. V., MBE. Born 9/3/40. Commd 12/7/65. Flt Lt 8/3/72. Retd PE 12/7/81.
LEARY N. O., DFC. Born 19/10/34. Commd 27/5/53. Sqn Ldr 1/1/69. Retd GD 1/11/85.
LEARY W. B. L., MBE. Born 19/8/23. Commd 16/3/45. Flt Lt 4/1/51. Retd GD 27/9/68.
LEATHAM G. H. Born 9/5/36. Commd 3/11/77. Sqn Ldr 1/1/91. Retd ENG 1/4/95.
LEATHERDALE F. R., DFC. Born 3/11/22. Commd 5/2/42. Sqn Ldr 1/4/56. Retd GD 3/11/65.
LEATHERS F. C. Born 20/12/20. Commd 13/7/61. Sqn Ldr 1/1/72. Retd ENG 2/11/74.
LEATHLEY F. Born 17/2/96. Commd 1/4/18. Flt Lt 30/6/22. Retd GD 27/1/25.
LEAVER G., CBE MIMgt MHSM. Born 27/10/34. Commd 9/8/66. Gp Capt 1/7/89. Retd MED(SEC) 1/7/93.
LEAVEY D. Born 11/2/34. Commd 20/1/56. Sqn Ldr 1/1/72. Retd GD 23/1/82.
LECKENBY I. P. Born 28/8/46. Commd 18/8/67. Flt Lt 18/8/70. Retd GD 1/7/78.
LECKEY R. G., MSc ARIC. Born 13/5/33. Commd 28/9/60. Flt Lt 28/12/61. Retd ADMIN 29/5/84.
LECKIE R., CB DSO DSC DFC. Born 16/4/90. Commd 1/8/19. A Cdre 1/1/37. Retd GD 6/4/42 rtg AVM.
LECKY-THOMPSON., AFC. Born 12/3/35. Commd 5/7/53. Sqn Ldr 1/1/69. Retd GD 20/9/75. Reinstated 3/9/81.
    Sqn Ldr 15/12/75. Retd GD 30/9/90.
LEDDY A. Born 12/4/25. Commd 26/11/69. Flt Lt 28/11/72. Retd PI 2/11/77.
LEDGARD The Rev. J. C., BA. Born 3/6/41. Commd 1/9/70. Retd 1/9/86. Wg Cdr.
LEDGER C. L. K. Born 21/12/39. Commd 22/8/59. Sqn Ldr 1/7/77. Retd ADMIN 21/12/94.
LEDGER R. Born 24/9/49. Commd 3/8/68. Fg Offr 10/8/70. Retd SEC 14/7/71.
LEDLIE E. P., MBE. Born 26/9/23. Commd 4/2/48. Wg Cdr 1/1/73. Retd RGT 18/1/74.
LEDWARD H. T. R. Born 3/3/27. Commd 26/5/54. Flt Lt 14/2/66. Retd GD 3/4/81.
LEDWARD J. Born 4/1/33. Commd 4/6/52. Sqn Ldr 1/1/84. Retd GD 4/9/93.
LEDWIDGE R. G., AFC*. Born 19/1/38. Commd 22/1/57. Flt Lt 24/7/62. Retd GD 22/2/76.
LEE A. Born 24/7/57. Commd 24/6/76. Flt Lt 24/12/81. Retd GD 11/2/90.
LEE A. L. Born 10/2/45. Commd 27/5/71. Flt Lt 27/5/73. Retd GD(G) 10/2/83.
LEE A. N., BSc. Born 16/4/65. Commd 11/1/85. Flt Lt 22/6/89. Retd ENG 14/9/96.
LEE B. A., BSc CEng MIEE. Born 5/10/49. Commd 26/2/71. Wg Cdr 1/1/81. Retd ENG 6/6/94.
LEE B. J. Born 24/2/32. Commd 9/2/66. Flt Lt 9/2/71. Retd GD 26/8/75.
LEE B. R. Born 13/12/54. Commd 4/11/82. Flt Lt 4/11/84. Retd GD(G) 1/4/93.
LEE B. R. Born 15/1/42. Commd 6/7/62. Gp Capt 1/1/90. Retd GD 27/7/96.
LEE C. H., BSc. Born 22/11/62. Commd 2/9/84. Flt Lt 2/3/87. Retd GD 14/9/96.
LEE C. L. Born 22/5/52. Commd 16/4/78. Sqn Ldr 1/1/89. Retd ADMIN 5/10/92.
LEE Sir David, GBE CB. Born 4/9/12. Commd 23/7/32. ACM 7/10/67. Retd GD 19/3/71.
LEE D. A., BSc. Born 14/9/51. Commd 15/9/69. Sqn Ldr 1/7/84. Retd ENG 14/9/89.
LEE D. E. Born 10/9/22. Commd 18/7/45. Flt Lt 10/4/57. Retd SEC 3/6/65.
LEE D. G., MBE. Born 7/11/45. Commd 20/10/67. Sqn Ldr 1/1/78. Retd GD 7/11/83.
LEE D. W. Born 16/1/38. Commd 28/7/59. Sqn Ldr 1/1/84. Retd GD 16/7/98.
LEE D. W. H. Born 28/10/30. Commd 30/9/53. Sqn Ldr 1/7/76. Retd GD 28/10/88.
LEE F. H. Born 21/2/38. Commd 3/8/62. Sqn Ldr 1/1/90. Retd GD 21/11/94.
LEE G., BSc. Born 2/3/25. Commd 3/1/46. Wg Cdr 1/7/63. Retd ENG 31/3/78.

LEE G. Born 5/5/39. Commd 10/2/64. Wg Cdr 1/7/80. Retd GD 3/10/89.
LEE G. A., CEng MIEE MRAeS MIMgt. Born 20/9/43. Commd 15/7/64. Sqn Ldr 1/7/77. Retd ENG 2/12/97.
LEE G. G. Born 11/5/28. Commd 27/7/49. Sqn Ldr 1/7/59. Retd GD 26/8/77.
LEE G. R. Born 1/6/27. Commd 27/8/59. Sqn Ldr 1/7/72. Retd SY 2/6/77.
LEE H. Born 24/8/96. Commd 14/3/40. Flt Lt 1/3/45. Retd ENG 5/8/49 rtg Sqn Ldr.
LEE J. E. Born 29/6/23. Commd 26/7/44. Flt Lt 26/1/48. Retd GD 29/6/66.
LEE J. F. Born 10/12/22. Commd 3/8/61. Flt Lt 3/8/64. Retd ENG 2/9/73.
LEE J. F. W. Born 20/3/20. Commd 17/5/56. Flt Lt 17/5/62. Retd ENG 20/6/73.
LEE J. G. J., CEng MRAeS MIMechE. Born 29/7/38. Commd 28/7/60. Sqn Ldr 1/1/74. Retd ENG 7/8/81.
LEE J. J., AFC BSc. Born 18/8/39. Commd 23/10/59. Sqn Ldr 1/1/72. Retd GD 1/9/73.
LEE J. W. Born 16/4/36. Commd 9/3/72. Sqn Ldr 1/7/87. Retd ADMIN 30/6/91.
LEE M. E. Born 7/11/42. Commd 4/11/82. Flt Lt 4/11/86. Retd ENG 10/6/93.
LEE M. E. Born 9/4/55. Commd 23/5/85. Sqn Ldr 1/7/94. Retd ENG 7/9/98.
LEE M. J. W., CBE BSc. Born 23/2/30. Commd 10/3/54. Gp Capt 1/1/78. Retd GD 7/4/84.
LEE N. C., MB BS MRCS LRCP DAvMed. Born 11/7/33. Commd 21/2/52. Sqn Ldr 19/7/71. Retd MED 30/8/74.
LEE N. P. Born 17/4/57. Commd 27/1/77. Flt Lt 27/7/82. Retd GD 24/11/88.
LEE O. R. Born 6/9/23. Commd 19/2/43. Flt Lt 19/8/46. Retd GD 20/12/47 rtg Sqn Ldr.
LEE P. A., MB ChB BAO DPH DIH. Born 11/6/11. Commd 7/9/35. Gp Capt 1/1/57. Retd MED 7/6/67.
LEE P. A. Born 4/4/37. Commd 26/11/60. Flt Lt 26/5/66. Retd GD 9/8/76.
LEE P. D., MBE. Born 24/9/20. Commd 10/5/48. Wg Cdr 1/1/63. Retd RGT 1/4/71.
LEE P. H., AIIP. Born 27/12/23. Commd 1/2/45. Sqn Ldr 1/1/70. Retd ENG 30/6/78.
LEE P. N. Born 1/1/20. Commd 7/7/44. Sqn Ldr 1/7/58. Retd GD 1/1/63.
LEE R. E. Born 20/10/29. Commd 28/7/60. Flt Lt 28/1/66. Retd GD 1/5/85.
LEE R. E. Born 4/10/48. Commd 24/4/70. Sqn Ldr 1/1/82. Retd GD 4/10/86.
LEE R. K., CEng MIMechE. Born 25/10/45. Commd 7/3/71. Flt Lt 7/8/74. Retd ENG 29/5/98.
LEE W. B., MBE BEM. Born 11/11/36. Commd 22/2/79. Sqn Ldr 1/7/88. Retd ENG 11/11/91.
LEE W. G. Born 30/12/43. Commd 21/5/65. Fg Offr 21/5/67. Retd GD 9/1/70.
LEE-POTTER J. P., MB BS MRCS LRCP DTM&H DCP MCPath. Born 30/8/34. Commd 3/1/60. Sqn Ldr 25/11/64.
  Retd MED 24/2/68.
LEE-PRESTON P. C. Born 23/4/47. Commd 25/2/66. Flt Lt 25/8/71. Retd GD 23/4/85.
LEECH B. J. Born 22/7/36. Commd 21/4/67. Flt Lt 21/4/73. Retd GD(G) 31/8/89.
LEECH J. W. Born 11/1/36. Commd 22/7/66. Flt Lt 22/7/72. Retd MAR 12/1/78.
LEEDHAM M. L., MIMgt. Born 18/11/39. Commd 19/12/61. Sqn Ldr 1/1/72. Retd SUP 18/11/77.
LEEDS P. A. Born 27/8/25. Commd 27/4/45. Flt Lt 27/10/48. Retd GD 2/9/75.
LEEDS P. F. Born 25/3/42. Commd 31/10/74. Wg Cdr 1/1/91. Retd PRT 31/10/92.
LEEFARR B., MIMgt. Born 6/9/35. Commd 22/4/55. Wg Cdr 1/1/76. Retd GD 6/9/90.
LEEMING G. H. Born 14/9/42. Commd 28/4/61. Sqn Ldr 1/7/78. Retd GD 1/10/90.
LEEMING R. D., FRCS LRCP&S(I) DLO. Born 15/6/31. Commd 7/2/60. Wg Cdr 2/9/71. Retd MED 1/10/76.
LEEMING Rev J. Born 10/11/34. Commd 1/6/64. Retd 11/11/84. Wg Cdr.
LEEMING T. Born 26/4/32. Commd 9/8/51. Flt Lt 28/11/56. Retd GD 27/7/70.
LEEMING-LATHAM L., MMedSc MB ChB DAvMed MFOM. Born 13/4/51. Commd 23/1/72. Wg Cdr 4/6/88. Retd
  MED 24/4/96.
LEES B. D., BSc CEng MIEE. Born 30/9/61. Commd 14/9/80. Flt Lt 15/10/86. Retd ENG 10/6/94.
LEES B. E. Born 15/11/29. Commd 1/3/62. Sqn Ldr 1/7/80. Retd ENG 15/11/89.
LEES C. Q., FIFA. Born 15/7/39. Commd 27/8/59. Sqn Ldr 1/1/72. Retd ADMIN 15/7/94.
LEES J. R., MBE. Born 14/10/35. Commd 9/4/57. Sqn Ldr 1/1/74. Retd GD 14/10/93.
LEES M. R. Born 25/12/47. Commd 23/2/68. Flt Lt 23/8/73. Retd GD 25/12/85.
LEES N., BA. Born 12/11/37. Commd 30/9/57. Sqn Ldr 1/7/69. Retd ENG 12/11/75.
LEES P. D. Born 12/4/61. Commd 29/7/83. Sqn Ldr 1/7/95. Retd GD 12/4/99.
LEES P. D. Born 6/11/55. Commd 27/2/75. Flt Lt 27/8/80. Retd GD 27/6/87.
LEES P. J. Born 16/11/46. Commd 10/12/65. Flt Lt 10/6/72. Retd GD 16/11/84.
LEES R. A. Born 29/10/32. Commd 28/7/53. Sqn Ldr 1/7/72. Retd GD 23/12/65.
LEES R. L., CB MBE FCIPD FIMgt. Born 27/2/31. Commd 9/4/52. AVM 1/1/83. Retd ADMIN 3/3/86.
LEESE A. D. W., IEng FIEIE. Born 16/1/34. Commd 30/5/69. Flt Lt 30/5/74. Retd ENG 16/1/94.
LEESE I. D. Born 22/10/57. Commd 23/10/86. Flt Lt 23/10/88. Retd SY 22/10/95.
LEGG A. E. Born 18/5/41. Commd 24/2/61. Sqn Ldr 1/1/74. Retd GD 18/5/79.
LEGG B. R., MBE. Born 7/1/24. Commd 3/11/60. Flt Lt 3/11/65. Retd RGT 9/12/69.
LEGG P. D., MA FIMgt MRAeS. Born 24/5/55. Commd 15/9/74. Wg Cdr 1/7/93. Retd GD 24/5/99.
LEGG S. J. E., BSc. Born 18/1/51. Commd 22/4/71. Sqn Ldr 1/1/86. Retd GD 6/5/88.
LEGGE A. F. Born 4/6/44. Commd 3/3/67. Fg Offr 3/9/67. Retd GD 19/12/68.
LEGGE P. N. Born 24/3/31. Commd 30/7/52. Sqn Ldr 1/7/62. Retd GD 24/3/69.
LEGGET E. H., MRAeS MIMgt. Born 28/6/30. Commd 1/8/51. Sqn Ldr 1/7/69. Retd GD 1/5/76.
LEGGETT A. J., OBE FBCS MIMgt. Born 9/11/30. Commd 18/2/54. Gp Capt 1/7/77. Retd ADMIN 5/4/83 rtg A Cdre.
LEGGETT C. J. Born 17/11/42. Commd 8/12/61. Wg Cdr 1/1/95. Retd GD 17/11/98.
LEGGETT D. N. J. P. Born 17/4/14. Commd 3/3/33. Wg Cdr 1/7/47. Retd ENG 19/6/51 rtg Gp Capt.
LEGGETT P. G. Born 14/2/21. Commd 31/8/40. Sqn Ldr 1/7/49. Retd GD 23/5/58.

LEGGETT R. W. Born 3/4/22. Commd 10/1/42. Wg Cdr 1/7/56. Retd GD 1/4/68.
LEGGOTT R. H. Born 6/9/30. Commd 24/9/64. Sqn Ldr 1/7/74. Retd ENG 6/9/92.
LEGGOTT S. P., BSc. Born 15/3/63. Commd 13/4/83. Flt Lt 15/1/87. Retd GD 15/7/96.
LEGH-SMITH J. R. Born 10/9/39. Commd 19/12/61. Gp Capt 1/1/89. Retd GD 10/9/94.
LEHEUP M. D., BA. Born 12/1/29. Commd 5/5/60. Flt Lt 5/5/66. Retd ENG 30/7/80.
LEIGH A. M. Born 23/1/46. Commd 21/3/69. Flt Lt 1/11/72. Retd GD 3/2/76.
LEIGH B. N. B. Born 31/3/48. Commd 1/8/69. Sqn Ldr 1/1/80. Retd ADMIN 31/3/86.
LEIGH J. M. Born 20/1/46. Commd 20/8/65. Wg Cdr 1/7/89. Retd GD 13/9/96.
LEIGH M. E. Born 18/8/43. Commd 14/6/63. Sqn Ldr 1/1/77. Retd EDN 18/8/81.
LEIGH U. D. B. Born 1/7/15. Commd 29/11/44. Fg Offr 29/11/46. Retd SUP 6/10/50 rtg Flt Offr.
LEIGHTON D. G., MIMgt. Born 15/10/34. Commd 17/1/69. Sqn Ldr 1/1/81. Retd ADMIN 15/10/92.
LEIGHTON G. S. Born 8/11/47. Commd 29/6/72. Flt Lt 29/12/78. Retd SUP 27/3/84.
LEIGHTON R. Born 16/11/33. Commd 30/7/52. Sqn Ldr 1/7/71. Retd GD 16/11/88.
LEIGHTON-PORTER S. E., BSc. Born 26/3/57. Commd 5/9/76. Sqn Ldr 1/1/92. Retd GD 26/3/95.
LEINSTER I. A., BSc. Born 18/8/29. Commd 8/5/52. Sqn Ldr 1/7/62. Retd GD 2/6/71.
LEIPNIK W. A. M. Born 26/4/61. Commd 4/11/82. Flt Lt 30/4/89. Retd GD(G) 7/12/92.
LEITCH A. H. Born 9/4/51. Commd 16/3/73. Flt Lt 16/3/76. Retd GD 4/8/87.
LEITCH D. G., MB ChB MRCP DCH. Born 17/5/39 Commd 15/10/62. Wg Cdr. 28/9/78. Retd MED 1/2/79.
LEITH D. I., BA. Born 12/1/38. Commd 1/1/63. Sqn Ldr 1/7/70. Retd EDN 19/4/74.
LEITH D. J., OBE. Born 6/11/25. Commd 22/6/45. Gp Capt 1/7/77. Retd GD 6/11/80.
LELLIOT R. G. Born 31/1/32. Commd 22/8/63. Flt Lt 16/6/68. Retd SEC 15/5/79.
LEMARE D. A. C. Born 11/8/46. Commd 28/4/67. Sqn Ldr 1/1/87. Retd GD 27/4/00.
LEMON B. J., MBE AFC FIMgt. Born 18/2/34. Commd 9/11/54. A Cdre 1/1/81. Retd GD 14/6/89.
LEMON G. T. Born 27/12/22. Commd 29/1/44. Flt Lt 1/12/55. Retd GD 30/12/68.
LEMON J. H., MB BS DAvMed. Born 4/6/32. Commd 10/9/52. Wg Cdr 17/8/71. Retd MED 17/8/74.
LEMON P. C., DSO DFC. Born 16/6/18. Comm 12/10/36. Sqn Ldr 1/8/47. Retd GD 1/12/57.
LENAGHAN P. Born 28/2/38. Commd 18/2/58. Flt Lt 15/2/65. Retd GD 28/2/93.
LENNON P. Born 17/3/34. Commd 5/11/52. Flt Lt 24/3/58. Retd GD 1/6/76.
LENNON P. C. C. Born 8/5/42. Commd 15/9/61. Fg Offr 15/9/63. Retd GD 5/5/67.
LENNON R. B. Born 30/11/51. Commd 27/9/73. Sqn Ldr 1/1/88. Retd GD 1/1/91.
LENNOX D. Born 27/2/19. Commd 22/5/42. Flt Lt 16/7/51. Retd ENG 1/5/61 rtg Sqn Ldr.
LENNOX D. S., OBE CEng MRAeS. Born 12/2/37. Commd 23/7/58. Gp Capt 1/7/80. Retd ENG 1/8/87.
LENTON W. S. Born 18/2/40. Commd 27/7/60. Flt Lt 2/7/63. Retd GD 18/2/78.
LEONARD A., OBE BEM. Born 15/3/42. Commd 14/8/80. Wg Cdr 1/7/93. Retd ENG 3/1/98.
LEONARD B. J., MCIPS MIMgt. Born 19/3/26. Commd 3/5/46. Wg Cdr 1/7/67. Retd SUP 31/3/77 rtg Gp Capt.
LEONARD G., BA. Born 24/4/64. Commd 2/9/84. Flt Lt 2/3/88. Retd ADMIN 14/3/97.
LEONARD G. H. J., DFC. Born 14/2/23. Commd 10/3/44. Sqn Ldr 1/7/61. Retd SEC 31/8/68.
LEONARD H. A. Born 23/4/33. Commd 26/3/53. Flt Lt 5/8/58. Retd GD 23/4/71.
LEONARD R. A. Born 19/12/15. Commd 10/12/42. Flt Lt 11/10/46. Retd ENG 1/12/62.
LEONARD W. Born 11/6/22. Commd 19/7/57. Sqn Ldr 1/1/70. Retd ENG 11/10/77.
LEONCZEK M. R., BSc. Born 5/5/61. Commd 30/10/83. Sqn Ldr 1/7/97. Retd GD 1/7/00.
LEPPARD D. E. Born 13/5/38. Commd 13/12/60. A Cdre 1/7/86. Retd GD 9/9/89.
LEPPARD R. W., OBE CEng MIERE MIMgt. Born 23/9/21. Commd 13/12/45. Gp Capt 1/7/76. Retd ENG 29/11/78.
LERWILL G. F., DFC. Born 12/3/15. Commd 15/3/35. Cp Capt 1/1/59. Retd GD 12/4/65.
LESLIE A. B. Born 26/11/35. Commd 21/3/78. Flt Lt 23/1/83. Retd ADMIN 6/4/90.
LESLIE D. M. Born 16/1/34. Commd 3/9/52. Wg Cdr 1/7/72. Retd GD 24/2/85.
LESLIE G. E., BSc. Born 30/3/29. Commd 19/12/52. Flt Lt 17/5/56. Retd GD 14/1/69.
LESLIE J. Born 13/1/55. Commd 27/3/75. Flt Lt 27/3/80. Retd GD 13/1/93.
LESLIE W. A. Born 26/5/12. Commd 26/5/41. Fg Offr 26/5/42. Retd ENG 18/10/47 rtg Flt Lt.
LETCHFORD C. W. G. Born 2/5/38. Commd 6/4/72. Flt Lt 6/4/74. Retd GD 13/6/78.
LETHEM D. A. Born 31/12/29. Commd 11/4/51. Sqn Ldr 1/1/61. Retd GD 24/9/76.
LETHER H. V., CBE. Born 5/6/45. Commd 4/10/63. Gp Capt 1/7/91. Retd GD 3/12/96.
LETTEN N. L. Born 27/2/12. Commd 1/5/39. Wg Cdr 1/1/55. Retd ENG 1/5/67.
LETTON M. H. Born 21/7/35. Commd 3/3/54. Flt Lt 3/9/59. Retd GD 21/7/73.
LEUCHARS C. G., BSc. Born 5/6/46. Commd 26/5/67. Flt Lt 26/5/70. Retd GD 14/3/96.
LEVENE I. Born 2/5/22. Commd 6/11/43. Flt Lt 26/12/57. Retd GD(G) 17/10/63.
LEVER R. A. Born 10/2/52. Commd 24/1/71. Flt Lt 24/12/76. Retd GD 10/2/90.
LEVERSON J. J. Born 1/11/37. Commd 1/6/72. Flt Lt 1/6/74. Retd GD(G) 1/6/80.
LEVETT G. Born 25/2/32. Commd 2/7/52. Sqn Ldr 1/7/66. Retd ENG 25/2/70.
LEVIN R. Born 10/10/20. Commd 25/8/60. Flt Lt 25/8/65. Retd ENG 6/4/68.
LEVINGSTON., The Rev P. O. W. , BA. Born 7/9/31. Commd 4/9/62. Retd 4/9/78. Wg Cdr.
LEVISEUR R. H. Born 9/10/23. Commd 19/6/47. Sqn Ldr 1/1/65. Retd GD 9/9/72.
LEVISTON A. M., BSc. Born 5/12/57. Commd 26/9/82. Sqn Ldr 1/1/95. Retd GD 26/9/98.
LEVISTON A. R. Born 19/12/43. Commd 30/5/69. Sqn Ldr 1/7/89. Retd ENG 2/6/93.
LEVITT A. W. Born 19/6/44. Commd 29/6/72. Gp Capt 1/7/93. Retd ENG 4/4/94.
LEVY M. H., MBE. Born 18/1/27. Commd 1/1/47. Sqn Ldr 1/1/57. Retd GD 26/10/68.

LEWARNE J. O. H., BA. Born 30/8/30. Commd 5/5/54. Flt Lt 3/12/56. Retd GD 5/5/70.
LEWELL P. R. Born 19/4/25. Commd 4/11/44. Flt Lt 4/5/48. Retd GD 19/4/63.
LEWENDON A. J., LLB. Born 16/3/53. Commd 31/7/83. Flt Lt 31/1/87. Retd ADMIN 24/4/92.
LEWENDON J. M. Born 14/4/30. Commd 12/12/51. Gp Capt 1/1/76. Retd ADMIN 31/12/83.
LEWENDON M. J. Born 16/8/49. Commd 10/2/72. Flt Lt 17/2/77. Retd GD 18/10/87.
LEWER J. H. Born 19/2/41. Commd 3/8/62. Flt Lt 3/2/68. Retd GD 19/2/79.
LEWER J. S. Born 5/6/37. Commd 21/3/69. Sqn Ldr 30/11/80. Retd MED(SEC) 7/4/88.
LEWIN E. R. Born 6/4/13. Commd 29/8/42. Flt Lt 10/11/55. Retd SUP 10/6/62.
LEWIN P. Born 31/8/32. Commd 28/2/52. Sqn Ldr 1/7/86. Retd GD 31/8/92.
LEWINGTON D. I. Born 1/7/55. Commd 22/11/73. Sqn Ldr 1/1/86. Retd GD(G) 10/9/93.
LEWINGTON E. J. Born 21/10/22. Commd 3/1/46. Flt Lt 4/1/51. Retd GD 21/10/65.
LEWINGTON G. E. Born 20/2/45. Commd 5/3/65. Flt Lt 5/9/70. Retd GD 26/12/72.
LEWINGTON L. Born 17/8/17. Commd 21/2/40. Sqn Ldr 1/7/50. Retd. ENG 1/1/55 rtg Wg Cdr.
LEWINS D. M. Born 10/8/59. Commd 12/7/79. Sqn Ldr 1/7/91. Retd GD 10/8/97.
LEWIS A. E. Born 30/1/19. Commd 27/8/59. Sqn Ldr 1/1/70. Retd ENG 28/2/76.
LEWIS A. G., MBE. Born 23/6/20. Commd 1/3/45. Sqn Ldr 1/10/55. Retd ENG 26/10/62.
LEWIS A. O. Born 24/12/16. Commd 5/3/53. Sqn Ldr 1/7/61. Retd ENG 24/12/71.
LEWIS A. R. Born 11/10/30. Commd 28/7/53. Flt Lt 28/1/56. Retd GD 11/10/68.
LEWIS B., MIMgt. Born 5/10/24. Commd 13/9/45. Wg Cdr 1/1/71. Retd GD 5/11/75.
LEWIS B. A. Born 14/4/31. Commd 27/3/52. Flt Lt 27/12/57. Retd GD 14/11/68.
LEWIS B. D. B., DFM AFM. Born 16/1/15. Commd 16/5/42. Flt Lt 16/11/46. Retd GD(G) 16/1/65.
LEWIS B. H. J., BSc. Born 6/9/37. Commd 3/12/58. Flt Lt 4/1/66. Retd GD 6/9/75.
LEWIS C. B. Born 29/7/28. Commd 28/6/51. Flt Lt 10/10/56. Retd GD 14/2/63.
LEWIS C. G. Born 1/12/20. Commd 1/10/43. Wg Cdr 1/7/59. Retd GD 1/12/67.
LEWIS D. Born 29/9/50. Commd 23/4/87. Sqn Ldr 1/7/97. Retd ENG 1/10/99.
LEWIS D., MB ChB DObstRCOG. Born 18/10/39. Commd 13/8/72. Sqn Ldr 20/4/70, Retd MED 16/12/77.
LEWIS D. G. Born 26/9/29. Commd 6/12/51. Flt Lt 27/3/57. Retd GD 25/8/70.
LEWIS D. G., DFC. Born 8/5/11. Commd 10/6/32. Gp Capt 1/7/50. Retd GD 6/5/58 rtg A Cdre.
LEWIS D. H. Born 6/5/51. Commd 24/1/74. Sqn Ldr 1/1/89. Retd GD 1/10/97.
LEWIS D. I., AFC. Born 4/3/43. Commd 28/4/61. Wg Cdr 1/7/81. Retd GD 17/6/93.
LEWIS D. J., MSc BA PGCE. Born 1/3/59. Commd 11/9/83. Sqn Ldr 1/1/94. Retd ADMIN 11/9/99.
LEWIS D. J. Born 10/6/29. Commd 5/7/53. Flt Lt 11/12/58. Retd GD 10/6/84.
LEWIS D. M., MB ChB MRCGP DAvMed. Born 22/8/59. Commd 13/8/79. Sqn Ldr 1/8/88. Retd MED 31/1/89.
  Re-entered 3/7/89. Wg Cdr 1/8/96. Retd MED 22/8/99.
LEWIS D. R. Born 11/8/31. Commd 22/8/51. Flt Lt 22/2/56. Retd GD 6/7/87.
LEWIS E. W. Born 15/2/30. Commd 26/3/52. Flt Lt 7/8/57. Retd GD 14/11/70.
LEWIS G., MIMgt. Born 13/11/25. Commd 9/6/55. Sqn Ldr 1/7/69. Retd PRT 1/2/74.
LEWIS G. G. Born 17/1/31. Commd 6/12/51. Flt Lt 5/6/57. Retd GD 24/4/68.
LEWIS G. J., MA MEd BA MCIPD PGCE. Born 20/7/53. Commd 28/9/80. Sqn Ldr 1/7/89. Retd ADMIN 14/9/96.
LEWIS G. L. C. Born 13/10/48. Commd 10/9/70. Flt Lt 10/3/76. Retd GD 13/10/86.
LEWIS G. N., AFC. Born 7/6/31. Commd 16/7/52. Sqn Ldr 1/1/63. Retd GD 1/3/75.
LEWIS H. E., MRCS LRCP. Born 4/11/26. Commd 2/4/51. Wg Cdr 29/8/63. Retd MED 2/4/67.
LEWIS H. E. Born 5/5/24. Commd 15/9/60. Sqn Ldr 1/7/75. Retd ENG 30/9/77.
LEWIS H. E. Born 8/9/35. Commd 6/5/64. Flt Lt 6/5/70. Retd GD 1/10/83.
LEWIS H. P. Born 9/7/47. Commd 24/4/70. Flt Lt 7/1/74. Retd GD 30/9/77.
LEWIS J. Born 26/9/18. Commd 24/4/42. Sqn Ldr 1/7/69. Retd GD(G) 26/9/73.
LEWIS J. A. Born 5/6/25. Commd 19/7/51. Flt Lt 10/11/55. Retd GD(G) 10/10/72.
LEWIS J. A. H. Born 6/8/34. Commd 19/12/59. Flt Lt 19/6/64. Retd GD 24/1/68.
LEWIS J. C. W., BA. Born 20/9/14. Commd 16/2/48. Sqn Ldr 16/1/52. Retd EDN 1/9/65.
LEWIS J. E. Born 3/6/19. Commd 30/7/42. Flt Offr 30/1/47. Retd SEC 10/7/54.
LEWIS J. G., MBE. Born 29/10/28. Commd 16/7/52. Flt Lt 12/12/57. Retd GD 18/3/69.
LEWIS J. G. Born 11/9/40. Commd 19/7/84. Flt Lt 19/7/88. Retd ENG 1/3/96.
LEWIS J. H., MA LMSSA DPH. Born 17/4/10. Commd 4/1/37. Gp Capt 1/10/57. Retd MED 1/12/65.
LEWIS J. W., DFM. Born 20/1/16. Commd 21/11/41. Sqn Ldr 1/8/47. Retd GD 20/1/58.
LEWIS J. R. Born 3/7/23. Commd 19/7/51. Flt Lt 19/1/56. Retd RGT 3/7/68.
LEWIS J. T. S., AFC. Born 19/9/37. Commd 29/7/58. Sqn Ldr 1/7/68. Retd GD 1/2/72.
LEWIS K. G., CEng FRAeS FIEE FIMgt. Born 19/3/30. Commd 21/2/52. Gp Capt 1/1/76. Retd ENG 19/3/85.
LEWIS K. J. Born 31/3/31. Commd 17/6/52. Flt Lt 2/10/57. Retd GD 1/4/68.
LEWIS K. L. Born 25/4/23. Commd 17/6/44. Wg Cdr 1/1/72. Retd GD 23/4/77.
LEWIS L. W. C., MIMgt. Born 1/12/16. Commd 3/3/44. Wg Cdr 1/1/59. Retd PRT 1/12/68.
LEWIS M., MSc BSc CEng MIEE. Born 10/12/49. Commd 8/9/74. Wg Cdr 1/7/90. Retd ENG 7/5/94.
LEWIS N. R., MA MB BCh MRCS LRCP DPhysMed. Born 21/7/25. Commd 29/9/52. Wg Cdr 2/4/65. Retd MED 29/9/86.
LEWIS P., MIMgt. Born 9/10/33. Commd 11/6/63. Sqn Ldr 1/1/71. Retd SEC 1/1/76.
LEWIS P. E., DFC. Born 20/5/17. Commd 25/10/37. Sqn Ldr 1/9/45. Retd GD 25/5/58 rtg Wg Cdr.
LEWIS P. G. Born 7/1/48. Commd 27/5/71. Sqn Ldr 1/7/83. Retd GD(G) 8/2/87.

LEWIS P. H., OBE. Born 25/8/31. Commd 17/12/52. Wg Cdr 1/7/69. Retd GD 26/8/81. Reinstated on Retired List 28/8/86.
LEWIS P. H. T., OBE BEng CEng FIMechE MRAeS MIMgt. Born 24/10/25. Commd 6/6/46. Gp Capt 1/1/74. Retd ENG 24/10/80.
LEWIS P. J., LLB FCIPD FBIFM. Born 21/1/56. Commd 17/7/77. Gp Capt 1/1/96. Retd ADMIN 21/2/00.
LEWIS P. J. H., AFC. Born 10/1/33. Commd 6/4/54. Sqn Ldr 1/7/64. Retd GD 2/2/74.
LEWIS P. R., MA CEng MRAeS MIMgt. Born 16/6/35. Commd 30/9/55. Sqn Ldr 1/1/72. Retd ENG 6/2/88.
LEWIS R., BSc. Born 16/11/40. Commd 1/10/62. Sqn Ldr 1/7/72. Retd ENG 18/1/80.
LEWIS R. A. Born 27/9/26. Commd 19/11/52. Flt Lt 15/4/58. Retd GD 28/5/68.
LEWIS R. A. Born 11/8/42. Commd 5/8/64. Flt Lt 28/1/70. Retd ENG 11/8/80.
LEWIS R. A., BA. Born 31/8/30. Commd 20/8/58. Sqn Ldr 17/2/63. Retd ADMIN 31/8/85.
LEWIS R. A. Born 25/3/44. Commd 16/9/71. Wg Cdr 1/1/90. Retd ENG 30/11/00.
LEWIS R. C. J. Born 24/5/61. Commd 24/7/81. Flt Lt 24/1/87. Retd GD 25/5/00.
LEWIS R. J., BSc. Born 14/3/15. Commd 21/6/40. Gp Capt 1/1/63. Retd ENG 2/11/68.
LEWIS R. O., MBE MIMgt. Born 9/6/45. Commd 26/8/66. Sqn Ldr 1/1/80. Retd SY(RGT) 9/6/89.
LEWIS R. P. Born 30/10/47. Commd 11/11/71. Flt Lt 11/5/77. Retd GD 26/7/87.
LEWIS R. P. R. Born 2/5/24. Commd 4/10/44. Flt Lt 4/4/48. Retd GD 2/11/48.
LEWIS R. R. Born 1/7/42. Commd 27/1/61. Flt Lt 27/7/71. Retd GD 15/9/72.
LEWIS R. R. Born 22/10/58. Commd 19/9/76. Fg Offr 20/9/80. Retd SUP 3/9/82.
LEWIS S. A., BSc. Born 2/7/45. Commd 28/9/64. Flt Lt 15/10/70. Retd ENG 27/10/72.
LEWIS S. C. Born 12/2/51. Commd 4/9/81. Flt Lt 4/9/83. Retd GD(G) 2/5/91.
LEWIS S. K. Born 11/9/44. Commd 10/12/65. Flt Lt 11/3/70. Retd GD 12/9/92.
LEWIS S. R. Born 10/5/11. Commd 7/9/44. Flt Lt 29/6/50. Retd SUP 31/10/57.
LEWIS T. C. Born 4/10/30. Commd 11/2/65. Flt Lt 11/2/70. Retd ENG 1/9/76.
LEWIS T. G. Born 4/4/16. Commd 9/6/55. Flt Lt 18/11/58. Retd GD(G) 4/4/71.
LEWIS T. J. Born 20/1/63. Commd 25/5/89. Flt Lt 6/9/88. Retd GD 14/10/95.
LEWIS W. D. Born 10/9/13. Commd 29/6/44. Sqn Ldr 1/7/65. Retd SEC 10/9/68.
LEWIS W. E. Born 31/12/14. Commd 27/10/55. Flt Lt 27/10/58. Retd ENG 31/12/70.
LEWIS W. R. Born 20/7/44. Commd 24/6/65. Sqn Ldr 1/1/82. Retd GD 8/4/88.
LEWIS-LLOYD J. Born 24/6/31. Commd 30/7/52. Sqn Ldr 1/7/61. Retd GD 14/8/64.
LEWRY A. M. Born 26/11/52. Commd 28/10/76. Flt Lt 28/4/81. Retd GD 9/8/92.
LEY K. A. M. M. Born 11/5/43. Commd 3/8/61. Sqn Ldr 1/7/79. Retd RGT 11/5/87.
LEYLAND M., BSc. Born 20/11/35. Commd 6/1/69. Sqn Ldr 30/11/71. Retd ADMIN 20/11/85.
LEYLAND R. G. Born 5/11/45. Commd 30/8/84. Flt Lt 1/3/87. Retd GD 2/4/93.
LEYLAND R. H. Born 22/1/30. Commd 30/12/54. Sqn Ldr 1/1/82. Retd GD 1/4/84.
LEZEMORE R. B. Born 24/5/14. Commd 9/7/53. Flt Lt 9/7/56. Retd ENG 24/5/69.
LIDBETTER G. H. Born 10/8/39. Commd 6/4/72. Sqn Ldr 1/1/87. Retd GD 10/8/94.
LIDDELL D. Born 12/1/39. Commd 7/6/68. Sqn Ldr 1/7/86. Retd GD 12/1/94.
LIDDELL G. K. H. Born 18/8/22. Commd 11/9/52. Flt Lt 11/3/57. Retd SEC 31/10/64.
LIDDELL H. M., AFC BA. Born 27/9/24. Commd 14/4/49. Sqn Ldr 1/7/71. Retd GD 27/9/82.
LIDDIARD B., MIMgt. Born 23/7/30. Commd 19/7/51. Wg Cdr 1/1/80. Retd GD 31/10/83.
LIDDIARD M. T. N., OBE MIMgt. Born 25/12/34. Commd 26/7/55. Wg Cdr 1/1/75. Retd SUP 1/11/79.
LIDDLE A. G., BSc. Born 6/8/36. Commd 28/11/56. Flt Lt 2/7/60. Retd GD 30/10/68.
LIDDLE W. Born 7/9/27. Commd 17/5/56. Flt Lt 17/11/60. Retd GD 11/1/71.
LIDSTONE H. R. G. Born 9/3/13. Commd 28/3/46. Sqn Ldr 1/1/57. Retd SUP 9/3/62.
LIDSTONE J. H. Born 20/11/39. Commd 21/2/69. Flt Lt 21/2/71. Retd SEC 5/5/78.
LIDSTONE R. W. Born 9/10/30. Commd 30/7/52. Sqn Ldr 1/7/68. Retd SEC 7/6/75.
LIGGAT A. M. S. Born 9/5/58. Commd 6/6/78. Sqn Ldr 1/7/92. Retd GD 9/5/96.
LIGGINS R. O. Born 11/6/53. Commd 8/2/81. Flt Lt 8/8/85. Retd ENG 2/6/93.
LIGGITT D. J. Born 10/3/40. Commd 25/7/60. Wg Cdr 1/7/77. Retd GD 1/11/88.
LIGHT D. C., MRCS LRCP DMRD. Born 3/10/13. Commd 3/4/39. Gp Capt 1/1/60. Retd MED 1/3/74.
LIGHT G. A., BA. Born 19/10/58. Commd 15/5/79. Fg Offr 15/4/79. Retd SY 24/1/82.
LIGHT O. C. S. Born 24/4/31. Commd 14/9/64. Flt Lt 29/11/68. Retd SEC 7/3/73.
LIGHTBODY P. D. Born 14/7/64. Commd 6/5/83. Flt Lt 6/11/88. Retd GD 9/2/93.
LIGHTFOOT R. D., AFC. Born 30/3/40. Commd 1/8/61. A Cdre 1/7/87. Retd GD 28/6/93.
LIGHTOWLERS A. Born 5/3/23. Commd 10/3/44. Sqn Ldr 1/7/57. Retd GD 5/6/72.
LILBURN J. L. Born 22/9/19. Commd 11/7/43. Flt Lt 11/7/47. Retd GD 22/9/62.
LILES A. J., MBE. Born 19/11/31. Commd 14/1/53. Sqn Ldr 1/7/63. Retd ENG 26/10/76.
LILES T. N. F. Born 10/12/42. Commd 30/7/63. Flt Lt 30/1/66. Retd GD 10/12/80.
LILLEY C. G., MBE FIMgt MInstPS. Born 7/7/24. Commd 7/4/44. Gp Capt. 1/7/74. Retd SUP 7/7/79.
LILLEY D. S. Born 12/6/30. Commd 30/7/52. Sqn Ldr 1/7/63. Retd SUP 2/8/80.
LILLEY E. C. J., MHCIMA. Born 19/1/55. Commd 8/4/82. Sqn Ldr 1/7/93. Retd ADMIN 1/6/98.
LILLEY G. Born 1/7/43. Commd 5/7/73. Flt Lt 5/7/75. Retd ADMIN 5/7/82.
LILLEY K. G. Born 25/4/41. Commd 18/12/62. Sqn Ldr 1/7/72. Retd GD 10/8/85.
LILLEY R. L. Born 6/1/43. Commd 17/12/63. Sqn Ldr 1/1/74. Retd ADMIN 6/1/81.
LILLEY S. R. Born 11/6/23. Commd 21/6/56. Flt Lt 21/6/62. Retd GD 1/10/68.

LILLEYSTONE J. T., MIMgt. Born 25/12/21. Commd 12/9/42. Wg Cdr 1/7/68. Retd GD 25/12/76.
LILLY L. G. W. Born 1/8/17. Commd 15/3/39. Sqn Ldr 1/7/53. Retd SUP 2/9/61 rtg Wg Cdr.
LIM C. S., MCIT MILT MIDPM MIMgt. Born 22/2/31. Commd 28/7/53. Wg Cdr 1/1/73. Retd SUP 22/2/86.
LIMB B. J. M., QGM. Born 7/6/36. Commd 8/1/59. Sqn Ldr 1/7/84. Retd GD 7/6/92.
LIMB M. A., BA. Born 27/12/40. Commd 15/11/89. Flt Lt 23/11/69. Retd GD 2/4/93.
LIMBREY B. M., MSc. Born 26/8/44. Commd 17/9/72. Wg Cdr 1/7/86. Retd ADMIN 2/4/91.
LINALE J. R. Born 27/7/35. Commd 10/3/60. Flt Lt 10/9/64. Retd GD 5/8/80.
LINCOLN T. G., DFC MIMgt. Born 5/11/22. Commd 24/3/44. Flt Lt 24/3/50. Retd SUP 3/4/73 rtg Sqn Ldr.
LINCOLN W. D. Born 24/6/24. Commd 1/7/52. Sqn Ldr 1/7/72. Retd GD 1/7/76.
LIND R. E., DFC. Born 13/1/18. Commd 7/6/44. Flt Lt 7/6/50. Retd GD(G) 13/1/73.
LINDER G. R. Born 15/3/38. Commd 16/12/66. Sqn Ldr 1/7/78. Retd SUP 20/11/88.
LINDLEY A. J. Born 30/1/46. Commd 23/1/64. Flt Lt 20/6/70. Retd GD 30/1/84.
LINDLEY R. F. Born 21/7/47. Commd 2/12/66. Flt Lt 2/6/72. Retd GD 25/8/76.
LINDLEY The Venerable R. A., CBE BA. Born 21/11/20. Commd 12/9/46. Retd 29/11/70. Wg Cdr.
LINDO R. W., BSc. Born 14/4/49. Commd 22/4/71. Sqn Ldr 1/1/85. Retd GD 1/2/88.
LINDSAY A. H. Born 8/7/26. Commd 29/4/53. Flt Lt 16/8/61. Retd GD 21/10/68.
LINDSAY G. J., BA PGCE. Born 28/11/63. Commd 18/8/91. Flt Lt 18/2/94. Retd ADMIN 10/11/96.
LINDSAY I. D., MA MSc MB BChir MRCGP DRCOG DAvMed AFOM. Born 1/3/48. Commd 26/10/70. Gp Capt 1/1/97. Retd MED 12/12/99.
LINDSAY I. R., CBE MSc MB ChB DPH MFOM. Born 17/8/25. Commd 12/8/48. A Cdre 1/1/83. Retd MED 9/1/88.
LINDSAY W. R. S. Born 20/10/38. Commd 25/6/65. Flt Lt 17/3/71. Retd GD 20/10/93.
LINDSEY A. M. Born 26/1/39. Commd 22/3/63. Sqn Ldr 1/1/77. Retd GD(G) 7/9/93.
LINDSEY-HALLS D. J., BA MIMgt. Born 12/8/40. Commd 18/8/61. Wg Cdr 1/7/81. Retd GD 1/10/87.
LINE C. R. Born 5/4/55. Commd 13/12/79. Fg Offr 13/6/82. Retd GD(G) 1/8/85.
LINE K. M. Born 24/2/33. Commd 26/3/52. Flt Lt 7/3/62. Retd GD 11/9/71.
LINE R. C. Born 20/2/59. Commd 25/9/80. Flt Lt 25/3/86. Retd GD 20/2/97.
LINES A. Born 12/7/23. Commd 21/12/67. Flt Lt 21/12/72. Retd ENG 16/10/76.
LINES A. N. Born 14/2/46. Commd 19/10/72. Flt Lt 2/6/77. Retd GD(G) 15/7/85.
LINES C. Born 13/12/43. Commd 25/5/71. Flt Lt 27/11/76. Retd GD 31/12/93.
LINES J. A. Born 28/9/50. Commd 9/12/71. Flt Lt 9/6/77. Retd GD 28/9/88.
LINES P. J. Born 17/5/35. Commd 15/9/61. Flt Lt 1/4/66. Retd GD 12/5/89.
LINES R. P. Born 9/7/38. Commd 21/11/67. Flt Lt 14/12/74. Retd ADMIN 14/12/80.
LINFOOT J. A. Born 1/6/24. Commd 10/9/60. Flt Lt 10/9/65. Retd GD(G) 24/12/71.
LINFORD G. P. Born 16/3/50. Commd 28/10/68. Flt Lt 1/2/76. Retd ADMIN 20/8/77.
LINFORD R. J., OBE. Born 3/6/24. Commd 5/5/45. Wg Cdr 1/7/66. Retd GD 5/5/80.
LING C. W. M., DFC. Born 27/6/11. Commd 25/7/31. Wg Cdr 12/4/45. Retd GD 5/6/46 rtg Gp Capt.
LING H. T. N. Born 19/11/25. Commd 26/12/51. Flt Lt 26/6/56. Retd GD 19/11/85.
LINGARD B. R. Born 10/4/29. Commd 27/8/64. Flt Lt 27/8/69. Retd GD 21/12/74.
LINGARD D. I. Born 16/4/44. Commd 7/1/71. Flt Lt 7/7/76. Retd GD 16/4/99.
LINGARD R., DFC. Born 16/10/22. Commd 25/4/43. Sqn Ldr 1/7/54. Retd GD 16/10/61.
LINGWOOD K. E. Born 1/12/24. Commd 6/1/56. Flt Lt 6/1/56. Retd GD(G) 11/5/73.
LINGWOOD-WHITE F. S. G., BA. Born 17/5/29. Commd 27/10/54. Flt Lt 5/10/60. Retd GD 22/7/67.
LINK D. Born 18/6/23. Commd 2/9/44. Fg Offr 2/3/45. Retd GD 14/7/47 rtg Flt Lt.
LINNELL R. J. Born 19/10/63. Commd 10/2/83. Flt Lt 10/8/88. Retd GD 17/12/96.
LINNEY D. W., AFC. Born 8/8/47. Commd 15/9/67. Sqn Ldr 1/7/82. Retd GD 8/8/85.
LINNIT R. W. Born 1/6/08. Commd 19/8/40. Flt Lt 1/1/43. Retd GD 4/6/48 rtg Sqn Ldr.
LINTELL M. J., BSc CEng MRAeS. Born 2/10/29. Commd 10/7/52. Sqn Ldr 1/7/62. Retd ENG 29/12/73.
LINTHUNE V. H., DFC. Born 18/4/18. Commd 18/2/42. Sqn Ldr 1/1/51. Retd GD 18/11/57.
LINTON M. G. Born 30/1/36. Commd 9/12/53. Sqn Ldr 1/1/91. Retd GD 1/1/94.
LINTOTT A. G., MCIPS. Born 17/11/31. Commd 12/2/53. Wg Cdr 1/1/76. Retd SUP 17/11/86.
LINTOTT D. P., BA. Born 13/9/40. Commd 29/4/71. Flt Lt 29/4/73. Retd GD 30/9/78.
LIPPETT B. D. Born 29/1/30. Commd 31/12/52. Flt Lt 26/5/58. Retd GD 16/1/84.
LIQUORISH A. W. Born 10/7/10. Commd 2/10/41. Fg Offr 1/10/42. Retd SUP 9/8/46 rtg Flt Lt.
LISETT T. S. Born 4/2/55. Commd 15/3/84. Flt Lt 15/3/86. Retd ENG 4/2/93.
LISHER B. J., MB BS DAvMed. Born 25/11/43. Commd 24/1/66. Sqn Ldr 5/6/74. Retd MED 24/1/82.
LISHMAN C. W. P. Born 14/5/13. Commd 25/2/44. Sqn Ldr 1/4/58. Retd SEC 7/6/68.
LISHMAN P. J. S. Born 16/12/43. Commd 4/10/63. Flt Lt 4/4/69. Retd GD 21/5/85.
LISKUTIN M., DFC AFC. Born 23/8/19. Commd 3/7/43. Sqn Ldr 1/1/57. Retd GD 23/8/62.
LISLE E. J., DFC*. Born 9/5/20. Commd 9/8/41. Sqn Ldr 1/1/54. Retd GD 9/5/63.
LISTER C. E. Born 13/10/08. Commd 19/11/41. Fg Offr 8/3/43. Retd ASD 15/11/45.
LISTER C. W. M., MIMgt. Born 8/9/31. Commd 2/7/52. Sqn Ldr 1/1/67. Retd GD 17/1/77.
LISTER H. J. Born 8/3/16. Commd 6/2/43. Flt Lt 6/8/46. Retd GD 8/3/71.
LISTER J. A., MB ChB MRCPsych DPM. Born 4/10/33. Commd 26/3/53. Wg Cdr 21/11/72. Retd MED 15/8/76.
LISTER K., DFC. Born 7/8/21. Commd 21/7/42. Wg Cdr 1/1/60. Retd GD 7/2/68.
LISTER T. H. W. Born 23/11/18. Commd 24/6/43. Flt Lt 19/6/52. Retd GD(G) 10/3/61.
LISTON E. G., BSc. Born 20/9/51. Commd 11/8/74. Sqn Ldr 1/7/86. Retd GD 1/7/86.

LITHGOW P. Born 17/11/24. Commd 13/3/46. Sqn Ldr 1/7/59. Retd RGT 1/10/69.
LITTLE A. J. Born 17/12/45. Commd 27/2/70. Wg Cdr 1/7/90. Retd ADMIN 17/12/00.
LITTLE A. S., BSc. Born 8/5/39. Commd 30/9/58. Sqn Ldr 1/1/72. Retd ENG 8/5/77.
LITTLE A. S. Born 16/6/29. Commd 1/10/57. Sqn Ldr 1/1/78. Retd GD 3/1/80.
LITTLE B. V., MBE. Born 7/5/28. Commd 2/7/52. Flt Lt 27/11/57. Retd GD 2/5/79.
LITTLE G. D. Born 10/9/40. Commd 2/3/78. Sqn Ldr 1/1/88. Retd ADMIN 1/1/90.
LITTLE H. E. Born 8/12/07. Commd 1/7/43. Flt Lt 8/4/48. Retd SUP 7/8/48. Re-employed 12/11/48 to 12/11/56.
LITTLE M. J., MBE FIMgt. Born 2/4/30. Commd 1/10/58. Gp Capt 1/7/79. Retd GD(G) 2/6/82.
LITTLE P. C. Born 26/12/33. Commd 21/10/53. Sqn Ldr 1/1/65. Retd GD 9/5/74.
LITTLE R. Born 17/2/58. Commd 12/10/78. Flt Lt 10/3/85. Retd OPS SPT 29/1/99.
LITTLE R. G., MBE. Born 30/5/19. Commd 5/4/43. Wg Cdr 1/7/59. Retd ENG 30/5/77.
LITTLE S. H. Born 9/2/43. Commd 20/9/69. Flt Lt 20/9/73. Retd GD 9/2/81.
LITTLE T. W., BSc ACGI. Born 14/7/08. Commd 4/4/39. Sqn Ldr 1/10/46. Retd EDN 14/7/68.
LITTLE W. Born 10/2/52. Commd 29/6/72. Flt Lt 29/12/77. Retd GD 1/5/85.
LITTLEBOY W. E., MBE CEng MRAeS MIMgt. Born 4/9/32. Commd 2/11/55. Sqn Ldr 1/1/68. Retd ENG 4/9/87.
LITTLEFIELD D. B. Born 19/6/34. Commd 26/5/61. Flt Lt 1/4/66. Retd GD 19/6/72.
LITTLEJOHN R. J. Born 7/5/29. Commd 11/4/51. Sqn Ldr 1/1/62. Retd GD 2/4/82.
LITTLEJOHN R. K., MA MCIPD. Born 17/3/46. Commd 10/4/68. Wg Cdr 1/1/87. Retd ADMIN 14/3/97.
LITTLER L. R. Born 10/2/35. Commd 2/10/58. Sqn Ldr 1/1/70. Retd SUP 10/10/70.
LITTLER M. R. Born 9/1/49. Commd 3/7/80. Sqn Ldr 1/1/91. Retd GD 14/3/96.
LITTLER R. T. Born 11/6/43. Commd 22/6/70. Flt Lt 22/9/71. Retd GD 30/11/74.
LITTLER W. T. Born 15/5/31. Commd 11/2/65. Flt Lt 11/2/71. Retd ENG 15/5/76.
LITTLEWOOD G. C. B. Born 31/8/09. Commd 29/8/46. Flt Lt 4/1/51. Retd SUP 2/12/57.
LITTLEWOOD H., DFM. Born 25/8/12. Commd 20/1/42. Flt Lt 1/1/43. Retd GD 17/4/54.
LITTLEWOOD M. Born 29/1/64. Commd 20/12/90. Flt Lt 20/12/92. Retd ENG 14/9/96.
LIVERMORE N. K., BA. Born 7/1/57. Commd 20/3/80. Flt Lt 2/6/81. Retd GD 1/10/97.
LIVERMORE R., AFM. Born 13/12/23. Commd 10/2/56. Flt Lt 10/2/61. Retd GD 2/7/68.
LIVERSIDGE B. M. W. Born 7/5/44. Commd 25/8/67. Wg Cdr 1/1/85. Retd SY(RGT) 9/5/89.
LIVESEY N. J., BSc. Born 2/12/58. Commd 18/10/81. Flt Lt 18/7/82. Retd GD 18/10/97.
LIVESEY P. J. Born 4/6/61. Commd 31/1/80. Flt Lt 31/7/85. Retd GD 27/10/91.
LIVETT D. J., MBE. Born 29/4/22. Commd 11/4/57. Flt Lt 11/4/60. Retd SUP 5/8/72.
LIVETT E. Born 6/4/20. Commd 5/12/43. Flt Lt 18/8/48. Retd GD 17/4/63.
LIVINGSTON G., MB ChB MFCM MFOM DPH DIH. Born 2/8/28. Commd 5/5/58. AVM 1/1/85. Retd MED 16/4/89.
LIVINGSTON N. Born 8/7/63. Commd 11/10/84. Flt Lt 11/4/90. Retd GD 31/5/01.
LIVINGSTON R. J. Born 14/7/41. Commd 23/9/66. Sqn Ldr 1/7/78. Retd GD(G) 10/11/92.
LIVINGSTONE S., BSc MIMgt. Born 14/2/59. Commd 6/9/81. Sqn Ldr 1/1/89. Retd ADMIN 14/3/96.
LLEWELLYN D. G., BSc. Born 14/12/60. Commd 16/9/79. Fg Offr 15/4/81. Retd GD 14/11/83.
LLEWELLYN-SMITH M. Born 17/12/56. Commd 8/10/87. Flt Lt 8/10/89. Retd ADMIN 8/10/95.
LLOYD A., AFC. Born 16/10/16. Commd 20/8/43. Sqn Ldr 1/7/54. Retd GD 13/1/60.
LLOYD A., CEng MRAeS. Born 27/6/20. Commd 27/2/43. Wg Cdr 1/7/67. Retd ENG 2/7/70.
LLOYD A. G., MMar. Born 28/11/30. Commd 31/1/66. Flt Lt 31/1/72. Retd SUP 31/1/82.
LLOYD B. E. Born 16/12/44. Commd 31/10/63. Flt Lt 31/1/70. Retd SEC 12/2/77.
LLOYD D., CEng MIEE MRAeS. Born 29/12/39. Commd 18/7/61. Sqn Ldr 1/7/70. Retd ENG 30/9/79. rtg Wg Cdr.
LLOYD D. A. O. Born 27/3/23. Commd 18/7/46. Flt Lt 13/11/57. Retd GD 27/3/66.
LLOYD D. C. A., CB FIMgt. Born 5/11/28. Commd 5/4/50. AVM 1/1/76. Retd GD 28/5/83.
LLOYD D. G. Born 29/4/47. Commd 25/2/66. Sqn Ldr 1/1/83. Retd GD 7/12/91.
LLOYD D. M. Born 21/6/36. Commd 6/9/56. Sqn Ldr 1/1/74. Retd SEC 1/3/79.
LLOYD D. P. Born 24/7/35. Commd 29/7/54. Flt Lt 13/4/60. Retd GD 31/1/73.
LLOYD E. N., BSc. Born 22/10/30. Commd 10/9/52. Sqn Ldr 22/10/62. Retd EDN 22/10/68.
LLOYD G. K. N., AFC MRAeS MIMgt. Born 24/4/23. Commd 20/5/42. Wg Cdr 1/7/59. Retd GD 30/11/68.
LLOYD J. Born 27/4/31. Commd 21/5/52. Flt Lt 29/4/59. Retd GD 27/5/92.
LLOYD J. D. Born 12/7/47. Commd 2/8/68. Flt Lt 2/8/71. Retd GD 22/6/99.
LLOYD J. D. Born 12/2/33. Commd 4/10/51. Sqn Ldr 1/7/65. Retd GD 12/2/93.
LLOYD J. R. Born 5/12/40. Commd 24/3/61. Sqn Ldr 1/7/73. Retd GD 5/12/78.
LLOYD K. F. Born 22/6/28. Commd 3/11/51. Flt Lt 3/5/56. Retd GD 22/6/83.
LLOYD K. T. Born 18/12/45. Commd 29/4/71. Sqn Ldr 1/7/85. Retd ADMIN 20/4/96.
LLOYD M. G. Born 4/10/47. Commd 15/9/67. Wg Cdr 1/1/88. Retd GD 7/8/98.
LLOYD M. H. Born 21/1/62. Commd 19/11/87. Flt Lt 27/8/90. Retd GD 14/3/96.
LLOYD M. J., BSc. Born 12/8/55. Commd 7/11/76. Flt Lt 7/2/80. Retd ADMIN 12/8/93.
LLOYD M. J. Born 21/2/21. Commd 1/1/43. Flt Lt 1/7/46. Retd GD 21/2/64.
LLOYD P. R. J., BSc. Born 21/8/54. Commd 22/8/76. Sqn Ldr 1/1/88. Retd GD 22/8/92.
LLOYD P. U. Born 14/7/24. Commd 26/7/51. Flt Lt 13/11/57. Retd SEC 27/2/65.
LLOYD R. A. Born 27/3/27. Commd 23/6/60. Flt Lt 23/6/66. Retd SUP 2/12/69.
LLOYD R. B. Born 4/2/40. Commd 25/7/60. Sqn Ldr 1/7/70. Retd GD 31/7/79.
LLOYD R. H. Born 11/9/39. Commd 13/12/60. Sqn Ldr 1/1/74. Retd GD 11/9/94.
LLOYD R. I. Born 30/5/37. Commd 26/11/60. Sqn Ldr 1/7/85. Retd GD 30/9/87.

LLOYD R. J. C. Born 25/12/47. Commd 21/3/67. Flt Lt 21/3/76. Retd GD(G) 25/12/85.
LLOYD R. S. Born 21/10/26. Commd 23/8/46. Wg Cdr 1/7/64. Retd GD 1/11/75.
LLOYD R. S. R., BSc FCIPD FIMgt DipEd. Born 24/4/36. Commd 4/9/59. Gp Capt 1/1/88. Retd ADMIN 24/4/94.
LLOYD T. E. L., AFC. Born 16/2/37. Commd 29/12/54. Sqn Ldr 25/12/71. Retd GD 16/2/94.
LLOYD T. J. Born 2/7/54. Commd 20/9/79. Sqn Ldr 1/1/90. Retd ENG 1/1/93.
LLOYD W. A. C. Born 19/7/28. Commd 29/3/56. Flt Lt 29/9/60. Retd SEC 19/7/83.
LLOYD W. F. Born 24/1/23. Commd 10/11/43. Sqn Ldr 1/1/59. Retd SEC 4/1/73.
LLOYD W. F., MBE. Born 20/6/47. Commd 13/9/70. Sqn Ldr 1/1/80. Retd ENG 13/9/88.
LLOYD W. S., OBE FIMgt. Born 4/8/18. Commd 27/12/42. Gp Capt 1/1/68. Retd SEC 4/8/73.
LLOYD-JONES D. E. Born 1/10/18. Commd 22/11/46. Flt Lt 22/5/51. Retd SUP 1/10/67.
LLOYD-MORRISON S. G., AFC BSc. Born 2/8/45. Commd 20/8/67. Sqn Ldr 1/1/83. Retd GD 20/8/89.
LLOYD-ROACH D. J., BSc. Born 30/6/60. Commd 9/11/78. Sqn Ldr 1/1/90. Retd ENG 30/6/98.
LOADER C. G., AFC. Born 25/12/14. Commd 26/1/43. Flt Lt 26/7/46. Retd GD 18/9/53 rtg Sqn Ldr.
LOADER R. B., MBE. Born 16/3/23. Commd 5/3/59. Flt Lt 27/2/63. Retd ENG 16/3/78.
LOASBY B. L. Born 1/6/32. Commd 14/11/59. Flt Lt 14/5/65. Retd GD 1/6/70.
LOAT J., AFC. Born 25/8/20. Commd 17/9/38. Sqn Ldr 1/7/70. Retd GD 25/8/75.
LOBBAN I. C. Born 2/10/48. Commd 6/5/81. Flt Lt 15/2/74. Retd GD 6/5/89.
LOBLE S. J. Born 3/5/48. Commd 6/4/72. Flt Lt 6/10/78. Retd GD(G) 13/12/87.
LOBLEY B. Born 28/8/46. Commd 28/3/91. Flt Lt 28/3/95. Retd ENG 30/6/00.
LOBLEY C. Born 7/6/06. Commd 2/5/41. Sqn Ldr 1/8/47. Retd ENG 10/10/53.
LOBLEY G. V., CEng FIEE FRAeS. Born 29/3/31. Commd 22/7/55. A Cdre 1/7/78. Retd ENG 1/5/86.
LOBLEY J. V., MBE MIMgt. Born 30/5/39. Commd 10/12/57. Wg Cdr 1/7/74. Retd GD 31/12/77.
LOBO R. B. M., DPhysEd. Born 28/10/47. Commd 9/3/72. Sqn Ldr 1/7/87. Retd ADMIN 1/7/90.
LOCK A. A. Born 5/5/31. Commd 15/2/51. Flt Lt 17/5/56. Retd GD 5/5/69.
LOCK A. W. Born 13/2/31. Commd 20/12/51. Flt Lt 4/4/57. Retd GD 13/2/69.
LOCK B., BEM. Born 10/4/07. Commd 22/4/43. Sqn Ldr 1/1/53. Retd ENG 10/4/57.
LOCK D. A. Born 12/5/31. Commd 26/10/50. Sqn Ldr 1/1/65. Retd GD 12/5/69.
LOCK F. J. H. C., CEng MIMechE MRAeS MIMgt. Born 27/1/33. Commd 24/5/53. Wg Cdr 1/7/74. Retd ENG 27/1/88.
LOCK P. C. R., MBE. Born 26/7/23. Commd 19/8/65. Sqn Ldr 18/12/76. Retd MED(T) 26/7/78.
LOCK P. J. Born 9/2/45. Commd 11/11/65. Wg Cdr 1/1/94. Retd ENG 9/2/00.
LOCK T. N., BSc. Born 10/11/55. Commd 31/8/75. Flt Lt 14/5/79. Retd GD 15/7/90.
LOCKE D. R., OBE. Born 7/12/23. Commd 9/7/43. Gp Capt 1/7/70. Retd GD 7/12/78.
LOCKE G. H. Born 11/10/40. Commd 24/9/64. Sqn Ldr 1/1/75. Retd GD(G) 11/10/95.
LOCKE J. E., BA. Born 13/6/74. Commd 5/10/97. Fg Offr 5/4/98. Retd OPS SPT 29/6/99.
LOCKE M. A., MIMgt. Born 26/3/43. Commd 12/1/62. Sqn Ldr 1/1/75. Retd GD 13/11/96.
LOCKE P. D. Born 8/1/42. Commd 14/8/64. Flt Lt 9/2/68. Retd GD 8/1/80. Re-entrant 27/10/82. Sqn Ldr 1/7/88. Retd GD 8/1/97.
LOCKE T. F. Born 13/7/45. Commd 1/3/68. Flt Lt 4/5/72. Retd GD 13/7/89.
LOCKETT E. B., BSc CEng MRAeS. Born 3/10/45. Commd 3/10/68. Wg Cdr 1/1/88. Retd ENG 3/3/91.
LOCKETT P. Born 16/1/42. Commd 19/8/71. Flt Lt 13/1/78. Retd ADMIN 3/5/87.
LOCKETT R. J., CEng MRAeS. Born 29/8/39. Commd 18/7/61. Wg Cdr 1/1/80. Retd ENG 1/12/87.
LOCKHART D. S., DFC. Born 26/2/33. Commd 4/10/51. Sqn Ldr 1/7/65. Retd GD 27/8/76.
LOCKHART R. E. Born 12/3/25. Commd 31/3/45. Sqn Ldr 1/7/67. Retd GD 30/6/76.
LOCKHURST T. E., MBE. Born 17/7/42. Commd 3/11/77. Sqn Ldr 1/1/85. Retd ENG 16/7/97.
LOCKIE D. I. Born 25/6/51. Commd 19/6/70. Flt Lt 19/12/75. Retd GD 22/10/94.
LOCKWOOD G. Born 24/8/33. Commd 16/7/52. Flt Lt 12/12/57. Retd GD(G) 24/8/93.
LOCKWOOD G. A. Born 21/1/35. Commd 17/3/67. Flt Lt 3/7/72. Retd MED(SEC) 31/1/75.
LOCKWOOD G. J., MBE MIMgt. Born 19/4/23. Commd 20/2/43. Flt Lt 20/2/48. Retd SEC 19/4/75.
LOCKWOOD R. J. Born 22/2/18. Commd 28/10/43. Flt Lt 28/4/48. Retd SEC 14/3/67 rtg Sqn Ldr.
LOCKWOOD T. Born 12/3/25. Commd 25/2/44. Sqn Ldr 1/1/61. Retd SEC 12/9/81.
LOCKWOOD V. C., MIMgt MRAeS. Born 6/6/49. Commd 25/6/65. Wg Cdr 1/7/90. Retd GD 30/9/91.
LOCKYEAR K. O., MRAeS. Born 7/4/20. Commd 15/4/43. Wg Cdr 1/7/60. Retd ENG 13/7/68.
LOCKYER D. E. C., BEM CEng MIERE. Born 1/10/19. Commd 28/2/46. Sqn Ldr 1/10/56. Retd ENG 13/3/71.
LOCKYER F. R., OBE. Born 28/6/29. Commd 26/7/50. Gp Capt 1/7/69. Retd GD 5/3/76.
LODGE A. M., BSc CertED. Born 26/6/56. Commd 20/5/79. Flt Lt 20/9/82. Retd ADMIN 20/5/01.
LODGE T. F. Born 2/11/41. Commd 1/7/63. Sqn Ldr 1/1/74. Retd GD 2/11/79.
LOEB R. M. Born 28/2/47. Commd 22/3/81. Flt Lt 22/3/85. Retd ADMIN 30/9/87.
LOFFHAGEN D. A., MBE. Born 11/11/32. Commd 14/7/53. Wg Cdr 1/7/71. Retd SEC 16/6/74.
LOFTHOUSE A. J. Born 19/11/48. Commd 23/2/68. Flt Lt 23/8/73. Retd GD 9/4/86.
LOFTHOUSE B. W., ACIS. Born 27/4/25. Commd 25/8/44. Wg Cdr 1/1/64. Retd GD 27/2/76.
LOFTHOUSE C. J., OBE DFC. Born 26/9/19. Commd 6/5/41. Sqn Ldr 1/1/54. Retd GD 1/7/66.
LOFTING P. J. D. Born 16/8/21. Commd 12/1/44. Fg Offr 20/5/48. Retd GD 1/11/55.
LOFTING R. G., AFC. Born 28/10/21. Commd 22/9/43. Wg Cdr 1/1/62. Retd GD 28/3/75.
LOFTS D. Born 21/6/32. Commd 10/10/58. Sqn Ldr 1/1/72. Retd ADMIN 21/6/87.
LOFTS P. D. Born 5/11/62. Commd 20/5/82. Sqn Ldr 1/1/97. Retd GD 5/11/00.

LOGAN A. M., BA. Born 6/3/54. Commd 25/7/76. Flt Lt 1/12/79. Retd REGT 17/1/81.
LOGAN D. J. C. Born 23/8/11. Commd 3/6/41. Flt Lt 1/9/45. Retd ENG 22/10/53.
LOGAN H., MBE. Born 20/11/18. Commd 25/3/54. Flt Lt 25/3/57. Retd GD(G) 20/11/68.
LOGAN I. E. D. B., MIMgt. Born 21/1/34. Commd 24/9/52. Sqn Ldr 1/1/76. Retd ADMIN 20/5/92.
LOGAN J. J. F. M., AFM. Born 3/3/24. Commd 3/5/56. Flt Lt 3/11/59. Retd GD 13/7/68.
LOGAN K. G. Born 30/8/40. Commd 21/12/62. Flt Lt 1/7/68. Retd GD 30/8/95.
LOGAN L. J. Born 13/8/18. Commd 29/5/48. Sqn Ldr 1/7/59. Retd SUP 13/8/64.
LOGAN P. S. Born 27/11/43. Commd 22/5/64. Sqn Ldr 1/1/93. Retd GD 29/5/00.
LOGAN R. H. Born 6/8/31. Commd 13/6/74. Sqn Ldr 1/7/83. Retd ADMIN 6/8/85.
LOGAN R. N. Born 25/5/55. Commd 30/1/80. Sqn Ldr 1/1/85. Retd ADMIN 25/5/96.
LOGAN S. E. K., BSc. Born 9/12/43. Commd 1/8/66. Sqn Ldr 8/6/73. Retd ADMIN 1/8/82.
LOGAN S. T., BSc. Born 17/3/44. Commd 30/8/66. Flt Lt 30/5/68. Retd GD 2/12/97.
LOHAN K. H. Born 13/10/22. Commd 25/4/42. Sqn Ldr 1/4/56. Retd GD 13/10/65.
LOHSE K. R. Born 25/6/48. Commd 30/5/69. Flt Lt 30/11/75. Retd SY(RGT) 30/4/88.
LOLE R. W. Born 16/11/52. Commd 1/6/72. Flt Lt 1/12/77. Retd GD 16/2/91.
LOMAS D. J. Born 1/2/27. Commd 6/11/47. Sqn Ldr 1/1/60. Retd GD 3/12/76.
LOMAS J. G. Born 16/4/30. Commd 20/12/51. Flt Lt 4/4/57. Retd GD 16/4/68.
LOMAS R. L., OBE. Born 27/2/46. Commd 14/2/69. Wg Cdr 1/7/87. Retd GD 28/10/90.
LOMAS R. W., BSc CEng FIMgt MRAeS. Born 5/9/32. Commd 9/12/54. Gp Capt 1/7/78. Retd ENG 17/10/81.
LONDESBOROUGH A. Born 11/3/43. Commd 19/6/64. Flt Lt 19/12/69. Retd GD 3/4/88.
LONERGAN W. J. Born 3/9/37. Commd 15/2/60. Flt Lt 15/8/65. Retd GD 15/2/76.
LONG B. C., LLB MIMgt ACIS. Born 24/6/32. Commd 28/6/51. Flt Lt 10/10/56. Retd SEC 23/10/70.
LONG C., MBE MIMgt. Born 7/2/31. Commd 2/1/67. Sqn Ldr 1/7/77. Retd ADMIN 7/2/86.
LONG C. J. Born 5/1/47. Commd 2/8/68. Flt Lt 2/8/71. Retd GD 5/1/85.
LONG D., BSc. Born 3/10/40. Commd 4/12/64. Flt Lt 4/9/66. Retd GD 14/9/80.
LONG G. A. Born 5/11/11. Commd 6/9/45. Sqn Ldr 1/1/60. Retd SUP 3/12/66.
LONG I. J., BSc. Born 28/4/65. Commd 11/9/83. Flt Lt 15/1/89. Retd GD 15/7/98.
LONG J. A. W., AFC FIMgt. Born 14/4/22. Commd 19/10/42. Gp Capt 1/1/67. Retd GD 31/3/77.
LONG J. J. F. Born 21/3/20. Commd 12/2/44. Wg Cdr 1/7/66. Retd ENG 1/1/76.
LONG J. R., BA. Born 11/11/48. Commd 25/7/71. Flt Lt 25/7/72. Retd ADMIN 25/7/75. Re-entered 1/4/76. Wg Cdr 1/7/95. Retd ADMIN 30/9/96.
LONG J. T. C. Born 14/1/33. Commd 29/10/52. Flt Lt 24/3/58. Retd GD 14/1/71.
LONG M. A. Born 9/12/38. Commd 15/7/58. Flt Lt 16/4/64. Retd GD 9/12/93.
LONG P. R., RMN. Born 17/11/50. Commd 30/4/81. Flt Lt 30/10/87. Retd GD(G) 29/12/96.
LONG R. A. D. Born 26/6/41. Commd 14/6/63. Flt Lt 4/5/72. Retd GD 22/4/94.
LONG R. C. Born 26/8/31. Commd 8/10/70. Sqn Ldr 1/7/81. Retd ENG 30/3/84.
LONG R. G. Born 15/4/49. Commd 16/9/76. Flt Lt 23/7/79. Retd ENG 30/5/88.
LONG R. J. Born 5/4/45. Commd 30/4/81. Flt Lt 30/4/85. Retd GD(G) 31/7/87.
LONG S., OBE MA BSc. Born 20/8/59. Commd 8/5/83. Wg Cdr 1/1/98. Retd ENG 1/1/01.
LONG S. L. Born 19/7/51. Commd 17/5/79. Flt Lt 27/9/84. Retd GD(G) 9/8/96.
LONG T. J., CEng MRAeS. Born 18/11/23. Commd 25/8/60. Sqn Ldr 1/7/72. Retd ENG 1/10/77.
LONG V. E., AFC. Born 26/6/21. Commd 21/12/42. Sqn Ldr 1/7/52. Retd GD 26/6/64.
LONG W. R. H. Born 6/3/35. Commd 16/4/57. Sqn Ldr 1/7/87. Retd GD(G) 1/7/90.
LONGBONE N. J., MA. Born 1/12/29. Commd 5/8/59. Wg Cdr 1/1/78. Retd SUP 1/12/84.
LONGDEN A. G., CEng MIMechE MRAeS. Born 29/3/31. Commd 23/1/52. Gp Capt 1/7/76. Retd ENG 20/3/86.
LONGDEN D. A., MBE CEng MIEE MRAeS. Born 11/9/41. Commd 8/10/80. Wg Cdr 1/7/91. Retd ENG 11/4/93.
LONGDEN E. J., AFC. Born 13/12/23. Commd 24/1/52. Sqn Ldr 1/1/69. Retd GD 1/6/78.
LONGDEN J. P. Born 30/3/47. Commd 22/11/73. Flt Lt 22/5/76. Retd GD 9/8/88.
LONGDON S. J. Born 7/8/59. Commd 26/6/90. Flt Lt 21/6/92. Retd ENG 21/6/98.
LONGHURST B. M. Born 11/8/49. Commd 31/7/70. Flt Lt 31/7/73. Retd GD 3/10/78.
LONGHURST D. N., BSc. Born 31/10/61. Commd 14/9/80. Flt Lt 15/10/84. Retd GD 31/10/99.
LONGHURST E. Born 25/10/21. Commd 26/5/60. Flt Lt 26/5/66. Retd ENG 24/10/73.
LONGHURST J. Born 16/6/33. Commd 27/2/52. Sqn Ldr 1/7/82. Retd GD 16/6/88.
LONGHURST R. Born 28/11/44. Commd 22/11/84. Flt Lt 22/11/88. Retd GD(G) 30/9/96.
LONGLEY R. D. Born 4/9/45. Commd 19/12/63. Wg Cdr 1/1/89. Retd GD(G) 3/4/92.
LONGLEY R. G. Born 31/3/24. Commd 29/5/45. Wg Cdr 1/7/66. Retd SUP 1/6/74.
LONGMAN B. D., OBE CEng MRAeS MIEE MIMgt. Born 25/2/45. Commd 15/7/66. Wg Cdr 1/7/86. Retd ENG 25/2/00.
LONGMIRE K., BA. Born 27/11/57. Commd 11/4/85. Sqn Ldr 1/7/94. Retd ADMIN 25/1/96.
LONGMUIR J. J. Born 16/1/42. Commd 11/1/79. Sqn Ldr 1/1/94. Retd GD 29/2/96.
LONGSTAFF B. N. Born 5/1/43. Commd 18/11/66. Flt Lt 15/10/70. Retd GD(G) 5/1/93.
LONGSTAFF D. J. Born 6/5/32. Commd 28/7/60. Flt Lt 1/4/66. Retd GD(G) 1/10/73.
LONGSTAFF R. B. Born 7/8/42. Commd 24/2/67. Sqn Ldr 1/1/77. Retd SUP 1/11/84.
LONGSTAFF R. J., OBE. Born 19/10/17. Commd 13/3/47. Wg Cdr 1/7/68. Retd SEC 19/10/72.
LOOSELEY K. D. Born 18/12/46. Commd 14/7/66. Flt Lt 8/3/72. Retd GD 10/1/98.
LOOSELEY M. Born 7/8/53. Commd 4/5/72. Flt Lt 4/11/77. Retd GD 29/7/00.

LOPES C. A. Born 17/9/27. Commd 24/2/67. Flt Lt 24/2/72. Retd ENG 17/9/85.
LORAM W. H. Born 12/6/35. Commd 3/11/77. Sqn Ldr 1/7/86. Retd ENG 12/6/95.
LORD D. V. Born 10/8/36. Commd 3/12/54. Flt Lt 3/6/60. Retd GD 10/8/91.
LORD G. Born 15/8/25. Commd 20/1/51. Flt Lt 20/10/55. Retd GD 11/5/70.
LORD H. Born 28/12/20. Commd 9/9/54. Flt Lt 3/10/59. Retd ENG 2/6/73.
LORD J. Born 6/8/26. Commd 29/3/50. Flt Lt 29/9/53. Retd GD 7/2/73.
LORD R. K. Born 29/12/29. Commd 9/8/51. Flt Lt 28/11/56. Retd GD 29/12/67.
LORIGAN M. P. Born 20/4/39. Commd 26/8/66. Flt Lt 14/11/71. Retd GD(G) 8/4/80.
LORIMER H., OBE MIMgt. Born 2/7/22. Commd 15/8/44. Wg Cdr 1/7/63. Retd SUP 2/7/77.
LORIMER J. M. Born 18/6/20. Commd 29/3/45. Flt Lt 30/6/49. Retd GD 19/6/63.
LORRAINE C. J. Born 10/7/54. Commd 13/6/74. Sqn Ldr 1/7/86. Retd GD 10/7/92.
LORRIMAN B., BSc. Born 30/10/40. Commd 19/6/64. Sqn Ldr 1/7/71. Retd GD 2/3/80.
LORRIMAN G. A. Born 29/1/17. Commd 16/9/43. Sqn Ldr 1/7/54. Retd ENG 1/6/68.
LORTON J. A. Born 10/11/29. Commd 2/2/68. Flt Lt 1/1/73. Retd GD 16/11/73.
LOS R., MBE MRAeS MIMgt. Born 28/6/17. Commd 11/2/42. Wg Cdr 1/1/59. Retd ENG 4/4/70.
LOTEN A. D. Born 21/9/18. Commd 29/6/50. Sqn Ldr 1/1/62. Retd SEC 21/9/73.
LOTINGA R. E. Born 16/5/53. Commd 4/5/72. Sqn Ldr 1/7/87. Retd GD 1/3/92.
LOTT D. C. Born 8/5/40. Commd. 1/8/61. Sqn Ldr 1/7/73. Retd GD 8/5/78.
LOTT E. J. Born 14/12/17. Commd 8/12/52. Flt Lt 8/12/52. Retd SEC 14/12/72.
LOTT M. A. Born 15/5/42. Commd 8/6/62. Flt Lt 8/12/67. Retd GD 31/1/76.
LOTT W. R. Born 6/12/16. Commd 14/5/43. Sqn Ldr 1/1/62. Retd SUP 7/12/71.
LOUBERT J. A. R. R. Born 21/5/32. Commd 15/10/62. Flt Lt 15/10/62. Retd GD 15/7/64.
LOUDON K., CEng MRAeS. Born 28/1/28. Commd 14/8/62. Sqn Ldr 14/8/67. Retd ADMIN 31/3/79. Reinstated
    9/4/80. Sqn Ldr 23/8/68. Retd ADMIN 28/1/88.
LOUDON S. M. Born 23/3/62. Commd 8/4/82. Flt Lt 15/9/88. Retd SUP 14/3/97.
LOUGH A. E. Born 14/8/20. Commd 19/12/55. Sqn Ldr 1/1/72. Retd ADMIN 14/8/75.
LOUGHBOROUGH I. P. G., MBE MIMgt. Born 30/6/43. Commd 19/12/63. Wg Cdr 1/7/87. Retd RGT 1/7/90.
LOUIS P. G., DFC DFM. Born 31/5/18. Commd 21/11/41. Wg Cdr 1/7/52. Retd GD 17/2/55.
LOVATT P., BA FIMgt. Born 16/11/24. Commd 1/5/47. Sqn Ldr 1/1/60. Retd RGT 16/11/79.
LOVE D. B., BJur MCIPD. Born 9/9/47. Commd17/1/72. Gp Capt1/1/97. Retd ADMIN 3/6/00.
LOVE J. M. Born 23/4/33. Commd 27/2/52. Sqn Ldr 1/1/66. Retd GD 23/10/91.
LOVE J. R. Born 27/2/24. Commd 6/1/50. Flt Lt 6/7/52. Retd GD 27/2/67.
LOVE P. V. Born 13/10/31. Commd 16/7/52. Flt Lt 2/10/58. Retd ENG 13/10/69.
LOVEDAY B. W. Born 3/11/42. Commd 9/3/62. Flt Lt 9/2/68. Retd GD 3/11/80.
LOVEDAY D. V. Born 30/5/43. Commd 24/6/65. Sqn Ldr 1/1/77. Retd GD 23/8/80.
LOVEDAY E. C. Born 23/11/30. Commd 28/7/53. Sqn Ldr 1/1/68. Retd GD 23/11/68.
LOVEDAY R., MA CEng MRAeS. Born 19/7/36. Commd 30/9/55. Sqn Ldr 1/7/67. Retd ENG 30/6/89.
LOVEGROVE C. F. Born 14/1/45. Commd 15/7/66. Sqn Ldr 1/1/79. Retd ADMIN 14/1/83.
LOVEGROVE G. B. Born 6/4/43. Commd 24/2/61. Sqn Ldr 1/1/76. Retd GD 6/4/84. Re-entered 27/3/87. Sqn Ldr
    22/12/78. Retd GD 6/4/00.
LOVEGROVE G. B. Born 6/12/41. Commd 16/2/61. Flt Lt 16/5/67. Retd GD(G) 16/6/73.
LOVEGROVE J. M. Born 1/7/19. Commd 6/10/41. Flt Offr 1/9/45. Retd SEC 7/6/52.
LOVEGROVE M. C. Born 12/8/43. Commd 14/11/76. Flt Lt 14/11/80. Retd ENG 14/11/92.
LOVEGROVE P. L. Born 19/11/24. Commd 9/12/48. Sqn Ldr 1/7/64. Retd GD 30/3/68.
LOVEJOY E. W., DFC. Born 14/2/20. Commd 3/3/43. Flt Lt 4/12/50. Retd GD 10/9/65.
LOVEJOY F., MBE. Born 24/3/44. Commd 5/4/79. Sqn Ldr 1/1/88. Retd ENG 24/3/99.
LOVELACE R. E. Born 26/6/19. Commd 19/1/50. Sqn Ldr 1/1/61. Retd ENG 26/6/74.
LOVELAND A. S., MIMgt. Born 9/11/29. Commd 13/12/50. Sqn Ldr 1/7/63. Retd SUP 9/11/67.
LOVELAND R. S., CEng MRAeS. Born 29/11/20. Commd 19/8/42. Wg Cdr 1/7/58. Retd ENG 29/11/75.
LOVELESS G. E. W., MBE. Born 3/3/18. Commd 1/7/57. Sqn Ldr 1/7/66. Retd CAT 3/1/75.
LOVELL A. G. Born 7/10/27. Commd 6/12/51. Flt Lt 13/4/60. Retd SEC 31/1/68.
LOVELL F. W. Born 18/6/29. Commd 17/9/52. Flt Lt 17/9/56. Retd SUP 17/9/68.
LOVELL J. W. Born 26/2/16. Commd 18/9/39. Wg Cdr 1/1/56. Retd SUP 28/1/61.
LOVELL K. A. Born 11/6/24. Commd 22/8/49. Flt Lt 18/5/58. Retd GD 31/8/68.
LOVENBURY L. M. Born 25/11/18. Commd 3/5/51. Sqn Ldr 1/7/63. Retd SUP 28/4/73.
LOVERIDGE D. C. E., CDipAF. Born 7/5/39. Commd 14/8/70. Sqn Ldr 1/7/82. Retd ENG 24/10/94.
LOVERIDGE D. J., OBE FIMgt. Born 21/10/37. Commd 28/7/59. A Cdre 1/1/88. Retd GD 14/4/91.
LOVERIDGE F. J., AFM. Born 4/12/23. Commd 30/7/59. Flt Lt 30/7/62. Retd GD 30/7/71 rtg Sqn Ldr.
LOVERIDGE G. E., OBE. Born 28/4/09. Commd 5/6/41. Wg Cdr 1/1/54. Retd ENG 28/4/64.
LOVERIDGE P. A. Born 20/7/45. Commd 15/7/66. Sqn Ldr 1/1/83. Retd ENG 14/3/96.
LOVERING P. R. Born 17/6/53. Commd 26/11/81. Sqn Ldr 1/7/90. Retd ENG 6/1/96.
LOVERING T. E. Born 20/12/36. Commd 21/10/66. Flt Lt 21/10/68. Retd PE 12/1/74.
LOVESEY J. C. Born 7/2/09. Commd 12/11/42. Flt Lt 2/9/45. Retd ENG 14/11/55.
LOVETT A. J. Born 5/12/44. Commd 11/8/67. Sqn Ldr 1/1/82. Retd GD 1/5/99.
LOVETT A. M. Born 1/1/35. Commd 12/11/57. Sqn Ldr 1/1/80. Retd GD 1/1/94.
LOVETT C. B., BA CEng MRAeS. Born 10/4/40. Commd 17/7/62. Sqn Ldr 1/7/77. Retd ENG 27/9/88.

LOVETT D. M., MVO. Born 30/10/31. Commd 17/3/58. Sqn Ldr 1/1/79. Retd GD 31/10/81.
LOVETT K. J., CBE. Born 4/8/35. Commd 17/3/54. A Cdre 1/7/86. Retd GD 5/4/91.
LOVETT M. S. Born 28/1/38. Commd 17/10/59. Wg Cdr 1/7/81. Retd GD 30/9/88.
LOW I. N. Born 18/1/57. Commd 18/12/80. Flt Lt 18/6/87. Retd SY 14/8/96.
LOW J. H. Born 3/11/22. Commd 1/10/43. Wg Cdr 1/7/70. Retd ADMIN 3/11/77.
LOW R. A. C. Born 21/4/57. Commd 22/2/79. Wg Cdr 1/7/96. Retd GD 21/4/01.
LOWDEN R. W. Born 1/6/15. Commd 3/2/44. Sqn Ldr 1/1/55. Retd ENG 2/6/64 rtg Wg Cdr.
LOWDON J. G. Born 12/4/41. Commd 26/10/62. Flt Lt 8/1/69. Retd GD 12/4/79.
LOWE Sir Douglas, GCB DFC AFC. Born 14/3/22. Commd 4/1/43. ACM 3/11/75. Retd GD 22/8/83.
LOWE D. R. Born 21/5/33. Commd 16/4/57. Wg Cdr 1/1/78. Retd GD 9/4/88.
LOWE D. W., FIMgt. Born 2/2/29. Commd 9/4/52. Gp Capt 1/1/80. Retd GD 2/2/83.
LOWE E. W. Born 10/11/19. Commd 18/12/43. Flt Lt 18/6/47. Retd GD 6/6/53.
LOWE G., CBE DFC AFC. Born 30/9/35. Gp Capt 1/7/54. Retd GD 11/12/65.
LOWE G. Born 6/11/38. Commd 24/6/71. Sqn Ldr 1/7/77. Retd ENG 18/7/80.
LOWE G. M. Born 5/3/49. Commd 11/11/71. Flt Lt 22/4/78. Retd SY 3/5/87.
LOWE H. H. Born 21/12/12. Commd 13/8/41. Sqn Ldr 1/7/50. Retd GD(G) 2/3/58.
LOWE M. R. Born 14/10/31. Commd 21/10/66. Sqn Ldr 1/1/82. Retd ENG 10/1/84.
LOWE P. D. Born 4/7/23. Commd 19/3/43. Flt Lt 15/4/49. Retd GD 29/1/63.
LOWE P. P. W. Born 16/11/40. Commd 23/12/60. Sqn Ldr 1/1/77. Retd GD 1/1/80.
LOWE R. F., MRCS LRCP DCP. Born 27/5/18. Commd 25/5/42. Wg Cdr 23/10/63. Retd MED 17/2/66.
LOWE The Rev T., MA. Born 1/3/39. Commd 6/10/77. Retd 1/3/94 Wg Cdr.
LOWERY A. J., CEng MIEE MRAeS MIMgt. Born 26/3/36. Commd 23/7/58. A Cdre 1/7/88. Retd ENG 31/8/92.
LOWERY D. J., AFC. Born 13/12/25. Commd 17/3/55. Sqn Ldr 1/9/65. Retd GD 21/12/74.
LOWERY H. J. L. Born 5/5/25. Commd 2/7/64. Flt Lt 2/7/67. Retd GD 12/11/73.
LOWES D. W. Born 17/4/28. Commd 26/7/50. Flt Lt 26/7/55. Retd SEC 17/4/66.
LOWES M. S. Born 16/2/52. Commd 6/4/72. Flt Lt 6/10/77. Retd GD 12/12/81.
LOWLES I. E., MB ChB MRCOG. Born 3/4/49. Commd 8/8/71. Sqn Ldr 7/8/79. Retd MED 8/2/88.
LOWNDES R. L., BSc. Born 16/7/57. Commd 8/2/81. Flt Lt 8/11/82. Retd GD 5/4/01.
LOWRIE B. Born 12/2/54. Commd 8/9/77. Sqn Ldr 1/1/89. Retd ADMIN 12/2/92.
LOWRY D. H., BSc. Born 10/9/42. Commd 11/11/73. Sqn Ldr 1/7/83. Retd GD(G) 30/9/90.
LOWRY K. G. Born 8/4/20. Commd 23/3/50. Sqn Ldr 1/1/63. Retd ENG 29/9/73.
LOWRY P., CEng FIEE FIERE MRAeS. Born 2/9/28. Commd 18/7/71. Sqn Ldr 18/7/71. Retd ENG 2/9/92.
LOWRY W. A., FINucE. Born 14/9/22. Commd 21/9/50. Wg Cdr 1/7/72. Retd ENG 14/9/77.
LOWTHER J. R. Born 26/11/14. Commd 28/2/57. Flt Lt 28/2/60. Retd ACB 11/10/63.
LOWTHER W. B., BA. Born 13/2/32. Commd 6/3/61. Wg Cdr 1/7/79. Retd GD 13/10/86.
LOWTON A. L. Born 5/8/38. Commd 24/9/64. Flt Lt 24/9/66. Retd GD 1/7/77.
LOXTON J. A., BA. Born 5/7/31. Commd 28/10/55. Sqn Ldr 17/2/63. Retd EDN 28/10/71.
LOYNES R. A. Born 12/11/52. Commd 19/7/84. Sqn Ldr 1/1/92. Retd GD 19/7/98.
LUBY J. S. Born 31/5/21. Commd 26/10/44. Flt Lt 26/4/48. Retd GD 3/5/76.
LUCAS A. M. Born 19/3/56. Commd 22/5/75. Flt Lt 22/11/80. Retd GD 26/2/88.
LUCAS D., MIMgt. Born 3/12/23. Commd 7/5/53. Wg Cdr 1/1/71. Retd ADMIN 1/3/78.
LUCAS D. G., AFC MBA BA. Born 5/7/37. Commd 16/12/58. Wg Cdr 1/1/75. Retd GD 1/1/78. Reinstated 28/1/81. Wg Cdr 28/1/78. Retd GD 1/12/87.
LUCAS E. D. Born 28/3/33. Commd 21/5/52. Sqn Ldr 1/1/71. Retd GD 28/3/91.
LUCAS G. A., OBE. Born 26/1/34. Commd 24/9/52. Gp Capt 1/7/80. Retd ADMIN 28/1/90.
LUCAS G. H. Born 24/2/32. Commd 6/2/52. Flt Lt 14/8/57. Retd GD 1/5/69.
LUCAS I. T. Born 13/9/48. Commd 28/2/85. Flt Lt 28/2/89. Retd ENG 31/3/94.
LUCAS K. P., MNI. Born 23/4/24. Commd 9/7/56. Wg Cdr 1/1/71. Retd MAR 23/4/79.
LUCAS M. Born 23/10/48. Commd 20/9/79. Flt Lt 20/9/81. Retd ENG 20/9/87.
LUCAS R. G., MSc BSc. Born 30/7/55. Commd 2/9/73. Sqn Ldr 1/1/86. Retd ENG 30/7/93.
LUCAS The Venerable B. H., CB BA. Born 20/1/40. Commd 22/6/70. Retd 31/10/95 AVM.
LUCAS W. C. Born 26/8/09. Commd 25/1/45. Flt Lt 25/7/48. Retd SUP 27/8/64. Re-appointed 1/3/66 to 1/9/70.
LUCIE F. J. F. Born 28/3/15. Commd 31/12/41. Flt Lt 1/9/45. Retd GD(G) 31/3/60 rtg Sqn Ldr.
LUCIE-SMITH H. J. Born 7/12/11. Commd 19/4/38. Wg Cdr 1/7/54. Retd SUP 1/10/63.
LUCK D. C. Born 21/3/30. Commd 13/12/50. Gp Capt 1/7/73. Retd GD 21/3/85.
LUCKHAM R. J., BSc. Born 26/1/54. Commd 12/8/79. Sqn Ldr 1/7/90. Retd ENG 31/3/94.
LUCKHURST T. E., MBE. Born 17/7/42. Commd 3/11/77. Sqn Ldr 1/1/85. Retd ENG 16/7/97.
LUCKING J. W., AFC. Born 13/6/34. Commd 27/5/53. Sqn Ldr 1/1/69. Retd GD 16/3/89.
LUCKING R. R. Born 15/9/38. Commd 25/7/60. Sqn Ldr 1/1/85. Retd GD 15/9/93.
LUCKINS G. Born 7/10/25. Commd 24/1/52. Flt Lt 15/5/57. Retd GD 7/1/74.
LUCY K. P. F. Born 20/8/19. Commd 29/7/44. Flt Lt 29/1/48. Retd SEC 2/2/55.
LUDFORD J. S. Born 18/12/51. Commd 16/11/72. Sqn Ldr 1/7/87. Retd GD 18/3/91.
LUDGATE F. E., CEng FIEE. Born 7/2/15. Commd 20/6/40. Gp Capt 1/7/58. Retd ENG 7/2/70.
LUDGATE L. G. Born 22/7/27. Commd 8/4/49. Wg Cdr 1/1/72. Retd SUP 24/3/78.
LUDIKAR M. Born 28/1/20. Commd 24/5/44. Sqn Ldr 1/7/71. Retd SEC 28/1/75.

LUDLOW B. P., MMedSci MB BS MRAeS MRCS DAvMed LRCP AFOM. Born 4/3/55. Commd 18/11/75. Wg Cdr 1/8/92. Retd MED 4/3/99.
LUDLOW V. J., MSc CEng MIEE. Born 13/4/34. Commd 24/12/64. Sqn Ldr 24/12/71. Retd ADMIN 1/10/76.
LUERY D. J. Born 27/3/30. Commd 5/5/60. Wg Cdr 1/7/80. Retd SUP 27/3/85.
LUFFMAN F. T. Born 28/11/26. Commd 5/5/60. Sqn Ldr 1/7/77. Retd SUP 28/11/78.
LUFFMAN G. Born 11/6/35. Commd 5/5/54. Sqn Ldr 1/7/70. Retd ADMIN 11/6/93.
LUGG A., MBE. Born 20/9/19. Commd 8/7/42. Sqn Offr 1/7/53. Retd SEC 21/6/57.
LUKE D. O., MIMgt. Born 31/3/23. Commd 19/6/42. Wg Cdr 1/1/61. Retd GD 31/3/78.
LUKE J. C. O., CBE BSc. Born 7/8/49. Commd 23/9/68. A Cdre 1/1/98. Retd ADMIN 1/9/00.
LUMB B. E. Born 15/5/16. Commd 14/7/43. Gp Capt 1/1/67. Retd SEC 1/6/71.
LUMB C. P., CBE. Born 30/10/43. Commd 6/9/63. A Cdre 1/1/90. Retd GD 30/10/95.
LUMB R. J., BSc. Born 12/12/43. Commd 28/9/64. Wg Cdr 1/1/90. Retd GD 10/6/93.
LUMSDEN I. A. Born 22/9/56. Commd 17/5/79. Wg Cdr 1/7/94. Retd SY 28/8/96.
LUMSDEN J. G., OBE AFC FIMgt. Born 21/12/40. Commd 31/7/62. A Cdre 1/7/90. Retd GD 10/6/96.
LUNAN T. D. A. Born 28/4/23. Commd 11/8/44. Sqn Ldr 1/4/56. Retd GD 3/2/67.
LUND B., BA. Born 16/6/31. Commd 21/10/53. Wg Cdr 1/7/71. Retd EDN 1/11/75.
LUND C. B. Born 24/2/32. Commd 3/6/65. Sqn Ldr 1/1/83. Retd ENG 1/11/86.
LUND F. R. Born 15/10/30. Commd 12/12/51. Flt Lt 11/11/54. Retd GD 15/10/69.
LUND R. A. Born 3/11/47. Commd 3/5/68. Sqn Ldr 1/7/84. Retd GD(G) 1/7/87.
LUNDY F. K. Born 28/12/31. Commd 6/12/51. Flt Lt 5/6/57. Retd GD 11/4/70.
LUNGLEY S. D. Born 29/1/60. Commd 28/6/79. Wg Cdr 1/7/97. Retd GD 1/7/00.
LUNN L. G., AFC. Born 27/1/23. Commd 14/9/43. Sqn Ldr 1/1/66. Retd GD 27/1/79.
LUNN R. Born 24/2/47. Commd 28/10/66. Wg Cdr 1/1/91. Retd GD 14/9/96.
LUNT C. C., BA. Born 26/11/60. Commd 11/9/83. Sqn Ldr 1/7/94. Retd GD 11/11/99.
LUNT J. D., BA. Born 13/3/41. Commd 9/9/63. Gp Capt 1/1/87. Retd GD 13/4/96.
LUPA H. T., BSc MB ChB DAvMed MRAeS. Born 2/2/59. Commd 6/10/81. Wg Cdr 2/8/97. Retd MED 7/10/99.
LUPTON K. V. Born 17/10/26. Commd 20/11/58. Flt Lt 20/11/63. Retd GD 29/3/69.
LUSCOMBE M. W. J. Born 11/11/28. Commd 3/6/65. Flt Lt 3/6/68. Retd GD 11/11/78.
LUSH N. A. Born 18/7/22. Commd 16/12/45. Flt Lt 30/6/49. Retd GD 18/7/65.
LUSHER H. G. Born 31/1/49. Commd 16/8/68. Sqn Ldr 1/1/89. Retd GD 1/1/92.
LUSSEY D. Born 19/12/45. Commd 22/7/66. Flt Lt 15/12/72. Retd SY 19/12/83.
LUTER B. C., MA. Born 23/5/36. Commd 12/9/58. Sqn Ldr 12/3/69. Retd ADMIN 23/5/93.
LUTKIN J. R. Born 30/8/46. Commd 20/9/68. Flt Lt 13/9/72. Retd GD 3/4/76.
LUTMAN A. J. A. Born 12/5/31. Commd 1/10/58. Sqn Ldr 1/7/69. Retd ADMIN 25/8/82.
LUTO A. T., CEng MIEE MIMgt. Born 16/6/32. Commd 20/12/57. Sqn Ldr 1/7/67. Retd ENG 16/6/87.
LUXMORE F. L., DFC. Born 4/8/97. Commd 1/4/18. Flt Lt 30/6/21. Retd GD 3/8/29.
LUXTON J. D., BEM. Born 14/9/43. Commd 8/9/77. Sqn Ldr 1/1/86. Retd ENG 14/9/97.
LUXTON P. A., BEng. Born 17/6/62. Commd 18/3/84. Sqn Ldr 1/7/94. Retd GD 17/6/00.
LYALL R. W. Born 9/1/43. Commd 24/2/61. Flt Lt 24/8/66. Retd GD 9/1/81.
LYDALL R. Born 3/2/38. Commd 6/7/62. Sqn Ldr 1/1/72. Retd GD 12/5/92.
LYDDON-JONES G. D. Born 8/3/35. Commd 19/9/59. Flt Lt 4/5/65. Retd GD(G) 17/8/79.
LYDIATE B. W. Born 28/3/33. Commd 29/12/51. Sqn Ldr 1/7/83. Retd GD 1/11/87.
LYDON B. B., DFC. Born 5/6/23. Commd 20/12/43. Flt Lt 16/10/51. Retd GD 1/2/63.
LYLE A., MBE. Born 16/3/19. Commd 12/9/46. Wg Cdr 1/1/69. Retd SUP 3/4/70.
LYNAS C. T., OBE FIIP MIMgt. Born 24/6/20. Commd 24/11/43. Wg Cdr 1/1/68. Retd ENG 30/6/73.
LYNCH D. Born 27/1/31. Commd 26/7/51. Flt Lt 14/3/61. Retd RGT 27/1/69.
LYNCH J. Born 1/4/13. Commd 2/9/45. Flt Lt 4/1/51. Retd SUP 3/4/55.
LYNCH J. M. Born 17/4/30. Commd 17/1/52. Flt Lt 8/5/57. Retd GD 17/4/68.
LYNCH P. A. Born 26/3/37. Commd 26/3/64. Sqn Ldr 1/7/72. Retd ADMIN 4/9/76.
LYNCH P. R. G., MBE. Born 6/8/10. Commd 30/10/42. Sqn Ldr 1/7/51. Retd SUP 15/8/59 rtg Wg Cdr.
LYNCH W., CEng MIMechE MRAeS. Born 29/8/43. Commd 26/5/67. Sqn Ldr 1/7/78. Retd ENG 29/8/83.
LYNDON R. J. Born 16/4/37. Commd 11/11/65. Flt Lt 6/10/71. Retd GD(G) 1/4/86.
LYNE M. D., CB AFC** MRAeS. Born 23/3/19. Commd 29/7/39. AVM 1/7/66. Retd GD 10/4/71.
LYNHAM C. R., BA. Born 5/4/74. Commd 2/8/95. Fg Offr 15/7/95. Retd GD 13/5/00.
LYNN G. S., MBE MIMgt. Born 18/7/44. Commd 2/8/73. Wg Cdr 1/1/88. Retd ENG 31/3/94.
LYNN J. R. Born 14/7/29. Commd 29/7/54. Flt Lt 5/2/60. Retd GD 27/4/70.
LYNN T. Born 24/6/43. Commd 12/1/62. Flt Lt 26/7/67. Retd GD 22/10/75.
LYON A. F., BA. Born 8/2/36. Commd 10/12/57. Flt Lt 18/6/63. Retd GD 8/2/94.
LYON R. T. F., CEng MIMechE MIProdE MRAeS CDipAF. Born 23/8/28. Commd 11/2/53. Sqn Ldr 1/1/67. Retd 23/8/78. Reinstated 9/9/81 to 9/9/84.
LYONS C. W., AFM. Born 19/12/24. Commd 4/6/59. Sqn Ldr 1/7/73. Retd GD 19/12/79.
LYONS D. Born 4/6/59. Commd 15/6/83. Sqn Ldr 1/7/93. Retd ENG 4/6/99.
LYONS D. S. H. Born 11/3/30. Commd 25/5/50. Sqn Ldr 1/1/64. Retd GD 11/3/85.
LYONS J. H. J., BSc MCIPD. Born 22/8/56. Commd 13/4/80. Sqn Ldr 1/7/94. Retd ADMIN 2/12/96.
LYONS J. P. Born 14/3/33. Commd 26/3/64. Flt Lt 26/3/70. Retd ADMIN 30/11/86.
LYONS T. R. H. Born 4/2/33. Commd 27/2/52. Flt Lt 26/6/56. Retd GD 4/2/71. Reinstated 17/9/80 to 1/5/84.

LYSTER D. G., DSO DFC AFC*. Born 16/4/11. Commd 1/4/40. Gp Capt 1/1/56. Retd GD 7/1/61.
LYTHABY R. Born 26/4/45. Commd 24/6/71. Wg Cdr 1/1/92. Retd ENG 26/4/00.
LYTHGOE M. R. Born 21/8/47. Commd 11/8/67. Flt Lt 11/2/73. Retd GD 9/5/76.
LYTTLE R. I. S. Born 1/6/50. Commd 24/6/71. Flt Lt 1/12/75. Retd GD 22/10/94.
LYWOOD G. E. G. Born 25/2/04. Commd 30/7/25. Sqn Ldr 1/4/37. Retd GD 1/2/38. Re-employed 1/1/40. Wg Cdr
    27/4/42. Retd 14/10/45 rtg Gp Capt.

# M

M'KENZIE-HALL J. E., MVO. Born 7/6/23. Commd 27/2/43. Flt Lt 26/5/55. Retd GD 6/3/64 rtg Sqn Ldr.
MAAN M. H., MSc BSc MIMgt. Born 15/9/45. Commd 1/3/68. Wg Cdr 1/1/85. Retd ENG 14/3/96.
MABBETT D. W., BSc. Born 26/8/58. Commd 5/9/76. Sqn Ldr 1/1/89. Retd GD 26/9/96.
MABBOTT J. E. Born 1/3/43. Commd 1/10/69. Sqn Ldr 1/1/82. Retd GD 1/3/86.
MABBOTT R. G. S. Born 21/1/35. Commd 10/9/70. Wg Cdr 1/7/90. Retd ADMIN 24/7/91.
MABEN A., LDS. Born 21/8/12. Commd 7/1/35. Sqn Ldr 1/7/46. Retd DEL 14/5/50.
MABLY J. R., MA. Born 11/7/22. Commd 4/4/61. Sqn Ldr 6/3/63. Retd EDN 22/9/70.
MacALLISTER J. D., LRCS LRCP. Born 1/6/21. Commd 23/11/53. Wg Cdr 21/1/66. Retd MED 19/9/77.
MacANGUS A., BSc. Born 6/4/61. Commd 5/9/82. Flt Lt 15/10/83. Retd GD 5/3/91.
MACARTE M. A. Born 4/4/54. Commd 6/12/87. Flt Lt 6/11/85. Retd ADMIN 9/5/96.
MACAULAY J. M., MBE MCSP. Born 8/10/20. Commd 19/7/56. Sqn Ldr 31/8/66. Retd MED(T) 6/9/68.
MACAULAY J. W. Born 4/8/66. Commd 16/6/88. Flt Lt 16/12/93. Retd GD 14/9/96.
MACAULAY L. K., BA. Born 27/10/58. Commd 28/9/80. Sqn Ldr 1/1/94. Retd ADMIN 31/7/00.
MACAULEY G. W. Born 5/4/55. Commd 5/4/79. Flt Lt 5/10/84. Retd GD 27/11/94.
MACAUSLAND G. H. Born 17/2/56. Commd 11/9/86. Flt Lt 11/9/88. Retd ENG 11/9/94.
MacBEAN A. Born 3/7/51. Commd 10/2/72. Sqn Ldr 1/1/87. Retd SUP 1/1/90.
MacBEAN A. A. Born 12/8/23. Commd 16/3/45. Flt Lt 4/6/53. Retd GD 1/5/66.
MacBEAN J. A. M., MBE FINucE. Born 24/7/20. Commd 23/9/43. Wg Cdr 1/7/65. Retd ENG 24/7/75.
MACBRAYNE D. Born 8/11/48. Commd 24/4/70. Sqn Ldr 1/1/84. Retd GD 8/11/92.
MacBRAYNE K. J. Born 13/8/42. Commd 7/6/68. Flt Lt 7/6/70. Retd GD 13/7/74.
MacCALLUM G. W., BA. Born 23/5/48. Commd 9/8/79. Sqn Ldr 1/7/86. Retd ENG 1/10/90.
MacCONNACHIE A. Born 8.3.31. Commd 31/12/52. Sqn Ldr 1/7/71. Retd GD(G) 8/3/86
MacCORKINDALE P. B., OBE. Born 11/6/24. Commd 17/6/45. Gp Capt 1/1/73. Retd GD 3/5/75.
MacDERMID M. Born 11/11/27. Commd 14/11/50. Wg Cdr 1/1/71. Retd GD 1/9/79.
MacDERMOT N. A. Born 25/4/35. Commd 4/1/56. Flt Lt 4/7/61. Retd GD 28/2/70.
MacDONALD A. J., BA. Born 7/11/45. Commd 30/8/66. Flt Lt 30/5/68. Retd GD 22/4/83.
MacDONALD A. R., MSc BA MCIPS MIMgt. Born 12/6/44. Commd 15/7/66. Sqn Ldr 1/1/78. Retd SUP 1/11/84.
MacDONALD C. M. Born 14/9/12. Commd 13/11/41. Flt Lt 20/11/45. Retd ENG 27/12/51.
MacDONALD C. S., MIMgt. Born 15/9/26. Commd 23/8/46. Wg Cdr 1/1/66. Retd GD 26/2/71.
MacDONALD D. A., DFM*. Born 24/6/19. Commd 23/10/42. Flt Lt 7/8/47. Retd SUP 7/12/54.
MacDONALD D. A. F. Born 19/7/24. Commd 6/2/44. Flt Lt 6/2/50. Retd GD(G) 19/4/63. Re-employed 4/1/65. Sqn Ldr 1/7/76. Retd 10/3/82.
MacDONALD D. C., BSc. Born 23/10/64. Commd 11/9/83. APO 11/9/83. Retd GD 1/2/88.
MacDONALD E. P., Commd 13/7/40. Sqn Offr 1/7/53. Retd SEC 15/1/55.
MACDONALD G. A. Born 14/11/20. Commd 24/1/63. Flt Lt 24/1/68. Retd ENG 14/11/73.
MacDONALD G. D., CEng FRAeS FIMgt. Born 20/5/26. Commd 27/9/50. Gp Capt 1/1/74. Retd ENG 20/7/81.
MACDONALD I. A. Born 25/3/60. Commd 11/1/79. Sqn Ldr 1/7/91. Retd GD 25/3/98.
MacDONALD I. N. M., AFC. Born 1/9/18. Commd 17/12/38. Wg Cdr 1/7/51. Retd GD 29/3/60.
MACDONALD I. T., MA. Born 22/12/47. Commd 17/1/72. Flt Lt 17/10/73. Retd ADMIN 22/7/76.
MACDONALD J. Born 23/2/47. Commd 25/2/66. Flt Lt 8/3/72. Retd GD 21/4/73.
MacDONALD J., DFC MBE. Born 20/8/19. Commd 15/4/44. Wg Cdr 1/1/66. Retd GD 11/7/67.
MACDONALD J. A., BSc. Born 28/8/32. Commd 2/2/56. Sqn Ldr 2/8/66. Retd ADMIN 28/3/86.
MACDONALD J. A. Born 12/3/65. Commd 8/12/83. Fg Offr 8/6/86. Retd GD(G) 7/7/88.
MACDONALD J. H., MSc FInstPet. Born 29/10/44. Commd 23/1/64. Wg Cdr 1/1/88. Retd SUP 29/10/99.
MacDONALD J. N., MBE. Born 25/8/21. Commd 18/4/44. Sqn Ldr 1/7/60. Retd GD 4/4/75.
MACDONALD M. J. A. Born 16/6/57. Commd 2/6/77. Sqn Ldr 1/1/89. Retd GD 14/9/96.
MACDONALD N. A. Born 27/4/42. Commd 15/8/85. Flt Lt 15/8/89. Retd SUP 2/4/93.
MACDONALD R. P. Born 14/2/41. Commd 6/5/65. Flt Lt 6/12/68. Retd SUP 14/2/79.
MacDONALD R.McD., MBE. Born 8/5/25. Commd 9/6/48. Gp Capt 1/7/73. Retd SEC 27/3/76.
MACDONALD W. Born 4/7/25. Commd 23/12/61. Sqn Ldr 1/1/73. Retd GD 5/7/77.
MACDONALD-BENNETT T. I. Born 28/2/45. Commd 31/1/64. Flt Lt 31/7/69. Retd GD 3/11/72.
MacDOUGALL D. J., AFC. Born 26/7/25. Commd 30/7/52. Sqn Ldr 1/9/65. Retd GD 26/7/76.
MACDOUGALL N., MBE. Born 31/8/44. Commd 18/10/79. Sqn Ldr 1/1/90. Retd SY 14/9/96.
MACDOUGALL N. R. H. Born 16/7/47. Commd 17/2/67. Sqn Ldr 1/7/86. Retd GD 12/3/93.
MACE B. H. Born 22/3/32. Commd 2/7/52. Flt Lt 5/11/58. Retd GD 22/3/70.
MACE J. L., MIDPM MIMgt. Born 13/4/37. Commd 8/7/65. Wg Cdr 1/7/84. Retd SUP 13/4/94.
MACE J. R., BA DPhysEd. Born 19/10/35. Commd 14/5/63. Wg Cdr 1/7/86. Retd ADMIN 19/10/90.
MACE K. B. Born 8/6/43. Commd 28/7/64. Sqn Ldr 1/1/73. Retd GD 8/6/81. Reinstated on Retired List 3/9/85.
MACEVOY R. I. Born 17/11/43. Commd 2/8/68. Wg Cdr 1/7/94. Retd OPS SPT 1/1/98.
MACEY E. H., OBE Born 4/4/36. Commd 23/2/55. AVM 1/7/85. Retd GD 9/4/91.

MACFADYEN I. D., CB OBE FRAeS. Born 19/2/42. Commd 30/7/63. AM 26/8/94. Retd GD 19/2/99.
MACFARLANE A. J. M. Born 5/10/09. Commd 24/6/42. Flt Offr 24/12/46. Retd SEC 13/8/61.
MacFARLANE G. A., MBE MIMgt. Born 17/3/23. Commd 3/8/50. Wg Cdr 1/7/66. Retd SUP 1/11/67.
MACFARLANE G. J. Born 25/2/59. Commd 15/6/83. Flt Lt 15/12/88. Retd GD 14/2/99.
MacFARLANE G. N. W., BA CEng MIEE. Born 2/6/20. Commd 26/3/42. Sqn Ldr 1/1/54. Retd ENG 17/8/63.
MacFARLANE N. G., DSO. Born 5/12/15. Commd 7/3/38. Wg Cdr 1/1/51. Retd GD 18/4/58.
MACFARLANE N. I. Born 22/7/56. Commd 11/5/78. Flt Lt 27/8/82. Retd GD 23/12/96.
MacGIBBON G. B., MB ChB. Born 30/10/08. Commd 7/9/35. Sqn Ldr 7/3/45. Retd MED 7/9/46 rtg Wg Cdr.
MacGOWAN W. E. Born 13/2/34. Commd 23/9/66. Flt Lt 23/9/72. Retd GD 20/8/84.
MacGREGOR A., BA MCIT MILT MIMgt. Born 30/7/32. Commd 27/7/54. Sqn Ldr 1/1/67. Retd GD 30/7/87.
MACGREGOR A. N. Born 18/7/44. Commd 31/1/64. Gp Capt 1/1/92. Retd GD 18/11/99.
MacGREGOR I. Born 30/11/31. Commd 11/3/65. Sqn Ldr 1/1/77. Retd ADMIN 10/7/82.
MacGREGOR J. P. Born 8/12/28. Commd 8/11/51. Flt Lt 23/2/57. Retd GD 8/12/83.
MacGREGOR S. W., BA. Born 31/1/36. Commd 6/8/63. Sqn Ldr 25/9/69. Retd EDN 6/8/79.
MACHEJ S. J., DFC. Born 23/9/19. Commd 1/9/45. Sqn Ldr 1/7/55. Retd GD 19/12/58.
MACHEN P. C., MA MSc CEng MIEE. Born 24/11/36. Commd 30/9/56. Sqn Ldr 1/7/68. Retd ENG 24/11/74.
MACHIN D. Born 26/5/09. Commd 1/9/41. Flt Offr 1/9/45. Retd CAT 2/6/58 rtg Sqn Offr.
MACHIN P. J. Born 2/11/26. Commd 4/7/51. Flt Lt 18/6/58. Retd GD(G) 2/11/64.
MACHRAY J. Born 22/2/33. Commd 1/3/57. Wg Cdr 1/1/77. Retd ENG 22/2/88.
MacINNES D. M., MCIPS MIMgt. Born 13/8/39. Commd 29/7/65. Sqn Ldr 1/1/76. Retd SUP 1/1/79. Reinstated 27/8/80. Sqn Ldr 27/8/77. Retd SUP 1/6/90.
MACINTOSH A. G. Born 16/3/47. Commd 19/7/84. Flt Lt 19/7/88. Retd GD(G) 14/3/96.
MACINTYRE J. S., MA. Born 14/11/32. Commd 11/4/57. Sqn Ldr 21/6/63. Retd ADMIN 14/11/87.
MACINTYRE T. A. Born 5/7/37. Commd 27/2/56. Gp Capt 1/1/79. Retd GD(G) 6/9/89.
MacIVER D. Born 16/6/24. Commd 3/11/44. Wg Cdr 1/7/62. Retd GD 29/1/72.
MACK D. R., MBA BSc CEng MIEE. Born 24/9/57. Commd 5/9/82. Sqn Ldr 1/1/91. Retd ENG 26/2/95.
MACK R. G. Born 21/8/93. Commd 1/4/18. Flt Lt 1/4/18. Retd GD 19/2/21.
MACKAY A. A. Born 14/7/38. Commd 13/12/60. Flt Lt 26/2/64. Retd GD 14/7/76.
MACKAY A. J., MBE DFC. Born 5/2/22. Commd 19/1/45. Wg Cdr 1/1/65. Retd SUP 25/11/72.
MACKAY A. S. G., BSc. Born 15/4/53. Commd 15/11/72. Sqn Ldr 1/7/88. Retd ENG 1/7/91.
MACKAY D. M., BA. Born 10/10/60. Commd 25/11/84. Flt Lt 25/5/88. Retd OPS SPT 25/11/00.
MACKAY D. W. D., AFC BSc. Born 22/3/57. Commd 21/10/79. Sqn Ldr 1/1/91. Retd GD 21/10/95.
MACKAY E. D. Born 23/12/23. Commd 28/7/44. Sqn Ldr 1/10/55. Retd GD 8/9/73.
MACKAY E. O., MBE MIMgt. Born 26/10/18. Commd 15/11/43. Wg Cdr 1/7/67. Retd GD(G) 12/3/71.
MACKAY F. D. Born 17/1/59. Commd 27/3/80. Flt Lt 5/7/86. Retd ADMIN 17/1/97.
MACKAY F. G., BSc. Born 25/5/19. Commd 21/7/43. Sqn Ldr 1/1/55. Retd GD 25/5/74.
MACKAY G. A., MBE. Born 28/12/39. Commd 2/8/73. Sqn Ldr 1/1/83. Retd ENG 28/12/89.
MACKAY G. D. Born 10/3/18. Commd 19/7/51. Flt Lt 1/8/58. Retd SUP 1/11/63.
MACKAY L. W. Born 17/6/64. Commd 19/12/85. Flt Lt 19/6/91. Retd GD 14/3/97.
MacKAY N. F. Born 1/1/33. Commd 17/1/52. Flt Lt 24/7/57. Retd GD 1/1/71.
MACKAY N. G. Born 7/1/57. Commd 15/10/81. Sqn Ldr 1/7/93. Retd SUP 14/3/97.
MACKAY S. M., AFC. Born 17/11/22. Commd 20/5/42. Wg Cdr 1/7/58. Retd GD 31/3/62.
MACKAY W. D., MCSP GradDipPhysio. Born 19/4/47. Commd 2/6/77. Flt Lt 2/6/83. Retd MED(T) 2/6/85. Re-entered 2/3/87. Sqn Ldr 2/3/91. Retd MED(T) 6/6/97.
MACKENZIE D., DFC. Born 9/3/12. Commd 12/10/36. Wg Cdr 1/7/52. Retd GD 12/10/56.
MACKENZIE G. C. Born 20/10/56. Commd 28/6/79. Sqn Ldr 1/1/92. Retd SUP 26/2/01.
MACKENZIE H. D. Born 15/10/45. Commd 10/6/66. Sqn Ldr 1/7/78. Retd GD 26/6/96.
MACKENZIE I. J., CEng MIERE MIMgt. Born 26/7/40. Commd 22/10/63. Sqn Ldr 1/1/75. Retd ENG 31/3/84.
MACKENZIE J. Born 7/11/49. Commd 27/3/86. Flt Lt 27/3/90. Retd ENG 2/6/93.
MacKENZIE J. L., Commd 25/10/73. Flt Lt 9/3/80. Retd GD(G) 24/10/81. Transferred to Reserve. 25/10/81. Reinstated 9/11/83
MACKENZIE K. Born 1/1/31. Commd 28/7/67. Flt Lt 28/7/68. Retd EDN 28/7/75.
MACKENZIE K. C. Born 12/7/38. Commd 4/12/67. Flt Lt 13/10/71. Retd SEC 7/9/74.
MACKENZIE K. I. Born 22/12/42. Commd 11/5/62. Flt Lt 11/11/67. Retd GD 22/1/80.
MACKENZIE K. J. Born 13/7/48. Commd 24/6/84. Flt Lt 10/9/74. Retd GD 31/12/89.
MACKENZIE K. P. Born 21/12/17. Commd 17/12/38. Wg Cdr 1/7/50. Retd GD 29/5/59.
MACKENZIE K. T. W. Born 27/2/18. Commd 23/3/50. Sqn Ldr 1/1/60. Retd ENG 2/3/68.
MACKENZIE K. W., DFC AFC AE FIMgt. Born 8/6/16. Commd 24/4/40. Wg Cdr 1/1/54. Retd GD 1/7/67.
MACKENZIE P. S. Born 22/5/39. Commd 22/1/63. Flt Lt 22/1/69. Retd SUP 22/5/89.
MACKENZIE R. M., DSO DFC AFC. Born 8/9/16. Commd 23/8/37. Wg Cdr 1/1/52. Retd GD 20/8/58.
MACKENZIE R. P. Born 27/1/55. Commd 5/1/78. Flt Lt 5/7/84. Retd GD(G) 20/6/93.
MACKENZIE T. A. Born 13/6/28. Commd 12/12/48. Flt Lt 12/12/54. Retd GD 13/6/66.
MACKENZIE W. R., DSC. Born 6/5/93. Commd 1/4/18. Flt Lt 1/4/18. Retd GD 2/11/21.
MACKENZIE-CROOKS R. B. Born 4/1/43. Commd 30/7/43. Sqn Ldr 1/1/73. Retd GD 2/6/80.
MACKEY A. E., BEM. Born 28/5/16. Commd 6/9/45. Sqn Ldr 1/7/56. Retd SUP 10/8/67.
MACKEY D. J. Born 15/3/59. Commd 20/9/79. Flt Lt 20/3/86. Retd SUP 16/3/94.

MACKEY J., BDS LDSRCS FISM FIMgt. Born 24/10/36. Commd 17/5/56. AVM 1/1/88. Retd DEL 14/4/97.
MACKEY P. E. A. Born 21/2/21. Commd 13/8/44. Sqn Ldr 1/1/73. Retd SEC 21/6/75.
MACKICHAN A. S., MSc BSc CEng FIMechE FRAeS. Born 6/9/43. Commd 15/7/65. Gp Capt 1/7/88. Retd ENG 6/9/98.
MACKIE A. C. L., CBE DFC*. Born 3/8/22. Commd 11/5/41. A Cdre 1/7/66. Retd GD 30/9/68.
MACKIE D. F. Born 20/9/22. Commd 11/8/45. Flt Lt 29/11/51. Retd GD 1/9/57.
MACKIE G. Born 28/8/21. Commd 12/11/43. Wg Cdr 1/7/61. Retd GD 29/6/72.
MACKIE H. Born 30/1/35. Commd 23/3/68. Flt Lt 15/4/70. Retd GD 31/8/74.
MACKIE I. G. Born 2/12/35. Commd 23/3/55. Flt Lt 1/3/61. Retd GD 23/3/87.
MACKIE N. A. J., DSO DFC* MIMgt. Born 22/12/20. Commd 30/11/40. Wg Cdr 1/7/57. Retd GD 22/12/67.
MACKIE W. S., MSc BSc BEng CEng MIIE MIEE. Born 6/2/62. Commd 3/8/88. Flt Lt 15/7/91. Retd ENG 6/2/01.
MACKINLAY G., CEng MIEE. Born 10/12/42. Commd 15/7/65. Wg Cdr 1/7/80. Retd ENG 10/12/97.
MACKINNON A. J. Born 8/3/30. Commd 1/8/51. Wg cdr 1/7/74. Retd GD 26/8/84.
MacKINNON M. S. Born 12/3/32. Commd 16/9/55. Fg Offr 16/9/57. Retd GD 22/12/59.
MACKINNON N. J. Born 10/2/43. Commd 26/11/81. Flt Lt 26/11/85. Retd OPS SPT 10/2/98.
MACKINNON R. J. N. Born 7/12/54. Commd 28/2/80. Wg Cdr 1/7/97. Retd ADMIN 11/5/00.
MacKINNON W. Born 21/12/23. Commd 31/3/45. Flt Lt 4/6/53. Retd GD 1/11/67.
MACKINTOSH A. M., BSc. Born 6/6/30. Commd 18/11/53. Gp Capt 1/1/76. Retd ENG 31/12/82.
MACKINTOSH E. K., MA CEng MIEE. Born 5/7/36. Commd 30/9/55. Sqn Ldr 1/7/67. Retd ENG 5/7/74.
MACKINTOSH J. Born 6/1/23. Commd 10/2/45. Sqn Ldr 1/1/57. Retd GD 6/1/72.
MACKINTOSH M. F. Born 1/9/21. Commd 9/6/43. Flt Lt 20/4/55. Retd GD(G) 19/12/57.
MACKLEY B. Born 29/10/32. Commd 23/8/51. Flt Lt 1/6/62. Retd GD(G) 30/1/72.
MACKREATH J., BSc. Born 28/4/51. Commd 9/9/69. Gp Capt 1/7/97. Retd ENG 2/4/99.
MacKRETH A. J. B. Born 21/7/12. Commd 31/7/43. Flt Lt 31/7/45. Retd GD 18/11/45.
MacLACHLAN A. C., MRCGP DPH DIH. Born 17/4/31. Commd 26/9/54. Wg Cdr 16/8/67. Retd MED 3/2/78.
MACLACHLAN A. J. C., CEng MRAeS. Born 19/10/41. Commd 2/3/61. Wg Cdr 1/7/88. Retd ENG 19/10/96.
MACLACHLAN M. R. F. Born 30/11/39. Commd 6/3/63. Flt Lt 9/5/67. Retd PRT 1/10/75.
MACLACHLAN N. K. Born 1/1/38. Commd 6/7/62. Flt Lt 12/11/69. Retd GD 13/3/78.
MACLACHLAN R., AFC. Born 4/6/23. Commd 28/9/51. Sqn Ldr 1/1/68. Retd GD 4/6/83.
MACLAINE M. J., AFC. Born 26/8/46. Commd 5/11/70. Sqn Ldr 1/1/84. Retd GD 20/7/92.
MacLAREN I. N. Born 13/2/18. Commd 26/6/39. Flt Lt 29/11/51. Retd GD(G) 31/3/62.
MacLAREN M. Born 20/6/45. Commd 19/8/66. Flt Lt 14/5/72. Retd GD 20/6/86.
MACLAREN R. B., MB ChB DIH. Born 23/10/29. Commd 3/3/57. Wg Cdr 3/3/70. Retd MED 3/3/73.
MacLAUGHLIN D. S., BSc. Born 14/12/40. Commd 25/9/62. Flt Lt 25/7/66. Retd ENG 11/10/72.
MACLEAN E. J., MBE. Born 11/5/49. Commd 19/9/71. Wg Cdr 1/7/90. Retd ENG 19/2/01.
MACLEAN H., BSc. Born 14/11/43. Commd 28/9/64. Sqn Ldr 1/1/76. Retd GD 14/11/81.
MACLEAN J., MBE MIMgt. Born 16/6/26. Commd 23/6/60. Wg Cdr 1/1/76. Retd SY 27/5/77.
MACLEAN J. E. B. B., DSC. Born 26/10/94. Commd 1/4/18. Flt Lt 1/4/18. Retd GD 10/12/24.
MacLEARY I. S. Born 20/8/36. Commd 9/5/66. Flt Lt 9/5/71. Retd ADMIN 9/5/82.
MacLENNAN A. O. Born 20/9/44. Commd 22/5/70. Sqn Ldr 1/7/85. Retd SY(RGT) 1/7/88.
MacLENNAN D. Born 24/7/35. Commd 3/7/56. Gp Capt 1/1/81. Retd GD 7/4/90.
MacLENNAN The Rev D. A. F., OBE BD. Born 6/5/34. Commd 5/8/64. Retd 6/11/89. Wg Cdr.
MacLEOD A. M., MB ChB DPM. Born 9/5/27. Commd 18/9/55. Wg Cdr 23/8/62. Retd MED 8/4/68.
MACLEOD The Rev A. M., MA. Born 12/7/20. Commd 18/11/47. Retd 12/7/75. Wg Cdr.
MACLEOD C. J., BSc. Born 1/2/36. Commd 16/4/63. Sqn Ldr 19/2/68. Retd ADMIN 16/4/82.
MACLEOD D. F., CEng MIEE. Born 2/11/38. Commd 24/9/59. Gp Capt 1/7/91. Retd ENG 1/7/94.
MACLEOD D. H. Born 25/7/61. Commd 20/10/83. Sqn Ldr 1/1/93. Retd GD 25/7/99.
MacLEOD D. H., MB ChB DTM&H. Born 5/10/32. Commd 3/11/56. Wg Cdr 3/11/69. Retd MED 2/4/80.
MACLEOD G. G. Born 17/5/46. Commd 23/4/87. Flt Lt 23/4/91. Retd ENG 2/4/93.
MACLEOD I. S. Born 27/4/61. Commd 28/2/80. Flt Lt 28/8/86. Retd GD(G) 1/6/93.
MacLEOD I. S., BA BA MIDPM MBCS. Born 23/6/42. Commd 18/8/61. Flt Lt 18/2/67. Retd GD 1/10/88.
MacLEOD M. D. Born 22/4/37. Commd 10/3/77. Sqn Ldr 1/1/86. Retd ENG 5/10/92.
MacLEOD M. M. Born 15/1/51. Commd 3/12/70. Sqn Ldr 1/7/83. Retd GD 15/1/89.
MACLEOD N., BSc. Born 10/5/54. Commd 30/10/72. Wg Cdr 1/7/90. Retd ADMIN 5/12/93.
MACLEOD N., OBE. Born 31/3/46. Commd 4/5/72. Gp Capt 1/1/94. Retd ADMIN 14/3/96.
MacLEOD N. R. Born 19/12/41. Commd 12/12/59. Sqn Ldr 1/7/73. Retd GD 19/12/79.
MACLEOD R. M., IEng MILT AMRAeS. Born 17/6/57. Commd 30/8/84. Sqn Ldr 1/7/96. Retd SUP 8/4/00.
MacLEOD W., DFM. Born 2/9/16. Commd 25/4/43. Flt Lt 6/12/47. Retd GD(G) 28/9/68.
MacLEOD W. J. R. Born 3/2/51. Commd 10/9/70. Flt Lt 10/3/76. Retd GD 3/2/89.
MACMASTER J. Born 15/5/22. Commd 5/9/57. Flt Lt 1/4/63. Retd GD 15/5/77.
MACMILLAN C. A. Born 11/3/43. Commd 16/11/61. Sqn Ldr 1/1/80. Retd GD(G) 31/3/94.
MacMILLAN D. R. Born 23/9/39. Commd 2/8/81. Flt Lt 12/11/70. Retd GD 31/10/89.
MACMILLAN I. C., MA. Born 15/6/41. Commd 17/8/64. Wg Cdr 1/7/84. Retd GD 15/6/96.
MACMILLAN-BELL H. I. Born 22/10/33. Commd 8/4/53. Fg Offr 3/3/55. Retd GD 1/10/57.
MACNAB A. J., MA BCom FCMA MInstAM MIMgt AMS. Born 18/8/54. Commd 14/1/73. Sqn Ldr 1/7/87. Retd ADMIN 4/5/00.

MacNEILL The Rev C. C., OBE BA. Born 27/9/30. Commd 7/6/62. Retd 6/6/84. Wg Cdr.
MacNICOL N. R. Born 24/1/32. Commd 15/12/53. Flt Lt 15/6/56. Retd GD 1/1/76.
MacNISH N. K. Born 6/8/42. Commd 24/2/61. Flt Lt 9/2/68. Retd GD 31/10/81.
MACPHERSON A. M. Born 3/1/61. Commd 23/10/86. Sqn Ldr 1/1/97. Retd OPS SPT 1/1/00.
MACPHERSON C. S. Born 24/5/43. Commd 3/8/62. Flt Lt 3/2/68. Retd GD 5/12/75.
MACPHERSON D. A., BA. Born 12/1/47. Commd 16/1/72. Flt Lt 16/10/75. Retd SEC 3/10/78.
MACPHERSON I. A. Born 18/10/36. Commd 5/7/73. Sqn Ldr 1/7/88. Retd ENG 18/10/94.
MacPHERSON I. S., DFC. Born 1/11/28. Commd 14/12/49. Sqn Ldr 1/1/61. Retd GD 10/1/70.
MacPHERSON J. D. V. Born 18/3/26. Commd 17/1/52. Wg Cdr 1/1/69. Retd GD 7/8/79.
MACPHERSON J. H., MIMgt. Born 14/3/44. Commd 18/7/63. Sqn Ldr 1/1/75. Retd SUP 30/8/95.
MacQUILLAN P. A. Born 10/5/43. Commd 29/3/62. Plt Offr 20/3/63. Retd ENG 19/12/64.
MACRAE A. Born 9/5/60. Commd 17/7/87. Flt Lt 21/11/89. Retd ENG 9/5/98.
MACRAE A. S. Born 6/7/40. Commd 31/8/62. Flt Lt 24/3/65. Retd GD 6/7/78.
MACRAE I. R. Born 16/2/36. Commd 11/11/71. Sqn Ldr 1/1/87. Retd ADMIN 1/1/89.
MacRAE J. P. R. Born 12/12/32. Commd 11/8/53. Flt Lt 5/10/60. Retd GD 12/12/70.
MACRAE J. R. A., BSc. Born 7/7/57. Commd 12/8/79. Sqn Ldr 1/1/91. Retd GD 7/4/98.
MACRAE K., MBE. Born 8/10/19. Commd 28/7/49. Wg Cdr 1/1/66. Retd SUP 8/10/74.
MacRAE M. K. Born 17/10/20. Commd 22/6/50. Gp Capt 1/7/72. Retd SEC 17/10/85.
MACRO E. L., OBE MIMgt. Born 5/3/20. Commd 3/4/39. Wg Cdr 1/7/59. Retd SUP 31/5/69.
MacTAGGART J. G. Born 12/1/42. Commd 15/9/61. Flt Lt 15/3/67. Retd GD 12/1/80.
MacTAGGART W. K., CBE BSc CEng FIMechE FRAeS FIMgt. Born 15/1/29. Commd 1/4/52. AVM 1/1/78. Retd ENG 7/5/80.
MADDEN F. A. P. Born 31/7/26. Commd 21/11/50. Sqn Ldr 1/1/66. Retd GD 28/11/75.
MADDEN J. M., MSc CEng MIEE. Born 17/12/52. Commd 25/9/71. Wg Cdr 1/1/89. Retd ENG 1/1/92.
MADDEN P. Born 11/3/34. Commd 6/4/72. Flt Lt 6/4/75. Retd GD 10/4/79.
MADDERN T., BA. Born 13/4/38. Commd 23/9/59. Wg Cdr 1/1/80. Retd GD 6/4/83.
MADDEX N. W. S. Born 26/9/37. Commd 4/11/82. Sqn Ldr 1/7/90. Retd ENG 4/11/92.
MADDIESON D. A. Born 3/7/29. Commd 12/3/64. Flt Lt 12/3/69. Retd GD 4/7/78.
MADDIESON G. S. Born 9/12/54. Commd 8/5/86. Sqn Ldr 1/1/94. Retd ENG 9/12/98.
MADDOCK T. W. Born 20/6/22. Commd 16/10/43. Flt Lt 16/4/47. Retd GD 20/6/65.
MADDOCKS B. J. Born 12/7/42. Commd 18/10/62. Wg Cdr 1/1/91. Retd GD 2/4/93.
MADDOX A. D. Born 3/3/51. Commd 16/3/73. Flt Lt 16/3/76. Retd GD 23/2/83.
MADDOX C. J., BSc. Born 20/8/38. Commd 14/10/71. Sqn Ldr 14/4/78. Retd EDN 14/10/79.
MADDOX D. A. Born 17/3/24. Commd 21/1/45. Gp Capt 1/1/68. Retd GD 17/3/79.
MADELIN I. Born 12/4/31. Commd 18/6/52. Gp Capt 1/7/79. Retd GD 12/7/86.
MADEN W. B. Born 13/2/38. Commd 15/12/59. Flt Lt 15/6/62. Retd GD 21/5/65.
MADER E. C. Born 25/3/19. Commd 23/5/63. Flt Lt 23/5/66. Retd GD(G) 15/6/73.
MADER P. R., BSc. Born 24/2/54. Commd 17/9/72. Sqn Ldr 1/1/89. Retd ADMIN 24/2/92.
MADERSON C. W. Born 12/10/19. Commd 24/4/43. Sqn Ldr 1/7/67. Retd SEC 12/10/64.
MADGE A. W., MSc BSc MRAeS. Born 18/9/61. Commd 2/9/79. Wg Cdr 1/1/97. Retd ENG 1/1/00.
MADGE E. W. Born 21/2/38. Commd 13/12/79. Sqn Ldr 1/1/87. Retd ENG 21/2/96.
MADOC-JONES H., BA. Born 29/11/29. Commd 11/1/50. Wg Cdr 1/1/71. Retd SEC 29/11/79.
MAEER K. W. Born 15/9/46. Commd 28/4/65. Flt Lt 17/3/71. Retd GD 25/9/92.
MAFFETT S. A. H. Born 18/2/41. Commd 19/12/61. Sqn Ldr 1/7/70. Retd GD 18/2/79.
MAGEE D. J. Born 19/8/44. Commd 14/6/63. Wg Cdr 1/1/91. Retd GD 2/4/93.
MAGEE F. Born 17/9/15. Commd 25/8/60. Flt Lt 25/8/63. Retd ENG 26/2/67.
MAGEE G. D. Born 30/12/51. Commd 14/10/71. Sqn Ldr 1/1/86. Retd GD 30/12/89.
MAGEE K. F. Born 11/7/58. Commd 11/1/79. Flt Lt 11/7/84. Retd GD 11/7/96.
MAGEE M. F., MIMgt. Born 12/6/34. Commd 17/9/53. Sqn Ldr 1/7/66. Retd ADMIN 12/6/92.
MAGEE M. J., BSc. Born 27/5/59. Commd 5/9/94. Sqn Ldr 1/7/93. Retd GD 27/5/97.
MAGGS C. A. Born 12/3/65. Commd 18/11/90. Flt Lt 18/11/90. Retd GD 14/9/96.
MAGGS E. A. Born 21/3/23. Commd 6/1/45. Flt Lt 19/11/53. Retd GD 28/7/68.
MAGGS K. J. Born 1/5/22. Commd 27/1/55. Flt Lt 27/1/61. Retd GD 1/5/77.
MAGGS W. J., CB OBE MA. Born 2/2/14. Commd 2/1/39. AVM 1/1/67. Retd SUP 10/10/69.
MAGILL P. Born 25/3/47. Commd 21/2/74. Flt Lt 21/2/76. Retd GD 25/3/85.
MAGILL P. G. Born 22/1/45. Commd 31/1/64. Flt Lt 30/10/69. Retd GD 18/6/75.
MAGILL T. N., BA. Born 8/12/59. Commd 11/12/83. Flt Lt 11/6/87. Retd SUP 14/9/96.
MAGOR D. H. Born 27/10/30. Commd 25/5/50. Gp Capt 1/1/78. Retd GD 2/8/83.
MAGUIRE F. M. Born 24/2/39. Commd 25/6/64. Flt Lt 1/7/69. Retd GD 7/3/77.
MAGUIRE J. H., MBE. Born 4/3/19. Commd 16/12/43. Sqn Ldr 1/1/56. Retd ENG 22/3/68.
MAGUIRE R. C., BA. Born 28/3/66. Commd 18/2/90. Flt Lt 18/8/93. Retd SY 31/8/96.
MAGURN J. P. Born 5/5/30. Commd 18/2/54. Flt Lt 1/1/61. Retd PRT 29/4/69.
MAHENDRAN R. Born 31/8/33. Commd 3/2/65. Sqn Ldr 1/7/71. Retd GD 3/2/81.
MAHER B. J. L. Born 15/8/39. Commd 1/8/63. Flt Lt 1/8/64. Retd GD 14/2/76.
MAHER T. M., BEng. Born 23/5/61. Commd 2/8/85. Sqn Ldr 1/1/96. Retd ENG 23/5/99.
MAHGHAN C. G., CB CBE AFC. Born 3/2/23. Commd 16/3/47. AV-M 1/1/75. Retd GD 3/3/78.

MAHON A. G. Born 11/2/42. Commd 17/12/63. Flt Lt 25/7/66. Retd GD 11/2/80.
MAHON A. W. L., MBE CEng MRAeS. Born 4/12/14. Commd 7/10/43. Wg Cdr 1/1/64. Retd ENG 4/6/67.
MAHONEY M., MB ChB FRCS(Glas). Born 18/7/34. Commd 8/8/62. A Cdre 2/5/94. Retd MED 1/1/97.
MAHONEY M. F., MA BSc. Born 25/1/57. Commd 12/8/79. Sqn Ldr 1/7/88. Retd GD 12/8/95.
MAIDMAN N. Born 23/9/35. Commd 7/5/64. Flt Lt 1/7/68. Retd ENG 23/1/74.
MAIDMENT L. J., DFM. Born 27/3/19. Commd 21/9/42. Flt Lt 21/3/46. Retd GD 9/5/53.
MAILLARD P. B. Born 24/5/33. Commd 27/2/52. Sqn Ldr 1/7/86. Retd GD 14/10/87.
MAIN B. J., MMar. Born 26/7/37. Commd 14/9/65. Wg Cdr 1/7/80. Retd MAR 1/4/86.
MAIN D. MacP. Born 27/2/44. Commd 2/8/68. Sqn Ldr 1/1/76. Retd ENG 27/2/82.
MAIN J. B., CB OBE BSc CEng FIEE FIIE(elec). FRAeS. Born 28/1/41. Commd 30/9/60. AVM 1/1/94. Retd ENG
    12/4/96.
MAINPRICE M. C. Born 1/6/17. Commd 23/1/39. Sqn Ldr 1/8/47. Retd SUP 3/2/60.
MAIR J. W., MVO MSc CEng MRAeS. Born 11/6/36. Commd 19/2/63. Wg Cdr 1/7/76. Retd ENG 23/7/86.
MAIR L. Born 21/1/34. Commd 29/4/53. Air Cdre 1/1/83. Retd GD 1/5/87.
MAIR T. J., MA MEd. Born 11/11/16. Commd 6/1/49. Gp Capt 1/7/68. Retd EDN 11/11/71.
MAISEY J. H., LLB FCIS. Born 25/7/23. Commd 28/8/42. Wg Cdr 1/7/73. Retd ADMIN 31/12/76.
MAISH W. B., MRAeS. Born 21/1/34. Commd 29/4/53. Air Cdre 1/1/83. Retd GD 1/5/87.
MAISNER A., CB CBE AFC. Born 26/7/21. Commd 1/9/48. A Cdre 1/1/72. Retd GD 14/1/77 rtg AVM.
MAITLAND J. E. Born 1/4/33. Commd 15/12/53. Gp Capt 1/7/80. Retd GD 1/5/93.
MAITLAND J. R. Born 11/10/14. Commd 3/9/46. Sqn Ldr 1/4/56. Retd GD 6/6/58.
MAITLAND P. J., AFC. Born 31/5/39. Commd 15/12/59. Sqn Ldr 1/1/68. Retd GD 23/9/77.
MAITLAND-TITTERTON L., MIMgt. Born 28/5/31. Commd 12/9/63. Flt Lt 12/9/69. Retd ENG 28/5/89.
MAJOR D. R. Born 11/8/40. Commd 22/8/61. Sqn Ldr 1/7/86. Retd GD 13/12/93.
MAJOR G. H. Born 26/9/09. Commd 11/5/43. Flt Lt 13/9/50. Retd SUP 28/2/59.
MAJOR P. C. A. Born 24/9/24. Commd 4/5/50. Wg Cdr 1/7/72. Retd GD 24/9/79.
MAJOR P. C. J. Born 11/4/53. Commd 19/3/81. Sqn Ldr 1/7/89. Retd ENG 26/12/95.
MAJOR R. J. Born 3/12/34. Commd 1/4/58. Sqn Ldr 1/1/77. Retd PI 18/10/85.
MAJOR W. T., MA. Born 13/4/23. Commd 14/5/45. Flt Lt 2/1/61. Retd EDN 9/1/63.
MAKEPEACE R. M. T. Born 28/12/41. Commd 3/1/64. Flt Lt 9/2/68. Retd GD 28/12/79.
MAKINSON-SANDERS J. M. F. Born 18/2/47. Commd 1/3/68. Flt Lt 1/3/71. Retd GD 26/5/72.
MALCOLM R. A., BSc., Born 6/11/47. Commd 1/9/70. Flt Lt 1/12/70. Retd GD 1/9/82.
MALIN D. P., DFC. Born 1/5/37. Commd 1/4/58. Flt Lt 1/10/60. Retd GD 19/4/69.
MALIN I. G. L. Born 30/8/54. Commd 5/7/73. Flt Lt 5/1/79. Retd GD 10/4/88.
MALING J. P. Born 10/10/31. Commd 30/7/80. Sqn Ldr 30/5/68. Retd SUP 10/4/92.
MALINGS R.C., BA. Born 29/1/26. Commd 26/9/57. Flt Lt 26/9/63. Retd ADMIN 29/1/86.
MALINS H. R. Born 12/4/11. Commd 7/10/43. Flt Lt 7/4/47. Retd ENG 12/5/58.
MALINS L. A., DSO DFC. Born 20/6/20. Commd 10/6/41. Gp Capt 1/7/61. Retd GD 1/3/66.
MALINS W. E. V., DFC. Born 26/9/15. Commd 4/6/38. Wg Cdr 1/7/51. Retd GD 8/5/52.
MALLABAND P. D., BSc. Born 1/12/50. Commd 15/9/69. Flt Lt 15/12/73. Retd GD 24/5/75.
MALLEN I. Born 26/4/43. Commd 28/4/65. Flt Lt 17/3/71. Retd GD 1/9/82.
MALLET M. H. Born 4/5/20. Commd 15/4/57. Flt Lt 15/4/57. Retd SEC 4/5/75.
MALLETT D. R. Born 21/7/24. Commd 25/2/44. Sqn Ldr 1/1/59. Retd GD 31/8/63.
MALLETT E., MA. Born 23/10/25. Commd 20/9/48. Sqn Ldr 1/1/65. Retd SUP 31/7/68.
MALLETT F. A. Born 17/8/33. Commd 6/4/54. Wg Cdr 1/1/70. Retd GD 10/1/76.
MALLINDER A. Born 23/7/34. Commd 18/8/61. Flt Lt 26/7/67. Retd GD 23/7/72.
MALLINSON J. D., AFC. Born 12/2/13. Commd 19/8/39. Wg Cdr 1/1/55. Retd ENG 29/8/64.
MALLINSON J. M. Born 25/11/33. Commd 27/10/67. Flt Lt 27/10/69. Retd GD(G) 27/10/75.
MALLINSON L., BEM. Born 16/6/16. Commd 25/8/55. Sqn Ldr 1/1/67. Retd ENG 16/6/73.
MALLINSON P. Born 24/10/35. Commd 2/2/68. Flt Lt 8/3/72. Retd GD 9/8/73.
MALLISON J. E. Born 1/8/23. Commd 3/8/61. Flt Lt 3/8/66. Retd GD(G) 1/8/74.
MALLORIE T. W., BSc. Born 7/12/54. Commd 16/9/73. Sqn Ldr 1/7/85. Retd GD 7/12/93.
MALONE D. Born 23/6/39. Commd 17/7/64. Flt Lt 8/1/69. Retd GD 23/6/77.
MALONE E. A. Born 20/11/49. Commd 22/6/75. Wg Cdr 1/7/91. Retd ADMIN 14/3/96.
MALONE M., MA. Born 17/7/53. Commd 25/9/71. Sqn Ldr 1/7/84. Retd GD 1/3/92.
MALONEY G. M., FIMgt. Born 2/2/24. Commd 19/5/44. Gp Capt 1/1/73. Retd GD 27/3/76.
MALONEY G. T. O. Born 4/5/22. Commd 22/6/45. Sqn Ldr 1/7/60. Retd ADMIN 30/3/77.
MALONEY T., CEng MIEE MRAeS. Born 23/11/35. Commd 3/4/58. Wg Cdr 1/7/78. Retd ENG 23/11/93.
MALPASS C. P., MB BS MRCS LRCP FRCS(Glas). Born 31/7/37. Commd 11/1/65. Sqn Ldr 15/6/72. Retd MED
    31/7/76.
MALPASS D. J., BSc FIMgt. Born 17/9/34. Commd 6/12/56. Gp Capt 1/1/83. Retd ADMIN 27/4/86.
MALSTER A. A. Born 6/12/15. Commd 17/8/40. Flt Lt 1/9/45. Retd SEC 5/6/55 rtg Sqn Ldr.
MALTBY M. J., BA. Born 23/6/39. Commd 1/1/61. Sqn Ldr 1/1/74. Retd GD 2/10/77.
MALYON J. N., BSc MIMgt MCIPD. Born 28/12/31. Commd 28/8/55. Sqn Ldr 25/2/65. Retd EDN 25/8/71.
MAMMEN J. H. Born 22/10/28. Commd 22/1/52. Flt Lt 22/7/56. Retd GD 22/10/66.
MANCLARK R. J., LLB. Born 17/5/52. Commd 11/8/74. Flt Lt 11/11/75. Retd GD 11/8/90.
MANDER J. G., MB BS. Born 5/10/27. Commd 29/6/53. Wg Cdr 2/6/64. Retd MED 29/6/69.

MANDER M., BA. Born 16/1/62. Commd 31/8/80. Plt Off 15/10/81. Retd GD 15/8/84.
MANDER R. M. J. Born 15/11/46. Commd 1/11/79. Flt Lt 21/12/81. Retd ENG 16/6/97.
MANDER S. G. Born 28/8/49. Commd 1/4/71. Sqn Ldr 1/7/86. Retd GD 7/4/01.
MANDERSON D. J. H., BSc. Born 17/12/50. Commd 13/9/70. Sqn Ldr 1/1/85. Retd ENG 17/12/88.
MANFIELD S. L. Born 25/11/10. Commd 18/7/42. Sqn Ldr 1/7/51. Retd SUP 25/11/59.
MANLEY A. Born 23/6/12. Commd 30/6/41. Flt Lt 1/9/45. Retd ENG 23/6/67.
MANLEY R. B. Born 5/10/42. Commd 12/7/62. Flt Lt 12/10/68. Retd SEC 1/10/75.
MANN A. H. Born 5/8/48. Commd 1/8/69. Flt Lt 1/2/75. Retd SY 5/8/86.
MANN A. S., DFC. Born 14/6/19. Commd 5/9/37. Gp Capt 1/1/67. Retd GD 14/6/74.
MANN J. Born 23/10/22. Commd 1/4/46. Flt Lt 29/6/50. Retd GD 31/7/73.
MANN J. R., MBE BSc. Born 27/9/52. Commd 30/10/72. Sqn Ldr 1/1/89. Retd GD 1/1/92.
MANN M. C. Born 19/3/53. Commd 25/9/71. Wg Cdr 1/7/88. Retd GD 1/7/90.
MANN S. P. Born 29/7/57. Commd 1/11/79. Flt Lt 1/5/85. Retd GD(G) 29/7/95.
MANN T., BA. Born 1/2/33. Commd 9/6/55. Sqn Ldr 4/3/66. Retd EDN 6/9/71.
MANN W. Born 1/7/25. Commd 15/3/5. Fg Offr 15/3/53. Retd SEC 12/10/55.
MANNERS J. G. Born 19/3/32. Commd 8/10/70. Sqn Ldr 1/7/82. Retd ENG 30/4/90.
MANNERS W. J. E. Born 4/8/24. Commd 25/8/44. Flt Lt 29/11/51. Retd GD 1/3/68.
MANNERS-SPENCER J. M., BSc. Born 1/11/39. Commd 1/10/62. Flt Lt 1/7/64. Retd GD 6/10/72.
MANNING B. Born 20/9/41. Commd 14/8/64. Flt Lt 15/4/70. Retd GD 1/7/87.
MANNING E. M. Born 4/5/18. Commd 9/6/55. Sqn Ldr 1/1/66. Retd SUP 2/9/70.
MANNING E. T. J., OBE CEng MRAeS MIMgt. Born 1/3/30. Commd 11/6/53. Gp Capt 1/7/80. Retd ENG 10/9/82.
MANNING G. A. K., MB BCh MRCGP DRCOG MRAeS. Born 4/4/55. Commd 14/2/78. Wg Cdr 1/8/93. Retd MED 14/2/94.
MANNING J. F., AFC ALCM. Born 6/3/21. Commd 28/7/43. Wg Cdr 1/1/60. Retd GD 6/3/68.
MANNING J. G. Born 24/5/09. Commd 13/3/47. Fg Offr 13/3/47. Retd SUP 21/6/48.
MANNING P. Born 13/11/42. Commd 31/10/69. Sqn Ldr 1/7/79. Retd ADMIN 2/6/96.
MANNING R. I., DFC. Born 16/5/18. Commd 14/7/43. Sqn Ldr 1/7/56. Retd ENG 17/8/63.
MANNING R. J. Born 5/3/37. Commd 29/7/58. Wg Cdr 1/1/79. Retd GD 1/4/91.
MANNING S. C. Born 11/9/54. Commd 13/3/73. Flt Lt 15/9/78. Retd GD 8/12/88.
MANNING W. E. Born 10/1/31. Commd 17/5/62. Flt Lt 1/4/66. Retd SUP 5/6/90.
MANNING-FOX J. H. Born 17/12/07. Commd 15/12/28. Fg Offr 8/7/30. Retd GD 7/7/34.
MANNINGS E. J. Born 9/5/47. Commd 5/3/65. Sqn Ldr 1/1/84. Retd GD 9/5/91.
MANNINGS G. N. Born 13/4/25. Commd 11/6/53. Sqn Ldr 1/1/73. Retd GD 13/4/83.
MANNINGS R. P. Born 21/11/33. Commd 16/12/53. Flt Lt 16/6/58. Retd GD 21/11/71.
MANNION C. J. M. Born 8/4/49. Commd 20/9/68. Flt Lt 20/3/74. Retd GD 8/6/87.
MANNS K. R., OBE. Born 8/10/14. Commd 22/11/43. Wg Cdr 1/7/60. Retd ADMIN 13/4/70.
MANOCHA S. D. H. Born 4/10/39. Commd 19/1/66. Wg Cdr 1/1/85. Retd ENG 2/4/90.
MANS K. D. R. Born 10/2/46. Commd 26/5/67. Flt Lt 18/2/70. Retd GD 5/1/77.
MANSBRIDGE P. A. Born 26/2/37. Commd 8/6/62. Flt Lt 26/7/67. Retd GD 1/5/74.
MANSER A. G. Born 27/3/20. Commd 8/4/44. Flt Lt 7/6/51. Retd GD 31/7/61.
MANSER R. C. H. Born 23/7/43. Commd 17/12/65. Sqn Ldr 1/1/89. Retd GD 22/9/94.
MANSER R. J. Born 8/12/44. Commd 13/2/86. Flt Lt 13/8/90. Retd ENG 31/5/92.
MANSFIELD B. R. Born 13/3/49. Commd 16/8/68. Flt Lt 16/2/74. Retd GD 1/7/87.
MANSFIELD E. A., MA MSc CEng MRAeS. Born 14/4/32. Commd 26/9/53. Gp Capt 1/7/77. Retd ENG 14/4/89.
MANSFIELD G. W. Born 21/9/49. Commd 29/8/72. Flt Lt 29/11/72. Retd GD 26/10/77.
MANSFIELD K. P. Born 11/7/59. Commd 23/10/78. Flt Lt 15/12/87. Retd ENG 31/3/94.
MANSFIELD R. A., MSc BSc (Eur Ing) CEng MBCS. Born 27/1/56. Commd 15/9/74. Sqn Ldr 1/7/91. Retd ENG 27/1/01.
MANSFIELD R. J. Born 1/4/14. Commd 9/5/40. Sqn Ldr 1/8/47. Retd GD 9/5/57.
MANSON J. McG. C. Born 20/3/41. Commd 26/11/60. Flt Lt 26/5/71. Retd GD 20/3/79.
MANSON M. LeM. Born 18/12/15. Commd 13/12/41. Sqn Ldr 1/1/52. Retd ENG 15/9/52.
MANSON R. E. B. Born 6/3/23. Commd 28/3/42. Sqn Ldr 1/7/54. Retd GD 31/8/68.
MANSON R. J. M., MMar MNI. Born 31/3/25. Commd 24/4/57. Sqn Ldr 24/4/65. Retd MAR 1/6/79.
MANTLE The Rev W. E., MA. Born 16/5/17. Commd 1/9/43. Retd 26/8/73 Gp Capt.
MANTON G. A. L. Born 18/6/10. Commd 26/6/31. Gp Capt 1/1/49. Retd GD 26/6/60.
MANTON S. R. Born 17/1/55. Commd 8/9/77. Flt Lt 8/3/83. Retd GD 14/2/93.
MANVILLE C. P. Born 9/3/41. Commd 19/12/61. Sqn Ldr 1/7/72. Retd GD 1/12/89.
MANVILLE K. D. Born 25/4/44. Commd 3/7/80. Sqn Ldr 1/1/89. Retd SUP 14/3/00.
MAPLE The Rev D. C. Born 30/7/24. Commd 22/8/71. Retd 13/11/75 Sqn Ldr.
MAPP C. Born 12/1/10. Commd 4/9/41. Flt Lt 21/3/45. Retd ENG 10/4/46 rtg Sqn Ldr.
MAPP N. J., MIMgt. Born 29/1/33. Commd 9/4/53. Sqn Ldr 1/1/70. Retd GD 10/9/91.
MARCH B. J., BSc LLB. Born 14/11/36. Commd 14/8/62. Sqn Ldr 1/7/73. Retd EDN 14/8/78.
MARCH V. R. Born 12/5/50. Commd 15/9/69. Flt Lt 15/10/75. Retd ENG 12/5/91.
MARCHANT D. J. S., MBE BSc. Born 29/7/37. Commd 28/9/60. Sqn Ldr 1/7/85. Retd GD 29/7/95.
MARCHANT D. W., BDS. Born 15/2/42. Commd 16/4/63. A Cdre 1/1/94. Retd DEL 2/1/96.
MARCHANT R. J. Born 14/9/34. Commd 9/4/53. Flt Lt 26/8/58. Retd GD 14/9/72.

MARCHBANK C. D., BSc. Born 23/5/61. Commd 13/2/83. Flt Lt 13/11/84. Retd GD 14/3/96.
MARCHINGTON F., MIEE DipEE. Born 9/11/37. Commd 24/2/67. Wg Cdr 1/7/89. Retd ENG 1/3/93.
MAREK G. J. Born 28/4/50. Commd 28/9/89. Flt Lt 28/9/93. Retd SUP 14/3/96.
MARENGO-ROWE A. J., MB BS MRCS LRCP. Born 20/8/36. Commd 4/2/64. Flt Lt 1/1/63. Retd MED 30/9/67.
MARETT P. L. P. Born 2/6/06. Commd 11/12/26. Sqn Ldr 1/2/38. Retd GD 13/2/48 rtg Wg Cdr.
MARFLEET A. C. Born 26/8/13. Commd 5/11/40. Sqn Ldr 1/7/52. Retd SUP 26/8/62.
MARGAILLAN R. M. Born 5/4/35. Commd 10/2/56. Flt Lt 7/3/62. Retd GD 5/4/73.
MARGETTS A. Born 25/4/31. Commd 17/12/52. Flt Lt 21/10/59. Retd GD 12/5/69.
MARGETTS D. Born 6/9/21. Commd 5/1/45. Flt Lt 1/3/52. Retd GD 3/5/62.
MARGETTS P. R., BSc. Born 14/1/61. Commd 2/9/79. Flt Lt 15/4/84. Retd GD 21/3/00.
MARGIOTTA G. J. Born 28/12/51. Commd 13/9/70. Flt Lt 12/2/80. Retd GD 29/7/94.
MARGIOTTA G. L., BA. Born 29/8/39. Commd 9/9/63. Wg Cdr 1/1/92. Retd GD 6/7/94.
MARKER T. J., AFC. Born 19/7/41. Commd 12/7/68. Flt Lt 4/1/71. Retd GD 19/7/96.
MARKEY A. H. C., CEng MRAeS FINucE MIMgt. Born 16/8/21. Commd 21/10/43. Wg Cdr 1/7/63. Retd ENG 1/11/77.
MARKEY M. C., MA. Born 9/10/39. Commd 9/11/60. Wg Cdr 1/7/77. Retd ADMIN 26/4/80.
MARKEY M. J. W. Born 2/6/40. Commd 10/2/59. Wg Cdr 1/1/86. Retd SY 3/4/93.
MARKEY P. D., OBE MSc BA FCIPS FILT FIMgt. Born 28/3/43. Commd 17/12/64. AVM 1/7/95. Retd SUP 28/8/97.
MARKS B. J., OBE FCA. Born 30/4/31. Commd 13/7/59. Wg Cdr 1/7/74. Retd ADMIN 24/7/86.
MARKS K. G., AACCA. Born 30/6/24. Commd 12/9/43. Sqn Ldr 1/4/58. Retd SEC 30/6/62.
MARKS M. H., MBE CEng MRAeS MInstD MIMgt. Born 17/4/63. Commd 28/2/88. Sqn Ldr 1/7/95. Retd ENG 17/4/01.
MARKS N. J. Born 5/11/58. Commd 11/9/77. Flt Lt 4/3/84. Retd GD 2/11/86. Re-entered 12/10/87. Flt Lt 22/1/85. Retd GD 5/11/96.
MARKS P. C. Born 11/3/59. Commd 15/6/83. Sqn Ldr 1/7/94. Retd ADMIN 9/8/99.
MARKS T. J. Born 25/9/45. Commd 5/11/65. Flt Lt 25/3/71. Retd GD 2/6/76.
MARKWELL E. Born 17/8/23. Commd 11/2/44. Sqn Ldr 1/1/68. Retd GD 29/3/78.
MARLAND R. C., BL. Born 17/8/40. Commd 22/4/63. Flt Lt 20/1/68. Retd GD 22/4/79.
MARLOW D. C. Born 23/9/46. Commd 1/3/68. Flt Lt 1/3/71. Retd GD 23/9/83.
MARLOW D. E. G. Born 31/1/26. Commd 25/10/46. Flt Lt 29/6/50. Retd GD 31/7/63.
MARLOW-SPALDING M. J. Born 13/5/47. Commd 6/4/72. Gp Capt 1/1/94. Retd ENG 14/3/97.
MARMAN C. S., MMar. Born 25/7/46. Commd 24/3/74. Flt Lt 24/3/74. Retd GD 14/3/96.
MARMAN P. G., AFC. Born 12/3/21. Commd 31/7/44. Sqn Ldr 1/10/55. Retd GD 29/9/62.
MARMENT H. V., MIMgt. Born 10/9/36. Commd 9/7/55. Sqn Ldr 1/1/85. Retd ADMIN 1/9/89.
MARMION J. C., OBE FIMgt. Born 25/3/24. Commd 30/6/44. Gp Capt 1/7/70. Retd GD 25/3/79.
MARMONT A. E. Born 27/8/29. Commd 10/3/64. Flt Lt 10/3/64. Retd GD 10/3/72.
MARNANE W. R., BA. Born 5/11/44. Commd 19/8/65. Sqn Ldr 1/1/84. Retd GD(G) 31/8/94.
MARQUIS L. W. Born 23/3/31. Commd 21/2/60. Flt Lt 21/2/74. Retd GD(G) 11/9/76.
MARQUIS R. J. Born 10/3/59. Commd 9/5/91. Flt Lt 9/5/93. Retd ADMIN 31/10/95.
MARR D. G., MBE CEng MRAeS MIMgt. Born 7/2/38. Commd 2/2/60. Wg Cdr 1/7/78. Retd ENG 3/4/91.
MARR D. S. B., AFC* BSc MRAeS. Born 12/11/40. Commd 9/9/63. Wg Cdr 1/7/78. Retd GD 1/7/81.
MARR J. Born 20/8/19. Commd 21/10/54. Sqn Ldr 1/7/68. Retd ENG 20/8/69.
MARR P. M. Born 31/3/15. Commd 24/1/45. Flt Offr 2/7/52. Retd SEC 16/9/61.
MARREN L. Born 21/10/19. Commd 12/12/46. Sqn Ldr 1/7/67. Retd SUP 21/10/74.
MARRIOTT G. Born 9/10/32. Commd 10/9/52. Flt Lt 25/12/75. Retd GD 9/10/92.
MARRIOTT G. T., BTech. Born 12/1/43. Commd 6/11/67. Sqn Ldr 1/7/79. Retd ENG 6/11/83.
MARRIOTT J. F. H. Born 25/5/34. Commd 26/7/55. Wg Cdr 1/1/78. Retd GD 3/4/88.
MARRIOTT M. B. R. Born 3/11/44. Commd 29/11/63. Sqn Ldr 1/1/93. Retd GD 31/10/00.
MARRIOTT N., DFC. Born 4/1/22. Commd 26/2/44. Sqn Ldr 1/10/54. Retd GD 24/3/61.
MARRIOTT W. H. E. Born 4/8/11. Commd 6/6/41. Sqn Ldr 1/7/49. Retd SEC 24/1/59. rtg Wg Cdr.
MARRIOTT W. J., OBE. Born 26/7/24. Commd 25/8/44. Wg Cdr 1/7/60. Retd GD 28/2/76.
MARRISON S. Born 17/9/11. Commd 28/11/40. Flt Lt 9/8/45. Retd ENG 20/11/47 rtg Sqn Ldr.
MARRS A. W. Born 6/3/42. Commd 9/9/63. Flt Lt 9/3/68. Retd GD 6/3/80.
MARSDEN B. P., BSc. Born 24/10/29. Commd 21/2/52. Sqn Ldr 1/1/63. Retd ENG 24/10/67.
MARSDEN C. R. Born 16/4/39. Commd 22/2/63. Sqn Ldr 1/1/79. Retd GD 28/7/90.
MARSDEN H. Born 16/11/28. Commd 29/4/71. Sqn Ldr 1/7/83. Retd ADMIN 15/3/85.
MARSDEN H. N. Born 27/7/27. Commd 16/12/43. Sqn Ldr 1/7/58. Retd ENG 20/2/74.
MARSDEN J., MBE. Born 20/11/18. Commd 6/9/56. Flt Lt 6/9/59. Retd CAT 20/11/73.
MARSDEN J. R. Born 10/11/41. Commd 19/6/70. Sqn Ldr 1/7/77. Retd ENG 22/7/93.
MARSDEN J. W., BSc MRINA. Born 26/1/50. Commd 14/10/71. Sqn Ldr 1/7/92. Retd OPS SPT 30/10/00.
MARSDEN M. R. Born 5/3/16. Commd 5/6/58. Flt Offr 5/6/63. Retd PRT 5/9/67.
MARSDEN T. E., BSc. Born 26/11/46. Commd 19/11/72. Flt Lt 19/8/74. Retd GD 31/3/95.
MARSDEN W. Born 18/1/36. Commd 30/4/59. Flt Lt 15/2/65. Retd GD 29/9/89.
MARSH A. J. Born 24/6/16. Commd 17/12/53. Flt Lt 17/12/56. Retd SEC 30/7/64.
MARSH D. A. Born 18/7/43. Commd 1/11/63. Sqn Ldr 1/7/89. Retd GD 18/7/00.
MARSH D. H. Born 6/8/31. Commd 20/12/51. Flt Lt 4/4/57. Retd GD 6/8/91.

MARSH D. T. Born 6/4/33. Commd 25/8/55. Flt Lt 21/10/59. Retd EDN 26/1/66.
MARSH E. P. Born 12/8/30. Commd 17/1/52. Flt Lt 24/7/57. Retd GD 12/8/68.
MARSH J. C. Born 19/1/46. Commd 26/5/67. Flt Lt 18/2/70. Retd GD 24/2/77.
MARSH J. S. Born 23/10/22. Commd 23/7/43. Flt Lt 23/1/47. Retd GD 23/10/60 rtg Sqn Ldr.
MARSH L., DFM. Born 29/10/21. Commd 30/11/44. Sqn Ldr 1/1/69. Retd SY 29/10/76.
MARSH M. J., OBE. Born 30/4/31. Commd 20/1/51. Wg Cdr 1/7/74. Retd GD 30/4/86.
MARSH N. Born 18/7/47. Commd 28/4/67. Sqn Ldr 1/7/83. Retd ENG 18/7/97.
MARSH P. A. Born 9/4/32. Commd 10/9/52. Flt Lt 7/2/58. Retd GD 9/4/70.
MARSH P. E. Born 6/1/21. Commd 6/2/56. Flt Lt 6/2/56. Retd CAT 17/1/67.
MARSH P. E. Born 18/10/33. Commd 17/1/52. Flt Lt 22/5/57. Retd GD(G) 17/5/80.
MARSH P. M., OBE. Born 24/6/25. Commd 9/6/45. Wg Cdr 1/1/65. Retd GD 24/6/78.
MARSH S. Born 15/4/24. Commd 12/2/53. Flt Lt 12/8/56. Retd GD 15/4/82.
MARSH T. P. Born 24/11/50. Commd 25/2/72. Sqn Ldr 1/1/87. Retd GD 1/1/90.
MARSHALL A. C., MIMechE MRAeS. Born 29/4/22. Commd 23/9/43. Sqn Ldr 1/4/56. Retd ENG 30/6/64.
MARSHALL A. F. Born 18/11/36. Commd 27/10/54. Flt Lt 1/3/61. Retd GD 2/3/87.
MARSHALL A. J. Born 5/11/34. Commd 28/2/57. Flt Lt 21/6/63. Retd GD(G) 1/5/64.
MARSHALL A. K., AFC. Born 27/8/19. Commd 10/3/44. Sqn Ldr 1/1/56. Retd GD 21/8/59.
MARSHALL A. R. Born 16/11/23. Commd 7/9/61. Flt Lt 1/7/73. Retd ENG 16/10/75.
MARSHALL A. S. Born 21/1/55. Commd 28/8/75. Flt Lt 28/2/81. Retd GD 14/3/96.
MARSHALL B. E. Born 25/2/33. Commd 3/6/65. Flt Lt 1/9/70. Retd MED(SEC) 13/3/76.
MARSHALL D. Born 24/3/33. Commd 3/4/59. Flt Lt 3/4/63. Retd ADMIN 19/2/77.
MARSHALL D., BA. Born 12/3/37. Commd 27/8/58. Sqn Ldr 27/2/69. Retd EDN 3/10/78.
MARSHALL D., MIEH MIMgt. Born 7/2/35. Commd 9/10/75. Sqn Ldr 21/4/84. Retd MED(T) 1/4/89.
MARSHALL D. A., BEM. Born 14/4/38. Commd 20/11/75. Flt Lt 20/11/80. Retd SUP 14/8/88.
MARSHALL D. B. Born 21/12/45. Commd 6/11/64. Flt Lt 6/10/71. Retd GD 1/1/75.
MARSHALL D. F. Born 13/9/38. Commd 10/2/59. Sqn Ldr 1/7/71. Retd GD 13/11/77.
MARSHALL E. E. H. Born 24/3/19. Commd 11/2/52. Flt Lt 11/2/52. Retd RGT 12/7/58.
MARSHALL E. W. T. Born 3/9/31. Commd 12/6/51. Flt Lt 12/3/56. Retd GD 3/9/89.
MARSHALL F. G. Born 27/11/35. Commd 1/12/54. Sqn Ldr 1/1/68. Retd GD 16/4/76.
MARSHALL F. W. C., BA DPhysEd MIMgt. Born 11/2/39. Commd 10/9/63. Wg Cdr 1/7/78. Retd ADMIN 9/11/90.
MARSHALL G. Born 30/10/42. Commd 29/3/68. Sqn Ldr 1/1/85. Retd GD 1/11/93.
MARSHALL H., AFC. Born 24/6/24. Commd 17/5/56. Flt Lt 17/5/62. Retd GD 31/3/74 rtg Sqn Ldr.
MARSHALL H., OBE DFC. Born 19/5/31. Commd 20/6/51. Gp Capt 1/1/80. Retd GD 19/5/86.
MARSHALL I. Born 26/8/36. Commd 23/12/60. Wg Cdr 1/1/90. Retd GD 1/1/93.
MARSHALL J., MBE MIMgt. Born 2/9/20. Commd 17/6/54. Sqn Ldr 1/7/65. Retd ENG 1/6/73.
MARSHALL J., CBE MVO BEng CEng MRAeS. Born 12/4/35. Commd 27/9/57. Air Cdre 1/7/83. Retd ENG 1/5/88.
MARSHALL J. A. Born 31/10/41. Commd 6/7/62. Flt Lt 1/7/69. Retd GD 31/10/79.
MARSHALL J. C. Born 23/11/27. Commd 13/2/64. Sqn Ldr 1/7/74. Retd ENG 23/11/87.
MARSHALL J. C. W. Born 20/8/42. Commd 29/11/63. Wg Cdr 1/1/97. Retd GD 20/8/97.
MARSHALL J. D. Born 13/7/49. Commd 9/12/71. Sqn Ldr 1/7/90. Retd GD 13/7/99.
MARSHALL J. McE. Born 8/4/20. Commd 25/2/43. Flt Lt 5/9/48. Retd SEC 25/4/64.
MARSHALL J. W., OBE. Born 24/11/39. Commd 11/8/67. Wg Cdr 1/1/84. Retd GD 31/3/95.
MARSHALL K. Born 8/10/45. Commd 3/3/67. Sqn Ldr 1/7/78. Retd GD 8/10/83.
MARSHALL L. Born 24/10/21. Commd 17/10/57. Flt Lt 1/4/63. Retd ENG 25/7/63.
MARSHALL L. H. Born 11/7/08. Commd 19/8/43. Flt Lt 19/2/47. Retd ENG 11/7/57.
MARSHALL L. J., MBE. Born 23/1/46. Commd 18/8/67. Wg Cdr 1/7/84. Retd GD 23/1/90
MARSHALL N. G. S. Born 7/3/23. Commd 31/5/49. Wg Cdr 1/7/61. Retd GD 7/3/78.
MARSHALL N. P. H. Born 2/3/54. Commd 28/7/88. Flt Lt 28/7/90. Retd ENG 1/4/93.
MARSHALL P. F., CB OBE. Born 4/11/20. Commd 10/6/42. A Cdre 1/7/69. Retd SEC 1/9/73.
MARSHALL P. M., FCIPD. Born 3/8/37. Commd 6/9/56. Gp Capt 1/1/88. Retd ADMIN 30/9/91.
MARSHALL R., OBE. Born 16/9/21. Commd 9/11/43. Wg Cdr 1/7/66. Retd GD(G) 17/8/76.
MARSHALL R. Born 14/5/56. Commd 28/8/75. Flt Lt 28/2/81. Retd GD 14/5/94.
MARSHALL R. A. Born 22/10/48. Commd 1/7/68. Flt Lt 12/7/74. Retd GD(G) 21/10/86.
MARSHALL R. A. Born 23/6/43. Commd 3/10/69. Sqn Ldr 1/1/93. Retd GD 22/10/97.
MARSHALL R. B. D. Born 29/11/30. Commd 12/12/51. Flt Lt 28/4/58. Retd GD 19/7/68.
MARSHALL R. H. Born 1/9/31. Commd 7/9/61. Sqn Ldr 1/7/74. Retd ENG 6/11/82.
MARSHALL R. J. Born 24/8/24. Commd 29/1/46. Flt Lt 2/4/52. Retd RGT 24/8/62.
MARSHALL R. W. Born 19/1/15. Commd 9/5/41. Wg Cdr 1/7/58. Retd SEC 15/6/66.
MARSHALL S. A., MB BCh BAO DavMed. Born 26/9/36. Commd 27/11/63. Wg Cdr 7/6/75. Retd MED 26/9/94.
MARSHALL S. J. Born 24/1/25. Commd 18/6/44. Flt Lt 18/12/47. Retd GD 24/1/64.
MARSHALL S. O. O. Born 23/9/22. Commd 14/8/50. Sqn Ldr 1/1/61. Retd SUP 24/4/68.
MARSHALL T. B. Born 13/6/55. Commd 22/11/73. Flt Lt 6/4/80. Retd GD(G) 30/9/82.
MARSHALL V. E. Born 14/8/16. Commd 6/8/35. Sqn Ldr 31/5/47. Retd GD 14/2/58 rtg Wg Cdr.
MARSHALL W. G., FAAI MIMgt. Born 1/1/35. Commd 29/7/65. Sqn Ldr 1/1/78. Retd SEC 1/10/81.
MARSHALL-HARDY R. F. Born 20/5/19. Commd 26/10/43. Sqn Ldr 1/4/55. Retd GD 20/5/62.
MARSHALL-HASDELL D. J. Born 6/1/54. Commd 16/11/72. Sqn Ldr 1/7/84. Retd GD 25/1/86.

MARSHFIELD M. J., BA. Born 5/4/56. Commd 8/2/81. Flt Lt 8/5/83. Retd ADMIN 11/12/88.
MARSHMAN E. D. Born 11/6/07. Commd 27/8/44. Fg Offr 27/2/45. Retd ASD 14/12/45.
MARSKELL P. R., BSc. Born 11/2/55. Commd 2/9/73. Flt Lt 15/10/77. Retd GD 15/7/88.
MARSON M. J. C. Born 18/4/39. Commd 31/7/58. Flt Lt 14/11/66. Retd GD 13/4/77.
MARSTON P., MBE BA MRAeS. Born 18/3/42. Commd 11/11/71. Sqn Ldr 1/1/89. Retd GD 18/3/97.
MARSTON S. W. Born 9/10/48. Commd 3/5/68. Flt Lt 3/11/73. Retd GD 1/2/88.
MART K., BEng. Born 16/4/61. Commd 28/8/83. Sqn Ldr 1/1/95. Retd ENG 16/4/99.
MARTER A. D. Born 9/6/46. Commd 2/4/65. Sqn Ldr 1/7/84. Retd ENG 26/2/99.
MARTIN A. G. Born 5/5/40. Commd 11/10/84. Flt Lt 1/3/87. Retd SUP 5/5/95.
MARTIN A. G., BSc. Born 1/8/61. Commd 5/2/84. Flt Lt 5/8/86. Retd GD 5/2/96.
MARTIN A. H., CEng MIMechE. Born 17/7/24. Commd 10/9/51. Flt Lt 10/3/54. Retd ENG 9/2/66.
MARTIN A. I. J. Born 8/2/33. Commd 17/1/69. Flt Lt 17/1/74. Retd ENG 8/2/88.
MARTIN A. M. Born 5/4/41. Commd 23/2/68. Wg Cdr 1/1/87. Retd GD 5/4/93.
MARTIN A. P., BSc. Born 15/1/58. Commd 11/12/83. Sqn Ldr 1/7/96. Retd SUP 11/12/99.
MARTIN A. R. Born 27/5/28. Commd 1/8/51. Wg Cdr 1/7/69. Retd ADMIN 1/12/76.
MARTIN B. S. Born 17/8/20. Commd 24/4/42. Wg Cdr 1/7/60. Retd GD 29/10/74.
MARTIN C. A. Born 18/3/03. Commd 13/1/41. Sqn Ldr 1/8/47. Retd ENG 31/10/53.
MARTIN C. E. H., CEng MRAeS MIMgt. Born 16/8/31. Commd 18/7/63. Sqn Ldr 1/7/73. Retd ENG 16/8/81.
MARTIN C. G. A. Born 28/1/25. Commd 4/4/59. Flt Lt 25/7/66. Retd GD 18/5/75.
MARTIN C. J., MSc BSc(Eng) CEng MIEE. Born 27/10/50. Commd 19/11/72. Flt Lt 19/2/76. Retd ENG 1/10/89.
MARTIN D. Born 19/8/20. Commd 6/3/53. Flt Lt 6/3/58. Retd GD 19/8/70.
MARTIN D. A. Born 17/1/46. Commd 2/8/68. Sqn Ldr 1/7/78. Retd GD 1/3/99.
MARTIN D. C. Born 14/10/42. Commd 9/3/62. Sqn Ldr 1/1/75. Retd GD 14/10/83.
MARTIN D. D., OBE BSc. Born 4/7/20. Commd 6/3/39. Sqn Ldr 1/1/49. Retd GD 1/7/73 rtg Wg Cdr.
MARTIN D. D. Born 5/10/47. Commd 6/4/72. Flt Lt 6/10/77. Retd GD 13/12/87.
MARTIN D. F., MIMgt. Born 11/2/21. Commd 23/10/43. Sqn Ldr 1/7/65. Retd GD(G) 11/2/76.
MARTIN D. J. G., BA MRAeS MIMgt. Born 27/2/30. Commd 9/8/55. Sqn Ldr 1/7/67. Retd GD 3/1/85.
MARTIN D. J. Y., MIMgt. Born 9/9/49. Commd 2/6/77. Sqn Ldr 1/1/84. Retd SY 9/9/87.
MARTIN F. B., DFM. Born 2/5/21. Commd 19/6/44. Flt Lt 21/7/61. Retd GD 30/3/68.
MARTIN F. R., BA. Born 21/8/34. Commd 9/8/57. Flt Lt 26/2/64. Retd EDN 25/12/65.
MARTIN G. E. Born 7/11/19. Commd 17/6/54. Sqn Ldr 1/1/63. Retd ENG 5/7/69.
MARTIN G. G., MBE. Born 28/4/54. Commd 18/1/73. Gp Capt 1/7/95. Retd ADMIN 6/12/98.
MARTIN G. N., BSc. Born 13/10/34. Commd 21/8/58. Sqn Ldr 1/7/69. Retd ADMIN 21/8/85.
MARTIN H. B., MIMgt. Born 20/5/47. Commd 24/6/71. Sqn Ldr 1/1/85. Retd SUP 11/2/97.
MARTIN H. F. Born 21/6/16. Commd 1/9/45. Flt Lt 1/9/45. Retd GD 21/6/66.
MARTIN H. L. Born 15/9/29. Commd 2/7/52. Flt Lt 27/11/57. Retd GD 5/2/68.
MARTIN H. V. Born 22/7/30. Commd 4/6/52. Sqn Ldr 1/7/83. Retd GD 2/7/87.
MARTIN H. W., DFM. Born 17/2/20. Commd 13/7/42. Flt Lt 13/1/47. Retd SEC 17/2/63 rtg Sqn Ldr.
MARTIN I. R., AFC*. Born 4/2/32. Commd 4/7/51. Gp Capt 1/7/72. Retd GD 31/5/75.
MARTIN J. A., MBE MIIM MIMgt. Born 21/8/32. Commd 18/1/84. Sqn Ldr 20/5/81. Retd ENG 21/2/92.
MARTIN J. C. P. Born 26/9/60. Commd 6/11/80. Sqn Ldr 1/7/94. Retd OPS SPT 26/9/98.
MARTIN J. D., BA. Born 19/9/46. Commd 2/4/65. Wg Cdr 1/1/90. Retd GD 14/1/01.
MARTIN J. F. Born 26/8/23. Commd 2/8/43. Flt Lt 2/9/46. Retd GD 26/8/66.
MARTIN J. F. S., AFC BSc. Born 13/12/38. Commd 28/9/60. Gp Capt 1/7/89. Retd GD 1/7/91.
MARTIN J. H., DFC. Born 24/7/24. Commd 28/2/57. Flt Lt 28/2/63. Retd GD 24/7/74.
MARTIN J. H., MIMgt. Born 25/3/29. Commd 12/12/51. Wg Cdr 1/7/81. Retd SUP 1/7/84.
MARTIN J. L. Born 27/6/32. Commd 7/5/52. Flt Lt 2/10/57. Retd GD 27/12/70.
MARTIN J. S., CBE BDS. Born 14/4/31. Commd 16/9/56. A Cdre 1/7/86. Retd DEL 31/12/90.
MARTIN K., OBE BA. Born 21/10/24. Commd 4/12/50. Gp Capt 1/1/72. Retd ENG 21/4/82.
MARTIN L. G. P., CBE FIMgt. Born 28/7/20. Commd 8/3/43. A Cdre 1/7/72. Retd GD 27/11/76.
MARTIN L. H. Born 7/4/07. Commd 10/4/41. Flt Lt 21/3/45. Retd ENG 30/12/45 rtg Sqn Ldr.
MARTIN L. S. Born 6/1/21. Commd 27/4/44. Wg Cdr 1/7/69. Retd ENG 6/1/76.
MARTIN M. F. Born 12/3/39. Commd 2/5/59. Flt Lt 2/11/64. Retd GD 12/3/77.
MARTIN P. Born 20/4/52. Commd 16/2/89. Flt Lt 16/2/93. Retd ENG 3/4/93.
MARTIN P. G. Born 20/7/33. Commd 4/6/44. Fg Offr 4/6/64. Retd ENG 10/10/69 rtg Flt Lt.
MARTIN P. G. Born 4/2/34. Commd 15/10/52. Sqn Ldr 1/1/69. Retd SUP 4/2/73.
MARTIN P. J., BSc. Born 31/8/43. Commd 29/11/81. Sqn Ldr 1/1/90. Retd ENG 14/9/96.
MARTIN P. S., DFC. Born 13/10/35. Commd 17/12/57. Sqn Ldr 1/7/66. Retd GD 25/1/69.
MARTIN R. Born 28/1/06. Commd 25/4/40. Wg Cdr 1/7/48. Retd SEC 28/1/58.
MARTIN R. F., DFC* AFC. Born 26/7/18. Commd 29/7/39. Wg Cdr 1/1/51. Retd GD 1/7/53.
MARTIN R. F. H. Born 17/2/23. Commd 7/3/42. Sqn Ldr 1/1/53. Retd GD 17/2/66.
MARTIN R. J. Born 30/1/33. Commd 9/4/52. Sqn Ldr 1/7/82. Retd GD(G) 30/1/88.
MARTIN R. J. W. Born 8/7/20. Commd 17/8/50. Flt Lt 17/2/55. Retd RGT 5/5/68 rtg Sqn Ldr.
MARTIN R. M. Born 14/9/21. Commd 27/4/40. Gp Capt 1/7/69. Retd SEC 16/4/75.
MARTIN S. R. Born 11/3/32. Commd 17/12/52. Flt Lt 17/6/55. Retd GD 26/4/61.
MARTIN S. E., MILT. Born 5/5/45. Commd 9/3/66. Sqn Ldr 1/1/84. Retd SUP 5/5/00.

MARTIN S. H., OBE. Born 9/11/19. Commd 1/5/42. Wg Cdr 1/7/58. Retd GD 2/6/68.
MARTIN S. J., BSc. Born 24/11/55. Commd 15/9/74. Flt Lt 15/10/78. Retd GD 15/7/89.
MARTIN S. L. Born 22/7/56. Commd 5/4/79. Flt Lt 5/10/84. Retd GD 30/4/96.
MARTIN S. V., BSc CEng MRAeS DLUT. Born 13/4/50. Commd 8/11/68. Wg Cdr 1/7/87. Retd ENG 1/7/90.
MARTIN T. C. D. Born 5/11/38. Commd 7/5/64. Flt Lt 10/2/67. Retd ENG 5/11/76.
MARTIN T. G. Born 26/12/14. Commd 26/9/57. Flt Lt 1/4/63. Retd ENG 26/12/70.
MARTIN T. J. Born 22/2/36. Commd 17/3/67. Flt Lt 17/3/69. Retd GD 17/3/75.
MARTIN T. T. Born 14/1/47. Commd 23/9/65. Sqn Ldr 1/7/80. Retd SY 14/1/85.
MARTIN W. B. Born 21/6/59. Commd 18/11/78. Flt Lt 18/11/83. Retd GD 1/7/89.
MARTIN W. D., BA. Born 4/7/44. Commd 16/1/67. Sqn Ldr 1/1/76. Retd GD 1/5/84.
MARTIN W. D. E. Born 9/1/22. Commd 21/6/56. Flt Lt 21/6/62. Retd GD 1/3/68.
MARTIN W. L. Born 19/9/14. Commd 15/7/43. Flt Lt 5/4/49. Retd SEC 1/3/68.
MARTIN-JONES I. L., MSc. Born 14/3/29. Commd 18/10/51. Wg Cdr 1/1/69. Retd ENG 14/3/84.
MARTIN-POPE A. Born 7/9/28. Commd 6/3/67. Sqn Ldr 1/7/77. Retd ENG 7/9/89.
MARTIN-SMITH P. R. Born 10/8/46. Commd 18/8/67. Wg Cdr 1/1/90. Retd GD 14/3/97.
MARTINDALE A. R., CB BA FIMgt. Born 20/1/30. Commd 3/5/51. AVM 1/1/83. Retd SUP 20/1/85.
MARTINDALE I. C. Born 3/12/45. Commd 5/6/66. Fg Offr 6/5/68. Retd GD 6/6/70.
MARTINDALE J. H. Born 17/9/44. Commd 1/4/71. Flt Lt 1/4/73. Retd SUP 28/6/75.
MARTINS M. D. Born 11/2/33. Commd 4/5/72. Flt Lt 4/5/76. Retd GD(G) 11/5/88.
MARTYN A. G. Born 17/3/26. Commd 27/2/47. Sqn Ldr 1/7/67. Retd SUP 8/10/74.
MARTYN C. A. Born 9/5/55. Commd 17/9/72. Sqn Ldr 1/7/87. Retd GD 1/8/95.
MARTYN K. P. Born 30/3/28. Commd 8/11/68. Flt Lt 8/11/71. Retd GD 1/4/76.
MARTYN R. D. Born 15/4/33. Commd 28/2/54. Wg Cdr 1/7/75. Retd ADMIN 6/7/77.
MARTYN W. J. Born 18/4/23. Commd 10/12/47. Flt Lt 12/8/56. Retd GD 31/3/62.
MARWOOD H. Born 15/11/05. Commd 10/6/41. Flt Lt 1/9/45. Retd RGT 23/4/48 rtg Sqn Ldr.
MARWOOD I. F., BSc(Eng). Born 11/11/53. Commd 2/9/73. Sqn Ldr 1/1/85. Retd ENG 11/11/91.
MARWOOD K. M., AFM. Born 4/1/30. Commd 10/11/53. Wg Cdr 1/1/77. Retd GD 4/1/85.
MASEFIELD B. J. Born 19/5/43. Commd 28/6/76. Sqn Ldr 1/7/91. Retd GD 31/12/93.
MASEFIELD R. M. Born 12/7/43. Commd 17/5/62. Sqn Ldr 1/7/80. Retd GD 12/7/87.
MASHEDER M. A. Born 4/3/47. Commd 17/2/67. Flt Lt 17/8/72. Retd GD 4/3/85.
MASHITER J. Born 10/8/11. Commd 13/8/41. Sqn Ldr 1/8/47. Retd ENG 11/8/60.
MASKELL C. J., BSc CEng MIMechE. Born 2/10/44. Commd 15/7/66. Gp Capt 1/1/90. Retd ENG 14/9/96.
MASKELL H. H. A. Born 27/1/14. Commd 25/5/50. Flt Lt 25/11/53. Retd CAT 27/1/61.
MASKELL N. W., CEng FIEE MRAeS FIMgt. Born 10/4/20. Commd 16/8/41. Gp Capt 1/7/65. Retd ENG 10/4/75.
MASLEN K. C. Born 2/3/21. Commd 16/8/44. Flt Lt 13/11/57. Retd GD 30/1/69.
MASLIN D. Born 2/1/42. Commd 18/12/62. Flt Lt 18/6/65. Retd GD 1/7/70.
MASON A. L. Born 31/8/18. Commd 3/3/42. Flt Lt 20/11/50. Retd SEC 21/11/61.
MASON A. R., MRIN. Born 23/9/29. Commd 12/9/51. Gp Capt 1/1/74. Retd GD 23/9/84.
MASON B. Born 13/3/31. Commd 24/10/51. Flt Lt 13/4/60. Retd GD(G) 13/3/86.
MASON B. H. D. Born 19/3/35. Commd 17/6/54. Sqn Ldr 1/1/72. Retd GD 31/1/84.
MASON B. I., OBE FIMgt. Born 17/5/37. Commd 1/4/58. Wg Cdr 1/1/80. Retd ADMIN 25/4/90.
MASON B. J., MA MIMgt. Born 22/1/35. Commd 12/9/58. Sqn Ldr 12/3/65. Retd EDN 12/9/74.
MASON B.T., MBE. Born 8/3/46. Commd 20/9/79. Flt Lt 20/9/81. Retd ENG 19/9/87. Re-entrant 16/10/89. Sqn Ldr 1/1/92. Retd ENG 14/3/96.
MASON D., BSc. Born 17/2/62. Commd 14/10/84. Sqn Ldr 1/1/98. Retd GD 1/1/01.
MASON D. Born 25/1/35. Commd 29/7/65. Sqn Ldr 3/10/73. Retd EDN 1/11/75.
MASON D. R., MBE LLB. Born 15/3/59. Commd 20/12/80. Wg Cdr 1/1/96. Retd GD 1/1/99.
MASON D. R. Born 10/4/46. Commd 9/3/72. Sqn Ldr 1/7/83. Retd GD 10/1/87.
MASON F. K. Born 4/9/28. Commd 11/4/51. Fg Offr 11/4/53. Retd GD(G) 20/7/56.
MASON G. A., DFC FIMgt. Born 20/12/21. Commd 20/8/42. A Cdre 1/1/72. Retd GD 26/3/77.
MASON G. E. Born 3/3/33. Commd 21/11/51. Flt Lt 6/3/57. Retd GD 3/3/71.
MASON G. J. A. Born 24/11/05. Commd 26/5/42. Fg Offr 1/1/43. Retd ENG 9/3/46 rtg Flt Lt.
MASON G. L. Born 14/11/45. Commd 22/9/64. Sqn Ldr 1/1/76. Retd SUP 1/10/79.
MASON I. M. Born 9/4/44. Commd 17/12/65. Flt Lt 17/3/71. Retd GD 22/10/94.
MASON J. Born 3/2/48. Commd 23/9/66. Sqn Ldr 1/7/84. Retd SUP 1/7/96.
MASON J. K. F., CBE MD BChir MRCPath DCP DMJ DTM&H. Born 19/12/19. Commd 12/8/43. Gp Capt 1/7/63. Retd MED 14/8/73.
MASON J. S., CBE CEng MRAeS. Born 25/10/17. Commd 20/9/40. A Cdre 1/1/69 Retd ENG 5/12/72.
MASON J. W. Born 25/2/16. Commd 5/11/42. Flt Lt 5/5/46. Retd ENG 9/1/54.
MASON K. Born 19/2/48. Commd 14/2/69. Sqn Ldr 1/1/84. Retd GD 1/7/00.
MASON M. D. Born 5/7/39. Commd 22/8/59. Fg Offr 22/8/62. Retd GD(G) 20/11/66. Reinstated 26/8/70. Sqn Ldr 17/7/89. Retd GD(G) 3/5/94.
MASON M. D. L., BSc CEng MIEE MIMechE MRAeS MIMgt. Born 1/6/38. Commd 30/7/59. Sqn Ldr 1/1/71. Retd ENG 1/6/76.
MASON M. S., OBE. Born 24/5/45. Commd 23/11/78. Gp Capt 1/7/95. Retd ENG 28/9/96.

MASON N. C., MA MSc MB BChir DAvMed AFOM. Born 17/3/46. Commd 29/4/68. Wg Cdr 10/9/84. Retd MED 29/4/90.
MASON N. J. Born 1/4/30. Commd 1/8/51. Fg Offr 1/8/53. Retd SEC 1/5/57.
MASON P. F., MB ChB FRCS(Edin) DAvMed. Born 5/11/59. Commd 21/7/81. Wg Cdr 1/8/97. Retd MED 1/10/99.
MASON P. H. Born 14/7/16. Commd 10/5/46. Flt Lt 29/11/51. Retd RGT 23/6/58.
MASON P. J. Born 18/4/38. Commd 11/6/60. Sqn Ldr 1/7/83. Retd GD 18/4/93.
MASON P. J., BA. Born 8/6/61. Commd 2/9/79. Sqn Ldr 1/7/93. Retd ADMIN 14/9/96.
MASON P. J. D. Born 20/9/50. Commd 20/12/73. Sqn Ldr 1/7/88. Retd GD 14/11/91.
MASON R. A., CB CBE MA. Born 22/10/32. Commd 29/6/56. AVM 1/1/86. Retd ADMIN 22/4/89.
MASON R. J. Born 9/3/51. Commd 5/11/70. Flt Lt 5/5/75. Retd GD 2/2/82.
MASON R. L., BSc. Born 4/9/30. Commd 18/2/54. Sqn Ldr 1/1/65. Retd ENG 4/9/80.
MASON R. S., MBE ACIS. Born 12/3/20. Commd 18/3/43. Wg Cdr 1/7/62. Retd SEC 13/1/68.
MASON S. Born 30/6/24. Commd 29/10/64. Flt Lt 29/10/67. Retd GD 30/6/84.
MASON S. B. Born 22/5/58. Commd 29/7/83. Flt Lt 19/8/86. Retd GD 22/5/96.
MASON T. Born 27/8/37. Commd 28/2/56. Sqn Ldr 1/7/70. Retd GD 27/8/84.
MASON T. C. W. Born 20/5/36. Commd 10/2/72. Flt Lt 10/2/78. Retd ENG 16/4/91.
MASON W. M., DSO DFC. Born 2/6/14. Commd 10/1/42. Wg Cdr 1/7/54. Retd GD 5/7/61.
MASSEY A. J. Born 7/1/67. Commd 31/7/86. Fg Offr 31/7/88. Retd GD 1/7/91.
MASSEY C., MCIPD MIMgt. Born 30/7/33. Commd 11/12/52. Sqn Ldr 1/1/68. Retd ADMIN 24/9/76.
MASSEY C. J. Born 4/12/45. Commd 22/5/70. Flt Lt 22/11/75. Retd GD 20/1/92.
MASSEY G. W. Born 31/8/22. Commd 11/2/44. Sqn Ldr 1/10/54. Retd GD 31/8/71.
MASSEY R. G., MIMgt. Born 10/12/42. Commd 22/7/71. Sqn Ldr 1/7/83. Retd ADMIN 10/12/97.
MASSEY W. J., MBE. Born 21/4/32. Commd 9/4/52. Wg Cdr 1/1/81. Retd GD 2/1/86.
MASSIE G. A. Born 11/5/30. Commd 14/11/51. Wg Cdr 1/1/72. Retd GD 14/5/83.
MASSIE G. W. S. Born 21/4/42. Commd 12/1/61. Flt Lt 1/7/68. Retd SEC 28/6/73.
MASTERMAN C. S., CEng MRAeS MIMechE. Born 29/6/42. Commd 24/9/64. Sqn Ldr 1/1/75. Retd ENG 29/6/80.
MASTERMAN D. L., MA. Born 7/7/41. Commd 6/9/65. Sqn Ldr 1/1/78. Retd GD 6/9/81.
MASTERMAN P. G. Born 7/3/35. Commd 19/8/53. Wg Cdr 1/1/78. Retd GD 1/1/86.
MASTERS B. M. Born 20/11/28. Commd 4/8/54. Flt Lt 21/10/59. Retd GD 20/11/83.
MASTERS E. V., MBE. Born 24/5/09. Commd 16/7/40. Wg Cdr 1/1/52. Retd SEC 29/6/64.
MASTERS M. C. H., BA. Born 24/11/59. Commd 26/9/82. Flt Lt 26/12/83. Retd GD 26/9/98.
MASTERS M. I., BSc. Born 27/3/47. Commd 17/12/72. Flt Lt 17/6/73. Retd GD 11/9/74.
MASTERS S. M. Born 16/8/61. Commd 14/8/80. Sqn Ldr 1/7/93. Retd GD 1/10/98.
MASTERTON R. G., BSc MB ChB MRCPath MIMgt DipGUM. Born 19/4/53. Commd 14/5/74. Sqn Ldr 1/8/83. Retd MED 19/4/91.
MASTIN P. J. Born 5/9/28. Commd 23/9/66. Flt Lt 8/1/69. Retd SEC 23/9/74.
MATCHAM G. M. Born 30/3/25. Commd 1/10/50. Wg Cdr 1/7/66. Retd GD 30/3/80.
MATES W. A. J., MDA MCIPS. Born 1/11/48. Commd 31/6/70. Sqn Ldr 1/1/83. Retd SUP 18/12/90.
MATHER D. A., BA. Born 7/12/67. Commd 15/9/85. Flt Lt 15/1/91. Retd GD 15/7/00.
MATHERS B. H. Born 18/2/35. Commd 18/5/56. Sqn Ldr 1/7/72. Retd SUP 18/2/93.
MATHERS D. K. Born 22/4/22. Commd 12/4/45. Flt Lt 4/6/53. Retd GD 26/4/77.
MATHESON J. A. Born 9/11/20. Commd 5/3/43. Flt Lt 6/3/58. Retd GD 31/8/68.
MATHESON N. G. Born 10/3/50. Commd 26/2/71. Wg Cdr 1/1/90. Retd GD 10/3/94.
MATHEWS A. T., BSc CEng MRAeS. Born 22/3/13. Commd 26/9/39. Wg Cdr 1/7/55. Retd EDN 22/3/68.
MATHEWS J., CEng MRAeS MIEE MIMgt. Born 5/12/22. Commd 17/2/44. A Cdre 1/1/75. Retd ENG 1/11/77.
MATHEWS M. F. J., AFC. Born 8/8/22. Commd 25/9/42. Wg Cdr 1/1/63. Retd GD 8/8/77.
MATHIAS A. J. Born 20/2/23. Commd 29/12/53. Sqn Ldr 1/4/61. Retd EDN 24/11/66.
MATHIAS D. A., BSc. Born 9/8/46. Commd 3/11/74. Flt Lt 3/8/78. Retd ADMIN 6/11/82.
MATHIE A. R. C. Born 10/5/44. Commd 24/6/65. Wg Cdr 1/7/89. Retd GD 3/4/92.
MATHIESON D. Born 12/12/59. Commd 14/8/80. Flt Lt 14/2/86. Retd GD 12/12/97.
MATHIESON K. R., BSc. Born 9/4/41. Commd 1/10/62. Sqn Ldr 1/1/76. Retd GD 9/4/79.
MATON J. C. Born 1/7/44. Commd 1/4/71. Sqn Ldr 1/1/80. Retd ADMIN 1/1/83.
MATSON H. J. D., AFC. Born 10/10/15. Commd 27/6/38. Sqn Ldr 1/9/45. Retd GD 27/12/58 rtg Wg Cdr.
MATSON K. E., BA DipEd. Born 22/9/40. Commd 2/1/67. Wg Cdr 1/1/85. Retd ADMIN 5/4/91.
MATSON R. E. Born 3/1/40. Commd 12/7/63. Flt Lt 12/1/69. Retd GD 1/10/90.
MATTEY G. L., CBE DFC AFC. Born 10/3/18. Commd 15/6/40. Gp Capt 1/7/63. Retd GD 2/6/66.
MATTHEW A. L., DFC. Born 28/3/22. Commd 31/8/43. Sqn Ldr 1/7/57. Retd GD 28/3/65.
MATTHEWMAN D. G. Born 5/6/61. Commd 26/9/90. Flt Lt 26/9/92. Retd ADMIN 20/2/97.
MATTHEWS A. G. Born 17/2/29. Commd 24/9/52. Flt Lt 21/2/58. Retd GD 17/2/67.
MATTHEWS A. P., OBE. Born 7/9/48. Commd 1/8/69. Gp Capt 1/7/89. Retd SUP 1/4/91.
MATTHEWS A. R. Born 28/9/45. Commd 6/5/66. Wg Cdr 1/1/91. Retd GD 31/3/94.
MATTHEWS C. D. Born 13/9/25. Retd 24/1/52. Flt Lt 1/10/58. Retd SUP 5/10/68.
MATTHEWS D. C., BSc. Born 19/7/54. Commd 6/3/77. Sqn Ldr 1/7/84. Retd 11/3/89. Re-entrant 7/1/91. Sqn Ldr 29/4/86. Retd GD 14/3/96.
MATTHEWS D. J. Born 25/1/38. Commd 27/2/67. Flt Lt 29/6/74. Retd ENG 29/6/80.
MATTHEWS D. J. P., DFC. Born 15/3/22. Commd 9/8/43. Sqn Ldr 1/7/66. Retd GD(G) 29/9/70.

MATTHEWS D. O., BPharm FDS BDS LDSRCS. Born 21/8/34. Commd 7/2/58. A Cdre 1/7/90. Retd DEL 14/8/93.
MATTHEWS E., OBE. Born 9/8/27. Commd 13/2/52. Wg Cdr 1/7/69. Retd GD 3/4/77.
MATTHEWS G. C. Born 3/11/09. Commd 11/8/41. Flt Lt 1/9/45. Retd ENG 3/11/58 rtg Sqn Ldr.
MATTHEWS G. J. Born 30/6/20. Commd 30/9/43. Wg Cdr 1/1/65. Retd SUP 13/7/74.
MATTHEWS G. L. Born 24/3/61. Commd 5/4/79. Flt Lt 5/10/84. Retd GD 1/4/87.
MATTHEWS G. R. Born 18/9/44. Commd 4/12/64. Flt Lt 4/5/72. Retd GD 7/10/76.
MATTHEWS I. D. Born 10/7/49. Commd 11/8/77. Sqn Ldr 1/1/87. Retd ENG 1/1/90.
MATTHEWS J. Born 28/10/38. Commd 29/11/63. Flt Lt 9/2/68. Retd GD 28/10/76.
MATTHEWS J. B. Born 21/7/20. Commd 5/11/52. Sqn Ldr 1/7/73. Retd GD 21/7/84.
MATTHEWS J. G., CBE AFC. Born 5/1/24. Commd 20/9/47. A Cdre 1/7/74. Retd GD 2/8/77.
MATTHEWS L. T. Born 20/10/46. Commd 11/9/64. Flt Lt 10/3/70. Retd GD 22/10/76.
MATTHEWS L. U., MIMgt. Born 20/3/26. Commd 17/7/46. Gp Capt 1/1/75. Retd GD 16/5/78.
MATTHEWS M. J., BA MBCS MIMgt. Born 25/9/32. Commd 14/12/54. Wg Cdr Retd ADMIN. 14/8/87.
MATTHEWS N. Born 8/1/36. Commd 11/3/65. Sqn Ldr 1/1/84. Retd GD(G) 8/1/91.
MATTHEWS N. Born 21/4/61. Commd 18/3/87. Sqn Ldr 1/1/95. Retd ENG 21/4/99.
MATTHEWS P. B. Born 11/6/16. Commd 30/3/44. Flt Lt 30/9/48. Retd GD(G) 11/6/69.
MATTHEWS R. L. Born 31/10/26. Commd 12/2/53. Flt Lt 12/8/56. Retd GD(G) 2/11/82.
MATTHEWS R. T. Born 14/12/21. Commd 19/5/49. Sqn Ldr 1/1/64. Retd SUP 14/12/76.
MATTHEWS S. I. Born 3/8/46. Commd 29/11/68. Sqn Ldr 1/1/95. Retd GD 31/5/98.
MATTHEWSON D. A. J. Born 27/5/43. Commd 2/4/65. Flt Lt 2/10/70. Retd GD 6/10/72.
MATTICK A. A., MSc BSc. Born 16/4/48. Commd 12/12/71. Sqn Ldr 12/6/79. Retd ADMIN 6/1/95.
MATTICK A. D. Born 10/9/23. Commd 26/9/57. Sqn Ldr 1/7/75. Retd ENG 29/4/78.
MATTIMOE I. C., BSc. Born 24/6/52. Commd 13/9/70. Sqn Ldr 1/7/84. Retd GD 24/6/90.
MATTOCK A. V. Born 9/12/23. Commd 23/9/44. Flt Lt 18/10/49. Retd GD 5/1/67.
MATTOCK J. E. Born 10/5/14. Commd 30/9/42. Sqn Offr 1/7/53. Retd SUP 10/5/63.
MAUD J. M. Born 22/12/25. Commd 27/4/45. Wg Cdr 1/1/65. Retd GD 7/8/76.
MAUDE A. F. Born 6/7/23. Commd 30/12/42. Flt Lt 30/12/44. Retd GD(G) 1/2/74.
MAUDE J. V., CEng MIMechE MRAeS. Born 20/8/37. Commd 28/7/60. Sqn Ldr 1/7/69. Retd ENG 19/8/89.
MAUGHAM H. B. Born 28/6/06. Commd 11/12/26. Fg Offr 8/10/28. Retd GD 25/3/31.
MAUGHAN C. G., CB CBE AFC. Born 3/3/23. Commd 14/3/49. AVM 1/1/75. Retd GD 3/3/78.
MAUGHAN M., MSc BSc. Born 16/7/48. Commd 13/2/72. Sqn Ldr 13/4/79. Retd ADMIN 13/2/91.
MAULE J. D., AFC. Born 8/6/22. Commd 1/10/43. Flt Lt 1/4/47. Retd GD 28/6/68.
MAULTBY J. M., BA. Born 17/12/36. Commd 2/10/58. Sqn Ldr 1/1/71. Retd GD 17/12/94.
MAUND H. G. Born 8/5/39. Commd 29/2/60. Flt Lt 25/7/66. Retd GD(G) 8/5/77.
MAUNDER M. J. Born 2/3/43. Commd 3/11/69. Wg Cdr 1/7/86. Retd ENG 30/6/98.
MAUNDER R. A. Born 26/7/37. Commd 5/11/70. Flt Lt 5/11/72. Retd SUP 5/11/79.
MAUNDERS D. A. Born 12/9/23. Commd 25/8/55. Flt Lt 25/8/61. Retd GD 31/12/68.
MAUNSELL-THOMAS J. R. Born 11/8/37. Commd 29/7/58. Flt Lt 29/1/61. Retd GD 9/11/68.
MAURICE D. J., FCA. Born 26/11/39. Commd 10/12/63. Wg Cdr 1/7/78. Retd SEC 1/7/81.
MAURICE-JONES D. W., MA. Born 10/8/37. Commd 24/8/59. Gp Capt 1/7/84. Retd GD 10/8/94.
MAURICE-JONES H. S. Born 29/9/13. Commd 11/6/37. Gp Capt 1/1/62. Retd SEC 29/9/68.
MAVIN A. V. Born 30/12/40. Commd 6/9/68. Flt Lt 6/9/70. Retd GD 10/1/91.
MAVOR R. I. D. Born 23/10/66. Commd 27/3/86. Sqn Ldr 1/1/98. Retd GD 1/2/99.
MAW J. M. T. Born 21/6/36. Commd 22/1/55. Flt Lt 18/10/62. Retd GD 4/8/81.
MAWBY A. Born 17/10/34. Commd 9/7/57. Flt Lt 17/1/68. Retd GD(G) 10/6/83.
MAWBY A. J., OBE BSc. Born 8/12/44. Commd 30/8/66. Wg Cdr 1/1/87. Retd GD 8/12/00.
MAWDSLEY D. E. Born 25/9/43. Commd 21/10/66. Wg Cdr 1/1/81. Retd ENG 21/5/93.
MAWDSLEY J. Born 1/11/13. Commd 22/4/43. Flt Lt 22/10/46. Retd ENG 1/5/54.
MAWER J. Born 22/3/29. Commd 20/10/50. Sqn Ldr 1/1/64. Retd SUP 22/9/88.
MAWHINNEY J. Born 7/8/43. Commd 17/12/64. Sqn Ldr 1/7/75. Retd GD 7/8/81.
MAWSON E. F. P. Born 1/7/57. Commd 24/7/81. Sqn Ldr 1/7/91. Retd ENG 1/7/95.
MAWSON S. J., BDS MIMgt. Born 28/1/48. Commd 5/1/69. Wg Cdr 24/1/84. Retd DEL 11/5/93.
MAX R. D., DSO DFC. Born 24/11/18. Commd 23/8/38. Gp Capt 1/1/60. Retd GD 24/11/68.
MAXEY I. H., MSc BA. Born 28/10/43. Commd 26/11/81. Sqn Ldr 1/1/90. Retd ENG 6/4/96.
MAXWELL A. M. L., LLB. Born 16/5/38. Commd 15/12/59. Wg Cdr 1/7/87. Retd GD 28/10/90.
MAXWELL I. A., BSc. Born 30/6/50. Commd 13/9/70. Sqn Ldr 1/1/87. Retd GD 1/1/90.
MAXWELL J. Born 22/5/21. Commd 15/5/42. Wg Cdr 1/7/69. Retd GD(G) 30/3/78.
MAXWELL T. J., DFC. Born 10/6/24. Commd 28/7/44. Flt Lt 4/2/56. Retd GD(G) 28/7/76.
MAXWELL W. A., MB BS FRCS(Edin) MRCS(Eng) LRCP. Born 26/7/52. Commd 5/12/72. Wg Cdr 9/2/90. Retd
  MED 1/10/91.
MAY A. Born 13/2/18. Commd 13/5/42. Sqn Ldr 1/1/54. Retd ENG 24/2/67.
MAY A. J., MBE. Born 26/4/10. Commd 11/6/53. Flt Lt 11/6/56. Retd ENG 26/5/65.
MAY D. McM. Born 6/2/20. Commd 7/11/46. Fg Offr 7/11/47. Retd SEC 7/4/50.
MAY D. R. Born 6/4/31. Commd 30/7/52. Flt Lt 27/12/57. Retd GD 6/4/69.
MAY D. T. Born 18/4/38. Commd 24/7/61. Flt Lt 1/4/66. Retd GD 15/3/72.
MAY J. A. G., CB CBE. Born 12/11/41. Commd 9/3/62. AVM 1/1/93. Retd GD 12/4/97.

MAY J. W., DFC. Born 8/7/22. Commd 17/4/43. Flt Lt 17/10/46. Retd GD 18/1/50.
MAY J. W. Born 6/11/34. Commd 24/11/60. Flt Lt 24/11/60. Retd GD 1/4/69.
MAY M. M. Born 7/1/55. Commd 11/5/80. Flt Lt 8/3/81. Retd RGT 30/9/81.
MAY N. Born 4/11/46. Commd 17/2/67. Sqn Ldr 1/1/87. Retd GD 27/7/00.
MAY N. P. Born 17/8/34. Commd 13/12/55. Flt Lt 13/6/58. Retd GD 2/11/68.
MAY P. Born 25/11/25. Commd 28/11/46. Flt Lt 17/5/56. Retd RGT 29/5/59.
MAYALL P. V., CBE FIMgt. Born 18/4/31. Commd 31/8/51. A Cdre 1/1/83. Retd GD 18/4/86.
MAYBURY P. L., MA MB BCh FFCM MFOM. Born 10/8/28. Commd 24/10/54. Gp Capt 1/1/76. Retd MED
    11/12/82 rtg A Cdre.
MAYCOCK R. E. Born 14/4/26. Commd 18/5/61. Flt Lt 18/5/67. Retd ENG 14/4/86.
MAYDWELL W. S. G., DSO DFC. Born 18/7/13. Commd 19/5/37. Wg Cdr 1/10/46. Retd GD 12/3/58 rtg Gp Capt.
MAYER W. L. M., AFC. Born 1/7/41. Commd 31/1/64. Wg Cdr 1/1/82. Retd GD 30/6/92.
MAYERS B. J. W. Born 25/3/46. Commd 27/3/75. Flt Lt 27/3/77. Retd GD 25/3/84.
MAYERS C. Born 27/3/21. Commd 8/1/44. Flt Lt 7/4/58. Retd GD 31/7/68.
MAYES H. E. B. Born 17/6/36. Commd 9/4/57. Sqn Ldr 1/7/69. Retd GD 7/11/75.
MAYES J. E. C. Born 24/2/34. Commd 9/11/54. Sqn Ldr 1/7/65. Retd GD 30/10/71.
MAYES M. W. Born 18/6/21. Commd 24/2/44. Flt Lt 4/6/53. Retd GD(G) 15/6/65.
MAYES P. W. Born 9/9/36. Commd 2/5/59. Wg Cdr 1/1/78. Retd GD 9/11/91.
MAYES R., BSc. Born 11/6/46. Commd 8/9/69. Flt Lt 8/6/71. Retd GD 23/12/86.
MAYES R. W., OBE PhD BSc CChem FRSC. Born 15/8/43. Commd 14/8/77. Wg Cdr 1/1/95. Retd MED(T) 15/8/99.
MAYHEW J. B. Born 26/7/31. Commd 11/9/56. Flt Lt 11/3/62. Retd GD 26/7/69.
MAYLE P. R., MBE. Born 18/11/23. Commd 17/7/46. Sqn Ldr 1/1/62. Retd ENG 28/11/70.
MAYNARD G. Born 17/4/23. Commd 27/3/45. Flt Lt 24/1/66. Retd GD 18/4/73.
MAYNARD G. J. D., CBE. Born 30/6/42. Commd 17/12/63. A Cdre 1/7/90. Retd SUP 30/6/97.
MAYNARD J. C., BA. Born 16/3/60. Commd 3/10/78. Flt Lt 15/10/82. Retd GD 3/10/98.
MAYNARD J. J. Born 18/4/34. Commd 26/11/52. Wg Cdr 1/1/75. Retd GD 18/10/89.
MAYNARD L. C., OBE MIMgt. Born 7/7/22. Commd 13/12/43. Wg Cdr 1/7/61. Retd GD 9/1/69.
MAYNARD L. H., CBE. Born 2/4/07. Commd 18/4/40. Gp Offr 1/7/52. Retd SEC 23/6/62.
MAYNARD M. J., BSc. Born 23/2/37. Commd 1/2/60. Sqn Ldr 1/8/67. Retd EDN 1/2/76.
MAYNARD M. R. Born 28/2/59. Commd 24/9/92. Flt Lt 24/9/98. Retd MED(T) 31/10/00.
MAYNARD P., BSc. Born 2/6/57. Commd 17/8/80. Flt Lt 17/5/82. Retd GD 17/8/96.
MAYNE J. L. Born 30/7/52. Commd 11/9/86. Flt Lt 11/9/88. Retd GD 16/2/97.
MAYNE K. M. Born 12/10/57. Commd 20/9/79. Sqn Ldr 1/1/90. Retd ADMIN 1/11/95.
MAYNE L. S. H. Born 17/10/46. Commd 6/10/69. Wg Cdr 1/7/92. Retd ADMIN 14/3/97.
MAYNER B. G. Born 31/8/34. Commd 30/7/52. Sqn Ldr 1/7/83. Retd GD 31/8/89.
MAYNERD D., BSc. Born 28/5/47. Commd 19/2/73. Flt Lt 19/5/73. Retd GD 20/7/77.
MAYO A. M., MSc CEng MIERE MITD CertEd. Born 12/8/42. Commd 11/8/77. Sqn Ldr 1/1/84. Retd ADMIN
    2/10/88.
MAYO J. M. A. Born 18/3/47. Commd 18/4/74. Wg Cdr 1/1/88. Retd SUP 15/11/96.
MAYS E. J. Born 14/7/42. Commd 15/10/81. Sqn Ldr 1/7/91. Retd ENG 14/7/98.
MAYS J. S. Born 12/7/37. Commd 20/8/55. Wg Cdr 1/7/80. Retd SUP 15/6/90.
MAZURK J. E. Born 22/2/45. Commd 15/7/66. Flt Lt 15/1/69. Retd GD 4/3/75.
McADAM D. W., DFC. Born 18/5/17. Commd 20/6/43. Sqn Ldr 1/10/54. Retd GD 12/7/60.
McADAM P. A. Born 29/5/31. Commd 9/4/53. Commd 9/4/53. Flt Lt 18/8/58. Retd GD 29/5/69.
McALEESE J. Born 21/1/51. Commd 11/11/71. Fg Offr 11/11/73. Retd GD 30/8/75.
McALISTER D. Born 1/3/45. Commd 17/2/67. Flt Lt 4/11/70. Retd GD 2/3/76.
McALLEN K. A., AFC. Born 6/1/23. Commd 3/12/59. Flt Lt 3/12/62. Retd GD 2/7/68.
McALLISTER C., MBE LHA FIMgt. Born 2/3/21. Commd 23/8/56. Gp Capt 1/1/73. Retd MED(SEC) 2/3/76.
McALLISTER C. P. Born 11/9/18. Commd 27/3/47. Flt Lt 27/9/51. Retd SUP 13/9/67.
McALLISTER D. Born 8/4/50. Commd 19/9/71. Sqn Ldr 1/1/81. Retd ADMIN 8/4/88.
McALLISTER V. S., MA. Born 19/7/17. Commd 16/2/49. Sqn Ldr 20/3/59. Retd EDN 10/5/72.
McANDREW S., CEng MIMechE MRAeS. Born 23/11/44. Commd 15/7/66. Sqn Ldr 1/7/79. Retd ENG 14/3/96.
McARDLE L., DFC. Born 18/8/21. Commd 5/3/41. Wg Cdr 1/7/59. Retd GD 30/7/65.
McARDLE M. P. Born 2/5/44. Commd 29/11/63. Flt Lt 29/5/69. Retd GD 15/8/70.
McAREAVEY H. I. B. Born 26/3/42. Commd 22/2/63. Flt Lt 8/1/69. Retd GD 28/3/79.
McARTHUR D. A. Born 26/5/34. Commd 5/4/55. Sqn Ldr 1/7/64. Retd GD 26/5/72.
McARTHUR J. A., AFC. Born 14/2/30. Commd 11/4/51. Sqn Ldr 1/1/59. Retd GD 14/2/68.
McARTHUR R. Born 11/8/21. Commd 12/8/54. Flt Lt 28/1/59. Retd GD 11/8/73.
McARTHUR W. P. Born 2/2/44. Commd 7/2/71. Sqn Ldr 1/7/83. Retd ENG 7/2/89.
McATHEY G., BA. Born 19/4/37. Commd 6/2/67. Sqn Ldr 8/10/75. Retd ADMIN 4/4/89.
McAULEY G. M. Born 23/6/44. Commd 25/6/65. Flt Lt 23/12/69. Retd GD 1/11/77.
McAULIFFE K. M. F. Born 31/12/53. Commd 9/10/75. Sqn Ldr 1/1/88. Retd GD 31/12/91.
McAUSLAN D. N., BSc. Born 29/5/36. Commd 1/10/57. Sqn Ldr 1/1/71. Retd GD 1/6/84.
McAVOY The Rev G. B., MBE MA BA. Born 9/6/41. Commd 7/10/68. Retd 31/12/95 Wg Cdr.
McBEATH M. Born 4/12/42. Commd 19/1/64. Flt Lt 19/7/68. Retd GD 28/6/93.
McBOYLE J. H., BSc. Born 13/12/54. Commd 20/5/79. Flt Lt 20/8/79. Retd GD 17/12/88.

McBRIDE I. A. D., BSc. Born 21/8/39. Commd 1/10/62. A Cdre 1/7/89. Retd GD 3/7/91.
McBRIEN T. Born 27/4/53. Commd 8/12/83. Flt Lt 8/12/85. Retd ENG 8/12/97.
McBURNEY K. M. Born 3/3/46. Commd 18/8/67. Sqn Ldr 1/1/80. Retd GD 3/3/97.
McCABE B. A. Born 18/10/23. Commd 1/4/45. Flt Lt 27/5/54. Retd GD 22/7/65.
McCABE E. T., OBE CEng MRAeS. Born 7/5/14. Commd 17/8/40. Gp Capt 1/1/60. Retd ENG 7/5/69.
McCABE J. Born 10/6/50. Commd 15/8/89. Flt Lt 15/8/69. Retd ADMIN 30/7/93.
McCABE J., OBE. Born 1/6/34. Commd 4/6/52. Wg Cdr 1/1/85. Retd GD 31/1/87.
McCABE M. J. Born 31/8/36. Commd 23/7/58. Sqn Ldr 1/1/68. Retd ENG 29/7/77. Reinstated 29/10/79. Sqn Ldr 3/4/70. Retd ENG 31/8/91.
McCAFFERTY J. B., MB BS DMRD FRCR. Born 23/4/34. Commd 20/9/59. Wg Cdr 24/7/72. Retd MED 1/5/79.
McCAFFREY W. F. Born 8/1/32. Commd 3/11/60. Flt Lt 3/11/65. Retd PI 2/11/85.
McCAIG D. P. F., MBE AFC. Born 4/10/22. Commd 4/7/43. Flt Lt 4/7/45. Retd GD 3/3/47. Re-employed 8/5/50. Sqn Ldr 1/4/56. Retd GD 4/10/65.
McCAIG P. E., MA. Born 18/8/32. Commd 14/10/59. Sqn Ldr 1/1/70. Retd ADMIN 4/5/84.
McCAIRNS C. J. Born 7/3/48. Commd 1/3/68. Sqn Ldr 1/1/78. Retd GD 7/3/86.
McCALL D. E. M. Born 14/2/24. Commd 25/7/45. Flt Offr 4/12/52. Retd SEC 14/8/66 rtg Sqn Offr.
McCALL D. R., BSc MinstP CEng MIEE MIERE. Born 14/8/24. Commd 16/6/48. Wg Cdr 1/4/69. Retd EDN 7/11/75.
McCALL S. D. Born 27/5/65. Commd 30/8/84. Flt Lt 20/2/90. Retd GD 14/3/96.
McCALLUM D. F. Born 24/9/20. Commd 19/9/49. Sqn Ldr 1/10/55. Retd GD 18/3/62.
McCALLUM H. H. Born 12/8/23. Commd 2/9/43. Flt Lt 2/3/47. Retd ENG 22/8/57.
McCALLUM J. M., AFC. Born 7/11/19. Commd 11/1/45. Flt Lt 19/8/68. Retd GD 27/11/74.
McCALLUM J. S. Born 11/12/19. Commd 23/12/44. Flt Lt 23/6/48. Retd GD 11/2/62.
McCALLUM K. R. Born 18/3/46. Commd 20/9/68. Sqn Ldr 1/1/88. Retd GD 10/6/90.
McCALLUM M. W. Born 4/6/32. Commd 9/11/54. Flt Lt 5/10/60. Retd GD 9/10/70.
McCALLUM N. K., DFC AFC. Born 24/9/20. Commd 1/9/45. Sqn Ldr 1/1/50. Retd GD 25/4/58.
McCAMBRIDGE D. Born 22/4/58. Commd 11/9/77. Flt Lt 4/5/85. Retd GD 21/3/92.
McCAMBRIDGE P. A. Born 10/12/58. Commd 2/2/78. Flt Lt 2/8/83. Retd GD 12/12/88.
McCANDLESS B. C., CB CBE MSc BSc CEng FIEE FRAeS. Born 14/05/44. Commd 15/7/65. AVM 1/1/96. Retd ENG 14/5/99.
McCANDLESS D. C. Born 29/3/45. Commd 27/3/86. Flt Lt 27/3/90. Retd ENG 29/3/00.
McCANN C. J. Born 19/7/50. Commd 22/8/76. Sqn Ldr 18/4/82. Retd LGL 17/9/85.
McCANN D. F. P. Born 15/5/38. Commd 29/4/71. Sqn Ldr 1/7/89. Retd ENG 15/5/93.
McCANN D. G., BA. Born 1/12/30. Commd 6/10/53. Sqn Ldr 1/1/63. Retd GD 1/10/69.
McCANN D. T., OBE. Born 1/12/32. Commd 9/4/52. Wg Cdr 1/1/75. Retd GD 31/7/89.
McCANN M. C., MISM MILT. Born 2/2/49. Commd 27/3/86. Sqn Ldr 1/7/96. Retd SUP 7/1/99.
McCANN. R. E. Born 24/8/50. Commd 24/8/72. Flt Lt 24/2/79. Retd GD(G) 24/8/88.
McCARRY K. J., BSc. Born 30/3/64. Commd 29/9/83. Flt Lt 15/1/88. Retd GD 15/10/98.
McCARTHEY J. V. Born 27/10/40. Commd 31/7/62. Flt Lt 31/1/65. Retd GD 15/1/72.
McCARTHY B. Born 15/4/29. Commd 1/9/47. Flt Lt 26/5/57. Retd GD 15/4/67.
McCARTHY B., DPhysEd. MHCIMA MIMgt. Born 11/5/26. Commd 18/5/55. Sqn Ldr 1/7/76. Retd CAT 1/7/79.
McCARTHY D. Born 23/3/44. Commd 23/3/67. Flt Lt 23/9/72. Retd GD 6/4/76.
McCARTHY J. Born 21/10/21. Commd 14/4/45. Flt Lt 7/6/51. Retd SEC 31/10/64. Re-employed 1/8/69 to 2/3/76.
McCARTHY J., BSc. Born 28/5/31. Commd 28/1/54. Gp Capt 1/1/80. Retd ADMIN 2/9/85.
McCARTHY J. P., MIMgt. Born 28/6/20. Commd 22/9/55. Sqn Ldr 1/7/66. Retd ENG 23/7/73.
McCARTHY J. V. Born 27/10/40. Commd 31/7/62. Flt Lt 31/1/65. Retd GD 15/1/72.
McCARTHY M. D. Born 28/3/47. Commd 23/3/67. Sqn Ldr 1/7/82. Retd SUP 28/3/91.
McCARTHY R. F. Born 15/4/34. Commd 27/2/70. Sqn Ldr 1/1/81. Retd GD(G) 30/4/85.
McCARTHY R. J., BSc. Born 3/8/55. Commd 1/9/74. Sqn Ldr 1/7/90. Retd GD 3/8/99.
McCARTHY J., MBE. Born 29/9/46. Commd 2/3/78. Wg Cdr 1/7/95. Retd GD 11/2/01.
McCARTNEY A. Born 25/12/14. Commd 15/10/42. Flt Lt 4/6/53. Retd GD(G) 31/12/65.
McCARTNEY J. Born 1/10/46. Commd 1/8/69. Flt Lt 1/11/73. Retd ENG 18/8/77.
McCARTNEY J. A. Born 29/1/68. Commd 16/6/88. Flt Lt 16/12/94. Retd ADMIN 14/3/97.
McCARTNEY R. J. Born 4/9/44. Commd 27/9/73. Wg Cdr 1/1/86. Retd ADMIN 1/11/88.
McCARTY R. S. Born 16/1/25. Commd 25/4/51. Flt Lt 14/11/56. Retd GD 16/10/66.
McCASKIE T. B., OBE MIMgt. Born 24/11/23. Commd 1/12/44. Wg Cdr 1/7/65. Retd ADMIN 28/5/76.
McCAUGHEY J. R., BSc. Born 12/9/51. Commd 15/9/69. Sqn Ldr 1/7/83. Retd GD 1/1/89.
McCAUSLAND A. G. Born 8/8/33. Commd 27/9/51. Flt Lt 17/6/57. Retd GD 8/8/76.
McCAUSLAND W. J., AFM. Born 4/6/24. Commd 27/5/54. Flt Lt 26/5/59. Retd GD 30/9/67.
McCHESNEY W. E. Born 2/2/10. Commd 17/6/41. Flt Lt 1/1/52. Retd SEC 29/11/58.
McCLARTY J. J. W., CEng MIEE. Born 16/1/46. Commd 27/6/71. Gp Capt 1/1/94. Retd ENG 14/9/96.
McCLAY M. P. Born 1/7/20. Commd 10/11/41. Flt Offr 1/9/45. Retd SEC 13/10/51.
McCLEAN F. W. Born 15/1/20. Commd 5/5/60. Flt Lt 5/5/65. Retd ENG 7/10/67.
McCLEERY C. W. V., MA CEng MIEE. Born 1/2/35. Commd 25/9/54. Sqn Ldr 1/1/68. Retd ENG 2/2/85.
McCLELLAND G. G. Born 14/1/18. Commd 29/4/54. Sqn Ldr 1/7/66. Retd PRT 11/7/70.
McCLELLAND I. W. Born 29/3/59. Commd 22/5/80. Flt Lt 22/2/86. Retd GD 17/5/96.
McCLEMENT D. J. Born 6/6/43. Commd 20/8/65. Flt Lt 20/2/71. Retd GD 28/10/81.

McCLEN D., AFC. Born 25/11/32. Commd 27/9/51. Gp Capt 1/1/72. Retd GD 1/9/75.
McCLORY F., OBE. Born 27/5/29. Commd 6/12/51. Gp Capt 1/7/79. Retd GD 2/10/82.
McCLUGGAGE W. Born 24/12/25. Commd 20/5/53. Flt Lt 15/9/58. Retd GD 3/5/69.
MCCLUGGAGE W. A., MSc BSc. Born 12/6/55. Commd 1/9/74. Wg Cdr 1/7/94. Retd ENG 12/6/99.
MCCLUNEY J. G. Born 3/11/37. Commd 1/4/58. Sqn Ldr 1/7/68. Retd GD 1/6/01.
MCCLURE-HALL G., MA BA MIMgt. Born 26/1/48. Commd 1/6/72. Gp Capt 1/1/92. Retd MED SEC 14/3/96.
MCCLUSKEY C. J., MB ChB FRCOG. Born 6/3/40. Commd 22/4/63. Gp Capt 1/10/89. Retd MED 14/9/96.
McCLUSKEY P. D. Born 31/7/34 Commd 4/3/71 Flt Lt 4/3/73. Retd PRT 4/3/79.
MCCLUSKEY R., AFC DPhysEd. Born 23/5/39. Commd 31/10/61. Wg Cdr 1/1/83. Retd ADMIN 3/10/93.
MCCLYMONT D., BSc. Born 5/7/59. Commd 26/7/81. Sqn Ldr 1/1/92. Retd GD 26/7/97.
MCCLYMONT G. J. Born 15/7/58. Commd 17/5/79. Sqn Ldr 1/7/91. Retd GD 15/7/96.
McCLYMONT W. Born 23/8/18. Commd 26/10/43. Sqn Ldr 1/7/55. Retd GD 29/3/58.
McCOLL A. H. McN. Born 28/8/20. Commd 22/2/44. Sqn Ldr 1/7/58. Retd GD 28/9/68.
McCOMAS J. F. Born 27/5/34. Commd 1/4/53. Flt Lt 2/11/59. Retd GD 27/5/72.
McCOMBIE I. L. Born 14/9/23. Commd 26/11/43. Wg Cdr 1/1/66. Retd GD 1/10/76.
MCCOMBIE I. M., BSc. Born 18/6/65. Commd 28/10/86. Flt Lt 26/4/89. Retd GD 26/10/98.
McCOMBIE J. W., CBE. Born 25/5/10. Commd 2/9/41. Gp Capt 1/1/60. Retd ENG 25/5/65.
McCOMISKY J. Born 26/7/47. Commd 17/5/79. Flt Lt 17/5/81. Retd ADMIN 17/5/87.
McCONCHIE R. P. Born 9/6/33. Commd 30/1/52. Flt Lt 16/6/57. Retd GD 9/6/71.
McCONE H. Born 1/9/34. Commd 2/7/64. Flt Lt 2/7/66. Retd SEC 30/9/72.
McCONKIE R. K. Born 14/7/39. Commd 21/4/67. Flt Lt 21/4/69. Retd GD(G) 14/7/77.
McCONNELL H. D. Born 19/3/30. Commd 1/6/63. Wg Cdr 1/7/76. Retd PRT 3/1/79.
MCCONNELL J. W., MIMgt. Born 6/12/22. Commd 17/4/47. Sqn Ldr 1/7/68. Retd SUP 6/12/77.
MCCONNELL P. E. Born 2/9/38. Commd 11/9/58. Flt Lt 15/2/65. Retd ADMIN 2/9/76.
McCONNON D., BA. Born 27/5/33. Commd 7/9/56. Sqn Ldr 7/3/66. Retd EDN 8/9/73.
MCCORD A. W., IEng. Born 18/7/39. Commd 3/11/77. Sqn Ldr 1/7/87. Retd ENG 18/7/97.
McCORD B. Born 24/2/44. Commd 16/6/69. Sqn Ldr 1/7/80. Retd SY 16/6/85.
McCORD T. N. Born 10/10/42. Commd 24/4/64. Flt Lt 12/11/69. Retd GD 14/1/73.
McCORKLE J. F., AFM. Born 10/12/21. Commd 10/8/55. Flt Lt 10/8/60. Retd GD 2/3/65.
MCCORMACK J. J. Born 8/6/33. Commd 9/3/66. Flt Lt 9/3/72. Retd GD(G) 8/6/88.
MCCORMICK A. M. Born 7/3/32. Commd 17/7/58. Flt Lt 17/1/63. Retd GD 25/7/69.
MCCORMICK D. G., BSc MInstP. Born 30/9/45. Commd 16/1/72. Flt Lt 16/10/72. Retd GD 30/9/00.
MCCORMICK J. C. H., MSc BSc. Born 31/10/61. Commd 22/7/84. Flt Lt 22/1/88. Retd ENG 30/9/96.
MCCORMICK M. J. Born 14/6/36. Commd 23/7/35. Sqn Ldr 1/1/89. Retd GD 14/6/94.
MCCORMICK R. P. Born 11/10/33. Commd 17/5/62. Sqn Ldr 1/7/77. Retd GD(G) 12/10/83.
MCCOUBREY I. A., MB ChB FFOM FIMgt MRCGP DAvMed MRAeS. Born 8/7/46. Commd 24/7/67. A Cdre 1/7/96.
    Retd MED 18/4/97.
MCCOURT J., MBE. Born 9/8/41. Commd 13/12/79. Sqn Ldr 1/7/88. Retd ENG 10/5/95.
McCOURT M. A. Born 13/11/15. Commd 8/4/43. Flt Lt 8/10/47. Retd SUP 24/10/53.
McCOY R. Born 22/8/42. Commd 11/10/84. Flt Lt 11/10/88. Retd ENG 31/3/94.
McCRACKEN A. W., MB ChB MCPath DCP DTM&H. Born 24/11/31. Commd 3/3/57. Sqn Ldr 1/4/62. Retd MED
    30/3/68.
MCCRAE D. I., MA. Born 29/11/41. Commd 7/12/65. Wg Cdr 1/1/91. Retd GD 29/11/96.
MCCRAN J. B. Born 28/4/49. Commd 22/9/88. Flt Lt 22/9/92. Retd ADMIN 14/3/96.
MCCRANN R. J. D. Born 29/5/35. Commd 6/2/64. Flt Lt 21/10/59. Retd GD 29/5/93.
McCREA W. E., DFC BSc. Born 3/4/21. Commd 27/3/43. Wg Cdr 1/7/64. Retd EDN 13/5/72.
McCREADY L. L. J. Born 19/1/53. Commd 12/4/73. Sqn Ldr 1/1/86. Retd GD 7/10/86.
MCCREANNEY T., MBE. Born 23/12/60. Commd 16/12/86. Sqn Ldr 1/7/90. Retd ENG 15/7/99.
McCREERY A. J. Born 10/4/37. Commd 5/6/56. ACdre 1/1/86. Retd GD 11/3/88.
McCREITH S., AFC* MRAeS. Born 11/6/19. Commd 3/7/42. Wg Cdr 1/1/58. Retd GD 11/6/66.
MCCRIMMON N. A. Born 5/10/41. Commd 25/7/59. Sqn Ldr 1/7/72. Retd GD 5/10/79. Re-entered 29/10/80.
    Sqn Ldr 25/7/73. Retd GD 5/10/96.
McCRINDLE M. K., BSc DPhysEd FIMgt. Born 28/4/32. Commd 18/11/54. Wg Cdr 1/1/74. Retd SUP 7/4/85.
McCRORIE J. D. Born 22/1/38. Commd 16/11/61. Sqn Ldr 1/7/74. Retd PRT 1/10/75.
MCCRORIE R. F. Born 30/4/42. Commd 21/10/65. Sqn ldr 1/1/77. Retd ADMIN 30/6/96.
McCRUDDEN K. M. Born 10/3/16. Commd 16/4/35. Flt Lt 1/3/45. Retd GD(G) 10/3/66 rtg Sqn Ldr.
MCCULLAGH E. A., MIMgt. Born 22/5/31. Commd 12/3/52. Sqn Ldr 1/7/65. Retd GD(G) 22/5/86.
MCCULLOCH I. J. Born 4/9/46. Commd 23/3/66. Sqn Ldr 1/1/84. Retd ADMIN 1/11/89.
MCCULLOCH J. D. C. Born 28/8/20. Commd 18/11/54. Sqn Ldr 1/7/69. Retd SEC 28/8/75.
MCCULLOCH J. W., BEng. Born 28/11/39. Commd 30/9/59. Wg Cdr 1/7/77. Retd ENG 28/11/94.
MCCULLOCH R. A., BA. Born 9/5/50. Commd 24/3/74. Sqn Ldr 1/1/86. Retd ADMIN 24/3/90.
MCCULLOCH T. Born 14/6/40. Commd 20/12/73. Flt Lt 20/12/75. Retd SEC 20/12/81.
MCCULLOCH T. A. Born 30/8/22. Commd 2/12/44. Sqn Ldr 1/10/55. Retd GD 30/8/71.
MCCULLOUCH S. D. Born 13/4/47. Commd 18/11/66. Wg Cdr 1/1/85. Retd GD(G) 13/4/91.
McCUMISKEY G. P., DPhysEd. Born 8/3/26. Commd 16/5/51. Flt Lt 16/5/55. Retd PE 14/5/67.

McCUNN W. J., BSc CEng MIERE DipSoton. Born 12/3/72. Commd 12/9/61. Sqn Ldr 12/3/72. Retd ADMIN 20/1/89.
McCURDY R., DFC*. Born 19/9/18. Commd 4/10/42. Sqn Ldr 1/1/64. Retd GD(G) 30/3/76.
MCCUTCHEON G., BSc. Born 2/9/64. Commd 8/5/88. Flt Lt 8/11/90. Retd SY 8/8/94.
MCCUTCHEON G., MCIPD MIMgt. Born 22/9/34. Commd 30/8/66. Sqn Ldr 1/7/77. Retd ADMIN 22/2/92.
MCDADE B., BA. Born 17/8/49. Commd 8/9/77. Sqn Ldr 1/1/85. Retd ENG 1/1/88.
McDEAN W. Born 13/9/19. Commd 29/8/45. Sqn Ldr 1/1/54. Retd RGT 30/4/61.
McDERMOTT A. R., BSc CEng MRAeS. Born 2/1/41. Commd 9/11/64. Sqn Ldr 1/7/76. Retd ENG 9/11/80.
MCDERMOTT J. G. S. Born 24/1/45. Commd 23/10/86. Flt Lt 23/10/90. Retd SUP 14/3/96.
McDERMOTT K. T., BA. Born 20/11/34. Commd 22/5/59. Wg Cdr 1/1/77. Retd ADMIN 14/2/85.
McDERMOTT P. A. C., DFC DFM. Born 4/3/20. Commd 7/4/42. Wg Cdr 1/1/57. Retd GD 30/4/66.
McDICKEN A. A. Born 15/3/45. Commd 1/4/66. Sqn Ldr 1/7/76. Retd GD 10/1/81.
McDILL J. M., MIMgt. Born 7/2/30. Commd 26/11/64. Sqn Ldr 1/7/77. Retd ADMIN 7/2/88.
MCDINNES J. K., BSc. Born 27/8/62. Commd 11/12/83. Flt Lt 11/6/86. Retd GD 14/9/96.
McDONALD A. P. Born 6/10/29. Commd 6/1/49. Flt Lt 10/4/56. Retd GD 6/10/67.
McDONALD A. W. Born 30/9/33. Commd 9/4/52. Wg Cdr 1/7/79. Retd GD 6/10/84.
McDONALD B. A. D. McK., AFC*. Born 9/5/30. Commd 4/6/59. Sqn Ldr 1/7/71. Retd GD 9/5/90.
McDONALD D., MBE MA BD. Born 6/3/29. Commd 6/8/63. Sqn Ldr 14/2/66. Retd ADMIN 6/8/82.
McDONALD F. J. Born 28/5/44. Commd 31/1/64. Flt Lt 31/7/69. Retd GD 26/7/75.
MCDONALD G. M. Born 13/4/51. Commd 14/1/88. Flt Lt 14/1/92. Retd ADMIN 14/3/96.
McDONALD I. Born 6/2/38. Commd 22/10/63. Sqn Ldr 9/10/74. Retd EDN 1/10/79.
MCDONALD I. Born 23/9/32. Commd 14/8/56. Sqn Ldr 1/1/84. Retd GD 23/9/92.
McDONALD I. A. Born 21/12/20. Commd 7/11/51. Flt Lt 16/8/61. Retd GD(G) 7/8/65.
McDONALD J., FIMgt. Born 13/12/33. Commd 17/9/53. Gp Capt 1/7/80. Retd SUP 18/4/84.
McDONALD J. D. Born 13/7/03. Commd 10/1/41. Flt Lt 1/3/42. Retd ENG 20/1/46 rtg Sqn Ldr.
McDONALD J. E. Born 1/3/30. Commd 5/5/51 Sqn Ldr 1/1/62. Retd GD 28/11/75 rtg Wg Cdr.
McDONALD K. Born 21/6/33. Commd 5/4/55. Flt Lt 13/11/57. Retd GD 21/6/71 rtg Sqn Ldr.
McDONALD K. J., OBE DFC. Born 1/3/14. Commd 13/7/36. Gp Capt 1/1/56. Retd GD 12/11/57.
MCDONALD M. Born 10/8/56. Commd 12/10/78. Sqn Ldr 1/7/88. Retd GD 10/8/94.
McDONALD M. M. Born 16/11/42. Commd 29/10/60. Flt Lt 15/4/70. Retd GD(G) 16/11/80.
McDONALD R. Born 23/8/24. Commd 17/3/45. Wg Cdr 1/1/69. Retd PE 1/12/72.
McDONALD S. G., MHCIMA. Born 5/8/32. Commd 1/10/60. Sqn Ldr 1/7/69. Retd CAT 14/10/83.
McDONALD W., DFC FCIS. Born 30/5/21. Comd 7/10/43. Sqn Ldr 1/7/69. Retd SEC 28/1/76.
MCDONALD-GIBSON J. H. Born 25/5/49. Commd 20/5/82. Flt Lt 20/11/88. Retd OPS SPT 18/1/98.
MCDONALD-WEBB I. D. Born 8/9/60. Commd 22/5/80. Sqn Ldr 1/7/94. Retd GD 8/9/98.
McDONNELL A. J. Born 22/9/23. Commd 11/12/44. Sqn Ldr 1/1/71. Retd GD 25/6/73.
MCDONNELL D. K. L., OBE. Born 27/1/46. Commd 31/1/64. Gp Capt 1/1/94. Retd GD 28/2/01.
McDONNELL F. E., OBE. Born 9/2/16. Commd 8/9/43. Wg Cdr 1/7/54. Retd SUP 31/5/61.
McDONNELL J. Born 28/4/04. Commd 17/4/47. Fg Offr 17/4/47. Retd SUP 17/1/49 rtg Flt Lt.
McDONNELL J. F. Born 29/3/23. Commd 30/11/44. Flt Lt 10/11/55. Retd GD 8/1/66.
McDONNELL J. P. Born 26/4/28. Commd 22/7/50. Wg Cdr 1/1/72. Retd RGT 27/4/78.
McDONNELL J. J. Born 21/5/23. Commd 24/2/67. Flt Lt 24/2/72. Retd ENG 1/3/78.
MCDONNELL N. J. Born 13/2/56. Commd 22/5/80. Sqn Ldr 1/6/90. Retd GD 1/8/99.
McDONOUGH J. I. Born 8/1/25. Commd 8/10/44. Wg Cdr 1/7/74. Retd SEC 6/10/78.
McDOUGALL A. D. Born 17/10/50. Commd 17/7/70. Flt Lt 17/1/77. Retd ADMIN 17/10/88.
McDOUGALL C. N., DFC. Born 17/3/35. Commd 30/4/62. Sqn Ldr 1/1/82. Retd GD 6/2/89.
McDOUGALL D. J. Born 24/5/48. Commd 9/12/71. Flt Lt 9/6/77. Retd GD 14/3/97.
McDOUGALL J. S. Born 26/3/50. Commd 24/4/70. Sqn Ldr 1/1/83. Retd SY(PRT) 26/3/88.
McDOUGALL M. R. L. Born 10/10/45. Commd 10/6/66. Flt Lt 4/5/72. Retd GD 25/4/76.
MCDOWELL C. B. Born 15/1/47. Commd 16/12/66. Sqn Ldr 1/7/80. Retd ENG 16/12/00.
McDOWELL S. R. Born 28/12/27. Commd 17/7/58. Flt Lt 17/7/64. Retd SEC 26/11/66.
McEACHERN W. H., DFC DFM. Born 16/5/24. Commd 4/6/59. Sqn Ldr 1/1/70. Retd GD 31/5/73.
McELHAW T. J., BA MIMgt. Born 14/10/26. Commd 3/5/46. Wg Cdr 1/1/65. Retd GD 14/10/81.
McELLIGOTT D. P., AM MBE BA. Born 26/5/25. Commd 17/7/46. Flt Lt 17/7/52. Retd RGT 31/12/66.
McELWAIN J. D. deS., OBE BSc CEng MRAeS. Born 7/9/17. Commd 20/9/40. Wg Cdr 1/7/56. Retd ENG 21/9/74.
McENERY J. N. Born 12/12/44. Commd 18/11/66. Sqn Ldr 1/1/84. Retd SUP 1/10/91.
MCERLEAN L., BSc. Born 18/10/58. Commd 30/10/83. Sqn Ldr 1/7/95. Retd SUP 30/10/99.
McEVOY J. Born 24/6/31. Commd 15/11/51. Sqn Ldr 1/1/82. Retd GD 24/6/89.
MCEVOY J. R. N., MBE. Born 11/4/40. Commd 1/8/61. Sqn Ldr 1/7/76. Retd GD 11/4/95.
McEWAN A. R. Born 22/12/38. Commd 22/5/75. Sqn Ldr 1/1/86. Retd ADMIN 1/10/87.
MCEWAN P. D. Born 8/12/42. Commd 28/2/64. Flt Lt 15/4/70. Retd GD 11/5/97.
McEWEN N. D., AFC FIMgt. Born 7/11/33. Commd 3/9/52. A Cdre 1/1/84. Retd GD 2/8/87.
McEWEN R. A. Born 29/11/34. Commd 3/6/65. Wg Cdr 1/7/81. Retd SUP 29/11/89.
McEWEN W. Born 25/8/23. Commd 6/1/55. Flt Lt 6/1/58. Retd GD 25/8/73.
McFADYEN M. A., BSc. Born 25/10/48. Commd 15/9/69. Flt Lt 15/10/70. Retd ENG 25/10/86.
McFADZEAN J. B., BSc. Born 27/7/58. Commd 22/3/81. Flt Lt 22/6/81. Retd GD 5/6/90.

McFARLAND J. Born 19/9/24. Commd 21/6/56. Sqn Ldr 1/7/71. Retd GD 19/9/82.
McFARLANE C. W. R. Born 26/5/48. Commd 22/9/69. Flt Lt 26/5/75. Retd ENG 2/8/76.
McFARLANE The Rev I. M., BA. Born 16/9/46. Commd 5/4/81. Retd 4/10/91 Sqn Ldr.
McFARLANE N. Born 23/11/33. Commd 16/7/52. Flt Lt 16/8/61. Retd GD 12/2/74.
McFARLANE R., DSO DFC*. Born 12/7/14. Commd 3/11/41. Gp Capt 1/7/56. Retd GD 30/6/62.
McFARLANE S. C. Born 13/4/35. Commd 1/11/79. Flt Lt 1/11/82. Retd ADMIN 10/8/87.
McFETRIDGE W. Born 9/1/17. Commd 16/11/43. Flt Lt 16/5/47. Retd GD 9/1/60.
MCGAHAN P. J., MISM MIMgt. Born 3/12/55. Commd 22/5/75. Wg Cdr 1/1/94. Retd ADMIN 4/12/98.
McGARRY P., BA. Born 29/6/31. Commd 21/7/55. Sqn Ldr 17/2/63. Retd EDN 20/9/71.
McGARRY T. P., OBE DFC. Born 6/3/19. Commd 21/9/42. Gp Capt 1/7/68. Retd GD 9/3/74.
McGARVEY J., MBE BSc. Born 21/3/37. Commd 25/7/57. Sqn Ldr 1/1/69. Retd ENG 31/12/76 rtg Wg Cdr.
McGEE P. C. T. Born 6/3/22. Commd 9/8/44. Flt Lt 18/2/52. Retd SUP 17/9/66.
McGEORGE W. Born 30/1/45. Commd 21/12/67. Flt Lt 9/3/74. Retd SEC 28/6/75.
MCGEOUGH P. J. R. Born 28/3/46. Commd 13/2/86. Sqn Ldr 1/1/96. Retd ENG 14/9/96.
MCGETTIGAN F. H. P. Born 23/8/42. Commd 19/7/84. Sqn Ldr 1/1/92. Retd SUP 23/8/97.
McGETTRICK J. J. Born 10/11/48. Commd 8/12/83. Flt Lt 8/12/87. Retd ADMIN 1/9/90.
McGHEE C. B., DFC. Born 26/9/21. Commd 7/3/42. Flt Lt 7/9/45. Retd ENG 18/6/55 rtg Sqn Ldr.
McGIBBON C. W., BSc. Born 10/1/46. Commd 27/10/70. Flt Lt 27/7/71. Retd GD 5/9/91.
McGILCHRIST D. G. Born 23/5/39. Commd 21/7/61. Flt Lt 21/1/67. Retd GD 23/5/77.
McGILL B. J. Born 8/2/34. Commd 26/7/55. Wg Cdr 1/1/74. Retd SUP 2/9/80.
MCGILL D. P. K., OBE CEng MRAeS. Born 31/8/42. Commd 15/7/64. A Cdre 1/7/92. Retd ENG 5/4/95.
McGINTY M. T., BSc. Born 27/2/51. Commd 25/9/71. Wg Cdr 1/1/87. Retd PRT 8/12/91.
McGLASHAN K. B., AFC. Born 28/8/20. Commd 18/3/39. Sqn Ldr 1/1/49. Retd GD 29/8/58.
MCGLENNON D. M. Born 6/1/65. Commd 8/5/88. Flt Lt 8/5/94. Retd ADMIN 1/11/96.
McGONIGLE F., MBE. Born 16/7/20. Commd 9/1/45. Wg Cdr 1/7/67. Retd SUP 16/7/75.
MCGONIGLE N. Born 1/1/58. Commd 5/9/76. Wg Cdr 1/1/96. Retd OPS SPT 21/4/01.
McGOUGH W. H., MIMgt. Born 1/4/25. Commd 21/10/65. Flt Lt 21/10/71. Retd GD(G) 1/4/80 rtg Sqn Ldr.
McGOWAN A., MA. Born 18/11/59. Commd 18/10/81. Sqn Ldr 1/1/91. Retd SY 14/3/96.
McGOWAN G. Born 24/3/17. Commd 27/8/52. Flt Lt 27/8/57. Retd GD(G) 3/5/67.
McGOWAN R. B. Born 17/9/18. Commd 7/5/44. Sqn Ldr 1/7/56. Retd GD 27/11/58.
McGOWAN R. C. Born 26/5/49. Commd 12/7/68. Flt Lt 12/1/74. Retd GD 16/9/78.
McGOWAN R. R., AFC. Born 1/7/23. Commd 2/4/43. Sqn Ldr 1/1/57. Retd GD 1/1/67.
McGRAIL R. Born 19/1/22. Commd 16/1/47. Flt Lt 1/1/53. Retd SUP 21/9/73.
MCGRAN A. J. V., IEng. Born 23/9/34. Commd 19/8/71. Sqn Ldr 1/7/87. Retd ENG 23/9/94.
McGRANAGHAN J. A., MA. Born 3/12/40. Commd 9/9/63. Flt Lt 9/6/65. Retd GD 22/2/74.
McGRATH A., BA. Born 3/10/39. Commd 23/3/66. Sqn Ldr 1/1/85. Retd GD(G) 2/4/91.
McGRATH A. P. Born 12/9/43. Commd 24/6/65. Fg Offr 24/12/65. Retd SUP 19/9/70.
McGRATH H. P. Born 10/1/42. Commd 8/7/43. Sqn Ldr 1/7/54. Retd ENG 10/9/62.
McGRATH K. E. Born 1/7/13. Commd 29/3/42. Fg Offr 7/3/47. Retd GD(G) 1/11/53.
McGRATH P. A., AFC. Born 14/6/21. Commd 17/3/43. Flt Lt 17/9/46. Retd GD 14/6/54.
McGRATH T. Born 14/10/21. Commd 2/10/47. Flt Lt 2/4/52. Retd SEC 11/11/60.
MCGRATH W. J. Born 17/5/48. Commd 27/2/70. Wg Cdr 1/1/91. Retd SUP 5/12/96.
McGREEVY T., OBE CEng FIMgt MRAeS. Born 10/5/18. Commd 15/12/41. Gp Capt 1/7/67. Retd ENG 10/5/73.
MCGREGOR A., BA. Born 25/7/59. Commd 11/4/82. Sqn Ldr 1/7/96. Retd OPS SPT 1/7/99.
McGREGOR A. D. Born 3/5/34. Commd 17/12/52. Flt Lt 12/5/58. Retd GD(G) 1/2/73.
MCGREGOR A. E. I. Born 17/2/45. Commd 8/1/65. Sqn Ldr 1/7/77. Retd GD 14/3/97.
McGREGOR A. J., DSO AE. Born 23/11/20. Commd 18/6/40. Wg Cdr 1/1/71. Retd GD(G) 23/11/76.
MCGREGOR D. R. H., MRAeS. Born 29/8/42. Commd 30/7/63. Gp Capt 1/7/84. Retd GD 28/7/93.
MCGREGOR G. L. Born 26/12/59. Commd 11/10/84. Sqn Ldr 1/7/97. Retd OPS SPT 1/7/00.
McGREGOR I. F., BSc. Born 17/6/55. Commd 15/9/74. Flt Lt 30/5/78. Retd GD 15/1/91.
MCGREGOR I. J. Born 18/10/15. Commd 6/1/44. Flt Lt 26/5/55. Retd GD(G) 9/7/66.
MCGREGOR I. M., MA. Born 17/2/56. Commd 30/10/83. Sqn Ldr 1/1/92. Retd ADMIN 30/10/99.
McGREGOR M. D., MA. Born 5/10/12. Commd 3/11/43. Wg Offr 1/1/64. Retd EDN 5/10/67.
McGREGOR R. R. Born 5/10/43. Commd 28/4/65. Flt Lt 4/11/70. Retd GD 1/4/78.
McGREGOR S. M. Born 7/4/21. Commd 16/3/47. Wg Cdr 7/7/64. Retd GD 7/7/64.
McGREGOR-EDWARDS N., BA. Born 3/4/51. Commd 3/1/71. Sqn Ldr 1/7/87. Retd ADMIN 1/7/90.
McGRORY J. I., MBE. Born 31/7/27. Commd 14/12/44. Sqn Ldr 1/1/66. Retd GD 31/7/76.
McGRORY J. M. Born 2/5/39. Commd 3/11/77. Sqn Ldr 1/1/88. Retd GD 3/10/93.
McGRORY W. J. Born 22/1/34. Commd 24/9/52. Flt Lt 1/4/58. Retd GD(G) 6/4/83.
McGUIGAN R. J. A. Born 25/10/31. Commd 22/11/56. Wg Cdr 1/1/75. Retd ENG 27/10/81.
MCGUINNESS G. P., BSc. Born 20/2/63. Commd 22/7/84. Flt Lt 22/1/87. Retd GD 14/4/92.
McGUIRE A. B., MBE. Born 16/5/28. Commd 5/4/50. A Cdre 1/1/80. Retd SY 1/8/81.
McGUIRE A. C. Born 22/5/21. Commd 23/2/44. Flt Lt 23/8/47. Retd GD 22/2/66.
McGUIRE E. J., MB BS FFCM MFOM MRAeS FIMgt. Born 7/12/24. Commd 29/6/50. A Cdre 18/1/75. Retd MED 2/4/81.
McGUIRE R. P. Born 21/9/52. Commd 12/7/79. Flt Lt 7/4/82. Retd GD 21/9/90.

McGUIRK T. Born 18/11/24. Commd 5/11/59. Sqn Ldr 1/1/75. Retd GD(G) 31/8/77.
MCHENDRY J. Born 4/9/43. Commd 11/4/85. Flt Lt 11/4/89. Retd ADMIN 14/3/96.
McHUGH A. L. Born 14/1/44. Commd 6/4/62. Sqn Ldr 1/1/73. Retd GD 15/1/82.
MCILROY C. D. R. Born 28/2/55. Commd 17/7/75. Sqn Ldr 1/1/89. Retd GD 28/2/93.
McILROY W. A., BSc CEng MRAeS AFIMA, Born 17/9/21. Commd 25/8/42. Sqn Ldr 1/1/58. Retd ENG 18/5/76.
McILWAINE G. L., BSc. Born 18/8/42. Commd 28/9/64. Fg Offr 15/4/65. Retd GD 23/9/67.
McILWRAITH A., LLB MIMgt. Born 23/4/28. Commd 4/2/64. Sqn Ldr 1/7/71. Retd ADMIN 23/4/83.
McINNES A. Born 24/2/46. Commd 11/2/65. Sqn Ldr 1/1/78. Retd SY 24/2/84.
McINROY T. Born 13/10/10. Commd 11/2/43. Flt Lt 29/6/50. Retd GD(G) 13/10/65.
MCINTEE B. M., BSc. Born 23/9/44. Commd 28/9/64. Wg Cdr 1/1/87. Retd ENG 1/10/93.
McINTOSH A. A., DFC MA. Born 13/8/19. Commd 15/3/43. Gp Capt 1/7/67. Retd EDN 13/8/74.
McINTOSH E. A. Born 30/10/30. Commd 10/3/59. Sqn Ldr 1/7/70. Retd ADMIN 30/10/87.
McINTOSH G. J., AFC. Born 19/2/36. Commd 26/8/63. Sqn Ldr 1/1/73. Retd GD 10/9/89.
McINTOSH The Rev H. N. M., MA. Born 24/8/22. Commd 22/3/61. Retd 22/3/66 Wg Cdr.
McINTOSH I. C. R. Born 7/6/32. Commd 6/4/54. Sqn Ldr 1/1/69. Retd GD 26/8/77.
McINTYRE A. G., AFC. Born 4/1/17. Commd 9/4/40. Sqn Ldr 1/7/56. Retd GD 30/1/59.
McINTYRE A. J. Born 16/4/36. Commd 19/8/65. Flt Lt 19/8/67. Retd GD 17/4/86.
McINTYRE D. Born 19/11/33. Commd 27/7/54. Flt Lt 27/1/57. Retd GD 1/5/68.
McINTYRE D. M. Born 10/1/50. Commd 27/2/70. Flt Lt 27/8/75. Retd GD 10/1/88.
MCINTYRE D. R. Born 24/7/40. Commd 3/11/77. Sqn Ldr 1/1/90. Retd ENG 24/7/95.
MCINTYRE I. G., MSc BDS FDSRCSEd MGDSRCS(Eng) DDPHRCS FIMgt. Born 9/7/43. Commd 17/9/61. AVM 1/7/97. Retd DEL 20/4/01.
MCINTYRE M. E., BSc. Born 26/9/51. Commd 7/11/76. Sqn Ldr 1/1/87. Retd ENG 7/11/92.
MCINTYRE R. S., FCIS MBCS. Born 18/6/40. Commd 1/4/65. Wg Cdr 1/1/85. Retd ADMIN 18/6/95.
McINTYRE T. F. Born 2/7/30. Commd 12/7/62. Flt Lt 12/7/68. Retd ENG 2/1/73.
McINTYRE W. J. J. H. Born 28/6/43. Commd 1/10/65. Flt Lt 17/3/71. Retd ADMIN 28/6/98.
MCKAVANAGH The Rev D. J., MA BD AKC. Born 2/3/51. Commd 26/1/87. Retd 31/12/99 Sqn Ldr.
McKAY A. Born 10/2/46. Commd 26/5/67. Gp Capt 1/1/87. Retd GD 10/2/90.
McKAY D. Born 9/3/33. Commd 4/10/51. Sqn Ldr 1/1/73. Retd GD(G) 11/10/74.
MCKAY D. S. Born 17/11/50. Commd 30/3/89. Flt Lt 30/3/93. Retd OPS SPT 6/6/00.
MCKAY G. W. Born 2/10/45. Commd 28/4/65. Flt Lt 28/10/70. Retd GD 14/9/96.
McKAY I. F., BSc. Born 27/6/51. Commd 13/11/72. Sqn Ldr 1/7/85. Retd GD 27/6/89.
McKAY J. T., LHA MIMgt. Born 27/5/29. Commd 8/7/65. Flt Lt 28/4/69. Retd MED(SEC) 9/11/74 rtg Sqn Ldr.
McKAY R. Born 8/9/20. Commd 9/9/54. Flt Lt 9/9/57. Retd SUP 8/9/75.
MCKAY R., CEng MIMechE MRAeS. Born 14/8/34. Commd 9/11/65. Sqn Ldr 1/1/83. Retd ENG 14/8/92.
McKAY R. A. Born 26/10/20. Commd 28/8/47. Sqn Ldr 1/4/55. Retd GD(G) 31/10/70 rtg Wg Cdr.
McKEATING G. E. D., BSc. Born 15/5/50. Commd 15/9/69. Sqn Ldr 1/7/85. Retd GD 1/7/88.
McKECHNIE E. M., CBE MRCS LRCP. Born 20/8/17. Commd 22/6/44. A Cdre 1/7/72. Retd MED 29/10/76.
McKEE I. K., AFC*. Born 5/4/34. Commd 21/10/53. Gp Capt 1/1/87. Retd GD 5/4/89.
MCKEE W. L., MIMgt. Born 28/3/40. Commd 25/7/60. Wg Cdr 1/1/85. Retd GD 28/3/95.
McKEEVER L. Born 4/2/27. Commd 21/10/66. Flt Lt 21/10/72. Retd SUP 4/2/83.
McKELLAR P. Born 14/6/42. Commd 22/5/64. Flt Lt 22/11/69. Retd GD 14/6/80.
McKELVIE A. S., MBE MIIM MIMgt. Born 18/11/35. Commd 4/5/72. Sqn Ldr 1/1/84. Retd SUP 3/1/91.
McKELVIE K. J. Born 29/1/50. Commd 18/4/74. Flt Lt 18/12/77. Retd GD 29/1/90.
MCKENDRICK D. I. Born 26/6/45. Commd 19/6/64. Sqn Ldr 1/7/80. Retd GD 6/7/99.
MCKENNA D. H. T., BSc. Born 15/9/60. Commd 8/10/81. Flt Lt 15/10/84. Retd GD 14/9/96.
McKENNA J., MIMgt. Born 26/9/31. Commd 27/1/55. Sqn Ldr 1/7/69. Retd SEC 1/7/75.
McKENNA J. F. Born 7/10/38. Commd 18/8/61. Fg Offr 18/8/63. Retd GD 26/2/65.
McKENNA J. R. Born 18/12/13. Commd 5/5/54. Flt Lt 8/10/59. Retd ENG 18/12/63.
MCKENNA S. M. Born 3/4/63. Commd 5/5/90. Flt Lt 15/2/93. Retd ENG 3/4/01.
McKENNA T., BSc. Born 4/12/34. Commd 10/9/63. Sqn Ldr 1/1 71. Retd ENG 4/12/92.
McKENNEY R. R., DFC. Born 3/7/21. Commd 30/7/49. Flt Lt 30/1/52. Retd GD(G) 31/7/70.
MCKENZIE I., BA CEng MIEE MRAeS. Born 1/4/39. Commd 18/7/61. Sqn Ldr 1/7/73. Retd ENG 1/10/94.
McKENZIE I., BSc MB ChB DAvMed. Born 9/5/55. Commd 14/2/83. Wg Cdr 3/5/95. Retd MED 14/9/96.
McKENZIE J., CEng MIMechE MRAeS. Born 24/3/37. Commd 10/9/63. Sqn Ldr 15/2/70. Retd EDN 10/9/79.
McKENZIE J. Born 12/7/47. Commd 1/8/69. Sqn Ldr 1/7/84. Retd ENG 12/7/91.
McKENZIE L. B., MB ChB. Born 9/3/31. Commd 14/10/56. Wg Cdr 14/10/69. Retd MED 14/10/72.
McKENZIE L. E., DFC. Born 23/6/20. Commd 3/3/43. Sqn Ldr 1/7/65. Retd GD(G) 23/6/75.
MCKEON A. J. M., CBE AFC. Born 3/2/44. Commd 21/12/62. A Cdre 1/1/92. Retd GD 22/12/95.
McKEOWN D. M., MBE MIIM MIMgt. Born 10/8/34. Commd 23/3/65. Wg Cdr 1/7/82. Retd ENG 1/5/85.
MCKEOWN G. M. Born 30/10/54. Commd 21/2/74. Sqn Ldr 1/7/89. Retd OPS SPT 30/10/98.
McKEOWN. I., MBE. Born 12/7/25. Commd 28/2/57. Sqn Ldr 1/1/70. Retd ADMIN 12/7/83.
MCKEOWN J. D. P. Born 22/9/51. Commd 4/5/72. Flt Lt 12/4/77. Retd OPS SPT 1/1/98.
McKEOWN Rev J. K., BA. Born 13/4/10. Commd 15/7/41. Retd 15/3/63 Wg Cdr.
MCKERLIE HOLLIST B. Born 10/6/61. Commd 7/10/91. Flt Lt 11/7/87. Retd GD 2/3/96.

MCKIE-SMITH S. Born 12/6/45. Commd 28/11/69. Flt Lt 28/5/75. Retd GD 14/7/87. Reinstated 1/3/91. Flt Lt 13/1/79. Retd GD 1/8/94.
MCKILLEN J. D. B. Born 7/10/45. Commd 26/4/84. Sqn Ldr 1/7/94. Retd ADMIN 5/4/99.
MCKINLAY K. P., MB BS MRCP MRCS LRCP. Born 17/6/57. Commd 28/5/86. Wg Cdr 4/8/94. Retd MED 15/10/97.
MCKINLAY P., MA BEd. Born 24/3/50. Commd 20/5/79. Sqn Ldr 1/1/86. Retd ADMIN 1/2/96.
McKINLAY R. C., AFC. Born 30/4/42. Commd 30/7/63. Wg Cdr 1/7/78. Retd GD 1/7/81.
McKINLEY D. C., CB CBE DFC AFC*. Born 18/9/13. Commd 5/9/37. AVM 1/1/63. Retd GD 26/3/68.
McKINLEY J. P. J. Born 3/8/11. Commd 17/3/41. Sqn Ldr 1/4/56. Retd ENG 11/3/67.
McKINLEY M. S. J. Born 2/10/41. Commd 31/7/62. Sqn Ldr 1/1/73. Retd GD 2/10/79.
McKINNON P. D. Born 22/7/42. Commd 6/5/65. Flt Lt 2/10/71. Retd GD 2/2/81.
McKINSTRY P. E. G. Born 30/12/33. Commd 6/4/54. Flt Lt 6/4/59. Retd SUP 6/7/67.
McKNIGHT R. J. N., BA. Born 22/3/36. Commd 14/10/63. Flt Lt 14/10/63. Retd GD 22/3/74.
McLACHLAN A. C. Born 19/7/45. Commd 2/3/78. Flt Lt 2/3/80. Retd GD 26/11/84.
McLACHLAN A. L. Born 3/12/30. Commd 26/5/55. Flt Lt 26/11/60. Retd GD(G) 3/12/68. Reinstated 20/9/71. Flt Lt 13/9/63. Retd GD(G) 3/12/88.
McLACHLAN G. G., MBE. Born 3/10/34. Commd 10/12/52. Wg Cdr 1/1/81. Retd GD 3/10/89.
MCLACHLAN P., MSc BEng CEng MIEE. Born 13/5/61. Commd 10/6/84. Wg Cdr 1/1/98. Retd ENG 1/1/00.
McLACHLAN T. A. G. Born 27/12/25. Commd 14/4/49. Sqn Ldr 1/1/60. Retd GD 30/12/68.
McLARDY W. Born 12/6/33. Commd 9/4/52. Flt Lt 5/9/57. Retd GD 12/6/71.
MCLAREN B. K. Born 21/5/34. Commd 16/4/57. Wg Cdr 1/1/84. Retd GD 21/5/92.
MCLAREN C. A. B., MB ChB FFARCS. Born 11/2/28. Commd 30/3/53. A Cdre 1/6/87. Retd MED 11/2/93.
McLAREN J. Born 11/12/45. Commd 16/8/68. Flt Lt 16/2/74. Retd GD 24/9/76.
McLAREN J. C. E. Born 2/8/28. Commd 27/10/67. Sqn Ldr 1/7/80. Retd ENG 2/8/84.
MCLAREN M. R. Born 23/12/60. Commd 16/6/88. Sqn Ldr 1/7/96. Retd OPS SPT 1/7/99.
MCLAREN S. A. Born 16/3/61. Commd 8/4/82. Sqn Ldr 1/1/94. Retd GD 16/3/99.
McLAUGHLAN The Rev K. B., BD PhL. Born 3/5/30. Commd 3/7/67. Retd 30/11/87. Wg Cdr.
McLAUCHLAN R. H. Born 11/4/21. Commd 1/7/45. Flt Lt 19/11/53. Retd GD 1/10/68.
McLAUGHLIN C., MBE. Born 12/5/09. Commd 9/7/53. Flt Offr 9/7/56. Retd CAT 29/7/61.
McLAUGHLIN G. Born 22/2/53. Commd 1/11/79. Flt Lt 29/9/82. Retd GD(G) 22/2/91.
MCLAUGHLIN M. Born 13/3/48. Commd 7/3/71. Gp Capt 1/7/90. Retd PRT 8/3/92.
McLAUGHLIN P. C. Born 7/10/41. Commd 21/12/62. Flt Lt 1/7/68. Retd GD 7/10/79.
MCLAUGHLIN R. Born 15/1/40. Commd 24/8/72. Wg Cdr 1/1/91. Retd GD(G) 15/1/95.
McLAUGHLIN R. P., MIMgt. Born 23/9/30. Commd 22/10/54. Flt Lt 22/4/60. Retd GD 29/6/70.
MCLAUGHLIN S., AFC BSc. Born 1/12/59. Commd 9/11/78. Flt Lt 15/4/81. Retd GD 1/12/97.
MCLEA C. D. Born 1/12/44. Commd 29/4/71. Flt Lt 1/4/74. Retd GD 14/9/96.
McLEAN A. H., BSc. Born 3/9/50. Commd 9/9/69. Sqn Ldr 1/1/85. Retd GD 3/9/88.
McLEAN A. I. Born 13/12/31. Commd 19/8/71. Flt Lt 19/8/73. Retd SUP 3/12/86.
McLEAN A. K. Born 8/2/30. Commd 19/8/53. Flt Lt 25/2/59. Retd GD 26/8/73.
McLEAN D., PhD CEng MIEE. Born 22/1/36. Commd 27/6/58. Sqn Ldr 27/6/70. Retd EDN 27/6/74.
McLEAN G. Born 6/7/41. Commd 17/7/70. Sqn Ldr 1/1/78. Retd ENG 1/1/81.
McLEAN G. M. Born 2/12/21. Commd 24/8/43. Wg Cdr 1/1/62. Retd ENG 2/12/76.
McLEAN I. Born 10/4/40. Commd 3/1/64. Flt Lt 22/5/71. Retd GD 13/4/77.
MCLEAN I. J. Born 5/3/62. Commd 5/2/81. Sqn Ldr 1/7/94. Retd GD 5/3/00.
MCLEAN K. Born 21/8/51. Commd 22/6/89. Flt Lt 22/6/93. Retd MED SEC 14/3/96.
McLEAN Q. Born 4/1/43. Commd 24/4/70. Flt Lt 4/5/72. Retd GD(G) 4/1/81. Re-entrant 22/4/87. Flt Lt 20/8/78. Retd GD(G) 14/3/96.
McLEAN W. T. Born 3/12/41. Commd 31/1/64. Flt Lt 4/5/72. Retd GD 31/8/75.
McLEISH I. Born 10/8/46. Commd 21/1/66. Flt Lt 21/7/72. Retd GD 10/8/84.
MCLELLAN A. M. K. Born 28/10/53. Commd 31/7/86. Flt Lt 31/7/88. Retd ENG 31/7/00.
McLELLAN J. P. Born 21/4/21. Commd 9/8/56. Flt Lt 9/8/56. Retd SUP 21/4/71.
MCLELLAN M. J., BSc. Born 26/10/52. Commd 30/10/72. Flt Lt 15/4/80. Retd ENG 1/4/95.
MCLELLAN R., AFC BSc MRAeS. Born 20/1/51. Commd 24/3/74. Wg Cdr 1/1/90. Retd GD 1/6/93.
McLEOD G., AFC. Born 27/9/46. Commd 2/8/68. Wg Cdr 1/7/84. Retd GD 27/9/90.
McLEOD H. G., DFC. Born 27/10/15. Commd 3/7/42. Flt Lt 3/1/47. Retd GD(G) 8/11/65.
McLEOD J., FIMgt. Born 29/3/33. Commd 6/4/54. Gp Capt 1/7/77. Retd GD 29/3/93.
McLEOD J. H. Born 6/7/45. Commd 19/8/71. Flt Lt 19/8/73. Retd GD(G) 6/7/83.
McLEOD M. Born 12/10/02. Commd 2/5/40. Sqn Ldr 1/8/47. Retd SUP 24/10/53.
McLEOD P., CEng MRAeS. Born 29/3/33. Commd 6/4/54. Wg Cdr 1/1/76. Retd ENG 25/1/84.
McLEOD The Rev R., MA BD. Born 7/11/01. Commd 31/7/44. Retd 7/2/73 Wg Cdr.
McLOUGHLIN A. J. Born 1/1/47. Commd 17/12/64. Flt Lt 17/6/70. Retd GD 4/1/77.
McLOUGHLIN E. J. Born 7/11/94. Commd 1/4/18. Flt Lt 30/6/22. Retd GD 31/3/28 recalled 11/11/39 to 26/2/48.
McLOUGHLIN G. A., BEM. Born 10/2/17. Commd 20/12/45. Flt Lt 4/1/51. Retd MAR 11/2/66.
McLOUGHLIN J. E., MBE. BEM. Born 26/1/31. Commd 17/3/67. Sqn Ldr 1/7/76. Retd SY 2/4/84.
McLUCKIE R. Born 8/5/39. Commd 8/6/62. Flt Lt 1/4/66. Retd GD 8/5/75.
McLURCAN D. C. Born 8/10/34. Commd 27/1/67. Flt Lt 27/1/73. Retd ADMIN 6/11/76.
MCLUSKIE I. R., OBE MSc. Born 30/8/48. Commd 2/6/67. Gp Capt 1/1/97. Retd GD 7/4/00.

MCMAHON D., BSc. Born 1/3/62. Commd 31/7/83. Flt Lt 31/1/87. Retd ENG 31/3/94.
McMAHON G. F., DFM. Born 2/9/20. Commd 27/4/44. Wg Cdr 1/7/60. Retd PRT 20/12/68.
MCMAHON M., BSc. Born 21/12/58. Commd 29/8/77. Sqn Ldr 1/7/93. Retd ENG 26/5/97.
McMASTER H., AFC AFM. Born 29/8/24. Commd 25/8/49. Sqn Ldr 1/7/63. Retd GD 14/5/73.
McMASTER L. Born 21/3/29. Commd 29/10/52. Flt Lt 15/8/62. Retd GD 21/3/87.
MCMASTER T. H. L. Born 25/6/48. Commd 20/9/79. Sqn Ldr 1/1/89. Retd ENG 3/9/99.
MCMELLIN G. F., OBE BSc. Born 6/11/40. Commd 1/10/62. Gp Capt 1/1/90. Retd GD 6/11/95.
McMICHAEL A. F. Born 18/6/35. Commd 13/7/61. Wg Cdr 1/1/78. Retd GD(G) 18/6/90.
McMILLAN A. Born 29/10/32. Commd 12/7/51. Flt Lt 13/11/57. Retd GD 29/10/70.
McMILLAN E. L., CBE AFC. Born 4/3/16. Commd 30/4/41. Gp Capt 1/7/58. Retd GD 4/6/66.
McMILLAN M., MSc BEng CEng MIEE. Born 28/2/60. Commd 2/8/85. Sqn Ldr 1/1/96. Retd ENG 31/7/99.
McMINN J. M., BSc CEng MRAeS. Born 16/10/30. Commd 15/10/52. Gp Capt 1/1/79. Retd GD 30/7/83.
McMORLAND J. Born 15/12/31. Commd 24/12/64. Flt Lt 24/12/65. Retd EDN 25/10/68.
McMULLEN E. L., MBE. Born 14/6/20. Commd 13/6/44. Sqn Ldr 1/7/52. Retd RGT 14/6/65.
McMULLEN H. D. Born 29/4/44. Commd 1/4/66. Flt Lt 1/10/72. Retd GD(G) 29/4/82.
McMURRAY G. B. N. Born 8/5/35. Commd 1/10/57. Flt Lt 26/2/64. Retd GD 3/10/76.
MCMURRAY W. A. Born 24/7/52. Commd 20/12/90. Flt Lt 20/12/94. Retd ENG 3/4/95.
McNABNEY V., GM. Born 27/9/25. Commd 16/9/50. Gp Capt 1/1/72. Retd GD 27/9/80.
MCNAE C. Born 29/11/48. Commd 23/3/67. Flt Lt 23/9/72. Retd GD 14/3/96.
McNAIR I. S. Born 27/8/32. Commd 26/5/55. Flt Lt 26/11/60. Retd GD 31/12/70.
McNAIR R. D., MIMgt. Born 29/12/24. Commd 19/12/49. Wg Cdr 1/1/70. Retd SUP 19/9/74.
MCNALLY L. C., CEng MIEE MRAeS. Born 16/9/38. Commd 24/11/60. Sqn Ldr 1/7/77. Retd ENG 31/8/94.
McNALLY N. F., BSc. Born 1/7/18. Commd 16/2/44. Flt Offr 7/4/48. Retd EDN 1/3/52.
McNAMARA P. T., BA. Born 9/12/53. Commd 17/9/72. Flt Lt 15/10/76. Retd GD 25/8/77.
MCNAMARA P. V. P. Born 17/2/44. Commd 10/5/90. Flt Lt 10/5/94. Retd ENG 17/2/01.
McNAUGHTAN J. M. Born 14/2/47. Commd 21/1/66. Flt Lt 21/7/71. Retd GD 14/2/85.
McNAUGHTON S. Born 16/5/48. Commd 25/9/80. Sqn Ldr 1/1/88. Retd ADMIN 29/1/90.
MCNEE I. R., MBE. Born 25/6/42. Commd 9/12/76. Sqn Ldr 1/1/85. Retd ENG 25/6/97.
MCNEIL I., MA. Born 8/9/56. Commd 15/3/87. Flt Lt 15/9/90. Retd ADMIN 29/7/92.
MCNEIL I. W. P. Born 30/9/45. Commd 3/3/67. A Cdre 1/7/96. Retd OPS SPT 7/8/99.
McNEILE A. D. C. Born 24/4/44. Commd 3/8/62. Sqn Ldr 1/1/76. Retd GD 24/2/79.
McNEILE M. A., AFC. Born 21/1/27. Commd 16/4/47. Sqn Ldr 1/1/57. Retd GD 30/7/76.
McNEILL J. E., BEM. Born 3/12/17. Commd 6/9/56. Sqn Ldr 1/7/66. Retd ENG 3/12/72.
McNEILL K. Born 15/7/39. Commd 22/7/66. Flt Lt 8/11/69. Retd ENG 15/7/77.
McNEISH The Rev J. Born 13/9/34. Commd 31/1/66. Retd 26/8/72 Sqn Ldr.
McNICHOL D., MIMgt. Born 25/3/24. Commd 28/5/47. Wg Cdr 1/7/68. Retd SUP 6/7/74.
McNICHOLL A. L. Born 23/9/42. Commd 1/4/66. Flt Lt 1/10/71. Retd GD 3/8/76.
MCNISH A. F., BA. Born 2/5/57. Commd 9/11/80. Wg Cdr 1/1/96. Retd ADMIN 1/1/99.
McPARTLIN M. J. Born 9/11/42. Commd 20/5/82. Flt Lt 1/3/87. Retd SUP 1/11/87.
McPHAIL G. J. Born 25/3/21. Commd 1/12/44. Flt Lt 19/9/57. Retd GD(G) 29/12/73.
McPHEE A., MIMgt. Born 11/6/46. Commd 4/5/72. Sqn Ldr 1/7/85. Retd ADMIN 30/9/98.
McPHEE J., AFC. Born 3/8/19. Commd 16/10/42. Flt Lt 4/12/52. Retd GD 1/6/68.
MCPHEE K. J., BA CEng FIEE. Born 18/8/39. Commd 24/9/59. Gp Capt 1/7/88. Retd ENG 18/8/94.
McPHERSON G., AFM. Born 15/10/10. Commd 16/4/41. Sqn Ldr 1/7/53. Retd GD(G) 15/10/60.
McPHIE R. A. Born 6/7/22. Commd 4/3/46. Sqn Ldr 1/7/56. Retd GD 6/7/65.
MCQUADE L. P., BA. Born 5/9/54. Commd 30/8/78. Sqn Ldr 1/1/91. Retd GD 30/8/94.
MCQUIGG C. J. W., BA. Born 17/4/46. Commd 11/4/85. Sqn Ldr 1/1/96. Retd GD 17/4/01.
McQUILLAN A. R., BA. Born 12/1/33. Commd 11/10/51. Sqn Ldr 1/1/63. Retd GD 22/4/77.
MCQUILLAN C. J., OBE CEng MRAeS. Born 15/5/41. Commd 17/5/62. Gp Capt 1/1/88. Retd ENG 15/5/96.
MCQUILLAN D. Born 5/10/44. Commd 24/6/65. Wg Cdr 1/7/87. Retd GD 14/9/96.
McQUINN D. E. Born 30/9/37. Commd 1/11/57. Fg Offr 1/11/57. Retd GD 19/7/63.
MCRAE J. Born 14/5/41. Commd 4/10/63. Sqn Ldr 1/1/75. Retd GD 8/10/94.
McROBB J. McK. Born 14/6/28. Commd 27/8/64. Sqn Ldr 1/1/80. Retd SUP 14/6/83.
McROBB K. D., AFC. Born 26/3/33. Commd 28/3/53. Sqn Ldr 1/7/80. Retd GD 8/11/87.
MCROBBIE G. L. Born 16/6/44. Commd 22/2/63. A Cdre 1/7/92. Retd GD 1/12/98.
McROBERTS D. D., MA. Born 28/3/57. Commd 18/11/79. Flt Lt 18/2/82. Retd ADMIN 1/6/90.
McRORY J. P., MB BCh BAO DPH. Born 13/12/23. Commd 26/11/51. Wg Cdr 1/4/62. Retd MED 20/4/68.
McSORLEY D. F. H. Born 17/5/44. Commd 7/2/67. Flt Lt 17/8/72. Retd GD 31/10/82.
MCSORLEY T. Born 23/1/42. Commd 10/2/72. Flt Lt 10/2/74. Retd GD 23/1/97.
McSWEENEY D. W. Born 4/1/30. Commd 13/2/52. Flt Lt 1/10/67. Retd GD 4/1/68.
MCTAGGART P. P., BEd. Born 4/2/60. Commd 26/4/87. Flt Lt 26/10/90. Retd ADMIN 1/12/96.
McTAVISH D. I., MBE. Born 23/1/35. Commd 23/6/67. Sqn Ldr 1/1/75. Retd ENG 23/1/90.
MCTEER A. H. Born 10/10/44. Commd 17/3/67. Sqn Ldr 1/7/85. Retd GD(G) 14/8/94.
MCTEER D., MIMgt. Born 21/4/47. Commd 2/8/68. Gp Capt 1/7/94. Retd ADMIN 14/9/96.
MCTEER M. M., MSc BA MIDPM MBCS. Born 26/8/54. Commd 20/9/79. Sqn Ldr 1/1/90. Retd SUP 16/1/99.
McTEER T. Born 21/8/19. Commd 31/10/63. Flt Lt 31/10/66. Retd PE 21/8/74.

MCTIGHE M. G. Born 12/8/49. Commd 15/8/85. Flt Lt 15/8/89. Retd ENG 2/5/94.
McTURK J. McE. Born 1/12/22. Commd 1/5/52. Flt Lt 14/11/56. Retd GD 14/10/70.
McVIE J. Born 16/10/33. Commd 10/4/56. Sqn Ldr 1/1/64. Retd GD 16/10/71.
McVITIE A. McK. Born 8/2/28. Commd 10/1/51. Sqn Ldr 1/1/61. Retd GD 29/2/68.
McWICKER J. S., AFM. Born 25/2/24. Commd 4/5/50. Flt Lt 4/11/53. Retd GD 1/10/68.
McWILLIAM A. C., DPhysEd. Born 17/11/23. Commd 3/2/51. Flt Lt 22/5/57. Retd PE 31/1/67.
McWILLIAM D. McK., OBE CEng FRAeS. Born 11/10/19. Commd 23/3/50. Gp Capt 1/7/70. Retd ENG 12/8/72.
McWILLIAMS J. B. Born 8/10/21. Commd 16/10/42. Sqn Ldr 1/7/53. Retd GD 8/10/64.
MEACHAM H. W. Born 30/10/21. Commd 24/9/59. Flt Lt 24/9/64. Retd ENG 30/10/73.
MEACHAM R. L. Born 17/3/44. Commd 17/1/85. Sqn Ldr 1/7/93. Retd ADMIN 17/3/99.
MEAD C. Born 22/7/41. Commd 10/11/61. Flt Lt 22/1/67. Retd GD 22/7/79.
MEAD D. J., BSc Born 30/3/49. Commd 24/9/67. Flt Lt 15/10/72. Retd GD 30/3/87.
MEAD S. B. Born 21/3/32. Commd 4/7/51. Fg Offr 3/5/53. Retd GD 1/8/70.
MEADER J. C. Born 6/2/34. Commd 11/4/54. Wg Cdr 1/7/78. Retd GD(G) 6/2/89.
MEADLEY B. A. F. Born 27/4/30. Commd 12/12/51. Flt Lt 12/6/54. Retd GD 27/4/68.
MEADOWS C. J. Born 17/3/47. Commd 18/12/80. Flt Lt 18/12/82. Retd GD 7/12/96.
MEADOWS F. W. G. Born 15/10/23. Commd 13/2/58. Sqn Ldr 1/7/72. Retd GD 15/10/83.
MEADOWS J., OBE MIMgt. Born 20/7/29. Commd 11/4/51. Gp Capt 1/7/76. Retd SUP 21/7/79.
MEADOWS L., MBE. Born 9/8/22. Commd 24/1/52. Sqn Ldr 1/7/73. Retd GD 9/12/76.
MEADOWS M., AFC. Born 4/2/33. Commd 8/11/51. Flt Lt 23/2/57. Retd GD 4/2/71.
MEADOWS N. R. Born 6/1/53. Commd 1/7/82. Flt Lt 15/6/86. Retd ADMIN 29/11/93.
MEADS R. H. F. Born 20/9/61. Commd 14/8/80. Flt Lt 14/2/87. Retd SUP 1/10/91.
MEADWELL D. M. Born 14/12/41. Commd 8/12/61. Wg Cdr 1/1/93. Retd GD 14/12/96.
MEAGHER J. K., CEng MRAeS. Born 1/11/56. Commd 28/2/80. Gp Capt 1/1/00. Retd ENG 10/1/01.
MEAKIN C. J. Born 5/11/43. Commd 13/10/61. Wg Cdr 1/1/89. Retd GD 21/7/92.
MEALING D. L., DFM. Born 8/7/19. Commd 5/7/43. Flt Lt 5/1/47. Retd GD 9/5/53.
MEARS J. A., AFM. Born 16/6/19. Commd 28/1/60. Flt Lt 28/1/65. Retd GD(G) 16/6/77.
MEARS W. A., BA. Born 11/3/34. Commd 17/12/52. Gp Capt 1/7/80. Retd GD 9/4/86.
MEATON R. A. H., BA. Born 9/3/51. Commd 24/1/72. Flt Lt 1/12/76. Retd SEC 3/2/79.
MEATS E. N., CBE BSc. Born 11/12/29. Commd 19/8/53. A Cdre 1/1/80. Retd ADMIN 11/12/84.
MEATYARD M. J. Born 19/3/51. Commd 4/2/71. Flt Lt 4/8/77. Retd GD(G) 19/3/89.
MECKIFF J. L. Born 20/9/33. Commd 31/7/45. Sqn Ldr 1/7/57. Retd GD 20/9/66.
MEDCALF D. Born 30/5/58. Commd 10/5/90. Flt Lt 10/5/92. Retd ADMIN 15/9/98.
MEDCRAFT A. J. Born 3.3.48. Commd 2/2/78. Flt Lt 15/10/80. Retd SY 28/12/86.
MEDD-SYGROVE B. F. Born 30/9/57. Commd 6/7/80. Flt Lt 6/7/86. Retd ADMIN 31/3/94.
MEDDINGS E. J. Born 5/6/23. Commd 4/5/50. Flt Lt 19/11/53. Retd GD 1/6/68.
MEDHURST I. B. Born 8/11/42. Commd 12/9/63. Sqn Ldr 1/7/92. Retd ADMIN 31/7/96.
MEDHURST P. W. Born 26/7/50. Commd 25/2/72. Flt Lt 25/2/75. Retd GD 26/7/88.
MEDLAND C. G. Born 9/5/44. Commd 28/2/66. Flt Lt 28/2/70. Retd GD 9/7/82 rtg Sqn Ldr.
MEDLAND L. G., MSc CEng MRAeS MIMgt. Born 3/11/35. Commd 1/2/63. Sqn Ldr 1/1/70. Retd ENG 3/11/93.
MEDWAY P. W. Born 21/2/49. Commd 2/6/77. Flg Off 2/6/77. Retd SY 1/7/78.
MEDWORTH J. C. O. Born 3/10/18. Commd 25/4/43. Flt Lt 25/6/52. Retd GD(G) 1/8/64.
MEE E. D., MBE. Born 9/4/24. Commd 25/3/54. Flt Lt 17/5/56. Retd GD 9/4/84.
MEE R. I. Born 19/7/16. Commd 25/8/55. Sqn Ldr 1/1/68. Retd ENG 19/7/71.
MEE V. A., BSc. Born 2/6/50. Commd 14/12/72. Sqn Ldr 1/1/91. Retd GD 19/1/97.
MEEHAN J. Born 6/7/46. Commd 23/9/66. Wg Cdr 1/1/87. Retd GD 14/3/96.
MEEHAN K. T. Born 20/4/33. Commd 24/1/52. Sqn Ldr 1/1/66. Retd GD 20/4/71.
MEEHAN M. Born 12/12/19. Commd 2/10/43. Wg Cdr 1/1/57. Retd RGT 1/4/61.
MEEK J. B. S., MIMgt. Born 24/5/38. Commd 28/7/59. Wg CDR 1/7/79. Retd ADMIN 24/5/93.
MEEK S. A., BSc. Born 8/3/65. Commd 19/7/87. Flt Lt 19/1/89. Retd GD 23/5/89.
MEEKS J. E., MRAeS. Born 8/9/32. Commd 19/4/51. Flt Lt 25/1/57. Retd ENG 8/9/70.
MEELBOOM D. J. A. Born 6/8/45. Commd 1/8/72. Flt Lt 1/12/77. Retd GD 2/4/93.
MEES W. C. Born 21/12/10. Commd 14/10/41. Flt Lt 13/9/44. Retd ENG 24/12/46 rtg Sqn Ldr.
MEGARRY J. B. Born 7/12/54. Commd 12/2/76. Sqn Ldr 1/1/88. Retd GD 7/12/92.
MEGGS H. G. Born 6/6/32. Commd 28/9/61. Flt Lt 28/9/66. Retd GD 1/10/76.
MEICHAN W. F., CEng MRAeS. Born 16/1/29. Commd 30/7/53. Sqn Ldr 1/1/66. Retd GD 30/4/77.
MEIKLEJOHN A. A. Born 13/9/38. Commd 9/3/66. Flt Lt 4/5/72. Retd ENG 24/7/77.
MEIKLEJOHN I. R., BA. Born 10/4/47. Commd 10/1/71. Flt Lt 10/10/74. Retd GD(G) 10/10/93.
MEIKLEJOHN J. S. Born 2/1/21. Commd 19/3/43. Sqn Ldr 1/1/56. Retd GD 30/3/68.
MEJOR J. G., DFC. Born 12/7/21. Commd 20/3/42. Sqn Ldr 1/1/53. Retd GD 12/7/64.
MELBOURNE A. P. Born 14/6/25. Commd 25/5/45. Sqn Ldr 1/1/62. Retd GD 26/8/77.
MELDON M. Born 14/8/47. Commd 28/4/67. Flt Lt 28/10/72. Retd GD 4/11/84.
MELDRUM R. S. Born 26/4/37. Commd 8/1/59. Flt Lt 15/2/65. Retd GD 1/9/65.
MELDRUM R. S., MCIPS, MIMgt. Born 4/11/38. Commd 15/7/58. Sqn Ldr 1/7/70. Retd SUP 8/8/78.
MELLERS J., DFC. Born 15/3/25. Commd 16/3/45. Gp Capt 1/1/71. Retd GD 13/7/73.
MELLET P. C., MBE. Born 24/2/24. Commd 28/1/44. Sqn Ldr 1/7/57. Retd GD 24/2/73.

MELLING P., BSc CEng MRAeS ACGI. Born 6/12/47. Commd 22/3/81. Sqn Ldr 1/1/88. Retd ENG 16/6/00.
MELLISH P. J., MBE. Born 2/4/33. Commd 29/12/51. Wg Cdr 1/7/82. Retd GD 30/9/91.
MELLOR E. V., MBE MRAeS. Born 4/1/29. Commd 26/7/50. Gp Capt 1/1/76. Retd GD 4/1/84.
MELLOR H. L., AFC. Born 31/10/18. Commd 19/1/43. Sqn Ldr 1/7/59. Retd GD 31/7/62.
MELLOR P. R., DFC*. Born 11/5/21. Commd 14/3/42. Flt Lt 19/4/45. Retd GD(G) 11/5/67.
MELLOR S. I. Born 19/7/48. Commd 18/1/73. Flt Lt 18/7/75. Retd GD 19/7/86.
MELLOR S. S. Born 22/2/25. Commd 4/10/56. Sqn Ldr 1/7/73. Retd GD(G) 22/2/83.
MELLOR T. K., MB BCh BDS FDSRCPS FRCS(Ed). Born 17/11/54. Commd 8/1/84. Wg Cdr 13/2/92. Retd DEL 8/1/00.
MELLORS W. C. Born 28/2/49. Commd 20/9/79. Flt Lt 20/9/81. Retd ADMIN 30/9/94.
MELROSE D. G. A., MBE. Born 28/5/22. Commd 25/4/43. Wg Cdr 1/7/68. Retd SEC 8/4/75.
MELROSE J. F. C., DFC. Born 11/2/20. Commd 20/8/41. Wg Cdr 1/1/61. Retd GD 10/4/72 rtg Gp Capt.
MELSOM C. J., BSc. Born 26/12/38. Commd 19/2/63. Flt Lt 19/11/66. Retd ENG 19/2/79.
MELTON N. H. Born 18/6/44. Commd 30/4/67. Flt Lt 30/4/71. Retd GD 30/4/89.
MELVILLE K. I. Born 7/12/61. Commd 11/4/85. Flt Lt 11/10/91. Retd SUP 31/3/94.
MELVILLE R. K. C. Born 28/10/38. Commd 25/7/60. Flt Lt 6/3/63. Retd GD 28/12/69.
MELVILLE-JACKSON G. H., DFC BA. Born 23/11/19. Commd 22/6/40. Wg Cdr 1/1/58. Retd GD 29/9/68.
MELVIN A. L., BSc. Born 15/5/33. Commd 8/8/56. Sqn Ldr 25/4/66. Retd ADMIN 15/5/93.
MELVIN N. Born 19/8/19. Commd 27/2/47. Flt Lt 27/8/51. Retd GD(G) 29/10/66.
MELVIN W. J. Born 1/1/44. Commd 1/3/71. Sqn Ldr 1/1/83. Retd ADMIN 3/7/87.
MENEAR G. H. Born 7/6/26. Commd 2/10/58. Flt Lt 2/10/63. Retd GD(G) 7/6/76.
MENEZES G. L. Born 25/8/41. Commd 29/3/68. Flt Lt 4/11/70. Retd GD 25/8/79.
MENZIES A. R. Born 31/10/34. Commd 13/7/59. Flt Lt 6/3/63. Retd PE 19/6/73.
MENZIES P. D. Born 5/4/24. Commd 2/3/45. Sqn Ldr 1/7/55. Retd GD 31/3/75.
MENZIES R. C. Born 2/9/16. Commd 15/6/42. Flt Lt 3/10/49. Retd GD 11/11/58.
MENZIES S. H., MB ChB. Born 30/7/54. Commd 19/7/77. Sqn Ldr 20/8/85. Retd MED 19/7/93.
MERCER A. Born 28/7/17. Commd 26/1/42. Sqn Ldr 1/1/54. Retd ENG 29/10/66.
MERCER B. P. W., AFC*. Born 19/1/29. Commd 29/1/48. Sqn Ldr 1/1/60. Retd GD 19/1/67.
MERCER I. H., LMSSA MFCH DPH. Born 29/12/20. Commd 2/5/46. Gp Capt 1/7/72. Retd MED 1/3/78.
MERCER J. D. Born 8/5/23. Commd 17/1/49. Flt Lt 13/4/60. Retd GD 26/3/62.
MERCER M. J. Born 18/8/33. Commd 30/7/52. Flt Lt 5/11/58. Retd GD 18/8/88.
MERCER P. R., MSc BSc CEng MIEE. Born 5/1/54. Commd 3/9/72. Sqn Ldr 1/7/85. Retd ENG 1/4/93.
MERCER R. N. Born 9/2/47. Commd 8/12/83. Sqn Ldr 1/1/92. Retd ADMIN 1/7/93.
MERCER T. J. Born 20/2/43. Commd 14/6/63. Flt Lt 14/12/68. Retd GD 28/12/73.
MERCER W. H. Born 29/5/19. Commd 27/5/54. Flt Lt 22/7/57. Retd GD 6/3/64.
MERCH-CHAMMON E., MBE CEng MIERE. Born 22/3/18. Commd 14/4/41. Wg Cdr 1/7/63. Retd ENG 6/7/67.
MERCHANT C. F. P., CEng MIERE MIMgt. Born 5/11/42. Commd 15/7/64. Wg Cdr 1/7/83. Retd ENG 5/11/86.
MEREDITH R. G. Born 5/6/38. Commd 28/7/59. Sqn Ldr 1/1/70. Retd SUP 1/10/87.
MEREDITH W. D. Born 2/8/17. Commd 15/1/44. Fg Offr 30/11/47. Retd GD 14/12/54 rtg Flt Lt.
MERIDEW K. J. Born 17/7/64. Commd 15/3/84. Fg Offr 15/9/86. Retd GD(G) 30/4/88.
MERIFIELD P. J. Born 15/10/48. Commd 16/8/68. Flt Lt 16/2/74. Retd GD 1/10/94.
MERRELL D., BSc Dip Soton. Born 2/10/37. Commd 1/1/63. Sqn Ldr 1/3/69. Retd EDN 1/1/79.
MERRETT K. D. Born 26/7/33. Commd 17/1/52. Flt Lt 22/5/57. Retd GD 26/7/88.
MERRICK C. S. Born 24/11/68. Commd 5/5/88. Flt Lt 24/3/95. Retd ADMIN 14/3/97.
MERRICK R. H., BA. Born 29/12/50. Commd 15/9/69. Flt Lt 15/4/76. Retd SEC 1/9/79.
MERRIFIELD A. J., MB BS FFARCS MRCS LRCP MIBiol DA. Born 4/8/26. Commd 1/5/51. A Cdre 1/1/82. Retd MED 1/6/87.
MERRIFIELD W. G. J. Born 3/9/20. Commd 2/9/45. Sqn Ldr 1/7/60. Retd SEC 1/7/68.
MERRILL E. Born 15/12/16. Commd 21/5/41. Flt Lt 1/9/45. Retd SUP 18/12/53 rtg Sqn Ldr.
MERRILL M. Born 6/8/59. Commd 22/2/79. Flt Lt 22/8/84. Retd GD 6/8/97.
MERRIMAN D. A. P., MA BA. Born 6/12/37. Commd 31/7/61. Sqn Ldr 1/7/71. Retd GD 1/2/88.
MERRIMAN E. W., CBE DFM FIMgt. Born 12/8/20. Commd 15/12/42. A Cdre 1/7/71. Retd GD 1/5/74.
MERRIMAN H. A., CBE AFC* FRAeS. Born 17/5/29. Commd 1/8/51. AVM 1/1/81. Retd GD 20/10/84.
MERRIMAN J. L. Born 27/6/46. Commd 21/10/66. Sqn Ldr 1/1/82. Retd OPS SPT 2/6/99.
MERRIMAN P. A., BSc. Born 25/4/43. Commd 15/7/65. Sqn Ldr 1/1/74. Retd ENG 14/5/81.
MERRITT B. W. Born 22/6/42. Commd 8/10/70. Flt Lt 8/10/72. Retd GD 22/6/80.
MERRITT G. W. M., BEM MIMgt. Born 22/5/16. Commd 29/4/42. Wg Cdr 1/7/64. Retd ENG 31/10/70.
MERRITT J. C., MB BS MRCGP DRCOG DAvMed. Born 22/10/48. Commd 27/7/70. Wg Cdr 11/7/87. Retd MED 6/11/88.
MERRY J. E. N. Born 18/4/36. Commd 22/1/55. Sqn Ldr 1/1/67. Retd GD 9/8/77.
MERRY J. F. Born 27/10/34. Commd 5/4/55. Sqn Ldr 1/1/68. Retd GD 27/10/89.
MERVYN-JONES C. F., DFO DFC. Born 12/5/18. Commd 15/6/40. Wg Cdr 1/7/52. Retd GD 14/5/60.
MESSAGE S. A. Born 7/4/13. Commd 30/1/47. Plt Offr 30/1/47. Retd SUP 1/11/48.
MESTON P. Born 23/12/16. Commd 31/7/37. Wg Cdr 1/1/49. Retd GD 30/6/58.
METCALF M. J. Born 7/1/54. Commd 9/12/91. Sqn Ldr 1/7/84. Retd GD 7/1/92. rtg Wg Cdr.
METCALF V. K., DFC. Born 30/11/25. Commd 1/3/57. Wg Cdr 1/1/67. Retd GD 1/5/76.

METCALFE F. D. Born 1/1/23. Commd 23/4/47. Wg Cdr 1/1/75. Retd SEC 1/1/78.
METCALFE G. Born 9/4/29. Commd 23/1/64. Flt Lt 23/1/69. Retd GD(G) 10/4/79.
METCALFE N. E. Born 16/2/20. Commd 1/11/43. Sqn Ldr 1/1/55. Retd GD 16/2/63.
METCALFE P. J., MIMgt. Born 6/6/34. Commd 29/10/64. Sqn Ldr 1/7/79. Retd ENG 6/6/94.
METCALFE R. Born 16/2/47. Commd 25/2/66. Wg Cdr 1/7/90. Retd GD 31/3/95.
METHERELL M. J., BA. Born 5/6/37. Commd 2/10/58. Wg Cdr 1/1/81. Retd GD 5/6/92.
METTERS L. J. Born 29/12/21. Commd 4/3/45. Flt Lt 19/11/53. Retd GD 3/1/65.
MEWES A. Born 11/2/53. Commd 2/2/75. Sqn Ldr 1/1/89. Retd ENG 1/1/92.
MEWIS W. D., MBE. Born 17/11/19. Commd 4/7/57. Sqn Ldr 1/7/68. Retd ENG 27/2/71.
MEYER B. G., DFC. Born 17/8/17. Commd 9/8/37. Sqn Ldr 1/7/70. Retd SEC 1/7/73.
MEYER K. Born 21/1/15. Commd 17/3/55. Flt Lt 17/3/58. Retd ENG 22/1/70.
MEYER M. S. Born 17/2/45. Commd 9/12/76. Wg Cdr 1/7/93. Retd ADMIN 17/5/00.
MEYER R. H., BSc. Born 26/4/59. Commd 9/11/80. Sqn Ldr 1/1/90. Retd SY 14/3/97.
MEYER R. J. Born 27/9/45. Commd 19/6/70. Flt Lt 17/10/76. Retd GD(G) 1/4/88.
MEYER T. P. Born 27/6/23. Commd 27/8/45. Flt Lt 27/2/48. Retd GD 27/6/66.
MEYERS T. K. Born 11/12/30. Commd 22/12/53. Flt Lt 21/10/59. Retd GD 11/12/68.
MEYNELL C. S., BSc. Born 15/2/53. Commd 17/9/72. Flt Lt 15/4/79. Retd ENG 9/8/83.
MEYRICK R. R. F. Born 27/6/36. Commd 26/1/56. Sqn Ldr 1/7/71. Retd SUP 1/10/77.
MIALL M. J. D. Born 25/9/42. Commd 12/1/62. Sqn Ldr 1/7/88. Retd GD 19/4/00.
MICALLEF D., MCIT MILT MIMgt. Born 11/1/45. Commd 26/8/66. Wg Cdr 1/1/92. Retd SUP 11/1/00.
MICALLEF-EYNAUD M. A. Born 11/10/48. Commd 27/2/70. Sqn Ldr 1/1/80. Retd GD 11/10/86.
MICHAEL J. J. Born 7/8/19. Commd 13/3/47. Sqn Ldr 1/1/67. Retd SEC 28/2/73.
MICHAELS T. J. Born 9/11/42. Commd 12/7/63. Flt Lt 12/1/69. Retd GD 1/1/75.
MICHIE I. G. Born 3/8/31. Commd 17/1/52. Flt Lt 24/7/57. Retd GD 3/8/69.
MICKLEBURGH G. H., MITD. Born 11/11/28. Commd 31/12/62. Wg Cdr 1/7/77. Retd GD(G) 11/5/85.
MICKLEBURGH-SAUNDERS R. J. Born 1/6/13. Commd 29/4/43. Flt Lt 29/10/46. Retd ENG 5/12/53.
MIDDA M., BDS FDSRCS. Born 24/2/37. Commd 6/1/63. Sqn Ldr 13/11/65. Retd DEL 31/8/71.
MIDDLEBROOK G., MBE. Born 13/9/26. Commd 25/10/46. Wg Cdr 1/7/67. Retd GD 11/9/76.
MIDDLEBROOK P. T. Born 7/2/37. Commd 26/5/61. Flt Lt 10/2/67. Retd GD 9/9/79.
MIDDLEMAS R. Born 7/2/54. Commd 10/3/77. Flt Lt 10/9/82. Retd GD 15/12/92.
MIDDLEMIST M. J. Born 18/2/31. Commd 11/11/50. Wg Cdr 1/1/72. Retd GD 10/12/85.
MIDDLETON A. Born 15/7/33. Commd 20/3/52. Flt Lt 17/12/58. Retd SUP 26/6/64.
MIDDLETON A. Born 6/4/36. Commd 18/11/66. Wg Cdr 1/7/83. Retd ADMIN 18/10/87.
MIDDLETON A. R., DSO DFC. Born 23/4/17. Commd 13/5/42. Sqn Ldr 1/1/52. Retd GD 23/3/58.
MIDDLETON B. D., BA. Born 19/4/55. Commd 16/9/73. Flt Lt 15/10/79. Retd ADMIN 22/2/83.
MIDDLETON C. L. Born 25/4/39. Commd 9/2/62. Flt Lt 9/8/67. Retd GD 1/6/79.
MIDDLETON G. W. Born 18/9/62. Commd 25/2/82. Flt Lt 25/8/87. Retd GD 18/9/00.
MIDDLETON H. K. W., BA FIMgt MCIPD. Born 7/2/44. Commd 15/7/66. Gp Capt 1/1/89. Retd ADMIN 30/6/93.
MIDDLETON J. Born 19/10/29. Commd 28/6/50. Flt Lt 14/5/56. Retd GD 19/10/67.
MIDDLETON J., MBE MIMgt. Born 3/5/27. Commd 24/9/64. Sqn Ldr 1/1/76. Retd ENG 31/3/78.
MIDDLETON J. B., BSc. Born 25/2/55. Commd 1/7/74. Flt Lt 15/10/78. Retd GD 25/1/94.
MIDDLETON J. G. Born 16/3/34. Commd 21/5/52. Flt Lt 16/10/57. Retd GD 16/3/93.
MIDDLETON J. S., DFC. Born 1/3/18. Commd 29/8/42. Flt Lt 28/2/47. Retd GD(G) 1/3/68.
MIDDLETON K. S., LLB. Born 25/10/45. Commd 18/8/67. Sqn Ldr 1/7/82. Retd ADMIN 1/7/85.
MIDDLETON L. M. Born 23/10/12. Commd 23/7/32. Plt Offr 23/7/32. Retd GD 5/4/33.
MIDDLETON N. Born 9/3/29. Commd 25/6/66. Flt Lt 25/6/71. Retd SUP 9/7/83.
MIDDLETON P. G. Born 24/1/45. Commd 24/6/76. Wg Cdr 1/7/94. Retd OPS SPT 1/7/99.
MIDDLETON P. G. Born 15/9/26. Commd 15/5/46. Wg Cdr 1/1/67. Retd GD 20/12/75.
MIDDLETON R., AFC. Born 11/8/06. Commd 2/5/40. Sqn Ldr 23/11/43. Retd GD 11/7/46 rtg Wg Cdr.
MIDDLETON R. J., BSc. Born 21/9/49. Commd 2/1/77. Sqn Ldr 1/1/89. Retd GD(G) 2/1/93.
MIDDLETON W. I. C., MBE. Born 1/3/37. Commd 18/6/62. Sqn Ldr 1/1/76. Retd SUP 26/10/82.
MIDDLETON Y. M. Born 1/7/35. Commd 14/10/59. Fg Offr 14/10/59. Retd CAT 23/7/64.
MIDDLETON-JONES D. L. Born 23/9/29. Commd 3/9/52. Flt Lt 10/3/58. Retd GD 22/10/72. Reinstated 3/9/80.
  Flt Lt 23/5/68. Retd GD 23/9/89.
MIDDLEWEEK C. A. T. Born 4/8/32. Commd 15/6/61. Sqn Ldr 1/7/77. Retd GD(G) 4/8/87.
MIDDLEWICK J. N., BEd DPhysEd. Born 25/10/47. Commd 11/4/74. Sqn Ldr 1/7/89. Retd ADMIN 1/7/92.
MIDWINTER R. H., BSc MRAeS. Born 25/4/54. Commd 3/9/72. Sqn Ldr 1/7/87. Retd GD 25/6/92.
MIDWOOD J. Born 22/12/20. Commd 23/1/42. Wg Cdr 1/1/57. Retd GD 12/9/66.
MIERS R. J. P. Born 5/10/31. Commd 28/9/51. Gp Capt 1/7/78. Retd GD 7/10/81.
MIGHALL R. T. W., OBE MSc BA. Born 4/7/40. Commd 19/12/61. Wg Cdr 1/7/80. Retd SUP 2/4/93.
MILBORROW G. C., MS MIMgt. Born 2/8/40. Commd 6/10/60. Sqn Ldr 1/1/72. Retd SUP 2/8/78.
MILBURN E. J., BA. Born 18/2/64. Commd 26/4/87. Flt Lt 26/10/90. Retd ADMIN 1/8/99.
MILEMAN D. Born 25/7/38. Commd 14/2/66. Flt Lt 14/2/66. Retd GD 25/7/76.
MILES A. F. Born 5/9/51. Commd 15/2/77. Flt Lt 15/2/83. Retd ADMIN 14/2/93.
MILES A. P., BSc. Born 20/8/37. Commd 17/10/71. Sqn Ldr 1/1/78. Retd ENG 30/9/93.
MILES C. G. Born 25/4/15. Commd 9/8/37. Sqn Ldr 1/9/45. Retd ENG 5/5/64 rtg Wg Cdr.

MILES C. G., BA. Born 6/5/56. Commd 25/2/79. Flt Lt 25/5/80. Retd GD 25/2/95.
MILES C. R., MBE. Born 27/4/32. Commd 18/7/63. Sqn Ldr 1/7/77. Retd ENG 27/4/92.
MILES D. B. G., MBE. Born 28/3/18. Commd 14/1/40. Sqn Ldr 1/8/47. Retd ENG 1/10/50.
MILES D. M. Born 16/8/45. Commd 28/11/67. Plt Offr 28/11/68. Retd GD 20/7/69.
MILES G. C. M., MA MSc. Born 1/4/36. Commd 25/9/54. Sqn Ldr 1/7/66. Retd ENG 1/4/74.
MILES H. G. K. Born 24/3/22. Commd 24/11/60. Sqn Ldr 1/7/71. Retd SEC 1/10/74.
MILES J. E. Born 5/7/09. Commd 12/11/42. Fg Offr 12/5/43. Retd ENG 25/11/45 rtg Flt Lt.
MILES J. T., BA. Born 20/7/33. Commd 9/8/54. Sqn Ldr 1/1/77. Retd GD 6/1/86.
MILES K. F. G. E. Born 14/8/40. Commd 19/12/61. Wg Cdr 1/1/87. Retd GD 31/3/97.
MILES K. H., AFC MIMgt. Born 13/9/23. Commd 27/5/44. Wg Cdr 1/1/62. Retd GD 31/8/73.
MILES K. V. Born 19/11/18. Commd 15/4/43. Flt Lt 15/10/46. Retd ENG 8/9/53.
MILES L. A. Born 27/3/19. Commd 7/5/53. Sqn Ldr 1/7/65. Retd ENG 4/12/71.
MILES M. J. Born 21/5/26. Commd 4/7/51. Flt Lt 17/10/56. Retd GD 25/5/76.
MILES M. W. Born 24/2/39. Commd 8/11/62. Sqn Ldr 1/1/74. Retd ADMIN 15/9/82.
MILES P. R. Born 28/11/59. Commd 30/3/89. Flt Lt 30/3/91. Retd ENG 14/3/97.
MILES R. Born 3/3/29. Commd 27/8/52. Flt Lt 29/4/59. Retd GD 3/3/89.
MILES R. M. Born 8/2/42. Commd 9/7/66. Sqn Ldr 1/7/76. Retd ENG 8/2/80.
MILES T., AFC. Born 1/2/41. Commd 4/12/64. Flt Lt 4/6/70. Retd GD 17/8/80.
MILL P. D. Born 16/11/58. Commd 22/5/80. Flt Lt 22/11/86. Retd SY 16/11/96.
MILLAR A. C. M. Born 25/8/19. Commd 7/11/40. Sqn Ldr 1/1/54. Retd GD 25/3/59.
MILLAR D. G., BSc. Born 3/4/50. Commd 6/1/71. Wg Cdr 1/7/87. Retd GD 1/7/90.
MILLAR G. H., CEng MIERE. Born 23/5/23. Commd 11/2/44. Wg Cdr 1/7/73. Retd ENG 23/5/79.
MILLAR G. M. Born 7/7/19. Commd 25/11/43. Sqn Ldr 1/1/56. Retd ENG 7/7/70.
MILLAR I. P., MSc BSc CEng MRAeS. Born 8/8/58. Commd 12/2/79. Sqn Ldr 1/1/91. Retd ENG 1/4/97.
MILLAR J. H., BA. Born 26/1/58. Commd 5/9/76. Flt Lt 15/10/82. Retd ADMIN 1/9/85.
MILLAR L. R., BSc. Born 30/6/41. Commd 9/9/63. Flt Lt 9/12/64. Retd GD 9/9/79.
MILLAR M. J. Born 1/1/50. Commd 9/12/71. Flt Lt 9/6/77. Retd GD 26/2/83.
MILLAR M. K. Born 2/2/42. Commd 25/2/66. Flt Lt 25/3/71. Retd GD 4/10/81.
MILLAR P., CB FRAeS MInstD. Born 20/06/42. Commd 30/7/63. AVM 1/1/95. Retd GD 31/5/98.
MILLAR W. I. Born 15/11/48. Commd 24/2/67. Sqn Ldr 1/1/79. Retd SUP 17/11/88.
MILLARD I. J. Born 13/7/44. Commd 20/10/67. Sqn Ldr 1/7/82. Retd ENG 13/6/93.
MILLARD L. E., BSc. Born 18/5/63. Commd 22/7/84. Plt Offr 22/7/84. Retd GD 28/1/85.
MILLARD P. Born 1/4/37. Commd 20/8/55. Flt Lt 1/3/61. Retd GD 1/4/75.
MILLARD P., DPhysEd. Born 10/3/46. Commd 7/8/67. Sqn Ldr 1/1/81. Retd ADMIN 1/9/85.
MILLARD V. F. E. Born 20/10/34. Commd 27/2/70. Sqn Ldr 1/1/83. Retd GD(G) 31/7/89.
MILLER A. Born 26/3/14. Commd 10/1/38. Wg Cdr 1/7/50. Retd SUP 20/4/59.
MILLER A. D., MRAeS. Born 17/4/16. Commd 1/4/40. Wg Cdr 1/1/56. Retd ENG 31/8/63 rtg Gp Capt.
MILLER A. T. Born 15/1/44. Commd 8/1/65. Flt Lt 8/7/70. Retd GD 1/6/94.
MILLER A. V. Born 16/8/37. Commd 23/9/66. Flt Lt 23/9/68. Retd GD 16/8/95.
MILLER C. Born 23/4/59. Commd 20/7/78. Wg Cdr 1/7/95. Retd GD 9/4/01.
MILLER C. E. C. Born 29/4/34. Commd 17/5/60. Flt Lt 17/5/60. Retd GD 13/3/64.
MILLER C. J. Born 17/5/42. Commd 30/8/62. Sqn Ldr 1/7/91. Retd OPS SPT 17/5/97.
MILLER D. Born 31/3/61. Commd 7/10/91. Flt Lt 27/7/88. Retd GD(G) 14/3/96.
MILLER D. Born 25/3/38. Commd 11/11/66. Flt Lt 26/7/69. Retd GD(G) 1/11/85.
MILLER D. G. Born 3/9/37. Commd 4/8/64. Flt Lt 8/1/69. Retd GD 6/6/80.
MILLER D. S., BA. Born 20/9/49. Commd 8/11/68. Sqn Ldr 1/7/84. Retd GD 20/3/87.
MILLER E. C. Born 5/1/31. Commd 6/12/51. Flt Lt 27/3/57. Retd GD(G) 7/7/81.
MILLER G. C., BTech. Born 29/12/57. Commd 28/9/80. Flt Lt 28/12/80. Retd GD 28/9/96.
MILLER H. Born 6/2/21. Commd 28/7/43. Wg Cdr 1/7/64. Retd GD 14/2/76.
MILLER I. E., MIMgt. Born 3/7/21. Commd 12/5/41. Wg Cdr 1/1/61. Retd SEC 3/11/73.
MILLER J., CBE DFC AFC FCA. Born 3/12/21. Commd 3/7/42. A Cdre 1/7/66. Retd GD 5/4/69.
MILLER J. A. Born 18/7/34. Commd 9/7/57. Sqn Ldr 1/1/80. Retd GD 18/7/84.
MILLER J. I. Born 12/2/32. Commd 17/5/51. Sqn Ldr 1/1/67. Retd GD 16/4/70.
MILLER J. J., CB BL. Born 27/4/28. Commd 6/9/47. AVM 1/1/79. Retd ADMIN 27/4/83.
MILLER J. W., CEng MRAeS. Born 22/4/21. Commd 25/1/45. Sqn Ldr 1/10/56. Retd ENG 30/3/78.
MILLER M. H., CBE AFC. Born 14/1/28. Commd 29/9/49. A Cdre 1/7/76. Retd GD 22/8/81.
MILLER P. A., BSc(Eng) CEng MRAeS ACGI. Born 15/1/46. Commd 1/1/67. Sqn Ldr 1/7/79. Retd ENG 15/1/90.
MILLER P. C., CEng MIMechE. Born 7/10/36. Commd 16/11/59. Wg Cdr 1/7/77. Retd ENG 3/4/90.
MILLER P. E. Born 2/1/45. Commd 19/12/63. Sqn Ldr 1/7/81. Retd GD(G) 2/1/89.
MILLER P. J., BSc(Eng) CEng MRAeS. Born 10/9/39. Commd 20/9/60. A Cdre 1/7/90. Retd ENG 11/12/93.
MILLER P. L. Born 21/12/35. Commd 14/1/54. Sqn Ldr 1/1/72. Retd GD 21/12/89.
MILLER R. Born 23/3/42. Commd 15/3/84. Sqn Ldr 1/7/94. Retd ADMIN 1/7/97.
MILLER R. Born 6/9/38. Commd 8/6/62. Flt Lt 1/7/68. Retd GD 13/2/78. Reinstated 11/1/84. Flt Lt 29/5/74. Retd GD 6/9/93.
MILLER R., MBA BA MIMgt. Born 18/10/33. Commd 6/5/55. Sqn Ldr 1/1/73. Retd GD 1/10/78. Reinstated 11/11/81. Sqn Ldr 11/2/76. Retd GD 18/10/91.

MILLER R. A. Born 11/8/21. Commd 15/1/43. Sqn Ldr 1/7/73. Retd GD 11/8/76.
MILLER R. A., OBE FIMgt FRAeS. Born 12/7/36. Commd 2/4/57. A Cdre 1/1/83. Retd GD 1/3/84.
MILLER R. C. Born 5/1/43. Commd 26/5/67. Sqn Ldr 1/7/82. Retd ENG 1/7/85.
MILLER R. E., BA PGCE FRGS. Born 20/12/47. Commd 2/8/68. Flt Lt 2/2/74. Retd GD 1/5/76. Reinstated 1/10/80. Flt
  Lt 5/7/78. Retd GD(G) 22/5/95.
MILLER S., BSc. Born 25/6/41. Commd 6/1/64. Sqn Ldr 1/7/74. Retd GD 3/3/78.
MILLER S. J., CEng MIMechE MRAeS. Born 12/9/40. Commd 17/7/62. Sqn Ldr 1/1/74. Retd ENG 12/9/95.
MILLER T. F. K., BSc. Born 14/5/45. Commd 22/9/65. Flt Lt 15/10/68. Retd GD 14/5/83.
MILLER T. W. L., AFC. Born 11/12/52. Commd 1/6/72. Sqn Ldr 1/1/84. Retd GD 11/12/90.
MILLER The Rev J. G., BEd. Born 29/3/40. Commd 22/5/83. Retd 31/10/88. Sqn Ldr.
MILLER W. H., DFC. Born 27/9/21. Commd 27/10/43. Flt Lt 27/4/47. Retd GD 18/9/56.
MILLER W. J. Born 31/7/37. Commd 7/7/67. Flt Lt 12/11/69. Retd GD 1/4/76.
MILLICAN The Rev J. A., MA. Born 25/2/23. Commd 6/3/50. Retd 1/10/61 Sqn Ldr.
MILLIGAN D., BSc. Born 11/1/56. Commd 23/4/87. Sqn Ldr 1/1/94. Retd ENG 1/3/99.
MILLIGAN F. Born 11/3/39. Commd 31/7/62. Sqn Ldr 1/7/72. Retd GD 1/3/94.
MILLIGAN G. M., BA. Born 9/12/47. Commd 6/12/70. Sqn Ldr 6/6/78. Retd ADMIN 6/12/86.
MILLIGAN J. Born 8/9/37. Commd 22/8/59. Sqn Ldr 1/1/74. Retd GD 13/8/88.
MILLIGAN J. L., MA MB BCh MRCS LRCP MRCP DPhysMed. Born 28/3/27. Commd 3/1/52. Wg Cdr 4/7/63. Retd
  MED 17/12/68.
MILLIGAN M. J., CBE FRAeS. Born 18/8/38. Commd 2/4/57. A Cdre 1/1/88. Retd GD 18/8/93.
MILLIKIN P. M., MBE. Born 7/3/46. Commd 8/1/65. Sqn Ldr 1/7/92. Retd GD 1/6/01.
MILLINGTON N. D., MSc BChD BDS MGDSRCS(Eng). Born 22/6/58. Commd 1/2/81. Flt Lt 10/12/81. Retd DEL 10/
  12/86. Re-entered 11/12/87. Wg Cdr 17/12/94. Retd DEL 10/2/98.
MILLINGTON R. J., MIMgt. Born 18/8/38. Commd 24/1/74. Flt Lt 24/1/78. Retd GD(G) 20/8/84. Reinstated
  16/6/86. Flt Lt 19/11/79. Retd GD(G) 19/8/91.
MILLINGTON T. J. Born 14/1/65. Commd 24/6/90. Fg Offr 24/6/92. Retd ADMIN 27/6/96.
MILLINS T. Born 8/12/62. Commd 30/7/92. Flt Lt 30/7/94. Retd ENG 14/9/96.
MILLIS O. J., MBE. Born 13/2/08. Commd 23/4/53. Flt Lt 23/4/56. Retd RGT 1/5/58.
MILLMAN A. R. Born 4/9/31. Commd 19/4/51. Flt Lt 17/10/56. Retd GD 4/9/69.
MILLMAN B., MBE. Born 19/5/10. Commd 14/1/43. Flt Lt 4/12/52. Retd SUP 6/6/59.
MILLNER R. Born 13/7/62. Commd 28/4/84. Flt Lt 29/4/89. Retd ENG 21/5/94.
MILLO J. R. Born 12/2/51. Commd 24/1/74. Flt Lt 24/7/79. Retd GD 14/9/96.
MILLOY P. D. G., MEng BSc. Born 6/9/47. Commd 16/1/72. Wg Cdr 1/7/90. Retd ENG 4/6/99.
MILLS A. Born 23/11/21. Commd 24/9/44. Flt Lt 24/9/50. Retd PE 1/2/68.
MILLS A. Born 25/10/16. Commd 3/4/39. Wg Cdr 1/7/59. Retd SUP 29/10/66.
MILLS A. A. K. Born 1/9/40. Commd 10/11/61. Flt Lt 10/5/67. Retd GD 1/9/78.
MILLS A. J., AFC. Born 27/10/17. Commd 20/12/43. Flt Lt 20/6/47. Retd GD 29/3/58.
MILLS A. R., MBE. Born 16/9/40. Commd 13/12/79. Sqn Ldr 1/1/88. Retd ENG 31/5/97.
MILLS B. C. Born 5/1/31. Commd 12/12/51. Sqn Ldr 1/1/66. Retd GD 14/1/69.
MILLS B. J. Born 13/12/51. Commd 6/4/72. Sqn Ldr 1/7/82. Retd GD 13/12/89.
MILLS C. Born 15/7/55. Commd 20/12/90. Flt Lt 20/12/94. Retd OPS SPT 31/12/00.
MILLS C. J., BA. Born 5/2/65. Commd 4/10/83. Flt Lt 15/1/89. Retd GD 17/10/98.
MILLS D. C. Born 7/4/31. Commd 4/6/52. Sqn Ldr 1/7/86. Retd GD 1/7/89.
MILLS D. H. Born 23/5/30. Commd 12/12/51. Sqn Ldr 1/7/65. Retd GD 16/4/73.
MILLS D. R. S. Born 9/6/30. Commd 28/2/52. Flt Lt 5/9/57. Retd GD 9/6/68.
MILLS D. T. Born 5/7/32. Commd 28/11/51. Sqn Ldr 1/1/67. Retd GD 1/10/74.
MILLS H. A., BEM. Born 11/9/19. Commd 23/3/50. Gp Capt 1/7/71. Retd ENG 2/3/74.
MILLS H. F. B. Born 2/5/1900. Commd 9/12/43. Flt Lt 9/12/43. Retd MED(T) 21/12/45 rtg Flt Lt.
MILLS H. W., DFM. Born 24/2/20. Commd 6/4/43. Flt Lt 6/4/45. Retd GD(G) 24/2/75 rtg Sqn Ldr.
MILLS J. A. Born 5/9/56. Commd 4/9/81. Flt Lt 9/6/85. Retd GD(G) 23/9/94.
MILLS J. E. Born 30/4/43. Commd 3/5/68. Flt Lt 3/11/74. Retd SUP 27/11/83.
MILLS J. M., BSc Dip Soton. Born 7/7/34. Commd 27/9/57. Wg Cdr 23/3/75. Retd EDN 6/12/75.
MILLS K. Born 13/8/31. Commd 2/7/52. Flt Lt 27/11/57. Retd GD 2/7/88.
MILLS K. W., AFC BSc. Born 30/8/41. Commd 17/8/64. Gp Capt 1/1/90. Retd GD 30/8/93.
MILLS L. C. Born 13/2/35. Commd 24/5/63. Flt Lt 1/10/58. Retd GD 13/2/73 rtg Sqn Ldr.
MILLS M. H., BSc CEng MIEE MinstP. Born 9/3/38. Commd 25/9/59. Sqn Ldr 1/1/68. Retd ENG 9/3/76.
MILLS O. Born 7/3/29. Commd 25/8/60. Sqn Ldr 1/7/80. Retd ADMIN 7/3/84.
MILLS P. S., CEng MRAeS. Born 1/9/22. Commd 9/7/44. Sqn Ldr 1/1/53. Retd ENG 1/2/75.
MILLS R., MBE MA MSc BA JP. Born 8/8/26. Commd 13/2/47. Sqn Ldr 7/7/61. Retd EDN 25/2/67.
MILLS R. Born 10/11/15. Commd 21/6/56. Sqn Ldr 1/1/66. Retd SEC 1/1/68.
MILLS R. B. Born 27/4/41. Commd 5/4/79. Sqn Ldr 1/1/91. Retd ENG 27/4/96.
MILLS R. F. Born 31/3/34. Commd 28/1/54. Wg Cdr 1/7/76. Retd GD 31/3/89.
MILLS R. H. F. Born 20/9/18. Commd 1/2/49. Flt Lt 22/12/49. Retd SEC 20/9/73.
MILLS R. L., OBE. Born 24/4/21. Commd 2/6/49. Wg Cdr 1/7/64. Retd ENG 20/4/76.
MILLS R. S. Born 1/4/33. Commd 6/12/51. Sqn Ldr 1/7/75. Retd ADMIN 1/4/78.
MILLS R. T. Born 10/11/24. Commd 15/5/47. Sqn Ldr 1/7/63. Retd SUP 4/1/70.

MILLS T. J. Born 28/9/36. Commd 8/4/60. Fg Offr 8/4/61. Retd GD 1/7/66.
MILLS V. R., MHCIMA. Born 5/8/30. Commd 24/2/67. Flt Lt 24/2/72. Retd ADMIN 1/2/77.
MILLS W. H., DFC. Born 28/7/20. Commd 22/7/42. Wg Cdr 1/7/58. Retd GD 28/7/67.
MILLSON A. E., DSO DFC. Born 18/4/21. Commd 3/4/41. Sqn Ldr 1/7/61. Retd GD 30/8/67 rtg Wg Cdr.
MILLWARD G. W., CEng MIEE. Born 20/9/42. Commd 14/9/65. Sqn Ldr 1/1/75. Retd ENG 14/9/81.
MILLWARD P. Born 16/2/60. Commd 8/9/83. Sqn Ldr 1/7/96. Retd OPS SPT 1/7/99.
MILNE A. R., DPhysEd. Born 26/11/48. Commd 13/9/70. Flt Lt 3/6/75. Retd GD 7/12/82.
MILNE D. Born 16/10/13. Commd 20/2/43. Fg Offr 20/8/43. Retd ENG 27/1/47 rtg Flt Lt.
MILNE D., MA MIMgt. Born 9/3/30. Commd 10/5/53. Wg Cdr 1/7/74. Retd ADMIN 6/4/82.
MILNE D. F., BSc. Born 4/12/56. Commd 30/8/78. Sqn Ldr 1/7/94. Retd GD 4/12/00.
MILNE D. J., MIMgt. Born 30/10/32. Commd 28/2/57. Flt Lt 1/3/63. Retd PI 22/4/81.
MILNE G. C. Born 7/1/45. Commd 18/11/66. Wg Cdr 1/1/86. Retd GD(G) 7/11/94.
MILNE M. S. Born 18/11/22. Commd 28/7/60. Flt Lt 28/7/63. Retd GD 17/5/73.
MILNE W. C., FIMgt. Born 11/2/29. Commd 22/8/51. A Cdre 1/1/80. Retd GD 11/2/84.
MILNER D. C. Born 4/10/23. Commd 21/4/45. Flt Lt 7/6/51. Retd GD 4/10/78.
MILNER D. H. Born 30/1/41. Commd 28/2/85. Flt Lt 28/2/89. Retd ENG 30/1/96.
MILNER G. S., BSc. Born 20/4/64. Commd 26/10/86. Flt Lt 26/4/89. Retd GD 14/3/96.
MILNER P. Born 29/4/34. Commd 5/7/68. Sqn Ldr 1/1/75. Retd ENG 29/4/94.
MILNES P. R. Born 18/3/58. Commd 4/9/81. Flt Lt 11/3/84. Retd GD 23/9/99.
MILNES S. D., MB BS MRCGP MRCS(Eng) LRCP DAvMed DIMC AFOM MRAeS. Born 16/2/48. Commd 9/5/71. Wg Cdr 20/6/88. Retd MED 14/3/97.
MILSOM R. A. Born 20/4/15. Commd 2/4/40. Sqn Ldr 1/7/53. Retd SUP 29/4/64.
MILSOM R. J., OBE. Born 9/12/43. Commd 17/12/64. Wg Cdr 1/1/85. Retd GD 8/12/98.
MILTON F. H. P. Born 18/9/21. Commd 9/11/47. Sqn Ldr 1/1/52. Retd RGT 29/5/58.
MILTON G. J., BSc. Born 23/7/55. Commd 19/3/78. Flt Lt 19/12/79. Retd GD 19/3/90.
MILTON I. Born 21/12/52. Commd 10/2/72. Flt Lt 10/8/77. Retd GD 1/5/90.
MILTON R. B. G. Born 24/1/47. Commd 1/3/68. Sqn Ldr 1/1/82. Retd GD 2/9/86.
MILWARD P. H. Born 17/8/43. Commd 6/5/66. Flt Lt 4/5/72. Retd GD 13/12/81.
MILWARD R. A., OBE DFC*. Born 7/10/16. Commd 16/4/35. Wg Cdr 1/7/47. Retd GD 2/5/59.
MIMMACK S. B. Born 18/6/44. Commd 1/4/65. Sqn Ldr 1/1/82. Retd GD(G) 18/6/88.
MINARDS R. P., LLB. Born 21/7/44. Commd 20/8/67. Flt Lt 20/11/68. Retd GD 20/8/89.
MINETT R. W. Born 24/4/24. Commd 29/3/45. Sqn Ldr 1/7/72. Retd GD 1/8/73.
MINGAYE B. Born 15/9/31. Commd 17/5/51. Flt Lt 6/9/56. Retd GD 15/9/69.
MINIHANE T. R. Born 10/4/26. Commd 29/6/50. Sqn Ldr 1/1/60. Retd ENG 15/5/64.
MINNIGIN G. A. F., DCM MM. Born 21/8/20. Commd 15/11/48. Wg Cdr 1/7/62. Retd RGT 21/8/75.
MINNIS H. Born 31/1/26. Commd 22/2/46. Sqn Ldr 1/7/56. Retd GD 31/1/64.
MINNS D. G. Born 16/5/32. Commd 16/9/71. Flt Lt 16/9/73. Retd ENG 31/3/79.
MINNS P., BA. Born 23/8/19. Commd 4/1/50. Flt Lt 1/9/45. Retd ENG 11/1/62 rtg Sqn Ldr.
MINSHULL J. S. Born 24/12/54. Commd 26/9/91. Flt Lt 26/9/95. Retd ENG 20/4/98.
MINTER J. M. Born 6/12/34. Commd 9/6/54. Sqn Ldr 1/1/69. Retd SUP 1/4/88.
MINTER P. C., CEng MIEE MIMgt. Born 9/1/47. Commd 1/8/69. Sqn Ldr 1/7/87. Retd ENG 9/1/91.
MINTER R. H. Born 30/11/10. Commd 17/12/41. Fg Offr 22/3/43. Retd ENG 28/12/45 rtg Flt Lt.
MINTON K. H., BSc(Econ) FIMgt. Born 13/1/45. Commd 3/3/67. A Cdre 1/7/91. Retd ADMIN 2/12/94.
MINTON L. A. Born 28/7/40. Commd 15/2/73. Flt Lt 15/2/75. Retd SUP 15/2/81. Reinstated 11/5/83. Sqn Ldr 1/1/87. Retd SUP 31/7/90.
MISKELLY I. D. Born 16/9/58. Commd 16/12/79. Flt Lt 16/10/86. Retd SUP 16/9/96.
MITCHAM D. T. Born 11/6/46. Commd 21/1/68. Flt Lt 21/7/75. Retd SUP 11/6/87.
MITCHELL A. A. Born 12/9/21. Commd 9/7/59. Flt Lt 9/7/64. Retd ENG 12/9/76.
MITCHELL A. L., BDS. Born 20/9/40. Commd 24/4/62. Wg Cdr 29/7/77. Retd DEL 20/9/78.
MITCHELL A. P. Born 2/6/48. Commd 28/7/67. Sqn Ldr 1/1/89. Retd ADMIN 1/8/95.
MITCHELL A. S. Born 18/10/32. Commd 1/3/56. Flt Lt 11/5/62. Retd GD 20/7/71.
MITCHELL A. T., MB BS MRCP(UK). Born 15/2/57. Commd 5/10/79. Wg Cdr 10/8/94. Retd MED 5/10/95.
MITCHELL B. Born 17/5/48. Commd 7/6/73. Flt Lt 7/12/78. Retd GD 22/10/94.
MITCHELL B. K. Born 1/12/43. Commd 17/3/67. Flt Lt 17/6/73. Retd ADMIN 29/11/82.
MITCHELL B. T., MIDPM MCIPS MIMgt. Born 17/9/33. Commd 31/7/56. Wg Cdr 1/7/75. Retd SUP 17/9/92.
MITCHELL B. W. Born 16/4/42. Commd 24/4/64. Flt Lt 5/5/90. Retd GD 6/8/93.
MITCHELL C., BA. Born 11/5/43. Commd 28/7/64. Sqn Ldr 1/7/72. Retd GD 11/5/87.
MITCHELL C. A. Born 28/5/45. Commd 8/9/77. Flt Lt 8/9/81. Retd ENG 8/9/85.
MITCHELL C. C., CEng MIMechE MRAeS. Born 22/8/39. Commd 28/7/60. Wg Cdr 1/7/78. Retd ENG 22/8/94.
MITCHELL C. E. Born 18/10/07. Commd 3/7/40. Flt Lt 10/8/43. Retd ENG 25/3/46 rtg Sqn Ldr.
MITCHELL C. H. A. Born 28/12/24. Commd 16/6/44. Sqn Ldr 1/4/55. Retd GD 28/12/67.
MITCHELL C. N. C. Born 25/9/25. Commd 20/7/50. Sqn Ldr 1/1/60. Retd GD 25/9/80.
MITCHELL Sir Dennis, KBE CVO DFC* AFC. Born 26/5/18. Commd 30/7/38. Gp Capt 1/7/56. Retd GD 14/3/62 rtg Hon. A Cdre.
MITCHELL D. Born 6/2/33. Commd 16/7/52. Flt Lt 12/12/57. Retd GD 6/2/71.
MITCHELL D. A. Born 21/11/43. Commd 25/3/64. Sqn Ldr 1/7/76. Retd GD 23/7/82.

MITCHELL D. C., MBE. Born 3/11/24. Commd 25/5/45. Wg Cdr 1/1/65. Retd GD 29/9/72.
MITCHELL D. J. Born 3/6/26. Commd 22/2/46. Sqn Ldr 1/1/60. Retd GD 1/6/68.
MITCHELL E. T. Born 28/1/30. Commd 17/3/67. Flt Lt 17/3/72. Retd ENG 2/10/74.
MITCHELL F. A. Born 9/11/56. Commd 1/12/77. Flt Lt 9/4/84. Retd GD(G) 1/12/85. Re-entered 18/10/91. Flt Lt 6/6/89. Retd OPS SPT 3/3/01.
MITCHELL F. W. Born 12/2/38. Commd 28/7/59. A Cdr 1/1/89. Retd GD 20/9/92.
MITCHELL G. Born 23/10/12. Commd 14/2/41. Flt Lt 27/8/44. Retd ASD 30/1/46 rtg Sqn Ldr.
MITCHELL G., MB ChB MRCP MRCP(Edin). Born 10/4/32. Commd 19/5/56. Sqn Ldr 1/4/62. Retd MED 26/11/66.
MITCHELL G. D., OBE BA. Born 23/1/35. Commd 28/7/60. Wg Cdr 1/1/78. Retd GD 23/1/90.
MITCHELL G. D. Born 8/9/27. Commd 28/8/50. Flt Lt 28/2/55. Retd GD 8/9/82.
MITCHELL G. F. Born 28/4/42. Commd 14/8/70. Sqn Ldr 1/7/89. Retd ADMIN 1/9/93.
MITCHELL G. G. Born 10/5/37. Commd 12/12/59. Flt Lt 12/6/65. Retd GD 25/8/75.
MITCHELL G. H. C. Born 29/8/29. Commd 6/11/47. Flt Lt 26/5/55. Retd 31/12/74. Reinstated 8/10/79 to 29/8/87. rtg Sqn Ldr.
MITCHELL G. H. E., CBE BA. Born 14/6/37. Commd 4/7/57. A Cdre 1/1/88. Retd ADMIN 14/6/92.
MITCHELL G. M. Born 17/7/62. Commd 19/12/91. Flt Lt 19/12/93. Retd ADMIN 15/11/96.
MITCHELL H. F. S., DFC. Born 2/11/16. Commd 21/3/43. Flt Lt 19/7/53. Retd GD(G) 9/3/62.
MITCHELL H. G. Born 1/5/30. Commd 12/11/55. Flt Lt 12/5/61. Retd GD 18/4/84 rtg Sqn Ldr.
MITCHELL I. A. Born 25/12/41. Commd 5/6/67. Sqn Ldr 1/1/79. Retd ENG 25/12/82.
MITCHELL J. Born 26/3/30. Commd 27/2/52. Wg Cdr 1/1/74. Retd GD 23/10/82.
MITCHELL J. B., CBE AFC. Born 24/11/30. Commd 11/6/53. A Cdre 1/1/82. Retd GD 2/7/84.
MITCHELL J. E. F., DFC. Born 27/11/18. Commd 28/7/42. Sqn Ldr 1/7/57. Retd GD 19/4/58.
MITCHELL J. H. Born 15/9/21. Commd 27/1/55. Sqn Ldr 1/7/69. Retd ENG 30/9/71.
MITCHELL J. L., LVO DFC AFC AE. Born 12/11/18. Commd 21/4/40. A Cdre 1/7/68. Retd GD 1/9/74.
MITCHELL J. N., MSc MB BS MFOM DAvMed. Born 21/12/35. Commd 28/4/63. Gp Capt 1/1/85. Retd MED 31/7/85.
MITCHELL J. N. S., MB ChB FRCP DCH. Born 16/12/26. Commd 29/9/50. Gp Capt 29/9/70. Retd MED 12/1/80.
MITCHELL J. R. Born 15/8/55. Commd 15/3/84. Flt Lt 15/3/86. Retd ADMIN 15/8/93.
MITCHELL J. T. Born 29/8/31. Commd 27/5/53. Flt Lt 11/11/58. Retd GD 29/8/69.
MITCHELL J. W. Born 17/5/31. Commd 11/4/63. Sqn Ldr 1/7/74. Retd SUP 30/11/84.
MITCHELL N. Born 20/1/46. Commd 15/10/81. Sqn Ldr 1/7/91. Retd ENG 15/9/00.
MITCHELL P., MBE. Born 8/9/42. Commd 4/7/69. Wg Cdr 1/7/92. Retd ENG 8/9/97.
MITCHELL P. D. Born 11/3/32. Commd 3/1/43. Flt Lt 31/7/46. Retd GD 11/3/77.
MITCHELL P. M. Born 17/11/22. Commd 30/6/44. Sqn Ldr 1/1/55. Retd GD 9/12/61.
MITCHELL R. Born 22/5/40. Commd 18/12/62. Sqn Ldr 1/7/75. Retd SUP 1/7/78.
MITCHELL R. A. K., BSc. Born 30/9/44. Commd 26/5/67. Sqn Ldr 1/7/74. Retd ENG 1/6/76.
MITCHELL R. C., MBE Born 14/10/18. Commd 9/7/53. Sqn Ldr 1/7/63. Retd ENG 18/4/70.
MITCHELL R. F. Born 13/2/33. Commd 22/5/61. Sqn Ldr 1/7/79. Retd ADMIN 13/2/88.
MITCHELL R. H. Born 25/6/33. Commd 24/2/67. Flt Lt 1/1/73. Retd ENG 1/10/74.
MITCHELL R. J., MBE CEng MIEE. Born 23/2/19. Commd 18/7/41. Sqn Ldr 1/1/53. Retd ENG 23/1/56.
MITCHELL R. P. G. Born 5/12/33. Commd 13/8/52. Flt Lt 20/7/58. Retd GD 5/4/72.
MITCHELL R. S. Born 8/12/29. Commd 28/6/51. Sqn Ldr 1/7/64. Retd GD 26/2/85.
MITCHELL T. A. Born 15/9/49. Commd 3/10/74. Flt Lt 3/4/80. Retd GD 20/5/90.
MITCHELL T. S. Born 10/4/37. Commd 19/7/57. Flt Lt 3/12/63. Retd SUP 11/2/66.
MITCHELL V. D. Born 25/4/35. Commd 26/5/67. Sqn Ldr 1/7/77. Retd GD(G) 25/4/85.
MITCHELL V. M. Born 1/6/57. Commd 3/7/80. Flt Lt 3/1/87. Retd SUP 4/3/89.
MITCHELL W. Born 25/2/17. Commd 26/11/43. Flt Lt 26/5/47. Retd GD 1/9/50.
MITCHELMORE A. Born 12/10/16. Commd 25/9/43. Sqn Ldr 1/1/55. Retd GD(G) 31/8/61.
MITCHEM M. M., DFM. Born 15/9/20. Commd 9/10/44. Flt Lt 9/4/49. Retd SUP 15/9/75.
MITCHENER A. W., MCIPS. Born 27/3/32. Commd 2/10/67. Sqn Ldr 1/7/73. Retd SUP 6/8/83.
MITCHISON B., MSc BSc. Born 18/12/62. Commd 5/9/82. Sqn Ldr 1/1/97. Retd ENG 18/12/00.
MLEJNECKY F. Born 10/12/18. Commd 20/10/43. Flt Lt 7/6/51. Retd GD 28/10/68.
MOBBERLEY D., AFC. Born 24/2/26. Commd 19/6/52. Sqn Ldr 1/8/65. Retd GD 3/9/68.
MOCK D. E. K. Born 2/5/23. Commd 28/8/42. Sqn Ldr 1/1/57. Retd GD 24/9/65.
MOCKFORD M. D., OBE. Born 21/9/34. Commd 19/8/65. Wg Cdr Retd PI 21/9/89.
MOFFAT A. Born 17/4/36. Commd 3/8/62. Sqn Ldr 1/7/87. Retd GD 17/4/96.
MOFFAT D. F., OBE. Born 21/10/28. Commd 16/1/52. Gp Capt 1/1/74. Retd GD 29/3/78.
MOFFAT D. F. Born 1/11/35. Commd 3/1/56. Flt Lt 3/7/61. Retd GD 2/11/79.
MOFFAT H. J., AFC. Born 26/6/33. Commd 27/2/52. Sqn Ldr 1/1/70. Retd GD 21/6/73.
MOFFAT J. R., CEng MIProdE. Born 6/4/46. Commd 17/12/72. Wg Cdr 1/7/88. Retd ENG 6/4/91.
MOFFAT P. M. Born 19/2/41. Commd 3/7/80. Flt Lt 3/7/85. Retd ENG 30/3/94.
MOFFAT W. Born 23/7/54. Commd 8/5/86. Flt Lt 8/5/88. Retd OPS SPT 8/5/00.
MOFFATT A. Born 24/4/50. Commd 14/2/69. Flt Lt 14/8/74. Retd GD 28/9/74.
MOFFATT G. W. Born 15/3/37. Commd 21/7/61. Sqn Ldr 1/7/72. Retd GD 4/5/88.
MOFFETT I. F. Born 11/4/47. Commd 29/7/65. Sqn ldr 1/7/83. Retd GD(G) 11/4/91.
MOFFETT M. T., MSc BSc. Born 5/6/47. Commd 16/10/72. Wg Cdr 1/7/86. Retd ENG 1/7/89.

MOFFITT A. J. Born 27/11/64. Commd 8/12/83. Fg Off 2/6/86. Retd SUP 19/1/90.
MOFFITT F. J. Born 30/11/40. Commd 22/2/63. Flt Lt 1/8/72. Retd GD 30/11/90.
MOGER B. Born 3/2/35. Commd 15/9/60. Sqn Ldr 1/1/72. Retd SEC 1/1/75.
MOHAMMED H. A. Born 27/9/47. Commd 4/6/87. Flt Lt 4/6/91. Retd OPS SPT 31/1/99.
MOIR A. D., OBE BSc MRIN. Born 3/11/46. Commd 23/3/69. Wg Cdr 1/1/88. Retd GD 10/5/94.
MOIR I., BSc CEng MIEE MRAeS. Born 31/8/42. Commd 15/7/63. Sqn Ldr 1/1/75. Retd ENG 31/8/80.
MOIR J. McG., MA. Born 28/3/44. Commd 28/9/64. Flt Lt 15/4/67. Retd GD 14/4/72.
MOLE B. F. Born 9/9/43. Commd 1/3/68. Sqn Ldr 1/7/81. Retd ADMIN 1/10/86.
MOLENDO S. B. Born 13/5/22. Commd 8/6/49. Flt Lt 19/6/52. Retd GD 13/5/68.
MOLES J. G., MIMgt. Born 2/11/26. Commd 25/8/60. Sqn Ldr 1/7/71. Retd ENG 1/9/78.
MOLES J. W., BEM. Born 21/4/25. Commd 14/11/57. Flt Lt 14/11/63. Retd ENG 17/1/70.
MOLESWORTH D. W., CEng MIEE MRAeS. Born 13/3/30. Commd 28/7/53. Sqn Ldr 1/7/67. Retd ENG 13/9/92.
MOLESWORTH J. E. N. Born 28/4/26. Commd 19/3/47. Flt Lt 17/5/56. Retd RGT 31/8/58.
MOLLAND A. Born 1/11/36. Commd 25/3/55. Flt Lt 7/8/64. Retd GD 1/11/74.
MOLLAND H. Born 13/12/32. Commd 17/5/51. Flt Lt 22/5/57. Retd GD 13/12/69.
MOLLISON A. Born 21/1/21. Commd 7/4/55. Sqn Ldr 1/7/66. Retd ENG 21/10/72.
MOLLISON K. B. Born 25/7/33. Commd 26/4/62. Flt Lt 26/4/62. Retd GD 25/7/88.
MOLLOY B., ACIS MIMgt. Born 18/5/31. Commd 31/10/71. Sqn Ldr 31/10/71. Retd SUP 18/5/91.
MOLLOY G. J., BA. Born 10/11/58. Commd 17/8/80. Sqn Ldr 1/7/89. Retd GD 1/10/99.
MOLLOY M. A. Born 21/4/41. Commd 14/6/63. Gp Capt 1/7/90. Retd GD 22/1/97.
MOLLOY M. H. T., MBE. Born 29/3/17. Commd 26/11/42. Sqn Ldr 1/1/54. Retd SEC 1/7/72.
MOLONEY P. A. Born 20/4/59. Commd 12/10/78. Flt Lt 12/4/84. Retd GD 20/4/97.
MOLONEY P. S. Born 17/5/38. Commd 22/9/58. Flt Lt 14/4/65. Retd SUP 17/5/76.
MOLONEY T. F., AFM. Born 10/8/26. Commd 18/11/66. Flt Lt 18/11/71. Retd REG 2/10/79.
MOLYNEAUX M. Born 6/1/47. Commd 18/11/66. Flt Lt 18/3/73. Retd GD(G) 25/4/80.
MOLYNEUX R. Born 22/1/25. Commd 16/3/45. Flt Lt 4/1/51. Retd GD 1/5/68.
MONAGHAN G. A. Born 3/2/48. Commd 11/8/67. Wg Cdr 1/7/87. Retd GD 4/5/01.
MONAGHAN G. M. J., BTech. Born 30/11/56. Commd 30/8/78. Sqn Ldr 1/1/89. Retd GD 30/11/94.
MONAGHAN S. H. Born 7/7/48. Commd 28/2/69. Flt Lt 28/2/72. Retd GD 17/7/92.
MONAHAN J. D. Born 23/6/49. Commd 25/10/73. Plt Offr 12/8/74 Retd PRT 17/10/75.
MONCASTER C. J., BSc. Born 8/4/54. Commd 17/9/72. Wg Cdr 1/1/94. Retd GD 8/4/98.
MONFORT G. R. Born 3/9/44. Commd 25/4/69. Flt Lt 25/10/75. Retd OPS SPT 3/2/00.
MONICO J. D. Born 24/1/21. Commd 15/4/43. Fg Offr 17/3/45. Retd ENG 9/1/47 rtg Flt Lt.
MONK B. Born 17/3/44. Commd 5/11/70. Sqn Ldr 1/1/79. Retd GD 1/4/90.
MONK D. Born 3/6/43. Commd 14/4/69. Sqn Ldr 1/1/79. Retd ENG 1/6/89.
MONK G. C. W. Born 3/9/13. Commd 27/9/45. Sqn Ldr 1/1/56. Retd ENG 10/9/68.
MONK K. L., MCIPD. Born 20/6/34. Commd 5/11/70. Sqn Ldr 1/1/78. Retd ENG 22/12/89.
MONK M. A. N. Born 1/10/47. Commd 2/2/68. Flt Lt 23/5/74. Retd GD(G) 1/10/85.
MONK M. J. Born 4/9/43. Commd 8/1/65. Flt Lt 8/7/70. Retd GD 1/10/76.
MONK M. R., MBE. Born 4/2/21. Commd 7/2/55. Sqn Ldr 1/7/67. Retd PI 1/8/74.
MONK W. G. Born 11/7/23. Commd 7/7/55. Flt Lt 25/2/60. Retd GD 31/5/72.
MONKHOUSE K. E. J., MA CEng FIEE. Born 2/6/38. Commd 30/9/58. Air Cdre 1/1/87. Retd ENG 2/6/93.
MONKS D., OBE CEng MRAeS. Born 15/5/17. Commd 15/4/43. Wg Cdr 1/1/66. Retd ENG 15/5/72.
MONKS M. R., FIMgt. Born 2/11/38. Commd 22/8/59. Gp Capt 1/7/85. Retd GD 30/11/89.
MONSON K. G., MIMgt. Born 26/3/36. Commd 12/11/54. Wg Cdr 1/7/73. Retd GD 11/7/78.
MONTAGU-SMITH A. M., DL. Born 17/7/15. Commd 15/3/35. Wg Cdr 1/7/47. Retd GD 1/1/61 rtg Gp Capt.
MONTAGUE E. Born 29/5/26. Commd 8/4/57. Sqn Ldr 1/1/65. Retd SEC 8/5/68.
MONTAGUE G. T., CertEd. Born 22/7/44. Commd 20/12/73. Sqn Ldr 1/1/89. Retd SUP 22/7/99.
MONTAGUE P. Born 24/4/16. Commd 18/1/48. Flt Lt 4/6/53. Retd SUP 1/5/65.
MONTAGUE R. M. B., BSc. Born 1/6/39. Commd 22/5/62. A Cdre 1/7/90. Retd ADMIN 1/6/94.
MONTALTO R. Born 20/8/18. Commd 14/5/53. Flt Lt 14/4/59. Retd SUP 20/8/66.
MONTEITH D. J., BA. Born 7/11/51. Commd 13/9/70. Flt Lt 13/6/76. Retd RGT 6/7/80.
MONTEITH-HODGE D., MIMgt. Born 11/9/27. Commd 10/9/52. Sqn Ldr 1/7/65. Retd PE 14/4/73.
MONTGOMERIE I. E. D. Born 31/5/40. Commd 13/12/60. Flt Lt 13/6/63. Retd GD 30/8/71.
MONTGOMERY A., BA. Born 16/12/32. Commd 6/8/63. Sqn Ldr 9/2/68. Retd ADMIN 6/8/79.
MONTGOMERY A. C., OBE MA. Born 1/8/46. Commd 6/10/69. Gp Capt 1/1/95. Retd GD 3/1/97.
MONTGOMERY B. G., BA. Born 31/10/31. Commd 20/11/56. Flt Lt 20/8/58. Retd GD 24/7/72.
MONTGOMERY C. M. Born 28/4/45. Commd 24/4/64. Flt Lt 24/10/69. Retd GD 22/10/82.
MONTGOMERY D. A., MB BS MRCS LRCP DCP MRCPath. Born 24/3/33. Commd 11/8/57. Wg Cdr 11/8/70. Retd MED 11/8/73.
MONTGOMERY D. M., BA. Born 18/2/47. Commd 22/6/70. Flt Lt 22/3/72. Retd GD 1/4/75.
MONTGOMERY G. P. F., MBE. Born 9/6/39. Commd 8/9/77. Sqn Ldr 1/1/85. Retd ENG 8/6/92.
MONTGOMERY R. A. Born 15/1/17. Commd 6/1/42. Flt Lt 1/9/45. Retd ENG 15/1/66.
MONTGOMERY R. S., BSc. Born 25/10/49. Commd 16/12/79. Flt Lt 16/12/80. Retd ADMIN 16/12/95.
MONTGOMERY-SAUNDERS F. W. L. Born 26/8/28. Commd 10/11/49. Flt Lt 21/9/55. Retd GD 26/8/66.
MOODY D. W. Born 26/3/28. Commd 13/1/72. Flt Lt 13/1/75. Retd ENG 5/4/79.

MOODY H. Born 30/1/22. Commd 17/3/67. Flt Lt 17/3/70. Retd ENG 23/9/72.
MOODY R. Born 20/3/20. Commd 18/8/43. Flt Lt 18/2/47. Retd GD 25/9/55.
MOON H. H. Born 21/6/19. Commd 27/4/41. Sqn Ldr 1/8/47. Retd GD 29/7/58.
MOON P. A. H. Born 9/6/20. Commd 2/2/52. Gp Capt 1/1/70. Retd SEC 9/6/75.
MOON. A. J. F. Born 26/10/41. Commd 6/4/62. Flt Lt 1/7/68. Retd GD 23/8/75.
MOONEY A. G. P. Born 18/1/40. Commd 16/9/71. Flt Lt 16/9/73. Retd SEC 16/9/79.
MOONEY D. L., MVO. Born 21/3/41. Commd 15/9/61. Sqn Ldr 1/7/88. Retd GD 22/3/91.
MOONEY F. C. Born 21/2/50. Commd 2/8/90. Fg Offr 2/8/90. Retd ENG 1/6/93.
MOONEY G. Born 6/11/38. Commd 27/5/71. Flt Lt 27/5/73. Retd GD 30/9/76.
MOONEY J. Born 23/12/45. Commd 28/6/79. Flt Lt 28/6/81. Retd GD 1/3/94.
MOONEY P. M. Born 13/10/49. Commd 11/4/85. Flt Lt 11/4/89. Retd SY 31/3/94.
MOONEY R. T., BSc. Born 26/9/38. Commd 8/6/62. Sqn Ldr 1/7/72. Retd GD 26/9/93.
MOORCROFT B., DSO DFC MA. Born 26/4/21. Commd 5/6/43. Wg Cdr 1/7/61. Retd GD 26/10/68.
MOORCROFT G. E. Born 19/2/37. Commd 22/7/71. Flt Lt 16/4/74. Retd ENG 22/7/79.
MOORCROFT P. Born 10/10/58. Commd 29/3/90. Flt Lt 29/3/92. Retd ADMIN 29/3/00.
MOORE A. Born 28/12/47. Commd 28/7/88. Flt Lt 28/7/92. Retd SY 31/10/95.
MOORE A. C., CEng MRAeS MIEE MIMgt. Born 15/10/21. Commd 15/3/46. Wg Cdr 1/1/67. Retd GD 1/8/73.
MOORE A. G. Born 9/2/38. Commd 26/10/62. Flt Lt 26/4/68. Retd GD 31/10/89.
MOORE B. A., MA MSc MIEE. Born 23/8/57. Commd 5/8/76. Sqn Ldr 1/1/87. Retd ENG 18/12/90.
MOORE B. D., OBE BSc CEng MRAeS MIMgt. Born 28/3/25. Commd 18/10/50. Gp Capt 1/7/73. Retd ENG 28/10/78.
MOORE C. Born 6/11/29. Commd 18/11/66. Flt Lt 18/11/69. Retd GD 1/5/76.
MOORE C. D., CEng MIEE. Born 16/10/08. Commd 5/11/40. Wg Cdr 1/1/49. Retd ENG 16/10/63.
MOORE C. M. Born 2/4/42. Commd 17/3/67. Gp Capt 1/7/89. Retd ADMIN 3/4/96.
MOORE C. S., CB OBE. Born 27/2/10. Commd 20/12/30. A Cdre 1/7/54. Retd GD 23/7/62 rtg AVM.
MOORE C. T., CBE. Born 1/1/43. Commd 17/12/64. Gp Capt 1/1/86. Retd GD 2/4/93.
MOORE D. Born 28/6/23. Commd 1/10/43. Flt Lt 19/11/53. Retd GD 18/11/64.
MOORE D. Born 8/11/35. Commd 23/11/78. Flt Lt 23/11/81. Retd SY 24/10/87.
MOORE D. McL. Born 7/5/20. Commd 22/9/49. Sqn Ldr 1/1/61. Retd ENG 12/10/73.
MOORE D. H., MBE. Born 25/9/35. Commd 12/12/59. Sqn Ldr 1/1/86. Retd GD 3/1/95.
MOORE D. R., BSc. Born 18/6/62. Commd 28/4/84. Flt Lt 29/10/87. Retd ENG 14/9/96.
MOORE E. T. Born 13/6/25. Commd 15/12/44. Gp Capt 1/7/76. Retd SUP 13/6/80.
MOORE F. A. Born 4/8/24. Commd 8/7/54. Flt Lt 7/7/59. Retd GD 4/8/79.
MOORE F. T., MIPM MIMgt. Born 2/10/34. Commd 12/7/62. Wg Cdr 1/7/80. Retd ADMIN 20/4/85.
MOORE G. A. Born 7/8/41. Commd 4/2/71. Sqn Ldr 1/1/87. Retd GD 7/8/96.
MOORE G. Born 18/5/30. Commd 24/1/52. Flt Lt 15/5/57. Retd GD 10/1/76.
MOORE G. C. Born 19/7/32. Commd 5/11/52. Flt Lt 24/3/58. Retd GD 22/3/74.
MOORE G. J. T. Born 27/4/41. Commd 3/7/80. Sqn Ldr 1/1/90. Retd SUP 26/2/94.
MOORE G. R., MA CEng MRAeS MIERE DipEl. Born 18/9/27. Commd 25/11/48. Sqn Ldr 1/1/61. Retd ENG 18/9/65.
MOORE G. S., MSc. Born 5/6/41. Commd 12/6/62. Wg Cdr 1/1/91. Retd SUP 6/10/91.
MOORE J. Born 6/10/28. Commd 12/9/50. Flt Lt 12/3/55. Retd GD 6/10/85.
MOORE J. C., BSc CEng MIEE ACGI. Born 16/9/40. Commd 30/9/59. Sqn Ldr 1/1/70. Retd ENG 16/9/78.
MOORE J. C., Commd 17/6/40. Flt Offr 1/9/45. Retd SEC 27/8/50 rtg Sqn Offr.
MOORE J. M., Commd 24/11/67. Flt Lt 19/9/74. Retd GD (G) 2/2/87.
MOORE K. B. Born 13/1/46. Commd 4/12/64. Gp Capt 1/7/88. Retd GD 18/4/91.
MOORE K. M., CEng MIERE. Born 3/10/31. Commd 23/3/66. Flt Lt 1/7/68. Retd ENG 23/3/74.
MOORE L. Born 21/4/18. Commd 4/12/43. Sqn Ldr 1/10/54. Retd GD 21/9/58.
MOORE M. Born 18/4/37. Commd 27/2/56. Wg Cdr 1/7/76. Retd GD 1/10/86.
MOORE M. A. Born 18/10/32. Commd 14/12/54. Plt Offr 14/12/54. Retd GD 6/9/56.
MOORE M. A. Born 29/12/44. Commd 4/5/72. Sqn Ldr 1/1/81. Retd ADMIN 29/12/88.
MOORE M. B. Born 24/9/30. Commd 20/12/51. Flt Lt 5/11/58. Retd GD 8/9/70.
MOORE M. J. Born 10/5/33. Commd 19/9/54. Flt Lt 16/8/61. Retd GD 4/10/78.
MOORE N. C., MD BCh MRCPsych DPM. Born 1/8/38. Commd 24/9/62. Wg Cdr 3/8/78. Retd MED 5/11/83.
MOORE N. D. Born 4/2/53. Commd 10/2/72. Sqn Ldr 1/1/85. Retd SUP 4/2/91.
MOORE P. J. Born 29/9/46. Commd 19/8/66. Gp Capt 1/7/91. Retd GD 7/1/95.
MOORE P. M., MILT. Born 19/7/44. Commd 25/2/82. Sqn Ldr 1/7/90. Retd SUP 27/11/95.
MOORE R. Born 29/12/40. Commd 18/12/62. Sqn Ldr 1/1/84. Retd GD 7/12/93.
MOORE R. C. Born 13/12/42. Commd 30/7/63. Wg Cdr 1/1/87. Retd GD 13/12/97.
MOORE R. D. Born 16/10/22. Commd 5/3/43. Flt Lt 5/5/49. Retd GD 20/10/49.
MOORE R. F., BEM. Born 25/2/37. Commd 9/10/75. Sqn Ldr 1/1/86. Retd ENG 1/5/91.
MOORE R. J. Born 1/10/47. Commd 23/3/67. Flt Lt 23/9/72. Retd GD 14/5/90.
MOORE R. M. Born 13/5/44. Commd 13/1/67. Flt Lt 13/7/72. Retd GD 26/9/82.
MOORE R. P. Born 5/12/35. Commd 28/11/69. Flt Lt 11/5/72. Retd GD 17/12/73.
MOORE T., MA BSc MINucE MIMgt. Born 27/4/17. Commd 23/9/43. Sqn Ldr 1/1/59. Retd ENG 27/4/66.
MOORE T., DFC. Born 15/10/18. Commd 24/2/44. Sqn Ldr 1/1/68. Retd GD(G) 15/10/73.

MOORE T. P. Y. Born 9/7/05. Commd 1/4/18. Sqn Ldr 1/7/29. Retd GD 11/2/31.
MOORE T. S. Born 16/8/41. Commd 9/8/79. Sqn Ldr 1/1/87. Retd ADMIN 21/6/96.
MOORE W. J. Born 26/12/63. Commd 19/7/84. Flt Lt 19/1/90. Retd GD 14/3/97.
MOOREHOUSE M. G., BSc(Eng) MIIM ACGI. Born 8/1/38. Commd 14/4/69. Sqn Ldr 1/7/79. Retd ENG 14/4/85.
MOORES D. S., BSc. Born 14/10/50. Commd 1/11/71. Flt Lt 1/2/73. Retd GD 20/12/88.
MOORES F. S., DFC. Born 1/12/15. Commd 21/6/43. Flt Lt 21/12/46. Retd ENG 15/9/53.
MOORES G. J. E., OBE. Born 11/7/31. Commd 14/10/51. Wg Cdr 1/7/70. Retd GD 29/5/76.
MOORES P. W., BSc. Born 16/5/48. Commd 1/9/71. Sqn Ldr 1/7/80. Retd ENG 31/10/87.
MOORHEAD M. D., BSc. Born 13/6/46. Commd 28/9/64. Flt Lt 22/6/72. Retd ENG 30/3/78.
MOORHOUSE A. G. Born 27/3/19. Commd 8/7/54. Sqn Ldr 1/7/67. Retd ENG 27/3/74.
MOORHOUSE G. H. Born 27/9/24. Commd 20/4/50. Flt Lt 20/10/53. Retd GD 27/9/62.
MOORS E. H. Born 26/12/30. Commd 25/5/50. Sqn Ldr 1/1/64. Retd GD 27/5/69.
MORALEE G. C. Born 3/10/23. Commd 6/1/45. Flt Lt 6/7/48. Retd GD 3/4/69.
MORALEE P. J. Born 26/5/46. Commd 27/2/70. Sqn Ldr 1/1/84. Retd SY 1/10/88. re-entered 27/2/70. Sqn Ldr
   28/5/86. Retd OPS SPT 26/5/01.
MORAN J. Born 10/4/42. Commd 19/6/86. Sqn Ldr 1/7/92. Retd ADMIN 1/7/98.
MORAN L. E., DFC. Born 23/7/20. Commd 8/8/43. Sqn Ldr 1/1/61. Retd GD 27/11/64.
MORAN M. F., MB Bch MChOtol BAO DLO MRAeS. Born 18/4/27. Commd 24/10/54. AVM 17/10/88. Retd MED
   3/12/91
MORAN S. F. Born 22/12/23. Commd 3/5/46. Flt Lt 29/6/50. Retd GD 25/12/66.
MORBLY-HARDINGE W. P. Born 18/6/32. Commd 6/9/68. Flt Lt 6/9/73. Retd ENG 13/7/82.
MOREAU R. D. Born 19/2/26. Commd 25/5/50. Sqn Ldr 1/7/68. Retd PI 13/9/80.
MORECOMBE L. G. Born 9/1/33. Commd 24/1/52. Flt Lt 15/8/57. Retd GD 9/1/88.
MORELAND A. C. Born 6/10/10. Commd 25/4/41. Sqn Ldr 1/7/49. Retd SUP 25/10/59.
MORELAND D. H., FIMgt. Born 2/11/30. Commd 3/11/51. Flt Lt 3/5/56. Retd ADMIN 2/11/68. Reemployed
   26/2/71. Sqn Ldr 1/1/79. Retd 16/4/84.
MOREN L. A. Born 22/6/28. Commd 6/10/60. Sqn Ldr 1/1/78. Retd GD 1/8/78.
MORFILL E. R. Born 19/2/12. Commd 2/8/41. Sqn Ldr 1/7/53. Retd ENG 19/8/61.
MORFILL P. F., DFM. Born 11/12/14. Commd 15/1/42. Sqn Ldr 1/7/53. Retd GD 4/2/58.
MORFORD D. J. Born 28/3/29. Commd 17/5/62. Sqn Ldr 1/7/73. Retd ENG 28/3/89.
MORGAN A. I., BSc. Born 8/4/37. Commd 2/10/58. Sqn Ldr 1/7/68. Retd GD 11/12/77.
MORGAN A. J. M., OBE CEng MIERE MIMgt. Born 13/1/22. Commd 29/5/43. Wg Cdr 1/1/62. Retd ENG 30/11/72.
MORGAN A. M., MB BChir DO FRCS. Born 6/10/30. Commd 5/5/57. Gp Capt 5/5/80. Retd MED 1/3/83.
MORGAN A. P., DFC. Born 23/2/17. Commd 22/6/42. Wg Cdr 1/7/57. Retd GD 23/2/64.
MORGAN B., MBE. Born 15/6/10. Commd 21/8/41. Wg Cdr 1/7/55. Retd SEC 15/6/62.
MORGAN B. Born 24/11/41. Commd 11/5/62. Flt Lt 11/11/67. Retd GD 1/10/76.
MORGAN B. C. Born 12/12/53. Commd 27/3/86. Flt Lt 27/3/88. Retd SUP 14/3/96.
MORGAN B. E., MBE DPhysEd. Born 4/3/35. Commd 21/9/59. Sqn Ldr 1/7/71. Retd SUP 7/2/88.
MORGAN B. V. Born 8/4/26. Commd 23/12/54. Flt Offr 7/2/62. Retd SUP 15/7/65.
MORGAN C. J., AFC* FIMgt. Born 10/3/25. Commd 7/7/49. Wg Cdr 1/7/74. Retd GD 10/3/80.
MORGAN C. W. Born 15/3/35. Commd 3/10/70. Flt Lt 8/10/75. Retd GD 15/2/78.
MORGAN D. J. Born 5/3/36. Commd 7/5/64. Flt Lt 7/5/66. Retd ENG 5/3/74. Reinstated 1/4/81. Flt Lt 3/6/73. Retd
   ENG 23/2/91.
MORGAN D. R. Born 21/5/44. Commd 4/7/85. Sqn Ldr 1/7/91. Retd GD 21/5/00.
MORGAN D. R., BA. Born 6/11/17. Commd 25/8/47. Wg Cdr 1/7/63. Retd EDN 16/4/68.
MORGAN G., BSc. Born 5/3/52. Commd 2/9/73. Flt Lt 2/12/74. Retd GD 5/3/90.
MORGAN G. I., BSc CEng MIProdE. Born 26/11/54. Commd 17/1/82. Sqn Ldr 1/1/91. Retd ENG 17/1/98.
MORGAN G. L. O., DPhysEd. Born 28/3/28. Commd 1/8/52. Flt Lt 21/8/63. Retd SUP 2/10/81.
MORGAN G. O., DPhysEd. Born 15/10/41. Commd 30/8/66. Wg Cdr 1/7/90. Retd ADMIN 15/10/96.
MORGAN G. R. T., MA CEng MRAeS. Born 24/2/40. Commd 30/9/59. Wg Cdr 1/7/79. Retd ENG 31/10/92.
MORGAN G. W. Born 12/4/24. Commd 16/11/61. Sqn Ldr 1/1/75. Retd ENG 12/4/78.
MORGAN H. E. Born 2/1/47. Commd 14/8/80. Flt Lt 14/8/82. Retd ENG 14/8/88.
MORGAN H. S. Born 11/6/28. Commd 26/9/57. Flt Lt 26/3/61. Retd GD 29/3/69.
MORGAN H. T. Born 8/8/15. Commd 1/5/39. Gpt Capt 1/7/61. Retd SUP 8/8/70.
MORGAN I. L. Born 17/3/42. Commd 24/3/61. Wg Cdr 1/1/90. Retd GD 17/3/97.
MORGAN J. Born 11/6/45. Commd 17/12/65. Wg Cdr 1/7/85. Retd GD 8/6/90.
MORGAN J. A., CBE. Born 1/9/31. Commd 15/12/53. ACdre 1/1/84. Retd GD 1/1/87.
MORGAN J. A. Born 26/1/39. Commd 28/7/60. Gp Capt 1/7/87. Retd ENG 26/1/94.
MORGAN J. A. F. Born 21/3/16. Commd 8/10/42. Sqn Ldr 1/1/54. Retd ENG 21/3/71 rtg Wg Cdr.
MORGAN J. C. Born 9/9/30. Commd 26/7/51. Flt Lt 14/11/56. Retd GD 12/3/71.
MORGAN J. D. Born 20/7/52. Commd 17/1/85. Flt Lt 17/7/87. Retd ENG 17/1/93.
MORGAN J. D. Born 26/2/20. Commd 20/5/43. Flt Lt 10/7/47. Retd ENG 30/6/55.
MORGAN J. G. Born 25/8/29. Commd 24/6/53. Sqn Ldr 1/1/68. Retd GD 25/8/84.
MORGAN J. L. Born 6/8/45. Commd 24/6/76. Wg Cdr 1/1/97. Retd GD 6/8/00.
MORGAN J. M., DFC. Born 8/12/16. Commd 9/7/37. Wg Cdr 1/1/55. Retd GD 13/12/63.
MORGAN J. M., BSc. Born 23/8/35. Commd 18/12/56. Flt Lt 8/7/59. Retd GD 23/8/73.

MORGAN J. R. Born 5/4/38. Commd 28/7/59. Sqn Ldr 1/1/69. Retd GD 30/6/81.
MORGAN J. T. Born 16/2/29. Commd 23/10/56. Flt Lt 23/4/62. Retd GD 16/2/67.
MORGAN J. T. Born 18/6/45. Commd 8/1/65. Flt Lt 8/7/70. Retd GD 11/8/76.
MORGAN J. V., BSc. Born 15/9/48. Commd 19/9/71. Wg Cdr 1/7/93. Retd SUP 29/11/99.
MORGAN K. C. Born 25/6/33. Commd 9/8/51. Flt Lt 11/11/63. Retd GD 11/11/71.
MORGAN K. J. W. Born 14/10/35. Commd 6/1/54. Flt Lt 6/7/59. Retd GD(G) 14/10/90.
MORGAN L., CEng MRAeS MIMgt. Born 13/11/23. Commd 8/3/44. Gp Capt 1/1/73. Retd ENG 11/1/75.
MORGAN L. R. Born 19/6/34. Commd 5/4/55. Sqn Ldr 1/7/68. Retd GD 5/9/76.
MORGAN M. C. W., BA MB BChir DA LRCP MRCS. Born 1/6/36. Commd 3/9/62. Flt Lt 3/9/62. Retd MED 9/4/67.
MORGAN M. L. Born 11/2/45. Commd 26/5/67. Sqn Ldr 1/1/93. Retd ADMIN 1/1/96.
MORGAN M. W., ACII. Born 20/4/44. Commd 3/5/68. Sqn Ldr 1/1/86. Retd GD(G) 31/3/94.
MORGAN N. Born 21/2/46. Commd 25/2/66. Sqn Ldr 1/1/92. Retd GD 18/5/96.
MORGAN P. Born 19/6/31. Commd 16/7/52. Flt Lt 12/12/57. Retd GD 31/7/76.
MORGAN P. Born 11/6/41. Commd 14/6/63. Flt Lt 14/12/68. Retd GD 11/6/79.
MORGAN P. K., BA. Born 19/10/43. Commd 6/1/69. Flt Lt 6/1/70. Retd EDN 17/8/74.
MORGAN R. Born 30/9/18. Commd 28/3/46. Sqn Ldr 1/1/57. Retd SUP 30/9/61.
MORGAN R. A. Born 15/4/26. Commd 9/8/48 Sqn Ldr 1/1/70. Retd SY 1/10/76.
MORGAN R. G., MIMgt. Born 9/5/35. Commd 31/7/56. Wg Cdr 1/1/73. Retd ADMIN 2/4/80.
MORGAN R. J. L., CEng MRAeS MIMgt. Born 14/8/41. Commd 17/7/62. Sqn Ldr 1/7/76. Retd ENG 1/4/89.
MORGAN R. R. Born 5/8/35. Commd 22/7/66. Sqn Ldr 1/1/81. Retd GD 5/8/90.
MORGAN S. H. Born 30/4/44. Commd 28/11/69. Sqn Ldr 1/1/95. Retd GD 30/4/99.
MORGAN S. K., CEng MIEE. Born 2/4/37. Commd 7/11/58. Gp Capt 1/1/84. Retd ENG 7/5/88.
MORGAN S. P., BSc. Born 21/10/53. Commd 3/9/72. Sqn Ldr 1/1/81. Retd GD 21/10/91.
MORGAN T. Born 27/1/25. Commd 25/8/55. Flt Lt 25/8/61. Retd GD 28/9/68.
MORGAN T. E., Commd 4/3/71. Flt Lt 10/7/77. Retd GD(G) 26/9/78. Reinstated 9/4/80. Flt Lt 21/1/79. Retd GD(G) 31/1/86.
MORGAN T. J., CEng. Born 7/4/37. Commd 30/7/59. Gp Capt 1/1/80. Retd ENG 7/4/87.
MORGAN T. R. Born 28/5/34. Commd 26/7/55. A Cdre 1/1/82. Retd ADMIN 9/11/85.
MORGAN V. J. Born 5/7/27. Commd 9/3/50. Wg Cdr 1/7/68. Retd GD 5/7/82.
MORGAN W. B. C. Born 30/11/25. Commd 6/3/42. Flt Lt 6/9/55. Retd GD 2/5/68.
MORGAN W. G., CB CBE FCCA ACMA. Born 13/8/14. Commd 29/7/39. AVM 1/7/67. Retd SEC 16/8/69.
MORGAN W. W. Born 19/12/50. Commd 25/2/72. Flt Lt 25/2/75. Retd GD 25/2/88.
MORGAN-JONES J. I., MBE. Born 4/6/34. Commd 19/11/53. Wg Cdr 1/1/79. Retd SY(RGT) 20/4/89.
MORGANS A. W. Born 17/7/34. Commd 3/6/65. Sqn Ldr 1/1/84. Retd GD 1/5/87.
MORGANS J. M. C. Born 2/2/33. Commd 4/10/57. Flt Lt 4/4/57. Retd GD 2/2/88.
MORGANTI D. J. Born 7/10/34. Commd 12/3/64. Sqn Ldr 1/7/80. Retd GD 7/10/94.
MORIARTY P. D. R. Born 17/4/40. Commd 1/3/68. Sqn Ldr 1/7/81. Retd ADMIN 1/10/86.
MORISON I. C. Born 15/5/58. Commd 20/7/78. Sqn Ldr 1/7/90. Retd GD 13/9/96.
MORISON R. B., DFC AFC. Born 7/12/20. Commd 23/12/39. Gp Capt 1/7/59. Retd GD 31/7/65.
MORISON R. T., CBE. Born 20/8/16. Commd 19/7/40. AVM 1/1/70. Retd ENG 19/4/72.
MORLEY B. G. Born 3/2/31. Commd 16/7/52. Flt Lt 12/12/57. Retd GD(G) 3/2/86.
MORLEY D. Born 14/3/47. Commd 14/7/66. Flt Lt 8/3/72. Retd GD 28/8/76.
MORLEY G. E., MB ChB DIH. Born 1/10/27. Commd 3/1/52. Wg Cdr 5/10/64. Retd MED 21/1/71.
MORLEY J. F. Born 6/1/42. Commd 22/2/79. Flt Lt 22/2/82. Retd GD 20/7/92.
MORLEY J. H. Born 13/7/02. Commd 31/10/41. Flt Lt 1/9/45. Retd SUP 12/5/48 rtg Sqn Ldr.
MORLEY J. R., MBE. Born 13/12/36. Commd 6/4/72. Sqn Ldr 1/1/87. Retd ENG 13/12/94.
MORLEY P. Born 24/8/33. Commd 15/6/53. Flt Lt 17/9/58. Retd GD 24/8/88.
MORLEY P. R. Born 24/10/46. Commd 3/3/67. Wg Cdr 1/1/89. Retd GD 14/9/96.
MORLEY The Rev J., AKC. Born 5/11/43. Commd 8/1/77. Retd 8/5/93 Wg Cdr.
MORLEY R. E., DFC. Born 24/5/24. Commd 10/10/44. Sqn Ldr 1/1/56. Retd GD 24/5/62.
MORLEY R. H., MBE. Born 11/4/23. Commd 30/5/45. Sqn Ldr 1/1/56. Retd GD 11/4/66.
MORLEY R. J. Born 4/8/47. Commd 4/3/71. Flt Lt 12/8/77. Retd ADMIN 1/1/76.
MORLEY-MOWER G. F., DFC AFC. Born 5/5/18. Commd 29/11/37. Wg Cdr 1/1/53. Retd GD 15/8/68.
MORONEY W. J., RMN. Born 20/2/37. Commd 17/3/67. Gp Capt 1/7/89. Retd MED(SEC) 9/12/91.
MORRELL P. Born 22/4/17. Commd 12/7/40. Sqn Ldr 1/7/62. Retd ENG 16/5/72.
MORRELL P. B. Born 4/4/46. Commd 1/3/68. Wg Cdr 1/7/88. Retd SUP 27/11/00.
MORRELL P. R. Born 5/12/32. Commd 24/10/51. Sqn Ldr 1/1/68. Retd GD 1/7/71.
MORRELL S. T. Born 16/11/48. Commd 31/7/70. Flt Lt 31/7/73. Retd GD 7/9/74.
MORRIS Sir Alec, KBE CB BSc CEng FIEE FRAeS DipEl. Born 11/3/26. Commd 8/2/49. AM 1/7/81. Retd ENG 1/7/83.
MORRIS A. G., BSc CEng MIEE. Born 7/4/55. Commd 16/9/73. Sqn Ldr 1/1/91. Retd ENG 17/5/98.
MORRIS A. R., BA. Born 1/11/54. Commd 2/9/73. Sqn Ldr 1/7/86. Retd GD 1/11/92.
MORRIS A. S. Born 14/10/37. Commd 22/2/63. Flt Lt 25/7/66. Retd GD 14/10/75.
MORRIS A. S. J., MIMgt Born 6/6/18. Commd 30/1/47. Sqn Ldr 1/7/66. Retd SEC 30/9/71.
MORRIS B., MCIPD MIMgt. Born 18/1/36. Commd 19/8/71. Sqn Ldr 1/7/89. Retd ADMIN 24/11/91.
MORRIS B. Born 25/2/43. Commd 29/3/62. Flt Lt 29/9/68. Retd ENG 29/3/69.

MORRIS B. A. Born 19/12/47. Commd 24/3/83. Flt Lt 24/3/87. Retd ENG 31/3/94.
MORRIS B. G., OBE. Born 30/3/13. Commd 16/3/34. Wg Cdr 1/10/46. Retd GD 19/6/54.
MORRIS B. S., OBE AFC. Born 21/8/45. Commd 28/2/64. Gp Capt 1/7/90. Retd GD 30/9/00.
MORRIS C. Born 26/4/33. Commd 26/6/56. Wg Cdr 1/1/82. Retd ENG 11/9/86.
MORRIS C. H. Born 26/8/55. Commd 21/4/77. Sqn Ldr 1/7/88. Retd ADMIN 26/8/93.
MORRIS D., BA MRAeS. Born 20/9/31. Commd 9/4/53. Sqn Ldr 1/1/68. Retd GD 9/7/89.
MORRIS D. B., BSc. Born 14/8/36. Commd 16/1/72. Sqn Ldr 16/1/72. Retd ENG 14/8/94.
MORRIS D. G. Born 28/3/42. Commd 26/11/60. Wg Cdr 1/1/88. Retd GD 1/7/95.
MORRIS D. G. A. Born 20/6/22. Commd 19/7/56. Flt Lt 12/4/60. Retd GD(G) 20/6/77.
MORRIS D. H., DFM. Born 2/10/20. Commd 31/10/43. Flt Lt 7/6/51. Retd PI 31/7/74.
MORRIS D. L., FFA MIMgt. Born 30/3/53. Commd 2/8/73. Sqn Ldr 1/1/90. Retd ADMIN 1/1/93.
MORRIS D. M., BSc(Eng) CEng MIEE MRAeS. Born 4/1/43. Commd 30/9/61. Wg Cdr 1/1/90. Retd ENG 30/1/97.
MORRIS E., FAAI MIMgt. Born 18/6/38. Commd 1/11/56. Wg Cdr 1/1/79. Retd ADMIN 5/4/88.
MORRIS E. J., CB CBE DSO DFC FIMgt. Born 6/4/15. Commd 5/9/37. A Cdre 1/1/63. Retd GD 16/7/68.
MORRIS E. W. J., MIMgt. Born 21/9/28. Commd 6/4/50. Wg Cdr 1/1/69. Retd GD 21/9/83.
MORRIS F. N. Born 21/12/13. commd 17/6/40. Sqn Ldr 1/7/56. Retd SEC 8/1/63.
MORRIS G. Born 7/9/41. Commd 14/8/80. Sqn Ldr 1/7/90. Retd ENG 1/8/93.
MORRIS G. E. Born 22/4/17. Commd 7/4/40. Wg Cdr 1/7/53. Retd GD(G) 29/5/70.
MORRIS G. M. Born 8/8/41. Commd 12/7/62. Wg Cdr 1/1/86. Retd ADMIN 2/7/94.
MORRIS G. W. Born 12/12/42. Commd 24/3/61. Sqn Ldr 1/7/94. Retd GD 14/9/96.
MORRIS H. D. Born 7/12/31. Commd 30/7/64. Flt Lt 30/7/70. Retd ADMIN 18/1/84.
MORRIS H. R. Born 22/11/34. Commd 31/3/64. Sqn Ldr 1/7/84. Retd GD(G) 22/11/89.
MORRIS J., CBE BSc. Born 8/7/36. Commd 1/10/57. AVM 1/1/90. Retd GD 1/1/92.
MORRIS J., Commd 27/11/52. Flt Offr 27/11/58. Retd SEC 1/5/68.
MORRIS J. B. Born 24/2/49. Commd 24/4/80. Flt Lt 24/4/82. Retd ADMIN 24/4/88.
MORRIS J. E. Born 12/9/32. Commd 29/10/69. Sqn Ldr 1/1/76. Retd ENG 13/12/84.
MORRIS J. R. Born 15/11/39. Commd 22/7/71. Sqn Ldr 1/7/79. Retd GD(G) 1/5/86.
MORRIS J. T., MSc BSc CEng MIEE MRAeS MIMgt. Born 16/3/20. Commd 17/10/41. Wg Cdr 1/7/56. Retd ENG 16/3/75.
MORRIS K. Born 6/12/36. Commd 3/5/68. Flt Lt 6/10/71. Retd GD(G) 20/7/88.
MORRIS K. E., BA. Born 4/4/70. Commd 10/10/93. Fg Offr 10/10/92. Retd GD 13/10/95.
MORRIS K. J H., BA. Born 26/6/57. Commd 19/9/76. Sqn Ldr 1/1/87. Retd SY 31/3/90.
MORRIS K. L. Born 8/7/25. Commd 19/10/45. Sqn Ldr 1/1/61. Retd GD 19/7/83.
MORRIS L. C. Born 6/10/10. Commd 4/4/43. Fg Offr 4/10/43. Retd ENG 29/1/46.
MORRIS L. J., MHCIMA. Born 30/10/16. Commd 2/8/45. Wg Cdr 1/1/60. Retd CAT 30/10/71.
MORRIS L. P., Commd 9/3/76. Flt Lt 9/12/79. Retd ADMIN 1/6/86.
MORRIS M. R. Born 8/5/54. Commd 11/9/86. Flt Lt 11/9/88. Retd SY 11/9/94.
MORRIS N. C. Born 17/10/29. Commd 21/10/66. Flt Lt 21/10/71. Retd ENG 31/1/81.
MORRIS P. G. Born 29/6/25. Commd 7/9/61. Flt Lt 7/9/64. Retd GD 2/7/68.
MORRIS P. J., BEM. Born 13/5/23. Commd 4/2/48. Flt Lt 4/8/52. Retd SY 13/5/82.
MORRIS P. L. Born 26/2/47. Commd 9/3/66. Sqn Ldr 1/7/90. Retd GD(G) 14/9/96.
MORRIS R., OBE MA CEng FIEE DipEl. Born 6/7/24. Commd 11/11/43. Gp Capt 1/1/70. Retd ENG 30/3/77.
MORRIS R. Born 30/12/43. Commd 19/6/64. Flt Lt 17/3/71. Retd GD 30/12/81.
MORRIS R. E., MBE. Born 16/9/17. Commd 27/3/47. Sqn Ldr 1/7/58. Retd SUP 17/6/70.
MORRIS R. H. Born 10/3/49. Commd 29/8/72. Flt Lty 29/8/76. Retd PE 31/12/79.
MORRIS R. H. J. Born 28/11/37. Commd 20/11/56. Flt Lt 20/5/62. Retd GD 28/11/75.
MORRIS R. I. Born 26/10/39. Commd 19/12/61. Sqn Ldr 1/7/70. Retd GD 15/12/79.
MORRIS R. J. Born 6/12/47. Commd 28/10/66. Sqn Ldr 1/1/80. Retd GD 6/12/84.
MORRIS S. J., BA. Born 10/12/51. Commd 25/9/71. Gp Capt 1/7/95. Retd ADMIN 3/12/97.
MORRIS S. P. Born 13/5/50. Commd 8/10/70. Flt Lt 8/4/76. Retd GD 20/5/81.
MORRIS T. F. Born 19/2/20. Commd 29/9/41. Flt Lt 27/12/50. Retd SEC 4/9/61.
MORRIS T. G. Born 12/6/35. Commd 30/5/59. Sqn Ldr 1/7/72. Retd GD 12/6/90.
MORRIS T. W. Born 9/7/28. Commd 30/9/49. Flt Lt 28/8/55. Retd GD 9/7/66.
MORRIS The Rev K. R. Born 20/7/35. Commd 15/9/65. Retd 26/2/83. Wg Cdr.
MORRIS W. J., MRAeS MIMgt. Born 8/7/22. Commd 17/6/44. Sqn Ldr 1/7/71. Retd GD 31/3/77.
MORRIS-TURNER J. M., Commd 27/7/72. Flt Lt 13/1/79. Retd GD(G) 2/8/89.
MORRISH D. C., BA. Born 28/12/32. Commd 12/9/56. Sqn Ldr 12/3/64. Retd EDN 31/12/72.
MORRISH P. J. Born 16/4/27. Commd 18/7/61. Fg Offr 18/7/63. Retd SEC 1/11/63.
MORRISON D. J., MEd BSc PGCE CBiol MIBiol MCIPD. Born 16/10/51. Commd 20/1/80. Sqn Ldr 1/1/88. Retd ADMIN 20/1/96.
MORRISON D. M. Born 3/12/43. Commd 21/5/65. Flt Lt 26/9/71. Retd GD 13/4/76.
MORRISON D. M. Born 28/7/22. Commd 14/6/42. Flt Lt 16/3/53. Retd GD(G) 28/7/77 rtg Sqn Ldr.
MORRISON D. P. Born 4/7/21. Commd 27/7/43. Sqn Ldr 1/4/55. Retd GD 4/7/64.
MORRISON The Rev F. G. Born 12/2/37. Commd 6/6/66. Retd 6/6/82 Wg Cdr.
MORRISON G. M., MBE. Born 9/12/33. Commd 21/10/53. Sqn Ldr 1/1/65. Retd GD 9/12/71.
MORRISON I. N., BSc. Born 17/12/65. Commd 3/1/88. Flt Lt 3/7/90. Retd GD 14/3/97.

MORRISON J., MB BSc ChB MRCGP. Born 6/10/41. Commd 29/6/64. Sqn Ldr 15/8/72. Retd MED 19/7/80.
MORRISON P. J., MIMgt. Born 31/7/41. Commd 16/4/63. Flt Lt 31/7/68. Retd REG 31/7/79. rtg Sqn Ldr.
MORRISON W. J. O., AFC MRAeS. Born 15/10/23. Commd 8/11/44. Gp Capt 1/1/67. Retd GD 14/2/73.
MORRISS R. A., Commd 11/12/58. Sqn Ldr 1/7/73. Retd ADMIN 1/7/76.
MORRISSEY B. M. Born 10/5/15. Commd 25/7/44. Flt Lt 10/11/55. Retd GD(G) 4/8/60.
MORRISSEY M. J. Born 20/9/34. Commd 12/11/57. Flt Lt 21/5/63. Retd GD 20/9/72.
MORROW M. McA. Born 6/3/42. Commd 25/11/63. Fg Offr 3/10/65. Retd GD 27/11/68.
MORS P. L. Born 16/5/45. Commd 28/9/64. Sqn Ldr 1/1/77. Retd ENG 16/5/83.
MORSE R. B. J. S. Born 11/12/17. Commd 4/4/45. Flt Lt 7/6/51. Retd RGT 30/9/58.
MORTEN P. G. Born 8/12/30. Commd 17/10/57. Flt Lt 17/4/62. Retd GD 30/8/69.
MORTER D. Born 8/7/30. Commd 21/3/51. Flt Lt 21/9/55. Retd GD 8/7/68.
MORTIMER B. W. Born 26/4/38. Commd 12/7/63. Sqn Ldr 1/7/74. Retd GD(G) 1/7/77.
MORTIMER The Rev C. P. Born 18/4/38. Commd 27/3/77. Retd 30/6/93 Wg Cdr.
MORTIMER E. L. Born 19/2/26. Commd 3/12/56. Flt Lt 3/12/56. Retd PRT 30/6/66.
MORTIMER I., BSc. Born 12/5/49. Commd 19/2/73. Sqn Ldr 1/1/83. Retd GD 19/2/89.
MORTIMER J. C. S. Born 4/12/44. Commd 8/5/86. Sqn Ldr 1/7/94. Retd ENG 14/3/96.
MORTIMER K. Born 14/5/44. Commd 22/7/71. Flt Lt 22/7/73. Retd ENG 25/7/83.
MORTIMER M. Born 11/5/32. Commd 8/7/65. Flt Lt 9/7/71 / Retd SY 1/10/76.
MORTIMORE G. T. Born 8/1/24. Commd 23/7/43. Flt Lt 23/1/47. Retd GD 8/1/70.
MORTLOCK D. F. Born 21/4/36. Commd 12/9/63. Gp Capt 1/1/84. Retd SUP 28/7/86.
MORTLOCK G. E. Born 29/12/25. Commd 11/10/51. Flt Lt 25/1/57. Retd GD 1/10/75.
MORTON A. M., BSc. Born 7/12/37. Commd 11/11/59. Sqn Ldr 1/7/70. Retd ADMIN 29/5/76.
MORTON C. C. R. Born 12/4/25. Commd 4/6/64. Sqn Ldr 1/1/77. Retd ENG 12/4/85.
MORTON F. de C. G. Born 22/4/18. Commd 27/4/41. Flt Lt 9/6/47. Retd SEC 1/7/55 rtg Sqn Ldr.
MORTON G. S. Born 17/2/46. Commd 8/1/65. Flt Lt 8/7/70. Retd GD(G) 1/3/74.
MORTON J. E., MSc BTech CEng MRAeS CertEd. Born 2/2/49. Commd 2/1/77. Sqn Ldr 1/7/85. Retd ADMIN 14/3/96.
MORTON R. M., CEng MRAeS MIMgt. Born 26/5/21. Commd 19/8/42. Wg Cdr 1/1/60. Retd ENG 14/6/71.
MORTON S. J. Born 7/2/45. Commd 31/1/64. Sqn Ldr 1/1/85. Retd GD 14/9/96.
MORTON W. H. Born 9/2/20. Commd 30/1/47. Fg Offr 30/1/49. Retd SEC 18/1/52.
MOSELEY A. G. Born 11/4/25. Commd 14/6/49. Flt Lt 14/12/53. Retd GD 21/9/64.
MOSELEY D. A. R. Born 20/9/24. Commd 19/10/59. Flt Lt 19/10/59. Retd ADMIN 20/9/82.
MOSES H. H., MBE. Born 5/5/39. Commd 3/9/60. Gp Capt 1/1/90. Retd GD 5/1/95.
MOSEY E., MBE. Born 3/10/13. Commd 18/11/54. Flt Lt 18/11/57. Retd ENG 3/10/68.
MOSLEY C. P. Born 15/7/61. Commd 11/6/81. Flt Lt 11/12/86. Retd GD 15/1/93.
MOSS A., DFM. Born 26/8/20. Commd 26/9/57. Sqn Ldr 1/7/71. Retd ENG 26/8/75.
MOSS B. G. Born 3/1/37. Commd 10/1/37. Sqn Ldr 1/1/86. Retd ENG 23/2/92.
MOSS G., OBE AFC. Born 22/6/23. Commd 29/4/44. Gp Capt 1/1/71. Retd GD 3/11/73.
MOSS I. E., CEng MRAeS. Born 5/2/27. Commd 20/2/72. Sqn Ldr 20/2/72. Retd ENG 22/4/90.
MOSS J. B., Commd 22/7/68. Plt Offr 22/7/68. Retd CAT 29/12/68.
MOSS M. Born 6/6/35. Commd 24/8/72. Sqn Ldr 1/7/82. Retd ADMIN 26/7/85.
MOSS P., MCSP. Born 30/1/30. Commd 2/3/61. Wg Cdr 1/7/76. Retd MED 28/10/77.
MOSS P. S. Born 23/7/44. Commd 9/8/63. Plt Offr 9/8/64. Retd GD 19/8/65.
MOSSFORD A. R., LGSM ARCM. Born 28/7/38. Commd 8/8/74. Sqn Ldr 18/8/84. Retd DM 14/4/95.
MOSSMAN G. K., CBE. Born 10/10/27. Commd 27/4/49. Gp Capt 1/7/73. Retd SUP 1/2/78.
MOSSMAN P. J. Born 28/6/42. Commd 16/12/63. Plt Offr 21/3/64. Retd GD(G) 1/10/65.
MOTT A. J., MBE. Born 12/5/16. Commd 7/4/42. Sqn Ldr 1/7/51. Retd GD 19/6/59.
MOTT A. J., OBE CEng FIEE MRAeS. Born 27/2/08. Commd 15/2/40. Wg Cdr 1/7/47. Retd ENG 27/2/63.
MOTT B. W. Born 4/3/35. Commd 2/2/68. Sqn Ldr 8/10/75. Retd ADMIN 2/4/84.
MOTT W. H. M. Born 19/9/44. Commd 17/12/65. Flt Lt 8/1/69. Retd GD 19/9/88.
MOTTERSHEAD J. K. Born 12/12/36. Commd 13/10/61. Flt Lt 1/4/66. Retd GD 8/9/76.
MOULD A. J., MBE. Born 22/3/11. Commd 26/10/36. Sqn Ldr 1/7/63. Retd GD(G) 1/1/63 rtg Wg Cdr.
MOULD H. J., CEng MRAeS. Born 29/9/26. Commd 29/4/54. Sqn Ldr 1/7/65. Retd ENG 1/10/76.
MOULD J. E. M., CBE. Born 12/11/14. Commd 23/1/39. A Cdre 1/7/66. Retd SUP 29/1/70.
MOULD S. G. Born 3/6/49. Commd 31/7/70. Flt Lt 31/7/73. Retd GD 7/2/88.
MOULD T. W., BEM. Born 11/12/20. Commd 27/8/59. Flt Lt 27/8/64. Retd ENG 11/12/76.
MOULDEN K. A. Born 27/12/32. Commd 26/12/51. Flt Lt 26/6/46. Retd GD 27/12/70.
MOULE A. L., BSc. Born 6/12/47. Commd 14/5/73. Sqn Ldr 1/1/85. Retd GD 14/6/98.
MOULE D. E., DFC. Born 28/12/56. Commd 6/11/80. Sqn Ldr 1/7/89. Retd GD 7/7/97.
MOULE D. G. Born 27/10/32. Commd 26/3/52. Wg Cdr 1/7/83. Retd GD 1/1/87.
MOULES P. L., BA. Born 27/3/50. Commd 15/9/69. Wg Cdr 1/7/86. Retd GD 27/3/91.
MOULES P. S., AFC. Born 23/4/23. Commd 8/2/43. Flt Lt 8/2/48. Retd GD 23/4/83.
MOULL A. P., BA. Born 27/4/35. Commd 25/2/64. Flt Lt 13/2/69. Retd SUP 8/1/83.
MOULTON J. E. Born 22/3/43. Commd 14/6/63. Wg Cdr 1/1/85. Retd SUP 22/3/98.
MOULTON L. H., CB DFC CEng FIEE FIMgt. Born 3/12/15. Commd 26/4/41. AVM 1/1/69. Retd ENG 15/3/71.
MOUNFIELD P. A., MB BS MRCOG. Born 4/12/31. Commd 8/9/57. Wg Cdr 8/9/70. Retd MED 8/9/73.

MOUNSEY E. R., DFC. Born 21/7/21. Commd 1/4/44. Flt Lt 1/10/47. Retd SEC 15/8/65.
MOUNSEY J. A. B., MBE MRCS LRCP FIMgt. Born 14/9/20. Commd 23/5/46. Gp Capt 1/1/67. Retd MED 31/3/78.
MOUNSEY J. S. Born 29/10/28. Commd 18/2/60. Flt Lt 18/2/65. Retd ENG 18/2/68.
MOUNSEY The Rev W. L. F., BD. Born 31/10/51. Commd 17/5/81. Retd 31/7/90 Sqn Ldr.
MOUNT C. J., CBE DSO DFC BA. Born 14/12/13. Commd 26/12/36. A Cdre 1/1/58. Retd GD 26/12/66.
MOUNTAIN D. Born 20/10/41. Commd 11/5/78. Flt Lt 11/5/80. Retd ENG 11/5/86.
MOUNTAIN J. B., MBE. Born 6/10/30. Commd 6/12/51. Wg Cdr 1/1/71. Retd GD 30/5/78.
MOUNTAIN P. Born 18/11/38. Commd 20/11/75. Flt Lt 20/11/78. Retd GD 3/9/89.
MOUNTER D. J., BSc. Born 6/2/43. Commd 8/4/68. Flt Lt 6/10/71. Retd ENG 16/6/89.
MOUNTFORD J. C. M., AFC. Born 20/2/21. Commd 10/7/39. Sqn Ldr 1/1/49. Retd GD 25/3/58.
MOUNTNEY M. C., Commd 27/8/87. Fg Offr 18/7/88. Retd ADMIN 1/2/91.
MOWAT J. Born 14/3/47. Commd 5/11/65. Flt Lt 4/5/72. Retd GD 2/6/76.
MOWBRAY F. J., CEng MIEE. Born 19/12/09. Commd 24/7/41. Wg Cdr 1/7/54. Retd ENG 19/12/64.
MOWBRAY R. G., BSc. Born 8/1/58. Commd 28/9/80. Flt Lt 28/12/81. Retd GD 28/9/96.
MOXAM L. R., MBE. Born 24/9/31. Commd 27/6/51. Sqn Ldr 1/1/63. Retd GD 31/12/64.
MOXEY B. W., BSc. Born 12/11/51. Commd 13/9/70. Sqn Ldr 1/1/81. Retd ADMIN 12/11/89.
MOXLEY The Rev C. E., MA. Born 28/10/09. Commd 1/9/44. Retd 21/10/50 recalled 1/12/52 to 16/10/65 Gp Capt.
MOXON R. H. Born 9/2/44. Commd 11/11/65. Flt Lt 9/2/71. Retd ADMIN 9/2/82.
MOXON W. A. Born 21/11/23. Commd 18/11/54. Flt Lt 18/11/60. Retd GD 31/7/73.
MOY D. B., BA. Born 31/10/33. Commd 1/1/63. Sqn Ldr 1/3/68. Retd ADMIN 1/1/79.
MOYCE D. J. Born 28/1/32. Commd 30/4/62. Wg Cdr 1/7/77. Retd GD(G) 28/1/87.
MOYES D. D. Born 1/4/34. Commd 8/5/53. Flt Lt 10/9/58. Retd GD 30/9/77. Reinstated 3/6/81. Flt Lt 14/5/62. Retd GD 1/4/89.
MOYES W., MBE. Born 6/1/25. Commd 30/9/48. Sqn Ldr 1/4/56. Retd ENG 6/1/80.
MUDDLE A. R. Born 27/6/35. Commd 4/5/72. Sqn Ldr 1/7/84. Retd ENG 8/8/86.
MUDE K. H., DFM. Born 2/2/22. Commd 16/7/4. Sqn Ldr 1/7/60. Retd GD 30/6/73.
MUDFORD J. J. Born 9/5/29. Commd 16/12/52. Sqn Ldr 1/7/63. Retd GD 16/12/68.
MUDGE R. F. Born 10/11/33. Commd 18/3/53. Wg Cdr 1/7/70. Retd GD 26/1/82.
MUDGE R. P. Born 13/3/21. Commd 22/10/59. Sqn Ldr 1/1/72. Retd ENG 30/8/75.
MUGFORD C. F. Born 6/3/35. Commd 22/7/53. Flt Lt 28/7/59. Retd GD 31/3/74.
MUGFORD D. M. T., BSc. Born 20/11/41. Commd 10/4/67. Sqn Ldr 1/1/74. Retd ENG 10/4/83.
MUGRIDGE C. A. Born 26/5/43. Commd 14/6/63. Flt Lt 14/12/68. Retd GD 2/3/76.
MUGRIDGE J. R. Born 23/12/42. Commd 17/12/64. Flt Lt 17/12/69. Retd SUP 21/7/83.
MUIR D. W. F. Born 15/4/26. Commd 22/2/46. Flt Lt 22/8/49. Retd GD 15/4/64.
MUIR J. Born 5/1/34. Commd 21/10/66. Flt Lt 21/10/71. Retd ENG 5/1/89.
MUIR J. S. C. Born 23/10/37. Commd 10/2/56. Wg Cdr 1/1/81. Retd GD 23/10/92.
MUIR R. W. Born 19/8/40. Commd 25/1/63. Flt Lt 8/1/69. Retd GD 2/10/78.
MUIRHEAD G. K., DFM. Born 22/3/20. Commd 10/6/41. Sqn Ldr 1/7/57. Retd GD 22/3/69.
MULCAHY P. L. Born 28/4/58. Commd 22/2/79. Sqn Ldr 1/7/89. Retd GD 17/12/96.
MULDOWNEY A. J. Born 8/2/60. Commd 23/4/87. Flt Lt 23/4/89. Retd ENG 8/2/98.
MULGREW K. Born 25/12/56. Commd 20/12/90. Flt Lt 20/12/92. Retd GD 5/1/01.
MULHALL T. A. Born 29/9/51. Commd 15/8/85. Sqn Ldr 1/7/95. Retd ENG 22/1/98.
MULHEARN The Rev K. J. Born 12/8/26. Commd 18/10/61. Retd 18/10/77 Gp Capt.
MULHOLLAND H. Born 3/5/10. Commd 6/9/46. Flt Lt 6/9/46. Retd PRT 6/11/59 rtg Sqn Ldr.
MULINDER W. D., AFC. Born 23/1/34. Commd 29/3/63. Wg Cdr 1/1/79. Retd GD 24/9/88.
MULKERN A. M. M., BSc. Commd 23/9/68. Sqn Ldr 1/1/83. Retd ADMIN 1/1/86.
MULKERN P. F. Born 30/9/44. Commd 25/2/66. Sqn Ldr 1/1/93. Retd GD 12/4/95.
MULLAN J. A., BEM. Born 8/3/42. Commd 23/5/85. Sqn Ldr 1/7/94. Retd ADMIN 8/3/97.
MULLAN J. P. Born 2/8/47. Commd 16/5/71. Flt Lt 4/5/72. Retd GD 14/3/97.
MULLANEY J. M., FIMgt LHSM. Born 17/6/34. Commd 22/5/70. Wg Cdr 1/1/85. Retd MED(SEC) 3/1/87.
MULLARKEY D., MBE. Born 29/8/28. Commd 5/4/50. Wg Cdr 1/7/64. Retd GD 9/4/81.
MULLEN A. B. Born 13/12/43. Commd 9/3/62. Sqn Ldr 1/7/74. Retd SUP 9/9/76.
MULLEN B. J., BSc. Born 16/11/47. Commd 1/11/71. Flt Lt 1/8/73. Retd GD 1/4/92.
MULLEN J. Born 28/1/20. Commd 14/3/57. Sqn Ldr 1/7/67. Retd ENG 31/7/70.
MULLEN J. V. Born 26/3/47. Commd 29/4/71. Flt Lt 3/12/84. Retd GD(G) 4/4/95.
MULLEN J. V. Born 26/3/47. Commd 29/4/71. Flt Lt 3/12/84. Retd GD(G) 4/4/95.
MULLEN N. H. Born 27/4/26. Commd 12/3/64. Flt Lt 12/3/67. Retd GD 17/1/76.
MULLEN P. J. P., MB ChB. Born 24/5/57. Commd 18/10/77. Wg Cdr 1/9/94. Retd MED 14/3/96.
MULLEN T. A. F. Born 22/4/47. Commd 1/3/68. Flt Lt 6/10/71. Retd GD 22/4/91.
MULLEN W. F., BA CEng FIEE FRAeS. Born 24/12/36. Commd 24/7/57. Gp Capt 1/1/81. Retd ENG 6/4/90.
MULLER J. E., BSc. Born 31/3/38. Commd 25/1/71. Flt Lt 25/1/71. Retd EDN 2/9/72.
MULLER M. E. Born 27/7/48. Commd 31/8/78. Flt Lt 31/8/82. ADMIN 1/5/94.
MULLETT C., MBE. Born 24/5/22. Commd 25/6/65. Flt Lt 25/6/71. Retd ADMIN 28/1/78.
MULLEY J. L., BSc. Born 18/6/45. Commd 2/3/70. Flt Lt 2/6/73. Retd ENG 2/3/86.
MULLIGAN S. K. Born 17/1/36. Commd 27/6/59. Flt Lt 27/12/64. Retd GD 1/5/79.
MULLINEAUX R. H., FIMgt. Born 12/12/25. Commd 29/6/50. Gp Capt 1/1/76. Retd GD 3/4/79.

MULLINGER J. R. Born 25/4/44. Commd 1/4/71. Sqn Ldr 1/1/92. Retd ADMIN 25/4/00.
MULLINGS W. M. Born 17/5/22. Commd 10/3/49. Flt Lt 19/11/53. Retd PE 3/5/64.
MULLINS R. D., AFC. Born 1/3/25. Commd 1/9/44. Wg Cdr 1/1/66. Retd PE 1/9/73.
MULLOOLY J. B. Born 30/5/33. Commd 28/1/53. Flt Lt 17/6/58. Retd GD(G) 9/8/87.
MULROONEY P. L., MB BCh FFA Dip Soton DA. Born 8/6/26. Commd 29/8/54. Wg Cdr 26/10/63. Retd MED 26/9/70.
MULVENNEY W., BA. Born 1/12/40. Commd 6/8/63. Wg Cdr 1/7/85. Retd ADMIN 1/2/91.
MUMBY L. R., OBE. Born 3/8/14. Commd 2/1/39. Gp Capt 1/1/62. Retd SUP 3/8/69.
MUMFORD A., CVO OBE. Born 8/3/36. Commd 9/4/57. Gp Capt 1/7/80. Retd GD 1/6/88.
MUMFORD J. S., BDS. Born 5/11/39. Commd 24/7/62. Wg Cdr 12/12/76. Retd DEL 24/7/78.
MUMFORD P. Born 21/6/37. Commd 15/9/65. Flt Lt 4/1/71. Retd GD(G) 22/12/87.
MUMMERY B. W., BSc. Born 20/6/39. Commd 27/6/59. Flt Lt 27/12/64. Retd GD 5/11/78.
MUNCASTER A. Born 31/3/51. Commd 21/9/72. Flt Lt 21/3/79. Retd GD(G) 1/4/80.
MUNCASTER G. A. Born14/6/30. Commd 17/12/52. Sqn Ldr 1/7/62. Retd GD 21/5/76.
MUNCASTER G. S. Born 19/12/24. Commd 27/1/45. Flt Lt 7/6/51. Retd SUP 19/12/62.
MUNDAY A. J., BDS LDSRCS. Born 24/10/32. Commd 14/9/58. Wg Cdr 17/3/71. Retd DEL 1/3/91.
MUNDAY A. R., OBE. Born 25/11/23. Commd 27/10/44. Wg Cdr 1/1/63. Retd GD 28/3/78.
MUNDAY B. Born 10/7/42. Commd 3/11/77. Flt Lt 3/11/79. Retd GD 31/3/94.
MUNDAY D. A. P., MIMgt. Born 5/11/36. Commd 30/7/57. Sqn Ldr 1/1/68. Retd SUP 5/11/74.
MUNDAY J. R. Born 9/4/48. Commd 2/1/70. Flt Lt 2/7/75. Retd GD 9/4/86.
MUNDAY K. N. Born 27/12/39. Commd 14/8/80. Flt Lt 14/8/83. Retd GD 27/12/94.
MUNDAY V. D., BSc. Born 2/9/39. Commd 19/2/63. Sqn Ldr 1/7/73. Retd SUP 2/9/94.
MUNDEN M. A. Born 5/11/32. Commd 13/9/51. Flt Lt 4/1/57. Retd GD 15/12/83.
MUNDY A. H. Born 31/5/20. Commd 31/5/43. Flt Lt 30/11/46. Retd GD 30/11/60.
MUNDY C. P. Born 5/7/23. Commd 20/8/43. Sqn Ldr 1/1/57. Retd GD 31/7/58.
MUNDY D. Born 5/9/43. Commd 8/1/76. Sqn Ldr 1/7/83. Retd ADMIN 8/1/90. Re-entered 2/9/94. Sqn Ldr 23/2/88. Retd ADMIN 5/9/99.
MUNDY D. Born 5/9/43. Commd 8/1/76. Sqn Ldr 1/7/83. Retd ADMIN 8/1/90.
MUNDY D. A. P., AMIMgt. Born 5/11/36. Commd 30/7/57. Sqn Ldr 1/1/68. Retd SUP 5/11/74.
MUNDY J. D., DFC. Born 14/5/19. Commd 23/1/39. Sqn Ldr 1/8/47. Retd GD 14/5/58.
MUNDY R. F. Born 7/5/35. Commd 9/4/57. Wg Cdr 1/7/73. Retd GD 28/7/89.
MUNGAVIN The Rev G. C. Born 26/2/27. Commd 6/3/62. Retd 6/3/75 Wg Cdr.
MUNN B. P. Born 4/2/47. Commd 7/7/67. Fg Offr 7/7/69. Retd GD 3/10/70.
MUNN B. R. H. Born 26/11/22. Commd 2/10/43. Flt Lt 2/4/47. Retd GD 26/11/65.
MUNN K. A. A. Born 3/4/25. Commd 31/3/45. Sqn Ldr 1/7/72. Retd GD 3/4/76.
MUNNELLY H. M. Born 20/6/62. Commd 30/8/84. Sqn Ldr 1/7/95. Retd GD 20/6/00.
MUNNS R. C., MA CEng MIEE. Born 12/10/53. Commd 2/11/75. Sqn Ldr 1/1/86. Retd ENG 2/11/94.
MUNNS S. A. E., OBE DFM. Born 30/5/19. Commd 5/2/42. Wg Cdr 1/7/58. Retd GD 30/5/74.
MUNRO A. D., BEM. Born 15/10/21. Commd 21/7/55. Sqn Ldr 1/1/69. Retd ENG 15/10/76.
MUNRO A. J. Born 4/5/30. Commd 13/8/52. Flt Lt 9/1/58. Retd GD 4/7/71.
MUNRO A. L. D., BSc. Born 11/10/41. Commd 22/9/63. Sqn Ldr 1/1/81. Retd ENG 2/4/92.
MUNRO The Rev A. W., MA BD. Born 7/8/49. Commd 11/6/78. Retd 11/6/94 Wg Cdr.
MUNRO C. A., BSc(Eng). Born 15/1/62. Commd 14/9/80. Flt Lt 15/4/85. Retd GD 15/1/00.
MUNRO D. G., AFM. Born 4/3/24. Commd 17/3/55. Flt Lt 17/3/61. Retd GD 28/6/68.
MUNRO J., AFC. Born 2/3/23. Commd 7/9/44. Sqn Ldr 1/7/63. Retd GD 16/7/68.
MUNRO J. Born 7/3/34. Commd 1/1/64. Sqn Ldr 1/7/74. Retd GD 1/9/87.
MUNRO M. R., BSc CEng MRAeS. Born 18/2/48. Commd 18/9/66. Wg Cdr 1/1/88. Retd ENG 1/8/98.
MUNRO P. Born 15/11/18. Commd 4/3/54. Flt Lt 4/3/57. Retd SEC 16/11/67.
MUNRO R. V. A., AFC*. Born 8/6/31. Commd 6/12/51. Sqn Ldr 1/1/69. Retd GD 23/4/76.
MUNSLOW C. H. J. Born 18/4/40. Commd 25/2/65. Flt Lt 25/2/69. Retd SUP 18/4/78. Reinstated 11/6/79. Flt Lt 20/4/70. Retd SUP 19/4/90.
MUNSLOW W., BEng. Born 24/3/61. Commd 13/7/90. Flt Lt 15/7/93. Retd ENG 24/3/99.
MUNSON D. H. G., BSc CEng MRAeS. Born 15/11/25. Commd 18/7/49. Sqn Ldr 1/1/57. Retd ENG 15/11/80.
MUNT M. H. Born 4/1/31. Commd 5/7/53. Flt Lt 29/4/59. Retd GD 4/1/69.
MUNYARD R. S., AFC. Born 10/3/43. Commd 19/8/66. Flt Lt 1/3/69. Retd GD 10/3/81.
MURCHIE I. T. A., MSc MIMechE FRAeS. Born 11/12/22. Commd 15/4/43. Wg Cdr 1/1/60. Retd ENG 22/6/68.
MURCHIE J. W. Born 4/4/17. Commd 31/1/44. Flt Lt 31/7/48. Retd SUP 16/6/66 rtg Sqn Ldr.
MURCUTT B. J., MIMgt. Born 3/4/34. Commd 8/7/65. Sqn Ldr 1/7/80. Retd SY 9/4/85.
MURDEN M. A., CEng MIMechE MIProdE MRAeS. Born 1/12/35. Commd 24/7/57. Sqn Ldr 1/7/66. Retd ENG 29/12/73.
MURDOCH C. J. B., AFM. Born 16/5/25. Commd 18/10/62. Flt Lt 18/10/65. Retd GD 31/3/74.
MURDOCH M. A. Born 22/8/54. Commd 17/5/79. Sqn Ldr 1/7/90. Retd GD 1/6/97.
MURDOCK A. E. Born 9/12/14. Commd 30/5/46. Flt Lt 30/11/50. Retd SEC 9/12/63.
MURDOCK B. Born 7/9/47. Commd 20/12/73. Flt Lt 3/4/76. Retd GD 22/4/94.
MURFITT K. P. Born 20/8/32. Commd 2/1/54. Flt Lt 5/10/60. Retd GD 20/8/87.
MURKIN D. A., BEM. Born 8/2/32. Commd 29/7/65. Flt Lt 29/7/71. Retd SY 7/8/82.

MURKOWSKI A. S. Born 19/4/20. Commd 17/5/56. Flt Lt 17/5/59. Retd GD 19/4/75.
MURLAND H. F., MIMgt. Born 12/4/23. Commd 12/7/44. Sqn Ldr 1/7/65. Retd SEC 4/4/70.
MURLEY H. T., DFC AFC* MRAeS. Born 9/9/23. Commd 10/5/44. Wg Cdr 1/1/62. Retd GD 31/3/75.
MURPHY A. Born 11/8/56. Commd 16/9/76. Sqn Ldr 1/1/89. Retd GD 1/5/95.
MURPHY B. M. P., BSc MRAeS. Born 16/9/41. Commd 4/10/65. Sqn Ldr 1/7/91. Retd GD 16/9/96.
MURPHY D. H., BA FRCS(Glas) MRCS LRCP. Born 31/7/30. Commd 7/7/57. Gp Capt 1/2/82. Retd MED 8/7/86.
MURPHY D. T. Born 8/2/31. Commd 12/1/61. Flt Lt 12/1/66. Retd GD 8/2/88.
MURPHY F. E., MBE. Born 17/1/12. Commd 3/12/42. Sqn Ldr 1/10/55. Retd ENG 17/1/68.
MURPHY G., MIMgt. Born 29/5/23. Commd 7/8/42. Sqn Ldr 1/1/55. Retd GD 1/2/71.
MURPHY J. C. Born 12/1/48. Commd 23/9/66. Wg Cdr 1/1/88. Retd SY 31/3/94.
MURPHY J. E. T., OBE. Born 18/3/17. Commd 23/1/39. Sqn Ldr 1/7/48. Retd SUP 27/5/53 rtg Wg Cdr.
MURPHY J. J., OBE CEng MIMechE. Born 26/10/06. Commd 10/10/30. A Cdre 1/1/58. Retd ENG 21/10/61.
MURPHY J. J. Born 2/8/57. Commd 12/10/78. Flt Lt 12/4/84. Retd GD 25/6/90.
MURPHY J. N. Born 25/12/28. Commd 13/12/50. Flt Lt 13/6/53. Retd GD 25/12/66.
MURPHY K. P. Born 12/2/24. Commd 3/6/57. Flt Lt 1/3/61. Retd SUP 2/12/75.
MURPHY M. J., IEng. Born 24/12/40. Commd 9/2/66. Sqn Ldr 1/7/76. Retd ENG 24/12/95.
MURPHY M. L. Born 7/5/60. Commd 8/4/82. Flt Lt 8/10/87. Retd GD 11/8/89.
MURPHY P. B., CEng MIEE. Born 5/1/42. Commd 23/6/67. Wg Cdr 1/7/84. Retd ENG 29/12/95.
MURPHY S. D. A., BDS. Born 10/11/38. Commd 9/6/63. Wg Cdr 9/6/76. Retd DEL 29/6/88.
MURPHY S. P., MA CEng MIEE MIMgt. Born 9/12/51. Commd 13/9/70. Wg Cdr 1/7/90. Retd ENG 14/9/96.
MURPHY T. G. Born 4/11/32. Commd 23/8/51. Flt Lt 30/11/59. Retd GD 1/10/76.
MURPHY T. J. Born 4/3/13. Commd 15/5/58. Flt Lt 15/5/63. Retd ENG 15/5/68.
MURPHY W. Born 23/12/19. Commd 15/10/43. Sqn Ldr 1/4/56. Retd ENG 27/6/70.
MURRAY A. D., AFC. Born 18/11/46. Commd 2/6/67. Flt Lt 2/12/72. Retd GD 7/4/79.
MURRAY A. R., MA CEng MRAeS. Born 1/12/30. Commd 26/9/53. Gp Capt 1/7/81. Retd ENG 3/4/85.
MURRAY A. S., BSc. Born 12/6/47. Commd 20/4/71. Sqn Ldr 1/1/84. Retd GD 30/12/88.
MURRAY C., OBE. Born 28/5/15. Commd 23/1/39. Gp Capt 1/7/66. Retd SUP 28/5/70.
MURRAY C., BSc. Born 24/2/41. Commd 25/1/63. Flt Lt 3/10/67. Retd ENG 24/8/82.
MURRAY C. G. Born 19/5/45. Commd 4/6/64. Flt Lt 20/10/70. Retd GD(G) 19/5/83.
MURRAY D., MB BS MRCP. Born 29/5/43. Commd 16/9/63. Gp Capt 19/8/91. Retd MED 14/3/96.
MURRAY D. C., MA. Born 6/8/41. Commd 11/3/62. Fg Offr 15/4/63. Retd GD 14/9/65.
MURRAY F. G. Born 27/2/25. Commd 6/3/57. Flt Lt 21/8/63. Retd SUP 26/6/72.
MURRAY G. S. Born 22/11/22. Commd 25/5/44. Sqn Ldr 1/7/70. Retd GD 1/5/73.
MURRAY I. R. Born 28/1/47. Commd 11/4/85. Sqn Ldr 20/12/94. Retd MED(T) 16/8/98.
MURRAY J. MacL., ACA. Born 18/7/01. Commd 10/11/24. Sqn Ldr 1/12/38. Retd SEC 10/11/41 rtg Wg Cdr.
MURRAY J. R. Born 9/9/35. Commd 9/7/57. Sqn Ldr 1/7/70. Retd GD 6/1/84.
MURRAY K. F. C. Born 11/3/55. Commd 3/7/80. Sqn Ldr 1/1/90. Retd SUP 11/3/95.
MURRAY L. C. Born 15/10/19. Commd 17/12/43. Flt Lt 29/11/51. Retd GD(G) 2/10/63.
MURRAY M. J. Born 5/2/53. Commd 27/1/77. Sqn Ldr 1/1/88. Retd ADMIN 9/8/98.
MURRAY M. R. Born 1/9/34. Commd 15/6/53. Sqn Ldr 1/7/90. Retd GD 29/7/93.
MURRAY P. A. L. Born 16/5/21. Commd 22/8/41. Flt Lt 1/9/45. Retd SEC 29/1/56.
MURRAY P. G. E., MRAeS FIMgt. Born 22/5/37. Commd 22/7/66. Wg Cdr 1/1/79. Retd MED(T) 1/12/86.
MURRAY P. S., BSc. Born 25/7/52. Commd 6/4/72. Sqn Ldr 1/1/85. Retd GD 17/1/86.
MURRAY R. A., MBE MIMgt. Born 19/5/40. Commd 9/3/62. Wg Cdr 1/7/84. Retd SY 16/5/91.
MURRAY R. S. Born 14/11/23. Commd 23/8/56. Flt Lt 23/8/62. Retd GD 14/11/73.
MURRAY T. C., DSO DFC*. Born 31/5/18. Commd 17/12/38. Wg Cdr 1/7/50. Retd GD 13/5/59.
MURRAY T. G. Born 30/9/30. Commd 24/9/64. Flt Lt 24/9/69. Retd GD(G) 31/1/76.
MURRAY T. J. Born 4/12/43. Commd 16/9/67. Gp Capt 1/7/93. Retd GD 4/12/98.
MURRAY-ROCHARD A. L., OBE. Born 2/5/25. Commd 7/3/46. Wg Cdr 1/1/64. Retd ENG 30/11/78.
MURRELL G. M. Born 14/4/37. Commd 8/10/70. Sqn Ldr 1/7/80. Retd GD 25/5/84.
MURRIE The Rev J., BD. Born 13/1/26. Commd 1/9/54. Retd 1/9/70 Wg Cdr.
MURROW J. S. Born 22/5/29. Commd 11/3/65. Sqn Ldr 1/7/76. Retd GD 22/5/87.
MURTAGH M. L., BA. Born 12/2/53. Commd 18/10/81. Flt Lt 18/1/85. Retd ADMIN 18/10/97.
MURTON B., BSc. Born 7/4/40. Commd 2/1/67. Sqn Ldr 2/2/73. Retd ADMIN 1/11/77.
MURTY J. K., BSc. Born 12/5/50. Commd 3/10/68. Sqn Ldr 1/7/85. Retd GD 13/7/00.
MURZYN J. F. Born 10/7/19. Commd 14/11/57. Flt Lt 14/11/60. Retd GD(G) 11/9/65.
MUSE R. W. Born 24/4/45. Commd 13/1/67. Flt Lt 13/7/72. Retd OPS SPT 15/12/98.
MUSGRAVE A. B., BSc. Born 5/2/29. Commd 16/6/53. Sqn Ldr 1/1/61. Retd GD 16/6/69.
MUSGRAVE C. M. Born 27/10/42. Commd 15/7/63. Wg Cdr 1/1/79. Retd ENG 1/1/82.
MUSGRAVE J. R., MC. Born 15/11/15. Commd 11/10/41. Flt Lt 11/10/43. Retd LGL 1/11/49.
MUSGRAVE J. R., DSO TD. Born 22/6/18. Commd 12/11/41. Gp Capt 1/1/67. Retd GD 31/3/70.
MUSGRAVE W. Born 27/12/22. Commd 17/2/47. Flt Lt 9/6/52. Retd GD 26/7/61.
MUSGROVE A. C., AFC*. Born 10/1/20. Commd 29/3/48. Sqn Ldr 1/9/65. Retd GD 1/2/73.
MUSGROVE S. A. Born 11/11/33. Commd 12/3/52. Flt Lt 10/7/57. Retd GD 11/11/71.
MUSHENS A. Born 25/7/34. Commd 8/10/52. Flt Lt 6/3/58. Retd GD 25/7/89.
MUSKER C. N., CEng MIMechE. Born 3/8/30. Commd 24/3/69. Wg Cdr 1/1/75. Retd ENG 2/4/82.

MUSSARD R. W., MSc BSc CEng MIMechE. Born 25/1/50. Commd 26/2/71. Sqn Ldr 1/7/85. Retd ENG 1/10/92.
MUSTARD J. E. M., BSc. Born 5/5/47. Commd 1/9/70. Sqn Ldr 1/1/86. Retd GD 1/1/89.
MUTCH J., CBE CEng FIMechE. Born 13/3/07. Commd 28/7/28. A Cdre 1/1/56. Retd ENG 1/10/58.
MUTCH P., MSc BEd. Born 27/6/58. Commd 23/9/79. Sqn Ldr 1/1/89. Retd ADMIN 14/3/97.
MUTCH T. Born 22/7/24. Commd 14/2/63. Flt Lt 14/2/66. Retd GD 1/11/73.
MUTSAARS J. A. B. Born 2/11/31. Commd 26/3/59. Wg Cdr 1/1/79. Retd GD 2/11/88.
MUTTON R. F. Born 18/4/10. Commd 17/4/47. Flt Lt 19/6/52. Retd SUP 10/1/56.
MYALL D. M. Born 18/1/45. Commd 2/8/68. Flt Lt 1/7/79. Retd 18/1/00.
MYATT W. G., AFC. Born 17/4/24. Commd 26/2/45. Flt Lt 26/8/48. Retd GD 17/4/62.
MYERS A. B. Born 12/1/70. Commd 30/3/89. Flt Lt 30/9/93. Retd GD 21/12/96.
MYERS F. J. Born 28/7/24. Commd 7/5/53. Sqn Ldr 1/9/65. Retd GD 31/3/74.
MYERS G. Born 28/5/25. Commd 22/5/45. Sqn Ldr 1/7/56. Retd GD 2/7/74.
MYERS J. R., LLB. Born 2/5/36. Commd 10/10/58. Wg Cdr 1/1/81. Retd ADMIN 1/12/91.
MYERS J. R. Born 29/5/45. Commd 10/1/69. Flt Lt 10/7/74. Retd GD 19/8/84.
MYERS L. E. Born 6/12/48. Commd 22/12/67. Flt Lt 22/6/73. Retd GD 6/12/86.
MYERS N. Born 14/3/14. Commd 17/4/47. Sqn Ldr 1/1/70. Retd SUP 1/1/73.
MYLES W. S. Born 6/4/37. Commd 21/10/66. Flt Lt 27/1/69. Retd SEC 6/4/75.

# N

NADIN J. L. Born 3/11/48. Commd 8/6/84. Sqn Ldr 1/7/92. Retd SUP 14/3/96.
NADIN W. V., AFC. Born 24/5/23. Commd 18/2/60. Flt Lt 1/4/63. Retd GD 24/5/83.
NAGLE P. M. Born 4/6/38. Commd 3/9/60. Flt Lt 3/3/66. Retd GD 4/6/76.
NAIDO B. S. Born 11/5/40. Commd 10/11/61. Sqn Ldr. 1/1/74. Retd GD 11/5/78.
NAILARD A. C. L., BSc. Born 22/5/61. Commd 16/9/79. Flt Lt 15/10/83. Retd GD 22/2/96.
NAILE L. S. Born 18/2/29. Commd 19/4/51. Flt Lt 17/10/56. Retd GD 18/2/67.
NAILER R. G., OBE CEng, FIMechE. Born 6/5/45. Commd 15/7/66. Gp Capt 1/7/89. Retd ENG 1/9/91.
NAIRN R. McF. Born 22/12/29. Commd 6/6/57. Flt Lt 7/3/62. Retd GD 22/12/67.
NAISH D. J. Born 14/9/31. Commd 11/3/65. Fg Offr 2/11/66. Retd MED(T) 20/9/69.
NANCARROW J. H. Born 14/5/14. Commd 12/9/38. Gp Capt 1/7/58. Retd SUP 12/6/70.
NANCE C. T., OBE MA CEng MIMechE MRAeS. Born 27/3/19. Commd 10/1/41. A Cdre 1/7/66. Retd ENG 27/3/76.
NANCE E. J., OBE. Born 30/3/36. Commd 17/12/57. Wg Cdr 1/7/73. Retd GD 7/7/78.
NANNERY C. J. Born 6/5/47. Commd 8/1/76. Sqn Ldr 1/7/83. Retd SUP 19/3/88.
NAPIER J. J. Born 11/4/43. Commd 2/6/67. Flt Lt 2/6/71. Retd GD 4/6/83.
NAPIER M. J. W., BSc(Eng). Born 20/9/59. Commd 4/9/78. Sqn Ldr 1/1/92. Retd GD 20/9/97.
NAPIER R. W., MBE. Born 4/5/32. Commd 22/7/66. Sqn Ldr 1/1/75. Retd ENG 17/7/82.
NAPLES W. B. B., MIMgt. Born 25/12/20. Commd 9/10/42. Sqn Ldr 1/10/55. Retd GD 25/12/69.
NARDONE S. G. Born 22/6/65. Commd 15/2/90. Flt Lt 3/3/92. Retd GD 14/3/96.
NARSEY A. K., BEng. Born 23/1/61. Commd 3/8/88. Flt Lt 15/7/91. Retd ENG 23/1/99.
NASH A. Born 31/7/46. Commd 2/12/66. Flt Lt 2/6/72. Retd GD 1/10/89.
NASH A. STJ. Born 22/4/65. Commd 26/4/84. Flt Lt 26/10/89. Retd GD 14/3/97.
NASH C. C., BA. Born 11/4/46. Commd 12/4/73. Wg Cdr 1/7/90. Retd OPS SPT 11/4/01.
NASH F. C. Born 26/12/41. Commd 17/7/70. Flt Lt 17/7/72. Retd GD(G) 26/12/79.
NASH J. A. Born 28/6/57. Commd 23/11/78. Sqn Ldr 1/7/91. Retd GD 5/4/99.
NASH J. M. Born 19/5/36. Commd 27/7/61. Sqn Ldr 1/1/72. Retd GD 4/11/86.
NASH L., BSc. Born 9/12/40. Commd 6/9/63. Flt Lt 18/12/67. Retd GD 18/6/79.
NASH L. A., CEng MRAeS. Born 8/12/32. Commd 22/7/55. Wg Cdr 1/1/76. Retd ENG 30/4/83.
NASH M. A., MBA BSc. Born 12/7/57. Commd 14/9/75. Sqn Ldr 1/1/88. Retd SY 12/7/95.
NASH M. C. Born 26/1/33. Commd 12/7/51. Flt Lt 11/1/57. Retd GD 26/1/88.
NASH M. R., AFC. Born 14/4/31. Commd 4/6/52. Sqn Ldr 1/7/66. Retd GD 3/2/76.
NASH P. Born 14/4/56. Commd 27/3/75. Flt Lt 27/9/81. Retd GD(G) 14/4/94.
NASH P. J., MB ChB FFARCS DA. Born 21/4/44. Commd 29/6/64. Sqn Ldr 30/7/73. Retd MED 3/1/76.
NASH R. A. Born 3/11/24. Commd 19/12/47. Wg Cdr 1/7/70. Retd GD 2/4/74.
NASH T. H. S. Born 23/7/38. Commd 28/11/60. Flt Lt 28/5/66. Retd GD 28/11/76.
NASH T. J., OBE AFC FIMgt MRAeS. Born 21/5/37. Commd 28/1/58. Gp Capt 1/7/80. Retd GD 31/10/83.
NAST M. J. Born 3/12/22. Commd 13/7/61. Flt Lt 13/7/64. Retd GD 14/10/72.
NATION B. H. G. Born 15/5/18. Commd 24/9/44. Flt Lt 24/3/48. Retd GD 15/5/61.
NATTRASS D. H., BSc MCIT MILT. Born 7/6/57. Commd 3/5/81. Flt Lt 3/11/84. Retd SUP 14/9/96.
NATTRASS T., CBE AFC*. Born 21/4/41. Commd 11/6/60. A Cdre 1/1/89. Retd GD 2/11/91.
NAUGHTON The Rev E. B. Born 26/1/34. Commd 18/7/66. Retd 18/7/85. Wg Cdr.
NAYAR V. K. Born 30/12/41. Commd 8/7/65. Sqn Ldr 1/1/75. Retd SUP 1/10/85.
NAYLOR B. F., MBE. Born 10/6/30. Commd 22/9/67. Flt Lt 22/9/69. Retd REG 10/6/79.
NAYLOR C., OBE. Born 27/5/32. Commd 18/2/54. Wg Cdr 1/7/75. Retd SUP 27/5/87.
NAYLOR M. L., AFC. Born 9/2/47. Commd 21/1/66. Sqn Ldr 1/1/83. Retd GD 1/1/86.
NAYLOR P. W., CEng MIMechE MRAeS. Born 17/5/39. Commd 18/7/61. Sqn Ldr 1/1/72. Retd ENG 20/7/91.
NAYLOR R. Born 7/11/20. Commd 9/6/55. Sqn Ldr 1/1/65. Retd GD(G) 1/6/70.
NAZ P. G., OBE. Born 2/6/35. Commd 8/7/53. A Cdre 1/1/87. Retd GD 4/9/90.
NEAL A. E., AFC FIMgt. Born 17/7/48. Commd 21/4/67. A Cdre 1/7/96. Retd GD 18/5/01.
NEAL D. Born 14/5/24. Commd 18/2/60. Flt Lt 18/2/65. Retd GD 14/5/79.
NEAL J. S. Born 13/5/38. Commd 1/4/76. Sqn Ldr 1/1/91. Retd GD 1/1/94.
NEAL K. L. H., BA. Born 3/2/51. Commd 24/9/72. Flt Lt 24/6/76. Retd GD(G) 31/3/82.
NEAL L. A., MD MB BCh MRCGP DRCOG. Born 4/1/58. Commd 1/8/82. Sqn Ldr 1/8/87. Retd MED 1/8/90. Re-entered 18/10/91. Wg Cdr 18/10/96. Retd MED 1/11/00.
NEAL N. McD., MBE. Born 9/5/22. Commd 1/5/47. Wg Cdr 1/7/73. Retd SUP 6/7/75.
NEAL P. M. Born 1/7/18. Commd 2/9/42. Sqn Offr 1/1/51. Retd SEC 21/10/58.
NEALE A., MBE. Born 9/1/42. Commd 23/11/78. Sqn Ldr 1/1/89. Retd REG 2/4/93.
NEALE A., OBE. Born 1/9/32. Commd 28/7/53. Gp Capt 1/1/80. Retd GD 2/9/86.
NEALE J. C. Born 8/2/35. Commd 17/1/69. Flt Lt 6/10/71. Retd GD 1/3/74.
NEALEY J. R. Born 15/6/36. Commd 1/12/77. Sqn Ldr 1/1/88. Retd ENG 15/6/94.
NEATE K. S. Born 23/7/26. Commd 4/6/64. Sqn Ldr 1/1/77. Retd GD 23/7/84.

NEATE R. G. Born 5/7/18. Commd 12/2/44. Wg Cdr 1/7/61. Retd SEC 30/10/64.
NEDVED V., MBE DFC. Born 27/3/17. Commd 2/8/40. Sqn Ldr 1/7/55. Retd GD 1/10/58 rtg Wg Cdr.
NEEDHAM A. Born 15/5/24. Commd 14/11/49. Flt Lt 24/10/57. Retd SEC 31/8/68.
NEEDHAM A. J. Born 21/10/44. Commd 13/2/64. Gp Capt 1/1/91. Retd GD(G) 21/10/94.
NEEDHAM D. A., BA. Born 27/9/41. Commd 30/7/63. Gp Capt 1/1/90. Retd GD 1/2/94.
NEEDHAM D. E. B. Born 30/3/32. Commd 27/11/55. Flt Lt 6/3/63. Retd SUP 12/1/71.
NEEDHAM D. G. Born 30/4/53. Commd 21/8/72. Sqn Ldr 1/1/84. Retd GD 30/4/91.
NEEDHAM J. R. M., MIMgt. Born 28/12/40. Commd 29/7/65. Sqn Ldr 1/7/79. Retd SUP 28/12/95.
NEEDHAM R. S., MIMgt. Born 7/4/17. Commd 4/7/42. Sqn Ldr 1/1/64. Retd GD(G) 7/4/75.
NEEDHAM R. W. L. Born 18/6/23. Commd 3/6/44. Flt Lt 26/1/59. Retd SEC 18/6/72.
NEIGHBOUR A. J. Born 14/10/47. Commd 29/8/72. Flt Lt 29/8/76. Retd ADMIN 29/8/77. Reinstated 25/9/83.
    Sqn Ldr 1/7/88. Retd ADMIN 31/3/94.
NEIL D. J. Born 29/2/28. Commd 26/5/60. Flt Lt 26/5/65. Retd GD 1/1/76.
NEIL M. J., MBE. Born 18/6/33. Commd 17/1/52. Sqn Ldr 1/7/65. Retd GD 1/1/94.
NEIL P. I. A. Born 29/9/50. Commd 25/2/72. Sqn Ldr 1/7/83. Retd GD 29/9/88.
NEIL R. Born 22/6/26. Commd 23/8/46. Gp Capt 1/1/75. Retd GD 22/6/81.
NEILL A., BSc. Born 27/1/61. Commd 5/9/82. Sqn Ldr 1/1/94. Retd GD 27/1/99.
NEILL C. E. Born 21/12/33. Commd 20/12/51. Sqn Ldr 1/1/69. Retd GD 31/1/71.
NEILSON D.E. Born 15/6/38. Commd 3/11/77. Sqn Ldr 1/1/89. Retd ENG 11/12/91.
NEL L. H. A. Born 11/6/36. Commd 1/4/58. Flt Lt 16/8/61. Retd GD 13/6/69.
NELLIST G., MIMgt. Born 20/11/21. Commd 5/8/43. Flt Lt 4/12/52. Retd GD 1/5/74.
NELSON A. F. Born 23/4/40. Commd 22/5/75. Flt Lt 22/5/78. Retd GD 23/4/95.
NELSON A. G. Born 12/1/30. Commd 26/5/60. Flt Lt 26/5/66. Retd ENG 25/1/85.
NELSON C. R., MA. Born 14/4/51. Commd 6/7/80. Sqn Ldr 1/1/88. Retd ADMIN 14/3/96.
NELSON C. T. M., MBE MIMgt. Born 30/3/40. Commd 15/9/61. Wg Cdr 1/1/88. Retd ADMIN 01/10/92.
NELSON D. H. Born 5/7/19. Commd 9/12/54. Sqn Ldr 1/1/64. Retd GD 5/7/74.
NELSON E. L. Born 23/7/21. Commd 5/8/44. Sqn Ldr 1/1/69. Retd SUP 23/7/76.
NELSON I. H. Born 24/2/39. Commd 29/4/58. Sqn Ldr 1/1/75. Retd GD 1/1/78.
NELSON P. A. Born 30/5/40. Commd 13/12/60. Flt Lt 13/6/63. Retd GD 30/5/78.
NELSON P. E., AFC. Born 27/2/24. Commd 27/2/51. Sqn Ldr 1/7/69. Retd GD 27/2/84.
NELSON Sir Richard, KCB OBE MD. Born 14/11/07. Commd 20/8/34. AM 1/1/63. Retd MED 19/2/67.
NELSON R. B. Born 28/4/37. Commd 17/12/57. Sqn Ldr 1/1/69. Retd GD 18/12/81. Re-entered 19/4/85. Sqn Ldr
    3/5/72. Retd GD 28/4/97.
NELSON T. G., MA. Born 10/7/32. Commd 1/10/54. Sqn Ldr 1/4/66. Retd EDN 25/9/73.
NELSON T. J., MIMgt. Born 20/12/35. Commd 30/7/57. Sqn Ldr 1/7/66. Retd GD 4/4/80.
NELSON-EDWARDS G. H., DFC. Born 8/3/18. Commd 26/9/39. Wg Cdr 1/7/53. Retd GD 30/9/60.
NEO C. K., BSc CEng MRAeS. Born 28/4/47. Commd 1/8/69 Sqn Ldr 1/7/80. Retd ENG 28/4/85.
NEQUEST D., OBE. Born 30/5/46. Commd 5/3/65. Wg Cdr 1/1/90. Retd GD 20/10/96.
NESBITT B. D. Born 23/6/46. Commd 10/6/66. Sqn Ldr 1/1/81. Retd GD(G) 1/7/87.
NESBITT J. R. Born 31/3/29. Commd 30/7/53. Flt Lt 30/1/58. Retd GD 3/8/76.
NESBITT R. C. Born 27/12/28. Commd 8/11/62. Sqn Ldr 1/1/80. Retd GD 2/12/80.
NESS A. M. Born 29/4/59. Commd 20/7/78. Fg Offr 20/1/81. Retd GD(G) 22/11/82.
NESS G. G. Born 28/1/27. Commd 7/5/52. Flt Lt 2/10/57. Retd GD 1/8/75 rtg Sqn Ldr.
NESS Sir Charles., KCB CBE CBIM MCIPD. Born 4/4/24. Commd 8/9/44. AM 1/7/80. Retd 18/7/83.
NETHERTON-SINCLAIR D. A., BA DPhysEd MCIPD. Born 21/7/46. Commd 29/8/72. Sqn Ldr 28/2/77. Retd ADMIN
    29/8/88.
NETTLESHIP G. W., MRIN MIMgt. Born 18/12/28. Commd 4/6/52. Flt Lt 30/10/57. Retd GD 18/12/83.
NETTLEY R. E. W., BA. Born 9/11/27. Commd 25/5/50. Wg Cdr 1/7/67. Retd GD 14/3/78.
NEUBROCH H., OBE FIMgt. Born 7/5/23. Commd 14/5/43. Gp Capt 1/1/66. Retd GD 7/5/78.
NEVE A. C. P., MBE MIMgt. Born 12/11/23. Commd 1/1/45. Sqn Ldr 1/7/61. Retd SEC 12/11/83.
NEVE R., CEng MRAeS. Born 21/11/39. Commd 28/7/60. Sqn Ldr 1/7/69. Retd ENG 21/11/77. Reinstated 3/6/81. Sqn
    Ldr 11/1/73. Retd ENG 21/11/94.
NEVE W. J. Born 2/5/20. Commd 19/8/42. Sqn Ldr 1/1/63. Retd ENG 4/7/70.
NEVELL V. H. Born 12/9/07. Commd 8/10/42. Flt Lt 8/10/47. Retd SEC 30/6/58.
NEVES R. E. H. Born 5/11/32. Commd 28/7/53. Gp Capt 1/7/83. Retd ADMIN 5/11/87.
NEVILL J. E., OBE FIMgt MRAeS. Born 27/10/35. Commd 31/7/56. Air Cdre 1/7/82. Retd GD 3/4/89.
NEVILLE A. J., DFC. Born 22/11/20. Commd 27/5/42. Sqn Ldr 1/1/67. Retd GD 22/11/75.
NEVILLE J. Born 14/10/33. Commd 3/3/54. Flt Lt 3/9/59. Retd GD 14/10/71.
NEVILLE R. E., MIMgt. Born 15/9/32. Commd 21/5/52. Gp Capt 1/1/78. Retd GD(G) 31/10/81.
NEVILLE R. E., AFC. Born 21/5/44. Commd 5/3/65. Flt Lt 4/11/70. Retd GD 23/10/84.
NEVILLE T. M. Born 4/7/52. Commd 7/1/71. Sqn Ldr 1/1/85. Retd GD 4/9/90.
NEVISON W. Born 30/10/42. Commd 28/7/64. Wg Cdr 1/1/90. Retd GD 2/4/93.
NEW P. A. Born 16/11/48. Commd 2/6/67. Sqn Ldr 1/1/85. Retd GD 1/7/88.
NEW R. Born 22/10/25. Commd 12/12/47. Wg Cdr 1/7/65. Retd GD 12/12/67.
NEW W. G. Born 10/12/14. Commd 10/5/37. Sqn Ldr 1/9/45. Retd GD 10/2/58 rtg Wg Cdr.
NEWALL D. Born 4/3/43. Commd 28/7/64. Flt Lt 10/2/67. Retd GD 18/10/75.

NEWALL E. R. Born 17/11/44. Commd 8/1/65. Flt Lt 22/8/70. Retd GD(G) 17/11/82. Re-entered 5/5/87. Flt Lt
7/2/75. Retd OPS SPT 29/4/99.
NEWBERRY G., OBE. Born 24/12/18. Commd 13/2/42. Wg Cdr 1/7/56. Retd GD 26/6/73 rtg Gp Capt.
NEWBERRY T. W. Born 13/6/14. Commd 26/6/41. Sqn Ldr 1/8/47. Retd GD 3/7/57.
NEWBERRY D. E., BSc. Born 26/5/55. Commd 2/9/73. Flt Lt 15/10/77. Retd GD 26/5/93.
NEWBERY J. H., DFC. Born 14/1/24. Commd 6/2/51. Sqn Ldr 1/1/75. Retd GD 14/1/82.
NEWBERY M. J. Born 26/10/56. Commd 14/7/77. Flt Lt 14/1/83. Retd GD 26/10/94.
NEWBOLD S. P., BSc. Born 1/10/57. Commd 28/9/80. Flt Lt 28/12/81. Retd GD 28/9/92.
NEWBOULD A. M., BA. Born 3/4/34. Commd 3/8/55. Sqn Ldr 3/2/64. Retd EDN 30/6/78.
NEWBROOK J. C. Born 9/1/15. Commd 15/2/45. Flt Lt 4/6/53. Retd SUP 2/7/64.
NEWBURY C. H. Born 6/7/16. Commd 8/8/46. Sqn Ldr 1/1/71. Retd SUP 30/6/73.
NEWBURY D. J. Born 5/2/33. Commd 22/11/56. Wg Cdr 1/1/80. Retd ADMIN 5/5/91.
NEWBURY R. D., BSc. Born 5/1/44. Commd 17/5/63. Sqn Ldr 1/7/77. Retd ENG 5/1/85.
NEWBY A. J. Born 27/8/13. Commd 27/9/45. Fg Offr 27/3/46. Retd ENG 3/9/46.
NEWBY G. W. E., MCIPD MIMgt. Born 30/8/22. Commd 15/4/44. Wg Cdr 1/1/66. Retd ADMIN 30/3/77.
NEWBY J. C., MIMgt. Born 26/4/30. Commd 26/7/51. Wg Cdr 1/1/67. Retd GD 18/11/72.
NEWELL D., OBE FIMgt. Born 15/6/24. Commd 11/2/44. Gp Capt 1/7/71. Retd GD(G) 4/4/76.
NEWELL D. L. Born 15/11/22. Commd 3/1/52. Flt Lt 13/10/48. Retd SUP 16/11/73.
NEWELL R. G. Born 16/4/32. Commd 15/8/51. Sqn Ldr 1/1/75. Retd GD 16/4/87.
NEWEY V. H., BSc. Born 10/5/60. Commd 23/5/82. Flt Lt 23/11/85. Retd ADMIN 24/9/88.
NEWING A. G. Born 23/4/33. Commd 27/2/52. Flt Lt 21/10/59. Retd GD 23/4/71.
NEWING L. R. Born 1/2/08. Commd 11/4/46. Fg Offr 21/8/46. Retd ENG 4/9/47.
NEWINGTON-IRVING N. J. N. Born 24/3/38. Commd 28/7/60. Flt Lt 1/4/66. Retd SEC 3/8/67.
NEWITT A. E., DFC. Born 1/8/17. Commd 25/10/37. Sqn Ldr 1/1/51. Retd GD 29/11/57 rtg Wg Cdr.
NEWLAND J. C. Born 10/10/44. Commd 15/7/66. Wg Cdr 1/1/85. Retd ADMIN 10/10/88.
NEWLANDS R. M. Born 4/11/36. Commd 10/9/70. Flt Lt 10/9/72. Retd SUP 10/9/78.
NEWMAN B. E. Born 27/12/39. Commd 11/5/62. Fg Offr 11/5/64. Retd GD 25/10/64.
NEWMAN B. H. Born 1/2/37. Commd 9/10/75. Sqn Ldr 1/1/84. Retd SUP 1/2/87.
NEWMAN C. J. Born 24/3/15. Commd 5/5/55. Sqn Ldr 31/12/63. Retd MED(T) 24/3/68.
NEWMAN C. J. V., LDS. Born 8/4/40. Commd 20/9/59. Wg Cdr 1/7/76. Retd DEL 8/4/78.
NEWMAN C. R., MB BS MRCP. Born 17/3/35. Commd 6/11/60. Wg Cdr 17/8/72. Retd MED 1/1/73.
NEWMAN C. R. Born 4/6/39. Commd 22/7/71. Flt Lt 22/7/72. Retd EDN 2/10/79.
NEWMAN C. W. McN., OBE DFC*. Born 2/12/17. Commd 30/7/38. Wg Cdr 1/1/50. Retd GD 2/12/64.
NEWMAN D. A. Born 21/11/33. Commd 23/9/66. Flt Lt 23/9/71. Retd ENG 21/11/88.
NEWMAN E. Born 12/11/29. Commd 5/11/52. Sqn Ldr 1/7/76. Retd GD 12/11/89.
NEWMAN G. S. Born 3/8/36. Commd 30/7/64. Wg Cdr 1/1/84. Retd GD(G) 1/8/88.
NEWMAN H. W. A., CEng MRAeS. Born 2/3/20. Commd 19/8/42. Sqn Ldr 1/7/53. Retd ENG 2/3/75.
NEWMAN K., MBE. Born 4/8/31. Commd 4/2/53. Sqn Ldr 1/1/70. Retd GD 9/9/86.
NEWMAN K. J., MBE DFC. Born 4/7/22. Commd 25/2/44. Wg Cdr 1/1/69. Retd SEC 10/11/73.
NEWMAN M. C. Born 27/4/27. Commd 4/7/51. Sqn Ldr 1/1/60. Retd GD 27/4/65.
NEWMAN M. J. Born 11/7/31. Commd 21/5/53. Sqn Ldr 1/1/68. Retd SUP 11/7/88.
NEWMAN N. J. Born 17/1/47. Commd 4/9/81. Sqn Ldr 1/1/91. Retd ENG 15/4/97.
NEWMAN P. M., OBE. Born 13/6/35. Commd 24/2/67. Wg Cdr 1/7/81. Retd ADMIN 2/4/87.
NEWMAN R. A. Born 15/6/28. Commd 3/5/68. Sqn Ldr 1/7/82. Retd ENG 15/6/86.
NEWMAN R. A. Born 20/10/42. Commd 21/7/65. Sqn Ldr 1/7/90. Retd GD 20/10/97.
NEWMAN R. D. Born 23/11/43. Commd 9/12/71. Flt Lt 9/12/73. Retd GD(G) 14/3/96.
NEWMAN R. H. Born 3/10/34. Commd 6/5/65. Sqn Ldr 1/7/82. Retd GD 1/5/89.
NEWMAN T. C. M., MA. Born 27/6/55. Commd 30/10/77. Sqn Ldr 1/1/89. Retd GD 30/10/93.
NEWMAN T. J. Born 1/3/30. Commd 9/8/51. Wg Cdr 1/1/72. Retd GD 1/3/85.
NEWMAN T. M. Born 15/7/42. Commd 4/10/63. Flt Lt 15/1/68. Retd GD 15/7/80.
NEWMAN T. P., BSc. Born 23/3/48. Commd 3/1/69. Sqn Ldr 1/1/82. Retd GD 2/3/86.
NEWMAN W. A., BA BA ACIS. Born 21/10/37. Commd 17/8/59. Wg Cdr 1/1/80. Retd GD 18/8/88.
NEWNHAM P. R. Born 28/4/61. Commd 30/4/81. Flt Lt 30/10/85. Retd GD 1/6/92.
NEWNS A. F. P., CEng MIEE MIMgt. Born 7/3/45. Commd 16/6/74. Wg Cdr 1/7/90. Retd ENG 16/6/93.
NEWRICK C. W., MA MB BChir FRCPath DCP. Born 23/6/37. Commd 2/9/64. Gp Capt 29/6/86. Retd MED 14/9/96.
NEWSOME C. P., BEd MCIPD. Born 20/3/56. Commd 21/10/79. Sqn Ldr 1/1/88. Retd ADMIN 14/3/96.
NEWSOME P. R. Born 10/1/33. Commd 4/6/52. Sqn Ldr 1/1/65. Retd GD 1/5/76.
NEWTON A. C. Born 30/8/60. Commd 13/12/79. Flt Lt 13/6/84. Retd GD 1/4/96.
NEWTON A. J., BEM. Born 24/12/45. Commd 16/6/88. Flt Lt 16/6/92. Retd ENG 3/4/93.
NEWTON B. H., CB OBE FIMgt. Born 1/4/32. Commd 28/7/53. AVM 1/1/85. Retd GD 9/6/89.
NEWTON B. V. Born 25/11/18. Commd 10/7/43. Flt Lt 10/1/47. Retd GD 11/6/53.
NEWTON D. R. Born 6/11/36. Commd 8/10/63. Flt Lt 8/10/63. Retd GD 8/10/79.
NEWTON D. W. Born 21/9/30. Commd 23/4/52. Flt Lt 5/11/58. Retd GD 15/9/72.
NEWTON E. J. C., BA. Born 5/11/56. Commd 14/10/84. Flt Lt 14/4/87. Retd ADMIN 1/10/89. Re-entered 5/3/90.
Flt Lt 16/9/87. Retd ADMIN 18/3/01.
NEWTON F. A. B., MBE MRAeS MIMgt. Born 26/12/17. Commd 2/1/45. Sqn Ldr 1/1/56. Retd GD 5/4/72.

NEWTON G. A., MBE. Born 23/9/30. Commd 19/12/63. Flt Lt 19/12/69. Retd SEC 4/10/75.
NEWTON G. S. Born 4/5/31. Commd 6/12/51. Wg Cdr 1/1/83. Retd GD 30/8/91.
NEWTON J. K., MSc BSc CEng MIMechE MRAeS. Born 22/4/45. Commd 15/7/66. Gp Capt 1/1/90. Retd ENG 22/4/00.
NEWTON J. M. Born 1/6/56. Commd 17/7/75. Flt Lt 17/1/81. Retd GD 1/6/94.
NEWTON J. R. Born 15/7/50. Commd 1/6/72. Flt Lt 1/12/77. Retd GD 15/7/88.
NEWTON P. A., BSc. Born 27/8/50. Commd 4/5/70. Flt Lt 15/4/73. Retd GD 27/8/88.
NEWTON P. C. Born 27/12/40. Commd 8/6/62. Flt Lt 15/4/70. Retd GD 4/1/72.
NEWTON P. E. Born 13/5/33. Commd 24/7/57. Sqn Ldr 1/7/67. Retd ENG 13/5/71.
NEWTON R. J., BSc(Eng). Born 24/7/45. Commd 26/9/66. Flt Lt 24/1/68. Retd GD 25/10/97.
NEWTON S. A. E. Born 17/9/29. Commd 16/11/51. Wg Cdr 1/7/69. Retd GD 17/10/79.
NEWTON T. H., DSC. Born 1/12/93. Commd 1/4/18. Sqn Ldr 12/12/28. Retd GD 31/12/30.
NEWTON T. J. B. Born 6/1/40. Commd 26/10/62. Flt Lt 26/4/68. Retd GD 10/7/78.
NEWTON W. Born 16/4/13. Commd 1/8/43. Flt Lt 7/6/51. Retd SEC 8/5/65.
NEWTON W. J. Born 3/10/33. Commd 23/7/52. Flt Lt 10/1/63. Retd GD 21/3/75.
NEYHAUL N. J., BA. Born 20/10/60. Commd 4/1/83. Flt Lt 4/7/86. Retd GD(G) 20/12/95.
NIAS T. J., IEng MIIE. Born 10/9/41. Commd 17/7/62. Wg Cdr 1/1/86. Retd ENG 10/9/96.
NIBLETT D. R., MCIPD. Born 13/5/43. Commd 22/9/67. Sqn Ldr 1/1/85. Retd SY 3/4/93.
NIBLOCK L. N. Born 12/6/39. Commd 8/6/84. Flt Lt 1/3/87. Retd GD 23/10/90.
NICE B. A. Born 5/12/31. Commd 5/5/54. Flt Lt 5/11/59. Retd GD 15/2/71.
NICHOL A. J. Born 12/11/63. Commd 4/12/86. Flt Lt 21/8/89. Retd GD 14/3/96.
NICHOL C. R. Born 13/5/60. Commd 11/1/79. Flt Lt 11/7/84. Retd GD 13/5/98.
NICHOL G. R., BSc. Born 11/6/51. Commd 2/9/73. Flt Lt 2/6/74. Retd GD 14/12/90
NICHOL R. S. Born 30/10/21. Commd 20/12/44. Wg Cdr 1/7/61. Retd GD 12/7/70.
NICHOL W. E. Born 10/12/27. Commd 14/11/51. Flt Lt 14/5/56. Retd GD 7/6/68.
NICHOLAS A. F., MBE. Born 10/4/29. Commd 3/5/56. Wg Cdr 1/7/77. Retd GD 10/4/84.
NICHOLAS A. J., OBE MRAeS. Born 3/7/96. Commd 18/3/36. Sqn Ldr 1/6/45. Retd ENG 16/3/51. rtg Gp Capt.
NICHOLAS E. F. Born 4/4/16. Commd 2/10/44. Flt Lt 2/4/48. Retd GD(G) 20/5/71 rtg Sqn Ldr.
NICHOLAS H. J. H. Born 3/7/20. Commd 2/2/56. Flt Lt 2/2/59. Retd RGT 19/8/67.
NICHOLAS J. A. Born 26/12/23. Commd 25/8/44. Sqn Ldr 1/4/58. Retd SEC 31/3/62.
NICHOLAS K. E. Born 5/4/38. Commd 26/5/67. Sqn Ldr 1/1/89. Retd GD 22/9/92.
NICHOLAS R. J. K. Born 30/9/25. Commd 10/11/49. Flt Lt 8/1/59. Retd GD 31/3/69.
NICHOLLS A. C., MIMgt. Born 3/1/34. Commd 24/1/63. Wg Cdr 1/7/80. Retd ADMIN 31/10/88.
NICHOLLS C. A. Born 19/10/50. Commd 22/5/70. Sqn Ldr 1/1/86. Retd GD 1/1/89.
NICHOLLS C. E. Born 21/9/50. Commd 10/1/69. Flt Lt 10/7/74. Retd GD 1/11/75.
NICHOLLS C. H. Born 3/11/52. Commd 1/4/71. Flt Lt 1/10/76. Retd GD 1/10/81.
NICHOLLS D. H., MA MRAeS. Born 7/10/41. Commd 9/11/64. Gp Capt 1/7/91. Retd GD 7/10/96.
NICHOLLS Sir John., KCB CBE DFC AFC. Born 5/7/26. Commd 14/6/46. AM 1/1/78. Retd GD 31/7/80.
NICHOLLS J. A. Born 31/7/10. Commd 17/1/41. Flt Lt 1/7/43. Retd ENG 8/1/46 rtg Sqn Ldr.
NICHOLLS P. M. Born 4/12/44. Commd 29/12/64. Flt Lt 11/12/71. Retd SUP 7/6/93.
NICHOLLS S., AFM. Born 26/3/26. Commd 15/5/58. Flt Lt 15/5/63. Retd GD 26/3/76.
NICHOLS A. Born 18/4/49. Commd 4/6/87. Fg Off 13/9/86. Retd MED 4/6/90
NICHOLS B. Born 18/6/61. Commd 26/11/81. Sqn Ldr 1/7/97. Retd OPS SPT 1/7/00.
NICHOLS B. A. Born 27/12/49. Commd 10/3/77. Flt Lt 10/3/79. Retd GD 18/5/86.
NICHOLS B. G. Born 16/3/39. Commd 18/2/58. Flt Lt 21/8/63. Retd GD 20/11/69. Reinstated 19/3/79. Flt Lt 19/3/79. Retd GD 2/4/90.
NICHOLS C. E., BSc. Born 30/11/43. Commd 28/9/64. Flt Lt 15/4/67. Retd PI 30/11/81.
NICHOLS D. A. G. Born 5/9/42. Commd 31/10/74. Flt Lt 31/10/76. Retd PI 6/9/85.
NICHOLS E. Born 20/2/47. Commd 29/8/72. Flt Lt 24/2/75. Retd GD 14/9/96.
NICHOLS G. C., DFC. Born 19/6/24. Commd 20/11/43. Flt Lt 20/5/47. Retd GD 26/4/50.
NICHOLS G. H. M. Born 25/3/13. Commd 8/5/41. Sqn Ldr 1/7/53. Retd GD(G) 25/3/63.
NICHOLS J. A. Born 27/5/39. Commd 18/8/61. Flt Lt 18/2/67. Retd GD 27/5/94.
NICHOLS M. J., MIISec. Born 3/7/51. Commd 10/9/70. Flt Lt 1/8/76. Retd SY(PRT) 3/7/89.
NICHOLS M. R. Born 7/2/46. Commd 31/10/69. Sqn Ldr 1/1/78. Retd GD 14/9/96.
NICHOLS P. D. H., CEng MIMechE. Born 13/9/36. Commd 23/7/58. Sqn Ldr 1/7/67. Retd ENG 13/9/74.
NICHOLS T. W. Born 20/9/35. Commd 18/8/61. Flt Lt 18/2/67. Retd GD 2/5/77.
NICHOLSON A. A., CBE LVO MA FRAeS. Born 27/6/46. Commd 22/9/65. AVM 1/1/99. Retd GD 27/6/00.
NICHOLSON A. A. N., CBE AE FIMgt. Born 8/3/19. Commd 3/10/39. A Cdre 1/1/66. Retd GD 11/12/70.
NICHOLSON A. C. M., BA. Born 20/6/44. Commd 28/9/64. Flt Lt 15/4/69. Retd GD 19/7/84.
NICHOLSON A. N., OBE PhD MD DSc MB ChB FRCPath FRCP FRCP(Edin) FFOM FRAeS. Born 26/7/34. Commd 4/9/60. A Cdre 18/7/90. Retd MED 1/6/99.
NICHOLSON C. E. Born 21/8/23. Commd 6/7/49. Flt Lt 6/7/53. Retd SEC 24/6/64.
NICHOLSON G. D., BA. Born 15/12/62. Commd 2/9/84. Flt Lt 2/3/88. Retd SUP 14/6/96.
NICHOLSON H. B. Born 11/10/32. Commd 8/10/52. Sqn Ldr 1/7/78. Retd GD(G) 1/2/83.
NICHOLSON I. G. Born 28/2/42. Commd 24/4/64. Fg Offr 24/4/66. Retd GD 24/8/68.
NICHOLSON J. M. Born 8/5/22. Commd 20/11/42. Flt Lt 24/12/48. Retd GD 19/6/54.

NICHOLSON M. H. Born 1/7/18. Commd 13/12/44. Flt Offr 29/11/51. Retd SEC 2/6/61.
NICHOLSON M. J. Born 27/9/49. Commd 28/2/82. Wg Cdr 1/7/99. Retd ADMIN 23/1/01.
NICHOLSON R. P. Born 14/12/27. Commd 14/11/51. Sqn Ldr 1/7/67. Retd GD 15/8/78.
NICHOLSON S. J. Born 15/3/59. Commd 21/6/90. Flt Lt 21/6/92. Retd SUP 14/3/96.
NICHOLSON W. F., FIMgt. Born 9/12/31. Commd 16/7/52. Wg Cdr 1/1/77. Retd GD(G) 21/1/80.
NICKERSON G. J., MIIE(elec). Born 12/3/47. Commd 1/7/82. Flt Lt 1/3/87. Retd ENG 1/1/92.
NICKLEN F. J. Born 25/3/37. Commd 12/12/59. Flt Lt 1/4/66. Retd GD(G) 25/3/75.
NICKLES F. R. Born 27/5/15. Commd 6/9/45. Sqn Ldr 1/1/66. Retd SUP 27/5/72.
NICKLES N. F. Born 2/3/53. Commd 6/4/72. Flt Lt 6/10/77. Retd GD 2/3/91.
NICKLIN J. G. Born 15/11/30. Commd 10/12/52. Flt Lt 17/8/58. Retd GD 15/11/68.
NICKOLLS M. H. Born 8/7/18. Commd 27/10/43. Sqn Ldr 1/7/66. Retd SEC 9/8/68.
NICKS J., BA. Born 30/7/32. Commd 10/9/70. Flt Lt 10/9/74. Retd ENG 3/8/82.
NICKS M., MA BL. Born 30/3/45. Commd 13/8/72. Wg Cdr 13/8/82. Retd LGL 16/9/91.
NICKSON R. E., FIMgt. Born 27/4/40. Commd 1/8/61. Wg Cdr 1/1/83. Retd GD 27/4/95.
NICKSON V. J., AFC MIMgt. Born 11/3/32. Commd 11/10/51. Sqn Ldr 1/1/66. Retd GD 24/11/73.
NICOL B. E., MBE BA. Born 1/2/32. Commd 1/2/56. Gp Capt 1/1/84. Retd ADMIN 30/8/86.
NICOL D. J., MSc MCIT MILT DPhysEd. Born 22/12/44. Commd 13/9/70. Wg Cdr 1/1/88. Retd SUP 13/9/92.
NICOL J. Born 19/3/36. Commd 29/7/55. Flt Lt 29/1/61. Retd PI 20/3/84.
NICOL J. B., MBE BEM. Born 20/11/21 Commd 18/7/63. Flt Lt 18/7/68. Retd PRT 3/4/80.
NICOL L. A. Born 2/8/62. Commd 30/4/81. Flt Lt 30/10/86. Retd GD 17/12/99.
NICOLL C. A. Born 7/6/20. Commd 7/10/40. Sqn Ldr 1/7/70. Retd GD 7/6/75.
NICOLL D. A. P., BSc MB ChB. Born 30/4/52. Commd 6/4/78. Wg Cdr 4/8/93. Retd MED 14/3/96.
NICOLL G. F. Born 11/9/29. Commd 14/8/70. Sqn Ldr 1/7/85. Retd GD 11/9/89.
NICOLL I. T., BSc CEng MRAeS MIMgt. Born 31/3/38. Commd 30/9/57. Gp Capt 1/7/88. Retd ENG 31/3/93.
NICOLLE B. P. Born 27/12/40. Commd 31/7/62. Wg Cdr 1/1/84. Retd GD 2/4/93.
NICOLLE B. R. Born 27/3/43. Commd 13/10/61. Sqn Ldr 1/1/91. Retd GD 31/3/93.
NICOLSON D. A. V., DFM. Born 12/1/24. Commd 30/7/44. Sqn Ldr 1/7/56. Retd RGT 12/1/69.
NIEASS E. L., MBE. Born 2/7/24. Commd 17/6/45. Wg Cdr 1/1/71. Retd GD 2/7/79.
NIEL E. C. Born 29/5/33. Commd 8/1/56. Flt Lt 7/8/64. Retd SEC 6/9/73 rtg Sqn Ldr.
NIELAND I. R. J., BA. Born 5/5/36. Commd 28/1/58. Wg Cdr 1/1/82. Retd GD 7/5/87.
NIELD R., CBE. Born 24/4/37. Commd 19/12/59. Gp Capt 1/1/86. Retd GD 23/1/92.
NIELSEN D. N. Born 9/1/20. Commd 2/6/43. Flt Lt 2/12/46. Retd ENG 8/5/54.
NIEZRECKI W. T., AFC DFM. Born 9/3/20. Commd 17/12/53. Sqn Ldr 1/1/72. Retd GD 9/3/75.
NIGHTINGALE A. L., BSc(Eng). Born 3/4/62. Commd 31/8/80. Flt Lt 15/10/84. Retd GD 3/4/00.
NIGHTINGALE H. H. Born 5/3/40. Commd 28/4/61. Sqn Ldr 1/1/76. Retd GD 1/7/78.
NIGHTINGALE J. H. Born 25/2/33. Commd 11/4/58. Sqn Lrd 1/1/74. Retd ENG 1/6/77.
NIGHTINGALE V. E. Born 14/10/40. Commd 8/12/61. Sqn Ldr 1/1/77. Retd GD 1/1/80.
NISBET D. J. Born 19/9/39. Commd 6/5/83. Flt Lt 6/5/87. Retd GD(G) 19/9/95.
NISBET G. McL., BSc(Eng). Born 20/4/52. Commd 11/5/75. Wg Cdr 1/1/91. Retd ENG 27/11/98.
NIVEN D. S. R. Born 23/11/26. Commd 16/11/61. Sqn Ldr 1/7/72. Retd ENG 19/8/78.
NIVEN J., DFC. Born 12/4/20. Commd 29/4/42. Sqn Ldr 1/10/55. Retd GD 3/9/58.
NIX S. W. Born 20/9/30. Commd 29/10/64. Sqn Ldr 1/1/86. Retd ENG 1/1/89.
NIXON A. F. Born 19/9/38. Commd 1/8/61. Flt Lt 26/2/64. Retd GD 19/9/76.
NIXON D. P. M., MA. Born 12/5/40. Commd 1/10/62. Flt Lt 1/1/64. Retd GD 1/6/70.
NIXON E. J. Born 20/6/28. Commd 21/12/67. Flt Lt 21/12/72. Retd ENG 20/6/86.
NIXON F. Born 25/7/27. Commd 15/12/49. Sqn Ldr 1/7/62. Retd GD 12/1/76.
NIXON F. B. Born 12/4/32. Commd 17/9/52. Flt Lt 22/5/57. Retd GD 23/5/70.
NIXON J. D. Born 13/11/31. Commd 5/2/57. Flt Lt 7/8/62. Retd GD 14/5/71.
NIXON K. C. D., AFC. Born 31/10/23. Commd 17/1/45. Gp Capt 1/1/69. Retd GD 18/10/75.
NIXON M. A. Born 3/2/40. Commd 12/7/62. Sqn Ldr 1/4/75. Retd ENG 20/5/86.
NIXON P. M. B. Born 6/6/45. Commd 28/5/66. Gp Capt 1/1/92. Retd GD(G) 14/9/96.
NOAKE E. L., BEM. Born 8/1/23. Commd 9/3/66. Flt Lt 9/3/71. Retd ENG 1/7/71.
NOAKES J. Born 19/3/21. Commd 16/5/57. Sqn Ldr 1/7/69. Retd ENG 19/11/73.
NOAKES J. E. P. Born 31/7/40. Commd 17/7/70. Flt Lt 17/7/72. Retd ENG 1/4/78.
NOBLE B. A. Born 8/2/57. Commd 13/12/79. Flt Lt 1/8/83. Retd SUP 8/2/95.
NOBLE B. J., AFC. Born 11/11/29. Commd 16/11/51. Sqn Ldr 1/7/62. Retd GD 12/12/83.
NOBLE D. Born 14/11/48. Commd 21/3/69. Flt Lt 1/4/75. Retd ENG 1/11/77. Reinstated 25/11/81. Sqn Ldr 1/7/87.
 Retd ENG 1/7/90.
NOBLE E. Born 16/6/28. Commd 30/3/61. Sqn Ldr 1/7/74. Retd GD(G) 26/10/77.
NOBLE K. G., BSc. Born 15/6/59. Commd 17/8/80. Sqn Ldr 1/7/92. Retd GD 15/6/97.
NOBLE M. A. Born 2/7/34. Commd 5/4/55. Sqn Ldr 1/7/65. Retd GD 2/7/72.
NOBLE P. R., BSc. Born 24/8/54. Commd 7/1/74. Flt Lt 15/10/78. Retd GD 1/1/87.
NOBLE The Rev R., BA BD. Born 28/9/43. Commd 26/9/71. Retd 28/9/98 Wg Cdr.
NOBLE R. F., DFC. Born 27/8/18. Commd 13/10/41. Sqn Ldr 1/7/49. Retd GD 16/2/58.
NOCKELS R. L. Born 25/3/30. Commd 3/6/65. Flt Lt 3/6/70. Retd ENG 1/12/83.
NOCKLES A. G., BSc. Born 21/2/52. Commd 30/3/75. Flt Lt 30/6/76. Retd GD 30/9/91.

NOCKOLDS M. D. S. Born 10/12/45. Commd 2/6/77. Sqn Ldr 1/7/91. Retd GD 30/11/93.
NOKES D. J. Born 2/2/20. Commd 3/11/41. Flt Lt 19/2/46. Retd ENG 10/10/53.
NOLAN B. N. Born 20/12/41. Commd 23/9/66. Sqn Ldr 1/1/77. Retd GD 26/4/79.
NOLAN F. P., BSc. Born 22/7/53. Commd 23/5/82. Sqn Ldr 1/7/91. Retd ENG 25/10/94.
NOLAN G. L. Born 22/11/53. Commd 3/9/72. Sqn Ldr 1/1/88. Retd SUP 22/11/91.
NOLAN J. Born 9/10/11. Commd 13/5/43. Sqn Ldr 1/7/60. Retd ENG 9/1/67.
NOLAN M. P. Born 1/9/34. Commd 25/2/53. Flt Lt 17/8/58. Retd GD 1/9/92.
NOLAN T. J. Born 6/3/48. Commd 20/9/68. Flt Lt 20/3/74. Retd GD 6/3/86.
NOON A. J., CEng BSc MIMechE MRAeS. Born 4/2/30. Commd 26/9/53. Sqn Ldr 1/7/63. Retd ENG 4/2/68.
NOOTT D. A. C. Born 25/9/39. Commd 9/1/64. Flt Lt 18/9/68. Retd GD 25/9/77.
NORBURY E. G. Born 2/11/44. Commd 3/3/67. Sqn Ldr 1/1/82. Retd GD 2/11/99.
NORCROSS H. S. L. T., DFC. Born 7/1/17. Commd 14/1/43. Sqn Ldr 1/7/56. Retd GD(G) 7/1/73.
NORCROSS T. R. Born 17/7/32. Commd 28/11/51. Sqn Ldr 1/1/82. Retd GD 30/9/82.
NORFOLK A. H. J., AFC. Born 15/12/44. Commd 31/1/64. Flt Lt 4/5/72. Retd GD 1/4/92.
NORGAN K. A., BSc. Born 25/11/42. Commd 12/1/62. Flt Lt 12/7/67. Retd GD 6/5/72. Re-entered 6/9/76. Sqn Ldr 1/7/87. Retd ENG 25/11/97.
NORMAN A. A. Born 8/1/33. Commd 26/3/52. Sqn Ldr 1/7/70. Retd GD 6/12/84.
NORMAN A. P., DFC. Born 19/5/24. Commd 10/12/43. Wg Cdr 1/1/68. Retd GD 30/10/72.
NORMAN E. H. A., BEM. Born 9/10/40. Commd 10/3/77. Sqn Ldr 1/7/90. Retd GD 13/12/96.
NORMAN F. L. G., FHCIMA MIMgt. Born 30/7/25. Commd 9/4/52. Sqn Ldr 1/1/74. Retd CAT 4/10/75.
NORMAN G. P. Born 10/3/22. Commd 28/5/46. Flt Lt 6/9/55. Retd GD(G) 31/8/68.
NORMAN I. A. W. Born 20/5/63. Commd 23/9/82. Sqn Ldr 1/1/96. Retd GD 21/5/01.
NORMAN K. P. Born 5/1/30. Commd 9/4/52. Flt Lt 21/10/59. Retd GD 28/3/70.
NORMAN M. J. Born 14/5/31. Commd 6/12/51. Flt Lt 22/5/57. Retd GD 14/7/91.
NORMAN M. J. S., MBE. Born 4/8/30. Commd 26/9/51. Wg Cdr 1/7/72. Retd GD 4/8/85.
NORMAN N. G. E. Born 22/7/35. Commd 23/9/66. Flt Lt 23/9/72. Retd SUP 1/11/74.
NORMAN P. B. Born 10/7/31. Commd 17/5/62. Flt Lt 17/5/68. Retd ENG 2/4/82.
NORMAN R. F. Born 9/11/33. Commd 16/7/52. Sqn Ldr 1/7/79. Retd GD 9/11/88.
NORMAN S. C., CEng MIMechE. Born 14/1/35. Commd 19/2/59. Sqn Ldr 1/7/66. Retd ENG 19/2/75.
NORMILE J. P. Born 14/10/51. Commd 15/12/88. Flt Lt 15/12/92. Retd ENG 3/4/93.
NORREYS W. L. Born 15/4/23. Commd 26/3/45. Flt Lt 10/11/55. Retd GD 15/4/66.
NORRIE S. D. Born 20/11/54. Commd 28/8/75. Flt Lt 28/2/81. Retd GD 20/11/92.
NORRIS A. H. Born 22/9/13. Commd 23/1/43. Flt Lt 30/6/49. Retd SEC 22/9/60.
NORRIS The Rev B. J., BA. Born 28/6/46. Commd 17/5/81. Retd 31/12/86 Sqn Ldr.
NORRIS D. F. G. Born 23/6/23. Commd 19/7/51. Sqn Ldr 1/7/62. Retd GD 23/6/78.
NORRIS E. R. Born 29/9/36. Commd 14/1/65. Sqn Ldr 1/1/73. Retd GD 30/4/87.
NORRIS G. B. H., CBE FFA FIMgt. Born 10/6/26. Commd 9/8/47. Gp Capt 1/7/74. Retd SEC 10/6/81.
NORRIS G. L. Born 20/9/40. Commd 6/7/62. Flt Lt 6/1/68. Retd GD 20/9/78.
NORRIS M. A., MBE. Born 17/1/44. Commd 25/6/65. Flt Lt 17/3/71. Retd GD 26/1/73. Re-entered 22/3/74. Wg Cdr 1/1/91. Retd GD 17/1/99.
NORRIS P., MB ChB. Born 28/9/28. Commd 30/3/53. Wg Cdr 16/1/65. Retd MED 30/3/69.
NORRIS R. A. D. Born 22/2/47. Commd 1/3/68. Sqn Ldr 1/7/79. Retd GD 22/2/91.
NORRISS D. K. Born 17/6/46. Commd 8/1/65. A Cdre 1/1/96. Retd GD 15/6/00.
NORRISS Sir Peter., KBE CB AFC MA FRAeS. Born 22/4/44. Commd 5/1/66. AM 30/10/98. Retd GD 22/3/01.
NORRISS R. C., BSc. Born 7/11/50. Commd 15/9/69. Flt Lt 15/4/74. Retd GD 7/11/88.
NORSWORTHY R. J., CEng MIEE DUS MIMgt. Born 8/1/34. Commd 7/9/56. Wg Cdr 1/7/71. Retd ENG 31/3/78.
NORTH B. P., MBE MIMgt. Born 17/1/40. Commd 7/5/64. Sqn Ldr 1/1/72. Retd ENG 1/4/78. Reinstated 7/11/79. Wg Cdr 1/7/85. Retd ENG 23/6/90.
NORTH C. A. Born 30/5/13. Commd 30/8/41. Flt Lt 18/11/55. Retd SEC 26/10/68 rtg Sqn Ldr.
NORTH D. E. Born 2/12/44. Commd 15/7/66. Gp Capt 1/1/91. Retd GD 1/9/97.
NORTH G. N., AFC. Born 9/12/15. Commd 3/8/41. Sqn Ldr 1/8/47. Retd GD 1/4/58.
NORTH G. P., OBE. Born 25/1/44. Commd 11/7/62. Wg Cdr 1/7/85. Retd GD 31/3/94.
NORTH J. L. Born 7/4/58. Commd 11/1/79. Flt Lt 11/7/85. Retd GD(G) 7/4/96.
NORTH M. A. Born 28/8/62. Commd 11/12/83. Flt Lt 11/12/88. Retd ADMIN 14/3/96.
NORTH N. M., MBE. Born 27/12/22. Commd 2/9/44. Flt Lt 17/5/56. Retd GD 18/10/67. Re-employed SUP 21/12/69 to 28/6/75 and re-instated 19/12/79 to 27/12/82.
NORTH P. G., MA BA. Born 1/3/47. Commd 8/2/81. Sqn Ldr 1/1/88. Retd ADMIN 14/9/96.
NORTH R. J. Born 30/10/47. Commd 27/2/70. Flt Lt 27/8/72. Retd GD 30/10/91.
NORTH R. P. Born 1/9/33. Commd 30/4/52. Flt Lt 24/11/57. Retd GD 1/9/70.
NORTH R. W. H. Born 10/3/50. Commd 31/10/69. Sqn Ldr 1/1/88. Retd GD 1/1/91.
NORTH V. M., BA. Born 18/12/47. Commd 8/4/79. Sqn Ldr 1/1/86. Retd ADMIN 8/6/87.
NORTH-LEWIS C. D., DSO DFC*. Born 13/3/18. Commd 4/12/40. A Cdre 1/1/64. Retd GD 1/2/71.
NORTHCOTE R., OBE BA. Born 21/10/45. Commd 15/7/66. Gp Capt 1/7/89. Retd GD 9/4/91.
NORTHCOTT D. S. Born 8/11/29. Commd 22/7/70. Fg Offr 22/7/70. Retd ENG 1/11/74.
NORTHEY H., MVO. Born 27/11/46. Commd 2/8/68. Wg Cdr 1/1/92. Retd GD 2/5/98.
NORTHMORE L. N. Born 21/8/18. Commd 11/12/42. Sqn Ldr 1/10/55. Retd GD 18/8/58.

NORTHMORE W. J. J., CBE CEng MIERE MRAeS. Born 10/7/29. Commd 8/2/51. A Cdre 1/1/82. Retd 10/7/84.
NORTHWOOD R. J. Born 9/3/38. Commd 25/6/66. Sqn Ldr 1/1/81. Retd GD 9/3/93.
NORTON D. M. Born 1/7/19. Commd 6/10/41. Flt Offr 1/9/45. Retd SEC 21/10/59.
NORTON G. E. Born 23/12/30. Commd 1/4/53. Flt Lt 21/10/59. Retd GD 2/10/71.
NORTON H. G. P. Born 3/7/45. Commd 25/2/66. Sqn Ldr 1/1/83. Retd GD 1/1/86.
NORTON J., ACIS. Born 12/7/31. Commd 9/8/60. Wg Cdr 1/7/79. Retd GD 21/11/81.
NORTON W. H. W., MBE. Born 17/4/33. Commd 17/1/52. Sqn Ldr 1/7/66. Retd GD 17/4/93.
NORTON W. L., BSc. Born 10/1/40. Commd 1/10/62. Sqn Ldr 1/7/71. Retd GD 1/10/78.
NORTON-SMITH P., CBE DFC AFC. Born 18/5/15. Commd 2/11/40. Sqn Ldr 1/7/59. Retd GD 8/6/65.
NOTMAN E. J. Born 26/12/67. Commd 10/5/90. Fg Offr 10/5/92. Retd GD 31/3/94.
NOTMAN R. F. Born 25/6/30. Commd 19/8/65. Sqn Ldr 1/1/77. Retd SUP 10/9/82.
NOTTAGE G. W., LLB. Born 6/3/45. Commd 3/3/67. Wg Cdr 1/7/87. Retd GD 31/12/92.
NOTTAGE S. M. Born 1/7/18. Commd 4/12/40. Sqn Offr 1/1/51. Retd SEC 12/3/52.
NOTTINGHAM J. Born 1/1/40. Commd 31/7/62. Sqn Ldr 1/1/76. Retd GD 1/1/79.
NOUJAIM S. C. J. Born 23/12/60. Commd 29/7/83. Flt Lt 29/1/89. Retd GD 14/2/99.
NOWAKOWSKI J. Born 26/3/21. Commd 15/10/46. Sqn Ldr 1/7/57. Retd GD 27/3/64.
NOWELL J. Born 25/7/41. Commd 27/3/70. Flt Lt 8/3/72. Retd GD 25/7/79.
NOWELL J. W. Born 12/5/32. Commd 28/7/53. Sqn Ldr 1/7/64. Retd GD 3/7/70.
NOWELL N. Born 14/1/31. Commd 22/7/71. Flt Lt 22/7/77. Retd SEC 1/5/81.
NOYCE B. F. Born 7/3/22. Commd 20/3/52. Flt Offr 20/9/56. Retd SEC 20/2/60.
NOYCE D. J., BA. Born 11/11/39. Commd 15/1/63. Gp Capt 1/7/85. Retd SY(PRT) 2/1/90.
NOYCE N. A., MBE. Born 8/2/22. Commd 29/8/42. Wg Cdr 1/7/72. Retd GD(G) 15/3/77.
NOYCE P. K. Born 14/2/23. Commd 6/3/52. Sqn Ldr 1/7/62. Retd SEC 1/9/66.
NOYES K. W. T., MBE. Born 17/11/35. Commd 7/1/71. Sqn Ldr 1/7/80. Retd SY 17/11/93.
NOYES L. B., AFC. Born 20/11/09. Commd 1/4/40. Sqn Ldr 1/7/51. Retd GD(G) 14/1/60 rtg Wg Cdr.
NUDDS C. Born 3/7/48. Commd 15/2/73. Flt Lt 17/11/75. Retd GD(G) 30/7/86. Reinstated 5/10/87. Flt LT 18/2/77. Retd GD(G) 6/1/92.
NUGENT N. A. D. Born 6/11/26. Commd 16/6/53. Wg Cdr 1/7/70. Retd GD 30/10/76.
NUGENT S. G. Born 17/3/63. Commd 26/9/90. Flt Lt 26/9/92. Retd OPS SPT 17/3/01.
NUNN A. B. C. Born 24/5/14. Commd 31/12/41. Sqn Ldr 1/8/47. Retd GD 25/12/54.
NUNN B. E., OBE BA. Born 6/8/41. Commd 1/10/62. Gp Capt 1/1/87. Retd GD 7/4/93.
NUNN I. D. Born 6/1/25. Commd 7/9/61. Sqn Ldr 1/1/77. Retd ENG 6/1/80.
NUNN J. L., DFC BSc MRAeS. Born 11/4/19. Commd 3/10/39. Wg Cdr 1/1/54. Retd GD 11/4/66.
NUNN J. M. Born 14/1/36. Commd 22/10/54. Wg Cdr 1/7/79. Retd GD 22/9/89.
NURSAW D. Born 27/5/29. Commd 26/7/50. Flt Lt 26/1/53. Retd GD 27/5/67.
NURSE W. F. Born 7/11/20. Commd 15/4/44. Flt Lt 15/4/50. Retd SUP 13/4/62 rtg Sqn Ldr.
NUSSEY A. S. Born 25/8/48. Commd 27/2/70. Sqn Ldr 1/7/83. Retd GD 13/4/96.
NUTKINS J. H., BSc. Born 5/11/41. Commd 22/9/65. Sqn Ldr 1/1/75. Retd GD 21/12/82.
NUTT P. J., CEng MRAeS. Born 4/3/44. Commd 15/7/65. Gp Capt 1/7/86. Retd ENG 1/7/89.
NUTT R. D. Born 5/8/35. Commd 11/2/55. Flt Lt 7/3/62. Retd GD 5/8/73.
NUTTALL A. Born 2/4/29. Commd 16/12/66. Flt Lt 16/12/72. Retd GD(G) 2/4/87.
NUTTALL J. A. Born 10/9/54. Commd 20/9/79. Sqn Ldr 1/1/92. Retd GD 1/10/97.
NUTTALL R., OBE CEng MRAeS FIMgt. Born 7/5/19. Commd 8/7/43. Wg Cdr 1/1/64. Retd ENG 16/1/75 rtg Gp Capt.
NUTTALL W. C., BA. Born 11/11/37. Commd 13/10/64. Sqn Ldr 13/4/70. Retd ADMIN 13/10/80.
NUTTER R. Born 3/8/45. Commd 31/1/64. Flt Lt 15/4/70. Retd GD 3/8/83.

# O

O'BRIAN P. G. St.G., OBE DFC*. Born 16/9/17. Commd 18/12/37. Gp Capt 1/7/56. Retd GD 18/7/59.
O'BRIEN C. M. P., BA. Born 5/10/48. Commd 1/11/71. Sqn Ldr 1/7/90. Retd GD 16/10/00.
O'BRIEN D. C. T. Born 30/3/45. Commd 27/10/67. Flt Lt 30/3/72. Retd GD 4/5/76.
O'BRIEN E. T. Born 26/1/51. Commd 6/4/72. Sqn Ldr 1/1/89. Retd GD(G) 1/1/92.
O'BRIEN G. P. Born 16/3/31. Commd 28/11/51. Sqn Ldr 1/1/66. Retd GD 9/8/75.
O'BRIEN J. D. Born 15/5/30. Commd 23/12/61. Wg Cdr 1/7/80. Retd ENG 12/5/85.
O'BRIEN J. J. Born 19/7/18. Commd 17/6/54. Flt Lt 17/6/57. Retd GD(G) 25/5/71.
O'BRIEN J. J. Born 1/12/37. Commd 15/6/61. Flt Lt 19/11/66. Retd GD 21/11/76.
O'BRIEN J. L. Born 24/9/07. Commd 8/11/40. Sqn Ldr 1/9/45. Retd ENG 10/10/53 rtg Wg Cdr.
O'BRIEN J. P., BA. Born 23/5/34. Commd 26/5/67. Sqn Ldr 1/1/74. Retd ENG 7/4/87.
O'BRIEN J. W. A. Born 21/6/47. Commd 14/8/70. Flt Lt 14/2/77. Retd GD(G) 31/3/86.
O'BRIEN K. S., MBE. Born 7/7/25. Commd 12/9/56. Sqn Ldr 1/9/65. Retd GD 8/9/82.
O'BRIEN N. G., MBE. Born 28/3/13. Commd 26/9/41. Wg Cdr 1/7/59. Retd ENG 1/8/63.
O'BRIEN R. P., CB OBE BA FRAeS. Born 1/11/41. Commd 31/7/62. AVM 1/7/92. Retd GD 5/12/98.
O'BRIEN T. M. Born 8/7/50. Commd 10/5/90. Flt Lt 10/5/94. Retd OPS SPT 10/9/00.
O'CALLAGHAN B. A. Born 1/1/24. Commd 7/7/54. Flt Lt 7/7/59. Retd GD 9/12/68.
O'CARROLL J. J. Born 22/8/28. Commd 12/4/73. Flt Lt 12/4/78. Retd ENG 19/9/85.
O'CARROLL J. V. Born 14/2/54. Commd 8/8/74. Flt Lt 23/2/81. Retd OPS SPT 14/2/99.
O'CONNOR I. M., BSc MB MCh BAO DPH DOMS. Born 5/7/18. Commd 2/4/51. Gp Capt 2/4/65. Retd MED 5/7/83.
O'CONNOR M. J., OBE. Born 8/12/46. Commd 1/3/68. Wg Cdr 1/1/88. Retd GD 2/12/96.
O'CONNOR P. D. T., CEng MRAeS. Born 7/3/37. Commd 30/7/59. Sqn Ldr 1/7/68. Retd ENG 7/3/75.
O'CONNOR S., DFC AFC AFM. Born 26/5/22. Commd 21/10/54. Sqn Ldr 1/9/65. Retd GD 26/5/77.
O'DOHERTY P. J. Born 28/2/42. Commd 13/2/69. Flt Lt 24/6/73. Retd GD(G) 28/2/80.
O'DONNELL J., MA. Born 22/6/47. Commd 17/7/77. Sqn Ldr 1/1/89. Retd ADMIN 17/7/93.
O'DONNELL M. Born 29/9/27. Commd 1/7/50. Flt Lt 1/1/55. Retd GD 31/8/79.
O'DONNELL P. Born 6/4/25. Commd 27/9/51. Flt Lt 13/6/58. Retd SUP 6/4/74.
O'DONNELL R. E., BSc AIB. Born 20/12/44. Commd 9/4/72. Sqn Ldr 1/1/85. Retd ADMIN 20/12/99.
O'DONOGHUE E. Born 15/11/23. Commd 30/4/43. Flt Lt 20/3/51. Retd GD(G) 19/2/76.
O'DONOVAN G. P. Born 7/3/31. Commd 15/10/52. Sqn Ldr 1/1/71. Retd GD 1/1/71.
O'DONOVAN G. W., DSO DFC. Born 24/3/21. Commd 27/2/43. Sqn Ldr 1/7/52. Retd GD 30/6/61.
O'DONOVAN M. Born 16/7/46. Commd 1/11/79. Flt Lt 13/8/73. Retd GD 9/11/85.
O'DWYER D. Born 4/4/42. Commd 23/6/67. Wg Cdr 1/7/86. Retd SUP 5/5/97.
O'DWYER-RUSSELL J. D., OBE. Born 31/8/30. Commd 31/8/50. Wg Cdr 1/1/73. Retd SY 31/8/85.
O'DWYER-RUSSELL T. D. Born 20/10/55. Commd 27/3/75. Flt Lt 22/10/80. Retd GD 8/2/91.
O'FLINN P. Born 6/6/36. Commd 30/7/64. Flt Lt 24/6/77. Retd GD(G) 25/9/82.
O'FLYNN F. J. Born 16/2/43. Commd 25/1/63. Sqn Ldr 1/7/75. Retd GD 4/6/95.
O'FLYNN F. M. G. Born 10/1/24. Commd 3/9/66. Flt Lt 23/9/72. Retd SEC 15/1/74.
O'FLYNN P. Born 15/12/56. Commd 30/9/81. Flt Lt 13/7/84. Retd ENG 29/12/94.
O'GRADY M. J. Born 29/8/38. Commd 24/4/70. Wg Cdr 1/1/88. Retd GD(G) 29/8/93.
O'HAGAN M., CEng MIERE. Born 7/8/24. Commd 1/11/45. Sqn Ldr 1/7/59. Retd ENG 19/9/64.
O'HAGAN M. P. A. Born 1/2/44. Commd 21/10/65. Wg Cdr 1/1/88. Retd GD(G) 2/12/96.
O'HAGAN V. W. J., BA CertEd. Born 16/7/41. Commd 1/8/66. Sqn Ldr 1/3/72. Retd ADMIN 1/8/88. Re-entered
   11/12/89. Sqn Ldr 11/7/73. Retd ADMIN 16/7/96.
O'HANLON M. J. Born 1/10/47. Commd 12/3/87. Flt Lt 12/3/91. Retd OPS SPT 8/10/99.
O'HARA J., AFC. Born 20/10/19. Commd 16/12/44. Flt Lt 16/6/48. Retd GD(G) 20/10/75.
O'HARA R. MCM. Born 14/4/39. Commd 12/10/75. Flt Lt 12/10/81. Retd GD(G) 14/4/94.
O'HARE B., BCom MITD MIMgt. Born 20/5/34. Commd 30/12/58. Wg Cdr 1/7/78. Retd ADMIN 1/10/84.
O'LEARY D., DFC. Born 8/10/20. Commd 27/9/42. Sqn Ldr 1/1/56. Retd GD(G) 8/4/71.
O'LEARY D. A. Born 6/6/33. Commd 8/10/70. Flt Lt 8/10/73. Retd GD(G) 6/6/93.
O'LEARY D. A. Born 18/4/25. Commd 8/11/51. Flt Lt 6/3/57. Retd GD(G) 7/1/78.
O'LEARY J. D. Born 10/1/21. Commd 12/5/43. Flt Lt 12/5/45. Retd GD(G) 1/2/73.
O'LEARY M. J. Born 28/11/31. Commd 3/8/61. Flt Lt 3/8/67. Retd GD 28/11/91.
O'LEARY T. O. Born 4/10/29. Commd 20/12/57. Flt Lt 20/12/63. Retd GD 28/3/69.
O'LOUGHLIN B. D. Born 10/6/66. Commd 23/5/85. Flt Lt 23/11/90. Retd GD 14/3/96.
O'MAHONY J. P. S. Born 18/10/30. Commd 30/8/50. Sqn Ldr 1/1/68. Retd GD 15/4/76.
O'MAHONY O. R. Born 10/7/39. Commd 20/8/65. Flt Lt 6/7/68. Retd GD 10/7/77.
O'MALLEY F. Born 3/12/29. Commd 28/5/66. Flt Lt 28/5/72. Retd ADMIN 1/3/83.
O'MALLEY F. P. Born 17/7/16. Commd 29/7/43. Sqn Ldr 1/7/54. Retd ENG 17/7/72.
O'MARA R. J., BSc. Born 8/1/66. Commd 8/6/87. Flt lt 15/1/91. Retd GD 1/5/96.
O'NEILL A. M. J., CEng FIMechE FRAeS. Born 27/3/43. Commd 6/4/62. Gp Capt 1/7/88. Retd ENG 6/8/94.

O'NEILL B. Born 10/12/46. Commd 1/6/72. Flt Lt 30/9/78. Retd GD(G) 14/8/88.
O'NEILL C. O. Born 11/7/52. Commd 29/6/72. Flt Lt 9/12/78. Retd GD(G) 11/7/90.
O'NEILL D. W. J., MRCS LRCP. Born 11/6/23. Commd 17/10/46. Flt Lt 10/8/47. Retd MED 30/4/54 rtg Sqn Ldr.
O'NEILL E. Born 9/2/16. Commd 9/11/50. Sqn Ldr 1/1/66. Retd SEC 1/7/70.
O'NEILL H. F., DFC*. Born 19/9/20. Commd 29/8/38. Gp Capt 1/1/62. Retd GD 3/12/66.
O'NEILL J. Born 11/4/14. Commd 12/9/38. Wg Cdr 1/1/51. Retd SUP 15/9/58.
O'NEILL J. Born 31/5/47. Commd 5/11/70. Flt Lt 1/4/74. Retd GD 31/5/85.
O'NEILL J. A., FC. Born 7/10/15. Commd 15/3/35. Wg Cdr 1/7/47. Retd GD 29/11/57 rtg Gp Capt.
O'NEILL J. P. H., MBE AFC. Born 6/1/31. Commd 24/1/52. Wg Cdr 1/1/74. Retd GD 1/4/85.
O'NEILL K. B., BSc CEng MIMechE MRAeS. Born 5/8/40. Commd 17/10/71. Sqn Ldr 1/7/89. Retd ENG 5/8/95.
O'NEILL M. J. Born 29/6/32. Commd 24/1/52. Flt Lt 15/5/57. Retd GD(G) 27/3/73.
O'NEILL M. T. C., MIMgt. Born 5/10/43. Commd 4/7/69. Sqn Ldr 1/2/93. Retd SUP 1/2/93.
O'NEILL P. J. Born 17/3/27. Commd 25/8/60. Fg Offr 25/8/60. Retd SEC 25/7/65.
O'NEILL S. J., MBE. Born 1/12/28. Commd 19/12/63. Sqn Ldr 1/7/76. Retd ENG 2/7/82.
O'NEILL T. J. Born 12/6/53. Commd 5/2/81. Flt Lt 4/3/85. Retd ENG 30/3/92.
O'NEILL W. I., MIMgt. Born 15/7/23. Commd 21/4/44. Wg Cdr 1/7/73. Retd SY 20/11/76.
O'REGAN C. A. Born 12/12/20. Commd 19/7/57. Sqn Ldr 1/7/72. Retd ENG 12/12/75.
O'REILLY B. J., MB ChB. Born 2/11/54. Commd 20/1/76. Wg Cdr 1/8/92. Retd MED 14/3/96.
O'REILLY C., OBE. Born 1/4/28. Commd 21/12/48. Wg Cdr 1/1/71. Retd SUP 1/4/83.
O'REILLY F. Born 23/7/49. Commd 27/7/89. Flt Lt 27/7/93. Retd SUP 9/9/96.
O'REILLY J. J. Born 2/7/32. Commd 15/9/60. Flt Lt 15/3/65. Retd GD 2/7/70.
O'REILLY M. J., BA. Born 4/9/54. Commd 20/1/80. Sqn Ldr 1/1/95. Retd GD 1/2/99.
O'REILLY P. J., CB BSc CEng FIEE FRAeS. Born 26/4/46. Commd 19/5/69. AVM 1/7/96. Retd ENG 24/4/99.
O'RIORDAN J. A. Born 14/9/25. Commd 30/4/59. Flt Lt 30/10/63. Retd GD 31/3/70.
O'ROURKE M. J. Born 26/10/38. Commd 28/5/57. Flt Lt 19/6/64. Retd GD 20/1/68.
O'SHEA N. Born 20/12/28. Commd 24/9/52. Sqn Ldr 1/7/70. Retd GD 3/1/76.
O'SHEA P. R., BEng. Born 6/6/58. Commd 2/8/85. Flt Lt 15/7/88. Retd ENG 6/6/96.
O'SHEA The Rev S. M. Born 26/6/23. Commd 15/4/58. Retd 15/10/74 Wg Cdr.
O'SULLIVAN J. B. P., MA. Born 30/5/33. Commd 22/11/56. Gp Capt 1/7/84. Retd ADMIN 5/9/87.
O'SULLIVAN J. H. Born 21/8/20. Commd 6/10/60. Flt Lt 6/10/63. Retd SEC 21/8/68.
O'SULLIVAN J. T., OBE. Born 26/10/19. Commd 23/2/42. Gp Capt 1/1/64. Retd RGT 21/5/66.
O'SULLIVAN K. M. Born 24/2/52. Commd 14/8/70. Fg Offr 14/8/72. Retd GD 12/9/75.
O'SULLIVAN V. F., MIMgt. Born 11/11/42. Commd 26/10/62. Sqn Ldr 1/1/74. Retd GD 18/5/86.
O'TOOLE E. F., MBE CEng MIEE MRAeS MIMgt. Born 3/9/35. Commd 7/9/61. Sqn Ldr 11/4/84. Retd ENG 3/9/94.
O'TOOLE E. H., MBE MIMgt. Born 2/3/21. Commd 30/11/43. Wg Cdr 1/1/63. Retd SEC 6/5/72.
O'TOOLE L. Born 23/10/32. Commd 3/9/80. Sqn Ldr 2/11/71. Retd SUP 23/4/92.
OAKDEN D. I. Born 12/6/34. Commd 15/11/55. Gp Capt 1/7/80. Retd GD 8/3/88.
OAKES C. W. Born 9/12/1900. Commd 17/1/41. Flt Lt 1/9/45. Retd ENG 15/3/48 rtg Sqn Ldr.
OAKES E. R. Born 12/4/23. Commd 14/11/57. Flt Lt 1/4/63. Retd GD 1/9/67.
OAKES M. S., BSc. Born 11/7/54. Commd 17/9/72. Flt Lt 15/4/77. Retd GD 2/2/93.
OAKES P. A., BSc. Born 24/5/66. Commd 30/8/87. Flt Lt 28/2/90. Retd GD 14/3/97.
OAKES S. L. Born 1/12/41. Commd 1/6/72. Sqn Ldr 1/7/79. Retd SY 1/6/86.
OAKEY T. W., AFC BSc. Born 20/10/24. Commd 4/9/50. Wg Cdr 1/1/62. Retd GD 20/10/79.
OAKLEY D., BSc. Born 16/4/50. Commd 15/9/69. Flt Lt 15/12/73. Retd GD 16/4/88.
OAKLEY J., OBE. Born 11/12/20. Commd 9/11/43. Gp Capt 1/7/71. Retd GD(G) 11/12/75.
OAKLEY P. A., MBE. Born 5/7/23. Commd 6/6/52. Sqn Ldr 1/1/63. Retd GD 8/7/67.
OAKLEY S., MSc BA MCIPS MILDM. Born 4/4/49. Commd 23/9/68. Sqn Ldr 1/1/87. Retd SUP 31/3/94.
OAKLEY W. W. Born 17/2/14. Commd 24/7/46. Fg Offr 24/7/47. Retd SEC 17/4/55.
OART J. H. Born 22/7/43. Commd 20/10/83. Flt Lt 20/10/87. Retd ENG 2/7/93.
OATES A. S. H. Born 3/3/11. Commd 17/9/45. Fg Offr 19/1/46. Retd ASD 28/9/46.
OATES L. H., MBE. Born 19/6/12. Commd 30/11/41. Sqn Ldr 1/7/54. Retd ENG 19/6/67 rtg Wg Cdr.
OATES N. A., BA. Born 11/2/57. Commd 15/9/74. Flt Lt 15/10/80. Retd ENG 9/8/83.
OATES V. Born 18/5/23. Commd 3/8/61. Sqn Ldr 1/7/71. Retd GD 30/9/77.
OATEY A. H., DUS CEng MIEE. Born 29/11/35. Commd 24/7/57. Sqn Ldr 1/7/66. Retd ENG 2/5/79.
OATEY W. R. Born 26/2/34. Commd 6/9/55. Sqn Ldr 1/7/69. Retd GD 30/6/76.
OBERTELLI A. J. A. Born 20/1/49. Commd 24/6/71. Flt Lt 24/12/75. Retd GD 8/3/87.
OBOLEWICZ A. Born 1/1/18. Commd 26/5/60. Flt Lt 26/5/63. Retd CAT 3/1/73.
OCKLEFORD C. E., LDS RCS(Edin). Born 23/12/19. Commd 9/1/42. Gp Capt 1/1/65. Retd DEL 1/12/83.
ODBERT R. M., BSc MB ChB MRCGP DCH DRCOG DAvMed MRAeS. Born 6/4/50. Commd 4/9/73. Sqn Ldr 1/8/82. Retd MED 6/4/50.
ODDEY M. J. L., BSc CEng MIMechE MIMgt. Born 1/12/58. Commd 1/9/77. Wg Cdr 1/1/94. Retd ENG 1/1/97.
ODDY S. J., BSc. Born 31/3/51. Commd 1/8/69. Sqn Ldr 1/1/85. Retd GD 31/3/89.
ODELL G. E. Born 15/7/05. Commd 3/7/41. Flt Lt 1/1/44. Retd ENG 1/12/45 rtg Flt Lt.
ODLING P. J. Born 3/3/35. Commd 24/6/53. Sqn Ldr 1/1/68. Retd GD 1/12/75.
OFFORD R. E. Born 11/10/32. Commd 31/5/51. Flt Lt 28/11/56. Retd GD 17/10/69.
OFFORD R. J., AFC FIMgt. Born 17/9/31. Commd 8/8/52. A Cdre 1/7/80. Retd GD 17/9/86.

OFFORD R. J., BCom. Born 10/6/60. Commd 15/8/82. Sqn Ldr 1/1/94. Retd GD 15/8/98.
OGDEN G. Born 17/8/44. Commd 6/5/65. Wg Cdr 1/1/85. Retd ADMIN 19/8/93.
OGIER T. H. Born 17/7/49. Commd 8/9/77. Flt Lt 24/5/80. Retd ENG 17/7/87.
OGILVIE H., AFC. Born 14/11/20. Commd 21/2/45. Sqn Ldr 1/7/57. Retd GD 23/4/68.
OGILVIE I. M., MB ChB MFCM DPH. Born 5/8/26. Commd 3/5/49. A Cdre 1/5/78. Retd MED 1/8/80.
OGILVIE J. G. Born 2/10/46. Commd 18/8/67. Sqn Ldr 1/1/76. Retd GD 1/1/80.
OGILVIE T., BSc. Born 16/1/32. Commd 25/9/62. Wg Cdr 1/7/77. Retd ENG 14/9/86.
OGLE J. R. N., MIMgt. Born 1/5/41. Commd 18/12/62. Sqn Ldr 1/1/76. Retd SUP 2/6/82.
OKE G. J. Born 2/5/36. Commd 10/3/60. Sqn Ldr 1/7/74. Retd SUP 2/5/91.
OLD D. G. Born 19/6/30. Commd 15/6/61. Flt Lt 15/6/67. Retd RGT 14/10/80.
OLD D. M., BSc. Born 12/10/51. Commd 13/9/70. Sqn Ldr 1/7/86. Retd GD 12/10/89.
OLD L. R. Born 24/8/21. Commd 19/8/42. Wg Cdr 1/1/62. Retd ENG 10/8/74.
OLDFIELD A. J. Born 11/6/41. Commd 15/9/61. Flt Lt 11/12/66. Retd GD 11/6/79.
OLDFIELD D., BA. Born 27/10/56. Commd 8/4/79. Sqn Ldr 1/1/87. Retd ADMIN 14/3/96.
OLDFIELD J. E. Born 17/6/45. Commd 2/6/67. Sqn Ldr 1/7/91. Retd GD 3/2/97.
OLDHAM J. B. Born 19/12/44. Commd 14/8/64. Flt Lt 14/2/70. Retd GD 31/12/75.
OLDING R. C., CBE DSC. Born 29/11/32. Commd 6/10/57. Gp Capt 1/1/79. Retd GD 31/12/84.
OLDLAND E. F., BSc. Born 11/6/19. Commd 23/7/48. Sqn Ldr 23/12/53. Retd EDN 21/2/63.
OLDROYD A. W., DFC AFC. Born 20/9/16. Commd 29/6/36. Wg Cdr 1/7/47. Retd GD 20/9/63.
OLIVE R. B., AFC. Born 20/3/30. Commd 2/2/56. Sqn Ldr 1/7/83. Retd GD 20/3/88.
OLIVER A. J. W., OBE FIMgt. Born 11/4/23. Commd 6/6/45. Gp Capt 1/1/69. Retd SUP 1/5/74.
OLIVER A. R., BA MIQA AMRAeS. Born 11/12/38. Commd 13/12/60. Wg Cdr 1/1/86. Retd ENG 5/6/90.
OLIVER B. R., DFC. Born 23/4/33. Commd 20/11/56. Sqn Ldr 1/1/67. Retd GD 7/4/77.
OLIVER C. E. Born 5/12/24. Commd 13/2/47. Sqn Ldr 1/7/59. Retd SUP 5/12/61.
OLIVER D., GM. Born 12/2/24. Commd 29/7/63. Flt Lt 9/10/66. Retd GD 12/2/84.
OLIVER D. R., MB ChB. Born 25/11/27. Commd 11/4/56. Flt Lt 11/4/57. Retd MED 30/3/61.
OLIVER D. R., DFC MIMgt. Born 20/2/22. Commd 11/8/43. Sqn Ldr 1/1/56. Retd GD 20/12/71.
OLIVER D. S. Born 26/9/39. Commd 1/4/68. Flt Lt 7/8/69. Retd ENG 23/10/80.
OLIVER E. J. Born 20/5/49. Commd 31/8/75. Sqn Ldr 1/1/90. Retd ADMIN 1/9/93.
OLIVER G. W., MIMgt. Born 15/2/23. Commd 5/8/44. Wg Cdr 1/1/68. Retd GD(G) 15/3/73.
OLIVER H. W. Born 17/1/41. Commd 29/10/63. Sqn Ldr 1/7/78. Retd GD 1/7/81.
OLIVER J. Born 2/1/24. Commd 3/2/45. Flt Lt 3/8/48. Retd GD 4/4/62.
OLIVER J. F., OBE. Born 23/11/17. Commd 7/6/43. Wg Cdr 1/1/60. Retd RGT 23/11/72.
OLIVER J. R., MSc MBCS. Born 11/12/38. Commd 13/12/60. Wg Cdr 1/7/80. Retd GD 25/9/89.
OLIVER K. H., LDSRCS. Born 16/2/34. Commd 25/10/59. Wg Cdr 1/8/72. Retd DEL 31/8/80.
OLIVER K. L. Born 5/3/54. Commd 19/12/61. Fg Offr 19/12/91. Retd ENG 3/4/93.
OLIVER K. M. Born 12/12/28. Commd 13/7/49. Gp Capt 1/7/72. Retd REGT 12/12/78.
OLIVER K. P., BSc. Born 12/4/51. Commd 13/9/70. Sqn Ldr 1/7/86. Retd GD 11/7/89.
OLIVER M. A. Born 9/1/62. Commd 4/9/81. Flt Lt 4/3/87. Retd GD 28/2/00.
OLIVER M. E. Born 20/2/51. Commd 29/4/71. Sqn Ldr 1/1/86. Retd ADMIN 20/2/89.
OLIVER M. S., MSc BSc. Born 4/8/47. Commd 18/9/66. Gp Capt 1/1/91. Retd SUP 7/10/97.
OLIVER N. W. J., MB BS DObstRCOG MRCP. Born 6/8/33. Commd 16/6/57. Wg Cdr 9/5/70. Retd MED 1/1/70.
OLIVER P. A., MIDPM MIMgt. Born 27/12/39. Commd 22/5/70. Sqn Ldr 1/7/82. Retd SUP 5/1/86.
OLIVER P. L. Born 30/6/30. Commd 13/9/50. Sqn Ldr 1/1/62. Retd GD 30/6/68.
OLIVER P. M. Born 5/9/47. Commd 9/3/72. Fg Offr 9/3/74. Retd GD 18/9/76.
OLLIFF N. J., BSc. Born 20/9/47. Commd 19/5/74. Flt Lt 19/2/77. Retd ENG 1/4/81.
OLLIFFE A. I. Born 20/9/20. Commd 6/1/55. Flt Lt 6/1/58. Retd GD 20/9/70.
OLLIVER T., MBE. Born 3/7/21. Commd 15/6/61. Sqn Ldr 1/7/73. Retd ENG 3/7/76.
OLLIVERE., MSc BDS. Born 16/4/47. Commd 8/12/74. Gp Capt 6/8/97. Retd DEL 15/10/99.
OLSON W. H. Born 10/2/25. Commd 1/4/45. Sqn Ldr 1/1/62. Retd GD 27/4/68.
OLVER M. K. Born 31/1/47. Commd 30/5/69. Flt Lt 4/8/64. Retd GD(G) 14/3/96.
ONGLEY C. G. Born 3/6/33. Commd 30/1/52. Flt Lt 29/5/57. Retd GD 13/12/71.
ONGLEY W. K., MBE MIMgt. Born 3/12/16. Commd 8/6/41. Sqn Ldr 1/1/62. Retd GD(G) 3/12/74.
ONLEY M. J, BSc. Born 12/5/59. Commd 17/1/82. Sqn Ldr 1/1/92. Retd GD 17/1/98.
ONSLOW G. H. Born 4/10/28. Commd 29/7/49. Flt Lt 20/11/58. Retd RGT 5/3/68.
OOUNG S. Born 3/10/59. Commd 6/5/83. Wg Cdr 1/7/98. Retd GD 1/10/00.
OPENSHAW D., BSc. Born 12/5/34. Commd 24/8/56. Sqn Ldr 24/2/66. Retd EDN 24/8/72.
OPENSHAW I. K., BSc. Born 11/7/31. Commd 16/1/72. Sqn Ldr 16/1/72. Retd ENG 11/7/93.
OPIE B. W., FCIPD FIMgt. Born 5/11/31. Commd 17/12/52. A Cdre 1/7/80. Retd ADMIN 3/4/85.
ORAM K. M. Born 13/7/43. Commd 27/3/86. Flt Lt 27/3/90. Retd ENG 31/3/94.
ORANGE N. G., MBE. Born 15/6/35. Commd 23/9/66. Sqn Ldr 1/7/80. Retd ADMIN 16/4/89.
ORBELL P. A., MA MIMgt. Born 13/10/27. Commd 5/11/52. Sqn Ldr 5/5/62. Retd ADMIN 13/10/85.
ORCHARD D. F. Born 29/6/24. Commd 1/10/43. Sqn Ldr 1/7/56. Retd GD 29/6/62.
ORCHARD H. F. Born 7/1/23. Commd 3/6/43. Sqn Ldr 1/1/56. Retd SUP 26/12/61.
ORCHARD N. A., MSc BDS MGDSRCS (Eng). Born 26/10/47. Commd 14/9/69. Wg Cdr 26/11/84. Retd DEL
14/3/97.

ORCHARD R. D. S., MBE. Born 7/2/22. Commd 2/5/44. Gp Capt 1/7/73. Retd GD(G) 7/2/77.
ORD G. E., CBE FIMgt. Born 19/8/31. Commd 21/5/52. Gp Capt 1/1/77. Retd GD 30/12/84.
ORD I. G. L. Born 14/2/44. Commd 28/4/65. Sqn Ldr 1/1/78. Retd GD 14/2/82.
ORGAN C. C., MBE TD. Born 10/5/16. Commd 3/9/45. Sqn Ldr 1/7/54. Retd RGT 13/12/57.
ORME B. M. Born 25/10/45. Commd 29/10/64. Fg Offr 29/4/67. Retd ENG 2/1/71.
ORME C. J. Born 18/6/46. Commd 17/12/64. Sqn Ldr 1/7/78. Retd ENG 14/3/96.
ORME J. P., CEng MIMechE. Born 15/3/38. Commd 19/9/71. Flt Lt 19/9/72. Retd ENG 29/9/89.
ORME K. P., AFC BSc MRAeS. Born 17/3/43. Commd 17/4/64. Sqn Ldr 1/1/75. Retd GD 17/3/81.
ORMEROD A. J. Born 22/2/48. Commd 7/1/71. Fg Offr 7/1/73. Retd GD 15/5/75.
ORMEROD J. A. Born 29/3/21. Commd 9/7/41. Sqn Ldr 1/1/59. Retd GD 29/3/64.
ORMEROD J. M. Born 23/1/23. Commd 4/6/64. Flt Lt 4/6/69. Retd ENG 1/11/69.
ORMISTON T. McN., DFC. Born 30/11/17. Commd 17/4/39. Sqn Ldr 1/10/54. Retd GD 26/11/57.
ORMROD W., CBE MSc CEng MRAeS. Born 21/1/26. Commd 22/2/46. A Cdre 1/1/75. Retd ENG 3/5/77.
ORMSHAW B. H. Born 29/11/34. Commd 20/2/59. Flt Lt 26/7/67. Retd ENG 20/2/75.
ORR B. J. Born 23/7/46. Commd 1/4/65. Sqn Ldr 1/1/90. Retd GD(G) 31/5/93.
ORR J. S., MBE. Born 1/1/43. Commd 1/4/76. Sqn Ldr 1/1/92. Retd GD 1/2/98.
ORR J. S., OBE. Born 21/9/10. Commd 25/7/40. Wg Cdr 1/7/56. Retd SEC 21/9/61.
ORR K. B. Born 16/11/18. Commd 14/1/41. Sqn Ldr 1/1/57. Retd GD 12/6/59.
ORR M. K. Born 5/12/27. Commd 30/9/50. Flt Lt 10/2/57. Retd GD 7/12/66.
ORR N. W. Born 16/11/19. Commd 14/1/41. Sqn Ldr 1/7/54. Retd GD 9/9/58.
ORR W. R. Born 21/8/13. Commd 13/9/42. Flt Lt 13/3/46. Retd ENG 1/1/54.
ORREY M. I. Born 14/10/30. Commd 3/5/51. Sqn Ldr 1/7/70. Retd GD(G) 15/2/85.
ORRICK R. Born 4/9/22. Commd 1/4/45. Flt Lt 10/11/55. Retd GD(G) 7/9/72.
ORRINGE D. A. Born 26/4/44. Commd 24/4/64. Flt Lt 24/10/69. Retd GD 29/11/75.
ORROCK R. K., DFM FIMgt. Born 18/1/21. Commd 21/12/40. A Cdre 1/7/72. Retd GD 18/1/76.
ORSLER T. B. Born 17/12/32. Commd 29/10/52. Flt Lt 14/8/59. Retd SUP 1/8/78.
ORTON A. A. Born 10/8/46. Commd 19/8/66. Flt Lt 4/5/72. Retd GD 10/8/84.
ORTON P. D. Born 4/9/32. Commd 28/7/53. Flt Lt 28/1/56. Retd GD 30/12/59.
ORWIN C. W., CEng MRAeS MIMgt. Born 13/2/23. Commd 23/2/50. Wg Cdr 1/1/72. Retd ENG 31/3/77.
ORYTL R., BSc. Born 16/1/60. Commd 11/9/83. Flt Lt 7/11/88. Retd GD 14/3/97.
OSBORN D. R. Born 23/10/33. Commd 26/3/52. Flt Lt 7/8/57. Retd GD 23/10/71.
OSBORN M. P. Born 19/12/40. Commd 30/5/59. Sqn Ldr 1/7/80. Retd GD(G) 19/12/95.
OSBORN P. Born 1/1/48. Commd 28/2/69. Flt Lt 28/2/72. Retd GD 2/11/87.
OSBORN P. D. Born 19/11/29. Commd 17/5/51. Sqn Ldr 1/7/67. Retd GD 31/5/74.
OSBORN T. G. R., CBE. Born 17/4/36. Commd 14/7/54. A Cdre 1/7/88. Retd GD 17/4/91.
OSBORNE A. F., DFC. Born 20/5/22. Commd 7/7/42. Sqn Ldr 1/1/52. Retd GD 1/12/60.
OSBORNE C. E. W. Born 8/5/31. Commd 19/1/70. Sqn Ldr 1/1/77. Retd GD 8/5/89.
OSBORNE D. G., BA. Born 7/9/48. Commd 22/6/70. Flt Lt 22/3/72. Retd GD 30/8/74.
OSBORNE I. W. S., DPhys Ed. Born 16/12/45. Commd 13/9/70. Flt Lt 13/9/74. Retd ADMIN 1/10/82.
OSBORNE M. Born 14/9/33. Commd 13/12/55. Flt Lt 18/8/59. Retd GD 28/4/70.
OSBORNE N. G., BSc. Born 5/12/51. Commd 13/9/70. Sqn Ldr 1/7/85. Retd GD 5/12/89.
OSBORNE P. B., DFC. Born 17/7/23. Commd 29/11/48. Sqn Ldr 1/7/74. Retd GD 30/6/78.
OSBORNE P. E. Born 28/6/46. Commd 3/3/67. Flt Lt 3/9/69. Retd GD 28/6/84.
OSBORNE P. R. P. Born 22/5/28. Commd 1/12/49. Flt Lt 2/11/55. Retd GD 22/5/66.
OSBORNE R. A., CertEd. Born 9/4/46. Commd 22/4/79. Sqn Ldr 1/7/91. Retd ADMIN 3/8/00.
OSBORNE R. W. Born 6/7/40. Commd 26/5/61. Flt Lt 26/11/66. Retd GD 1/11/77.
OSBORNE R. W. Born 21/4/46. Commd 2/4/65. Flt Lt 2/10/70. Retd GD 21/4/84.
OSBORNE S. C. Born 31/1/43. Commd 1/3/62. Flt Lt 8/1/69. Retd GD(G) 30/1/96.
OSBORNE S. R. Born 8/7/65. Commd 19/7/84. Flt Lt 19/1/90. Retd GD 14/3/96.
OSBORNE T. F. Born 24/5/46. Commd 11/6/81. Flt Lt 11/6/84. Retd GD 1/8/86.
OSMENT D. E. T. Born 14/10/16. Commd 7/3/38. Sqn Ldr 1/8/47. Retd SEC 14/10/65.
OSMENT D. G., MBE. Born 2/2/33. Commd 12/3/64. Sqn Ldr 1/7/74. Retd GD 13/11/81.
OSTERBERG R. D., FCIS MBCS. Born 22/4/30. Commd 19/6/52. Gp Capt 1/1/77. Retd SEC 23/9/78.
OSTRIDGE C. P. Born 24/12/29. Commd 17/1/52. Flt Lt 8/5/57. Retd GD 24/12/67.
OSTROWSKI J. S., OBE. Born 9/9/05. Commd 1/3/47. Flt Lt 1/3/47. Retd SE 13/10/62 rtg Wg Cdr.
OSWALD T. J. Born 11/2/43. Commd 20/8/65. Sqn Ldr 1/7/88. Retd GD 11/2/98.
OSWELL Q. M. B. Born 30/10/35. Commd 10/4/56. Wg Cdr 1/1/81. Retd GD 30/10/90.
OSZCZYK M. S., BSc CertEd. Born 8/4/55. Commd 6/9/81. Flt Lt 6/9/82. Retd ADMIN 6/9/97.
OTLEY L. J. Born 7/10/24. Commd 24/3/44. Flt Lt 24/9/47. Retd GD 21/12/63 rtg Sqn Ldr.
OTRIDGE B. Born 1/3/50. Commd 30/5/69. Sqn Ldr 1/7/87. Retd ENG 1/7/90.
OTRIDGE D. Born 5/4/43. Commd 10/6/66. Flt Lt 14/2/69. Retd GD 5/4/98.
OTTAWAY K. P., BA MCIPD. Born 9/12/54. Commd 24/3/44. Sqn Ldr 1/1/89. Retd SY 9/12/92.
OTTER G. R., MBE. Born 5/8/16. Commd 6/9/56. Sqn Ldr 1/1/66. Retd ENG 23/12/72.
OTTEWILL P. G., AFC GM. Born 5/11/15. Commd 19/6/41. Gp Capt 1/7/60. Retd GD 6/11/65.
OUGHTON G. J., BSc CEng MRAeS. Born 8/11/45. Commd 15/7/66. Gp Capt 1/7/92. Retd ENG 22/10/94.
OULTON P.D. Born 6/9/37. Commd 28/7/59. A Cdre 1/1/89. Retd GD 6/9/92.

OUSTON R. J. Born 2/1/37. Commd 16/4/57. Wg Cdr 1/7/88. Retd GD 13/1/91.
OUTEN D. R. Born 28/11/52. Commd 11/7/74. Sqn Ldr 1/7/91. Retd ADMIN 17/3/97.
OVEL W. E., BSc. Born 13/10/50. Commd 15/9/69. Sqn Ldr 1/7/85. Retd GD 14/3/96.
OVENDEN D. A., RVM IEng FIIE(elec) MIMgt. Born 7/9/43. Commd 14/8/80. Sqn Ldr 1/7/89. Retd ENG 25/10/97.
OVENDEN L. R. J., AFC. Born 28/8/17. Commd 15/1/41. Sqn Ldr 1/8/47. Retd GD 26/8/58.
OVENS J. L. P. Born 18/7/80. Commd 6/12/51. Sqn Offr 1/7/66. Retd SEC 1/7/69.
OVER F., MA MSc BA AFIMA. Born 20/11/32. Commd 2/3/57. Sqn Ldr 1/11/68. Retd EDN 23/10/75.
OVERALL R. H. T. Born 23/5/31. Commd 17/12/52. Sqn Ldr 1/1/67. Retd ADMIN 23/5/86.
OVEREND A. P. J., BA. Born 1/7/43. Commd 31/10/66. Fg Offr 11/11/66. Retd EDN 12/7/68.
OVERSBY G. Born 15/12/12. Commd 6/11/41. Flt Lt 4/11/46. Retd ENG 28/4/58.
OVERTON C. R. Born 16/6/14. Commd 4/11/43. Sqn Ldr 1/10/55. Retd ENG 16/6/63.
OVERY L. R. Born 13/8/34. Commd 13/2/60. Flt Lt 13/8/65. Retd GD 22/9/75.
OWEN A. Born 5/5/56. Commd 11/8/77. Flt Lt 24/3/81. Retd GD 1/7/86.
OWEN A. J., DFC* AFC DFM. Born 8/7/22. Commd 11/3/43. Wg Cdr 1/1/60. Retd GD 8/7/69.
OWEN C. R. W. Born 20/10/25. Commd 7/7/52. Flt Lt 7/7/52. Retd ENG 20/10/63.
OWEN D., BA. Born 7/9/40. Commd 31/3/64. Sqn Ldr 31/3/73. Retd ADMIN 31/3/80.
OWEN D. C. Born 2/12/31. Commd 6/9/79. Sqn Ldr 9/7/75. Retd ADMIN 2/12/86.
OWEN D. P. Born 15/2/50. Commd 9/8/85. Flt Lt 26/9/89. Retd ENG 6/3/93.
OWEN E. I. Born 14/9/20. Commd 23/4/45. Flt Lt 11/8/55. Retd GD 2/7/68.
OWEN G. M., MBE. Born 26/4/17. Commd 1/9/41. Wg Offr 1/7/61. Retd CAT 10/7/63.
OWEN G. W. Born 20/4/17. Commd 17/7/46. Fg Offr 17/7/47. Retd RGT 25/5/49.
OWEN H. Born 4/6/21. Commd 20/9/44. Flt Lt 4/1/51. Retd SEC 15/7/55.
OWEN J. H. Born 3/2/44. Commd 26/3/64. Sqn Ldr 1/1/79. Retd ADMIN 3/2/88.
OWEN J. K., CEng MIMech E MRAeS. Born 17/4/38. Commd 30/7/59. Sqn Ldr 1/1/71. Retd ENG 17/4/76.
OWEN J. R. Born 19/1/45. Commd 27/3/80. Flt Lt 27/3/80. Retd ENG 1/10/94.
OWEN J. R., AFC. Born 15/9/37. Commd 28/7/59. Sqn Ldr 1/7/68. Retd GD 15/9/75.
OWEN J. S. Born 6/10/18. Commd 29/3/39. Wg Cdr 1/7/54. Retd GD 10/6/64 rtg Gp Capt.
OWEN M. C. Born 30/3/48. Commd 17/2/67. Flt Lt 17/8/73. Retd GD(G) 30/9/78.
OWEN M. J., MSc BSc CEng MIEE MRIN MRAeS MIMgt ACGI. Born 17/3/43. Commd 6/10/74. Sqn Ldr 1/7/84. Retd ENG 15/4/94.
OWEN N. C., MCIPD MIMgt. Born 15/9/45. Commd 7/7/69. Sqn Ldr 1/1/86. Retd RGT 7/7/91.
OWEN N. T. Born 8/7/20. Commd 29/3/44. Flt Lt 17/3/49. Retd GD(G) 26/12/53.
OWEN P. C. Born 9/11/57. Commd 8/12/83. Sqn Ldr 1/1/93. Retd ADMIN 2/12/97.
OWEN P. L. T., OBE MA DipSoton CEng FIEE. Born 16/12/33. Commd 26/9/53. A Cdre 1/7/78. Retd ENG 3/4/81.
OWEN P. S. Born 7/9/47. Commd 23/6/67. Gp Capt 1/7/92. Retd GD 1/4/00.
OWEN R. C., CEng MIEE DipElEng. Born 7/7/49. Commd 17/10/71. Wg Cdr 1/1/90. Retd ENG 7/12/96.
OWEN R. L. Born 18/4/50. Commd 27/3/75. Flt Lt 9/8/79. Retd PI 14/5/89.
OWEN W. K., BA. Born 29/11/65. Commd 16/9/84. Flt Lt 15/1/90. Retd GD 15/7/99.
OWEN W. R., DFC. Born 11/6/19. Commd 6/12/41. Sqn Ldr 1/1/51. Retd GD 28/1/59.
OWEN W. T., BA. Born 13/7/27. Commd 10/2/49. Wg Cdr 1/1/70. Retd SEC 1/11/74.
OWENS D. T., FIMgt. Born 30/9/23. Commd 2/2/45. Gp Capt 1/7/73. Retd SUP 30/6/77.
OWENS D. W. L. Born 13/10/31. Commd 11/9/52. Gp Capt 1/7/84. Retd GD(G) 1/7/87.
OWENS W. D. Born 10/6/54. Commd 27/8/87. Flt Lt 27/8/89. Retd SUP 14/3/96.
OWENS W. J. Born 25/6/21. Commd 23/12/61. Flt Lt 23/12/66. Retd ENG 31/12/74.
OWER P. C., MSc BDS MGDSRCS(Ed) MGDSRCS(Eng). Born 24/12/55. Commd 22/6/80. Wg Cdr 28/2/92. Retd DEL 22/6/96.
OWERS A. J., BA. Born 14/3/62. Commd 25/1/82. Sqn Ldr 1/7/96. Retd GD 1/12/00.
OWGAN D. F. Born 23/12/40. Commd 5/11/70. Flt Lt 5/11/72. Retd GD(G) 22/12/78.
OXBORROW G. E. Born 28/12/55. Commd 17/8/80. Sqn Ldr 1/1/90. Retd ADMIN 14/3/96.
OXBORROW M. D. Born 30/5/52. Commd 11/1/79. Flt Lt 21/2/83. Retd GD 20/12/97.
OXBORROW R. J., AHSM. Born 5/12/45. Commd 3/7/80. Sqn Ldr 1/1/87. Retd MED(SEC) 1/8/92.
OXBY D. A., DSO DFC DFM*. Born 10/6/20. Commd 31/10/42. Wg Cdr 1/7/57. Retd GD 11/3/69.
OXENHAM D. O. Born 29/9/25. Commd 14/12/50. Sqn Ldr 1/1/67. Retd GD 25/9/75.
OXER H. F., MA MB BChir MRCS FFARCS LRCP DA. Born 16/4/32. Commd 14/10/58. Wg Cdr 13/10/71. Retd MED 10/9/75.
OXLEE D. D., OBE. Born 3/7/34. Commd 29/7/65. Wg Cdr 1/1/81. Retd PI 10/1/86.
OXLEE G. J., OBE BA MRAeS MIMgt. Born 30/3/36. Commd 21/10/65. Gp Capt 1/1/85. Retd PI 9/8/87.
OXLEY C. D. A., AFC MIMgt. Born 10/9/23. Commd 6/1/45. Wg Cdr 1/1/74. Retd GD(G) 31/3/77.
OXLEY J. D., BSc CEng MIEE. Born 23/7/24. Commd 17/9/57. Sqn Ldr 1/1/63. Retd ENG 1/6/78.
OXLEY J. F. Born 20/11/41. Commd 27/1/61. Flt Lt 9/2/68. Retd GD(G) 14/9/92.
OXLEY M. Born 13/7/29. Commd 3/11/60. Flt Lt 3/11/65. Retd GD 1/6/68.
OXLEY R. G. Born 31/1/45. Commd 3/3/67. Flt Lt 12/11/69. Retd GD 7/5/76.
OXTOBY P. A. Born 2/8/24. Commd 1/11/43. Sqn Ldr 1/7/59. Retd CAT 30/5/70.
OYSTON J. K., MB BS FRCS. Born 13/1/25. Commd 29/9/50. Wg Cdr 1/4/62. Retd MED 1/11/69.
OZANNE D. T. F. Born 26/5/34. Commd 26/7/55. Flt Lt 29/4/59. Retd GD 26/5/72.
OZANNE J. F. Born 28/11/30. Commd 18/10/62. Sqn Ldr 1/1/78. Retd ENG 28/11/83.

O'HARA L., MBE. Born 6/6/36. Commd 18/7/60. Wg Cdr 1/1/75. Retd SUP 16/11/82.

# P

PACK J. M., CBE. Born 5/3/31. Commd 14/4/53. A Cdre 1/1/78. Retd GD 1/8/86.
PACKER D. G. L., BSc DipSoton CEng MIEE MIMgt. Born 3/10/30. Commd 24/9/52. Wg Cdr 3/10/70. Retd EDN 3/1/76.
PACKER F. W. J. Born 19/3/30. Commd 21/11/51. Flt Lt 6/3/57. Retd GD 19/3/68.
PACKMAN D., FInstPet FIMgt FCIPS FRGS. Born 26/8/38. Commd 15/12/59. Gp Capt 1/7/85. Retd SUP 23/5/87.
PACKMAN R. E. E. Born 23/7/32. Commd 27/3/70. Flt Lt 27/3/76. Retd SEC 1/4/78.
PACKWOOD E. W. H., ACIS MIMgt. Born 8/9/27. Commd 17/3/49. Gp Capt. 1/7/77. Retd SEC 8/9/79.
PADBURY D. W. Born 22/7/30. Commd 13/2/52. Sqn Ldr 1/7/76. Retd GD 22/7/88.
PADDON A. E., BEd. Born 24/1/51. Commd 3/9/78. Sqn Ldr 1/1/89. Retd ADMIN 1/10/94.
PADFIELD F. C., CBE BSc CEng FIEE FRAeS. Born 30/10/22. Commd 13/12/45. A Cdre 1/7/72. Retd ENG 30/10/77.
PADGET P. I., LDS. Born 4/4/19. Commd 3/10/41. Wg Cdr 1/1/57. Retd DEL 31/10/72.
PADLEY P. G. Born 3/9/33. Commd 8/9/54. Wg Cdr 1/7/70. Retd GD 15/6/73.
PAGE A. M., BA. Born 21/10/56. Commd 5/5/77. Flt Lt 15/10/79. Retd GD 14/8/88.
PAGE C. I. Born 10/12/54. Commd 18/4/74. Flt Lt 14/9/80. Retd GD(G) 28/5/82. Reinstated 25/4/84. Flt Lt 12/8/82. Retd GD(G) 14/3/96.
PAGE G. J. Born 7/11/30. Commd 21/8/54. Sqn Ldr 1/7/66. Retd GD 14/3/74.
PAGE G. M. B., BSc. Born 2/10/46. Commd 6/10/69. Wg Cdr 1/1/89. Retd GD 14/9/96.
PAGE J. S. Born 2/7/47. Commd 2/1/70. Sqn Ldr 1/1/88. Retd SY 14/3/96.
PAGE M. D., BSc. Born 22/9/61. Commd 29/4/84. Flt Lt 29/10/87. Retd SUP 14/9/96.
PAGE R. J., MIMgt. Born 8/8/24. Commd 13/6/46. Sqn Ldr 1/1/60. Retd RGT 15/7/78.
PAGE R. S. Born 11/5/58. Commd 4/9/81. Flt Lt 4/3/88. Retd SUP 31/3/94.
PAGE S. L., BSc MIMgt. Born 30/12/21. Commd 27/3/43. Wg Cdr 1/7/65. Retd ADMIN 30/12/76.
PAGE T. J., DFM. Born 24/1/22. Commd 19/7/44. Sqn Ldr 1/4/58. Retd SEC 10/5/68.
PAGE T. S., CEng MIEE. Born 10/11/43. Commd 15/7/65. Sqn Ldr 1/7/76. Retd ADMIN 10/11/87.
PAGE W. F., OBE AFC FIMgt. Born 21/1/33. Commd 23/4/52. Gp Capt 1/1/77. Retd GD 2/1/91.
PAGET J. W. F. Born 29/5/29. Commd 5/7/53. Flt Lt 25/11/58. Retd GD 4/4/70.
PAICE R. H. Born 22/5/38. Commd 10/11/61. Flt Lt 1/4/66. Retd GD 1/4/78.
PAIN E. J. Born 20/6/34. Commd 7/1/71. Fg Offr 7/1/71. Retd ENG 14/1/76 rtg Flt Lt.
PAIN H. Born 27/8/21. Commd 18/11/43. Flt Lt 17/4/46. Retd GD(G) 31/8/73 rtg Sqn Ldr.
PAIN K. V. Born 8/1/38. Commd 16/5/74. Sqn Ldr 1/1/86. Retd ADMIN 14/10/89.
PAIN R. C. Born 27/8/25. Commd 26/3/59. Sqn Ldr 1/1/74. Retd GD 27/4/76.
PAINES D. A. M. Born 14/7/31. Commd 10/12/52. Flt Lt 29/4/59. Retd GD 6/5/72.
PAINTER A. S. Born 7/1/37. Commd 6/9/63. Sqn Ldr 1/1/76. Retd GD 18/6/79.
PAINTER K. P. Born 20/4/38. Commd 23/1/64. Flt Lt 8/8/66. Retd ADMIN 20/4/76.
PAINTING C. H. Born 11/1/29. Commd 3/11/51 Flt Lt 3/5/56. Retd GD 11/1/87.
PAISEY M. A. C., BA. Born 6/8/64. Commd 5/9/82. Flt Lt 15/10/86. Retd GD 15/7/97.
PAISH C. M., BA. Born 1/4/37. Commd 2/10/58. Sqn Ldr 1/7/68. Retd GD 10/10/88.
PAISLEY C. J., MIDPM. Born 27/5/46. Commd 23/9/66. Sqn Ldr 1/1/80. Retd SUP 27/5/90.
PAISLEY E. J., CEng MRAeS MIMechE. Born 13/1/33. Commd 8/2/57. Sqn Ldr 1/7/65. Retd ENG 8/2/73.
PAKES F. Born 7/8/19. Commd 29/4/43. Wg Cdr 1/7/69. Retd ENG 7/8/74.
PAKULA K., BSc. Born 7/2/20. Commd 5/4/49. Flt Lt 4/12/52. Retd GD(G) 22/11/65.
PALETHORPE H. W. O. Born 29/3/09. Commd 1/4/40. Flt Lt 1/4/42. Retd GD 21/12/45.
PALEY M. A. Born 25/8/41. Commd 12/3/60. Wg Cdr 1/1/86. Retd GD 25/6/94.
PALFREY M. J. Born 29/7/45. Commd 16/9/76. Flt Lt 16/9/78. Retd ENG 16/9/84.
PALFREYMAN C. R., MB BS FRCS DOMS. Born 19/4/05. Commd 1/12/30. Wg Cdr 1/9/41. Retd MED 9/4/47 rtg Gp Capt.
PALIN G. R., PhD BSc CEng MRAeS. Born 23/4/30. Commd 28/10/55. Wg Cdr 28/3/70. Retd EDN 30/9/75.
PALIN Sir Roger., KCB OBE MA FRAeS FCIPD. Born 8/7/38. Commd 21/1/63. ACM 22/4/91. Retd GD 1/7/93.
PALLISTER C. A. J. Born 19/10/39. Commd 14/11/59. Sqn Ldr 1/1/74. Retd GD 19/10/77.
PALLISTER M. A., BA MB BChir MRCGP MFCM MRCS LRCP DTM&H DPH DIH. Born 5/10/30. Commd 3/3/57. A Cdre 1/1/85. Retd MED 5/4/89.
PALLOT C. G. Born 17/11/18. Commd 17/6/54. Sqn Ldr 1/1/63. Retd ENG 17/11/73.
PALMER A., MIMgt. Born 27/3/21. Commd 29/6/44. Sqn Ldr 1/7/70. Retd SEC 27/3/76.
PALMER A. G. Born 11/9/10. Commd 10/8/44. Flt Lt 29/6/50. Retd SUP 6/1/58.
PALMER A. V. E. Born 11/10/23. Commd 3/4/45. Wg Cdr 1/1/65. Retd GD 2/4/74.
PALMER A. V. H., OBE. Born 23/5/22. Commd 28/7/49. Wg Cdr 1/1/68. Retd ENG 23/5/77.
PALMER A. V. M., MBE. Born 20/3/40. Commd 3/6/65. Sqn Ldr 1/1/75. Retd ADMIN 20/3/78.
PALMER B. Born 14/11/32. Commd 12/2/53. Wg Cdr 1/1/76. Retd GD(G) 4/12/82.
PALMER B. G., BA BEd. Born 20/8/47. Commd 9/4/72. Wg Cdr 1/7/90. Retd GD(G) 31/3/94.
PALMER B. J., BA. Born 18/5/20. Commd 19/10/49. Sqn Ldr 19/11/59. Retd EDN 1/11/64.

PALMER C. R., MBE AFC. Born 31/7/22. Commd 30/12/45. Sqn Ldr 1/7/66. Retd GD 1/4/73.
PALMER D. J., BSc. Born 18/12/50. Commd 28/8/73. Sqn Ldr 1/7/84. Retd ENG 14/9/90.
PALMER G. A. W. Born 6/12/32. Commd 26/3/64. Sqn Ldr 1/7/78. Retd ADMIN 12/5/89.
PALMER G. P. Born 22/11/38. Commd 17/3/67. Flt Lt 17/3/73. Retd ENG 1/9/76.
PALMER J., MBE. Born 11/9/18. Commd 15/4/43. Flt Lt 15/10/46. Retd ENG 19/6/54.
PALMER J. F. Born 17/11/19. Commd 22/8/46. Sqn Ldr 1/7/62. Retd ENG 16/11/74.
PALMER J. H. Born 9/6/28. Commd 27/7/49. Sqn Ldr 1/1/59. Retd GD 9/7/71 rtg Wg Cdr.
PALMER J. K., OBE. Born 10/6/30. Commd 27/9/51. Gp Capt 1/1/80. Retd GD 5/3/83.
PALMER L. J. Born 27/9/20. Commd 19/3/43. Sqn Ldr 1/7/54. Retd GD 1/4/61.
PALMER L. O. Born 3/6/13. Commd 12/8/43. Sqn Ldr 1/7/60. Retd ENG 3/6/69.
PALMER L. V., DPhysEd. Born 31/12/43. Commd 14/9/65. Wg Cdr 1/1/86. Retd ADMIN 14/3/96.
PALMER M. J. S. Born 23/11/42. Commd 23/6/67. A Cdre 1/7/91. Retd ENG 1/5/94.
PALMER R. C. Born 25/5/33. Commd 1/6/72. Flt Lt 1/6/75. Retd GD 25/5/88.
PALMER R. S. Born 2/2/33. Commd 21/11/51. Sqn Ldr 1/1/66. Retd SEC 2/2/71.
PALMER R. V., MIMgt Born 8/2/20. Commd 12/6/50. Sqn Ldr 1/1/60. Retd SEC 8/5/72.
PALMER S. J., MIMgt. Born 17/2/19. Commd 23/8/45. Sqn Ldr 1/7/62. Retd SEC 17/2/74.
PALMER S. J., OBE DFC MIMgt. Born 21/9/22. Commd 3/9/43. Wg Cdr 1/7/66. retd ADMIN 21/11/77.
PALMER S. J. J., MIMgt. Born 11/7/23. Commd 29/9/43. Flt Lt 15/12/49. Retd SEC 20/4/74.
PALMER T. J. Born 17/1/12. Commd 13/2/47. Fg Offr 13/2/47. Retd SUP 28/6/48.
PALMER T. J. Born 9/5/20. Commd 12/9/47. Sqn Ldr 1/7/68. Retd SEC 9/5/75.
PALMER W. J. Born 21/12/43. Commd 8/12/83. Sqn Ldr 31/12/96. Retd ENG 31/7/98.
PAMPLIN B. P. Born 27/4/35. Commd 7/3/54. Wg Cdr 1/7/72. Retd GD(G) 3/4/82.
PANKHURST D. M. Born 30/5/28. Commd 19/3/62. Flt Lt 19/3/62. Retd GD 23/9/72.
PANTER W. J. Born 27/6/26. Commd 1/10/64. Flt Lt 1/10/64. Retd GD(G) 1/9/82.
PANTING P. D., BA. Born 3/5/24. Commd 24/10/45. Sqn Ldr 11/6/59. Retd EDN 31/8/68.
PANTON A. D., CB OBE DFC. Born 2/11/16. Commd 18/12/37. A Cdre 1/7/67. Retd GD 18/12/72.
PANTON I. E. Born 25/4/53. Commd 18/1/73. Flt Lt 28/6/79. Retd ADMIN 25/4/91.
PANTON I. H., FIMgt MInstAM. Born 23/12/28. Commd 23/4/53. Gp Capt 1/7/79. Retd GD 23/12/83.
PANTON S. E. Born 29/11/12. Commd 28/11/46. Sqn Ldr 1/7/56. Retd SUP 29/11/61.
PAPPIN V. G. H., BEd. Born 19/5/58. Commd 9/11/80. Flt Lt 9/11/84. Retd ADMIN 9/11/89.
PAPWORTH P. M. Born 5/5/33. Commd 5/4/55. Wg Cdr 1/7/75. Retd GD 1/10/83.
PAPWORTH P. R. Born 20/5/38. Commd 14/3/57. Flt Lt 14/6/63. Retd SEC 5/11/69.
PAPWORTH R. D. J., MB ChB DA. Born 5/1/41. Commd 18/7/71. Wg Cdr 5/5/79. Retd MED 20/8/87.
PARDO P. J. Born 4/7/49. Commd 8/10/70. Flt Lt 4/1/75. Retd GD 5/7/75.
PARFIT K. J., FIMgt MCIPD. Born 20/3/24. Commd 3/9/43. Gp Capt 1/7/71. Retd GD 31/3/78.
PARFIT S. M., BSc. Born 31/3/64. Commd 30/3/86. Flt Lt 30/9/89. Retd ADMIN 14/9/96.
PARFITT D. T. Born 25/5/27. Commd 7/10/48. Flt Lt 7/4/52. Retd GD 5/7/75.
PARFITT I. G. Born 23/7/43. Commd 21/7/65. Flt Lt 11/8/70. Retd GD 15/5/84.
PARFITT R. Born 7/10/28. Commd 9/4/52. Flt Lt 9/10/54. Retd GD 25/5/56.
PARFITT R. A., ACMA. Born 17/10/23. Commd 22/3/45. Sqn Ldr 1/1/58. Retd GD 17/1/67.
PARFITT S. J. R., BSc. Born 22/12/90. Commd 30/9/73. Sqn Ldr 1/1/87. Retd GD 22/12/90.
PARHAM W. J., MBE. Born 16/2/18. Commd 30/8/45. Gp Capt 1/1/70. Retd SUP 16/2/73.
PARIS R. N. Born 4/12/24. Commd 26/2/51. Flt Lt 10/11/55. Retd GD 4/12/79.
PARISH G. E. Born 14/12/11. Commd 7/8/41. Fg Offr 7/8/41. Retd GD 22/2/46.
PARK A. J., CBE. Born 7/10/34. Commd 27/5/53. A Cdre 1/7/88. Retd GD 1/7/94.
PARK A. J. Born 10/6/48. Commd 1/8/69. Sqn Ldr 1/7/82. Retd GD 10/11/86.
PARK K. W. Born 23/3/55. Commd 6/10/77. Sqn Ldr 1/1/94. Retd GD 19/6/99.
PARK L., DFC. Born 7/5/22. Commd 30/10/43. Sqn Ldr 1/1/68. Retd GD(G) 31/3/77.
PARKER A. D., BSc. Born 3/10/22. Commd 11/1/76. Flt Lt 11/4/77. Retd GD 11/1/92.
PARKER A. F. B. Born 3/10/22. Commd 6/9/56. Flt Lt 6/9/62. Retd GD 28/12/63.
PARKER A. P. Born 10/10/44. Commd 31/1/64. Flt Lt 31/7/69. Retd GD 12/8/70.
PARKER A. S. BA. Born 16/6/28. Commd 6/3/52. Sqn Ldr 6/9/61. Retd EDN 21/11/67.
PARKER C. J., BSc. Born 16/12/54. Commd 7/1/74. Flt Lt 15/4/78. Retd GD 15/7/88.
PARKER D. A., CEng MRAeS. Born 13/2/33. Commd 22/5/59. Wg Cdr 1/7/77. Retd ENG 17/12/83.
PARKER D. E. Born 9/3/31. Commd 21/10/66. Sqn Ldr 19/10/76. Retd MED(T) 1/6/80.
PARKER D. J. Born 21/7/36. Commd 13/2/60. Flt Lt 13/8/65. Retd GD 1/5/89.
PARKER D. M., MBE MB ChB. Born 6/5/29. Commd 21/11/54. Wg Cdr 4/5/67. Retd MED 21/11/70.
PARKER E. R. Born 15/5/37. Commd 24/1/74. Flt Lt 24/1/78. Retd GD(G) 29/11/82.
PARKER F. E., FIIE. Born 15/6/48. Commd 5/7/73. Wg Cdr 1/7/93. Retd ENG 14/3/97.
PARKER G. A., CEng MRAeS. Born 4/2/29. Commd 5/11/52. Flt Lt 5/11/57. Retd ENG 5/11/68.
PARKER G. B. Born 19/9/57. Commd 26/11/81. Flt Lt 26/5/87. Retd GD 19/1/89.
PARKER G. E. Born 16/6/10. Commd 24/10/41. Flt Lt 18/11/57. Retd SEC 28/6/62.
PARKER G. R., MSc BSc. Born 6/12/40. Commd 31/12/63. Wg Cdr 1/1/84. Retd ADMIN 6/12/95.
PARKER G. S. Born 28/3/25. Commd 8/10/48. Flt Lt 21/3/54. Retd GD 30/9/60.
PARKER H. B. Born 26/6/29. Commd 23/8/56. Fg Offr 23/11/58. Retd SEC 2/6/61.
PARKER H. J., OBE DFM MRAeS. Born 13/2/20. Commd 1/5/42. Wg Cdr 1/7/60. Retd ENG 1/3/75.

PARKER H. M., FAAI MIMgt. Born 3/12/31. Commd 31/5/51. Wg Cdr 1/1/81. Retd ADMIN 2/11/85.
PARKER J. A., MBE. Born 22/5/21. Commd 27/1/44. Gp Capt 1/7/68. Retd ENG 27/3/76.
PARKER J. C. L. Born 29/4/46. Commd 1/3/68. Flt Lt 8/3/72. Retd GD 10/1/75.
PARKER J. E. Born 15/2/53. Commd 15/12/88. Flt Lt 15/12/92. Retd ENG 17/4/93.
PARKER J. F. Born 10/4/08. Commd 7/8/41. Fg Offr 29/8/42. Retd ENG 14/4/46 rtg Flt Lt.
PARKER J. I., AFC. Born 14/9/22. Commd 18/12/43. Wg Cdr 1/7/59. Retd GD 14/9/69.
PARKER J. J. Born 12/5/31. Commd 9/4/52. Sqn Ldr 1/7/67. Retd GD 9/12/75.
PARKER J. J. Born 25/3/36. Commd 29/11/63. Flt Lt 26/7/67. Retd GD 25/3/74.
PARKER J. R. Born 12/4/39. Commd 4/11/63. Flt Lt 29/7/67. Retd PI 12/4/77.
PARKER J. W. Born 9/12/48. Commd 21/2/74. Sqn Ldr 1/7/83. Retd ADMIN 9/12/86.
PARKER J. W. G. Born 12/11/20. Commd 11/7/43. Wg Cdr 1/7/68. Retd ENG 12/11/75.
PARKER L. H. T., CEng MRAeS. Born 6/3/33. Commd 8/2/57. Wg Cdr 1/7/75. Retd ENG 4/2/86.
PARKER M. A., BSc. Born 11/7/63. Commd 30/8/81. Flt Lt 15/4/86. Retd GD 3/11/00.
PARKER M. J., BSc. Born 6/3/51. Commd 3/9/70. Sqn Ldr 1/7/84. Retd ENG 6/3/89.
PARKER N. A. Born 26/2/31. Commd 9/3/50. Flt Lt 18/2/58. Retd GD 26/2/69.
PARKER O. B. Born 11/11/16. Commd 7/1/43. Wg Cdr 1/7/61. Retd ENG 11/11/71.
PARKER R. Born 26/1/43. Commd 24/3/61. Wg Cdr 1/7/87. Retd GD 26/1/98.
PARKER R. Born 14/7/15. Commd 26/11/53. Sqn Ldr 1/1/64. Retd SUP 14/7/70.
PARKER R. C. Born 16/5/31. Commd 25/5/50 Gp Capt 1/1/79. Retd GD 16/5/86.
PARKER R. G. Born 8/12/49. Commd 20/10/85. Flt Lt 20/10/85. Retd ADMIN 20/10/91.
PARKER S., FInstPet. Born 13/3/34. Commd 28/7/63. Sqn Ldr 1/7/73. Retd SUP 6/10/81.
PARKER S. C. B., DFC MCIPS MIMgt. Born 9/12/22. Commd 20/8/44. Wg Cdr 1/7/71. Retd SUP 9/12/77.
PARKER T. E. Born 25/6/63. Commd 4/11/82. Flt Lt 31/3/89. Retd SUP 14/3/96.
PARKER W. D. Born 19/8/22. Commd 4/9/58. Flt Lt 4/9/61. Retd PI 19/9/74.
PARKER W. I., MIMgt. Born 24/5/40. Commd 18/5/61. Flt Lt 28/12/66. Retd GD 8/10/70. Re-employed 11/7/69. Retd ADMIN Sqn Ldr 6/4/83.
PARKER W. M. Born 19/6/34. Commd 26/10/61. Wg Cdr 1/7/79. Retd GD 19/6/89.
PARKER-ASHLEY A. N. S., MA BSc MRAeS. Born 18/11/38. Commd 9/9/63. Wg Cdr 1/1/78. Retd GD 12/9/83.
PARKER-EATON R. G., MBE MIMgt. Born 21/11/31. Commd 26/10/50. Wg Cdr 1/7/67. Retd SUP 13/7/74.
PARKER-HOARE M. J. Born 12/2/35. Commd 9/2/66. Flt Lt 9/2/72. Retd ADMIN 30/9/78.
PARKES A., BSc. Born 20/1/33. Commd 22/1/54. Gp Capt 1/1/80. Retd GD 20/1/91.
PARKES W. B. Born 27/4/19. Commd 18/2/53. Flt Lt 18/8/46. Retd PI 26/6/50.
PARKHOUSE R. C. L. Born 4/2/21. Commd 7/3/40. Sqn Ldr 1/1/54. Retd SEC 31/8/73.
PARKIN A. G. Born 25/5/47. Commd 29/7/65. Sqn Ldr 1/1/84. Retd GD(G) 1/3/93.
PARKIN C. S. Born 28/8/38. Commd 15/12/59. Sqn Ldr 1/1/70. Retd SUP 28/8/76.
PARKIN E. G. Born 21/4/17. Commd 26/5/40. Flt Lt 1/12/53. Retd GD(G) 21/4/72.
PARKIN H. V. Born 3/9/17. Commd 5/10/43. Flt Lt 27/5/54. Retd GD 1/4/62.
PARKIN J. Born 27/5/42. Commd 31/1/80. Sqn Ldr 1/7/90. Retd ENG 14/3/96.
PARKIN L. W. R., MBE MIMgt. Born 22/5/32. Commd 9/3/62. Sqn Ldr 1/1/84. Retd ENG 22/5/92.
PARKIN M. Born 31/7/49. Commd 22/5/75. Sqn Ldr 1/7/86. Retd GD 15/4/95.
PARKIN N. D., MB BS MRCS LRCP MRCPath DCP. Born 12/8/31. Commd 2/7/52. Wg Cdr 11/6/72. Retd MED 23/5/76.
PARKIN R. D., MBE MMAR. Born 11/2/32. Commd 13/11/62. Wg Cdr 1/1/77. Retd MAR 13/11/80.
PARKINSON C. L., MA. Born 26/3/29. Commd 10/9/51. A Cdre 1/1/77. Retd ENG 14/8/79.
PARKINSON D. Born 18/5/38. Commd 2/4/64. Flt Lt 1/7/69. Retd GD 5/5/76.
PARKINSON D., DFM MIMgt. Born 27/8/24. Commd 13/11/44. Sqn Ldr 1/1/71. Retd SEC 23/7/79.
PARKINSON D. J. Born 5/9/35. Commd 12/3/60. Flt Lt 12/9/65. Retd GD 5/9/90.
PARKINSON J. Born 10/5/45. Commd 22/11/84. Flt Lt 22/11/88. Retd SUP 12/7/93.
PARKINSON J. B. Born 29/11/34. Commd 16/11/56. Gp Capt 1/7/81. Retd GD 1/1/87.
PARKINSON R. C. C., FHCIMA FIMgt. Born 24/10/43. Commd 9/3/66. Wg Cdr 1/7/85. Retd ADMIN 2/6/93.
PARKINSON R. K. Born 12/11/23. Commd 3/11/44. Sqn Ldr 1/4/55. Retd GD 12/11/66.
PARKINSON T. W. Born 10/5/45. Commd 15/7/66. Wg Cdr 1/1/81. Retd ENG 12/12/84.
PARKS H. E., DPhysEd. Born 23/12/24. Commd 13/8/52. Flt Lt 13/8/56. Retd PE 1/4/72 rtg Sqn Ldr.
PARKS P. J., MBE. Born 1/1/20. Commd 22/9/49. Sqn Ldr 1/7/61. Retd ENG 1/1/75.
PARKYN J. E. Born 16/12/47. Commd 24/6/76. Flt Lt 24/6/78. Retd ADMIN 6/12/85.
PARLOUR A. W., DFC. Born 3/9/22. Commd 24/8/43. Flt Lt 27/7/47. Retd GD 1/10/60.
PARMEE R. J., MIMgt. Born 12/5/48. Commd 18/1/73. Sqn Ldr 1/7/87. Retd ADMIN 1/9/99.
PARMINTER L. M. T. Born 12/2/64. Commd 8/12/83. Flt Lt 2/6/90. Retd SUP 31/1/91.
PARNABY G. S. A., OBE. Born 12/3/13. Commd 16/3/34. Gp Capt 1/7/51. Retd GD 1/10/58.
PARNABY J. D., BA LLB. Born 1/7/41. Commd 26/5/70. Wg Cdr 1/1/89. Retd ADMIN 1/7/96.
PARNELL F. G. Born 26/12/40. Commd 8/4/82. Flt Lt 1/3/87. Retd ENG 26/12/95.
PARNELL J. T. W. Born 25/9/10. Commd 25/4/40. Fg Offr 4/1/41. Retd ASD 3/12/45 rtg Sqn Ldr.
PARNELL M. A., BSc MRAeS MRIN. Born 6/7/55. Commd 16/9/73. Flt Lt 15/4/78. Retd GD 25/7/93.
PARR A. W., AFC. Born 17/10/33. Commd 23/7/52. Wg Cdr 1/7/73. Retd GD 29/5/88.
PARR D. Born 9/10/49. Commd 8/8/69. Sqn Ldr 1/1/87. Retd SUP 9/10/90.
PARR G. Born 26/8/39. Commd 24/2/64. Flt Lt 4/11/70. Retd GD 7/10/79.

PARR G. E. R. Born 23/11/19. Commd 26/8/42. Sqn Ldr 1/7/53. Retd GD 20/11/59.
PARR J. J. E. Born 12/2/49. Commd 27/2/70. Wg Cdr 1/7/90. Retd GD 14/9/96.
PARR J. L., AIB. Born 17/10/42. Commd 4/9/87. Wg Cdr 1/1/91. Retd ADMIN 1/7/93.
PARR J. M. Born 29/11/32. Commd 20/10/55. Sqn Ldr 1/7/80. Retd ADMIN 17/1/89.
PARR R. I. Born 29/12/44. Commd 18/11/66. Fg Offr 29/12/67. Retd GD(G) 14/2/70.
PARRATT D. Born 3/4/29. Commd 14/12/49. Gp Capt 1/7/73. Retd GD 4/3/80.
PARRATT R., MBE. Born 8/9/34. Commd 24/5/53. Sqn Ldr 1/7/79. Retd GD 8/9/92.
PARRINI A. L. Born 11/9/46. Commd 25/6/66. Sqn Ldr 1/7/83. Retd SUP 11/9/90.
PARROTT D. N. H. Born 26/1/18. Commd 2/6/44. Flt Lt 18/9/48. Retd GD(G) 26/1/73.
PARROTT P. L., DFC* AFC. Born 28/6/20. Commd 27/6/38. Wg Cdr 1/1/54. Retd GD 10/7/65.
PARRY C. H. Born 18/3/25. Commd 17/11/44. Gp Capt 1/1/77. Retd GD 18/3/80.
PARRY D. G., MBE BA. Born 18/5/62. Commd 31/8/80. Wg Cdr 1/1/97. Retd ADMIN 1/10/99.
PARRY D. J., DFC. Born 8/10/21. Commd 10/9/43. Flt Lt 10/9/49. Retd GD(G) 8/10/71.
PARRY D. J., MRAeS. Born 28/12/34. Commd 10/2/56. Sqn Ldr 1/1/68. Retd GD 28/12/72.
PARRY D. M. Born 12/7/33. Commd 1/8/69. Sqn Ldr 1/7/79. Retd SEC 12/7/83.
PARRY G. F., CEng MIEE. Born 1/4/38. Commd 23/1/64. Gp Capt 1/1/85. Retd ENG 10/4/88.
PARRY G. R. Born 11/12/54. Commd 16/2/89. Flt Lt 16/2/91. Retd ENG 16/2/97.
PARRY I. E., MIMgt. Born 22/12/21. Commd 15/10/43. Sqn Ldr 1/7/60. Retd SUP 1/10/70.
PARRY I. J. Born 22/5/38. Commd 6/10/77. Flt Lt 6/10/83. Retd MED(SEC) 22/5/88.
PARRY I. S., BSc MS CEng MIEE. Born 10/5/38. Commd 30/9/57. Wg Cdr 1/7/74. Retd ENG 19/12/81.
PARRY I. T. Born 8/9/41. Commd 20/7/66. Flt Lt 1/7/69. Retd GD 8/9/96.
PARRY J. K., BSc. Born 21/12/40. Commd 2/10/61. Sqn Ldr 1/7/70. Retd GD 21/12/78.
PARRY M. L. P. Born 4/12/40. Commd 22/3/63. Flt Lt 4/6/66. Retd GD 29/4/78.
PARRY N. M. S. Born 25/11/43. Commd 12/7/63. Flt Lt 8/9/70. Retd GD 3/1/76.
PARRY P. W. P., MBE. Born 19/3/48. Commd 29/3/68. Sqn Ldr 1/1/81. Retd RGT 19/6/92.
PARRY R. Born 30/11/62. Commd 2/2/84. Flt Lt 2/8/89. Retd GD 14/3/96.
PARRY R. D. Born 17/12/48. Commd 31/7/70. Flt Lt 31/7/73. Retd GD 17/12/86.
PARRY W. G. Born 17/3/27. Commd 3/1/51. Sqn Ldr 1/1/72. Retd GD(G) 4/9/75.
PARRY-DAVIES D. O. Born 3/3/24. Commd 30/3/45. Wg Cdr 1/7/63. Retd GD 29/6/78.
PARRY-EVANS Sir David., GCB CBE. Born 19/7/35. Commd 4/12/56. ACM 1/7/89. Retd GD 29/2/92.
PARRY-EVANS R. Born 31/10/23. Commd 16/7/56. Flt Lt 16/7/56. Retd CAT 11/3/67.
PARSLEY R. R. C., OBE. Born 22/3/43. Commd 17/12/65. Wg Cdr 1/7/84. Retd GD 22/3/98.
PARSLOE C. F. M. Born 20/11/23. Commd 23/4/47. Flt Lt 23/10/51. Retd RGT 29/12/59.
PARSLOW A., IEng FRAeS. Born 5/9/37. Commd 1/9/85. Sqn Ldr 1/1/88. Retd ENG 25/10/91.
PARSONS B. K. Born 11/9/45. Commd 6/9/63. Wg Cdr 1/7/84. Retd ENG 2/2/83.
PARSONS B. W., CBE DFC AFC FIMgt. Born 12/4/20. Commd 5/12/42. A Cdre 1/7/70. Retd GD 26/8/75.
PARSONS C. A., MB BS FRCS FRCR LRCP DMRD. Born 1/10/40. Commd 10/9/62. Sqn Ldr 18/2/71. Retd MED 1/10/76.
PARSONS C. H. J., TD. Born 29/3/20. Commd 31/10/47. Sqn Ldr 1/7/52. Retd RGT 15/11/58.
PARSONS C. J., MIMgt. Born 6/2/45. Commd 6/5/65. Wg Cdr 1/1/88. Retd ADMIN 24/1/98.
PARSONS C. K., BSc. Born 7/6/43. Commd 19/11/64. Flt Lt 6/6/67. Retd GD 29/3/74.
PARSONS D. Born 1/10/52. Commd 15/8/85. Flt Lt 15/8/87. Retd SUP 14/3/96.
PARSONS D. G. Born 5/11/27. Commd 6/8/47. Flt Lt 7/1/53. Retd GD 23/10/58.
PARSONS D. L. Born 2/5/34. Commd 14/12/54. Sqn Ldr 1/7/65. Retd GD 31/12/71.
PARSONS D. W., MVO FIMgt. Born 27/11/35. Commd 12/1/55. Wg Cdr 1/7/72. Retd GD 3/4/80.
PARSONS E. Born 14/9/39. Commd 14/5/60. Flt Lt 14/11/65. Retd GD 5/2/78.
PARSONS E. A. Born 21/1/37. Commd 3/5/68. Sqn Ldr 1/1/78. Retd ADMIN 1/4/84.
PARSONS F. H., BA. Born 1/9/23. Commd 24/9/63. Sqn Ldr 24/3/67. Retd EDN 24/9/79.
PARSONS G. C., MSc BSc ARCS. Born 20/8/42. Commd 28/9/80. Sqn Ldr 1/1/88. Retd ADMIN 20/8/97.
PARSONS J. B., MB BS MRCS LRCP FFARCS. Born 21/1/26. Commd 4/1/51. Wg Cdr 26/6/63. Retd MED 25/12/68.
PARSONS J. D. Born 13/2/28. Commd 1/6/49. Flt Lt 8/1/59. Retd GD 13/2/66.
PARSONS M., MBE DPhysEd. Born 18/6/44. Commd 19/8/68. Sqn Ldr 1/7/81. Retd ADMIN 1/5/94.
PARSONS P. I. Born 28/2/49. Commd 31/7/70. Flt Lt 31/7/76. Retd SY 28/2/93.
PARSONS P. M. Born 26/11/20. Commd 30/10/45. Flt Offr 3/10/51. Retd SEC 5/6/65.
PARSONS R. M. Born 10/7/60. Commd 6/5/83. Sqn Ldr 1/1/91. Retd ENG 1/9/98.
PARSONS S. R., OBE CEng MRAeS. Born 28/7/39. Commd 7/5/64. Gp Capt 1/7/82. Retd ENG 26/11/84.
PARTINGTON G. R., BEM. Born 13/11/42. Commd 2/2/65. Sqn Ldr 1/1/78. Retd ENG 2/2/83.
PARTINGTON J. A., MBE BSc. Born 8/6/38. Commd 13/11/62. Wg Cdr 1/7/79. Retd ENG 8/6/93.
PARTINGTON T. G., BSc(Eng). Born 17/5/55. Commd 2/9/73. Flt Lt 15/10/77. Retd GD 15/7/88.
PARTRIDGE B. C., MBE. Born 1/11/22. Commd 29/3/56. Sqn Ldr 1/1/70. Retd ENG 31/10/73.
PARTRIDGE B. L. Born 9/10/22. Commd 1/1/43. Wg Cdr 1/1/59. Retd GD 9/7/61.
PARTRIDGE D. J. Born 24/12/71. Commd 17/9/90. Fg Offr 15/7/92. Retd GD 1/5/95.
PARTRIDGE J. E., DSO DFC*. Born 23/3/14. Commd 1/5/42. Sqn Ldr 1/7/58. Retd SEC 6/4/69 rtg Wg Cdr.
PARTRIDGE J. M. Born 10/9/26. Commd 25/8/60. Sqn Ldr 1/1/72. Retd ENG 10/9/81.
PARTRIDGE R. H. Born 27/11/44. Commd 25/3/64. Flt Lt 12/11/69. Retd GD 30/9/78.

PARTRIDGE R. W. Born 22/2/54. Commd 1/12/77. Flt Lt 1/6/84. Retd SUP 15/8/93.
PARTRIDGE R. W., BSc. Born 21/7/56. Commd 3/1/82. Flt Lt 23/6/82. Retd ENG 11/2/93.
PARTRIDGE S. J. Born 7/4/57. Commd 28/10/76. Flt Lt 28/4/83. Retd SY 7/4/95.
PASCALL A. R. J. Born 23/9/39. Commd 23/6/64. Wg Cdr 1/1/80. Retd ADMIN 22/7/87.
PASCO D. Born 21/9/37. Commd 17/10/59. Sqn Ldr 1/7/71. Retd GD 30/10/76.
PASCOE D. T. C., CEng MIEE. Born 8/4/17. Commd 18/7/46. Sqn Ldr 28/8/59. Retd ENG 8/4/72.
PASCOE P. W., AFC. Born 18/1/34. Commd 5/11/52. Flt Lt 24/3/58. Retd GD 30/9/77.
PASCOE S. V. Born 2/10/18. Commd 5/11/42. Flt Lt 17/5/56. Retd GD(G) 29/3/61.
PASH N. E. Born 25/1/20. Commd 27/9/46. Flt Lt 19/11/53. Retd GD 7/10/61.
PASKETT G. Born 16/6/46. Commd 4/12/64. Flt Lt 4/6/70. Retd GD 3/12/75.
PASS D. M., BA. Born 7/8/35. Commd 8/8/58. Sqn Ldr 8/2/68. Retd ADMIN 7/8/93.
PASS L., MBE. Born 26/4/22. Commd 6/10/60. Sqn Ldr 1/1/70. Retd GD 30/7/73.
PASSBY D. C., BA DipEd. Born 9/5/33. Commd 26/1/56. Sqn Ldr 22/6/65. Retd ADMIN 9/5/88.
PASSFIELD R. F. Born 17/8/32. Commd 13/9/51. Sqn Ldr 1/7/80. Retd GD 17/8/92.
PATCHETT C. H. Born 19/12/50. Commd 28/11/74. Flt Lt 28/5/80. Retd GD 12/8/90.
PATCHING E. J. Born 22/7/61. Commd 8/9/83. Flt Lt 8/3/89. Retd GD 22/10/99.
PATERSON A. W. Born 17/7/26. Commd 25/10/46. Flt Lt 25/4/50. Retd GD 21/1/59.
PATERSON C. R. Born 19/9/38. Commd 25/7/60. Sqn Ldr 1/7/70. Retd GD 19/9/93.
PATERSON D. F. M., BA. Born 27/2/54. Commd 14/11/76. Flt Lt 14/8/77. Retd GD 14/11/88.
PATERSON D. S. Born 11/7/20. Commd 20/12/57. Flt Lt 20/12/63. Retd CAT 17/7/70.
PATERSON G. H., DPhysEd. Born 18/9/29. Commd 21/12/52. Flt Lt 21/12/57. Retd PE 4/1/68 rtg Sqn Ldr.
PATERSON J., LLB. Born 7/5/40. Commd 10/2/59. Flt Lt 12/8/64. Retd GD 7/5/78.
PATERSON J. G., MB ChB FRCR DMRD. Born 14/7/37. Commd 3/3/63. Wg Cdr 7/9/75. Retd MED 3/3/79.
PATERSON L. C., MSc BSc CPhys MInstP CEng. Born 10/9/50. Commd 25/5/80. Wg Cdr 1/1/94. Retd ADMIN 25/5/96.
PATERSON M., LLB. Born 5/1/57. Commd 17/8/80. Flt Lt 17/11/80. Retd GD 14/3/96.
PATERSON M., DFC. Born 15/4/15. Commd 5/2/41. Wg Cdr 1/1/55. Retd GD 9/12/66.
PATERSON N. S. Born 14/1/22. Commd 17/7/46. Flt Lt 19/11/53. Retd RGT 25/1/67.
PATON A. B. Born 19/5/23. Commd 9/9/47. Flt Lt 26/11/53. Retd GD(G) 19/5/73.
PATON B. J. Born 7/8/50. Commd 15/9/69. Sqn Ldr 1/1/87. Retd GD 1/1/90.
PATON D. McL., MRAeS MIMgt. Born 17/8/44. Commd 17/5/63. Wg Cdr 1/7/88. Retd GD 1/10/91.
PATON G. Born 25/1/58. Commd 26/11/81. Sqn Ldr 1/1/94. Retd GD 1/1/97.
PATON J. A. Born 20/6/22. Commd 9/7/44. Sqn Ldr 1/1/58. Retd GD 28/2/61.
PATON M. A. Born 10/10/62. Commd 11/5/86. Flt Lt 11/5/92. Retd ADMIN 2/9/99.
PATON N., BEd MHCIMA. Born 30/3/48. Commd 20/1/80. Fg Off 20/4/79. Retd ADMIN 14/4/81.
PATRICK D. A. Born 2/10/23. Commd 23/2/49. Flt Lt 14/10/52. Retd GD 30/6/67.
PATRICK D. R. Born 9/7/29. Commd 12/9/50. Sqn Ldr 1/1/61. Retd GD 5/7/76.
PATRICK G. A. Born 7/11/30. Commd 20/12/51. Flt Lt 8/12/66. Retd GD 18/4/72.
PATRICK H. N. Born 22/10/43. Commd 14/8/64. Sqn Ldr 1/1/83. Retd GD 30/9/89.
PATRICK I. W. Born 26/9/42. Commd 2/2/68. Sqn Ldr 1/1/90. Retd GD(G) 19/12/92.
PATRICK J. W. Born 9/10/24. Commd 8/9/44. Flt Lt 8/3/48. Retd GD 9/10/62.
PATRICK K. B. Born 3/8/45. Commd 3/3/67. Sqn Ldr 1/7/81. Retd GD 1/7/84.
PATRICK R. A. Born 21/3/44. Commd 6/5/65. Flt Lt 8/3/72. Retd GD(G) 21/3/82.
PATRICK R. C., DFC* AFC. Born 8/10/17. Commd 14/12/38. Wg Cdr 1/7/55. Retd GD 10/10/64.
PATRICK R. I. Born 9/12/47. Commd 11/8/67. Flt Lt 11/5/73. Retd GD 6/10/85.
PATTEN D. A. R. Born 24/7/22. Commd 14/3/49. Sqn Ldr 1/1/65. Retd ADMIN 24/7/82.
PATTEN H. P. F. Born 15/10/17. Commd 9/1/38. Flt Lt 28/3/47. Retd GD(G) 28/5/64 rtg Sqn Ldr.
PATTEN T. J., MA. Born 23/3/41. Commd 30/12/63. Sqn Ldr 1/1/76. Retd SEC 30/3/81.
PATTEN V. E. G., MIMgt. Born 23/1/39. Commd 10/9/63. Wg Cdr 1/7/83. Retd ENG 1/8/89.
PATTERSON A. H. R. Born 8/10/29. Commd 21/6/56. Flt Lt 21/12/59. Retd GD 30/9/77.
PATTERSON D. H. Born 21/7/51. Commd 4/2/71. Sqn Ldr 1/7/88. Retd GD 1/7/91.
PATTERSON E. J. A., OBE. Born 14/5/23. Commd 28/8/42. Wg Cdr 1/1/61. Retd GD 31/3/78.
PATTERSON G. Born 30/10/23. Commd 2/10/50. Flt Lt 26/9/56. Retd GD 31/3/62.
PATTERSON H., MBE. Born 18/3/20. Commd 14/1/48. Flt Lt 14/7/51. Retd SUP 3/4/57.
PATTERSON J. Born 20/12/15. Commd 8/10/42. Flt Lt 8/4/46. Retd ENG 23/12/64.
PATTERSON J. A. Born 28/11/20. Commd 24/3/44. Flt Lt 7/6/51. Retd SEC 28/11/69.
PATTERSON J. R., CEng MIEE. Born 30/6/43. Commd 18/7/63. Wg Cdr 1/1/88. Retd ENG 18/7/97.
PATTERSON L. J., BSc. Born 8/10/58. Commd 15/5/79. Flt Lt 15/4/82. Retd GD 8/10/96.
PATTERSON M., MBE. Born 30/4/39. Commd 26/10/62. Sqn Ldr 1/7/77. Retd GD 14/5/90.
PATTERSON M. G., MSc BSc(Eurlng) CEng MRAeS. Born 13/10/53. Commd 17/9/72. Sqn Ldr 1/1/85. Retd ENG 3/12/96.
PATTERSON P. J., MRIN MIMgt. Born 18/10/36. Commd 28/2/56. Wg Cdr 1/1/80. Retd GD 10/12/86.
PATTERSON R. Born 16/8/36. Commd 5/3/57. Flt Lt 6/3/63. Retd GD 10/9/76.
PATTERSON R. Born 3/9/44. Commd 7/7/67. Flt Lt 7/1/73. Retd GD 31/3/95.
PATTERSON R. A. Born 13/8/20. Commd 1/9/45. Sqn Ldr 1/10/54. Retd GD 13/8/63.
PATTERSON S. Born 7/3/23. Commd 28/5/66. Flt Lt 28/5/71. Retd ENG 7/3/78.

PATTIE A. S., CBE FHCIMA. Born 10/3/17. Commd 17/10/41. Gp Capt 1/7/66. Retd CAT 10/3/72.
PATTINSON A. G. S. Born 5/5/31. Commd 27/6/51. Flt Lt 27/12/55. Retd GD 9/1/60.
PATTINSON I. D., OBE MA CEng MIEE MRAeS DipEL. Born 21/2/28. Commd 19/2/51. Wg Cdr 1/1/75. Retd ENG 4/1/83.
PATTINSON R. W. B. Born 17/1/42. Commd 14/9/64. Flt Lt 4/5/72. Retd GD 14/9/80.
PATTISON F. Born 2/5/50. Commd 28/7/88. Flt Lt 28/7/92. Retd ENG 1/9/00.
PATTISON G. E. Born 16/12/48. Commd 7/1/73. Flt Lt 4/3/76. Retd MAR 1/4/86.
PATTISON J. Born 9/3/29. Commd 28/3/63. Sqn Ldr 10/10/73. Retd MED(SEC) 28/5/75.
PATTON J. W. Born 11/6/25. Commd 24/11/67. Flt Lt 24/11/72. Retd SEC 11/6/75.
PATTRICK R. V., BEM. Born 19/5/25. Commd 30/7/59. Wg Cdr 1/1/77. Retd ENG 28/4/79.
PAUL D. M. Born 22/5/40. Commd 19/12/61. Wg Cdr 1/7/91. Retd GD 2/6/95.
PAUL F. M. Born 9/7/96. Commd 1/4/18. Flt Lt 1/1/22. Retd GD 17/4/26.
PAUL G. J. C., CB DFC. Born 31/10/07. Commd 20/6/27. A Cdre 1/1/54. Retd GD 6/10/58.
PAUL G. W. Born 22/9/27. Commd 1/12/54. Flt Lt 1/10/67. Retd GD 17/8/70.
PAUL I. S. M., DipEl. Born 19/11/13. Commd 26/2/53. Flt Lt 26/2/58. Retd ENG 15/12/69.
PAUL R. E., AFC. Born 11/3/22. Commd 10/4/42. Sqn Ldr 1/7/54. Retd GD 11/3/71.
PAULETTE P. D. A. Born 8/9/30. Commd 28/2/57. Flt Lt 28/8/61. Retd GD 8/9/68.
PAVELEY R. G., BEd. Born 8/1/35. Commd 9/2/55. Flt Lt 10/8/60. Retd GD 8/1/73. Reinstated 15/4/81. Flt Lt 15/11/68. Retd GD 6/5/90.
PAVEY C. W. J. Born 8/10/16. Commd 30/7/46. Flt Lt 20/7/54. Retd GD(G) 8/10/73.
PAVEY F. T. Born 1/7/20. Commd 16/11/61. Flt Lt 16/11/64. Retd GD 1/7/75.
PAVEY The Rev M. T., ALCD. Born 29/2/32. Commd 1/1/64. Retd 1/1/80. Wg Cdr.
PAVEY R. E. Born 26/1/44. Commd 19/4/63. Wg Cdr 1/1/84. Retd GD(G) 31/3/94.
PAVIS E. J., DPhysEd. Born 8/4/36. Commd 14/8/62. Sqn Ldr 1/1/80. Retd ADMIN 1/2/86.
PAWLEY D. E., BA MCIPD. Born 15/4/39. Commd 10/9/63. Sqn Ldr 10/9/75. Retd ADMIN 20/10/84.
PAWSON A. W., MIMgt. Born 25/5/19. Commd 21/4/44. Wg Cdr 1/7/62. Retd ENG 20/5/75.
PAWSON G. I. Born 19/10/14. Commd 16/3/34. Wg Cdr 1/1/53. Retd SEC 26/11/60.
PAWSON J. B. Born 29/6/40. Commd 5/6/69. Wg Cdr 1/7/83. Retd GD(G) 14/7/85.
PAWSON T. W. Born 4/5/32. Commd 7/9/61. Wg Cdr 1/1/79. Retd GD 31/12/83.
PAXTON J. L. Born 1/6/31. Commd 3/8/51. Wg Cdr 1/7/80. Retd SUP 2/6/84.
PAXTON T. R. Born 26/5/50. Commd 14/2/69. Sqn Ldr 1/7/88. Retd GD 1/7/91.
PAYLING J. D. Born 13/7/30. Commd 28/7/49. Gp Capt. 1/7/72. Retd GD 7/4/79.
PAYN A. J., OBE. Born 11/9/18. Commd 17/12/38. Wg Cdr 1/1/51. Retd GD 11/9/67.
PAYN A. L. Born 1/11/61. Commd 5/2/81. Wg Cdr 1/1/98. Retd ADMIN 1/1/01.
PAYNE A. V. Born 13/5/44. Commd 1/4/66. Flt Lt 1/10/71. Retd GD 29/8/98.
PAYNE B. E. N. Born 12/3/32. Commd 22/1/54. Sqn Ldr 1/7/71. Retd SUP 1/8/85.
PAYNE D. Born 7/6/36. Commd 12/3/60. Flt Lt 12/9/65. Retd GD 7/6/74.
PAYNE F. L. Born 23/9/10. Commd 7/11/40. Flt Lt 1/4/46. Retd ENG 28/4/47 rtg Sqn Ldr.
PAYNE F. P. G. Born 24/9/14. Commd 25/5/44. Flt Lt 22/11/47. Retd GD 21/9/53.
PAYNE G. Born 19/1/25. Commd 6/6/57. Flt Lt 1/4/63. Retd GD 1/10/68.
PAYNE G. W. Born 14/2/29. Commd 26/7/50. Sqn Ldr 1/1/62. Retd GD 14/2/84.
PAYNE H. W. Born 25/5/10. Commd 27/1/44. Flt Lt 30/4/55. Retd GD(G) 31/3/62.
PAYNE The Rev J. M., MA. Born 13/2/17. Commd 7/12/44. Retd 7/3/72 Gp Capt.
PAYNE K. W. Born 12/8/29. Commd 17/5/51. Sqn Ldr 1/1/64. Retd GD 12/8/84.
PAYNE M. A. Born 19/12/37. Commd 29/6/72. Flt Lt 29/6/74. Retd ENG 14/1/85.
PAYNE M. A. Born 7/3/56. Commd 27/3/86. Fg Offr 23/11/84. Retd SUP 11/6/88.
PAYNE M. T. Born 9/5/35. Commd 19/8/58. Flt Lt 24/9/65. Retd GD 22/5/74.
PAYNE N. G., DFC. Born 31/1/22. Commd 3/9/42. Sqn Ldr 1/1/59. Retd SEC 1/1/66.
PAYNE R., AFC. Born 24/1/44. Commd 22/3/63. Flt Lt 22/9/68. Retd GD 24/1/82.
PAYNE R. A., BA. Born 3/5/60. Commd 15/8/82. Flt Lt 15/11/83. Retd GD 15/8/98.
PAYNE R. E. G. Born 20/11/25. Commd 25/10/50. Sqn Ldr 1/7/63. Retd GD 19/3/76.
PAYNE R. H. Born 20/5/20. Commd 25/2/42. Sqn Ldr 1/7/66. Retd GD 2/7/68.
PAYNE R. J. Born 10/5/31. Commd 17/10/71. Flt Lt 17/5/74. Retd ENG 10/5/89.
PAYNE R. L., MIMgt. Born 20/6/34. Commd 23/9/65. Sqn Ldr 1/7/79. Retd ADMIN 10/8/87.
PAYNE R. N., MA BA. Born 1/12/38. Commd 30/9/57. Wg Cdr 1/7/79. Retd ENG 28/9/94.
PAYNE R. W., AFC. Born 23/9/22. Commd 15/10/44. Wg Cdr 1/1/60. Retd GD 23/9/77.
PAYNE S. G. E. Born 25/10/18. Commd 15/6/44. Flt Lt 15/12/47. Retd ENG 29/12/61.
PAYNE S. R. Born 1/5/61. Commd 15/10/81. Flt Lt 15/4/88. Retd ADMIN 14/3/97.
PAYTON D. Born 19/3/44. Commd 31/1/64. Sqn Ldr 1/1/77. Retd GD 19/3/82.
PEACE B. W. Born 12/6/28. Commd 12/8/52. Flt Lt 12/5/58. Retd GD 12/6/66.
PEACE N. A. Born 20/8/29. Commd 3/10/69. Sqn Ldr 1/1/79. Retd ENG 20/8/87.
PEACEY A. W. D. Born 6/3/29. Commd 5/12/51. Sqn Ldr 1/1/68. Retd GD 25/6/76.
PEACH A. P. W. Born 15/6/35. Commd 30/4/57. Sqn Ldr 1/7/70. Retd GD 4/6/76.
PEACH R. M., MRIN. Born 6/1/43. Commd 28/10/66. Wg Cdr 1/1/85. Retd GD 2/4/93.
PEACHEY M. J., BSc CEng MIMechE. Born 4/1/43. Commd 15/7/65. Sqn Ldr 1/1/74. Retd ENG 21/8/76.
PEACOCK D. A., DFC. Born 28/12/17. Commd 21/12/36. Sqn Ldr 1/7/50. Retd GD 7/2/58 rtg Wg Cdr.

PEACOCK J. A. Born 18/11/34. Commd 21/10/66. Flt Lt 12/11/69. Retd GD(G) 18/11/94.
PEACOCK J. H. Born 23/1/32. Commd 27/6/63. Flt Lt 27/6/63. Retd GD 15/8/68.
PEACOCK P. Born 30/7/52. Commd 15/3/73. Wg Cdr 1/1/88. Retd ADMIN 1/1/91.
PEACOCK P. G., CBE BSc. Born 27/3/29. Commd 26/10/50. A Cdre 1/7/80. Retd GD 27/3/84.
PEACOCK T. C. W. Born 4/10/21. Commd 22/10/59. Sqn Ldr 1/7/70. Retd GD 4/10/76.
PEACOCK T. H. Born 20/6/44. Commd 20/1/64. Flt Lt 11/12/69. Retd GD 3/9/76.
PEACOCK T. J., LLB. Born 15/11/55. Commd 17/8/80. Flt Lt 5/6/84. Retd SY 17/8/96.
PEACOCK W. T. Born 7/4/35. Commd 27/3/70. Flt Lt 4/5/72. Retd SUP 1/5/85.
PEACOCK-EDWARDS R. S., CBE AFC FRAeS FIMgt. Born 27/1/45. Commd 21/5/65. A Cdre 1/7/94. Retd GD 27/1/00.
PEAKE A. D. Born 16/11/33. Commd 4/2/53. Flt Lt 1/7/58. Retd SUP 29/5/76.
PEAKE Dame Felicity Hyde., DBE. Born 1/7/13. Commd 25/4/41. A Cdt 1/2/49. Retd SEC 29/7/50.
PEAKE F. Born 17/5/15. Commd 18/3/43. Sqn Ldr 1/1/63. Retd ENG 7/5/70.
PEAKER A. B., CEng MRAeS. Born 25/6/22. Commd 17/1/44. Wd Cdr 1/1/69. Retd ENG 25/6/77.
PEAKER M. G. Born 20/5/39. Commd 24/11/59. Gp Capt 1/1/84. Retd GD 20/5/94.
PEAKMAN R., BSc. Born 4/7/41. Commd 13/10/64. Sqn Ldr 13/4/74. Retd ADMIN 22/10/94.
PEAPLE T. D. Born 22/4/38. Commd 19/1/66. Flt Lt 8/1/69. Retd ENG 1/8/91.
PEARCE A. A., MRAeS. Born 11/5/22. Commd 6/7/44. Sqn Ldr 1/4/55. Retd GD 31/8/68.
PEARCE A. C., MSc BSc PGCE DIC. Born 1/7/13. Commd 28/9/83. Sqn Ldr 1/1/93. Retd ADMIN 28/9/99.
PEARCE A. F. Born 19/9/43. Commd 11/11/65. Sqn Ldr 1/7/79. Retd GD(G) 19/9/87.
PEARCE A. G. Born 8/6/40. Commd 31/7/62. Sqn Ldr 1/1/72. Retd GD 8/6/95.
PEARCE B. P. J. Born 29/5/46. Commd 26/5/67. Sqn Ldr 1/1/78. Retd ENG 29/5/84.
PEARCE C. F., CEng MIEE. Born 4/8/13. Commd 15/7/33. Wg Cdr 1/7/47. Retd ENG 1/11/52 rtg Gp Capt.
PEARCE D. Born 1/7/19. Commd 10/2/43. Flt Offr 26/5/53. Retd GD(G) 28/2/58.
PEARCE F. W., DFC. Born 8/5/21. Commd 18/7/44. Sqn Ldr 1/1/67. Retd GD 8/11/75.
PEARCE G. A. Born 27/3/36. Commd 12/11/54. Flt Lt 1/3/61. Retd GD 27/3/74.
PEARCE G. C. Born 7/3/36. Commd 22/1/54. Flt Lt 7/8/64. Retd GD 28/10/86.
PEARCE G. M., BA. Born 27/4/35. Commd 5/5/54. Sqn Ldr 1/1/71. Retd GD 1/8/77.
PEARCE J. Born 10/2/47. Commd 9/12/76. Wg Cdr 1/1/93. Retd ADMIN 13/11/00.
PEARCE J. F. L., MBE. Born 24/9/26. Commd 11/3/65. Sqn Ldr 1/7/75. Retd ENG 24/9/84.
PEARCE J. H. Born 6/6/24. Commd 26/11/43. Sqn Ldr 1/4/55. Retd GD 1/5/68.
PEARCE M. J., BSc. Born 27/2/51. Commd 19/5/69. Sqn Ldr 1/1/84. Retd GD 27/2/89.
PEARCE R. A. Born 18/2/37. Commd 18/8/61. Flt Lt 1/4/66. Retd GD 29/9/73.
PEARCE R. D. Born 11/3/21. Commd 4/10/43. Sqn Ldr 1/7/70. Retd GD 11/3/76.
PEARCE R. S. Born 1/6/60. Commd 4/9/81. Sqn Ldr 1/7/93. Retd GD 1/6/98.
PEARCE W. E. R. Born 22/7/57. Commd 15/6/83. Flt Lt 5/8/85. Retd GD 22/7/95.
PEARMAN L., MBE MM. Born 29/3/21. Commd 11/6/44. Wg Cdr 1/1/61. Retd SUP 1/6/68.
PEARS H., DFC. Born 30/5/23. Commd 10/11/42. Sqn Ldr 1/1/53. Retd GD 30/5/66.
PEARSE J. G. Born 22/5/14. Commd 1/5/42. Wg Cdr 1/7/60. Retd SEC 18/1/69.
PEARSE W. J., CEng MRAeS. Born 5/3/37. Commd 11/10/60. Wg Cdr 1/7/79. Retd ENG 16/4/89.
PEARSE W. T. D. Born 14/11/32. Commd 10/5/73. Sqn Ldr Ldr 1/1/87. Retd ENG 25/4/92.
PEARSON A. D. G. Born 1/3/37. Commd 27/7/72. Sqn Ldr 27/1/76. Retd ADMIN 3/1/88.
PEARSON C. R. Born 7/3/60. Commd 11/5/78. Flt Lt 11/11/83. Retd GD 1/10/90.
PEARSON E. Born 16/11/34. Commd 29/10/52. Sqn Ldr 1/7/65. Retd GD 22/2/79.
PEARSON F., TD BL. Born 25/10/09. Commd 24/10/55. Wg Cdr 24/10/68. Retd LGL 25/10/72.
PEARSON F. J. C. Born 16/1/31. Commd 18/6/52. Flt Lt 13/11/57. Retd GD 5/5/78.
PEARSON F. MacC. Born 17/3/39. Commd 12/11/57. Wg Cdr 1/1/81. Retd GD 17/3/94.
PEARSON F. R. Born 25/4/31. Commd 28/6/51. Flt Lt 10/10/56. Retd GD 25/4/69.
PEARSON G. Born 12/3/14. Commd 25/11/43. Flt Lt 25/5/47. Retd SEC 21/7/62.
PEARSON G. Born 31/3/31. Commd 19/7/51. Sqn Ldr 1/1/65. Retd GD 28/11/75.
PEARSON G. S., MBE ACIS MIMgt. Born 6/11/46. Commd 27/5/71. Wg Cdr 1/7/88. Retd ADMIN 19/6/93.
PEARSON I. D. Born 11/12/44. Commd 9/3/72. Flt Lt 3/5/77. Retd ADMIN 1/9/78.
PEARSON J. D., BSc. Born 30/1/54. Commd 9/10/75. Flt Lt 15/4/78. Retd GD 15/7/89.
PEARSON J. McL. Born 14/3/20. Commd 25/5/49. Flt Lt 4/12/52. Retd GD(G) 18/3/75.
PEARSON J. P. Born 21/7/42. Commd 6/4/72. Flt Lt 6/4/74. Retd GD 1/11/93.
PEARSON J. W. Born 25/1/48. Commd 1/8/69. Sqn Ldr 1/1/86. Retd GD(G) 01/10/92.
PEARSON M. F. V. Born 30/7/17. Commd 28/12/44. Sqn Ldr 1/1/55. Retd RGT 6/5/58.
PEARSON M. L., MEng. Born 18/12/70. Commd 14/12/89. Fg Offr 15/1/92. Retd ENG 5/8/97.
PEARSON N. A. J. Born 20/3/65. Commd 15/3/84. Flt Lt 15/9/89. Retd GD 14/3/96.
PEARSON R. A. J. Born 10/3/38. Commd 28/2/57. Wg Cdr 1/7/77. Retd SUP 10/3/93.
PEARSON R. F., MBE. Born 2/12/23. Commd 5/12/43. Wg Cdr 1/1/75. Retd ENG 2/12/78.
PEARSON R. J. H., AFC. Born 2/5/24. Commd 28/9/44. Flt Lt 16/1/50. Retd GD(G) 8/6/54.
PEARSON R. M. Born 9/9/30. Commd 1/8/51. Flt Lt 1/8/56. Retd SUP 9/9/68.
PEARSON R. S. Born 4/2/59. Commd 11/6/81. Sqn Ldr 1/6/90. Retd GD 1/2/97.
PEARSON S. D. Born 5/11/61. Commd 6/11/80. Sqn Ldr 1/1/93. Retd GD 5/11/99.
PEARSON S. W. Born 3/3/45. Commd 27/9/73. Flt Lt 27/9/75. Retd SY 11/7/82.

PEARSON T. Born 22/9/52. Commd 17/12/64. Flt Lt 9/2/68. Retd GD 22/9/80.
PEARSON T. A. Born 23/3/39. Commd 15/12/59. Wg Cdr 1/7/78. Retd GD 29/9/89.
PEART H. Born 21/11/42. Commd 25/2/88. Flt Lt 25/2/92. Retd ENG 2/5/93.
PEART J. W. Born 10/1/63. Commd 10/5/90. Flt Lt 10/5/92. Retd ADMIN 10/1/01.
PEART R., AFC. Born 7/9/46. Commd 14/7/66. Sqn Ldr 1/7/78. Retd GD 8/11/84.
PEART-JACKSON W. J. P. Born 10/5/28. Commd 2/5/61. Sqn Ldr 27/8/69. Retd ADMIN 2/9/77.
PEARTON F. W., FIMgt. Born 25/10/22. Commd 26/5/60. Flt Lt 26/5/63. Retd ENG 2/6/73.
PEASE A. K. F., BSc. Born 16/2/62. Commd 15/7/82. Sqn Ldr 1/7/96. Retd GD 16/2/00.
PEASE E. I., MBE CEng MIEE AMIMgt. Born 1/4/34. Commd 20/12/57. Wg Cdr 1/7/72. Retd ENG 19/4/84.
PEASLEY G. K., AFC. Born 4/6/33. Commd 19/7/51. Gp Capt 1/1/79. Retd GD 2/9/84.
PEASLEY W. R., DFC. Born 1/5/20. Commd 17/6/42. Flt Lt 22/5/49. Retd GD 19/11/54.
PEAT K. S. Born 27/8/23. Commd 20/1/45. Flt Lt 20/7/48. Retd GD 27/8/61.
PEATY B., BSc. Born 20/7/38. Commd 26/10/62. Flt Lt 26/4/68. Retd GD 10/7/78.
PEBERDY R. J., OBE CEng MIEE. Born 19/8/31. Commd 22/7/55. Gp Capt 1/1/81. Retd ENG 4/10/83.
PECK G., AFC BSc. Born 27/9/49. Commd 3/10/68. Sqn Ldr 1/7/80. Retd GD 12/2/83.
PECK G. C., AFC. Born 1/12/22. Commd 12/1/61. Sqn Ldr 1/7/73. Retd GD 1/12/77.
PECK R. E. F. Born 4/4/23. Commd 22/9/49. Sqn Ldr 1/1/69. Retd ENG 26/3/76.
PECK R. J. Born 13/11/47. Commd 27/2/70. Flt Lt 27/8/75. Retd GD 13/11/85.
PECKETT D. S., MEng BSc CEng MIEE. Born 24/5/48. Commd 28/2/69. Wg Cdr 1/7/87. Retd ENG 31/3/94.
PEDDER Sir Ian, KCB OBE DFC. Born 2/5/26. Commd 21/12/45. AM 1/1/82. Retd GD 15/3/85.
PEDEN W. Born 14/6/34. Commd 23/9/82. Flt Lt 23/9/85. Retd ENG 29/12/89.
PEDLEY M. G. F., OBE DSO DFC. Born 17/11/15. Commd 6/8/35. Wg Cdr 1/7/47. Retd GD 31/12/57 rtg Gp Capt.
PEDLEY N. M. Born 11/10/46. Commd 19/8/66. Flt Lt 4/5/72. Retd GD 21/9/86.
PEDLEY T. F., BSc CEng MRAeS. Born 25/5/56. Commd 14/1/79. Sqn Ldr 1/7/87. Retd ENG 9/12/96.
PEDRICK D. W., BA MBCS. Born 2/4/46. Commd 23/9/66. Wg Cdr 1/1/87. Retd ENG 2/4/90.
PEEBLES A. D. Born 5/11/40. Commd 11/6/60. Flt Lt 11/12/65. Retd GD 5/11/78.
PEEBLES J. S. Born 9/11/20. Commd 10/8/48. Flt Lt 10/8/56. Retd MAR 20/6/57.
PEEKE-VOUT J. M. Born 9/6/46. Commd 19/1/66. Flt Lt 19/7/72. Retd ENG 28/3/75.
PEEL G. W. Born 20/12/13. Commd 1/1/34. Wg Cdr 5/10/45. Retd ENG 25/1/46 rtg Gp Capt.
PEEL J., BA FIMgt FInstPET MCIPS. Born 8/1/31. Commd 12/12/51. Gp Capt 1/7/74. Retd SUP 1/7/81.
PEEL J. R. A., DSO DFC. Born 17/10/11. Commd 23/7/32. Wg Cdr 1/10/46. Retd GD 20/1/48 rtg Gp Capt.
PEELE R. A. Born 5/5/46. Commd 2/8/68. Flt Lt 2/2/71. Retd GD 8/11/75.
PEER R. C., MBE. Born 13/5/44. Commd 10/3/69. Sqn Ldr 1/7/83. Retd ENG 13/5/99.
PEET E. D. Born 8/5/43. Commd 9/2/62. Flt Lt 9/8/67. Retd GD 8/5/80.
PEET W. W., DFC. Born 24/7/20. Commd 11/7/49. Flt Lt 1/8/55. Retd GD(G) 9/3/65.
PEFFERS F. G. C. Born 23/11/29. Commd 13/9/51. Sqn Ldr 1/1/68. Retd GD 2/3/76.
PEGG B. P. R. Born 10/9/30. Commd 24/1/52. Flt Lt 13/11/57. Retd GD 1/12/82.
PEGG R. F. Born 17/7/42. Commd 24/8/72. Flt Lt 24/8/74. Retd GD(G) 24/8/80.
PEGNALL B. E. A. Born 15/4/44. Commd 3/3/67. A Cdre 1/7/92. Retd GD 14/12/95.
PEILE C. T. B., MRAeS. Born 21/5/32. Commd 28/7/53. Wg Cdr 1/1/77. Retd GD 22/5/90.
PEIRSE Sir Richard., KCVO CB. Born 16/3/31. Commd 9/4/52. AVM 1/7/82. Retd GD 16/6/88.
PEIRSE R. E. Born 21/7/44. Commd 21/5/65. Fg Offr 21/5/67. Retd GD 17/11/68.
PELCOT A. F. Born 31/1/53. Commd 28/7/88. Flt Lt 28/7/92. Retd SY 5/8/96.
PELLANT The Rev W. R. G., AKC. Born 2/2/14. Commd 21/4/48. Retd 24/10/71 Gp Capt.
PELLING A. H. Born 21/5/33. Commd 27/6/66. Flt Lt 22/7/68. Retd ENG 22/7/74.
PELLS D. E. W. Born 29/10/41. Commd 19/4/63. Flt Lt 19/10/68. Retd GD 30/4/94.
PELLY A. E. Born 5/12/23. Commd 27/5/43. Sqn Ldr 1/10/56. Retd SEC 10/2/69.
PELLY M. L. Born 1/7/18. Commd 15/3/50. Fg Offr 15/3/52. Retd SEC 1/6/54.
PEMBERTON A. J. R. Born 15/4/25. Commd 29/9/50. Sqn Ldr 1/1/72. Retd GD(G) 15/4/83.
PEMBERTON A. M. Born 24/4/57. Commd 28/10/76. Flt Lt 28/4/82. Retd GD 24/4/95.
PEMBERTON B. M., MIMgt. Born 12/5/28. Commd 28/10/63. Sqn Ldr 1/7/69. Retd SUP 18/5/79.
PEMBERTON C. M. G. Born 1/2/51. Commd 8/8/69. Flt Lt 8/2/75. Retd GD 4/10/77.
PEMBERTON D. L. Born 13/2/37. Commd 27/9/73. Sqn Ldr 1/7/84. Retd GD(G) 7/10/91.
PEMBERTON J. Born 6/3/21. Commd 28/12/44. Flt Lt 11/5/60. Retd GD 24/1/62.
PEMBERTON-PIGOTT T. N. J., MCIT MILT. Born 14/11/46. Commd 13/8/72. Wg Cdr 1/1/90. Retd SUP 2/4/01.
PEMBREY T. E. C. Born 7/6/50. Commd 23/2/72. FLT LT 25/2/75. Retd GD 6/7/87.
PENDER H. K. Born 12/8/59. Commd 15/8/85. Flt Lt 15/2/87. Retd GD 14/9/96.
PENDLEBURY B. A. Born 16/12/32. Commd 4/3/71. Flt Lt 4/3/73. Retd SUP 16/12/87.
PENDLEBURY P. Born 4/7/32. Commd 26/3/64. Sqn Ldr 1/1/85. Retd ADMIN 20/1/87.
PENDLETON G. Born 19/6/39. Commd 24/2/61. Flt Lt 24/8/66. Retd GD 19/6/77.
PENDRED G. L. Born 8/3/24. Commd 13/11/43. Gp Capt 1/1/69. Retd GD 16/4/73.
PENDREGAUST R. Born 8/5/82. Commd 24/7/81. Flt Lt 24/1/87. Retd GD 8/3/92.
PENDRY J. B. Born 1/3/37. Commd 19/8/65. Flt Lt 18/5/71. Retd GD 18/5/84.
PENFOLD A. B. Born 25/2/47. Commd 14/9/65. Flt Lt 1/3/71. Retd GD 8/1/83.
PENFOLD P. D. Born 20/9/34. Commd 5/4/55. Sqn Ldr 1/7/67. Retd GD 20/9/84.
PENGELLY G. R. Born 19/4/35. Commd 7/7/55. A Cdre 1/7/85. Retd SUP 29/1/90.

PENGILLEY D. R., BTech MRAeS. Born 17/10/46. Commd 28/2/72. Sqn Ldr 1/1/85. Retd GD 28/2/88.
PENKETH W. J., BSc. Born 26/1/48. Commd 1/9/71. Wg Cdr 1/7/97. Retd ENG 17/12/99.
PENLEY-MARTIN J. R. Born 27/3/33. Commd 30/4/52. Flt Lt 6/11/57. Retd GD 27/3/76.
PENLEY-MARTIN J. R. M. Born 7/4/59. Commd 25/2/88. Flt Lt 25/2/90. Retd ENG 7/4/97.
PENMAN D. J., OBE DSO DFC. Born 14/10/19. Commd 30/11/37. Wg Cdr 1/7/67. Retd GD 14/10/74.
PENMAN G. H. Born 19/11/27. Commd 17/5/62. Sqn Ldr 1/1/77. Retd GD(G) 19/5/83.
PENMAN J. McA., MB ChB MRCPsych DPM. Born 8/3/33. Commd 4/9/58. Wg Cdr 24/9/71. Retd MED 6/10/76.
PENMAN J. O. R., BSc CEng MIEE MRAeS. Born 17/4/37. Commd 7/12/61. Wg Cdr 1/7/86. Retd ENG 6/4/89.
PENN K. Born 8/4/33. Commd 19/7/51. Flt Lt 9/11/56. Retd GD(G) 8/4/88.
PENNA C., DFM. Born 10/6/22. Commd 29/1/44. Sqn Ldr 1/1/70. Retd SEC 10/6/72.
PENNELL C. W., MBE MIMgt. Born 11/10/41. Commd 31/10/69. Gp Capt 1/1/90. Retd PRT 12/10/91.
PENNELL M. E., BSc. Born 26/2/43. Commd 30/9/62. Sqn Ldr 1/1/74. Retd ENG 26/2/81.
PENNEY B. J. Born 28/2/54. Commd 10/5/90. Flt Lt 10/5/94. Retd ENG 14/3/96.
PENNEY N. W., DFC. Born 4/10/22. Commd 28/8/43. Flt Lt 4/12/52. Retd GD 30/1/65.
PENNEY R. Born 18/6/43. Commd 11/4/85. Flt Lt 11/4/89. Retd ENG 20/4/93.
PENNIALL R. G., MBE. Born 3/9/32. Commd 14/5/53. Wg Cdr 1/1/76. Retd ADMIN 1/8/87.
PENNING R. C. Born 24/11/19. Commd 11/9/42. Sqn Ldr 1/7/52. Retd GD 10/7/59.
PENNINGTON G. C. Born 4/7/57. Commd 26/9/90. Flt Lt 26/9/92. Retd ENG 16/11/98.
PENNINGTON G. H., OBE BSc CEng MIEE MRAeS. Born 29/12/21. Commd 12/9/49. Wg Cdr 29/12/62. Retd EDN 7/1/68.
PENNINGTON G. J. Born 12/10/55. Commd 8/6/84. Flt Lt 8/6/86. Retd ADMIN 15/12/92.
PENNY C. R., BSc. Born 8/8/38. Commd 21/12/62. Flt Lt 1/1/66. Retd GD 30/11/74.
PENNY F. C. B., AFM. Born 3/7/22. Commd 27/5/54. Flt Lt 27/5/57. Retd GD 1/10/68.
PENNY H. A., OBE FIMgt. Born 1/2/22. Commd 18/12/42. Gp Capt 1/1/68. Retd SEC 5/1/70.
PENNY J. A. Born 19/7/22. Commd 5/2/48. Flt Lt 5/8/51. Retd SEC 19/7/71.
PENNY J. C. Born 22/12/21. Commd 30/10/42. Sqn Ldr 1/7/73. Retd ADMIN 31/3/77.
PENNY K. C. Born 23/3/31. Commd 14/1/53. Flt Lt 3/6/58. Retd GD 8/4/69.
PENNY L. Born 7/2/15. Commd 18/7/44. Sqn Ldr 1/1/57. Retd CAT 15/3/65 rtg Wg Cdr.
PENNY L. S., BA. Born 8/6/40. Commd 19/12/61. Wg Cdr 1/7/78. Retd GD 1/7/81.
PENNY S. D., BA BSc CEng MBCS MIEE MRAeS. Born 3/1/58. Commd 19/9/76. Wg Cdr 1/7/94. Retd ENG 1/7/97.
PENNYFATHER P. R., MIMgt. Born 1/5/24. Commd 15/12/44. Sqn Ldr 1/10/57. Retd SEC 1/5/79.
PENRICE C., BSc. Born 9/4/59. Commd 17/3/79. Sqn Ldr 1/7/92. Retd GD 23/6/98.
PENROSE A., DFC* CGM. Born 6/5/20. Commd 21/4/45. Flt Lt 5/10/54. Retd GD(G) 1/4/65.
PENROSE J. D., DLC CEng FRAeS FRSA. Born 1/5/30. Commd 19/6/50. Flt Lt 13/11/57. Retd GD 30/9/61.
PENRY K. R., MIMgt. Born 28/12/21. Commd 20/11/42. Wg Cdr 1/1/59. Retd GD 28/12/68.
PENTON-VOAK B. E. Born 11/8/40. Commd 22/2/63. Sqn Ldr 1/7/87. Retd ADMIN 11/8/95.
PENTON-VOAK M. J. Born 15/1/43. Commd 8/6/62. Wg Cdr 1/1/91. Retd GD 15/1/98.
PENTYCROSS F. A. Born 4/3/17. Commd 27/6/36. Sqn Ldr 1/8/47. Retd GD 27/3/60.
PENWARDEN G. W. F. Born 17/3/07. Commd 1/10/41. Sqn Ldr 1/8/47. Retd ENG 17/4/57.
PEPPER A. C. Born 9/9/41. Commd 20/9/79. Sqn Ldr 1/7/89. Retd SUP 19/6/93.
PEPPER D. J. S., CEng MRAeS MIMgt. Born 12/11/39. Commd 2/2/65. Sqn Ldr 1/7/76. Retd ENG 2/2/87.
PEPPER S. P. Born 23/9/51. Commd 4/3/71. Flt Lt 4/9/76. Retd GD 23/9/89.
PERCIVAL S. H., BEd. Born 22/4/48. Commd 29/8/72. Sqn Ldr 1/7/89. Retd ADMIN 14/3/96.
PERCY T. E., BSc. Born 5/7/44. Commd 18/8/68. Flt Lt 18/5/70. Retd GD 31/1/76.
PERDUE G. S. Born 4/9/24. Commd 2/5/69. Flt Lt 27/3/55. Retd GD 4/9/62.
PERERA M. D. M. Born 28/9/32. Commd 29/12/65. Flt Lt 29/12/65. Retd SUP 29/12/81.
PERFECT A. A., MIMgt. Born 15/6/43. Commd 5/7/68. Wg Cdr 1/1/94. Retd OPS SPT 4/4/00.
PERIGO J. D. Born 23/9/34. Commd 13/2/64. Sqn Ldr 1/1/85. Retd ADMIN 26/7/87.
PERKIN K. A. Born 6/5/18. Commd 19/8/40. Sqn Ldr 1/7/53. Retd GD 29/10/58.
PERKIN-BALL R. W. K. Born 24/8/44. Commd 25/10/73. Flt Lt 25/10/75. Retd GD(G) 24/8/82.
PERKINS C. T. Born 26/5/47. Commd 21/4/77. Sqn Ldr 1/1/98. Retd GD 26/5/01.
PERKINS D. A. Born 8/10/25. Commd 21/12/45. Sqn Ldr 1/1/57. Retd GD 28/1/77.
PERKINS H. Born 23/4/09. Commd 29/1/42. Fg Offr 27/11/42. Retd ENG 15/1/46 rtg Flt Lt.
PERKINS I. M., MBE MRCS MFCM LRCP FIMgt. Born 15/12/20. Commd 30/7/48. AVM 31/3/78. Retd MED 15/12/80.
PERKINS L. J. Born 12/12/31. Commd 27/8/52. Flt Lt 23/1/58. Retd GD 12/12/69.
PERKINS M. Born 29/9/36. Commd 29/7/58. Sqn Ldr 1/7/70. Retd SUP 14/1/83.
PERKINS N. J. Born 18/1/60. Commd 22/2/79. Flt Lt 22/8/85. Retd GD(G) 22/8/87. Re-entered 19/4/91. Flt Lt 17/10/86. Retd OPS SPT 1/10/97.
PERKINS R. C, MBE. Born 20/3/35. Commd 16/11/61. Wg Cdr 1/7/80. Retd SEC 30/7/83.
PERKINS R. H. Born 29/8/24. Commd 29/3/45. Flt Lt 3/2/53. Retd GD 3/1/66.
PERKINS R. L., BA. Born 12/1/47. Commd 13/9/71. Plt Offr 13/9/71. Retd SEC 17/1/72.
PERKINS S. J., OBE AFC FIMgt. Born 13/4/23. Commd 3/7/42. Gp Capt 1/1/69. Retd GD 1/11/75.
PERKINS S. J. B. Born 6/8/56. Commd 15/6/83. Flt Lt 15/12/89. Retd GD(G) 1/1/96.
PERKS G. D., DFC. Born 19/9/18. Commd 9/3/43. Flt Lt 14/9/47. Retd GD 27/7/58.
PERKS M. J. Born 8/8/48. Commd 17/1/69. Flt Lt 21/5/75. Retd SUP 8/8/86.

PERKS R. I., CEng MIERE. Born 26/12/21. Commd 31/5/43. Wg Cdr 1/7/67. Retd ENG 29/6/74.
PERKS T. A. N. Born 25/11/48. Commd 7/6/73. Flt Lt 13/8/78. Retd GD(G) 19/4/87.
PERMAN A. E., ACIS. Born 9/7/31. Commd 3/6/65. Flt Lt 3/6/70. Retd SEC 9/7/75.
PEROU R. L. Born 8/7/37. Commd 12/8/59. Fg Offr 12/8/59. Retd ENG 18/1/64.
PEROWNE B. I. S., AFC. Born 25/12/22. Commd 30/4/43. Sqn Ldr 1/1/60. Retd GD 25/6/73.
PERRETT G. E., CEng MRAeS. Born 10/4/24. Commd 19/7/51. Sqn Ldr 1/1/64. Retd ENG 20/7/74.
PERRETT M W., MInstPS. Born 10/1/36. Commd 14/10/75. Flt Lt 14/10/75. Retd SUP 2/2/86.
PERRETT M. J., OBE. Born 7/11/44. Commd 29/11/63. Gp Capt 1/7/94. Retd GD 31/5/01.
PERRIDGE M. J., BSc CEng MIEE. Born 8/8/42. Commd 15/7/63. Gp Capt 1/7/90. Retd ENG 31/3/94.
PERRIN D. R., OBE DFC. Born 19/1/21. Commd 17/6/43. Wg Cdr 1/1/73. Retd SEC 19/1/76.
PERRIN D. S. Born 11/4/15. Commd 12/11/42. Wg Cdr 1/1/60. Retd ENG 11/4/70.
PERRIN F. Born 31/8/16. Commd 14/11/46. Sqn Ldr 1/7/62. Retd SUP 15/3/69.
PERRIN G. M., MBE. Born 1/10/33. Commd 18/6/52. Sqn Ldr 1/7/68. Retd GD 27/2/76.
PERRIN J. E. Born 23/4/20. Commd 23/3/50. Sqn Ldr 1/1/72. Retd ENG 22/4/73.
PERRIN N. A., BA CEng FRAeS. Born 30/9/30. Commd 29/11/51. AVM 1/7/84. Retd ENG 1/7/86.
PERRINS W. J. Born 13/8/55. Commd 17/7/75. Flt Lt 17/1/81. Retd GD 13/1/94.
PERRIS A. J. B. Born 27/12/44. Commd 19/8/66. Flt Lt 4/11/70. GD 1/1/76.
PERROTT D. J. S. Born 25/11/42. Commd 29/6/72. Sqn Ldr 1/1/81. Retd ENG 14/7/86.
PERROTT P. J., AFC. Born 22/5/33. Commd 13/2/52. Flt Lt 12/6/57. Retd GD 22/5/71.
PERRY A. D. Born 2/11/29. Commd 17/5/62. Sqn Ldr 1/7/77. Retd GD 2/11/87.
PERRY B. V. Born 7/6/46. Commd 18/8/67. Flt Lt 18/8/70. Retd GD 4/10/77. Reinstated 27/7/81. Sqn Ldr 1/7/86. Retd GD 1/7/89.
PERRY C., BSc. Born 17/10/59. Commd 5/2/84. Flt Lt 5/8/86. Retd GD 5/2/00.
PERRY C. C. Born 18/11/55. Commd 8/12/83. Sqn Ldr 1/7/93. Retd SY 1/7/96.
PERRY D. J., MBE. Born 31/8/26. Commd 2/8/50. Sqn Ldr 1/1/75. Retd GD 30/3/78.
PERRY E. A. Born 23/3/44. Commd 5/2/65. Flt Lt 23/9/69. Retd GD 1/5/76.
PERRY F. G. Born 30/6/13. Commd 21/10/54. Flt Lt 21/10/57. Retd ENG 2/7/68.
PERRY F. G. Born 30/1/34. Commd 4/6/52. Flt Lt 30/10/57. Retd GD 6/4/59.
PERRY G. L., MS BSc CEng MRAeS MIMgt ACGI. Born 31/12/44. Commd 22/9/63. Wg Cdr 1/1/81. Retd ENG 1/1/84.
PERRY I. A. Born 18/3/09. Commd 28/1/43. Sqn Ldr 1/7/60. Retd SUP 18/3/64.
PERRY K. H., DSO AFC. Born 25/3/22. Commd 22/10/43. Sqn Ldr 1/7/55. Retd GD 25/3/65.
PERRY P. J., MSc BSc(Eng) CEng MRAeS. Born 22/9/39. Commd 30/9/59. Wg Cdr 1/1/79. Retd ENG 19/1/90.
PERRY P. N., AFC*. Born 7/1/38. Commd 28/2/56. Flt Lt 21/8/63. Retd GD 24/11/78.
PERRY R. C., MBE. Born 14/7/34. Commd 22/7/66. Wg Cdr 1/7/85. Retd ENG 1/10/91.
PERRY R. G. Born 10/3/29. Commd 26/7/50. Sqn Ldr 1/7/59. Retd GD 1/9/74.
PERRY R. N. Born 2/5/46. Commd 1/4/65. Sqn Ldr 1/7/76. Retd GD(G) 2/5/90.
PERRY R. S. N., MA. Born 8/9/49. Commd 22/4/71. Gp Capt 1/1/91. Retd SUP 1/5/92.
PERRY S. G. Born 20/2/34. Commd 25/2/53. Wg Cdr 1/1/74. Retd GD 30/8/80.
PERRY T. D. Born 26/12/33. Commd 13/2/52. Sqn Ldr 1/1/68. Retd GD 26/12/88.
PERRYMAN N. F. Born 3/7/15. Commd 30/6/43. Sqn Ldr 1/7/63. Retd GD(G) 28/8/65.
PERT G. Born 2/9/56. Commd 11/5/89. Flt Lt 11/5/91. Retd ENG 11/5/97.
PERTWEE H. R. P., DFC MIMgt. Born 15/2/23. Commd 7/2/42. Sqn Ldr 1/1/51. Retd SUP 15/2/72.
PESIKAKA D. B., BSc CEng MIEE. Born 2/7/19. Commd 5/8/42. Sqn Ldr 1/1/56. Retd ENG 2/7/74.
PETCH C. S. F., MSc BSc. Born 26/10/58. Commd 29/8/77. Sqn Ldr 1/1/90. Retd ENG 1/5/00.
PETERS A. D. A. Born 14/9/23. Commd 25/11/53. Flt Lt 25/11/58. Retd GD 11/4/68.
PETERS A. J. Born 7/3/54. Commd 24/4/80. Sqn Ldr 1/7/94. Retd GD 14/3/96.
PETERS C. E., DFC. Born 15/2/21. Commd 28/7/43. Flt Lt 26/5/55. Retd GD 28/9/68.
PETERS D. B. Born 4/10/58. Commd 11/1/79. Sqn Ldr 11/7/84. Retd GD 4/10/96.
PETERS E. A. Born 29/7/30. Commd 12/12/51. Sqn Ldr 1/1/62. Retd GD 29/7/68.
PETERS G. F. Born 14/10/29. Commd 26/3/53. Sqn Ldr 1/1/69. Retd GD 22/5/76.
PETERS J. G., BSc. Born 30/12/61. Commd 14/9/80. Sqn Ldr 1/7/97. Retd GD 1/7/00.
PETERS J. P. E. Born 6/3/22. Commd 22/6/42. Sqn Ldr 1/1/54. Retd GD 19/10/64.
PETERS L. J. Born 1/2/13. Commd 2/12/41. Flt Lt 4/9/45. Retd ENG 20/9/47 rtg Sqn Ldr.
PETERS P., OBE DFC. Born 29/12/16. Commd 26/3/38. Wg Cdr 1/7/52. Retd GD 17/1/72.
PETERS P. H. J., AFC. Born 1/11/31. Commd 4/4/51. Sqn Ldr 1/7/61. Retd GD 12/6/85.
PETERS P. W., DFC AFC. Born 24/1/16. Commd 6/3/39. Sqn Ldr 1/8/47. Retd GD 3/3/53.
PETERS R. G., CB. Born 22/8/40. Commd 1/8/61. AVM 1/1/91. Retd GD 1/7/93.
PETERS R. S. Born 17/3/26. Commd 20/12/46. Sqn Ldr 1/1/58. Retd GD 17/3/64.
PETERSON C. M. Born 2/4/20. Commd 28/2/46. Flt Lt 15/12/49. Retd ENG 27/6/53.
PETERSON R. V. Born 17/9/20. Commd 26/9/57. Sqn Ldr 1/7/68. Retd ENG 18/9/73.
PETGRAVE-JOHNSON A. G., BA. Born 14/4/35. Commd 12/2/54. Flt Lt 13/4/60. Retd GD 31/3/61.
PETHARD J. W. G. Born 2/8/42. Commd 23/3/61. Flt Lt 24/9/66. Retd GD 1/10/88.
PETHERAM C. J., MIMgt. Born 3/4/28. Commd 27/9/49. Sqn Ldr 1/7/59. Retd GD 4/4/78.
PETHICK A. F., DFC. Born 19/4/20. Commd 14/7/42. Flt Lt 14/7/48. Retd SEC 20/4/64.
PETHICK M. Born 26/12/33. Commd 24/9/52. Sqn Ldr 1/1/75. Retd GD(G) 17/11/77.

PETR F. Born 26/11/18. Commd 22/9/55. Flt Lt 22/9/61. Retd GD(G) 5/5/72.
PETRE B. Born 26/10/46. Commd 4/7/85. Flt Lt 4/7/89. Retd ENG 6/12/97.
PETRE G. W., DFC AFC. Born 17/12/16. Commd 30/7/38. Gp Capt 1/1/57. Retd GD 17/12/66.
PETRIE I. J. N., BSc. Born 24/3/59. Commd 9/11/80. Flt Lt 9/8/81. Retd ENG 11/3/90.
PETRIE K. R. Born 29/2/36. Commd 2/9/55. Wg Cdr 1/1/80. Retd GD 1/3/91.
PETRIE M. A. Born 20/10/59. Commd 5/2/81. Flt Lt 1/6/85. Retd GD 6/3/90.
PETTERSON G. C. Born 7/1/27. Commd 3/6/54. Flt Lt 3/12/56. Retd GD 9/1/65.
PETTET M. J., CEng MRAeS. Born 30/5/34. Commd 26/9/53. Sqn Ldr 1/7/67. Retd ENG 1/6/84.
PETTIFER J. K., MA CEng MIEE. Born 18/5/35. Commd 26/9/53. Wg Cdr 1/1/72. Retd ENG 10/6/85.
PETTIFER M. I., OBE BSc. Born 4/11/48. Commd 24/1/71. Gp Capt 1/7/97. Retd ADMIN 1/6/01.
PETTIFER W. E. Born 12/9/22. Commd 11/3/43. Wg Cdr 1/1/61. Retd GD 25/5/68.
PETTINGER D. C., MIMgt. Born 4/9/33. Commd 1/10/62. Sqn Ldr 1/1/70. Retd GD 15/10/83
PETTIT A. C. Born 15/7/15. Commd 20/8/43. Flt Lt 11/11/54. Retd PE 28/8/63.
PETTIT B. D. Born 30/3/33. Commd 21/8/61. Flt Lt 21/8/61. Retd GD 30/3/91.
PETTMAN L. O. Born 26/5/30. Commd 26/11/64. Flt Lt 26/11/65. Retd EDN 26/11/72.
PETTS J. E. Born 4/5/33. Commd 17/12/52. Sqn Ldr 1/1/80. Retd GD 5/5/91.
PETTS N. R. Born 2/5/34. Commd 2/7/84. Flt Lt 19/11/78. Retd GD 2/5/92.
PETTY D. A., MA MA CertEd. Born 28/10/45. Commd 30/7/72. Sqn Ldr 30/1/79. Retd ADMIN 14/3/96.
PETTY S. H. Born 20/8/55. Commd 11/8/77. Flt Lt 11/2/83. Retd GD 31/3/87.
PEXTON B. L. Born 18/6/34. Commd 24/2/55. Wg Cdr 1/1/74. Retd SY 31/12/85.
PEXTON D. L., MIMgt. Born 28/11/35. Commd 22/1/55. Sqn Ldr 1/7/71. Retd ADMIN 27/4/87.
PEYCKE E. C. Born 11/11/48. Commd 10/1/69. Flt Lt 10/7/74. Retd GD 1/1/77.
PFANDER K. N. Born 18/6/48. Commd 10/9/70. Fg Offr 10/9/72. Retd GD 25/1/75.
PHAIR The Rev E. N. Born 5/10/15. Commd 24/3/43. Retd 24/10/53 Sqn Ldr.
PHARAOH M. H. Born 8/6/38. Commd 30/7/59. Wg Cdr 1/7/89. Retd ENG 8/11/93.
PHEASANT V. A., MBE. Born 2/7/40. Commd 24/9/64. Sqn Ldr 1/1/74. Retd GD 6/1/85.
PHILBEY B. Born 25/7/29. Commd 8/11/50. Flt Lt 14/5/56. Retd GD 25/7/67.
PHILIP A. C., MBE. Born 19/12/11. Commd 22/7/41. Sqn Ldr 1/7/53. Retd SEC 24/2/61.
PHILIP P. H. Born 22/2/27. Commd 11/6/53. Sqn Ldr 1/7/67. Retd GD 22/2/82.
PHILIP R. J. Born 21/9/42. Commd 28/2/85. Sqn Ldr 1/7/93. Retd ADMIN 21/9/97.
PHILLIP E. M. Born 22/7/20. Commd 29/7/42. Flt Offr 29/1/47. Retd SEC 14/5/53.
PHILLIPS A. Born 8/3/23. Commd 16/9/44. Sqn Ldr 1/7/55. Retd GD 8/3/66.
PHILLIPS A. D. S., OBE FIMgt. Born 14/8/20. Commd 4/4/46. Gp Capt 1/7/70. Retd ENG 3/7/73.
PHILLIPS A. J. Born 23/12/40. Commd 18/8/61. Flt Lt 23/12/67. Retd GD(G) 23/2/81. Reinstated 30/4/90. Flt Lt 30/4/88. Retd GD(G) 23/12/95.
PHILLIPS A. L., BA. Born 22/9/43. Commd 26/5/67. Flt Lt 24/10/70. Retd ENG 22/9/81.
PHILLIPS B. A., MBE MRAeS. Born 30/3/28. Commd 27/7/49. Sqn Ldr 1/1/62. Retd ENG 30/3/66.
PHILLIPS C. H. P. Born 31/1/20. Commd 19/6/43. Flt Lt 19/12/46. Retd GD 31/1/63.
PHILLIPS C. J. Born 16/5/34. Commd 14/12/54. Gp Capt 1/1/79. Retd GD 2/4/88.
PHILLIPS C. M., BA. Born 18/7/44. Commd 9/10/64. Flt Lt 9/4/70. Retd GD 18/7/94.
PHILLIPS D. B., BA BSc. Born 18/2/34. Commd 22/8/58. Sqn Ldr 17/5/67. Retd ADMIN 17/7/76. Reinstated 22/10/79. Sqn Ldr 22/8/70. Retd ADMIN 18/2/89.
PHILLIPS D. H., OBE. Born 6/9/44. Commd 17/12/65. Gp Capt 1/7/89. Retd GD 27/11/93.
PHILLIPS D. J., CEng MRAeS MIMgt. Born 15/2/35. Commd 27/2/58. Wg Cdr 1/7/75. Retd ENG 3/4/79.
PHILLIPS D. L., MM. Born 12/3/20. Commd 19/8/43. Flt Lt 23/7/48. Retd GD 22/9/54.
PHILLIPS D. M. Born 23/8/35. Commd 14/4/54. Flt Lt 7/7/61. Retd SUP 15/2/67.
PHILLIPS D. R., FIFA ACIS. Born 9/11/44. Commd 30/7/64. Wg Cdr 1/1/87. Retd ADMIN 4/4/90.
PHILLIPS E., DFC. Born 4/11/22. Commd 11/8/43. Flt Lt 4/12/52. Retd GD 28/9/68.
PHILLIPS F. C. Born 29/9/85. Commd 16/11/18. Retd GD 8/5/20. Recalled 28/8/39. Flt Lt 5/12/40. Retd 15/9/43.
PHILLIPS F. H. Born 10/4/17. Commd 3/8/43. Flt Lt 29/1/52. Retd GD(G) 10/5/56.
PHILLIPS G. M., MBE. Born 5/7/24. Commd 26/9/51. Sqn Ldr 1/1/69. Retd GD 5/7/79.
PHILLIPS G. T., BSc. Born 9/10/45. Commd 25/7/71. Sqn Ldr 1/7/84. Retd ADMIN 1/2/98.
PHILLIPS G. W., BSc. Born 1/2/52. Commd 2/9/84. Sqn Ldr 1/1/93. Retd GD 1/10/97.
PHILLIPS H. Born 4/1/35. Commd 17/1/52. Flt Lt 16/11/63. Retd GD 30/9/75.
PHILLIPS H. D. Born 12/3/01. Commd 24/4/41. Flt Lt 24/12/44. Retd ENG 14/6/46 rtg Sqn Ldr.
PHILLIPS J. F. Born 11/3/42. Commd 29/10/64. Sqn Ldr 1/7/76. Retd GD(G) 1/10/89.
PHILLIPS J. H., MIMgt. Born 16/1/25. Commd 3/5/46. Wg Cdr 1/7/64. Retd ADMIN 16/12/69. Re-employed 20/1/72 to 16/1/82. Sqn Ldr 6/5/58.
PHILLIPS J. J. Born 1/5/43. Commd 15/10/81. Flt Lt 15/10/86. Retd ENG 1/2/98.
PHILLIPS J. S. S. Born 20/12/35. Commd 5/11/62. Sqn Ldr 1/7/73. Retd GD 7/4/81.
PHILLIPS J. W. Born 23/9/17. Commd 20/10/44. Flt Lt 20/10/50. Retd GD(G) 15/9/62.
PHILLIPS K. Born 19/9/53. Commd 1/12/77. Sqn Ldr 1/7/86. Retd ADMIN 19/9/91.
PHILLIPS K. H. Born 11/4/21. Commd 6/12/56. Flt Lt 6/12/59. Retd ENG 26/9/64.
PHILLIPS M. J., MB ChB DCP DTM&H MRCPath. Born 24/2/31. Commd 8/2/56. Wg Cdr 8/2/69. Retd MED 30/6/72.
PHILLIPS M. J., BSc(Eng). Born 5/7/44. Commd 28/9/64. Flt Lt 5/7/67. Retd GD 5/7/82.

PHILLIPS M. T. Born 4/5/44. Commd 17/12/65. Gp Capt 1/1/94. Retd GD 14/3/96.
PHILLIPS N. R., BSc. Born 25/12/46. Commd 15/9/71. Sqn Ldr 1/7/84. Retd ENG 15/9/87.
PHILLIPS O. R., MIMgt. Born 9/3/28. Commd 11/6/52. Sqn Ldr 1/1/63. Retd GD 24/9/76.
PHILLIPS P. Born 27/11/29. Commd 26/8/66. Flt Lt 26/8/69. Retd GD 31/12/76.
PHILLIPS P. C., BSc. Born 16/12/29. Commd 24/1/52. Wg Cdr 1/7/72. Retd ENG 21/1/81.
PHILLIPS P. K. Born 8/5/45. Commd 2/3/78. Sqn Ldr 1/1/88. Retd SUP 2/3/92.
PHILLIPS R. Born 16/6/24. Commd 23/8/50. Sqn Ldr 1/4/61. Retd EDN 1/9/73.
PHILLIPS R. Born 12/12/21. Commd 12/12/44. Flt Lt 7/7/59. Retd GD 14/8/66.
PHILLIPS R. H. Born 18/2/10. Commd 9/12/43. Flt Lt 9/6/47. Retd ENG 1/9/50.
PHILLIPS R. J. Born 16/3/19. Commd 10/10/46. Wg Cdr 1/1/69. Retd SUP 30/9/72.
PHILLIPS S. A. Born 12/3/60. Commd 11/1/79. Sqn Ldr 1/1/91. Retd GD 12/3/98.
PHILLIPS S. B. Born 1/5/14. Commd 11/2/44. Fg Offr 5/11/48. Retd GD(G) 18/6/50 rtg Flt Lt.
PHILLIPS T. Born 4/12/14. Commd 6/6/40. Wg Cdr 1/1/56. Retd SEC 21/6/61.
PHILLIPS T. Born 4/10/33. Commd 28/11/69. Sqn Ldr 1/1/80. Retd ENG 5/11/85.
PHILLIPSON J. MCD., BA. Born 28/1/62. Commd 14/9/80. Flt Lt 15/10/84. Retd GD 15/7/95.
PHILLIPSON P. R. Born 26/9/55. Commd 19/3/81. Flt Lt 16/5/85. Retd OPS SPT 26/9/99.
PHILLPOTTS M. J., AMBCS. Born 19/11/46. Commd 5/1/70. Sqn Ldr 1/1/81. Retd ENG 1/10/92.
PHILO P. D. G., MILDM MCIT MILT MIMgt. Born 15/1/38. Commd 5/5/60. Retd ENG 15/1/76. Reinstated
    25/11/80. Sqn Ldr 1/1/88. Retd ENG 15/1/93.
PHILP G. Born 11/10/46. Commd 21/4/77. Sqn Ldr 1/1/88. Retd GD 30/10/96.
PHILP W. A. Born 28/4/32. Commd 11/6/52. Sqn Ldr 1/1/65. Retd ADMIN 6/9/77.
PHILPOTT A. J. Born 13/3/53. Commd 22/11/84. Flt Lt 22/11/86. Retd ENG 22/11/92.
PHILPOTT I. M. Born 18/8/35. Commd 21/10/54. Flt Lt 21/10/60. Retd RGT 18/8/73.
PHILPOTT R. J. Born 16/7/19. Commd 18/11/41. Sqn Ldr 1/1/68. Retd GD(G) 16/7/75.
PHILPOTT W. F. Born 29/3/20. Commd 15/9/60. Flt Lt 15/9/65. Retd ENG 29/3/75.
PHIPPEN J. Born 6/9/36. Commd 20/6/63. Sqn Ldr 1/7/71. Retd SEC 2/10/79.
PHIPPS A. R. P. Born 8/11/39. Commd 25/7/60. Wg Cdr 1/1/77. Retd GD 9/11/84.
PHIPPS L. W., CB AFC. Born 17/4/30. Commd 26/10/50. AVM 1/1/80. Retd GD 20/4/84.
PHYSICK M. J. Born 12/3/61. Commd 16/9/79. Sqn Ldr 1/1/96. Retd GD 22/12/99.
PICHEL-JUAN M. Born 2/3/48. Commd 26/8/76. Flt Lt 1/12/75. Retd GD 19/11/93.
PICK R. E., CEng MIM ARSM. Born 23/2/33. Commd 30/12/63. Sqn Ldr 1/1/70. Retd ENG 23/5/91.
PICK S. J. Born 1/7/55. Commd 17/1/85. Sqn Ldr 1/1/92. Retd SUP 1/1/95.
PICK W. M. H. Born 23/9/15. Commd 8/7/43. Flt Lt 8/1/47. Retd ENG 15/9/53.
PICKARD A. C., BA. Born 18/3/61. Commd 31/7/83. Flt Lt 31/1/86. Retd GD 30/4/00.
PICKARD C. F. Born 23/3/28. Commd 14/12/49. Gp Capt 1/7/75. Retd GD 4/4/80.
PICKARD H. H., MBE BSc. Born 18/12/21. Commd 11/11/43. A Cdre 1/7/73. Retd ADMIN 18/12/76.
PICKAVANCE M. J. Born 3/1/61. Commd 3/10/79. Flt Lt 11/3/89. Retd GD 3/1/99.
PICKAVANCE P., CEng MRAeS. Born 6/9/34. Commd 5/6/67. Sqn Ldr 1/1/78. Retd ENG 5/6/83.
PICKEN B. W., MIMgt. Born 24/7/30. Commd 4/7/51. Sqn Ldr 1/1/75. Retd GD(G) 6/4/83.
PICKERELL I. W. Born 26/3/51. Commd 21/10/81. Sqn Ldr 1/1/86. Retd GD 24/8/91.
PICKERING J. H. T. Born 11/8/14. Commd 31/8/36. Wg Cdr 1/1/49. Retd GD(G) 31/5/68.
PICKERING J. M. Born 25/2/48. Commd 3/11/77. Sqn Ldr 1/1/91. Retd ENG 14/3/97.
PICKERSGILL J. N. M. Born 5/8/31. Commd 28/7/53. Flt Lt 22/5/57. Retd GD 5/8/69.
PICKETT R. E. Born 15/12/54. Commd 22/5/75. Flt Lt 22/11/80. Retd GD 16/12/95.
PICKING A. W., MVO. Born 31/7/31. Commd 28/9/51. Sqn Ldr 1/1/65. Retd GD 31/1/71.
PICKMERE O. D. Born 25/4/26. Commd 6/12/51. Flt Lt 27/3/57. Retd GD 4/8/66.
PICKNETT A. J., DFC. Born 28/1/21. Commd 14/2/40. Wg Cdr 1/1/56. Retd GD 28/1/68.
PICKTHALL C. R. Born 30/12/49. Commd 24/8/72. Sqn Ldr 1/1/87. Retd GD(G) 14/3/96.
PICKTHALL M. A. Born 4/11/45. Commd 20/8/65. Flt Lt 20/2/71. Retd GD 19/11/88.
PICKUP K. H., LDSRCS. Born 4/6/14. Commd 25/6/43. Wg Cdr 7/6/63. Retd DEL 31/5/70.
PICTON R. S., MSc BSc. Born 20/4/46. Commd 17/10/71. Sqn Ldr 17/4/77. Retd ADMIN 17/10/87.
PIDDLESDEN M. O. Born 29/9/32. Commd 23/8/51. Flt Lt 23/2/57. Retd GD 29/1/72.
PIELOW A. N., MIMgt. Born 17/7/44. Commd 5/9/69. Flt Lt 7/3/76. Retd ADMIN 1/7/94.
PIERCE B. A. J. Born 27/7/28. Commd 5/7/68. Sqn Ldr 1/7/78. Retd ENG 4/4/85.
PIERCE C. G. H., BA. Born 29/7/31. Commd 9/4/52. Gp Capt 1/7/80. Retd ADMIN 6/4/83.
PIERCE D. H. Born 22/5/37. Commd 8/5/56. Flt Lt 7/5/62. Retd GD 7/5/78.
PIERCE D. J. B., MBE. Born 2/6/38. Commd 17/1/60. Gp Capt 1/1/91. Retd GD 1/1/93.
PIERCE D. P., MIEH. Born 30/12/60. Commd 4/6/87. Flt Lt 4/6/93. Retd MED(T) 31/10/95.
PIERCE E. W. Born 16/12/07. Commd 9/2/42. Flt Lt 1/9/45. Retd ENG 28/8/52 rtg Sqn Ldr.
PIERCE F. S. J. Born 26/9/27. Commd 13/3/48. Flt Lt 11/11/54. Retd GD 26/9/65.
PIERCE S. L., MBE. Born 1/3/32. Commd 30/7/52. Sqn Ldr 1/7/78. Retd GD 1/3/90.
PIERCE T. R. B., CBE. Born 14/9/19. Commd 4/4/38. A Cdre 1/1/66. Retd GD 3/10/70.
PIERCEY V. G. Born 14/7/21. Commd 6/6/46. Wg Cdr 1/7/67. Retd ENG 14/7/76.
PIERSE J. W. Born 12/11/34. Commd 2/7/64. Flt Lt 2/7/70. Retd GD 16/1/74.
PIERSON M. J. W., MBE MRAeS MBCS MMS MIMgt. Born 6/10/31. Commd 24/5/53. Gp Capt 1/1/80. Retd GD 14/7/
    86.

PIESING C. C. Born 8/2/14. Commd 13/3/47. Flt Lt 29/11/51. Retd CAT 11/3/52.
PIFF B. S. J., MBE. Born 22/9/20. Commd 13/8/41. Sqn Ldr 1/7/55. Retd GD 22/9/63.
PIFF R. E. G., CEng MRAeS. Born 20/3/16. Commd 11/2/42. Wg Cdr 1/1/59. Retd ENG 11/4/71.
PIGDON J. E. Born 27/9/29. Commd 13/2/52. Sqn Ldr 1/7/68. Retd GD 27/2/76.
PIGGOTT D. F. St J. Born 9/9/15. Commd 17/8/39. Flt Lt 27/11/45. Retd SUP 8/12/61 rtg Sqn Ldr.
PIKE D., BSc ACGI. Born 28/11/43. Commd 22/9/63. Flt Lt 15/4/68. Retd GD 28/11/81.
PIKE D. H. O., MIMgt. Born 26/5/22. Commd 3/4/59. Flt Lt 3/4/64. Retd ENG 26/5/77 rtg Sqn Ldr.
PIKE D. J. Born 22/5/38. Commd 30/12/59. Flt Lt 30/6/65. Retd GD 1/9/71.
PIKE E. Born 10/4/22. Commd 9/6/55. Flt Lt 9/6/60. Retd GD 1/10/68.
PIKE F. W., MBE. Born 7/9/42. Commd 19/10/65. Wg Cdr 1/1/82. Retd ENG 19/10/87.
PIKE H. E. Born 23/8/20. Commd 24/10/46. Sqn Ldr 1/1/68. Retd SUP 23/8/75.
PIKE J. E., PhD MSc BSc. Born 27/6/45. Commd 14/6/71. Flt Lt 3/10/73. Retd ENG 1/12/78.
PIKE J. R., CEng MIMechE MRAeS. Born 28/6/35. Commd 10/8/65. Sqn Ldr 1/1/77. Retd ENG 30/4/90.
PIKE P. C. G., MIMgt. Born 3/8/50. Commd 3/10/74. Sqn Ldr 1/7/86. Retd GD 20/5/90.
PIKE R. G. Born 12/7/43. Commd 28/7/64. Flt Lt 28/1/67. Retd GD 12/7/81.
PIKE W. F. J. Born 6/11/30. Commd 30/4/50. Sqn Ldr 1/1/76. Retd GD 14/10/84.
PIKE W. M. Born 12/10/48. Commd 3/12/74. Flg Off 31/12/76. Retd SEC 29/7/78.
PILBEAM K. A. Born 22/10/35. Commd 18/10/62. Wg Cdr 1/1/88. Retd GD 22/10/93.
PILCHER C. E. C., BSc. Born 10/9/47. Commd 2/8/68. Flt Lt 2/5/73. Retd ENG 21/3/75.
PILCHER R. D. Born 9/6/25. Commd 28/7/45. Sqn Ldr 1/1/60. Retd GD 8/1/76.
PILCHER-CLAYTON J. K. Born 15/10/11. Commd 23/9/41. Sqn Ldr 1/7/55. Retd ENG 15/10/60.
PILE B. L., BA. Born 7/8/52. Commd 17/9/72. Wg Cdr 1/7/90. Retd OPS SPT 1/11/98.
PILE R. L. C., LLM FIMLS DMLM. Born 11/10/40. Commd 2/6/77. Sqn Ldr 27/3/87. Retd MED(T) 12/11/90.
PILGRAM G. R., CEng MRAeS MMS. Born 6/12/35. Commd 5/7/68. Sqn Ldr 1/1/77. Retd ENG 16/2/91.
PILGREM R. A. Born 26/2/30. Commd 22/7/71. Flt Lt 22/7/76. Retd ENG 7/9/82.
PILGRIM-MORRIS G. J., BSc(Econ) FInstAM. Born 19/5/45. Commd 18/8/67. Wg Cdr 1/7/89. Retd ADMIN
    19/5/01.
PILGRIM-MORRIS J. S. Born 30/12/36. Commd 16/10/58. Wg Cdr 1/7/81. Retd GD 6/9/86.
PILKINGTON A. J. Born 3/1/42. Commd 6/5/66. Sqn Ldr 1/7/80. Retd GD 3/1/97.
PILKINGTON J. L., BSc(Eng). Born 26/11/51. Commd 16/9/73. Wg Cdr 1/7/93. Retd ENG 20/9/99.
PILKINGTON M. G. Born 29/12/51. Commd 20/7/78. Sqn Ldr 1/1/92. Retd GD 14/3/97.
PILKINGTON M. J., CB CBE. Born 9/10/37. Commd 17/11/58. AVM 1/7/86. Retd GD 18/12/92.
PILKINGTON P. P. Born 20/11/29. Commd 26/8/66. Flt Lt 26/8/69. Retd GD 6/1/76.
PILLAI S. N., BSc. Born 19/11/60. Commd 14/9/80. Flt Lt 15/1/86. Retd GD 27/9/99.
PILLEY R. Born 12/8/46. Commd 26/5/67. Flt Lt 18/2/70. Retd GD 2/6/78.
PIMM D. M. J. Born 2/5/46. Commd 16/9/76. Sqn Ldr 1/1/88. Retd ENG 24/8/92.
PINCHES L. J. E. Born 12/10/40. Commd 14/5/60. Flt Lt 14/11/65. Retd GD 12/10/78.
PINCHIN R. P. Born 26/4/57. Commd 24/6/76. Flt Lt 24/12/81. Retd GD 3/10/93.
PINDER S. P. H., MB BS DAvMed DFFP. Born 15/2/53. Commd 13/4/86. Wg Cdr 13/4/92. Retd MED 14/3/96.
PINE D. Born 2/9/24. Commd 6/10/44. Sqn Ldr 1/7/55. Retd GD 2/7/76.
PINE R. D. H. Born 25/6/49. Commd 25/2/72. Flt Lt 25/2/75. Retd GD 28/4/89.
PINFOLD H. M. Born 5/2/13. Commd 14/9/34. Gp Capt 1/7/53. Retd GD 1/10/58.
PINGREE B. J. W., MSc BSc MB ChB. Born 13/8/38. Sqn Ldr 5/2/74. Retd MED 4/2/75.
PINK A. W., OBE. Born 8/8/17. Commd 19/6/47. Wg Cdr 1/1/56. Retd PRT 8/8/67.
PINK J. R. Born 27/4/39. Commd 4/5/57. Gp Capt 1/7/84. Retd SUP 27/4/94.
PINK N. R. Born 3/8/29. Commd 5/7/68. Flt Lt 5/7/73. Retd ENG 3/8/79.
PINK T. J., OBE MCIPD. Born 22/8/46. Commd 16/1/72. Gp Capt 1/1/94. Retd ADMIN 22/8/96.
PINKEY K. Born 27/8/39. Commd 14/10/71. Sqn Ldr 1/7/90. Retd ENG 27/8/94.
PINKS C. N. R. Born 6/2/23. Commd 26/3/59. Flt Lt 1/4/63. Retd GD 6/2/78.
PINN D. L., MBE. Born 28/11/25. Commd 14/4/49. Sqn Ldr 1/1/59. Retd GD 30/9/75.
PINNELL C. P. Born 11/5/44. Commd 9/11/70. Wg Cdr 1/4/81. Retd LGL 9/11/86.
PINNER K. S. R., MIMgt. Born 15/7/33. Commd 6/2/67. Sqn Ldr 1/7/73. Retd ADMIN 28/2/86.
PINNEY P. G., CVO. Born 27/8/39. Commd 13/12/60. Gp Capt 1/7/86. Retd GD 22/5/94.
PINNINGTON A. Born 31/12/44. Commd 27/2/75. Flt Lt 27/2/77. Retd GD 8/6/96.
PINNINGTON J. F. Born 3/2/24. Commd 8/1/45. Wg Cdr 1/1/61. Retd GD 31/3/73 rtg Gp Capt.
PINNOCK R. E. Born 21/1/23. Commd 13/7/61. Sqn Ldr 1/1/74. Retd ENG 21/1/78.
PINTCHES J. R. Born 15/9/31. Commd 20/12/51. Flt Lt 14/5/58. Retd GD 15/9/86.
PIPE G. K. Born 17/8/45. Commd 25/3/64. Flt Lt 25/9/69. Retd GD 2/7/82.
PIPE P. J. Born 16/2/33. Commd 3/4/56. Sqn Ldr 1/1/77. Retd GD 16/2/91.
PIPER A. H., DFC. Born 4/4/16. Commd 5/6/41. Sqn Ldr 1/8/47. Retd GD 24/1/58.
PIPER A. L. Born 10/4/51. Commd 6/10/77. Flt Lt 15/10/79. Retd ENG 10/4/89.
PIPER C. Born 24/2/40. Commd 21/1/66. Flt Lt 8/3/72. Retd GD(G) 1/1/75.
PIPER C. J. Born 1/5/48. Commd 30/5/69. Fg Offr 1/5/71. Retd ENG 10/4/75.
PIPER J. F. G. Born 15/8/22. Commd 17/3/55. Plt Offr 17/3/55. Retd GD 28/5/60.
PIPER K. R. Born 29/7/37. Commd 5/12/63. Flt Lt 15/4/70. Retd GD(G) 10/9/79.
PIPER L. R. Born 8/1/38. Commd 1/10/60. Sqn Ldr 1/7/75. Retd GD 8/1/96.

PIPER R., MBE. Born 23/6/41. Commd 6/9/68. Sqn Ldr 1/7/80. Retd GD 29/6/91.
PIPER R. J. Born 4/3/33. Commd 6/12/51. Flt Lt 27/3/57. Retd GD 24/9/75.
PIPER S. A. J., MBE. Born 5/10/25. Commd 18/10/62. Sqn Ldr 1/1/74. Retd GD 5/10/83.
PIPPET E. F., OBE. Born 23/10/15. Commd 15/3/35. Wg Cdr 1/7/47. Retd GD 23/10/70 rtg Gp Capt.
PIPPET T. F. Born 20/8/08. Commd 18/3/41. Fg Offr 15/3/42. Retd ASD 3/11/45 rtg Sqn Ldr.
PIRIE Sir Gordon., CVO CBE. Born 10/2/18. Commd 30/7/38. Wg Cdr 26/4/45. Retd GD 29/11/46 rtg Gp Capt.
PITCAIRN-HILL F. C. Born 17/11/30. Commd 26/11/52. Flt Lt 5/10/60. Retd GD(G) 17/11/85.
PITCAIRN-HILL T. H. Born 26/12/15. Commd 19/3/42. Sqn Ldr 1/7/53. Retd ENG 28/10/68.
PITCHER A., CEng MIMechE MIMgt. Born 13/3/30. Commd 15/11/51. Wg Cdr 1/7/74. Retd ENG 5/12/81.
PITCHER G. Born 3/7/41. Commd 12/1/62. Flt Lt 3/1/67. Retd GD 28/2/73.
PITCHER P. C. Born 31/7/48. Commd 19/8/66. Flt Lt 4/5/72. Retd GD 9/10/95.
PITCHFORK G. R., MBE BA FRAeS. Born 4/2/39. Commd 1/8/61. A Cdre 1/1/90. Retd GD 3/10/94.
PITICK G. Born 26/9/44. Commd 17/2/67. Flt Lt 17/8/72. Retd GD 1/10/84.
PITKIN J. M., BSc CEng MRAeS. Born 1/11/62. Commd 31/8/80. Sqn Ldr 1/1/92. Retd ENG 1/11/99.
PITMAN D. C. J. Born 30/1/32. Commd 16/12/66. Flt Lt 16/12/71. Retd SUP 1/7/82.
PITMAN R. J. G., MSc. Born 30/10/34. Commd 23/10/62. Sqn Ldr 30/9/72. Retd EDN 1/10/79.
PITT A. J., MSc BSc(Eng) CEng MRAeS. Born 20/7/39. Commd 30/9/58. Gp Capt 1/7/85. Retd ENG 20/7/94.
PITT J. G. Born 3/2/65. Commd 11/9/86. Flt Lt 11/3/93. Retd ADMIN 14/9/96.
PITT M. R. Born 13/3/50. Commd 14/8/70. Sqn Ldr 1/7/86. Retd GD 1/7/89.
PITT R., AFM. Born 10/8/18. Commd 25/3/42. Sqn Ldr 1/1/68. Retd GD(G) 10/8/76.
PITT-BROWN W., CBE DFC* AFC FIMgt. Born 3/7/18. Commd 30/7/38. A Cdre 1/7/61. Retd GD 3/4/69.
PITTAWAY R. A. Born 25/10/47. Commd 2/6/67. Sqn Ldr 1/7/85. Retd GD 14/9/96.
PITTAWAY S. F. Born 19/12/60. Commd 20/10/83. Flt Lt 1/10/87. Retd GD 20/6/99.
PITTS A. Born 8/12/47. Commd 2/12/66. Flt Lt 2/6/72. Retd GD 10/1/99.
PITTS R. F. Born 24/8/58. Commd 11/9/86. Flt Lt 11/9/88. Retd GD(G) 24/8/96.
PITTS R. J. M. Born 2/8/59. Commd 6/11/80. Flt Lt 6/5/86. Retd GD 1/1/01.
PITTSON K. T. Born 2/5/49. Commd 8/6/84. Sqn Ldr 1/1/95. Retd ADMIN 15/11/99.
PLACE R. T. Born 15/4/27. Commd 8/10/52. Flt Lt 6/3/58. Retd GD 27/5/68.
PLAISTOW C. M. Born 3/7/30. Commd 14/11/51. Flt Lt 14/5/56. Retd GD 2/8/73.
PLANK N. F. Born 3/2/39. Commd 8/8/74. Flt Lt 8/8/76. Retd ENG 7/4/83.
PLANT M. E. Born 20/6/42. Commd 14/8/70. Flt Lt 14/8/72. Retd GD 20/6/97.
PLANT R. Born 7/12/65. Commd 28/2/85. Flt Lt 28/8/91. Retd SUP 14/3/97.
PLANTEROSE P.J., MVO. Born 16/2/39. Commd 30/9/58. Gp Capt 1/1/90. Retd GD 20/4/92.
PLASIL J. F. Born 15/6/17. Commd 12/3/53. Flt Lt 12/3/58. Retd GD(G) 15/6/67.
PLATER L. W., BA. Born 27/12/47. Commd 9/12/71. Sqn Ldr 1/7/85. Retd GD 1/7/88.
PLATER R. F. Born 30/8/27. Commd 1/11/50. Flt Lt 1/5/55. Retd GD 30/3/68.
PLATT B. D. Born 12/3/24. Commd 27/10/55. Flt Lt 27/10/61. Retd PI 12/3/79.
PLATT E. A., BA. Born 30/10/33. Commd 25/8/55. Sqn Ldr 30/4/63. Retd EDN 30/10/71.
PLATT J. C., MIMgt. Born 5/6/22. Commd 2/10/43. Wg Cdr 1/1/69. Retd GD(G) 5/6/77.
PLATT K. J. G., CEng MIEE. Born 5/10/49. Commd 26/2/71. Sqn Ldr 1/7/83. Retd GD 24/10/87.
PLATTS F. J., OBE FIMS. Born 15/5/32. Commd 30/7/64. Wg Cdr 1/1/80. Retd GD(G) 1/1/85.
PLATTS J. T., MSc BEng. Born 24/10/62. Commd 16/2/86. Flt Lt 16/8/88. Retd ADMIN 14/3/97.
PLAYER B. C., CBE. Born 6/2/22. Commd 29/3/45. A Cdre 1/1/74. Retd PRT 26/3/76.
PLAYLE L. C. W. Born 16/2/52. Commd 29/4/71. Flt Lt 29/10/76. Retd GD 16/2/90.
PLEASANCE H. P., OBE DFC*. Born 12/4/14. Commd 11/5/36. Gp Capt 1/7/55. Retd GD 1/12/60.
PLEASANT A. M. Born 26/3/39. Commd 19/2/76. Flt Lt 19/2/81. Retd GD(G) 5/5/93.
PLEDGER P. V., OBE. Born 24/3/27. Commd 8/4/49. Gp Capt 1/1/68. Retd GD 2/1/70.
PLENDERLEITH B. C. Born 27/9/50. Commd 8/12/83. Flt Lt 8/12/85. Retd ADMIN 14/3/97.
PLESSIS R. J. N. Born 1/7/37. Retd 30/10/61. Flt Lt 30/10/61. Retd GD 17/2/68.
PLESTED I. J. Born 16/7/47. Commd 21/5/65. Flt Lt 21/11/70. Retd GD 15/12/84.
PLEWS J. G., BA. Born 5/8/46. Commd 11/5/78. Flt Lt 11/5/80. Retd GD 21/11/98.
PLIMMER H. L., DFC*. Born 3/3/12. Commd 4/4/42. Sqn Ldr 1/7/53. Retd PE 1/9/60.
PLIMMER M. Born 6/8/39. Commd 19/1/66. Sqn Ldr 1/7/76. Retd ENG 1/7/79.
PLINSTON F. A., DFC. Born 29/4/19. Commd 17/12/38. Sqn Ldr 1/6/45. Retd GD 16/5/58.
PLOSZEK H. R., AFC. Born 6/5/36. Commd 17/12/57. Sqn Ldr 1/7/69. Retd GD 18/6/90.
PLOWMAN C. G., CEng MIMechE MRAeS. Born 17/5/37. Commd 25/9/59. Gp Capt 1/1/85. Retd ENG 17/5/92.
PLOWMAN K. F. Born 18/1/23. Commd 13/6/46. Flt Lt 13/6/52. Retd RGT 18/1/61.
PLOWMAN P. E. Born 26/10/39. Commd 4/4/59. Sqn Ldr 1/7/73. Retd SUP 8/11/82.
PLOWMAN R. L., LDSRCS. Born 28/8/57. Commd 30/9/79. Wg Cdr 1/12/94. Retd DEL 30/9/95.
PLOWMAN R. T. F., BA. Born 10/7/28. Commd 12/10/52. Sqn Ldr 1/7/62. Retd GD 12/10/68.
PLOWMAN W. A. Born 4/3/16. Commd 19/7/45. Sqn Ldr 1/1/54. Retd SUP 5/6/60.
PLOWMAN W. S., BA MCIPD. Born 11/2/48. Commd 31/8/78. Sqn Ldr 1/7/85. Retd ADMIN 14/3/97.
PLOWRIGHT H. D. W., MB BS MRCS MRCOG LRCP DObstRCOG. Born 26/3/34. Commd 12/6/60. Sqn Ldr 16/3/64. Retd MED 2/8/69.
PLOWS D. M., BSc. Born 28/3/46. Commd 14/4/67. Flt Lt 1/6/71. Retd GD 3/2/76.
PLUCK M. F. E. W. Born 30/11/44. Commd 2/4/65. Flt Lt 2/10/70. Retd GD 30/11/82.

PLUCK N. S., MIMgt. Born 10/8/30. Commd 21/2/52. Sqn Ldr 1/7/66. Retd SEC 1/7/69.
PLUMB A. A. Born 4/11/36. Commd 25/10/73. Sqn Ldr 1/7/83. Retd PI 4/10/83.
PLUMB F. A. Born 3/1/33. Commd 13/9/51. Sqn Ldr 1/1/67. Retd GD 31/1/71.
PLUMB K. J., BSc. Born 1/12/52. Commd 20/1/80. Sqn Ldr 1/1/88. Retd ADMIN 14/3/97.
PLUMB R. G., FCCS. Born 7/4/17. Commd 21/2/57. Flt Lt 23/9/59. Retd SEC 4/4/70.
PLUMBLEY E. P. Born 4/10/21. Commd 5/9/57. Flt Lt 26/11/61. Retd ENG 30/12/72.
PLUME J. M. Born 16/5/58. Commd 22/11/84. Flt Lt 14/5/89. Retd ADMIN 9/7/00.
PLUME M. A. P. Born 4/7/16. Commd 1/3/62. Flt Lt 1/3/65. Retd CAT 31/12/71.
PLUME P. S., BTech CEng MIMechE. Born 29/1/50. Commd 2/9/73. Sqn Ldr 1/1/83. Retd ENG 2/9/89.
PLUMLEY J. H., BSc. Born 9/5/48. Commd 3/1/69. Wg Cdr 1/1/94. Retd GD 5/5/00.
PLUMMER A. J. W. Born 8/8/42. Commd 25/10/87. Flt Lt 25/10/89. Retd ADMIN 19/8/91.
PLUMMER B., MBE. Born 1/1/36. Commd 18/8/54. Sqn Ldr 1/7/81. Retd GD 1/1/96.
PLUMMER J. H. C., MBE FIMgt MBCS. Born 30/5/23. Commd 23/10/43. A Cdre 1/1/74. Retd ADMIN 1/9/76.
PLUMMER K. G., BSc. Born 2/1/56. Commd 15/10/78. Sqn Ldr 1/1/91. Retd GD 14/9/96.
PLUMMER R. A., MCIPS. Born 9/7/42. Commd 29/3/68. Gp Capt 1/7/90. Retd SUP 9/7/97.
PLUNKETT P. A., BSc. Born 7/2/42. Commd 14/9/64. Flt Lt 14/6/66. Retd GD 14/9/80.
PLUNKETT P. N. O., BSc. Born 28/8/45. Commd 5/1/66. Gp Capt 1/1/90. Retd GD 30/9/98.
POATE C. D. Born 30/7/50. Commd 26/2/71. Fg Offr 26/2/72. Retd GD 15/6/73.
POCKNELL D. Born 1/10/19. Commd 5/4/43. Sqn Ldr 1/7/56. Retd ENG 1/10/68.
POCOCK D. A., CBE. Born 5/7/20. Commd 25/7/41. AVM 1/1/73. Retd RGT 5/7/75.
POCOCK R. C. Born 23/9/18. Commd 5/3/43. Flt Lt 5/9/46. Retd GD 15/10/57 rtg Sqn Ldr.
POCOCK R. E. Born 8/6/28. Commd 26/12/51. Flt Lt 14/11/56. Retd GD 8/6/83.
POCOCK R. W., MIMgt. Born 11/5/30. Commd 30/7/53. Wg Cdr 1/7/75. Retd SUP 21/4/84.
PODEVIN C. Born 4/1/12. Commd 12/8/43. Fg Offr 12/2/44. Retd ENG 9/2/46.
PODGER C. J. Born 3/5/34. Commd 12/7/55. Sqn Ldr 1/1/68. Retd GD 1/5/82.
PODMORE W. F., MIMgt. Born 18/8/20. Commd 30/8/62. Flt Lt 30/8/67. Retd ENG 18/8/75.
POGMORE J. R., MB BS MRCS MRCOG LRCP DObstRCOG. Born 12/6/42. Commd 22/4/63. Wg Cdr 2/1/80. Retd
   MED 12/6/80.
POIL The Rev R. W., AKC. Born 9/11/30. Commd 17/1/52. Retd 10/12/76 Wg Cdr.
POINTER A. R. B., MBE. Born 15/10/17. Commd 18/4/43. Flt Lt 18/10/46. Retd GD(G) 2/8/69.
POLAK E. Born 22/2/20. Commd 12/4/44. Flt Lt 27/5/54. Retd GD(G) 22/2/75.
POLAND E. R. Born 20/4/25. Commd 29/4/44. Flt Lt 4/12/52. Retd SUP 1/2/58.
POLDEN D. B., DFM. Born 29/1/23. Commd 10/9/43. Sqn Ldr 1/7/67. Retd GD(G) 2/10/76.
POLE F. G., CEng MIMechE MRAeS MIMgt. Born 26/7/36. Commd 12/9/58. Flt Lt 21/6/64. Retd ENG 21/8/77.
POLE F. G., BSc. Born 25/5/47. Commd 6/10/69. Sqn Ldr 1/1/83. Retd GD 1/1/86.
POLHILL J. Born 29/9/12. Commd 31/12/41. Sqn Ldr 1/10/55. Retd ENG 29/9/67.
POLL J. N. Born 19/12/06. Commd 22/4/43. Fg Offr 4/3/44. Retd ASD 13/11/48 rtg Flt Lt.
POLLARD B. D., BA. Born 8/10/31. Commd 23/9/55. Sqn Ldr 23/3/63. Retd EDN 23/9/71.
POLLARD D. W., BSc. Born 20/11/46. Commd 26/5/67. Flt Lt 18/11/71. Retd ENG 16/10/75.
POLLARD E. H. Born 3/2/18. Commd 14/9/44. Sqn Ldr 1/1/56. Retd ENG 12/3/73.
POLLARD J. T. Born 14/2/31. Commd 15/10/52. Flt Lt 5/11/58. Retd GD 14/2/69.
POLLARD K. Born 5/4/20. Commd 11/9/43. Flt Lt 19/6/52. Retd RGT 5/4/65.
POLLARD K. G. Born 17/10/37. Commd 13/10/61. Sqn Ldr 1/7/72. Retd GD 7/4/79.
POLLARD N. A. Born 18/12/28. Commd 22/7/50. Wg Cdr 1/7/77. Retd SY 13/11/82.
POLLARD N. J., MCIPS. Born 10/9/43. Commd 24/6/65. Sqn Ldr 1/1/80. Retd SUP 10/9/87.
POLLEY I. W. M., CEng MIMechE. Born 13/9/37. Commd 10/12/63. Sqn Ldr 1/1/71. Retd ENG 10/12/79.
POLLINGTON J. E., MIMgt. Born 27/1/23. Commd 5/10/50. Wg Cdr 1/7/65. Retd GD 31/3/73.
POLLITT A. M., MBE. Born 18/5/15. Commd 19/4/41. Sqn Ldr 1/7/60. Retd GD(G) 28/5/70.
POLLOCK A. R. Born 13/3/36. Commd 10/4/56. Flt Lt 10/10/58. Retd GD 24/10/68.
POLLOCK D. P. Born 10/9/38. Commd 9/4/60. Wg Cdr 1/7/77. Retd GD(G) 10/9/93.
POLLOCK H. A., MBE MIMgt. Born 9/11/21. Commd 9/5/46. Sqn Ldr 1/1/63. Retd ENG 1/12/77.
POLLOCK H. A. J. Born 9/4/24. Commd 7/11/44. Flt Lt 14/12/54. Retd GD(G) 16/5/65.
POLLOCK J. Born 17/6/25. Commd 9/7/59. Flt Lt 9/7/65. Retd ACB 30/4/66.
POLLOCK J. Born 24/2/34. Commd 3/12/70. Flt Lt 3/12/73. Retd GD 24/5/92.
POLLOCK N. J. C., OBE. Born 5/1/18. Commd 29/6/41. Sqn Ldr 1/7/54. Retd SEC 7/1/65.
POLLOCK N. R., MBE. Born 29/12/23. Commd 21/10/54. Sqn Ldr 1/7/70. Retd GD 30/4/84.
POLLOCK S. J. C. Born 10/9/46. Commd 9/3/72. Flt Lt 9/3/77. Retd ENG 15/11/87.
POLWARTH J. B., BA. Born 23/12/59. Commd 7/11/82. Flt Lt 7/2/83. Retd GD 1/4/93.
POMEROY C. A. Born 3/12/42. Commd 14/7/66. Sqn Ldr 1/7/80. Retd GD 3/12/80.
POMFORD J. A. Born 27/9/32. Commd 20/12/51. Flt Lt 4/4/57. Retd GD 27/9/70.
POMFRET C. J., BSc(Tech) CEng MIMechE MIMgt. Born 13/12/54. Commd 16/9/73. Sqn Ldr 1/7/86. Retd ENG
   27/3/96.
POMFRET S. Born 1/7/31. Commd 2/5/51. Wg Cdr 1/7/68. Retd GD 1/7/87.
POND A. H. D., AFC. Born 15/12/14. Commd 1/12/42. Sqn Ldr 1/7/53. Retd SEC 17/12/63.
POND G. R. Born 20/4/29. Commd 1/11/50. Flt Lt 1/5/55. Retd GD 14/11/75.
POND M. R. Born 25/2/39. Commd 31/10/69. Flt Lt 31/10/71. Retd ENG 1/4/78.

PONSFORD R. A., LRAM ARCM. Born 22/10/19. Commd 28/3/59. Sqn Ldr 13/12/67. Retd DM 22/10/74.
PONTET-PICCOLOMINI D. R. A. Born 25/3/19. Commd 4/9/58. Flt Lt 4/9/61. Retd GD(G) 30/9/69.
PONTING A. J., LLB. Born 21/1/35. Commd 25/11/60. Flt Lt 18/2/70. Retd SUP 10/2/78.
PONTON W. H. Born 24/8/20. Commd 19/1/46. Sqn Ldr 1/1/68. Retd GD(G) 24/8/75.
POOK B. T. T. Born 3/9/08. Commd 26/11/40. Sqn Ldr 1/8/47. Retd ENG 14/8/53.
POOK H. A. Born 11/10/09. Commd 25/11/41. Sqn Ldr 1/1/53. Retd ENG 11/10/58.
POOK J. J., MBE DFC. Born 20/4/45. Commd 15/7/66. Sqn Ldr 1/1/79. Retd GD 15/6/97.
POOL G. L. Born 19/9/23. Commd 28/5/47. Flt Lt 19/11/53. Retd GD 27/6/65.
POOL I. Born 3/9/59. Commd 9/5/91. Flt Lt 9/5/93. Retd GD(G) 14/3/96.
POOLE A. N. Born 28/1/45. Commd 31/10/74. Sqn Ldr 1/7/91. Retd GD(G) 1/4/94.
POOLE D. Born 2/5/50. Commd 6/11/72. Flt Lt 11/11/76. Retd GD(G) 26/8/86.
POOLE D. Born 1/8/16. Commd 21/10/54. Flt Lt 21/10/57. Retd SEC 1/8/73.
POOLE D. R., BSc. Born 17/5/60. Commd 6/9/81. Sqn Ldr 1/7/91. Retd GD 17/5/98.
POOLE F. A. G., MA BSc. Born 22/2/21. Commd 1/1/50. Sqn Ldr 1/11/55. Retd EDN 15/9/61.
POOLE F. W. Born 14/3/20. Commd 17/5/56. Flt Lt 17/5/62. Retd SEC 25/6/65.
POOLE G. M. Born 9/2/34. Commd 24/2/67. Flt Lt 24/2/72. Retd GD 19/4/79.
POOLE J. Born 16/6/21. Commd 1/11/56. Sqn Ldr 1/1/69. Retd ENG 16/6/76.
POOLE J. V. Born 5/8/31. Commd 7/10/55. Flt Lt 25/4/61. Retd GD 25/4/77. Reinstated 15/11/79 to 15/8/84.
POOLE N. P. Born 18/5/47. Commd 11/8/67. Sqn Ldr 1/7/84. Retd GD 2/1/99.
POOLE P. B. Born 1/7/21. Commd 29/10/53. Fg Offr 29/10/55. Retd SEC 15/3/57.
POOLE R. Born 15/11/13. Commd 19/9/44. Flt Lt 19/6/52. Retd RGT 1/5/58.
POOLE R. S. G. Born 24/5/27. Commd 20/12/46. Flt Lt 4/1/51. Retd GD 31/10/75.
POOLER M. J. Born 23/2/49. Commd 27/2/70. Flt Lt 27/8/75. Retd GD 23/2/91.
POOLEY A. F. V. Born 21/5/46. Commd 31/10/69. Sqn Ldr 1/1/86. Retd GD 16/6/91.
POOLEY J. D. A. Born 8/11/32. Commd 23/4/52. Flt Lt 19/9/57. Retd GD 8/11/70.
POOLEY T. T. Born 9/10/45. Commd 7/11/85. Sqn Ldr 1/7/96. Retd ENG 23/3/01.
POOTS R. Born 26/11/51. Commd 21/2/74. Sqn Ldr 1/7/88. Retd GD 1/7/91.
POPAY H. I., DFM*. Born 1/1/19. Commd 31/3/42. Sqn Ldr 1/10/55. Retd GD 1/1/62.
POPE B. J. Born 10/10/58. Commd 23/8/80. Flt Lt 22/10/82. Retd SUP 1/7/89.
POPE B. T. Born 4/12/40. Commd 27/7/72. Sqn Ldr 25/11/77. Retd ADMIN 27/7/81.
POPE C. A., MA PGCE FRGS MCIPD DipEdTech. Born 18/3/55. Commd 8/4/79. Sqn Ldr 1/7/89. Retd ADMIN 8/4/01.
POPE F. C. Born 21/6/99. Commd 9/5/40. Sqn Ldr 10/4/46. Retd ENG 1/9/50 rtg Wg Cdr.
POPE F. R., MBE. Born 29/3/15. Commd 22/4/43. Sqn Ldr 1/7/56. Retd ENG 31/3/65.
POPE G. B. Born 8/3/17. Commd 5/6/43. Sqn Ldr 1/1/65. Retd SUP 8/3/74.
POPE I. G., MHCIMA. Born 9/3/53. Commd 30/3/75. Sqn Ldr 1/1/88. Retd ADMIN 30/3/91.
POPE J. C., CB CBE CEng FIMechE FRAeS. Born 27/4/11. Commd 17/12/32. AVM 1/7/64. Retd ENG 29/9/66.
POPE J. R., BSc. Born 14/5/52. Commd 13/9/70. Sqn Ldr 1/7/87. Retd GD 1/7/90.
POPE K. Born 28/8/53. Commd 16/5/74. Flt Lt 17/8/80. Retd GD(G) 28/8/92.
POPE L. C. Born 29/3/28. Commd 14/5/53. Flt Lt 14/11/56. Retd GD 29/3/66.
POPE L. D., DFC. Born 1/1/22. Commd 24/6/43. Sqn Ldr 1/1/68. Retd GD 1/8/73.
POPE L. R. Born 18/12/30. Commd 28/6/51. Flt Lt 14/5/58. Retd SEC 28/12/68.
POPE R. Born 24/2/39. Commd 1/4/66. Flt Lt 1/10/70. Retd GD 7/6/77.
POPE R. D. G. Born 1/11/22. Commd 31/7/58. Flt Lt 31/7/53. Retd GD 1/11/77.
POPE W. H., OBE. Born 27/7/21. Commd 31/7/42. A Cdre 1/7/73. Retd GD(G) 27/7/76.
POPE W. J., OBE CEng MRAeS MIMgt. Born 4/12/19. Commd 19/8/42. Wg Cdr 1/1/60. Retd ENG 4/12/74.
POPEJOY G. E. Born 13/4/13. Commd 8/4/43. Sqn Ldr 1/1/57. Retd ENG 13/4/68.
POPPITT B. P., MIMgt. Born 6/7/35. Commd 25/9/62. Sqn Ldr 1/1/71. Retd ENG 25/9/75.
POPPLE J. R. Born 23/11/56. Commd 25/11/82. Sqn Ldr 1/7/96. Retd SUP 19/12/97.
POPPLE R. T., MBE MCIPD MIMgt. Born 26/1/31. Commd 19/6/52. Wg Cdr 1/7/76. Retd SEC 1/9/78.
PORTEOUS T. C., AFC. Born 23/7/38. Commd 15/12/59. Sqn Ldr 1/1/69. Retd GD 27/8/75.
PORTER A. H., OBE CEng MRAeS FIMgt. Born 14/9/12. Commd 20/2/41. Gp Capt 1/7/62. Retd ENG 14/9/66.
PORTER A. V. Born 26/8/41. Commd 29/11/63. Flt Lt 1/7/69. Retd GD 28/2/70.
PORTER E. J., BSc. Born 21/1/58. Commd 31/8/75. Flt Lt 15/10/81. Retd ADMIN 15/7/91.
PORTER E. O. Born 3/7/17. Commd 30/7/38. Sqn Ldr 1/3/42. Retd GD 28/1/48.
PORTER G., BA. Born 15/10/24. Commd 23/8/50. Sqn Ldr 15/10/58. Retd EDN 11/9/65.
PORTER H. R., CEng MRAeS. Born 26/6/14. Commd 12/11/42. Sqn Ldr 1/7/53. Retd ENG 26/6/69.
PORTER J. A., OBE BA. Born 20/11/42. Commd 9/2/62. Gp Capt 1/1/90. Retd GD 2/4/93.
PORTER J. A., OBE BSc DipSoton CEng FIEE FRAeS. Born 29/9/34. Commd 26/9/53. AVM 1/7/84. Retd ENG 6/2/89.
PORTER J. W. Born 20/4/40. Commd 24/4/64. Sqn Ldr 1/7/75. Retd GD 1/7/78.
PORTER Sir Kenneth, KCB CBE CEng FIEE FRAeS CBIM. Born 19/11/12. Commd 17/12/32. AM 1/7/67. Retd ENG 8/6/70.
PORTER L. J. Born 3/10/20. Commd 18/10/47. Flt Lt 4/1/51. Retd GD(G) 27/9/75.
PORTER M. D. Born 27/5/35. Commd 10/4/56. Flt Lt 5/11/58. Retd GD 10/4/92.
PORTER M. J. Born 14/10/37. Commd 15/12/59. Sqn Ldr 1/1/73. Retd ADMIN 30/11/90.

PORTER W. Born 4/6/23. Commd 24/4/45. Flt Lt 4/1/51. Retd GD 29/10/61.
PORTER The Rev W. W., BD. Born 2/3/27. Commd 20/10/65. Retd 20/10/81 Wg Cdr.
POSKITT L. A. Born 23/11/18. Commd 24/12/44. Fg Offr 24/12/45. Retd GD(G) 26/9/52 rtg Flt Lt.
POSTANCE R., CEng MIERE. Born 29/7/44. Commd 24/1/63. Flt Lt 24/7/69. Retd ENG 29/7/82.
POSTLETHWAITE J. P. Born 29/11/35. Commd 2/4/57. Sqn Ldr 1/1/70. Retd GD 1/10/77.
POTESTA T. C., OBE. Born 9/6/38. Commd 5/11/59. Gp Capt 1/1/86. Retd ADMIN 9/11/89.
POTHAN G. M. Born 19/6/31. Commd 4/11/51. Flt Lt 1/11/61. Retd CAT 16/11/70.
POTOCKI W. J., DFC. Born 9/6/19. Commd 1/11/45. Sqn Ldr 1/7/53. Retd GD 31/5/56.
POTTAGE J., OBE. Born 23/11/38. Commd 16/1/60. Wg Cdr 1/7/84. Retd GD(G) 23/11/93.
POTTER A. Born 8/11/31. Commd 13/8/52. Sqn Ldr 1/1/81. Retd GD 8/11/89.
POTTER A. W. Born 9/10/33. Commd 8/7/53. Sqn Ldr 1/1/79. Retd GD 9/10/88.
POTTER B. Born 15/5/39. Commd 15/12/59. Flt Lt 15/8/62. Retd GD 31/7/69.
POTTER C. E. Born 25/3/40. Commd 13/12/79. Sqn Ldr 1/1/89. Retd ENG 25/3/95.
POTTER C. J., BSc. Born 23/3/53. Commd 28/9/80. Sqn Ldr 1/1/87. Retd ENG 28/3/97.
POTTER D. D. Born 9/5/30. Commd 19/7/51. Flt Lt 22/6/59. Retd GD 30/9/77.
POTTER D. M., BA. Born 16/5/34. Commd 8/10/70. Flt Lt 8/10/71. Retd EDN 3/1/76.
POTTER G. J. Born 9/3/38. Commd 18/8/61. Flt Lt 25/7/66. Retd GD 9/3/93.
POTTER I. P. G., BSc CEng MIEE. Born 17/2/49. Commd 27/2/70. Sqn Ldr 1/1/86. Retd ENG 1/5/94.
POTTER J., MA MSc MBCS MRAeS. Born 23/12/43. Commd 6/9/65. Sqn Ldr 28/6/74. Retd ADMIN 30/1/82.
POTTER J. E. Born 23/12/11. Commd 9/4/41. Wg Cdr 1/7/56. Retd ENG 23/6/65.
POTTER J. G., MDA BSc. Born 7/1/54. Commd 18/11/73. Wg Cdr 1/1/92. Retd SUP 16/7/95.
POTTER J. R., BSc. Born 16/2/92. Commd 26/9/71. Sqn Ldr 1/7/88. Retd GD 31/3/93.
POTTER M. A. G. Born 29/11/11. Commd 25/8/41. Sqn Offr 1/1/51. Retd SEC 2/12/60.
POTTER M. G., DFC. Born 27/12/14. Commd 8/11/42. Flt Lt 8/5/46. Retd GD 11/9/53.
POTTER M. W., BSc. Born 9/8/47. Commd 2/8/68. Sqn Ldr 1/7/79. Retd ENG 29/4/86.
POTTER R. A. Born 13/5/45. Commd 11/3/68. Flt Lt 11/6/71. Retd SEC 31/5/75.
POTTER S. B., BSc. Born 1/5/57. Commd 2/3/80. Sqn Ldr 1/7/89. Retd GD 1/10/96.
POTTLE W. M., BSc. Born 25/12/37. Commd 4/9/59. Sqn Ldr 4/3/70. Retd EDN 25/12/75.
POTTS A. N. Born 30/9/62. Commd 11/4/85. Flt Lt 11/10/90. Retd GD 14/3/96.
POTTS A. T. Born 10/6/44. Commd 12/7/79. Sqn Ldr 1/1/90. Retd SUP 10/6/99.
POTTS C. J. Born 1/7/22. Commd 9/12/42. Flt Offr 28/5/49. Retd SEC 14/6/55.
POTTS J. A. Born 21/11/43. Commd 31/8/62. Flt Lt 15/4/71. Retd ADMIN 18/3/94.
POTTS N. H. Born 15/4/15. Commd 17/7/43. Sqn Ldr 1/1/55. Retd SEC 4/9/61.
POUGHER-HEMSLEY P. R., BA FCIPD MIMgt MRAeS. Born 30/4/48. Commd 28/2/69. Wg Cdr 1/1/90. Retd GD 14/3/97.
POULSON A. Born 28/11/19. Commd 1/3/51. Sqn Ldr 1/7/61. Retd SEC 28/1/69.
POULSON H. F. Born 18/2/20. Commd 21/6/43. Sqn Ldr 1/7/59. Retd ENG 18/2/75.
POULTER J. M., BSc. Born 1/8/45. Commd 16/1/72. Wg Cdr 1/1/88. Retd ADMIN 1/8/00.
POULTER K. Born 31/7/46. Commd 25/6/65. Flt Lt 25/3/71. Retd GD 14/3/96.
POULTER L. G. Born 25/4/47. Commd 28/2/69. Flt Lt 8/3/72. Retd GD 25/4/85.
POULTER R. A., MS BSc. Born 9/2/46. Commd 26/5/67. Sqn Ldr 1/7/76. Retd ENG 9/2/84.
POULTER R. G. Born 29/2/24. Commd 13/9/51. Flt Lt 22/5/57. Retd GD 30/8/66.
POULTON B. J., AFC. Born 3/5/44. Commd 6/4/62. A Cdre 1/1/96. Retd GD 2/5/97.
POUNDS B., BEM. Born 4/5/29. Commd 30/1/70. Flt Lt 30/1/74. Retd ENG 5/5/79.
POUNTAIN S. G., CEng MRAeS MIMgt. Born 6/1/30. Commd 4/2/53. Wg Cdr 1/7/73. Retd ENG 15/5/80.
POUNTNEY F. K. Born 9/2/43. Commd 8/10/70. Wg Cdr 1/7/87. Retd GD(G) 11/4/91.
POVAH A. J. Born 11/10/20. Commd 23/8/56. Flt Lt 10/8/60. Retd GD 1/5/68.
POVEY C. F. Born 2/7/07. Commd 20/10/41. Flt Lt 1/9/45. Retd ENG 2/7/56 rtg Sqn Ldr.
POVEY K. C. Born 7/4/31. Commd 27/6/51. Flt Lt 14/11/56. Retd GD 8/6/71.
POVEY R. W., MB BS FRCS LRCP. Born 11/4/21. Commd 19/8/56. A Cdre 1/1/79. Retd MED 24/10/83.
POWELL A., OBE. Born 12/8/14. Commd 14/6/40. Wg Cdr 1/1/58. Retd SEC 12/8/69.
POWELL A. E. Born 19/6/46. Commd 28/7/67. Sqn Ldr 1/7/78. Retd ADMIN 19/6/90.
POWELL A. G., CEng MIEE. Born 22/4/13. Commd 17/12/32. A Cdre 1/7/59. Retd ENG 4/2/69.
POWELL A. I. Born 16/7/07. Commd 29/5/43. Flt Lt 29/11/46. Retd GD(G) 15/5/57.
POWELL D. J., OBE BA MInstPet MIMgt. Born 15/7/43. Commd 8/11/67. Wg Cdr 1/7/84. Retd SUP 15/7/93.
POWELL E. Born 3/2/30. Commd 21/9/50. Sqn Ldr 1/1/67. Retd GD 3/2/85.
POWELL F. W. Born 27/9/09. Commd 25/9/52. Sqn Ldr 1/7/61. Retd ENG 27/9/64.
POWELL G. Born 20/12/19. Commd 17/6/45. Flt Lt 30/6/49. Retd GD 18/5/58.
POWELL G. R. Born 15/6/26. Commd 28/7/67. Flt Lt 28/7/72. Retd ENG 7/10/75.
POWELL H. F. Born 5/12/10. Commd 27/5/43. Wg Cdr 1/1/63. Retd ENG 12/1/66.
POWELL J. F., OBE MA. Born 12/6/15. Commd 18/4/39. AVM 1/7/68. Retd EDN 4/5/72.
POWELL J. R. Born 2/10/24. Commd 4/5/50. Sqn Ldr 1/1/61. Retd GD 1/10/73.
POWELL L. G. Born 2/5/54. Commd 17/9/72. Sqn Ldr 1/7/91. Retd ENG 2/5/98.
POWELL M. Born 10/7/40. Commd 6/7/62. Sqn Ldr 1/7/89. Retd GD 15/5/94.
POWELL M. B., MIMgt. Born 12/5/38. Commd 26/5/67. Sqn Ldr 1/7/83. Retd ENG 12/5/96.
POWELL R. F. B. Born 30/10/20. Commd 23/4/42. Wg Cdr 1/7/56. Retd GD 30/10/67.

POWELL R. G., MIMgt. Born 19/1/46. Commd 31/1/64. Wg Cdr 1/1/90. Retd GD 22/4/94.
POWER A. G. Born 15/10/11. Commd 20/4/44. Flt Lt 20/10/47. Retd ENG 10/11/56.
POWER F. Born 5/2/62. Commd 19/3/81. Flt Lt 19/9/87. Retd OPS SPT 5/2/00.
POWER G. H. D. A., MRCS LRCP. Born 12/6/23. Commd 3/8/44. Sqn Ldr 17/1/59. Retd MED 1/11/66.
POWER J. Born 12/4/37. Commd 23/9/66. Flt Lt 23/9/68. Retd GD 12/4/75.
POWER M. Born 25/12/51. Commd 28/7/88. Flt Lt 28/7/92. Retd GD(G) 9/8/96.
POWER M. D., MA. Born 7/2/52. Commd 24/6/73. Flt Lt 15/10/74. Retd GD 23/12/82.
POWIS B. R. Born 24/6/26. Commd 23/9/65. Flt Lt 23/9/68. Retd GD 31/7/82.
POWLES E. C., AFC. Born 19/4/21. Commd 21/4/45. Flt Lt 30/6/49. Retd GD 22/6/53.
POWLES R. T. Born 6/4/57. Commd 8/9/77. Flt Lt 8/3/84. Retd SY 6/4/85.
POWLEY R. H., MSc. Born 30/12/44. Commd 6/5/65. Gp Capt 1/1/92. Retd SUP 3/12/96.
POWLING R. H. C. Born 2/11/20. Commd 12/9/40. Wg Cdr 1/1/61. Retd GD 1/6/73.
POWNALL D. J. Born 7/4/32. Commd 17/5/51. Sqn Ldr 1/7/64. Retd SY 7/4/87.
POWNER W. H., DPhysEd. Born 7/7/29. Commd 18/4/56. Sqn Ldr 1/7/70. Retd PE 7/7/79.
POYNDER S. C. R. Born 27/8/50. Commd 4/2/71. Flt Lt 4/8/76. Retd GD 1/6/78.
POYNTER L. W., OBE CEng FIMechE MRAeS MIMgt. Born 4/1/41. Commd 11/4/63. Gp Capt 1/7/89. Retd ENG 29/6/96.
POYSER G. F. Born 10/5/32. Commd 27/7/54. Wg Cdr 1/7/76. Retd GD 10/5/87.
POYSER J. Born 17/7/23. Commd 11/1/44. Flt Lt 11/7/47. Retd GD 17/7/61.
POZYCZKA T. A., MB BS MROG. Born 11/9/48. Commd 27/1/69. Wg Cdr 22/12/85. Retd MED 11/9/86.
PRAGNELL D. J. Born 9/1/37. Commd 10/3/77. Flt Lt 10/3/81. Retd ENG 3/4/87.
PRAGNELL G. R. Born 8/5/31. Commd 2/7/52. Flt Lt 21/10/59. Retd GD 8/5/69.
PRANDLE A. L. Born 28/3/13. Commd 23/4/43. Fg Offr 19/6/48. Retd GD(G) 19/7/51 rtg Sqn Ldr.
PRATCHETT I. A. V., LLB IEng. Born 7/9/39. Commd 22/3/81. Flt Lt 22/3/83. Retd ENG 22/3/97.
PRATLEY C. W., OBE CEng FIEE. Born 7/11/45. Commd 26/5/67. Gp Capt 1/7/97. Retd ENG 7/11/00.
PRATT A. E. J. Born 23/6/99. Commd 2/5/27. Wg Cdr 14/6/44. Retd GD 1/1/48 rtg Gp Capt.
PRATT B. C. Born 22/10/37. Commd 29/9/55. Wg Cdr 1/1/85. Retd GD(G) 30/8/88.
PRATT B. G. Born 24/2/34. Commd 15/6/53. Flt Lt 17/9/58. Retd GD 24/2/72.
PRATT C. W. Born 23/6/43. Commd 23/6/67. Wg Cdr 1/1/88. Retd ADMIN 1/10/91.
PRATT G., DFM. Born 23/11/24. Commd 15/2/45. Sqn Ldr 1/1/72. Retd PI 30/11/74.
PRATT G. L. Born 25/8/33. Commd 25/9/52. Flt 27/2/59. Retd RGT 10/11/70 rtg Sqn Ldr.
PRATT J. W., MHCIMA. Born 15/7/21. Commd 7/9/61. Flt Lt 7/9/67. Retd CAT 16/6/73.
PRATT P. L. Born 22/3/58. Commd 12/10/78. Flt Lt 12/4/84. Retd GD 1/3/89.
PRATT R. W., BSc. Born 30/11/43. Commd 30/8/66. Flt Lt 30/11/67. Retd GD 29/7/72.
PRATT S. J., MCIPD MIMgt. Born 9/1/36. Commd 4/4/54. Sqn Ldr 1/7/68. Retd GD 25/11/75.
PRATT W. C. Born 16/8/23. Commd 17/12/53. Flt Lt 17/12/59. Retd GD(G) 1/9/72.
PRATT W. E. Born 22/6/20. Commd 11/7/46. Flt Lt 11/1/51. Retd SEC 30/9/67.
PRATTIS P. A. Born 8/5/44. Commd 24/4/64. Flt Lt 4/11/70. Retd GD 8/5/82.
PREDDY L., AFC. Born 24/9/20. Commd 16/4/43. Wg Cdr 1/7/58. Retd GD 24/9/63.
PREECE C. D., OBE AFC. Born 30/4/26. Commd 22/1/48. Gp Capt 1/1/78. Retd GD 30/4/84.
PREECE C. P. Born 12/11/52. Commd 9/3/72. Flt Lt 9/3/77. Retd GD 12/3/82.
PREECE J. M. Born 7/10/36. Commd 13/12/56. Sqn Ldr 1/1/72. Retd GD 1/1/75.
PREECE M. R. Born 29/8/91. Commd 1/4/18. Fg Offr 2/4/18. Retd SUP 18/4/25. Recalled 1/1/39 to 31/8/41.
PRENTICE J. M., BSc. Born 20/1/54. Commd 19/6/77. Flt Lt 19/3/78. Retd GD 19/12/93.
PRENTICE J. T., MIMgt. Born 25/4/20. Commd 5/4/43. Wg Cdr 1/7/60. Retd SUP 26/1/71.
PRENTON The Rev C. G. Born 8/4/33. Commd 1/1/63. Retd 21/8/83 Wg Cdr.
PRESCOTT F. B. Born 7/8/49. Commd 11/7/74. Sqn Ldr 1/1/87. Retd GD 24/3/90. Re-entered 19/8/91. Sqn Ldr 28/5/88. Retd GD 26/2/00.
PRESCOTT M. E., BA FCIS FCIPD MIMgt. Born 5/1/53. Commd 28/12/80. Flt Lt 28/12/82. Retd ADMIN 9/1/91.
PRESLAND P. N. Born 3/4/43. Commd 28/7/64. Gp Capt 1/7/88. Retd GD 1/6/93.
PRESNAIL A. P. Born 16/5/26. Commd 15/6/50. Sqn Ldr 1/7/59. Retd GD 3/7/79.
PRESS C. H., CEng MRAeS. Born 3/6/15. Commd 14/12/35. Gp Capt 1/7/57. Retd ENG 3/6/70.
PRESS L. G., OBE AFC**. Born 1/3/19. Commd 21/10/41. Wg Cdr 1/1/58. Retd GD 1/7/69.
PRESSLEY P. L. W., AFC. Born 23/2/32. Commd 26/9/51. Sqn Ldr 1/7/71. Retd GD 31/10/88.
PREST R. Born 24/12/49. Commd 20/6/68. Flt Lt 20/3/74. Retd GD 4/1/80.
PRESTON C. J. Born 2/5/35. Commd 21/10/53. Flt Lt 21/4/59. Retd GD 8/5/73.
PRESTON D. A., MIMgt. Born 24/5/23. Commd 11/1/44. Sqn Ldr 1/1/73. Retd ADMIN 30/3/78.
PRESTON J. M. Born 5/8/30. Commd 11/4/51. Flt Lt 11/1/54. Retd GD 14/5/60.
PRESTON J. S., FIMgt. Born 11/12/33. Commd 20/12/51. Gp Capt 1/7/79. Retd GD 20/1/84.
PRESTON M. H. Born 7/7/45. Commd 6/11/64. Flt Lt 6/5/70. Retd GD 12/1/77.
PRESTON P., BEd MCIPD MRAeS. Born 12/8/52. Commd 30/10/83. Sqn Ldr 1/1/90. Retd ADMIN 14/3/96.
PRESTON P. P. Born 16/4/59. Commd 24/7/81. Flt Lt 24/1/87. Retd GD 14/3/96.
PRESTON R. B. Born 25/8/38. Commd 23/3/61. Flt Lt 25/10/66. Retd PI 8/6/84.
PRESTON T. S., BSc. Born 14/4/13. Commd 4/4/39. Flt Lt 1/6/47. Retd EDN 25/9/48.
PREW R. A., MRAeS. Born 7/12/12. Commd 15/5/40. Sqn Ldr 1/1/52. Retd ENG 28/8/58.
PREWETT C. L. Born 25/5/40. Commd 6/12/70. Flt Lt 6/12/72. Retd ENG 30/10/81.

PRICE A. C. Born 14/5/42. Commd 5/11/70. Flt Lt 5/11/72. Retd GD(G) 14/5/80.
PRICE A. C., BSc. Born 1/8/57. Commd 31/8/75. Flt Lt 15/10/81. Retd GD(G) 20/2/88.
PRICE A. J., BSc BSc. Born 22/7/61. Commd 5/2/80. Flt Lt 15/1/86. Retd GD(G) 31/5/92.
PRICE A. R. Born 23/2/40. Commd 22/5/70. Sqn Ldr 1/7/78. Retd ENG 7/4/91.
PRICE A. S. Born 16/1/46. Commd 1/3/68. Sqn Ldr 1/1/83. Retd GD 30/4/89.
PRICE A. W. Born 3/8/36. Commd 20/11/56. Flt Lt 20/5/62. Retd GD 3/8/74.
PRICE B. H., BSc. Born 3/2/32. Commd 8/5/56. Gp Capt 1/7/76. Retd ENG 3/2/89.
PRICE B. W., OBE MSc BSc FIMgt MRAeS. Born 9/1/42. Commd 12/11/63. Wg Cdr 1/1/78. Retd SUP 9/1/97.
PRICE C. F. Born 25/7/16. Commd 3/7/41. Flt Lt 1/1/55. Retd RGT 25/7/66.
PRICE C. P, MA. Born 28/12/44. Commd 13/8/72. Sqn Ldr 13/8/77. Retd LGL 8/1/82.
PRICE The Rev D., BA. Born 30/1/23. Commd 4/1/56. Retd 6/9/68 Sqn Ldr.
PRICE D. J., MSc BSc. Born 11/11/51. Commd 20/5/79. Flt Lt 20/5/80. Retd ADMIN 4/1/91.
PRICE D. R. Born 15/2/47. Commd 10/12/65 . Flt Lt 10/6/71. Retd GD 4/8/72.
PRICE D. S., MBE. Born 10/6/25. Commd 6/11/52. Flt Lt 17/5/56. Retd GD 24/3/61.
PRICE F. H. Born 8/11/11. Commd 10/12/42. Sqn Ldr 1/7/54. Retd SUP 29/11/60.
PRICE The Rev F. W., BA. Born 22/4/22. Commd 11/11/52. Retd 11/11/68 Wg Cdr.
PRICE G. Born 8/6/24. Commd 3/11/60. Flt Lt 3/11/65. Retd ENG 8/6/76.
PRICE G. C. Born 19/6/30. Commd 25/11/53. Sqn Ldr 1/1/78. Retd GD 19/6/88.
PRICE H. T. Born 9/8/27. Commd 27/7/49. Wg Cdr 1/1/69. Retd GD 15/11/77.
PRICE J., BSc AFIMA. Born 6/12/33. Commd 22/11/57. Wg Cdr 1/1/83. Retd ADMIN 2/4/87.
PRICE J. A. Born 24/3/53. Commd 11/9/86. Flt Lt 11/12/88. Retd GD 11/9/94.
PRICE J. A. B. Born 26/4/63. Commd 8/4/82. Flt Lt 8/10/87. Retd GD 13/3/92.
PRICE J. D. H. Born 3/6/30. Commd 1/12/50. Flt Lt 25/3/57. Retd GD 19/6/68.
PRICE J. L., AFC MRAeS FIMgt. Born 18/8/29. Commd 13/12/50. Gp Capt. 1/1/73. Retd GD 3/1/80.
PRICE J. S. B., CBE. Born 11/2/38. Commd 15/12/59. Gp Capt. 1/7/81. Retd GD 12/5/87.
PRICE J. W., CBE FIMgt MRAeS. Born 26/1/30. Commd 26/7/50. AVM 1/1/83. Retd GD 1/8/84.
PRICE K. O. N. Born 22/8/42. Commd 17/12/63. Flt Lt 4/11/70. Retd GD 22/8/80.
PRICE N. F. Born 12/4/44. Commd 27/8/64. Flt Lt 27/2/71. Retd ENG 12/4/83.
PRICE N. R. C. Born 29/5/31. Commd 9/4/52. Wg Cdr 1/7/67. Retd GD 18/1/78.
PRICE N. S. Born 16/3/14. Commd 28/3/47. Flt Lt 28/9/51. Retd SUP 30/9/58.
PRICE P. J., BSc. Born 7/8/58. Commd 5/2/84. Sqn Ldr 1/7/95. Retd ADMIN 28/8/96.
PRICE P. W. McL. Born 28/8/49. Commd 23/2/68. Sqn Ldr 1/7/83. Retd GD 28/8/87. Re-entered 2/9/88. Wg Cdr 1/7/93. Retd GD 14/9/96.
PRICE R. A., MBE. Born 8/3/30. Commd 1/10/54. Flt Lt 1/4/60. Retd GD 8/3/92.
PRICE R. C. Born 5/2/24. Commd 25/8/60. Sqn Ldr 1/7/71. Retd ENG 5/2/79.
PRICE R. G., DFC* FIMgt MIPM. Born 9/1/22. Commd 31/8/42. Gp Capt 1/1/66. Retd GD 9/4/73.
PRICE R. G., CB FIMgt. Born 18/7/28. Commd 27/7/49. AVM 1/1/82. Retd GD 1/1/84.
PRICE R. L., MBA MIMgt. Born 21/10/57. Commd 14/4/85. Flt Lt 14/4/90. Retd ADMIN 14/3/97.
PRICE R. W. Born 31/8/21. Commd 5/9/44. Sqn Ldr 1/1/67. Retd GD 31/8/73.
PRICE S. T. G., AFM. Born 12/10/25. Commd 15/12/49. Sqn Ldr 1/1/60. Retd GD 31/3/75.
PRICE T. Born 1/3/47. Commd 2/6/67. Flt Lt 2/12/72. Retd GD 1/3/85.
PRICE T. R., BSc. Born 18/11/62. Commd 14/10/84. Flt Lt 14/4/87. Retd GD 14/10/96.
PRICE W. L., MB BCh. Born 21/4/16. Commd 18/7/41. Sqn Ldr 9/8/48. Retd MED 28/1/50.
PRICE W. S., MBE MIMgt. Born 30/3/29. Commd 19/1/50. Sqn Ldr 1/7/67. Retd SEC 3/4/79.
PRICE-REES T. E. Born 12/12/43. Commd 20/10/67. Flt Lt 15/7/71. Retd GD 1/11/75.
PRICE-WALKER C. D. Born 30/8/42. Commd 28/2/80. Flt Lt 28/2/80. Retd ENG 5/2/97.
PRICHARD D. L., DSO. Born 15/11/16. Commd 16/8/39. Wg Cdr 1/7/54. Retd GD 29/11/63.
PRICHARD G. W. Born 30/5/41. Commd 26/10/62. Flt Lt 15/4/70. Retd GD 30/5/79.
PRICKETT F. M., MRAeS. Born 13/7/16. Commd 20/4/50. Sqn Ldr 1/7/61. Retd ENG 13/7/71.
PRICKETT Sir Thomas O., KCB DSO DFC. Born 31/7/13. Commd 9/1/38. ACM 1/5/69. Retd GD 1/10/70.
PRIDDLE A. L., BSc. Born 29/12/58. Commd 6/9/81. Flt Lt 6/12/81. Retd GD 6/9/97.
PRIDE I. McC., MBE. Born 13/1/45. Commd 14/8/64. Flt Lt 14/5/72. Retd OPS SPT 13/1/00.
PRIDEAUX J. A. Born 6/4/39. Commd 4/4/59. Gp Capt 1/1/86. Retd GD 21/4/90.
PRIDMORE D. W. R. Born 23/12/22. Commd 8/3/54. Sqn Ldr 1/1/73. Retd ADMIN 23/12/77.
PRIER R. G., DFC. Born 25/10/12. Commd 16/12/33. Wg Cdr 1/10/46. Retd GD 21/1/58.
PRIEST B., BA. Born 17/10/40. Commd 31/7/62. Sqn Ldr 1/1/73. Retd GD 8/4/79.
PRIEST J. R. Born 8/1/30. Commd 10/10/63. Flt Lt 10/10/68. Retd GD 18/9/69.
PRIEST J. S. D. Born 24/12/49. Commd 20/9/68. Flt Lt 16/2/74. Retd GD 4/1/80.
PRIEST P. W., BMet. Born 7/4/35. Commd 14/3/57. Flt Lt 12/6/61. Retd ENG 30/5/73 rtg Sqn Ldr.
PRIESTLEY D. E., MSc CEng FIEE FCIPD. Born 28/5/34. Commd 7/9/56. Gp Capt 1/7/83. Retd ADMIN 28/5/89.
PRIESTLEY H. Born 6/5/23. Commd 7/10/44. Flt Lt 26/5/55. Retd GD(G) 31/5/70.
PRIESTLEY I. Born 10/6/39. Commd 20/9/79. Sqn Ldr 1/9/79. Retd SY 10/6/94.
PRIESTLEY J. C. Born 3/6/32. Commd 7/1/71. Sqn Ldr 1/7/82. Retd SY 3/6/87.
PRIESTLEY V., MIMgt. Born 24/7/28. Commd 24/11/60. Sqn Ldr 1/1/73. Retd ENG 3/4/75.
PRIMAVESI B. A., CVO FIMgt MRAeS. Born 24/5/21. Commd 19/8/39. Gp Capt 1/7/63. Retd GD 24/5/76.
PRIMER R. Born 1/4/16. Commd 6/9/43. Flt Lt 1/1/50. Retd GD(G) 1/4/66.

PRIMROSE J., AFC DPhysEd. Born 24/3/25. Commd 17/12/51. Sqn Ldr 1/7/58. Retd GD 2/7/68. Re-instated 22/10/80 to 24/3/85.
PRINCE E. J., MBE. Born 29/12/07. Commd 17/10/41. Flt Lr 4/6/53. Retd CAT 29/6/65 rtg Sqn Ldr.
PRINCE H. J. D., AFC. Born 28/2/34. Commd 3/3/54. Sqn Ldr 1/1/70. Retd GD 15/3/86.
PRINCE J. T. Born 6/9/40. Commd 2/5/59. Flt Lt 20/6/69. Retd GD 6/9/95.
PRINCE J. W. Born 11/9/08. Commd 31/12/46. Flt Lt 7/6/51. Retd SUP 1/1/52.
PRINCE M. J. Born 11/5/60. Commd 15/12/88. Flt Lt 15/12/90. Retd ENG 11/5/98.
PRINCE R. M. Born 13/1/37. Commd 15/3/73. Sqn Ldr 1/1/87. Retd GD 13/1/92.
PRINCE R. S. Born 1/5/56. Commd 16/6/88. Flt Lt 16/6/90. Retd ENG 16/6/96.
PRING A. J. Born 16/11/12. Commd 22/9/49. Sqn Ldr 1/1/58. Retd ENG 16/11/61.
PRING R. M. Born 4/12/45. Commd 1/7/82. Flt Lt 1/7/85. Retd GD 4/12/00.
PRINGLE Sir Charles, KBE MA FEng Hon FRAeS. Born 6/6/19. Commd 4/4/41. AM 1/7/73. Retd ENG 6/6/76.
PRINGLE H. J., AFC. Born 10/9/08. Commd 28/7/28. Gp Capt 1/7/47. Retd GD 28/9/57.
PRINGLE M. A. Born 12/12/33. Commd 11/6/52. Sqn Ldr 1/1/72. Retd GD 3/11/81.
PRINGLE R. Born 24/8/47. Commd 9/12/71. Flt Lt 9/6/77. Retd GD 19/9/79.
PRINGUER D. C. Born 16/7/40. Commd 9/7/60. Flt Lt 9/1/66. Retd GD 16/7/95.
PRINT C. P., MSc. Born 16/1/60. Commd 25/11/84. Flt Lt 25/5/87. Retd OPS SPT 25/11/00.
PRIOR A. R. J., MBE BSc MB BS. Born 3/11/52. Commd 19/11/74. Wg Cdr 1/8/92. Retd MED 2/4/98.
PRIOR B. M. G. Born 5/11/32. Commd 24/2/52. Flt Lt 14/11/58. Retd GD(G) 5/11/92.
PRIOR F. R. J. Born 13/4/37. Commd 19/6/70. Sqn Ldr 1/1/77. Retd ENG 13/12/90.
PRIOR H. Born 18/2/36. Commd 4/3/71. Sqn Ldr 1/1/86. Retd GD 6/2/91.
PRIOR I. R., BA AMBCS. Born 11/3/44. Commd 25/3/64. Wg Cdr 1/1/89. Retd GD 26/11/94.
PRIOR K. S., MB BS FRCGP MFOM MRCS(Eng) LRCP DAvMed. Born 23/8/40. Commd 13/8/62. A Cdre 1/7/92. Retd MED 14/3/96.
PRIOR M. R. Born 23/8/60. Commd 27/3/80. Sqn Ldr 1/7/92. Retd GD 23/8/98.
PRIOR P. E., OBE AFC. Born 3/11/21. Commd 16/3/43. Wg Cdr 1/7/64. Retd GD 30/5/77.
PRIOR P. N., MBE BA. Born 15/11/33. Commd 3/9/59. Wg Cdr 1/7/78. Retd SUP 25/4/81.
PRIOR R. G. Born 2/3/30. Commd 21/2/52. Flt Lt 21/2/58. Retd GD(G) 20/7/68.
PRIOR V. Born 9/4/32. Commd 12/11/57. Flt Lt 21/5/63. Retd GD 28/12/77.
PRISSICK H. Born 19/11/52. Commd 25/9/71. Sqn Ldr 1/7/88. Retd GD 20/4/93.
PRITCHARD A. Born 12/5/29. Commd 23/9/66. Flt Lt 23/9/69. Retd GD 12/5/76.
PRITCHARD A. R., MSc BEng CEng MIMechE. Born 10/8/52. Commd 16/5/72. Sqn Ldr 1/7/85. Retd ENG 1/5/91.
PRITCHARD A. W., FCIPD FIMgt. Born 8/7/40. Commd 27/6/59. Gp Capt 1/7/88. Retd ADMIN 8/1/97.
PRITCHARD D. Born 25/4/44. Commd 6/9/63. Flt Lt 6/3/69. Retd GD 25/4/82.
PRITCHARD D. B. Born 19/10/19. Commd 23/10/42. Sqn Ldr 1/1/57. Retd GD 14/3/61.
PRITCHARD D. M. Born 23/9/60. Commd 18/12/80. Sqn Ldr 1/7/93. Retd GD 23/9/98.
PRITCHARD G. S. B., MA CEng MRAeS. Born 23/4/41. Commd 30/9/60. Wg Cdr 1/7/84. Retd ENG 23/4/96.
PRITCHARD J. E. Born 24/2/42. Commd 28/4/61. Flt Lt 13/1/72. Retd GD 24/2/80.
PRITCHARD M., MIMgt. Born 25/4/44. Commd 31/10/63. Sqn Ldr 1/7/74. Retd ADMIN 3/10/97.
PRITCHARD N. Born 9/7/19. Commd 17/3/49. Sqn Ldr 1/7/61. Retd SEC 9/7/74.
PRITCHARD-SMITH S. Born 6/11/23. Commd 3/6/53. Flt Lt 14/5/58. Retd CAT 6/11/72.
PRITCHETT A. J., BSc. Born 6/6/61. Commd 4/1/83. Flt Lt 4/10/84. Retd GD 14/3/96.
PRITCHETT P. N. B. Born 19/5/21. Commd 21/11/44. Flt Lt 21/5/48. Retd GD 19/5/64.
PRITT M. G. Born 9/3/43. Commd 1/12/69. Sqn Ldr 1/7/83. Retd ADMIN 9/3/99.
PROBERT C. G. Born 19/1/40. Commd 4/11/81. Flt Lt 13/4/67. Retd GD(G) 12/12/86. Reinstated 4/11/81-12/12/86.
PROBERT H. A., MBE MA. Born 23/12/26. Commd 4/11/48. A Cdre 1/7/76. Retd ADMIN 1/10/78.
PROBERT R. J., MIMgt. Born 18/7/30. Commd 24/7/52. Sqn Ldr 1/7/65. Retd SUP 3/4/81.
PROBERT R. L. Born 25/7/40. Commd 9/4/60. Flt Lt 9/10/65. Retd GD 25/7/78.
PROBERT T. V. Born 15/10/30. Commd 13/9/51. Flt Lt 4/1/57. Retd GD 15/10/68.
PROBERT V. C. M. Born 24/2/35. Commd 1/8/69. Flt Lt 6/10/71. Retd ADMIN 1/8/77.
PROBYN P. J., FIMgt. Born 23/1/24. Commd 6/9/47. G Capt 1/1/71. Retd SUP 31/3/78.
PROCOPIDES M. D., BSc. Born 1/6/50. Commd 7/11/76. Sqn Ldr 1/7/86. Retd GD 1/1/01.
PROCTER G. H. H., CBE. Born 9/8/06. Commd 17/12/27. Gp Capt 1/7/47. Retd ENG 12/6/58.
PROCTER J. H., MBE BA. Born 5/7/37. Commd 4/9/59. Sqn Ldr 4/3/68. Retd EDN 4/9/75.
PROCTER K. J. M., BSc (Eur Ing) CEng FIEE FRAeS FIMgt. Born 7/3/44. Commd 30/9/62. A Cdre 1/1/97. Retd ENG 7/4/00.
PROCTOR C. T., BA CEng MIEE. Born 19/12/37. Commd 28/7/60. Flt Lt 19/10/65. Retd ENG 4/7/90.
PROCTOR D. A. Born 5/3/32. Commd 17/5/51. Flt Lt 19/12/56. Retd GD 7/5/70.
PROCTOR G. P. Born 3/2/29. Commd 23/6/60. Wg Cdr 1/7/81. Retd ENG 3/2/87.
PROCTOR J. W. Born 27/3/20. Commd 5/11/43. Flt Lt 10/1/50. Retd GD 25/12/63.
PROCTOR R. G., MBE. Born 22/12/24. Commd 17/6/45. Wg Cdr 1/7/65. Retd SUP 22/12/79.
PROCTOR R. S., BSc CEng MIEE. Born 5/6/46. Commd 26/5/70. Sqn Ldr 1/7/79. Retd ENG 26/5/86.
PROFIT G. R., OBE AFC MRAeS. Born 31/10/40. Commd 23/6/61. A Cdre 1/7/87. Retd GD 2/11/90.
PROOPS R. A., FIMLT. Born 23/1/30. Commd 1/2/62. Sqn Ldr 25/6/73. Retd MED(T) 30/10/75.
PROSSER C. J., BEng. Born 11/5/68. Commd 17/2/91. Fg Off 17/2/89. Retd GD 21/10/92.

PROSSER W. H. Born 31/5/34. Commd 11/11/60. Flt Lt 11/11/60. Retd GD 30/7/65.
PROSSER-HIGDON D. R. Born 28/3/27. Commd 25/8/54. Wg Cdr 1/1/69. Retd PRT 8/6/76 rtg Gp Capt.
PROTHERO F. J. Born 5/5/22. Commd 15/6/50. Flt Lt 15/12/53. Retd GD 28/7/73.
PROTHERO R. M., MRAeS MIMgt. Born 30/5/39. Commd 25/7/60. Wg Cdr 1/1/84. Retd GD 30/5/94.
PROUD P., BA. Born 16/1/32. Commd 19/8/54. Sqn Ldr 17/2/63. Retd EDN 30/8/70.
PROUDLOCK J. R. C. Born 20/10/16. Commd 4/12/42. Gp Capt 1/1/65. Retd PRT 29/6/68.
PROUDLOVE F. W. Born 15/3/15. Commd 14/1/42. Flt Lt 1/9/45. Retd ENG 1/8/53.
PROUT C. D., BSc. Born 26/12/59. Commd 26/9/82. Flt Lt 26/12/85. Retd ENG 26/9/87.
PROUT K. E., IEng FIIE. Born 27/1/51. Commd 5/2/81. Sqn Ldr 1/7/90. Retd ENG 10/10/99.
PROUT R. A., BSc. Born 6/7/47. Commd 28/10/73. Flt Lt 28/1/75. Retd GD 19/3/81.
PROVAN G. G. Born 30/9/40. Commd 31/10/74. Flt Lt 31/10/76. Retd SY 31/10/82.
PROVINS N. P., MIMgt. Born 26/3/20. Commd 2/3/61. Flt Lt 2/3/66. Retd ENG 31/3/75.
PROWTING N. H. Born 6/7/22. Commd 21/11/47. Flt Lt 4/12/52. Retd GD 3/1/64.
PRUNIER A. P., BSc. Born 29/10/48. Commd 5/2/84. Sqn Ldr 1/1/89. Retd ADMIN 5/2/00.
PRYCE G. O., AIIP. Born 26/4/20. Commd 6/10/60. Flt Lt 6/10/65. Retd ENG 8/4/72.
PRYCE K. E., BA. Born 26/10/41. Commd 11/10/70. Sqn Ldr 1/7/83. Retd SUP 1/7/96.
PRYCE R. N., CEng MIEE. Born 19/11/21. Commd 22/11/56. Sqn Ldr 1/7/66. Retd ENG 19/11/76.
PRYDE N. W. W. Born 8/4/24. Commd 27/10/44. Flt Lt 27/4/48. Retd GD 29/4/67.
PRYOR A. D. Born 29/4/95. Commd 1/4/18. Gp Capt 1/7/38. Retd GD 27/11/41 rtg A Cdre.
PRYOR-JONES A. J. W. Born 30/5/42. Commd 11/1/79. Flt Lt 11/1/82. Retd GD 9/11/96.
PUCKERING J. N. Born 3/8/36. Commd 16/12/58. Sqn Ldr 1/7/67. Retd GD 3/8/74.
PUDDY R. J. Born 5/11/52. Commd 20/1/80. Sqn Ldr 1/1/88. Retd ADMIN 14/3/96.
PUDNEY K. W. Born 21/5/45. Commd 8/1/76. Sqn Ldr 1/1/87. Retd MED(SEC) 1/9/92. rtg Wg Cdr.
PUDWELL J. S. Born 4/1/31. Commd 11/11/50. Flt Lt 11/5/55. Retd GD(G) 4/1/93.
PUGH D. J., MA DCAe. Born 17/1/34. Commd 26/9/53. Gp Capt 1/7/81. Retd ENG 17/1/89.
PUGH D. T. S. Born 7/2/13. Commd 3/8/44. Flt Lt 19/3/48. Retd ENG 23/3/68.
PUGH G. A. W., BDS. Born 13/10/44. Commd 1/6/72. Sqn Ldr 10/1/75. Retd DEL 1/9/76.
PUGH H. Born 7/10/23. Commd 26/11/43. Flt Lt 26/11/49. Retd SEC 5/3/62.
PUGH H. A., BSc. Born 4/4/56. Commd 28/8/79. Flt Lt 12/11/80. Retd GD 12/8/95.
PUGH J. D. Born 20/3/34. Commd 14/12/54. Wg Cdr 1/7/72. Retd GD 16/9/87.
PUGH J. R. Born 27/4/47. Commd 18/8/67. Flt Lt 4/11/70. Retd GD 28/8/75.
PUGH K. W. T., AFC CEng MRAeS FIMgt. Born 22/8/20. Commd 18/10/41. Gp Capt 1/7/61. Retd GD 22/8/72.
PUGH M. A. P., OBE AFC. Born 27/4/33. Commd 28/2/52. Wg Cdr 1/7/77. Retd GD 27/4/93.
PUGH P. M. D., MIMgt. Born 20/9/48. Commd 16/12/66. Flt Lt 16/6/73. Retd SUP 1/9/77. Re-entered 3/3/81.
    Sqn Ldr 1/7/84. Retd SUP 5/3/97.
PUGH R. M., AFC. Born 25/6/21. Commd 23/10/39. Sqn Ldr 1/1/51. Retd GD 28/9/68.
PULFORD J. F. Born 30/3/61. Commd 8/10/87. Flt Lt 8/10/89. Retd ADMIN 31/5/99.
PULFREY A. J. Born 11/11/48. Commd 17/7/70. Wg Cdr 1/1/89. Retd GD 25/4/01.
PULFREY J. M. Born 20/2/60. Commd 17/5/79. Flt Lt 17/11/85. Retd GD 17/5/86. Re-entered 16/5/90. Flt Lt
    15/11/89. Retd OPS SPT 19/2/01.
PULL S. J. Born 2/11/46. Commd 6/5/66. Flt Lt 6/11/71. Retd GD 2/11/84.
PULLAN J. R., OBE FCA. Born 17/1/14. Commd 29/7/39. Wg Cdr 1/7/55. Retd SEC 6/3/61.
PULLAN M. G. A. Born 7/4/49. Commd 29/6/72. Flt Lt 29/12/77. Retd GD 13/3/88.
PULLEN F. F., MBE. Born 29/11/46. Commd 23/9/68. Sqn Ldr 1/7/85. Retd SUP 14/3/96.
PULLEN J. A., MIMgt. Born 20/1/38. Commd 24/6/71. Sqn Ldr 1/7/82. Retd ENG 20/1/88.
PULLEN L. R. Born 24/3/20. Commd 6/6/57. Flt Lt 6/6/60. Retd ENG 6/6/70.
PULLEN S. K. Born 14/5/62. Commd 15/10/81. Flt Lt 15/4/87. Retd GD 14/5/00.
PULLEY N. S. Born 3/5/32. Commd 9/4/52. Flt Lt 15/2/65. Retd GD(G) 31/12/85.
PULLEYBLANK B. A. Born 15/3/47. Commd 10/5/73. Flt Lt 10/5/75. Retd GD 14/3/96.
PULLIN R. W. Born 31/7/33. Commd 10/9/70. Flt Lt 10/9/74. Retd GD 14/1/76.
PUNCHER C. L. G., MBE. Born 28/5/11. Commd 30/10/42. Sqn Ldr 1/7/51. Retd SUP 28/5/60.
PURCELL J. Born 5/1/38. Commd 29/7/58. Sqn Ldr 1/1/69. Retd SUP 5/1/76.
PURCELL J. D., AFC. Born 8/7/26. Commd 31/7/50. Flt Lt 16/5/56. Retd GD 28/10/65.
PURCHASE G. W., BSc. Born 21/5/52. Commd 13/9/70. Flt Lt 15/4/75. Retd GD 21/5/90.
PURCHASE W., MBE. Born 19/11/36. Commd 7/1/58. Sqn Ldr 1/1/73. Retd GD 19/11/94.
PURDIE M. J. Born 5/11/44. Commd 17/12/65. Wg Cdr 1/1/83. Retd GD 31/3/94.
PURDUE E. G. Born 16/4/22. Commd 22/8/63. Sqn Ldr 1/1/72. Retd ENG 25/8/73.
PURDY R. B. Born 22/4/43. Commd 17/7/64. Flt Lt 17/1/70. Retd GD 22/4/81.
PURKIS E. F. J., CEng MRAeS MIMgt. Born 26/2/40. Commd 15/7/63. Flt Lt 26/7/67. Retd ENG 26/2/78.
PURNELL I. J. Born 7/9/48. Commd 5/8/76. Wg Cdr 1/1/90. Retd ENG 10/8/96.
PURNELL T. L. G. Born 29/4/62. Commd 30/4/81. Flt Lt 30/10/86. Retd GD 29/4/00.
PURSE J. M., BSc. Born 9/5/61. Commd 26/9/82. Flt Lt 26/12/83. Retd GD 9/9/99.
PURSER B. L., MIMgt. Born 13/5/23. Commd 4/12/42. Sqn Ldr 1/1/67. Retd PI 31/12/77.
PURSER H. E., ACIS. Born 28/1/36. Commd 22/10/59. Wg Cdr 1/1/83. Retd ADMIN 12/8/86.
PURSER M. M., BSc CEng MRAeS. Born 10/7/44. Commd 22/9/63. Sqn Ldr 1/1/77. Retd ENG 10/7/82.
PURT M. B. D. Born 5/4/50. Commd 31/7/70. Flt Lt 31/7/73. Retd GD 27/7/79.

PURVES G. F. Born 21/10/22. Commd 27/3/43. Flt Lt 15/3/47. Retd SEC 30/3/62.
PUSEY C. H., MBE. Born 8/12/12. Commd 18/7/46. Sqn Ldr 1/7/57. Retd SUP 28/4/67.
PUSEY F. R., OBE MIMgt. Born 5/3/20. Commd 21/4/45. Wg Cdr 1/7/62. Retd GD(G) 5/3/75.
PUSEY W. A. S. Born 31/8/40. Commd 8/9/83. Flt Lt 8/9/87. Retd GD(G) 31/8/95.
PYE A. C., DPhysEd. Born 6/2/27. Commd 18/4/56. Flt Lt 18/4/60. Retd PE 20/1/71.
PYE A. J. Born 4/5/47. Commd 9/2/66. A Cdre 1/1/97. Retd SUP 2/12/99.
PYE C. R., MSc BSc CEng MRAeS. Born 1/6/46. Commd 2/7/72. Gp Capt 1/1/95. Retd ENG 14/9/96.
PYE K. A. Born 17/1/31. Commd 26/3/52. Flt Lt 31/7/57. Retd GD 17/1/69.
PYLE G. S. Born 24/6/44. Commd 3/3/67. Sqn Ldr 1/7/78. Retd GD 24/6/82.
PYLE M. W. Born 7/3/43. Commd 15/7/66. Flt Lt 15/7/68. Retd GD 6/4/76.
PYM J. M. E., AFC. Born 2/12/41. Commd 18/12/62. Sqn Ldr 1/1/78. Retd GD 1/1/81. Reinstated on Retired List 13/11/88.
PYNE A. R., BA. Born 5/10/46. Commd 28/2/72. Flt Lt 28/5/73. Retd GD 28/2/88.
PYNE G. L., MIMgt. Born 10/5/31. Commd 30/5/61. Sqn Ldr 1/7/75. Retd SUP 1/9/83.
PYNN D., BSc. Born 3/2/48. Commd 4/6/72. Sqn Ldr 1/1/84. Retd GD 4/6/88.
PYPER G. D., BSc. Born 5/11/49. Commd 17/1/72. Sqn Ldr 1/7/83. Retd GD 17/1/88.
PYPER H. H. Born 7/5/54. Commd 20/12/73. Wg Cdr 1/7/90. Retd OPS SPT 13/2/99.
PYPER J. Born 21/6/45. Commd 15/7/66. Sqn Ldr 1/7/80. Retd GD 1/7/89.
PYPER S. E., BSc. Born 12/12/51. Commd 14/11/76. Flt Lt 14/2/80. Retd GD(G) 19/7/87.
PYRAH R. E. Born 23/3/31. Commd 14/4/53. Flt Lt 17/5/56. Retd GD 23/3/69.
PYSDEN G. T. Born 2/8/30. Commd 18/5/61. Sqn Ldr 1/7/71. Retd ENG 15/8/84.

# Q

QUAID C. F., FInstPet MIMgt. Born 29/12/42. Commd 12/3/64. Sqn Ldr 1/7/76. Retd SUP 26/5/82.
QUAID P. D. Born 27/2/40. Commd 14/8/70. Flt Lt 14/8/72. Retd GD 14/8/78.
QUAIFE C. M., OBE. Born 15/3/35. Commd 9/4/57. Wg Cdr 1/1/78. Retd GD 1/2/86.
QUAINTMERE P. J. Born 29/9/41. Commd 12/4/66. Sqn Ldr 1/1/77. Retd GD(G) 29/3/94.
QUANT J. A., MB BS BDS FDSRCS(Eng) MRCS(Eng) LRCP. Born 19/1/33. Commd 16/6/57. A Cdre 1/1/85. Retd DEL 6/4/90.
QUANT P., MHCIMA. Born 17/2/33. Commd 22/5/59. Sqn Ldr 1/1/69. Retd CAT 22/5/75.
QUANTICK D. J. Born 1/8/46. Commd 22/11/73. Flt Lt 22/11/75. Retd GD(G) 1/8/91.
QUARMBY D. A., BEng CEng MIEE. Born 9/6/60. Commd 16/9/84. Flt Lt 30/12/87. Retd ENG 9/6/98.
QUARTERMAINE R. W., MSc CEng MRAeS. Born 10/4/35. Commd 25/7/56. Wg Cdr 1/7/76. Retd MED 8/4/87.
QUARTERMAN R. J. Born 4/2/35. Commd 31/1/54. Wg Cdr 1/7/74. Retd GD 3/4/81.
QUARTLY A. F., BSc. Born 3/1/44. Commd 22/9/64. Flt Lt 6/6/67. Retd GD 29/3/74.
QUATERMASS-LEWIS G. M. Born 21/11/35. Commd 12/1/55. Flt Lt 31/5/61. Retd RGT 21/1/74.
QUAYLE C. E. G. Born 8/12/32. Commd 28/7/53. Sqn Ldr 1/7/69. Retd SUP 1/10/79.
QUELCH N., ACCS. Born 7/1/15. Commd 12/2/43. Sqn Ldr 1/1/55. Retd SEC 23/3/63.
QUERZANI J. F. G. R. Born 16/5/36. Commd 1/8/69. Sqn Ldr 1/7/81. Retd GD 13/9/89.
QUESTED E., MBE. Born 25/8/11. Commd 22/1/42. Fg Offr 22/3/43. Retd ENG 26/7/46.
QUICK D. A. G., BSc. Born 23/5/52. Commd 13/9/70. Sqn Ldr 1/1/85. Retd ADMIN 23/5/90.
QUICK D. M. Born 14/11/44. Commd 19/11/87. Flt Lt 19/11/89. Retd ADMIN 5/4/99.
QUICK F. C. Born 23/3/20. Commd 21/10/54. Sqn Ldr 1/1/71. Retd SEC 23/3/75.
QUICK G. H. Born 21/3/23. Commd 19/1/44. Sqn Ldr 1/1/58. Retd GD 21/3/66.
QUICK G. J., BSc. Born 13/11/49. Commd 15/9/69. Flt Lt 15/6/75. Retd GD(G) 1/7/82. Re-entered 19/10/87. Flt Lt 3/10/80. Retd GD(G) 24/7/96.
QUICK M. C. Born 22/1/47. Commd 4/12/86. Flt Lt 4/12/88. Retd GD(G) 14/3/96.
QUICK M. E. H., MIMgt. Born 9/3/40. Commd 27/3/75. Flt Lt 27/3/80. Retd ENG 31/3/83.
QUILL T. C. Born 6/10/18. Commd 29/7/42. Wg Cdr 1/7/62. Retd GD(G) 6/10/68.
QUIN K. C. Born 15/6/39. Commd 13/12/60. Flt Lt 13/6/63. Retd GD 15/3/77 rtg Sqn Ldr.
QUIN P. L., OBE LLB FIMgt MCIPD. Born 15/1/33. Commd 7/12/56. Gp Capt 1/7/82. Retd ADMIN 10/3/84.
QUINCEY N. J. Born 12/8/49. Commd 13/2/86. Sqn Ldr 1/7/94. Retd MED(SEC) 10/12/98.
QUINE J. D. Born 16/4/25. Commd 4/7/57. Flt Lt 1/4/63. Retd GD 15/4/76.
QUINLAN M. A., BSc. Born 16/5/62. Commd 14/10/84. Flt Lt 14/4/87. Retd GD 14/10/00.
QUINLAN P. J. Born 5/6/43. Commd 8/1/76. Flt Lt 8/1/78. Retd GD 2/4/93.
QUINN A. E. Born 8/8/19. Commd 21/9/44. Flt Lt 30/6/49. Retd PRT 1/12/62.
QUINN G. W., BA. Born 27/4/41. Commd 23/11/78. Flt Lt 23/11/88. Retd ENG 24/7/91.
QUINN J., DFC*. Born 14/6/19. Commd 28/12/41. Gp Capt 1/1/64. Retd GD 20/10/69.
QUINN P. N. Born 15/4/43. Commd 21/1/66. Fg Offr 21/1/68. Retd GD 1/3/69.
QUINN P. R., BA. Born 27/4/34. Commd 29/10/64. Sqn Ldr 1/7/75. Retd MED 1/9/87.
QUINN S. E. Born 16/5/14. Commd 17/6/42. Flt Lt 14/2/47. Retd SUP 20/10/55.
QUINNELL J. P. Born 19/7/47. Commd 16/8/68. Flt Lt 16/2/74. Retd GD 9/9/75.
QUINTIN-BAXENDALE B. W. Born 5/1/40. Commd 10/3/77. Sqn Ldr 1/1/91. Retd GD 5/1/95.
QUINTON A. A. G., MRCS LRCP DAvMed AFOM. Born 14/3/42. Commd 16/9/63. Wg Cdr 31/7/80. Retd MED 1/9/88.
QUINTON C. D., MIMgt. Born 19/5/29. Commd 8/2/54. Wg Cdr 1/1/75. Retd SEC 4/4/81.
QUINTON J. B., BSc MInstP MIMgt. Born 9/6/34. Commd 1/3/56. Gp Capt. 1/1/75. Retd ENG 29/9/79.
QUINTRELL G. H. A. Born 17/7/36. Commd 28/5/66. Flt Lt 28/5/68. Retd PRT 1/12/73.

# R

RABAN M. C., AFC. Born 16/2/20. Commd 9/10/39. Wg Cdr 1/1/55. Retd GD 16/2/67.
RABBITTS H. W. Born 4/8/20. Commd 25/8/55. Sqn Ldr 1/7/67. Retd ENG 4/8/70.
RABY K. W. Born 24/5/30. Commd 2/7/52. Flt Lt 27/11/57. Retd GD 1/7/64.
RABY P., FCCS. Born 3/6/14. Commd 17/4/39. Wg Cdr 1/1/57. Retd SEC 31/10/63.
RACE F. G. Born 12/8/28. Commd 5/11/70. Flt Lt 5/11/72. Retd ENG 12/8/83.
RACKHAM M. A. Born 22/4/52. Commd 22/5/75. Flt Lt 22/11/80. Retd GD 3/2/91.
RACKHAM R. D. Born 6/5/45. Commd 20/7/78. Sqn Ldr 1/1/87. Retd ENG 14/3/96.
RACKSTRAW A. Born 30/5/37. Commd 1/4/58. Wg Cdr 1/7/76. Retd SUP 18/10/87.
RADBOURNE B. M., BSc MB ChB DA FFARCS. Born 1/7/23. Commd 9/12/48. Wg Cdr 9/12/60. Retd MED 1/5/63.
RADCLIFFE N. Born 18/10/33. Commd 21/10/66. Flt Lt 21/10/72. Retd SUP 31/10/74.
RADD J. Born 20/6/16. Commd 1/2/48. Flt Lt 1/2/48. Retd PE 5/8/64.
RADFORD H. R. Born 25/4/28. Commd 26/7/50. Sqn Ldr 1/7/58. Retd GD 28/12/63.
RADFORD L. P. G. Born 22/7/60. Commd 22/2/79. Flt Lt 22/8/83. Retd GD 5/11/89.
RADFORD P. J. Born 6/11/38. Commd 22/11/73. Flt Lt 22/11/78. Retd ADMIN 5/11/84.
RADFORTH A. M. Born 31/12/54. Commd 15/3/73. Sqn Ldr 1/1/88. Retd OPS SPT 31/12/98.
RADFORTH M. A. Born 3/7/42. Commd 30/7/63. Gp Capt 1/1/89. Retd GD 3/7/98.
RADICE J. V., OBE MIMgt. Born 18/12/30. Commd 27/6/51. Wg Cdr 1/1/70. Retd GD 27/4/85.
RADLEY B., CEng MRAeS. Born 6/1/23. Commd 7/9/45. Flt Lt 30/6/49. Retd GD 1/8/52.
RADLEY R. S., DFC AFC FIMgt. Born 18/3/19. Commd 10/8/40. Gp Capt 1/7/60. Retd GD 18/3/74.
RADNOR A. E. Born 10/1/33. Commd 23/8/51. Wg Cdr 1/7/72. Retd GD 10/1/91.
RADTKE J. W. J. Born 10/2/19. Commd 29/7/48. Flt Lt 18/5/56. Retd GD(G) 10/7/68.
RAE C. N. Born 16/2/57. Commd 24/6/84. Flt Lt 25/10/82. Retd GD 30/4/88.
RAE I. E. Born 30/3/46. Commd 23/2/68. Flt Lt 20/9/73. Retd GD 1/11/74.
RAE J., MVO. Born 14/7/36. Commd 14/10/71. Sqn Ldr 1/1/84. Retd ENG 4/7/94.
RAE K. McK. Born 14/6/38. Commd 24/2/61. Sqn Ldr 1/1/87. Retd GD 14/6/96.
RAE T. McM., AFM. Born 29/7/25. Commd 18/5/61. Flt Lt 18/5/64. Retd GD 29/7/83.
RAE W. C., CB. Born 22/6/40. Commd 23/12/58. AVM 1/1/92. Retd GD 22/6/95.
RAEBURN P. D. Born 2/12/34. Commd 13/12/55. Sqn Ldr 1/7/65. Retd GD 1/10/80.
RAEBURN R. M. Born 27/5/31. Commd 7/3/51. Sqn Ldr 1/7/69. Retd GD 3/5/77.
RAESIDE J. F. Born 5/7/38. Commd 13/12/60. Sqn Ldr 1/7/71. Retd ADMIN 9/1/78.
RAESIDE J. M. Born 6/1/24. Commd 29/7/65. Flt Lt 29/7/70. Retd GD(G) 6/1/79.
RAFFEL J. W., BSc CEng MIMechE MIEE MINucE. Born 19/1/34. Commd 17/6/62. Sqn Ldr 1/1/68. Retd ENG 17/7/78. Re-instated 3/12/79 to 14/1/85.
RAFFERTY M. D. Born 8/6/25. Commd 21/5/47. Sqn Ldr 1/7/57. Retd GD 4/6/73.
RAFTERY R. G. Born 18/1/31. Commd 17/5/51. Flt Lt 6/9/56. Retd GD 27/4/70.
RAGG W. L. Born 2/5/42. Commd 15/3/79. Sqn Ldr 1/1/89. Retd GD 2/11/97.
RAGLAN J. B. Born 19/12/36. Commd 9/7/60. Sqn Ldr 1/1/76. Retd GD 19/12/91.
RAIKES P. F. J. Born 3/5/38. Commd 18/7/63. Wg Cdr 1/1/81. Retd GD(G) 3/5/93.
RAIMONDO J. V., MSc BSc. Born 29/11/47. Commd 1/8/69. Sqn Ldr 1/1/80. Retd ENG 1/10/87.
RAINBIRD T. Born 26/9/31. Commd 5/3/57. Flt Lt 5/9/62. Retd GD 7/4/72.
RAINBOW, A. D. Born 26/12/32. Commd 5/9/69. Flt Lt 5/9/73. Retd ENG 31/3/87.
RAINBOW C.A., ACIS. Born 5/3/37. Commd 28/7/59. Gp Capt 1/7/81. Retd ADMIN 11/11/86.
RAINBOW E., BSc Dip Soton CEng MIEE MIMgt. Born 27/8/33. Commd 22/12/55. Wg Cdr 1/1/74. Retd ENG 30/9/83.
RAINE P. D., MSc BSc CEng MIEE. Born 21/11/62. Commd 29/1/82. Sqn Ldr 1/7/94. Retd ENG 21/11/00.
RAINE P. J. W., DFC. Born 2/11/21. Commd 21/12/42. Flt Lt 21/6/46. Retd SEC 1/7/60.
RAINE-BISHOP N. N., BSc CEng MIMeche. Born 19/11/64. Commd 5/9/82. Fg Offr 15/4/84. Retd ENG 12/7/86.
RAISON R. M., BA PGCE. Born 29/9/51. Commd 23/10/86. Sqn Ldr 1/7/93. Retd ADMIN 14/3/96.
RAIT D. M. Born 2/12/47. Commd 2/2/78. Wg Cdr 1/1/97. Retd ENG 1/12/00.
RAJAPAKSHA H. Born 7/3/34. Commd 19/6/67. Flt Lt 19/6/67. Retd GD 15/12/73.
RAKE A. C. Born 7/9/57. Commd 14/7/77. Flt Lt 14/1/83. Retd GD 18/6/96.
RAKE D. S. V., OBE AFC*. Born 26/5/22. Commd 19/6/42. Gp Capt 1/7/64. Retd GD 26/3/76.
RALEY A. J., MBE. Born 6/6/35. Commd 4/9/61. Wg Cdr 1/1/80. Retd GD 6/6/91.
RALLS A. W., BA. Born 7/9/54. Commd 8/2/81. Sqn Ldr 1/1/92. Retd SUP 14/3/97.
RALPH A., BSc. Born 21/5/59. Commd 29/11/81. Flt Lt 28/2/83. Retd GD 29/11/97.
RALPH J. A. Born 10/11/30. Commd 23/12/53. Flt Lt 23/12/59. Retd GD(G) 10/11/92.
RAMAGE L. M. Born 6/11/57. Commd 31/1/80. Sqn Ldr 1/7/94. Retd GD 14/9/96.
RAMIREZ R., AFC. Born 26/4/24. Commd 7/7/49. Wg Cdr 1/1/67. Retd GD 28/12/72.
RAMSAY A. C. Born 16/5/30. Commd 24/1/52. Sqn Ldr 1/7/63. Retd GD 17/5/84.
RAMSAY A. W. D. Born 9/12/25. Commd 6/9/51. Flt Lt 14/11/56. Retd PRT 9/12/72.

RAMSAY I. A. Born 30/7/41. Commd 4/2/71. Sqn Ldr 1/1/86. Retd GD(G) 16/9/94.
RAMSAY I. G. Born 16/6/46. Commd 11/2/65. Sqn Ldr 1/1/77. Retd GD(G) 22/10/94.
RAMSAY J. G. Born 23/1/32. Commd 13/8/52. Flt Lt 9/1/58. Retd GD 1/12/85.
RAMSAY N. H. D., DFC. Born 29/7/19. Commd 19/3/41. Flt Lt 1/9/45. Retd GD 29/7/62.
RAMSBOTTOM A., MIDPM. Born 8/5/48. Commd 13/1/67. Sqn Ldr 1/7/80. Retd ADMIN 8/5/86.
RAMSBOTTOM B. D., BDS. Born 2/4/47. Commd 29/9/68. Wg Cdr 10/6/83. Retd DEL 2/4/85.
RAMSBOTTOM D. H. Born 24/6/19. Commd 28/7/49. Sqn Ldr 1/1/64. Retd SEC 31/10/67.
RAMSBOTTOM R. W. Born 23/9/32. Commd 31/1/51. Flt Lt 31/10/56. Retd GD 23/9/70.
RAMSBOTTOM T. A. Born 13/6/40. Commd 28/4/64. Flt Lt 4/11/70. Retd ENG 28/4/83.
RAMSDALE R. Born 21/5/33. Commd 12/3/52. Flt Lt 2/4/62. Retd GD 2/4/78.
RAMSDEN A., AFM. Born 26/1/23. Commd 14/3/57. Flt Lt 14/3/63. Retd GD 29/6/68.
RAMSDEN D. R., BSc. Born 18/2/56. Commd 30/10/77. Flt Lt 30/1/79. Retd GD 30/10/89.
RAMSEY I. A. F. Born 28/10/49. Commd 15/1/79. Flt Lt 15/1/81. Retd SY 31/1/94.
RAMSEY N. G. C., DFC. Born 16/12/19. Commd 2/2/42. Flt Lt 20/7/48. Retd GD 4/3/61.
RAMSEY S. Born 27/9/59. Commd 15/6/83. Sqn Ldr 1/1/92. Retd ENG 8/2/98.
RAMSHAW F. M. Born 25/6/43. Commd 19/4/63. Sqn Ldr 1/7/93. Retd GD 23/4/97.
RAMSHAW G. D., BSc CEng Dip Soton MIEE. Born 5/2/34. Commd 24/8/56. Wg Cdr 24/2/74. Retd ADMIN
   29/9/84.
RAMUS A. A. Born 21/11/29. Commd 11/4/51. Wg Cdr 1/1/68. Retd GD 15/7/85.
RANASINGHE D. J. C., MIMgt. Born 25/9/30. Commd 28/2/66. Sqn Ldr 1/1/72. Retd SUP 3/7/84.
RANCE B. H., MSc MB ChB MFOM. Born 20/9/29. Commd 16/6/57. Wg Cdr 16/6/70. Retd MED 16/7/83.
RANCE F. S. Born 2/6/43. Commd 6/4/62. Gp Capt 1/7/90. Retd GD 2/6/98.
RAND M. D. Born 22/5/43. Commd 3/1/64. Flt Lt 4/5/72. Retd GD 25/6/76.
RANDALL A. M. Born 11/5/61. Commd 2/9/79. Sqn Ldr 1/7/93. Retd GD 11/5/99.
RANDALL B. A. Born 17/8/36. Commd 5/7/68. Flt Lt 5/7/70. Retd ENG 5/7/76.
RANDALL D. J. Born 13/4/50. Commd 3/7/83. Flt Lt 12/6/75. Retd GD 19/4/88.
RANDALL H. C., DFC. Born 2/9/18. Commd 29/7/39. Wg Cdr 1/1/52. Retd GD 2/9/65.
RANDALL N. O., BA. Born 11/5/50. Commd 22/8/76. Sqn Ldr 1/1/84. Retd ADMIN 22/8/92.
RANDALL R. W. Born 10/1/33. Commd 9/10/58. Sqn Ldr 1/1/69. Retd SY(PRT) 15/11/73.
RANDEL J. Born 16/11/45. Commd 15/6/83. Flt Lt 15/6/87. Retd ENG 17/6/94.
RANDELL A. R. Born 2/2/24. Commd 11/7/49. Sqn Ldr 1/1/70. Retd GD(G) 18/3/78.
RANDELL E. J. Born 10/4/30. Commd 18/6/64. Sqn Ldr 1/7/78. Retd GD 10/4/88.
RANDELL J. R. F., DFC. Born 27/6/99. Commd 1/4/18. Flt Lt 1/7/25. Retd GD 3/3/28. Recalled 26/8/39 to
   30/11/47 rtg Sqn Ldr.
RANDLE R. R., PhD BSc CEng MIEE. Born 5/7/29. Commd 9/12/54. Wg Cdr 1/7/69. Retd ENG 1/7/72.
RANDLE W. S. O., CBE AFC DFM FRAeS FIMgt. Born 17/5/21. Commd 30/3/43. Gp Capt 1/1/64. Retd GD 1/4/72.
RANDLES S. Born 25/4/56. Commd 1/12/77. Wg Cdr 1/1/96. Retd GD 25/4/00.
RANDOLPH P. McD. Born 16/5/29. Commd 5/4/50. Wg Cdr 1/7/69. Retd SUP 1/10/77.
RANDS A. J. Born 6/3/64. Commd 6/5/83. Flt Lt 6/11/88. Retd GD 14/3/96.
RANDS E. G., FIMgt. Born 19/2/14. Commd 13/10/37. Gp Capt 1/7/59. Retd SEC 28/7/69.
RANDS J. E., OBE. Born 23/11/59. Commd 5/4/79. Sqn Ldr 1/1/91. Retd GD 23/11/97.
RANKIN A. F. Born 5/3/32. Commd 19/11/52. Flt Lt 5/11/58. Retd GD 1/11/75.
RANKIN C. L. Born 23/7/39. Commd 25/6/57. Flt Lt 31/1/63. Retd GD 1/10/78.
RANKIN M. E. Born 7/11/33. Commd 27/7/54. Sqn Ldr 1/1/65. Retd GD 11/11/71.
RANKIN R. Born 3/4/33. Commd 17/3/54. Flt Lt 17/9/59. Retd GD 3/4/71.
RANKINE S. K., BSc. Born 22/11/52. Commd 25/9/71. Sqn Ldr 1/1/85. Retd ENG 1/10/91.
RANSCOMBE G. L. Born 27/9/29. Commd 9/4/52. Flt Lt 26/5/55. Retd GD 30/9/66.
RANSCOMBE J. W. Born 1/7/27. Commd 3/8/61. Flt Lt 3/8/67. Retd SUP 1/6/74.
RANSLEY B. M. Born 29/8/32. Commd 17/1/69. Wg Cdr 1/7/88. Retd PRT 1/7/91.
RANSLEY R. A. Born 19/4/18. Commd 9/8/37. Flt Lt 1/9/45. Retd SEC 19/4/73.
RANSOM D. C. Born 8/4/33. Commd 26/3/52. Flt Lt 7/8/57. Retd GD(G) 8/4/93.
RANSOM G., MSc BA. Born 25/7/43. Commd 17/1/82. Sqn Ldr 1/1/91. Retd ENG 25/7/98.
RANSOM W. H. Born 11/8/21. Commd 8/2/44. Sqn Ldr 1/7/61. Retd GD(G) 11/8/76.
RANSOME R. L. Born 26/9/61. Commd 11/6/81. Flt Lt 11/12/86. Retd GD 26/9/99.
RANSON G. Born 12/2/43. Commd 26/4/84. Flt Lt 26/4/88. Retd ENG 2/4/93.
RAPHAEL B., AFC. Born 3/9/43. Commd 21/12/62. Sqn Ldr 1/7/76. Retd GD 31/3/94.
RAPHAEL W. G. Born 18/7/19. Commd 1/9/45. Flt Lt 1/9/45. Retd GD 31/3/62.
RAPKINS L. B. Born 14/10/41. Commd 14/8/70. Flt Lt 13/10/72. Retd GD(G) 16/12/74.
RAPLEY C. Born 14/7/57. Commd 16/2/86. Flt Lt 16/8/89. Retd ENG 14/3/97.
RAPSON A. H. Born 21/8/45. Commd 16/8/68. Flt Lt 16/2/74. Retd GD 6/5/85.
RAPSON P. E., DFC. Born 21/11/15. Commd 10/4/42. Flt Lt 5/7/50. Retd SEC 1/9/62.
RATCLIFFE D. Born 13/11/61. Commd 24/4/80. Flt Lt 24/10/85. Retd GD 12/5/99.
RATCLIFFE P. C. B. Born 29/4/23. Commd 6/9/47. Sqn Ldr 1/1/60. Retd SUP 1/1/62.
RATCLIFFE R. H. Born 27/1/25. Commd 4/10/56. Plt Offr 4/10/56. Retd GD 30/9/59.
RATCLIFFE W. D. Born 31/1/26. Commd 11/7/47. Sqn Ldr 1/1/59. Retd RGT 30/10/65.
RATHBONE C. W. H. Born 16/5/53. Commd 1/6/72. Sqn Ldr 1/7/89. Retd GD 1/7/92.

RATHMELL C. W., DFC. Born 19/10/20. Commd 6/2/44. Sqn Ldr 1/7/70. Retd SUP 3/12/70.
RATNARAJA E. C. L. M. Born 25/4/40. Commd 5/4/61. Flt Lt 15/6/67. Retd SEC 6/3/73.
RATTUE J. M., MSc BSc. Born 28/12/56. Commd 2/3/80. Sqn Ldr 1/7/90. Retd ADMIN 14/3/96.
RAVEN G. W. Born 18/1/63. Commd 30/8/84. Fg Off 12/11/85. Retd SUP 1/10/88.
RAVEN J. Born 17/3/13. Commd 1/2/40. Fg Offr 13/3/47. Retd SUP 5/12/56 rtg Sqn Ldr.
RAVENHALL J. M. Born 8/2/47. Commd 20/8/65. Flt Lt 20/2/71. Retd GD 23/6/92.
RAVENHILL S. M. Born 27/12/15. Commd 13/1/48. Sqn Ldr 1/7/52. Retd SUP 27/12/72.
RAVENSCROFT K. Born 17/12/32. Commd 17/10/57. Flt Lt 17/4/62. Retd GD 17/12/92.
RAW R. Born 22/4/26. Commd 21/5/52. Flt Lt 1/9/59. Retd MAR 3/4/68.
RAWCLIFFE E. C. Born 12/10/27. Commd 8/11/51. Flt Lt 23/2/57. Retd GD 2/4/69.
RAWLES G. K., BSc. Born 22/10/56. Commd 25/5/80. Flt Lt 25/8/81. Retd GD 11/11/96.
RAWLINGS P. A. Born 23/12/46. Commd 2/4/65. Flt Lt 20/10/70. Retd GD 1/1/77.
RAWLINS S. J., DFC FIMgt. Born 25/7/21. Commd 5/8/39. Gp Capt 1/1/66. Retd GD 27/3/76.
RAWLINSON A. C., OBE DFC* AFC. Born 31/7/18. Commd 1/9/45. Wg Cdr 1/7/52. Retd GD 13/11/61 rtg Gp Capt.
RAWLINSON H., DFC. Born 14/4/20. Commd 3/7/41. Flt Lt 16/5/48. Retd GD 25/8/65.
RAWLL C. C. G., MB ChB DTPH. Born 18/8/30. Commd 29/8/54. Wg Cdr 29/8/67. Retd MED 5/9/70.
RAWTHORNE C. Born 18/7/53. Commd 5/7/73. Sqn Ldr 1/1/86. Retd GD 18/7/91.
RAY A. P., MSc BSc CEng MIEE MRAeS MIMgt MCIPD. Born 25/8/38. Commd 31/12/63. Sqn Ldr 23/4/70. Retd
    ADMIN 1/3/84.
RAY D. W. Born 19/12/33. Commd 21/5/52. Flt Lt 16/10/57. Retd GD 19/12/71 rtg Sqn Ldr.
RAY E. G. Born 31/10/35. Commd 21/4/67. Sqn Ldr 1/7/81. Retd ENG 31/8/88.
RAY F. G. A. Born 10/9/37. Commd 6/9/63. Flt Lt 8/1/69. Retd GD 10/9/75.
RAY J. A. Born 6/3/33. Commd 11/3/65. Sqn Ldr 14/5/76. Retd MED(SEC) 18/3/85.
RAY J. M. A. Born 2/5/26. Commd 21/9/56. Sqn Ldr 1/1/73. Retd RGT 9/7/80.
RAY P. R. Born 22/6/45. Commd 11/8/67. Wg Cdr 1/1/91. Retd GD 5/7/99.
RAY R. L. G., AFC. Born 6/7/25. Commd 1/3/49. Sqn Ldr 1/7/72. Retd GD 6/7/80.
RAYBOULD K. Born 9/5/36. Commd 27/5/71. Sqn Ldr 1/7/85. Retd ADMIN 2/1/91.
RAYDEN R. S. Born 12/8/16. Commd 18/7/43. Sqn Ldr 1/1/66. Retd ENG 12/8/70.
RAYFIELD G., BA CIMS FMS FInstAM MIMgt. Born 25/3/43. Commd 24/6/65. Wg Cdr 1/1/93. Retd GD 20/12/97.
RAYMENT A. G. Born 8/5/44. Commd 24/4/64. Sqn Ldr 1/7/80. Retd GD 2/4/93.
RAYMOND P. E., BSc. Born 25/9/24. Commd 24/1/45. Gp Capt 1/1/72. Retd ADMIN 26/3/77.
RAYMOND-BARKER G. G. C. Born 30/4/26. Commd 25/10/46. Flt Lt 19/6/52. Retd GD 22/3/68.
RAYMONT G. J. Born 10/6/48. Commd 19/9/70. Flt Lt 10/3/77. Retd SY 10/6/86.
RAYNER A. Born 12/4/61. Commd 8/12/83. Flt Lt 20/2/92. Retd RGT 20/2/92.
RAYNER C. M. Born 9/9/52. Commd 20/12/73. Sqn Ldr 1/7/84. Retd GD 9/9/90.
RAYNER G. W., BA. Born 12/5/29. Commd 26/10/50. Wg Cdr 1/7/68. Retd EDN 12/5/79.
RAYNER H. J., DFC AFC. Born 15/7/14. Commd 22/5/41. Wg Cdr 1/7/54. Retd GD 29/9/61.
RAYNER H. R., MSc MBCS. Born 5/9/50. Commd 19/9/71. Sqn Ldr 1/7/84. Retd SUP 30/9/89.
RAYNER K. E. J. Born 5/1/38. Commd 29/10/60. Sqn Ldr 1/7/72. Retd GD 5/1/76. Re-instated 6/3/77. Retd
    31/7/83.
RAYNER M. O., OBE CEng MRAeS MIMgt. Born 26/2/19. Commd 28/3/46. Wg Cdr 1/7/62. Retd ENG 18/5/74.
RAYNER P. R., AFC. Born 15/1/34. Commd 17/2/53. Flt Lt 10/3/58. Retd GD 2/10/78.
RAYNHAM H. D., AFC. Born 2/11/39. Commd 21/3/84. Flt Lt 3/2/81. Retd GD 2/11/94.
RAYNOR R. N., BA BTech. CEng MRAeS MIMgt. Born 22/11/53. Commd 30/9/73. Sqn Ldr 1/1/84. Retd ENG
    22/11/91.
RAYSON J., OBE AFC. Born 11/6/21. Commd 6/7/42. Wg Cdr 1/1/58. Retd GD 1/4/68.
RAYSON M. J., LVO. Born 19/7/30. Commd 24/10/51. A Cdre 1/7/82. Retd GD 19/7/85.
REA A. P., MMAR. Born 16/6/35. Commd 28/4/64. Sqn Ldr 1/7/78. Retd SUP 16/6/92.
REA P. B. Born 6/8/23. Commd 1/4/49. Flt Lt 25/2/53. Retd GD 31/3/62.
REA T. J., BA. Born 12/2/50. Commd 16/12/79. Flt Lt 16/12/80. Retd ADMIN 16/12/95.
READ A. C. L. Born 17/7/44. Commd 14/1/65. Flt Lt 15/4/71. Retd SEC 10/8/74.
READ A. R. Born 5/6/38. Commd 15/12/59. Gp Capt 1/7/86. Retd SUP 11/2/89.
READ C. A. Born 25/7/27. Commd 7/5/52. Flt Lt 7/2/58. Retd GD 25/7/65.
READ D. Born 12/4/20. Commd 15/2/45. Sqn Ldr 1/1/61. Retd SUP 11/6/65.
READ D. Born 11/10/24. Commd 12/4/51. Flt Lt 1/1/53. Retd PRT 18/2/59.
READ D. C. Born 8/4/37. Commd 2/12/55. Gp Capt 1/1/84. Retd GD 3/6/87.
READ D. G. Born 12/3/37. Commd 8/8/60. Flt Lt 8/2/66. Retd GD 8/8/76.
READ D. J., MA MCIPD MIMgt. Born 25/2/33. Commd 24/8/56. Gp Capt 1/1/80. Retd ADMIN 16/11/87.
READ D. J. Born 31/10/42. Commd 6/6/66. Sqn Ldr 1/1/83. Retd ADMIN 5/6/86.
READ G. J. Born 6/1/24. Commd 10/7/45. Sqn Ldr 1/7/60. Retd GD 7/1/75.
READ H. G. Born 28/8/20. Commd 14/10/42. Sqn Ldr 1/1/70. Retd SEC 28/8/75.
READ J. A., CertEd. Born 4/5/50. Commd 29/8/72. Sqn Ldr 1/7/89. Retd ADMIN 7/4/01.
READ J. S. Born 13/10/20. Commd 17/5/43. Sqn Ldr 1/7/67. Retd SUP 13/10/75.
READ The Rev J. R. J., BA. Born 15/3/39. Commd 30/4/72. Retd 30/4/88, Wg Cdr.
READ K. R. L. Born 26/10/39. Commd 19/12/61. Flt Lt 7/8/64. Retd GD 26/10/77. Re-entered 2/4/80. Sqn Ldr
    1/1/91. Retd GD 26/10/99.

READ M. G. Born 27/3/30. Commd 17/5/51. Flt Lt 6/9/56. Retd GD 25/7/70.
READ M. S. Born 21/7/31. Commd 23/5/51. Flt Lt 15/3/56. Retd GD 21/7/69.
READ N. R. Born 28/5/36. Commd 29/4/58. Sqn Ldr 1/1/77. Retd GD 3//10/87.
READE C. S. Born 28/4/15. Commd 17/8/39. Sqn Ldr 1/8/47. Retd SUP 17/5/64.
READE M. Born 28/11/30. Commd 23/11/53. Sqn Ldr 1/7/67. Retd GD 30/4/76.
READER B. A. Born 17/11/32. Commd 6/4/54. Flt Lt 14/11/56. Retd GD 17/11/70.
READER D. C., PhD BSc MB BS MRCS LRCP. Born 7/6/35. Commd 3/3/63. Gp Capt 3/3/86. Retd MED 2/1/99.
READER D. M., MA CEng FIMgt MRAeS. Born 11/4/34. Commd 26/9/53. A Cdre 1/7/81. Retd ENG 27/6/86.
READFERN P. A. Born 13/9/56. Commd 15/12/79. Wg Cdr 1/7/96. Retd GD 1/12/00.
READHEAD N. J. Born 25/2/56. Commd 14/7/77. Fg Offr 14/7/79. Retd GD 6/1/82.
READING J. H., MB BS MRCS LRCP DTM&H. Born 26/4/26. Commd 1/9/52. Wg Cdr 31/1/64. Retd MED 1/9/68.
READING R. W., MCIPS MIMgt. Born 24/2/50. Commd 2/5/69. Sqn Ldr 1/7/84. Retd SUP 24/2/88.
READMAN A. B. Born 3/5/40. Commd 5/11/70. Sqn Ldr 5/5/77. Retd ADMIN 5/11/80.
READMAN E., MBCS. Born 2/2/32. Commd 25/6/66. Flt Lt 25/6/71. Retd ENG 1/2/84.
READYHOOF K. C. Born 10/5/30. Commd 28/6/51. Flt Lt 10/10/56. Retd GD 10/5/68.
REASON D. J., MIMgt. Born 11/7/42. Commd 31/1/64. Wg Cdr 1/7/88. Retd ADMIN 25/10/92.
REAY G. E., DFM. Born 29/8/22. Commd 10/1/45. Flt Lt 10/7/48. Retd GD 29/8/65.
REAY W., MSc BDS FDSRCS(Ed) MOrthRCSE LDS DOrthRCS. Born 6/9/45. Commd 16/4/74. Gp Capt 22/12/92. Retd
    DEL 16/4/96.
REDDIN G. Born 25/9/31. Commd 16/7/52. Flt Lt 17/7/61. Retd GD 13/8/70.
REDDING J. S. Born 20/9/30. Commd 28/6/51. Sqn Ldr 1/7/76. Retd GD 20/9/88.
REDDING R. F., MBE. Born 5/6/25. Commd 22/9/44. Wg Cdr 1/7/70. Retd GD 3/4/76.
REDDISH J. Born 15/2/24. Commd 10/4/51. Sqn Ldr 1/7/73. Retd GD 15/2/79.
REDDY P. E. Born 12/11/42. Commd 17/12/63. Flt Lt 26/7/67. Retd GD 12/11/80.
REDDYHOFF F. D., BSc. Born 15/1/31. Commd 31/8/64. Sqn Ldr 1/3/68. Retd EDN 9/5/81.
REDFERN A., BA. Born 29/7/31. Commd 4/9/59. Wg Cdr 1/1/74. Retd MAR 1/1/77.
REDFERN J. C., DPhysEd. Born 24/7/46. Commd 18/1/73. Flt Lt 18/7/79. Retd SY(PRT) 3/7/88.
REDFERN R. H., McV. Born 5/5/25. Commd 3/11/49. Gp Capt 1/7/72. Retd GD 5/5/80.
REDFORD J. Born 6/9/41. Commd 8/6/62. Flt Lt 8/12/67. Retd GD 6/9/79.
REDGRAVE M. St. J. Born 6/2/52. Commd 23/4/87. Flt Lt 23/4/89. Retd GD 31/3/97.
REDLEY T. A. Born 26/6/25. Commd 14/11/49. Sqn Ldr 1/1/63. Retd SUP 26/6/82.
REDMAN A. R. Born 20/9/33. Commd 21/5/52. Sqn Ldr 1/7/84. Retd GD 29/5/87.
REDMAN H. G. Born 30/4/21. Commd 10/5/46. Flt Lt 29/12/52. Retd RGT 30/4/66.
REDMOND C. F. S. Born 18/8/42. Commd 17/12/64. Flt Lt 26/7/67. Retd GD 13/7/74.
REDMOND D. J. Born 8/5/23. Commd 19/7/56. Sqn Ldr 1/7/66. Retd ENG 8/5/78.
REDMOND T. Born 27/6/48. Commd 4/7/85. Flt Lt 4/7/89. Retd GD(G) 29/7/94.
REDMONDS C. Born 9/6/33. Commd 7/7/55. Flt Lt 9/2/57. Retd GD 9/6/71.
REDMORE M. A. Born 22/6/42. Commd 11/5/62. Sqn Ldr 1/7/74. Retd GD 22/6/97.
REECE J. R. Born 11/6/34. Commd 8/10/70. Flt Lt 8/10/73. Retd GD 4/7/84.
REECE R. A., DFC DFM. Born 2/11/14. Commd 9/8/40. Sqn Ldr 1/8/47. Retd GD 21/2/58.
REED A. C., OBE MA. Born 6/5/35. Commd 1/10/57. Wg Cdr 1/7/81. Retd GD 15/4/87.
REED A. D., BSc. Born 16/5/60. Commd 19/6/83. Sqn Ldr 1/7/93. Retd GD 19/6/99.
REED A. G., IEng FIIE MIMgt. Born 14/6/45. Commd 1/4/76. Wg Cdr 1/7/99. Retd ENG 14/6/00.
REED A. J. H. Born 21/12/41. Commd 3/8/62. Flt Lt 8/1/69. Retd GD 21/12/79.
REED D. W. M. Born 12/3/34. Commd 9/7/55. Flt Lt 15/8/62. Retd GD 1/10/80.
REED G. E. Born 24/10/10. Commd 11/2/43. Fg Offr 11/8/43. Retd ASD 8/1/46 rtg Flt Lt.
REED I. P. Born 27/9/20. Commd 1/6/42. Flt Lt 29/6/50. Retd RGT 27/10/65.
REED K. B. Born 21/5/39. Commd 1/7/82. Flt Lt 1/3/87. Retd ADMIN 28/1/90.
REED M. B., MIMgt. Born 5/6/31. Commd 7/6/60. Sqn Ldr 1/1/70. Retd SUP 15/8/84.
REED P. F., OBE CEng MRAeS. Born 26/4/23. Commd 20/2/43. Wg Cdr 1/1/69. Retd ENG 6/4/74.
REED P. J., BSc. Born 10/2/63. Commd 10/11/85. Flt Lt 10/5/89. Retd ADMIN 1/11/96.
REED S., MIDPM MCIPS. Born 15/3/40. Commd 19/12/61. Wg Cdr 1/7/86. Retd SUP 15/3/95.
REED T. A., BSc. Born 1/5/44. Commd 15/7/66. Sqn Ldr 1/7/75. Retd ENG 11/11/75.
REED T. W. Born 7/3/19. Commd 27/10/55. Fg Offr 27/10/58. Retd ENG 9/10/61.
REED-PURVIS H., CB OBE BSc. Born 1/7/28. Commd 19/7/51. AVM 1/1/80. Retd SY 4/9/83.
REEDER F. E., CEng MIEE MIMgt. Born 15/9/20. Commd 2/12/43. Sqn Ldr 1/7/66. Retd ENG 1/5/73.
REEDER M. P. Born 2/6/61. Commd 30/8/84. Flt Lt 1/3/91. Retd ADMIN 30/11/96.
REEDER R. W. Born 7/10/22. Commd 14/1/44. Flt Lt 19/6/52. Retd GD 31/3/74.
REEH D., BSc. Born 17/1/51. Commd 15/9/69. Sqn Ldr 1/7/82. Retd GD 1/7/85.
REEKIE G. L. Born 20/8/44. Commd 14/7/66. Sqn Ldr 1/1/87. Retd GD 20/8/99.
REEN P. J. Born 23/6/23. Commd 4/10/45. Sqn Ldr 1/7/56. Retd ENG 29/9/61.
REEP M. F. Born 24/3/39. Commd 2/5/69. Sqn Ldr 1/7/83. Retd GD(G) 6/4/90.
REEP T. C., ACA. Born 22/9/04. Commd 11/6/28. Wg Cdr 1/7/48. Retd SEC 25/2/55.
REES B. G. Born 17/4/49. Commd 2/11/88. Sqn Ldr 1/7/97. Retd ENG 31/10/99.
REES C. D. Born 17/4/53. Commd 2/9/73. Sqn Ldr 1/1/90. Retd ADMIN 1/1/93.
REES C. D. Born 23/3/32. Commd 1/10/60. Sqn Ldr 1/7/78. Retd RGT 8/6/84.

REES D. Born 28/7/58. Commd 29/11/81. Flt Lt 29/11/85. Retd PRT 2/4/92.
REES D. L., DPhysEd. Born 23/4/54. Commd 3/7/80. Flt Lt 17/1/83. Retd GD 1/7/93.
REES D. W., BSc. Born 28/11/48. Commd 1/9/70. Wg Cdr 1/7/88. Retd GD 19/5/92.
REES E. I. Born 16/9/56. Commd 19/3/81. Sqn Ldr 30/5/95. Retd SY 10/11/96.
REES G., CEng MIEE MRAeS. Born 1/8/29. Commd 27/2/52. Gp Capt 1/7/78. Retd ENG 13/4/84.
REES G. M. Born 12/8/36. Commd 19/8/71. Sqn Ldr 1/1/83. Retd ENG 1/10/87.
REES G. T. Born 3/9/18. Commd 17/10/57. Sqn Ldr 1/7/66. Retd ENG 31/10/70.
REES H., OBE BSc CEng MIEE. Born 11/9/49. Commd 28/9/70. Gp Capt 2/3/90. Retd ENG 11/9/93.
REES H. K. Born 2/2/21. Commd 13/1/42. Wg Cdr 1/7/58. Retd GD 2/2/68.
REES J., FIMgt MRAeS. Born 30/6/25. Commd 3/3/45. Gp Capt 1/1/74. Retd SUP 1/1/76.
REES J., AFC. Born 13/2/22. Commd 7/6/44. Flt Lt 7/12/47. Retd GD 21/10/56.
REES J. V. Born 30/9/15. Commd 15/10/53. Sqn Ldr 23/1/64. Retd MED(T) 30/9/70.
REES K. M. Born 14/2/46. Commd 18/8/67. Flt Lt 18/2/73. Retd SUP 2/4/75.
REES O. R. Born 7/12/47. Commd 24/11/67. Sqn Ldr 1/1/95. Retd GD 14/9/96.
REES R. A., MA DCAe CEng MIEE. Born 26/1/36. Commd 30/9/55. Flt Lt 21/8/63. Retd ENG 26/1/74.
REES R. J., BSc MIMgt. Born 15/6/32. Commd 25/8/55. Wg Cdr 1/1/84. Retd 15/6/87 ADMIN.
REES S. A. L., CEng MIMechE MRAeS MIMgt. Born 23/1/29. Commd 5/12/51. Gp Capt. 1/7/73. Retd ENG 11/8/79.
REES S. C. Born 22/4/61. Commd 5/5/88. Flt Lt 3/1/94. Retd ADMIN 14/3/97.
REES S. T. Born 24/10/59. Commd 19/2/88. Flt lt 28/10/86. Retd GD 25/11/95.
REES V., DFC. Born 7/8/17. Commd 21/1/38. Wg Cdr 1/1/52. Retd GD 7/8/72.
REES V. Born 2/12/40. Commd 21/3/62.. Sqn Ldr 1/1/74. Retd SUP 1/7/79.
REES V. J., MBE MA BSC DipEl. Born 18/6/23. Commd 20/3/47. Sqn Ldr 24/8/59. Retd EDN 24/8/65.
REEVE J. D. Born 19/6/34. Commd 16/7/57. Flt Lt 1/4/63. Retd GD 5/2/77.
REEVE K. A. Born 22/5/27. Commd 4/4/51. Flt Lt 4/10/55. Retd GD 22/5/65.
REEVE M. P. J., MIMgt. Born 5/9/28. Commd 2/6/49. Gp Capt 1/7/75. Retd ADMIN 5/9/83.
REEVE R. J. Born 18/12/47. Commd 1/3/68. Sqn Ldr 1/7/80. Retd GD 26/5/98.
REEVE S. Born 18/3/22. Commd 23/12/61. Flt Lt 23/12/66. Retd SUP 29/4/72.
REEVE T. J. Born 21/4/62. Commd 30/6/91. Flt Lt 24/10/89. Retd GD 14/3/96.
REEVE W. G. Born 29/1/20. Commd 28/7/43. Sqn Ldr 1/7/69. Retd SEC 13/5/72.
REEVES A. J. W., CEng MRAeS. Born 6/9/38. Commd 28/7/60. Wg Cdr 1/7/76. Retd ENG 16/5/91.
REEVES B. M. Born 15/11/55. Commd 13/12/79. Flt Lt 13/8/85. Retd SY 13/8/95.
REEVES D. V. Born 27/4/19. Commd 6/10/60. Sqn Ldr 1/1/71. Retd ENG 27/4/74.
REEVES E. E., MBE. Born 1/12/28. Commd 25/8/49. Wg Cdr 1/1/70. Retd GD 10/1/79.
REEVES F. J. Born 8/3/27. Commd 15/12/49. Sqn Ldr 1/7/72. Retd GD 8/3/83.
REEVES M. J. Born 8/1/53. Commd 22/11/73. Flt Lt 22/5/79. Retd GD 8/1/91.
REFFOLD C. N. Born 9/5/52. Commd 16/9/71. Flt Lt 16/3/77. Retd GD 25/10/86.
REGAN E. J. Born 10/5/20. Commd 25/7/43. Flt Lt 20/9/49. Retd ENG 10/5/69.
REGAN J. Q., MA LLB. Born 17/9/43. Commd 23/9/68. Sqn Ldr 23/3/76. Retd ADMIN 16/9/94.
REGAN T. P., MSc CEng MIEE MRAeS. Born 30/10/39. Commd 18/7/61. Gp Capt 1/7/81. Retd ENG 3/7/83.
REGESTER M. J. C. Born 16/6/25. Commd 19/10/45. Flt Lt 19/10/51. Retd SUP 16/6/63.
REID A. G. Born 18/7/24. Commd 13/5/44. Sqn Ldr 1/1/55. Retd GD 18/7/62.
REID B. A., MB ChB MRCOG MRCGP MFFP DCH. Born 3/4/57. Commd 24/2/81. Wg Cdr 1/8/94. Retd MED 14/3/96.
REID B. K. Born 2/10/39. Commd 25/3/64. Flt Lt 15/4/70. Retd GD 2/10/71.
REID C. A. W. Born 24/3/42. Commd 21/12/62. Wg Cdr 1/1/83. Retd GD 22/4/94.
REID D. C., MRAeS. Born 20/4/43. Commd 22/2/63. Wg Cdr 1/1/90. Retd GD 20/4/98.
REID D. C. Born 3/5/52. Commd 4/2/71. Sqn Ldr 1/7/88. Retd GD 1/7/91.
REID D. E. MACD., BSc. Born 8/2/59. Commd 9/11/80. Sqn Ldr 1/7/92. Retd GD 29/7/97.
REID D. F. S. Born 25/1/49. Commd 29/3/68. Flt Lt 29/9/79. Retd ADMIN 13/12/96.
REID D. W. Born 10/2/43. Commd 19/8/71. Sqn Ldr 1/7/80. Retd ENG 5/9/88.
REID G. F., DFC FIMgt. Born 15/2/18. Commd 2/7/40. Gp Capt 1/7/61. Retd GD 19/4/68.
REID G. G. Born 2/9/48. Commd 28/2/69. Sqn Ldr 1/7/81. Retd GD 1/1/83.
REID G. M., DFC. Born 5/11/22. Commd 20/7/44. Flt Lt 20/1/48. Retd GD 28/9/49.
REID H. Born 24/7/43. Commd 31/1/64. Gp Capt 1/7/95. Retd GD 24/9/99.
REID I. A., MA. Born 2/5/37. Commd 1/5/61. Sqn Ldr 1/1/68. Retd GD 2/5/95.
REID J. Born 17/7/40. Commd 20/7/78. Flt Lt 20/7/81. Retd GD 16/1/93.
REID J. A. Born 28/2/54. Commd 10/5/90. Flt Lt 10/5/92. Retd OPS SPT 10/11/99.
REID J. A. R. M., CEng FRAeS FINucE FIMgt. Born 21/7/17. Commd 9/7/38. Gp Capt 1/1/59. Retd ENG 17/8/72.
REID J. C. Born 11/8/47. Commd 16/8/68. Flt Lt 16/2/74. Retd GD 11/12/86.
REID K. Born 19/7/46. Commd 5/2/65. Sqn Ldr 1/1/83. Retd GD 19/7/90.
REID M. Born 29/6/43. Commd 3/3/67. Flt Lt 8/3/72. Retd SUP 24/4/82.
REID M. Born 31/3/39. Commd 31/8/78. Flt Lt 31/8/82. Retd ADMIN 31/1/85.
REID M. C. Born 18/5/42. Commd 30/1/70. Sqn Ldr 1/1/77. Retd ENG 18/10/80.
REID M. D. C. Born 11/5/30. Commd 15/9/60. Sqn Ldr 1/7/80. Retd ADMIN 11/5/85.
REID P. D., BSc. Born 25/12/60. Commd 30/10/83. Flt Lt 30/4/85. Retd GD 30/10/95.
REID R. Born 25/2/14. Commd 10/7/47. Sqn Ldr 1/7/62. Retd CAT 28/9/68.

REID R. G. Born 30/9/18. Commd 17/8/39. Sqn Ldr 1/7/48. Retd SUP 30/1/55.
REID R. L., CBE CEng MIMechE. Born 17/2/35. Commd 31/12/62. A Cdre 1/7/83. Retd ENG 16/5/88.
REILLEY M. I. S. Born 5/9/45. Commd 15/9/67. Flt Lt 15/3/73. Retd GD 14/9/96.
REILLY D. P. Born 17/7/33. Commd 20/5/53. Gp Capt 1/7/84. Retd GD 25/6/85.
REILLY I., OBE BA. Born 7/4/44. Commd 17/12/65. Wg Cdr 1/7/85. Retd GD 14/3/96.
REILLY N. M. Born 13/8/22. Commd 28/3/45. Sqn Ldr 1/1/71. Retd GD 20/8/77.
REINECK C. H., OBE. Born 23/5/37. Commd 26/8/57. A Cdre 1/7/85. Retd GD 1/9/90.
REITH C. G. Born 23/2/30. Commd 7/5/52. Flt Lt 2/10/57. Retd GD 6/10/67.
REIZ J. M. Born 4/8/56. Commd 16/9/76. Flt Lt 20/1/83. Retd ADMIN 5/8/86.
REJDER B., FIMgt. Born 11/12/24. Commd 3/11/44. Wg Cdr 1/1/62. Retd GD 11/12/79.
RELF B. R. F., DipEurHum AIPM. Born 23/12/42. Commd 18/8/61. Sqn Ldr 1/1/81. Retd OPS SPT 23/12/97.
RELF J. A. Born 23/5/43. Commd 15/7/64. Sqn Ldr 1/7/78. Retd ENG 3/4/82.
RELFE R. I., BSc. Born 27/2/51. Commd 13/9/70. Sqn Ldr 1/7/85. Retd ADMIN 27/2/89.
RELPH W., OBE. Born 15/8/13. Commd 22/9/49. Wg Cdr 27/2/65. Retd MED(T) 15/8/68.
REMFRY K. R. M., MBE. Born 19/3/21. Commd 4/5/45. Flt Lt 19/5/52. Retd GD 7/5/70.
REMINGTON N. R. Born 1/10/44. Commd 29/1/72. Flt Lt 29/12/77. Retd GD 14/2/88.
REMLINGER M. J. Born 3/1/48. Commd 28/2/69. Gp Capt 1/1/94. Retd GD 15/5/01.
REMNANT D. McL. Born 16/5/30. Commd 17/6/53. Flt Lt 21/10/58. Retd ADMIN 31/12/82.
RENAUD-WRIGHT M. St. J. Born 24/3/17. Commd 5/11/42. Flt Lt 5/5/46. Retd ENG 1/1/60.
RENFREW S. C. Born 30/6/46. Commd 13/1/67. Sqn Ldr 1/7/91. Retd SUP 29/3/96.
RENKIN P. H. Born 28/9/19. Commd 8/6/49. Gp Capt 1/7/71. Retd SUP 12/12/73.
RENNIE C. A., DFM. Born 29/12/19. Commd 19/1/43. Wg Cdr 1/1/59. Retd GD 29/12/74.
RENNIE J., MA BSc FCIPD FIMgt. Born 12/10/40. Commd 6/1/69. Gp Capt 1/1/89. Retd ADMIN 15/7/95.
RENOWDEN The Venerable G. R., CB BA LTh. Born 13/8/29. Commd 15/1/58. Retd 8/10/88. AVM.
RENSHAW E. C. Born 13/9/40. Commd 4/7/69. Flt Lt 4/7/71. Retd ENG 18/3/72.
RENSHAW G. R. Born 10/9/31. Commd 31/5/51. Flt Lt 20/9/56. Retd GD 8/8/65.
RENSHAW J., BSc. Born 20/6/59. Commd 28/9/80. Plt Offr 28/12/78. Retd ENG 31/3/82.
RENSHAW J. D. E. Born 7/1/30. Commd 14/4/53. Flt Lt 14/4/58. Retd SEC 7/7/68.
RENSHAW J. L. Born 27/7/53. Commd 14/1/88. Flt Lt 14/1/90. Retd ENG 14/1/96.
RENSHAW S. J. Born 22/4/51. Commd 26/11/81. Flt Lt 26/5/88. Retd OPS SPT 27/7/97.
RENTON H. F., CB LLD MA. Born 13/3/31. Commd 9/6/55. A Cdre 1/7/80. Retd ADMIN 13/3/86.
RENTON R. A. Born 25/12/38. Commd 31/8/60. Sqn Ldr 1/1/73. Retd GD 2/10/77.
RENWICK A. W. Born 20/6/49. Commd 22/9/69. Fg Offr 22/3/72. Retd ENG 30/1/76.
RENWICK C. H., DPhysEd. Born 3/9/35. Commd 13/11/62. Wg Cdr 1/1/86. Retd ADMIN 19/1/89.
RENYARD B., CEng MIMechE MRAeS MIMgt. Born 8/4/38. Commd 28/7/60. Wg Cdr 1/7/76. Retd ENG 3/5/90.
REST P. A. Born 14/12/37. Commd 28/9/60. Flt Lt 28/3/71. Retd GD 28/9/76.
RETALLACK M., MBE. Born 25/4/27. Commd 14/11/57. Flt Lt 14/5/62. Retd GD 25/4/87.
REVELL The Rev. A., BA. Born 14/5/26. Commd 5/3/64. Retd 24/9/80. Gp Capt.
REVELL J. D., BSc. Born 11/7/44. Commd 15/7/66. Sqn Ldr 1/1/80. Retd ENG 11/7/88.
REVILL R., BA. Born 10/1/42. Commd 10/5/71. Sqn Ldr 10/10/76. Retd ADMIN 1/1/94.
REVITT E. D., DFC. Born 18/10/19. Commd 20/9/42. Sqn Ldr 1/1/64. Retd GD(G) 31/1/67.
REVNELL B. J. Born 4/3/33. Commd 6/12/51. Sqn Ldr 1/7/68. Retd GD 1/7/71.
REX A. J., BSc. Born 12/5/54. Commd 30/5/76. Flt Lt 20/8/77. Retd GD 14/3/89.
REXFORD-WELCH S. C., MA MSc MRCS LRCP. Born 27/10/15. Commd 1/6/49. Gp Capt 13/7/68. Retd MED 27/10/80.
REY M. Born 24/11/33. Commd 26/5/67. Sqn Ldr 1/1/75. Retd ENG 1/4/79.
REYNER K., FIMgt FITD. Born 26/11/35. Commd 26/7/56. Gp Capt 1/7/82. Retd SY 18/6/86.
REYNISH T. K. D. Born 11/10/39. Commd 8/2/91. Sqn Ldr 8/2/91. Retd GD 11/10/94.
REYNOLDS A. J. Born 15/4/46. Commd 10/6/66. Flt Lt 8/3/72. Retd GD 1/10/76.
REYNOLDS A. L. Born 2/3/49. Commd 6/4/72. Sqn Ldr 1/1/85. Retd GD 6/7/88.
REYNOLDS B. R. Born 5/8/35. Commd 9/12/53. Sqn Ldr 1/1/70. Retd GD 5/8/90.
REYNOLDS C., DFC. Born 6/10/21. Commd 2/8/44. Flt Lt 16/5/49. Retd GD(G) 31/3/62.
REYNOLDS D. A. Born 16/4/15. Commd 4/11/43. Sqn Ldr 1/7/62. Retd ENG 15/8/64.
REYNOLDS E. Born 9/3/31. Commd 15/12/53. Flt Lt 15/6/56. Retd GD 1/7/58.
REYNOLDS G. F. Born 21/4/34. Commd 21/10/66. Wg Cdr 1/1/84. Retd SUP 21/4/89.
REYNOLDS G. L., BSc. Born 12/11/43. Commd 13/4/64. Flt Lt 15/4/67. Retd GD 12/4/75.
REYNOLDS J., DPhysEd. Born 2/4/33. Commd 28/2/57. Gp Capt 1/1/85. Retd ADMIN 2/4/88.
REYNOLDS J. C., MB BS MRCS MRCP. Born 8/4/51. Commd 20/2/73. Sqn Ldr 13/7/81. Retd MED 23/8/89.
REYNOLDS J. R. Born 28/2/33. Commd 22/7/71. Flt Lt 22/7/73. Retd ENG 22/7/79.
REYNOLDS J. T. Born 21/12/29. Commd 26/3/52. Flt Lt 26/9/56. Retd GD 21/12/67.
REYNOLDS N. S. B., BEM. Born 5/10/22. Commd 11/2/65. Flt Lt 11/2/70. Retd ENG 5/10/77.
REYNOLDS P., DFC*. Born 23/10/21. Commd 11/5/41. Wg Cdr 1/7/57. Retd GD 23/10/68.
REYNOLDS P. Born 22/1/44. Commd 22/2/63. Sqn Ldr 1/1/81. Retd GD 1/7/84.
REYNOLDS P. A., CertEd. Born 4/7/46. Commd 17/10/71. Wg Cdr 1/1/92. Retd ADMIN 13/9/96.
REYNOLDS P. F. Born 21/12/34. Commd 14/1/65. Flt Lt 14/1/71. Retd SUP 1/11/75.
REYNOLDS P. G. H. Born 18/10/16. Commd 1/11/44. Flt Lt 16/5/60. Retd GD(G) 25/11/66.

REYNOLDS P. J. Born 1/2/44. Commd 16/8/68. Flt Lt 16/2/74. Retd GD 6/5/87.
REYNOLDS S., BA. Born 1/1/49. Commd 22/2/71. Flt Lt 22/5/74. Retd ADMIN 22/2/87.
REYNOLDS S. K. Born 10/11/42. Commd 5/9/69. Sqn Ldr 1/7/76. Retd GD 6/6/84.
REYNOLDS T. F., CEng MIMechE. Born 17/6/36. Commd 17/11/58. Gp Capt 1/7/83. Retd ENG 18/6/86.
RHIND H. A. Born 12/3/44. Commd 15/7/65. Flt Lt 15/7/70. Retd ENG 27/11/76.
RHIND J. R. Born 10/5/28. Commd 31/1/51. Sqn Ldr 1/1/63. Retd GD 12/1/67.
RHODES A. D. Born 28/6/56. Commd 4/6/87. Flt Lt 4/6/89. Retd GD(G) 4/6/95.
RHODES A. F. P. Born 4/4/45. Commd 1/4/66. Flt Lt 1/10/71. Retd GD 3/1/76.
RHODES D. B. D., MBE CEng MRAeS MIMgt. Born 13/12/20. Commd 26/9/57. Sqn Ldr 1/7/68. Retd ENG 5/6/75.
RHODES G. K. Born 27/6/34. Commd 18/11/66. Sqn Ldr 1/1/79. Retd ENG 1/10/85.
RHODES I. A. Born 8/3/32. Commd 4/3/63. Flt Lt 5/2/70. Retd GD 4/7/83.
RHODES K. D., BA MIMgt. Born 29/6/44. Commd 24/6/65. Wg Cdr 1/7/84. Retd GD 30/3/94.
RHODES M. D. Born 6/4/36. Commd 23/6/67. Wg Cdr 1/7/84. Retd ENG 6/4/94.
RHODES R. G., MBE AFC. Born 11/7/29. Commd 9/3/66. Sqn Ldr 1/7/76. Retd GD 11/7/89.
RHODES R. H. N., AFC MRAeS. Born 1/12/43. Commd 26/10/62. Wg Cdr 1/1/82. Retd GD 6/1/86.
RHODES R. L. Born 27/3/47. Commd 24/7/81. Flt Lt 24/7/83. Retd GD 24/7/89.
RHODES W. Born 30/11/43. Commd 22/3/63. Flt Lt 8/1/69. Retd GD 27/8/81.
RHYDDERCH R. D., MB BCh FFARCS DA. Born 26/5/44. Commd 15/9/69. Sqn Ldr 5/9/73. Retd MED 1/12/78.
RICCOMINI G. C. Born 23/3/23. Commd 20/11/43. Sqn Ldr 1/1/66. Retd GD(G) 31/3/76.
RICE B., BEM. Born 2/5/39. Commd 1/7/82. Sqn Ldr 1/7/91. Retd SY 1/7/94.
RICE D. J. C. Born 7/5/42. Commd 22/3/63. Flt lt 22/9/68. Retd GD 7/5/80.
RICE E. A., OBE MB BCh. Born 4/5/04. Commd 16/8/26. A Cdre 1/7/59. Retd MED 3/9/63.
RICE K. N. Born 6/6/25. Commd 17/8/45. Sqn Ldr 1/1/57. Retd GD 6/6/68.
RICE L. G. Born 14/10/23. Commd 27/8/59. Flt Lt 27/8/64. Retd ENG 30/4/76.
RICE P. D. Born 20/1/46. Commd 23/9/66. Flt Lt 23/3/72. Retd GD 13/3/76.
RICE R. G. Born 22/12/20. Commd 23/7/56. Flt Lt 23/7/56. Retd SEC 30/12/72.
RICE V. J., BA IEng. Born 7/6/42. Commd 3/7/80. Sqn Ldr 1/7/88. Retd ENG 7/6/97.
RICH N. L., BSc. Born 21/12/53. Commd 17/9/72. Sqn Ldr 1/1/89. Retd GD 15/5/92.
RICH P. C. A., MIMgt. Born 23/11/14. Commd 18/9/40. Wg Cdr 1/7/61. Retd SUP 24/1/70.
RICHARD D. M., CBE MRAeS. Born 19/10/33. Commd 27/7/54. Air Cdre 1/7/84. Retd GD 19/10/88.
RICHARDS A. C., DFC. Born 23/6/21. Commd 26/1/43. Wg Cdr 1/7/62. Retd GD 23/6/76.
RICHARDS A. J., OBE. Born 21/5/38. Commd 10/7/57. Wg Cdr 1/7/72. Retd GD 21/6/77.
RICHARDS B. Born 2/5/50. Commd 26/9/90. Flt Lt 26/9/94. Retd ENG 3/3/01.
RICHARDS D., BA. Born 13/11/31. Commd 15/11/55. Sqn Ldr 1/7/64. Retd GD 15/11/71.
RICHARDS D. Born 7/7/39. Commd 23/12/58. Sqn Ldr 1/1/73. Retd ENG 7/7/77.
RICHARDS D. A., DFC. Born 2/4/23. Commd 28/5/44. Flt Lt 28/11/47. Retd GD 1/5/68.
RICHARDS D. V. T., MBE. Born 9/5/09. Commd 2/12/43. Sqn Ldr 1/7/53. Retd SEC 9/5/58.
RICHARDS E. Born 15/1/25. Commd 15/12/49. Sqn Ldr 1/7/71. Retd PI 30/6/78.
RICHARDS G., AFC. Born 11/12/20. Commd 5/7/43. Sqn Ldr 1/7/66. Retd GD 11/12/75.
RICHARDS G. A. T., MA. Born 18/6/18. Commd 15/3/41. Wg Cdr 1/1/67. Retd EDN 9/9/69.
RICHARDS G. E. A. Born 8/2/36. Commd 22/10/59. Flt Lt 22/1/66. Retd SUP 8/2/74.
RICHARDS G. T. G. Born 30/9/23. Commd 4/11/44. Sqn Ldr 1/10/55. Retd GD 1/4/61.
RICHARDS I. J. Born 12/9/07. Commd 24/11/41. Flt Lt 1/9/45. Retd ENG 10/3/58 rtg Sqn Ldr.
RICHARDS J. Born 12/7/39. Commd 16/7/84. Sqn Ldr 1/1/92. Retd GD 12/7/94.
RICHARDS J., BSc. Born 16/3/35. Commd 5/7/60. Sqn Ldr 9/6/70. Retd EDN 14/8/75.
RICHARDS J., BA DPhysEd. Born 12/5/34. Commd 7/9/56. Sqn Ldr 7/3/64. Retd EDN 9/9/75.
RICHARDS J. M. Born 20/4/42. Commd 24/2/61. Flt Lt 24/8/66. Retd GD 14/2/76.
RICHARDS J. T. G., MA, MIMgt. Born 1/10/35. Commd 11/4/58. Sqn Ldr 14/4/66. Retd EDN 26/6/74.
RICHARDS K. D. Born 10/2/45. Commd 22/5/64. Flt Lt 22/11/69. Retd GD 10/2/00.
RICHARDS M. Born 25/1/45. Commd 10/9/70. Flt Lt 3/12/76. Retd PRT 29/9/78.
RICHARDS M. J., MRIN MIMgt. Born 20/12/33. Commd 9/4/52. Wg Cdr 1/1/79. Retd GD 30/4/85.
RICHARDS P. B. M. Born 27/4/42. Commd 28/7/64. Gp Capt 1/7/87. Retd SUP 27/4/97.
RICHARDS R. B. Born 5/9/42. Commd 19/4/63. Wg Cdr 1/1/86. Retd GD 2/1/93.
RICHARDS R. E. Born 23/1/52. Commd 7/1/71. Flt Lt 7/7/77. Retd GD(G) 23/1/90.
RICHARDS R. G. H. Born 3/5/44. Commd 28/2/80. Flt Lt 28/2/84. Retd ENG 3/5/88.
RICHARDS The Rev R. J., BA. Born 25/1/16. Commd 19/1/43. Retd 25/1/71 Wg Cdr.
RICHARDS R. R. V., BA. Born 17/4/28. Commd 19/10/49. Sqn Ldr 1/7/62. Retd SEC 17/4/66.
RICHARDS R. S. Born 26/8/28. Commd 9/4/52. Flt Lt 9/1/58. Retd GD 27/8/66.
RICHARDS S. M., BSc. Born 11/3/53. Commd 25/9/71. Sqn Ldr 1/7/88. Retd ENG 1/7/91.
RICHARDS S. W., MBE. Born 17/6/43. Commd 17/7/70. Wg Cdr 1/1/84. Retd ADMIN 17/6/87.
RICHARDSON A. Born 12/12/42. Commd 14/2/65. Flt Lt 6/12/69. Retd GD 12/12/80.
RICHARDSON A. Born 26/1/39. Commd 9/12/76. Sqn Ldr 9/12/82. Retd MED(T) 9/12/84.
RICHARDSON A. G. Born 3/1/33. Commd 6/4/59. Flt Lt 6/4/59. Retd GD 3/1/93.
RICHARDSON A. G. Born 28/8/51. Commd 13/9/70. Flt Lt 22/1/79. Retd GD 28/8/89.
RICHARDSON A. J. Born 4/5/28. Commd 8/11/51. Sqn Ldr 1/1/69. Retd GD(G) 2/8/80.
RICHARDSON A. M., BSc. Born 21/2/63. Commd 2/9/84. Flt Lt 2/3/88. Retd ADMIN 14/9/96.

RICHARDSON A. P. Born 26/11/19. Commd 29/1/44. Flt Lt 24/9/47. Retd GD 17/7/58.
RICHARDSON B. Born 27/7/45. Commd 5/2/65. Fg Offr 5/2/67. Retd GD 28/2/70.
RICHARDSON B. T., MBE. Born 24/2/51. Commd 23/4/87. Sqn Ldr 1/1/97. Retd ADMIN 21/4/98.
RICHARDSON C. G. Born 10/7/34. Commd 5/4/55. Sqn Ldr 1/1/71. Retd GD 1/1/74.
RICHARDSON C. H., MILT DipMgmt. Born 25/1/58. Commd 19/9/76. Flt Lt 19/3/83. Retd SUP 25/1/99.
RICHARDSON D. Born 28/7/35. Commd 31/5/56. Flt Lt 20/10/61. Retd SUP 1/3/78.
RICHARDSON D. A. Born 11/10/49. Commd 22/7/71. Fg Offr 22/7/73. Retd GD 2/9/76.
RICHARDSON D. J., BSc. Born 16/9/51. Commd 29/4/84. Sqn Ldr 1/7/88. Retd ADMIN 14/3/97.
RICHARDSON D. L. Born 21/6/53. Commd 17/9/72. Flt Lt 7/4/80. Retd GD 21/6/91.
RICHARDSON D. L. Born 15/7/26. Commd 21/6/50. Flt Lt 21/12/54. Retd GD 2/3/76.
RICHARDSON F. R. J., DFM AIIP. Born 26/8/23. Commd 10/10/44. Wg Cdr 1/7/70. Retd ENG 26/8/81.
RICHARDSON F. W. Born 27/8/27. Commd 8/7/53. Flt Lt 25/1/57. Retd GD 17/4/67.
RICHARDSON G. Born 16/9/49. Commd 30/5/69. Sqn Ldr 1/7/81. Retd GD 16/9/87.
RICHARDSON G. L., BSc. Born 16/5/53. Commd 13/2/77. Flt Lt 13/8/79. Retd SUP 13/2/93.
RICHARDSON J., MBE AFC FIMgt. Born 26/2/24. Commd 27/3/45. Gp Capt 1/1/68. Retd GD 26/9/75.
RICHARDSON J. Born 17/4/34. Commd 19/1/66. Sqn Ldr 19/1/78. Retd MED(T) 20/5/86.
RICHARDSON J. B., DFC. Born 7/4/15. Commd 26/1/44. Flt Lt 26/7/47. Retd GD 21/8/58.
RICHARDSON J. E. Born 18/9/23. Commd 25/5/45. Flt Lt 4/12/52. Retd GD 26/6/67.
RICHARDSON J. F. Born 18/2/30. Commd 20/12/51. Flt Lt 22/5/57. Retd GD 18/2/73.
RICHARDSON J. J. D., BA CEng MRAeS MIMgt. Born 27/6/29. Commd 12/7/62. Sqn Ldr 1/1/73. Retd ENG 27/6/89.
RICHARDSON J. W. Born 3/9/33. Commd 21/1/54. Sqn Ldr 1/7/68. Retd GD 30/9/73.
RICHARDSON K. E., OBE. Born 21/10/27. Commd 8/4/49. Gp Capt 1/7/73. Retd GD 21/10/82.
RICHARDSON K. P., BA. Born 11/12/44. Commd 11/8/77. Sqn Ldr 1/1/85. Retd ADMIN 31/3/94.
RICHARDSON K. R., OBE DFC MIMgt. Born 30/1/22. Commd 26/10/44. Wg Cdr 1/7/61. Retd GD 30/1/77.
RICHARDSON L. C. M. Born 7/4/07. Commd 7/10/43. Flt Lt 7/4/47. Retd ENG 10/11/61.
RICHARDSON N. J. Born 2/4/22. Commd 7/5/47. Flt Lt 4/6/53. Retd GD 2/7/65.
RICHARDSON P. D., BA MISM MIMgt. Born 4/11/61. Commd 29/4/84. Flt Lt 29/10/87. Retd OPS SPT 29/4/00.
RICHARDSON P. D. Born 13/7/15. Commd 23/12/42. Flt Lt 19/2/47. Retd GD 1/4/58.
RICHARDSON R. Born 3/4/47. Commd 13/1/67. Flt Lt 13/7/72. Retd GD 3/4/85.
RICHARDSON R. A. Born 23/7/21. Commd 21/2/48. Flt Lt 4/6/53. Retd GD 2/4/68.
RICHARDSON S. A. Born 14/9/61. Commd 30/4/81. Sqn Ldr 1/1/96. Retd GD 14/9/99.
RICHARDSON V., RM. Born 8/7/44. Commd 6/10/74. Sqn Offr 28/4/83. Retd 18/5/95.
RICHARDSON W. A., BSc CEng MIMechE. Born 2/3/42. Commd 15/7/63. Gp Capt 1/1/86. Retd ENG 25/2/89.
RICHES H. F. Born 24/3/22. Commd 19/10/49. Sqn Ldr 1/7/60. Retd MAR 8/7/61.
RICHFORD H. C., DFC. Born 30/8/23. Commd 21/8/44. Sqn Ldr 1/1/58. Retd GD 10/10/66.
RICHMOND D. E. Born 24/8/37. Commd 5/3/57. Sqn Ldr 1/1/74. Retd ENG 24/8/87.
RICHMOND G. Born 4/5/43. Commd 5/7/68. Sqn Ldr 1/7/76. Retd ENG 2/11/83.
RICHMOND K. A. Born 6/6/30. Commd 23/9/53. Sqn Ldr 23/3/64. Retd ADMIN 6/6/85.
RICHMOND P. Born 20/2/39. Commd 7/7/64. Flt Lt 19/8/64. Retd GD 20/2/77.
RICHMOND R. C. Born 14/3/05. Commd 29/12/30. Wg Cdr 1/7/47. Retd ENG 7/8/49 rtg Gp Capt.
RICHMOND S. P. Born 18/1/48. Commd 28/2/69. Sqn Ldr 1/1/81. Retd SUP 17/7/86.
RICHMOND W. Born 21/9/24. Commd 24/11/60. Flt Lt 24/11/63. Retd ADMIN 1/9/76.
RICKABY A. J. Born 13/4/41. Commd 2/3/61. Sqn Ldr 1/1/75. Retd SEC 13/4/79.
RICKARD D. K. Born 15/7/70. Commd 28/4/61. Sqn Ldr 1/1/72. Retd GD 15/7/78.
RICKARD F. P. Born 21/4/38. Commd 4/2/71. Flt Lt 4/2/73. Retd GD 1/1/90.
RICKARD F. W. Born 26/11/21. Commd 30/1/45. Flt Lt 11/6/53. Retd GD 10/5/67.
RICKARD P. E. Born 12/1/48. Commd 19/8/66. Sqn Ldr 1/7/83. Retd GD 1/7/86.
RICKARDS F. B. Born 16/8/29. Commd 5/12/51. Flt Lt 5/6/56. Retd GD 31/1/76 rtg Sqn Ldr.
RICKETS P. M., MBE. Born 16/3/23. Commd 30/4/45. Flt Lt 17/5/56. Retd SUP 16/3/79.
RICKETT R. C. A. Born 16/3/27. Commd 26/3/64. Flt Lt 26/3/67. Retd GD 3/7/73.
RICKETTS H. P. Born 29/6/13. Commd 10/12/42. Flt Lt 10/6/46. Retd ENG 19/3/47 rtg Sqn Ldr.
RICKETTS M. P. Born 26/6/33. Commd 6/4/72. Flt Lt 6/4/78. Retd ADMIN 6/4/84.
RICKINSON J. Born 31/7/41. Commd 7/11/85. Flt Lt 7/11/87. Retd ENG 31/7/96.
RICKWOOD R. P., MBE. Born 18/4/36. Commd 2/8/68. Sqn Ldr 1/1/77. Retd ENG 5/1/79.
RIDDELL G., BSc. Born 1/6/60. Commd 4/1/79. Sqn Ldr 1/1/94. Retd GD 31/3/99.
RIDDELL M. A. D., DFC DFM. Born 25/7/21. Commd 31/7/42. Flt Lt 31/1/46. Retd GD 26/7/54 rtg Sqn Ldr.
RIDDELL M. E. M. Born 13/7/13. Commd 27/10/41. Wg Offr 1/7/52. Retd SEC 13/6/68.
RIDDELL T. Born 23/5/51. Commd 2/1/75. Sqn Ldr 1/1/86. Retd GD 23/9/90.
RIDDETT G. O., BSc. Born 27/12/46. Commd 18/4/69. Flt Lt 15/4/71. Retd GD 1/4/89.
RIDE M. M. Born 31/12/26. Commd 28/2/51. Flt Lt 16/2/57. Retd GD 17/10/66.
RIDEAL E. C., OBE. Born 23/6/20. Commd 7/1/42. Sqn Ldr 1/1/56. Retd SEC 23/6/69.
RIDER W. J., BEd. Born 18/10/14. Commd 21/1/43. Sqn Ldr 1/7/63. Retd ENG 6/8/66.
RIDGE A. A. G., AFC. Born 12/12/24. Commd 17/10/57. Flt Lt 2/12/63. Retd GD 31/3/71.
RIDGEWAY F., MBE. Born 16/1/20. Commd 18/8/43. Wg Cdr 1/1/66. Retd SEC 1/2/74.
RIDGEWELL R. J. Born 8/1/18. Commd 8/7/54. Fl Lt 8/7/60. Retd GD(G) 11/4/74.

RIDGLEY M. G. Born 4/7/33. Commd 13/2/52. Flt Lt 12.6/57. Retd GD 4/7/71.
RIDGWAY C. A. Born 19/8/23. Commd 22/9/50. Flt Lt 22/9/54. Retd GD(G) 31/1/69.
RIDLER A. W., MA. Born 2/7/58. Commd 1/4/90. Flt Lt 1/10/91. Retd ADMIN 14/3/97.
RIDLEY C. R. A., BSc. Born 22/9/59. Commd 19/6/83. Flt Lt 19/12/85. Retd GD 21/3/00.
RIDLEY J. W., CEng MRAeS MIMgt. Born 30/5/23. Commd 2/10/58. Sqn Ldr 1/7/73. Retd ENG 26/3/77.
RIDLEY K. C. Born 2/7/56. Commd 19/7/84. Flt Lt 19/7/86. Retd GD 3/12/96.
RIDLEY N. M., MBE. Born 28/9/31. Commd 12/8/54. Wg Cdr 1/7/72. Retd SUP 29/9/81.
RIDLEY R. A., BSc. Born 16/11/42. Commd 15/7/64. Sqn Ldr 1/1/76. Retd ENG 16/11/80.
RIDLEY R. G. Born 23/2/27. Commd 9/3/50. Sqn Ldr 1/1/65. Retd GD 23/2/85.
RIDOUT H. J. Born 9/11/30. Commd 12/12/51. Sqn Ldr 1/7/60. Retd GD 9/11/68.
RIDOUT T. A. F. Born 5/2/23. Commd 20/6/45. Flt Lt 29/6/50. Retd GD 23/6/57.
RIDPATH F. T. Born 5/9/30. Commd 26/3/52. Flt Lt 14/9/60. Retd GD(G) 5/9/80.
RIGBY D. G. L. Born 31/5/26. Commd 16/7/52. Flt Lt 12/12/57. Retd GD 31/5/64.
RIGBY D. H. Born 17/5/34. Commd 29/10/52. Flt Lt 24/3/58. Retd GD 17/5/72.
RIGBY D. S. Born 27/4/45. Commd 21/1/66. Sqn Ldr 1/7/90. Retd GD 14/3/97.
RIGBY F. M. Born 17/11/29. Commd 20/12/51. Flt Lt 22/5/57. Retd GD 17/11/67.
RIGBY J. C. H., BA. Born 26/1/55. Commd 2/3/80. Flt Lt 2/6/83. Retd SY 1/10/93.
RIGBY P. Born 18/2/52. Commd 28/2/85. Flt Lt 28/2/87. Retd ENG 1/7/94.
RIGBY W. T. L. Born 16/10/23. Commd 29/6/50. Sqn Ldr 1/7/71. Retd GD 16/10/78.
RIGDEN K. F., BA. Born 2/8/54. Commd 30/10/77. Flt Lt 30/7/79. Retd GD 30/10/89.
RIGG E. C., MBE AFC MRAeS. Born 21/4/26. Commd 25/10/46. Wg Cdr 1/7/65. Retd GD 18/5/76.
RIGG H. W. J., AFC MRAeS. Born 28/7/34. Commd 10/4/56. Wg Cdr 1/7/76. Retd GD 12/7/85.
RIGG M. D. Born 9/6/43. Commd 14/7/66. Flt Lt 14/1/72. Retd GD 7/4/76.
RIGG S. M., MB ChB. Born 9/1/16. Commd 13/5/41. Wg Cdr 1/1/56. Retd MED 30/12/61.
RIGGS G. Born 5/10/12. Commd 7/6/44. Flt Lt 1/1/55. Retd SUP 1/5/54.
RILETT C. T. Born 8/4/17. Commd 24/6/43. Sqn Ldr 1/1/62. Retd ENG 8/4/72 rtg Wg Cdr.
RILEY B. A. Born 14/8/33. Commd 18/6/52. Wg Cdr 1/1/78. Retd GD 1/5/87.
RILEY D. Born 29/5/32. Commd 16/4/54. Flt Lt 13/4/60. Retd GD 15/6/72.
RILEY D., BSc. Born 4/12/35. Commd 20/10/69. Sqn Ldr 3/10/73. Retd ADMIN 4/12/85.
RILEY D. C. Born 8/8/58. Commd 21/4/77. Sqn Ldr 1/7/90. Retd GD 8/8/96.
RILEY D. G. Born 15/4/33. Commd 17/1/52. Wg Cdr 1/7/79. Retd GD 27/6/92.
RILEY D. J., BSc. Born 1/3/63. Commd 25/11/84. Flt Lt 25/5/87. Retd GD 1/3/01.
RILEY G. G. Born 24/11/60. Commd 13/12/79. Sqn Ldr 1/7/92. Retd GD 24/11/98.
RILEY H. R., CEng FIMgt MIERE MRAeS. Born 18/2/29. Commd 22/3/51. Gp Capt 1/7/73. Retd ENG 6/11/82.
RILEY J. A., MBE. Born 13/6/28. Commd 14/2/63. Sqn Ldr 1/7/74. Retd ENG 5/11/77. Re-instated 25/3/81 to 1/12/84.
RILEY J. J. Born 26/11/56. Commd 23/11/78. Sqn Ldr 1/1/91. Retd OPS SPT 26/11/00.
RILEY J. T. Born 12/2/22. Commd 2/11/44. Flt Lt 17/9/51. Retd GD 12/2/65.
RILEY L. J., BA. Born 28/5/23. Commd 6/11/52. Sqn Ldr 1/7/67. Retd GD 30/9/73.
RILEY P. M. Born 26/9/40. Commd 1/8/61. Sqn Ldr 1/7/70. Retd GD 31/12/77.
RILEY R. J. Born 24/4/27. Commd 2/6/47. Sqn Ldr 1/1/60. Retd SUP 24/4/65.
RILEY S. C. Born 15/6/51. Commd 28/11/69. Flt Lt 28/5/75. Retd GD 30/6/88.
RILEY T. Born 20/8/30. Commd 13/1/56. Flt Lt 14/5/61. Retd GD 20/8/68. Re-employed GD(G) 13/9/74 to 11/2/75.
RILEY T. J. Born 1/10/57. Commd 10/3/77. Flt Lt 10/9/82. Retd GD 1/10/95.
RILEY W. A. Born 27/5/48. Commd 7/6/68. Sqn Ldr 1/1/80. Retd ENG 27/5/86.
RILEY W. L. Born 29/3/22. Commd 22/10/43. Flt Lt 30/10/53. Retd SUP 31/3/62.
RIMER F. J. Born 30/1/08. Commd 17/1/40. Sqn Ldr 1/7/51. Retd ENG 30/11/57.
RIMINGTON R. Born 27/8/31. Commd 14/11/51. Sqn Ldr 1/7/63. Retd GD 27/8/69.
RIMINI F. M., BEM. Born 10/3/34. Commd 27/3/70. Sqn Ldr 16/8/80. Retd MED(T) 4/1/88.
RIMMER B. A. Born 12/6/29. Commd 23/2/54. Flt Lt 23/8/59. Retd GD 8/11/77.
RIMMER F. Born 24/7/23. Commd 4/9/46. Sqn Ldr 1/1/61. Retd GD 24/2/67.
RIMMER T. Born 3/11/21. Commd 27/1/44. Flt Lt 27/7/47. Retd ENG 26/4/56 rtg Sqn Ldr.
RING M. M. D., BEM. Born 25/4/24. Commd 12/3/64. Flt Lt 12/3/69. Retd SUP 25/4/79.
RINGER A. W., CBE MVO AFC* MIMgt. Born 22/8/21. Commd 17/1/45. Gp Capt 1/1/71. Retd GD 17/9/76.
RINGLAND D. C. M., BSc. Born 15/1/53. Commd 28/1/73. Sqn Ldr 1/7/85. Retd GD 28/1/97.
RINGROSE G. E., BSc. Born 19/10/30. Commd 5/11/52. Sqn Ldr 1/1/63. Retd ENG 5/11/68.
RIORDAN D. P., DFC. Born 17/9/32. Commd 19/7/51. Flt Lt 29/4/59. Retd GD 17/9/87.
RIORDAN M. H., BA. Born 21/11/33. Commd 5/10/56. Sqn Ldr 31/7/64. Retd EDN 3/1/68.
RIORDAN R. D. Born 18/12/43. Commd 21/9/72. Sqn Ldr 1/1/90. Retd GD(G) 18/12/94.
RIPLEY M. B. H., CEng. Born 25/2/38. Commd 6/8/63. Sqn Ldr 1/7/76. Retd ENG 20/1/89.
RIPPENGAL A. V., DFC DFM. Born 13/9/22. Commd 3/9/43. Flt Lt 7/6/51. Retd GD 13/9/77.
RIPPIN G. W. Born 17/8/34. Commd 30/7/52. Sqn Ldr 1/1/80. Retd GD 17/8/89.
RISBY A. E. Born 6/1/25. Commd 17/5/62. Sqn Ldr 1/7/71. Retd GD 31/1/74.
RISDALE N. L., DFC BSc. Born 9/4/59. Commd 28/12/80. Sqn Ldr 1/7/90. Retd GD 9/4/97.
RISELEY E. A. Born 26/1/23. Commd 16/6/44. Sqn Ldr 1/1/55. Retd GD 26/1/78.

RISELEY-PRICHARD R. A., MA BM BCh FFCM FIMgt. Born 19/2/25. Commd 1/3/51. AVM 1/1/81. Retd MED 19/2/85.
RITCHIE F. G. Born 19/5/20. Commd 16/2/45. Flt Lt 16/8/48. Retd GD(G) 29/6/62.
RITCHIE P., LLB. Born 16/10/35. Commd 28/11/58. Wg Cdr 16/10/73. Retd LGL 28/11/74.
RITCHIE P. W. Born 27/3/47. Commd 11/8/67. Flt Lt 11/2/73. Retd GD 1/7/90.
RITCHIE W. B. C., MBE. Born 8/1/33. Commd 21/5/52. Sqn Ldr 1/7/83. Retd GD 8/1/91.
RITCHLEY K., CBE AFC. Born 26/4/16. Commd 9/5/42. Gp Capt 1/1/61. Retd GD 17/5/71.
RIVERS J. L. S. Born 16/12/22. Commd 11/4/57. Sqn Ldr 1/7/70. Retd ENG 22/7/82.
RIVETT F. L. Born 13/10/37. Commd 24/4/56. Flt Lt 21/8/63. Retd GD 31/10/64.
RIX D. A. Born 9/4/44. Commd 12/7/63. Flt Lt 30/4/69. Retd GD 9/4/82 rtg Sqn Ldr.
RIXOM J. A., BSc. Born 24/6/32. Commd 1/3/61. A Cdre 1/1/81. Retd ENG 24/8/87.
RIXON J. J. Born 22/7/52. Commd 8/5/86. Flt Lt 8/5/88. Retd SUP 14/3/96.
RIXSON S. R. Born 19/5/52. Commd 9/10/75. Sqn Ldr 1/7/89. Retd GD 14/9/96.
ROACH A. Born 15/5/23. Commd 9/1/46. Flt Lt 15/12/53. Retd GD 15/5/66.
ROACH C. J. Born 28/4/44. Commd 21/4/67. Flt Lt 6/9/73. Retd GD(G) 1/7/92.
ROACHE R. B., DFC*. Born 16/7/21. Commd 19/2/41. Gp Capt 1/7/65. Retd GD 14/2/70.
ROBB B. S. Born 11/12/56. Commd 2/2/84. Flt Lt 14/3/86. Retd GD 1/6/98.
ROBB E. J. L. Born 17/4/14. Commd 21/8/41. Sqn Ldr 1/7/55. Retd ENG 17/4/63.
ROBB G. P., MBE. Born 7/12/24. Commd 13/12/68. Flt Lt 13/12/73. Retd ENG 7/12/84.
ROBB J. W. Born 7/1/38. Commd 25/7/59. Flt Lt 25/1/65. Retd GD 25/7/85.
ROBB R. C., OBE MB ChB MFCM DPhysMed DPH DIH. Born 30/5/22. Commd 17/10/46. A Cdre 1/1/73. Retd MED 1/7/76.
ROBBIE P. J., OBE. Born 11/4/46. Commd 3/3/67. Gp Capt 1/7/94. Retd GD 14/8/96.
ROBBINS F. M., CEng MIEE. Born 12/7/36. Commd 23/7/58. Sqn Ldr 1/1/68. Retd ENG 29/12/79.
ROBBINS J. A. Born 16/8/34. Commd 14/2/56. Flt Lt 14/8/61. Retd GD 16/8/72.
ROBBINS J. S., ACT(Bath) FHCIMA. Born 5/9/34. Commd 2/10/62. Sqn Ldr 1/7/74. Retd ADMIN 29/9/84.
ROBERSON N. J. Born 27/9/40. Commd 25/6/66. Flt Lt 8/1/69. Retd GD 27/9/95.
ROBERSON S. C. Born 16/2/36. Commd 17/6/54. Sqn Ldr 1/7/85. Retd GD 16/2/94.
ROBERT P. W., DFC. Born 1/9/09. Commd 27/2/44. Flt Lt 29/12/50. Retd CAT 5/9/64.
ROBERTS A. Born 14/11/45. Commd 26/5/67. Flt Lt 18/2/70. Retd GD 14/11/83.
ROBERTS A. J., BSc MB BS MRCGP DAvMed. Born 23/4/60. Commd 15/12/82. Wg Cdr 1/2/99. Retd MED 15/12/00.
ROBERTS A. J. Born 29/10/29. Commd 20/12/51. Flt Lt 8/4/57. Retd GD 29/10/67.
ROBERTS A. J. Born 25/8/57. Commd 15/3/79. Flt Lt 27/12/82. Retd GD 25/8/95.
ROBERTS A. J. A., DFC. Born 23/12/15. Commd 24/4/41. Sqn Ldr 1/8/47. Retd GD 23/12/57.
ROBERTS A. L., CB CBE AFC FRAeS. Born 19/5/38. Commd 16/12/58. AVM 1/1/87. Retd GD 5/4/94.
ROBERTS A. L. N. Born 20/5/28. Commd 14/8/70. Flt Lt 14/8/73. Retd GD 20/5/83.
ROBERTS A. M., AFC. Born 16/4/47. Commd 18/8/67. Sqn Ldr 1/7/80. Retd GD 16/4/85.
ROBERTS A. W., DPhysEd. Born 9/5/28. Commd 5/5/54. Wg Cdr 1/1/80. Retd ADMIN 14/6/83.
ROBERTS B. E. Born 16/8/81. Commd 5/8/76. Flt Lt 5/8/78. Retd ENG 5/8/84.
ROBERTS B. E. W. Born 18/1/17. Commd 29/7/53. Sqn Ldr 1/1/69. Retd GD(G) 1/9/70.
ROBERTS B. H., BEM. Born 6/4/21. Commd 27/4/61. Flt Lt 27/4/66. Retd SEC 1/4/70.
ROBERTS C. Born 9/2/49. Commd 31/7/70. Flt Lt 31/7/73. Retd GD 9/2/87.
ROBERTS C. E., BA. Born 9/3/09. Commd 20/4/50. Sqn Ldr 1/1/61. Retd SEC 9/3/63.
ROBERTS C. F. Born 13/4/45. Commd 22/5/64. Flt Lt 22/11/69. Retd GD 1/11/79.
ROBERTS C. P. Born 22/5/38. Commd 18/12/56. Sqn Ldr 1/7/89. Retd GD 22/5/96.
ROBERTS D. Born 22/8/29. Commd 8/10/52. Flt Lt 26/8/57. Retd GD 22/8/67.
ROBERTS D., DFC AFC. Born 6/5/23. Commd 20/2/43. Gp Capt 1/7/64. Retd GD 6/5/78.
ROBERTS D., BEng. Born 1/3/58. Commd 18/11/79. Flt Lt 18/2/81. Retd GD 1/10/97.
ROBERTS D., MBCS MCIPD CertEd. Born 13/11/43. Commd 30/10/83. Sqn Ldr 1/7/90. Retd ADMIN 1/11/95.
ROBERTS D. A. Born 20/11/35. Commd 27/1/77. Flt Lt. 27/1/82. Retd ADMIN 20/9/86.
ROBERTS D. P., MA MRAeS. Born 1/11/24. Commd 1/12/44. Sqn Ldr 1/10/56. Retd ENG 10/4/65.
ROBERTS D. W., BSc. Born 13/8/49. Commd 20/1/80. Sqn Ldr 1/7/91. Retd ADMIN 14/3/97.
ROBERTS E. Born 20/10/47. Commd 8/12/83. Flt Lt 8/12/87. Retd ADMIN 10/3/91.
ROBERTS E., MBE. Born 30/4/09. Commd 4/3/54. Flt Lt 4/3/57. Retd GD 30/4/64.
ROBERTS E. H. Born 7/8/29. Commd 3/9/52. Sqn Ldr 1/7/69. Retd GD 7/8/84.
ROBERTS E. S., MIMgt. Born 17/10/20. Commd 3/5/56. Sqn Ldr 1/7/65. Retd ENG 31/10/70.
ROBERTS E. W. Born 12/11/16. Commd 29/5/46. Flt Lt 29/11/50. Retd SEC 28/5/64.
ROBERTS F. Born 14/7/22. Commd 26/5/60. Flt Lt 26/5/63. Retd GD(G) 14/7/77.
ROBERTS F. E. Born 1/7/16. Commd 3/2/40. Sqn Offr 1/7/54. Retd SUP 26/8/55.
ROBERTS G., MA. Born 12/3/32. Commd 11/8/53. Sqn Ldr 1/7/62. Retd GD 7/4/72.
ROBERTS G. D. Born 10/4/45. Commd 14/7/66. Sqn Ldr 1/7/80. Retd GD 1/2/92.
ROBERTS G. P. Born 8/6/25. Commd 31/8/45. Wg Cdr 1/7/71. Retd GD 9/12/75.
ROBERTS H. D., BSc(Eng). Born 20/9/59. Commd 4/9/78. Flt Lt 15/10/82. Retd GD 13/4/93.
ROBERTS H. G. Born 9/9/12. Commd 28/5/45. Fg Offr 10/3/54. Retd GD(G) 11/6/60.
ROBERTS I. F. Born 16/8/49. Commd 8/8/69. Flt Lt 8/2/75. Retd GD 4/10/88.

ROBERTS J., DFM. Born 10/9/22. Commd 14/11/43. Flt Lt 14/5/47. Retd GD 10/9/60.
ROBERTS The Rev J. C., BA. Born 8/10/50. Commd 26/6/77. Retd 26/6/93 Wg Cdr.
ROBERTS J. G., DFC DFM. Born 25/2/21. Commd 10/7/42. Wg Cdr 1/1/58. Retd GD 26/7/60.
ROBERTS J. K. Born 19/8/15. Commd 24/11/43. Sqn Ldr 1/4/55. Retd GD 13/12/57.
ROBERTS J. L., MBE. Born 10/8/33. Commd 6/6/57. Wg Cdr 1/7/77. Retd PRT 10/8/91.
ROBERTS J. L. Born 11/10/37. Commd 2/3/61. Flt Lt 5/10/65. Retd SY 1/10/77.
ROBERTS J. M., CEng MIMechE MRAeS MIMgt. Born 20/10/29. Commd 28/10/56. Gp Capt 1/1/79. Retd ENG 20/10/84.
ROBERTS J. N. Born 24/12/35. Commd 9/2/66. Sqn Ldr 1/1/73. Retd PRT 1/10/74.
ROBERTS K. C., AFC. Born 26/5/18. Commd 24/11/37. Wg Cdr 1/1/52. Retd GD 2/6/65.
ROBERTS L. A. Born 10/1/16. Commd 21/9/50. Sqn Ldr 1/7/59. Retd ENG 10/1/74.
ROBERTS M. C. Born 5/6/43. Commd 17/12/65. Sqn Ldr 1/1/76. Retd SUP 14/6/84.
ROBERTS The Rev M. G., BA. Born 22/9/13. Commd 1/11/46. Retd 22/9/68 Wg Cdr.
ROBERTS M. H. W. Born 18/9/40. Commd 3/2/64. Sqn Ldr 1/7/80. Retd SUP 2/4/93.
ROBERTS N. J., FISM MInstAM MIMgt. Born 17/2/55. Commd 15/8/85. Sqn Ldr 1/1/96. Retd ADMIN 15/8/99.
ROBERTS P. Born 6/9/57. Commd 24/6/76. Gp Capt 1/1/99. Retd OPS SPT 12/4/01.
ROBERTS P. A. Born 3/2/31. Commd 4/7/51. Wg Cdr 1/7/73. Retd GD 20/6/85.
ROBERTS P. A. B., MSc BSc CEng MRAeS MIQA. Born 25/7/51. Commd 25/2/72. Sqn Ldr 1/1/84. Retd ENG 01/10/90.
ROBERTS P. B. Born 2/6/34. Commd 4/2/53. Flt Lt 24/6/58. Retd GD 2/6/92.
ROBERTS P. E. Born 4/6/39. Commd 22/7/71. Flt Lt 22/7/73. Retd ENG 4/6/81.
ROBERTS P. H. P. Born 20/8/22. Commd 28/11/43. Sqn Ldr 1/10/54. Retd GD 21/11/60.
ROBERTS P. J. Born 1/5/60. Commd 17/5/79. Sqn Ldr 1/1/96. Retd GD 6/6/00.
ROBERTS P. J., MB BS MRCS LRCP DA. Born 10/10/46. Commd 8/8/71. Wg Cdr 21/1/87. Retd MED 18/12/92.
ROBERTS P. K. Born 22/1/56. Commd 15/3/84. Flt Lt 15/3/86. Retd ENG 1/6/94.
ROBERTS P. M. Born 12/3/58. Commd 27/1/77. Flt Lt 27/7/82. Retd GD 1/6/89.
ROBERTS R. A. P. Born 27/1/03. Commd 15/8/23. Flt Lt 29/5/29. Retd GD 25/8/35.
ROBERTS R. D., OBE CEng MRAeS FIMgt. Born 29/3/20. Commd 19/8/42. Gp Capt 1/7/70. Retd ENG 29/3/75.
ROBERTS R. E. Born 11/3/41. Commd 13/12/79. Sqn Ldr 1/1/88. Retd ENG 16/9/93.
ROBERTS R. J., MBE. Born 11/5/32. Commd 14/4/53. Sqn Ldr 1/7/64. Retd GD 24/1/86.
ROBERTS R. L. A., DFM. Born 25/5/25. Commd 19/9/44. Gp Capt 1/7/74. Retd ADMIN 25/5/80.
ROBERTS R. V. Born 11/1/10. Commd 17/4/47. Fg Offr 17/4/49. Retd SUP 6/1/50.
ROBERTS S. B. Born 18/6/37. Commd 26/3/64. Flt Lt 25/7/70. Retd GD(G) 1/6/81.
ROBERTS S. G., BA. Born 3/8/57. Commd 23/9/79. Flt Lt 23/12/81 Pl. Retd Pl 13/12/82.
ROBERTS T. A., DFC. Born 21/6/21. Commd 1/5/42. Flt Lt 1/11/45. Retd ENG 15/5/55.
ROBERTS T. K. Born 30/9/37. Commd 11/11/71. Flt Lt 11/11/73. Retd GD(G) 12/11/76.
ROBERTS V. J., MInstAM(Dip) MIMgt. Born 24/5/43. Commd 8/10/70. Flt Lt 8/10/72. Retd SEC 24/5/81 rtg Sqn Ldr.
ROBERTS W. A. B., OBE. Born 4/7/44. Commd 29/11/63. Wg Cdr 1/1/87. Retd GD 4/7/00.
ROBERTS W. J., OBE CEng FIERE DipEl. Born 19/5/23. Commd 14/10/43. Wg Cdr 1/7/61. Retd ENG 19/5/73.
ROBERTS W. J. H. Born 12/10/21. Commd 13/7/44. Gp Capt 1/1/68. Retd GD 30/1/77.
ROBERTS W. R. Born 6/4/20. Commd 23/9/43. Sqn Ldr 1/1/63. Retd ENG 7/4/75.
ROBERTSHAW K., LLB. Born 18/3/43. Commd 6/9/65. Wg Cdr 1/1/85. Retd GD 31/3/93.
ROBERTSHAW R. J., BSc. Born 24/10/56. Commd 31/8/75. Flt Lt 15/10/79. Retd GD 15/3/91.
ROBERTSHAW S. Born 1/10/57. Commd 11/4/85. Flt Lt 11/4/87. Retd GD(G) 1/10/95.
ROBERTSON A., MITD MIPM MIMgt. Born 13/1/35. Commd 22/5/59. Wg Cdr 1/7/79. Retd ADMIN 21/10/87.
ROBERTSON A. J. L. Born 19/4/45. Commd 24/4/70. Sqn Ldr 1/1/82. Retd GD(G) 1/12/85.
ROBERTSON A. R., BSc. Born 26/3/84. Commd 11/9/77. Flt Lt 11/6/78. Retd GD 11/9/93.
ROBERTSON B. H. Born 1/7/14. Commd 16/6/41. Flt Lt 1/9/45. Retd SEC 20/8/51.
ROBERTSON C. D. Born 26/6/60. Commd 15/2/90. Flt Lt 25/7/92. Retd ENG 31/3/99.
ROBERTSON D. C., BSc. Born 7/2/63. Commd 2/9/84. Sqn Ldr 1/1/98. Retd GD 7/2/01.
ROBERTSON D. G. W. Born 14/9/24. Commd 3/5/51. Flt Lt 1/11/56. Retd GD 14/9/62.
ROBERTSON D. H. Born 20/5/30. Commd 9/11/55. Flt Lt 1/10/67. Retd GD 2/7/69.
ROBERTSON D. S. T., MBE. Born 5/5/24. Commd 4/10/51. Sqn Ldr 1/7/62. Retd ADMIN 1/9/77.
ROBERTSON E. Born 24/9/43. Commd 20/7/78. Flt Lt 20/7/80. Retd GD(G) 20/7/86.
ROBERTSON E. S., CEng MRAeS MIMgt. Born 18/6/19. Commd 19/8/42. Wg Cdr 1/7/70. Retd ENG 18/6/74.
ROBERTSON F. H. Born 10/8/24. Commd 29/12/44. Flt Lt 29/12/50. Retd GD(G) 10/8/74.
ROBERTSON G. Born 3/2/35. Commd 17/12/52. Sqn Ldr 1/1/66. Retd GD 10/3/89.
ROBERTSON G., MPhil BA CEng MIEE. Born 9/5/48. Commd 28/2/69. Wg Cdr 1/7/90. Retd ENG 4/12/98.
ROBERTSON G. Born 23/7/43. Commd 28/2/85. Sqn Ldr 1/7/94. Retd ENG 24/10/97.
ROBERTSON G. A., CBE BA FRAeS FRSA. Born 22/2/45. Commd 15/7/66. AM 18/3/96. Retd GD 9/12/98.
ROBERTSON G. B., AFC BSc. Born 18/11/41. Commd 22/9/63. Wg Cdr 1/7/77. Retd GD 1/7/80.
ROBERTSON G. M. Born 24/3/47. Commd 25/8/67. Fg Offr 25/2/70. Retd ENG 14/9/72.
ROBERTSON H. D. Born 18/3/15. Commd 27/3/44. Flt Lt 6/10/48. Retd ENG 21/4/64.
ROBERTSON I. K. Born 7/1/31. Commd 21/1/54. Flt Lt 8/6/59. Retd GD 7/1/69.
ROBERTSON I. M. Born 26/9/45. Commd 15/7/66. Wg Cdr 1186. Retd GD 26/9/00.

ROBERTSON I. McK., BSc MBCS. Born 23/4/43. Commd 10/7/67. Sqn Ldr 1/7/79. Retd ENG 10/7/83.
ROBERTSON J. MacG. Born 14/4/26. Commd 8/4/49. Gp Capt 1/1/71. Retd GD 26/5/72.
ROBERTSON J. N. Born 19/12/27. Commd 16/2/53. Flt Lt 5/11/58. Retd GD 16/2/69.
ROBERTSON K. F. Born 25/12/38. Commd 16/11/59. Sqn Ldr 1/7/71. Retd GD 28/1/72.
ROBERTSON L. A., MBE. Born 15/6/23. Commd 15/5/42. Flt Lt 1/8/51. Retd GD 31/7/57.
ROBERTSON M. J., BSc CEng MRAeS. Born 21/7/48. Commd 13/9/71. Flt Lt 15/4/76. Retd ENG 13/9/87.
ROBERTSON N. A. Born 18/7/46. Commd 23/9/66. Flt Lt 4/5/72. Retd GD 1/4/89.
ROBERTSON N. D., BA. Born 11/5/56. Commd 6/10/75. Flt Lt 15/10/78. Retd GD 15/7/90.
ROBERTSON P. W., MD ChB. Born 6/11/23. Commd 12/8/48. Wg Cdr 1/5/60. Retd MED 30/12/67.
ROBERTSON R. F., MIMgt. Born 17/10/35. Commd 30/7/57. Gp Capt 1/7/79. Retd SUP 5/5/90.
ROBERTSON R. J. Born 23/11/23. Commd 8/11/62. Sqn Ldr 1/7/72. Retd ENG 15/5/75.
ROBERTSON R. McC., MA. Born 9/12/22. Commd 17/4/45. Sqn Ldr 17/8/61. Retd EDN 19/5/71.
ROBERTSON R. S., MBE. Born 1/2/34. Commd 5/11/70. Sqn Ldr 1/1/80. Retd ADMIN 17/6/84.
ROBERTSON V. C. Born 31/8/39. Commd 2/10/61. Sqn Ldr 1/1/74. Retd GD 1/10/88.
ROBERTSON W. D., CBE. Born 24/6/22. Commd 10/7/43. A Cdre 1/1/69. Retd GD 29/1/77.
ROBINS E. A. Born 27/3/10. Commd 3/10/46. Flt Lt 11/11/54. Retd SUP 11/10/66.
ROBINS I. H. R., MBE MRAeS MIMgt. Born 10/4/39. Commd 18/2/58. Wg Cdr 1/1/86. Retd GD 31/5/90.
ROBINS V. A., DFC. Born 19/6/22. Commd 15/4/43. Sqn Ldr 1/7/65. Retd GD 20/6/73.
ROBINSON A. Born 5/6/16. Commd 21/6/45. Flt Lt 21/12/49. Retd CAT 5/6/71.
ROBINSON A. J. Born 6/4/37. Commd 29/7/55. Sqn Ldr 1/1/83. Retd GD 27/7/91.
ROBINSON A. R. Born 13/3/41. Commd 21/5/65. Flt Lt 21/11/71. Retd GD(G) 29/11/94.
ROBINSON A. T. Born 3/5/20. Commd 29/7/50. Retd RGT 11/2/58.
ROBINSON B. Born 29/12/33. Commd 26/10/61. Fg Offr 26/10/61. Retd GD 25/7/65.
ROBINSON B. L., FIMgt. Born 2/7/36. Commd 7/12/54. AVM 1/7/89. Retd GD 2/7/91.
ROBINSON B. N., MIPM MIMgt. Born 12/1/25. Commd 10/5/46. Sqn Ldr 1/1/73. Retd SEC 1/11/73.
ROBINSON C. Born 25/1/33. Commd 3/9/52. Flt Lt 21/10/58. Retd GD 25/1/71.
ROBINSON C. A. Born 8/6/61. Commd 14/1/82. Flt Lt 14/7/87. Retd GD 14/3/96.
ROBINSON C. A. Born 31/8/48. Commd 8/11/68. Sqn Ldr 1/7/83. Retd RGT 1/10/90.
ROBINSON C. B. G., AFC. Born 29/9/11. Commd 7/9/36. Wg Cdr 1/10/46. Retd GD 20/4/48.
ROBINSON C. I. Born 6/7/43. Commd 14/9/64. Flt Lt 14/3/70. Retd GD 31/3/93.
ROBINSON C. P. Born 26/11/37. Commd 22/1/57. Flt Lt 7/8/64. Retd GD 29/4/78.
ROBINSON C. R. N. Born 30/7/54. Commd 5/7/73. Flt Lt 5/1/79. Retd GD 7/1/79.
ROBINSON D. A. Born 17/4/50. Commd 10/2/72. Plt Offr 10/2/72. Retd GD(G) 26/6/73.
ROBINSON D. B. Born 26/7/27. Commd 8/4/49. Wg Cdr 1/1/63. Retd GD 26/7/82 rtg Gp Capt.
ROBINSON D. C., FIMgt MInst PS. Born 12/11/28. Commd 5/4/50. A Cdre 1/7/78. Retd SUP 12/11/83.
ROBINSON D. E. Born 8/10/42. Commd 2/5/69. Flt Lt 30/8/75. Retd SUP 7/1/85.
ROBINSON D. G., MBE FTCL LRAM ARCO(CHM) ARCM. Born 4/9/31. Commd 18/3/60. Flt Lt 18/3/66. Retd DM 9/2/72.
ROBINSON D. G. Born 14/9/41. Commd 25/1/63. Sqn Ldr 1/7/75. Retd GD 14/9/79.
ROBINSON D. McI. Born 16/9/35. Commd 20/8/55. Sqn Ldr 1/1/68. Retd GD 16/9/73.
ROBINSON E., OBE. Born 20/1/22. Commd 6/11/42. Sqn Ldr 1/4/55. Retd GD 20/1/65.
ROBINSON E. T., BEM. Born 29/4/22. Commd 6/10/60. Sqn Ldr 1/1/70. Retd ENG 7/7/72.
ROBINSON F. G. M., MBE CEng FRAeS MIMechE. Born 5/6/28. Commd 5/12/51. A Cdre 1/7/81. Retd ENG 1/7/83.
ROBINSON G. G. Born 8/4/21. Commd 21/10/43. Sqn Ldr 1/7/69. Retd GD(G) 30/3/78.
ROBINSON G. H. Born 12/6/22. Commd 29/6/43. Flt Lt 14/1/51. Retd GD 28/6/66.
ROBINSON H. B. Born 13/7/20. Commd 19/1/42. Flt Lt 14/7/49. Retd GD(G) 25/8/61.
ROBINSON H. R. Born 18/3/32. Commd 6/12/51. Sqn Ldr 1/7/72. Retd GD(G) 9/12/83.
ROBINSON I. D., BSc CEng MIMechE. Born 29/6/57. Commd 2/1/75. Flt Lt 15/4/81. Retd ENG 29/6/95.
ROBINSON I. G., BA. Born 14/4/56. Commd 19/6/83. Flt Lt 19/12/85. Retd GD 19/6/99.
ROBINSON I. L. J., CEng MRAeS MIMgt. Born 17/6/20. Commd 25/8/55. Sqn Ldr 1/7/67. Retd ENG 17/6/75.
ROBINSON J., DPhysEd. Born 28/3/31. Commd 13/4/56. Flt Lt 13/4/60. Retd PE 13/4/62.
ROBINSON J. Born 11/6/13. Commd 21/3/41. Sqn Ldr 1/7/53. Retd SEC 11/6/62.
ROBINSON J. A., AFC MRAeS. Born 8/3/32. Commd 17/12/52. Wg Cdr 1/1/72. Retd GD 3/1/78.
ROBINSON J. B., AFC. Born 29/3/34. Commd 10/9/52. Sqn Ldr 1/1/71. Retd GD 31/2/75.
ROBINSON J. H. Born 29/9/21. Commd 15/9/60. Flt Lt 15/9/65. Retd ENG 6/4/68.
ROBINSON J. H. Born 16/2/33. Commd 8/10/70. Sqn Ldr 1/1/84. Retd ENG 21/4/92.
ROBINSON J. L., MA BA BA CertEd. Born 9/3/37. Commd 13/9/70. Wg Cdr 1/7/85. Retd ADMIN 25/10/89.
ROBINSON J. M. Born 24/2/31. Commd 24/6/55. Flt Lt 6/3/63. Retd GD(G) 24/8/92.
ROBINSON J. R., AFC. Born 2/8/19. Commd 20/10/41. Sqn Ldr 1/1/52. Retd GD 2/8/62.
ROBINSON J. S. Born 6/6/42. Commd 17/12/63. Sqn Ldr 1/1/75. Retd GD 6/6/82.
ROBINSON K., BSc. Born 20/3/41. Commd 1/3/62. Wg Cdr 1/7/86. Retd SY(PRT) 1/7/88.
ROBINSON K. H. A. Born 6/12/34. Commd 24/4/70. Flt Lt 24/4/75. Retd ENG 26/4/75.
ROBINSON K. W., MB BCh MRCGP DRCOG DAvMed. Born 9/3/47. Commd 25/11/68. Sqn Ldr 16/8/77. Retd MED 27/5/85.
ROBINSON L. A. Born 26/9/34. Commd 8/9/58. Sqn Ldr 1/1/90. Retd GD 26/9/92.
ROBINSON L. T. Born 24/11/23. Commd 2/6/44. Flt Lt 29/6/50. Retd GD 24/11/66.

ROBINSON L. W. Born 30/9/24. Commd 8/11/62. Flt Lt 8/11/67. Retd GD(G) 1/10/74.
ROBINSON M . W. Born 31/12/48. Commd 24/6/71. Flt Lt 24/12/76. Retd GD 31/12/86.
ROBINSON M., BSc CEng MRAeS. Born 22/3/57. Commd 17/7/87. Sqn Ldr 1/7/96. Retd ENG 10/4/00.
ROBINSON M. H., BSc. Born 28/5/35. Commd 5/2/57. Flt Lt 5/11/58. Retd GD 15/4/64.
ROBINSON M. I., BSc. Born 9/12/60. Commd 11/9/83. Flt Lt 11/3/86. Retd GD 16/12/95.
ROBINSON M. J., BTech CEng MIMechE. Born 14/2/59. Commd 13/2/83. Sqn Ldr 1/1/93. Retd ENG 13/2/99.
ROBINSON M. L. R., MA. Born 27/6/59. Commd 4/9/78. Flt Lt 15/10/82. Retd GD 27/6/97.
ROBINSON M. M. J., CB FIMgt. Born 11/2/27. Commd 7/4/48. AVM 1/7/80. Retd GD 1/7/82.
ROBINSON N. Born 26/4/22. Commd 18/8/44. Flt Lt 10/7/48. Retd GD 31/3/62.
ROBINSON P. B. Born 6/7/26. Commd 16/5/49. Sqn Ldr 1/1/61. Retd RGT 6/10/67.
ROBINSON P. G., BSc. Born 24/10/44. Commd 15/7/66. Sqn Ldr 1/1/78. Retd ENG 24/12/88.
ROBINSON P. H. J. Born 26/4/34. Commd 28/3/60. Sqn Ldr 1/1/73. Retd GD 26/4/89.
ROBINSON P. N. Born 15/4/45. Commd 11/11/65. Wg Cdr 1/7/88. Retd ENG 14/4/98.
ROBINSON P. T., BA BSc. Born 9/6/38. Commd 8/8/58. Sqn Ldr 9/12/67. Retd ADMIN 9/6/76.
ROBINSON R., MBE. Born 21/6/21. Commd 20/9/49. Sqn Ldr 1/7/69. Retd SEC 21/6/81.
ROBINSON R. G. Born 2/6/24. Commd 30/7/64. Flt Lt 30/7/67. Retd GD 10/6/82.
ROBINSON R. M. Born 3/9/44. Commd 11/9/64. Flt Lt 8/3/72. Retd GD 29/9/88.
ROBINSON R. P. Born 5/12/44. Commd 20/8/65. Sqn Ldr 1/7/86. Retd GD 2/4/93.
ROBINSON S., FCA MIMgt. Born 26/1/16. Commd 29/7/39. Wg Cdr 1/1/56. Retd SEC 29/7/63.
ROBINSON T., BSc. Born 31/7/63. Commd 22/6/86. Flt Lt 22/12/88. Retd GD 22/6/98.
ROBINSON T. Born 23/5/45. Commd 23/9/68. Flt Lt 23/3/73. Retd ENG 31/3/76.
ROBINSON T. A., MBE. Born 15/12/24. Commd 11/1/51. Wg Cdr 1/7/70. Retd GD 15/12/82.
ROBINSON T. B. Born 1/10/19. Commd 26/3/42. Sqn Ldr 1/7/54. Retd ENG 1/6/63.
ROBINSON T. D. Born 22/9/64. Commd 15/3/84. Flt Lt 15/9/89. Retd GD 10/12/96.
ROBINSON W., MBE. Born 10/1/17. Commd 23/9/43. Sqn Ldr 1/1/62. Retd ENG 11/10/69.
ROBINSON W. E., MBE MIMgt. Born 1/1/21. Commd 18/5/61. Sqn Ldr 1/7/69. Retd ENG 11/4/79.
ROBINSON W. W., CEng MIEE. Born 22/1/45. Commd 15/7/65. Gp Capt 1/1/91. Retd ENG 14/9/96.
ROBINSON-BROWN S. J. Born 18/12/57. Commd 5/4/79. Flt Lt 13/9/85. Retd SY 1/10/87.
ROBSON A. J. R., DFC. Born 27/7/22. Commd 13/3/44. Flt Lt 13/9/47. Retd SEC 31/12/65.
ROBSON A. N. Born 8/4/35. Commd 7/5/59. Sqn Ldr 1/1/74. Retd ADMIN 1/7/80.
ROBSON B., MSc BSc CEng MRAeS. Born 20/8/38. Commd 30/9/58. Wg Cdr 1/1/80. Retd ENG 3/10/92.
ROBSON F. Born 16/12/19. Commd 24/10/41. Flt Lt 19/2/46. Retd ENG 19/4/55.
ROBSON J. Born 4/8/46. Commd 12/3/87. Sqn Ldr 1/1/98. Retd GD 1/7/99.
ROBSON J. D., MA. Born 25/10/31. Commd 17/10/54. Sqn Ldr 1/1/68. Retd SEC 1/1/71.
ROBSON K., MIMgt. Born 30/6/33. Commd 10/10/63. Wg Cdr 1/7/80. Retd ENG 3/7/84.
ROBSON K. Born 9/3/59. Commd 8/9/77. Flt Lt 8/3/83. Retd GD 9/3/97.
ROBSON N. Born 21/8/24. Commd 28/4/45. Sqn Ldr 1/7/71. Retd GD(G) 23/5/78.
ROBSON R. Born 2/7/45. Commd 17/7/64. Flt Lt 17/1/70. Retd GD 4/10/92.
ROBSON R. A. M., MIMgt AIL. Born 23/9/52. Commd 3/12/70. Sqn Ldr 1/1/84. Retd ADMIN 31/1/90.
ROBSON R. H., MA. Born 2/8/29. Commd 12/12/51. Flt Lt 12/6/54. Retd GD 30/8/67.
ROBSON R. M., OBE FIMgt. Born 22/4/35. Commd 28/7/55. AVM 1/7/87. Retd GD 7/11/87.
ROBSON S. M. Born 21/4/46. Commd 8/8/69. Sqn Ldr 1/1/85. Retd ENG 1/1/88.
ROBSON T. D., BA MIMgt DipEd. Born 23/9/42. Commd 13/6/66. Sqn Ldr 1/1/87. Retd ADMIN 7/4/97.
ROBSON W., BA. Born 2/5/36. Commd 27/8/58. Flt Lt 12/1/65. Retd GD 23/6/77.
ROCH J. W., DFC. Born 30/10/13. Commd 5/11/42. Sqn Ldr 1/10/57. Retd SEC 12/11/68.
ROCHARD E. B. Born 3/7/23. Commd 16/5/49. Flt Lt 7/6/51. Retd RGT 29/2/60.
ROCHE J. P. Born 10/8/28. Commd 29/3/68. Fg Offr 29/3/68. Retd SEC 2/6/73.
ROCHE P. J. Born 21/8/29. Commd 23/12/61. Flt Lt 23/12/67. Retd GD 21/8/84.
ROCHE T. J., BA. Born 30/3/60. Commd 4/8/78. Sqn Ldr 1/7/91. Retd GD 30/3/98.
ROCHESTER E., MIMgt. Born 10/8/35. Commd 26/5/61. Gp Capt 1/7/82. Retd GD(G) 19/9/89.
ROCHESTER G. W. Born 15/3/28. Commd 18/9/47. Flt Lt 10/11/55. Retd RGT 15/3/66.
ROCHFORT B. J. J., FCIPD FIMgt. Born 7/7/38. Commd 4/10/56. Wg Cdr 1/1/77. Retd SY 7/7/86.
ROCHFORT J. Born 22/4/45. Commd 4/12/64. Flt Lt 4/6/70. Retd GD 1/4/87.
ROCK K. G., FCIPD MIMgt. Born 7/10/34. Commd 14/5/60. Flt Lt 14/11/65. Retd GD 2/4/75.
ROCKALL R. M. Born 4/6/33. Commd 15/9/60. Flt Lt 15/3/65. Retd GD 4/6/71.
ROCKEL L. A. Born 11/4/45. Commd 21/7/65. Flt Lt 8/3/72. Retd GD 29/4/77.
ROCKINGHAM P. Born 4/8/20. Commd 22/9/55. Flt Lt 22/9/61. Retd GD(G) 4/8/70.
ROCKLIFFE E. A. Born 7/12/20. Commd 29/9/41. Sqn Ldr 1/7/53. Retd GD 1/1/58.
RODDA S. G. Born 27/2/46. Commd 11/11/71. Wg Cdr 1/1/94. Retd GD 27/2/01.
RODDIS S. T. E., BSc. Born 3/5/48. Commd 11/3/73. Flt Lt 11/6/73. Retd GD 1/9/89.
RODEN R. F. Born 31/12/27. Commd 30/9/53. Flt Lt 7/7/59. Retd GD 30/5/70.
RODEN T. G. V., MRCS LRCP DPH. Born 8/1/20. Commd 14/11/40. Wg Cdr 23/2/62. Retd MED 23/1/63.
RODGER M. W., BA. Born 29/5/35. Commd 27/4/70. Sqn Ldr 31/12/72. Retd ADMIN 27/4/87.
RODGER R. H. Born 11/7/10. Commd 14/1/43. Flt Lt 27/10/58. Retd SUP 16/2/62.
RODGERS D. L., BA. Born 18/11/47. Commd 21/1/66. Wg Cdr 1/1/87. Retd GD 18/11/91.
RODGERS I. A. Born 8/4/43. Commd 9/12/65. Sqn Ldr 1/7/79. Retd ADMIN 1/7/82.

RODGERS J. B., MSc BSc CEng FIMA FCA MRAeS. Born 5/10/30. Commd 28/5/57. Wg Cdr 28/7/73. Retd ADMIN 28/4/76.
RODGERS J. D. Born 23/1/63. Commd 16/12/82. Sqn Ldr 1/1/98. Retd OPS SPT 23/1/01.
RODGERS M. M., BCom. Born 16/9/26. Commd 17/5/50. Flt Offr 17/11/55. Retd SEC 29/7/60.
RODGERS P. J., MBE. Born 25/11/43. Commd 9/8/63. Gp Capt 1/1/97. Retd OPS SPT 25/11/98.
RODWAY J. Born 4/11/46. Commd 11/9/64. Plt Offr 11/9/65. Retd GD 2/9/66.
ROE M. Born 27/6/44. Commd 20/9/68. Flt Lt 20/3/74. Retd GD 31/12/84.
ROE Sir Rex., GCB AFC. Born 4/5/25. Commd 29/3/45. ACM 1/12/78. Retd GD 1/8/81.
ROE S. J. B. Born 21/6/18. Commd 19/10/43. Sqn Ldr 1/7/63. Retd PE 21/6/73.
ROEBUCK A. F. Born 30/6/45. Commd 5/3/65. Flt Lt 5/9/70. Retd GD 29/3/74.
ROEBUCK R. F., FCIS. Born 6/9/42. Commd 9/12/65. Sqn Ldr 1/7/80. Retd ADMIN 18/6/93.
ROFFEY H. H. Born 28/2/24. Commd 18/4/44. Sqn Ldr 1/7/60. Retd GD 28/2/79.
ROGAN T. J. Born 21/9/41. Commd 12/1/62. Flt Lt 1/7/68. Retd GD 31/8/80.
ROGERS A. C. Born 26/1/41. Commd 5/3/65. Flt Lt 5/9/70. Retd GD 24/3/73.
ROGERS A. P. Born 20/11/54. Commd 3/10/74. Fg Offr 3/4/77. Retd ADMIN 17/2/78.
ROGERS B. A. Born 25/1/34. Commd 26/7/55. Flt Lt 26/7/60. Retd SEC 25/1/72.
ROGERS B. N. Born 16/11/37. Commd 29/7/58. Sqn Ldr 1/7/69. Retd GD 1/2/90.
ROGERS C. Born 16/2/54. Commd 2/8/90. Flt Lt 2/8/94. Retd ENG 14/9/96.
ROGERS C. A. Born 19/8/1900. Commd 19/6/42. Flt Lt 2/9/45. Retd ENG 25/10/48.
ROGERS C. G., DFC. Born 16/2/23. Commd 22/1/43. Flt Lt 22/7/46. Retd GD 22/8/64.
ROGERS D. R. Born 27/8/58. Commd 5/4/79. Flt Lt 5/10/84. Retd GD 5/4/87.
ROGERS E. W. Born 27/7/47. Commd 8/10/87. Flt Lt 8/10/91. Retd ENG 6/6/00.
ROGERS G. A. Born 23/12/51. Commd 12/4/73. Flt Lt 12/10/78. Retd GD 16/1/82.
ROGERS G. B. Born 17/4/40. Commd 19/8/58. Wg Cdr 1/7/77. Retd GD(G) 6/3/85.
ROGERS G. F., BA MCIPD. Born 7/5/52. Commd 28/12/71. Sqn Ldr 1/1/86. Retd ADMIN 1/10/89.
ROGERS G. W. Born 23/12/17. Commd 8/6/54. Flt Lt 8/6/59. Retd ENG 23/12/61.
ROGERS Sir John, KCB CBE CBIM FRAeS. Born 11/1/28. Commd 5/4/50. ACM 1/1/84. Retd GD 31/3/86.
ROGERS J. Born 27/8/22. Commd 27/1/43. Flt Offr 27/1/48. Retd GD(G) 15/3/52.
ROGERS J. E. G. Born 17/12/29. Commd 2/7/52. Flt Lt 4/5/60. Retd SUP 25/7/73.
ROGERS J. H., AFC MIMgt. Born 6/2/24. Commd 1/10/43. Wg Cdr 1/7/61. Retd GD 29/10/76.
ROGERS J. K., OBE FIMgt. Born 20/1/24. Commd 20/8/43. Gp Capt 1/1/71. Retd GD(G) 31/3/78.
ROGERS J. N. Born 30/4/52. Commd 1/8/74. Flt Lt 4/9/76. Retd GD 11/9/79.
ROGERS J. P. Born 8/4/46. Commd 9/10/75. Gp Capt 21/3/94. Retd ADMIN 20/1/96.
ROGERS J. S., BEng. Born 5/7/73. Commd 6/4/97. Fg Offr 6/4/96. Retd GD 19/7/00.
ROGERS K. B., DFC AFC. Born 11/10/22. Commd 11/9/43. Wg Cdr 1/1/59. Retd GD 16/7/66.
ROGERS L., BSc. Born 16/9/46. Commd 11/5/71. Flt Lt 11/2/72. Retd GD 11/5/87.
ROGERS L. R. Born 21/10/19. Commd 29/6/50. Sqn Ldr 1/7/64 Retd SUP 20/9/68.
ROGERS M. A., OBE. Born 3/10/47. Commd 30/5/71. Gp Capt 1/7/95. Retd ENG 11/12/99.
ROGERS M. H., MB ChB MFCM DRCOG AFOM FIMgt. Born 26/7/30. Commd 29/8/54. A Cdre 1/7/81. Retd MED 5/4/85.
ROGERS M. J. Born 12/4/26. Commd 16/11/51. Flt Lt 16/5/56. Retd GD 12/4/64.
ROGERS N. C. Born 14/11/58. Commd 18/10/81. Sqn Ldr 1/1/94. Retd GD 18/10/97.
ROGERS P. A., DipPE. Born 24/12/46. Commd 22/8/71. Flt Lt 22/8/75. Retd ADMIN 22/8/87.
ROGERS P. C. H. Born 22/10/61. Commd 6/11/80. Flt Lt 6/5/86. Retd GD 3/1/99.
ROGERS P. F., OBE BA. Born 28/5/32. Commd 28/2/52. Gp Capt 1/7/78. Retd GD 2/10/86.
ROGERS P. J., BA. Born 13/11/49. Commd 13/9/70. Sqn Ldr 1/1/85. Retd GD 1/1/88.
ROGERS P. L. Born 11/8/42. Commd 30/8/62. Flt Lt 8/1/69. Retd ADMIN 11/8/80.
ROGERS P. M. Born 5/7/37. Commd 30/5/69. Flt Lt 30/5/71. Retd GD 26/7/74.
ROGERS R. J. Born 8/11/46. Commd 11/9/64. Flt Lt 11/3/70. Retd GD 10/11/96.
ROGERS R. J. Born 19/9/34. Commd 10/9/52. Wg Cdr 1/7/79. Retd GD 31/8/86.
ROGERS R. M., MIMgt. Born 31/3/20. Commd 24/3/39. Sqn Ldr 1/1/61. Retd SUP 31/3/75.
ROGERS R. S. Born 21/11/50. Commd 30/1/70. Flt Lt 30/7/75. Retd GD 21/11/88.
ROGERS S. F. Born 23/6/08. Commd 1/12/41. Fg Offr 14/12/44. Retd ENG 19/6/46.
ROGERS T. G. P. Born 3/8/06. Retd 17/12/41. Fg Offr 1/11/42. Retd ENG 9/2/47 rtg Flt Lt.
ROGERS T. V. Born 19/9/43. Commd 22/3/63. Wg Cdr 1/1/86. Retd GD 19/9/98.
ROGERS V. Born 18/1/22. Commd 22/10/59. Flt Lt 22/10/62. Retd ENG 18/1/77.
ROGERS W. E. Born 14/1/11. Commd 24/12/41. Fg Offr 1/10/42. Retd RGT 3/4/46.
ROGERS W. G., MBE. Born 26/12/14. Commd 3/12/42. Flt Lt 16/8/61. Retd ENG 26/12/71.
ROGERSON A. C., MA. Born 1/5/37. Commd 3/9/59. Sqn Ldr 1/3/68. Retd ADMIN 18/1/77.
ROGERSON A. W. Born 30/3/12. Commd 3/7/41. Flt Lt 1/9/45. Retd RGT 12/4/57 rtg Sqn Ldr.
ROGERSON C. S., BA. Born 8/12/61. Commd 2/9/84. Sqn Ldr 1/1/93. Retd ADMIN 2/9/00.
ROGERSON J. T. G., MB ChB FFARCS DA. Born 28/1/40. Commd 3/2/65. Gp Capt 22/4/86. Retd MED 11/10/95.
ROGERSON P. H. Born 23/1/20. Commd 24/2/44. Flt Lt 24/8/47. Retd ENG 1/1/59.
ROKOSZ S. T., AFC. Born 9/11/18. Commd 28/11/47. Flt Lt 18/5/56. Retd GD 29/1/58.
ROLFE C. I. Born 18/11/13. Commd 1/4/40. Sqn Ldr 1/8/47. Retd GD 1/4/56.
ROLFE G. D. Born 26/4/42. Commd 18/8/61. Sqn Ldr 1/7/76. Retd GD 26/7/80.

ROLFE G. H., CVO CBE. Born 10/12/40. Commd 31/7/62. Gp Capt 1/1/83. Retd GD 10/12/95.
ROLFE P. J. A. Born 9/12/47. Commd 30/5/69. Flt Lt 30/11/74. Retd GD 30/6/85.
ROLFE P.P. Born 19/5/42. Commd 31/1/64. Sqn Ldr 1/7/74. Retd GD 19/5/80.
ROLLIN N. Born 4/10/22. Commd 28/2/44. Wg Cdr 1/7/71. Retd SUP 30/3/77.
ROLLINS J. W., MBBS MRCPhys MRCS LRCP DPM. Born 27/9/35. Commd 12/6/60. Gp Capt 12/12/82. Retd MED 27/9/85.
ROLLINS M. S. Born 3/2/33. Commd 9/4/52. Flt Lt 20/7/58. Retd PI 8/12/84
ROLLO T. R. D. Born 15/12/46. Commd 2/2/68. Flt Lt 12/4/74. Retd SEC 31/8/74.
ROLLO W. S. Born 17/5/43. Commd 24/1/63. Sqn Ldr 1/1/76. Retd SUP 17/5/84.
ROLPH D. A., MBE. Born 20/9/34. Commd 5/11/52. Gp Capt 1/7/86. Retd GD 8/5/89.
ROLPH T. C., BSc. Born 14/10/53. Commd 8/1/76. Flt Lt 15/4/79. Retd GD 8/1/92.
ROMAN P. M. Born 14/7/44. Commd 14/7/66. Flt Lt 15/4/70. Retd GD 14/4/82.
ROMNEY F. C. Born 31/7/29. Commd 14/10/51. Sqn Ldr 1/1/63. Retd GD 2/8/79.
RONAYNE D. C. Born 13/6/42. Commd 12/7/63. Flt Lt 12/1/69. Retd GD 6/1/80.
RONDEL G. J. Born 23/1/29. Commd 2/1/52. Flt Lt 2/10/57. Retd GD 23/1/67.
RONDOT M. J. Born 7/2/48. Commd 22/12/67. Sqn Ldr 1/7/86. Retd GD(G) 4/7/92.
ROOKE W. D. Born 7/4/23. Commd 16/5/57. Flt Lt 16/11/60. Retd GD 30/5/64.
ROOM C. A. Born 15/2/20. Commd 29/6/50. Sqn Ldr 1/1/61. Retd SEC 14/10/67.
ROOM P. A., MBE BSc. Born 12/5/52. Commd 25/9/71. Flt Lt 23/9/79. Retd ENG 19/11/82.
ROOME D. C., OBE FRAeS. Born 30/11/46. Commd 21/7/65. Gp Capt 1/1/97. Retd GD 6/4/01.
ROOMS P. L. P. Born 19/8/40. Commd 18/7/61. Sqn Ldr 1/7/70. Retd ENG 19/8/78 rtg Wg Cdr.
ROOMS W. S., OBE BSc (Eur Ing) CEng MIEE MRAeS. Born 17/7/54. Commd 17/9/72. Gp Capt 1/1/96. Retd ENG 29/4/99.
ROONEY E. S. Born 27/6/22. Commd 11/5/43. Flt Lt 11/5/45. Retd GD 17/7/46. Re-employed 3/10/49. Sqn Ldr 1/7/60. Retd 6/8/65.
ROONEY J., BSc. Born 16/10/53. Commd 7/11/76. Flt Lt 7/8/77. Retd GD 30/4/00.
ROONEY M. A., DFC. Born 6/4/21. Commd 11/1/44. Flt Lt 27/5/60. Retd GD 6/4/76.
ROONEY P., BA DPhysEd. Born 15/2/46. Commd 19/8/68. Wg Cdr 1/1/96. Retd ADMIN 8/4/01.
ROOTES J. G., BSc. Born 25/3/46. Commd 26/5/67. Sqn Ldr 1/1/77. Retd ENG 25/3/84.
ROOTHAM J. Born 18/3/22. Commd 5/5/60. Flt Lt 5/5/65. Retd ENG 2/6/73.
ROOUM J. E., CBE AFC. Born 14/10/42. Commd 23/12/60. A Cdr 1/7/91. Retd GD 11/11/97.
ROPE B. A. Born 9/9/44. Commd 26/4/84. Sqn Ldr 1/7/92. Retd ENG 9/9/99.
ROPER C. F. K., AFM. Born 17/10/22. Commd 17/6/54. Flt Lt 17/6/60. Retd GD 1/1/65.
ROPER N., OBE ACIS. Born 3/5/34. Commd 17/6/63. Gp Capt 1/7/80. Retd ADMIN 1/8/84.
RORK G. D., CEng MRAeS. Born 16/7/39. Commd 25/6/66. Sqn Ldr 1/1/75. Retd ENG 24/7/89.
ROSBOTTOM P. M., CEng MRAeS. Born 16/7/39. Commd 25/6/66. Sqn Ldr 1/1/75. Retd ENG 24/7/89.
ROSCILLI G. A., CEng MIProdE MRAeS. Born 1/9/40. Commd 14/9/65. Sqn Ldr 1/7/76. Retd ENG 2/7/93.
ROSCOE B. J., BSc. Born 26/8/55. Commd 17/7/77. Flt Lt 17/10/78. Retd GD 17/7/89.
ROSCOE C. W. Born 21/5/51. Commd 22/6/89. Flt Lt 22/6/91. Retd ADMIN 22/6/97.
ROSCOE G. R., DFM. Born 14/3/20. Commd 28/2/46. Wg Cdr 1/7/65. Retd ENG 26/4/69.
ROSE A. E. Born 30/1/44. Commd 8/8/69. Fg Offr 8/8/71. Retd GD 1/6/73.
ROSE B., MBE MMar. Born 11/6/21. Commd 4/1/50. Sqn Ldr 4/1/58. Retd MAR 4/1/66.
ROSE I. A. Born 10/6/62. Commd 24/7/81. Sqn Ldr 1/7/92. Retd GD 10/6/00.
ROSE J., OBE MIISec. Born 15/9/45. Commd 21/10/66. Gp Capt 1/7/91. Retd ADMIN 20/7/97.
ROSE L., CEng FRAeS FIMgt. Born 15/9/14. Commd 15/12/34. Gp Capt 1/7/64. Retd ENG 15/9/69.
ROSE L. G., BSc. Born 7/9/45. Commd 18/7/66. Flt Lt 1/7/69. Retd GD 21/12/74.
ROSE M. A. Born 6/1/42. Commd 28/4/61. Flt Lt 1/7/68. Retd GD 6/1/80.
ROSE N. E., AFC* MIMgt. Born 30/5/24. Commd 27/5/54. Sqn Ldr 1/1/68. Retd GD 30/5/84.
ROSE O. M., MBE. Born 25/8/32. Commd 11/2/65. Sqn Ldr 1/7/77. Retd ENG 11/4/92.
ROSE P. W. Born 21/7/30. Commd 9/4/52. Flt Lt 9/4/57. Retd SEC 21/7/68.
ROSE R. Born 12/10/23. Commd 13/7/61. Flt Lt 13/7/66. Retd ENG 1/12/73.
ROSE R. I. L. Born 22/11/31. Commd 14/4/53. Flt Lt 14/10/55. Retd GD 28/3/69.
ROSE S. A., BA. Born 25/11/56. Commd 20/5/79. Flt Lt 20/8/82. Retd ADMIN 26/4/83.
ROSE V. Born 17/11/20. Commd 26/9/57. Sqn Ldr 1/7/68. Retd ENG 17/11/70.
ROSEDALE J. R. Born 10/3/54. Commd 23/4/87. Flt Lt 23/4/89. Retd ENG 3/4/93.
ROSEFIELD L. Born 8/8/33. Commd 18/6/52. Flt Lt 14/5/58. Retd SUP 8/8/73.
ROSENORN-LANNG M. J. Born 5/2/31. Commd 23/2/51. Sqn Ldr 1/1/70. Retd GD 5/2/86.
ROSEVEARE L. A., MIMgt. Born 30/10/33. Commd 9/4/53. Sqn Ldr 1/1/69. Retd GD 5/9/86.
ROSS A. Born 31/7/13. Commd 4/2/43. Fg Offr 1/4/45. Retd SEC 18/2/58 rtg Flt Lt.
ROSS A. Born 24/9/37. Commd 2/3/61. Sqn Ldr 1/7/73. Retd ADMIN 5/6/89.
ROSS A. J., BSc. Born 6/1/61. Commd 2/9/79. Sqn Ldr 1/7/94. Retd GD 6/1/99.
ROSS A. J. Born 24/2/40. Commd 13/12/60. Sqn Ldr 1/7/69. Retd GD 24/2/78.
ROSS A. N., BSc. Born 19/3/66. Commd 2/9/84. Flt Lt 15/1/90. Retd GD 15/7/99.
ROSS A. Q. M., BA. Born 4/2/42. Commd 31/7/62. Flt Lt 15/2/65. Retd GD 30/11/74.
ROSS C. J. Born 13/6/30. Commd 17/3/67. Flt Lt 17/3/72. Retd GD(G) 25/9/75.
ROSS C. W. Born 23/2/29. Commd 1/3/62. Sqn Ldr 1/1/74. Retd SEC 23/2/79.

ROSS D., FInstAM MCIPD. Born 30/9/42. Commd 5/1/78. Sqn Ldr 1/7/89. Retd ADMIN 12/7/97.
ROSS D. H. Born 24/2/23. Commd 13/2/47. Flt Lt 19/11/53. Retd GD 22/3/62.
ROSS G., BSc. Born 17/7/31. Commd 30/6/54. Gp Capt 1/7/80. Retd GD 17/10/86.
ROSS G. B., MA. Born 6/6/49. Commd 10/4/68. Flt Lt 15/4/72. Retd GD 3/2/81.
ROSS G. I. M. Born 26/5/26. Commd 17/11/47. Flt Lt 4/12/52. Retd RGT 26/5/64.
ROSS H. J. Born 8/9/10. Commd 14/10/41. Flt Lt 1/10/42. Retd ENG 26/4/46 rtg Flt Lt.
ROSS I. B. Born 8/4/31. Commd 31/5/51. Sqn Ldr 1/1/81. Retd ADMIN 8/4/86.
ROSS I. J. Born 28/3/37. Commd 14/5/63. Fg Offr 14/5/63. Retd EDN 31/8/66.
ROSS J., AFC. Born 13/11/23. Commd 5/5/47. Sqn Ldr 1/7/58. Retd GD 13/11/66.
ROSS J. Born 15/12/31. Commd 5/7/68. Sqn Ldr 1/1/80. Retd ADMIN 19/11/86.
ROSS J. A. G., MVO. Born 15/8/28. Commd 2/1/52. Sqn Ldr 1/7/64. Retd GD 5/6/76.
ROSS J. B., MB ChB DTM&H. Born 3/7/12. Commd 3/1/38. A Cdre 1/7/64. Retd MED 16/6/70.
ROSS J. H., MBE. Born 21/11/31. Commd 24/9/64. Sqn Ldr 1/1/77. Retd ENG 21/5/92.
ROSS M. G., MILT. Born 4/6/55. Commd 8/11/90. Flt Lt 8/11/94. Retd SUP 14/9/96.
ROSS N., MB ChB DRCOG DAvMed. Born 16/2/60. Commd 18/12/80. Wg Cdr 1/8/97. Retd MED 16/2/01.
ROSS N. F., BSc. Born 27/3/59. Commd 27/9/79. Flt Lt 15/10/81. Retd GD 22/1/93.
ROSS P. S. Born 20/3/46. Commd 1/10/65. Flt Lt 1/4/71. Retd GD 1/11/76.
ROSS T. A. Born 11/7/13. Commd 6/4/46. Flt Lt 11/11/54. Retd SEC 1/4/66.
ROSS T. G. Born 15/5/12. Commd 30/5/46. Fg Offr 30/5/46. Retd ASD 10/11/47.
ROSS W. G., AFC. Born 3/2/11. Commd 1/5/42. Flt Lt 1/5/44. Retd GD 24/1/47.
ROSS-SMITH J. M., CEng MIMechE MIProdE MRAeS MIMgt. Born 12/2/35. Commd 14/9/65. Wg Cdr 1/7/80. Retd ENG 1/6/87.
ROSSER M. J., MB BS DAvMed. Born 5/11/48. Commd 26/10/70. Wg Cdr 15/7/88. Retd MED 9/2/89.
ROSSER W. J., DFC. Born 18/2/17. Commd 7/8/41. Flt Lt 27/5/54. Retd SEC 20/2/72.
ROSSIE M. D. Born 17/6/38. Commd 14/11/59. Flt Lt 14/5/65. Retd GD 17/6/93.
ROSTRON J. D. Born 14/7/41. Commd 18/11/81. Flt Lt 3/4/93. Retd GD 2/4/93.
ROTHERAM R. C., OBE DFC. Born 27/8/17. Commd 30/7/38. Wg Cdr 1/7/50. Retd GD 27/8/72.
ROTHERY D. R. Born 30/1/34. Commd 26/11/52. Sqn Ldr 1/1/72. Retd GD 30/1/92.
ROTHWELL I. P. Born 4/12/33. Commd 23/7/52. Flt Lt 13/4/60. Retd GD 4/12/71.
ROTHWELL M. J. Born 19/1/49. Commd 27/5/71. Flt Lt 27/11/76. Retd GD 8/2/87.
ROTHWELL T. A. Born 1/6/10. Commd 26/12/46. Plt Offr 26/12/46. Retd SUP 30/3/48.
ROUGEAU R. G. Born 22/2/34. Commd 29/1/58. Fg Offr 29/1/58. Retd GD 26/9/64.
ROUGH M. J. A. Born 17/1/47. Commd 2/12/66. Sqn Ldr 1/1/83. Retd GD 1/1/86.
ROUGH N. M. Born 28/8/44. Commd 6/10/69. Sqn Ldr 1/1/92. Retd GD 22/4/94.
ROUGHTON J. G. A. Born 14/3/39. Commd 8/7/65. Sqn Ldr 1/7/80. Retd ADMIN 18/10/93.
ROUGIER L. V. Born 23/7/98. Commd 25/3/43. Flt Lt 12/7/45. Retd ASD 30/10/45.
ROUND P. Born 19/10/61. Commd 8/12/83. Fg Off 17/5/86. Retd ADMIN 31/3/89.
ROUND P. M., LLB. Born 20/8/52. Commd 13/2/77. Sqn Ldr 1/1/91. Retd SY 14/9/96.
ROURKE P. J. Born 14/3/35. Commd 19/8/53. Flt Lt 25/12/58. Retd GD 14/3/73.
ROURKE T. K., MIMgt. Born 21/12/23. Commd 26/11/43. Sqn Ldr 1/1/59. Retd SUP 21/6/76.
ROURKE T. W. Born 4/2/48. Commd 15/9/67. Flt Lt 15/3/73. Retd GD 22/7/76.
ROUSE G. G. Born 17/12/22. Commd 4/9/58. Flt Lt 4/9/63. Retd ENG 31/5/73.
ROUSELL R. H. Born 27/2/26. Commd 20/10/49. Flt Lt 20/4/53. Retd GD 14/9/68.
ROUSSEAU N. A. B. Born 8/10/42. Commd 11/5/78. Sqn Ldr 1/7/94. Retd GD 1/7/98.
ROUSSEL G. T. Born 10/6/20. Commd 16/1/50. Flt Lt 16/1/56. Retd SUP 10/6/69.
ROUTH J. E., MRCS LRCP DPH. Born 23/7/25. Commd 24/11/50. Wg Cdr 3/5/63. Retd MED 28/4/76.
ROUTIER J. S. Born 15/1/29. Commd 12/9/63. Flt Lt 12/9/68. Retd ENG 15/6/82.
ROUTLEDGE B. L. Born 21/5/50. Commd 4/3/71. Fg Offr 4/9/73. Retd PI 30/6/77.
ROUTLEDGE G. C. Born 21/7/46. Commd 15/10/81. Flt Lt 1/3/87. Retd ENG 19/9/87.
ROUTLEDGE J., MIMgt. Born 22/6/35. Commd 28/5/66. Wg Cdr 1/7/85. Retd ADMIN 25/10/89.
ROWBOTHAM B., DFC. Born 3/7/25. Commd 25/6/53. Sqn Ldr 1/1/67. Retd GD 31/3/74.
ROWDEN A. H. Born 22/7/15. Commd 17/4/47. Flt Lt 17/10/51. Retd SEC 22/7/64.
ROWDEN B. P., BEM MIMgt. Born 1/8/26. Commd 8/4/53. Sqn Ldr 1/1/65. Retd GD 2/12/75.
ROWE B. E., MBE. Born 11/8/30. Commd 12/9/63. Sqn Ldr 1/7/76. Retd ENG 6/7/87.
ROWE C., MIMgt. Born 4/4/35. Commd 27/9/57. Wg Cdr 1/7/84. Retd GD(G) 4/9/90.
ROWE C. G. Born 5/3/22. Commd 12/12/42. Flt Lt 7/10/48. Retd GD 5/3/77.
ROWE C. J. Born 11/1/43. Commd 5/7/68. Gp Capt 1/1/90. Retd SUP 11/1/96.
ROWE D. F. Born 1/10/38. Commd 25/8/67. Sqn Ldr 1/1/82. Retd GD 10/4/91.
ROWE D. H. G. Born 7/6/43. Commd 17/12/65. Flt Lt 8/1/69. Retd GD 9/8/75.
ROWE D. H. W. Born 23/11/40. Commd 20/11/75. Sqn Ldr 1/7/91. Retd SUP 30/4/95.
ROWE D. J., LVO. Born 12/9/32. Commd 27/8/52. Sqn Ldr 1/1/74. Retd GD 12/3/92.
ROWE E. M. C. Born 1/1/30. Commd 4/7/51. Flt Lt 21/3/58. Retd GD 30/8/80.
ROWE J. E. Born 21/5/23. Commd 12/6/58. Flt Lt 12/6/63. Retd SEC 3/4/74.
ROWE K. A., BSc. Born 15/12/52. Commd 14/1/74. Flt Lt 15/10/77. Retd ENG 3/12/85.
ROWE K. O. Born 14/9/31. Commd 2/7/52. Flt Lt 14/5/58. Retd GD(G) 14/9/86.
ROWE L. E. Born 25/9/24. Commd 30/6/44. Flt Lt 30/12/47. Retd GD 29/6/68.

ROWE L. E., BSc(Eng). Born 26/10/31. Commd 30/1/58. Wg Cdr 1/1/76. Retd ENG 1/5/82.
ROWE L. W. H. Born 23/11/30. Commd 13/8/52. Wg Cdr 1/7/71. Retd GD 23/11/85.
ROWE M. P., MB BCh DAvMed. Born 22/8/44. Commd 9/5/71. Sqn Ldr 9/8/76. Retd MED 6/2/90.
ROWE R. Born 26/5/20. Commd 16/4/45. Flt Lt 18/5/56. Retd CAT 26/5/73.
ROWE R. G., MA CEng MRAeS. Born 10/3/27. Commd 24/8/50. Wg Cdr. 1/7/71. Retd ENG 5/2/75.
ROWE T., IEng MCIPS. Born 13/12/42. Commd 9/3/72. Wg Cdr 1/7/88. Retd SUP 22/5/93.
ROWE T. H. Born 28/11/20. Commd 14/11/49. Flt Lt 14/11/49. Retd SUP 28/11/69.
ROWELL J. D. Born 1/8/28. Commd 30/5/51. Sqn Ldr 1/7/61. Retd GD 1/4/73.
ROWELL K. Born 30/8/25. Commd 7/7/55. Sqn Ldr 1/7/70. Retd ADMIN 27/10/76.
ROWELL P. A., AFC. Born 27/9/19. Commd 6/1/42. Flt Lt 1/9/45. Retd GD 1/4/50.
ROWELL P. W. Born 14/11/45. Commd 3/5/68. Flt Lt 3/11/73. Retd GD 2/9/75.
ROWLAND A. D., BA MCIPS. Born 23/2/37. Commd 22/7/66. Wg Cdr 1/7/83. Retd SUP 20/11/89.
ROWLAND B., MA. Born 2/10/20. Commd 31/7/57. Sqn Ldr 5/11/58. Retd ADMIN 2/10/75.
ROWLAND C. J., BSc(Eng) CEng MRAeS. Born 9/8/42. Commd 30/9/61. Wg Cdr 1/1/79. Retd ENG 4/4/93.
ROWLAND D. M. Born 24/2/24. Commd 20/2/50. Flt Lt 19/6/52. Retd GD 24/2/84.
ROWLAND G. C. Born 1/9/19. Commd 25/5/50. Wg Cdr 1/7/70. Retd SEC 1/1/75.
ROWLANDS Sir John, KBE BSc CEng FRAeS MInstP. Born 23/9/15. Commd 4/4/39. AM 1/7/71. Retd ENG 1/7/73.
ROWLAND J. D. G., AFC. Born 26/4/39. Commd 25/7/60. Flt Lt 25/1/68. Retd GD 26/4/94.
ROWLAND J. N., DSO DFC*. Born 28/12/19. Commd 7/3/40. Flt Lt 7/9/43. Retd GD 2/1/47.
ROWLANDS B. A., MBE. Born 24/1/44. Commd 5/2/65. Flt Lt 6/10/71. Retd GD(G) 30/9/89.
ROWLANDS G. F. R. Born 25/3/50. Commd 27/3/70. Flt Lt 27/9/75. Retd GD 25/3/88.
ROWLANDS J. A., MSc CEng MIMechE MRAeS. Born 15/2/40. Commd 18/7/61. Wg Cdr 1/1/78. Retd ENG 2/9/94.
ROWLANDS J. B. Born 20/3/20. Commd 22/12/44. Flt Lt 22/6/48. Retd GD 20/3/74.
ROWLANDS P., BSc MB BCh MRCP DCH. Born 25/9/30. Commd 21/8/55. Wg Cdr 4/8/68. Retd MED 21/8/71.
ROWLANDS P. G. Born 16/1/50. Commd 14/9/75. Wg Cdr 1/7/90. Retd ADMIN 7/1/97.
ROWLANDS R. Born 23/8/50. Commd 24/7/81. Flt Lt 24/7/83. Retd ENG 27/2/90.
ROWLANDS R. E. Born 13/9/33. Commd 11/10/51. Flt Lt 1/3/61. Retd GD 1/2/71.
ROWLEY E. Born 30/9/43. Commd 21/10/65. Sqn Ldr 1/7/79. Retd ENG 30/9/98.
ROWLEY M. J. B. Born 13/12/39. Commd 18/7/61. Wg Cdr 1/1/80. Retd ENG 1/1/90.
ROWLEY P. S. Born 11/1/30. Commd 4/7/69. Flt Lt 4/7/72. Retd GD(G) 2/4/75.
ROWLEY R. L. Born 10/2/47. Commd 27/5/71. Flt Lt 27/11/75. Retd GD 13/6/89.
ROWLEY W. E. Born 13/9/29. Commd 21/10/66. Sqn Ldr 1/1/79. Retd ENG 14/11/81.
ROWLEY W. H. Born 23/2/29. Commd 8/11/51. Sqn Ldr 1/1/78. Retd ADMIN 12/8/85.
ROWNEY J. F. Born 14/1/22. Commd 18/10/62. Flt Lt 18/10/67. Retd ENG 1/9/77.
ROWNEY N. A. Born 11/12/12. Commd 14/3/41. Flt Lt 1/9/45. Retd ENG 23/5/54.
ROWNTREE C. G., BSc CEng MIMechE. Born 26/3/46. Commd 28/9/64. Wg Cdr 1/1/87. Retd ENG 6/5/90.
ROWNTREE M. P. Born 22/4/45. Commd 8/7/65. Sqn Ldr 1/7/83. Retd ENG 1/10/89.
ROWORTH D. W. Born 5/7/35. Commd 26/10/59. Flt Lt 26/4/61. Retd GD 30/9/77.
ROWSON D. J. Born 23/2/47. Commd 27/7/72. Flt Lt 27/1/78. Retd GD 5/11/89.
ROXBERRY A. E. Born 1/7/30. Commd 7/12/50. Fg Offr 7/12/52. Retd SEC 2/5/55.
ROXBERRY D. K. Born 21/12/26. Commd 14/6/46. Sqn Ldr 1/1/57. Retd GD 3/10/75.
ROXBURGH D. A., MB ChB DMRD. Born 24/2/39. Commd 23/9/63. Wg Cdr 1/12/78. Retd MED 2/2/81.
ROXBURGH E. M. Born 13/12/27. Commd 16/10/52. Flt Lt 16/10/58. Retd SEC 17/1/69.
ROXBURGH I. D., AFC AFM. Born 5/9/17. Commd 26/3/41. Sqn Ldr 1/1/51. Retd GD 1/11/57.
ROY J. G. Born 26/10/33. Commd 25/10/73. Flt Lt 25/10/76. Retd GD 26/4/84.
ROY L. T. Born 17/11/29. Commd 18/5/61. Sqn Ldr 1/7/72. Retd SUP 2/9/81.
ROYAL E. G. Born 18/6/20. Commd 12/8/54. Sqn Ldr 1/7/69. Retd GD(G) 18/6/75.
ROYLE A. P., BEng. Born 9/10/59. Commd 4/1/83. Flt Lt 4/7/83. Retd GD 4/1/99.
ROYLE G. A., MSc BSc. Born 21/3/61. Commd 16/9/79. Sqn Ldr 1/1/92. Retd ENG 21/3/99.
ROYLE P., MB BS FFARCS. Born 31/1/53. Commd 2/9/75. Wg Cdr 4/8/90. Retd MED 21/3/93.
RUBENSTEIN M., MSc CEng MRAeS. Born 16/12/53. Commd 10/6/84. Flt Lt 10/12/82. Retd ENG 10/6/00.
RUDD A. W. Born 24/6/29. Commd 2/7/52. Flt Lt 8/1/58. Retd GD 22/1/68.
RUDD D. I. Born 24/6/48. Commd 20/5/82. Sqn Ldr 1/1/92. Retd ADMIN 31/3/94.
RUDD M. C., AFC. Born 12/5/49. Commd 1/4/69. A Cdre 1/7/95. Retd GD 3/12/97.
RUDD P. C. Born 18/9/18. Commd 10/12/42. Flt Lt 10/6/47. Retd RGT 26/8/58 rtg Sqn Ldr.
RUDDICK D. R., MA. Born 23/4/39. Commd 1/10/62. Wg Cdr 1/7/77. Retd GD 1/7/80.
RUDIN J., BSc(Eng). Born 20/10/37. Commd 26/11/60. Sqn Ldr 1/1/83. Retd GD 1/1/96.
RUDOLPH F. R. C. Born 6/11/40. Commd 30/5/69. Wg Cdr 1/7/84. Retd ADMIN 11/7/94.
RUFF C. E., MBE. Born 20/9/19. Commd 20/10/55. Sqn Ldr 1/7/65. Retd ENG 20/9/74.
RUFF P. J., MBE. Born 11/7/33. Commd 8/7/65. Sqn Ldr 1/1/79. Retd SY 15/3/87.
RUFFLE D. M. Born 5/7/30. Commd 2/7/52. Flt Lt 17/12/59. Retd SEC 5/7/68.
RUGG D. E. Born 3/10/24. Commd 6/3/52. Sqn Ldr 1/1/69. Retd GD 3/10/84.
RULE A. E. Born 8/3/43. Commd 13/1/67. Flt Lt 13/7/72. Retd GD 1/8/90.
RULE D. W., MBE. Born 23/1/29. Commd 26/5/67. Wg Cdr 1/1/81. Retd ADMIN 26/2/83.
RULE T. W. Born 4/6/43. Commd 27/10/67. Flt Lt 27/4/74. Retd SUP 11/7/83.
RUMBLE H., DFC. Born 29/1/22. Commd 11/2/44. Flt Lt 11/8/47. Retd GD 29/1/77.

RUMBOL R. W. Born 3/10/32. Commd 31/5/51. Flt Lt 28/11/56. Retd GD 3/10/70.
RUMBOLD The Rev B. J., CertEd. Born 30/6/43. Commd 20/6/77. Retd 1/9/94 Wg Cdr.
RUMP F., CBE. Born 10/5/13. Commd 3/3/33. Gp Capt 1/7/51. Retd GD 15/8/67 rtg A Cdre.
RUNACRES K. B. Born 30/8/40. Commd 27/7/72. Sqn Ldr 1/7/82. Retd ENG 30/8/95.
RUNCHMAN F. E. Born 11/1/22. Commd 29/11/43. Sqn Ldr 1/4/55. Retd GD 22/2/65.
RUNDLE A. F. Born 2/11/46. Commd 1/4/69. Fg Offr 1/4/71. Retd GD 16/12/71.
RUSE D. E. McG. Born 14/9/24. Commd 19/1/56. Sqn Offr 1/7/67. Retd SEC 18/10/75.
RUSE N. F. Born 23/2/13. Commd 10/11/41. Wg Cdr 1/1/60. Retd ENG 23/2/65.
RUSH F. C. I. Born 7/11/53. Commd 20/7/78. Flt Lt 20/1/84. Retd GD 1/10/95.
RUSH J. M., BA. Born 20/5/41. Commd 11/11/71. Sqn Ldr 1/1/89. Retd GD(G) 20/5/96.
RUSH W. J., MBE BA. Born 10/5/43. Commd 24/6/76. Wg Cdr 1/7/90. Retd ENG 3/4/97.
RUSHER D. H. S., DSO. Born 18/3/15. Commd 15/12/34. Wg Cdr 1/7/47. Retd GD 1/1/48.
RUSHFORTH G. W. Born 1/6/27. Commd 27/8/52. Sqn Ldr 1/7/64. Retd GD 1/2/80.
RUSHFORTH R. N. Born 2/12/28. Commd 9/3/66. Sqn Ldr 1/1/77. Retd ENG 3/12/82.
RUSHMERE M. J. Born 5/6/48. Commd 27/3/70. Flt Lt 5/6/75. Retd SUP 5/6/88.
RUSHTON P. Born 3/12/51. Commd 24/8/72. Flt Lt 1/9/78. Retd GD 9/2/82.
RUSHTON W. L. Born 8/6/33. Commd 19/8/71. Sqn Ldr 1/7/82. Retd ENG 8/6/93.
RUSHWORTH D. W. Born 25/2/30. Commd 18/5/61. Flt Lt 18/5/67. Retd SEC 31/7/68.
RUSHWORTH G. F. Born 12/2/36. Commd 24/3/61. Flt Lt 10/2/67. Retd GD 12/2/74.
RUSKELL K., MBE DFC. Born 14/6/22. Commd 9/10/42. Sqn Ldr 1/7/54. Retd ADMIN 1/9/76.
RUSKELL R. M. F. Born 18/7/48. Commd 2/6/67. Flt Lt 2/12/72. Retd GD 28/2/76.
RUSSELL A., BA. Born 1/10/50. Commd 27/3/86. Flt Lt 27/3/90. Retd GD 14/3/96.
RUSSELL A. Born 1/10/12. Commd 1/4/45. Flt Lt 14/11/56. Retd SEC 1/10/67.
RUSSELL A. J. Born 23/12/30. Commd 1/3/62. Flt Lt 1/3/68. Retd ENG 1/9/73.
RUSSELL A. K. M. Born 21/9/38. Commd 27/1/67. Wg Cdr 1/7/87. Retd ADMIN 31/12/91.
RUSSELL B. Born 14/10/50. Commd 2/11/88. Flt Lt 2/11/92. Retd ADMIN 13/1/96.
RUSSELL B. E. Born 29/5/33. Commd 6/5/55. Sqn Ldr 1/1/71. Retd GD 30/9/78. Reinstated 7/5/80. Sqn Ldr
    8/8/72. Retd GD 15/3/88.
RUSSELL F. T., MBE. Born 16/3/17. Commd 25/11/43. Gp Capt 1/7/67. Retd SEC 12/8/72.
RUSSELL G. L., BSc. Born 22/9/48. Commd 1/2/87. Flt Lt 1/2/87. Retd ADMIN 14/12/96.
RUSSELL G. O., DFC. Born 17/6/17. Commd 17/7/43. Sqn Ldr 1/7/54. Retd GD 23/10/57.
RUSSELL H., MBE. Born 20/7/09. Commd 6/9/47. Sqn Ldr 1/7/60. Retd SUP 20/7/64.
RUSSELL J. D. Born 25/7/20. Commd 9/2/43. Flt Lt 13/6/51. Retd GD(G) 17/12/69.
RUSSELL J. H. Born 17/7/37. Commd 25/1/63. Sqn Ldr 1/1/75. Retd SUP 2/10/78.
RUSSELL J. T. A. Born 20/6/32. Commd 16/7/52. Sqn Ldr 1/1/77. Retd GD 16/6/86.
RUSSELL L. D. A. Born 31/5/40. Commd 30/5/59. Flt Lt 30/11/64. Retd GD 1/7/77.
RUSSELL L. J. Born 29/1/30. Commd 13/12/50. Sqn Ldr 1/1/59. Retd GD 30/10/70 rtg Wg Cdr.
RUSSELL M. E. J. Born 15/6/40. Commd 21/7/61. Flt Lt 21/1/67. Retd GD 1/10/81.
RUSSELL M. I. Born 31/3/34. Commd 27/8/52. Flt Lt 14/5/58. Retd GD 2/3/63.
RUSSELL M. J., OBE. Born 28/3/47. Commd 23/9/66. Wg Cdr 1/7/87. Retd GD 14/12/96.
RUSSELL M. W. J. Born 14/5/44. Commd 15/7/65. Sqn Ldr 1/7/83. Retd ENG 1/10/85.
RUSSELL P. Born 10/2/24. Commd 14/2/63. Flt Lt 14/2/66. Retd GD(G) 10/2/72.
RUSSELL R. B. Born 11/12/45. Commd 22/7/81. Flt Lt 22/1/77. Retd GD 8/3/87.
RUSSELL R. H. Born 25/7/28. Commd 2/8/50. Sqn Ldr 1/1/64. Retd GD 16/12/68.
RUSSELL R. J., AFC. Born 30/4/32. Commd 28/1/53. Sqn Ldr 1/7/86. Retd GD 23/2/91.
RUSSELL R. M., BA. Born 1/12/44. Commd 26/11/81. Sqn Ldr 1/1/90. Retd ADMIN 31/7/98.
RUSSELL T. A. E. Born 29/3/21. Commd 6/8/43. Flt Lt 1/1/49. Retd PRT 1/10/65.
RUSSELL W. Born 4/10/42. Commd 28/2/80. Sqn Ldr 1/1/91. Retd GD(G) 12/7/96.
RUSSELL W. B., MB ChB DRCOG DAvMed DPH MFOM. Born 18/5/33. Commd 24/5/59. Gp Capt 1/1/83. Retd MED
    21/9/85.
RUSSELL-BISHOP R. G. Born 16/9/13. Commd 29/6/50. Sqn Ldr 29/6/62. Retd MED(T) 4/12/67.
RUSSELL-SMITH C. P., BSc CEng MRAeS. Born 16/11/41. Commd 24/9/63. Sqn Ldr 1/1/72. Retd ENG 16/11/96.
RUSSELL-SMITH S. J. Born 27/9/24. Commd 30/6/44. Flt Lt 16/8/61. Retd GD(G) 28/11/73.
RUSSUM K., AFC. Born 12/10/22. Commd 9/9/44. Wg Cdr 1/1/68. Retd GD 25/3/77.
RUST J. D. Born 5/1/39. Commd 25/7/60. Wg Cdr 1/1/78. Retd GD 1/2/82.
RUST V. R. Born 25/3/29. Commd 7/7/55. Flt Lt 7/1/59. Retd GD 25/3/84.
RUSTIN C. C., BSc CEng MRAeS. Born 14/5/32. Commd 14/11/57. Wg Cdr 1/1/74. Retd GD 14/5/87.
RUSTON A. M., CBE DFC. Born 2/3/20. Commd 8/10/39. A Cdre 1/1/65. Retd GD 2/4/70.
RUSTON C. Born 29/3/47. Commd 10/12/65. Flt Lt 3/8/72. Retd GD 14/3/96.
RUSTON N. D. Born 14/4/50. Commd 30/7/92. Fg Offr 30/7/92. Retd ENG 31/3/94.
RUSTON P. E., MCIPS MIMgt. Born 2/10/34. Commd 30/8/60. Wg Cdr 1/7/76. Retd SUP 18/4/86.
RUTHEN P. L., MBE BSc CEng MRAeS. Born 13/7/34. Commd 1/10/57. Sqn Ldr 29/3/71. Retd ADMIN 13/7/92.
RUTHERFORD B. E. Born 22/3/25. Commd 17/1/51. Flt Lt 17/10/56. Retd GD 29/8/65.
RUTHERFORD D. A., BA. Born 7/5/53. Commd 25/6/66. Sqn Ldr 1/7/80. Retd MAR 1/4/86.
RUTHERFORD I. Born 5/4/39. Commd 7/1/58. Flt Lt 9/7/62. Retd GD 5/4/95.
RUTHVEN J. C. Born 31/8/37. Commd 16/12/66. Flt Lt 16/12/68. Retd GD(G) 31/8/93.

RUTLEDGE B. Born 22/11/38. Commd 12/3/60. Wg Cdr 1/1/87. Retd GD 22/11/93.
RUTLEDGE G. A., BA. Born 24/11/47. Commd 28/2/69. Flt Lt 28/2/72. Retd GD 14/7/92.
RUTLEY F. G., BSc. Born 26/6/63. Commd 30/8/87. Flt Lt 30/8/88. Retd ADMIN 14/3/97.
RUTSON G. M. Born 14/8/45. Commd 5/11/65. Flt Lt 5/5/71. Retd GD 15/2/76.
RUTTER I. T., MBE. Born 8/8/24. Commd 6/9/56. Sqn Ldr 1/7/68. Retd GD 8/8/84.
RUXTON T. E. Born 25/9/21. Commd 5/5/54. Flt Lt 5/5/58. Retd ADMIN 25/9/76.
RYALL K. J., DFC MIMgt. Born 8/11/23. Commd 4/11/43. Wg Cdr 1/1/69. Retd GD 31/3/78.
RYALL M., CEng CPhys MInstP. Born 17/7/44. Commd 10/3/69. Gp Capt 1/1/99. Retd ENG 17/9/99.
RYALL P. J. Born 15/4/33. Commd 17/5/56. Flt Lt 11/10/62. Retd GD 1/9/85.
RYAN B. F. Born 6/1/22. Commd 4/9/43. Sqn Ldr 1/4/56. Retd GD 30/1/71.
RYAN J. A. Born 21/5/26. Commd 14/6/46. Wg Cdr 1/1/64. Retd GD 1/11/75.
RYAN K. J., OBE. Born 8/10/25. Commd 15/12/49. Wg Cdr 1/7/67. Retd GD 8/10/83.
RYAN M. A. F. Born 28/7/36. Commd 17/12/57. Wg Cdr 1/1/77. Retd GD 19/4/84.
RYAN M. C. Born 19/7/37. Commd 2/2/68. Flt Lt 2/2/70. Retd SEC 2/2/76.
RYAN P. A. Born 14/7/42. Commd 13/7/61. Gp Capt 1/1/86. Retd SY 12/2/94.
RYAN P. W. Born 18/6/39. Commd 30/5/59. Flt Lt 30/11/64. Retd GD 18/6/77.
RYAN T. P. F., MHCIMA. Born 8/7/46. Commd 4/9/67. Flt Lt 4/9/72. Retd ADMIN 1/9/76.
RYAN W. A. Born 18/2/20. Commd 17/5/56. Flt Lt 17/5/62. Retd GD(G) 30/4/66.
RYAN W. F. Born 20/9/23. Commd 2/10/58. Flt Lt 2/10/64. Retd PRT 5/1/74 rtg Sqn Ldr.
RYANS P. T., CEng MIMechE MRAeS. Born 31/5/32. Commd 3/8/55. Gp Capt 1/7/79. Retd ENG 7/4/84.
RYANS R. B. Born 3/7/44. Commd 21/12/62. Flt Lt 21/6/68. Retd GD 3/7/82.
RYCROFT D. H., CEng MIEE. Born 11/12/42. Commd 6/1/69. Flt Lt 4/5/72. Retd ENG 11/12/97.
RYDER A. N. Born 25/5/50. Commd 17/7/70. Flt Lt 17/1/76. Retd GD 12/7/78.
RYDER D. J. Born 13/3/20. Commd 8/4/44. Sqn Ldr 1/7/66. Retd SUP 13/3/75.
RYDER E. J., MSc. Born 26/8/14. Commd 26/12/37. Wg Cdr 1/7/48. Retd ENG 1/9/66.
RYDER R. E. T., BSc. Born 5/2/51. Commd 15/9/69. Sqn Ldr 1/7/84. Retd ENG 6/12/89.
RYDER S. F. Born 22/5/31. Commd 23/4/52. Flt Lt 14/11/56. Retd GD 22/5/69.
RYE W. J., AFC. Born 11/10/08. Commd 26/8/40. Sqn Ldr 1/1/51. Retd GD(G) 11/10/58 rtg Wg Cdr.
RYGALSKI S. A. Born 3/3/63. Commd 13/8/82. Sqn Ldr 1/7/96. Retd SUP 3/3/01.
RYLE A. E., OBE AFC FIMgt. Born 5/6/35. Commd 27/2/58. Sqn Ldr 1/7/68. Retd GD 5/6/95.
RYLES D. S. Born 12/7/32. Commd 13/8/52. Flt Lt 9/1/58. Retd GD 12/7/70. Re-instated 23/12/81 to 1/7/85.
RYMARZ R. J. G., MA MSc BSc CertEd. Born 15/12/49. Commd 18/4/71. Wg Cdr 1/7/88. Retd ADMIN 14/9/96.

# S

SAADY D. J., BA. Born 27/6/38. Commd 30/9/58. Sqn Ldr 1/1/70. Retd ENG 27/6/76.
SAAR R. C., MBE MIMgt. Born 30/5/39. Commd 7/1/58. Sqn Ldr 1/1/71. Retd GD 30/5/77.
SABAN J. T. Born 15/8/30. Commd 17/3/55. Wg Cdr 1/1/76. Retd SUP 15/8/85.
SABBEN J. M. H., BMet CEng MRAeS. Born 9/12/40. Commd 12/3/63. Wg Cdr 1/7/79. Retd ENG 12/3/85.
SABIN J. R., BSc CEng MIEE. Born 1/11/44. Commd 13/9/71. Sqn Ldr 1/1/82. Retd GD 13/9/87.
SABINE M. S. Born 8/2/40. Commd 1/8/61. Sqn Ldr 1/7/75. Retd GD 1/7/78.
SABOURIN P. C., BA. Born 23/4/60. Commd 7/11/82. Flt Lt 7/8/86. Retd ENG 7/11/87.
SACHEDINA K. A., BSc. Born 4/2/61. Commd 26/9/82. Sqn Ldr 1/1/97. Retd GD 1/1/00.
SACKETT P. D. M. Born 22/4/41. Commd 6/4/62. Fg Offr 6/4/64. Retd GD 14/5/65.
SADDLETON D. S., BA. Born 13/2/38. Commd 16/1/72. Sqn Ldr 16/7/75. Retd ADMIN 19/12/87.
SADDLETON P. E. J. Born 29/12/33. Commd 4/4/54. Wg Cdr 1/1/75. Retd GD(G) 25/11/85.
SADLER A. E. Born 18/4/27. Commd 31/1/51. Sqn Ldr 1/1/64. Retd GD 18/4/85.
SADLER A. G. Born 25/4/33. Commd 29/9/51. Flt Lt 15/1/57. Retd GD 25/4/71.
SADLER B., BSc. Born 11/4/58. Commd 28/9/80. Flt Lt 28/6/81. Retd GD 31/1/93.
SADLER E. C. Born 29/2/32. Commd 23/4/52. Flt Lt 19/9/57. Retd GD 29/2/92.
SADLER G. B., MSc BSc CEng MRAeS MBCS MIMgt. Born 19/11/51. Commd 13/9/70. Sqn Ldr 1/7/85. Retd ENG 1/12/92.
SADLER I. F. Born 3/6/49. Commd 15/8/77. Sqn Ldr 1/1/88. Retd SY 15/8/93.
SADLER J. Born 6/12/09. Commd 14/10/43. Flt Lt 14/4/48. Retd SEC 21/9/53.
SADLER J. M. Born 15/7/44. Commd 5/2/81. Sqn Ldr 1/7/92. Retd ENG 17/6/96.
SADLER J. R. Born 22/4/43. Commd 22/2/63. Flt Lt 22/8/68. Retd GD 9/11/81.
SADLER W. R. Born 26/2/09. Commd 20/3/29. Wg Cdr 1/10/46. Retd GD 25/3/54 rtg Gp Capt.
SADLER-HALL M. M., MA. Born 28/12/35. Commd 14/9/65. Flt Lt 14/9/66. Retd EDN 1/10/71.
SAER J. M. H. Born 1/4/51. Commd 23/9/79. Flt Lt 23/9/83. Retd ADMIN 23/9/95.
SAGE D. J., BA. Born 11/12/45. Commd 17/1/72. Flt Lt 17/10/75. Retd ENG 17/1/88.
SAGE G. D. Born 11/11/32. Commd 17/7/70. Flt Lt 1/7/72. Retd PI 1/9/84.
SAIFURRAHMAN Z. A., BSc CEng MRAeS. Born 20/2/47. Commd 1/8/69. Flt Lt 13/7/73. Retd ENG 20/2/85.
SAKER J. Born 8/10/34. Commd 10/9/52. Flt Lt 23/3/58. Retd GD 8/10/92.
SAKER R. N. J., MBE CDipAF. Born 24/12/31. Commd 29/3/51. Wg Cdr 1/1/80. Retd GD 16/5/83.
SALE M. J., MIMgt. Born 7/12/43. Commd 31/10/69. Wg Cdr 1/1/88. Retd SUP 1/5/93.
SALISBURY J., BSc MInstP MCIPD AIPM. Born 10/6/37. Commd 13/11/62. Sqn Ldr 24/3/70. Retd ADMIN 13/11/82. Reinstated 31/8/83. Sqn Ldr 24/3/70. Retd ADMIN 22/5/91.
SALISBURY K. J. Born 20/11/16. Commd 15/5/47. Sqn Ldr 1/4/58. Retd SEC 30/11/71.
SALISBURY K. W. N. Born 4/11/48. Commd 31/7/70. Fg Offr 31/7/71. Retd SEC 31/12/75 rtg Flt Lt.
SALKELD D., BSc. Born 3/11/28. Commd 20/10/49. Wg Cdr 1/7/67. Retd ENG 11/12/75.
SALKELD P. Born 13/4/51. Commd 7/1/71. Fg Offr 7/1/73. Retd GD 23/11/73.
SALMON J. F., BA. Born 14/11/43. Commd 30/9/63. Flt Lt 15/10/69. Retd ENG 4/9/71.
SALMON R. D. Born 7/6/62. Commd 30/4/81. Flt Lt 30/10/86. Retd GD 23/6/89.
SALMON R. S., MIMgt. Born 25/3/24. Commd 21/6/44. Gp Capt 1/7/72. Retd GD 7/4/79.
SALMON S. E., CEng MIEE MRAeS. Born 25/1/40. Commd 18/7/61. Sqn Ldr 1/1/71. Retd ENG 11/2/77.
SALMOND J. J. W. Born 20/12/26. Commd 14/6/46. Flt Lt 15/12/49. Retd GD 2/5/50.
SALMOND J. S. R. Born 20/6/31. Commd 14/4/53. Flt Lt 14/10/55. Retd GD 20/6/86.
SALT G. S. Born 23/4/45. Commd 9/8/79. Flt Lt 9/8/81. Retd GD(G) 9/8/87.
SALT R. M., MBE AFC. Born 25/7/32. Commd 14/4/53. Sqn Ldr 1/7/66. Retd GD 25/7/70.
SALTER A. Born 15/6/34. Commd 5/4/55. Gp Capt 1/7/83. Retd GD 15/6/89.
SALTER A. G., DFC. Born 13/7/16. Commd 10/5/37. Sqn Ldr 1/8/52. Retd GD 27/1/58.
SALTER D. G., CEng MIEE. Born 26/5/24. Commd 24/10/43. Sqn Ldr 1/1/56. Retd ENG 26/11/77.
SALTER G. A. Born 17/9/23. Commd 10/4/51. Flt Lt 10/10/54. Retd GD 9/4/73.
SALTER L. A. Born 22/2/43. Commd 3/10/69. Fg Offr 14/3/72. Retd GD(G) 3/10/73.
SALTER R. M. Born 19/12/45. Commd 30/4/81. Flt Lt 30/4/85. Retd ENG 22/9/97.
SALTER T. A., MBE BSc(Eng) CEng MRAeS MIMgt DNCL. Born 13/5/42. Commd 1/9/64. Wg Cdr 1/1/87. Retd ENG 13/5/97.
SALUSBURY D. J., BA. Born 6/9/43. Commd 6/6/66. Gp Capt 1/7/94. Retd SY 1/9/96.
SALWEY C. H. Born 5/8/34. Commd 26/7/55. Sqn Ldr 1/1/66. Retd GD 5/8/92.
SAMARASINGHE S. N. Born 4/5/26. Commd 28/2/66. Flt Lt 28/2/66. Retd SEC 17/11/81.
SAMBROOK G. Born 6/8/47. Commd 1/3/68. Flt Lt 1/3/71. Retd GD 6/8/85.
SAMES C. R. Born 2/10/46. Commd 28/2/85. Flt Lt 28/2/89. Retd ADMIN 1/4/92.
SAMES D. W., BSc. Born 25/5/35. Commd 28/9/60. Sqn Ldr 1/1/68. Retd GD 21/9/84.
SAMPLE W. C. H. M. Born 27/9/50. Commd 27/3/70. Flt Lt 27/9/75. Retd GD 14/9/76.
SAMPSON C. F. J., BSc AMBCS. Born 6/4/46. Commd 13/9/70. Wg Cdr 1/7/90. Retd ADMIN 14/3/96.

SAMPSON D. P., DFC. Born 5/2/22. Commd 16/7/42. Sqn Ldr 1/7/51. Retd GD 5/2/65 rtg Wg Cdr.
SAMPSON I. W. Born 24/9/40. Commd 6/7/62. Sqn Ldr 1/1/81. Retd GD 24/9/95.
SAMPSON J. A. Born 5/2/31. Commd 10/12/52. Flt Lt 1/11/61. Retd GD 3/11/67.
SAMPSON J. R., AFC. Born 1/5/46. Commd 13/5/88. Flt Lt 23/12/71. Retd GD 14/5/94.
SAMPSON R. B. Born 24/1/15. Commd 13/4/44. Flt Lt 13/10/47. Retd ENG 24/1/64.
SAMPSON T. R. Born 7/5/46. Commd 24/4/64. Sqn Ldr 1/1/81. Retd GD(G) 7/5/91.
SAMUEL D. L., DPhysEd. Born 10/5/38. Commd 3/1/63. Sqn Ldr 1/1/74. Retd PE 3/7/79.
SAMUELS D. M. A. Born 30/7/32. Commd 14/4/53. Flt Lt 14/10/55. Retd GD 30/7/70.
SAMUELS T. C. Born 31/5/19. Commd 17/1/50. Flt Lt 29/11/51. Retd GD 15/7/62.
SAND R. P. D. Born 26/8/35. Commd 2/10/53. Flt Lt 5/10/60. Retd GD(G) 26/8/73. Reinstated 3/12/80. Flt Lt 12/1/68. Retd GD(G) 26/8/90.
SANDBACH L. Born 23/9/26. Commd 27/9/51. Flt Lt 11/1/57. Retd GD 3/11/69.
SANDEMAN C. A. Born 19/4/47. Commd 20/10/83. Sqn Ldr 1/7/92. Retd ENG 2/1/99.
SANDERS A. A. J., DFC AFC. Born 30/9/20. Commd 7/3/40. Wg Cdr 1/1/54. Retd GD 30/9/67.
SANDERS A. E. Born 25/8/29. Commd 15/9/50. Flt Lt 5/6/56. Retd GD 25/8/67.
SANDERS J. F., BSc. Born 28/5/11. Commd 25/4/39. Gp Capt 1/1/64. Retd EDN 28/2/69.
SANDERS M. F. Born 8/9/45. Commd 16/9/76. Sqn Ldr 1/7/84. Retd ENG 2/12/96.
SANDERS N. B. Born 1/6/41. Commd 22/8/63. Flt Lt 15/4/70. Retd SUP 1/6/79.
SANDERS P. J. G. Born 4/2/44. Commd 24/6/65. Flt Lt 24/12/67. Retd GD 4/9/82.
SANDERS P. T., MSc. BA. Born 27/2/50. Commd 8/9/77. Sqn Ldr 1/1/84. Retd ADMIN 27/8/88.
SANDERS R. F. Born 30/11/45. Commd 4/6/72. Sqn Ldr 1/7/84. Retd ENG 4/6/88.
SANDERS R. S., DFC AFC*. Born 14/12/22. Commd 20/11/42. Wg Cdr 1/1/58. Retd GD 14/12/77.
SANDERSON C. Born 5/7/22. Commd 9/5/44. Flt Lt 19/8/49. Retd GD(G) 5/7/22.
SANDERSON C. E., BA. Born 16/12/60. Commd 16/9/79. Flt Lt 15/4/86. Retd SUP 1/10/89.
SANDERSON C. P. Born 20/8/31. Commd 2/7/52. Sqn Ldr 1/7/67. Retd GD 1/4/71.
SANDERSON F. A. S. Born 8/3/33. Commd 23/9/65. Flt Lt 23/9/71. Retd SUP 8/8/80.
SANDERSON G. Born 24/6/30. Commd 14/2/63. Flt Lt 14/2/69. Retd ADMIN 24/6/85.
SANDERSON M. D. Born 21/8/40. Commd 19/10/62. Flt Lt 19/5/67. Retd ENG 19/10/81.
SANDERSON P. R. Born 19/9/27. Commd 8/4/49. Sqn Ldr 1/7/60. Retd GD 28/6/68.
SANDERSON P. R. Born 18/7/29. Commd 24/9/64. Flt Lt 24/9/69. Retd ENG 1/9/73.
SANDERSON R., BA MBA. Born 8/4/42. Commd 6/8/63. Sqn Ldr 6/8/75. Retd ADMIN 2/10/82.
SANDERSON S. P. Born 15/4/56. Commd 14/8/80. Sqn Ldr 1/7/87. Retd ENG 15/4/94.
SANDERSON-MILLER A. F. J. Born 5/1/18. Commd 17/9/42. Flt Lt 7/4/48. Retd SUP 26/1/67.
SANDERSON-MILLER M. S. Born 25/3/42. Commd 30/1/75. Sqn Ldr 1/1/84. Retd ENG 21/4/88.
SANDFORD B. V. Born 24/8/43. Commd 24/6/65. Flt Lt 24/12/67. Retd GD 2/4/76.
SANDFORD J., BSc MRAeS DCAe. Born 20/5/24. Commd 10/9/47. Wg Cdr 20/5/65. Retd EDN 1/8/70.
SANDFORD R. F. Born 22/10/45. Commd 26/5/67. Flt Lt 18/2/70. Retd GD 7/10/76.
SANDLE J. R. Born 30/8/32. Commd 6/4/54. Sqn Ldr 1/7/66. Retd SUP 30/8/70.
SANDMANN G. Born 14/1/28. Commd 12/2/54. Flt Lt 21/10/59. Retd GD 13/10/69.
SANDOE R. J. Born 30/11/39. Commd 30/3/65. Sqn Ldr 1/7/76. Retd ENG 30/11/95.
SANDOM C. W., MSc BEng CEng MIEE. Born 24/7/61. Commd 7/8/87. Flt Lt 15/7/90. Retd ENG 9/9/00.
SANDON R. A. Born 8/9/62. Commd 11/5/89. Flt Lt 11/5/91. Retd OPS SPT 12/6/98.
SANDS J. Born 27/7/24. Commd 29/6/50. Sqn Ldr 1/7/60. Retd GD 23/7/76.
SANDS L. Born 16/7/22. Commd 14/4/60. Flt Lt 14/4/60. Retd GD 16/7/77 rtg Sqn Ldr.
SANDS P. L. Born 20/9/30. Commd 26/8/66. Flt Lt 26/8/71. Retd ENG 8/8/74.
SANDS R. P. Born 30/8/45. Commd 1/4/65. Sqn Ldr 1/1/86. Retd GD(G) 30/8/89.
SANDYS J. F. Born 6/7/34. Commd 5/7/66. Sqn Ldr 1/7/82. Retd GD 7/8/89.
SANFORD F. Born 13/11/18. Commd 23/6/43. Sqn Ldr 1/4/55. Retd GD 1/5/58.
SANFORD-CASEY B. M., BA. Born 7/5/45. Commd 17/3/65. Wg Cdr 1/1/90. Retd GD 13/8/94.
SANKEY C. V. Born 28/2/33. Commd 27/9/51. Sqn Ldr 1/1/70. Retd GD 7/5/76.
SANSOM A. C. StQ., MBE. Born 25/9/18. Commd 15/9/60. Flt Lt 15/9/63. Retd ENG 7/4/73.
SANSOM F. B. Born 5/7/39. Commd 29/7/65. Sqn Ldr 1/7/74. Retd ENG 5/7/77.
SANSOM M. D. Born 4/8/31. Commd 5/7/51. Sqn Ldr 1/1/67. Retd ADMIN 4/11/85.
SANSOME G. E., CEng MIMechE MRAeS. Born 25/2/28. Commd 4/4/61. Sqn Ldr 1/7/67. Retd ENG 25/8/91.
SANSOME N. F. E. Born 22/9/37. Commd 15/2/73. Flt Lt 15/2/77. Retd GD(G) 22/9/87.
SAPSFORD J. W., CEng MIMechE MIMgt. Born 28/6/29. Commd 3/10/61. Sqn Ldr 1/1/70. Retd ENG 3/10/77.
SARBUTT D. W., BEM. Born 1/4/16. Commd 26/9/57. Sqn Ldr 1/1/66. Retd ENG 16/1/71.
SAREL A. R. Born 5/5/07. Commd 11/12/26. Sqn Ldr 1/10/38. Retd GD 1/5/40.
SARGEANT A. R. Born 1/3/34. Commd 29/4/53. Sqn Ldr 1/1/67. Retd GD 28/1/77.
SARGEANT B. Born 7/6/41. Commd 23/9/66. Flt Lt 1/7/69. Retd GD(G) 7/6/79.
SARGEANT R. A. Born 24/4/46. Commd 14/7/66. Wg Cdr 1/1/91. Retd GD 20/7/96.
SARGEANT R. M., CEng MIEE. Born 23/2/29. Commd 5/9/57. Sqn Ldr 1/7/65. Retd ENG 23/2/89.
SARGENT D. Born 18/2/44. Commd 7/6/68. Sqn Ldr 1/1/86. Retd GD 11/3/99.
SARGENT D. M. Born 21/11/36. Commd 24/1/63. Sqn Ldr 1/7/74. Retd ADMIN 18/10/87.
SARGENT D. S. Born 15/6/29. Commd 26/5/60. Flt Lt 26/5/66. Retd ENG 15/12/79.
SARGENT J. Born 19/5/48. Commd 1/8/69. Flt Lt 8/3/72. Retd GD 19/5/86.

SARGENT K. G. Born 5/8/21. Commd 6/12/56. Flt Lt 23/11/61. Retd GD 5/8/76.
SARGENT M. W. Born 2/10/48. Commd 21/3/69. Flt Lt 19/7/75. Retd SEC 1/4/78.
SARGENT R. H. Born 16/12/47. Commd 2/8/68. Sqn Ldr 1/1/81. Retd GD 16/12/91.
SARJEANT C. J. Born 22/12/54. Commd 4/6/87. Flt Lt 4/6/89. Retd GD 22/12/98.
SATCHWELL G. F., MRAeS. Born 8/1/21. Commd 1/11/41. Wg Cdr 1/7/60. Retd ENG 14/10/61.
SATHERLEY A. Born 24/9/14. Commd 21/9/50. Flt Lt 21/3/54. Retd ENG 15/10/66.
SATOW A. R. Born 1/3/27. Commd 2/3/49. Sqn Ldr 1/1/58. Retd GD 1/3/65.
SATTERLY R. D. Born 1/11/31. Commd 29/3/62. Flt Lt 29/3/66. Retd PRT 1/11/69.
SATTERTHWAITE W. E., OBE CEng MIEE. Born 1/8/16. Commd 16/3/44. Wg Cdr 1/1/62. Retd ENG 12/9/71.
SAUNBY C. C. Born 21/10/44. Commd 15/7/66. Flt Lt 15/1/69. Retd GD 29/8/74.
SAUNDBY R. P., MMedSci MB ChB MFCM MFOM MRAeS. Born 31/5/32. Commd 26/3/54. A Cdre 1/7/86. Retd MED 31/5/91.
SAUNDERS A. E. Born 25/2/52. Commd 20/1/80. Flt Lt 20/1/84. Retd ADMIN 20/1/96.
SAUNDERS A. F. Born 9/2/32. Commd 5/3/57. Flt Lt 6/3/63. Retd GD 6/5/76.
SAUNDERS C. Born 22/6/14. Commd 18/11/40. Sqn Ldr 1/8/47. Retd SEC 22/6/63.
SAUNDERS D., CEng MIERE DipEl. Born 18/11/27. Commd 11/6/53. Sqn Ldr 1/7/63. Retd ENG 1/7/66.
SAUNDERS D. A., CBE MSc BSc CEng FIEE. Born 14/11/33. Commd 10/1/57. AVM 1/7/87. Retd ENG 5/4/90.
SAUNDERS D. J., CBE MSc BSc CEng FIMechE FRAeS. Born 12/6/43. Commd 15/7/64. AVM 1/7/91. Retd ENG 1/9/97.
SAUNDERS D. M. C. Born 21/7/55. Commd 30/1/75. Flt Lt 30/7/81. Retd ADMIN 17/9/85.
SAUNDERS E. J., IEng MIIE. Born 1/7/56. Commd 22/11/84. Sqn Ldr 1/7/95. Retd ENG 15/10/00.
SAUNDERS E. M. Born 11/12/65. Commd 8/11/90. Flt Lt 8/5/96. Retd GD 10/2/00.
SAUNDERS F. A. Born 17/2/15. Commd 20/5/43. Flt Lt 20/11/46. Retd GD 1/9/57.
SAUNDERS F. E. Born 11/4/12. Commd 17/5/56. Flt Lt 17/5/59. Retd ENG 11/2/67.
SAUNDERS J. Born 10/9/36. Commd 31/8/62. Flt Lt 29/2/68. Retd GD 15/5/78.
SAUNDERS J. D., BSc. Born 19/5/41. Commd 9/11/64. Flt Lt 9/2/66. Retd GD 19/5/96.
SAUNDERS J. R. Born 14/9/22. Commd 1/11/41. Gp Capt 1/1/66. Retd GD 15/3/70.
SAUNDERS M. G. Born 10/5/45. Commd 5/2/65. Wg Cdr 1/1/90. Retd GD 10/5/00.
SAUNDERS N. J. Born 20/7/54. Commd 17/9/72. Fg Offr 2/9/75. Retd GD 20/10/77.
SAUNDERS P., DFC. Born 28/9/17. Commd 18/5/41. Sqn Ldr 1/1/53. Retd GD 26/1/58.
SAUNDERS R. F. Born 17/5/33. Commd 8/5/53. Gp Capt 1/7/81. Retd GD 17/5/88.
SAUNDERS R. H. G., CENG MIMechE MIEE. Born 30/1/25. Commd 13/11/62. Sqn Ldr 13/5/66. Retd EDN 13/11/78.
SAUNDERS R. L., MA. Born 24/8/07. Commd 4/7/39. Sqn Ldr 1/9/47. Retd EDN 1/9/67.
SAUNDERS R. M. Born 5/5/39. Commd 26/8/66. Sqn Ldr 1/7/78. Retd SEC 7/8/81.
SAUNDERS R. T., CBE. Born 15/10/25. Commd 21/12/45. Gp Capt 1/7/67. Retd GD 1/7/71.
SAUNDERS R. V. Born 20/3/09. Commd 30/7/43. Fg Offr 30/1/44. Retd ENG 3/11/45.
SAUNDERS T. B. J., MBE. Born 17/9/30. Commd 21/6/56. Sqn Ldr 1/7/69. Retd GD 13/6/84.
SAUNDERS W. R. Born 18/12/09. Commd 5/11/40. Flt Lt 1/9/45. Retd ENG 30/12/57 rtg Sqn Ldr.
SAUNDERS W. W., MBE AFC MIMgt. Born 30/10/21. Commd 10/4/42. Wg Cdr 1/1/67. Retd GD 4/5/72.
SAUNDERS-DAVIES D. A. P., FIMgt. Born 9/12/24. Commd 23/9/44. Gp Capt 1/1/71. Retd GD 29/3/76.
SAUZIER J. R. D., OBE CEng MIERE. Born 23/8/43. Commd 15/7/65. Wg Cdr 1/1/83. Retd ENG 23/8/87.
SAVAGE A. P. Born 9/4/13. Commd 28/6/45. Fg Offr 28/6/46. Retd GD 29/5/54.
SAVAGE G. P. J., BA. Born 6/5/42. Commd 16/9/76. Flt Lt 16/9/78. Retd ENG 16/9/84.
SAVAGE J. D. C., MSc BSc. Born 26/1/62. Commd 5/9/82. Sqn Ldr 1/1/98. Retd ENG 1/1/01.
SAVAGE M. H. Born 2/6/22. Commd 27/1/45. Sqn Ldr 1/10/55. Retd GD 16/9/60.
SAVAGE T. I. B. Born 14/3/69. Commd 17/1/85. Fg Offr 29/3/87. Retd SY 1/10/90 rtg Flt Lt.
SAVIGAR N. J. L. Born 28/7/52. Commd 19/3/73. Wg Cdr 1/7/87. Retd GD 28/7/90.
SAVILL M. S. Born 4/2/37. Commd 9/7/62. Flt Lt 28/7/65. Retd GD 28/1/73.
SAVILLE H. W. Born 18/3/16. Commd 11/8/54. Flt Lt 11/8/59. Retd GD(G) 10/4/66.
SAVILLE I., BSc. Born 12/7/55. Commd 15/9/74. Flt Lt 15/4/79. Retd GD 14/9/96.
SAVVA E. Born 6/6/22. Commd 2/7/47. Sqn Ldr 1/7/58. Retd SEC 26/1/63.
SAW A. J. A., BSc CEng MRAeS MIEE. Born 26/11/41. Commd 15/7/63. Sqn Ldr 1/1/72. Retd ENG 26/11/80.
SAWARD D., OBE. Born 6/6/13. Commd 28/7/34. Wg Cdr 8/10/43. Retd ENG 8/8/45 rtg Gp Capt.
SAWDEN D. Born 26/8/32. Commd 19/7/51. Sqn Ldr 1/1/63. Retd GD 9/4/84.
SAWLE THOMAS M. I. Born 12/8/43. Commd 12/7/63. Flt Lt 20/6/70. Retd GD 12/8/84.
SAWYER A. V., DFC. Born 28/12/12. Commd 16/12/33. Wg Cdr 28/10/43. Retd GD 13/8/46 rtg Gp Capt.
SAWYER D. J., MRAeS. Born 4/3/41. Commd 31/7/62. Flt Lt 31/1/65. Retd GD 30/10/82.
SAWYER H. G., AFC. Born 27/8/99. Commd 1/4/18. Sqn Ldr 1/4/35. Retd GD 1/3/37.
SAWYER J. H. Born 20/7/21. Commd 22/11/43. Flt Lt 22/5/47. Retd GD 20/7/76.
SAWYER J. N., CBE. Born 29/10/34. Commd 5/4/55. Gp Capt 1/1/84. Retd GD 29/10/89.
SAWYER J. S. Born 26/3/30. Commd 9/6/49. Sqn Ldr 1/1/77. Retd ENG 26/8/88.
SAWYER L. R. Born 24/8/34. Commd 10/9/52. Flt Lt 14/5/58. Retd GD 24/8/72.
SAWYER M. N., AFC. Born 16/12/37. Commd 18/1/56. Sqn Ldr 1/1/83. Retd GD 20/12/88.
SAWYER P. G., AFC. Born 15/4/27. Commd 20/10/49. Sqn Ldr 1/7/59. Retd GD 15/4/82.
SAWYER P. J. Born 28/1/35. Commd 13/12/55. Sqn Ldr 1/1/68. Retd GD 1/10/76.

SAWYER R., MBE. Born 4/6/26. Commd 27/8/59. Wg Cdr 1/7/75. Retd SUP 31/10/78.
SAWYER R. G., MA BSc MIMgt. Born 15/3/36. Commd 22/11/57. Sqn Ldr 5/12/66. Retd EDN 1/10/78.
SAXBY G. Born 18/8/10. Commd 25/11/43. Flt Lt 25/5/47. Retd ENG 18/5/65.
SAXBY G., BSc AIIP. Born 4/11/25. Commd 16/12/66. Sqn Ldr 13/2/72. Retd EDN 1/5/74.
SAXBY R. L., BSc. Born 26/3/35. Commd 20/12/57. Sqn Ldr 20/6/68. Retd EDN 12/9/73.
SAXTON D. W., MB ChB MRCOG. Born 4/6/52. Commd 16/7/74. Sqn Ldr 15/8/83. Retd MED 1/12/90.
SAXTON K. L. W., MBE MIMgt. Born 25/2/28. Commd 28/7/60. Sqn Ldr 1/7/73. Retd ENG 16/4/76.
SAXTON P. J., BA. Born 6/8/47. Commd 1/1/67. Flt Lt 15/10/70. Retd GD 1/2/77.
SAY D. I. Born 3/11/47. Commd 7/7/67. Plt Offr 7/7/68. Retd GD 2/5/69.
SAYE J. G. Born 3/10/37. Commd 16/12/58. Gp Capt 1/1/82. Retd GD 21/1/90.
SAYER M. H. W., BSc CEng MIEE. Born 5/2/39. Commd 30/9/58. Sqn Ldr 7/4/72. Retd ENG 5/2/94.
SAYER M. J., FRIN. Born 17/8/43. Commd 9/3/62. Sqn Ldr 1/1/74. Retd GD 13/3/00.
SAYER M. R. Born 28/11/03. Commd 1/7/43. Fg Offr 1/7/43. Retd SUP 10/10/46.
SAYER R. Born 10/1/43. Commd 5/2/81. Sqn Ldr 1/7/89. Retd ADMIN 1/10/93.
SAYERS G. F. H., DFC AFC. Born 30/6/11. Commd 30/10/42. Flt Lt 30/10/44. Retd GD 27/5/47 rtg Sqn Ldr.
SAYERS J. L., DFC*. Born 21/2/21. Commd 17/11/49. Sqn Ldr 1/1/69. Retd GD(G) 31/8/71.
SAYERS R. C. Born 23/7/38. Commd 6/8/60. Flt Lt 6/2/66. Retd GD 23/7/76.
SAYERS R. W. Born 13/4/07. Commd 25/8/41. Flt Lt 1/9/45. Retd ENG 23/11/49.
SAYFRITZ H. V. Born 3/12/22. Commd 14/7/44. Wg Cdr 1/1/63. Retd GD 18/3/77.
SCALES E. J. Born 24/3/33. Commd 25/10/51. Sqn Ldr 1/1/71. Retd GD 31/5/84.
SCAMBLER J. A., FIMgt. Born 8/7/32. Commd 26/3/52. Gp Capt 1/7/76. Retd GD 3/4/85.
SCAMMELL N. R. Born 14/1/47. Commd 1/8/69. Flt Lt 8/3/72. Retd GD 19/5/86.
SCAMMELLS J. R. Born 13/10/18. Commd 30/5/46. Flt Lt 4/1/51. Retd GD(G) 13/10/71 rtg Sqn Ldr.
SCANDRETT B. J., CBE AFC. Born 14/12/16. Commd 28/8/42. Gp Capt 1/1/65. Retd GD 14/12/71.
SCANDRETT C. F., MIMgt. Born 25/5/15. Commd 27/10/55. Flt Lt 27/10/61. Retd ENG 25/5/71.
SCANLON F. P., MSc BSc. Born 13/12/58. Commd 11/9/77. Sqn Ldr 1/1/90. Retd ENG 13/12/96.
SCANLON J. T., CEng FIMgt MRAeS. Born 22/3/22. Commd 21/10/42. Gp Capt 1/7/67. Retd ENG 22/3/77.
SCARD G. T., BA. Born 13/5/45. Commd 3/1/64. Wg Cdr 1/1/91. Retd GD 13/5/00.
SCARFF B. H. Born 9/11/20. Commd 24/2/43. Sqn Ldr 1/1/71. Retd GD 15/5/74.
SCARGILL P. N. Born 23/1/50. Commd 27/2/70. Fg Offr 27/8/72. Retd SEC 4/1/75.
SCARLETT A. P. Born 22/11/46. Commd 28/7/67. Sqn Ldr 1/7/85. Retd SUP 18/9/90.
SCARLETT R. Born 8/9/29. Commd 18/9/50. Flt Lt 5/6/56. Retd GD 8/9/67.
SCARLETT R. W. J. Born 16/9/21. Commd 10/12/43. Sqn Ldr 1/1/67. Retd GD 7/4/73.
SCARRATT R. G. Born 13/4/21. Commd 31/7/58. Sqn Ldr 1/7/69. Retd SEC 1/10/71.
SCASE E. H., MBE. Born 22/7/38. Commd 27/9/73. Sqn Ldr 1/7/82. Retd ADMIN 23/7/88.
SCATES E. A. Born 19/1/23. Commd 5/5/60. Flt Lt 5/5/63. Retd GD(G) 19/1/78.
SCATES R. W. Born 7/3/17. Commd 27/2/58. Sqn Ldr 1/1/67. Retd ENG 7/3/73.
SCEATS J. M. Born 12/5/33. Commd 26/3/53. Flt Lt 26/9/57. Retd GD 12/5/71.
SCHAUER B. J. A. Born 6/5/32. Commd 23/10/56. Flt Lt 22/4/62. Retd GD 6/5/70.
SCHENK K. S. R. Born 23/9/68. Commd 10/5/90. Fg Offr 10/11/92. Retd ADMIN 14/3/97.
SCHIMMEL A. A. Born 8/4/51. Commd 22/7/71. Flt Lt 22/1/77. Retd GD 8/4/89.
SCHLUSSLER K. A., BE. Born 17/9/39. Commd 21/1/66. Flt Lt 24/11/69. Retd GD 20/7/75.
SCHOFIELD A. E., CEng MIEE MIMgt. Born 27/8/20. Commd 12/9/45. Gp Capt 1/7/75. Retd ENG 30/7/77.
SCHOFIELD A. V. Born 11/5/35. Commd 11/3/68. Wg Cdr 1/1/87. Retd PRT 11/5/90.
SCHOFIELD B. S. Born 13/9/41. Commd 20/9/79. Sqn Ldr 1/1/90. Retd ADMIN 13/9/97.
SCHOFIELD The Rev E. P., MA BD. Born 9/3/21. Commd 15/1/53. Retd 15/1/71 Wg Cdr.
SCHOFIELD J. F. Born 7/4/32. Commd 6/12/51. Flt Lt 27/3/57. Retd GD 7/4/45.
SCHOFIELD J. M. Born 14/1/54. Commd 9/8/79. Flt Lt 26/10/81. Retd SUP 14/1/92.
SCHOFIELD M. L. Born 6/3/45. Commd 19/6/64. Wg Cdr 1/1/85. Retd GD 6/3/89.
SCHOFIELD N. B., MBE BSc CEng MIMechE MRIN. Born 11/9/53. Commd 17/9/72. Sqn Ldr 1/1/88. Retd ENG 11/9/91.
SCHOFIELD R. A. Born 17/5/23. Commd 11/6/43. Sqn Ldr 1/7/53. Retd GD 17/5/66 rtg Wg Cdr.
SCHOFIELD R. R. Born 16/7/18. Commd 15/5/47. Flt Lt 27/5/54. Retd ENG 16/1/64.
SCHOFIELD T. J., BSc(Eng). Born 9/5/60. Commd 18/3/84. Flt Lt 18/9/87. Retd RGT 11/5/90.
SCHOLEFIELD J. N., MIMgt. Born 28/12/47. Commd 16/9/76. Wg Cdr 1/7/91. Retd ADMIN 1/5/98.
SCHOLES K. Born 28/1/20. Commd 12/3/43. Sqn Ldr 1/7/54. Retd GD 28/1/63.
SCHOLES M., MBE DFM. Born 17/10/24. Commd 29/8/44. Wg Cdr 1/7/67. Retd ADMIN 25/3/78.
SCHOLLAR A. J., MCIPD. Born 17/1/35. Commd 2/2/56. Wg Cdr 1/1/75. Retd ADMIN 2/4/87.
SCHONER N. J., MSc BSc. Born 13/9/61. Commd 6/10/83. Flt Lt 22/7/88. Retd ENG 13/4/00.
SCHOOLING N. J. Born 14/3/35. Commd 16/1/72. Sqn Ldr 16/1/72. Retd SUP 16/1/88.
SCHRANZ P. J., FRCSEd(Orth) MRCS(Eng) LRCP. Born 23/2/58. Commd 15/2/79. Wg Cdr 1/8/95. Retd MED 30/11/96.
SCHROETER N. S., MMar MNI. Born 1/4/48. Commd 30/3/75. Flt Lt 30/3/75. Retd GD 14/12/96.
SCHUCK K. Born 6/3/21. Commd 1/12/44. Flt Lt 15/10/52. Retd GD 19/6/65.
SCHULMAN C. J., DFM. Born 9/8/17. Commd 12/1/43. Flt Lt 31/8/56. Retd GD(G) 19/2/69.
SCHULTZ K., BSc. Born 11/2/51. Commd 15/9/69. Sqn Ldr 1/1/87. Retd GD 3/1/89.

SCHWAIGER I. L. Born 24/5/30. Commd 1/8/51. Sqn Ldr 1/7/60. Retd GD 24/6/68.
SCHYNS M. G. B. Born 18/2/22. Commd 1/12/49. Flt Lt 20/3/61. Retd SEC 18/2/79.
SCILLEY H. G. A., CEng MRaeS. Born 11/11/14. Commd 3/10/41. Wg Cdr 1/1/59. Retd ENG 11/11/69.
SCOBBIE D. M. Born 8/7/38. Commd 15/9/60. Flt Lt 26/7/67. Retd GD 8/7/76.
SCOFIELD K. H., BSc. Born 5/1/56. Commd 20/1/80. Flt Lt 12/12/82. Retd GD(G) 1/10/87.
SCOGGINS I. M., MA CEng MRaeS. Born 28/7/36. Commd 30/9/55. Sqn Ldr 1/7/67. Retd ENG 28/7/74.
SCORER C., DFC. Born 4/11/16. Commd 5/1/42. Sqn Ldr 1/1/50. Retd GD 4/11/57.
SCORER L., DFC. Born 18/4/19. Commd 30/3/42. Flt Lt 19/6/52. Retd GD 25/5/62.
SCOREY A. T. Born 28/11/26. Commd 14/2/51. Flt Lt 17/3/57. Retd GD 15/1/67.
SCOTCHMER L. E. H., OBE. Born 29/10/23. Commd 14/5/43. Gp Capt 1/1/69. Retd GD 30/3/78.
SCOTHERN D. Born 4/1/42. Commd 10/3/77. Sqn Ldr 1/1/88. Retd ENG 4/1/97.
SCOTHERN M., CertEd. Born 20/9/45. Commd 12/10/78. Sqn Ldr 1/1/87. Retd ENG 3/4/97.
SCOTLAND A., MBE. Born 16/11/36. Commd 2/2/68. Sqn Ldr 1/7/76. Retd GD 1/5/87.
SCOTT A., AFC. Born 25/12/03. Commd 14/8/40. Flt Lt 17/7/46. Retd SEC 19/7/47. Re-employed 15/11/48. Sqn Ldr 1/7/52. Retd 15/11/56.
SCOTT A., MBE. Born 11/5/23. Commd 14/3/49. Sqn Ldr 1/1/73. Retd GD 11/5/83.
SCOTT A. D., BSc CEng MRaeS. Born 20/9/39. Commd 30/9/59. Flt Lt 15/4/66. Retd ENG 20/9/94.
SCOTT A. G., MBE. Born 26/11/21. Commd 26/11/43. Sqn Ldr 1/1/65. Retd GD(G) 1/1/71.
SCOTT A. G., CEng MIEE. Born 20/4/48. Commd 17/9/72. Sqn Ldr 1/7/80. Retd ENG 31/5/86.
SCOTT A. H., DFM. Born 27/7/21. Commd 13/3/43. Sqn Ldr 1/7/69. Retd GD(G) 27/7/76.
SCOTT A. M. Born 20/12/21. Commd 5/9/42. Flt Lt 3/10/48. Retd SEC 12/9/67.
SCOTT A. R., DFC* MIMgt. Born 21/11/19. Commd 2/6/47. Wg Cdr 1/1/59. Retd GD 21/11/74.
SCOTT B. C., AFC. Born 27/12/51. Commd 24/6/71. Sqn Ldr 1/7/85. Retd GD 27/12/89.
SCOTT C. Born 18/3/39. Commd 11/8/77. Flt Lt 11/8/78. Retd ADMIN 28/11/88.
SCOTT C. F. S. Born 1/6/08. Commd 28/1/43. Flt Lt 2/9/45. Retd ENG 1/6/57.
SCOTT C. L. M. Born 31/5/27. Commd 27/7/49. Flt Lt 27/1/52. Retd GD 31/5/65.
SCOTT D. H. Born 7/7/36. Commd 17/12/57. Sqn Ldr 1/7/72. Retd GD 1/7/75.
SCOTT D. I., MBE FRIN FIMgt. Born 24/7/32. Commd 19/4/51. Gp Capt 1/1/84. Retd GD 27/10/86.
SCOTT D. J., MA BA MB BChir MRCP DCH. Born 25/10/50. Commd 9/1/72. Wg Cdr 9/9/88. Retd MED 9/1/89.
SCOTT D. M., BA. Born 31/5/60. Commd 12/10/79. Sqn Ldr 1/1/92. Retd ADMIN 14/3/96.
SCOTT D. M. Born 20/10/21. Commd 27/1/43. Flt Offr 24/2/56. Retd SEC 5/8/62.
SCOTT D. N., BSc. Born 27/3/58. Commd 27/9/78. Flt Lt 15/4/81. Retd GD 30/9/00.
SCOTT D. R., DFC AFC. Born 12/7/21. Commd 7/9/43. Flt Lt 7/3/47. Retd GD 12/7/67.
SCOTT D. S. Born 21/4/20. Commd 4/11/43. Flt Lt 4/5/47. Retd ENG 1/12/64.
SCOTT D. S. M., AFC. Born 17/1/16. Commd 18/11/40. Sqn Ldr 1/7/50. Retd GD 20/3/59.
SCOTT D. W., MBE CEng MRaeS. Born 19/4/25. Commd 4/2/48. Wg Cdr 1/1/69. Retd ENG 12/4/79.
SCOTT E., MBE. Born 18/2/11. Commd 7/9/44. Flt Lt 7/3/47. Retd ENG 30/9/67.
SCOTT E. J. Born 5/3/34. Commd 18/2/53. Sqn Ldr 1/7/81. Retd GD 15/4/87.
SCOTT F., MBE FIMgt. Born 2/12/32. Commd 17/1/52. Gp Capt 1/7/76. Retd GD 4/4/80.
SCOTT F. G., BA MHSM MCIPD. Born 25/11/38. Commd 8/9/77. Flt Lt 8/9/82. Retd MED(SEC) 25/11/93.
SCOTT G. Born 7/12/04. Commd 10/12/42. Fg Offr 10/12/42. Retd ENG 1/9/47 rtg Flt Lt.
SCOTT G., BSc. Born 14/10/37. Commd 22/1/59. Sqn Ldr 4/10/72. Retd EDN 10/3/75.
SCOTT G. K., DFC. Born 20/8/20. Commd 5/10/39. Sqn Ldr 1/7/54. Retd ENG 20/9/76.
SCOTT H. C., MBE. Born 8/7/15. Commd 3/6/42. Sqn Ldr 1/1/56. Retd GD(G) 27/3/61.
SCOTT I. F., BA. Born 4/3/47. Commd 1/9/70. Flt Lt 1/6/71. Retd GD 1/9/82.
SCOTT I. G., ACMA. Born 16/3/33. Commd 20/6/63. Sqn Ldr 1/7/74. Retd ADMIN 1/11/77.
SCOTT I. L. Born 6/6/24. Commd 1/10/43. Sqn Ldr 1/1/56. Retd GD 6/6/62.
SCOTT I. P. Born 29/12/50. Commd 21/9/72. Flt Lt 21/3/78. Retd GD 29/12/88.
SCOTT I. W. Born 29/9/47. Commd 1/7/82. Flt Lt 1/7/84. Retd GD 1/7/91.
SCOTT J., MCIPS MIMgt. Born 25/3/42. Commd 27/1/67. Wg Cdr 1/1/89. Retd SUP 25/3/97.
SCOTT J. Born 5/11/17. Commd 14/12/43. Flt Lt 10/11/55. Retd GD(G) 31/12/65.
SCOTT J. F. H. Born 11/3/22. Commd 22/4/45. Wg Cdr 1/1/72. Retd SUP 11/3/77.
SCOTT J. H. L. Born 26/1/44. Commd 28/9/62. Fg Offr 28/9/64. Retd GD 14/11/67.
SCOTT J. R. Born 28/7/28. Commd 8/5/50. Flt Lt 1/6/59. Retd GD 1/6/67.
SCOTT J. S. Born 5/1/13. Commd 18/12/43. Flt Lt 18/12/45. Retd GD 4/7/46.
SCOTT J. S. W., DPhysEd. Born 2/2/46. Commd 19/8/68. Sqn Ldr 1/1/88. Retd ADMIN 2/4/97.
SCOTT K. F. Born 12/3/22. Commd 21/6/56. Flt Lt 21/6/59. Retd GD 1/3/74 rtg Sqn Ldr.
SCOTT L. Born 14/9/21. Commd 20/4/50. Flt Lt 20/10/53. Retd GD 14/9/76.
SCOTT L. J. Born 24/5/35. Commd 7/1/81. Flt Lt 15/3/73. Retd GD 24/5/93.
SCOTT L. K. Born 7/11/47. Commd 29/3/68. Fg Offr 29/3/70. Retd GD 13/1/72.
SCOTT P., BEM. Born 17/4/17. Commd 11/4/57. Flt Lt 1/4/63. Retd ENG 17/4/72.
SCOTT P. Born 21/6/46. Commd 2/1/70. Flt Lt 2/7/76. Retd ADMIN 11/8/85.
SCOTT P. H. L., AFC. Born 27/2/24. Commd 21/1/45. A Cdre 1/1/73. Retd GD 29/3/77.
SCOTT P. J., MSc BSc. Born 24/1/58. Commd 5/9/76. Sqn Ldr 1/1/90. Retd ENG 7/4/01.
SCOTT P. R. Born 24/4/58. Commd 11/6/81. Flt Lt 11/12/87. Retd GD(G) 9/2/97.
SCOTT R. Born 1/2/56. Commd 19/7/84. Flt Lt 13/5/87. Retd ADMIN 1/2/94.

SCOTT R. A. Born 30/12/35. Commd 12/12/59. Flt Lt 13/1/67. Retd GD 29/1/76.
SCOTT R. E., LLB. Born 17/1/58. Commd 31/8/75. Flt Lt 15/10/79. Retd GD 1/4/88.
SCOTT R. G., AFC. Born 13/2/32. Commd 14/1/60. Sqn Ldr 1/7/77. Retd GD 30/9/82.
SCOTT R. J., MA. Born 18/8/33. Commd 24/2/55. Sqn Ldr 18/2/63. Retd EDN 1/9/71.
SCOTT R. J. S., BA. Born 18/7/39. Commd 18/7/61. Sqn Ldr 1/7/80. Retd ENG 18/3/92.
SCOTT R. T. D. Born 25/5/22. Commd 20/7/50. Sqn Ldr 1/7/67. Retd GD 25/5/77.
SCOTT R. W., CEng MIMechE MRAeS. Born 17/12/37. Commd 23/7/58. Wg Cdr 1/7/77. Retd ENG 3/7/79.
SCOTT S. Born 23/2/56. Commd 9/5/91. Flt Lt 9/5/95. Retd ENG 1/10/99.
SCOTT T. F., CEng MIMechE. Born 3/9/37. Commd 2/5/66. Sqn Ldr 14/5/72. Retd ADMIN 2/5/76.
SCOTT T. I., BEM. Born 31/10/38. Commd 18/4/74. Sqn Ldr 1/1/84. Retd ENG 18/8/90.
SCOTT T. McM., BA MIMgt. Born 12/3/34. Commd 5/9/69. Wg Cdr 1/7/85. Retd ADMIN 1/2/90.
SCOTT W. A., MBE. Born 21/10/18. Commd 9/8/45. Sqn Ldr 1/7/66. Retd SEC 9/6/73.
SCOTT W. J., BSc. Born 13/4/53. Commd 7/10/73. Sqn Ldr 1/7/87. Retd ADMIN 25/11/00.
SCOTT W. L. Born 26/3/55. Commd 25/9/83. Flt Lt 23/5/79. Retd GD 1/12/89.
SCOTT W. L. M. Born 16/3/24. Commd 12/11/43. Gp Capt 1/7/68. Retd GD 16/3/79.
SCOTT W. P., CEng MIEE. Born 23/3/40. Commd 15/7/63. Wg Cdr 1/1/78. Retd ENG 6/1/81.
SCOTT W. T. Born 26/10/11. Commd 3/12/42. Sqn Ldr 1/7/62. Retd ENG 26/10/67.
SCOTT-NELSON R. J., Dip PE. Born 23/5/44. Commd 16/8/70. Flt Lt 16/8/74. Retd ADMIN 16/8/86.
SCOTT-SKINNER S. M. Born 7/2/51. Commd 16/3/73. Flt Lt 16/3/76. Retd GD 7/2/89.
SCOTTING P. A. Born 8/8/61. Commd 20/6/91. Flt Lt 20/6/93. Retd ADMIN 4/12/96.
SCOTTON A. H. Born 22/2/34. Commd 27/2/52. Flt Lt 26/6/57. Retd GD(G) 26/4/80.
SCOULLER D. C., AFC MRAeS. Born 9/4/35. Commd 30/7/57. Gp Capt 1/7/83. Retd GD 9/4/89.
SCOWEN B. J., DFC. Born 29/4/21. Commd 11/11/44. Wg Cdr 1/1/69. Retd GD 4/7/72.
SCRAGG W. A. Born 8/1/42. Commd 14/5/60. Sqn Ldr 1/7/91. Retd GD 8/1/97.
SCRANCHER P. J. Born 24/12/48. Commd 26/9/90. Flt Lt 26/9/92. Retd SUP 1/1/00.
SCREECH P. V., BA. Born 1/11/54. Commd 11/12/83. Sqn Ldr 1/1/92. Retd ADMIN 11/12/00.
SCRIMGEOUR D., McL CBE. Born 14/5/27. Commd 3/9/47. A Cdre 1/7/76. Retd GD 14/5/82.
SCRIMGEOUR J., MBE BEM. Born 12/2/20. Commd 23/2/50. Sqn Ldr 1/7/58. Retd SEC 31/8/68.
SCRIMSHAW K. A. Born 29/5/61. Commd 19/12/91. Fg Offr 19/6/94. Retd ADMIN 23/1/97.
SCRIVEN A. W. Born 4/11/29. Commd 19/6/70. Flt Lt 19/6/72. Retd SUP 4/11/87.
SCRIVENER F. M. H. Born 26/3/24. Commd 28/5/57. Sqn Ldr 1/7/69. Retd SUP 30/6/78.
SCRIVENER R. J. Born 8/3/44. Commd 29/11/63. Flt Lt 29/5/69. Retd GD 8/3/88.
SCRIVENS E. R., MIMgt. Born 26/8/18. Commd 30/12/43. Sqn Ldr 1/1/62. Retd ENG 9/9/73.
SCROGGS T. W. M. Born 1/11/32. Commd 14/12/54. Flt Lt 14/12/59. Retd ADMIN 1/11/87.
SCULLION J. L., MIMgt. Born 30/10/31. Commd 16/11/61. Wg Cdr 1/1/80. Retd ENG 29/4/83.
SCULLION P. J., MIMgt. Born 7/4/45. Commd 21/1/73. Sqn Ldr 1/1/81. Retd ENG 14/3/97.
SCUTT J. B. Born 20/4/20. Commd 9/7/59. Sqn Ldr 1/7/70. Retd ENG 30/4/73.
SEABOURNE E. W., DFC. Born 26/8/19. Commd 12/8/41. Sqn Ldr 1/8/47. Retd SEC 2/12/60.
SEABROOK G. L., CB FCA. Born 25/8/09. Commd 7/6/33. AVM 1/1/64. Retd SEC 29/6/66.
SEABROOK S. E. Born 5/2/22. Commd 5/5/60. Sqn Ldr 1/7/70. Retd ENG 9/9/72.
SEABY E. W., ACIS. Born 25/4/38. Commd 6/9/68. Flt Lt 6/9/70. Retd ADMIN 6/9/76.
SEAGER K. D. Born 13/12/63. Commd 24/3/83. Flt Lt 24/9/88. Retd GD 14/3/96.
SEALE D. R., MBIM. Born 14/4/32. Commd 24/1/52. Wg Cdr 1/1/75. Retd GD 5/11/85.
SEALEY A. D. Born 4/2/69. Commd 2/11/88. Flt Lt 2/5/94. Retd GD 30/3/00.
SEALEY H. G., MVO. Born 9/2/26. Commd 10/2/52. Sqn Ldr 1/7/67. Retd GD 8/5/76.
SEALY J. L. Born 4/6/39. Commd 18/8/61. Fg Offr 18/8/63. Retd GD 25/9/65.
SEAMAN G. Born 27/4/41. Commd 21/4/77. Flt Lt 21/4/80. Retd GD 22/4/94.
SEAR D. A. Born 13/7/21. Commd 18/11/54. Sqn Ldr 1/7/66. Retd ENG 13/1/77.
SEARLE J. F., BSc CEng MIMechE. Born 13/8/43. Commd 29/8/72. Sqn Ldr 1/7/90. Retd ENG 31/3/94.
SEARLE N. F., MRAeS. Born 19/2/20. Commd 23/9/43. Wg Cdr 1/1/61. Retd ENG 4/5/68.
SEARLE P. E. Born 6/4/43. Commd 4/3/71. Sqn Ldr 1/7/79. Retd SUP 6/4/98.
SEARLE R. E. Born 1/6/46. Commd 22/7/71. Sqn Ldr 1/7/80. Retd ENG 1/6/90.
SEARLE R. J., CEng MRAeS. Born 18/3/36. Commd 25/2/64. Sqn Ldr 1/7/81. Retd ENG 21/3/90.
SEARLE R. W. Born 3/5/46. Commd 5/3/65. Flt Lt 5/9/70. Retd GD 1/1/80.
SEARS R. H. Born 27/11/44. Commd 2/2/84. Sqn Ldr 1/1/93. Retd ADMIN 27/11/99.
SEARS R. W. Born 25/2/48. Commd 28/2/69. Sqn Ldr 1/7/85. Retd GD 25/2/89.
SEATON C. M. Born 19/11/44. Commd 26/4/84. Flt Lt 1/3/87. Retd GD 22/6/99.
SEATON D. H., DFC AFC*. Born 19/5/21. Commd 20/8/41. Gp Capt 1/7/60. Retd GD 20/5/64.
SEATON D. J., MBE. Born 8/8/45. Commd 7/6/68. Sqn Ldr 1/7/81. Retd ENG 8/6/97.
SEATON D. J., BSc. Born 18/4/53. Commd 30/8/78. Sqn Ldr 1/1/89. Retd ENG 30/8/94.
SEAWARD P. V. A. Born 17/9/46. Commd 16/12/66. Flt Lt 25/2/73. Retd ADMIN 17/9/84.
SEBLEY T. P. H. Born 7/11/50. Commd 4/3/71. Sqn Ldr 1/7/86. Retd SY 14/9/96.
SEBRIGHT A. L. Born 20/5/32. Commd 28/6/51. Sqn Ldr 1/1/64. Retd GD 12/11/76.
SECKER R. L. Born 22/8/12. Commd 18/10/43. Flt Lt 18/4/47. Retd ENG 29/3/55.
SEDDON H. Born 6/3/50. Commd 4/5/72. Sqn Ldr 1/1/93. Retd GD 14/9/96.
SEDGLEY B. A. Born 17/4/25. Commd 24/1/52. Flt Lt 18/8/57. Retd GD 17/4/63.

SEDGWICK P. A., BSc. Born 18/2/39. Commd 1/10/62. Sqn Ldr 1/7/71. Retd GD 1/10/78.
SEDMAN D. M. Born 10/4/45. Commd 10/12/65. Wg Cdr 1/7/91. Retd GD 10/4/00.
SEEGER J. E. R. Born 21/6/42. Commd 24/3/61. Flt Lt 24/9/66. Retd GD 30/1/73.
SEEKINGS M. R. J. Born 23/9/33. Commd 9/4/57. Flt Lt 9/4/62. Retd SEC 15/2/68.
SEELEY A. H. Born 20/9/31. Commd 30/7/52. Flt Lt 27/12/57. Retd GD 20/9/69.
SEFTON J. Born 23/1/49. Commd 31/7/70. Flt Lt 31/7/73. Retd GD 22/10/94.
SEFTON J. L. Born 24/4/11. Commd 18/9/40. Sqn Ldr 1/8/47. Retd SEC 1/8/58.
SEGGER W. M. Born 5/12/13. Commd 22/9/41. Flt Offr 29/9/45. Retd SUP 18/1/63 rtg Sqn Offr.
SEIDELIN R., MA DM BCh MRCP DPM. Born 24/1/24. Commd 29/9/50. Wg Cdr 13/12/60. Retd MED 13/12/68.
SELBY F. Born 4/3/29. Commd 17/5/51. Flt Lt 6/9/56. Retd GD 4/3/67.
SELBY M. J. Born 24/1/47. Commd 28/11/69. Wg Cdr 1/7/94. Retd GD 14/3/96.
SELBY R. C., MCIPS MIMgt. Born 13/4/32. Commd 17/5/62. Sqn Ldr 1/7/73. Retd SUP 3/10/78.
SELBY-DAVIES R., BA. Born 9/9/42. Commd 13/6/71. Flt Lt 13/3/75. Retd OPS SPT 9/9/97.
SELBY-GREEN A. G. Born 19/1/59. Commd 19/7/84. Flt Lt 19/7/86. Retd GD 6/9/89.
SELDON F. P. Born 18/1/58. Commd 15/2/90. Flt Lt 15/2/92. Retd OPS SPT 28/7/98.
SELDON J. L., MA MSc. Born 4/12/35. Commd 25/9/54. Sqn Ldr 1/1/69. Retd ENG 4/12/73.
SELDON P. R. Born 15/7/32. Commd 6/12/51. Flt Lt 27/3/57. Retd GD 15/7/87.
SELDON R. J. B. Born 11/9/30. Commd 21/4/54. Flt Lt 16/8/61. Retd RGT 22/5/70.
SELF A. W., MSc. Born 14/3/42. Commd 9/3/72. Sqn Ldr 15/10/80. Retd ADMIN 2/10/84.
SELF F. J. A., MA. Born 26/6/56. Commd 15/10/78. Flt Lt 15/10/84. Retd ADMIN 15/10/86.
SELLAR J. C., BDS. Born 15/4/47. Commd 18/12/67. Sqn Ldr 23/12/74. Retd DEL 1/10/76.
SELLARS N. A. Born 4/1/20. Commd 29/11/37. Wg Cdr 1/7/58. Retd GD 1/10/68.
SELLARS R. J., MHCIMA. Born 10/4/33. Commd 17/1/52. Sqn Ldr 1/7/73. Retd ADMIN 1/7/76.
SELLER M. A. E. Born 8/2/40. Commd 13/10/61. Wg Cdr 1/1/81. Retd GD 26/10/90.
SELLERS B., BSc CEng MIMechE MRAeS MIMgt. Born 30/12/38. Commd 30/9/57. Sqn Ldr 1/7/71. Retd ENG
  30/9/80.
SELVARAJAH G. Born 21/1/41. Commd 29/12/69. Flt Lt 29/12/69. Retd GD(G) 21/1/96.
SELVARATNAM S., CEng MIEE MRAeS MIMgt AMIMechE. Born 25/9/44. Commd 13/4/80. Sqn Ldr 1/1/89. Retd ENG
  14/3/97.
SELVES M. J. Born 27/7/46. Commd 8/1/65. Flt Lt 8/7/70. Retd GD 27/7/85.
SELWAY A. D. M. Born 8/8/48. Commd 27/3/70. Fg Offr 13/8/72. Retd SY 10/7/76.
SEMARK A. M. Born 22/11/42. Commd 6/7/62. Flt Lt 1/7/68. Retd GD 22/11/80.
SEMMENS W. C. Born 22/11/28. Commd 18/11/66. Flt Lt 18/11/71. Retd SUP 22/11/78.
SEMPLE A. W. Born 14/10/44. Commd 3/3/67. Wg Cdr 1/1/91. Retd GD 10/10/00.
SEMPLE I. Born 22/11/35. Commd 14/7/54. Gp Capt 1/7/85. Retd GD 31/7/89.
SEMPLE N. Born 3/9/46. Commd 26/5/67. Flt Lt 18/8/72. Retd ENG 3/10/78.
SENIOR G. G., BA. Born 29/10/49. Commd 12/8/79. Flt Lt 12/8/81. Retd ADMIN 12/8/89.
SENIOR J. A. Born 9/6/20. Commd 29/8/45. Flt Lt 30/11/60. Retd RGT 9/6/65.
SENIOR J. E., BSc. Born 17/1/46. Commd 28/9/64. Flt Lt 15/10/69. Retd GD 17/1/84.
SENIOR R. Born 10/2/29. Commd 12/9/51. Sqr Ldr 1/7/77. Retd GD 10/2/84.
SENIOR S. E., MBE. Born 10/4/60. Commd 13/8/82. Sqn Ldr 1/7/93. Retd ADMIN 12/4/98.
SENTANCE G. A., MBE FCIS FCCS MIMgt. Born 29/6/15. Commd 21/11/41. Wg Cdr 1/1/59. Retd SEC 3/4/68.
SEPHTON A. J., BSc. Born 13/1/50. Commd 15/9/69. Flt Lt 15/4/74. Retd GD 1/7/89.
SEPPINGS C. E. Born 21/6/21. Commd 18/9/47. Flt Lt 1/1/55. Retd PRT 31/8/63.
SERCOMBE C. B. Born 14/10/24. Commd 14/4/49. Flt Lt 14/10/52. Retd GD 31/1/62.
SERCOMBE S. P. R. Born 15/6/20. Commd 4/11/44. Flt Lt 5/11/58. Retd SEC 2/7/75.
SERGEANT R. E. Born 8/11/41. Commd 4/11/82. Sqn Ldr 1/1/92. Retd ENG 8/11/96.
SERGEANT R. H., AE MIMgt. Born 30/6/20. Commd 11/10/41. Sqn Ldr 1/10/55. Retd GD 30/6/69.
SERRELL-COOKE J., MIMgt. Born 9/7/34. Commd 14/12/54. Sqn Ldr 1/1/79. Retd ADMIN 14/9/84.
SEVERN J. G. Born 15/9/17. Commd 17/5/56. Flt Lt 17/5/62. Retd SUP 30/5/70.
SEVERN P. J. Born 4/12/42. Commd 10/1/61. Flt Lt 26/7/67. Retd GD 1/7/77.
SEVERNE Sir John, KCVO OBE AFC DL. Born 15/8/25. Commd 19/10/45. AVM 1/7/78. Retd GD 15/8/80.
SEVERS A. D. Born 12/4/65. Commd 15/3/84. Flt Lt 15/9/89. Retd GD 14/3/96.
SEWARD D. J., AFC CBIM. Born 25/1/31. Commd 25/10/50. Gp Capt 1/7/79. Retd GD 25/1/81.
SEWARD R. F. Born 12/2/53. Commd 21/6/90. Flt Lt 21/6/94. Retd ENG 14/9/96.
SEWART A. Born 21/1/19. Commd 26/4/45. Flt Lt 26/10/49. Retd GD(G) 1/12/63 rtg Sqn Ldr.
SEWELL E. Born 12/9/19. Commd 25/3/54. Flt Lt 25/3/57. Retd GD(G) 12/9/69.
SEWELL E. F. W. Born 10/1/21. Commd 6/2/44. Flt Lt 7/6/51. Retd GD 19/7/55.
SEWELL J., BA FRGS. Born 14/6/40. Commd 14/5/62. Wg Cdr 1/7/87. Retd GD 6/12/92.
SEWELL J. E., MBE MIMgt. Born 4/2/28. Commd 9/8/51. Wg Cdr 1/1/67. Retd GD 8/4/78. rtg Gp Capt.
SEWELL J. P., MB BS DLO. Born 14/5/07. Commd 21/5/40. Gp Capt 1/1/59. Retd MED 21/5/72.
SEWELL M. K., DFC AFC. Born 22/3/14. Commd 4/6/38. Wg Cdr 1/7/47. Retd GD 4/4/61.
SEXSTONE C. L. Born 2/7/48. Commd 12/3/72. Gp Capt 1/7/94. Retd ADMIN 14/9/94.
SEXTON K. R. F., MBE CEng MIProdE MRAeS. Born 17/10/37. Commd 9/2/66. Sqn Ldr 1/1/77. Retd ENG 24/12/91.
SEYD M. V. Born 25/10/40. Commd 18/12/62. Flt Lt 26/7/67. Retd GD 25/10/78.
SEYMOUR A. C. P. Born 1/11/39. Commd 28/3/63. A Cdre 1/7/90. Retd SY 1/1/94.

SEYMOUR C. C. B. Born 12/9/38. Commd 21/8/62. Wg Cdr 1/1/80. Retd GD 14/9/92.
SEYMOUR C. R. Born 1/7/45. Commd 3/3/67. Wg Cdr 1/7/86. Retd SUP 1/7/89.
SEYMOUR D. W. Born 29/4/37. Commd 29/8/60. Sqn Ldr 1/3/71. Retd ADMIN 29/4/92.
SEYMOUR J. M. Born 17/8/39. Commd 9/4/72. Flt Lt 9/10/76. Retd ADMIN 9/4/88.
SEYMOUR P. J., OBE FIMgt. Born 26/5/43. Commd 24/6/65. Gp Capt 1/1/90. Retd ADMIN 22/4/94.
SEYMOUR R. G. Born 28/11/18. Commd 24/7/42. Wg Cdr 1/7/58. Retd ENG 28/11/76.
SEYMOUR-COOKE T. C., DFC AFC DFM. Born 23/7/21. Commd 2/8/41. Flt Lt 22/10/47. Retd GD 19/7/52 rtg Sqn Ldr.
SHACKELL J. M. Born 6/5/53. Commd 14/12/72. Wg Cdr 1/7/92. Retd OPS SPT 1/2/01.
SHACKLETON J. Born 15/6/20. Commd 24/5/51. Flt Lt 24/11/55. Retd GD(G) 20/6/62.
SHACKLEY G. J., MSc BSc CEng MIEE. Born 9/4/45. Commd 6/9/81. Sqn Ldr 1/1/90. Retd ENG 6/9/97.
SHADBOLT B. M. Born 26/10/37. Commd 3/7/56. Flt Lt 3/1/62. Retd GD 1/8/64.
SHAFE A. C., AFC. Born 13/5/22. Commd 16/3/44. Sqn Ldr 1/7/68. Retd GD 13/5/77.
SHAKESPEAR J. G. W. Born 13/7/20. Commd 20/6/56. Flt Lt 20/6/56. Retd SEC 1/12/63. Re-employed 29/4/71 to 13/7/75.
SHAKESPEARE R. Born 8/3/30. Commd 23/10/62. Sqn Ldr 23/10/67. Retd EDN 23/10/78.
SHALLCROSS P. S. Born 24/8/28. Commd 13/2/64. Flt Lt 13/2/69. Retd ENG 21/4/76.
SHAMBROOK P., BEng. Born 14/12/56. Commd 2/8/85. Flt Lt 15/7/88. Retd ENG 14/12/94.
SHANAHAN D. W., DFC. Born 4/6/20. Commd 25/6/42. Flt Lt 28/1/46. Retd GD 8/7/63.
SHANKLAND D. Born 7/8/46. Commd 12/2/68. Sqn Ldr 1/7/96. Retd GD 2/4/01.
SHANKS C. J. A. Born 22/1/52. Commd 4/2/71. Flt Lt 4/8/76. Retd GD 22/4/89.
SHANKS C. R., DFC. Born 10/4/20. Commd 16/6/44. Flt Lt 13/3/51. Retd GD 28/9/68.
SHANNON D. M., OBE. Born 18/2/45. Commd 28/4/65. Gp Capt 1/1/95. Retd GD 28/2/00.
SHANNON H., DFC. Born 9/11/18. Commd 27/7/40. Sqn Ldr 1/1/53. Retd GD 12/12/57.
SHANNON M. S., BSc MEd. Born 28/6/38. Commd 31/12/63. Sqn Ldr 1/3/71. Retd ADMIN 14/8/82.
SHANNON T. S., BSc. Born 30/9/60. Commd 2/9/79. Sqn Ldr 1/1/92. Retd ENG 30/9/98.
SHAPLAND J. A., BA. Born 25/11/65. Commd 14/6/86. Flt Lt 15/1/90. Retd GD 14/3/96.
SHARKEY J. B., BA. Born 23/8/42. Commd 19/9/71. Wg Cdr 1/1/89. Retd SUP 19/9/93.
SHARMA A., MB ChB DTM&H. Born 14/10/51. Commd 31/3/88. Wg Cdr 28/9/90. Retd MED 29/10/96.
SHARMA R. K. Born 7/12/39. Commd 29/11/63. Flt Lt 29/5/69. Retd GD 13/8/79.
SHARMAN A. J., AFC. Born 5/2/24. Commd 1/10/43. Sqn Ldr 1/7/54. Retd GD 13/10/59.
SHARMAN B. B. Born 14/7/29. Commd 28/6/50. Flt Lt 14/5/56. Retd GD 14/7/67.
SHARMAN E. V. Born 8/10/22. Commd 27/10/46. Flt Lt 10/12/56. Retd GD 6/4/62.
SHARMAN M. R. Born 13/11/51. Commd 29/4/71. Flt Lt 29/10/76. Retd GD 14/4/89.
SHARP A. L., MIMgt. Born 27/5/22. Commd 10/8/43. Wg Cdr 1/1/62. Retd SEC 28/9/68.
SHARP A. T., BA. Born 10/3/18. Commd 5/10/53. Flt Lt 13/11/57. Retd PI 10/3/73.
SHARP C., MSc MB BS MRCGP MRCP MRCS DCH DAvMed AFOM MRAeS. Born 5/3/52. Commd 29/10/78. Wg Cdr 5/4/89. Retd MED 23/7/95.
SHARP C. G., FCA. Born 28/1/07. Commd 2/6/30. Gp Capt 1/7/52. Retd SEC 2/3/62.
SHARP D. J., AFC BSc. Born 23/10/45. Commd 2/4/65. Sqn Ldr 1/1/83. Retd GD 23/10/00.
SHARP D. J. T., DFC. Born 30/8/18. Commd 24/7/39. Sqn Ldr 1/7/55. Retd GD 30/9/58.
SHARP E. Born 23/12/32. Commd 27/9/51. Flt Lt 11/1/57. Retd GD 30/6/73.
SHARP F. Born 24/5/25. Commd 29/4/57. Flt Lt 29/4/57. Retd GD 19/5/69.
SHARP G. R., PhD MB ChB. Born 11/4/35. Commd 30/9/62. Wg Cdr 30/9/72. Retd MED 16/3/82.
SHARP J. A. H. Born 25/8/52. Commd 19/3/78. Wg Cdr 1/1/96. Retd ENG 1/5/98.
SHARP J. S., BEng. Born 9/6/57. Commd 16/9/84. Flt Lt 11/10/86. Retd ENG 9/6/95.
SHARP J. T. Born 11/5/29. Commd 21/11/51. Sqn Ldr 1/1/77. Retd GD 11/5/84.
SHARP K. G., DSC. Born 25/1/13. Commd 23/12/35. Sqn Ldr 1/1/61. Retd SEC 30/4/63.
SHARP P. A. Born 6/10/54. Commd 1/9/92. Flt Lt 27/1/95. Retd MED(T) 14/9/96.
SHARP P. E., CEng MIEE. Born 6/9/40. Commd 7/3/65. Sqn Ldr 1/7/78. Retd ENG 1/7/81.
SHARP R. J. Born 15/12/47. Commd 31/7/70. Gp Capt 1/1/95. Retd GD 1/11/96.
SHARP W. T. H. Born 2/2/10. Commd 22/2/42. Sqn Ldr 1/1/51. Retd CAT 22/2/59 rtg Wg Cdr.
SHARPE C. D. Born 3/11/31. Commd 30/7/52. Sqn Ldr 1/7/61. Retd GD 24/6/66.
SHARPE C. E., BA. Born 15/1/58. Commd 28/12/80. Flt Lt 28/12/86. Retd ADMIN 28/12/88. Re-entered 4/7/89. Flt Lt 28/6/84. Retd ADMIN 13/10/96.
SHARPE D. E. Born 24/6/23. Commd 27/2/44. Flt Lt 27/8/47. Retd ENG 24/7/61.
SHARPE D. E. Born 8/5/41. Commd 19/6/70. Flt Lt 19/6/72. Retd ENG 1/10/84.
SHARPE D. I. Born 20/4/58. Commd 29/11/81. Sqn Ldr 1/1/90. Retd ENG 29/11/97.
SHARPE D. R., BSc. Born 9/6/57. Commd 13/5/76. Flt Lt 15/10/81. Retd ENG 20/7/90.
SHARPE G. C., BA. Born 18/10/44. Commd 23/3/67. Flt Lt 23/9/72. Retd GD 18/10/00.
SHARPE G. M., MA CEng MIEE MRAeS MIMgt. Born 21/4/38. Commd 30/9/58. Sqn Ldr 1/1/95. Retd ENG 21/4/96.
SHARPE H. C., BEM. Born 15/9/19. Commd 29/1/43. Flt Lt 7/6/51. Retd GD(G) 1/4/65.
SHARPE K. A. Born 9/10/20. Commd 29/4/43. Sqn Ldr 1/7/54. Retd ENG 4/1/64.
SHARPE M. C. Born 10/1/42. Commd 27/1/61. Sqn Ldr 1/7/74. Retd GD 10/1/97.
SHARPE M. F. Born 2/10/36. Commd 13/2/60. Sqn Ldr 1/1/79. Retd ADMIN 1/10/87.

SHARPE P. Born 15/8/30. Commd 2/9/52. Flt Lt 14/8/57. Retd GD 15/8/68.
SHARPE S. D. Born 26/4/32. Commd 2/5/69. Sqn Ldr 1/7/77. Retd GD(G) 1/5/82.
SHARPE W. G. D. Born 7/4/29. Commd 21/5/52. Flt Lt 16/10/57. Retd GD 30/10/67.
SHARPLES A. O., MBE. Born 9/12/15. Commd 29/6/50. Flt Lt 29/12/53. Retd GD 6/1/66.
SHARPLES D., BA MCIPD MIMgt. Born 1/7/41. Commd 22/2/71. Wg Cdr 1/7/88. Retd SY 1/7/96.
SHARPLES E. J. Born 21/9/23. Commd 15/2/45. Sqn Ldr 1/7/70. Retd GD 21/9/78.
SHARRATT J. G. Born 4/2/17. Commd 18/6/42. Sqn Ldr 1/7/52. Retd SEC 4/2/72.
SHAW A. Born 28/12/41. Commd 12/3/60. Sqn Ldr 1/7/87. Retd GD 28/12/96.
SHAW A. G., BSc(Eng) CEng MIEE. Born 6/8/40. Commd 30/9/59. Gp Capt 1/7/91. Retd ENG 6/8/95.
SHAW A. G. Born 24/8/33. Commd 4/7/64. Sqn Ldr 4/7/71. Retd EDN 4/7/73.
SHAW A. T. Born 21/9/23. Commd 19/5/49. Sqn Ldr 1/7/62. Retd GD 30/6/78.
SHAW B., MSc BSc CEng MIMechE MRAeS MIMgt. Born 1/4/51. Commd 15/9/69. Sqn Ldr 1/1/85. Retd ENG 1/5/90.
SHAW B. W. B., MA DCAe CEng MIMechE MRAeS. Born 22/2/27. Commd 5/11/52. Sqn Ldr 1/1/62. Retd ENG 5/11/68.
SHAW C. F. Born 4/8/43. Commd 29/8/72. Wg Cdr 1/1/96. Retd ADMIN 14/9/96.
SHAW C. J., BSc(Eng). Born 7/11/34. Commd 26/9/53. Sqn Ldr 1/7/70. Retd ENG 27/1/86.
SHAW C. P. Born 25/5/44. Commd 17/7/64. Flt Lt 17/3/71. Retd GD 25/5/82.
SHAW CLOSE C. C., BA. Born 22/1/22. Commd 23/10/51. Sqn Ldr 23/8/58. Retd EDN 28/4/64.
SHAW D., BA. Born 19/10/36. Commd 20/9/60. Sqn Ldr 20/3/69. Retd ADMIN 20/9/76.
SHAW D. A., BSc CEng MRAeS. Born 7/6/53. Commd 3/10/76. Sqn Ldr 1/7/91. Retd ENG 3/10/98.
SHAW D. C. Born 11/3/23. Commd 13/3/46. Flt Lt 4/6/54. Retd GD 25/9/68.
SHAW D. S., OBE. Born 14/4/42. Commd 21/10/66. Wg Cdr 1/1/84. Retd GD 1/12/86.
SHAW E. J., AFC. Born 28/4/26. Commd 25/10/46. Wg Cdr 1/1/78. Retd GD 1/5/80.
SHAW G. A., BSc. Born 12/7/61. Commd 16/10/80. Sqn Ldr 1/7/91. Retd ADMIN 14/3/96.
SHAW G. W., MBE. Born 30/7/27. Commd 24/2/67. Flt Lt 24/2/73. Retd PRT 31/5/75.
SHAW H. F. Born 28/2/22. Commd 27/1/44. Wg Cdr 1/1/65. Retd GD(G) 10/8/73.
SHAW H. J. Born 2/1/33. Commd 9/8/51. Sqn Ldr 1/7/67. Retd GD 24/4/76.
SHAW J. Born 6/7/28. Commd 13/2/52. Flt Lt 13/11/56. Retd GD 6/7/66.
SHAW J. C. Born 27/7/16. Commd 8/10/42. Sqn Ldr 1/7/59. Retd ENG 13/8/66.
SHAW J. L., MBE. Born 4/6/33. Commd 3/8/61. Sqn Ldr 1/7/79. Retd GD 4/6/88.
SHAW K. D., MBE MSc FCIS. Born 22/11/47. Commd 11/11/71. Wg Cdr 1/7/88. Retd ADMIN 2/4/96.
SHAW K. G. Born 3/7/23. Commd 24/9/44. Flt Lt 7/6/51. Retd GD 4/9/62.
SHAW K. W. Born 11/8/55. Commd 24/7/81. Flt Lt 24/7/83. Retd GD 1/12/95.
SHAW M., CEng MRAeS. Born 8/3/36. Commd 24/7/57. Flt Lt 6/3/63. Retd ENG 1/10/77.
SHAW M., BA. Born 18/9/33. Commd 9/8/57. Sqn Ldr 9/2/67. Retd ADMIN 26/11/85.
SHAW M. J. A., DSO FIMgt. Born 20/4/20. Commd 4/6/38. Gp Capt 1/7/64. Retd GD 12/4/75.
SHAW M. J. F., CBE. Born 11/4/37. Commd 28/7/59. Gp Capt 1/7/79. Retd GD 6/4/92.
SHAW M. P. G. L. Born 16/12/41. Commd 18/12/62. Sqn Ldr 1/7/77. Retd GD 1/11/80.
SHAW P. A. T. Born 8/12/35. Commd 17/3/67. Flt Lt 17/3/69. Retd GD 30/8/75.
SHAW P. J., BSc. Born 20/5/50. Commd 22/8/71. Sqn Ldr 1/7/86. Retd ADMIN 1/7/89.
SHAW P. R. Born 13/5/60. Commd 26/11/81. Flt Lt 26/5/87. Retd GD 1/4/90.
SHAW P. W. Born 5/7/24. Commd 1/10/43. Sqn Ldr 1/1/58. Retd GD 1/6/68.
SHAW R. H., DFC. Born 6/7/12. Commd 23/7/32. Gp Capt 1/1/52. Retd GD 18/3/54.
SHAW S. Born 16/11/35. Commd 1/10/62. Flt Lt 1/4/68. Retd GD 25/2/72.
SHAW T. J. H., BSc CEng MIMechE. Born 15/12/45. Commd 1/10/70. Sqn Ldr 1/7/83. Retd ENG 15/12/00.
SHAW W. Born 1/8/14. Commd 24/10/46. Fg Offr 24/10/47. Retd ENG 27/1/48.
SHAW-BROWN K. M., DFC. Born 18/12/20. Commd 15/5/44. Flt Lt 26/8/48. Retd SEC 29/8/68.
SHAWE M. P. Born 6/3/25. Commd 4/2/48. Sqn Ldr 1/7/65. Retd RGT 6/3/80.
SHEARD M. S., MSc BSc CEng MIEE. Born 16/11/62. Commd 13/9/81. Wg Cdr 1/1/97. Retd ENG 16/11/00.
SHEARDOWN R. D., OBE. Born 8/10/11. Commd 3/6/41. Sqn Ldr 1/7/53. Retd SEC 9/8/58.
SHEARER J., OBE. Born 28/2/30. Commd 14/4/53. Wg Cdr 1/1/73. Retd SUP 19/12/84.
SHEARER R., DPhysEd. Born 13/7/30. Commd 2/1/52. Flt Lt 13/7/56. Retd PE 13/7/68.
SHEARER T. Born 11/5/51. Commd 4/5/72. Sqn Ldr 1/7/86. Retd SY(RGT) 1/7/89.
SHEARMAN A. Born 1/9/59. Commd 20/3/90. Flt Lt 29/3/92. Retd SUP 13/9/96.
SHEARN M. R., BSc. Born 22/9/47. Commd 13/9/70. Sqn Ldr 15/1/79. Retd ADMIN 13/9/86.
SHEARS P. E., BSc. Born 9/4/66. Commd 15/9/86. Flt Lt 15/1/93. Retd ADMIN 14/9/96.
SHEARWOOD M., AIIP. Born 17/8/39. Commd 4/7/66. Flt Lt 4/7/72. Retd ENG 4/7/82.
SHEARWOOD P. D., MBE. Born 23/9/21. Commd 14/4/44. Sqn Ldr 1/4/56. Retd GD 23/9/70.
SHEASBY R. K. Born 13/1/38. Commd 22/1/57. Flt Lt 15/8/62. Retd GD 1/2/79.
SHEATH J. M. Born 16/3/38. Commd 4/6/64. Sqn Ldr 1/1/81. Retd GD 1/1/86.
SHEDDEN The Rev J., CBE BD. Born 23/6/43. Commd 3/3/86. Retd 23/6/98. Gp Capt.
SHEEHAN A. J., MB BS FRCS DLO. Born 19/1/34. Commd 7/3/63. Wg Cdr 24/12/74. Retd MED 6/1/81.
SHEEHAN M. J. Born 1/2/40. Commd 22/5/70. Wg Cdr 1/1/90. Retd MED(SEC) 1/11/93.
SHEEHAN W. J. L., DFC MRAeS MIMgt. Born 7/6/21. Commd 25/7/44. Wg Cdr 1/7/61. Retd GD 29/9/72.
SHEELEY G. J. Born 26/7/53. Commd 14/7/77. Flt Lt 14/1/82. Retd GD 1/4/85.

SHEELEY I. M. Born 21/3/57. Commd 14/7/77. Wg Cdr 1/7/96. Retd OPS SPT 21/3/01.
SHEEN D. J. Born 18/10/41. Commd 28/4/61. Flt Lt 26/7/67. Retd GD 18/10/79.
SHEEN T. A., DFC. Born 6/11/21. Commd 8/6/44. Flt Lt 8/12/47. Retd GD 28/9/68.
SHEFFIELD C. J. Born 12/6/45. Commd 11/10/84. Flt Lt 11/10/88. Retd ENG 12/6/00.
SHEFFIELD I. V. Born 15/9/46. Commd 7/1/71. Fg Offr 7/1/73. Retd GD 22/7/75.
SHEFFIELD R. J. Born 6/4/47. Commd 11/4/85. Flt Lt 11/4/89. Retd GD(G) 14/3/96.
SHEILD H. J., DFC*. Born 30/9/16. Commd 1/9/45. Sqn Ldr 1/7/49. Retd GD 30/9/58.
SHELBOURN R. J. Born 7/12/46. Commd 12/7/68. Flt Lt 12/1/74. Retd GD 4/4/78.
SHELDON J. G., BSc(Econ). Born 28/11/36. Commd 2/10/58. Gp Capt 1/7/87. Retd GD 29/7/94.
SHELDON K. J. Born 8/8/45. Commd 1/12/77. Sqn Ldr 1/1/90. Retd ADMIN 8/8/00.
SHELDRAKE R. J., BSc. Born 30/1/49. Commd 1/11/71. Flt Lt 1/8/75. Retd ENG 1/11/87.
SHELL K. E., BSc CEng MRAeS. Born 20/10/45. Commd 26/5/67. Sqn Ldr 1/7/79. Retd ENG 20/10/89.
SHELLEY D. Born 20/10/21. Commd 30/11/50. Wg Cdr 1/7/71. Retd GD(G) 6/11/76.
SHELLEY E. A. Born 6/5/33. Commd 26/8/66. Flt Lt 26/8/71. Retd GD 8/11/75.
SHELLEY G. H. D. Born 4/8/27. Commd 31/5/30. Sqn Ldr 1/1/64. Retd GD 1/9/73.
SHELLEY J. A. F., BA MIMgt. Born 19/1/30. Commd 15/12/49. Wg Cdr 1/7/68. Retd GD 19/1/85.
SHELLEY K. D. Born 23/3/54. Commd 21/12/89. Flt Lt 21/12/93. Retd ENG 6/2/96.
SHELLEY L. P. Born 18/6/25. Commd 10/5/46. Flt Lt 10/5/52. Retd RGT 29/5/59.
SHELLEY P. A. J., MBE DPhys Ed. Born 23/5/23. Commd 15/7/43. Gp Capt 1/7/75. Retd EDN 29/3/78.
SHELLEY P. C. Born 8/12/32. Commd 24/6/71. Flt Lt 24/6/76. Retd ADMIN 6/4/87.
SHELLEY T. G. Born 23/2/26. Commd 30/7/52. Flt Lt 27/12/56. Retd GD 1/5/67.
SHELTON E. R. A., MIMgt. Born 30/10/26. Commd 23/8/46. Sqn Ldr 1/1/60. Retd SEC 26/7/75.
SHELTON J. R., BA MBCS. Born 3/2/55. Commd 7/11/76. Sqn Ldr 1/1/89. Retd SUP 3/2/93.
SHELTON-SMITH K. C., BEng. Born 24/3/60. Commd 1/7/82. Flt Lt 13/8/86. Retd ENG 24/9/98.
SHENTON J. H. Born 8/2/26. Commd 24/4/50. Flt Lt 11/11/54. Retd GD 24/4/66.
SHENTON R. T. Born 10/11/27. Commd 12/3/64. Sqn Ldr 31/8/74. Retd MED 1/6/78.
SHEPARD G. R. A., MSc BSc CEng MIEE. Born 24/3/45. Commd 14/9/66. Sqn Ldr 15/1/77. Retd ADMIN 24/3/83.
SHEPARD M. J. W. Born 19/12/44. Commd 18/11/66. Sqn Ldr 1/7/79. Retd ENG 19/12/82. Re-entered 3/1/86. Sqn
    Ldr 15/7/82. Retd ENG 19/12/99.
SHEPARD R. W. R., BEM. Born 14/10/11. Commd 25/3/54. Sqn Ldr 1/7/63. Retd ENG 14/10/66.
SHEPHARD I., CEng MIEE. Born 25/9/41. Commd 15/7/63. Sqn Ldr 1/7/74. Retd ENG 25/9/79.
SHEPHARD R. G., MA. Born 11/3/47. Commd 27/10/70. Flt Lt 27/1/74. Retd ADMIN 14/3/96.
SHEPHERD A. Born 5/10/22. Commd 15/9/47. Flt Lt 25/11/53. Retd GD 5/10/67.
SHEPHERD A. E. Born 19/2/26. Commd 22/2/46. Sqn Ldr 1/7/56. Retd GD 1/3/75.
SHEPHERD D. N., DFC. Born 31/10/20. Commd 23/7/41. Wg Cdr 1/1/59. Retd GD 30/11/64.
SHEPHERD J. M. P. Born 12/8/36. Commd 23/9/66. Flt Lt 23/9/72. Retd GD(G) 11/1/90.
SHEPHERD J. R., OBE DFC. Born 30/3/22. Commd 17/5/41. Wg Cdr 1/7/66. Retd GD 30/3/77.
SHEPHERD J. W. Born 14/6/20. Commd 3/6/46. Sqn Ldr 1/7/57. Retd SEC 1/6/73.
SHEPHERD R. C., DFC. Born 27/4/19. Commd 2/11/42. Sqn Ldr 1/1/71. Retd SUP 27/4/74.
SHEPHERD R. G. Born 5/8/18. Commd 4/3/43. Flt Lt 4/9/46. Retd ENG 5/8/73.
SHEPHERD R. W., MCIPS AIDPM. Born 21/3/37. Commd 11/4/63. Wg Cdr 1/7/89. Retd SUP 22/7/91.
SHEPHERD S. G., BSc. Born 23/4/45. Commd 28/9/64. Flt Lt 15/10/68. Retd GD 31/8/74.
SHEPHERD-SMITH M. A. Born 2/10/41. Commd 11/6/60. Sqn Ldr 1/1/79. Retd GD 2/12/96.
SHEPPARD A. J., AFC. Born 8/4/39. Commd 25/7/60. Wg Cdr 1/1/90. Retd GD 8/4/94.
SHEPPARD B. Born 21/2/32. Commd 13/8/52. Flt Lt 1/10/67. Retd GD 31/3/74.
SHEPPARD C. W. Born 18/8/08. Commd 11/3/41. Sqn Ldr 1/8/47. Retd ENG 4/5/56.
SHEPPARD J. D. Born 24/5/39. Commd 19/10/72. Flt Lt 19/10/74. Retd GD(G) 19/10/80.
SHEPPARD P. B. Born 30/8/31. Commd 25/6/66. Flt Lt 25/6/71. Retd GD 30/9/84.
SHEPPARD R. F. Born 10/12/22. Commd 12/11/51. Wg Cdr 1/7/73. Retd ADMIN 10/12/77.
SHEPPARD T. H., MBE. Born 16/10/33. Commd 27/5/54. Sqn Ldr 1/7/64. Retd GD 27/2/76.
SHEPPARD W. P. Born 8/9/31. Commd 16/1/52. Flt Lt 16/7/56. Retd GD 10/12/70.
SHEPPERSON D. A. Born 29/6/39. Commd 27/1/67. Sqn Ldr 1/1/74. Retd SUP 29/6/77.
SHEPPHARD A. Born 11/2/29. Commd 10/7/52. Flt Lt 22/6/59. Retd GD 1/7/75 rtg Sqn Ldr.
SHERBURN J., DFC. Born 18/8/24. Commd 19/6/47. Flt Lt 15/4/57. Retd GD 18/8/62.
SHERET G. L., MA. Born 29/5/28. Commd 6/9/50. Wg Cdr 1/1/68. Retd GD 6/11/70.
SHERISTON J. H. Born 9/6/21. Commd 14/9/43. Sqn Ldr 1/7/58. Retd GD 9/8/76.
SHERLOCK B. A. Born 4/4/34. Commd 1/11/56. Sqn Ldr 1/1/85. Retd GD 1/3/88.
SHERLOCK W. P. Born 29/11/33. Commd 13/8/52. Sqn Ldr 1/1/75. Retd GD 29/11/88.
SHERMAN-BALL G. A., FIMgt. Born 7/6/34. Commd 12/8/54. Gp Capt 1/1/85. Retd ADMIN 1/10/87.
SHERRARD J. L., BEM MIMgt. Born 18/4/21. Commd 28/2/46. Wg Cdr 1/7/66. Retd ENG 14/9/74.
SHERRIFF H. M., MB ChB FRCS. Born 13/4/41. Commd 1/4/63. Wg Cdr 10/8/80. Retd MED 8/5/82.
SHERRIFF P. A. Born 11/1/63. Commd 8/6/84. Flt Lt 1/6/89. Retd GD 14/9/96.
SHERRINGTON A. S. Born 27/9/42. Commd 29/3/62. Flt Lt 29/6/68. Retd SEC 30/4/71.
SHERRINGTON C. F., BSc. Born 16/9/52. Commd 17/1/74. Flt Lt 15/10/75. Retd GD 27/4/77.
SHERRINGTON T. B., CB OBE FIMgt MHCIMA. Born 30/9/42. Commd 12/9/63. AVM 1/1/92. Retd ADMIN
    30/9/97.

SHERWIN B. Born 18/10/22. Commd 1/6/45. Sqn Ldr 1/4/56. Retd GD 27/5/66.
SHERWIN V. G. Born 29/5/23. Commd 6/6/57. Flt Lt 1/4/63. Retd GD 31/3/69.
SHERWOOD C. A. Born 4/10/21. Commd 24/6/44. Sqn Ldr 1/10/57. Retd SEC 4/10/73.
SHEVELS A. A. Born 22/4/46. Commd 8/9/77. Sqn Ldr 1/7/87. Retd ENG 22/4/01.
SHEVLIN B. J. M. Born 19/3/48. Commd 26/5/67. Flt Lt 4/11/73. Retd SUP 19/3/89.
SHEWRY M. Born 17/7/48. Commd 1/8/69. Sqn Ldr 1/7/85. Retd SY(RGT) 1/7/89.
SHIEBER N. W. Born 25/4/38. Commd 5/8/76. Sqn Ldr 1/7/89. Retd ADMIN 25/4/90.
SHIELDS D. Born 16/12/50. Commd 17/5/79. Flt Lt 17/5/81. Retd ADMIN 16/12/88.
SHIELDS F. L. Born 22/12/28. Commd 6/10/60. Sqn Ldr 1/7/75. Retd ENG 22/6/84.
SHIELDS G. Born 10/6/43. Commd 24/6/65. Sqn Ldr 1/1/78. Retd GD 10/6/81.
SHIELDS M. H., FIMgt. Born 4/3/45. Commd 24/11/67. Gp Capt 1/7/93. Retd OPS SPT 4/3/00.
SHIELDS M. T. C. Born 21/12/19. Commd 1/6/42. Flt Lt 1/12/46. Retd SEC 21/12/74.
SHIELDS W. Born 11/7/24. Commd 2/8/51. Sqn Ldr 1/7/68. Retd GD 11/7/82.
SHIELLS I. M. Born 26/4/56. Commd 22/5/80. Flt Lt 18/7/83. Retd GD 14/9/96.
SHIELS J. P. Born 19/3/38. Commd 23/9/65. Flt Lt 23/9/67. Retd GD 2/5/75.
SHILLITO J. A. Born 21/10/18. Commd 13/9/45. Sqn Ldr 1/7/66. Retd SEC 30/8/69.
SHILTON P. R. Born 7/8/53. Commd 18/1/73. Plt Offr 18/1/74. Retd GD 14/9/47.
SHIMELL C. R., MSc BSc CEng MIMechE ACGI. Born 2/5/54. Commd 3/9/72. Sqn Ldr 1/1/86. Retd ENG 2/5/92.
SHIMMONS R. W. Born 24/12/44. Commd 15/7/66. Wg Cdr 1/7/85. Retd GD 6/8/89.
SHINE M. E. Born 10/1/35. Commd 10/12/52. Sqn Ldr 1/1/65. Retd GD 31/5/76.
SHINGLES A. G., DFC. Born 18/10/22. Commd 18/10/44. Flt Lt 18/4/48. Retd GD 25/11/67.
SHINNIE G. M., DFC. Born 14/6/20. Commd 17/3/42. Wg Cdr 1/7/64. Retd GD(G) 5/7/75.
SHIPLEY E., MA MRAeS. Born 2/11/10. Commd 3/4/33. Wg Cdr 1/7/47. Retd ENG 3/4/54 rtg Gp Capt.
SHIPLEY G. V. Born 10/7/36. Commd 7/12/54. Flt Lt 15/6/60. Retd GD 10/7/74.
SHIPMAN K. E. W. Born 18/6/35. Commd 24/2/55. Sqn Ldr 1/7/70. Retd GD 1/7/73.
SHIPMAN N. M. Born 14/6/31. Commd 12/7/62. Flt Lt 12/7/68. Retd ADMIN 13/7/68. Re-instated 30/4/80 to
    13/7/85.
SHIPPEN J. M., BSc. Born 24/2/61. Commd 29/7/83. Sqn Ldr 1/7/99. Retd ENG 26/11/00.
SHIPTON A. J. Born 20/11/33. Commd 4/9/58. Wg Cdr 1/7/77. Retd SEC 1/12/78.
SHIPWAY G. T. Born 2/11/33. Commd 30/1/52. Flt Lt 29/5/57. Retd GD 2/11/71.
SHIRLEY M. J., AMIMgt. Born 11/3/33. Commd 3/5/54. Sqn Ldr 1/7/68. Retd ADMIN 1/12/78.
SHIRREFF A. C. Born 12/2/19. Commd 22/1/51. Sqn Ldr 1/1/51. Retd GD 1/5/58.
SHOEBRIDGE R. B. Born 14/9/42. Commd 31/1/64. Flt Lt 6/10/71. Retd GD 14/9/80.
SHOOLBRAID W. G. H. Born 20/4/28. Commd 4/9/58. Sqn Ldr 1/1/69. Retd ENG 4/11/78.
SHOPLAND A. W., BSc. Born 2/11/63. Commd 19/7/87. Flt Lt 19/1/90. Retd GD 14/9/96.
SHORE G. B., BSc. Born 3/2/30. Commd 15/10/52. Wg Cdr 3/9/70. Retd EDN 21/11/81.
SHORE W. A., BA. Born 13/3/51. Commd 6/10/74. Flt Lt 6/7/78. Retd SY 19/1/85.
SHOREMAN A. Born 3/1/15. Commd 28/5/42. Flt Lt 28/4/47. Retd GD(G) 3/1/65.
SHORRICK N., BSc MCIPD MIMgt. Born 25/2/33. Commd 20/9/57. Wg Cdr 1/1/84. Retd ADMIN 23/9/87.
SHORROCK G. C., MBE. Born 12/9/41. Commd 30/7/63. Sqn Ldr 1/7/75. Retd GD 12/9/79.
SHORROCK K. J. Born 17/3/33. Commd 27/8/52. Sqn Ldr 1/1/64. Retd GD 19/4/77.
SHORROCKS C. E. Born 17/3/65. Commd 17/3/69. Flt Lt 17/3/69. Retd REG 31/10/79.
SHORT A. F., OBE MCIPD. Born 25/2/44. Commd 20/6/63. Gp Capt 1/7/88. Retd ADMIN 25/2/94.
SHORT B. E. Born 27/3/30. Commd 25/6/53. Flt Lt 25/12/57. Retd GD 27/3/66 rtg Sqn Ldr.
SHORT C. D., BSc. Born 24/9/49. Commd 23/9/68. Flt Lt 15/10/74. Retd ENG 22/9/81.
SHORT C. J. G. Born 23/2/22. Commd 25/3/44. Sqn Ldr 1/1/55. Retd GD 29/7/66.
SHORT D. A. W. Born 15/7/26. Commd 30/7/59. Flt Lt 30/7/64. Retd ENG 31/7/75.
SHORT D. J. Born 11/10/36. Commd 13/11/61. Fg Offr 3/11/63. Retd GD 27/1/68.
SHORT F. D. Born 25/3/43. Commd 11/9/64. Flt Lt 4/5/72. Retd GD 5/3/76.
SHORT F. R., MA. Born 18/11/17. Commd 3/1/51. Wg Cdr 1/1/66. Retd EDN 2/12/72.
SHORT H. Born 25/12/44. Commd 14/2/69. Sqn Ldr 1/1/80. Retd GD 25/6/90.
SHORT J. A. V., MIMgt. Born 12/1/24. Commd 24/8/44. Gp Capt 1/7/76. Retd GD(G) 31/3/78.
SHORT J. C. Born 16/5/57. Commd 4/9/81. Flt Lt 16/7/84. Retd GD(G) 23/6/95.
SHORT J. H., ACMA. Born 14/7/37. Commd 21/10/65. Sqn Ldr 1/7/73. Retd ADMIN 14/7/77.
SHORT M., MBE AFC. Born 5/9/25. Commd 1/4/52. Gp Capt 1/7/74. Retd GD 5/12/80.
SHORT M. A. Born 31/5/62. Commd 24/4/80. Sqn Ldr 1/1/93. Retd ADMIN 22/11/00.
SHORT R. M. Born 24/2/36. Commd 14/10/71. Flt Lt 14/10/73. Retd SUP 14/10/79.
SHORTER B. Born 2/12/47. Commd 21/4/67. Sqn Ldr 1/1/81. Retd SUP 2/12/91.
SHORTHOUSE A. Q. Born 17/4/30. Commd 26/2/53. Flt Lt 26/8/57. Retd GD 17/4/68.
SHOTTON J. Born 10/3/33. Commd 8/7/65. Wg Cdr 1/1/85. Retd ADMIN 10/3/88.
SHREEVE C. J. Born 18/5/48. Commd 7/6/68. Flt Lt 7/12/74. Retd ENG 31/8/77.
SHREEVE P. A., BSc. Born 6/8/51. Commd 15/9/69. Flt Lt 15/10/75. Retd ENG 31/8/78.
SHRIMPTON P. H. W. D. Born 30/7/37. Commd 29/7/58. Sqn Ldr 1/7/68. Retd SUP 30/11/77.
SHUBROOK D. C., MA. Born 31/12/42. Commd 20/8/67. Sqn Ldr 9/7/78. Retd ADMIN 20/8/83.
SHUSTER R. C., AFC. Born 2/9/44. Commd 15/7/66. Flt Lt 15/1/69. Retd GD 26/9/97.
SHUTLER M. J., BA. Born 13/8/47. Commd 13/12/68. Flt Lt 13/8/74. Retd ENG 1/1/87.

SHUTT S., BSc. Born 21/3/57. Commd 19/9/76. Sqn Ldr 1/1/93. Retd GD 1/1/96.
SHUTTLEWORTH F. N., MB ChB DOMS. Born 18/8/13. Commd 24/10/39. Gp Capt 1/7/61. Retd MED 1/4/64.
SIBBALD M. C. Born 19/10/45. Commd 5/3/65. Flt Lt 4/5/72. Retd GD 12/6/73.
SIBBONS F. T. Born 5/12/10. Commd 24/11/41. Flt Lt 3/12/46. Retd SUP 5/12/59 rtg Sqn Ldr.
SIBLEY J. C. Born 7/8/47. Commd 25/4/69. Flt Lt 25/10/74. Retd GD 1/11/75.
SIBLEY M. E. Born 8/2/37. Commd 3/7/80. Flt Lt 3/7/82. Retd GD 28/3/88.
SIBREE B. O. Born 21/8/22. Commd 23/7/43. Flt Lt 23/7/45. Retd GD 1/7/75.
SIDDLE P. Born 18/12/23. Commd 6/10/60. Flt Lt 6/10/65. Retd ENG 31/3/78 rtg Sqn Ldr.
SIDDLE V. J. Born 19/5/42. Commd 17/5/63. Plt Offr 16/9/64. Retd SUP 30/12/66.
SIDDONS G. A. Born 30/6/55. Commd 10/3/77. Flt Lt 30/7/83. Retd GD(G) 30/6/93.
SIDDOWAY A. P. Born 26/6/57. Commd 13/8/82. Flt Lt 19/1/85. Retd GD(G) 1/4/96.
SIDEBOTHAM B. Born 6/2/41. Commd 10/10/63. Wg Cdr 1/1/78. Retd GD 22/5/93.
SIDEBOTTOM T. G., OBE FCIS FCIPD. Born 11/11/43. Commd 16/6/69. Gp Capt 1/7/89. Retd ADMIN 27/10/94.
SIDEY Sir Ernest., KBE CB MD ChB MFCM DPH. Born 2/1/13. Commd 4/1/37. AM 1/1/71. Retd MED 15/2/74.
SIDEY R. M., CEng MIMechE. Born 12/6/25. Commd 25/9/62. Sqn Ldr 1/7/71. Retd ENG 12/6/83.
SIDLOW H. Born 27/9/29. Commd 27/8/52. Flt Lt 23/1/58. Retd GD 2/4/84.
SIDWELL T. V. Born 6/12/33. Commd 6/2/52. Flt Lt 2/1/61. Retd GD(G) 2/1/77. Reinstated 20/5/81. Flt Lt 20/5/65. Retd GD(G) 6/12/88.
SIEDLE L. D. C. Born 7/12/46. Commd 11/3/65. Flt Lt 7/1/72. Retd RGT 25/8/72.
SIERWALD R. C. Born 2/3/42. Commd 30/7/63. Sqn Ldr 1/1/76. Retd GD 2/6/97.
SIEVWRIGHT J. M. Born 8/10/26. Commd 25/5/53. Flt Lt 24/3/60. Retd GD(G) 14/10/65. Reinstated on Active List 6/12/71. Sqn Ldr 1/1/76. Retd GD(G) 8/10/86.
SIGLEY G. C. Born 29/12/45. Commd 6/2/77. Sqn Ldr 1/1/88. Retd GD 14/9/96.
SILANDER S. Born 25/5/45. Commd 8/6/84. Flt Lt 1/3/87. Retd GD 1/5/94.
SILCOX J. F. Born 28/9/46. Commd 2/4/65. Flt Lt 4/11/70. Retd GD 20/10/76.
SILK A. E. T. Born 12/9/32. Commd 4/3/71. Sqn Ldr 1/7/80. Retd GD 29/2/84.
SILK D. J., MA PhD CEng FIEE. Born 15/12/43. Commd 30/9/62. Wg Cdr 1/1/78. Retd ENG 15/12/84 rtg Gp Capt.
SILLARS R. B., FIMgt. Born 16/4/23. Commd 1/5/43. Gp Capt 1/1/69. Retd GD 22/9/73.
SILLENCE M. Born 2/4/42. Commd 24/1/63. Sqn Ldr 1/1/74. Retd ADMIN 2/4/80.
SILLINCE B. Born 15/5/27. Commd 15/5/58. Sqn Ldr 1/7/71. Retd ENG 2/5/78.
SILLITOE C. S. Born 19/4/33. Commd 26/3/52. Flt Lt 13/4/60. Retd GD 19/4/71.
SILLS B. T., MIMgt. Born 21/3/36. Commd 9/4/57. A Cdre 1/1/86. Retd GD 6/7/91.
SILVANI M. J. Born 4/7/31. Commd 1/5/52. Flt Lt 11/5/58. Retd GD 14/7/69.
SILVER C. S., CEng MIEE MRAeS. Born 15/10/31. Commd 7/6/51. Wg Cdr 1/1/74. Retd ENG 15/10/81.
SILVERTAND J. M. Born 16/7/44. Commd 1/4/66. Fg Offr 1/4/68. Retd GD 1/7/71.
SILVESTER A. E., MA FIMgt. Born 21/8/29. Commd 22/10/52. Gp Capt 1/1/75. Retd EDN 14/1/81.
SIM J. K., OBE AFC. Born 2/9/40. Commd 12/7/59. Gp Capt 1/1/84. Retd GD 21/4/87.
SIM J. W., GM MA. Born 1/8/10. Commd 4/4/39. Gp Capt 1/1/62. Retd EDN 31/12/64.
SIM S. R. Born 5/10/21. Commd 21/5/44. Sqn Ldr 1/4/55. Retd GD 18/5/74.
SIM V. A., MBE. Born 16/9/44. Commd 11/67. Sqn Ldr 1/1/79. Retd ADMIN 10/12/96.
SIMCOCK S. W. Born 21/11/25. Commd 20/4/50. Flt Lt 16/8/53. Retd GD 1/2/68.
SIMES D. A. Born 2/9/12. Commd 21/4/44. Flt Lt 21/10/47. Retd GD(G) 1/9/59 rtg Sqn Ldr.
SIMICH M. F. R. Born 6/10/45. Commd 21/4/67. Flt Lt 21/10/72. Retd GD 29/6/74.
SIMKIN D. P. M. Born 17/12/23. Commd 7/7/49. Sqn Ldr 1/7/60. Retd GD 1/7/63.
SIMKINS K. I., BSc. Born 28/8/47. Commd 1/9/70. Flt Lt 1/6/71. Retd GD 1/3/76.
SIMMONDS E. L. Born 1/6/22. Commd 13/1/52. Flt Lt 13/7/55. Retd GD 22/4/64.
SIMMONDS J. E. Born 8/12/20. Commd 23/4/41. Sqn Ldr 1/7/54. Retd GD 16/12/68.
SIMMONDS J. J., MIMgt. Born 13/2/31. Commd 18/8/54. Wg Cdr 1/7/75. Retd SUP 30/6/84.
SIMMONDS P. A. A. Born 9/4/37. Commd 23/6/61. Flt Lt 26/7/67. Retd GD 13/7/76.
SIMMONS D. C. H., CBE AFC MA FIMgt. Born 11/12/21. Commd 14/3/42. A Cdre 1/7/70. Retd GD 11/12/76.
SIMMONS D. J., LDSRCS MIMgt. Born 2/10/32. Commd 25/9/60. Wg Cdr 9/10/72. Retd DEL 2/10/91.
SIMMONS D. R. Born 9/10/18. Commd 16/2/42. Flt Lt 1/9/45. Retd GD 9/10/61.
SIMMONS E. N. Born 22/11/20. Commd 22/9/44. Flt Lt 22/3/48. Retd GD 22/11/75.
SIMMONS I. A. Born 11/7/29. Commd 1/8/51. Sqn Ldr 1/1/60. Retd GD 27/7/67.
SIMMONS J. N. Born 24/12/30. Commd 31/8/50. Sqn Ldr 1/1/79. Retd GD 24/12/88.
SIMMONS L. H. Born 27/9/21. Commd 10/5/46. Sqn Ldr 1/7/71. Retd RGT 8/4/72.
SIMMONS Sir Michael., KCB AFC. Born 8/5/37. Commd 29/7/58. AM 3/4/89. Retd GD 5/12/92.
SIMMONS P. J. Born 24/3/34. Commd 5/11/70. Sqn Ldr 1/1/80. Retd ENG 11/9/84.
SIMMONS R. O. Born 11/7/20. Commd 12/3/43. Flt Lt 19/11/53. Retd GD(G) 11/7/75.
SIMMS D. A. G., BSc. Born 19/12/52. Commd 11/7/76. Flt Lt 10/9/78. Retd ADMIN 3/10/78.
SIMMS J. B. Born 29/7/35. Commd 5/11/70. Sqn Ldr 28/10/81. Retd MED(SEC) 31/8/86.
SIMMS J. G. Born 8/2/25. Commd 28/1/54. Sqn Ldr 1/1/68. Retd GD 31/10/77.
SIMMS P. J. Born 20/8/40. Commd 29/9/87. Flt Lt 13/5/76. Retd ADMIN 29/9/95.
SIMON B. J. Born 7/8/45. Commd 26/5/67. Wg Cdr 1/7/87. Retd SUP 14/9/96.
SIMONIS H. R. Born 7/5/38. Commd 6/8/60. Flt Lt 6/2/66. Retd GD 1/10/81.
SIMONS C. A. E., FIMgt. Born 15/7/27. Commd 2/3/49. Gp Capt 1/7/70. Retd GD 13/11/82.

SIMONS R. W. B., OBE MILDM MIMgt. Born 12/2/32. Commd 6/6/57. Gp Capt 1/7/84. Retd SUP 1/7/89.
SIMONS T. A. Born 15/10/05. Commd 18/7/41. Sqn Ldr 1/8/47. Retd SUP 24/10/53.
SIMPKIN M. L., OBE MCIPD. Born 9/6/47. Commd 22/1/67. Gp Capt 1/7/91. Retd ADMIN 27/4/94.
SIMPSON A. Born 28/4/46. Commd 4/1/68. Flt Lt 1/12/75. Retd OPS SPT 1/6/98.
SIMPSON A. B. Born 12/6/33. Commd 28/6/51. Flt Lt 10/10/56. Retd GD 31/5/93.
SIMPSON A. D. Born 9/5/54. Commd 17/7/75. Sqn Ldr 1/7/88. Retd ADMIN 9/5/92.
SIMPSON A. J., BA. Born 10/3/67. Commd 1/9/85. Flt Lt 15/1/91. Retd GD 14/9/96.
SIMPSON A. W., BSc CEng MIEE MIMgt. Born 28/11/33. Commd 23/10/59. Sqn Ldr 1/7/68. Retd ENG 28/11/93.
SIMPSON A. W. Born 3/10/43. Commd 1/11/63. Flt Lt 1/7/69. Retd GD 21/6/76.
SIMPSON B. Born 24/11/44. Commd 11/6/81. Flt Lt 11/6/85. Retd ENG 14/4/89.
SIMPSON B. S. Born 3/3/50. Commd 26/2/71. Flt Lt 26/8/76. Retd SUP 1/9/78.
SIMPSON C. A., AFC. Born 29/3/31. Commd 21/11/50. Wg Cdr 1/1/74. Retd GD 3/4/85.
SIMPSON C. E., DFC. Born 22/6/20. Commd 21/10/41. Sqn Ldr 1/7/60. Retd GD 30/3/68.
SIMPSON C. E., MSc MB ChB MFOM MFCM. Born 24/9/29. Commd 6/3/55. AVM 1/7/86. Retd MED 3/4/89.
SIMPSON D. A., BA DPhilTrans. Born 4/3/33. Commd 24/11/55. Sqn Ldr 24/5/65. Retd ADMIN 4/3/88.
SIMPSON D. C., BA MIL DipTrans. Born 5/11/45. Commd 24/9/67. Sqn Ldr 1/7/88. Retd ADMIN 22/10/94.
SIMPSON D. C., MB ChB FRCS LRCP. Born 15/6/56. Commd 24/11/85. Wg Cdr 10/4/94. Retd MED 14/3/96.
SIMPSON D. J. Born 25/3/32. Commd 18/5/61. Flt Lt 18/5/66. Retd GD(G) 1/1/83.
SIMPSON E. V. C. Born 25/9/18. Commd 23/3/50. Wg Cdr 1/7/70. Retd ENG 25/9/73.
SIMPSON G. A. D., MIMgt. Born 22/3/28. Commd 3/1/51. Wg Cdr 1/1/71. Retd GD 1/10/76.
SIMPSON G. P. Born 6/7/36. Commd 11/2/55. Sqn Ldr 1/1/82. Retd GD 6/7/91.
SIMPSON H R., MA PhD CEng FBCS MIEE. Born 17/6/35. Commd 25/9/54. Gp Capt 1/7/74. Retd ENG 1/10/80.
SIMPSON H. Born 1/5/14. Commd 11/9/41. Sqn Ldr 1/1/53. Retd ENG 1/5/63.
SIMPSON J., BA MSc. Born 15/5/35. Commd 18/7/63. Sqn Ldr 18/4/71. Retd ADMIN 4/11/85.
SIMPSON J. A., DFC AFC. Born 15/10/18. Commd 25/5/43. Sqn Ldr 1/1/54. Retd GD 20/12/57.
SIMPSON J. C., MBE MSc DipUS FINucE MInstP MIMgt. Born 4/4/27. Commd 18/7/49. Sqn Ldr 1/7/63. Retd 27/11/76.
SIMPSON J. H., MBE. Born 19/7/55. Commd 18/4/74. Sqn Ldr 1/1/89. Retd GD(G) 19/7/93.
SIMPSON J. H., DFC. Born 23/5/20. Commd 3/3/42. Flt Lt 3/9/45. Retd GD 15/7/48 rtg Wg Cdr.
SIMPSON J. H. Born 22/9/48. Commd 11/10/84. Flt Lt 1/10/88. Retd ENG 19/12/96.
SIMPSON J. M. Born 15/4/28. Commd 30/3/61. Flt Lt 30/3/66. Retd GD 15/4/73.
SIMPSON K. C. H. Born 9/5/40. Commd 19/12/61. Sqn Ldr 1/7/73. Retd GD 1/6/79.
SIMPSON K. W. Born 23/9/23. Commd 11/11/44. Gp Capt 1/7/70. Retd GD 1/10/76.
SIMPSON M. J. Born 29/5/51. Commd 30/1/70. Flt Lt 13/6/76. Retd GD(G) 2/6/81.
SIMPSON M. R. Born 4/6/40. Commd 17/7/64. Flt Lt 15/4/70. Retd GD 2/4/93.
SIMPSON P. J. H. Born 8/6/39. Commd 14/12/72. Flt Lt 14/12/74. Retd SEC 14/12/80.
SIMPSON R. A. Born 19/4/17. Commd 27/2/58. Sqn Ldr 1/7/68. Retd ENG 19/4/72.
SIMPSON R. A. L. Born 8/5/18. Commd 10/8/44. Sqn Ldr 1/1/59. Retd SEC 6/3/65.
SIMPSON R. C., CBE. Born 30/6/24. Commd 3/8/49. Gp Capt 1/7/70. Retd GD 30/6/80. Retd A Cdre.
SIMPSON R. G., BTech. Born 25/9/56. Commd 17/8/80. Flt Lt 17/11/80. Retd GD 17/8/96.
SIMPSON S. B. Born 18/5/24. Commd 17/10/44. Sqn Ldr 1/7/55. Retd GD 18/5/62.
SIMPSON S. G. Born 22/2/23. Commd 30/6/44. Flt Lt 30/12/47. Retd GD 22/2/66.
SIMPSON W. G., OBE MCIPS MCIT MILT MIMgt. Born 12/5/48. Commd 1/8/69. Wg Cdr 1/1/85. Retd SUP 11/12/88.
SIMPSON W. J., DFC MIMgt. Born 31/5/23. Commd 7/12/48. Wg Cdr 1/1/61. Retd GD 11/4/74.
SIMS A. G., BA. Born 18/7/41. Commd 24/7/81. Sqn Ldr 1/1/89. Retd ADMIN 18/7/96.
SIMS A. G. Born 18/6/50. Commd 26/2/71. Flt Lt 26/2/74. Retd GD 19/6/80.
SIMS G., BA. Born 28/4/54. Commd 11/9/77. Sqn Ldr 1/1/89. Retd GD 11/9/93.
SIMS G. N., DFC MIMgt. Born 25/12/22. Commd 20/8/44. Wg Cdr 1/7/65. Retd GD 25/4/74.
SIMS H. H., MRAeS. Born 25/2/08. Commd 7/11/40. Wg Cdr 1/7/48. Retd ENG 25/2/63.
SIMS J. F., MIMgt. Born 27/8/33. Commd 19/4/60. Sqn Ldr 1/1/70. Retd SUP 27/8/88.
SIMS J. L. M. Born 10/5/39. Commd 11/5/62. Sqn Ldr 1/7/72. Retd GD 1/10/81. Reinstated 9/3/83. Sqn Ldr 6/12/73. Retd GD 31/8/89.
SIMS J. R., MBE MA. Born 18/5/24. Commd 6/4/45. Flt Lt 22/6/52. Retd GD 18/5/67 rtg Sqn Ldr.
SIMS M., MISM MHSM CertMHS. Born 29/12/49. Commd 30/3/89. Flt Lt 30/3/93. Retd MED(SEC) 14/3/96.
SIMS M. R. Born 5/1/08. Commd 15/6/44. Flt Lt 8/12/54. Retd GD(G) 29/11/58.
SIMS M. R. C. Born 9/6/42. Commd 18/12/62. Flt Lt 18/4/68. Retd GD 9/6/82.
SIMS P. G. D., BSc(Eng) CEng MIMechE MRAeS MIMgt. Born 9/11/38. Commd 24/9/63. Sqn Ldr 1/1/72. Retd ENG 24/9/82. Reinstated 21/7/86. Sqn Ldr 27/10/75. Retd ENG 4/9/90
SIMS T. R., MSc. Born 17/10/37. Commd 12/3/64. Sqn Ldr 1/1/72. Retd ENG 26/9/81.
SINCLAIR A. J. Born 25/4/36. Commd 26/11/60. Flt Lt 1/4/66. Retd GD 25/4/74.
SINCLAIR A. R., BA. Born 20/7/51. Commd 15/9/69. Sqn Ldr 1/7/84. Retd GD 20/7/89.
SINCLAIR G. A., BSc. Born 21/11/54. Commd 1/8/76. Sqn Ldr 1/7/96. Retd GD 21/11/98.
SINCLAIR G. L., DFC. Born 15/8/16. Commd 1/3/37. Wg Cdr 1/1/51. Retd GD 23/12/57.
SINCLAIR I. R. Born 20/3/39. Commd 15/12/59. Flt Lt 15/8/62. Retd GD 20/3/77.
SINCLAIR J. Born 13/11/19. Commd 22/6/40. Flt Lt 6/11/45. Retd GD 4/8/61.

SINCLAIR J. G. Born 6/5/19. Commd 22/9/49. Flt Lt 11/11/54. Retd SUP 6/5/68.
SINCLAIR J. J., MIMgt AIIP. Born 23/8/27. Commd 26/8/66. Sqn Ldr 1/7/81. Retd ENG 23/8/85.
SINCLAIR J. W. S., DFC. Born 29/6/18. Commd 6/12/40. Flt Lt 1/9/45. Retd GD 4/2/58.
GC SINCLAIR Sir Laurence, KCB CBE DSO*. Born 13/6/08. Commd 28/7/28. AVM 1/7/52. Retd GD 29/7/60.
SINCLAIR P. Born 27/3/23. Commd 7/9/61. Flt Lt 7/9/67. Retd SEC 1/5/74.
SINCLAIR P. L., MIMgt. Born 17/9/43. Commd 27/2/70. Sqn Ldr 1/1/88. Retd OPS SPT 13/4/01.
SINCLAIR R. E. Born 8/12/45. Commd 2/4/65. Sqn Ldr 1/1/89. Retd GD 1/6/98.
SINCLAIR W. C., AFC. Born 4/9/19. Commd 23/7/42. Sqn Ldr 1/1/52. Retd GD 4/9/74.
SINCLAIR-DAY I. E. Born 3/1/32. Commd 17/10/57. Flt Lt 17/2/63. Retd GD(G) 13/3/71.
SINDALL T. H. Born 8/7/41. Commd 31/7/62. Sqn Ldr 1/7/73. Retd GD 6/1/79.
SINEL M. L. Born 31/1/33. Commd 6/4/54. Sqn Ldr 1/1/63. Retd GD 31/1/71.
SINFIELD A. T. Born 1/8/39. Commd 30/4/81. Sqn Ldr 1/7/94. Retd ADMIN 31/3/99.
SINGH A., BSc. Born 16/7/57. Commd 14/9/75. Flt Lt 15/4/80. Retd GD 15/7/90.
SINGH V. Born 1/9/31. Commd 8/10/52. Flt Lt 1/3/61. Retd GD 1/9/69.
SINGLETON A. P., MBE MIMgt. Born 8/4/43. Commd 19/12/63. Wg Cdr 1/1/83. Retd ADMIN 15/5/93.
SINGLETON D. F. K., BA MSc CEng MIEE. Born 15/12/47. Commd 24/9/67. Sqn Ldr 1/1/80. Retd ENG 15/12/85.
SINGLETON J. R. M. Born 27/3/44. Commd 22/7/66. Flt Lt 27/3/71. Retd SEC 1/11/72. Re-entered 18/6/80.
  Wg Cdr 1/7/96. Retd ADMIN 6/7/98.
SINGLETON P. H. Born 25/10/35. Commd 26/10/61. Sqn Ldr 1/1/77. Retd GD 31/5/88.
SINGLETON P. M., MCIPD. Born 15/12/49. Commd 1/8/69. Wg Cdr 1/1/90. Retd OPS SPT 9/7/99.
SINGLETON S. D., CEng MRAeS. Born 6/12/20. Commd 7/1/43. Wg Cdr 1/7/65. Retd ENG 6/12/75.
SINGLETON S. L. Born 15/10/49. Commd 7/6/68. Fg Offr 21/9/70. Retd GD 7/6/74. Re-entered 30/8/79. Wg Cdr
  1/7/96. Retd ADMIN 22/12/99.
SINGLETON-HOBBS G. A. Born 23/9/53. Commd 28/10/76. Flt Lt 28/4/83. Retd ADMIN 4/8/98.
SINKER A., BSc. Born 26/7/41. Commd 9/9/63. Flt Lt 9/6/65. Retd GD 9/9/79.
SINKER D. R. G., BSc. Born 2/3/60. Commd 18/3/84. Flt Lt 18/9/86. Retd GD 18/12/00.
SINKINSON I., BA. Born 19/6/46. Commd 26/8/66. Wg Cdr 1/1/91. Retd ENG 11/12/96.
SIRCUS R J. Born 15/2/48. Commd 19/6/70. Flt Lt 17/10/76. Retd ADMIN 1/8/80.
SISE G. D., DSO* DFC*. Born 21/1/17. Commd 5/5/44. Gp Capt 1/7/58. Retd GD 26/1/67.
SISMORE E. B., DSO DFC** AFC AE FIMgt. Born 23/6/21. Commd 29/8/42. A Cdre 1/7/71. Retd GD 23/6/76.
SITUNAYAKE S. M. V. Born 25/3/31. Commd 28/9/64. Sqn Ldr 1/7/70. Retd GD. 1/11/87.
SIUDA W. L. Born 4/10/15. Commd 4/10/48. Flt Lt 4/10/48. Retd GD(G) 20/10/70.
SIVITER C. E. Born 16/5/48. Commd 30/5/69. Flt Lt 16/11/73. Retd GD 27/12/75.
SIVITER D. Born 19/3/31. Commd 26/3/53. Flt Lt 5/8/58. Retd GD 19/3/69.
SIVYER S. W., BSc. Born 10/10/54. Commd 3/8/86. Flt Lt 3/8/85. Retd ADMIN 10/3/87.
SIZELAND G. E., MBE. Born 27/7/29. Commd 24/11/67. Sqn Ldr 1/7/80. Retd ADMIN 27/2/84.
SIZER G. H. Born 16/3/23. Commd 26/11/43. Sqn Ldr 1/7/54. Retd GD 16/3/66.
SIZER W. M., DFC*. Born 23/2/20. Commd 7/5/38. Sqn Ldr 1/1/50. Retd GD 23/2/63 rtg Wg Cdr.
SKEA A. F., MA. Born 10/4/41. Commd 22/2/63. Sqn Ldr 1/1/75. Retd GD 10/4/79.
SKEA P. E. Born 21/12/42. Commd 16/9/81. Sqn Ldr 1/1/84. Retd ENG 30/9/94.
SKEHILL J. M. Born 1/7/15. Commd 17/11/41. Flt Offr 1/9/45. Retd SEC 29/5/53.
SKELLAND D. J. Born 17/12/33. Commd 27/1/67. Sqn Ldr 1/1/77. Retd SUP 17/12/90.
SKELLERN C. I. B., BEd FITD qs. Born 28/3/41. Commd 5/10/66. Wg Cdr 1/7/87. Retd ADMIN 13/7/94.
SKELLEY M. H. Born 1/7/18. Commd 9/12/42. Flt Offr 9/12/47. Retd SEC 7/2/55.
SKELLEY R. P. Born 20/3/38. Commd 16/12/58. A Cdre 1/7/90. Retd GD 1/7/93.
SKELLON R. C. Born 13/3/16. Commd 19/1/39. Wg Cdr 1/1/57. Retd SEC 28/4/62.
SKELTON C. D. Born 3/4/11. Commd 8/11/44. Sqn Ldr 1/1/62. Retd GD(G) 20/4/66.
SKELTON S. S. Born 20/4/29. Commd 3/8/49. Flt Lt 3/7/55. Retd GD 20/7/67.
SKERRETT C. G. H. Born 6/11/25. Commd 3/11/60. Sqn Ldr 1/10/66. Retd EDN 1/1/72.
SKILLICORN B. W., AFC. Born 16/2/43. Commd 7/12/64. Flt Lt 12/11/69. Retd GD 15/2/98.
SKILLINGS D. H. A. Born 6/2/15. Commd 17/1/40. Flt Lt 1/1/43. Retd GD 28/4/58 rtg Sqn Ldr.
SKILTON J. A., DFC. Born 24/6/20. Commd 3/3/44. Flt Lt 3/9/47. Retd GD 27/5/58.
SKINGSLEY Sir Anthony., GBE KCB MA. Born 19/10/33. Commd 6/9/55. ACM 1/5/89. Retd GD 31/12/92.
SKINNER A. H., MIMgt. Born 30/8/38. Commd 19/9/58. Sqn Ldr 1/1/73. Retd GD 2/10/77.
SKINNER D. Born 15/12/18. Commd 5/9/57. Flt Lt 6/4/61. Retd GD(G) 14/12/75.
SKINNER D. Born 30/10/29. Commd 20/1/51. Flt Lt 20/7/55. Retd GD 29/2/84.
SKINNER D. A. Born 8/4/43. Commd 11/8/67. Flt Lt 4/5/72. Retd GD 9/8/76.
SKINNER E. J. Born 21/1/29. Commd 11/3/53. Flt Lt 7/3/62. Retd GD 22/1/67.
SKINNER G., CBE MSc BSc CEng FILT FIMechE FIMgt MRAeS. Born 16/9/45. Commd 28/9/64. AVM 1/7/99. Retd
  ENG 16/9/00.
SKINNER H. H., FIMgt. Born 4/8/32. Commd 26/1/55. Wg Cdr 1/7/76. Retd GD 4/8/87.
SKINNER H. M. Born 5/5/34. Commd 2/9/55. Flt Lt 2/3/61. Retd GD 5/5/72.
SKINNER J. D., PhD BTech AdvDipEd(Open). Born 2/1/44. Commd 13/9/70. Wg Cdr 1/7/89. Retd ADMIN 11/4/99.
SKINNER J. D. Born 12/12/32. Commd 31/3/60. Wg Cdr 1/7/79. Retd ADMIN 12/12/87.
SKINNER K. E. Born 18/5/44. Commd 5/11/65. Wg Cdr 1/1/88. Retd GD 9/12/96.
SKINNER P. D. Born 27/2/41. Commd 27/1/61. Flt Lt 27/7/66. Retd GD 28/9/74.

SKINNER R. J. Born 31/5/24. Commd 4/5/50. Sqn Ldr 1/7/70. Retd GD(G) 31/5/79.
SKINNER T. A., MB BS. Born 7/1/58. Commd 19/2/84. Wg Cdr 19/2/96. Retd MED 31/3/00.
SKIPP J. S. Born 31/5/55. Commd 9/8/79. Flt Lt 6/10/81. Retd GD 14/3/97.
SKIPSEY M. R., BSc. Born 3/5/39. Commd 19/4/63. Sqn Ldr 1/1/71. Retd Eng 30/1/79.
SKITCH R. E., DFC. Born 8/7/22. Commd 30/1/42. Sqn Ldr 1/4/55. Retd GD 5/9/55.
SKLIROS The Rev M. P., MA. Born 15/4/33. Commd 15/8/65. Retd 15/9/77 Sqn Ldr.
SKOYLES R. W., BA. Born 27/1/60. Commd 20/10/80. Sqn Ldr 1/7/94. Retd ADMIN 12/4/97.
SKRINE J. R. Born 22/12/23. Commd 21/6/45. Flt Lt 21/12/48. Retd GD 22/12/66.
SKUODAS L. J., BEd BSc. Born 8/9/58. Commd 14/10/84. Flt Lt 14/4/84. Retd ADMIN 14/10/00.
SLACK A. J., BSc. Born 26/10/59. Commd 29/11/81. Flt Lt 29/5/85. Retd ADMIN 19/1/91.
SLACK G. W. Born 3/10/09. Commd 29/11/45. Fg Offr 29/11/46. Retd ENG 5/7/50 Flt Lt.
SLACK M. R. G., BSc. Born 7/5/57. Commd 24/9/75. Sqn Ldr 1/1/90. Retd ENG 2/3/96.
SLACK R. A., CEng MRAeS. Born 18/4/43. Commd 26/5/67. Sqn Ldr 1/7/76. Retd ENG 18/4/81.
SLADDEN D. L. Born 20/7/21. Commd 1/9/45. Wg Cdr 1/1/54. Retd RGT 24/9/60.
SLADDEN R. E. A. Born 9/10/29. Commd 18/9/68. Flt Lt 20/8/58. Retd GD 9/10/84.
SLADE D. G. Born 10/8/29. Commd 30/7/52. Gp Capt 1/7/70. Retd GD 10/12/82.
SLADE D. R., BSc. Born 16/1/34. Commd 23/9/63. Flt Lt 18/11/63. Retd ENG 23/9/79.
SLADE H. G., CBE AFC. Born 2/10/21. Commd 20/6/42. Gp Capt 1/7/72. Retd GD 2/10/76 rtg A Cdre.
SLADE R. G. S. Born 1/10/39. Commd 1/8/61. Sqn Ldr 1/1/76. Retd GD 1/1/79.
SLADEN The Rev P., MA. Born 22/3/50. Commd 11/12/77. Retd 11/12/99 Wg Cdr.
SLADER E. D., BSc. Born 13/5/58. Commd 9/11/80. Flt Lt 9/5/82. Retd GD 9/11/96.
SLANEY G. H. W. Born 16/2/32. Commd 13/8/52. Flt Lt 16/8/61. Retd GD 16/2/70.
SLATER A., BA. Born 7/4/58. Commd 18/10/81. Sqn Ldr 1/1/96. Retd OPS SPT 1/1/99.
SLATER C. E., MBE DFC AFC. Born 9/4/22. Commd 25/8/55. Sqn Ldr 1/7/67. Retd GD 5/3/77.
SLATER E. W. Born 28/2/13. Commd 21/10/54. Flt Lt 21/10/57. Retd ENG 28/2/68.
SLATER F. W. Born 6/3/23. Commd 20/6/63. Flt Lt 20/6/66. Retd ENG 18/10/73.
SLATER G., MSc BSc CEng MIEE MRAeS. Born 26/12/50. Commd 23/9/68. Sqn Ldr 1/7/81. Retd ENG 26/12/88.
SLATER J. C. Born 12/5/53. Commd 5/7/68. Fg Offr 5/1/71. Retd SUP 15/12/72.
SLATER J. K. Born 11/9/48. Commd 3/5/68. Flt Lt 3/11/73. Retd GD 4/4/78.
SLATER K. G. Born 17/9/26. Commd 29/8/51. Sqn Ldr 14/2/66. Retd EDN 10/2/67.
SLATER R. J. Born 13/2/45. Commd 4/2/71. Gp Capt 1/7/91. Retd ADMIN 13/2/00.
SLATER S., DSO OBE DFC*. Born 29/9/21. Commd 10/4/43. Gp Capt 1/1/65. Retd GD 1/7/70.
SLATER S. A. Born 7/12/50. Commd 16/11/72. Sqn Ldr 1/1/85. Retd GD 7/12/88.
SLATER T. G. Born 13/10/59. Commd 21/12/89. Flt Lt 21/12/91. Retd OPS SPT 21/12/97.
SLATTER A. T. Born 28/4/38. Commd 20/6/63. Flt Lt 1/4/66. Retd GD 28/4/76.
SLATTER C., BSc(Eng). Born 29/9/49. Commd 2/7/72. Sqn Ldr 1/1/87. Retd GD 18/9/00.
SLATTER D. A., MBE. Born 28/2/34. Commd 11/10/79. Sqn Ldr 1/1/86. Retd ADMIN 28/2/92.
SLATTERY D. P. Born 2/5/25. Commd 23/3/50. Flt Lt 27/5/54. Retd GD 2/5/63.
SLAUGHTER F. W. Born 21/11/22. Commd 17/9/43. Sqn Ldr 1/7/54. Retd GD 21/11/77.
SLAWSON P. R. Born 19/12/45. Commd 28/2/69. Sqn Ldr 1/7/80. Retd ENG 19/12/83.
SLAYTER R. P. Born 20/5/37. Commd 16/12/58. Wg Cdr 1/1/88. Retd SUP 20/5/92.
SLEDGE D. J., BSc CEng MIMechE MRAeS. Born 18/6/33. Commd 25/9/54. Gp Capt 1/7/77. Retd ENG 3/4/87.
SLEDMERE F. W., AFC FIMgt. Born 3/4/22. Commd 18/12/43. Gp Capt 1/1/69. Retd GD 3/4/75.
SLEEMAN E. Born 28/12/18. Commd 26/7/43. Sqn Ldr 1/7/56. Retd GD 11/7/58.
SLESSOR J. A. G., CVO DL. Born 14/8/25. Commd 19/10/45. Gp Capt 1/1/70. Retd GD 31/1/78.
SLINGER A. P., OBE. Born 19/6/35. Commd 13/7/61. Wg Cdr 1/1/81. Retd GD 19/6/93.
SLINGSBY G. G. Born 24/7/28. Commd 19/11/50. Sqn Ldr 1/1/76. Retd GD 24/7/86.
SLINN G. K., BSc. Born 4/1/40. Commd 7/9/66. Sqn Ldr 1/7/74. Retd ENG 4/1/95.
SLOAN C. H., AFC. Born 24/7/26. Commd 20/10/46. Sqn Ldr 1/7/56. Retd GD 24/10/65.
SLOAN D., DFC MIMgt. Born 23/2/21. Commd 1/5/42. Sqn Ldr 1/7/63. Retd SEC 1/11/74.
SLOAN R. A., BTech. Born 15/5/55. Commd 8/1/78. Flt Lt 8/10/78. Retd GD 8/1/94.
SLOAN R. W., BSc. Born 6/4/20. Commd 14/5/43. Wg Cdr 29/12/66. Retd EDN 6/4/75.
SLOAN S. N., MVO DFC. CGM. Born 25/10/22. Commd 24/5/43. Flt Lt 24/11/46. Retd GD 17/8/51.
SLOAN W. J. P. Born 30/8/02. Commd 19/12/23. Fg Offr 19/6/25. Retd GD 20/11/31 rtg Sqn Ldr.
SLOANE I. R. F., BSc. Born 19/9/52. Commd 2/10/72. Flt Lt 15/4/78. Retd ENG 20/11/81.
SLOCOMBE P. H. Born 5/10/46. Commd 2/7/77. Flt Lt 27/1/79. Retd MED(SEC) 21/12/85.
SLOCUM G. D. Born 21/11/46. Commd 10/6/66. Sqn Ldr 1/7/80. Retd GD 21/11/84.
SLOGROVE R. P., BA. Born 1/11/45. Commd 15/7/66. Flt Lt 15/10/70. Retd SUP 10/3/76 rtg Sqn Ldr.
SLOSS D. J. Born 16/12/44. Commd 14/8/80. Flt Lt 14/8/82. Retd GD(G) 1/10/88.
SLOSS I., CEng FRAeS. Born 3/8/46. Commd 2/10/66. A Cdre 1/1/97. Retd ENG 2/4/00.
SLOSS R. P., MA. Born 5/11/27. Commd 25/8/54. Wg Cdr 1/4/69. Retd EDN 1/4/73.
SLOUGH D. Born 14/11/40. Commd 24/6/76. Sqn Ldr 1/1/86. Retd ADMIN 1/10/87.
SLY K. B. Born 24/2/24. Commd 23/10/51. Flt Lt 11/11/54. Retd GD 30/3/63.
SMAIL T. W., DFC. Born 16/8/23. Commd 18/12/42. Flt Lt 22/2/50. Retd GD 29/12/67.
SMAILES A. A., AFC. Born 10/5/23. Commd 20/12/43. Wg Cdr 1/1/60. Retd GD 8/1/65.
SMAILES R. A. C. Born 28/12/37. Commd 20/12/56. Flt Lt 20/12/62. Retd RGT 31/12/71.

SMALE A. M. Born 20/6/62. Commd 30/4/81. Flt Lt 30/10/86. Retd GD 1/10/89.
SMALE D. J., MBE MIMgt. Born 13/5/36. Commd 17/7/70. Wg Cdr 1/7/90. Retd ADMIN 26/5/92.
SMALE K. C. Born 26/8/25. Commd 11/10/51. Flt Lt 25/1/57. Retd GD 28/9/68.
SMALE L. W. Born 27/4/14. Commd 26/9/57. Flt Lt 26/9/60. Retd SEC 24/5/67.
SMALES K. P., DSO DFC FIMgt. Born 7/1/17. Commd 18/5/37. Gp Capt 1/7/58. Retd GD 21/3/68.
SMALL A. Born 13/11/35. Commd 26/9/57. Sqn Ldr 1/1/68. Retd ENG 13/11/80.
SMALL A. R. Born 30/5/30. Commd 25/10/51. Flt Lt 13/11/57. Retd GD 30/5/85.
SMALL I. Mack., BA. Born 15/5/56. Commd 19/9/76. Flt Lt 15/4/80. Retd GD 15/7/90.
SMALL I. T. Born 10/6/33. Commd 26/3/52. Sqn Ldr 1/1/71. Retd GD 1/11/84.
SMALL J. A., BA. Born 24/1/49. Commd 13/2/72. Sqn Ldr 1/1/90. Retd ADMIN 13/7/96.
SMALL K. A. Born 9/12/32. Commd 4/10/51. Flt Lt 5/11/58. Retd GD 9/12/70.
SMALL M. F. Born 1/8/45. Commd 6/11/80. Sqn Ldr 1/7/94. Retd ENG 14/6/96.
SMALL R., BA. Born 18/1/47. Commd 9/12/71. Flt Lt 9/6/77. Retd GD 14/3/96.
SMALL S. J. Born 12/5/63. Commd 8/4/82. Fg Offr 8/10/84. Retd GD(G) 11/7/86.
SMALL V. W., MIMgt. Born 18/9/33. Commd 26/11/52. Gp Capt 1/1/85. Retd GD 18/9/88.
SMALL W., DFC. Born 18/3/23. Commd 9/11/43. Flt Lt 6/7/56. Retd GD(G) 30/3/74.
SMALLEY J. E. Born 11/10/20. Commd 19/11/42. Gp Capt 1/1/73. Retd SUP 10/11/75.
SMALLEY R. G. Born 10/2/32. Commd 23/8/51. Wg Cdr 1/1/72. Retd GD 30/9/85.
SMALLMAN A. P., DSO AFC. Born 27/6/19. Commd 7/11/40. Wg Cdr 1/1/56. Retd GD 18/3/57.
SMART A. M. Born 8/3/40. Commd 6/9/63. Sqn Ldr 1/7/74. Retd GD 8/3/80.
SMART D. M. Born 30/9/45. Commd 20/5/82. Sqn Ldr 1/7/90. Retd ADMIN 27/2/97.
SMART G. A., MBE AFC. Born 24/4/37. Commd 15/4/55. Air Cdre 1/1/87. Retd GD 8/4/89.
SMART G. J., MSc BDS MGDSRCS(Ed) LDSRCS. Born 12/5/54. Commd 22/2/81. Wg Cdr 3/8/89. Retd DEL 22/2/97.
SMART H. S., BA. Born 5/4/45. Commd 14/7/69. Flt Lt 14/10/70. Retd GD 22/10/94.
SMART M. C. N., AFC. Born 9/11/26. Commd 3/9/47. Gp Capt 1/1/75. Retd GD 6/12/81.
SMART M. D., BA FCIPD. Born 18/3/42. Commd 15/12/60. AVM 1/9/96. Retd ADMIN 25/4/98.
SMART R. E. Born 6/12/15. Commd 26/6/43. Sqn Ldr 1/1/56. Retd SEC 3/1/70.
SMART R. J. R. Born 24/8/57. Commd 5/4/79. Flt Lt 16/9/82. Retd GD 24/10/95.
SMART R. T., MIMgt. Born 28/4/16. Commd 1/5/47. Sqn Ldr 1/7/58. Retd SUP 28/4/74.
SMEATON G. T., OBE. Born 30/10/27. Commd 9/12/48. A Cdre 1/1/79. Retd GD 7/7/79.
SMEATON L. W. Born 9/2/19. Commd 26/10/43. Flt Lt 26/5/55. Retd Pl 9/2/74.
SMEDLEY A. W. A. Born 8/6/31. Commd 14/3/57. Sqn Ldr 1/7/67. Retd GD 24/9/76.
SMEDLEY K. J. Born 12/12/19. Commd 20/3/44. Sqn Ldr 1/7/63. Retd ENG 12/12/74.
SMEDLEY W. M., OBE CEng MRAeS. Born 14/4/20. Commd 19/8/42. Gp Capt 1/7/66. Retd ENG 14/4/75.
SMEETH E. F. Born 10/10/23. Commd 1/10/53. Flt Lt 29/6/50. Retd GD 10/10/83.
SMEETON J. Born 20/7/21. Commd 19/7/51. Flt Lt 19/1/55. Retd ENG 28/4/62.
SMEETON R., OBE. Born 4/7/30. Commd 9/6/55. Wg Cdr 1/7/78. Retd ENG 3/4/84.
SMERDON G. R. B., BSc. Born 4/8/61. Commd 19/6/83. Flt Lt 19/12/85. Retd GD 4/3/00.
SMERDON R. E. W. Born 25/11/22. Commd 3/7/43. Sqn Ldr 1/1/56. Retd GD 25/11/71.
SMERDON T. R. Born 22/2/31. Commd 17/3/67. Sqn Ldr 1/1/78. Retd ENG 12/8/85.
SMETHURST H. C., BA. Born 17/4/60. Commd 4/9/78. Flt Lt 15/10/82. Retd GD 15/7/93.
SMIRTHWAITE S. M., BSc. Born 19/2/58. Commd 17/8/80. Flt Lt 17/11/81. Retd GD 17/8/96.
SMIRTHWAITE S. P., BSc. Born 30/6/55. Commd 16/9/73. Flt Lt 15/4/78. Retd GD 15/7/88.
SMITH A., BSc. Born 22/1/58. Commd 23/9/79. Flt Lt 23/12/80. Retd GD 12/1/93.
SMITH A., MBE. Born 21/12/39. Commd 29/6/72. Sqn Ldr 1/1/80. Retd ADMIN 21/12/94.
SMITH The Rt Rev Mgr A. Born 29/3/41. Commd 18/9/77. Retd 21/4/97. Gp. Capt.
SMITH A. C. Born 25/5/25. Commd 21/2/52. Flt Lt 21/8/55. Retd GD 25/5/63.
SMITH A. C. L. Born 9/7/26. Commd 10/10/63. Flt Lt 10/10/68. Retd GD 9/7/82.
SMITH A. D. B. Born 16/7/24. Commd 29/9/44. Sqn Ldr 1/1/56. Retd GD 16/7/67.
SMITH A. E., CEng MIMechE. Born 1/7/37. Commd 24/9/64. Flt Lt 24/9/66. Retd ENG 1/7/75.
SMITH A. G. Born 16/4/62. Commd 18/12/80. Flt Lt 18/6/86. Retd GD 14/9/96.
SMITH A. G., AFC. Born 25/12/10. Commd 18/9/40. Sqn Ldr 1/7/50. Retd GD(G) 3/3/59.
SMITH A. G. Born 3/12/42. Commd 9/9/63. Flt Lt 17/3/71. Retd GD 3/12/80.
SMITH A. I. A. Born 1/4/40. Commd 4/4/59. Sqn Ldr 1/1/70. Retd GD 1/4/78.
SMITH A. J. Born 11/1/31. Commd 17/12/52. Flt Lt 12/5/58. Retd GD(G) 11/1/86.
SMITH A. J. Born 23/2/14. Commd 10/6/39. Flt Lt 14/1/43. Retd GD 28/3/46 rtg Sqn Ldr.
SMITH A. J. Born 12/6/47. Commd 26/9/85. Flt Lt 26/9/87. Retd GD 27/1/99.
SMITH A. J. E. Born 16/7/46. Commd 21/10/66. Fg Offr 21/4/69. Retd RGT 16/9/72.
SMITH A. J. F., MBE. Born 5/10/26. Commd 29/5/52. Sqn Ldr 1/7/68. Retd GD 5/10/87.
SMITH A. M. Born 6/6/40. Commd 21/4/77. Sqn Ldr 1/7/92. Retd ENG 6/6/95.
SMITH A. M. Born 31/1/25. Commd 12/10/55. Flt Offr 12/10/59. Retd CAT 17/3/62.
SMITH A. M. Born 5/10/67. Commd 9/5/91. Fg Offr 10/10/93. Retd ADMIN 14/3/97.
SMITH A. M. W. Born 24/6/28. Commd 8/8/62. Flt Lt 1/4/66. Retd RGT 11/7/71.
SMITH A. P. D. Born 28/7/46. Commd 14/7/66. Flt Lt 14/1/72. Retd GD 14/3/96.
SMITH A. R. Born 27/12/42. Commd 18/1/73. Sqn Ldr 1/7/81. Retd ADMIN 15/6/96.

SMITH A. R. S., DFC FIMgt. Born 18/5/23. Commd 2/1/44. Flt Lt 2/7/47. Retd GD 13/4/59.
SMITH A. W. S. Born 16/5/47. Commd 21/7/65. Fg Offr 21/7/67. Retd GD 17/2/69.
SMITH The Rev B. Born 15/7/44. Commd 18/9/77. Retd 15/7/95 Gp Capt.
SMITH B., BA. Born 12/6/37. Commd 30/12/55. Sqn Ldr 1/7/73. Retd GD 30/4/88.
SMITH B. D., BSc CEng ARIC MRAeS. Born 7/5/24. Commd 2/9/53. Wg Cdr 1/7/72. Retd ENG 28/2/76.
SMITH B. E. Born 26/5/37. Commd 9/12/65. Sqn Ldr 15/9/73. Retd EDN 26/5/75.
SMITH B. H. Born 3/6/44. Commd 4/5/72. Flt Lt 2/5/79. Retd GD(G) 3/6/82. Re-entrant 1/6/87. Sqn Ldr 1/7/92. Retd GD(G) 14/3/96.
SMITH B. I. Born 17/8/59. Commd 5/1/78. Sqn Ldr 1/7/90. Retd GD 17/8/97.
SMITH B. M., BSc. Born 27/7/21. Commd 1/9/53. Wg Cdr 17/10/61. Retd EDN 11/6/66.
SMITH B. N. Born 5/8/28. Commd 31/1/51. Fg Offr 31/1/52. Retd GD 11/12/54.
SMITH B. S. Born 7/2/61. Commd 4/12/86. Flt Lt 12/5/89. Retd GD 7/2/99.
SMITH B. S. Born 31/3/33. Commd 15/6/53. Flt Lt 14/10/58. Retd GD 9/7/71.
SMITH C. A. Born 25/2/44. Commd 19/5/69. Sqn Ldr 1/7/77. Retd ENG 19/5/85.
SMITH C. C. Born 12/11/21. Commd 12/6/58. Sqn Ldr 1/7/69. Retd ENG 17/3/78.
SMITH C. D., MBE DFC. Born 31/12/20. Commd 18/8/44. Flt Lt 4/12/52. Retd GD(G) 5/4/63.
SMITH C. D., MA. Born 14/4/49. Commd 15/9/69. Wg Cdr 1/7/88. Retd ADMIN 14/3/96.
SMITH C. E. Born 3/1/40. Commd 29/7/68. Flt Lt 24/6/73. Retd ENG 24/1/81.
SMITH C. F., AFC. Born 21/2/13. Commd 30/5/42. Flt Lt 30/5/44. Retd GD 6/12/46.
SMITH C. J., BTech. Born 14/12/51. Commd 3/11/74. Sqn Ldr 1/7/87. Retd GD 3/11/90.
SMITH C. J., MBE. Born 22/1/11. Commd 27/3/47. Flt Lt 27/9/51. Retd SUP 22/1/68.
SMITH C. J. Born 17/8/60. Commd 6/11/80. Flt Lt 8/2/87. Retd GD 14/9/87.
SMITH C. J. D., BSc. Born 12/5/58. Commd 17/8/80. Sqn Ldr 1/1/90. Retd ENG 17/8/96.
SMITH C. R. Born 1/12/30. Commd 24/9/64. Sqn Ldr 1/7/75. Retd ENG 1/12/88.
SMITH C. W. Born 17/5/35. Commd 3/12/70. Sqn Ldr 1/7/85. Retd ADMIN 17/5/90.
SMITH D., MBA MSc BSc MCIPD MIMgt. Born 15/11/57. Commd 22/7/84. Sqn Ldr 1/7/90. Retd ADMIN 28/2/97.
SMITH D., BSc. Born 30/4/38. Commd 15/2/60. Flt Lt 15/8/65. Retd GD 30/4/76.
SMITH D. Born 10/4/46. Commd 5/7/68. Flt Lt 21/11/74. Retd SY 10/4/84.
SMITH D. Born 14/2/39. Commd 3/11/77. Flt Lt 3/11/82. Retd ENG 15/2/89.
SMITH D. Born 10/11/42. Commd 25/6/66. Wg Cdr 1/1/86. Retd ENG 1/10/89.
SMITH D. A., BSc. Born 27/2/52. Commd 3/9/72. Sqn Ldr 1/7/84. Retd ENG 27/2/90.
SMITH D. A. Born 25/9/21. Commd 27/4/61. Flt Lt 27/4/66. Retd ENG 25/9/73.
SMITH D. C. Born 21/2/45. Commd 19/7/84. Sqn Ldr 1/7/94. Retd ADMIN 17/5/96.
SMITH D. C., OBE. Born 17/9/42. Commd 8/6/62. Gp Capt 1/7/90. Retd GD 8/6/93.
SMITH D. E. S., MBCS MIMgt. Born 26/4/30. Commd 14/1/60 Wg Cdr 1/7/76. Retd ADMIN 26/4/85.
SMITH D. F. Born 13/9/33. Commd 3/1/61. Sqn Ldr 1/1/72. Retd SUP 3/1/77.
SMITH D. F. Born 3/2/30. Commd 17/12/52. Sqn Ldr 1/1/62. Retd GD 19/3/76.
SMITH D. G. Born 29/4/47. Commd 7/6/68. Flt Lt 7/12/73. Retd GD 30/4/76.
SMITH D. H. Born 31/3/38. Commd 6/7/59. Sqn Ldr 1/7/71. Retd GD 24/4/88.
SMITH D. J. Born 4/7/33. Commd 10/10/63. Flt Lt 1/4/66. Retd SEC 10/10/71.
SMITH D. J. Born 1/9/24. Commd 21/10/54. Sqn Ldr 1/7/73. Retd GD 1/3/77.
SMITH D. J., MB BS MRCS LRCP. Born 25/6/35. Commd 12/6/60. Wg Cdr 14/5/73. Retd MED 12/6/76.
SMITH D. J. Born 14/6/33. Commd 27/8/52. Sqn Ldr 1/1/69. Retd GD 23/4/88.
SMITH D. M., OBE. Born 21/8/36. Commd 27/8/64. Gp Capt 1/1/85. Retd ADMIN 27/10/89.
SMITH D. M. Born 1/7/24. Commd 5/7/51. Fg Offr 5/7/53. Retd SEC 6/11/54.
SMITH D. P. J., CBE DFC. Born 17/5/22. Commd 22/6/43. Gp Capt 1/1/67. Retd GD(G) 26/3/77.
SMITH D. R. Born 10/9/40. Commd 1/4/71. Flt Lt 1/4/73. Retd GD(G) 1/10/87.
SMITH D. S. Born 30/8/30. Commd 2/5/51. Sqn Ldr 1/7/63. Retd GD 19/12/75.
SMITH D. W. Born 29/6/24. Commd 9/6/45. Wg Cdr 1/1/63. Retd GD 29/4/78.
SMITH D. W., BSc. Born 2/6/44. Commd 16/1/67. Flt Lt 16/4/68. Retd GD 29/5/76.
SMITH D. W. H., AFC. Born 23/2/24. Commd 12/11/43. Gp Capt 1/7/69. Retd GD 27/11/70.
SMITH E. D., BSc. Born 4/4/18. Commd 7/6/40. Gp Capt 1/7/61. Retd ENG 15/9/69.
SMITH E. D., DFC. Born 18/9/56. Commd 5/8/76. Sqn Ldr 1/1/93. Retd GD 1/1/96.
SMITH E. G. Born 11/1/15. Commd 30/8/41. Sqn Ldr 1/7/51. Retd GD(G) 15/1/62.
SMITH E. J. Born 10/8/20. Commd 19/12/59. Flt Lt 19/12/65. Retd ENG 15/3/69.
SMITH E. J. Born 20/2/42. Commd 23/3/67. Sqn Ldr 1/1/89. Retd GD 2/2/97.
SMITH E. J. E., OBE. Born 2/10/34. Commd 31/7/56. Wg Cdr 1/7/71. Retd GD 1/7/74.
SMITH E. S. Born 12/5/18. Commd 12/6/40. Sqn Ldr 1/7/52. Retd GD 31/12/57.
SMITH F. Born 27/4/21. Commd 24/2/44. Flt Lt 24/8/47. Retd GD 27/4/64.
SMITH F. A., MCIPS MIMgt. Born 22/12/29. Commd 4/10/51. Wg Cdr 1/7/75. Retd SUP 4/4/80.
SMITH F. J., BA MIMgt DPhysEd. Born 3/9/32. Commd 26/1/56. Wg Cdr 1/1/79. Retd ADMIN 2/4/85.
SMITH F. L. Born 28/5/21. Commd 7/12/44. Flt Lt 9/12/55. Retd GD(G) 13/4/76.
SMITH F. R. Born 6/2/20. Commd 20/4/50. Flt Lt 20/10/54. Retd SEC 20/4/70.
SMITH F. W. M. Born 5/12/32. Commd 27/9/71. Flt Lt 11/5/57. Retd GD 30/4/93.
SMITH G. Born 6/6/31. Commd 8/7/65. Flt Lt 8/7/71. Retd PRT 14/4/72.
SMITH G. Born 4/9/22. Commd 31/7/58. Sqn Ldr 1/7/70. Retd ENG 4/9/73.

SMITH G. Born 5/9/38. Commd 30/1/75. Flt Lt 30/1/80. Retd GD(G) 31/12/84.
SMITH G. A. Born 6/12/35. Commd 19/1/66. Flt Lt 19/1/68. Retd ENG 19/1/74.
SMITH G. A. Born 30/4/39. Commd 4/11/82. Flt Lt 1/3/87. Retd ENG 30/4/94.
SMITH G. A. R., BEng. Born 30/1/64. Commd 2/8/85. Flt Lt 1/11/90. Retd ENG 2/12/95.
SMITH G. C., OBE AFC. Born 11/4/45. Commd 6/5/66. Gp Capt 1/7/89. Retd GD 18/4/93.
SMITH G. D. Born 31/7/41. Commd 8/12/83. Sqn Ldr 1/7/94. Retd ENG 1/7/97.
SMITH G. F. Born 17/5/44. Commd 14/6/63. Sqn Ldr 1/1/80. Retd GD 29/7/93.
SMITH G. G. Born 19/4/21. Commd 26/5/46. Flt Lt 25/11/48. Retd GD 1/10/55.
SMITH G. H. Born 5/8/25. Commd 27/1/55. Flt Lt 27/1/61. Retd SEC 6/8/70.
SMITH G. H. Born 12/5/23. Commd 13/10/48. Flt Lt 27/8/67. Retd GD 12/5/78. Reinstated 28/8/79 to 12/5/83.
SMITH G. J. E., BSc. Born 9/10/49. Commd 1/11/71. Flt Lt 1/2/73. Retd GD 1/11/91.
SMITH G. L. Born 13/1/31. Commd 3/1/51. Flt Lt 10/11/55. Retd PI 13/1/86.
SMITH G. M. Born 14/5/46. Commd 25/2/82. Sqn Ldr 1/7/91. Retd SUP 6/4/98.
SMITH G. McD., MBE BSc. Born 17/6/48. Commd 20/1/71. Flt Lt 20/10/73. Retd ENG 31/3/94.
SMITH G. N., CEng MRAeS MIEE. Born 25/3/37. Commd 30/7/59. Sqn Ldr 1/7/68. Retd ENG 25/3/75.
SMITH G. N., MCSP Dip TP. Born 5/8/50. Commd 30/4/81. Fg Off 30/4/83. Retd MED(T) 1/9/86.
SMITH G. P. Born 27/3/55. Commd 5/8/76. Flt Lt 5/2/83. Retd SY 27/3/93.
SMITH G. T. Born 5/12/18. Commd 31/1/46. Flt Lt 31/7/49. Retd ENG 5/12/53.
SMITH G. T. Born 25/2/38. Commd 14/3/57. Flt Lt 19/6/63. Retd SEC 30/8/69.
SMITH G. T. Born 6/9/37. Commd 23/6/67. Sqn Ldr 1/1/87. Retd GD 17/1/90.
SMITH G. W. Born 9/10/52. Commd 28/2/85. Flt Lt 28/2/87. Retd ENG 1/10/93.
SMITH G. W., MBE. Born 19/12/19. Commd 25/10/43. Sqn Ldr 1/7/66. Retd GD 3/12/68.
SMITH G. W. Born 22/6/42. Commd 17/7/75. Flt Lt 17/7/77. Retd ENG 17/7/83.
SMITH G. W. T., MA MB BChir MRCS LRCP FRCS(Edin) DO. Born 18/3/37. Commd 20/9/59. Wg Cdr 19/6/68. Retd MED 20/9/75.
SMITH H., DFC AFC. Born 17/4/23. Commd 9/2/44. Wg Cdr 1/7/62. Retd GD 18/4/68.
SMITH H. B. Born 8/1/49. Commd 11/11/71. Sqn Ldr 1/7/86. Retd SUP 1/7/89.
SMITH H. C. Born 30/10/37. Commd 24/6/71. Flt Lt 24/6/73. Retd ENG 1/10/85.
SMITH H. D., MIMgt FInst Pet. Born 7/7/24. Commd 8/9/44. Sqn Ldr 1/7/65. Retd SUP 10/10/78.
SMITH H. J., MBE DFC. Born 8/10/18. Commd 20/10/42. Flt Lt 30/7/47. Retd CAT 15/2/61.
SMITH H. J., BSc. Born 14/5/32. Commd 13/8/52. Flt Lt 18/5/58. Retd GD 1/5/86.
SMITH H. R., BA CEng MRAeS. Born 30/9/42. Commd 30/9/61. Wg Cdr 1/7/89. Retd ENG 2/8/93.
SMITH H. R. Born 8/7/22. Commd 11/8/44. Flt Lt 11/2/48. Retd GD 5/8/60.
SMITH I. D. Born 3/4/49. Commd 20/9/68. Flt Lt 20/3/74. Retd GD 29/5/86.
SMITH The Rev I. C. Born 11/2/39. Commd 16/1/72. Retd 8/3/83. Sqn Ldr.
SMITH I. E. Born 22/12/23. Commd 16/5/45. Wg Cdr 1/1/68. Retd SUP 1/11/72.
SMITH I. G. Born 4/9/54. Commd 6/10/77. Flt Lt 6/4/83. Retd GD 28/3/93.
SMITH I. P., BSc CEng MRAeS. Born 16/3/46. Commd 26/5/67. Sqn Ldr 1/7/80. Retd ENG 16/9/84.
SMITH I. R. G. Born 13/5/20. Commd 12/11/41. Sqn Ldr 1/1/63. Retd ENG 13/1/73.
SMITH J. Born 24/9/41. Commd 11/8/67. Sqn Ldr 1/7/76. Retd ADMIN 3/4/82. Re-entered 5/11/90. Sqn Ldr 2/2/85. Retd ADMIN 5/6/98.
SMITH J., BSc BM BCh MRCPath DCP. Born 2/8/39. Commd 20/1/64. Wg Cdr 2/9/79. Retd MED 20/1/82.
SMITH J. Born 24/9/41. Commd 9/7/66. Sqn Ldr 1/7/76. Retd ADMIN 2/4/82.
SMITH J., BA. Born 17/8/62. Commd 10/11/85. Flt Lt 10/5/89. Retd ADMIN 10/11/91.
SMITH J. A. Born 4/4/30. Commd 29/3/50. Flt Lt 29/9/54. Retd GD 4/4/68.
SMITH J. A. Born 4/6/38. Commd 26/5/60. Flt Lt 10/2/67. Retd GD 4/6/76.
SMITH J. A. Born 10/5/25. Commd 11/1/51. Sqn Ldr 1/1/68. Retd GD 10/5/80.
SMITH J. C. I. Born 13/10/58. Commd 22/3/81. Sqn Ldr 1/7/94. Retd ADMIN 14/3/97.
SMITH J. D., MEd BSc. Born 26/6/36. Commd 20/2/59. Sqn Ldr 17/5/68. Retd ADMIN 18/9/82.
SMITH J. E., CB CBE AFC. Born 8/6/24. Commd 6/3/50. AVM 1/1/78. Retd GD 3/4/81.
SMITH J. E. Born 11/11/43. Commd 2/2/84. Flt Lt 2/2/88. Retd ADMIN 14/3/97.
SMITH J. F. Born 19/2/22. Commd 6/10/60. Sqn Ldr 1/7/73. Retd ENG 1/10/75.
SMITH J. F., CEng MIMechE MRAeS. Born 11/10/38. Commd 30/7/59. Wg Cdr 1/1/78. Retd ENG 13/10/81.
SMITH J. M. Born 6/11/71. Commd 5/10/95. Plt Offr 5/10/96. Retd GD 26/7/97.
SMITH J. M., BSc. Born 11/8/60. Commd 25/10/87. Flt Lt 11/8/88. Retd GD(G) 21/3/91.
SMITH J. M. Born 12/9/27. Commd 4/9/58. Sqn Ldr 1/1/70. Retd ENG 13/1/73.
SMITH J. P. Born 22/3/37. Commd 10/2/72. Flt Lt 10/2/74. Retd GD 22/3/95.
SMITH J. R. Born 8/12/46. Commd 19/6/70. Flt Lt 30/1/74. Retd GD 4/11/75.
SMITH J. R. Born 31/12/37. Commd 2/1/67. Flt Lt 23/12/71. Retd ADMIN 13/2/82.
SMITH J. W. C. Born 17/2/15. Commd 22/4/43. Flt Lt 22/10/46. Retd ENG 17/2/64.
SMITH J. W. G., CBE DFC. Born 11/5/22. Commd 10/11/42. Gp Capt 1/1/72. Retd GD(G) 11/5/77.
SMITH J. W. G. Born 26/3/36. Commd 22/8/58. Flt Lt 26/7/64. Retd GD 22/8/74.
SMITH J. W. R. Born 23/10/14. Commd 30/1/47. Fg Offr 30/1/49. Retd SUP 1/9/52.
SMITH K. Born 20/1/24. Commd 11/5/45. Sqn Ldr 1/1/57. Retd GD 20/1/67.
SMITH K., BSc. Born 1/4/48. Commd 18/9/96. Wg Cdr 1/7/90. Retd GD 7/10/98.
SMITH K. B. Born 9/10/28. Commd 1/8/51. Plt Offr 1/8/51. Retd GD 14/6/52.

SMITH K. B. Born 29/7/50. Commd 30/5/69. Flt Lt 30/11/74. Retd GD 29/1/83.
SMITH K. C., BEM. Born 22/10/21. Commd 12/6/58. Flt Lt 12/6/64. Retd ENG 4/8/73.
SMITH K. E. Born 31/7/40. Commd 5/4/71. Flt Lt 5/4/71. Retd SUP 5/10/79.
SMITH K. G. Born 30/11/56. Commd 27/1/77. Sqn Ldr 1/1/89. Retd GD 11/11/95.
SMITH K. P., BA. Born 16/5/47. Commd 11/8/69. Flt Lt 11/8/75. Retd GD 17/1/76. Re-entered 8/2/79. Wg Cdr 1/7/94. Retd OPS SPT 8/2/01.
SMITH K. R. Born 29/5/58. Commd 6/11/80. Flt Lt 21/4/86. Retd ADMIN 30/4/94.
SMITH K. W. E. Born 6/5/53. Commd 22/7/71. Sqn Ldr 1/7/87. Retd RGT 16/2/91.
SMITH L. Born 28/5/28. Commd 25/6/66. Flt Lt 25/6/71. Retd SEC 31/5/74.
SMITH L. C. J., OBE. Born 16/4/10. Commd 30/12/39. Wg Cdr 1/1/52. Retd SEC 29/6/63.
SMITH L. F. Born 13/4/23. Commd 26/3/59. Flt Lt 26/3/64. Retd GD 7/4/73.
SMITH L. O. Born 17/2/26. Commd 31/5/50. Sqn Ldr 1/1/73. Retd GD(G) 17/2/86.
SMITH M. F. Born 9/2/29. Commd 9/4/52. Flt Lt 5/11/58. Retd GD 2/12/75.
SMITH M. H. Born 8/2/38. Commd 28/7/59. Gp Capt 1/7/82. Retd GD 1/2/89.
SMITH M. J., BSc. Born 27/7/38. Commd 22/8/61. Sqn Ldr 22/2/69. Retd ADMIN 27/7/93.
SMITH M. J., MCIPD MIMgt. Born 4/6/46. Commd 8/9/69. Wg Cdr 1/1/87. Retd ADMIN 5/11/90.
SMITH M. J. Born 8/4/47. Commd 24/11/67. Flt Lt 24/5/73. Retd GD 22/4/94.
SMITH M. J. M. Born 26/11/44. Commd 7/7/67. Flt Lt 7/7/74. Retd SUP 8/5/83.
SMITH M. L., BA. Born 22/4/46. Commd 28/10/66. Wg Cdr 1/7/90. Retd GD 3/12/96.
SMITH M. R., CBE. Born 28/5/39. Commd 15/12/59. Gp Capt 1/1/89. Retd GD 1/8/93.
SMITH M. R., MIMgt. Born 28/2/53. Commd 19/10/75. Sqn Ldr 1/7/84. Retd PRT 19/10/91.
SMITH M. T. Born 16/6/47. Commd 9/5/91. Flt Lt 9/5/95. Retd ADMIN 22/7/98.
SMITH M. V. Born 19/6/46. Commd 26/5/67. Flt Lt 18/2/70. Retd GD 30/11/77.
SMITH N. B. Born 21/6/43. Commd 15/7/66. Flt Lt 15/1/69. Retd GD 20/6/81.
SMITH N. C. R., BSc. Born 16/5/52. Commd 20/2/75. Flt Lt 15/10/80. Retd ENG 20/2/91.
SMITH N. F. G., BA FIMgt MInstPkg MCIPS. Born 13/2/33. Commd 20/11/52. Wg Cdr 1/1/72. Retd SUP 26/5/78.
SMITH N. H. J., DFC. Born 15/4/18. Commd 1/5/39. Flt Lt 1/9/45. Retd GD 29/3/58 rtg Wg Cdr.
SMITH N. J., MSc BSc. Born 19/5/56. Commd 8/1/84. Sqn Ldr 1/1/93. Retd ENG 8/1/00.
SMITH N. S. Born 21/11/31. Commd 27/3/52. Flt Lt 27/12/57. Retd GD 21/11/69.
SMITH P., MBA BTech. Born 19/9/53. Commd 3/9/72. Sqn Ldr 1/7/88. Retd GD 14/9/96.
SMITH P., MBE FIMgt MCIPD. Born 29/2/24. Commd 29/4/44. Gp Capt 1/7/69. Retd GD 1/3/79.
SMITH P. Born 15/4/43. Commd 24/6/65. Sqn Ldr 1/1/75. Retd GD 15/4/81.
SMITH P. A., BSc FRIN. Born 18/2/47. Commd 1/3/68. Gp Capt 1/1/94. Retd GD 13/1/01.
SMITH P. A. Born 13/11/46. Commd 22/8/71. Flt Lt 22/11/74. Retd ENG 22/8/87.
SMITH P. B. Born 16/11/30. Commd 19/3/52. Flt Lt 19/9/56. Retd GD 16/11/68.
SMITH P. B. Born 6/11/60. Commd 6/11/80. Flt Lt 6/5/87. Retd GD(G) 1/10/91.
SMITH P. C. Born 26/9/48. Commd 7/1/71. Flt Lt 7/7/76. Retd GD 14/3/96.
SMITH P. C. C. Born 20/2/31. Commd 30/6/50. Flt Lt 29/1/59. Retd GD 1/11/68.
SMITH P. D. B., LLB. Born 31/1/31. Commd 11/5/51. Flt Lt 11/5/57. Retd SEC 31/7/59.
SMITH P. F., MBE. Born 8/1/18. Commd 15/1/42. Wg Cdr 1/1/61. Retd SEC 8/1/68.
SMITH P. G. Born 25/12/46. Commd 25/4/69. Flt Lt 25/10/74. Retd GD 20/8/76.
SMITH P. G., CEng MRAeS. Born 16/3/20. Commd 10/2/49. Wg Cdr 1/7/65. Retd ENG 1/11/72.
SMITH P. J. Born 12/7/32. Commd 11/10/51. Grp Capt 1/7/77. Retd SY 12/7/87.
SMITH P. J. Born 27/2/44. Commd 19/6/70. Flt Lt 19/6/72. Retd GD 8/4/76.
SMITH P. J., CEng MIEE. Born 29/6/42. Commd 28/2/66. Sqn Ldr 1/7/76. Retd ENG 28/2/82.
SMITH R. Born 26/3/33. Commd 28/6/51. Flt Lt 10/10/56. Retd GD 15/8/74.
SMITH R., FIMgt MCIT MILT. Born 10/8/28. Commd 12/12/51. Gp Capt 1/7/76. Retd SUP 10/8/83.
SMITH R. A., BSc. Born 3/12/54. Commd 31/1/80. Flt Lt 29/5/86. Retd GD(G) 1/10/96.
SMITH R. A. Born 22/7/32. Commd 25/6/66. Flt Lt 25/6/71. Retd GD 22/7/90.
SMITH R. A., MA FIMgt FCIPD. Born 9/1/37. Commd 22/8/58. Gp Capt 1/1/86. Retd ADMIN 30/9/90.
SMITH R. A. Born 19/11/39. Commd 2/5/59. Flt Lt 2/11/64. To Reserve GD 14/1/71. Re-employed 30/4/72. Retd SUP 1/7/78.
SMITH R. B., DPhysEd. Born 7/3/44. Commd 19/8/68. Sqn Ldr 1/1/81. Retd GD 7/1/97.
SMITH R. B. Born 24/10/41. Commd 26/5/61. Sqn Ldr 1/7/78. Retd GD 1/8/90.
SMITH R. B. Born 27/12/41. Commd 11/7/61. Flt Lt 11/1/67. Retd GD 7/9/73.
SMITH R. C. Born 3/9/43. Commd 5/2/65. Sqn Ldr 1/1/87. Retd GD 3/9/00.
SMITH R. D. D., MIMgt. Born 9/8/30. Commd 17/7/51. Sqn Ldr 1/1/63. Retd GD 17/8/73.
SMITH R. F. L. H. Born 2/11/48. Commd 8/4/73. Sqn Ldr 1/1/85. Retd ADMIN 15/4/89.
SMITH R. G. Born 18/10/23. Commd 12/9/58. Flt Lt 1/4/63. Retd GD 1/8/68.
SMITH R. G. Born 26/1/19. Commd 27/3/42. Sqn Ldr 1/7/54. Retd GD 3/7/59.
SMITH R. G., MA MIMgt. Born 12/5/54. Commd 3/9/72. Wg Cdr 1/7/89. Retd RGT 1/7/92.
SMITH R. H., FIMgt. Born 11/7/42. Commd 26/5/61. Gp Capt 1/1/88. Retd ADMIN 11/7/97.
SMITH R. H. Born 22/5/21. Commd 17/4/42. Flt Lt 27/5/54. Retd GD(G) 5/10/67.
SMITH R. H., DFC. Born 28/4/17. Commd 19/11/42. Sqn Ldr 1/1/55. Retd GD 28/2/58.
SMITH R. H., OBE. Born 14/9/17. Commd 14/9/37. Wg Cdr 1/1/49. Retd GD 29/9/59.
SMITH R. H., OBE CEng MIEE MIMgt. Born 24/2/21. Commd 22/8/46. Gp Capt 1/1/74. Retd ENG 30/3/78.

SMITH R. J. Born 12/5/42. Commd 22/5/80. Flt Lt 22/5/83. Retd GD 2/4/93.
SMITH R. J. Born 10/8/32. Commd 19/4/51. Sqn Ldr 1/7/63. Retd GD 10/8/70.
SMITH R. J. D. Born 3/6/42. Commd 8/6/62. Flt Lt 8/12/67. Retd GD 28/8/76.
SMITH R. K. Born 13/6/45. Commd 28/11/69. Flt Lt 17/8/73. Retd GD 14/6/77.
SMITH R. L., BSc MInst P. Born 8/5/34. Commd 20/5/59. Gp Capt 1/1/77. Retd ENG 2/5/87.
SMITH R. M., BSc. Born 13/3/44. Commd 30/5/71. Sqn Ldr 1/7/78. Retd ENG 13/3/99.
SMITH R. M. Born 14/7/29. Commd 17/1/51. Flt Lt 14/11/56. Retd GD 14/7/67.
SMITH R. M. Born 11/10/36. Commd 4/9/59. Wg Cdr 1/7/79. Retd ADMIN 6/4/83.
SMITH R. N., OBE. Born 24/12/15. Commd 14/9/34. Wg Cdr 1/7/47. Retd GD 30/6/57.
SMITH R. S. Born 31/7/44. Commd 15/7/65. Sqn Ldr 1/1/77. Retd ENG 31/7/82. Reinstated 24/4/87. Sqn Ldr
    28/9/81. Retd ENG 11/10/90.
SMITH R. T. D., AFM. Born 13/2/21. Commd 4/9/58. Flt Lt 4/9/63. Retd PE 22/8/74 rtg Sqn Ldr.
SMITH R. W. Born 22/11/25. Commd 21/9/50. Flt Lt 21/3/54. Retd GD 23/11/73.
SMITH R. W., DBE CEng MIMechE MRAeS. Born 1/6/37. Commd 30/4/59. Wg Cdr 1/7/75. Retd ENG 25/9/91.
SMITH R. W. Born 17/5/45. Commd 27/10/67. Flt Lt 24/2/74. Retd GD(G) 17/5/83.
SMITH S. Born 30/10/53. Commd 20/12/73. Flt Lt 20/6/79. Retd GD 30/10/91.
SMITH S. A. Born 9/11/45. Commd 11/11/65. Flt Lt 11/5/71. Retd GD(G) 9/11/83.
SMITH S. C. Born 7/9/52. Commd 30/8/73. Sqn Ldr 1/1/88. Retd GD 1/10/97.
SMITH S. C., MBE MIIM MIMgt. Born 26/7/25. Commd 18/6/56. Sqn Ldr 1/1/72. Retd MAR 26/7/79.
SMITH S. C., BSc. Born 5/5/56. Commd 14/1/79. Flt Lt 14/10/80. Retd GD 14/1/87.
SMITH S. C. Born 9/11/61. Commd 20/10/83. Flt Lt 20/4/90. Retd ADMIN 14/3/97.
SMITH S. E. Born 23/10/60. Commd 24/7/81. Sqn Ldr 1/7/96. Retd GD 1/7/99.
SMITH S. E., MBE MBA BEd MCIPD MIMgt. Born 13/6/56. Commd 23/5/82. Wg Cdr 1/1/95. Retd ADMIN 20/9/99.
SMITH S. G. Born 1/3/14. Commd 28/2/57. Flt Lt 28/2/60. Retd ACB 1/1/66.
SMITH S. J. Born 19/3/44. Commd 29/4/71. Sqn Ldr 1/7/80. Retd ENG 31/7/93.
SMITH S. K. Born 3/8/59. Commd 5/1/78. Sqn Ldr 1/7/90. Retd OPS SPT 5/12/98.
SMITH S. L. Born 29/3/60. Commd 11/1/79. Sqn Ldr 1/7/95. Retd GD 1/7/98.
SMITH S. P., MIMgt. Born 26/4/21. Commd 13/11/43. Sqn Ldr 15/2/65. Retd EDN 4/9/75.
SMITH S. R. F. Born 8/3/61. Commd 28/7/94. Flt Lt 28/7/96. Retd OPS SPT 11/5/00.
SMITH S. R. R. Born 25/6/14. Commd 19/10/34. Wg Cdr 1/7/47. Retd GD 25/6/58.
SMITH S. W., MBE. Born 19/1/27. Commd 12/3/52. Flt Lt 1/3/61. Retd GD 19/1/77.
SMITH S. W. G., BSc. Born 13/6/23. Commd 23/12/43. Sqn Ldr 1/7/56. Retd EDN 11/1/73.
YSMITH T. D. Born 2/7/36. Commd 26/8/66. Fg Offr 26/8/66. Retd GD(G) 18/7/69.
SMITH T. G. Born 11/12/19. Commd 16/8/41. Flt Lt 31/1/47. Retd GD 2/9/50.
SMITH T. G. Born 1/10/36. Commd 1/11/79. Flt Lt 1/11/82. Retd GD(G) 1/10/88.
SMITH T. J., BSc CEng FIMechE MRAeS. Born 20/12/42. Commd 4/1/71. Wg Cdr 1/7/91. Retd ENG 1/10/93.
SMITH T. M. Born 5/6/41. Commd 15/2/73. Sqn Ldr 1/1/81. Retd SUP 15/2/90.
SMITH T. R. C. Born 27/8/43. Commd 12/7/63. Sqn Ldr 1/1/82. Retd GD 3/4/96.
SMITH V. G., LLB(Lond) LLB BL. Born 25/7/33. Commd 4/4/60. Sqn Ldr 1/1/65. Retd EDN 4/4/73.
SMITH W. Born 29/5/56. Commd 31/8/78. Wg Cdr 1/1/94. Retd ADMIN 29/5/00.
SMITH W. Born 21/1/16. Commd 6/9/45. Flt Lt 29/6/50. Retd SUP 31/8/63.
SMITH W. Born 13/5/25. Commd 13/2/52. Sqn Ldr 1/7/73. Retd GD 30/4/76.
SMITH W. Born 22/9/56. Commd 30/8/84. Flt Lt 18/2/87. Retd SUP 22/4/94.
SMITH W. G. Born 11/12/21. Commd 16/9/44. Sqn Ldr 1/7/55. Retd GD 11/12/64.
SMITH W. H. Born 5/10/18. Commd 29/8/45. Fg Offr 29/8/46. Retd RGT 5/5/50 rtg Flt Lt.
SMITH W. H., MB BS FRCR MRCS LRCP DMR(D). Born 21/4/47. Commd 22/1/68. Wg Cdr 2/7/84. Retd MED
    21/4/85.
SMITH W. H. H. Born 28/8/08. Commd 2/12/40. Flt Lt 6/12/44. Retd ENG 6/1/46 rtg Sqn Ldr.
SMITH W. J., DFC. Born 9/2/13. Commd 13/7/36. Wg Cdr 1/10/46. Retd GD 14/2/58.
SMITH W. M., MB ChB MRCGP. Born 28/2/44. Commd 25/7/66. Sqn Ldr 1/7/75. Retd MED 25/7/82.
SMITH-CARINGTON J. H., AFC. Born 26/10/21. Commd 14/3/42. Wg Cdr 1/7/60. Retd GD 26/10/71.
SMITHER M. J. B. Born 24/8/39. Commd 18/7/61. Sqn Ldr 1/7/70. Retd ENG 3/1/78.
SMITHSON F. M. Born 4/12/23. Commd 8/4/44. Flt Lt 10/11/55. Retd GD 4/12/66.
SMITHSON P. C., MSc BEd. Born 25/5/54. Commd 17/1/82. Wg Cdr 1/1/98. Retd ADMIN 5/12/98.
SMITHSON W. J. Born 2/11/33. Commd 20/12/51. Flt Lt 4/4/57. Retd GD(G) 17/1/73.
SMITZ A. J., DFC. Born 12/10/11. Commd 26/3/40. Sqn Ldr 1/1/60. Retd GD(G) 1/8/60.
SMORTHIT N. M., BSc. Born 23/8/62. Commd 2/4/84. Flt Lt 15/1/87. Retd GD 23/8/00.
SMOUT P. F., AFC DPhysEd. Born 1/6/47. Commd 19/8/68. Wg Cdr 1/7/97. Retd ADMIN 3/7/99.
SMULOVIC P. S. V., BSc. Born 22/11/46. Commd 15/6/83. Sqn Ldr 1/7/95. Retd ENG 24/1/98.
SMURTHWAITE R., CEng MIEE. Born 2/1/18. Commd 8/10/42. Sqn Ldr 1/7/53. Retd ENG 1/9/70.
SMUTS J. A. Born 24/9/36. Commd 18/2/58. Flt Lt 18/2/65. Retd GD(G) 24/9/74.
SMYTH A. J. M., OBE DFC BSc. Born 17/2/15. Commd 21/2/37. Gp Capt 1/7/55. Retd GD 6/10/61.
SMYTH A. T. Born 28/3/54. Commd 7/7/80. Wg Cdr 1/1/95. Retd ADMIN 9/7/98.
SMYTH D. F. Born 23/10/39. Commd 6/5/83. Flt Lt 6/5/87. Retd SY 23/10/94.
SMYTH G. H. Born 5/6/24. Commd 20/4/50. Sqn Ldr 1/1/75. Retd GD 5/6/79.
SMYTH G. T. Born 4/5/12. Commd 5/11/42. Flt Lt 5/5/46. Retd ENG 15/9/59 rtg Sqn Ldr.

SMYTH J. A., BChD. Born 21/10/57. Commd 1/10/78. Wg Cdr 14/3/93. Retd DEL 21/10/96.
SMYTH P. A. Born 20/12/25. Commd 29/3/56. Sqn Ldr 1/1/68. Retd ADMIN 20/12/83.
SMYTH P. N. Born 21/9/27. Commd 19/7/56. Sqn Ldr 1/1/72. Retd ENG 14/5/80.
SMYTH R. H., AFC. Born 27/1/22. Commd 5/8/42. Sqn Ldr 1/7/54. Retd GD 31/10/61.
SMYTH R. J. V., DFC. Born 14/2/20. Commd 24/6/41. Wg Cdr 1/1/59. Retd GD 14/2/67.
SMYTH T. A. Born 7/5/35. Commd 3/12/54. Flt Lt 3/6/60. Retd GD 7/5/73.
SMYTH W. L., MBE MIMgt. Born 12/9/25. Commd 26/12/51. Wg Cdr 1/7/68. Retd GD 12/9/80.
SMYTHE D. W. Born 11/7/10. Commd 22/2/29. Gp Capt 1/1/49. Retd ENG 29/5/59.
SMYTHE G. Born 25/9/24. Commd 11/11/50. Flt Lt 11/5/55. Retd GD 3/4/74.
SMYTHE P. J. Born 17/3/36. Commd 15/4/55. Flt Lt 1/3/61. Retd GD 17/3/91.
SMYTHE R. F. W. Born 27/2/34. Commd 27/1/67. Fg Offr 27/1/67. Retd RGT 29/9/72.
SMYTHE W. V. Born 21/10/20. Commd 10/3/44. Flt Lt 9/7/56. Retd GD(G) 23/5/69.
SNADDEN W. R. Born 19/2/42. Commd 28/2/64. Flt Lt 28/8/69. Retd GD 19/2/80.
SNAPE B. R. R., OBE. Born 9/11/08. Commd 12/12/41. Sqn Ldr 1/7/52. Retd SEC 15/4/58.
SNAPE D. E. Born 9/6/23. Commd 10/2/45. Flt Lt 10/8/48. Retd GD 31/3/62.
SNAPE K. R. Born 23/4/37. Commd 19/2/57. Flt Lt 19/8/62. Retd GD(G) 23/4/75.
SNAPE R. A. Born 19/6/51. Commd 10/2/72. Flt Lt 22/6/78. Retd ADMIN 19/12/89.
SNARE R. T. F. Born 23/9/32. Commd 26/9/51. Sqn Ldr 1/1/65. Retd GD 23/9/70.
SNEDDON H. M. Born 17/5/24. Commd 26/5/60. Sqn Ldr 1/7/71. Retd ENG 1/9/73.
SNEDDON J. Born 25/7/30. Commd 21/11/51. Flt Lt 13/11/57. Retd GD 25/10/68.
SNEDDON M. I., BSc CEng MIEE. Born 7/7/59. Commd 26/9/82. Flt Lt 1/11/85. Retd ENG 26/9/98.
SNEDDON P. A., BSc. Born 25/1/51. Commd 8/4/73. Sqn Ldr 1/1/84. Retd GD 8/4/89.
SNEDDON T. J. Born 30/3/42. Commd 8/12/61. Wg Cdr 1/7/84. Retd GD 22/12/89.
SNEE J. J. Born 8/6/19. Commd 25/2/44. Flt Lt 25/2/46. Retd GD(G) 8/6/74.
SNELGROVE P. S. Born 28/12/47. Commd 11/10/84. Flt Lt 11/10/88. Retd SUP 1/10/93.
SNELL A. M., BA CertEd. Born 7/8/53. Commd 2/11/88. Flt Lt 2/11/90. Retd ADMIN 2/11/96.
SNELL J. D. Born 3/7/46. Commd 18/8/67. Sqn Ldr 1/1/82. Retd GD 3/7/91.
SNELL P. R., BA. Born 12/9/54. Commd 6/11/77. Sqn Ldr 1/7/90. Retd GD 1/6/95.
SNELL R. J., AFM. Born 24/4/22. Commd 4/7/57. Sqn Ldr 1/7/73. Retd GD 24/4/77.
SNELL R. W. K. Born 12/3/36. Commd 22/10/54. Flt Lt 7/3/62. Retd GD 12/3/74.
SNELL S. Born 9/7/19. Commd 10/2/45. Flt Lt 23/3/47. Retd ENG 7/11/53.
SNELL V. A. Born 8/2/69. Commd 29/3/90. Plt Offr 13/7/90. Retd ADMIN 15/11/91.
SNELLER J. A. J., MA CEng MRAeS. Born 6/3/57. Commd 1/7/82. Wg Cdr 1/1/96. Retd ENG 6/3/01.
SNELLER K. G., AFC. Born 3/10/20. Commd 21/6/56. Sqn Ldr 1/7/72. Retd GD 25/10/75.
SNELLER R. G. J., DFC. Born 25/11/21. Commd 21/6/50. Flt Lt 21/12/54. Retd GD 30/3/68.
SNELLING G. E., MIMgt. Born 12/11/25. Commd 9/2/66. Sqn Ldr 1/7/77. Retd ENG 12/11/83.
SNELLING M. H. B., AFC MA. Born 12/12/41. Commd 30/9/60. Flt Lt 22/2/66. Retd GD 29/12/73.
SNELLING R. F. S., CEng MIMechE. Born 22/8/35. Commd 11/6/63. Flt Lt 10/2/67. Retd ENG 22/8/93.
SNOOK P., MBE. Born 14/1/43. Commd 11/8/67. Flt Lt 12/11/69. Retd GD 14/1/00.
SNOOKES W. C. Born 2/2/32. Commd 26/12/51. Flt Lt 26/6/56. Retd GD 2/3/70.
SNOW D. B. Born 15/10/53. Commd 18/1/73. Sqn Ldr 1/1/88. Retd GD 15/10/91.
SNOW I. P. Born 30/11/47. Commd 27/1/77. Sqn Ldr 1/7/84. Retd SUP 1/10/89.
SNOW J. W. Born 8/10/21. Commd 20/4/50. Fg Offr 20/4/51. Retd ENG 12/10/54.
SNOWDEN J. S., BA. Born 12/4/49. Commd 15/3/73. Sqn Ldr 1/1/84. Retd GD(G) 14/3/96.
SNOWDEN R. W. Born 29/4/48. Commd 11/9/86. Flt Lt 11/9/90. Retd ENG 21/10/99.
SNOWDON E. Born 8/2/18. Commd 6/11/58. Flt Lt 6/11/64. Retd ENG 1/6/66.
SOAMES-WARING D. Born 25/4/31. Commd 3/5/68. Flt Lt 3/5/71. Retd GD 3/7/73.
SOAR D. E. Born 3/11/28. Commd 19/8/65. Sqn Ldr 1/1/76. Retd ENG 6/8/80.
SODEN E., BSc. Born 27/7/42. Commd 30/9/61. Flt Lt 9/2/68. Retd ENG 29/12/73.
SOFFE C. R., BSc. Born 1/6/65. Commd 28/8/83. Flt Lt 15/1/89. Retd GD 15/7/98.
SOLE M. A. Born 23/9/50. Commd 20/9/69. Fg Offr 20/3/72. Retd GD(G) 22/11/74.
SOLIS P. Born 15/5/39. Commd 27/5/68. Flt Lt 17/3/71. Retd AD 15/5/94.
SOLLEY D. C., BSc. Born 26/5/62. Commd 11/9/83. Flt Lt 11/3/87. Retd ADMIN 5/12/87.
SOLLITT A. G. Born 11/4/46. Commd 26/5/67. Sqn Ldr 1/1/76. Retd GD 27/7/99.
SOLLITT S., AFC. Born 27/10/21. Commd 29/6/50. Flt Lt 29/12/53. Retd GD 2/1/68.
SOLOMON S. P. E. Born 25/12/50. Commd 1/1/71. Sqn Ldr 1/7/85. Retd GD 25/12/88.
SOMERFIELD B. M. Born 8/1/19. Commd 12/9/46. Sqn Ldr 1/10/56. Retd ENG 27/3/64.
SOMERFIELD P. J. Born 25/4/45. Commd 5/2/65. Flt Lt 6/10/71. Retd GD 22/10/94.
SOMERS W., AFC. Born 1/1/24. Commd 31/7/51. Sqn Ldr 1/1/71. Retd GD 1/1/82.
SOMERS-JOCE D. R. Born 30/3/32. Commd 28/6/51. Flt Lt 9/3/57. Retd GD 29/5/76.
SOMERVELL M. J. S., CEng MRAeS MIMgt. Born 15/6/30. Commd 4/8/53. Wg Cdr 1/7/74. Retd ENG 17/6/80.
SOMERVILLE P. C. Born 4/11/41. Commd 1/11/79. Sqn Ldr 1/1/92. Retd SY 27/6/94.
SOMMER V. M. Born 1/7/20. Commd 25/8/41. Sqn Offr 1/7/50. Retd SEC 16/9/57.
SOUCH G. Born 6/7/29. Commd 11/4/51. Fg Offr 11/4/52. Retd GD 12/3/53.
SOULSBY R. Born 11/6/26. Commd 23/1/59. Flt Lt 18/3/64. Retd EDN 25/5/66.
SOULSBY R. N. Born 10/2/45. Commd 28/2/64. Flt Lt 28/8/69. Retd GD 10/2/83.

SOUNESS F. S., DFC. Born 31/8/30. Commd 17/5/51. Flt Lt 6/9/56. Retd GD 31/12/69. Reinstated 18/6/80 to 31/8/87.
SOUTAR Sir Charles., KBE MB BS LMSSA MFCM DPH DIH. Born 12/6/20. Commd 2/5/46. AM 31/3/78. Retd MED 12/6/81.
SOUTER J. O. Born 6/11/27. Commd 25/8/60. Sqn Ldr 1/7/72. Retd ADMIN 6/11/82.
SOUTER K. P. Born 12/6/19. Commd 6/7/42. Flt Lt 9/1/50. Retd GD 25/4/58.
SOUTH G. J., DSO DFC FIMgt. Born 21/10/22. Commd 28/2/43. Gp Capt 1/1/66. Retd GD 2/3/73.
SOUTH P. G., BA. Born 26/6/25. Commd 10/3/45. Gp Capt 1/1/68. Retd GD 14/8/71.
SOUTHALL J. D. Born 20/12/19. Commd 20/5/44. Flt Lt 20/5/47. Retd ENG 15/10/56.
SOUTHAM T. H. Born 15/8/49. Commd 7/6/73. Sqn Ldr 1/1/86. Retd GD 1/7/94.
SOUTHCOMBE W. R. Born 11/12/42. Commd 22/3/63. Wg Cdr 1/1/88. Retd GD 31/3/99.
SOUTHERN D. F. Born 3/7/92. Commd 3/7/31. Sqn Ldr 1/7/86. Retd GD 3/7/92.
SOUTHERN J. M. Born 27/6/58. Commd 1/7/82. Flt Lt 27/5/85. Retd GD 20/4/92.
SOUTHERN P., BSc. Born 27/9/61. Commd 20/1/85. Flt Lt 20/7/87. Retd GD 20/1/01.
SOUTHERN S. Born 28/4/60. Commd 17/5/79. Sqn Ldr 1/7/97. Retd ADMIN 30/6/99.
SOUTHERN T. Born 17/9/18. Commd 22/9/41. Flt Offr 1/9/45. Retd SEC 17/5/56.
SOUTHGATE H. C., CB CBE. Born 30/10/21. Commd 23/9/43. AVM 1/1/74. Retd SUP 30/10/76.
SOUTHGATE M. R. Born 1/6/33. Commd 22/7/54. Sqn Ldr 1/1/71. Retd GD 25/6/86.
SOUTHON V. A. Born 3/4/29. Commd 13/12/50. Flt Lt 13/6/53. Retd GD 3/4/67.
SOUTHWELL B. G. Born 14/1/32. Commd 19/7/51. Flt Lt 14/11/56. Retd GD 14/1/70.
SOUTHWELL D. W. Born 31/7/23. Commd 7/11/46. Flt Lt 7/5/51. Retd SEC 6/2/58.
SOUTHWELL F. R. Born 26/11/24. Commd 20/4/50. Wg Cdr 1/7/71. Retd SEC 11/8/81.
SOUTHWICK E. E., BEM. Born 20/4/30. Commd 12/4/73. Sqn Ldr 1/1/83. Retd ENG 12/2/87.
SOUTHWOOD D. R., AFC BSc. Born 15/6/55. Commd 2/9/73. Sqn Ldr 1/7/89. Retd GD 15/6/99.
SOUTHWOULD B. W., BA. Born 26/6/45. Commd 29/11/63. Flt Lt 29/5/69. Retd GD 26/6/00.
SOWDEN E. H., MBE MIMgt. Born 24/9/15. Commd 13/5/43. Wg Cdr 1/1/62. Retd ENG 24/9/70.
SOWDEN P. Born 31/10/31. Commd 27/8/64. Wg Cdr 1/7/81. Retd ADMIN 1/2/80.
SOWDEN P. J., CEng MRAeS. Born 14/10/38. Commd 30/7/59. Sqn Ldr 1/7/78. Retd ENG 17/2/89.
SOWDEN R. E., BSc. Born 7/11/56. Commd 15/10/78. Sqn Ldr 1/7/92. Retd ENG 1/12/96.
SOWELLS E. J., MBE. Born 17/9/43. Commd 27/7/72. Wg Cdr 1/7/89. Retd ENG 15/1/94.
SOWELLS W. T. Born 16/5/39. Commd 1/7/82. Sqn Ldr 1/1/92. Retd ENG 16/5/94.
SOWERBY R. F., MB ChB MRCGP DavMed MFOM. Born 17/6/31. Commd 5/4/59. Gp Capt 1/1/82. Retd MED 7/9/84.
SOWERBY W. B., MVO. Born 1/3/33. Commd 4/7/51. Sqn Ldr 1/7/78. Retd GD 28/11/86.
SOWLER D. J., AFC. Born 22/4/44. Commd 24/6/65. Sqn Ldr 1/7/76. Retd GD 30/9/81.
SOWMAN P. N. Born 26/12/13. Commd 1/1/37. Wg Cdr 1/7/50. Retd SUP 31/8/59.
SOWOOD P. J., MA PhD MBA BM BCh DAvMed. Born 23/2/53. Commd 20/1/76. Wg Cdr 1/8/92. Retd MED 20/1/96.
SOWREY Sir Frederick, KCB CBE AFC. Born 14/9/22. Commd 20/8/41. AM 1/1/78. Retd GD 5/4/80.
SOWREY J. A., DFC AFC MRAeS. Born 5/1/20. Commd 7/3/40. Gp Capt 1/7/61. Retd GD 18/6/68 rtg A Cdre.
SPALDING I. R. M. Born 27/8/48. Commd 1/8/69. Gp Capt 1/1/94. Retd ADMIN 14/3/96.
SPALDING M. B. Born 15/8/23. Commd 21/4/44. Wg Cdr 1/7/63. Retd GD 1/10/68.
SPANDLER R. B. Born 13/8/37. Commd 21/8/68. Sqn Ldr 1/1/79. Retd ADMIN 13/8/95.
SPANDLEY T. A. Born 25/12/60. Commd 31/1/80. Sqn Ldr 1/1/90. Retd GD 25/12/98.
SPANNER C. A. Born 2/8/42. Commd 12/1/62. Sqn Ldr 1/1/77. Retd GD 18/12/95.
SPARKES P. Born 20/2/65. Commd 16/6/88. Flt Lt 16/12/93. Retd GD 14/3/97.
SPARKES P. D., BSc CEng MIEE. Born 12/2/40. Commd 10/12/63. Sqn Ldr 1/7/74. Retd ENG 1/10/88.
SPARKES R. G., MBE DFC. Born 12/5/22. Commd 12/11/43. Wg Cdr 1/1/69. Retd GD(G) 31/3/77.
SPARKES R. M. Born 5/4/33. Commd 19/7/51. Wg Cdr 1/7/70. Retd GD 18/7/87.
SPARKES R. W., MBE DFC MIMgt. Born 11/3/21. Commd 3/9/43. Wg Cdr 1/7/68. Retd SUP 11/3/76.
SPARKS J. P., AE BSc CEng MRAeS. Born 30/9/23. Commd 24/2/45. Sqn Ldr 1/7/62. Retd ENG 30/3/78.
SPARKS M., LRCP LRFPS. Born 9/8/16. Commd 25/7/41. Sqn Capt 1/1/66. Retd MED 9/8/74.
SPARKS M. J., MIMgt. Born 13/5/35. Commd 25/6/66. Sqn Ldr 1/7/75. Retd SUP 10/6/81.
SPARKS M. N., AFC. Born 30/12/20. Commd 20/9/47. Flt Lt 29/6/50. Retd GD 13/11/67.
SPARKS W., MBE. Born 10/10/19. Commd 26/6/43. Flt Lt 19/6/52. Retd GD(G) 10/10/74.
SPARROW E. M., DFC AFC MIMgt. Born 18/2/22. Commd 8/5/42. Wg Cdr 1/1/60. Retd GD 18/2/69.
SPARROW M. J. Born 4/3/32. Commd 10/9/52. Sqn Ldr 1/1/69. Retd GD 1/5/76.
SPATCHER J. L., AFC. Born 12/1/33. Commd 6/4/54. Sqn Ldr 1/7/63. Retd GD 12/1/71.
SPEAIGHT P. D. Born 20/5/49. Commd 13/8/82. Flt Lt 13/8/84. Retd ENG 13/8/90.
SPEAKE P. J. Born 1/7/29. Commd 1/6/61. Flt Offr 1/6/63. Retd SEC 18/7/63.
SPEAKMAN N. A. Born 21/6/61. Commd 8/12/83. Flt Lt 8/6/89. Retd GD 1/10/00.
SPEAR C. W. P. Born 27/4/43. Commd 15/7/64. Wg Cdr 1/7/89. Retd ENG 27/4/98.
SPEAR J. R., BSc. Born 30/3/58. Commd 5/9/76. Flt Lt 15/10/80. Retd GD 14/9/96.
SPEAREY W. W. Born 16/5/20. Commd 11/9/42. Sqn Ldr 1/1/71. Retd PI 16/5/75.
SPEARS P. A., AFC. Born 14/4/50. Commd 19/6/70. Sqn Ldr 1/7/87. Retd GD 1/7/90.
SPEED B. N. J., OBE FIMgt MIL. Born 16/9/40. Commd 6/8/60. A Cdre 1/7/87. Retd GD 16/9/95.

SPEED M. D. Born 6/12/44. Commd 28/9/62. Gp Capt 1/7/90. Retd GD 31/3/94.
SPEEDIE A. Born 24/4/21. Commd 14/2/46. Sqn Ldr 1/7/60. Retd ENG 24/4/71.
SPEER K. G. Born 21/6/28. Commd 14/1/53. Flt Lt 3/6/58. Retd GD 25/8/68.
SPEIGHT M. J., BSc. Born 16/7/64. Commd 10/11/85. Flt Lt 10/5/88. Retd GD 26/5/99.
SPEIGHT W., MBE. Born 11/1/46. Commd 1/7/82. Sqn Ldr 1/7/91. Retd GD 7/9/98.
SPEIRS J. P. Born 7/4/32. Commd 25/6/57. Flt Lt 6/3/63. Retd GD 25/3/73.
SPENCE A., BTech. Born 16/9/57. Commd 8/2/81. Flt Lt 8/5/81. Retd GD 7/12/93.
SPENCE A. J., MBE FIMgt. Born 9/5/21. Commd 13/3/47. Gp Capt 1/7/71. Retd SUP 9/5/76.
SPENCE B. G., BA IEng. Born 27/9/44. Commd 12/7/79. Sqn Ldr 1/1/92. Retd ENG 19/5/97.
SPENCE E. L. Born 1/7/37. Commd 27/4/60. Flt Offr 7/8/64. Retd CAT 31/12/65.
SPENCE J. F. Born 8/2/43. Commd 22/5/70. Sqn Ldr 1/1/82. Retd GD(G) 9/2/89.
SPENCE J. U. Born 21/12/28. Commd 18/5/55. Sqn Ldr 1/1/67. Retd ENG 29/3/84.
SPENCE N. M. Born 25/6/43. Commd 1/6/72. Sqn Ldr 1/1/84. Retd GD(G) 1/10/86.
SPENCER A. W. Born 20/12/29. Commd 7/5/52. Sqn Ldr 1/1/79. Retd GD(G) 20/12/89.
SPENCER C. Born 29/11/32. Commd 11/5/59. Wg Cdr 1/1/73. Retd SUP 14/2/76.
SPENCER C. L. B. Born 9/8/20. Commd 14/3/46. Wg Cdr 1/7/68. Retd ENG 4/4/75.
SPENCER C. R., AFC DFM. Born 10/9/16. Commd 10/7/43. Flt Lt 9/6/50. Retd GD(G) 14/5/63.
SPENCER C. R. C. Born 16/10/25. Commd 6/12/46. Sqn Ldr 1/7/56. Retd GD 1/2/68.
SPENCER D. E. Born 29/12/22. Commd 29/3/45. Gp Capt 1/1/75. Retd SUP 29/12/77.
SPENCER D. G. Born 15/2/28. Commd 18/9/48. Flt Lt 8/5/57. Retd GD 11/5/67.
SPENCER F. A., OBE MCIPS FIMgt. Born 22/11/27. Commd 31/7/58. Gp Capt 1/7/78. Retd SUP 22/11/82.
SPENCER F. L. Born 19/5/19. Commd 3/7/44. Sqn Ldr 1/4/56. Retd GD 18/11/58.
SPENCER G. B., MIMgt. Born 7/12/33. Commd 20/12/51. Sqn Ldr 1/7/64. Retd GD 1/6/86.
SPENCER J., MBE. Born 6/10/33. Commd 5/3/57. Wg Cdr 1/7/79. Retd GD 1/11/85.
SPENCER J. D., BA. Born 29/3/29. Commd 27/8/64. Sqn Ldr 1/7/77. Retd ADMIN 29/3/84.
SPENCER J. H., CBE AFC MCIPD. Born 2/10/39. Commd 3/6/58. A Cdre 1/7/90. Retd GD 2/10/95.
SPENCER J. R., ACIS. Born 11/5/50. Commd 7/6/73. Sqn Ldr 1/1/84. Retd ADMIN 2/4/94.
SPENCER J. R. C. Born 17/5/24. Commd 13/1/44. Sqn Ldr 1/7/57. Retd ENG 17/5/73.
SPENCER K., BA MInstAM(Dip). Born 6/8/46. Commd 13/2/72. Sqn Ldr 1/1/84. Retd ADMIN 2/12/96.
SPENCER L. V., OBE. Born 7/4/08. Commd 15/8/33. Wg Cdr 1/10/46. Retd GD 7/4/55 rtg Gp Capt.
SPENCER M. Born 28/1/50. Commd 30/4/81. Flt Lt 30/4/83. Retd ENG 11/7/85.
SPENCER P. D. Born 15/12/54. Commd 30/6/78. Wg Cdr 1/7/93. Retd GD 31/10/98.
SPENCER R. E. Born 14/5/30. Commd 7/5/52. Flt Lt 2/10/57. Retd GD 2/9/71.
SPENCER T. D., MBE. Born 29/12/16. Commd 26/2/42. Sqn Ldr 1/1/53. Retd ENG 29/12/65.
SPERANDEO F. Born 17/7/30. Commd 21/10/65. Sqn Ldr 1/7/76. Retd ADMIN 6/4/83.
SPERRING P. J. Born 15/6/49. Commd 2/1/75. Wg Cdr 1/7/90. Retd ENG 30/4/94.
SPIBY D. W., DFM. Born 7/7/21. Commd 1/10/43. Flt Lt 7/6/51. Retd GD(G) 1/5/69.
SPICE P. C. Born 18/11/22. Commd 23/12/44. Wg Cdr 1/7/69. Retd ENG 18/11/77.
SPICER M. J., BSc. Born 11/10/36. Commd 22/8/61. Flt Lt 10/6/63. Retd EDN 1/9/68.
SPIERS G. W., MBE AE CEng MRAeS MIMgt. Born 5/1/21. Commd 29/3/40. Sqn Ldr 1/7/52. Retd ENG 31/7/76.
SPIERS P. Born 15/6/31. Commd 29/3/68. Flt Lt 29/3/71. Retd GD 15/6/86.
SPIERS P. H. Born 14/12/13. Commd 15/6/44. Flt Lt 3/10/51. Retd ENG 16/4/56.
SPIERS R. J., MB BS MRCS LRCP DAvMed. Born 18/5/51. Commd 21/11/71. Wg Cdr 9/7/89. Retd MED 23/3/90.
SPIERS R. J., OBE FRAeS. Born 8/11/28. Commd 14/12/49. A Cdre 1/1/79. Retd GD 8/11/83.
SPIEWAKOWSKI M. J. Born 8/7/48. Commd 7/2/72. Sqn Ldr 1/7/82. Retd ENG 8/7/86.
SPIGHT B. F. Born 12/11/34. Commd 5/5/60. Flt Lt 5/11/64. Retd GD 12/11/72.
SPIGHT P. J. U. Born 12/12/44. Commd 11/5/78. Sqn Ldr 1/7/91. Retd ADMIN 12/12/98.
SPIKINS B. C. Born 29/3/55. Commd 23/9/39. Sqn Ldr 1/80. Retd GD 18/10/85.
SPILLANE J. P., OBE CEng MIMechE MRAeS DCAe. Born 18/11/18. Commd 10/11/42. Wg Cdr 1/7/60. Retd ENG 5/7/66.
SPILSBURY D. A. Born 6/5/45. Commd 11/9/64. Wg Cdr 1/1/91. Retd GD 12/7/99.
SPILSBURY D. R., MRAeS. Born 28/1/15. Commd 28/10/43. Wg Cdr 1/7/65. Retd ENG 11/8/70.
SPINK D. J. Born 1/1/33. Commd 27/9/51. Sqn Ldr 1/7/67. Retd GD 1/1/71.
SPINK P. L. Born 3/11/47. Commd 30/1/68. Flt Lt 25/5/74. Retd GD 3/11/00.
SPINKS A. J., BSc. Born 4/4/33. Commd 14/11/57. Wg Cdr 1/7/72. Retd ENG 30/11/88.
SPINKS L. G. Born 10/2/30. Commd 23/9/66. Flt Lt 23/9/71. Retd GD 10/2/85.
SPINKS S. J. Born 4/5/27. Commd 24/9/59. Sqn Ldr 1/1/71. Retd ADMIN 4/5/82.
SPITTAL M. J., MB ChB. Born 15/2/60. Commd 19/11/81. Wg Cdr 1/8/97. Retd MED 1/10/98.
SPITTLES T. W. Born 14/5/34. Commd 24/5/53. Sqn Ldr 1/1/87. Retd GD 14/5/89.
SPOFFORTH J. S. Born 29/3/40. Commd 21/10/66. Flt Lt 21/1/73. Retd ADMIN 4/7/82.
SPOFFORTH P. A. M. Born 6/8/47. Commd 2/8/68. Sqn Ldr 1/7/82. Retd GD 6/8/85.
SPONG D. B., BSc. Born 4/1/55. Commd 30/9/73. Flt Lt 15/10/76. Retd GD 7/4/88.
SPOONER C. Born 9/12/25. Commd 27/6/51. Flt Lt 27/12/55. Retd GD 9/12/79.
SPOONER R. H. Born 19/3/46. Commd 8/11/68. Wg Cdr 1/1/90. Retd ADMIN 14/3/96.
SPOONER R. J. S., AFC. Born 6/3/22. Commd 17/9/43. Wg Cdr 1/1/60. Retd GD 2/5/68.
SPOOR S. J., AFC. Born 20/11/43. Commd 6/5/66. Sqn Ldr 1/7/81. Retd GD 24/1/88.

SPOTTISWOOD J. Born 21/12/10. Commd 16/11/44. Fg Offr 11/7/45. Retd ASD 21/12/45.
SPOTTISWOOD J. D., CB CVO AFC MA. Born 27/5/34. Commd 11/6/52. AVM 1/1/84. Retd GD 27/5/89.
SPRACKLING B. J., DFC. Born 9/7/22. Commd 3/8/43. Sqn Ldr 1/7/57. Retd GD 9/7/65.
SPRACKLING J. M. Born 11/12/38. Commd 7/1/58. Wg Cdr 1/1/83. Retd GD 4/11/89.
SPRAGG B. J., DFC. Born 2/12/23. Commd 14/4/44. Wg Cdr 1/7/69. Retd GD 1/5/74.
SPRAGG E. G. Born 1/12/12. Commd 18/7/42. Sqn Ldr 1/7/57. Retd SUP 1/12/67.
SPRAGG R. E. Born 15/2/32. Commd 29/10/64. Sqn Ldr 1/10/71. Retd EDN 29/10/72.
SPRAGUE D. J. Born 6/11/59. Commd 20/9/79. Sqn Ldr 1/1/94. Retd GD 1/3/99.
SPREADBURY J. A. Born 12/5/29. Commd 28/11/49. Flt Lt 27/12/55. Retd GD 12/5/67.
SPRECKLEY G. C. Born 10/3/44. Commd 12/7/63. Sqn Ldr 1/1/92. Retd GD 10/3/99.
SPRENT J. C. Born 10/9/31. Commd 27/6/51. Gp Capt 1/1/78. Retd GD 30/4/86.
SPRINGATE L. T., AFM. Born 18/5/43. Commd 29/4/77. Flt Lt 29/4/73. Retd GD 18/5/81.
SPRINGETT R., FRAeS MILT. Born 9/04/44. Commd 26/3/64. Gp Capt 1/7/93. Retd SUP 9/4/99.
SPRINGETT R. J., OBE BSc BA. Born 13/5/38. Commd 1/1/61. Gp Capt 1/7/92. Retd GD 13/2/94.
SPRINKS P. L. E., MIMgt. Born 24/9/41. Commd 2/8/68. Sqn Ldr 1/7/77. Retd ENG 1/7/80. Re-entered 8/12/82. Wg Cdr 1/1/91. Retd ENG 1/2/97.
SPROSEN B. J. Born 21/1/39. Commd 22/2/63. Wg Cdr 1/7/84. Retd GD 21/10/88.
SPRULES R. K. Born 4/5/34. Commd 24/2/67. Flt Lt 4/5/72. Retd ENG 24/2/75.
SPURDENS C. N., DFC AFC. Born 23/3/21. Commd 5/2/43. Sqn Ldr 1/7/52. Retd GD 19/9/58.
SPURGEON J. H., DFC* AFC. Born 10/3/16. Commd 23/6/42. Flt Lt 23/12/45. Retd GD(G) 10/3/71 rtg Sqn Ldr.
SPURLING T. A. Born 3/8/34. Commd 30/12/55. Flt Lt 30/6/61. Retd GD 3/8/72.
SPURR C. B. Born 16/8/24. Commd 8/7/54. Flt Lt 8/1/58. Retd GD 15/5/64.
SPURRELL G. L., MPhil BA MCIPS. Born 7/3/40. Commd 13/2/64. Gp Capt 1/7/91. Retd SUP 7/3/95.
SPURWAY B. Born 7/1/39. Commd 5/11/70. Sqn Ldr 1/7/84. Retd GD 18/7/89.
SQUIRE G. L. G., FIMgt. Born 1/1/34. Commd 22/7/66. Sqn Ldr 1/7/84. Retd 1/1/93.
SQUIRE P. C., MSc BSc(Eng) CEng MRAeS. Born 16/8/37. Commd 22/8/58. Wg Cdr 1/7/78. Retd ADMIN 22/8/91.
SQUIRE R. Born 10/11/50. Commd 8/10/70. Flt Lt 16/1/77. Retd ADMIN 12/2/77.
SQUIRE R. F. G. Born 10/4/26. Commd 12/12/51. Flt Lt 12/6/56. Retd GD 10/10/69.
SQUIRES B. W. Born 14/10/42. Commd 2/1/75. Flt Lt 2/1/77. Retd ADMIN 15/11/87.
SQUIRES D. H., BSc. Born 1/12/52. Commd 6/7/80. Flt Lt 6/10/82. Retd SUP 2/4/93.
SQUIRES E. J. J. Born 9/7/22. Commd 10/2/45. Sqn Ldr 1/7/53. Retd PRT 31/3/62.
SQUIRES P. J., MSc BEng CEng MIEE. Born 20/12/52. Commd 13/4/80. Sqn Ldr 1/1/91. Retd ENG 1/10/99.
SQUIRES S. B. Born 27/5/59. Commd 28/7/88. Flt Lt 28/7/90. Retd ADMIN 27/5/98.
SQUIRRELL C. R. R. Born 12/3/23. Commd 26/5/60. Sqn Ldr 1/7/72. Retd ENG 30/10/76.
St AUBYN B. J. Born 20/1/32. Commd 6/4/54. Gp Capt 1/1/79. Retd GD 8/11/85.
ST GEORGE CAREY G. M., BA. Born 11/2/60. Commd 5/2/84. Flt Lt 5/5/86. Retd SUP 14/3/96.
ST. CLAIR B. E. Born 17/10/33. Commd 23/7/52. Wg Cdr 1/1/75. Retd GD 1/2/84.
ST. JOHN BROWN T. Born 9/3/34. Commd 8/10/52. Sqn Ldr 1/1/70. Retd SEC 22/10/74.
STABLEFORD B. T. Born 29/1/43. Commd 17/12/64. Flt Lt 8/1/69. Retd GD 31/5/70.
STABLER A. M. Born 20/1/32. Commd 23/4/52. Sqn Ldr 1/7/70. Retd GD 1/10/73.
STABLES A. J., CBE FRAeS. Born 1/3/45. Commd 3/3/67. AVM 1/1/95. Retd GD 29/1/01.
STABLES D. H., MA. Born 26/10/33. Commd 3/9/62. Wg Cdr 1/7/75. Retd ADMIN 4/4/88.
STACEY A. C. E., MBBS MRCGP MRCS LRCP DCH DRCOG DAvMed. Born 4/11/46. Commd 2/8/68. Sqn Ldr 8/6/80. Retd MED 6/4/86.
STACEY A. D. Born 7/3/32. Commd 9/7/54. Sqn Ldr 1/1/70. Retd GD 7/3/87.
STACEY C. C. D., BSc. Born 20/3/50. Commd 23/9/68. Wg Cdr 1/1/92. Retd OPS SPT 24/7/98.
STACEY C. F. Born 20/5/47. Commd 11/8/67. Flt Lt 11/2/73. Retd GD 25/9/75.
STACEY F. P. S. Born 6/3/16. Commd 16/4/44. Sqn Ldr 1/7/63. Retd PRT 29/5/60.
STACEY J. N., CBE DSO DFC FIMgt. Born 14/9/20. Commd 17/9/38. AVM 1/1/74. Retd GD 1/1/76.
STACEY P. M. Born 22/7/17. Commd 13/3/45. Flt Lt 14/8/55. Retd GD(G) 14/5/61.
STACEY T. B. Born 9/3/36. Commd 14/2/63. Flt Lt 16/5/68. Retd GD(G) 9/3/94.
STAFF F. R. C., MBE. Born 23/3/24. Commd 24/6/44. Sqn Ldr 1/1/57. Retd GD 23/7/67.
STAFF W. J. Born 20/9/34. Commd 16/4/80. Flt Lt 17/5/77. Retd ENG 6/4/93.
STAFF-BRETT J. Born 20/12/14. Commd 4/3/43. Wg Cdr 1/1/59. Retd ENG 25/5/68.
STAFFERTON P., MCIPD AIIP. Born 2/12/42. Commd 2/6/67. Sqn Ldr 1/7/82. Retd ENG 2/12/97.
STAFFORD J. W. Born 11/6/50. Commd 4/3/71. Sqn Ldr 1/1/84. Retd ENG 11/6/88.
STAGG A. J. F., OBE MRAeS MIMgt. Born 15/3/32. Commd 10/10/63. Sqn Ldr 1/1/74. Retd ENG 2/4/76.
STAGG C. M. Born 25/11/51. Commd 10/4/73. Sqn Ldr 1/1/85. Retd GD 5/5/90.
STAGG G. A. H. Born 8/6/44. Commd 6/12/70. Sqn Ldr 1/1/81. Retd GD(G) 12/4/90.
STAGG J. G., MIMgt. Born 24/1/36. Commd 16/2/61. Wg Cdr 1/7/80. Retd ADMIN 15/10/88.
STAINES H. C., ACA. Born 17/10/14. Commd 10/6/38. Sqn Ldr 1/6/45. Retd SEC 20/7/48 rtg Wg Cdr.
STAINTON R., BSc. Born 4/9/35. Commd 30/8/60. Sqn Ldr 1/7/74. Retd ADMIN 4/9/93.
STAITE T. J. Born 14/8/16. Commd 17/4/47. Flt Lt 29/11/51. Retd SUP 29/2/64 rtg Sqn Ldr.
STALEY J. R. Born 17/5/26. Commd 16/7/52. Flt Lt 12/12/57. Retd GD 4/3/68.
STALEY R. L. Born 4/8/35. Commd 23/1/64. Flt Lt 1/4/71. Retd GD 4/8/73.
STALEY R. V. Born 23/4/28. Commd 26/9/51. Flt Lt 26/3/54. Retd GD 1/5/59.

STALKER R. H. Born 21/1/33. Commd 25/10/51. Flt Lt 25/4/57. Retd GD 26/1/71.
STALLAN D. C. Born 3/5/42. Commd 3/8/62. Flt Lt 3/2/68. Retd GD 9/6/79.
STALLWOOD G. Born 27/8/52. Commd 16/6/92. Flt Lt 16/6/94. Retd GD 18/7/00.
STALLWORTHY H. E., MBE. Born 18/6/09. Commd 12/6/44. Flt Lt 12/12/47. Retd ENG 18/6/58.
STAMER P. T. Born 19/11/51. Commd 25/9/71. Flt Lt 14/4/80. Retd PI 11/7/89.
STAMFORD M. C. Born 4/5/23. Commd 19/5/44. Sqn Ldr 1/7/62. Retd PE 14/9/68.
STAMFORD M. C. R., MBA BA MIMgt. Born 30/1/56. Commd 19/9/74. Flt Lt 27/7/82. Retd ADMIN 15/10/96.
STAMMERS C. V., OBE. Born 6/2/08. Commd 7/11/40. Wg Cdr 1/1/49. Retd ENG 6/2/62.
STAMMERS H. J. Born 25/1/19. Commd 9/8/43. Flt Lt 9/2/47. Retd GD 12/2/53.
STAMMERS J. B., BA. Born 28/3/62. Commd 5/2/84. Flt Lt 5/8/86. Retd GD 28/10/91.
STAMP P. A. Born 11/5/44. Commd 29/11/63. Wg Cdr 1/7/85. Retd SUP 17/9/94.
STAMP P. G. Born 22/8/46. Commd 2/12/66. Sqn Ldr 1/1/79. Retd ENG 22/8/84.
STAMP R. A. Born 16/3/13. Commd 28/3/46. Flt Lt 28/9/50. Retd SUP 6/5/54.
STAMP R. J. M., MA. Born 8/12/44. Commd 25/7/71. Flt Lt 25/10/73. Retd ADMIN 25/7/87.
STAMPER C. Born 23/12/20. Commd 17/7/42. Flt 11/5/46. Retd ENG 23/3/54.
STANBRIDGE Sir Brian, KCVO CBE AFC. Born 6/7/24. Commd 14/1/44. AVM 1/1/76. Retd GD 6/7/79.
STANBRIDGE T. F. S. Born 27/6/27. Commd 19/8/71. Flt Lt 19/8/74. Retd SY 27/6/87.
STANDEN B. E. Born 1/8/32. Commd 13/6/61. Flt Lt 13/6/61. Retd GD 13/6/77.
STANDEN K. J. Born 13/4/34. Commd 24/5/53/ Flt Lt 10/9/58. Retd GD 3/4/76.
STANDHAM C. F. Born 24/10/42. Commd 16/12/66. Flt Lt 16/6/73. Retd ENG 30/8/82.
STANDING M. G. T., MIMgt. Born 8/3/44. Commd 27/8/64. Sqn Ldr 1/1/76. Retd ADMIN 8/3/82.
STANDING P. A. Born 28/1/47. Commd 8/10/70. Sqn Ldr 1/1/85. Retd GD 22/4/94.
STANDLEY S., BA. Born 12/12/40. Commd 22/9/63. Sqn Ldr 1/1/73. Retd GD 23/9/79.
STANFORD F. G. Born 28/4/26. Commd 22/3/51. Sqn Ldr 1/7/74. Retd GD 28/4/81.
STANFORD K. J., DFM. Born 5/1/20. Commd 1/9/45. Sqn Ldr 1/1/51. Retd GD 5/1/63.
STANFORD R. K., BEd MCIPD. Born 11/7/52. Commd 5/2/84. Flt Lt 5/8/83. Retd ADMIN 1/2/97.
STANGER G. A. B. Born 20/2/33. Commd 8/10/70. Flt Lt 8/10/73. Retd GD 17/4/84.
STANGROOM D. A., AFC. Born 19/10/41. Commd 9/2/62. Wg Cdr 1/1/86. Retd GD 19/10/96.
STANIER B. Born 6/7/44. Commd 8/5/86. Flt Lt 8/5/90. Retd SY 2/4/93.
STANIFORD W. A. Born 30/4/55. Commd 8/8/74. Sqn Ldr 1/7/86. Retd GD(G) 2/5/87.
STANIFORTH J. I. Born 12/2/38. Commd 4/10/63. Wg Cdr 1/1/86. Retd GD 12/2/94.
STANLEY D. J. Born 28/2/49. Commd 2/6/77. Gp Capt 1/7/95. Retd ADMIN 1/11/99.
STANLEY D. R., BA. Born 18/4/46. Commd 18/8/67. Sqn Ldr 1/1/81. Retd GD 18/4/84.
STANLEY D. T., OBE. Born 6/5/14. Commd 31/12/41. Sqn Ldr 1/7/55. Retd ENG 6/5/69.
STANLEY K. Born 19/4/45. Commd 3/1/64. Flt Lt 4/5/72. Retd GD 1/9/79.
STANLEY R. A., MB BS FRCS LRCP. Born 8/1/46. Commd 27/7/70. Wg Cdr 12/1/85. Retd MED 8/1/96.
STANLEY R. L., MBE. Born 5/5/28. Commd 16/5/49. Sqn Ldr 1/7/63. Retd RGT 7/5/74.
STANMORE R. Born 11/9/34. Commd 25/6/66. Flt Lt 25/6/72. Retd GD(G) 1/10/80.
STANNARD B. M. Born 3/11/55. Commd 28/10/76. Sqn Ldr 1/1/89. Retd ADMIN 11/4/95.
STANNARD D. G. Born 21/9/35. Commd 29/3/56. Flt Lt 24/10/61. Retd GD 30/6/92.
STANNARD H. G. Born 25/2/24. Commd 6/9/56. Flt Lt 6/9/62. Retd GD(G) 31/10/64.
STANNARD J. H., AFC. Born 11/8/23. Commd 27/2/58. Sqn Ldr 1/7/71. Retd GD 11/8/83.
STANNARD P. W., OBE BSc. Born 20/6/44. Commd 22/9/63. Wg Cdr 1/1/89. Retd GD 22/4/94.
STANNING P. Born 1/1/32. Commd 10/12/52. Flt Lt 5/5/58. Retd GD 2/6/77 rtg Sqn Ldr.
STANNIS J. S. Born 16/12/14. Commd 3/3/48. Flt Lt 17/4/53. Retd ADMIN 19/7/88.
STANSFELD P. W., CBE DFC. Born 18/5/09. Commd 19/5/35. Gp Capt 1/7/47. Retd GD 13/12/57.
STANSFIELD B., OBE. Born 28/12/25. Commd 1/10/52. Wg Cdr 1/7/66. Retd GD 1/3/80.
STANSFIELD C. E. Born 7/4/14. Commd 24/10/40. Flt Lt 24/10/43. Retd GD(G) 7/4/64 rtg Sqn Ldr.
STANSFIELD R. Born 28/5/24. Commd 28/1/44. Sqn Ldr 1/1/57. Retd GD 28/5/62.
STANTON R. H., MVO MRAeS MRIN. Born 6/1/45. Commd 21/1/66. Sqn Ldr 1/1/92. Retd GD 14/3/96.
STANTON S. Born 17/6/51. Commd 25/2/72. Sqn Ldr 1/1/85. Retd GD 17/6/88.
STANTON T. A. Born 28/1/23. Commd 18/12/42. Flt Lt 18/12/47. Retd GD 28/1/66.
STANTON V. H. Born 9/5/26. Commd 4/7/57. Sqn Ldr 1/7/68. Retd GD 29/10/75.
STANWAY M. I. Born 12/1/30. Commd 20/4/50. Wg Cdr 1/1/73. Retd GD 12/1/85.
STANYON D. Born 16/9/33. Commd 29/9/54. Wg Cdr 1/7/74. Retd ADMIN 19/7/88.
STAPLEFORD H. P., CEng FIMechE MRAeS. Born 14/1/20. Commd 19/8/42. Gp Capt 1/7/64. Retd ENG 7/4/68.
STAPLES J., CEng MIEE. Born 10/11/35. Commd 13/7/61. Sqn Ldr 1/7/70. Retd ENG 10/11/73.
STAPLES J. E., DFM. Born 12/1/21. Commd 30/11/43. Flt Lt 30/5/47. Retd GD 28/9/68.
STAPLES T. N., OBE DFM. Born 12/1/20. Commd 27/6/41. Wg Cdr 1/7/58. Retd GD(G) 6/9/65.
STAPLETON D. C., CB CBE DFC AFC. Born 15/1/18. Commd 18/5/36. AVM 1/7/63. Retd GD 16/7/68.
STAPLETON E. J. Born 10/9/28. Commd 8/11/62. Flt Lt 8/11/68. Retd SEC 5/10/74.
STAPLETON E. J., MBE MInstPet MCIPS MIMgt. Born 5/1/45. Commd 3/3/67. Wg Cdr 1/7/84. Retd SUP 5/1/89.
STAPLETON F. G. Born 3/3/24. Commd 21/10/65. Flt Lt 21/10/70. Retd ENG 2/10/74.
STAPLETON L. A. Born 20/8/26. Commd 6/4/50. Sqn Ldr 1/9/65. Retd GD 31/10/73.
STAPLETON P. J. Born 5/3/04. Commd 16/12/25. Fg Offr 16/6/27. Retd GD 1/4/32.
STAPLETON W., CBE. Born 27/6/20. Commd 20/8/38. Wg Cdr 1/7/54. Retd GD 12/9/64.

STAPLEY V. A., OBE DFC. Born 22/2/22. Commd 19/4/44. Wg Cdr 1/1/67. Retd GD(G) 22/2/77.
STAPPARD J. A., AFC. Born 28/4/29. Commd 26/9/54. Sqn Ldr 1/1/68. Retd GD 28/6/92.
STARK F. H. B. Born 6/7/33. Commd 27/5/53. Sqn Ldr 1/7/67. Retd GD 12/11/76.
STARK L. W. F., DFC* AFC. Born 16/11/20. Commd 12/6/43. Flt Lt 12/12/46. Retd GD 16/11/63 rtg Sqn Ldr.
STARK R. A., MIMgt. Born 20/9/34. Commd 9/5/54. Sqn Ldr 1/7/69. Retd ADMIN 3/4/82.
STARK R. F., MB ChB. Born 16/12/23. Commd 30/10/43. Wg Cdr 8/11/63. Retd MED 2/1/70.
STARKEY D. A. J., MIMgt. Born 24/12/29. Commd 22/10/53. Gp Capt 1/1/77. Retd SUP 24/12/84.
STARKEY F. E. Born 23/9/31. Commd 26/3/52. Flt Lt 7/8/57 Retd GD(G) 28/4/78.
STARKEY I. D., BA. Born 11/1/48. Commd 27/3/70. Sqn Ldr 1/1/84. Retd ADMIN 1/1/87.
STARLING J. Born 22/12/61. Commd 26/3/92. Flt Lt 26/3/94. Retd SUP 12/4/96.
STARLING M. C. Born 23/6/42. Commd 29/11/63. Sqn Ldr 1/7/88. Retd GD 23/6/00.
STARLING N. A., BA. Born 1/4/63. Commd 5/9/82. Flt Lt 15/10/88. Retd ENG 6/10/91.
STARLING R. F., DFC. Born 10/5/22. Commd 27/2/42. Wg Cdr 1/7/58. Retd GD 10/5/64.
STARR W. K., DPhysEd. Born 16/5/43. Commd 6/12/70. Fg Offr 6/12/70. Retd EDN 17/8/74.
START D. A. Born 1/11/36. Commd 25/6/66. Flt Lt 25/6/68. Retd GD 1/11/74.
STATHAM C. R., LLB. Born 7/8/50. Commd 25/2/79. Wg Cdr 1/1/93. Retd ADMIN 14/3/97.
STATHAM G. A., MBE. Born 25/4/26. Commd 26/3/52. Flt Lt 31/7/57. Retd GD 25/4/86.
STATHAM H. R. Born 21/7/97. Commd 21/7/41. Fg Offr 21/7/41. Retd ASD 28/10/46 rtg Flt Lt.
STATHAM R. H. G. Born 22/3/36. Commd 4/12/56. Flt Lt 12/6/62. Retd GD 22/3/74.
STAVELEY A. T. Born 12/9/14. Commd 1/3/37. Wg Cdr 1/7/52. Retd GD 12/9/61.
STAVERS L. W. Born 17/8/18. Commd 22/2/42. Flt Lt 22/6/47. Retd SEC 17/8/67.
STAVERT C. M., AFC. Born 10/8/21. Commd 26/6/39. Sqn Ldr 1/7/53. Retd GD 15/8/64.
STEAD B. A., BSc CEng MRAeS MIMgt ACGI. Born 20/4/33. Commd 8/11/53. Wg Cdr 1/7/69. Retd GD 1/2/73.
STEAN P. M. Born 26/2/41. Commd 23/12/58. A Cdre 1/1/90. Retd GD 2/4/96.
STEAR Sir Michael., KCB CBE MA FRAeS. Born 11/10/38. Commd 1/10/62. ACM 27/8/92. Retd GD 11/10/96.
STEDMAN D. W. S. Born 20/11/27. Commd 5/12/51. Flt Lt 5/6/56. Retd GD 19/8/73.
STEED F. S., CEng MIEE. Born 7/12/19. Commd 8/5/41. Flt Lt 1/9/45. Retd ENG 27/10/56 rtg Sqn Ldr.
STEED M. W. Born 13/3/42. Commd 6/7/62. Flt Lt 6/1/68. Retd GD(G) 30/12/82.
STEED R. E. Born 3/11/25. Commd 1/5/52. Sqn Ldr 1/1/62. Retd GD 13/12/75.
STEED R. J. Born 7/2/34. Commd 24/9/52. Sqn Ldr 1/1/85. Retd GD 7/2/89.
STEEDMAN A., AFC. Born 10/9/23. Commd 20/2/45. Wg Cdr 1/7/62. Retd GD 29/9/72.
STEEDMAN H. A. J., OBE. Born 19/4/15. Commd 22/4/43. Gp Capt 1/7/67. Retd ENG 19/4/70.
STEEL A. J. Born 29/4/44. Commd 15/7/66. Flt Lt 15/1/69. Retd GD 29/4/82.
STEEL D. J., MBE BSc. Born 2/3/61. Commd 15/8/82. Sqn Ldr 1/1/93. Retd GD 2/3/99.
STEEL M. K. Born 24/10/43. Commd 4/10/63. Flt Lt 1/7/69. Retd GD 9/1/94.
STEEL N. G. Born 27/12/36. Commd 17/12/57. Flt Lt 17/6/60. Retd GD 18/11/68.
STEEL W. Born 20/1/29. Commd 1/2/62. Flt Lt 1/2/67. Retd CAT 6/10/72.
STEEL W. H., BEng. Born 13/9/65. Commd 25/9/88. Flt Lt 25/3/91. Retd GD 14/3/96.
STEELE A. G., CBE AFC*. Born 2/10/23. Commd 16/4/43. A Cdre 1/7/72. Retd GD 1/7/78.
STEELE A. J. Born 27/12/48. Commd 15/9/67. Flt Lt 15/3/73. Retd GD 1/10/88.
STEELE G. Born 11/9/21. Commd 11/6/43. Flt Lt 11/12/46. Retd GD 4/6/65.
STEELE J. Born 22/10/42. Commd 11/4/85. Flt Lt 11/4/89. Retd ENG 22/10/97.
STEELE J. C. Born 27/8/23. Commd 20/2/43. Sqn Ldr 1/7/54. Retd GD 19/7/66.
STEELE P. F. Born 25/5/33. Commd 6/12/51. Wg Cdr 1/7/79. Retd GD 1/10/81.
STEELE R. J. Born 26/2/16. Commd 11/8/44. Sqn Ldr 1/7/63. Retd PE 26/2/71.
STEELE W. P., BSc. Born 7/7/34. Commd 4/2/64. Sqn Ldr 1/7/68. Retd ADMIN 6/11/86.
STEELE-MORGAN M. D. Born 17/10/29. Commd 4/10/56. Flt Lt 5/10/60. Retd GD(G) 30/6/70.
STEEN B. A., MBE. Born 1/8/47. Commd 18/1/73. Sqn Ldr 1/1/84. Retd GD 17/5/88.
STEENSON J. E. Born 3/12/47. Commd 2/8/68. Sqn Ldr 1/7/80. Retd GD 3/1/85.
STEER C. W., BEM. Born 25/9/14. Commd 1/5/43. Flt Lt 1/11/46. Retd ENG 10/2/58.
STEER D. G. Born 3/5/47. Commd 5/4/79. Flt Lt 5/4/81. Retd GD 1/10/89.
STEER E. R. A. Born 8/12/23. Commd 12/8/54. Flt Lt 12/2/58. Retd GD 22/5/68.
STEER G. W., MBE. Born 11/3/22. Commd 23/6/60. Sqn Ldr 1/1/69. Retd ENG 11/3/77.
STEER J. H., OBE. Born 8/6/07. Commd 3/8/40. Sqn Ldr 1/8/47. Retd ENG 8/6/56.
STEER J. W. M., MSc. Born 10/11/27. Commd 18/4/50. Sqn Ldr 1/1/63. Retd ENG 27/5/78.
STEER M. J., FCIPD FIMgt. Born 21/5/47. Commd 10/7/90. Gp Capt 1/1/90. Retd ADMIN 2/12/97.
STEER M. J. W. Born 28/9/59. Commd 8/9/83. Flt Lt 8/3/89. Retd GD 14/3/96.
STEER R. J. R. Born 15/11/14. Commd 17/10/57. Flt Lt 1/4/63. Retd ENG 18/5/69.
STEER W. H. Born 1/4/49. Commd 26/9/83. Flt Lt 26/9/89. Retd ENG 3/4/92.
STEFF-LANGSTON J. A., MBE FIMgt. Born 5/11/26. Commd 25/10/46. Gp Capt 1/1/69. Retd GD 10/6/78.
STEGGALL G. Born 20/3/31. Commd 25/5/50. Flt Lt 6/10/56. Retd GD 1/9/84.
STEGGLES R. H. Born 18/3/21. Commd 21/1/67. Flt Lt 27/1/72. Retd ENG 1/1/74.
STEIB D. E. Born 1/7/20. Commd 27/10/41. Flt Offr 1/9/45. Retd SEC 24/6/53.
STEIN E. D. Born 6/5/38. Commd 23/9/59. Gp Capt 1/1/93. Retd GD 6/7/93.
STEIN N. J. A., BA. Born 13/7/60. Commd 6/9/81. Flt Lt 6/12/82. Retd GD 14/3/96.
STEINFURTH O. R. Born 20/9/19. Commd 4/8/41. Flt Offr 1/9/45. Retd SEC 1/10/64.

STELLMACHER C. A., BSc. Born 13/8/45. Commd 6/9/81. Sqn Ldr 1/1/88. Retd ADMIN 26/10/96.
STENNER A. B., BSc. Born 14/4/33. Commd 20/10/55. Sqn Ldr 20/4/63. Retd EDN 7/7/71.
STENNETT R. A. Born 25/7/47. Commd 13/12/79. Flt Lt 13/12/81. Retd GD 30/8/88.
STENNING S. A. Born 1/9/58. Commd 31/8/78. Sqn Ldr 1/1/91. Retd SY 14/3/96.
STENSON R., BA. Born 20/1/46. Commd 20/8/65. Flt Lt 20/2/71. Retd OPS SPT 18/5/98.
STEPHEN C. D. Born 15/3/43. Commd 28/4/67. Sqn Ldr 1/1/77. Retd GD 15/3/81.
STEPHEN H. F. Born 3/5/17. Commd 6/10/59. Flt Lt 6/10/65. Retd ENG 19/8/67.
STEPHENS A. Born 22/1/32. Commd 23/12/61. Flt Lt 23/12/67. Retd GD 22/1/87.
STEPHENS A. R. Born 3/4/35. Commd 19/7/57. Flt Lt 1/7/61. Retd PRT 1/10/66.
STEPHENS A. T., LLB. Born 19/11/35. Commd 23/10/59. Wg Cdr 1/1/80. Retd ADMIN 19/11/90.
STEPHENS A.B., BA MIMgt. Born 24/6/38. Commd 31/7/62. Gp Capt 1/1/90. Retd GD 18/6/92.
STEPHENS C. M., BSc. Born 11/10/57. Commd 19/9/76. Sqn Ldr 1/7/87. Retd GD 12/12/89.
STEPHENS E. L. Born 21/3/16. Commd 25/8/55. Sqn Ldr 4/6/65. Retd MED(T) 3/4/72.
STEPHENS F. C. Born 26/7/34. Commd 13/6/62. Flt Lt 1/10/67. Retd GD 13/6/84.
STEPHENS F. P., MB BS MRCS LRCP DPM. Born 22/12/27. Commd 27/10/52. Wg Cdr 6/1/64. Retd MED 27/10/68.
STEPHENS G. R., MSc BSc CEng MRAeS ACGI. Born 24/4/45. Commd 28/9/64. Sqn Ldr 1/7/80. Retd ENG 1/7/83.
STEPHENS H. O. Born 7/3/20. Commd 19/6/41. Sqn Ldr 1/1/58. Retd ENG 20/6/73.
STEPHENS I. G. C., CEng MIEE. Born 5/4/21. Commd 12/4/51. Sqn Ldr 1/7/60. Retd ENG 19/12/64.
STEPHENS J. A. T. Born 16/12/58. Commd 9/8/79. Sqn Ldr 1/1/93. Retd GD 16/4/97.
STEPHENS J. B. Born 14/1/26. Commd 27/6/51. Flt Lt 27/12/54. Retd GD 14/1/69.
STEPHENS M. A. Born 12/12/43. Commd 7/1/71. Wg Cdr 1/7/90. Retd SY 1/2/93.
STEPHENS M. C., BSc. Born 18/1/63. Commd 3/2/84. Sqn Ldr 1/1/97. Retd GD 18/1/01.
STEPHENS M. J. Born 6/10/59. Commd 24/3/83. Flt Lt 19/1/89. Retd OPS SPT 18/5/98.
STEPHENS M. M., DSO DFC**. Born 20/10/19. Commd 23/12/39. Gp Capt 1/7/58. Retd GD 10/11/60.
STEPHENS M. R. Born 24/5/55. Commd 16/5/74. Flt Lt 16/11/79. Retd GD 24/5/93.
STEPHENS R., MBE. Born 24/11/20. Commd 19/8/42. Sqn Ldr 1/1/55. Retd ENG 28/11/70.
STEPHENS R. D. Born 14/5/14. Commd 2/1/39. Gp Capt 1/1/65. Retd SUP 14/5/69.
STEPHENS R. J., BSc CEng FIEE. Born 18/10/44. Commd 3/10/66. Wg Cdr 1/1/89. Retd ENG 18/10/00.
STEPHENS T. G., BA. Born 26/4/32. Commd 5/5/55. Sqn Ldr 17/2/65. Retd EDN 6/7/70.
STEPHENS T. W., BSc. Born 12/6/42. Commd 10/7/67. Sqn Ldr 1/3/74. Retd EDN 15/11/83.
STEPHENS W. C., DFM. Born 27/7/16. Commd 30/3/43. Flt Lt 14/1/52. Retd GD(G) 5/7/67.
STEPHENS W. L. Born 19/3/10. Commd 29/10/42. Fg Offr 29/6/43. Retd ASD 27/11/46 rtg Flt Lt.
STEPHENSON A. D. G., DFC AFC. Born 17/4/18. Commd 6/10/38. Flt Lt 1/9/45. Retd GD 3/12/57 rtg Sqn Ldr.
STEPHENSON A. H. Born 13/8/36. Commd 5/2/57. Sqn Ldr 1/7/72. Retd GD 13/2/93.
STEPHENSON D. J. A., MHCIMA. Born 25/6/46. Commd 14/4/69. Sqn Ldr 1/7/79. Retd ADMIN 14/3/96.
STEPHENSON E. V. Born 20/10/14. Commd 2/5/44. Flt Lt 14/11/56. Retd SUP 20/10/63.
STEPHENSON G., DFC AFC. Born 23/3/16. Commd 15/6/43. Flt Lt 15/12/46. Retd GD 16/2/58.
STEPHENSON G. D. Born 1/7/21. Commd 21/3/45. Flt Offr 1/1/50. Retd PRT 24/9/55.
STEPHENSON G. G. Born 5/6/36. Commd 20/12/57. Flt Lt 2/1/60. Retd GD 27/5/66.
STEPHENSON H. Born 23/3/59. Commd 8/4/82. Fg Offr 11/2/83. Retd PI 1/12/86.
STEPHENSON J. W. N. Born 10/12/36. Commd 28/11/69. Flt Lt 8/3/72. Retd GD(G) 11/1/91.
STEPHENSON L. J. Born 8/11/37. Commd 28/7/67. Flt Lt 12/4/73. Retd GD(G) 31/5/85.
STEPHENSON M. J. Born 18/8/46. Commd 1/3/68. Sqn Ldr 1/7/80. Retd SUP 18/8/83.
STEPHENSON M. P. Born 24/4/59. Commd 24/7/81. Flt Lt 24/1/88. Retd SUP 11/10/91.
STEPHENSON M. P. H. Born 21/9/25. Commd 17/13/45. Flt Lt 29/11/51. Retd GD 1/2/57.
STEPHENSON P. J. T., DFC. Born 25/8/18. Commd 18/6/40. Sqn Ldr 1/9/45. Retd GD 31/7/55 rtg Wg Cdr.
STEPHENSON R. V. Born 4/1/28. Commd 8/4/49. Sqn Ldr 1/1/62. Retd GD 4/1/66.
STEPHENSON T. B., CB DipEl. Born 18/8/26. Commd 13/9/45. AVM 1/1/80. Retd ENG 9/10/82.
STEPHENSON W. Born 26/4/24. Commd 19/9/44. Wg Cdr 1/7/66. Retd GD 30/3/78.
STEPHENSON-OLIVER J. N. Born 28/7/38. Commd 8/1/57. Wg Cdr 1/7/79 Retd GD 11/5/85.
STEPNEY M. S. Born 1/6/47. Commd 8/9/83. Sqn Ldr 1/7/92. Retd SUP 14/3/96.
STEPNIEWSKI T. Z., BEM. Born 2/4/23. Commd 5/12/63. Flt Lt 5/12/66. Retd GD(G) 1/7/74.
STEPTOE B. E., BA MIMgt. Born 14/12/32. Commd 29/12/53. Sqn Ldr 1/1/68. Retd SEC 28/2/71.
STERLING N. Born 24/8/31. Commd 10/9/52. Flt Lt 7/2/58. Retd GD 19/10/70.
STERLING S. C. Born 22/2/34. Commd 22/1/57. Sqn Ldr 1/1/70. Retd GD 24/3/76.
STERN P. A. P. Born 9/12/41. Commd 12/7/63. Flt Lt 12/1/69. Retd GD 9/12/79.
STERNE G. Born 17/4/34. Commd 26/11/52. Flt Lt 2/6/58. Retd GD 17/4/92.
STEUART T. S. Born 23/12/08. Commd 12/2/43. Flt Lt 11/2/48. Retd GD(G) 23/3/59.
STEVEN D. A. Born 4/6/57. Commd 21/4/77. Flt Lt 21/10/82. Retd GD 4/6/95.
STEVEN W. Born 5/12/21. Commd 22/9/49. Wg Cdr 1/7/69. Retd SUP 5/12/76.
STEVENS A. C. Born 30/8/53. Commd 1/6/72. Flt Lt 1/12/77. Retd GD 1/9/82.
STEVENS A. H. Born 26/2/33. Commd 19/12/63. Flt Lt 19/12/68. Retd ENG 4/11/72.
STEVENS A. R. Born 20/3/31. Commd 31/8/50. Flt Lt 31/8/56. Retd SEC 20/3/69.
STEVENS B. A. Born 6/3/28. Commd 17/1/49. Flt Lt 6/5/55. Retd GD 1/4/73.
STEVENS The Rev B. R., MA LLM. Born 7/8/49. Commd 13/9/87. Retd 13/9/93 Sqn Ldr.

STEVENS C. D. Born 19/5/47. Commd 2/8/68. Sqn Ldr 1/1/86. Retd GD 14/3/96.
STEVENS C. F. Born 18/9/33. Commd 27/8/52. Flt Lt 14/5/58. Retd GD 18/9/70.
STEVENS D. B. L., MIMgt. Born 4/2/42. Commd 23/12/61. Sqn Ldr 1/1/73. Retd SUP 1/5/84.
STEVENS D. G., BSc MB BS MRCGP MRCPsych. Born 22/4/51. Commd 18/11/75. Wg Cdr 4/2/93. Retd MED 14/3/96.
STEVENS D. J., CEng MRAeS. Born 16/8/39. Commd 6/2/67. Sqn Ldr 1/1/76. Retd ENG 16/8/94.
STEVENS E. R. Born 27/1/31. Commd 11/2/64. Sqn Ldr 1/7/76. Retd ENG 4/4/80.
STEVENS F. J. W. Born 3/11/26. Commd 17/1/52. Sqn Ldr 1/7/65. Retd GD 30/9/77.
STEVENS G. Born 21/8/17. Commd 16/1/43. Flt Lt 16/7/46. Retd GD(G) 4/5/68.
STEVENS I. H., MA. Born 28/4/63. Commd 30/8/81. Flt Lt 15/4/88. Retd ADMIN 7/7/91.
STEVENS I. P. Born 15/11/30. Commd 1/8/51. Wg Cdr 1/7/76. Retd SUP 12/6/82.
STEVENS J. D. Born 7/4/30. Commd 23/2/55. Sqn Ldr 1/1/67. Retd GD 30/4/76.
STEVENS J. E., MBE BSc CEng MRAeS MIMgt. Born 30/5/48. Commd 19/9/71. Wg Cdr 1/7/96. Retd ENG 10/4/99.
STEVENS J. F. V. Born 12/1/15. Commd 14/2/46. Flt Lt 4/1/51. Retd SUP 12/12/53.
STEVENS J. M. S. Born 29/2/24. Commd 13/1/54. Fg Offr 13/1/54. Retd CAT 22/1/57.
STEVENS M. Born 25/8/45. Commd 4/5/72. Flt Lt 4/11/78. Retd GD(G) 15/11/93.
STEVENS M. M. J., DFC. Born 1/11/15. Commd 15/3/35. Sqn Ldr 1/12/40. Retd GD 10/12/45 rtg Wg Cdr.
STEVENS M. R. Born 14/1/49. Commd 13/1/72. Flt Lt 13/7/77. Retd GD 20/9/87.
STEVENS M. R. J., BSc(Eng) CEng MIEE MRAeS. Born 16/7/40. Commd 30/9/60. Sqn Ldr 1/1/72. Retd ENG 16/7/95.
STEVENS P. D. B., BA FIMgt. Born 17/9/20. Commd 29/10/38. Gp Capt 1/7/64. Retd GD 17/10/72.
STEVENS P. E., MB BS MRCP(UK). Born 13/7/56. Commd 18/10/77. Sqn Ldr 1/8/86. Retd MED 13/7/94.
STEVENS P. J., OBE MD MRCPath ChB DCP DTM&H. Born 11/8/26. Commd 29/9/50. Wg Cdr 1/4/62. Retd MED 30/6/70.
STEVENS P. J. Born 26/1/53. Commd 22/5/75. Flt Lt 22/11/80. Retd GD 3/2/91.
STEVENS R. Born 14/12/30. Commd 7/9/61. Sqn Ldr 1/7/72. Retd SUP 31/8/74.
STEVENS The Rev R. W., AKC. Born 15/12/36. Commd 2/9/63. Retd 2/9/79. Wg Cdr.
STEVENS W., MIMgt. Born 26/1/20. Commd 28/2/46. Sqn Ldr 1/1/56. Retd ENG 28/4/73.
STEVENS W. C. H. Born 1/11/11. Commd 5/6/42. Sqn Ldr 1/7/60. Retd ENG 29/8/63.
STEVENS W. F. J., MBE DFC AFC. Born 1/11/18. Commd 10/7/43. Sqn Ldr 1/7/62. Retd GD 1/11/73.
STEVENS-HOARE P. Born 7/11/22. Commd 21/10/54. Flt Lt 21/4/58. Retd GD(G) 23/10/70.
STEVENSON A. Born 24/8/15. Commd 12/6/47. Flt Lt 12/12/50. Retd ENG 24/11/62.
STEVENSON A. G. Born 20/9/36. Commd 17/5/63. Flt Lt 12/11/67. Retd GD 20/9/94.
STEVENSON A. L. Born 11/5/20. Commd 21/6/56. Sqn Ldr 1/1/72. Retd GD 11/5/77.
STEVENSON B. L., DPhysEd. Born 27/7/48. Commd 24/4/77. Sqn Ldr 1/7/90. Retd ADMIN 31/3/94.
STEVENSON C., BSc. Born 6/11/54. Commd 8/1/78. Flt Lt 8/4/80. Retd ENG 27/5/85.
STEVENSON D. A. Born 21/11/22. Commd 30/10/43. Flt Lt 30/4/47. Retd GD 2/6/54.
STEVENSON D. A., BSc. Born 7/4/33. Commd 18/10/55. Sqn Ldr 1/7/65. Retd GD 18/10/71.
STEVENSON D. L., DFC. Born 13/10/20. Commd 2/8/41. Sqn Ldr 1/1/57. Retd GD 13/10/69.
STEVENSON G. P. Born 6/5/20. Commd 6/3/52. Sqn Ldr 1/1/62. Retd ENG 20/3/76.
STEVENSON J. Born 4/7/32. Commd 28/6/51. Sqn Ldr 1/1/78. Retd GD 4/7/90.
STEVENSON J. C. Born 5/12/12. Commd 19/4/37. Wg Cdr 1/7/52. Retd GD 18/2/60.
STEVENSON J. M., CBE FCIT FILT FCIPS FIMgt. Born 27/7/26. Commd 13/3/47. A Cdre 1/7/75. Retd SUP 27/7/81.
STEVENSON N., MHCIMA. Born 15/6/24. Commd 2/7/47. Sqn Ldr 1/7/69. Retd CAT 15/6/79.
STEVENSON P. E. A., MRAeS. Born 24/5/22. Commd 10/10/46. Flt Lt 10/4/50. Retd ENG 1/12/61.
STEVENSON P. R., CEng MIEE. Born 3/7/43. Commd 6/11/67. Sqn Ldr 1/7/76. Retd ENG 6/11/89.
STEVENSON R. M., BSc CEng MIEE MIMgt. Born 20/12/47. Commd 1/11/70. Retd ENG 1/11/86.
STEVENSON R. W. H. Born 4/6/18. Commd 21/1/38. Sqn Ldr 1/6/45. Retd GD 26/10/48.
STEVENSON S. T. Born 2/2/14. Commd 13/8/41. Flt Lt 1/9/45. Retd ENG 13/2/48.
STEWARD I. B. M., BSc. Born 1/11/49. Commd 13/10/71. Sqn Ldr 1/7/80. Retd ENG 1/11/87.
STEWARD M. J. Born 15/10/37. Commd 16/1/60. Flt Lt 16/7/65. Retd GD 13/8/78.
STEWART A. R., MBE. Born 17/6/17. Commd 23/2/50. Sqn Ldr 1/7/59. Retd SEC 1/12/70.
STEWART A. W. J. Born 19/5/51. Commd 25/2/72. Wg Cdr 1/1/93. Retd GD 6/4/98.
STEWART C. E., BSc MCIPS. Born 13/9/61. Commd 5/2/84. Sqn Ldr 1/1/92. Retd SUP 5/2/00.
STEWART C. G. Born 2/4/26. Commd 30/4/53. Flt Lt 30/4/53. Retd GD 30/4/69.
STEWART D. Born 29/1/42. Commd 1/4/65. Wg Cdr 1/1/88. Retd GD 29/1/97.
STEWART D., CEng FRAeS. Born 3/1/29. Commd 4/2/64. Grp Capt 1/7/76. Retd ENG 3/1/86.
STEWART D. McG. Born 16/9/19. Commd 18/10/45. Flt Lt 19/11/53. Retd GD(G) 30/9/64.
STEWART D. McL. Born 6/1/41. Commd 2/7/64. Sqn Ldr 1/7/78. Retd SUP 1/7/84.
STEWART D. R., MA. Born 7/2/40. Commd 26/2/63. Sqn Ldr 1/1/74. Retd SEC 26/5/81.
STEWART G., BA. Born 24/9/42. Commd 27/1/61. Wg Cdr 1/1/85. Retd GD(G) 14/3/96.
STEWART G. Born 14/6/48. Commd 27/7/72. Flt Lt 13/1/79. Retd GD(G) 11/1/88.
STEWART G. H., BSc. Born 14/5/22. Commd 19/7/44. Sqn Ldr 1/1/59. Retd GD 31/7/68.
STEWART H. Born 26/10/43. Commd 10/3/77. Wg Cdr 1/7/98. Retd GD 23/8/00.
STEWART I. G. Born 1/3/47. Commd 4/11/82. Sqn Ldr 1/7/94. Retd ENG 13/7/97.
STEWART I. G. M. Born 29/4/33. Commd 19/12/63. Sqn Ldr 1/7/84. Retd GD 29/4/93.

STEWART I. McL., LMSSA DPM. Born 15/1/27. Commd 7/1/54. Sqn Ldr 7/1/61. Retd MED 29/10/62.
STEWART J., MRIN. Born 9/3/35. Commd 6/1/64. Sqn Ldr 1/7/83. Retd GD 12/4/90.
STEWART J. A., BA. Born 26/9/45. Commd 31/1/64. Wg Cdr 1/1/85. Retd GD 26/9/89.
STEWART J. A., BEng. Born 13/1/61. Commd 1/8/86. Flt Lt 15/7/89. Retd ENG 13/1/99.
STEWART J. A., BA. Born 8/3/57. Commd 6/10/94. Flt Lt 6/10/96. Retd GD 22/5/01.
STEWART J. F. Born 22/10/25. Commd 20/7/45. Gp Capt 1/7/77. Retd GD 22/1/81.
STEWART J. G. Born 17/5/62. Commd 15/8/85. Flt Lt 31/1/90. Retd SUP 17/5/00.
STEWART J. M. Born 3/5/53. Commd 9/12/76. Sqn Ldr 1/7/90. Retd ADMIN 3/5/97.
STEWART K. A. Born 15/6/31. Commd 18/11/66. Flt Lt 18/11/71. Retd ENG 29/6/74.
STEWART K. J. Born 25/3/22. Commd 5/9/42. Flt Lt 21/3/51. Retd GD 7/8/63.
STEWART L., BDS. Born 9/7/40. Commd 18/9/60. Sqn Ldr 5/6/70. Retd DEL 9/7/78.
STEWART M., FIMgt. Born 26/2/42. Commd 3/8/62. Wg Cdr 1/7/85. Retd GD 2/4/93.
STEWART M. Born 13/3/62. Commd 8/4/82. Sqn Ldr 1/7/94. Retd OPS SPT 13/3/00.
STEWART N. R. Born 26/1/46. Commd 5/2/65. Sqn Ldr 1/1/97. Retd GD 26/1/01.
STEWART P. C. Born 13/6/32. Commd 13/6/66. Flt Lt 26/7/76. Retd GD 1/11/84.
STEWART P. M. G. Born 8/12/36. Commd 29/10/57. Flt Lt 29/4/63. Retd GD 24/7/69. Reinstated 22/6/70. Flt Lt
   22/6/70. Retd GD 8/12/94.
STEWART R., MCIPS MIMgt. Born 8/12/22. Commd 31/10/63. Sqn Ldr 1/1/74. Retd SUP 8/12/77.
STEWART S. Born 3/7/11. Commd 8/5/44. Fg Offr 20/8/46. Retd ENG 17/11/47. Re-employed 1/3/49. Flt Lt
   18/5/56. Retd 29/7/63.
STEWART S. G. Born 12/2/57. Commd 31/8/75. Sqn Ldr 1/7/90. Retd GD 1/10/95.
STEWART S. H. Born 22/7/44. Commd 21/4/77. Flt Lt 21/4/79. Retd GD 31/12/94.
STEWART T. W. Born 21/10/32. Commd 9/10/75. Fg Offr 9/10/75. Retd SEC 17/10/78.
STEWART-RATTRAY I. J. Born 7/2/38. Commd 28/5/66. Sqn Ldr 1/1/76. Retd GD 1/1/79.
STEWART-SMITH J. T. Born 8/10/39. Commd 19/8/65. Flt Lt 2/12/67. Retd SEC 11/7/70.
STICK D. H., CEng MRAeS. Born 28/8/38. Commd 16/4/63. Sqn Ldr 1/1/76. Retd ENG 16/4/82.
STICKINGS T. J. Born 27/3/35. Commd 7/6/68. Flt Lt 7/6/70. Retd ENG 21/6/76.
STICKLAND G. C., MRAeS. Born 8/7/16. Commd 9/5/40. Sqn Ldr 1/7/52. Retd ENG 31/8/63.
STICKLAND R. E., BA. Born 1/7/37. Commd 13/2/64. Wg Cdr 1/1/79. Retd ENG 22/10/88.
STICKLEY E. G., TEng FSERT. Born 14/3/43. Commd 24/8/72. Sqn Ldr 1/7/80. Retd ENG 14/3/87.
STIFF P. A. Born 28/7/21. Commd 18/9/42. Flt Lt 18/3/46. Retd SEC 1/11/53.
STILES B. N. Born 13/11/22. Commd 12/2/44. Flt Lt 4/1/51. Retd GD 5/8/62.
STILL J. B. Born 16/3/54. Commd 7/6/73. Flt Lt 7/12/79. Retd GD(G) 16/3/92.
STILLMAN D. J., DPhysEd. Born 19/4/47. Commd 10/1/71. Sqn Ldr 1/1/89. Retd ADMIN 1/5/94.
STILLWELL F. Born 8/8/23. Commd 5/3/46. Sqn Ldr 1/7/58. Retd GD 31/12/74.
STILWELL N. S. E. Born 3/1/62. Commd 11/6/81. Flt Lt 11/12/86. Retd GD 14/3/96.
STIMPSON C. W. Born 3/12/49. Commd 26/2/71. Flt Lt 26/2/74. Retd GD 22/5/81.
STIMSON R. Born 14/3/19. Commd 21/2/46. Wg Cdr 1/7/68. Retd SUP 28/6/69.
STINCHCOMBE A. B., FIMgt. Born 26/7/27. Commd 8/4/49. Gp Capt 1/7/72. Retd GD 1/1/77.
STINGEMORE G. P. Born 24/1/60. Commd 8/5/86. Flt Lt 13/1/89. Retd GD 24/3/99.
STINTON D., MBE MRAeS. Born 9/12/27. Commd 8/6/53. Sqn Ldr 1/1/63. Retd GD 8/6/69.
STINTON J. G. Born 1/12/30. Commd 24/1/52. Flt Lt 15/5/57. Retd GD 1/12/68.
STIRLAND G. Born 10/2/10. Commd 5/4/43. Sqn Ldr 1/7/62. Retd ENG 1/7/65.
STIRLING J. C., DPhysEd MIMgt. Born 23/9/42. Commd 27/4/65. Sqn Ldr 1/1/79. Retd GD 1/5/93.
STIRRUP J., MBE MIMgt. Born 4/10/26. Commd 25/5/50. Wg Cdr 1/7/67. Retd GD 4/4/81.
STIRRUP M. A. Born 16/9/44. Commd 11/10/70. Flt Lt 11/10/76. Retd ADMIN 6/5/77.
STIRZAKER P. J. Born 6/11/43. Commd 5/9/69. Flt Lt 3/4/72. Retd RGT 6/11/81.
STOALING A. P. Born 26/11/53. Commd 16/5/74. Flt Lt 16/11/79. Retd GD 26/11/91.
STOAT B. E., MBE. Born 8/2/32. Commd 13/8/52. Flt Lt 20/2/58. Retd GD 6/10/72.
STOBART B. A. W. Born 9/11/25. Commd 14/3/47. Sqn Ldr 1/7/58. Retd GD 9/11/63.
STOCK B., MIMgt. Born 19/7/33. Commd 8/8/69. Sqn Ldr 25/3/54. Wg Cdr 1/7/84. Retd ADMIN 13/6/87.
STOCK C. J. Born 23/10/41. Commd 24/1/63. Sqn Ldr 1/1/79. Retd GD(G) 1/1/82.
STOCKER E. E., DSO DFC CEng MIMechE. Born 31/8/22. Commd 19/1/43. Flt Lt 19/7/46. Retd GD 10/9/56.
STOCKER J. A. Born 24/5/32. Commd 26/8/54. Gp Capt 1/1/82. Retd GD 17/9/84.
STOCKER T. A. J., MBE MSc DipEl FIMgt. Born 30/10/22. Commd 11/1/43. Gp Capt 1/7/69. Retd ENG 16/12/72.
STOCKHAM J. J. Born 2/9/54. Commd 5/7/73. Fg Offr 5/7/75. Retd GD 7/8/78.
STOCKILL J. A., BA. Born 15/8/48. Commd 31/7/70. Flt Lt 31/1/76. Retd SEC 29/3/78.
STOCKING R. Born 24/1/23. Commd 22/10/59. Sqn Ldr 1/7/74. Retd ENG 10/7/76.
STOCKINGS J. D., BSc. Born 26/2/65. Commd 19/7/87. Flt Lt 19/1/90. Retd GD 19/7/99.
STOCKLEY T. P. Born 14/6/41. Commd 17/12/63. Sqn Ldr 1/1/76. Retd GD 14/6/79.
STOCKMAN B. T., MBE. Born 23/4/33. Commd 8/7/71. Flt Lt 8/7/71. Retd GD(G) 23/4/88.
STOCKS G. A., DFC* Born 17/2/23. Commd 29/12/42. Sqn Ldr 1/7/64. Retd GD(G) 31/3/77.
STOCKS M. Born 23/5/52. Commd 4/7/57. Flt Lt 4/1/62. Retd GD(G) 25/10/86.
STOCKTING J., BSc DipEL CEng MIEE MRAeS. Born 15/11/28. Commd 27/10/54. Wg Cdr 1/7/73. ENG Retd
   11/4/81.
STOCKTON B. J., BA. Born 1/6/27. Commd 29/8/56. Wg Cdr 1/1/72. Retd EDN 2/5/79.

STOCKWELL G. D. Born 3/10/28. Commd 2/9/50. Flt Lt 7/11/57. Retd GD 3/10/66.
STOCKWELL J. M. Born 25/6/39. Commd 8/12/61. Flt Lt 1/4/66. Retd GD 25/6/77.
STODDART P. J., BSc. Born 5/12/59. Commd 4/1/83. Flt Lt 4/10/85. Retd ENG 1/3/91.
STODDART-STONES G. Born 9/9/21. Commd 29/10/43. Flt Lt 4/1/51. Retd GD 9/9/64.
STODDART-STONES R. C. E. Born 6/1/15. Commd 30/8/51. Flt Offr 30/8/57. Retd SUP 23/4/66.
STOKER D. J., MB BS MRCS MRCP. Born 22/3/28. Commd 3/7/52. Wg Cdr 15/6/64. Retd MED 3/7/68.
STOKER W. I. C. Born 6/11/35. Commd 17/12/57. Wg Cdr 1/1/75. Retd GD 18/1/86.
STOKER W. L. Born 12/12/34. Commd 1/3/68. Flt Lt 12/2/73. Retd MED(SEC) 12/12/73.
STOKES B. J., IEng FIIE. Born 1/6/47. Commd 31/8/78. Wg Cdr 1/1/96. Retd ENG 4/12/99.
STOKES B. P. L. Born 17/3/39. Commd 6/4/62. Sqn Ldr 1/7/85. Retd GD 17/3/94.
STOKES D. G. Born 15/10/13. Commd 28/7/34. Gp Capt 1/1/51. Retd GD 12/6/59.
STOKES E. V., CBE BSc CEng MinstP FRAeS. Born 17/10/15. Commd 4/4/39. A Cdre 1/1/66. Retd ENG 19/4/71.
STOKES F. Born 27/7/27. Commd 3/7/50. Sqn Ldr 1/1/63. Retd GD 1/1/66.
STOKES F. J. Born 22/8/46. Commd 28/10/66. Flt Lt 8/3/72. Retd GD 14/3/96.
STOKES J. A., BSc CEng MIEE. Born 27/10/62. Commd 1/10/84. Sqn Ldr 1/1/94. Retd ENG 27/10/00.
STOKES J. E., MBE. Born 21/1/36. Commd 21/10/65. Sqn Ldr 1/1/74. Retd ENG 1/10/94.
STOKES L. R., DFC. Born 13/9/01. Commd 13/3/26. Wg Cdr 1/6/43. Retd GD 17/5/44 rtg Gp Capt.
STOKES The Rev M. J. Born 2/12/34. Commd 24/6/68. Retd 2/12/89. Wg Cdr.
STOKES M. J. Born 3/1/46. Commd 26/5/67. Wg Cdr 1/1/94. Retd GD 2/4/97.
STOKES P. D., MA CEng MRAeS. Born 2/7/40. Commd 30/9/60. Wg Cdr 1/1/78. Retd ENG 1/5/89.
STOKES R. C. W. Born 10/11/30. Commd 28/6/50. Sqn Ldr 1/1/77. Retd GD 4/11/85.
STOKES R. J. S., MBE MSc BSc. Born 21/2/53. Commd 3/9/72. Wg Cdr 1/7/87. Retd ENG 22/1/91.
STOKLE N., BA CEng MIEE. Born 3/11/12. Commd 31/1/46. Flt Lt 31/7/48. Retd ENG 3/11/61.
STOLTON A. T. Born 29/1/63. Commd 14/1/82. Flt Lt 14/7/88. Retd ADMIN 14/3/97.
STONE D. R., MCIPS MIMgt. Born 25/1/33. Commd 21/5/53. Sqn Ldr 1/1/88. Retd SUP 25/1/91.
STONE D. S. Born 4/4/48. Commd 24/4/67. Flt Lt 21/10/73. Retd SUP 14/6/75.
STONE E. N., MBE MMar. Born 6/12/20. Commd 4/1/50. Wg Cdr 1/7/64. Retd MAR 4/10/72.
STONE G. E. J. Born 6/7/52. Commd 29/6/72. Sqn Ldr 1/7/88. Retd ADMIN 1/7/91.
STONE J. Born 28/4/45. Commd 29/11/68. Sqn Ldr 1/7/80. Retd GD 28/9/86.
STONE J. L. Born 21/6/26. Commd 4/7/64. Sqn Ldr 4/1/69. Retd EDN 4/7/74.
STONE J. L. H. B. Born 16/4/34. Commd 17/7/70. Sqn Ldr 1/7/83. Retd ENG 16/4/92.
STONE N. L. M., MINucE MIMgt. Born 13/5/20. Commd 6/6/57. Sqn Ldr 1/7/74. Retd ENG 3/7/76.
STONE P. T., BSc. Born 12/2/64. Commd 5/9/82. FO 4/10/83. Retd ENG 10/4/87.
STONE R., OBE MIMgt. Born 27/7/21. Commd 19/8/42. Gp Capt 1/1/70. Retd ENG 27/7/76.
STONE R. C. Born 30/12/58. Commd 14/1/82. Flt Lt 14/7/88. Retd SUP 4/5/97.
STONE R. D., AFC. Born 30/4/33. Commd 11/10/51. A Cdre 1/7/81. Retd GD 22/8/83.
STONE R. D., OBE. Born 4/4/46. Commd 28/4/67. Wg Cdr 1/1/89. Retd GD 4/4/01.
STONEHOUSE G. G. Born 11/8/30. Commd 20/12/62. Flt Lt 20/12/68. Retd SEC 1/11/72.
STONEMAN W. J., DFM MIMgt. Born 8/9/23. Commd 26/10/44. Sqn Ldr 1/1/71. Retd SEC 8/9/79.
STONER J. F. B. Born 30/4/19. Commd 18/11/43. Wg Cdr 1/7/61. Retd ENG 30/4/74.
STONER M. B., AFC. Born 29/8/47. Commd 28/2/69. Wg Cdr 1/7/91. Retd GD 14/9/96.
STONER M. P. Born 1/2/56. Commd 20/5/82. Flt Lt 11/12/84. Retd GD(G) 1/2/94.
STONER R. A., BSc. Born 11/4/63. Commd 2/9/84. Flt Lt 2/3/87. Retd GD 11/4/01.
STONES A. J. Born 5/2/42. Commd 11/5/62. Fg Offr 11/5/64. Retd GD 30/5/69.
STONES C. E. Born 10/4/24. Commd 30/1/47. Flt Lt 4/12/52. Retd GD 10/4/62.
STONES J. Born 19/8/25. Commd 12/1/61. Flt Lt 12/1/64. Retd GD 17/6/67.
STONES S., MBE. Born 2/7/25. Commd 31/10/63. Sqn Ldr 1/1/74. Retd SUP 2/7/83.
STONHAM J. F. G., DFC. Born 5/11/22. Commd 20/11/43. Sqn Ldr 1/7/58. Retd GD 5/11/71.
STONOR Sir Thomas, KCB BSc. Born 5/3/36. Commd 23/9/59. AM 30/9/88. Retd GD 19/10/91.
STORAR A. A., MBE. Born 26/4/14. Commd 9/11/42. Wg Cdr 1/1/62. Retd SUP 26/4/70.
STORER J. S. Born 15/10/62. Commd 23/5/85. Sqn Ldr 1/7/97. Retd GD 21/1/01.
STORER R. A. E., BSc. Born 9/11/33. Commd 25/9/56. Wg Cdr 1/1/75. Retd GD 9/11/88.
STOREY E. S. Born 2/4/21. Commd 11/9/43. Sqn Ldr 1/7/57. Retd GD 2/4/64.
STOREY G. J., OBE AFC FIMgt. Born 6/7/23. Commd 21/8/43. Gp Capt 1/7/67. Retd GD 6/1/69.
STOREY P. J., OBE FCIS MIMgt. Born 12/9/41. Commd 31/3/64. Wg Cdr 1/7/82. Retd ADMIN 12/9/92.
STORRS R. Born 4/3/67. Commd 12/3/87. Fg Offr 12/3/89. Retd GD 5/10/90.
STORY J. F. Born 31/12/19. Commd 19/8/42. Flt Lt 19/2/46. Retd ENG 31/12/68.
STOTT B. J. Born 20/10/37. Commd 14/8/56. Flt Lt 26/2/64. Retd GD 20/10/75.
STOTT D. F. Born 30/5/33. Commd 17/7/56. Flt Lt 6/2/63. Retd SEC 10/4/72.
STOTT J. E. Born 30/5/50. Commd 19/12/85. Flt Lt 19/12/89. Retd GD(G) 14/3/96.
STOUT A. R. Born 9/1/38. Commd 4/10/63. Flt Lt 1/4/71. Retd GD 9/1/76.
STOVES W. Born 25/5/17. Commd 16/6/43. Flt Lt 31/1/47. Retd GD 1/3/50.
STOW D. R. Born 8/7/35. Commd 24/11/60. Flt Lt 25/7/66. Retd SEC 8/7/73.
STOWE J. R. Born 9/4/17. Commd 10/4/43. Wg Cdr 1/1/60. Retd SUP 9/4/72.
STOWELL P. T. Born 6/12/30. Commd 27/6/51. Flt Lt 27/3/56. Retd GD 6/12/73.
STRACHAN A. Born 7/3/59. Commd 17/5/79. Flt Lt 17/11/84. Retd GD 7/3/97.

STRACHAN C. H. Born 14/8/35. Commd 25/7/56. Sqn Ldr 1/1/68. Retd ENG 14/8/73.
STRACHAN I. W., MBE AFC FRAeS. Born 3/5/38. Commd 28/7/59. Wg Cdr 1/7/77. Retd GD 3/5/93.
STRACHAN J. S., BSc. Born 2/2/60. Commd 17/10/80. Flt Lt 15/10/84. Retd ADMIN 22/7/85.
STRACHAN M. Born 31/5/54. Commd 24/6/76. Flt Lt 11/11/82. Retd ADMIN 31/5/92.
STRACHAN R. W. S. Born 28/3/33. Commd 12/4/73. Flt Lt 12/4/77. Retd GD(G) 2/4/93.
STRACHAN V. F. Born 16/6/45. Commd 6/5/66. Flt Lt 8/3/72. Retd GD 16/6/83.
STRAFFORD H. Born 28/12/36. Commd 14/2/63. Sqn Ldr 1/7/70. Retd GD 1/10/77.
STRAFFORD R. A. Born 13/7/34. Commd 2/10/58. Sqn Ldr 1/7/70. Retd GD 1/10/77.
STRANG F. A., MBE BEd. Born 3/5/58. Commd 10/6/84. Flt Lt 10/12/86. Retd ADMIN 30/6/94.
STRANGE D. J. Born 10/2/11. Commd 10/6/43. Fg Offr 10/2/44. Retd ENG 14/2/46.
STRANGE G., MIMgt. Born 26/4/22. Commd 10/2/43. Wg Cdr 1/1/61. Retd GD 2/7/74.
STRANGE J. E. Born 14/5/23. Commd 16/6/44. Flt Lt 27/5/54. Retd GD 17/4/68.
STRANGEWAY E. J., AFC. Born 2/5/26. Commd 3/5/46. Wg Cdr 1/1/68. Retd GD 27/9/75.
STRATTON D. R., MIMgt. Born 1/3/25. Commd 5/1/45. Sqn Ldr 1/4/56. Retd GD 30/11/75.
STRATTON G. F., MRCS LRCP DAvMed. Born 31/3/46. Commd 26/9/66. Flt Lt 29/12/71. Retd MED 29/12/76. Re-
    entered 5/11/80. Wg Cdr 4/4/85. Retd MED 14/3/97.
STRATTON G. J. Born 7/6/28. Commd 2/3/61. Flt Lt 2/3/66. Retd ENG 7/6/83.
STRATTON J. G., AFM. Born 15/11/23. Commd 6/1/55. Flt Lt 6/1/61. Retd GD 1/8/68.
STRATTON N. Born 12/5/42. Commd 26/3/64. Flt Lt 12/5/69. Retd SUP 16/7/71.
STRAUGHAN B. J. J. Born 20/1/33. Commd 16/7/52. Sqn Ldr 1/1/71. Retd GD 20/1/88.
STRAUGHAN G. A., MSc. Born 20/2/49. Commd 24/3/74. Sqn Ldr 1/7/83. Retd ENG 1/7/91.
STRAUGHTON R., DPhysEd. Born 14/10/38. Commd 2/4/65. Flt Lt 2/2/69. Retd ADMIN 24/5/76.
STRAW D. P. E. Born 6/9/42. Commd 11/5/62. Wg Cdr 1/7/88. Retd GD 6/9/97.
STRAWSON C. R. Born 17/12/33. Commd 3/9/52. Sqn Ldr 1/1/79. Retd GD 17/12/88.
STREET G. N., OBE. Born 11/3/17. Commd 3/4/39. Wt Cdr 1/1/57. Retd SUP 3/4/67.
STREET H. G. Born 22/9/20. Commd 21/6/56. Sqn Ldr 1/1/68. Retd ENG 22/9/82.
STREET J. A. Born 16/3/21. Commd 14/10/44. Flt Lt 13/11/57. Retd GD 17/2/69.
STREET R. Born 7/4/23. Commd 16/10.43. Sqn Ldr 1/1/57. Retd GD 7/4/66.
STREET R. J. Born 2/6/24. Commd 26/11/43. Gp Capt. 1/7/75. Retd GD(G) 2/6/79.
STREETER A. H., MBE. Born 1/5/11. Commd 10/12/42. Sqn Ldr 1/10/55. Retd ENG 1/5/66.
STREETER J. F. Born 14/4/53. Commd 27/2/75. Flt Lt 27/8/80. Retd GD 14/10/91.
STRETCH A. G., DFM. Born 27/8/20. Commd 3/6/44. Flt Lt 3/12/47. Retd GD 17/11/54.
STRETEN M. W., BSc. Born 12/2/43. Commd 22/9/63. Wg Cdr 1/1/82. Retd GD 12/2/98.
STRETTON R. S. J. Born 13/8/29. Commd 19/12/52. Flt Lt 13/2/61. Retd GD 13/2/69.
STREVENS C. J., BDS. Born 5/3/44. Commd 28/12/66. Wg Cdr 23/12/82. Retd DEL 28/12/82.
STRICKLAND A. W. Born 19/6/24. Commd 10/3/44. Sqn Ldr 1/7/56. Retd GD 4/7/68.
STRICKLAND D. Born 21/5/51. Commd 25/8/71. Wg Cdr 1/7/91. Retd ADMIN 31/5/98.
STRICKLAND V. J. Born 9/8/41. Commd 24/2/61. Flt Lt 24/8/66. Retd GD 9/8/80.
STRIKE I. D. Born 20/1/35. Commd 8/5/53. Sqn Ldr 1/1/85. Retd GD 21/10/86.
STRINGER B. Born 5/1/30. Commd 6/12/56. Sqn Ldr; 1/1/74. Retd GD(G) 31/1/78.
STRINGFELLOW C. H., MBE. Born 16/1/24. Commd 9/7/59. Sqn Ldr 1/1/72. Retd ENG 11/10/77.
STRONG C. J. Born 3/8/32. Commd 9/4/52. Wg Cdr 1/7/80. Retd GD 3/8/87.
STRONG D. M., CB AFC. Born 30/9/13. Commd 6/1/36. A Cdre 1/1/60. Retd GD 6/4/66.
STRONG J. F., MBE. Born 8/3/33. Commd 6/12/51. Wg Cdr 1/1/74. Retd GD 1/10/77.
STRONG W. I. N. Born 9/6/03. Commd 13/3/26. Plt Offr 13/3/26. Retd GD 20/4/27.
STRONG W. J. Born 4/11/20. Commd 13/6/46. Flt Lt 13/12/50. Retd RGT 8/6/74.
STRONGE F. W. T. Born 17/5/38. Commd 29/11/63. Flt Lt 8/1/69. Retd ADMIN 17/5/76.
STRONGMAN E., BSc. Born 23/11/49. Commd 23/9/68. Sqn Ldr 1/7/83. Retd GD 24/11/86.
STROUD A. E. Born 24/10/29. Commd 25/8/49. Wg Cdr 1/1/73. Retd GD 15/7/83.
STROUD H. M. Born 30/4/37. Commd 28/7/59. Wg Cdr 1/1/82. Retd ADMIN 5/10/90.
STROUD J. K. Born 22/2/34. Commd 23/6/67. Flt Lt 8/3/72. Retd ENG 23/6/75.
STROUD K. Born 21/3/46. Commd 7/6/68. Flt Lt 7/12/74. Retd GD(G) 1/10/91.
STROUD M. H. McM. Born 16/12/45. Commd 5/4/79. Flt Lt 5/4/81. Retd GD(AEO) 7/12/87.
STRUDWICK A. S. R., CB DFC. Born 16/4/21. Commd 9/6/42. A Cdre 1/7/67. Retd GD 29/3/76.
STRUTHERS I., BSc. Born 3/8/50. Commd 18/4/71. Flt Lt 15/4/74. Retd GD 20/11/81.
STUART A. F. Born 29/8/50. Commd 27/3/70. Wg Cdr 1/7/90. Retd GD 15/1/00.
STUART D. J. Born 16/10/33. Commd 10/3/54. Flt Lt 16/10/60. Retd GD 16/10/71.
STUART D. W., MB BS FRCS (Edin) FRCS DLO. Born 23/12/21. Commd 27/2/47. Wg Cdr 27/2/59. Retd MED
    28/11/60.
STUART E. M., BSc. Born 9/10/53. Commd 13/2/77. Wg Cdr 1/1/92. Retd ADMIN 27/9/96.
STUART J. C. Born 7/12/19. Commd 20/1/44. Flt Lt 20/7/47. Retd GD 8/6/64.
STUART J. C., DFC. Born 5/3/21. Commd 25/6/44. Sqn Ldr 1/1/54. Retd GD 3/4/64.
STUART J. E., MBE. Born 31/7/30. Commd 26/3/53. Sqn Ldr 1/1/76. Retd ADMIN 5/9/81.
STUART J. R. Born 11/9/30. Commd 19/7/57. Sqn Ldr 1/7/71. Retd GD(G) 1/10/74.
STUART M. D. Born 2/10/31. Commd 2/7/52. Flt Lt 5/11/58. Retd GD 2/10/69.
STUART T. B., CEng MIMechE MIProdE. Born 4/3/32. Commd 19/5/69. Sqn Ldr 1/7/79. Retd ENG 4/3/93.

STUART The Venerable H. J., CB MA. Born 16/11/26. Commd 18/5/55. Retd 11/7/83. AVM.
STUART-PAUL Sir Roland., KBE. Born 7/11/34. Commd 10/4/56. AM 7/11/89. Retd GD 1/4/92.
STUBBINGS D. H. Born 25/12/21. Commd 17/10/57. Sqn Ldr 1/7/69. Retd ENG 15/4/72.
STUBBINGTON J. E. G., CEng MIEE MRAeS. Born 17/5/40. Commd 18/7/61. Wg Cdr 1/7/83. Retd ENG 1/3/85.
STUBBS B. H. Born 5/1/30. Commd 30/1/52. Flt Lt 29/5/57. Retd GD 5/1/68.
STUBBS K. Born 9/5/40. Commd 26/10/62. Wg Cdr 1/7/84. Retd SUP 9/5/95.
STUBBS R. H. Born 2/1/25. Commd 3/11/44. Sqn Ldr 1/7/72. Retd GD 2/10/75.
STUBINGS R. A. Born 26/7/26. Commd 15/6/50. Sqn Ldr 1/7/60. Retd GD 30/4/76.
STUDWELL H. E., BEM. Born 30/9/28. Commd 30/7/59. Wg Cdr 1/7/78. Retd ENG 30/9/83.
STUMP E. R., CEng MIEE MRAeS. Born 7/6/28. Commd 4/10/56. Flt Lt 4/4/60. Retd ENG 7/6/66 rtg Sqn Ldr.
STUNELL P. Born 10/4/47. Commd 20/10/83. Flt Lt 20/10/87. Retd ENG 14/9/96.
STUPPLES D. W., BA MSc CEng MIEE. Born 15/12/43. Commd 6/4/72. Sqn Ldr 1/1/79. Retd ENG 1/10/84.
STURGEON A. R., MRAeS. Born 24/11/22. Commd 14/3/44. Flt Lt 14/9/47. Retd ENG 24/11/60.
STURGEON B. Born 15/3/43. Commd 16/9/76. Sqn Ldr 1/1/86. Retd ADMIN 31/3/99.
STURGEON D. W. Born 4/12/19. Commd 4/12/42. Flt Lt 4/6/46. Retd GD 12/2/58.
STURGESS A. P. Born 25/11/54. Commd 20/10/83. Flt Lt 20/10/85. Retd OPS SPT 25/11/98.
STURGESS I. T. Born 25/5/49. Commd 27/2/70. Flt Lt 27/2/73. Retd GD 25/5/87.
STURGESS M. I. Born 9/7/56. Commd 20/10/83. Wg Cdr 1/7/97. Retd ENG 9/7/00.
STURGESS T. N. Born 25/12/46. Commd 27/5/78. Sqn Ldr 1/7/91. Retd SUP 14/3/96.
STURMAN A. V. H. Born 25/7/23. Commd 1/6/45. Flt Lt 4/6/53. Retd GD 22/12/69.
STURMAN G. G. Born 23/6/44. Commd 23/3/67. Flt Lt 23/9/72. Retd GD 31/10/82.
STURNHAM B. J., LRAM ARCM. Born 29/3/35. Commd 21/12/67. Flt Lt 17/3/73. Retd DM 30/4/77.
STURROCK D., MB ChB MSc. Born 3/5/26. Commd 1/3/51. Gp Capt 1/3/73. Retd MED 28/3/75.
STURT C. J., OBE MIMgt. Born 6/1/39. Commd 28/7/59. Gp Capt 1/1/84. Retd GD 12/11/90.
STURT P. G. Born 25/1/42. Commd 31/7/62. Gp Capt 1/1/91. Retd GD 26/8/96.
STUTTARD J. Born 8/3/49. Commd 20/9/68. Flt Lt 20/3/74. Retd GD 3/3/81.
STYLES A. F. Born 10/10/36. Commd 2/8/68. Flt Lt 17/3/71. Retd GD 2/8/76.
STYLES A. J. P., BSc. Born 14/4/45. Commd 15/7/66. Sqn Ldr 1/7/77. Retd ENG 14/4/83.
STYLES F. R. Born 7/2/39. Commd 15/12/59. Wg Cdr 1/1/84. Retd GD 7/2/94.
STYLES J. C. Born 14/11/46. Commd 22/7/71. Sqn Ldr 1/1/80. Retd SY 14/11/90. Re-entered 1/10/91. Sqn Ldr
   18/11/80. Retd ADMIN 14/9/99.
STYLES K. L. Born 24/3/33. Commd 27/8/52. Sqn Ldr 1/1/66. Retd GD 29/3/71.
STYLES L. F. Born 18/4/15. Commd 3/4/39. Sqn Ldr 1/8/47. Retd SUP 18/4/64 rtg Wg Cdr.
STYLES P. L., BA. Born 5/9/34. Commd 14/8/70. Fg Offr 14/8/70. Retd ENG 30/3/78 rtg Flt Lt.
SUDLOW R. A. A. Born 1/4/50. Commd 31/7/70. Flt Lt 31/1/74. Retd GD 1/4/88.
SUFFOLK R. N. Born 17/7/52. Commd 9/3/72. Flt Lt 9/9/77. Retd GD 17/7/90.
SUFFOLK T. F. Born 15/10/44. Commd 21/7/65. Wg Cdr 1/1/90. Retd GD(G) 2/4/94.
SUGDEN R. B. Born 5/11/51. Commd 22/7/71. Fg Offr 22/7/73. Retd GD 14/9/76.
SUGG M. R. Born 17/2/33. Commd 23/3/66. Flt Lt 23/3/71. Retd SUP 30/9/79.
SUGGATE J. R., BSc. Born 18/1/27. Commd 25/4/62. Wg Cdr 1/7/72. Retd ENG 18/1/82.
SULAIMAN BIN S. Born 25/3/34. Commd 1/4/58. Flt Lt 1/3/61. Retd GD 30/9/65.
SULLIVAN D. G. Born 15/4/33. Commd 14/3/57. Gp Capt 1/7/80. Retd ADMIN 15/4/89.
SULLIVAN J. B. Born 30/3/33. Commd 10/12/52. Flt Lt 29/4/59. Retd GD 29/8/64.
SULLIVAN J. I. H. Born 26/1/15. Commd 6/10/41. Flt Offr 1/9/45. Retd SEC 14/11/57.
SULLIVAN M. Born 21/12/36. Commd 26/5/67. Wg Cdr 1/7/90. Retd SUP 4/1/91.
SULLIVAN M. Born 5/7/54. Commd 21/3/74. Sqn Ldr 1/1/87. Retd SUP 5/7/92.
SULLY D. S., BEng. Born 6/1/60. Commd 4/7/82. Flt Lt 4/4/84. Retd GD 4/7/98.
SUMMERS J. J. Born 25/3/63. Commd 15/3/84. Flt Lt 21/7/90. Retd SUP 1/11/96.
SUMMERS J. R. Born 20/10/35. Commd 23/9/65. Sqn Ldr 1/7/73. Retd SEC 1/11/78.
SUMMERS N. J., MSc BSc. Born 9/3/63. Commd 30/8/81. Sqn Ldr 1/1/95. Retd ENG 26/10/98.
SUMMERS P. G., BA MEng. Born 5/6/45. Commd 1/3/68. Sqn Ldr 1/1/82. Retd ENG 1/10/86.
SUMMERS R. G. B., OBE. Born 18/10/21. Commd 7/6/42. Wg Cdr 1/1/58. Retd GD 18/10/68.
SUMMERS T. J. Born 13/7/47. Commd 1/8/69. Flt Lt 1/2/72. Retd GD 13/7/85.
SUMNER A. J., MA. Born 17/5/52. Commd 13/9/70. Flt Lt 15/4/75. Retd GD 15/7/85. Reinstated 22/1/86. Flt Lt
   22/10/75. Retd GD 17/5/90.
SUMNER A. W. Born 7/12/47. Commd 17/2/67. Wg Cdr 1/7/91. Retd GD 1/7/97.
SUMNER D. G. Born 22/2/54. Commd 15/10/81. Flt Lt 15/10/83. Retd OPS SPT 22/2/98.
SUMNER D. P. T. Born 17/8/43. Commd 25/3/64. Flt Lt 15/4/70. Retd GD 17/8/81.
SUMNER S. A. Born 2/6/33. Commd 17/1/52. Flt Lt 24/7/57. Retd GD 3/6/76. Reinstated on Active List 1/4/81. Retd
   GD 17/10/86.
SUNDARAM V. K., BSc. Born 9/4/44. Commd 2/8/71. Flt Lt 2/2/75. Retd ADMIN 2/12/85.
SUNDERLAND R. Born 10/12/52. Commd 1/6/72. Sqn Ldr 1/7/85. Retd GD 10/12/90.
SUNLEY A. W. Born 13/5/43. Commd 14/8/70. Flt Lt 24/3/74. Retd GD 13/5/76.
SUNNUCKS P. J. Born 9/7/32. Commd 19/4/51. Wg Cdr 1/7/79. Retd GD 9/7/84.
SUREN I. E. Born 5/4/29. Commd 2/8/50. Sqn Ldr 1/7/60. Retd GD 17/2/68.
SURMAN P. J. Born 9/11/35. Commd 8/7/54. Sqn Ldr 1/1/67. Retd SEC 9/11/73.

SURTEES G. C., MA BSc. Born 16/6/61. Commd 30/10/83. Flt Lt 30/4/87. Retd ADMIN 14/3/96.
SURTEES W., DFC. Born 16/7/14. Commd 26/3/38. Wg Cdr 1/1/53. Retd GD 1/12/57.
SUSANS B. Born 20/4/49. Commd 3/7/80. Sqn Ldr 1/1/89. Retd ENG 28/12/96.
SUSSUM G. E. Born 20/6/39. Commd 18/2/58. Sqn Ldr 1/7/73. Retd GD 2/9/89.
SUTCLIFFE C., OBE CEng MIMechE MSc. Born 8/11/24. Commd 17/1/51. Gp Capt. 1/7/76. Retd ENG 31/5/79.
SUTCLIFFE D. W., MBE. Born 4/3/43. Commd 31/10/63. Wg Cdr 1/7/84. Retd SY 5/1/95.
SUTCLIFFE G. D. Born 19/6/22. Commd 23/1/43. Sqn Ldr 1/10/54. Retd GD 19/6/71.
SUTCLIFFE R., MIMgt. Born 24/11/27. Commd 14/1/65. Flt Lt 14/1/71. Retd PRT 1/11/72.
SUTHERLAND D. J. L., BSc. Born 4/5/55. Commd 30/10/83. Flt Lt 30/4/87. Retd ADMIN 30/10/99.
SUTHERLAND G., BSc. Born 22/3/33. Commd 24/4/57. Sqn Ldr 24/7/66. Retd GD 24/4/73.
SUTHERLAND G. B. Born 18/4/09. Commd 2/11/42. Flt Lt 2/5/46. Retd SEC 6/1/58.
SUTHERLAND G. MacL, MIMgt. Born 28/1/30. Commd 29/11/51. Wg Cdr 1/1/79. Retd SY 1/12/83.
SUTHERLAND J. D. M. Born 9/1/05. Commd 15/2/40. Wg Cdr 1/7/51. Retd ENG 9/1/57.
SUTHERLAND J. G. Born 14/8/49. Commd 26/2/71. Fg Offr 26/2/72. Retd SUP 20/8/76.
SUTHERLAND J. G. Born 21/12/55. Commd 28/10/76. Flt Lt 28/4/82. Retd GD 29/12/84.
SUTHERLAND J. W., AFC. Born 1/4/23. Commd 2/3/49. Sqn Ldr 1/1/62. Retd GD 1/5/70.
SUTHERLAND J. W., MA. Born 11/5/46. Commd 16/8/70. Wg Cdr 1/1/88. Retd ADMIN 14/3/97.
SUTHERLAND M. A., MBE. Born 23/7/33. Commd 26/2/53. Gp Capt 1/7/79. Retd GD 23/7/88.
SUTHERLAND M. J., BSc. Born 27/8/62. Commd 31/8/80. Flt Lt 15/10/84. Retd GD 14/9/96.
SUTHERLAND M. J., BSc. Born 16/2/51. Commd 13/9/70. Plt Offr 15/7/74. Retd SUP 25/2/75.
SUTHERLAND R., MSc BSc. Born 10/1/52. Commd 13/6/71. Flt Lt 15/1/76. Retd ADMIN 10/1/90.
SUTHERLAND T. G. G. Born 12/7/34. Commd 19/2/76. Flt Lt 19/2/79. Retd PI 17/4/89.
SUTHERLAND W. J. Born 15/12/18. Commd 7/8/43. Sqn Ldr 1/1/54. Retd GD 7/2/58.
SUTHERLAND-EARL T. L. Born 6/4/30. Commd 23/9/65. Flt Lt 23/9/71. Retd ENG 6/4/85.
SUTTIE A. J., MInstAM. Born 18/4/49. Commd 23/11/78. Sqn Ldr 1/1/87. Retd ADMIN 31/1/97.
SUTTLE C. E. P., OBE BSc CEng FIEE FRCO DNCL. Born 9/7/13. Commd 17/10/39. Gp Capt 9/7/59. Retd EDN 9/7/73 rtg A Cdre.
SUTTON D. H., CBE. Born 3/12/20. Commd 14/12/38. A Cdr 1/7/71. Retd GD 31/12/75.
SUTTON G. E. Born 18/2/31. Commd 19/7/57. Flt Lt 19/1/62. Retd GD 31/7/68.
SUTTON H. T., OBE DFC. Born 21/1/14. Commd 19/10/34. Wg Cdr 1/7/57. Retd SEC 17/2/66 rtg Gp Capt.
SUTTON I., MBE CEng MRAeS MIMgt. Born 6/5/24. Commd 17/10/57. Sqn Ldr 1/7/71. Retd ENG 9/5/78.
SUTTON Sir John., KCB. Born 9/7/32. Commd 22/3/51. AM 1/1/86. Retd GD 5/7/89.
SUTTON J. C. K., MBE. CEng MRAeS. Born 23/6/15. Commd 15/5/41. Sqn Ldr 1/1/52. Retd ENG 23/6/70 rtg Wg Cdr.
SUTTON J. D. D. Born 4/3/35. Commd 22/5/70. Flt Lt 22/5/73. Retd GD 2/6/76.
SUTTON M. P. J. Born 1/11/45. Commd 21/1/66. Flt Lt 3/6/71. Retd GD 2/11/82.
SUTTON P. Born 25/11/36. Commd 7/5/64. Sqn Ldr 1/7/73. Retd ENG 25/11/94.
SUTTON P. D., MB BS FRCR DMR(D). Born 29/6/21. Commd 16/1/47. A Cdre 1/1/80. Retd MED 30/6/83.
SUTTON R. J. Born 18/10/47. Commd 14/2/91. Flt Lt 14/2/93. Retd GD 19/10/98.
SUTTON W. A. Born 5/10/22. Commd 23/6/44. Flt Lt 23/12/47. Retd GD 28/11/58.
SVENSSON I. A. G. Born 29/5/31. Commd 30/7/52. Sqn Ldr 1/1/64. Retd GD 29/5/69.
SVETLIK L. Born 23/3/17. Commd 28/2/42. Flt Lt 18/5/56. Retd GD(G) 28/7/66.
SWABY S. J. Born 29/12/43. Commd 16/12/82. Flt Lt 16/12/85. Retd GD(G) 14/3/96.
SWAFFER D. C. Born 10/5/46. Commd 15/3/79. Flt Lt 15/3/81. Retd GD 30/1/96.
SWAFFIELD J. Born 3/6/24. Commd 30/12/44. Sqn Ldr 1/1/61. Retd CAT 1/10/66.
SWAFFIELD N. Born 5/8/41. Commd 13/12/68. Sqn Ldr 1/1/85. Retd SUP 1/1/88.
SWAIN B. L. Born 5/11/45. Commd 11/5/78. Wg Cdr 1/7/91. Retd ADMIN 5/11/00.
SWAIN C de P. D. Born 8/5/26. Commd 1/10/56. Flt Lt 23/2/56. Retd ADMIN 1/10/80.
SWAIN C. M. Born 19/3/38. Commd 29/6/72. Plt Offr 29/12/72. Retd GD(G) 2/10/74.
SWAIN G. G., BA. Born 19/8/47. Commd 25/2/68. Flt Lt 8/3/72. Retd GD(G) 19/8/91.
SWAIN J. Born 26/2/41. Commd 19/12/61. Flt Lt 19/6/64. Retd GD 1/9/73.
SWAIN J. A. Born 27/2/35. Commd 11/6/60. Flt Lt 11/12/65. Retd GD 27/2/73.
SWAIN J. G. G., BDS. Born 20/1/46. Commd 28/12/66. Wg Cdr 18/12/81. Retd DEL 8/6/98.
SWAITHES C. W. C. Born 12/12/34. Commd 25/1/66. Sqn Ldr 1/1/73. Retd SUP 1/6/92.
SWALES F. L. Born 28/2/28. Commd 25/4/51. Flt Lt 25/1/57. Retd GD 28/2/66.
SWALWELL L. C. Born 27/1/28. Commd 14/12/49. Gp Capt 1/1/73. Retd GD 1/11/75.
SWAN A. J., MBE QGM MIExpE. Born 5/11/42. Commd 23/11/78. Sqn Ldr 1/1/89. Retd ENG 1/6/92.
SWAN D. A., FCIS. Born 23/10/34. Commd 20/6/61. Sqn Ldr 1/1/72. Retd SEC 10/7/79.
SWANCOTT N. A. J. Born 22/4/63. Commd 24/11/81. Flt Lt 26/5/87. Retd GD 1/10/90.
SWANN R. N. Born 20/7/41. Commd 8/12/61. Sqn Ldr 1/1/76. Retd GD 20/7/79.
SWANSON B. G. Born 29/2/32. Commd 19/7/51. Wg Cdr 1/7/83. Retd GD 1/3/87.
SWANSON S. J. Born 7/6/30. Commd 24/2/67. Flt Lt 24/2/70. Retd GD 7/6/88.
SWANWICK G. W. Born 10/11/15. Commd 7/10/41. Wg Cdr 1/1/60. Retd SEC 30/4/70.
SWAPP G. D., OBE MA. Born 25/5/31. Commd 21/10/54. Wg Cdr 1/1/70. Retd ADMIN 31/12/83.
SWARBRICK D. L. Born 17/5/30. Commd 18/5/61. Sqn Ldr 1/1/78. Retd ENG 17/5/80.
SWART D. W., OBE MIMgt. Born 9/8/25. Commd 20/12/51. Wg Cdr 1/1/65. Retd GD 1/10/74.

SWART L., CBE AFC. Born 28/11/32. Commd 12/7/51. A Cdre 1/7/80. Retd GD 28/11/87.
SWASH M. G. Born 27/5/44. Commd 15/6/83. Sqn Ldr 1/7/91. Retd ENG 27/9/96.
SWASH W. P. Born 3/9/38. Commd 9/8/63. Flt Lt 26/7/67. Retd GD(G) 3/9/76.
SWATTON B. P. Born 11/4/41. Commd 18/12/62. Wg Cdr 1/1/81. Retd SUP 2/4/93.
SWATTON P. J. Born 4/5/35. Commd 13/5/53. Sqn Ldr 1/1/86. Retd GD 3/2/89.
SWEENEY A. E., AFC. Born 11/1/22. Commd 19/5/44. Wg Cdr 1/1/70. Retd GD 6/2/77.
SWEENEY C. M. Born 15/11/48. Commd 4/3/71. Gp Capt 1/7/95. Retd GD 31/1/01.
SWEENEY L. J. Born 27/5/27. Commd 7/7/49. Sqn Ldr 1/1/68. Retd GD 27/5/85.
SWEENEY M. Born 11/4/53. Commd 9/12/71. Flt Lt 9/6/77. Retd GD 20/4/83.
SWEET I. D., MSc BSc. Born 2/4/49. Commd 4/10/71. Sqn Ldr 1/7/83. Retd ENG 1/10/90.
SWEET J., BA. Born 25/9/29. Commd 21/5/52. Sqn Ldr 1/1/65. Retd GD 1/1/68.
SWEETING J., MA. Born 27/7/37. Commd 29/12/65. Flt Lt 29/9/68. Retd ADMIN 27/7/92.
SWEETING J. M. Born 5/8/38d. Commd 2/5/68. Fg Offr 2/5/68. Retd GD 1/1/70.
SWEETING R. F., DFC. Born 16/3/20. Commd 17/5/41. Sqn Ldr 1/7/49. Retd GD 21/5/58.
SWEETLOVE G. G., MBE. Born 20/4/26. Commd 12/1/61. Sqn Ldr 1/1/75. Retd GD 21/4/76.
SWEETMAN J. E. Born 3/3/48. Commd 2/12/66. Flt Lt 2/6/72. Retd GD 3/3/86.
SWEPSON D. Born 1/2/33. Commd 28/1/53. Flt Lt 17/8/58. Retd GD 1/2/71.
SWETMAN K. M., TD. Born 9/5/44. Commd 13/4/86. Flt Lt 13/12/87. Retd ADMIN 13/4/98.
SWETTENHAM W. A. Born 27/2/33. Commd 8/11/51. Flt Lt 23/2/57. Retd GD(G) 27/2/71.
SWIFT A. N., BA. Born 12/9/56. Commd 14/9/75. Flt Lt 15/10/79. Retd GD 15/7/90.
SWIFT D. J. Born 5/4/32. Commd 17/7/61. Flt Lt 17/7/61. Retd GD 17/7/65.
SWIFT D. S. Born 2/11/44. Commd 6/12/65. Flt Lt 26/2/72. Retd GD(G) 2/11/82.
SWIFT G. R. Born 14/8/45. Commd 5/2/65. Flt Lt 5/8/70. Retd GD 4/4/78.
SWINBURN W. H., AIIP. Born 23/2/20. Commd 2/6/44. Flt Lt 2/6/46. Retd ENG 23/2/75.
SWINDEN J., MSc BSc CEng MIEE. Born 8/6/41. Commd 30/9/62. Wg Cdr 1/1/85. Retd ENG 2/4/93.
SWINDLE E. S. Born 13/2/57. Commd 22/11/84. Flt Lt 18/6/87. Retd ENG 13/2/95.
SWINDLEHURST P. W., CEng FCIPD MIMechE MRAeS. Born 11/6/36. Commd 17/5/60. Wg Cdr 1/1/73. Retd ENG 17/10/87.
SWINEY M. J. E., OBE. Born 19/8/26. Commd 14/6/46. A Cdre 1/1/74. Retd GD 3/4/80.
SWINGLEHURST F. H. Born 22/4/20. Commd 27/10/41. Flt Lt 19/2/46. Retd ENG 5/1/54.
SWINHOE M. H. Born 31/12/45. Commd 3/3/67. Sqn Ldr 1/7/82. Retd GD 31/12/89.
SWINNERTON D. Born 17/9/53. Commd 9/11/89. Fg Offr 9/11/89. Retd SUP 1/6/93 rtg Flt Lt.
SWINSCOE B. D., BSc. Born 21/6/48. Commd 28/2/69. Flt Lt 28/11/73. Retd ENG 30/9/76.
SWIRES R. I., MB ChB DAvMed. Born 30/11/33. Commd 15/2/59. Wg Cdr 17/6/71. Retd MED 15/2/75.
SYDENHAM J. R. Born 28/4/20. Commd 16/10/46. Flt Lt 16/4/51. Retd SEC 24/7/54.
SYDNEY J., MIMgt. Born 29/2/20. Commd 8/10/42. Sqn Ldr 1/1/63. Retd ENG 16/2/74.
SYDNEY P. H. Born 19/1/21. Commd 14/10/42. Flt Offr 24/2/50. Retd SEC 16/2/55.
SYKES F., MBE. Born 26/8/17. Commd 27/10/55. Sqn Ldr 1/1/65. Retd ENG 18/10/67.
SYKES L. J., CEng MIMechE MRAeS. Born 6/1/35. Commd 25/10/57. Wg Cdr 1/7/77. Retd ENG 30/4/86.
SYKES M. J. Born 9/5/44. Commd 23/3/64. Flt Lt 25/9/69. Retd GD 9/5/82.
SYKES N. Born 26/6/33. Commd 8/2/57. Wg Cdr 1/1/71. Retd ENG 1/1/74.
SYKES R. L. Born 15/3/23. Commd 7/8/45. Flt Lt 4/6/53. Retd GD(G) 15/3/78.
SYLVESTER P. A. M., OBE BEM MIMgt. Born 10/11/20. Commd 25/5/50. Wg Cdr 1/7/69. Retd SUP 10/4/75.
SYME J. Born 13/6/19. Commd 6/9/45. Sqn Ldr 1/1/56. Retd ENG 21/9/74.
SYME T. S., DFC DPhysEd. Born 28/5/28. Commd 6/4/50. Sqn Ldr 1/7/62. Retd GD 27/4/68.
SYMES D. B. Born 2/12/45. Commd 28/4/67. Gp Capt 1/7/91. Retd GD 2/4/98.
SYMES G. D., BA. Born 7/10/49. Commd 15/9/69. Sqn Ldr 1/1/83. Retd ADMIN 10/4/01.
SYMES K. A., BEM. Born 13/4/32. Commd 17/3/67. Sqn Ldr 1/1/78. Retd ADMIN 13/4/82.
SYMES L. Born 2/4/30. Commd 28/11/51. Sqn Ldr 2/4/71. Retd GD 18/3/77.
SYMES L. F. Born 27/3/24. Commd 6/8/43. Sqn Ldr 24/10/62. Retd EDN 28/6/78.
SYMES P. J. Born 30/5/38. Commd 15/12/59. Sqn Ldr 1/7/75. Retd SEC 1/7/78.
SYMMANS T. Born 29/4/48. Commd 25/4/69. Plt Offr 29/4/69. Retd GD 19/8/70. Re-entered 1/11/81. Flt Lt 1/11/87. Retd OPS SPT 1/11/97.
SYMONDS D. C., AFC. Born 10/4/50. Commd 7/6/68. Wg Cdr 1/1/85. Retd GD 10/4/89.
SYMONDS E. J. G. Born 1/5/15. Commd 17/8/39. Flt Lt 2/7/47. Retd SUP 1/5/64 rtg Sqn Ldr.
SYMONDS J. B., MCIPD. Born 18/6/42. Commd 21/10/65. A Cdre 1/7/94. Retd ADMIN 18/6/97.
SYMONDS K. W. P., AFM. Born 20/8/24. Commd 26/10/61. Sqn Ldr 1/7/74. Retd ENG 20/8/82.
SYMONDS P. C., OBE FIMgt MRAeS. Born 5/3/40. Commd 7/5/64. Gp Capt 1/1/90. Retd ENG 5/3/96.
SYMONDSON B. F. Born 7/4/37. Commd 27/11/55. Sqn Ldr 1/1/69. Retd ADMIN 7/12/77.
SYMONS A. J. P., MIMgt. Born 26/9/40. Commd 11/10/70. Sqn Ldr 1/1/82. Retd ADMIN 11/10/90.
SYMONS B. R. Born 18/4/47. Commd 17/2/67. Sqn Ldr 1/7/92. Retd GD 18/4/00.
SYMONS D. Born 1/1/36. Commd 30/7/57. Wg Cdr 1/7/85. Retd GD 2/7/87.
SYMONS F. Born 10/4/38. Commd 27/10/67. Flt Lt 7/10/72. Retd SUP 19/3/91.
SYMONS J. C. Born 11/3/35. Commd 7/5/64. Sqn Ldr 1/1/72. Retd ENG 8/4/85.
SYNDERCOMBE M. R. L. Born 16/5/58. Commd 2/6/77. Sqn Ldr 1/1/94. Retd GD 1/1/97.
SYNNOTT B. P. Born 20/10/45. Commd 15/7/66. Wg Cdr 1/1/82. Retd GD 1/1/85.

SYVRET-THOMPSON D. G. Born 27/7/30. Commd 9/7/54. Flt Lt 28/7/65. Retd GD 2/11/82.
SZOTA B. Born 16/10/18. Commd 7/2/57. Sqn Ldr 1/7/70. Retd GD 16/10/73.

# T

TABARD P. G. Born 13/2/21. Commd 15/6/44. Flt Lt 11/11/54. Retd GD 18/1/63.
TABBERER N. J. H. Born 21/8/37. Commd 18/1/56. Flt Lt 16/8/61. Retd GD 21/8/75 rtg Sqn Ldr.
TABER T. E. Born 27/6/20. Commd 1/8/43. Flt Lt 21/11/50. Retd SEC 27/6/69.
TABERHAM M. C., BEng. Born 29/6/58. Commd 19/9/76. Flt Lt 15/10/80. Retd GD 29/2/92.
TABERNACLE J. M. Born 20/4/30. Commd 1/8/51. Flt Lt 11/11/54. Retd GD 20/7/68.
TABOR K. J. Born 29/7/25. Commd 25/5/45. Sqn Ldr 1/4/56. Retd GD 29/7/63.
TACEY A. Born 13/8/23. Commd 27/5/54. Flt Lt 27/5/60. Retd GD 1/8/68.
TACON E. W., CBE DSO MVO DFC* AFC*. Born 6/12/17. Commd 11/5/39. A Cdre 1/7/63. Retd GD 15/2/71.
TACQ A. R. L. Born 10/1/18. Commd 24/3/44. Flt Lt 7/6/51. Retd GD(G) 19/2/68.
TAGG J. K. S. Born 3/11/38. Commd 8/5/60. Flt Lt 26/7/67. Retd GD 3/11/76.
TAGGART A. W. McM, AFC BA MRAeS. Born 26/9/45. Commd 1/4/66. Sqn Ldr 1/7/80. Retd GD 6/1/93.
TAGGART M. P., BSc. Born 2/10/54. Commd 16/9/73. Flt Lt 15/4/78. Retd GD 14/9/96.
TAGGESELL C. W. Born 5/2/17. Commd 27/5/44. Sqn Ldr 1/1/67. Retd ENG 5/2/73.
TAILBY A. J., BSc. Born 19/3/58. Commd 7/1/76. Sqn Ldr 1/1/90. Retd GD 19/3/96.
TAINSH G. H. Born 30/1/47. Commd 1/3/68. Flt Lt 6/10/71. Retd GD 16/12/75.
TAIT A. P. W. Born 12/2/40. Commd 1/10/60. Flt Lt 26/7/67. Retd GD 7/9/78.
TAIT J., LLB. Born 21/4/34. Commd 6/7/60. Sqn Ldr 13/12/71. Retd EDN 30/9/78.
TAIT J. B., DSO*** DFC*. Born 9/12/16. Commd 1/8/36. Gp Capt 1/1/53. Retd GD 9/12/66.
TAIT P. C. Born 3/12/42. Commd 9/3/62. Flt Lt 9/9/67. Retd GD 3/12/80.
TAIT S. A. Born 5/8/81. Commd 20/10/83. Flt Lt 20/4/89. Retd GD 17/7/00.
TAIT T. R. V. Born 14/2/12. Commd 23/2/42. Sqn Ldr 1/10/55. Retd ENG 20/8/66.
TAIT W. A. K. Born 21/1/34. Commd 15/6/53. Flt Lt 12/9/58. Retd GD 4/9/72.
TAIT W. A. M. Born 27/7/41. Commd 23/6/61. Sqn Ldr 1/1/73. Retd GD 27/7/79.
TAIT W. B. Born 2/5/37. Commd 17/7/64. Flt Lt 9/2/68. Retd GD 27/1/79.
TAIT W. C. Born 27/1/44. Commd 20/5/68. Flt Lt 4/5/72. Retd ADMIN 20/5/87.
TAITE R. G. Born 30/6/42. Commd 9/2/62. Flt Lt 9/8/67. Retd GD 30/6/79.
TALBOT E. C. S., BSc. Born 22/8/46. Commd 7/1/68. Flt Lt 15/4/70. Retd GD 2/3/76.
TALBOT E. W., DFC*. Born 10/7/22. Commd 24/1/42. Wg Cdr 1/1/60. Retd GD 10/7/69.
TALBOT G. A. Born 3/9/34. Commd 10/4/56. Sqn Ldr 1/7/68. Retd GD 28/11/75.
TALBOT G. S., BA. Born 13/10/32. Commd 5/10/56. Sqn Ldr 5/7/64. Retd EDN 5/10/72.
TALBOT-WILLIAMS A. T., MA. Born 29/5/24. Commd 26/6/44. Gp Capt 1/1/66. Retd GD 30/4/71.
TALL E. H. Born 2/5/25. Commd 1/4/65. Flt Lt 1/4/68. Retd GD 1/11/77.
TALLACK L. E. Born 20/11/61. Commd 8/6/84. Flt Lt 2/3/89. Retd GD 14/9/96.
TALLETT A. S., MCIPD. Born 14/4/31. Commd 17/5/51. Wg Cdr 1/7/71. Retd GD 30/6/85.
TALLISS J. G. Born 18/7/30. Commd 6/12/51. Flt Lt 5/6/57. Retd GD 18/7/68. Reinstated 17/12/80. Flt Lt 4/11/70.
    Retd GD 19/10/90.
TALTON H. Born 4/3/33. Commd 22/8/61. Wg Cdr 1/7/76. Retd GD(G) 4/3/88.
TAMBLIN P. A. Born 25/9/45. Commd 11/10/84. Flt Lt 11/10/88. Retd ENG 10/4/93.
TAMBLIN P. J., CB BA CIMgt. Born 11/1/26. Commd 11/7/51. A Cdre 1/1/77. Retd ADMIN 22/4/80.
TAMBLING D. W. Born 20/7/21. Commd 27/2/47. Sqn Ldr 1/1/64. Retd SUP 20/7/71.
TAME F. W. Born 24/8/18. Commd 16/1/47. Wg Cdr 1/1/64. Retd SUP 19/10/68.
TAME P. A. Born 23/8/45. Commd 10/12/65. Fg Offr 10/12/68. Retd GD(G) 1/10/71.
TAME P. H. Born 10/1/43. Commd 22/2/63. Sqn Ldr 1/1/77. Retd GD 8/6/97.
TAMS F. A. B., OBE. Born 19/2/14. Commd 1/4/40. Wg Cdr 1/1/54. Retd GD 20/2/59.
TAMSETT C. H. Born 30/11/17. Commd 20/11/43. Wg Cdr 1/1/61. Retd SUP 13/9/69.
TANNER A. T. Born 5/12/23. Commd 9/8/48. Flt Lt 20/11/53. Retd GD 5/10/68.
TANNER B. D. Born 6/4/35. Commd 28/7/60. Wg Cdr 1/1/80. Retd GD 19/6/84.
TANNER C. E., DPhysEd. Born 20/11/40. Commd 1/9/64. Flt Lt 1/9/68. Retd PE 28/2/73.
TANNER D. W. Born 29/8/46. Commd 1/4/71. Flt Lt 1/10/76. Retd GD 14/12/96.
TANNER D. W., DFC. Born 21/5/29. Commd 26/10/50. Sqn Ldr 1/1/62. Retd GD 25/6/76.
TANNER J. R. Born 29/11/22. Commd 27/3/45. Gp Capt 1/7/74. Retd GD 31/3/77.
TANNER M. R. Born 30/6/42. Commd 17/9/63. Sqn Ldr 1/1/75. Retd GD 30/6/80.
TAPLIN F. M. N., OBE. Born 11/7/24. Commd 16/3/47. Wg Cdr 1/7/65. Retd GD 11/7/79.
TAPLIN R. K., MBE BSc(Econ) FILT MCIPS MIMIS MBCS MIL MRAeS MIMgt. Born 3/12/48. Commd 27/1/70.
    Wg Cdr 1/1/97. Retd SUP 25/2/00.
TAPPER K. F. W., MBE. Born 25/5/21. Commd 17/4/43. Wg Cdr 1/1/58. Retd GD 15/10/66.
TAPSTER I. R., MCIPD. Born 9/6/30. Commd 1/8/51. Gp Capt 1/7/72. Retd SEC 1/8/74.
TARGETT R. A., MBE. Born 30/10/19. Commd 13/7/45. Wg Cdr 1/7/63. Retd CAT 6/8/66.
TARGETT S. R. Born 18/3/62. Commd 4/9/81. Sqn Ldr 1/7/95. Retd SUP 18/3/00.
TARLING R. G. R. Born 7/8/16. Commd 24/11/41. Flt Lt 1/9/45. Retd GD(G) 29/11/58.

TARLTON S. W., MB BS MRCS LRCP MRCPath DCP DTM&H. Born 5/1/32. Commd 11/8/57. Wg Cdr 26/7/70. Retd MED 11/8/73.
TARRAN O. A. Born 18/12/27. Commd 16/7/52. Flt Lt 12/12/57. Retd GD 21/1/76 rtg Sqn Ldr.
TARRANT D. L. Born 27/11/40. Commd 11/8/77. Flt Lt 11/8/82. Retd GD(G) 1/11/88.
TARRANT K. W. J., DFC*. Born 30/12/17. Commd 17/8/40. Gp Capt 1/1/68. Retd GD 29/12/70.
TARRY A. W. Born 24/2/22. Commd 25/2/44. Wg Cdr 1/1/60. Retd GD 28/9/68.
TARWID A. S., MBE. Born 15/10/21. Commd 23/4/53. Sqn Ldr 1/1/67. Retd GD 15/10/76.
TASKER D. Born 14/9/15. Commd 24/5/43. Sqn Ldr 1/1/61. Retd GD(G) 28/11/64.
TASKER D. R., BA. Born 10/9/50. Commd 11/10/84. Sqn Ldr 1/1/91. Retd ENG 11/10/98.
TASKER J. C. Born 24/11/33. Commd 18/2/60. Sqn Ldr 1/7/74. Retd SUP 24/11/92.
TASKER T. M. Born 13/9/47. Commd 19/6/70. Sqn Ldr 1/1/86. Retd GD(G) 13/9/91.
TASSELL D. M., BSc. Born 10/11/61. Commd 26/4/84. Sqn Ldr 1/7/96. Retd ENG 10/11/99.
TASWELL H., OBE MIMgt. Born 19/2/18. Commd 24/10/44. Wg Cdr 1/7/67. Retd PRT 19/2/73.
TATE A. Born 19/9/33. Commd 28/3/60. Sqn Ldr 1/1/66. Retd GD 19/9/71.
TATE F. H., AFM. Born 25/9/23. Commd 17/5/62. Flt Lt 17/5/65. Retd GD 25/9/78.
TATE J. S. Born 21/8/40. Commd 10/11/61. Flt Lt 10/5/67. Retd GD 3/9/76.
TATE P. Born 10/3/92. Commd 14/11/51. Flt Lt 14/5/56. Retd GD 31/12/92.
TATTERSALL J., BSc. Born 7/1/31. Commd 9/12/54. Sqn Ldr 9/6/65. Retd EDN 10/1/81.
TATTON R. I. Born 26/10/47. Commd 28/6/81. Sqn Ldr 1/1/87. Retd GD(G) 1/10/89.
TAUNTON R. E. Born 25/1/49. Commd 21/2/69. Flt Lt 26/6/75. Retd SY 25/1/87.
TAVANYAR E. A. Born 1/7/21. Commd 24/8/50. Flt Offr 24/8/56. Retd SEC 1/3/57.
TAVANYAR T. G., BA. Born 24/7/66. Commd 8/5/88. Flt Lt 8/11/91. Retd SUP 14/9/96.
TAVNER C. C., MIPR. Born 9/1/39. Commd 19/9/59. Wg Cdr 1/1/86. Retd GD 9/1/94.
TAYLER G. G., CEng MIERE. Born 12/5/16. Commd 27/9/40. Sqn Ldr 1/1/52. Retd ENG 30/5/64.
TAYLER J. S. Born 27/10/36. Commd 4/5/72. Flt Lt 4/5/75. Retd GD(G) 29/7/89.
TAYLER R. H. Born 27/1/32. Commd 31/5/51. Flt Lt 10/7/58. Retd GD 1/8/74.
TAYLOR A. Born 31/8/33. Commd 9/4/52. Sqn Ldr 1/7/68. Retd GD 31/8/71.
TAYLOR A. Born 11/12/39. Commd 9/10/64. Plt Offr 9/10/65. Retd GD 21/8/66.
TAYLOR A., MSc. Born 16/5/31. Commd 2/7/52. Sqn Ldr 5/7/67. Retd EDN 26/10/75.
TAYLOR A. Born 8/1/43. Commd 24/1/74. Flt Lt 24/1/76. Retd SY 24/1/83.
TAYLOR A. A. Born 22/3/21. Commd 14/5/45. Sqn Ldr 1/7/58. Retd GD 22/3/71.
TAYLOR A. G. S., BA MCollP MCIPD AdDipEd. Born 24/5/53. Commd 17/8/80. Flt Lt 17/8/81. Retd ADMIN 17/8/96.
TAYLOR A. I. J. Born 4/10/50. Commd 14/1/88. Flt Lt 14/1/90. Retd ENG 2/8/93.
TAYLOR A. J. Born 22/9/48. Commd 8/10/87. Flt Lt 8/10/89. Retd ADMIN 14/3/96.
TAYLOR A. J., BEng. Born 6/6/62. Commd 16/9/84. Flt Lt 3/5/89. Retd ENG 6/8/00.
TAYLOR A. J., BA. Born 24/12/40. Commd 18/5/65. Sqn Ldr 1/7/85. Retd ADMIN 28/6/86.
TAYLOR A. M., BSc. Born 29/3/47. Commd 17/1/72. Sqn Ldr 1/7/86. Retd GD 1/7/89.
TAYLOR A. R. Born 25/2/22. Commd 19/10/44. Flt Lt 19/4/48. Retd GD 31/5/68.
TAYLOR A. R., BSc. Born 26/1/49. Commd 27/2/70. Sqn Ldr 1/1/80. Retd ENG 26/1/89.
TAYLOR A. S. H., MInstAM. Born 3/1/46. Commd 8/9/69. Sqn Ldr 1/1/81. Retd SY 8/11/85.
TAYLOR A. T. H., BSc MIMgt. Born 3/10/39. Commd 2/10/61. Sqn Ldr 1/1/73. Retd GD 14/5/82.
TAYLOR A. W. Born 20/6/38. Commd 11/6/81. Flt Lt 11/12/83. Retd GD(G) 20/6/93.
TAYLOR B., BA. Born 9/5/38. Commd 6/4/62. Flt Lt 7/7/63. Retd GD 10/5/88.
TAYLOR B. Born 22/4/44. Commd 2/65. Sqn Ldr 1/1/77. Retd GD 22/4/88.
TAYLOR B. C. Born 5/4/31. Commd 25/8/67. Flt Lt 25/8/73. Retd ADMIN 30/4/76.
TAYLOR B. P. Born 3/1/53. Commd 6/4/72. Sqn Ldr 1/7/89. Retd GD 1/7/92.
TAYLOR B. T. Born 27/9/39. Commd 29/4/58. Flt Lt 5/11/63. Retd GD 3/4/79. Reinstated 21/9/84. Flt Lt 25/4/69. Retd GD 15/12/90.
TAYLOR C. Born 18/2/22. Commd 8/7/54. Sqn Ldr 1/7/68. Retd GD 18/2/77.
TAYLOR C. Born 23/1/17. Commd 9/4/43. Flt Lt 1/10/51. Retd GD(G) 29/11/61 rtg Sqn Ldr.
TAYLOR C. C. Born 3/3/33. Commd 15/12/53. Wg Cdr 1/1/85. Retd ADMIN 3/3/88.
TAYLOR C. E. B. Born 27/7/36. Commd 5/5/58. Sqn Ldr 1/1/82. Retd GD 27/7/91.
TAYLOR C. H. Born 22/8/29. Commd 18/1/50. Sqn Ldr 1/7/62. Retd GD 22/8/67.
TAYLOR C. J., MBE. Born 18/5/44. Commd 10/6/66. Sqn Ldr 1/1/80. Retd GD 6/8/98.
TAYLOR C. R., OBE. Born 25/12/10. Commd 24/3/33. Wg Cdr 4/7/44. Retd GD 6/4/46 rtg Gp Capt.
TAYLOR C. R. V. Born 8/9/32. Commd 26/12/51. Flt Lt 14/11/56. Retd GD 8/11/75.
TAYLOR D. Born 14/7/31. Commd 19/1/66. Sqn Ldr 1/7/77. Retd ENG 14/7/81.
TAYLOR D. Born 9/6/54. Commd 27/7/72. Flt Lt 27/1/79. Retd GD(G) 9/6/92.
TAYLOR D. Born 13/6/17. Commd 14/6/44. Wg Cdr 1/7/67. Retd SUP 13/6/72.
TAYLOR D. A., DFC*. Born 29/4/21. Commd 14/8/39. Sqn Ldr 1/7/49. Retd GD 19/9/58.
TAYLOR D. A. Born 21/1/26. Commd 29/6/50. Sqn Ldr 1/1/60. Retd GD 21/1/76.
TAYLOR D. A. Born 31/12/58. Commd 12/10/78. Sqn Ldr 1/1/90. Retd GD 31/1/96.
TAYLOR D. A. J., BEM CEng MRAeS. Born 8/7/22. Commd 28/7/60. Sqn Ldr 1/1/72. Retd ENG 30/6/78.
TAYLOR D. B. Born 6/3/34. Commd 7/5/52. Flt Lt 2/10/57. Retd GD 1/5/84.
TAYLOR D. E. Born 7/4/30. Commd 28/11/51. Flt Lt 28/5/56. Retd GD 31/1/68.

TAYLOR D. H., BSc. Born 10/11/34. Commd 26/3/56. Sqn Ldr 1/1/69. Retd GD 10/11/72.
TAYLOR D. H. Born 6/11/43. Commd 28/4/67. Flt Lt 26/4/70. Retd GD 5/11/76.
TAYLOR D. H. E. Born 16/9/25. Commd 21/5/46. Sqn Ldr 1/1/61. Retd GD 5/3/76.
TAYLOR D. I. W., FIFA. Born 12/12/50. Commd 28/12/80. Flt Lt 4/7/84. Retd ADMIN 17/9/89.
TAYLOR D. J. Born 5/4/44. Commd 8/1/69. Sqn Ldr 1/7/85. Retd GD 29/11/93.
TAYLOR D. J. Born 13/1/31. Commd 18/5/70. Sqn Ldr 1/1/74. Retd ADMIN 22/5/82.
TAYLOR D. J. Born 3/9/50. Commd 25/2/72. Wg Cdr 1/7/90. Retd SUP 14/5/94.
TAYLOR D. J. J. Born 4/1/27. Commd 13/9/50. Flt Lt 13/3/55. Retd GD 4/1/85.
TAYLOR D. J. W. Born 5/2/40. Commd 13/12/60. Flt Lt 13/6/63. Retd GD 21/8/64.
TAYLOR D. L., BSc MRAeS ACGI. Born 7/11/17. Commd 8/7/42. Sqn Ldr 1/1/57. Retd ENG 7/11/69.
TAYLOR D. L. Born 24/8/45. Commd 2/4/65. Flt Lt 8/4/72. Retd SUP 24/8/83.
TAYLOR D. M. Born 31/1/27. Commd 7/10/48. Sqn Ldr 1/7/60. Retd GD 11/2/76.
TAYLOR D. Mc. Born 18/12/40. Commd 29/6/72. Flt Lt 29/6/74. Retd ENG 3/11/77.
TAYLOR D. P., BSc. Born 26/3/66. Commd 16/9/84. Flt Lt 15/1/90. Retd GD 15/7/99.
TAYLOR D. W. Born 10/7/30. Commd 28/6/66. Flt Lt 26/8/72 Retd SUP 29/4/78.
TAYLOR D. W., BSc. Born 26/8/49. Commd 27/2/70. Flt Lt 27/11/74. Retd ENG 26/8/87.
TAYLOR E. A., BA. Born 31/8/29. Commd 26/9/50. Wg Cdr 1/1/68. Retd GD 3/4/80.
TAYLOR E. C., DFC Born 24/10/23. Commd 13/12/44. Sqn Ldr 1/1/73. Retd GD 18/7/78.
TAYLOR E. W., BA DPhysEd. Born 27/6/22. Commd 24/4/47. Sqn Ldr 1/1/60. Retd PE 2/5/63.
TAYLOR F. H. Born 10/11/42. Commd 10/12/75. Sqn Ldr 1/7/87. Retd ENG 10/12/91.
TAYLOR G. Born 29/5/34. Commd 16/7/52. Sqn Ldr 1/1/67. Retd GD 27/11/76.
TAYLOR G. Born 7/11/29. Commd 1/3/57. Flt Lt 1/3/61. Retd GD 26/6/84.
TAYLOR G. C., BSc. Born 21/9/44. Commd 8/9/69. Sqn Ldr 8/3/77. Retd ADMIN 8/9/85.
TAYLOR G. D. Born 24/5/28. Commd 28/6/55. Flt Lt 1/3/61. Retd GD 24/5/83.
TAYLOR G. L. Born 28/6/24. Commd 12/6/52. Flt Lt 1/7/56. Retd PRT 22/4/70.
TAYLOR G. P., CEng MRAeS MIEE. Born 2/3/40. Commd 17/7/62. Sqn Ldr 1/7/72. Retd ENG 2/3/78.
TAYLOR G. S., BSc. Born 16/10/27. Commd 22/12/49. Flt Lt 10/11/52. Retd GD 16/10/65.
TAYLOR G. T. Born 14/3/24. Commd 4/6/47. Flt Lt 25/3/56. Retd GD 31/3/62.
TAYLOR G. T. Born 6/3/43. Commd 15/7/66. Sqn Ldr 1/1/97. Retd GD 30/10/97.
TAYLOR G. W. Born 20/1/33. Commd 4/10/51. Flt Lt 1/11/61. Retd GD 20/12/72.
TAYLOR H. Born 3/9/11. Commd 28/5/41. Flt Lt 1/9/45. Retd ASD 25/11/49.
TAYLOR H. Born 25/12/21. Commd 4/10/45. Flt Lt 4/4/49. Retd GD 10/12/66.
TAYLOR H. Born 1/7/29. Commd 2/5/51. Flt Lt 2/11/55. Retd GD 1/7/67.
TAYLOR H. L., CEng MIMechE. Born 18/9/19. Commd 8/7/42. Wg Cdr 1/1/71. Retd ENG 18/9/77.
TAYLOR H. N. Born 13/2/38. Commd 9/3/62. Flt Lt 1/7/69. Retd GD 20/10/77.
TAYLOR H. W., DFC. Born 27/8/20. Commd 24/10/41. Sqn Ldr 1/1/58. Retd GD 27/8/75.
TAYLOR J. Born 7/5/33. Commd 26/3/52. Flt Lt 1/8/57. Retd GD 8/5/71.
TAYLOR J. Born 5/12/41. Commd 28/2/85. Sqn Ldr 1/7/93. Retd ENG 5/12/96.
TAYLOR J. C. E. Born 10/5/59. Commd 15/3/84. Fg Offr 15/9/86. Retd GD(G) 14/5/89.
TAYLOR J. D., CEng MIMechE. Born 12/3/34. Commd 12/4/65. Sqn Ldr 1/7/71. Retd ENG 2/3/93.
TAYLOR J. J. Born 18/8/22. Commd 29/8/44. Flt Lt 4/10/48. Retd GD 22/9/67.
TAYLOR J. J. T. Born 20/4/51. Commd 16/3/76. Retd GD 31/12/84.
TAYLOR J. K. I. Born 2/4/35. Commd 14/11/71. Sqn Ldr 4/9/83. Retd ADMIN 14/11/87.
TAYLOR J. M. Born 5/7/19. Commd 29/7/39. Flt Lt 3/9/41. Retd GD 24/2/46.
TAYLOR J. M. Born 10/10/29. Commd 4/9/51. Flt Lt 30/1/61. Retd GD 31/7/64.
TAYLOR J. N. H. Born 7/7/54. Commd 2/9/73. Sqn Ldr 1/1/91. Retd ADMIN 1/1/94.
TAYLOR J. V., MBE. Born 13/10/24. Commd 25/12/58. Wg Cdr 1/7/75. Retd GD(G) 28/2/83.
TAYLOR J. W. J. Born 21/3/33. Commd 4/6/52. Sqn Ldr 1/1/64. Retd GD 21/6/92.
TAYLOR K. B. Born 13/10/49. Commd 3/12/70. Sqn Ldr 1/1/83. Retd GD 14/3/97.
TAYLOR L. C. Born 25/6/26. Commd 15/10/53. Flt Lt 15/4/57. Retd GD 30/9/77.
TAYLOR L. E. K., BA. Born 23/2/70. Commd 1/12/96. Fg Offr 1/6/96. Retd SUP 28/3/00.
TAYLOR L. I. A. Born 21/1/28. Commd 27/7/49. Sqn Ldr 1/7/61. Retd GD 30/5/64.
TAYLOR L. W., BSc. Born 6/7/55. Commd 6/3/77. Flt Lt 6/12/78. Retd GD 6/3/89.
TAYLOR M. Born 15/8/58. Commd 15/2/90. Flt Lt 15/2/92. Retd ENG 31/3/94.
TAYLOR M. Born 13/5/30. Commd 5/9/57. Flt Lt 5/3/62. Retd GD 28/3/69.
TAYLOR M. A., BEM. Born 30/7/36. Commd 12/4/73. Sqn Ldr 1/7/84. Retd ENG 30/7/95.
TAYLOR M. B. Born 13/2/60. Commd 23/4/78. Flt Lt 23/10/83. Retd GD 18/4/87.
TAYLOR M. B., BDS. Born 21/6/45. Commd 20/1/74. Wg Cdr 13/2/83. Retd DEL 20/1/90.
TAYLOR M. C. Born 26/6/39. Commd 6/4/62. Sqn Ldr 1/1/75. Retd GD 1/1/78.
TAYLOR M. D. Born 20/4/47. Commd 9/2/66. Flt Lt 18/6/72. Retd GD(G) 1/10/75.
TAYLOR M. F. H. Born 17/7/45. Commd 8/6/84. Sqn Ldr 1/7/97. Retd ADMIN 2/7/99.
TAYLOR M. F. W., BSc. Born 1/6/53. Commd 26/4/72. Flt Lt 15/10/78. Retd GD 1/6/91.
TAYLOR M. H., MSc BSc CEng MIEE. Born 30/9/30. Commd 2/1/62. Wg Cdr 1/1/79. Retd ADMIN 28/8/83.
TAYLOR M. J., BSc. Born 9/4/54. Commd 3/9/72. Sqn Ldr 1/1/91. Retd GD 9/4/98.
TAYLOR M. J. Born 25/10/31. Commd 4/6/52. Sqn Ldr 1/1/67. Retd GD 1/1/70.
TAYLOR M. J. Born 23/8/39. Commd 11/11/71. Sqn Ldr 1/1/85. Retd GD 7/2/90.

TAYLOR M. J. C. Born 2/6/33. Commd 1/12/54. Wg Cdr 1/7/79. Retd GD 2/6/88.
TAYLOR M. S., BSc CEng MRAeS. Born 7/3/49. Commd 27/2/70. Wg Cdr 1/1/87. Retd ENG 14/3/96.
TAYLOR N. H. Born 7/1/34. Commd 10/12/52. Flt Lt 5/5/58. Retd GD(G) 4/9/89.
TAYLOR N. I. Born 20/9/33. Commd 19/10/80. Sqn Ldr 1/7/84. Retd ADMIN 25/1/87.
TAYLOR N. R. Born 3/9/60. Commd 19/7/84. Flt Lt 19/1/89. Retd GD 19/3/00.
TAYLOR N. S. Born 1/11/21. Commd 21/11/44. Flt Lt 21/5/48. Retd GD 29/3/68
TAYLOR O. G., MA CEng FIMgt MIEE. Born 11/5/28 Commd 25/11/48. Wg Cdr 1/7/63. Retd ENG 11/5/65.
TAYLOR P. Born 15/11/46. Commd 15/9/67. Flt Lt 15/3/73. Retd GD 1/5/93.
TAYLOR P., OBE CEng MRAeS. Born 26/8/33. Commd 24/9/64. Wg Cdr 1/7/76. Retd ENG 26/8/83.
TAYLOR P. Born 1/12/47. Commd 21/4/67. Flt Lt 29/7/73. Retd GD(G) 1/12/85.
TAYLOR P. C., OBE BA. Born 6/7/45. Commd 23/9/66. Wg Cdr 1/7/87. Retd SUP 6/1/00.
TAYLOR P. F., BA. Born 9/2/62. Commd 14/10/84. Flt Lt 14/4/87. Retd GD 14/10/00.
TAYLOR P. G. Born 6/6/22. Commd 11/1/43. Flt Lt 15/7/47. Retd SEC 11/6/55.
TAYLOR P. G., MA FIMgt. Born 6/10/35. Commd 12/9/58. Gp Capt 1/7/84. Retd ADMIN 4/4/88.
TAYLOR P. L. Born 25/6/57. Commd 14/7/77. Flt Lt 14/1/83. Retd GD 2/7/87.
TAYLOR P. P. W., CBE AFC. Born 2/1/37. Commd 29/7/58. A Cdre 1/1/84. Retd GD 1/1/87.
TAYLOR P. R. Born 13/10/21. Commd 4/3/43. Sqn Ldr 1/1/54. Retd ENG 10/5/58.
TAYLOR P. T., AFC. Born 28/11/29. Commd 21/4/54. Sqn Ldr 1/1/69. Retd GD 1/7/73.
TAYLOR P. W., MIMgt. Born 27/10/39. Commd 24/4/70. Flt Lt 24/4/77. Retd MED(SEC) 8/1/33. Reinstated
      28/9/83. Sqn Ldr 1/7/85. Retd MED(SEC) 28/9/88.
TAYLOR R. Born 7/2/40. Commd 29/4/58. Sqn Ldr 1/1/76. Retd GD 1/5/94.
TAYLOR R. Born 19/4/52. Commd 4/3/71. Sqn Ldr 1/1/89. Retd GD 1/1/92.
TAYLOR R. B. Born 5/6/30. Commd 27/8/52. Flt Lt 23/1/58. Retd GD 22/5/76.
TAYLOR R. C. Born 4/3/33. Commd 9/4/52. Sqn Ldr 1/7/65. Retd GD 1/6/73.
TAYLOR R. C. Born 1/1/67. Commd 31/7/86. Act Plt Offr 31/7/86. Retd GD 22/3/87.
TAYLOR R. D. G., BSc. Born 25/2/41. Commd 19/6/64. Flt Lt 19/9/65. Retd GD 15/2/96.
TAYLOR R. E. T. Born 25/1/28. Commd 1/7/53. Flt Lt 26/11/58. Retd GD 6/1/69.
TAYLOR R. F. Born 1/10/14. Commd 18/11/43. Sqn Ldr 1/7/58. Retd ENG 1/10/69.
TAYLOR R. G. Born 24/5/44. Commd 20/8/65. Sqn Ldr 1/7/76. Retd GD 24/5/88.
TAYLOR R. H., MRAeS. Born 2/4/21. Commd 19/8/42. Sqn Ldr 1/7/54. Retd ENG 20/12/69.
TAYLOR R. H. W. Born 12/12/25. Commd 16/12/66. Flt Lt 16/12/69. Retd GD 14/1/76.
TAYLOR Rev R. H., BA. Born 10/7/27. Commd 1/6/61. Retd 10/4/83 Wg Cdr.
TAYLOR R. I., BSc. Born 5/6/51. Commd 8/9/74. Sqn Ldr 1/7/88. Retd ENG 31/1/95.
TAYLOR R. J. M. Born 17/11/44. Commd 26/10/62. Sqn Ldr 1/1/78. Retd OPS SPT 4/2/99.
TAYLOR R. K., MIMgt. Born 7/10/30. Commd 17/1/52. Sqn Ldr 1/7/67. Retd GD 28/11/75.
TAYLOR R. M., BSc. Born 30/12/49. Commd 3/1/71. Flt Lt 15/10/72. Retd GD 30/12/87.
TAYLOR R. P., BSc(Eng) CEng MIMechE MIMgt. Born 17/3/36. Commd 12/3/60. Wg Cdr 1/7/79. Retd ENG 4/2/89.
TAYLOR R. R., OBE MBE DL. Born 14/6/32. Commd 28/6/51. Sqn Ldr 1/7/66. Retd GD 30/6/73.
TAYLOR R. S. Born 14/6/47. Commd 6/5/66. Flt Lt 4/5/72. Retd GD 14/6/85.
TAYLOR R. W., BSc. Born 26/3/58. Commd 28/9/80. Sqn Ldr 1/1/93. Retd GD 28/9/96.
TAYLOR S. Born 5/7/22. Commd 20/10/55. Flt Lt 22/2/59. Retd ENG 2/6/73.
TAYLOR S. Born 20/1/18. Commd 21/10/54. Sqn Ldr 5/3/65. Retd MED(T) 8/7/68.
TAYLOR S. C., CBE Born 22/4/20. Commd 21/9/44. Gp Capt 1/7/69. Retd ENG 22/4/75.
TAYLOR S. C., BSc BDS MGDSRCS(Eng). Born 23/12/52. Commd 25/9/71. Sqn Ldr 22/5/87. Retd DEL 23/3/92.
TAYLOR S. D., MCIPD. Born 17/9/30. Commd 4/1/54. Wg Cdr 1/1/83. Retd GD 17/9/85.
TAYLOR S. E. Born 6/2/17. Commd 1/1/51. Flt Lt 17/5/56. Retd CAT 17/11/58.
TAYLOR S. J. Born 30/10/64. Commd 16/6/88. Fg Offr 12/10/88. Retd ADMIN 30/11/91.
TAYLOR S. L. Born 25/2/21. Commd 21/11/42. Flt Lt 21/11/47. Retd SEC 29/7/60.
TAYLOR S. McM., BSc. Born 3/8/37. Commd 23/9/59. Wg Cdr 1/1/85. Retd GD 6/12/91.
TAYLOR T. Born 2/1/19. Commd 5/8/42. Sqn Ldr 1/1/53. Retd ENG 2/1/74.
TAYLOR T. C. Born 27/12/32. Commd 4/10/51. Sqn Ldr 1/1/66. Retd GD 27/12/70.
TAYLOR T. D. Born 18/4/44. Commd 22/5/64. Flt Lt 12/11/69. Retd GD 18/4/82.
TAYLOR T. H. Born 6/7/42. Commd 19/6/64. Flt Lt 1/7/69. Retd GD 1/8/94.
TAYLOR T. H. Born 1/11/20. Commd 9/8/41. Wg Cdr 1/1/68. Retd GD 1/11/75.
TAYLOR The Rev T. R. B., MA. Born 23/1/23. Commd 18/8/49. Retd 18/8/65 Wg Cdr.
TAYLOR V. W. C., DFC. Born 26/7/19. Commd 1/5/42. Flt Lt 1/11/46. Retd SEC 12/12/53 rtg Sqn Ldr.
TAYLOR W. Born 16/5/20. Commd 25/3/43. Flt Lt 25/9/46. Retd ENG 30/7/53.
TAYLOR W. C., OBE CEng MRAeS. Born 3/6/20. Commd 19/8/42. A Cdre 1/1/72. Retd ENG 3/6/75.
TAYLOR W. F. Born 20/10/35. Commd 7/3/61. Flt Lt 1/4/66. Retd GD 29/1/75.
TAYLOR W. G. Born 30/5/39. Commd 21/4/77. Flt Lt 21/4/80. Retd GD(G) 30/5/94.
TAYLOR W. H., DUS CEng MIEE. Born 8/8/31. Commd 2/9/53. Sqn Ldr 1/7/65. Retd ENG 2/9/69.
TAYLOR W. J., OBE MRAeS. Born 31/1/51. Commd 22/11/73. Gp Capt 1/7/93. Retd ENG 6/4/01.
TAYLOR W. S., MSc CEng. Born 24/1/53. Commd 13/2/77. Sqn Ldr 1/7/86. Retd ENG 13/2/96.
TAYLOR W. W. Born 24/1/31. Commd 29/4/71. Flt Lt 29/4/76. Retd ENG 24/1/92.
TEAGER J. E. W., OBE AFC. Born 12/8/21. Commd 28/9/43. Gp Capt 1/7/70. Retd GD 16/7/75.
TEAGER J. F. N. Born 21/3/58. Commd 21/4/77. Wg Cdr 1/7/94. Retd GD 1/1/98.

TEALE C., BSc. Born 26/6/60. Commd 4/9/78. Flt Lt 15/10/82. Retd GD 7/6/89.
TEAR R. C., MBE BSc(Eng) CEng MIMechE MRAeS. Born 11/6/30. Commd 6/5/53. Gp Capt 1/7/79. Retd ENG 2/4/85.
TEASDALE R. J., BDS. Born 21/6/38. Commd 13/7/66. Wg Cdr 11/1/78. Retd DEL 24/6/96.
TEATHER J. B. Born 27/10/44. Commd 31/1/64. Flt Lt 12/11/69. Retd GD 27/10/83.
TEBB B. A. Born 27/5/45. Commd 29/11/63. Sqn Ldr 1/7/79. Retd GD 27/5/83.
TEBBIT D. F. J. Born 23/7/14. Commd 14/8/43. Sqn Ldr 1/7/55. Retd GD(G) 23/4/65 rtg Wg Cdr.
TEBBOTH J. G. Born 25/4/31. Commd 29/7/65. Flt Lt 11/4/70. Retd MED(T) 4/9/75.
TEBBS C. R. Born 25/6/45. Commd 4/5/72. Sqn Ldr 1/7/81. Retd ADMIN 1/12/88.
TEBBS J. W., BA. Born 26/1/35. Commd 2/1/62. Wg Cdr 1/7/84. Retd ADMIN 3/8/87.
TEBBS N. A. Born 22/6/38. Commd 7/12/61. Flt Lt 1/4/66. Retd GD 22/6/76.
TEBBUTT K., AFC. Born 7/8/23. Commd 12/11/43. Sqn Ldr 1/1/55. Retd GD 16/9/61.
TEDDER C. J. Born 4/3/24. Commd 16/9/44. Sqn Ldr 1/7/55. Retd GD 4/3/73.
TEHAN B. M. Born 6/2/33. Commd 18/6/52. Sqn Ldr 1/1/66. Retd GD 27/10/73.
TELFER-SMITH S. R., MBA BSc DIC. Born 10/8/60. Commd 29/9/85. Sqn Ldr 1/1/92. Retd ADMIN 14/3/96.
TELFORD A. M. Born 12/8/58. Commd 8/9/77. Flt Lt 8/3/84. Retd SY 12/8/96.
TELFORD C. M. Born 29/12/24. Commd 29/12/49. Flt Lt 29/6/53. Retd GD 29/12/62.
TELFORD F. G. Born 14/12/40. Commd 15/9/67. Flt Lt 6/10/71. Retd GD(G) 14/12/78.
TELFORD J. K. Born 11/1/29. Commd 27/1/67. Flt Lt 27/1/72. Retd SEC 12/1/74.
TELFORD M. Born 9/2/30. Commd 4/7/64. Sqn Ldr 5/10/68. Retd EDN 31/8/72.
TELFORD M. A., AFC. Born 20/1/36. Commd 9/6/54. Flt Lt 28/7/65. Retd GD 3/10/78.
TELLIS R. C. L. Born 27/6/40. Commd 23/7/67. Flt Lt 23/9/72. Retd GD 27/6/95.
TEMPERO K. Born 4/9/23. Commd 28/1/45. Sqn Ldr 1/7/61. Retd GD(G) 31/3/77.
TEMPERTON A. Born 21/2/27. Commd 2/5/51. Flt Lt 2/11/55. Retd GD 6/4/76.
TEMPLE A. I., MSc BA. Born 24/7/48. Commd 12/3/72. Wg Cdr 1/7/91. Retd SUP 14/3/97.
TEMPLE G. F. Born 7/1/22. Commd 20/4/50. Flt Lt 20/4/56. Retd GD(G) 7/9/62.
TEMPLE T. C. Born 22/12/33. Commd 15/6/53. Sqn Ldr 1/1/78. Retd PI 2/12/84.
TEMPLE-SMITH M. N. Born 10/8/57. Commd 24/7/81. Flt Lt 24/1/87. Retd GD 23/3/97.
TEMPLEMAN-ROOKE B. A., DSO DFC* AFC. Born 13/6/21. Commd 15/8/43. Sqn Ldr 1/1/54. Retd GD 13/6/71 rtg Wg Cdr.
TEMPLETON J. B. Born 19/11/36. Commd 21/10/64. Flt Lt 21/10/64. Retd GD 25/5/67.
TEMPLETON R. J. Born 14/5/16. Commd 8/1/47. Sqn Ldr 1/1/60. Retd CAT 14/5/66.
TEMPLETON W. V., BSc CEng MRAeS MIEE. Born 24/1/40. Commd 30/9/59. Sqn Ldr 1/1/76. Retd ENG 2/4/91.
TEMPLING B. C. Born 10/2/18. Commd 13/12/45. Flt Lt 15/12/49. Retd ENG 10/12/63.
TENISON-COLLINS J. A., BSc. Born 24/7/58. Commd 11/9/77. Flt Lt 15/4/82. Retd GD 24/7/96.
TENNANT E. A., DFC. Born 25/2/22. Commd 3/12/42. Flt Lt 3/6/46. Retd GD 16/6/53 rtg Sqn Ldr.
TERNOUTH M. L. Born 25/10/49. Commd 4/7/69. Flt Lt 4/1/75. Retd GD 25/10/87. Re-entered 1/3/89. Sqn Ldr 1/7/96. Retd GD 4/3/01.
TERRETT A. L. Born 24/10/39. Commd 19/12/61. Gp Capt 1/7/92. Retd GD 24/10/94.
TERRETT P. E., OBE LLB. Born 8/2/34. Commd 30/1/58. Gp Capt 1/1/81. Retd ADMIN 18/7/88.
TERRY Sir Colin., KBE CB BSc(Eng) CEng FRAeS FRSA FILT FCGI. Born 8/8/43. Commd 30/9/62. AM 11/7/97. Retd ENG 7/8/99.
TERRY C. J. Born 21/10/50. Commd 4/3/71. Flt Lt 4/9/76. Retd GD 1/3/94.
TERRY Sir Peter., GCB AFC. Born 18/10/26. Commd 17/7/46. ACM 1/3/81. Retd GD 18/10/84.
TERRY R. B., BSc CEng MRAeS. Born 16/8/29. Commd 15/11/51. Sqn Ldr 1/7/62. Retd ENG 16/8/67.
TETLEY J. F. H. Born 5/2/32. Commd 14/4/53. AVM 1/7/84. Retd GD 3/4/87.
TETLEY W. Born 17/11/12. Commd 6/6/44. Fg Offr 20/9/51. Retd CAT 3/12/64.
TETLOW H. H. Born 22/3/23. Commd 27/8/59. Flt Lt 27/8/65. Retd ENG 10/12/74.
TETLOW P. E. Born 9/8/24. Commd 8/6/61. Flt Lt 30/3/64. Retd GD(G) 5/7/68.
TETTMAR R. E., MB BS MRCPath MRCS LRCP DPath. Born 28/6/47. Commd 10/11/69. Sqn Ldr 26/7/78. Retd MED 10/11/85.
TEW B. Born 13/12/33. Commd 20/1/56. Sqn Ldr 1/1/78. Retd GD(G) 1/12/85.
TEW D. H. Born 22/4/24. Commd 19/7/56. Sqn Ldr 1/7/69. Retd GD 22/4/82.
TEW M. R. N., BSc. Born 27/9/47. Commd 11/5/71. Sqn Ldr 1/7/82. Retd GD 21/6/99.
TEW P. A. Born 13/2/47. Commd 28/2/69. Flt Lt 8/3/72. Retd GD 13/2/85.
THACKER J., BSc. Born 8/9/53. Commd 17/7/72. Sqn Ldr 1/7/86. Retd ADMIN 17/7/93.
THACKER J. H. Born 6/3/20. Commd 24/10/45. Sqn Ldr 1/7/56. Retd RGT 28/1/61.
THACKER R. Born 16/11/32. Commd 13/9/51. Flt Lt 30/1/57. Retd GD 30/1/74.
THACKRAY H. W. Born 16/9/15. Commd 10/3/44. Sqn Ldr 1/1/57. Retd SEC 16/9/64.
THAIN G. T., DFC. Born 12/7/18. Commd 3/11/40. Wg Cdr 1/1/55. Retd GD 26/8/65.
THAIN J. W., MRAeS. Born 29/6/19. Commd 27/4/44. Flt Lt 11/5/48. Retd ENG 12/1/63.
THAIN M. C. Born 8/1/44. Commd 30/5/69. Flt Lt 15/11/71. Retd GD 8/1/83. Reinstated 3/7/85. Flt Lt 9/5/74. Retd GD 22/10/94.
THATCHER M. Born 25/6/44. Commd 7/7/67. Sqn Ldr 1/1/84. Retd GD 25/6/94.
THATCHER M. F., AFM. Born 23/5/37. Commd 3/10/69. Flt Lt 4/5/72. Retd GD 14/1/75.
THAYER F. E., MBE MIMgt. Born 4/4/21. Commd 5/2/43. Sqn Ldr 1/1/66. Retd GD(G) 4/4/74.

THEAKSON A. E. Born 16/5/34. Commd 6/6/64. Flt Lt 6/6/66. Retd GD 6/6/72.
THEED A. J. M. Born 20/7/40. Commd 25/8/60. Flt Lt 27/7/67. Retd RGT 20/7/78.
THEOBALD D. A. Born 19/11/49. Commd 1/4/71. Flt Lt 1/10/76. Retd GD 30/1/81.
THEOBALD R. M. Born 4/10/33. Commd 29/10/64. Sqn Ldr 1/7/79. Retd ENG 4/10/89.
THILTHORPE R. Born 18/11/43. Commd 8/12/61. Sqn Ldr 1/1/77. Retd GD 15/10/87.
THIRD D., MSc BSc CEng MIEE. Born 23/6/41. Commd 1/8/66. Sqn Ldr 6/10/71. Retd ADMIN 1/8/82.
THIRKETTLE A., BSc FIMgt. Born 22/11/31. Commd 24/9/52. Gp Capt 1/1/73. Retd ENG 25/9/76.
THIRLE J., AFC. Born 8/1/32. Commd 12/9/56. Sqn Ldr 1/1/67. Retd PE 12/9/72.
THIRLWALL C., OBE AFC BA. Born 11/7/44. Commd 14/8/64. Gp Capt 1/7/94. Retd GD 11/7/99.
THIRLWELL J. D., OBE DFC. Born 31/10/19. Commd 7/3/40. Gp Capt 1/1/61. Retd GD 20/7/68.
THIRNBECK J. R. Born 16/9/29. Commd 11/4/51. Sqn Ldr 1/7/64. Retd SEC 16/9/67.
THISTLETHWAITE K. Born 24/9/55. Commd 15/3/84. Wg Cdr 1/7/96. Retd SUP 24/9/99.
THOLEN P. J. Born 5/3/61. Commd 24/4/80. Flt Lt 24/10/85. Retd GD 9/1/92.
THOM M. I., MA CEng MRAeS MIEE. Born 24/5/35. Commd 25/9/54. Gp Capt 1/1/76. Retd ENG 1/6/78.
THOMAS A. Born 9/3/44. Commd 25/9/80. Sqn Ldr 1/7/94. Retd SUP 7/1/98.
THOMAS A. C., BA DPhysEd. Born 10/6/36. Commd 10/9/63. Sqn Ldr 17/10/71. Retd EDN 10/9/79.
THOMAS A. F. Born 7/4/10. Commd 30/8/41. Flt Lt 26/5/55. Retd CAT 24/5/62.
THOMAS A. L. Born 16/12/30. Commd 1/4/53. Flt Lt 5/11/56. Retd GD 16/12/68.
THOMAS A. R. Born 26/2/45. Commd 14/6/63. Sqn Ldr 1/1/85. Retd GD 22/12/95.
THOMAS A. T. Born 16/4/35. Commd 14/8/70. Flt Lt 14/8/72. Retd SY 1/10/76.
THOMAS A. V. Born 25/12/31. Commd 25/9/56. Flt Lt 25/3/62. Retd GD 25/12/89.
THOMAS A. W. G. Born 27/5/22. Commd 5/8/44. Flt Lt 22/7/48. Retd GD 31/3/74.
THOMAS B. Born 7/1/26. Commd 23/2/50. Flt Lt 27/5/54. Retd GD(G) 7/1/69.
THOMAS B. Born 15/6/63. Commd 8/11/90. Flt Lt 8/11/92. Retd ADMIN 14/3/97.
THOMAS B. A. Born 4/12/31. Commd 2/5/59. Flt Lt 2/11/64. Retd GD 28/11/69.
THOMAS C. Born 17/6/23. Commd 18/10/51. Sqn Ldr 1/7/74. Retd GD 17/6/83.
THOMAS C. B. Born 24/12/47. Commd 13/9/70. Flt Lt 13/3/76. Retd GD 15/7/76.
THOMAS C. P., BSc Born 9/9/33. Commd 10/2/59. Flt Lt 15/8/62. Retd GD 7/11/74.
THOMAS C. S., BA MIMgt. Born 16/11/42. Commd 14/9/64. Gp Capt 1/7/92. Retd GD 10/2/96.
THOMAS D. Born 10/5/22. Commd 19/6/43. Flt Lt 14/11/48. Retd GD 1/5/61.
THOMAS D. A., CEng MRAeS MIMgt. Born 10/6/18. Commd 2/6/49. Sqn Ldr 1/1/59. Retd ENG 11/6/68.
THOMAS D. A. Born 21/2/43. Commd 17/7/64. Flt Lt 4/5/72. Retd GD 21/2/81.
THOMAS D. B., BSc. Born 22/10/26. Commd 29/6/49. Wg Cdr 1/1/70. Retd EDN 20/9/73.
THOMAS D. C. Born 26/12/37. Commd 7/1/58. Sqn Ldr 1/7/72. Retd GD 26/12/95.
THOMAS D. D. Born 15/3/46. Commd 29/3/68. Flt Lt 29/9/73. Retd GD 15/3/87.
THOMAS D. H., MSc. Born 8/1/44. Commd 30/8/66. Sqn Ldr 1/7/78. Retd GD 30/8/88.
THOMAS D. J. Born 29/6/37. Commd 27/8/64. Flt Lt 27/8/66. Retd GD 25/6/75.
THOMAS D. L., BSc. Born 31/3/40. Commd 14/9/65. Sqn Ldr 14/3/75. Retd EDN 14/9/81.
THOMAS D. L. J. Born 4/7/45. Commd 29/11/63. Flt Lt 29/5/69. Retd GD 1/11/79.
THOMAS D. M. Born 1/8/20. Commd 23/6/60. Flt Lt 23/6/66. Retd PRT 16/1/76.
THOMAS D. V. H., OBE. Born 13/5/09. Commd 1/9/45. Sqn Ldr 1/1/61. Retd GD(G) 13/5/64.
THOMAS E. B. Born 27/3/31. Commd 26/12/51. Sqn Ldr 1/1/67. Retd GD 19/12/75.
THOMAS E. B. Born 2/10/23. Commd 1/5/44. Flt Lt 1/5/46. Retd GD(G) 9/8/72.
THOMAS E. J. M., DPhysEd. Born 13/2/34. Commd 25/9/62. Sqn Ldr 1/7/74. Retd ADMIN 13/2/89.
THOMAS E. L. Born 28/2/36. Commd 25/6/66. Sqn Ldr 1/7/81. Retd GD 31/7/87.
THOMAS F. A., DFC AFC FIMgt. Born 30/10/21. Commd 10/11/42. Wg Cdr 1/1/63. Retd GD 1/10/73 rtg Gp Capt.
THOMAS F. B. Born 8/2/36. Commd 3/8/61. Flt Lt 1/4/66. Retd ADMIN 30/4/76.
THOMAS F. D. Born 17/8/22. Commd 21/1/53. Flt Lt 21/7/56. Retd GD 1/7/73.
THOMAS F. M. Born 10/10/15. Commd 15/3/35. Wg Cdr 1/7/47. Retd GD 29/12/58.
THOMAS F. W. Born 4/8/13. Commd 21/10/35. Flt Lt 1/6/45. Retd SEC 1/5/48 rtg Sqn Ldr.
THOMAS G. Born 28/4/54. Commd 15/2/73. Sqn Ldr 1/1/88. Retd GD 14/12/93.
THOMAS G., BSc. Born 5/4/40. Commd 14/9/64. Flt Lt 14/6/66. Retd GD 14/9/80.
THOMAS G. J. R. Born 10/2/50. Commd 29/8/72. Flt Lt 29/8/76. Retd ADMIN 29/8/88.
THOMAS H. Born 2/1/35. Commd 1/4/53. Flt Lt 21/10/59. Retd GD 2/1/90.
THOMAS H., AFC. Born 30/12/15. Commd 29/8/42. Sqn Ldr 1/1/54. Retd GD(G) 30/12/65.
THOMAS H. A. Born 21/5/42. Commd 12/7/63. Flt Lt 12/1/69. Retd GD 2/4/93.
THOMAS H. S. Born 3/10/19. Commd 6/6/57. Sqn Ldr 1/7/69. Retd ENG 5/4/72.
THOMAS I. Born 16/9/36. Commd 8/4/65. Fg Offr 8/4/65. Retd RGT 7/1/70.
THOMAS I. Born 17/12/41. Commd 9/2/62. Sqn Ldr 1/1/77. Retd GD 1/1/80.
THOMAS I. E. Born 8/6/25. Commd 18/10/51. Flt Lt 18/4/55. Retd GD 31/7/64.
THOMAS I. J. Born 15/3/33. Commd 3/1/61. Wg Cdr 1/1/78. Retd ADMIN 29/9/85.
THOMAS The Rev I. M., MA. Born 3/1/50. Commd 2/1/77. Retd 3/1/01. Wg Cdr.
THOMAS J., MBE. Born 10/3/31. Commd 9/4/52. Sqn Ldr 1/7/74. Retd GD 10/3/93.
THOMAS J. Born 13/4/17. Commd 17/10/57. Flt Lt 1/4/63. Retd ENG 15/7/67.
THOMAS J. A. Born 15/6/38. Commd 30/7/59. Flt Lt 30/1/63. Retd GD 24/4/89.
THOMAS J. B. P. Born 28/3/11. Commd 3/3/33. Wg Cdr 1/7/47. Retd GD 21/10/49 rtg Gp Capt.

THOMAS J. E., MA. Born 10/2/23. Commd 8/4/53. Sqn Ldr 8/10/60. Retd EDN 21/7/67.
THOMAS J. F., BA. Born 29/12/43. Commd 21/4/67. Wg Cdr 1/1/86. Retd ADMIN 3/1/89.
THOMAS J. M., MEng BSc. Born 15/9/45. Commd 1/9/71. Flt Lt 1/8/73. Retd ENG 26/10/79.
THOMAS J. V., BSc. Born 4/6/47. Commd 2/7/72. Flt Lt 2/10/73. Retd GD 2/7/88.
THOMAS K. D., BSc. Born 26/7/49. Commd 23/9/68. Sqn Ldr 1/7/95. Retd GD 31/8/99.
THOMAS K. I., MBE. Born 10/6/14. Commd 14/1/42. Sqn Ldr 1/7/53. Retd ENG 10/6/63.
THOMAS M. Born 4/9/18. Commd 24/3/44. Flt Lt 4/1/51. Retd SEC 23/10/65.
THOMAS M. Born 24/10/42. Commd 3/8/62. Flt Lt 1/7/69. Retd GD 31/1/76.
THOMAS M. Born 4/9/18. Commd 3/6/42. Flt Offr 3/12/46. Retd SEC 21/3/61.
THOMAS M. E. Born 18/1/43. Commd 13/1/67. Flt Lt 13/7/72. Retd GD 28/6/75. Re-instated 5/6/78. Retd 3/9/85.
THOMAS M. G. Born 13/5/34. Commd 5/4/55. Sqn Ldr 1/1/72. Retd GD 14/5/88.
THOMAS M. K., MSc BDS MGDSRCS(Eng). Born 17/4/54. Commd 10/9/78. Wg Cdr 12/1/91. Retd DEL 10/12/95.
THOMAS M. O., MEd MSc Dip Soton. Born 1/11/34. Commd 7/9/56. Sqn Ldr 1/5/65. Retd ADMIN 4/5/83.
THOMAS M. P., BSc CEng MRAeS. Born 23/8/40. Commd 18/5/65. Sqn Ldr 1/7/75. Retd ENG 18/5/82.
THOMAS N. C., CEng MIEE MRAeSae. Born 29/4/41. Commd 17/7/62. Sqn Ldr 1/7/71. Retd ENG 29/4/79.
THOMAS N. N., MA CEng Dip El MIEE. Born 28/9/31. Commd 26/9/53. Wg Cdr 1/1/75. Retd ENG 28/9/86.
THOMAS O. G., AFC. Born 17/3/20. Commd 1/12/44. Flt Lt 1/6/48. Retd GD(G) 26/8/67.
THOMAS P., AFC. Born 21/2/26. Commd 17/12/45. Sqn Ldr 1/1/63. Retd GD 1/1/66.
THOMAS P. E. H., AFC. Born 13/12/19. Commd 3/11/40. Wg Cdr 1/7/58. Retd GD 6/2/65.
THOMAS P. H. Born 25/2/29. Commd 14/1/53. Fg Offr 28/4/55. Retd GD 5/6/59.
THOMAS P. J., MBE. Born 4/3/36. Commd 3/12/59. Sqn Ldr 1/7/70. Retd GD 29/11/86.
THOMAS P. M., BA. Born 30/7/44. Commd 28/3/67. Flt Lt 28/3/69. Retd GD 31/3/93.
THOMAS P. M. H. Born 21/8/32. Commd 10/12/52. Flt Lt 18/10/60. Retd GD 9/4/75.
THOMAS P. W., BSc. Born 5/8/57. Commd 12/8/79. Flt Lt 12/11/79. Retd GD 28/1/88.
THOMAS R. D. Born 22/2/35. Commd 22/7/66. Flt Lt 22/7/71. Retd ENG 1/12/73.
THOMAS R. G., MBE CEng MRAeS MIMgt. Born 26/8/19. Commd 5/10/50. Wg Cdr 1/1/68. Retd ENG 1/5/75.
THOMAS R. H., DFC. Born 5/7/20. Commd 17/1/45. Flt Lt 14/10/60. Retd GD(G) 1/5/75 rtg Sqn Ldr.
THOMAS R. J. M. Born 27/5/47. Commd 21/1/66. Sqn Ldr 1/7/93. Retd GD 27/5/98.
THOMAS R. L., MRAeS. Born 31/3/37. Commd 1/4/58. Sqn Ldr 1/1/69. Retd GD 31/3/75.
THOMAS R. M., OBE AFC FRAeS. Born 3/5/49. Commd 27/2/70. Gp Capt 1/7/95. Retd GD 1/8/99.
THOMAS R. M. Born 19/6/40. Commd 17/7/64. Flt Lt 17/1/70. Retd GD 1/4/80.
THOMAS R. S., BTech. Born 6/5/49. Commd 2/8/71. Sqn Ldr 1/7/85. Retd GD 1/7/88.
THOMAS R. W. Born 10/7/23. Commd 15/6/61. Flt Lt 15/6/64. Retd GD 10/7/83.
THOMAS S. E., MBE. Born 20/6/53. Commd 19/7/84. Sqn Ldr 1/1/91. Retd GD 1/8/00.
THOMAS S. J., AFC*. Born 11/4/20. Commd 2/1/42. Flt Lt 23/8/47. Retd GD 31/3/62 rtg Sqn Ldr.
THOMAS T. Born 17/12/17. Commd 3/2/44. Sqn Ldr 1/7/55. Retd ENG 1/4/76.
THOMAS T. J., MBE Born 30/4/23. Commd 20/8/44. Wg Cdr 1/7/71. Retd ENG 30/4/78.
THOMAS The Rev T. J. S., BA. Born 17/12/21. Commd 8/10/51. Retd 22/12/76 Gp Capt.
THOMAS T. P. Born 5/12/14. Commd 29/9/41. Flt Lt 18/7/48. Retd GD(G) 5/12/64.
THOMAS V., MB BCh MRCGP DRCOG DAvMed AFOM. Born 18/5/45. Commd 22/1/68. Wg Cdr 16/1/87. Retd MED 18/5/95.
THOMAS W., BEM. Born 21/3/30. Commd 27/8/64. Sqn Ldr 1/7/80. Retd ENG 21/3/90.
THOMAS The Rev W. A., BA. Born 8/11/11. Commd 4/11/41. Retd 18/11/66 Gp Capt.
THOMAS W. E., OBE AFC. Born 15/6/21. Commd 26/1/41. Wg Cdr 1/7/60. Retd GD 1/5/67.
THOMAS W. E. Born 16/5/21. Commd 3/7/42. Flt Lt 3/1/46. Retd PI 16/5/76.
THOMAS W. E. W., MIMgt. Born 6/2/25. Commd 31/7/58. Sqn Ldr 1/1/71. Retd SEC 1/8/79.
THOMAS W. J., BSc. Born 22/11/18. Commd 8/11/59. Sqn Ldr 8/3/61. Retd EDN 6/9/67.
THOMAS W. J. Born 16/3/11. Commd 16/3/44. Flt Lt 16/9/47. Retd ENG 19/12/48. Re-employed 5/1/53 to 5/1/58.
THOMAS W. K. Born 17/2/17. Commd 12/9/42. Sqn Ldr 1/7/70. Retd SEC 30/6/73.
THOMPSON A. Born 27/4/23. Commd 4/10/51. Sqn Ldr 1/1/62. Retd ENG 1/1/65.
THOMPSON A., BSc CEng MIEE. Born 24/9/47. Commd 2/9/73. Sqn Ldr 1/7/81. Retd ENG 2/9/89.
THOMPSON A., BSc. Born 7/2/49. Commd 13/9/71. Wg Cdr 1/1/93. Retd GD 7/2/99.
THOMPSON A. B., CEng MRAeS. Born 5/12/25. Commd 6/3/52. Gp Capt 1/7/72. Retd ENG 9/12/75.
THOMPSON A. C., BA. Born 13/2/61. Commd 11/9/83. Flt Lt 11/3/86. Retd ADMIN 4/7/87.
THOMPSON A. I., MIMgt Born 12/6/23. Commd 6/10/44. Wg Cdr 1/7/72. Retd GD 12/6/78.
THOMPSON A. J. Born 25/7/29. Commd 20/3/52. Flt Lt 27/9/57. Retd GD 25/7/72 rtg Sqn Ldr.
THOMPSON A. L. C. Born 22/5/26. Commd 21/5/46. Gp Capt 1/1/77. Retd PRT 1/3/80.
THOMPSON A. R., MBE MPhil BA FIMgt MCIPD. Born 6/1/46. Commd 15/4/66. Gp Capt 1/1/89. Retd ADMIN 10/5/94.
THOMPSON B. Born 18/8/29. Commd 21/5/52. Flt Lt 16/10/57. Retd GD 16/10/67.
THOMPSON B. A. W. Born 4/12/44. Commd 27/5/71. Flt Lt 18/9/77. Retd SUP 9/11/86.
THOMPSON B. D. Born 25/5/32. Commd 11/4/54. Sqn Ldr 1/7/77. Retd GD(G) 1/9/82.
THOMPSON C. F. P. Born 28/9/25. Commd 13/6/46. Sqn Ldr 1/1/59. Retd GD 28/6/68.
THOMPSON C. J. Born 20/2/45. Commd 5/2/65. Flt Lt 5/8/70. Retd GD 21/2/76.
THOMPSON C. R. Born 4/10/37. Commd 22/5/70. Flt Lt 22/5/72. Retd SUP 22/11/75.
THOMPSON C. V., MS BSc CEng. Born 27/5/44. Commd 15/7/65. A Cdre 1/7/91. Retd ENG 27/9/96.

THOMPSON D., BEM. Born 16/7/29. Commd 24/2/67. Flt Lt 24/2/72. Retd PRT 1/4/73.
THOMPSON D. W. Born 4/6/37. Commd 31/3/64. Sqn Ldr 1/1/74. Retd SUP 4/5/83.
THOMPSON G., BA. Born 20/8/29. Commd 25/8/54. Sqn Ldr 1/1/65. Retd SUP 6/11/65.
THOMPSON G. A. Born 22/8/47. Commd 21/1/66. Sqn Ldr 1/1/79. Retd GD 22/8/85.
THOMPSON G. C. Born 6/11/41. Commd 22/2/63. Flt Lt 22/8/68. Retd GD 6/11/96.
THOMPSON H., MIMgt. Born 30/11/48. Commd 31/10/74. Sqn Ldr 1/1/85. Retd PRT 1/10/89.
THOMPSON J. Born 6/8/14. Commd 30/1/47. Fg Offr 30/1/49. Retd SUP 1/9/52.
THOMPSON J. Born 22/4/30. Commd 5/7/53. Flt Lt 7/4/55. Retd GD 28/2/69.
THOMPSON J. A. Born 5/4/49. Commd 11/6/81. Flt Lt 11/6/83. Retd SUP 11/6/89.
THOMPSON J. E., MBE. Born 11/5/16. Commd 17/4/40. Flt Lt 29/4/48. Retd SEC 7/12/49 rtg Sqn Ldr.
THOMPSON J. E. Born 3/8/34. Commd 26/5/67. Sqn Ldr 1/7/81. Retd ENG 1/8/90.
THOMPSON J. W. C. Born 18/3/39. Commd 2/5/69. Fg Offr 2/11/71. Retd ENG 1/7/75.
THOMPSON K. S. Born 28/10/62. Commd 14/1/82. Sqn Ldr 1/1/96. Retd OPS SPT 28/10/00.
THOMPSON L. D. Born 9/1/61. Commd 23/9/82. Flt Lt 23/3/89. Retd SY 1/2/93.
THOMPSON M. O. Born 11/5/21. Commd 13/6/46. Flt Lt 13/6/52. Retd RGT 11/9/64.
THOMPSON N. J., MA BA. Born 26/1/48. Commd 30/3/80. Flt Lt 30/3/81. Retd ADMIN 30/3/96.
THOMPSON P. A. Born 6/1/43. Commd 9/10/64. Flt Lt 6/7/68. Retd GD 21/9/74.
THOMPSON P. A. S., OBE DFC. Born 18/11/22. Commd 8/11/41. Wg Cdr 1/1/60. Retd GD 18/11/69.
THOMPSON P. D., DFC AE MIMgt. Born 7/9/20. Commd 24/8/40. Wg Cdr 1/7/56. Retd GD 7/9/75 rtg Gp Capt.
THOMPSON P. D. Born 3/3/43. Commd 17/12/65. Flt Lt 17/6/68. Retd GD 3/9/70.
THOMPSON P. F., DFC. Born 3/3/21. Commd 6/3/44. Flt Lt 6/4/97. Retd GD 3/3/64.
THOMPSON P. J. Born 24/10/31. Commd 26/12/51. Sqn Ldr 1/1/70. Retd GD 1/2/85.
THOMPSON P. R. Born 24/6/63. Commd 9/12/84. Flt Lt 14/3/96. Retd GD(G) 14/3/96.
THOMPSON R. R. Born 25/12/41. Commd 23/12/60. Flt Lt 23/6/66. Retd GD 25/12/79.
THOMPSON R. G. Born 29/8/29. Commd 10/1/50. Flt Lt 11/11/54. Retd GD 29/8/67.
THOMPSON R. J., DFC. Born 18/1/25. Commd 17/11/44. Flt Lt 17/5/48. Retd GD 17/1/63.
THOMPSON R. J. Born 19/4/35. Commd 7/5/64. Wg Cdr 1/7/81. Retd ENG 31/12/85.
THOMPSON R. J. Born 25/8/39. Commd 2/1/70. Flt Lt 2/1/72. Retd PI 2/1/78.
THOMPSON R. M., MSERT. Born 26/11/56. Commd 4/7/85. Sqn Ldr 1/7/95. Retd ADMIN 26/11/00.
THOMPSON R. P. Born 31/8/55. Commd 16/9/73. Sqn Ldr 1/1/91. Retd ADMIN 29/1/94.
THOMPSON R. W. P., CEng MRAeS MIMgt. Born 3/9/19. Commd 10/2/49. Sqn Ldr 1/7/60. Retd ENG 6/4/74.
THOMPSON S. E. Born 11/4/14. Commd 9/9/51. Flt Lt 10/9/51. Retd SEC 11/4/69.
THOMPSON S. W., BSc. Born 8/3/63. Commd 19/7/87. Flt Lt 19/1/90. Retd GD 24/9/96.
THOMPSON T. L., BSc. Born 8/11/18. Commd 30/12/42. Sqn Ldr 9/3/55. Retd EDN 1/2/68.
THOMPSON T. L., MIMgt. Born 24/7/23. Commd 25/1/51. Sqn Ldr 1/1/67. Retd GD 20/4/73.
THOMPSON T. P. Born 3/4/29. Commd 4/6/52. Sqn Ldr 1/7/63. Retd GD 8/1/68.
THOMPSON V. Born 21/3/47. Commd 10/11/74. Wg Cdr 1/1/96. Retd GD(G) 14/9/96.
THOMPSON V. R., AFC. Born 12/10/31. Commd 2/7/52. Sqn Ldr 1/7/69. Retd GD 1/7/72.
THOMPSON W. L. Born 20/3/27. Commd 7/5/53. Flt Lt 7/11/57. Retd GD 20/3/87.
THOMPSTONE R. R. Born 19/7/21. Commd 29/5/52. Flt Lt 14/6/61. Retd SUP 30/4/66.
THOMSON A., CEng MIEE. Born 23/8/30. Commd 28/7/60. Sqn Ldr 1/7/68. Retd ENG 29/1/83.
THOMSON A. D., DFC. Born 15/4/21. Commd 18/4/43. Flt Lt 18/10/46. Retd GD 15/4/76.
THOMSON A. D., BSc. Born 10/10/53. Commd 30/9/73. Flt Lt 15/10/78. Retd ENG 24/3/86.
THOMSON A. R. Born 12/5/33. Commd 1/12/53. Flt Lt 19/12/58. Retd GD 12/5/71.
THOMSON A. S. Born 24/3/22. Commd 3/10/49. Flt Lt 26/8/56. Retd GD 19/7/66.
THOMSON A. V. Born 5/12/27. Commd 7/5/52. Flt Lt 2/10/57. Retd GD 29/3/69.
THOMSON C. A. P., DFC. Born 19/6/23. Commd 7/4/44. Flt Lt 29/9/57. Retd SEC 11/12/67.
THOMSON C. R., BSc CEng MIEE. Born 31/7/61. Commd 18/3/84. Sqn Ldr 1/7/95. Retd ENG 18/3/00.
THOMSON D. A. Born 12/1/45. Commd 23/3/67. Wg Cdr 1/7/89. Retd GD 14/3/96.
THOMSON G. C., BSc. Born 15/7/60. Commd 26/9/82. Flt Lt 26/12/83. Retd GD 26/9/98.
THOMSON G. E. Born 9/2/31. Commd 29/12/51. Flt Lt 29/6/56. Retd GD 9/2/69.
THOMSON H. G., AFC. Born 7/2/31. Commd 13/5/53. Flt Lt 5/11/58. Retd GD 31/8/72.
THOMSON I. Born 25/7/36. Commd 5/6/56. Gp Capt 1/7/82. Retd GD 23/6/90.
THOMSON I. D. L. Born 12/2/42. Commd 29/11/63. Sqn Ldr 1/1/81. Retd GD 12/2/97.
THOMSON I. R., MBE. Born 12/9/44. Commd 10/5/90. Flt Lt 10/5/94. Retd ENG 21/1/99.
THOMSON J. Born 9/5/38. Commd 16/5/74. Sqn Ldr 16/5/74. Retd ENG 28/5/90.
THOMSON J. A. Born 18/1/16. Commd 25/11/35. Sqn Ldr 1/9/45. Retd GD 18/12/57 rtg Wg Cdr.
THOMSON J. A. S. Born 17/9/29. Commd 1/8/51. Wg Cdr 1/1/73. Retd GD 17/9/84.
THOMSON J. D., MSc BSc CEng MIEE DIC. Born 21/5/47. Commd 14/11/76. Sqn Ldr 1/7/84. Retd ADMIN 17/9/94.
THOMSON J. I. S. Born 16/6/33. Commd 25/7/59. Flt Lt 13/5/66. Retd GD(G) 10/3/68.
THOMSON J. K. B., BSc. Born 10/10/53. Commd 26/10/75. Flt Lt 26/7/77. Retd GD 26/10/87.
THOMSON J. P. A., MA MSc. Born 3/7/38. Commd 30/9/58. Sqn Ldr 1/1/72. Retd ENG 30/11/90.
THOMSON K. G. Born 25/3/17. Commd 23/9/43. Wg Cdr 1/1/61. Retd ENG 7/4/70.
THOMSON L. A. J. Born 2/2/61. Commd 29/7/91. Flt Lt 29/7/93. Retd SUP 14/2/97.
THOMSON P. A., AFC. Born 26/6/24. Commd 1/2/45. Wg Cdr 1/7/67. Retd GD 29/6/74.

THOMSON R. Born 2/5/23. Commd 10/12/45. Sqn Ldr 1/7/57. Retd GD(G) 1/10/63.
THOMSON R. C. P. Born 14/10/21. Commd 17/9/43. Gp Capt 1/7/65. Retd GD 14/10/76.
THOMSON T. R. Born 18/11/21. Commd 17/4/43. Sqn Ldr 1/1/70. Retd GD(G) 18/11/76.
THOMSON W. M. S., MB ChB DCH. Born 3/12/25. Commd 3/3/49. Wg Cdr 1/4/62. Retd MED 18/3/68.
THORBURN A. R. Born 26/11/10. Commd 10/12/42. Fg Offr 11/3/44. Retd ENG 21/3/49 rtg Flt Lt.
THORBURN G. G., OBE BA. Born 2/9/30. Commd 19/8/54. Gp Capt 1/1/82. Retd ADMIN 4/11/84.
THORBURN N. R., BDS. Born 22/7/57. Commd 12/3/78. Wg Cdr 10/12/92. Retd DEL 22/7/95.
THORINGTON S. Born 17/3/57. Commd 10/3/77. Sqn Ldr 1/1/92. Retd ADMIN 17/3/95.
THORLEY L. R. Born 21/11/45. Commd 15/10/81. Sqn Ldr 1/7/97. Retd ENG 18/10/00.
THORLEY M. A., MRAeS. Born 5/12/44. Commd 15/10/81. Wg Cdr 1/7/89. Retd ENG 27/4/96.
THORMAN D. L. Born 6/7/21. Commd 22/1/43. Flt Lt 6/6/49. Retd GD 6/7/64.
THORN G. W., MBE. Born 5/9/16. Commd 15/11/45. Sqn Ldr 1/7/67. Retd CAT 12/9/69.
THORN P. F. C. A. Born 15/7/27. Commd 5/2/62. Flt Lt 5/2/62. Retd GD 19/2/88.
THORN T. G., AFC FRAes. Born 21/9/42. Commd 28/7/64. A Cdre 1/7/90. Retd GD 28/12/95.
THORNALLEY A. H. Born 20/7/23. Commd 22/1/45. Wg Cdr 1/7/70. Retd SUP 29/3/78.
THORNBERRY S. C. C. Born 19/2/50. Commd 2/1/70. Flt Lt 2/7/75. Retd GD 19/2/88.
THORNBOROUGH R. J. Born 29/5/22. Commd 9/7/43. Flt Lt 11/2/49. Retd GD 29/5/67.
THORNE A. C. Born 3/1/35. Commd 15/2/72. Flt Lt 15/2/78. Retd MAR 10/4/86.
THORNE B. A. R. Born 12/2/39. Commd 27/2/75. Sqn Ldr 1/7/86. Retd SUP 12/2/94.
THORNE J. B., OBE FIMgt. Born 25/3/37. Commd 22/10/59. Air Cdre 1/1/88. Retd ADMIN 1/1/90.
THORNE J. N. Born 22/4/24. Commd 12/11/43. Sqn Ldr 1/10/55. Retd GD 30/9/65.
THORNE N. C., AFC*. Born 6/6/24. Commd 26/11/43. Wg Cdr 1/7/59. Retd GD 6/6/71.
THORNE P. D., OBE AFC** MRAeS. Born 3/6/23. Commd 3/7/42. A Cdre 1/7/74. Retd GD 3/6/78.
THORNE R. E. J. Born 27/9/46. Commd 20/10/83. Flt Lt 20/10/87. Retd ENG 1/1/97.
THORNE-THORNE L. Born 28/4/43. Commd 8/10/70. Fg Offr 9/1/73. Retd SEC 30/8/75.
THORNEYCROFT G. N. Born 1/1/34. Commd 6/2/56. Flt Lt 26/2/64. Retd GD 1/7/66.
THORNHAM A. B. Born 9/7/59. Commd 18/12/80. Sqn Ldr 1/1/94. Retd ADMIN 9/7/97.
THORNHILL C., DFC. Born 13/4/14. Commd 16/4/44. Flt Lt 16/10/47. Retd GD 20/7/53.
THORNICROFT E. F., AFC DFM. Born 28/9/13. Commd 24/9/41. Sqn Ldr 1/8/47. Retd ENG 28/9/68 rtg Wg Cdr.
THORNLEY G. A. Born 16/10/15. Commd 8/4/59. Sqn Ldr 14/2/66. Retd EDN 8/4/75.
THORNLEY H. V. Born 15/3/18. Commd 9/8/45. Flt Lt 9/2/49. Retd GD(G) 15/4/68.
THORNLEY J. F., BEM IEng FIEIE. Born 5/4/45. Commd 24/3/83. Sqn Ldr 1/7/93. Retd ENG 2/4/99.
THORNTHWAITE A. P. Born 16/2/51. Commd 3/12/70. Sqn Ldr 1/7/88. Retd GD 1/7/91.
THORNTON A. E. Born 10/10/57. Commd 11/6/81. Flt Lt 6/7/86. Retd SY 10/10/95.
THORNTON D. L. F., OBE. Born 12/4/28. Commd 11/4/51. A Cdre 1/1/80. Retd GD 12/4/83.
THORNTON E. Born 14/9/20. Commd 17/5/62. Sqn Ldr 1/7/72. Retd SUP 14/9/73.
THORNTON G. F., DFC. Born 17/6/22. Commd 25/9/42. Flt Lt 25/3/46. Retd GD(G) 21/12/49.
THORNTON J. B., OBE. Born 30/11/33. Commd 26/11/52. Wg Cdr 1/1/77. Retd GD 24/1/89.
THORNTON J. G. Born 26/12/41. Commd 18/8/61. Flt Lt 18/2/67. Retd GD 26/12/79.
THORNTON J. H. E. Born 2/3/36. Commd 4/9/57. Flt Lt 5/10/60. Retd GD 12/9/82.
THORNTON M. E. Born 17/2/48. Commd 16/9/71. Wg Cdr 1/7/90. Retd SY 1/3/94.
THORNTON P. D., BEng. Born 3/7/60. Commd 2/8/85. Flt Lt 21/10/89. Retd ENG 31/3/94.
THORNTON P. J. Born 7/12/44. Commd 19/8/71. Flt Lt 19/2/78. Retd ADMIN 3/7/83.
THORNTON R. C., MBE MIMgt. Born 10/10/16. Commd 23/8/45. Flt Lt 23/8/51. Retd SEC 15/10/74.
THORNTON R. W., MBE. Born 27/2/14. Commd 1/2/45. Flt Lt 27/10/61. Retd ENG 7/1/67.
THORNTON T. Born 17/8/34. Commd 16/1/61. Wg Cdr 1/7/80. Retd GD 17/8/89.
THORNTON Z. Born 1/7/16. Commd 29/9/41. Flt Offr 1/9/45. Retd SEC 30/11/51.
THORNTON-HENSHAW G. St.J. M., MCIPD. Born 25/11/54. Commd 8/1/76. Sqn Ldr 1/7/87. Retd ADMIN 25/5/93.
THOROGOOD A. N. J. Born 29/12/56. Commd 27/2/83. Sqn Ldr 1/1/96. Retd GD 27/2/99.
THOROGOOD L. A., DFC. Born 13/5/19. Commd 14/8/41. Flt Lt 14/2/45. Retd GD(G) 1/6/64 rtg Sqn Ldr.
THORP R. J. Born 12/3/23. Commd 16/9/44. Gp Capt 1/1/70. Retd SUP 12/3/78.
THORPE A. A. P., MIMgt. Born 26/10/42. Commd 23/5/63. Wg Cdr 1/7/86. Retd ENG 10/4/97.
THORPE G. S. E. Born 30/8/41. Commd 5/4/79. Sqn Ldr 1/7/89. Retd ENG 30/8/96.
THORPE H. R. Born 19/8/11. Commd 4/10/45. Flt Lt 15/12/49. Retd ENG 19/8/66 rtg Sqn Ldr.
THORPE J. W., AFC. Born 19/3/45. Commd 22/3/63. Gp Capt 1/1/96. Retd GD 10/4/99.
THORPE M. P., BSc. Born 18/6/62. Commd 14/10/84. Flt Lt 14/4/88. Retd ENG 14/10/00.
THORPE P. N. Born 6/12/32. Commd 19/2/64. Sqn Ldr 1/1/83. Retd GD 6/12/92.
THORPE R., MRCS LRCP. Born 6/10/02. Commd 2/9/26. Wg Cdr 1/3/41. Retd MED 7/10/51 rtg Gp Capt.
THORPE R. B. Born 2/3/35. Commd 9/5/54. Fg Offr 9/5/56. Retd GD 19/12/61.
THRASHER A. H. W. Born 9/4/30. Commd 11/1/51. Flt Lt 15/2/54. Retd GD 9/4/68.
THREADGOULD A., AFC. Born 8/8/46. Commd 10/10/65. Gp Capt 1/7/91. Retd GD 1/12/95.
THREAPLETON M. R. Born 9/5/55. Commd 20/5/82. Flt Lt 29/6/84. Retd GD 2/10/87.
THRELFALL T. J., BA. Born 12/12/34. Commd 10/2/54. Flt Lt 9/6/61. Retd GD 29/5/71.
THRIPP G., OBE. Born 27/12/12. Commd 16/12/33. Wg Cdr 15/3/45. Retd GD 25/3/47.
THROP K., CEng MIEE. Born 6/8/36. Commd 23/3/66. Sqn Ldr 1/1/74. Retd ENG 28/10/91.

THROWER B. S. Born 2/6/46. Commd 28/8/75. Wg Cdr 1/7/91. Retd ENG 31/10/97.
THROWER G. Born 15/1/31. Commd 26/6/51. Flt Lt 10/10/56. Retd GD 19/1/69.
THRUSH J. P. Born 13/10/20. Commd 17/2/44. Sqn Ldr 1/1/56. Retd SEC 16/6/61.
THRUSSELL B. Born 19/3/31. Commd 17/12/52. Flt Lt 17/6/55. Retd GD 19/3/69.
THURBON M. T., CEng MRAeS MIERE MIEE. Born 28/2/33. Commd 1/3/56. Wg Cdr 1/7/72. Retd ENG 26/7/75.
THURLEY A. P., AFC. Born 25/8/54. Commd 22/5/75. Sqn Ldr 1/7/88. Retd GD 25/2/94.
THURLOW P. R. Born 24/2/45. Commd 24/11/67. Flt Lt 21/8/71. Retd GD 19/5/76.
THURSTON G. L., MA. Born 13/11/45. Commd 8/2/69. Wg Cdr 1/1/90. Retd GD 12/2/96.
THURSTON N., LVO. Born 25/9/47. Commd 12/7/68. Wg Cdr 1/1/82. Retd GD 14/9/96.
THURSTON N. C. Born 13/12/31. Commd 31/5/31. Wg Cdr 1/7/84. Retd GD(G) 13/12/91.
THWAITE A. R. Born 12/12/33. Commd 21/4/67. Sqn Ldr 1/7/78. Retd ENG 31/12/83.
THWAITE W. Born 11/10/29. Commd 1/3/62. Flt Lt 1/3/68. Retd SEC 1/9/73.
THWAITES G. J., MBE MIMgt. Born 27/4/21. Commd 25/9/46. Sqn Ldr 1/7/63. Retd SEC 28/7/70.
TIBBLE M. R. Born 12/7/44. Commd 28/9/62. Flt Lt 28/3/68. Retd GD 28/2/76.
TICKELL C. R. B. Born 9/12/35. Commd 9/4/57. Sqn Ldr 1/1/70. Retd GD 8/9/77.
TICKNER D. Born 28/8/32. Commd 10/10/51. Flt Lt 1/2/60. Retd GD(G) 5/4/83.
TIDBALL C. J. Born 6/6/45. Commd 3/3/67. Sqn Ldr 1/1/81. Retd GD 6/6/00.
TIDMAN W. A. Born 8/12/20. Commd 13/3/47. Wg Cdr 1/7/71. Retd SUP 26/1/76.
TIDY D. P., MA. Born 17/4/23. Commd 13/11/62. Sqn Ldr 15/2/65. Retd EDN 30/7/66.
TIERNAN F. Born 30/6/46. Commd 8/1/65. Wg Cdr 1/1/91. Retd GD 18/7/00.
TIERNEY H. F. Born 28/9/38. Commd 28/10/76. Sqn Ldr 1/1/87. Retd SUP 28/9/93.
TIERNEY J. E. Born 3/6/31. Commd 27/7/54. Flt Lt 27/7/59. Retd SUP 3/6/69.
TIERNEY R., BSc. Born 17/9/41. Commd 6/9/65. Sqn Ldr 1/1/73. Retd GD 21/9/91.
TILBROOK P. G. Born 20/6/16. Commd 31/10/40. Sqn Ldr 1/8/47. Retd GD 1/1/58.
TILFORD D. C., MBE MRIN. Born 3/11/37. Commd 2/10/58. Sqn Ldr 1/1/86. Retd GD 3/11/92.
TILFORD R. S. Born 26/4/43. Commd 9/2/62. Flt Lt 9/8/67. Retd GD 27/8/76.
TILL M. A. C. Born 6/4/19. Commd 22/6/46. Flt Lt 29/11/51. Retd SEC 12/5/59.
TILLARD L. R. W. Born 20/11/04. Commd 31/7/24. Flt Lt 5/3/30. Retd GD 7/5/36.
TILLEARD J. R. Born 5/9/20. Commd 22/9/49. Sqn Ldr 1/1/59. Retd ENG 17/1/62.
TILLER B. R. Born 8/6/31. Commd 24/1/63. Wg Cdr 1/1/85. Retd ENG 8/6/89.
TILLEY D., BSc. Born 7/8/73. Commd 2/11/92. A Plt Offr 2/11/92. Retd GD 30/10/94.
TILLMAN A. K., CEng MIEE. Born 21/5/38. Commd 30/7/59. Wg Cdr 1/7/84. Retd GD 16/7/91.
TILLOTSON N. J. Born 27/12/43. Commd 28/9/62. Flt Lt 28/3/68. Retd GD 27/12/81.
TILLOTSON R. G. W. Born 3/9/42. Commd 23/5/63. Flt Lt 1/4/70. Retd GD 3/9/80.
TILSLEY E. C. F. Born 23/8/26. Commd 11/4/57. Flt Lt 11/10/61. Retd GD 1/1/73.
TILSLEY L. Born 1/7/22. Commd 13/6/45. Fg Offr 13/6/47. Retd SEC 4/3/54.
TILSON D. R. Born 12/1/41. Commd 7/6/68. Wg Cdr 1/1/92. Retd ENG 12/1/96.
TILSTONE P. J., MIMgt. Born 1/10/48. Commd 17/7/70. Sqn Ldr 1/7/85. Retd GD 01/10/92.
TILY C. N. J., MSc MBCS DIC AFIMA., Born 1/10/38. Commd 20/9/60. Sqn Ldr 20/3/71. Retd ADMIN 1/10/85.
TILY M. F. Born 3/4/40. Commd 17/7/70. Flt Lt 17/7/76. Retd MED SEC 3/1/79.
TIMBERS C. J. Born 30/6/68. Commd 17/9/89. Flt Lt 15/1/94. Retd ADMIN 12/6/98.
TIMBERS M. D. Born 24/11/33. Commd 17/10/59. Sqn Ldr 1/1/73. Retd GD 24/11/88.
TIMEWELL G. C. Born 25/9/23. Commd 22/9/55. Flt Lt 22/9/61. Retd GD 25/9/73.
TIMILTY J. Born 16/7/24. Commd 23/9/44. Flt Lt 19/8/49. Retd GD 12/12/62.
TIMLETT R. J. Born 18/10/25. Commd 26/9/51. Flt Lt 26/3/56. Retd GD 18/10/63.
TIMMINS D. L. Born 3/9/14. Commd 18/10/42. Flt Lt 18/4/48. Retd SEC 3/9/63.
TIMMS G. Born 5/2/49. Commd 27/2/70. Sqn Ldr 1/1/82. Retd GD 1/3/86.
TIMMS G. W., MBE. Born 13/7/32. Commd 27/8/52. Wg Cdr 1/7/82. Retd GD 13/7/94.
TIMMS N. J., BEd. Born 22/7/46. Commd 22/9/74. Sqn Ldr 1/7/85. Retd ADMIN 31/3/94.
TIMMS W., MIMgt. Born 6/5/18. Commd 17/6/54. Sqn Ldr 1/7/67. Retd ENG 6/5/73.
TINDAL N. H. J. Born 7/3/11. Commd 10/10/31. Wg Cdr 1/10/46. Retd GD 20/3/48 rtg Gp Capt.
TINDALE A. B. Born 20/4/44. Commd 30/7/64. Sqn Ldr 1/7/80. Retd SUP 5/11/94.
TINDALE M. Born 23/4/39. Commd 14/6/63. Flt Lt 14/12/68. Retd GD 26/2/79.
TINDALL P. L. Born 15/11/30. Commd 14/11/51. Sqn Ldr 1/7/68. Retd GD 1/7/71.
TINGAY C. D., MBE AFC. Born 20/9/55. Commd 31/8/78. Sqn Ldr 1/1/90. Retd GD 20/9/93.
TINGLE M. W., MBE. Born 13/2/40. Commd 6/11/64. Sqn Ldr 1/1/78. Retd GD 31/5/85.
TINGLE N. B., BA. Born 17/8/50. Commd 26/2/71. Sqn Ldr 1/7/83. Retd ADMIN 17/8/94.
TINKLER C., MBE. Born 21/2/25. Commd 28/1/60. Flt Lt 28/1/65. Retd GD 21/2/74.
TINLEY M. F. J., CBE AE FIMgt. Born 28/7/31. Commd 30/8/50. Gp Capt 1/7/76. Retd GD 10/5/83.
TINSLEY I. C., BDS LDSRCS. Born 9/2/45. Commd 8/9/63. Wg Cdr 25/7/81. Retd DEL 9/2/83.
TINSLEY M. U. Born 15/8/13. Commd 10/4/41. Flt Lt 1/9/45. Retd ENG 1/9/53. rtg Sqn Ldr.
TINSON M. S. Born 17/10/06. Commd 16/4/66. Flt Lt 17/10/69. Retd GD 18/4/81.
TIPPELL E. A. Born 23/8/23. Commd 15/12/44. Sqn Ldr 1/4/56. Retd GD 23/11/66.
TIPPEN M. W. Born 3/5/36. Commd 21/8/55. Wg Cdr 1/7/78. Retd GD(G) 1/8/90.
TIPPER G. J., MHCIMA. Born 25/11/46. Commd 25/11/68. Sqn Ldr 1/7/84. Retd ADMIN 14/3/96.
TIPPER M. S. Born 10/5/40. Commd 7/7/67. Flt Lt 4/5/72. Retd GD 10/5/78.

TIPPETT C. M. Born 23/10/51. Commd 28/9/80. Sqn Ldr 1/7/95. Retd ADMIN 1/7/98.
TIPTON J. E., DFC* LLB. Born 15/9/17. Commd 13/7/42. Wg Cdr 1/1/58. Retd GD 30/9/65.
TISBURY J. A., MBE MIMgt. Born 7/1/45. Commd 27/1/77. Sqn Ldr 1/7/85. Retd ADMIN 6/4/98.
TISDALE D. N. P. Born 27/5/52. Commd 18/10/81. Sqn Ldr 1/7/90. Retd SUP 14/3/97.
TISLEY G. F., BEM FIMgt. Born 4/11/21. Commd 28/7/49. Wg Cdr 1/7/66. Retd SEC 5/4/75.
TITCHEN B. J., FIMgt MRIN. Born 4/8/45. Commd 28/4/65. Gp Capt 1/1/94. Retd GD 4/8/00.
TITE I. D. C., AFC. Born 13/5/36. Commd 29/7/58. Sqn Ldr 1/7/70. Retd GD 29/3/75.
TITTERTON M. V. Born 30/8/44. Commd 22/5/64. Flt Lt 22/11/69. Retd GD 31/10/75.
TIVENAN W. H. Born 30/10/28. Commd 18/5/61. Sqn Ldr 1/7/80. Retd ENG 30/10/86.
TIWANA K. S. Born 14/7/49. Commd 31/7/86. Flt Lt 31/7/88. Retd ENG 31/7/94.
TIWARI A., MSc. Born 26/12/46. Commd 11/7/76. Flt Lt 11/1/78. Retd ENG 11/7/93.
TIWARI I. B., MB BS FRCS(Ed). Born 13/11/35. Commd 24/3/69. Gp Capt 4/4/85. Retd MED 2/12/97.
TIZZARD A. P., AFM. Born 5/3/26. Commd 14/1/65. Flt Lt 14/1/68. Retd GD 3/11/73.
TIZZARD D. W. Born 11/11/51. Commd 5/8/76. Flt Lt 19/4/80. Retd GD 28/3/90.
TOAL K. G. Born 25/5/43. Commd 4/12/64. Flt Lt 4/5/72. Retd GD 25/5/81.
TOAL S., BSc. Born 16/11/44. Commd 5/5/68. Flt Lt 5/2/70. Retd GD 25/5/76.
TODD A. G. Born 5/2/07. Commd 17/2/44. Fg Offr 17/2/44. Retd ENG 29/12/45.
TODD B., MBE. Born 17/4/44. Commd 15/7/65. Wg Cdr 1/8/83. Retd ENG 12/2/97.
TODD B. Born 9/11/31. Commd 12/9/63. Flt Lt 12/9/68. Retd GD 18/1/86.
TODD D. E. Born 24/8/30. Commd 3/7/53. Sqn Ldr 1/7/66. Retd GD 4/7/69.
TODD G. P. Born 30/4/43. Commd 22/8/63. Wg Cdr 1/7/86. Retd SUP 30/9/90.
TODD G. R. Born 10/12/60. Commd 24/7/81. Flt Lt 24/1/87. Retd GD 14/3/96.
TODD J. O., MB ChB MRCPsych MRCGP DAvMed AFOM. Born 24/9/56. Commd 18/10/77. Wg Cdr 1/8/93. Retd
    MED 14/3/96.
TODD M. D. Born 5/2/43. Commd 28/4/61. Wg Cdr 1/7/82. Retd GD 3/10/90.
TODD P. R. Born 22/5/38. Commd 26/8/66. Flt Lt 13/11/71. Retd GD(G) 11/5/82.
TODD R. H., MIMgt. Born 25/9/21. Commd 10/5/46. Wg Cdr 1/7/66. Retd SUP 25/9/76.
TODD R. M., MB ChB FRCS. Born 18/11/31. Commd 4/2/57. Wg Cdr 4/2/70. Retd MED 4/2/73.
TODD W. Born 10/4/12. Commd 4/11/43. Flt Lt 4/5/47. Retd ENG 1/3/58.
TODD W. D. Born 6/2/29. Commd 16/11/61. Wg Cdr 1/7/83. Retd GD(G) 6/2/89.
TODMAN D. A. W., DFC. Born 6/6/30. Commd 13/5/53. Sqn Ldr 1/7/66. Retd GD 1/10/69.
TOFTS S. W., MA BA PGCE CertEd. Born 19/11/55. Commd 20/1/80. Wg Cdr 1/7/95. Retd ADMIN 31/1/99.
TOGNERI R., MSc BA BSc. Born 10/11/50. Commd 15/9/69. Sqn Ldr 1/7/86. Retd GD 10/11/94.
TOLAN E. P., DFM MIMgt. Born 10/5/23. Commd 20/3/44. Sqn Ldr 1/7/66. Retd SUP 30/8/75.
TOLCHER A. R. Born 24/2/36. Commd 2/5/55. Gp Capt 1/7/85. Retd GD 24/4/92.
TOLFREE D. J., MIOSH. Born 9/7/31. Commd 21/10/66. Flt Lt 21/10/71. Retd ENG 4/6/90.
TOLHURST A. C. Born 10/6/38. Commd 25/7/60. Gp Capt 1/1/84. Retd GD 14/11/88.
TOLLADAY B. E., BA. Born 11/6/43. Commd 17/12/64. Sqn Ldr 1/1/85. Retd ENG 2/5/93.
TOLMAN P. A., AFC. Born 22/8/52. Commd 3/12/70. Sqn Ldr 1/1/86. Retd GD 22/8/89.
TOM M. D. Born 14/6/43. Commd 21/12/62. Flt Lt 15/4/70. Retd GD 15/4/76.
TOMALIN A. M. Born 2/5/43. Commd 17/12/65. Sqn Ldr 1/1/79. Retd GD 2/5/98.
TOMALIN S. W. StJ., ACIS MIMgt. Born 23/12/29. Commd 23/10/59. Sqn Ldr 1/7/71. Retd SUP 23/10/75.
TOMBLESON D. A. L., BA MRAeS. Born 4/4/46. Commd 1/3/68. Wg Cdr 1/1/85. Retd ENG 4/4/90.
TOMBLESON W. T. Born 18/3/12. Commd 17/3/49. Flt Lt 17/9/52. Retd 21/4/59.
TOMBLIN H. C. W. Born 6/9/18. Commd 7/10/43. Sqn Ldr 1/7/63. Retd SUP 1/6/74.
TOMES J. N., CBE BA. Born 7/2/13. Commd 24/8/33. A Cdre 1/7/57. Retd GD 23/3/63.
TOMKINS M. G., MBE MCIPD. Born 5/10/31. Commd 30/7/52. A Cdre 1/7/84. Retd ADMIN 5/10/86.
TOMKINS S. J., BEng. Born 18/3/46. Commd 20/8/67. Sqn Ldr 1/1/82. Retd GD 18/3/90.
TOMLIN R. A., MBE. Born 18/12/25. Commd 1/11/50. Wg Cdr 1/7/68. Retd GD 31/8/73.
TOMLIN R. C. Born 13/5/50. Commd 4/5/70. Sqn Ldr 1/1/88. Retd GD 7/9/92.
TOMLINS D. Born 18/10/32. Commd 8/10/70. Flt Lt 8/10/73. Retd GD 27/3/77.
TOMLINSON A. J. W. Born 1/7/27. Commd 18/11/53. Flt Offr 18/11/57. Retd CAT 29/8/64.
TOMLINSON B. J., BSc. Born 19/1/35. Commd 3/4/59. Sqn Ldr 21/2/67. Retd EDN 3/4/75.
TOMLINSON C. A., AFC* MRAeS. Born 26/5/24. Commd 11/11/43. Sqn Ldr 1/7/56. Retd GD 1/6/68.
TOMLINSON G. C., OBE DFC. Born 1/12/07. Commd 29/8/31. Wg Cdr 17/11/43. Retd GD 19/7/46 rtg Gp Capt.
TOMLINSON G. J., BSc. Born 22/3/50. Commd 9/8/71. Sqn Ldr 1/7/84. Retd GD 9/1/86.
TOMLINSON M. A. Born 6/12/42. Commd 5/9/69. Flt Lt 5/9/71. Retd GD 6/12/80.
TOMLINSON M. C. Born 23/2/33. Commd 24/10/51. Flt Lt 1/6/64. Retd GD 1/6/72.
TOMLINSON M. I. Born 26/9/59. Commd 7/11/85. Flt Lt 7/11/87. Retd GD 26/9/99.
TOMLINSON N. F. Born 21/4/21. Commd 8/7/54. Flt Lt 6/8/59. Retd SUP 14/8/73.
TOMLINSON P. F., BEd. Born 20/9/49. Commd 4/11/73. Flt Lt 4/8/76. Retd ADMIN 4/11/89.
TOMLINSON R. Born 9/4/29. Commd 29/10/64. Sqn Ldr 23/5/71. Retd EDN 29/10/72.
TOMLINSON S. Born 8/9/54. Commd 3/7/80. Flt Lt 30/6/83. Retd SUP 8/9/92.
TOMLINSON W., BEM. Born 20/11/19. Commd 22/9/55. Sqn Ldr 1/1/67. Retd PRT 20/11/74.
TOMPKINS G. J., MBE. Born 20/6/32. Commd 28/6/51. Flt Lt 10/10/56. Retd GD 28/6/70.
TOMPKINS K. W. Born 23/9/48. Commd 10/2/72. Fg Offr 10/2/72. Retd SEC 11/12/72.

TOMPKINS R. C., MBE. Born 2/7/34. Commd 26/7/55. Wg Cdr 1/7/82. Retd GD 2/7/89.
TOMPKINS R. N., LDSRCS. Born 27/6/37. Commd 23/10/60. Wg Cdr 19/11/72. Retd DEL 15/8/92.
TOMPKINSON D. J. Born 30/3/32. Commd 5/5/54. Flt Lt 1/10/67. Retd GD 30/3/88.
TOMPSON G. L. Born 14/3/49. Commd 7/1/71. Sqn Ldr 1/7/84. Retd GD 17/12/87.
TONES M. D. Born 1/1/44. Commd 31/10/69. Wg Cdr 1/1/87. Retd GD 16/6/92.
TONG R. C., OBE. Born 23/6/40. Commd 18/2/60. Gp Capt 1/7/91. Retd ADMIN 23/6/95.
TONKIN S. M., MA. Born 1/11/59. Commd 18/4/79. Flt Lt 15/10/84. Retd ADMIN 1/8/89.
TONKINSON B. J. Born 4/5/36. Commd 4/1/56. Flt Lt 6/3/63. Retd GD 2/8/69.
TONKS J. E. W. Born 27/4/18. Commd 6/11/58. Flt Lt 6/11/63. Retd ENG 27/4/73.
TOOGOOD G. Born 27/6/09. Commd 1/1/42. Sqn Ldr 1/1/49. Retd ENG 27/6/58.
TOOGOOD H. Born 5/2/20. Commd 24/10/41. Flt Lt 19/2/47. Retd SEC 1/3/62.
TOOGOOD W. G., BEM. Born 27/3/20. Commd 5/4/43. Sqn Ldr 1/1/55. Retd ENG 2/5/70.
TOOGOOD W. R. Born 5/3/48. Commd 16/12/66. Sqn Ldr 1/1/91. Retd OPS SPT 1/5/98.
TOOMER H. S. Born 20/3/23. Commd 9/7/59. Sqn Ldr 1/1/71. Retd ENG 20/2/78.
TOOMEY J. P., MA. Born 15/9/34. Commd 12/7/57. Sqn Ldr 15/3/64. Retd EDN 12/7/73.
TOON D. A., CBE. Born 11/4/25. Commd 29/7/48. Gp Capt 1/1/72. Retd GD 11/12/80.
TOOTAL P. S. E., OBE. Born 7/6/41. Commd 18/12/62. Gp Capt 1/1/85. Retd GD 7/4/93.
TOOTELL W. Born 20/8/31. Commd 13/9/51. Sqn Ldr 1/7/69. Retd SUP 23/7/86.
TOOTS R. I. Born 15/2/56. Commd 7/11/85. Flt Lt 7/5/92. Retd ADMIN 8/7/97.
TOOZE R. R. Born 21/6/41. Commd 19/9/71. Sqn Ldr 1/1/88. Retd ADMIN 21/6/96.
TOPAZ T. K. Born 27/2/34. Commd 3/6/65. Flt Lt 3/6/70. Retd GD 7/12/74.
TOPHAM A. G. Born 8/2/33. Commd 6/6/57. Sqn Ldr 1/1/69. Retd GD 21/7/86.
TOPHAM C. R., BSc. Born 21/1/57. Commd 31/8/75. Sqn Ldr 1/7/90. Retd GD 21/1/95.
TOPHAM D. O. Born 23/3/38. Commd 18/11/66. Flt Lt 4/2/70. Retd SUP 15/12/76.
TOPHAM K. D. Born 21/4/63. Commd 26/8/90. Flt Lt 4/10/90. Retd OPS SPT 21/4/01.
TOPHAM M., MA. Born 26/7/28. Commd 17/11/49. Sqn Ldr 1/12/65. Retd EDN 14/7/67.
TOPHAM M. W., MBE. Born 27/4/38. Commd 23/11/78. Flt Lt 23/11/83. Retd ENG 27/4/96.
TOPHAM R. Born 8/3/30. Commd 9/8/51. Sqn Ldr 1/7/72. Retd GD(G) 8/3/85.
TOPLISS G. W., DFC. Born 20/7/14. Commd 10/1/38. Wg Cdr 1/1/51. Retd GD 10/10/61.
TOPP K. F., MSc CEng MRAeS. Born 8/8/35. Commd 26/9/71. Sqn Ldr 26/9/71. Retd ENG 26/9/87.
TOPP R. A. Born 15/8/24. Commd 25/3/46. Sqn Ldr 1/1/61. Retd ENG 31/10/75.
TOPP R. L., AFC**. Born 15/5/23. Commd 22/9/44. A Cdre 1/7/70. Retd GD 31/3/78.
TOPPER L. Born 27/7/21. Commd 14/11/43. Flt Lt 4/12/52. Retd GD 18/5/65.
TOPPING I. B. Born 15/3/34. Commd 18/6/52. Sqn Ldr 1/1/67. Retd GD 15/3/72.
TORDOFF L. W., MBE. Born 27/1/11. Commd 22/8/41. Flt Lt 1/9/45. Retd SUP 1/9/50 rtg Sqn Ldr.
TORODE A. S., OBE MB ChB FRCP DPhysMed. Born 15/6/41. Commd 20/1/64. Gp Capt 6/10/90. Retd MED 14/3/96.
TORPY G. L., MBE. Born 14/9/32. Commd 20/12/51. Flt Lt 22/5/57. Retd GD 1/9/73.
TORRENS R. G., OBE BSc CEng MRAeS MIMgt. Born 27/5/58. Commd 5/9/76. Wg Cdr 1/1/93. Retd ENG 3/4/99.
TOSH D. A., BMet. Born 6/11/61. Commd 11/9/83. Flt Lt 11/3/87. Retd ADMIN 29/10/96.
TOSHNEY J. J., BSc. Born 15/4/50. Commd 30/10/72. Flt Lt 15/4/76. Retd ENG 30/10/88.
TOSSELL J. H., FCIPS FIMgt MCIT MILT. Born 15/8/35. Commd 24/1/63. Air Cdre 1/7/86. Retd SUP 31/5/89.
TOTTMAN S. H. Born 25/4/31. Commd 14/4/53. Wg Cdr 1/7/74. Retd SUP 28/6/82.
TOUGH M. R. Born 8/3/15. Commd 27/1/43. Flt Offr 27/1/48. Retd GD(G) 8/3/65.
TOULL G. R., MSc BSc CEng FIEE MIMgt. Born 13/12/31. Commd 18/2/54. Gp Capt 1/7/75. Retd ENG 26/4/83.
TOURLE M. J., MCIPS MIMgt. Born 26/8/41. Commd 30/7/59. Wg Cdr 1/1/84. Retd SUP 25/4/93.
TOUT E. S. T., MBE. Born 6/1/27. Commd 24/9/64. Sqn Ldr 1/1/76. Retd ENG 3/4/79.
TOUZEL M. Born 26/1/57. Commd 5/8/76. Flt Lt 5/2/82. Retd GD 16/4/95.
TOVEY B. A. Born 25/8/30. Commd 17/2/58. Sqn Ldr 1/1/80. Retd GD(G) 25/8/85.
TOWEY J. V., OBE BA MIMgt. Born 15/9/33. Commd 12/7/57. Wg Cdr 1/1/74. Retd ADMIN 22/12/85.
TOWLE C. M. Born 13/9/46. Commd 11/7/74. Fg Offr 15/10/74. Retd SEC 17/3/79.
TOWLER B. A. Born 22/5/43. Commd 4/10/63. Flt Lt 29/1/69. Retd GD 2/11/76.
TOWLER B. M. Born 29/3/59. Commd 2/2/78. Sqn Ldr 1/7/92. Retd SUP 17/2/96.
TOWLER C. O., DSM. Born 7/7/90. Commd 1/4/18. Flt Lt 1/7/27. Retd GD 11/4/33.
TOWLER J. B., FIMgt. Born 23/8/23. Commd 15/10/43. Wg Cdr 1/7/66. Retd GD 15/2/77.
TOWLER J. L. W. Born 22/11/24. Commd 4/9/46. A Cdre 1/7/74. Retd GD 29/4/78.
TOWN C. G. Born 14/1/30. Commd 27/2/75. Flt Lt 27/2/78. Retd SUP 27/2/88.
TOWNEND G., BSc PGCE. Born 27/4/67. Commd 3/9/89. Flt Lt 15/1/92. Retd ADMIN 5/8/99.
TOWNEND I. A. Born 30/1/61. Commd 26/11/81. Sqn Ldr 1/7/96. Retd ADMIN 1/7/99.
TOWNEND-DYSON E. B. Born 19/10/08. Commd 30/8/41. Sqn Ldr 1/7/49. Retd SEC 30/11/57.
TOWNLEY C., MA BA MIMgt MCIPD. Born 7/9/34. Commd 12/9/61. Sqn Ldr 12/9/73. Retd ADMIN 14/10/84.
TOWNLEY C. P. Born 8/10/17. Commd 28/8/41. Flt Lt 1/9/45. Retd ENG 8/10/73.
TOWNLEY R., BSc. Born 13/9/31. Commd 5/2/68. Flt Lt 5/2/68. Retd EDN 6/2/73.
TOWNS D., BEM MInstPet. Born 20/11/50. Commd 2/11/88. Flt Lt 2/11/92. Retd SUP 1/8/96.
TOWNSEND B. K., DFC. Born 28/9/15. Commd 5/1/40. Flt Lt 20/7/46. Retd GD 25/10/70 rtg Sqn Ldr.
TOWNSEND D. Born 10/9/23. Commd 1/12/44. Flt Lt 1/6/48. Retd GD 10/9/66.

TOWNSEND D. F. Born 8/4/24. Commd 23/8/45. Flt Lt 1/1/56. Retd SEC 31/5/69.
TOWNSEND G. R. Born 11/3/19. Commd 12/11/43. Flt Lt 12/5/48. Retd SEC 30/11/55 rtg Sqn Ldr.
TOWNSEND J. A. Born 2/7/36. Commd 17/5/56. Flt Lt 17/5/62. Retd SEC 14/10/75.
TOWNSEND J. E. Born 13/3/20. Commd 11/4/42. Sqn Ldr 1/1/55. Retd GD 30/6/58.
TOWNSEND J. F. Born 20/1/13. Commd 2/4/63. Flt Lt 2/4/56. Retd ENG 31/8/67.
TOWNSEND J. G. Born 12/2/44. Commd 24/6/71. Flt Lt 24/6/73. Retd GD(G) 1/5/85.
TOWNSEND J. W. Born 25/9/30. Commd 22/7/71. Flt Lt 22/7/72. Retd EDN 30/9/78.
TOWNSEND M. E., MA. Born 29/7/23. Commd 11/2/44. Sqn Ldr 1/1/59. Retd GD 2/3/68.
TOWNSEND R. M. Born 26/9/51. Commd 13/1/72. Plt Offr 13/1/73. Retd GD 3/10/73.
TOWNSON J., MBE. Born 23/8/24. Commd 22/11/44. Sqn Ldr 1/4/56. Retd GD 23/8/73.
TOY R. D., IEng MIIE. Born 23/4/39. Commd 9/3/72. Wg Cdr 1/1/92. Retd ENG 1/1/95.
TOYNE C. V., MBE. Born 5/12/07. Commd 10/1/45. Flt Offr 4/12/52. Retd SUP 22/4/60.
TOYNE S., MBE. Born 8/1/32. Commd 21/9/55. Sqn Ldr 1/1/67. Retd GD 31/8/87.
TOZER C. S. Born 9/2/22. Commd 29/10/43. Flt Lt 29/4/47. Retd GD 18/5/48.
TRACY A. J., BA. Born 28/2/59. Commd 29/8/77. Flt Lt 15/4/82. Retd GD 15/7/92.
TRACY J. P. Born 31/12/48. Commd 29/3/69. Fg Offr 21/3/71. Retd GD 26/9/73.
TRACY R. F. Born 16/7/23. Commd 8/5/45. Sqn Ldr 1/7/68. Retd GD 16/7/78.
TRAGHEIM J. A. Born 24/10/30. Commd 23/9/65. Flt Lt 23/9/70. Retd ENG 1/2/75.
TRAHAIR F. T., MBE FCCS. Born 13/5/16. Commd 28/6/45. Sqn Ldr 1/1/57. Retd SEC 13/5/65.
TRAINER E. J. Born 23/10/23. Commd 1/2/50. Flt Lt 3/5/56. Retd GD 28/10/66.
TRANT H. B., MBE. Born 14/12/23. Commd 3/9/53. Wg Cdr 1/7/77. Retd ADMIN 19/1/80.
TRANTER N. A. Born 27/6/22. Commd 12/6/58. Flt Lt 12/6/63. Retd GD(G) 1/10/75.
TRANTER S. G. R., BSc. Born 4/4/58. Commd 12/8/79. Sqn Ldr 1/7/90. Retd GD 4/4/96608225.
TRANTHAM I. D. Born 11/4/44. Commd 8/4/82. Sqn Ldr 1/7/91. Retd ENG 1/9/94.
TRATHEN A. M. Born 23/10/34. Commd 7/5/64. Sqn Ldr 1/1/73. Retd ENG 1/1/76.
TRAVERS D. C. Born 16/2/39. Commd 29/10/62. Fg Offr 26/6/63. Retd GD 17/8/86.
TRAVERS D. L. M., LDS. Born 8/8/17. Commd 18/1/45. Gp Capt 1/1/67. Retd DEL 20/11/69.
TRAVERS P. R., MB BS MRCS LRCP DPhysMed. Born 16/2/19. Commd 17/6/43. Wg Cdr 18/8/57. Retd MED
    9/1/66.
TRAVERSE A. J., DSM. Born 10/7/23. Commd 25/9/52. Sqn Ldr 1/1/71. Retd GD(G) 26/1/77.
TRAVIS E. B., BA. Born 22/3/26. Commd 6/11/62. Sqn Ldr 14/2/66. Retd EDN 6/11/73.
TRAVIS R. C., MBE BSc CEng FIEE FRAeS. Born 26/8/30. Commd 21/12/52. Gp Capt 1/7/79. Retd ADMIN 4/4/85.
TRAYLOR A. G. Born 2/10/44. Commd 29/11/63. Sqn Ldr 1/7/82. Retd GD 2/10/99.
TREADWELL E. A., BSc. Born 28/11/46. Commd 20/4/71. Flt Lt 20/1/72. Retd GD 30/8/75.
TREDRE A. F., MB BS MRCP MRCS. Born 15/10/34. Commd 3/2/64. Gp Capt 3/2/84. Retd MED 14/2/89.
TREEN M. A. Born 29/9/40. Commd 28/4/67. Flt Lt 15/4/70. Retd GD 1/1/76.
TREGASKIS N. R. Born 27/10/42. Commd 3/8/62. Sqn Ldr 1/7/77. Retd GD 27/10/80.
TREGEAR R. M., CEng MIEE MRAeS. Born 12/6/31. Commd 30/12/63. Sqn Ldr 1/1/69. Retd ENG 12/6/91.
TRELOAR G. H. L., CEng MRAeS. Born 6/6/27. Commd 16/5/51. Wg Cdr 1/1/75. Retd ENG 1/9/78.
TREMBLING G. E. J., DFM. Born 18/2/24. Commd 7/7/54. Flt Lt 7/7/59. Retd GD 2/1/69.
TRENCH B. W. Born 17/1/44. Commd 22/7/66. Wg Cdr 1/1/88. Retd SUP 6/8/98.
TREVAINS C. J., OBE. Born 27/5/26. Commd 15/12/49. Wg Cdr 1/7/67. Retd GD 3/4/80.
TREVAINS G. E., CEng MIEE. Born 12/1/22. Commd 22/9/49. Wg Cdr 1/7/67. Retd ENG 1/2/79.
TREVASKUS R Born 3/7/46. Commd 11/1/79. Fl Lt 11/1/81. Retd GD 19/1/93.
TREVELYAN R. F. Born 16/9/19. Commd 4/11/43. Flt Lt 4/5/47. Retd ENG 22/11/47.
TREVELYAN R. S. Born 14/11/20. Commd 24/12/48. Flt Lt 24/12/48. Retd RGT 1/10/57.
TREVERTON V. J., BSc. Born 24/10/56. Commd 31/8/75. Sqn Ldr 1/7/89. Retd GD 24/10/94.
TREVIS A. C. E. Born 6/7/44. Commd 13/1/67. Flt Lt 13/7/72. Retd GD 22/8/82.
TREW D. H. Born 16/5/30. Commd 1/1/61. Sqn Ldr 23/9/71. Retd ADMIN 14/9/82.
TREWEEK A. Born 26/3/31. Commd 23/1/58. Flt Lt 28/10/58. Retd GD 1/5/84.
TREWENACK R. W. L., AFC. Born 26/3/24. Commd 4/4/50. Flt Lt 19/11/53. Retd GD 11/2/68 rtg Sqn Ldr.
TREWIN I. A., (Eur Ing) CEng MIEE. Born 5/11/44. Commd 9/11/65. Wg Cdr 1/0/88. Retd ENG 17/5/99.
TREWINNARD L. P. Born 9/8/49. Commd 31/7/70. Flt Lt 31/7/73. Retd GD 31/3/95.
TRIBE D. H., MIMgt. Born 27/11/30. Commd 2/7/64. Wg Cdr 1/1/83. Retd ADMIN 3/4/85.
TRICCAS A. P. P. Born 29/6/36. Commd 10/3/77. Sqn Ldr 1/7/90. Retd ENG 1/7/93.
TRICE K. M. Born 20/2/29. Commd 3/7/67. Sqn Ldr 1/1/74. Retd ADMIN 20/2/84.
TRICK P. A. R., CEng MRAeS MIMgt. Born 11/9/19. Commd 26/9/57. Sqn Ldr 1/1/71. Retd ENG 11/9/74.
TRICKER G. E. Born 16/4/24. Commd 15/2/45. Sqn Ldr 1/1/57. Retd GD 10/2/68.
TRICKETT C. L., DFC. Born 19/7/13. Commd 31/3/41. Sqn Ldr 1/8/47. Retd GD 19/7/56.
TRIGG C. J., MBE MSc BSc CEng MRAeS MIMgt. Born 26/10/54. Commd 2/9/73. Wg Cdr 1/1/92. Retd ENG
    26/10/98.
TRIGG N. E., CEng MRAeS MIMechE. Born 9/9/36. Commd 28/7/60. Wg Cdr 1/7/64. Retd ENG 16/12/77.
TRIGG R. Born 22/2/33. Commd 27/6/59. Flt Lt 27/12/69. Retd GD 6/2/75.
TRIGG R. S., DFC. Born 14/3/22. Commd 23/4/40. Flt Lt 19/11/53. Retd GD 31/8/62.
TRILLO W. Born 13/4/36. Commd 9/12/71. Sqn Ldr 1/1/86. Retd ENG 8/7/90.
TRIMBLE E. N. Born 28/7/44. Commd 31/8/78. Wg Cdr 1/7/90. Retd ADMIN 31/5/94.

TRIMMER R. M., PhD MSc BDS. Born 9/6/41. Commd 30/12/62. Wg Cdr 26/11/77. Retd DEL 16/8/85.
TRINDER R. R. S. Born 16/4/51. Commd 15/9/69. Sqn Ldr 1/7/83. Retd GD 16/4/89.
TRIPLOW P. H. J. Born 9/4/32. Commd 19/7/56. Flt Lt 19/1/61. Retd GD 9/4/70.
TRIPP G. T., OBE BA. Born 13/7/33. Commd 12/3/52. Gp Capt 1/7/80. Retd GD 17/4/86.
TRIPP M. J. Born 6/2/43. Commd 16/12/68. Flt Lt 22/10/73. Retd GD(G) 18/3/83. Re-entrant 26/9/84. Flt Lt
    2/5/75. Retd GD(G) 14/3/96.
TRIPP R. N. Born 17/4/44. Commd 22/5/64. Flt Lt 22/11/69. Retd 30/9/76.
TRIPTREE D. W., AFC. Born 24/9/16. Commd 15/4/39. Wg Cdr 1/7/54. Retd GD 6/11/63.
TRITTON J. W., AFC. Born 13/11/31. Commd 15/8/51. Gp Capt 1/1/81. Retd GD 4/8/87.
TROAKE M. S., CEng MRAeS. Born 21/8/31. Commd 10/10/51. Sqn Ldr 1/7/66. Retd ENG 4/10/75. Reinstated
    19/8/81. Sqn Ldr 16/5/72. Retd ENG 27/9/88.
TROBE K. M. W. Born 22/5/22. Commd 9/7/43. Flt Lt 19/11/53. Retd GD 22/5/77.
TRODD N. H. Born 22/9/11. Commd 23/4/53. Sqn Ldr 1/7/62. Retd ENG 30/9/66.
TROKE C. B. Born 22/7/45. Commd 11/8/67. Wg Cdr 1/7/91. Retd GD 22/7/00.
TROMP J. E. Born 14/8/23. Commd 5/5/60. Flt Lt 5/5/65. Retd RGT 10/8/68.
TROTMAN A. J. Born 14/6/48. Commd 19/8/66. Flt Lt 19/2/72. Retd GD 14/6/86.
TROTMAN A. J. E. Born 27/8/50. Commd 13/4/80. Sqn Ldr 1/1/88. Retd ADMIN 14/3/97.
TROTMAN D. A., AFC FIMgt. Born 28/11/21. Commd 19/6/42. A Cdre 1/1/68. Retd GD 28/11/76.
TROTMAN J., OBE. Born 6/7/15. Commd 1/5/39. Wg Cdr 1/1/58. Retd SUP 1/8/72.
TROTTER D. Born 11/5/44. Commd 18/7/63. Flt Lt 20/3/70. Retd GD 11/5/82.
TROTTER E. W. Born 14/9/35. Commd 9/3/72. Sqn Ldr 1/7/83. Retd ENG 2/4/88.
TROTTER K. Born 7/8/17. Commd 6/6/57. Flt Lt 6/6/60. Retd PE 5/12/70. rtg Sqn Ldr.
TROTTER K. R. A., BSc(Eng) CEng MIEE. Born 31/12/42. Commd 30/2/62. Gp Capt 1/1/90. Retd ENG 18/4/95.
TROTTER P. I. W. Born 2/5/18. Commd 17/7/46. Flt Lt 19/6/52. Retd RGT 8/8/54.
TROTTER R., DFC. Born 22/6/22. Commd 19/7/44. Flt Lt 19/1/48. Retd PI 17/10/72.
TROTTER R. W. D. Born 18/7/47. Commd 21/5/65. Wg Cdr 1/7/88. Retd GD 31/10/92.
TROUGHTON-SMITH S. H. Born 19/11/20. Commd 31/10/38. Wg Cdr 1/1/62. Retd SUP 1/9/67.
TROUP H. B., MRCS LRCP. Born 25/5/94. Commd 6/6/18. Sqn Ldr 6/6/28. Retd MED 3/2/32.
TROWBRIDGE K. R., BSc. Born 23/8/50. Commd 3/10/72. Flt Lt 3/1/74. Retd GD 3/10/88.
TROWERN F. A., OBE AFC MIMgt. Born 28/8/32. Commd 26/7/51. Wg Cdr 1/7/76. Retd GD 1/9/83.
TROWERN R. M. Born 12/9/36. Commd 15/12/59. Wg Cdr 1/1/87. Retd GD 30/11/89.
TROWN E. Born 16/11/33. Commd 31/12/52. Flt Lt 12/2/60. Retd GD 11/12/71.
TRUBSHAW E. B., MVO. Born 29/1/24. Commd 5/12/43. Flt Lt 5/6/47. Retd GD 22/4/50.
TRUELOVE O. J., MBE CEng FRAeS MIMechE. Born 24/10/37. Commd 30/7/59. A Cdre 1/7/86. Retd ENG
    10/11/89.
TRUELOVE P. A. Born 4/1/33. Commd 4/3/63. Sqn Ldr 18/4/70. Retd ADMIN 4/1/88.
TRUEMAN D. A. Born 7/9/42. Commd 20/11/75. Sqn Ldr 1/1/84. Retd GD 7/9/97.
TRUEMAN D. W. Born 26/2/43. Commd 4/6/64. Sqn Ldr 1/1/78. Retd GD 26/2/81.
TRUEMAN G. F. R., BSc CEng MIProdE. Born 16/1/38. Commd 1/9/70. Sqn Ldr 1/1/77. Retd ENG 1/9/86. Reinstated
    16/11/87. Sqn Ldr 18/3/78. Retd ENG 10/7/90.
TRUEPENNY L. K. Born 30/1/35. Commd 4/2/71. Flt Lt 4/2/76. Retd SUP 30/1/93.
TRULUCK V. G. Born 18/11/35. Commd 5/7/68. Flt Lt 5/7/70. Retd ENG 5/7/76.
TRUMBLE A. J., OBE. Born 15/12/15. Commd 15/3/35. Gp Capt 1/1/56. Retd GD 3/5/66.
TRUMPER M. G., CEng MIMechE MRAeS. Born 9/6/38. Commd 12/12/59. Wg Cdr 1/1/79. Retd ENG 9/6/93.
TRUMPESS B. E. Born 21/6/32. Commd 7/9/56. Sqn Ldr 7/3/66. Retd EDN 7/9/72.
TRUNDLE L. Born 27/9/17. Commd 19/7/57. Sqn Ldr 1/1/66. Retd ENG 25/5/72.
TRUSCOTT E. M. Born 2/3/42. Commd 9/2/62. Flt Lt 9/8/67. Retd GD 12/5/69.
TRUSCOTT J. A. W. Born 2/5/45. Commd 20/12/90. Flt Lt 20/12/94. Retd ADMIN 7/4/96.
TRUSCOTT J. C. Born 31/1/20. Commd 30/6/42. Flt Lt 30/12/45. Retd GD 27/1/47.
TRUSCOTT T. T., BSc. Born 9/1/34. Commd 30/1/58. Sqn Ldr 9/8/68. Retd EDN 5/5/75.
TRUSLER D. G. M. Born 2/7/45. Commd 28/4/65. Flt Lt 28/10/70. Retd GD 8/12/76.
TRUSSLER J. D., BA. Born 6/12/40. Commd 24/6/71. Wg Cdr 1/7/89. Retd ENG 9/12/95.
TUCK A. J. Born 12/3/02. Commd 24/11/41. Flt Lt 1/1/43. Retd ASD 4/1/47 rtg Sqn Ldr.
TUCK D. T., CEng MIEE. Born 14/7/46. Commd 26/10/75. Sqn Ldr 1/1/89. Retd ENG 1/10/96.
TUCK J. Born 15/4/18. Commd 5/6/43. Sqn Ldr 1/1/58. Retd SUP 29/7/72.
TUCKER D. E., FINucE. Born 17/11/23. Commd 16/5/57. Sqn Ldr 1/1/70. Retd ENG 1/8/74.
TUCKER D. K., MSc CEng MRAeS MIEE. Born 13/10/38. Commd 18/7/61. Sqn Ldr 1/1/71. Retd ENG 14/10/75.
TUCKER D. R., BA. Born 13/6/48. Commd 11/7/74. Flt Lt 27/9/76. Retd ENG 13/6/86.
TUCKER E. G. F. Born 16/7/25. Commd 23/6/44. Sqn Ldr 1/1/60. Retd GD(G) 18/3/77.
TUCKER H. L., MBE. Born 14/5/11. Commd 10/9/43. Sqn Ldr 1/1/52. Retd SUP 4/6/66.
TUCKER J. Born 30/4/33. Commd 16/9/53. Sqn Ldr 1/1/67. Retd GD 30/4/71.
TUCKER J. A. Born 9/11/33. Commd 21/5/52. Sqn Ldr 1/7/70. Retd GD 1/7/73.
TUCKER J. A. Born 6/10/29. Commd 15/12/53. Flt Lt 14/11/56. Retd GD 6/10/67.
TUCKER J. M., DPhysEd. Born 6/5/40. Commd 18/5/65. Flt Lt 4/5/72. Retd PE 18/5/81.
TUCKER J. McD. Born 9/12/15. Commd 1/7/42. Sqn Offr 1/1/54. Retd SEC 27/11/60.
TUCKER J. R., FIMgt. Born 30/1/30. Commd 13/2/52. Wg Cdr 1/7/69. Retd GD 30/1/85.

TUCKER M. J. Born 30/10/43. Commd 23/11/78. Flt Lt 23/11/83. Retd ENG 30/10/88.
TUCKER R. C. Born 21/4/38. Commd 6/4/72. Sqn Ldr 1/7/87. Retd ENG 21/4/93.
TUCKER S. S. P., BSc. Born 18/3/59. Commd 28/12/80. Flt Lt 28/9/82. Retd ENG 25/10/89.
TUCKER V. P., BA. Born 2/4/60. Commd 19/7/87. Flt Lt 19/7/87. Retd ADMIN 14/3/97.
TUCKER W. H., AFC. Born 6/6/22. Commd 10/7/45. Sqn Ldr 1/7/72. Retd GD 31/7/73.
TUCKEY J. T. Born 18/7/32. Commd 6/4/54. Sqn Ldr 1/7/72. Retd ADMIN 18/7/87.
TUCKFIELD H. Born 12/5/13. Commd 18/10/43. Fg Offr 1/7/44. Retd ENG 22/12/46.
TUCKFIELD L. S. Born 17/4/63. Commd 19/7/84. Flt Lt 19/7/89. Retd GD 17/4/01.
TUDNO-JONES M. Born 3/5/63. Commd 15/3/84. Flt Lt 15/9/90. Retd ADMIN 14/3/97.
TUDOR E. W. D. Born 2/12/32. Commd 6/12/51. Flt Lt 27/3/57. Retd GD(G) 2/12/70. Reinstated 11/1/74. Flt Lt 6/5/60. Retd GD(G) 11/1/90.
TUDOR H. M. H., DFC AFC. Born 6/10/22. Commd 19/6/42. Gp Capt 1/1/62. Retd GD 3/9/66.
TUFF J. M. Born 6/9/64. Commd 19/12/85. Flt Lt 23/4/92. Retd ADMIN 2/4/93.
TUFFIN P. E. Born 27/3/44. Commd 21/2/74. Sqn Ldr 1/1/82. Retd ENG 1/1/85. Reinstated 8/12/86. Sqn Ldr 8/12/83. Retd ENG 5/6/93.
TUFFIN R. Born 24/9/27. Commd 2/3/49. Flt Lt 4/12/53. Retd GD 1/4/65.
TUFFS N. R., MBE. Born 4/9/53. Commd 13/1/92. Sqn Ldr 1/7/85. Retd GD 15/12/91.
TUFT W. J., MBE MCIPD FIMgt. Born 12/8/21. Commd 22/4/43. Gp Capt 1/1/71. Retd ADMIN 12/8/76.
TUHILL P. J., DFC. Born 15/2/12. Commd 3/8/43. Flt Lt 4/1/51. Retd GD(G) 1/3/62.
TUKE L. L. Born 13/11/27. Commd 8/4/49. Sqn Ldr 1/1/58. Retd GD 7/4/68.
TUKE P. Born 10/10/33. Commd 23/7/52. Flt Lt 11/5/58. Retd GD 30/11/70.
TULETT G. A. Born 25/5/35. Commd 17/12/64. Sqn Ldr 24/9/72. Retd EDN 2/4/79.
TULIP J. A. Born 21/8/34. Commd 5/11/52. Flt Lt 26/7/67. Retd GD 1/4/73.
TULK J. A. Born 16/8/30. Commd 9/4/52. Flt Lt 9/10/54. Retd GD 6/10/68.
TULL G. A. Born 16/7/25. Commd 2/8/51. Sqn Ldr 1/1/74. Retd GD 16/7/83.
TULLO M. B. Born 2/2/39. Commd 28/4/60. Sqn Ldr 1/1/72. Retd ADMIN 1/12/82.
TUNBRIDGE P. A., (Eur Ing) CEng MIMechE. Born 1/12/21. Commd 30/1/47. Flt Lt 30/11/51. Retd ENG 17/7/55.
TUNLEY N. E. Born 17/2/43. Commd 15/9/67. Flt Lt 15/3/73. Retd GD 22/10/94.
TUNNAH J. E., BEM MIMgt. Born 9/2/41. Commd 24/1/74. Flt Lt 24/1/76. Retd RGT 10/7/84.
TUNNICLIFF R. Born 4/2/29. Commd 25/8/67. Flt Lt 25/8/72. Retd SEC 6/7/79.
TUNNICLIFFE A. R. Born 11/8/33. Commd 30/7/57. Flt Lt 15/2/63. Retd GD 3/5/73.
TUNNICLIFFE R. E. Born 22/2/30. Commd 6/1/64. Flt Lt 4/5/72. Retd GD(G) 6/1/83.
TUNSTALL P. D. Born 1/12/18. Commd 24/11/37. Sqn Ldr 1/8/47. Retd GD 3/12/57.
TUPPEN H. J., BDS LDSRCS. Born 9/10/33. Commd 7/6/59. Gp Capt 1/7/82. Retd DEL 9/4/94.
TURBIN R. W. Born 17/6/37. Commd 10/4/56. Flt Lt 6/3/63. Retd GD 17/6/75.
TURFERY P., MBE MIMgt. Born 6/2/43. Commd 19/10/72. Gp Capt 1/7/88. Retd ADMIN 1/3/90.
TURFF M. F. Born 8/9/48. Commd 19/9/71. Flt Lt 19/9/76. Retd ENG 19/9/87.
TURFREY G. P. Born 25/11/48. Commd 29/3/68. Flt Lt 29/9/73. Retd GD 1/5/94.
TURGOOSE R., BSc. Born 19/10/39. Commd 2/10/61. Sqn Ldr 1/1/73. Retd GD 19/10/94.
TURK E. P., MB BChir MRCPath. Born 15/4/48. Commd 26/10/70. Wg Cdr 23/6/87. Retd MED 14/3/96.
TURLEY G. J., DFM. Born 25/11/23. Commd 8/7/54. Sqn Ldr 1/1/69. Retd GD 1/6/73.
TURNBULL A., BSc. Born 7/8/59. Commd 6/9/81. Flt Lt 6/12/83. Retd ENG 1/10/87.
TURNBULL E. Born 10/7/23. Commd 26/5/60. Flt Lt 26/5/65. Retd ENG 9/7/77.
TURNBULL G. J., BSc MB ChB MRCP MRCPsych. Born 22/12/48. Commd 29/11/70. Wg Cdr 1/8/87. Retd MED 20/8/93.
TURNBULL I. F. Born 11/9/53. Commd 9/3/72. Flt Lt 5/8/78. Retd GD(G) 11/9/91.
TURNBULL J. D. Born 25/12/21. Commd 24/6/43. Flt Lt 31/12/56. Retd SUP 3/7/66.
TURNBULL J. G. Born 23/3/47. Commd 1/3/68. Flt Lt 1/3/71. Retd GD 19/4/83.
TURNBULL K., BSc. Born 6/6/61. Commd 2/9/79. Flt Lt 15/4/84. Retd GD 6/6/99.
TURNBULL L. J. Born 1/1/26. Commd 21/10/54. Flt Lt 21/10/60. Retd GD 1/1/76.
TURNBULL R. T. Born 30/7/43. Commd 9/3/62. Sqn Ldr 1/1/94. Retd GD 30/7/98.
TURNBULL T. R. C. Born 22/2/36. Commd 21/7/55. Sqn Ldr 1/7/71. Retd SEC 1/7/74.
TURNBULL W. N. O. Born 5/7/57. Commd 19/8/91. Flt Lt 15/12/80. Retd ENG 3/11/92.
TURNER A., MBE MIMgt. Born 14/11/40. Commd 28/5/66. Wg Cdr 1/7/88. Retd GD 4/7/95.
TURNER A. D., FIMgt. Born 30/5/37. Commd 18/12/56. Gp Capt 1/1/84. Retd GD 1/12/88.
TURNER A. D. H., BSc. Born 2/9/46. Commd 8/8/68. Flt Lt 18/2/73. Retd GD 2/9/84.
TURNER A. J. Born 30/12/40. Commd 6/7/62. Flt Lt 6/1/68. Retd GD 30/12/78.
TURNER B. L. StC., FIMgt. Born 15/9/32. Commd 14/12/54. Wg Cdr 1/7/80. Retd ADMIN 31/10/88.
TURNER C. A. Born 5/2/34. Commd 5/7/53. Sqn Ldr 1/7/66. Retd GD 5/2/89.
TURNER C. F. L., BEM. Born 23/10/16. Commd 1/4/43. Sqn Ldr 1/7/55. Retd ENG 21/12/68.
TURNER C. J., BSc. Born 5/6/48. Commd 4/1/68. Sqn Ldr 1/7/81. Retd GD 1/8/92.
TURNER C. McA., BSc. Born 5/11/50. Commd 3/1/74. Flt Lt 15/10/75. Retd GD 3/1/90.
TURNER C. R., AFC. Born 2/9/17. Commd 30/7/42. Sqn Ldr 1/1/54. Retd GD 7/1/58.
TURNER D. G. L. Born 20/9/44. Commd 21/3/69. Flt Lt 8/3/72. Retd GD 7/9/89.
TURNER D. J., MSc BEng CEng MIMechE. Born 15/1/63. Commd 16/9/84. Sqn Ldr 1/1/95. Retd ENG 15/1/01.
TURNER D. J. Born 8/2/36. Commd 6/1/64. Flt Lt 1/4/66. Retd GD 8/2/74.

TURNER D. J., BSc(Eng) CEng MIMechE. Born 8/8/34. Commd 1/2/60. Sqn Ldr 1/7/70. Retd ENG 1/8/88.
TURNER D. M., BA. Born 31/12/53. Commd 19/6/77. Flt Lt 19/3/79. Retd GD 14/3/97.
TURNER D. W. T., BA. Born 10/4/33. Commd 19/11/52. Flt Lt 15/4/58. Retd GD 10/4/92.
TURNER E., DSC. Born 1/1/22. Commd 18/10/56. Flt Lt 18/10/56. Retd MAR 1/12/63.
TURNER E. C., MRAeS. Born 25/4/30. Commd 1/4/53. Sqn Ldr 1/1/66. Retd GD 19/12/75.
TURNER G. Born 27/7/14. Commd 10/10/46. Fg Offr 10/10/48. Retd SUP 20/12/49 rtg Flt Lt.
TURNER G., BEM MIMgt. Born 22/6/29. Commd 16/11/61. Sqn Ldr 1/1/73. Retd ADMIN 23/9/82.
TURNER G. C., MRAeS. Born 22/1/10. Commd 2/9/41. Wg Cdr 1/1/57. Retd ENG 22/3/62.
TURNER G. C., MB ChB FRCP DCH. Born 13/5/32. Commd 17/8/58. A Cdre 8/4/89. Retd MED 6/4/92.
TURNER G. E. Born 16/2/28. Commd 1/7/53. Flt Lt 11/12/58. Retd GD 1/7/76.
TURNER G. F., DFC. Born 10/4/21. Commd 15/5/42. Sqn Ldr 1/1/54. Retd GD 10/4/64.
TURNER G. M., AFC. Born 29/9/33. Commd 27/7/54. Sqn Ldr 1/7/65. Retd GD 27/7/68.
TURNER G. R. Born 5/1/23. Commd 20/5/42. Sqn Ldr 1/1/53. Retd SEC 5/1/66. Re-employed Flt Lt 20/2/71 to 27/4/76.
TURNER G. R. Born 14/6/47. Commd 11/7/74. Sqn Ldr 1/1/81. Retd ENG 14/6/85.
TURNER G. W., OBE DFM. Born 3/12/19. Commd 20/7/42. Wg Cdr 1/7/60. Retd GD 3/12/74.
TURNER H. T., DFC. Born 23/4/21. Commd 27/10/43. Flt Lt 27/4/47. Retd GD 14/6/76.
TURNER H. W. Born 24/5/22. Commd 4/5/50. Flt Lt 4/11/53. Retd GD 24/5/65.
TURNER I. R., MMar. Born 21/3/20. Commd 19/10/49. Sqn Ldr 19/10/57. Retd MAR 19/10/65.
TURNER J., MSc BSc CEng MRAeS. Born 18/9/45. Commd 22/10/72. Gp Capt 1/1/92. Retd ENG 15/6/99.
TURNER J., BA. Born 11/10/52. Commd 26/4/72. Sqn Ldr 1/1/87. Retd GD 11/10/90.
TURNER J. Born 1/7/19. Commd 17/11/43. Flt Offr 17/11/49. Retd SUP 20/5/54.
TURNER J. A., BEd. Born 12/3/62. Commd 11/9/83. Flt Lt 11/3/87. Retd ADMIN 12/3/00.
TURNER J. A. Born 5/7/41. Commd 3/9/62. Flt Lt 5/1/67. Retd GD 5/7/79.
TURNER J. A. Born 15/3/30. Commd 23/2/50. Wg Cdr 1/1/70. Retd ADMIN 15/3/85.
TURNER J. H. Born 1/10/22. Commd 20/3/43. Gp Capt 1/7/68. Retd ADMIN 1/10/77.
TURNER J. H., MVO. Born 11/4/34. Commd 26/7/55. Wg Cdr 1/1/76. Retd GD 11/5/84.
TURNER J. McC. Born 15/3/47. Commd 8/6/84. Fg Off 8/6/83. Retd ADMIN 1/12/87.
TURNER J. N. Born 1/10/37. Commd 1/4/58. Flt Lt 1/3/61. Retd GD 1/10/75.
TURNER L. H., BEng. Born 16/2/54. Commd 19/7/87. Flt Lt 19/1/90. Retd ADMIN 14/3/97.
TURNER M., MIMgt. Born 3/11/28. Commd 16/10/52. Sqn Ldr 1/7/68. Retd ADMIN 7/11/83.
TURNER M. C., MIMgt. Born 16/6/38. Commd 25/7/60. Sqn Ldr 1/7/72. Retd GD 9/4/90.
TURNER M. J. Born 4/6/43. Commd 28/8/75. Sqn Ldr 1/1/86. Retd ENG 30/11/87.
TURNER N. M., BA. Born 16/6/55. Commd 9/10/77. Flt Lt 9/1/80. Retd SY 10/4/96.
TURNER P., CB. Born 29/12/24. Commd 30/4/45. AVM 1/7/76. Retd SEC 29/12/79.
TURNER P. Born 11/2/48. Commd 11/10/70. Fg Offr 24/11/71. Retd GD 31/1/72.
TURNER P. E. Born 8/4/92. Commd 26/12/51. Sqn Ldr 1/1/79. Retd GD 8/4/92.
TURNER P. J., BSc. Born 15/9/45. Commd 17/1/72. Flt Lt 17/10/73. Retd GD 12/5/88.
TURNER The Venerable P. R., CB MTh BA AKC. Born 8/3/42. Commd 22/6/70. Retd 13/12/98 AMV.
TURNER P. R., BA. Born 25/12/54. Commd 14/8/77. Flt Lt 14/11/78. Retd GD 14/8/89.
TURNER P. W. Born 24/5/60. Commd 15/1/83. Flt Lt 4/12/86. Retd GD(G) 13/12/86.
TURNER P. W. Born 19/6/48. Commd 29/3/68. Wg Cdr 1/1/86. Retd SUP 1/1/89.
TURNER R. Born 19/6/45. Commd 2/12/66. Sqn Ldr 1/7/80. Retd GD 30/4/94.
TURNER R. A. N., CEng MIMechE. Born 17/10/29. Commd 14/8/61. Sqn Ldr 26/2/64. Retd EDN 21/9/68.
TURNER R. A. P. Born 28/8/14. Commd 18/4/41. Sqn Ldr 1/8/47. Retd SEC 1/4/55.
TURNER R. E. Born 12/5/36. Commd 10/8/55. Wg Cdr 1/7/76. Retd GD 10/2/82.
TURNER R. E. Born 31/8/42. Commd 1/10/60. Wg Cdr 1/7/83. Retd GD 31/8/86.
TURNER R. M., MBE. Born 12/8/38. Commd 30/9/58. Sqn Ldr 1/7/69. Retd GD 12/8/76.
TURNER S., BSc. Born 15/8/59. Commd 29/8/77. Sqn Ldr 1/7/93. Retd ENG 15/8/97.
TURNER S. C. Born 8/8/60. Commd 25/2/82. Sqn Ldr 1/1/96. Retd GD 1/1/99.
TURNER S. C., CEng MIEE MIMgt. Born 13/7/20. Commd 18/7/46. Sqn Ldr 1/1/57. Retd ENG 13/7/70.
TURNER S., BA. Born 23/3/57. Commd 2/10/75. Wg Cdr 1/7/94. Retd GD 5/4/96.
TURNER W. A., MSc MRAeS. Born 1/5/38. Commd 5/7/60. Flt Lt 5/1/63. Retd ADMIN 5/7/76.
TURNER W. L. Born 23/3/19. Commd 6/11/41. Flt Lt 19/11/51. Retd ENG 5/9/57.
TURNER W. R. Born 25/1/20. Commd 17/7/46. Fg Offr 17/7/48. Retd RGT 10/1/56.
TURNHAM J. A. Born 14/5/33. Commd 20/12/57. Wg Cdr 1/7/77. Retd ADMIN 14/5/88.
TURNILL T. W. Born 22/7/34. Commd 10/4/56. Sqn Ldr 1/1/67. Retd GD 22/7/92.
TURPIN R. H., OBE. Born 17/8/36. Commd 27/10/67. Wg Cdr 1/7/91. Retd GD 1/7/94.
TURPY J. R. Born 4/4/45. Commd 2/3/64. Sqn Ldr 1/7/79. Retd ADMIN 4/4/89.
TUSON J. W., MSc CEng MIMechE MIEE MRAeS. Born 28/2/31. Commd 2/10/54. Wd Cdr 1/7/71. Retd ENG 28/2/86.
TUSON R. L. B. Born 9/4/36. Commd 2/5/59. Sqn Ldr 1/7/71. Retd GD 9/4/91.
TUTHILL A. R. Born 17/8/28. Commd 13/7/61. Flt Lt 13/7/66. Retd ENG 1/2/69.
TUTHILL D. E., MBE. Born 29/9/33. Commd 30/1/52. Sqn Ldr 1/7/79. Retd GD 29/9/91.
TUTIN F. Born 3/5/37. Commd 1/12/77. Sqn Ldr 1/7/88. Retd ENG 2/7/90.
TUTT J. R. Born 14/5/51. Commd 24/4/70. Flt Lt 24/10/76. Retd RGT 1/7/78.

TUTTON P. E. Born 30/8/32. Commd 18/10/62. Flt Lt 18/10/67. Retd GD(G) 30/8/87.
TUXFORD R., AFC. Born 30/3/49. Commd 27/2/70. Sqn Ldr 1/1/80 Retd GD 30/3/87.
TUXWORTH N. C. Born 12/4/10. Commd 30/7/41. Sqn Ldr 1/7/52. Retd SEC 1/2/58.
TWEEDIE D. Born 19/11/19. Commd 30/7/53. Sqn Ldr 1/7/63. Retd ENG 1/8/74.
TWEEDIE J. M. Born 5/2/31. Commd 5/11/70. Flt Lt 5/11/73. Retd GD 23/4/76.
TWEEDIE K. A., MBE CEng MIEE. Born 24/3/16. Commd 11/4/46. Sqn Ldr 1/10/56. Retd ENG 24/3/71.
TWEEDLEY J. McM., MBE. Born 17/9/36. Commd 27/3/75. Sqn Ldr 1/1/86. Retd ENG 1/5/89.
TWELFTREE J. C. Born 22/5/35. Commd 15/5/57. Flt Lt 6/3/63. Retd GD 17/7/65.
TWELVETREE T. Born 21/6/62. Commd 11/6/81. Flt Lt 11/12/86. Retd GD 21/6/00.
TWIBILL M. T., MMAR MNI. Born 5/8/26. Commd 9/10/56. Sqn Ldr 9/10/64. Retd MAR 5/8/81.
TWIDLE H. W., MBE. Born 12/5/15. Commd 18/2/57. Flt Lt 18/2/57. Retd CAT 4/5/68.
TWIGG A. Born 22/5/27. Commd 3/9/47. Wg Cdr 1/1/66. Retd GD 3/10/78.
TWIGGER A. R. Born 18/8/23. Commd 13/6/51. Sqn Ldr 1/1/67. Retd GD 18/8/83.
TWISS B. C., MA CEng MIMechE DCAe. Born 18/4/26. Commd 31/8/48. Sqn Ldr 1/1/58. Retd ENG 4/5/65.
TWIST J. N., BA. Born 15/4/56. Commd 20/5/79. Flt Lt 20/8/82. Retd SUP 31/8/84.
TWITCHETT S. P., MIMgt. Born 9/2/22. Commd 26/9/57. Sqn Ldr 1/1/70. Retd ENG 7/8/76.
TWYMAN C. D., BSc. Born 6/6/46. Commd 13/4/66. Sqn Ldr 1/7/80. Retd SUP 6/6/84.
TYACK E. W., CBE FRAeS. Born 23/4/44. Commd 22/5/64. A Cdre 1/1/92. Retd GD 3/12/99.
TYACK G. E., MTech BSc CEng MIEE MBCS MIMgt. Born 23/12/40. Commd 10/9/63. Wg Cdr 1/7/79. Retd ENG 29/9/97.
TYDEMAN R. J. Born 10/3/48. Commd 28/2/69. Sqn Ldr 1/7/81. Retd GD 21/1/89.
TYE A. C., MIMgt. Born 28/5/26. Commd 18/4/39. A Cdre 1/7/61. Retd GD 28/5/81.
TYE J. Born 9/6/38. Commd 26/10/62. Flt Lt 26/4/68. Retd GD 9/1/81.
TYLDESLEY A. M., MRAeS. Born 22/12/33. Commd 17/8/55. Sqn Ldr 1/7/66. Retd GD 22/12/88.
TYLER G. A., BA. Born 18/4/42. Commd 14/9/64. Flt Lt 14/6/66. Retd GD 14/9/80.
TYLER J. C. Born 18/1/30. Commd 8/7/65. Flt Lt 8/7/70. Retd SY 26/8/77.
TYLER J. D., MBE. Born 23/5/49. Commd 27/3/70. Sqn Ldr 1/7/85. Retd GD 14/3/97.
TYLER M. W. R. H. Born 31/8/24. Commd 14/1/46. Sqn Ldr 1/1/60. Retd GD 8/10/67.
TYLER P. G., OBE FIMgt. Born 21/12/19. Commd 31/10/39. A Cdre 1/1/71. Retd SUP 27/1/73.
TYLER R. C. Born 21/1/33. Commd 10/12/52. Flt Lt 5/5/58. Retd GD 21/1/71.
TYLER W., DFC. Born 18/5/20. Commd 21/8/42. Flt Lt 21/2/46. Retd GD 18/5/63.
TYNDALL F. E., CBE. Born 4/1/13. Commd 18/4/39. A Cdre 1/7/61. Retd ENG 22/3/68.
TYNDALL W. F. C. Born 18/4/42. Commd 24/6/65. Flt Lt 9/2/68. Retd GD 30/9/80.
TYRRELL G. M. Born 26/9/44. Commd 16/6/69. Flt Lt 16/3/71. Retd GD 16/6/91.
TYRRELL J. J. Born 7/4/35. Commd 26/7/55. Flt Lt 14/5/58. Retd GD 1/1/69.
TYRRELL M. J. M., MMar. Born 17/10/40. Commd 6/1/69. Wg Cdr 1/7/84. Retd MAR 1/4/86.
TYSON J. Born 24/4/24. Commd 3/11/44. Sqn Ldr 1/7/58. Retd GD 24/4/73.
TYSON P. N., BSc. Born 9/4/62. Commd 13/5/81. Flt Lt 15/10/84. Retd GD 15/7/95.
TYSON-WOODCOCK P. J. E. Born 24/7/40. Commd 9/12/65. Sqn Ldr 1/7/78. Retd ADMIN 31/8/90.
TYZAZK J. E. V., CBE. Born 11/1/04. Commd 10/1/29. Wg Cdr 31/7/42. Retd SUP 9/2/46 rtg Gp Capt.

# U

UDY R. J. Born 21/6/41. Commd 1/2/62. Flt Lt 1/7/69. Retd GD(G) 21/6/79.
UNDERDOWN M. Born 26/7/42. Commd 1/4/66. Flt Lt 28/8/68. Retd GD 26/7/80.
UNDERDOWN P. J. Born 12/1/31. Commd 14/4/53. Flt Lt 14/10/55. Retd GD 12/1/69.
UNDERHILL C. D., BSc. Born 25/10/52. Commd 28/1/73. Flt Lt 15/4/76. Retd GD 25/10/90.
UNDERHILL P. W., BTech CEng MIMechE. Born 19/5/48. Commd 5/12/73. Sqn Ldr 1/1/84. Retd ENG 5/12/89.
UNDERWOOD J. K. Born 9/1/20. Commd 18/12/43. Flt Lt 18/6/47. Retd GD 29/1/58.
UNDERWOOD M. H. Born 18/4/33. Commd 12/4/73. Sqn Ldr 1/7/82. Retd ENG 2/1/86.
UNDERWOOD P. G., BSc. Born 2/9/58. Commd 17/8/80. Flt Lt 17/5/82. Retd GD 2/9/96.
UNDERWOOD R. J. Born 1/7/28. Commd 24/9/64. Fg Offr 24/9/65. Retd CAT 31/1/68.
UNDERWOOD S. C. Born 21/5/59. Commd 28/2/80. Flt Lt 28/8/85. Retd GD 21/10/99.
UNDERWOOD S. T., OBE. Born 4/4/17. Commd 5/12/41. Wg Cdr 1/7/55. Retd GD 4/4/72.
UNDERWOOD T. H. Born 31/3/43. Commd 23/12/61. Wg Cdr 1/1/84. Retd ADMIN 1/1/94.
UNDERWOOD T. M. Born 10/2/26. Commd 23/1/60. Flt Lt 23/1/65. Retd GD(G) 30/6/78.
UNDERWOOD W. B., MBE MIMgt. Born 9/10/32. Commd 15/5/58. Sqn Ldr 1/1/69. Retd SUP 16/1/84.
UNSTED B. G. W. Born 2/7/32. Commd 1/4/53. Flt Lt 17/3/59. Retd GD 2/7/70.
UNSWORTH G. W., BA. Born 15/1/31. Commd 26/3/53. Flt Lt 26/6/54. Retd GD 15/1/69.
UNWIN C. R., MBE DPhysEd. Born 3/6/39. Commd 18/5/65. Flt Lt 8/3/72. Retd GD 18/5/81. Reinstated 24/3/86.
 Flt Lt 11/1/77. Retd GD 9/10/93.
UNWIN G. C., DSO DFM*. Born 18/1/13. Commd 31/7/41. Wg Cdr 1/1/54. Retd GD 18/1/61.
UNWIN J. N. B. Born 18/6/24. Commd 8/9/44. Sqn Ldr 1/7/55. Retd GD 18/6/67.
UNWIN R. F. B. Born 3/2/13. Commd 12/6/47. Fg Offr 12/6/47. Retd SEC 5/9/48.
UPFOLD P. E. Born 6/8/32. Commd 28/11/74. Sqn Ldr 21/11/82. Retd MED 6/8/87.
UPRICHARD J. L., CBE. Born 31/12/43. Commd 8/3/65. A Cdre 1/7/94. Retd GD 31/12/98.
UPRICHARD R. J. H., MA MIMgt. Born 31/12/22. Commd 9/7/43. Gp Capt 1/7/68. Retd GD 31/12/73.
UPSHALL F. W. Born 4/5/07. Commd 15/10/41. Sqn Ldr 1/1/49. Retd ENG 4/5/56.
UPSON P. A., BSc. Born 28/4/60. Commd 4/9/78. Flt Lt 15/8/85. Retd SY(RGT) 16/12/88.
UPTON C. E., MSc MCIT MILT. Born 11/2/43. Commd 17/12/65. Wg Cdr 1/1/82. Retd SUP 14/4/91.
UPTON G. T. G. Born 18/10/25. Commd 19/10/45. Flt Lt 4/4/51. Retd GD 18/10/63.
UPTON R. T., MBE. Born 8/6/26. Commd 5/7/68. Flt Lt 1/1/73. Retd GD 25/10/78.
UREN E. F., CEng MIMechE. Born 1/6/40. Commd 18/7/61. Wg Cdr 1/7/79. Retd ENG 1/6/90.
UREN J. C. Born 27/3/60. Commd 22/2/79. Sqn Ldr 1/1/98. Retd GD 1/1/01.
URQUHART J. M., MB ChB DPH. Born 1/10/18. Commd 2/7/42. Gp Capt 1/7/63. Retd MED 3/10/68.
URRY F. A. Born 6/1/22. Commd 5/7/68. Flt Lt 1/1/73. Retd ENG 5/7/78.
URRY M. W. Born 13/8/41. Commd 2/1/75. Sqn Ldr 1/1/84. Retd ENG 2/1/86.
USHER D. C., DFC DFM. Born 18/1/20. Commd 5/12/43. Sqn Ldr 1/1/54. Retd GD 19/1/63.
USHERWOOD W. P., MCIPS. Born 19/10/27. Commd 1/10/57. Sqn Ldr 1/7/67. Retd SUP 3/1/80.
USSHER C. W. J., MRCS LRCP. Born 13/7/22. Commd 2/12/47. Flt Lt 2/12/48. Retd MED 1/4/53 rtg Sqn Ldr.
UTTLEY J. R. S., MSc CEng MIMechE. Born 2/4/46. Commd 21/1/73. Sqn Ldr 1/7/85. Retd ENG 21/1/89.
UTTON K. H. G. Born 30/4/22. Commd 16/3/45. Flt Lt 16/9/48. Retd GD 9/5/65.

# V

VACQUIER A. T., CEng MIEE. Born 28/1/20. Commd 5/6/42. Wg Cdr 1/7/67. Retd ENG 28/1/75.
VALE D. L., BSc. Born 21/1/50. Commd 28/2/72. Flt Lt 28/11/75. Retd GD(G) 28/2/88.
VALE G. G. Born 4/7/47. Commd 23/11/78. Sqn Ldr 1/1/92. Retd ENG 13/4/96.
VALE J. B. Born 2/8/34. Commd 27/5/53. Flt Lt 17/9/58. Retd GD(G) 2/8/89.
VALE N. Born 11/3/33. Commd 18/3/53. Sqn Ldr 1/1/84. Retd GD 11/3/88.
VALE P. N., BSc. Born 16/6/50. Commd 25/2/72. Flt Lt 25/11/76. Retd ENG 1/9/00.
VALENTINE D. G. A. Born 6/7/18. Commd 3/8/44. Gp Capt 1/7/69. Retd SUP 6/7/73.
VALENTINE D. J. B. Born 26/8/36. Commd 13/7/61. Gp Capt 1/7/86. Retd ADMIN 2/5/91.
VALENTINE L. F. Born 18/3/20. Commd 6/3/44. Flt Lt 6/3/50. Retd SEC 18/3/75.
VALENTINE M. C. Born 23/9/45. Commd 9/12/65. Wg Cdr 1/1/87. Retd OPS SPT 23/9/00.
VALENTINE M. R. Born 26/12/23. Commd 16/10/44. Flt Lt 2/4/49. Retd SEC 31/3/62.
VALENTINE R. G. Born 11/11/34. Commd 27/3/56. Flt Lt 19/6/62. Retd GD 11/11/72 rtg Sqn Ldr.
VALLANCE C. G., BSc. Born 6/8/48. Commd 15/6/70. Sqn Ldr 1/1/82. Retd ENG 6/8/86.
VAN DER VEEN M., MA CEng FIEE. Born 22/1/46. Commd 28/9/64. AVM 1/1/96. Retd ENG 3/1/98.
VAN GEENE R. G. Born 24/8/49. Commd 29/11/68. Flt Lt 29/5/75. Retd GD 24/8/87.
VAN HINSBERGH P. J. Born 31/1/22. Commd 11/4/57. Sqn Ldr 1/1/72. Retd GD 31/1/82.
VAN PUYENBROEK J. E. Born 27/6/18. Commd 14/12/42. Sqn Ldr 1/1/59. Retd ENG 27/3/63.
VAN REE G., BDS. Born 27/5/51. Commd 3/9/72. Wg Cdr 6/12/87. Retd DEL 8/6/96.
VAN TOEN R. Born 13/5/20. Commd 14/3/42. Flt Lt 25/9/45. Retd GD(G) 12/4/59.
VAN WARMELO W., MBE BSc. Born 16/3/36. Commd 5/3/57. Wg Cdr 1/1/85. Retd GD 27/2/87.
VAN WYK P. D. Born 2/7/37. Commd 27/2/60. Flt Lt 27/11/60. Retd GD 1/10/64.
VANGUCCI P. C., AFC FIMgt. Born 29/8/31. Commd 11/1/51. Gp Capt 1/7/77. Retd GD 5/11/84.
VANSTONE D. J., FIMgt. Born 13/4/19. Commd 1/6/44. Gp Capt 1/7/67. Retd ENG 13/4/74.
VANT W. J. Born 28/6/48. Commd 14/8/70. Wg Cdr 1/7/88. Retd GD(G) 1/10/92.
VARCOE D. H. Born 1/7/23. Commd 12/10/55. Flt Offr 12/4/61. Retd SEC 12/5/67.
VARDY S. J., MB ChB FRCSEd. Born 7/8/53. Commd 5/11/79. Wg Cdr 1/8/96. Retd MED 2/4/00.
VAREY A. J. Born 24/1/47. Commd 1/3/68. Wg Cdr 1/7/85. Retd ENG 8/5/91.
VAREY H. R. S. Born 9/8/50. Commd 19/6/70. Flt Lt 17/10/76. Retd SEC 7/4/79.
VARLEY G. W., BSc FRCS(Ed) MB ChB. Born 30/5/58. Commd 25/9/80. Sqn Ldr 1/8/89. Retd MED 25/9/96.
VARLEY P. W. R. Born 19/1/24. Commd 27/4/45. Flt Lt 29/6/50. Retd GD 28/4/55.
VARLEY R. W., ACIS. Born 20/4/32. Commd 2/8/51. Sqn Ldr 1/1/71. Retd ADMIN 1/10/77.
VARTY L. Born 3/12/25. Commd 26/3/52. Flt Lt 31/7/57. Retd GD 3/12/63.
VARY C. E. Born 28/2/43. Commd 19/11/62. Wg Cdr 1/7/90. Retd GD 3/3/97.
VASEY C. A., FIMgt. Born 20/9/28. Commd 11/4/51. Gp Capt 1/7/76. Retd GD 21/1/82.
VASSE D. G. Born 17/6/25. Commd 28/7/45. Sqn Ldr 1/1/57. Retd GD 29/6/68.
VATCHER A. R., SRN RNT. Born 11/3/35. Commd 11/11/65. Flt Lt 11/11/71. Retd MED(T) 31/8/74.
VAUGHAN A. H., OBE BA. Born 3/12/49. Commd 15/9/69. A Cdre 1/1/97. Retd ADMIN 1/2/99.
VAUGHAN B. R. Born 5/3/37. Commd 12/1/61. Sqn Ldr 1/1/73. Retd SEC 7/4/81.
VAUGHAN J. C. Born 9/1/25. Commd 2/1/51. Sqn Ldr 1/1/66. Retd GD(G) 9/1/83.
VAUGHAN K. H. Born 29/6/22. Commd 7/6/44. Flt Lt 7/12/47. Retd GD 29/6/77.
VAUGHAN M. C. M., CBE. Born 12/6/16. Commd 24/6/43. Gp Capt 1/7/65. Retd SEC 8/1/73 rtg A Cdre.
VAUGHAN S. A. Born 12/10/56. Commd 22/11/84. Sqn Ldr 1/7/94. Retd ENG 1/7/97.
VAUGHAN-LANE T., MB ChB FRCS. Born 9/4/47. Commd 27/1/69. Sqn Ldr 10/7/77. Retd MED 9/6/85.
VAUGHNLEY A. G. Born 5/2/62. Commd 28/9/89. Flt Lt 28/9/91. Retd GD 5/2/00.
VAUTIER B. Born 20/7/52. Commd 27/2/75. Flt Lt 27/8/81. Retd ADMIN 4/11/90.
VAUTIER E. A. Born 21/2/22. Commd 19/10/44. Sqn Ldr 1/1/59. Retd CAT 14/12/67.
VAUX J. M. S. Born 27/4/22. Commd 28/5/43. Sqn Ldr 1/7/58. Retd GD 27/4/65.
VAUX S. D. Born 1/4/50. Commd 8/10/87. Flt Lt 8/10/91. Retd SUP 1/2/97.
VEAL P. J. Born 25/6/38. Commd 28/7/59. Sqn Ldr 1/7/82. Retd GD 25/6/95.
VEALE A. Born 2/4/26. Commd 21/12/45. Wg Cdr 1/7/63. Retd GD 15/5/76.
VEALL J. J. Born 21/9/26. Commd 2/3/49. Flt Lt 9/6/52. Retd GD 21/9/69.
VEARNCOMBE M. G. Born 8/8/55. Commd 22/2/79. Wg Cdr 1/1/97. Retd ADMIN 1/2/98.
VELLA J. F., MIMgt. Born 6/5/33. Commd 6/4/54. Wg Cdr 1/1/80. Retd SUP 27/11/84.
VELTMAN D. R., BA. Born 15/7/44. Commd 20/10/83. Flt Lt 20/10/85. Retd ADMIN 20/10/91.
VENABLES W. A., MBE. Born 31/10/19. Commd 2/6/49. Flt Lt 2/12/52. Retd SEC 31/7/66.
VENDRELL J., MMar. Born 19/1/17. Commd 12/7/56. Sqn Ldr 12/7/64. Retd MAR 19/1/72.
VENIER A. L., MVO Born 14/5/30. Commd 20/12/51. Wg Cdr 1/1/84. Retd GD 14/5/85.
VENMAN A. J. Born 12/2/38. Commd 2/1/75. Sqn Ldr 2/1/87. Retd MED(T) 12/2/93.
VENN K. F., CEng MRAeS MIMgt DCAe. Born 30/1/21. Commd 19/8/42. Wg Cdr 1/7/59. Retd ENG 31/5/69.
VENN M. G. P., OBE MB BS MFOM DAvMed MRAeS MIMgt. Born 29/4/31. Commd 6/1/57. A Cdre 1/7/84. Retd MED 1/2/85.

VENN S. W. A. Born 17/2/08. Commd 1/8/41. Flt Lt 1/1/44. Retd ENG 20/1/46 rtg Sqn Ldr.
VENTHAM V., BSc. Born 30/1/34. Commd 23/8/55. Flt Lt 23/5/57. Retd GD 30/1/72.
VENTURA M. R. C. Born 12/10/37. Commd 2/8/68. Flt Lt 2/8/70. Retd SUP 2/8/76.
VENUS L. C. Born 22/7/58. Commd 19/10/81. Sqn Ldr 1/1/94. Retd ADMIN 19/10/97.
VERDEN G. Born 15/1/99. Commd 1/4/18. Fg Offr 1/4/18. Retd GD 5/4/22.
VERDON-ROE R. Born 23/7/25. Commd 29/1/46. Flt Lt 6/2/54. Retd GD 1/7/57.
VERE R. P. Born 12/6/37. Commd 15/9/61. Flt Lt 25/7/66. Retd GD(G) 3/10/78.
VERGNANO P. N. Born 7/11/52. Commd 30/3/75. Sqn Ldr 1/7/86. Retd ADMIN 14/3/97.
VERITY H. B., DSO* DFC MA. Born 6/4/18. Commd 8/11/38. Gp Capt 1/7/58 Retd GD 2/6/65.
VERNON A. R., MB BS. Born 27/4/55. Commd 18/11/75. Sqn Ldr 1/8/84. Retd MED 1/2/86.
VERNON F. H., MBE. Born 22/12/20. Commd 30/1/58. Flt Lt 1/4/63 Retd ENG 12/1/76.
VERNON F. L. A., MRCS LRCP FRCOG. Born 17/10/18. Commd 4/1/54. Gp Capt 1/12/66. Retd MED 1/2/70.
VERNON J. Born 8/4/37. Commd 4/1/56. Sqn Ldr 1/1/70. Retd GD 6/2/91.
VERNON P. A. Born 9/10/48. Commd 29/4/71. Sqn Ldr 1/1/86. Retd GD 1/1/89.
VERNON R. K., BEM. Born 15/9/47. Commd 8/9/83. Flt Lt 8/9/87. Retd ENG 2/12/98.
VERRALL W. H. Born 22/12/19. Commd 22/9/55. Sqn Ldr 1/7/67. Retd ENG 27/12/74.
VERRALLS W. A., DFC. Born 18/3/14. Commd 8/5/43. Flt Lt 21/2/56. Retd GD(G) 18/3/69.
VERRIER P. C., DPhysEd. Born 5/10/37. Commd 8/12/64. Flt Lt 9/2/68. Retd PE 27/5/81.
VERRIL M. Born 8/2/42. Commd 22/5/64. Sqn Ldr 1/1/93. Retd GD 28/11/95.
VESELY V., DFC AFC. Born 20/9/13. Commd 17/8/40. Sqn Ldr 1/1/58. Retd GD(G) 3/10/68.
VICK J. W., DFC. Born 30/1/17. Commd 10/8/44. Wg Cdr 1/1/66. Retd GD(G) 17/2/72.
VICKERS A. G. W. Born 2/1/25. Commd 2/3/61. Flt Lt 2/3/66. Retd GD 1/6/73. Reinstated 19/10/78 to 2/1/83.
VICKERS D. R., MBE BA CEng MIMechE MIMgt. Born 28/1/42. Commd 13/10/64. Wg Cdr 1/7/77. Retd ENG
  13/10/83.
VICKERS F. J. Born 21/4/23. Commd 4/6/44. Sqn Ldr 1/7/56. Retd GD 31/3/62.
VICKERS M. A., AFC. Born 22/5/23. Commd 1/10/47. Sqn Ldr 1/7/67. Retd GD 22/5/78.
VICKERY J. E., MA. Born 30/12/34. Commd 1/10/57. Gp Capt 1/1/86. Retd GD 30/12/89.
VICKERY L. D. Born 14/2/16. Commd 10/6/39. Wg Cdr 1/1/63. Retd SEC 14/4/66.
VICKERY L. J. Born 17/9/21. Commd 6/9/56. Sqn Ldr 1/1/69. Retd ENG 15/9/73.
VICKERY R. A. Born 2/4/28. Commd 30/7/52. Flt Lt 27/12/57. Retd GD 2/4/66.
VIDOT C. C., MRCS LRCP DPH. Born 13/10/18. Commd 16/5/46. Wg Cdr 10/8/60. Retd MED 10/8/62.
VIELLE E. E., OBE MRAeS. Born 29/4/13. Commd 28/7/34. Gp Capt 1/1/51 Retd GD 14/11/57.
VIEROD D. Born 23/10/29. Commd 3/5/68. Flt Lt 3/5/73. Retd ENG 23/10/87.
VIGAR J. A. Born 5/4/31. Commd 22/10/53. Flt Lt 22/10/57. Retd GD 11/9/64.
VIGORS T. A., DFC. Born 22/3/21. Commd 23/12/39. Sqn Ldr 24/1/44. Retd GD 8/11/46 rtg Wg Cdr.
VIMPANY R. N., MBE. Born 18/4/23. Commd 28/12/43. Sqn Ldr 1/1/64. Retd GD 1/1/67.
VINALES J. Born 8/8/45. Commd 28/4/65. Sqn Ldr 1/1/83. Retd GD 1/7/94.
VINCE D. G. Born 3/5/24. Commd 13/3/46. Flt Lt 13/3/52. Retd RGT 3/5/62.
VINCENT F., OBE MWSOM MIMgt. Born 13/7/24. Commd 31/12/44. Gp Capt. 1/1/75. Retd SEC 13/7/79.
VINCENT H. A. Born 14/3/59. Commd 8/11/89. Flt Lt 9/11/91. Retd ADMIN 23/4/94.
VINCENT H. McC. Born 12/5/24. Commd 9/3/50. Flt Lt 27/5/54. Retd GD 12/5/67.
VINCENT J. C., BSc. Born 30/9/54. Commd 3/9/72. Wg Cdr 1/1/95. Retd GD 30/9/98.
VINCENT M. D. Born 3/4/47. Commd 22/3/67. Flt Lt 23/9/72. Retd GD 8/12/76.
VINCENT R. E., BSc CEng MRAeS MIMgt. Born 27/7/49. Commd 24/9/72. Sqn Ldr 1/1/84. Retd ENG 24/9/88.
VINCENT R. J., MIMgt. Born 27/10/29. Commd 28/6/51. Sqn Ldr 1/1/67. Retd GD 1/7/73.
VINCENTI J. H., MD. Born 26/12/26. Commd 5/7/54. Sqn Ldr 2/12/61. Retd MED 22/2/65.
VINCENTI N., MD FRCS FRCS(Glas) DLO. Born 4/12/26. Commd 5/2/56. Gp Capt 20/2/73. Retd MED 5/2/84.
VINE A. W., MBE AFC AFM. Born 1/2/23. Commd 4/7/57. Sqn Ldr 1/1/67. Retd GD 12/3/77.
VINE A. W. Born 21/2/42. Commd 27/1/67. Flt Lt 27/1/69. Retd GD 9/4/83.
VINE D. C. Born 27/7/49. Commd 7/11/85. Sqn Ldr 1/1/92. Retd GD 14/3/97.
VINE E., AFC*. Born 16/2/22. Commd 24/1/52. Flt Lt 15/5/57. Retd GD 1/11/74.
VINEY E. C. Born 16/6/43. Commd 21/5/65. Flt Lt 12/11/69. Retd GD 16/6/81.
VINEY R. C. Born 13/3/40. Commd 17/7/62. Sqn Ldr 1/7/77. Retd ENG 13/3/95.
VINNICOMBE K. Born 7/2/36. Commd 3/1/61. Sqn Ldr 29/10/73. Retd ADMIN 7/2/94.
VIRASINGHE I. A. K. Born 26/1/34. Commd 15/9/65. Flt Lt 15/9/65. Retd SEC 6/2/75.
VIRGO I., MSc BTech CEng MRAes. Born 22/10/52. Commd 25/9/71. Sqn Ldr 1/7/87. Retd ENG 31/7/96.
VISAGIE P. W., LLB. Born 1/12/48. Commd 30/6/74. Wg Cdr 1/12/84. Retd LGL 30/6/90.
VITTLES S. R. Born 18/3/42. Commd 19/6/64. Flt Lt 19/12/69. Retd GD 1/7/75.
VIVASH E. P., BA MIMgt. Born 26/8/35. Commd 2/10/57. Sqn Ldr 2/4/66. Retd ADMIN 26/8/85.
VIVIAN H. D. Born 4/4/22. Commd 22/7/42. Flt Offr 22/1/47. Retd SEC 20/8/57.
VIVIAN J. A., MA. Born 7/12/26. Commd 11/2/63. Flt Lt 28/7/65. Retd ADMIN 13/2/79.
VIZARD A. E. Born 23/4/54. Commd 21/4/77. Flt Lt 21/10/82. Retd GD 2/1/93.
VOADEN J. H., CEng MIEE MIMgt. Born 28/9/35. Commd 17/5/60. Sqn Ldr 1/7/67. Retd ENG 17/5/76.
VOCKINS V. V. Born 28/9/17. Commd 17/10/41. Sqn Ldr 1/7/62. Retd ENG 28/9/72.
VOLLBORTH P. W. Born 21/3/33. Commd 5/12/51. Sqn Ldr 1/7/68. Retd ADMIN 4/10/84.
VOLLER E. B. Born 17/3/36. Commd 30/7/57. Flt Lt 26/2/64. Retd GD 17/3/74.

VOLWERK J. M. Born 17/8/45. Commd 15/8/85. Sqn Ldr 1/7/92. Retd ADMIN 14/3/96.
VON BAUMANN A. G. Born 10/6/23. Commd 27/10/55. Flt Lt 27/10/61. Retd GD 31/12/77.
VON PATZELT M. G. Born 23/12/19. Commd 6/5/43. Sqn Ldr 1/1/60. Retd SEC 23/12/68.
VOSPER J. R. Born 31/3/13. Commd 19/11/42. Flt Lt 19/5/46. Retd ENG 31/3/62.
VOUSDEN R. J. C., MRAeS. Born 4/3/44. Commd 9/8/63. Sqn Ldr 1/7/81. Retd GD 1/1/96.
VOUTE N. M. Born 15/4/49. Commd 28/11/69. Flt Lt 15/10/74. Retd GD 15/4/87.
VOYLE A. J., BSc. Born 9/11/41. Commd 15/7/63. Sqn Ldr 1/7/75. Retd ENG 9/11/79.
VOYSEY A., BSc. Born 27/6/57. Commd 14/9/75. Sqn Ldr 1/7/89. Retd ENG 27/6/95.
VOYSEY F. W. Born 13/12/27. Commd 15/12/49. Flt Lt 15/6/53. Retd GD 26/7/68.
VRACAS B. H., BA. Born 14/7/56. Commd 15/9/74. Flt Lt 15/10/78. Retd GD 1/12/85.
VYE H. J. Born 8/9/21. Commd 6/1/55. Flt Lt 6/1/58. Retd GD 20/5/76.

# W

WADAMS G. V., AFC. Born 19/5/24. Commd 29/3/45. Flt Lt 7/6/51. Retd GD 3/11/62.
WADDELL A. D., MBE MCIT MILT. Born 25/5/47. Commd 21/10/66. Wg Cdr 1/7/85. Retd SUP 14/3/97.
WADDELL C. P. Born 26/9/15. Commd 8/7/41. Wg Cdr 1/1/54. Retd GD(G) 20/7/65.
WADDELL R. G. Born 1/8/22. Commd 17/7/58. Sqn Ldr 1/1/70. Retd GD 31/3/74.
WADDICOR A. E., DFC DFM. Born 24/12/19. Commd 14/1/44. Flt Lt 14/7/47. Retd GD(G) 23/1/65.
WADDINGHAM J. Born 28/6/27. Commd 30/7/53. Flt Lt 30/1/58. Retd GD 28/6/70.
WADDINGTON B. Born 29/11/48. Commd 4/7/69. Flt Lt 4/1/75. Retd GD 9/6/86.
WADDINGTON J. F., AFC. Born 13/11/42. Commd 7/7/67. Sqn Ldr 1/7/87. Retd GD 22/4/94.
WADDINGTON W. D. B., DFC. Born 8/8/19. Commd 25/8/40. Flt Lt 1/9/45. Retd GD 8/8/62 rtg Sqn Ldr.
WADE B. R. M., DFC. Born 15/9/21. Commd 9/10/39. Wg Cdr 1/1/59. Retd GD 15/9/68.
WADE G. M., MBE. Born 17/12/22. Commd 9/11/43. Flt Lt 4/1/51. Retd SEC 10/4/62.
WADE G. N. Born 15/8/38. Commd 31/7/62. Flt Lt 15.2.65. Retd GD(G) 16/8/75.
WADE J. M., BA. Born 6/12/38. Commd 25/10/73. Flt Lt 25/10/75. Retd GD(G) 25/10/81. Reinstated 13/10/86. Flt Lt 13/10/80. Retd GD(G) 24/1/90.
WADE J. P. A., DFC. Born 11/7/23. Commd 27/11/43. Flt Lt 4/1/51. Retd SUP 21/8/57.
WADE N. L., DFC. Born 11/7/23. Commd 27/11/45. Flt Lt 27/11/49. SUP 16/1/65.
WADE Sir Ruthven, KCB DFC. Born 15/7/20. Commd 23/12/39. ACM 31/3/76. Retd GD 31/3/78.
WADE R. D. Born 7/7/50. Commd 15/8/85. Flt Lt 15/8/89. Retd GD 31/3/94.
WADEY G. D. Born 28/5/33. Commd 2/3/59. Flt Lt 1/3/61. Retd GD 28/5/93.
WADLEY M. E., BA MIMgt CertEd. Born 17/12/37. Commd 3/10/61. Wg Cdr 1/1/87. Retd ADMIN 1/11/91.
WADLEY R. E. A. Born 19/9/36. Commd 27/4/65. Sqn Ldr 1/1/91. Retd ADMIN 1/1/94.
WADSWORTH D. A. Born 24/2/44. Commd 24/6/65. Sqn Ldr 1/7/74. Retd GD 31/3/94.
WAGGETT A. V. Born 29/9/33. Commd 27/2/70. Sqn Ldr 1/7/81. Retd ENG 29/9/88.
WAGHORN C. P., MSc BA MCIT MILT. Born 6/10/54. Commd 17/6/79. Sqn Ldr 1/7/90. Retd SUP 17/6/95.
WAGHORN E. W. Born 27/7/25. Commd 26/3/64. Flt Lt 26/4/69. Retd PE 1/2/74.
WAGNER F. P. G. Born 26/1/35. Commd 20/1/56. Flt Lt 20/7/61. Retd GD(G) 27/1/72. Re-employed Flt Lt 5/4/74 to 1/4/78.
WAGNER P. R., MB BS MRCS LRCP. Born 10/8/23. Commd 1/9/49. Wg Cdr 1/4/62. Retd MED 1/9/65.
WAGSTAFF L. E. Born 8/5/37. Commd 18/5/55. Flt Lt 1/8/61. Retd GD 8/5/65.
WAGSTAFF M. F. Born 10/10/41. Commd 23/9/65. Sqn Ldr 1/7/75. Retd SEC 10/2/79.
WAGSTAFF R., BSc. Born 5/2/40. Commd 30/6/62. Flt Lt 30/6/67. Retd ENG 31/3/80.
WAGSTAFFE B., IEng AMRAeS. Born 28/5/35. Commd 5/7/68. Sqn Ldr 1/7/77. Retd ENG 28/5/90.
WAIN M. R., BA. Born 7/7/42. Commd 22/7/68. Wg Cdr 1/7/87. Retd ENG 22/7/90.
WAIN R. M. Born 9/8/33. Commd 28/9/54. Flt Lt 28/3/59. Retd GD 5/4/75.
WAINMAN H., BA. Born 17/1/42. Commd 10/11/61. Flt Lt 12/10/71. Retd GD 16/1/94.
WAINWRIGHT E. H. Born 19/3/24. Commd 3/11/44. Sqn Ldr 1/1/71. Retd GD(G) 28/10/77.
WAINWRIGHT G. C., BSc MRAeS. Born 19/9/16. Commd 21/6/40. Wg Cdr 1/7/56. Retd ENG 24/12/64.
WAINWRIGHT J. A., DSO. Born 8/11/21. Commd 13/5/44. Flt Lt 13/11/47. Retd GD 8/11/65.
WAINWRIGHT M. T., AFC. Born 15/3/19. Commd 27/9/37. Sqn Ldr 1/7/53. Retd GD 31/3/58.
WAINWRIGHT N. D. Born 2/10/58. Commd 31/8/78. Sqn Ldr 1/1/93. Retd GD 10/6/00.
WAINWRIGHT R. N. Born 18/4/52. Commd 25/9/71. Flt Lt 9/3/80. Retd GD 18/4/90.
WAINWRIGHT W. A., BSc. Born 5/7/43. Commd 14/9/64. Sqn Ldr 1/1/76. Retd GD 5/7/81.
WAITE B. Born 22/10/47. Commd 9/2/81. Sqn Ldr 1/7/94. Retd ADMIN 1/7/97.
WAITE E., MRAeS. Born 5/6/23. Commd 4/5/50. Wg Cdr 1/7/71. Retd ENG 30/3/77.
WAITE G., MIMgt. Born 12/12/18. Commd 5/10/44. Wg Cdr 1/7/62. Retd SUP 27/2/71.
WAITE G. W. Born 4/9/45. Commd 20/8/65. Flt Lt 6/10/71. Retd GD 4/9/00.
WAITE W. E., MBE. Born 14/4/31. Commd 26/3/52. Sqn Ldr 1/7/64. Retd GD 1/12/73 rtg Wg Cdr.
WAITING J. E. Born 4/1/27. Commd 26/7/51. Flt Lt 14/11/56. Retd GD 14/2/70.
WAITT C. B., BA. Born 4/8/58. Commd 29/11/81. Wg Cdr 1/7/96. Retd SUP 1/7/99.
WAKEFIELD A. J., CEng MIMechE MIOSH. Born 12/12/36. Commd 30/5/71. Sqn Ldr 1/7/90. Retd ENG 12/12/94.
WAKEFIELD C. P. Born 28/11/33. Commd 13/8/52. Flt Lt 9/1/58. Retd GD 28/11/71.
WAKEFIELD D. C. Born 21/6/36. Commd 23/3/66. Flt Lt 23/3/68. Retd PE 11/8/73.
WAKEFIELD D. K., BSc. Born 20/4/49. Commd 2/1/70. Flt Lt 15/10/72. Retd GD 20/4/87.
WAKEFIELD W. J. N. Born 26/3/08. Commd 5/5/41. Flt Lt 1/9/45. Retd SEC 1/10/57.
WAKEFORD D. B. W., CEng MIMechE. Born 10/2/35. Commd 7/11/58. Wg Cdr 1/7/80. Retd ENG 6/12/85.
WAKEFORD Sir Richard, KCB MVO OBE AFC. Born 20/4/22. Commd 7/3/42. AM 1/7/75. Retd GD 31/3/78.
WAKELIN R. H. W. Born 4/4/43. Commd 24/6/65. Sqn Ldr 1/7/77. Retd SUP 4/4/81.
WAKELY B., BSc. Born 9/4/47. Commd 28/2/69. Gp Capt 1/1/99. Retd ENG 18/9/00.
WAKELY P. A., MB BS MRCS LRCP. Born 12/8/44. Commd 13/9/65. Sqn Ldr 26/6/74. Retd MED 24/1/76.
WAKEMAN R., DFC. Born 14/10/18. Commd 8/9/44. Flt Lt 19/6/55. Retd GD(G) 10/6/69.

WAKERLEY D. G., BSc BChD LDS. Born 9/5/35. Commd 22/11/57. Wg Cdr 22/7/66. Retd DEL 4/3/77.
WAKLING B. G. E. Born 14/4/44. Commd 21/12/62. Sqn Ldr 1/1/75. Retd GD 21/12/82.
WALDECK A. C. Born 3/10/40. Commd 2/8/68. Flt Lt 2/8/70. Retd GD(G) 5/10/77.
WALDEN C. T. Born 21/2/27. Commd 19/7/51. Wg Cdr 1/7/68. Retd GD 30/10/70.
WALDEN G. F., DFC. Born 14/4/21. Commd 29/7/45. Sqn Ldr 1/7/70. Retd GD(G) 14/4/76.
WALDING J. K., BA. Born 16/9/37. Commd 29/10/60. Flt Lt 29/4/66. Retd GD 12/7/76.
WALDREN F. S., DFC. Born 27/5/15. Commd 17/10/42. Flt Lt 17/4/47. Retd SEC 26/6/64 rtg Sqn Ldr.
WALDWYN C. R., MSc BSc CEng MIIE(mech) MRAeS. Born 11/12/60. Commd 4/2/81. Sqn Ldr 1/7/94. Retd ENG 11/12/98.
WALENTOWICZ J. Born 4/8/20. Commd 7/1/48. Flt Lt 10/11/55. Retd GD 1/10/69.
WALES D. H., AFC. Born 11/6/22. Commd 23/7/41. Flt Lt 17/12/51. Retd GD 4/3/63.
WALES K. C. G., BSc CEng MIMechE MRAeS. Born 18/11/33. Commd 25/1/71. Flt Lt 25/8/70. Retd ENG 25/1/87.
WALES W. H. N. Born 22/12/19. Commd 24/2/67. Flt Lt 24/2/70. Retd ENG 24/2/77.
WALFORD G. B., OBE. Born 13/4/16. Commd 10/5/37. Gp Capt 1/1/58. Retd GD 31/3/67.
WALKER A., BSc. Born 9/10/49. Commd 1/11/71. Sqn Ldr 1/1/86. Retd GD 1/1/89.
WALKER A. Born 29/6/56. Commd 16/2/89. Flt Lt 17/9/94. Retd MED(T) 14/9/96.
WALKER A. A. Born 6/3/39. Commd 16/12/68. Sqn Ldr 1/12/68. Retd GD 6/4/89.
WALKER A. C. Born 3/9/16. Commd 25/5/55. Sqn Ldr 1/1/68. Retd ENG 3/9/73.
WALKER A. C., BEM. Born 9/3/29. Commd 29/3/68. Sqn Ldr 1/1/78. Retd SUP 18/5/82.
WALKER A. D. Born 24/7/39. Commd 30/5/59. Sqn Ldr 1/7/74. Retd SUP 1/10/86.
WALKER A. E. Born 28/6/20. Commd 3/8/61. Flt Lt 3/8/67. Retd RGT 1/6/74.
WALKER A. F., BSc. Born 11/9/56. Commd 13/5/76. Sqn Ldr 1/7/88. Retd GD 15/6/96.
WALKER A. R., BSc. Born 10/11/59. Commd 5/1/86. Flt Lt 15/3/90. Retd ENG 10/11/97.
WALKER B. C. Born 9/7/35. Commd 17/3/55. Sqn Ldr 1/7/72. Retd ADMIN 19/5/89.
WALKER C. B. Born 25/12/50. Commd 13/5/81. Sqn Ldr 1/7/89. Retd GD(G) 14/3/96.
WALKER C. P. Born 28/4/62. Commd 11/5/89. Flt Lt 12/2/92. Retd OPS SPT 28/4/00.
WALKER C. S. Born 21/2/14. Commd 6/1/44. Flt Lt 6/7/47. Retd GD 1/3/52.
WALKER D. B. Born 30/7/32. Commd 29/12/51. Flt Lt 25/4/57. Retd GD 30/7/70.
WALKER D. C. Born 26/12/17. Commd 2/1/39. Sqn Ldr 1/7/48. Retd SUP 26/12/66 rtg Wg Cdr.
WALKER D. G., AFC. Born 24/12/24. Commd 8/4/44. Wg Cdr 1/1/62. Retd GD 12/8/78.
WALKER E. E. Born 27/2/22. Commd 23/2/45. Sqn Ldr 1/7/66. Retd GD 27/2/77.
WALKER F. P., OBE AFC*. Born 26/8/20. Commd 25/12/45. Wg Cdr 1/7/61. Retd GD 1/8/64.
WALKER G. B. Born 15/12/30. Commd 12/10/54. Flt Lt 12/4/60. Retd GD 12/10/70.
WALKER G. F., BSc. Born 5/11/42. Commd 15/7/63. Sqn Ldr 1/7/72. Retd ENG 15/11/75.
WALKER G. N. Born 10/10/40. Commd 12/1/62. Sqn Ldr 1/7/74. Retd GD 10/10/95.
WALKER G. R., AFC. Born 4/3/22. Commd 22/2/46. Flt Lt 4/1/51. Retd GD 4/3/77.
WALKER H. G. A. Born 28/6/55. Commd 2/2/78. Flt Lt 2/8/83. Retd GD 14/3/96.
WALKER H. H., BEM. Born 15/7/38. Commd 18/4/74. Sqn Ldr 1/1/85. Retd ENG 15/7/93.
WALKER H. J. Born 5/9/45. Commd 14/10/71. Flt Lt 14/10/73. Retd GD 5/9/83.
WALKER H. R. Born 16/4/06. Commd 5/11/41. Flt Lt 1/1/43. Retd GD 14/7/48.
WALKER I. D. Born 21/3/56. Commd 17/5/79. Sqn Ldr 1/1/92. Retd ADMIN 17/5/95.
WALKER Sir John., KCB CBE AFC FRAeS. Born 26/5/36. Commd 31/7/56. AM 18/10/91. Retd GD 5/1/95.
WALKER J. F. Born 11/3/23. Commd 11/2/44. Sqn Ldr 1/4/56. Retd GD 11/3/72.
WALKER J. G. Born 6/4/39. Commd 9/3/62. Fg Offr 25/7/63. Retd RGT 27/5/68.
WALKER J. J. Born 12/4/29. Commd 28/2/49. Flt Lt 2/2/55. Retd GD 12/4/67.
WALKER J. L., AFC. Born 26/1/22. Commd 24/1/44. Sqn Ldr 1/7/68. Retd GD 26/1/77.
WALKER J. M. Born 3/11/44. Commd 13/2/64. Gp Capt 1/1/88. Retd SUP 14/9/96.
WALKER J. N. Born 12/1/46. Commd 5/6/67. Sqn Ldr 1/7/77. Retd ENG 12/1/84.
WALKER J. S. Born 27/7/42. Commd 8/6/62. Flt Lt 8/12/67. Retd GD 3/2/76.
WALKER K. Born 11/3/34. Commd 23/8/55. Sqn Ldr 1/1/88. Retd GD 1/1/91.
WALKER M. D. Born 9/3/45. Commd 25/3/64. Flt Lt 25/9/69. Retd GD 22/4/94.
WALKER M. J. Born 24/2/53. Commd 15/10/81. Flt Lt 15/10/84. Retd GD(G) 15/4/91.
WALKER M. J. C., BA. Born 15/12/28. Commd 28/9/55. Flt Lt 28/9/55. Retd GD 6/10/69.
WALKER M. J. H., BA MCIT MILT MIMgt. Born 20/7/34. Commd 13/12/55. Wg Cdr 1/1/76. Retd SUP 1/3/89.
WALKER M. V., MA. Born 17/5/33. Commd 14/10/59. Sqn Ldr 1/7/73. Retd ADMIN 17/5/88.
WALKER N. E. D. Born 15/12/35. Commd 16/4/54. Flt Lt 16/10/59. Retd GD 15/12/73.
WALKER N. E. N. Born 11/8/32. Commd 1/10/54. Flt Lt 1/10/67. Retd GD(G) 11/8/70.
WALKER P. F. H. Born 5/3/39. Commd 25/7/60. Sqn Ldr 1/7/72. Retd GD 5/3/77.
WALKER P. G. Born 21/7/29. Commd 30/7/52. Flt Lt 30/4/55. Retd GD 22/7/67.
WALKER R. Born 26/5/29. Commd 8/2/49. Flt Lt 12/1/55. Retd GD 4/12/57.
WALKER R. Born 14/7/39. Commd 20/9/81. Flt Lt 20/10/78. Retd ADMIN 20/9/89.
WALKER R. B., MBE. Born 22/9/20. Commd 6/9/45. Flt Lt 6/9/51. Retd SEC 1/5/64.
WALKER R. B. Born 13/11/44. Commd 24/2/67. Flt Lt 31/8/72. Retd ADMIN 13/11/82.
WALKER R. D. Born 11/7/34. Commd 2/7/52. Sqn Ldr 1/1/67. Retd GD 11/7/72.
WALKER R. J. E., CEng MIMechE MRAeS. Born 19/12/23. Commd 6/1/44. Sqn Ldr 1/1/56. Retd ENG 16/1/74.
WALKER R. K. Born 14/5/43. Commd 13/6/71. Flt Lt 13/6/71. Retd EDN 14/1/76.

WALKER R. L. Born 30/3/20. Commd 22/5/47. Wg Cdr 1/7/69. Retd SUP 1/8/74.
WALKER R. M. Born 7/11/43. Commd 3/8/62. Sqn Ldr 1/1/89. Retd GD 6/9/96.
WALKER R. P. H., BSc. Born 14/11/49. Commd 28/2/72. Flt Lt 28/5/73. Retd GD 28/2/88.
WALKER R. T. Born 15/9/31. Commd 23/2/55. Flt Lt 18/6/61. Retd GD 6/10/70.
WALKER S., SRN RCNT RNT. Born 1/3/37. Commd 10/5/73. Fg Offr 30/8/74. Retd MED(T) 11/9/76.
WALKER S., AFC. Born 15/7/24. Commd 13/5/44. Gp Capt 1/1/72. Retd GD 15/7/79.
WALKER S., BA. Born 7/4/52. Commd 13/9/70. Flt Lt 15/10/75. Retd GD 10/5/82.
WALKER S. G. Born 11/7/58. Commd 13/8/82. Flt Lt 13/2/89. Retd OPS SPT 12/4/98.
WALKER S. L. Born 27/11/50. Commd 24/2/74. Sqn Ldr 1/1/87. Retd SUP 14/3/96.
WALKER S. T., MBE BSc. Born 13/4/61. Commd 2/9/79. Flt Lt 15/10/83. Retd GD 13/4/99.
WALKER S. T. E. Born 25/4/49. Commd 27/2/70. Flt Lt 27/2/73. Retd GD 17/9/75.
WALKER T. W., MBE. Born 9/4/63. Commd 2/9/84. Sqn Ldr 1/7/94. Retd GD 9/4/01.
WALKER W. D. Born 22/2/26. Commd 20/4/50. Flt Lt 26/5/55. Retd GD 22/2/68.
WALKER-ARNOTT D. A., BSc MRAeS ACGI. Born 24/2/22. Commd 13/1/44. Sqn Ldr 1/7/55. Retd ENG 15/4/61.
WALKER-NORTHWOOD P. A. Born 4/9/67. Commd 4/6/87. Flt Lt 4/12/92. Retd GD 14/3/97.
WALKERLEY R. A., BTech. Born 7/1/50. Commd 15/9/69. Sqn Ldr 1/1/86. Retd ENG 1/1/89.
WALKINGTON I. R., BA. Born 5/12/27. Commd 9/12/48. Wg Cdr 1/7/70. Retd SEC 4/3/75.
WALL A. J., CEng MRAeS. Born 7/4/58. Commd 20/5/82. Sqn Ldr 1/1/91. Retd ENG 7/12/97.
WALL A. L. Born 1/11/40. Commd 18/12/62. Sqn Ldr 1/1/75. Retd GD 12/1/80.
WALL B. L. E. Born 13/12/28. Commd 13/12/50. Sqn Ldr 1/1/63. Retd SEC 6/3/76.
WALL F. J. J. Born 11/10/26. Commd 21/11/51. Flt Lt 21/5/56. Retd GD 30/11/70.
WALL G. P., MBA BSc(Eng) CEng MRAes. Born 3/2/61. Commd 23/11/81. Wg Cdr 1/7/98. Retd ENG 1/12/00.
WALL J. Born 16/9/23. Commd 14/11/49. Sqn Ldr 1/4/61. Retd EDN 31/10/70.
WALL L. F. E. Born 20/1/14. Commd 21/9/40. Flt Offr 29/11/48. Retd SEC 1/12/67.
WALL L. T., MSc MRCGP DRCOG LMSSA AFOM. Born 25/4/43. Commd 1/3/71. Wg Cdr 1/3/85. Retd MED 1/3/87.
WALL S. A. Born 31/3/64. Commd 15/3/84. Flt Lt 15/9/89. Retd GD 2/4/01.
WALLACE A. B. Born 11/5/47. Commd 31/10/69. Sqn Ldr 1/1/86. Retd GD 21/2/93.
WALLACE A. F., CBE DFC. Born 22/8/21. Commd 23/12/40. Gp Capt 1/7/61. Retd GD 15/6/69.
WALLACE A. F., AFC. Born 23/11/20. Commd 11/9/42. Sqn Ldr 1/7/67. Retd GD 23/11/75.
WALLACE B. Born 7/12/34. Commd 21/4/67. Flt Lt 21/4/69. Retd ENG 21/4/75.
WALLACE D. B., MBE. Born 14/3/48. Commd 10/6/66. Wg Cdr 1/1/95. Retd GD 31/5/01.
WALLACE D. O. W. Born 30/9/46. Commd 4/5/72. Wg Cdr 1/1/87. Retd ADMIN 14/3/96.
WALLACE The Rev D. S. Born 5/9/25. Commd 20/1/51. Retd 5/9/80. Wg Cdr.
WALLACE H. C., OBE. Born 24/7/16. Commd 11/7/41. Wg Cdr 30/4/68. Retd MED(SEC) 24/1/73.
WALLACE I. R., BSc. Born 7/11/34. Commd 20/9/57. Sqn Ldr 3/9/67. Retd EDN 20/9/73.
WALLACE J. A. Born 15/7/22. Commd 20/10/55. Flt Lt 1/3/59. Retd ENG 1/5/76.
WALLACE J. E. V., BSc(Eng). Born 27/9/43. Commd 14/4/69. Sqn Ldr 1/7/77. Retd ENG 14/4/91.
WALLACE J. R., BSc. Born 7/1/33. Commd 13/6/71. Sqn Ldr 13/6/71. Retd ENG 13/10/89.
WALLACE J. S. McC., MBE. Born 21/5/24. Commd 16/9/44. Flt Lt 16/3/48. Retd GD 21/5/67.
WALLACE M. F., BSc. Born 6/12/54. Commd 6/3/77. Flt Lt 6/12/78. Retd GD 21/9/93.
WALLACE M. W., BA. Born 6/5/28. Commd 26/10/50. Sqn Ldr 1/7/63. Retd SEC 27/11/74.
WALLACE N. A. Born 29/7/51. Commd 13/1/72. Flt Lt 13/7/77. Retd GD 28/10/88.
WALLACE R. Born 12/1/26. Commd 26/3/52. Sqn Ldr 1/7/67. Retd GD 1/9/76.
WALLACE R. L., CBE AFC. Born 28/2/09. Commd 14/12/29. Gp Capt 1/7/47. Retd GD 28/4/53.
WALLANE E. L. Born 27/7/22. Commd 8/8/43. Sqn Ldr 1/1/54. Retd GD 27/7/65.
WALLBANK D. J. Born 5/5/53. Commd 14/12/72. Flt Lt 14/6/79. Retd GD(G) 5/5/91.
WALLBANK H. Born 21/4/25. Commd 7/5/52. Sqn Ldr 1/7/73. Retd GD 21/4/83.
WALLBANK N. Born 13/5/25. Commd 3/3/45. Flt Lt 3/3/51. Retd RGT 3/5/59.
WALLBUTTON B. C., CEng FIEE. Born 11/12/34. Commd 22/8/58. Sqn Ldr 30/7/67. Retd ADMIN 12/4/91.
WALLEN G. S. Born 20/9/38. Commd 6/5/65. Sqn Ldr 1/1/76. Retd ADMIN 20/9/93.
WALLER A. D., LDS. Born 20/10/41. Commd 18/9/60. Sqn Ldr 17/9/69. Retd DEL 31/12/74.
WALLER D. E. Born 5/7/29. Commd 4/6/52. Flt Lt 21/1/59. Retd SUP 14/1/68.
WALLER D. M., FIMgt. Born 6/7/37. Commd 29/7/58. A Cdre 1/1/85. Retd SUP 1/8/90.
WALLER D. R. Born 10/5/45. Commd 5/11/70. Sqn Ldr 1/1/85. Retd SUPPLY 19/8/87.
WALLER E. A., BA CEng MIEE MBCS. Born 31/8/46. Commd 13/9/70. Flt Lt 13/12/73. Retd ENG 13/9/86.
WALLER I. M. Born 27/12/34. Commd 18/3/53. Flt Lt 29/4/59. Retd GD 27/12/72.
WALLER P. F., BA. Born 8/7/50. Commd 26/10/86. Fg Off 26/4/86. Retd ADMIN 21/8/88.
WALLER P. J. C. Born 3/10/49. Commd 27/5/71. Fg Offr 27/5/73. Retd GD 4/1/74.
WALLIKER D. J., CBE. Born 26/1/19. Commd 17/4/39. A Cdre 1/1/70. Retd SUP 26/1/74.
WALLIKER J. A. Born 24/8/47. Commd 28/2/69. Sqn Ldr 1/7/78. Retd GD 11/12/85.
WALLIKER P. A., BA. Born 12/2/44. Commd 17/12/65. Flt Lt 17/9/68. Retd GD 12/2/82.
WALLINGTON R. M. A. Born 22/3/44. Commd 17/7/64. Flt Lt 4/11/70. Retd GD 15/4/77.
WALLINGTON W. J. Born 29/6/27. Commd 16/9/71. Flt Lt 16/9/76. Retd ADMIN 29/6/82.
WALLINGTON W. P. Born 19/12/34. Commd 28/1/53. Flt Lt 5/11/58. Retd GD 1/1/90.
WALLIS B. Born 21/8/30. Commd 9/4/52. Flt Lt 21/8/57. Retd GD 21/8/71.

WALLIS E. F., MBE. Born 13/3/30. Commd 13/2/52. Sqn Ldr 1/1/76. Retd GD 13/3/88.
WALLIS G. E. Born 17/11/37. Commd 14/8/65. Flt Lt 14/8/67. Retd GD 18/2/75.
WALLIS J. G. Born 14/10/28. Commd 22/7/50. Fg Offr 22/7/52. Retd RGT 7/12/58.
WALLIS K. H., MRAeS. Born 26/4/16. Commd 1/12/40. Wg Cdr 1/7/58. Retd ENG 30/5/64.
WALLIS P. Born 14/11/41. Commd 21/7/61. Sqn Ldr 1/1/87. Retd GD 14/11/96.
WALLIS P. E. Born 31/5/47. Commd 17/10/71. Flt Lt 17/4/76. Retd ENG 17/10/87.
WALLIS R. Born 10/7/42. Commd 17/12/63. Sqn Ldr 1/7/88. Retd ADMIN 15/9/95.
WALLIS R. J. Born 25/10/46. Commd 20/10/67. Wg Cdr 1/1/88. Retd SUP 14/3/97.
WALLIS T. T. Born 16/10/35. Commd 19/9/55. Gp Capt 1/1/87. Retd RGT 6/4/90.
WALLS J. A. Born 14/8/43. Commd 27/1/77. Sqn Ldr 1/7/91. Retd GD 14/8/98.
WALMSLEY C. R., MBE. Born 18/11/21. Commd 15/9/60. Sqn Ldr 1/1/69. Retd ENG 20/11/71.
WALMSLEY F., MIMgt. Born 21/12/29. Commd 28/12/51. Sqn Ldr 1/7/74. Retd ADMIN 1/9/82.
WALMSLEY H. E., DFC*. Born 14/12/22. Commd 4/1/43. Gp Capt 1/7/63. Retd GD 14/10/71.
WALMSLEY I. H. F. Born 1/4/29. Commd 26/7/50. Sqn Ldr 1/7/65. Retd GD 1/4/71.
WALMSLEY J. Born 19/12/46. Commd 3/1/64. Wg Cdr 1/1/90. Retd GD 1/11/94.
WALMSLEY J. D. Born 14/2/44. Commd 10/6/66. Sqn Ldr 1/7/79. Retd GD 1/12/89.
WALMSLEY M. J. P., MVO. Born 22/6/31. Commd 17/12/52. Sqn Ldr 1.1.63. Retd GD 22/6/69.
WALMSLEY P., BSc. Born 17/6/56. Commd 14/8/77. Sqn Ldr 1/1/88. Retd GD 28/3/91.
WALPOLE J. J. Born 26/10/42. Commd 28/3/63. Sqn Ldr 1/7/78. Retd GD(G) 1/7/81.
WALPOLE N. J. R., OBE. Born 20/2/34. Commd 14/12/54. Gp Capt 1/1/80. Retd GD 31/7/88.
WALSH D. B. Born 16/11/45. Commd 17/7/70. Flt Lt 17/1/76. Retd GD 22/10/94.
WALSH G. A. Born 8/6/47. Commd 24/7/81. Sqn Ldr 1/1/89. Retd ADMIN 14/3/97.
WALSH J. F. Born 27/9/61. Commd 20/9/88. Flt Lt 5/11/86. Retd ADMIN 6/4/93.
WALSH J. N. Born 18/4/24. Commd 13/7/61. Flt Lt 13/7/64. Retd GD 23/4/69.
WALSH J. P., BA. Born 29/5/47. Commd 22/8/71. Flt Lt 22/11/72. Retd GD 30/9/75.
WALSH J. W. Born 16/5/29. Commd 16/1/52. Flt Lt 4/2/59. Retd GD(G) 16/5/67.
WALSH K. M. Born 2/9/44. Commd 24/4/70. Sqn Ldr 1/1/82. Retd GD(G) 3/12/85. Reinstated on Retired List 22/1/88.
WALSH M., MBE. Born 1/7/12. Commd 17/6/40. Sqn Offr 1/2/49. Retd SUP 1/5/56.
WALSH N. R., BSc. Born 13/5/61. Commd 27/3/83. Flt Lt 27/6/84. Retd GD 30/10/99.
WALSH P. Born 11/11/42. Commd 12/4/73. Flt Lt 12/4/75. Retd GD 10/11/97.
WALSHE N. R. Born 30/3/52. Commd 5/7/73. Flt Lt 30/3/79. Retd GD(G) 2/5/80.
WALSTER R. A., BSc. Born 2/2/48. Commd 24/9/67. Sqn Ldr 1/1/86. Retd ENG 2/2/92.
WALTER D. Born 26/5/31. Commd 9/7/53. Flt Lt 13/4/60. Retd SUP 26/5/69 rtg Sqn Ldr.
WALTER D. J. Born 11/9/25. Commd 25/8/55. Flt Lt 25/8/61. Retd GD 1/10/68.
WALTER E. J. Born 23/12/34. Commd 30/7/57. Flt Lt 30/7/62. Retd SEC 16/1/65.
WALTER J. N., MBE CEng MIMechE. Born 2/1/35. Commd 5/10/56. Gp Capt 1/7/79. Retd ENG 5/10/87.
WALTER N. E. Born 30/10/36. Commd 22/7/71. Sqn Ldr 3/10/79. Retd ADMIN 22/7/85.
WALTER N. W. Born 5/7/25. Commd 26/5/45. Sqn Ldr 1/7/70. Retd SUP 29/1/77.
WALTERS B. S., AFC. Born 7/8/49. Commd 17/7/70. Flt Lt 17/1/76. Retd GD 7/8/86.
WALTERS J. K. Born 15/3/40. Commd 24/3/61. Gp Capt 1/1/87. Retd GD 15/3/95.
WALTERS M. Born 3/7/26. Commd 20/7/50. Flt Lt 20/1/54. Retd GD 1/8/68.
WALTERS P., MTech CEng MIEE MRAeS. Born 20/3/42. Commd 15/7/64. Sqn Ldr 1/7/74. Retd ENG 20/3/97.
WALTERS R. H., CEng MRAeS MIEE. Born 2/1/32. Commd 24/2/55. Wg Cdr 1/7/78. Retd ENG 1/6/90.
WALTERS-MORGAN W. M. Born 7/4/35. Commd 17/5/56. Sqn Ldr 1/1/68. Retd PRT 7/4/73.
WALTHAM D. L. Born 29/8/33. Commd 21/5/52. Flt Lt 26/11/57. Retd GD 29/8/71.
WALTHAM J. D. Born 12/2/36. Commd 10/9/70. Sqn Ldr 1/1/82. Retd GD 18/3/86.
WALTON A. Born 9/9/30. Commd 30/3/52. Flt Lt 29/10/57. Retd GD 9/9/68.
WALTON A. D. Born 1/4/49. Commd 20/10/67. Flt Lt 20/4/73. Retd GD 1/4/87.
WALTON B. K. Born 6/10/40. Commd 2/5/59. Sqn Ldr 1/7/71. Retd GD 6/10/78.
WALTON D. Born 14/4/44. Commd 11/4/85. Flt Lt 11/4/89. Retd ENG 14/12/90.
WALTON D. E., DFC. Born 16/5/22. Commd 27/3/44. Flt Lt 27/9/47. Retd GD 16/5/65.
WALTON E. J., MIMgt ACIS. Born 19/12/35. Commd 15/2/56. Sqn Ldr 1/7/68. Retd SEC 19/12/73.
WALTON H. A. Born 14/11/15. Commd 8/7/43. Sqn Ldr 1/7/60. Retd ENG 31/8/68.
WALTON J., CEng MIMechE MRAeS. Born 6/7/31. Commd 28/3/66. Sqn Ldr 1/7/74. Retd ENG 6/7/89.
WALTON J., MBE. Born 20/6/39. Commd 19/8/65. Sqn Ldr 1/7/77. Retd PRT 14/2/91.
WALTON J. H., AFC. Born 14/3/23. Commd 5/8/43. Gp Capt 1/7/67. Retd GD 5/4/72.
WALTON J. T., MBE. Born 4/7/31. Commd 6/9/68. Sqn Ldr 1/7/78. Retd ENG 30/10/82.
WALTON P. R. Born 29/12/36. Commd 15/2/56. Flt Lt 15/8/61. Retd GD 29/12/74.
WALTON P. R. C. Born 8/3/52. Commd 22/5/70. Sqn Ldr 1/1/85. Retd ADMIN 7/6/89.
WALTON R., AFC. Born 17/1/22. Commd 18/12/42. Flt Lt 18/6/47. Retd SEC 17/1/71.
WALTON R. D. Born 10/3/22. Commd 19/6/42. Wg Cdr 1/1/61. Retd GD 28/7/68 rtg Gp Capt.
WALTON S. B., BEM. Born 21/9/31. Commd 14/8/70. Flt Lt 14/8/73. Retd SEC 20/9/75.
WALTON W. C., DFC. Born 23/12/20. Commd 26/3/42. Flt Lt 26/9/45. Retd GD 16/6/53.
WALWYN-JAMES D. H., MA BSc DPhil DCAe CEng MRAeS FRIC. Born 18/5/28. Commd 11/6/56. Wg Cdr 1/4/69. Retd EDN 14/5/69.

WANDZILAK S., OBE DFC AFC. Born 23/7/17. Commd 1/9/48. Gp Capt 1/1/67. Retd GD 23/7/72.
WANKLYN D. C., AIIP. Born 28/6/25. Commd 21/3/51. Flt Lt 21/9/55. Retd ENG 5/5/79.
WANSTALL B. N., OBE AIPD. Born 5/11/29. Commd 27/6/51. Wg Cdr 1/1/75. Retd GD 8/5/82.
WANT N. D., OBE. Born 9/6/35. Commd 1/10/54. Wg Cdr 1/1/80. Retd GD 1/9/91.
WAPLE C. A., BSc. Born 2/9/76. Commd 1/9/97. Fg Offr 15/7/97. Retd GD 2/5/00.
WAPLINGTON R. J. W. Born 10/10/36. Commd 23/7/58. Flt Lt 15/2/65. Retd ENG 12/8/67.
WAPPAT F., BEM. Born 22/6/30. Commd 7/1/71. Sqn Ldr 1/1/79. Retd ADMIN 16/5/84.
WARBOYS K. J. Born 22/6/43. Commd 3/1/64. Flt Lt 3/7/69. Retd GD 1/9/76.
WARBURTON K. C. Born 12/8/22. Commd 31/5/48. Fg Offr 19/5/50. Retd GD 9/10/54.
WARBURTON P. L. Born 30/7/61. Commd 8/12/83. Flt Lt 11/3/91. Retd GD 30/7/99.
WARBURTON R. G. Born 10/5/42. Commd 31/7/86. Flt Lt 31/7/90. Retd ENG 10/5/97.
WARBURTON S. A. Born 28/1/41. Commd 24/3/61. Sqn Ldr 1/7/72. Retd GD 7/2/95.
WARD A. Born 29/4/35. Commd 2/3/61. Sqn Ldr 1/7/72. Retd GD 11/5/84.
WARD A. F., OBE. Born 6/6/12. Commd 2/12/40. Gp Capt 1/7/58. Retd ENG 6/6/67.
WARD A. S., BSc. Born 16/9/55. Commd 30/10/77. Flt Lt 30/1/79. Retd GD 4/2/90.
WARD A. W., MBE BSc. Born 1/1/49. Commd 6/12/70. Wg Cdr 1/7/95. Retd ADMIN 23/5/00.
WARD B. A., BSc DIC ARCS MRAeS. Born 29/9/26. Commd 10/2/49. Gp Capt 1/1/75. Retd ENG 31/3/77.
WARD B. C. Born 15/5/37. Commd 7/5/64. Sqn Ldr 1/1/74. Retd MED 16/5/87.
WARD C. D. Born 12/4/57. Commd 21/6/90. Flt Lt 21/6/92. Retd ENG 21/6/98.
WARD C. E. Born 20/1/58. Commd 8/9/77. Flt Lt 17/12/83. Retd ADMIN 2/11/89.
WARD C. J. Born 19/9/33. Commd 31/10/74. Flt Lt 31/10/79. Retd GD(G) 19/9/94.
WARD C. J. Born 5/7/19. Commd 1/11/56. Sqn Ldr 1/1/68. Retd ENG 29/4/72.
WARD C. R., MBE BSc. Born 12/11/44. Commd 4/1/71. Wg Cdr 1/7/86. Retd ENG 10/5/93.
WARD C. W. Born 31/5/25. Commd 24/1/52. Sqn Ldr 1/1/67. Retd GD 31/5/76.
WARD D., BA BSc. Born 21/9/42. Commd 6/9/65. Sqn Ldr 1/1/86. Retd GD 21/9/00.
WARD D., MA MIMgt. Born 20/1/34. Commd 22/2/60. Gp Capt 1/7/84. Retd GD 20/1/89.
WARD D. A., BSc MRAeS. Born 7/7/28. Commd 17/11/49. Sqn Ldr 1/1/61. Retd ENG 7/7/66.
WARD D. A. Born 9/10/26. Commd 15/5/47. Sqn Ldr 1/1/62. Retd GD 13/7/67.
WARD D. J. Born 23/2/26. Commd 11/8/48. Wg Cdr 1/1/73. Retd GD 23/8/83.
WARD D. J., BA. Born 19/4/54. Commd 25/2/79. Flt Lt 25/5/81. Retd ADMIN 31/7/88.
WARD D. S. Born 25/9/33. Commd 14/11/59. Flt Lt 14/5/65. Retd GD 1/9/74.
WARD D.A., MIMgt. Born 17/2/36. Commd 17/3/67. Sqn Ldr 1/7/79. Retd ADMIN 1/6/87.
WARD E., BA MB BCh MFCM DPH. Born 30/7/26. Commd 1/9/52. Gp Capt 1/1/74. Retd MED 1/2/77.
WARD E. Born 20/10/39. Commd 8/5/64. Flt Lt 8/5/68. Retd SUP 8/9/70.
WARD E. W. Born 22/1/41. Commd 29/3/68. Flt Lt 12/7/93.
WARD G. E., MBE. Born 2/3/55. Commd 23/11/78. Sqn Ldr 1/7/90. Retd GD(G) 1/7/93.
WARD G. R., MSc. Born 27/4/43. Commd 8/9/69. Flt Lt 8/3/70. Retd ENG 8/11/75.
WARD J., BSc CEng MRAeS ACGI MICE. Born 7/8/33. Commd 16/1/57. Wg Cdr 1/7/76. Retd ENG 24/12/77.
WARD J. Born 28/7/22. Commd 1/8/50. Flt Lt 23/10/56. Retd GD 7/12/66.
WARD J. Born 19/4/28. Commd 12/8/54. Sqn Ldr 1/1/77. Retd GD 19/4/88.
WARD J. A., AFC FIMgt. Born 29/4/43. Commd 8/6/62. Wg Cdr 1/1/84. Retd GD 2/4/93.
WARD J. A. Born 18/10/39. Commd 21/12/67. Flt Lt 11/2/71. Retd SUP 18/10/77.
WARD J. C. W., BMet. Born 16/6/59. Commd 2/5/80. Flt Lt 15/4/83. Retd GD 16/6/97.
WARD J. H. Born 8/5/15. Commd 9/7/38. Flt Lt 1/4/47. Retd LGL 15/3/49 rtg Sqn Ldr.
WARD J. L. Born 23/5/48. Commd 22/5/75. Sqn Ldr 1/7/87. Retd ADMIN 17/5/95.
WARD J. M. Born 14/3/42. Commd 11/11/71. Flt Lt 11/11/73. Retd GD(G) 1/4/87.
WARD J. R. Born 27/11/41. Commd 11/9/64. Sqn Ldr 1/1/94. Retd GD 27/11/96.
WARD J. R. Born 31/10/30. Commd 13/5/53. Gp Capt 1/1/81. Retd GD 26/8/83.
WARD K. A. Born 3/3/35. Commd 8/7/53. Flt Lt 8/1/59. Retd GD 3/3/73 rtg Sqn Ldr.
WARD K. M. M., LLB. Born 21/6/56. Commd 14/10/81. Flt Lt 21/1/84. Retd SY 2/10/85.
WARD L. H. Born 17/12/19. Commd 17/4/47. Flt Lt 29/11/51. Retd SUP 17/8/53.
WARD L. M. Born 5/5/56. Commd 8/5/85. Flt Lt 15/8/85. Retd SUP 5/5/94.
WARD L. W., BA. Born 22/3/32. Commd 9/9/59. Sqn Ldr 9/9/69. Retd ADMIN 22/3/92.
WARD M., CEng MIEE. Born 15/10/37. Commd 9/12/65. Sqn Ldr 1/1/74. Retd ENG 2/4/88.
WARD M. C. Born 20/10/44. Commd 9/8/63. Flt Lt 1/7/69. Retd GD 14/6/75.
WARD M. D. Born 6/1/47. Commd 2/12/68. Sqn Ldr 1/1/81. Retd ENG 6/1/85.
WARD M. G. Born 5/7/40. Commd 23/6/67. Sqn Ldr 1/7/74. Retd SEC 5/7/78.
WARD M. J. Born 24/4/46. Commd 26/5/67. Sqn Ldr 1/7/81. Retd ENG 24/4/90.
WARD M. J. Born 15/1/47. Commd 11/10/84. Flt Lt 11/10/88. Retd OPS SPT 24/8/98.
WARD M. T. Born 17/4/50. Commd 6/4/72. Flt Lt 6/10/78. Retd GD(G) 11/6/88.
WARD M. W., OBE MB BS FRCS(Edin). Born 2/10/40. Commd 11/3/68. Gp Capt 6/7/89. Retd MED 23/10/96.
WARD N. A., BSc. Born 19/11/55. Commd 13/4/80. Flt Lt 13/1/83. Retd GD(G) 13/4/96.
WARD N. A., BSc. Born 2/2/53. Commd 28/12/71. Flt Lt 15/4/76. Retd GD 2/2/91.
WARD O. A. Born 22/9/18. Commd 17/1/49. Gp Capt 1/1/67. Retd RGT 22/9/73.
WARD P. Born 6/5/33. Commd 26/11/56. Flt Lt 2/6/58. Retd GD 11/6/72.
WARD P. A. Born 5/9/33. Commd 3/10/69. Flt Lt 3/10/72. Retd GD(G) 4/10/74.

WARD R., MIMgt. Born 11/2/34. Commd 8/7/52. Flt Lt 20/11/57. Retd GD 11/8/72.
WARD The Rev R. A. P. Born 17/1/53. Commd 19/7/82. Retd 19/7/98. Wg Cdr.
WARD R. J., BSc. Born 25/7/59. Commd 17/8/80. Sqn Ldr 1/1/95. Retd GD 11/6/98.
WARD R. J. Born 6/7/41. Commd 30/7/63. Wg Cdr 1/1/87. Retd GD 6/4/96.
WARD S. Born 23/1/30. Commd 29/12/51. Wg Cdr 1/1/80. Retd GD 17/11/84.
WARD S. J., BSc. Born 5/10/65. Commd 29/1/86. Flt Lt 15/1/90. Retd GD 15/7/99.
WARD T. Born 31/8/25. Commd 19/12/63. Flt Lt 19/12/66. Retd GD 28/3/69.
WARD T. C., BSc. Born 23/12/38. Commd 25/3/64. Sqn Ldr 1/7/78. Retd GD 1/7/81.
WARD T. D., FIMgt. Born 20/7/30. Commd 11/6/53. G Capt 1/1/73. Retd ENG 1/11/78.
WARD W. Born 15/7/45. Commd 28/11/69. Flt Lt 4/5/72. Retd GD 15/7/83.
WARD-DUTTON I. Born 8/8/41. Commd 24/11/67. Wg Cdr 1/1/85. Retd ENG 8/8/91.
WARD-SUMNER M. D., MBE. Born 27/10/06. Commd 21/7/41. Sqn Offr 1/7/50. Retd SEC 18/3/56.
WARDELL A. Born 23/6/24. Commd 21/10/66. Flt Lt 21/10/71. Retd ENG 23/6/79.
WARDELL H. H. Born 12/9/16. Commd 15/1/42. Sqn Ldr 1/7/61. Retd ENG 30/6/65.
WARDEN G. M. Born 14/2/25. Commd 14/2/25. Flt Lt 12/3/67. Retd GD 16/1/76.
WARDEN K. E. Born 30/3/34. Commd 13/8/52. Flt Lt 9/1/58. Retd GD 27/4/79.
WARDEN R. H., BSc. Born 10/5/50. Commd 12/12/71. Flt Lt 12/3/76. Retd SEC 2/10/79.
WARDHAUGH R. C. Born 2/1/49. Commd 27/2/70. Sqn Ldr 1/1/83. Retd GD 2/1/87.
WARDILL D. H., CEng MIEE MIMechE. Born 3/3/36. Commd 8/8/58. Gp Capt 1/7/79. Retd ENG 3/3/91.
WARDILL J. C., MIMgt. Born 23/12/20. Commd 26/11/41. Sqn Ldr 1/1/60. Retd SUP 23/12/75.
WARDILL J. D., BA MB BChir DMRD. Born 15/11/31. Commd 13/4/58. Sqn Ldr 13/4/63. Retd MED 1/10/68.
WARDLAW K. Born 19/6/47. Commd 26/9/90. Flt Lt 26/9/94. Retd ADMIN 31/3/99.
WARDLE J. C. R., MMedSci MB BS MRCS LRCP DRCOG. Born 2/5/31. Commd 17/9/72. Wg Cdr 7/4/74. Retd MED 2/11/89.
WARDLE P. R., BSc. Born 25/10/41. Commd 19/8/63. Flt Lt 19/12/68. Retd ENG 19/10/81.
WARDMAN C. T. Born 11/9/13. Commd 1/1/37. Sqn Ldr 1/12/43. Retd SUP 5/3/46 rtg Wg Cdr.
WARDROP A. L. Born 20/12/30. Commd 12/9/63. Sqn Ldr 1/1/74. Retd ENG 1/10/85.
WARDROP R. E., FINucE. Born 8/9/18. Commd 4/8/43. Sqn Ldr 1/1/59. Retd ENG 6/9/75.
WARE A. Born 27/4/44. Commd 15/7/66. Wg Cdr 1/1/90. Retd GD 27/4/00.
WARE A. S. Born 3/4/20. Commd 27/2/44. Flt Lt 27/8/47. Retd GD 12/10/62.
WARE C. C. Born 4/11/40. Commd 24/8/70. Flt Lt 12/7/65. Retd GD 4/11/95.
WARE C. C. G. Born 8/9/16. Commd 4/5/50. Flt Lt 4/11/54. Retd SUP 24/6/62.
WARE D. R., MBE DFC AFC. Born 13/9/22. Commd 5/11/43. Sqn Ldr 1/10/54. Retd GD 15/2/64.
WARE E. M., DFC. Born 24/10/16. Commd 24/10/36. Sqn Ldr 1/6/41. Retd GD 30/8/50 rtg Wg Cdr.
WARE G. W. H., DFM. Born 28/2/19. Commd 22/7/43. Wg Cdr 1/7/70. Retd ENG 1/11/73.
WARE M. H. Born 1/10/22. Commd 3/7/43. Sqn Ldr 1/1/67. Retd GD 1/10/77.
WARE M. W., BA MIMgt. Born 10/11/32. Commd 3/10/66. Sqn Ldr 1/9/73. Retd ADMIN 12/4/83.
WAREHAM F. Born 14/2/50. Commd 13/2/87. Flt Lt 12/3/91. Retd SUP 2/4/00.
WAREHAM P. J., BEd. Born 23/11/53. Commd 19/3/78. Flt Lt 19/6/78. Retd GD 14/3/96.
WAREHAM R. J. E. Born 11/5/22. Commd 4/5/50. Sqn Ldr 1/1/72. Retd GD 11/5/82.
WARGENT M. G. Born 10/2/46. Commd 5/3/65. Sqn Ldr 1/7/82. Retd GD 10/9/90.
WARHAFTIG W., MBE CEng FIMechE FRAeS FIMgt. Born 29/4/26. Commd 18/4/51. Gp Capt 1/1/75. Retd ENG 29/4/81.
WARING S. L. Born 5/10/45. Commd 25/6/65. Flt Lt 25/12/70. Retd GD 5/10/83.
WARMINGTON W. I., DFC. Born 17/5/22. Commd 11/3/43. Flt Lt 17/5/56. Retd GD 3/11/63.
WARNE D. W., MRAeS. Born 20/3/26. Commd 11/10/51. Sqn Ldr 1/1/69. Retd GD 20/3/84.
WARNE P. C. Born 9/10/31. Commd 29/10/52. Flt Lt 3/3/59. Retd GD 9/10/69.
WARNE P. F. Born 8/3/41. Commd 25/8/67. Flt Lt 18/11/73. Retd SEC 3/5/75.
WARNEFORD D., MBE. Born 12/6/42. Commd 23/11/78. Sqn Ldr 1/1/88. Retd ENG 14/3/96.
WARNER A. Born 31/1/40. Commd 30/5/69. Sqn Ldr 1/1/78. Retd ENG 1/4/90.
WARNER A. E. Born 13/6/33. Commd 8/11/51. Flt Lt 23/2/57. Retd GD 24/2/73.
WARNER B. J. Born 22/6/49. Commd 31/7/86. Flt Lt 31/7/90. Retd ADMIN 14/3/96.
WARNER C. E. Born 12/12/23. Commd 20/11/58. Flt Lt 20/11/63. Retd GD 3/10/64.
WARNER D. B. Born 14/5/32. Commd 5/7/53. Flt Lt 5/11/58. Retd GD 14/5/70.
WARNER D. L., BSc. Born 14/2/56. Commd 15/9/74. Sqn Ldr 1/7/86. Retd GD 1/10/88.
WARNER D. M. Born 21/5/18. Commd 28/11/48. Flt Lt 27/5/54. Retd GD(G) 1/8/63.
WARNER I. Born 7/5/21. Commd 18/12/43. Flt Offr 8/12/49. Retd SEC 11/8/51.
WARNER K. B. Born 19/11/28. Commd 2/5/51. Sqn Ldr 1/7/68. Retd SUP 19/11/83.
WARNER M. P. Born 22/7/43. Commd 24/8/72. Flt Lt 24/8/72. Retd SY 1/2/93.
WARNER N. G. Born 7/1/43. Commd 17/12/64. Sqn Ldr 1/7/73. Retd GD 9/1/75.
WARNER R. T. Born 20/5/46. Commd 11/5/78. Flt Lt 11/5/80. Retd GD 11/5/86.
WARNER T. F. Born 14/6/44. Commd 17/5/63. Flt Lt 17/11/68. Retd GD 1/1/76.
WARNES N. J., MBE LRAM ARCM. Born 6/7/28. Commd 28/3/60. Sqn Ldr 30/7/71. Retd DM 15/9/73.
WARNOCK J. D. Born 17/8/54. Commd 11/6/81. Sqn Ldr 1/7/91. Retd SUP 1/7/94.
WARNOCK J. S., MIMgt. Born 22/4/45. Commd 18/11/66. Sqn Ldr 1/7/80. Retd ADMIN 1/7/83.
WARNOCK J. T. D., BSc. Born 2/2/54. Commd 8/1/78. Flt Lt 8/10/78. Retd GD 8/1/90.

WARNOCK T. S. Born 27/12/44. Commd 23/9/66. Flt Lt 23/3/72. Retd GD(G) 27/12/82.
WARR C. B. Born 12/10/24. Commd 4/1/45. Flt Lt 27/5/54. Retd GD 31/3/67.
WARREN A. Y., MSc MB BS MRCPath. Born 30/6/59. Commd 24/9/84. Sqn Ldr 1/8/93. Retd MED 4/5/01.
WARREN C., MBE DFC. Born 15/11/18. Commd 1/10/39. Sqn Ldr 1/6/45. Retd GD 14/12/57 rtg Wg Cdr.
WARREN D., MBE. Born 30/12/35. Commd 21/10/66. Wg Cdr 1/1/85. Retd ADMIN 1/7/88.
WARREN D. C. Born 24/3/44. Commd 25/4/69. Flt Lt 1/1/73. Retd GD 22/10/94.
WARREN D. E., BA MIMgt. Born 21/5/31. Commd 1/10/57. Wg Cdr 1/1/76. Retd ADMIN 6/2/86.
WARREN D. G., DFC. Born 11/7/16. Commd 7/10/35. Flt Lt 11/12/46. Retd GD(G) 11/7/66 rtg Wg Cdr.
WARREN D. H. Born 9/9/29. Commd 30/7/52. Gp Capt 1/7/75. Retd GD 9/9/84.
WARREN D. J. Born 4/12/44. Commd 3/10/66. Sqn Ldr 1/1/75. Retd ADMIN 6/4/85.
WARREN G. F. P. Born 24/1/91. Commd 1/4/18. Fg Offr 24/6/26. Retd SUP 27/12/28 rtg Sqn Ldr.
WARREN G. G. Born 20/5/23. Commd 24/9/59. Flt Lt 24/9/62. Retd GD 30/9/66.
WARREN J. Born 24/1/43. Commd 28/4/65. Sqn Ldr 1/1/80. Retd GD 4/5/94.
WARREN J. C. A. Born 5/8/27. Commd 15/9/60. Sqn Ldr 1/1/74. Retd ENG 1/12/76.
WARREN J. J. Born 18/7/37. Commd 17/3/67. Flt Lt 18/7/92. Retd GD 18/7/92.
WARREN J. W., BEM. Born 23/11/20. Commd 21/6/56. Sqn Ldr 1/1/68. Retd ENG 23/11/75.
WARREN P. A. Born 26/3/58. Commd 21/4/77. Flt Lt 21/10/82. Retd GD 30/8/88.
WARREN P. F. F., BA. Born 23/9/33. Commd 5/10/56. Sqn Ldr 5/4/65. Retd EDN 5/10/72.
WARREN P. H., BSc. Born 22/3/61. Commd 20/1/85. Flt Lt 20/7/88. Retd GD(G) 19/1/90.
WARREN P. J., BEng. Born 7/8/49. Commd 24/3/74. Sqn Ldr 1/7/96. Retd GD 21/11/00.
WARREN P. J. Born 11/9/46. Commd 20/10/67. Sqn Ldr 1/7/79. Retd GD 11/9/84.
WARREN R. J. Born 3/10/32. Commd 13/8/52. Flt Lt 9/1/58. Retd GD 3/10/70.
WARREN R. S. Born 16/3/25. Commd 23/8/56. Flt Lt 23/2/61. Retd GD 2/1/68.
WARREN T. A. Born 2/1/23. Commd 25/9/43. Sqn Ldr 1/4/56. Retd GD 2/1/78.
WARREN T. B. Born 28/7/33. Commd 28/1/53. Flt Lt 29/4/59. Retd GD 27/1/72.
WARREN V. J. Born 17/12/22. Commd 19/3/44. Flt Lt 19/3/50. Retd GD(G) 12/9/64.
WARREN W. H. Born 17/1/02. Commd 9/5/40. Flt Lt 1/3/45. Retd ENG 30/5/54 rtg Sqn Ldr.
WARREN-SMITH C. D., BSc MB BS FRCS. Born 23/2/51. Commd 20/2/73. Wg Cdr 11/1/90. Retd MED 1/1/92.
WARREN-WILSON J. P., BA. Born 6/10/54. Commd 24/7/77. Sqn Ldr 1/7/87. Retd GD 24/7/93.
WARRICK N. M., FIAP MIMgt. Born 18/4/56. Commd 27/2/75. Wg Cdr 1/1/97. Retd OPS SPT 19/4/01.
WARRINGTON L., BA BSc. Born 21/2/55. Commd 3/9/72. Sqn Ldr 1/1/90. Retd ENG 21/2/93.
WARRINGTON L. M. Born 22/1/49. Commd 31/7/70. Flt Lt 31/7/73. Retd GD 22/6/87.
WARRINGTON V. L., OBE MA. Born 2/7/34. Commd 11/9/57. Air Cdre 1/7/84. Retd GD 1/8/88.
WARSAP B. L., OBE. Born 2/12/38. Commd 18/12/56. Wg Cdr 1/7/80. Retd GD 2/12/93.
WARTON K. F. Born 13/3/40. Commd 9/7/59. Flt Lt 19/2/65. Retd GD 13/3/78.
WARWICK C. B. L., MBE. Born 10/12/16. Commd 10/6/44. Sqn Ldr 1/7/66. Retd GD(G) 10/12/73.
WARWICK J. L. Born 11/6/28. Commd 1/3/62. Flt Lt 1/3/68. Retd PE 16/6/78.
WARWICK M. Born 16/1/45. Commd 8/9/83. Sqn Ldr 1/7/91. Retd ENG 1/3/93.
WARWICK P. H. Born 13/6/21. Commd 27/5/54. Flt Lt 26/5/59. Retd GD 13/6/68.
WARWICK R. A., OBE MIMgt. Born 16/10/28. Commd 71/11/51. Wg Cdr 1/1/76. Retd GD 16/10/83.
WARWICK-SPAUL C. B. R., MIMgt. Born 11/11/18. Commd 17/4/39. Sqn Ldr 1/1/68. Retd SUP 11/11/73.
WARWOOD M. Born 26/7/37. Commd 24/9/64. Sqn Ldr 1/1/73. Retd GD(G) 30/4/83.
WASHBOURN R. O. Born 20/2/33. Commd 22/8/61. Sqn Ldr 1/7/71. Retd ENG 20/2/88.
WASHBOURNE A. E. Born 5/9/47. Commd 3/1/82. Flt Lt 24/12/76. Retd GD 3/1/89.
WASHINGTON F. J. Born 14/7/33. Commd 26/7/51. Flt Lt 24/4/57. Retd GD 17/10/84.
WASHINGTON I. P. Born 12/3/33. Commd 16/12/66. Flt Lt 16/12/71. Retd GD 12/3/89.
WASHINGTON-SMITH J. P. Born 22/9/51. Commd 31/8/78. Wg Cdr 1/7/93. Retd ENG 1/10/99.
WASHINGTON-SMITH M. H., BEd. Born 20/7/55. Commd 8/1/78. Wg Cdr 1/1/94. Retd ADMIN 14/3/97.
WASLEY R. J. Born 4/3/24. Commd 23/1/45. Wg Cdr 1/7/69. Retd SEC 30/6/78.
WASS E. A., AE MIMgt. Born 8/10/20. Commd 9/11/44. Sqn Ldr 1/1/59. Retd SUP 8/10/75.
WASSELL R. A. Born 28/10/48. Commd 11/10/70. Sqn Ldr 1/7/86. Retd ENG 14/3/97.
WATERER E. C., MIMgt. Born 22/3/24. Commd 21/1/45. Sqn Ldr 1/4/56. Retd GD 22/3/73.
WATERFALL E. J. Born 27/10/47. Commd 1/8/70. Flt Lt 1/8/72. Retd GD 7/10/78.
WATERFALL R. T. F., MBE. Born 2/8/27. Commd 20/9/48. Wg Cdr 1/1/74. Retd SY 4/8/81.
WATERFIELD C. D., MIMgt. Born 17/10/33. Commd 26/3/52. Wg Cdr 1/1/74. Retd GD 1/1/85.
WATERHOUSE C., BSc. Born 5/5/65. Commd 1/4/85. Flt Lt 15/1/89. Retd GD 15/7/98.
WATERHOUSE I. J. Born 21/11/44. Commd 8/4/82. Sqn Ldr 1/7/90. Retd ENG 10/1/97.
WATERKEYN P. H., OBE DFC. Born 29/10/19. Commd 21/10/41. Wg Cdr 1/7/59. Retd GD 1/10/73 rtg Gp Capt.
WATERMAN D. G. G., FIL. Born 14/11/35. Commd 1/4/58. Sqn Ldr 1/7/74. Retd ADMIN 29/4/91.
WATERMEYER A. E. Born 24/9/66. Commd 19/6/88. Fl Lt 19/6/94. Retd ADMIN 14/9/96.
WATERS A. P. J. Born 19/8/29. Commd 8/9/49. Flt Lt 8/3/53. Retd GD 19/8/67.
WATERS B. L. Born 30/9/36. Commd 14/12/55. Sqn Ldr 1/1/69. Retd GD 30/9/74.
WATERS G. J. Born 8/4/34. Commd 16/9/53. Flt Lt 13/4/60. Retd GD 8/4/72.
WATERS I. F. Born 14/8/43. Commd 23/11/78. Sqn Ldr 1/1/89. Retd ENG 31/3/93.
WATERS I. R., MRCS LRCP. Born 12/3/16. Commd 24/2/44. Flt Lt 24/2/44. Retd MED 14/9/48 rtg Sqn Ldr.
WATERS J., MHCIMA. Born 5/5/37. Commd 6/9/56. Wg Cdr 1/1/76. Retd ADMIN 6/5/77.

WATERS J. C. Born 31/10/33. Commd 14/12/54. Sqn Ldr 1/1/66. Retd GD 31/10/71.
WATERS J. D., CEng MRAeS. Born 13/8/42. Commd 15/7/65. Gp Capt 1/1/91. Retd ENG 14/9/96.
WATERS L. Born 25/8/35. Commd 19/6/70. Flt Lt 19/6/72. Retd SUP 19/6/78.
WATERS R. C. J. Born 5/7/20. Commd 29/8/38. Sqn Ldr 1/1/52. Retd SEC 26/8/67.
WATERS R. D. Born 24/6/57. Commd 11/7/81. Flt Lt 11/12/86. Retd GD 9/2/97.
WATERS R. S., MBE. Born 23/9/44. Commd 7/1/75. Wg Cdr 1/7/92. Retd GD(G) 31/3/94.
WATERSON M. R. G. Born 19/11/40. Commd 26/10/62. Flt Lt 26/4/68. Retd GD 19/11/78.
WATERWORTH A. Born 11/6/43. Commd 27/5/71. Flt Lt 27/5/73. Retd GD 6/12/74. Re-employed 4/11/76. Flt Lt 25/
    4/75. Retd ADMIN 4/11/84.
WATFORD B., AFC. Born 19/3/24. Commd 5/1/45. Sqn Ldr 1/7/71. Retd GD 19/6/84.
WATKIN E. W. Born 9/8/33. Commd 13/2/52. Flt Lt 12/6/57. Retd GD(G) 9/8/93.
WATKIN G. Born 17/4/49. Commd 2/2/70. Wg Cdr 1/7/94. Retd OPS SPT 31/1/98.
WATKIN-JONES H., DFC. Born 8/3/23. Commd 1/1/49. Sqn Ldr 1/1/59. Retd GD 8/3/66.
WATKINS A. R., BA MIMgt. Born 3/4/37. Commd 19/2/56. Wg Cdr 1/1/77. Retd GD 1/9/87.
WATKINS D. G. Born 30/4/30. Commd 2/7/52. Flt Lt 27/11/57. Retd GD 9/12/75.
WATKINS D. J., DFC. Born 8/11/21. Commd 24/11/44. Flt Lt 4/12/52. Retd GD(G) 1/5/65.
WATKINS M. Born 16/9/41. Commd 24/11/67. Sqn Ldr 1/7/87. Retd GD 8/12/95.
WATKINS M. J. Born 17/5/45. Commd 10/5/71. Wg Cdr 1/1/92. Retd ADMIN 19/6/93.
WATKINS M. R., BSc. Born 24/1/39. Commd 11/10/63. Flt Lt 11/10/66 Retd GD 21/8/78.
WATKINS M. W. Born 21/6/46. Commd 4/12/64. Flt Lt 4/11/70. Retd GD 28/2/85.
WATKINS T. Born 10/1/18. Commd 24/4/42. Flt Lt 18/9/49. Retd GD(G) 10/1/68.
WATKINS W. M., OBE. Born 3/11/37. Commd 11/9/61. Gp Cpt 1/7/92. Retd GD 3/11/92.
WATLING P. R., BSc. Born 3/9/54. Commd 2/9/73. Sqn Ldr 1/1/88. Retd GD 3/9/92.
WATRET W. Born 14/8/22. Commd 15/9/60. Sqn Ldr 1/1/73. Retd ENG 14/8/77.
WATSON A., BSc. Born 1/2/36. Commd 20/2/59. Flt Lt 20/11/62. Retd ENG 20/2/75.
WATSON A. H. Born 28/10/22. Commd 23/11/44. Sqn Ldr 1/1/71. Retd GD(G) 31/3/77.
WATSON A. L., BA MBCS. Born 9/5/34. Commd 13/12/55. Wg Cdr 1/7/72. Retd SUP 9/5/89.
WATSON A. M., BSc. Born 20/10/43. Commd 30/8/66. Wg Cdr 1/7/90. Retd GD 20/10/98.
WATSON A. V. Born 16/4/42. Commd 19/3/65. Flt Lt 19/9/68. Retd GD 16/4/80.
WATSON B. R. Born 26/9/44. Commd 5/1/70. Wg Cdr 1/7/91. Retd ADMIN 25/8/96.
WATSON B. W. Born 13/3/30. Commd 16/12/51. Flt Lt 27/3/57. Retd GD(G) 13/3/88.
WATSON C. C. Born 9/8/42. Commd 9/12/76. Sgn Ldr 1/1/82. Retd ADMIN 10/7/85.
WATSON C. J., MBE CEng MIEE MRAeS. Born 11/7/38. Commd 30/7/59. Gp Capt 1/7/89. Retd ENG 11/7/93.
WATSON C. M. G., MBE. Born 5/11/17. Commd 18/5/44. Sqn Ldr 1/10/57. Retd SEC 5/4/72.
WATSON C. W. D. Born 7/3/45. Commd 26/5/67. Flt Lt 18/2/70. Retd GD 1/5/84.
WATSON D., CEng MIEE MRAeS. Born 8/5/40. Commd 19/12/63. Gp Capt 1/7/91. Retd ENG 8/5/95.
WATSON D. Born 5/2/44. Commd 5/7/73. Sqn Ldr 1/7/90. Retd ENG 6/1/96.
WATSON D. A. Born 10/3/30. Commd 12/3/52. Sqn Ldr 1/1/69. Retd GD 10/9/91.
WATSON D. F. D., BA. Born 23/12/46. Commd 1/10/65. Flt Lt 1/4/71. Retd GD 31/12/86.
WATSON D. Q., DFC MIMgt. Born 1/6/15. Commd 1/5/42. Wg Cdr 1/7/59. Retd SEC 15/6/70.
WATSON D. R. McK., MBE MIMgt. Born 28/4/33. Commd 13/8/52. Gp Capt 1/1/79. Retd GD 28/4/88.
WATSON E. E. Born 11/2/22. Commd 22/4/44. Sqn Ldr 1/10/57. Retd ADMIN 11/2/82.
WATSON F. Born 14/11/29. Commd 11/3/65. Flt Lt 11/3/68. Retd GD 31/7/76.
WATSON F. C. Born 25/1/19. Commd 15/4/43. Sqn Ldr 1/4/56. Retd ENG 2/12/67.
WATSON G., BSc CEng MRAes. Born 30/10/26. Commd 17/3/49. A Cdre 1/7/74. Retd ENG 8/4/78.
WATSON G. Born 26/4/34. Commd 10/12/57. Sqn Ldr 1/1/69. Ret GD 13/7/87.
WATSON G. C., MBE BEM. Born 5/5/25. Commd 29/10/64. Sqn Ldr 1/7/75. Retd ENG 5/5/80.
WATSON G. C., AIPM. Born 24/6/47. Commd 2/8/73. Flt Lt 22/11/79. Retd ADMIN 16/4/89.
WATSON G. M., BSc. Born 23/2/55. Commd 30/10/77. Flt Lt 30/7/79. Retd GD 30/11/89.
WATSON G. V., MRAeS. Born 12/11/18. Commd 15/4/43. Sqn Ldr 1/1/62. Retd ENG 23/1/71.
WATSON H. E. E. Born 15/7/30. Commd 24/9/52. Flt Lt 21/2/58. Retd GD 30/9/77.
WATSON J. Born 10/3/49. Commd 21/3/69. Sqn Ldr 1/1/89. Retd SUP 10/3/93.
WATSON J. Born 5/8/47. Commd 10/12/65. Flt Lt 10/6/71. Retd GD 13/9/75.
WATSON J., AFC. Born 26/8/39. Commd 14/11/59. Sqn Ldr 1/7/72. Retd GD 12/10/79.
WATSON J. A. Born 4/4/25. Commd 24/5/51. Sqn Ldr 1/1/68. Retd GD 1/7/73.
WATSON J. A. Born 10/5/34. Commd 4/7/69. Flt Lt 4/7/75. Retd GD(G) 15/11/84.
WATSON K. Born 24/6/56. Commd 9/12/76. Flg Offr 1/5/78. Retd ADMIN 30/6/82.
WATSON K. I. Born 8/4/32. Commd 2/8/51. Wg Cdr 1/1/73. Retd GD 18/11/86.
WATSON K. R., FIMLS. Born 7/2/39. Commd 8/1/76. Sqn Ldr 25/8/86. Retd MED(T) 1/7/90.
WATSON K. T., DFC. Born 13/8/15. Commd 21/2/42. Sqn Ldr 1/8/47. Retd GD 30/11/51.
WATSON L. Born 16/11/21. Commd 27/4/61. Flt Lt 27/4/66. Retd ENG 16/11/71.
WATSON M. Born 26/6/33. Commd 7/8/59. Flt Lt 7/8/63. Retd PE 7/8/75.
WATSON M. J., BSc(Eng). Born 9/8/45. Commd 20/1/80. Flt Lt 20/7/76. Retd ADMIN 20/1/96.
WATSON M. W. B., MRCS LRCP DObstRCOG. Born 19/4/27. Commd 3/7/52. Wg Cdr 13/5/64. Retd MED 3/7/68.
WATSON P. A. Born 5/11/38. Commd 25/8/60. Flt Lt 25/2/67. Retd ENG 5/11/76.
WATSON P. H., MA. Born 7/6/34. Commd 1/9/70. Flt Lt 1/9/70. Retd GD(G) 14/2/79.

WATSON P. K., BA MRAeS. Born 29/9/27. Commd 24/5/49. Sqn Ldr 1/1/62. Retd ENG 29/9/65.
WATSON P. L., FIMgt DPhysEd. Born 11/2/46. Commd 16/8/70. Gp Capt 1/1/98. Retd ADMIN 11/2/01.
WATSON P. M., BSc. Born 25/7/62. Commd 14/9/80. Flt Lt. Retd GD 15/7/95.
WATSON P. R. Born 14/2/41. Commd 22/5/75. Wg Cdr 1/7/90. Retd ADMIN 14/2/98.
WATSON R. L. Born 7/2/33. Commd 27/9/51. Wg Cdr 1/7/70. Retd GD 1/2/78.
WATSON R. W. Born 5/6/32. Commd 27/8/52. Wg Cdr 1/1/74. Retd GD 1/12/84.
WATSON S. Born 26/8/34. Commd 27/5/53. Flt Lt 17/9/58. Retd GD 26/8/71.
WATSON S. W., IEng MIIE. Born 19/11/46. Commd 15/3/84. Sqn Ldr 1/7/97. Retd ENG 31/1/98.
WATSON T. H., BA. Born 7/6/35. Commd 23/10/56. Gp Capt 1/7/80. Ret GD 8/4/87.
WATSON T. J. Born 11/12/51. Commd 16/3/73. Sqn Ldr 1/1/84. Retd SUP 11/12/89.
WATSON T. M. Born 15/12/36. Commd 6/5/65. Sqn Ldr 1/1/75. Retd ADMIN 19/11/77.
WATSON W. Born 7/7/21. Commd 5/3/46. Flt Lt 5/3/52. Retd SEC 6/3/76.
WATT B. A. Born 31/5/50. Commd 28/2/71. Wg Cdr 1/7/87. Retd SUP 1/7/90.
WATT B. M. W., BSc. Born 28/7/42. Commd 10/9/63. Flt Lt 10/9/69. Retd SEC 14/9/73.
WATT D. R. Born 3/11/22. Commd 3/7/42. Wg Cdr 1/7/70. Retd ENG 1/12/77.
WATT F., BSc. Born 1/1/44. Commd 20/10/66. Flt Lt 5/4/71. Retd GD 30/10/75.
WATT H. J., MA. Born 20/1/59. Commd 9/11/80. Flt Lt 9/2/81. Retd GD 20/1/97.
WATT J. Born 6/10/23. Commd 9/5/44. Flt Lt 10/11/55. Retd GD 29/3/69.
WATT J., MBE. Born 10/6/27. Commd 3/11/60. Sqn Ldr 1/1/74. Retd ENG 2/10/79.
WATT J. A. Born 15/12/33. Commd 8/10/52. Flt Lt 6/3/58. Retd GD 6/11/64.
WATT J. D. Born 23/3/51. Commd 18/4/74. Sqn Ldr 1/7/87. Retd ENG 14/3/96.
WATT J. G. Born 8/10/45. Commd 19/8/66. Flt Lt 4/5/72. Retd GD 8/10/83.
WATT J. J. Born 19/2/33. Commd 27/2/52. Flt Lt 26/6/57. Retd GD 19/2/71.
WATT J. R., DFC. Born 25/9/09. Commd 25/6/40. Flt Lt 1/9/45. Retd GD(G) 25/9/59 rtg Sqn Ldr.
WATT M. A., RMN. Born 23/4/57. Commd 17/7/87. Flt Lt 8/9/92. Retd MED(SEC) 14/3/96.
WATT R. Born 7/3/15. Commd 3/12/42. Sqn Ldr 1/7/53. Retd SUP 15/9/62.
WATT T. B. Born 30/9/20. Commd 25/5/44. Flt Lt 27/5/46. Retd Pl 30/9/75.
WATTERS P. T., MB BCh BAO FFARCS DA. Born 19/8/30. Commd 13/4/58. Wg Cdr 13/10/68. Retd MED 15/4/75.
WATTERS T. W. Born 24/4/33. Commd 20/3/52. Wg Cdr 1/7/77. Retd SUP 24/4/86.
WATTERSON M. E. Born 28/10/42. Commd 26/5/67. Fg Offr 26/5/67. Retd ENG 9/8/69.
WATTON A. J., DFC. Born 10/4/17. Commd 28/4/42. Flt Lt 6/7/49. Retd GD(G) 10/4/72.
WATTON P. J. L., MBE CEng MRAeS. Born 14/6/35. Commd 2/11/56. Sqn Ldr 1/1/68. Retd ENG 23/4/86.
WATTS A. F. Born 9/9/35. Commd 22/7/71. Flt Lt 22/7/73. Retd GD(G) 22/7/79.
WATTS A. R. M., OBE BA. Born 7/9/16. Commd 3/2/47. Wg Cdr 1/1/59. Retd EDN 8/9/66.
WATTS D. A. Born 3/4/59. Commd 19/6/86. Flt Lt 19/6/88. Retd ENG 1/2/94.
WATTS D. A. Born 26/10/31. Commd 4/11/53. Flt Lt 9/5/57. Retd GD 16/2/73.
WATTS E. J., MBE. Born 8/4/09. Commd 24/10/40. Wg Cdr 1/1/53. Retd ENG 27/5/64.
WATTS F. H. A., DFC. Born 26/2/20. Commd 13/12/43. Flt Lt 18/12/47. Retd GD 14/7/64.
WATTS H. D. Born 22/1/56. Commd 22/5/75. Sqn Ldr 1/7/86. Retd ADMIN 7/6/91.
WATTS J. A., BA. Born 19/5/55. Commd 16/9/73. Flt Lt 15/10/77. Retd GD 16/7/84.
WATTS J. M. Born 11/10/23. Commd 28/5/52. Flt Lt 10/2/55. Retd ADMIN 20/2/82.
WATTS J. R. Born 28/7/32. Commd 15/12/53. Wg Cdr 1/7/73. Retd ADMIN 28/5/84.
WATTS J. W. Born 29/9/33. Commd 2/2/68. Flt Lt 8/3/72. Retd GD 30/3/78.
WATTS M. Born 25/4/09. Commd 11/8/41. Flt Offr 11/11/54. Retd SEC 10/8/62.
WATTS M. E. T. Born 13/12/13. Commd 21/5/47. Flt Lt 21/11/51. Retd SUP 31/12/62.
WATTS M. H. F. Born 23/12/47. Commd 24/4/70. Flt Lt 23/1/74. Retd GD 22/10/94.
WATTS M. J. Born 7/12/32. Commd 23/12/52. Sqn Ldr 1/1/69. Retd GD 1/1/72.
WATTS M. W., BSc MIMgt. Born 26/5/35. Commd 27/8/58. Sqn Ldr 1/7/66. Retd ENG 13/12/88.
WATTS R. F., BA. Born 13/9/14. Commd 4/6/38. Gp Capt 1/7/57. Retd GD 4/10/64.
WATTS R. J. Born 7/8/47. Commd 2/8/68. Flt Lt 2/8/71. Retd GD 24/9/86.
WATTS T. R. Born 17/4/52. Commd 22/7/71. Sqn Ldr 1/7/83. Retd GD 17/4/89.
WATTS-PHILLIPS J. E., OBE BSc MRAeS. Born 11/8/34. Commd 1/10/57. Wg Cdr 1/1/79. Retd GD 17/2/82.
WAUCHOPE F. A. Born 22/2/59. Commd 3/7/80. Fg Offr 3/1/83. Retd SY 23/4/83.
WAUGH W. J. Born 9/3/17. Commd 1/5/39. Flt Lt 1/9/45. Retd SUP 9/3/66 rtg Sqn Ldr.
WAY D. H., LHA MIMgt. Born 27/5/35. Commd 19/1/66. Wg Cdr 1/1/83. Retd MED SEC 28/12/85.
WAY P. D. Born 31/3/59. Commd 23/3/81. Sqn Ldr 1/7/91. Retd ADMIN 31/3/97.
WEARDEN S. F., BEng. Born 27/5/56. Commd 8/4/79. Sqn Ldr 1/1/92. Retd ENG 8/4/95.
WEARING S. H. Born 25/1/56. Commd 9/10/75. Flt Lt 9/4/81. Retd GD 21/7/88.
WEATHERALL K. Born 28/3/27. Commd 25/6/66. Flt Lt 25/6/69. Retd ENG 18/8/78.
WEATHERHEAD E. P. Born 27/12/39. Commd 24/6/76. Sqn Ldr 1/1/89. Retd ADMIN 1/1/90.
WEATHERILL P. G., BEM. Born 9/9/48. Commd 2/11/88. Flt Lt 2/11/92. Retd ADMIN 14/3/97.
WEATHERILT P. F. Born 7/7/36. Commd 24/7/57. Sqn Ldr 1/7/66. Retd ENG 7/7/74.
WEATHERLY B. D. Born 8/10/32. Commd 31/5/51. Wg Cdr 1/1/77. Retd GD 8/10/82.
WEATHERSTON S. A. Born 15/3/54. Commd 11/7/74. Sqn Ldr 1/1/85. Retd GD 15/3/92.
WEAVER A. Born 17/7/40. Commd 18/12/62. Sqn Ldr 1/7/79. Retd ADMIN 1/6/87.
WEAVER A. V. Born 7/4/42. Commd 9/3/62. Flt Lt 9/9/67. Retd GD 7/4/80.

WEAVER B. J., OBE. Born 12/5/35. Commd 7/5/64. Wg Cdr 1/1/78. Retd ENG 12/5/89.
WEAVER G. T., MBE. Born 24/3/39. Commd 27/3/70. Flt Lt 27/3/72. Retd ENG 1/10/92.
WEAVER I. W. Born 31/1/60. Commd 6/6/89. Flt Lt 31/1/85. Retd GD 4/12/97.
WEAVER P. A., BSc CEng MIMgt MRAeS MMS. Born 12/10/52. Commd 13/9/70. Sqn Ldr 1/1/82. Retd ENG 12/10/90.
WEAVER-SMITH M., MSc CDip AF AIPD. Born 27/11/31. Commd 9/3/56. Sqn Ldr 17/2/63. Retd ADMIN 27/11/86.
WEAVILL A. D., BEd. Born 19/4/54. Commd 30/10/77. Sqn Ldr 1/1/87. Retd SY 30/10/93.
WEBB A. Born 23/1/16. Commd 18/4/45. Fg Offr 28/7/48. Retd SEC 8/5/52.
WEBB A. C. Born 4/6/40. Commd 13/10/61. Flt Lt 1/4/66. Retd GD 1/5/76.
WEBB A. E. P., AFC. Born 14/3/43. Commd 9/2/62. Wg Cdr 1/7/86. Retd GD 2/4/93.
WEBB B. Born 16/8/31. Commd 28/2/57. Sqn Ldr 1/7/67. Retd GD 1/7/70.
WEBB B. P. Born 26/3/46. Commd 11/10/84. Flt Lt 11/10/88. Retd OPS SPT 26/3/01.
WEBB D. Born 22/12/46. Commd 1/3/68. Sqn Ldr 1/1/83. Retd GD 22/4/94.
WEBB D. Born 16/4/47. Commd 21/1/66. Flt Lt 4/5/72. Retd GD 1/10/86.
WEBB D. B., DFC. Born 30/5/20. Commd 17/11/42. Sqn Ldr 1/7/53. Retd GD 30/5/63.
WEBB D. F. Born 14/6/31. Commd 5/9/55. Flt Lt 7/3/62. Retd GD 5/9/69.
WEBB D. F. Born 26/8/16. Commd 18/11/54. Flt Lt 18/11/57. Retd CAT 30/4/69.
WEBB D. G., DFM. Born 14/12/23. Commd 30/5/44. Wg Cdr 1/1/66. Retd SEC 20/6/78.
WEBB D. J. Born 22/9/46. Commd 28/2/69. Flt Lt 23/5/73. Retd ENG 8/4/74.
WEBB D. J. Born 18/4/41. Commd 21/10/65. Flt Lt 8/4/72. Retd SUP 12/1/81.
WEBB E. A. H., DMS FISM MInstAM MCIPD MIMgt. Born 18/4/43. Commd 23/7/80. Sqn Ldr 1/7/88. Retd ADMIN 18/4/98.
WEBB E. A. N., CEng MIEE. Born 22/1/17. Commd 1/11/45. Sqn Ldr 1/7/58. Retd ENG 22/1/66.
WEBB E. J. Born 23/8/22. Commd 3/7/44. Sqn Ldr 1/1/55. Retd GD 23/8/65.
WEBB F. J. Born 19/6/17. Commd 7/6/51. Flt Lt 7/12/55. Retd RGT 27/2/58.
WEBB G. S. R. Born 13/12/25. Commd 2/7/52. Sqn Ldr 1/7/71. Retd GD 31/10/75.
WEBB H. Born 30/12/20. Commd 18/5/61. Flt Lt 18/5/64. Retd PRT 30/12/67.
WEBB J. Born 23/11/51. Commd 20/9/71. Sqn Ldr 1/1/88. Retd GD 14/4/91.
WEBB J. A. L., DFC. Born 25/3/20. Commd 15/5/44. Flt Lt 19/2/48. Retd SEC 23/5/75.
WEBB J. F., MIMgt. Born 10/2/29. Commd 3/8/50. Wg Cdr 1/7/76. Retd SEC 3/7/79.
WEBB J. G., CEng MRAeS MIMgt. Born 17/11/18. Commd 26/5/44. Wg Cdr 1/1/65. Retd ENG 17/11/73.
WEBB J. J. Born 10/4/37. Commd 21/6/60. Flt Lt 21/8/63. Retd GD 2/2/68.
WEBB M. F. D. Born 24/3/46. Commd 22/5/64. Sqn Ldr 1/1/84. Retd GD 24/3/90.
WEBB M. J., BA MIDPM AMBCS. Born 4/8/39. Commd 25/7/60. Gp Capt 1/1/89. Retd GD 4/8/94.
WEBB M. J. Born 15/9/33. Commd 2/7/52. Sqn Ldr 1/7/69. Retd GD 27/5/77.
WEBB M. J. Born 21/10/49. Commd 25/7/71. Wg Cdr 1/1/91. Retd ADMIN 14/3/97.
WEBB P. C., CBE DFC. Born 10/3/18. Commd 1/9/45. Gp Capt 1/7/63. Retd GD 18/3/73 rtg A Cdre.
WEBB P. M. G. Born 13/11/40. Commd 21/7/65. Flt Lt 19/3/68. Retd SY (PRT) 13/11/78.
WEBB P. R. Born 31/12/44. Commd 7/5/64. Sqn Ldr 1/1/78. Retd GD(G) 31/12/88.
WEBB P. R. A., MIMgt. Born 11/11/34. Commd 24/9/52. Wg Cdr 1/7/80. Retd GD 1/9/86.
WEBB R. B. Born 27/3/57. Commd 15/3/79. Sqn Ldr 1/1/89. Retd GD 27/3/95.
WEBB R. J. Born 13/4/33. Commd 11/10/51. Flt Lt 25/1/57. Retd GD 13/4/71.
WEBB R. K. Born 28/6/39. Commd 3/6/58. Flt Lt 5/12/63. Retd GD 1/10/85.
WEBB R. T., BM MRCGP DRCOG DAvMed. Born 15/11/54. Commd 1/8/79. Wg Cdr 1/8/92. Retd MED 1/8/95.
WEBB T. M., AFC MRAeS. Born 22/4/42. Commd 24/2/61. Gp Capt 1/7/87. Retd GD 3/4/93.
WEBB W. E., MIMgt. Born 17/11/29. Commd 24/1/63. Sqn Ldr 1/7/74. Retd ENG 17/11/89.
WEBBER L. B. Born 4/9/14. Commd 3/12/42. Sqn Ldr 1/7/54. Retd ENG 4/9/63.
WEBBER M. J., AFC BSc. Born 16/4/39. Commd 21/9/60. Wg Cdr 1/1/74. Retd GD 2/10/77.
WEBLEY E. J. Born 20/9/38. Commd 6/11/67. Sqn Ldr 1/7/80. Retd SUP 20/9/93.
WEBLEY S. K. Born 3/12/55. Commd 12/10/78. Flt Lt 12/4/84. Retd GD 12/6/94.
WEBSTER A. Born 28/7/30. Commd 25/9/52. Flt Lt 26/3/56. Retd GD 28/7/68.
WEBSTER A. H., DFM. Born 16/7/17. Commd 7/3/41. Sqn Ldr 1/7/51. Retd SEC 17/7/66.
WEBSTER A. J. Born 17/9/20. Commd 16/9/44. Wg Cdr 1/7/70. Retd GD(G) 17/9/75.
WEBSTER A. K. Born 6/11/42. Commd 28/7/64. Flt Lt 10/2/67. Retd GD 6/11/80.
WEBSTER A. M. Born 2/10/22. Commd 29/3/62. Flt Lt 29/3/65. Retd GD 86/6/73.
WEBSTER C. J. Born 6/6/44. Commd 18/9/63. Sqn Ldr 1/1/74. Retd GD(G) 6/6/82.
WEBSTER C. M. F. Born 6/11/29. Commd 20/10/49. Flt Lt 20/4/53. GD 6/11/89.
WEBSTER C. S. Born 3/5/65. Commd 22/9/88. Flt Lt 22/3/95. Retd SUP 14/3/97.
WEBSTER D. J. Born 8/4/24. Commd 19/10/49. Flt Lt 19/10/55. Retd SEC 16/6/63.
WEBSTER D. S., MBE. Born 29/2/56. Commd 27/1/77. Flt Lt 2/7/83. Retd OPS SPT 31/1/00.
WEBSTER J. J., AFC. Born 14/10/20. Commd 19/6/42. Sqn Ldr 1/7/66. Retd GD 10/5/68.
WEBSTER M. Born 15/4/35. Commd 29/10/57. Flt Lt 29/4/63. Retd GD 15/4/73 rtg Sqn Ldr.
WEBSTER M., MBE. Born 12/7/27. Commd 23/2/51. Sqn Ldr 1/7/75. Retd GD 12/7/82.
WEBSTER R., MSc CEng MIEE. Born 24/12/32. Commd 22/5/62. Sqn Ldr 22/1/69. Retd ADMIN 21/10/85.
WEBSTER R. A. Born 6/10/42. Commd 2/1/75. Flt Lt 2/1/77. Retd GD(G) 2/1/83.
WEBSTER R. E. Born 25/6/29. Commd 14/12/49. Sqn Ldr 1/1/61. Retd GD 25/6/67.

WEBSTER R. E., MB BS MRCPath. Born 27/1/59. Commd 9/4/85. Sqn Ldr 27/11/88. Retd MED 14/3/96.
WEBSTER R. J., MBE. Born 30/9/56. Commd 14/1/88. Sqn Ldr 1/1/97. Retd OPS SPT 1/6/01.
WEBSTER R. K., MSc BDS. Born 3/10/44. Commd 8/9/63. Sqn Ldr 22/12/71. Retd DEL 21/9/79.
WEBSTER R. M., CEng MIEE MRAeS. Born 19/6/42. Commd 15/7/63. Wg Cdr 1/1/90. Retd ENG 27/9/94.
WEBSTER S. M. R. Born 24/11/30. Commd 19/11/52. Flt Lt 15/4/58. Retd GD 1/5/70.
WEDDERBURN A. C., MBE DPhysEd. Born 30/10/30. Commd 23/4/52. Sqn Ldr 1/1/70. Retd GD 30/10/90.
WEDDLE I. Born 21/3/38. Commd 15/12/59. Wg Cdr 1/1/86. Retd GD 4/5/92.
WEDGE R. E., CBE BSc FRAeS MInstD. Born 22/6/44. Commd 5/1/66. Gp Capt 1/7/91. Retd GD 1/2/00.
WEDGWOOD P. W. Born 6/1/21. Commd 23/5/63. Flt Lt 23/5/66. Retd SEC 1/8/68.
WEEDEN B. A. Born 25/3/34. Commd 14/12/54. Sqn Ldr 1/7/64. Retd GD 29/8/73.
WEEDING D. E., CEng MIMechE MRAeS. Born 30/8/30. Commd 24/9/52. Sqn Ldr 1/1/63. Retd ENG 22/10/68.
WEEDON H. F. Born 31/7/27. Commd 3/6/65. Flt Lt 3/6/68. Retd GD 31/7/82.
WEEDON R. C. Born 26/8/29. Commd 8/11/51. Flt Lt 23/2/57. Retd GD 30/4/76.
WEEKES C. D. Born 14/2/28. Commd 11/4/51. Flt Lt 16/12/58. Retd GD(G) 14/2/66.
WEEKS D. T. Born 4/12/30. Commd 1/8/68. Flt Lt 1/8/74. Retd ENG 9/1/81.
WEEKS E. T. Born 23/3/32. Commd 28/6/51. Wg Cdr 1/1/78. Retd GD 23/3/87.
WEEKS R. L., CEng MRAeS. Born 31/10/39. Commd 22/5/62. Sqn Ldr 1/7/73. Retd ENG 22/5/78.
WEEKS S. G. Born 28/12/61. Commd 15/6/83. Flt Lt 18/12/89. Retd GD(G) 14/3/96.
WEERASINGHE N. E. Born 3/1/31. Commd 12/12/51. Fg Offr 12/12/51. Retd GD 21/5/55.
WEETMAN A. Born 24/1/23. Commd 6/12/56. Flt Lt 6/12/62. Retd GD 28/3/70.
WEIGALL S. H. D. Born 7/3/28. Commd 5/4/50. Wg Cdr 1/1/67. Retd ADMIN 2/8/80.
WEIGHT C. D. Born 27/9/56. Commd 31/1/80. Flt Lt 2/8/84. Retd GD(G) 27/9/94.
WEIGHTMAN W. A. Born 1/10/25. Commd 12/7/56. Flt Lt 10/2/58. Retd RGT 13/5/70.
WEIL T. O., DFC. Born 25/3/17. Commd 25/9/42. Flt Lt 26/3/46. Retd GD(G) 25/3/64.
WEINDLING M. R. Born 14/1/48. Commd 21/3/69. Sqn Ldr 1/7/84. Retd ENG 14/1/92.
WEIR A. A. Born 2/10/30. Commd 25/10/53. Wg Cdr 1/1/78. Retd GD(G) 9/4/85.
WEIR A. A. McP. Born 24/4/40. Commd 9/3/62. Flt Lt 9/9/67. Retd GD 24/4/78.
WEIR C. F. Born 22/1/24. Commd 12/3/52. Flt Lt 10/7/56. Retd GD 18/9/67.
WEIR D. M. Born 1/4/33. Commd 10/9/52. Flt Lt 7/2/58. Retd GD 1/4/71.
WEIR I. Born 21/11/36. Commd 1/10/60. Sqn Ldr 1/7/88. Retd GD 1/8/89.
WEIR N. A. Born 4/4/59. Commd 24/11/85. Flt Lt 6/4/88. Retd GD 14/3/96.
WEIR R. S., AFC DPhysEd. Born 1/5/53. Commd 17/7/77. Flt Lt 17/1/83. Retd GD 17/7/93.
WEISS A. P. W. Born 24/9/37. Commd 16/11/59. Flt Lt 9/12/64. Retd GD 25/8/66.
WEISS R. M. J. Born 9/9/63. Commd 17/1/85. Flt Lt 17/7/90. Retd GD 18/12/92.
WELBY P. J., MIMgt. Born 29/4/32. Commd 14/12/54. Wg Cdr 1/1/80. Retd SUP 9/2/85.
WELCH A. H. E., DFC TD CEng MIEE MRAeS MIMgt. Born 30/1/21. Commd 6/4/44. Sqn Ldr 1/10/54. Retd GD 26/11/75.
WELCH A. L., BSc CEng MRAeS. Born 5/5/43. Commd 9/10/67. Sqn Ldr 1/7/77. Retd ENG 9/11/86.
WELCH E. C. A. Born 23/8/32. Commd 26/7/51. Flt Lt 14/11/56. Retd GD 23/8/70.
WELCH F. I., AFC. Born 23/2/34. Commd 23/4/52. Sqn Ldr 1/1/64. Retd GD 26/2/94.
WELCH J., DFC. Born 13/9/19. Commd 3/7/41. Sqn Ldr 1/1/51. Retd GD 26/12/58 rtg Wg Cdr.
WELCH J. Born 17/1/32. Commd 7/5/52. Flt Lt 14/5/58. Retd GD 17/1/70.
WELCH W. H. Born 15/1/44. Commd 30/8/84. Flt Lt 30/8/88. Retd SY 1/10/91.
WELCOMME R. G., CEng MRAeS. Born 18/2/22. Commd 17/2/44. Wg Cdr 1/7/65. Retd ENG 18/2/77.
WELDING T. E., MBE. Born 31/10/16. Commd 1/7/43. Sqn Ldr 1/7/56. Retd ENG 31/10/73.
WELFARE D., DFC*. Born 14/9/22. Commd 17/1/42. Flt Lt 19/4/48. Retd GD 17/6/62.
WELFORD F. L., DFC. Born 23/5/21. Commd 13/9/46. Sqn Ldr 1/1/57. Retd GD 23/5/64.
WELFORD L. Born 26/7/34. Commd 16/1/60. Sqn Ldr 1/1/70. Retd GD 30/9/78.
WELHAM J. B., CEng MIMechE MIMgt. Born 9/4/48. Commd 28/2/69. Sqn Ldr 1/7/79. Retd ENG 9/4/86.
WELLEN W. M. J., MBE. Born 29/9/26. Commd 17/10/57. Flt Lt 1/4/63. Retd GD 30/9/75.
WELLER A. G., AFC. Born 19/4/25. Commd 21/1/45. Sqn Ldr 1/7/58. Retd GD 19/4/63.
WELLER B. I., MSc BDS MGDSRCS(Ed) LDSRCS(Eng). Born 22/11/56. Commd 23/11/80. Wg Cdr 12/2/93. Retd DEL 23/11/96.
WELLER J. B. Born 19/12/43. Commd 6/4/62. Flt Lt 6/10/67. Retd GD 31/3/94.
WELLER M. G., MBE BEM. Born 31/3/31. Commd 24/1/63. Flt Lt 24/1/69. Retd ENG 19/10/69.
WELLER P. F. Born 19/10/09. Commd 10/7/41. Wg Cdr 1/1/55. Retd ENG 8/12/59.
WELLER P. L., MA BA. Born 5/11/41. Commd 27/3/80. Sqn Ldr 1/1/87. Retd ADMIN 1/1/90.
WELLER R. B. Born 15/2/13. Commd 15/6/44. Sqn Ldr 1/4/57. Retd SEC 15/3/68.
WELLER V. A., BA BSc PGCE. Born 12/1/55. Commd 14/8/77. Sqn Ldr 1/1/88. Retd ADMIN 14/3/97.
WELLERD J. A. Born 14/11/33. Commd 3/9/52. Sqn Ldr 1/1/71. Retd GD 4/5/79.
WELLICOME B. W. Born 28/12/26. Commd 25/10/46. Sqn Ldr 1/7/61. Retd GD 13/4/68.
WELLINGHAM J. B., MA CEng FRAeS FIMgt. Born 21/6/25. Commd 14/2/46. A Cdre 1/1/72. Retd ENG 31/3/78.
WELLINGS I. G. Born 18/6/44. Commd 22/5/64. Wg Cdr 1/7/90. Retd GD 14/9/96.
WELLINGS N. D. Born 5/3/66. Commd 19/11/87. Flt Lt 19/5/94. Retd SUP 26/3/01.
WELLINGTON R. T. Born 21/2/35. Re-commd 24/11/65. Flt Lt 24/11/65. Retd GD 18/5/76.
WELLS A. S. Born 9/9/55. Commd 11/1/79. Flt Lt 11/7/84. Retd GD 5/11/88.

WELLS D. Born 28/7/36. Commd 17/1/69. Sqn Ldr 29/1/80. Retd MED(SEC) 28/2/85.
WELLS E. P., DSO DFC*. Born 26/7/16. Commd 1/9/45. Gp Capt 1/1/59. Retd GD 15/6/60.
WELLS F. Born 27/4/34. Commd 1/2/62. Flt Lt 1/4/66. Retd GD 27/4/72.
WELLS G. Born 15/2/34. Commd 11/6/60. Sqn Ldr 1/7/85. Retd GD 14/8/86.
WELLS G. C. D., MA CEng MRAeS. Born 26/2/38. Commd 30/9/56. Sqn Ldr 1/1/68. Retd ENG 26/2/76.
WELLS J., MCIPS. Born 26/4/42. Commd 2/1/70. Wg Cdr 1/7/87. Retd SUP 1/9/97.
WELLS J. C. A., SRN RMN RNT. Born 12/2/38. Commd 9/10/67. Flt Lt 9/10/73. Retd MED(T) 29/9/75.
WELLS J. T., MIMgt. Born 1/12/33. Commd 16/4/54. Sqn Ldr 1/7/79. Retd ADMIN 1/12/88.
WELLS J. W., BSc. Born 11/12/62. Commd 2/9/84. Flt Lt 2/9/89. Retd ENG 11/12/00.
WELLS K. J., DFC. Born 26/11/24. Commd 27/5/44. Wg Cdr 1/1/65. Retd GD 8/2/77.
WELLS M. P. Born 20/10/30. Commd 21/3/51. Sqn Ldr 1/7/61. Retd GD 20/10/68.
WELLS O. J. Born 10/3/22. Commd 22/10/41. Wg Cdr 1/1/56. Retd GD 28/4/56.
WELLS P. J. Born 31/5/25. Commd 16/2/45. Gp Capt 1/7/72. Retd GD 1/10/77.
WELLS R. Born 18/11/32. Commd 6/2/52. Flt Lt 14/8/57. Retd GD 1/7/76 rtg Sqn Ldr.
WELLS R. J. Born 14/9/35. Commd 3/3/54. Sqn Ldr 1/1/67. Retd GD 17/6/77.
WELLS R. N. Born 7/8/09. Commd 3/3/41. Sqn Ldr 1/8/47. Retd ENG 7/8/58.
WELLS R. W., BA. Born 8/12/61. Commd 19/8/90. Flt Lt 19/2/94. Retd ADMIN 14/3/96.
WELLS W. J. E., BA. Born 25/3/49. Commd 22/7/84. Flt Lt 24/4/86. Retd ADMIN 25/4/93.
WELLS W. J. G. Born 17/6/33. Commd 27/8/62. Sqn Ldr 1/7/84. Retd GD 6/12/85.
WELLSPRING P. J. C., BSc. Born 19/9/39. Commd 28/11/66. Flt Lt 28/8/70. Retd GD(G) 28/11/82.
WELLUM G. H. A., DFC. Born 4/8/21. Commd 23/10/39. Flt Lt 1/9/45. Retd GD 30/6/61 rtg Sqn Ldr.
WELPLY P. M. C. Born 3/5/34. Commd 25/3/54. Wg Cdr 1/1/81. Retd ADMIN 30/10/84.
WELSH J. Born 13/10/36. Commd 5/2/57. Flt Lt 15/8/62. Retd GD 13/10/74.
WELSH M., BSc. Born 8/12/65. Commd 1/4/86. Flt Lt 15/1/89. Retd GD 15/7/99.
WELSH S. A. Born 19/2/42. Commd 11/8/67. Flt Lt 11/2/74. Retd GD(G) 1/5/83.
WELSTEAD E. H. Born 30/8/41. Commd 11/5/62. Fg Offr 11/5/64. Retd GD 28/1/72.
WELTON A. J. Born 18/2/42. Commd 23/9/66. Sqn Ldr 11/7/86. Retd SUP 18/2/97.
WELTON R. L., SRN RCNT RNT. Born 18/6/21. Commd 17/7/70. Flt Lt 17/7/76. Retd MED(T) 31/7/76.
WELVAERT A. L. S., AFM. Born 27/7/17. Commd 27/3/52. Flt Lt 27/9/55. Retd GD(G) 27/2/65.
WENHAM P. L., BSc. Born 16/5/59. Commd 11/9/77. Flt Lt 15/4/82. Retd GD 16/5/97.
WENHAM W. T. Born 30/8/26. Commd 28/6/60. Flt Lt 28/7/65. Retd ENG 1/9/77.
WENSLEY E. Born 16/6/36. Commd 28/5/66. Wg Cdr 1/7/83. Retd SY(PRT) 9/1/89.
WENSLEY G. Born 2/8/42. Commd 4/10/63. Wg Cdr 1/1/84. Retd GD 2/8/97.
WERB D. G. Born 19/4/42. Commd 28/7/64. Wg Cdr 1/1/85. Retd GD 18/4/94.
WERE J. M. Born 4/2/29. Commd 5/9/69. Flt Lt 5/9/73. Retd SUP 5/9/74.
WESKETT B. W., MIMgt. Born 8/7/31. Commd 14/4/53. Sqn Ldr 1/1/65. Retd GD(G) 8/7/69. Re-employed 19/2/71-6/11/71.
WESLEY C. J. Born 15/11/48. Commd 22/12/67. Sqn Ldr 1/1/96. Retd GD 1/7/00.
WESSON P. G., BA. Born 8/5/57. Commd 22/3/81. Flt Lt 22/6/81. Retd GD 22/3/97.
WEST A. E. Born 31/7/28. Commd 18/9/47. Flt Lt 19/6/54. Retd RGT 31/7/66.
WEST A. G. Born 25/7/15. Commd 10/1/42. Wg Cdr 1/1/62. Retd SUP 7/8/70.
WEST A. M., BSc. Born 19/4/49. Commd 15/9/69. Sqn Ldr 1/7/82. Retd ADMIN 12/7/87.
WEST B. L., MIMgt. Born 13/2/35. Commd 17/3/55. Flt Lt 17/3/61. Retd SEC 13/2/73.
WEST C. D. P. Born 26/10/44. Commd 11/9/64. Flt Lt 15/4/70. Retd GD 28/8/75.
WEST D. R., DFC. Born 1/1/21. Commd 27/3/39. Flt Lt 1/9/45. Retd GD 1/12/61 rtg Sqn Ldr.
WEST D. R., OBE CEng MRAeS MIEE. Born 20/5/35. Commd 30/7/59. Gp Capt 1/1/85. Retd ENG 1/1/87.
WEST D. R., MA CEng MRAeS. Born 3/5/38. Commd 6/8/80. Sqn Ldr 23/9/75. Retd ENG 1/6/92.
WEST F. P. Born 9/2/30. Commd 30/7/52. Sqn Ldr 1/7/75. Retd SUP 3/1/89.
WEST F. P. Born 11/7/23. Commd 7/2/45. Flt Offr 29/11/51. Retd GD 1/10/55.
WEST F. T., FIMgt. Born 4/12/32. Commd 13/9/51. Wg Cdr 1/1/74. Retd GD 2/4/86.
WEST G. T. Born 12/12/38. Commd 28/11/60. Sqn Ldr 1/1/73. Retd GD 12/12/76.
WEST H. J., DSO DFC. Born 17/4/23. Commd 27/2/44. Sqn Ldr 1/1/58. Retd GD 17/4/72.
WEST H. R. A. Born 19/7/21. Commd 21/4/44. Sqn Ldr 1/1/67. Retd GD(G) 1/7/69.
WEST I. J. Born 31/7/58. Commd 17/7/87. Sqn Ldr 1/1/95. Retd ADMIN 1/5/00.
WEST I. W., MHCIMA. Born 22/9/53. Commd 8/1/78. Sqn Ldr 1/1/89. Retd ADMIN 8/1/94.
WEST J. G. Born 21/2/43. Commd 27/9/73. Flt Lt 27/9/74. Retd ENG 27/9/81.
WEST J. S., BEd. Born 25/12/53. Commd 18/3/84. Sqn Ldr 1/7/94. Retd ADMIN 14/3/97.
WEST K. D. Born 22/11/53. Commd 8/10/87. Flt Lt 8/10/89. Retd SUP 8/10/95.
WEST L. J. T., AFC. Born 7/4/08. Commd 25/4/40. Sqn Ldr 1/8/47. Retd GD 1/9/55.
WEST L. N., MBE CEng MRAeS MIMgt. Born 19/3/20. Commd 10/2/49. Wg Cdr 1/7/68. Retd ENG 9/3/75.
WEST M. E. Born 9/1/41. Commd 25/8/67. Sqn Ldr 1/1/78. Retd SUP 2/4/93.
WEST M. J. Born 3/10/33. Commd 31/7/58. Wg Cdr 1/1/75. Retd ADMIN 11/2/86.
WEST P. Born 13/7/51. Commd 4/9/90. Sqn Ldr 4/9/88. Retd ENG 20/9/96.
WEST P. Born 22/5/36. Commd 7/5/64. Sqn Ldr 1/7/71. Retd ENG 22/5/94.
WEST P. J., MBE. Born 21/7/33. Commd 28/1/60. Wg Cdr 1/7/80. Retd GD 2/9/85.
WEST P. R., BSc. Born 16/5/51. Commd 13/11/72. Flt Lt 15/4/74. Retd GD 16/5/89.

WEST P. T., OBE CEng MIEE MRAeS. Born 28/1/40. Commd 20/8/60. Wg Cdr 1/7/84. Retd ENG 28/1/95.
WEST R. J. Born 16/9/47. Commd 28/2/69. Sqn Ldr 1/7/80. Retd ADMIN 16/9/85.
WEST S. J. Born 13/3/30. Commd 11/4/51. Sqn Ldr 1/1/59. Retd GD 10/6/77.
WEST T. A. Born 15/9/31. Commd 8/5/53. Flt Lt 26/8/58. Retd GD 15/9/69.
WEST-JONES G. S. Born 21/5/24. Commd 3/6/44. Flt Lt 3/12/47. Retd GD 21/5/62.
WESTBROOK L. H. Born 21/4/23. Commd 16/1/45. Flt Lt 19/11/53. Retd GD 28/6/68.
WESTBY N., MBE DFC AFC. Born 29/8/23. Commd 1/6/44. Flt Lt 1/12/47. Retd GD 29/8/66.
WESTCOTT D. A. Born 21/9/22. Commd 29/4/44. Flt Lt 23/5/48. Retd GD 21/9/77.
WESTCOTT J. J. Born 4/6/34. Commd 29/3/68. Flt Lt 29/3/70. Retd ENG 5/6/74.
WESTELL H. L. Born 23/10/32. Commd 12/7/51. Flt Lt 13/11/61. Retd GD 4/11/75.
WESTERMAN A. G. Born 8/7/22. Commd 6/8/43. Flt Lt 6/2/47. Retd GD 12/8/68.
WESTERN H. J. B. Born 7/5/35. Commd 26/10/61. Flt Lt 1/4/66. Retd GD 7/5/73.
WESTHEAD W. A. Born 13/2/29. Commd 4/6/52. Sqn Ldr 1/7/69. Retd GD 13/2/84.
WESTLAKE G. H., DSO DFC FIMgt. Born 21/4/18. Commd 24/8/40. Gp Capt 1/7/61. Retd GD 25/7/69.
WESTLEY M. D. Born 15/3/37. Commd 10/2/59. Flt Lt 1/4/66. Retd SEC 15/3/75.
WESTLEY P. W., BA. Born 20/11/52. Commd 17/1/82. Flt Lt 17/1/83. Retd ADMIN 14/3/96.
WESTOBY B.J. Born 24/12/32. Commd 27/9/51. Gp Capt 1/7/78. Retd GD 24/12/91.
WESTON C. T., BEng. Born 29/1/69. Commd 6/9/87. Flt Lt 15/1/94. Retd ENG 6/4/00.
WESTON D. Born 20/1/31. Commd 6/1/51. Flt Lt 25/7/56. Retd GD 20/1/74.
WESTON D. J., BSc. Born 29/5/50. Commd 15/9/69. Sqn Ldr 1/7/85. Retd GD 1/7/88.
WESTON E. J. Born 5/12/21. Commd 28/8/42. Flt Lt 22/4/46. Retd GD 30/5/68.
WESTON F. G., MBE. Born 13/10/07. Commd 17/1/42. Flt Lt 1/9/45. Retd ENG 9/5/53.
WESTON G. A. C. Born 10/10/55. Commd 27/3/80. Flt Lt 5/6/82. Retd GD 3/12/97.
WESTON G. E. Born 14/1/15. Commd 21/2/46. Flt Lt 21/8/50. Retd SUP 16/2/64.
WESTON I. Born 25/3/46. Commd 5/3/65. Flt Lt 5/9/70. Retd GD 3/12/85.
WESTON I. F. Born 25/3/32. Commd 17/12/52. Sqn Ldr 1/7/67. Retd GD 1/7/70.
WESTON The Rev I. J., MBE. Born 28/4/45. Commd 18/9/77. Retd 28/4/00 Wg Cdr.
WESTON J. R., BSc. Born 18/2/58. Commd 18/10/81. Flt Lt 18/7/82. Retd GD 18/10/97.
WESTON K. J. Born 7/6/45. Commd 9/12/76. Sqn Ldr 1/7/89. Retd ENG 31/3/94.
WESTON M. R. Born 5/2/35. Commd 9/7/57. Flt Lt 17/1/63. Retd Pl 10/9/76.
WESTON P. J. Born 11/9/62. Commd 26/4/84. Flt Lt 21/10/87. Retd GD 11/4/01.
WESTON R. I. Born 5/11/21. Commd 14/5/59. Flt Lt 14/5/59. Retd ENG 30/9/61.
WESTWELL D. K. Born 29/1/37. Commd 5/12/63. Sqn Ldr 1/7/73. Retd ADMIN 2/2/87.
WESTWOOD C. Born 10/4/32. Commd 29/4/53. Flt Lt 30/9/58. Retd GD 1/9/77.
WESTWOOD D. B., AFC. Born 27/5/30. Commd 5/9/69. Flt Lt 5/9/72. Retd GD 30/5/84.
WESTWOOD H. C., OBE. Born 28/10/04. Commd 30/5/40. Wg Cdr 1/7/47. Retd GD(G) 28/10/56.
WESTWOOD H. J. Born 11/10/21. Commd 4/6/56. Flt Lt 4/6/56. Retd GD(G) 11/10/76.
WETHERELL I. Born 17/4/33. Commd 28/11/74. Flt Lt 28/11/77. Retd GD(G) 3/6/85.
WETTON D. N. Born 12/11/38. Commd 25/7/60. Flt Lt 25/1/63. Retd GD 12/11/76.
WETTON G. R. Born 21/8/32. Commd 29/7/65. Flt Lt 29/7/70. Retd GD 21/8/87.
WEVILL P., MMar. Born 24/11/18. Commd 19/10/49. Wg Cdr 1/1/62. Retd MAR 24/11/73.
WHALEY L. E. S., DFC. Born 15/1/14. Commd 21/6/42. Sqn Ldr 1/7/52. Retd SEC 16/7/60.
WHALEY R. K. J., BA. Born 17/2/44. Commd 24/6/65. Flt Lt 24/12/67. Retd GD 24/4/76. Reinstated 22/4/81. Flt Lt 22/12/72. Retd GD 6/8/93.
WHALLEY F. Born 31/1/32. Commd 22/8/51. Flt Lt 22/2/56. Retd GD 31/1/70.
WHARRAD M. F. Born 2/10/44. Commd 4/7/69. Flt Lt 6/10/71. Retd GD 31/12/76.
WHARRIER I., BSc. Born 8/8/62. Commd 5/9/82. Flt Lt 5/11/87. Retd ENG 8/8/00.
WHARTON A. N. R., MCIPS. Born 5/8/48. Commd 27/2/70. Sqn Ldr 1/1/83. Retd SUP 5/8/92.
WHARTON B. K., MRCS LRCP DPM. Born 9/12/27. Commd 27/4/53. Wg Cdr 3/4/65. Retd MED 27/4/70.
WHARTON N. J. Born 8/1/46. Commd 19/6/64. Flt Lt 19/12/69. Retd GD 8/1/84.
WHATLEY A. E. Born 20/2/24. Commd 7/7/54. Flt Lt 7/7/59. Retd GD 1/10/68.
WHATLING D. Born 5/1/47. Commd 1/10/65. Sqn Ldr 1/1/81. Retd GD 11/8/84.
WHATLING L. Born 30/5/51. Commd 4/2/71. Flt Lt 4/8/76. Retd GD 13/10/81. Reinstated 24/11/82. Flt Lt 16/9/77. Retd GD 11/6/90.
WHEALE R. D. J., MBE BA AKC MIMgt. Born 7/12/37. Commd 8/12/64. Sqn Ldr 2/6/69. Retd ADMIN 7/12/93.
WHEATLEY P. E. Born 28/5/56. Commd 10/3/77. Flt Lt 10/9/82. Retd GD 28/5/94.
WHEATLEY R. A. Born 2/6/21. Commd 26/2/54. Flt Lt 26/2/59. Retd ENG 28/8/63.
WHEATLEY R. B. Born 10/8/60. Commd 23/4/87. Sqn Ldr 9/5/97. Retd GD 10/8/98.
WHEATLEY T. M. K. Born 29/4/44. Commd 26/10/62. Sqn Ldr 1/1/77. Retd GD 29/4/99.
WHEATON B. C. Born 13/4/34. Commd 26/8/66. Flt Lt 26/8/68. Retd ENG 26/8/74.
WHEELDON D. A. A. Born 8/6/55. Commd 8/8/74. Sqn Ldr 1/7/87. Retd SUP 27/2/96.
WHEELDON G. R., AFC. Born 28/12/16. Commd 5/5/43. Sqn Ldr 1/1/54. Retd SEC 28/12/65.
WHEELER A. E. C., DFC*. Born 29/1/18. Commd 9/6/41. Sqn Ldr 1/7/49. Retd GD 28/12/57.
WHEELER A. J., BSc. Born 4/4/60. Commd 18/10/81. Flt Lt 10/10/87. Retd OPS SPT 7/4/00.
WHEELER B. V. Born 7/1/48. Commd 2/8/68. Sqn Ldr 1/7/82. Retd GD 7/1/86.
WHEELER D. A., LLB. Born 22/2/47. Commd 8/1/65. Sqn Ldr 1/1/84. Retd GD 1/1/87.

WHEELER D. J., BSc. Born 28/3/66. Commd 2/9/84. Flt Lt 15/1/90. Retd GD 15/1/00.
WHEELER G. C., BSc. Born 4/8/39. Commd 4/12/64. Flt Lt 4/9/66. Retd GD 11/7/72.
WHEELER J. A. Born 28/9/33. Commd 2/7/52. Sqn Ldr 1/1/70. Retd GD 28/11/75. Reinstated 1/4/80. Sqn Ldr 5/5/74. Retd GD 28/9/88.
WHEELER J. P. Born 15/6/24. Commd 12/11/43. Flt Lt 27/12/56. Retd ENG 30/7/68.
WHEELER J. R., MIMgt. Born 5/10/38. Commd 7/1/58. Wg Cdr 1/1/90. Retd GD 5/10/93.
WHEELER L. E., BEd. Born 22/1/50. Commd 7/12/75. Flt Lt 7/9/78. Retd ADMIN 12/7/85.
WHEELER L. W. F. Born 4/7/30. Commd 21/5/52. AVM 1/7/83. Retd GD 2/7/84.
WHEELER Sir Neil, GCB CBE DSO DFC* AFC FRAeS. Born 8/7/17. Commd 31/7/37. ACM 11/3/72. Retd GD 3/1/76.
WHEELER P. A. Born 28/9/45. Commd 31/3/70. Flt Lt 30/6/73. Retd ENG 31/3/86.
WHEELER R. L. Born 21/4/36. Commd 26/8/66. Flt Lt 26/8/68. Retd GD 26/8/74.
WHEELER R. R. Born 30/7/21. Commd 10/10/44. Flt Lt 11/8/48. Retd GD 30/8/64.
WHEELER T. W. Born 27/4/43. Commd 24/4/83. Flt Lt 24/3/87. Retd ENG 28/4/93.
WHEELER W. J. Born 4/5/27. Commd 21/10/66. Flt Lt 21/10/71. Retd ENG 29/1/72.
WHEELER W. M. Born 19/10/27. Commd 9/8/51. Sqn Ldr 1/7/69. Retd GD 15/11/75.
WHEELEY J. M. Born 11/6/42. Commd 1/2/62. Flt Lt 1/8/68. Retd ADMIN 11/6/80.
WHEELIKER P. G., MBA FIFA MIMgt. Born 10/6/52. Commd 25/5/80. Flt Lt 25/8/83. Retd SUP 2/4/93.
WHELAN A. R., BA. Born 13/10/34. Commd 8/8/58. Flt Lt 30/6/64. Retd GD 8/8/74.
WHELAN J. B. D. Born 21/7/44. Commd 8/1/76. Flt Lt 8/1/78. Retd ADMIN 8/1/84.
WHELAN J. F. Born 31/5/35. Commd 30/7/57. Flt Lt 15/2/63. Retd GD 31/5/93.
WHELAN P. N. Born 12/2/56. Commd 22/5/80. Flt Lt 22/11/85. Retd GD 21/1/96.
WHELLER J. V. Born 14/2/47. Commd 25/2/66. Flt Lt 25/8/72. Retd GD(G) 14/2/88.
WHERRETT M. J. Born 3/2/49. Commd 18/4/69. Flt Lt 13/9/74. Retd GD 14/3/96.
WHERRY G. H., OBE DFC. Born 13/12/18. Commd 3/5/37. Wg Cdr 1/7/51. Retd GD 13/5/68.
WHERRY I. L. Born 22/7/44. Commd 13/2/64. Flt Lt 20/6/70. Retd GD(G) 22/7/82.
WHICHELO A. E. Born 29/10/18. Commd 23/6/44. Flt Lt 23/12/48. Retd SEC 29/12/62.
WHIGHT M. G. Born 21/4/46. Commd 26/4/84. Sqn Ldr 1/7/93. Retd ENG 14/3/96.
WHIGHT R. A. Born 30/1/48. Commd 17/2/67. Wg Cdr 1/1/90. Retd GD 14/9/96.
WHILEY K. C. H., MBE. Born 31/10/22. Commd 10/7/45. Sqn Ldr 1/1/62. Retd ENG 1/6/73.
WHIPPY S. W. Born 21/8/31. Commd 5/9/57. Sqn Ldr 1/7/77. Retd ADMIN 11/5/84.
WHITAKER A. J. W. Born 23/4/33. Commd 27/7/54. Sqn Ldr 1/7/64. Retd GD 23/4/71.
WHITAKER C. L. Born 22/2/46. Commd 26/5/67. Wg Cdr 1/7/86. Retd GD 23/2/90.
WHITAKER D., CEng MIMechE. Born 16/2/39. Commd 1/8/66. Wg Cdr 1/7/88. Retd ENG 16/7/94.
WHITAKER E. J. Born 5/1/49. Commd 2/12/66. Sqn Ldr 1/7/89. Retd GD 14/3/97.
WHITAKER J. G., BSc CEng MRAeS. Born 14/4/26. Commd 6/11/47. Gp Capt 1/1/74. Retd ENG 14/8/79.
WHITAKER P. K. Born 2/5/17. Commd 11/4/46. Flt Lt 29/6/50. Retd ENG 2/5/66.
WHITAKER P. L., DFC. Born 21/9/19. Commd 23/1/38. Sqn Ldr 1/8/47. Retd GD 5/9/58.
WHITBREAD J. E. Born 24/9/45. Commd 19/6/86. Flt Lt 19/6/90. Retd ENG 1/6/93.
WHITBREAD P. C. A. Born 20/1/48. Commd 14/10/71. Sqn Ldr 1/1/90. Retd GD 1/12/00.
WHITBREAD P. H., MIMechE. Born 11/1/30. Commd 4/7/60. Sqn Ldr 1/7/67. Retd ENG 5/7/89.
WHITBURN C. H. Born 8/2/20. Commd 21/4/45. Flt Lt 30/6/49. Retd GD 8/2/63.
WHITBY D. E., MBE. Born 1/6/21. Commd 23/9/65. Sqn Ldr 1/1/76. Retd ENG 1/6/81.
WHITBY M. S. Born 11/12/46. Commd 20/8/65. Flt Lt 4/5/72. Retd PI 31/12/83.
WHITBY P. G. Born 13/9/16. Commd 10/5/37. Flt Lt 1/12/42. Retd SEC 27/9/65 rtg Sqn Ldr.
WHITCHURCH A. R., MMar. Born 19/12/35. Commd 31/3/64. Sqn Ldr 2/10/74. Retd MAR 1/4/86.
WHITCHURCH P. A. Born 28/4/65. Commd 19/7/84. Fg Offr 19/1/87. Retd GD(G) 1/5/90.
WHITE A., MBE FIMgt MCIPD. Born 2/7/23. Commd 12/6/47. Gp Capt 1/7/71. Retd SEC 4/5/74.
WHITE A. D. M. Born 26/3/45. Commd 2/3/78. Flt Lt 2/3/80. Retd GD 23/3/86.
WHITE A. E. Born 27/1/38. Commd 7/11/62. Flt Lt 4/5/72. Retd GD 1/5/74.
WHITE A. J. Born 6/11/28. Commd 27/1/67. Flt Lt 27/1/72. Retd ENG 6/11/86.
WHITE A. J. Born 13/3/42. Commd 6/4/62. Flt Lt 6/10/67. Retd GD 13/3/80.
WHITE A. J., BA. Born 2/1/49. Commd 22/9/74. Sqn Ldr 1/1/84. Retd ADMIN 22/9/90.
WHITE A. J. Born 12/3/61. Commd 26/11/81. Flt Lt 26/5/87. Retd GD 31/8/89.
WHITE A. M., MSc BSc MInstP. Born 11/11/34. Commd 4/9/67. Sqn Ldr 4/3/71. Retd ADMIN 4/9/83.
WHITE C. B. Born 31/1/20. Commd 9/8/45. Wg Cdr 1/7/64. Retd ENG 15/4/71.
WHITE C. R. Born 2/3/24. Commd 6/10/45. Flt Lt 30/6/49. Retd GD 2/9/68.
WHITE C. S., BA. Born 11/9/56. Commd 26/11/78. Flt Lt 26/8/80. Retd GD 26/11/86.
WHITE C.F., DPhysEd. Born 9/2/40. Commd 31/12/63. Flt Lt 31/12/67. Retd ADMIN 31/6/82.
WHITE C.P. Born 13/10/49. Commd 27/2/70. Flt Lt 27/8/75. Retd GD 13/10/87.
WHITE D., DFC. Born 6/6/22. Commd 8/11/41. Flt Lt 1/9/45. Retd GD 11/4/54 rtg Sqn Ldr.
WHITE D. A., MB ChB FRCS FFARCS DRCOG. Born 7/12/48. Commd 14/3/82. Wg Cdr 14/3/88. Retd MED 14/3/98.
WHITE D. A. C. Born 28/8/42. Commd 31/10/69. Flt Lt 4/5/72. Retd OPS SPT 28/2/98.
WHITE D. B. Born 3/2/34. Commd 24/9/52. Wg Cdr 1/1/77. Retd GD 10/8/87.
WHITE D. J. Born 19/1/55. Commd 20/9/79. Sqn Ldr 1/7/91. Retd GD(G) 22/5/95.

WHITE D. J., MB BS FRCOG. Born 1/6/22. Commd 5/8/52. Gp Capt 8/4/71. Retd MED 2/4/85.
WHITE D. S. Born 5/6/27. Commd 27/7/49. Sqn Ldr 1/1/59. Retd GD 1/3/68.
WHITE D. W. Born 10/6/23. Commd 25/8/44. Flt Lt 6/1/52. Retd GD 3/7/62.
WHITE E. J., DFM. Born 25/10/22. Commd 23/2/45. Sqn Ldr 1/7/53. Retd SUP 26/10/73.
WHITE F. H., MIMgt. Born 20/9/25. Commd 19/8/65. Sqn Ldr 1/1/76. Retd ENG 20/9/78.
WHITE F. W. L., MBE BSc. Born 3/12/35. Commd 27/11/58. Sqn Ldr 1/7/67. Retd ENG 3/5/75.
WHITE G. A., CB AFC LLB FRAeS. Born 11/3/32. Commd 17/3/54. AVM 1/1/83. Retd GD 3/4/87.
WHITE G. A. Born 30/1/60. Commd 5/5/88. Flt Lt 5/5/94. Retd MED(T) 14/9/96.
WHITE G. E., MIMgt. Born 19/7/21. Commd 17/3/67. Flt Lt 17/3/72. Retd ENG 1/5/77.
WHITE G. E., MBE. Born 6/5/35. Commd 19/1/66. Flt Lt 8/1/69. Retd ENG 19/1/74.
WHITE H. F. Born 8/1/18. Commd 30/4/59. Sqn Ldr 28/8/68. Retd MED(T) 24/10/70.
WHITE H. J. Born 27/5/22. Commd 28/7/60. Flt Lt 28/7/63. Retd SEC 30/9/67.
WHITE I., AInstAM. Born 5/1/62. Commd 30/10/83. Flt Lt 30/4/89. Retd ADMIN 14/3/96.
WHITE J. Born 25/1/32. Commd 15/6/64. Sqn Ldr 1/7/74. Retd GD(G) 21/4/86.
WHITE J. B., MA. Born 4/4/37. Commd 20/9/55. Wg Cdr 1/1/75. Retd ENG 10/12/79.
WHITE J. C. Born 9/11/21. Commd 21/6/56. Sqn Ldr 1/7/70. Retd ENG 1/3/78.
WHITE J. F., BA. Born 19/6/44. Comd 16/2/69. Flt Lt 16/5/70. Retd GD 28/2/76.
WHITE J. F. Born 17/8/42. Commd 6/9/63. Flt Lt 6/3/69. Retd GD 17/8/76.
WHITE J. J. Born 19/1/25. Commd 10/3/60. Flt Lt 10/3/65. Retd GD 28/9/68.
WHITE J. K., MInstAM. Born 6/1/38. Commd 2/2/68. Sqn Ldr 1/7/76. Retd ADMIN 6/1/93.
WHITE J. R. Born 5/8/20. Commd 6/7/55. Flt Lt 1/12/59. Retd GD(G) 1/11/73.
WHITE J. V. Born 2/8/16. Commd 21/6/45. Fg Offr 30/1/47. Retd SUP 26/7/47 rtg Flt Lt.
WHITE J. W. Born 28/3/30. Commd 15/10/52. Flt Lt 6/3/63. Retd GD 20/11/71.
WHITE J. W., MBE CEng MRAeS. Born 29/1/14. Commd 25/4/40. Gp Capt 1/1/58. Retd ENG 12/11/66.
WHITE K. G., MIMgt. Born 2/12/22. Commd 15/9/60. Sqn Ldr 1/7/72. Retd ADMIN 30/4/77.
WHITE K. J., BSc. Born 10/4/64. Commd 26/10/86. Flt Lt 26/4/90. Retd SUP 14/3/97.
WHITE L. D. Born 18/4/58. Commd 23/5/85. Flt Lt 23/5/87. Retd GD 18/4/96.
WHITE L. E. Born 3/8/38. Commd 9/2/62. Sqn Ldr 1/7/89. Retd GD 3/8/93.
WHITE M. Born 16/8/24. Commd 4/9/48. Flt Lt 29/12/53. Retd GD 16/8/68.
WHITE M. J. Born 2/2/43. Commd 28/4/61. Gp Capt 1/1/91. Retd GD 2/1/96.
WHITE M. J. F. Born 12/6/35. Commd 9/4/57. Sqn Ldr 1/7/70. Retd GD 1/7/73.
WHITE M. V. Born 20/10/49. Commd 21/3/69. Flt Lt 21/9/75. Retd GD(G) 20/10/87.
WHITE M. W. Born 6/7/43. Commd 17/7/70. Sqn Ldr 1/7/78. Retd SY 6/7/87.
WHITE N. K., BSc MB ChB. Born 18/9/56. Commd 25/9/80. Sqn Ldr 1/8/89. Retd MED 29/5/97.
WHITE R. C. Born 12/6/52. Commd 1/6/72. Flt Lt 1/12/77. Retd GD 12/6/90.
WHITE R. D. R., BSc. Born 7/6/58. Commd 26/7/81. Flt Lt 20/10/81. Retd GD 20/10/00.
WHITE R. G. J., OBE. Born 5/10/13. Commd 10/1/38. Wg Cdr 1/1/49. Retd SUP 1/8/50.
WHITE R. J., BSc CEng MRAeS. Born 4/9/42. Commd 15/7/64. Sqn Ldr 1/7/76. Retd ENG 31/5/98.
WHITE R. J., MIMgt. Born 11/1/31. Commd 9/3/50. Wg Cdr 1/7/80. Retd ADMIN 11/1/86.
WHITE R. R. G. Born 3/3/19. Commd 19/8/42. Sqn Ldr 1/1/63. Retd ENG 16/11/74.
WHITE R. W., MBE. Born 17/10/46. Commd 18/11/66. Wg Cdr 1/1/91. Retd OPS SPT 1/12/00.
WHITE R. W., BSc. Born 1/10/42. Commd 15/7/64. Flt Lt 15/10/68. Retd ENG 5/10/69.
WHITE S. E. Born 18/10/59. Commd 5/4/79. Flt Lt 5/10/85. Retd GD(G) 1/6/86.
WHITE S. G. R., MRAeS. Born 25/1/20. Commd 15/7/43. Sqn Ldr 1/1/55. Retd ENG 12/10/63.
WHITE S. J. Born 18/2/36. Commd 26/11/60. Flt Lt 1/4/66. Retd GD 3/10/79.
WHITE S. M. F. Born 6/2/16. Commd 23/12/43. Sqn Ldr 1/1/57. Retd SEC 19/7/64.
WHITE T. A., BSc. Born 2/5/62. Commd 12/3/87. Flt Lt 2/9/91. Retd ENG 2/5/00.
WHITE T. P., CB CEng FIEE. Born 1/5/32. Commd 1/7/54. AVM 1/7/83. Retd ENG 1/5/87.
WHITE V. G. B. Born 21/10/09. Commd 31/7/41. Flt Lt 1/7/44. Retd ENG 20/12/45 rtg Sqn Ldr.
WHITE W. B., DPhysEd MIMgt. Born 27/5/31. Commd 12/9/56. Wg Cdr 1/1/74. Retd ADMIN 24/12/85.
WHITE W. R. J. Born 8/5/21. Commd 30/3/43. Sqn Ldr 1/1/71. Retd GD 8/5/76.
WHITEAR G. S. Born 20/3/47. Commd 2/8/68. Flt Lt 6/10/71. Retd GD 1/9/77.
WHITEHEAD D. J. B., AFC. Born 4/10/23. Commd 18/6/46. Wg Cdr 1/7/63. Retd GD 4/10/78.
WHITEHEAD F. L., MD CM. Born 20/11/09. Commd 29/3/36. Sqn Ldr 1/12/41. Retd MED 30/8/46 rtg Wg Cdr.
WHITEHEAD G. E., BSc. Born 5/9/44. Commd 19/9/71. Sqn Ldr 1/7/88. Retd ENG 5/9/99.
WHITEHEAD H. A. L. Born 27/7/36. Commd 23/11/78. Sqn Ldr 1/7/89. Retd ENG 29/5/92.
WHITEHEAD L. J. Born 14/8/56. Commd 28/11/74. Sqn Ldr 1/1/88. Retd SY 14/11/95.
WHITEHEAD M. D., BTech. Born 4/7/59. Commd 26/9/82. Sqn Ldr 1/7/94. Retd GD 1/5/01.
WHITEHEAD P. F. Born 28/2/52. Commd 10/5/73. Flt Lt 10/11/78. Retd GD 28/2/90.
WHITEHOUSE L. J. Born 6/7/54. Commd 19/12/85. Flt Lt 19/12/87. Retd ADMIN 19/12/93.
WHITEHOUSE T. F. Born 21/8/42. Commd 30/7/64. Flt Lt 30/1/71. Retd ENG 10/6/76.
WHITEHURST G. R., BSc. Born 26/1/53. Commd 25/7/76. Flt Lt 25/10/77. Retd GD 25/4/97.
WHITEIGHT L. J. S. Born 1/11/22. Commd 23/8/56. Sqn Ldr 1/7/71. Retd GD 23/3/76.
WHITELAW P. T. Born 6/5/30. Commd 2/7/52. Flt Lt 14/5/58. Retd GD 6/5/68.

WHITELEGG J. W., MBE BSc CEng MIMechE MIEE MRAeS. Born 6/6/16. Commd 27/9/45. Sqn Ldr 1/1/58. Retd ENG 1/1/64.
WHITELEGG P. J. Born 3/3/58. Commd 2/8/90. Flt Lt 2/8/92. Retd ENG 2/8/98.
WHITELEY A. M. Born 24/8/55. Commd 28/6/79. Sqn Ldr 1/7/89. Retd ENG 24/8/99.
WHITELEY D. L. Born 15/6/40. Commd 16/1/60. Sqn Ldr 1/7/71. Retd GD 15/6/78.
WHITELEY F. G. Born 25/3/03. Commd 14/3/40. Sqn Ldr 24/4/45. Retd ENG 6/8/46 rtg Wg Cdr.
WHITELEY G. E., DSO. Born 22/5/16. Commd 22/10/42. Flt Lt 22/2/46. Retd SEC 23/5/65.
WHITELEY H. Born 23/9/14. Commd 9/8/41. Sqn Ldr 1/7/52. Retd ENG 23/9/63.
WHITELEY M. C., CEng MRAeS MIMgt. Born 15/5/35. Commd 25/7/56. Sqn Ldr 1/7/66. Retd ENG 15/5/73.
WHITELOCK C. F. Born 20/3/14. Commd 30/3/42. Sqn Ldr 1/1/53. Retd ENG 20/12/61.
WHITEMAN D. M. Born 27/4/44. Commd 22/5/64. Flt Lt 15/4/70. Retd GD 10/3/76.
WHITEMAN M. N. Born 28/4/37. Commd 14/5/57. Sqn Ldr 1/1/72. Retd GD 28/4/75.
WHITESIDE B. Born 24/10/17. Commd 13/3/46. Flt Lt 13/9/50. Retd RGT 26/2/58.
WHITESIDE T. C. D., MBE PhD MB ChB MRCP FRAeS FIMgt. Born 2/7/21. Commd 11/7/46. Gp Capt 25/2/68. Retd MED 15/5/79.
WHITEWRIGHT I. S., BA. Born 2/10/27. Commd 10/12/63. Sqn Ldr 10/6/67. Retd EDN 10/12/79.
WHITFIELD E. J. Born 30/6/14. Commd 31/12/52. Flt Lt 1/1/57. Retd PRT 16/12/69.
WHITFIELD E. N. Born 30/1/18. Commd 6/1/44. Flt Lt 6/7/48. Retd SEC 1/9/62.
WHITFIELD G. F. Born 19/1/27. Commd 19/12/63. Flt Lt 19/12/66. Retd. GD 19/1/82.
WHITFIELD J. J. Born 6/8/45. Commd 5/2/65. Gp Capt 1/7/90. Retd GD 2/7/94.
WHITFIELD N. M. Born 7/2/37. Commd 18/3/81. Flt Lt 13/10/79. Retd ENG 24/10/87.
WHITFIELD P. C., MA BA MCIPD. Born 31/7/37. Commd 1/1/63. Sqn Ldr 27/10/70. Retd ADMIN 1/10/77.
WHITFORD I. R. Born 1/10/35. Commd 7/12/54. Sqn Ldr 1/7/67. Retd GD 31/12/74.
WHITFORD T. J. Born 12/10/32. Commd 23/8/51. Flt Lt 23/2/57. Retd GD 12/10/70.
WHITING A. Born 5/4/35. Commd 11/5/78. Flt Lt 11/5/81. Retd ENG 17/4/87.
WHITING T. A., DFC. Born 31/8/17. Commd 17/1/40. Wg Cdr 1/7/54. Retd GD 6/11/67.
WHITINGTON R. B. Born 20/12/27. Commd 19/12/63. Sqn Ldr 1/7/75. Retd ENG 1/7/80.
WHITLING N. R. W. Born 31/3/37. Commd 16/12/58. Sqn Ldr 1/7/69. Retd GD 14/12/75.
WHITLOCK A. J., OBE. Born 25/9/24. Commd 12/5/47. Gp Capt 1/7/70. Retd GD 25/9/82.
WHITLOCK J. E., OBE DFC. Born 19/12/21. Commd 20/9/43. Wg Cdr 1/1/62. Retd GD 18/9/72.
WHITMAN D. C. Born 11/1/33. Commd 5/4/55. Wg Cdr 1/1/74. Retd GD 11/1/88.
WHITMAN R. D. Born 9/1/33. Commd 20/12/51. Flt Lt 21/10/59. Retd GD 9/1/71.
WHITMELL M. A., BSc. Born 31/10/59. Commd 18/10/81. Flt Lt 18/7/85. Retd SUP 4/3/86.
WHITNEY B. H., BSc. Born 11/3/39. Commd 2/8/60. Flt Lt 2/2/65. Retd ENG 6/3/66.
WHITNEY G. D. Born 25/10/28. Commd 10/9/56. Wg Cdr 1/7/79. Retd PRT 2/6/81.
WHITNEY J. M. Born 26/4/38. Commd 17/7/70. Flt Lt 17/7/72. Retd SUP 17/7/79.
WHITSON A. C., MIMgt. Born 7/5/32. Commd 15/12/53. Sqn Ldr 1/1/68. Retd GD 1/1/71.
WHITSTON J. R. Born 8/8/46. Commd 5/2/65. Wg Cdr 1/1/88. Retd GD 1/2/01.
WHITSUN-JONES D. D. Born 1/2/23. Commd 3/9/43. Flt Lt 3/3/47. Retd GD 1/5/62.
WHITTAKER A. W., CEng MIMechE MRAeS MIEE. Born 25/8/34. Commd 10/10/60. Wg Cdr 1/1/76. Retd ENG 30/9/83.
WHITTAKER C. R. Born 13/3/58. Commd 5/2/81. Sqn Ldr 1/7/94. Retd GD 5/4/99.
WHITTAKER D., CB MBE. Born 25/6/33. Commd 20/3/52. AVM 1/7/86. Retd GD 4/4/89.
WHITTAKER G. Born 4/8/24. Commd 7/4/44. Flt Lt 7/10/47. Retd GD 26/8/58.
WHITTAKER G. L. Born 25/6/41. Commd 11/11/71. Flt Lt 11/11/73. Retd GD(G) 11/11/79.
WHITTAKER J. R. Born 13/12/07. Commd 1/11/43. Fg Offr 1/11/43. Retd ENG 4/8/47 rtg Flt Lt.
WHITTAKER K. Born 29/4/55. Commd 9/8/79. Flt Lt 9/2/85. Retd GD 6/5/95.
WHITTAKER N. S. Born 2/7/31. Commd 24/9/53. Flt Lt 26/11/58. Retd GD 2/7/69.
WHITTAKER P. Born 20/5/52. Commd 5/4/79. Sqn Ldr 1/1/94. Retd GD(G) 14/3/96.
WHITTAKER P. J. Born 16/2/25. Commd 26/8/45. Sqn Ldr 1/7/59. Retd GD 16/2/63.
WHITTAKER R. A. Born 1/2/46. Commd 7/1/71. Flt Lt 7/7/77. Retd GD(G) 14/9/86.
WHITTAKER R. N., MBE. Born 27/3/33. Commd 10/4/52. Air Cdre 1/7/84. Retd SUP 27/3/88.
WHITTAKER T. B., MBE. Born 25/11/17. Commd 3/5/56. Sqn Ldr 1/1/66. Retd PRT 1/9/70.
WHITTAKER W. A. Born 21/8/42. Commd 7/6/68. Wg Cdr 1/7/90. Retd ENG 12/4/93.
WHITTAM J. R. Born 25/2/34. Commd 27/7/54. Sqn Ldr 1/1/64. Retd GD 25/2/72.
WHITTAM R. Born 2/10/21. Commd 5/12/42. Wg Cdr 1/1/61. Retd GD 2/10/76 rtg Gp Capt.
WHITTEN E. W. Born 31/1/32. Commd 31/10/61. Flt Lt 31/10/61. Retd ENG 12/10/67.
WHITTICASE R. J., BA. Born 23/5/44. Commd 10/12/65. Flt Lt 10/6/71. Retd GD 23/5/82.
WHITTINGHAM H. W., MA MB ChB MRCS LRCP DTM&H. Born 11/10/14. Commd 28/9/39. Gp Capt 1/1/60. Retd MED 11/10/72.
WHITTINGHAM I. C. Born 26/10/58. Commd 2/2/84. Sqn Ldr 1/7/92. Retd ADMIN 1/7/97.
WHITTINGHAM J. Born 14/4/55. Commd 16/5/74. Wg Cdr 1/7/94. Retd GD 14/6/99.
WHITTINGHAM L. F., OBE. Born 10/10/23. Commd 17/4/44. Wg Cdr 1/7/74. Retd GD 10/10/78.
WHITTINGHAM T. H., MITD. Born 8/2/34. Commd 3/4/56. Gp Capt 1/1/86. Retd GD 31/3/86.
WHITTINGTON L. M., AFC. Born 13/11/21. Commd 6/4/43. Flt Lt 6/10/46. Retd GD 22/8/53 rtg Sqn Ldr.
WHITTINGTON R. S. Born 12/11/24. Commd 14/7/44. Sqn Ldr 1/4/56. Retd GD 12/11/67.

WHITTLE G. G., DFM. Born 15/9/23. Commd 27/9/43. Sqn Ldr 1/1/56. Retd GD 28/12/61.
WHITTLE J., DFC. Born 3/7/19. Commd 1/5/42. Sqn Ldr 1/7/65. Retd GD 9/4/68.
WHITTLE P. S. Born 21/2/15. Commd 23/3/50. Flt Lt 23/9/53. Retd SUP 22/2/64.
WHITTLE R., CEng MRAeS. Born 14/9/38. Commd 2/1/62. Flt Lt 1/5/66. Retd ENG 2/1/78.
WHITTLE T. J. Born 10/11/46. Commd 6/5/68. Flt Lt 2/3/73. Retd GD 14/8/90.
WHITTOME K. J. Born 6/8/34. Commd 19/11/52. Flt Lt 15/4/58. Retd GD 6/8/72.
WHITTON B., MBE. Born 27/5/48. Commd 11/10/84. Sqn Ldr 1/7/94. Retd ADMIN 14/3/97.
WHITTON D. J., MBE BA. Born 28/2/23. Commd 29/5/45. Flt Lt 3/9/53. Retd SEC 1/10/64.
WHITTON J. G., BSc. Born 2/1/51. Commd 30/9/73. Sqn Ldr 1/7/86. Retd GD 27/12/89.
WHITWAM A. S. J. Born 19/10/30. Commd 15/12/53. Flt Lt 15/6/56. Retd GD 9/8/75 rtg Sqn Ldr.
WHITWELL J. K. Born 5/2/29. Commd 15/2/51. Sqn Ldr 1/1/63. Retd ENG 26/6/65.
WHITWORTH R. E. S. Born 12/1/36. Commd 27/8/64. Wg Cdr 1/7/79. Retd SUP 31/12/82.
WHOLEY R. E. Born 16/2/45. Commd 22/5/64. Wg Cdr 1/1/88. Retd GD 3/2/01.
WHYBRAY E. D., DFC. Born 27/12/20. Commd 12/4/43. Sqn Ldr 1/7/56. Retd GD 27/12/63.
WHYBRO M. J. Born 19/11/41. Commd 12/1/62. Sqn Ldr 1/7/79. Retd GD 1/10/94.
WHYBROW P. G., BA. Born 1/7/14. Commd 10/3/41. Sqn Offr 1/1/50. Retd SY 1/9/93.
WHYMAN A. J. Born 18/3/16. Commd 18/6/44. Sqn Ldr 1/7/62. Retd GD(G) 19/3/66.
WHYNACHT K. A., DFC AFC. Born 30/11/23. Commd 8/8/47. Sqn Ldr 1/1/75. Retd GD(G) 30/11/78.
WHYTE A., FIISec MIOSH MIMgt. Born 29/7/42. Commd 4/12/64. Wg Cdr 1/7/91. Retd SY 1/9/93.
WHYTE A. B., MSc CEng MIEE MRAeS. Born 12/11/25. Commd 19/10/49. Wg Cdr 17/2/71. Retd EDN 13/7/73.
WHYTE A. J., BSc. Born 12/4/60. Commd 5/2/84. Flt Lt 5/8/86. Retd GD 17/12/96.
WHYTE R. A. Born 13/6/30. Commd 16/11/51. Sqn Ldr 1/7/62. Retd GD 14/12/71.
WHYTE S. G. Born 26/5/63. Commd 11/6/81. Flt Lt 11/12/87. Retd ADMIN 9/8/91.
WHYTE W. L. Born 19/1/46. Commd 2/12/66. Wg Cdr 1/1/86. Retd GD 26/11/97.
WICK K. L. Born 14/3/31. Commd 17/1/69. Flt Lt 17/1/73. Retd ENG 30/11/74. Reinstated 22/10/80. Sqn Ldr 1/1/87. Retd ENG 31/7/89.
WICKENS S. G. Born 12/1/64. Commd 29/7/83. Flt Lt 12/10/90. Retd SUP 14/3/96.
WICKES A. J. Born 8/2/44. Commd 17/5/63. Flt Lt 8/1/69. Retd GD 1/10/77.
WICKES N. A., DFC AFC. Born 30/7/24. Commd 16/2/49. Sqn Ldr 1/7/57. Retd GD 30/7/67.
WICKHAM A. A., BA BA FIMgt. Born 21/10/35. Commd 12/1/55. Wg Cdr 1/1/74. Retd GD 21/10/90.
WICKMAN P. R. Born 6/10/52. Commd 16/5/74. Flt Lt 16/11/79. Retd GD 6/10/90.
WICKS C. H. Born 18/11/17. Commd 28/1/43. Sqn Ldr 1/7/62. Retd ENG 18/11/73.
WICKS F. F., CBE DFC. Born 5/9/07. Commd 14/12/29. Gp Capt 1/7/47. Retd GD 1/4/57.
WICKSON A. Born 1/5/10. Commd 27/5/47. Flt Lt 27/11/51. Retd SUP 1/5/67.
WICKSON K. M., MIMgt. Born 23/12/24. Commd 14/7/44. Sqn Ldr 1/1/58. Retd GD 23/12/67.
WICKSON W. J. H., MBE. Born 10/11/25. Commd 3/11/60. Sqn Ldr 1/1/74. Retd ENG 10/11/83.
WIDD P. L. Born 15/11/39. Commd 28/3/63. Flt Lt 1/7/69. Retd SEC 14/2/76.
WIDDESS J. D. McM., MBE. Born 16/9/44. Commd 25/3/64. Sqn Ldr 1/7/79. Retd GD 16/9/00.
WIDDICOMBE R. A. L. Born 29/5/27. Commd 11/11/65. Flt Lt 11/11/70. Retd ENG 29/5/82.
WIDDISON G. C. Born 12/6/21. Commd 15/12/52. Flt Lt 15/12/52. Retd ENG 3/11/61.
WIDDOWS S. C., CB DFC. Born 4/10/09. Commd 25/7/31. A Cdre 1/1/55. Retd GD 29/12/58.
WIDDOWSON M. K. Born 10/5/46. Commd 25/3/64. A Cdre 1/7/92. Retd GD 14/9/96.
WIDMER J. F. M. Born 3/6/23. Commd 29/10/43. Sqn Ldr 1/1/68. Retd GD 16/6/74.
WIER T., AFC. Born 2/1/20. Commd 12/10/48. Flt Lt 12/10/48. Retd GD(G) 2/1/75.
WIGGINS B. D., MBE BSc CEng MIMechE MRAeS MIMgt. Born 7/7/29. Commd 5/12/60. Wg Cdr 1/7/75. Retd ENG 13/11/79.
WIGGINS R. M. Born 14/4/46. Commd 31/3/70. Sqn Ldr 1/7/86. Retd ENG 1/10/89.
WIGGINS T. E. Born 18/3/37. Commd 22/8/62. Sqn Ldr 1/1/71. Retd GD 18/3/95.
WIGGLE J. G. Born 29/5/55. Commd 30/9/73. Sqn Ldr 1/7/86. Retd GD 20/5/96.
WIGHT-BOYCOTT A. B., OBE. Born 7/4/46. Commd 3/3/67. Gp Capt 1/1/95. Retd GD 14/9/96.
WIGHT-BOYCOTT C. M., CBE DSO* MA. Born 18/8/10. Commd 28/9/37. A Cdre 1/7/58. Retd GD 1/7/64.
WIGHTMAN C. L. Born 4/4/38. Commd 6/1/61. Flt Lt 6/7/65. Retd GD 16/4/66.
WIGHTMAN R. A. Born 3/10/36. Commd 4/12/58. Flt Lt 14/2/66. Retd GD 4/12/74.
WIGHTMAN W. K., AFC. Born 13/1/24. Commd 28/1/44. Flt Lt 28/7/47. Retd GD 1/6/77.
WIGHTON J. P. Born 28/8/30. Commd 27/2/52. Flt Lt 26/6/57. Retd GD 6/6/71.
WIGLEY A. E. L. Born 10/3/21. Commd 22/5/44. Sqn Ldr 1/1/69. Retd SUP 10/3/76.
WIGMORE B. T. Born 14/1/41. Commd 27/7/64. Wg Cdr 1/7/79. Retd GD(G) 4/7/89.
WIGMORE W. I. C. Born 18/12/38. Commd 14/4/59. Sqn Ldr 1/7/86. Retd GD 27/2/91.
WIKELEY J. D., MCIPS MIMgt. Born 2/2/25. Commd 30/4/72. Sqn Ldr 30/4/72. Retd SUP 2/2/85.
WILBERFORCE B. D., MB ChB MRCS LRVP. Born 11/8/16. Commd 18/11/43. Wg Cdr 1/4/62. Retd MED 1/7/69.
WILBRAHAM W. H. Born 12/4/37. Commd 18/8/61. Flt Lt 1/4/66. Retd GD 19/1/91.
WILBY D. J. G., AFC. Born 20/5/47. Commd 21/7/65. A Cdre 1/7/96. Retd GD 24/7/00.
WILBY P. J., CEng MRAeS. Born 17/12/37. Commd 29/10/64. Sqn Ldr 5/8/72. Retd EDN 17/12/75.
WILCOCK A. H. Born 21/3/18. Commd 13/1/44. Flt Lt 13/7/47. Retd GD(G) 30/6/62.
WILCOCK C. J. M. Born 6/7/44. Commd 9/8/63. Sqn Ldr 1/7/77. Retd GD 12/3/89.
WILCOCK J. Born 6/6/33. Commd 27/1/67. Sqn Ldr 1/1/78. Retd ENG 7/6/83.

WILCOCK J. R., AFC. Born 3/2/23. Commd 28/3/45. Sqn Ldr 1/1/61. Retd GD 28/9/68.
WILCOCK M. D. Born 24/9/63. Commd 23/4/87. Flt Lt 21/8/93. Retd ADMIN 31/10/96.
WILCOCK P. J., MBE. Born 5/2/49. Commd 24/8/72. Sqn Ldr 1/7/83. Retd GD 3/1/89.
WILCOX A. T. Born 30/5/16. Commd 2/8/45. Flt Lt 4/1/51. Retd SUP 30/8/64.
WILCOX B. Born 6/7/33. Commd 29/11/65. Flt Lt 29/11/65. Retd GD 6/7/88.
WILCOX J. R. Born 9/1/22. Commd 12/9/58. Sqn Ldr 15/4/70. Retd ADMIN 9/1/82.
WILCOX L. J. C., AFC AFM. Born 14/1/24. Commd 21/2/69. Flt Lt 21/2/72. Retd GD(G) 21/2/79.
WILCOX N. H. Born 21/7/40. Commd 11/5/62. Flt Lt 11/11/67. Retd GD 1/11/68.
WILCOX P. H., MBE. Born 28/9/43. Commd 23/3/63. Sqn Ldr 1/1/81. Retd GD 1/10/00.
WILCOX R. J. V. Born 26/10/44. Commd 21/8/68. Gp Capt 1/1/91. Retd ADMIN 31/3/94.
WILCOX W. J. Born 11/8/32. Commd 9/12/76. Flt Lt 9/12/79. Retd ADMIN 30/9/89.
WILD F. J., CEng MIMechE. Born 26/1/33. Commd 21/10/55. Gp Capt 1/1/76. Retd ENG 21/6/86.
WILD G. L., BSc. Born 11/5/65. Commd 30/8/54. Flt Lt 25/12/92. Retd ADMIN 14/9/96.
WILD J. Born 15/7/27. Commd 1/10/52. Gp Capt 1/7/75. Retd GD 2/4/80.
WILD J. G. Born 8/9/40. Commd 14/7/66. Sqn Ldr 1/7/87. Retd GD 2/4/93.
WILD J. M., BA. Born 21/9/56. Commd 18/11/79. Flt Lt 18/5/83. Retd SY 18/11/95.
WILD M. S. Born 31/8/35. Commd 21/10/53. Gp Capt 1/1/89. Retd GD 4/7/89.
WILD N. N., LLB. Born 6/4/48. Commd 27/4/70. Flt Lt 27/1/74. Retd SEC 1/4/78.
WILD P. R., AFC. Born 29/7/34. Commd 18/8/54. Flt Lt 5/10/60. Retd GD 29/7/72. Reinstated 5/11/80 to 31/7/84.
WILDE A. Born 21/4/29. Commd 13/12/51. Gp Capt 1/7/79. Retd SUP 21/4/84.
WILDE C. D. Born 8/9/33. Commd 9/2/66. Sqn Ldr 1/7/81. Retd ENG 8/9/91.
WILDE P. H. Born 26/7/22. Commd 30/9/43. Flt Lt 30/3/47. Retd ENG 2/8/55.
WILDE P. J. Born 31/10/32. Commd 17/5/51. Flt Lt 6/9/56. Retd GD 1/5/74.
WILDEMAN M., BA. Born 6/9/61. Commd 25/11/84. Flt Lt 25/5/86. Retd GD 25/11/96.
WILDER S. R. Born 1/2/63. Commd 22/11/84. APO 22/11/84. Retd GD 6/9/85.
WILDERS R. H. J. Born 24/8/25. Commd 2/7/52. Flt Lt 3/6/59. Retd SEC 8/3/69.
WILDERSPIN K. L., BSc CEng MIEE MRAeS DLUT. Born 29/9/94. Commd 16/9/73. Gp Capt 20/12/96. Retd ENG 4/12/98.
WILDGUST P. G. Born 30/12/31. Commd 7/5/52. Flt Lt 2/10/57. Retd GD 30/12/69.
WILDIG R. B. Born 5/3/22. Commd 4/4/49. Flt Lt 30/1/57. Retd GD 6/8/65.
WILDIN B. A. Born 2/7/52. Commd 2/2/31. Flt Lt 21/10/59. Retd GD 21/9/86.
WILDING A., MSc CEng MIMechE MRAeS. Born 28/9/27. Commd 7/11/82. Flt Lt 23/10/73. Retd ADMIN 30/9/76.
WILDING A.C, BSc. Born 20/3/59. Commd 7/11/82. Wg Cdr 1/7/96. Retd ENG 11/7/99.
WILDING R. G., AFM. Born 3/5/20. Commd 27/1/55. Flt Lt 27/1/61. Retd GD 29/6/68.
WILDING S. W., CBE. Born 3/8/19. Commd 30/8/43. A Cdre 1/7/71. Retd SUP 3/8/74.
WILDMAN J. C. Born 1/2/45. Commd 1/3/68. Wg Cdr 1/1/87. Retd ENG 11/12/96.
WILDMAN W. A., MBE. Born 17/6/11. Commd 24/5/43. Sqn Ldr 1/7/55. Retd ENG 17/6/66.
WILDRIDGE D. B., BSc. Born 4/4/51. Commd 15/9/69. Flt Lt 15/4/74. Retd GD 4/4/89.
WILDS P. J. Born 2/5/33. Commd 11/2/65. Sqn Ldr 1/1/80. Retd GD 1/8/84.
WILDSMITH D. A. Born 31/10/42. Commd 9/8/63. Flt Lt 9/8/68. Retd GD 1/7/76.
WILES C. W. Born 26/2/22. Commd 27/2/47. Flt Lt 11/11/54. Retd GD 26/2/65.
WILES R. A., BSc MCIPD MIMgt PGCE. Born 30/10/32. Commd 23/11/56. Wg Cdr 1/7/78. Retd ADMIN 30/10/87.
WILKES I. F., BSc. Born 20/2/56. Commd 1/9/74. Flt Lt 15/10/78. Retd GD 15/7/89.
WILKES J. D. Born 2/7/40. Commd 1/4/70. Sqn Ldr 1/1/83. Retd ADMIN 1/8/84. Reinstated 1/10/85. Sqn Ldr 2/3/84. Retd ADMIN 1/4/88.
WILKES V. T. M., DFC. Born 29/1/21. Commd 31/12/44. Flt Lt 7/6/51. Retd SUP 15/8/54.
WILKEY R. C. Born 22/12/49. Commd 3/10/74. Sqn Ldr 1/1/88. Retd OPS SPT 18/9/98.
WILKIE I. H. Born 23/6/37. Commd 17/7/58. Wg Cdr 1/7/81. Retd ADMIN 17/7/87.
WILKIE P., MBE. Born 16/3/29. Commd 21/10/65. Sqn Ldr 1/1/77. Retd ENG 13/4/79.
WILKIN L. Born 24/1/48. Commd 24/2/67. Sqn Ldr 1/1/82. Retd GD(G) 11/10/85.
WILKINS C. J., BSc. Born 10/11/51. Commd 13/9/70. Flt Lt 15/4/77. Retd GD(G) 23/9/80.
WILKINS F. J., MA CEng MRAeS MIMechE. Born 20/3/24. Commd 21/6/50. Sqn Ldr 21/6/60. Retd EDN 21/6/66.
WILKINS N. E., DFC MIMgt. Born 10/1/25. Commd 25/3/44. Wg Cdr 1/1/63. Retd GD 3/1/76.
WILKINS P. A., FIMgt MIPM '. Born 30/6/45. Commd 31/10/63. Gp Capt 1/7/91. Retd ADMIN 14/6/94.
WILKINS R. J. Born 3/10/30. Commd 10/3/60. Flt Lt 10/9/63. Retd GD 3/10/68.
WILKINS R. M. Born 14/11/32. Commd 13/9/51. Flt Lt 24/4/57. Retd GD 30/6/91.
WILKINSON A., MBE. Born 29/4/23. Commd 19/6/52. Sqn Ldr 1/7/68. Retd SUP 29/4/78.
WILKINSON A. C. Born 19/2/34. Commd 22/5/59. Sqn Ldr 22/9/69. Retd EDN 8/10/74.
WILKINSON A. L. Born 18/8/35. Commd 30/6/54. Sqn Ldr 1/7/67. Retd SUP 18/8/73.
WILKINSON A. T. B., MBE BA FIMgt MRAeS MCIPS MIMIS. Born 19/4/43. Commd 30/1/70. Wg Cdr 1/1/96. Retd SUP 19/4/98.
WILKINSON C. E., BSc. Born 10/6/36. Commd 30/9/58. Wg Cdr 1/1/77. Retd GD 28/1/84.
WILKINSON C. J., BSc. Born 6/7/65. Commd 11/9/83. Flt Lt 15/1/89. Retd GD 15/7/98.
WILKINSON C. J. Born 9/10/07. Commd 18/2/43. Fg Offr 3/12/43. Retd ENG 23/11/45 rtg Flt Lt.
WILKINSON C. S., FCA. Born 16/6/43. Commd 17/12/64. Flt Lt 15/4/70. Retd GD 14/4/71.
WILKINSON D. Born 11/10/11. Commd 27/5/43. Sqn Ldr 1/1/55. Retd ENG 12/12/64.

WILKINSON D. J., BSc. Born 23/3/49. Commd 27/1/70. Sqn Ldr 1/7/82. Retd GD 25/2/89.
WILKINSON E. A. F. Born 14/7/37. Commd 11/2/65. Sqn Ldr 1/7/83. Retd ADMIN 14/7/87.
WILKINSON F. B., BEM. Born 30/3/22. Commd 15/9/60. Flt Lt 15/9/65. Retd ENG 4/7/73.
WILKINSON G. Born 27/12/34. Commd 2/3/61. Sqn Ldr 1/1/73. Retd ENG 27/12/92.
WILKINSON G. C., AFC. Born 7/11/26. Commd 29/12/48. Flt Lt 21/12/54. Retd GD 1/7/59.
WILKINSON I. D., FIMgt. Born 8/4/32. Commd 27/7/54. A Cdre 1/7/81. Retd SUP 4/8/84.
WILKINSON J., AFC. Born 21/9/31. Commd 30/7/52. Acdre 1/7/83. Retd GD 1/8/86.
WILKINSON J. H. Born 22/11/21. Commd 27/3/47. Sqn Ldr 1/7/61. Retd SUP 1/3/69. Re-employed 3/1/72 to
  28/6/75.
WILKINSON J. H. B. Born 26/8/35. Commd 27/1/61. Flt Lt 1/7/68. Retd GD 25/8/73.
WILKINSON J. N. Born 22/10/45. Commd 17/7/64. Flt Lt 4/5/72. Retd GD 12/12/98.
WILKINSON J. N., BA. Born 17/2/62. Commd 14/9/80. Flt Lt 15/10/86. Retd SUP 1/10/89.
WILKINSON K. G., BSc. Born 29/9/46. Commd 13/9/70. Wg Cdr 1/7/90. Retd GD(G) 1/1/97.
WILKINSON K. J. Born 31/1/29. Commd 12/12/51. Flt Lt 12/12/56. Retd SUP 31/1/67 rtg Sqn Ldr.
WILKINSON P. A., MRCS LRCP. Born 3/3/11. Commd 3/5/37. Gp Capt 1/10/57. Retd MED 3/12/69.
WILKINSON P. J., CVO MA FRAeS. Born 8/6/38. Commd 10/1/57. Plt Offr 8/3/57. Retd GD(G) 21/10/58.
  Re-entered 11/9/61. A Cdre 1/7/91. Retd GD 30/10/96.
WILKINSON R. E., LRAM ARCM. Born 28/1/42. Commd 9/12/76. Wg Cdr 1/7/95. Retd DM 1/6/98.
WILKINSON R. J., FIMgt. Born 20/4/34. Commd 24/9/52. Gp Capt 1/1/78. Retd SUP 6/5/88.
WILKINSON R. M. Born 9/1/22. Commd 19/12/42. Flt Lt 17/10/50. Retd GD(G) 13/7/69.
WILKINSON R. S. Born 17/2/39. Commd 28/1/58. Flt Lt 30/7/63. Retd GD 17/2/77.
WILKINSON S. Born 24/2/21. Commd 6/3/45. Sqn Ldr 1/1/72. Retd GD 1/9/73.
WILKINSON T. H. Born 23/8/40. Commd 9/12/76. Flt Lt 9/12/81. Retd SUP 3/2/85.
WILKINSON W., OBE CEng FIMgt MIEE. Born 9/5/18. Commd 29/4/43. Gp Capt 1/1/67. Retd ENG 9/5/73.
WILKINSON W. A., MIMgt. Born 16/11/23. Commd 1/4/44. Wg Cdr 1/7/75. Retd ADMIN 29/3/78.
WILKINSON W. H., MRCS LRCP. Born 5/5/25. Commd 29/6/53. Wg Cdr 29/6/64. Retd MED 29/6/69.
WILKINSON W. H. G. Born 9/2/30. Commd 26/3/64. Flt Lt 26/3/70. Retd PE 2/10/71.
WILKS B. P., BEM MLitt. Born 21/12/42. Commd 20/5/82. Fl Lt 20/5/86. Retd ADMIN 21/12/97.
WILKS C. E. Born 26/4/29. Commd 4/10/51. Flt Lt 14/7/57. Retd GD 22/6/74.
WILKS J. E. G. Born 19/8/19. Commd 31/1/46. Flt Lt 7/6/51. Retd ENG 22/5/63.
WILL B. V., BSc. Born 2/1/47. Commd 24/4/77. Sqn Ldr 1/7/85. Retd ADMIN 24/4/93.
WILL J. A., MBE. Born 18/2/26. Commd 20/12/51. Flt Lt 4/4/57. Retd GD 18/2/69.
WILLANS R. J., MIMgt. Born 31/8/33. Commd 19/12/63. Sqn Ldr 1/1/78. Retd ENG 6/4/85.
WILLBOND T. C. Born 15/11/46. Commd 11/11/65. Gp Capt 1/1/90. Retd GD(G) 14/9/96.
WILLCOCKS H. J., DCAe. Born 27/3/20. Commd 30/11/50. Sqn Ldr 1/7/60. Retd ENG 31/8/68.
WILLCOX L. G., MIMgt. Born 11/11/35. Commd 16/9/53. Sqn Ldr 1/7/68. Retd GD 15/5/86.
WILLCOX L. T. H. Born 1/12/44. Commd 6/11/64. Flt Lt 6/5/70. Retd GD 21/7/76.
WILLDER K. B. S., CBE BSc CEng FIEE. Born 12/1/18. Commd 31/3/40. A Cdre 1/7/64. Retd ENG 12/1/73.
WILLETS D. F. Born 13/11/36. Commd 28/10/76. Flt Lt 28/10/77. Retd ADMIN 23/8/83.
WILLETTS W. J. Born 19/2/17. Commd 5/10/44. Flt Lt 5/4/48. Retd ENG 29/9/62 rtg Sqn Ldr.
WILLEY J. R. Born 3/1/47. Commd 1/4/66. Sqn Ldr 1/7/82. Retd GD 1/7/85.
WILLEY R. St. J. F. Born 22/11/33. Commd 24/6/53. Flt Lt 21/10/59. Retd GD 22/11/71.
WILLIAMS A., BSc DCAe MRAeS. Born 5/2/29. Commd 30/9/54. Wg Cdr 30/9/69. Retd EDN 2/3/76.
WILLIAMS A. E. Born 4/6/13. Commd 28/2/57. Flt Lt 28/2/60. Retd ACB 1/11/65.
WILLIAMS A. F. Born 15/9/36. Commd 24/8/55. Flt Lt 24/2/60. Retd GD 18/5/67.
WILLIAMS A. F. E., ACIS. Born 6/8/51. Commd 13/2/77. Wg Cdr 1/7/94. Retd ADMIN 14/9/96.
WILLIAMS A. G. Born 6/2/44. Commd 24/6/65. Sqn Ldr 1/1/74. Retd ADMIN 6/2/82.
WILLIAMS A. H. Born 10/3/49. Commd 9/7/79. Flt Lt 16/3/75. Retd GD 22/10/94.
WILLIAMS A. P., BA. Born 9/6/60. Commd 7/5/92. Flt Lt 7/5/94. Retd ADMIN 14/3/97.
WILLIAMS B. Born 27/1/45. Commd 14/1/88. Flt Lt 14/1/92. Retd ADMIN 30/4/98.
WILLIAMS B. Born 17/8/47. Commd 21/10/66. Flt Lt 25/2/73. Retd GD(G) 2/4/75.
WILLIAMS B. G., MSc BA FIMgt. Born 14/4/33. Commd 25/8/55. Gp Capt 1/1/76. Retd SUP 3/4/82.
WILLIAMS C., OBE. Born 24/10/30. Commd 30/7/53. Wg Cdr 1/7/74. Retd GD 27/8/84.
WILLIAMS C. D., BSc. Born 27/6/62. Commd 2/9/84. Sqn Ldr 1/7/97. Retd GD 2/9/00.
WILLIAMS C. J., BChD MIMgt. Born 25/7/55. Commd 30/10/77. Sqn Ldr 16/3/84. Retd DEL 31/5/89.
WILLIAMS C. J. A. Born 26/8/37. Commd 7/2/57. Sqn Ldr 1/1/86. Retd GD 26/8/87.
WILLIAMS C. L. Born 29/12/29. Commd 30/7/52. Flt Lt 2/3/58. Retd GD 18/9/68.
WILLIAMS D. Born 27/5/33. Commd 21/11/51. Sqn Ldr 1/7/75. Retd GD 27/5/93.
WILLIAMS D., OBE BSc CEng MRAeS. Born 22/6/39. Commd 22/8/61. Gp Capt 1/1/86. Retd ENG 22/6/94.
WILLIAMS D. Born 10/12/32. Commd 25/10/57. Sqn Ldr 25/10/68. Retd EDN 25/10/73.
WILLIAMS D., MA DCAe. Born 12/5/33. Commd 26/9/53. Sqn Ldr 1/7/66. Retd ENG 12/5/71.
WILLIAMS D. A., AFC. Born 19/12/44. Commd 28/4/65. Gp Capt 1/1/91. Retd GD 28/7/00.
WILLIAMS D. B., DFC. Born 30/3/14. Commd 4/7/42. Flt Lt 4/1/46. Retd GD 23/9/53.
WILLIAMS D. C., OBE. Born 6/11/46. Commd 18/8/67. Wg Cdr 1/1/90. Retd GD 7/9/00.
WILLIAMS D. G., BA. Born 12/7/40. Commd 12/3/63. Sqn Ldr 12/9/71. Retd EDN 12/3/79.
WILLIAMS D. G. Born 28/6/27. Commd 22/8/63. Wg Cdr 1/7/77. Retd MED(SEC) 21/7/79.

WILLIAMS D. H. Born 4/4/28. Commd 27/7/49. Sqn Ldr 1/7/59. Retd GD 1/9/72.
WILLIAMS D. H., MIMgt. Born 16/8/20. Commd 21/9/50. Sqn Ldr 1/7/63. Retd SUP 16/8/73.
WILLIAMS D. J., BA. Born 19/12/37. Commd 7/8/59. Flt Lt 26/2/64. Retd EDN 8/5/65.
WILLIAMS D. J., BSc CEng MRAeS. Born 7/5/32. Commd 29/4/54. Wg Cdr 1/7/71. Retd ENG 22/4/85.
WILLIAMS D. L., BSc CEng MIEE. Born 15/9/41. Commd 5/10/70. Wg Cdr 1/1/87. Retd ENG 15/9/96.
WILLIAMS D. M., MA MSc. Born 23/6/55. Commd 30/8/78. Wg Cdr 1/1/91. Retd SUP 30/8/94.
WILLIAMS D. M. Born 22/1/22. Commd 25/1/51. Gp Capt 1/1/72. Retd SEC 22/1/77.
WILLIAMS D. S. Born 24/8/30. Commd 8/4/63. Sqn Ldr 1/7/74. Retd ADMIN 24/8/87.
WILLIAMS D. W. Born 31/7/27. Commd 21/11/51. Sqn Ldr 1/7/67. Retd GD 29/10/75.
WILLIAMS E., MIMgt. Born 14/12/22. Commd 14/11/48. Flt Lt 29/6/50. Retd ADMIN 31/12/82.
WILLIAMS E. C. A. Born 9/11/42. Commd 9/2/66. Flt Lt 30/4/72. Retd ADMIN 31/3/94.
WILLIAMS E. H. C. Born 7/6/30. Commd 10/4/52. Sqn Ldr 1/7/62. Retd GD 7/6/68.
WILLIAMS E. I. Born 22/7/16. Commd 23/7/42. Sqn Ldr 1/1/54. Retd SEC 7/10/67.
WILLIAMS E. M. Born 10/6/25. Commd 8/9/44. Flt Lt 4/12/52. Retd GD 31/12/68.
WILLIAMS E. M. Born 12/12/17. Commd 12/1/49. Flt Lt 12/1/55. Retd SEC 23/8/69.
WILLIAMS E. S. Born 15/7/24. Commd 20/7/50. Flt Lt 20/1/54. Retd GD 30/4/63.
WILLIAMS E. S., CBE. Born 27/9/24. Commd 7/7/49. A Cdre 1/7/79. Retd GD 23/11/81.
WILLIAMS F. J. B., MB ChB FRCR DMRD. Born 1/2/42. Commd 16/9/63. Sqn Ldr 4/8/72. Retd MED 1/2/80.
WILLIAMS The Rev G. Born 8/3/36. Commd 3/9/68. Retd 31/8/90 Wg Cdr.
WILLIAMS G. C., AFC* FRAeS. Born 4/6/31. Commd 17/12/57. AVM 1/7/87. Retd GD 4/4/91.
WILLIAMS G. E., CEng MRAeS. Born 29/9/29. Commd 5/12/51. Sqn Ldr 1/7/65. Retd ENG 2/6/81.
WILLIAMS G. H., LVO. Born 6/3/39. Commd 14/5/60. Sqn Ldr 1/1/72. Retd GD 16/6/95.
WILLIAMS G. J. Born 13/11/52. Commd 9/3/72. Sqn Ldr 1/7/81. Retd GD 13/11/90.
WILLIAMS G. J. C. Born 24/9/30. Commd 4/2/57. Flt Lt 7/7/61. Retd SEC 22/1/73.
WILLIAMS G. J. K., MBE. Born 11/4/42. Commd 11/4/64. Flt Lt 11/10/67. Retd GD 11/4/80.
WILLIAMS G. L. Born 25/6/19. Commd 10/1/46. Sqn Ldr 1/7/65. Retd ENG 9/4/74.
WILLIAMS H. Born 4/6/41. Commd 28/4/67. Flt Lt 28/10/72. Retd GD 2/4/93.
WILLIAMS H. C. J. Born 11/7/43. Commd 12/7/63. Flt Lt 12/1/69. Retd GD 11/7/87.
WILLIAMS H. M. Born 11/9/54. Commd 22/5/75. Sqn Ldr 1/1/91. Retd GD 11/9/98.
WILLIAMS H. R. Born 28/11/22. Commd 19/8/44. Gp Capt 1/7/66. Retd GD 8/2/71.
WILLIAMS H. W. T. Born 25/2/16. Commd 26/3/42. Flt Lt 4/6/53. Retd GD(G) 25/2/71.
WILLIAMS I. A., BEd. Born 16/1/58. Commd 5/2/84. Sqn Ldr 1/1/98. Retd ADMIN 1/1/01.
WILLIAMS I. D., BA. Born 14/4/37. Commd 11/6/63. Sqn Ldr 11/12/73. Retd EDN 11/10/81.
WILLIAMS I. G., MIMgt. Born 28/4/21. Commd 22/9/55. Sqn Ldr 1/7/63. Retd ENG 28/4/76.
WILLIAMS I. S., BSc. Born 22/6/58. Commd 27/3/83. Flt Lt 27/6/85. Retd SUP 22/3/96.
WILLIAMS J. Born 14/11/22. Commd 24/2/55. Flt Lt 24/2/61. Retd GD 9/9/70.
WILLIAMS J. Born 6/12/46. Commd 1/11/81. Flt Lt 1/11/86. Retd ENG 1/11/97.
WILLIAMS J. A., OBE. Born 3/3/29. Commd 13/12/50. Wg Cdr 1/7/75. Retd GD 3/3/84.
WILLIAMS J. A. Born 19/2/23. Commd 4/5/50. Flt Lt 19/11/53. Retd GD 19/4/63.
WILLIAMS J. A. Born 31/5/48. Commd 5/11/70. Flt Lt 6/5/77. Retd ADMIN 20/7/86.
WILLIAMS J. A. Born 29/12/25. Commd 29/3/51. Flt Lt 16/11/54. Retd GD 30/12/75.
WILLIAMS J. A. Born 15/9/26. Commd 7/3/51. Sqn Ldr 1/7/67. Retd GD 15/9/86.
WILLIAMS J. D., MIMgt. Born 26/11/25. Commd 25/5/50. Wg Cdr 1/1/68. Retd GD 5/1/77.
WILLIAMS J. E., BA. Born 8/5/27. Commd 4/8/64. Sqn Ldr 10/2/67. Retd ADMIN 22/8/86.
WILLIAMS J. E. F., CBE MMAR. Born 9/6/28. Commd 30/4/54. Gp Capt 1/7/80. Retd MAR 9/6/84.
WILLIAMS J. G., MBE. Born 16/4/46. Commd 2/4/65. Wg Cdr 1/7/96. Retd GD 16/1/01.
WILLIAMS J. G., BSc. Born 26/10/30. Commd 6/11/52. Sqn Ldr 26/10/63. Retd ADMIN 21/10/76.
WILLIAMS J. H. H. Born 15/9/20. Commd 15/1/45. Flt Lt 15/1/51. Retd GD(G) 15/9/70.
WILLIAMS J. K., BA. Born 2/5/56. Commd 6/11/77. Sqn Ldr 1/1/89. Retd GD 2/5/00.
WILLIAMS J. K. Born 17/4/22. Commd 15/6/50. Sqn Ldr 1/1/67. Retd GD 30/6/76.
WILLIAMS J. M., BSc. Born 1/5/54. Commd 30/10/72. Flt Lt 15/10/75. Retd ENG 25/6/86.
WILLIAMS J. N., OBE CEng MIEE. Born 4/1/23. Commd 21/5/43. Gp Capt 1/7/74. Retd ENG 4/1/78.
WILLIAMS J. P. E. Born 20/9/20. Commd 13/2/56. Flt Lt 13/2/56. Retd SEC 29/9/75.
WILLIAMS J. R. Born 29/6/22. Commd 10/10/63. Flt Lt 10/10/66. Retd ENG 28/8/71.
WILLIAMS J. W., BSc. Born 30/1/38. Commd 26/11/60. Flt Lt 26/5/66. Retd GD 30/1/94.
WILLIAMS K., MIMgt. Born 24/2/44. Commd 14/8/80. Sqn Ldr 1/1/92. Retd MED(SEC) 25/9/98.
WILLIAMS K. E. Born 24/3/26. Commd 14/6/46. Wg Cdr 1/7/66. Retd GD 21/7/73.
WILLIAMS K. G., BA MRCS LRCP. Born 23/6/26. Commd 27/10/56. Flt Lt 27/10/51. Retd MED 1/5/57 rtg Sqn Ldr.
WILLIAMS K. J. Born 19/9/43. Commd 30/1/70. Sqn Ldr 1/7/79. Retd ENG 1/11/93.
WILLIAMS K. L. D. Born 5/5/43. Commd 23/11/78. Sqn Ldr 1/7/89. Retd ADMIN 5/5/98.
WILLIAMS M. Born 30/7/37. Commd 26/11/56. Flt Lt 3/1/62. Retd GD 30/7/75.
WILLIAMS M. A. Born 22/9/53. Commd 8/8/74. Wg Cdr 1/1/94. Retd GD 1/7/99.
WILLIAMS M. A. Born 16/12/59. Commd 22/2/79. Flt Lt 22/8/84. Retd GD 16/12/97.
WILLIAMS M. D. Born 23/3/50. Commd 17/5/79. Sqn Ldr 1/7/90. Retd ENG 14/3/96.
WILLIAMS M. F. Born 19/4/42. Commd 6/5/81. Flt Lt 12/8/68. Retd GD 2/4/93.
WILLIAMS M. G., CEng MIEE. Born 7/3/33. Commd 8/2/57. Sqn Ldr 1/1/68. Retd ENG 13/2/74.

WILLIAMS M. G. E., AFC. Born 6/11/24. Commd 12/6/45. Flt Lt 12/12/48. Retd GD 8/4/64.
WILLIAMS M. J. Born 15/11/45. Commd 26/4/84. Sqn Ldr 1/7/92. Retd ADMIN 19/7/94.
WILLIAMS M. J., CEng MIEE MRAeS MIMgt. Born 4/11/42. Commd 11/3/65. Sqn Ldr 1/7/77. Retd ENG 4/11/80.
WILLIAMS M. J., BSc ARTC. Born 8/9/30. Commd 9/8/55. Sqn Ldr 1/1/70. Retd GD 8/9/85.
WILLIAMS M. R., MA FIMgt. Born 9/8/29. Commd 31/8/54. ACdre 1/1/78. Retd GD 9/8/84.
WILLIAMS M. T. Born 7/9/35. Commd 14/2/58. Fg Offr 4/3/60. Retd GD 11/3/64.
WILLIAMS M. W. Born 2/1/36. Commd 20/8/58. Flt Lt 7/8/64. Retd GD 15/9/67.
WILLIAMS N., MBE. Born 5/12/06. Commd 20/10/41. Sqn Offr 1/1/52. Retd SEC 22/9/56.
WILLIAMS N. H. Born 25/12/43. Commd 17/5/63. Wg Cdr 1/7/87. Retd OPS SPT 25/12/98.
WILLIAMS N. M., BA. Born 9/10/26. Commd 17/11/49. Sqn Ldr 1/4/61. Retd EDN 30/4/66.
WILLIAMS N. R., AFC. Born 10/3/33. Commd 15/11/51. Sqn Ldr 1/7/65. Retd GD 10/3/71.
WILLIAMS O. M., CEng MRAeS. Born 25/6/48. Commd 28/2/69. Sqn Ldr 1/1/80. Retd ENG 25/6/86.
WILLIAMS P. Born 26/5/37. Commd 28/4/61. Fg Offr 28/4/63. Retd GD 30/7/65.
WILLIAMS P. D., BTech. Born 18/1/51. Commd 11/8/74. Sqn Ldr 1/7/88. Retd GD 14/7/92.
WILLIAMS P. F., DPhysEd. Born 19/7/31. Commd 6/1/58. Wg Cdr 1/1/75. Retd ADMIN 6/7/85.
WILLIAMS P. G., BSc. Born 23/2/54. Commd 3/8/75. Flt Lt 3/5/77. Retd GD 23/2/92.
WILLIAMS P. V. Born 15/1/24. Commd 7/5/53. Flt Lt 13/11/57. Retd GD 6/9/69.
WILLIAMS R., BSc(Eng). Born 30/6/40. Commd 30/9/59. Sqn Ldr 1/1/71. Retd ENG 30/6/95.
WILLIAMS R. A., BSc. Born 24/2/68. Commd 7/1/90. Flt Lt 7/7/92. Retd GD 7/10/93.
WILLIAMS R. A. Born 6/8/22. Commd 20/6/43. Wg Cdr 1/7/66. Retd EDN 1/7/73.
WILLIAMS R. C., BSc. Born 29/9/53. Commd 28/9/80. Sqn Ldr 1/1/91. Retd SUP 14/11/96.
WILLIAMS R. C., MB ChB MRCS LRCP DAvMed. Born 27/3/33. Commd 15/2/59. Wg Cdr 15/2/72. Retd MED 5/7/76.
WILLIAMS R. C., MB ChB DAvMed. Born 31/7/51. Commd 18/7/72. Wg Cdr 24/9/88. Retd MED 31/7/89.
WILLIAMS R. E. Born 31/1/41. Commd 1/8/61. Gp Capt 1/1/90. Retd GD 29/2/96.
WILLIAMS R. G., BA. Born 15/11/52. Commd 25/9/71. Wg Cdr 1/7/91. Retd SUP 14/3/97.
WILLIAMS R. G. C. Born 3/8/39. Commd 6/7/62. Sqn Ldr 1/7/84. Retd GD 3/8/94.
WILLIAMS R. G. L. Born 19/6/43. Commd 17/12/65. Sqn Ldr 1/1/73. Retd GD 19/6/81.
WILLIAMS R. H. Born 15/9/35. Commd 16/9/53. Flt Lt 13/4/60. Retd GD 15/9/73.
WILLIAMS R. H. Born 19/4/33. Commd 29/12/51. Flt Lt 2/1/62. Retd GD 1/7/76.
WILLIAMS R. J. Born 23/2/13. Commd 27/5/42. Sqn Ldr 1/7/57. Retd GD(G) 17/4/59.
WILLIAMS R. J. R. Born 30/12/24. Commd 31/3/45. Sqn Ldr 1/7/56. Retd GD 10/6/77.
WILLIAMS R. McC., DFC. Born 10/4/21. Commd 20/10/42. Flt Lt 14/3/51. Retd GD 10/4/76.
WILLIAMS R. S. Born 5/12/36. Commd 28/2/56. Sqn Ldr 1/1/73. Retd GD 3/4/87.
WILLIAMS R. T. Born 11/2/36. Commd 12/1/67. Sqn Ldr 1/1/73. Retd GD 11/2/91.
WILLIAMS R. T., BSc. Born 17/4/29. Commd 24/10/51. Flt Lt 24/7/55. Retd ENG 2/9/80.
WILLIAMS S. Born 17/4/22. Commd 30/12/42. Sqn Ldr 1/1/72. Retd SUP 17/4/73.
WILLIAMS S. B. Born 31/10/41. Commd 9/12/65. Sqn Ldr 1/1/75. Retd ENG 2/11/82.
WILLIAMS S. C. Born 30/11/21. Commd 18/10/62. Flt Lt 18/10/65. Retd GD 30/11/76.
WILLIAMS S. D. P. Born 4/12/60. Commd 31/1/80. Flt Lt 31/7/85. Retd GD 13/9/88.
WILLIAMS S. R., BA BEd. Born 27/5/51. Commd 8/12/83. Sqn Ldr 1/1/91. Retd ADMIN 1/1/94.
WILLIAMS T., MBE. Born 26/7/18. Commd 29/7/48. Sqn Ldr 1/1/58. Retd SEC 26/7/65.
WILLIAMS T. C., MA. Born 30/4/25. Commd 4/1/56. Sqn Ldr 17/8/61. Retd EDN 22/12/67.
WILLIAMS T. C. Born 30/9/25. Commd 14/1/65. Flt Lt 14/1/68. Retd GD 30/9/75.
WILLIAMS T. G., BSc. Born 4/6/60. Commd 4/9/78. Flt Lt 15/4/84. Retd GD 4/6/98.
WILLIAMS T. I., BEM. Born 30/12/19. Commd 15/6/61. Sqn Ldr 1/7/71. Retd SEC 30/12/74.
WILLIAMS T. J. C. Born 21/12/28. Commd 27/8/52. Sqn Ldr 1/1/70. Retd GD 31/10/75.
WILLIAMS T. R. D., BSc. Born 11/8/44. Commd 30/7/72. Sqn Ldr 30/1/75. Retd ADMIN 30/10/88.
WILLIAMS T. W. Born 17/8/20. Commd 4/4/45. Flt Lt 18/5/51. Retd CAT 1/7/75.
WILLIAMS W. B., LDS. Born 19/6/24. Commd 19/6/47. Wg Cdr 1/4/62. Retd DEL 8/3/73.
WILLIAMS W. M. Born 1/7/30. Commd 22/2/57. Flt Offr 27/2/61. Retd CAT 27/3/65.
WILLIAMSON B. T. Born 18/12/50. Commd 21/2/74. Sqn Ldr 1/7/88. Retd OPS SPT 29/4/01.
WILLIAMSON C. K. Born 29/7/30. Commd 4/10/50. Flt Lt 4/4/55. Retd GD 25/7/68.
WILLIAMSON C. M., MA MSc CEng MRAeS CDipAF. Born 16/4/55. Commd 24/9/76. Wg Cdr 1/7/94. Retd ENG 6/4/01.
WILLIAMSON C. R. Born 2/4/46. Commd 20/8/65. Wg Cdr 1/1/90. Retd GD 9/8/97.
WILLIAMSON D. L. Born 17/8/59. Commd 26/11/81. Flt Lt 26/5/88. Retd SY 28/7/93.
WILLIAMSON E. C., BA FIMgt. Born 21/4/40. Commd 31/7/62. Gp Capt 1/7/88. Retd SY 1/8/93.
WILLIAMSON F. W., AFC. Born 10/7/20. Commd 28/10/43. Sqn Ldr 1/7/56. Retd SEC 10/7/69.
WILLIAMSON I. G. Born 31/3/35. Commd 8/11/68. Flt Lt 8/11/70. Retd SUP 1/5/74.
WILLIAMSON J. A. Born 1/7/14. Commd 8/7/42. Flt Offr 8/1/47. Retd SEC 18/6/51.
WILLIAMSON J. H. S. Born 8/2/34. Commd 29/10/52. Flt Lt 24/3/58. Retd GD 8/2/72.
WILLIAMSON J. I. T. Born 25/11/23. Commd 3/8/50. Flt Lt 3/2/54. Retd GD 21/4/56.
WILLIAMSON J. S. Born 29/10/28. Commd 18/10/62. Flt Lt 18/10/68. Retd ENG 1/6/79.
WILLIAMSON M. C. Born 12/12/47. Commd 28/2/69. Sqn Ldr 1/1/93. Retd GD 14/3/96.
WILLIAMSON M. E. Born 12/10/44. Commd 9/7/72. Wg Cdr 1/1/90. Retd ADMIN 14/9/96.

WILLIAMSON M. E., OBE. Born 13/4/37. Commd 28/7/59. Gp Capt 1/1/86. Retd GD 2/7/88.
WILLIAMSON P. P., BSc. Born 3/1/43. Commd 6/9/65. Sqn Ldr 1/7/92. Retd GD 31/12/95.
WILLIAMSON R., DFM. Born 8/3/22. Commd 30/11/43. Flt Lt 30/11/49. Retd SEC 25/6/55.
WILLIAMSON R. D. Born 2/12/31. Commd 19/8/53. Sqn Ldr 1/1/64. Retd GD 2/12/69.
WILLIAMSON W. H. Born 5/11/28. Commd 9/1/52. Wg Cdr 1/7/67. Retd ENG 1/7/70.
WILLIAMSON W. M., BA DipPE. Born 18/10/48. Commd 22/8/71. Flt Lt 22/8/75. Retd ADMIN 22/8/87.
WILLIAMSON-NOBLE S. M. D., MA MS CEng FRAeS. Born 18/5/43. Commd 30/9/62. A Cdre 1/1/93. Retd ENG 1/8/97.
WILLIES D. A. Born 6/2/41. Commd 14/5/60. Flt Lt 1/4/70. Retd GD(G) 29/10/91.
WILLIMENT A. R. Born 13/5/36. Commd 8/11/68. Wg Cdr 1/7/88. Retd MED(T) 1/1/93.
WILLING M. J. Born 24/8/43. Commd 13/10/61. Flt Lt 9/2/68. Retd GD 8/4/77. Rtg Sqn Ldr.
WILLINGALE D. J. Born 20/3/46. Commd 28/4/67. Flt Lt 16/4/77. Retd GD(G) 25/1/94.
WILLINGS A. L. Born 3/7/34. Commd 5/4/55. Flt Lt 14/5/58. Retd GD 7/4/79.
WILLIS A. F. Born 16/2/20. Commd 3/5/56. Sqn Ldr 1/7/67. Retd SUP 16/2/75.
WILLIS A. P. Born 12/2/49. Commd 21/12/67. Sqn Ldr 1/1/89. Retd SUP 14/3/96.
WILLIS A. R. Born 5/12/58. Commd 3/2/85. Flt Lt 14/3/83. Retd GD 5/12/96.
WILLIS A. S., CEng MRAeS. Born 6/12/25. Commd 23/1/52. Wg Cdr 1/1/71. Retd ENG 19/8/77.
WILLIS B. H. P. Born 17/7/33. Commd 29/4/53. Flt Lt 13/4/60. Retd GD 17/7/71.
WILLIS C. J. Born 15/6/56. Commd 23/10/86. Flt Lt 10/1/89. Retd ADMIN 14/3/96.
WILLIS C. V. D., DSO OBE DFC. Born 9/11/16. Commd 30/7/38. Gp Capt 1/7/56. Retd GD 3/3/65 rtg A Cdre.
WILLIS D., MCSP GradDipPhysio. Born 23/4/39. Commd 21/2/74. Sqn Ldr 3/2/85. Retd MED(T) 20/9/91.
WILLIS D. G., BA. Born 22/8/26. Commd 6/9/56. Flt Lt 6/3/60. Retd GD(G) 8/4/66.
WILLIS D. J., AFC. Born 14/6/39. Commd 25/7/60. Sqn Ldr 1/7/71. Retd GD 14/6/77.
WILLIS D. J. R., MBE CEng MIMechE. Born 13/8/25. Commd 4/9/58. Flt Lt 4/9/63. Retd ENG 5/9/73.
WILLIS G. Born 30/4/30. Commd 13/12/52. Sqn Ldr 1/1/66. Retd GD 1/1/69.
WILLIS G. C. S. Born 31/7/08. Commd 27/10/41. Flt Lt 1/7/44. Retd ENG 16/1/46. rtg Sqn Ldr.
WILLIS G. F. Born 7/3/49. Commd 31/8/78. Sqn Ldr 1/1/91. Retd GD(G) 1/1/93.
WILLIS G. W., FInstPet MIMgt. Born 21/2/25. Commd 14/5/49. Wg Cdr 1/7/74. Retd SUP 21/2/80.
WILLIS Sir John., GBE KCB. Born 27/10/37. Commd 29/7/58. ACM 4/4/95. Retd GD 10/1/98.
WILLIS J. M., BSc. Born 10/4/42. Commd 1/9/65. Flt Lt 1/6/67. Retd GD 22/10/94.
WILLIS R. D. Born 16/5/29. Commd 7/9/61. Sqn Ldr 1/1/74. Retd ENG 19/5/79.
WILLIS-FLEMING R. C. Born 11/12/36. Commd 18/2/58. WgCdr 1/7/84. Retd GD(G) 11/12/91.
WILLIS-RICHARDS J. W., MBE. Born 15/10/19. Commd 10/6/41. Sqn Ldr 1/1/58. Retd GD 15/10/62.
WILLISON D. J., BSc. Born 4/7/43. Commd 17/8/64. Gp Capt 1/1/89. Retd GD 7/4/93.
WILLMAN W. T., BA MIMgt. Born 16/11/42. Commd 28/7/64. Sqn Ldr 1/1/73. Retd GD 18/12/82 rtg Wg Cdr.
WILLMER C. J. Born 9/4/47. Commd 2/12/66. Sqn Ldr 1/1/85. Retd GD 1/1/88.
WILLMOTT B. Born 26/10/46. Commd 1/3/68. Flt Lt 4/5/72. Retd GD 26/10/84.
WILLMOTT G. Born 12/8/29. Commd 5/1/60. Sqn Ldr 1/7/72. Retd SUP 15/4/91.
WILLMOTT J. Born 19/2/52. Commd 16/3/73. Flt Lt 16/3/76. Retd GD 19/2/80.
WILLMOTT J. R. M. Born 30/6/41. Commd 28/9/61. Sqn Ldr 1/1/73. Retd ENG 30/6/79.
WILLMOTT N. P. Born 29/9/51. Commd 14/10/71. Wg Cdr 1/1/89. Retd OPS SPT 1/10/99.
WILLMOTT R. A. Born 26/6/44. Commd 2/2/84. Flt Lt 2/2/88. Retd ADMIN 2/12/97.
WILLMOTT T. W., DFC. Born 28/7/17. Commd 4/3/42. Sqn Ldr 1/4/56. Retd GD 5/8/60.
WILLOUGHBY D. F. Born 21/2/40. Commd 3/8/62. Flt Lt 15/4/70. Retd GD 21/2/95.
WILLOUGHBY M. L., BSc. Born 30/9/48. Commd 1/12/71. Sqn Ldr 1/7/88. Retd ENG 1/12/93.
WILLOUGHBY-CRISP G. A. Born 5/9/44. Commd 29/4/71. Flt Lt 29/4/73. Retd GD 12/9/91.
WILLOX K. W., BA MHCIMA. Born 25/1/58. Commd 20/1/80. Flt Lt 20/10/83. Retd ADMIN 20/1/87.
WILLS A. M., CVO OBE. Born 21/9/43. Commd 28/7/64. Gp Capt 1/7/83. Retd GD 31/3/94.
WILLS A. P., DFC. Born 14/4/22. Commd 23/7/41. Sqn Ldr 1/7/50. Retd GD 27/4/52.
WILLS K. E., CEng MIMechE MRAeS. Born 8/1/26. Commd 4/5/50. Sqn Ldr 1/7/62. Retd ENG 10/1/76.
WILLS R. E. Born 3/11/46. Commd 2/6/67. Flt Lt 2/12/72. Retd GD 3/11/84.
WILLS R. P., BSc. Born 7/12/57. Commd 16/12/79. Flt Lt 16/3/81. Retd GD 9/10/89.
WILLSMER M. J. Born 18/4/45. Commd 12/7/68. Flt Lt 12/1/74. Retd GD 14/3/96.
WILLSON G. R., MBE. Born 11/11/26. Commd 24/10/46. Sqn Ldr 1/7/60. Retd GD 31/12/84.
WILLSON J. D., MBE BSc MICE. Born 9/12/30. Commd 2/5/55. Sqn Ldr 1/1/65. Retd ACB 8/4/69.
WILLSON J. R. Born 22/5/42. Commd 27/1/61. Sqn Ldr 1/1/74. Retd GD 22/5/86.
WILLSON R. A. Born 12/6/46. Commd 5/3/65. Flt Lt 24/12/70. Retd GD 17/3/77.
WILLSON-PEPPER A. C. Born 7/6/31. Commd 14/7/53. Flt Lt 17/1/58. Retd GD 7/6/68.
WILLY K. R., CBE BA FBCS MMS MCIPS. Born 25/1/25. Commd 30/1/47. A Cdre 1/1/74. Retd SUP 25/1/80.
WILMOT A. G., CEng MIEE MIMgt. Born 10/7/22. Commd 15/2/51. Wg Cdr 1/1/68. Retd ENG 10/7/77.
WILMOT C. J. Born 27/6/34. Commd 13/12/55. Flt Lt 13/6/58. Retd GD 1/10/71.
WILMOT J. C., MRAeS MIMgt. Born 14/3/42. Commd 12/1/61. Sqn Ldr 1/1/76. Retd GD(G) 30/9/88.
WILMOTT C. J. Born 26/7/36. Commd 14/1/65. Flt Lt 26/7/67. Retd SEC 26/7/74.
WILMSHURST A. K. Born 28/7/30. Commd 13/2/52. Sqn Ldr 1/7/69. Retd GD. 1/9/77.
WILMSHURST-SMITH S. M. Born 11/1/56. Commd 27/2/75. Sqn Ldr 1/1/88. Retd ADMIN 28/6/93.
WILSHIRE P. J. Born 29/11/40. Commd 20/11/75. Flt Lt 20/11/77. Retd GD(G) 20/11/83.

WILSON Sir Andrew., KCB AFC FRAeS. Born 27/2/41. Commd 31/7/62. ACM 16/4/93. Retd GD 26/8/95.
WILSON A. D. Born 21/12/42. Commd 25/6/65. Flt Lt 25/12/70. Retd GD 8/3/81.
WILSON A. E. Born 19/1/34. Commd 16/9/71. Sqn Ldr 1/1/80. Retd SUP 19/1/84.
WILSON A. H. P., CEng MRAeS MIEE. Born 21/10/36. Commd 23/7/58. Sqn Ldr 1/1/69. Retd ENG 21/10/74.
WILSON A. J. Born 29/6/38. Commd 27/1/64. Flt Lt 27/1/64. Retd GD 11/2/65.
WILSON A. J. Born 1/7/51. Commd 30/1/70. Flt Lt 30/7/75. Retd GD 1/7/89.
WILSON A. J. H., MIMgt. Born 11/2/23. Commd 27/3/47. Wg Cdr 1/7/74. Retd SUP 11/2/78.
WILSON A. L., MSc BSc CEng MBCS. Born 26/7/58. Commd 25/1/77. Wg Cdr 1/1/96. Retd ENG 1/1/99.
WILSON A. L., AFC. Born 3/11/23. Commd 16/11/44. Sqn Ldr 1/1/66. Retd GD 1/7/73.
WILSON A. P., LLB. Born 19/8/52. Commd 25/2/79. Wg Cdr 1/1/92. Retd SY 14/3/96.
WILSON A. R., DSO. Born 22/9/19. Commd 2/3/41. Wg Cdr 1/1/58. Retd GD 22/9/74.
WILSON A. R., MB ChB MFCM DAvMed. Born 22/2/32. Commd 3/11/57. Wg Cdr 3/11/70. Retd MED 1/1/75.
WILSON A. R. Born 1/5/39. Commd 11/4/57. Sqn Ldr 1/7/70. Retd SEC 1/7/73.
WILSON A. R. E. Born 4/5/34. Commd 13/7/61. Flt Lt 1/4/66. Retd SEC 4/5/72.
WILSON B. Born 22/4/39. Commd 5/2/57. Wg Cdr 1/1/80. Retd GD 16/12/89.
WILSON B. Born 21/1/33. Commd 11/10/51. Flt Lt 25/1/57. Retd GD 21/1/71.
WILSON B. A. Born 14/11/40. Commd 28/4/65. Flt Lt 1/7/69. Retd GD 3/5/78.
WILSON B. C. F. Born 26/4/33. Commd 5/11/70. Wg Cdr 1/7/85. Retd GD(G) 26/4/93.
WILSON B. G. R. Born 31/12/59. Commd 1/11/79. Flt Lt 1/5/85. Retd GD 31/12/97.
WILSON C. B. Born 23/2/43. Commd 23/2/64. Fg Offr 23/2/65. Retd GD 23/4/67.
WILSON D., MDA MCIPS. Born 22/1/48. Commd 7/3/71. Wg Cdr 1/7/91. Retd SUP 14/3/97.
WILSON D. C., McH. Born 2/1/52. Commd 1/6/72. Flt Lt 1/12/77. Retd GD 29/10/82.
WILSON D. F., BA. Born 24/5/50. Commd 13/2/72. Wg Cdr 1/1/88. Retd ADMIN 25/10/96.
WILSON D. J. Born 5/3/45. Commd 31/1/64. Flt Lt 4/11/70. Retd GD 1/9/76.
WILSON D. S. Born 22/5/45. Commd 29/11/63. Sqn Ldr 1/1/81. Retd GD 1/2/85.
WILSON E. Born 27/9/23. Commd 5/5/44. Flt Lt 5/11/47. Retd GD 28/12/64.
WILSON E. R., BSc. Born 18/1/53. Commd 14/9/75. Flt Lt 14/6/78. Retd GD(G) 14/9/91.
WILSON F. M. Born 4/7/42. Commd 21/1/74. Flt Lt 8/6/67. Retd GD 28/7/72.
WILSON G. B., BSc CEng MIEE. Born 26/3/32. Commd 23/9/55. Wg Cdr 1/7/73. Retd ENG 1/1/81.
WILSON G. E., BA. Born 12/5/27. Commd 25/9/62. Sqn Ldr 15/2/65. Retd ADMIN 25/9/78. Reinstated 6/8/80 to 12/5/84.
WILSON G. J., MC. Born 14/8/26. Commd 17/7/47. Wg Cdr 1/1/71. Retd RGT 14/8/84.
WILSON G. K., BSc. Born 16/3/60. Commd 7/11/82. Sqn Ldr 1/7/95. Retd GD 7/11/98.
WILSON G. S., PhD MSc BDS DGDPRCS. Born 9/11/42. Commd 28/7/63. Gp Capt 1/1/88. Retd DEL 4/11/93.
WILSON G. W., MIMgt. Born 20/9/24. Commd 22/8/63. Sqn Ldr 1/7/73. Retd ENG 20/9/79.
WILSON H. A. Born 12/11/38. Commd 9/2/62. Wg Cdr 1/1/83. Retd GD 3/1/90.
WILSON H. F., FHCIMA. Born 23/11/17. Commd 7/6/43. Sqn Ldr 1/7/65. Retd CAT 14/11/72.
WILSON I. A. B., MBE MBCS. Born 14/5/49. Commd 31/7/70. Sqn Ldr 1/1/87. Retd GD(G) 17/6/94.
WILSON I. K. A. G. Born 1/4/42. Comm 21/5/65. Flt Lt 4/5/72. Retd GD 8/2/81.
WILSON I. N. Born 25/4/24. Commd 10/3/44. Flt Lt 28/12/47. Retd GD 13/5/67.
WILSON I. T. Born 17/11/20. Commd 24/5/44. Sqn Ldr 1/4/56. Retd GD 17/11/63.
WILSON J. Born 15/6/37. Commd 24/2/67. Sqn Ldr 1/1/74. Retd ADMIN 12/11/87.
WILSON J. B., MSc BSc. Born 28/2/31. Commd 24/9/52. Sqn Ldr 7/7/66. Retd EDN 12/10/74.
WILSON J. C. Born 6/3/33. Commd 26/3/59. Sqn Ldr 1/7/71. Retd GD 6/3/91.
WILSON J. D. Born 18/3/26. Commd 18/3/53. Flt Lt 24/7/58. Retd GD 23/9/68.
WILSON J. D. Born 24/12/33. Commd 27/10/67. Flt Lt 12/11/69. Retd GD 24/12/88.
WILSON J. E. S. Born 7/10/22. Commd 14/3/49. Wg Cdr 1/1/62. Retd SY 26/3/77.
WILSON J. F. Born 5/2/26. Commd 14/3/47. Flt Lt 7/6/51. Retd GD 5/2/64.
WILSON J. G. Born 28/10/40. Commd 3/11/77. Sqn Ldr 1/1/85. Retd ENG 28/10/95.
WILSON J. G. Born 21/9/19. Commd 10/11/42. Sqn Ldr 1/4/55. Retd GD 17/7/59.
WILSON J. G. Born 16/1/17. Commd 28/3/46. Sqn Ldr 1/1/57. Retd SUP 31/5/63 rtg Wg Cdr.
WILSON J. H. M., BSc. Born 4/1/66. Commd 30/8/87. Flt Lt 28/2/90. Retd GD 14/3/97.
WILSON J. H. W. Born 3/3/33. Commd 18/6/52. Sqn Ldr 1/7/80. Retd GD 3/3/91.
WILSON The Venerable J. H. CB MA. Born 14/2/24. Commd 10/10/50. Retd 15/9/80. AVM.
WILSON J. S. Born 21/6/47. Commd 2/8/68. Wg Cdr 1/7/90. Retd GD 20/5/98.
WILSON J. U., MB BS. Born 18/3/55. Commd 19/7/77. Sqn Ldr 1/2/86. Retd MED 9/9/93.
WILSON J. W., MBE. Born 9/9/14. Commd 16/5/57. Sqn Ldr 1/7/65. Retd ENG 9/9/69.
WILSON J. W., BSc(Eng). Born 5/8/32. Commd 24/8/59. Flt lt 24/5/61. Reg GD(G) 5/8/90.
WILSON K. Born 20/3/21. Commd 16/3/45. Flt Lt 14/11/55. Retd SUP 25/7/64.
WILSON K. C. Born 3/7/20. Commd 17/5/43. Sqn Ldr 1/7/54. Retd GD 19/8/67.
WILSON K. H., AFM. Born 23/4/24. Commd 14/1/54. Flt Lt 14/1/60. Retd GD 30/6/65.
WILSON K. J. Born 28/2/30. Commd 26/11/52. Sqn Ldr 1/1/66. Retd GD 1/7/73.
WILSON L. B. Born 16/3/19. Commd 28/2/46. Flt Lt 29/6/50. Retd ENG 24/7/54.
WILSON L. D., DSO DFC AFC. Born 31/3/17. Commd 19/12/36. Wg Cdr 1/1/51. Retd GD 30/9/59.
WILSON L. R. Born 9/12/63. Commd 30/8/84. Flt Lt 1/3/91. Retd ADMIN 20/7/91.
WILSON M. A., BSc. Born 23/12/65. Commd 15/9/86. Flt Lt 15/1/91. Retd GD 15/7/00.

WILSON M. A. S., MA. Born 5/2/49. Commd 14/7/69. Flt Lt 14/4/73. Retd SEC 27/6/75.
WILSON M. C. G. Born 23/4/43. Commd 28/7/64. A Cdre 1/1/92. Retd SUP 14/9/96.
WILSON M. E. Born 24/8/47. Commd 6/1/69. Wg Cdr 1/7/94. Retd ENG 6/4/01.
WILSON M. G. Born 7/7/50. Commd 26/2/71. Sqn Ldr 1/7/85. Retd GD 7/7/88.
WILSON M. J., BA. Born 29/10/32. Commd 3/8/55. Sqn Ldr 17/2/63. Retd EDN 3/8/71.
WILSON M. P. Born 15/9/40. Commd 26/10/61. Flt Lt 15/11/67. Retd SUP 15/11/77.
WILSON M. R., BSc. Born 24/3/57. Commd 14/9/75. Flt Lt 15/4/80. Retd GD 30/9/92.
WILSON N. Born 16/9/34. Commd 25/9/54. Flt Lt 4/6/62. Retd GD 16/9/72.
WILSON P. Born 8/9/31. Commd 14/11/51. Flt Lt 14/5/56. Retd GD 8/9/69.
WILSON P. A. Born 28/5/55. Commd 20/9/79. Flt Lt 25/10/81. Retd GD 28/5/93.
WILSON P. D., MIMgt. Born 3/6/47. Commd 6/4/72. Wg Cdr 1/7/91. Retd ADMIN 14/9/96.
WILSON P. F. Born 26/7/23. Commd 29/12/49. Flt Lt 26/5/55. Retd GD 30/7/67.
WILSON P. G. C., AFC MRAeS. Born 23/4/29. Commd 26/9/51. Gp Capt 1/7/73. Retd GD 23/12/81.
WILSON P. M. Born 7/1/38. Commd 1/2/62. Sqn Ldr 1/7/78. Retd ADMIN 21/5/90.
WILSON P. M., OBE CEng MRAeS MIMgt. Born 17/4/31. Commd 25/3/54. Gp Capt 1/7/74. Retd ENG 28/5/77.
WILSON P. R., BSc AMRAeS. Born 24/4/59. Commd 4/7/82. Flt Lt 4/4/84. Retd GD 31/8/98.
WILSON R. Born 5/7/36. Commd 31/7/55. Sqn Ldr 1/1/68. Retd GD 5/7/74.
WILSON R. C. Born 15/6/48. Commd 22/12/67. Wg Cdr 1/7/89. Retd GD 28/3/93.
WILSON R. G. Born 1/1/50. Commd 10/2/72. Fg Offr 10/2/74. Retd GD 13/1/76.
WILSON R. J., MTech CEng MIMechE MRAeS. Born 12/4/38. Commd 30/7/59. Sqn Ldr 1/1/70. Retd ENG 4/11/78. Reinstated 16/4/80. Sqn Ldr 13/6/71. Retd ENG 1/7/90.
WILSON R. L., CEng MIEE. Born 3/4/43. Commd 26/5/67. Wg Cdr 1/1/92. Retd ENG 2/8/93.
WILSON R. L. Born 9/10/47. Commd 28/4/67. Fg Offr 28/4/69. Retd GD 2/12/71.
WILSON R. M., BA MRAeS MIMgt. Born 22/4/44. Commd 29/11/63. Sqn Ldr 1/7/81. Retd GD 22/4/99.
WILSON R. N. Born 8/5/32. Commd 5/12/60. Sqn Ldr 1/7/68. Retd GD 1/4/73.
WILSON R. P., MIMgt. Born 23/3/20. Commd 27/3/47. Wg Cdr 1/7/69. Retd SUP 30/9/72.
WILSON R. R. Born 7/1/22. Commd 7/2/47. Fg Offr 16/2/49. Retd GD 12/9/52.
WILSON R. V. Born 8/5/45. Commd 27/11/65. Flt Lt 4/5/72. Retd GD 12/4/76.
WILSON R. V. W., BSc. Born 16/5/46. Commd 17/9/67. Sqn Ldr 1/7/81. Retd ENG 16/5/90.
WILSON S., BSc. Born 14/10/58. Commd 29/8/77. Sqn Ldr 1/1/91. Retd GD 14/10/96.
WILSON S. G. W. Born 29/6/45. Commd 25/6/65. Flt Lt 17/3/71. Retd GD 25/4/76.
WILSON S. J., BSc. Born 18/1/62. Commd 10/11/85. Flt Lt 10/5/89. Retd SUP 15/12/90.
WILSON S. P. Born 11/2/47. Commd 16/11/72. Flt Lt 16/5/77. Retd GD 1/5/91.
WILSON S. R., MIMgt. Born 19/1/33. Commd 12/9/63. Sqn Ldr 1/1/74. Retd ADMIN 31/3/85.
WILSON T. A. Born 5/8/43. Commd 12/1/62. Flt Lt 12/7/67. Retd GD 15/4/76.
WILSON T. H. W., CEng MRAeS MIEE. Born 20/7/38. Commd 9/3/66. Sqn Ldr 1/1/73. Retd ENG 29/9/81.
WILSON T. M., BEM. Born 23/9/32. Commd 4/7/69. Sqn Ldr 1/7/80. Retd ADMIN 24/9/82.
WILSON The Rev T.I. Born 25/10/30. Commd 16/1/57. Retd 8/11/85. Wg Cdr.
WILSON W. Born 17/6/23. Commd 10/3/41. Sqn Ldr 1/7/71. Retd GD 17/6/81.
WILSON W., BSc. Born 1/2/54. Commd 8/4/79. Flt Lt 8/1/83. Retd ADMIN 1/5/85.
WILSON W. D. M., BSc. Born 29/10/62. Commd 11/12/83. Flt Lt 11/6/86. Retd GD 29/10/00.
WILSON W. J. Born 17/10/40. Commd 4/9/81. Sqn Ldr 1/1/90. Retd SY 7/10/95.
WILSON W. J. Mc., AFM. Born 19/6/24. Commd 17/5/56. Sqn Ldr 1/7/71. Retd GD 1/10/77.
WILSON-CLARK F. K. Born 15/2/43. Commd 8/6/62. Flt Lt 9/2/68. Retd GD 15/2/81.
WILTON A. E. Born 30/6/25. Commd 7/9/53. Wg Cdr 1/1/72. Retd SUP 1/7/76.
WILTON J. A. P. Born 8/12/07. Commd 7/1/43. Fg Offr 7/7/43. Retd ASD 15/9/46 rtg Sqn Ldr.
WILTON M. S. J. Born 23/3/17. Commd 4/4/38. Flt Lt 1/9/45. Retd SEC 19/10/52 rtg Sqn Ldr.
WILTON-JONES A. M. Born 8/4/49. Commd 18/1/73. Plt Offr 19/4/73. Retd PI 28/2/75.
WILTSHIER J. R., DPhysEd. Born 15/12/23. Commd 8/8/51. Flt Lt 8/8/55. Retd ADMIN 31/8/65.
WILTSHIRE J., OBE CEng MIMechE MRAeS MIMgt. Born 22/12/31. Commd 16/5/57. Wg Cdr 1/7/78. Retd ENG 31/8/86.
WILTSHIRE J. R., DPhysEd. Born 15/12/23. Commd 8/8/51. Flt Lt 8/8/55. Retd PE 31/8/65.
WILTSHIRE P. A. Born 5/7/61. Commd 15/10/81. Flt Lt 15/4/87. Retd GD 14/3/96.
WIMBLEDON F. H. C. Born 29/9/10. Commd 23/2/42. Flt Lt 5/3/52. Retd GD(G) 29/6/65.
WINCH A. G. W., DFC. Born 23/4/17. Commd 16/10/43. Flt Lt 16/4/47. Retd SEC 30/7/53.
WINCH C. A. H. Born 28/6/21. Commd 9/1/43. Flt Lt 9/7/46. Retd GD 31/12/55.
WINCH G. E., CBE FIMgt. Born 27/7/35. Commd 3/5/56. A Cdre 1/7/87. Retd SY 27/7/90.
WINCH H. J. Born 20/4/18. Commd 15/2/39. Sqn Ldr 1/7/43. Retd ENG 1/5/46 rtg Wg Cdr.
WINCHURCH J. C. G. Born 29/5/37. Commd 23/1/64. Sqn Ldr 1/1/78. Retd ADMIN 10/4/82.
WINDEATT M. C. Born 23/11/40. Commd 17/5/79. Flt Lt 17/5/82. Retd GD 19/1/94.
WINDER K. J. Born 4/5/20. Commd 13/3/47. Sqn Ldr 1/1/68. Retd SUP 4/5/75.
WINDER P. D. Born 31/5/50. Commd 16/9/71. Flt Lt 16/3/77. Retd GD 31/5/88.
WINDER P. L. Born 1/8/43. Commd 17/5/63. Flt Lt 17/11/68. Retd GD 4/9/70.
WINDLE M. N., ADC MA CEng MIMechE. Born 15/6/43. Commd 30/9/61. Gp Capt 1/1/83. Retd ENG 10/10/86.
WINDLE R. E., AFC. Born 30/3/22. Commd 21/2/44. Flt Lt 21/8/47. Retd GD 30/6/61.
WINDSOR B. J. Born 12/9/33. Commd 28/9/54. Flt Lt 1/3/61. Retd GD 30/9/64.

WINDSOR G. E. J., BEd. Born 23/3/58. Commd 19/6/83. Sqn Ldr 1/1/89. Retd ADMIN 23/6/89.
WINDSOR P. J., BSc CEng MRAeS. Born 20/7/59. Commd 26/9/82. Sqn Ldr 1/7/94. Retd ENG 26/9/98.
WINEPRESS F. J. Born 17/1/22. Commd 21/12/44. Sqn Ldr 1/7/69. Retd SUP 25/6/73.
WINFIELD D., BSc CertEd. Born 23/9/52. Commd 9/11/80. Sqn Ldr 1/1/90. Retd ADMIN 14/3/96.
WINFIELD R. G. Born 21/1/25. Commd 3/12/59. Sqn Ldr 1/1/76. Retd GD 21/1/83.
WING L., MBE BA MIMgt. Born 28/10/32. Commd 12/7/51. AC 1/1/85. Retd GD 28/10/87.
WING W. A. Born 6/10/20. Commd 9/12/54. Flt Lt 9/12/60. Retd GD(G) 8/10/68. Re-instated on the Active List 5/4/71. Flt Lt 6/6/63. Retd 1/2/78.
WING W. M. G., MBE DFM. Born 12/2/19. Commd 31/8/42. Sqn Ldr 1/1/54. Retd SEC 22/7/67.
WINGATE J. B. Born 25/8/24. Commd 11/2/44. Flt Lt 11/8/47. Retd GD 25/8/62.
WINGATE N. R. J., AFC. Born 26/5/34. Commd 28/11/60. Sqn Ldr 1/1/81. Retd GD 5/4/85.
WINGFIELD J. D. T. Born 12/9/39. Commd 25/7/60. Sqn Ldr 1/1/73. Retd GD 30/4/74.
WINKLEY C. H. Born 9/7/55. Commd 6/11/80. Flt Lt 6/5/87. Retd SY 31/3/94.
WINKS H. Born 18/10/22. Commd 6/1/55. Flt Lt 6/1/61. Retd GD 15/8/68.
WINKS S. W. Born 26/11/16. Commd 9/7/59. Flt Lt 9/7/62. Retd ENG 28/11/70.
WINKWORTH R. J., LDSRCS. Born 4/5/37. Commd 9/6/63. Gp Capt 1/1/84. Retd DEL 9/6/94.
WINLOW R. S. Born 3/1/22. Commd 9/8/47. Sqn Ldr 1/7/59. Retd SUP 14/12/63.
WINN A. H., BA. Born 15/1/25. Commd 21/7/54. Sqn Ldr 8/1/62. Retd EDN 6/12/68.
WINN S. Born 31/12/18. Commd 9/18/47. Flt Lt 19/6/52. Retd SEC 30/9/67.
WINN S. B. Born 3/9/24. Commd 11/9/44. Sqn Ldr 1/1/55. Retd GD 14/1/57.
WINN-MORGAN T. M., BSc. Born 28/5/56. Commd 15/9/74. Wg Cdr 1/7/94. Retd ENG 1/8/96.
WINNING R. M. J. Born 14/3/43. Commd 5/12/43. Sqn Ldr 1/7/87. Retd OPS SPT 14/3/98.
WINSHIP J. H. A. Born 15/9/31. Commd 28/12/51. Wg Cdr 1/1/66. Retd GD 15/9/69.
WINSKILL Sir Archie., KCVO CBE DFC* AE MRAeS. Born 24/1/17. Commd 15/8/40. A Cdre 1/7/63. Retd GD 18/12/68.
WINSLADE S. E. Born 5/4/45. Commd 22/5/64. Flt Lt 16/1/73. Retd GD(G) 5/4/83.
WINSLAND C. G., OBE. Born 21/6/46. Commd 26/5/67. A Cdre 1/7/94. Retd ADMIN 13/5/99.
WINSTANLEY K. Born 8/3/39. Commd 26/5/61. Sqn Ldr 1/7/74. Retd GD 1/7/77.
WINSTON D. G. Born 8/9/34. Commd 13/1/72. Flt Lt 13/1/77. Retd GD(G) 7/3/86.
WINSTONE T. J. Born 6/9/44. Commd 31/1/64. Flt Lt 4/11/70. Retd GD 31/1/76.
WINTER C. B. Born 12/1/54. Commd 30/1/75. Sqn Ldr 1/1/88. Retd SY 14/3/96.
WINTER C. R., DFC. Born 2/6/23. Commd 5/12/43. Sqn Ldr 1/1/55. Retd GD 11/10/56.
WINTER D. Born 18/5/39. Commd 12/2/59. Flt Lt 12/5/65. Retd SEC 8/10/74.
WINTER E. Born 11/6/42. Commd 25/6/66. Flt Lt 25/6/68. Retd GD 31/1/75.
WINTER K. R. Born 9/5/40. Commd 1/8/61. Wg Cdr 1/1/85. Retd GD 9/5/95.
WINTER L. H., MBE. Born 24/10/17. Commd 18/9/39. Flt Lt 1/3/45. Retd SUP 7/4/61 rtg Sqn Ldr.
WINTER T. J. Born 13/1/24. Commd 17/10/57. Sqn Ldr 1/7/71. Retd PRT 26/5/73.
WINTER Y. E., BSc. Born 1/7/20. Commd 12/10/55. Flt Offr 12/4/61. Retd SEC 12/8/67.
WINTERBOTTOM D. Born 30/4/31. Commd 26/7/51. Sqn Ldr 1/1/84. Retd GD 30/4/93.
WINTERBOTTOM D. F. Born 6/1/23. Commd 26/9/57. Flt Lt 26/9/63. Retd SEC 1/8/70.
WINTERBOURNE J. S., MBE AFC. Born 16/1/25. Commd 7/5/53. Sqn Ldr 1/7/72. Retd GD 24/1/85.
WINTERBOURNE S. J. Born 12/12/57. Commd 3/11/77. Sqn Ldr 1/7/90. Retd ADMIN 12/6/97.
WINTERFORD D. A. Born 4/7/23. Commd 3/3/44. Sqn Ldr 1/7/57. Retd GD 12/2/67.
WINTERHALDER V. N., BSc. Born 23/11/41. Commd 15/7/64. Flt Lt 22/5/68. Retd ENG 23/11/79.
WINTERS A. L. Born 3/5/35. Commd 28/5/66. Flt Lt 28/5/72. Retd PRT 1/4/76.
WINTERS I. J. E. Born 30/4/66. Commd 14/1/88. Flt Lt 12/3/92. Retd ADMIN 14/9/96.
WINTERSGILL D. Born 13/12/42. Commd 20/7/65. Flt Lt 65/10/71. Retd ENG 20/7/81.
WINTERTON I. T., CEng MIEE. Born 9/6/38. Commd 18/10/62. Flt Lt 14/11/67. Retd ENG 9/6/76.
WINTERTON R. M., MSc BSc CPhys MInstP MIMgt. Born 24/6/54. Commd 8/4/79. Wg Cdr 1/7/94. Retd ADMIN 14/3/97.
WIRDNAM A. R. J. Born 15/9/38. Commd 26/10/62. Flt Lt 26/4/67. Retd GD 10/7/78.
WIRDNAM K. A. C. Born 13/9/28. Commd 1/8/51. A Cdre 1/7/76. Retd GD 13/9/83.
WISBY W. G. Born 13/8/14. Commd 26/11/53. Flt Lt 26/11/56. Retd ENG 13/8/69.
WISE A. M. Born 9/12/58. Commd 19/7/84. Flt Lt 19/1/91. Retd ADMIN 3/1/93.
WISE A. N., LVO MBE BA. Born 1/8/43. Commd 17/12/65. Gp Capt 1/7/90. Retd GD 1/8/98.
WISEMAN E. A. Born 14/4/18. Commd 10/10/46. Sqn Ldr 1/1/59. Retd SUP 13/7/68.
WISEMAN H. Born 1/7/24. Commd 12/1/49. Flt Offr 12/1/55. Retd SUP 30/9/55.
WISEMAN N., BSc MIExpE DipEd AIL. Born 22/7/46. Commd 2/5/71. Wg Cdr 1/7/89. Retd ENG 14/9/96.
WISEMAN R. A., BSc. Born 26/6/54. Commd 13/2/77. Flt Lt 13/5/78. Retd GD 14/3/97.
WISEMAN W. E., MBE DFC. Born 14/3/20. Commd 21/2/45. Flt Lt 21/8/48. Retd GD 3/10/53.
WISHART R., BSc. Born 10/7/55. Commd 3/9/72. Flt Lt 15/4/80. Retd ENG 15/7/88.
WISHART S. R. Born 22/8/45. Commd 16/9/71. Flt Lt 16/3/77. Retd GD 29/7/77.
WISMARK M. R. S., MBE. Born 22/10/34. Commd 25/7/56. Wg Cdr 1/7/74. Retd ENG 2/9/75.
WISTOW D. J., MBE. Born 2/2/24. Commd 23/3/51. Sqn Ldr 1/1/70. Retd GD 1/4/73.
WITCHALL S. C. Born 5/4/24. Commd 28/7/60. Flt Lt 28/7/63. Retd GD 5/4/84.
WITCHELL W. J. H. Born 14/3/17. Commd 8/7/48. Sqn Ldr 1/1/52. Retd RGT 31/3/58.

WITHERINGTON A. A. Born 29/9/20. Commd 31/8/44. Gp Capt 1/1/67. Retd PRT 29/9/75.
WITHEROW J. H., MCIPD MIMgt. Born 10/6/27. Commd 1/6/49. Sqn Ldr 1/1/67. Retd SY 10/6/82.
WITHEROW M. S., FIMgt. Born 17/8/36. Commd 21/6/56. A Cdre 1/7/86. Retd RGT 23/11/90.
WITHERS A. F. Born 14/1/44. Commd 26/5/67. Flt Lt 15/4/70. Retd GD 4/1/86.
WITHERS P. A. G. Born 5/5/23. Commd 29/5/43. Sqn Ldr 1/1/53. Retd GD 10/6/61.
WITHERS R. B. Born 3/12/30. Commd 13/7/61. Flt Lt 13/7/67. Retd SEC 20/9/69.
WITHERS W. F. G., MBE. Born 28/10/11. Commd 20/11/41. Sqn Ldr 1/1/53. Retd ENG 28/1/59.
WITHERS W. F. M., DFC. Born 12/1/46. Commd 18/8/68. Sqn Ldr 1/1/87. Retd GD 26/9/91.
WITHEY V. R. Born 11/10/21. Commd 15/8/44. Wg Cdr 1/7/67. Retd SUP 27/3/76.
WITHINGTON A. M. Born 17/9/36. Commd 15/4/55. Sqn Ldr 1/1/71. Retd GD 17/9/74.
WITHINGTON B., BSc. Born 12/1/51. Commd 22/9/74. Sqn Ldr 1/7/83. Retd ADMIN 9/12/90.
WITTIN-HAYDEN L. J., DFC AFC. Born 23/11/19. Commd 15/11/44. Sqn Ldr 1/1/68. Retd GD 30/9/70.
WITTON H. Born 15/12/29. Commd 10/9/69. Sqn Ldr 1/7/80. Retd ENG 30/10/81.
WITTS D. R. Born 27/9/40. Commd 23/3/67. Flt Lt 1/1/70. Retd GD(G) 28/11/88.
WITTS S. M., MB ChB DRCOG. Born 23/11/59. Commd 31/1/88. Flt Lt 31/1/88. Retd MED 6/7/88.
WOBER H. A., MB BS MFOM DRCOG DAvMed MRAeS. Born 6/6/39. Commd 10/9/62. A Cdre 1/1/92. Retd MED 1/6/97.
WOLFF J. M., MBE. Born 16/1/38. Commd 7/6/68. Flt Lt 7/6/70. Retd GD 7/6/76.
WOLLASTON K. F. Born 19/2/35. Commd 11/6/63. Sqn Ldr 1/7/72. Retd CAT 11/6/79.
WOLLERT C. A. L. Born 29/7/28. Commd 28/6/51. Flt Lt 10/10/56. Retd GD 1/3/68.
WOLLEY J. H., MBE. Born 3/4/31. Commd 28/9/51. Sqn Ldr 1/1/70. Retd GD 3/4/93.
WOLSEY A. K. Born 18/7/49. Commd 27/5/71. Sqn Ldr 1/7/85. Retd ADMIN 30/9/97.
WOLSEY W. E., FCA. Born 23/6/15. Commd 11/6/37. Gp Capt 1/7/58. Retd SEC 23/6/71.
WOLSTENHOLE A. Born 10/8/32. Commd 5/7/53. Flt Lt 7/3/62. Retd GD(G) 10/8/87.
WOLSTENHOLME H. Born 14/1/32. Commd 22/8/51. Sqn Ldr 1/1/62. Retd GD 14/4/71 rtg Wg Cdr.
WOLSTENHOLME R. A. Born 11/3/32. Commd 10/9/52. Flt Lt 7/2/58. Retd GD 11/3/70.
WOMACK J., BSc. Born 11/5/49. Commd 17/1/72. Flt Lt 17/10/75. Retd SUP 17/1/88.
WOMPHREY P. Born 29/10/39. Commd 17/9/57. Sqn Ldr 1/1/71. Retd GD 29/10/90.
WOOBERRY D. E. Born 22/1/36. Commd 24/7/57. Flt Lt 15/4/62. Retd ENG 8/6/70.
WOOD A. C. M. Born 31/7/52. Commd 26/10/62. Flt Lt 4/5/72. Retd GD 31/7/76.
WOOD A. H., BSc. Born 8/11/31. Commd 24/2/55. Sqn Ldr 17/2/63. Retd EDN 11/11/70.
WOOD A. L., AFC. Born 12/5/07. Commd 1/4/40. Flt Lt 1/4/42. Retd GD 9/8/46 rtg Sqn Ldr.
WOOD A. MCF. Born 3/8/46. Commd 27/3/75. Sqn Ldr 1/7/89. Retd GD(G) 14/9/96.
WOOD A. S., BSc. Born 29/3/59. Commd 1/2/87. Flt Lt 1/8/86. Retd ADMIN 14/3/97.
WOOD A. W. Born 1/10/63. Commd 19/12/91. Flt Lt 19/12/93. Retd ENG 15/3/99.
WOOD A. W. Born 10/3/45. Commd 26/11/64. Flt Lt 15/4/71. Retd SUP 5/7/75.
WOOD B. Born 22/10/49. Commd 23/9/68. Plt Offr 8/11/71. Retd GD 6/4/73.
WOOD B. L., OBE. Born 11/12/36. Commd 30/12/54. Gp Capt 1/1/90. Retd GD 1/2/91.
WOOD C. C. Born 26/9/48. Commd 29/6/72. Plt Offr 29/6/73. Retd GD 8/2/74.
WOOD C. L. Born 2/2/42. Commd 11/6/81. Flt Lt 11/6/86. Retd ENG 31/3/94.
WOOD C. R. S. Born 24/11/41. Commd 15/7/64. Wg Cdr 1/7/88. Retd ENG 11/10/99.
WOOD D., OBE MIMgt. Born 5/10/19. Commd 30/5/44. Wg Cdr 1/7/65. Retd GD 5/10/74.
WOOD D., BA FTCL LGSM ARCM. Born 3/11/37. Commd 28/6/79. Sqn Ldr 5/7/88. Retd DM 1/5/91.
WOOD D. Born 30/12/23. Commd 30/11/44. Sqn Ldr 1/1/56. Retd GD 30/12/61.
WOOD D. Born 17/7/30. Commd 26/8/66. Sqn Ldr 1/1/85. Retd GD 17/7/85.
WOOD D. A. Born 15/1/53. Commd 15/3/73. Fg Offr 15/9/75. Retd SY 18/8/76.
WOOD D. A. Born 30/1/28. Commd 23/4/53. Sqn Ldr 1/1/63. Retd GD 9/7/73.
WOOD D. A. Born 6/3/34. Commd 5/2/57. Sqn Ldr 1/7/80. Retd ADMIN 10/7/86.
WOOD D. A., BA. Born 20/3/42. Commd 1/10/67. Sqn Ldr 5/7/75. Retd ADMIN 5/1/83.
WOOD D. D. Born 22/2/48. Commd 5/4/79. Flt Lt 5/4/81. Retd GD 30/11/91.
WOOD D. G. Born 20/3/32. Commd 4/10/56. Flt Lt 4/4/61. Retd GD 1/5/75.
WOOD D. G. Born 20/3/32. Commd 4/10/56. Flt Lt 4/4/61. Retd GD(G) 1/5/75. Re-instated 23/4/80 to 1/5/85.
WOOD D. H., MIMgt. Born 26/2/30. Commd 12/12/51. Wg Cdr 1/7/76. Retd GD 12/11/84.
WOOD D. J., CEng MRAeS. Born 5/2/19. Commd 28/10/43. Sqn Ldr 1/10/55. Retd ENG 8/2/69.
WOOD D. L., BSc CEng MIEE MRAeS. Born 13/6/21. Commd 18/3/43. Sqn Ldr 1/1/54. Retd ENG 10/8/61.
WOOD E. Born 2/1/35. Commd 29/7/55. Flt Lt 16/8/61. Retd GD 2/1/73.
WOOD E. G. Born 13/10/37. Commd 2/4/57. Sqn Ldr 1/7/69. Retd GD 30/9/80.
WOOD E. J. C. Born 21/1/36. Commd 4/7/69. Sqn Ldr 1/1/76. Retd ENG 4/7/77.
WOOD E. T. Born 11/6/24. Commd 15/12/44. Sqn Ldr 1/7/59. Retd GD 12/6/68.
WOOD F. J. H., MBE. Born 14/6/18. Commd 29/7/49. Sqn Ldr. 1/7/60. Retd SEC 14/6/73.
WOOD F. R., AFC. Born 31/3/25. Commd 15/12/49. Flt Lt 19/11/53. Retd GD 31/3/63.
WOOD G., CBE. Born 3/9/39. Commd 1/10/64. A Cdre 1/7/91. Retd GD(G) 3/9/94.
WOOD G. P. Born 29/6/60. Commd 29/1/87. Flt Lt 23/4/89. Retd SUP 29/6/98.
WOOD H. Born 25/7/08. Commd 30/6/41. Flt Lt 1/9/45. Retd ENG 25/7/57 rtg Sqn Ldr.
WOOD H. R. Born 1/4/20. Commd 2/10/58. Flt Lt 2/10/63. Retd ENG 4/7/70.
WOOD H. W. Born 24/5/23. Commd 26/6/44. Flt Lt 7/6/51. Retd PE 29/1/53.

WOOD I. Born 4/3/46. Commd 18/8/70. Flt Lt 18/2/76. Retd GD 17/8/86.
WOOD I. J. Born 11/6/48. Commd 27/5/68. Fg Offr 10/8/70. Retd SEC 2/2/74.
WOOD J., DFM. Born 4/8/13. Commd 31/7/41. Wg Cdr 1/7/47. Retd GD 2/5/58.
WOOD J. B. H. Born 7/11/39. Commd 19/12/61. Flt Lt 10/2/67. Retd GD 7/11/77.
WOOD J. E. Born 11/3/23. Commd 23/12/43. Flt Lt 27/5/54. Retd PE 11/3/71.
WOOD J. F., BA. Born 12/8/41. Commd 7/7/67. Flt Lt 12/1/70. Retd GD 12/8/79. Re-entered 13/8/80. Flt Lt 13/1/71. Retd GD 12/8/96.
WOOD J. M., CEng MIEE. Born 11/5/43. Commd 21/1/66. Flt Lt 21/7/72. Retd ENG 5/10/87.
WOOD J. P., CBE. Born 7/3/32. Commd 1/3/51. A Cdre 1/1/79. Retd ADMIN 1/4/83.
WOOD J. W. Born 6/3/21. Commd 8/12/42. Sqn Ldr 1/1/55. Retd SEC 6/3/64.
WOOD J. W., MBE. Born 14/1/17. Commd 22/7/44. Wg Cdr 1/1/69. Retd GD(G) 14/1/74.
WOOD K. E. Born 11/8/22. Commd 27/8/59. Sqn Ldr 1/1/73. Retd PRT 27/2/76.
WOOD K. G., BSc. Born 29/6/43. Commd 27/10/68. Sqn Ldr 1/7/88. Retd GD 22/6/93.
WOOD L., MBE DFM. Born 7/7/14. Commd 12/2/41. Wg Cdr 1/1/66. Retd ENG 7/7/69.
WOOD L. D. Born 9/10/29. Commd 31/10/69. Flt Lt 31/10/74. Retd GD(G) 29/6/83.
WOOD M., BSc. Born 5/8/53. Commd 6/3/77. Flt Lt 6/12/78. Retd GD 6/3/89.
WOOD M. A. Born 4/11/40. Commd 17/12/63. Gp Capt 1/1/90. Retd GD 4/11/90.
WOOD M. E. Born 4/10/48. Commd 2/6/67. Sqn Ldr 1/7/83. Retd GD 6/11/86.
WOOD M. H., MBE. Born 11/9/44. Commd 10/12/65. Wg Cdr 1/1/94. Retd GD 10/10/97.
WOOD M. J. Born 14/2/56. Commd 23/11/78. Flt Lt 2/1/83. Retd SY 14/2/94.
WOOD M. L. Born 30/12/46. Commd 10/12/65. Flt Lt 4/5/72. Retd GD 28/9/73.
WOOD M. P., BSc. Born 19/3/57. Commd 12/10/78. Flt Lt 15/10/79. Retd GD 10/6/95.
WOOD M. S., BA. Born 26/10/61. Commd 30/10/83. Flt Lt 30/4/87. Retd OPS SPT 30/10/99.
WOOD P., MBE. Born 10/8/57. Commd 24/3/83. Wg Cdr 1/7/94. Retd SY 14/3/96.
WOOD P. C. Born 23/11/39. Commd 31/8/62. Flt Lt 29/2/68. Retd GD 15/5/78.
WOOD P. D. Born 27/7/23. Commd 11/8/44. Wg Cdr 1/1/72. Retd GD(G) 1/12/77.
WOOD P. D. J., DFC. Born 27/5/22. Commd 9/6/47. Wg Cdr 1/1/58. Retd GD 30/3/68.
WOOD P. E. Born 17/7/29. Commd 27/10/55. Flt Lt 21/10/59. Retd ENG 1/12/61.
WOOD P. J. Born 17/10/48. Commd 16/8/68. Flt Lt 16/2/74. Retd GD 17/10/86.
WOOD P. L., CEng MRAeS. Born 3/8/38. Commd 28/4/64. Wg Cdr 1/7/90. Retd ENG 18/2/94.
WOOD P. R. Born 8/4/44. Commd 28/4/65. Sqn Ldr 1/1/78. Retd GD 8/4/82.
WOOD R., BSc(Eng) CEng MRAeS. Born 26/9/41. Commd 30/9/61. Wg Cdr 1/7/79. Retd ENG 3/4/93.
WOOD R., MBE. Born 15/5/14. Commd 14/11/46. Sqn Ldr 1/1/62. Retd SUP 15/5/69.
WOOD R., MIMgt. Born 15/5/21. Commd 28/8/46. Wg Cdr 1/1/72. Retd GD(G) 13/4/74.
WOOD R. A., MBE MCIT MILT. Born 25/11/43. Commd 13/2/64. Wg Cdr 1/1/83. Retd SUP 25/11/87.
WOOD R. B. Born 23/2/45. Commd 4/11/82. Sqn Ldr 1/7/91. Retd ENG 20/8/98.
WOOD R. C., OBE AFC. Born 11/11/29. Commd 18/6/76. Gp Capt 1/1/80. Retd GD 7/11/84.
WOOD R. F. Born 10/3/38. Commd 3/9/60. Flt Lt 1/4/71. Retd GD 4/2/76.
WOOD R. H., OBE. Born 24/1/36. Commd 1/2/56. AVM 1/1/88. Retd GD 3/4/90.
WOOD R. J., BSc CEng MIEE. Born 19/6/45. Commd 15/7/66. Sqn Ldr 1/1/77 Retd ENG 19/6/83.
WOOD R. R. Born 14/11/27. Commd 4/2/71. Flt Lt 4/2/74. Retd SUP 14/11/82.
WOOD R. S., McP. Born 12/5/47. Commd 25/2/66. Flt Lt 6/10/71. Retd GD 12/5/85.
WOOD S. J., BSc. Born 1/2/53. Commd 25/9/71. Sqn Ldr 1/1/87. Retd GD 1/2/91.
WOOD T. A. K. Born 6/11/32. Commd 28/6/51. Flt Lt 10/1/57. Retd GD 6/11/92.
WOOD T. C., DFC. Born 20/6/16. Commd. 20/8/42. Sqn Ldr 1/1/51. Retd GD 3/1/58.
WOOD T. C. Born 2/6/21. Commd 6/9/56. Flt Lt 6/9/59. Retd ADMIN 2/6/76.
WOOD W. Born 22/7/40. Commd 31/7/62. Sqn Ldr 1/7/71. Retd GD 22/7/78.
WOOD W. C., AFC AFM. Born 25/12/21. Commd 20/4/50. Flt Lt 20/10/53. Retd GD 1/5/61.
WOOD W. J. H. Born 8/9/44. Commd 17/10/71. Sqn Ldr 1/7/84. Retd ENG 17/10/87.
WOOD W. R. Born 11/7/20. Commd 6/11/58. Flt Lt 6/11/63. Retd RGT 11/7/75.
WOODACRE R. W. Born 23/5/39. Commd 9/7/59. Flt Lt 10/2/67. Retd GD 14/9/68.
WOODARD J. F., CBE FIMgt. Born 5/6/31. Commd 30/9/53. Gp Capt 1/7/77. Retd GD 5/6/84.
WOODBERRY M. A. S. Born 10/4/38. Commd 10/9/70. Sqn Ldr 1/7/88. Retd ADMIN 10/4/93.
WOODBRIDGE D. A. S., MBE MRAeS. Born 14/1/20. Commd 15/4/43. Sqn Ldr 1/7/58. Retd ENG 1/10/63.
WOODCOCK A. D., DFC* MRAeS. Born 26/2/23. Commd 10/12/43. Wg Cdr 1/7/60 Retd GD 4/9/69.
WOODCOCK A. W. D., MBE. Born 8/6/24. Commd 20/2/45. Wg Cdr 1/1/72. Retd ADMIN 29/3/79.
WOODCOCK B. N., BTech. Born 3/2/48. Commd 10/4/68. Sqn Ldr 1/7/78. Retd ENG 4/5/01.
WOODCOCK J. A., BDS. Born 14/7/58. Commd 22/2/81. Sqn Ldr 16/1/86. Retd DEL 22/2/86.
WOODCOCK J. D. Born 12/2/18. Commd 24/3/43. Flt Lt 24/9/47. Retd GD(G) 25/4/69.
WOODCRAFT R. G., AFC. Born 29/8/13. Commd 2/5/40. Sqn Ldr 1/7/53. Retd GD(G) 29/8/63.
WOODCRAFT R. W. Born 4/11/20. Commd 19/8/42. Sqn Ldr 1/7/59. Retd ENG 4/11/75.
WOODFIELD R. W. Born 31/5/48. Commd 15/8/85. Flt Lt 15/8/89. Retd ENG 1/2/95.
WOODFORD A.A.G., CB BA. Born 6/1/39. Commd 28/7/59. AVM 1/1/88. Retd GD 2/6/92.
WOODGATE L. Born 3/7/28. Commd 4/6/64. Flt Lt 4/6/69. Retd ENG 1/8/78. Reinstated 4/3/81 to 4/3/84.
WOODHAM P. R. Born 25/3/26. Commd 14/1/53. Sqn Ldr 1/7/71. Retd GD 3/8/74.

WOODHAMS M. W. Born 16/11/31. Commd 17/5/51. Flt Lt 6/9/56. Retd GD 10/10/64.
WOODHEAD R. W. A. Born 8/4/39. Commd 13/12/60. Sqn Ldr 1/7/77. Retd GD 8/4/94.
WOODHOUSE C. H. D. Born 4/7/45. Commd 25/1/71. Flt Lt 16/1/74. Retd GD(G) 19/7/89.
WOODHOUSE G. Born 23/12/40. Commd 22/5/80. Flt Lt 22/5/83. Retd GD 9/7/91.
WOODHOUSE J. E. Born 4/11/46. Commd 2/11/88. Flt Lt 2/11/92. Retd ENG 1/5/93.
WOODHOUSE J. M., BA. Born 22/12/65. Commd 10/11/91. Flt Lt 10/5/94. Retd ADMIN 14/3/96.
WOODHOUSE R. Born 13/11/20. Commd 14/1/44. Flt Lt 14/7/47. Retd GD(G) 7/2/56.
WOODHOUSE R. Born 25/5/32. Commd 7/5/52. Flt Lt 2/10/57. Retd GD 25/5/70.
WOODHOUSE S. H. Born 4/2/31. Commd 1/3/51. Sqn Ldr 1/1/63. Retd SEC 4/2/69.
WOODHOUSE W. K. Born 4/12/51. Commd 26/3/72. Sqn Ldr 1/1/85. Retd SY(RGT) 4/12/89.
WOODIER J. L. Born 6/3/33. Commd 18/11/66. Flt Lt 18/11/72. Retd SEC 16/12/72.
WOODING G. P. C., BA. Born 1/1/51. Commd 15/9/69. Wg Cdr 1/1/88. Retd ADMIN 7/12/91.
WOODING R. J., DPhysEd. Born 21/6/49. Commd 16/8/70. Sqn Ldr 1/1/88. Retd ADMIN 1/10/91.
WOODIWISS M. J. Born 9/9/42. Commd 4/2/71. Flt Lt 6/4/75. Retd ADMIN 5/12/82.
WOODLEY G. J., OBE. Born 18/5/46. Commd 1/3/68. A Cdre 1/1/96. Retd ENG 31/12/96.
WOODLEY G. V. Born 18/8/36. Commd 25/6/66. Flt Lt 4/11/70. Retd SUP 18/8/74.
WOODLEY M. E. Born 2/9/46. Commd 2/8/68. Sqn Ldr 1/7/81. Retd GD 2/9/90.
WOODLEY R. J. R. Born 7/7/23. Commd 6/9/56. Sqn Ldr 1/7/69. Retd GD 3/9/73.
WOODMAN A. W. K. Born 4/4/27. Commd 20/6/51. Flt Lt 20/12/55. Retd GD 4/4/65.
WOODMAN C. M., BA. Born 17/4/56. Commd 14/1/79. Wg Cdr 1/7/93. Retd ADMIN 23/8/95.
WOODMAN D. D., MA BA CEng MIEE MRAeS. Born 18/5/54. Commd 3/9/72. Wg Cdr 1/7/91. Retd ENG 1/7/94.
WOODMAN P. M. Born 2/1/44. Commd 2/3/78. Sqn Ldr 1/7/89. Retd GD 23/12/96.
WOODRUFF A. F. Born 27/11/56. Commd 6/5/83. Flt Lt 14/10/85. Retd SY 27/11/94.
WOODRUFF D. B. Born 30/6/33. Commd 6/2/52. Flt Lt 29/4/60. Retd GD 18/9/70.
WOODS A. E. G., AFC. Born 19/1/23. Commd 24/3/44. Wg Cdr 1/7/65. Retd GD 1/7/75.
WOODS A. J., BA. Born 30/9/38. Commd 9/3/72. Wg Cdr 1/7/89. Retd ADMIN 30/9/93.
WOODS C. Born 1/7/43. Commd 11/5/62. Flt Lt 11/11/67. Retd GD 31/12/74.
WOODS D., CBE CEng MRAeS MIMgt. Born 10/4/24. Commd 7/4/46. Gp Capt 1/7/72. Retd ENG 28/8/76.
WOODS D. J., MBCS MIMgt. Born 14/9/32. Commd 15/12/53. Gp Capt 1/7/84. Retd SUP 14/9/87.
WOODS G. Born 5/5/36. Commd 7/12/61. Wg Cdr 1/1/79. Retd GD(G) 16/12/81. Reinstated on Retired List
    24/11/89.
WOODS G. C. Born 4/5/46. Commd 21/7/65. Flt Lt 21/1/71. Retd GD 18/12/73.
WOODS G. P. Born 15/4/35. Commd 19/8/53. Sqn Ldr 1/7/80. Retd GD 15/4/93.
WOODS J., CChem MRSC. Born 28/8/37. Commd 25/7/71. Sqn Ldr 1/1/80. Retd ENG 28/8/95.
WOODS J. Born 18/9/41. Commd 22/2/63. Flt Lt 22/8/68. Retd GD 18/9/79.
WOODS J. C. Born 16/8/22. Commd 25/2/44. Wg Cdr 1/7/66. Retd GD 6/3/76.
WOODS J. J., DFC. Born 6/3/20. Commd 7/2/42. Sqn Ldr 1/7/54. Retd GD 6/3/63.
WOODS J. R., BSc. Born 26/9/50. Commd 28/2/72. Sqn Ldr 1/1/84. Retd GD 26/9/88.
WOODS J. W. Born 16/12/28. Commd 5/7/68. Flt Lt 5/7/73. Retd ENG 16/12/89.
WOODS K. B., BSc DipEl. Born 10/11/21. Commd 31/10/41. Sqn Ldr 10/11/55. Retd EDN 31/8/63.
WOODS L. A. Born 2/3/50. Commd 11/11/71. Sqn Ldr 1/1/84. Retd ADMIN 2/3/88.
WOODS P. A. A., MSc. Born 3/11/45. Commd 18/8/67. Wg Cdr 1/7/87. Retd SUP 14/3/97.
WOODS P. R. Born 20/7/38. Commd 24/7/71. Sqn Ldr 1/7/80. Retd ENG 20/7/93.
WOODS P. R., ACIS. Born 7/5/39. Commd 13/7/61. Sqn Ldr 1/7/71. Retd ADMIN 1/10/80.
WOODS R. D. Born 2/12/53. Commd 11/8/77. Flt Lt 11/2/83. Retd GD 14/3/97.
WOODS R. J. A. Born 15/5/20. Commd 13/5/44. Sqn Ldr 1/9/65. Retd GD 15/5/68.
WOODS T. A. Born 14/7/58. Commd 15/8/85. Sqn Ldr 1/7/95. Retd ENG 20/5/99.
WOODS W. E. Born 5/11/31. Commd 17/12/52. Flt Lt 17/6/55. Retd GD 5/11/69.
WOODWARD B. S. A., MIMgt. Born 12/12/31. Commd 7/2/52. Sqn Ldr 1/7/70. Retd GD 30/4/83.
WOODWARD C. J., DFC. Born 2/3/17. Commd 31/12/42. Sqn Ldr 1/7/51. Retd GD 8/11/57.
WOODWARD D. A. Born 12/6/52. Commd 25/9/71. Plt Offr 25/9/73. Retd GD 25/9/74.
WOODWARD D. A., BA. Born 7/4/56. Commd 2/3/80. Flt Lt 2/9/83. Retd SUP 2/3/96.
WOODWARD F. H., ACIS. Born 27/2/21. Commd 22/9/44. Flt Lt 22/9/50. Retd SEC 28/2/55.
WOODWARD P., MBE. Born 7/4/38. Commd 7/1/58. Flt Lt 7/8/64. Retd GD 30/9/78.
WOODWARD R. A. Born 7/10/14. Commd 17/5/56. Flt Lt 17/5/59. Retd ENG 16/9/66.
WOODWARD R. C. Born 7/1/43. Commd 23/12/60. Wg Cdr 1/1/85. Retd GD 2/4/93.
WOODYATT A. P. Born 21/9/15. Commd 9/9/39. Sqn Ldr 1/1/49. Retd SUP 11/9/61.
WOOFF K. C. Born 19/6/59. Commd 29/7/83. Flt Lt 29/1/89. Retd GD 13/9/99.
WOOLCOCK P. R. Born 26/1/25. Commd 28/7/44. Flt Lt 11/11/54. Retd GD 16/1/76.
WOOLDRIDGE D. Born 28/2/44. Commd 4/7/69. Sqn Ldr 1/1/82. Retd GD 2/7/93.
WOOLDRIDGE M. Born 3/11/41. Commd 18/12/65. Flt Lt 8/3/72. Retd GD 22/10/94.
WOOLDRIDGE M. G. L., MA. Born 15/7/50. Commd 19/2/73. Wg Cdr 1/7/91. Retd SUP 14/3/97.
WOOLER K. Born 19/4/54. Commd 6/10/77. Flt Lt 6/4/83. Retd GD 1/5/90.
WOOLF D. Born 24/1/39. Commd 21/2/69. Flt Lt 25/12/74. Retd MED(SEC) 22/2/77.
WOOLFORD K. C., BA. Born 15/3/44. Commd 29/7/65. Sqn Ldr 1/7/79. Retd GD 1/7/82.

WOOLFORD P. R., MBA (Eur Ing) CEng FRSA MRAeS MInstD MIMgt. Born 25/4/44. Commd 27/3/70. Wg Cdr 1/7/88. Retd ENG 25/4/99.
WOOLFORD R. F. Born 12/8/33. Commd 19/8/71. Sqn Ldr 19/2/78. Retd ADMIN 13/8/86.
WOOLFREY A. G. J. Born 12/11/31. Commd 19/6/52. Sqn Ldr 1/7/82. Retd GD 12/5/92.
WOOLFREY A. R. G. Born 7/10/09. Commd 2/5/40. Sqn Ldr 1/7/49. Retd SUP 7/10/58.
WOOLGAR D. C. Born 18/9/40. Commd 26/8/66. Flt Lt 7/12/68. Retd ENG 18/9/78.
WOOLLAM R. J. Born 2/7/47. Commd 29/6/72. Flt Lt 29/12/77. Retd GD 13/3/88.
WOOLLER J. Born 10/8/22. Commd 3/11/60. Sqn Ldr 1/1/73. Retd ENG 10/8/77.
WOOLLETT R. Born 1/5/30. Commd 5/9/57. Flt Lt 5/3/62. Retd GD 19/1/63.
WOOLLEY F. C., MBE. Born 4/5/10. Commd 16/5/40. Wg Cdr 1/7/53. Retd ENG 4/9/62.
WOOLLEY F. E. Born 14/3/13. Commd 12/12/46. Flt Lt 12/6/51. Retd SUP 14/3/62 rtg Sqn Ldr.
WOOLLEY G. A., OBE AFC. Born 16/5/45. Commd 21/7/65. Gp Capt 1/1/94. Retd GD 14/3/96.
WOOLLEY G. W. E., DFC. Born 5/1/12. Commd 24/8/42. Sqn Ldr 1/1/54. Retd ENG 1/3/61.
WOOLLEY H. H., MBE. Born 18/7/31. Commd 16/12/51. Sqn Ldr 1/1/71. Retd GD(G) 18/7/86.
WOOLLEY J. C., BSc. Born 15/6/35. Commd 25/9/45. Flt Lt 15/4/61. Retd ENG 28/12/67.
WOOLLEY J. M. Born 9/7/47. Commd 16/8/68. Sqn Ldr 1/7/81. Retd GD 9/7/85.
WOOLLEY R. Born 26/5/56. Commd 7/11/91. Flt Lt 7/11/95. Retd MED(SEC) 15/10/97.
WOOLLEY W. Born 19/9/32. Commd 30/7/52. Flt Lt 27/12/57. Retd GD 19/9/91.
WOOLLIAMS W. G., MBE. Born 10/1/06. Commd 28/11/25. Sqn Ldr 1/4/37. Retd GD 9/3/40. RAFVR 21/7/41 to 10/2/54 rtg Wg Cdr.
WOOLLISCROFT D. G., MB BS MRCGP DRCOG DAvMed AFOM. Born 1/2/57. Commd 21/8/80. Wg Cdr 1/8/94. Retd MED 21/8/96.
WOOLMAN M. A. Born 6/10/66. Commd 25/2/88. Flt Lt 25/8/93. Retd GD 14/3/97.
WOOLSTON P. C. G., BEM. Born 11/8/20. Commd 27/10/55. Sqn Ldr 1/1/69. Retd GD(G) 30/4/74.
WOOLVEN C. G., CEng MRAeS. Born 17/1/20. Commd 27/4/44. Sqn Ldr 1/7/65. Retd ENG 17/9/70.
WOOLVEN R. E. Born 1/1/31. Commd 19/9/59. Sqn Ldr 1/1/71. Retd GD 21/10/78.
WOOSTER J. L. Born 20/5/31. Commd 10/10/51. Flt Lt 10/4/56. Retd GD 20/5/69.
WOOTTON D. G., FIMLS MRIC. Born 17/11/39. Commd 27/3/70. Flt Lt 27/3/76. Retd MED(T) 31/12/77.
WOOTTON H. A. O. Born 6/12/06. Commd 6/11/39. Sqn Ldr 1/8/47. Retd SEC 31/12/53 rtg Wg Cdr.
WORBY I. A. N. Born 6/9/28. Commd 5/4/50. Gp Capt 1/7/77. Retd GD 29/5/82.
WORDSWORTH J. C. R., MHCIMA. Born 15/6/27. Commd 15/8/62. Flt Lt 14/2/66. Retd CAT 20/11/74.
WORLEY D. C. Born 21/1/67. Commd 27/8/87. Flt Lt 27/2/93. Retd GD 14/9/96.
WORMALD I. A. Born 31/3/38. Commd 10/11/61. Sqn Ldr 1/1/74. Retd GD 1/1/77. Reinstated 11/10/76 to 11/10/87.
WORRALL G. G. Born 7/7/33. Commd 13/8/52. Flt Lt 9/1/58. Retd GD 7/7/72.
WORRALL J. A., OBE MIMgt. Born 21/6/27. Commd 7/12/49. Wg Cdr 1/1/65. Retd GD 22/6/82.
WORSELL G. A. W., BA. Born 1/5/30. Commd 19/8/53. Sqn Ldr 17/2/63. Retd EDN 19/8/69.
WORSLEY G. A. Born 6/12/34. Commd 8/9/69. Sqn Ldr 1/7/79. Retd SY 8/9/85.
WORSLEY W. E. Born 6/11/35. Commd 27/4/61. Flt Lt 1/7/68. Retd SUP 12/1/75 rtg Sqn Ldr.
WORT M. J., MB BS BMedSci FFARCS. Born 26/2/53. Commd 17/9/74. Wg Cdr 20/7/91. Retd MED 21/10/91.
WORT P. L. Born 8/10/32. Commd 27/8/52. Flt Lt 23/1/58. Retd GD 20/8/76.
WORTH A. J. S. Born 29/7/48. Commd 10/2/72. Flt Lt 15/7/75. Retd GD(G) 29/7/86.
WORTH A. M., BDS LDSRCS. Born 12/9/43. Commd 23/8/61. Flt Lt 23/12/64. Retd DEL 28/9/68.
WORTHINGTON D. R., CEng MIEE MRAeS MIMgt. Born 10/8/33. Commd 22/7/55. Sqn Ldr 1/7/66. Retd ENG 14/12/71.
WORTHINGTON I. J., BA CEng MIEE. Born 22/4/40. Commd 30/9/59. Wg Cdr 1/7/82. Retd ENG 1/3/94.
WORTHINGTON I. R. Born 23/11/51. Commd 9/12/71. Flt Lt 25/11/78. Retd SY(RGT) 23/11/89.
WORTHINGTON P. L. B., PhD MSc BSc BSc. Born 20/3/44. Commd 20/1/80. Flt Lt 20/1/81. Retd ADMIN 1/1/85.
WORTHINGTON P. M., MBE. Born 8/10/28. Commd 27/7/49. Sqn Ldr 1/1/61. Retd GD 8/10/66.
WORTHINGTON P. S. Born 20/6/37. Commd 3/10/69. Sqn Ldr 1/1/76. Retd GD(G) 1/1/79.
WORTHINGTON R. B., MBE. Born 6/4/15. Commd 16/12/43. Sqn Ldr 1/1/70. Retd SEC 1/1/73.
WORTHY E. A. Born 23/10/21. Commd 24/4/43. Flt Lt 5/10/60. Retd GD(G) 31/1/76.
WORTLEY M. G. Born 24/7/41. Commd 22/2/63. Flt Lt 22/8/68. Retd GD 24/7/96.
WOSKETT S. W. K., AFM MIMgt. Born 24/10/28. Commd 19/12/59. Sqn Ldr 1/1/77. Retd ADMIN 24/10/83.
WOTHERSPOON A. S. Born 16/3/30. Commd 27/9/51. Flt Lt 11/1/57. Retd GD 16/3/68.
WRAGG K. H. Born 31/8/15. Commd 3/5/55. Flt Lt 9/5/60. Retd GD(G) 31/8/70.
WRAIGHT M. J. Born 27/4/33. Commd 17/1/52. Sqn Ldr 1/1/71. Retd GD 27/4/88.
WRANGHAM J. Born 4/12/32. Commd 26/3/52. Flt Lt 31/7/57. Retd GD 22/3/71.
WRATTEN Sir William., GBE CB AFC CIMgt FRAeS. Born 15/8/39. Commd 13/12/60. ACM 1/9/94. Retd GD 5/11/97.
WRAY A. F. Born 12/2/35. Commd 14/1/53. Wg Cdr 1/1/76. Retd GD 16/6/81.
WRAY C. D. Born 30/10/16. Commd 22/3/45. Flt Lt 4/1/51. Retd SUP 30/10/69.
WRAY P., BSc CEng MIEE. Born 24/5/46. Commd 26/5/67. Wg Cdr 1/1/82. Retd ENG 10/12/86.
WREN C. G. Born 4/5/48. Commd 23/2/68. Flt Lt 23/8/73. Retd GD 4/5/82.
WREN D. Born 2/6/21. Commd 30/7/59. Flt Lt 27/2/63. Retd ENG 4/9/71.
WREN R. J. Born 6/7/59. Commd 11/8/77. Sqn Ldr 1/7/93. Retd GD 8/5/98.

WRIDE G. B. Born 16/5/53. Commd 21/12/89. Flt Lt 21/12/93. Retd ENG 1/11/94.
WRIGHT A. Born 5/4/24. Commd 8/9/43. Sqn Ldr 1/7/55. Retd GD 5/4/73.
WRIGHT A. A. H. Born 1/8/22. Commd 25/5/50. Sqn Ldr 1/1/70. Retd GD 1/8/73.
WRIGHT A. B. Born 29/5/46. Commd 29/10/64. Fg Offr 7/5/67. Retd RGT 1/9/71.
WRIGHT A. C. Born 30/3/24. Commd 18/9/48. Flt Lt 3/7/54. Retd GD 30/3/67.
WRIGHT A. G., DFC. Born 3/8/11. Commd 16/10/43. Sqn Ldr 1/7/53. Retd SUP 3/8/60.
WRIGHT A. J., BA MIMgt. Born 1/1/42. Commd 24/2/61. Sqn Ldr 1/1/79. Retd GD 1/7/98.
WRIGHT A. J., DFC* MRIN MIMgt. Born 27/7/22. Commd 6/11/42. Wg Cdr 1/1/66. Retd GD(G) 3/1/76.
WRIGHT A. J. W. Born 8/10/40. Commd 26/5/61. Flt Lt 26/11/66. Retd GD 8/10/78.
WRIGHT A. L., CEng MRAeS. Born 20/9/27. Commd 27/6/57. Wg Cdr 1/1/77. Retd EDN 19/5/79.
WRIGHT A. O., MBE CEng MRAeS. Born 8/10/37. Commd 30/7/59. Wg Cdr 1/7/88. Retd ENG 8/10/90.
WRIGHT A. R., DFC* AFC. Born 12/2/20. Commd 23/10/39. Wg Cdr 1/7/52. Retd GD 12/2/67 rtg Gp Capt.
WRIGHT A. W. A. Born 4/8/31. Commd 27/6/51. Flt Lt 27/12/55. Retd GD 4/8/89.
WRIGHT B. A., CBE AFC. Born 22/11/40. Commd 11/9/64. Gp Capt 1/1/84. Retd GD 22/11/95.
WRIGHT B. W., BA. Born 19/3/57. Commd 22/3/81. Flt Lt 22/6/81. Retd GD 12/2/91.
WRIGHT The Rev C. E. Born 6/11/08. Commd 12/11/42. Retd 12/11/62 Wg Cdr.
WRIGHT C. H. Born 8/4/37. Commd 3/11/60. Sqn Ldr 1/1/72. Retd GD 12/7/90.
WRIGHT C. J., BA MIMgt. Born 15/10/57. Commd 22/3/81. Flt Lt 22/9/84. Retd ADMIN 22/3/97.
WRIGHT D., MMar. Born 24/6/35. Commd 9/3/62. Flt Lt 9/9/67. Retd GD 24/6/93.
WRIGHT D. Born 30/6/26. Commd 13/8/52. Flt Lt 9/1/58. Retd GD 29/6/68.
WRIGHT D., MIMgt. Born 23/11/33. Commd 13/8/52. Flt Lt 20/2/58. Retd GD 23/11/71.
WRIGHT D., AFC. Born 28/9/28. Commd 27/7/49. Wg Cdr 1/1/65. Retd GD 28/9/83.
WRIGHT D. B. Born 4/12/30. Commd 19/8/53. Flt Lt 20/2/59. Retd GD 15/1/64.
WRIGHT D. D. Born 11/5/38. Commd 26/5/67. Flt Lt 30/10/69. Retd ADMIN 11/5/76.
WRIGHT D. G. M., AFC. Born 3/9/24. Commd 6/9/56. Sqn Ldr 1/1/74. Retd GD 1/1/83.
WRIGHT D. H., LDSRCS. Born 5/5/36. Commd 22/5/60. Wg Cdr 17/4/73. Retd DEL 15/6/93.
WRIGHT D. K., DPhysEd. Born 20/6/35. Commd 7/2/57. Gp Capt 1/1/91. Retd ADMIN 20/4/91.
WRIGHT D. W. Born 16/2/38. Commd 24/11/60. Sqn Ldr 1/1/72. Retd SUP 1/8/78.
WRIGHT D. W. Born 29/9/57. Commd 20/1/85. Fg Offr 20/1/87. Retd ADMIN 30/4/90.
WRIGHT E. H. Born 15/4/32. Commd 27/8/52. Sqn Ldr 1/1/67. Retd GD 3/9/85.
WRIGHT E. W., CBE DFC DFM. Born 21/9/19. Commd 18/12/40. A Cdre 1/7/66. Retd GD 21/7/73.
WRIGHT F. Born 3/11/19. Commd 13/2/47. Flt Lt 13/8/51. Retd SUP 6/11/68.
WRIGHT F. C., MBE MIPM. Born 22/1/23. Commd 9/7/43. Sqn Ldr 1/1/70. Retd ADMIN 22/1/78.
WRIGHT F. G., BEM. Born 7/2/35. Commd 24/2/67. Flt Lt 24/2/73. Retd PRT 2/4/75.
WRIGHT G. C. Born 29/2/48. Commd 22/4/73. Flt Lt 22/10/73. Retd GD 11/3/78.
WRIGHT G. J. Born 13/12/14. Commd 15/12/34. Wg Cdr 1/7/47. Retd GD 1/11/49 rtg Gp Capt.
WRIGHT G. J. Born 13/2/40. Commd 28/10/68. Sqn Ldr 1/7/78. Retd CAT 28/10/84.
WRIGHT G. W. F. Born 5/1/46. Commd 18/8/67. Flt Lt 18/8/70. Retd GD 24/4/75.
WRIGHT H. H., DFM. Born 30/4/22. Commd 9/12/42. Flt Lt 4/6/51. Retd GD(G) 1/2/62.
WRIGHT H. T. Born 3/9/17. Commd 6/6/44. Flt Lt 6/12/47. Retd ENG 31/12/64.
WRIGHT I. H. Born 4/10/41. Commd 20/10/68. Sqn Ldr 1/7/79. Retd GD 10/7/83.
WRIGHT I. M., BSc. Born 15/4/61. Commd 2/9/79. Flt Lt 15/10/83. Retd GD 15/4/99.
WRIGHT J., MBE. Born 28/11/41. Commd 16/9/71. Wg Cdr 1/1/88. Retd MED(SEC) 30/6/90.
WRIGHT J. Born 15/11/33. Commd 14/12/54. Sqn Ldr 1/7/68. Retd GD 15/11/71.
WRIGHT J. S. Born 9/3/20. Commd 10/3/45. Sqn Ldr 1/1/68. Retd SEC 9/9/75.
WRIGHT J. W. F. Born 11/5/26. Commd 21/12/45. Flt Lt 30/6/49. Retd GD 26/10/52.
WRIGHT K. B. Born 8/12/23. Commd 11/2/44. Flt Lt 11/8/47. Retd GD 8/12/61.
WRIGHT K. W., MBE DFM. Born 19/4/16. Commd 20/10/55. Flt Lt 5/4/59. Retd GD(G) 30/8/69.
WRIGHT L. H., MBE MIMgt. Born 5/5/31. Commd 17/5/62. Sqn Ldr 1/7/75. Retd ADMIN 19/1/84.
WRIGHT L. J. Born 5/8/06. Commd 29/1/42. Sqn Ldr 1/7/56. Retd ENG 5/8/61.
WRIGHT L. J. Born 11/3/28. Commd 17/5/51. Sqn Ldr 1/7/62. Retd GD 25/10/75.
WRIGHT M. A. B. K. Born 3/7/53. Commd 16/9/71. Flt Lt 16/3/77. Retd GD 3/1/92.
WRIGHT M. C. Born 31/5/39 Commd 13/12/60. Flt Lt 13/6/63. Retd GD 31/12/69.
WRIGHT M. C. ST.J. Born 31/12/41. Commd 24/2/67. Sqn Ldr 1/7/81. Retd ENG 31/12/96.
WRIGHT M. D., MBE. Born 25/6/27. Commd 30/8/48. Wg Cdr 1/1/73. Retd PRT 1/6/78.
WRIGHT M. H. Born 29/1/49. Commd 31/3/70. Flt Lt 31/3/75. Retd GD 14/3/96.
WRIGHT N. Born 26/2/29. Commd 23/2/50. Flt Lt 18/5/59. Retd GD 26/2/67.
WRIGHT N., BSc. Born 8/4/35. Commd 25/2/64. Sqn Ldr 25/3/70. Retd ADMIN 25/2/83.
WRIGHT N. J. Born 4/10/41. Commd 28/7/60. Wg Cdr 1/7/83. Retd ADMIN 4/10/91.
WRIGHT O. D., BA. Born 15/4/49. Commd 8/11/68. Wg Cdr 1/1/94. Retd GD 14/3/97.
WRIGHT P. Born 29/11/38. Commd 25/11/78. Flt Lt 23/11/84. Retd SY 1/10/86.
WRIGHT P. C. Born 9/10/45. Commd 2/8/68. Fg Offr 9/11/70. Retd GD(G) 6/4/74.
WRIGHT P. D., BA. Born 4/7/26. Commd 4/10/50. Wg Cdr 1/7/63. Retd GD 1/11/80. rtg Gp Capt.
WRIGHT P. H. F. Born 12/7/32. Commd 10/4/56. Flt Lt 10/10/61. Retd GD 10/10/75.
WRIGHT P. J. Born 18/5/32. Commd 28/11/51. Sqn Ldr 1/7/65. Retd GD 14/8/72.
WRIGHT P. J. Born 18/3/48. Commd 19/8/66. Sqn Ldr 1/1/81. Retd GD 18/3/86.

WRIGHT P. M. Born 5/2/63. Commd 20/5/82. Flt Lt 20/11/87. Retd GD 29/11/91.
WRIGHT R. Born 28/7/35. Commd 27/1/67. Sqn Ldr 1/7/82. Retd ENG 3/11/85.
WRIGHT R. C. Born 23/1/43. Commd 28/7/64. Sqn Ldr 1/1/78. Retd GD 2/4/93.
WRIGHT R. E. Born 5/4/10. Commd 4/11/43. Fg Offr 6/10/44. Retd ENG 23/3/46.
WRIGHT R. H. Born 23/11/21. Commd 13/7/61. Flt Lt 13/7/66. Retd ENG 5/4/75.
WRIGHT R. J. Born 20/7/44. Commd 5/11/70. Flt Lt 1/4/74. Retd GD 20/7/82.
WRIGHT R. M. Born 14/7/39. Commd 11/5/62. Flt Lt 11/11/67. Retd GD 14/7/97.
WRIGHT R. St. L. Born 7/5/28. Commd 28/2/57. Sqn Ldr 1/7/68. Retd GD 15/7/72.
WRIGHT R. W., MB ChB. Born 11/1/23. Commd 22/9/44. Wg Cdr 5/9/64. Retd MED 12/2/68.
WRIGHT R. W. J. Born 2/5/36. Commd 10/8/55. Sqn Ldr 1/7/81. Retd GD 2/7/89.
WRIGHT S. G., DFC. Born 6/7/22. Commd 16/8/46. Flt Lt 29/6/50. Retd GD 7/7/55.
WRIGHT S. G. Born 20/5/37. Commd 24/4/61. Flt Lt 25/5/61. Retd GD 24/4/77.
WRIGHT S. J. Born 12/3/35. Commd 23/11/78. Flt Lt 23/11/83. Retd PI 4/1/86.
WRIGHT S. R. A. Born 25/6/51. Commd 8/4/82. Sqn Ldr 1/7/92. Retd ADMIN 30/9/99.
WRIGHT T. B., BA. Born 10/2/43. Commd 22/7/71. Wg Cdr 1/1/86. Retd ENG 10/2/98.
WRIGHT W. J. R. Born 19/3/35. Commd 23/5/63. Flt Lt 26/10/69. Retd GD(G) 20/2/79.
WRIGHT W. W., BA BA DipEd. Born 5/10/42. Commd 8/1/68. Wg Cdr 1/1/87. Retd ADMIN 29/8/94.
WRIGHT-NOOTH P. H. Born 24/10/26. Commd 3/8/66. Flt Lt 15/3/68. Retd ADMIN 3/8/82.
WRIGHTON P. J., MRIN. Born 27/10/44. Commd 14/7/66. Wg Cdr 1/7/88. Retd GD 2/4/93.
WRIGLEY H. A. Born 21/6/03. Commd 15/10/27. Wg Cdr 1/10/46. Retd SUP 13/9/52.
WRIGLEY S. A. Born 19/3/44. Commd 15/7/66. Gp Capt 1/1/96. Retd GD 19/3/99.
WRINCH N. P. H. Born 11/10/53. Commd 6/9/81. Fg Off 5/8/78. Retd GD 9/12/81.
WYATT A. R., MSc. Born 2/2/45. Commd 16/9/76. Sqn Ldr 1/7/84. Retd ADMIN 16/9/89.
WYATT A. StC. Born 24/8/27. Commd 1/6/50. Sqn Ldr 1/1/61. Retd GD 24/9/76.
WYATT A. V. Born 15/2/43. Commd 21/1/66. Sqn Ldr 1/1/92. Retd GD 15/2/98.
WYATT D. A. Born 3/2/61. Commd 31/1/80. Sqn Ldr 1/1/92. Retd GD 4/2/98.
WYATT D. P. P., BSc. Born 19/2/66. Commd 11/10/84. Flt Lt 15/1/90. Retd GD 15/7/99.
WYATT D. R., MBE. Born 3/10/40. Commd 15/3/79. Sqn Ldr 1/1/89. Retd ENG 3/10/95.
WYATT G. M., DFC. Born 24/9/15. Commd 30/9/35. Wg Cdr 1/7/47. Retd GD 24/9/55 rtg Gp Capt.
WYATT J. W., BSc CEng MRAeS. Born 27/2/37. Commd 30/9/56. Wg Cdr 1/7/76. Retd ENG 30/8/80.
WYATT S. G., BSc. Born 16/3/61. Commd 11/9/83. Flt Lt 11/3/86. Retd GD 14/3/97.
WYATT S. J. Born 21/8/53. Commd 11/8/77. Flt Lt 11/2/83. Retd GD 1/10/98.
WYDRA S. P., BSc. Born 6/2/53. Commd 13/11/72. Flt Lt 15/10/74. Retd GD 15/7/85.
WYER E. J. Born 11/12/47. Commd 31/7/70. Sqn Ldr 1/1/84. Retd GD 12/12/91.
WYER R. F. E. Born 22/11/43. Commd 22/3/63. Flt Lt 22/9/68. Retd GD 2/12/75.
WYLAM B. B. Born 28/9/35. Commd 27/1/55. Flt Lt 1/3/61. Retd SEC 28/9/73.
WYLD H. Born 28/1/33. Commd 9/4/52. Flt Lt 5/9/57. Retd GD 28/1/76.
WYLD J. R. Born 16/3/31. Commd 9/4/52. Flt Lt 5/9/57. Sqn Ldr 1/7/69. Retd GD 30/9/77.
WYLDE R. C. Born 25/9/29. Commd 10/12/52. Flt Lt 5/5/58. Retd GD 23/6/68.
WYLIE M. D. Born 13/12/46. Commd 2/8/68. Wg Cdr 1/1/96. Retd GD 31/1/01.
WYLIE M. D., DFC. Born 28/2/22. Commd 15/1/41. Wg Cdr 1/1/58. Retd GD 30/8/69 rtg Gp Capt.
WYLLIE D. G. V. Born 13/1/30. Commd 1/12/53. Flt Lt 1/3/61. Retd GD 1/12/69.
WYLLIE H. A., LDSRCS. Born 17/6/33. Commd 20/11/60. Sqn Ldr 20/7/65. Retd DEL 26/8/70.
WYMAN A. R. A. Born 21/1/33. Commd 5/9/69. Flt Lt 5/9/71. Retd ENG 5/9/77.
WYN-JONES E. W., BSc. Born 9/3/56. Commd 6/9/81. Wg Cdr 1/1/96. Retd ADMIN 7/4/00.
WYNELL-MAYOW J. Born 21/4/21. Commd 1/11/56. Sqn Ldr 1/1/69. Retd ENG 21/4/76.
WYNESS J. A., MA. Born 11/5/56. Commd 19/7/87. Flt Lt 19/1/87. Retd ADMIN 2/10/91.
WYNESS R. F., DFM. Born 2/10/12. Commd 3/10/40. Sqn ldr 1/8/47. Retd GD 2/10/55.
WYNN D. I., MBE CertEd. Born 25/12/47. Commd 4/5/72. Sqn Ldr 1/1/88. Retd ADMIN 1/5/00.
WYNN L. L. W. Born 13/12/12. Commd 10/10/46. Fg Offr 10/10/47. Retd SUP 12/5/58.
WYNN M. J., DPhysEd. Born 3/10/40. Commd 31/1/66. Wg Cdr 1/7/81. Retd ADMIN 31/1/88.
WYNN-PARRY C. B., MBE MA DM BCh FRCP DPhysMed. Born 11/10/24. Commd 7/10/48. Gp Capt 1/5/68. Retd
    MED 3/4/76.
WYNNE D. J. Born 5/6/38. Commd 2/7/62. Flt Lt 16/8/63. Retd GD 8/9/67.
WYNNE D. T. Born 26/2/36. Commd 10/2/72. Flt Lt 10/2/75. Retd ADMIN 1/9/87.
WYNNE G. Born 2/5/24. Commd 10/3/44. Flt Lt 10/3/49. Retd GD 2/5/67.
WYNNE J. E. Born 31/1/43. Commd 26/5/60. Sqn Ldr 1/1/71. Retd ENG 31/1/81.
WYNNE J. G., DFC. Born 8/5/21. Commd 19/12/41. Wg Cdr 1/7/60. Retd GD 28/7/73.
WYNNE-POWELL G. T., DFC. 22/3/15. Commd 19/6/35. Wg Cdr 1/7/47. Retd GD 4/3/58.
WYPER D. J., MB ChB DRCOG DAvMed MRAeS. Born 13/2/51. Commd 14/5/74. Wg Cdr 18/2/90. Retd MED
    19/9/96.
WYRILL R. P. S. Born 20/5/16. Commd 7/10/35. Wg Cdr 1/7/47. Retd GD 29/12/59.
WYSE D. Born 2/6/52. Commd 7/11/91. Fg Offr 7/11/91. Retd SUP 7/1/96.
WYVER C. C. Born 4/7/47. Commd 25/4/69. Flt Lt 4/1/73. Retd GD 12/5/88.

# Y

YAPP A. R. E., CEng MIEE MRAeS. Born 16/10/36. Commd 30/5/59. Sqn Ldr 1/1/72. Retd GD 6/2/75.
YARDLEY J. H. G. Born 9/6/11. Commd 17/2/45. Flt Lt 17/2/51. Retd SUP 12/5/58.
YARRAM M. F., BSc. Born 24/6/47. Commd 26/5/70. Sqn Ldr 1/7/81. Retd SUP 1/6/00.
YARRONTON P. G. Born 30/9/24. Commd 11/8/44. Flt Lt 14/1/49. Retd GD 14/4/57.
YARROW S. W. S., MIMgt. Born 18/2/41. Commd 18/12/62. Wg Cdr 1/7/85. Retd GD 18/2/96.
YARROW T. B. J., MBE BSc. Born 27/5/49. Commd 15/9/69. Wg Cdr 1/1/94. Retd GD 14/3/97.
YARWOOD T., MInstAM MIMgt. Born 1/8/39. Commd 16/5/74. Sqn Ldr 1/7/85. Retd ADMIN 1/8/94.
YATES B. Born 22/7/39. Commd 24/6/71. Flt Lt 24/6/73. Retd ENG 24/6/79.
YATES C. Born 18/3/95. Commd 24/6/43. Flt Lt 24/6/47. Retd ASD 28/6/48.
YATES C. E. J., BSc. Born 1/2/57. Commd 17/8/79. Sqn Ldr 1/7/90. Retd GD 13/10/95.
YATES D. N. Born 3/2/23. Commd 30/10/43. Flt Lt 4/12/52. Retd GD 2/8/63. Re-instated on active list 20/1/64. Retd 10/12/75 rtg Sqn Ldr.
YATES D. P., OBE. Born 9/7/46. Commd 18/11/66. Gp Capt 1/1/99. Retd ENG 2/1/01.
YATES G. W. Born 21/2/21. Commd 31/3/60. Flt Lt 31/3/63. Retd ENG 1/5/73.
YATES H. F. Born 9/8/15. Commd 2/8/45. Flt Lt 4/1/51. Retd SEC 24/10/53.
YATES J. A., BEM. Born 10/7/35. Commd 24/2/67. Flt Lt 24/2/72. Retd ENG 19/12/86.
YATES J. A. Born 22/6/51. Commd 22/10/72. Sqn Ldr 1/7/85. Retd ADMIN 1/10/91.
YATES J. B., CEng MRAeS. Born 29/9/17. Commd 19/8/42. Wg Cdr 1/7/58. Retd ENG 30/3/68.
YATES J. F. W., DFC. Born 29/9/22. Commd 8/4/43. Flt Lt 8/10/46. Retd GD 30/9/55.
YATES J. R. Born 25/4/24. Commd 3/11/45. Sqn Ldr 1/7/55. Retd GD 14/8/65.
YATES J. W. L. Born 4/9/27. Commd 7/8/59. Sqn Ldr 30/12/66. Retd EDN 7/8/75.
YATES M. J., BSc. Born 19/3/57. Commd 28/12/80. Sqn Ldr 1/1/89. Retd ADMIN 14/3/97.
YATES P. M. Born 13/1/49. Commd 28/10/66. Sqn Ldr 1/1/83. Retd GD(G) 13/1/87.
YATES P. N. Born 18/6/34. Commd 22/8/59. Flt Lt 22/2/65. Retd GD 31/8/72.
YATES P. W. Born 22/2/55. Commd 9/12/76. Flt Lt 30/4/83. Retd GD(G) 22/2/93.
YATES R. Born 20/2/45. Commd 22/2/63. Sqn Ldr 1/1/88. Retd GD 21/7/98.
YATES R. G. Born 19/8/49. Commd 1/6/72. Flt Lt 6/6/75. Retd GD 19/8/87.
YATES V. W. Born 19/7/44. Commd 15/7/66. Flt Lt 15/1/69. Retd GD 3/7/70.
YATES W. H. Born 1/11/31. Commd 25/2/53. Flt Lt 7/3/62. Retd GD(G) 2/11/82.
YATES-EARL J. E. Born 31/10/19. Commd 11/2/43. Sqn Ldr 1/7/59. Retd GD(G) 31/10/74.
YAXLEY R. E., MIMgt. Born 22/10/24. Commd 14/1/57. Flt Lt 24/4/60. Retd SUP 22/10/79.
YEARDLEY J. N. Born 11/4/48. Commd 4/6/87. Flt Lt 4/6/91. Retd ENG 1/7/93.
YEARWOOD G. De L. Born 2/10/34. Commd 12/3/60. Sqn Ldr 1/7/82. Retd GD(AEO) 2/10/89.
YEARWOOD H. G. Born 26/4/21. Commd 10/12/42. Sqn Ldr 1/7/52. Retd RGT 1/10/58.
YEATES A. G. Born 5/11/45. Commd 6/11/67. Gp Capt 1/1/89. Retd ENG 2/4/94.
YEATS P. N. Born 21/3/59. Commd 4/84. Flt Lt 19/10/83. Retd GD 21/3/97.
YEE Y. S., BSc CEng MIMechE MRAeS. Born 30/11/44. Commd 9/11/80. Flt Lt 9/11/78. Retd ENG 9/11/96.
YELDHAM R. E. D. Born 23/4/34. Commd 9/4/52. Flt Lt 5/9/57. Retd GD 23/4/71.
YELDHAM, A., MBE. Born 12/6/53. Commd 27/7/72. Wg Cdr 1/7/89. Retd ADMIN 1/11/92.
YEO C. J., AFC. Born 24/5/46. Commd 10/12/65. Sqn Ldr 1/7/78. Retd GD 17/11/78.
YEO P. G. R. Born 24/10/37. Commd 10/8/61. Wg Cdr 1/1/81. Retd GD 30/9/83.
YEOMANS J. A., MIMgt. Born 25/3/23. Commd 28/3/46. Wg Cdr 1/1/66. Retd GD 25/9/76.
YEOMANS K. T. Born 29/7/29. Commd 27/2/52. Flt Lt 27/11/57. Retd GD 29/7/67.
YERBY R. K. Born 17/6/45. Commd 26/4/84. Sqn Ldr 1/7/94. Retd ENG 14/6/96.
YETMAN F. B., BA. Born 12/2/28. Commd 4/10/50. A Cdre 1/7/78. Retd GD 1/5/79.
YORK A. E. C., BA. Born 22/10/22. Commd 8/1/52. Gp Capt 1/7/70. Retd EDN 27/10/73.
YORK D. A. Born 5/12/36. Commd 12/6/57. Fg Offr 17/9/59. Retd GD 6/12/65.
YORK G. A. Born 1/7/41. Commd 7/6/64. Flt Lt 1/1/67. Retd GD 1/7/79. Re-entrant 6/7/86. Flt Lt 4/1/74. Retd GD 1/7/96.
YORK H. Born 4/5/19. Commd 2/3/43. Flt Lt 2/3/49. Retd SEC 4/5/68.
YORK M. W., MSc CEng MIEE. Born 28/10/46. Commd 3/2/71. Flt Lt 3/11/72. Retd ENG 6/9/80.
YORK V. W., DFC. Born 4/3/21. Commd 11/6/44. Wg Cdr 1/7/70. Retd SUP 4/3/76.
YOUD W. E. Born 8/9/26. Commd 18/6/52. Flt Lt 17/12/57. Retd GD 8/9/64.
YOUDAN D., MIMgt. Born 20/7/35. Commd 8/7/54. Wg Cdr 1/1/78. Retd SUP 3/4/84.
YOUINGS A. W. Born 11/4/10. Commd 3/6/41. Fg Offr 5/8/42. Retd ENG 27/11/45 rtg Sqn Ldr.
YOULDON K. C., CEng MIMechE. Born 26/7/33. Commd 24/9/59. Wg Cdr 1/7/79. Retd ENG 26/12/88.
YOUNG A. C. M. N. Born 30/12/42. Commd 6/7/62. Flt Lt 15/4/70. Retd GD 20/12/93.
YOUNG A. G., 15/9/38. Commd 20/12/60. Flt Lt 1/4/66. Retd 15/9/76.
YOUNG A. J. Born 21/2/60. Commd 22/2/79. Flt Lt 22/8/84. Retd GD 1/4/90.
YOUNG A. M., BA. Born 22/5/59. Commd 4/9/78. Flt Lt 14/10/82. Retd GD 22/8/97.

YOUNG A. V. M. Born 8/3/50. Commd 25/2/72. Fg Offr 25/2/73. Retd SEC 20/9/75.
YOUNG B. Born 27/1/47. Commd 1/3/68. Sqn Ldr 1/7/82. Retd GD 1/7/91.
YOUNG B. C. Born 24/2/47. Commd 17/1/69. Flt Lt 27/11/75. Retd GD(G) 24/2/85.
YOUNG D. C. Born 4/3/36. Commd 8/1/59. Sqn Ldr 1/1/72. Retd GD 1/6/77.
YOUNG D. H. Born 7/8/22. Commd 22/10/41. Sqn Ldr 1/4/55. Retd GD 7/8/65.
YOUNG D. J. Born 27/4/47. Commd 2/12/66. Flt Lt 2/6/72. Retd GD 27/4/85.
YOUNG D. R. Born 23/12/26. Commd 3/5/46. Wg Cdr 1/1/69. Retd GD 8/11/75.
YOUNG F. Born 8/10/08. Commd 17/4/47. Flt Lt 17/10/51. Retd SUP 15/7/58.
YOUNG G. A. Born 12/6/45. Commd 1/10/65. Sqn Ldr 1/1/79. Retd GD 12/6/83.
YOUNG G. D., MSc BSc CEng MIEE. Born 29/8/41. Commd 22/10/63. Sqn Ldr 28/3/73. Retd EDN 22/10/79.
YOUNG G. E. Born 11/5/25. Commd 4/10/77. Flt Lt 1/1/56. Retd GD 23/9/77.
YOUNG G. K., MBE BSc CEng MCIPD MRAeS. Born 10/12/32. Commd 1/7/61. Wg Cdr 1/7/80. Retd ADMIN 1/8/82.
YOUNG G. L. Born 30/1/47. Commd 1/2/89. Sqn Ldr 1/7/99. Retd GD 18/9/00.
YOUNG G. P. Born 23/2/25. Commd 22/1/45. Flt Lt 21/7/48. Retd GD 23/2/63.
YOUNG G. W. V. Born 10/4/17. Commd 20/10/55. Flt Lt 20/10/58. Retd ENG 9/2/65.
YOUNG H. M. Born 19/8/49. Commd 30/5/69. Flt Lt 30/11/74. Retd GD 19/9/92.
YOUNG I., BSc. Born 31/10/46. Commd 19/11/72. Sqn Ldr 1/7/81. Retd GD 1/9/89.
YOUNG I. F., MB ChB DMRD. Born 6/5/31. Commd 6/5/56. Sqn Ldr 1/4/62. Retd MED 6/4/68.
YOUNG J., OBE. Born 16/9/42. Commd 22/8/71. Wg Cdr 1/7/86. Retd ADMIN 2/10/91.
YOUNG J. A. Born 13/9/32. Commd 31/5/51. Flt Lt 5/10/60. Retd GD 3/10/71 rtg Sqn Ldr.
YOUNG J. G. P. Born 3/8/34. Commd 5/11/52. Flt Lt 1/3/61. Retd GD 1/2/78.
YOUNG J. M., MBE. Born 12/7/36. Commd 19/6/70. Sqn Ldr 1/7/77. Retd ADMIN 10/8/87.
YOUNG J. R. Born 15/10/30. Commd 4/6/53. Flt Lt 19/11/58. Retd GD 29/3/69.
YOUNG J. R. Born 21/10/22. Commd 3/12/43. Sqn Ldr 1/1/72. Retd GD 31/3/74.
YOUNG J. W. C. N. Born 21/9/15. Commd 3/4/39. Wg Cdr 1/7/56. Retd SUP 31/5/61.
YOUNG L. Born 16/4/1900. Commd 1/4/22. Wg Cdr 1/4/39. Retd GD 8/12/46.
YOUNG L. C., DFC. Born 1/6/20. Commd 3/2/44. Flt Lt 27/6/51. Retd GD 27/9/55.
YOUNG M., MBE. Born 25/10/45. Commd 24/4/70. Wg Cdr 1/7/89. Retd GD 2/7/93.
YOUNG M., BSc(Eng). Born 28/12/45. Commd 28/9/64. Sqn Ldr 1/1/81. Retd GD 14/10/85. Re-entered 3/8/90. Sqn Ldr 21/10/85. Retd GD 30/5/01.
YOUNG M. J. R., MA BA CertEd MCIPD. Born 28/1/47. Commd 24/1/74. Flt Lt 8/6/80. Retd GD(G) 1/10/89. Re-entered 13/3/91. Flt Lt 18/11/81. Retd OPS SPT 1/6/98.
YOUNG M. M., MBE. Born 3/2/27. Commd 8/7/54. Flt Lt 8/1/58. Retd GD 4/8/73.
YOUNG P. Born 8/10/47. Commd 28/11/74. Flt Lt 28/5/77 Retd GD 8/10/85.
YOUNG P., MBE. Born 1/7/14. Commd 22/7/42. Flt Offr 22/1/47. Retd SEC 23/6/52.
YOUNG P. A. Born 27/7/44. Commd 8/10/87. Flt Lt 8/10/91. Retd ENG 2/7/93.
YOUNG P. J. Born 28/5/25. Commd 26/5/54. Sqn Ldr 1/1/66. Retd GD 10/12/76.
YOUNG P. J. J. Born 14/4/51. Commd 1/4/71. Sqn Ldr 1/7/86. Retd GD 1/7/89.
YOUNG P. W. F. Born 23/4/41. Commd 3/1/68. Flt Lt 14/10/73. Retd SUP 2/7/80.
YOUNG R. B., BSc. Born 17/12/48. Commd 13/6/71. Flt Lt 15/10/72. Retd GD 13/6/87.
YOUNG R. I., AFC. Born 23/1/26. Commd 30/10/50. Flt Lt 11/11/54. Retd GD 23/1/64.
YOUNG R. J., BEM. Born 9/2/48. Commd 22/5/80. Flt Lt 22/5/82. Retd SUP 20/5/88.
YOUNG R. S. E., BSc. Born 8/7/60. Commd 10/2/82. Flt Lt 15/10/84. Retd GD 14/9/95.
YOUNG R. W. Born 5/6/42. Commd 20/9/68. Flt Lt 12/5/72. Retd GD 1/4/76.
YOUNG R. W. R., MBE CEng MRAeS MIMgt. Born 28/2/35. Commd 25/7/56. Wg Cdr 1/7/75 Retd ENG 3/4/85.
YOUNG S., Born 3/10/59. Doc 6/5/83. Wg Cdr 1/7/98. Retd GD 1/10/00.
YOUNG S. H. Born 17/11/22. Commd 20/3/52. Flt Offr 20/3/58. Retd SEC 18/1/65.
YOUNG T. B., BSc CEng MIEE. Born 20/10/59. Commd 6/9/81. Sqn Ldr 1/7/90. Retd ENG 20/10/97.
YOUNG T. G., OBE BEng MRAeS. Born 17/6/11. Commd 29/9/33. Wg Cdr 1/7/47. Retd ENG 20/6/63 rtg Gp Capt.
YOUNG W. A., MIMgt. Born 8/10/19. Commd 9/7/38. Sqn Ldr 1/7/53. Retd GD 4/4/71.
YOUNG W. B. C. Born 25/6/22. Commd 14/11/44. Sqn Ldr 1/7/57. Retd GD 31/8/63.
YOUNG W. F., AFC. Born 26/12/19. Commd 31/7/42. Sqn Ldr 1/7/54. Retd GD 20/4/59.
YOUNG W. S. Born 18/10/13. Commd 19/6/42. Sqn Ldr 1/7/52. Retd SUP 18/1/69.
YOUNGER W. G. W. Born 5/4/18. Commd 14/11/46. Flt Lt 14/5/51. Retd SUP 5/10/67.
YUILLE J., FCCA. Born 24/11/13. Commd 17/12/42. Flt Lt 4/1/51. Retd SEC 21/12/62.
YULE A. J. Born 1/9/57. Commd 6/11/80. Sqn Ldr 1/7/90. Retd GD 7/7/96.
YULE L. J. Born 14/2/21. Commd 24/11/52. Flt Lt 13/2/55. Retd SEC 14/2/76.
YULE M. R. Born 30/6/42. Commd 17/12/63. Wg Cdr 1/7/85. Retd SUP 7/7/96.

# Z

ZAJAC W. J. Born 17/12/18. Commd 3/1/49. Flt Lt 3/1/49. Retd GD(G) 20/1/74.
ZALA E. D., AFC. Born 16/5/23. Commd 28/5/43. Sqn Ldr 1/7/68. Retd GD 31/3/74.
ZANKER M. W. Born 16/2/62. Commd 26/11/81. Flt Lt 26/5/87. Retd GD 16/2/00.
ZARRAGA H. P. Born 9/2/40. Commd 14/8/64. Flt Lt 14/2/70. Retd GD 1/7/80.
ZAVALA-SUAREZ C. M. R., MIMgt. Born 19/4/26. Commd 11/12/64. Flt Lt 12/2/63. Retd SUP 19/4/83.
ZBROZEK F., MSc BSc. Born 22/10/47. Commd 2/9/73. Sqn Ldr 2/3/79. Retd ADMIN 2/9/89.
ZELENY A. P., MBE. Born 11/10/14. Commd 23/6/41. Flt Lt 10/11/50. Retd GD(G) 15/11/71 rtg Sqn Ldr.
ZINKUS V. J., BA MILT. Born 5/9/57. Commd 31/1/80. Flt Lt 31/7/86. Retd SUP 24/9/95.
ZMITROWICZ K. Born 8/9/24. Commd 4/6/64. Flt Lt 4/6/67. Retd GD 29/6/74.
ZMITROWICZ Z. Born 12/6/22. Commd 2/3/61. Flt Lt 2/3/64. Retd GD 12/6/73.
ZOTOV D. V., MBE. Born 2/11/39. Commd 19/12/61. Sqn Ldr 1/1/72. Retd GD 3/12/76.
ZOTOV N. V., CEng MIEE. Born 20/12/45. Commd 30/11/64. Sqn Ldr 1/7/79. Retd ENG 23/4/93.

# LIST OF RETIRED OFFICERS OF
# THE PRINCESS MARY'S ROYAL AIR FORCE
# NURSING SERVICE

A'COURT M. E. SRN. Born 28/3/19. Sqn Offr 31/5/57. Retd 31/5/61.
AITCHISON B. M. SRN. Born 6/5/14. Sister 15/5/40. Retd 6/11/45.
ALDERSON G. P. SRN SCM. Born 30/11/36. Sqn Offr 6/7/70. Retd 1/10/71.
AMBROSE L. A. SRN. Born 5/5/32. Sqn Offr 22/5/69. Retd 31/7/71.
ANDERSON K. SRN. Born 1/7/37. Flt Offr 14/9/64. Retd 19/8/67.
ARIS M. S. SRN. Born 1/12/18. Sqn Offr 2/11/55. Retd 26/11/60.
ARNOLD P. A. SRN. Born 17/3/42. Flt Offr 8/5/68. Retd 4/7/75.
ASHTON D. F. MacD. SRN. Born 21/6/30. Sqn Offr 7/1/68. Retd 5/11/73.
ATKINSON J. W. ARRC SRN. Born 2/10/09. Sister 31/3/37. Retd 10/4/47 rtg Senior Sister.
AYLWARD S. J. SRN SCM. Born 9/4/31. Sqn Offr 5/11/66. Retd 9/6/73.
BADGER A. E. SRN. Born 25/11/09. Sister 5/9/40. Retd 2/10/50 Rtg Senior Sister.
BAKER S. M. ARRC SRN. Born 2/12/31. Sqn Offr 2/5/65. Retd 22/7/75.
BALDOCK G. A. Born 30/6/41. Sqn Ldr 15/11/76. Retd 28/7/82.
BALDWIN P. A. SRN SCM. Born 1/7/31. Flt Offr 14/8/63. Retd 15/4/67.
BALDWIN R. SRN SCM. Born 8/3/35. Sqn Offr 9/8/69. Retd 13/12/71.
BECKWITH C. A. ARRC RM. Born 8/1/52. Sqn Ldr 4/3/88. Retd 14/3/96.
BENNETT J. M. SCM. Born 27/4/57. Flt Lt 7/4/83. Retd 8/7/87.
BENNETT K. M. SRN. Born 4/3/22. Flt Offr 28/6/50. Retd 6/7/58.
BENNETT M. M. Born 5/10/45. Sqn Ldr 13/5/83. Retd 10/9/88.
BIRD M. T. ARRC SRN. Born 1/6/25. Sqn Ldr 3/11/62. Retd 1/6/80.
BLACKWOOD M. F. SRN. Born 8/8/05. Sqn Offr 14/6/52. Retd 14/9/60.
BLAKE O. C. RRC SRN RNT. Born 10/7/20. Wg Offr 1/7/65. Retd 12/9/67.
BOASE J. N. M. ARRC. Born 27/9/44. Sqn Ldr 9/12/77. Retd 27/9/88.
BONSEY B. M. N. ARRC SRN. Born 22/2/24. Sqn Offr 3/11/62. Retd 4/11/76.
BOWLER R. A. SRN SCM. Born 18/5/36. Flt Offr 3/2/66. Retd 31/5/71.
BRADLEY M. M. SRN RFN SCM. Born 2/9/13. Sqn Offr 26/3/54. Retd 26/9/68.
BREWSTER-LIDDLE J. J. G. Born 11/9/56. Fg Offr 2/1/90. Retd 1/1/96.
BROWN H. C. SRN. Born 7/3/11. Sister 1/4/41. Retd 19/7/50.
BROWN J. B. ARRC SRN SCM. Born 8/11/29. Sqn Offr 5/4/66. Retd 18/11/73.
BROWN M. RM. Born 27/2/43. Sqn Ldr 18/8/79. Retd 17/9/88.
BRUCE J. H. ARRC SCM. Born 5/3/50. Sqn Ldr 1/6/85. Retd 15/2/86.
BRUMPTON N. J. Born 2/8/58. Sqn Ldr 7/4/92. Retd 1/10/95.
BUDGE M. A. SRN SCM. Born 19/11/13. Sqn Offr 15/6/55. Retd 15/12/68.
BULL C. P. I. ARRC RM. Born 22/12/35. Wg Cdr 1/1/85. Retd 22/12/90.
BUNCE F. C. SRN SCM. Born 25/4/17. Sqn Offr 25/5/58. Retd 3/8/64.
BURTON M. M. SRN. Born 2/10/06. Sqn Offr 5/8/55. Retd 10/11/59.
BYRNE S. P. A. SRN. Born 19/7/10. Sister 16/10/40. Retd 17/6/49 rtg Senior Sister.
CAPEWELL C. E. SRN. Born 19/9/34. Sqn Offr 19/5/69. Retd 20/12/69.
CARMICHAEL I. R. ARRC SRN SCM. Born 18/11/27. Sqn Offr 10/2/69. Retd 10/2/75.
CARTWRIGHT J. SRN. Born 1/7/24. Flt Offr 17/11/60. Retd 5/5/67.
CASTLE M. A. SRN SCM. Born 8/7/38. Flt Offr 3/12/64. Retd 26/6/70.
CAYGILL M. RRC SRN SCM. Born 5/6/16. Gp Offr 1/7/69. Retd 5/6/73.
CHANDLER M. F. R. SRN. Born 22/10/19. Flt Offr 13/6/49. Retd 4/4/52.
CHAPMAN I. M. ARRC SRN. Born 22/3/04. Sqn Offr 8/12/52. Retd 1/6/59.
CHEEL Z. M. ARRC. Born 9/11/29. Wg Cdr 1/7/79. Retd 9/11/84.
CHINNERY G. E. ARRC SRN. Born 13/11/05. Wg Offr 1/7/56. Retd 26/11/60.
CHURCH E. J. SRN RM. Born 7/5/59. Sqn Ldr 6/3/93. Retd 14/3/96.
CLARKSON S. E. Born 29/1/53. Sqn Ldr 18/5/86. Retd 20/4/91.
COGGINS V. M. SRN. Born 10/2/19. Sqn Offr 4/7/62. Retd 20/2/74.
COGHLAN A. J. ARRC SRN. Born 15/5/20. Wg Offr 1/7/70. Retd 15/5/75.
COLAM P. F. ARRC SRN SCM. Born 14/11/27. Sqn Offr 3/5/64. Retd 3/5/70.
COOKSON H. M. ARRC SRN. Born 23/4/21. Sqn Offr 1/4/62. Retd 13/9/74.
COOPER J. RM. Born 4/7/47. Sqn Ldr 31/5/83. Retd 3/5/91.
CORAM M. P. E. SRN SCM. Born 24/12/29. Sqn Offr 7/10/67. Retd 29/10/73.
COUSINS S. J. SRN. Born 28/1/57. Sqn Ldr 24/10/91. Retd 14/3/96.
COWDEN C. E. SRN. Born 17/2/30. Flt Offr 29/7/68. Retd 31/10/72.

COX A. C. W. RRC. Born 18/8/48. Sqn Ldr 11/4/88. Retd 22/5/88.
CROSSLAND B. A. SRN. Born 28/2/53. Sqn Ldr 9/4/87. Retd 14/3/96.
CROSTHWAITE R. G. C. SRN. Born 28/5/15. Flt Offr 12/10/50. Retd 21/1/52.
CUFF J. M. SRN. Born 18/9/28. Flt Offr 2/2/57. Retd 25/3/60.
DANIELS J. M. SRN. Born 22/1/19. Sqn Offr 5/6/61. Retd 5/6/65.
DAVERN C. C. SCM. Born 26/12/30. Sqn Offr 12/11/67. Retd 24/11/78.
DAVIES G. M. ARRC SRN RSCN. Born 28/4/14. Sqn Offr 9/1/53. Retd 28/4/69.
DAVIES M. D. SRN. Born 11/6/34. Flt Offr 5/1/67. Retd 3/6/75.
DENNETT E. D. ARRC. Born 31/7/31. Wg Cdr 1/7/80. Retd 29/4/85.
DOUGLAS J. SRN. Born 14/8/30. Sqn Offr 8/7/67. Retd 10/7/73.
DUCAT-AMOS B. M. CB RRC. Born 2/2/21. A Cdt 1/7/72. Retd 29/11/78.
DUNCAN M. B. SRN RFN. Born 25/2/19. Sqn Offr 5/6/62. Retd 29/6/68.
DUNN M. K. ARRC SRN SCM. Born 22/10/22. Sqn Offr 3/7/64. Retd 23/10/72.
DURAND I. M. L. SRN. Born 15/12/13. Sister 15/3/40. Retd 4/4/45.
DUTCH B. J. SRN. Born 1/7/25. Sqn Offr 1/4/62. Retd 8/10/67.
DUTHIE I. M. SRN SCM. Born 1/7/28. Flt Offr 1/4/62. Retd 31/7/65.
EASTBURN E. A. Born 15/10/58. Sqn Ldr 30/5/93. Retd 13/11/99.
EASTON K. H. SRN SCM. Born 29/6/33. Sqn Offr 20/10/68. Retd 20/10/74.
EASY P. J. Born 2/12/47. Sqn Ldr 12/2/82. Retd 13/8/88.
EDMUNDS-JONES J. RRC RSCN. Born 24/5/38. Sqn Offr 19/3/78. Retd 31/12/88.
EILLEY E. M. SRN RMN. Born 23/5/36. Sqn Offr 1/5/71. Retd 26/10/74.
ELLIS P. M. SRN. Born 1/7/28. Flt Offr 3/5/58. Retd 7/4/62.
EMERSON J. M. ARRC SRN. Born 3/5/21. Wg Offr 1/7/68. Retd 10/10/70.
FERN M. C. SRN SCM. Born 20/3/38. Sqn Offr 3/4/73. Retd 29/6/80.
FINUCANE E. M. SRN RFN. Born 6/1/14. Sqn Offr 11/6/56. Retd 6/1/67.
FIRTH M. J. SRN. Born 4/9/24. Flt Offr 20/9/52. Retd 1/3/60.
FIRTH S. M. RRC SCM. Born 24/1/31. Gp Capt 1/1/82. Retd 1/9/87.
FLEMING R. A. SRN. Born 21/7/56. Flt Lt 12/7/82. Retd 17/5/85.
FRANCIS D. SRN. Born 26/4/22. Sqn Offr 22/7/57. Retd 15/7/70.
FRASER C. A. SRN. Born 1/7/34. Flt Offr 4/7/62. Retd 30/7/67.
FROUDE H. RM. Born 23/1/51. Sqn Ldr 1/6/85. Retd 10/11/93.
FRUDE M. J. MBE SCM. Born 26/9/27. Sqn Ldr 5/8/68. Retd 26/9/82.
FUDGE L. M. RM. Born 12/11/47. Commd 31/10/71. Sqn Ldr 4/9/81. Retd 14/3/97.
FURLONG D. M. SRN. Born 11/7/52. Sqn Ldr 1/1/86. Retd 25/1/92.
GALL M. R. RRC SRN. Born 28/3/03. Gp Offr 1/7/54. Retd 24/5/60.
GIBBONS O. E. V. MBE SRN. Born 28/2/15. Sister 1/4/41. Retd 9/9/50.
GILES Dame Pauline. DBE RRC SRN SCM. Born 17/9/12. A Cdt 1/9/66. Retd 12/10/70.
GLASSBOROW S. A. SRN. Born 21/5/25. Sqn Offr 1/7/62. Retd 21/10/72.
GOLDING A. B. ARRC. Born 2/10/32. Wg Cdr 1/1/85. Retd 1/1/88.
GOOD D. M. ARRC SRN. Born 7/9/09. Sister 1/9/38. Retd 16/6/50 rtg Senior Sister.
GOODFELLOW N. S. RM. Born 3/7/43. Sqn Ldr 22/6/81. Retd 5/7/98.
GOSTLING M. P. RRC. Born 7/5/24. Wg Offr 1/7/76. Retd 7/5/79.
GOULDING C. R. SRN. Born 3/12/23. Sqn Offr 5/11/60. Retd 2/12/76.
GOWSELL D. A. S. W. SRN. Born 1/7/26. Flt Offr 5/3/56. Retd 19/10/58.
GRAHAM M. R. SRN. Born 1/4/17. Flt Offr 9/12/49. Retd 28/9/52.
GREEN E. M. SRN. Born 26/7/15. Sqn Offr 27/11/53. Retd 10/5/56.
GRIFFITH J. D. SRN. Born 1/7/27. Sqn Offr 1/4/62. Retd 25/8/66.
GUINNESS E. M. SRN. Born 3/9/06. Flt Offr 1/2/49. Retd 8/4/57.
GULLIVER V. J. SRN SCM. Born 17/2/41. Flt Offr 4/12/69. Retd 5/7/75.
GUMLEY C. J. G. RRC SCM RNT. Born 24/9/27. Wg Offr 1/1/69. Retd 1/9/79.
GURNEY M. C. SRN. Born 3/5/14. Sister 14/9/40. Retd 11/9/45.
GWYTHER M. E. SRN. Born 3/10/31. Sqn Offr 10/11/66. Retd 1/9/71.
HALE M. E. ARRC SRN. Born 30/7/08. Sister 31/7/40. Retd 7/11/48 rtg Senior Sister.
HALL A. R. Born 21/3/41. Sqn Ldr 1/5/75. Retd 6/7/95.
HANCOCK E. M. RRC RM. Born 5/4/37. Gp Capt 1/7/89. Retd 5/4/94.
HAND V. M. RRC. Born 2/4/44. Flt Lt 2/10/69. Retd 2/10/71. Re-entered 10/7/72. A Cdre 1/7/95. Retd 1/7/97.
HANSON G. H. Born 9/11/47. Sqn Ldr 1/7/85. Retd 11/1/87.
HARDY K. SRN. Born 21/8/12. Sister 4/7/40. Retd 31/7/49 rtg Senior Sister.
HARPER M. SRN. Born 18/11/08. Sister 1/4/41. Retd 31/8/50.
HARRIS E. M. ARRC DN RCNT RNT. Born 26/6/29. Sqn Offr 8/8/70. Retd 26/6/84.
HARRIS I. J. CB RRC SCM. Born 26/9/26. A Cdre 1/1/82. Retd 26/11/84.
HARRIS M. A. SRN RSCN. Born 18/1/33. Flt Offr 12/11/70.
HARRISON C. B. DN. Born 13/12/35. Sqn Ldr 17/3/73. Retd 1/10/85.
HARRISON M. J. SRN SCM. Born 27/6/33. Sqn Offr 4/4/71. Retd 20/4/74.
HAWKE G. L. ARRC SRN. Born 14/5/25. Sqn Ldr 3/5/64. Retd 14/5/80.
HAWKINS M. A. ARRC SRN. Born 26/12/05. Sister 3/10/39. Retd 9/11/48 rtg Senior Sister.

HAYES K. B. ARRC SRN. Born 2/2/25. Sqn Offr 16/2/63. Retd 2/2/80.
HAZELGROVE A. SRN SCM. Born 10/8/35. Flt Offr 8/4/65. Retd 3/1/69.
HERD M. E. SRN SCM. Born 31/5/40. Sqn Ldr 24/7/74. Retd 7/9/80.
HEWITT E. J. M. ARRC SRN SCM. Born 14/5/09. Sqn Offr 1/2/49. Retd 1/10/52.
HIGGINS J. M. RRC SRN SCM. Born 16/12/12. Wg Offr 1/1/61. Retd 2/4/68.
HIGGS M. ARRC SRN. Born 1/10/29. Sqn Offr 30/10/65. Retd 1/7/77.
HINSON P. J. SRN. Born 4/1/58. Sqn Ldr 21/5/92. Retd 14/3/96.
HIRST R. B. SRN SCM. Born 25/6/39. Flt Offr 8/2/67. Retd 31/1/73.
HOGLAND J. R. ARRC SRN. Born 1/7/20. Sqn Offr 21/7/57. Retd 12/6/65.
HOLLIDAY G. ARRC. Born 23/2/50. Sqn Ldr 25/9/88. Retd 14/3/96.
HOLLINGDALE P. M. SRN SRCN. Born 23/10/25. Sqn Offr 22/6/63. Retd 30/4/69.
HOLT E. B. SCM. Born 8/7/47. Flt Offr 3/12/64. Retd 29/8/81.
HOPE D. P. SRN. Born 1/7/24. Sqn Offr 1/4/62. Retd 25/11/66.
HOPKINS K. J. ARRC SCM. Born 19/10/37. Sqn Ldr 13/8/74. Retd 7/2/82.
HORN A. M. SRN. Born 27/1/13. Sister 1/5/40. Retd 1/4/45.
HORSFORD E. E. SRN. Born 9/10/98. Sister 17/12/26. Retd 4/6/34.
HOYLE H. ARRC RM. Born 19/10/60. Commd 3/2/85. Sqn Ldr 16/6/94. Retd 3/2/01.
HUTCHINS D. ARRC SRN SCM. Born 20/7/30. Sqn Offr 23/9/67. Retd 23/9/75.
IBBOTT B. A. SRN SCM. Born 1/8/38. Flt Offr 3/12/64. Retd 3/12/70.
JAMIESON L. N. ARRC SRN. Born 23/7/10. Sister 1/10/39. Retd 1/12/48 rtg Senior Sister.
JOHNS B. M. A. ARRC SRN. Born 1/8/21. Sqn Offr 7/7/58. Retd 1/8/74.
JOHNSON F. M. SRN RFN. Born 30/3/21. Sqn Offr 27/5/58. Retd 1/6/66.
JOHNSON K. D. SRN. Born 11/2/02. Sister 27/1/33. Retd 7/4/46 rtg Matron.
JOHNSTON M. E. ARRC RM. Born 7/8/33. Sqn Ldr 15/11/69. Retd 7/8/88.
JONES G. RRC SRN. Born 3/7/11. Gp Offr 15/7/63. Retd 3/7/68.
JOY S. N. ARRC SCM RSCN. Born 24/2/38. Sqn Ldr 2/8/78. Retd 5/6/83.
JOY W. E. ARRC RSCN. Born 6/4/52. Sqn Ldr 22/1/88. Retd 25/6/94.
KEEBLE C. L. RM. Born 23/2/60. Sqn Ldr 14/5/93. Retd 14/3/96.
KELL H. E. AARC SCM. Born 6/6/45. Sqn Ldr 1/7/80. Retd 25/1/87.
KEMP H. M. SRN SCM. Born 21/3/30. Sqn Offr 16/7/66. Retd 12/8/73.
KENEFICK L. M. SRN. Born 16/10/17. Sqn Offr 20/6/58. Retd 31/3/59.
KENT D. M. SRN. Born 5/2/21. Flt Offr 21/3/53. Retd 13/8/60.
KIDMAN E. F. RM. Born 17/5/47. Sqn Ldr 22/3/83. Retd 15/12/92.
KING A. G. SRN RNT. Born 21/4/37. Flt Offr 4/12/63. Retd 31/8/71.
KING E. E. E. SRN. Born 3/7/13. Sqn Offr 24/6/57. Retd 20/7/66.
KING I. E. ARRC SCM. Born 31/1/31. Sqn Ldr 21/7/67. Retd 31/1/86.
KINGSTON M. A. SRN. Born 16/4/16. Sqn Offr 1/4/62. Retd 16/4/71.
KIRK M. L. SRN. Born 5/3/26. Flt Offr 1/12/55. Retd 20/11/60.
KIRKHAM O. A. SRN. Born 1/7/26. Sqn Offr 1/4/62. Retd 16/11/66.
KNOX E. M. ARRC SRN. Born 3/12/08. Sqn Offr 1/5/49. Retd 12/1/51.
KRUSIN A. M. ARRC SRN RSCN SCM. Born 16/1/13. Gp Offr 1/7/66. Retd 22/4/69.
LA-ROCHE A. SCM. Born 25/6/52. Flt Offr 15/9/79. Retd 1/8/85.
LANE D. E. MBE ARRC. Born 22/10/23. Sqn Offr 15/7/66. Retd 22/10/78.
LAURENCE R. Born 26/3/54. Sqn Ldr 23/5/91. Retd 31/8/00.
LAY E. ARRC SRN. Born 8/1/17. Sqn Offr 5/7/54. Retd 8/1/67.
LEACHMAN D. M. ARRC SRN. Born 21/6/09. Sister 25/1/39. Retd 19/4/48 rtg Senior Sister.
LEIPER J. SRN. Born 7/11/11. Sister 4/1/40. Retd 20/7/49 rtg Senior Sister.
LEVICK C. ARRC. Born 5/10/42. Sqn Offr 23/2/78. Retd 7/2/85.
LEWIS-BOWEN A. J. RM. Born 10/2/53. Commd 29/1/79. Sqn Ldr 11/8/88. Retd 28/1/95.
LUMLEY M. O. ARRC SRN. Born 24/11/18. Wg Offr 1/1/68. Retd 24/11/73.
MacBAIN C. M. C. SRN. Born 6/8/15. Flt Offr 1/2/49. Retd 14/2/52.
MacFIE A. K. ARRC SRN. Born 10/8/06. Sqn Offr 1/2/49. Retd 29/9/51.
MacKAY D. E. SRN. Born 25/3/13. Sister 6/3/40. Retd 5/3/45.
MacMILLAN M. SRN. Born 1/7/21. Flt Offr 11/6/60. Retd 13/10/64.
MALLALIEU J. M. ARRC SRN. Born 25/10/05. Sister 9/1/38. Retd 31/10/48 rtg Senior Sister.
MANNING R. C. RM. Born 11/10/41. Wg Cdr 1/1/88. Retd 11/10/96.
MAPP Y. E. RM. Born 14/3/41. Sqn Ldr 5/6/82. Retd 26/11/88.
MARSH M. A. SRN SCM. Born 1/7/19. Sqn Offr 1/10/60. Retd 1/10/64.
MARTIN E. E. SRN. Born 3/10/30. Flt Offr 1/11/60. Retd 29/3/65.
MASON C. M. SRN. Born 21/5/33. Sqn Offr 27/9/69. Retd 13/2/71.
MASSAM R. ARRC SRN. Born 28/7/19. Wg Offr 1/7/70. Retd 28/7/74.
MATCHETT J. K. SRN. Born 11/9/27. Sqn Offr 16/2/63. Retd 16/2/69.
McCABE I. M. Born 14/2/39. Sqn Ldr 4/1/75. Retd 1/6/83.
McCARDLE J. SRN RFN SCM. Born 7/12/12. Sqn Offr 8/1/55. Retd 8/1/68.
McCREADY N. SRN. Born 1/7/23. Flt Offr 14/9/57. Retd 1/8/60.
MCCULLOCH J. Born 24/12/57. Sqn Ldr 18/2/93. Retd 1/8/98.

McLEAN M. McK. SRN. Born 27/9/23. Flt Offr 16/5/59. Retd 31/8/61.
McLUCKIE M. D. SRN. Born 9/4/37. Flt Offr 6/4/66. Retd 31/12/72.
McNAIR M. K. SRN RFN. Born 18/4/16. Wg Offr 1/1/67. Retd 18/4/71.
McPHAIL A. ARRC SRN. Born 1/7/17. Sqn Offr 30/8/60. Retd 24/7/65.
McPHERSON M. S. SRN RSCN. Born 20/10/12. Sqn Offr 9/6/54. Retd 20/10/65.
McTEAR V. L. Born 1/7/37. Sqn Offr 17/12/72. Retd 4/2/79.
METCALFE J. ARRC SRN SCM. Born 19/7/27. Sqn Offr 1/2/66. Retd 1/2/72.
METCALFE J. CB RRC SRN SCM. Born 8/1/23. A Cdre 1/1/79. Retd 29/11/81.
MILLAR M. M. SCM. Born 30/11/34. Wg Cdr 1/7/80. Retd 1/7/83.
MILLER R. B. F. SRN. Born 9/8/07. Sqn Offr 1/2/49. Retd 9/8/60 rtg Wg Offr.
MITCHELL L. M. SRN. Born 26/2/12. Sister 1/8/40. Retd 12/4/45.
MOENS A. R. SRN. Born 4/2/25. Sqn Offr 1/4/62. Retd 15/4/63.
MOFFATT A. RRC SRN. Born 24/4/25. Sqn Ldr 19/8/68. Retd 24/4/80.
MORGAN G. Born 29/10/52. Flt Lt 25/3/86. Retd 12/12/88.
MORGAN K. A. SCM. Born 8/12/43. Sqn Offr 4/1/79. Retd 2/2/86.
MORRIS D. P. SRN. Born 6/9/22. Sqn Offr 1/4/62. Retd 6/1/68.
MOSELEY P. M. SCM RSCN. Born 21/1/41. Sqn Offr 15/12/80. Retd 24/11/81.
MYLES A. P. Born 29/12/44. Flt Lt 8/4/77. Retd 29/12/82.
NEEHAM D. R. Born 9/7/48. Sqn Ldr 4/7/84. Retd 6/2/89.
NEWBROOK W. A. SRN. Born 20/3/18. Sqn Offr 20/11/59. Retd 20/11/66.
NEWTON C. A. SRN. Born 1/7/34. Flt Offr 6/10/61. Retd 14/11/63.
NEWTON C. M. SRN. Born 31/12/60. Sqn Ldr 18/5/95. Retd 14/3/96.
O'CONNOR M. M. RRC SRN SCM. Born 26/4/25. Gp Capt 1/7/76. Retd 26/4/80.
O'DONOVAN M. SRN. Born 18/2/18. Flt Offr 1/2/49. Retd 23/10/54.
O'KEEFFE J. J. Born 16/4/42. Sqn Ldr 6/4/85. Retd 31/3/93.
O'LEARY T. P. Born 30/7/40. Flt Lt 4/4/81. Retd 4/4/87.
O'REGAN T. S. SRN. Born 5/2/11. Sqn Offr 28/8/52. Retd 28/8/62.
OAKMAN J. ARRC. Born 6/1/54. Sqn Ldr 12/12/87. Retd 14/3/96.
ORR A. M. RRC RSCN. Born 22/7/35. Wg Cdr 1/7/88. Retd 1/1/92.
OSBORNE D. B. SRN RSCN. Born 30/3/57. Sqn Ldr 24/1/94. Retd 14/3/96.
OVENS E. R. K. SRN SCM. Born 27/3/21. Sqn Offr 21/11/65. Retd 21/11/71.
OXBOROUGH C. V. ARRC. Born 15/9/34. Sqn Offr 24/6/74. Retd 24/6/84.
PAGE M. M. SRN. Born 1/7/28. Flt Offr 1/10/57. Retd 18/2/62.
PARKER B. J. SRN RFN. Born 1/7/30. Flt Offr 1/10/60. Retd 5/9/66.
PARTINGTON R. A. L. RRC RM. Born 14/6/33. Commd 11/11/57. Wg Cdr 1/1/80. Retd 14/6/88.
PASIFULL D. F. SRN RSCN. Born 1/7/05. Sqn Offr 12/3/54. Retd 24/3/61.
PEDDER M. E. Born 11/4/40. Wg Cdr 1/7/85. Retd 11/4/95.
PENNY F. A. SRN. Born 19/6/41. Sqn Offr 17/12/74. Retd 18/11/75.
PENROSE R. A. RRC SRN. Born 18/6/25. Wg Cdr 1/1/73. Retd 18/6/80.
PERKINS J. B. BA DN RNT CertEd. Born 31/10/48. Sqn Ldr 13/4/92. Retd 14/3/97.
PERKINS S. J. Born 24/3/33. Sqn Ldr 30/10/72. Retd 7/4/83.
PETTIFER S. M. SRN. Born 27/2/48. Flt Offr 15/8/73. Retd 1/1/80.
PIRIE M. L. ARRC SCM. Born 16/5/42. Sqn Offr 11/4/78. Retd 9/6/85.
POULTER J. R. SRN. Born 15/3/47. Flt Lt 13/3/82. Retd 22/2/86.
PRICE C. V. RRC SRN. Born 2/12/16. Sqn Offr 4/10/60. Retd 2/12/71.
PROUD E. B. ARRC RM. Born 22/5/52. Sqn Ldr 23/7/88. Retd 28/6/97.
REED A. A. RRC. Born 25/1/30. A Cdre 1/1/85. Retd 25/8/85.
REILLY P. J. Born 18/11/57. Sqn Ldr 23/7/92. Retd 14/9/96.
ROBINSON P. SCM. Born 29/3/44. Sqn Offr 2/6/79. Retd 23/2/87.
RODDY A. SRN. Born 1/7/25. Flt Offr 23/7/57. Retd 5/12/64.
ROE B. A. SRN. Born 1/7/30. Flt Offr 29/5/58. Retd 30/11/61.
ROQUES L. M. ARRC SRN. Born 1/1/12. Wg Offr 1/1/61. Retd 10/4/61.
ROSE M. F. SRN SCM. Born 2/2/32. Sqn Offr 21/3/67. Retd 2/7/72.
RUSSELL D. D. SRN. Born 28/7/18. Flt Offr 23/7/49. Retd 20/9/54.
RYAN E. F. T. H. SRN. Born 28/2/14. Sqn Offr 6/1/54. Retd 10/10/57.
SABINI D. L. SRN. Born 14/11/53. Sqn Ldr 26/2/89. Retd 7/10/89.
SANDISON E. A. RRC. Born 23/11/40. Gp Capt 1/1/88. Retd 30/11/91.
SANSOME A. J. SRN. Born 10/9/54. Sqn Ldr 6/1/88. Retd 3/10/92.
SCOFIELD A. J. ARRC. Born 1/7/48. Wg Cdr 1/1/92. Retd 1/7/98.
SCOTT L. R. Born 9/1/55. Flt Lt 23/9/81. Retd 21/2/83.
SCOTT M. M. SRN. Born 1/7/31. Flt Offr 1/4/62. Retd 1/8/64.
SEXTON R. ARRC RM. Born 9/9/52. Sqn Ldr 3/7/86. Retd 3/2/89.
SHANNON F. Born 16/3/53. Sqn Ldr 20/12/90. Retd 2/11/96.
SHAW M. J. MSc BSc CertEd(RNT). Born 23/2/48. Sqn Ldr 3/12/92. Retd 7/5/99.
SHAW M. M. RRC RM. Born 7/4/33. Gp Capt 1/1/85. Retd 31/8/88.
SHELDON M. A. ARRC. Born 19/10/25. Sqn Offr 20/9/67. Retd 19/10/80.

SHIMELL J. M. Born 11/6/50. Flt Offr 15/8/79. Retd 31/8/85.
SILCOCK V. M. J. RRC SRN. Born 17/10/20. Wg Offr 1/1/68. Retd 31/1/70.
SILVERTHORNE E. RM. Born 13/6/35. Sqn Offr 2/12/73. Retd 2/12/79.
SIMACEK J. J. Born 11/7/46. Flt Lt 3/4/82. Retd 1/5/87.
SIMKIN M. J. SRN SCM. Born 29/1/39. Flt Offr 4/1/67. Retd 17/11/73.
SIMPSON G. M. C. RRC. Born 12/8/42. Wg Cdr 1/7/85. Retd 13/3/89.
SIMPSON J. ARRC. Born 30/9/40. Sqn Offr 29/10/76. Retd 15/9/85.
SINKER J. E. SRN RM. Born 12/6/50. Sqn Ldr 22/5/85. Retd 7/5/89.
SLADE C. E. SRN SCM. Born 22/5/35. Sqn Offr 9/2/69. Retd 12/7/69.
SMALL I. A. SRN. Born 20/3/23. Flt Offr 1/5/55. Retd 9/1/60.
SMEDLEY J. D. RRC. Born 17/3/28. Wg Cdr 1/7/78. Retd 17/3/83.
SMITH T. A. RRC. Born 21/11/43. Sqn Ldr 11/1/87. Retd 14/3/97.
SOPER B. SRN. Born 15/2/22. Sqn Offr 26/2/59. Retd 23/9/59.
SOUTHERN-ROBERTS D. SRN. Born 22/1/42. Sqn Ldr 6/4/84. Retd 6/10/85.
STACEY R. C. RM. Born 20/12/56. Commd 9/6/85. Sqn Ldr 19/3/93. Retd 14/3/97.
STAINER S. M. SRN. Born 29/9/40. Flt Offr 1/9/66. Retd 31/8/70.
STALKER M. MacD. ARRC SRN. Born 1/7/29. Flt Offr 20/12/56. Retd 7/8/63.
STEEL I. B. SRN SCM. Born 11/6/22. Sqn Offr 15/9/61. Retd 4/4/72.
STEER P. Born 27/3/56. Flt Lt 16/1/93. Retd 14/3/96.
STEWART J. M. SCM RSCN. Born 16/1/34. Sqn Offr 31/5/72. Retd 4/10/81.
STONES P. ARRC RM. Born 24/11/35. Sqn Offr 13/4/76. Retd 24/11/90.
SURRIDGE P. D. MBE ARRC RM. Born 24/4/43. Sqn Ldr 12/1/77. Retd 9/10/94.
SWINDLEHURST P. A. SRN. Born 5/12/40. Sqn Ldr 15/12/74. Retd 1/8/80.
SYKES J. E. A. SRN. Born 10/6/35. Flt Offr 3/10/62. Retd 22/9/63.
TAIT I. J. SRN RFN. Born 1/7/25. Flt Offr 11/11/61. Retd 1/6/65.
TAYLOR A. M. SRN RSCN. Born 7/12/29. Sqn Offr 6/2/67. Retd 20/2/72.
TAYLOR J. L. Born 18/5/48. Flt Lt 7/8/79. Retd 22/6/84.
TEED N. S. MBE SRN. Born 4/5/05. Sister 31/3/37. Retd 5/7/48 rtg Senior Sister.
THOMAS K. SRN SCM. Born 26/5/13. Sqn Offr 10/2/51. Retd 10/2/65.
TIBBIT D. G. W. Born 1/10/50. Flt Lt 22/5/81. Retd 1/10/88.
TILBROOK E. M. RRC SRN. Born 1/7/02. Wg Offr 1/7/52. Retd 14/7/57.
TOOP J. M. SRN. Born 13/4/28. Sqn Offr 1/5/71. Retd 1/5/77.
TRICK D. M. RRC SRN. Born 14/1/13. Wg Offr 26/6/63. Retd 14/1/68.
TUCKER D. R. Born 11/6/53. Sqn Ldr 20/2/90. Retd 14/9/96.
TYLER M. H. RSCN. Born 13/4/35. Sqn Offr 8/5/79. Retd 11/8/85.
UPFOLD M. M. A. ARRC RM. Born 13/2/36. Sqn Ldr 8/2/75. Retd 8/2/88.
UTLEY S. RRC. Born 1/1/46. Wg Cdr 1/7/89. Retd 14/12/96.
WALKER E. K. Born 20/1/56. Flt Lt 20/8/83. Retd 13/11/86.
WALSH D. M. SRN. Born 1/7/31. Flt Offr 7/11/60. Retd 6/2/64.
WALSH M. B. ARRC SRN. Born 15/8/20. Wg Offr 1/1/70. Retd 15/8/75.
WALSH M. D. SRN SCM. Born 12/4/28. Sqn Offr 23/2/69. Retd 23/2/75.
WATSON A. SRN. Born 25/3/40. Flt Offr 6/2/67. Retd 7/11/70.
WATSON E. M. SRN. Born 18/1/27. Sqn Offr 29/4/67. Retd 29/4/77.
WATSON J. A. SRN. Born 10/6/42. Sqn Offr 22/1/76. Retd 28/5/76.
WATT M. V. SRN. Born 2/3/31. Sqn Offr 1/6/66. Retd 2/6/81.
WEEKS L. Born 8/1/48. Sqn Ldr 5/4/87. Retd 1/10/87.
WELBY M. M. C. SRN. Born 1/7/34. Flt Offr 1/4/62. Retd 21/10/66.
WELFORD A. M. RRC RM. Born 25/6/45. Wg Cdr 1/7/92. Retd 25/6/00.
WESTMAN D. M. BA RNT SCM. Born 3/9/46. Sqn Ldr 27/3/80. Retd 15/9/85.
WHITE N. A. SRN. Born 1/7/21. Flt Offr 18/6/59. Retd 11/11/61.
WILLCOX F. H. ARRC SRN. Born 24/4/12. Flt Offr 1/2/49. Retd 1/4/52.
WILLIAMSON Dame Alice Mary. DBE RRC SRN. Born 18/1/03. A Cdt 1/9/56. Retd 1/9/59.
WILLLIAMS E. E. R. SRN. Born 7/4/20. Flt Offr 7/3/54. Retd 17/3/85.
WILSON M. SRN SCM. Born 1/5/39. Flt Offr 28/4/66. Retd 26/6/73.
WINTER C. SRN. Born 16/12/46. Sqn Offr 22/7/82. Retd 14/3/96.
WOOD M. MBE SRN. Born 14/6/28. Sqn Offr 14/2/63. Retd 3/12/67.
WOOD M. J. SRN SCM. Born 1/7/36. Flt Offr 4/4/63. Retd 20/3/67.
WOODBRIDGE V. T. Born 12/10/59. Sqn Ldr 24/9/94. Retd 14/9/96.
WRIGHT D. H. SRN. Born 28/2/20. Sqn Offr 9/8/56. Retd 31/1/59.
WRIGHT S. W. SRN. Born 4/12/39. Flt Offr 20/5/70. Retd 31/3/76.
WRIGHT V. D. ARRC SCM. Born 19/4/36. Sqn Ldr 9/12/73. Retd 5/6/83.
WYATT J. B. Born 3/6/43. Sqn Ldr 8/11/86. Retd 21/3/88.
WYATT K. N. SRN. Born 4/3/24. Sqn Offr 1/4/62. Retd 10/4/67.
YENDELL A. B. RRC SRN. Born 1/7/06. Sqn Offr 6/2/52. Retd 6/5/61.
YOUNG M. J. ARRC SRN RSCN. Born 30/8/28. Sqn Offr 31/12/67. Retd 12/6/73.

# OBITUARY

Retired Officers whose deaths have been reported since July 2000

### ROYAL AIR FORCE

| Name | Date of Death | Name | Date of Death |
|---|---|---|---|
| ACONS S. J. Sqn Ldr | 9.4.01 | BROWN F. MIMgt Flt Lt | 1.9.00 |
| ADAMS F. J. Flt Lt | 9.11.00 | BROWN R. N. S. BA Sqn Ldr | 15.7.00 |
| ALLEN G. Flt Lt | 19.2.01 | BROWNLOW R. J. BSc Flt Lt | 29.8.00 |
| ALTON J. L. Sqn Ldr | 25.10.00 | BUCHANAN R. J. T. AFC Sqn Ldr | 25.4.01 |
| AMSDEN A. S. MRCS LRCP Gp Capt | 15.3.01 | BUCKLAND G. W. DFC Wg Cdr | 10.7.00 |
| ANDERSON A. R. L. Sqn Ldr | 13.8.00 | BULLOCK I. B. Sqn Ldr | 11.10.00 |
| ANDERSON M. M. Flt Lt | 5.4.01 | BURGE G. P. Flt Lt | 16.2.01 |
| ANDREW H. Sqn Ldr | 7.5.01 | BUTLER A. W. J. Sqn dr | 23.3.01 |
| ANDREW T. A. F. Flt Lt | 13.4.01 | CAIRNS R. MBE Sqn Ldr | 8.2.00 |
| ANDREWS H. W. G. DFC Wg Cdr | 29.3.01 | CARLING B. R. Flt Lt | 20.12.00 |
| ANSTEE P. J. Wg Cdr | 25.8.00 | CARR J. W. DFC Sqn Ldr | 24.3.01 |
| ARBURY K. W. C. Flt Lt | 23.3.01 | CARTRIDGE D. L. DSO DFC* Wg Cdr | 5.7.00 |
| ARMSTRONG E. MBE Flt Lt | 15.7.00 | CASTLE R. B. DFC Flt Lt | 13.1.01 |
| ARNOLD I. Flt Lt | 22.7.00 | CASWELL A. W. CBE CEng MRAeS | |
| ARNOTT D. A. DFC AFC FIMgt A Cdre | 1.3.01 | Gp Capt | 28.11.00 |
| BAGNALL D. R. DSO DFC Wg Cdr | 29.12.00 | CHAMBERLAIN L. T. Flt Lt | 27.11.00 |
| BAILEY L. A. Sqn Ldr | 28.3.01 | CHAPMAN A. F. Sqn Ldr | 20.6.00 |
| BAKER A. K. Flt Lt | 8.12.00 | CHAPMAN G. K. DFM Flt Lt | 2.3.01 |
| BALL H. Wg Cdr | 28.2.01 | COLLIER J. B. Sqn Ldr | 23.7.00 |
| BANCROFT-WILSON G. M. Sqn Ldr | 3.6.01 | COLLO J. C. Flt Lt | 16.2.01 |
| BARFORD J. E. Flt Lt | 10.5.01 | CONSTABLE-MAXWELL M. H. DSO | |
| BARGH P. C. DFC Sqn Ldr | 30.6.00 | DFC MA Wg Cdr | 15.8.00 |
| BARNARD D. A. MBE Sqn Ldr | 4.12.00 | COOBAN E. P. Sqn Ldr | 24.1.01 |
| BARRELL W. A. AFC AFM Sqn Ldr | 24.2.01 | COOK G. R. Wg Cdr | 12.6.01 |
| BARRETT G. P. MBE Wg Cdr | 27.3.01 | COOKE D. S. E. MA Sqn Ldr | 28.2.01 |
| BAXTER R. Flt Lt | 1.9.00 | COOKE F. E. Flt Lt | 22.8.00 |
| BAYLIS J. F. H. Flt Lt | 30.4.00 | COPPOCK B. A. Flt Lt | 17.12.00 |
| BEADNELL A. G. Wg Cdr | 9.9.00 | CORBISHLEY J. OBE AFC ACIS | |
| BEER R. H. W. Sqn Ldr | 20.2.01 | ACA(NZ) MIMgt Gp Capt | 2.5.01 |
| BENNETT A. L. FIMgt Gp Capt | 20.4.01 | CORDERY A. S. Flt Lt | 16.1.01 |
| BERE G. A. Sqn Ldr | 8.9.00 | CRITCHLOW J. L. BA CEng Wg Cdr | 22.6.00 |
| BERRY H. MBE Flt Lt | 21.3.01 | CROUCH R. DFC Sqn Ldr | 21.3.01 |
| BERRY R. CBE DSO DFC* A Cdre | 13.8.00 | CRUTCHLEY J. J. S. Sqn Ldr | 3.5.01 |
| BETTY T. V. CEng MRAeS MIMgt | | CUSWORTH A. P. Flt Lt | 4.3.01 |
| FINucE Sqn Ldr | 29.5.01 | DALE H. Flt Lt | 13.2.01 |
| BILLINGTON W. MBE Sqn Ldr | 1.4.01 | DAVENPORT V. S. BEM Flt Lt | 8.8.00 |
| BISHOP L. H. Flt Lt | 10.5.00 | DAVID M. I. OBE FIMgt A Cdre | 27.8.00 |
| BISHOP W. J. MBE Sqn Ldr | 12.12.00 | DAVIES E. G. Wg Cdr | 20.12.00 |
| BLISS T. H. Flt Lt | 26.11.00 | DAVIES I. AFC Sqn Ldr | 7.2.01 |
| BLYTHE J. A. CEng MRAeS Sqn Ldr | 11.10.00 | DAVISON J. Flt Lt | 9.8.00 |
| BOATMAN D. W. MRCS LRCP DPH | | DAVISON M. R. DFC Flt Lt | 3.4.01 |
| Gp Capt | 19.3.01 | DAW W. H. J. MBE Sqn Ldr | 15.12.00 |
| BOLLAND G. A. CBE Gp Capt | 20.1.01 | DAWKINS B. H. Sqn Ldr | 9.1.01 |
| BOOTH G. E. Sqn Ldr | 3.9.00 | de BURTON B. MBE MIMgt Wg Cdr | 29.12.00 |
| BOURNE W. J. BSc MIEE Wg Cdr | 28.5.01 | de VAL L. A. Flt Lt | 18.7.00 |
| BOWERS R. A. J. Sqn Ldr | 25.2.01 | DEAN A. H. BSc Sqn Ldr | 11.12.00 |
| BOYD J. N. B. AFC Sqn Ldr | 11.1.01 | DEBENHAM F. E. AFC Sqn Ldr | 23.3.01 |
| BOYD The Rev W. T. MA Gp Capt | 14.8.00 | DERWENT H. L. AFC Wg Cdr | 9.1.01 |
| BRABAZON W. J. Flt Lt | 8.1.01 | DESEMONIE J. V. Sqn Ldr | 24.10.00 |
| BRAND R. Flt Lt | 25.4.01 | DEVAS W. G. CBE DFC AFC Gp Capt | 13.4.01 |
| BRIDGES R. C. Sqn Ldr | 16.6.01 | DICKINSON B. G. OBE A Cdre | 7.2.01 |
| BRITTAIN H. G. DFC AFC Sqn Ldr | 19.6.00 | DICKINSON R. N. BEM Flt Lt | 15.3.01 |
| BROMLEY C. W. DFC AFC Wg Cdr | 25.1.01 | DOBSON P. DSO DFC AFC Wg Cdr | 26.12.00 |

| Name | Date of Death | Name | Date of Death |
|------|---------------|------|---------------|
| DONKIN P. L. CBE DSO A Cdre | 12.7.00 | HALL W. J. Flt Lt | 14.10.00 |
| DONOVAN C. J. Sqn Ldr | 24.11.00 | HAMMOND J. P. Sqn Ldr | 20.11.00 |
| DOWLING J. R. MBE DFC* AFC | | HANKINS A. J. BSc CEng MIEE DipEl | |
| Wg Cdr | 14.7.00 | Sqn Ldr | 11.8.00 |
| DRAPER D. AFC Flt Lt | 28.7.00 | HARDING W. F. Flt Lt | 15.1.01 |
| DULIEU R. H. D. Sqn Ldr | 6.3.01 | HARGREAVES B. I. Flt Lt | 10.3.00 |
| DUNCAN J. R. Wg Cdr | 19.1.01 | HARRIS G. W. MA Sqn Ldr | 14.2.01 |
| DUNKLEY A. G. H. Sqn Ldr | 1.2.01 | HARRIS N. T. Wg Cdr | 24.6.00 |
| DUTT E. R. AFC Wg Cdr | 1.7.00 | HARRIS W. I. AFC Wg Cdr | 28.8.00 |
| EASTMEAD S. A. Flt Lt | 5.3.01 | HARRISON I. A. Flt Lt | 27.5.01 |
| EDWARDS J. Flt Lt | 12.8.00 | HARVEY C. C. MBE Flt Lt | 29.8.00 |
| ELLARD A. W. Fg Offr | 23.6.00 | HATTON J. E. Sqn Ldr | 17.10.00 |
| ELMES H. D. MBE Sqn Ldr | 15.3.01 | HATTON T. G. Flt Lt | 21.9.00 |
| ELTRINGHAM J. C. BA Sqn Ldr | 14.5.01 | HAYR Sir Kenneth. KCB KBE AFC* AM | 2.6.01 |
| ENGLISH R. G. Flt Lt | 3.9.00 | HAYWOOD D. Flt Lt | 16.10.00 |
| EVANS K. G. Sqn Ldr | 22.12.00 | HEATON J. H. Sqn Ldr | 24.6.00 |
| EVANS S. L. Flt Lt | 1.9.00 | HEMMING E. F. MIMgt Wg Cdr | 29.9.00 |
| EVERETT D. J. Sqn Ldr | 23.7.00 | HENTON D. F. BA Flt Lt | 2.7.00 |
| FALK E. H. R. Wg Cdr | 7.2.01 | HEPBURN A. J. MIMgt Sqn Ldr | 12.12.00 |
| FANE de SALIS A. R. OBE Gp Capt | 24.3.01 | HEWAT R. M. MRCS LRCP DOMS | |
| FARMER R. G. Flt Lt | 21.9.00 | Gp Capt | 16.2.01 |
| FIDLER G. T. J. DFC Flt Lt | 21.11.00 | HIPPMAN V. V. Flt Lt | 23.9.00 |
| FIDLIN W. J. Flt Lt | 29.3.01 | HODGE S. R. Wg Cdr | 5.9.00 |
| FIELD R. A. Wg Cdr | 11.3.01 | HOLDEN E. DFC Wg Cdr | 27.1.01 |
| FITTON T. E. J. CBE MRAeS A Cdre | 31.8.00 | HOLDER Sir Paul KBE CB DSO DFC | |
| FLOWERDEW L. L. CEng FRAeS FIMgt | | MSc PhD FRAeS AM | 22.4.01 |
| Gp Capt | 12.1.01 | HOLGATE G. W. Flt Lt | 28.8.00 |
| FOOT Rev L. F. Wg Cdr | 6.5.01 | HOLGATE S. G. Flt Lt | 5.8.00 |
| FORSYTH I. R. Sqn Ldr | 16.6.00 | HOLLAND A. L. MBE AFM Sqn Ldr | 24.11.00 |
| FOSTER A. E. OBE CEng MRAeS | | HOLLOWAY C. T. E. Sqn Ldr | 29.12.00 |
| Gp Capt | 14.2.01 | HOLMES T. Flt Lt | 22.11.00 |
| FOWLER D. S. MBE Gp Capt | 10.8.00 | HONE D. T. Flt Lt | 24.12.00 |
| FRANCIS B. J. Sqn Offr | 23.10.00 | HOOPER A. M. Sqn Ldr | 30.7.00 |
| FRITH C. J. Sqn Ldr | 10.12.00 | HOPE P. W. BA Wg Cdr | 23.3.01 |
| FROST N. H. DFC Flt Lt | 3.9.00 | HOPKINSON H. DSO Sqn Ldr | 3.7.00 |
| FRY R. H. DFC BA Wg Cdr | 24.1.01 | HORTON R. J. Flt Lt | 7.4.01 |
| FURNIVAL R. Flt Lt | 9.3.01 | HOSEGOOD G. G. Flt Lt | 19.8.00 |
| GABILLIA R. H. Flt Lt | 17.11.00 | HOWELL E. A. OBE DFC Wg Cdr | 4.8.00 |
| GALLANDERS D. DFC DFM Sqn Ldr | 1.6.01 | HOWELL R. A. AFC Sqn Ldr | 25.6.00 |
| GARDNER M. E. Sqn Ldr | 7.6.01 | HOWELL R. Flt Lt | 18.6.00 |
| GARRARD L. Flt Lt | 16.2.01 | HUDDY L. G. Flt Lt | 26.11.00 |
| GARSTIN J. H. AFC Wg Cdr | 14.8.00 | HUDSON R. A. Flt Lt | 8.11.00 |
| GARTON W. F. Flt Lt | 23.12.00 | HUGHES J. J. Sqn Ldr | 21.1.01 |
| GATES J. W. L. Flt Lt | 3.1.01 | HUGHES R. G. Flt Lt | 18.10.00 |
| GEORGE R. G. Flt Lt | 12.8.00 | HUNTER A. K. OBE BSc MSc Gp Capt | 18.4.01 |
| GIBB J. S. E. Flt Lt | 27.7.00 | HUNTINGDON J. R. AFC DFM Flt Lt | 2.9.00 |
| GIBBARD V. G. AFC Flt Lt | 17.3.01 | HURRING V. J. R. DFC Flt Lt | 6.9.00 |
| GILL W. A. DFC Sqn Ldr | 17.7.00 | IVEY L. Flt Lt | 8.1.01 |
| GILLIES A. J. Flt Lt | 20.5.01 | JACKSON J. A. G. CBE DFC AFC FIMgt | |
| GILROY J. P. Flt Lt | 13.6.01 | A Cdre | 12.11.00 |
| GOODE W. A. Flt Lt | 17.2.01 | JACKSON J. D. MIMgt Sqn Ldr | 15.3.01 |
| GOODING K. H. CB OBE AVM | 4.8.01 | JAMIESON W. M. MBE Wg Cdr | 14.12.00 |
| GOODSELL G. S. Wg Cdr | 28.7.00 | JARVIS J. A. DFC AFC Wg Cdr | 4.6.01 |
| GOUGH A. H. Flt Lt | 22.3.01 | JENKINS F. V. B. Sqn Ldr | 22.3.01 |
| GOULD R. H. MBE MA Sqn Ldr | 22.1.01 | JENKINS H. L. MD BS Gp Capt | 2.3.01 |
| GOWING R. MBE Wg Cdr | 19.3.01 | JENKINS J. G. DFC MIMgt MCIPD | |
| GREEN A. R. Flt Lt | 14.1.01 | Sqn Ldr | 17.2.00 |
| GROVES H. A. Flt Lt | 2.10.00 | JENKINS J. R. R. MRCS LRCP Gp Capt | 9.3.01 |
| GUMBRELL H. W. Flt Lt | 24.8.00 | JENKINSON F. Flt Lt | 7.11.00 |
| GUTTERIDGE The Rev R. J. C. MA | | JOHNSTONE A. V. R. CB DFC AE AVM | 13.12.00 |
| Wg Cdr | 30.11.00 | JOLLY J. D. MBE MA Wg Cdr | 14.3.01 |
| HAIG H. J. L. Sqn Ldr | 9.5.01 | JONES A. G. Flt Lt | 15.4.01 |
| HALL D. R. J. Wg Cdr | 7.6.00 | JONES D. A. Flt Lt | 1.5.01 |

| Name | Date of Death | Name | Date of Death |
|---|---|---|---|
| JONES F. R. MB BS FRCPath DTM&H DCP A Cdre | 18.7.00 | MILROY E. Sqn Ldr | 9.5.01 |
| JONES H. Flt Lt | 20.8.00 | MITCHELL D. D. Sqn Ldr | 5.2.01 |
| JONES J. H. Flt Lt | 14.8.00 | MITCHELL D. L. Sqn Ldr | 17.4.01 |
| JONES The Rev A. A. B. Wg Cdr | 1.6.00 | MITCHELL J. H. MBCS Gp Capt | 22.2.01 |
| JUDGE J. W. MBE Sqn Ldr | 30.5.01 | MITCHELL W. O. DFC Wg Cdr | 17.8.00 |
| KENTISH J. N. CBE DFC FIMgt Gp Capt | 12.6.00 | MOLYNEAUX H. Sqn Ldr | 11.6.01 |
| KILBURN J. W. Flt Lt | 9.12.00 | MOODY A. J. Gp Capt | 12.11.00 |
| KINSEY D. E. Flt Lt | 24.4.01 | MOORE P. D. M. A Cdre | 17.3.01 |
| KIRK H. B. Sqn Ldr | 4.11.00 | MORAN T. F. Sqn Ldr | 9.3.01 |
| KUDREWICZ B. J. AFC Flt Lt | 13.4.01 | MORGAN R. B. DFC Sqn Ldr | 27.3.01 |
| LADYMAN S. C. Wg Cdr | 9.7.00 | MORGAN W. H. Flt Lt | 22.1.01 |
| LAINE E. J. CBE DFC Gp Capt | 22.4.01 | MORRIS R. J. A. CB MB ChB MFCM DPH AVM | 10.6.00 |
| LAING M. F. Sqn Ldr | 18.8.00 | MOSS N. R. OBE MIMgt Wg Cdr | 31.7.00 |
| LAURENT T. M. AFM Sqn Ldr | 17.12.00 | MUDWAY W. L. Sqn Ldr | 19.3.01 |
| LAWRENCE D. J. Flt Lt | 22.8.00 | MUNNS R. DFC Wg Cdr | 2.1.01 |
| LAWRENCE F. H. Sqn Ldr | 6.1.01 | MURRAY A. D. DFC Gp Capt | 30.1.01 |
| LAWSON A. M. Sqn Ldr | 1.6.01 | MURRAY A. E. D. Flt Lt | 30.1.01 |
| LESTER G. T. Wg Cdr | 3.6.00 | MURRAY J. DFM Flt Lt | 1.4.01 |
| LEVIEN E. D. DSO DFC Gp Capt | 14.10.00 | MURRAY J. W. B. MIMgt Sqn Ldr | 25.4.01 |
| LEWIS D. A. Sqn Ldr | 5.1.01 | MacDONALD J. C. CB CBE DFC* AFC A Cdre | 26.9.00 |
| LEWIS R. J. BSc Sqn Ldr | 29.10.00 | McCANN. P. O. MBIM Sqn Ldr | 29.11.00 |
| LEWIS W. L. Sqn Ldr | 25.11.00 | McCORMACK J. V. Sqn Ldr | 23.3.01 |
| LINFORD J. H. Flt Lt | 1.3.01 | McGUIRE J. OBE DFC Wg Cdr | 29.5.01 |
| LOFTUS J. A. Flt Lt | 12.4.01 | McKAY J. P. BSc DCAe Sqn Ldr | 25.1.01 |
| LOMAS, J. D. Wg Cdr Wg Cdr | 14.1.01 | McKAY K. D. Wg Cdr | 3.2.01 |
| LOWE F. C. CEng MIERE MRAeS Wg Cdr | 14.3.01 | McKAY S. T. Sqn Ldr | 19.4.01 |
| LUDLAM A. Flt Lt | 21.9.00 | McLEAN N. C. BSc DipSoton Wg Cdr | 13.10.00 |
| LUNSON E. A. BA Wg Cdr | 17.9.00 | McNABB H. F. DFC Sqn Ldr | 6.9.00 |
| LYWOOD A. M. G. DFC Wg Cdr | 7.2.01 | McROBBIE W. OBE AFC AE Wg Cdr | 4.6.01 |
| MACDONALD N. W. V. U. Sqn Ldr | 6.5.01 | McROSTIE J. S. Wg Cdr | 23.6.00 |
| MACKIE M. J. BEM Wg Cdr | 17.10.00 | McVITTIE A. R. J. Flt Lt | 3.9.00 |
| MADARO A. L. Flt Lt | 20.6.00 | NESBITT T. BSc Wg Cdr | 2.1.01 |
| MAGUIRE Sir Harold KCB DSO OBE AM | 1.2.01 | NEWBON L. A. Flt Lt | 24.1.01 |
| MANN A. R. Flt Lt | 30.9.00 | NICHOLAS T. V. DFC Sqn ldr | 23.2.01 |
| MANSON M. K. DFC DFM Flt Lt | 26.4.01 | NUGENT P. E. Sqn Ldr | 24.4.01 |
| MARLOW L. S. OBE Wg Cdr | 9.11.00 | NUNWICK F. H. E. MBE Wg Cdr | 21.5.01 |
| MARSHALL D. A. W. Flt Lt | 12.10.00 | NUTTALL R. Flt Lt | 13.6.00 |
| MARTIN D. G. Flt Lt | 22.11.00 | O'CONNOR L. P. OBE MRAeS Wg Cdr | 6.10.00 |
| MARTIN G. C. Flt Lt | 7.6.00 | O'CONNOR P. J. CB OBE MD BCh FRCP(Edin) FRCPsych DPM AVM | 5.3.01 |
| MARVIN G. P. CBE Gp Capt | 22.9.00 | O'DONOVAN G. V. Flt Lt | 5.1.01 |
| MASON A. C. C. BSc Flt Lt | 27.2.01 | O'KEEFFE P. F. AFM Flt Lt | 12.4.01 |
| MASON J. R. MIMgt Gp Capt | 15.8.00 | OHRBERG D. L. Sqn Ldr | 9.1.01 |
| MASON W. R. Flt Lt | 15.10.00 | OLLIVER W. O. Flt Lt | 27.12.00 |
| MATHERS R. W. DFC Wg Cdr | 21.8.00 | ORBELL A. J. Wg Cdr | 20.12.00 |
| MATYEAR A. D. Sqn Ldr | 27.1.01 | OSBON L. A. E. MBE DFC FIMgt Wg Cdr | 20.3.01 |
| MAY B. J. Wg Cdr | 13.3.01 | OURY A. J. Flt Lt | 25.6.00 |
| MAYHEW A. E. MIERE Sqn Ldr | 10.6.01 | OUTEN S. R. Flt Lt | 5.2.01 |
| MEARS R. S. Flt Lt | 18.3.01 | OWEN E. DFM Flt Lt | 8.6.01 |
| MEHARG B. G. OBE AFC* Wg Cdr | 17.7.00 | OWEN J. S. AFC Sqn Ldr | 1.1.01 |
| METCALFE J. W. W. Flt Lt | 12.8.00 | OWEN M. MBE Sqn Ldr | 24.2.01 |
| MEYER V. J. H. Sqn Ldr | 23.4.01 | PAGE A. G. DSO DFC* Wg Cdr | 3.8.00 |
| MICHIE W. D. J. CB A Cdre | 7.2.01 | PAGE B. C. DPhysEd Flt Lt | 30.6.00 |
| MIEDZYBRODZKI L. R. AFC Sqn Ldr | 18.1.01 | PAINE M. A. Sqn Ldr | 29.4.01 |
| MILES T. Wg Cdr | 23.6.00 | PALMER J. D. OBE BSc CEng MIEE DipEl Gp Capt | 15.4.01 |
| MILLAR J. G. LVO DFC Sqn Ldr | 19.5.01 | PARKER T. C. OBE Wg Cdr | 6.7.00 |
| MILLATT L. C. Flt Lt | 14.9.00 | PARKINSON W. C. R. Flt Lt | 8.10.00 |
| MILLS S. E. D. CB CBE FCA A Cdre | 19.1.01 | PARSONS E. F. J. Sqn Ldr | 1.1.01 |
| MILNE G. W. Flt Lt | 3.6.01 | PARTRIDGE G. A. Flt Lt | 15.4.01 |
| MILNER W. J. Sqn Ldr | 26.10.00 | | |

| Name | Date of Death | Name | Date of Death |
|------|---------------|------|---------------|
| PASSMORE P. M. CEng MIEE MIMgt Sqn Ldr | 20.6.00 | SAMMELS A. J. H. Wg Cdr | 21.5.01 |
| PATTON H. Flt Lt | 15.1.01 | SAUNDERS D. B. Sqn Ldr | 7.6.01 |
| PEART A. E. AFRAeS Sqn Ldr | 17.11.00 | SCOTT J. O. CEng MRAeS MIMgt Sqn Ldr | 4.7.01 |
| PECKOWSKI J. W. DFC Flt Lt | 27.3.01 | SCOTT-GURNEY E. T. Wg Cdr | 16.11.00 |
| PEGG J. D. Sqn Ldr | 22.11.00 | SHARMAN W. L. Sqn Ldr | 9.1.00 |
| PENMAN M. DFM Sqn Ldr | 13.8.00 | SHARPE J. W. Sqn Ldr | 12.2.01 |
| PERRY T. R. MBE MIMgt Wg Cdr | 11.4.01 | SHEEN D. F. B. DFC* Gp Capt | 24.4.01 |
| PERRY T. Sqn Ldr | 29.9.00 | SHIPP P. B. MIMgt Wg Cdr | 24.2.01 |
| PETRIE P. D. DFC Sqn Ldr | 23.3.01 | SHORE C. B. Sqn Ldr | 17.3.01 |
| PETTY G. G. DSO DFC AFC Gp Capt | 15.8.00 | SILLS C. J. Sqn Ldr | 10.7.01 |
| PICKERING E. W. Sqn Ldr | 21.9.00 | SILVANUS The Rev D. G. Wg Cdr | 15.5.00 |
| PIERCE R. H. Flt Lt | 12.2.01 | SIMMS R. M. Flt Lt | 5.3.01 |
| PIRRIE A. W. Flt Lt | 16.12.00 | SIMPSON C. H. CBE MA A Cdre | 20.7.00 |
| PLANT A. F. DFM CEng MIEE Sqn Ldr | 3.7.00 | SIMPSON N. F. OBE Gp Capt | 8.4.01 |
| PRATT T. E. Flt Lt | 28.4.01 | SKERMER G. J. Flt Lt | 6.1.01 |
| PRICE A. W. Flt Lt | 7.10.00 | SKILLMAN K. C. Sqn Ldr | 16.12.00 |
| PRICHARD R. J. P. CB CBE DFC AFC A Cdre | 26.4.01 | SLATER B. W. AFC Sqn Ldr | 15.4.01 |
| PRISMALL D. G. Flt Lt | 16.10.00 | SMITH E. M. B. MB ChB Wg Cdr | 27.1.01 |
| PRITCHARD E. C. Sqn Ldr | 21.2.01 | SMITH H. S. Sqn Ldr | 24.11.00 |
| PULVERMACHER M. E. MA DipEl Wg Cdr | 27.5.00 | SMITH P. D. Flt Lt | 21.12.00 |
| PURVIS W. D. MA Sqn Ldr | 14.1.01 | SMITH T. S. C. Sqn Ldr | 22.6.01 |
| PUXLEY W. A. J. Flt Lt | 28.8.00 | SOREL-CAMERON R. CBE AFC A Cdre | 30.3.01 |
| RABA V. Sqn Ldr | 27.6.00 | SPACKMAN D. A. Gp Capt | 10.7.00 |
| RAPLEY G. W. C. Sqn Ldr | 15.2.01 | STACEY E. AFC, MIMgt Sqn Ldr | 12.7.01 |
| RATCLIFFE B. O. Wg Cdr | 25.10.00 | STAFFORD E. Flt Lt | 5.2.01 |
| RAWSTRON G. C. Flt Lt | 5.8.00 | STAUNTON G. H. C. Flt Lt | 25.10.00 |
| RAY W. E. Flt Lt | 1.10.00 | STEINER F. Sqn Ldr | 4.6.00 |
| READING G. Sqn Ldr | 14.9.00 | STEPHENS Dame Anne. DBE AE A Cmdt | 26.7.00 |
| REEVE C. G. OBE Wg Cdr | 27.12.00 | STEVENS N. R. MBE Sqn Ldr | 19.1.01 |
| REEVE R. MIMgt Sqn Ldr | 6.11.00 | STEVENSON J. Sqn Ldr | 26.4.01 |
| REID D. W. Sqn Ldr | 3.10.00 | STEWART A. W. B. BSc CEng MIEE Sqn Ldr | 7.9.00 |
| REID J. F. M. Sqn Ldr | 9.10.00 | STILL C. G. Flt Lt | 1.1.01 |
| RETIEF P. J. T. Sqn Ldr | 19.6.01 | STIRLING G. C. MIMgt Sqn Ldr | 15.2.01 |
| REVELL J. D. T. CBE Gp Capt | 22.4.01 | STOCKER H. F. Sqn Ldr | 19.10.00 |
| RHYS M. H. CBE AFC Gp Capt | 16.6.01 | STONE R. G. Gp Capt | 21.12.00 |
| RICE F. G. MA Gp Capt | 22.8.00 | STONEMAN W. B. Sqn Ldr | 29.3.01 |
| RICHARDS G. Flt Lt | 12.2.01 | STOYLE K. BSc Sqn Ldr | 3.12.00 |
| RICHARDS H. G. OBE Flt Lt | 17.11.00 | STRINGFELLOW P. BSc MIMgt Sqn Ldr | 10.4.01 |
| RICHARDSON D. R. MB BS FRCS LRCP Wg Cdr | 19.9.00 | STUBBS F. H. AFC DFM Wg Cdr | 3.10.00 |
| RICKERBY A. MIMgt AMPIM Flt Lt | 5.1.01 | TATTERSALL D. R. DFM Flt Lt | 30.3.01 |
| RIDGEWAY M. V. Gp Capt | 18.2.01 | TAYLOR A. M. BA Wg Cdr | 2.2.01 |
| RILEY K. Flt Lt | 24.11.00 | TAYLOR C. J. Flt Lt | 28.6.01 |
| RITCHIE W. W. T. OBE AFC Gp Capt | 21.10.00 | TAYLOR D. T. Sqn Ldr | 1.11.00 |
| ROBERTS A. Sqn Ldr | 2.8.00 | TAYLOR L. C. Flt Lt | 28.4.01 |
| ROBERTS D. G. MBE MM Gp Capt | 3.5.01 | TAYLOR S. G. MRAeS Gp Capt | 10.11.00 |
| ROBERTS D. N. CBE AFC A Cdre | 25.10.00 | TEE J. H. AFM Flt Lt | 24.8.00 |
| ROBERTS G. MBE Sqn Ldr | 30.11.00 | THIRLWALL G. E. CB MSc BEng CEng FRAeS FIMgt AVM | 19.10.00 |
| ROGERS J. T. Sqn Ldr | 27.12.00 | THOMAS E. Flt Lt | 11.8.00 |
| ROGERS K. C. Sqn Ldr | 2.5.01 | THOMAS I. OBE DFC FIMgt Gp Capt | 29.9.00 |
| ROGERS K. W. Sqn Ldr | 12.7.00 | THOMAS J. O. Sqn Ldr | 13.4.01 |
| ROSE A. J. Fg Offr | 3.7.00 | THOMAS R. G. Sqn Ldr | 15.10.00 |
| ROTHWELL J. CEng MIEE Wg Cdr | 14.3.01 | THOMAS T. W. BA CEng MRAeS Sqn Ldr | 2.6.01 |
| ROWE K. S. Wg Cdr | 7.3.01 | THOMPSON H. H. AFC Sqn Ldr | 5.7.00 |
| ROWSON D. W. BSc CEng MIEE Gp Capt | 30.3.01 | THOMPSON M. P. Wg Cdr | 13.5.01 |
| RUSHEN G. N. Gp Capt | 8.3.01 | TICEHURST J. G. Sqn Ldr | 10.4.01 |
| RYAN J. E. Wg Cdr | 3.1.01 | TIPPER S. Sqn Ldr | 18.3.01 |
| RYDEN D. MBE MIMgt Sqn Ldr | 6.5.01 | TIPPING P. A. AFC Wg Cdr | 16.6.00 |
| SALMON R. R. Sqn Ldr | 20.11.00 | | |

| Name | Date of Death |
|------|---------------|
| TITTERTON J. W. CEng MRAeS Sqn Ldr | 11.6.01 |
| TOMBLIN F. J. Wg Cdr | 10.5.01 |
| TOMKINS R. E. BA Sqn Ldr | 24.8.00 |
| TOMLINSON I. M. BSc Flt Lt | 13.5.01 |
| TOTTEY G. A. MBE MIMgt Sqn Ldr | 22.6.01 |
| TRAYFORD G. W. Sqn Ldr | 12.3.01 |
| TROWBRIDGE A. P. AFC Sqn Ldr | 1.7.01 |
| TUCKER A. J. Flt Lt | 28.1.01 |
| TUCKER J. A. G. OBE MRAeS Sqn Ldr | 3.4.01 |
| TURNBULL G. F. OBE AFC Wg Cdr | 8.9.00 |
| TURNER G. Sqn Ldr | 23.12.00 |
| TURNER J. F. Sqn Ldr | 23.8.00 |
| TURNER-ETTLINGER D. M. Sqn Ldr | 23.1.01 |
| VALENTINE K. A. Sqn Ldr | 2.3.01 |
| VAUGHAN-EDMONDS T. Sqn Ldr | 13.10.00 |
| WAKEFIELD G. W. Sqn Ldr | 26.10.00 |
| WALBANK S. D. AFC Flt Lt | 23.4.01 |
| WALKER A. B. Wg Cdr | 2.3.01 |
| WALKER J. F. MBE Sqn Ldr | 5.3.01 |
| WALKER R. J. DSO Gp Capt | 11.6.01 |
| WALLIS K. E. Flt Lt | 27.6.01 |
| WARING S. A. MBE Flt Lt | 1.7.00 |
| WARR R. H. Sqn Ldr | 13.3.01 |
| WARREN A. McL Flt Lt | 26.12.00 |
| WASHBROOK A. DFC AFC Sqn Ldr | 25.8.00 |
| WATERS J. M. MBE Flt Lt | 23.4.01 |
| WATKINS-FIELD J. L. MA Flt Lt | 21.8.00 |
| WATSON H. L. E. Wg Cdr | 24.4.01 |
| WEAVER F. H. Q. AFC Sqn Ldr | 1.10.00 |
| WEBB P. A. BEM Sqn Ldr | 8.2.01 |
| WEIGHILL R. H. G. CBE DFC A Cdre | 27.10.00 |
| WEST J. A. AFC BSc Wg Cdr | 9.12.00 |
| WHELAN J. Flt Lt | 24.1.01 |
| WHELLENS J. Flt Lt | 25.3.01 |
| WHITE D. C. Flt Lt | 7.2.01 |
| WHITE E. L. J. W. Flt Lt | 26.1.01 |
| WHITE M. C. R. CBE Gp Capt | 10.9.00 |
| WHITE SPUNNER The Rev A. E. S. OBE Wg Cdr | 18.10.00 |
| WIGMORE W. E. Flt Lt | 3.7.00 |
| WILCOX H. C. G. Sqn Ldr | 15.2.01 |
| WILDIG L. J. C. DFM Flt Lt | 14.6.00 |
| WILLIAMS A. G. DFC Sqn Ldr | 14.3.01 |
| WILLIAMS C. Wg Cdr | 9.9.00 |
| WILLIAMS D. C. MB BCh FRCS(Edin) Wg Cdr | 17.10.00 |
| WILLIAMS D. J. BSc Wg Cdr | 22.11.00 |
| WILLIAMS J. M. MBE Sqn Ldr | 4.2.01 |
| WILLIAMSON K. M. Flt Lt | 24.2.01 |
| WILLIS G. E. DFC AFC Wg Cdr | 26.4.01 |
| WILSON G. D. MA Flt Lt | 7.1.01 |
| WOLLERTON G. Sqn Ldr | 2.7.01 |
| WOODCOCK W. Flt Lt | 2.11.00 |
| WOODWARD V. C. DFC* Wg Cdr | 26/5/00 |
| WORTH D. Sqn Ldr | 4.11.00 |
| WRIGHT D. P. Fg Offr | 23.3.01 |
| WRIGHT F. C. D. DFC Wg Cdr | 3.2.01 |
| WYLLIE J. M. DFM Flt Lt | 14.3.01 |
| WYNN G. Wg Cdr | 7.3.01 |
| YOUNG L. C. Wg Cdr | 22.11.00 |

| Name | Date of Death |
|------|---------------|
| **Princess Mary's Royal Air Force Nursing Service** | |
| HOLT B. RRC SRN Wg Offr | 8.5.01 |
| LOWREY Dame Alice. DBE RRC SRN A Cdt | 19.5.01 |
| McGREGOR H. SRN Sqn Offr | 19.11.00 |

Printed in the United Kingdom by The Stationery Office
TJ 005475   C14   10/2001   655888   19585